SAINT THOMAS AQUINAS

# SUMMA THEOLOGIAE
# SECUNDA SECUNDAE, 1–91

Translated by Fr. Laurence Shapcote, OP

SUMMA THEOLOGIAE

Volume 17
Latin/English Edition of the Works of St. Thomas Aquinas

AQUINAS INSTITUTE | EMMAUS ACADEMIC
GREEN BAY, WI | STEUBENVILLE, OH

We would like to thank Kevin Bergdorf, Patricia Lynch, Josh and Holly Harnisch, Fr. Brian McMaster, Dr. Brian Cutter, and the Studentate Community of the Dominican Province of St. Albert the Great, USA, for their support. This series is dedicated to Marcus Berquist, Rose Johanna Trumbull, John and Mary Deignan, Thomas and Eleanor Sullivan, Ann C. Arcidi, the Very Rev. Romanus Cessario, OP, STM, and Fr. John T. Feeney and his sister Mary.

Published with the ecclesiastical approval of
The Most Reverend Paul D. Etienne, DD, STL
Bishop of Cheyenne
Given on November 10, 2012

PUBLISHER'S CATALOGING-IN-PUBLICATION DATA

Thomas Aquinas, St., 1225–1274
  Summa Theologiae Secunda Secundae Pars, q. 1-91 / Saint Thomas Aquinas; edited by The Aquinas Institute;
  translated by Fr. Laurence Shapcote, OP
  p. 880 cm.
  ISBN 978-1-62340-010-1

1. Thomas, Aquinas, Saint, 1225?–1274 — Summa theologiae — Secunda Secundae — 1-91. 2. Catholic Church — Doctrines — Early works to 1800. 3. Theology, Doctrinal — Early works to 1800. I. Title. II. Series

BX1749.T512 2015
230′.2--dc23                                                      2012953834

## NOTES ON THE TEXT

### Latin Text of St. Thomas

The Latin text used in this volume is based on the Leonine Edition, transcribed and revised by The Aquinas Institute.

### English Translation of St. Thomas

The English translation of the Summa Theologiae was prepared by Fr. Laurence Shapcote, OP (1864–1947), of the English Dominican Province. It has been edited and revised by The Aquinas Institute.

The Aquinas Institute requests your assistance in the continued perfection of these texts.
If you discover any errors, please send us a note by email: editor@theaquinasinstitute.org

DEDICATED WITH LOVE TO
OUR LADY OF MT. CARMEL

# Contents

xvii

# SUMMA THEOLOGIAE
# SECUNDA SECUNDAE, 1–91

# Prologue

Post communem considerationem de virtutibus et vitiis et aliis ad materiam moralem pertinentibus, necesse est considerare singula in speciali, sermones enim morales universales sunt minus utiles, eo quod actiones in particularibus sunt. Potest autem aliquid in speciali considerari circa moralia dupliciter, uno modo, ex parte ipsius materiae moralis, puta cum consideratur de hac virtute vel hoc vitio; alio modo, quantum ad speciales status hominum, puta cum consideratur de subditis et praelatis, de activis et contemplativis, vel quibuscumque aliis differentiis hominum.

Primo ergo considerabimus specialiter de his quae pertinent ad omnes hominum status; secundo vero, specialiter de his quae pertinent ad determinatos status.

Est autem considerandum circa primum quod, si seorsum determinaremus de virtutibus, donis, vitiis et praeceptis, oporteret idem multoties dicere, qui enim sufficienter vult tractare de hoc praecepto, *non moechaberis*, necesse habet inquirere de adulterio, quod est quoddam peccatum, cuius etiam cognitio dependet ex cognitione oppositae virtutis. Erit igitur compendiosior et expeditior considerationis via si simul sub eodem tractatu consideratio procedit de virtute et dono sibi correspondente, et vitiis oppositis, et praeceptis affirmativis vel negativis. Erit autem hic considerationis modus conveniens ipsis vitiis secundum propriam speciem, ostensum est enim supra quod vitia et peccata diversificantur specie secundum materiam vel obiectum, non autem secundum alias differentias peccatorum, puta cordis, oris et operis, vel secundum infirmitatem, ignorantiam et malitiam, et alias huiusmodi differentias; est autem eadem materia circa quam et virtus recte operatur et vitia opposita a rectitudine recedunt. Sic igitur tota materia morali ad considerationem virtutum reducta, omnes virtutes sunt ulterius reducendae ad septem,

quarum tres sunt theologicae, de quibus primo est agendum; aliae vero quatuor sunt cardinales, de quibus posterius agetur.

Virtutum autem intellectualium una quidem est prudentia, quae inter cardinales virtutes continetur et numeratur; ars vero non pertinet ad moralem, quae circa agibilia versatur, cum ars sit recta ratio factibilium, ut supra dictum est; aliae vero tres intellectuales virtutes, scilicet sapientia, intellectus et scientia, communicant etiam in nomine cum donis quibusdam spiritus sancti, unde simul etiam de eis considerabitur in consideratione donorum virtutibus correspondentium.

Aliae vero virtutes morales omnes aliqualiter reducuntur ad virtutes cardinales, ut ex supradictis patet, unde in consideratione alicuius virtutis cardinalis con-

After a general consideration of virtues, vices, and other things pertaining to moral matters, it is necessary to consider each of them in particular. For universal moral discourse is less useful, since actions are singulars. Particular moral matters can be considered in two ways: first, with respect to the moral matter itself, for example, this virtue or that vice; second, with respect to the special states of men, for example, subjects and prelates, people in active or contemplative life, and so on for other differences of men.

Therefore, first we will consider in particular everything that pertains to people of whatever state, second, what pertains to people in special states of life.

It should first be remarked that, if we were to treat virtues, gifts, vices and commandments separately, we would have to say the same thing many times over. For, if you were adequately to treat the commandment *Do not commit adultery*, you would have to examine adultery, which is a particular sin, and to understand it you must understand the opposite virtue. Therefore, it will be a briefer and quicker to treat together the virtue and the gift corresponding to it, along with the opposite vices and the affirmative and negative commandments. This is the most convenient procedure for treating vices in their proper species, for it was shown above that vices and sins differ in species according to their matter or object, not according to other factors differentiating sins, such as by thought, word and deed, or by way of weakness, ignorance or malice, and other such differentiations. But virtues act correctly with regard to the same matter as the opposite vices deviate from. Therefore, as all moral matters are reduced to the consideration of the virtues, all the virtues are furthermore reduced to seven:

of which three are theological, which will be treated first, and the other four are cardinal, which will be treated afterwards.

As for intellectual virtues, one is prudence, which is included and numbered among the cardinal virtues. Art, which has to do with making things, does not pertain to morals, as was said above. The other three intellectual virtues, i.e., wisdom, understanding and knowledge, share names with some gifts of the Holy Spirit. So they will be treated along with the gifts corresponding to virtues.

All the other moral virtues are somehow reducible to the cardinal virtues, as was shown previously. So along with each cardinal virtue we will treat also all the virtues that are

1

siderabuntur etiam omnes virtutes ad eam qualitercumque pertinentes et vitia opposita. Et sic nihil moralium erit praetermissum.

in some way related to it, as well as the contrary vices. In this way nothing pertaining to morals will be omitted.

# QUESTION 1

## FAITH

Circa virtutes igitur theologicas primo erit considerandum de fide; secundo, de spe; tertio, de caritate.

Circa fidem vero quadruplex consideratio occurrit, prima quidem de ipsa fide; secunda de donis intellectus et scientiae sibi correspondentibus; tertia de vitiis oppositis; quarta de praeceptis ad hanc virtutem pertinentibus.

Circa fidem vero primo erit considerandum de eius obiecto; secundo, de eius actu; tertio, de ipso habitu fidei.

Circa primum quaeruntur decem.

Primo, utrum obiectum fidei sit veritas prima.

Secundo, utrum obiectum fidei sit aliquid complexum vel incomplexum, idest res aut enuntiabile.

Tertio, utrum fidei possit subesse falsum.

Quarto, utrum obiectum fidei possit esse aliquid visum.

Quinto, utrum possit esse aliquid scitum.

Sexto, utrum credibilia debeant distingui per certos articulos.

Septimo, utrum iidem articuli subsint fidei secundum omne tempus.

Octavo, de numero articulorum.

Nono, de modo tradendi articulos in symbolo.

Decimo, cuius sit fidei symbolum constituere.

Having to treat now of the theological virtues, we shall begin with faith, second we shall speak of hope, and third, of charity.

The treatise on faith will be fourfold: (1) Of faith itself; (2) Of the corresponding gifts, knowledge and understanding; (3) Of the opposite vices; (4) Of the precepts pertaining to this virtue.

About faith itself we shall consider: (1) its object; (2) its act; (3) the habit of faith.

Under the first head there are ten points of inquiry:

(1) Whether the object of faith is the First Truth?

(2) Whether the object of faith is something complex or incomplex, i.e., whether it is a thing or a proposition?

(3) Whether anything false can come under faith?

(4) Whether the object of faith can be anything seen?

(5) Whether it can be anything known?

(6) Whether the things to be believed should be divided into a certain number of articles?

(7) Whether the same articles are of faith for all times?

(8) Of the number of articles;

(9) Of the manner of embodying the articles in a symbol;

(10) Who has the right to propose a symbol of faith?

# Article 1

*Whether the object of faith is the first truth?*

**AD PRIMUM SIC PROCEDITUR.** Videtur quod obiectum fidei non sit veritas prima. Illud enim videtur esse obiectum fidei quod nobis proponitur ad credendum. Sed non solum proponuntur nobis ad credendum ea quae pertinent ad divinitatem, quae est veritas prima; sed etiam ea quae pertinent ad humanitatem Christi et Ecclesiae sacramenta et creaturarum conditionem. Ergo non solum veritas prima est fidei obiectum.

**PRAETEREA**, fides et infidelitas sunt circa idem, cum sint opposita. Sed circa omnia quae in sacra Scriptura continentur potest esse infidelitas, quidquid enim horum homo negaverit, infidelis reputatur. Ergo etiam fides est circa omnia quae in sacra Scriptura continentur. Sed ibi multa continentur de hominibus et de aliis rebus

**OBJECTION 1**: It would seem that the object of faith is not the First Truth. For it seems that the object of faith is that which is proposed to us to be believed. Now not only things pertaining to the Godhead, i.e., the First Truth, are proposed to us to be believed, but also things concerning Christ's human nature, and the sacraments of the Church, and the condition of creatures. Therefore the object of faith is not only the First Truth.

**OBJ. 2**: Further, faith and unbelief have the same object since they are opposed to one another. Now unbelief can be about all things contained in Holy Writ, for whichever one of them a man denies, he is considered an unbeliever. Therefore faith also is about all things contained in Holy Writ. But there are many things therein, concerning man

3

creatis. Ergo obiectum fidei non solum est veritas prima, sed etiam veritas creata.

**Praeterea**, fides caritati condividitur, ut supra dictum est. Sed caritate non solum diligimus Deum, qui est summa bonitas, sed etiam diligimus proximum. Ergo fidei obiectum non est solum veritas prima.

**Sed contra** est quod Dionysius dicit, VII cap. de Div. Nom., quod *fides est circa simplicem et semper existentem veritatem*. Haec autem est veritas prima. Ergo obiectum fidei est veritas prima.

**Respondeo** dicendum quod cuiuslibet cognoscitivi habitus obiectum duo habet, scilicet id quod materialiter cognoscitur, quod est sicut materiale obiectum; et id per quod cognoscitur, quod est formalis ratio obiecti. Sicut in scientia geometriae materialiter scita sunt conclusiones; formalis vero ratio sciendi sunt media demonstrationis, per quae conclusiones cognoscuntur.

Sic igitur in fide, si consideremus formalem rationem obiecti, nihil est aliud quam veritas prima, non enim fides de qua loquimur assentit alicui nisi quia est a Deo revelatum; unde ipsi veritati divinae innititur tanquam medio. Si vero consideremus materialiter ea quibus fides assentit, non solum est ipse Deus, sed etiam multa alia. Quae tamen sub assensu fidei non cadunt nisi secundum quod habent aliquem ordinem ad Deum, prout scilicet per aliquos divinitatis effectus homo adiuvatur ad tendendum in divinam fruitionem. Et ideo etiam ex hac parte obiectum fidei est quodammodo veritas prima, inquantum nihil cadit sub fide nisi in ordine ad Deum, sicut etiam obiectum medicinae est sanitas, quia nihil medicina considerat nisi in ordine ad sanitatem.

**Ad primum** ergo dicendum quod ea quae pertinent ad humanitatem Christi et ad sacramenta Ecclesiae vel ad quascumque creaturas cadunt sub fide inquantum per haec ordinamur ad Deum. Et eis etiam assentimus propter divinam veritatem.

**Et similiter** dicendum est ad secundum, de omnibus illis quae in sacra Scriptura traduntur.

**Ad tertium** dicendum quod etiam caritas diligit proximum propter Deum; et sic obiectum eius proprie est ipse Deus, ut infra dicetur.

and other creatures. Therefore the object of faith is not only the First Truth, but also created truth.

**Obj. 3**: Further, faith is condivided with charity, as stated above (I-II, Q. 62, A. 3). Now by charity we love not only God, who is the sovereign Good, but also our neighbor. Therefore the object of Faith is not only the First Truth.

**On the contrary**, Dionysius says (*Div. Nom.* vii) that *faith is about the simple and everlasting truth*. Now this is the First Truth. Therefore the object of faith is the First Truth.

**I answer that**, The object of every cognitive habit includes two things: first, that which is known materially, and is the material object, so to speak, and, second, that whereby it is known, which is the formal aspect of the object. Thus in the science of geometry, the conclusions are what is known materially, while the formal aspect of the science is the mean of demonstration, through which the conclusions are known.

Accordingly if we consider, in faith, the formal aspect of the object, it is nothing else than the First Truth. For the faith of which we are speaking, does not assent to anything, except because it is revealed by God. Hence the mean on which faith is based is the Divine Truth. If, however, we consider materially the things to which faith assents, they include not only God, but also many other things, which, nevertheless, do not come under the assent of faith, except as bearing some relation to God, inasmuch as, to wit, through certain effects of the Divine operation, man is helped on his journey towards the enjoyment of God. Consequently from this point of view also the object of faith is, in a way, the First Truth, inasmuch as nothing comes under faith except in relation to God, even as the object of the medical art is health, for it considers nothing save in relation to health.

**Reply Obj. 1**: Things concerning Christ's human nature, and the sacraments of the Church, or any creatures whatever, come under faith, insofar as by them we are directed to God, and inasmuch as we assent to them on account of the Divine Truth.

**The same answer** applies to the Second Objection, as regards all things contained in Holy Writ.

**Reply Obj. 3**: Charity also loves our neighbor on account of God, so that its object, properly speaking, is God, as we shall show further on (Q. 25, A. 1).

# Article 2

*Whether the object of faith is something complex, by way of a proposition?*

**AD SECUNDUM SIC PROCEDITUR.** Videtur quod obiectum fidei non sit aliquid complexum per modum enuntiabilis. Obiectum enim fidei est veritas prima, sicut dictum est. Sed prima veritas est aliquid incomplexum. Ergo obiectum fidei non est aliquid complexum.

**PRAETEREA,** expositio fidei in symbolo continetur. Sed in symbolo non ponuntur enuntiabilia, sed res, non enim dicitur ibi quod Deus sit omnipotens, sed, *credo in Deum omnipotentem.* Ergo obiectum fidei non est enuntiabile, sed res.

**PRAETEREA,** fidei succedit visio, secundum illud I ad Cor. XIII, *videmus nunc per speculum in aenigmate, tunc autem facie ad faciem.* Sed visio patriae est de incomplexo, cum sit ipsius divinae essentiae. Ergo etiam fides viae.

**SED CONTRA,** fides est media inter scientiam et opinionem. Medium autem et extrema sunt eiusdem generis. Cum igitur scientia et opinio sint circa enuntiabilia, videtur quod similiter fides sit circa enuntiabilia. Et ita obiectum fidei, cum fides sit circa enuntiabilia, est aliquid complexum.

**RESPONDEO** dicendum quod cognita sunt in cognoscente secundum modum cognoscentis. Est autem modus proprius humani intellectus ut componendo et dividendo veritatem cognoscat, sicut in primo dictum est. Et ideo ea quae sunt secundum se simplicia intellectus humanus cognoscit secundum quandam complexionem, sicut e converso intellectus divinus incomplexe cognoscit ea quae sunt secundum se complexa.

Sic igitur obiectum fidei dupliciter considerari potest. Uno modo, ex parte ipsius rei creditae, et sic obiectum fidei est aliquid incomplexum, scilicet res ipsa de qua fides habetur. Alio modo, ex parte credentis, et secundum hoc obiectum fidei est aliquid complexum per modum enuntiabilis.

Et ideo utrumque vere opinatum fuit apud antiquos, et secundum aliquid utrumque est verum.

**AD PRIMUM** ergo dicendum quod ratio illa procedit de obiecto fidei ex parte ipsius rei creditae.

**AD SECUNDUM** dicendum quod in symbolo tanguntur ea de quibus est fides inquantum ad ea terminatur actus credentis, ut ex ipso modo loquendi apparet. Actus autem credentis non terminatur ad enuntiabile, sed ad rem, non enim formamus enuntiabilia nisi ut per ea de rebus cognitionem habeamus, sicut in scientia, ita et in fide.

**AD TERTIUM** dicendum quod visio patriae erit veritatis primae secundum quod in se est, secundum illud I Ioan. III, *cum apparuerit, similes ei erimus et videbimus eum sicuti est.* Et ideo visio illa erit non per modum

**OBJECTION 1:** It would seem that the object of faith is not something complex by way of a proposition. For the object of faith is the First Truth, as stated above (A. 1). Now the First Truth is something simple. Therefore the object of faith is not something complex.

**OBJ. 2:** Further, the exposition of faith is contained in the symbol. Now the symbol does not contain propositions, but things: for it is not stated therein that God is almighty, but: *I believe in God . . . almighty.* Therefore the object of faith is not a proposition but a thing.

**OBJ. 3:** Further, faith is succeeded by vision, according to 1 Cor. 13:12: *We see now through a glass in a dark manner: but then face to face.* But the object of the heavenly vision is something simple, for it is the Divine Essence. Therefore the faith of the wayfarer is also.

**ON THE CONTRARY,** Faith is a mean between science and opinion. Now the mean is in the same genus as the extremes. Since, then, science and opinion are about propositions, it seems that faith is likewise about propositions; so that its object is something complex.

**I ANSWER THAT,** The thing known is in the knower according to the mode of the knower. Now the mode proper to the human intellect is to know the truth by synthesis and analysis, as stated in the First Part (Q. 85, A. 5). Hence things that are simple in themselves, are known by the intellect with a certain amount of complexity, just as on the other hand, the Divine intellect knows, without any complexity, things that are complex in themselves.

Accordingly the object of faith may be considered in two ways. First, as regards the thing itself which is believed, and thus the object of faith is something simple, namely the thing itself about which we have faith. Second, on the part of the believer, and in this respect the object of faith is something complex by way of a proposition.

Hence in the past both opinions have been held with a certain amount of truth.

**REPLY OBJ. 1:** This argument considers the object of faith on the part of the thing believed.

**REPLY OBJ. 2:** The symbol mentions the things about which faith is, insofar as the act of the believer is terminated in them, as is evident from the manner of speaking about them. Now the act of the believer does not terminate in a proposition, but in a thing. For as in science we do not form propositions, except in order to have knowledge about things through their means, so is it in faith.

**REPLY OBJ. 3:** The object of the heavenly vision will be the First Truth seen in itself, according to 1 John 3:2: *We know that when He shall appear, we shall be like to Him: because we shall see Him as He is*: hence that vision will not

enuntiabilis, sed per modum simplicis intelligentiae. Sed per fidem non apprehendimus veritatem primam sicut in se est. Unde non est similis ratio.

be by way of a proposition but by way of a simple understanding. On the other hand, by faith, we do not apprehend the First Truth as it is in itself. Hence the comparison fails.

# Article 3

*Whether anything false can come under faith?*

AD TERTIUM SIC PROCEDITUR. Videtur quod fidei possit subesse falsum. Fides enim condividitur spei et caritati. Sed spei potest aliquid subesse falsum, multi enim sperant se habituros vitam aeternam qui non habebunt. Similiter etiam et caritati, multi enim diliguntur tanquam boni qui tamen boni non sunt. Ergo etiam fidei potest aliquid subesse falsum.

PRAETEREA, Abraham credidit Christum nasciturum, secundum illud Ioan. VIII, *Abraham, pater vester, exultavit ut videret diem meum.* Sed post tempus Abrahae Deus poterat non incarnari, sola enim sua voluntate carnem accepit, et ita esset falsum quod Abraham de Christo credidit. Ergo fidei potest subesse falsum.

PRAETEREA, fides antiquorum fuit quod Christus esset nasciturus, et haec fides duravit in multis usque ad praedicationem Evangelii. Sed Christo iam nato, antequam praedicare inciperet, falsum erat Christum nasciturum. Ergo fidei potest subesse falsum.

PRAETEREA, unum de pertinentibus ad fidem est ut aliquis credat sub sacramento altaris verum corpus Christi contineri. Potest autem contingere, quando non recte consecratur, quod non est ibi verum corpus Christi, sed solum panis. Ergo fidei potest subesse falsum.

SED CONTRA, nulla virtus perficiens intellectum se habet ad falsum secundum quod est malum intellectus, ut patet per Philosophum, in VI Ethic. Sed fides est quaedam virtus perficiens intellectum, ut infra patebit. Ergo ei non potest subesse falsum.

RESPONDEO dicendum quod nihil subest alicui potentiae vel habitui aut etiam actui, nisi mediante ratione formali obiecti, sicut color videri non potest nisi per lucem, et conclusio sciri non potest nisi per medium demonstrationis. Dictum est autem quod ratio formalis obiecti fidei est veritas prima. Unde nihil potest cadere sub fide nisi inquantum stat sub veritate prima. Sub qua nullum falsum stare potest, sicut nec non ens sub ente, nec malum sub bonitate. Unde relinquitur quod fidei non potest subesse aliquod falsum.

OBJECTION 1: It would seem that something false can come under faith. For faith is condivided with hope and charity. Now something false can come under hope, since many hope to have eternal life, who will not obtain it. The same may be said of charity, for many are loved as being good, who, nevertheless, are not good. Therefore something false can be the object of faith.

OBJ. 2: Further, Abraham believed that Christ would be born, according to John 8:56: *Abraham your father rejoiced that he might see My day: he saw it, and was glad.* But after the time of Abraham, God might not have taken flesh, for it was merely because He willed that He did, so that what Abraham believed about Christ would have been false. Therefore the object of faith can be something false.

OBJ. 3: Further, the ancients believed in the future birth of Christ, and many continued so to believe, until they heard the preaching of the Gospel. Now, when once Christ was born, even before He began to preach, it was false that Christ was yet to be born. Therefore something false can come under faith.

OBJ. 4: Further, it is a matter of faith, that one should believe that the true Body of Christ is contained in the Sacrament of the altar. But it might happen that the bread was not rightly consecrated, and that there was not Christ's true Body there, but only bread. Therefore something false can come under faith.

ON THE CONTRARY, No virtue that perfects the intellect is related to the false, considered as the evil of the intellect, as the Philosopher declares (*Ethic.* vi, 2). Now faith is a virtue that perfects the intellect, as we shall show further on (Q. 4, AA. 2, 5). Therefore nothing false can come under it.

I ANSWER THAT, Nothing comes under any power, habit or act, except by means of the formal aspect of the object: thus color cannot be seen except by means of light, and a conclusion cannot be known save through the mean of demonstration. Now it has been stated (A. 1) that the formal aspect of the object of faith is the First Truth; so that nothing can come under faith, save insofar as it stands under the First Truth, under which nothing false can stand, as neither can non-being stand under being, nor evil under goodness. It follows therefore that nothing false can come under faith.

**Ad primum** ergo dicendum quod, quia verum est bonum intellectus, non autem est bonum appetitivae virtutis, ideo omnes virtutes quae perficiunt intellectum excludunt totaliter falsum, quia de ratione virtutis est quod se habeat solum ad bonum. Virtutes autem perficientes partem appetitivam non excludunt totaliter falsum, potest enim aliquis secundum iustitiam aut temperantiam agere aliquam falsam opinionem habens de eo circa quod agit. Et ita, cum fides perficiat intellectum, spes autem et caritas appetitivam partem, non est similis ratio de eis.

Et tamen neque etiam spei subest falsum. Non enim aliquis sperat se habiturum vitam aeternam secundum propriam potestatem (hoc enim esset praesumptionis), sed secundum auxilium gratiae, in qua si perseveraverit, omnino infallibiliter vitam aeternam consequetur.

Similiter etiam ad caritatem pertinet diligere Deum in quocumque fuerit. Unde non refert ad caritatem utrum in isto sit Deus qui propter Deum diligitur.

**Ad secundum** dicendum quod Deum non incarnari, secundum se consideratum, fuit possibile etiam post tempus Abrahae. Sed secundum quod cadit sub praescientia divina, habet quandam necessitatem infallibilitatis, ut in primo dictum est. Et hoc modo cadit sub fide. Unde prout cadit sub fide, non potest esse falsum.

**Ad tertium** dicendum quod hoc ad fidem credentis pertinebat post Christi nativitatem quod crederet eum quandoque nasci. Sed illa determinatio temporis, in qua decipiebatur, non erat ex fide, sed ex coniectura humana. Possibile est enim hominem fidelem ex coniectura humana falsum aliquid aestimare. Sed quod ex fide falsum aestimet, hoc est impossibile.

**Ad quartum** dicendum quod fides credentis non refertur ad has species panis vel illas, sed ad hoc quod verum corpus Christi sit sub speciebus panis sensibilis quando recte fuerit consecratum. Unde si non sit recte consecratum, fidei non suberit propter hoc falsum.

**Reply Obj. 1**: Since the true is the good of the intellect, but not of the appetitive power, it follows that all virtues which perfect the intellect, exclude the false altogether, because it belongs to the nature of a virtue to bear relation to the good alone. On the other hand those virtues which perfect the appetitive faculty, do not entirely exclude the false, for it is possible to act in accordance with justice or temperance, while having a false opinion about what one is doing. Therefore, as faith perfects the intellect, whereas hope and charity perfect the appetitive part, the comparison between them fails.

Nevertheless neither can anything false come under hope, for a man hopes to obtain eternal life, not by his own power (since this would be an act of presumption), but with the help of grace; and if he perseveres therein he will obtain eternal life surely and infallibly.

In like manner it belongs to charity to love God, wherever He may be; so that it matters not to charity, whether God be in the individual whom we love for God's sake.

**Reply Obj. 2**: That God would not take flesh, considered in itself was possible even after Abraham's time, but insofar as it stands in God's foreknowledge, it has a certain necessity of infallibility, as explained in the First Part (Q. 14, AA. 13, 15): and it is thus that it comes under faith. Hence insofar as it comes under faith, it cannot be false.

**Reply Obj. 3**: After Christ's birth, to believe in Him, was to believe in Christ's birth at some time or other. The fixing of the time, wherein some were deceived, was not due to their faith, but to a human conjecture. For it is possible for a believer to have a false opinion through a human conjecture, but it is quite impossible for a false opinion to be the outcome of faith.

**Reply Obj. 4**: The faith of the believer is not directed to such and such accidents of bread, but to the fact that the true body of Christ is under the appearances of sensible bread, when it is rightly consecrated. Hence if it be not rightly consecrated, it does not follow that anything false comes under faith.

# Article 4

*Whether the object of faith can be something seen?*

**Ad quartum sic proceditur.** Videtur quod obiectum fidei sit aliquid visum. Dicit enim dominus Thomae, Ioan. XX, *quia vidisti me, credidisti.* Ergo et de eodem est visio et fides.

**Praeterea**, apostolus, I ad Cor. XIII, dicit, *videmus nunc per speculum in aenigmate.* Et loquitur de cognitione fidei. Ergo id quod creditur videtur.

**Praeterea**, fides est quoddam spirituale lumen. Sed quolibet lumine aliquid videtur. Ergo fides est de rebus visis.

**Objection 1**: It would seem that the object of faith is something seen. For Our Lord said to Thomas (John 20:29): *Because thou hast seen Me, Thomas, thou hast believed.* Therefore vision and faith regard the same object.

**Obj. 2**: Further, the Apostle, while speaking of the knowledge of faith, says (1 Cor 13:12): *We see now through a glass in a dark manner.* Therefore what is believed is seen.

**Obj. 3**: Further, faith is a spiritual light. Now something is seen under every light. Therefore faith is of things seen.

PRAETEREA, quilibet sensus visus nominatur, ut Augustinus dicit, in libro de Verb. Dom. Sed fides est de auditis, secundum illud ad Rom. X, *fides ex auditu*. Ergo fides est de rebus visis.

SED CONTRA est quod apostolus dicit, ad Heb. XI, quod *fides est argumentum non apparentium*.

RESPONDEO dicendum quod fides importat assensum intellectus ad id quod creditur. Assentit autem alicui intellectus dupliciter. Uno modo, quia ad hoc movetur ab ipso obiecto, quod est vel per seipsum cognitum, sicut patet in principiis primis, quorum est intellectus; vel est per aliud cognitum, sicut patet de conclusionibus, quarum est scientia. Alio modo intellectus assentit alicui non quia sufficienter moveatur ab obiecto proprio, sed per quandam electionem voluntarie declinans in unam partem magis quam in aliam. Et si quidem hoc fit cum dubitatione et formidine alterius partis, erit opinio, si autem fit cum certitudine absque tali formidine, erit fides.

Illa autem videri dicuntur quae per seipsa movent intellectum nostrum vel sensum ad sui cognitionem. Unde manifestum est quod nec fides nec opinio potest esse de visis aut secundum sensum aut secundum intellectum.

AD PRIMUM ergo dicendum quod Thomas *aliud vidit et aliud credidit. Hominem vidit et Deum credens confessus est, cum dixit, dominus meus et Deus meus.*

AD SECUNDUM dicendum quod ea quae subsunt fidei dupliciter considerari possunt. Uno modo, in speciali, et sic non possunt esse simul visa et credita, sicut dictum est. Alio modo, in generali, scilicet sub communi ratione credibilis. Et sic sunt visa ab eo qui credit, non enim crederet nisi videret ea esse credenda, vel propter evidentiam signorum vel propter aliquid huiusmodi.

AD TERTIUM dicendum quod lumen fidei facit videre ea quae creduntur. Sicut enim per alios habitus virtutum homo videt illud quod est sibi conveniens secundum habitum illum, ita etiam per habitum fidei inclinatur mens hominis ad assentiendum his quae conveniunt rectae fidei et non aliis.

AD QUARTUM dicendum quod auditus est verborum significantium ea quae sunt fidei, non autem est ipsarum rerum de quibus est fides. Et sic non oportet ut huiusmodi res sint visae.

OBJ. 4: Further, *Every sense is a kind of sight*, as Augustine states (*De Verb. Domini*, Serm. xxxiii). But faith is of things heard, according to Rom. 10:17: *Faith . . . cometh by hearing*. Therefore faith is of things seen.

ON THE CONTRARY, The Apostle says (Heb 11:1) that *faith is the evidence of things that appear not*.

I ANSWER THAT, Faith implies assent of the intellect to that which is believed. Now the intellect assents to a thing in two ways. First, through being moved to assent by its very object, which is known either by itself (as in the case of first principles, which are held by the habit of understanding), or through something else already known (as in the case of conclusions which are held by the habit of science). Second the intellect assents to something, not through being sufficiently moved to this assent by its proper object, but through an act of choice, whereby it turns voluntarily to one side rather than to the other: and if this be accompanied by doubt or fear of the opposite side, there will be opinion, while, if there be certainty and no fear of the other side, there will be faith.

Now those things are said to be seen which, of themselves, move the intellect or the senses to knowledge of them. Wherefore it is evident that neither faith nor opinion can be of things seen either by the senses or by the intellect.

REPLY OBJ. 1: Thomas *saw one thing, and believed another: he saw the Man, and believing Him to be God, he made profession of his faith, saying: My Lord and my God.*

REPLY OBJ. 2: Those things which come under faith can be considered in two ways. First, in particular; and thus they cannot be seen and believed at the same time, as shown above. Second, in general, that is, under the common aspect of credibility; and in this way they are seen by the believer. For he would not believe unless, on the evidence of signs, or of something similar, he saw that they ought to be believed.

REPLY OBJ. 3: The light of faith makes us see what we believe. For just as, by the habits of the other virtues, man sees what is becoming to him in respect of that habit, so, by the habit of faith, the human mind is directed to assent to such things as are becoming to a right faith, and not to assent to others.

REPLY OBJ. 4: Hearing is of words signifying what is of faith, but not of the things themselves that are believed; hence it does not follow that these things are seen.

# Article 5

*Whether those things that are of faith can be an object of science ?*

AD QUINTUM SIC PROCEDITUR. Videtur quod ea quae sunt fidei possint esse scita. Ea enim quae non sciuntur videntur esse ignorata, quia ignorantia scientiae opponitur. Sed ea quae sunt fidei non sunt ignorata,

OBJECTION 1: It would seem that those things that are of faith can be an object of science. For where science is lacking there is ignorance, since ignorance is the opposite of science. Now we are not in ignorance of those things

horum enim ignorantia ad infidelitatem pertinet, secundum illud I ad Tim. I, *ignorans feci in incredulitate mea.* Ergo ea quae sunt fidei possunt esse scita.

**PRAETEREA**, scientia per rationes acquiritur. Sed ad ea quae sunt fidei a sacris auctoribus rationes inducuntur. Ergo ea quae sunt fidei possunt esse scita.

**PRAETEREA**, ea quae demonstrative probantur sunt scita, quia *demonstratio est syllogismus faciens scire.* Sed quaedam quae in fide continentur sunt demonstrative probata a philosophis, sicut Deum esse, et Deum esse unum, et alia huiusmodi. Ergo ea quae sunt fidei possunt esse scita.

**PRAETEREA**, opinio plus distat a scientia quam fides, cum fides dicatur esse media inter opinionem et scientiam. Sed *opinio et scientia possunt esse aliquo modo de eodem*, ut dicitur in I Poster. Ergo etiam fides et scientia.

**SED CONTRA** est quod Gregorius dicit, quod *apparentia non habent fidem, sed agnitionem.* Ea ergo de quibus est fides agnitionem non habent. Sed ea quae sunt scita habent agnitionem. Ergo de his quae sunt scita non potest esse fides.

**RESPONDEO** dicendum quod omnis scientia habetur per aliqua principia per se nota, et per consequens visa. Et ideo oportet quaecumque sunt scita aliquo modo esse visa.

Non autem est possibile quod idem ab eodem sit creditum et visum, sicut supra dictum est. Unde etiam impossibile est quod ab eodem idem sit scitum et creditum. Potest tamen contingere ut id quod est visum vel scitum ab uno, sit creditum ab alio. Ea enim quae de Trinitate credimus nos visuros speramus, secundum illud I ad Cor. XIII, *videmus nunc per speculum in aenigmate, tunc autem facie ad faciem*, quam quidem visionem iam Angeli habent, unde quod nos credimus illi vident. Et similiter potest contingere ut id quod est visum vel scitum ab uno homine, etiam in statu viae, sit ab alio creditum, qui hoc demonstrative non novit.

Id tamen quod communiter omnibus hominibus proponitur ut credendum est communiter non scitum. Et ista sunt quae simpliciter fidei subsunt. Et ideo fides et scientia non sunt de eodem.

**AD PRIMUM** ergo dicendum quod infideles eorum quae sunt fidei ignorantiam habent, quia nec vident aut sciunt ea in seipsis, nec cognoscunt ea esse credibilia. Sed per hunc modum fideles habent eorum notitiam, non quasi demonstrative, sed inquantum per lumen fidei videntur esse credenda, ut dictum est.

we have to believe, since ignorance of such things savors of unbelief, according to 1 Tim. 1:13: *I did it ignorantly in unbelief.* Therefore things that are of faith can be an object of science.

**OBJ. 2**: Further, science is acquired by reasons. Now sacred writers employ reasons to inculcate things that are of faith. Therefore such things can be an object of science.

**OBJ. 3**: Further, things which are demonstrated are an object of science, since a *demonstration is a syllogism that produces science.* Now certain matters of faith have been demonstrated by the philosophers, such as the Existence and Unity of God, and so forth. Therefore things that are of faith can be an object of science.

**OBJ. 4**: Further, opinion is further from science than faith is, since faith is said to stand between opinion and science. Now *opinion and science can, in a way, be about the same object*, as stated in *Poster Analytics* (i). Therefore, faith and science can be about the same object also.

**ON THE CONTRARY**, Gregory says (*Hom. xxvi in Evang.*) that *when a thing is manifest, it is the object, not of faith, but of perception.* Therefore things that are of faith are not the object of perception, whereas what is an object of science is the object of perception. Therefore there can be no faith about things which are an object of science.

**I ANSWER THAT**, All science is derived from self-evident and therefore *seen* principles; wherefore all objects of science must needs be, in a fashion, seen.

Now as stated above (A. 4), it is impossible that one and the same thing should be believed and seen by the same person. Hence it is equally impossible for one and the same thing to be an object of science and of belief for the same person. It may happen, however, that a thing which is an object of vision or science for one, is believed by another: since we hope to see some day what we now believe about the Trinity, according to 1 Cor. 13:12: *We see now through a glass in a dark manner; but then face to face*: which vision the angels possess already; so that what we believe, they see. In like manner it may happen that what is an object of vision or scientific knowledge for one man, even in the state of a wayfarer, is, for another man, an object of faith, because he does not know it by demonstration.

Nevertheless that which is proposed to be believed equally by all, is equally unknown by all as an object of science: such are the things which are of faith simply. Consequently faith and science are not about the same things.

**REPLY OBJ. 1**: Unbelievers are in ignorance of things that are of faith, for neither do they see or know them in themselves, nor do they know them to be credible. The faithful, on the other hand, know them, not as by demonstration, but by the light of faith which makes them see that they ought to believe them, as stated above (A. 4, ad 2, 3).

**AD SECUNDUM** dicendum quod rationes quae inducuntur a sanctis ad probandum ea quae sunt fidei non sunt demonstrativae, sed persuasiones quaedam manifestantes non esse impossibile quod in fide proponitur. Vel procedunt ex principiis fidei, scilicet ex auctoritatibus sacrae Scripturae, sicut Dionysius dicit, II cap. de Div. Nom. Ex his autem principiis ita probatur aliquid apud fideles sicut etiam ex principiis naturaliter notis probatur aliquid apud omnes. Unde etiam theologia scientia est, ut in principio operis dictum est.

**AD TERTIUM** dicendum quod ea quae demonstrative probari possunt inter credenda numerantur, non quia de ipsis sit simpliciter fides apud omnes, sed quia praeexiguntur ad ea quae sunt fidei, et oportet ea saltem per fidem praesupponi ab his qui horum demonstrationem non habent.

**AD QUARTUM** dicendum quod, sicut Philosophus ibidem dicit, a diversis hominibus de eodem omnino potest haberi scientia et opinio, sicut et nunc dictum est de scientia et fide. Sed ab uno et eodem potest quidem haberi fides et scientia de eodem secundum quid, scilicet subiecto, sed non secundum idem, potest enim esse quod de una et eadem re aliquis aliquid sciat et aliquid aliud opinetur; et similiter de Deo potest aliquis demonstrative scire quod sit unus, et credere quod sit trinus. Sed de eodem secundum idem non potest esse simul in uno homine scientia nec cum opinione nec cum fide, alia tamen et alia ratione. Scientia enim cum opinione simul esse non potest simpliciter de eodem, quia de ratione scientiae est quod id quod scitur existimetur esse impossibile aliter se habere; de ratione autem opinionis est quod id quod quis existimat, existimet possibile aliter se habere. Sed id quod fide tenetur, propter fidei certitudinem, existimatur etiam impossibile aliter se habere, sed ea ratione non potest simul idem et secundum idem esse scitum et creditum, quia scitum est visum et creditum est non visum, ut dictum est.

**REPLY OBJ. 2**: The reasons employed by holy men to prove things that are of faith, are not demonstrations; they are either persuasive arguments showing that what is proposed to our faith is not impossible, or else they are proofs drawn from the principles of faith, i.e., from the authority of Holy Writ, as Dionysius declares (*Div. Nom.* ii). Whatever is based on these principles is as well proved in the eyes of the faithful, as a conclusion drawn from self-evident principles is in the eyes of all. Hence again, theology is a science, as we stated at the outset of this work (P. I, Q. 1, A. 2).

**REPLY OBJ. 3**: Things which can be proved by demonstration are reckoned among the articles of faith, not because they are believed simply by all, but because they are a necessary presupposition to matters of faith, so that those who do not know them by demonstration must know them first of all by faith.

**REPLY OBJ. 4**: As the Philosopher says (*Poster.* i), science and opinion about the same object can certainly be in different men, as we have stated above about science and faith; yet it is possible for one and the same man to have science and faith about the same thing relatively, i.e., in relation to the object, but not in the same respect. For it is possible for the same person, about one and the same object, to know one thing and to think another: and, in like manner, one may know by demonstration the unity of the Godhead, and, by faith, the Trinity. On the other hand, in one and the same man, about the same object, and in the same respect, science is incompatible with either opinion or faith, yet for different reasons. Because science is incompatible with opinion about the same object simply, for the reason that science demands that its object should be deemed impossible to be otherwise, whereas it is essential to opinion, that its object should be deemed possible to be otherwise. Yet that which is the object of faith, on account of the certainty of faith, is also deemed impossible to be otherwise; and the reason why science and faith cannot be about the same object and in the same respect is because the object of science is something seen whereas the object of faith is the unseen, as stated above.

# Article 6

*Whether those things that are of faith should be divided into certain articles?*

**AD SEXTUM SIC PROCEDITUR**. Videtur quod credibilia non sint per certos articulos distinguenda. Eorum enim omnium quae in sacra Scriptura continentur est fides habenda. Sed illa non possunt reduci ad aliquem certum numerum, propter sui multitudinem. Ergo superfluum videtur articulos fidei distinguere.

**PRAETEREA**, materialis distinctio, cum in infinitum fieri possit, est ab arte praetermittenda. Sed formalis

**OBJECTION 1**: It would seem that those things that are of faith should not be divided into certain articles. For all things contained in Holy Writ are matters of faith. But these, by reason of their multitude, cannot be reduced to a certain number. Therefore it seems superfluous to distinguish certain articles of faith.

**OBJ. 2**: Further, material differences can be multiplied indefinitely, and therefore art should take no notice of

ratio obiecti credibilis est una et indivisibilis, ut supra dictum est, scilicet veritas prima, et sic secundum rationem formalem credibilia distingui non possunt. Ergo praetermittenda est credibilium materialis distinctio per articulos.

**Praeterea**, sicut a quibusdam dicitur, *articulus est indivisibilis veritas de Deo arctans nos ad credendum.* Sed credere est voluntarium, quia, sicut Augustinus dicit, *nullus credit nisi volens.* Ergo videtur quod inconvenienter distinguantur credibilia per articulos.

**Sed contra** est quod Isidorus dicit, *articulus est perceptio divinae veritatis tendens in ipsam.* Sed perceptio divinae veritatis competit nobis secundum distinctionem quandam, quae enim in Deo unum sunt in nostro intellectu multiplicantur. Ergo credibilia debent per articulos distingui.

**Respondeo** dicendum quod nomen *articuli* ex Graeco videtur esse derivatum. *Arthron* enim in Graeco, quod in Latino *articulus* dicitur, significat quandam coaptationem aliquarum partium distinctarum. Et ideo particulae corporis sibi invicem coaptatae dicuntur membrorum articuli. Et similiter in grammatica apud Graecos dicuntur articuli quaedam partes orationis coaptatae aliis dictionibus ad exprimendum earum genus, numerum vel casum. Et similiter in rhetorica articuli dicuntur quaedam partium coaptationes, dicit enim Tullius, in IV Rhet., quod *articulus dicitur cum singula verba intervallis distinguuntur caesa oratione, hoc modo, acrimonia, voce, vultu adversarios perterruisti.*

Unde et credibilia fidei Christianae dicuntur per articulos distingui inquantum in quasdam partes dividuntur habentes aliquam coaptationem ad invicem. Est autem obiectum fidei aliquid non visum circa divina, ut supra dictum est. Et ideo ubi occurrit aliquid speciali ratione non visum, ibi est specialis articulus, ubi autem multa secundum eandem rationem sunt incognita, ibi non sunt articuli distinguendi. Sicut aliam difficultatem habet ad videndum quod Deus sit passus, et aliam quod mortuus resurrexerit, et ideo distinguitur articulus resurrectionis ab articulo passionis. Sed quod sit passus, mortuus et sepultus, unam et eandem difficultatem habent, ita quod, uno suscepto, non est difficile alia suscipere, et propter hoc omnia haec pertinent ad unum articulum.

**Ad primum** ergo dicendum quod aliqua sunt credibilia de quibus est fides secundum se; aliqua vero sunt credibilia de quibus non est fides secundum se, sed solum in ordine ad alia, sicut etiam in aliis scientiis quaedam proponuntur ut per se intenta, et quaedam ad manifestationem aliorum. Quia vero fides principaliter est de his quae videnda speramus in patria, secundum illud Heb. XI, *fides est substantia sperandarum rerum;* ideo per se ad fidem pertinent illa quae directe nos ordinant ad vitam aeternam, sicut sunt tres personae,

them. Now the formal aspect of the object of faith is one and indivisible, as stated above (A. 1), viz. the First Truth, so that matters of faith cannot be distinguished in respect of their formal object. Therefore no notice should be taken of a material division of matters of faith into articles.

**Obj. 3**: Further, it has been said by some that *an article is an indivisible truth concerning God, exacting our belief.* Now belief is a voluntary act, since, as Augustine says (*Tract. xxvi in Joan.*), *no man believes against his will.* Therefore it seems that matters of faith should not be divided into articles.

**On the contrary**, Isidore says: *An article is a glimpse of Divine truth, tending thereto.* Now we can only get a glimpse of Divine truth by way of analysis, since things which in God are one, are manifold in our intellect. Therefore matters of faith should be divided into articles.

**I answer that**, the word *article* is apparently derived from the Greek; for the Greek *arthron* which the Latin renders *articulus*, signifies a fitting together of distinct parts: wherefore the small parts of the body which fit together are called the articulations of the limbs. Likewise, in the Greek grammar, articles are parts of speech which are affixed to words to show their gender, number or case. Again in rhetoric, articles are parts that fit together in a sentence, for Tully says (*Rhet.* iv) that an article is composed of words each pronounced singly and separately, thus: *Your passion, your voice, your look, have struck terror into your foes.*

Hence matters of Christian faith are said to contain distinct articles, insofar as they are divided into parts, and fit together. Now the object of faith is something unseen in connection with God, as stated above (A. 4). Consequently any matter that, for a special reason, is unseen, is a special article; whereas when several matters are unknown under the same aspect, we are not to distinguish various articles. Thus one encounters one difficulty in seeing that God suffered, and another in seeing that He rose again from the dead, wherefore the article of the Resurrection is distinct from the article of the Passion. But that He suffered, died and was buried, present the same difficulty, so that if one be accepted, it is not difficult to accept the others; wherefore all these belong to one article.

**Reply Obj. 1**: Some things proposed to our belief are in themselves of faith, while others are of faith, not in themselves but only in relation to others: even as in sciences certain propositions are put forward on their own account, while others are put forward in order to manifest others. Now, since the chief object of faith consists in those things which we hope to see in the fatherland, according to Heb. 11:2: *Faith is the substance of things to be hoped for*, it follows that those things are in themselves of faith, which order us directly to eternal life. Such are the Trinity

omnipotentia Dei, mysterium incarnationis Christi, et alia huiusmodi. Et secundum ista distinguuntur articuli fidei. Quaedam vero proponuntur in sacra Scriptura ut credenda non quasi principaliter intenta, sed ad praedictorum manifestationem, sicut quod Abraham habuit duos filios, quod ad tactum ossium Elisaei suscitatus est mortuus, et alia huiusmodi, quae narrantur in sacra Scriptura in ordine ad manifestationem divinae maiestatis vel incarnationis Christi. Et secundum talia non oportet articulos distinguere.

**AD SECUNDUM** dicendum quod ratio formalis obiecti fidei potest accipi dupliciter. Uno modo, ex parte ipsius rei creditae. Et sic ratio formalis omnium credibilium est una, scilicet veritas prima. Et ex hac parte articuli non distinguuntur. Alio modo potest accipi formalis ratio credibilium ex parte nostra. Et sic ratio formalis credibilis est ut sit non visum. Et ex hac parte articuli fidei distinguuntur, ut visum est.

**AD TERTIUM** dicendum quod illa definitio datur de articulo magis secundum quandam etymologiam nominis prout habet derivationem Latinam, quam secundum eius veram significationem prout a Graeco derivatur. Unde non est magni ponderis. Potest tamen dici quod, licet ad credendum necessitate coactionis nullus arctetur, cum credere sit voluntarium; arctatur tamen necessitate finis, quia *accedentem ad Deum oportet credere, et sine fide impossibile est placere Deo*, ut apostolus dicit, Heb. XI.

of Persons, the omnipotence of God, the mystery of Christ's Incarnation, and the like: and these are distinct articles of faith. On the other hand certain things in Holy Writ are proposed to our belief, not chiefly on their own account, but for the manifestation of those mentioned above: for instance, that Abraham had two sons, that a dead man rose again at the touch of Eliseus' bones, and the like, which are related in Holy Writ for the purpose of manifesting the Divine majesty or the Incarnation of Christ: and such things should not form distinct articles.

**REPLY OBJ. 2**: The formal aspect of the object of faith can be taken in two ways: first, on the part of the thing believed, and thus there is one formal aspect of all matters of faith, viz. the First Truth: and from this point of view there is no distinction of articles. Second, the formal aspect of matters of faith, can be considered from our point of view; and thus the formal aspect of a matter of faith is that it is something unseen; and from this point of view there are various distinct articles of faith, as we saw above.

**REPLY OBJ. 3**: This definition of an article is taken from an etymology of the word as derived from the Latin, rather than in accordance with its real meaning, as derived from the Greek: hence it does not carry much weight. Yet even then it could be said that although faith is exacted of no man by a necessity of coercion, since belief is a voluntary act, yet it is exacted of him by a necessity of end, since *he that cometh to God must believe that He is*, and *without faith it is impossible to please God*, as the Apostle declares (Heb 11:6).

# Article 7

*Whether the articles of faith have increased in course of time?*

**AD SEPTIMUM SIC PROCEDITUR**. Videtur quod articuli fidei non creverint secundum temporum successionem. Quia, ut apostolus dicit, ad Heb. XI, *fides est substantia sperandarum rerum*. Sed omni tempore sunt eadem speranda. Ergo omni tempore sunt eadem credenda.

**PRAETEREA**, in scientiis humanitus ordinatis per successionem temporum augmentum factum est propter defectum cognitionis in primis qui scientias invenerunt, ut patet per philosophum, in II Metaphys. Sed doctrina fidei non est inventa humanitus, sed tradita a Deo. *Dei enim donum est*, ut dicitur Ephes. II. Cum igitur in Deum nullus defectus scientiae cadat, videtur quod a principio cognitio credibilium fuerit perfecta, et quod non creverit secundum successionem temporum.

**PRAETEREA**, operatio gratiae non minus ordinate procedit quam operatio naturae. Sed natura semper initium sumit a perfectis ut Boetius dicit, in libro de

**OBJECTION 1**: It would seem that the articles of faith have not increased in course of time. Because, as the Apostle says (Heb 11:1), *faith is the substance of things to be hoped for*. Now the same things are to be hoped for at all times. Therefore, at all times, the same things are to be believed.

**OBJ. 2**: Further, development has taken place, in sciences devised by man, on account of the lack of knowledge in those who discovered them, as the Philosopher observes (*Metaph.* ii). Now the doctrine of faith was not devised by man, but was delivered to us by God, as stated in Eph. 2:8: *It is the gift of God*. Since then there can be no lack of knowledge in God, it seems that knowledge of matters of faith was perfect from the beginning and did not increase as time went on.

**OBJ. 3**: Further, the operation of grace proceeds in orderly fashion no less than the operation of nature. Now nature always makes a beginning with perfect things, as

Consol. Ergo etiam videtur quod operatio gratiae a perfectis initium sumpserit, ita quod illi qui primo tradiderunt fidem perfectissime eam cognoverunt.

PRAETEREA, sicut per apostolos ad nos fides Christi pervenit, ita etiam in veteri testamento per priores patres ad posteriores devenit cognitio fidei, secundum illud Deut. XXXII, *interroga patrem tuum et annuntiabit tibi.* Sed apostoli plenissime fuerunt instructi de mysteriis, acceperunt enim, *sicut tempore prius, ita et ceteris abundantius,* ut dicit Glossa, super illud Rom. VIII, *nos ipsi primitias spiritus habentes.* Ergo videtur quod cognitio credibilium non creverit per temporum successionem.

SED CONTRA est quod Gregorius dicit, quod *secundum incrementa temporum crevit scientia sanctorum patrum, et quanto viciniores adventui salvatoris fuerunt, tanto sacramenta salutis plenius perceperunt.*

RESPONDEO dicendum quod ita se habent in doctrina fidei articuli fidei sicut principia per se nota in doctrina quae per rationem naturalem habetur. In quibus principiis ordo quidam invenitur, ut quaedam in aliis implicite contineantur, sicut omnia principia reducuntur ad hoc sicut ad primum, *impossibile est simul affirmare et negare,* ut patet per philosophum, in IV Metaphys. Et similiter omnes articuli implicite continentur in aliquibus primis credibilibus, scilicet ut credatur Deus esse et providentiam habere circa hominum salutem, secundum illud ad Heb. XI, *accedentem ad Deum oportet credere quia est, et quod inquirentibus se remunerator sit.* In esse enim divino includuntur omnia quae credimus in Deo aeternaliter existere, in quibus nostra beatitudo consistit, in fide autem providentiae includuntur omnia quae temporaliter a Deo dispensantur ad hominum salutem, quae sunt via in beatitudinem. Et per hunc etiam modum aliorum subsequentium articulorum quidam in aliis continentur, sicut in fide redemptionis humanae implicite continetur et incarnatio Christi et eius passio et omnia huiusmodi.

Sic igitur dicendum est quod, quantum ad substantiam articulorum fidei, non est factum eorum augmentum per temporum successionem, quia quaecumque posteriores crediderunt continebantur in fide praecedentium patrum, licet implicite. Sed quantum ad explicationem, crevit numerus articulorum, quia quaedam explicite cognita sunt a posterioribus quae a prioribus non cognoscebantur explicite. Unde Dominus Moysi dicit, Exod. VI, *ego sum Deus Abraham, Deus Isaac, Deus Iacob, et nomen meum Adonai non indicavi eis.* Et David dicit, *super senes intellexi.* Et apostolus dicit, ad Ephes. III, *aliis generationibus non est agnitum myste-*

Boethius states (*De Consol.* iii). Therefore it seems that the operation of grace also began with perfect things, so that those who were the first to deliver the faith, knew it most perfectly.

OBJ. 4: Further, just as the faith of Christ was delivered to us through the apostles, so too, in the Old Testament, the knowledge of faith was delivered by the early fathers to those who came later, according to Deut. 32:7: *Ask thy father, and he will declare to thee.* Now the apostles were most fully instructed about the mysteries, for *they received them more fully than others, even as they received them earlier,* as a gloss says on Rom. 8:23: *Ourselves also who have the first fruits of the Spirit.* Therefore it seems that knowledge of matters of faith has not increased as time went on.

ON THE CONTRARY, Gregory says (*Hom. xvi in Ezech.*) that *the knowledge of the holy fathers increased as time went on . . . and the nearer they were to Our Savior's coming, the more fully did they receive the mysteries of salvation.*

I ANSWER THAT, The articles of faith stand in the same relation to the doctrine of faith, as self-evident principles to a teaching based on natural reason. Among these principles there is a certain order, so that some are contained implicitly in others; thus all principles are reduced, as to their first principle, to this one: *The same thing cannot be affirmed and denied at the same time,* as the Philosopher states (*Metaph.* iv, text. 9). In like manner all the articles are contained implicitly in certain primary matters of faith, such as God's existence, and His providence over the salvation of man, according to Heb. 11: *He that cometh to God, must believe that He is, and is a rewarder to them that seek Him.* For the existence of God includes all that we believe to exist in God eternally, and in these our happiness consists; while belief in His providence includes all those things which God dispenses in time, for man's salvation, and which are the way to that happiness: and in this way, again, some of those articles which follow from these are contained in others: thus faith in the Redemption of mankind includes belief in the Incarnation of Christ, His Passion and so forth.

Accordingly we must conclude that, as regards the substance of the articles of faith, they have not received any increase as time went on: since whatever those who lived later have believed, was contained, albeit implicitly, in the faith of those Fathers who preceded them. But there was an increase in the number of articles believed explicitly, since to those who lived in later times some were known explicitly which were not known explicitly by those who lived before them. Hence the Lord said to Moses (Exod 6:2, 3): *I am the God of Abraham, the God of Isaac, the God of Jacob . . . and My name Adonai I did not show them:* David also said (Ps 118:100): *I have had understanding above ancients:*

*rium Christi sicut nunc revelatum est sanctis apostolis eius et prophetis.*

**AD PRIMUM** ergo dicendum quod semper fuerunt eadem speranda apud omnes. Quia tamen ad haec speranda homines non pervenerunt nisi per Christum, quanto a Christo fuerunt remotiores secundum tempus, tanto a consecutione sperandorum longinquiores, unde apostolus dicit, ad Heb. XI, *iuxta fidem defuncti sunt omnes isti, non acceptis repromissionibus, sed a longe eas respicientes.* Quanto autem aliquid a longinquioribus videtur, tanto minus distincte videtur. Et ideo bona speranda distinctius cognoverunt qui fuerunt adventui Christi vicini.

**AD SECUNDUM** dicendum quod profectus cognitionis dupliciter contingit. Uno modo, ex parte docentis, qui in cognitione proficit, sive unus sive plures, per temporum successionem. Et ista est ratio augmenti in scientiis per rationem humanam inventis. Alio modo, ex parte addiscentis, sicut magister qui novit totam artem non statim a principio tradit eam discipulo, quia capere non posset, sed paulatim, condescendens eius capacitati. Et hac ratione profecerunt homines in cognitione fidei per temporum successionem. Unde apostolus, ad Gal. III, comparat statum veteris testamenti pueritiae.

**AD TERTIUM** dicendum quod ad generationem naturalem duae causae praeexiguntur, scilicet agens et materia. Secundum igitur ordinem causae agentis, naturaliter prius est quod est perfectius, et sic natura a perfectis sumit exordium, quia imperfecta non ducuntur ad perfectionem nisi per aliqua perfecta praeexistentia. Secundum vero ordinem causae materialis, prius est quod est imperfectius, et secundum hoc natura procedit ab imperfecto ad perfectum. In manifestatione autem fidei Deus est sicut agens, qui habet perfectam scientiam ab aeterno, homo autem est sicut materia recipiens influxum Dei agentis. Et ideo oportuit quod ab imperfectis ad perfectum procederet cognitio fidei in hominibus. Et licet in hominibus quidam se habuerint per modum causae agentis, quia fuerunt fidei doctores; tamen *manifestatio spiritus datur talibus ad utilitatem communem,* ut dicitur I ad Cor. XII. Et ideo tantum dabatur patribus qui erant instructores fidei de cognitione fidei, quantum oportebat pro tempore illo populo tradi vel nude vel in figura.

**AD QUARTUM** dicendum quod ultima consummatio gratiae facta est per Christum, unde et tempus eius dicitur *tempus plenitudinis,* ad Gal. IV. Et ideo illi qui fuerunt propinquiores Christo vel ante, sicut Ioannes Baptista, vel post, sicut apostoli, plenius mysteria fidei cognoverunt. Quia et circa statum hominis hoc videmus, quod perfectio est in iuventute, et tanto habet homo per-

and the Apostle says (Eph 3:5) that the mystery of Christ, *in other generations was not known, as it is now revealed to His holy apostles and prophets.*

**REPLY OBJ. 1:** Among men the same things were always to be hoped for. But as they did not acquire this hope save through Christ, the further they were removed from Christ in point of time, the further they were from obtaining what they hoped for. Hence the Apostle says (Heb 11:13): *All these died according to faith, not having received the promises, but beholding them afar off.* Now the further off a thing is the less distinctly is it seen; wherefore those who were nigh to Christ's advent had a more distinct knowledge of the good things to be hoped for.

**REPLY OBJ. 2:** Progress in knowledge occurs in two ways. First, on the part of the teacher, be he one or many, who makes progress in knowledge as time goes on: and this is the kind of progress that takes place in sciences devised by man. Second, on the part of the learner; thus the master, who has perfect knowledge of the art, does not deliver it all at once to his disciple from the very outset, for he would not be able to take it all in, but he condescends to the disciple's capacity and instructs him little by little. It is in this way that men made progress in the knowledge of faith as time went on. Hence the Apostle (Gal 3:24) compares the state of the Old Testament to childhood.

**REPLY OBJ. 3:** Two causes are requisite before actual generation can take place, an agent, namely, and matter. In the order of the active cause, the more perfect is naturally first; and in this way nature makes a beginning with perfect things, since the imperfect is not brought to perfection, except by something perfect already in existence. On the other hand, in the order of the material cause, the imperfect comes first, and in this way nature proceeds from the imperfect to the perfect. Now in the manifestation of faith, God is the active cause, having perfect knowledge from all eternity; while man is likened to matter in receiving the influx of God's action. Hence, among men, the knowledge of faith had to proceed from imperfection to perfection; and, although some men have been after the manner of active causes, through being doctors of faith, nevertheless *the manifestation of the Spirit is given to such men for the common good,* according to 1 Cor. 12:7; so that the knowledge of faith was imparted to the Fathers who were instructors in the faith, so far as was necessary at the time for the instruction of the people, either openly or in figures.

**REPLY OBJ. 4:** The ultimate consummation of grace was effected by Christ, wherefore the time of His coming is called the *time of fullness* (Gal 4:4). Hence those who were nearest to Christ, whether before, like John the Baptist, or after, like the apostles, had a fuller knowledge of the mysteries of faith; for even with regard to man's state we find that the perfection of manhood comes in youth, and

fectiorem statum vel ante vel post, quanto est iuventuti propinquior.

that a man's state is all the more perfect, whether before or after, the nearer it is to the time of his youth.

# Article 8

*Whether the articles of faith are suitably formulated?*

AD OCTAVUM SIC PROCEDITUR. Videtur quod inconvenienter articuli fidei enumerentur. Ea enim quae possunt ratione demonstrativa sciri non pertinent ad fidem ut apud omnes sint credibilia, sicut supra dictum est. Sed Deum esse unum potest esse scitum per demonstrationem, unde et philosophus hoc in XII Metaphys. probat, et multi alii philosophi ad hoc demonstrationes induxerunt. Ergo Deum esse unum non debet poni unus articulus fidei.

PRAETEREA, sicut de necessitate fidei est quod credamus Deum omnipotentem, ita etiam quod credamus eum omnia scientem et omnibus providentem; et circa utrumque eorum aliqui erraverunt. Debuit ergo inter articulos fidei fieri mentio de sapientia et providentia divina, sicut et de omnipotentia.

PRAETEREA, eadem est notitia Patris et Filii, secundum illud Ioan. XIV, *qui videt me videt et patrem*. Ergo unus tantum articulus debet esse de Patre et Filio; et, eadem ratione, de Spiritu Sancto.

PRAETEREA, persona Patris non est minor quam Filii et Spiritus Sancti. Sed plures articuli ponuntur circa personam Spiritus Sancti, et similiter circa personam Filii. Ergo plures articuli debent poni circa personam Patris.

PRAETEREA, sicuti personae patris et personae spiritus sancti aliquid appropriatur, ita et personae filii secundum divinitatem. Sed in articulis ponitur aliquod opus appropriatum patri, scilicet opus creationis; et similiter aliquod opus appropriatum spiritui sancto, scilicet quod *locutus est per prophetas*. Ergo etiam inter articulos fidei debet aliquod opus appropriari filio secundum divinitatem.

PRAETEREA, sacramentum Eucharistiae specialem habet difficultatem prae multis articulis. Ergo de ea debuit poni specialis articulus. Non videtur ergo quod articuli sufficienter enumerentur.

SED IN CONTRARIUM est auctoritas Ecclesiae sic enumerantis.

RESPONDEO dicendum quod, sicut dictum est, illa per se pertinent ad fidem quorum visione in vita aeterna perfruemur, et per quae ducemur in vitam ae-

OBJECTION 1: It would seem that the articles of faith are unsuitably formulated. For those things, which can be known by demonstration, do not belong to faith as to an object of belief for all, as stated above (A. 5). Now it can be known by demonstration that there is one God; hence the Philosopher proves this (*Metaph.* xii, text. 52) and many other philosophers demonstrated the same truth. Therefore that *there is one God* should not be set down as an article of faith.

OBJ. 2: Further, just as it is necessary to faith that we should believe God to be almighty, so is it too that we should believe Him to be *all-knowing* and *provident for all*, about both of which points some have erred. Therefore, among the articles of faith, mention should have been made of God's wisdom and providence, even as of His omnipotence.

OBJ. 3: Further, to know the Father is the same thing as to know the Son, according to John 14:9: *He that seeth Me, seeth the Father also.* Therefore there ought to be but one article about the Father and Son, and, for the same reason, about the Holy Spirit.

OBJ. 4: Further, the Person of the Father is no less than the Person of the Son, and of the Holy Spirit. Now there are several articles about the Person of the Holy Spirit, and likewise about the Person of the Son. Therefore there should be several articles about the Person of the Father.

OBJ. 5: Further, just as certain things are said by appropriation, of the Person of the Father and of the Person of the Holy Spirit, so too is something appropriated to the Person of the Son, in respect of His Godhead. Now, among the articles of faith, a place is given to a work appropriated to the Father, viz. the creation, and likewise, a work appropriated to the Holy Spirit, viz. that *He spoke by the prophets.* Therefore the articles of faith should contain some work appropriated to the Son in respect of His Godhead.

OBJ. 6: Further, the sacrament of the Eucharist presents a special difficulty over and above the other articles. Therefore it should have been mentioned in a special article: and consequently it seems that there is not a sufficient number of articles.

ON THE CONTRARY stands the authority of the Church who formulates the articles thus.

I ANSWER THAT, As stated above (AA. 4, 6), to faith those things in themselves belong, the sight of which we shall enjoy in eternal life, and by which we are brought to

ternam. Duo autem nobis ibi videnda proponuntur, scilicet occultum divinitatis, cuius visio nos beatos facit; et mysterium humanitatis Christi, per quem *in gloriam filiorum Dei accessum habemus*, ut dicitur ad Rom. V. Unde dicitur Ioan. XVII, *haec est vita aeterna, ut cognoscant te, Deum verum, et quem misisti Iesum Christum.* Et ideo prima distinctio credibilium est quod quaedam pertinent ad maiestatem divinitatis; quaedam vero pertinent ad mysterium humanitatis Christi, quod est *pietatis sacramentum*, ut dicitur I ad Tim. III.

Circa maiestatem autem divinitatis tria nobis credenda proponuntur. Primo quidem, unitas divinitatis, et ad hoc pertinet primus articulus. Secundo, Trinitas personarum, et de hoc sunt tres articuli secundum tres personas. Tertio vero proponuntur nobis opera divinitatis propria. Quorum primum pertinet ad esse naturae, et sic proponitur nobis articulus creationis. Secundum vero pertinet ad esse gratiae, et sic proponuntur nobis sub uno articulo omnia pertinentia ad sanctificationem humanam. Tertium vero pertinet ad esse gloriae, et sic ponitur alius articulus de resurrectione carnis et de vita aeterna. Et ita sunt septem articuli ad divinitatem pertinentes.

Similiter etiam circa humanitatem Christi ponuntur septem articuli. Quorum primus est de incarnatione sive de conceptione Christi; secundus de nativitate eius ex virgine; tertius de passione eius et morte et sepultura; quartus est de descensu ad Inferos; quintus est de resurrectione; sextus de ascensione; septimus de adventu ad iudicium. Et sic in universo sunt quatuordecim.

Quidam tamen distinguunt duodecim articulos fidei, sex pertinentes ad divinitatem et sex pertinentes ad humanitatem. Tres enim articulos trium personarum comprehendunt sub uno, quia eadem est cognitio trium personarum. Articulum vero de opere glorificationis distinguunt in duos, scilicet in resurrectionem carnis et gloriam animae. Similiter articulum conceptionis et nativitatis coniungunt in unum.

**AD PRIMUM** ergo dicendum quod multa per fidem tenemus de Deo quae naturali ratione investigare philosophi non potuerunt, puta circa providentiam eius et omnipotentiam, et quod ipse solus sit colendus. Quae omnia continentur sub articulo unitatis Dei.

**AD SECUNDUM** dicendum quod ipsum nomen divinitatis importat provisionem quandam, ut in primo libro dictum est. Potentia autem in habentibus intellectum non operatur nisi secundum voluntatem et cognitionem. Et ideo omnipotentia Dei includit quodammodo omnium scientiam et providentiam, non enim posset omnia quae vellet in istis inferioribus agere nisi ea cognosceret et eorum providentiam haberet.

eternal life. Now two things are proposed to us to be seen in eternal life: viz. the secret of the Godhead, to see which is to possess happiness; and the mystery of the humanity of Christ, *by Whom we have access* to the glory of the sons of God, according to Rom. 5:2. Hence it is written (John 17:3): *This is eternal life: that they may know Thee, the . . . true God, and Jesus Christ Whom Thou hast sent.* Wherefore the first distinction in matters of faith is that some concern the majesty of the Godhead, while others pertain to the mystery of Christ's humanity, which is the *mystery of godliness* (1 Tim 3:16).

Now with regard to the majesty of the Godhead, three things are proposed to our belief: first, the unity of the Godhead, to which the first article refers; second, the trinity of the Persons, to which three articles refer, corresponding to the three Persons; and third, the works proper to the Godhead, the first of which refers to the order of nature, in relation to which the article about the creation is proposed to us; the second refers to the order of grace, in relation to which all matters concerning the sanctification of man are included in one article; while the third refers to the order of glory, and in relation to this another article is proposed to us concerning the resurrection of the dead and life everlasting. Thus there are seven articles referring to the Godhead.

In like manner, with regard to Christ's human nature, there are seven articles, the first of which refers to Christ's incarnation or conception; the second, to His virginal birth; the third, to His Passion, death and burial; the fourth, to His descent into hell; the fifth, to His resurrection; the sixth, to His ascension; the seventh, to His coming for the judgment, so that in all there are fourteen articles.

Some, however, distinguish twelve articles, six pertaining to the Godhead, and six to the humanity. For they include in one article the three about the three Persons; because we have one knowledge of the three Persons: while they divide the article referring to the work of glorification into two, viz. the resurrection of the body, and the glory of the soul. Likewise they unite the conception and nativity into one article.

**REPLY OBJ. 1:** By faith we hold many truths about God, which the philosophers were unable to discover by natural reason, for instance His providence and omnipotence, and that He alone is to be worshiped, all of which are contained in the one article of the unity of God.

**REPLY OBJ. 2:** The very name of the Godhead implies a kind of watching over things, as stated in the First Part (Q. 13, A. 8). Now in beings having an intellect, power does not work save by the will and knowledge. Hence God's omnipotence includes, in a way, universal knowledge and providence. For He would not be able to do all He wills in things here below, unless He knew them, and exercised His providence over them.

AD TERTIUM dicendum quod patris et filii et spiritus sancti est una cognitio quantum ad unitatem essentiae, quae pertinet ad primum articulum. Quantum vero ad distinctionem personarum, quae est per relationes originis, quodammodo in cognitione patris includitur cognitio filii, non enim esset pater si filium non haberet, quorum nexus est Spiritus Sanctus. Et quantum ad hoc bene moti sunt qui posuerunt unum articulum trium personarum. Sed quia circa singulas personas sunt aliqua attendenda circa quae contingit esse errorem, quantum ad hoc de tribus personis possunt poni tres articuli. Arius enim credidit patrem omnipotentem et aeternum, sed non credidit filium coaequalem et consubstantialem patri, et ideo necessarium fuit apponere articulum de persona filii ad hoc determinandum. Et eadem ratione contra Macedonium necesse fuit ponere articulum tertium de persona spiritus sancti. Et similiter etiam conceptio Christi et nativitas, et etiam resurrectio et vita aeterna, secundum unam rationem possunt comprehendi sub uno articulo, inquantum ad unum ordinantur, et secundum aliam rationem possunt distingui, inquantum seorsum habent speciales difficultates.

AD QUARTUM dicendum quod filio et spiritui sancto convenit mitti ad sanctificandam creaturam, circa quod plura credenda occurrunt. Et ideo circa personam filii et spiritus sancti plures articuli multiplicantur quam circa personam patris, qui nunquam mittitur, ut in primo dictum est.

AD QUINTUM dicendum quod sanctificatio creaturae per gratiam et consummatio per gloriam fit etiam per donum caritatis, quod appropriatur spiritui sancto, et per donum sapientiae, quod appropriatur filio. Et ideo utrumque opus pertinet et ad filium et ad spiritum sanctum per appropriationem secundum rationes diversas.

AD SEXTUM dicendum quod in sacramento Eucharistiae duo possunt considerari. Unum scilicet quod sacramentum est, et hoc habet eandem rationem cum aliis effectibus gratiae sanctificantis. Aliud est quod miraculose ibi corpus Christi continetur, et sic concluditur sub omnipotentia, sicut et omnia alia miracula, quae omnipotentiae attribuuntur.

REPLY OBJ. 3: We have but one knowledge of the Father, Son, and Holy Spirit, as to the unity of the Essence, to which the first article refers: but, as to the distinction of the Persons, which is by the relations of origin, knowledge of the Father does indeed, in a way, include knowledge of the Son, for He would not be Father, had He not a Son; the bond whereof being the Holy Spirit. From this point of view, there was a sufficient motive for those who referred one article to the three Persons. Since, however, with regard to each Person, certain points have to be observed, about which some happen to fall into error, looking at it in this way, we may distinguish three articles about the three Persons. For Arius believed in the omnipotence and eternity of the Father, but did not believe the Son to be coequal and consubstantial with the Father; hence the need for an article about the Person of the Son in order to settle this point. In like manner it was necessary to appoint a third article about the Person of the Holy Spirit, against Macedonius. In the same way Christ's conception and birth, just as the resurrection and life everlasting, can from one point of view be united together in one article, insofar as they are ordained to one end; while, from another point of view, they can be distinct articles, inasmuch as each one separately presents a special difficulty.

REPLY OBJ. 4: It belongs to the Son and Holy Spirit to be sent to sanctify the creature; and about this several things have to be believed. Hence it is that there are more articles about the Persons of the Son and Holy Spirit than about the Person of the Father, Who is never sent, as we stated in the First Part (Q. 43, A. 4).

REPLY OBJ. 5: The sanctification of a creature by grace, and its consummation by glory, is also effected by the gift of charity, which is appropriated to the Holy Spirit, and by the gift of wisdom, which is appropriated to the Son: so that each work belongs by appropriation, but under different aspects, both to the Son and to the Holy Spirit.

REPLY OBJ. 6: Two things may be considered in the sacrament of the Eucharist. One is the fact that it is a sacrament, and in this respect it is like the other effects of sanctifying grace. The other is that Christ's body is miraculously contained therein and thus it is included under God's omnipotence, like all other miracles which are ascribed to God's almighty power.

# Article 9

*Whether it is suitable for the articles of faith to be embodied in a symbol?*

AD NONUM SIC PROCEDITUR. Videtur quod inconvenienter articuli fidei in symbolo ponantur. Sacra enim Scriptura est regula fidei, cui nec addere nec subtrahere licet, dicitur enim Deut. IV, *non addetis ad verbum quod*

OBJECTION 1: It would seem that it is unsuitable for the articles of faith to be embodied in a symbol. Because Holy Writ is the rule of faith, to which no addition or subtraction can lawfully be made, since it is written (Deut 4:2): *You shall*

*vobis loquor, neque auferetis ab eo.* Ergo illicitum fuit aliquod symbolum constituere quasi regulam fidei, post sacram Scripturam editam.

**PRAETEREA,** sicut apostolus dicit, ad Ephes. IV, *una est fides.* Sed symbolum est professio fidei. Ergo inconvenienter traditur multiplex symbolum.

**PRAETEREA,** confessio fidei quae in symbolo continetur pertinet ad omnes fideles. Sed non omnibus fidelibus convenit credere *in Deum,* sed solum illis qui habent fidem formatam. Ergo inconvenienter symbolum fidei traditur sub hac forma verborum, *credo in unum Deum.*

**PRAETEREA,** descensus ad inferos est unus de articulis fidei, sicut supra dictum est. Sed in symbolo patrum non fit mentio de descensu ad inferos. Ergo videtur insufficienter collectum.

**PRAETEREA,** sicut Augustinus dicit, exponens illud Ioan. XIV, *creditis in Deum, et in me credite,* Petro aut Paulo credimus, sed non dicimur credere nisi *in Deum.* Cum igitur Ecclesia Catholica sit pure aliquid creatum, videtur quod inconvenienter dicatur, *in unam, sanctam, catholicam et apostolicam Ecclesiam.*

**PRAETEREA,** symbolum ad hoc traditur ut sit regula fidei. Sed regula fidei debet omnibus proponi et publice. Quodlibet igitur symbolum deberet in Missa cantari, sicut symbolum patrum. Non videtur ergo esse conveniens editio articulorum fidei in symbolo.

**SED CONTRA** est quod Ecclesia universalis non potest errare, quia spiritu sancto gubernatur, qui est spiritus veritatis, hoc enim promisit dominus discipulis, Ioan. XVI, dicens, *cum venerit ille spiritus veritatis, docebit vos omnem veritatem.* Sed symbolum est auctoritate universalis Ecclesiae editum. Nihil ergo inconveniens in eo continetur.

**RESPONDEO** dicendum quod, sicut apostolus dicit, ad Heb. XI, *accedentem ad Deum oportet credere.* Credere autem non potest aliquis nisi ei veritas quam credat proponatur. Et ideo necessarium fuit veritatem fidei in unum colligi, ut facilius posset omnibus proponi, ne aliquis per ignorantiam a fidei veritate deficeret. Et ab huiusmodi collectione sententiarum fidei nomen symboli est acceptum.

**AD PRIMUM** ergo dicendum quod veritas fidei in sacra Scriptura diffuse continetur et variis modis, et in quibusdam obscure; ita quod ad eliciendum fidei veritatem ex sacra Scriptura requiritur longum studium et exercitium, ad quod non possunt pervenire omnes illi quibus necessarium est cognoscere fidei veritatem, quorum plerique, aliis negotiis occupati, studio vacare non possunt. Et ideo fuit necessarium ut ex sententiis

*not add to the word that I speak to you, neither shall you take away from it.* Therefore it was unlawful to make a symbol as a rule of faith, after the Holy Writ had once been published.

**OBJ. 2**: Further, according to the Apostle (*Eph 4:5*) there is but *one faith.* Now the symbol is a profession of faith. Therefore it is not fitting that there should be more than one symbol.

**OBJ. 3**: Further, the confession of faith, which is contained in the symbol, concerns all the faithful. Now the faithful are not all competent to believe *in God,* but only those who have living faith. Therefore it is unfitting for the symbol of faith to be expressed in the words: *I believe in one God.*

**OBJ. 4**: Further, the descent into hell is one of the articles of faith, as stated above (A. 8). But the descent into hell is not mentioned in the symbol of the Fathers. Therefore the latter is expressed inadequately.

**OBJ. 5**: Further, Augustine (*Tract. xxix in Joan.*) expounding the passage, *You believe in God, believe also in Me* (John 14:1) says: We believe *Peter* or *Paul,* but we speak only of believing '*in*' God. Since then the Catholic Church is merely a created being, it seems unfitting to say: *in the one, holy, catholic, and apostolic Church.*

**OBJ. 6**: Further, a symbol is drawn up that it may be a rule of faith. Now a rule of faith ought to be proposed to all, and that publicly. Therefore every symbol, besides the symbol of the Fathers, should be sung at Mass. Therefore it seems unfitting to publish the articles of faith in a symbol.

**ON THE CONTRARY,** The universal Church cannot err, since she is governed by the Holy Spirit, Who is the Spirit of truth: for such was Our Lord's promise to His disciples (John 16:13): *When He, the Spirit of truth, is come, He will teach you all truth.* Now the symbol is published by the authority of the universal Church. Therefore it contains nothing defective.

**I ANSWER THAT,** As the Apostle says (Heb 11:6), *he that cometh to God, must believe that He is.* Now a man cannot believe, unless the truth be proposed to him that he may believe it. Hence the need for the truth of faith to be collected together, so that it might the more easily be proposed to all, lest anyone might stray from the truth through ignorance of the faith. It is from its being a collection of maxims of faith that the symbol takes its name.

**REPLY OBJ. 1**: The truth of faith is contained in Holy Writ, diffusely, under various modes of expression, and sometimes obscurely, so that, in order to gather the truth of faith from Holy Writ, one needs long study and practice, which are unattainable by all those who require to know the truth of faith, many of whom have no time for study, being busy with other affairs. And so it was necessary to gather together a clear summary from the sayings of Holy Writ, to

sacrae Scripturae aliquid manifestum summarie colligeretur quod proponeretur omnibus ad credendum. Quod quidem non est additum sacrae Scripturae, sed potius ex sacra Scriptura assumptum.

**AD SECUNDUM** dicendum quod in omnibus symbolis eadem fidei veritas docetur. Sed ibi oportet populum diligentius instrui de fidei veritate ubi errores insurgunt, ne fides simplicium per haereticos corrumpatur. Et haec fuit causa quare necesse fuit edere plura symbola. Quae in nullo alio differunt nisi quod in uno plenius explicantur quae in alio continentur implicite, secundum quod exigebat haereticorum instantia.

**AD TERTIUM** dicendum quod confessio fidei traditur in symbolo quasi ex persona totius Ecclesiae, quae per fidem unitur. Fides autem Ecclesiae est fides formata, talis enim fides invenitur in omnibus illis qui sunt numero et merito de Ecclesia. Et ideo confessio fidei in symbolo traditur secundum quod convenit fidei formatae, ut etiam si qui fideles fidem formatam non habent, ad hanc formam pertingere studeant.

**AD QUARTUM** dicendum quod de descensu ad inferos nullus error erat exortus apud haereticos, et ideo non fuit necessarium aliquam explicationem circa hoc fieri. Et propter hoc non reiteratur in symbolo patrum, sed supponitur tanquam praedeterminatum in symbolo apostolorum. Non enim symbolum sequens abolet praecedens, sed potius illud exponit, ut dictum est.

**AD QUINTUM** dicendum quod, si dicatur *in sanctam Ecclesiam Catholicam*, est hoc intelligendum secundum quod fides nostra refertur ad spiritum sanctum, qui sanctificat Ecclesiam, ut sit sensus, *credo in spiritum sanctum sanctificantem Ecclesiam.* Sed melius est et secundum communiorem usum, ut non ponatur ibi in, sed simpliciter dicatur *sanctam Ecclesiam Catholicam*, sicut etiam Leo Papa dicit.

**AD SEXTUM** dicendum quod, quia symbolum patrum est declarativum symboli apostolorum, et etiam fuit conditum fide iam manifestata et Ecclesia pacem habente, propter hoc publice in Missa cantatur. Symbolum autem apostolorum, quod tempore persecutionis editum fuit, fide nondum publicata, occulte dicitur in prima et in completorio, quasi contra tenebras errorum praeteritorum et futurorum.

be proposed to the belief of all. This indeed was no addition to Holy Writ, but something taken from it.

**REPLY OBJ. 2**: The same doctrine of faith is taught in all the symbols. Nevertheless, the people need more careful instruction about the truth of faith, when errors arise, lest the faith of simple-minded persons be corrupted by heretics. It was this that gave rise to the necessity of formulating several symbols, which nowise differ from one another, save that on account of the obstinacy of heretics, one contains more explicitly what another contains implicitly.

**REPLY OBJ. 3**: The confession of faith is drawn up in a symbol as if from the person of the whole Church, which is united together by faith. Now the faith of the Church is living faith; since such is the faith to be found in all those who are of the Church not only outwardly but also by merit. Hence the confession of faith is expressed in a symbol, in a manner that is in keeping with living faith, so that even if some of the faithful lack living faith, they should endeavor to acquire it.

**REPLY OBJ. 4**: No error about the descent into hell had arisen among heretics, so that there was no need to be more explicit on that point. For this reason it is not repeated in the symbol of the Fathers, but is supposed as already settled in the symbol of the Apostles. For a subsequent symbol does not cancel a preceding one; rather does it expound it, as stated above (ad 2).

**REPLY OBJ. 5**: If we say: *'in'* the holy Catholic Church, this must be taken as verified insofar as our faith is directed to the Holy Spirit, Who sanctifies the Church; so that the sense is: I believe in the Holy Spirit sanctifying the Church. But it is better and more in keeping with the common use, to omit the 'in,' and say simply, *the holy Catholic Church*, as Pope Leo observes.

**REPLY OBJ. 6**: Since the symbol of the Fathers is an explanation of the symbol of the Apostles, and was drawn up after the faith was already spread abroad, and when the Church was already at peace, it is sung publicly in the Mass. On the other hand the symbol of the Apostles, which was drawn up at the time of persecution, before the faith was made public, is said secretly at Prime and Compline, as though it were against the darkness of past and future errors.

# Article 10

*Whether it belongs to the sovereign pontiff to draw up a symbol of faith?*

**AD DECIMUM SIC PROCEDITUR**. Videtur quod non pertineat ad summum pontificem fidei symbolum ordinare. Nova enim editio symboli necessaria est propter

**OBJECTION 1**: It would seem that it does not belong to the Sovereign Pontiff to draw up a symbol of faith. For a new edition of the symbol becomes necessary in order to

explicationem articulorum fidei, sicut dictum est. Sed in veteri testamento articuli fidei magis ac magis explicabantur secundum temporum successionem propter hoc quod veritas fidei magis manifestabatur secundum maiorem propinquitatem ad Christum, ut supra dictum est. Cessante ergo tali causa in nova lege, non debet fieri maior ac maior explicatio articulorum fidei. Ergo non videtur ad auctoritatem summi pontificis pertinere nova symboli editio.

**PRAETEREA**, illud quod est sub anathemate interdictum ab universali Ecclesia non subest potestati alicuius hominis. Sed nova symboli editio interdicta est sub anathemate auctoritate universalis Ecclesiae. Dicitur enim in gestis primae Ephesinae synodi quod, *perlecto symbolo Nicaenae synodi, decrevit sancta synodus aliam fidem nulli licere proferre vel conscribere vel componere praeter definitam a sanctis patribus qui in Nicaea congregati sunt cum spiritu sancto,* et subditur anathematis poena; et idem etiam reiteratur in gestis Chalcedonensis synodi. Ergo videtur quod non pertineat ad auctoritatem summi pontificis nova editio symboli.

**PRAETEREA**, Athanasius non fuit summus pontifex, sed Alexandrinus patriarcha. Et tamen symbolum constituit quod in Ecclesia cantatur. Ergo non magis videtur pertinere editio symboli ad summum pontificem quam ad alios.

**SED CONTRA** est quod editio symboli facta est in synodo generali. Sed huiusmodi synodus auctoritate solius summi pontificis potest congregari, ut habetur in decretis, dist. XVII. Ergo editio symboli ad auctoritatem summi pontificis pertinet.

**RESPONDEO** dicendum quod, sicut supra dictum est, nova editio symboli necessaria est ad vitandum insurgentes errores. Ad illius ergo auctoritatem pertinet editio symboli ad cuius auctoritatem pertinet sententialiter determinare ea quae sunt fidei, ut ab omnibus inconcussa fide teneantur. Hoc autem pertinet ad auctoritatem summi pontificis, *ad quem maiores et difficiliores Ecclesiae quaestiones referuntur* ut dicitur in decretis, dist. XVII. Unde et dominus, Luc. XXII, Petro dixit, quem summum pontificem constituit, *ego pro te rogavi, Petre, ut non deficiat fides tua, et tu aliquando conversus confirma fratres tuos.* Et huius ratio est quia una fides debet esse totius Ecclesiae, secundum illud I ad Cor. I, *idipsum dicatis omnes, et non sint in vobis schismata.* Quod servari non posset nisi quaestio fidei de fide exorta determinaretur per eum qui toti Ecclesiae praeest, ut sic eius sententia a tota Ecclesia firmiter teneatur. Et ideo ad solam auctoritatem summi pontificis pertinet nova editio symboli, sicut et omnia alia quae pertinent ad totam Ecclesiam, ut congregare synodum generalem et alia huiusmodi.

explain the articles of faith, as stated above (A. 9). Now, in the Old Testament, the articles of faith were more and more explained as time went on, by reason of the truth of faith becoming clearer through greater nearness to Christ, as stated above (A. 7). Since then this reason ceased with the advent of the New Law, there is no need for the articles of faith to be more and more explicit. Therefore it does not seem to belong to the authority of the Sovereign Pontiff to draw up a new edition of the symbol.

**OBJ. 2**: Further, no man has the power to do what is forbidden under pain of anathema by the universal Church. Now it was forbidden under pain of anathema by the universal Church, to make a new edition of the symbol. For it is stated in the acts of the first council of Ephesus (P. ii, Act. 6) that *after the symbol of the Nicene council had been read through, the holy synod decreed that it was unlawful to utter, write or draw up any other creed, than that which was defined by the Fathers assembled at Nicaea together with the Holy Spirit,* and this under pain of anathema. The same was repeated in the acts of the council of Chalcedon (P. ii, Act. 5). Therefore it seems that the Sovereign Pontiff has no authority to publish a new edition of the symbol.

**OBJ. 3**: Further, Athanasius was not the Sovereign Pontiff, but patriarch of Alexandria, and yet he published a symbol which is sung in the Church. Therefore it does not seem to belong to the Sovereign Pontiff any more than to other bishops, to publish a new edition of the symbol.

**ON THE CONTRARY**, The symbol was drawn up by a general council. Now such a council cannot be convoked otherwise than by the authority of the Sovereign Pontiff, as stated in the Decretals. Therefore it belongs to the authority of the Sovereign Pontiff to draw up a symbol.

**I ANSWER THAT**, As stated above (Obj. 1), a new edition of the symbol becomes necessary in order to set aside the errors that may arise. Consequently to publish a new edition of the symbol belongs to that authority which is empowered to decide matters of faith finally, so that they may be held by all with unshaken faith. Now this belongs to the authority of the Sovereign Pontiff, *to whom the more important and more difficult questions that arise in the Church are referred,* as stated in the Decretals. Hence our Lord said to Peter whom he made Sovereign Pontiff (Luke 22:32): *I have prayed for thee, Peter, that thy faith fail not, and thou, being once converted, confirm thy brethren.* The reason of this is that there should be but one faith of the whole Church, according to 1 Cor. 1:10: *That you all speak the same thing, and that there be no schisms among you*: and this could not be secured unless any question of faith that may arise be decided by him who presides over the whole Church, so that the whole Church may hold firmly to his decision. Consequently it belongs to the sole authority of the Sovereign Pontiff to publish a new edition of the symbol, as do all other matters which concern the whole Church, such as to convoke a general council and so forth.

**AD PRIMUM** ergo dicendum quod in doctrina Christi et apostolorum veritas fidei est sufficienter explicata. Sed quia perversi homines apostolicam doctrinam et ceteras Scripturas *pervertunt ad sui ipsorum perditionem*, sicut dicitur II Pet. ult.; ideo necessaria est, temporibus procedentibus, explanatio fidei contra insurgentes errores.

**AD SECUNDUM** dicendum quod prohibitio et sententia synodi se extendit ad privatas personas, quarum non est determinare de fide. Non enim per huiusmodi sententiam synodi generalis ablata est potestas sequenti synodo novam editionem symboli facere, non quidem aliam fidem continentem, sed eandem magis expositam. Sic enim quaelibet synodus observavit, ut sequens synodus aliquid exponeret supra id quod praecedens synodus exposuerat, propter necessitatem alicuius haeresis insurgentis. Unde pertinet ad summum pontificem, cuius auctoritate synodus congregatur et eius sententia confirmatur.

**AD TERTIUM** dicendum quod Athanasius non composuit manifestationem fidei per modum symboli, sed magis per modum cuiusdam doctrinae, ut ex ipso modo loquendi apparet. Sed quia integram fidei veritatem eius doctrina breviter continebat, auctoritate summi pontificis est recepta, ut quasi regula fidei habeatur.

**REPLY OBJ. 1**: The truth of faith is sufficiently explicit in the teaching of Christ and the apostles. But since, according to 2 Pet. 3:16, some men are so evil-minded as *to pervert* the apostolic teaching and other doctrines and Scriptures *to their own destruction*, it was necessary as time went on to express the faith more explicitly against the errors which arose.

**REPLY OBJ. 2**: This prohibition and sentence of the council was intended for private individuals, who have no business to decide matters of faith: for this decision of the general council did not take away from a subsequent council the power of drawing up a new edition of the symbol, containing not indeed a new faith, but the same faith with greater explicitness. For every council has taken into account that a subsequent council would expound matters more fully than the preceding council, if this became necessary through some heresy arising. Consequently this belongs to the Sovereign Pontiff, by whose authority the council is convoked, and its decision confirmed.

**REPLY OBJ. 3**: Athanasius drew up a declaration of faith, not under the form of a symbol, but rather by way of an exposition of doctrine, as appears from his way of speaking. But since it contained briefly the whole truth of faith, it was accepted by the authority of the Sovereign Pontiff, so as to be considered as a rule of faith.

# QUESTION 2

## THE ACT OF FAITH

Deinde considerandum est de actu fidei. Et primo, de actu interiori; secundo, de actu exteriori.

Circa primum quaeruntur decem.

Primo, quid sit credere, quod est actus interior fidei.

Secundo, quot modis dicatur.

Tertio, utrum credere aliquid supra rationem naturalem sit necessarium ad salutem.

Quarto, utrum credere ea ad quae ratio naturalis pervenire potest sit necessarium.

Quinto, utrum sit necessarium ad salutem credere aliqua explicite.

Sexto, utrum ad credendum explicite omnes aequaliter teneantur.

Septimo, utrum habere explicitam fidem de Christo semper sit necessarium ad salutem.

Octavo, utrum credere Trinitatem explicite sit de necessitate salutis.

Nono, utrum actus fidei sit meritorius.

Decimo, utrum ratio humana diminuat meritum fidei.

We must now consider the act of faith, and (1) the internal act; (2) the external act.

Under the first head there are ten points of inquiry:

(1) What is *to believe*, which is the internal act of faith?

(2) In how many ways is it expressed?

(3) Whether it is necessary for salvation to believe in anything above natural reason?

(4) Whether it is necessary to believe those things that are attainable by natural reason?

(5) Whether it is necessary for salvation to believe certain things explicitly?

(6) Whether all are equally bound to explicit faith?

(7) Whether explicit faith in Christ is always necessary for salvation?

(8) Whether it is necessary for salvation to believe in the Trinity explicitly?

(9) Whether the act of faith is meritorious?

(10) Whether human reason diminishes the merit of faith?

# Article 1

### *Whether to believe is to think with assent?*

**Ad primum sic proceditur.** Videtur quod credere non sit *cum assensione cogitare*. Cogitatio enim importat quandam inquisitionem, dicitur enim cogitare quasi *simul agitare*. Sed Damascenus dicit, in IV Lib., quod *fides est non inquisitus consensus.* Ergo cogitare non pertinet ad actum fidei.

**Praeterea,** fides in ratione ponitur, ut infra dicetur. Sed cogitare est actus cogitativae potentiae, quae pertinet ad partem sensitivam, ut in primo dictum est. Ergo cogitatio ad fidem non pertinet.

**Praeterea,** credere est actus intellectus, quia eius obiectum est verum. Sed assentire non videtur esse actus intellectus, sed voluntatis, sicut et consentire, ut supra dictum est. Ergo credere non est cum assensione cogitare.

**In contrarium** est quod Augustinus sic definit credere in libro de Praed. Sanct.

**Respondeo** dicendum quod cogitare tripliciter sumi potest. Uno modo, communiter pro qualibet actuali consideratione intellectus, sicut Augustinus dicit, in XIV

**Objection 1**: It would seem that to believe is not to think with assent. Because the Latin word *cogitatio* implies a research, for *cogitare* seems to be equivalent to *coagitare*, i.e., *to discuss together.* Now Damascene says (*De Fide Orth.* iv) that faith is *an assent without research.* Therefore thinking has no place in the act of faith.

**Obj. 2**: Further, faith resides in the reason, as we shall show further on (Q. 4, A. 2). Now to cogitate is an act of the cogitative power, which belongs to the sensitive faculty, as stated in the First Part (Q. 78, A. 4). Therefore thought has nothing to do with faith.

**Obj. 3**: Further, to believe is an act of the intellect, since its object is truth. But assent seems to be an act not of the intellect, but of the will, even as consent is, as stated above (I-II, Q. 15, A. 1, ad 3). Therefore to believe is not to think with assent.

**On the contrary,** This is how *to believe* is defined by Augustine (*De Praedest. Sanct.* ii).

**I answer that,** *To think* can be taken in three ways. First, in a general way for any kind of actual consideration of the intellect, as Augustine observes (*De Trin.* xiv,

23

de Trin., *hanc nunc dico intelligentiam qua intelligimus cogitantes.* Alio modo dicitur cogitare magis proprie consideratio intellectus quae est cum quadam inquisitione, antequam perveniatur ad perfectionem intellectus per certitudinem visionis. Et secundum hoc Augustinus, XV de Trin., dicit quod *Dei filius non cogitatio dicitur, sed verbum Dei dicitur. Cogitatio quippe nostra proveniens ad id quod scimus atque inde formata verbum nostrum verum est. Et ideo verbum Dei sine cogitatione debet intelligi, non aliquid habens formabile, quod possit esse informe.* Et secundum hoc cogitatio proprie dicitur motus animi deliberantis nondum perfecti per plenam visionem veritatis. Sed quia talis motus potest esse vel animi deliberantis circa intentiones universales, quod pertinet ad intellectivam partem; vel circa intentiones particulares, quod pertinet ad partem sensitivam, ideo cogitare secundo modo sumitur pro actu intellectus deliberantis; tertio modo, pro actu virtutis cogitativae.

Si igitur cogitare sumatur communiter, secundum primum modum, sic hoc quod dicitur *cum assensione cogitare* non dicit totam rationem eius quod est credere, nam per hunc modum etiam qui considerat ea quae scit vel intelligit cum assensione cogitat. Si vero sumatur cogitare secundo modo, sic in hoc intelligitur tota ratio huius actus qui est credere. Actuum enim ad intellectum pertinentium quidam habent firmam assensionem absque tali cogitatione, sicut cum aliquis considerat ea quae scit vel intelligit, talis enim consideratio iam est formata. Quidam vero actus intellectus habent quidem cogitationem informem absque firma assensione, sive in neutram partem declinent, sicut accidit dubitanti; sive in unam partem magis declinent sed tenentur aliquo levi signo, sicut accidit suspicanti; sive uni parti adhaereant, tamen cum formidine alterius, quod accidit opinanti. Sed actus iste qui est credere habet firmam adhaesionem ad unam partem, in quo convenit credens cum sciente et intelligente, et tamen eius cognitio non est perfecta per manifestam visionem, in quo convenit cum dubitante, suspicante et opinante. Et sic proprium est credentis ut cum assensu cogitet, et per hoc distinguitur iste actus qui est credere ab omnibus actibus intellectus qui sunt circa verum vel falsum.

**AD PRIMUM** ergo dicendum quod fides non habet inquisitionem rationis naturalis demonstrantis id quod creditur. Habet tamen inquisitionem quandam eorum per quae inducitur homo ad credendum, puta quia sunt dicta a Deo et miraculis confirmata.

**AD SECUNDUM** dicendum quod cogitare non sumitur hic prout est actus cogitativae virtutis, sed prout pertinet ad intellectum, ut dictum est.

**AD TERTIUM** dicendum quod intellectus credentis determinatur ad unum non per rationem, sed per volun-

7): *By understanding I mean now the faculty whereby we understand when thinking.* Second, *to think* is more strictly taken for that consideration of the intellect, which is accompanied by some kind of inquiry, and which precedes the intellect's arrival at the stage of perfection that comes with the certitude of sight. In this sense Augustine says (*De Trin.* xv, 16) that *the Son of God is not called the Thought, but the Word of God. When our thought realizes what we know and takes form therefrom, it becomes our word. Hence the Word of God must be understood without any thinking on the part of God, for there is nothing there that can take form, or be unformed.* In this way thought is, properly speaking, the movement of the mind while yet deliberating, and not yet perfected by the clear sight of truth. Since, however, such a movement of the mind may be one of deliberation either about universal notions, which belongs to the intellectual faculty, or about particular matters, which belongs to the sensitive part, hence it is that *to think* is taken second for an act of the deliberating intellect, and third for an act of the cognitive power.

Accordingly, if *to think* be understood broadly according to the first sense, then *to think with assent*, does not express completely what is meant by *to believe*: since, in this way, a man thinks with assent even when he considers what he knows by science, or understands. If, on the other hand, *to think* be understood in the second way, then this expresses completely the nature of the act of believing. For among the acts belonging to the intellect, some have a firm assent without any such kind of thinking, as when a man considers the things that he knows by science, or understands, for this consideration is already formed. But some acts of the intellect have unformed thought devoid of a firm assent, whether they incline to neither side, as in one who *doubts*; or incline to one side rather than the other, but on account of some slight motive, as in one who *suspects*; or incline to one side yet with fear of the other, as in one who *opines*. But this act *to believe*, cleaves firmly to one side, in which respect belief has something in common with science and understanding; yet its knowledge does not attain the perfection of clear sight, wherein it agrees with doubt, suspicion and opinion. Hence it is proper to the believer to think with assent: so that the act of believing is distinguished from all the other acts of the intellect, which are about the true or the false.

**REPLY OBJ. 1:** Faith has not that research of natural reason which demonstrates what is believed, but a research into those things whereby a man is induced to believe, for instance that such things have been uttered by God and confirmed by miracles.

**REPLY OBJ. 2:** *To think* is not taken here for the act of the cognitive power, but for an act of the intellect, as explained above.

**REPLY OBJ. 3:** The intellect of the believer is determined to one object, not by the reason, but by the will,

tatem. Et ideo assensus hic accipitur pro actu intellectus secundum quod a voluntate determinatur ad unum.

wherefore assent is taken here for an act of the intellect as determined to one object by the will.

# Article 2

*Whether the act of faith is suitably distinguished as believing God, believing in a God, and believing in God?*

**AD SECUNDUM SIC PROCEDITUR.** Videtur quod inconvenienter distinguatur actus fidei per hoc quod est *credere Deo, credere Deum et credere in Deum.* Unius enim habitus unus est actus. Sed fides est unus habitus, cum sit una virtus. Ergo inconvenienter ponuntur plures actus eius.

**PRAETEREA**, illud quod est commune omni actui fidei non debet poni ut particularis actus fidei. Sed credere Deo invenitur communiter in quolibet actu fidei, quia fides innititur primae veritati. Ergo videtur quod inconvenienter distinguatur a quibusdam aliis actibus fidei.

**PRAETEREA**, illud quod convenit etiam non fidelibus non potest poni fidei actus. Sed credere Deum esse convenit etiam infidelibus. Ergo non debet poni inter actus fidei.

**PRAETEREA**, moveri in finem pertinet ad voluntatem, cuius obiectum est bonum et finis. Sed credere non est actus voluntatis, sed intellectus. Ergo non debet poni differentia una eius quod est credere *in Deum*, quod importat motum in finem.

**SED CONTRA** est quod Augustinus hanc distinctionem ponit, in libris de Verb. Dom., et super Ioan.

**RESPONDEO** dicendum quod actus cuiuslibet potentiae vel habitus accipitur secundum ordinem potentiae vel habitus ad suum obiectum. Obiectum autem fidei potest tripliciter considerari. Cum enim credere ad intellectum pertineat prout est a voluntate motus ad assentiendum, ut dictum est, potest obiectum fidei accipi vel ex parte ipsius intellectus, vel ex parte voluntatis intellectum moventis.

Si quidem ex parte intellectus, sic in obiecto fidei duo possunt considerari, sicut supra dictum est. Quorum unum est materiale obiectum fidei. Et sic ponitur actus fidei *credere Deum*, quia, sicut supra dictum est, nihil proponitur nobis ad credendum nisi secundum quod ad Deum pertinet. Aliud autem est formalis ratio obiecti, quod est sicut medium propter quod tali credibili assentitur. Et sic ponitur actus fidei *credere Deo*, quia, sicut supra dictum est, formale obiectum fidei est veritas prima, cui inhaeret homo ut propter eam creditis assentiat.

**OBJECTION 1**: It would seem that the act of faith is unsuitably distinguished as *believing God, believing in a God, and believing in God*. For one habit has but one act. Now faith is one habit since it is one virtue. Therefore it is unreasonable to say that there are three acts of faith.

**OBJ. 2**: Further, that which is common to all acts of faith should not be reckoned as a particular kind of act of faith. Now *to believe God* is common to all acts of faith, since faith is founded on the First Truth. Therefore it seems unreasonable to distinguish it from certain other acts of faith.

**OBJ. 3**: Further, that which can be said of unbelievers, cannot be called an act of faith. Now unbelievers can be said to believe in a God. Therefore it should not be reckoned an act of faith.

**OBJ. 4**: Further, movement towards the end belongs to the will, whose object is the good and the end. Now to believe is an act, not of the will, but of the intellect. Therefore *to believe in God*, which implies movement towards an end, should not be reckoned as a species of that act.

**ON THE CONTRARY** is the authority of Augustine who makes this distinction (*De Verb. Dom.*, Serm. lxi; *Tract. xxix in Joan.*).

**I ANSWER THAT**, The act of any power or habit depends on the relation of that power or habit to its object. Now the object of faith can be considered in three ways. For, since *to believe* is an act of the intellect, insofar as the will moves it to assent, as stated above (A. 1, ad 3), the object of faith can be considered either on the part of the intellect, or on the part of the will that moves the intellect.

If it be considered on the part of the intellect, then two things can be observed in the object of faith, as stated above (Q. 1, A. 1). One of these is the material object of faith, and in this way an act of faith is *to believe in a God*; because, as stated above (ibid.) nothing is proposed to our belief, except inasmuch as it is referred to God. The other is the formal aspect of the object, for it is the medium on account of which we assent to such and such a point of faith; and thus an act of faith is *to believe God*, since, as stated above (ibid.) the formal object of faith is the First Truth, to Which man gives his adhesion, so as to assent for Its sake to whatever he believes.

Si vero consideretur tertio modo obiectum fidei, secundum quod intellectus est motus a voluntate, sic ponitur actus fidei *credere in Deum*, veritas enim prima ad voluntatem refertur secundum quod habet rationem finis.

**AD PRIMUM** ergo dicendum quod per ista tria non designantur diversi actus fidei, sed unus et idem actus habens diversam relationem ad fidei obiectum.

**ET PER HOC** etiam patet responsio ad secundum.

**AD TERTIUM** dicendum quod credere Deum non convenit infidelibus sub ea ratione qua ponitur actus fidei. Non enim credunt Deum esse sub his conditionibus quas fides determinat. Et ideo nec vere Deum credunt, quia, ut philosophus dicit, IX Metaphys., in simplicibus defectus cognitionis est solum in non attingendo totaliter.

**AD QUARTUM** dicendum quod, sicut supra dictum est, voluntas movet intellectum et alias vires animae in finem. Et secundum hoc ponitur actus fidei credere in Deum.

Third, if the object of faith be considered insofar as the intellect is moved by the will, an act of faith is *to believe in God*. For the First Truth is referred to the will, through having the aspect of an end.

**REPLY OBJ. 1**: These three do not denote different acts of faith, but one and the same act having different relations to the object of faith.

**THIS SUFFICES** for the Reply to the Second Objection.

**REPLY OBJ. 3**: Unbelievers cannot be said *to believe in a God* as we understand it in relation to the act of faith. For they do not believe that God exists under the conditions that faith determines; hence they do not truly believe in a God, since, as the Philosopher observes (*Metaph.* ix, text. 22) to know simple things defectively is not to know them at all.

**REPLY OBJ. 4**: As stated above (I-II, Q. 9, A. 1) the will moves the intellect and the other powers of the soul to the end: and in this respect an act of faith is *to believe in God*.

# Article 3

### Whether it is necessary for salvation to believe?

**AD TERTIUM SIC PROCEDITUR.** Videtur quod credere non sit necessarium ad salutem. Ad salutem enim et perfectionem cuiuslibet rei ea sufficere videntur quae conveniunt ei secundum suam naturam. Sed ea quae sunt fidei excedunt naturalem hominis rationem, cum sint non apparentia, ut supra dictum est. Ergo credere non videtur esse necessarium ad salutem.

**PRAETEREA**, periculose homo assentit illis in quibus non potest iudicare utrum illud quod ei proponitur sit verum vel falsum, secundum illud Iob XII, *nonne auris verba diiudicat?* Sed tale iudicium homo habere non potest in his quae sunt fidei, quia non potest homo ea resolvere in principia prima, per quae de omnibus iudicamus. Ergo periculosum est talibus fidem adhibere. Credere ergo non est necessarium ad salutem.

**PRAETEREA**, salus hominis in Deo consistit, secundum illud Psalm., *salus autem iustorum a domino. Sed invisibilia Dei per ea quae facta sunt intellecta conspiciuntur; sempiterna quoque virtus eius et divinitas*, ut dicitur Rom. I. Quae autem conspiciuntur intellectu non creduntur. Ergo non est necessarium ad salutem ut homo aliqua credat.

**SED CONTRA** est quod dicitur Heb. XI, *sine fide impossibile est placere Deo.*

**RESPONDEO** dicendum quod in omnibus naturis ordinatis invenitur quod ad perfectionem naturae infe-

**OBJECTION 1**: It would seem unnecessary for salvation to believe anything above the natural reason. For the salvation and perfection of a thing seem to be sufficiently insured by its natural endowments. Now matters of faith, surpass man's natural reason, since they are things unseen as stated above (Q. 1, A. 4). Therefore to believe seems unnecessary for salvation.

**OBJ. 2**: Further, it is dangerous for man to assent to matters, wherein he cannot judge whether that which is proposed to him be true or false, according to Job 12:11: *Doth not the ear discern words?* Now a man cannot form a judgment of this kind in matters of faith, since he cannot trace them back to first principles, by which all our judgments are guided. Therefore it is dangerous to believe in such matters. Therefore to believe is not necessary for salvation.

**OBJ. 3**: Further, man's salvation rests on God, according to Ps. 36:39: *But the salvation of the just is from the Lord.* Now *the invisible things of God are clearly seen, being understood by the things that are made; His eternal power also and Divinity*, according to Rom. 1:20: and those things which are clearly seen by the understanding are not an object of belief. Therefore it is not necessary for man's salvation, that he should believe certain things.

**ON THE CONTRARY**, It is written (Heb 11:6): *Without faith it is impossible to please God.*

**I ANSWER THAT**, Wherever one nature is subordinate to another, we find that two things concur towards the

rioris duo concurrunt, unum quidem quod est secundum proprium motum; aliud autem quod est secundum motum superioris naturae. Sicut aqua secundum motum proprium movetur ad centrum, secundum autem motum lunae movetur circa centrum secundum fluxum et refluxum, similiter etiam orbes planetarum moventur propriis motibus ab occidente in orientem, motu autem primi orbis ab oriente in occidentem. Sola autem natura rationalis creata habet immediatum ordinem ad Deum. Quia ceterae creaturae non attingunt ad aliquid universale, sed solum ad aliquid particulare, participantes divinam bonitatem vel in essendo tantum, sicut inanimata, vel etiam in vivendo et cognoscendo singularia, sicut plantae et animalia, natura autem rationalis, inquantum cognoscit universalem boni et entis rationem, habet immediatum ordinem ad universale essendi principium.

Perfectio ergo rationalis creaturae non solum consistit in eo quod ei competit secundum suam naturam, sed etiam in eo quod ei attribuitur ex quadam supernaturali participatione divinae bonitatis. Unde et supra dictum est quod ultima beatitudo hominis consistit in quadam supernaturali Dei visione. Ad quam quidem visionem homo pertingere non potest nisi per modum addiscentis a Deo doctore, secundum illud Ioan. VI, *omnis qui audit a patre et didicit venit ad me.* Huius autem disciplinae fit homo particeps non statim, sed successive, secundum modum suae naturae. Omnis autem talis addiscens oportet quod credat, ad hoc quod ad perfectam scientiam perveniat, sicut etiam philosophus dicit quod *oportet addiscentem credere.*

Unde ad hoc quod homo perveniat ad perfectam visionem beatitudinis praeexigitur quod credat Deo tanquam discipulus magistro docenti.

**AD PRIMUM** ergo dicendum quod, quia natura hominis dependet a superiori natura, ad eius perfectionem non sufficit cognitio naturalis, sed requiritur quaedam supernaturalis, ut supra dictum est.

**AD SECUNDUM** dicendum quod, sicut homo per naturale lumen intellectus assentit principiis, ita homo virtuosus per habitum virtutis habet rectum iudicium de his quae conveniunt virtuti illi. Et hoc modo etiam per lumen fidei divinitus infusum homini homo assentit his quae sunt fidei, non autem contrariis. Et ideo *nihil* periculi vel *damnationis inest his qui sunt in Christo Iesu,* ab ipso illuminati per fidem.

**AD TERTIUM** dicendum quod invisibilia Dei altiori modo, quantum ad plura, percipit fides quam ratio naturalis ex creaturis in Deum procedens. Unde dicitur Eccli. III, *plurima super sensum hominis ostensa sunt tibi.*

perfection of the lower nature, one of which is in respect of that nature's proper movement, while the other is in respect of the movement of the higher nature. Thus water by its proper movement moves towards the centre (of the earth), while according to the movement of the moon, it moves round the centre by ebb and flow. In like manner the planets have their proper movements from west to east, while in accordance with the movement of the first heaven, they have a movement from east to west. Now the created rational nature alone is immediately subordinate to God, since other creatures do not attain to the universal, but only to something particular, while they partake of the Divine goodness either in being only, as inanimate things, or also in living, and in knowing singulars, as plants and animals; whereas the rational nature, inasmuch as it apprehends the universal notion of good and being, is immediately related to the universal principle of being.

Consequently the perfection of the rational creature consists not only in what belongs to it in respect of its nature, but also in that which it acquires through a supernatural participation of Divine goodness. Hence it was said above (I-II, Q. 3, A. 8) that man's ultimate happiness consists in a supernatural vision of God: to which vision man cannot attain unless he be taught by God, according to John 6:45: *Every one that hath heard of the Father and hath learned cometh to Me.* Now man acquires a share of this learning, not indeed all at once, but by little and little, according to the mode of his nature: and every one who learns thus must needs believe, in order that he may acquire science in a perfect degree; thus also the Philosopher remarks (*De Soph. Elench.* i, 2) that *it behooves a learner to believe.*

Hence in order that a man arrive at the perfect vision of heavenly happiness, he must first of all believe God, as a disciple believes the master who is teaching him.

**REPLY OBJ. 1:** Since man's nature is dependent on a higher nature, natural knowledge does not suffice for its perfection, and some supernatural knowledge is necessary, as stated above.

**REPLY OBJ. 2:** Just as man assents to first principles, by the natural light of his intellect, so does a virtuous man, by the habit of virtue, judge aright of things concerning that virtue; and in this way, by the light of faith which God bestows on him, a man assents to matters of faith and not to those which are against faith. Consequently *there is no danger or condemnation to them that are in Christ Jesus,* and whom He has enlightened by faith.

**REPLY OBJ. 3:** In many respects faith perceives the invisible things of God in a higher way than natural reason does in proceeding to God from His creatures. Hence it is written (Sir 3:25): *Many things are shown to thee above the understandings of man.*

# Article 4

*Whether it is necessary to believe those things which can be proved by natural reason?*

AD QUARTUM SIC PROCEDITUR. Videtur quod ea quae ratione naturali probari possunt non sit necessarium credere. In operibus enim Dei nihil superfluum invenitur, multo minus quam in operibus naturae. Sed ad id quod per unum potest fieri superflue apponitur aliud. Ergo ea quae per naturalem rationem cognosci possunt superfluum esset per fidem accipere.

PRAETEREA, ea necesse est credere de quibus est fides. Sed non est de eodem scientia et fides, ut supra habitum est. Cum igitur scientia sit de omnibus illis quae naturali ratione cognosci possunt, videtur quod non oporteat credere ea quae per naturalem rationem probantur.

PRAETEREA, omnia scibilia videntur esse unius rationis. Si igitur quaedam eorum proponuntur homini ut credenda, pari ratione omnia huiusmodi necesse esset credere. Hoc autem est falsum. Non ergo ea quae per naturalem rationem cognosci possunt necesse est credere.

SED CONTRA est quia necesse est Deum credere esse unum et incorporeum, quae naturali ratione a philosophis probantur.

RESPONDEO dicendum quod necessarium est homini accipere per modum fidei non solum ea quae sunt supra rationem, sed etiam ea quae per rationem cognosci possunt. Et hoc propter tria. Primo quidem, ut citius homo ad veritatis divinae cognitionem perveniat. Scientia enim ad quam pertinet probare Deum esse et alia huiusmodi de Deo, ultimo hominibus addiscenda proponitur, praesuppositis multis aliis scientiis. Et sic non nisi post multum tempus vitae suae homo ad Dei cognitionem perveniret. Secundo, ut cognitio Dei sit communior. Multi enim in studio scientiae proficere non possunt, vel propter hebetudinem ingenii; vel propter alias occupationes et necessitates temporalis vitae; vel etiam propter torporem addiscendi. Qui omnino a Dei cognitione fraudarentur nisi proponerentur eis divina per modum fidei. Tertio modo, propter certitudinem. Ratio enim humana in rebus divinis est multum deficiens, cuius signum est quia philosophi, de rebus humanis naturali investigatione perscrutantes, in multis erraverunt et sibi ipsis contraria senserunt. Ut ergo esset indubitata et certa cognitio apud homines de Deo, oportuit quod divina eis per modum fidei traderentur, quasi a Deo dicta, qui mentiri non potest.

AD PRIMUM ergo dicendum quod investigatio naturalis rationis non sufficit humano generi ad cognitionem

OBJECTION 1: It would seem unnecessary to believe those things which can be proved by natural reason. For nothing is superfluous in God's works, much less even than in the works of nature. Now it is superfluous to employ other means, where one already suffices. Therefore it would be superfluous to receive by faith, things that can be known by natural reason.

OBJ. 2: Further, those things must be believed, which are the object of faith. Now science and faith are not about the same object, as stated above (Q. 1, AA. 4, 5). Since therefore all things that can be known by natural reason are an object of science, it seems that there is no need to believe what can be proved by natural reason.

OBJ. 3: Further, all things knowable scientifically would seem to come under one head: so that if some of them are proposed to man as objects of faith, in like manner the others should also be believed. But this is not true. Therefore it is not necessary to believe those things which can be proved by natural reason.

ON THE CONTRARY, It is necessary to believe that God is one and incorporeal: which things philosophers prove by natural reason.

I ANSWER THAT, It is necessary for man to accept by faith not only things which are above reason, but also those which can be known by reason: and this for three motives. First, in order that man may arrive more quickly at the knowledge of Divine truth. Because the science to whose province it belongs to prove the existence of God, is the last of all to offer itself to human research, since it presupposes many other sciences: so that it would not be until late in life that man would arrive at the knowledge of God. The second reason is, in order that the knowledge of God may be more general. For many are unable to make progress in the study of science, either through dullness of mind, or through having a number of occupations, and temporal needs, or even through laziness in learning, all of whom would be altogether deprived of the knowledge of God, unless Divine things were brought to their knowledge under the guise of faith. The third reason is for the sake of certitude. For human reason is very deficient in things concerning God. A sign of this is that philosophers in their researches, by natural investigation, into human affairs, have fallen into many errors, and have disagreed among themselves. And consequently, in order that men might have knowledge of God, free of doubt and uncertainty, it was necessary for Divine matters to be delivered to them by way of faith, being told to them, as it were, by God Himself Who cannot lie.

REPLY OBJ. 1: The researches of natural reason do not suffice mankind for the knowledge of Divine matters, even

divinorum etiam quae ratione ostendi possunt. Et ideo non est superfluum ut talia credantur.

**AD SECUNDUM** dicendum quod de eodem non potest esse scientia et fides apud eundem. Sed id quod est ab uno scitum potest esse ab alio creditum, ut supra dictum est.

**AD TERTIUM** dicendum quod, si omnia scibilia conveniant in ratione scientiae, non tamen conveniunt in hoc quod aequaliter ordinent ad beatitudinem. Et ideo non aequaliter omnia proponuntur ut credenda.

of those that can be proved by reason: and so it is not superfluous if these others be believed.

**REPLY OBJ. 2**: Science and faith cannot be in the same subject and about the same object: but what is an object of science for one, can be an object of faith for another, as stated above (Q. 1, A. 5).

**REPLY OBJ. 3**: Although all things that can be known by science are of one common scientific aspect, they do not all alike lead man to beatitude: hence they are not all equally proposed to our belief.

# Article 5

*Whether man is bound to believe anything explicitly?*

**AD QUINTUM SIC PROCEDITUR.** Videtur quod non teneatur homo ad credendum aliquid explicite. Nullus enim tenetur ad id quod non est in eius potestate. Sed credere aliquid explicite non est in hominis potestate, dicitur enim Rom. X, *quomodo credent ei quem non audierunt? Quomodo audient sine praedicante? Quomodo autem praedicabunt nisi mittantur?* Ergo credere aliquid explicite homo non tenetur.

**PRAETEREA,** sicut per fidem ordinamur in Deum, ita et per caritatem. Sed ad servandum praecepta caritatis homo non tenetur, sed sufficit sola praeparatio animi, sicut patet in illo praecepto domini quod ponitur Matth. V, *si quis percusserit te in una maxilla, praebe ei et aliam,* et in aliis consimilibus, ut Augustinus exponit, in libro de Serm. Dom. in monte. Ergo etiam non tenetur homo explicite aliquid credere, sed sufficit quod habeat animum paratum ad credendum ea quae a Deo proponuntur.

**PRAETEREA,** bonum fidei in quadam obedientia consistit, secundum illud Rom. I, *ad obediendum fidei in omnibus gentibus.* Sed ad virtutem obedientiae non requiritur quod homo aliqua determinata praecepta observet, sed sufficit quod habeat promptum animum ad obediendum, secundum illud Psalm., *paratus sum, et non sum turbatus, ut custodiam mandata tua.* Ergo videtur quod etiam ad fidem sufficiat quod homo habeat promptum animum ad credendum ea quae ei divinitus proponi possent, absque hoc quod explicite aliquid credat.

**SED CONTRA** est quod dicitur ad Heb. XI, *accedentem ad Deum oportet credere quia est, et quod inquirentibus se remunerator est.*

**RESPONDEO** dicendum quod praecepta legis quae homo tenetur implere dantur de actibus virtutum qui sunt via perveniendi ad salutem. Actus autem virtutis, sicut supra dictum est, sumitur secundum habitudinem habitus ad obiectum. Sed in obiecto cuiuslibet virtutis

**OBJECTION 1**: It would seem that man is not bound to believe anything explicitly. For no man is bound to do what is not in his power. Now it is not in man's power to believe a thing explicitly, for it is written (Rom 10:14, 15): *How shall they believe Him, of whom they have not heard? And how shall they hear without a preacher? And how shall they preach unless they be sent?* Therefore man is not bound to believe anything explicitly.

**OBJ. 2**: Further, just as we are directed to God by faith, so are we by charity. Now man is not bound to keep the precepts of charity, and it is enough if he be ready to fulfill them: as is evidenced by the precept of Our Lord (Matt 5:39): *If one strike thee on one cheek, turn to him also the other*; and by others of the same kind, according to Augustine's exposition (*De Serm. Dom. in Monte* xix). Therefore neither is man bound to believe anything explicitly, and it is enough if he be ready to believe whatever God proposes to be believed.

**OBJ. 3**: Further, the good of faith consists in obedience, according to Rom. 1:5: *For obedience to the faith in all nations.* Now the virtue of obedience does not require man to keep certain fixed precepts, but it is enough that his mind be ready to obey, according to Ps. 118:60: *I am ready and am not troubled; that I may keep Thy commandments.* Therefore it seems enough for faith, too, that man should be ready to believe whatever God may propose, without his believing anything explicitly.

**ON THE CONTRARY**, It is written (Heb 11:6): *He that cometh to God, must believe that He is, and is a rewarder to them that seek Him.*

**I ANSWER THAT**, The precepts of the Law, which man is bound to fulfill, concern acts of virtue which are the means of attaining salvation. Now an act of virtue, as stated above (I-II, Q. 60, A. 5) depends on the relation of the habit to its object. Again two things may be considered in the

duo possunt considerari, scilicet id quod est proprie et per se virtutis obiectum, quod necessarium est in omni actu virtutis; et iterum id quod per accidens sive consequenter se habet ad propriam rationem obiecti. Sicut ad obiectum fortitudinis proprie et per se pertinet sustinere pericula mortis et aggredi hostes cum periculo propter bonum commune, sed quod homo armetur vel ense percutiat in bello iusto, aut aliquid huiusmodi faciat, reducitur quidem ad obiectum fortitudinis, sed per accidens.

Determinatio igitur virtuosi actus ad proprium et per se obiectum virtutis est sub necessitate praecepti, sicut et ipse virtutis actus. Sed determinatio actus virtuosi ad ea quae accidentaliter vel secundario se habent ad proprium et per se virtutis obiectum non cadit sub necessitate praecepti nisi pro loco et tempore. Dicendum est ergo quod fidei obiectum per se est id per quod homo beatus efficitur, ut supra dictum est. Per accidens autem vel secundario se habent ad obiectum fidei omnia quae in Scriptura divinitus tradita continentur, sicut quod Abraham habuit duos filios, quod David fuit filius Isai, et alia huiusmodi.

Quantum ergo ad prima credibilia, quae sunt articuli fidei, tenetur homo explicite credere, sicut et tenetur habere fidem. Quantum autem ad alia credibilia, non tenetur homo explicite credere, sed solum implicite vel in praeparatione animi, inquantum paratus est credere quidquid in divina Scriptura continetur. Sed tunc solum huiusmodi tenetur explicite credere quando hoc ei constiterit in doctrina fidei contineri.

**AD PRIMUM** ergo dicendum quod, si in potestate hominis esse dicatur aliquid excluso auxilio gratiae, sic ad multa tenetur homo ad quae non potest sine gratia reparante, sicut ad diligendum Deum et proximum; et similiter ad credendum articulos fidei. Sed tamen hoc potest homo cum auxilio gratiae. Quod quidem auxilium quibuscumque divinitus datur, misericorditer datur; quibus autem non datur, ex iustitia non datur, in poenam praecedentis peccati, saltem originalis peccati; ut Augustinus dicit, in libro de Cor. et gratia.

**AD SECUNDUM** dicendum quod homo tenetur ad determinate diligendum illa diligibilia quae sunt proprie et per se caritatis obiecta, scilicet Deus et proximus. Sed obiectio procedit de illis praeceptis caritatis quae quasi consequenter pertinent ad obiectum caritatis.

**AD TERTIUM** dicendum quod virtus obedientiae proprie in voluntate consistit. Et ideo ad actum obedientiae sufficit promptitudo voluntatis subiecta praecipienti, quae est proprium et per se obiectum obedientiae. Sed hoc praeceptum vel illud per accidens vel consequenter se habet ad proprium et per se obiectum obedientiae.

object of any virtue; namely, that which is the proper and direct object of that virtue, and that which is accidental and consequent to the object properly so called. Thus it belongs properly and directly to the object of fortitude, to face the dangers of death, and to charge at the foe with danger to oneself, for the sake of the common good: yet that, in a just war, a man be armed, or strike another with his sword, and so forth, is reduced to the object of fortitude, but indirectly.

Accordingly, just as a virtuous act is required for the fulfilment of a precept, so is it necessary that the virtuous act should terminate in its proper and direct object: but, on the other hand, the fulfilment of the precept does not require that a virtuous act should terminate in those things which have an accidental or secondary relation to the proper and direct object of that virtue, except in certain places and at certain times. We must, therefore, say that the direct object of faith is that whereby man is made one of the Blessed, as stated above (Q. 1, A. 8): while the indirect and secondary object comprises all things delivered by God to us in Holy Writ, for instance that Abraham had two sons, that David was the son of Jesse, and so forth.

Therefore, as regards the primary points or articles of faith, man is bound to believe them, just as he is bound to have faith; but as to other points of faith, man is not bound to believe them explicitly, but only implicitly, or to be ready to believe them, insofar as he is prepared to believe whatever is contained in the Divine Scriptures. Then alone is he bound to believe such things explicitly, when it is clear to him that they are contained in the doctrine of faith.

**REPLY OBJ. 1**: If we understand those things alone to be in a man's power, which we can do without the help of grace, then we are bound to do many things which we cannot do without the aid of healing grace, such as to love God and our neighbor, and likewise to believe the articles of faith. But with the help of grace we can do this, for this help to whomsoever it is given from above it is mercifully given; and from whom it is withheld it is justly withheld, as a punishment of a previous, or at least of original, sin, as Augustine states (*De Corr. et Grat.* v, vi ).

**REPLY OBJ. 2**: Man is bound to love definitely those lovable things which are properly and directly the objects of charity, namely, God and our neighbor. The objection refers to those precepts of charity which belong, as a consequence, to the objects of charity.

**REPLY OBJ. 3**: The virtue of obedience is seated, properly speaking, in the will; hence promptness of the will subject to authority, suffices for the act of obedience, because it is the proper and direct object of obedience. But this or that precept is accidental or consequent to that proper and direct object.

# Article 6

*Whether all are equally bound to have explicit faith?*

**AD SEXTUM SIC PROCEDITUR.** Videtur quod aequaliter omnes teneantur ad habendum fidem explicitam. Ad ea enim quae sunt de necessitate salutis omnes tenentur, sicut patet de praeceptis caritatis. Sed explicatio credendorum est de necessitate salutis, ut dictum est. Ergo omnes aequaliter tenentur ad explicite credendum.

**PRAETEREA**, nullus debet examinari de eo quod explicite credere non tenetur. Sed quandoque etiam simplices examinantur de minimis articulis fidei. Ergo omnes tenentur explicite omnia credere.

**PRAETEREA**, si minores non tenentur habere fidem explicitam, sed solum implicitam, oportet quod habeant fidem implicitam in fide maiorum. Sed hoc videtur esse periculosum, quia posset contingere quod illi maiores errarent. Ergo videtur quod minores etiam debeant habere fidem explicitam. Sic ergo omnes aequaliter tenentur ad explicite credendum.

**SED CONTRA** est quod dicitur Iob I, quod *boves arabant et asinae pascebantur iuxta eos*, quia videlicet minores, qui significantur per asinos, debent in credendis adhaerere maioribus, qui per boves significantur; ut Gregorius exponit, in II Moral.

**RESPONDEO** dicendum quod explicatio credendorum fit per revelationem divinam, credibilia enim naturalem rationem excedunt. Revelatio autem divina ordine quodam ad inferiores pervenit per superiores, sicut ad homines per Angelos, et ad inferiores Angelos per superiores, ut patet per Dionysium, in Cael. Hier. Et ideo, pari ratione, explicatio fidei oportet quod perveniat ad inferiores homines per maiores. Et ideo sicut superiores Angeli, qui inferiores illuminant, habent pleniorem notitiam de rebus divinis quam inferiores, ut dicit Dionysius, XII cap. Cael. Hier.; ita etiam superiores homines, ad quos pertinet alios erudire, tenentur habere pleniorem notitiam de credendis et magis explicite credere.

**AD PRIMUM** ergo dicendum quod explicatio credendorum non aequaliter quantum ad omnes est de necessitate salutis, quia plura tenentur explicite credere maiores, qui habent officium alios instruendi, quam alii.

**AD SECUNDUM** dicendum quod simplices non sunt examinandi de subtilitatibus fidei nisi quando habetur suspicio quod sint ab haereticis depravati, qui in his quae ad subtilitatem fidei pertinent solent fidem simplicium depravare. Si tamen inveniuntur non pertinaciter perversae doctrinae adhaerere, si in talibus ex simplicitate deficiant, non eis imputatur.

**OBJECTION 1**: It would seem that all are equally bound to have explicit faith. For all are bound to those things which are necessary for salvation, as is evidenced by the precepts of charity. Now it is necessary for salvation that certain things should be believed explicitly. Therefore all are equally bound to have explicit faith.

**OBJ. 2**: Further, no one should be put to test in matters that he is not bound to believe. But simple persons are sometimes tested in reference to the slightest articles of faith. Therefore all are bound to believe everything explicitly.

**OBJ. 3**: Further, if the simple are bound to have, not explicit but only implicit faith, their faith must needs be implied in the faith of the learned. But this seems unsafe, since it is possible for the learned to err. Therefore it seems that the simple should also have explicit faith; so that all are, therefore, equally bound to have explicit faith.

**ON THE CONTRARY**, It is written (Job 1:14): *The oxen were ploughing, and the asses feeding beside them*, because, as Gregory expounds this passage (*Moral.* ii, 17), the simple, who are signified by the asses, ought, in matters of faith, to stay by the learned, who are denoted by the oxen.

**I ANSWER THAT**, The unfolding of matters of faith is the result of Divine revelation: for matters of faith surpass natural reason. Now Divine revelation reaches those of lower degree through those who are over them, in a certain order; to men, for instance, through the angels, and to the lower angels through the higher, as Dionysius explains (*Cael. Hier.* iv, vii). In like manner therefore the unfolding of faith must needs reach men of lower degree through those of higher degree. Consequently, just as the higher angels, who enlighten those who are below them, have a fuller knowledge of Divine things than the lower angels, as Dionysius states (*Coel. Hier.* xii), so too, men of higher degree, whose business it is to teach others, are under obligation to have fuller knowledge of matters of faith, and to believe them more explicitly.

**REPLY OBJ. 1**: The unfolding of the articles of faith is not equally necessary for the salvation of all, since those of higher degree, whose duty it is to teach others, are bound to believe explicitly more things than others are.

**REPLY OBJ. 2**: Simple persons should not be put to the test about subtle questions of faith, unless they be suspected of having been corrupted by heretics, who are wont to corrupt the faith of simple people in such questions. If, however, it is found that they are free from obstinacy in their heterodox sentiments, and that it is due to their simplicity, it is no fault of theirs.

**Ad tertium** dicendum quod minores non habent fidem implicitam in fide maiorum nisi quatenus maiores adhaerent doctrinae divinae, unde et apostolus dicit, I ad Cor. IV, *imitatores mei estote, sicut et ego Christi.* Unde humana cognitio non fit regula fidei, sed veritas divina. A qua si aliqui maiorum deficiant, non praeiudicat fidei simplicium, qui eos rectam fidem habere credunt, nisi pertinaciter eorum erroribus in particulari adhaereant contra universalis Ecclesiae fidem, quae non potest deficere, domino dicente, Luc. XXII, *ego pro te rogavi, Petre, ut non deficiat fides tua.*

**Reply Obj. 3**: The simple have no faith implied in that of the learned, except insofar as the latter adhere to the Divine teaching. Hence the Apostle says (1 Cor 4:16): *Be ye followers of me, as I also am of Christ.* Hence it is not human knowledge, but the Divine truth that is the rule of faith: and if any of the learned stray from this rule, he does not harm the faith of the simple ones, who think that the learned believe aright; unless the simple hold obstinately to their individual errors, against the faith of the universal Church, which cannot err, since Our Lord said (Luke 22:32): *I have prayed for thee, Peter, that thy faith fail not.*

# Article 7

*Whether it is necessary for the salvation of all to believe explicitly in the mystery of Christ?*

**Ad septimum sic proceditur.** Videtur quod credere explicite mysterium Christi non sit de necessitate salutis apud omnes. Non enim tenetur homo explicite credere ea quae Angeli ignorant, quia explicatio fidei fit per revelationem divinam, quae pervenit ad homines mediantibus Angelis, ut dictum est. Sed etiam Angeli mysterium incarnationis ignoraverunt, unde quaerebant in Psalm., *quis est iste rex gloriae?* Et Isaiae LXIII, *quis est iste qui venit de Edom?* Ut Dionysius exponit, cap. VII Cael. Hier. Ergo ad credendum explicite mysterium incarnationis homines non tenebantur.

**Praeterea**, constat beatum Ioannem Baptistam de maioribus fuisse, et propinquissimum Christo, de quo dominus dicit, Matth. XI, quod *inter natos mulierum nullus maior eo surrexit.* Sed Ioannes Baptista non videtur Christi mysterium explicite cognovisse, cum a Christo quaesierit, *tu es qui venturus es, an alium expectamus?* Ut habetur Matth. XI. Ergo non tenebantur etiam maiores ad habendum explicitam fidem de Christo.

**Praeterea**, multi gentilium salutem adepti sunt per ministerium Angelorum, ut Dionysius dicit, IX cap. Cael. Hier. Sed gentiles non habuerunt fidem de Christo nec explicitam nec implicitam, ut videtur, quia nulla eis revelatio facta est. Ergo videtur quod credere explicite Christi mysterium non fuerit omnibus necessarium ad salutem.

**Sed contra** est quod Augustinus dicit, in libro de Cor. et gratia, *illa fides sana est qua credimus nullum hominem, sive maioris sive parvae aetatis, liberari a contagio mortis et obligatione peccati nisi per unum mediatorem Dei et hominum Iesum Christum.*

**Respondeo** dicendum quod, sicut supra dictum est, illud proprie et per se pertinet ad obiectum fidei per quod homo beatitudinem consequitur. Via autem

**Objection 1**: It would seem that it is not necessary for the salvation of all that they should believe explicitly in the mystery of Christ. For man is not bound to believe explicitly what the angels are ignorant about: since the unfolding of faith is the result of Divine revelation, which reaches man by means of the angels, as stated above (A. 6; I, Q. 111, A. 1). Now even the angels were in ignorance of the mystery of the Incarnation: hence, according to the commentary of Dionysius (*Cael. Hier.* vii), it is they who ask (Ps 23:8): *Who is this king of glory?* and (Isa 63:1): *Who is this that cometh from Edom?* Therefore men were not bound to believe explicitly in the mystery of Christ's Incarnation.

**Obj. 2**: Further, it is evident that John the Baptist was one of the teachers, and most nigh to Christ, Who said of him (Matt 11:11) that *there hath not risen among them that are born of women, a greater than he.* Now John the Baptist does not appear to have known the mystery of Christ explicitly, since he asked Christ (Matt 11:3): *Art Thou He that art to come, or look we for another?* Therefore even the teachers were not bound to explicit faith in Christ.

**Obj. 3**: Further, many gentiles obtained salvation through the ministry of the angels, as Dionysius states (*Cael. Hier.* ix). Now it would seem that the gentiles had neither explicit nor implicit faith in Christ, since they received no revelation. Therefore it seems that it was not necessary for the salvation of all to believe explicitly in the mystery of Christ.

**On the contrary**, Augustine says (*De Corr. et Gratia* vii; Ep. cxc): *Our faith is sound if we believe that no man, old or young is delivered from the contagion of death and the bonds of sin, except by the one Mediator of God and men, Jesus Christ.*

**I answer that**, As stated above (A. 5; Q. 1, A. 8), the object of faith includes, properly and directly, that thing through which man obtains beatitude. Now the mystery of

hominibus veniendi ad beatitudinem est mysterium incarnationis et passionis Christi, dicitur enim Act. IV, *non est aliud nomen datum hominibus in quo oporteat nos salvos fieri.* Et ideo mysterium incarnationis Christi aliqualiter oportuit omni tempore esse creditum apud omnes, diversimode tamen secundum diversitatem temporum et personarum. Nam ante statum peccati homo habuit explicitam fidem de Christi incarnatione secundum quod ordinabatur ad consummationem gloriae, non autem secundum quod ordinabatur ad liberationem a peccato per passionem et resurrectionem, quia homo non fuit praescius peccati futuri. Videtur autem incarnationis Christi praescius fuisse per hoc quod dixit, *propter hoc relinquet homo patrem et matrem et adhaerebit uxori suae,* ut habetur Gen. II; et hoc apostolus, ad Ephes. V, dicit *sacramentum magnum esse in Christo et Ecclesia;* quod quidem sacramentum non est credibile primum hominem ignorasse.

Post peccatum autem fuit explicite creditum mysterium Christi non solum quantum ad incarnationem, sed etiam quantum ad passionem et resurrectionem, quibus humanum genus a peccato et morte liberatur. Aliter enim non praefigurassent Christi passionem quibusdam sacrificiis et ante legem et sub lege. Quorum quidem sacrificiorum significatum explicite maiores cognoscebant, minores autem sub velamine illorum sacrificiorum, credentes ea divinitus esse disposita de Christo venturo, quodammodo habebant velatam cognitionem. Et sicut supra dictum est, ea quae ad mysteria Christi pertinent tanto distinctius cognoverunt quanto Christo propinquiores fuerunt.

Post tempus autem gratiae revelatae tam maiores quam minores tenentur habere fidem explicitam de mysteriis Christi; praecipue quantum ad ea quae communiter in Ecclesia sollemnizantur et publice proponuntur, sicut sunt articuli incarnationis, de quibus supra dictum est. Alias autem subtiles considerationes circa incarnationis articulos tenentur aliqui magis vel minus explicite credere secundum quod convenit statui et officio uniuscuiusque.

**AD PRIMUM** ergo dicendum quod *Angelos non omnino latuit mysterium regni Dei,* sicut Augustinus dicit, V super Gen. ad Litt. Quasdam tamen rationes huius mysterii perfectius cognoverunt Christo revelante.

**AD SECUNDUM** dicendum quod Ioannes Baptista non quaesivit de adventu Christi in carnem quasi hoc ignoraret, cum ipse hoc expresse confessus fuerit, dicens, *ego vidi, et testimonium perhibui quia hic est filius Dei,* ut habetur Ioan. I. Unde non dixit, *tu es qui venisti?* Sed, *tu es qui venturus es?* Quaerens de futuro, non de praeterito. Similiter non est credendum quod ignoraverit eum ad passionem venturum, ipse enim dixerat, *ecce agnus Dei, qui tollit peccata mundi,* praenuntians eius immolationem futuram; et cum hoc prophetae alii

Christ's Incarnation and Passion is the way by which men obtain beatitude; for it is written (Acts 4:12): *There is no other name under heaven given to men, whereby we must be saved.* Therefore belief of some kind in the mystery of Christ's Incarnation was necessary at all times and for all persons, but this belief differed according to differences of times and persons. The reason of this is that before the state of sin, man believed, explicitly in Christ's Incarnation, insofar as it was intended for the consummation of glory, but not as it was intended to deliver man from sin by the Passion and Resurrection, since man had no foreknowledge of his future sin. He does, however, seem to have had foreknowledge of the Incarnation of Christ, from the fact that he said (Gen 2:24): *Wherefore a man shall leave father and mother, and shall cleave to his wife,* of which the Apostle says (Eph 5:32) that *this is a great sacrament . . . in Christ and the Church,* and it is incredible that the first man was ignorant about this sacrament.

But after sin, man believed explicitly in Christ, not only as to the Incarnation, but also as to the Passion and Resurrection, whereby the human race is delivered from sin and death: for they would not, else, have foreshadowed Christ's Passion by certain sacrifices both before and after the Law, the meaning of which sacrifices was known by the learned explicitly, while the simple folk, under the veil of those sacrifices, believed them to be ordained by God in reference to Christ's coming, and thus their knowledge was covered with a veil, so to speak. And, as stated above (Q. 1, A. 7), the nearer they were to Christ, the more distinct was their knowledge of Christ's mysteries.

After grace had been revealed, both learned and simple folk are bound to explicit faith in the mysteries of Christ, chiefly as regards those which are observed throughout the Church, and publicly proclaimed, such as the articles which refer to the Incarnation, of which we have spoken above (Q. 1, A. 8). As to other minute points in reference to the articles of the Incarnation, men have been bound to believe them more or less explicitly according to each one's state and office.

**REPLY OBJ. 1**: *The mystery of the Kingdom of God was not entirely hidden from the angels,* as Augustine observes (*Gen ad lit.* v, 19), yet certain aspects thereof were better known to them when Christ revealed them to them.

**REPLY OBJ. 2**: It was not through ignorance that John the Baptist inquired of Christ's advent in the flesh, since he had clearly professed his belief therein, saying: *I saw, and I gave testimony, that this is the Son of God* (John 1:34). Hence he did not say: *Art Thou He that hast come?* but *Art Thou He that art to come?* thus saying about the future, not about the past. Likewise it is not to be believed that he was ignorant of Christ's future Passion, for he had already said (John 1:39): *Behold the Lamb of God, behold Him who taketh away the sins of the world,* thus foretelling His future immolation;

ante praedixerint, sicut praecipue patet in Isaiae LIII. Potest igitur dici, sicut Gregorius dicit, quod inquisivit ignorans an ad Infernum esset in propria persona descensurus. Sciebat autem quod virtus passionis eius extendenda erat usque ad eos qui in Limbo detinebantur, secundum illud Zach. IX, *tu quoque in sanguine testamenti tui emisisti vinctos de lacu in quo non est aqua*. Nec hoc tenebatur explicite credere, antequam esset impletum, quod per seipsum deberet descendere.

Vel potest dici, sicut Ambrosius dicit, super Luc., quod non quaesivit ex dubitatione seu ignorantia, sed magis ex pietate. Vel potest dici, sicut Chrysostomus dicit, quod non quaesivit quasi ipse ignoraret, sed ut per Christum satisfieret eius discipulis. Unde et Christus ad discipulorum instructionem respondit, signa operum ostendens.

**AD TERTIUM** dicendum quod multis gentilium facta fuit revelatio de Christo, ut patet per ea quae praedixerunt. Nam Iob XIX dicitur, *scio quod redemptor meus vivit*. Sibylla etiam praenuntiavit quaedam de Christo, ut Augustinus dicit. Invenitur etiam in historiis Romanorum quod tempore Constantini Augusti et Irenae matris eius inventum fuit quoddam sepulcrum in quo iacebat homo auream laminam habens in pectore in qua scriptum erat, *Christus nascetur ex virgine et credo in eum. O sol, sub Irenae et Constantini temporibus iterum me videbis*. Si qui tamen salvati fuerunt quibus revelatio non fuit facta, non fuerunt salvati absque fide mediatoris. Quia etsi non habuerunt fidem explicitam, habuerunt tamen fidem implicitam in divina providentia, credentes Deum esse liberatorem hominum secundum modos sibi placitos et secundum quod aliquibus veritatem cognoscentibus ipse revelasset, secundum illud Iob XXXV, *qui docet nos super iumenta terrae*.

and since other prophets had foretold it, as may be seen especially in Isaiah 53. We may therefore say with Gregory (*Hom. xxvi in Evang.*) that he asked this question, being in ignorance as to whether Christ would descend into hell in His own Person. But he did not ignore the fact that the power of Christ's Passion would be extended to those who were detained in Limbo, according to Zach. 9:11: *Thou also, by the blood of Thy testament hast sent forth Thy prisoners out of the pit, wherein there is no water*; nor was he bound to believe explicitly, before its fulfilment, that Christ was to descend thither Himself.

It may also be replied that, as Ambrose observes in his commentary on Luke 7:19, he made this inquiry, not from doubt or ignorance but from devotion: or again, with Chrysostom (*Hom. xxxvi in Matth.*), that he inquired, not as though ignorant himself, but because he wished his disciples to be satisfied on that point, through Christ: hence the latter framed His answer so as to instruct the disciples, pointing to the signs of His works.

**REPLY OBJ. 3**: Many of the Gentiles received revelations of Christ, as is clear from their predictions. Thus we read (Job 19:25): *I know that my Redeemer liveth*. The Sibyl too foretold certain things about Christ, as Augustine states (*Contra Faust.* xiii, 15). Moreover, we read in the history of the Romans, that at the time of Constantine Augustus and his mother Irene a tomb was discovered, wherein lay a man on whose breast was a golden plate with the inscription: *Christ shall be born of a virgin, and in Him, I believe. O sun, during the lifetime of Irene and Constantine, thou shalt see me again*. If, however, some were saved without receiving any revelation, they were not saved without faith in a Mediator, for, though they did not believe in Him explicitly, they did, nevertheless, have implicit faith through believing in Divine providence, since they believed that God would deliver mankind in whatever way was pleasing to Him, and according to the revelation of the Spirit to those who knew the truth, as stated in Job 35:11: *Who teacheth us more than the beasts of the earth.*

# Article 8

*Whether it is necessary for salvation to believe explicitly in the Trinity?*

**AD OCTAVUM SIC PROCEDITUR**. Videtur quod credere Trinitatem explicite non fuerit de necessitate salutis. Dicit enim apostolus, ad Heb. XI, *credere oportet accedentem ad Deum quia est, et quia inquirentibus se remunerator est*. Sed hoc potest credi absque fide Trinitatis. Ergo non oportebat explicite fidem de Trinitate habere.

**PRAETEREA**, dominus dicit, Ioan. XVII, *pater, manifestavi nomen tuum hominibus*, quod exponens Au-

**OBJECTION 1**: It would seem that it was not necessary for salvation to believe explicitly in the Trinity. For the Apostle says (Heb 11:6): *He that cometh to God must believe that He is, and is a rewarder to them that seek Him*. Now one can believe this without believing in the Trinity. Therefore it was not necessary to believe explicitly in the Trinity.

**OBJ. 2**: Further our Lord said (John 17:5, 6): *Father, I have manifested Thy name to men*, which words Augustine

gustinus dicit, *non illud nomen tuum quo vocaris Deus, sed illud quo vocaris pater meus*. Et postea subdit etiam, *in hoc quod Deus fecit hunc mundum, notus in omnibus gentibus; in hoc quod non est cum diis falsis colendus, notus in Iudaea Deus; in hoc vero quod pater est huius Christi per quem tollit peccatum mundi, hoc nomen eius, prius occultum, nunc manifestavit eis*. Ergo ante Christi adventum non erat cognitum quod in deitate esset paternitas et filiatio. Non ergo Trinitas explicite credebatur.

**PRAETEREA**, illud tenemur explicite credere in Deo quod est beatitudinis obiectum. Sed obiectum beatitudinis est bonitas summa, quae potest intelligi in Deo etiam sine personarum distinctione. Ergo non fuit necessarium credere explicite Trinitatem.

**SED CONTRA** est quod in veteri testamento multipliciter expressa est Trinitas personarum, sicut statim in principio Gen. dicitur, ad expressionem Trinitatis, *faciamus hominem ad imaginem et similitudinem nostram*. Ergo a principio de necessitate salutis fuit credere Trinitatem.

**RESPONDEO** dicendum quod mysterium Christi explicite credi non potest sine fide Trinitatis, quia in mysterio Christi hoc continetur quod filius Dei carnem assumpserit, quod per gratiam spiritus sancti mundum renovaverit, et iterum quod de spiritu sancto conceptus fuerit. Et ideo eo modo quo mysterium Christi ante Christum fuit quidem explicite creditum a maioribus, implicite autem et quasi obumbrate a minoribus, ita etiam et mysterium Trinitatis. Et ideo etiam post tempus gratiae divulgatae tenentur omnes ad explicite credendum mysterium Trinitatis. Et omnes qui renascuntur in Christo hoc adipiscuntur per invocationem Trinitatis, secundum illud Matth. ult., *euntes, docete omnes gentes, baptizantes eos in nomine patris et filii et spiritus sancti*.

**AD PRIMUM** ergo dicendum quod illa duo explicite credere de Deo omni tempore et quoad omnes necessarium fuit. Non tamen est sufficiens omni tempore et quoad omnes.

**AD SECUNDUM** dicendum quod ante Christi adventum fides Trinitatis erat occulta in fide maiorum. Sed per Christum manifestata est mundo per apostolos.

**AD TERTIUM** dicendum quod summa bonitas Dei secundum modum quo nunc intelligitur per effectus, potest intelligi absque Trinitate personarum. Sed secundum quod intelligitur in seipso, prout videtur a beatis, non potest intelligi sine Trinitate personarum. Et iterum ipsa missio personarum divinarum perducit nos in beatitudinem.

expounds (*Tract.* cvi) as follows: *Not the name by which Thou art called God, but the name whereby Thou art called My Father*, and further on he adds: *In that He made this world, God is known to all nations; in that He is not to be worshiped together with false gods, 'God is known in Judea'; but, in that He is the Father of this Christ, through Whom He takes away the sin of the world, He now makes known to men this name of His, which hitherto they knew not.* Therefore before the coming of Christ it was not known that Paternity and Filiation were in the Godhead: and so the Trinity was not believed explicitly.

**OBJ. 3**: Further, that which we are bound to believe explicitly of God is the object of heavenly happiness. Now the object of heavenly happiness is the sovereign good, which can be understood to be in God, without any distinction of Persons. Therefore it was not necessary to believe explicitly in the Trinity.

**ON THE CONTRARY**, In the Old Testament the Trinity of Persons is expressed in many ways; thus at the very outset of Genesis it is written in manifestation of the Trinity: *Let us make man to Our image and likeness* (Gen 1:26). Therefore from the very beginning it was necessary for salvation to believe in the Trinity.

**I ANSWER THAT**, It is impossible to believe explicitly in the mystery of Christ, without faith in the Trinity, since the mystery of Christ includes that the Son of God took flesh; that He renewed the world through the grace of the Holy Spirit; and again, that He was conceived by the Holy Spirit. Wherefore just as, before Christ, the mystery of Christ was believed explicitly by the learned, but implicitly and under a veil, so to speak, by the simple, so too was it with the mystery of the Trinity. And consequently, when once grace had been revealed, all were bound to explicit faith in the mystery of the Trinity: and all who are born again in Christ, have this bestowed on them by the invocation of the Trinity, according to Matt. 28:19: *Going therefore teach ye all nations, baptizing them in the name of the Father, and of the Son and of the Holy Spirit.*

**REPLY OBJ. 1**: Explicit faith in those two things was necessary at all times and for all people: but it was not sufficient at all times and for all people.

**REPLY OBJ. 2**: Before Christ's coming, faith in the Trinity lay hidden in the faith of the learned, but through Christ and the apostles it was shown to the world.

**REPLY OBJ. 3**: God's sovereign goodness as we understand it now through its effects, can be understood without the Trinity of Persons: but as understood in itself, and as seen by the Blessed, it cannot be understood without the Trinity of Persons. Moreover the mission of the Divine Persons brings us to heavenly happiness.

# Article 9

*Whether to believe is meritorious?*

AD NONUM SIC PROCEDITUR. Videtur quod credere non sit meritorium. Principium enim merendi est caritas, ut supra dictum est. Sed fides est praeambula ad caritatem, sicut et natura. Ergo, sicut actus naturae non est meritorius (quia naturalibus non meremur), ita etiam nec actus fidei.

PRAETEREA, credere medium est inter opinari et scire vel considerare scita. Sed consideratio scientiae non est meritoria; similiter autem nec opinio. Ergo etiam neque credere est meritorium.

PRAETEREA, ille qui assentit alicui rei credendo aut habet causam sufficienter inducentem ipsum ad credendum, aut non. Si habet sufficiens inductivum ad credendum, non videtur hoc ei esse meritorium, quia non est ei iam liberum credere et non credere. Si autem non habet sufficiens inductivum ad credendum, levitatis est credere, secundum illud Eccli. XIX, *qui cito credit levis est corde*, et sic non videtur esse meritorium. Ergo credere nullo modo est meritorium.

SED CONTRA est quod dicitur ad Heb. XI, quod sancti *per fidem adepti sunt repromissiones*. Quod non esset nisi credendo mererentur. Ergo ipsum credere est meritorium.

RESPONDEO dicendum quod, sicut supra dictum est, actus nostri sunt meritorii inquantum procedunt ex libero arbitrio moto a Deo per gratiam. Unde omnis actus humanus qui subiicitur libero arbitrio, si sit relatus in Deum, potest meritorius esse. Ipsum autem credere est actus intellectus assentientis veritati divinae ex imperio voluntatis a Deo motae per gratiam, et sic subiacet libero arbitrio in ordine ad Deum. Unde actus fidei potest esse meritorius.

AD PRIMUM ergo dicendum quod natura comparatur ad caritatem, quae est merendi principium, sicut materia ad formam. Fides autem comparatur ad caritatem sicut dispositio praecedens ultimam formam. Manifestum est autem quod subiectum vel materia non potest agere in virtute formae, neque etiam dispositio praecedens, antequam forma adveniat. Sed postquam forma advenerit, tam subiectum quam dispositio praecedens agit in virtute formae, quae est principale agendi principium, sicut calor ignis agit in virtute formae substantialis. Sic ergo neque natura neque fides sine caritate possunt producere actum meritorium, sed caritate superveniente, actus fidei fit meritorius per caritatem, sicut et actus naturae et naturalis liberi arbitrii.

AD SECUNDUM dicendum quod in scientia duo possunt considerari, scilicet ipse assensus scientis ad rem scitam, et consideratio rei scitae. Assensus autem scien-

OBJECTION 1: It would seem that to believe is not meritorious. For the principle of all merit is charity, as stated above (I-II, Q. 114, A. 4). Now faith, like nature, is a preamble to charity. Therefore, just as an act of nature is not meritorious, since we do not merit by our natural gifts, so neither is an act of faith.

OBJ. 2: Further, belief is a mean between opinion and scientific knowledge or the consideration of things scientifically known. Now the considerations of science are not meritorious, nor on the other hand is opinion. Therefore belief is not meritorious.

OBJ. 3: Further, he who assents to a point of faith, either has a sufficient motive for believing, or he has not. If he has a sufficient motive for his belief, this does not seem to imply any merit on his part, since he is no longer free to believe or not to believe: whereas if he has not a sufficient motive for believing, this is a mark of levity, according to Ecclus. 19:4: *He that is hasty to give credit, is light of heart*, so that, seemingly, he gains no merit thereby. Therefore to believe is by no means meritorious.

ON THE CONTRARY, It is written (Heb 11:33) that the saints *by faith . . . obtained promises*, which would not be the case if they did not merit by believing. Therefore to believe is meritorious.

I ANSWER THAT, As stated above (I-II, Q. 114, AA. 3, 4), our actions are meritorious insofar as they proceed from the free-will moved with grace by God. Therefore every human act proceeding from the free-will, if it be referred to God, can be meritorious. Now the act of believing is an act of the intellect assenting to the Divine truth at the command of the will moved by the grace of God, so that it is subject to the free-will in relation to God; and consequently the act of faith can be meritorious.

REPLY OBJ. 1: Nature is compared to charity which is the principle of merit, as matter to form: whereas faith is compared to charity as the disposition which precedes the ultimate form. Now it is evident that the subject or the matter cannot act save by virtue of the form, nor can a preceding disposition, before the advent of the form: but after the advent of the form, both the subject and the preceding disposition act by virtue of the form, which is the chief principle of action, even as the heat of fire acts by virtue of the substantial form of fire. Accordingly neither nature nor faith can, without charity, produce a meritorious act; but, when accompanied by charity, the act of faith is made meritorious thereby, even as an act of nature, and a natural act of the free-will.

REPLY OBJ. 2: Two things may be considered in science: namely the scientist's assent to a scientific fact and his consideration of that fact. Now the assent of science is

tiae non subiicitur libero arbitrio, quia sciens cogitur ad assentiendum per efficaciam demonstrationis. Et ideo assensus scientiae non est meritorius. Sed consideratio actualis rei scitae subiacet libero arbitrio, est enim in potestate hominis considerare vel non considerare. Et ideo consideratio scientiae potest esse meritoria, si referatur ad finem caritatis, idest ad honorem Dei vel utilitatem proximi. Sed in fide utrumque subiacet libero arbitrio. Et ideo quantum ad utrumque actus fidei potest esse meritorius. Sed opinio non habet firmum assensum, est enim quoddam debile et infirmum, secundum Philosophum, in I Poster. Unde non videtur procedere ex perfecta voluntate. Et sic ex parte assensus non multum videtur habere rationem meriti. Sed ex parte considerationis actualis potest meritoria esse.

**AD TERTIUM** dicendum quod ille qui credit habet sufficiens inductivum ad credendum, inducitur enim auctoritate divinae doctrinae miraculis confirmatae, et, quod plus est, interiori instinctu Dei invitantis. Unde non leviter credit. Tamen non habet sufficiens inductivum ad sciendum. Et ideo non tollitur ratio meriti.

not subject to free-will, because the scientist is obliged to assent by force of the demonstration, wherefore scientific assent is not meritorious. But the actual consideration of what a man knows scientifically is subject to his free-will, for it is in his power to consider or not to consider. Hence scientific consideration may be meritorious if it be referred to the end of charity, i.e., to the honor of God or the good of our neighbor. On the other hand, in the case of faith, both these things are subject to the free-will so that in both respects the act of faith can be meritorious: whereas in the case of opinion, there is no firm assent, since it is weak and infirm, as the Philosopher observes (*Poster.* i, 33), so that it does not seem to proceed from a perfect act of the will: and for this reason, as regards the assent, it does not appear to be very meritorious, though it can be as regards the actual consideration.

**REPLY OBJ. 3**: The believer has sufficient motive for believing, for he is moved by the authority of Divine teaching confirmed by miracles, and, what is more, by the inward instinct of the Divine invitation: hence he does not believe lightly. He has not, however, sufficient reason for scientific knowledge, hence he does not lose the merit.

# Article 10

*Whether reasons in support of what we believe lessen the merit of faith?*

**AD DECIMUM SIC PROCEDITUR**. Videtur quod ratio inducta ad ea quae sunt fidei diminuat meritum fidei. Dicit enim Gregorius, in quadam homilia, quod *fides non habet meritum cui humana ratio praebet experimentum*. Si ergo ratio humana sufficienter experimentum praebens totaliter excludit meritum fidei, videtur quod qualiscumque ratio humana inducta ad ea quae sunt fidei diminuat meritum fidei.

**PRAETEREA**, quidquid diminuit rationem virtutis diminuit rationem meriti, quia *felicitas virtutis est praemium* ut etiam philosophus dicit, in I Ethic. Sed ratio humana videtur diminuere rationem virtutis ipsius fidei, quia de ratione fidei est quod sit non apparentium, ut supra dictum est; quanto autem plures rationes inducuntur ad aliquid, tanto minus est non apparens. Ergo ratio humana inducta ad ea quae sunt fidei meritum fidei diminuit.

**PRAETEREA**, contrariorum contrariae sunt causae. Sed id quod inducitur in contrarium fidei auget meritum fidei, sive sit persecutio cogentis ad recedendum a fide, sive etiam sit ratio aliqua hoc persuadens. Ergo ratio coadiuvans fidem diminuit meritum fidei.

**SED CONTRA** est quod I Petri III dicitur, *parati semper ad satisfactionem omni poscenti vos rationem de ea*

**OBJECTION 1**: It would seem that reasons in support of what we believe lessen the merit of faith. For Gregory says (*Hom. xxvi in Evang.*) that *there is no merit in believing what is shown by reason*. If, therefore, human reason provides sufficient proof, the merit of faith is altogether taken away. Therefore it seems that any kind of human reasoning in support of matters of faith, diminishes the merit of believing.

**OBJ. 2**: Further, whatever lessens the measure of virtue, lessens the amount of merit, since *happiness is the reward of virtue*, as the Philosopher states (*Ethic.* i, 9). Now human reasoning seems to diminish the measure of the virtue of faith, since it is essential to faith to be about the unseen, as stated above (Q. 1, AA. 4, 5). Now the more a thing is supported by reasons the less is it unseen. Therefore human reasons in support of matters of faith diminish the merit of faith.

**OBJ. 3**: Further, contrary things have contrary causes. Now an inducement in opposition to faith increases the merit of faith whether it consist in persecution inflicted by one who endeavors to force a man to renounce his faith, or in an argument persuading him to do so. Therefore reasons in support of faith diminish the merit of faith.

**ON THE CONTRARY**, It is written (1 Pet 3:15): *Being ready always to satisfy every one that asketh you a reason of*

*quae in vobis est fide et spe.* Non autem ad hoc induceret apostolus si per hoc meritum fidei diminueretur. Non ergo ratio diminuit meritum fidei.

RESPONDEO dicendum quod, sicut dictum est, actus fidei potest esse meritorius inquantum subiacet voluntati non solum quantum ad usum, sed etiam quantum ad assensum. Ratio autem humana inducta ad ea quae sunt fidei dupliciter potest se habere ad voluntatem credentis. Uno quidem modo, sicut praecedens, puta cum quis aut non haberet voluntatem, aut non haberet promptam voluntatem ad credendum, nisi ratio humana induceretur. Et sic ratio humana inducta diminuit meritum fidei, sicut etiam supra dictum est quod passio praecedens electionem in virtutibus moralibus diminuit laudem virtuosi actus. Sicut enim homo actus virtutum moralium debet exercere propter iudicium rationis, non propter passionem; ita credere debet homo ea quae sunt fidei non propter rationem humanam, sed propter auctoritatem divinam. Alio modo ratio humana potest se habere ad voluntatem credentis consequenter. Cum enim homo habet promptam voluntatem ad credendum, diligit veritatem creditam, et super ea excogitat et amplectitur si quas rationes ad hoc invenire potest. Et quantum ad hoc ratio humana non excludit meritum fidei, sed est signum maioris meriti, sicut etiam passio consequens in virtutibus moralibus est signum promptioris voluntatis, ut supra dictum est. Et hoc significatur Ioan. IV, ubi Samaritani ad mulierem, per quam ratio humana figuratur, dixerunt, *iam non propter tuam loquelam credimus.*

AD PRIMUM ergo dicendum quod Gregorius loquitur in casu illo quando homo non habet voluntatem credendi nisi propter rationem inductam. Quando autem homo habet voluntatem credendi ea quae sunt fidei ex sola auctoritate divina, etiam si habeat rationem demonstrativam ad aliquid eorum, puta ad hoc quod est Deum esse, non propter hoc tollitur vel minuitur meritum fidei.

AD SECUNDUM dicendum quod rationes quae inducuntur ad auctoritatem fidei non sunt demonstrationes quae in visionem intelligibilem intellectum humanum reducere possunt. Et ideo non desinunt esse non apparentia. Sed removent impedimenta fidei, ostendendo non esse impossibile quod in fide proponitur. Unde per tales rationes non diminuitur meritum fidei nec ratio fidei. Sed rationes demonstrativae inductae ad ea quae sunt fidei, praeambula tamen ad articulos, etsi diminuant rationem fidei, quia faciunt esse apparens id quod proponitur; non tamen diminuunt rationem caritatis, per quam voluntas est prompta ad ea credendum etiam si non apparerent. Et ideo non diminuitur ratio meriti.

AD TERTIUM dicendum quod ea quae repugnant fidei, sive in consideratione hominis sive in exteriori

*that faith and hope which is in you.* Now the Apostle would not give this advice, if it would imply a diminution in the merit of faith. Therefore reason does not diminish the merit of faith.

I ANSWER THAT, As stated above (A. 9), the act of faith can be meritorious, insofar as it is subject to the will, not only as to the use, but also as to the assent. Now human reason in support of what we believe, may stand in a twofold relation to the will of the believer. First, as preceding the act of the will; as, for instance, when a man either has not the will, or not a prompt will, to believe, unless he be moved by human reasons: and in this way human reason diminishes the merit of faith. In this sense it has been said above (I-II, Q. 24, A. 3, ad 1; Q. 77, A. 6, ad 2) that, in moral virtues, a passion which precedes choice makes the virtuous act less praiseworthy. For just as a man ought to perform acts of moral virtue, on account of the judgment of his reason, and not on account of a passion, so ought he to believe matters of faith, not on account of human reason, but on account of the Divine authority. Second, human reasons may be consequent to the will of the believer. For when a man's will is ready to believe, he loves the truth he believes, he thinks out and takes to heart whatever reasons he can find in support thereof; and in this way human reason does not exclude the merit of faith but is a sign of greater merit. Thus again, in moral virtues a consequent passion is the sign of a more prompt will, as stated above (I-II, Q. 24, A. 3, ad 1). We have an indication of this in the words of the Samaritans to the woman, who is a type of human reason: *We now believe, not for thy saying* (John 4:42).

REPLY OBJ. 1: Gregory is referring to the case of a man who has no will to believe what is of faith, unless he be induced by reasons. But when a man has the will to believe what is of faith on the authority of God alone, although he may have reasons in demonstration of some of them, e.g., of the existence of God, the merit of his faith is not, for that reason, lost or diminished.

REPLY OBJ. 2: The reasons which are brought forward in support of the authority of faith, are not demonstrations which can bring intellectual vision to the human intellect, wherefore they do not cease to be unseen. But they remove obstacles to faith, by showing that what faith proposes is not impossible; wherefore such reasons do not diminish the merit or the measure of faith. On the other hand, though demonstrative reasons in support of the preambles of faith, but not of the articles of faith, diminish the measure of faith, since they make the thing believed to be seen, yet they do not diminish the measure of charity, which makes the will ready to believe them, even if they were unseen; and so the measure of merit is not diminished.

REPLY OBJ. 3: Whatever is in opposition to faith, whether it consist in a man's thoughts, or in outward per-

persecutione, intantum augent meritum fidei inquantum ostenditur voluntas magis prompta et firma in fide. Et ideo martyres maius fidei meritum habuerunt non recedentes a fide propter persecutiones; et etiam sapientes maius meritum fidei habent non recedentes a fide propter rationes philosophorum vel haereticorum contra fidem inductas. Sed ea quae conveniunt fidei non semper diminuunt promptitudinem voluntatis ad credendum. Et ideo non semper diminuunt meritum fidei.

secution, increases the merit of faith, insofar as the will is shown to be more prompt and firm in believing. Hence the martyrs had more merit of faith, through not renouncing faith on account of persecution; and even the wise have greater merit of faith, through not renouncing their faith on account of the reasons brought forward by philosophers or heretics in opposition to faith. On the other hand things that are favorable to faith, do not always diminish the promptness of the will to believe, and therefore they do not always diminish the merit of faith.

# QUESTION 3

## THE OUTWARD ACT OF FAITH

Deinde considerandum est de exteriori fidei actu, qui est confessio. Et circa hoc quaeruntur duo.

Primo, utrum confessio sit actus fidei.
Secundo, utrum confessio sit necessaria ad salutem.

We must now consider the outward act, viz. the confession of faith: under which head there are two points of inquiry:

(1) Whether confession is an act of faith?
(2) Whether confession of faith is necessary for salvation?

# Article 1

*Whether confession is an act of faith?*

**AD PRIMUM SIC PROCEDITUR**. Videtur quod confessio non sit actus fidei. Non enim idem actus pertinet ad diversas virtutes. Sed confessio pertinet ad poenitentiam, cuius ponitur pars. Ergo non est actus fidei.

**PRAETEREA**, ab hoc quod homo confiteatur fidem retrahitur interdum per timorem, vel etiam propter aliquam confusionem, unde et apostolus, ad Ephes. ult., petit orari pro se ut detur sibi *cum fiducia notum facere mysterium Evangelii*. Sed non recedere a bono propter confusionem vel timorem pertinet ad fortitudinem, quae moderatur audacias et timores. Ergo videtur quod confessio non sit actus fidei, sed magis fortitudinis vel constantiae.

**PRAETEREA**, sicut per fidei fervorem inducitur aliquis ad confitendum fidem exterius, ita etiam inducitur ad alia exteriora bona opera facienda, dicitur enim Gal. V quod *fides per dilectionem operatur*. Sed alia exteriora opera non ponuntur actus fidei. Ergo etiam neque confessio.

**SED CONTRA** est quod, II ad Thess. I, super illud, *et opus fidei in virtute*, dicit Glossa, *idest confessionem, quae proprie est opus fidei*.

**RESPONDEO** dicendum quod actus exteriores illius virtutis proprie sunt actus ad cuius fines secundum suas species referuntur, sicut ieiunare secundum suam speciem refertur ad finem abstinentiae, quae est compescere carnem, et ideo est actus abstinentiae.

Confessio autem eorum quae sunt fidei secundum suam speciem ordinatur sicut ad finem ad id quod est fidei, secundum illud II ad Cor. IV, *habentes eundem spiritum fidei credimus, propter quod et loquimur*, exterior enim locutio ordinatur ad significandum id quod in corde concipitur. Unde sicut conceptus interior eorum quae sunt fidei est proprie fidei actus, ita etiam et exterior confessio.

**OBJECTION 1**: It would seem that confession is not an act of faith. For the same act does not belong to different virtues. Now confession belongs to penance of which it is a part. Therefore it is not an act of faith.

**OBJ. 2**: Further, man is sometimes deterred by fear or some kind of confusion, from confessing his faith: wherefore the Apostle (Eph 6:19) asks for prayers that it may be granted him *with confidence, to make known the mystery of the gospel*. Now it belongs to fortitude, which moderates daring and fear, not to be deterred from doing good on account of confusion or fear. Therefore it seems that confession is not an act of faith, but rather of fortitude or constancy.

**OBJ. 3**: Further, just as the ardor of faith makes one confess one's faith outwardly, so does it make one do other external good works, for it is written (Gal 5:6) that *faith . . . worketh by charity*. But other external works are not reckoned acts of faith. Therefore neither is confession an act of faith.

**ON THE CONTRARY**, A gloss explains the words of 2 Thess. 1:11, *and the work of faith in power* as referring to *confession which is a work proper to faith*.

**I ANSWER THAT**, Outward actions belong properly to the virtue to whose end they are specifically referred: thus fasting is referred specifically to the end of abstinence, which is to tame the flesh, and consequently it is an act of abstinence.

Now confession of those things that are of faith is referred specifically as to its end, to that which concerns faith, according to 2 Cor. 4:13: *Having the same spirit of faith . . . we believe, and therefore we speak also*. For the outward utterance is intended to signify the inward thought. Wherefore, just as the inward thought of matters of faith is properly an act of faith, so too is the outward confession of them.

**Ad primum** ergo dicendum quod triplex est confessio quae in Scripturis laudatur. Una est confessio eorum quae sunt fidei. Et ista est proprius actus fidei, utpote relata ad fidei finem, sicut dictum est. Alia est confessio gratiarum actionis sive laudis. Et ista est actus latriae, ordinatur enim ad honorem Deo exterius exhibendum, quod est finis latriae. Tertia est confessio peccatorum. Et haec ordinatur ad deletionem peccati, quae est finis poenitentiae. Unde pertinet ad poenitentiam.

**Ad secundum** dicendum quod removens prohibens non est causa per se, sed per accidens, ut patet per Philosophum, in VIII Phys. Unde fortitudo, quae removet impedimentum confessionis fidei, scilicet timorem vel erubescentiam, non est proprie et per se causa confessionis, sed quasi per accidens.

**Ad tertium** dicendum quod fides interior, mediante dilectione, causat omnes exteriores actus virtutum mediantibus aliis virtutibus, imperando, non eliciendo. Sed confessionem producit tanquam proprium actum, nulla alia virtute mediante.

**Reply Obj. 1**: A threefold confession is commended by the Scriptures. One is the confession of matters of faith, and this is a proper act of faith, since it is referred to the end of faith as stated above. Another is the confession of thanksgiving or praise, and this is an act of *latria*, for its purpose is to give outward honor to God, which is the end of *latria*. The third is the confession of sins, which is ordained to the blotting out of sins, which is the end of penance, to which virtue it therefore belongs.

**Reply Obj. 2**: That which removes an obstacle is not a direct, but an indirect, cause, as the Philosopher proves (*Phys.* viii, 4). Hence fortitude which removes an obstacle to the confession of faith, viz. fear or shame, is not the proper and direct cause of confession, but an indirect cause, so to speak.

**Reply Obj. 3**: Inward faith, with the aid of charity, causes all outward acts of virtue, by means of the other virtues, commanding, but not eliciting them; whereas it produces the act of confession as its proper act, without the help of any other virtue.

# Article 2

### Whether confession of faith is necessary for salvation?

**Ad secundum sic proceditur.** Videtur quod confessio fidei non sit necessaria ad salutem. Illud enim videtur ad salutem sufficere per quod homo attingit finem virtutis. Sed finis proprius fidei est coniunctio humanae mentis ad veritatem divinam, quod potest etiam esse sine exteriori confessione. Ergo confessio fidei non est necessaria ad salutem.

**Praeterea**, per exteriorem confessionem fidei homo fidem suam alii homini patefacit. Sed hoc non est necessarium nisi illis qui habent alios in fide instruere. Ergo videtur quod minores non teneantur ad fidei confessionem.

**Praeterea**, illud quod potest vergere in scandalum et turbationem aliorum non est necessarium ad salutem, dicit enim apostolus, I ad Cor. X, *sine offensione estote Iudaeis et gentibus et Ecclesiae Dei.* Sed per confessionem fidei quandoque ad perturbationem infideles provocantur. Ergo confessio fidei non est necessaria ad salutem.

**Sed contra** est quod apostolus dicit, ad Rom. X, *corde creditur ad iustitiam, ore autem confessio fit ad salutem.*

**Respondeo** dicendum quod ea quae sunt necessaria ad salutem cadunt sub praeceptis divinae legis. Confessio autem fidei, cum sit quoddam affirmativum, non potest cadere nisi sub praecepto affirmativo. Unde eo modo est de necessariis ad salutem quo modo potest cadere sub praecepto affirmativo divinae legis. Praecepta

**Objection 1**: It would seem that confession of faith is not necessary for salvation. For, seemingly, a thing is sufficient for salvation, if it is a means of attaining the end of virtue. Now the proper end of faith is the union of the human mind with Divine truth, and this can be realized without any outward confession. Therefore confession of faith is not necessary for salvation.

**Obj. 2**: Further, by outward confession of faith, a man reveals his faith to another man. But this is unnecessary save for those who have to instruct others in the faith. Therefore it seems that the simple folk are not bound to confess the faith.

**Obj. 3**: Further, whatever may tend to scandalize and disturb others, is not necessary for salvation, for the Apostle says (1 Cor 10:32): *Be without offense to the Jews and to the gentiles and to the Church of God.* Now confession of faith sometimes causes a disturbance among unbelievers. Therefore it is not necessary for salvation.

**On the contrary**, The Apostle says (Rom 10:10): *With the heart we believe unto justice; but with the mouth, confession is made unto salvation.*

**I answer that**, Things that are necessary for salvation come under the precepts of the Divine law. Now since confession of faith is something affirmative, it can only fall under an affirmative precept. Hence its necessity for salvation depends on how it falls under an affirmative precept of the Divine law. Now affirmative precepts as stated above (I-

autem affirmativa, ut supra dictum est, non obligant ad semper, etsi semper obligent, obligant autem pro loco et tempore et secundum alias circumstantias debitas secundum quas oportet actum humanum limitari ad hoc quod sit actus virtutis.

Sic igitur confiteri fidem non semper neque in quolibet loco est de necessitate salutis, sed aliquo loco et tempore, quando scilicet per omissionem huius confessionis subtraheretur honor debitus Deo, vel etiam utilitas proximis impendenda; puta si aliquis interrogatus de fide taceret, et ex hoc crederetur vel quod non haberet fidem vel quod fides non esset vera, vel alii per eius taciturnitatem averterentur a fide. In huiusmodi enim casibus confessio fidei est de necessitate salutis.

**AD PRIMUM** ergo dicendum quod finis fidei, sicut et aliarum virtutum, referri debet ad finem caritatis, qui est amor Dei et proximi. Et ideo quando honor Dei vel utilitas proximi hoc exposcit, non debet esse contentus homo ut per fidem suam ipse veritati divinae coniungatur; sed debet fidem exterius confiteri.

**AD SECUNDUM** dicendum quod in casu necessitatis, ubi fides periclitatur, quilibet tenetur fidem suam aliis propalare, vel ad instructionem aliorum fidelium sive confirmationem, vel ad reprimendum infidelium insultationem. Sed aliis temporibus instruere homines de fide non pertinet ad omnes fideles.

**AD TERTIUM** dicendum quod, si turbatio infidelium oriatur de confessione fidei manifesta absque aliqua utilitate fidei vel fidelium, non est laudabile in tali casu fidem publice confiteri, unde dominus dicit, Matth. VII, *nolite sanctum dare canibus, neque margaritas vestras spargere ante porcos, ne conversi dirumpant vos.* Sed si utilitas aliqua fidei speretur aut necessitas adsit, contempta turbatione infidelium, debet homo fidem publice confiteri. Unde Matth. XV dicitur quod, cum discipuli dixissent domino quod Pharisaei, audito eius verbo, scandalizati sunt, dominus respondit, *sinite illos,* scilicet turbari, *caeci sunt et duces caecorum.*

II, Q. 71, A. 5, ad 3; I-II, Q. 88, A. 1, ad 2) do not bind for always, although they are always binding; but they bind as to place and time according to other due circumstances, in respect of which human acts have to be regulated in order to be acts of virtue.

Thus then it is not necessary for salvation to confess one's faith at all times and in all places, but in certain places and at certain times, when, namely, by omitting to do so, we would deprive God of due honor, or our neighbor of a service that we ought to render him: for instance, if a man, on being asked about his faith, were to remain silent, so as to make people believe either that he is without faith, or that the faith is false, or so as to turn others away from the faith; for in such cases as these, confession of faith is necessary for salvation.

**REPLY OBJ. 1**: The end of faith, even as of the other virtues, must be referred to the end of charity, which is the love of God and our neighbor. Consequently when God's honor and our neighbor's good demand, man should not be contented with being united by faith to God's truth, but ought to confess his faith outwardly.

**REPLY OBJ. 2**: In cases of necessity where faith is in danger, every one is bound to proclaim his faith to others, either to give good example and encouragement to the rest of the faithful, or to check the attacks of unbelievers: but at other times it is not the duty of all the faithful to instruct others in the faith.

**REPLY OBJ. 3**: There is nothing commendable in making a public confession of one's faith, if it causes a disturbance among unbelievers, without any profit either to the faith or to the faithful. Hence Our Lord said (Matt 7:6): *Give not that which is holy to dogs, neither cast ye your pearls before swine . . . lest turning upon you, they tear you.* Yet, if there is hope of profit to the faith, or if there be urgency, a man should disregard the disturbance of unbelievers, and confess his faith in public. Hence it is written (Matt 15:12) that when the disciples had said to Our Lord that the Pharisee, when they heard this word, were scandalized, He answered: *Let them alone, they are blind, and leaders of the blind.*

# QUESTION 4

## THE VIRTUE ITSELF OF FAITH

Deinde considerandum est de ipsa fidei virtute. Et primo quidem, de ipsa fide; secundo, de habentibus fidem; tertio, de causa fidei; quarto, de effectibus eius.

Circa primum quaeruntur octo.

Primo, quid sit fides.

Secundo, in qua vi animae sit sicut in subiecto.

Tertio, utrum forma eius sit caritas.

Quarto, utrum eadem numero sit fides formata et informis.

Quinto, utrum fides sit virtus.

Sexto, utrum sit una virtus.

Septimo, de ordine eius ad alias virtutes.

Octavo, de comparatione certitudinis eius ad certitudinem virtutum intellectualium.

We must now consider the virtue itself of faith, and, in the first place, faith itself; second, those who have faith; third, the cause of faith; fourth, its effects.

Under the first head there are eight points of inquiry:

(1) What is faith?

(2) In what power of the soul does it reside?

(3) Whether its form is charity?

(4) Whether living (formata) faith and lifeless (informis) faith are one identically?

(5) Whether faith is a virtue?

(6) Whether it is one virtue?

(7) Of its relation to the other virtues;

(8) Of its certitude as compared with the certitude of the intellectual virtues.

# Article 1

*Whether this is a fitting definition of faith: "faith is the substance of things to be hoped for, the evidence of things that appear not"?*

**AD PRIMUM SIC PROCEDITUR**. Videtur quod sit incompetens fidei definitio quam apostolus ponit, ad Heb. XI, dicens, *est autem fides substantia sperandarum rerum, argumentum non apparentium*. Nulla enim qualitas est substantia. Sed fides est qualitas, cum sit virtus theologica, ut supra dictum est. Ergo non est substantia.

**PRAETEREA**, diversarum virtutum diversa sunt obiecta. Sed res speranda est obiectum spei. Non ergo debet poni in definitione fidei tanquam eius obiectum.

**PRAETEREA**, fides magis perficitur per caritatem quam per spem, quia caritas est forma fidei, ut infra dicetur. Magis ergo poni debuit in definitione fidei res diligenda quam res speranda.

**PRAETEREA**, idem non debet poni in diversis generibus. Sed substantia et argumentum sunt diversa genera non subalternatim posita. Ergo inconvenienter fides dicitur esse substantia et argumentum.

**PRAETEREA**, per argumentum veritas manifestatur eius ad quod inducitur argumentum. Sed illud dicitur esse apparens cuius veritas est manifestata. Ergo videtur implicari oppositio in hoc quod dicitur *argumentum non apparentium*. Inconvenienter ergo describitur fides.

**IN CONTRARIUM** sufficit auctoritas apostoli.

**OBJECTION 1**: It would seem that the Apostle gives an unfitting definition of faith (Heb 11:1) when he says: *Faith is the substance of things to be hoped for, the evidence of things that appear not*. For no quality is a substance: whereas faith is a quality, since it is a theological virtue, as stated above (I-II, Q. 62, A. 3). Therefore it is not a substance.

**OBJ. 2**: Further, different virtues have different objects. Now things to be hoped for are the object of hope. Therefore they should not be included in a definition of faith, as though they were its object.

**OBJ. 3**: Further, faith is perfected by charity rather than by hope, since charity is the form of faith, as we shall state further on (A. 3). Therefore the definition of faith should have included the thing to be loved rather than the thing to be hoped for.

**OBJ. 4**: Further, the same thing should not be placed in different genera. Now *substance* and *evidence* are different genera, and neither is subalternate to the other. Therefore it is unfitting to state that faith is both *substance* and *evidence*.

**OBJ. 5**: Further, evidence manifests the truth of the matter for which it is adduced. Now a thing is said to be apparent when its truth is already manifest. Therefore it seems to imply a contradiction to speak of *evidence of things that appear not*: and so faith is unfittingly defined.

**ON THE CONTRARY**, The authority of the Apostle suffices.

RESPONDEO dicendum quod, licet quidam dicant praedicta apostoli verba non esse fidei definitionem, tamen, si quis recte consideret, omnia ex quibus fides potest definiri in praedicta descriptione tanguntur, licet verba non ordinentur sub forma definitionis, sicut etiam apud philosophos praetermissa syllogistica forma syllogismorum principia tanguntur.

Ad cuius evidentiam considerandum est quod, cum habitus cognoscantur per actus et actus per obiecta, fides, cum sit habitus quidam, debet definiri per proprium actum in comparatione ad proprium obiectum. Actus autem fidei est credere, qui, sicut supra dictum est, actus est intellectus determinati ad unum ex imperio voluntatis. Sic ergo actus fidei habet ordinem et ad obiectum voluntatis, quod est bonum et finis; et ad obiectum intellectus, quod est verum. Et quia fides, cum sit virtus theologica, sicut supra dictum est, habet idem pro obiecto et fine, necesse est quod obiectum fidei et finis proportionaliter sibi correspondeant. Dictum est autem supra quod veritas prima est obiectum fidei secundum quod ipsa est non visa et ea quibus propter ipsam inhaeretur. Et secundum hoc oportet quod ipsa veritas prima se habeat ad actum fidei per modum finis secundum rationem rei non visae. Quod pertinet ad rationem rei speratae, secundum illud apostoli, ad Rom. VIII, *quod non videmus speramus*, veritatem enim videre est ipsam habere; non autem sperat aliquis id quod iam habet, sed spes est de hoc quod non habetur, ut supra dictum est. Sic igitur habitudo actus fidei ad finem, qui est obiectum voluntatis, significatur in hoc quod dicitur, *fides est substantia rerum sperandarum*. Substantia enim solet dici prima inchoatio cuiuscumque rei, et maxime quando tota res sequens continetur virtute in primo principio, puta si dicamus quod prima principia indemonstrabilia sunt substantia scientiae, quia scilicet primum quod in nobis est de scientia sunt huiusmodi principia, et in eis virtute continetur tota scientia. Per hunc ergo modum dicitur fides esse substantia rerum sperandarum, quia scilicet prima inchoatio rerum sperandarum in nobis est per assensum fidei, quae virtute continet omnes res sperandas. In hoc enim speramus beatificari quod videbimus aperta visione veritatem cui per fidem adhaeremus, ut patet per ea quae supra de felicitate dicta sunt.

Habitudo autem actus fidei ad obiectum intellectus, secundum quod est obiectum fidei, designatur in hoc quod dicitur, *argumentum non apparentium*. Et sumitur argumentum pro argumenti effectu, per argumentum enim intellectus inducitur ad adhaerendum alicui vero; unde ipsa firma adhaesio intellectus ad veritatem fidei non apparentem vocatur hic argumentum. Unde alia littera habet convictio, quia scilicet per auctoritatem divinam intellectus credentis convincitur ad assentiendum

I ANSWER THAT, Though some say that the above words of the Apostle are not a definition of faith, yet if we consider the matter aright, this definition overlooks none of the points in reference to which faith can be defined, albeit the words themselves are not arranged in the form of a definition, just as the philosophers touch on the principles of the syllogism, without employing the syllogistic form.

In order to make this clear, we must observe that since habits are known by their acts, and acts by their objects, faith, being a habit, should be defined by its proper act in relation to its proper object. Now the act of faith is to believe, as stated above (Q. 2, AA. 2, 3), which is an act of the intellect determinate to one object of the will's command. Hence an act of faith is related both to the object of the will, i.e., to the good and the end, and to the object of the intellect, i.e., to the true. And since faith, through being a theological virtue, as stated above (I-II, Q. 62, A. 2), has one same thing for object and end, its object and end must, of necessity, be in proportion to one another. Now it has been already stated (Q. 1, AA. 1, 4) that the object of faith is the First Truth, as unseen, and whatever we hold on account thereof: so that it must needs be under the aspect of something unseen that the First Truth is the end of the act of faith, which aspect is that of a thing hoped for, according to the Apostle (Rom 8:25): *We hope for that which we see not*: because to see the truth is to possess it. Now one hopes not for what one has already, but for what one has not, as stated above (I-II, Q. 67, A. 4). Accordingly the relation of the act of faith to its end which is the object of the will, is indicated by the words: *Faith is the substance of things to be hoped for*. For we are wont to call by the name of substance, the first beginning of a thing, especially when the whole subsequent thing is virtually contained in the first beginning; for instance, we might say that the first self-evident principles are the substance of science, because, to wit, these principles are in us the first beginnings of science, the whole of which is itself contained in them virtually. In this way then faith is said to be the *substance of things to be hoped for*, for the reason that in us the first beginning of things to be hoped for is brought about by the assent of faith, which contains virtually all things to be hoped for. Because we hope to be made happy through seeing the unveiled truth to which our faith cleaves, as was made evident when we were speaking of happiness (I-II, Q. 3, A. 8; I-II, Q. 4, A. 3).

The relationship of the act of faith to the object of the intellect, considered as the object of faith, is indicated by the words, *evidence of things that appear not*, where *evidence* is taken for the result of evidence. For evidence induces the intellect to adhere to a truth, wherefore the firm adhesion of the intellect to the non-apparent truth of faith is called *evidence* here. Hence another reading has *conviction*, because to wit, the intellect of the believer is convinced by Divine authority, so as to assent to what it sees not.

his quae non videt. Si quis ergo in formam definitionis huiusmodi verba reducere velit, potest dicere quod *fides est habitus mentis, qua inchoatur vita aeterna in nobis, faciens intellectum assentire non apparentibus.*

Per hoc autem fides ab omnibus aliis distinguitur quae ad intellectum pertinent. Per hoc enim quod dicitur *argumentum*, distinguitur fides ab opinione, suspicione et dubitatione, per quae non est prima adhaesio intellectus firma ad aliquid. Per hoc autem quod dicitur *non apparentium*, distinguitur fides a scientia et intellectu, per quae aliquid fit apparens. Per hoc autem quod dicitur *substantia sperandarum rerum*, distinguitur virtus fidei a fide communiter sumpta, quae non ordinatur ad beatitudinem speratam.

Omnes autem aliae definitiones quaecumque de fide dantur, explicationes sunt huius quam apostolus ponit. Quod enim dicit Augustinus, *fides est virtus qua creduntur quae non videntur*; et quod dicit Damascenus, quod *fides est non inquisitus consensus*; et quod alii dicunt, quod *fides est certitudo quaedam animi de absentibus supra opinionem et infra scientiam*; idem est ei quod apostolus dicit, argumentum non apparentium. Quod vero Dionysius dicit, VII cap. de Div. Nom., quod *fides est manens credentium fundamentum, collocans eos in veritate et in ipsis veritatem*, idem est ei quod dicitur, substantia sperandarum rerum.

**AD PRIMUM** ergo dicendum quod substantia non sumitur hic secundum quod est genus generalissimum contra alia genera divisum, sed secundum quod in quolibet genere invenitur quaedam similitudo substantiae, prout scilicet primum in quolibet genere, continens in se alia virtute, dicitur esse substantia illorum.

**AD SECUNDUM** dicendum quod, cum fides pertineat ad intellectum secundum quod imperatur a voluntate, oportet quod ordinetur, sicut ad finem, ad obiecta illarum virtutum quibus perficitur voluntas. Inter quas est spes, ut infra patebit. Et ideo in definitione fidei ponitur obiectum spei.

**AD TERTIUM** dicendum quod dilectio potest esse et visorum et non visorum, et praesentium et absentium. Et ideo res diligenda non ita proprie adaptatur fidei sicut res speranda, cum spes sit semper absentium et non visorum.

**AD QUARTUM** dicendum quod substantia et argumentum, secundum quod in definitione fidei ponuntur, non important diversa genera fidei neque diversos actus, sed diversas habitudines unius actus ad diversa obiecta, ut ex dictis patet.

**AD QUINTUM** dicendum quod argumentum quod sumitur ex propriis principiis rei facit rem esse apparentem. Sed argumentum quod sumitur ex auctoritate divina non facit rem in se esse apparentem. Et tale argumentum ponitur in definitione fidei.

Accordingly if anyone would reduce the foregoing words to the form of a definition, he may say that *faith is a habit of the mind, whereby eternal life is begun in us, making the intellect assent to what is non-apparent.*

In this way faith is distinguished from all other things pertaining to the intellect. For when we describe it as *evidence*, we distinguish it from opinion, suspicion, and doubt, which do not make the intellect adhere to anything firmly; when we go on to say, *of things that appear not*, we distinguish it from science and understanding, the object of which is something apparent; and when we say that it is *the substance of things to be hoped for*, we distinguish the virtue of faith from faith commonly so called, which has no reference to the beatitude we hope for.

Whatever other definitions are given of faith, are explanations of this one given by the Apostle. For when Augustine says (*Tract. xl in Joan.*: QQ. *Evang. ii*, qu. 39) that *faith is a virtue whereby we believe what we do not see*, and when Damascene says (*De Fide Orth.* iv, 11) that *faith is an assent without research*, and when others say that *faith is that certainty of the mind about absent things which surpasses opinion but falls short of science*, these all amount to the same as the Apostle's words: *Evidence of things that appear not*; and when Dionysius says (*Div. Nom.* vii) that *faith is the solid foundation of the believer, establishing him in the truth, and showing forth the truth in him*, comes to the same as *substance of things to be hoped for*.

**REPLY OBJ. 1**: *Substance* here does not stand for the supreme genus condivided with the other genera, but for that likeness to substance which is found in each genus, inasmuch as the first thing in a genus contains the others virtually and is said to be the substance thereof.

**REPLY OBJ. 2**: Since faith pertains to the intellect as commanded by the will, it must needs be directed, as to its end, to the objects of those virtues which perfect the will, among which is hope, as we shall prove further on (Q. 18, A. 1). For this reason the definition of faith includes the object of hope.

**REPLY OBJ. 3**: Love may be of the seen and of the unseen, of the present and of the absent. Consequently a thing to be loved is not so adapted to faith, as a thing to be hoped for, since hope is always of the absent and the unseen.

**REPLY OBJ. 4**: *Substance* and *evidence* as included in the definition of faith, do not denote various genera of faith, nor different acts, but different relationships of one act to different objects, as is clear from what has been said.

**REPLY OBJ. 5**: Evidence taken from the proper principles of a thing, make it apparent, whereas evidence taken from Divine authority does not make a thing apparent in itself, and such is the evidence referred to in the definition of faith.

# Article 2

*Whether faith resides in the intellect as in a subject?*

**AD SECUNDUM SIC PROCEDITUR.** Videtur quod fides non sit in intellectu sicut in subiecto. Dicit enim Augustinus, in libro de Praed. Sanct., quod *fides in credentium voluntate consistit.* Sed voluntas est alia potentia ab intellectu. Ergo fides non est in intellectu sicut in subiecto.

**PRAETEREA,** assensus fidei ad aliquid credendum provenit ex voluntate Deo obediente. Tota ergo laus fidei ex obedientia esse videtur. Sed obedientia est in voluntate. Ergo et fides. Non ergo est in intellectu.

**PRAETEREA,** intellectus est vel speculativus vel practicus. Sed fides non est in intellectu speculativo, qui, cum *nihil dicat de imitabili et fugiendo,* ut dicitur in III de Anima, non est principium operationis, fides autem est quae *per dilectionem operatur,* ut dicitur ad Gal. V. Similiter etiam nec in intellectu practico, cuius obiectum est verum contingens factibile vel agibile, obiectum enim fidei est verum aeternum, ut ex supradictis patet. Non ergo fides est in intellectu sicut in subiecto.

**SED CONTRA** est quod fidei succedit visio patriae, secundum illud I ad Cor. XIII, *videmus nunc per speculum in aenigmate, tunc autem facie ad faciem.* Sed visio est in intellectu. Ergo et fides.

**RESPONDEO** dicendum quod, cum fides sit quaedam virtus, oportet quod actus eius sit perfectus. Ad perfectionem autem actus qui ex duobus activis principiis procedit requiritur quod utrumque activorum principiorum sit perfectum, non enim potest bene secari nisi et secans habeat artem et serra sit bene disposita ad secandum. Dispositio autem ad bene agendum in illis potentiis animae quae se habent ad opposita est habitus, ut supra dictum est. Et ideo oportet quod actus procedens ex duabus talibus potentiis sit perfectus habitu aliquo praeexistente in utraque potentiarum. Dictum est autem supra quod credere est actus intellectus secundum quod movetur a voluntate ad assentiendum, procedit enim huiusmodi actus et a voluntate et ab intellectu. Quorum uterque natus est per habitum perfici, secundum praedicta. Et ideo oportet quod tam in voluntate sit aliquis habitus quam in intellectu, si debeat actus fidei esse perfectus, sicut etiam ad hoc quod actus concupiscibilis sit perfectus, oportet quod sit habitus prudentiae in ratione et habitus temperantiae in concupiscibili. Credere autem est immediate actus intellectus, quia obiectum huius actus est verum, quod proprie pertinet ad intellectum. Et ideo necesse est quod fides, quae est proprium principium huius actus, sit in intellectu sicut in subiecto.

**OBJECTION 1:** It would seem that faith does not reside in the intellect. For Augustine says (*De Praedest. Sanct.* v) that *faith resides in the believer's will.* Now the will is a power distinct from the intellect. Therefore faith does not reside in the intellect.

**OBJ. 2:** Further, the assent of faith to believe anything, proceeds from the will obeying God. Therefore it seems that faith owes all its praise to obedience. Now obedience is in the will. Therefore faith is in the will, and not in the intellect.

**OBJ. 3:** Further, the intellect is either speculative or practical. Now faith is not in the speculative intellect, since this is *not concerned with things to be sought or avoided,* as stated in *De Anima* iii, 9, so that it is not a principle of operation, whereas *faith . . . worketh by charity* (Gal 5:6). Likewise, neither is it in the practical intellect, the object of which is some true, contingent thing, that can be made or done. For the object of faith is the Eternal Truth, as was shown above (Q. 1, A. 1). Therefore faith does not reside in the intellect.

**ON THE CONTRARY,** Faith is succeeded by the heavenly vision, according to 1 Cor. 13:12: *We see now through a glass in a dark manner; but then face to face.* Now vision is in the intellect. Therefore faith is likewise.

**I ANSWER THAT,** Since faith is a virtue, its act must needs be perfect. Now, for the perfection of an act proceeding from two active principles, each of these principles must be perfect: for it is not possible for a thing to be sawn well, unless the sawyer possess the art, and the saw be well fitted for sawing. Now, in a power of the soul, which is related to opposite objects, a disposition to act well is a habit, as stated above (I-II, Q. 49, A. 4, ad 1, 2, 3). Wherefore an act that proceeds from two such powers must be perfected by a habit residing in each of them. Again, it has been stated above (Q. 2, AA. 1, 2) that to believe is an act of the intellect inasmuch as the will moves it to assent. And this act proceeds from the will and the intellect, both of which have a natural aptitude to be perfected in this way. Consequently, if the act of faith is to be perfect, there needs to be a habit in the will as well as in the intellect: even as there needs to be the habit of prudence in the reason, besides the habit of temperance in the concupiscible faculty, in order that the act of that faculty be perfect. Now, to believe is immediately an act of the intellect, because the object of that act is *the true,* which pertains properly to the intellect. Consequently faith, which is the proper principle of that act, must needs reside in the intellect.

**AD PRIMUM** ergo dicendum quod Augustinus fidem accipit pro actu fidei, qui dicitur consistere in credentium voluntate inquantum ex imperio voluntatis intellectus credibilibus assentit.

**AD SECUNDUM** dicendum quod non solum oportet voluntatem esse promptam ad obediendum, sed etiam intellectum esse bene dispositum ad sequendum imperium voluntatis, sicut oportet concupiscibilem esse bene dispositam ad sequendum imperium rationis. Et ideo non solum oportet esse habitum virtutis in voluntate imperante, sed etiam in intellectu assentiente.

**AD TERTIUM** dicendum quod fides est in intellectu speculativo sicut in subiecto, ut manifeste patet ex fidei obiecto. Sed quia veritas prima, quae est fidei obiectum, est finis omnium desideriorum et actionum nostrarum, ut patet per Augustinum, in I de Trin.; inde est quod per dilectionem operatur. Sicut etiam intellectus speculativus extensione fit practicus, ut dicitur in III de anima.

**REPLY OBJ. 1**: Augustine takes faith for the act of faith, which is described as depending on the believer's will, insofar as his intellect assents to matters of faith at the command of the will.

**REPLY OBJ. 2**: Not only does the will need to be ready to obey but also the intellect needs to be well disposed to follow the command of the will, even as the concupiscible faculty needs to be well disposed in order to follow the command of reason; hence there needs to be a habit of virtue not only in the commanding will but also in the assenting intellect.

**REPLY OBJ. 3**: Faith resides in the speculative intellect, as evidenced by its object. But since this object, which is the First Truth, is the end of all our desires and actions, as Augustine proves (*De Trin.* i, 8), it follows that faith worketh by charity just as the speculative intellect becomes practical by extension (*De Anima* iii, 10).

# Article 3

*Whether charity is the form of faith?*

**AD TERTIUM SIC PROCEDITUR**. Videtur quod caritas non sit forma fidei. Unumquodque enim sortitur speciem per suam formam. Eorum ergo quae ex opposito dividuntur sicut diversae species unius generis, unum non potest esse forma alterius. Sed fides et caritas dividuntur ex opposito, I ad Cor. XIII, sicut diversae species virtutis. Ergo caritas non potest esse forma fidei.

**PRAETEREA**, forma et id cuius est forma sunt in eodem, quia ex eis fit unum simpliciter. Sed fides est in intellectu, caritas autem in voluntate. Ergo caritas non est forma fidei.

**PRAETEREA**, forma est principium rei. Sed principium credendi ex parte voluntatis magis videtur esse obedientia quam caritas, secundum illud ad Rom. I, *ad obediendum fidei in omnibus gentibus*. Ergo obedientia magis est forma fidei quam caritas.

**SED CONTRA** est quod unumquodque operatur per suam formam. Fides autem *per dilectionem operatur*. Ergo dilectio caritatis est forma fidei.

**RESPONDEO** dicendum quod, sicut ex superioribus patet, actus voluntarii speciem recipiunt a fine, qui est voluntatis obiectum. Id autem a quo aliquid speciem sortitur se habet ad modum formae in rebus naturalibus. Et ideo cuiuslibet actus voluntarii forma quodammodo est finis ad quem ordinatur, tum quia ex ipso recipit speciem; tum etiam quia modus actionis oportet quod respondeat proportionaliter fini. Manifestum est autem ex praedictis quod actus fidei ordinatur ad obiectum voluntatis, quod est bonum, sicut ad finem. Hoc autem

**OBJECTION 1**: It would seem that charity is not the form of faith. For each thing derives its species from its form. When therefore two things are opposite members of a division, one cannot be the form of the other. Now faith and charity are stated to be opposite members of a division, as different species of virtue (1 Cor 13:13). Therefore charity is not the form of faith.

**OBJ. 2**: Further, a form and the thing of which it is the form are in one subject, since together they form one simply. Now faith is in the intellect, while charity is in the will. Therefore charity is not the form of faith.

**OBJ. 3**: Further, the form of a thing is a principle thereof. Now obedience, rather than charity, seems to be the principle of believing, on the part of the will, according to Rom. 1:5: *For obedience to the faith in all nations*. Therefore obedience rather than charity, is the form of faith.

**ON THE CONTRARY**, Each thing works through its form. Now faith works through charity. Therefore the love of charity is the form of faith.

**I ANSWER THAT**, As appears from what has been said above (I-II, Q. 1, A. 3; I-II, Q. 18, A. 6), voluntary acts take their species from their end which is the will's object. Now that which gives a thing its species, is after the manner of a form in natural things. Wherefore the form of any voluntary act is, in a manner, the end to which that act is directed, both because it takes its species therefrom, and because the mode of an action should correspond proportionately to the end. Now it is evident from what has been said (A. 1), that the act of faith is directed to the object

bonum quod est finis fidei, scilicet bonum divinum, est proprium obiectum caritatis. Et ideo caritas dicitur forma fidei, inquantum per caritatem actus fidei perficitur et formatur.

**AD PRIMUM** ergo dicendum quod caritas dicitur esse forma fidei inquantum informat actum ipsius. Nihil autem prohibet unum actum a diversis habitibus informari, et secundum hoc ad diversas species reduci ordine quodam, ut supra dictum est, cum de actibus humanis in communi ageretur.

**AD SECUNDUM** dicendum quod obiectio illa procedit de forma intrinseca. Sic autem caritas non est forma fidei, sed prout informat actum eius, ut supra dictum est.

**AD TERTIUM** dicendum quod etiam ipsa obedientia, et similiter spes et quaecumque alia virtus posset praecedere actum fidei, formatur a caritate, sicut infra patebit. Et ideo ipsa caritas ponitur forma fidei.

of the will, i.e., the good, as to its end: and this good which is the end of faith, viz. the Divine Good, is the proper object of charity. Therefore charity is called the form of faith insofar as the act of faith is perfected and formed by charity.

**REPLY OBJ. 1**: Charity is called the form of faith because it quickens the act of faith. Now nothing hinders one act from being quickened by different habits, so as to be reduced to various species in a certain order, as stated above (I-II, Q. 18, AA. 6, 7; I-II, Q. 61, A. 2) when we were treating of human acts in general.

**REPLY OBJ. 2**: This objection is true of an intrinsic form. But it is not thus that charity is the form of faith, but in the sense that it quickens the act of faith, as explained above.

**REPLY OBJ. 3**: Even obedience, and hope likewise, and whatever other virtue might precede the act of faith, is quickened by charity, as we shall show further on (Q. 23, A. 8), and consequently charity is spoken of as the form of faith.

# Article 4

*Whether lifeless faith can become living, or living faith, lifeless?*

**AD QUARTUM SIC PROCEDITUR**. Videtur quod fides informis non fiat formata, nec e converso. Quia ut dicitur I ad Cor. XIII, *cum venerit quod perfectum est, evacuabitur quod ex parte est*. Sed fides informis est imperfecta respectu formatae. Ergo, adveniente fide formata, fides informis excluditur, ut non sit unus habitus numero.

**PRAETEREA**, illud quod est mortuum non fit vivum. Sed fides informis est mortua, secundum illud Iac. II, *fides sine operibus mortua est*. Ergo fides informis non potest fieri formata.

**PRAETEREA**, gratia Dei adveniens non habet minorem effectum in homine fideli quam in infideli. Sed adveniens homini infideli causat in eo habitum fidei. Ergo etiam adveniens fideli qui habebat prius habitum fidei informis causat in eo alium habitum fidei.

**PRAETEREA**, sicut Boetius dicit, accidentia alterari non possunt. Sed fides est quoddam accidens. Ergo non potest eadem fides quandoque esse formata et quandoque informis.

**SED CONTRA** est quod Iac. II, super illud, *fides sine operibus mortua est*, dicit Glossa, quibus reviviscit. Ergo fides quae erat prius mortua et informis fit formata et vivens.

**RESPONDEO** dicendum quod circa hoc fuerunt diversae opiniones. Quidam enim dixerunt quod alius est habitus fidei formatae et informis, sed, adveniente fide formata, tollitur fides informis. Et similiter, homine post fidem formatam peccante mortaliter, succedit alius ha-

**OBJECTION 1**: It would seem that lifeless faith does not become living, nor living faith lifeless. For, according to 1 Cor. 13:10, *when that which is perfect is come, that which is in part shall be done away*. Now lifeless faith is imperfect in comparison with living faith. Therefore when living faith comes, lifeless faith is done away, so that they are not one identical habit.

**OBJ. 2**: Further, a dead thing does not become a living thing. Now lifeless faith is dead, according to James 2:20: *Faith without works is dead*. Therefore lifeless faith cannot become living.

**OBJ. 3**: Further, God's grace, by its advent, has no less effect in a believer than in an unbeliever. Now by coming to an unbeliever it causes the habit of faith. Therefore when it comes to a believer, who hitherto had the habit of lifeless faith, it causes another habit of faith in him.

**OBJ. 4**: Further, as Boethius says (*In Categ. Arist.* i), accidents cannot be altered. Now faith is an accident. Therefore the same faith cannot be at one time living, and at another, lifeless.

**ON THE CONTRARY**, A gloss on the words, *Faith without works is dead* (Jas 2:20) adds, *by which it lives once more*. Therefore faith which was lifeless and without form hitherto, becomes formed and living.

**I ANSWER THAT**, There have been various opinions on this question. For some have said that living and lifeless faith are distinct habits, but that when living faith comes, lifeless faith is done away, and that, in like manner, when a man sins mortally after having living faith, a new habit

bitus fidei informis a Deo infusus. Sed hoc non videtur esse conveniens quod gratia adveniens homini aliquod Dei donum excludat, neque etiam quod aliquod Dei donum homini infundatur propter peccatum mortale.

Et ideo alii dixerunt quod sunt quidem diversi habitus fidei formatae et informis, sed tamen, adveniente fide formata, non tollitur habitus fidei informis, sed simul manet in eodem cum habitu fidei formatae. Sed hoc etiam videtur inconveniens quod habitus fidei informis in habente fidem formatam remaneat otiosus.

Et ideo aliter dicendum quod idem est habitus fidei formatae et informis. Cuius ratio est quia habitus diversificatur secundum illud quod per se ad habitum pertinet. Cum autem fides sit perfectio intellectus, illud per se ad fidem pertinet quod pertinet ad intellectum, quod autem pertinet ad voluntatem non per se pertinet ad fidem, ita quod per hoc diversificari possit habitus fidei. Distinctio autem fidei formatae et informis est secundum id quod pertinet ad voluntatem, idest secundum caritatem, non autem secundum illud quod pertinet ad intellectum. Unde fides formata et informis non sunt diversi habitus.

**AD PRIMUM** ergo dicendum quod verbum apostoli est intelligendum quando imperfectio est de ratione imperfecti. Tunc enim oportet quod, adveniente perfecto, imperfectum excludatur, sicut, adveniente aperta visione, excluditur fides, de cuius ratione est ut sit non apparentium. Sed quando imperfectio non est de ratione rei imperfectae, tunc illud numero idem quod erat imperfectum fit perfectum, sicut pueritia non est de ratione hominis, et ideo idem numero qui erat puer fit vir. Informitas autem fidei non est de ratione fidei, sed per accidens se habet ad ipsam, ut dictum est. Unde ipsamet fides informis fit formata.

**AD SECUNDUM** dicendum quod illud quod facit vitam animalis est de ratione ipsius, quia est forma essentialis eius, scilicet anima. Et ideo mortuum vivum fieri non potest, sed aliud specie est quod est mortuum et quod est vivum. Sed id quod facit fidem esse formatam vel vivam non est de essentia fidei. Et ideo non est simile.

**AD TERTIUM** dicendum quod gratia facit fidem non solum quando fides de novo incipit esse in homine, sed etiam quandiu fides durat, dictum est enim supra quod Deus semper operatur iustificationem hominis, sicut sol semper operatur illuminationem aeris. Unde gratia non minus facit adveniens fideli quam adveniens infideli, quia in utroque operatur fidem, in uno quidem confirmando eam et perficiendo, in alio de novo creando.

Vel potest dici quod hoc est per accidens, scilicet propter dispositionem subiecti, quod gratia non causat fidem in eo qui habet. Sicut e contrario secundum pec-

of lifeless faith is infused into him by God. But it seems unfitting that grace should deprive man of a gift of God by coming to him, and that a gift of God should be infused into man, on account of a mortal sin.

Consequently others have said that living and lifeless faith are indeed distinct habits, but that, all the same, when living faith comes the habit of lifeless faith is not taken away, and that it remains together with the habit of living faith in the same subject. Yet again it seems unreasonable that the habit of lifeless faith should remain inactive in a person having living faith.

We must therefore hold differently that living and lifeless faith are one and the same habit. The reason is that a habit is differentiated by that which directly pertains to that habit. Now since faith is a perfection of the intellect, that pertains directly to faith, which pertains to the intellect. Again, what pertains to the will, does not pertain directly to faith, so as to be able to differentiate the habit of faith. But the distinction of living from lifeless faith is in respect of something pertaining to the will, i.e., charity, and not in respect of something pertaining to the intellect. Therefore living and lifeless faith are not distinct habits.

REPLY OBJ. 1: The saying of the Apostle refers to those imperfect things from which imperfection is inseparable, for then, when the perfect comes the imperfect must needs be done away. Thus with the advent of clear vision, faith is done away, because it is essentially of the things that appear not. When, however, imperfection is not inseparable from the imperfect thing, the same identical thing which was imperfect becomes perfect. Thus childhood is not essential to man and consequently the same identical subject who was a child, becomes a man. Now lifelessness is not essential to faith, but is accidental thereto as stated above. Therefore lifeless faith itself becomes living.

REPLY OBJ. 2: That which makes an animal live is inseparable from an animal, because it is its substantial form, viz. the soul: consequently a dead thing cannot become a living thing, and a living and a dead thing differ specifically. On the other hand that which gives faith its form, or makes it live, is not essential to faith. Hence there is no comparison.

REPLY OBJ. 3: Grace causes faith not only when faith begins anew to be in a man, but also as long as faith lasts. For it has been said above (I, Q. 104, A. 1; I-II, Q. 109, A. 9) that God is always working man's justification, even as the sun is always lighting up the air. Hence grace is not less effective when it comes to a believer than when it comes to an unbeliever: since it causes faith in both, in the former by confirming and perfecting it, in the latter by creating it anew.

We might also reply that it is accidental, namely on account of the disposition of the subject, that grace does not cause faith in one who has it already: just as, on the other

catum mortale non tollit gratiam ab eo qui eam amisit per peccatum mortale praecedens.

**AD QUARTUM** dicendum quod per hoc quod fides formata fit informis non mutatur ipsa fides, sed mutatur subiectum fidei, quod est anima, quod quandoque quidem habet fidem sine caritate, quandoque autem cum caritate.

hand, a second mortal sin does not take away grace from one who has already lost it through a previous mortal sin.

**REPLY OBJ. 4**: When living faith becomes lifeless, faith is not changed, but its subject, the soul, which at one time has faith without charity, and at another time, with charity.

# Article 5

## *Whether faith is a virtue?*

**AD QUINTUM SIC PROCEDITUR**. Videtur quod fides non sit virtus. Virtus enim ordinatur ad bonum, nam *virtus est quae bonum facit habentem*, ut dicit philosophus, in II Ethic. Sed fides ordinatur ad verum. Ergo fides non est virtus.

**PRAETEREA**, perfectior est virtus infusa quam acquisita. Sed fides, propter sui imperfectionem, non ponitur inter virtutes intellectuales acquisitas, ut patet per philosophum, in VI Ethic. Ergo multo minus potest poni virtus infusa.

**PRAETEREA**, fides formata et informis sunt eiusdem speciei, ut dictum est. Sed fides informis non est virtus, quia non habet connexionem cum aliis virtutibus. Ergo nec fides formata est virtus.

**PRAETEREA**, gratiae gratis datae et fructus distinguuntur a virtutibus. Sed fides enumeratur inter gratias gratis datas, I ad Cor. XII, et similiter inter fructus, ad Gal. V. Ergo fides non est virtus.

**SED CONTRA** est quod homo per virtutes iustificatur, nam *iustitia est tota virtus*, ut dicitur in V Ethic. Sed per fidem homo iustificatur, secundum illud ad Rom. V, *iustificati ergo ex fide pacem habemus* et cetera. Ergo fides est virtus.

**RESPONDEO** dicendum quod, sicut ex supradictis patet, virtus humana est per quam actus humanus redditur bonus. Unde quicumque habitus est semper principium boni actus, potest dici virtus humana. Talis autem habitus est fides formata. Cum enim credere sit actus intellectus assentientis vero ex imperio voluntatis, ad hoc quod iste actus sit perfectus duo requiruntur. Quorum unum est ut infallibiliter intellectus tendat in suum bonum, quod est verum, aliud autem est ut infallibiliter ordinetur ad ultimum finem, propter quem voluntas assentit vero. Et utrumque invenitur in actu fidei formatae. Nam ex ratione ipsius fidei est quod intellectus semper feratur in verum, quia fidei non potest subesse falsum, ut supra habitum est, ex caritate autem, quae format fidem, habet anima quod infallibiliter voluntas ordinetur in bonum finem. Et ideo fides formata est virtus.

**OBJECTION 1**: It would seem that faith is not a virtue. For virtue is directed to the good, since *it is virtue that makes its subject good*, as the Philosopher states (*Ethic.* ii, 6). But faith is directed to the true. Therefore faith is not a virtue.

**OBJ. 2**: Further, infused virtue is more perfect than acquired virtue. Now faith, on account of its imperfection, is not placed among the acquired intellectual virtues, as the Philosopher states (*Ethic.* vi, 3). Much less, therefore, can it be considered an infused virtue.

**OBJ. 3**: Further, living and lifeless faith are the same species, as stated above (A. 4). Now lifeless faith is not a virtue, since it is not connected with the other virtues. Therefore neither is living faith a virtue.

**OBJ. 4**: Further, the gratuitous graces and the fruits are distinct from the virtues. But faith is numbered among the gratuitous graces (1 Cor 12:9) and likewise among the fruits (Gal 5:23). Therefore faith is not a virtue.

**ON THE CONTRARY**, Man is justified by the virtues, since *justice is all virtue*, as the Philosopher states (*Ethic.* v, 1). Now man is justified by faith according to Rom. 5:1: *Being justified therefore by faith let us have peace*, etc. Therefore faith is a virtue.

**I ANSWER THAT**, As shown above, it is by human virtue that human acts are rendered good; hence, any habit that is always the principle of a good act, may be called a human virtue. Such a habit is living faith. For since to believe is an act of the intellect assenting to the truth at the command of the will, two things are required that this act may be perfect: one of which is that the intellect should infallibly tend to its object, which is the true; while the other is that the will should be infallibly directed to the last end, on account of which it assents to the true: and both of these are to be found in the act of living faith. For it belongs to the very essence of faith that the intellect should ever tend to the true, since nothing false can be the object of faith, as proved above (Q. 1, A. 3): while the effect of charity, which is the form of faith, is that the soul ever has its will directed to a good end. Therefore living faith is a virtue.

Fides autem informis non est virtus, quia etsi habeat perfectionem debitam actus fidei informis ex parte intellectus, non tamen habet perfectionem debitam ex parte voluntatis. Sicut etiam si temperantia esset in concupiscibili et prudentia non esset in rationali, temperantia non esset virtus, ut supra dictum est, quia ad actum temperantiae requiritur et actus rationis et actus concupiscibilis, sicut ad actum fidei requiritur actus voluntatis et actus intellectus.

AD PRIMUM ergo dicendum quod ipsum verum est bonum intellectus, cum sit eius perfectio. Et ideo inquantum per fidem intellectus determinatur ad verum, fides habet ordinem in bonum quoddam. Sed ulterius, inquantum fides formatur per caritatem, habet etiam ordinem ad bonum secundum quod est voluntatis obiectum.

AD SECUNDUM dicendum quod fides de qua philosophus loquitur innititur rationi humanae non ex necessitate concludenti, cui potest subesse falsum. Et ideo talis fides non est virtus. Sed fides de qua loquimur innititur veritati divinae quae est infallibilis, et ita non potest ei subesse falsum. Et ideo talis fides potest esse virtus.

AD TERTIUM dicendum quod fides formata et informis non differunt specie sicut in diversis speciebus existentes, differunt autem sicut perfectum et imperfectum in eadem specie. Unde fides informis, cum sit imperfecta, non pertingit ad perfectam rationem virtutis, nam *virtus est perfectio quaedam*, ut dicitur in VII Physic.

AD QUARTUM dicendum quod quidam ponunt quod fides quae connumeratur inter gratias gratis datas est fides informis. Sed hoc non convenienter dicitur. Quia gratiae gratis datae, quae ibi enumerantur, non sunt communes omnibus membris Ecclesiae, unde apostolus ibi dicit, *divisiones gratiarum sunt*; et iterum, alii datur hoc, alii datur illud. Fides autem informis est communis omnibus membris Ecclesiae, quia informitas non est de substantia eius, secundum quod est donum gratuitum. Unde dicendum est quod fides ibi sumitur pro aliqua fidei excellentia, sicut pro constantia fidei, ut dicit Glossa, vel pro sermone fidei.

Fides autem ponitur fructus secundum quod habet aliquam delectationem in suo actu, ratione certitudinis. Unde ad Gal. V, ubi enumerantur fructus, exponitur fides *de invisibilibus certitudo.*

On the other hand, lifeless faith is not a virtue, because, though the act of lifeless faith is duly perfect on the part of the intellect, it has not its due perfection as regards the will: just as if temperance be in the concupiscible, without prudence being in the rational part, temperance is not a virtue, as stated above (I-II, Q. 65, A. 1), because the act of temperance requires both an act of reason, and an act of the concupiscible faculty, even as the act of faith requires an act of the will, and an act of the intellect.

REPLY OBJ. 1: The truth is itself the good of the intellect, since it is its perfection: and consequently faith has a relation to some good insofar as it directs the intellect to the true. Furthermore, it has a relation to the good considered as the object of the will, inasmuch as it is formed by charity.

REPLY OBJ. 2: The faith of which the Philosopher speaks is based on human reasoning in a conclusion which does not follow, of necessity, from its premisses; and which is subject to be false: hence such like faith is not a virtue. On the other hand, the faith of which we are speaking is based on the Divine Truth, which is infallible, and consequently its object cannot be anything false; so that faith of this kind can be a virtue.

REPLY OBJ. 3: Living and lifeless faith do not differ specifically, as though they belonged to different species. But they differ as perfect and imperfect within the same species. Hence lifeless faith, being imperfect, does not satisfy the conditions of a perfect virtue, for *virtue is a kind of perfection* (*Phys.* vii, text. 18).

REPLY OBJ. 4: Some say that faith which is numbered among the gratuitous graces is lifeless faith. But this is said without reason, since the gratuitous graces, which are mentioned in that passage, are not common to all the members of the Church: wherefore the Apostle says: *There are diversities of graces*, and again, *To one is given* this grace and *to another* that. Now lifeless faith is common to all members of the Church, because its lifelessness is not part of its substance, if we consider it as a gratuitous gift. We must, therefore, say that in that passage, faith denotes a certain excellency of faith, for instance, *constancy in faith*, according to a gloss, or the *word of faith*.

Faith is numbered among the fruits, insofar as it gives a certain pleasure in its act by reason of its certainty, wherefore the gloss on the fifth chapter to the Galatians, where the fruits are enumerated, explains faith as being *certainty about the unseen.*

# Article 6

*Whether faith is one virtue?*

**AD SEXTUM SIC PROCEDITUR.** Videtur quod non sit una fides. Sicut enim *fides est donum Dei*, ut dicitur ad Ephes. II, ita etiam sapientia et scientia inter dona Dei computantur, ut patet Isaiae XI. Sed sapientia et scientia differunt per hoc quod sapientia est de aeternis, scientia vero de temporalibus, ut patet per Augustinum, XII de Trin. Cum igitur fides sit et de aeternis et de quibusdam temporalibus, videtur quod non sit una fides, sed distinguatur in partes.

**PRAETEREA,** confessio est actus fidei, ut supra dictum est. Sed non est una et eadem confessio fidei apud omnes, nam quod nos confitemur factum antiqui patres confitebantur futurum, ut patet Isaiae VII, *ecce virgo concipiet.* Ergo non est una fides.

**PRAETEREA,** fides est communis omnibus fidelibus Christi. Sed unum accidens non potest esse in diversis subiectis. Ergo non potest esse una fides omnium.

**SED CONTRA** est quod apostolus dicit, ad Ephes. IV, *unus dominus, una fides.*

**RESPONDEO** dicendum quod fides, si sumatur pro habitu, dupliciter potest considerari. Uno modo, ex parte obiecti. Et sic est una fides, obiectum enim formale fidei est veritas prima, cui inhaerendo credimus quaecumque sub fide continentur. Alio modo, ex parte subiecti. Et sic fides diversificatur secundum quod est diversorum. Manifestum est autem quod fides, sicut et quilibet alius habitus, ex formali ratione obiecti habet speciem, sed ex subiecto individuatur. Et ideo, si fides sumatur pro habitu quo credimus, sic fides est una specie, et differens numero in diversis.

Si vero sumatur pro eo quod creditur, sic etiam est una fides. Quia idem est quod ab omnibus creditur, et si sint diversa credibilia quae communiter omnes credunt, tamen omnia reducuntur ad unum.

**AD PRIMUM** ergo dicendum quod temporalia quae in fide proponuntur non pertinent ad obiectum fidei nisi in ordine ad aliquod aeternum, quod est veritas prima, sicut supra dictum est. Et ideo fides una est de temporalibus et aeternis. Secus autem est de sapientia et scientia, quae considerant temporalia et aeterna secundum proprias rationes utrorumque.

**AD SECUNDUM** dicendum quod illa differentia praeteriti et futuri non contingit ex aliqua diversitate rei creditae, sed ex diversa habitudine credentium ad unam rem creditam, ut etiam supra habitum est.

**AD TERTIUM** dicendum quod illa ratio procedit ex diversitate fidei secundum numerum.

**OBJECTION 1**: It would seem that faith is not one. For just as faith is *a gift of God* according to Eph. 2:8, so also wisdom and knowledge are numbered among God's gifts according to Isa. 11:2. Now wisdom and knowledge differ in this, that wisdom is about eternal things, and knowledge about temporal things, as Augustine states (*De Trin.* xii, 14, 15). Since, then, faith is about eternal things, and also about some temporal things, it seems that faith is not one virtue, but divided into several parts.

**OBJ. 2**: Further, confession is an act of faith, as stated above (Q. 3, A. 1). Now confession of faith is not one and the same for all: since what we confess as past, the fathers of old confessed as yet to come, as appears from Isa. 7:14: *Behold a virgin shall conceive.* Therefore faith is not one.

**OBJ. 3**: Further, faith is common to all believers in Christ. But one accident cannot be in many subjects. Therefore all cannot have one faith.

**ON THE CONTRARY**, The Apostle says (*Eph 4:5*): *One Lord, one faith.*

**I ANSWER THAT**, If we take faith as a habit, we can consider it in two ways. First on the part of the object, and thus there is one faith. Because the formal object of faith is the First Truth, by adhering to which we believe whatever is contained in the faith. Second, on the part of the subject, and thus faith is differentiated according as it is in various subjects. Now it is evident that faith, just as any other habit, takes its species from the formal aspect of its object, but is individualized by its subject. Hence if we take faith for the habit whereby we believe, it is one specifically, but differs numerically according to its various subjects.

If, on the other hand, we take faith for that which is believed, then, again, there is one faith, since what is believed by all is one same thing: for though the things believed, which all agree in believing, be diverse from one another, yet they are all reduced to one.

**REPLY OBJ. 1**: Temporal matters which are proposed to be believed, do not belong to the object of faith, except in relation to something eternal, viz. the First Truth, as stated above (Q. 1, A. 1). Hence there is one faith of things both temporal and eternal. It is different with wisdom and knowledge, which consider temporal and eternal matters under their respective aspects.

**REPLY OBJ. 2**: This difference of past and future arises, not from any difference in the thing believed, but from the different relationships of believers to the one thing believed, as also we have mentioned above (I-II, Q. 103, A. 4; I-II, Q. 107, A. 1, ad 1).

**REPLY OBJ. 3**: This objection considers numerical diversity of faith.

# Article 7

*Whether faith is the first of the virtues?*

**AD SEPTIMUM SIC PROCEDITUR.** Videtur quod fides non sit prima inter virtutes. Dicitur enim Luc. XII, in Glossa super illud, *dico vobis amicis meis,* quod *fortitudo est fidei fundamentum.* Sed fundamentum est prius eo cuius est fundamentum. Ergo fides non est prima virtus.

**PRAETEREA,** quaedam Glossa dicit, super illum Psalmum, *noli aemulari,* quod *spes introducit ad fidem.* Spes autem est virtus quaedam, ut infra dicetur. Ergo fides non est prima virtutum.

**PRAETEREA,** supra dictum est quod intellectus credentis inclinatur ad assentiendum his quae sunt fidei ex obedientia ad Deum. Sed obedientia etiam est quaedam virtus. Non ergo fides est prima virtus.

**PRAETEREA,** fides informis non est fundamentum, sed fides formata, sicut in Glossa dicitur, I ad Cor. III. Formatur autem fides per caritatem, ut supra dictum est. Ergo fides a caritate habet quod sit fundamentum. Caritas ergo est magis fundamentum quam fides, nam fundamentum est prima pars aedificii. Et ita videtur quod sit prior fide.

**PRAETEREA,** secundum ordinem actuum intelligitur ordo habituum. Sed in actu fidei actus voluntatis, quem perficit caritas, praecedit actum intellectus, quem perficit fides, sicut causa, quae praecedit effectum. Ergo caritas praecedit fidem. Non ergo fides est prima virtutum.

**SED CONTRA** est quod apostolus dicit, ad Heb. XI, quod *fides est substantia sperandarum rerum.* Sed substantia habet rationem primi. Ergo fides est prima inter virtutes.

**RESPONDEO** dicendum quod aliquid potest esse prius altero dupliciter, uno modo, per se; alio modo, per accidens. Per se quidem inter omnes virtutes prima est fides. Cum enim in agibilibus finis sit principium, ut supra dictum est, necesse est virtutes theologicas, quarum obiectum est ultimus finis, esse priores ceteris virtutibus. Ipse autem ultimus finis oportet quod prius sit in intellectu quam in voluntate, quia voluntas non fertur in aliquid nisi prout est in intellectu apprehensum. Unde cum ultimus finis sit quidem in voluntate per spem et caritatem, in intellectu autem per fidem, necesse est quod fides sit prima inter omnes virtutes, quia naturalis cognitio non potest attingere ad Deum secundum quod est obiectum beatitudinis, prout tendit in ipsum spes et caritas.

Sed per accidens potest aliqua virtus esse prior fide. Causa enim per accidens est per accidens prior. Removere autem prohibens pertinet ad causam per accidens, ut patet per philosophum, in VIII Physic. Et secundum hoc aliquae virtutes possunt dici per accidens priores

**OBJECTION 1**: It would seem that faith is not the first of the virtues. For a gloss on Luke 12:4, *I say to you My friends,* says that *fortitude is the foundation of faith.* Now the foundation precedes that which is founded thereon. Therefore faith is not the first of the virtues.

**OBJ. 2**: Further, a gloss on Ps. 36, *Be not emulous,* says that hope *leads on to faith.* Now hope is a virtue, as we shall state further on (Q. 17, A. 1). Therefore faith is not the first of the virtues.

**OBJ. 3**: Further, it was stated above (A. 2) that the intellect of the believer is moved, out of obedience to God, to assent to matters of faith. Now obedience also is a virtue. Therefore faith is not the first virtue.

**OBJ. 4**: Further, not lifeless but living faith is the foundation, as a gloss remarks on 1 Cor. 3:11. Now faith is formed by charity, as stated above (A. 3). Therefore it is owing to charity that faith is the foundation: so that charity is the foundation yet more than faith is (for the foundation is the first part of a building) and consequently it seems to precede faith.

**OBJ. 5**: Further, the order of habits is taken from the order of acts. Now, in the act of faith, the act of the will which is perfected by charity, precedes the act of the intellect, which is perfected by faith, as the cause which precedes its effect. Therefore charity precedes faith. Therefore faith is not the first of the virtues.

**ON THE CONTRARY**, The Apostle says (Heb 11:1) that *faith is the substance of things to be hoped for.* Now the substance of a thing is that which comes first. Therefore faith is first among the virtues.

**I ANSWER THAT,** One thing can precede another in two ways: first, by its very nature; second, by accident. Faith, by its very nature, precedes all other virtues. For since the end is the principle in matters of action, as stated above (I-II, Q. 13, A. 3; I-II, Q. 34, A. 4, ad 1), the theological virtues, the object of which is the last end, must needs precede all the others. Again, the last end must of necessity be present to the intellect before it is present to the will, since the will has no inclination for anything except insofar as it is apprehended by the intellect. Hence, as the last end is present in the will by hope and charity, and in the intellect, by faith, the first of all the virtues must, of necessity, be faith, because natural knowledge cannot reach God as the object of heavenly bliss, which is the aspect under which hope and charity tend towards Him.

On the other hand, some virtues can precede faith accidentally. For an accidental cause precedes its effect accidentally. Now that which removes an obstacle is a kind of accidental cause, according to the Philosopher (*Phys.* viii, 4): and in this sense certain virtues may be said to precede

fide, inquantum removent impedimenta credendi, sicut fortitudo removet inordinatum timorem impedientem fidem; humilitas autem superbiam, per quam intellectus recusat se submittere veritati fidei. Et idem potest dici de aliquibus aliis virtutibus, quamvis non sint verae virtutes nisi praesupposita fide, ut patet per Augustinum, in libro contra Iulianum.

UNDE PATET responsio ad primum.

AD SECUNDUM dicendum quod spes non potest universaliter introducere ad fidem. Non enim potest spes haberi de aeterna beatitudine nisi credatur possibile, quia impossibile non cadit sub spe, ut ex supradictis patet. Sed ex spe aliquis introduci potest ad hoc quod perseveret in fide, vel quod fidei firmiter adhaereat. Et secundum hoc dicitur spes introducere ad fidem.

AD TERTIUM dicendum quod obedientia dupliciter dicitur. Quandoque enim importat inclinationem voluntatis ad implendum divina mandata. Et sic non est specialis virtus, sed generaliter includitur in omni virtute, quia omnes actus virtutum cadunt sub praeceptis legis divinae, ut supra dictum est. Et hoc modo ad fidem requiritur obedientia. Alio modo potest accipi obedientia secundum quod importat inclinationem quandam ad implendam mandata secundum quod habent rationem debiti. Et sic obedientia est specialis virtus, et est pars iustitiae, reddit enim superiori debitum obediendo sibi. Et hoc modo obedientia sequitur fidem, per quam manifestatur homini quod Deus sit superior, cui debeat obedire.

AD QUARTUM dicendum quod ad rationem fundamenti non solum requiritur quod sit primum, sed etiam quod sit aliis partibus aedificii connexum, non enim esset fundamentum nisi ei aliae partes aedificii cohaererent. Connexio autem spiritualis aedificii est per caritatem, secundum illud Coloss. III, *super omnia caritatem habete, quae est vinculum perfectionis*. Et ideo fides sine caritate fundamentum esse non potest, nec tamen oportet quod caritas sit prior fide.

AD QUINTUM dicendum quod actus voluntatis praeexigitur ad fidem, non tamen actus voluntatis caritate informatus, sed talis actus praesupponit fidem, quia non potest voluntas perfecto amore in Deum tendere nisi intellectus rectam fidem habeat circa ipsum.

faith accidentally, insofar as they remove obstacles to belief. Thus fortitude removes the inordinate fear that hinders faith; humility removes pride, whereby a man refuses to submit himself to the truth of faith. The same may be said of some other virtues, although there are no real virtues, unless faith be presupposed, as Augustine states (*Contra Julian.* iv, 3).

THIS SUFFICES for the Reply to the First Objection.

REPLY OBJ. 2: Hope cannot lead to faith absolutely. For one cannot hope to obtain eternal happiness, unless one believes this possible, since hope does not tend to the impossible, as stated above (I-II, Q. 40, A. 1). It is, however, possible for one to be led by hope to persevere in faith, or to hold firmly to faith; and it is in this sense that hope is said to lead to faith.

REPLY OBJ. 3: Obedience is twofold: for sometimes it denotes the inclination of the will to fulfill God's commandments. In this way it is not a special virtue, but is a general condition of every virtue; since all acts of virtue come under the precepts of the Divine law, as stated above (I-II, Q. 100, A. 2); and thus it is requisite for faith. In another way, obedience denotes an inclination to fulfill the commandments considered as a duty. In this way it is a special virtue, and a part of justice: for a man does his duty by his superior when he obeys him: and thus obedience follows faith, whereby man knows that God is his superior, Whom he must obey.

REPLY OBJ. 4: To be a foundation a thing requires not only to come first, but also to be connected with the other parts of the building: since the building would not be founded on it unless the other parts adhered to it. Now the connecting bond of the spiritual edifice is charity, according to Col. 3:14: *Above all . . . things have charity which is the bond of perfection*. Consequently faith without charity cannot be the foundation: and yet it does not follow that charity precedes faith.

REPLY OBJ. 5: Some act of the will is required before faith, but not an act of the will quickened by charity. This latter act presupposes faith, because the will cannot tend to God with perfect love, unless the intellect possesses right faith about Him.

# Article 8

*Whether faith is more certain than science and the other intellectual virtues?*

AD OCTAVUM SIC PROCEDITUR. Videtur quod fides non sit certior scientia et aliis virtutibus intellectualibus. Dubitatio enim opponitur certitudini, unde videtur illud esse certius quod minus potest habere de dubita-

OBJECTION 1: It would seem that faith is not more certain than science and the other intellectual virtues. For doubt is opposed to certitude, wherefore a thing would seem to be the more certain, through being less doubtful,

tione; sicut est albius quod est nigro impermixtius. Sed intellectus et scientia, et etiam sapientia, non habent dubitationem circa ea quorum sunt, credens autem interdum potest pati motum dubitationis et dubitare de his quae sunt fidei. Ergo fides non est certior virtutibus intellectualibus.

**PRAETEREA**, visio est certior auditu. Sed *fides est ex auditu*, ut dicitur ad Rom. X, in intellectu autem et scientia et sapientia includitur quaedam intellectualis visio. Ergo certior est scientia vel intellectus quam fides.

**PRAETEREA**, quanto aliquid est perfectius in his quae ad intellectum pertinent, tanto est certius. Sed intellectus est perfectior fide, quia per fidem ad intellectum pervenitur, secundum illud Isaiae VII, *nisi credideritis, non intelligetis*, secundum aliam litteram. Et Augustinus dicit etiam de scientia, XIV de Trin., quod *per scientiam roboratur fides*. Ergo videtur quod certior sit scientia vel intellectus quam fides.

**SED CONTRA** est quod apostolus dicit, I ad Thess. II, *cum accepissetis a nobis verbum auditus*, scilicet per fidem, *accepistis illud non ut verbum hominum, sed, sicut vere est, verbum Dei*. Sed nihil certius verbo Dei. Ergo scientia non est certior fide, nec aliquid aliud.

**RESPONDEO** dicendum quod, sicut supra dictum est, virtutum intellectualium duae sunt circa contingentia, scilicet prudentia et ars. Quibus praefertur fides in certitudine, ratione suae materiae, quia est de aeternis, quae non contingit aliter se habere. Tres autem reliquae intellectuales virtutes, scilicet sapientia, scientia et intellectus, sunt de necessariis, ut supra dictum est. Sed sciendum est quod sapientia, scientia et intellectus dupliciter dicuntur, uno modo, secundum quod ponuntur virtutes intellectuales a philosopho, in VI Ethic.; alio modo, secundum quod ponuntur dona spiritus sancti. Primo igitur modo, dicendum est quod certitudo potest considerari dupliciter. Uno modo, ex causa certitudinis, et sic dicitur esse certius illud quod habet certiorem causam. Et hoc modo fides est certior tribus praedictis, quia fides innititur veritati divinae, tria autem praedicta innituntur rationi humanae. Alio modo potest considerari certitudo ex parte subiecti, et sic dicitur esse certius quod plenius consequitur intellectus hominis. Et per hunc modum, quia ea quae sunt fidei sunt supra intellectum hominis, non autem ea quae subsunt tribus praedictis, ideo ex hac parte fides est minus certa. Sed quia unumquodque iudicatur simpliciter quidem secundum causam suam; secundum autem dispositionem quae est ex parte subiecti iudicatur secundum quid, inde est quod fides est simpliciter certior, sed alia sunt certiora secundum quid, scilicet quoad nos. Similiter etiam, si accipiantur tria praedicta secundum quod sunt

just as a thing is the whiter, the less it has of an admixture of black. Now understanding, science and also wisdom are free of any doubt about their objects; whereas the believer may sometimes suffer a movement of doubt, and doubt about matters of faith. Therefore faith is no more certain than the intellectual virtues.

**OBJ. 2**: Further, sight is more certain than hearing. But *faith* is *through hearing* according to Rom. 10:17; whereas understanding, science and wisdom imply some kind of intellectual sight. Therefore science and understanding are more certain than faith.

**OBJ. 3**: Further, in matters concerning the intellect, the more perfect is the more certain. Now understanding is more perfect than faith, since faith is the way to understanding, according to another version of Isa. 7:9: *If you will not believe, you shall not understand*: and Augustine says (*De Trin.* xiv, 1) that *faith is strengthened by science*. Therefore it seems that science or understanding is more certain than faith.

**ON THE CONTRARY**, The Apostle says (1 Thess 2:15): *When you had received of us the word of the hearing*, i.e., by faith . . . *you received it not as the word of men, but, as it is indeed, the word of God*. Now nothing is more certain than the word of God. Therefore science is not more certain than faith; nor is anything else.

**I ANSWER THAT**, As stated above (I-II, Q. 57, A. 4, ad 2) two of the intellectual virtues are about contingent matter, viz. prudence and art; to which faith is preferable in point of certitude, by reason of its matter, since it is about eternal things, which never change, whereas the other three intellectual virtues, viz. wisdom, science and understanding, are about necessary things, as stated above (I-II, Q. 57, A. 5, ad 3). But it must be observed that wisdom, science and understanding may be taken in two ways: first, as intellectual virtues, according to the Philosopher (*Ethic.* vi, 2, 3); second, for the gifts of the Holy Spirit. If we consider them in the first way, we must note that certitude can be looked at in two ways. First, on the part of its cause, and thus a thing which has a more certain cause, is itself more certain. In this way faith is more certain than those three virtues, because it is founded on the Divine truth, whereas the aforesaid three virtues are based on human reason. Second, certitude may be considered on the part of the subject, and thus the more a man's intellect lays hold of a thing, the more certain it is. In this way, faith is less certain, because matters of faith are above the human intellect, whereas the objects of the aforesaid three virtues are not. Since, however, a thing is judged simply with regard to its cause, but relatively, with respect to a disposition on the part of the subject, it follows that faith is more certain simply, while the others are more certain relatively, i.e., for us. Likewise if these three be taken as gifts received in this present life, they are related to faith as to their principle

dona praesentis vitae, comparantur ad fidem sicut ad principium quod praesupponunt. Unde etiam secundum hoc fides est eis certior.

**Ad primum** ergo dicendum quod illa dubitatio non est ex parte causae fidei, sed quoad nos, inquantum non plene assequimur per intellectum ea quae sunt fidei.

**Ad secundum** dicendum quod, ceteris paribus, visio est certior auditu. Sed si ille a quo auditur multum excedit visum videntis, sic certior est auditus quam visus. Sicut aliquis parvae scientiae magis certificatur de eo quod audit ab aliquo scientissimo quam de eo quod sibi secundum suam rationem videtur. Et multo magis homo certior est de eo quod audit a Deo, qui falli non potest, quam de eo quod videt propria ratione, quae falli potest.

**Ad tertium** dicendum quod perfectio intellectus et scientiae excedit cognitionem fidei quantum ad maiorem manifestationem, non tamen quantum ad certiorem inhaesionem. Quia tota certitudo intellectus vel scientiae secundum quod sunt dona, procedit a certitudine fidei, sicut certitudo cognitionis conclusionum procedit ex certitudine principiorum. Secundum autem quod scientia et sapientia et intellectus sunt virtutes intellectuales, innituntur naturali lumini rationis, quod deficit a certitudine verbi Dei, cui innititur fides.

which they presuppose: so that again, in this way, faith is more certain.

**Reply Obj. 1**: This doubt is not on the side of the cause of faith, but on our side, insofar as we do not fully grasp matters of faith with our intellect.

**Reply Obj. 2**: Other things being equal sight is more certain than hearing; but if (the authority of) the person from whom we hear greatly surpasses that of the seer's sight, hearing is more certain than sight: thus a man of little science is more certain about what he hears on the authority of an expert in science, than about what is apparent to him according to his own reason: and much more is a man certain about what he hears from God, Who cannot be deceived, than about what he sees with his own reason, which can be mistaken.

**Reply Obj. 3**: The gifts of understanding and knowledge are more perfect than the knowledge of faith in the point of their greater clearness, but not in regard to more certain adhesion: because the whole certitude of the gifts of understanding and knowledge, arises from the certitude of faith, even as the certitude of the knowledge of conclusions arises from the certitude of premisses. But insofar as science, wisdom and understanding are intellectual virtues, they are based upon the natural light of reason, which falls short of the certitude of God's word, on which faith is founded.

# QUESTION 5

## THOSE WHO HAVE FAITH

Deinde considerandum est de habentibus fidem. Et circa hoc quaeruntur quatuor.

Primo, utrum Angelus aut homo in prima sui conditione habuerit fidem.

Secundo, utrum Daemones habeant fidem.

Tertio, utrum haeretici errantes in uno articulo fidei habeant fidem de aliis articulis.

Quarto, utrum fidem habentium unus alio habeat maiorem fidem.

We must now consider those who have faith: under which head there are four points of inquiry:

(1) Whether there was faith in the angels, or in man, in their original state?

(2) Whether the demons have faith?

(3) Whether those heretics who err in one article, have faith in others?

(4) Whether among those who have faith, one has it more than another?

## Article 1

*Whether there was faith in the angels, or in man, in their original state?*

**AD PRIMUM SIC PROCEDITUR.** Videtur quod Angelus aut homo in sua prima conditione fidem non habuerit. Dicit enim Hugo de sancto Victore, *quia homo oculum contemplationis non habet, Deum et quae in Deo sunt videre non valet.* Sed Angelus in statu primae conditionis, ante confirmationem vel lapsum, habuit oculum contemplationis, videbat enim res in verbo, ut Augustinus dicit, in II super Gen. ad Litt. Et similiter primus homo in statu innocentiae videtur habuisse oculum contemplationis apertum, dicit enim Hugo de sancto Victore, in suis sententiis, quod *novit homo, in primo statu, creatorem suum non ea cognitione quae foris auditu solo percipitur, sed ea quae intus per inspirationem ministratur, non ea qua Deus modo a credentibus absens fide quaeritur, sed ea qua per praesentiam contemplationis manifestius cernebatur.* Ergo homo vel Angelus in statu primae conditionis fidem non habuit.

**PRAETEREA,** cognitio fidei est aenigmatica et obscura, secundum illud I ad Cor. XIII, *videmus nunc per speculum in aenigmate.* Sed in statu primae conditionis non fuit aliqua obscuritas neque in homine neque in Angelo, quia tenebrositas est poena peccati. Ergo fides in statu primae conditionis esse non potuit neque in homine neque in Angelo.

**PRAETEREA,** apostolus dicit, ad Rom. X, quod *fides est ex auditu.* Sed hoc locum non habuit in primo statu angelicae conditionis aut humanae, non enim erat ibi auditus ab alio. Ergo fides in statu illo non erat neque in homine neque in Angelo.

**SED CONTRA** est quod apostolus dicit, ad Heb. XI, *accedentem ad Deum oportet credere.* Sed Angelus et

**OBJECTION 1:** It would seem that there was no faith, either in the angels, or in man, in their original state. For Hugh of S. Victor says in his Sentences (*De Sacram.* i, 10) that *man cannot see God or things that are in God, because he closes his eyes to contemplation.* Now the angels, in their original state, before they were either confirmed in grace, or had fallen from it, had their eyes opened to contemplation, since they saw things in the Word, according to Augustine (*Gen ad lit.* ii, 8). Likewise the first man, while in the state of innocence, seemingly had his eyes open to contemplation; for Hugh of St. Victor says (*De Sacram.* i, 6) that *in his original state man knew his Creator, not by the mere outward perception of hearing, but by inward inspiration, not as now believers seek an absent God by faith, but by seeing Him clearly present to their contemplation.* Therefore there was no faith in the angels and man in their original state.

**OBJ. 2:** Further, the knowledge of faith is dark and obscure, according to 1 Cor. 13:13: *We see now through a glass in a dark manner.* Now in their original state there was not obscurity either in the angels or in man, because it is a punishment of sin. Therefore there could be no faith in the angels or in man, in their original state.

**OBJ. 3:** Further, the Apostle says (Rom 10:17) that *faith . . . cometh by hearing.* Now this could not apply to angels and man in their original state; for then they could not hear anything from another. Therefore, in that state, there was no faith either in man or in the angels.

**ON THE CONTRARY,** It is written (Heb 11:6): *He that cometh to God, must believe.* Now the original state of angels

59

homo in sui prima conditione erant in statu accedendi ad Deum. Ergo fide indigebant.

**RESPONDEO** dicendum quod quidam dicunt quod in Angelis ante confirmationem et lapsum, et in homine ante peccatum, non fuit fides, propter manifestam contemplationem quae tunc erat de rebus divinis. Sed cum fides sit *argumentum non apparentium*, secundum apostolum; et *per fidem credantur ea quae non videntur*, ut Augustinus dicit, illa sola manifestatio excludit fidei rationem per quam redditur apparens vel visum id de quo principaliter est fides. Principale autem obiectum fidei est veritas prima, cuius visio beatos facit et fidei succedit. Cum igitur Angelus ante confirmationem, et homo ante peccatum, non habuit illam beatitudinem qua Deus per essentiam videtur; manifestum est quod non habuit sic manifestam cognitionem quod excluderetur ratio fidei.

Unde quod non habuit fidem, hoc esse non potuit nisi quod penitus ei erat ignotum illud de quo est fides. Et si homo et Angelus fuerunt creati in puris naturalibus, ut quidam dicunt, forte posset teneri quod fides non fuit in Angelo ante confirmationem nec in homine ante peccatum, cognitio enim fidei est supra naturalem cognitionem de Deo non solum hominis, sed etiam Angeli.

Sed quia in primo iam diximus quod homo et Angelus creati sunt cum dono gratiae, ideo necesse est dicere quod per gratiam acceptam et nondum consummatam fuerit in eis inchoatio quaedam speratae beatitudinis, quae quidem inchoatur in voluntate per spem et caritatem, sed in intellectu per fidem, ut supra dictum est. Et ideo necesse est dicere quod Angelus ante confirmationem habuerat fidem, et similiter homo ante peccatum. Sed tamen considerandum est quod in obiecto fidei est aliquid quasi formale, scilicet veritas prima super omnem naturalem cognitionem creaturae existens; et aliquid materiale, sicut id cui assentimus inhaerendo primae veritati. Quantum ergo ad primum horum, communiter fides est in omnibus habentibus cognitionem de Deo, futura beatitudine nondum adepta, inhaerendo primae veritati. Sed quantum ad ea quae materialiter credenda proponuntur, quaedam sunt credita ab uno quae sunt manifeste scita ab alio, etiam in statu praesenti, ut supra dictum est. Et secundum hoc etiam potest dici quod Angelus ante confirmationem et homo ante peccatum quaedam de divinis mysteriis manifesta cognitione cognoverunt quae nunc non possumus cognoscere nisi credendo.

**AD PRIMUM** ergo dicendum quod, quamvis dicta Hugonis de sancto Victore magistralia sint et robur auctoritatis non habeant, tamen potest dici quod contemplatio quae tollit necessitatem fidei est contemplatio

and man was one of approach to God. Therefore they had need of faith.

**I ANSWER THAT,** Some say that there was no faith in the angels before they were confirmed in grace or fell from it, and in man before he sinned, by reason of the manifest contemplation that they had of Divine things. Since, however, *faith is the evidence of things that appear not*, according to the Apostle (Heb 11:2), and since *by faith we believe what we see not*, according to Augustine (*Tract. xl in Joan.*; *QQ. Evang. ii*, qu. 39), that manifestation alone excludes faith, which renders apparent or seen the principal object of faith. Now the principal object of faith is the First Truth, the sight of which gives the happiness of heaven and takes the place of faith. Consequently, as the angels before their confirmation in grace, and man before sin, did not possess the happiness whereby God is seen in His Essence, it is evident that the knowledge they possessed was not such as to exclude faith.

It follows then, that the absence of faith in them could only be explained by their being altogether ignorant of the object of faith. And if man and the angels were created in a purely natural state, as some hold, perhaps one might hold that there was no faith in the angels before their confirmation in grace, or in man before sin, because the knowledge of faith surpasses not only a man's but even an angel's natural knowledge about God.

Since, however, we stated in the First Part (Q. 62, A. 3; Q. 95, A. 1) that man and the angels were created with the gift of grace, we must needs say that there was in them a certain beginning of hoped-for happiness, by reason of grace received but not yet consummated, which happiness was begun in their will by hope and charity, and in the intellect by faith, as stated above (Q. 4, A. 7). Consequently we must hold that the angels had faith before they were confirmed, and man, before he sinned. Nevertheless we must observe that in the object of faith, there is something formal, as it were, namely the First Truth surpassing all the natural knowledge of a creature, and something material, namely, the thing to which we assent while adhering to the First Truth. With regard to the former, before obtaining the happiness to come, faith is common to all who have knowledge of God, by adhering to the First Truth: whereas with regard to the things which are proposed as the material object of faith, some are believed by one, and known manifestly by another, even in the present state, as we have shown above (Q. 1, A. 5; Q. 2, A. 4, ad 2). In this respect, too, it may be said that the angels before being confirmed, and man, before sin, possessed manifest knowledge about certain points in the Divine mysteries, which now we cannot know except by believing them.

**REPLY OBJ. 1:** Although the words of Hugh of S. Victor are those of a master, and have the force of an authority, yet it may be said that the contemplation which removes the need of faith is heavenly contemplation, whereby the

patriae, qua supernaturalis veritas per essentiam videtur. Hanc autem contemplationem non habuit Angelus ante confirmationem nec homo ante peccatum. Sed eorum contemplatio erat altior quam nostra, per quam, magis de propinquo accedentes ad Deum, plura manifeste cognoscere poterant de divinis effectibus et mysteriis quam nos possumus. Unde non inerat eis fides qua ita quaereretur Deus absens sicut a nobis quaeritur. Erat enim eis magis praesens per lumen sapientiae quam sit nobis, licet nec eis esset ita praesens sicut est beatis per lumen gloriae.

**AD SECUNDUM** dicendum quod in statu primae conditionis hominis vel Angeli non erat obscuritas culpae vel poenae. Inerat tamen intellectui hominis et Angeli quaedam obscuritas naturalis, secundum quod omnis creatura tenebra est comparata immensitati divini luminis. Et talis obscuritas sufficit ad fidei rationem.

**AD TERTIUM** dicendum quod in statu primae conditionis non erat auditus ab homine exterius loquente, sed a Deo interius inspirante, sicut et prophetae audiebant, secundum illud Psalm., *audiam quid loquatur in me dominus Deus.*

supernatural truth is seen in its essence. Now the angels did not possess this contemplation before they were confirmed, nor did man before he sinned: yet their contemplation was of a higher order than ours, for by its means they approached nearer to God, and had manifest knowledge of more of the Divine effects and mysteries than we can have knowledge of. Hence faith was not in them so that they sought an absent God as we seek Him: since by the light of wisdom He was more present to them than He is to us, although He was not so present to them as He is to the Blessed by the light of glory.

**REPLY OBJ. 2:** There was no darkness of sin or punishment in the original state of man and the angels, but there was a certain natural obscurity in the human and angelic intellect, insofar as every creature is darkness in comparison with the immensity of the Divine light: and this obscurity suffices for faith.

**REPLY OBJ. 3:** In the original state there was no hearing anything from man speaking outwardly, but there was from God inspiring inwardly: thus the prophets heard, as expressed by the Ps. 84:9: *I will hear what the Lord God will speak in me.*

# Article 2

*Whether in the demons there is faith?*

**AD SECUNDUM SIC PROCEDITUR.** Videtur quod in Daemonibus non sit fides. Dicit enim Augustinus, in libro de Praed. Sanct., quod *fides consistit in credentium voluntate.* Haec autem voluntas bona est qua quis vult credere Deo. Cum igitur in Daemonibus non sit aliqua voluntas deliberata bona, ut in primo dictum est, videtur quod in Daemonibus non sit fides.

**PRAETEREA,** fides est quoddam donum divinae gratiae, secundum illud Ephes. II, *gratia estis salvati per fidem, donum enim Dei est.* Sed Daemones dona gratuita amiserunt per peccatum, ut dicitur in Glossa, super illud Osee III, *ipsi respiciunt ad deos alienos, et diligunt vinacia uvarum.* Ergo fides in Daemonibus post peccatum non remansit.

**PRAETEREA,** infidelitas videtur esse gravius inter peccata, ut patet per Augustinum, super illud Ioan. XV, *si non venissem, et locutus eis non fuissem, peccatum non haberent, nunc autem excusationem non habent de peccato suo.* Sed in quibusdam hominibus est peccatum infidelitatis. Si igitur fides esset in Daemonibus, aliquorum hominum peccatum esset gravius peccato Daemonum. Quod videtur esse inconveniens. Non ergo fides est in Daemonibus.

**SED CONTRA** est quod dicitur Iac. II, *Daemones credunt et contremiscunt.*

**OBJECTION 1:** It would seem that the demons have no faith. For Augustine says (*De Praedest. Sanct.* v) that *faith depends on the believer's will*: and this is a good will, since by it man wishes to believe in God. Since then no deliberate will of the demons is good, as stated above (I, Q. 64, A. 2, ad 5), it seems that in the demons there is no faith.

**OBJ. 2:** Further, faith is a gift of Divine grace, according to Eph. 2:8: *By grace you are saved through faith . . . for it is the gift of God.* Now, according to a gloss on Hosea 3:1, *They look to strange gods, and love the husks of the grapes,* the demons lost their gifts of grace by sinning. Therefore faith did not remain in the demons after they sinned.

**OBJ. 3:** Further, unbelief would seem to be graver than other sins, as Augustine observes (*Tract. lxxxix in Joan.*) on John 15:22, *If I had not come and spoken to them, they would not have sin: but now they have no excuse for their sin.* Now the sin of unbelief is in some men. Consequently, if the demons have faith, some men would be guilty of a sin graver than that of the demons, which seems unreasonable. Therefore in the demons there is no faith.

**ON THE CONTRARY,** It is written (Jas 2:19): *The devils . . . believe and tremble.*

RESPONDEO dicendum quod, sicut supra dictum est, intellectus credentis assentit rei creditae non quia ipsam videat vel secundum se vel per resolutionem ad prima principia per se visa, sed propter imperium voluntatis. Quod autem voluntas moveat intellectum ad assentiendum potest contingere ex duobus. Uno modo, ex ordine voluntatis ad bonum, et sic credere est actus laudabilis. Alio modo, quia intellectus convincitur ad hoc quod iudicet esse credendum his quae dicuntur, licet non convincatur per evidentiam rei. Sicut si aliquis propheta praenuntiaret in sermone domini aliquid futurum, et adhiberet signum mortuum suscitando, ex hoc signo convinceretur intellectus videntis ut cognosceret manifeste hoc dici a Deo, qui non mentitur; licet illud futurum quod praedicitur in se evidens non esset, unde ratio fidei non tolleretur.

Dicendum est ergo quod in fidelibus Christi laudatur fides secundum primum modum. Et secundum hoc non est in Daemonibus, sed solum secundo modo. Vident enim multa manifesta indicia ex quibus percipiunt doctrinam Ecclesiae esse a Deo; quamvis ipsi res ipsas quas Ecclesia docet non videant, puta Deum esse trinum et unum, vel aliquid huiusmodi.

AD PRIMUM ergo dicendum quod Daemonum fides est quodammodo coacta ex signorum evidentia. Et ideo non pertinet ad laudem voluntatis ipsorum quod credunt.

AD SECUNDUM dicendum quod fides quae est donum gratiae inclinat hominem ad credendum secundum aliquem affectum boni, etiam si sit informis. Unde fides quae est in Daemonibus non est donum gratiae; sed magis coguntur ad credendum ex perspicacitate naturalis intellectus.

AD TERTIUM dicendum quod hoc ipsum Daemonibus displicet quod signa fidei sunt tam evidentia ut per ea credere compellantur. Et ideo in nullo malitia eorum minuitur per hoc quod credunt.

I ANSWER THAT, As stated above (Q. 1, A. 4; Q. 2, A. 1), the believer's intellect assents to that which he believes, not because he sees it either in itself, or by resolving it to first self-evident principles, but because his will commands his intellect to assent. Now, that the will moves the intellect to assent, may be due to two causes. First, through the will being directed to the good, and in this way, to believe is a praiseworthy action. Second, because the intellect is convinced that it ought to believe what is said, though that conviction is not based on objective evidence. Thus if a prophet, while preaching the word of God, were to foretell something, and were to give a sign, by raising a dead person to life, the intellect of a witness would be convinced so as to recognize clearly that God, Who lieth not, was speaking, although the thing itself foretold would not be evident in itself, and consequently the essence of faith would not be removed.

Accordingly we must say that faith is commended in the first sense in the faithful of Christ: and in this way faith is not in the demons, but only in the second way, for they see many evident signs, whereby they recognize that the teaching of the Church is from God, although they do not see the things themselves that the Church teaches, for instance that there are three Persons in God, and so forth.

REPLY OBJ. 1: The demons are, in a way, compelled to believe, by the evidence of signs, and so their will deserves no praise for their belief.

REPLY OBJ. 2: Faith, which is a gift of grace, inclines man to believe, by giving him a certain affection for the good, even when that faith is lifeless. Consequently the faith which the demons have, is not a gift of grace. Rather are they compelled to believe through their natural intellectual acumen.

REPLY OBJ. 3: The very fact that the signs of faith are so evident, that the demons are compelled to believe, is displeasing to them, so that their malice is by no means diminished by their belief.

# Article 3

*Whether a heretic who disbelieves one article of faith can have lifeless faith in the other articles?*

AD TERTIUM SIC PROCEDITUR. Videtur quod haereticus qui discredit unum articulum fidei possit habere fidem informem de aliis articulis. Non enim intellectus naturalis haeretici est potentior quam intellectus catholici. Sed intellectus catholici indiget adiuvari, ad credendum quemcumque articulum fidei, dono fidei. Ergo videtur quod nec haeretici aliquos articulos credere possint sine dono fidei informis.

OBJECTION 1: It would seem that a heretic who disbelieves one article of faith, can have lifeless faith in the other articles. For the natural intellect of a heretic is not more able than that of a catholic. Now a catholic's intellect needs the aid of the gift of faith in order to believe any article whatever of faith. Therefore it seems that heretics cannot believe any articles of faith without the gift of lifeless faith.

PRAETEREA, sicut sub fide continentur multi articuli fidei, ita sub una scientia, puta geometria, continentur multae conclusiones. Sed homo aliquis potest habere scientiam geometriae circa quasdam geometricas conclusiones, aliis ignoratis. Ergo homo aliquis potest habere fidem de aliquibus articulis fidei, alios non credendo.

PRAETEREA, sicut homo obedit Deo ad credendum articulos fidei, ita etiam ad servanda mandata legis. Sed homo potest esse obediens circa quaedam mandata et non circa alia. Ergo potest habere fidem circa quosdam articulos et non circa alios.

SED CONTRA, sicut peccatum mortale contrariatur caritati, ita discredere unum articulum contrariatur fidei. Sed caritas non remanet in homine post unum peccatum mortale. Ergo neque fides postquam discredit unum articulum fidei.

RESPONDEO dicendum quod haereticus qui discredit unum articulum fidei non habet habitum fidei neque formatae neque informis.

Cuius ratio est quia species cuiuslibet habitus dependet ex formali ratione obiecti, qua sublata, species habitus remanere non potest. Formale autem obiectum fidei est veritas prima secundum quod manifestatur in Scripturis sacris et doctrina Ecclesiae. Unde quicumque non inhaeret, sicut infallibili et divinae regulae, doctrinae Ecclesiae, quae procedit ex veritate prima in Scripturis sacris manifestata, ille non habet habitum fidei, sed ea quae sunt fidei alio modo tenet quam per fidem. Sicut si aliquis teneat mente aliquam conclusionem non cognoscens medium illius demonstrationis, manifestum est quod non habet eius scientiam, sed opinionem solum. Manifestum est autem quod ille qui inhaeret doctrinae Ecclesiae tanquam infallibili regulae, omnibus assentit quae Ecclesia docet. Alioquin, si de his quae Ecclesia docet quae vult tenet et quae vult non tenet, non iam inhaeret Ecclesiae doctrinae sicut infallibili regulae, sed propriae voluntati. Et sic manifestum est quod haereticus qui pertinaciter discredit unum articulum non est paratus sequi in omnibus doctrinam Ecclesiae (si enim non pertinaciter, iam non est haereticus, sed solum errans). Unde manifestum est quod talis haereticus circa unum articulum fidem non habet de aliis articulis, sed opinionem quandam secundum propriam voluntatem.

AD PRIMUM ergo dicendum quod alios articulos fidei, de quibus haereticus non errat, non tenet eo modo sicut tenet eos fidelis, scilicet simpliciter inhaerendo primae veritati, ad quod indiget homo adiuvari per habitum fidei, sed tenet ea quae sunt fidei propria voluntate et iudicio.

AD SECUNDUM dicendum quod in diversis conclusionibus unius scientiae sunt diversa media per quae probantur, quorum unum potest cognosci sine alio. Et

OBJ. 2: Further, just as faith contains many articles, so does one science, viz. geometry, contain many conclusions. Now a man may possess the science of geometry as to some geometrical conclusions, and yet be ignorant of other conclusions. Therefore a man can believe some articles of faith without believing the others.

OBJ. 3: Further, just as man obeys God in believing the articles of faith, so does he also in keeping the commandments of the Law. Now a man can obey some commandments, and disobey others. Therefore he can believe some articles, and disbelieve others.

ON THE CONTRARY, Just as mortal sin is contrary to charity, so is disbelief in one article of faith contrary to faith. Now charity does not remain in a man after one mortal sin. Therefore neither does faith, after a man disbelieves one article.

I ANSWER THAT, Neither living nor lifeless faith remains in a heretic who disbelieves one article of faith.

The reason of this is that the species of every habit depends on the formal aspect of the object, without which the species of the habit cannot remain. Now the formal object of faith is the First Truth, as manifested in Holy Writ and the teaching of the Church, which proceeds from the First Truth. Consequently whoever does not adhere, as to an infallible and Divine rule, to the teaching of the Church, which proceeds from the First Truth manifested in Holy Writ, has not the habit of faith, but holds that which is of faith otherwise than by faith. Even so, it is evident that a man whose mind holds a conclusion without knowing how it is proved, has not scientific knowledge, but merely an opinion about it. Now it is manifest that he who adheres to the teaching of the Church, as to an infallible rule, assents to whatever the Church teaches; otherwise, if, of the things taught by the Church, he holds what he chooses to hold, and rejects what he chooses to reject, he no longer adheres to the teaching of the Church as to an infallible rule, but to his own will. Hence it is evident that a heretic who obstinately disbelieves one article of faith, is not prepared to follow the teaching of the Church in all things; but if he is not obstinate, he is no longer in heresy but only in error. Therefore it is clear that such a heretic with regard to one article has no faith in the other articles, but only a kind of opinion in accordance with his own will.

REPLY OBJ. 1: A heretic does not hold the other articles of faith, about which he does not err, in the same way as one of the faithful does, namely by adhering simply to the Divine Truth, because in order to do so, a man needs the help of the habit of faith; but he holds the things that are of faith, by his own will and judgment.

REPLY OBJ. 2: The various conclusions of a science have their respective means of demonstration, one of which may be known without another, so that we may know some

ideo homo potest scire quasdam conclusiones unius scientiae, ignoratis aliis. Sed omnibus articulis fidei inhaeret fides propter unum medium, scilicet propter veritatem primam propositam nobis in Scripturis secundum doctrinam Ecclesiae intellectis sane. Et ideo qui ab hoc medio decidit totaliter fide caret.

**AD TERTIUM** dicendum quod diversa praecepta legis possunt referri vel ad diversa motiva proxima, et sic unum sine alio servari potest. Vel ad unum motivum primum, quod est perfecte obedire Deo, a quo decidit quicumque unum praeceptum transgreditur, secundum illud Iac. II, *qui offendit in uno factus est omnium reus.*

conclusions of a science without knowing the others. On the other hand faith adheres to all the articles of faith by reason of one mean, viz. on account of the First Truth proposed to us in Scriptures, according to the teaching of the Church who has the right understanding of them. Hence whoever abandons this mean is altogether lacking in faith.

**REPLY OBJ. 3**: The various precepts of the Law may be referred either to their respective proximate motives, and thus one can be kept without another; or to their primary motive, which is perfect obedience to God, in which a man fails whenever he breaks one commandment, according to James 2:10: *Whosoever shall . . . offend in one point is become guilty of all.*

# Article 4

### *Whether faith can be greater in one man than in another?*

**AD QUARTUM SIC PROCEDITUR**. Videtur quod fides non possit esse maior in uno quam in alio. Quantitas enim habitus attenditur secundum obiecta. Sed quicumque habet fidem credit omnia quae sunt fidei, quia qui deficit ab uno totaliter amittit fidem, ut supra dictum est. Ergo videtur quod fides non possit esse maior in uno quam in alio.

**PRAETEREA**, ea quae sunt in summo non recipiunt magis neque minus. Sed ratio fidei est in summo, requiritur enim ad fidem quod homo inhaereat primae veritati super omnia. Ergo fides non recipit magis et minus.

**PRAETEREA**, ita se habet fides in cognitione gratuita sicut intellectus principiorum in cognitione naturali, eo quod articuli fidei sunt prima principia gratuitae cognitionis, ut ex dictis patet. Sed intellectus principiorum aequaliter invenitur in omnibus hominibus. Ergo et fides aequaliter invenitur in omnibus fidelibus.

**SED CONTRA**, ubicumque invenitur parvum et magnum, ibi invenitur maius et minus. Sed in fide invenitur magnum et parvum, dicit enim dominus Petro, Matth. XIV, *modicae fidei, quare dubitasti?* Et mulieri dixit, Matth. XV, *mulier, magna est fides tua.* Ergo fides potest esse maior in uno quam in alio.

**RESPONDEO** dicendum quod, sicut supra dictum est, quantitas habitus ex duobus attendi potest, uno modo, ex obiecto; alio modo, secundum participationem subiecti.

Obiectum autem fidei potest dupliciter considerari, uno modo, secundum formalem rationem; alio modo, secundum ea quae materialiter credenda proponuntur. Formale autem obiectum fidei est unum et simplex scili-

**OBJECTION 1**: It would seem that faith cannot be greater in one man than in another. For the quantity of a habit is taken from its object. Now whoever has faith believes everything that is of faith, since by failing in one point, a man loses his faith altogether, as stated above (A. 3). Therefore it seems that faith cannot be greater in one than in another.

**OBJ. 2**: Further, those things which consist in something supreme cannot be *more* or *less*. Now faith consists in something supreme, because it requires that man should adhere to the First Truth above all things. Therefore faith cannot be *more* or *less*.

**OBJ. 3**: Further, faith is to knowledge by grace, as the understanding of principles is to natural knowledge, since the articles of faith are the first principles of knowledge by grace, as was shown above (Q. 1, A. 7). Now the understanding of principles is possessed in equal degree by all men. Therefore faith is possessed in equal degree by all the faithful.

**ON THE CONTRARY**, Wherever we find great and little, there we find more or less. Now in the matter of faith we find great and little, for Our Lord said to Peter (Matt 14:31): *O thou of little faith, why didst thou doubt?* And to the woman he said (Matt 15: 28): *O woman, great is thy faith!* Therefore faith can be greater in one than in another.

**I ANSWER THAT**, As stated above (I-II, Q. 52, AA. 1, 2; I-II, Q. 112, A. 4), the quantity of a habit may be considered from two points of view: first, on the part of the object; second, on the part of its participation by the subject.

Now the object of faith may be considered in two ways: first, in respect of its formal aspect; second, in respect of the material object which is proposed to be believed. Now the formal object of faith is one and simple, namely the

cet veritas prima, ut supra dictum est. Unde ex hac parte fides non diversificatur in credentibus, sed est una specie in omnibus, ut supra dictum est. Sed ea quae materialiter credenda proponuntur sunt plura, et possunt accipi vel magis vel minus explicite. Et secundum hoc potest unus homo plura explicite credere quam alius. Et sic in uno potest esse maior fides secundum maiorem fidei explicationem.

Si vero consideretur fides secundum participationem subiecti, hoc contingit dupliciter. Nam actus fidei procedit et ex intellectu et ex voluntate, ut supra dictum est. Potest ergo fides in aliquo dici maior uno modo ex parte intellectus, propter maiorem certitudinem et firmitatem, alio modo ex parte voluntatis, propter maiorem promptitudinem seu devotionem vel confidentiam.

**AD PRIMUM** ergo dicendum quod ille qui pertinaciter discredit aliquid eorum quae sub fide continentur non habet habitum fidei, quem tamen habet ille qui non explicite omnia credit, sed paratus est omnia credere. Et secundum hoc ex parte obiecti unus habet maiorem fidem quam alius, inquantum plura explicite credit, ut dictum est.

**AD SECUNDUM** dicendum quod de ratione fidei est ut veritas prima omnibus praeferatur. Sed tamen eorum qui eam omnibus praeferunt quidam certius et devotius se ei subiiciunt quam alii. Et secundum hoc fides est maior in uno quam in alio.

**AD TERTIUM** dicendum quod intellectus principiorum consequitur ipsam naturam humanam, quae aequaliter in omnibus invenitur. Sed fides consequitur donum gratiae, quod non est aequaliter in omnibus, ut supra dictum est. Unde non est eadem ratio.

Et tamen secundum maiorem capacitatem intellectus, unus magis cognoscit virtutem principiorum quam alius.

First Truth, as stated above (Q. 1, A. 1). Hence in this respect there is no diversity of faith among believers, but it is specifically one in all, as stated above (Q. 4, A. 6). But the things which are proposed as the matter of our belief are many and can be received more or less explicitly; and in this respect one man can believe explicitly more things than another, so that faith can be greater in one man on account of its being more explicit.

If, on the other hand, we consider faith from the point of view of its participation by the subject, this happens in two ways, since the act of faith proceeds both from the intellect and from the will, as stated above (Q. 2, AA. 1, 2; Q. 4, A. 2). Consequently a man's faith may be described as being greater, in one way, on the part of his intellect, on account of its greater certitude and firmness, and, in another way, on the part of his will, on account of his greater promptitude, devotion, or confidence.

**REPLY OBJ. 1**: A man who obstinately disbelieves a thing that is of faith, has not the habit of faith, and yet he who does not explicitly believe all, while he is prepared to believe all, has that habit. In this respect, one man has greater faith than another, on the part of the object, insofar as he believes more things, as stated above.

**REPLY OBJ. 2**: It is essential to faith that one should give the first place to the First Truth. But among those who do this, some submit to it with greater certitude and devotion than others; and in this way faith is greater in one than in another.

**REPLY OBJ. 3**: The understanding of principles results from man's very nature, which is equally shared by all: whereas faith results from the gift of grace, which is not equally in all, as explained above (I-II, Q. 112, A. 4). Hence the comparison fails.

Nevertheless the truth of principles is more known to one than to another, according to the greater capacity of intellect.

# QUESTION 6

## THE CAUSE OF FAITH

Deinde considerandum est de causa fidei. Et circa hoc quaeruntur duo.

Primo, utrum fides sit homini infusa a Deo.

Secundo, utrum fides informis sit donum.

We must now consider the cause of faith, under which head there are two points of inquiry:

(1) Whether faith is infused into man by God?

(2) Whether lifeless faith is a gift of God?

# Article 1

*Whether faith is infused into man by God?*

**AD PRIMUM SIC PROCEDITUR**. Videtur quod fides non sit homini infusa a Deo. Dicit enim Augustinus, XIV de Trin., quod *per scientiam gignitur in nobis fides, nutritur, defenditur et roboratur*. Sed ea quae per scientiam in nobis gignuntur magis videntur acquisita esse quam infusa. Ergo fides non videtur in nobis esse ex infusione divina.

**PRAETEREA**, illud ad quod homo pertingit audiendo et videndo videtur esse ab homine acquisitum. Sed homo pertingit ad credendum et videndo miracula et audiendo fidei doctrinam, dicitur enim Ioan. IV, *cognovit pater quia illa hora erat in qua dixit ei Iesus, filius tuus vivit, et credidit ipse et domus eius tota*; et Rom. X dicitur quod *fides est ex auditu*. Ergo fides habetur ab homine tanquam acquisita.

**PRAETEREA**, illud quod consistit in hominis voluntate ab homine potest acquiri. Sed fides consistit in credentium voluntate, ut Augustinus dicit, in libro de Praed. Sanct. Ergo fides potest esse ab homine acquisita.

**SED CONTRA** est quod dicitur ad Ephes. II, *gratia estis salvati per fidem, et non ex vobis, ne quis glorietur, Dei enim donum est*.

**RESPONDEO** dicendum quod ad fidem duo requiruntur. Quorum unum est ut homini credibilia proponantur, quod requiritur ad hoc quod homo aliquid explicite credat. Aliud autem quod ad fidem requiritur est assensus credentis ad ea quae proponuntur. Quantum igitur ad primum horum, necesse est quod fides sit a Deo. Ea enim quae sunt fidei excedunt rationem humanam, unde non cadunt in contemplatione hominis nisi Deo revelante. Sed quibusdam quidem revelantur immediate a Deo, sicut sunt revelata apostolis et prophetis, quibusdam autem proponuntur a Deo mittente fidei praedicatores, secundum illud Rom. X, *quomodo praedicabunt nisi mittantur?*

**OBJECTION 1**: It would seem that faith is not infused into man by God. For Augustine says (*De Trin.* xiv) that *science begets faith in us, and nourishes, defends and strengthens it*. Now those things which science begets in us seem to be acquired rather than infused. Therefore faith does not seem to be in us by Divine infusion.

**OBJ. 2**: Further, that to which man attains by hearing and seeing, seems to be acquired by him. Now man attains to belief, both by seeing miracles, and by hearing the teachings of faith: for it is written (John 4:53): *The father . . . knew that it was at the same hour, that Jesus said to him, Thy son liveth; and himself believed, and his whole house*; and (Rom 10:17) it is said that *faith is through hearing*. Therefore man attains to faith by acquiring it.

**OBJ. 3**: Further, that which depends on a man's will can be acquired by him. But *faith depends on the believer's will*, according to Augustine (*De Praedest. Sanct.* v). Therefore faith can be acquired by man.

**ON THE CONTRARY**, It is written (*Eph 2:8, 9*): *By grace you are saved through faith, and that not of yourselves . . . that no man may glory . . . for it is the gift of God.*

**I ANSWER THAT**, Two things are requisite for faith. First, that the things which are of faith should be proposed to man: this is necessary in order that man believe anything explicitly. The second thing requisite for faith is the assent of the believer to the things which are proposed to him. Accordingly, as regards the first of these, faith must needs be from God. Because those things which are of faith surpass human reason, hence they do not come to man's knowledge, unless God reveal them. To some, indeed, they are revealed by God immediately, as those things which were revealed to the apostles and prophets, while to some they are proposed by God in sending preachers of the faith, according to Rom. 10:15: *How shall they preach, unless they be sent?*

Quantum vero ad secundum, scilicet ad assensum hominis in ea quae sunt fidei, potest considerari duplex causa. Una quidem exterius inducens, sicut miraculum visum, vel persuasio hominis inducentis ad fidem. Quorum neutrum est sufficiens causa, videntium enim unum et idem miraculum, et audientium eandem praedicationem, quidam credunt et quidam non credunt. Et ideo oportet ponere aliam causam interiorem, quae movet hominem interius ad assentiendum his quae sunt fidei.

Hanc autem causam Pelagiani ponebant solum liberum arbitrium hominis, et propter hoc dicebant quod initium fidei est ex nobis, inquantum scilicet ex nobis est quod parati sumus ad assentiendum his quae sunt fidei; sed consummatio fidei est a Deo, per quem nobis proponuntur ea quae credere debemus. Sed hoc est falsum. Quia cum homo, assentiendo his quae sunt fidei, elevetur supra naturam suam, oportet quod hoc insit ei ex supernaturali principio interius movente, quod est Deus. Et ideo fides quantum ad assensum, qui est principalis actus fidei, est a Deo interius movente per gratiam.

**AD PRIMUM** ergo dicendum quod per scientiam gignitur fides et nutritur per modum exterioris persuasionis, quae fit ab aliqua scientia. Sed principalis et propria causa fidei est id quod interius movet ad assentiendum.

**AD SECUNDUM** dicendum quod etiam ratio illa procedit de causa proponente exterius ea quae sunt fidei, vel persuadente ad credendum vel verbo vel facto.

**AD TERTIUM** dicendum quod credere quidem in voluntate credentium consistit, sed oportet quod voluntas hominis praeparetur a Deo per gratiam ad hoc quod elevetur in ea quae sunt supra naturam, ut supra dictum est.

As regards the second, viz. man's assent to the things which are of faith, we may observe a twofold cause, one of external inducement, such as seeing a miracle, or being persuaded by someone to embrace the faith: neither of which is a sufficient cause, since of those who see the same miracle, or who hear the same sermon, some believe, and some do not. Hence we must assert another internal cause, which moves man inwardly to assent to matters of faith.

The Pelagians held that this cause was nothing else than man's free-will: and consequently they said that the beginning of faith is from ourselves, inasmuch as, to wit, it is in our power to be ready to assent to things which are of faith, but that the consummation of faith is from God, Who proposes to us the things we have to believe. But this is false, for, since man, by assenting to matters of faith, is raised above his nature, this must needs accrue to him from some supernatural principle moving him inwardly; and this is God. Therefore faith, as regards the assent which is the chief act of faith, is from God moving man inwardly by grace.

**REPLY OBJ. 1**: Science begets and nourishes faith, by way of external persuasion afforded by science; but the chief and proper cause of faith is that which moves man inwardly to assent.

**REPLY OBJ. 2**: This argument again refers to the cause that proposes outwardly the things that are of faith, or persuades man to believe by words or deeds.

**REPLY OBJ. 3**: To believe does indeed depend on the will of the believer: but man's will needs to be prepared by God with grace, in order that he may be raised to things which are above his nature, as stated above (Q. 2, A. 3).

# Article 2

*Whether lifeless faith is a gift of God?*

**AD SECUNDUM SIC PROCEDITUR**. Videtur quod fides informis non sit donum Dei. Dicitur enim Deut. XXXII, quod *Dei perfecta sunt opera*. Fides autem informis est quiddam imperfectum. Ergo fides informis non est opus Dei.

**PRAETEREA**, sicut actus dicitur deformis propter hoc quod caret debita forma, ita etiam fides dicitur informis propter hoc quod caret debita forma. Sed actus deformis peccati non est a Deo, ut supra dictum est. Ergo neque etiam fides informis est a Deo.

**PRAETEREA**, quaecumque Deus sanat totaliter sanat, dicitur enim Ioan. VII, *si circumcisionem accipit homo in sabbato ut non solvatur lex Moysi, mihi indignamini quia*

**OBJECTION 1**: It would seem that lifeless faith is not a gift of God. For it is written (Deut 32:4) that *the works of God are perfect*. Now lifeless faith is something imperfect. Therefore it is not the work of God.

**OBJ. 2**: Further, just as an act is said to be deformed through lacking its due form, so too is faith called lifeless (informis) when it lacks the form due to it. Now the deformed act of sin is not from God, as stated above (I-II, Q. 79, A. 2, ad 2). Therefore neither is lifeless faith from God.

**OBJ. 3**: Further, whomsoever God heals, He heals wholly: for it is written (John 7:23): *If a man receive circumcision on the sabbath-day, that the law of Moses may*

*totum hominem salvum feci in sabbato.* Sed per fidem homo sanatur ab infidelitate. Quicumque ergo donum fidei a Deo accipit simul sanatur ab omnibus peccatis. Sed hoc non fit nisi per fidem formatam. Ergo sola fides formata est donum Dei. Non ergo fides informis.

**SED CONTRA** est quod quaedam Glossa dicit, I ad Cor. XIII, quod *fides quae est sine caritate est donum Dei.* Sed fides quae est sine caritate est fides informis. Ergo fides informis est donum Dei.

**RESPONDEO** dicendum quod informitas privatio quaedam est. Est autem considerandum quod privatio quandoque quidem pertinet ad rationem speciei, quandoque autem non, sed supervenit rei iam habenti propriam speciem. Sicut privatio debitae commensurationis humorum est de ratione speciei ipsius aegritudinis, tenebrositas autem non est de ratione speciei ipsius diaphani, sed supervenit. Quia igitur cum assignatur causa alicuius rei, intelligitur assignari causa eius secundum quod in propria specie existit, ideo quod non est causa privationis non potest dici esse causa illius rei ad quam pertinet privatio sicut existens de ratione speciei ipsius, non enim potest dici causa aegritudinis quod non est causa distemperantiae humorum. Potest tamen aliquid dici esse causa diaphani quamvis non sit causa obscuritatis, quae non est de ratione speciei diaphani.

Informitas autem fidei non pertinet ad rationem speciei ipsius fidei, cum fides dicatur informis propter defectum cuiusdam exterioris formae, sicut dictum est. Et ideo illud est causa fidei informis quod est causa fidei simpliciter dictae. Hoc autem est Deus, ut dictum est. Unde relinquitur quod fides informis sit donum Dei.

**AD PRIMUM** ergo dicendum quod fides informis, etsi non sit perfecta simpliciter perfectione virtutis, est tamen perfecta quadam perfectione quae sufficit ad fidei rationem.

**AD SECUNDUM** dicendum quod deformitas actus est de ratione speciei ipsius actus secundum quod est actus moralis, ut supra dictum est, dicitur enim actus deformis per privationem formae intrinsecae, quae est debita commensuratio circumstantiarum actus. Et ideo non potest dici causa actus deformis Deus, qui non est causa deformitatis, licet sit causa actus inquantum est actus.

Vel dicendum quod deformitas non solum importat privationem debitae formae, sed etiam contrariam dispositionem. Unde deformitas se habet ad actum sicut falsitas ad fidem. Et ideo sicut actus deformis non est a Deo, ita nec aliqua fides falsa. Et sicut fides informis est a Deo, ita etiam actus qui sunt boni ex genere, quamvis non sint caritate formati, sicut plerumque in peccatoribus contingit.

*not be broken; are you angry at Me because I have healed the whole man on the sabbath-day?* Now faith heals man from unbelief. Therefore whoever receives from God the gift of faith, is at the same time healed from all his sins. But this is not done except by living faith. Therefore living faith alone is a gift of God: and consequently lifeless faith is not from God.

**ON THE CONTRARY,** A gloss on 1 Cor. 13:2 says that *the faith which lacks charity is a gift of God.* Now this is lifeless faith. Therefore lifeless faith is a gift of God.

**I ANSWER THAT,** Lifelessness is a privation. Now it must be noted that privation is sometimes essential to the species, whereas sometimes it is not, but supervenes in a thing already possessed of its proper species: thus privation of the due equilibrium of the humors is essential to the species of sickness, while darkness is not essential to a diaphanous body, but supervenes in it. Since, therefore, when we assign the cause of a thing, we intend to assign the cause of that thing as existing in its proper species, it follows that what is not the cause of privation, cannot be assigned as the cause of the thing to which that privation belongs as being essential to its species. For we cannot assign as the cause of a sickness, something which is not the cause of a disturbance in the humors: though we can assign as cause of a diaphanous body, something which is not the cause of the darkness, which is not essential to the diaphanous body.

Now the lifelessness of faith is not essential to the species of faith, since faith is said to be lifeless through lack of an extrinsic form, as stated above (Q. 4, A. 4). Consequently the cause of lifeless faith is that which is the cause of faith strictly so called: and this is God, as stated above (A. 1). It follows, therefore, that lifeless faith is a gift of God.

**REPLY OBJ. 1:** Lifeless faith, though it is not simply perfect with the perfection of a virtue, is, nevertheless, perfect with a perfection that suffices for the essential notion of faith.

**REPLY OBJ. 2:** The deformity of an act is essential to the act's species, considered as a moral act, as stated above (I, Q. 48, A. 1, ad 2; I-II, Q. 18, A. 5): for an act is said to be deformed through being deprived of an intrinsic form, viz. the due commensuration of the act's circumstances. Hence we cannot say that God is the cause of a deformed act, for He is not the cause of its deformity, though He is the cause of the act as such.

We may also reply that deformity denotes not only privation of a due form, but also a contrary disposition, wherefore deformity is compared to the act, as falsehood is to faith. Hence, just as the deformed act is not from God, so neither is a false faith; and as lifeless faith is from God, so too, acts that are good generically, though not quickened by charity, as is frequently the case in sinners, are from God.

**AD TERTIUM** dicendum quod ille qui accipit a Deo fidem absque caritate non simpliciter sanatur ab infidelitate, quia non removetur culpa praecedentis infidelitatis, sed sanatur secundum quid, ut scilicet cesset a tali peccato. Hoc autem frequenter contingit, quod aliquis desistit ab uno actu peccati, etiam Deo hoc faciente, qui tamen ab actu alterius peccati non desistit, propria iniquitate suggerente. Et per hunc modum datur aliquando a Deo homini quod credat, non tamen datur ei caritatis donum, sicut etiam aliquibus absque caritate datur donum prophetiae vel aliquid simile.

**REPLY OBJ. 3**: He who receives faith from God without charity, is healed from unbelief, not entirely (because the sin of his previous unbelief is not removed) but in part, namely, in the point of ceasing from committing such and such a sin. Thus it happens frequently that a man desists from one act of sin, through God causing him thus to desist, without desisting from another act of sin, through the instigation of his own malice. And in this way sometimes it is granted by God to a man to believe, and yet he is not granted the gift of charity: even so the gift of prophecy, or the like, is given to some without charity.

# QUESTION 7

## THE EFFECTS OF FAITH

Deinde considerandum est de effectibus fidei. Et circa hoc quaeruntur duo.

Primo, utrum timor sit effectus fidei.

Secundo, utrum purificatio cordis sit effectus fidei.

We must now consider the effects of faith: under which head there are two points of inquiry:

(1) Whether fear is an effect of faith?

(2) Whether the heart is purified by faith?

## Article 1

*Whether fear is an effect of faith?*

**AD PRIMUM SIC PROCEDITUR.** Videtur quod timor non sit effectus fidei. Effectus enim non praecedit causam. Sed timor praecedit fidem, dicitur enim Eccli. II, *qui timetis Deum, credite illi.* Ergo timor non est effectus fidei.

**PRAETEREA,** idem non est causa contrariorum. Sed timor et spes sunt contraria, ut supra dictum est, *fides autem generat spem*, ut dicitur in Glossa, Matth. I. Ergo non est causa timoris.

**PRAETEREA,** contrarium non est causa contrarii. Sed obiectum fidei est quoddam bonum, quod est veritas prima, obiectum autem timoris est malum, ut supra dictum est. Actus autem habent speciem ex obiectis, secundum supradicta. Ergo fides non est causa timoris.

**SED CONTRA** est quod dicitur Iac. II, *Daemones credunt et contremiscunt.*

**RESPONDEO** dicendum quod timor est quidam motus appetitivae virtutis, ut supra dictum est. Omnium autem appetitivorum motuum principium est bonum vel malum apprehensum. Unde oportet quod timoris et omnium appetitivorum motuum sit principium aliqua apprehensio. Per fidem autem fit in nobis quaedam apprehensio de quibusdam malis poenalibus quae secundum divinum iudicium inferuntur, et per hunc modum fides est causa timoris quo quis timet a Deo puniri, qui est timor servilis.

Est etiam causa timoris filialis, quo quis timet separari a Deo, vel quo quis refugit se Deo comparare reverendo ipsum; inquantum per fidem hanc existimationem habemus de Deo, quod sit quoddam immensum et altissimum bonum, a quo separari est pessimum et cui velle aequari est malum. Sed primi timoris, scilicet servilis, est causa fides informis. Sed secundi timoris, scilicet filialis, est causa fides formata, quae per caritatem facit hominem Deo inhaerere et ei subiici.

**OBJECTION 1:** It would seem that fear is not an effect of faith. For an effect does not precede its cause. Now fear precedes faith: for it is written (Sir 2:8): *Ye that fear the Lord, believe in Him.* Therefore fear is not an effect of faith.

**OBJ. 2:** Further, the same thing is not the cause of contraries. Now fear and hope are contraries, as stated above (I-II, Q. 23, A. 2): and faith begets hope, as a gloss observes on Matt. 1:2. Therefore fear is not an effect of faith.

**OBJ. 3:** Further, one contrary does not cause another. Now the object of faith is a good, which is the First Truth, while the object of fear is an evil, as stated above (I-II, Q. 42, A. 1). Again, acts take their species from the object, according to what was stated above (I-II, Q. 18, A. 2). Therefore faith is not a cause of fear.

**ON THE CONTRARY,** It is written (Jas 2:19): *The devils . . . believe and tremble.*

**I ANSWER THAT,** Fear is a movement of the appetitive power, as stated above (I-II, Q. 41, A. 1). Now the principle of all appetitive movements is the good or evil apprehended: and consequently the principle of fear and of every appetitive movement must be an apprehension. Again, through faith there arises in us an apprehension of certain penal evils, which are inflicted in accordance with the Divine judgment. In this way, then, faith is a cause of the fear whereby one dreads to be punished by God; and this is servile fear.

It is also the cause of filial fear, whereby one dreads to be separated from God, or whereby one shrinks from equalling oneself to Him, and holds Him in reverence, inasmuch as faith makes us appreciate God as an unfathomable and supreme good, separation from which is the greatest evil, and to which it is wicked to wish to be equalled. Of the first fear, viz. servile fear, lifeless faith is the cause, while living faith is the cause of the second, viz. filial fear, because it makes man adhere to God and to be subject to Him by charity.

71

**AD PRIMUM** ergo dicendum quod timor Dei non potest universaliter praecedere fidem, quia si omnino eius ignorantiam haberemus quantum ad praemia vel poenas de quibus per fidem instruimur, nullo modo eum timeremus. Sed supposita fide de aliquibus articulis fidei, puta de excellentia divina, sequitur timor reverentiae, ex quo sequitur ulterius ut homo intellectum suum Deo subiiciat ad credendum omnia quae sunt promissa a Deo. Unde ibi sequitur, *et non evacuabitur merces vestra.*

**AD SECUNDUM** dicendum quod idem secundum contraria potest esse contrariorum causa, non autem idem secundum idem. Fides autem generat spem secundum quod facit nobis existimationem de praemiis quae Deus retribuit iustis. Est autem causa timoris secundum quod facit nobis aestimationem de poenis quas peccatoribus infliget.

**AD TERTIUM** dicendum quod obiectum fidei primum et formale est bonum quod est veritas prima. Sed materialiter fidei proponuntur credenda etiam quaedam mala, puta quod malum sit Deo non subiici vel ab eo separari, et quod peccatores poenalia mala sustinebunt a Deo. Et secundum hoc fides potest esse causa timoris.

**REPLY OBJ. 1:** Fear of God cannot altogether precede faith, because if we knew nothing at all about Him, with regard to rewards and punishments, concerning which faith teaches us, we should nowise fear Him. If, however, faith be presupposed in reference to certain articles of faith, for example the Divine excellence, then reverential fear follows, the result of which is that man submits his intellect to God, so as to believe in all the Divine promises. Hence the text quoted continues: *And your reward shall not be made void.*

**REPLY OBJ. 2:** The same thing in respect of contraries can be the cause of contraries, but not under the same aspect. Now faith begets hope, insofar as it enables us to appreciate the prize which God awards to the just, while it is the cause of fear, insofar as it makes us appreciate the punishments which He intends to inflict on sinners.

**REPLY OBJ. 3:** The primary and formal object of faith is the good which is the First Truth; but the material object of faith includes also certain evils; for instance, that it is an evil either not to submit to God, or to be separated from Him, and that sinners will suffer penal evils from God: in this way faith can be the cause of fear.

# Article 2

*Whether faith has the effect of purifying the heart?*

**AD SECUNDUM SIC PROCEDITUR.** Videtur quod purificatio cordis non sit effectus fidei. Puritas enim cordis praecipue in affectu consistit. Sed fides in intellectu est. Ergo fides non causat cordis purificationem.

**PRAETEREA**, illud quod causat cordis purificationem non potest simul esse cum impuritate. Sed fides simul potest esse cum impuritate peccati, sicut patet in illis qui habent fidem informem. Ergo fides non purificat cor.

**PRAETEREA**, si fides aliquo modo purificaret cor humanum, maxime purificaret hominis intellectum. Sed intellectum non purificat ab obscuritate, cum sit cognitio aenigmatica. Ergo fides nullo modo purificat cor.

**SED CONTRA** est quod dicit Petrus, Act. XV, *fide purificans corda eorum.*

**RESPONDEO** dicendum quod impuritas uniuscuiusque rei consistit in hoc quod rebus vilioribus immiscetur, non enim dicitur argentum esse impurum ex permixtione auri, per quam melius redditur, sed ex permixtione plumbi vel stanni. Manifestum est autem quod rationalis creatura dignior est omnibus temporalibus et corporalibus creaturis. Et ideo impura redditur ex hoc quod temporalibus se subiicit per amorem. A qua quidem impuritate purificatur per contrarium motum, dum scilicet tendit in id quod est supra se, scilicet in Deum. In quo

**OBJECTION 1:** It would seem that faith does not purify the heart. For purity of the heart pertains chiefly to the affections, whereas faith is in the intellect. Therefore faith has not the effect of purifying the heart.

**OBJ. 2:** Further, that which purifies the heart is incompatible with impurity. But faith is compatible with the impurity of sin, as may be seen in those who have lifeless faith. Therefore faith does not purify the heart.

**OBJ. 3:** Further, if faith were to purify the human heart in any way, it would chiefly purify the intellect of man. Now it does not purify the intellect from obscurity, since it is a veiled knowledge. Therefore faith nowise purifies the heart.

**ON THE CONTRARY,** Peter said (Acts 15:9): *Purifying their hearts by faith.*

**I ANSWER THAT,** A thing is impure through being mixed with baser things: for silver is not called impure, when mixed with gold, which betters it, but when mixed with lead or tin. Now it is evident that the rational creature is more excellent than all transient and corporeal creatures; so that it becomes impure through subjecting itself to transient things by loving them. From this impurity the rational creature is purified by means of a contrary movement, namely, by tending to that which is above it, viz. God. The first beginning of this movement is faith: since

quidem motu primum principium est fides, *accedentem enim ad Deum oportet credere*, ut dicitur Heb. XI. Et ideo primum principium purificationis cordis est fides, quae si perficiatur per caritatem formatam, perfectam purificationem causat.

**AD PRIMUM** ergo dicendum quod ea quae sunt in intellectu sunt principia eorum quae sunt in affectu, inquantum scilicet bonum intellectum movet affectum.

**AD SECUNDUM** dicendum quod fides etiam informis excludit quandam impuritatem sibi oppositam, scilicet impuritatem erroris, quae contingit ex hoc quod intellectus humanus inordinate inhaeret rebus se inferioribus, dum scilicet vult secundum rationes rerum sensibilium metiri divina. Sed quando per caritatem formatur, tunc nullam impuritatem secum compatitur, *quia universa delicta operit caritas*, ut dicitur Prov. X.

**AD TERTIUM** dicendum quod obscuritas fidei non pertinet ad impuritatem culpae, sed magis ad naturalem defectum intellectus humani, secundum statum praesentis vitae.

*he that cometh to God must believe that He is*, according to Heb. 11:6. Hence the first beginning of the heart's purifying is faith; and if this be perfected through being quickened by charity, the heart will be perfectly purified thereby.

**REPLY OBJ. 1**: Things that are in the intellect are the principles of those which are in the appetite, insofar as the apprehended good moves the appetite.

**REPLY OBJ. 2**: Even lifeless faith excludes a certain impurity which is contrary to it, viz. that of error, and which consists in the human intellect, adhering inordinately to things below itself, through wishing to measure Divine things by the rule of sensible objects. But when it is quickened by charity, then it is incompatible with any kind of impurity, because *charity covereth all sins* (Prov 10:12).

**REPLY OBJ. 3**: The obscurity of faith does not pertain to the impurity of sin, but rather to the natural defect of the human intellect, according to the present state of life.

# QUESTION 8

## THE GIFT OF UNDERSTANDING

Deinde considerandum est de dono intellectus et scientiae, quae respondent virtuti fidei. Et circa donum intellectus quaeruntur octo.

Primo, utrum intellectus sit donum spiritus sancti.

Secundo, utrum possit simul esse in eodem cum fide.

Tertio, utrum intellectus qui est donum sit speculativus tantum, vel etiam practicus.

Quarto, utrum omnes qui sunt in gratia habeant donum intellectus.

Quinto, utrum hoc donum inveniatur in aliquibus absque gratia.

Sexto, quomodo se habeat donum intellectus ad alia dona.

Septimo, de eo quod respondet huic dono in beatitudinibus.

Octavo, de eo quod respondet ei in fructibus.

We must now consider the gifts of understanding and knowledge, which respond to the virtue of faith. With regard to the gift of understanding there are eight points of inquiry:

(1) Whether understanding is a gift of the Holy Spirit?

(2) Whether it can be together with faith in the same person?

(3) Whether the understanding which is a gift of the Holy Spirit is only speculative, or practical also?

(4) Whether all who are in a state of grace have the gift of understanding?

(5) Whether this gift is to be found in those who are without grace?

(6) Of the relationship of the gift of understanding to the other gifts.

(7) Which of the beatitudes corresponds to this gift?

(8) Which of the fruits?

# Article 1

*Whether understanding is a gift of the Holy Spirit?*

**Ad primum sic proceditur.** Videtur quod intellectus non sit donum spiritus sancti. Dona enim gratuita distinguuntur a donis naturalibus, superadduntur enim eis. Sed intellectus est quidam habitus naturalis in anima, quo cognoscuntur principia naturaliter nota, ut patet in VI Ethic. Ergo non debet poni donum spiritus sancti.

**Praeterea**, dona divina participantur a creaturis secundum earum proportionem et modum, ut patet per Dionysium, in libro de Div. Nom. Sed modus humanae naturae est ut non simpliciter veritatem cognoscat, quod pertinet ad rationem intellectus, sed discursive, quod est proprium rationis, ut patet per Dionysium, in VII cap. de Div. Nom. Ergo cognitio divina quae hominibus datur magis debet dici donum rationis quam intellectus.

**Praeterea**, in potentiis animae intellectus contra voluntatem dividitur, ut patet in III de anima. Sed nullum donum spiritus sancti dicitur voluntas. Ergo etiam nullum donum spiritus sancti debet dici intellectus.

**Sed contra** est quod dicitur Isaiae XI, *requiescet super eum spiritus domini, spiritus sapientiae et intellectus.*

**Objection 1**: It would seem that understanding is not a gift of the Holy Spirit. For the gifts of grace are distinct from the gifts of nature, since they are given in addition to the latter. Now understanding is a natural habit of the soul, whereby self-evident principles are known, as stated in *Ethic.* vi, 6. Therefore it should not be reckoned among the gifts of the Holy Spirit.

**Obj. 2**: Further, the Divine gifts are shared by creatures according to their capacity and mode, as Dionysius states (*Div. Nom.* iv). Now the mode of human nature is to know the truth, not simply (which is a sign of understanding), but discursively (which is a sign of reason), as Dionysius explains (*Div. Nom.* vii). Therefore the Divine knowledge which is bestowed on man, should be called a gift of reason rather than a gift of understanding.

**Obj. 3**: Further, in the powers of the soul the understanding is condivided with the will (*De Anima* iii, 9, 10). Now no gift of the Holy Spirit is called after the will. Therefore no gift of the Holy Spirit should receive the name of understanding.

**On the contrary**, It is written (Isa 11:2): *The Spirit of the Lord shall rest upon him, the Spirit of wisdom and of understanding.*

75

**Respondeo** dicendum quod nomen intellectus quandam intimam cognitionem importat, dicitur enim *intelligere* quasi *intus legere*. Et hoc manifeste patet considerantibus differentiam intellectus et sensus, nam cognitio sensitiva occupatur circa qualitates sensibiles exteriores; cognitio autem intellectiva penetrat usque ad essentiam rei, obiectum enim intellectus est *quod quid est*, ut dicitur in III de anima.

Sunt autem multa genera eorum quae interius latent, ad quae oportet cognitionem hominis quasi intrinsecus penetrare. Nam sub accidentibus latet natura rerum substantialis, sub verbis latent significata verborum, sub similitudinibus et figuris latet veritas figurata: res etiam intelligibiles sunt quodammodo interiores respectu rerum sensibilium quae exterius sentiuntur, et in causis latent effectus et e converso. Unde respectu horum omnium potest dici intellectus.

Sed cum cognitio hominis a sensu incipiat, quasi ab exteriori, manifestum est quod quanto lumen intellectus est fortius, tanto potest magis ad intima penetrare. Lumen autem naturale nostri intellectus est finitae virtutis, unde usque ad determinatum aliquid pertingere potest. Indiget igitur homo supernaturali lumine ut ulterius penetret ad cognoscendum quaedam quae per lumen naturale cognoscere non valet. Et illud lumen supernaturale homini datum vocatur donum intellectus.

**Ad primum** ergo dicendum quod per lumen naturale nobis inditum statim cognoscuntur quaedam principia communia quae sunt naturaliter nota. Sed quia homo ordinatur ad beatitudinem supernaturalem, ut supra dictum est, necesse est quod homo ulterius pertingat ad quaedam altiora. Et ad hoc requiritur donum intellectus.

**Ad secundum** dicendum quod discursus rationis semper incipit ab intellectu et terminatur ad intellectum, ratiocinamur enim procedendo ex quibusdam intellectis, et tunc rationis discursus perficitur quando ad hoc pervenimus ut intelligamus illud quod prius erat ignotum. Quod ergo ratiocinamur ex aliquo praecedenti intellectu procedit. Donum autem gratiae non procedit ex lumine naturae, sed superadditur ei, quasi perficiens ipsum. Et ideo ista superadditio non dicitur ratio, sed magis intellectus, quia ita se habet lumen superadditum ad ea quae nobis supernaturaliter innotescunt sicut se habet lumen naturale ad ea quae primordialiter cognoscimus.

**Ad tertium** dicendum quod voluntas nominat simpliciter appetitivum motum, absque determinatione alicuius excellentiae. Sed intellectus nominat quandam excellentiam cognitionis penetrandi ad intima. Et ideo supernaturale donum magis nominatur nomine intellectus quam nomine voluntatis.

**I answer that,** Understanding implies an intimate knowledge, for *intelligere* is the same as *intus legere*. This is clear to anyone who considers the difference between intellect and sense, because sensitive knowledge is concerned with external sensible qualities, whereas intellective knowledge penetrates into the very essence of a thing, because the object of the intellect is *what a thing is*, as stated in *De Anima* iii, 6.

Now there are many kinds of things that are hidden within, to find which human knowledge has to penetrate within, so to speak. Thus, under the accidents lies hidden the nature of the substantial reality, under words lies hidden their meaning; under likenesses and figures the truth they denote lies hidden (because the intelligible world is enclosed within as compared with the sensible world, which is perceived externally), and effects lie hidden in their causes, and vice versa. Hence we may speak of understanding with regard to all these things.

Since, however, human knowledge begins with the outside of things, as it were, it is evident that the stronger the light of the understanding, the further can it penetrate into the heart of things. Now the natural light of our understanding is of finite power; wherefore it can reach to a certain fixed point. Consequently, man needs a supernatural light in order to penetrate further still so as to know what it cannot know by its natural light: and this supernatural light which is bestowed on man is called the gift of understanding.

**Reply Obj. 1**: The natural light instilled within us manifests only certain general principles, which are known naturally. But since man is ordained to supernatural happiness, as stated above (Q. 2, A. 3; I-II, Q. 3, A. 8), man needs to reach to certain higher truths, for which he requires the gift of understanding.

**Reply Obj. 2**: The discourse of reason always begins from an understanding and ends at an understanding; because we reason by proceeding from certain understood principles, and the discourse of reason is perfected when we come to understand what hitherto we ignored. Hence the act of reasoning proceeds from something previously understood. Now a gift of grace does not proceed from the light of nature, but is added thereto as perfecting it. Wherefore this addition is not called reason but understanding, since the additional light is in comparison with what we know supernaturally, what the natural light is in regard to those things which we know from the first.

**Reply Obj. 3**: Will denotes simply a movement of the appetite without indicating any excellence; whereas understanding denotes a certain excellence of a knowledge that penetrates into the heart of things. Hence the supernatural gift is called after the understanding rather than after the will.

# Article 2

*Whether the gift of understanding is compatible with faith?*

**Ad secundum sic proceditur**. Videtur quod donum intellectus non simul habeatur cum fide. Dicit enim Augustinus, in libro Octogintatrium trium Quaest., *id quod intelligitur intelligentis comprehensione finitur*. Sed id quod creditur non comprehenditur, secundum illud apostoli, ad Philipp. III, *non quod iam comprehenderim aut perfectus sim*. Ergo videtur quod fides et intellectus non possint esse in eodem.

**Praeterea**, omne quod intelligitur intellectu videtur. Sed fides est de non apparentibus, ut supra dictum est. Ergo fides non potest simul esse in eodem cum intellectu.

**Praeterea**, intellectus est certior quam scientia. Sed scientia et fides non possunt esse de eodem, ut supra habitum est. Multo ergo minus intellectus et fides.

**Sed contra** est quod Gregorius dicit, in libro Moral., quod *intellectus de auditis mentem illustrat*. Sed aliquis habens fidem potest esse illustratus mente circa audita, unde dicitur Luc. ult. quod Dominus *aperuit discipulis suis sensum ut intelligerent Scripturas*. Ergo intellectus potest simul esse cum fide.

**Respondeo** dicendum quod hic duplici distinctione est opus, una quidem ex parte fidei; alia autem ex parte intellectus.

Ex parte quidem fidei, distinguendum est quod quaedam per se et directe cadunt sub fide, quae naturalem rationem excedunt, sicut Deum esse trinum et unum, filium Dei esse incarnatum. Quaedam vero cadunt sub fide quasi ordinata ad ista secundum aliquem modum, sicut omnia quae in Scriptura divina continentur.

Ex parte vero intellectus, distinguendum est quod dupliciter dici possumus aliqua intelligere. Uno modo, perfecte, quando scilicet pertingimus ad cognoscendum essentiam rei intellectae, et ipsam veritatem enuntiabilis intellecti, secundum quod in se est. Et hoc modo ea quae directe cadunt sub fide intelligere non possumus, durante statu fidei. Sed quaedam alia ad fidem ordinata etiam hoc modo intelligi possunt.

Alio modo contingit aliquid intelligi imperfecte, quando scilicet ipsa essentia rei, vel veritas propositionis, non cognoscitur quid sit aut quomodo sit, sed tamen cognoscitur quod ea quae exterius apparent veritati non contrariantur; inquantum scilicet homo intelligit quod propter ea quae exterius apparent non est recedendum ab his quae sunt fidei. Et secundum hoc nihil prohibet,

**Objection 1**: It would seem that the gift of understanding is incompatible with faith. For Augustine says (*83 Questions*, Q. 15) that *the thing which is understood is bounded by the comprehension of him who understands it*. But the thing which is believed is not comprehended, according to the word of the Apostle to the Philippians 3:12: *Not as though I had already comprehended, or were already perfect*. Therefore it seems that faith and understanding are incompatible in the same subject.

**Obj. 2**: Further, whatever is understood is seen by the understanding. But faith is of things that appear not, as stated above (Q. 1, A. 4; Q. 4, A. 1). Therefore faith is incompatible with understanding in the same subject.

**Obj. 3**: Further, understanding is more certain than science. But science and faith are incompatible in the same subject, as stated above (Q. 1, AA. 4, 5). Much less, therefore, can understanding and faith be in the same subject.

**On the contrary**, Gregory says (*Moral.* i, 15) that *understanding enlightens the mind concerning the things it has heard*. Now one who has faith can be enlightened in his mind concerning what he has heard; thus it is written (Luke 24:27, 32) that Our Lord *opened the scriptures* to his disciples, *that they might understand them*. Therefore understanding is compatible with faith.

**I answer that**, We need to make a twofold distinction here: one on the side of faith, the other on the part of understanding.

On the side of faith the distinction to be made is that certain things, of themselves, come directly under faith, such as the mystery of three Persons in one God, and the incarnation of God the Son; whereas other things come under faith, through being subordinate, in one way or another, to those just mentioned, for instance, all that is contained in the Divine Scriptures.

On the part of understanding the distinction to be observed is that there are two ways in which we may be said to understand. In one way, perfectly, when we arrive at knowing the essence of the thing we understand, and the very truth considered in itself of the proposition understood. In this way, so long as the state of faith lasts, we cannot understand those things which are the direct object of faith: although certain other things that are subordinate to faith can be understood even in this way.

In another way we understand a thing imperfectly, when the essence of a thing or the truth of a proposition is not known as to its quiddity or mode of being, and yet we know that whatever be the outward appearances, they do not contradict the truth, insofar as we understand that we ought not to depart from matters of faith, for the sake of things that appear externally. In this way, even during the

durante statu fidei, intelligere etiam ea quae per se sub fide cadunt.

**Et per hoc** patet responsio ad obiecta. Nam primae tres rationes procedunt secundum quod aliquid perfecte intelligitur. Ultima autem ratio procedit de intellectu eorum quae ordinantur ad fidem.

state of faith, nothing hinders us from understanding even those things which are the direct object of faith.

**This suffices** for the replies to the objections: for the first three argue in reference to perfect understanding, while the last refers to the understanding of matters subordinate to faith.

# Article 3

*Whether the gift of understanding is merely speculative or also practical?*

**Ad tertium sic proceditur.** Videtur quod intellectus qui ponitur donum spiritus sancti non sit practicus, sed speculativus tantum. Intellectus enim, ut Gregorius dicit, in I Moral., *altiora quaedam penetrat.* Sed ea quae pertinent ad intellectum practicum non sunt alta, sed quaedam infima, scilicet singularia, circa quae sunt actus. Ergo intellectus qui ponitur donum non est intellectus practicus.

**Praeterea,** intellectus qui est donum est dignius aliquid quam intellectus qui est virtus intellectualis. Sed intellectus qui est virtus intellectualis est solum circa necessaria, ut patet per Philosophum, in VI Ethic. Ergo multo magis intellectus qui est donum est solum circa necessaria. Sed intellectus practicus non est circa necessaria, sed circa contingentia aliter se habere, quae opere humano fieri possunt. Ergo intellectus qui est donum non est intellectus practicus.

**Praeterea,** donum intellectus illustrat mentem ad ea quae naturalem rationem excedunt. Sed operabilia humana, quorum est practicus intellectus, non excedunt naturalem rationem, quae dirigit in rebus agendis, ut ex supradictis patet. Ergo intellectus qui est donum non est intellectus practicus.

**Sed contra** est quod dicitur in Psalm., *intellectus bonus omnibus facientibus eum.*

**Respondeo** dicendum quod, sicut dictum est, donum intellectus non solum se habet ad ea quae primo et principaliter cadunt sub fide, sed etiam ad omnia quae ad fidem ordinantur. Operationes autem bonae quendam ordinem ad fidem habent, nam *fides per dilectionem operatur,* ut apostolus dicit, ad Gal. V. Et ideo donum intellectus etiam ad quaedam operabilia se extendit, non quidem ut circa ea principaliter versetur; sed inquantum in agendis regulamur *rationibus aeternis, quibus conspiciendis et consulendis,* secundum Augustinum, XII de Trin., *inhaeret superior ratio,* quae dono intellectus perficitur.

**Ad primum** ergo dicendum quod operabilia humana, secundum quod in se considerantur, non habent

**Objection 1**: It would seem that understanding, considered as a gift of the Holy Spirit, is not practical, but only speculative. For, according to Gregory (*Moral.* i, 32), *understanding penetrates certain more exalted things.* But the practical intellect is occupied, not with exalted, but with inferior things, viz. singulars, about which actions are concerned. Therefore understanding, considered as a gift, is not practical.

**Obj. 2**: Further, the gift of understanding is something more excellent than the intellectual virtue of understanding. But the intellectual virtue of understanding is concerned with none but necessary things, according to the Philosopher (*Ethic.* vi, 6). Much more, therefore, is the gift of understanding concerned with none but necessary matters. Now the practical intellect is not about necessary things, but about things which may be otherwise than they are, and which may result from man's activity. Therefore the gift of understanding is not practical.

**Obj. 3**: Further, the gift of understanding enlightens the mind in matters which surpass natural reason. Now human activities, with which the practical intellect is concerned, do not surpass natural reason, which is the directing principle in matters of action, as was made clear above (I-II, Q. 58, A. 2; I-II, Q. 71, A. 6). Therefore the gift of understanding is not practical.

**On the contrary**, It is written (Ps 110:10): *A good understanding to all that do it.*

**I answer that,** As stated above (A. 2), the gift of understanding is not only about those things which come under faith first and principally, but also about all things subordinate to faith. Now good actions have a certain relationship to faith: since *faith worketh through charity,* according to the Apostle (Gal 5:6). Hence the gift of understanding extends also to certain actions not as though these were its principal object, but insofar as the rule of our actions is the eternal law, to which *the higher reason, which is perfected by the gift of understanding, adheres by contemplating and consulting it,* as Augustine states (*De Trin.* xii, 7).

**Reply Obj. 1**: The things with which human actions are concerned are not surpassingly exalted considered in

aliquam excellentiae altitudinem. Sed secundum quod referuntur ad regulam legis aeternae et ad finem beatitudinis divinae, sic altitudinem habent, ut circa ea possit esse intellectus.

AD SECUNDUM dicendum quod hoc ipsum pertinet ad dignitatem doni quod est intellectus, quod intelligibilia aeterna vel necessaria considerat non solum secundum quod in se sunt, sed etiam secundum quod sunt regulae quaedam humanorum actuum, quia quanto virtus cognoscitiva ad plura se extendit, tanto nobilior est.

AD TERTIUM dicendum quod regula humanorum actuum est et ratio humana et lex aeterna, ut supra dictum est. Lex autem aeterna excedit naturalem rationem. Et ideo cognitio humanorum actuum secundum quod regulantur a lege aeterna, excedit rationem naturalem, et indiget supernaturali lumine doni spiritus sancti.

themselves, but, as referred to the rule of the eternal law, and to the end of Divine happiness, they are exalted so that they can be the matter of understanding.

REPLY OBJ. 2: The excellence of the gift of understanding consists precisely in its considering eternal or necessary matters, not only in themselves, but also as they are rules of human actions, because a cognitive virtue is the more excellent according to the greater extent of its object.

REPLY OBJ. 3: The rule of human actions is the human reason and the eternal law, as stated above (I-II, Q. 71, A. 6). Now the eternal law surpasses human reason: so that the knowledge of human actions as ruled by the eternal law surpasses the natural reason, and requires the supernatural light of a gift of the Holy Spirit.

# Article 4

*Whether the gift of understanding is in all who are in a state of grace?*

AD QUARTUM SIC PROCEDITUR. Videtur quod donum intellectus non insit omnibus hominibus habentibus gratiam. Dicit enim Gregorius, II Moral., quod donum intellectus datur contra *hebetudinem mentis*. Sed multi habentes gratiam adhuc patiuntur mentis hebetudinem. Ergo donum intellectus non est in omnibus habentibus gratiam.

PRAETEREA, inter ea quae ad cognitionem pertinent sola fides videtur esse necessaria ad salutem, quia *per fidem Christus habitat in cordibus nostris*, ut dicitur ad Ephes. III. Sed non omnes habentes fidem habent donum intellectus, immo *qui credunt, debent orare ut intelligant*, sicut Augustinus dicit, in libro de Trin. Ergo donum intellectus non est necessarium ad salutem. Non ergo est in omnibus habentibus gratiam.

PRAETEREA, ea quae sunt communia omnibus habentibus gratiam nunquam ab habentibus gratiam subtrahuntur. Sed gratia intellectus et aliorum donorum *aliquando se utiliter subtrahit, quandoque* enim, *dum sublimia intelligendo in elationem se animus erigit, in rebus imis et vilibus gravi hebetudine pigrescit*, ut Gregorius dicit, in II Moral. Ergo donum intellectus non est in omnibus habentibus gratiam.

SED CONTRA est quod dicitur in Psalm., *nescierunt neque intellexerunt, in tenebris ambulant*. Sed nullus habens gratiam ambulat in tenebris, secundum illud Ioan. VIII, *qui sequitur me non ambulat in tenebris*. Ergo nullus habens gratiam caret dono intellectus.

OBJECTION 1: It would seem that the gift of understanding is not in all who are in a state of grace. For Gregory says (*Moral.* ii, 49) that the gift of understanding is given as a remedy against *dulness of mind*. Now many who are in a state of grace suffer from dulness of mind. Therefore the gift of understanding is not in all who are in a state of grace.

OBJ. 2: Further, of all the things that are connected with knowledge, faith alone seems to be necessary for salvation, since *by faith Christ dwells in our hearts*, according to Eph. 3:17. Now the gift of understanding is not in everyone that has faith; indeed, *those who have faith ought to pray that they may understand*, as Augustine says (*De Trin.* xv, 27). Therefore the gift of understanding is not necessary for salvation: and, consequently, is not in all who are in a state of grace.

OBJ. 3: Further, those things which are common to all who are in a state of grace are never withdrawn from them. Now the grace of understanding and of the other gifts *sometimes withdraws itself profitably*, for, *at times, when the mind is puffed up with understanding sublime things, it becomes sluggish and dull in base and vile things*, as Gregory observes (*Moral.* ii, 49). Therefore the gift of understanding is not in all who are in a state of grace.

ON THE CONTRARY, It is written (Ps 81:5): *They have not known or understood, they walk on in darkness*. But no one who is in a state of grace walks in darkness, according to John 8:12: *He that followeth Me, walketh not in darkness*. Therefore no one who is in a state of grace is without the gift of understanding.

**RESPONDEO** dicendum quod in omnibus habentibus gratiam necesse est esse rectitudinem voluntatis, quia *per gratiam praeparatur voluntas hominis ad bonum*, ut Augustinus dicit. Voluntas autem non potest recte ordinari in bonum nisi praeexistente aliqua cognitione veritatis, quia obiectum voluntatis est bonum intellectum, ut dicitur in III de Anima. Sicut autem per donum caritatis Spiritus Sanctus ordinat voluntatem hominis ut directe moveatur in bonum quoddam supernaturale, ita etiam per donum intellectus illustrat mentem hominis ut cognoscat veritatem quandam supernaturalem, in quam oportet tendere voluntatem rectam.

Et ideo, sicut donum caritatis est in omnibus habentibus gratiam gratum facientem, ita etiam donum intellectus.

**AD PRIMUM** ergo dicendum quod aliqui habentes gratiam gratum facientem possunt pati hebetudinem circa aliqua quae sunt praeter necessitatem salutis. Sed circa ea quae sunt de necessitate salutis sufficienter instruuntur a spiritu sancto, secundum illud I Ioan. II, *unctio docet vos de omnibus*.

**AD SECUNDUM** dicendum quod etsi non omnes habentes fidem plene intelligant ea quae proponuntur credenda, intelligunt tamen ea esse credenda, et quod ab eis pro nullo est deviandum.

**AD TERTIUM** dicendum quod donum intellectus nunquam se subtrahit sanctis circa ea quae sunt necessaria ad salutem. Sed circa alia interdum se subtrahit, ut non omnia ad liquidum per intellectum penetrare possint, ad hoc quod superbiae materia subtrahatur.

**I ANSWER THAT,** In all who are in a state of grace, there must be rectitude of the will, since *grace prepares man's will for good*, according to Augustine (*Contra Julian. Pelag.* iv, 3). Now the will cannot be rightly directed to good, unless there be already some knowledge of the truth, since the object of the will is good understood, as stated in *De Anima* iii, 7. Again, just as the Holy Spirit directs man's will by the gift of charity, so as to move it directly to some supernatural good; so also, by the gift of understanding, He enlightens the human mind, so that it knows some supernatural truth, to which the right will needs to tend.

Therefore, just as the gift of charity is in all of those who have sanctifying grace, so also is the gift of understanding.

**REPLY OBJ. 1:** Some who have sanctifying grace may suffer dulness of mind with regard to things that are not necessary for salvation; but with regard to those that are necessary for salvation, they are sufficiently instructed by the Holy Spirit, according to 1 John 2:27: *His unction teacheth you of all things.*

**REPLY OBJ. 2:** Although not all who have faith understand fully the things that are proposed to be believed, yet they understand that they ought to believe them, and that they ought nowise to deviate from them.

**REPLY OBJ. 3:** With regard to things necessary for salvation, the gift of understanding never withdraws from holy persons: but, in order that they may have no incentive to pride, it does withdraw sometimes with regard to other things, so that their mind is unable to penetrate all things clearly.

# Article 5

*Whether the gift of understanding is found also in those who have not sanctifying grace?*

**AD QUINTUM SIC PROCEDITUR**. Videtur quod intellectus donum inveniatur etiam in non habentibus gratiam gratum facientem. Augustinus enim, exponens illud Psalm., *concupivit anima mea desiderare iustificationes tuas*, dicit quod *praevolat intellectus, sequitur tardus aut nullus affectus*. Sed in omnibus habentibus gratiam gratum facientem est promptus affectus, propter caritatem. Ergo donum intellectus potest esse in his qui non habent gratiam gratum facientem.

**PRAETEREA**, Danielis X dicitur quod *intelligentia opus est in visione* prophetica, et ita videtur quod prophetia non sit sine dono intellectus. Sed prophetia potest esse sine gratia gratum faciente, ut patet Matth. VII, ubi dicentibus, *in nomine tuo prophetavimus*, respondetur,

**OBJECTION 1:** It would seem that the gift of understanding is found also in those who have not sanctifying grace. For Augustine, in expounding the words of Ps. 118:20: *My soul hath coveted to long for Thy justifications*, says: *Understanding flies ahead, and man's will is weak and slow to follow.* But in all who have sanctifying grace, the will is prompt on account of charity. Therefore the gift of understanding can be in those who have not sanctifying grace.

**OBJ. 2:** Further, it is written (Dan 10:1) that *there is need of understanding in a prophetic vision*, so that, seemingly, there is no prophecy without the gift of understanding. But there can be prophecy without sanctifying grace, as evidenced by Matt. 7:22, where those who say: *We have*

*nunquam novi vos.* Ergo donum intellectus potest esse sine gratia gratum faciente.

**PRAETEREA**, donum intellectus respondet virtuti fidei, secundum illud Isaiae VII, secundum aliam litteram, *nisi credideritis, non intelligetis.* Sed fides potest esse sine gratia gratum faciente. Ergo etiam donum intellectus.

**SED CONTRA** est quod dominus dicit, Ioan. VI, *omnis qui audivit a patre et didicit, venit ad me.* Sed per intellectum audita addiscimus vel penetramus, ut patet per Gregorium, in I Moral. Ergo quicumque habet intellectus donum venit ad Christum. Quod non est sine gratia gratum faciente. Ergo donum intellectus non est sine gratia gratum faciente.

**RESPONDEO** dicendum quod, sicut supra dictum est, dona spiritus sancti perficiunt animam secundum quod est bene mobilis a spiritu sancto. Sic ergo intellectuale lumen gratiae ponitur donum intellectus, inquantum intellectus hominis est bene mobilis a spiritu sancto. Huius autem motus consideratio in hoc est quod homo apprehendat veritatem circa finem. Unde nisi usque ad hoc moveatur a spiritu sancto intellectus humanus ut rectam aestimationem de fine habeat, nondum assecutus est donum intellectus; quantumcumque ex illustratione spiritus alia quaedam praeambula cognoscat.

Rectam aut aestimationem de ultimo fine non habet nisi ille qui circa finem non errat, sed ei firmiter inhaeret tanquam optimo. Quod est solum habentis gratiam gratum facientem, sicut etiam in moralibus rectam aestimationem habet homo de fine per habitum virtutis. Unde donum intellectus nullus habet sine gratia gratum faciente.

**AD PRIMUM** ergo dicendum quod Augustinus intellectum nominat quamcumque illustrationem intellectualem. Quae tamen non pertingit ad perfectam doni rationem nisi usque ad hoc mens hominis deducatur ut rectam aestimationem habeat homo circa finem.

**AD SECUNDUM** dicendum quod intelligentia quae necessaria est ad prophetiam est quaedam illustratio mentis circa ea quae prophetis revelantur. Non est autem illustratio mentis circa aestimationem rectam de ultimo fine, quae pertinet ad donum intellectus.

**AD TERTIUM** dicendum quod fides importat solum assensum ad ea quae proponuntur. Sed intellectus importat quandam perceptionem veritatis, quae non potest esse circa finem nisi in eo qui habet gratiam gratum facientem, ut dictum est. Et ideo non est similis ratio de intellectu et fide.

*prophesied in Thy name*, are answered with the words: *I never knew you.* Therefore the gift of understanding can be without sanctifying grace.

**OBJ. 3**: Further, the gift of understanding responds to the virtue of faith, according to Isa. 7:9, following another reading: *If you will not believe, you shall not understand.* Now faith can be without sanctifying grace. Therefore the gift of understanding can be without it.

**ON THE CONTRARY**, Our Lord said (John 6:45): *Every one that hath heard of the Father, and hath learned, cometh to Me.* Now it is by the intellect, as Gregory observes (*Moral.* i, 32), that we learn or understand what we hear. Therefore whoever has the gift of understanding comes to Christ, which is impossible without sanctifying grace. Therefore the gift of understanding cannot be without sanctifying grace.

**I ANSWER THAT**, As stated above (I-II, Q. 68, AA. 1, 2) the gifts of the Holy Spirit perfect the soul, according as it is amenable to the motion of the Holy Spirit. Accordingly, then, the intellectual light of grace is called the gift of understanding, insofar as man's understanding is easily moved by the Holy Spirit, the consideration of which movement depends on a true apprehension of the end. Therefore, unless the human intellect be moved by the Holy Spirit so far as to have a right estimate of the end, it has not yet obtained the gift of understanding, however much the Holy Spirit may have enlightened it in regard to other truths that are preambles to the faith.

Now to have a right estimate about the last end one must not be in error about the end, and must adhere to it firmly as to the greatest good: and no one can do this without sanctifying grace; even as in moral matters a man has a right estimate about the end through a habit of virtue. Therefore no one has the gift of understanding without sanctifying grace.

**REPLY OBJ. 1**: By understanding Augustine means any kind of intellectual light, that, however, does not fulfill all the conditions of a gift, unless the mind of man be so far perfected as to have a right estimate about the end.

**REPLY OBJ. 2**: The understanding that is requisite for prophecy is a kind of enlightenment of the mind with regard to the things revealed to the prophet: but it is not an enlightenment of the mind with regard to a right estimate about the last end, which belongs to the gift of understanding.

**REPLY OBJ. 3**: Faith implies merely assent to what is proposed, but understanding implies a certain perception of the truth, which perception, except in one who has sanctifying grace, cannot regard the end, as stated above. Hence the comparison fails between understanding and faith.

81

# Article 6

*Whether the gift of understanding is distinct from the other gifts?*

**AD SEXTUM SIC PROCEDITUR.** Videtur quod donum intellectus non distinguatur ab aliis donis. Quorum enim opposita sunt eadem, ipsa quoque sunt eadem. Sed sapientiae opponitur stultitia, hebetudini intellectus, praecipitationi consilium, ignorantiae scientia, ut patet per Gregorium, II Moral. Non videntur autem differre stultitia, hebetudo, ignorantia et praecipitatio. Ergo nec intellectus distinguitur ab aliis donis.

**PRAETEREA**, intellectus qui ponitur virtus intellectualis differt ab aliis intellectualibus virtutibus per hoc sibi proprium, quod est circa principia per se nota. Sed donum intellectus non est circa aliqua principia per se nota, quia ad ea quae naturaliter per se cognoscuntur sufficit naturalis habitus primorum principiorum; ad ea vero quae sunt supernaturalia sufficit fides, quia articuli fidei sunt sicut prima principia in supernaturali cognitione, sicut dictum est. Ergo donum intellectus non distinguitur ab aliis donis intellectualibus.

**PRAETEREA**, omnis cognitio intellectiva vel est speculativa vel practica. Sed donum intellectus se habet ad utrumque, ut dictum est. Ergo non distinguitur ab aliis donis intellectualibus, sed omnia in se complectitur.

**SED CONTRA** est quod quaecumque connumerantur ad invicem oportet esse aliquo modo ab invicem distincta, quia distinctio est principium numeri. Sed donum intellectus connumeratur aliis donis, ut patet Isaiae XI. Ergo donum intellectus est distinctum ab aliis donis.

**RESPONDEO** dicendum quod distinctio doni intellectus ab aliis tribus donis, scilicet pietate, fortitudine et timore, manifesta est, quia donum intellectus pertinet ad vim cognoscitivam, illa vero tria pertinent ad vim appetitivam.

Sed differentia huius doni intellectus ad alia tria, scilicet sapientiam, scientiam et consilium, quae etiam ad vim cognoscitivam pertinent, non est adeo manifesta. Videtur autem quibusdam quod donum intellectus distinguatur a dono scientiae et consilii per hoc quod illa duo pertineant ad practicam cognitionem, donum vero intellectus ad speculativam. A dono vero sapientiae, quod etiam ad speculativam cognitionem pertinet, distinguitur in hoc quod ad sapientiam pertinet iudicium, ad intellectum vero capacitas intellectus eorum quae proponuntur, sive penetratio ad intima eorum. Et secundum hoc supra numerum donorum assignavimus.

Sed diligenter intuenti, donum intellectus non solum se habet circa speculanda, sed etiam circa operanda,

**OBJECTION 1**: It would seem that the gift of understanding is not distinct from the other gifts. For there is no distinction between things whose opposites are not distinct. Now wisdom is contrary to folly, understanding is contrary to dulness, counsel is contrary to rashness, knowledge is contrary to ignorance, as Gregory states (*Moralia* ii, 49). But there would seem to be no difference between folly, dulness, ignorance and rashness. Therefore neither does understanding differ from the other gifts.

**OBJ. 2**: Further, the intellectual virtue of understanding differs from the other intellectual virtues in that it is proper to it to be about self-evident principles. But the gift of understanding is not about any self-evident principles, since the natural habit of first principles suffices in respect of those matters which are naturally self-evident: while faith is sufficient in respect of such things as are supernatural, since the articles of faith are like first principles in supernatural knowledge, as stated above (Q. 1, A. 7). Therefore the gift of understanding does not differ from the other intellectual gifts.

**OBJ. 3**: Further, all intellectual knowledge is either speculative or practical. Now the gift of understanding is related to both, as stated above (A. 3). Therefore it is not distinct from the other intellectual gifts, but comprises them all.

**ON THE CONTRARY**, When several things are enumerated together they must be, in some way, distinct from one another, because distinction is the origin of number. Now the gift of understanding is enumerated together with the other gifts, as appears from Isa. 11:2. Therefore the gift of understanding is distinct from the other gifts.

**I ANSWER THAT**, The difference between the gift of understanding and three of the others, viz. piety, fortitude, and fear, is evident, since the gift of understanding belongs to the cognitive power, while the three belong to the appetitive power.

But the difference between this gift of understanding and the remaining three, viz. wisdom, knowledge, and counsel, which also belong to the cognitive power, is not so evident. To some, it seems that the gift of understanding differs from the gifts of knowledge and counsel, in that these two belong to practical knowledge, while the gift of understanding belongs to speculative knowledge; and that it differs from the gift of wisdom, which also belongs to speculative knowledge, in that wisdom is concerned with judgment, while understanding renders the mind apt to grasp the things that are proposed, and to penetrate into their very heart. And in this sense we have assigned the number of the gifts, above (I-II, Q. 68, A. 4).

But if we consider the matter carefully, the gift of understanding is concerned not only with speculative, but also

ut dictum est, et similiter etiam donum scientiae circa utrumque se habet, ut infra dicetur. Et ideo oportet aliter eorum distinctionem accipere. Omnia enim haec quatuor dicta ordinantur ad supernaturalem cognitionem, quae in nobis per fidem fundatur. Fides autem est *ex auditu*, ut dicitur Rom. X. Unde oportet aliqua proponi homini ad credendum non sicut visa, sed sicut audita, quibus per fidem assentiat. Fides autem primo quidem et principaliter se habet ad veritatem primam; secundario, ad quaedam circa creaturas consideranda; et ulterius se extendit etiam ad directionem humanorum operum, secundum quod *per dilectionem operatur*, ut ex dictis patet.

Sic igitur circa ea quae fidei proponuntur credenda duo requiruntur ex parte nostra. Primo quidem, ut intellectu penetrentur vel capiantur, et hoc pertinet ad donum intellectus. Secundo autem oportet ut de eis homo habeat iudicium rectum, ut aestimet his esse inhaerendum et ab eorum oppositis recedendum. Hoc igitur iudicium, quantum ad res divinas, pertinet ad donum sapientiae; quantum vero ad res creatas, pertinet ad donum scientiae; quantum vero ad applicationem ad singularia opera, pertinet ad donum consilii.

**AD PRIMUM** ergo dicendum quod praedicta differentia quatuor donorum manifeste competit distinctioni eorum quae Gregorius ponit eis esse opposita. Hebetudo enim acuitati opponitur. Dicitur autem per similitudinem intellectus acutus quando potest penetrare ad intima eorum quae proponuntur. Unde hebetudo mentis est per quam mens ad intima penetrare non sufficit. Stultus autem dicitur ex hoc quod perverse iudicat circa communem finem vitae. Et ideo proprie opponitur sapientiae, quae facit rectum iudicium circa universalem causam. Ignorantia vero importat defectum mentis etiam circa quaecumque particularia. Et ideo opponitur scientiae, per quam homo habet rectum iudicium circa particulares causas, scilicet circa creaturas. Praecipitatio vero manifeste opponitur consilio, per quod homo ad actionem non procedit ante deliberationem rationis.

**AD SECUNDUM** dicendum quod donum intellectus est circa prima principia cognitionis gratuitae, aliter tamen quam fides. Nam ad fidem pertinet eis assentire, ad donum vero intellectus pertinet penetrare mente ea quae dicuntur.

**AD TERTIUM** dicendum quod donum intellectus pertinet ad utramque cognitionem, scilicet speculativam et practicam, non quantum ad iudicium, sed quantum ad apprehensionem, ut capiantur ea quae dicuntur.

with practical matters, as stated above (A. 3), and likewise, the gift of knowledge regards both matters, as we shall show further on (Q. 9, A. 3), and consequently, we must take their distinction in some other way. For all these four gifts are ordained to supernatural knowledge, which, in us, takes its foundation from faith. Now faith is *through hearing* (Rom 10:17). Hence some things must be proposed to be believed by man, not as seen, but as heard, to which he assents by faith. But faith, first and principally, is about the First Truth, secondarily, about certain considerations concerning creatures, and furthermore extends to the direction of human actions, insofar as it *works through charity*, as appears from what has been said above (Q. 4, A. 2, ad 3).

Accordingly, on the part of the things proposed to faith for belief, two things are requisite on our part: first that they be penetrated or grasped by the intellect, and this belongs to the gift of understanding. Second, it is necessary that man should judge these things aright, that he should esteem that he ought to adhere to these things, and to withdraw from their opposites: and this judgment, with regard to Divine things, belongs to the gift of wisdom, but with regard to created things, belongs to the gift of knowledge, and as to its application to individual actions, belongs to the gift of counsel.

**REPLY OBJ. 1**: The foregoing difference between those four gifts is clearly in agreement with the distinction of those things which Gregory assigns as their opposites. For dulness is contrary to sharpness, since an intellect is said, by comparison, to be sharp, when it is able to penetrate into the heart of the things that are proposed to it. Hence it is dulness of mind that renders the mind unable to pierce into the heart of a thing. A man is said to be a fool if he judges wrongly about the common end of life, wherefore folly is properly opposed to wisdom, which makes us judge aright about the universal cause. Ignorance implies a defect in the mind, even about any particular things whatever, so that it is contrary to knowledge, which gives man a right judgment about particular causes, viz. about creatures. Rashness is clearly opposed to counsel, whereby man does not proceed to action before deliberating with his reason.

**REPLY OBJ. 2**: The gift of understanding is about the first principles of that knowledge which is conferred by grace; but otherwise than faith, because it belongs to faith to assent to them, while it belongs to the gift of understanding to pierce with the mind the things that are said.

**REPLY OBJ. 3**: The gift of understanding is related to both kinds of knowledge, viz. speculative and practical, not as to the judgment, but as to apprehension, by grasping what is said.

# Article 7

*Whether the sixth beatitude, "blessed are the clean of heart, for they shall see God," responds to the gift of understanding?*

**AD SEPTIMUM SIC PROCEDITUR**. Videtur quod dono intellectus non respondeat beatitudo sexta, scilicet, *beati mundo corde, quoniam ipsi Deum videbunt*. Munditia enim cordis maxime videtur pertinere ad affectum. Sed donum intellectus non pertinet ad affectum, sed magis ad vim intellectivam. Ergo praedicta beatitudo non respondet dono intellectus.

**PRAETEREA**, Act. XV dicitur, *fide purificans corda eorum*. Sed per purificationem cordis acquiritur munditia cordis. Ergo praedicta beatitudo magis pertinet ad virtutem fidei quam ad donum intellectus.

**PRAETEREA**, dona spiritus sancti perficiunt hominem in praesenti vita. Sed visio Dei non pertinet ad vitam praesentem, ipsa enim beatos facit, ut supra habitum est. Ergo sexta beatitudo, continens Dei visionem, non pertinet ad donum intellectus.

**SED CONTRA** est quod Augustinus dicit, in libro de Serm. Dom. in monte, *sexta operatio spiritus sancti, quae est intellectus, convenit mundis corde, qui purgato oculo possunt videre quod oculus non vidit*.

**RESPONDEO** dicendum quod in sexta beatitudine, sicut et in aliis, duo continentur, unum per modum meriti, scilicet munditia cordis; aliud per modum praemii, scilicet visio Dei, ut supra dictum est. Et utrumque pertinet aliquo modo ad donum intellectus.

Est enim duplex munditia. Una quidem praeambula et dispositiva ad Dei visionem, quae est depuratio affectus ab inordinatis affectionibus, et haec quidem munditia cordis fit per virtutes et dona quae pertinent ad vim appetitivam. Alia vero munditia cordis est quae est quasi completiva respectu visionis divinae, et haec quidem est munditia mentis depuratae a phantasmatibus et erroribus, ut scilicet ea quae de Deo proponuntur non accipiantur per modum corporalium phantasmatum, nec secundum haereticas perversitates. Et hanc munditiam facit donum intellectus.

Similiter etiam duplex est Dei visio. Una quidem perfecta, per quam videtur Dei essentia. Alia vero imperfecta, per quam, etsi non videamus de Deo quid est, videmus tamen quid non est, et tanto in hac vita Deum perfectius cognoscimus quanto magis intelligimus eum excedere quidquid intellectu comprehenditur. Et utraque Dei visio pertinet ad donum intellectus, prima quidem ad donum intellectus consummatum, secundum quod erit in patria; secunda vero ad donum intellectus inchoatum, secundum quod habetur in via.

**OBJECTION 1**: It would seem that the sixth beatitude, *Blessed are the clean of heart, for they shall see God*, does not respond to the gift of understanding, because cleanness of heart seems to belong chiefly to the appetite. But the gift of understanding belongs not to the appetite, but rather to the intellectual power. Therefore the aforesaid beatitude does not respond to the gift of understanding.

**OBJ. 2**: Further, it is written (Acts 15:9): *Purifying their hearts by faith*. Now cleanness of heart is acquired by the heart being purified. Therefore the aforesaid beatitude is related to the virtue of faith rather than to the gift of understanding.

**OBJ. 3**: Further, the gifts of the Holy Spirit perfect man in the present state of life. But the sight of God does not belong to the present life, since it is that which gives happiness to the blessed, as stated above (I-II, Q. 3, A. 8). Therefore the sixth beatitude which comprises the sight of God does not respond to the gift of understanding.

**ON THE CONTRARY**, Augustine says (*De Serm. Dom. in Monte* i, 4): *The sixth work of the Holy Spirit which is understanding, is applicable to the clean of heart, whose eye being purified, they can see what eye hath not seen.*

**I ANSWER THAT**, Two things are contained in the sixth beatitude, as also in the others. One by way of merit, namely, cleanness of heart; the other by way of reward, viz. the sight of God, as stated above (I-II, Q. 69, AA. 2, 4), and each of these, in some way, responds to the gift of understanding.

For cleanness is twofold. One is a preamble and a disposition to seeing God, and consists in the heart being cleansed of inordinate affections: and this cleanness of heart is effected by the virtues and gifts belonging to the appetitive power. The other cleanness of heart is a kind of complement to the sight of God; such is the cleanness of the mind that is purged of phantasms and errors, so as to receive the truths which are proposed to it about God, no longer by way of corporeal phantasms, nor infected with heretical misrepresentations: and this cleanness is the result of the gift of understanding.

Again, the sight of God is twofold. One is perfect, whereby God's Essence is seen: the other is imperfect, whereby, though we see not what God is, yet we see what He is not; and whereby, the more perfectly do we know God in this life, the more we understand that He surpasses all that the mind comprehends. Each of these visions of God belongs to the gift of understanding; the first, to the gift of understanding in its state of perfection, as possessed in heaven; the second, to the gift of understanding in its state of inchoation, as possessed by wayfarers.

**ET PER HOC** patet responsio ad obiecta. Nam primae duae rationes procedunt de prima munditia. Tertia vero de perfecta Dei visione, dona autem et hic nos perficiunt secundum quandam inchoationem, et in futuro implebuntur, ut supra dictum est.

**THIS SUFFICES** for the replies to the objections: for the first two arguments refer to the first kind of cleanness; while the third refers to the perfect vision of God. Moreover, the gifts both perfect us in this life by way of inchoation, and will be fulfilled, as stated above (I-II, Q. 69, A. 2).

# Article 8

*Whether faith, among the fruits, responds to the gift of understanding?*

**AD OCTAVUM SIC PROCEDITUR.** Videtur quod in fructibus fides non respondeat dono intellectus. Intellectus enim est fructus fidei, dicitur enim Isaiae VII, *nisi credideritis, non intelligetis*, secundum aliam litteram, ubi nos habemus, *si non credideritis, non permanebitis*. Non ergo fides est fructus intellectus.

**PRAETEREA**, prius non est fructus posterioris. Sed fides videtur esse prior intellectu, quia fides est fundamentum totius spiritualis aedificii, ut supra dictum est. Ergo fides non est fructus intellectus.

**PRAETEREA**, plura sunt dona pertinentia ad intellectum quam pertinentia ad appetitum. Sed inter fructus ponitur tantum unum pertinens ad intellectum, scilicet fides, omnia vero alia pertinent ad appetitum. Ergo fides non magis videtur respondere intellectui quam sapientiae vel scientiae seu consilio.

**SED CONTRA** est quod finis uniuscuiusque rei est fructus eius. Sed donum intellectus videtur principaliter ordinari ad certitudinem fidei, quae ponitur fructus, dicit enim Glossa, ad Gal. V, quod fides quae est fructus est *de invisibilibus certitudo*. Ergo in fructibus fides respondet dono intellectus.

**RESPONDEO** dicendum quod, sicut supra dictum est, cum de fructibus ageretur, fructus spiritus dicuntur quaedam ultima et delectabilia quae in nobis proveniunt ex virtute spiritus sancti. Ultimum autem delectabile habet rationem finis, qui est proprium obiectum voluntatis. Et ideo oportet quod id quod est ultimum et delectabile in voluntate sit quodammodo fructus omnium aliorum quae pertinent ad alias potentias.

Secundum hoc ergo doni vel virtutis perficientis aliquam potentiam potest accipi duplex fructus, unus quidem pertinens ad suam potentiam; alius autem quasi ultimus, pertinens ad voluntatem. Et secundum hoc dicendum est quod dono intellectus respondet pro proprio fructu fides, idest fidei certitudo, sed pro ultimo fructu respondet ei gaudium, quod pertinet ad voluntatem.

**OBJECTION 1**: It would seem that, among the fruits, faith does not respond to the gift of understanding. For understanding is the fruit of faith, since it is written (Isa 7:9) according to another reading: *If you will not believe you shall not understand*, where our version has: *If you will not believe, you shall not continue*. Therefore fruit is not the fruit of understanding.

**OBJ. 2**: Further, that which precedes is not the fruit of what follows. But faith seems to precede understanding, since it is the foundation of the entire spiritual edifice, as stated above (Q. 4, AA. 1, 7). Therefore faith is not the fruit of understanding.

**OBJ. 3**: Further, more gifts pertain to the intellect than to the appetite. Now, among the fruits, only one pertains to the intellect; namely, faith, while all the others pertain to the appetite. Therefore faith, seemingly, does not pertain to understanding more than to wisdom, knowledge or counsel.

**ON THE CONTRARY**, The end of a thing is its fruit. Now the gift of understanding seems to be ordained chiefly to the certitude of faith, which certitude is reckoned a fruit. For a gloss on Gal. 5:22 says that the faith which is a fruit *is certitude about the unseen*. Therefore faith, among the fruits, responds to the gift of understanding.

**I ANSWER THAT**, The fruits of the Spirit, as stated above (I-II, Q. 70, A. 1), when we were discussing them, are so called because they are something ultimate and delightful, produced in us by the power of the Holy Spirit. Now the ultimate and delightful has the nature of an end, which is the proper object of the will: and consequently that which is ultimate and delightful with regard to the will, must be, after a fashion, the fruit of all the other things that pertain to the other powers.

Accordingly, therefore, to this kind of gift of virtue that perfects a power, we may distinguish a double fruit: one, belonging to the same power; the other, the last of all as it were, belonging to the will. In this way we must conclude that the fruit which properly responds to the gift of understanding is faith, i.e., the certitude of faith; while the fruit that responds to it last of all is joy, which belongs to the will.

**AD PRIMUM** ergo dicendum quod intellectus est fructus fidei quae est virtus. Sic autem non accipitur fides cum dicitur fructus, sed pro quadam certitudine fidei, ad quam homo pervenit per donum intellectus.

**AD SECUNDUM** dicendum quod fides non potest universaliter praecedere intellectum, non enim posset homo assentire credendo aliquibus propositis nisi ea aliqualiter intelligeret. Sed perfectio intellectus consequitur fidem quae est virtus, ad quam quidem intellectus perfectionem sequitur quaedam fidei certitudo.

**AD TERTIUM** dicendum quod cognitionis practicae fructus non potest esse in ipsa, quia talis cognitio non scitur propter se, sed propter aliud. Sed cognitio speculativa habet fructum in seipsa, scilicet certitudinem eorum quorum est. Et ideo dono consilii, quod pertinet solum ad practicam cognitionem, non respondet aliquis fructus proprius. Donis autem sapientiae, intellectus et scientiae, quae possunt etiam ad speculativam cognitionem pertinere, respondet solum unus fructus, qui est certitudo significata nomine fidei. Plures autem fructus ponuntur pertinentes ad partem appetitivam, quia, sicut iam dictum est, ratio finis, quae importatur in nomine fructus, magis pertinet ad vim appetitivam quam intellectivam.

**REPLY OBJ. 1**: Understanding is the fruit of faith, taken as a virtue. But we are not taking faith in this sense here, but for a kind of certitude of faith, to which man attains by the gift of understanding.

**REPLY OBJ. 2**: Faith cannot altogether precede understanding, for it would be impossible to assent by believing what is proposed to be believed, without understanding it in some way. However, the perfection of understanding follows the virtue of faith: which perfection of understanding is itself followed by a kind of certainty of faith.

**REPLY OBJ. 3**: The fruit of practical knowledge cannot consist in that very knowledge, since knowledge of that kind is known not for its own sake, but for the sake of something else. On the other hand, speculative knowledge has its fruit in its very self, which fruit is the certitude about the thing known. Hence the gift of counsel, which belongs only to practical knowledge, has no corresponding fruit of its own: while the gifts of wisdom, understanding and knowledge, which can belong also to speculative knowledge, have but one corresponding fruit, which is certainly denoted by the name of faith. The reason why there are several fruits pertaining to the appetitive faculty, is because, as already stated, the character of end, which the word fruit implies, pertains to the appetitive rather than to the intellective part.

# QUESTION 9

## THE GIFT OF KNOWLEDGE

Deinde considerandum est de dono scientiae. Et circa hoc quaeruntur quatuor.

Primo, utrum scientia sit donum.

Secundo, utrum sit circa divina.

Tertio, utrum sit speculativa vel practica.

Quarto, quae beatitudo ei respondeat.

We must now consider the gift of knowledge, under which head there are four points of inquiry:

(1) Whether knowledge is a gift?

(2) Whether it is about Divine things?

(3) Whether it is speculative or practical?

(4) Which beatitude responds to it?

# Article 1

*Whether knowledge is a gift?*

**AD PRIMUM SIC PROCEDITUR.** Videtur quod scientia non sit donum. Dona enim spiritus sancti naturalem facultatem excedunt. Sed scientia importat effectum quendam naturalis rationis, dicit enim philosophus, in I Poster., quod demonstratio est *syllogismus faciens scire*. Ergo scientia non est donum spiritus sancti.

**PRAETEREA,** dona spiritus sancti sunt communia omnibus sanctis, ut supra dictum est. Sed Augustinus, XIV de Trin., dicit quod *scientia non pollent fideles plurimi, quamvis polleant ipsa fide*. Ergo scientia non est donum.

**PRAETEREA,** donum est perfectius virtute, ut supra dictum est. Ergo unum donum sufficit ad perfectionem unius virtutis. Sed virtuti fidei respondet donum intellectus, ut supra dictum est. Ergo non respondet ei donum scientiae. Nec apparet cui alii virtuti respondeat. Ergo, cum dona sint perfectiones virtutum, ut supra dictum est, videtur quod scientia non sit donum.

**SED CONTRA** est quod Isaiae XI computatur inter septem dona.

**RESPONDEO** dicendum quod gratia est perfectior quam natura, unde non deficit in his in quibus homo per naturam perfici potest. Cum autem homo per naturalem rationem assentit secundum intellectum alicui veritati, dupliciter perficitur circa veritatem illam, primo quidem, quia capit eam; secundo, quia de ea certum iudicium habet.

Et ideo ad hoc quod intellectus humanus perfecte assentiat veritati fidei duo requiruntur. Quorum unum est quod sane capiat ea quae proponuntur, quod pertinet ad donum intellectus, ut supra dictum est. Aliud autem est ut habeat certum et rectum iudicium de eis, discernendo

**OBJECTION 1**: It would seem that knowledge is not a gift. For the gifts of the Holy Spirit surpass the natural faculty. But knowledge implies an effect of natural reason: for the Philosopher says (*Poster.* i, 2) that a demonstration is *a syllogism which produces knowledge*. Therefore knowledge is not a gift of the Holy Spirit.

**OBJ. 2**: Further, the gifts of the Holy Spirit are common to all holy persons, as stated above (Q. 8, A. 4; I-II, Q. 68, A. 5). Now Augustine says (*De Trin.* xiv, 1) that *many of the faithful lack knowledge though they have faith*. Therefore knowledge is not a gift.

**OBJ. 3**: Further, the gifts are more perfect than the virtues, as stated above (I-II, Q. 68, A. 8). Therefore one gift suffices for the perfection of one virtue. Now the gift of understanding responds to the virtue of faith, as stated above (Q. 8, A. 2). Therefore the gift of knowledge does not respond to that virtue, nor does it appear to which other virtue it can respond. Since, then, the gifts are perfections of virtues, as stated above (I-II, Q. 68, AA. 1, 2), it seems that knowledge is not a gift.

**ON THE CONTRARY**, Knowledge is reckoned among the seven gifts (Isa 11:2).

**I ANSWER THAT**, Grace is more perfect than nature, and, therefore, does not fail in those things wherein man can be perfected by nature. Now, when a man, by his natural reason, assents by his intellect to some truth, he is perfected in two ways in respect of that truth: first, because he grasps it; second, because he forms a sure judgment on it.

Accordingly, two things are requisite in order that the human intellect may perfectly assent to the truth of the faith: one of these is that he should have a sound grasp of the things that are proposed to be believed, and this pertains to the gift of understanding, as stated above

scilicet credenda non credendis. Et ad hoc necessarium est donum scientiae.

**AD PRIMUM** ergo dicendum quod certitudo cognitionis in diversis naturis invenitur diversimode, secundum diversam conditionem uniuscuiusque naturae. Nam homo consequitur certum iudicium de veritate per discursum rationis, et ideo scientia humana ex ratione demonstrativa acquiritur. Sed in Deo est certum iudicium veritatis absque omni discursu per simplicem intuitum, ut in primo dictum est, et ideo divina scientia non est discursiva vel ratiocinativa, sed absoluta et simplex. Cui similis est scientia quae ponitur donum spiritus sancti, cum sit quaedam participativa similitudo ipsius.

**AD SECUNDUM** dicendum quod circa credenda duplex scientia potest haberi. Una quidem per quam homo scit quid credere debeat, discernens credenda a non credendis, et secundum hoc scientia est donum, et convenit omnibus sanctis. Alia vero est scientia circa credenda per quam homo non solum scit quid credi debeat, sed etiam scit fidem manifestare et alios ad credendum inducere et contradictores revincere. Et ista scientia ponitur inter gratias gratis datas, quae non datur omnibus, sed quibusdam. Unde Augustinus, post verba inducta, subiungit, *aliud est scire tantummodo quid homo credere debeat, aliud scire quemadmodum hoc ipsum et piis opituletur et contra impios defendatur.*

**AD TERTIUM** dicendum quod dona sunt perfectiora virtutibus moralibus et intellectualibus. Non sunt autem perfectiora virtutibus theologicis, sed magis omnia dona ad perfectionem theologicarum virtutum ordinantur sicut ad finem. Et ideo non est inconveniens si diversa dona ad unam virtutem theologicam ordinantur.

(Q. 8, A. 6); while the other is that he should have a sure and right judgment on them, so as to discern what is to be believed, from what is not to be believed, and for this the gift of knowledge is required.

**REPLY OBJ. 1**: Certitude of knowledge varies in various natures, according to the various conditions of each nature. Because man forms a sure judgment about a truth by the discursive process of his reason: and so human knowledge is acquired by means of demonstrative reasoning. On the other hand, in God, there is a sure judgment of truth, without any discursive process, by simple intuition, as was stated in the First Part (Q. 14, A. 7); wherefore God's knowledge is not discursive, or argumentative, but absolute and simple, to which that knowledge is likened which is a gift of the Holy Spirit, since it is a participated likeness thereof.

**REPLY OBJ. 2**: A twofold knowledge may be had about matters of belief. One is the knowledge of what one ought to believe by discerning things to be believed from things not to be believed: in this way knowledge is a gift and is common to all holy persons. The other is a knowledge about matters of belief, whereby one knows not only what one ought to believe, but also how to make the faith known, how to induce others to believe, and confute those who deny the faith. This knowledge is numbered among the gratuitous graces, which are not given to all, but to some. Hence Augustine, after the words quoted, adds: *It is one thing for a man merely to know what he ought to believe, and another to know how to dispense what he believes to the godly, and to defend it against the ungodly.*

**REPLY OBJ. 3**: The gifts are more perfect than the moral and intellectual virtues; but they are not more perfect than the theological virtues; rather are all the gifts ordained to the perfection of the theological virtues, as to their end. Hence it is not unreasonable if several gifts are ordained to one theological virtue.

# Article 2

*Whether the gift of knowledge is about divine things?*

**AD SECUNDUM SIC PROCEDITUR**. Videtur quod scientiae donum sit circa res divinas. Dicit enim Augustinus, XIV de Trin., quod per scientiam, *gignitur fides, nutritur et roboratur.* Sed fides est de rebus divinis, quia obiectum fidei est veritas prima, ut supra habitum est. Ergo et donum scientiae est de rebus divinis.

**PRAETEREA**, donum scientiae est dignius quam scientia acquisita. Sed aliqua scientia acquisita est circa res divinas, sicut scientia metaphysicae. Ergo multo magis donum scientiae est circa res divinas.

**OBJECTION 1**: It would seem that the gift of knowledge is about Divine things. For Augustine says (*De Trin.* xiv, 1) that knowledge *begets, nourishes and strengthens faith.* Now faith is about Divine things, because its object is the First Truth, as stated above (Q. 1, A. 1). Therefore the gift of knowledge also is about Divine things.

**OBJ. 2**: Further, the gift of knowledge is more excellent than acquired knowledge. But there is an acquired knowledge about Divine things, for instance, the science of metaphysics. Much more therefore is the gift of knowledge about Divine things.

**PRAETEREA**, sicut dicitur Rom. I, *invisibilia Dei per ea quae facta sunt intellecta conspiciuntur*. Si igitur est scientia circa res creatas, videtur quod etiam sit circa res divinas.

**SED CONTRA** est quod Augustinus, XIV de Trin., dicit, *rerum divinarum scientia proprie sapientia nuncupetur, humanarum autem proprie scientiae nomen obtineat*.

**RESPONDEO** dicendum quod certum iudicium de re aliqua maxime datur ex sua causa. Et ideo secundum ordinem causarum oportet esse ordinem iudiciorum, sicut enim causa prima est causa secundae, ita per causam primam iudicatur de causa secunda. De causa autem prima non potest iudicari per aliam causam. Et ideo iudicium quod fit per causam primam est primum et perfectissimum.

In his autem in quibus aliquid est perfectissimum, nomen commune generis appropriatur his quae deficiunt a perfectissimo, ipsi autem perfectissimo adaptatur aliud speciale nomen, ut patet in logicis. Nam in genere convertibilium illud quod significat *quod quid est*, speciali nomine *definitio* vocatur, quae autem ab hoc deficiunt convertibilia existentia nomen commune sibi retinent, scilicet quod *propria* dicuntur.

Quia igitur nomen scientiae importat quandam certitudinem iudicii, ut dictum est; si quidem certitudo iudicii fit per altissimam causam, habet speciale nomen, quod est sapientia, dicitur enim sapiens in unoquoque genere qui novit altissimam causam illius generis, per quam potest de omnibus iudicare. Simpliciter autem sapiens dicitur qui novit altissimam causam simpliciter, scilicet Deum. Et ideo cognitio divinarum rerum vocatur sapientia. Cognitio vero rerum humanarum vocatur scientia, quasi communi nomine importante certitudinem iudicii appropriato ad iudicium quod fit per causas secundas. Et ideo, sic accipiendo scientiae nomen, ponitur donum distinctum a dono sapientiae. Unde donum scientiae est solum circa res humanas, vel circa res creatas.

**AD PRIMUM** ergo dicendum quod, licet ea de quibus est fides sint res divinae et aeternae, tamen ipsa fides est quoddam temporale in animo credentis. Et ideo scire quid credendum sit pertinet ad donum scientiae. Scire autem ipsas res creditas secundum seipsas per quandam unionem ad ipsas pertinet ad donum sapientiae. Unde donum sapientiae magis respondet caritati, quae unit mentem hominis Deo.

**AD SECUNDUM** dicendum quod ratio illa procedit secundum quod nomen scientiae communiter sumitur.

**OBJ. 3**: Further, according to Rom. 1:20, *the invisible things of God . . . are clearly seen, being understood by the things that are made*. If therefore there is knowledge about created things, it seems that there is also knowledge of Divine things.

**ON THE CONTRARY**, Augustine says (*De Trin*. xiv, 1): *The knowledge of Divine things may be properly called wisdom, and the knowledge of human affairs may properly receive the name of knowledge*.

**I ANSWER THAT**, A sure judgment about a thing is formed chiefly from its cause, and so the order of judgments should be according to the order of causes. For just as the first cause is the cause of the second, so ought the judgment about the second cause to be formed through the first cause: nor is it possible to judge of the first cause through any other cause; wherefore the judgment which is formed through the first cause, is the first and most perfect judgment.

Now in those things where we find something most perfect, the common name of the genus is appropriated for those things which fall short of the most perfect, and some special name is adapted to the most perfect thing, as is the case in Logic. For in the genus of convertible terms, that which signifies *what a thing is*, is given the special name of *definition*, but the convertible terms which fall short of this, retain the common name, and are called *proper* terms.

Accordingly, since the word knowledge implies certitude of judgment as stated above (A. 1), if this certitude of the judgment is derived from the highest cause, the knowledge has a special name, which is wisdom: for a wise man in any branch of knowledge is one who knows the highest cause of that kind of knowledge, and is able to judge of all matters by that cause: and a wise man *absolutely*, is one who knows the cause which is absolutely highest, namely God. Hence the knowledge of Divine things is called *wisdom*, while the knowledge of human things is called *knowledge*, this being the common name denoting certitude of judgment, and appropriated to the judgment which is formed through second causes. Accordingly, if we take knowledge in this way, it is a distinct gift from the gift of wisdom, so that the gift of knowledge is only about human or created things.

**REPLY OBJ. 1**: Although matters of faith are Divine and eternal, yet faith itself is something temporal in the mind of the believer. Hence to know what one ought to believe, belongs to the gift of knowledge, but to know in themselves the very things we believe, by a kind of union with them, belongs to the gift of wisdom. Therefore the gift of wisdom corresponds more to charity which unites man's mind to God.

**REPLY OBJ. 2**: This argument takes knowledge in the generic acceptation of the term: it is not thus that knowl-

Sic autem scientia non ponitur speciale donum, sed secundum quod restringitur ad iudicium quod fit per res creatas.

**AD TERTIUM** dicendum quod, sicut supra dictum est, quilibet cognoscitivus habitus formaliter quidem respicit medium per quod aliquid cognoscitur, materialiter autem id quod per medium cognoscitur. Et quia id quod est formale potius est, ideo illae scientiae quae ex principiis mathematicis concludunt circa materiam naturalem, magis cum mathematicis connumerantur, utpote eis similiores, licet quantum ad materiam magis conveniant cum naturali, et propter hoc dicitur in II Physic. quod sunt *magis naturales*. Et ideo, cum homo per res creatas Deum cognoscit, magis videtur hoc pertinere ad scientiam, ad quam pertinet formaliter, quam ad sapientiam, ad quam pertinet materialiter. Et e converso, cum secundum res divinas iudicamus de rebus creatis, magis hoc ad sapientiam quam ad scientiam pertinet.

edge is a special gift, but according as it is restricted to judgments formed through created things.

**REPLY OBJ. 3**: As stated above (Q. 1, A. 1), every cognitive habit regards formally the mean through which things are known, and materially, the things that are known through the mean. And since that which is formal is of most account, it follows that those sciences which draw conclusions about physical matter from mathematical principles, are reckoned rather among the mathematical sciences; though, as to their matter they have more in common with physical sciences: and for this reason it is stated in *Phys.* ii, 2 that they are *more akin to physics*. Accordingly, since man knows God through His creatures, this seems to pertain to *knowledge*, to which it belongs formally, rather than to *wisdom*, to which it belongs materially: and, conversely, when we judge of creatures according to Divine things, this pertains to *wisdom* rather than to *knowledge*.

# Article 3

*Whether the gift of knowledge is practical knowledge?*

**AD TERTIUM SIC PROCEDITUR**. Videtur quod scientia quae ponitur donum sit scientia practica. Dicit enim Augustinus, XII de Trin., quod *actio qua exterioribus rebus utimur scientiae deputatur*. Sed scientia cui deputatur actio est practica. Ergo scientia quae est donum est scientia practica.

**PRAETEREA**, Gregorius dicit, in I Moral., *nulla est scientia si utilitatem pietatis non habet, et valde inutilis est pietas si scientiae discretione caret*. Ex quo habetur quod scientia dirigit pietatem. Sed hoc non potest competere scientiae speculativae. Ergo scientia quae est donum non est speculativa, sed practica.

**PRAETEREA**, dona spiritus sancti non habentur nisi a iustis, ut supra habitum est. Sed scientia speculativa potest haberi etiam ab iniustis, secundum illud Iac. ult., *scienti bonum et non facienti, peccatum est illi*. Ergo scientia quae est donum non est speculativa, sed practica.

**SED CONTRA** est quod Gregorius dicit, in I Moral., *scientia in die suo convivium parat, quia in ventre mentis ignorantiae ieiunium superat*. Sed ignorantia non tollitur totaliter nisi per utramque scientiam, scilicet et speculativam et practicam. Ergo scientia quae est donum est et speculativa et practica.

**RESPONDEO** dicendum quod, sicut supra dictum est, donum scientiae ordinatur, sicut et donum intellectus, ad certitudinem fidei. Fides autem primo et principaliter in speculatione consistit, inquantum scilicet inhaeret primae veritati. Sed quia prima veritas est etiam ultimus

**OBJECTION 1**: It would seem that the knowledge, which is numbered among the gifts, is practical knowledge. For Augustine says (*De Trin.* xii, 14) that *knowledge is concerned with the actions in which we make use of external things*. But the knowledge which is concerned about actions is practical. Therefore the gift of knowledge is practical.

**OBJ. 2**: Further, Gregory says (*Moral.* i, 32): *Knowledge is naught if it hath not its use for piety . . . and piety is very useless if it lacks the discernment of knowledge*. Now it follows from this authority that knowledge directs piety. But this cannot apply to a speculative science. Therefore the gift of knowledge is not speculative but practical.

**OBJ. 3**: Further, the gifts of the Holy Spirit are only in the righteous, as stated above (Q. 9, A. 5). But speculative knowledge can be also in the unrighteous, according to James 4:17: *To him . . . who knoweth to do good, and doth it not, to him it is a sin*. Therefore the gift of knowledge is not speculative but practical.

**ON THE CONTRARY**, Gregory says (*Moral.* i, 32): *Knowledge on her own day prepares a feast, because she overcomes the fast of ignorance in the mind*. Now ignorance is not entirely removed, save by both kinds of knowledge, viz. speculative and practical. Therefore the gift of knowledge is both speculative and practical.

**I ANSWER THAT**, As stated above (Q. 9, A. 8), the gift of knowledge, like the gift of understanding, is ordained to the certitude of faith. Now faith consists primarily and principally in speculation, inasmuch as it is founded on the First Truth. But since the First Truth is also the last end for

finis, propter quem operamur, inde etiam est quod fides ad operationem se extendit, secundum illud Gal. V, *fides per dilectionem operatur.*

Unde etiam oportet quod donum scientiae primo quidem et principaliter respiciat speculationem, inquantum scilicet homo scit quid fide tenere debeat. Secundario autem se extendit etiam ad operationem, secundum quod per scientiam credibilium, et eorum quae ad credibilia consequuntur, dirigimur in agendis.

**AD PRIMUM** ergo dicendum quod Augustinus loquitur de dono scientiae secundum quod se extendit ad operationem, attribuitur enim ei actio, sed non sola nec primo. Et hoc etiam modo dirigit pietatem.

**UNDE PATET** solutio ad secundum.

**AD TERTIUM** dicendum quod, sicut dictum est de dono intellectus quod non quicumque intelligit habet donum intellectus, sed qui intelligit quasi ex habitu gratiae; ita etiam de dono scientiae est intelligendum quod illi soli donum scientiae habeant qui ex infusione gratiae certum iudicium habent circa credenda et agenda, quod in nullo deviat a rectitudine iustitiae. Et haec est scientia sanctorum, de qua dicitur Sap. X, *iustum deduxit dominus per vias rectas et dedit illi scientiam sanctorum.*

the sake of which our works are done, hence it is that faith extends to works, according to Gal. 5:6: *Faith . . . worketh by charity.*

The consequence is that the gift of knowledge also, primarily and principally indeed, regards speculation, insofar as man knows what he ought to hold by faith; yet, secondarily, it extends to works, since we are directed in our actions by the knowledge of matters of faith, and of conclusions drawn therefrom.

**REPLY OBJ. 1:** Augustine is speaking of the gift of knowledge, insofar as it extends to works; for action is ascribed to knowledge, yet not action solely, nor primarily: and in this way it directs piety.

**HENCE** the Reply to the Second Objection is clear.

**REPLY OBJ. 3:** As we have already stated (Q. 8, A. 5) about the gift of understanding, not everyone who understands, has the gift of understanding, but only he that understands through a habit of grace: and so we must take note, with regard to the gift of knowledge, that they alone have the gift of knowledge, who judge aright about matters of faith and action, through the grace bestowed on them, so as never to wander from the straight path of justice. This is the knowledge of holy things, according to Wis. 10:10: *She conducted the just . . . through the right ways . . . and gave him the knowledge of holy things.*

# Article 4

*Whether the third beatitude, "blessed are they that mourn, for they shall be consoled," corresponds to the gift of knowledge?*

**AD QUARTUM SIC PROCEDITUR.** Videtur quod scientiae non respondeat tertia beatitudo, scilicet, *beati qui lugent, quoniam ipsi consolabuntur.* Sicut enim malum est causa tristitiae et luctus, ita etiam bonum est causa laetitiae. Sed per scientiam principalius manifestantur bona quam mala, quae per bona cognoscuntur, *rectum* enim *est iudex sui ipsius et obliqui,* ut dicitur in I de Anima. Ergo praedicta beatitudo non convenienter respondet scientiae.

**PRAETEREA,** consideratio veritatis est actus scientiae. Sed in consideratione veritatis non est tristitia, sed magis gaudium, dicitur enim Sap. VIII, *non habet amaritudinem conversatio illius, nec taedium convictus illius, sed laetitiam et gaudium.* Ergo praedicta beatitudo non convenienter respondet dono scientiae.

**PRAETEREA,** donum scientiae prius consistit in speculatione quam in operatione. Sed secundum quod consistit in speculatione, non respondet sibi luctus, quia intellectus speculativus *nihil dicit de imitabili et fugiendo,* ut dicitur in III de Anima; neque dicit aliquid laetum

**OBJECTION 1:** It would seem that the third beatitude, *Blessed are they that mourn, for they shall be consoled,* does not correspond to the gift of knowledge. For, even as evil is the cause of sorrow and grief, so is good the cause of joy. Now knowledge brings good to light rather than evil, since the latter is known through evil: for *the straight line rules both itself and the crooked line* (*De Anima* i, 5). Therefore the aforesaid beatitude does not suitably correspond to the gift of knowledge.

**OBJ. 2:** Further, consideration of truth is an act of knowledge. Now there is no sorrow in the consideration of truth; rather is there joy, since it is written (Wis 8:16): *Her conversation hath no bitterness, nor her company any tediousness, but joy and gladness.* Therefore the aforesaid beatitude does not suitably correspond with the gift of knowledge.

**OBJ. 3:** Further, the gift of knowledge consists in speculation, before operation. Now, insofar as it consists in speculation, sorrow does not correspond to it, since the speculative intellect *is not concerned about things to be sought or avoided* (*De Anima* iii, 9). Therefore the aforesaid

et triste. Ergo praedicta beatitudo non convenienter ponitur respondere dono scientiae.

**SED CONTRA** est quod Augustinus dicit, in libro de Serm. Dom. in monte, *scientia convenit lugentibus, qui didicerunt quibus malis vincti sunt, quae quasi bona petierunt.*

**RESPONDEO** dicendum quod ad scientiam proprie pertinet rectum iudicium creaturarum. Creaturae autem sunt ex quibus homo occasionaliter a Deo avertitur, secundum illud Sap. XIV, *creaturae factae sunt in odium, et in muscipulam pedibus insipientium,* qui scilicet rectum iudicium de his non habent, dum aestimant in eis esse perfectum bonum; unde in eis finem constituendo, peccant et verum bonum perdunt. Et hoc damnum homini innotescit per rectum iudicium de creaturis, quod habetur per donum scientiae.

Et ideo beatitudo luctus ponitur respondere dono scientiae.

**AD PRIMUM** ergo dicendum quod bona creata non excitant spirituale gaudium nisi quatenus referuntur ad bonum divinum, ex quo proprie consurgit gaudium spirituale. Et ideo directe quidem spiritualis pax, et gaudium consequens, respondet dono sapientiae. Dono autem scientiae respondet quidem primo luctus de praeteritis erratis; et consequenter consolatio, dum homo per rectum iudicium scientiae creaturas ordinat in bonum divinum. Et ideo in hac beatitudine ponitur luctus pro merito, et consolatio consequens pro praemio. Quae quidem inchoatur in hac vita, perficitur autem in futura.

**AD SECUNDUM** dicendum quod de ipsa consideratione veritatis homo gaudet, sed de re circa quam considerat veritatem potest tristari quandoque. Et secundum hoc luctus scientiae attribuitur.

**AD TERTIUM** dicendum quod scientiae secundum quod in speculatione consistit, non respondet beatitudo aliqua, quia beatitudo hominis non consistit in consideratione creaturarum, sed in contemplatione Dei. Sed aliqualiter beatitudo hominis consistit in debito usu creaturarum et ordinata affectione circa ipsas, et hoc dico quantum ad beatitudinem viae. Et ideo scientiae non attribuitur aliqua beatitudo pertinens ad contemplationem; sed intellectui et sapientiae, quae sunt circa divina.

beatitude is not suitably reckoned to correspond with the gift of knowledge.

**ON THE CONTRARY,** Augustine says (*De Serm. Dom. in Monte* iv): *Knowledge befits the mourner, who has discovered that he has been mastered by the evil which he coveted as though it were good.*

**I ANSWER THAT,** Right judgment about creatures belongs properly to knowledge. Now it is through creatures that man's aversion from God is occasioned, according to Wis. 14:11: *Creatures . . . are turned to an abomination . . . and a snare to the feet of the unwise,* of those, namely, who do not judge aright about creatures, since they deem the perfect good to consist in them. Hence they sin by placing their last end in them, and lose the true good. It is by forming a right judgment of creatures that man becomes aware of the loss (of which they may be the occasion), which judgment he exercises through the gift of knowledge.

Hence the beatitude of sorrow is said to correspond to the gift of knowledge.

**REPLY OBJ. 1:** Created goods do not cause spiritual joy, except insofar as they are referred to the Divine good, which is the proper cause of spiritual joy. Hence spiritual peace and the resulting joy correspond directly to the gift of wisdom: but to the gift of knowledge there corresponds, in the first place, sorrow for past errors, and, in consequence, consolation, since, by his right judgment, man directs creatures to the Divine good. For this reason sorrow is set forth in this beatitude, as the merit, and the resulting consolation, as the reward; which is begun in this life, and is perfected in the life to come.

**REPLY OBJ. 2:** Man rejoices in the very consideration of truth; yet he may sometimes grieve for the thing, the truth of which he considers: it is thus that sorrow is ascribed to knowledge.

**REPLY OBJ. 3:** No beatitude corresponds to knowledge, insofar as it consists in speculation, because man's beatitude consists, not in considering creatures, but in contemplating God. But man's beatitude does consist somewhat in the right use of creatures, and in well-ordered love of them: and this I say with regard to the beatitude of a wayfarer. Hence beatitude relating to contemplation is not ascribed to knowledge, but to understanding and wisdom, which are about Divine things.

# QUESTION 10

## UNBELIEF IN GENERAL

Consequenter considerandum est de vitiis oppositis. Et primo, de infidelitate, quae opponitur fidei; secundo, de blasphemia, quae opponitur confessioni; tertio, de ignorantia et hebetudine, quae opponuntur scientiae et intellectui.

Circa primum, considerandum est de infidelitate in communi; secundo, de haeresi, tertio, de apostasia a fide.

Circa primum quaeruntur duodecim.

Primo, utrum infidelitas sit peccatum.

Secundo, in quo sit sicut in subiecto.

Tertio, utrum sit maximum peccatorum.

Quarto, utrum omnis actio infidelium sit peccatum.

Quinto, de speciebus infidelitatis.

Sexto, de comparatione earum ad invicem.

Septimo, utrum cum infidelibus sit disputandum de fide.

Octavo, utrum sint cogendi ad fidem.

Nono, utrum sit eis communicandum.

Decimo, utrum possint Christianis fidelibus praeesse.

Undecimo, utrum ritus infidelium sint tolerandi.

Duodecimo, utrum pueri infidelium sint invitis parentibus baptizandi.

In due sequence we must consider the contrary vices: first, unbelief, which is contrary to faith; second, blasphemy, which is opposed to confession of faith; third, ignorance and dulness of mind, which are contrary to knowledge and understanding.

As to the first, we must consider (1) unbelief in general; (2) heresy; (3) apostasy from the faith.

Under the first head there are twelve points of inquiry:

(1) Whether unbelief is a sin?

(2) What is its subject?

(3) Whether it is the greatest of sins?

(4) Whether every action of unbelievers is a sin?

(5) Of the species of unbelief;

(6) Of their comparison, one with another;

(7) Whether we ought to dispute about faith with unbelievers?

(8) Whether they ought to be compelled to the faith?

(9) Whether we ought to have communications with them?

(10) Whether unbelievers can have authority over Christians?

(11) Whether the rites of unbelievers should be tolerated?

(12) Whether the children of unbelievers are to be baptized against their parents' will?

# Article 1

*Whether unbelief is a sin?*

**AD PRIMUM SIC PROCEDITUR**. Videtur quod infidelitas non sit peccatum. Omne enim peccatum est contra naturam, ut patet per Damascenum, in II libro. Sed infidelitas non videtur esse contra naturam, dicit enim Augustinus, in libro de Praed. Sanct., quod *posse habere fidem, sicut posse habere caritatem, naturae est hominum, habere autem fidem, quemadmodum habere caritatem, gratiae est fidelium*. Ergo non habere fidem, quod est infidelem esse, non est peccatum.

**PRAETEREA**, nullus peccat in eo quod vitare non potest, quia omne peccatum est voluntarium. Sed non est in potestate hominis quod infidelitatem vitet, quam vitare non potest nisi fidem habendo, dicit enim apostolus, ad Rom. X, *quomodo credent ei quem non audierunt? Quomodo autem audient sine praedicante?* Ergo infidelitas non videtur esse peccatum.

**OBJECTION 1**: It would seem that unbelief is not a sin. For every sin is contrary to nature, as Damascene proves (*De Fide Orth.* ii, 4). Now unbelief seems not to be contrary to nature; for Augustine says (*De Praedest. Sanct.* v) that *to be capable to having faith, just as to be capable of having charity, is natural to all men; whereas to have faith, even as to have charity, belongs to the grace of the faithful.* Therefore not to have faith, which is to be an unbeliever, is not a sin.

**OBJ. 2**: Further, no one sins in that which he cannot avoid, since every sin is voluntary. Now it is not in a man's power to avoid unbelief, for he cannot avoid it unless he have faith, because the Apostle says (Rom 10:14): *How shall they believe in Him, of Whom they have not heard? And how shall they hear without a preacher?* Therefore unbelief does not seem to be a sin.

**PRAETEREA**, sicut supra dictum est, sunt septem vitia capitalia, ad quae omnia peccata reducuntur. Sub nullo autem horum videtur contineri infidelitas. Ergo infidelitas non est peccatum.

**SED CONTRA**, virtuti contrariatur vitium. Sed fides est virtus, cui contrariatur infidelitas. Ergo infidelitas est peccatum.

**RESPONDEO** dicendum quod infidelitas dupliciter accipi potest. Uno modo, secundum puram negationem, ut dicatur infidelis ex hoc solo quod non habet fidem. Alio modo potest intelligi infidelitas secundum contrarietatem ad fidem, quia scilicet aliquis repugnat auditui fidei, vel etiam contemnit ipsam, secundum illud Isaiae LIII, *quis credidit auditui nostro?* Et in hoc proprie perficitur ratio infidelitatis. Et secundum hoc infidelitas est peccatum.

Si autem accipiatur infidelitas secundum negationem puram, sicut in illis qui nihil audierunt de fide, non habet rationem peccati, sed magis poenae, quia talis ignorantia divinorum ex peccato primi parentis est consecuta. Qui autem sic sunt infideles damnantur quidem propter alia peccata, quae sine fide remitti non possunt, non autem damnantur propter infidelitatis peccatum. Unde dominus dicit, Ioan. XV, *si non venissem, et locutus eis non fuissem, peccatum non haberent*, quod exponens Augustinus dicit quod *loquitur de illo peccato quo non crediderunt in Christum.*

**AD PRIMUM** ergo dicendum quod habere fidem non est in natura humana, sed in natura humana est ut mens hominis non repugnet interiori instinctui et exteriori veritatis praedicationi. Unde infidelitas secundum hoc est contra naturam.

**AD SECUNDUM** dicendum quod ratio illa procedit de infidelitate secundum quod importat simplicem negationem.

**AD TERTIUM** dicendum quod infidelitas secundum quod est peccatum, oritur ex superbia, ex qua contingit quod homo intellectum suum non vult subiicere regulis fidei et sano intellectui patrum. Unde Gregorius dicit, XXXI Moral., quod *ex inani gloria oriuntur novitatum praesumptiones.*

Quamvis posset dici quod, sicut virtutes theologicae non reducuntur ad virtutes cardinales, sed sunt priores eis; ita etiam vitia opposita virtutibus theologicis non reducuntur ad vitia capitalia.

**OBJ. 3**: Further, as stated above (I-II, Q. 84, A. 4), there are seven capital sins, to which all sins are reduced. But unbelief does not seem to be comprised under any of them. Therefore unbelief is not a sin.

**ON THE CONTRARY**, Vice is opposed to virtue. Now faith is a virtue, and unbelief is opposed to it. Therefore unbelief is a sin.

**I ANSWER THAT**, Unbelief may be taken in two ways: first, by way of pure negation, so that a man be called an unbeliever, merely because he has not the faith. Second, unbelief may be taken by way of opposition to the faith; in which sense a man refuses to hear the faith, or despises it, according to Isa. 53:1: *Who hath believed our report?* It is this that completes the notion of unbelief, and it is in this sense that unbelief is a sin.

If, however, we take it by way of pure negation, as we find it in those who have heard nothing about the faith, it bears the character, not of sin, but of punishment, because such like ignorance of Divine things is a result of the sin of our first parent. If such like unbelievers are damned, it is on account of other sins, which cannot be taken away without faith, but not on account of their sin of unbelief. Hence Our Lord said (John 15:22) *If I had not come, and spoken to them, they would not have sin*; which Augustine expounds (*Tract. lxxxix in Joan.*) *as referring to the sin whereby they believed not in Christ.*

**REPLY OBJ. 1**: To have the faith is not part of human nature, but it is part of human nature that man's mind should not thwart his inner instinct, and the outward preaching of the truth. Hence, in this way, unbelief is contrary to nature.

**REPLY OBJ. 2**: This argument takes unbelief as denoting a pure negation.

**REPLY OBJ. 3**: Unbelief, insofar as it is a sin, arises from pride, through which man is unwilling to subject his intellect to the rules of faith, and to the sound interpretation of the Fathers. Hence Gregory says (*Moral.* xxxi, 45) that *presumptuous innovations arise from vainglory.*

It might also be replied that just as the theological virtues are not reduced to the cardinal virtues, but precede them, so too, the vices opposed to the theological virtues are not reduced to the capital vices.

# Article 2

*Whether unbelief is in the intellect as its subject?*

**AD SECUNDUM SIC PROCEDITUR.** Videtur quod infidelitas non sit in intellectu sicut in subiecto. Omne enim peccatum in voluntate est, ut Augustinus dicit, in libro de duabus Anim. Sed infidelitas est quoddam peccatum, ut dictum est. Ergo infidelitas est in voluntate, non in intellectu.

**PRAETEREA**, infidelitas habet rationem peccati ex eo quod praedicatio fidei contemnitur. Sed contemptus ad voluntatem pertinet. Ergo infidelitas est in voluntate.

**PRAETEREA**, II ad Cor. XI, super illud, *ipse Satanas transfigurat se in Angelum lucis*, dicit Glossa quod, *si Angelus malus se bonum fingat, etiam si credatur bonus, non est error periculosus aut morbidus, si facit vel dicit quae bonis Angelis congruunt.* Cuius ratio esse videtur propter rectitudinem voluntatis eius qui ei inhaeret intendens bono Angelo adhaerere. Ergo totum peccatum infidelitatis esse videtur in perversa voluntate. Non ergo est in intellectu sicut in subiecto.

**SED CONTRA**, contraria sunt in eodem subiecto. Sed fides, cui contrariatur infidelitas, est in intellectu sicut in subiecto. Ergo et infidelitas in intellectu est.

**RESPONDEO** dicendum quod, sicut supra dictum est, peccatum dicitur esse in illa potentia quae est principium actus peccati. Actus autem peccati potest habere duplex principium. Unum quidem primum et universale, quod imperat omnes actus peccatorum, et hoc principium est voluntas, quia omne peccatum est voluntarium. Aliud autem principium actus peccati est proprium et proximum, quod elicit peccati actum, sicut concupiscibilis est principium gulae et luxuriae, et secundum hoc gula et luxuria dicuntur esse in concupiscibili. Dissentire autem, qui est proprius actus infidelitatis, est actus intellectus, sed moti a voluntate, sicut et assentire.

Et ideo infidelitas, sicut et fides, est quidem in intellectu sicut in proximo subiecto, in voluntate autem sicut in primo motivo. Et hoc modo dicitur omne peccatum esse in voluntate.

**UNDE PATET** responsio ad primum.

**AD SECUNDUM** dicendum quod contemptus voluntatis causat dissensum intellectus, in quo perficitur ratio infidelitatis. Unde causa infidelitatis est in voluntate, sed ipsa infidelitas est in intellectu.

**AD TERTIUM** dicendum quod ille qui credit malum Angelum esse bonum non dissentit ab eo quod est fidei, quia *sensus corporis fallitur, mens vero non removetur a vera rectaque sententia*, ut ibidem dicit Glossa. Sed si aliquis Satanae adhaereret cum incipit ad sua ducere,

**OBJECTION 1**: It would seem that unbelief is not in the intellect as its subject. For every sin is in the will, according to Augustine (*De Duabus Anim.* x, xi). Now unbelief is a sin, as stated above (A. 1). Therefore unbelief resides in the will and not in the intellect.

**OBJ. 2**: Further, unbelief is sinful through contempt of the preaching of the faith. But contempt pertains to the will. Therefore unbelief is in the will.

**OBJ. 3**: Further, a gloss on 2 Cor. 11:14 *Satan . . . transformeth himself into an angel of light*, says that if *a wicked angel pretend to be a good angel, and be taken for a good angel, it is not a dangerous or an unhealthy error, if he does or says what is becoming to a good angel.* This seems to be because of the rectitude of the will of the man who adheres to the angel, since his intention is to adhere to a good angel. Therefore the sin of unbelief seems to consist entirely in a perverse will: and, consequently, it does not reside in the intellect.

**ON THE CONTRARY**, Things which are contrary to one another are in the same subject. Now faith, to which unbelief is opposed, resides in the intellect. Therefore unbelief also is in the intellect.

**I ANSWER THAT**, As stated above (I-II, Q. 74, AA. 1, 2), sin is said to be in the power which is the principle of the sinful act. Now a sinful act may have two principles: one is its first and universal principle, which commands all acts of sin; and this is the will, because every sin is voluntary. The other principle of the sinful act is the proper and proximate principle which elicits the sinful act: thus the concupiscible is the principle of gluttony and lust, wherefore these sins are said to be in the concupiscible. Now dissent, which is the act proper to unbelief, is an act of the intellect, moved, however, by the will, just as assent is.

Therefore unbelief, like faith, is in the intellect as its proximate subject. But it is in the will as its first moving principle, in which way every sin is said to be in the will.

**HENCE** the Reply to the First Objection is clear.

**REPLY OBJ. 2**: The will's contempt causes the intellect's dissent, which completes the notion of unbelief. Hence the cause of unbelief is in the will, while unbelief itself is in the intellect.

**REPLY OBJ. 3**: He that believes a wicked angel to be a good one, does not dissent from a matter of faith, because *his bodily senses are deceived, while his mind does not depart from a true and right judgment* as the gloss observes. But, according to the same authority, to adhere to Satan when he

idest ad mala et falsa, tunc non careret peccato, ut ibidem dicitur.

begins to invite one to his abode, i.e., wickedness and error, is not without sin.

# Article 3

*Whether unbelief is the greatest of sins?*

**AD TERTIUM SIC PROCEDITUR.** Videtur quod infidelitas non sit maximum peccatorum. Dicit enim Augustinus, et habetur V, qu. I, *utrum Catholicum pessimis moribus alicui haeretico in cuius vita, praeter id quod haereticus est, non inveniunt homines quod reprehendant, praeponere debeamus, non audeo praecipitare sententiam.* Sed haereticus est infidelis. Ergo non est simpliciter dicendum quod infidelitas sit maximum peccatorum.

**PRAETEREA,** illud quod diminuit vel excusat peccatum non videtur esse maximum peccatum. Sed infidelitas excusat vel diminuit peccatum, dicit enim apostolus, I ad Tim. I, *prius fui blasphemus et persecutor et contumeliosus, sed misericordiam consecutus sum, quia ignorans feci in incredulitate.* Ergo infidelitas non est maximum peccatum.

**PRAETEREA,** maiori peccato debetur maior poena, secundum illud Deut. XXV, *pro mensura peccati erit et plagarum modus.* Sed maior poena debetur fidelibus peccantibus quam infidelibus, secundum illud ad Heb. X, *quanto magis putatis deteriora mereri supplicia qui filium Dei conculcaverit, et sanguinem testamenti pollutum duxerit, in quo sanctificatus est?* Ergo infidelitas non est maximum peccatum.

**SED CONTRA** est quod Augustinus dicit, exponens illud Ioan. XV, *si non venissem, et locutus eis non fuissem, peccatum non haberent: Magnum,* inquit, *quoddam peccatum sub generali nomine vult intelligi. Hoc enim est peccatum,* scilicet infidelitatis, *quo tenentur cuncta peccata.* Infidelitas ergo est maximum omnium peccatorum.

**RESPONDEO** dicendum quod omne peccatum formaliter consistit in aversione a Deo, ut supra dictum est. Unde tanto aliquod peccatum est gravius quanto per ipsum homo magis a Deo separatur. Per infidelitatem autem maxime homo a Deo elongatur, quia nec veram Dei cognitionem habet; per falsam autem cognitionem ipsius non appropinquat ei, sed magis ab eo elongatur.

Nec potest esse quod quantum ad quid Deum cognoscat qui falsam opinionem de ipso habet, quia id quod ipse opinatur non est Deus. Unde manifestum est quod peccatum infidelitatis est maius omnibus peccatis quae contingunt in perversitate morum. Secus autem est de peccatis quae opponuntur aliis virtutibus theologicis, ut infra dicetur.

**AD PRIMUM** ergo dicendum quod nihil prohibet peccatum quod est gravius secundum suum genus esse

**OBJECTION 1:** It would seem that unbelief is not the greatest of sins. For Augustine says (*De Bapt. contra Donat.* iv, 20): *I should hesitate to decide whether a very wicked Catholic ought to be preferred to a heretic, in whose life one finds nothing reprehensible beyond the fact that he is a heretic.* But a heretic is an unbeliever. Therefore we ought not to say absolutely that unbelief is the greatest of sins.

**OBJ. 2:** Further, that which diminishes or excuses a sin is not, seemingly, the greatest of sins. Now unbelief excuses or diminishes sin: for the Apostle says (1 Tim 1:12, 13): *I . . . before was a blasphemer, and a persecutor and contumelious; but I obtained . . . mercy . . . because I did it ignorantly in unbelief.* Therefore unbelief is not the greatest of sins.

**OBJ. 3:** Further, the greater sin deserves the greater punishment, according to Deut. 25:2: *According to the measure of the sin shall the measure also of the stripes be.* Now a greater punishment is due to believers than to unbelievers, according to Heb. 10:29: *How much more, do you think, he deserveth worse punishments, who hath trodden under foot the Son of God, and hath esteemed the blood of the testament unclean, by which he was sanctified?* Therefore unbelief is not the greatest of sins.

**ON THE CONTRARY,** Augustine, commenting on John 15:22, *If I had not come, and spoken to them, they would not have sin,* says (*Tract. lxxxix in Joan.*): *Under the general name, he refers to a singularly great sin.* For this, viz. infidelity, *is the sin to which all others may be traced.* Therefore unbelief is the greatest of sins.

**I ANSWER THAT,** Every sin consists formally in aversion from God, as stated above (I-II, Q. 71, A. 6; I-II, Q. 73, A. 3). Hence the more a sin severs man from God, the graver it is. Now man is more than ever separated from God by unbelief, because he has not even true knowledge of God: and by false knowledge of God, man does not approach Him, but is severed from Him.

Nor is it possible for one who has a false opinion of God, to know Him in any way at all, because the object of his opinion is not God. Therefore it is clear that the sin of unbelief is greater than any sin that occurs in the perversion of morals. This does not apply to the sins that are opposed to the theological virtues, as we shall state further on (Q. 20, A. 3; Q. 34, A. 2, ad 2; Q. 39, A. 2, ad 3).

**REPLY OBJ. 1:** Nothing hinders a sin that is more grave in its genus from being less grave in respect of some cir-

minus grave secundum aliquas circumstantias. Et propter hoc Augustinus noluit praecipitare sententiam de malo Catholico et haeretico alias non peccante, quia peccatum haeretici, etsi sit gravius ex genere, potest tamen ex aliqua circumstantia alleviari; et e converso peccatum Catholici ex aliqua circumstantia aggravari.

**AD SECUNDUM** dicendum quod infidelitas habet et ignorantiam adiunctam, et habet renisum ad ea quae sunt fidei, et ex hac parte habet rationem peccati gravissimi. Ex parte autem ignorantiae habet aliquam rationem excusationis, et maxime quando aliquis ex malitia non peccat, sicut fuit in apostolo.

**AD TERTIUM** dicendum quod infidelis pro peccato infidelitatis gravius punitur quam alius peccator pro quocumque alio peccato, considerato peccati genere. Sed pro alio peccato, puta pro adulterio, si committatur a fideli et ab infideli, ceteris paribus, gravius peccat fidelis quam infidelis, tum propter notitiam veritatis ex fide; tum etiam propter sacramenta fidei quibus est imbutus, quibus peccando contumeliam facit.

cumstances. Hence Augustine hesitated to decide between a bad Catholic, and a heretic not sinning otherwise, because although the heretic's sin is more grave generically, it can be lessened by a circumstance, and conversely the sin of the Catholic can, by some circumstance, be aggravated.

**REPLY OBJ. 2:** Unbelief includes both ignorance, as an accessory thereto, and resistance to matters of faith, and in the latter respect it is a most grave sin. In respect, however, of this ignorance, it has a certain reason for excuse, especially when a man sins not from malice, as was the case with the Apostle.

**REPLY OBJ. 3:** An unbeliever is more severely punished for his sin of unbelief than another sinner is for any sin whatever, if we consider the kind of sin. But in the case of another sin, e.g., adultery, committed by a believer, and by an unbeliever, the believer, other things being equal, sins more gravely than the unbeliever, both on account of his knowledge of the truth through faith, and on account of the sacraments of faith with which he has been satiated, and which he insults by committing sin.

# Article 4

*Whether every act of an unbeliever is a sin?*

**AD QUARTUM SIC PROCEDITUR.** Videtur quod quaelibet actio infidelis sit peccatum. Quia super illud Rom. XIV, *omne quod non est ex fide peccatum est*, dicit Glossa, *omnis infidelium vita est peccatum*. Sed ad vitam infidelium pertinet omne quod agunt. Ergo omnis actio infidelis est peccatum.

**PRAETEREA,** fides intentionem dirigit. Sed nullum bonum potest esse quod non est ex intentione recta. Ergo in infidelibus nulla actio potest esse bona.

**PRAETEREA,** corrupto priori, corrumpuntur posteriora. Sed actus fidei praecedit actus omnium virtutum. Ergo, cum in infidelibus non sit actus fidei, nullum bonum opus facere possunt, sed in omni actu suo peccant.

**SED CONTRA** est quod Cornelio adhuc infideli existenti dictum est quod acceptae erant Deo eleemosynae eius. Ergo non omnis actio infidelis est peccatum, sed aliqua actio eius est bona.

**RESPONDEO** dicendum quod, sicut supra dictum est, peccatum mortale tollit gratiam gratum facientem, non autem totaliter corrumpit bonum naturae. Unde, cum infidelitas sit quoddam mortale peccatum, infideles quidem gratia carent, remanet tamen in eis aliquod bonum naturae. Unde manifestum est quod infideles non possunt operari opera bona quae sunt ex gratia, scilicet

**OBJECTION 1:** It would seem that each act of an unbeliever is a sin. Because a gloss on Rom. 14:23, *All that is not of faith is sin*, says: *The whole life of unbelievers is a sin.* Now the life of unbelievers consists of their actions. Therefore every action of an unbeliever is a sin.

**OBJ. 2:** Further, faith directs the intention. Now there can be no good save what comes from a right intention. Therefore, among unbelievers, no action can be good.

**OBJ. 3:** Further, when that which precedes is corrupted, that which follows is corrupted also. Now an act of faith precedes the acts of all the virtues. Therefore, since there is no act of faith in unbelievers, they can do no good work, but sin in every action of theirs.

**ON THE CONTRARY,** It is said of Cornelius, while yet an unbeliever (Acts 10:4, 31), that his alms were acceptable to God. Therefore not every action of an unbeliever is a sin, but some of his actions are good.

**I ANSWER THAT,** As stated above (I-II, Q. 85, AA. 2, 4) mortal sin takes away sanctifying grace, but does not wholly corrupt the good of nature. Since therefore, unbelief is a mortal sin, unbelievers are without grace indeed, yet some good of nature remains in them. Consequently it is evident that unbelievers cannot do those good works which proceed from grace, viz. meritorious works; yet they can, to

opera meritoria, tamen opera bona ad quae sufficit bonum naturae aliqualiter operari possunt.

Unde non oportet quod in omni suo opere peccent, sed quandocumque aliquod opus operantur ex infidelitate, tunc peccant. Sicut enim habens fidem potest aliquod peccatum committere in actu quem non refert ad fidei finem, vel venialiter vel etiam mortaliter peccando; ita etiam infidelis potest aliquem actum bonum facere in eo quod non refert ad finem infidelitatis.

**AD PRIMUM** ergo dicendum quod verbum illud est intelligendum vel quia vita infidelium non potest esse sine peccato, cum peccata sine fide non tollantur. Vel quia quidquid agunt ex infidelitate peccatum est. Unde ibi subditur, *quia omnis infideliter vivens vel agens vehementer peccat.*

**AD SECUNDUM** dicendum quod fides dirigit intentionem respectu finis ultimi supernaturalis. Sed lumen etiam naturalis rationis potest dirigere intentionem respectu alicuius boni connaturalis.

**AD TERTIUM** dicendum quod per infidelitatem non corrumpitur totaliter in infidelibus ratio naturalis, quin remaneat in eis aliqua veri cognitio, per quam possunt facere aliquod opus de genere bonorum. De Cornelio tamen sciendum est quod infidelis non erat, alioquin eius operatio accepta non fuisset Deo, cui sine fide nullus potest placere. Habebat autem fidem implicitam, nondum manifestata Evangelii veritate. Unde ut eum in fide plene instrueret, mittitur ad eum Petrus.

a certain extent, do those good works for which the good of nature suffices.

Hence it does not follow that they sin in everything they do; but whenever they do anything out of their unbelief, then they sin. For even as one who has the faith, can commit an actual sin, venial or even mortal, which he does not refer to the end of faith, so too, an unbeliever can do a good deed in a matter which he does not refer to the end of his unbelief.

**REPLY OBJ. 1**: The words quoted must be taken to mean either that the life of unbelievers cannot be sinless, since without faith no sin is taken away, or that whatever they do out of unbelief, is a sin. Hence the same authority adds: *Because every one that lives or acts according to his unbelief, sins grievously.*

**REPLY OBJ. 2**: Faith directs the intention with regard to the supernatural last end: but even the light of natural reason can direct the intention in respect of a connatural good.

**REPLY OBJ. 3**: Unbelief does not so wholly destroy natural reason in unbelievers, but that some knowledge of the truth remains in them, whereby they are able to do deeds that are generically good. With regard, however, to Cornelius, it is to be observed that he was not an unbeliever, else his works would not have been acceptable to God, whom none can please without faith. Now he had implicit faith, as the truth of the Gospel was not yet made manifest: hence Peter was sent to him to give him fuller instruction in the faith.

# Article 5

*Whether there are several species of unbelief?*

**AD QUINTUM SIC PROCEDITUR**. Videtur quod non sint plures infidelitatis species. Cum enim fides et infidelitas sint contraria, oportet quod sint circa idem. Sed formale obiectum fidei est veritas prima, a qua habet unitatem, licet multa materialiter credat. Ergo etiam obiectum infidelitatis est veritas prima, ea vero quae discredit infidelis materialiter se habent in infidelitate. Sed differentia secundum speciem non attenditur secundum principia materialia, sed secundum principia formalia. Ergo infidelitatis non sunt diversae species secundum diversitatem eorum in quibus infideles errant.

**PRAETEREA**, infinitis modis potest aliquis a veritate fidei deviare. Si igitur secundum diversitates errorum diversae species infidelitatis assignentur, videtur sequi quod sint infinitae infidelitatis species. Et ita huiusmodi species non sunt considerandae.

**OBJECTION 1**: It would seem that there are not several species of unbelief. For, since faith and unbelief are contrary to one another, they must be about the same thing. Now the formal object of faith is the First Truth, whence it derives its unity, although its matter contains many points of belief. Therefore the object of unbelief also is the First Truth; while the things which an unbeliever disbelieves are the matter of his unbelief. Now the specific difference depends not on material but on formal principles. Therefore there are not several species of unbelief, according to the various points which the unbeliever disbelieves.

**OBJ. 2**: Further, it is possible to stray from the truth of faith in an infinite number of ways. If therefore the various species of unbelief correspond to the number of various errors, it would seem to follow that there is an infinite number of species of unbelief, and consequently, that we ought not to make these species the object of our consideration.

**PRAETEREA**, idem non invenitur in diversis speciebus. Sed contingit aliquem esse infidelem ex eo quod errat circa diversa. Ergo diversitas errorum non facit diversas species infidelitatis. Sic igitur infidelitatis non sunt plures species.

**SED CONTRA** est quod unicuique virtuti opponuntur plures species vitiorum, *bonum* enim *contingit uno modo, malum vero multipliciter*, ut patet per Dionysium, IV cap. de Div. Nom., et per Philosophum, in II Ethic. Sed fides est una virtus. Ergo ei opponuntur plures infidelitatis species.

**RESPONDEO** dicendum quod quaelibet virtus consistit in hoc quod attingat regulam aliquam cognitionis vel operationis humanae, ut supra dictum est. Attingere autem regulam est uno modo circa unam materiam, sed a regula deviare contingit multipliciter. Et ideo uni virtuti multa vitia opponuntur. Diversitas autem vitiorum quae unicuique virtuti opponitur potest considerari dupliciter. Uno modo, secundum diversam habitudinem ad virtutem. Et secundum hoc determinatae sunt quaedam species vitiorum quae opponuntur virtuti, sicut virtuti morali opponitur unum vitium secundum excessum ad virtutem, et aliud vitium secundum defectum a virtute. Alio modo potest considerari diversitas vitiorum oppositorum uni virtuti secundum corruptionem diversorum quae ad virtutem requiruntur. Et secundum hoc uni virtuti, puta temperantiae vel fortitudini, opponuntur infinita vitia, secundum quod infinitis modis contingit diversas circumstantias virtutis corrumpi, ut a rectitudine virtutis recedatur. Unde et Pythagorici malum posuerunt infinitum.

Sic ergo dicendum est quod, si infidelitas attendatur secundum comparationem ad fidem, diversae sunt infidelitatis species et numero determinatae. Cum enim peccatum infidelitatis consistat in renitendo fidei, hoc potest contingere dupliciter. Quia aut renititur fidei nondum susceptae, et talis est infidelitas Paganorum sive gentilium. Aut renititur fidei Christianae susceptae, vel in figura, et sic est infidelitas Iudaeorum; vel in ipsa manifestatione veritatis, et sic est infidelitas haereticorum. Unde in generali possunt assignari tres praedictae species infidelitatis.

Si vero distinguantur infidelitatis species secundum errorem in diversis quae ad fidem pertinent, sic non sunt determinatae infidelitatis species, possunt enim errores in infinitum multiplicari, ut patet per Augustinum, in libro de haeresibus.

**AD PRIMUM** ergo dicendum quod formalis ratio alicuius peccati potest accipi dupliciter. Uno modo, secundum intentionem peccantis, et sic id ad quod convertitur peccans est formale obiectum peccati; et ex hoc diversificantur eius species. Alio modo, secundum rationem mali, et sic illud bonum a quo receditur est formale obiectum peccati; sed ex hac parte peccatum

**OBJ. 3**: Further, the same thing does not belong to different species. Now a man may be an unbeliever through erring about different points of truth. Therefore diversity of errors does not make a diversity of species of unbelief: and so there are not several species of unbelief.

**ON THE CONTRARY**, Several species of vice are opposed to each virtue, because *good happens in one way, but evil in many ways*, according to Dionysius (*Div. Nom.* iv) and the Philosopher (*Ethic.* ii, 6). Now faith is a virtue. Therefore several species of vice are opposed to it.

**I ANSWER THAT**, As stated above (I-II, Q. 55, A. 4; I-II, Q. 64, A. 1), every virtue consists in following some rule of human knowledge or operation. Now conformity to a rule happens one way in one matter, whereas a breach of the rule happens in many ways, so that many vices are opposed to one virtue. The diversity of the vices that are opposed to each virtue may be considered in two ways, first, with regard to their different relations to the virtue: and in this way there are determinate species of vices contrary to a virtue: thus to a moral virtue one vice is opposed by exceeding the virtue, and another, by falling short of the virtue. Second, the diversity of vices opposed to one virtue may be considered in respect of the corruption of the various conditions required for that virtue. In this way an infinite number of vices are opposed to one virtue, e.g., temperance or fortitude, according to the infinite number of ways in which the various circumstances of a virtue may be corrupted, so that the rectitude of virtue is forsaken. For this reason the Pythagoreans held evil to be infinite.

Accordingly we must say that if unbelief be considered in comparison to faith, there are several species of unbelief, determinate in number. For, since the sin of unbelief consists in resisting the faith, this may happen in two ways: either the faith is resisted before it has been accepted, and such is the unbelief of pagans or heathens; or the Christian faith is resisted after it has been accepted, and this either in the figure, and such is the unbelief of the Jews, or in the very manifestation of truth, and such is the unbelief of heretics. Hence we may, in a general way, reckon these three as species of unbelief.

If, however, the species of unbelief be distinguished according to the various errors that occur in matters of faith, there are not determinate species of unbelief: for errors can be multiplied indefinitely, as Augustine observes (*De Haeresibus*).

**REPLY OBJ. 1**: The formal aspect of a sin can be considered in two ways. First, according to the intention of the sinner, in which case the thing to which the sinner turns is the formal object of his sin, and determines the various species of that sin. Second, it may be considered as an evil, and in this case the good which is forsaken is the formal object of the sin; which however does not derive its species

non habet speciem, immo privatio est speciei. Sic igitur dicendum est quod infidelitatis obiectum est veritas prima sicut a qua recedit, sed formale eius obiectum sicut ad quod convertitur est sententia falsa quam sequitur; et ex hac parte eius species diversificantur. Unde sicut caritas est una, quae inhaeret summo bono, sunt autem diversa vitia caritati opposita, quae per conversionem ad diversa bona temporalia recedunt ab uno summo bono, et iterum secundum diversas habitudines inordinatas ad Deum; ita etiam fides est una virtus, ex hoc quod adhaeret uni primae veritati; sed infidelitatis species sunt multae, ex hoc quod infideles diversas falsas sententias sequuntur.

AD SECUNDUM dicendum quod obiectio illa procedit de distinctione specierum infidelitatis secundum diversa in quibus erratur.

AD TERTIUM dicendum quod sicut fides est una quia multa credit in ordine ad unum, ita infidelitas potest esse una, etiam si in multis erret, inquantum omnia habent ordinem ad unum. Nihil tamen prohibet hominem diversis infidelitatis speciebus errare, sicut etiam potest unus homo diversis vitiis subiacere et diversis corporalibus morbis.

from this point of view, in fact it is a privation. We must therefore reply that the object of unbelief is the First Truth considered as that which unbelief forsakes, but its formal aspect, considered as that to which unbelief turns, is the false opinion that it follows: and it is from this point of view that unbelief derives its various species. Hence, even as charity is one, because it adheres to the Sovereign Good, while there are various species of vice opposed to charity, which turn away from the Sovereign Good by turning to various temporal goods, and also in respect of various inordinate relations to God, so too, faith is one virtue through adhering to the one First Truth, yet there are many species of unbelief, because unbelievers follow many false opinions.

REPLY OBJ. 2: This argument considers the various species of unbelief according to various points in which errors occur.

REPLY OBJ. 3: Since faith is one because it believes in many things in relation to one, so may unbelief, although it errs in many things, be one insofar as all those things are related to one. Yet nothing hinders one man from erring in various species of unbelief, even as one man may be subject to various vices, and to various bodily diseases.

# Article 6

*Whether the unbelief of pagans or heathens is graver than other kinds?*

AD SEXTUM SIC PROCEDITUR. Videtur quod infidelitas gentilium sive Paganorum sit gravior ceteris. Sicut enim corporalis morbus tanto est gravior quanto saluti principalioris membri contrariatur, ita peccatum tanto videtur esse gravius quanto contrariatur ei quod est principalius in virtute. Sed principalius in fide est fides unitatis divinae, a qua deficiunt gentiles, multitudinem deorum credentes. Ergo eorum infidelitas est gravissima.

PRAETEREA, inter haereticos tanto haeresis aliquorum detestabilior est quanto in pluribus et principalioribus veritati fidei contradicunt, sicut haeresis Arii, qui separavit divinitatem, detestabilior fuit quam haeresis Nestorii, qui separavit humanitatem Christi a persona filii Dei. Sed gentiles in pluribus et principalioribus recedunt a fide quam Iudaei et haeretici, quia omnino nihil de fide recipiunt. Ergo eorum infidelitas est gravissima.

PRAETEREA, omne bonum est diminutivum mali. Sed aliquod bonum est in Iudaeis, quia confitentur vetus testamentum esse a Deo. Bonum etiam est in haereticis, quia venerantur novum testamentum. Ergo minus peccant quam gentiles, qui utrumque testamentum detestantur.

OBJECTION 1: It would seem that the unbelief of heathens or pagans is graver than other kinds. For just as bodily disease is graver according as it endangers the health of a more important member of the body, so does sin appear to be graver, according as it is opposed to that which holds a more important place in virtue. Now that which is most important in faith, is belief in the unity of God, from which the heathens deviate by believing in many gods. Therefore their unbelief is the gravest of all.

OBJ. 2: Further, among heresies, the more detestable are those which contradict the truth of faith in more numerous and more important points: thus, the heresy of Arius, who severed the Godhead, was more detestable than that of Nestorius who severed the humanity of Christ from the Person of God the Son. Now the heathens deny the faith in more numerous and more important points than Jews and heretics; since they do not accept the faith at all. Therefore their unbelief is the gravest.

OBJ. 3: Further, every good diminishes evil. Now there is some good in the Jews, since they believe in the Old Testament as being from God, and there is some good in heretics, since they venerate the New Testament. Therefore they sin less grievously than heathens, who receive neither Testament.

**Sed contra** est quod dicitur II Pet. II, *melius erat illis non cognoscere viam iustitiae quam post cognitam retrorsum converti.* Sed gentiles non cognoverunt viam iustitiae, haeretici autem et Iudaei aliqualiter cognoscentes deseruerunt. Ergo eorum peccatum est gravius.

**Respondeo** dicendum quod in infidelitate, sicut dictum est, duo possunt considerari. Quorum unum est comparatio eius ad fidem. Et ex hac parte aliquis gravius contra fidem peccat qui fidei renititur quam suscepit quam qui renititur fidei nondum susceptae, sicut gravius peccat qui non implet quod promisit quam si non impleat quod nunquam promisit. Et secundum hoc infidelitas haereticorum, qui profitentur fidem Evangelii et ei renituntur corrumpentes ipsam, gravius peccant quam Iudaei, qui fidem Evangelii nunquam susceperunt. Sed quia susceperunt eius figuram in veteri lege, quam male interpretantes corrumpunt, ideo etiam ipsorum infidelitas est gravius peccatum quam infidelitas gentilium, qui nullo modo fidem Evangelii susceperunt.

Aliud quod in infidelitate consideratur est corruptio eorum quae ad fidem pertinent. Et secundum hoc, cum in pluribus errent gentiles quam Iudaei, et Iudaei quam haeretici, gravior est infidelitas gentilium quam Iudaeorum, et Iudaeorum quam haereticorum, nisi forte quorundam, puta Manichaeorum, qui etiam circa credibilia plus errant quam gentiles.

Harum tamen duarum gravitatum prima praeponderat secundae quantum ad rationem culpae. Quia infidelitas habet rationem culpae, ut supra dictum est, magis ex hoc quod renititur fidei quam ex hoc quod non habet ea quae fidei sunt, hoc enim videtur, ut dictum est, magis ad rationem poenae pertinere unde, simpliciter loquendo, infidelitas haereticorum est pessima.

**Et per hoc** patet responsio ad obiecta.

**On the contrary,** It is written (2 Pet 2:21): *It had been better for them not to have known the way of justice, than after they have known it, to turn back.* Now the heathens have not known the way of justice, whereas heretics and Jews have abandoned it after knowing it in some way. Therefore theirs is the graver sin.

**I answer that,** As stated above (A. 5), two things may be considered in unbelief. One of these is its relation to faith: and from this point of view, he who resists the faith after accepting it, sins more grievously against faith, than he who resists it without having accepted it, even as he who fails to fulfill what he has promised, sins more grievously than if he had never promised it. In this way the unbelief of heretics, who confess their belief in the Gospel, and resist that faith by corrupting it, is a more grievous sin than that of the Jews, who have never accepted the Gospel faith. Since, however, they accepted the figure of that faith in the Old Law, which they corrupt by their false interpretations, their unbelief is a more grievous sin than that of the heathens, because the latter have not accepted the Gospel faith in any way at all.

The second thing to be considered in unbelief is the corruption of matters of faith. In this respect, since heathens err on more points than Jews, and these in more points than heretics, the unbelief of heathens is more grievous than the unbelief of the Jews, and that of the Jews than that of the heretics, except in such cases as that of the Manichees, who, in matters of faith, err even more than heathens do.

Of these two gravities the first surpasses the second from the point of view of guilt; since, as stated above (A. 1) unbelief has the character of guilt, from its resisting faith rather than from the mere absence of faith, for the latter as was stated (A. 1) seems rather to bear the character of punishment. Hence, speaking absolutely, the unbelief of heretics is the worst.

**This suffices** for the Replies to the Objections.

# Article 7

*Whether one ought to dispute with unbelievers in public?*

**Ad septimum sic proceditur.** Videtur quod non sit cum infidelibus publice disputandum. Dicit enim apostolus, II ad Tim. II, *noli verbis contendere, ad nihilum enim utile est nisi ad subversionem audientium.* Sed disputatio publica cum infidelibus fieri non potest sine contentione verborum. Ergo non est publice disputandum cum infidelibus.

**Praeterea,** lex Marciani Augusti, per canones confirmata, sic dicit, *iniuriam facit iudicio religiosissimae synodi, si quis semel iudicata ac recte disposita revolvere et publice disputare contendit.* Sed omnia quae ad fidem

**Objection 1:** It would seem that one ought not to dispute with unbelievers in public. For the Apostle says (2 Tim 2:14): *Contend not in words, for it is to no profit, but to the subverting of the hearers.* But it is impossible to dispute with unbelievers publicly without contending in words. Therefore one ought not to dispute publicly with unbelievers.

**Obj. 2:** Further, the law of Martianus Augustus confirmed by the canons expresses itself thus: *It is an insult to the judgment of the most religious synod, if anyone ventures to debate or dispute in public about matters which have once*

pertinent sunt per sacra Concilia determinata. Ergo graviter peccat, iniuriam synodo faciens, si quis de his quae sunt fidei publice disputare praesumat.

**PRAETEREA**, disputatio argumentis aliquibus agitur. Sed argumentum est ratio rei dubiae faciens fidem. Ea autem quae sunt fidei, cum sint certissima, non sunt in dubitationem adducenda. Ergo de his quae sunt fidei non est publice disputandum.

**SED CONTRA** est quod Act. IX dicitur quod *Saulus invalescebat et confundebat Iudaeos; et quod loquebatur gentibus et disputabat cum Graecis.*

**RESPONDEO** dicendum quod in disputatione fidei duo sunt consideranda, unum quidem ex parte disputantis; aliud autem ex parte audientium. Ex parte quidem disputantis est consideranda intentio. Si enim disputet tanquam de fide dubitans, et veritatem fidei pro certo non supponens, sed argumentis experiri intendens, procul dubio peccat, tanquam dubius in fide et infidelis. Si autem disputet aliquis de fide ad confutandum errores, vel etiam ad exercitium, laudabile est.

Ex parte vero audientium considerandum est utrum illi qui disputationem audiunt sint instructi et firmi in fide, aut simplices et in fide titubantes. Et coram quidem sapientibus in fide firmis nullum periculum est disputare de fide. Sed circa simplices est distinguendum. Quia aut sunt sollicitati sive pulsati ab infidelibus, puta Iudaeis vel haereticis sive Paganis, nitentibus corrumpere in eis fidem, aut omnino non sunt sollicitati super hoc, sicut in terris in quibus non sunt infideles.

In primo casu necessarium est publice disputare de fide, dummodo inveniantur aliqui ad hoc sufficientes et idonei, qui errores confutare possint. Per hoc enim simplices in fide firmabuntur; et tolletur infidelibus decipiendi facultas; et ipsa taciturnitas eorum qui resistere deberent pervertentibus fidei veritatem esset erroris confirmatio. Unde Gregorius, in II Pastoral., *sicut incauta locutio in errorem pertrahit, ita indiscretum silentium eos qui erudiri poterant in errore derelinquit.*

In secundo vero casu periculosum est publice disputare de fide coram simplicibus; quorum fides ex hoc est firmior quod nihil diversum audierunt ab eo quod credunt. Et ideo non expedit eis ut verba infidelium audiant disceptantium contra fidem.

**AD PRIMUM** ergo dicendum quod apostolus non prohibet totaliter disputationem, sed inordinatam, quae magis fit contentione verborum quam firmitate sententiarum.

*been judged and disposed of.* Now all matters of faith have been decided by the holy councils. Therefore it is an insult to the councils, and consequently a grave sin to presume to dispute in public about matters of faith.

**OBJ. 3**: Further, disputations are conducted by means of arguments. But an argument is a reason in settlement of a dubious matter: whereas things that are of faith, being most certain, ought not to be a matter of doubt. Therefore one ought not to dispute in public about matters of faith.

**ON THE CONTRARY**, It is written (Acts 9:22, 29) that *Saul increased much more in strength, and confounded the Jews,* and that *he spoke . . . to the gentiles and disputed with the Greeks.*

**I ANSWER THAT**, In disputing about the faith, two things must be observed: one on the part of the disputant; the other on the part of his hearers. On the part of the disputant, we must consider his intention. For if he were to dispute as though he had doubts about the faith, and did not hold the truth of faith for certain, and as though he intended to probe it with arguments, without doubt he would sin, as being doubtful of the faith and an unbeliever. On the other hand, it is praiseworthy to dispute about the faith in order to confute errors, or for practice.

On the part of the hearers we must consider whether those who hear the disputation are instructed and firm in the faith, or simple and wavering. As to those who are well instructed and firm in the faith, there can be no danger in disputing about the faith in their presence. But as to simple-minded people, we must make a distinction; because either they are provoked and molested by unbelievers, for instance, Jews or heretics, or pagans who strive to corrupt the faith in them, or else they are not subject to provocation in this matter, as in those countries where there are no unbelievers.

In the first case it is necessary to dispute in public about the faith, provided there be those who are equal and adapted to the task of confuting errors; since in this way simple people are strengthened in the faith, and unbelievers are deprived of the opportunity to deceive, while if those who ought to withstand the perverters of the truth of faith were silent, this would tend to strengthen error. Hence Gregory says (*Pastor.* ii, 4): *Even as a thoughtless speech gives rise to error, so does an indiscreet silence leave those in error who might have been instructed.*

On the other hand, in the second case it is dangerous to dispute in public about the faith, in the presence of simple people, whose faith for this very reason is more firm, that they have never heard anything differing from what they believe. Hence it is not expedient for them to hear what unbelievers have to say against the faith.

**REPLY OBJ. 1**: The Apostle does not entirely forbid disputations, but such as are inordinate, and consist of contentious words rather than of sound speeches.

**Ad secundum** dicendum quod lex illa prohibet publicam disputationem de fide quae procedit ex dubitatione fidei, non autem illam quae est ad fidei conservationem.

**Ad tertium** dicendum quod non debet disputari de his quae sunt fidei quasi de eis dubitando, sed propter veritatem manifestandam et errores confutandos. Oportet enim ad fidei confirmationem aliquando cum infidelibus disputare, quandoque quidem defendendo fidem, secundum illud I Pet. III, *parati semper ad satisfactionem omni poscenti vos rationem de ea quae est in vobis spe et fide*; quandoque autem ad convincendos errantes, secundum illud ad Tit. I, *ut sit potens exhortari in doctrina sana, et eos qui contradicunt arguere.*

**Reply Obj. 2**: That law forbade those public disputations about the faith, which arise from doubting the faith, but not those which are for the safeguarding thereof.

**Reply Obj. 3**: One ought to dispute about matters of faith, not as though one doubted about them, but in order to make the truth known, and to confute errors. For, in order to confirm the faith, it is necessary sometimes to dispute with unbelievers, sometimes by defending the faith, according to 1 Pet. 3:15: *Being ready always to satisfy everyone that asketh you a reason of that hope and faith which is in you.* Sometimes again, it is necessary, in order to convince those who are in error, according to Titus 1:9: *That he may be able to exhort in sound doctrine and to convince the gainsayers.*

# Article 8

*Whether unbelievers ought to be compelled to the faith?*

**Ad octavum sic proceditur.** Videtur quod infideles nullo modo compellendi sint ad fidem. Dicitur enim Matth. XIII quod servi patrisfamilias in cuius agro erant zizania seminata quaesierunt ab eo, *vis imus et colligimus ea?* Et ipse respondit, *non, ne forte, colligentes zizania, eradicetis simul cum eis triticum.* Ubi dicit Chrysostomus, *haec dixit dominus prohibens occisiones fieri. Nec enim oportet interficere haereticos, quia si eos occideritis, necesse est multos sanctorum simul subverti.* Ergo videtur quod pari ratione nec aliqui infideles sint ad fidem cogendi.

**Praeterea,** in Decretis, dist. XLV, sic dicitur, *de Iudaeis praecepit sancta synodus nemini deinceps ad credendum vim inferre.* Ergo pari ratione nec alii infideles sunt ad fidem cogendi.

**Praeterea,** Augustinus dicit quod cetera potest homo nolens, *credere nonnisi volens.* Sed voluntas cogi non potest. Ergo videtur quod infideles non sint ad fidem cogendi.

**Praeterea,** Ezech. XVIII dicitur ex persona Dei, *nolo mortem peccatoris.* Sed nos debemus voluntatem nostram conformare divinae, ut supra dictum est. Ergo etiam nos non debemus velle quod infideles occidantur.

**Sed contra** est quod dicitur Luc. XIV, *exi in vias et saepes et compelle intrare, ut impleatur domus mea.* Sed homines in domum Dei, idest in Ecclesiam, intrant per fidem. Ergo aliqui sunt compellendi ad fidem.

**Objection 1**: It would seem that unbelievers ought by no means to be compelled to the faith. For it is written (Matt 13:28) that the servants of the householder, in whose field cockle had been sown, asked him: *Wilt thou that we go and gather it up?* and that he answered: *No, lest perhaps gathering up the cockle, you root up the wheat also together with it*: on which passage Chrysostom says (*Hom. xlvi in Matth.*): *Our Lord says this so as to forbid the slaying of men. For it is not right to slay heretics, because if you do you will necessarily slay many innocent persons.* Therefore it seems that for the same reason unbelievers ought not to be compelled to the faith.

**Obj. 2**: Further, we read in the Decretals (*Dist. xlv can., De Judaeis*): *The holy synod prescribes, with regard to the Jews, that for the future, none are to be compelled to believe.* Therefore, in like manner, neither should unbelievers be compelled to the faith.

**Obj. 3**: Further, Augustine says (*Tract. xxvi in Joan.*) that it is possible for a man to do other things against his will, but *he cannot believe unless he is willing.* Therefore it seems that unbelievers ought not to be compelled to the faith.

**Obj. 4**: It is said in God's person (Ezek 18:32 ): *I desire not the death of the sinner.* Now we ought to conform our will to the Divine will, as stated above (I-II, Q. 19, AA. 9, 10). Therefore we should not even wish unbelievers to be put to death.

**On the contrary**, It is written (Luke 14:23): *Go out into the highways and hedges, and compel them to come into my house.* Now men enter into the house of God, i.e., into Holy Church, by faith. Therefore some ought to be compelled to the faith.

RESPONDEO dicendum quod infidelium quidam sunt qui nunquam susceperunt fidem, sicut gentiles et Iudaei. Et tales nullo modo sunt ad fidem compellendi, ut ipsi credant, quia credere voluntatis est. Sunt tamen compellendi a fidelibus, si facultas adsit, ut fidem non impediant vel blasphemiis, vel malis persuasionibus, vel etiam apertis persecutionibus. Et propter hoc fideles Christi frequenter contra infideles bellum movent, non quidem ut eos ad credendum cogant (quia si etiam eos vicissent et captivos haberent, in eorum libertate relinquerent an credere vellent), sed propter hoc ut eos compellant ne fidem Christi impediant.

Alii vero sunt infideles qui quandoque fidem susceperunt et eam profitentur, sicut haeretici vel quicumque apostatae. Et tales sunt etiam corporaliter compellendi ut impleant quod promiserunt et teneant quod semel susceperunt.

AD PRIMUM ergo dicendum quod per illam auctoritatem quidam intellexerunt esse prohibitam non quidem excommunicationem haereticorum, sed eorum occisionem, ut patet per auctoritatem Chrysostomi inductam. Et Augustinus, ad Vincentium, de se dicit, *haec primitus mea sententia erat, neminem ad unitatem Christi esse cogendum, verbo esse agendum, disputatione pugnandum. Sed haec opinio mea non contradicentium verbis, sed demonstrantium superatur exemplis. Legum enim terror ita profuit ut multi dicant, gratias domino, qui vincula nostra dirupit.* Quod ergo dominus dicit, *sinite utraque crescere usque ad messem,* qualiter intelligendum sit apparet ex hoc quod subditur, *ne forte, colligentes zizania, eradicetis simul cum eis et triticum.* Ubi satis ostendit, sicut Augustinus dicit (contra Epist. Parmen.), *cum metus iste non subest, idest quando ita cuiusque crimen notum est et omnibus execrabile apparet ut vel nullos prorsus, vel non tales habeat defensores per quos possit schisma contingere, non dormiat severitas disciplinae.*

AD SECUNDUM dicendum quod Iudaei, si nullo modo susceperunt fidem, non sunt cogendi ad fidem. Si autem susceperunt fidem, *oportet ut fidem necessitate cogantur retinere,* sicut in eodem capitulo dicitur.

AD TERTIUM dicendum quod, sicut *vovere est voluntatis,* reddere autem est necessitatis, ita accipere fidem est voluntatis, sed tenere iam acceptam est necessitatis. Et ideo haeretici sunt compellendi ut fidem teneant. Dicit enim Augustinus, ad Bonifacium comitem, *ubi est quod isti clamare consueverunt, liberum est credere vel non credere, cui vim Christus intulit? Agnoscant in Paulo prius cogentem Christum et postea docentem.*

AD QUARTUM dicendum quod, sicut in eadem epistola Augustinus dicit, *nullus nostrum vult aliquem*

I ANSWER THAT, Among unbelievers there are some who have never received the faith, such as the heathens and the Jews: and these are by no means to be compelled to the faith, in order that they may believe, because to believe depends on the will: nevertheless they should be compelled by the faithful, if it be possible to do so, so that they do not hinder the faith, by their blasphemies, or by their evil persuasions, or even by their open persecutions. It is for this reason that Christ's faithful often wage war with unbelievers, not indeed for the purpose of forcing them to believe, because even if they were to conquer them, and take them prisoners, they should still leave them free to believe, if they will, but in order to prevent them from hindering the faith of Christ.

On the other hand, there are unbelievers who at some time have accepted the faith, and professed it, such as heretics and all apostates: such should be submitted even to bodily compulsion, that they may fulfill what they have promised, and hold what they, at one time, received.

REPLY OBJ. 1: Some have understood the authority quoted to forbid, not the excommunication but the slaying of heretics, as appears from the words of Chrysostom. Augustine too, says (*Ep. ad Vincent. xciii*) of himself: *It was once my opinion that none should be compelled to union with Christ, that we should deal in words, and fight with arguments. However this opinion of mine is undone, not by words of contradiction, but by convincing examples. Because fear of the law was so profitable, that many say: Thanks be to the Lord Who has broken our chains asunder.* Accordingly the meaning of Our Lord's words, *Suffer both to grow until the harvest,* must be gathered from those which precede, *lest perhaps gathering up the cockle, you root the wheat also together with it.* For, Augustine says (*Contra Ep. Parmen.* iii, 2) *these words show that when this is not to be feared, that is to say, when a man's crime is so publicly known, and so hateful to all, that he has no defenders, or none such as might cause a schism, the severity of discipline should not slacken.*

REPLY OBJ. 2: Those Jews who have in no way received the faith, ought not by no means to be compelled to the faith: if, however, they have received it, *they ought to be compelled to keep it,* as is stated in the same chapter.

REPLY OBJ. 3: Just as *taking a vow is a matter of will,* and keeping a vow, a matter of obligation, so acceptance of the faith is a matter of the will, whereas keeping the faith, once one has received it, is a matter of obligation. Wherefore heretics should be compelled to keep the faith. Thus Augustine says to the Count Boniface (*Ep. clxxxv*): *What do these people mean by crying out continually: 'We may believe or not believe just as we choose. Whom did Christ compel?' They should remember that Christ at first compelled Paul and afterwards taught Him.*

REPLY OBJ. 4: As Augustine says in the same letter, *none of us wishes any heretic to perish. But the house of*

*haereticum perire. Sed aliter non meruit habere pacem domus David, nisi Absalom filius eius in bello quod contra patrem gerebat fuisset extinctus. Sic Ecclesia Catholica, si aliquorum perditione ceteros colligit, dolorem materni sanat cordis tantorum liberatione populorum.*

*David did not deserve to have peace, unless his son Absalom had been killed in the war which he had raised against his father. Thus if the Catholic Church gathers together some of the perdition of others, she heals the sorrow of her maternal heart by the delivery of so many nations.*

# Article 9

*Whether it is lawful to communicate with unbelievers?*

**AD NONUM SIC PROCEDITUR**. Videtur quod cum infidelibus possit communicari. Dicit enim apostolus, I ad Cor. X, *si quis vocat vos infidelium ad coenam, et vultis ire, omne quod vobis apponitur manducate.* Et Chrysostomus dicit, *ad mensam Paganorum si volueris ire, sine ulla prohibitione permittimus.* Sed ad coenam alicuius ire est ei communicare. Ergo licet infidelibus communicare.

**PRAETEREA**, apostolus dicit, I ad Cor. V, *quid mihi est de his qui foris sunt iudicare?* Foris autem sunt infideles. Cum igitur per iudicium Ecclesiae aliquorum communio fidelibus inhibeatur, videtur quod non sit inhibendum fidelibus cum infidelibus communicare.

**PRAETEREA**, dominus non potest uti servo nisi ei communicando saltem verbo, quia dominus movet servum per imperium. Sed Christiani possunt habere servos infideles, vel Iudaeos vel etiam Paganos sive Saracenos. Ergo possunt licite cum eis communicare.

**SED CONTRA** est quod dicitur Deut. VII, *non inibis cum eis foedus, nec misereberis eorum, neque sociabis cum eis connubia.* Et super illud Lev. XV, *mulier quae redeunte mense* etc., dicit Glossa, *sic oportet ab idololatria abstinere ut nec idololatras nec eorum discipulos contingamus, nec cum eis communionem habeamus.*

**RESPONDEO** dicendum quod communio alicuius personae interdicitur fidelibus dupliciter, uno modo, in poenam illius cui communio fidelium subtrahitur; alio modo, ad cautelam eorum quibus interdicitur ne alii communicent. Et utraque causa ex verbis apostoli accipi potest, I ad Cor. V. Nam postquam sententiam excommunicationis protulit, subdit pro ratione, *nescitis quia modicum fermentum totam massam corrumpit?* Et postea rationem subdit ex parte poenae per iudicium Ecclesiae illatae, cum dicit, *nonne de his qui intus sunt vos iudicatis?*

Primo igitur modo non interdicit Ecclesia fidelibus communionem infidelium qui nullo modo fidem Christianam receperunt, scilicet Paganorum vel Iudaeorum,

**OBJECTION 1**: It would seem that it is lawful to communicate with unbelievers. For the Apostle says (1 Cor 10:27): *If any of them that believe not, invite you, and you be willing to go, eat of anything that is set before you.* And Chrysostom says (*Hom. xxv super Epist. ad Heb.*): *If you wish to go to dine with pagans, we permit it without any reservation.* Now to sit at table with anyone is to communicate with him. Therefore it is lawful to communicate with unbelievers.

**OBJ. 2**: Further, the Apostle says (1 Cor 5:12): *What have I to do to judge them that are without?* Now unbelievers are without. When, therefore, the Church forbids the faithful to communicate with certain people, it seems that they ought not to be forbidden to communicate with unbelievers.

**OBJ. 3**: Further, a master cannot employ his servant, unless he communicate with him, at least by word, since the master moves his servant by command. Now Christians can have unbelievers, either Jews, or pagans, or Saracens, for servants. Therefore they can lawfully communicate with them.

**ON THE CONTRARY**, It is written (Deut 7:2, 3): *Thou shalt make no league with them, nor show mercy to them; neither shalt thou make marriages with them*: and a gloss on Lev. 15:19, *The woman who at the return of the month,* etc. says: *It is so necessary to shun idolatry, that we should not come in touch with idolaters or their disciples, nor have any dealings with them.*

**I ANSWER THAT**, Communication with a particular person is forbidden to the faithful, in two ways: first, as a punishment of the person with whom they are forbidden to communicate; second, for the safety of those who are forbidden to communicate with others. Both motives can be gathered from the Apostle's words (1 Cor 5:6). For after he had pronounced sentence of excommunication, he adds as his reason: *Know you not that a little leaven corrupts the whole lump?* and afterwards he adds the reason on the part of the punishment inflicted by the sentence of the Church when he says (1 Cor 5:12): *Do not you judge them that are within?*

Accordingly, in the first way the Church does not forbid the faithful to communicate with unbelievers, who have not in any way received the Christian faith, viz. with pagans

quia non habet de eis iudicare spirituali iudicio, sed temporali, in casu cum, inter Christianos commorantes, aliquam culpam committunt et per fideles temporaliter puniuntur. Sed isto modo, scilicet in poenam, interdicit Ecclesia fidelibus communionem illorum infidelium qui a fide suscepta deviant, vel corrumpendo fidem, sicut haeretici, vel etiam totaliter a fide recedendo, sicut apostatae. In utrosque enim horum excommunicationis sententiam profert Ecclesia.

Sed quantum ad secundum modum, videtur esse distinguendum secundum diversas conditiones personarum et negotiorum et temporum. Si enim aliqui fuerint firmi in fide, ita quod ex communione eorum cum infidelibus conversio infidelium magis sperari possit quam fidelium a fide aversio; non sunt prohibendi infidelibus communicare qui fidem non susceperunt, scilicet Paganis vel Iudaeis, et maxime si necessitas urgeat. Si autem sint simplices et infirmi in fide, de quorum subversione probabiliter timeri possit, prohibendi sunt ab infidelium communione, et praecipue ne magnam familiaritatem cum eis habeant, vel absque necessitate eis communicent.

**AD PRIMUM** ergo dicendum quod dominus illud praecipit de illis gentibus quarum terram ingressuri erant Iudaei, qui erant proni ad idololatriam, et ideo timendum erat ne per continuam conversationem cum eis alienarentur a fide. Et ideo ibidem subditur, *quia seducet filium tuum ne sequatur me.*

**AD SECUNDUM** dicendum quod Ecclesia in infideles non habet iudicium quoad poenam spiritualem eis infligendam. Habet tamen iudicium super aliquos infideles quoad temporalem poenam infligendam, ad quod pertinet quod Ecclesia aliquando, propter aliquas speciales culpas, subtrahit aliquibus infidelibus communionem fidelium.

**AD TERTIUM** dicendum quod magis est probabile quod servus, qui regitur imperio domini, convertatur ad fidem domini fidelis, quam e converso. Et ideo non est prohibitum quin fideles habeant servos infideles. Si tamen domino periculum immineret ex communione talis servi, deberet eum a se abiicere, secundum illud mandatum domini, Matth. V et XVIII, *si pes tuus scandalizaverit te, abscinde eum et proiice abs te.*

and Jews, because she has not the right to exercise spiritual judgment over them, but only temporal judgment, in the case when, while dwelling among Christians they are guilty of some misdemeanor, and are condemned by the faithful to some temporal punishment. On the other hand, in this way, i.e., as a punishment, the Church forbids the faithful to communicate with those unbelievers who have forsaken the faith they once received, either by corrupting the faith, as heretics, or by entirely renouncing the faith, as apostates, because the Church pronounces sentence of excommunication on both.

With regard to the second way, it seems that one ought to distinguish according to the various conditions of persons, circumstances and time. For some are firm in the faith; and so it is to be hoped that their communicating with unbelievers will lead to the conversion of the latter rather than to the aversion of the faithful from the faith. These are not to be forbidden to communicate with unbelievers who have not received the faith, such as pagans or Jews, especially if there be some urgent necessity for so doing. But in the case of simple people and those who are weak in the faith, whose perversion is to be feared as a probable result, they should be forbidden to communicate with unbelievers, and especially to be on very familiar terms with them, or to communicate with them without necessity.

**REPLY OBJ. 1**: With regard to the argument in the contrary sense the reply is that the Lord gave this command in reference to those nations into whose territory the Jews were about to enter. For the latter were inclined to idolatry, so that it was to be feared lest, through frequent dealings with those nations, they should be estranged from the faith: hence the text goes on (Deut 7:4): *For she will turn away thy son from following Me.*

**REPLY OBJ. 2**: The Church does not exercise judgment against unbelievers in the point of inflicting spiritual punishment on them: but she does exercise judgment over some of them in the matter of temporal punishment. It is under this head that sometimes the Church, for certain special sins, withdraws the faithful from communication with certain unbelievers.

**REPLY OBJ. 3**: There is more probability that a servant who is ruled by his master's commands, will be converted to the faith of his master who is a believer, than if the case were the reverse: and so the faithful are not forbidden to have unbelieving servants. If, however, the master were in danger, through communicating with such a servant, he should send him away, according to Our Lord's command (Matt 18:8): *If . . . thy foot scandalize thee, cut it off, and cast it from thee.*

# Article 10

*Whether unbelievers may have authority or dominion over the faithful?*

**AD DECIMUM SIC PROCEDITUR**. Videtur quod infideles possint habere praelationem vel dominium supra fideles. Dicit enim apostolus, I ad Tim. VI, *quicumque sunt sub iugo servi dominos suos omni honore dignos arbitrentur*, et quod loquatur de infidelibus patet per hoc quod subdit, *qui autem fideles habent dominos non contemnant*. Et I Pet. II dicitur, *servi, subditi estote in omni timore dominis, non tantum bonis et modestis, sed etiam dyscolis*. Non autem hoc praeciperetur per apostolicam doctrinam nisi infideles possent fidelibus praeesse. Ergo videtur quod infideles possint praeesse fidelibus.

**PRAETEREA**, quicumque sunt de familia alicuius principis subsunt ei. Sed fideles aliqui erant de familiis infidelium principum, unde dicitur ad Philipp. IV, *salutant vos omnes sancti, maxime autem qui de Caesaris domo sunt*, scilicet Neronis, qui infidelis erat. Ergo infideles possunt fidelibus praeesse.

**PRAETEREA**, sicut Philosophus dicit, in I Polit., servus est instrumentum domini in his quae ad humanam vitam pertinent, sicut et minister artificis est instrumentum artificis in his quae pertinent ad operationem artis. Sed in talibus potest fidelis infideli subiici, possunt enim fideles infidelium coloni esse. Ergo infideles possunt fidelibus praefici etiam quantum ad dominium.

**SED CONTRA** est quod ad eum qui praeest pertinet habere iudicium super eos quibus praeest. Sed infideles non possunt iudicare de fidelibus, dicit enim apostolus, I ad Cor. VI, *audet aliquis vestrum, habens negotium adversus alterum, iudicari apud iniquos, idest infideles, et non apud sanctos?* Ergo videtur quod infideles fidelibus praeesse non possint.

**RESPONDEO** dicendum quod circa hoc dupliciter loqui possumus. Uno modo, de dominio vel praelatione infidelium super fideles de novo instituenda. Et hoc nullo modo permitti debet. Cedit enim hoc in scandalum et in periculum fidei, de facili enim illi qui subiiciuntur aliorum iurisdictioni immutari possunt ab eis quibus subsunt ut sequantur eorum imperium, nisi illi qui subsunt fuerint magnae virtutis. Et similiter infideles contemnunt fidem si fidelium defectus cognoscant. Et ideo apostolus prohibuit quod fideles non contendant iudicio coram iudice infideli. Et ideo nullo modo permittit Ecclesia quod infideles acquirant dominium super fideles, vel qualitercumque eis praeficiantur in aliquo officio.

Alio modo possumus loqui de dominio vel praelatione iam praeexistenti. Ubi considerandum est quod

**OBJECTION 1**: It would seem that unbelievers may have authority or dominion over the faithful. For the Apostle says (1 Tim 6:1): *Whosoever are servants under the yoke, let them count their masters worthy of all honor*: and it is clear that he is speaking of unbelievers, since he adds (1 Tim 6:2): *But they that have believing masters, let them not despise them*. Moreover it is written (1 Pet 2:18): *Servants be subject to your masters with all fear, not only to the good and gentle, but also to the forward*. Now this command would not be contained in the apostolic teaching unless unbelievers could have authority over the faithful. Therefore it seems that unbelievers can have authority over the faithful.

**OBJ. 2**: Further, all the members of a prince's household are his subjects. Now some of the faithful were members of unbelieving princes' households, for we read in the Epistle to the Philippians (4:22): *All the saints salute you, especially they that are of Caesar's household*, referring to Nero, who was an unbeliever. Therefore unbelievers can have authority over the faithful.

**OBJ. 3**: Further, according to the Philosopher (*Polit.* i, 2) a slave is his master's instrument in matters concerning everyday life, even as a craftsman's laborer is his instrument in matters concerning the working of his art. Now, in such matters, a believer can be subject to an unbeliever, for he may work on an unbeliever's farm. Therefore unbelievers may have authority over the faithful even as to dominion.

**ON THE CONTRARY**, Those who are in authority can pronounce judgment on those over whom they are placed. But unbelievers cannot pronounce judgment on the faithful, for the Apostle says (1 Cor 6:1): *Dare any of you, having a matter against another, go to be judged before the unjust*, i.e., unbelievers, *and not before the saints?* Therefore it seems that unbelievers cannot have authority over the faithful.

**I ANSWER THAT**, This question may be considered in two ways. First, we may speak of dominion or authority of unbelievers over the faithful as of a thing to be established for the first time. This ought by no means to be allowed, since it would provoke scandal and endanger the faith, for subjects are easily influenced by their superiors to comply with their commands, unless the subjects are of great virtue: moreover unbelievers hold the faith in contempt, if they see the faithful fall away. Hence the Apostle forbade the faithful to go to law before an unbelieving judge. And so the Church altogether forbids unbelievers to acquire dominion over believers, or to have authority over them in any capacity whatever.

Second, we may speak of dominion or authority, as already in force: and here we must observe that dominion

dominium et praelatio introducta sunt ex iure humano, distinctio autem fidelium et infidelium est ex iure divino. Ius autem divinum, quod est ex gratia, non tollit ius humanum, quod est ex naturali ratione. Et ideo distinctio fidelium et infidelium, secundum se considerata, non tollit dominium et praelationem infidelium supra fideles.

Potest tamen iuste per sententiam vel ordinationem Ecclesiae, auctoritatem Dei habentis, tale ius dominii vel praelationis tolli, quia infideles merito suae infidelitatis merentur potestatem amittere super fideles, qui transferuntur in filios Dei sed hoc quidem Ecclesia quandoque facit, quandoque autem non facit.

In illis enim infidelibus qui etiam temporali subiectione subiiciuntur Ecclesiae et membris eius, hoc ius Ecclesiae statuit, ut servus Iudaeorum, statim factus Christianus, a servitute liberetur, nullo pretio dato, si fuerit vernaculus, idest in servitute natus; et similiter si, infidelis existens, fuerit emptus ad servitium. Si autem fuerit emptus ad mercationem, tenetur eum infra tres menses exponere ad vendendum. Nec in hoc iniuriam facit Ecclesia, quia, cum ipsi Iudaei sint servi Ecclesiae, potest disponere de rebus eorum; sicut etiam principes saeculares multas leges ediderunt erga suos subditos in favorem libertatis. In illis vero infidelibus qui temporaliter Ecclesiae vel eius membris non subiacent, praedictum ius Ecclesia non statuit, licet posset instituere de iure. Et hoc facit ad scandalum vitandum. Sicut etiam dominus, Matth. XVII, ostendit quod poterat se a tributo excusare quia *liberi sunt filii*, sed tamen mandavit tributum solvi ad scandalum vitandum. Ita etiam et Paulus, cum dixisset quod servi dominos suos honorarent, subiungit, *ne nomen domini et doctrina blasphemetur.*

**Unde patet** responsio ad primum.

**Ad secundum** dicendum quod illa praelatio Caesaris praeexistebat distinctioni fidelium ab infidelibus, unde non solvebatur per conversionem aliquorum ad fidem. Et utile erat quod aliqui fideles locum in familia imperatoris haberent, ad defendendum alios fideles, sicut beatus Sebastianus Christianorum animos, quos in tormentis videbat deficere, confortabat, et adhuc latebat sub militari chlamyde in domo Diocletiani.

**Ad tertium** dicendum quod servi subiiciuntur dominis suis ad totam vitam, et subditi praefectis ad omnia negotia, sed ministri artificum subduntur eis ad aliqua specialia opera. Unde periculosius est quod infideles accipiant dominium vel praelationem super fideles quam quod accipiant ab eis ministerium in aliquo artificio. Et ideo permittit Ecclesia quod Christiani possint colere terras Iudaeorum, quia per hoc non habent necesse conversari cum eis. Salomon etiam expetiit a rege Tyri

and authority are institutions of human law, while the distinction between faithful and unbelievers arises from the Divine law. Now the Divine law which is the law of grace, does not do away with human law which is the law of natural reason. Wherefore the distinction between faithful and unbelievers, considered in itself, does not do away with dominion and authority of unbelievers over the faithful.

Nevertheless this right of dominion or authority can be justly done away with by the sentence or ordination of the Church who has the authority of God: since unbelievers in virtue of their unbelief deserve to forfeit their power over the faithful who are converted into children of God. This the Church does sometimes, and sometimes not.

For among those unbelievers who are subject, even in temporal matters, to the Church and her members, the Church made the law that if the slave of a Jew became a Christian, he should forthwith receive his freedom, without paying any price, if he should be a *vernaculus*, i.e., born in slavery; and likewise if, when yet an unbeliever, he had been bought for his service: if, however, he had been bought for sale, then he should be offered for sale within three months. Nor does the Church harm them in this, because since those Jews themselves are subject to the Church, she can dispose of their possessions, even as secular princes have enacted many laws to be observed by their subjects, in favor of liberty. On the other hand, the Church has not applied the above law to those unbelievers who are not subject to her or her members, in temporal matters, although she has the right to do so: and this, in order to avoid scandal, for as Our Lord showed (Matt 17:25, 26) that He could be excused from paying the tribute, because *the children are free*, yet He ordered the tribute to be paid in order to avoid giving scandal. Thus Paul too, after saying that servants should honor their masters, adds, *lest the name of the Lord and His doctrine be blasphemed.*

**This suffices** for the Reply to the First Objection.

**Reply Obj. 2:** The authority of Caesar preceded the distinction of faithful from unbelievers. Hence it was not cancelled by the conversion of some to the faith. Moreover it was a good thing that there should be a few of the faithful in the emperor's household, that they might defend the rest of the faithful. Thus the Blessed Sebastian encouraged those whom he saw faltering under torture, and, the while, remained hidden under the military cloak in the palace of Diocletian.

**Reply Obj. 3:** Slaves are subject to their masters for their whole lifetime, and are subject to their overseers in everything: whereas the craftsman's laborer is subject to him for certain special works. Hence it would be more dangerous for unbelievers to have dominion or authority over the faithful, than that they should be allowed to employ them in some craft. Wherefore the Church permits Christians to work on the land of Jews, because this does not entail their living together with them. Thus Solomon

magistros operum ad ligna caedenda, ut habetur III Reg. V. Et tamen si ex tali communicatione vel convictu subversio fidelium timeretur, esset penitus interdicendum.

besought the King of Tyre to send master workmen to hew the trees, as related in 3 Kings 5:6. Yet, if there be reason to fear that the faithful will be perverted by such communications and dealings, they should be absolutely forbidden.

# Article 11

*Whether the rites of unbelievers ought to be tolerated?*

AD UNDECIMUM SIC PROCEDITUR. Videtur quod ritus infidelium non sint tolerandi. Manifestum est enim quod infideles in suis ritibus peccant eos servando. Sed peccato consentire videtur qui non prohibet cum prohibere possit, ut habetur in Glossa Rom. I, super illud, *non solum qui faciunt, sed etiam qui consentiunt facientibus.* Ergo peccant qui eorum ritus tolerant.

PRAETEREA, ritus Iudaeorum idololatriae comparantur, quia super illud Gal. V, *nolite iterum iugo servitutis contineri,* dicit Glossa, *non est levior haec legis servitus quam idololatriae.* Sed non sustineretur quod idololatriae ritum aliqui exercerent, quinimmo Christiani principes templa idolorum primo claudi, et postea dirui fecerunt, ut Augustinus narrat, XVIII de Civ. Dei. Ergo etiam ritus Iudaeorum tolerari non debent.

PRAETEREA, peccatum infidelitatis est gravissimum, ut supra dictum est. Sed alia peccata non tolerantur, sed lege puniuntur, sicut adulterium, furtum et alia huiusmodi. Ergo etiam ritus infidelium tolerandi non sunt.

SED CONTRA est quod in Decretis, dist. XLV, Can. *qui sincera,* dicit Gregorius de Iudaeis, *omnes festivitates suas, sicut hactenus ipsi et patres eorum per longa colentes tempora tenuerunt, liberam habeant observandi celebrandique licentiam.*

RESPONDEO dicendum quod humanum regimen derivatur a divino regimine, et ipsum debet imitari. Deus autem, quamvis sit omnipotens et summe bonus, permittit tamen aliqua mala fieri in universo, quae prohibere posset, ne, eis sublatis, maiora bona tollerentur, vel etiam peiora mala sequerentur. Sic igitur et in regimine humano illi qui praesunt recte aliqua mala tolerant, ne aliqua bona impediantur, vel etiam ne aliqua mala peiora incurrantur, sicut Augustinus dicit, in II de ordine, *aufer meretrices de rebus humanis, turbaveris omnia libidinibus.* Sic igitur, quamvis infideles in suis ritibus peccent, tolerari possunt vel propter aliquod bonum quod ex eis provenit, vel propter aliquod malum quod vitatur. Ex hoc autem quod Iudaei ritus suos observant, in quibus olim praefigurabatur veritas fidei quam tenemus, hoc bonum provenit quod testimonium fidei nostrae habemus ab hostibus, et quasi in figura

OBJECTION 1: It would seem that rites of unbelievers ought not to be tolerated. For it is evident that unbelievers sin in observing their rites: and not to prevent a sin, when one can, seems to imply consent therein, as a gloss observes on Rom. 1:32: *Not only they that do them, but they also that consent to them that do them.* Therefore it is a sin to tolerate their rites.

OBJ. 2: Further, the rites of the Jews are compared to idolatry, because a gloss on Gal. 5:1, *Be not held again under the yoke of bondage,* says: *The bondage of that law was not lighter than that of idolatry.* But it would not be allowable for anyone to observe the rites of idolatry, in fact Christian princes at first caused the temples of idols to be closed, and afterwards, to be destroyed, as Augustine relates (*De Civ. Dei* xviii, 54). Therefore it follows that even the rites of Jews ought not to be tolerated.

OBJ. 3: Further, unbelief is the greatest of sins, as stated above (A. 3). Now other sins such as adultery, theft and the like, are not tolerated, but are punishable by law. Therefore neither ought the rites of unbelievers to be tolerated.

ON THE CONTRARY, Gregory says, speaking of the Jews: *They should be allowed to observe all their feasts, just as hitherto they and their fathers have for ages observed them.*

I ANSWER THAT, Human government is derived from the Divine government, and should imitate it. Now although God is all-powerful and supremely good, nevertheless He allows certain evils to take place in the universe, which He might prevent, lest, without them, greater goods might be forfeited, or greater evils ensue. Accordingly in human government also, those who are in authority, rightly tolerate certain evils, lest certain goods be lost, or certain greater evils be incurred: thus Augustine says (*De Ordine* ii, 4): *If you do away with harlots, the world will be convulsed with lust.* Hence, though unbelievers sin in their rites, they may be tolerated, either on account of some good that ensues therefrom, or because of some evil avoided. Thus from the fact that the Jews observe their rites, which, of old, foreshadowed the truth of the faith which we hold, there follows this good—that our very enemies bear witness to our faith, and that our faith is represented in a figure, so to

nobis repraesentatur quod credimus. Et ideo in suis ritibus tolerantur.

Aliorum vero infidelium ritus, qui nihil veritatis aut utilitatis afferunt, non sunt aliqualiter tolerandi, nisi forte ad aliquod malum vitandum, scilicet ad vitandum scandalum vel dissidium quod ex hoc posset provenire, vel impedimentum salutis eorum, qui paulatim, sic tolerati, convertuntur ad fidem. Propter hoc enim etiam haereticorum et Paganorum ritus aliquando Ecclesia toleravit, quando erat magna infidelium multitudo.

**ET PER HOC** patet responsio ad obiecta.

speak. For this reason they are tolerated in the observance of their rites.

On the other hand, the rites of other unbelievers, which are neither truthful nor profitable are by no means to be tolerated, except perchance in order to avoid an evil, e.g., the scandal or disturbance that might ensue, or some hindrance to the salvation of those who if they were unmolested might gradually be converted to the faith. For this reason the Church, at times, has tolerated the rites even of heretics and pagans, when unbelievers were very numerous.

**THIS SUFFICES** for the Replies to the Objections.

# Article 12

*Whether the children of Jews and other unbelievers ought to be baptized against their parents' will?*

**AD DUODECIMUM SIC PROCEDITUR.** Videtur quod pueri Iudaeorum et aliorum infidelium sint baptizandi parentibus invitis. Maius enim est vinculum matrimoniale quam ius patriae potestatis, quia ius patriae potestatis potest per hominem solvi, cum filiusfamilias emancipatur; vinculum autem matrimoniale non potest solvi per hominem, secundum illud Matth. XIX, *quod Deus coniunxit homo non separet.* Sed propter infidelitatem solvitur vinculum matrimoniale, dicit enim apostolus, I ad Cor. VII, *quod si infidelis discedit, discedat, non enim servituti subiectus est frater aut soror in huiusmodi*; et canon dicit quod si coniux infidelis non vult sine contumelia sui creatoris cum altero stare, quod alter coniugum non debet ei cohabitare. Ergo multo magis propter infidelitatem tollitur ius patriae potestatis in suos filios. Possunt ergo eorum filii baptizari eis invitis.

**PRAETEREA**, magis debet homini subveniri circa periculum mortis aeternae quam circa periculum mortis temporalis. Sed si aliquis videret hominem in periculo mortis temporalis et ei non ferret auxilium, peccaret. Cum ergo filii Iudaeorum et aliorum infidelium sint in periculo mortis aeternae si parentibus relinquuntur, qui eos in sua infidelitate informant, videtur quod sint eis auferendi et baptizandi et in fidelitate instruendi.

**PRAETEREA**, filii servorum sunt servi et in potestate dominorum. Sed Iudaei sunt servi regum et principum. Ergo et filii eorum. Reges igitur et principes habent potestatem de filiis Iudaeorum facere quod voluerint. Nulla ergo erit iniuria si eos baptizent invitis parentibus.

**PRAETEREA**, quilibet homo magis est Dei, a quo habet animam, quam patris carnalis, a quo habet corpus.

**OBJECTION 1**: It would seem that the children of Jews and of other unbelievers ought to be baptized against their parents' will. For the bond of marriage is stronger than the right of parental authority over children, since the right of parental authority can be made to cease, when a son is set at liberty; whereas the marriage bond cannot be severed by man, according to Matt. 19:6: *What . . . God hath joined together let no man put asunder.* And yet the marriage bond is broken on account of unbelief: for the Apostle says (1 Cor 7:15): *If the unbeliever depart, let him depart. For a brother or sister is not under servitude in such cases*: and a canon says that if the unbelieving partner is unwilling to abide with the other, without insult to their Creator, then the other partner is not bound to cohabitation. Much more, therefore, does unbelief abrogate the right of unbelieving parents' authority over their children: and consequently their children may be baptized against their parents' will.

**OBJ. 2**: Further, one is more bound to succor a man who is in danger of everlasting death, than one who is in danger of temporal death. Now it would be a sin, if one saw a man in danger of temporal death and failed to go to his aid. Since, then, the children of Jews and other unbelievers are in danger of everlasting death, should they be left to their parents who would imbue them with their unbelief, it seems that they ought to be taken away from them and baptized, and instructed in the faith.

**OBJ. 3**: Further, the children of a bondsman are themselves bondsmen, and under the power of his master. Now the Jews are bondsmen of kings and princes: therefore their children are also. Consequently kings and princes have the power to do what they will with Jewish children. Therefore no injustice is committed if they baptize them against their parents' wishes.

**OBJ. 4**: Further, every man belongs more to God, from Whom he has his soul, than to his carnal father, from whom

Non ergo est iniustum si pueri Iudaeorum carnalibus parentibus auferantur et Deo per Baptismum consecrentur.

**Praeterea**, Baptismus efficacior est ad salutem quam praedicatio, quia per Baptismum statim tollitur peccati macula, reatus poenae, et aperitur ianua caeli. Sed si periculum sequitur ex defectu praedicationis, imputatur ei qui non praedicavit, ut habetur Ezech. III, et XXXIII de eo qui *videt gladium venientem et non insonuerit tuba*. Ergo multo magis, si pueri Iudaeorum damnentur propter defectum Baptismi, imputatur ad peccatum eis qui potuerunt baptizare et non baptizaverunt.

**Sed contra**, nemini facienda est iniuria. Fieret autem Iudaeis iniuria si eorum filii baptizarentur eis invitis, quia amitterent ius patriae potestatis in filios iam fideles. Ergo eis invitis non sunt baptizandi.

**Respondeo** dicendum quod maximam habet auctoritatem Ecclesiae consuetudo, quae semper est in omnibus aemulanda. Quia et ipsa doctrina Catholicorum doctorum ab Ecclesia auctoritatem habet, unde magis standum est auctoritati Ecclesiae quam auctoritati vel Augustini vel Hieronymi vel cuiuscumque doctoris. Hoc autem Ecclesiae usus nunquam habuit quod Iudaeorum filii invitis parentibus baptizarentur, quamvis fuerint retroactis temporibus multi Catholici principes potentissimi, ut Constantinus, Theodosius, quibus familiares fuerunt sanctissimi episcopi, ut Sylvester Constantino et Ambrosius Theodosio, qui nullo modo hoc praetermisissent ab eis impetrare, si hoc esset consonum rationi. Et ideo periculosum videtur hanc assertionem de novo inducere, ut praeter consuetudinem in Ecclesia hactenus observatam, Iudaeorum filii invitis parentibus baptizarentur.

Et huius ratio est duplex. Una quidem propter periculum fidei. Si enim pueri nondum usum rationis habentes Baptismum susciperent, postmodum, cum ad perfectam aetatem pervenirent, de facili possent a parentibus induci ut relinquerent quod ignorantes susceperunt. Quod vergeret in fidei detrimentum.

Alia vero ratio est quia repugnat iustitiae naturali. Filius enim naturaliter est aliquid patris. Et primo quidem a parentibus non distinguitur secundum corpus, quandiu in matris utero continetur. Postmodum vero, postquam ab utero egreditur, antequam usum liberi arbitrii habeat, continetur sub parentum cura sicut sub quodam spirituali utero. Quandiu enim usum rationis non habet puer, non differt ab animali irrationali. Unde sicut bos vel equus est alicuius ut utatur eo cum voluerit, secundum ius civile, sicut proprio instrumento; ita de iure naturali est quod filius, antequam habeat usum rationis, sit sub cura patris. Unde contra iustitiam

he has his body. Therefore it is not unjust if Jewish children be taken away from their parents, and consecrated to God in Baptism.

**Obj. 5**: Further, Baptism avails for salvation more than preaching does, since Baptism removes forthwith the stain of sin and the debt of punishment, and opens the gate of heaven. Now if danger ensue through not preaching, it is imputed to him who omitted to preach, according to the words of Ezech. 33:6 about the man who *sees the sword coming and sounds not the trumpet*. Much more therefore, if Jewish children are lost through not being baptized are they accounted guilty of sin, who could have baptized them and did not.

**On the contrary**, Injustice should be done to no man. Now it would be an injustice to Jews if their children were to be baptized against their will, since they would lose the rights of parental authority over their children as soon as these were Christians. Therefore these should not be baptized against their parents' will.

**I answer that**, The custom of the Church has very great authority and ought to be jealously observed in all things, since the very doctrine of catholic doctors derives its authority from the Church. Hence we ought to abide by the authority of the Church rather than by that of an Augustine or a Jerome or of any doctor whatever. Now it was never the custom of the Church to baptize the children of the Jews against the will of their parents, although at times past there have been many very powerful catholic princes like Constantine and Theodosius, with whom most holy bishops have been on most friendly terms, as Sylvester with Constantine, and Ambrose with Theodosius, who would certainly not have failed to obtain this favor from them if it had been at all reasonable. It seems therefore hazardous to repeat this assertion, that the children of Jews should be baptized against their parents' wishes, in contradiction to the Church's custom observed hitherto.

There are two reasons for this custom. One is on account of the danger to the faith. For children baptized before coming to the use of reason, afterwards when they come to perfect age, might easily be persuaded by their parents to renounce what they had unknowingly embraced; and this would be detrimental to the faith.

The other reason is that it is against natural justice. For a child is by nature part of its father: thus, at first, it is not distinct from its parents as to its body, so long as it is enfolded within its mother's womb; and later on after birth, and before it has the use of its free-will, it is enfolded in the care of its parents, which is like a spiritual womb, for so long as man has not the use of reason, he differs not from an irrational animal; so that even as an ox or a horse belongs to someone who, according to the civil law, can use them when he likes, as his own instrument, so, according to the natural law, a son, before coming to the use of reason, is under his father's care. Hence it would

naturalem esset si puer, antequam habeat usum rationis, a cura parentum subtrahatur, vel de eo aliquid ordinetur invitis parentibus. Postquam autem incipit habere usum liberi arbitrii, iam incipit esse suus, et potest, quantum ad ea quae sunt iuris divini vel naturalis, sibi ipsi providere. Et tunc est inducendus ad fidem non coactione, sed persuasione; et potest etiam invitis parentibus consentire fidei et baptizari, non autem antequam habeat usum rationis. Unde de pueris antiquorum patrum dicitur quod *salvati sunt in fide parentum*, per quod datur intelligi quod ad parentes pertinet providere filiis de sua salute, praecipue antequam habeant usum rationis.

**AD PRIMUM** ergo dicendum quod in vinculo matrimoniali uterque coniugum habet usum liberi arbitrii, et uterque potest invito altero fidei assentire. Sed hoc non habet locum in puero antequam habeat usum rationis. Sed postquam habet usum rationis, tunc tenet similitudo, si converti voluerit.

**AD SECUNDUM** dicendum quod a morte naturali non est aliquis eripiendus contra ordinem iuris civilis, puta, si aliquis a suo iudice condemnetur ad mortem temporalem, nullus debet eum violenter eripere. Unde nec aliquis debet irrumpere ordinem iuris naturalis, quo filius est sub cura patris, ut eum liberet a periculo mortis aeternae.

**AD TERTIUM** dicendum quod Iudaei sunt servi principum servitute civili, quae non excludit ordinem iuris naturalis vel divini.

**AD QUARTUM** dicendum quod homo ordinatur ad Deum per rationem, per quam eum cognoscere potest. Unde puer, antequam usum rationis habeat, naturali ordine ordinatur in Deum per rationem parentum, quorum curae naturaliter subiacet; et secundum eorum dispositionem sunt circa ipsum divina agenda.

**AD QUINTUM** dicendum quod periculum quod sequitur de praedicatione omissa non imminet nisi eis quibus commissum est officium praedicandi, unde in Ezechiel praemittitur, *speculatorem dedi te filiis Israel*. Providere autem pueris infidelium de sacramentis salutis pertinet ad parentes eorum. Unde eis imminet periculum si, propter subtractionem sacramentorum, eorum parvuli detrimentum salutis patiantur.

be contrary to natural justice, if a child, before coming to the use of reason, were to be taken away from its parents' custody, or anything done to it against its parents' wish. As soon, however, as it begins to have the use of its free-will, it begins to belong to itself, and is able to look after itself, in matters concerning the Divine or the natural law, and then it should be induced, not by compulsion but by persuasion, to embrace the faith: it can then consent to the faith, and be baptized, even against its parents' wish; but not before it comes to the use of reason. Hence it is said of the children of the fathers of old that they were saved in the faith of their parents; whereby we are given to understand that it is the parents' duty to look after the salvation of their children, especially before they come to the use of reason.

**REPLY OBJ. 1**: In the marriage bond, both husband and wife have the use of the free-will, and each can assent to the faith without the other's consent. But this does not apply to a child before it comes to the use of reason: yet the comparison holds good after the child has come to the use of reason, if it is willing to be converted.

**REPLY OBJ. 2**: No one should be snatched from natural death against the order of civil law: for instance, if a man were condemned by the judge to temporal death, nobody ought to rescue him by violence: hence no one ought to break the order of the natural law, whereby a child is in the custody of its father, in order to rescue it from the danger of everlasting death.

**REPLY OBJ. 3**: Jews are bondsmen of princes by civil bondage, which does not exclude the order of natural or Divine law.

**REPLY OBJ. 4**: Man is directed to God by his reason, whereby he can know Him. Hence a child before coming to the use of reason, in the natural order of things, is directed to God by its parents' reason, under whose care it lies by nature: and it is for them to dispose of the child in all matters relating to God.

**REPLY OBJ. 5**: The peril that ensues from the omission of preaching, threatens only those who are entrusted with the duty of preaching. Hence it had already been said (Ezek 3:17): *I have made thee a watchman to the children of Israel*. On the other hand, to provide the sacraments of salvation for the children of unbelievers is the duty of their parents. Hence it is they whom the danger threatens, if through being deprived of the sacraments their children fail to obtain salvation.

# Question 11

Deinde considerandum est de haeresi. Circa quam quaeruntur quatuor.

Primo, utrum haeresis sit infidelitatis species.
Secundo, de materia eius circa quam est.
Tertio, utrum haeretici sint tolerandi.
Quarto, utrum revertentes sint recipiendi.

We must now consider heresy: under which head there are four points of inquiry:

(1) Whether heresy is a kind of unbelief?
(2) Of the matter about which it is;
(3) Whether heretics should be tolerated?
(4) Whether converts should be received?

## Article 1

*Whether heresy is a species of unbelief?*

**AD PRIMUM SIC PROCEDITUR.** Videtur quod haeresis non sit infidelitatis species. Infidelitas enim in intellectu est, ut supra dictum est. Sed haeresis non videtur ad intellectum pertinere, sed magis ad vim appetitivam. Dicit enim Hieronymus, et habetur in decretis, XXIV, qu. III, *haeresis Graece ab electione dicitur, quod scilicet eam sibi unusquisque eligat disciplinam quam putat esse meliorem*, electio autem est actus appetitivae virtutis, ut supra dictum est. Ergo haeresis non est infidelitatis species.

**PRAETEREA,** vitium praecipue accipit speciem a fine, unde philosophus dicit, in V Ethic., quod *ille qui moechatur ut furetur, magis est fur quam moechus.* Sed finis haeresis est commodum temporale, et maxime principatus et gloria, quod pertinet ad vitium superbiae vel cupiditatis, dicit enim Augustinus, in libro de Util. Cred., quod *haereticus est qui alicuius temporalis commodi, et maxime gloriae principatusque sui gratia, falsas ac novas opiniones vel gignit vel sequitur.* Ergo haeresis non est species infidelitatis, sed magis superbiae.

**PRAETEREA,** infidelitas, cum sit in intellectu, non videtur ad carnem pertinere. Sed haeresis pertinet ad opera carnis, dicit enim apostolus, ad Gal. V, *manifesta sunt opera carnis, quae sunt fornicatio, immunditia*; et inter cetera postmodum subdit, dissensiones, sectae, quae sunt idem quod haereses. Ergo haeresis non est infidelitatis species.

**SED CONTRA** est quod falsitas veritati opponitur. Sed *haereticus est qui falsas vel novas opiniones vel gignit vel sequitur.* Ergo opponitur veritati, cui fides innititur. Ergo sub infidelitate continetur.

**RESPONDEO** dicendum quod nomen haeresis, sicut dictum est, electionem importat. Electio autem, ut supra dictum est, est eorum quae sunt ad finem, praesupposito

**OBJECTION 1:** It would seem that heresy is not a species of unbelief. For unbelief is in the understanding, as stated above (Q. 10, A. 2). Now heresy would seem not to pertain to the understanding, but rather to the appetitive power; for Jerome says on Gal. 5:19: *The works of the flesh are manifest: Heresy is derived from a Greek word meaning choice, whereby a man makes choice of that school which he deems best.* But choice is an act of the appetitive power, as stated above (I-II, Q. 13, A. 1). Therefore heresy is not a species of unbelief.

**OBJ. 2:** Further, vice takes its species chiefly from its end; hence the Philosopher says (*Ethic.* v, 2) that *he who commits adultery that he may steal, is a thief rather than an adulterer.* Now the end of heresy is temporal profit, especially lordship and glory, which belong to the vice of pride or covetousness: for Augustine says (*De Util. Credendi* i) that *a heretic is one who either devises or follows false and new opinions, for the sake of some temporal profit, especially that he may lord and be honored above others.* Therefore heresy is a species of pride rather than of unbelief.

**OBJ. 3:** Further, since unbelief is in the understanding, it would seem not to pertain to the flesh. Now heresy belongs to the works of the flesh, for the Apostle says (Gal 5:19): *The works of the flesh are manifest, which are fornication, uncleanness,* and among the others, he adds, *dissensions, sects,* which are the same as heresies. Therefore heresy is not a species of unbelief.

**ON THE CONTRARY,** Falsehood is contrary to truth. Now a heretic is one who devises or follows false or new opinions. Therefore heresy is opposed to the truth, on which faith is founded; and consequently it is a species of unbelief.

**I ANSWER THAT,** The word heresy as stated in the first objection denotes a choosing. Now choice as stated above (I-II, Q. 13, A. 3) is about things directed to the end, the end

fine. In credendis autem voluntas assentit alicui vero tanquam proprio bono, ut ex supradictis patet. Unde quod est principale verum habet rationem finis ultimi, quae autem secundaria sunt habent rationem eorum quae sunt ad finem.

Quia vero quicumque credit alicuius dicto assentit, principale videtur esse, et quasi finis, in unaquaque credulitate ille cuius dicto assentitur, quasi autem secundaria sunt ea quae quis tenendo vult alicui assentire. Sic igitur qui recte fidem Christianam habet sua voluntate assentit Christo in his quae vere ad eius doctrinam pertinent.

A rectitudine igitur fidei Christianae dupliciter aliquis potest deviare. Uno modo, quia ipsi Christo non vult assentire, et hic habet quasi malam voluntatem circa ipsum finem. Et hoc pertinet ad speciem infidelitatis Paganorum et Iudaeorum. Alio modo, per hoc quod intendit quidem Christo assentire, sed deficit in eligendo ea quibus Christo assentiat, quia non eligit ea quae sunt vere a Christo tradita, sed ea quae sibi propria mens suggerit.

Et ideo haeresis est infidelitatis species pertinens ad eos qui fidem Christi profitentur, sed eius dogmata corrumpunt.

**Ad primum** ergo dicendum quod hoc modo electio pertinet ad infidelitatem sicut et voluntas ad fidem, ut supra dictum est.

**Ad secundum** dicendum quod vitia habent speciem ex fine proximo, sed ex fine remoto habent genus et causam. Sicut cum aliquis moechatur ut furetur, est ibi quidem species moechiae ex proprio fine et obiecto, sed ex fine ultimo ostenditur quod moechia ex furto oritur, et sub eo continetur sicut effectus sub causa vel sicut species sub genere, ut patet ex his quae supra de actibus dicta sunt in communi. Unde et similiter in proposito finis proximus haeresis est adhaerere falsae sententiae propriae, et ex hoc speciem habet. Sed ex fine remoto ostenditur causa eius, scilicet quod oritur ex superbia vel cupiditate.

**Ad tertium** dicendum quod, sicut haeresis dicitur ab *eligendo*, ita secta a *sectando*, sicut Isidorus dicit, in libro Etymol., et ideo haeresis et secta idem sunt. Et utrumque pertinet ad opera carnis, non quidem quantum ad ipsum actum infidelitatis respectu proximi obiecti, sed ratione causae, quae est vel appetitus finis indebiti, secundum quod oritur ex superbia vel cupiditate, ut dictum est; vel etiam aliqua phantastica illusio, quae est errandi principium, ut etiam philosophus dicit, in IV Metaphys. Phantasia autem quodammodo ad carnem pertinet, inquantum actus eius est cum organo corporali.

being presupposed. Now, in matters of faith, the will assents to some truth, as to its proper good, as was shown above (Q. 4, A. 3): wherefore that which is the chief truth, has the character of last end, while those which are secondary truths, have the character of being directed to the end.

Now, whoever believes, assents to someone's words; so that, in every form of unbelief, the person to whose words assent is given seems to hold the chief place and to be the end as it were; while the things by holding which one assents to that person hold a secondary place. Consequently he that holds the Christian faith aright, assents, by his will, to Christ, in those things which truly belong to His doctrine.

Accordingly there are two ways in which a man may deviate from the rectitude of the Christian faith. First, because he is unwilling to assent to Christ: and such a man has an evil will, so to speak, in respect of the very end. This belongs to the species of unbelief in pagans and Jews. Second, because, though he intends to assent to Christ, yet he fails in his choice of those things wherein he assents to Christ, because he chooses not what Christ really taught, but the suggestions of his own mind.

Therefore heresy is a species of unbelief, belonging to those who profess the Christian faith, but corrupt its dogmas.

**Reply Obj. 1**: Choice regards unbelief in the same way as the will regards faith, as stated above.

**Reply Obj. 2**: Vices take their species from their proximate end, while, from their remote end, they take their genus and cause. Thus in the case of adultery committed for the sake of theft, there is the species of adultery taken from its proper end and object; but the ultimate end shows that the act of adultery is both the result of the theft, and is included under it, as an effect under its cause, or a species under its genus, as appears from what we have said about acts in general (I-II, Q. 18, A. 7). Wherefore, as to the case in point also, the proximate end of heresy is adherence to one's own false opinion, and from this it derives its species, while its remote end reveals its cause, viz. that it arises from pride or covetousness.

**Reply Obj. 3**: Just as heresy is so called from its being a *choosing*, so does sect derive its name from its being a *cutting off* (*secando*), as Isidore states (*Etym.* viii, 3). Wherefore heresy and sect are the same thing, and each belongs to the works of the flesh, not indeed by reason of the act itself of unbelief in respect of its proximate object, but by reason of its cause, which is either the desire of an undue end in which way it arises from pride or covetousness, as stated in the second objection, or some illusion of the imagination (which gives rise to error, as the Philosopher states in *Metaph.* iv; *Ed. Did.* iii, 5), for this faculty has a certain connection with the flesh, inasmuch as its act is independent on a bodily organ.

# Article 2

*Whether heresy is properly about matters of faith?*

AD SECUNDUM SIC PROCEDITUR. Videtur quod haeresis non sit proprie circa ea quae sunt fidei. Sicut enim sunt haereses et sectae in Christianis, ita etiam fuerunt in Iudaeis et Pharisaeis, sicut Isidorus dicit, in libro Etymol. Sed eorum dissensiones non erant circa ea quae sunt fidei. Ergo haeresis non est circa ea quae sunt fidei sicut circa propriam materiam.

PRAETEREA, materia fidei sunt res quae creduntur. Sed haeresis non solum est circa res, sed etiam circa verba, et circa expositiones sacrae Scripturae. Dicit enim Hieronymus quod *quicumque aliter Scripturam intelligit quam sensus spiritus sancti efflagitat, a quo scripta est, licet ab Ecclesia non recesserit, tamen haereticus appellari potest*, et alibi dicit quod *ex verbis inordinate prolatis fit haeresis*. Ergo haeresis non est proprie circa materiam fidei.

PRAETEREA, etiam circa ea quae ad fidem pertinent inveniuntur quandoque sacri doctores dissentire, sicut Hieronymus et Augustinus circa cessationem legalium. Et tamen hoc est absque vitio haeresis. Ergo haeresis non est proprie circa materiam fidei.

SED CONTRA est quod Augustinus dicit, contra Manichaeos, *qui in Ecclesia Christi morbidum aliquid pravumque quid sapiunt, si correcti ut sanum rectumque sapiant, resistant contumaciter, suaque pestifera et mortifera dogmata emendare nolunt, sed defendere persistunt, haeretici sunt.* Sed pestifera et mortifera dogmata non sunt nisi illa quae opponuntur dogmatibus fidei, per quam *iustus vivit*, ut dicitur Rom. I. Ergo haeresis est circa ea quae sunt fidei sicut circa propriam materiam.

RESPONDEO dicendum quod de haeresi nunc loquimur secundum quod importat corruptionem fidei Christianae. Non autem ad corruptionem fidei Christianae pertinet si aliquis habeat falsam opinionem in his quae non sunt fidei, puta in geometricalibus vel in aliis huiusmodi, quae omnino ad fidem pertinere non possunt, sed solum quando aliquis habet falsam opinionem circa ea quae ad fidem pertinent.

Ad quam aliquid pertinet dupliciter, sicut supra dictum est, uno modo, directe et principaliter, sicut articuli fidei; alio modo, indirecte et secundario, sicut ea ex quibus sequitur corruptio alicuius articuli. Et circa utraque potest esse haeresis, eo modo quo et fides.

AD PRIMUM ergo dicendum quod sicut haereses Iudaeorum et Pharisaeorum erant circa opiniones aliquas

OBJECTION 1: It would seem that heresy is not properly about matters of faith. For just as there are heresies and sects among Christians, so were there among the Jews, and Pharisees, as Isidore observes (*Etym.* viii, 3, 4, 5). Now their dissensions were not about matters of faith. Therefore heresy is not about matters of faith, as though they were its proper matter.

OBJ. 2: Further, the matter of faith is the thing believed. Now heresy is not only about things, but also about works, and about interpretations of Holy Writ. For Jerome says on Gal. 5:20 that *whoever expounds the Scriptures in any sense but that of the Holy Spirit by Whom they were written, may be called a heretic, though he may not have left the Church*: and elsewhere he says that *heresies spring up from words spoken amiss*. Therefore heresy is not properly about the matter of faith.

OBJ. 3: Further, we find the holy doctors differing even about matters pertaining to the faith, for example Augustine and Jerome, on the question about the cessation of the legal observances: and yet this was without any heresy on their part. Therefore heresy is not properly about the matter of faith.

ON THE CONTRARY, Augustine says against the Manichees: *In Christ's Church, those are heretics, who hold mischievous and erroneous opinions, and when rebuked that they may think soundly and rightly, offer a stubborn resistance, and, refusing to mend their pernicious and deadly doctrines, persist in defending them.* Now pernicious and deadly doctrines are none but those which are contrary to the dogmas of faith, whereby *the just man liveth* (Rom 1:17). Therefore heresy is about matters of faith, as about its proper matter.

I ANSWER THAT, We are speaking of heresy now as denoting a corruption of the Christian faith. Now it does not imply a corruption of the Christian faith, if a man has a false opinion in matters that are not of faith, for instance, in questions of geometry and so forth, which cannot belong to the faith by any means; but only when a person has a false opinion about things belonging to the faith.

Now a thing may be of the faith in two ways, as stated above (I, Q. 32, A. 4; I-II, Q. 1, A. 6, ad 1; I-II, Q. 2, A. 5), in one way, directly and principally, e.g., the articles of faith; in another way, indirectly and secondarily, e.g., those matters, the denial of which leads to the corruption of some article of faith; and there may be heresy in either way, even as there can be faith.

REPLY OBJ. 1: Just as the heresies of the Jews and Pharisees were about opinions relating to Judaism or Phar-

ad Iudaismum vel Pharisaeam pertinentes, ita etiam Christianorum haereses sunt circa ea quae pertinent ad fidem Christi.

**AD SECUNDUM** dicendum quod ille dicitur aliter exponere sacram Scripturam quam Spiritus Sanctus efflagitat qui ad hoc expositionem sacrae Scripturae intorquet quod contrariatur ei quod est per spiritum sanctum revelatum. Unde dicitur Ezech. XIII de falsis prophetis quod *perseveraverunt confirmare sermonem,* scilicet per falsas expositiones Scripturae. Similiter etiam per verba quae quis loquitur suam fidem profitetur, est enim confessio actus fidei, ut supra dictum est. Et ideo si sit inordinata locutio circa ea quae sunt fidei, sequi potest ex hoc corruptio fidei. Unde Leo Papa in quadam epistola ad Proterium episcopum Alexandrinum, dicit, *quia inimici Christi crucis omnibus et verbis nostris insidiantur et syllabis, nullam illis vel tenuem occasionem demus qua nos Nestoriano sensui congruere mentiantur.*

**AD TERTIUM** dicendum quod, sicut Augustinus dicit, et habetur in decretis, XXIV, qu. III, *si qui sententiam suam, quamvis falsam atque perversam, nulla pertinaci animositate defendunt, quaerunt autem cauta sollicitudine veritatem, corrigi parati cum invenerint, nequaquam sunt inter haereticos deputandi,* quia scilicet non habent electionem contradicentem Ecclesiae doctrinae. Sic ergo aliqui doctores dissensisse videntur vel circa ea quorum nihil interest ad fidem utrum sic vel aliter teneatur; vel etiam in quibusdam ad fidem pertinentibus quae nondum erant per Ecclesiam determinata. Postquam autem essent auctoritate universalis Ecclesiae determinata, si quis tali ordinationi pertinaciter repugnaret, haereticus censeretur. Quae quidem auctoritas principaliter residet in summo pontifice. Dicitur enim XXIV, qu. I, *quoties fidei ratio ventilatur, arbitror omnes fratres nostros et coepiscopos non nisi ad Petrum, idest sui nominis auctoritatem, referre debere.* Contra cuius auctoritatem nec Hieronymus nec Augustinus nec aliquis sacrorum doctorum suam sententiam defendit. Unde dicit Hieronymus, *haec est fides, Papa beatissime, quam in Catholica didicimus Ecclesia. In qua si minus perite aut parum caute forte aliquid positum est, emendari cupimus a te, qui Petri fidem et sedem tenes. Si autem haec nostra confessio apostolatus tui iudicio comprobatur, quicumque me culpare voluerit, se imperitum vel malevolum, vel etiam non Catholicum sed haereticum, comprobabit.*

isaism, so also heresies among Christians are about matter touching the Christian faith.

**REPLY OBJ. 2:** A man is said to expound Holy Writ in another sense than that required by the Holy Spirit, when he so distorts the meaning of Holy Writ, that it is contrary to what the Holy Spirit has revealed. Hence it is written (Ezek 13:6) about the false prophets: *They have persisted to confirm what they have said,* viz. by false interpretations of Scripture. Moreover a man professes his faith by the words that he utters, since confession is an act of faith, as stated above (Q. 3, A. 1). Wherefore inordinate words about matters of faith may lead to corruption of the faith; and hence it is that Pope Leo says in a letter to Proterius, Bishop of Alexandria: *The enemies of Christ's cross lie in wait for our every deed and word, so that, if we but give them the slightest pretext, they may accuse us mendaciously of agreeing with Nestorius.*

**REPLY OBJ. 3:** As Augustine says (*Ep. xliii*) and we find it stated in the *Decretals* (xxiv, qu. 3, can. Dixit Apostolus): *By no means should we accuse of heresy those who, however false and perverse their opinion may be, defend it without obstinate fervor, and seek the truth with careful anxiety, ready to mend their opinion, when they have found the truth,* because, to wit, they do not make a choice in contradiction to the doctrine of the Church. Accordingly, certain doctors seem to have differed either in matters the holding of which in this or that way is of no consequence, so far as faith is concerned, or even in matters of faith, which were not as yet defined by the Church; although if anyone were obstinately to deny them after they had been defined by the authority of the universal Church, he would be deemed a heretic. This authority resides chiefly in the Sovereign Pontiff. For we read: *Whenever a question of faith is in dispute, I think that all our brethren and fellow bishops ought to refer the matter to none other than Peter, as being the source of their name and honor,* against whose authority neither Jerome nor Augustine nor any of the holy doctors defended their opinion. Hence Jerome says (*Exposit. Symbol*): *This, most blessed Pope, is the faith that we have been taught in the Catholic Church. If anything therein has been incorrectly or carelessly expressed, we beg that it may be set aright by you who hold the faith and see of Peter. If, however, this, our profession, be approved by the judgment of your apostleship, whoever may blame me, will prove that he himself is ignorant, or malicious, or even not a catholic but a heretic.*

# Article 3

*Whether heretics ought to be tolerated?*

**AD TERTIUM SIC PROCEDITUR**. Videtur quod haeretici sint tolerandi. Dicit enim apostolus, II ad Tim. II, *servum Dei oportet mansuetum esse, cum modestia corripientem eos qui resistunt veritati, ne quando det illis poenitentiam Deus ad cognoscendam veritatem, et resipiscant a laqueis Diaboli.* Sed si haeretici non tolerantur, sed morti traduntur, aufertur eis facultas poenitendi. Ergo hoc videtur esse contra praeceptum apostoli.

**PRAETEREA**, illud quod est necessarium in Ecclesia est tolerandum. Sed haereses sunt necessariae in Ecclesia, dicit enim apostolus, I ad Cor. XI, *oportet haereses esse, ut et qui probati sunt manifesti fiant in vobis.* Ergo videtur quod haeretici sunt tolerandi.

**PRAETEREA**, dominus mandavit, Matth. XIII, servis suis ut zizania permitterent crescere usque ad messem, quae est finis saeculi, ut ibidem exponitur. Sed per zizania significantur haeretici, secundum expositionem sanctorum. Ergo haeretici sunt tolerandi.

**SED CONTRA** est quod apostolus dicit, ad Tit. III, *haereticum hominem, post primam et secundam correptionem, devita, sciens quia subversus est qui eiusmodi est.*

**RESPONDEO** dicendum quod circa haereticos duo sunt consideranda, unum quidem ex parte ipsorum; aliud ex parte Ecclesiae. Ex parte quidem ipsorum est peccatum per quod meruerunt non solum ab Ecclesia per excommunicationem separari, sed etiam per mortem a mundo excludi. Multo enim gravius est corrumpere fidem, per quam est animae vita, quam falsare pecuniam, per quam temporali vitae subvenitur. Unde si falsarii pecuniae, vel alii malefactores, statim per saeculares principes iuste morti traduntur; multo magis haeretici, statim cum de haeresi convincuntur, possent non solum excommunicari, sed et iuste occidi.

Ex parte autem Ecclesiae est misericordia, ad errantium conversionem. Et ideo non statim condemnat, sed *post primam et secundam correctionem*, ut apostolus docet. Postmodum vero, si adhuc pertinax inveniatur, Ecclesia, de eius conversione non sperans, aliorum saluti providet, eum ab Ecclesia separando per excommunicationis sententiam; et ulterius relinquit eum iudicio saeculari a mundo exterminandum per mortem. Dicit enim Hieronymus, et habetur XXIV, qu. III, *resecandae sunt putridae carnes, et scabiosa ovis a caulis repellenda, ne tota domus, massa, corpus et pecora, ardeat, corrumpatur, putrescat, intereat. Arius in Alexandria una scintilla fuit, sed quoniam non statim oppressus est, totum orbem eius flamma populata est.*

**OBJECTION 1**: It seems that heretics ought to be tolerated. For the Apostle says (2 Tim 2:24, 25): *The servant of the Lord must not wrangle . . . with modesty admonishing them that resist the truth, if peradventure God may give them repentance to know the truth, and they may recover themselves from the snares of the devil.* Now if heretics are not tolerated but put to death, they lose the opportunity of repentance. Therefore it seems contrary to the Apostle's command.

**OBJ. 2**: Further, whatever is necessary in the Church should be tolerated. Now heresies are necessary in the Church, since the Apostle says (1 Cor 11:19): *There must be . . . heresies, that they . . . who are reproved, may be manifest among you.* Therefore it seems that heretics should be tolerated.

**OBJ. 3**: Further, the Master commanded his servants (Matt 13:30) to suffer the cockle to grow until the harvest, i.e., the end of the world, as a gloss explains it. Now holy men explain that the cockle denotes heretics. Therefore heretics should be tolerated.

**ON THE CONTRARY**, The Apostle says (Titus 3:10, 11): *A man that is a heretic, after the first and second admonition, avoid: knowing that he, that is such an one, is subverted.*

**I ANSWER THAT**, With regard to heretics two points must be observed: one, on their own side; the other, on the side of the Church. On their own side there is the sin, whereby they deserve not only to be separated from the Church by excommunication, but also to be severed from the world by death. For it is a much graver matter to corrupt the faith which quickens the soul, than to forge money, which supports temporal life. Wherefore if forgers of money and other evil-doers are forthwith condemned to death by the secular authority, much more reason is there for heretics, as soon as they are convicted of heresy, to be not only excommunicated but even put to death.

On the part of the Church, however, there is mercy which looks to the conversion of the wanderer, wherefore she condemns not at once, but *after the first and second admonition*, as the Apostle directs: after that, if he is yet stubborn, the Church no longer hoping for his conversion, looks to the salvation of others, by excommunicating him and separating him from the Church, and furthermore delivers him to the secular tribunal to be exterminated thereby from the world by death. For Jerome commenting on Gal. 5:9, *A little leaven*, says: *Cut off the decayed flesh, expel the mangy sheep from the fold, lest the whole house, the whole paste, the whole body, the whole flock, burn, perish, rot, die. Arius was but one spark in Alexandria, but as that spark was not at once put out, the whole earth was laid waste by its flame.*

**AD PRIMUM** ergo dicendum quod ad modestiam illam pertinet ut primo et secundo corripiatur. Quod si redire noluerit, iam pro subverso habetur, ut patet in auctoritate apostoli inducta.

**AD SECUNDUM** dicendum quod utilitas quae ex haeresibus provenit est praeter haereticorum intentionem, dum scilicet constantia fidelium comprobatur, ut apostolus dicit; et ut excutiamus pigritiam, divinas Scripturas sollicitius intuentes, sicut Augustinus dicit. Sed ex intentione eorum est corrumpere fidem, quod est maximi nocumenti. Et ideo magis respiciendum est ad id quod est per se de eorum intentione, ut excludantur; quam ad hoc quod est praeter eorum intentionem, ut sustineantur.

**AD TERTIUM** dicendum quod, sicut habetur in decretis, XXIV, qu. III, *aliud est excommunicatio, et aliud eradicatio. Excommunicatur enim ad hoc aliquis*, ut ait apostolus, *ut spiritus eius salvus fiat in die Domini*. Si tamen totaliter eradicentur per mortem haeretici, non est etiam contra mandatum domini, quod est in eo casu intelligendum quando non possunt extirpari zizania sine extirpatione tritici, ut supra dictum est, cum de infidelibus in communi ageretur.

**REPLY OBJ. 1**: This very modesty demands that the heretic should be admonished a first and second time: and if he be unwilling to retract, he must be reckoned as already *subverted*, as we may gather from the words of the Apostle quoted above.

**REPLY OBJ. 2**: The profit that ensues from heresy is beside the intention of heretics, for it consists in the constancy of the faithful being put to the test, and makes us shake off our sluggishness, and search the Scriptures more carefully, as Augustine states (*De Gen. cont. Manich.* i, 1). What they really intend is the corruption of the faith, which is to inflict very great harm indeed. Consequently we should consider what they directly intend, and expel them, rather than what is beside their intention, and so, tolerate them.

**REPLY OBJ. 3**: According to *Decret.* (xxiv, qu. iii, can. Notandum), *to be excommunicated is not to be uprooted. A man is excommunicated, as the Apostle says* (1 Cor 5:5) *that his spirit may be saved in the day of Our Lord.* Yet if heretics be altogether uprooted by death, this is not contrary to Our Lord's command, which is to be understood as referring to the case when the cockle cannot be plucked up without plucking up the wheat, as we explained above (Q. 10, A. 8, ad 1), when treating of unbelievers in general.

# Article 4

*Whether the Church should receive those who return from heresy?*

**AD QUARTUM SIC PROCEDITUR.** Videtur quod revertentes ab haeresi sint omnino ab Ecclesia recipiendi. Dicitur enim Ierem. III, ex persona domini, *fornicata es cum amatoribus multis, tamen revertere ad me, dicit dominus*. Sed Ecclesiae iudicium est iudicium Dei, secundum illud Deut. I, *ita parvum audietis ut magnum, neque accipietis cuiusquam personam, quia Dei iudicium est*. Ergo si aliqui fornicati fuerint per infidelitatem, quae est spiritualis fornicatio, nihilominus sunt recipiendi.

**PRAETEREA**, Dominus, Matth. XVIII, Petro mandat ut fratri peccanti dimittat non solum septies, *sed usque septuagies septies*, per quod intelligitur, secundum expositionem Hieronymi, quod quotiescumque aliquis peccaverit, est ei dimittendum. Ergo quotiescumque aliquis peccaverit in haeresim relapsus, erit ab Ecclesia suscipiendus.

**PRAETEREA**, haeresis est quaedam infidelitas. Sed alii infideles volentes converti ab Ecclesia recipiuntur. Ergo etiam haeretici sunt recipiendi.

**SED CONTRA** est quod decretalis dicit, quod *si aliqui, post abiurationem erroris, deprehensi fuerint in abiura-*

**OBJECTION 1**: It would seem that the Church ought in all cases to receive those who return from heresy. For it is written (Jer 3:1) in the person of the Lord: *Thou hast prostituted thyself to many lovers; nevertheless return to Me saith the Lord.* Now the sentence of the Church is God's sentence, according to Deut. 1:17: *You shall hear the little as well as the great: neither shall you respect any man's person, because it is the judgment of God.* Therefore even those who are guilty of the prostitution of unbelief which is spiritual prostitution, should be received all the same.

**OBJ. 2**: Further, Our Lord commanded Peter (Matt 18:22) to forgive his offending brother not only seven times, *but till seventy times seven times*, which Jerome expounds as meaning that a man should be forgiven as often as he has sinned. Therefore he ought to be received by the Church as often as he has sinned by falling back into heresy.

**OBJ. 3**: Further, heresy is a kind of unbelief. Now other unbelievers who wish to be converted are received by the Church. Therefore heretics also should be received.

**ON THE CONTRARY**, The Decretal Ad abolendam (*De Haereticis*, cap. ix) says that *those who are found to have*

*tam haeresim recidisse, saeculari iudicio sunt relinquendi. Non ergo ab Ecclesia sunt recipiendi.*

**RESPONDEO** dicendum quod Ecclesia, secundum domini institutionem, caritatem suam extendit ad omnes, non solum amicos, verum etiam inimicos et persequentes, secundum illud Matth. V, *diligite inimicos vestros, benefacite his qui oderunt vos.* Pertinet autem ad caritatem ut aliquis bonum proximi et velit et operetur. Est autem duplex bonum. Unum quidem spirituale, scilicet salus animae, quod principaliter respicit caritas, hoc enim quilibet ex caritate debet alii velle. Unde quantum ad hoc, haeretici revertentes, quotiescumque relapsi fuerint, ab Ecclesia recipiuntur ad poenitentiam, per quam impenditur eis via salutis.

Aliud autem est bonum quod secundario respicit caritas, scilicet bonum temporale, sicuti est vita corporalis, possessio mundana, bona fama, et dignitas ecclesiastica sive saecularis. Hoc enim non tenemur ex caritate aliis velle nisi in ordine ad salutem aeternam et eorum et aliorum. Unde si aliquid de huiusmodi bonis existens in uno impedire possit aeternam salutem in multis, non oportet quod ex caritate huiusmodi bonum ei velimus, sed potius quod velimus eum illo carere, tum quia salus aeterna praeferenda est bono temporali; tum quia bonum multorum praefertur bono unius. Si autem haeretici revertentes semper reciperentur ut conservarentur in vita et aliis temporalibus bonis, posset in praeiudicium salutis aliorum hoc esse, tum quia, si relaberentur alios inficerent; tum etiam quia, si sine poena evaderent, alii securius in haeresim relaberentur; dicitur enim Eccle. VIII, *ex eo quod non cito profertur contra malos sententia, absque timore ullo filii hominum perpetrant mala.*

Et ideo Ecclesia quidem primo revertentes ab haeresi non solum recipit ad poenitentiam, sed etiam conservat eos in vita; et interdum restituit eos dispensative ad ecclesiasticas dignitates quas prius habebant, si videantur vere conversi. Et hoc pro bono pacis frequenter legitur esse factum. Sed quando recepti iterum relabuntur, videtur esse signum inconstantiae eorum circa fidem. Et ideo ulterius redeuntes recipiuntur quidem ad poenitentiam, non tamen ut liberentur a sententia mortis.

**AD PRIMUM** ergo dicendum quod in iudicio Dei semper recipiuntur redeuntes, quia Deus scrutator est cordium, et vere redeuntes cognoscit. Sed hoc Ecclesia imitari non potest. Praesumit autem eos non vere reverti qui, cum recepti fuissent, iterum sunt relapsi. Et ideo eis viam salutis non denegat, sed a periculo mortis eos non tuetur.

*relapsed into the error which they had already abjured, must be left to the secular tribunal. Therefore they should not be received by the Church.*

**I ANSWER THAT,** In obedience to Our Lord's institution, the Church extends her charity to all, not only to friends, but also to foes who persecute her, according to Matt. 5:44: *Love your enemies; do good to them that hate you.* Now it is part of charity that we should both wish and work our neighbor's good. Again, good is twofold: one is spiritual, namely the health of the soul, which good is chiefly the object of charity, since it is this chiefly that we should wish for one another. Consequently, from this point of view, heretics who return after falling no matter how often, are admitted by the Church to Penance whereby the way of salvation is opened to them.

The other good is that which charity considers secondarily, viz. temporal good, such as life of the body, worldly possessions, good repute, ecclesiastical or secular dignity, for we are not bound by charity to wish others this good, except in relation to the eternal salvation of them and of others. Hence if the presence of one of these goods in one individual might be an obstacle to eternal salvation in many, we are not bound out of charity to wish such a good to that person, rather should we desire him to be without it, both because eternal salvation takes precedence of temporal good, and because the good of the many is to be preferred to the good of one. Now if heretics were always received on their return, in order to save their lives and other temporal goods, this might be prejudicial to the salvation of others, both because they would infect others if they relapsed again, and because, if they escaped without punishment, others would feel more assured in lapsing into heresy. For it is written (Eccl 8:11): *For because sentence is not speedily pronounced against the evil, the children of men commit evils without any fear.*

For this reason the Church not only admits to Penance those who return from heresy for the first time, but also safeguards their lives, and sometimes by dispensation, restores them to the ecclesiastical dignities which they may have had before, should their conversion appear to be sincere: we read of this as having frequently been done for the good of peace. But when they fall again, after having been received, this seems to prove them to be inconstant in faith, wherefore when they return again, they are admitted to Penance, but are not delivered from the pain of death.

**REPLY OBJ. 1:** In God's tribunal, those who return are always received, because God is a searcher of hearts, and knows those who return in sincerity. But the Church cannot imitate God in this, for she presumes that those who relapse after being once received, are not sincere in their return; hence she does not debar them from the way of salvation, but neither does she protect them from the sentence of death.

**AD SECUNDUM** dicendum quod dominus loquitur Petro de peccato in eum commisso, quod est semper dimittendum, ut fratri redeunti parcatur. Non autem intelligitur de peccato in proximum vel in Deum commisso, quod *non est nostri arbitrii dimittere*, ut Hieronymus dicit; sed in hoc est lege modus statutus, secundum quod congruit honori Dei et utilitati proximorum.

**AD TERTIUM** dicendum quod alii infideles, qui nunquam fidem acceperant, conversi ad fidem nondum ostendunt aliquod signum inconstantiae circa fidem, sicut haeretici relapsi. Et ideo non est similis ratio de utrisque.

**REPLY OBJ. 2**: Our Lord was speaking to Peter of sins committed against oneself, for one should always forgive such offenses and spare our brother when he repents. These words are not to be applied to sins committed against one's neighbor or against God, for it is not left to our discretion to forgive such offenses, as Jerome says on Matt. 18:15, *If thy brother shall offend against thee*. Yet even in this matter the law prescribes limits according as God's honor or our neighbor's good demands.

**REPLY OBJ. 3**: When other unbelievers, who have never received the faith are converted, they do not as yet show signs of inconstancy in faith, as relapsed heretics do; hence the comparison fails.

# QUESTION 12

Deinde considerandum est de apostasia. Et circa hoc quaeruntur duo.

Primo, utrum apostasia ad infidelitatem pertineat.

Secundo, utrum propter apostasiam a fide subditi absolvantur a dominio praesidentium apostatarum.

We must now consider apostasy: about which there are two points of inquiry:

(1) Whether apostasy pertains to unbelief?

(2) Whether, on account of apostasy from the faith, subjects are absolved from allegiance to an apostate prince?

## Article 1

*Whether apostasy pertains to unbelief?*

**AD PRIMUM SIC PROCEDITUR.** Videtur quod apostasia non pertineat ad infidelitatem. Illud enim quod est omnis peccati principium non videtur ad infidelitatem pertinere, quia multa peccata sine infidelitate existunt. Sed apostasia videtur esse omnis peccati principium, dicitur enim Eccli. X, *initium superbiae hominis apostatare a Deo*; et postea subditur, *initium omnis peccati superbia*. Ergo apostasia non pertinet ad infidelitatem.

**PRAETEREA**, infidelitas in intellectu consistit. Sed apostasia magis videtur consistere in exteriori opere vel sermone, aut etiam in interiori voluntate, dicitur enim Prov. VI, *homo apostata vir inutilis, gradiens ore perverso, annuit oculis, terit pede, digito loquitur, pravo corde machinatur malum, et in omni tempore iurgia seminat*. Si quis etiam se circumcideret, vel sepulcrum Mahumeti adoraret, apostata reputaretur. Ergo apostasia non pertinet directe ad infidelitatem.

**PRAETEREA**, haeresis, quia ad infidelitatem pertinet, est quaedam determinata species infidelitatis. Si ergo apostasia ad infidelitatem pertineret, sequeretur quod esset quaedam determinata species infidelitatis. Quod non videtur, secundum praedicta. Non ergo apostasia ad infidelitatem pertinet.

**SED CONTRA** est quod dicitur Ioan. VI, *multi ex discipulis eius abierunt retro*, quod est apostatare, de quibus supra dixerat Dominus: *sunt quidam ex vobis qui non credunt*. Ergo apostasia pertinet ad infidelitatem.

**RESPONDEO** dicendum quod apostasia importat retrocessionem quandam a Deo. Quae quidem diversimode fit, secundum diversos modos quibus homo Deo coniungitur. Primo namque coniungitur homo Deo per fidem; secundo, per debitam et subiectam voluntatem ad obediendum praeceptis eius; tertio, per aliqua specialia

**OBJECTION 1**: It would seem that apostasy does not pertain to unbelief. For that which is the origin of all sins, does not, seemingly, pertain to unbelief, since there are many sins without unbelief. Now apostasy seems to be the origin of every sin, for it is written (Sir 10:14): *The beginning of the pride of man is apostasy from God*, and further on, (Sir 10:15): *Pride is the beginning of all sin*. Therefore apostasy does not pertain to unbelief.

**OBJ. 2**: Further, unbelief is an act of the understanding: whereas apostasy seems rather to consist in some outward deed or utterance, or even in some inward act of the will, for it is written (Prov 6:12–14): *A man that is an apostate, an unprofitable man walketh with a perverse mouth. He winketh with the eyes, presseth with the foot, speaketh with the finger. With a wicked heart he deviseth evil, and at all times he soweth discord*. Moreover if anyone were to have himself circumcised, or to worship at the tomb of Mahomet, he would be deemed an apostate. Therefore apostasy does not pertain to unbelief.

**OBJ. 3**: Further, heresy, since it pertains to unbelief, is a determinate species of unbelief. If then, apostasy pertained to unbelief, it would follow that it is a determinate species of unbelief, which does not seem to agree with what has been said (Q. 10, A. 5). Therefore apostasy does not pertain to unbelief.

**ON THE CONTRARY**, It is written (John 6:67): *Many of his disciples went back*, i.e., apostatized, of whom Our Lord had said previously (John 6:65): *There are some of you that believe not*. Therefore apostasy pertains to unbelief.

**I ANSWER THAT**, Apostasy denotes a backsliding from God. This may happen in various ways according to the different kinds of union between man and God. For, in the first place, man is united to God by faith; second, by having his will duly submissive in obeying His commandments; third, by certain special things pertaining to supererogation

121

ad supererogationem pertinentia, sicut per religionem et clericaturam vel sacrum ordinem. Remoto autem posteriori remanet prius, sed non convertitur. Contingit ergo aliquem apostatare a Deo retrocedendo a religione quam professus est, vel ab ordine quem suscepit, et haec dicitur apostasia religionis seu ordinis. Contingit etiam aliquem apostatare a Deo per mentem repugnantem divinis mandatis. Quibus duabus apostasiis existentibus, adhuc potest remanere homo Deo coniunctus per fidem.

Sed si a fide discedat, tunc omnino a Deo retrocedere videtur. Et ideo simpliciter et absolute est apostasia per quam aliquis discedit a fide, quae vocatur apostasia perfidiae. Et per hunc modum apostasia simpliciter dicta ad infidelitatem pertinet.

AD PRIMUM ergo dicendum quod obiectio illa procedit de secunda apostasia, quae importat voluntatem a mandatis Dei resilientem, quae invenitur in omni peccato mortali.

AD SECUNDUM dicendum quod ad fidem pertinet non solum credulitas cordis, sed etiam protestatio interioris fidei per exteriora verba et facta, nam confessio est actus fidei. Et per hunc etiam modum quaedam exteriora verba vel opera ad infidelitatem pertinent, inquantum sunt infidelitatis signa, per modum quo signum sanitatis sanum dicitur. Auctoritas autem inducta, etsi possit intelligi de omni apostasia, verissime tamen convenit in apostasia a fide. Quia enim fides est *primum fundamentum sperandarum rerum*, et *sine fide impossibile est placere Deo*; sublata fide, nihil remanet in homine quod possit esse utile ad salutem aeternam; et propter hoc primo dicitur, *homo apostata vir inutilis*. Fides etiam est vita animae, secundum illud Rom. I, *iustus ex fide vivit*. Sicut ergo, sublata vita corporali, omnia membra et partes hominis a debita dispositione recedunt; ita, sublata vita iustitiae, quae est per fidem, apparet inordinatio in omnibus membris. Et primo quidem in ore, per quod maxime manifestatur cor; secundo, in oculis; tertio, in instrumentis motus; quarto, in voluntate, quae ad malum tendit. Et ex his sequitur quod iurgia seminet, alios intendens separare a fide, sicut et ipse recessit.

AD TERTIUM dicendum quod species alicuius qualitatis vel formae non diversificatur per hoc quod est terminus motus a quo vel ad quem, sed potius e converso secundum terminos motuum species attenduntur. Apostasia autem respicit infidelitatem ut terminum ad quem est motus recedentis a fide. Unde apostasia non importat determinatam speciem infidelitatis, sed quandam circumstantiam aggravantem, secundum illud II Pet. II, *melius erat eis veritatem non cognoscere quam post agnitam retroire.*

such as the religious life, the clerical state, or Holy Orders. Now if that which follows be removed, that which precedes, remains, but the converse does not hold. Accordingly a man may apostatize from God, by withdrawing from the religious life to which he was bound by profession, or from the Holy Order which he had received: and this is called *apostasy from religious life* or *Orders*. A man may also apostatize from God, by rebelling in his mind against the Divine commandments: and though man may apostatize in both the above ways, he may still remain united to God by faith.

But if he give up the faith, then he seems to turn away from God altogether: and consequently, apostasy simply and absolutely is that whereby a man withdraws from the faith, and is called *apostasy of perfidy*. In this way apostasy, simply so called, pertains to unbelief.

REPLY OBJ. 1: This objection refers to the second kind of apostasy, which denotes an act of the will in rebellion against God's commandments, an act that is to be found in every mortal sin.

REPLY OBJ. 2: It belongs to faith not only that the heart should believe, but also that external words and deeds should bear witness to the inward faith, for confession is an act of faith. In this way too, certain external words or deeds pertain to unbelief, insofar as they are signs of unbelief, even as a sign of health is said itself to be healthy. Now although the authority quoted may be understood as referring to every kind of apostate, yet it applies most truly to an apostate from the faith. For since faith is *the first foundation of things to be hoped for*, and since, without faith it is *impossible to please God*; when once faith is removed, man retains nothing that may be useful for the obtaining of eternal salvation, for which reason it is written (Prov 6:12): *A man that is an apostate, an unprofitable man*: because faith is the life of the soul, according to Rom. 1:17: *The just man liveth by faith*. Therefore, just as when the life of the body is taken away, man's every member and part loses its due disposition, so when the life of justice, which is by faith, is done away, disorder appears in all his members. First, in his mouth, whereby chiefly his mind stands revealed; second, in his eyes; third, in the instrument of movement; fourth, in his will, which tends to evil. The result is that *he sows discord*, endeavoring to sever others from the faith even as he severed himself.

REPLY OBJ. 3: The species of a quality or form are not diversified by the fact of its being the term wherefrom or whereto of movement: on the contrary, it is the movement that takes its species from the terms. Now apostasy regards unbelief as the term whereto of the movement of withdrawal from the faith; wherefore apostasy does not imply a special kind of unbelief, but an aggravating circumstance thereof, according to 2 Pet. 2:21: *It had been better for them not to know the truth, than after they had known it, to turn back.*

# Article 2

*Whether a prince forfeits his dominion over his subjects because of apostasy from the faith, so that they no longer owe him allegiance?*

AD SECUNDUM SIC PROCEDITUR. Videtur quod princeps propter apostasiam a fide non amittat dominium in subditos, quin ei teneantur obedire. Dicit enim Ambrosius quod *Iulianus imperator, quamvis esset apostata, habuit tamen sub se Christianos milites, quibus cum dicebat, producite aciem pro defensione reipublicae, obediebant ei.* Ergo propter apostasiam principis subditi non absolvuntur ab eius dominio.

PRAETEREA, apostata a fide infidelis est. Sed infidelibus dominis inveniuntur aliqui sancti viri fideliter servisse, sicut Ioseph Pharaoni, et Daniel Nabuchodonosor, et Mardochaeus Assuero. Ergo propter apostasiam a fide non est dimittendum quin principi obediatur a subditis.

PRAETEREA, sicut per apostasiam a fide receditur a Deo, ita per quodlibet peccatum. Si ergo propter apostasiam a fide perderent principes ius imperandi subditis fidelibus, pari ratione propter alia peccata hoc amitterent. Sed hoc patet esse falsum. Non ergo propter apostasiam a fide est recedendum ab obedientia principum.

SED CONTRA est quod Gregorius VII dicit, *nos, sanctorum praedecessorum statuta tenentes, eos qui excommunicatis fidelitate aut sacramento sunt constricti, apostolica auctoritate a sacramento absolvimus, et ne sibi fidelitatem observent omnibus modis prohibemus, quousque ad satisfactionem veniant.* Sed apostatae a fide sunt excommunicati, sicut et haeretici, ut dicit decretalis ad abolendam. Ergo principibus apostatantibus a fide non est obediendum.

RESPONDEO dicendum quod, sicut supra dictum est, infidelitas secundum seipsam non repugnat dominio, eo quod dominium introductum est de iure gentium, quod est ius humanum; distinctio autem fidelium et infidelium est secundum ius divinum, per quod non tollitur ius humanum. Sed aliquis per infidelitatem peccans potest sententialiter ius dominii amittere, sicut et quandoque propter alias culpas.

Ad Ecclesiam autem non pertinet punire infidelitatem in illis qui nunquam fidem susceperunt, secundum illud apostoli, I ad Cor. V, *quid mihi de his qui foris sunt iudicare?* Sed infidelitatem illorum qui fidem susceperunt potest sententialiter punire. Et convenienter in hoc puniuntur quod subditis fidelibus dominari non possint, hoc enim vergere posset in magnam fidei corruptionem; quia, ut dictum est, *homo apostata suo corde*

OBJECTION 1: It would seem that a prince does not so forfeit his dominion over his subjects, on account of apostasy from the faith, that they no longer owe him allegiance. For Ambrose says that *the Emperor Julian, though an apostate, nevertheless had under him Christian soldiers, who when he said to them, "Fall into line for the defense of the republic," were bound to obey.* Therefore subjects are not absolved from their allegiance to their prince on account of his apostasy.

OBJ. 2: Further, an apostate from the faith is an unbeliever. Now we find that certain holy men served unbelieving masters; thus Joseph served Pharaoh, Daniel served Nabuchodonosor, and Mardochai served Assuerus. Therefore apostasy from the faith does not release subjects from allegiance to their sovereign.

OBJ. 3: Further, just as by apostasy from the faith, a man turns away from God, so does every sin. Consequently if, on account of apostasy from the faith, princes were to lose their right to command those of their subjects who are believers, they would equally lose it on account of other sins: which is evidently not the case. Therefore we ought not to refuse allegiance to a sovereign on account of his apostatizing from the faith.

ON THE CONTRARY, Gregory VII says (Council, Roman V): *Holding to the institutions of our holy predecessors, we, by our apostolic authority, absolve from their oath those who through loyalty or through the sacred bond of an oath owe allegiance to excommunicated persons: and we absolutely forbid them to continue their allegiance to such persons, until these shall have made amends.* Now apostates from the faith, like heretics, are excommunicated, according to the Decretal. Therefore princes should not be obeyed when they have apostatized from the faith.

I ANSWER THAT, As stated above (Q. 10, A. 10), unbelief, in itself, is not inconsistent with dominion, since dominion is a device of the law of nations which is a human law: whereas the distinction between believers and unbelievers is of Divine right, which does not annul human right. Nevertheless a man who sins by unbelief may be sentenced to the loss of his right of dominion, as also, sometimes, on account of other sins.

Now it is not within the competency of the Church to punish unbelief in those who have never received the faith, according to the saying of the Apostle (1 Cor 5:12): *What have I to do to judge them that are without?* She can, however, pass sentence of punishment on the unbelief of those who have received the faith: and it is fitting that they should be punished by being deprived of the allegiance of their subjects: for this same allegiance might conduce to

*machinatur malum et iurgia seminat*, intendens homines separare a fide. Et ideo quam cito aliquis per sententiam denuntiatur excommunicatus propter apostasiam a fide, ipso facto eius subditi sunt absoluti a dominio eius et iuramento fidelitatis quo ei tenebantur.

**Ad primum** ergo dicendum quod illo tempore Ecclesia, in sui novitate, nondum habebat potestatem terrenos principes compescendi. Et ideo toleravit fideles Iuliano apostatae obedire in his quae non erant contra fidem, ut maius fidei periculum vitaretur.

**Ad secundum** dicendum quod alia ratio est de aliis infidelibus, qui nunquam fidem susceperunt, ut dictum est.

**Ad tertium** dicendum quod apostasia a fide totaliter separat hominem a Deo, ut dictum est, quod non contingit in quibuscumque aliis peccatis.

great corruption of the faith, since, as was stated above (A. 1, Obj. 2), *a man that is an apostate . . . with a wicked heart deviseth evil, and . . . soweth discord*, in order to sever others from the faith. Consequently, as soon as sentence of excommunication is passed on a man on account of apostasy from the faith, his subjects are *ipso facto* absolved from his authority and from the oath of allegiance whereby they were bound to him.

**Reply Obj. 1**: At that time the Church was but recently instituted, and had not, as yet, the power of curbing earthly princes; and so she allowed the faithful to obey Julian the apostate, in matters that were not contrary to the faith, in order to avoid incurring a yet greater danger.

**Reply Obj. 2**: As stated in the article, it is not a question of those unbelievers who have never received the faith.

**Reply Obj. 3**: Apostasy from the faith severs man from God altogether, as stated above (A. 1), which is not the case in any other sin.

# QUESTION 13

## THE SIN OF BLASPHEMY, IN GENERAL

Deinde considerandum est de peccato blasphemiae, quod opponitur confessioni fidei. Et primo, de blasphemia in generali; secundo, de blasphemia quae dicitur peccatum in spiritum sanctum.

Circa primum quaeruntur quatuor.

Primo, utrum blasphemia opponatur confessioni fidei.

Secundo, utrum blasphemia semper sit peccatum mortale.

Tertio, utrum blasphemia sit maximum peccatorum.

Quarto, utrum blasphemia sit in damnatis.

We must now consider the sin of blasphemy, which is opposed to the confession of faith; and (1) blasphemy in general, (2) that blasphemy which is called the sin against the Holy Spirit.

Under the first head there are four points of inquiry:

(1) Whether blasphemy is opposed to the confession of faith?

(2) Whether blasphemy is always a mortal sin?

(3) Whether blasphemy is the most grievous sin?

(4) Whether blasphemy is in the damned?

# Article 1

*Whether blasphemy is opposed to the confession of faith?*

**AD PRIMUM SIC PROCEDITUR.** Videtur quod blasphemia non opponatur confessioni fidei. Nam blasphemare est contumeliam vel aliquod convicium inferre in iniuriam creatoris. Sed hoc magis pertinet ad malevolentiam contra Deum quam ad infidelitatem. Ergo blasphemia non opponitur confessioni fidei.

**PRAETEREA,** ad Ephes. IV, super illud, *blasphemia tollatur a vobis,* dicit Glossa, *quae fit in Deum vel in sanctos.* Sed confessio fidei non videtur esse nisi de his quae pertinent ad Deum, qui est fidei obiectum. Ergo blasphemia non semper opponitur confessioni fidei.

**PRAETEREA,** a quibusdam dicitur quod sunt tres blasphemiae species, quarum una est cum attribuitur Deo quod ei non convenit; secunda est cum ab eo removetur quod ei convenit; tertia est cum attribuitur creaturae quod Deo appropriatur. Et sic videtur quod blasphemia non solum sit circa Deum, sed etiam circa creaturas. Fides autem habet Deum pro obiecto. Ergo blasphemia non opponitur confessioni fidei.

**SED CONTRA** est quod apostolus dicit, I ad Tim. I, *prius fui blasphemus et persecutor;* et postea subdit, *ignorans feci in incredulitate.* Ex quo videtur quod blasphemia ad infidelitatem pertineat.

**RESPONDEO** dicendum quod nomen blasphemiae importare videtur quandam derogationem alicuius excellentis bonitatis, et praecipue divinae. Deus autem, ut Dionysius dicit, I cap. de Div. Nom., est ipsa essentia bonitatis. Unde quidquid Deo convenit pertinet ad bonitatem ipsius; et quidquid ad ipsum non pertinet longe est

**OBJECTION 1:** It would seem that blasphemy is not opposed to the confession of faith. Because to blaspheme is to utter an affront or insult against the Creator. Now this pertains to ill-will against God rather than to unbelief. Therefore blasphemy is not opposed to the confession of faith.

**OBJ. 2:** Further, on Eph. 4:31, *Let blasphemy . . . be put away from you,* a gloss says, *that which is committed against God or the saints.* But confession of faith, seemingly, is not about other things than those pertaining to God, who is the object of faith. Therefore blasphemy is not always opposed to the confession of faith.

**OBJ. 3:** Further, according to some, there are three kinds of blasphemy. The first of these is when something unfitting is affirmed of God; the second is when something fitting is denied of Him; and the third, when something proper to God is ascribed to a creature, so that, seemingly, blasphemy is not only about God, but also about His creatures. Now the object of faith is God. Therefore blasphemy is not opposed to confession of faith.

**ON THE CONTRARY,** The Apostle says (1 Tim 1:12, 13): *I . . . before was a blasphemer and a persecutor,* and afterwards, *I did it ignorantly in* my *unbelief.* Hence it seems that blasphemy pertains to unbelief.

**I ANSWER THAT,** The word blasphemy seems to denote the disparagement of some surpassing goodness, especially that of God. Now God, as Dionysius says (*Div. Nom.* i), is the very essence of true goodness. Hence whatever befits God, pertains to His goodness, and whatever does not befit Him, is far removed from the perfection of goodness which

a ratione perfectae bonitatis, quae est eius essentia. Quicumque igitur vel negat aliquid de Deo quod ei convenit, vel asserit de eo quod ei non convenit, derogat divinae bonitati.

Quod quidem potest contingere dupliciter, uno quidem modo, secundum solam opinionem intellectus; alio modo, coniuncta quadam affectus detestatione, sicut e contrario fides Dei per dilectionem perficitur ipsius. Huiusmodi igitur derogatio divinae bonitatis est vel secundum intellectum tantum; vel etiam secundum affectum. Si consistat tantum in corde, est cordis blasphemia. Si autem exterius prodeat per locutionem, est oris blasphemia. Et secundum hoc blasphemia confessioni opponitur.

**AD PRIMUM** ergo dicendum quod ille qui contra Deum loquitur convicium inferre intendens, derogat divinae bonitati non solum secundum veritatem intellectus, sed etiam secundum pravitatem voluntatis detestantis et impedientis pro posse divinum honorem. Quod est blasphemia perfecta.

**AD SECUNDUM** dicendum quod sicut Deus in sanctis suis laudatur, inquantum laudantur opera quae Deus in sanctis efficit; ita et blasphemia quae fit in sanctos ex consequenti in Deum redundat.

**AD TERTIUM** dicendum quod secundum illa tria non possunt, proprie loquendo, distingui diversae species peccati blasphemiae. Attribuere enim Deo quod ei non convenit, vel removere ab eo quod ei convenit, non differt nisi secundum affirmationem et negationem. Quae quidem diversitas habitus speciem non distinguit, quia per eandem scientiam innotescit falsitas affirmationum et negationum, et per eandem ignorantiam utroque modo erratur, cum *negatio probetur per affirmationem*, ut habetur I Poster. Quod autem ea quae sunt Dei propria creaturis attribuantur, ad hoc pertinere videtur quod aliquid ei attribuatur quod ei non conveniat. Quidquid enim est Deo proprium est ipse Deus, attribuere ergo id quod Dei proprium est alicui creaturae est ipsum Deum dicere idem creaturae.

is His Essence. Consequently whoever either denies anything befitting God, or affirms anything unbefitting Him, disparages the Divine goodness.

Now this may happen in two ways. In the first way it may happen merely in respect of the opinion in the intellect; in the second way this opinion is united to a certain detestation in the affections, even as, on the other hand, faith in God is perfected by love of Him. Accordingly this disparagement of the Divine goodness is either in the intellect alone, or in the affections also. If it is in thought only, it is blasphemy of the heart, whereas if it betrays itself outwardly in speech it is blasphemy of the tongue. It is in this sense that blasphemy is opposed to confession of faith.

**REPLY OBJ. 1**: He that speaks against God, with the intention of reviling Him, disparages the Divine goodness, not only in respect of the falsehood in his intellect, but also by reason of the wickedness of his will, whereby he detests and strives to hinder the honor due to God, and this is perfect blasphemy.

**REPLY OBJ. 2**: Even as God is praised in His saints, insofar as praise is given to the works which God does in His saints, so does blasphemy against the saints, redound, as a consequence, against God.

**REPLY OBJ. 3**: Properly speaking, the sin of blasphemy is not in this way divided into three species: since to affirm unfitting things, or to deny fitting things of God, differ merely as affirmation and negation. For this diversity does not cause distinct species of habits, since the falsehood of affirmations and negations is made known by the same knowledge, and it is the same ignorance which errs in either way, since *negatives are proved by affirmatives*, according to *Poster*. i, 25. Again to ascribe to creatures things that are proper to God, seems to amount to the same as affirming something unfitting of Him, since whatever is proper to God is God Himself: and to ascribe to a creature, that which is proper to God, is to assert that God is the same as a creature.

# Article 2

*Whether blasphemy is always a mortal sin?*

**AD SECUNDUM SIC PROCEDITUR.** Videtur quod blasphemia non semper sit peccatum mortale. Quia super illud ad Col. III, *nunc autem deponite vos* etc., dicit Glossa, *post maiora prohibet minora*. Et tamen subdit de blasphemia. Ergo blasphemia inter peccata minora computatur, quae sunt peccata venialia.

**PRAETEREA**, omne peccatum mortale opponitur alicui praecepto Decalogi. Sed blasphemia non videtur

**OBJECTION 1**: It would seem that blasphemy is not always a mortal sin. Because a gloss on the words, *Now lay you also all away*, etc. (Col 3:8) says: *After prohibiting greater crimes he forbids lesser sins*: and yet among the latter he includes blasphemy. Therefore blasphemy is comprised among the lesser, i.e., venial, sins.

**OBJ. 2**: Further, every mortal sin is opposed to one of the precepts of the decalogue. But, seemingly, blasphemy is

alicui eorum opponi. Ergo blasphemia non est peccatum mortale.

**PRAETEREA**, peccata quae absque deliberatione committuntur non sunt mortalia, propter quod primi motus non sunt peccata mortalia, quia deliberationem rationis praecedunt, ut ex supradictis patet. Sed blasphemia quandoque absque deliberatione procedit. Ergo non semper est peccatum mortale.

**SED CONTRA** est quod dicitur Levit. XXIV, *qui blasphemaverit nomen domini, morte moriatur*. Sed poena mortis non infertur nisi pro peccato mortali. Ergo blasphemia est peccatum mortale.

**RESPONDEO** dicendum quod, sicut supra dictum est, peccatum mortale est per quod homo separatur a primo principio spiritualis vitae, quod est caritas Dei. Unde quaecumque caritati repugnant, ex suo genere sunt peccata mortalia. Blasphemia autem secundum genus suum repugnat caritati divinae, quia derogat divinae bonitati, ut dictum est, quae est obiectum caritatis. Et ideo blasphemia est peccatum mortale ex suo genere.

**AD PRIMUM** ergo dicendum quod Glossa illa non est sic intelligenda quasi omnia quae subduntur sint peccata minora. Sed quia, cum supra non expressisset nisi maiora, postmodum etiam quaedam minora subdit, inter quae etiam quaedam de maioribus ponit.

**AD SECUNDUM** dicendum quod, cum blasphemia opponatur confessioni fidei, ut dictum est, eius prohibitio reducitur ad prohibitionem infidelitatis, quae intelligitur in eo quod dicitur, *ego sum dominus Deus tuus* et cetera. Vel prohibetur per id quod dicitur, *non assumes nomen Dei tui in vanum*. Magis enim in vanum assumit nomen Dei qui aliquod falsum de Deo asserit quam qui per nomen Dei aliquod falsum confirmat.

**AD TERTIUM** dicendum quod blasphemia potest absque deliberatione ex subreptione procedere dupliciter. Uno modo, quod aliquis non advertat hoc quod dicit esse blasphemiam. Quod potest contingere cum aliquis subito ex aliqua passione in verba imaginata prorumpit, quorum significationem non considerat. Et tunc est peccatum veniale, et non habet proprie rationem blasphemiae. Alio modo, quando advertit hoc esse blasphemiam, considerans significata verborum. Et tunc non excusatur a peccato mortali, sicut nec ille qui ex subito motu irae aliquem occidit iuxta se sedentem.

not contrary to any of them. Therefore blasphemy is not a mortal sin.

**OBJ. 3**: Further, sins committed without deliberation, are not mortal: hence first movements are not mortal sins, because they precede the deliberation of the reason, as was shown above (I-II, Q. 74, AA. 3, 10). Now blasphemy sometimes occurs without deliberation of the reason. Therefore it is not always a mortal sin.

**ON THE CONTRARY**, It is written (Lev 24:16): *He that blasphemeth the name of the Lord, dying let him die.* Now the death punishment is not inflicted except for a mortal sin. Therefore blasphemy is a mortal sin.

**I ANSWER THAT**, As stated above (I-II, Q. 72, A. 5), a mortal sin is one whereby a man is severed from the first principle of spiritual life, which principle is the charity of God. Therefore whatever things are contrary to charity, are mortal sins in respect of their genus. Now blasphemy, as to its genus, is opposed to Divine charity, because, as stated above (A. 1), it disparages the Divine goodness, which is the object of charity. Consequently blasphemy is a mortal sin, by reason of its genus.

**REPLY OBJ. 1**: This gloss is not to be understood as meaning that all the sins which follow, are mortal, but that whereas all those mentioned previously are more grievous sins, some of those mentioned afterwards are less grievous; and yet among the latter some more grievous sins are included.

**REPLY OBJ. 2**: Since, as stated above (A. 1), blasphemy is contrary to the confession of faith, its prohibition is comprised under the prohibition of unbelief, expressed by the words: *I am the Lord thy God*, etc. (Exod 20:1). Or else, it is forbidden by the words: *Thou shalt not take the name of . . . God in vain* (Exod 20:7). Because he who asserts something false about God, takes His name in vain even more than he who uses the name of God in confirmation of a falsehood.

**REPLY OBJ. 3**: There are two ways in which blasphemy may occur unawares and without deliberation. In the first way, by a man failing to advert to the blasphemous nature of his words, and this may happen through his being moved suddenly by passion so as to break out into words suggested by his imagination, without heeding to the meaning of those words: this is a venial sin, and is not a blasphemy properly so called. In the second way, by adverting to the meaning of his words, and to their blasphemous nature: in which case he is not excused from mortal sin, even as neither is he who, in a sudden movement of anger, kills one who is sitting beside him.

# Article 3

*Whether the sin of blasphemy is the greatest sin?*

AD TERTIUM SIC PROCEDITUR. Videtur quod peccatum blasphemiae non sit maximum peccatum. *Malum* enim *dicitur quod nocet,* secundum Augustinum, in Enchirid. Sed magis nocet peccatum homicidii, quod perimit vitam hominis, quam peccatum blasphemiae, quod Deo nullum nocumentum potest inferre. Ergo peccatum homicidii est gravius peccato blasphemiae.

PRAETEREA, quicumque peierat inducit Deum testem falsitati, et ita videtur eum asserere esse falsum. Sed non quilibet blasphemus usque ad hoc procedit ut Deum asserat esse falsum. Ergo periurium est gravius peccatum quam blasphemia.

PRAETEREA, super illud Psalm., *nolite extollere in altum cornu vestrum,* dicit Glossa, *maximum est vitium excusationis peccati.* Non ergo blasphemia est maximum peccatum.

SED CONTRA est quod Isaiae XVIII, super illud, *ad populum terribilem,* etc., dicit Glossa, *omne peccatum, blasphemiae comparatum, levius est.*

RESPONDEO dicendum quod, sicut supra dictum est, blasphemia opponitur confessioni fidei. Et ideo habet in se gravitatem infidelitatis. Et aggravatur peccatum si superveniat detestatio voluntatis; et adhuc magis si prorumpat in verba; sicut et laus fidei augetur per dilectionem et confessionem.

Unde, cum infidelitas sit maximum peccatum secundum suum genus, sicut supra dictum est, consequens est quod etiam blasphemia sit peccatum maximum, ad idem genus pertinens et ipsum aggravans.

AD PRIMUM ergo dicendum quod homicidium et blasphemia si comparentur secundum obiecta in quae peccatur, manifestum est quod blasphemia, quae est directe peccatum in Deum, praeponderat homicidio, quod est peccatum in proximum. Si autem comparentur secundum effectum nocendi, sic homicidium praeponderat, plus enim homicidium nocet proximo quam blasphemia Deo. Sed quia in gravitate culpae magis attenditur intentio voluntatis perversae quam effectus operis, ut ex supradictis patet; ideo, cum blasphemus intendat nocumentum inferre honori divino, simpliciter loquendo gravius peccat quam homicida. Homicidium tamen primum locum tenet in peccatis inter peccata in proximum commissa.

AD SECUNDUM dicendum quod super illud ad Ephes. IV, *blasphemia tollatur a vobis,* dicit Glossa *peius est blasphemare quam peierare.* Qui enim peierat non dicit aut sentit aliquid falsum de Deo, sicut blasphemus, sed Deum adhibet testem falsitati non tanquam aesti-

OBJECTION 1: It would seem that the sin of blasphemy is not the greatest sin. For, according to Augustine (*Enchiridion* xii), *a thing is said to be evil because it does harm.* Now the sin of murder, since it destroys a man's life, does more harm than the sin of blasphemy, which can do no harm to God. Therefore the sin of murder is more grievous than that of blasphemy.

OBJ. 2: Further, a perjurer calls upon God to witness to a falsehood, and thus seems to assert that God is false. But not every blasphemer goes so far as to say that God is false. Therefore perjury is a more grievous sin than blasphemy.

OBJ. 3: Further, on Ps. 74:6, *Lift not up your horn on high,* a gloss says: *To excuse oneself for sin is the greatest sin of all.* Therefore blasphemy is not the greatest sin.

ON THE CONTRARY, On Isa. 18:2, *To a terrible people,* etc. a gloss says: *In comparison with blasphemy, every sin is slight.*

I ANSWER THAT, As stated above (A. 1), blasphemy is opposed to the confession of faith, so that it contains the gravity of unbelief: while the sin is aggravated if the will's detestation is added thereto, and yet more, if it breaks out into words, even as love and confession add to the praise of faith.

Therefore, since, as stated above (Q. 10, A. 3), unbelief is the greatest of sins in respect of its genus, it follows that blasphemy also is a very great sin, through belonging to the same genus as unbelief and being an aggravated form of that sin.

REPLY OBJ. 1: If we compare murder and blasphemy as regards the objects of those sins, it is clear that blasphemy, which is a sin committed directly against God, is more grave than murder, which is a sin against one's neighbor. On the other hand, if we compare them in respect of the harm wrought by them, murder is the graver sin, for murder does more harm to one's neighbor, than blasphemy does to God. Since, however, the gravity of a sin depends on the intention of the evil will, rather than on the effect of the deed, as was shown above (I-II, Q. 73, A. 8), it follows that, as the blasphemer intends to do harm to God's honor, absolutely speaking, he sins more grievously that the murderer. Nevertheless murder takes precedence, as to punishment, among sins committed against our neighbor.

REPLY OBJ. 2: A gloss on the words, *Let ... blasphemy be put away from you* (Eph 4:31) says: *Blasphemy is worse than perjury.* The reason is that the perjurer does not say or think something false about God, as the blasphemer does: but he calls God to witness to a falsehood, not that he deems

mans Deum esse falsum testem, sed tanquam sperans quod Deus super hoc non testificetur per aliquod evidens signum.

**AD TERTIUM** dicendum quod excusatio peccati est quaedam circumstantia aggravans omne peccatum, etiam ipsam blasphemiam. Et pro tanto dicitur esse maximum peccatum, quia quodlibet facit maius.

God a false witness, but in the hope, as it were, that God will not testify to the matter by some evident sign.

**REPLY OBJ. 3:** To excuse oneself for sin is a circumstance that aggravates every sin, even blasphemy itself: and it is called the most grievous sin, for as much as it makes every sin more grievous.

# Article 4

### *Whether the damned blaspheme?*

**AD QUARTUM SIC PROCEDITUR.** Videtur quod damnati non blasphement. Detinentur enim nunc aliqui mali a blasphemando propter timorem futurarum poenarum. Sed damnati has poenas experiuntur, unde magis eas abhorrent. Ergo multo magis a blasphemando compescuntur.

**PRAETEREA**, blasphemia, cum sit gravissimum peccatum, est maxime demeritorium. Sed in futura vita non est status merendi neque demerendi. Ergo nullus erit locus blasphemiae.

**PRAETEREA**, Eccle. XI dicitur quod *in quocumque loco lignum ceciderit, ibi erit*, ex quo patet quod post hanc vitam homini non accrescit nec meritum nec peccatum quod non habuit in hac vita. Sed multi damnabuntur qui in hac vita non fuerunt blasphemi. Ergo nec in futura vita blasphemabunt.

**SED CONTRA** est quod dicitur Apoc. XVI, *aestuaverunt homines aestu magno, et blasphemaverunt nomen domini habentis potestatem super has plagas*, ubi dicit Glossa quod *in Inferno positi, quamvis sciant se pro merito puniri, dolebunt tamen quod Deus tantam potentiam habeat quod plagas eis inferat.* Hoc autem esset blasphemia in praesenti. Ergo et in futuro.

**RESPONDEO** dicendum quod, sicut dictum est, ad rationem blasphemiae pertinet detestatio divinae bonitatis. Illi autem qui sunt in Inferno retinebunt perversam voluntatem, aversam a Dei iustitia, in hoc quod diligunt ea pro quibus puniuntur, et vellent eis uti si possent, et odiunt poenas quae pro huiusmodi peccatis infliguntur; dolent tamen de peccatis quae commiserunt, non quia ipsa odiant, sed quia pro eis puniuntur. Sic ergo talis detestatio divinae iustitiae est in eis interior cordis blasphemia. Et credibile est quod post resurrectionem erit in eis etiam vocalis blasphemia, sicut in sanctis vocalis laus Dei.

**AD PRIMUM** ergo dicendum quod homines deterrentur in praesenti a blasphemia propter timorem

**OBJECTION 1:** It would seem that the damned do not blaspheme. Because some wicked men are deterred from blaspheming now, on account of the fear of future punishment. But the damned are undergoing these punishments, so that they abhor them yet more. Therefore, much more are they restrained from blaspheming.

**OBJ. 2:** Further, since blasphemy is a most grievous sin, it is most demeritorious. Now in the life to come there is no state of meriting or demeriting. Therefore there will be no place for blasphemy.

**OBJ. 3:** Further, it is written (Eccl 11:3) that *the tree . . . in what place soever it shall fall, there shall it be*: whence it clearly follows that, after this life, man acquires neither merit nor sin, which he did not already possess in this life. Now many will be damned who were not blasphemous in this life. Neither, therefore, will they blaspheme in the life to come.

**ON THE CONTRARY,** It is written (Rev 16:9): *The men were scorched with great heat, and they blasphemed the name of God, Who hath power over these plagues*, and a gloss on these words says that *those who are in hell, though aware that they are deservedly punished, will nevertheless complain that God is so powerful as to torture them thus.* Now this would be blasphemy in their present state: and consequently it will also be in their future state.

**I ANSWER THAT,** As stated above (AA. 1, 3), detestation of the Divine goodness is a necessary condition of blasphemy. Now those who are in hell retain their wicked will which is turned away from God's justice, since they love the things for which they are punished, would wish to use them if they could, and hate the punishments inflicted on them for those same sins. They regret indeed the sins which they have committed, not because they hate them, but because they are punished for them. Accordingly this detestation of the Divine justice is, in them, the interior blasphemy of the heart: and it is credible that after the resurrection they will blaspheme God with the tongue, even as the saints will praise Him with their voices.

**REPLY OBJ. 1:** In the present life men are deterred from blasphemy through fear of punishment which they

poenarum quas se putant evadere. Sed damnati in Inferno non sperant se posse poenas evadere. Et ideo, tanquam desperati, feruntur ad omne ad quod eis perversa voluntas suggerit.

**Ad secundum** dicendum quod mereri et demereri pertinent ad statum viae. Unde bona in viatoribus sunt meritoria, mala vero demeritoria. In beatis autem bona non sunt meritoria, sed pertinentia ad eorum beatitudinis praemium. Et similiter mala in damnatis non sunt demeritoria, sed pertinent ad damnationis poenam.

**Ad tertium** dicendum quod quilibet in peccato mortali decedens fert secum voluntatem detestantem divinam iustitiam quantum ad aliquid. Et secundum hoc poterit ei inesse blasphemia.

think they can escape: whereas, in hell, the damned have no hope of escape, so that, in despair, they are borne towards whatever their wicked will suggests to them.

**Reply Obj. 2**: Merit and demerit belong to the state of a wayfarer, wherefore good is meritorious in them, while evil is demeritorious. In the blessed, on the other hand, good is not meritorious, but is part of their blissful reward, and, in like manner, in the damned, evil is not demeritorious, but is part of the punishment of damnation.

**Reply Obj. 3**: Whoever dies in mortal sin, bears with him a will that detests the Divine justice with regard to a certain thing, and in this respect there can be blasphemy in him.

# Question 14

## Blasphemy against the Holy Spirit

Deinde considerandum est in speciali de blasphemia in spiritum sanctum. Et circa hoc quaeruntur quatuor.

Primo, utrum blasphemia vel peccatum in spiritum sanctum sit idem quod peccatum ex certa malitia.

Secundo, de speciebus huius peccati.

Tertio, utrum sit irremissibile.

Quarto, utrum aliquis possit peccare in spiritum sanctum a principio, antequam alia peccata committat.

We must now consider in particular blasphemy against the Holy Spirit: under which head there are four points of inquiry:

(1) Whether blasphemy or the sin against the Holy Spirit is the same as the sin committed through certain malice?

(2) Of the species of this sin;

(3) Whether it can be forgiven?

(4) Whether it is possible to begin by sinning against the Holy Spirit before committing other sins?

# Article 1

*Whether the sin against the Holy Spirit is the same as the sin committed through certain malice?*

**Ad primum sic proceditur**. Videtur quod peccatum in spiritum sanctum non sit idem quod peccatum ex certa malitia. Peccatum enim in spiritum sanctum est peccatum blasphemiae, ut patet Matth. XII. Sed non omne peccatum ex certa malitia est peccatum blasphemiae, contingit enim multa alia peccatorum genera ex certa malitia committi. Ergo peccatum in spiritum sanctum non est idem quod peccatum ex certa malitia.

**Praeterea**, peccatum ex certa malitia dividitur contra peccatum ex ignorantia et contra peccatum ex infirmitate. Sed peccatum in spiritum sanctum dividitur contra peccatum in filium hominis, ut patet Matth. XII. Ergo peccatum in spiritum sanctum non est idem quod peccatum ex certa malitia, quia quorum opposita sunt diversa, ipsa quoque sunt diversa.

**Praeterea**, peccatum in spiritum sanctum est quoddam genus peccati cui determinatae species assignantur. Sed peccatum ex certa malitia non est speciale genus peccati, sed est quaedam conditio vel circumstantia generalis quae potest esse circa omnia peccatorum genera. Ergo peccatum in spiritum sanctum non est idem quod peccatum ex certa malitia.

**Sed contra** est quod Magister dicit, XLIII dist. II Lib. Sent., quod ille peccat in spiritum sanctum *cui malitia propter se placet*. Hoc autem est peccare ex certa malitia. Ergo idem videtur esse peccatum ex certa malitia quod peccatum in spiritum sanctum.

**Objection 1**: It would seem that the sin against the Holy Spirit is not the same as the sin committed through certain malice. Because the sin against the Holy Spirit is the sin of blasphemy, according to Matt. 12:32. But not every sin committed through certain malice is a sin of blasphemy: since many other kinds of sin may be committed through certain malice. Therefore the sin against the Holy Spirit is not the same as the sin committed through certain malice.

**Obj. 2**: Further, the sin committed through certain malice is condivided with sin committed through ignorance, and sin committed through weakness: whereas the sin against the Holy Spirit is condivided with the sin against the Son of Man (Matt 12:32). Therefore the sin against the Holy Spirit is not the same as the sin committed through certain malice, since things whose opposites differ, are themselves different.

**Obj. 3**: Further, the sin against the Holy Spirit is itself a generic sin, having its own determinate species: whereas sin committed through certain malice is not a special kind of sin, but a condition or general circumstance of sin, which can affect any kind of sin at all. Therefore the sin against the Holy Spirit is not the same as the sin committed through certain malice.

**On the contrary**, The Master says (*Sent.* ii, D, 43) that to sin against the Holy Spirit is *to take pleasure in the malice of sin for its own sake*. Now this is to sin through certain malice. Therefore it seems that the sin committed through certain malice is the same as the sin against the Holy Spirit.

**Respondeo** dicendum quod de peccato seu blasphemia in spiritum sanctum tripliciter aliqui loquuntur. Antiqui enim doctores, scilicet Athanasius, Hilarius, Ambrosius, Hieronymus et Chrysostomus dicunt esse peccatum in spiritum sanctum quando, ad litteram, aliquid blasphemum dicitur contra spiritum sanctum, sive *Spiritus Sanctus* accipiatur secundum quod est nomen essentiale conveniens toti Trinitati, cuius quaelibet persona et spiritus est et sanctus; sive prout est nomen personale unius in Trinitate personae. Et secundum hoc distinguitur, Matth. XII blasphemia in spiritum sanctum contra blasphemiam in filium hominis. Christus enim operabatur quaedam humanitus, comedendo, bibendo et alia huiusmodi faciendo; et quaedam divinitus, scilicet Daemones eiiciendo, mortuos suscitando, et cetera huiusmodi; quae quidem agebat et per virtutem propriae divinitatis, et per operationem spiritus sancti, quo secundum humanitatem erat repletus. Iudaei autem primo quidem dixerant blasphemiam in Filium hominis, cum dicebant eum *voracem, potatorem vini et publicanorum amatorem*, ut habetur Matth. XI. Postmodum autem blasphemaverunt in spiritum sanctum, dum opera quae ipse operabatur virtute propriae divinitatis et per operationem spiritus sancti, attribuebant principi Daemoniorum. Et propter hoc dicuntur in spiritum sanctum blasphemasse.

Augustinus autem, in libro de Verb. Dom., blasphemiam vel peccatum in spiritum sanctum dicit esse finalem impoenitentiam, quando scilicet aliquis perseverat in peccato mortali usque ad mortem. Quod quidem non solum verbo oris fit, sed etiam verbo cordis et operis, non uno sed multis. Hoc autem verbum, sic acceptum, dicitur esse contra spiritum sanctum, quia est contra remissionem peccatorum, quae fit per spiritum sanctum, qui est caritas patris et filii. Nec hoc dominus dixit Iudaeis quasi ipsi peccarent in spiritum sanctum, nondum enim erant finaliter impoenitentes. Sed admonuit eos ne, taliter loquentes, ad hoc pervenirent quod in spiritum sanctum peccarent. Et sic intelligendum est quod dicitur Marc. III, ubi, postquam dixerat, *qui blasphemaverit in spiritum sanctum* etc., subiungit Evangelista *quoniam dicebant, spiritum immundum habet.*

Alii vero aliter accipiunt, dicentes peccatum vel blasphemiam in spiritum sanctum esse quando aliquis peccat contra appropriatum bonum spiritus sancti, cui appropriatur bonitas, sicut patri appropriatur potentia et filio sapientia. Unde peccatum in patrem dicunt esse quando peccatur ex infirmitate; peccatum autem in filium, quando peccatur ex ignorantia; peccatum autem in spiritum sanctum, quando peccatur ex certa malitia, idest ex ipsa electione mali, ut supra expositum est.

**I answer that,** Three meanings have been given to the sin against the Holy Spirit. For the earlier doctors, viz. Athanasius (*Super Matth.* xii, 32), Hilary (Can. xii *in Matth.*), Ambrose (*Super Luc.* xii, 10), Jerome (*Super Matth.* xii), and Chrysostom (*Hom. xli in Matth.*), say that the sin against the Holy Spirit is literally to utter a blasphemy against *the Holy Spirit*, whether by Holy Spirit we understand the essential name applicable to the whole Trinity, each Person of which is a Spirit and is holy, or the personal name of one of the Persons of the Trinity, in which sense blasphemy against the Holy Spirit is distinct from the blasphemy against the Son of Man (Matt 12:32), for Christ did certain things in respect of His human nature, by eating, drinking, and such like actions, while He did others in respect of His Godhead, by casting out devils, raising the dead, and the like: which things He did both by the power of His own Godhead and by the operation of the Holy Spirit, of Whom He was full, according to his human nature. Now the Jews began by speaking blasphemy against the Son of Man, when they said (Matt 11:19) that He was *a glutton, a wine drinker, and a friend of publicans*: but afterwards they blasphemed against the Holy Spirit, when they ascribed to the prince of devils those works which Christ did by the power of His own Divine Nature and by the operation of the Holy Spirit.

Augustine, however (*De Verb. Dom.*, Serm. lxxi), says that blasphemy or the sin against the Holy Spirit, is final impenitence when, namely, a man perseveres in mortal sin until death, and that it is not confined to utterance by word of mouth, but extends to words in thought and deed, not to one word only, but to many. Now this word, in this sense, is said to be uttered against the Holy Spirit, because it is contrary to the remission of sins, which is the work of the Holy Spirit, Who is the charity both of the Father and of the Son. Nor did Our Lord say this to the Jews, as though they had sinned against the Holy Spirit, since they were not yet guilty of final impenitence, but He warned them, lest by similar utterances they should come to sin against the Holy Spirit: and it is in this sense that we are to understand Mark 3:29, 30, where after Our Lord had said: *But he that shall blaspheme against the Holy Spirit*, etc. the Evangelist adds, *because they said: He hath an unclean spirit.*

But others understand it differently, and say that the sin of blasphemy against the Holy Spirit, is a sin committed against that good which is appropriated to the Holy Spirit: because goodness is appropriated to the Holy Spirit, just a power is appropriated to the Father, and wisdom to the Son. Hence they say that when a man sins through weakness, it is a sin *against the Father*; that when he sins through ignorance, it is a sin *against the Son*; and that when he sins through certain malice, i.e., through the very choosing of evil, as explained above (I-II, Q. 78, AA. 1, 3), it is a sin *against the Holy Spirit*.

Quod quidem contingit dupliciter. Uno modo, ex inclinatione habitus vitiosi, qui malitia dicitur, et sic non est idem peccare ex malitia quod peccare in spiritum sanctum. Alio modo contingit ex eo quod per contemptum abiicitur et removetur id quod electionem peccati poterat impedire, sicut spes per desperationem, et timor per praesumptionem, et quaedam alia huiusmodi, ut infra dicetur. Haec autem omnia quae peccati electionem impediunt, sunt effectus spiritus sancti in nobis. Et ideo sic ex malitia peccare est peccare in spiritum sanctum.

Ad primum ergo dicendum quod, sicut confessio fidei non solum consistit in protestatione oris, sed etiam in protestatione operis; ita etiam blasphemia spiritus sancti potest considerari et in ore et in corde et in opere.

Ad secundum dicendum quod secundum tertiam acceptionem blasphemia in spiritum sanctum distinguitur contra blasphemiam in filium hominis secundum quod filius hominis est etiam filius Dei, idest *Dei virtus et Dei sapientia*. Unde secundum hoc, peccatum in filium hominis erit peccatum ex ignorantia vel ex infirmitate.

Ad tertium dicendum quod peccatum ex certa malitia secundum quod provenit ex inclinatione habitus, non est speciale peccatum, sed quaedam generalis peccati conditio. Prout vero est ex speciali contemptu effectus spiritus sancti in nobis, habet rationem specialis peccati. Et secundum hoc etiam peccatum in spiritum sanctum est speciale genus peccati. Et similiter secundum primam expositionem. Secundum autem secundam expositionem, non est speciale genus peccati, nam finalis impoenitentia potest esse circumstantia cuiuslibet generis peccati.

Now this may happen in two ways. First by reason of the very inclination of a vicious habit which we call malice, and, in this way, to sin through malice is not the same as to sin against the Holy Spirit. In another way it happens that by reason of contempt, that which might have prevented the choosing of evil, is rejected or removed; thus hope is removed by despair, and fear by presumption, and so on, as we shall explain further on (QQ. 20, 21). Now all these things which prevent the choosing of sin are effects of the Holy Spirit in us; so that, in this sense, to sin through malice is to sin against the Holy Spirit.

Reply Obj. 1: Just as the confession of faith consists in a protestation not only of words but also of deeds, so blasphemy against the Holy Spirit can be uttered in word, thought and deed.

Reply Obj. 2: According to the third interpretation, blasphemy against the Holy Spirit is condivided with blasphemy against the Son of Man, forasmuch as He is also the Son of God, i.e., the *power of God and the wisdom of God* (1 Cor 1:24). Wherefore, in this sense, the sin against the Son of Man will be that which is committed through ignorance, or through weakness.

Reply Obj. 3: Sin committed through certain malice, insofar as it results from the inclination of a habit, is not a special sin, but a general condition of sin: whereas, insofar as it results from a special contempt of an effect of the Holy Spirit in us, it has the character of a special sin. According to this interpretation the sin against the Holy Spirit is a special kind of sin, as also according to the first interpretation: whereas according to the second, it is not a species of sin, because final impenitence may be a circumstance of any kind of sin.

# Article 2

*Whether it is fitting to distinguish six kinds of sin against the Holy Spirit?*

Ad secundum sic proceditur. Videtur quod inconvenienter assignentur sex species peccati in spiritum sanctum, scilicet desperatio, praesumptio, impoenitentia, obstinatio, impugnatio veritatis agnitae et invidentia fraternae gratiae; quas species ponit Magister, XLIII dist. II Lib. Sent. Negare enim divinam iustitiam vel misericordiam ad infidelitatem pertinet. Sed per desperationem aliquis reiicit divinam misericordiam, per praesumptionem autem divinam iustitiam. Ergo unumquodque eorum potius est species infidelitatis quam peccati in spiritum sanctum.

Praeterea, impoenitentia videtur respicere peccatum praeteritum, obstinatio autem peccatum futurum. Sed praeteritum vel futurum non diversificant speciem

Objection 1: It would seem unfitting to distinguish six kinds of sin against the Holy Spirit, viz. despair, presumption, impenitence, obstinacy, resisting the known truth, envy of our brother's spiritual good, which are assigned by the Master (*Sent.* ii, D, 43). For to deny God's justice or mercy belongs to unbelief. Now, by despair, a man rejects God's mercy, and by presumption, His justice. Therefore each of these is a kind of unbelief rather than of the sin against the Holy Spirit.

Obj. 2: Further, impenitence, seemingly, regards past sins, while obstinacy regards future sins. Now past and future time do not diversify the species of virtues or vices,

virtutis vel vitii, secundum enim eandem fidem qua credimus Christum natum, antiqui crediderunt eum nasciturum. Ergo obstinatio et impoenitentia non debent poni duae species peccati in spiritum sanctum.

**PRAETEREA**, *veritas et gratia per Iesum Christum facta est*, ut habetur Ioan. I. Ergo videtur quod impugnatio veritatis agnitae et invidentia fraternae gratiae magis pertineant ad blasphemiam in filium hominis quam ad blasphemiam in spiritum sanctum.

**PRAETEREA**, Bernardus dicit, in libro de Dispensat. et Praecept., *quod nolle obedire est resistere spiritui sancto.* Glossa etiam dicit, Levit. X, quod *simulata poenitentia est blasphemia spiritus sancti.* Schisma etiam videtur directe opponi spiritui sancto, per quem Ecclesia unitur. Et ita videtur quod non sufficienter tradantur species peccati in spiritum sanctum.

**SED CONTRA**, Augustinus dicit, in libro de fide ad Petrum, quod illi qui desperant de indulgentia peccatorum, vel qui sine meritis de misericordia Dei praesumunt, peccant in spiritum sanctum. Et in Enchiridio dicit quod *qui in obstinatione mentis diem claudit extremum, reus est peccato in spiritum sanctum.* Et in libro de Verb. Dom. dicit quod impoenitentia est peccatum in spiritum sanctum. Et in libro de Serm. Dom. in monte dicit quod *invidiae facibus fraternitatem impugnare est* peccare in spiritum sanctum. Et in libro de unico Bapt. dicit quod *qui veritatem contemnit, aut circa fratres malignus est, quibus veritas revelatur; aut circa Deum ingratus, cuius inspiratione Ecclesia instruitur*; et sic videtur quod peccet in spiritum sanctum.

**RESPONDEO** dicendum quod, secundum quod peccatum in spiritum sanctum tertio modo accipitur, convenienter praedictae species ei assignantur. Quae distinguuntur secundum remotionem vel contemptum eorum per quae potest homo ab electione peccati impediri. Quae quidem sunt vel ex parte divini iudicii; vel ex parte donorum ipsius; vel etiam ex parte ipsius peccati. Avertitur enim homo ab electione peccati ex consideratione divini iudicii, quod habet iustitiam cum misericordia, et per spem, quae consurgit ex consideratione misericordiae remittentis peccata et praemiantis bona, et haec tollitur per desperationem, et iterum per timorem, qui insurgit ex consideratione divinae iustitiae punientis peccata; et hic tollitur per praesumptionem, dum scilicet aliquis se praesumit gloriam adipisci sine meritis, vel veniam sine poenitentia.

Dona autem Dei quibus retrahimur a peccato sunt duo. Quorum unum est agnitio veritatis, contra quod ponitur impugnatio veritatis agnitae, dum scilicet aliquis veritatem fidei agnitam impugnat ut licentius peccet. Aliud est auxilium interioris gratiae, contra quod ponitur invidentia fraternae gratiae, dum scilicet aliquis non

since it is the same faith whereby we believe that Christ was born, and those of old believed that He would be born. Therefore obstinacy and impenitence should not be reckoned as two species of sin against the Holy Spirit.

**OBJ. 3**: Further, *grace and truth came by Jesus Christ* (John 1:17). Therefore it seems that resistance of the known truth, and envy of a brother's spiritual good, belong to blasphemy against the Son rather than against the Holy Spirit.

**OBJ. 4**: Further, Bernard says (*De Dispens. et Praecept.* xi) that *to refuse to obey is to resist the Holy Spirit.* Moreover a gloss on Lev. 10:16, says that *a feigned repentance is a blasphemy against the Holy Spirit.* Again, schism is, seemingly, directly opposed to the Holy Spirit by Whom the Church is united together. Therefore it seems that the species of sins against the Holy Spirit are insufficiently enumerated.

**ON THE CONTRARY**, Augustine (*De Fide ad Petrum* iii) says that those who despair of pardon for their sins, or who without merits presume on God's mercy, sin against the Holy Spirit, and (*Enchiridion* lxxxiii) that *he who dies in a state of obstinacy is guilty of the sin against the Holy Spirit*, and (*De Verb. Dom.*, Serm. lxxi) that impenitence is a sin against the Holy Spirit, and (*De Serm. Dom. in Monte* xxii), that *to resist fraternal goodness with the brands of envy* is to sin against the Holy Spirit, and (*De Bap. contra Donat.* vi, 35) that *a man who spurns the truth is either envious of his brethren to whom the truth is revealed, or ungrateful to God, by Whose inspiration the Church is taught*, and therefore, seemingly, sins against the Holy Spirit.

**I ANSWER THAT**, The above species are fittingly assigned to the sin against the Holy Spirit taken in the third sense, because they are distinguished in respect of the removal or contempt of those things whereby a man can be prevented from sinning through choice. These things are either on the part of God's judgment, or on the part of His gifts, or on the part of sin. For, by consideration of the Divine judgment, wherein justice is accompanied with mercy, man is hindered from sinning through choice, both by hope, arising from the consideration of the mercy that pardons sins and rewards good deeds, which hope is removed by *despair*; and by fear, arising from the consideration of the Divine justice that punishes sins, which fear is removed by *presumption*, when, namely, a man presumes that he can obtain glory without merits, or pardon without repentance.

God's gifts whereby we are withdrawn from sin, are two: one is the acknowledgment of the truth, against which there is the *resistance of the known truth*, when, namely, a man resists the truth which he has acknowledged, in order to sin more freely: while the other is the assistance of inward grace, against which there is *envy of a brother's*

solum invidet personae fratris, sed etiam invidet gratiae Dei crescenti in mundo.

Ex parte vero peccati duo sunt quae hominem a peccato retrahere possunt. Quorum unum est inordinatio et turpitudo actus, cuius consideratio inducere solet in homine poenitentiam de peccato commisso. Et contra hoc ponitur impoenitentia, non quidem eo modo quo dicit permanentiam in peccato usque ad mortem, sicut supra impoenitentia accipiebatur (sic enim non esset speciale peccatum, sed quaedam peccati circumstantia); sed accipitur hic impoenitentia secundum quod importat propositum non poenitendi. Aliud autem est parvitas et brevitas boni quod quis in peccato quaerit, secundum illud Rom. VI, *quem fructum habuistis in quibus nunc erubescitis?* Cuius consideratio inducere solet hominem ad hoc quod eius voluntas in peccato non firmetur. Et hoc tollitur per obstinationem, quando scilicet homo firmat suum propositum in hoc quod peccato inhaereat. Et de his duobus dicitur Ierem. VIII, *nullus est qui agat poenitentiam super peccato suo, dicens, quid feci?* Quantum ad primum; *omnes conversi sunt ad cursum quasi equus impetu vadens ad praelium,* quantum ad secundum.

**AD PRIMUM** ergo dicendum quod peccatum desperationis vel praesumptionis non consistit in hoc quod Dei iustitia vel misericordia non credatur, sed in hoc quod contemnatur.

**AD SECUNDUM** dicendum quod obstinatio et impoenitentia non solum differunt secundum praeteritum et futurum, sed secundum quasdam formales rationes ex diversa consideratione eorum quae in peccato considerari possunt, ut dictum est.

**AD TERTIUM** dicendum quod gratiam et veritatem Christus fecit per dona spiritus sancti, quae hominibus dedit.

**AD QUARTUM** dicendum quod nolle obedire pertinet ad obstinationem; simulatio poenitentiae ad impoenitentiam; schisma ad invidentiam fraternae gratiae, per quam membra Ecclesiae uniuntur.

*spiritual good,* when, namely, a man is envious not only of his brother's person, but also of the increase of Divine grace in the world.

On the part of sin, there are two things which may withdraw man therefrom: one is the inordinateness and shamefulness of the act, the consideration of which is wont to arouse man to repentance for the sin he has committed, and against this there is *impenitence,* not as denoting permanence in sin until death, in which sense it was taken above (for thus it would not be a special sin, but a circumstance of sin), but as denoting the purpose of not repenting. The other thing is the smallness or brevity of the good which is sought in sin, according to Rom. 6:21: *What fruit had you therefore then in those things, of which you are now ashamed?* The consideration of this is wont to prevent man's will from being hardened in sin, and this is removed by *obstinacy,* whereby man hardens his purpose by clinging to sin. Of these two it is written (Jer 8:6): *There is none that doth penance for his sin, saying: What have I done?* as regards the first; and, *They are all turned to their own course, as a horse rushing to the battle,* as regards the second.

**REPLY OBJ. 1**: The sins of despair and presumption consist, not in disbelieving in God's justice and mercy, but in contemning them.

**REPLY OBJ. 2**: Obstinacy and impenitence differ not only in respect of past and future time, but also in respect of certain formal aspects by reason of the diverse consideration of those things which may be considered in sin, as explained above.

**REPLY OBJ. 3**: Grace and truth were the work of Christ through the gifts of the Holy Spirit which He gave to men.

**REPLY OBJ. 4**: To refuse to obey belongs to obstinacy, while a feigned repentance belongs to impenitence, and schism to the envy of a brother's spiritual good, whereby the members of the Church are united together.

# Article 3

*Whether the sin against the Holy Spirit can be forgiven?*

**AD TERTIUM SIC PROCEDITUR.** Videtur quod peccatum in spiritum sanctum non sit irremissibile. Dicit enim Augustinus, in libro de Verb. Dom., *de nullo desperandum est quandiu patientia domini ad poenitentiam adducit.* Sed si aliquod peccatum esset irremissibile, esset de aliquo peccatore desperandum. Ergo peccatum in spiritum sanctum non est irremissibile.

**OBJECTION 1**: It would seem that the sin against the Holy Spirit can be forgiven. For Augustine says (*De Verb. Dom.,* Serm. lxxi): *We should despair of no man, so long as Our Lord's patience brings him back to repentance.* But if any sin cannot be forgiven, it would be possible to despair of some sinners. Therefore the sin against the Holy Spirit can be forgiven.

PRAETEREA, nullum peccatum remittitur nisi per hoc quod anima sanatur a Deo. *Sed omnipotenti medico nullus insanabilis languor occurrit*, sicut dicit Glossa super illud Psalm., *qui sanat omnes infirmitates tuas.* Ergo peccatum in spiritum sanctum non est irremissibile.

PRAETEREA, liberum arbitrium se habet ad bonum et ad malum. Sed quandiu durat status viae, potest aliquis a quacumque virtute excidere, cum etiam Angelus de caelo ceciderit, unde dicitur Iob IV, *in Angelis suis reperit pravitatem, quanto magis qui habitant domos luteas?* Ergo pari ratione potest aliquis a quocumque peccato ad statum iustitiae redire. Ergo peccatum in spiritum sanctum non est irremissibile.

SED CONTRA est quod dicitur Matth. XII, *qui dixerit verbum contra spiritum sanctum, non remittetur ei neque in hoc saeculo neque in futuro.* Et Augustinus dicit, in libro de Serm. Dom. in monte, quod *tanta est labes huius peccati quod humilitatem deprecandi subire non potest.*

RESPONDEO dicendum quod secundum diversas acceptiones peccati in spiritum sanctum, diversimode irremissibile dicitur. Si enim dicatur peccatum in spiritum sanctum finalis impoenitentia, sic dicitur irremissibile quia nullo modo remittitur. Peccatum enim mortale in quo homo perseverat usque ad mortem, quia in hac vita non remittitur per poenitentiam, nec etiam in futuro dimittetur.

Secundum autem alias duas acceptiones dicitur irremissibile, non quia nullo modo remittatur, sed quia, quantum est de se, habet meritum ut non remittatur. Et hoc dupliciter. Uno modo, quantum ad poenam. Qui enim ex ignorantia vel infirmitate peccat, minorem poenam meretur, qui autem ex certa malitia peccat, non habet aliquam excusationem unde eius poena minuatur. Similiter etiam qui blasphemabat in filium hominis, eius divinitate nondum revelata, poterat habere aliquam excusationem propter infirmitatem carnis quam in eo aspiciebat, et sic minorem poenam merebatur, sed qui ipsam divinitatem blasphemabat, opera spiritus sancti Diabolo attribuens, nullam excusationem habebat unde eius poena diminueretur.

Et ideo dicitur, secundum expositionem Chrysostomi, hoc peccatum Iudaeis non remitti neque in hoc saeculo neque in futuro, quia pro eo passi sunt poenam et in praesenti vita per Romanos, et in futura vita in poena Inferni. Sicut etiam Athanasius inducit exemplum de eorum parentibus, qui primo quidem contra Moysen contenderunt propter defectum aquae et panis, et hoc dominus sustinuit patienter, habebant enim excusationem ex infirmitate carnis. Sed postmodum gravius peccaverunt quasi blasphemantes in spiritum sanctum, beneficia Dei qui eos de Aegypto eduxerat, idolo attribuentes, cum dixerunt, *hi sunt dii tui, Israel, qui te eduxerunt de terra Aegypti.* Et ideo dominus et tempora-

OBJ. 2: Further, no sin is forgiven, except through the soul being healed by God. But *no disease is incurable to an all-powerful physician*, as a gloss says on Ps. 102:3, *Who healeth all thy diseases.* Therefore the sin against the Holy Spirit can be forgiven.

OBJ. 3: Further, the free-will is indifferent to either good or evil. Now, so long as man is a wayfarer, he can fall away from any virtue, since even an angel fell from heaven, wherefore it is written (Job 4:18, 19): *In His angels He found wickedness: how much more shall they that dwell in houses of clay?* Therefore, in like manner, a man can return from any sin to the state of justice. Therefore the sin against the Holy Spirit can be forgiven.

ON THE CONTRARY, It is written (Matt 12:32): *He that shall speak against the Holy Spirit, it shall not be forgiven him, neither in this world, nor in the world to come*: and Augustine says (*De Serm. Dom. in Monte* i, 22) that *so great is the downfall of this sin that it cannot submit to the humiliation of asking for pardon.*

I ANSWER THAT, According to the various interpretations of the sin against the Holy Spirit, there are various ways in which it may be said that it cannot be forgiven. For if by the sin against the Holy Spirit we understand final impenitence, it is said to be unpardonable, since in no way is it pardoned: because the mortal sin wherein a man perseveres until death will not be forgiven in the life to come, since it was not remitted by repentance in this life.

According to the other two interpretations, it is said to be unpardonable, not as though it is nowise forgiven, but because, considered in itself, it deserves not to be pardoned: and this in two ways. First, as regards the punishment, since he that sins through ignorance or weakness, deserves less punishment, whereas he that sins through certain malice, can offer no excuse in alleviation of his punishment. Likewise those who blasphemed against the Son of Man before His Godhead was revealed, could have some excuse, on account of the weakness of the flesh which they perceived in Him, and hence, they deserved less punishment; whereas those who blasphemed against His very Godhead, by ascribing to the devil the works of the Holy Spirit, had no excuse in diminution of their punishment.

Wherefore, according to Chrysostom's commentary (*Hom. xlii in Matth.*), the Jews are said not to be forgiven this sin, neither in this world nor in the world to come, because they were punished for it, both in the present life, through the Romans, and in the life to come, in the pains of hell. Thus also Athanasius adduces the example of their forefathers who, first of all, wrangled with Moses on account of the shortage of water and bread; and this the Lord bore with patience, because they were to be excused on account of the weakness of the flesh: but afterwards they sinned more grievously when, by ascribing to an idol the favors bestowed by God Who had brought them out of Egypt, they blasphemed, so to speak, against the Holy

liter fecit eos puniri, quia *ceciderunt in die illo quasi tria millia hominum*; et in futurum eis poenam comminatur, dicens, *ego autem in die ultionis visitabo hoc peccatum eorum.*

Alio modo potest intelligi quantum ad culpam, sicut aliquis dicitur morbus incurabilis secundum naturam morbi, per quem tollitur id ex quo morbus potest curari, puta cum morbus tollit virtutem naturae, vel inducit fastidium cibi et medicinae; licet etiam talem morbum Deus possit curare. Ita etiam peccatum in spiritum sanctum dicitur irremissibile secundum suam naturam, inquantum excludit ea per quae fit remissio peccatorum. Per hoc tamen non praecluditur via remittendi et sanandi omnipotentiae et misericordiae Dei, per quam aliquando tales quasi miraculose spiritualiter sanantur.

**AD PRIMUM** ergo dicendum quod de nemine desperandum est in hac vita, considerata omnipotentia et misericordia Dei. Sed considerata conditione peccati, dicuntur aliqui *filii diffidentiae*, ut habetur ad Ephes. II.

**AD SECUNDUM** dicendum quod ratio illa procedit ex parte omnipotentiae Dei, non secundum conditionem peccati.

**AD TERTIUM** dicendum quod liberum arbitrium remanet quidem semper in hac vita vertibile, tamen quandoque abiicit a se id per quod verti potest ad bonum, quantum in ipso est. Unde ex parte sua peccatum est irremissibile, licet Deus remittere possit.

Spirit, saying (Exod 32:4): *These are thy gods, O Israel, that have brought thee out of the land of Egypt.* Therefore the Lord both inflicted temporal punishment on them, since *there were slain on that day about three and twenty thousand men* (Exod 32:28), and threatened them with punishment in the life to come, saying, (Exod 32:34): *I, in the day of revenge, will visit this sin . . . of theirs.*

Second, this may be understood to refer to the guilt: thus a disease is said to be incurable in respect of the nature of the disease, which removes whatever might be a means of cure, as when it takes away the power of nature, or causes loathing for food and medicine, although God is able to cure such a disease. So too, the sin against the Holy Spirit is said to be unpardonable, by reason of its nature, insofar as it removes those things which are a means towards the pardon of sins. This does not, however, close the way of forgiveness and healing to an all-powerful and merciful God, Who, sometimes, by a miracle, so to speak, restores spiritual health to such men.

**REPLY OBJ. 1**: We should despair of no man in this life, considering God's omnipotence and mercy. But if we consider the circumstances of sin, some are called (*Eph 2:2*) *children of despair.*

**REPLY OBJ. 2**: This argument considers the question on the part of God's omnipotence, not on that of the circumstances of sin.

**REPLY OBJ. 3**: In this life the free-will does indeed ever remain subject to change: yet sometimes it rejects that whereby, so far as it is concerned, it can be turned to good. Hence considered in itself this sin is unpardonable, although God can pardon it.

# Article 4

*Whether a man can sin first of all against the Holy Spirit without having committed other sins?*

**AD QUARTUM SIC PROCEDITUR.** Videtur quod homo non possit primo peccare in spiritum sanctum, non praesuppositis aliis peccatis. Naturalis enim ordo est ut ab imperfecto ad perfectum quis moveatur. Et hoc quidem in bonis apparet, secundum illud Proverb. IV, *iustorum semita quasi lux splendens crescit et proficit usque ad perfectum diem.* Sed perfectum dicitur in malis quod est maximum malum, ut patet per philosophum, in V Metaphys. Cum igitur peccatum in spiritum sanctum sit gravissimum, videtur quod homo ad hoc peccatum perveniat per alia peccata minora.

**PRAETEREA**, peccare in spiritum sanctum est peccare ex certa malitia, sive ex electione. Sed hoc non statim potest homo, antequam multoties peccaverit, dicit enim philosophus, in V Ethic., quod, si homo possit iniusta facere, non tamen potest statim operari sicut iniustus,

**OBJECTION 1**: It would seem that a man cannot sin first of all against the Holy Spirit, without having previously committed other sins. For the natural order requires that one should be moved to perfection from imperfection. This is evident as regards good things, according to Prov. 4:18: *The path of the just, as a shining light, goeth forwards and increases even to perfect day.* Now, in evil things, the perfect is the greatest evil, as the Philosopher states (*Metaph.* v, text. 21). Since then the sin against the Holy Spirit is the most grievous sin, it seems that man comes to commit this sin through committing lesser sins.

**OBJ. 2**: Further, to sin against the Holy Spirit is to sin through certain malice, or through choice. Now man cannot do this until he has sinned many times; for the Philosopher says (*Ethic.* v, 6, 9) that although a man is able to do unjust deeds, yet he cannot all at once do them as an

scilicet ex electione. Ergo videtur quod peccatum in spiritum sanctum non possit committi nisi post alia peccata.

**PRAETEREA**, poenitentia et impoenitentia sunt circa idem. Sed poenitentia non est nisi de peccatis praeteritis. Ergo etiam neque impoenitentia, quae est species peccati in spiritum sanctum. Peccatum ergo in spiritum sanctum praesupponit alia peccata.

**SED CONTRA** est quod *facile est in conspectu Dei subito honestare pauperem*, ut dicitur Eccli. XI. Ergo e contrario possibile est, secundum malitiam Daemonis suggerentis, ut statim aliquis inducatur in gravissimum peccatum, quod est in spiritum sanctum.

**RESPONDEO** dicendum quod, sicut dictum est, peccare in spiritum sanctum uno modo est peccare ex certa malitia. Ex certa autem malitia dupliciter peccare contingit, sicut dictum est. Uno modo, ex inclinatione habitus, quod non est proprie peccare in spiritum sanctum. Et hoc modo peccare ex certa malitia non contingit a principio, oportet enim actus peccatorum praecedere ex quibus causetur habitus ad peccandum inclinans. Alio modo potest aliquis peccare ex certa malitia abiiciendo per contemptum ea per quae homo retrahitur a peccando, quod proprie est peccare in spiritum sanctum, sicut dictum est. Et hoc etiam plerumque praesupponit alia peccata, quia sicut dicitur Proverb. XVIII, *impius, cum in profundum peccatorum venerit, contemnit.*

Potest tamen contingere quod aliquis in primo actu peccati in spiritum sanctum peccet per contemptum, tum propter libertatem arbitrii; tum etiam propter multas dispositiones praecedentes; vel etiam propter aliquod vehemens motivum ad malum et debilem affectum hominis ad bonum. Et ideo in viris perfectis hoc vix aut nunquam accidere potest quod statim a principio peccent in spiritum sanctum. Unde dicit Origenes, in I Periarch., *non arbitror quod aliquis ex his qui in summo perfectoque gradu constiterint, ad subitum evacuetur aut decidat, sed paulatim ac per partes eum decidere necesse est.*

Et eadem ratio est si peccatum in spiritum sanctum accipiatur ad litteram pro blasphemia spiritus sancti. Talis enim blasphemia de qua dominus loquitur, semper ex malitiae contemptu procedit.

Si vero per peccatum in spiritum sanctum intelligatur finalis impoenitentia, secundum intellectum Augustini, quaestionem non habet, quia ad peccatum in spiritum sanctum requiritur continuatio peccatorum usque in finem vitae.

**AD PRIMUM** ergo dicendum quod tam in bono quam in malo, ut in pluribus, proceditur ab imperfecto ad perfectum, prout homo proficit vel in bono vel in malo. Et tamen in utroque unus potest incipere a maiori quam alius. Et ita illud a quo aliquis incipit, potest esse perfectum in bono vel in malo secundum genus suum; licet

unjust man does, viz. from choice. Therefore it seems that the sin against the Holy Spirit cannot be committed except after other sins.

**OBJ. 3**: Further, repentance and impenitence are about the same object. But there is no repentance, except about past sins. Therefore the same applies to impenitence which is a species of the sin against the Holy Spirit. Therefore the sin against the Holy Spirit presupposes other sins.

**ON THE CONTRARY**, *It is easy in the eyes of God on a sudden to make a poor man rich* (Sir 11:23). Therefore, conversely, it is possible for a man, according to the malice of the devil who tempts him, to be led to commit the most grievous of sins which is that against the Holy Spirit.

**I ANSWER THAT**, As stated above (A. 1), in one way, to sin against the Holy Spirit is to sin through certain malice. Now one may sin through certain malice in two ways, as stated in the same place: first, through the inclination of a habit; but this is not, properly speaking, to sin against the Holy Spirit, nor does a man come to commit this sin all at once, inasmuch as sinful acts must precede so as to cause the habit that induces to sin. Second, one may sin through certain malice, by contemptuously rejecting the things whereby a man is withdrawn from sin. This is, properly speaking, to sin against the Holy Spirit, as stated above (A. 1); and this also, for the most part, presupposes other sins, for it is written (Prov 18:3) that *the wicked man, when he is come into the depth of sins, contemneth.*

Nevertheless it is possible for a man, in his first sinful act, to sin against the Holy Spirit by contempt, both on account of his free-will, and on account of the many previous dispositions, or again, through being vehemently moved to evil, while but feebly attached to good. Hence never or scarcely ever does it happen that the perfect sin all at once against the Holy Spirit: wherefore Origen says (*Peri Archon.* i, 3): *I do not think that anyone who stands on the highest step of perfection, can fail or fall suddenly; this can only happen by degrees and bit by bit.*

The same applies, if the sin against the Holy Spirit be taken literally for blasphemy against the Holy Spirit. For such blasphemy as Our Lord speaks of, always proceeds from contemptuous malice.

If, however, with Augustine (*De Verb. Dom.*, Serm. lxxi) we understand the sin against the Holy Spirit to denote final impenitence, it does not regard the question in point, because this sin against the Holy Spirit requires persistence in sin until the end of life.

**REPLY OBJ. 1**: Movement both in good and in evil is made, for the most part, from imperfect to perfect, according as man progresses in good or evil: and yet in both cases, one man can begin from a greater (good or evil) than another man does. Consequently, that from which a man begins can be perfect in good or evil according to its genus,

sit imperfectum secundum seriem processus hominis in melius vel in peius proficientis.

**AD SECUNDUM** dicendum quod ratio illa procedit de peccato ex malitia quando est ex inclinatione habitus.

**AD TERTIUM** dicendum quod, si accipiatur impoenitentia secundum intentionem Augustini, secundum quod importat permanentiam in peccato usque in finem, sic planum est quod impoenitentia praesupponit peccata, sicut et poenitentia. Sed si loquamur de impoenitentia habituali, secundum quod ponitur species peccati in spiritum sanctum, sic manifestum est quod impoenitentia potest esse etiam ante peccata, potest enim ille qui nunquam peccavit habere propositum vel poenitendi vel non poenitendi, si contingeret eum peccare.

although it may be imperfect as regards the series of good or evil actions whereby a man progresses in good or evil.

**REPLY OBJ. 2**: This argument considers the sin which is committed through certain malice, when it proceeds from the inclination of a habit.

**REPLY OBJ. 3**: If by impenitence we understand with Augustine (*De Verb. Dom.*, Serm. lxxi) persistence in sin until the end, it is clear that it presupposes sin, just as repentance does. If, however, we take it for habitual impenitence, in which sense it is a sin against the Holy Spirit, it is evident that it can precede sin: for it is possible for a man who has never sinned to have the purpose either of repenting or of not repenting, if he should happen to sin.

# QUESTION 15

## THE VICES OPPOSED TO KNOWLEDGE AND UNDERSTANDING

Deinde considerandum est de vitiis oppositis scientiae et intellectui. Et quia de ignorantia, quae opponitur scientiae, dictum est supra, cum de causis peccatorum ageretur; quaerendum est nunc de caecitate mentis et hebetudine sensus, quae opponuntur dono intellectus. Et circa hoc quaeruntur tria.

Primo, utrum caecitas mentis sit peccatum.
Secundo, utrum hebetudo sensus sit aliud peccatum a caecitate mentis.
Tertio, utrum haec vitia a peccatis carnalibus oriantur.

We must now consider the vices opposed to knowledge and understanding. Since, however, we have treated of ignorance which is opposed to knowledge, when we were discussing the causes of sins (I-II, Q. 76), we must now inquire about blindness of mind and dulness of sense, which are opposed to the gift of understanding; and under this head there are three points of inquiry:
(1) Whether blindness of mind is a sin?
(2) Whether dulness of sense is a sin distinct from blindness of mind?
(3) Whether these vices arise from sins of the flesh?

# Article 1

*Whether blindness of mind is a sin?*

**AD PRIMUM SIC PROCEDITUR.** Videtur quod caecitas mentis non sit peccatum. Illud enim quod excusat a peccato non videtur esse peccatum. Sed caecitas excusat a peccato, dicitur enim Ioan. IX, *si caeci essetis, non haberetis peccatum.* Ergo caecitas mentis non est peccatum.

**PRAETEREA,** poena differt a culpa. Sed caecitas mentis est quaedam poena, ut patet per illud quod habetur Isaiae VI, *excaeca cor populi huius*; non enim esset a Deo, cum sit malum, nisi poena esset. Ergo caecitas mentis non est peccatum.

**PRAETEREA,** omne peccatum est voluntarium, ut Augustinus dicit. Sed caecitas mentis non est voluntaria, quia ut Augustinus dicit, X Confess., *cognoscere veritatem lucentem omnes amant*; et Eccle. XI dicitur, *dulce lumen, et delectabile oculis videre solem.* Ergo caecitas mentis non est peccatum.

**SED CONTRA** est quod Gregorius, XXXI Moral., caecitatem mentis ponit inter vitia quae causantur ex luxuria.

**RESPONDEO** dicendum quod sicut caecitas corporalis est privatio eius quod est principium corporalis visionis, ita etiam caecitas mentis est privatio eius quod est principium mentalis sive intellectualis visionis. Cuius quidem principium est triplex. Unum quidem est lumen naturalis rationis. Et hoc lumen, cum pertineat ad speciem animae rationalis, nunquam privatur ab anima. Impeditur tamen quandoque a proprio actu per impedimenta virium inferiorum, quibus indiget intellectus

**OBJECTION 1**: It would seem that blindness of mind is not a sin. Because, seemingly, that which excuses from sin is not itself a sin. Now blindness of mind excuses from sin; for it is written (John 9:41): *If you were blind, you should not have sin.* Therefore blindness of mind is not a sin.

**OBJ. 2**: Further, punishment differs from guilt. But blindness of mind is a punishment as appears from Isa. 6:10, *Blind the heart of this people*, for, since it is an evil, it could not be from God, were it not a punishment. Therefore blindness of mind is not a sin.

**OBJ. 3**: Further, every sin is voluntary, according to Augustine (*De Vera Relig.* xiv). Now blindness of mind is not voluntary, since, as Augustine says (*Confess.* x), *all love to know the resplendent truth*, and as we read in Eccles. 11:7, *the light is sweet and it is delightful for the eyes to see the sun.* Therefore blindness of mind is not a sin.

**ON THE CONTRARY**, Gregory (*Moral.* xxxi, 45) reckons blindness of mind among the vices arising from lust.

**I ANSWER THAT,** Just as bodily blindness is the privation of the principle of bodily sight, so blindness of mind is the privation of the principle of mental or intellectual sight. Now this has a threefold principle. One is the light of natural reason, which light, since it pertains to the species of the rational soul, is never forfeit from the soul, and yet, at times, it is prevented from exercising its proper act, through being hindered by the lower powers which the human intellect needs in order to understand, for instance

humanus ad intelligendum, sicut patet in amentibus et furiosis, ut in primo dictum est.

Aliud autem principium intellectualis visionis est aliquod lumen habituale naturali lumini rationis superadditum. Et hoc quidem lumen interdum privatur ab anima. Et talis privatio est caecitas quae est poena, secundum quod privatio luminis gratiae quaedam poena ponitur. Unde dicitur de quibusdam, Sap. II, *excaecavit illos malitia eorum.*

Tertium principium visionis intellectualis est aliquod intelligibile principium per quod homo intelligit alia. Cui quidem principio intelligibili mens hominis potest intendere vel non intendere. Et quod ei non intendat contingit dupliciter. Quandoque quidem ex hoc quod habet voluntatem spontanee se avertentem a consideratione talis principii, secundum illud Psalm., *noluit intelligere ut bene ageret.* Alio modo, per occupationem mentis circa alia quae magis diligit, quibus ab inspectione huius principii mens avertitur, secundum illud Psalm., *supercecidit ignis,* scilicet concupiscentiae, *et non viderunt solem.* Et utroque modo caecitas mentis est peccatum.

**AD PRIMUM** ergo dicendum quod caecitas quae excusat a peccato est quae contingit ex naturali defectu non potentis videre.

**AD SECUNDUM** dicendum quod ratio illa procedit de secunda caecitate, quae est poena.

**AD TERTIUM** dicendum quod intelligere veritatem cuilibet est secundum se amabile. Potest tamen per accidens esse alicui odibile, inquantum scilicet per hoc homo impeditur ab aliis quae magis amat.

in the case of imbeciles and madmen, as stated in the First Part (Q. 84, AA. 7, 8).

Another principle of intellectual sight is a certain habitual light superadded to the natural light of reason, which light is sometimes forfeit from the soul. This privation is blindness, and is a punishment, insofar as the privation of the light of grace is a punishment. Hence it is written concerning some (Wis 2:21): *Their own malice blinded them.*

A third principle of intellectual sight is an intelligible principle, through which a man understands other things; to which principle a man may attend or not attend. That he does not attend thereto happens in two ways. Sometimes it is due to the fact that a man's will is deliberately turned away from the consideration of that principle, according to Ps. 35:4, *He would not understand, that he might do well*: whereas sometimes it is due to the mind being more busy about things which it loves more, so as to be hindered thereby from considering this principle, according to Ps. 57:9, *Fire,* i.e., of concupiscence, *hath fallen on them and they shall not see the sun.* In either of these ways blindness of mind is a sin.

**REPLY OBJ. 1**: The blindness that excuses from sin is that which arises from the natural defect of one who cannot see.

**REPLY OBJ. 2**: This argument considers the second kind of blindness which is a punishment.

**REPLY OBJ. 3**: To understand the truth is, in itself, beloved by all; and yet, accidentally it may be hateful to someone, insofar as a man is hindered thereby from having what he loves yet more.

# Article 2

*Whether dulness of sense is a sin distinct from blindness of mind?*

**AD SECUNDUM SIC PROCEDITUR**. Videtur quod hebetudo sensus non sit aliud a caecitate mentis. Unum enim uni est contrarium. Sed dono intellectus opponitur hebetudo, ut patet per Gregorium, in II Moral.; cui etiam opponitur caecitas mentis, eo quod intellectus principium quoddam visivum designat. Ergo hebetudo sensus est idem quod caecitas mentis.

**PRAETEREA**, Gregorius, in XXXI Moral., de hebetudine loquens, nominat eam *hebetudinem sensus circa intelligentiam.* Sed hebetari sensu circa intelligentiam nihil aliud esse videtur quam intelligendo deficere, quod pertinet ad mentis caecitatem. Ergo hebetudo sensus idem est quod caecitas mentis.

**PRAETEREA**, si in aliquo differunt, maxime videntur in hoc differre quod caecitas mentis est voluntaria, ut supra dictum est, hebetudo autem sensus est naturalis.

**OBJECTION 1**: It seems that dulness of sense is not a distinct sin from blindness of mind. Because one thing has one contrary. Now dulness is opposed to the gift of understanding, according to Gregory (*Moral.* ii, 49); and so is blindness of mind, since understanding denotes a principle of sight. Therefore dulness of sense is the same as blindness of mind.

**OBJ. 2**: Further, Gregory (*Moral.* xxxi, 45) in speaking of dulness describes it as *dulness of sense in respect of understanding.* Now dulness of sense in respect of understanding seems to be the same as a defect in understanding, which pertains to blindness of mind. Therefore dulness of sense is the same as blindness of mind.

**OBJ. 3**: Further, if they differ at all, it seems to be chiefly in the fact that blindness of mind is voluntary, as stated above (A. 1), while dulness of sense is a natural defect. But

Sed defectus naturalis non est peccatum. Ergo secundum hoc hebetudo sensus non esset peccatum. Quod est contra Gregorium, qui connumerat eam inter vitia quae ex gula oriuntur.

**SED CONTRA** est quod diversarum causarum sunt diversi effectus. Sed Gregorius, XXXI Moral., dicit quod hebetudo mentis oritur ex gula, caecitas autem mentis ex luxuria. Ergo sunt diversa vitia.

**RESPONDEO** dicendum quod hebes acuto opponitur. Acutum autem dicitur aliquid ex hoc quod est penetrativum. Unde et hebes dicitur aliquid ex hoc quod est obtusum, penetrare non valens. Sensus autem corporalis per quandam similitudinem penetrare dicitur medium inquantum ex aliqua distantia suum obiectum percipit; vel inquantum potest quasi penetrando intima rei percipere. Unde in corporalibus dicitur aliquis esse acuti sensus qui potest percipere sensibile aliquod ex remotis, vel videndo vel audiendo vel olfaciendo; et e contrario dicitur sensu hebetari qui non percipit nisi ex propinquo et magna sensibilia.

Ad similitudinem autem corporalis sensus dicitur etiam circa intelligentiam esse aliquis sensus, qui est aliquorum *primorum extremorum*, ut dicitur in VI Ethic., sicut etiam sensus est cognoscitivus sensibilium quasi quorundam principiorum cognitionis. Hic autem sensus qui est circa intelligentiam non percipit suum obiectum per medium distantiae corporalis, sed per quaedam alia media, sicut cum per proprietatem rei percipit eius essentiam, et per effectus percipit causam. Ille ergo dicitur esse acuti sensus circa intelligentiam qui statim ad apprehensionem proprietatis rei, vel etiam effectus, naturam rei comprehendit, et inquantum usque ad minimas conditiones rei considerandas pertingit. Ille autem dicitur esse hebes circa intelligentiam qui ad cognoscendam veritatem rei pertingere non potest nisi per multa ei exposita, et tunc etiam non potest pertingere ad perfecte considerandum omnia quae pertinent ad rei rationem.

Sic igitur hebetudo sensus circa intelligentiam importat quandam debilitatem mentis circa considerationem spiritualium bonorum, caecitas autem mentis importat omnimodam privationem cognitionis ipsorum. Et utrumque opponitur dono intellectus, per quem homo spiritualia bona apprehendendo cognoscit et ad eorum intima subtiliter penetrat. Habet autem hebetudo rationem peccati sicut et caecitas mentis, inquantum scilicet est voluntaria, ut patet in eo qui, affectus circa carnalia, de spiritualibus subtiliter discutere fastidit vel negligit.

**ET PER HOC** patet responsio ad obiecta.

a natural defect is not a sin: so that, accordingly, dulness of sense would not be a sin, which is contrary to what Gregory says (*Moral.* xxxi, 45), where he reckons it among the sins arising from gluttony.

**ON THE CONTRARY**, Different causes produce different effects. Now Gregory says (*Moral.* xxxi, 45) that dulness of sense arises from gluttony, and that blindness of mind arises from lust. Now these others are different vices. Therefore those are different vices also.

**I ANSWER THAT**, Dull is opposed to sharp: and a thing is said to be sharp because it can pierce; so that a thing is called dull through being obtuse and unable to pierce. Now a bodily sense, by a kind of metaphor, is said to pierce the medium, insofar as it perceives its object from a distance or is able by penetration as it were to perceive the smallest details or the inmost parts of a thing. Hence in corporeal things the senses are said to be acute when they can perceive a sensible object from afar, by sight, hearing, or scent, while on the other hand they are said to be dull, through being unable to perceive, except sensible objects that are near at hand, or of great power.

Now, by way of similitude to bodily sense, we speak of sense in connection with the intellect; and this latter sense is in respect of certain *primals and extremes*, as stated in *Ethic.* vi, even as the senses are cognizant of sensible objects as of certain principles of knowledge. Now this sense which is connected with understanding, does not perceive its object through a medium of corporeal distance, but through certain other media, as, for instance, when it perceives a thing's essence through a property thereof, and the cause through its effect. Consequently a man is said to have an acute sense in connection with his understanding, if, as soon as he apprehends a property or effect of a thing, he understands the nature or the thing itself, and if he can succeed in perceiving its slightest details: whereas a man is said to have a dull sense in connection with his understanding, if he cannot arrive at knowing the truth about a thing, without many explanations; in which case, moreover, he is unable to obtain a perfect perception of everything pertaining to the nature of that thing.

Accordingly dulness of sense in connection with understanding denotes a certain weakness of the mind as to the consideration of spiritual goods; while blindness of mind implies the complete privation of the knowledge of such things. Both are opposed to the gift of understanding, whereby a man knows spiritual goods by apprehending them, and has a subtle penetration of their inmost nature. This dulness has the character of sin, just as blindness of mind has, that is, insofar as it is voluntary, as evidenced in one who, owing to his affection for carnal things, dislikes or neglects the careful consideration of spiritual things.

**THIS SUFFICES** for the Replies to the Objections.

# Article 3

*Whether blindness of mind and dulness of sense arise from sins of the flesh?*

**AD TERTIUM SIC PROCEDITUR.** Videtur quod caecitas mentis et hebetudo sensus non oriantur ex vitiis carnalibus. Augustinus enim, in libro Retract., retractans illud quod dixerat in Soliloq., *Deus, qui non nisi mundos verum scire voluisti*, dicit quod *responderi potest multos etiam non mundos multa vera scire.* Sed homines maxime efficiuntur immundi per vitia carnalia. Ergo caecitas mentis et hebetudo sensus non causantur a vitiis carnalibus.

**PRAETEREA,** caecitas mentis et hebetudo sensus sunt defectus quidam circa partem animae intellectivam; vitia autem carnalia pertinent ad corruptionem carnis. Sed caro non agit in animam, sed potius e converso. Ergo vitia carnalia non causant caecitatem mentis et hebetudinem sensus.

**PRAETEREA,** unumquodque magis patitur a propinquiori quam a remotiori. Sed propinquiora sunt menti vitia spiritualia quam carnalia. Ergo caecitas mentis et hebetudo sensus magis causantur ex vitiis spiritualibus quam ex vitiis carnalibus.

**SED CONTRA** est quod Gregorius, XXXI Moral., dicit quod hebetudo sensus circa intelligentiam oritur ex gula, caecitas mentis ex luxuria.

**RESPONDEO** dicendum quod perfectio intellectualis operationis in homine consistit in quadam abstractione a sensibilium phantasmatibus. Et ideo quanto intellectus hominis magis fuerit liber ab huiusmodi phantasmatibus, tanto potius considerare intelligibilia poterit et ordinare omnia sensibilia, sicut et Anaxagoras dixit quod oportet intellectum esse immixtum ad hoc quod imperet, et agens oportet quod dominetur super materiam ad hoc quod possit eam movere. Manifestum est autem quod delectatio applicat intentionem ad ea in quibus aliquis delectatur, unde philosophus dicit, in X Ethic., quod unusquisque ea in quibus delectatur optime operatur, contraria vero nequaquam vel debiliter.

Vitia autem carnalia, scilicet gula et luxuria, consistunt circa delectationes tactus, ciborum scilicet et venereorum, quae sunt vehementissimae inter omnes corporales delectationes. Et ideo per haec vitia intentio hominis maxime applicatur ad corporalia, et per consequens debilitatur operatio hominis circa intelligibilia, magis autem per luxuriam quam per gulam, quanto delectationes venereorum sunt vehementiores quam ciborum. Et ideo ex luxuria oritur caecitas mentis, quae quasi totaliter spiritualium bonorum cognitionem excludit, ex gula autem hebetudo sensus, quae reddit hominem debilem circa huiusmodi intelligibilia. Et e converso oppositae virtutes, scilicet abstinentia et castitas, maxime disponunt hominem ad perfectionem

**OBJECTION 1**: It would seem that blindness of mind and dulness of sense do not arise from sins of the flesh. For Augustine (*Retract.* i, 4) retracts what he had said in his Soliloquies i, 1, *God Who didst wish none but the clean to know the truth*, and says that one might reply that *many, even those who are unclean, know many truths.* Now men become unclean chiefly by sins of the flesh. Therefore blindness of mind and dulness of sense are not caused by sins of the flesh.

**OBJ. 2**: Further, blindness of mind and dulness of sense are defects in connection with the intellective part of the soul: whereas carnal sins pertain to the corruption of the flesh. But the flesh does not act on the soul, but rather the reverse. Therefore the sins of the flesh do not cause blindness of mind and dulness of sense.

**OBJ. 3**: Further, all things are more passive to what is near them than to what is remote. Now spiritual vices are nearer the mind than carnal vices are. Therefore blindness of mind and dulness of sense are caused by spiritual rather than by carnal vices.

**ON THE CONTRARY**, Gregory says (*Moral.* xxxi, 45) that dulness of sense arises from gluttony and blindness of mind from lust.

**I ANSWER THAT**, The perfect intellectual operation in man consists in an abstraction from sensible phantasms, wherefore the more a man's intellect is freed from those phantasms, the more thoroughly will it be able to consider things intelligible, and to set in order all things sensible. Thus Anaxagoras stated that the intellect requires to be *detached* in order to command, and that the agent must have power over matter, in order to be able to move it. Now it is evident that pleasure fixes a man's attention on that which he takes pleasure in: wherefore the Philosopher says (*Ethic.* x, 4, 5) that we all do best that which we take pleasure in doing, while as to other things, we do them either not at all, or in a faint-hearted fashion.

Now carnal vices, namely gluttony and lust, are concerned with pleasures of touch in matters of food and sex; and these are the most impetuous of all pleasures of the body. For this reason these vices cause man's attention to be very firmly fixed on corporeal things, so that in consequence man's operation in regard to intelligible things is weakened—more, however, by lust than by gluttony, forasmuch as sexual pleasures are more vehement than those of the table. Wherefore lust gives rise to blindness of mind, which excludes almost entirely the knowledge of spiritual things, while dulness of sense arises from gluttony, which makes a man weak in regard to the same intelligible things. On the other hand, the contrary virtues, viz. abstinence and chastity, dispose man very much to the perfection

intellectualis operationis. Unde dicitur Dan. I, quod *pueris his*, scilicet abstinentibus et continentibus, *dedit Deus scientiam et disciplinam in omni libro et sapientia.*

**AD PRIMUM** ergo dicendum quod, quamvis aliqui vitiis carnalibus subditi possint quandoque subtiliter aliqua speculari circa intelligibilia, propter bonitatem ingenii naturalis vel habitus superadditi; tamen necesse est ut ab hac subtilitate contemplationis eorum intentio plerumque retrahatur propter delectationes corporales. Et ita immundi possunt aliqua vera scire sed ex sua immunditia circa hoc impediuntur.

**AD SECUNDUM** dicendum quod caro non agit in partem intellectivam alterando ipsam, sed impediendo operationem ipsius per modum praedictum.

**AD TERTIUM** dicendum quod vitia carnalia, quo magis sunt remota a mente, eo magis eius intentionem ad remotiora distrahunt. Unde magis impediunt mentis contemplationem.

of intellectual operation. Hence it is written (Dan 1:17) that *to these children* on account of their abstinence and continency, *God gave knowledge and understanding in every book, and wisdom.*

**REPLY OBJ. 1**: Although some who are the slaves of carnal vices are at times capable of subtle considerations about intelligible things, on account of the perfection of their natural genius, or of some habit superadded thereto, nevertheless, on account of the pleasures of the body, it must needs happen that their attention is frequently withdrawn from this subtle contemplation: wherefore the unclean can know some truths, but their uncleanness is a clog on their knowledge.

**REPLY OBJ. 2**: The flesh acts on the intellective faculties, not by altering them, but by impeding their operation in the aforesaid manner.

**REPLY OBJ. 3**: It is owing to the fact that the carnal vices are further removed from the mind, that they distract the mind's attention to more remote things, so that they hinder the mind's contemplation all the more.

# QUESTION 16

Deinde considerandum est de praeceptis pertinentibus ad praedicta. Et circa hoc quaeruntur duo.

Primo, de praeceptis pertinentibus ad fidem.
Secundo, de praeceptis pertinentibus ad dona scientiae et intellectus.

We must now consider the precepts pertaining to the aforesaid, and under this head there are two points of inquiry:
(1) The precepts concerning faith;
(2) The precepts concerning the gifts of knowledge and understanding.

# Article 1

*Whether in the Old Law there should have been given precepts of faith?*

**AD PRIMUM SIC PROCEDITUR**. Videtur quod in veteri lege dari debuerint praecepta credendi. Praeceptum enim est de eo quod est debitum et necessarium. Sed maxime necessarium est homini quod credat, secundum illud Heb. XI, *sine fide impossibile est placere Deo*. Ergo maxime oportuit praecepta dari de fide.

**PRAETEREA**, novum testamentum continetur in veteri sicut figuratum in figura, ut supra dictum est. Sed in novo testamento ponuntur expressa mandata de fide, ut patet Ioan. XIV, *creditis in Deum, et in me credite*. Ergo videtur quod in veteri lege etiam debuerint aliqua praecepta dari de fide.

**PRAETEREA**, eiusdem rationis est praecipere actum virtutis et prohibere vitia opposita. Sed in veteri lege ponuntur multa praecepta prohibentia infidelitatem, sicut Exod. XX, *non habebis deos alienos coram me*; et iterum Deut. XIII mandatur quod non audient verba prophetae aut somniatoris qui eos de fide Dei vellet divertere. Ergo in veteri lege etiam debuerunt dari praecepta de fide.

**PRAETEREA**, confessio est actus fidei, ut supra dictum est. Sed de confessione et promulgatione fidei dantur praecepta in veteri lege, mandatur enim Exod. XII quod filiis suis interrogantibus rationem assignent paschalis observantiae; et Deut. XIII mandatur quod ille qui disseminat doctrinam contra fidem occidatur. Ergo lex vetus praecepta fidei debuit habere.

**PRAETEREA**, omnes libri veteris testamenti sub lege veteri continentur, unde dominus, Ioan. XV, dicit in lege esse scriptum, *odio habuerunt me gratis*, quod tamen scribitur in Psalmo. Sed Eccli. II dicitur, *qui timetis do-*

**OBJECTION 1**: It would seem that, in the Old Law, there should have been given precepts of faith. Because a precept is about something due and necessary. Now it is most necessary for man that he should believe, according to Heb. 11:6, *Without faith it is impossible to please God.* Therefore there was very great need for precepts of faith to be given.

**OBJ. 2**: Further, the New Testament is contained in the Old, as the reality in the figure, as stated above (I-II, Q. 107, A. 3). Now the New Testament contains explicit precepts of faith, for instance John 14:1: *You believe in God; believe also in Me.* Therefore it seems that some precepts of faith ought to have been given in the Old Law also.

**OBJ. 3**: Further, to prescribe the act of a virtue comes to the same as to forbid the opposite vices. Now the Old Law contained many precepts forbidding unbelief: thus (Exod 20:3): *Thou shalt not have strange gods before Me,* and (Deut 13:1–3) they were forbidden to hear the words of the prophet or dreamer who might wish to turn them away from their faith in God. Therefore precepts of faith should have been given in the Old Law also.

**OBJ. 4**: Further, confession is an act of faith, as stated above (Q. 3, A. 1). Now the Old Law contained precepts about the confession and the promulgation of faith: for they were commanded (Exod 12:27) that, when their children should ask them, they should tell them the meaning of the paschal observance, and (Deut 13:9) they were commanded to slay anyone who disseminated doctrine contrary to faith. Therefore the Old Law should have contained precepts of faith.

**OBJ. 5**: Further, all the books of the Old Testament are contained in the Old Law; wherefore Our Lord said (John 15:25) that it was written in the Law: *They have hated Me without cause,* although this is found written in Ps. 34

*minum, credite illi.* Ergo in veteri lege fuerunt praecepta danda de fide.

**Sed contra** est quod apostolus, ad Rom. III, legem veterem nominat legem factorum, et dividit eam contra legem fidei. Ergo in lege veteri non fuerunt praecepta danda de fide.

**Respondeo** dicendum quod lex non imponitur ab aliquo domino nisi suis subditis, et ideo praecepta legis cuiuslibet praesupponunt subiectionem recipientis legem ad eum qui dat legem. Prima autem subiectio hominis ad Deum est per fidem, secundum illud Heb. XI, *accedentem ad Deum oportet credere quia est.* Et ideo fides praesupponitur ad legis praecepta. Et propter hoc Exod. XX id quod est fidei praemittitur ante legis praecepta, cum dicitur, *ego sum dominus Deus tuus, qui eduxi te de terra Aegypti.* Et similiter Deut. VI praemittitur, *audi, Israel, dominus Deus tuus unus est,* et postea statim incipit agere de praeceptis.

Sed quia in fide multa continentur ordinata ad fidem qua credimus Deum esse, quod est primum et principale inter omnia credibilia, ut dictum est; ideo, praesupposita fide de Deo, per quam mens humana Deo subiiciatur, possunt dari praecepta de aliis credendis, sicut Augustinus dicit, super Ioan., quod plurima sunt nobis de fide mandata, exponens illud, *hoc est praeceptum meum.* Sed in veteri lege non erant secreta fidei populo exponenda. Et ideo, supposita fide unius Dei, nulla alia praecepta sunt in veteri lege data de credendis.

**Ad primum** ergo dicendum quod fides est necessaria tanquam principium spiritualis vitae. Et ideo praesupponitur ad legis susceptionem.

**Ad secundum** dicendum quod ibi etiam dominus praesupponit aliquid de fide, scilicet fidem unius Dei, cum dicit, *creditis in Deum,* et aliquid praecipit, scilicet fidem incarnationis, per quam unus est Deus et homo; quae quidem fidei explicatio pertinet ad fidem novi testamenti. Et ideo subdit, *et in me credite.*

**Ad tertium** dicendum quod praecepta prohibitiva respiciunt peccata, quae corrumpunt virtutem. Virtus autem corrumpitur ex particularibus defectibus, ut supra dictum est. Et ideo, praesupposita fide unius Dei, in lege veteri fuerunt danda prohibitiva praecepta, quibus homines prohiberentur ab his particularibus defectibus per quos fides corrumpi posset.

**Ad quartum** dicendum quod etiam confessio vel doctrina fidei praesupponit subiectionem hominis ad Deum per fidem. Et ideo magis potuerunt dari praecepta in veteri lege pertinentia ad confessionem et doctrinam fidei quam pertinentia ad ipsam fidem.

and 68. Now it is written (Sir 2:8): *Ye that fear the Lord, believe Him.* Therefore the Old Law should have contained precepts of faith.

**On the contrary,** The Apostle (Rom 3:27) calls the Old Law the *law of works* which he contrasts with the *law of faith.* Therefore the Old Law ought not to have contained precepts of faith.

**I answer that,** A master does not impose laws on others than his subjects; wherefore the precepts of a law presuppose that everyone who receives the law is subject to the giver of the law. Now the primary subjection of man to God is by faith, according to Heb. 11:6: *He that cometh to God, must believe that He is.* Hence faith is presupposed to the precepts of the Law: for which reason (Exod 20:2) that which is of faith, is set down before the legal precepts, in the words, *I am the Lord thy God, Who brought thee out of the land of Egypt,* and, likewise (Deut 6:4), the words, *Hear, O Israel, the Lord thy God is one,* precede the recording of the precepts.

Since, however, faith contains many things subordinate to the faith whereby we believe that God is, which is the first and chief of all articles of faith, as stated above (Q. 1, AA. 1, 7), it follows that, if we presuppose faith in God, whereby man's mind is subjected to Him, it is possible for precepts to be given about other articles of faith. Thus Augustine expounding the words: *This is My commandment* (John 15:12) says (*Tract. lxxxiii in Joan.*) that we have received many precepts of faith. In the Old Law, however, the secret things of faith were not to be set before the people, wherefore, presupposing their faith in one God, no other precepts of faith were given in the Old Law.

**Reply Obj. 1:** Faith is necessary as being the principle of spiritual life, wherefore it is presupposed before the receiving of the Law.

**Reply Obj. 2:** Even then Our Lord both presupposed something of faith, namely belief in one God, when He said: *You believe in God,* and commanded something, namely, belief in the Incarnation whereby one Person is God and man. This explanation of faith belongs to the faith of the New Testament, wherefore He added: *Believe also in Me.*

**Reply Obj. 3:** The prohibitive precepts regard sins, which corrupt virtue. Now virtue is corrupted by any particular defect, as stated above (I-II, Q. 18, A. 4, ad 3; I-II, Q. 19, A. 6, ad 1, A. 7, ad 3). Therefore faith in one God being presupposed, prohibitive precepts had to be given in the Old Law, so that men might be warned off those particular defects whereby their faith might be corrupted.

**Reply Obj. 4:** Confession of faith and the teaching thereof also presuppose man's submission to God by faith: so that the Old Law could contain precepts relating to the confession and teaching of faith, rather than to faith itself.

**AD QUINTUM** dicendum quod in illa etiam auctoritate praesupponitur fides per quam credimus Deum esse, unde praemittit, *qui timetis Deum*, quod non posset esse sine fide. Quod autem addit, *credite illi*, ad quaedam credibilia specialia referendum est, et praecipue ad illa quae promittit Deus sibi obedientibus. Unde subdit, *et non evacuabitur merces vestra*.

**REPLY OBJ. 5**: In this passage again that faith is presupposed whereby we believe that God is; hence it begins, *Ye that fear the Lord*, which is not possible without faith. The words which follow—*believe Him*—must be referred to certain special articles of faith, chiefly to those things which God promises to them that obey Him, wherefore the passage concludes—*and your reward shall not be made void*.

# Article 2

*Whether the precepts referring to knowledge and understanding were fittingly set down in the Old Law?*

**AD SECUNDUM SIC PROCEDITUR.** Videtur quod in veteri lege inconvenienter tradantur praecepta pertinentia ad scientiam et intellectum. Scientia enim et intellectus ad cognitionem pertinent. Cognitio autem praecedit et dirigit actionem. Ergo praecepta ad scientiam et intellectum pertinentia debent praecedere praecepta pertinentia ad actionem. Cum ergo prima praecepta legis sint praecepta Decalogi, videtur quod inter praecepta Decalogi debuerunt tradi aliqua praecepta pertinentia ad scientiam et intellectum.

**PRAETEREA**, disciplina praecedit doctrinam, prius enim homo ab alio discit quam alium doceat. Sed dantur in veteri lege aliqua praecepta de doctrina, et affirmativa, ut praecipitur Deut. IV, *docebis ea filios ac nepotes tuos*; et etiam prohibitiva, sicut habetur Deut. IV, *non addetis ad verbum quod vobis loquor, neque auferetis ab eo*. Ergo videtur quod etiam aliqua praecepta dari debuerint inducentia hominem ad addiscendum.

**PRAETEREA**, scientia et intellectus magis videntur necessaria sacerdoti quam regi, unde dicitur Malach. II, *labia sacerdotis custodiunt scientiam, et legem requirunt ex ore eius*; et Osee IV dicitur, *quia scientiam repulisti, repellam te et ego, ne sacerdotio fungaris mihi*. Sed regi mandatur quod addiscat scientiam legis, ut patet Deut. XVII. Ergo multo magis debuit praecipi in lege quod sacerdotes legem addiscerent.

**PRAETEREA**, meditatio eorum quae ad scientiam et intellectum pertinent non potest esse in dormiendo. Impeditur etiam per occupationes extraneas. Ergo inconvenienter praecipitur, Deut. VI, *meditaberis ea sedens in domo tua, et ambulans in itinere, dormiens atque consurgens*. Inconvenienter ergo traduntur in veteri lege praecepta ad scientiam et intellectum pertinentia.

**SED CONTRA** est quod dicitur Deut. IV, *audientes universi praecepta haec, dicant, en populus sapiens et intelligens*.

**OBJECTION 1**: It would seem that the precepts referring to knowledge and understanding were unfittingly set down in the Old Law. For knowledge and understanding pertain to cognition. Now cognition precedes and directs action. Therefore the precepts referring to knowledge and understanding should precede the precepts of the Law referring to action. Since, then, the first precepts of the Law are those of the decalogue, it seems that precepts of knowledge and understanding should have been given a place among the precepts of the decalogue.

**OBJ. 2**: Further, learning precedes teaching, for a man must learn from another before he teaches another. Now the Old Law contains precepts about teaching—both affirmative precepts as, for example, (Deut 4:9), *Thou shalt teach them to thy sons*—and prohibitive precepts, as, for instance, (Deut 4:2), *You shall not add to the word that I speak to you, neither shall you take away from it*. Therefore it seems that man ought to have been given also some precepts directing him to learn.

**OBJ. 3**: Further, knowledge and understanding seem more necessary to a priest than to a king, wherefore it is written (Mal 2:7): *The lips of the priest shall keep knowledge, and they shall seek the law at his mouth*, and (Hos 4:6): *Because thou hast rejected knowledge, I will reject thee, that thou shalt not do the office of priesthood to Me*. Now the king is commanded to learn knowledge of the Law (Deut 17:18, 19). Much more therefore should the Law have commanded the priests to learn the Law.

**OBJ. 4**: Further, it is not possible while asleep to meditate on things pertaining to knowledge and understanding: moreover it is hindered by extraneous occupations. Therefore it is unfittingly commanded (Deut 6:7): *Thou shalt meditate upon them sitting in thy house, and walking on thy journey, sleeping and rising*. Therefore the precepts relating to knowledge and understanding are unfittingly set down in the Law.

**ON THE CONTRARY**, It is written (Deut 4:6): *That, hearing all these precepts, they may say, Behold a wise and understanding people*.

RESPONDEO dicendum quod circa scientiam et intellectum tria possunt considerari, primo quidem, acceptio ipsius; secundo, usus eius; tertio vero, conservatio ipsius. Acceptio quidem scientiae vel intellectus fit per doctrinam et disciplinam. Et utrumque in lege praecipitur. Dicitur enim Deut. VI, *erunt verba haec quae ego praecipio tibi, in corde tuo*, quod pertinet ad disciplinam, pertinet enim ad discipulum ut cor suum applicet his quae dicuntur. Quod vero subditur, *et narrabis ea filiis tuis*, pertinet ad doctrinam.

Usus vero scientiae vel intellectus est meditatio eorum quae quis scit vel intelligit. Et quantum ad hoc subditur, *et meditaberis sedens in domo tua*, et cetera.

Conservatio autem fit per memoriam. Et quantum ad hoc subdit, *et ligabis ea quasi signum in manu tua, eruntque et movebuntur inter oculos tuos, scribesque ea in limine et ostiis domus tuae.* Per quae omnia iugem memoriam mandatorum Dei significat, ea enim quae continue sensibus nostris occurrunt, vel tactu, sicut ea quae in manu habemus; vel visu, sicut ea quae ante oculos mentis sunt continue; vel ad quae oportet nos saepe recurrere, sicut ad ostium domus; a memoria nostra excidere non possunt. Et Deut. IV manifestius dicitur, *ne obliviscaris verborum quae viderunt oculi tui, et ne excidant de corde tuo cunctis diebus vitae tuae.*

Et haec etiam abundantius in novo testamento, tam in doctrina evangelica quam apostolica, mandata leguntur.

AD PRIMUM ergo dicendum quod, sicut dicitur Deut. IV, *haec est vestra sapientia et intellectus coram populis*, ex quo datur intelligi quod scientia et intellectus fidelium Dei consistit in praeceptis legis. Et ideo primo sunt proponenda legis praecepta; et postmodum homines sunt inducendi ad eorum scientiam vel intellectum. Et ideo praemissa praecepta non debuerunt poni inter praecepta Decalogi, quae sunt prima.

AD SECUNDUM dicendum quod etiam in lege ponuntur praecepta pertinentia ad disciplinam, ut dictum est. Expressius tamen praecipitur doctrina quam disciplina, quia doctrina pertinet ad maiores, qui sunt sui iuris, immediate sub lege existentes, quibus debent dari legis praecepta, disciplina autem pertinet ad minores, ad quos praecepta legis per maiores debent pervenire.

AD TERTIUM dicendum quod scientia legis est adeo annexa officio sacerdotis ut simul cum iniunctione officii intelligatur etiam et scientiae legis iniunctio. Et ideo non oportuit specialia praecepta dari de instructione sacerdotum. Sed doctrina legis Dei non adeo est annexa regali officio, quia rex constituitur super populum in tempora-

I ANSWER THAT, Three things may be considered in relation to knowledge and understanding: first, the reception thereof; second, the use; and third, their preservation. Now the reception of knowledge or understanding, is by means of teaching and learning, and both are prescribed in the Law. For it is written (Deut 6:6): *These words which I command thee . . . shall be in thy heart.* This refers to learning, since it is the duty of a disciple to apply his mind to what is said, while the words that follow—*and thou shalt tell them to thy children*—refer to teaching.

The use of knowledge and understanding is the meditation on those things which one knows or understands. In reference to this, the text goes on: *thou shalt meditate upon them sitting in thy house*, etc.

Their preservation is effected by the memory, and, as regards this, the text continues—*and thou shalt bind them as a sign on thy hand, and they shall be and shall move between thy eyes. And thou shalt write them in the entry, and on the doors of thy house.* Thus the continual remembrance of God's commandments is signified, since it is impossible for us to forget those things which are continually attracting the notice of our senses, whether by touch, as those things we hold in our hands, or by sight, as those things which are ever before our eyes, or to which we are continually returning, for instance, to the house door. Moreover it is clearly stated (Deut 4:9): *Forget not the words that thy eyes have seen and let them not go out of thy heart all the days of thy life.*

We read of these things also being commanded more notably in the New Testament, both in the teaching of the Gospel and in that of the apostles.

REPLY OBJ. 1: According to Deut. 4:6, *this is your wisdom and understanding in the sight of the nations.* By this we are given to understand that the wisdom and understanding of those who believe in God consist in the precepts of the Law. Wherefore the precepts of the Law had to be given first, and afterwards men had to be led to know and understand them, and so it was not fitting that the aforesaid precepts should be placed among the precepts of the decalogue which take the first place.

REPLY OBJ. 2: There are also in the Law precepts relating to learning, as stated above. Nevertheless teaching was commanded more expressly than learning, because it concerned the learned, who were not under any other authority, but were immediately under the law, and to them the precepts of the Law were given. On the other hand learning concerned the people of lower degree, and these the precepts of the Law have to reach through the learned.

REPLY OBJ. 3: Knowledge of the Law is so closely bound up with the priestly office that being charged with the office implies being charged to know the Law: hence there was no need for special precepts to be given about the training of the priests. On the other hand, the doctrine of God's law is not so bound up with the kingly office, be-

libus. Et ideo specialiter praecipitur ut rex instruatur de his quae pertinent ad legem Dei per sacerdotes.

AD QUARTUM dicendum quod illud praeceptum legis non est sic intelligendum quod homo dormiendo meditetur de lege Dei, sed quod dormiens, idest vadens dormitum, de lege Dei meditetur; quia ex hoc etiam homines dormiendo nanciscuntur meliora phantasmata, secundum quod pertranseunt motus a vigilantibus ad dormientes, ut patet per philosophum, in I Ethic. Similiter etiam mandatur ut in omni actu suo aliquis meditetur de lege, non quod semper actu de lege cogitet, sed quod omnia quae facit secundum legem moderetur.

cause a king is placed over his people in temporal matters: hence it is especially commanded that the king should be instructed by the priests about things pertaining to the law of God.

REPLY OBJ. 4: That precept of the Law does not mean that man should meditate on God's law by sleeping, but during sleep, i.e., that he should meditate on the law of God when he is preparing to sleep, because this leads to his having better phantasms while asleep, insofar as our movements pass from the state of vigil to the state of sleep, as the Philosopher explains (*Ethic.* i, 13). In like manner we are commanded to meditate on the Law in every action of ours, not that we are bound to be always actually thinking about the Law, but that we should regulate all our actions according to it.

# QUESTION 17

## HOPE, CONSIDERED IN ITSELF

Consequenter post fidem considerandum est de spe. Et primo, de ipsa spe; secundo, de dono timoris; tertio, de vitiis oppositis; quarto, de praeceptis ad hoc pertinentibus. Circa primum occurrit primo consideratio de ipsa spe; secundo, de subiecto eius.

Circa primum quaeruntur octo.

Primo, utrum spes sit virtus.

Secundo, utrum obiectum eius sit beatitudo aeterna.

Tertio, utrum unus homo possit sperare beatitudinem alterius per virtutem spei.

Quarto, utrum homo licite possit sperare in homine.

Quinto, utrum spes sit virtus theologica.

Sexto, de distinctione eius ab aliis virtutibus theologicis.

Septimo, de ordine eius ad fidem.

Octavo, de ordine eius ad caritatem.

After treating of faith, we must consider hope and (1) hope itself; (2) the gift of fear; (3) the contrary vices; (4) the corresponding precepts. The first of these points gives rise to a twofold consideration: (1) hope, considered in itself; (2) its subject.

Under the first head there are eight points of inquiry:

(1) Whether hope is a virtue?

(2) Whether its object is eternal happiness?

(3) Whether, by the virtue of hope, one man may hope for another's happiness?

(4) Whether a man may lawfully hope in man?

(5) Whether hope is a theological virtue?

(6) Of its distinction from the other theological virtues?

(7) Of its relation to faith;

(8) Of its relation to charity.

# Article 1

### Whether hope is a virtue?

**AD PRIMUM SIC PROCEDITUR.** Videtur quod spes non sit virtus. *Virtute* enim *nullus male utitur*; ut dicit Augustinus, in libro de Lib. Arb. Sed spe aliquis male utitur, quia circa passionem spei contingit esse medium et extrema, sicut et circa alias passiones. Ergo spes non est virtus.

**PRAETEREA,** nulla virtus procedit ex meritis, quia *virtutem Deus in nobis sine nobis operatur*, ut Augustinus dicit. Sed spes est *ex gratia et meritis proveniens*; ut Magister dicit, XXVI dist. III Lib. Sent. Ergo spes non est virtus.

**PRAETEREA,** *virtus est dispositio perfecti*; ut dicitur in VII Physic. Spes autem est dispositio imperfecti, scilicet eius qui non habet id quod sperat. Ergo spes non est virtus.

**SED CONTRA** est quod Gregorius, in I Moral., dicit quod per tres filias Iob significantur hae tres virtutes, fides, spes, caritas. Ergo spes est virtus.

**RESPONDEO** dicendum quod, secundum philosophum, in II Ethic., *virtus uniuscuiusque rei est quae bonum facit habentem et opus eius bonum reddit.* Oportet igitur, ubicumque invenitur aliquis actus hominis bonus, quod respondeat alicui virtuti humanae. In omnibus autem regulatis et mensuratis bonum consideratur per hoc quod aliquid propriam regulam attingit, sicut dicimus

**OBJECTION 1**: It would seem that hope is not a virtue. For *no man makes ill use of a virtue*, as Augustine states (*De Lib. Arb.* ii, 18). But one may make ill use of hope, since the passion of hope, like the other passions, is subject to a mean and extremes. Therefore hope is not a virtue.

**OBJ. 2**: Further, no virtue results from merits, since *God works virtue in us without us*, as Augustine states (*De Grat. et Lib. Arb.* xvii). But hope is *caused by grace and merits*, according to the Master (*Sent.* iii, D, 26). Therefore hope is not a virtue.

**OBJ. 3**: Further, *virtue is the disposition of a perfect thing* (*Phys.* vii, text. 17, 18). But hope is the disposition of an imperfect thing, of one, namely, that lacks what it hopes to have. Therefore hope is not a virtue.

**ON THE CONTRARY**, Gregory says (*Moral.* i, 33) that the three daughters of Job signify these three virtues, faith, hope and charity. Therefore hope is a virtue.

**I ANSWER THAT**, According to the Philosopher (*Ethic.* ii, 6) *the virtue of a thing is that which makes its subject good, and its work good likewise.* Consequently wherever we find a good human act, it must correspond to some human virtue. Now in all things measured and ruled, the good is that which attains its proper rule: thus we say that a coat is good if it neither exceeds nor falls short of its proper

vestem esse bonam quae nec excedit nec deficit a debita mensura. Humanorum autem actuum, sicut supra dictum est, duplex est mensura, una quidem proxima et homogenea, scilicet ratio; alia autem est suprema et excedens, scilicet Deus. Et ideo omnis actus humanus attingens ad rationem aut ad ipsum Deum est bonus. Actus autem spei de qua nunc loquimur attingit ad Deum. Ut enim supra dictum est, cum de passione spei ageretur, obiectum spei est bonum futurum arduum possibile haberi. Possibile autem est aliquid nobis dupliciter, uno modo, per nos ipsos; alio modo, per alios; ut patet in III Ethic. Inquantum igitur speramus aliquid ut possibile nobis per divinum auxilium, spes nostra attingit ad ipsum Deum, cuius auxilio innititur. Et ideo patet quod spes est virtus, cum faciat actum hominis bonum et debitam regulam attingentem.

**Ad primum** ergo dicendum quod in passionibus accipitur medium virtutis per hoc quod attingitur ratio recta, et in hoc etiam consistit ratio virtutis. Unde etiam et in spe bonum virtutis accipitur secundum quod homo attingit sperando regulam debitam, scilicet Deum. Et ideo spe attingente Deum nullus potest male uti, sicut nec virtute morali attingente rationem, quia hoc ipsum quod est attingere est bonus usus virtutis. Quamvis spes de qua nunc loquimur non sit passio, sed habitus mentis, ut infra patebit.

**Ad secundum** dicendum quod spes dicitur ex meritis provenire quantum ad ipsam rem expectatam, prout aliquis sperat se beatitudinem adepturum ex gratia et meritis. Vel quantum ad actum spei formatae. Ipse autem habitus spei, per quam aliquis expectat beatitudinem, non causatur ex meritis, sed pure ex gratia.

**Ad tertium** dicendum quod ille qui sperat est quidem imperfectus secundum considerationem ad id quod sperat obtinere, quod nondum habet, sed est perfectus quantum ad hoc quod iam attingit propriam regulam, scilicet Deum, cuius auxilio innititur.

measurement. But, as we stated above (Q. 8, A. 3, ad 3) human acts have a twofold measure; one is proximate and homogeneous, viz. the reason, while the other is remote and excelling, viz. God: wherefore every human act is good, which attains reason or God Himself. Now the act of hope, whereof we speak now, attains God. For, as we have already stated (I-II, Q. 40, A. 1), when we were treating of the passion of hope, the object of hope is a future good, difficult but possible to obtain. Now a thing is possible to us in two ways: first, by ourselves; second, by means of others, as stated in *Ethic.* iii. Wherefore, insofar as we hope for anything as being possible to us by means of the Divine assistance, our hope attains God Himself, on Whose help it leans. It is therefore evident that hope is a virtue, since it causes a human act to be good and to attain its due rule.

**Reply Obj. 1:** In the passions, the mean of virtue depends on right reason being attained, wherein also consists the essence of virtue. Wherefore in hope too, the good of virtue depends on a man's attaining, by hoping, the due rule, viz. God. Consequently man cannot make ill use of hope which attains God, as neither can he make ill use of moral virtue which attains the reason, because to attain thus is to make good use of virtue. Nevertheless, the hope of which we speak now, is not a passion but a habit of the mind, as we shall show further on (A. 5; Q. 18, A. 1).

**Reply Obj. 2:** Hope is said to arise from merits, as regards the thing hoped for, insofar as we hope to obtain happiness by means of grace and merits; or as regards the act of living hope. The habit itself of hope, whereby we hope to obtain happiness, does not flow from our merits, but from grace alone.

**Reply Obj. 3:** He who hopes is indeed imperfect in relation to that which he hopes to obtain, but has not as yet; yet he is perfect, insofar as he already attains his proper rule, viz. God, on Whose help he leans.

# Article 2

*Whether eternal happiness is the proper object of hope?*

**Ad secundum sic proceditur.** Videtur quod beatitudo aeterna non sit obiectum proprium spei. Illud enim homo non sperat quod omnem animi sui motum excedit, cum spei actus sit quidam animi motus. Sed beatitudo aeterna excedit omnem humani animi motum, dicit enim apostolus, I ad Cor. II, quod *in cor hominis non ascendit.* Ergo beatitudo non est proprium obiectum spei.

**Praeterea,** petitio est spei interpretativa, dicitur enim in Psalm., *revela domino viam tuam et spera in eo, et ipse faciet.* Sed homo petit a Deo licite non solum

**Objection 1:** It would seem that eternal happiness is not the proper object of hope. For a man does not hope for that which surpasses every movement of the soul, since hope itself is a movement of the soul. Now eternal happiness surpasses every movement of the human soul, for the Apostle says (1 Cor 2:9) that it hath not *entered into the heart of man.* Therefore happiness is not the proper object of hope.

**Obj. 2:** Further, prayer is an expression of hope, for it is written (Ps 36:5): *Commit thy way to the Lord, and trust in Him, and He will do it.* Now it is lawful for man to pray God

beatitudinem aeternam, sed etiam bona praesentis vitae tam spiritualia quam temporalia, et etiam liberationem a malis, quae in beatitudine aeterna non erunt, ut patet in oratione dominica, Matth. VI. Ergo beatitudo aeterna non est proprium obiectum spei.

**PRAETEREA**, spei obiectum est arduum. Sed in comparatione ad hominem multa alia sunt ardua quam beatitudo aeterna. Ergo beatitudo aeterna non est proprium obiectum spei.

**SED CONTRA** est quod apostolus dicit, ad Heb. VI, *habemus spem incedentem, idest incedere facientem, ad interiora velaminis, idest ad beatitudinem caelestem*; ut Glossa ibidem exponit. Ergo obiectum spei est beatitudo aeterna.

**RESPONDEO** dicendum quod, sicut dictum est, spes de qua loquimur attingit Deum innitens eius auxilio ad consequendum bonum speratum. Oportet autem effectum esse causae proportionatum. Et ideo bonum quod proprie et principaliter a Deo sperare debemus est bonum infinitum, quod proportionatur virtuti Dei adiuvantis, nam infinitae virtutis est proprium ad infinitum bonum perducere. Hoc autem bonum est vita aeterna, quae in fruitione ipsius Dei consistit, non enim minus aliquid ab eo sperandum est quam sit ipse, cum non sit minor eius bonitas, per quam bona creaturae communicat, quam eius essentia. Et ideo proprium et principale obiectum spei est beatitudo aeterna.

**AD PRIMUM** ergo dicendum quod beatitudo aeterna perfecte quidem in cor hominis non ascendit, ut scilicet cognosci possit ab homine viatore quae et qualis sit, sed secundum communem rationem, scilicet boni perfecti, cadere potest in apprehensione hominis. Et hoc modo motus spei in ipsam consurgit. Unde et signanter apostolus dicit quod spes incedit *usque ad interiora velaminis*, quia id quod speramus est nobis adhuc velatum.

**AD SECUNDUM** dicendum quod quaecumque alia bona non debemus a Deo petere nisi in ordine ad beatitudinem aeternam. Unde et spes principaliter quidem respicit beatitudinem aeternam; alia vero quae petuntur a Deo respicit secundario, in ordine ad beatitudinem aeternam. Sicut etiam fides respicit principaliter Deum, et secundario respicit ea quae ad Deum ordinantur, ut supra dictum est.

**AD TERTIUM** dicendum quod homini qui anhelat ad aliquid magnum, parvum videtur omne aliud quod est eo minus. Et ideo homini speranti beatitudinem aeternam, habito respectu ad istam spem, nihil aliud est arduum. Sed habito respectu ad facultatem sperantis, possunt etiam quaedam alia ei esse ardua. Et secundum hoc eorum potest esse spes in ordine ad principale obiectum.

not only for eternal happiness, but also for the goods, both temporal and spiritual, of the present life, and, as evidenced by the Lord's Prayer, to be delivered from evils which will no longer be in eternal happiness. Therefore eternal happiness is not the proper object of hope.

**OBJ. 3**: Further, the object of hope is something difficult. Now many things besides eternal happiness are difficult to man. Therefore eternal happiness is not the proper object of hope.

**ON THE CONTRARY**, The Apostle says (Heb 6:19) that we have hope *which entereth in*, i.e., maketh us to enter ... *within the veil*, i.e., into the happiness of heaven, according to the interpretation of a gloss on these words. Therefore the object of hope is eternal happiness.

**I ANSWER THAT**, As stated above (A. 1), the hope of which we speak now, attains God by leaning on His help in order to obtain the hoped for good. Now an effect must be proportionate to its cause. Wherefore the good which we ought to hope for from God properly and chiefly is the infinite good, which is proportionate to the power of our divine helper, since it belongs to an infinite power to lead anyone to an infinite good. Such a good is eternal life, which consists in the enjoyment of God Himself. For we should hope from Him for nothing less than Himself, since His goodness, whereby He imparts good things to His creature, is no less than His Essence. Therefore the proper and principal object of hope is eternal happiness.

**REPLY OBJ. 1**: Eternal happiness does not enter into the heart of man perfectly, i.e., so that it be possible for a wayfarer to know its nature and quality; yet, under the general notion of the perfect good, it is possible for it to be apprehended by a man, and it is in this way that the movement of hope towards it arises. Hence the Apostle says pointedly (Heb 6:19) that hope *enters in, even within the veil*, because that which we hope for is as yet veiled, so to speak.

**REPLY OBJ. 2**: We ought not to pray God for any other goods, except in reference to eternal happiness. Hence hope regards eternal happiness chiefly, and other things, for which we pray God, it regards secondarily and as referred to eternal happiness: just as faith regards God principally, and, secondarily, those things which are referred to God, as stated above (Q. 1, A. 1).

**REPLY OBJ. 3**: To him that longs for something great, all lesser things seem small; wherefore to him that hopes for eternal happiness, nothing else appears arduous, as compared with that hope; although, as compared with the capability of the man who hopes, other things besides may be arduous to him, so that he may have hope for such things in reference to its principal object.

# Article 3

*Whether one man may hope for another's eternal happiness?*

**AD TERTIUM SIC PROCEDITUR.** Videtur quod aliquis possit sperare alteri beatitudinem aeternam. Dicit enim apostolus, Philipp. I, *confidens hoc ipsum, quia qui coepit in vobis opus bonum perficiet usque in diem Christi Iesu.* Perfectio aut illius diei erit beatitudo aeterna. Ergo aliquis potest alteri sperare beatitudinem aeternam.

**PRAETEREA,** ea quae a Deo petimus speramus obtinere ab eo. Sed a Deo petimus quod alios ad beatitudinem aeternam perducat, secundum illud Iac. ult., *orate pro invicem ut salvemini.* Ergo possumus aliis sperare beatitudinem aeternam.

**PRAETEREA,** spes et desperatio sunt de eodem. Sed aliquis potest desperare de beatitudine aeterna alicuius, alioquin frustra diceret Augustinus, in libro de Verb. Dom., *de nemine esse desperandum dum vivit.* Ergo etiam potest aliquis sperare alteri vitam aeternam.

**SED CONTRA** est quod Augustinus dicit, in Enchirid., quod *spes non est nisi rerum ad eum pertinentium qui earum spem gerere perhibetur.*

**RESPONDEO** dicendum quod spes potest esse alicuius dupliciter. Uno quidem modo, absolute, et sic est solum boni ardui ad se pertinentis. Alio modo, ex praesuppositione alterius, et sic potest esse etiam eorum quae ad alium pertinent. Ad cuius evidentiam sciendum est quod amor et spes in hoc differunt quod amor importat quandam unionem amantis ad amatum; spes autem importat quendam motum sive protensionem appetitus in aliquod bonum arduum. Unio autem est aliquorum distinctorum, et ideo amor directe potest respicere alium, quem sibi aliquis unit per amorem, habens eum sicut seipsum. Motus autem semper est ad proprium terminum proportionatum mobili, et ideo spes directe respicit proprium bonum, non autem id quod ad alium pertinet. Sed praesupposita unione amoris ad alterum, iam aliquis potest desiderare et sperare aliquid alteri sicut sibi. Et secundum hoc aliquis potest sperare alteri vitam aeternam, inquantum est ei unitus per amorem. Et sicut est eadem virtus caritatis qua quis diligit Deum, seipsum et proximum, ita etiam est eadem virtus spei qua quis sperat sibi ipsi et alii.

**ET PER HOC** patet responsio ad obiecta.

**OBJECTION 1**: It would seem that one may hope for another's eternal happiness. For the Apostle says (Phil 1:6): *Being confident of this very thing, that He Who hath begun a good work in you, will perfect it unto the day of Jesus Christ.* Now the perfection of that day will be eternal happiness. Therefore one man may hope for another's eternal happiness.

**OBJ. 2**: Further, whatever we ask of God, we hope to obtain from Him. But we ask God to bring others to eternal happiness, according to James 5:16: *Pray for one another that you may be saved.* Therefore we can hope for another's eternal happiness.

**OBJ. 3**: Further, hope and despair are about the same object. Now it is possible to despair of another's eternal happiness, else Augustine would have no reason for saying (*De Verb. Dom.*, Serm. lxxi) that *we should not despair of anyone so long as he lives.* Therefore one can also hope for another's eternal salvation.

**ON THE CONTRARY**, Augustine says (*Enchiridion* viii) that *hope is only of such things as belong to him who is supposed to hope for them.*

**I ANSWER THAT**, We can hope for something in two ways: first, absolutely, and thus the object of hope is always something arduous and pertaining to the person who hopes. Second, we can hope for something, through something else being presupposed, and in this way its object can be something pertaining to someone else. In order to explain this we must observe that love and hope differ in this, that love denotes union between lover and beloved, while hope denotes a movement or a stretching forth of the appetite towards an arduous good. Now union is of things that are distinct, wherefore love can directly regard the other whom a man unites to himself by love, looking upon him as his other self: whereas movement is always towards its own term which is proportionate to the subject moved. Therefore hope regards directly one's own good, and not that which pertains to another. Yet if we presuppose the union of love with another, a man can hope for and desire something for another man, as for himself; and, accordingly, he can hope for another's eternal life, inasmuch as he is united to him by love, and just as it is the same virtue of charity whereby a man loves God, himself, and his neighbor, so too it is the same virtue of hope, whereby a man hopes for himself and for another.

**THIS SUFFICES** for the Replies to the Objections.

# Article 4

*Whether a man can lawfully hope in man?*

**AD QUARTUM SIC PROCEDITUR.** Videtur quod aliquis possit licite sperare in homine. Spei enim obiectum est beatitudo aeterna. Sed ad beatitudinem aeternam consequendam adiuvamur patrociniis sanctorum, dicit enim Gregorius, in I Dial., quod *praedestinatio iuvatur precibus sanctorum.* Ergo aliquis potest in homine sperare.

**PRAETEREA**, si non potest aliquis sperare in homine, non esset reputandum alicui in vitium quod in eo aliquis sperare non possit. Sed hoc de quibusdam in vitium dicitur, ut patet Ierem. IX, *unusquisque a proximo suo se custodiat, et in omni fratre suo non habeat fiduciam.* Ergo licite potest aliquis sperare in homine.

**PRAETEREA**, petitio est interpretativa spei, sicut dictum est. Sed licite potest homo aliquid petere ab homine. Ergo licite potest sperare de eo.

**SED CONTRA** est quod dicitur Ierem. XVII, *maledictus homo qui confidit in homine.*

**RESPONDEO** dicendum quod spes, sicut dictum est, duo respicit, scilicet bonum quod obtinere intendit; et auxilium per quod illud bonum obtinetur. Bonum autem quod quis sperat obtinendum habet rationem causae finalis; auxilium autem per quod quis sperat illud bonum obtinere habet rationem causae efficientis. In genere autem utriusque causae invenitur principale et secundarium. Principalis enim finis est finis ultimus; secundarius autem finis est bonum quod est ad finem. Similiter principalis causa agens est primum agens; secundaria vero causa efficiens est agens secundarium instrumentale. Spes autem respicit beatitudinem aeternam sicut finem ultimum; divinum autem auxilium sicut primam causam inducentem ad beatitudinem.

Sicut igitur non licet sperare aliquod bonum praeter beatitudinem sicut ultimum finem, sed solum sicut id quod est ad finem beatitudinis ordinatum; ita etiam non licet sperare de aliquo homine, vel de aliqua creatura, sicut de prima causa movente in beatitudinem; licet autem sperare de aliquo homine, vel de aliqua creatura, sicut de agente secundario et instrumentali, per quod aliquis adiuvatur ad quaecumque bona consequenda in beatitudinem ordinata. Et hoc modo ad sanctos convertimur; et ab hominibus aliqua petimus; et vituperantur illi de quibus aliquis confidere non potest ad auxilium ferendum.

**ET PER HOC** patet responsio ad obiecta.

**OBJECTION 1**: It would seem that one may lawfully hope in man. For the object of hope is eternal happiness. Now we are helped to obtain eternal happiness by the patronage of the saints, for Gregory says (*Dial.* i, 8) that *predestination is furthered by the saints' prayers.* Therefore one may hope in man.

**OBJ. 2**: Further, if a man may not hope in another man, it ought not to be reckoned a sin in a man, that one should not be able to hope in him. Yet this is reckoned a vice in some, as appears from Jer. 9:4: *Let every man take heed of his neighbor, and let him not trust in any brother of his.* Therefore it is lawful to trust in a man.

**OBJ. 3**: Further, prayer is the expression of hope, as stated above (A. 2, Obj. 2). But it is lawful to pray to a man for something. Therefore it is lawful to trust in him.

**ON THE CONTRARY**, It is written (Jer 17:5): *Cursed be the man that trusteth in man.*

**I ANSWER THAT,** Hope, as stated above (A. 1; I-II, Q. 40, A. 7), regards two things, viz. the good which it intends to obtain, and the help by which that good is obtained. Now the good which a man hopes to obtain, has the aspect of a final cause, while the help by which one hopes to obtain that good, has the character of an efficient cause. Now in each of these kinds of cause we find a principal and a secondary cause. For the principal end is the last end, while the secondary end is that which is referred to an end. In like manner the principal efficient cause is the first agent, while the secondary efficient cause is the secondary and instrumental agent. Now hope regards eternal happiness as its last end, and the Divine assistance as the first cause leading to happiness.

Accordingly, just as it is not lawful to hope for any good save happiness, as one's last end, but only as something referred to final happiness, so too, it is unlawful to hope in any man, or any creature, as though it were the first cause of movement towards happiness. It is, however, lawful to hope in a man or a creature as being the secondary and instrumental agent through whom one is helped to obtain any goods that are ordained to happiness. It is in this way that we turn to the saints, and that we ask men also for certain things; and for this reason some are blamed in that they cannot be trusted to give help.

**THIS SUFFICES** for the Replies to the Objections.

# Article 5

*Whether hope is a theological virtue?*

**AD QUINTUM SIC PROCEDITUR**. Videtur quod spes non sit virtus theologica. Virtus enim theologica est quae habet Deum pro obiecto. Sed spes non habet solum Deum pro obiecto, sed etiam alia bona quae a Deo obtinere speramus. Ergo spes non est virtus theologica.

**PRAETEREA**, virtus theologica non consistit in medio duorum vitiorum, ut supra habitum est. Sed spes consistit in medio praesumptionis et desperationis. Ergo spes non est virtus theologica.

**PRAETEREA**, expectatio pertinet ad longanimitatem, quae est pars fortitudinis. Cum ergo spes sit quaedam expectatio, videtur quod spes non sit virtus theologica, sed moralis.

**PRAETEREA**, obiectum spei est arduum. Sed tendere in arduum pertinet ad magnanimitatem, quae est virtus moralis. Ergo spes est virtus moralis, et non theologica.

**SED CONTRA** est quod, I ad Cor. XIII, connumeratur fidei et caritati quae sunt virtutes theologicae.

**RESPONDEO** dicendum quod, cum differentiae specificae per se dividant genus, oportet attendere unde habeat spes rationem virtutis, ad hoc quod sciamus sub qua differentia virtutis collocetur.

Dictum est autem supra quod spes habet rationem virtutis ex hoc quod attingit supremam regulam humanorum actuum; quam attingit et sicut primam causam efficientem, inquantum eius auxilio innititur; et sicut ultimam causam finalem, inquantum in eius fruitione beatitudinem expectat. Et sic patet quod spei, inquantum est virtus, principale obiectum est Deus. Cum igitur in hoc consistat ratio virtutis theologicae quod Deum habeat pro obiecto, sicut supra dictum est, manifestum est quod spes est virtus theologica.

**AD PRIMUM** ergo dicendum quod quaecumque alia spes adipisci expectat, sperat in ordine ad Deum sicut ad ultimum finem et sicut ad primam causam efficientem, ut dictum est.

**AD SECUNDUM** dicendum quod medium accipitur in regulatis et mensuratis secundum quod regula vel mensura attingitur; secundum autem quod exceditur regula, est superfluum; secundum autem defectum a regula, est diminutum. In ipsa autem regula vel mensura non est accipere medium et extrema. Virtus autem moralis est circa ea quae regulantur ratione sicut circa proprium obiectum, et ideo per se convenit ei esse in medio ex parte proprii obiecti. Sed virtus theologica est circa ipsam regulam primam, non regulatam alia regula, sicut circa proprium obiectum. Et ideo per se, et secundum proprium obiectum, non convenit virtuti theologicae esse in medio. Sed potest sibi competere

**OBJECTION 1**: It would seem that hope is not a theological virtue. For a theological virtue is one that has God for its object. Now hope has for its object not only God but also other goods which we hope to obtain from God. Therefore hope is not a theological virtue.

**OBJ. 2**: Further, a theological virtue is not a mean between two vices, as stated above (I-II, Q. 64, A. 4). But hope is a mean between presumption and despair. Therefore hope is not a theological virtue.

**OBJ. 3**: Further, expectation belongs to longanimity which is a species of fortitude. Since, then, hope is a kind of expectation, it seems that hope is not a theological, but a moral virtue.

**OBJ. 4**: Further, the object of hope is something arduous. But it belongs to magnanimity, which is a moral virtue, to tend to the arduous. Therefore hope is a moral, and not a theological virtue.

**ON THE CONTRARY**, Hope is enumerated (1 Cor 13) together with faith and charity, which are theological virtues.

**I ANSWER THAT**, Since specific differences, by their very nature, divide a genus, in order to decide under what division we must place hope, we must observe whence it derives its character of virtue.

Now it has been stated above (A. 1) that hope has the character of virtue from the fact that it attains the supreme rule of human actions: and this it attains both as its first efficient cause, inasmuch as it leans on its assistance, and as its last final cause, inasmuch as it expects happiness in the enjoyment thereof. Hence it is evident that God is the principal object of hope, considered as a virtue. Since, then, the very idea of a theological virtue is one that has God for its object, as stated above (I-II, Q. 62, A. 1), it is evident that hope is a theological virtue.

**REPLY OBJ. 1**: Whatever else hope expects to obtain, it hopes for it in reference to God as the last end, or as the first efficient cause, as stated above (A. 4).

**REPLY OBJ. 2**: In things measured and ruled the mean consists in the measure or rule being attained; if we go beyond the rule, there is excess, if we fall short of the rule, there is deficiency. But in the rule or measure itself there is no such thing as a mean or extremes. Now a moral virtue is concerned with things ruled by reason, and these things are its proper object; wherefore it is proper to it to follow the mean as regards its proper object. On the other hand, a theological virtue is concerned with the First Rule not ruled by another rule, and that Rule is its proper object. Wherefore it is not proper for a theological virtue, with regard to its proper object, to follow the mean, although this may happen to it accidentally with regard to something

per accidens, ratione eius quod ordinatur ad principale obiectum. Sicut fides non potest habere medium et extrema in hoc quod innitatur primae veritati, cui nullus potest nimis inniti, sed ex parte eorum quae credit, potest habere medium et extrema, sicut unum verum est medium inter duo falsa. Et similiter spes non habet medium et extrema ex parte principalis obiecti, quia divino auxilio nullus potest nimis inniti, sed quantum ad ea quae confidit aliquis se adepturum, potest ibi esse medium et extrema, inquantum vel praesumit ea quae sunt supra suam proportionem, vel desperat de his quae sunt sibi proportionata.

**Ad tertium** dicendum quod expectatio quae ponitur in definitione spei non importat dilationem, sicut expectatio quae pertinet ad longanimitatem, sed importat respectum ad auxilium divinum, sive illud quod speratur differatur, sive non differatur.

**Ad quartum** dicendum quod magnanimitas tendit in arduum sperans aliquid quod est suae potestatis. Unde proprie respicit operationem aliquorum magnorum. Sed spes, secundum quod est virtus theologica, respicit arduum alterius auxilio assequendum, ut dictum est.

that is referred to its principal object. Thus faith can have no mean or extremes in the point of trusting to the First Truth, in which it is impossible to trust too much; whereas on the part of the things believed, it may have a mean and extremes; for instance one truth is a mean between two falsehoods. So too, hope has no mean or extremes, as regards its principal object, since it is impossible to trust too much in the Divine assistance; yet it may have a mean and extremes, as regards those things a man trusts to obtain, insofar as he either presumes above his capability, or despairs of things of which he is capable.

**Reply Obj. 3**: The expectation which is mentioned in the definition of hope does not imply delay, as does the expectation which belongs to longanimity. It implies a reference to the Divine assistance, whether that which we hope for be delayed or not.

**Reply Obj. 4**: Magnanimity tends to something arduous in the hope of obtaining something that is within one's power, wherefore its proper object is the doing of great things. On the other hand hope, as a theological virtue, regards something arduous, to be obtained by another's help, as stated above (A. 1).

# Article 6

*Whether hope is distinct from the other theological virtues?*

**Ad sextum sic proceditur.** Videtur quod spes non sit virtus distincta ab aliis theologicis. Habitus enim distinguuntur secundum obiecta, ut supra dictum est. Sed idem est obiectum spei et aliarum virtutum theologicarum. Ergo spes non distinguitur ab aliis virtutibus theologicis.

**Praeterea,** in symbolo fidei, in quo fidem profitemur, dicitur, *expecto resurrectionem mortuorum et vitam futuri saeculi.* Sed expectatio futurae beatitudinis pertinet ad spem, ut supra dictum est. Ergo spes a fide non distinguitur.

**Praeterea,** per spem homo tendit in Deum. Sed hoc proprie pertinet ad caritatem. Ergo spes a caritate non distinguitur.

**Sed contra,** ubi non est distinctio ibi non est numerus. Sed spes connumeratur aliis virtutibus theologicis, dicit enim Gregorius, in I Moral., esse tres virtutes, fidem, spem et caritatem. Ergo spes est virtus distincta ab aliis theologicis.

**Respondeo** dicendum quod virtus aliqua dicitur theologica ex hoc quod habet Deum pro obiecto cui inhaeret. Potest autem aliquis alicui rei inhaerere dupliciter, uno modo, propter seipsum; alio modo, inquantum

**Objection 1**: It would seem that hope is not distinct from the other theological virtues. For habits are distinguished by their objects, as stated above (I-II, Q. 54, A. 2). Now the object of hope is the same as of the other theological virtues. Therefore hope is not distinct from the other theological virtues.

**Obj. 2**: Further, in the symbol of faith, whereby we make profession of faith, we say: *I expect the resurrection of the dead and the life of the world to come.* Now expectation of future happiness belongs to hope, as stated above (A. 5). Therefore hope is not distinct from faith.

**Obj. 3**: Further, by hope man tends to God. But this belongs properly to charity. Therefore hope is not distinct from charity.

**On the contrary**, There cannot be number without distinction. Now hope is numbered with the other theological virtues: for Gregory says (*Moral.* i, 16) that the three virtues are faith, hope, and charity. Therefore hope is distinct from the theological virtues.

**I answer that**, A virtue is said to be theological from having God for the object to which it adheres. Now one may adhere to a thing in two ways: first, for its own sake; second, because something else is attained thereby. Accordingly

ex eo ad aliud devenitur. Caritas igitur facit hominem Deo inhaerere propter seipsum, mentem hominis uniens Deo per affectum amoris.

Spes autem et fides faciunt hominem inhaerere Deo sicut cuidam principio ex quo aliqua nobis proveniunt. De Deo autem provenit nobis et cognitio veritatis et adeptio perfectae bonitatis. Fides ergo facit hominem Deo inhaerere inquantum est nobis principium cognoscendi veritatem, credimus enim ea vera esse quae nobis a Deo dicuntur. Spes autem facit Deo adhaerere prout est nobis principium perfectae bonitatis, inquantum scilicet per spem divino auxilio innitimur ad beatitudinem obtinendam.

**AD PRIMUM** ergo dicendum quod Deus secundum aliam et aliam rationem est obiectum harum virtutum, ut dictum est. Ad distinctionem autem habituum sufficit diversa ratio obiecti, ut supra habitum est.

**AD SECUNDUM** dicendum quod expectatio ponitur in symbolo fidei non quia sit actus proprius fidei, sed inquantum actus spei praesupponit fidem, ut dicetur, et sic actus fidei manifestantur per actus spei.

**AD TERTIUM** dicendum quod spes facit tendere in Deum sicut in quoddam bonum finale adipiscendum, et sicut in quoddam adiutorium efficax ad subveniendum. Sed caritas proprie facit tendere in Deum uniendo affectum hominis Deo, ut scilicet homo non sibi vivat sed Deo.

charity makes us adhere to God for His own sake, uniting our minds to God by the emotion of love.

On the other hand, hope and faith make man adhere to God as to a principle wherefrom certain things accrue to us. Now we derive from God both knowledge of truth and the attainment of perfect goodness. Accordingly faith makes us adhere to God, as the source whence we derive the knowledge of truth, since we believe that what God tells us is true: while hope makes us adhere to God, as the source whence we derive perfect goodness, i.e., insofar as, by hope, we trust to the Divine assistance for obtaining happiness.

**REPLY OBJ. 1**: God is the object of these virtues under different aspects, as stated above: and a different aspect of the object suffices for the distinction of habits, as stated above (I-II, Q. 54, A. 2).

**REPLY OBJ. 2**: Expectation is mentioned in the symbol of faith, not as though it were the proper act of faith, but because the act of hope presupposes the act of faith, as we shall state further on (A. 7). Hence an act of faith is expressed in the act of hope.

**REPLY OBJ. 3**: Hope makes us tend to God, as to a good to be obtained finally, and as to a helper strong to assist: whereas charity, properly speaking, makes us tend to God, by uniting our affections to Him, so that we live, not for ourselves, but for God.

# Article 7

*Whether hope precedes faith?*

**AD SEPTIMUM SIC PROCEDITUR.** Videtur quod spes praecedat fidem. Quia super illud Psalm., *spera in domino, et fac bonitatem*, dicit Glossa, *spes est introitus fidei, initium salutis*. Sed salus est per fidem, per quam iustificamur. Ergo spes praecedit fidem.

**PRAETEREA,** illud quod ponitur in definitione alicuius debet esse prius et magis notum. Sed spes ponitur in definitione fidei, ut patet Heb. XI, *fides est substantia rerum sperandarum*. Ergo spes est prior fide.

**PRAETEREA,** spes praecedit actum meritorium, dicit enim apostolus, I ad Cor. IX, quod *qui arat debet arare in spe fructus percipiendi*. Sed actus fidei est meritorius. Ergo spes praecedit fidem.

**SED CONTRA** est quod Matth. I dicitur, *Abraham genuit Isaac, idest fides spem*, sicut dicit Glossa.

**RESPONDEO** dicendum quod fides absolute praecedit spem. Obiectum enim spei est bonum futurum arduum possibile haberi. Ad hoc ergo quod aliquis speret, requiritur quod obiectum spei proponatur ei ut

**OBJECTION 1**: It would seem that hope precedes faith. Because a gloss on Ps. 36:3, *Trust in the Lord, and do good*, says: *Hope is the entrance to faith and the beginning of salvation*. But salvation is by faith whereby we are justified. Therefore hope precedes faith.

**OBJ. 2**: Further, that which is included in a definition should precede the thing defined and be more known. But hope is included in the definition of faith (Heb 11:1): *Faith is the substance of things to be hoped for*. Therefore hope precedes faith.

**OBJ. 3**: Further, hope precedes a meritorious act, for the Apostle says (1 Cor 9:10): *He that plougheth should plough in hope . . . to receive fruit*. But the act of faith is meritorious. Therefore hope precedes faith.

**ON THE CONTRARY**, It is written (Matt 1:2): *Abraham begot Isaac*, i.e., *Faith begot hope*, according to a gloss.

**I ANSWER THAT**, Absolutely speaking, faith precedes hope. For the object of hope is a future good, arduous but possible to obtain. In order, therefore, that we may hope, it is necessary for the object of hope to be proposed to us

possibile. Sed obiectum spei est uno modo beatitudo aeterna, et alio modo divinum auxilium, ut ex dictis patet. Et utrumque eorum proponitur nobis per fidem, per quam nobis innotescit quod ad vitam aeternam possumus pervenire, et quod ad hoc paratum est nobis divinum auxilium, secundum illud Heb. XI, *accedentem ad Deum oportet credere quia est, et quia inquirentibus se remunerator est.* Unde manifestum est quod fides praecedit spem.

**Ad primum** ergo dicendum quod, sicut Glossa ibidem subdit, spes dicitur introitus fidei, idest rei creditae, *quia per spem intratur ad videndum illud quod creditur.* Vel potest dici quod est introitus fidei quia per eam homo intrat ad hoc quod stabiliatur et perficiatur in fide.

**Ad secundum** dicendum quod in definitione fidei ponitur res speranda quia proprium obiectum fidei est non apparens secundum seipsum. Unde fuit necessarium ut quadam circumlocutione designaretur per id quod consequitur ad fidem.

**Ad tertium** dicendum quod non omnis actus meritorius habet spem praecedentem, sed sufficit si habeat concomitantem vel consequentem.

as possible. Now the object of hope is, in one way, eternal happiness, and in another way, the Divine assistance, as explained above (A. 2; A. 6, ad 3): and both of these are proposed to us by faith, whereby we come to know that we are able to obtain eternal life, and that for this purpose the Divine assistance is ready for us, according to Heb. 11:6: *He that cometh to God, must believe that He is, and is a rewarder to them that seek Him.* Therefore it is evident that faith precedes hope.

**Reply Obj. 1:** As the same gloss observes further on, *hope* is called *the entrance* to faith, i.e., of the thing believed, because *by hope we enter in to see what we believe.* Or we may reply that it is called the *entrance to faith,* because thereby man begins to be established and perfected in faith.

**Reply Obj. 2:** The thing to be hoped for is included in the definition of faith, because the proper object of faith, is something not apparent in itself. Hence it was necessary to express it in a circumlocution by something resulting from faith.

**Reply Obj. 3:** Hope does not precede every meritorious act; but it suffices for it to accompany or follow it.

# Article 8

## *Whether charity precedes hope?*

**Ad octavum sic proceditur.** Videtur quod caritas sit prior spe. Dicit enim Ambrosius, super illud Luc. XVII, *si habueritis fidem sicut granum sinapis, etc., ex fide est caritas, ex caritate spes.* Sed fides est prior caritate. Ergo caritas est prior spe.

**Praeterea,** Augustinus dicit, XIV de Civ. Dei, quod *boni motus atque affectus ex amore et sancta caritate veniunt.* Sed sperare, secundum quod est actus spei, est quidam bonus animi motus. Ergo derivatur a caritate.

**Praeterea,** Magister dicit, XXVI dist. III Lib. Sent., quod *spes ex meritis provenit, quae praecedunt non solum rem speratam, sed etiam spem, quam natura praeit caritas.* Caritas ergo est prior spe.

**Sed contra** est quod apostolus dicit, I ad Tim. I, *finis praecepti caritas est de corde puro et conscientia bona,* glossa, *idest spe.* Ergo spes est prior caritate.

**Respondeo** dicendum quod duplex est ordo. Unus quidem secundum viam generationis et materiae, secundum quem imperfectum prius est perfecto. Alius autem ordo est perfectionis et formae, secundum quem perfectum naturaliter prius est imperfecto. Secundum igitur primum ordinem spes est prior caritate. Quod sic patet. Quia spes, et omnis appetitivus motus, ex amore

**Objection 1:** It would seem that charity precedes hope. For Ambrose says on Luke 27:6, *If you had faith like to a grain of mustard seed,* etc.: *Charity flows from faith, and hope from charity.* But faith precedes charity. Therefore charity precedes hope.

**Obj. 2:** Further, Augustine says (*De Civ. Dei* xiv, 9) that *good emotions and affections proceed from love and holy charity.* Now to hope, considered as an act of hope, is a good emotion of the soul. Therefore it flows from charity.

**Obj. 3:** Further, the Master says (*Sent.* iii, D, 26) that hope proceeds from merits, which precede not only the thing hoped for, but also hope itself, which, in the order of nature, is preceded by charity. Therefore charity precedes hope.

**On the contrary,** The Apostle says (1 Tim 1:5): *The end of the commandment is charity from a pure heart, and a good conscience,* i.e., *from hope,* according to a gloss. Therefore hope precedes charity.

**I answer that,** Order is twofold. One is the order of generation and of matter, in respect of which the imperfect precedes the perfect: the other is the order of perfection and form, in respect of which the perfect naturally precedes the imperfect. In respect of the first order hope precedes charity: and this is clear from the fact that hope and all movements of the appetite flow from love, as stated above

derivatur, ut supra habitum est, cum de passionibus ageretur.

Amor autem quidam est perfectus, quidam imperfectus. Perfectus quidem amor est quo aliquis secundum se amatur, ut puta cui aliquis vult bonum, sicut homo amat amicum. Imperfectus amor est quo quis amat aliquid non secundum ipsum, sed ut illud bonum sibi ipsi proveniat, sicut homo amat rem quam concupiscit. Primus autem amor Dei pertinet ad caritatem, quae inhaeret Deo secundum seipsum, sed spes pertinet ad secundum amorem, quia ille qui sperat aliquid sibi obtinere intendit. Et ideo in via generationis spes est prior caritate. Sicut enim aliquis introducitur ad amandum Deum per hoc quod, timens ab ipso puniri, cessat a peccato, ut Augustinus dicit, super primam canonicam Ioan.; ita etiam et spes introducit ad caritatem, inquantum aliquis, sperans remunerari a Deo, accenditur ad amandum Deum et servandum praecepta eius. Sed secundum ordinem perfectionis caritas naturaliter prior est. Et ideo, adveniente caritate, spes perfectior redditur, quia de amicis maxime speramus. Et hoc modo dicit Ambrosius quod spes est ex caritate.

**UNDE PATET** responsio ad primum.

**AD SECUNDUM** dicendum quod spes, et omnis motus appetitivus, ex amore provenit aliquo, quo scilicet aliquis amat bonum expectatum. Sed non omnis spes provenit a caritate, sed solum motus spei formatae, qua scilicet aliquis sperat bonum a Deo ut ab amico.

**AD TERTIUM** dicendum quod Magister loquitur de spe formata, quam naturaliter praecedit caritas, et merita ex caritate causata.

(I-II, Q. 27, A. 4; I-II, Q. 28, A. 6, ad 2; I-II, Q. 40, A. 7) in the treatise on the passions.

Now there is a perfect, and an imperfect love. Perfect love is that whereby a man is loved in himself, as when someone wishes a person some good for his own sake; thus a man loves his friend. Imperfect love is that whereby a man love something, not for its own sake, but that he may obtain that good for himself; thus a man loves what he desires. The first love of God pertains to charity, which adheres to God for His own sake; while hope pertains to the second love, since he that hopes, intends to obtain possession of something for himself. Hence in the order of generation, hope precedes charity. For just as a man is led to love God, through fear of being punished by Him for his sins, as Augustine states (*In primam canon. Joan.* Tract. ix), so too, hope leads to charity, inasmuch as a man through hoping to be rewarded by God, is encouraged to love God and obey His commandments. On the other hand, in the order of perfection charity naturally precedes hope, wherefore, with the advent of charity, hope is made more perfect, because we hope chiefly in our friends. It is in this sense that Ambrose states (Obj. 1) that hope flows from charity.

**THIS SUFFICES** for the Reply to the First Objection.

**REPLY OBJ. 2**: Hope and every movement of the appetite proceed from some kind of love, whereby the expected good is loved. But not every kind of hope proceeds from charity, but only the movement of living hope, viz. that whereby man hopes to obtain good from God, as from a friend.

**REPLY OBJ. 3**: The Master is speaking of living hope, which is naturally preceded by charity and the merits caused by charity.

# QUESTION 18

## THE SUBJECT OF HOPE

Deinde considerandum est de subiecto spei. Et circa hoc quaeruntur quatuor.

Primo, utrum virtus spei sit in voluntate sicut in subiecto.

Secundo, utrum sit in beatis.

Tertio, utrum sit in damnatis.

Quarto, utrum in viatoribus habeat certitudinem.

We must now consider the subject of hope, under which head there are four points of inquiry:

(1) Whether the virtue of hope is in the will as its subject?

(2) Whether it is in the blessed?

(3) Whether it is in the damned?

(4) Whether there is certainty in the hope of the wayfarer?

# Article 1

*Whether hope is in the will as its subject?*

**AD PRIMUM SIC PROCEDITUR.** Videtur quod spes non sit in voluntate sicut in subiecto. Spei enim obiectum est bonum arduum, ut supra dictum est. Arduum autem non est obiectum voluntatis, sed irascibilis. Ergo spes non est in voluntate, sed in irascibili.

**PRAETEREA**, ad id ad quod unum sufficit, superflue apponitur aliud. Sed ad perficiendum potentiam voluntatis sufficit caritas, quae est perfectissima virtutum. Ergo spes non est in voluntate.

**PRAETEREA**, una potentia non potest simul esse in duobus actibus, sicut intellectus non potest simul multa intelligere. Sed actus spei simul esse potest cum actu caritatis. Cum ergo actus caritatis manifeste pertineat ad voluntatem, actus spei non pertinet ad ipsam. Sic ergo spes non est in voluntate.

**SED CONTRA**, anima non est capax Dei nisi secundum mentem; in qua est memoria, intelligentia et voluntas, ut patet per Augustinum, in libro de Trin. Sed spes est virtus theologica habens Deum pro obiecto. Cum igitur non sit neque in memoria neque in intelligentia, quae pertinent ad vim cognoscitivam, relinquitur quod sit in voluntate sicut in subiecto.

**RESPONDEO** dicendum quod, sicut ex praedictis patet, habitus per actus cognoscuntur. Actus autem spei est quidam motus appetitivae partis, cum sit eius obiectum bonum. Cum autem sit duplex appetitus in homine, scilicet appetitus sensitivus, qui dividitur per irascibilem et concupiscibilem, et appetitus intellectivus, qui dicitur voluntas, ut in primo habitum est; similes motus qui sunt in appetitu inferiori cum passione, in superiori sunt sine passione, ut ex supradictis patet. Actus autem virtutis spei non potest pertinere ad appetitum sensitivum, quia

**OBJECTION 1**: It would seem that hope is not in the will as its subject. For the object of hope is an arduous good, as stated above (Q. 17, A. 1; I-II, Q. 40, A. 1). Now the arduous is the object, not of the will, but of the irascible. Therefore hope is not in the will but in the irascible.

**OBJ. 2**: Further, where one suffices it is superfluous to add another. Now charity suffices for the perfecting of the will, which is the most perfect of the virtues. Therefore hope is not in the will.

**OBJ. 3**: Further, the one same power cannot exercise two acts at the same time; thus the intellect cannot understand many things simultaneously. Now the act of hope can be at the same time as an act of charity. Since, then, the act of charity evidently belongs to the will, it follows that the act of hope does not belong to that power: so that, therefore, hope is not in the will.

**ON THE CONTRARY**, The soul is not apprehensive of God save as regards the mind in which is memory, intellect and will, as Augustine declares (*De Trin.* xiv, 3, 6). Now hope is a theological virtue having God for its object. Since therefore it is neither in the memory, nor in the intellect, which belong to the cognitive faculty, it follows that it is in the will as its subject.

**I ANSWER THAT**, As shown above (I, Q. 87, A. 2), habits are known by their acts. Now the act of hope is a movement of the appetitive faculty, since its object is a good. And, since there is a twofold appetite in man, namely, the sensitive which is divided into irascible and concupiscible, and the intellective appetite, called the will, as stated in the First Part (Q. 82, A. 5), those movements which occur in the lower appetite are with passion, while those in the higher appetite are without passion, as shown above (I, Q. 87, A. 2, ad 1; I-II, Q. 22, A. 3, ad 3). Now the act

bonum quod est obiectum principale huius virtutis non est aliquod bonum sensibile, sed bonum divinum. Et ideo spes est in appetitu superiori, qui dicitur voluntas, sicut in subiecto, non autem in appetitu inferiori, ad quem pertinet irascibilis.

**AD PRIMUM** ergo dicendum quod irascibilis obiectum est arduum sensibile. Obiectum autem virtutis spei est arduum intelligibile; vel potius supra intellectum existens.

**AD SECUNDUM** dicendum quod caritas sufficienter perficit voluntatem quantum ad unum actum, qui est diligere. Requiritur autem alia virtus ad perficiendum ipsam secundum alium actum eius, qui est sperare.

**AD TERTIUM** dicendum quod motus spei et motus caritatis habent ordinem ad invicem, ut ex supradictis patet. Unde nihil prohibet utrumque motum simul esse unius potentiae. Sicut et intellectus potest simul multa intelligere ad invicem ordinata, ut in primo habitum est.

of the virtue of hope cannot belong to the sensitive appetite, since the good which is the principal object of this virtue, is not a sensible but a Divine good. Therefore hope resides in the higher appetite called the will, and not in the lower appetite, of which the irascible is a part.

**REPLY OBJ. 1:** The object of the irascible is an arduous sensible: whereas the object of the virtue of hope is an arduous intelligible, or rather superintelligible.

**REPLY OBJ. 2:** Charity perfects the will sufficiently with regard to one act, which is the act of loving: but another virtue is required in order to perfect it with regard to its other act, which is that of hoping.

**REPLY OBJ. 3:** The movement of hope and the movement of charity are mutually related, as was shown above (Q. 17, A. 8). Hence there is no reason why both movements should not belong at the same time to the same power: even as the intellect can understand many things at the same time if they be related to one another, as stated in the First Part (Q. 85, A. 4).

# Article 2

*Whether in the blessed there is hope?*

**AD SECUNDUM SIC PROCEDITUR.** Videtur quod spes sit in beatis. Christus enim a principio suae conceptionis fuit perfectus comprehensor. Sed ipse habuit spem, cum ex eius persona dicatur in Psalm., *in te, domine, speravi*, ut Glossa exponit. Ergo in beatis potest esse spes.

**PRAETEREA**, sicut adeptio beatitudinis est quoddam bonum arduum, ita etiam eius continuatio. Sed homines antequam beatitudinem adipiscantur habent spem de beatitudinis adeptione. Ergo postquam sunt beatitudinem adepti, possunt sperare beatitudinis continuationem.

**PRAETEREA**, per virtutem spei potest aliquis beatitudinem sperare non solum sibi sed etiam aliis, ut supra dictum est. Sed beati qui sunt in patria sperant beatitudinem aliis, alioquin non rogarent pro eis. Ergo in beatis potest esse spes.

**PRAETEREA**, ad beatitudinem sanctorum pertinet non solum gloria animae sed etiam gloria corporis. Sed animae sanctorum qui sunt in patria expectant adhuc gloriam corporis, ut patet Apoc. VI, et XII super Gen. ad Litt. Ergo spes potest esse in beatis.

**SED CONTRA** est quod apostolus dicit, ad Rom. VIII, *quod videt quis, quid sperat?* Sed beati fruuntur Dei visione. Ergo in eis spes locum non habet.

**OBJECTION 1:** It would seem that in the blessed there is hope. For Christ was a perfect comprehensor from the first moment of His conception. Now He had hope, since, according to a gloss, the words of Ps. 30:2, *In Thee, O Lord, have I hoped*, are said in His person. Therefore in the blessed there can be hope.

**OBJ. 2:** Further, even as the obtaining of happiness is an arduous good, so is its continuation. Now, before they obtain happiness, men hope to obtain it. Therefore, after they have obtained it, they can hope to continue in its possession.

**OBJ. 3:** Further, by the virtue of hope, a man can hope for happiness, not only for himself, but also for others, as stated above (Q. 17, A. 3). But the blessed who are in heaven hope for the happiness of others, else they would not pray for them. Therefore there can be hope in them.

**OBJ. 4:** Further, the happiness of the saints implies not only glory of the soul but also glory of the body. Now the souls of the saints in heaven, look yet for the glory of their bodies (Rev 6:10; Augustine, *Gen. ad lit.* xii, 35). Therefore in the blessed there can be hope.

**ON THE CONTRARY,** The Apostle says (Rom 8:24): *What a man seeth, why doth he hope for?* Now the blessed enjoy the sight of God. Therefore hope has no place in them.

**RESPONDEO** dicendum quod, subtracto eo quod dat speciem rei, solvitur species, et res non potest eadem remanere, sicut remota forma corporis naturalis, non remanet idem secundum speciem. Spes autem recipit speciem a suo obiecto principali, sicut et ceterae virtutes, ut ex supradictis patet. Obiectum autem principale eius est beatitudo aeterna secundum quod est possibilis haberi ex auxilio divino, ut supra dictum est.

Quia ergo bonum arduum possibile non cadit sub ratione spei nisi secundum quod est futurum, ideo, cum beatitudo iam non fuerit futura sed praesens, non potest ibi esse virtus spei. Et ideo spes, sicut et fides, evacuatur in patria, et neutrum eorum in beatis esse potest.

**AD PRIMUM** ergo dicendum quod Christus, etsi esset comprehensor, et per consequens beatus, quantum ad divinam fruitionem; erat tamen simul viator quantum ad passibilitatem naturae, quam adhuc gerebat. Et ideo gloriam impassibilitatis et immortalitatis sperare poterat. Non tamen ita quod haberet virtutem spei, quae non respicit gloriam corporis sicut principale obiectum, sed potius fruitionem divinam.

**AD SECUNDUM** dicendum quod beatitudo sanctorum dicitur vita aeterna, quia per hoc quod Deo fruuntur, efficiuntur quodammodo participes aeternitatis divinae, quae excedit omne tempus. Et ita continuatio beatitudinis non diversificatur per praesens, praeteritum et futurum. Et ideo beati non habent spem de continuatione beatitudinis, sed habent ipsam rem, quia non est ibi ratio futuri.

**AD TERTIUM** dicendum quod, durante virtute spei, eadem spe aliquis sperat beatitudinem sibi et aliis. Sed evacuata spe in beatis qua sperabant sibi beatitudinem, sperant quidem aliis beatitudinem, sed non virtute spei, sed magis ex amore caritatis. Sicut etiam qui habet caritatem Dei eadem caritate diligit proximum, et tamen aliquis potest diligere proximum non habens virtutem caritatis, alio quodam amore.

**AD QUARTUM** dicendum quod, cum spes sit virtus theologica habens Deum pro obiecto, principale obiectum spei est gloria animae, quae in fruitione divina consistit, non autem gloria corporis. Gloria etiam corporis, etsi habeat rationem ardui per comparationem ad naturam humanam, non habet tamen rationem ardui habenti gloriam animae. Tum quia gloria corporis est minimum quiddam in comparatione ad gloriam animae. Tum etiam quia habens gloriam animae habet iam sufficienter causam gloriae corporis.

**I ANSWER THAT**, If what gives a thing its species be removed, the species is destroyed, and that thing cannot remain the same; just as when a natural body loses its form, it does not remain the same specifically. Now hope takes its species from its principal object, even as the other virtues do, as was shown above (Q. 17, AA. 5, 6; I-II, Q. 54, A. 2): and its principal object is eternal happiness as being possible to obtain by the assistance of God, as stated above (Q. 17, A. 2).

Since then the arduous possible good cannot be an object of hope except insofar as it is something future, it follows that when happiness is no longer future, but present, it is incompatible with the virtue of hope. Consequently hope, like faith, is voided in heaven, and neither of them can be in the blessed.

**REPLY OBJ. 1**: Although Christ was a comprehensor and therefore blessed as to the enjoyment of God, nevertheless He was, at the same time, a wayfarer, as regards the passibility of nature, to which He was still subject. Hence it was possible for Him to hope for the glory of impassibility and immortality, yet not so as to have the virtue of hope, the principal object of which is not the glory of the body but the enjoyment of God.

**REPLY OBJ. 2**: The happiness of the saints is called eternal life, because through enjoying God they become partakers, as it were, of God's eternity which surpasses all time: so that the continuation of happiness does not differ in respect of present, past and future. Hence the blessed do not hope for the continuation of their happiness (for as regards this there is no future), but are in actual possession thereof.

**REPLY OBJ. 3**: So long as the virtue of hope lasts, it is by the same hope that one hopes for one's own happiness, and for that of others. But when hope is voided in the blessed, whereby they hoped for their own happiness, they hope for the happiness of others indeed, yet not by the virtue of hope, but rather by the love of charity. Even so, he that has Divine charity, by that same charity loves his neighbor, without having the virtue of charity, but by some other love.

**REPLY OBJ. 4**: Since hope is a theological virtue having God for its object, its principal object is the glory of the soul, which consists in the enjoyment of God, and not the glory of the body. Moreover, although the glory of the body is something arduous in comparison with human nature, yet it is not so for one who has the glory of the soul; both because the glory of the body is a very small thing as compared with the glory of the soul, and because one who has the glory of the soul has already the sufficient cause of the glory of the body.

# Article 3

*Whether hope is in the damned?*

**AD TERTIUM SIC PROCEDITUR.** Videtur quod in damnatis sit spes. Diabolus enim est et damnatus et princeps damnatorum, secundum illud Matth. XXV, *ite, maledicti, in ignem aeternum, qui paratus est Diabolo et Angelis eius.* Sed Diabolus habet spem, secundum illud Iob XL, *ecce spes eius frustrabitur eum.* Ergo videtur quod damnati habeant spem.

**PRAETEREA,** sicut fides potest esse formata et informis, ita et spes. Sed fides informis potest esse in Daemonibus et damnatis, secundum illud Iac. II, *Daemones credunt et contremiscunt.* Ergo videtur quod etiam spes informis potest esse in damnatis.

**PRAETEREA,** nulli hominum post mortem accrescit meritum vel demeritum quod in vita non habuit, secundum illud Eccle. XI, *si ceciderit lignum ad Austrum aut ad Aquilonem, in quocumque loco ceciderit ibi erit.* Sed multi qui damnabuntur habuerunt in hac vita spem, nunquam desperantes. Ergo etiam in futura vita spem habebunt.

**SED CONTRA** est quod spes causat gaudium, secundum illud Rom. XII, *spe gaudentes.* Sed damnati non sunt in gaudio, sed in dolore et luctu, secundum illud Isaiae LXV, *servi mei laudabunt prae exultatione cordis, et vos clamabitis prae dolore cordis et prae contritione spiritus ululabitis.* Ergo spes non est in damnatis.

**RESPONDEO** dicendum quod sicut de ratione beatitudinis est ut in ea quietetur voluntas, ita de ratione poenae est ut id quod pro poena infligitur voluntati repugnet. Non potest autem voluntatem quietare, vel ei repugnare, quod ignoratur. Et ideo Augustinus dicit, super Gen. ad Litt., quod Angeli perfecte beati esse non potuerunt in primo statu ante confirmationem, vel miseri ante lapsum, cum non essent praescii sui eventus, requiritur enim ad veram et perfectam beatitudinem ut aliquis certus sit de suae beatitudinis perpetuitate; alioquin voluntas non quietaretur.

Similiter etiam, cum perpetuitas damnationis pertineat ad poenam damnatorum, non vere haberet rationem poenae nisi voluntati repugnaret, quod esse non posset si perpetuitatem suae damnationis ignorarent. Et ideo ad conditionem miseriae damnatorum pertinet ut ipsi sciant quod nullo modo possunt damnationem evadere et ad beatitudinem pervenire, unde dicitur Iob XV, *non credit quod reverti possit de tenebris ad lucem.* Unde patet quod non possunt apprehendere beatitudinem ut bonum possibile, sicut nec beati ut bonum futurum. Et ideo neque in beatis neque in damnatis est spes. Sed in viatoribus sive sint in vita ista sive in Purgatorio, potest

**OBJECTION 1:** It would seem that there is hope in the damned. For the devil is damned and prince of the damned, according to Matt. 25:41: *Depart . . . you cursed, into everlasting fire, which was prepared for the devil and his angels.* But the devil has hope, according to Job 40:28, *Behold his hope shall fail him.* Therefore it seems that the damned have hope.

**OBJ. 2:** Further, just as faith is either living or dead, so is hope. But lifeless faith can be in the devils and the damned, according to James 2:19: *The devils . . . believe and tremble.* Therefore it seems that lifeless hope also can be in the damned.

**OBJ. 3:** Further, after death there accrues to man no merit or demerit that he had not before, according to Eccles. 11:3, *If the tree fall to the south, or to the north, in what place soever it shall fall, there shall it be.* Now many who are damned, in this life hoped and never despaired. Therefore they will hope in the future life also.

**ON THE CONTRARY,** Hope causes joy, according to Rom. 12:12, *Rejoicing in hope.* Now the damned have no joy, but sorrow and grief, according to Isa. 65:14, *My servants shall praise for joyfulness of heart, and you shall cry for sorrow of heart, and shall howl for grief of spirit.* Therefore no hope is in the damned.

**I ANSWER THAT,** Just as it is a condition of happiness that the will should find rest therein, so is it a condition of punishment, that what is inflicted in punishment, should go against the will. Now that which is not known can neither be restful nor repugnant to the will: wherefore Augustine says (*Gen ad lit.* xi, 17) that the angels could not be perfectly happy in their first state before their confirmation, or unhappy before their fall, since they had no foreknowledge of what would happen to them. For perfect and true happiness requires that one should be certain of being happy for ever, else the will would not rest.

In like manner, since the everlastingness of damnation is a necessary condition of the punishment of the damned, it would not be truly penal unless it went against the will; and this would be impossible if they were ignorant of the everlastingness of their damnation. Hence it belongs to the unhappy state of the damned, that they should know that they cannot by any means escape from damnation and obtain happiness. Wherefore it is written (Job 15:22): *He believeth not that he may return from darkness to light.* It is, therefore, evident that they cannot apprehend happiness as a possible good, as neither can the blessed apprehend it as a future good. Consequently there is no hope either in the

esse spes, quia utrobique apprehendunt beatitudinem ut futurum possibile.

**AD PRIMUM** ergo dicendum quod, sicut Gregorius dicit, XXXIII Moral., hoc dicitur de Diabolo secundum membra eius, quorum spes annullabitur. Vel si intelligatur de ipso Diabolo, potest referri ad spem qua sperat se de sanctis victoriam obtinere, secundum illud quod supra praemiserat, *habet fiduciam quod Iordanis influat in os eius.* Haec autem non est spes de qua loquimur.

**AD SECUNDUM** dicendum quod, sicut Augustinus dicit, in Enchirid., *fides est et malarum rerum et bonarum, et praeteritarum et praesentium et futurarum, et suarum et alienarum, sed spes non est nisi rerum bonarum futurarum ad se pertinentium.* Et ideo magis potest esse fides informis in damnatis quam spes, quia bona divina non sunt eis futura possibilia, sed sunt eis absentia.

**AD TERTIUM** dicendum quod defectus spei in damnatis non variat demeritum, sicut nec evacuatio spei in beatis auget meritum, sed utrumque contingit propter mutationem status.

blessed or in the damned. On the other hand, hope can be in wayfarers, whether of this life or in purgatory, because in either case they apprehend happiness as a future possible thing.

**REPLY OBJ. 1**: As Gregory says (*Moral.* xxxiii, 20) this is said of the devil as regards his members, whose hope will fail utterly: or, if it be understood of the devil himself, it may refer to the hope whereby he expects to vanquish the saints, in which sense we read just before (Job 40:18): *He trusteth that the Jordan may run into his mouth*: this is not, however, the hope of which we are speaking.

**REPLY OBJ. 2**: As Augustine says (*Enchiridion* viii), *faith is about things, bad or good, past, present, or future, one's own or another's; whereas hope is only about good things, future and concerning oneself.* Hence it is possible for lifeless faith to be in the damned, but not hope, since the Divine goods are not for them future possible things, but far removed from them.

**REPLY OBJ. 3**: Lack of hope in the damned does not change their demerit, as neither does the voiding of hope in the blessed increase their merit: but both these things are due to the change in their respective states.

# Article 4

*Whether there is certainty in the hope of a wayfarer?*

**AD QUARTUM SIC PROCEDITUR.** Videtur quod spes viatorum non habeat certitudinem. Spes enim est in voluntate sicut in subiecto. Sed certitudo non pertinet ad voluntatem, sed ad intellectum. Ergo spes non habet certitudinem.

**PRAETEREA**, *spes ex gratia et meritis provenit*, ut supra dictum est. Sed in hac vita scire per certitudinem non possumus quod gratiam habeamus, ut supra dictum est. Ergo spes viatorum non habet certitudinem.

**PRAETEREA**, certitudo esse non potest de eo quod potest deficere. Sed multi viatores habentes spem deficiunt a consecutione beatitudinis. Ergo spes viatorum non habet certitudinem.

**SED CONTRA** est quod *spes est certa expectatio futurae beatitudinis*, sicut Magister dicit, XXVI dist. III Sent. Quod potest accipi ex hoc quod dicitur II ad Tim. I, *scio cui credidi, et certus sum quia potens est depositum meum servare.*

**RESPONDEO** dicendum quod certitudo invenitur in aliquo dupliciter, scilicet essentialiter, et participative. Essentialiter quidem invenitur in vi cognoscitiva, participative autem in omni eo quod a vi cognoscitiva movetur infallibiliter ad finem suum; secundum quem modum dicitur quod natura certitudinaliter operatur,

**OBJECTION 1**: It would seem that there is no certainty in the hope of a wayfarer. For hope resides in the will. But certainty pertains not to the will but to the intellect. Therefore there is no certainty in hope.

**OBJ. 2**: Further, *hope is based on grace and merits*, as stated above (Q. 17, A. 1). Now it is impossible in this life to know for certain that we are in a state of grace, as stated above (I-II, Q. 112, A. 5). Therefore there is no certainty in the hope of a wayfarer.

**OBJ. 3**: Further, there can be no certainty about that which may fail. Now many a hopeful wayfarer fails to obtain happiness. Therefore wayfarer's hope has no certainty.

**ON THE CONTRARY**, *Hope is the certain expectation of future happiness*, as the Master states (*Sent.* iii, D, 26): and this may be gathered from 2 Tim. 1:12, *I know Whom I have believed, and I am certain that He is able to keep that which I have committed to Him.*

**I ANSWER THAT**, Certainty is found in a thing in two ways, essentially and by participation. It is found essentially in the cognitive power; by participation in whatever is moved infallibly to its end by the cognitive power. In this way we say that nature works with certainty, since it is moved by the Divine intellect which moves everything with

tanquam mota ab intellectu divino certitudinaliter movente unumquodque ad suum finem. Et per hunc etiam modum virtutes morales certius arte dicuntur operari, inquantum per modum naturae moventur a ratione ad suos actus. Et sic etiam spes certitudinaliter tendit in suum finem, quasi participans certitudinem a fide, quae est in vi cognoscitiva.

**UNDE PATET** responsio ad primum.

**AD SECUNDUM** dicendum quod spes non innititur principaliter gratiae iam habitae, sed divinae omnipotentiae et misericordiae, per quam etiam qui gratiam non habet eam consequi potest, ut sic ad vitam aeternam perveniat. De omnipotentia autem Dei et eius misericordia certus est quicumque fidem habet.

**AD TERTIUM** dicendum quod hoc quod aliqui habentes spem deficiant a consecutione beatitudinis, contingit ex defectu liberi arbitrii ponentis obstaculum peccati, non autem ex defectu divinae omnipotentiae vel misericordiae, cui spes innititur. Unde hoc non praeiudicat certitudini spei.

certainty to its end. In this way too, the moral virtues are said to work with greater certainty than art, inasmuch as, like a second nature, they are moved to their acts by the reason: and thus too, hope tends to its end with certainty, as though sharing in the certainty of faith which is in the cognitive faculty.

**THIS SUFFICES** for the Reply to the First Objection.

**REPLY OBJ. 2**: Hope does not trust chiefly in grace already received, but on God's omnipotence and mercy, whereby even he that has not grace, can obtain it, so as to come to eternal life. Now whoever has faith is certain of God's omnipotence and mercy.

**REPLY OBJ. 3**: That some who have hope fail to obtain happiness, is due to a fault of the free will in placing the obstacle of sin, but not to any deficiency in God's power or mercy, in which hope places its trust. Hence this does not prejudice the certainty of hope.

# QUESTION 19

## THE GIFT OF FEAR

Deinde considerandum est de dono timoris. Et circa hoc quaeruntur duodecim.

Primo, utrum Deus debeat timeri.

Secundo, de divisione timoris in timorem filialem, initialem, servilem et mundanum.

Tertio, utrum timor mundanus semper sit malus.

Quarto, utrum timor servilis sit bonus.

Quinto, utrum sit idem in substantia cum filiali.

Sexto, utrum adveniente caritate excludatur timor servilis.

Septimo, utrum timor sit initium sapientiae.

Octavo, utrum timor initialis sit idem in substantia cum timore filiali.

Nono, utrum timor sit donum spiritus sancti.

Decimo, utrum crescat crescente caritate.

Undecimo, utrum maneat in patria.

Duodecimo, quid respondeat ei in beatitudinibus et fructibus.

We must now consider the gift of fear, about which there are twelve points of inquiry:

(1) Whether God is to be feared?

(2) Of the division of fear into filial, initial, servile and worldly;

(3) Whether worldly fear is always evil?

(4) Whether servile fear is good?

(5) Whether it is substantially the same as filial fear?

(6) Whether servile fear departs when charity comes?

(7) Whether fear is the beginning of wisdom?

(8) Whether initial fear is substantially the same as filial fear?

(9) Whether fear is a gift of the Holy Spirit?

(10) Whether it grows when charity grows?

(11) Whether it remains in heaven?

(12) Which of the beatitudes and fruits correspond to it?

# Article 1

*Whether God can be feared?*

**AD PRIMUM SIC PROCEDITUR.** Videtur quod Deus timeri non possit. Obiectum enim timoris est malum futurum, ut supra habitum est. Sed Deus est expers omnis mali, cum sit ipsa bonitas. Ergo Deus timeri non potest.

**PRAETEREA**, timor spei opponitur. Sed spem habemus de Deo. Ergo non possumus etiam simul eum timere.

**PRAETEREA**, sicut Philosophus dicit, in II Rhet., *illa timemus ex quibus nobis mala proveniunt*. Sed mala non proveniunt nobis a Deo, sed ex nobis ipsis, secundum illud Osee XIII, *perditio tua, Israel, ex me auxilium tuum*. Ergo Deus timeri non debet.

**SED CONTRA** est quod dicitur Ierem. X, *quis non timebit te, o rex gentium?* Et Malach. I, *si ego dominus, ubi timor meus?*

**RESPONDEO** dicendum quod sicut spes habet duplex obiectum, quorum unum est ipsum bonum futurum cuius adeptionem quis expectat, aliud autem est auxilium alicuius per quem expectat se adipisci quod sperat; ita etiam et timor duplex obiectum habere potest, quorum unum est ipsum malum quod homo refugit, aliud autem est illud a quo malum provenire potest. Primo

**OBJECTION 1**: It would seem that God cannot be feared. For the object of fear is a future evil, as stated above (I-II, Q. 41, AA. 2, 3). But God is free of all evil, since He is goodness itself. Therefore God cannot be feared.

**OBJ. 2**: Further, fear is opposed to hope. Now we hope in God. Therefore we cannot fear Him at the same time.

**OBJ. 3**: Further, as the Philosopher states (*Rhet.* ii, 5), *we fear those things whence evil comes to us*. But evil comes to us, not from God, but from ourselves, according to Osee 13:9: *Destruction is thy own, O Israel: thy help is . . . in Me*. Therefore God is not to be feared.

**ON THE CONTRARY**, It is written (Jer 10:7): *Who shall not fear Thee, O King of nations?* and (Mal 1:6): *If I be a master, where is My fear?*

**I ANSWER THAT**, Just as hope has two objects, one of which is the future good itself, that one expects to obtain, while the other is someone's help, through whom one expects to obtain what one hopes for, so, too, fear may have two objects, one of which is the very evil which a man shrinks from, while the other is that from which the evil may come. Accordingly, in the first way God, Who is

igitur modo Deus, qui est ipsa bonitas, obiectum timoris esse non potest. Sed secundo modo potest esse obiectum timoris, inquantum scilicet ab ipso, vel per comparationem ad ipsum, nobis potest aliquod malum imminere.

Ab ipso quidem potest nobis imminere malum poenae, quod non est simpliciter malum, sed secundum quid, bonum autem simpliciter. Cum enim bonum dicatur in ordine ad finem, malum autem importat huius ordinis privationem; illud est malum simpliciter quod excludit ordinem a fine ultimo, quod est malum culpae. Malum autem poenae est quidem malum, inquantum privat aliquod particulare bonum, est tamen bonum simpliciter, inquantum dependet ab ordine finis ultimi.

Per comparationem autem ad Deum potest nobis malum culpae provenire, si ab eo separemur. Et per hunc modum Deus potest et debet timeri.

**AD PRIMUM** ergo dicendum quod ratio illa procedit secundum quod malum est timoris obiectum.

**AD SECUNDUM** dicendum quod in Deo est considerare et iustitiam, secundum quam peccantes punit; et misericordiam, secundum quam nos liberat. Secundum igitur considerationem iustitiae ipsius, insurgit in nobis timor, secundum autem considerationem misericordiae, consurgit in nobis spes. Et ita secundum diversas rationes Deus est obiectum spei et timoris.

**AD TERTIUM** dicendum quod malum culpae non est a Deo sicut ab auctore, sed est a nobis ipsis, inquantum a Deo recedimus. Malum autem poenae est quidem a Deo auctore inquantum habet rationem boni, prout scilicet est iustum, sed quod iuste nobis poena infligatur, hoc primordialiter ex merito nostri peccati contingit. Secundum quem modum dicitur Sap. I, quod *Deus mortem non fecit, sed impii manibus et verbis accersierunt illam.*

goodness itself, cannot be an object of fear; but He can be an object of fear in the second way, insofar as there may come to us some evil either from Him or in relation to Him.

From Him there comes the evil of punishment, but this is evil not absolutely but relatively, and, absolutely speaking, is a good. Because, since a thing is said to be good through being ordered to an end, while evil implies lack of this order, that which excludes the order to the last end is altogether evil, and such is the evil of fault. On the other hand the evil of punishment is indeed an evil, insofar as it is the privation of some particular good, yet absolutely speaking, it is a good, insofar as it is ordained to the last end.

In relation to God the evil of fault can come to us, if we be separated from Him: and in this way God can and ought to be feared.

**REPLY OBJ. 1**: This objection considers the object of fear as being the evil which a man shuns.

**REPLY OBJ. 2**: In God, we may consider both His justice, in respect of which He punishes those who sin, and His mercy, in respect of which He sets us free: in us the consideration of His justice gives rise to fear, but the consideration of His mercy gives rise to hope, so that, accordingly, God is the object of both hope and fear, but under different aspects.

**REPLY OBJ. 3**: The evil of fault is not from God as its author but from us, in for far as we forsake God: while the evil of punishment is from God as its author, insofar as it has character of a good, since it is something just, through being inflicted on us justly; although originally this is due to the demerit of sin: thus it is written (Wis 1:13, 16): *God made not death . . . but the wicked with works and words have called it to them.*

# Article 2

*Whether fear is fittingly divided into filial, initial, servile, and worldly fear?*

**AD SECUNDUM SIC PROCEDITUR.** Videtur quod inconvenienter dividatur timor in filialem, initialem, servilem et mundanum. Damascenus enim, in II Lib., ponit sex species timoris, scilicet segnitiem, erubescentiam, et alia de quibus supra dictum est, quae in hac divisione non tanguntur. Ergo videtur quod haec divisio timoris sit inconveniens.

**PRAETEREA**, quilibet horum timorum vel est bonus vel malus. Sed est aliquis timor, scilicet naturalis, qui neque bonus est moraliter, cum sit in Daemonibus, secundum illud Iac. II, *Daemones credunt et contremiscunt*; neque etiam est malus, cum sit in Christo, secundum illud Marc. XIV *coepit* Iesus *pavere et taedere.* Ergo timor insufficienter dividitur secundum praedicta.

**OBJECTION 1**: It would seem that fear is unfittingly divided into filial, initial, servile and worldly fear. For Damascene says (*De Fide Orth.* ii, 15) that there are six kinds of fear, viz. *laziness, shamefacedness,* etc. of which we have treated above (I-II, Q. 41, A. 4), and which are not mentioned in the division in question. Therefore this division of fear seems unfitting.

**OBJ. 2**: Further, each of these fears is either good or evil. But there is a fear, viz. natural fear, which is neither morally good, since it is in the demons, according to James 2:19, *The devils . . . believe and tremble,* nor evil, since it is in Christ, according to Mk. 14:33, Jesus *began to fear and be heavy.* Therefore the aforesaid division of fear is insufficient.

**Praeterea**, alia est habitudo filii ad patrem, et uxoris ad virum, et servi ad dominum. Sed timor filialis, qui est filii in comparatione ad patrem, distinguitur a timore servili, qui est servi per comparationem ad dominum. Ergo etiam timor castus, qui videtur esse uxoris per comparationem ad virum, debet distingui ab omnibus istis timoribus.

**Praeterea**, sicut timor servilis timet poenam, ita timor initialis et mundanus. Non ergo debuerunt ad invicem distingui isti timores.

**Praeterea**, sicut concupiscentia est boni, ita etiam timor est mali. Sed alia est concupiscentia oculorum, qua quis concupiscit bona mundi; alia est concupiscentia carnis, qua quis concupiscit delectationem propriam. Ergo etiam alius est timor mundanus, quo quis timet amittere bona exteriora; et alius est timor humanus, quo quis timet propriae personae detrimentum.

**Sed contra** est auctoritas Magistri, XXXIV dist. III Lib. Sent.

**Respondeo** dicendum quod de timore nunc agimus secundum quod per ipsum aliquo modo ad Deum convertimur vel ab eo avertimur. Cum enim obiectum timoris sit malum, quandoque homo propter mala quae timet a Deo recedit, et iste dicitur timor *humanus* vel *mundanus*. Quandoque autem homo per mala quae timet ad Deum convertitur et ei inhaeret. Quod quidem malum est duplex, scilicet malum poenae, et malum culpae.

Si igitur aliquis convertatur ad Deum et ei inhaereat propter timorem poenae, erit timor *servilis*. Si autem propter timorem culpae, erit timor *filialis*, nam filiorum est timere offensam patris. Si autem propter utrumque, est timor *initialis*, qui est medius inter utrumque timorem. Utrum autem malum culpae possit timeri, supra habitum est, cum de passione timoris ageretur.

**Ad primum** ergo dicendum quod Damascenus dividit timorem secundum quod est passio animae. Haec autem divisio timoris attenditur in ordine ad Deum, ut dictum est.

**Ad secundum** dicendum quod bonum morale praecipue consistit in conversione ad Deum, malum autem morale in aversione a Deo. Et ideo omnes praedicti timores vel important bonum morale vel malum. Sed timor naturalis praesupponitur bono et malo morali. Et ideo non connumeratur inter istos timores.

**Ad tertium** dicendum quod habitudo servi ad dominum est per potestatem domini servum sibi subiicientis, sed habitudo filii ad patrem, vel uxoris ad virum, est e converso per affectum filii se subdentis patri vel uxoris se coniungentis viro unione amoris. Unde timor filialis et castus ad idem pertinent, quia per

**Obj. 3**: Further, the relation of son to father differs from that of wife to husband, and this again from that of servant to master. Now filial fear, which is that of the son in comparison with his father, is distinct from servile fear, which is that of the servant in comparison with his master. Therefore chaste fear, which seems to be that of the wife in comparison with her husband, ought to be distinguished from all these other fears.

**Obj. 4**: Further, even as servile fear fears punishment, so do initial and worldly fear. Therefore no distinction should be made between them.

**Obj. 5**: Further, even as concupiscence is about some good, so is fear about some evil. Now *concupiscence of the eyes*, which is the desire for things of this world, is distinct from *concupiscence of the flesh*, which is the desire for one's own pleasure. Therefore *worldly fear*, whereby one fears to lose external goods, is distinct from *human fear*, whereby one fears harm to one's own person.

**On the contrary** stands the authority of the Master (*Sent.* iii, D, 34).

**I answer that**, We are speaking of fear now, insofar as it makes us turn, so to speak, to God or away from Him. For, since the object of fear is an evil, sometimes, on account of the evils he fears, man withdraws from God, and this is called *human* and *worldly* fear; while sometimes, on account of the evils he fears, he turns to God and adheres to Him. This latter evil is twofold, viz. evil of punishment, and evil of fault.

Accordingly if a man turn to God and adhere to Him, through fear of punishment, it will be *servile* fear; but if it be on account of fear of committing a fault, it will be *filial* fear, for it becomes a child to fear offending its father. If, however, it be on account of both, it will be *initial* fear, which is between both these fears. As to whether it is possible to fear the evil of fault, the question has been treated above (I-II, Q. 42, A. 3) when we were considering the passion of fear.

**Reply Obj. 1**: Damascene divides fear as a passion of the soul: whereas this division of fear is taken from its relation to God, as explained above.

**Reply Obj. 2**: Moral good consists chiefly in turning to God, while moral evil consists chiefly in turning away from Him: wherefore all the fears mentioned above imply either moral evil or moral good. Now natural fear is presupposed to moral good and evil, and so it is not numbered among these kinds of fear.

**Reply Obj. 3**: The relation of servant to master is based on the power which the master exercises over the servant; whereas, on the contrary, the relation of a son to his father or of a wife to her husband is based on the son's affection towards his father to whom he submits himself, or on the wife's affection towards her husband to whom

caritatis amorem Deus pater noster efficitur, secundum illud Rom. VIII, *accepistis spiritum adoptionis filiorum, in quo clamamus, abba, pater*; et secundum eandem caritatem dicitur etiam sponsus noster, secundum illud II ad Cor. XI, *despondi vos uni viro, virginem castam exhibere Christo.* Timor autem servilis ad aliud pertinet, quia caritatem in sua ratione non includit.

**AD QUARTUM** dicendum quod praedicti tres timores respiciunt poenam sed diversimode. Nam timor mundanus sive humanus respicit poenam a Deo avertentem, quam quandoque inimici Dei infligunt vel comminantur. Sed timor servilis et initialis respiciunt poenam per quam homines attrahuntur ad Deum, divinitus inflictam vel comminatam. Quam quidem poenam principaliter timor servilis respicit, timor autem initialis secundario.

**AD QUINTUM** dicendum quod eadem ratione homo a Deo avertitur propter timorem amittendi bona mundana, et propter timorem amittendi incolumitatem proprii corporis, quia bona exteriora ad corpus pertinent. Et ideo uterque timor hic pro eodem computatur, quamvis mala quae timentur sint diversa, sicut et bona quae concupiscuntur. Ex qua quidem diversitate provenit diversitas peccatorum secundum speciem, quibus tamen omnibus commune est a Deo abducere.

she binds herself in the union of love. Hence filial and chaste fear amount to the same, because by the love of charity God becomes our Father, according to Rom. 8:15, *You have received the spirit of adoption of sons, whereby we cry: Abba (Father)*; and by this same charity He is called our spouse, according to 2 Cor. 11:2, *I have espoused you to one husband, that I may present you as a chaste virgin to Christ*: whereas servile fear has no connection with these, since it does not include charity in its definition.

**REPLY OBJ. 4**: These three fears regard punishment but in different ways. For worldly or human fear regards a punishment which turns man away from God, and which God's enemies sometimes inflict or threaten: whereas servile and initial fear regard a punishment whereby men are drawn to God, and which is inflicted or threatened by God. Servile fear regards this punishment chiefly, while initial fear regards it secondarily.

**REPLY OBJ. 5**: It amounts to the same whether man turns away from God through fear of losing his worldly goods, or through fear of forfeiting the well-being of his body, since external goods belong to the body. Hence both these fears are reckoned as one here, although they fear different evils, even as they correspond to the desire of different goods. This diversity causes a specific diversity of sins, all of which alike however lead man away from God.

# Article 3

*Whether worldly fear is always evil?*

**AD TERTIUM SIC PROCEDITUR**. Videtur quod timor mundanus non semper sit malus. Ad timorem enim humanum pertinere videtur quod homines reveremur. Sed quidam vituperantur de hoc quod homines non reverentur, ut patet Luc. XVIII de illo iudice iniquo, *qui nec Deum timebat nec homines reverebatur.* Ergo videtur quod timor mundanus non semper sit malus.

**PRAETEREA**, ad timorem mundanum videntur pertinere poenae quae per potestates saeculares infliguntur. Sed per huiusmodi poenas provocamur ad bene agendum, secundum illud Rom. XIII, *vis non timere potestatem? Bonum fac, et habebis laudem ex illa.* Ergo timor mundanus non semper est malus.

**PRAETEREA**, illud quod inest nobis naturaliter non videtur esse malum, eo quod naturalia sunt nobis a Deo. Sed naturale est homini ut timeat proprii corporis detrimentum et amissionem bonorum temporalium, quibus praesens vita sustentatur. Ergo videtur quod timor mundanus non semper sit malus.

**SED CONTRA** est quod dominus dicit, Matth. X, *nolite timere eos qui corpus occidunt*, ubi timor mundanus

**OBJECTION 1**: It would seem that worldly fear is not always evil. Because regard for men seems to be a kind of human fear. Now some are blamed for having no regard for man, for instance, the unjust judge of whom we read (Luke 18:2) that he *feared not God, nor regarded man.* Therefore it seems that worldly fear is not always evil.

**OBJ. 2**: Further, worldly fear seems to have reference to the punishments inflicted by the secular power. Now such like punishments incite us to good actions, according to Rom. 13:3, *Wilt thou not be afraid of the power? Do that which is good, and thou shalt have praise from the same.* Therefore worldly fear is not always evil.

**OBJ. 3**: Further, it seems that what is in us naturally, is not evil, since our natural gifts are from God. Now it is natural to man to fear detriment to his body, and loss of his worldly goods, whereby the present life is supported. Therefore it seems that worldly fear is not always evil.

**ON THE CONTRARY**, Our Lord said (Matt 10:28): *Fear ye not them that kill the body*, thus forbidding worldly

prohibetur. Nihil autem divinitus prohibetur nisi malum. Ergo timor mundanus est malus.

**RESPONDEO** dicendum quod, sicut ex supradictis patet, actus morales et habitus ex obiectis et nomen et speciem habent. Proprium autem obiectum appetitivi motus est bonum finale. Et ideo a proprio fine omnis motus appetitivus et specificatur et nominatur. Si quis enim cupiditatem nominaret amorem laboris, quia propter cupiditatem homines laborant, non recte nominaret, non enim cupidi laborem quaerunt sicut finem, sed sicut id quod est ad finem, sicut finem autem quaerunt divitias, unde cupiditas recte nominatur desiderium vel amor divitiarum, quod est malum. Et per hunc modum amor mundanus proprie dicitur quo aliquis mundo innititur tanquam fini. Et sic amor mundanus semper est malus. Timor autem ex amore nascitur, illud enim homo timet amittere quod amat; ut patet per Augustinum, in libro Octoginta trium Quaest. Et ideo timor mundanus est qui procedit ab amore mundano tanquam a mala radice. Et propter hoc et ipse timor mundanus semper est malus.

**AD PRIMUM** ergo dicendum quod aliquis potest revereri homines dupliciter. Uno modo, inquantum est in eis aliquod divinum, puta bonum gratiae aut virtutis, vel saltem naturalis Dei imaginis, et hoc modo vituperantur qui homines non reverentur. Alio modo potest aliquis homines revereri inquantum Deo contrariantur. Et sic laudantur qui homines non reverentur, secundum illud Eccli. XLVIII, de Elia vel Elisaeo, *in diebus suis non pertimuit principem.*

**AD SECUNDUM** dicendum quod potestates saeculares, quando inferunt poenas ad retrahendum a peccato, in hoc sunt Dei ministri, secundum illud Rom. XIII, *minister enim Dei est, vindex in iram ei qui male agit.* Et secundum hoc timere potestatem saecularem non pertinet ad timorem mundanum, sed ad timorem servilem vel initialem.

**AD TERTIUM** dicendum quod naturale est quod homo refugiat proprii corporis detrimentum, vel etiam damna temporalium rerum, sed quod homo propter ista recedat a iustitia, est contra rationem naturalem. Unde etiam philosophus dicit, in III Ethic., quod quaedam sunt, scilicet peccatorum opera, ad quae nullo timore aliquis debet cogi, quia peius est huiusmodi peccata committere quam poenas quascumque pati.

fear. Now nothing but what is evil is forbidden by God. Therefore worldly fear is evil.

**I ANSWER THAT,** As shown above (I-II, Q. 1, A. 3; I-II, Q. 18, A. 1; I-II, Q. 54, A. 2) moral acts and habits take their name and species from their objects. Now the proper object of the appetite's movement is the final good: so that, in consequence, every appetitive movement is both specified and named from its proper end. For if anyone were to describe covetousness as love of work because men work on account of covetousness, this description would be incorrect, since the covetous man seeks work not as end but as a means: the end that he seeks is wealth, wherefore covetousness is rightly described as the desire or the love of wealth, and this is evil. Accordingly worldly love is, properly speaking, the love whereby a man trusts in the world as his end, so that worldly love is always evil. Now fear is born of love, since man fears the loss of what he loves, as Augustine states (*83 Questions*, Q. 33). Now worldly fear is that which arises from worldly love as from an evil root, for which reason worldly fear is always evil.

**REPLY OBJ. 1:** One may have regard for men in two ways. First insofar as there is in them something divine, for instance, the good of grace or of virtue, or at least of the natural image of God: and in this way those are blamed who have no regard for man. Second, one may have regard for men as being in opposition to God, and thus it is praiseworthy to have no regard for men, according as we read of Elias or Eliseus (Sir 48:13): *In his days he feared not the prince.*

**REPLY OBJ. 2:** When the secular power inflicts punishment in order to withdraw men from sin, it is acting as God's minister, according to Rom. 13:4, *For he is God's minister, an avenger to execute wrath upon him that doth evil.* To fear the secular power in this way is part, not of worldly fear, but of servile or initial fear.

**REPLY OBJ. 3:** It is natural for man to shrink from detriment to his own body and loss of worldly goods, but to forsake justice on that account is contrary to natural reason. Hence the Philosopher says (*Ethic.* iii, 1) that there are certain things, viz. sinful deeds, which no fear should drive us to do, since to do such things is worse than to suffer any punishment whatever.

# Article 4

*Whether servile fear is good?*

**AD QUARTUM SIC PROCEDITUR**. Videtur quod timor servilis non sit bonus. Quia cuius usus est malus, ipsum quoque malum est. Sed usus timoris servilis est malus, quia sicut Glossa dicit Rom. VIII, *qui timore aliquid facit, etsi bonum sit quod facit, non tamen bene facit*. Ergo timor servilis non est bonus.

**PRAETEREA**, illud quod ex radice peccati oritur non est bonum. Sed timor servilis oritur ex radice peccati, quia super illud Iob III, *quare non in vulva mortuus sum?* Dicit Gregorius, *cum ex peccato praesens poena metuitur, et amissa Dei facies non amatur, timor ex tumore est, non ex humilitate*. Ergo timor servilis est malus.

**PRAETEREA**, sicuti amori caritatis opponitur amor mercenarius, ita timori casto videtur opponi timor servilis. Sed amor mercenarius semper est malus. Ergo et timor servilis.

**SED CONTRA**, nullum malum est a spiritu sancto. Sed timor servilis est ex spiritu sancto, quia super illud Rom. VIII, *non accepistis spiritum servitutis* etc., dicit Glossa, *unus spiritus est qui facit duos timores, scilicet servilem et castum*. Ergo timor servilis non est malus.

**RESPONDEO** dicendum quod timor servilis ex parte servilitatis habet quod sit malus. Servitus enim libertati opponitur. Unde, cum liber sit *qui causa sui est*, ut dicitur in principio Metaphys. servus est qui non causa sui operatur, sed quasi ab extrinseco motus. Quicumque autem ex amore aliquid facit, quasi ex seipso operatur, quia ex propria inclinatione movetur ad operandum. Et ideo contra rationem servilitatis est quod aliquis ex amore operetur. Sic ergo timor servilis, inquantum servilis est, caritati contrariatur. Si ergo servilitas esset de ratione timoris, oporteret quod timor servilis simpliciter esset malus, sicut adulterium simpliciter est malum, quia id ex quo contrariatur caritati pertinet ad adulterii speciem.

Sed praedicta servilitas non pertinet ad speciem timoris servilis, sicut nec informitas ad speciem fidei informis. Species enim moralis habitus vel actus ex obiecto accipitur. Obiectum autem timoris servilis est poena; cui accidit quod bonum cui contrariatur poena ametur tanquam finis ultimus, et per consequens poena timeatur tanquam principale malum, quod contingit in non habente caritatem; vel quod ordinetur in Deum sicut in finem, et per consequens poena non timeatur tanquam principale malum, quod contingit in habente caritatem. Non enim tollitur species habitus per hoc quod eius obiectum vel finis ordinatur ad ulteriorem finem. Et ideo timor servilis secundum suam substantiam bonus est, sed servilitas eius mala est.

**OBJECTION 1**: It would seem that servile fear is not good. For if the use of a thing is evil, the thing itself is evil. Now the use of servile fear is evil, for according to a gloss on Rom. 8:15, *if a man do anything through fear, although the deed be good, it is not well done*. Therefore servile fear is not good.

**OBJ. 2**: Further, no good grows from a sinful root. Now servile fear grows from a sinful root, because when commenting on Job 3:11, *Why did I not die in the womb?* Gregory says (*Moral.* iv, 25): *When a man dreads the punishment which confronts him for his sin and no longer loves the friendship of God which he has lost, his fear is born of pride, not of humility*. Therefore servile fear is evil.

**OBJ. 3**: Further, just as mercenary love is opposed to the love of charity, so is servile fear, apparently, opposed to chaste fear. But mercenary love is always evil. Therefore servile fear is also.

**ON THE CONTRARY**, Nothing evil is from the Holy Spirit. But servile fear is from the Holy Spirit, since a gloss on Rom. 8:15, *You have not received the spirit of bondage*, etc. says: *It is the one same spirit that bestows two fears, viz. servile and chaste fear*. Therefore servile fear is not evil.

**I ANSWER THAT**, It is owing to its servility that servile fear may be evil. For servitude is opposed to freedom. Since, then, *what is free is cause of itself* (*Metaph.* i, 2), a slave is one who does not act as cause of his own action, but as though moved from without. Now whoever does a thing through love, does it of himself so to speak, because it is by his own inclination that he is moved to act: so that it is contrary to the very notion of servility that one should act from love. Consequently servile fear as such is contrary to charity: so that if servility were essential to fear, servile fear would be evil simply, even as adultery is evil simply, because that which makes it contrary to charity belongs to the species of adultery.

This servility, however, does not belong to the species of servile fear, even as neither does lifelessness to the species of lifeless faith. For the species of a moral habit or act is taken from the object. Now the object of servile fear is punishment, and it is by accident that, either the good to which the punishment is contrary, is loved as the last end, and that consequently the punishment is feared as the greatest evil, which is the case with one who is devoid of charity, or that the punishment is directed to God as its end, and that, consequently, it is not feared as the greatest evil, which is the case with one who has charity. For the species of a habit is not destroyed through its object or end being directed to a further end. Consequently servile fear is substantially good, but his servility is evil.

**AD PRIMUM** ergo dicendum quod verbum illud Augustini intelligendum est de eo qui facit aliquid timore servili inquantum est servilis, ut scilicet non amet iustitiam, sed solum timeat poenam.

**AD SECUNDUM** dicendum quod timor servilis secundum suam substantiam non oritur ex tumore. Sed eius servilitas ex tumore nascitur, inquantum scilicet homo affectum suum non vult subiicere iugo iustitiae per amorem.

**AD TERTIUM** dicendum quod amor mercenarius dicitur qui Deum diligit propter bona temporalia. Quod secundum se caritati contrariatur. Et ideo amor mercenarius semper est malus. Sed timor servilis secundum suam substantiam non importat nisi timorem poenae, sive timeatur ut principale malum, sive non timeatur ut malum principale.

**REPLY OBJ. 1**: This saying of Augustine is to be applied to a man who does something through servile fear as such, so that he loves not justice, and fears nothing but the punishment.

**REPLY OBJ. 2**: Servile fear as to its substance is not born of pride, but its servility is, inasmuch as man is unwilling, by love, to subject his affections to the yoke of justice.

**REPLY OBJ. 3**: Mercenary love is that whereby God is loved for the sake of worldly goods, and this is, of itself, contrary to charity, so that mercenary love is always evil. But servile fear, as to its substance, implies merely fear of punishment, whether or not this be feared as the principal evil.

# Article 5

*Whether servile fear is substantially the same as filial fear?*

**AD QUINTUM SIC PROCEDITUR**. Videtur quod timor servilis sit idem in substantia cum timore filiali. Ita enim videtur se habere timor filialis ad servilem sicut fides formata ad informem, quorum unum est cum peccato mortali, aliud vero non. Sed eadem secundum substantiam est fides formata et informis. Ergo etiam idem est secundum substantiam timor servilis et filialis.

**PRAETEREA**, habitus diversificantur secundum obiecta. Sed idem est obiectum timoris servilis et filialis, quia utroque timore timetur Deus. Ergo idem est secundum substantiam timor servilis et timor filialis.

**PRAETEREA**, sicut homo sperat frui Deo et etiam ab eo beneficia obtinere, ita etiam timet separari a Deo et poenas ab eo pati. Sed eadem est spes qua speramus frui Deo et qua speramus alia beneficia obtinere ab eo, ut dictum est. Ergo etiam idem est timor filialis, quo timemus separationem a Deo, et timor servilis, quo timemus ab eo puniri.

**SED CONTRA** est quod Augustinus, super Prim. Canonic. Ioan., dicit esse duos timores, unum servilem, et alium filialem vel castum.

**RESPONDEO** dicendum quod proprie obiectum timoris est malum. Et quia actus et habitus distinguuntur secundum obiecta, ut ex dictis patet, necesse est quod secundum diversitatem malorum etiam timores specie differant.

Differunt autem specie malum poenae, quod refugit timor servilis, et malum culpae, quod refugit timor filialis, ut ex supradictis patet. Unde manifestum est quod timor servilis et filialis non sunt idem secundum substantiam, sed differunt specie.

**OBJECTION 1**: It would seem that servile fear is substantially the same as filial fear. For filial fear is to servile fear the same apparently as living faith is to lifeless faith, since the one is accompanied by mortal sin and the other not. Now living faith and lifeless faith are substantially the same. Therefore servile and filial fear are substantially the same.

**OBJ. 2**: Further, habits are diversified by their objects. Now the same thing is the object of servile and of filial fear, since they both fear God. Therefore servile and filial fear are substantially the same.

**OBJ. 3**: Further, just as man hopes to enjoy God and to obtain favors from Him, so does he fear to be separated from God and to be punished by Him. Now it is the same hope whereby we hope to enjoy God, and to receive other favors from Him, as stated above (Q. 17, A. 2, ad 2). Therefore filial fear, whereby we fear separation from God, is the same as servile fear whereby we fear His punishments.

**ON THE CONTRARY**, Augustine (*In prim. canon. Joan.* Tract. ix) says that there are two fears, one servile, another filial or chaste fear.

**I ANSWER THAT**, The proper object of fear is evil. And since acts and habits are diversified by their objects, as shown above (I-II, Q. 54, A. 2), it follows of necessity that different kinds of fear correspond to different kinds of evil.

Now the evil of punishment, from which servile fear shrinks, differs specifically from evil of fault, which filial fear shuns, as shown above (A. 2). Hence it is evident that servile and filial fear are not the same substantially but differ specifically.

**AD PRIMUM** ergo dicendum quod fides formata et informis non differunt secundum obiectum, utraque enim fides et credit Deo et credit Deum, sed differunt solum per aliquod extrinsecum, scilicet secundum praesentiam et absentiam caritatis. Et ideo non differunt secundum substantiam. Sed timor servilis et filialis differunt secundum obiecta. Et ideo non est similis ratio.

**AD SECUNDUM** dicendum quod timor servilis et timor filialis non habent eandem habitudinem ad Deum, nam timor servilis respicit Deum sicut principium inflictivum poenarum; timor autem filialis respicit Deum non sicut principium activum culpae, sed potius sicut terminum a quo refugit separari per culpam. Et ideo ex hoc obiecto quod est Deus non consequuntur identitatem speciei. Quia etiam motus naturales secundum habitudinem ad aliquem terminum specie diversificantur, non enim est idem motus specie qui est ab albedine et qui est ad albedinem.

**AD TERTIUM** dicendum quod spes respicit Deum sicut principium tam respectu fruitionis divinae quam respectu cuiuscumque alterius beneficii. Non sic autem est de timore. Et ideo non est similis ratio.

**REPLY OBJ. 1**: Living and lifeless faith differ, not as regards the object, since each of them believes God and believes in a God, but in respect of something extrinsic, viz. the presence or absence of charity, and so they do not differ substantially. On the other hand, servile and filial fear differ as to their objects: and hence the comparison fails.

**REPLY OBJ. 2**: Servile fear and filial fear do not regard God in the same light. For servile fear looks upon God as the cause of the infliction of punishment, whereas filial fear looks upon Him, not as the active cause of guilt, but rather as the term wherefrom it shrinks to be separated by guilt. Consequently the identity of object, viz. God, does not prove a specific identity of fear, since also natural movements differ specifically according to their different relationships to some one term, for movement from whiteness is not specifically the same as movement towards whiteness.

**REPLY OBJ. 3**: Hope looks upon God as the principle not only of the enjoyment of God, but also of any other favor whatever. This cannot be said of fear; and so there is no comparison.

# Article 6

*Whether servile fear remains with charity?*

**AD SEXTUM SIC PROCEDITUR**. Videtur quod timor servilis non remaneat cum caritate. Dicit enim Augustinus, super Prim. Canonic. Ioan., quod *cum coeperit caritas habitare, pellitur timor, qui ei praeparavit locum*.

**PRAETEREA**, *caritas Dei diffunditur in cordibus nostris per spiritum sanctum, qui datus est nobis*, ut dicitur Rom. V. *Sed ubi spiritus domini, ibi libertas*, ut habetur II ad Cor. III. Cum ergo libertas excludat servitutem, videtur quod timor servilis expellatur caritate adveniente.

**PRAETEREA**, timor servilis ex amore sui causatur, inquantum poena diminuit proprium bonum. Sed amor Dei expellit amorem sui, facit enim contemnere seipsum, ut patet ex auctoritate Augustini, XIV de Civ. Dei, quod *amor Dei usque ad contemptum sui facit civitatem Dei*. Ergo videtur quod veniente caritate timor servilis tollatur.

**SED CONTRA** est quod timor servilis est donum spiritus sancti, ut supra dictum est. Sed dona spiritus sancti non tolluntur adveniente caritate, per quam Spiritus Sanctus in nobis habitat. Ergo veniente caritate non tollitur timor servilis.

**RESPONDEO** dicendum quod timor servilis ex amore sui causatur, quia est timor poenae, quae est detrimentum proprii boni. Unde hoc modo timor poenae potest stare cum caritate sicut et amor sui, eiusdem enim ratio-

**OBJECTION 1**: It would seem that servile fear does not remain with charity. For Augustine says (*In prim. canon. Joan.* Tract. ix) that *when charity takes up its abode, it drives away fear which had prepared a place for it.*

**OBJ. 2**: Further, *The charity of God is poured forth in our hearts, by the Holy Spirit, Who is given to us* (Rom 5:5). Now *where the Spirit of the Lord is, there is liberty* (2 Cor 3:17). Since then freedom excludes servitude, it seems that servile fear is driven away when charity comes.

**OBJ. 3**: Further, servile fear is caused by self-love, insofar as punishment diminishes one's own good. Now love of God drives away self-love, for it makes us despise ourselves: thus Augustine testifies (*De Civ. Dei* xiv, 28) that *the love of God unto the contempt of self builds up the city of God.* Therefore it seems that servile fear is driven out when charity comes.

**ON THE CONTRARY**, Servile fear is a gift of the Holy Spirit, as stated above (A. 4). Now the gifts of the Holy Spirit are not forfeited through the advent of charity, whereby the Holy Spirit dwells in us. Therefore servile fear is not driven out when charity comes.

**I ANSWER THAT**, Servile fear proceeds from self-love, because it is fear of punishment which is detrimental to one's own good. Hence the fear of punishment is consistent with charity, in the same way as self-love is: because it

nis est quod homo cupiat bonum suum et quod timeat eo privari.

Amor autem sui tripliciter se potest habere ad caritatem. Uno enim modo contrariatur caritati, secundum scilicet quod aliquis in amore proprii boni finem constituit. Alio vero modo in caritate includitur, secundum quod homo se propter Deum et in Deo diligit. Tertio modo a caritate quidem distinguitur, sed caritati non contrariatur, puta cum aliquis diligit quidem seipsum secundum rationem proprii boni, ita tamen quod in hoc proprio bono non constituat finem, sicut etiam et ad proximum potest esse aliqua alia specialis dilectio praeter dilectionem caritatis, quae fundatur in Deo, dum proximus diligitur vel ratione consanguinitatis vel alicuius alterius conditionis humanae, quae tamen referibilis sit ad caritatem.

Sic igitur et timor poenae includitur uno modo in caritate, nam separari a Deo est quaedam poena, quam caritas maxime refugit. Unde hoc pertinet ad timorem castum. Alio autem modo contrariatur caritati, secundum quod aliquis refugit poenam contrariam bono suo naturali sicut principale malum contrarium bono quod diligitur ut finis. Et sic timor poenae non est cum caritate. Alio modo timor poenae distinguitur quidem secundum substantiam a timore casto, quia scilicet homo timet malum poenale non ratione separationis a Deo, sed inquantum est nocivum proprii boni, nec tamen in illo bono constituitur eius finis, unde nec illud malum formidatur tanquam principale malum. Et talis timor poenae potest esse cum caritate. Sed iste timor poenae non dicitur esse servilis nisi quando poena formidatur sicut principale malum, ut ex dictis patet. Et ideo timor inquantum servilis non manet cum caritate, sed substantia timoris servilis cum caritate manere potest, sicut amor sui manere potest cum caritate.

**AD PRIMUM** ergo dicendum quod Augustinus loquitur de timore inquantum servilis est.

**ET SIC ETIAM** procedunt aliae duae rationes.

comes to the same that a man love his own good and that he fear to be deprived of it.

Now self-love may stand in a threefold relationship to charity. In one way it is contrary to charity, when a man places his end in the love of his own good. In another way it is included in charity, when a man loves himself for the sake of God and in God. In a third way, it is indeed distinct from charity, but is not contrary thereto, as when a man loves himself from the point of view of his own good, yet not so as to place his end in this his own good: even as one may have another special love for one's neighbor, besides the love of charity which is founded on God, when we love him by reason of usefulness, consanguinity, or some other human consideration, which, however, is referable to charity.

Accordingly fear of punishment is, in one way, included in charity, because separation from God is a punishment, which charity shuns exceedingly; so that this belongs to chaste fear. In another way, it is contrary to charity, when a man shrinks from the punishment that is opposed to his natural good, as being the principal evil in opposition to the good which he loves as an end; and in this way fear of punishment is not consistent with charity. In another way fear of punishment is indeed substantially distinct from chaste fear, when, to wit, a man fears a penal evil, not because it separates him from God, but because it is hurtful to his own good, and yet he does not place his end in this good, so that neither does he dread this evil as being the principal evil. Such fear of punishment is consistent with charity; but it is not called servile, except when punishment is dreaded as a principal evil, as explained above (AA. 2, 4). Hence fear considered as servile, does not remain with charity, but the substance of servile fear can remain with charity, even as self-love can remain with charity.

**REPLY OBJ. 1**: Augustine is speaking of fear considered as servile.

**AND SUCH** is the sense of the two other objections.

# Article 7

*Whether fear is the beginning of wisdom?*

**AD SEPTIMUM SIC PROCEDITUR.** Videtur quod timor non sit initium sapientiae. Initium enim est aliquid rei. Sed timor non est aliquid sapientiae, quia timor est in vi appetitiva, sapientia autem est in vi intellectiva. Ergo videtur quod timor non sit initium sapientiae.

**PRAETEREA**, nihil est principium sui ipsius. Sed *timor Dei ipse est sapientia*, ut dicitur Iob XXVIII. Ergo videtur quod timor Dei non sit initium sapientiae.

**OBJECTION 1**: It would seem that fear is not the beginning of wisdom. For the beginning of a thing is a part thereof. But fear is not a part of wisdom, since fear is seated in the appetitive faculty, while wisdom is in the intellect. Therefore it seems that fear is not the beginning of wisdom.

**OBJ. 2**: Further, nothing is the beginning of itself. *Now fear of the Lord, that is wisdom*, according to Job 28:28. Therefore it seems that fear of God is not the beginning of wisdom.

**PRAETEREA**, principio non est aliquid prius. Sed timore est aliquid prius, quia fides praecedit timorem. Ergo videtur quod timor non sit initium sapientiae.

**SED CONTRA** est quod dicitur in Psalm., *initium sapientiae timor domini.*

**RESPONDEO** dicendum quod initium sapientiae potest aliquid dici dupliciter, uno modo, quia est initium ipsius sapientiae quantum ad eius essentiam; alio modo, quantum ad eius effectum. Sicut initium artis secundum eius essentiam sunt principia ex quibus procedit ars, initium autem artis secundum eius effectum est unde incipit ars operari; sicut si dicamus quod principium artis aedificativae est fundamentum, quia ibi incipit aedificator operari.

Cum autem sapientia sit cognitio divinorum, ut infra dicetur, aliter consideratur a nobis et aliter a philosophis. Quia enim vita nostra ad divinam fruitionem ordinatur et dirigitur secundum quandam participationem divinae naturae, quae est per gratiam; sapientia secundum nos non solum consideratur ut est cognoscitiva Dei, sicut apud philosophos; sed etiam ut est directiva humanae vitae, quae non solum dirigitur secundum rationes humanas, sed etiam secundum rationes divinas, ut patet per Augustinum, XII de Trin. Sic igitur initium sapientiae secundum eius essentiam sunt prima principia sapientiae, quae sunt articuli fidei. Et secundum hoc fides dicitur sapientiae initium. Sed quantum ad effectum, initium sapientiae est unde sapientia incipit operari. Et hoc modo timor est initium sapientiae. Aliter tamen timor servilis, et aliter timor filialis. Timor enim servilis est sicut principium extra disponens ad sapientiam, inquantum aliquis timore poenae discedit a peccato, et per hoc habilitatur ad sapientiae effectum; secundum illud Eccli. I, *timor domini expellit peccatum.* Timor autem castus vel filialis est initium sapientiae sicut primus sapientiae effectus. Cum enim ad sapientiam pertineat quod humana vita reguletur secundum rationes divinas, hinc oportet sumere principium, ut homo Deum revereatur et se ei subiiciat, sic enim consequenter in omnibus secundum Deum regulabitur.

**AD PRIMUM** ergo dicendum quod ratio illa ostendit quod timor non est principium sapientiae quantum ad essentiam sapientiae.

**AD SECUNDUM** dicendum quod timor Dei comparatur ad totam vitam humanam per sapientiam Dei regulatam sicut radix ad arborem, unde dicitur Eccli. I, *radix sapientiae est timere dominum, rami enim illius longaevi.* Et ideo sicut radix virtute dicitur esse tota arbor, ita timor Dei dicitur esse sapientia.

**AD TERTIUM** dicendum quod, sicut dictum est, alio modo fides est principium sapientiae et alio modo timor. Unde dicitur Eccli. XXV, *timor Dei initium dilectionis eius, initium autem fidei agglutinandum est ei.*

**OBJ. 3**: Further, nothing is prior to the beginning. But something is prior to fear, since faith precedes fear. Therefore it seems that fear is not the beginning of wisdom.

**ON THE CONTRARY**, It is written in the Ps. 110:10: *The fear of the Lord is the beginning of wisdom.*

**I ANSWER THAT**, A thing may be called the beginning of wisdom in two ways: in one way because it is the beginning of wisdom itself as to its essence; in another way, as to its effect. Thus the beginning of an art as to its essence consists in the principles from which that art proceeds, while the beginning of an art as to its effect is that wherefrom it begins to operate: for instance we might say that the beginning of the art of building is the foundation because that is where the builder begins his work.

Now, since wisdom is the knowledge of Divine things, as we shall state further on (Q. 45, A. 1), it is considered by us in one way, and in another way by philosophers. For, seeing that our life is ordained to the enjoyment of God, and is directed thereto according to a participation of the Divine Nature, conferred on us through grace, wisdom, as we look at it, is considered not only as being cognizant of God, as it is with the philosophers, but also as directing human conduct; since this is directed not only by the human law, but also by the Divine law, as Augustine shows (*De Trin.* xii, 14). Accordingly the beginning of wisdom as to its essence consists in the first principles of wisdom, i.e., the articles of faith, and in this sense faith is said to be the beginning of wisdom. But as regards the effect, the beginning of wisdom is the point where wisdom begins to work, and in this way fear is the beginning of wisdom, yet servile fear in one way, and filial fear, in another. For servile fear is like a principle disposing a man to wisdom from without, insofar as he refrains from sin through fear of punishment, and is thus fashioned for the effect of wisdom, according to Ecclus. 1:27, *The fear of the Lord driveth out sin.* On the other hand, chaste or filial fear is the beginning of wisdom, as being the first effect of wisdom. For since the regulation of human conduct by the Divine law belongs to wisdom, in order to make a beginning, man must first of all fear God and submit himself to Him: for the result will be that in all things he will be ruled by God.

**REPLY OBJ. 1**: This argument proves that fear is not the beginning of wisdom as to the essence of wisdom.

**REPLY OBJ. 2**: The fear of God is compared to a man's whole life that is ruled by God's wisdom, as the root to the tree: hence it is written (Sir 1:25): *The root of wisdom is to fear the Lord, for the branches thereof are longlived.* Consequently, as the root is said to be virtually the tree, so the fear of God is said to be wisdom.

**REPLY OBJ. 3**: As stated above, faith is the beginning of wisdom in one way, and fear, in another. Hence it is written (Sir 25:16): *The fear of God is the beginning of love: and the beginning of faith is to be fast joined to it.*

# Article 8

*Whether initial fear differs substantially from filial fear?*

AD OCTAVUM SIC PROCEDITUR. Videtur quod timor initialis differat secundum substantiam a timore filiali. Timor enim filialis ex dilectione causatur. Sed timor initialis est principium dilectionis, secundum illud Eccli. XXV, *timor domini initium est dilectionis.* Ergo timor initialis est alius a filiali.

PRAETEREA, timor initialis timet poenam, quae est obiectum servilis timoris, et sic videtur quod timor initialis sit idem cum servili. Sed timor servilis est alius a filiali. Ergo etiam timor initialis est alius secundum substantiam a filiali.

PRAETEREA, medium differt eadem ratione ab utroque extremorum. Sed timor initialis est medium inter timorem servilem et timorem filialem. Ergo differt et a filiali et a servili.

SED CONTRA est quod perfectum et imperfectum non diversificant substantiam rei. Sed timor initialis et filialis differunt secundum perfectionem et imperfectionem caritatis, ut patet per Augustinum, in Prim. Canonic. Ioan. Ergo timor initialis non differt secundum substantiam a filiali.

RESPONDEO dicendum quod timor initialis dicitur ex eo quod est initium. Sed cum et timor servilis et timor filialis sint aliquo modo initium sapientiae, uterque potest aliquo modo initialis dici.

Sed sic non accipitur initialis secundum quod distinguitur a timore servili et filiali. Sed accipitur secundum quod competit statui incipientium, in quibus inchoatur quidam timor filialis per inchoationem caritatis; non tamen est in eis timor filialis perfecte, quia nondum pervenerunt ad perfectionem caritatis. Et ideo timor initialis hoc modo se habet ad filialem, sicut caritas imperfecta ad perfectam. Caritas autem perfecta et imperfecta non differunt secundum essentiam, sed solum secundum statum. Et ideo dicendum est quod etiam timor initialis, prout hic sumitur, non differt secundum essentiam a timore filiali.

AD PRIMUM ergo dicendum quod timor qui est initium dilectionis est timor servilis, qui *introducit caritatem sicut seta introducit linum,* ut Augustinus dicit. Vel, si hoc referatur ad timorem initialem, dicitur esse dilectionis initium non absolute, sed quantum ad statum caritatis perfectae.

AD SECUNDUM dicendum quod timor initialis non timet poenam sicut proprium obiectum, sed inquantum habet aliquid de timore servili adiunctum. Qui secundum substantiam manet quidem cum caritate, servilitate remota, sed actus eius manet quidem cum caritate imperfecta in eo qui non solum movetur ad bene agendum ex amore iustitiae, sed etiam ex timore poenae; sed iste

OBJECTION 1: It would seem that initial fear differs substantially from filial fear. For filial fear is caused by love. Now initial fear is the beginning of love, according to Ecclus. 25:16, *The fear of God is the beginning of love.* Therefore initial fear is distinct from filial fear.

OBJ. 2: Further, initial fear dreads punishment, which is the object of servile fear, so that initial and servile fear would seem to be the same. But servile fear is distinct from filial fear. Therefore initial fear also is substantially distinct from initial fear.

OBJ. 3: Further, a mean differs in the same ratio from both the extremes. Now initial fear is the mean between servile and filial fear. Therefore it differs from both filial and servile fear.

ON THE CONTRARY, Perfect and imperfect do not diversify the substance of a thing. Now initial and filial fear differ in respect of perfection and imperfection of charity, as Augustine states (*In prim. canon. Joan. Tract.* ix). Therefore initial fear does not differ substantially from filial fear.

I ANSWER THAT, Initial fear is so called because it is a beginning. Since, however, both servile and filial fear are, in some way, the beginning of wisdom, each may be called in some way, initial.

It is not in this sense, however, that we are to understand initial fear insofar as it is distinct from servile and filial fear, but in the sense according to which it belongs to the state of beginners, in whom there is a beginning of filial fear resulting from a beginning of charity, although they do not possess the perfection of filial fear, because they have not yet attained to the perfection of charity. Consequently initial fear stands in the same relation to filial fear as imperfect to perfect charity. Now perfect and imperfect charity differ, not as to essence but as to state. Therefore we must conclude that initial fear, as we understand it here, does not differ essentially from filial fear.

REPLY OBJ. 1: The fear which is a beginning of love is servile fear, which is *the herald of charity, just as the bristle introduces the thread,* as Augustine states (*Tract. ix in Ep. i Joan.*). Or else, if it be referred to initial fear, this is said to be the beginning of love, not absolutely, but relatively to the state of perfect charity.

REPLY OBJ. 2: Initial fear does not dread punishment as its proper object, but as having something of servile fear connected with it: for this servile fear, as to its substance, remains indeed, with charity, its servility being cast aside; whereas its act remains with imperfect charity in the man who is moved to perform good actions not only through love of justice, but also through fear of punishment, though

actus cessat in eo qui habet caritatem perfectam, quae *foras mittit timorem habentem poenam*, ut dicitur I Ioan. IV.

**AD TERTIUM** dicendum quod timor initialis est medium inter timorem filialem et servilem non sicut inter ea quae sunt unius generis; sed sicut imperfectum est medium inter ens perfectum et non ens, ut dicitur in II Metaphys.; quod tamen est idem secundum substantiam cum ente perfecto, differt autem totaliter a non ente.

this same act ceases in the man who has perfect charity, which *casteth out fear*, according to 1 John 4:18.

**REPLY OBJ. 3**: Initial fear is a mean between servile and filial fear, not as between two things of the same genus, but as the imperfect is a mean between a perfect being and a non-being, as stated in *Metaph.* ii, for it is the same substantially as the perfect being, while it differs altogether from non-being.

# Article 9

*Whether fear is a gift of the Holy Spirit?*

**AD NONUM SIC PROCEDITUR**. Videtur quod timor non sit donum spiritus sancti. Nullum enim donum spiritus sancti opponitur virtuti, quae etiam est a spiritu sancto, alioquin Spiritus Sanctus esset sibi contrarius. Sed timor opponitur spei, quae est virtus. Ergo timor non est donum spiritus sancti.

**PRAETEREA**, virtutis theologicae proprium est quod Deum habeat pro obiecto. Sed timor habet Deum pro obiecto, inquantum Deus timetur. Ergo timor non est donum, sed virtus theologica.

**PRAETEREA**, timor ex amore consequitur. Sed amor ponitur quaedam virtus theologica. Ergo etiam timor est virtus theologica, quasi ad idem pertinens.

**PRAETEREA**, Gregorius dicit, II Moral., quod timor datur contra superbiam. Sed superbiae opponitur virtus humilitatis. Ergo etiam timor sub virtute comprehenditur.

**PRAETEREA**, dona sunt perfectiora virtutibus, dantur enim in adiutorium virtutum, ut Gregorius dicit, II Moral. Sed spes est perfectior timore, quia spes respicit bonum, timor malum. Cum ergo spes sit virtus, non debet dici quod timor sit donum.

**SED CONTRA** est quod Isaiae XI timor domini enumeratur inter septem dona spiritus sancti.

**RESPONDEO** dicendum quod multiplex est timor, ut supra dictum est. Timor autem humanus, ut dicit Augustinus, in libro de gratia et Lib. Arb., non est donum Dei, hoc enim timore Petrus negavit Christum, sed ille timor de quo dictum est, *illum timete qui potest animam et corpus mittere in Gehennam.*

Similiter etiam timor servilis non est numerandus inter septem dona spiritus sancti, licet sit a spiritu sancto. Quia, ut Augustinus dicit, in libro de Nat. et gratia, potest habere annexam voluntatem peccandi, dona autem spiritus sancti non possunt esse cum voluntate peccandi, quia non sunt sine caritate, ut dictum est.

Unde relinquitur quod timor Dei qui numeratur inter septem dona spiritus sancti est timor filialis sive

**OBJECTION 1**: It would seem that fear is not a gift of the Holy Spirit. For no gift of the Holy Spirit is opposed to a virtue, which is also from the Holy Spirit; else the Holy Spirit would be in opposition to Himself. Now fear is opposed to hope, which is a virtue. Therefore fear is not a gift of the Holy Spirit.

**OBJ. 2**: Further, it is proper to a theological virtue to have God for its object. But fear has God for its object, insofar as God is feared. Therefore fear is not a gift, but a theological virtue.

**OBJ. 3**: Further, fear arises from love. But love is reckoned a theological virtue. Therefore fear also is a theological virtue, being connected with the same matter, as it were.

**OBJ. 4**: Further, Gregory says (*Moral.* ii, 49) that fear is bestowed as a remedy against pride. But the virtue of humility is opposed to pride. Therefore again, fear is a kind of virtue.

**OBJ. 5**: Further, the gifts are more perfect than the virtues, since they are bestowed in support of the virtues as Gregory says (*Moral.* ii, 49). Now hope is more perfect than fear, since hope regards good, while fear regards evil. Since, then, hope is a virtue, it should not be said that fear is a gift.

**ON THE CONTRARY**, The fear of the Lord is numbered among the seven gifts of the Holy Spirit (Isa 11:3).

**I ANSWER THAT**, Fear is of several kinds, as stated above (A. 2). Now it is not human fear, according to Augustine (*De Gratia et Lib. Arb.* xviii), that is a gift of God—for it was by this fear that Peter denied Christ—but that fear of which it was said (Matt 10:28): *Fear Him that can destroy both soul and body into hell.*

Again servile fear is not to be reckoned among the seven gifts of the Holy Spirit, though it is from Him, because according to Augustine (*De Nat. et Grat.* lvii) it is compatible with the will to sin: whereas the gifts of the Holy Spirit are incompatible with the will to sin, as they are inseparable from charity, as stated above (I-II, Q. 68, A. 5).

It follows, therefore, that the fear of God, which is numbered among the seven gifts of the Holy Spirit, is filial or

castus. Dictum est enim supra quod dona spiritus sancti sunt quaedam habituales perfectiones potentiarum animae quibus redduntur bene mobiles a spiritu sancto, sicut virtutibus moralibus potentiae appetitivae redduntur bene mobiles a ratione. Ad hoc autem quod aliquid sit bene mobile ab aliquo movente, primo requiritur ut sit ei subiectum, non repugnans, quia ex repugnantia mobilis ad movens impeditur motus. Hoc autem facit timor filialis vel castus, inquantum per ipsum Deum reveremur, et refugimus nos ipsi subducere. Et ideo timor filialis quasi primum locum tenet ascendendo inter dona spiritus sancti, ultimum autem descendendo; sicut Augustinus dicit, in libro de Serm. Dom. in monte.

AD PRIMUM ergo dicendum quod timor filialis non contrariatur virtuti spei. Non enim per timorem filialem timemus ne nobis deficiat quod speramus obtinere per auxilium divinum, sed timemus ab hoc auxilio nos subtrahere. Et ideo timor filialis et spes sibi invicem cohaerent et se invicem perficiunt.

AD SECUNDUM dicendum quod proprium et principale obiectum timoris est malum quod quis refugit. Et per hunc modum Deus non potest esse obiectum timoris, sicut supra dictum est. Est autem per hunc modum obiectum spei et aliarum virtutum theologicarum. Quia per virtutem spei non solum innitimur divino auxilio ad adipiscendum quaecumque alia bona; sed principaliter ad adipiscendum ipsum Deum, tanquam principale bonum. Et idem patet in aliis virtutibus theologicis.

AD TERTIUM dicendum quod ex hoc quod amor est principium timoris non sequitur quod timor Dei non sit habitus distinctus a caritate, quae est amor Dei, quia amor est principium omnium affectionum, et tamen in diversis habitibus perficimur circa diversas affectiones. Ideo tamen amor magis habet rationem virtutis quam timor, quia amor respicit bonum, ad quod principaliter virtus ordinatur secundum propriam rationem, ut ex supradictis patet. Et propter hoc etiam spes ponitur virtus. Timor autem principaliter respicit malum, cuius fugam importat. Unde est aliquid minus virtute theologica.

AD QUARTUM dicendum quod, sicut dicitur Eccli. X, *initium superbiae hominis apostatare a Deo*, hoc est nolle subdi Deo, quod opponitur timori filiali, qui Deum revereretur. Et sic timor excludit principium superbiae, propter quod datur contra superbiam. Nec tamen sequitur quod sit idem cum virtute humilitatis, sed quod sit principium eius, dona enim spiritus sancti sunt principia virtutum intellectualium et moralium, ut supra dictum est. Sed virtutes theologicae sunt principia donorum, ut supra habitum est.

UNDE PATET responsio ad quintum.

chaste fear. For it was stated above (I-II, Q. 68, AA. 1, 3) that the gifts of the Holy Spirit are certain habitual perfections of the soul's powers, whereby these are rendered amenable to the motion of the Holy Spirit, just as, by the moral virtues, the appetitive powers are rendered amenable to the motion of reason. Now for a thing to be amenable to the motion of a certain mover, the first condition required is that it be a non-resistant subject of that mover, because resistance of the movable subject to the mover hinders the movement. This is what filial or chaste fear does, since thereby we revere God and avoid separating ourselves from Him. Hence, according to Augustine (*De Serm. Dom. in Monte* i, 4) filial fear holds the first place, as it were, among the gifts of the Holy Spirit, in the ascending order, and the last place, in the descending order.

REPLY OBJ. 1: Filial fear is not opposed to the virtue of hope: since thereby we fear, not that we may fail of what we hope to obtain by God's help, but lest we withdraw ourselves from this help. Wherefore filial fear and hope cling together, and perfect one another.

REPLY OBJ. 2: The proper and principal object of fear is the evil shunned, and in this way, as stated above (A. 1), God cannot be an object of fear. Yet He is, in this way, the object of hope and the other theological virtues, since, by the virtue of hope, we trust in God's help, not only to obtain any other goods, but, chiefly, to obtain God Himself, as the principal good. The same evidently applies to the other theological virtues.

REPLY OBJ. 3: From the fact that love is the origin of fear, it does not follow that the fear of God is not a distinct habit from charity which is the love of God, since love is the origin of all the emotions, and yet we are perfected by different habits in respect of different emotions. Yet love is more of a virtue than fear is, because love regards good, to which virtue is principally directed by reason of its own nature, as was shown above (I-II, Q. 55, AA. 3, 4); for which reason hope is also reckoned as a virtue; whereas fear principally regards evil, the avoidance of which it denotes, wherefore it is something less than a theological virtue.

REPLY OBJ. 4: According to Ecclus. 10:14, *the beginning of the pride of man is to fall off from God*, that is to refuse submission to God, and this is opposed to filial fear, which reveres God. Thus fear cuts off the source of pride for which reason it is bestowed as a remedy against pride. Yet it does not follow that it is the same as the virtue of humility, but that it is its origin. For the gifts of the Holy Spirit are the origin of the intellectual and moral virtues, as stated above (I-II, Q. 68, A. 4), while the theological virtues are the origin of the gifts, as stated above (I-II, Q. 69, A. 4, ad 3).

THIS SUFFICES for the Reply to the Fifth Objection.

# Article 10

*Whether fear decreases when charity increases?*

**AD DECIMUM SIC PROCEDITUR**. Videtur quod crescente caritate diminuatur timor. Dicit enim Augustinus, super Prim. Canonic. Ioan., *quantum caritas crescit, tantum timor decrescit.*

**PRAETEREA**, crescente spe diminuitur timor. Sed crescente caritate crescit spes, ut supra habitum est. Ergo crescente caritate diminuitur timor.

**PRAETEREA**, amor importat unionem, timor autem separationem. Sed crescente unione diminuitur separatio. Ergo crescente amore caritatis diminuitur timor.

**SED CONTRA** est quod dicit Augustinus, in libro Octoginta trium Quaest., quod *Dei timor non solum inchoat, sed etiam perficit sapientiam, idest quae summe diligit Deum et proximum tanquam seipsum.*

**RESPONDEO** dicendum quod duplex est timor Dei, sicut dictum est, unus quidem filialis, quo quis timet offensam ipsius vel separationem ab ipso; alius autem servilis, quo quis timet poenam.

Timor autem filialis necesse est quod crescat crescente caritate, sicut effectus crescit crescente causa, quanto enim aliquis magis diligit aliquem, tanto magis timet eum offendere et ab eo separari.

Sed timor servilis, quantum ad servilitatem, totaliter tollitur caritate adveniente, remanet tamen secundum substantiam timor poenae, ut dictum est. Et iste timor diminuitur caritate crescente, maxime quantum ad actum, quia quanto aliquis magis diligit Deum, tanto minus timet poenam. Primo quidem, quia minus attendit ad proprium bonum, cui contrariatur poena. Secundo, quia firmius inhaerens magis confidit de praemio, et per consequens minus timet de poena.

**AD PRIMUM** ergo dicendum quod Augustinus loquitur de timore poenae.

**AD SECUNDUM** dicendum quod timor poenae est qui diminuitur crescente spe. Sed ea crescente crescit timor filialis, quia quanto aliquis certius expectat alicuius boni consecutionem per auxilium alterius, tanto magis veretur eum offendere vel ab eo separari.

**AD TERTIUM** dicendum quod timor filialis non importat separationem sed magis subiectionem ad ipsum, separationem autem refugit a subiectione ipsius. Sed quodammodo separationem importat per hoc quod non praesumit se ei adaequare, sed ei se subiicit. Quae etiam separatio invenitur in caritate, inquantum diligit Deum supra se et supra omnia. Unde amor caritatis augmentatus reverentiam timoris non minuit, sed auget.

**OBJECTION 1**: It seems that fear decreases when charity increases. For Augustine says (*In prim. canon. Joan. Tract.* ix): *The more charity increases, the more fear decreases.*

**OBJ. 2**: Further, fear decreases when hope increases. But charity increases when hope increases, as stated above (Q. 17, A. 8). Therefore fear decreases when charity increases.

**OBJ. 3**: Further, love implies union, whereas fear implies separation. Now separation decreases when union increases. Therefore fear decreases when the love of charity increases.

**ON THE CONTRARY**, Augustine says (*83 Questions*, Q. 36) that *the fear of God not only begins but also perfects wisdom, whereby we love God above all things, and our neighbor as ourselves.*

**I ANSWER THAT**, Fear is twofold, as stated above (AA. 2, 4); one is filial fear, whereby a son fears to offend his father or to be separated from him; the other is servile fear, whereby one fears punishment.

Now filial fear must needs increase when charity increases, even as an effect increases with the increase of its cause. For the more one loves a man, the more one fears to offend him and to be separated from him.

On the other hand, servile fear, as regards its servility, is entirely cast out when charity comes, although the fear of punishment remains as to its substance, as stated above (A. 6). This fear decreases as charity increases, chiefly as regards its act, since the more a man loves God, the less he fears punishment; first, because he thinks less of his own good, to which punishment is opposed; second, because, the faster he clings, the more confident he is of the reward, and, consequently the less fearful of punishment.

**REPLY OBJ. 1**: Augustine speaks there of the fear of punishment.

**REPLY OBJ. 2**: It is fear of punishment that decreases when hope increases; but with the increase of the latter filial fear increases, because the more certainly a man expects to obtain a good by another's help, the more he fears to offend him or to be separated from him.

**REPLY OBJ. 3**: Filial fear does not imply separation from God, but submission to Him, and shuns separation from that submission. Yet, in a way, it implies separation, in the point of not presuming to equal oneself to Him, and of submitting to Him, which separation is to be observed even in charity, insofar as a man loves God more than himself and more than aught else. Hence the increase of the love of charity implies not a decrease but an increase in the reverence of fear.

# Article 11

*Whether fear remains in heaven?*

AD UNDECIMUM SIC PROCEDITUR. Videtur quod timor non remaneat in patria. Dicitur enim Prov. I, *abundantia perfruetur, timore malorum sublato*, quod intelligitur de homine iam sapientia perfruente in beatitudine aeterna. Sed omnis timor est alicuius mali, quia malum est obiectum timoris, ut supra dictum est. Ergo nullus timor erit in patria.

PRAETEREA, homines in patria erunt Deo conformes, secundum illud I Ioan. III, *cum apparuerit, similes ei erimus.* Sed Deus nihil timet. Ergo homines in patria non habebunt aliquem timorem.

PRAETEREA, spes est perfectior quam timor, quia spes est respectu boni, timor respectu mali. Sed spes non erit in patria. Ergo nec timor erit in patria.

SED CONTRA est quod dicitur in Psalm., *timor domini sanctus permanet in saeculum.*

RESPONDEO dicendum quod timor servilis, sive timor poenae, nullo modo erit in patria, excluditur enim talis timor per securitatem aeternae beatitudinis, quae est de ipsius beatitudinis ratione, sicut supra dictum est.

Timor autem filialis, sicut augetur augmentata caritate, ita caritate perfecta perficietur. Unde non habebit in patria omnino eundem actum quem habet modo.

Ad cuius evidentiam sciendum est quod proprium obiectum timoris est malum possibile, sicut proprium obiectum spei est bonum possibile. Et cum motus timoris sit quasi fugae, importat timor fugam mali ardui possibilis, parva enim mala timorem non inducunt. Sicut autem bonum uniuscuiusque est ut in suo ordine consistat, ita malum uniuscuiusque est ut suum ordinem deserat. Ordo autem creaturae rationalis est ut sit sub Deo et supra ceteras creaturas. Unde sicut malum creaturae rationalis est ut subdat se creaturae inferiori per amorem, ita etiam malum eius est si non Deo se subiiciat, sed in ipsum praesumptuose insiliat vel contemnat. Hoc autem malum creaturae rationali secundum suam naturam consideratae possibile est, propter naturalem liberi arbitrii flexibilitatem, sed in beatis fit non possibile per gloriae perfectionem. Fuga igitur huius mali quod est Deo non subiici, ut possibilis naturae, impossibilis autem beatitudini, erit in patria. In via autem est fuga huius mali ut omnino possibilis. Et ideo Gregorius dicit, XVII Moral., exponens illud Iob XXVI, *columnae caeli contremiscunt et pavent ad nutum eius, ipsae,* inquit, *virtutes caelestium, quae hunc sine cessatione conspiciunt, in ipsa contemplatione contremiscunt. Sed idem tremor, ne eis poenalis sit, non timoris est sed admirationis,* quia scilicet admirantur Deum ut supra se existentem et eis incomprehensibilem. Augustinus etiam, in XIV de Civ.

OBJECTION 1: It would seem that fear does not remain in heaven. For it is written (Prov 1:33): *He . . . shall enjoy abundance, without fear of evils,* which is to be understood as referring to those who already enjoy wisdom in everlasting happiness. Now every fear is about some evil, since evil is the object of fear, as stated above (AA. 2, 5; I-II, Q. 42, A. 1). Therefore there will be no fear in heaven.

OBJ. 2: Further, in heaven men will be conformed to God, according to 1 John 3:2, *When He shall appear, we shall be like to Him.* But God fears nothing. Therefore, in heaven, men will have no fear.

OBJ. 3: Further, hope is more perfect than fear, since hope regards good, and fear, evil. Now hope will not be in heaven. Therefore neither will there be fear in heaven.

ON THE CONTRARY, It is written (Ps 18:10): *The fear of the Lord is holy, enduring for ever and ever.*

I ANSWER THAT, Servile fear, or fear of punishment, will by no means be in heaven, since such a fear is excluded by the security which is essential to everlasting happiness, as stated above (I-II, Q. 5, A. 4).

But with regard to filial fear, as it increases with the increase of charity, so is it perfected when charity is made perfect; hence, in heaven, it will not have quite the same act as it has now.

In order to make this clear, we must observe that the proper object of fear is a possible evil, just as the proper object of hope is a possible good: and since the movement of fear is like one of avoidance, fear implies avoidance of a possible arduous evil, for little evils inspire no fear. Now as a thing's good consists in its staying in its own order, so a thing's evil consists in forsaking its order. Again, the order of a rational creature is that it should be under God and above other creatures. Hence, just as it is an evil for a rational creature to submit, by love, to a lower creature, so too is it an evil for it, if it submit not to God, but presumptuously revolt against Him or contemn Him. Now this evil is possible to a rational creature considered as to its nature on account of the natural flexibility of the free-will; whereas in the blessed, it becomes impossible, by reason of the perfection of glory. Therefore the avoidance of this evil that consists in non-subjection to God, and is possible to nature, but impossible in the state of bliss, will be in heaven; while in this life there is avoidance of this evil as of something altogether possible. Hence Gregory, expounding the words of Job (26:11), *The pillars of heaven tremble, and dread at His beck,* says (*Moral.* xvii, 29): *The heavenly powers that gaze on Him without ceasing, tremble while contemplating: but their awe, lest it should be of a penal nature, is one not of fear but of wonder,* because, to wit, they wonder at God's supereminence and incomprehensibility.

Dei, hoc modo ponit timorem in patria, quamvis hoc sub dubio derelinquat. *Timor, inquit, ille castus permanens in saeculum saeculi, si erit in futuro saeculo, non erit timor exterrens a malo quod accidere potest; sed tenens in bono quod amitti non potest. Ubi enim boni adepti amor immutabilis est, profecto, si dici potest, mali cavendi timor securus est. Timoris quippe casti nomine ea voluntas significata est qua nos necesse erit nolle peccare, et non sollicitudine infirmitatis ne forte peccemus, sed tranquillitate caritatis cavere peccatum. Aut, si nullius omnino generis timor ibi esse poterit, ita fortasse timor in saeculum saeculi dictus est permanens, quia id permanebit quo timor ipse perducit.*

**AD PRIMUM** ergo dicendum quod in auctoritate praedicta excluditur a beatis timor sollicitudinem habens, de malo praecavens, non autem timor securus, ut Augustinus dicit.

**AD SECUNDUM** dicendum quod, sicut dicit Dionysius, IX cap. de Div. Nom., *eadem et similia sunt Deo et dissimilia, hoc quidem secundum contingentem non imitabilis imitationem*, idest inquantum secundum suum posse imitantur Deum, qui non est perfecte imitabilis; *hoc autem secundum hoc quod causata minus habent a causa, infinitis mensuris et incomparabilibus deficientia*. Unde non oportet quod, si Deo non convenit timor, quia non habet superiorem cui subiiciatur, quod propter hoc non conveniat beatis, quorum beatitudo consistit in perfecta subiectione ad Deum.

**AD TERTIUM** dicendum quod spes importat quendam defectum, scilicet futuritionem beatitudinis, quae tollitur per eius praesentiam. Sed timor importat defectum naturalem creaturae, secundum quod in infinitum distat a Deo, quod etiam in patria remanebit. Et ideo timor non evacuabitur totaliter.

Augustine also (*De Civ. Dei* xiv, 9) in this sense, admits fear in heaven, although he leaves the question doubtful. *If,* he says, *this chaste fear that endureth for ever and ever is to be in the future life, it will not be a fear that is afraid of an evil which might possibly occur, but a fear that holds fast to a good which we cannot lose. For when we love the good which we have acquired, with an unchangeable love, without doubt, if it is allowable to say so, our fear is sure of avoiding evil. Because chaste fear denotes a will that cannot consent to sin, and whereby we avoid sin without trembling lest, in our weakness, we fall, and possess ourselves in the tranquillity born of charity. Else, if no kind of fear is possible there, perhaps fear is said to endure for ever and ever, because that which fear will lead us to, will be everlasting.*

**REPLY OBJ. 1**: The passage quoted excludes from the blessed, the fear that denotes solicitude, and anxiety about evil, but not the fear which is accompanied by security.

**REPLY OBJ. 2**: As Dionysius says (*Div. Nom.* ix) *the same things are both like and unlike God. They are like by reason of a variable imitation of the Inimitable*—that is, because, so far as they can, they imitate God Who cannot be imitated perfectly—*they are unlike because they are the effects of a Cause of Whom they fall short infinitely and immeasurably*. Hence, if there be no fear in God (since there is none above Him to whom He may be subject) it does not follow that there is none in the blessed, whose happiness consists in perfect subjection to God.

**REPLY OBJ. 3**: Hope implies a certain defect, namely the futurity of happiness, which ceases when happiness is present: whereas fear implies a natural defect in a creature, insofar as it is infinitely distant from God, and this defect will remain even in heaven. Hence fear will not be cast out altogether.

# Article 12

*Whether poverty of spirit is the beatitude corresponding to the gift of fear?*

**AD DUODECIMUM SIC PROCEDITUR**. Videtur quod paupertas spiritus non sit beatitudo respondens dono timoris. Timor enim est initium spiritualis vitae, ut ex dictis patet. Sed paupertas pertinet ad perfectionem vitae spiritualis, secundum illud Matth. XIX, *si vis perfectus esse, vade et vende omnia quae habes, et da pauperibus*. Ergo paupertas spiritus non respondet dono timoris.

**PRAETEREA**, in Psalm. dicitur, *confige timore tuo carnes meas*, ex quo videtur quod ad timorem pertineat carnem reprimere. Sed ad repressionem carnis maxime videtur pertinere beatitudo luctus. Ergo beatitudo luctus

**OBJECTION 1**: It would seem that poverty of spirit is not the beatitude corresponding to the gift of fear. For fear is the beginning of the spiritual life, as explained above (A. 7): whereas poverty belongs to the perfection of the spiritual life, according to Matt. 19:21, *If thou wilt be perfect, go sell what thou hast, and give to the poor*. Therefore poverty of spirit does not correspond to the gift of fear.

**OBJ. 2**: Further, it is written (Ps 118:120): *Pierce Thou my flesh with Thy fear*, whence it seems to follow that it belongs to fear to restrain the flesh. But the curbing of the flesh seems to belong rather to the beatitude of mourning.

magis respondet dono timoris quam beatitudo paupertatis.

**PRAETEREA**, donum timoris respondet virtuti spei, sicut dictum est. Sed spei maxime videtur respondere beatitudo ultima, quae est, *beati pacifici, quoniam filii Dei vocabuntur*, quia, ut dicitur Rom. V, *gloriamur in spe gloriae filiorum Dei*. Ergo illa beatitudo magis respondet dono timoris quam paupertas spiritus.

**PRAETEREA**, supra dictum est quod beatitudinibus respondent fructus. Sed nihil in fructibus invenitur respondere dono timoris. Ergo etiam neque in beatitudinibus aliquid ei respondet.

**SED CONTRA** est quod Augustinus dicit, in libro de Serm. Dom. in Mont., *timor Dei congruit humilibus, de quibus dicitur, beati pauperes spiritu*.

**RESPONDEO** dicendum quod timori proprie respondet paupertas spiritus. Cum enim ad timorem filialem pertineat Deo reverentiam exhibere et ei subditum esse, id quod ex huiusmodi subiectione consequitur pertinet ad donum timoris. Ex hoc autem quod aliquis Deo se subiicit, desinit quaerere in seipso vel in aliquo alio magnificari nisi in Deo, hoc enim repugnaret perfectae subiectioni ad Deum. Unde dicitur in Psalm., *hi in curribus et hi in equis, nos autem in nomine Dei nostri invocabimus*. Et ideo ex hoc quod aliquis perfecte timet Deum, consequens est quod non quaerat magnificari in seipso per superbiam; neque etiam quaerat magnificari in exterioribus bonis, scilicet honoribus et divitiis; quorum utrumque pertinet ad paupertatem spiritus, secundum quod paupertas spiritus intelligi potest vel exinanitio inflati et superbi spiritus, ut Augustinus exponit; vel etiam abiectio temporalium rerum quae fit spiritu, idest propria voluntate per instinctum spiritus sancti, ut Ambrosius et Hieronymus exponunt.

**AD PRIMUM** ergo dicendum quod, cum beatitudo sit actus virtutis perfectae, omnes beatitudines ad perfectionem spiritualis vitae pertinent. In qua quidem perfectione principium esse videtur ut tendens ad perfectam spiritualium bonorum participationem terrena bona contemnat, sicut etiam timor primum locum habet in donis. Non autem consistit perfectio in ipsa temporalium desertione, sed haec est via ad perfectionem. Timor autem filialis, cui respondet beatitudo paupertatis, etiam est cum perfectione sapientiae, ut supra dictum est.

**AD SECUNDUM** dicendum quod directius opponitur subiectioni ad Deum, quam facit timor filialis, indebita magnificatio hominis vel in seipso vel in aliis rebus quam delectatio extranea. Quae tamen opponitur timori ex consequenti, quia qui Deum reveretur et ei subiicitur, non delectatur in aliis a Deo. Sed tamen delectatio non pertinet ad rationem ardui, quam respicit timor, sicut

Therefore the beatitude of mourning corresponds to the gift of fear, rather than the beatitude of poverty.

**OBJ. 3**: Further, the gift of fear corresponds to the virtue of hope, as stated above (A. 9, ad 1). Now the last beatitude which is, *Blessed are the peacemakers, for they shall be called the children of God*, seems above all to correspond to hope, because according to Rom. 5:2, *we . . . glory in the hope of the glory of the sons of God*. Therefore that beatitude corresponds to the gift of fear, rather than poverty of spirit.

**OBJ. 4**: Further, it was stated above (I-II, Q. 70, A. 2) that the fruits correspond to the beatitudes. Now none of the fruits correspond to the gift of fear. Neither, therefore, does any of the beatitudes.

**ON THE CONTRARY**, Augustine says (*De Serm. Dom. in Monte* i, 4): *The fear of the Lord is befitting the humble of whom it is said: Blessed are the poor in spirit*.

**I ANSWER THAT**, Poverty of spirit properly corresponds to fear. Because, since it belongs to filial fear to show reverence and submission to God, whatever results from this submission belongs to the gift of fear. Now from the very fact that a man submits to God, it follows that he ceases to seek greatness either in himself or in another but seeks it only in God. For that would be inconsistent with perfect subjection to God, wherefore it is written (Ps 19:8): *Some trust in chariots and some in horses; but we will call upon the name of . . . our God*. It follows that if a man fear God perfectly, he does not, by pride, seek greatness either in himself or in external goods, viz. honors and riches. In either case, this proceeds from poverty of spirit, insofar as the latter denotes either the voiding of a puffed up and proud spirit, according to Augustine's interpretation (*De Serm. Dom. in Monte* i, 4), or the renunciation of worldly goods which is done in spirit, i.e., by one's own will, through the instigation of the Holy Spirit, according to the expounding of Ambrose on Luke 6:20 and Jerome on Matt. 5:3.

**REPLY OBJ. 1**: Since a beatitude is an act of perfect virtue, all the beatitudes belong to the perfection of spiritual life. And this perfection seems to require that whoever would strive to obtain a perfect share of spiritual goods, needs to begin by despising earthly goods, wherefore fear holds the first place among the gifts. Perfection, however, does not consist in the renunciation itself of temporal goods; since this is the way to perfection: whereas filial fear, to which the beatitude of poverty corresponds, is consistent with the perfection of wisdom, as stated above (AA. 7, 10).

**REPLY OBJ. 2**: The undue exaltation of man either in himself or in another is more directly opposed to that submission to God which is the result of filial fear, than is external pleasure. Yet this is, in consequence, opposed to fear, since whoever fears God and is subject to Him, takes no delight in things other than God. Nevertheless, pleasure is not concerned, as exaltation is, with the arduous

magnificatio. Et ideo directe beatitudo paupertatis respondet timori, beatitudo autem luctus ex consequenti.

**Ad tertium** dicendum quod spes importat motum secundum habitudinem ad terminum ad quem tenditur, sed timor importat magis motum secundum habitudinem recessus a termino. Et ideo ultima beatitudo, quae est spiritualis perfectionis terminus, congrue respondet spei per modum obiecti ultimi, sed prima beatitudo, quae est per recessum a rebus exterioribus impedientibus divinam subiectionem, congrue respondet timori.

**Ad quartum** dicendum quod in fructibus illa quae pertinent ad moderatum usum vel abstinentiam a rebus temporalibus, videntur dono timoris convenire, sicut modestia, continentia et castitas.

character of a thing which fear regards: and so the beatitude of poverty corresponds to fear directly, and the beatitude of mourning, consequently.

**Reply Obj. 3**: Hope denotes a movement by way of a relation of tendency to a term, whereas fear implies movement by way of a relation of withdrawal from a term: wherefore the last beatitude which is the term of spiritual perfection, fittingly corresponds to hope, by way of ultimate object; while the first beatitude, which implies withdrawal from external things which hinder submission to God, fittingly corresponds to fear.

**Reply Obj. 4**: As regards the fruits, it seems that those things correspond to the gift of fear, which pertain to the moderate use of temporal things or to abstinence therefrom; such are modesty, continency and chastity.

# QUESTION 20

## DESPAIR

Deinde considerandum est de vitiis oppositis. Et primo, de desperatione; secundo, de praesumptione. Circa primum quaeruntur quatuor.

Primo, utrum desperatio sit peccatum.

Secundo, utrum possit esse sine infidelitate.

Tertio, utrum sit maximum peccatorum.

Quarto, utrum oriatur ex acedia.

We must now consider the contrary vices; (1) despair; (2) presumption. Under the first head there are four points of inquiry:

(1) Whether despair is a sin?

(2) Whether it can be without unbelief?

(3) Whether it is the greatest of sins?

(4) Whether it arises from sloth?

## Article 1

*Whether despair is a sin?*

**AD PRIMUM SIC PROCEDITUR.** Videtur quod desperatio non sit peccatum. Omne enim peccatum habet conversionem ad commutabile bonum cum aversione ab incommutabili bono; ut patet per Augustinum, in Lib. de Lib. Arb. Sed desperatio non habet conversionem ad commutabile bonum. Ergo non est peccatum.

**PRAETEREA,** illud quod oritur ex bona radice non videtur esse peccatum, quia *non potest arbor bona fructus malos facere,* ut dicitur Matth. VII. Sed desperatio videtur procedere ex bona radice, scilicet ex timore Dei, vel ex horrore magnitudinis propriorum peccatorum. Ergo desperatio non est peccatum.

**PRAETEREA,** si desperatio esset peccatum, in damnatis esset peccatum quod desperant. Sed hoc non imputatur eis ad culpam, sed magis ad damnationem. Ergo neque viatoribus imputatur ad culpam. Et ita desperatio non est peccatum.

**SED CONTRA,** illud per quod homines in peccata inducuntur videtur esse non solum peccatum, sed principium peccatorum. Sed desperatio est huiusmodi, dicit enim apostolus de quibusdam, ad Ephes. IV, *qui desperantes semetipsos tradiderunt impudicitiae in operationem omnis immunditiae et avaritiae.* Ergo desperatio non solum est peccatum, sed aliorum peccatorum principium.

**RESPONDEO** dicendum quod secundum philosophum, in VI Ethic., id quod est in intellectu affirmatio vel negatio est in appetitu prosecutio et fuga, et quod est in intellectu verum vel falsum est in appetitu bonum et malum. Et ideo omnis motus appetitivus conformiter se habens intellectui vero, est secundum se bonus, omnis autem motus appetitivus conformiter se habens intellectui falso, est secundum se malus et peccatum. Circa Deum autem vera existimatio intellectus est quod

**OBJECTION 1:** It would seem that despair is not a sin. For every sin includes conversion to a mutable good, together with aversion from the immutable good, as Augustine states (*De Lib. Arb.* ii, 19). But despair includes no conversion to a mutable good. Therefore it is not a sin.

**OBJ. 2:** Further, that which grows from a good root, seems to be no sin, because *a good tree cannot bring forth evil fruit* (Matt 7:18). Now despair seems to grow from a good root, viz. fear of God, or from horror at the greatness of one's own sins. Therefore despair is not a sin.

**OBJ. 3:** Further, if despair were a sin, it would be a sin also for the damned to despair. But this is not imputed to them as their fault but as part of their damnation. Therefore neither is it imputed to wayfarers as their fault, so that it is not a sin.

**ON THE CONTRARY,** That which leads men to sin, seems not only to be a sin itself, but a source of sins. Now such is despair, for the Apostle says of certain men (*Eph* 4:19): *Who, despairing, have given themselves up to lasciviousness, unto the working of all uncleanness and covetousness.* Therefore despair is not only a sin but also the origin of other sins.

**I ANSWER THAT,** According to the Philosopher (*Ethic.* vi, 2) affirmation and negation in the intellect correspond to search and avoidance in the appetite; while truth and falsehood in the intellect correspond to good and evil in the appetite. Consequently every appetitive movement which is conformed to a true intellect, is good in itself, while every appetitive movement which is conformed to a false intellect is evil in itself and sinful. Now the true opinion of the intellect about God is that from Him comes salvation to

ex ipso provenit hominum salus, et venia peccatoribus datur; secundum illud Ezech. XVIII, *nolo mortem peccatoris, sed ut convertatur et vivat.* Falsa autem opinio est quod peccatori poenitenti veniam deneget, vel quod peccatores ad se non convertat per gratiam iustificantem. Et ideo sicut motus spei, qui conformiter se habet ad existimationem veram, est laudabilis et virtuosus; ita oppositus motus desperationis, qui se habet conformiter existimationi falsae de Deo, est vitiosus et peccatum.

AD PRIMUM ergo dicendum quod in quolibet peccato mortali est quodammodo aversio a bono incommutabili et conversio ad bonum commutabile, sed aliter et aliter. Nam principaliter consistunt in aversione a bono incommutabili peccata quae opponuntur virtutibus theologicis, ut odium Dei, desperatio et infidelitas, quia virtutes theologicae habent Deum pro obiecto, ex consequenti autem important conversionem ad bonum commutabile, inquantum anima deserens Deum consequenter necesse est quod ad alia convertatur. Peccata vero alia principaliter consistunt in conversione ad commutabile bonum, ex consequenti vero in aversione ab incommutabili bono, non enim qui fornicatur intendit a Deo recedere, sed carnali delectatione frui, ex quo sequitur quod a Deo recedat.

AD SECUNDUM dicendum quod ex radice virtutis potest aliquid procedere dupliciter. Uno modo, directe ex parte ipsius virtutis, sicut actus procedit ex habitu, et hoc modo ex virtuosa radice non potest aliquod peccatum procedere; hoc enim sensu Augustinus dicit, in libro de Lib. Arb., quod *virtute nemo male utitur.* Alio modo procedit aliquid ex virtute indirecte sive occasionaliter. Et sic nihil prohibet aliquod peccatum ex aliqua virtute procedere, sicut interdum de virtutibus aliqui superbiunt, secundum illud Augustini, *superbia bonis operibus insidiatur ut pereant.* Et hoc modo ex timore Dei vel ex horrore propriorum peccatorum contingit desperatio, inquantum his bonis aliquis male utitur, occasionem ab eis accipiens desperandi.

AD TERTIUM dicendum quod damnati non sunt in statu sperandi, propter impossibilitatem reditus ad beatitudinem. Et ideo quod non sperant non imputatur eis ad culpam, sed est pars damnationis ipsorum. Sicut etiam in statu viae si quis desperaret de eo quod non est natus adipisci, vel quod non est debitum adipisci, non esset peccatum, puta si medicus desperat de curatione alicuius infirmi, vel si aliquis desperat se fore divitias adepturum.

mankind, and pardon to sinners, according to Ezech. 18:23, *I desire not the death of the sinner, but that he should be converted, and live*: while it is a false opinion that He refuses pardon to the repentant sinner, or that He does not turn sinners to Himself by sanctifying grace. Therefore, just as the movement of hope, which is in conformity with the true opinion, is praiseworthy and virtuous, so the contrary movement of despair, which is in conformity with the false opinion about God, is vicious and sinful.

REPLY OBJ. 1: In every mortal sin there is, in some way, aversion from the immutable good, and conversion to a mutable good, but not always in the same way. Because, since the theological virtues have God for their object, the sins which are contrary to them, such as hatred of God, despair and unbelief, consist principally in aversion from the immutable good; but, consequently, they imply conversion to a mutable good, insofar as the soul that is a deserter from God, must necessarily turn to other things. Other sins, however, consist principally in conversion to a mutable good, and, consequently, in aversion from the immutable good: because the fornicator intends, not to depart from God, but to enjoy carnal pleasure, the result of which is that he departs from God.

REPLY OBJ. 2: A thing may grow from a virtuous root in two ways: first, directly and on the part of the virtue itself; even as an act proceeds from a habit: and in this way no sin can grow from a virtuous root, for in this sense Augustine declared (*De Lib. Arb.* ii, 18, 19) that *no man makes evil use of virtue.* Second, a thing proceeds from a virtue indirectly, or is occasioned by a virtue, and in this way nothing hinders a sin proceeding from a virtue: thus sometimes men pride themselves of their virtues, according to Augustine (*Ep. ccxi*): *Pride lies in wait for good works that they may die.* In this way fear of God or horror of one's own sins may lead to despair, insofar as man makes evil use of those good things, by allowing them to be an occasion of despair.

REPLY OBJ. 3: The damned are outside the pale of hope on account of the impossibility of returning to happiness: hence it is not imputed to them that they hope not, but it is a part of their damnation. Even so, it would be no sin for a wayfarer to despair of obtaining that which he had no natural capacity for obtaining, or which was not due to be obtained by him; for instance, if a physician were to despair of healing some sick man, or if anyone were to despair of ever becoming rich.

# Article 2

*Whether there can be despair without unbelief?*

**AD SECUNDUM SIC PROCEDITUR.** Videtur quod desperatio sine infidelitate esse non possit. Certitudo enim spei a fide derivatur. Sed manente causa non tollitur effectus. Ergo non potest aliquis certitudinem spei amittere desperando nisi fide sublata.

**PRAETEREA,** praeferre culpam propriam bonitati vel misericordiae divinae est negare infinitatem divinae misericordiae vel bonitatis, quod est infidelitatis. Sed qui desperat culpam suam praefert misericordiae vel bonitati divinae, secundum illud Gen. IV, *maior est iniquitas mea quam ut veniam merear.* Ergo quicumque desperat est infidelis.

**PRAETEREA,** quicumque incidit in haeresim damnatam est infidelis. Sed desperans videtur incidere in haeresim damnatam, scilicet Novatianorum, qui dicunt peccata non remitti post Baptismum. Ergo videtur quod quicumque desperat sit infidelis.

**SED CONTRA** est quod remoto posteriori non removetur prius. Sed spes est posterior fide, ut supra dictum est. Ergo remota spe potest remanere fides. Non ergo quicumque desperat est infidelis.

**RESPONDEO** dicendum quod infidelitas pertinet ad intellectum, desperatio vero ad vim appetitivam. Intellectus autem universalium est, sed vis appetitiva movetur ad particularia, est enim motus appetitivus ab anima ad res, quae in seipsis particulares sunt. Contingit autem aliquem habentem rectam existimationem in universali circa motum appetitivum non recte se habere, corrupta eius aestimatione in particulari, quia necesse est quod ab aestimatione in universali ad appetitum rei particularis perveniatur mediante aestimatione particulari, ut dicitur in III de Anima; sicut a propositione universali non infertur conclusio particularis nisi assumendo particularem. Et inde est quod aliquis habens rectam fidem in universali deficit in motu appetitivo circa particulare, corrupta particulari eius aestimatione per habitum vel per passionem. Sicut ille qui fornicatur, eligendo fornicationem ut bonum sibi ut nunc, habet corruptam aestimationem in particulari, cum tamen retineat universalem aestimationem veram secundum fidem, scilicet quod fornicatio sit mortale peccatum. Et similiter aliquis, retinendo in universali veram aestimationem fidei, scilicet quod est remissio peccatorum in Ecclesia, potest pati motum desperationis, quasi sibi in tali statu existenti non sit sperandum de venia, corrupta aestimatione eius circa particulare. Et per hunc modum potest esse desperatio sine infidelitate, sicut et alia peccata mortalia.

**OBJECTION 1**: It would seem that there can be no despair without unbelief. For the certainty of hope is derived from faith; and so long as the cause remains the effect is not done away. Therefore a man cannot lose the certainty of hope, by despairing, unless his faith be removed.

**OBJ. 2**: Further, to prefer one's own guilt to God's mercy and goodness, is to deny the infinity of God's goodness and mercy, and so savors of unbelief. But whoever despairs, prefers his own guilt to the Divine mercy and goodness, according to Gen. 4:13: *My iniquity is greater than that I may deserve pardon.* Therefore whoever despairs, is an unbeliever.

**OBJ. 3**: Further, whoever falls into a condemned heresy, is an unbeliever. But he that despairs seems to fall into a condemned heresy, viz. that of the Novatians, who say that there is no pardon for sins after Baptism. Therefore it seems that whoever despairs, is an unbeliever.

**ON THE CONTRARY**, If we remove that which follows, that which precedes remains. But hope follows faith, as stated above (Q. 17, A. 7). Therefore when hope is removed, faith can remain; so that, not everyone who despairs, is an unbeliever.

**I ANSWER THAT,** Unbelief pertains to the intellect, but despair, to the appetite: and the intellect is about universals, while the appetite is moved in connection with particulars, since the appetitive movement is from the soul towards things, which, in themselves, are particular. Now it may happen that a man, while having a right opinion in the universal, is not rightly disposed as to his appetitive movement, his estimate being corrupted in a particular matter, because, in order to pass from the universal opinion to the appetite for a particular thing, it is necessary to have a particular estimate (*De Anima* iii, 2), just as it is impossible to infer a particular conclusion from an universal proposition, except through the holding of a particular proposition. Hence it is that a man, while having right faith, in the universal, fails in an appetitive movement, in regard to some particular, his particular estimate being corrupted by a habit or a passion, just as the fornicator, by choosing fornication as a good for himself at this particular moment, has a corrupt estimate in a particular matter, although he retains the true universal estimate according to faith, viz. that fornication is a mortal sin. In the same way, a man while retaining in the universal, the true estimate of faith, viz. that there is in the Church the power of forgiving sins, may suffer a movement of despair, to wit, that for him, being in such a state, there is no hope of pardon, his estimate being corrupted in a particular matter. In this way there can be despair, just as there can be other mortal sins, without unbelief.

**AD PRIMUM** ergo dicendum quod effectus tollitur non solum sublata causa prima, sed etiam sublata causa secunda. Unde motus spei auferri potest non solum sublata universali aestimatione fidei, quae est sicut causa prima certitudinis spei; sed etiam sublata aestimatione particulari, quae est sicut secunda causa.

**AD SECUNDUM** dicendum quod si quis in universali aestimaret misericordiam Dei non esse infinitam, esset infidelis. Hoc autem non existimat desperans, sed quod sibi in statu illo, propter aliquam particularem dispositionem, non sit de divina misericordia sperandum.

**ET SIMILITER** dicendum ad tertium quod Novatiani in universali negant remissionem peccatorum fieri in Ecclesia.

**REPLY OBJ. 1**: The effect is done away, not only when the first cause is removed, but also when the secondary cause is removed. Hence the movement of hope can be done away, not only by the removal of the universal estimate of faith, which is, so to say, the first cause of the certainty of hope, but also by the removal of the particular estimate, which is the secondary cause, as it were.

**REPLY OBJ. 2**: If anyone were to judge, in universal, that God's mercy is not infinite, he would be an unbeliever. But he who despairs judges not thus, but that, for him in that state, on account of some particular disposition, there is no hope of the Divine mercy.

**THE SAME ANSWER** applies to the Third Objection, since the Novatians denied, in universal, that there is remission of sins in the Church.

# Article 3

*Whether despair is the greatest of sins?*

**AD TERTIUM SIC PROCEDITUR**. Videtur quod desperatio non sit maximum peccatorum. Potest enim esse desperatio absque infidelitate, sicut dictum est. Sed infidelitas est maximum peccatorum, quia subruit fundamentum spiritualis aedificii. Ergo desperatio non est maximum peccatorum.

**PRAETEREA**, maiori bono maius malum opponitur; ut patet per philosophum, in VIII Ethic. Sed caritas est maior spe, ut dicitur I Cor. XIII. Ergo odium est maius peccatum quam desperatio.

**PRAETEREA**, in peccato desperationis est solum inordinata aversio a Deo. Sed in aliis peccatis est non solum aversio inordinata, sed etiam inordinata conversio. Ergo peccatum desperationis non est gravius, sed minus aliis.

**SED CONTRA**, peccatum insanabile videtur esse gravissimum, secundum illud Ierem. XXX, *insanabilis fractura tua, pessima plaga tua*. Sed peccatum desperationis est insanabile, secundum illud Ierem. XV, *plaga mea desperabilis renuit curari*. Ergo desperatio est gravissimum peccatum.

**RESPONDEO** dicendum quod peccata quae opponuntur virtutibus theologicis sunt secundum suum genus aliis peccatis graviora. Cum enim virtutes theologicae habeant Deum pro obiecto, peccata eis opposita important directe et principaliter aversionem a Deo. In quolibet autem peccato mortali principalis ratio mali et gravitas est ex hoc quod avertit a Deo, si enim posset esse conversio ad bonum commutabile sine aversione a Deo, quamvis esset inordinata, non esset peccatum mortale. Et ideo illud quod primo et per se habet aversionem a Deo est gravissimum inter peccata mortalia.

**OBJECTION 1**: It would seem that despair is not the greatest of sins. For there can be despair without unbelief, as stated above (A. 2). But unbelief is the greatest of sins because it overthrows the foundation of the spiritual edifice. Therefore despair is not the greatest of sins.

**OBJ. 2**: Further, a greater evil is opposed to a greater good, as the Philosopher states (*Ethic.* viii, 10). But charity is greater than hope, according to 1 Cor. 13:13. Therefore hatred of God is a greater sin than despair.

**OBJ. 3**: Further, in the sin of despair there is nothing but inordinate aversion from God: whereas in other sins there is not only inordinate aversion from God, but also an inordinate conversion. Therefore the sin of despair is not more but less grave than other sins.

**ON THE CONTRARY**, An incurable sin seems to be most grievous, according to Jer. 30:12: *Thy bruise is incurable, thy wound is very grievous*. Now the sin of despair is incurable, according to Jer. 15:18: *My wound is desperate so as to refuse to be healed*. Therefore despair is a most grievous sin.

**I ANSWER THAT**, Those sins which are contrary to the theological virtues are in themselves more grievous than others: because, since the theological virtues have God for their object, the sins which are opposed to them imply aversion from God directly and principally. Now every mortal sin takes its principal malice and gravity from the fact of its turning away from God, for if it were possible to turn to a mutable good, even inordinately, without turning away from God, it would not be a mortal sin. Consequently a sin which, first and of its very nature, includes aversion from God, is most grievous among mortal sins.

Virtutibus autem theologicis opponuntur infidelitas, desperatio et odium Dei. Inter quae odium et infidelitas, si desperationi comparentur, invenientur secundum se quidem, idest secundum rationem propriae speciei, graviora. Infidelitas enim provenit ex hoc quod homo ipsam Dei veritatem non credit; odium vero Dei provenit ex hoc quod voluntas hominis ipsi divinae bonitati contrariatur; desperatio autem ex hoc quod homo non sperat se bonitatem Dei participare. Ex quo patet quod infidelitas et odium Dei sunt contra Deum secundum quod in se est; desperatio autem secundum quod eius bonum participatur a nobis. Unde maius peccatum est, secundum se loquendo, non credere Dei veritatem, vel odire Deum, quam non sperare consequi gloriam ab ipso.

Sed si comparetur desperatio ad alia duo peccata ex parte nostra, sic desperatio est periculosior, quia per spem revocamur a malis et introducimur in bona prosequenda; et ideo, sublata spe, irrefrenate homines labuntur in vitia, et a bonis laboribus retrahuntur. Unde super illud Proverb. XXIV, *si desperaveris lapsus in die angustiae, minuetur fortitudo tua*, dicit Glossa, *nihil est execrabilius desperatione, quam qui habet et in generalibus huius vitae laboribus, et, quod peius est, in fidei certamine constantiam perdit*. Et Isidorus dicit, in libro de summo bono, *perpetrare flagitium aliquod mors animae est, sed desperare est descendere in Infernum*.

**ET PER HOC** patet responsio ad obiecta.

Now unbelief, despair and hatred of God are opposed to the theological virtues: and among them, if we compare hatred of God and unbelief to despair, we shall find that, in themselves, that is, in respect of their proper species, they are more grievous. For unbelief is due to a man not believing God's own truth; while the hatred of God arises from man's will being opposed to God's goodness itself; whereas despair consists in a man ceasing to hope for a share of God's goodness. Hence it is clear that unbelief and hatred of God are against God as He is in Himself, while despair is against Him, according as His good is partaken of by us. Wherefore strictly speaking it is a more grievous sin to disbelieve God's truth, or to hate God, than not to hope to receive glory from Him.

If, however, despair be compared to the other two sins from our point of view, then despair is more dangerous, since hope withdraws us from evils and induces us to seek for good things, so that when hope is given up, men rush headlong into sin, and are drawn away from good works. Wherefore a gloss on Prov. 24:10, *If thou lose hope being weary in the day of distress, thy strength shall be diminished*, says: *Nothing is more hateful than despair, for the man that has it loses his constancy both in the every day toils of this life, and, what is worse, in the battle of faith*. And Isidore says (*De Sum. Bono* ii, 14): *To commit a crime is to kill the soul, but to despair is to fall into hell*.

**THE RESPONSE** to the objections is evident.

# Article 4

*Whether despair arises from sloth?*

**AD QUARTUM SIC PROCEDITUR**. Videtur quod desperatio ex acedia non oriatur. Idem enim non procedit ex diversis causis. Desperatio autem futuri saeculi procedit ex luxuria; ut dicit Gregorius, XXXI Moral. Non ergo procedit ex acedia.

**PRAETEREA**, sicut spei opponitur desperatio, ita gaudio spirituali opponitur acedia. Sed gaudium spirituale procedit ex spe, secundum illud Rom. XII, *spe gaudentes*. Ergo acedia procedit ex desperatione, et non e converso.

**PRAETEREA**, contrariorum contrariae sunt causae. Sed spes, cui opponitur desperatio, videtur procedere ex consideratione divinorum beneficiorum, et maxime ex consideratione incarnationis, dicit enim Augustinus, XII de Trin., *nihil tam necessarium fuit ad erigendum spem nostram quam ut demonstraretur nobis quantum nos Deus diligeret. Quid vero huius rei isto indicio ma-*

**OBJECTION 1**: It would seem that despair does not arise from sloth. Because different causes do not give rise to one same effect. Now despair of the future life arises from lust, according to Gregory (*Moral.* xxxi, 45). Therefore it does not arise from sloth.

**OBJ. 2**: Further, just as despair is contrary to hope, so is sloth contrary to spiritual joy. But spiritual joy arises from hope, according to Romans, *rejoicing in hope* (12:12). Therefore sloth arises from despair, and not vice versa.

**OBJ. 3**: Further, contrary effects have contrary causes. Now hope, the contrary of which is despair, seems to proceed from the consideration of Divine favors, especially the Incarnation, for Augustine says (*De Trin.* xiii, 10): *Nothing was so necessary to raise our hope, than that we should be shown how much God loves us. Now what greater proof could we have of this than that God's Son should deign to unite*

*nifestius, quam quod Dei filius naturae nostrae dignatus est inire consortium?* Ergo desperatio magis procedit ex negligentia huius considerationis quam ex acedia.

**SED CONTRA** est quod Gregorius, XXXI Moral., desperationem enumerat inter ea quae procedunt ex acedia.

**RESPONDEO** dicendum quod, sicut supra dictum est, obiectum spei est bonum arduum possibile vel per se vel per alium. Dupliciter ergo potest in aliquo spes deficere de beatitudine obtinenda, uno modo, quia non reputat eam ut bonum arduum; alio modo, quia non reputat eam ut possibilem adipisci vel per se vel per alium. Ad hoc autem quod bona spiritualia non sapiunt nobis quasi bona, vel non videantur nobis magna bona, praecipue perducimur per hoc quod affectus noster est infectus amore delectationum corporalium, inter quas praecipuae sunt delectationes venereae, nam ex affectu harum delectationum contingit quod homo fastidit bona spiritualia, et non sperat ea quasi quaedam bona ardua. Et secundum hoc desperatio causatur ex luxuria.

Ad hoc autem quod aliquod bonum arduum non aestimet ut possibile sibi adipisci per se vel per alium, perducitur ex nimia deiectione; quae quando in affectu hominis dominatur, videtur ei quod nunquam possit ad aliquod bonum relevari. Et quia acedia est tristitia quaedam deiectiva spiritus, ideo per hunc modum desperatio ex acedia generatur.

Hoc autem est proprium obiectum spei, scilicet quod sit possibile, nam bonum et arduum etiam ad alias passiones pertinent. Unde specialius oritur ex acedia. Potest tamen oriri ex luxuria, ratione iam dicta.

**UNDE PATET** responsio ad primum.

**AD SECUNDUM** dicendum quod, sicut philosophus dicit, in II Rhetor., sicut spes facit delectationem, ita etiam homines in delectationibus existentes efficiuntur maioris spei. Et per hunc etiam modum homines in tristitiis existentes facilius in desperationem incidunt, secundum illud II ad Cor. II, *ne maiori tristitia absorbeatur qui eiusmodi est.* Sed tamen quia spei obiectum est bonum, in quod naturaliter tendit appetitus, non autem refugit ab eo naturaliter, sed solum propter aliquod impedimentum superveniens; ideo directius quidem ex spe oritur gaudium, desperatio autem e converso ex tristitia.

**AD TERTIUM** dicendum quod ipsa etiam negligentia considerandi divina beneficia ex acedia provenit. Homo enim affectus aliqua passione praecipue illa cogitat quae ad illam pertinent passionem. Unde homo in tristitiis constitutus non de facili aliqua magna et iucunda cogitat, sed solum tristia, nisi per magnum conatum se avertat a tristibus.

*Himself to our nature?* Therefore despair arises rather from the neglect of the above consideration than from sloth.

**ON THE CONTRARY,** Gregory (*Moral.* xxxi, 45) reckons despair among the effects of sloth.

**I ANSWER THAT,** As stated above (Q. 17, A. 1; I-II, Q. 40, A. 1), the object of hope is a good, difficult but possible to obtain by oneself or by another. Consequently the hope of obtaining happiness may be lacking in a person in two ways: first, through his not deeming it an arduous good; second, through his deeming it impossible to obtain either by himself, or by another. Now, the fact that spiritual goods taste good to us no more, or seem to be goods of no great account, is chiefly due to our affections being infected with the love of bodily pleasures, among which, sexual pleasures hold the first place: for the love of those pleasures leads man to have a distaste for spiritual things, and not to hope for them as arduous goods. In this way despair is caused by lust.

On the other hand, the fact that a man deems an arduous good impossible to obtain, either by himself or by another, is due to his being over downcast, because when this state of mind dominates his affections, it seems to him that he will never be able to rise to any good. And since sloth is a sadness that casts down the spirit, in this way despair is born of sloth.

Now this is the proper object of hope—that the thing is possible, because the good and the arduous regard other passions also. Hence despair is born of sloth in a more special way: though it may arise from lust, for the reason given above.

**THIS SUFFICES** for the Reply to the First Objection.

**REPLY OBJ. 2:** According to the Philosopher (*Rhet.* i, 11), just as hope gives rise to joy, so, when a man is joyful he has greater hope: and, accordingly, those who are sorrowful fall the more easily into despair, according to 2 Corinthians: *Lest . . . such an one be swallowed up by overmuch sorrow* (2:7). Yet, since the object of hope is good, to which the appetite tends naturally, and which it shuns, not naturally but only on account of some supervening obstacle, it follows that, more directly, hope gives birth to joy, while on the contrary despair is born of sorrow.

**REPLY OBJ. 3:** This very neglect to consider the Divine favors arises from sloth. For when a man is influenced by a certain passion he considers chiefly the things which pertain to that passion: so that a man who is full of sorrow does not easily think of great and joyful things, but only of sad things, unless by a great effort he turn his thoughts away from sadness.

# QUESTION 21

## PRESUMPTION

Deinde considerandum est de praesumptione. Et circa hoc quaeruntur quatuor.

Primo, quid sit obiectum praesumptionis cui innititur.

Secundo, utrum sit peccatum.

Tertio, cui opponatur.

Quarto, ex quo vitio oriatur.

We must now consider presumption, under which head there are four points of inquiry:

(1) What is the object in which presumption trusts?

(2) Whether presumption is a sin?

(3) To what is it opposed?

(4) From what vice does it arise?

# Article 1

*Whether presumption trusts in God or in our own power?*

**AD PRIMUM SIC PROCEDITUR.** Videtur quod praesumptio quae est peccatum in spiritum sanctum non innititur Deo, sed propriae virtuti. Quanto enim minor est virtus, tanto magis peccat qui ei nimis innititur. Sed minor est virtus humana quam divina. Ergo gravius peccat qui praesumit de virtute humana quam qui praesumit de virtute divina. Sed peccatum in spiritum sanctum est gravissimum. Ergo praesumptio quae ponitur species peccati in spiritum sanctum inhaeret virtuti humanae magis quam divinae.

**PRAETEREA,** ex peccato in spiritum sanctum alia peccata oriuntur, peccatum enim in spiritum sanctum dicitur malitia ex qua quis peccat. Sed magis videntur alia peccata oriri ex praesumptione qua homo praesumit de seipso quam ex praesumptione qua homo praesumit de Deo, quia amor sui est principium peccandi, ut patet per Augustinum, XIV de Civ. Dei. Ergo videtur quod praesumptio quae est peccatum in spiritum sanctum maxime innitatur virtuti humanae.

**PRAETEREA,** peccatum contingit ex conversione inordinata ad bonum commutabile. Sed praesumptio est quoddam peccatum. Ergo magis contingit ex conversione ad virtutem humanam, quae est bonum commutabile, quam ex conversione ad virtutem divinam, quae est bonum incommutabile.

**SED CONTRA** est quod sicut ex desperatione aliquis contemnit divinam misericordiam, cui spes innititur, ita ex praesumptione contemnit divinam iustitiam, quae peccatores punit. Sed sicut misericordia est in Deo, ita etiam et iustitia est in ipso. Ergo sicut desperatio est per aversionem a Deo, ita praesumptio est per inordinatam conversionem ad ipsum.

**RESPONDEO** dicendum quod praesumptio videtur importare quandam immoderantiam spei. Spei autem

**OBJECTION 1**: It would seem that presumption, which is a sin against the Holy Spirit, trusts, not in God, but in our own power. For the lesser the power, the more grievously does he sin who trusts in it too much. But man's power is less than God's. Therefore it is a more grievous sin to presume on human power than to presume on the power of God. Now the sin against the Holy Spirit is most grievous. Therefore presumption, which is reckoned a species of sin against the Holy Spirit, trusts to human rather than to Divine power.

**OBJ. 2**: Further, other sins arise from the sin against the Holy Spirit, for this sin is called malice which is a source from which sins arise. Now other sins seem to arise from the presumption whereby man presumes on himself rather than from the presumption whereby he presumes on God, since self-love is the origin of sin, according to Augustine (*De Civ. Dei* xiv, 28). Therefore it seems that presumption which is a sin against the Holy Spirit, relies chiefly on human power.

**OBJ. 3**: Further, sin arises from the inordinate conversion to a mutable good. Now presumption is a sin. Therefore it arises from turning to human power, which is a mutable good, rather than from turning to the power of God, which is an immutable good.

**ON THE CONTRARY**, Just as, through despair, a man despises the Divine mercy, on which hope relies, so, through presumption, he despises the Divine justice, which punishes the sinner. Now justice is in God even as mercy is. Therefore, just as despair consists in aversion from God, so presumption consists in inordinate conversion to Him.

**I ANSWER THAT**, Presumption seems to imply immoderate hope. Now the object of hope is an arduous possible

obiectum est bonum arduum possibile. Possibile autem est aliquid homini dupliciter, uno modo, per propriam virtutem; alio modo, non nisi per virtutem divinam. Circa utramque autem spem per immoderantiam potest esse praesumptio. Nam circa spem per quam aliquis de propria virtute confidit, attenditur praesumptio ex hoc quod aliquis tendit in aliquid ut sibi possibile quod suam facultatem excedit, secundum quod dicitur Iudith VI, *praesumentes de se humilias*. Et talis praesumptio opponitur virtuti magnanimitatis, quae medium tenet in huiusmodi spe.

Circa spem autem qua aliquis inhaeret divinae potentiae, potest per immoderantiam esse praesumptio in hoc quod aliquis tendit in aliquod bonum ut possibile per virtutem et misericordiam divinam quod possibile non est, sicut cum aliquis sperat se veniam obtinere sine poenitentia, vel gloriam sine meritis. Haec autem praesumptio est proprie species peccati in spiritum sanctum, quia scilicet per huiusmodi praesumptionem tollitur vel contemnitur adiutorium spiritus sancti per quod homo revocatur a peccato.

**AD PRIMUM** ergo dicendum quod, sicut supra dictum est, peccatum quod est contra Deum secundum suum genus est gravius ceteris peccatis. Unde praesumptio qua quis inordinate innititur Deo gravius peccatum est quam praesumptio qua quis innititur propriae virtuti. Quod enim aliquis innitatur divinae virtuti ad consequendum id quod Deo non convenit, hoc est diminuere divinam virtutem. Patet autem quod gravius peccat qui diminuit divinam virtutem quam qui propriam virtutem superextollit.

**AD SECUNDUM** dicendum quod ipsa etiam praesumptio qua quis de Deo inordinate praesumit amorem sui includit, quo quis proprium bonum inordinate desiderat. Quod enim multum desideramus, aestimamus nobis de facili per alios posse provenire, etiam si non possit.

**AD TERTIUM** dicendum quod praesumptio de divina misericordia habet et conversionem ad bonum commutabile, inquantum procedit ex desiderio inordinato proprii boni; et aversionem a bono incommutabili, inquantum attribuit divinae virtuti quod ei non convenit; per hoc enim avertitur homo a veritate divina.

good: and a thing is possible to a man in two ways: first by his own power; second, by the power of God alone. With regard to either hope there may be presumption owing to lack of moderation. As to the hope whereby a man relies on his own power, there is presumption if he tends to a good as though it were possible to him, whereas it surpasses his powers, according to Judith 6:15: *Thou humblest them that presume of themselves.* This presumption is contrary to the virtue of magnanimity which holds to the mean in this kind of hope.

But as to the hope whereby a man relies on the power of God, there may be presumption through immoderation, in the fact that a man tends to some good as though it were possible by the power and mercy of God, whereas it is not possible, for instance, if a man hope to obtain pardon without repenting, or glory without merits. This presumption is, properly, the sin against the Holy Spirit, because, to wit, by presuming thus a man removes or despises the assistance of the Holy Spirit, whereby he is withdrawn from sin.

**REPLY OBJ. 1**: As stated above (Q. 20, A. 3; I-II, Q. 73, A. 3) a sin which is against God is, in its genus, graver than other sins. Hence presumption whereby a man relies on God inordinately, is a more grievous sin than the presumption of trusting in one's own power, since to rely on the Divine power for obtaining what is unbecoming to God, is to depreciate the Divine power, and it is evident that it is a graver sin to detract from the Divine power than to exaggerate one's own.

**REPLY OBJ. 2**: The presumption whereby a man presumes inordinately on God, includes self-love, whereby he loves his own good inordinately. For when we desire a thing very much, we think we can easily procure it through others, even though we cannot.

**REPLY OBJ. 3**: Presumption on God's mercy implies both conversion to a mutable good, insofar as it arises from an inordinate desire of one's own good, and aversion from the immutable good, inasmuch as it ascribes to the Divine power that which is unbecoming to it, for thus man turns away from God's truth.

# Article 2

*Whether presumption is a sin?*

**AD SECUNDUM SIC PROCEDITUR.** Videtur quod praesumptio non sit peccatum. Nullum enim peccatum est ratio quod homo exaudiatur a Deo. Sed per praesumptionem aliqui exaudiuntur a Deo, dicitur enim

**OBJECTION 1**: It would seem that presumption is not a sin. For no sin is a reason why man should be heard by God. Yet, through presumption some are heard by God, for it is written (Jdt 9:17): *Hear me a poor wretch making*

Iudith IX, *exaudi me miseram deprecantem et de tua misericordia praesumentem*. Ergo praesumptio de divina misericordia non est peccatum.

**PRAETEREA**, praesumptio importat superexcessum spei. Sed in spe quae habetur de Deo non potest esse superexcessus, cum eius potentia et misericordia sint infinita. Ergo videtur quod praesumptio non sit peccatum.

**PRAETEREA**, id quod est peccatum non excusat a peccato. Sed praesumptio excusat a peccato, dicit enim Magister, XXII dist. II Lib. Sent., quod Adam minus peccavit quia sub spe veniae peccavit, quod videtur ad praesumptionem pertinere. Ergo praesumptio non est peccatum.

**SED CONTRA** est quod ponitur species peccati in spiritum sanctum.

**RESPONDEO** dicendum quod, sicut supra dictum est circa desperationem, omnis motus appetitivus qui conformiter se habet ad intellectum falsum est secundum se malus et peccatum. Praesumptio autem est motus quidam appetitivus, quia importat quandam spem inordinatam. Habet autem se conformiter intellectui falso, sicut et desperatio, sicut enim falsum est quod Deus poenitentibus non indulgeat, vel quod peccantes ad poenitentiam non convertat, ita falsum est quod in peccato perseverantibus veniam concedat, et a bono opere cessantibus gloriam largiatur; cui existimationi conformiter se habet praesumptionis motus.

Et ideo praesumptio est peccatum. Minus tamen quam desperatio, quanto magis proprium est Deo misereri et parcere quam punire, propter eius infinitam bonitatem. Illud enim secundum se Deo convenit, hoc autem propter nostra peccata.

**AD PRIMUM** ergo dicendum quod *praesumere* aliquando ponitur pro *sperare*, quia ipsa spes recta quae habetur de Deo praesumptio videtur si mensuretur secundum conditionem humanam. Non autem est praesumptio si attendatur immensitas bonitatis divinae.

**AD SECUNDUM** dicendum quod praesumptio non importat superexcessum spei ex hoc quod aliquis nimis speret de Deo, sed ex hoc quod sperat de Deo aliquid quod Deo non convenit. Quod etiam est minus sperare de eo, quia hoc est eius virtutem quodammodo diminuere, ut dictum est.

**AD TERTIUM** dicendum quod peccare cum proposito perseverandi in peccato sub spe veniae ad praesumptionem pertinet. Et hoc non diminuit, sed auget peccatum. Peccare autem sub spe veniae quandoque percipiendae cum proposito abstinendi a peccato et poenitendi de ipso, hoc non est praesumptionis, sed hoc peccatum diminuit, quia per hoc videtur habere voluntatem minus firmatam ad peccandum.

*supplication to Thee, and presuming of Thy mercy.* Therefore presumption on God's mercy is not a sin.

**OBJ. 2**: Further, presumption denotes excessive hope. But there cannot be excess of that hope which is in God, since His power and mercy are infinite. Therefore it seems that presumption is not a sin.

**OBJ. 3**: Further, that which is a sin does not excuse from sin: for the Master says (*Sent.* ii, D, 22) that Adam sinned less, because he sinned in the hope of pardon, which seems to indicate presumption. Therefore presumption is not a sin.

**ON THE CONTRARY**, It is reckoned a species of sin against the Holy Spirit.

**I ANSWER THAT**, As stated above (Q. 20, A. 1) with regard to despair, every appetitive movement that is conformed to a false intellect, is evil in itself and sinful. Now presumption is an appetitive movement, since it denotes an inordinate hope. Moreover it is conformed to a false intellect, just as despair is: for just as it is false that God does not pardon the repentant, or that He does not turn sinners to repentance, so is it false that He grants forgiveness to those who persevere in their sins, and that He gives glory to those who cease from good works: and it is to this estimate that the movement of presumption is conformed.

Consequently presumption is a sin, but less grave than despair, since, on account of His infinite goodness, it is more proper to God to have mercy and to spare, than to punish: for the former becomes God in Himself, the latter becomes Him by reason of our sins.

**REPLY OBJ. 1**: *Presumption* sometimes stands for *hope*, because even the right hope which we have in God seems to be presumption, if it be measured according to man's estate: yet it is not, if we look at the immensity of the goodness of God.

**REPLY OBJ. 2**: Presumption does not denote excessive hope, as though man hoped too much in God; but through man hoping to obtain from God something unbecoming to Him; which is the same as to hope too little in Him, since it implies a depreciation of His power; as stated above (A. 1, ad 1).

**REPLY OBJ. 3**: To sin with the intention of persevering in sin and through the hope of being pardoned, is presumptuous, and this does not diminish, but increases sin. To sin, however, with the hope of obtaining pardon some time, and with the intention of refraining from sin and of repenting of it, is not presumptuous, but diminishes sin, because this seems to indicate a will less hardened in sin.

# Article 3

*Whether presumption is more opposed to fear than to hope?*

AD TERTIUM SIC PROCEDITUR. Videtur quod praesumptio magis opponatur timori quam spei. Inordinatio enim timoris opponitur recto timori. Sed praesumptio videtur ad inordinationem timoris pertinere, dicitur enim Sap. XVII, *semper praesumit saeva perturbata conscientia*; et ibidem dicitur quod *timor est praesumptionis adiutorium*. Ergo praesumptio opponitur timori magis quam spei.

PRAETEREA, contraria sunt quae maxime distant. Sed praesumptio magis distat a timore quam a spe, quia praesumptio importat motum ad rem, sicut et spes; timor autem motum a re. Ergo praesumptio magis contrariatur timori quam spei.

PRAETEREA, praesumptio totaliter excludit timorem, non autem totaliter excludit spem, sed solum rectitudinem spei. Cum ergo opposita sint quae se interimunt, videtur quod praesumptio magis opponatur timori quam spei.

SED CONTRA est quod duo invicem opposita vitia contrariantur uni virtuti, sicut timiditas et audacia fortitudini. Sed peccatum praesumptionis contrariatur peccato desperationis, quod directe opponitur spei. Ergo videtur quod etiam praesumptio directius spei opponatur.

RESPONDEO dicendum quod, sicut Augustinus dicit, in IV contra Iulian., *omnibus virtutibus non solum sunt vitia manifesta discretione contraria, sicut prudentiae temeritas, verum etiam vicina quodammodo, nec veritate, sed quadam specie fallente similia, sicut prudentiae astutia*. Et hoc etiam philosophus dicit, in II Ethic., quod virtus maiorem convenientiam videtur habere cum uno oppositorum vitiorum quam cum alio, sicut temperantia cum insensibilitate et fortitudo cum audacia.

Praesumptio igitur manifestam oppositionem videtur habere ad timorem, praecipue servilem, qui respicit poenam ex Dei iustitia provenientem, cuius remissionem praesumptio sperat. Sed secundum quandam falsam similitudinem magis contrariatur spei, quia importat quandam inordinatam spem de Deo. Et quia directius aliqua opponuntur quae sunt unius generis quam quae sunt generum diversorum (nam contraria sunt in eodem genere), ideo directius praesumptio opponitur spei quam timori, utrumque enim respicit idem obiectum cui innititur, sed spes ordinate, praesumptio inordinate.

AD PRIMUM ergo dicendum quod sicut spes abusive dicitur de malo, proprie autem de bono, ita etiam praesumptio. Et secundum hunc modum inordinatio timoris praesumptio dicitur.

OBJECTION 1: It would seem that presumption is more opposed to fear than to hope. Because inordinate fear is opposed to right fear. Now presumption seems to pertain to inordinate fear, for it is written (Wis 17:10): *A troubled conscience always presumes grievous things*, and (Wis 17:11) that *fear is a help to presumption*. Therefore presumption is opposed to fear rather than to hope.

OBJ. 2: Further, contraries are most distant from one another. Now presumption is more distant from fear than from hope, because presumption implies movement to something, just as hope does, whereas fear denotes movement from a thing. Therefore presumption is contrary to fear rather than to hope.

OBJ. 3: Further, presumption excludes fear altogether, whereas it does not exclude hope altogether, but only the rectitude of hope. Since therefore contraries destroy one another, it seems that presumption is contrary to fear rather than to hope.

ON THE CONTRARY, When two vices are opposed to one another they are contrary to the same virtue, as timidity and audacity are opposed to fortitude. Now the sin of presumption is contrary to the sin of despair, which is directly opposed to hope. Therefore it seems that presumption also is more directly opposed to hope.

I ANSWER THAT, As Augustine states (*Contra Julian.* iv, 3), *every virtue not only has a contrary vice manifestly distinct from it, as temerity is opposed to prudence, but also a sort of kindred vice, alike, not in truth but only in its deceitful appearance, as cunning is opposed to prudence*. This agrees with the Philosopher who says (*Ethic.* ii, 8) that a virtue seems to have more in common with one of the contrary vices than with the other, as temperance with insensibility, and fortitude with audacity.

Accordingly presumption appears to be manifestly opposed to fear, especially servile fear, which looks at the punishment arising from God's justice, the remission of which presumption hopes for; yet by a kind of false likeness it is more opposed to hope, since it denotes an inordinate hope in God. And since things are more directly opposed when they belong to the same genus, than when they belong to different genera, it follows that presumption is more directly opposed to hope than to fear. For they both regard and rely on the same object, hope ordinately, presumption inordinately.

REPLY OBJ. 1: Just as hope is misused in speaking of evils, and properly applied in speaking of good, so is presumption: it is in this way that inordinate fear is called presumption.

**AD SECUNDUM** dicendum quod contraria sunt quae maxime distant in eodem genere. Praesumptio autem et spes important motum eiusdem generis, qui potest esse vel ordinatus vel inordinatus. Et ideo praesumptio directius contrariatur spei quam timori, nam spei contrariatur ratione propriae differentiae, sicut inordinatum ordinato; timori autem contrariatur ratione differentiae sui generis, scilicet motus spei.

**AD TERTIUM** dicendum quod quia praesumptio contrariatur timori contrarietate generis, virtuti autem spei contrarietate differentiae, ideo praesumptio excludit totaliter timorem etiam secundum genus, spem autem non excludit nisi ratione differentiae, excludendo eius ordinationem.

**REPLY OBJ. 2**: Contraries are things that are most distant from one another within the same genus. Now presumption and hope denote a movement of the same genus, which can be either ordinate or inordinate. Hence presumption is more directly opposed to hope than to fear, since it is opposed to hope in respect of its specific difference, as an inordinate thing to an ordinate one, whereas it is opposed to fear, in respect of its generic difference, which is the movement of hope.

**REPLY OBJ. 3**: Presumption is opposed to fear by a generic contrariety, and to the virtue of hope by a specific contrariety. Hence presumption excludes fear altogether even generically, whereas it does not exclude hope except by reason of its difference, by excluding its ordinateness.

# Article 4

### Whether presumption arises from vainglory?

**AD QUARTUM SIC PROCEDITUR**. Videtur quod praesumptio non causetur ex inani gloria. Praesumptio enim maxime videtur inniti divinae misericordiae. Misericordia autem respicit miseriam, quae opponitur gloriae. Ergo praesumptio non oritur ex inani gloria.

**PRAETEREA**, praesumptio opponitur desperationi. Sed desperatio oritur ex tristitia, ut dictum est. Cum igitur oppositorum oppositae sint causae, videtur quod oriatur ex delectatione. Et ita videtur quod oriatur ex vitiis carnalibus, quorum delectationes sunt vehementiores.

**PRAETEREA**, vitium praesumptionis consistit in hoc quod aliquis tendit in aliquod bonum quod non est possibile, quasi possibile. Sed quod aliquis aestimet possibile quod est impossibile, provenit ex ignorantia. Ergo praesumptio magis provenit ex ignorantia quam ex inani gloria.

**SED CONTRA** est quod Gregorius dicit, XXXI Moral., quod *praesumptio novitatum* est filia inanis gloriae.

**RESPONDEO** dicendum quod, sicut supra dictum est, duplex est praesumptio. Una quidem quae innititur propriae virtuti, attentans scilicet aliquid ut sibi possibile quod propriam virtutem excedit. Et talis praesumptio manifeste ex inani gloria procedit, ex hoc enim quod aliquis multam desiderat gloriam, sequitur quod attentet ad gloriam quaedam super vires suas. Et huiusmodi praecipue sunt nova, quae maiorem admirationem habent. Et ideo signanter Gregorius *praesumptionem novitatum* posuit filiam inanis gloriae.

Alia vero est praesumptio quae innititur inordinate divinae misericordiae vel potentiae, per quam sperat se obtinere gloriam sine meritis et veniam sine poenitentia. Et talis praesumptio videtur oriri directe ex superbia, ac

**OBJECTION 1**: It would seem that presumption does not arise from vainglory. For presumption seems to rely most of all on the Divine mercy. Now mercy (*misericordia*) regards unhappiness (*miseriam*) which is contrary to glory. Therefore presumption does not arise from vainglory.

**OBJ. 2**: Further, presumption is opposed to despair. Now despair arises from sorrow, as stated above (Q. 20, A. 4, ad 2). Since therefore opposites have opposite causes, presumption would seem to arise from pleasure, and consequently from sins of the flesh, which give the most absorbing pleasure.

**OBJ. 3**: Further, the vice of presumption consists in tending to some impossible good, as though it were possible. Now it is owing to ignorance that one deems an impossible thing to be possible. Therefore presumption arises from ignorance rather than from vainglory.

**ON THE CONTRARY**, Gregory says (*Moral.* xxxi, 45) that *presumption of novelties* is a daughter of vainglory.

**I ANSWER THAT**, As stated above (A. 1), presumption is twofold; one whereby a man relies on his own power, when he attempts something beyond his power, as though it were possible to him. Such like presumption clearly arises from vainglory; for it is owing to a great desire for glory, that a man attempts things beyond his power, and especially novelties which call for greater admiration. Hence Gregory states explicitly that *presumption of novelties* is a daughter of vainglory.

The other presumption is an inordinate trust in the Divine mercy or power, consisting in the hope of obtaining glory without merits, or pardon without repentance. Such like presumption seems to arise directly from pride, as

si ipse tanti se aestimet quod etiam eum peccantem Deus non puniat vel a gloria excludat.

**ET PER HOC** patet responsio ad obiecta.

though man thought so much of himself as to esteem that God would not punish him or exclude him from glory, however much he might be a sinner.

**THIS SUFFICES** for the Replies to the Objections.

# QUESTION 22

## THE PRECEPTS RELATING TO HOPE AND FEAR

Deinde considerandum est de praeceptis pertinentibus ad spem et timorem. Et circa hoc quaeruntur duo.

Primo, de praeceptis pertinentibus ad spem.

Secundo, de praeceptis pertinentibus ad timorem.

We must now consider the precepts relating to hope and fear: under which head there are two points of inquiry:

(1) The precepts relating to hope;

(2) The precepts relating to fear.

# Article 1

### Whether a precept of hope should be given?

**AD PRIMUM SIC PROCEDITUR**. Videtur quod nullum praeceptum sit dandum pertinens ad virtutem spei. Quod enim potest sufficienter fieri per unum, non oportet quod ad id aliquid aliud inducatur. Sed ad sperandum bonum sufficienter homo inducitur ex ipsa naturali inclinatione. Ergo non oportet quod ad hoc inducatur homo per legis praeceptum.

**PRAETEREA**, cum praecepta dentur de actibus virtutum, principalia praecepta debent dari de actibus principalium virtutum. Sed inter omnes virtutes principaliores sunt tres virtutes theologicae, scilicet spes, fides et caritas. Cum igitur principalia legis praecepta sint praecepta Decalogi, ad quae omnia alia reducuntur, ut supra habitum est; videtur quod, si de spe daretur aliquod praeceptum, quod deberet inter praecepta Decalogi contineri. Non autem continetur. Ergo videtur quod nullum praeceptum in lege debeat dari de actu spei.

**PRAETEREA**, eiusdem rationis est praecipere actum virtutis et prohibere actum vitii oppositi. Sed non invenitur aliquod praeceptum datum per quod prohibeatur desperatio, quae est opposita spei. Ergo videtur quod nec de spe conveniat aliquod praeceptum dari.

**SED CONTRA** est quod Augustinus dicit, super illud Ioan. XV, *hoc est praeceptum meum, ut diligatis invicem, de fide nobis quam multa mandata sunt; quam multa de spe.* Ergo de spe convenit aliqua praecepta dari.

**RESPONDEO** dicendum quod praeceptorum quae in sacra Scriptura inveniuntur quaedam sunt de substantia legis; quaedam vero sunt praeambula ad legem. Praeambula quidem sunt ad legem illa quibus non existentibus lex locum habere non potest. Huiusmodi autem sunt praecepta de actu fidei et de actu spei, quia per actum fidei mens hominis inclinatur ut recognoscat auctorem legis talem cui se subdere debeat; per spem vero praemii homo inducitur ad observantiam praeceptorum. Praecepta vero de substantia legis sunt quae homini

**OBJECTION 1**: It would seem that no precept should be given relating to the virtue of hope. For when an effect is sufficiently procured by one cause, there is no need to induce it by another. Now man is sufficiently induced by his natural inclination to hope for good. Therefore there is no need of a precept of the Law to induce him to do this.

**OBJ. 2**: Further, since precepts are given about acts of virtue, the chief precepts are about the acts of the chief virtues. Now the chief of all the virtues are the three theological virtues, viz. hope, faith and charity. Consequently, as the chief precepts of the Law are those of the decalogue, to which all others may be reduced, as stated above (I-II, Q. 100, A. 3), it seems that if any precept of hope were given, it should be found among the precepts of the decalogue. But it is not to be found there. Therefore it seems that the Law should contain no precept of hope.

**OBJ. 3**: Further, to prescribe an act of virtue is equivalent to a prohibition of the act of the opposite vice. Now no precept is to be found forbidding despair which is contrary to hope. Therefore it seems that the Law should contain no precept of hope.

**ON THE CONTRARY**, Augustine says on John 15:12, *This is My commandment, that you love one another (Tract. lxxxiii in Joan.)*: *How many things are commanded us about faith! How many relating to hope!* Therefore it is fitting that some precepts should be given about hope.

**I ANSWER THAT**, Among the precepts contained in Holy Writ, some belong to the substance of the Law, others are preambles to the Law. The preambles to the Law are those without which no law is possible: such are the precepts relating to the act of faith and the act of hope, because the act of faith inclines man's mind so that he believes the Author of the Law to be One to Whom he owes submission, while, by the hope of a reward, he is induced to observe the precepts. The precepts that belong to the substance of the Law are those which relate to right conduct

199

iam subiecto et ad obediendum parato imponuntur, pertinentia ad rectitudinem vitae. Et ideo huiusmodi praecepta statim in ipsa legis latione proponuntur per modum praeceptorum.

Spei vero et fidei praecepta non erant proponenda per modum praeceptorum, quia nisi homo iam crederet et speraret, frustra ei lex proponeretur. Sed sicut praeceptum fidei proponendum fuit per modum denuntiationis vel commemorationis, ut supra dictum est; ita etiam praeceptum spei in prima legis latione proponendum fuit per modum promissionis, qui enim obedientibus praemia promittit, ex hoc ipso incitat ad spem. Unde omnia promissa quae in lege continentur sunt spei excitativa.

Sed quia, lege iam posita, pertinet ad sapientes viros ut non solum inducant homines ad observantiam praeceptorum, sed etiam multo magis ad conservandum legis fundamentum; ideo post primam legis lationem in sacra Scriptura multipliciter inducuntur homines ad sperandum, etiam per modum admonitionis vel praecepti, et non solum per modum promissionis, sicut in lege, sicut patet in Psalm., *sperate in eo omnes congregationes populi*, et in multis aliis Scripturae locis.

**AD PRIMUM** ergo dicendum quod natura sufficienter inclinat ad sperandum bonum naturae humanae proportionatum. Sed ad sperandum supernaturale bonum oportuit hominem induci auctoritate legis divinae, partim quidem promissis, partim autem admonitionibus vel praeceptis. Et tamen ad ea etiam ad quae naturalis ratio inclinat, sicut sunt actus virtutum moralium, necessarium fuit praecepta legis divinae dari, propter maiorem firmitatem; et praecipue quia naturalis ratio hominis obtenebrata erat per concupiscentias peccati.

**AD SECUNDUM** dicendum quod praecepta Decalogi pertinent ad primam legis lationem. Et ideo inter praecepta Decalogi non fuit dandum praeceptum aliquod de spe, sed suffecit per aliquas promissiones positas inducere ad spem, ut patet in primo et quarto praecepto.

**AD TERTIUM** dicendum quod in illis ad quorum observationem homo tenetur ex ratione debiti, sufficit praeceptum affirmativum dari de eo quod faciendum est, in quibus prohibitiones eorum quae sunt vitanda intelliguntur. Sicut datur praeceptum de honoratione parentum, non autem prohibetur quod parentes dehonorentur, nisi per hoc quod dehonorantibus poena adhibetur in lege. Et quia debitum est ad humanam salutem ut speret homo de Deo, fuit ad hoc homo inducendus aliquo praedictorum modorum quasi affirmative, in quo intelligeretur prohibitio oppositi.

and are imposed on man already subject and ready to obey: wherefore when the Law was given these precepts were set forth from the very outset under the form of a command.

Yet the precepts of hope and faith were not to be given under the form of a command, since, unless man already believed and hoped, it would be useless to give him the Law: but, just as the precept of faith had to be given under the form of an announcement or reminder, as stated above (Q. 16, A. 1), so too, the precept of hope, in the first promulgation of the Law, had to be given under the form of a promise. For he who promises rewards to them that obey him, by that very fact, urges them to hope: hence all the promises contained in the Law are incitements to hope.

Since, however, when once the Law has been given, it is for a wise man to induce men not only to observe the precepts, but also, and much more, to safeguard the foundation of the Law, therefore, after the first promulgation of the Law, Holy Writ holds out to man many inducements to hope, even by way of warning or command, and not merely by way of promise, as in the Law; for instance, in the Ps. 61:9: *Hope in Him all ye congregation of the people*, and in many other passages of the Scriptures.

**REPLY OBJ. 1**: Nature inclines us to hope for the good which is proportionate to human nature; but for man to hope for a supernatural good he had to be induced by the authority of the Divine law, partly by promises, partly by admonitions and commands. Nevertheless there was need for precepts of the Divine law to be given even for those things to which natural reason inclines us, such as the acts of the moral virtues, for sake of insuring a greater stability, especially since the natural reason of man was clouded by the lusts of sin.

**REPLY OBJ. 2**: The precepts of the law of the decalogue belong to the first promulgation of the Law: hence there was no need for a precept of hope among the precepts of the decalogue, and it was enough to induce men to hope by the inclusion of certain promises, as in the case of the first and fourth commandments.

**REPLY OBJ. 3**: In those observances to which man is bound as under a duty, it is enough that he receive an affirmative precept as to what he has to do, wherein is implied the prohibition of what he must avoid doing: thus he is given a precept concerning the honor due to parents, but not a prohibition against dishonoring them, except by the law inflicting punishment on those who dishonor their parents. And since in order to be saved it is man's duty to hope in God, he had to be induced to do so by one of the above ways, affirmatively, so to speak, wherein is implied the prohibition of the opposite.

# Article 2

*Whether, in the Law, there should have been given a precept of fear?*

**Ad secundum sic proceditur.** Videtur quod de timore non fuerit dandum aliquod praeceptum in lege. Timor enim Dei est de his quae sunt praeambula ad legem, cum sit *initium sapientiae.* Sed ea quae sunt praeambula ad legem non cadunt sub praeceptis legis. Ergo de timore non est dandum aliquod praeceptum legis.

**Praeterea,** posita causa ponitur effectus. Sed amor est causa timoris, omnis enim timor ex aliquo amore procedit, ut Augustinus dicit, in libro octoginta trium quaest. Ergo, posito praecepto de amore, superfluum fuisset praecipere timorem.

**Praeterea,** timori aliquo modo opponitur praesumptio. Sed nulla prohibitio invenitur in lege de praesumptione data. Ergo videtur quod nec de timore aliquod praeceptum dari debuerit.

**Sed contra** est quod dicitur Deut. X, *et nunc, Israel, quid dominus Deus tuus petit a te, nisi ut timeas dominum Deum tuum?* Sed illud a nobis requirit quod nobis praecipit observandum. Ergo sub praecepto cadit quod aliquis timeat Deum.

**Respondeo** dicendum quod duplex est timor, scilicet servilis et filialis. Sicut autem aliquis inducitur ad observantiam praeceptorum legis per spem praemiorum, ita etiam inducitur ad legis observantiam per timorem poenarum, qui est timor servilis.

Et ideo sicut, secundum praedicta, in ipsa legis latione non fuit praeceptum dandum de actu spei, sed ad hoc fuerunt homines inducendi per promissa; ita nec de timore qui respicit poenam fuit praeceptum dandum per modum praecepti, sed ad hoc fuerunt homines inducendi per comminationem poenarum. Quod fuit factum et in ipsis praeceptis Decalogi, et postmodum consequenter in secundariis legis praeceptis.

Sed sicut sapientes et prophetae consequenter, intendentes homines stabilire in obedientia legis, documenta tradiderunt de spe per modum admonitionis vel praecepti, ita etiam et de timore.

Sed timor filialis, qui reverentiam exhibet Deo, est quasi quoddam genus ad dilectionem Dei, et principium quoddam omnium eorum quae in Dei reverentiam observantur. Et ideo de timore filiali dantur praecepta in lege sicut et de dilectione, quia utrumque est praeambulum ad exteriores actus qui praecipiuntur in lege, ad quos pertinent praecepta Decalogi. Et ideo in auctoritate legis inducta requiritur ab homine timor, et *ut ambulet in viis* Dei colendo ipsum, et *ut diligat ipsum.*

**Objection 1**: It would seem that, in the Law, there should not have been given a precept of fear. For the fear of God is about things which are a preamble to the Law, since it is the *beginning of wisdom.* Now things which are a preamble to the Law do not come under a precept of the Law. Therefore no precept of fear should be given in the Law.

**Obj. 2**: Further, given the cause, the effect is also given. Now love is the cause of fear, since every fear proceeds from some kind of love, as Augustine states (*83 Questions,* qu. 33). Therefore given the precept of love, it would have been superfluous to command fear.

**Obj. 3**: Further, presumption, in a way, is opposed to fear. But the Law contains no prohibition against presumption. Therefore it seems that neither should any precept of fear have been given.

**On the contrary**, It is written (Deut 10:12): *And now, Israel, what doth the Lord thy God require of thee, but that thou fear the Lord thy God?* But He requires of us that which He commands us to do. Therefore it is a matter of precept that man should fear God.

**I answer that,** Fear is twofold, servile and filial. Now just as man is induced, by the hope of rewards, to observe precepts of law, so too is he induced thereto by the fear of punishment, which fear is servile.

And just as according to what has been said (A. 1), in the promulgation of the Law there was no need for a precept of the act of hope, and men were to be induced thereto by promises, so neither was there need for a precept, under form of command, of fear which regards punishment, and men were to be induced thereto by the threat of punishment: and this was realized both in the precepts of the decalogue, and afterwards, in due sequence, in the secondary precepts of the Law.

Yet, just as wise men and the prophets who, consequently, strove to strengthen man in the observance of the Law, delivered their teaching about hope under the form of admonition or command, so too did they in the matter of fear.

On the other hand filial fear which shows reverence to God, is a sort of genus in respect of the love of God, and a kind of principle of all observances connected with reverence for God. Hence precepts of filial fear are given in the Law, even as precepts of love, because each is a preamble to the external acts prescribed by the Law and to which the precepts of the decalogue refer. Hence in the passage quoted in the argument On the contrary, man is required *to have fear, to walk in God's ways,* by worshipping Him, and *to love Him.*

**AD PRIMUM** ergo dicendum quod timor filialis est quoddam praeambulum ad legem non sicut extrinsecum aliquid, sed sicut principium legis, sicut etiam dilectio. Et ideo de utroque dantur praecepta, quae sunt quasi quaedam principia communia totius legis.

**AD SECUNDUM** dicendum quod ex amore sequitur timor filialis, sicut etiam et alia bona opera quae ex caritate fiunt. Et ideo sicut post praeceptum caritatis dantur praecepta de aliis actibus virtutum, ita etiam simul dantur praecepta de timore et amore caritatis. Sicut etiam in scientiis demonstrativis non sufficit ponere principia prima, nisi etiam ponantur conclusiones quae ex his sequuntur vel proxime vel remote.

**AD TERTIUM** dicendum quod inductio ad timorem sufficit ad excludendum praesumptionem, sicut etiam inductio ad spem sufficit ad excludendum desperationem, ut dictum est.

**REPLY OBJ. 1**: Filial fear is a preamble to the Law, not as though it were extrinsic thereto, but as being the beginning of the Law, just as love is. Hence precepts are given of both, since they are like general principles of the whole Law.

**REPLY OBJ. 2**: From love proceeds filial fear as also other good works that are done from charity. Hence, just as after the precept of charity, precepts are given of the other acts of virtue, so at the same time precepts are given of fear and of the love of charity, just as, in demonstrative sciences, it is not enough to lay down the first principles, unless the conclusions also are given which follow from them proximately or remotely.

**REPLY OBJ. 3**: Inducement to fear suffices to exclude presumption, even as inducement to hope suffices to exclude despair, as stated above (A. 1, ad 3).

# QUESTION 23

## CHARITY, CONSIDERED IN ITSELF

Consequenter considerandum est de caritate. Et primo, de ipsa caritate; secundo, de dono sapientiae ei correspondente. Circa primum consideranda sunt quinque, primo, de ipsa caritate; secundo, de obiecto caritatis; tertio, de actibus eius; quarto, de vitiis oppositis; quinto, de praeceptis ad hoc pertinentibus.

Circa primum est duplex consideratio, prima quidem de ipsa caritate secundum se; secunda de caritate per comparationem ad subiectum. Circa primum quaeruntur octo.

Primo, utrum caritas sit amicitia.

Secundo, utrum sit aliquid creatum in anima.

Tertio, utrum sit virtus.

Quarto, utrum sit virtus specialis.

Quinto, utrum sit una virtus.

Sexto, utrum sit maxima virtutum.

Septimo, utrum sine ea possit esse aliqua vera virtus.

Octavo, utrum sit forma virtutum.

In proper sequence, we must consider charity; and (1) charity itself; (2) the corresponding gift of wisdom. The first consideration will be fivefold: (1) Charity itself; (2) The object of charity; (3) Its acts; (4) The opposite vices; (5) The precepts relating thereto.

The first of these considerations will be twofold: (1) Charity, considered as regards itself; (2) Charity, considered in its relation to its subject. Under the first head there are eight points of inquiry:

(1) Whether charity is friendship?

(2) Whether it is something created in the soul?

(3) Whether it is a virtue?

(4) Whether it is a special virtue?

(5) Whether it is one virtue?

(6) Whether it is the greatest of the virtues?

(7) Whether any true virtue is possible without it?

(8) Whether it is the form of the virtues?

# Article 1

*Whether charity is friendship?*

**AD PRIMUM SIC PROCEDITUR**. Videtur quod caritas non sit amicitia. *Nihil enim est ita proprium amicitiae sicut convivere amico*; ut Philosophus dicit, in VIII Ethic. Sed caritas est hominis ad Deum et ad Angelos, *quorum non est cum hominibus conversatio*, ut dicitur Dan. II. Ergo caritas non est amicitia.

**PRAETEREA**, amicitia non est sine reamatione, ut dicitur in VIII Ethic. Sed caritas habetur etiam ad inimicos, secundum illud Matth. V, *diligite inimicos vestros*. Ergo caritas non est amicitia.

**PRAETEREA**, amicitiae tres sunt species, secundum philosophum, in VIII Ethic., scilicet amicitia *delectabilis, utilis* et *honesti*. Sed caritas non est amicitia utilis aut delectabilis, dicit enim Hieronymus, in Epist. ad Paulinum, quae ponitur in principio Bibliae, *illa est vera necessitudo, et Christi glutino copulata, quam non utilitas rei familiaris, non praesentia tantum corporum, non subdola et palpans adulatio, sed Dei timor et divinarum Scripturarum studia conciliant*. Similiter etiam non est amicitia honesti, quia caritate diligimus etiam peccatores; amicitia vero honesti non est nisi ad virtuosos, ut dicitur in VIII Ethic. Ergo caritas non est amicitia.

**OBJECTION 1**: It would seem that charity is not friendship. For *nothing is so appropriate to friendship as to dwell with one's friend*, according to the Philosopher (*Ethic.* viii, 5). Now charity is of man towards God and the angels, *whose dwelling is not with men* (Dan 2:11). Therefore charity is not friendship.

**OBJ. 2**: Further, there is no friendship without return of love (*Ethic.* viii, 2). But charity extends even to one's enemies, according to Matt. 5:44: *Love your enemies*. Therefore charity is not friendship.

**OBJ. 3**: Further, according to the Philosopher (*Ethic.* viii, 3) there are three kinds of friendship, directed respectively towards the delightful, the useful, or the virtuous. Now charity is not the friendship for the useful or delightful; for Jerome says in his letter to Paulinus which is to be found at the beginning of the Bible: *True friendship cemented by Christ, is where men are drawn together, not by household interests, not by mere bodily presence, not by crafty and cajoling flattery, but by the fear of God, and the study of the Divine Scriptures*. No more is it friendship for the virtuous, since by charity we love even sinners, whereas friendship based on the virtuous is only for virtuous men (*Ethic.* viii). Therefore charity is not friendship.

SED CONTRA est quod Ioan. XV dicitur, *iam non dicam vos servos, sed amicos meos.* Sed hoc non dicebatur eis nisi ratione caritatis. Ergo caritas est amicitia.

RESPONDEO dicendum quod, secundum Philosophum, in VIII Ethic., non quilibet amor habet rationem amicitiae, sed amor qui est cum benevolentia, quando scilicet sic amamus aliquem ut ei bonum velimus. Si autem rebus amatis non bonum velimus, sed ipsum eorum bonum velimus nobis, sicut dicimur amare vinum aut equum aut aliquid huiusmodi, non est amor amicitiae, sed cuiusdam concupiscentiae, ridiculum enim est dicere quod aliquis habeat amicitiam ad vinum vel ad equum.

Sed nec benevolentia sufficit ad rationem amicitiae, sed requiritur quaedam mutua amatio, quia amicus est amico amicus. Talis autem mutua benevolentia fundatur super aliqua communicatione.

Cum igitur sit aliqua communicatio hominis ad Deum secundum quod nobis suam beatitudinem communicat, super hac communicatione oportet aliquam amicitiam fundari. De qua quidem communicatione dicitur I ad Cor. I, *fidelis Deus, per quem vocati estis in societatem filii eius.* Amor autem super hac communicatione fundatus est caritas. Unde manifestum est quod caritas amicitia quaedam est hominis ad Deum.

AD PRIMUM ergo dicendum quod duplex est hominis vita. Una quidem exterior secundum naturam sensibilem et corporalem, et secundum hanc vitam non est nobis communicatio vel conversatio cum Deo et Angelis.

Alia autem est vita hominis spiritualis secundum mentem. Et secundum hanc vitam est nobis conversatio et cum Deo et cum Angelis. In praesenti quidem statu imperfecte, unde dicitur Philipp. III, *nostra conversatio in caelis est.* Sed ista conversatio perficietur in patria, quando *servi eius servient Deo et videbunt faciem eius,* ut dicitur Apoc. ult. Et ideo hic est caritas imperfecta, sed perficietur in patria.

AD SECUNDUM dicendum quod amicitia se extendit ad aliquem dupliciter. Uno modo, respectu sui ipsius, et sic amicitia nunquam est nisi ad amicum. Alio modo se extendit ad aliquem respectu alterius personae, sicut, si aliquis habet amicitiam ad aliquem hominem, ratione eius diligit omnes ad illum hominem pertinentes, sive filios sive servos sive qualitercumque ei attinentes.

Et tanta potest esse dilectio amici quod propter amicum amantur hi qui ad ipsum pertinent etiam si nos offendant vel odiant. Et hoc modo amicitia caritatis se extendit etiam ad inimicos, quos diligimus ex caritate in ordine ad Deum, ad quem principaliter habetur amicitia caritatis.

AD TERTIUM dicendum quod amicitia honesti non habetur nisi ad virtuosum sicut ad principalem perso-

ON THE CONTRARY, It is written (John 15:15): *I will not now call you servants . . . but My friends.* Now this was said to them by reason of nothing else than charity. Therefore charity is friendship.

I ANSWER THAT, According to the Philosopher (*Ethic.* viii, 2, 3) not every love has the character of friendship, but that love which is together with benevolence, when, to wit, we love someone so as to wish good to him. If, however, we do not wish good to what we love, but wish its good for ourselves, (thus we are said to love wine, or a horse, or the like), it is love not of friendship, but of a kind of concupiscence. For it would be absurd to speak of having friendship for wine or for a horse.

Yet neither does well-wishing suffice for friendship, for a certain mutual love is requisite, since friendship is between friend and friend: and this well-wishing is founded on some kind of communication.

Accordingly, since there is a communication between man and God, inasmuch as He communicates His happiness to us, some kind of friendship must needs be based on this same communication, of which it is written (1 Cor 1:9): *God is faithful: by Whom you are called unto the fellowship of His Son.* The love which is based on this communication, is charity: wherefore it is evident that charity is the friendship of man for God.

REPLY OBJ. 1: Man's life is twofold. There is his outward life in respect of his sensitive and corporeal nature: and with regard to this life there is no communication or fellowship between us and God or the angels.

The other is man's spiritual life in respect of his mind, and with regard to this life there is fellowship between us and both God and the angels, imperfectly indeed in this present state of life, wherefore it is written (Phil 3:20): *Our conversation is in heaven.* But this *conversation* will be perfected in heaven, when *His servants shall serve Him, and they shall see His face* (Rev 22:3, 4). Therefore charity is imperfect here, but will be perfected in heaven.

REPLY OBJ. 2: Friendship extends to a person in two ways: first in respect of himself, and in this way friendship never extends but to one's friends: second, it extends to someone in respect of another, as, when a man has friendship for a certain person, for his sake he loves all belonging to him, be they children, servants, or connected with him in any way.

Indeed so much do we love our friends, that for their sake we love all who belong to them, even if they hurt or hate us; so that, in this way, the friendship of charity extends even to our enemies, whom we love out of charity in relation to God, to Whom the friendship of charity is chiefly directed.

REPLY OBJ. 3: The friendship that is based on the virtuous is directed to none but a virtuous man as the

nam, sed eius intuitu diliguntur ad eum attinentes etiam si non sint virtuosi. Et hoc modo caritas, quae maxime est amicitia honesti, se extendit ad peccatores, quos ex caritate diligimus propter Deum.

principal person, but for his sake we love those who belong to him, even though they be not virtuous: in this way charity, which above all is friendship based on the virtuous, extends to sinners, whom, out of charity, we love for God's sake.

# Article 2

*Whether charity is something created in the soul?*

AD SECUNDUM SIC PROCEDITUR. Videtur quod caritas non sit aliquid creatum in anima. Dicit enim Augustinus, in VIII de Trin., *qui proximum diligit, consequens est ut ipsam dilectionem diligat. Deus autem dilectio est. Consequens est ergo ut praecipue Deum diligat.* Et in XV de Trin. dicit, *ita dictum est, Deus caritas est, sicut dictum est, Deus spiritus est.* Ergo caritas non est aliquid creatum in anima, sed est ipse Deus.

PRAETEREA, Deus est spiritualiter vita animae, sicut anima vita corporis, secundum illud Deut. XXX, *ipse est vita tua.* Sed anima vivificat corpus per seipsam. Ergo Deus vivificat animam per seipsum. Vivificat autem eam per caritatem, secundum illud I Ioan. III, *nos scimus quoniam translati sumus de morte ad vitam, quoniam diligimus fratres.* Ergo Deus est ipsa caritas.

PRAETEREA, nihil creatum est infinitae virtutis, sed magis omnis creatura est vanitas. Caritas autem non est vanitas, sed magis vanitati repugnat, et est infinitae virtutis, quia animam hominis ad bonum infinitum perducit. Ergo caritas non est aliquid creatum in anima.

SED CONTRA est quod Augustinus dicit, in III de Doct. Christ., *caritatem voco motum animi ad fruendum Deo propter ipsum.* Sed motus animi est aliquid creatum in anima. Ergo et caritas est aliquid creatum in anima.

RESPONDEO dicendum quod Magister perscrutatur hanc quaestionem in XVII dist. I Lib. Sent., et ponit quod caritas non est aliquid creatum in anima, sed est ipse Spiritus Sanctus mentem inhabitans. Nec est sua intentio quod iste motus dilectionis quo Deum diligimus sit ipse Spiritus Sanctus, sed quod iste motus dilectionis est a spiritu sancto non mediante aliquo habitu, sicut a spiritu sancto sunt alii actus virtuosi mediantibus habitibus aliarum virtutum, puta habitu spei aut fidei aut alicuius alterius virtutis. Et hoc dicebat propter excellentiam caritatis.

Sed si quis recte consideret, hoc magis redundat in caritatis detrimentum. Non enim motus caritatis ita procedit a spiritu sancto movente humanam mentem quod humana mens sit mota tantum et nullo modo sit principium huius motus, sicut cum aliquod corpus movetur ab aliquo exteriori movente. Hoc enim est contra rationem voluntarii, cuius oportet principium in ipso esse, sicut

OBJECTION 1: It would seem that charity is not something created in the soul. For Augustine says (*De Trin.* viii, 7): *He that loveth his neighbor, consequently, loveth love itself.* Now God is love. Therefore it follows that he loves God in the first place. Again he says (*De Trin.* xv, 17): *It was said: God is Charity, even as it was said: God is a Spirit.* Therefore charity is not something created in the soul, but is God Himself.

OBJ. 2: Further, God is the life of the soul spiritually just as the soul is the life of the body, according to Deut. 30:20: *He is thy life.* Now the soul by itself quickens the body. Therefore God quickens the soul by Himself. But He quickens it by charity, according to 1 John 3:14: *We know that we have passed from death to life, because we love the brethren.* Therefore God is charity itself.

OBJ. 3: Further, no created thing is of infinite power; on the contrary every creature is vanity. But charity is not vanity, indeed it is opposed to vanity; and it is of infinite power, since it brings the human soul to the infinite good. Therefore charity is not something created in the soul.

ON THE CONTRARY, Augustine says (*De Doctr. Christ.* iii, 10): *By charity I mean the movement of the soul towards the enjoyment of God for His own sake.* But a movement of the soul is something created in the soul. Therefore charity is something created in the soul.

I ANSWER THAT, The Master looks thoroughly into this question in Q. 17 of the First Book, and concludes that charity is not something created in the soul, but is the Holy Spirit Himself dwelling in the mind. Nor does he mean to say that this movement of love whereby we love God is the Holy Spirit Himself, but that this movement is from the Holy Spirit without any intermediary habit, whereas other virtuous acts are from the Holy Spirit by means of the habits of other virtues, for instance the habit of faith or hope or of some other virtue: and this he said on account of the excellence of charity.

But if we consider the matter aright, this would be, on the contrary, detrimental to charity. For when the Holy Spirit moves the human mind the movement of charity does not proceed from this motion in such a way that the human mind be merely moved, without being the principle of this movement, as when a body is moved by some extrinsic motive power. For this is contrary to the nature of a

supra dictum est. Unde sequeretur quod diligere non esset voluntarium. Quod implicat contradictionem, cum amor de sui ratione importet quod sit actus voluntatis.

Similiter etiam non potest dici quod sic moveat Spiritus Sanctus voluntatem ad actum diligendi sicut movetur instrumentum quod, etsi sit principium actus, non tamen est in ipso agere vel non agere. Sic enim etiam tolleretur ratio voluntarii, et excluderetur ratio meriti, cum tamen supra habitum sit quod dilectio caritatis est radix merendi. Sed oportet quod sic voluntas moveatur a spiritu sancto ad diligendum quod etiam ipsa sit efficiens hunc actum.

Nullus autem actus perfecte producitur ab aliqua potentia activa nisi sit ei connaturalis per aliquam formam quae sit principium actionis. Unde Deus, qui omnia movet ad debitos fines, singulis rebus indidit formas per quas inclinantur ad fines sibi praestitutos a Deo, et secundum hoc *disponit omnia suaviter*, ut dicitur Sap. VIII. Manifestum est autem quod actus caritatis excedit naturam potentiae voluntatis. Nisi ergo aliqua forma superadderetur naturali potentiae per quam inclinaretur ad dilectionis actum, secundum hoc esset actus iste imperfectior actibus naturalibus et actibus aliarum virtutum, nec esset facilis et delectabilis. Quod patet esse falsum, quia nulla virtus habet tantam inclinationem ad suum actum sicut caritas, nec aliqua ita delectabiliter operatur. Unde maxime necesse est quod ad actum caritatis existat in nobis aliqua habitualis forma superaddita potentiae naturali, inclinans ipsam ad caritatis actum, et faciens eam prompte et delectabiliter operari.

**AD PRIMUM** ergo dicendum quod ipsa essentia divina caritas est, sicut et sapientia est, et sicut bonitas est. Unde sicut dicimur boni bonitate quae Deus est, et sapientes sapientia quae Deus est, quia bonitas qua formaliter boni sumus est participatio quaedam divinae bonitatis, et sapientia qua formaliter sapientes sumus est participatio quaedam divinae sapientiae; ita etiam caritas qua formaliter diligimus proximum est quaedam participatio divinae caritatis. Hic enim modus loquendi consuetus est apud Platonicos, quorum doctrinis Augustinus fuit imbutus. Quod quidam non advertentes ex verbis eius sumpserunt occasionem errandi.

**AD SECUNDUM** dicendum quod Deus est vita effective et animae per caritatem et corporis per animam, sed formaliter caritas est vita animae, sicut et anima corporis. Unde per hoc potest concludi quod, sicut anima immediate unitur corpori, ita caritas animae.

**AD TERTIUM** dicendum quod caritas operatur formaliter. Efficacia autem formae est secundum virtutem agentis qui inducit formam. Et ideo quod caritas non

voluntary act, whose principle needs to be in itself, as stated above (I-II, Q. 6, A. 1): so that it would follow that to love is not a voluntary act, which involves a contradiction, since love, of its very nature, implies an act of the will.

Likewise, neither can it be said that the Holy Spirit moves the will in such a way to the act of loving, as though the will were an instrument, for an instrument, though it be a principle of action, nevertheless has not the power to act or not to act, for then again the act would cease to be voluntary and meritorious, whereas it has been stated above (I-II, Q. 114, A. 4) that the love of charity is the root of merit: and, given that the will is moved by the Holy Spirit to the act of love, it is necessary that the will also should be the efficient cause of that act.

Now no act is perfectly produced by an active power, unless it be connatural to that power by reason of some form which is the principle of that action. Wherefore God, Who moves all things to their due ends, bestowed on each thing the form whereby it is inclined to the end appointed to it by Him; and in this way He *ordereth all things sweetly* (Wis 8:1). But it is evident that the act of charity surpasses the nature of the power of the will, so that, therefore, unless some form be superadded to the natural power, inclining it to the act of love, this same act would be less perfect than the natural acts and the acts of the other powers; nor would it be easy and pleasurable to perform. And this is evidently untrue, since no virtue has such a strong inclination to its act as charity has, nor does any virtue perform its act with so great pleasure. Therefore it is most necessary that, for us to perform the act of charity, there should be in us some habitual form superadded to the natural power, inclining that power to the act of charity, and causing it to act with ease and pleasure.

**REPLY OBJ. 1**: The Divine Essence Itself is charity, even as It is wisdom and goodness. Wherefore just as we are said to be good with the goodness which is God, and wise with the wisdom which is God (since the goodness whereby we are formally good is a participation of Divine goodness, and the wisdom whereby we are formally wise, is a share of Divine wisdom), so too, the charity whereby formally we love our neighbor is a participation of Divine charity. For this manner of speaking is common among the Platonists, with whose doctrines Augustine was imbued; and the lack of adverting to this has been to some an occasion of error.

**REPLY OBJ. 2**: God is effectively the life both of the soul by charity, and of the body by the soul: but formally charity is the life of the soul, even as the soul is the life of the body. Consequently we may conclude from this that just as the soul is immediately united to the body, so is charity to the soul.

**REPLY OBJ. 3**: Charity works formally. Now the efficacy of a form depends on the power of the agent, who instills the form, wherefore it is evident that charity is not vanity.

est vanitas, sed facit effectum infinitum dum coniungit animam Deo iustificando ipsam, hoc demonstrat infinitatem virtutis divinae, quae est caritatis auctor.

But because it produces an infinite effect, since, by justifying the soul, it unites it to God, this proves the infinity of the Divine power, which is the author of charity.

# Article 3

*Whether charity is a virtue?*

AD TERTIUM SIC PROCEDITUR. Videtur quod caritas non sit virtus. Caritas enim est amicitia quaedam. Sed amicitia a philosophis non ponitur virtus, ut in libro Ethic. patet, neque enim connumeratur inter virtutes morales neque inter intellectuales. Ergo etiam neque caritas est virtus.

PRAETEREA, *virtus est ultimum potentiae*, ut dicitur in I de caelo. Sed caritas non est ultimum; sed magis gaudium et pax. Ergo videtur quod caritas non sit virtus; sed magis gaudium et pax.

PRAETEREA, omnis virtus est quidam habitus accidentalis. Sed caritas non est habitus accidentalis, cum sit nobilior ipsa anima; nullum autem accidens est nobilius subiecto. Ergo caritas non est virtus.

SED CONTRA est quod Augustinus dicit, in libro de moribus Eccles., *caritas est virtus quae, cum nostra rectissima affectio est, coniungit nos Deo, qua eum diligimus.*

RESPONDEO dicendum quod humani actus bonitatem habent secundum quod regulantur debita regula et mensura, et ideo humana virtus, quae est principium omnium bonorum actuum hominis, consistit in attingendo regulam humanorum actuum. Quae quidem est duplex, ut supra dictum est, scilicet humana ratio, et ipse Deus.

Unde sicut virtus moralis definitur per hoc quod est *secundum rationem rectam*, ut patet in II Ethic., ita etiam attingere Deum constituit rationem virtutis, sicut etiam supra dictum est de fide et spe. Unde, cum caritas attingit Deum, quia coniungit nos Deo, ut patet per auctoritatem Augustini inductam; consequens est caritatem esse virtutem.

AD PRIMUM ergo dicendum quod philosophus in VIII Ethic. non negat amicitiam esse virtutem, sed dicit quod est *virtus vel cum virtute*. Posset enim dici quod est virtus moralis circa operationes quae sunt ad alium, sub alia tamen ratione quam iustitia. Nam iustitia est circa operationes quae sunt ad alium sub ratione debiti legalis, amicitia autem sub ratione cuiusdam debiti amicabilis et moralis, vel magis sub ratione beneficii gratuiti, ut patet per Philosophum, in VIII Ethic. Potest tamen dici quod non est virtus per se ab aliis distincta. Non enim habet rationem laudabilis et honesti nisi ex obiecto, secundum scilicet quod fundatur super honestate virtutum, quod

OBJECTION 1: It would seem that charity is not a virtue. For charity is a kind of friendship. Now philosophers do not reckon friendship a virtue, as may be gathered from *Ethic.* viii, 1; nor is it numbered among the virtues whether moral or intellectual. Neither, therefore, is charity a virtue.

OBJ. 2: Further, *virtue is the ultimate limit of power* (*De Caelo et Mundo* i, 11). But charity is not something ultimate, this applies rather to joy and peace. Therefore it seems that charity is not a virtue, and that this should be said rather of joy and peace.

OBJ. 3: Further, every virtue is an accidental habit. But charity is not an accidental habit, since it is a more excellent thing than the soul itself: whereas no accident is more excellent than its subject. Therefore charity is not a virtue.

ON THE CONTRARY, Augustine says (*De Moribus Eccl.* xi): *Charity is a virtue which, when our affections are perfectly ordered, unites us to God, for by it we love Him.*

I ANSWER THAT, Human acts are good according as they are regulated by their due rule and measure. Wherefore human virtue which is the principle of all man's good acts consists in following the rule of human acts, which is twofold, as stated above (Q. 17, A. 1), viz. human reason and God.

Consequently just as moral virtue is defined as being *in accord with right reason*, as stated in *Ethic.* ii, 6, so too, the nature of virtue consists in attaining God, as also stated above with regard to faith, (Q. 4, A. 5) and hope (Q. 17, A. 1). Wherefore, it follows that charity is a virtue, for, since charity attains God, it unites us to God, as evidenced by the authority of Augustine quoted above.

REPLY OBJ. 1: The Philosopher (*Ethic.* viii) does not deny that friendship is a virtue, but affirms that it is *either a virtue or with a virtue*. For we might say that it is a moral virtue about works done in respect of another person, but under a different aspect from justice. For justice is about works done in respect of another person, under the aspect of the legal due, whereas friendship considers the aspect of a friendly and moral duty, or rather that of a gratuitous favor, as the Philosopher explains (*Ethic.* viii, 13). Nevertheless it may be admitted that it is not a virtue distinct of itself from the other virtues. For its praiseworthiness and virtuousness are derived merely from its object, insofar, to

patet ex hoc quod non quaelibet amicitia habet rationem laudabilis et honesti, sicut patet in amicitia delectabili et utilis. Unde amicitia virtuosa magis est aliquid consequens ad virtutes quam sit virtus. Nec est simile de caritate, quae non fundatur principaliter super virtute humana, sed super bonitate divina.

**AD SECUNDUM** dicendum quod eiusdem virtutis est diligere aliquem et gaudere de illo, nam gaudium amorem consequitur, ut supra habitum est, cum de passionibus ageretur. Et ideo magis ponitur virtus amor quam gaudium, quod est amoris effectus. Ultimum autem quod ponitur in ratione virtutis non importat ordinem effectus, sed magis ordinem superexcessus cuiusdam, sicut centum librae excedunt sexaginta.

**AD TERTIUM** dicendum quod omne accidens secundum suum esse est inferius substantia, quia substantia est ens per se, accidens autem in alio. Sed secundum rationem suae speciei, accidens quidem quod causatur ex principiis subiecti est indignius subiecto, sicut effectus causa. Accidens autem quod causatur ex participatione alicuius superioris naturae est dignius subiecto, inquantum est similitudo superioris naturae, sicut lux diaphano. Et hoc modo caritas est dignior anima, inquantum est participatio quaedam spiritus sancti.

wit, as it is based on the moral goodness of the virtues. This is evident from the fact that not every friendship is praiseworthy and virtuous, as in the case of friendship based on pleasure or utility. Wherefore friendship for the virtuous is something consequent to virtue rather than a virtue. Moreover there is no comparison with charity since it is not founded principally on the virtue of a man, but on the goodness of God.

**REPLY OBJ. 2**: It belongs to the same virtue to love a man and to rejoice about him, since joy results from love, as stated above (I-II, Q. 25, A. 2) in the treatise on the passions: wherefore love is reckoned a virtue, rather than joy, which is an effect of love. And when virtue is described as being something ultimate, we mean that it is last, not in the order of effect, but in the order of excess, just as one hundred pounds exceed sixty.

**REPLY OBJ. 3**: Every accident is inferior to substance if we consider its being, since substance has being in itself, while an accident has its being in another: but considered as to its species, an accident which results from the principles of its subject is inferior to its subject, even as an effect is inferior to its cause; whereas an accident that results from a participation of some higher nature is superior to its subject, insofar as it is a likeness of that higher nature, even as light is superior to the diaphanous body. In this way charity is superior to the soul, inasmuch as it is a participation of the Holy Spirit.

# Article 4

*Whether charity is a special virtue?*

**AD QUARTUM SIC PROCEDITUR.** Videtur quod caritas non sit virtus specialis. Dicit enim Hieronymus, *ut breviter omnem virtutis definitionem complectar, virtus est caritas, qua diligitur Deus et proximus.* Et Augustinus dicit, in libro de moribus Eccles., quod *virtus est ordo amoris.* Sed nulla virtus specialis ponitur in definitione virtutis communis. Ergo caritas non est specialis virtus.

**PRAETEREA**, illud quod se extendit ad opera omnium virtutum non potest esse specialis virtus. Sed caritas se extendit ad opera omnium virtutum, secundum illud I ad Cor. XIII, *caritas patiens est, benigna est,* et cetera. Extendit etiam se ad omnia opera humana, secundum illud I ad Cor. ult., *omnia opera vestra in caritate fiant.* Ergo caritas non est specialis virtus.

**PRAETEREA**, praecepta legis respondent actibus virtutum. Sed Augustinus, in libro de Perfect. Hum. Iust., dicit quod *generalis iussio est, diliges; et generalis prohibitio, non concupisces.* Ergo caritas cst generalis virtus.

**OBJECTION 1**: It would seem that charity is not a special virtue. For Jerome says: *Let me briefly define all virtue as the charity whereby we love God*: and Augustine says (*De Moribus Eccl.* xv) that *virtue is the order of love.* Now no special virtue is included in the definition of virtue in general. Therefore charity is not a special virtue.

**OBJ. 2**: Further, that which extends to all works of virtue, cannot be a special virtue. But charity extends to all works of virtue, according to 1 Cor. 13:4: *Charity is patient, is kind,* etc.; indeed it extends to all human actions, according to 1 Cor. 16:14: *Let all your things be done in charity.* Therefore charity is not a special virtue.

**OBJ. 3**: Further, the precepts of the Law refer to acts of virtue. Now Augustine says (*De Perfect. Human. Justit.* v) that, *Thou shalt love* is *a general commandment*, and *Thou shalt not covet*, a general prohibition. Therefore charity is a general virtue.

**Sed contra**, nullum generale connumeratur speciali. Sed caritas connumeratur specialibus virtutibus, scilicet fidei et spei, secundum illud I ad Cor. XIII, *nunc autem manent fides, spes, caritas, tria haec.* Ergo caritas est virtus specialis.

**Respondeo** dicendum quod actus et habitus specificantur per obiecta, ut ex supradictis patet. Proprium autem obiectum amoris est bonum, ut supra habitum est. Et ideo ubi est specialis ratio boni, ibi est specialis ratio amoris. Bonum autem divinum, inquantum est beatitudinis obiectum, habet specialem rationem boni. Et ideo amor caritatis, qui est amor huius boni, est specialis amor. Unde et caritas est specialis virtus.

**Ad primum** ergo dicendum quod caritas ponitur in definitione omnis virtutis, non quia sit essentialiter omnis virtus, sed quia ab ea dependent aliqualiter omnes virtutes, ut infra dicetur. Sicut etiam prudentia ponitur in definitione virtutum moralium, ut patet in II et VI Ethic., eo quod virtutes morales dependent a prudentia.

**Ad secundum** dicendum quod virtus vel ars ad quam pertinet finis ultimus, imperat virtutibus vel artibus ad quas pertinent alii fines secundarii, sicut militaris imperat equestri, ut dicitur in I Ethic. Et ideo, quia caritas habet pro obiecto ultimum finem humanae vitae, scilicet beatitudinem aeternam, ideo extendit se ad actus totius humanae vitae per modum imperii, non quasi immediate eliciens omnes actus virtutum.

**Ad tertium** dicendum quod praeceptum de diligendo dicitur esse iussio generalis, quia ad hoc reducuntur omnia alia praecepta sicut ad finem, secundum illud I ad Tim. I, *finis praecepti caritas est.*

**On the contrary,** Nothing general is enumerated together with what is special. But charity is enumerated together with special virtues, viz. hope and faith, according to 1 Cor. 13:13: *And now there remain faith, hope, charity, these three.* Therefore charity is a special virtue.

**I answer that,** Acts and habits are specified by their objects, as shown above (I-II, Q. 18, A. 2; I-II, Q. 54, A. 2). Now the proper object of love is the good, as stated above (I-II, Q. 27, A. 1), so that wherever there is a special aspect of good, there is a special kind of love. But the Divine good, inasmuch as it is the object of happiness, has a special aspect of good, wherefore the love of charity, which is the love of that good, is a special kind of love. Therefore charity is a special virtue.

**Reply Obj. 1:** Charity is included in the definition of every virtue, not as being essentially every virtue, but because every virtue depends on it in a way, as we shall state further on (AA. 7, 8). In this way prudence is included in the definition of the moral virtues, as explained in *Ethic.* ii, vi, from the fact that they depend on prudence.

**Reply Obj. 2:** The virtue or art which is concerned about the last end, commands the virtues or arts which are concerned about other ends which are secondary, thus the military art commands the art of horse-riding (*Ethic.* i). Accordingly since charity has for its object the last end of human life, viz. everlasting happiness, it follows that it extends to the acts of a man's whole life, by commanding them, not by eliciting immediately all acts of virtue.

**Reply Obj. 3:** The precept of love is said to be a general command, because all other precepts are reduced thereto as to their end, according to 1 Tim. 1:5: *The end of the commandment is charity.*

# Article 5

*Whether charity is one virtue?*

**Ad quintum sic proceditur.** Videtur quod caritas non sit una virtus. Habitus enim distinguuntur secundum obiecta. Sed duo sunt obiecta caritatis, Deus et proximus, quae in infinitum ab invicem distant. Ergo caritas non est una virtus.

**Praeterea**, diversae rationes obiecti diversificant habitum, etiam si obiectum sit realiter idem, ut ex supradictis patet. Sed multae sunt rationes diligendi Deum, quia ex singulis beneficiis eius perceptis debitores sumus dilectionis ipsius. Ergo caritas non est una virtus.

**Praeterea**, sub caritate includitur amicitia ad proximum. Sed Philosophus, in VIII Ethic., ponit diversas amicitiae species. Ergo caritas non est una virtus, sed multiplicatur in diversas species.

**Objection 1:** It would seem that charity is not one virtue. For habits are distinct according to their objects. Now there are two objects of charity—God and our neighbor—which are infinitely distant from one another. Therefore charity is not one virtue.

**Obj. 2:** Further, different aspects of the object diversify a habit, even though that object be one in reality, as shown above (Q. 17, A. 6; I-II, Q. 54, A. 2, ad 1). Now there are many aspects under which God is an object of love, because we are debtors to His love by reason of each one of His favors. Therefore charity is not one virtue.

**Obj. 3:** Further, charity comprises friendship for our neighbor. But the Philosopher reckons several species of friendship (*Ethic.* viii, 3, 11, 12). Therefore charity is not one virtue, but is divided into a number of various species.

**SED CONTRA**, sicut obiectum fidei est Deus, ita et caritatis. Sed fides est una virtus, propter unitatem divinae veritatis, secundum illud ad Ephes. IV, *una fides*. Ergo etiam caritas est una virtus, propter unitatem divinae bonitatis.

**RESPONDEO** dicendum quod caritas, sicut dictum est, est quaedam amicitia hominis ad Deum. Diversae autem amicitiarum species accipiuntur quidem uno modo secundum diversitatem finis, et secundum hoc dicuntur tres species amicitiae, scilicet amicitia utilis, delectabilis et honesti. Alio modo, secundum diversitatem communicationum in quibus amicitiae fundantur, sicut alia species amicitiae est consanguineorum, et alia concivium aut peregrinantium, quarum una fundatur super communicatione naturali, aliae super communicatione civili vel peregrinationis; ut patet per philosophum, in VIII Ethic.

Neutro autem istorum modorum caritas potest dividi in plura. Nam caritatis finis est unus, scilicet divina bonitas. Est etiam et una communicatio beatitudinis aeternae, super quam haec amicitia fundatur. Unde relinquitur quod caritas est simpliciter una virtus, non distincta in plures species.

**AD PRIMUM** ergo dicendum quod ratio illa directe procederet si Deus et proximus ex aequo essent caritatis obiecta. Hoc autem non est verum, sed Deus est principale obiectum caritatis, proximus autem ex caritate diligitur propter Deum.

**AD SECUNDUM** dicendum quod caritate diligitur Deus propter seipsum. Unde una sola ratio diligendi principaliter attenditur a caritate, scilicet divina bonitas, quae est eius substantia, secundum illud Psalm., *confitemini domino, quoniam bonus*. Aliae autem rationes ad diligendum inducentes, vel debitum dilectionis facientes, sunt secundariae et consequentes ex prima.

**AD TERTIUM** dicendum quod amicitiae humanae, de qua philosophus loquitur, est diversus finis et diversa communicatio. Quod in caritate locum non habet, ut dictum est. Et ideo non est similis ratio.

**ON THE CONTRARY**, Just as God is the object of faith, so is He the object of charity. Now faith is one virtue by reason of the unity of the Divine truth, according to Eph. 4:5: *One faith*. Therefore charity also is one virtue by reason of the unity of the Divine goodness.

**I ANSWER THAT**, Charity, as stated above (A. 1) is a kind of friendship of man for God. Now the different species of friendship are differentiated, first of all, in respect of a diversity of end, and in this way there are three species of friendship, namely friendship for the useful, for the delightful, and for the virtuous; second, in respect of the different kinds of communion on which friendships are based; thus there is one species of friendship between kinsmen, and another between fellow citizens or fellow travellers, the former being based on natural communion, the latter on civil communion or on the comradeship of the road, as the Philosopher explains (*Ethic.* viii, 12).

Now charity cannot be differentiated in either of these ways: for its end is one, namely, the goodness of God; and the fellowship of everlasting happiness, on which this friendship is based, is also one. Hence it follows that charity is simply one virtue, and not divided into several species.

**REPLY OBJ. 1**: This argument would hold, if God and our neighbor were equally objects of charity. But this is not true: for God is the principal object of charity, while our neighbor is loved out of charity for God's sake.

**REPLY OBJ. 2**: God is loved by charity for His own sake: wherefore charity regards principally but one aspect of lovableness, namely God's goodness, which is His substance, according to Ps. 105:1: *Give glory to the Lord for He is good*. Other reasons that inspire us with love for Him, or which make it our duty to love Him, are secondary and result from the first.

**REPLY OBJ. 3**: Human friendship of which the Philosopher treats has various ends and various forms of fellowship. This does not apply to charity, as stated above: wherefore the comparison fails.

# Article 6

*Whether charity is the most excellent of the virtues?*

**AD SEXTUM SIC PROCEDITUR.** Videtur quod caritas non sit excellentissima virtutum. Altioris enim potentiae altior est virtus, sicut et altior operatio. Sed intellectus est altior voluntate, et dirigit ipsam. Ergo fides, quae est in intellectu, est excellentior caritate, quae est in voluntate.

**PRAETEREA**, illud per quod aliud operatur, videtur eo esse inferius, sicut minister, per quem dominus

**OBJECTION 1**: It would seem that charity is not the most excellent of the virtues. Because the higher power has the higher virtue even as it has a higher operation. Now the intellect is higher than the will, since it directs the will. Therefore, faith, which is in the intellect, is more excellent than charity which is in the will.

**OBJ. 2**: Further, the thing by which another works seems the less excellent of the two, even as a servant, by

aliquid operatur, est inferior domino. *Sed fides per dilectionem operatur*, ut habetur ad Gal. V. Ergo fides est excellentior caritate.

PRAETEREA, illud quod se habet ex additione ad aliud, videtur esse perfectius. Sed spes videtur se habere ex additione ad caritatem, nam caritatis obiectum est bonum, spei autem obiectum est bonum arduum. Ergo spes est excellentior caritate.

SED CONTRA est quod dicitur I ad Cor. XIII, *maior horum est caritas.*

RESPONDEO dicendum quod, cum bonum in humanis actibus attendatur secundum quod regulantur debita regula, necesse est quod virtus humana, quae est principium bonorum actuum, consistat in attingendo humanorum actuum regulam. Est autem duplex regula humanorum actuum, ut supra dictum est, scilicet ratio humana et Deus, sed Deus est prima regula, a qua etiam humana ratio regulanda est. Et ideo virtutes theologicae, quae consistunt in attingendo illam regulam primam, eo quod earum obiectum est Deus, excellentiores sunt virtutibus moralibus vel intellectualibus, quae consistunt in attingendo rationem humanam. Propter quod oportet quod etiam inter ipsas virtutes theologicas illa sit potior quae magis Deum attingit.

Semper autem id quod est per se magis est eo quod est per aliud. Fides autem et spes attingunt quidem Deum secundum quod ex ipso provenit nobis vel cognitio veri vel adeptio boni, sed caritas attingit ipsum Deum ut in ipso sistat, non ut ex eo aliquid nobis proveniat. Et ideo caritas est excellentior fide et spe; et per consequens omnibus aliis virtutibus. Sicut etiam prudentia, quae attingit rationem secundum se, est excellentior quam aliae virtutes morales, quae attingunt rationem secundum quod ex ea medium constituitur in operationibus vel passionibus humanis.

AD PRIMUM ergo dicendum quod operatio intellectus completur secundum quod intellectum est in intelligente, et ideo nobilitas operationis intellectualis attenditur secundum mensuram intellectus. Operatio autem voluntatis, et cuiuslibet virtutis appetitivae, perficitur in inclinatione appetentis ad rem sicut ad terminum. Ideo dignitas operationis appetitivae attenditur secundum rem quae est obiectum operationis. Ea autem quae sunt infra animam nobiliori modo sunt in anima quam in seipsis, quia unumquodque est in aliquo per modum eius in quo est, ut habetur in libro de Causis, quae vero sunt supra animam nobiliori modo sunt in seipsis quam sint in anima. Et ideo eorum quae sunt infra nos nobilior est cognitio quam dilectio, propter quod Philosophus, in X Ethic., praetulit virtutes intellectuales moralibus. Sed eorum quae sunt supra nos, et praecipue

whom his master works, is beneath his master. Now *faith . . . worketh by charity*, according to Gal. 5:6. Therefore faith is more excellent than charity.

OBJ. 3: Further, that which is by way of addition to another seems to be the more perfect of the two. Now hope seems to be something additional to charity: for the object of charity is good, whereas the object of hope is an arduous good. Therefore hope is more excellent than charity.

ON THE CONTRARY, It is written (1 Cor 13:13): *The greater of these is charity.*

I ANSWER THAT, Since good, in human acts, depends on their being regulated by the due rule, it must needs be that human virtue, which is a principle of good acts, consists in attaining the rule of human acts. Now the rule of human acts is twofold, as stated above (A. 3), namely, human reason and God: yet God is the first rule, whereby, even human reason must be regulated. Consequently the theological virtues, which consist in attaining this first rule, since their object is God, are more excellent than the moral, or the intellectual virtues, which consist in attaining human reason: and it follows that among the theological virtues themselves, the first place belongs to that which attains God most.

Now that which is of itself always ranks before that which is by another. But faith and hope attain God indeed insofar as we derive from Him the knowledge of truth or the acquisition of good, whereas charity attains God Himself that it may rest in Him, but not that something may accrue to us from Him. Hence charity is more excellent than faith or hope, and, consequently, than all the other virtues, just as prudence, which by itself attains reason, is more excellent than the other moral virtues, which attain reason insofar as it appoints the mean in human operations or passions.

REPLY OBJ. 1: The operation of the intellect is completed by the thing understood being in the intellectual subject, so that the excellence of the intellectual operation is assessed according to the measure of the intellect. On the other hand, the operation of the will and of every appetitive power is completed in the tendency of the appetite towards a thing as its term, wherefore the excellence of the appetitive operation is gauged according to the thing which is the object of the operation. Now those things which are beneath the soul are more excellent in the soul than they are in themselves, because a thing is contained according to the mode of the container (*De Causis* xii). On the other hand, things that are above the soul, are more excellent in themselves than they are in the soul. Consequently it is better to know than to love the things that are beneath us; for which reason the Philosopher gave the preference

dilectio Dei, cognitioni praefertur. Et ideo caritas est excellentior fide.

**AD SECUNDUM** dicendum quod fides non operatur per dilectionem sicut per instrumentum, ut dominus per servum; sed sicut per formam propriam. Et ideo ratio non sequitur.

**AD TERTIUM** dicendum quod idem bonum est obiectum caritatis et spei, sed caritas importat unionem ad illud bonum, spes autem distantiam quandam ab eo. Et inde est quod caritas non respicit illud bonum ut arduum sicut spes, quod enim iam unitum est non habet rationem ardui. Et ex hoc apparet quod caritas est perfectior spe.

to the intellectual virtues over the moral virtues (*Ethic.* x, 7, 8): whereas the love of the things that are above us, especially of God, ranks before the knowledge of such things. Therefore charity is more excellent than faith.

**REPLY OBJ. 2:** Faith works by love, not instrumentally, as a master by his servant, but as by its proper form: hence the argument does not prove.

**REPLY OBJ. 3:** The same good is the object of charity and of hope: but charity implies union with that good, whereas hope implies distance therefrom. Hence charity does not regard that good as being arduous, as hope does, since what is already united has not the character of arduous: and this shows that charity is more perfect than hope.

# Article 7

*Whether any true virtue is possible without charity?*

**AD SEPTIMUM SIC PROCEDITUR.** Videtur quod sine caritate possit esse aliqua vera virtus. Virtutis enim proprium est bonum actum producere. Sed illi qui non habent caritatem faciunt aliquos bonos actus, puta dum nudum vestiunt, famelicum pascunt et similia operantur. Ergo sine caritate potest esse aliqua vera virtus.

**PRAETEREA**, caritas non potest esse sine fide, procedit enim *ex fide non ficta*, ut apostolus dicit, I Tim. I. Sed in infidelibus potest esse vera castitas, dum concupiscentias cohibent; et vera iustitia, dum recte iudicant. Ergo vera virtus potest esse sine caritate.

**PRAETEREA**, scientia et ars quaedam virtutes sunt, ut patet in VI Ethic. Sed huiusmodi inveniuntur in hominibus peccatoribus non habentibus caritatem. Ergo vera virtus potest esse sine caritate.

**SED CONTRA** est quod apostolus dicit, I ad Cor. XIII, *si distribuero in cibos pauperum omnes facultates meas, et si tradidero corpus meum ita ut ardeam, caritatem autem non habeam, nihil mihi prodest.* Sed virtus vera multum prodest, secundum illud Sap. VIII, *sobrietatem et iustitiam docet, prudentiam et virtutem, quibus in vita nihil est utilius hominibus.* Ergo sine caritate vera virtus esse non potest.

**RESPONDEO** dicendum quod virtus ordinatur ad bonum, ut supra habitum est. Bonum autem principaliter est finis, nam ea quae sunt ad finem non dicuntur bona nisi in ordine ad finem. Sicut ergo duplex est finis, unus ultimus et alius proximus, ita etiam est duplex bonum, unum quidem ultimum, et aliud proximum et particulare. Ultimum quidem et principale bonum hominis est Dei fruitio, secundum illud Psalm., *mihi adhaerere*

**OBJECTION 1:** It would seem that there can be true virtue without charity. For it is proper to virtue to produce a good act. Now those who have not charity, do some good actions, as when they clothe the naked, or feed the hungry and so forth. Therefore true virtue is possible without charity.

**OBJ. 2:** Further, charity is not possible without faith, since it comes of *an unfeigned faith*, as the Apostle says (1 Tim 1:5). Now, in unbelievers, there can be true chastity, if they curb their concupiscences, and true justice, if they judge rightly. Therefore true virtue is possible without charity.

**OBJ. 3:** Further, science and art are virtues, according to *Ethic.* vi. But they are to be found in sinners who lack charity. Therefore true virtue can be without charity.

**ON THE CONTRARY,** The Apostle says (1 Cor 13:3): *If I should distribute all my goods to the poor, and if I should deliver my body to be burned, and have not charity, it profiteth me nothing.* And yet true virtue is very profitable, according to Wis. 8:7: *She teacheth temperance, and prudence, and justice, and fortitude, which are such things as men can have nothing more profitable in life.* Therefore no true virtue is possible without charity.

**I ANSWER THAT,** Virtue is ordered to the good, as stated above (I-II, Q. 55, A. 4). Now the good is chiefly an end, for things directed to the end are not said to be good except in relation to the end. Accordingly, just as the end is twofold, the last end, and the proximate end, so also, is good twofold, one, the ultimate and universal good, the other proximate and particular. The ultimate and principal good of man is the enjoyment of God, according to Ps. 72:28: *It is good for*

*Deo bonum est*, et ad hoc ordinatur homo per caritatem. Bonum autem secundarium et quasi particulare hominis potest esse duplex, unum quidem quod est vere bonum, utpote ordinabile, quantum est in se, ad principale bonum, quod est ultimus finis; aliud autem est bonum apparens et non verum, quia abducit a finali bono. Sic igitur patet quod virtus vera simpliciter est illa quae ordinat ad principale bonum hominis, sicut etiam Philosophus, in VII Physic., dicit quod virtus est *dispositio perfecti ad optimum*. Et sic nulla vera virtus potest esse sine caritate.

Sed si accipiatur virtus secundum quod est in ordine ad aliquem finem particularem, sic potest aliqua virtus dici sine caritate, inquantum ordinatur ad aliquod particulare bonum. Sed si illud particulare bonum non sit verum bonum, sed apparens, virtus etiam quae est in ordine ad hoc bonum non erit vera virtus, sed falsa similitudo virtutis, sicut *non est vera virtus avarorum prudentia, qua excogitant diversa genera lucellorum; et avarorum iustitia, qua gravium damnorum metu contemnunt aliena; et avarorum temperantia, qua luxuriae, quoniam sumptuosa est, cohibent appetitum; et avarorum fortitudo, qua, ut ait Horatius, per mare pauperiem fugiunt, per saxa, per ignes*, ut Augustinus dicit, in IV Lib. contra Iulian. Si vero illud bonum particulare sit verum bonum, puta conservatio civitatis vel aliquid huiusmodi, erit quidem vera virtus, sed imperfecta, nisi referatur ad finale et perfectum bonum. Et secundum hoc simpliciter vera virtus sine caritate esse non potest.

**AD PRIMUM** ergo dicendum quod actus alicuius caritate carentis potest esse duplex. Unus quidem secundum hoc quod caritate caret, utpote cum facit aliquid in ordine ad id per quod caret caritate. Et talis actus semper est malus, sicut Augustinus dicit, in IV contra Iulian., quod actus infidelis, inquantum est infidelis, semper est peccatum; etiam si nudum operiat vel quidquid aliud huiusmodi faciat, ordinans ad finem suae infidelitatis.

Alius autem potest esse actus carentis caritate non secundum id quod caritate caret, sed secundum quod habet aliquod aliud donum Dei, vel fidem vel spem, vel etiam naturae bonum, quod non totum per peccatum tollitur, ut supra dictum est. Et secundum hoc sine caritate potest quidem esse aliquis actus bonus ex suo genere, non tamen perfecte bonus, quia deest debita ordinatio ad ultimum finem.

**AD SECUNDUM** dicendum quod, cum finis se habeat in agibilibus sicut principium in speculativis, sicut non potest esse simpliciter vera scientia si desit recta aestimatio de primo et indemonstrabili principio; ita non potest esse simpliciter vera iustitia aut vera castitas si desit ordinatio debita ad finem, quae est per caritatem, quantumcumque aliquis se recte circa alia habeat.

*me to adhere to God*, and to this good man is ordered by charity. Man's secondary and, as it were, particular good may be twofold: one is truly good, because, considered in itself, it can be directed to the principal good, which is the last end; while the other is good apparently and not truly, because it leads us away from the final good. Accordingly it is evident that simply true virtue is that which is directed to man's principal good; thus also the Philosopher says (*Phys.* vii, text. 17) that virtue is *the disposition of a perfect thing to that which is best*: and in this way no true virtue is possible without charity.

If, however, we take virtue as being ordered to some particular end, then we speak of virtue being where there is no charity, insofar as it is directed to some particular good. But if this particular good is not a true, but an apparent good, it is not a true virtue that is ordered to such a good, but a counterfeit virtue. Even so, as Augustine says (*Contra Julian.* iv, 3), *the prudence of the miser, whereby he devises various roads to gain, is no true virtue; nor the miser's justice, whereby he scorns the property of another through fear of severe punishment; nor the miser's temperance, whereby he curbs his desire for expensive pleasures; nor the miser's fortitude, whereby as Horace, says, 'he braves the sea, he crosses mountains, he goes through fire, in order to avoid poverty'* (*Epis.* lib, 1; *Ep. i*, 45). If, on the other hand, this particular good be a true good, for instance the welfare of the state, or the like, it will indeed be a true virtue, imperfect, however, unless it be referred to the final and perfect good. Accordingly no strictly true virtue is possible without charity.

**REPLY OBJ. 1**: The act of one lacking charity may be of two kinds; one is in accordance with his lack of charity, as when he does something that is referred to that whereby he lacks charity. Such an act is always evil: thus Augustine says (*Contra Julian.* iv, 3) that the actions which an unbeliever performs as an unbeliever, are always sinful, even when he clothes the naked, or does any like thing, and directs it to his unbelief as end.

There is, however, another act of one lacking charity, not in accordance with his lack of charity, but in accordance with his possession of some other gift of God, whether faith, or hope, or even his natural good, which is not completely taken away by sin, as stated above (Q. 10, A. 4; I-II, Q. 85, A. 2). In this way it is possible for an act, without charity, to be generically good, but not perfectly good, because it lacks its due order to the last end.

**REPLY OBJ. 2**: Since the end is in practical matters, what the principle is in speculative matters, just as there can be no strictly true science, if a right estimate of the first indemonstrable principle be lacking, so, there can be no strictly true justice, or chastity, without that due ordering to the end, which is effected by charity, however rightly a man may be affected about other matters.

213

AD TERTIUM dicendum quod scientia et ars de sui ratione important ordinem ad aliquod particulare bonum, non autem ultimum finem humanae vitae, sicut virtutes morales, quae simpliciter faciunt hominem bonum, ut supra dictum est. Et ideo non est similis ratio.

REPLY OBJ. 3: Science and art of their very nature imply a relation to some particular good, and not to the ultimate good of human life, as do the moral virtues, which make man good simply, as stated above (I-II, Q. 56, A. 3). Hence the comparison fails.

# Article 8

*Whether charity is the form of the virtues?*

AD OCTAVUM SIC PROCEDITUR. Videtur quod caritas non sit forma virtutum. Forma enim alicuius rei vel est exemplaris, vel est essentialis. Sed caritas non est forma exemplaris virtutum aliarum, quia sic oporteret quod aliae virtutes essent eiusdem speciei cum ipsa. Similiter etiam non est forma essentialis aliarum virtutum, quia non distingueretur ab aliis. Ergo nullo modo est forma virtutum.

PRAETEREA, caritas comparatur ad alias virtutes ut radix et fundamentum, secundum illud Ephes. III, *in caritate radicati et fundati*. Radix autem vel fundamentum non habet rationem formae, sed magis rationem materiae, quia est prima pars in generatione. Ergo caritas non est forma virtutum.

PRAETEREA, forma et finis et efficiens non incidunt in idem numero, ut patet in II Physic. Sed caritas dicitur finis et mater virtutum. Ergo non debet dici forma virtutum.

SED CONTRA est quod Ambrosius dicit caritatem esse formam virtutum.

RESPONDEO dicendum quod in moralibus forma actus attenditur principaliter ex parte finis, cuius ratio est quia principium moralium actuum est voluntas, cuius obiectum et quasi forma est finis. Semper autem forma actus consequitur formam agentis. Unde oportet quod in moralibus id quod dat actui ordinem ad finem, det ei et formam. Manifestum est autem secundum praedicta quod per caritatem ordinantur actus omnium aliarum virtutum ad ultimum finem. Et secundum hoc ipsa dat formam actibus omnium aliarum virtutum. Et pro tanto dicitur esse forma virtutum, nam et ipsae virtutes dicuntur in ordine ad actus formatos.

AD PRIMUM ergo dicendum quod caritas dicitur esse forma aliarum virtutum non quidem exemplariter aut essentialiter, sed magis effective, inquantum scilicet omnibus formam imponit secundum modum praedictum.

AD SECUNDUM dicendum quod caritas comparatur fundamento et radici inquantum ex ea sustentantur et nutriuntur omnes aliae virtutes, et non secundum rationem qua fundamentum et radix habent rationem causae materialis.

OBJECTION 1: It would seem that charity is not the true form of the virtues. Because the form of a thing is either exemplar or essential. Now charity is not the exemplar form of the other virtues, since it would follow that the other virtues are of the same species as charity: nor is it the essential form of the other virtues, since then it would not be distinct from them. Therefore it is in no way the form of the virtues.

OBJ. 2: Further, charity is compared to the other virtues as their root and foundation, according to Eph. 3:17: *Rooted and founded in charity*. Now a root or foundation is not the form, but rather the matter of a thing, since it is the first part in the making. Therefore charity is not the form of the virtues.

OBJ. 3: Further, formal, final, and efficient causes do not coincide with one another (*Phys.* ii, 7). Now charity is called the end and the mother of the virtues. Therefore it should not be called their form.

ON THE CONTRARY, Ambrose says that charity is the form of the virtues.

I ANSWER THAT, In morals the form of an act is taken chiefly from the end. The reason of this is that the principal of moral acts is the will, whose object and form, so to speak, are the end. Now the form of an act always follows from a form of the agent. Consequently, in morals, that which gives an act its order to the end, must needs give the act its form. Now it is evident, in accordance with what has been said (A. 7), that it is charity which directs the acts of all other virtues to the last end, and which, consequently, also gives the form to all other acts of virtue: and it is precisely in this sense that charity is called the form of the virtues, for these are called virtues in relation to *informed* acts.

REPLY OBJ. 1: Charity is called the form of the other virtues not as being their exemplar or their essential form, but rather by way of efficient cause, insofar as it sets the form on all, in the aforesaid manner.

REPLY OBJ. 2: Charity is compared to the foundation or root insofar as all other virtues draw their sustenance and nourishment therefrom, and not in the sense that the foundation and root have the character of a material cause.

**AD TERTIUM** dicendum quod caritas dicitur finis aliarum virtutum quia omnes alias virtutes ordinat ad finem suum. Et quia mater est quae in se concipit ex alio, ex hac ratione dicitur mater aliarum virtutum, quia ex appetitu finis ultimi concipit actus aliarum virtutum, imperando ipsos.

**REPLY OBJ. 3**: Charity is said to be the end of other virtues, because it directs all other virtues to its own end. And since a mother is one who conceives within herself and by another, charity is called the mother of the other virtues, because, by commanding them, it conceives the acts of the other virtues, by the desire of the last end.

# QUESTION 24

## THE SUBJECT OF CHARITY

Deinde considerandum est de caritate in comparatione ad subiectum. Et circa hoc quaeruntur duodecim.

Primo, utrum caritas sit in voluntate tanquam in subiecto.

Secundo, utrum caritas causetur in homine ex actibus praecedentibus, vel ex infusione divina.

Tertio, utrum infundatur secundum capacitatem naturalium.

Quarto, utrum augeatur in habente ipsam.

Quinto, utrum augeatur per additionem.

Sexto, utrum quolibet actu augeatur.

Septimo, utrum augeatur in infinitum.

Octavo, utrum caritas viae possit esse perfecta.

Nono, de diversis gradibus caritatis.

Decimo, utrum caritas possit diminui.

Undecimo, utrum caritas semel habita possit amitti.

Duodecimo, utrum amittatur per unum actum peccati mortalis.

We must now consider charity in relation to its subject, under which head there are twelve points of inquiry:

(1) Whether charity is in the will as its subject?

(2) Whether charity is caused in man by preceding acts or by a Divine infusion?

(3) Whether it is infused according to the capacity of our natural gifts?

(4) Whether it increases in the person who has it?

(5) Whether it increases by addition?

(6) Whether it increases by every act?

(7) Whether it increases indefinitely?

(8) Whether the charity of a wayfarer can be perfect?

(9) Of the various degrees of charity;

(10) Whether charity can diminish?

(11) Whether charity can be lost after it has been possessed?

(12) Whether it is lost through one mortal sin?

# Article 1

*Whether the will is the subject of charity?*

**AD PRIMUM SIC PROCEDITUR**. Videtur quod voluntas non sit subiectum caritatis. Caritas enim amor quidam est. Sed amor, secundum philosophum, est in concupiscibili. Ergo et caritas est in concupiscibili, et non in voluntate.

**PRAETEREA**, caritas est principalissima virtutum, ut supra dictum est. Sed subiectum virtutis est ratio. Ergo videtur quod caritas sit in ratione, et non in voluntate.

**PRAETEREA**, caritas se extendit ad omnes actus humanos, secundum illud I ad Cor. ult., *omnia vestra in caritate fiant*. Sed principium humanorum actuum est liberum arbitrium. Ergo videtur quod caritas maxime sit in libero arbitrio sicut in subiecto, et non in voluntate.

**SED CONTRA** est quod obiectum caritatis est bonum, quod etiam est obiectum voluntatis. Ergo caritas est in voluntate sicut in subiecto.

**RESPONDEO** dicendum quod, cum duplex sit appetitus, scilicet sensitivus et intellectivus, qui dicitur voluntas, ut in primo habitum est; utriusque obiectum est bonum, sed diversimode. Nam obiectum appetitus sensitivi est bonum per sensum apprehensum, obiectum

**OBJECTION 1**: It would seem that the will is not the subject of charity. For charity is a kind of love. Now, according to the Philosopher (*Topic.* ii, 3) love is in the concupiscible part. Therefore charity is also in the concupiscible and not in the will.

**OBJ. 2**: Further, charity is the foremost of the virtues, as stated above (Q. 23, A. 6). But the reason is the subject of virtue. Therefore it seems that charity is in the reason and not in the will.

**OBJ. 3**: Further, charity extends to all human acts, according to 1 Cor. 16:14: *Let all your things be done in charity*. Now the principle of human acts is the free-will. Therefore it seems that charity is chiefly in the free-will as its subject and not in the will.

**ON THE CONTRARY**, The object of charity is the good, which is also the object of the will. Therefore charity is in the will as its subject.

**I ANSWER THAT**, Since, as stated in the First Part (Q. 80, A. 2), the appetite is twofold, namely the sensitive, and the intellective which is called the will, the object of each is the good, but in different ways: for the object of the sensitive appetite is a good apprehended by sense,

vero appetitus intellectivi, vel voluntatis, est bonum sub communi ratione boni, prout est apprehensibile ab intellectu. Caritatis autem obiectum non est aliquod bonum sensibile, sed bonum divinum, quod solo intellectu cognoscitur. Et ideo caritatis subiectum non est appetitus sensitivus, sed appetitus intellectivus, idest voluntas.

**AD PRIMUM** ergo dicendum quod concupiscibilis est pars appetitus sensitivi, non autem appetitus intellectivi, ut in primo ostensum est. Unde amor qui est in concupiscibili est amor sensitivi boni. Ad bonum autem divinum, quod est intelligibile, concupiscibilis se extendere non potest, sed sola voluntas. Et ideo concupiscibilis subiectum caritatis esse non potest.

**AD SECUNDUM** dicendum quod voluntas etiam, secundum philosophum, in III de Anima, in ratione est. Et ideo per hoc quod caritas est in voluntate non est aliena a ratione. Tamen ratio non est regula caritatis, sicut humanarum virtutum, sed regulatur a Dei sapientia, et excedit regulam rationis humanae, secundum illud Ephes. III, *supereminentem scientiae caritatem Christi.* Unde non est in ratione neque sicut in subiecto, sicut prudentia; neque sicut in regulante, sicut iustitia vel temperantia; sed solum per quandam affinitatem voluntatis ad rationem.

**AD TERTIUM** dicendum quod liberum arbitrium non est alia potentia a voluntate, ut in primo dictum est. Et tamen caritas non est in voluntate secundum rationem liberi arbitrii, cuius actus est eligere, *electio* enim *est eorum quae sunt ad finem, voluntas autem est ipsius finis,* ut dicitur in III Ethic. Unde caritas, cuius obiectum est finis ultimus, magis debet dici esse in voluntate quam in libero arbitrio.

whereas the object of the intellective appetite or will is good under the universal aspect of good, according as it can be apprehended by the intellect. Now the object of charity is not a sensible good, but the Divine good which is known by the intellect alone. Therefore the subject of charity is not the sensitive, but the intellective appetite, i.e., the will.

**REPLY OBJ. 1**: The concupiscible is a part of the sensitive, not of the intellective appetite, as proved in the First Part (Q. 81, A. 2): wherefore the love which is in the concupiscible, is the love of sensible good: nor can the concupiscible reach to the Divine good which is an intelligible good; the will alone can. Consequently the concupiscible cannot be the subject of charity.

**REPLY OBJ. 2**: According to the Philosopher (*De Anima* iii, 9), the will also is in the reason: wherefore charity is not excluded from the reason through being in the will. Yet charity is regulated, not by the reason, as human virtues are, but by God's wisdom, and transcends the rule of human reason, according to Eph. 3:19: *The charity of Christ, which surpasseth all knowledge.* Hence it is not in the reason, either as its subject, like prudence is, or as its rule, like justice and temperance are, but only by a certain kinship of the will to the reason.

**REPLY OBJ. 3**: As stated in the First Part (Q. 83, A. 4), the free-will is not a distinct power from the will. Yet charity is not in the will considered as free-will, the act of which is to choose. For *choice is of things directed to the end, whereas the will is of the end itself* (*Ethic.* iii, 2). Hence charity, whose object is the last end, should be described as residing in the will rather than in the free-will.

# Article 2

*Whether charity is caused in us by infusion?*

**AD SECUNDUM SIC PROCEDITUR.** Videtur quod caritas non causetur in nobis ex infusione. Illud enim quod est commune omnibus creaturis, naturaliter hominibus inest. Sed sicut Dionysius dicit, in IV cap. de Div. Nom., *omnibus diligibile et amabile est bonum divinum,* quod est obiectum caritatis. Ergo caritas inest nobis naturaliter, et non ex infusione.

**PRAETEREA,** quanto aliquid est magis diligibile, tanto facilius diligi potest. Sed Deus est maxime diligibilis, cum sit summe bonus. Ergo facilius est ipsum diligere quam alia. Sed ad alia diligenda non indigemus aliquo habitu infuso. Ergo nec etiam ad diligendum Deum.

**PRAETEREA,** apostolus dicit, I ad Tim. I, *finis praecepti est caritas de corde bono et conscientia pura et fide*

**OBJECTION 1**: It would seem that charity is not caused in us by infusion. For that which is common to all creatures, is in man naturally. Now, according to Dionysius (*Div. Nom.* iv), the *Divine good,* which is the object of charity, *is for all an object of dilection and love.* Therefore charity is in us naturally, and not by infusion.

**OBJ. 2**: Further, the more lovable a thing is the easier it is to love it. Now God is supremely lovable, since He is supremely good. Therefore it is easier to love Him than other things. But we need no infused habit in order to love other things. Neither, therefore, do we need one in order to love God.

**OBJ. 3**: Further, the Apostle says (1 Tim 1:5): *The end of the commandment is charity from a pure heart, and a good*

*non ficta.* Sed haec tria pertinent ad actus humanos. Ergo caritas causatur in nobis ex actibus praecedentibus, et non ex infusione.

**Sed contra** est quod apostolus dicit, Rom. V, *caritas Dei diffusa est in cordibus nostris per spiritum sanctum, qui datus est nobis.*

**Respondeo** dicendum quod, sicut dictum est, caritas est amicitia quaedam hominis ad Deum fundata super communicationem beatitudinis aeternae. Haec autem communicatio non est secundum bona naturalia, sed secundum dona gratuita, quia, ut dicitur Rom. VI, *gratia Dei vita aeterna.* Unde et ipsa caritas facultatem naturae excedit. Quod autem excedit naturae facultatem non potest esse neque naturale neque per potentias naturales acquisitum, quia effectus naturalis non transcendit suam causam.

Unde caritas non potest neque naturaliter nobis inesse, neque per vires naturales est acquisita, sed per infusionem spiritus sancti, qui est amor patris et filii, cuius participatio in nobis est ipsa caritas creata, sicut supra dictum est.

**Ad primum** ergo dicendum quod Dionysius loquitur de dilectione Dei quae fundatur super communicatione naturalium bonorum, et ideo naturaliter omnibus inest. Sed caritas fundatur super quadam communicatione supernaturali. Unde non est similis ratio.

**Ad secundum** dicendum quod sicut Deus secundum se est maxime cognoscibilis, non tamen nobis, propter defectum nostrae cognitionis, quae dependet a rebus sensibilibus; ita etiam Deus in se est maxime diligibilis inquantum est obiectum beatitudinis, sed hoc modo non est maxime diligibilis a nobis, propter inclinationem affectus nostri ad visibilia bona. Unde oportet quod ad Deum hoc modo maxime diligendum nostris cordibus caritas infundatur.

**Ad tertium** dicendum quod cum caritas dicitur in nobis procedere *ex corde bono et conscientia pura et fide non ficta,* hoc referendum est ad actum caritatis, qui ex praemissis excitatur. Vel etiam hoc dicitur quia huiusmodi actus disponunt hominem ad recipiendum caritatis infusionem. Et similiter etiam dicendum est de eo quod Augustinus dicit, quod timor introducit caritatem, et de hoc quod dicitur in Glossa Matth. I, quod *fides generat spem, et spes caritatem.*

*conscience, and an unfeigned faith.* Now these three have reference to human acts. Therefore charity is caused in us from preceding acts, and not from infusion.

**On the contrary,** The Apostle says (Rom 5:5): *The charity of God is poured forth in our hearts by the Holy Spirit, Who is given to us.*

**I answer that,** As stated above (Q. 23, A. 1), charity is a friendship of man for God, founded upon the fellowship of everlasting happiness. Now this fellowship is in respect, not of natural, but of gratuitous gifts, for, according to Rom. 6:23, *the grace of God is life everlasting:* wherefore charity itself surpasses our natural facilities. Now that which surpasses the faculty of nature, cannot be natural or acquired by the natural powers, since a natural effect does not transcend its cause.

Therefore charity can be in us neither naturally, nor through acquisition by the natural powers, but by the infusion of the Holy Spirit, Who is the love of the Father and the Son, and the participation of Whom in us is created charity, as stated above (Q. 23, A. 2).

**Reply Obj. 1:** Dionysius is speaking of the love of God, which is founded on the fellowship of natural goods, wherefore it is in all naturally. On the other hand, charity is founded on a supernatural fellowship, so the comparison fails.

**Reply Obj. 2:** Just as God is supremely knowable in Himself yet not to us, on account of a defect in our knowledge which depends on sensible things, so too, God is supremely lovable in Himself, inasmuch as He is the object of happiness. But He is not supremely lovable to us in this way, on account of the inclination of our appetite towards visible goods. Hence it is evident that for us to love God above all things in this way, it is necessary that charity be infused into our hearts.

**Reply Obj. 3:** When it is said that in us charity proceeds from *a pure heart, and a good conscience, and an unfeigned faith,* this must be referred to the act of charity which is aroused by these things. Or again, this is said because the aforesaid acts dispose man to receive the infusion of charity. The same remark applies to the saying of Augustine (*Tract. ix in prim. canon. Joan.*): Fear leads to charity, and of a gloss on Matt. 1:2: *Faith begets hope, and hope charity.*

# Article 3

*Whether charity is infused according to the capacity of our natural gifts?*

**Ad tertium sic proceditur.** Videtur quod caritas infundatur secundum quantitatem naturalium. Dicitur enim Matth. XXV quod *dedit unicuique secundum*

**Objection 1:** It would seem that charity is infused according to the capacity of our natural gifts. For it is written (Matt 25:15) that *He gave to every one according*

*propriam virtutem.* Sed caritatem nulla virtus praecedit in homine nisi naturalis, quia sine caritate nulla est virtus, ut dictum est. Ergo secundum capacitatem virtutis naturalis infunditur homini caritas a Deo.

**PRAETEREA**, omnium ordinatorum ad invicem secundum proportionatur primo, sicut videmus quod in rebus materialibus forma proportionatur materiae, et in donis gratuitis gloria proportionatur gratiae. Sed caritas, cum sit perfectio naturae, comparatur ad capacitatem naturalem sicut secundum ad primum. Ergo videtur quod caritas infundatur secundum naturalium capacitatem.

**PRAETEREA**, homines et Angeli secundum eandem rationem caritatem participant, quia in utrisque est similis beatitudinis ratio, ut habetur Matth. XXII, et Luc. XX. Sed in Angelis caritas et alia dona gratuita sunt data secundum capacitatem naturalium; ut Magister dicit, III dist. II Lib. Sent. Ergo idem etiam videtur esse in hominibus.

**SED CONTRA** est quod dicitur Ioan. III, *spiritus ubi vult spirat*; et I ad Cor. XII, *haec omnia operatur unus et idem spiritus, dividens singulis prout vult.* Ergo caritas datur non secundum capacitatem naturalium, sed secundum voluntatem spiritus sua dona distribuentis.

**RESPONDEO** dicendum quod uniuscuiusque quantitas dependet a propria causa rei, quia universalior causa effectum maiorem producit. Caritas autem, cum superexcedat proportionem naturae humanae, ut dictum est, non dependet ex aliqua naturali virtute, sed ex sola gratia spiritus sancti eam infundentis. Et ideo quantitas caritatis non dependet ex conditione naturae vel ex capacitate naturalis virtutis, sed solum ex voluntate spiritus sancti distribuentis sua dona prout vult. Unde et apostolus dicit, ad Ephes. IV, *unicuique nostrum data est gratia secundum mensuram donationis Christi.*

**AD PRIMUM** ergo dicendum quod illa virtus secundum quam sua dona Deus dat unicuique, est dispositio vel praeparatio praecedens, sive conatus gratiam accipientis. Sed hanc etiam dispositionem vel conatum praevenit Spiritus Sanctus, movens mentem hominis vel plus vel minus secundum suam voluntatem. Unde et apostolus dicit, ad Coloss. I, *qui dignos nos fecit in partem sortis sanctorum in lumine.*

**AD SECUNDUM** dicendum quod forma non excedit proportionem materiae, sed sunt eiusdem generis. Similiter etiam gratia et gloria ad idem genus referuntur, quia gratia nihil est aliud quam quaedam inchoatio gloriae in nobis. Sed caritas et natura non pertinent ad idem genus. Et ideo non est similis ratio.

**AD TERTIUM** dicendum quod Angelus est naturae intellectualis, et secundum suam conditionem competit ei ut totaliter feratur in omne id in quod fertur, ut in primo habitum est. Et ideo in superioribus Angelis fuit

*to his own virtue.* Now, in man, none but natural virtue precedes charity, since there is no virtue without charity, as stated above (Q. 23, A. 7). Therefore God infuses charity into man according to the measure of his natural virtue.

**OBJ. 2**: Further, among things ordained towards one another, the second is proportionate to the first: thus we find in natural things that the form is proportionate to the matter, and in gratuitous gifts, that glory is proportionate to grace. Now, since charity is a perfection of nature, it is compared to the capacity of nature as second to first. Therefore it seems that charity is infused according to the capacity of nature.

**OBJ. 3**: Further, men and angels partake of happiness according to the same measure, since happiness is alike in both, according to Matt. 22:30 and Luke 20:36. Now charity and other gratuitous gifts are bestowed on the angels, according to their natural capacity, as the Master teaches (*Sent.* ii, D, 3). Therefore the same apparently applies to man.

**ON THE CONTRARY**, It is written (John 3:8): *The Spirit breatheth where He will*, and (1 Cor 12:11): *All these things one and the same Spirit worketh, dividing to every one according as He will.* Therefore charity is given, not according to our natural capacity, but according as the Spirit wills to distribute His gifts.

**I ANSWER THAT**, The quantity of a thing depends on the proper cause of that thing, since the more universal cause produces a greater effect. Now, since charity surpasses the proportion of human nature, as stated above (A. 2) it depends, not on any natural virtue, but on the sole grace of the Holy Spirit Who infuses charity. Wherefore the quantity of charity depends neither on the condition of nature nor on the capacity of natural virtue, but only on the will of the Holy Spirit Who *divides* His gifts *according as He will.* Hence the Apostle says (*Eph 4:7*): *To every one of us is given grace according to the measure of the giving of Christ.*

**REPLY OBJ. 1**: The virtue in accordance with which God gives His gifts to each one, is a disposition or previous preparation or effort of the one who receives grace. But the Holy Spirit forestalls even this disposition or effort, by moving man's mind either more or less, according as He will. Wherefore the Apostle says (Col 1:12): *Who hath made us worthy to be partakers of the lot of the saints in light.*

**REPLY OBJ. 2**: The form does not surpass the proportion of the matter. In like manner grace and glory are referred to the same genus, for grace is nothing else than a beginning of glory in us. But charity and nature do not belong to the same genus, so that the comparison fails.

**REPLY OBJ. 3**: The angel's is an intellectual nature, and it is consistent with his condition that he should be borne wholly whithersoever he is borne, as stated in the First Part (Q. 61, A. 6). Hence there was a greater effort in

maior conatus et ad bonum in perseverantibus et ad malum in cadentibus. Et ideo superiorum Angelorum persistentes facti sunt meliores et cadentes facti sunt peiores aliis. Sed homo est rationalis naturae, cui competit esse quandoque in potentia et quandoque in actu. Et ideo non oportet quod feratur totaliter in id in quod fertur; sed eius qui habet meliora naturalia potest esse minor conatus, et e converso. Et ideo non est simile.

the higher angels, both for good in those who persevered, and for evil in those who fell, and consequently those of the higher angels who remained steadfast became better than the others, and those who fell became worse. But man's is a rational nature, with which it is consistent to be sometimes in potentiality and sometimes in act: so that it is not necessarily borne wholly whithersoever it is borne, and where there are greater natural gifts there may be less effort, and vice versa. Thus the comparison fails.

# Article 4

### *Whether charity can increase?*

AD QUARTUM SIC PROCEDITUR. Videtur quod caritas augeri non possit. Nihil enim augetur nisi quantum. Duplex autem est quantitas, scilicet dimensiva, et virtualis. Quarum prima caritati non convenit, cum sit quaedam spiritualis perfectio. Virtualis autem quantitas attenditur secundum obiecta, secundum quae caritas non crescit, quia minima caritas diligit omnia quae sunt ex caritate diligenda. Ergo caritas non augetur.

PRAETEREA, illud quod est in termino non recipit augmentum. Sed caritas est in termino, quasi maxima virtutum existens et summus amor optimi boni. Ergo caritas augeri non potest.

PRAETEREA, augmentum quidam motus est. Ergo quod augetur movetur. Quod ergo augetur essentialiter movetur essentialiter. Sed non movetur essentialiter nisi quod corrumpitur vel generatur. Ergo caritas non potest augeri essentialiter, nisi forte de novo generetur vel corrumpatur, quod est inconveniens.

SED CONTRA est quod Augustinus dicit, super Ioan., quod *caritas meretur augeri, ut aucta mereatur et perfici.*

RESPONDEO dicendum quod caritas viae potest augeri. Ex hoc enim dicimur esse viatores quod in Deum tendimus, qui est ultimus finis nostrae beatitudinis. In hac autem via tanto magis procedimus quanto Deo magis propinquamus, cui non appropinquatur passibus corporis, sed affectibus mentis. Hanc autem propinquitatem facit caritas, quia per ipsam mens Deo unitur. Et ideo de ratione caritatis viae est ut possit augeri, si enim non posset augeri, iam cessaret viae processus. Et ideo apostolus caritatem viam nominat, dicens I ad Cor. XII, *adhuc excellentiorem viam vobis demonstro.*

AD PRIMUM ergo dicendum quod caritati non convenit quantitas dimensiva, sed solum quantitas virtualis. Quae non solum attenditur secundum numerum obiectorum, ut scilicet plura vel pauciora diligantur, sed etiam

OBJECTION 1: It would seem that charity cannot increase. For nothing increases save what has quantity. Now quantity is twofold, namely dimensive and virtual. The former does not befit charity which is a spiritual perfection, while virtual quantity regards the objects in respect of which charity does not increase, since the slightest charity loves all that is to be loved out of charity. Therefore charity does not increase.

OBJ. 2: Further, that which consists in something extreme receives no increase. But charity consists in something extreme, being the greatest of the virtues, and the supreme love of the greatest good. Therefore charity cannot increase.

OBJ. 3: Further, increase is a kind of movement. Therefore wherever there is increase there is movement, and if there be increase of essence there is movement of essence. Now there is no movement of essence save either by corruption or generation. Therefore charity cannot increase essentially, unless it happen to be generated anew or corrupted, which is unreasonable.

ON THE CONTRARY, Augustine says (*Tract. lxxiv in Joan.*) that *charity merits increase that by increase it may merit perfection.*

I ANSWER THAT, The charity of a wayfarer can increase. For we are called wayfarers by reason of our being on the way to God, Who is the last end of our happiness. In this way we advance as we get nigh to God, Who is approached, not by steps of the body but by the affections of the soul: and this approach is the result of charity, since it unites man's mind to God. Consequently it is essential to the charity of a wayfarer that it can increase, for if it could not, all further advance along the way would cease. Hence the Apostle calls charity the way, when he says (1 Cor 12:31): *I show unto you yet a more excellent way.*

REPLY OBJ. 1: Charity is not subject to dimensive, but only to virtual quantity: and the latter depends not only on the number of objects, namely whether they be in greater number or of greater excellence, but also on the intensity of

secundum intensionem actus, ut magis vel minus aliquid diligatur. Et hoc modo virtualis quantitas caritatis augetur.

**AD SECUNDUM** dicendum quod caritas est in summo ex parte obiecti, inquantum scilicet eius obiectum est summum bonum, et ex hoc sequitur quod ipsa sit excellentior aliis virtutibus. Sed non est omnis caritas in summo quantum ad intensionem actus.

**AD TERTIUM** dicendum quod quidam dixerunt caritatem non augeri secundum suam essentiam, sed solum secundum radicationem in subiecto, vel secundum fervorem.

Sed hi propriam vocem ignoraverunt. Cum enim sit accidens, eius esse est inesse, unde nihil est aliud ipsam secundum essentiam augeri quam eam magis inesse subiecto, quod est eam magis radicari in subiecto. Similiter etiam ipsa essentialiter est virtus ordinata ad actum, unde idem est ipsam augeri secundum essentiam et ipsam habere efficaciam ad producendum ferventioris dilectionis actum. Augetur ergo essentialiter non quidem ita quod esse incipiat vel esse desinat in subiecto, sicut obiectio procedit, sed ita quod magis in subiecto esse incipiat.

the act, namely whether a thing is loved more, or less; it is in this way that the virtual quantity of charity increases.

REPLY OBJ. 2: Charity consists in an extreme with regard to its object, insofar as its object is the Supreme Good, and from this it follows that charity is the most excellent of the virtues. Yet not every charity consists in an extreme, as regards the intensity of the act.

REPLY OBJ. 3: Some have said that charity does not increase in its essence, but only as to its radication in its subject, or according to its fervor.

But these people did not know what they were talking about. For since charity is an accident, its being is to be in something. So that an essential increase of charity means nothing else but that it is yet more in its subject, which implies a greater radication in its subject. Furthermore, charity is essentially a virtue ordained to act, so that an essential increase of charity implies ability to produce an act of more fervent love. Hence charity increases essentially, not by beginning anew, or ceasing to be in its subject, as the objection imagines, but by beginning to be more and more in its subject.

# Article 5

*Whether charity increases by addition?*

**AD QUINTUM SIC PROCEDITUR.** Videtur quod caritas augeatur per additionem. Sicut enim est augmentum secundum quantitatem corporalem, ita secundum quantitatem virtualem. Sed augmentum quantitatis corporalis fit per additionem, dicit enim philosophus, in I de Gen., quod *augmentum est praeexistenti magnitudini additamentum.* Ergo etiam augmentum caritatis, quod est secundum virtualem quantitatem, erit per additionem.

**PRAETEREA,** caritas in anima est quoddam spirituale lumen, secundum illud I Ioan. II, *qui diligit fratrem suum in lumine manet.* Sed lumen crescit in aere per additionem, sicut in domo lumen crescit alia candela superaccensa. Ergo etiam caritas crescit in anima per additionem.

**PRAETEREA,** augere caritatem ad Deum pertinet, sicut et ipsam creare, secundum illud II ad Cor. IX, *augebit incrementa frugum iustitiae vestrae.* Sed Deus primo infundendo caritatem aliquid facit in anima quod ibi prius non erat. Ergo etiam augendo caritatem aliquid ibi facit quod prius non erat. Ergo caritas augetur per additionem.

**SED CONTRA** est quod caritas est forma simplex. Simplex autem simplici additum non facit aliquid maius,

OBJECTION 1: It would seem that charity increases by addition. For just as increase may be in respect of bodily quantity, so may it be according to virtual quantity. Now increase in bodily quantity results from addition; for the Philosopher says (*De Gener.* i, 5) that *increase is addition to pre-existing magnitude.* Therefore the increase of charity which is according to virtual quantity is by addition.

OBJ. 2: Further, charity is a kind of spiritual light in the soul, according to 1 John 2:10: *He that loveth his brother abideth in the light.* Now light increases in the air by addition; thus the light in a house increases when another candle is lit. Therefore charity also increases in the soul by addition.

OBJ. 3: Further, the increase of charity is God's work, even as the causing of it, according to 2 Cor. 9:10: *He will increase the growth of the fruits of your justice.* Now when God first infuses charity, He puts something in the soul that was not there before. Therefore also, when He increases charity, He puts something there which was not there before. Therefore charity increases by addition.

ON THE CONTRARY, Charity is a simple form. Now nothing greater results from the addition of one simple

ut probatur in VI Physic. Ergo caritas non augetur per additionem.

**RESPONDEO** dicendum quod omnis additio est alicuius ad aliquid. Unde in omni additione oportet saltem praeintelligere distinctionem eorum quorum unum additur alteri, ante ipsam additionem. Si igitur caritas addatur caritati, oportet praesupponi caritatem additam ut distinctam a caritate cui additur, non quidem ex necessitate secundum esse, sed saltem secundum intellectum. Posset enim Deus etiam quantitatem corporalem augere addendo aliquam magnitudinem non prius existentem, sed tunc creatam, quae quamvis prius non fuerit in rerum natura, habet tamen in se unde eius distinctio intelligi possit a quantitate cui additur. Si igitur caritas addatur caritati, oportet praesupponere, ad minus secundum intellectum, distinctionem unius caritatis ab alia.

Distinctio autem in formis est duplex, una quidem secundum speciem; alia autem secundum numerum. Distinctio quidem secundum speciem in habitibus est secundum diversitatem obiectorum, distinctio vero secundum numerum est secundum diversitatem subiecti. Potest igitur contingere quod aliquis habitus per additionem augeatur dum extenditur ad quaedam obiecta ad quae prius se non extendebat, et sic augetur scientia geometriae in eo qui de novo incipit scire aliqua geometricalia quae prius nesciebat. Hoc autem non potest dici de caritate, quia etiam minima caritas se extendit ad omnia illa quae sunt ex caritate diligenda. Non ergo talis additio in augmento caritatis potest intelligi praesupposita distinctione secundum speciem caritatis additae ad eam cui superadditur.

Relinquitur ergo, si fiat additio caritatis ad caritatem, quod hoc fit praesupposita distinctione secundum numerum, quae est secundum diversitatem subiectorum, sicut albedo augetur per hoc quod album additur albo, quamvis hoc augmento non fiat aliquid magis album. Sed hoc in proposito dici non potest. Quia subiectum caritatis non est nisi mens rationalis, unde tale caritatis augmentum fieri non posset nisi per hoc quod una mens rationalis alteri adderetur, quod est impossibile. Quamvis etiam si esset possibile tale augmentum, faceret maiorem diligentem, non autem magis diligentem. Relinquitur ergo quod nullo modo caritas augeri potest per additionem caritatis ad caritatem, sicut quidam ponunt.

Sic ergo caritas augetur solum per hoc quod subiectum magis ac magis participat caritatem, idest secundum quod magis reducitur in actum illius et magis subditur illi. Hic enim est modus augmenti proprius cuiuslibet formae quae intenditur, eo quod esse huiusmodi formae totaliter consistit in eo quod inhaeret susceptibili. Et ideo, cum magnitudo rei consequitur esse ipsius, formam esse maiorem hoc est eam magis

thing to another, as proved in *Phys.* iii, text. 59, and *Metaph.* ii, 4. Therefore charity does not increase by addition.

**I ANSWER THAT,** Every addition is of something to something else: so that in every addition we must at least presuppose that the things added together are distinct before the addition. Consequently if charity be added to charity, the added charity must be presupposed as distinct from charity to which it is added, not necessarily by a distinction of reality, but at least by a distinction of thought. For God is able to increase a bodily quantity by adding a magnitude which did not exist before, but was created at that very moment; which magnitude, though not pre-existent in reality, is nevertheless capable of being distinguished from the quantity to which it is added. Wherefore if charity be added to charity we must presuppose the distinction, at least logical, of the one charity from the other.

Now distinction among forms is twofold: specific and numeric. Specific distinction of habits follows diversity of objects, while numeric distinction follows distinction of subjects. Consequently a habit may receive increase through extending to objects to which it did not extend before: thus the science of geometry increases in one who acquires knowledge of geometrical matters which he ignored hitherto. But this cannot be said of charity, for even the slightest charity extends to all that we have to love by charity. Hence the addition which causes an increase of charity cannot be understood, as though the added charity were presupposed to be distinct specifically from that to which it is added.

It follows therefore that if charity be added to charity, we must presuppose a numerical distinction between them, which follows a distinction of subjects: thus whiteness receives an increase when one white thing is added to another, although such an increase does not make a thing whiter. This, however, does not apply to the case in point, since the subject of charity is none other than the rational mind, so that such like an increase of charity could only take place by one rational mind being added to another; which is impossible. Moreover, even if it were possible, the result would be a greater lover, but not a more loving one. It follows, therefore, that charity can by no means increase by addition of charity to charity, as some have held to be the case.

Accordingly charity increases only by its subject partaking of charity more and more subject thereto. For this is the proper mode of increase in a form that is intensified, since the being of such a form consists wholly in its adhering to its subject. Consequently, since the magnitude of a thing follows on its being, to say that a form is greater is the same as to say that it is more in its subject, and not that another form is added to it: for this would be the case if the form,

inesse susceptibili, non autem aliam formam advenire. Hoc enim esset si forma haberet aliquam quantitatem ex seipsa, non per comparationem ad subiectum. Sic igitur et caritas augetur per hoc quod intenditur in subiecto, et hoc est ipsam augeri secundum essentiam, non autem per hoc quod caritas addatur caritati.

AD PRIMUM ergo dicendum quod quantitas corporalis habet aliquid inquantum est quantitas; et aliquid inquantum est forma accidentalis. Inquantum est quantitas, habet quod sit distinguibilis secundum situm vel secundum numerum. Et ideo hoc modo consideratur augmentum magnitudinis per additionem; ut patet in animalibus. Inquantum vero est forma accidentalis, est distinguibilis solum secundum subiectum. Et secundum hoc habet proprium augmentum, sicut et aliae formae accidentales, per modum intensionis eius in subiecto, sicut patet in his quae rarefiunt, ut probat Philosophus, in IV Physic. Et similiter etiam scientia habet quantitatem, inquantum est habitus, ex parte obiectorum. Et sic augetur per additionem, inquantum aliquis plura cognoscit. Habet etiam quantitatem, inquantum est quaedam forma accidentalis, ex eo quod inest subiecto. Et secundum hoc augetur in eo qui certius eadem scibilia cognoscit nunc quam prius. Similiter etiam et caritas habet duplicem quantitatem. Sed secundum eam quae est ex parte obiecti, non augetur, ut dictum est. Unde relinquitur quod per solam intensionem augeatur.

AD SECUNDUM dicendum quod additio luminis ad lumen potest intelligi in aere propter diversitatem luminarium causantium lumen. Sed talis distinctio non habet locum in proposito, quia non est nisi unum luminare influens lumen caritatis.

AD TERTIUM dicendum quod infusio caritatis importat quandam mutationem secundum habere caritatem et non habere, et ideo oportet quod aliquid adveniat quod prius non infuit. Sed augmentatio caritatis importat mutationem secundum minus aut magis habere. Et ideo non oportet quod aliquid insit quod prius non infuerit, sed quod magis insit quod prius minus inerat. Et hoc est quod facit Deus caritatem augendo, scilicet quod magis insit, et quod perfectius similitudo spiritus sancti participetur in anima.

of itself, had any quantity, and not in comparison with its subject. Therefore charity increases by being intensified in its subject, and this is for charity to increase in its essence; and not by charity being added to charity.

REPLY OBJ. 1: Bodily quantity has something as quantity, and something else, insofar as it is an accidental form. As quantity, it is distinguishable in respect of position or number, and in this way we have the increase of magnitude by addition, as may be seen in animals. But insofar as it is an accidental form, it is distinguishable only in respect of its subject, and in this way it has its proper increase, like other accidental forms, by way of intensity in its subject, for instance in things subject to rarefaction, as is proved in *Phys.* iv, 9. In like manner science, as a habit, has its quantity from its objects, and accordingly it increases by addition, when a man knows more things; and again, as an accidental form, it has a certain quantity through being in its subject, and in this way it increases in a man who knows the same scientific truths with greater certainty now than before. In the same way charity has a twofold quantity; but with regard to that which it has from its object, it does not increase, as stated above: hence it follows that it increases solely by being intensified.

REPLY OBJ. 2: The addition of light to light can be understood through the light being intensified in the air on account of there being several luminaries giving light: but this distinction does not apply to the case in point, since there is but one luminary shedding forth the light of charity.

REPLY OBJ. 3: The infusion of charity denotes a change to the state of having charity from the state of not having it, so that something must needs come which was not there before. On the other hand, the increase of charity denotes a change to more having from less having, so that there is need, not for anything to be there that was not there before, but for something to be more there that previously was less there. This is what God does when He increases charity, that is He makes it to have a greater hold on the soul, and the likeness of the Holy Spirit to be more perfectly participated by the soul.

# Article 6

*Whether charity increases through every act of charity?*

AD SEXTUM SIC PROCEDITUR. Videtur quod quolibet actu caritatis caritas augeatur. Quod enim potest id quod maius est, potest id quod minus est. Sed quilibet actus caritatis meretur vitam aeternam, quae maius est

OBJECTION 1: It would seem that charity increases through every act of charity. For that which can do what is more, can do what is less. But every act of charity can merit everlasting life; and this is more than a simple addition of

quam simplex caritatis augmentum, quia vita aeterna includit caritatis perfectionem. Ergo multo magis quilibet actus caritatis caritatem auget.

**PRAETEREA**, sicuti habitus virtutum acquisitarum generatur ex actibus, ita etiam augmentum caritatis causatur per actus caritatis. Sed quilibet actus virtuosus operatur ad virtutis generationem. Ergo etiam quilibet actus caritatis operatur ad caritatis augmentum.

**PRAETEREA**, Gregorius dicit quod *in via Dei stare retrocedere est*. Sed nullus, dum movetur actu caritatis, retrocedit. Ergo quicumque movetur actu caritatis, procedit in via Dei. Ergo quolibet actu caritatis caritas augetur.

**SED CONTRA** est quod effectus non excedit virtutem causae. Sed quandoque aliquis actus caritatis cum aliquo tepore vel remissione emittitur. Non ergo perducit ad excellentiorem caritatem, sed magis disponit ad minorem.

**RESPONDEO** dicendum quod augmentum spirituale caritatis quodammodo simile est augmento corporali. Augmentum autem corporale in animalibus et plantis non est motus continuus, ita scilicet quod, si aliquid tantum augetur in tanto tempore, necesse sit quod proportionaliter in qualibet parte illius temporis aliquid augeatur, sicut contingit in motu locali, sed per aliquod tempus natura operatur disponens ad augmentum et nihil augens actu, et postmodum producit in effectum id ad quod disposuerat, augendo animal vel plantam in actu. Ita etiam non quolibet actu caritatis caritas actu augetur, sed quilibet actus caritatis disponit ad caritatis augmentum, inquantum ex uno actu caritatis homo redditur promptior iterum ad agendum secundum caritatem; et, habilitate crescente, homo prorumpit in actum ferventiorem dilectionis, quo conetur ad caritatis profectum; et tunc caritas augetur in actu.

**AD PRIMUM** ergo dicendum quod quilibet actus caritatis meretur vitam aeternam, non quidem statim exhibendam, sed suo tempore. Similiter etiam quilibet actus caritatis meretur caritatis augmentum, non tamen statim augetur, sed quando aliquis conatur ad huiusmodi augmentum.

**AD SECUNDUM** dicendum quod etiam in generatione virtutis acquisitae non quilibet actus complet generationem virtutis, sed quilibet operatur ad eam ut disponens, et ultimus, qui est perfectior, agens in virtute omnium praecedentium, reducit eam in actum. Sicut etiam est in multis guttis cavantibus lapidem.

**AD TERTIUM** dicendum quod in via Dei procedit aliquis non solum dum actu caritas eius augetur, sed etiam dum disponitur ad augmentum.

charity, since it includes the perfection of charity. Much more, therefore, does every act of charity increase charity.

**OBJ. 2**: Further, just as the habits of acquired virtue are engendered by acts, so too an increase of charity is caused by an act of charity. Now each virtuous act conduces to the engendering of virtue. Therefore also each virtuous act of charity conduces to the increase of charity.

**OBJ. 3**: Further, Gregory says that *to stand still in the way to God is to go back*. Now no man goes back when he is moved by an act of charity. Therefore whoever is moved by an act of charity goes forward in the way to God. Therefore charity increases through every act of charity.

**ON THE CONTRARY**, The effect does not surpass the power of its cause. But an act of charity is sometimes done with tepidity or slackness. Therefore it does not conduce to a more excellent charity, rather does it dispose one to a lower degree.

**I ANSWER THAT**, The spiritual increase of charity is somewhat like the increase of a body. Now bodily increase in animals and plants is not a continuous movement, so that, to wit, if a thing increase so much in so much time, it need to increase proportionally in each part of that time, as happens in local movement; but for a certain space of time nature works by disposing for the increase, without causing any actual increase, and afterwards brings into effect that to which it had disposed, by giving the animal or plant an actual increase. In like manner charity does not actually increase through every act of charity, but each act of charity disposes to an increase of charity, insofar as one act of charity makes man more ready to act again according to charity, and this readiness increasing, man breaks out into an act of more fervent love, and strives to advance in charity, and then his charity increases actually.

**REPLY OBJ. 1**: Every act of charity merits everlasting life, which, however, is not to be bestowed then and there, but at its proper time. In like manner every act of charity merits an increase of charity; yet this increase does not take place at once, but when we strive for that increase.

**REPLY OBJ. 2**: Even when an acquired virtue is being engendered, each act does not complete the formation of the virtue, but conduces towards that effect by disposing to it, while the last act, which is the most perfect, and acts in virtue of all those that preceded it, reduces the virtue into act, just as when many drops hollow out a stone.

**REPLY OBJ. 3**: Man advances in the way to God, not merely by actual increase of charity, but also by being disposed to that increase.

# Article 7

*Whether charity increases indefinitely?*

AD SEPTIMUM SIC PROCEDITUR. Videtur quod caritas non augeatur in infinitum. Omnis enim motus est ad aliquem finem et terminum, ut dicitur in II Metaphys. Sed augmentum caritatis est quidam motus. Ergo tendit ad aliquem finem et terminum. Non ergo caritas in infinitum augetur.

PRAETEREA, nulla forma excedit capacitatem sui subiecti. Sed capacitas creaturae rationalis, quae est subiectum caritatis, est finita. Ergo caritas in infinitum augeri non potest.

PRAETEREA, omne finitum per continuum augmentum potest pertingere ad quantitatem alterius finiti quantumcumque maioris, nisi forte id quod accrescit per augmentum semper sit minus et minus; sicut Philosophus dicit, in III Physic., quod si uni lineae addatur quod subtrahitur ab alia linea quae in infinitum dividitur, in infinitum additione facta, nunquam pertingetur ad quandam determinatam quantitatem quae est composita ex duabus lineis, scilicet divisa et ea cui additur quod ex alia subtrahitur. Quod in proposito non contingit, non enim necesse est ut secundum caritatis augmentum sit minus quam prius; sed magis probabile est quod sit aequale aut maius. Cum ergo caritas patriae sit quiddam finitum, si caritas viae in infinitum augeri potest, sequitur quod caritas viae possit adaequare caritatem patriae, quod est inconveniens. Non ergo caritas viae in infinitum potest augeri.

SED CONTRA est quod apostolus dicit, ad Philipp. III. *Non quod iam acceperim, aut iam perfectus sim, sequor autem si quo modo comprehendam.* Ubi dicit Glossa, *nemo fidelium, etsi multum profecerit, dicat, sufficit mihi. Qui enim hoc dicit, exit de via ante finem.* Ergo semper in via caritas potest magis ac magis augeri.

RESPONDEO dicendum quod terminus augmento alicuius formae potest praefigi tripliciter. Uno modo, ex ratione ipsius formae, quae habet terminatam mensuram, ad quam cum perventum fuerit, non potest ultra procedi in forma, sed si ultra processum fuerit, pervenietur ad aliam formam, sicut patet in pallore, cuius terminos per continuam alterationem aliquis transit, vel ad albedinem vel ad nigredinem perveniens. Alio modo, ex parte agentis, cuius virtus non se extendit ad ulterius augendum formam in subiecto. Tertio, ex parte subiecti, quod non est capax amplioris perfectionis.

Nullo autem istorum modorum imponitur terminus augmento caritatis in statu viae. Ipsa enim caritas secundum rationem propriae speciei terminum augmenti non habet, est enim participatio quaedam infinitae caritatis, quae est Spiritus Sanctus. Similiter etiam causa

OBJECTION 1: It would seem that charity does not increase indefinitely. For every movement is towards some end and term, as stated in *Metaph.* ii, text. 8, 9. But the increase of charity is a movement. Therefore it tends to an end and term. Therefore charity does not increase indefinitely.

OBJ. 2: Further, no form surpasses the capacity of its subject. But the capacity of the rational creature who is the subject of charity is finite. Therefore charity cannot increase indefinitely.

OBJ. 3: Further, every finite thing can, by continual increase, attain to the quantity of another finite thing however much greater, unless the amount of its increase be ever less and less. Thus the Philosopher states (*Phys.* iii, 6) that if we divide a line into an indefinite number of parts, and take these parts away and add them indefinitely to another line, we shall never arrive at any definite quantity resulting from those two lines, viz. the one from which we subtracted and the one to which we added what was subtracted. But this does not occur in the case in point: because there is no need for the second increase of charity to be less than the first, since rather is it probable that it would be equal or greater. As, therefore, the charity of the blessed is something finite, if the charity of the wayfarer can increase indefinitely, it would follow that the charity of the way can equal the charity of heaven; which is absurd. Therefore the wayfarer's charity cannot increase indefinitely.

ON THE CONTRARY, The Apostle says (Phil 3:12): *Not as though I had already attained, or were already perfect; but I follow after, if I may, by any means apprehend,* on which words a gloss says: *Even if he has made great progress, let none of the faithful say: 'Enough.' For whosoever says this, leaves the road before coming to his destination.* Therefore the wayfarer's charity can ever increase more and more.

I ANSWER THAT, A term to the increase of a form may be fixed in three ways: first by reason of the form itself having a fixed measure, and when this has been reached it is no longer possible to go any further in that form, but if any further advance is made, another form is attained. An example of this is paleness, the bounds of which may, by continual alteration, be passed, either so that whiteness ensues, or so that blackness results. Second, on the part of the agent, whose power does not extend to a further increase of the form in its subject. Third, on the part of the subject, which is not capable of ulterior perfection.

Now, in none of these ways, is a limit imposed to the increase of man's charity, while he is in the state of the wayfarer. For charity itself considered as such has no limit to its increase, since it is a participation of the infinite charity which is the Holy Spirit. In like manner the cause

augens caritatem est infinitae virtutis, scilicet Deus. Similiter etiam ex parte subiecti terminus huic augmento praefigi non potest, quia semper, caritate excrescente, superexcrescit habilitas ad ulterius augmentum. Unde relinquitur quod caritatis augmento nullus terminus praefigi possit in hac vita.

**AD PRIMUM** ergo dicendum quod augmentum caritatis est ad aliquem finem, sed ille finis non est in hac vita, sed in futura.

**AD SECUNDUM** dicendum quod capacitas creaturae spiritualis per caritatem augetur, quia per ipsam cor dilatatur, secundum illud II ad Cor. VI, *cor nostrum dilatatum est.* Et ideo adhuc ulterius manet habilitas ad maius augmentum.

**AD TERTIUM** dicendum quod ratio illa procedit in his quae habent quantitatem eiusdem rationis, non autem in his quae habent diversam rationem quantitatis; sicut linea, quantumcumque crescat, non attingit quantitatem superficiei. Non est autem eadem ratio quantitatis caritatis viae, quae sequitur cognitionem fidei, et caritatis patriae, quae sequitur visionem apertam. Unde ratio non sequitur.

of the increase of charity, viz. God, is possessed of infinite power. Furthermore, on the part of its subject, no limit to this increase can be determined, because whenever charity increases, there is a corresponding increased ability to receive a further increase. It is therefore evident that it is not possible to fix any limits to the increase of charity in this life.

**REPLY OBJ. 1**: The increase of charity is directed to an end, which is not in this, but in a future life.

**REPLY OBJ. 2**: The capacity of the rational creature is increased by charity, because the heart is enlarged thereby, according to 2 Cor. 6:11: *Our heart is enlarged*; so that it still remains capable of receiving a further increase.

**REPLY OBJ. 3**: This argument holds good in those things which have the same kind of quantity, but not in those which have different kinds: thus however much a line may increase it does not reach the quantity of a superficies. Now the quantity of a wayfarer's charity which follows the knowledge of faith is not of the same kind as the quantity of the charity of the blessed, which follows open vision. Hence the argument does not prove.

# Article 8

*Whether charity can be perfect in this life?*

**AD OCTAVUM SIC PROCEDITUR**. Videtur quod caritas in hac vita non possit esse perfecta. Maxime enim haec perfectio in apostolis fuisset. Sed in eis non fuit, dicit enim apostolus, ad Philipp. III, *non quod iam comprehenderim aut perfectus sim.* Ergo caritas in hac vita perfecta esse non potest.

**PRAETEREA**, Augustinus dicit, in libro Octoginta trium Quaest., quod *nutrimentum caritatis est diminutio cupiditatis; perfectio, nulla cupiditas.* Sed hoc non potest esse in hac vita, in qua sine peccato vivere non possumus, secundum illud I Ioan. I, *si dixerimus quia peccatum non habemus, nos ipsos seducimus*, omne autem peccatum ex aliqua inordinata cupiditate procedit. Ergo in hac vita caritas perfecta esse non potest.

**PRAETEREA**, illud quod iam perfectum est non habet ulterius crescere. Sed caritas in hac vita semper potest augeri, ut dictum est. Ergo caritas in hac vita non potest esse perfecta.

**SED CONTRA** est quod Augustinus dicit, super Prim. Canonic. Ioan., *caritas cum fuerit roborata, perficitur, cum ad perfectionem pervenerit, dicit, cupio dissolvi et esse cum Christo.* Sed hoc possibile est in hac vita, sicut in Paulo fuit. Ergo caritas in hac vita potest esse perfecta.

**OBJECTION 1**: It would seem that charity cannot be perfect in this life. For this would have been the case with the apostles before all others. Yet it was not so, since the Apostle says (Phil 3:12): *Not as though I had already attained, or were already perfect.* Therefore charity cannot be perfect in this life.

**OBJ. 2**: Further, Augustine says (*83 Questions*, Q. 36) that *whatever kindles charity quenches cupidity, but where charity is perfect, cupidity is done away altogether.* But this cannot be in this world, wherein it is impossible to live without sin, according to 1 John 1:8: *If we say that we have no sin, we deceive ourselves.* Now all sin arises from some inordinate cupidity. Therefore charity cannot be perfect in this life.

**OBJ. 3**: Further, what is already perfect cannot be perfected any more. But in this life charity can always increase, as stated above (A. 7). Therefore charity cannot be perfect in this life.

**ON THE CONTRARY**, Augustine says (*In prim. canon. Joan.* Tract. v) *Charity is perfected by being strengthened; and when it has been brought to perfection, it exclaims, 'I desire to be dissolved and to be with Christ.'* Now this is possible in this life, as in the case of Paul. Therefore charity can be perfect in this life.

RESPONDEO dicendum quod perfectio caritatis potest intelligi dupliciter, uno modo, ex parte diligibilis; alio modo, ex parte diligentis. Ex parte quidem diligibilis perfecta est caritas ut diligatur aliquid quantum diligibile est. Deus autem tantum diligibilis est quantum bonus est. Bonitas autem eius est infinita. Unde infinite diligibilis est. Nulla autem creatura potest eum diligere infinite, cum quaelibet virtus creata sit finita. Unde per hunc modum nullius creaturae caritas potest esse perfecta, sed solum caritas Dei, qua seipsum diligit.

Ex parte vero diligentis caritas dicitur perfecta quando aliquis secundum totum suum posse diligit. Quod quidem contingit tripliciter. Uno modo, sic quod totum cor hominis actualiter semper feratur in Deum. Et haec est perfectio caritatis patriae, quae non est possibilis in hac vita, in qua impossibile est, propter humanae vitae infirmitatem, semper actu cogitare de Deo et moveri dilectione ad ipsum. Alio modo, ut homo studium suum deputet ad vacandum Deo et rebus divinis, praetermissis aliis nisi quantum necessitas praesentis vitae requirit. Et ista est perfectio caritatis quae est possibilis in via, non tamen est communis omnibus caritatem habentibus. Tertio modo, ita quod habitualiter aliquis totum cor suum ponat in Deo, ita scilicet quod nihil cogitet vel velit quod sit divinae dilectioni contrarium. Et haec perfectio est communis omnibus caritatem habentibus.

AD PRIMUM ergo dicendum quod apostolus negat de se perfectionem patriae. Unde Glossa ibi dicit quod *perfectus erat viator, sed nondum ipsius itineris perfectione perventor.*

AD SECUNDUM dicendum quod hoc dicitur propter peccata venialia. Quae non contrariantur habitui caritatis, sed actui, et ita non repugnant perfectioni viae, sed perfectioni patriae.

AD TERTIUM dicendum quod perfectio viae non est perfectio simpliciter. Et ideo semper habet quo crescat.

I ANSWER THAT, The perfection of charity may be understood in two ways: first with regard to the object loved, second with regard to the person who loves. With regard to the object loved, charity is perfect, if the object be loved as much as it is lovable. Now God is as lovable as He is good, and His goodness is infinite, wherefore He is infinitely lovable. But no creature can love Him infinitely since all created power is finite. Consequently no creature's charity can be perfect in this way; the charity of God alone can, whereby He loves Himself.

On the part of the person who loves, charity is perfect, when he loves as much as he can. This happens in three ways. First, so that a man's whole heart is always actually borne towards God: this is the perfection of the charity of heaven, and is not possible in this life, wherein, by reason of the weakness of human life, it is impossible to think always actually of God, and to be moved by love towards Him. Second, so that man makes an earnest endeavor to give his time to God and Divine things, while scorning other things except insofar as the needs of the present life demand. This is the perfection of charity that is possible to a wayfarer; but is not common to all who have charity. Third, so that a man gives his whole heart to God habitually, viz. by neither thinking nor desiring anything contrary to the love of God; and this perfection is common to all who have charity.

REPLY OBJ. 1: The Apostle denies that he has the perfection of heaven, wherefore a gloss on the same passage says that *he was a perfect wayfarer, but had not yet achieved the perfection to which the way leads.*

REPLY OBJ. 2: This is said on account of venial sins, which are contrary, not to the habit, but to the act of charity: hence they are incompatible, not with the perfection of the way, but with that of heaven.

REPLY OBJ. 3: The perfection of the way is not perfection simply, wherefore it can always increase.

# Article 9

*Whether charity is rightly distinguished into three degrees: beginning, progress, and perfection?*

AD NONUM SIC PROCEDITUR. Videtur quod inconvenienter distinguantur tres gradus caritatis, scilicet caritas *incipiens, proficiens* et *perfecta.* Inter principium enim caritatis et eius ultimam perfectionem sunt multi gradus medii. Non ergo unum solum medium debuit poni.

PRAETEREA, statim cum caritas incipit esse, incipit etiam proficere non ergo debet distingui caritas proficiens a caritate incipiente.

PRAETEREA, quantumcumque aliquis habeat in hoc mundo caritatem perfectam, potest etiam eius caritas

OBJECTION 1: It would seem unfitting to distinguish three degrees of charity, beginning, progress, and perfection. For there are many degrees between the beginning of charity and its ultimate perfection. Therefore it is not right to put only one.

OBJ. 2: Further, charity begins to progress as soon as it begins to be. Therefore we ought not to distinguish between charity as progressing and as beginning.

OBJ. 3: Further, in this world, however perfect a man's charity may be, it can increase, as stated above (A. 7). Now

augeri, ut dictum est. Sed caritatem augeri est ipsam proficere. Ergo caritas perfecta non debet distingui a caritate proficiente. Inconvenienter igitur praedicti tres gradus caritatis assignantur.

**SED CONTRA** est quod Augustinus dicit, super Prim. Canonic. Ioan., *caritas cum fuerit nata, nutritur*, quod pertinet ad incipientes; *cum fuerit nutrita, roboratur*, quod pertinet ad proficientes; *cum fuerit roborata, perficitur*, quod pertinet ad perfectos. Ergo est triplex gradus caritatis.

**RESPONDEO** dicendum quod spirituale augmentum caritatis considerari potest quantum ad aliquid simile corporali hominis augmento. Quod quidem quamvis in plurimas partes distingui possit, habet tamen aliquas determinatas distinctiones secundum determinatas actiones vel studia ad quae homo perducitur per augmentum, sicut infantilis aetas dicitur antequam habeat usum rationis; postea autem distinguitur alius status hominis quando iam incipit loqui et ratione uti; iterum tertius status eius est pubertatis, quando iam incipit posse generare; et sic inde quousque perveniatur ad perfectum.

Ita etiam et diversi gradus caritatis distinguuntur secundum diversa studia ad quae homo perducitur per caritatis augmentum. Nam primo quidem incumbit homini studium principale ad recedendum a peccato et resistendum concupiscentiis eius, quae in contrarium caritatis movent. Et hoc pertinet ad incipientes, in quibus caritas est nutrienda vel fovenda ne corrumpatur. Secundum autem studium succedit, ut homo principaliter intendat ad hoc quod in bono proficiat. Et hoc studium pertinet ad proficientes, qui ad hoc principaliter intendunt ut in eis caritas per augmentum roboretur. Tertium autem studium est ut homo ad hoc principaliter intendat ut Deo inhaereat et eo fruatur. Et hoc pertinet ad perfectos, qui *cupiunt dissolvi et esse cum Christo*.

Sicut etiam videmus in motu corporali quod primum est recessus a termino; secundum autem est appropinquatio ad alium terminum; tertium autem quies in termino.

**AD PRIMUM** ergo dicendum quod omnis illa determinata distinctio quae potest accipi in augmento caritatis, comprehenditur sub istis tribus quae dicta sunt. Sicut etiam omnis divisio continuorum comprehenditur sub tribus his, principio, medio et fine; ut philosophus dicit, in I de caelo.

**AD SECUNDUM** dicendum quod illis in quibus caritas incipit, quamvis proficiant, principalior tamen cura imminet ut resistant peccatis, quorum impugnatione inquietantur. Sed postea, hanc impugnationem minus sentientes, iam quasi securius ad profectum intendunt; ex una tamen parte facientes opus, et ex alia parte habentes manum ad gladium, ut dicitur in Esdra de aedificatoribus Ierusalem.

for charity to increase is to progress. Therefore perfect charity ought not to be distinguished from progressing charity: and so the aforesaid degrees are unsuitably assigned to charity.

**ON THE CONTRARY**, Augustine says (*In prim. canon. Joan.* Tract. v) *As soon as charity is born it takes food*, which refers to beginners, *after taking food, it waxes strong*, which refers to those who are progressing, *and when it has become strong it is perfected*, which refers to the perfect. Therefore there are three degrees of charity.

**I ANSWER THAT**, The spiritual increase of charity may be considered in respect of a certain likeness to the growth of the human body. For although this latter growth may be divided into many parts, yet it has certain fixed divisions according to those particular actions or pursuits to which man is brought by this same growth. Thus we speak of a man being an infant until he has the use of reason, after which we distinguish another state of man wherein he begins to speak and to use his reason, while there is again a third state, that of puberty when he begins to acquire the power of generation, and so on until he arrives at perfection.

In like manner the diverse degrees of charity are distinguished according to the different pursuits to which man is brought by the increase of charity. For at first it is incumbent on man to occupy himself chiefly with avoiding sin and resisting his concupiscences, which move him in opposition to charity: this concerns beginners, in whom charity has to be fed or fostered lest it be destroyed: in the second place man's chief pursuit is to aim at progress in good, and this is the pursuit of the proficient, whose chief aim is to strengthen their charity by adding to it: while man's third pursuit is to aim chiefly at union with and enjoyment of God: this belongs to the perfect who *desire to be dissolved and to be with Christ*.

In like manner we observe in local motion that at first there is withdrawal from one term, then approach to the other term, and third, rest in this term.

**REPLY OBJ. 1**: All these distinct degrees which can be discerned in the increase of charity, are comprised in the aforesaid three, even as every division of continuous things is included in these three—the beginning, the middle, and the end, as the Philosopher states (*De Caelo* i, 1).

**REPLY OBJ. 2**: Although those who are beginners in charity may progress, yet the chief care that besets them is to resist the sins which disturb them by their onslaught. Afterwards, however, when they come to feel this onslaught less, they begin to tend to perfection with greater security; yet with one hand doing the work, and with the other holding the sword as related in 2 Esdr. 4:17 about those who built up Jerusalem.

**AD TERTIUM** dicendum quod perfecti etiam in caritate proficiunt, sed non est ad hoc principalis eorum cura, sed iam eorum studium circa hoc maxime versatur ut Deo inhaereant. Et quamvis hoc etiam quaerant et incipientes et proficientes, tamen magis sentiunt circa alia sollicitudinem, incipientes quidem de vitatione peccatorum, proficientes vero de profectu virtutum.

**REPLY OBJ. 3**: Even the perfect make progress in charity: yet this is not their chief care, but their aim is principally directed towards union with God. And though both the beginner and the proficient seek this, yet their solicitude is chiefly about other things, with the beginner, about avoiding sin, with the proficient, about progressing in virtue.

# Article 10

*Whether charity can decrease?*

**AD DECIMUM SIC PROCEDITUR.** Videtur quod caritas possit diminui. Contraria enim nata sunt fieri circa idem. Sed diminutio et augmentum sunt contraria. Cum igitur caritas augeatur, ut dictum est supra, videtur quod etiam possit diminui.

**PRAETEREA,** Augustinus, X Confess., ad Deum loquens, dicit, *minus te amat qui tecum aliquid amat.* Et in libro Octoginta trium Quaest. dicit quod *nutrimentum caritatis est diminutio cupiditatis,* ex quo videtur quod etiam e converso augmentum cupiditatis sit diminutio caritatis. Sed cupiditas, qua amatur aliquid aliud quam Deus, potest in homine crescere. Ergo caritas potest diminui.

**PRAETEREA,** sicut Augustinus dicit, VIII super Gen. ad Litt., *non ita Deus operatur hominem iustum iustificando eum, ut, si abscesserit, maneat in absente quod fecit,* ex quo potest accipi quod eodem modo Deus operatur in homine caritatem eius conservando, quo operatur primo ei caritatem infundendo. Sed in prima caritatis infusione minus se praeparanti Deus minorem caritatem infundit. Ergo etiam in conservatione caritatis minus se praeparanti minorem caritatem conservat. Potest ergo caritas diminui.

**SED CONTRA** est quod caritas in Scriptura igni comparatur, secundum illud Cant. VIII, *lampades eius,* scilicet caritatis, *lampades ignis atque flammarum.* Sed ignis, quandiu manet, semper ascendit. Ergo caritas, quandiu manet, ascendere potest; sed descendere, idest diminui, non potest.

**RESPONDEO** dicendum quod quantitas caritatis quam habet in comparatione ad obiectum proprium, minui non potest, sicut nec augeri, ut supra dictum est.

Sed cum augeatur secundum quantitatem quam habet per comparationem ad subiectum, hic oportet considerare utrum ex hac parte diminui possit. Si autem diminuatur, oportet quod vel diminuatur per aliquem actum; vel per solam cessationem ab actu. Per cessationem quidem ab actu diminuuntur virtutes ex actibus acquisitae, et quandoque etiam corrumpuntur, ut supra dictum est, unde de amicitia Philosophus dicit, in VIII

**OBJECTION 1**: It would seem that charity can decrease. For contraries by their nature affect the same subject. Now increase and decrease are contraries. Since then charity increases, as stated above (A. 4), it seems that it can also decrease.

**OBJ. 2**: Further, Augustine, speaking to God, says (*Confess.* x) *He loves Thee less, who loves aught besides Thee*: and (*83 Questions*, Q. 36) he says that *what kindles charity quenches cupidity.* From this it seems to follow that, on the contrary, what arouses cupidity quenches charity. But cupidity, whereby a man loves something besides God, can increase in man. Therefore charity can decrease.

**OBJ. 3**: Further, as Augustine says (*Gen ad lit.* viii, 12) *God makes the just man, by justifying him, but in such a way, that if the man turns away from God, he no longer retains the effect of the Divine operation.* From this we may gather that when God preserves charity in man, He works in the same way as when He first infuses charity into him. Now at the first infusion of charity God infuses less charity into him that prepares himself less. Therefore also in preserving charity, He preserves less charity in him that prepares himself less. Therefore charity can decrease.

**ON THE CONTRARY**, In Scripture, charity is compared to fire, according to Cant 8:6: *The lamps thereof,* i.e., of charity, *are fire and flames.* Now fire ever mounts upward so long as it lasts. Therefore as long as charity endures, it can ascend, but cannot descend, i.e., decrease.

**I ANSWER THAT**, The quantity which charity has in comparison with its proper object, cannot decrease, even as neither can it increase, as stated above (A. 4, ad 2).

Since, however, it increases in that quantity which it has in comparison with its subject, here is the place to consider whether it can decrease in this way. Now, if it decrease, this must needs be either through an act, or by the mere cessation from act. It is true that virtues acquired through acts decrease and sometimes cease altogether through cessation from act, as stated above (I-II, Q. 53, A. 3). Wherefore the Philosopher says, in reference to friendship (*Ethic.* viii, 5)

Ethic., quod *multas amicitias inappellatio solvit*, idest non appellare amicum vel non colloqui ei. Sed hoc ideo est quia conservatio uniuscuiusque rei dependet ex sua causa; causa autem virtutis acquisitae est actus humanus; unde, cessantibus humanis actibus, virtus acquisita diminuitur et tandem totaliter corrumpitur. Sed hoc in caritate locum non habet, quia caritas non causatur ab humanis actibus, sed solum a Deo, ut supra dictum est. Unde relinquitur quod etiam cessante actu, propter hoc nec diminuitur nec corrumpitur, si desit peccatum in ipsa cessatione.

Relinquitur ergo quod diminutio caritatis non possit causari nisi vel a Deo, vel ab aliquo peccato. A Deo quidem non causatur aliquis defectus in nobis nisi per modum poenae, secundum quod subtrahit gratiam in poenam peccati. Unde nec ei competit diminuere caritatem nisi per modum poenae. Poena autem debetur peccato.

Unde relinquitur quod, si caritas diminuatur, quod causa diminutionis eius sit peccatum, vel effective vel meritorie. Neutro autem modo peccatum mortale diminuit caritatem, sed totaliter corrumpit ipsam, et effective, quia omne peccatum mortale contrariatur caritati, ut infra dicetur; et etiam meritorie, quia qui peccando mortaliter aliquid contra caritatem agit, dignum est ut Deus ei subtrahat caritatem.

Similiter etiam nec per peccatum veniale caritas diminui potest, neque effective, neque meritorie. Effective quidem non, quia ad ipsam caritatem non attingit. Caritas enim est circa finem ultimum, veniale autem peccatum est quaedam inordinatio circa ea quae sunt ad finem. Non autem diminuitur amor finis ex hoc quod aliquis inordinationem aliquam committit circa ea quae sunt ad finem, sicut aliquando contingit quod aliqui infirmi, multum amantes sanitatem, inordinate tamen se habent circa diaetae observationem; sicut etiam et in speculativis falsae opiniones circa ea quae deducuntur ex principiis, non diminuunt certitudinem principiorum. Similiter etiam veniale peccatum non meretur diminutionem caritatis. Cum enim aliquis delinquit in minori, non meretur detrimentum pati in maiori. Deus enim non plus se avertit ab homine quam homo se avertit ab ipso. Unde qui inordinate se habet circa ea quae sunt ad finem, non meretur detrimentum pati in caritate, per quam ordinatur ad ultimum finem.

Unde consequens est quod caritas nullo modo diminui possit, directe loquendo. Potest tamen indirecte dici diminutio caritatis dispositio ad corruptionem ipsius, quae fit vel per peccata venialia; vel etiam per cessationem ab exercitio operum caritatis.

**AD PRIMUM** ergo dicendum quod contraria sunt circa idem quando subiectum aequaliter se habet ad utrumque contrariorum. Sed caritas non eodem modo

*that want of intercourse*, i.e., the neglect to call upon or speak with one's friends, *has destroyed many a friendship*. Now this is because the safe-keeping of a thing depends on its cause, and the cause of human virtue is a human act, so that when human acts cease, the virtue acquired thereby decreases and at last ceases altogether. Yet this does not occur to charity, because it is not the result of human acts, but is caused by God alone, as stated above (A. 2). Hence it follows that even when its act ceases, it does not for this reason decrease, or cease altogether, unless the cessation involves a sin.

The consequence is that a decrease of charity cannot be caused except either by God or by some sinful act. Now no defect is caused in us by God, except by way of punishment, insofar as He withdraws His grace in punishment of sin. Hence He does not diminish charity except by way of punishment: and this punishment is due on account of sin.

It follows, therefore, that if charity decrease, the cause of this decrease must be sin either effectively or by way of merit. But mortal sin does not diminish charity, in either of these ways, but destroys it entirely, both effectively, because every mortal sin is contrary to charity, as we shall state further on (A. 12), and by way of merit, since when, by sinning mortally, a man acts against charity, he deserves that God should withdraw charity from him.

In like manner, neither can venial sin diminish charity either effectively or by way of merit. Not effectively, because it does not touch charity, since charity is about the last end, whereas venial sin is a disorder about things directed to the end: and a man's love for the end is nonetheless through his committing an inordinate act as regards the things directed to the end. Thus sick people sometimes, though they love health much, are irregular in keeping to their diet: and thus again, in speculative sciences, the false opinions that are derived from the principles, do not diminish the certitude of the principles. So too, venial sin does not merit diminution of charity; for when a man offends in a small matter he does not deserve to be mulcted in a great matter. For God does not turn away from man, more than man turns away from Him: wherefore he that is out of order in respect of things directed to the end, does not deserve to be mulcted in charity whereby he is ordered to the last end.

The consequence is that charity can by no means be diminished, if we speak of direct causality, yet whatever disposes to its corruption may be said to conduce indirectly to its diminution, and such are venial sins, or even the cessation from the practice of works of charity.

**REPLY OBJ. 1:** Contraries affect the same subject when that subject stands in equal relation to both. But charity does not stand in equal relation to increase and decrease.

se habet ad augmentum et diminutionem, potest enim habere causam augentem, sed non potest habere causam minuentem, sicut dictum est. Unde ratio non sequitur.

Ad secundum dicendum quod duplex est cupiditas. Una quidem qua finis in creaturis constituitur. Et haec totaliter mortificat caritatem, cum sit *venenum* ipsius, ut Augustinus dicit ibidem. Et hoc facit quod Deus minus ametur, scilicet quam debet amari ex caritate, non quidem caritatem diminuendo, sed eam totaliter tollendo. Et sic intelligendum est quod dicitur, *minus te amat qui tecum aliquid amat*, subditur enim, quod *non propter te amat*. Quod non contingit in peccato veniali, sed solum in mortali, quod enim amatur in peccato veniali, propter Deum amatur habitu, etsi non actu. Est autem alia cupiditas venialis peccati, quae semper diminuitur per caritatem, sed tamen talis cupiditas caritatem diminuere non potest, ratione iam dicta.

Ad tertium dicendum quod in infusione caritatis requiritur motus liberi arbitrii, sicut supra dictum est. Et ideo illud quod diminuit intensionem liberi arbitrii, dispositive operatur ad hoc quod caritas infundenda sit minor. Sed ad conservationem caritatis non requiritur motus liberi arbitrii, alioquin non remaneret in dormientibus. Unde per impedimentum intensionis motus liberi arbitrii non diminuitur caritas.

For it can have a cause of increase, but not of decrease, as stated above. Hence the argument does not prove.

Reply Obj. 2: Cupidity is twofold, one whereby man places his end in creatures, and this kills charity altogether, since it is its poison, as Augustine states (*Confess.* x). This makes us love God less (i.e., less than we ought to love Him by charity), not indeed by diminishing charity but by destroying it altogether. It is thus that we must understand the saying: *He loves Thee less, who loves aught beside Thee*, for he adds these words, *which he loveth not for Thee*. This does not apply to venial sin, but only to mortal sin: since that which we love in venial sin, is loved for God's sake habitually though not actually. There is another cupidity, that of venial sin, which is always diminished by charity: and yet this cupidity cannot diminish charity, for the reason given above.

Reply Obj. 3: A movement of the free-will is requisite in the infusion of charity, as stated above (I-II, Q. 113, A. 3). Wherefore that which diminishes the intensity of the free-will conduces dispositively to a diminution in the charity to be infused. On the other hand, no movement of the free-will is required for the safe-keeping of charity, else it would not remain in us while we sleep. Hence charity does not decrease on account of an obstacle on the part of the intensity of the free-will's movement.

# Article 11

*Whether we can lose charity when once we have it?*

Ad undecimum sic proceditur. Videtur quod caritas semel habita non possit amitti. Si enim amittitur, non amittitur nisi propter peccatum. Sed ille qui habet caritatem non potest peccare. Dicitur enim I Ioan. III, *omnis enim qui natus est ex Deo, peccatum non facit, quia semen ipsius in eo manet, et non potest peccare, quoniam ex Deo natus est.* Caritatem autem non habent nisi filii Dei, *ipsa* enim *est quae distinguit inter filios regni et filios perditionis*, ut Augustinus dicit, in XV de Trin. Ergo ille qui habet caritatem non potest eam amittere.

Praeterea, Augustinus dicit, in VIII de Trin., quod *dilectio, si non est vera, dilectio dicenda non est.* Sed sicut ipse dicit in Epist. ad Iulianum comitem, *caritas quae deseri potest, nunquam vera fuit.* Ergo neque caritas fuit. Si ergo caritas semel habeatur, nunquam amittitur.

Praeterea, Gregorius dicit, in homilia Pentecostes, quod *amor Dei magna operatur, si est, si desinit operari, caritas non est.* Sed nullus magna operando amittit caritatem. Ergo, si caritas insit, amitti non potest.

Objection 1: It would seem that we cannot lose charity when once we have it. For if we lose it, this can only be through sin. Now he who has charity cannot sin, for it is written (1 John 3:9): *Whosoever is born of God, committeth not sin; for His seed abideth in him, and he cannot sin, because he is born of God.* But none save the children of God have charity, for it is this which distinguishes *the children of God from the children of perdition*, as Augustine says (*De Trin.* xv, 17). Therefore he that has charity cannot lose it.

Obj. 2: Further, Augustine says (*De Trin.* viii, 7) that *if love be not true, it should not be called love.* Now, as he says again in a letter to Count Julian, *charity which can fail was never true.* Therefore it was no charity at all. Therefore, when once we have charity, we cannot lose it.

Obj. 3: Further, Gregory says in a homily for Pentecost (*In Evang. xxx*) that *God's love works great things where it is; if it ceases to work it is not charity.* Now no man loses charity by doing great things. Therefore if charity be there, it cannot be lost.

**PRAETEREA**, liberum arbitrium non inclinatur ad peccatum nisi per aliquod motivum ad peccandum. Sed caritas excludit omnia motiva ad peccandum, et amorem sui, et cupiditatem, et quidquid aliud huiusmodi est. Ergo caritas amitti non potest.

**SED CONTRA** est quod dicitur Apoc. II, *habeo adversum te pauca, quod caritatem primam reliquisti.*

**RESPONDEO** dicendum quod per caritatem Spiritus Sanctus in nobis habitat, ut ex supradictis patet. Tripliciter ergo possumus considerare caritatem. Uno modo, ex parte spiritus sancti moventis animam ad diligendum Deum. Et ex hac parte caritas impeccabilitatem habet ex virtute spiritus sancti, qui infallibiliter operatur quodcumque voluerit. Unde impossibile est haec duo simul esse vera, quod Spiritus Sanctus aliquem velit movere ad actum caritatis, et quod ipse caritatem amittat peccando, nam donum perseverantiae computatur inter *beneficia Dei quibus certissime liberantur quicumque liberantur*, ut Augustinus dicit, in libro de Praed. Sanct.

Alio modo potest considerari caritas secundum propriam rationem. Et sic caritas non potest nisi illud quod pertinet ad caritatis rationem. Unde caritas nullo modo potest peccare, sicut nec calor potest infrigidare; et sicut etiam iniustitia non potest bonum facere, ut Augustinus dicit, in libro de Serm. Dom. in monte.

Tertio modo potest considerari caritas ex parte subiecti, quod est vertibile secundum arbitrii libertatem. Potest autem attendi comparatio caritatis ad hoc subiectum et secundum universalem rationem qua comparatur forma ad materiam; et secundum specialem rationem qua comparatur habitus ad potentiam. Est autem de ratione formae quod sit in subiecto amissibiliter quando non replet totam potentialitatem materiae, sicut patet in formis generabilium et corruptibilium. Quia materia horum sic recipit unam formam quod remanet in ea potentia ad aliam formam, quasi non repleta tota materiae potentialitate per unam formam; et ideo una forma potest amitti per acceptionem alterius. Sed forma corporis caelestis, quia replet totam materiae potentialitatem, ita quod non remanet in ea potentia ad aliam formam, inamissibiliter inest. Sic igitur caritas patriae, quia replet totam potentialitatem rationalis mentis, inquantum scilicet omnis actualis motus eius fertur in Deum, inamissibiliter habetur. Caritas autem viae non sic replet potentialitatem sui subiecti, quia non semper actu fertur in Deum. Unde quando actu in Deum non fertur, potest aliquid occurrere per quod caritas amittatur.

Habitui vero proprium est ut inclinet potentiam ad agendum quod convenit habitui inquantum facit id vi-

**OBJ. 4:** Further, the free-will is not inclined to sin unless by some motive for sinning. Now charity excludes all motives for sinning, both self-love and cupidity, and all such things. Therefore charity cannot be lost.

**ON THE CONTRARY**, It is written (Rev 2:4): *I have somewhat against thee, because thou hast left thy first charity.*

**I ANSWER THAT**, The Holy Spirit dwells in us by charity, as shown above (A. 2; QQ. 23, 24). We can, accordingly, consider charity in three ways: first on the part of the Holy Spirit, Who moves the soul to love God, and in this respect charity is incompatible with sin through the power of the Holy Spirit, Who does unfailingly whatever He wills to do. Hence it is impossible for these two things to be true at the same time—that the Holy Spirit should will to move a certain man to an act of charity, and that this man, by sinning, should lose charity. For the gift of perseverance is reckoned among the blessings of God whereby *whoever is delivered, is most certainly delivered*, as Augustine says in his book on the Predestination of the saints (*De Dono Persev.* xiv).

Second, charity may be considered as such, and thus it is incapable of anything that is against its nature. Wherefore charity cannot sin at all, even as neither can heat cool, nor unrighteousness do good, as Augustine says (*De Serm. Dom. in Monte* ii, 24).

Third, charity can be considered on the part of its subject, which is changeable on account of the free-will. Moreover charity may be compared with this subject, both from the general point of view of form in comparison with matter, and from the specific point of view of habit as compared with power. Now it is natural for a form to be in its subject in such a way that it can be lost, when it does not entirely fill the potentiality of matter: this is evident in the forms of things generated and corrupted, because the matter of such things receives one form in such a way, that it retains the potentiality to another form, as though its potentiality were not completely satisfied with the one form. Hence the one form may be lost by the other being received. On the other hand the form of a celestial body which entirely fills the potentiality of its matter, so that the latter does not retain the potentiality to another form, is in its subject inseparably. Accordingly the charity of the blessed, because it entirely fills the potentiality of the rational mind, since every actual movement of that mind is directed to God, is possessed by its subject inseparably: whereas the charity of the wayfarer does not so fill the potentiality of its subject, because the latter is not always actually directed to God: so that when it is not actually directed to God, something may occur whereby charity is lost.

It is proper to a habit to incline a power to act, and this belongs to a habit, insofar as it makes whatever is

deri bonum quod ei convenit, malum autem quod ei repugnat. Sicut enim gustus diiudicat sapores secundum suam dispositionem, ita mens hominis diiudicat de aliquo faciendo secundum suam habitualem dispositionem, unde et philosophus dicit, in III Ethic., quod *qualis unusquisque est, talis finis videtur ei.* Ibi ergo caritas inamissibiliter habetur, ubi id quod convenit caritati non potest videri nisi bonum, scilicet in patria, ubi Deus videtur per essentiam, quae est ipsa essentia bonitatis. Et ideo caritas patriae amitti non potest. Caritas autem viae, in cuius statu non videtur ipsa Dei essentia, quae est essentia bonitatis, potest amitti.

**AD PRIMUM** ergo dicendum quod auctoritas illa loquitur secundum potestatem spiritus sancti, cuius conservatione a peccato immunes redduntur quos ipse movet quantum ipse voluerit.

**AD SECUNDUM** dicendum quod caritas quae deseri potest ex ipsa ratione caritatis, vera caritas non est. Hoc enim esset si hoc in suo amore haberet, quod ad tempus amaret et postea amare desineret quod non esset verae dilectionis. Sed si caritas amittatur ex mutabilitate subiecti, contra propositum caritatis, quod in suo actu includitur; hoc non repugnat veritati caritatis.

**AD TERTIUM** dicendum quod amor Dei semper magna operatur in proposito, quod pertinet ad rationem caritatis. Non tamen semper magna operatur in actu, propter conditionem subiecti.

**AD QUARTUM** dicendum quod caritas, secundum rationem sui actus, excludit omne motivum ad peccandum. Sed quandoque contingit quod caritas actu non agit. Et tunc potest intervenire aliquod motivum ad peccandum, cui si consentiatur, caritas amittitur.

suitable to it, to seem good, and whatever is unsuitable, to seem evil. For as the taste judges of savors according to its disposition, even so does the human mind judge of things to be done, according to its habitual disposition. Hence the Philosopher says (*Ethic.* iii, 5) that *such as a man is, so does the end appear to him.* Accordingly charity is inseparable from its possessor, where that which pertains to charity cannot appear otherwise than good, and that is in heaven, where God is seen in His Essence, which is the very essence of goodness. Therefore the charity of heaven cannot be lost, whereas the charity of the way can, because in this state God is not seen in His Essence, which is the essence of goodness.

**REPLY OBJ. 1**: The passage quoted speaks from the point of view of the power of the Holy Spirit, by Whose safeguarding, those whom He wills to move are rendered immune from sin, as much as He wills.

**REPLY OBJ. 2**: The charity which can fail by reason of itself is no true charity; for this would be the case, were its love given only for a time, and afterwards were to cease, which would be inconsistent with true love. If, however, charity be lost through the changeableness of the subject, and against the purpose of charity included in its act, this is not contrary to true charity.

**REPLY OBJ. 3**: The love of God ever works great things in its purpose, which is essential to charity; but it does not always work great things in its act, on account of the condition of its subject.

**REPLY OBJ. 4**: Charity by reason of its act excludes every motive for sinning. But it happens sometimes that charity is not acting actually, and then it is possible for a motive to intervene for sinning, and if we consent to this motive, we lose charity.

# Article 12

*Whether charity is lost through one mortal sin?*

**AD DUODECIMUM SIC PROCEDITUR.** Videtur quod caritas non amittatur per unum actum peccati mortalis. Dicit enim Origenes, in I Periarch., *si aliquando satietas capit aliquem ex his qui in summo perfectoque constiterint gradu, non arbitror quod ad subitum quis evacuetur aut decidat, sed paulatim ac per partes eum decidere necesse est.* Sed homo decidit caritatem amittens. Ergo caritas non amittitur per unum solum actum peccati mortalis.

**PRAETEREA**, Leo Papa dicit, in Serm. de passione, alloquens Petrum, *vidit in te dominus non fidem victam, non dilectionem aversam, sed constantiam fuisse turbatam. Abundavit fletus, ubi non defecit affectus, et fons caritatis lavit verba formidinis.* Et ex hoc accepit Bernardus quod dixit *in Petro caritatem non fuisse extinctam,*

**OBJECTION 1**: It would seem that charity is not lost through one mortal sin. For Origen says (*Peri Archon* i): *When a man who has mounted to the stage of perfection, is satiated, I do not think that he will become empty or fall away suddenly; but he must needs do so gradually and by little and little.* But man falls away by losing charity. Therefore charity is not lost through only one mortal sin.

**OBJ. 2**: Further, Pope Leo in a sermon on the Passion (lx) addresses Peter thus: *Our Lord saw in thee not a conquered faith, not an averted love, but constancy shaken. Tears abounded where love never failed, and the words uttered in trepidation were washed away by the fount of charity.* From this Bernard drew his assertion that *charity in Peter was not*

*sed sopitam*. Sed Petrus, negando Christum, peccavit mortaliter. Ergo caritas non amittitur per unum actum peccati mortalis.

PRAETEREA, caritas est fortior quam virtus acquisita. Sed habitus virtutis acquisitae non tollitur per unum actum peccati contrarium. Ergo multo minus caritas tollitur per unum actum peccati mortalis contrarium.

PRAETEREA, caritas importat dilectionem Dei et proximi. Sed aliquis committens aliquod peccatum mortale retinet dilectionem Dei et proximi, ut videtur, inordinatio enim affectionis circa ea quae sunt ad finem non tollit amorem finis, ut supra dictum est. Ergo potest remanere caritas ad Deum, existente peccato mortali per inordinatam affectionem circa aliquod temporale bonum.

PRAETEREA, virtutis theologicae obiectum est ultimus finis. Sed aliae virtutes theologicae, scilicet fides et spes, non excluduntur per unum actum peccati mortalis, immo remanent informes. Ergo etiam caritas potest remanere informis, etiam uno peccato mortali perpetrato.

SED CONTRA, per peccatum mortale fit homo dignus morte aeterna, secundum illud Rom. VI, *stipendia peccati mors*. Sed quilibet habens caritatem habet meritum vitae aeternae, dicitur enim Ioan. XIV, *si quis diligit me, diligetur a patre meo, et ego diligam eum, et manifestabo ei meipsum*; in qua quidem manifestatione vita aeterna consistit, secundum illud Ioan. XVII, *haec est vita aeterna, ut cognoscant te, verum Deum, et quem misisti, Iesum Christum*. Nullus autem potest esse simul dignus vita aeterna et morte aeterna. Ergo impossibile est quod aliquis habeat caritatem cum peccato mortali. Tollitur ergo caritas per unum actum peccati mortalis.

RESPONDEO dicendum quod unum contrarium per aliud contrarium superveniens tollitur. Quilibet autem actus peccati mortalis contrariatur caritati secundum propriam rationem, quae consistit in hoc quod Deus diligatur super omnia, et quod homo totaliter se illi subiiciat, omnia sua referendo in ipsum. Est igitur de ratione caritatis ut sic diligat Deum quod in omnibus velit se ei subiicere, et praeceptorum eius regulam in omnibus sequi, quidquid enim contrariatur praeceptis eius, manifeste contrariatur caritati. Unde de se habet quod caritatem excludere possit.

Et si quidem caritas esset habitus acquisitus ex virtute subiecti dependens, non oporteret quod statim per unum actum contrarium tolleretur. Actus enim non directe contrariatur habitui, sed actui, conservatio autem habitus in subiecto non requirit continuitatem actus, unde ex superveniente contrario actu non statim habitus acquisitus excluditur. Sed caritas, cum sit habitus infusus, dependet ex actione Dei infundentis, qui sic se habet in infusione et conservatione caritatis sicut sol in illuminatione aeris, ut dictum est. Et ideo, sicut lumen statim cessaret esse in aere quod aliquod obstaculum

*quenched, but cooled*. But Peter sinned mortally in denying Christ. Therefore charity is not lost through one mortal sin.

OBJ. 3: Further, charity is stronger than an acquired virtue. Now a habit of acquired virtue is not destroyed by one contrary sinful act. Much less, therefore, is charity destroyed by one contrary mortal sin.

OBJ. 4: Further, charity denotes love of God and our neighbor. Now, seemingly, one may commit a mortal sin, and yet retain the love of God and one's neighbor; because an inordinate affection for things directed to the end, does not remove the love for the end, as stated above (A. 10). Therefore charity towards God can endure, though there be a mortal sin through an inordinate affection for some temporal good.

OBJ. 5: Further, the object of a theological virtue is the last end. Now the other theological virtues, namely faith and hope, are not done away by one mortal sin, in fact they remain though lifeless. Therefore charity can remain without a form, even when a mortal sin has been committed.

ON THE CONTRARY, By mortal sin man becomes deserving of eternal death, according to Rom. 6:23: *The wages of sin is death*. On the other hand whoever has charity is deserving of eternal life, for it is written (John 14:21): *He that loveth Me, shall be loved by My Father: and I will love Him, and will manifest Myself to him*, in which manifestation everlasting life consists, according to John 17:3: *This is eternal life; that they may know Thee the . . . true God, and Jesus Christ Whom Thou hast sent*. Now no man can be worthy, at the same time, of eternal life and of eternal death. Therefore it is impossible for a man to have charity with a mortal sin. Therefore charity is destroyed by one mortal sin.

I ANSWER THAT, That one contrary is removed by the other contrary supervening. Now every mortal sin is contrary to charity by its very nature, which consists in man's loving God above all things, and subjecting himself to Him entirely, by referring all that is his to God. It is therefore essential to charity that man should so love God as to wish to submit to Him in all things, and always to follow the rule of His commandments; since whatever is contrary to His commandments is manifestly contrary to charity, and therefore by its very nature is capable of destroying charity.

If indeed charity were an acquired habit dependent on the power of its subject, it would not necessarily be removed by one mortal sin, for act is directly contrary, not to habit but to act. Now the endurance of a habit in its subject does not require the endurance of its act, so that when a contrary act supervenes the acquired habit is not at once done away. But charity, being an infused habit, depends on the action of God Who infuses it, Who stands in relation to the infusion and safekeeping of charity, as the sun does to the diffusion of light in the air, as stated above (A. 10, Obj. 3). Consequently, just as the light would cease

poneretur illuminationi solis, ita etiam caritas statim deficit esse in anima quod aliquod obstaculum ponitur influentiae caritatis a Deo in animam.

Manifestum est autem quod per quodlibet mortale peccatum, quod divinis praeceptis contrariatur, ponitur praedictae infusioni obstaculum, quia ex hoc ipso quod homo eligendo praefert peccatum divinae amicitiae, quae requirit ut Dei voluntatem sequamur, consequens est ut statim per unum actum peccati mortalis habitus caritatis perdatur. Unde et Augustinus dicit, VIII super Gen. ad Litt., quod *homo, Deo sibi praesente, illuminatur; absente autem, continuo tenebratur; a quo non locorum intervallis, sed voluntatis aversione disceditur.*

**AD PRIMUM** ergo dicendum quod verbum Origenis potest uno modo sic intelligi quod homo qui est in statu perfecto non subito procedit in actum peccati mortalis, sed ad hoc disponitur per aliquam negligentiam praecedentem. Unde et peccata venialia dicuntur esse dispositio ad mortale, sicut supra dictum est. Sed tamen per unum actum peccati mortalis, si eum commiserit, decidit, caritate amissa.

Sed quia ipse subdit, *si aliquis brevis lapsus acciderit, et cito resipiscat, non penitus ruere videtur,* potest aliter dici quod ipse intelligit eum penitus evacuari et decidere qui sic decidit ut ex malitia peccet. Quod non statim in viro perfecto a principio contingit.

**AD SECUNDUM** dicendum quod caritas amittitur dupliciter. Uno modo, directe, per actualem contemptum. Et hoc modo Petrus caritatem non amisit. Alio modo, indirecte, quando committitur aliquod contrarium caritati propter aliquam passionem concupiscentiae vel timoris. Et hoc modo Petrus, contra caritatem faciens, caritatem amisit, sed eam cito recuperavit.

**AD QUARTUM** dicendum quod non quaelibet inordinatio affectionis quae est circa ea quae sunt ad finem, idest circa bona creata, constituit peccatum mortale, sed solum quando est talis inordinatio quae repugnat divinae voluntati. Et hoc directe contrariatur caritati, ut dictum est.

**AD QUINTUM** dicendum quod caritas importat unionem quandam ad Deum, non autem fides neque spes. Omne autem peccatum mortale consistit in aversione a Deo, ut supra dictum est. Et ideo omne peccatum mortale contrariatur caritati. Non autem omne peccatum mortale contrariatur fidei vel spei, sed quaedam determinata peccata, per quae habitus fidei et spei tollitur, sicut et per omne peccatum mortale habitus caritatis. Unde patet quod caritas non potest remanere informis, cum sit ultima forma virtutum, ex hoc quod respicit Deum in ratione finis ultimi, ut dictum est.

at once in the air, were an obstacle placed to its being lit up by the sun, even so charity ceases at once to be in the soul through the placing of an obstacle to the outpouring of charity by God into the soul.

Now it is evident that through every mortal sin which is contrary to God's commandments, an obstacle is placed to the outpouring of charity, since from the very fact that a man chooses to prefer sin to God's friendship, which requires that we should obey His will, it follows that the habit of charity is lost at once through one mortal sin. Hence Augustine says (*Gen ad lit.* viii, 12) that *man is enlightened by God's presence, but he is darkened at once by God's absence, because distance from Him is effected not by change of place but by aversion of the will.*

**REPLY OBJ. 1:** This saying of Origen may be understood, in one way, that a man who is in the state of perfection, does not suddenly go so far as to commit a mortal sin, but is disposed thereto by some previous negligence, for which reason venial sins are said to be dispositions to mortal sin, as stated above (I-II, Q. 88, A. 3). Nevertheless he falls, and loses charity through the one mortal sin if he commits it.

Since, however, he adds: *If some slight slip should occur, and he recover himself quickly he does not appear to fall altogether,* we may reply in another way, that when he speaks of a man being emptied and falling away altogether, he means one who falls so as to sin through malice; and this does not occur in a perfect man all at once.

**REPLY OBJ. 2:** Charity may be lost in two ways; first, directly, by actual contempt, and, in this way, Peter did not lose charity. Second, indirectly, when a sin is committed against charity, through some passion of desire or fear; it was by sinning against charity in this way, that Peter lost charity; yet he soon recovered it.

**REPLY OBJ. 4:** Not every inordinate affection for things directed to the end, i.e., for created goods, constitutes a mortal sin, but only such as is directly contrary to the Divine will; and then the inordinate affection is contrary to charity, as stated.

**REPLY OBJ. 5:** Charity denotes union with God, whereas faith and hope do not. Now every mortal sin consists in aversion from God, as stated above (*Gen ad lit.* viii, 12). Consequently every mortal sin is contrary to charity, but not to faith and hope, but only certain determinate sins, which destroy the habit of faith or of hope, even as charity is destroyed by every moral sin. Hence it is evident that charity cannot remain lifeless, since it is itself the ultimate form regarding God under the aspect of last end as stated above (Q. 23, A. 8).

# QUESTION 25

## THE OBJECT OF CHARITY

Deinde considerandum est de obiecto caritatis. Circa quod duo consideranda occurrunt, primo quidem de his quae sunt ex caritate diligenda; secundo, de ordine diligendorum. Circa primum quaeruntur duodecim.

Primo, utrum solus Deus sit ex caritate diligendus, vel etiam proximus.

Secundo, utrum caritas sit ex caritate diligenda.

Tertio, utrum creaturae irrationales sint ex caritate diligendae.

Quarto, utrum aliquis possit ex caritate seipsum diligere.

Quinto, utrum corpus proprium.

Sexto, utrum peccatores sint ex caritate diligendi.

Septimo, utrum peccatores seipsos diligant.

Octavo, utrum inimici sint ex caritate diligendi.

Nono, utrum sint eis signa amicitiae exhibenda.

Decimo, utrum Angeli sint ex caritate diligendi.

Undecimo, utrum Daemones.

Duodecimo, de enumeratione diligendorum ex caritate.

We must now consider the object of charity; which consideration will be twofold: (1) The things we ought to love out of charity: (2) The order in which they ought to be loved. Under the first head there are twelve points of inquiry:

(1) Whether we should love God alone, out of charity, or should we love our neighbor also?

(2) Whether charity should be loved out of charity?

(3) Whether irrational creatures ought to be loved out of charity?

(4) Whether one may love oneself out of charity?

(5) Whether one's own body?

(6) Whether sinners should be loved out of charity?

(7) Whether sinners love themselves?

(8) Whether we should love our enemies out of charity?

(9) Whether we are bound to show them tokens of friendship?

(10) Whether we ought to love the angels out of charity?

(11) Whether we ought to love the demons?

(12) How to enumerate the things we are bound to love out of charity.

# Article 1

*Whether the love of charity stops at God, or extends to our neighbor?*

**AD PRIMUM SIC PROCEDITUR.** Videtur quod dilectio caritatis sistat in Deo, et non se extendat ad proximum. Sicut enim Deo debemus amorem, ita et timorem, secundum illud Deut. X, *et nunc, Israel, quid dominus Deus petit nisi ut timeas et diligas eum?* Sed alius est timor quo timetur homo, qui dicitur timor humanus; et alius timor quo timetur Deus, qui est vel servilis vel filialis; ut ex supradictis patet. Ergo etiam alius est amor caritatis, quo diligitur Deus; et alius est amor quo diligitur proximus.

**PRAETEREA,** Philosophus dicit, in VIII Ethic., quod *amari est honorari.* Sed alius est honor qui debetur Deo, qui est honor latriae; et alius est honor qui debetur creaturae, qui est honor duliae. Ergo etiam alius est amor quo diligitur Deus, et quo diligitur proximus.

**OBJECTION 1**: It would seem that the love of charity stops at God and does not extend to our neighbor. For as we owe God love, so do we owe Him fear, according to Deut. 10:12: *And now Israel, what doth the Lord thy God require of thee, but that thou fear . . . and love Him?* Now the fear with which we fear man, and which is called human fear, is distinct from the fear with which we fear God, and which is either servile or filial, as is evident from what has been stated above (Q. 10, A. 2). Therefore also the love with which we love God, is distinct from the love with which we love our neighbor.

**OBJ. 2**: Further, the Philosopher says (*Ethic.* viii, 8) that *to be loved is to be honored.* Now the honor due to God, which is known as latria, is distinct from the honor due to a creature, and known as dulia. Therefore again the love wherewith we love God, is distinct from that with which we love our neighbor.

237

**PRAETEREA**, spes generat caritatem; ut habetur in Glossa, Matth. I. Sed spes ita habetur de Deo quod reprehenduntur sperantes in homine, secundum illud Ierem. XVII, *maledictus homo qui confidit in homine*. Ergo caritas ita debetur Deo quod ad proximum non se extendat.

**SED CONTRA** est quod dicitur I Ioan. IV, *hoc mandatum habemus a Deo, ut qui diligit Deum, diligat et fratrem suum*.

**RESPONDEO** dicendum quod, sicut supra dictum est, habitus non diversificantur nisi ex hoc quod variat speciem actus, omnes enim actus unius speciei ad eundem habitum pertinent. Cum autem species actus ex obiecto sumatur secundum formalem rationem ipsius, necesse est quod idem specie sit actus qui fertur in rationem obiecti, et qui fertur in obiectum sub tali ratione, sicut est eadem specie visio qua videtur lumen, et qua videtur color secundum luminis rationem.

Ratio autem diligendi proximum Deus est, hoc enim debemus in proximo diligere, ut in Deo sit. Unde manifestum est quod idem specie actus est quo diligitur Deus, et quo diligitur proximus. Et propter hoc habitus caritatis non solum se extendit ad dilectionem Dei, sed etiam ad dilectionem proximi.

**AD PRIMUM** ergo dicendum quod proximus potest timeri dupliciter, sicut et amari. Uno modo, propter id quod est sibi proprium, puta cum aliquis timet tyrannum propter eius crudelitatem, vel cum amat ipsum propter cupiditatem acquirendi aliquid ab eo. Et talis timor humanus distinguitur a timore Dei, et similiter amor. Alio modo timetur homo et amatur propter id quod est Dei in ipso, sicut cum saecularis potestas timetur propter ministerium divinum quod habet ad vindictam malefactorum, et amatur propter iustitiam. Et talis timor hominis non distinguitur a timore Dei, sicut nec amor.

**AD SECUNDUM** dicendum quod amor respicit bonum in communi, sed honor respicit proprium bonum honorati, defertur enim alicui in testimonium propriae virtutis. Et ideo amor non diversificatur specie propter diversam quantitatem bonitatis diversorum, dummodo referuntur ad aliquod unum bonum commune, sed honor diversificatur secundum propria bona singulorum. Unde eodem amore caritatis diligimus omnes proximos, inquantum referuntur ad unum bonum commune, quod est Deus, sed diversos honores diversis deferimus, secundum propriam virtutem singulorum. Et similiter Deo singularem honorem latriae exhibemus, propter eius singularem virtutem.

**AD TERTIUM** dicendum quod vituperantur qui sperant in homine sicut in principali auctore salutis, non autem qui sperant in homine sicut in adiuvante ministerialiter sub Deo. Et similiter reprehensibile esset si quis

**OBJ. 3**: Further, hope begets charity, as a gloss states on Matt. 1:2. Now hope is so due to God that it is reprehensible to hope in man, according to Jer. 17:5: *Cursed be the man that trusteth in man.* Therefore charity is so due to God, as not to extend to our neighbor.

**ON THE CONTRARY**, It is written (1 John 4:21): *This commandment we have from God, that he, who loveth God, love also his brother.*

**I ANSWER THAT**, As stated above (Q. 17, A. 6; Q. 19, A. 3; I-II, Q. 54, A. 3) habits are not differentiated except their acts be of different species. For every act of the one species belongs to the same habit. Now since the species of an act is derived from its object, considered under its formal aspect, it follows of necessity that it is specifically the same act that tends to an aspect of the object, and that tends to the object under that aspect: thus it is specifically the same visual act whereby we see the light, and whereby we see the color under the aspect of light.

Now the aspect under which our neighbor is to be loved, is God, since what we ought to love in our neighbor is that he may be in God. Hence it is clear that it is specifically the same act whereby we love God, and whereby we love our neighbor. Consequently the habit of charity extends not only to the love of God, but also to the love of our neighbor.

**REPLY OBJ. 1**: We may fear our neighbor, even as we may love him, in two ways: first, on account of something that is proper to him, as when a man fears a tyrant on account of his cruelty, or loves him by reason of his own desire to get something from him. Such like human fear is distinct from the fear of God, and the same applies to love. Second, we fear a man, or love him on account of what he has of God; as when we fear the secular power by reason of its exercising the ministry of God for the punishment of evildoers, and love it for its justice: such like fear of man is not distinct from fear of God, as neither is such like love.

**REPLY OBJ. 2**: Love regards good in general, whereas honor regards the honored person's own good, for it is given to a person in recognition of his own virtue. Hence love is not differentiated specifically on account of the various degrees of goodness in various persons, so long as it is referred to one good common to all, whereas honor is distinguished according to the good belonging to individuals. Consequently we love all our neighbors with the same love of charity, insofar as they are referred to one good common to them all, which is God; whereas we give various honors to various people, according to each one's own virtue, and likewise to God we give the singular honor of latria on account of His singular virtue.

**REPLY OBJ. 3**: It is wrong to hope in man as though he were the principal author of salvation, but not, to hope in man as helping us ministerially under God. In like manner it would be wrong if a man loved his neighbor as though he

proximum diligeret tanquam principalem finem, non autem si quis proximum diligat propter Deum, quod pertinet ad caritatem.

were his last end, but not, if he loved him for God's sake; and this is what charity does.

# Article 2

*Whether we should love charity out of charity?*

**AD SECUNDUM SIC PROCEDITUR.** Videtur quod caritas non sit ex caritate diligenda. Ea enim quae sunt ex caritate diligenda, duobus praeceptis caritatis concluduntur, ut patet Matth. XXII. Sed sub neutro eorum caritas continetur, quia nec caritas est Deus nec est proximus. Ergo caritas non est ex caritate diligenda.

**PRAETEREA**, caritas fundatur super communicatione beatitudinis, ut supra dictum est. Sed caritas non potest esse particeps beatitudinis. Ergo caritas non est ex caritate diligenda.

**PRAETEREA**, caritas est amicitia quaedam, ut supra dictum est. Sed nullus potest habere amicitiam ad caritatem, vel ad aliquod accidens, quia huiusmodi reamare non possunt, quod est de ratione amicitiae, ut dicitur in VIII Ethic. Ergo caritas non est ex caritate diligenda.

**SED CONTRA** est quod Augustinus dicit, VIII de Trin., *qui diligit proximum, consequens est ut etiam ipsam dilectionem diligat.* Sed proximus diligitur ex caritate. Ergo consequens est ut etiam caritas ex caritate diligatur.

**RESPONDEO** dicendum quod caritas amor quidam est. Amor autem ex natura potentiae cuius est actus habet quod possit supra seipsum reflecti. Quia enim voluntatis obiectum est bonum universale, quidquid sub ratione boni continetur potest cadere sub actu voluntatis; et quia ipsum velle est quoddam bonum, potest velle se velle, sicut etiam intellectus, cuius obiectum est verum, intelligit se intelligere, quia hoc etiam est quoddam verum. Sed amor etiam ex ratione propriae speciei habet quod supra se reflectatur, quia est spontaneus motus amantis in amatum; unde ex hoc ipso quod amat aliquis, amat se amare.

Sed caritas non est simplex amor, sed habet rationem amicitiae, ut supra dictum est. Per amicitiam autem amatur aliquid dupliciter. Uno modo, sicut ipse amicus ad quem amicitiam habemus et cui bona volumus. Alio modo, sicut bonum quod amico volumus. Et hoc modo caritas per caritatem amatur, et non primo, quia caritas est illud bonum quod optamus omnibus quos ex caritate diligimus. Et eadem ratio est de beatitudine et de aliis virtutibus.

**AD PRIMUM** ergo dicendum quod Deus et proximus sunt illi ad quos amicitiam habemus. Sed in illorum dilectione includitur dilectio caritatis, diligimus enim

**OBJECTION 1**: It would seem that charity need not be loved out of charity. For the things to be loved out of charity are contained in the two precepts of charity (Matt 22:37–39): and neither of them includes charity, since charity is neither God nor our neighbor. Therefore charity need not be loved out of charity.

**OBJ. 2**: Further, charity is founded on the fellowship of happiness, as stated above (Q. 23, A. 1). But charity cannot participate in happiness. Therefore charity need not be loved out of charity.

**OBJ. 3**: Further, charity is a kind of friendship, as stated above (Q. 23, A. 1). But no man can have friendship for charity or for an accident, since such things cannot return love for love, which is essential to friendship, as stated in *Ethic.* viii. Therefore charity need not be loved out of charity.

**ON THE CONTRARY**, Augustine says (*De Trin.* viii, 8): *He that loves his neighbor, must, in consequence, love love itself.* But we love our neighbor out of charity. Therefore it follows that charity also is loved out of charity.

**I ANSWER THAT**, Charity is love. Now love, by reason of the nature of the power whose act it is, is capable of reflecting on itself; for since the object of the will is the universal good, whatever has the aspect of good, can be the object of an act of the will: and since to will is itself a good, man can will himself to will. Even so the intellect, whose object is the true, understands that it understands, because this again is something true. Love, however, even by reason of its own species, is capable of reflecting on itself, because it is a spontaneous movement of the lover towards the beloved, wherefore from the moment a man loves, he loves himself to love.

Yet charity is not love simply, but has the nature of friendship, as stated above (Q. 23, A. 1). Now by friendship a thing is loved in two ways: first, as the friend for whom we have friendship, and to whom we wish good things: second, as the good which we wish to a friend. It is in the latter and not in the former way that charity is loved out of charity, because charity is the good which we desire for all those whom we love out of charity. The same applies to happiness, and to the other virtues.

**REPLY OBJ. 1**: God and our neighbor are those with whom we are friends, but love of them includes the loving of charity, since we love both God and our neighbor, insofar

proximum et Deum inquantum hoc amamus, ut nos et proximus Deum diligamus, quod est caritatem habere.

AD SECUNDUM dicendum quod caritas est ipsa communicatio spiritualis vitae, per quam ad beatitudinem pervenitur. Et ideo amatur sicut bonum desideratum omnibus quos ex caritate diligimus.

AD TERTIUM dicendum quod ratio illa procedit secundum quod per amicitiam amantur illi ad quos amicitiam habemus.

as we love ourselves and our neighbor to love God, and this is to love charity.

REPLY OBJ. 2: Charity is itself the fellowship of the spiritual life, whereby we arrive at happiness: hence it is loved as the good which we desire for all whom we love out of charity.

REPLY OBJ. 3: This argument considers friendship as referred to those with whom we are friends.

# Article 3

*Whether irrational creatures also ought to be loved out of charity?*

AD TERTIUM SIC PROCEDITUR. Videtur quod etiam creaturae irrationales sint ex caritate diligendae. Per caritatem enim maxime conformamur Deo. Sed Deus diligit creaturas irrationales ex caritate, *diligit enim omnia quae sunt*, ut habetur Sap. XI; et omne quod diligit, seipso diligit, qui est caritas. Ergo et nos debemus creaturas irrationales ex caritate diligere.

PRAETEREA, caritas principaliter fertur in Deum, ad alia autem se extendit secundum quod ad Deum pertinent. Sed sicut creatura rationalis pertinet ad Deum inquantum habet similitudinem imaginis, ita etiam creatura irrationalis inquantum habet similitudinem vestigii. Ergo caritas etiam se extendit ad creaturas irrationales.

PRAETEREA, sicut caritatis obiectum est Deus, ita et fidei. Sed fides se extendit ad creaturas irrationales, inquantum credimus caelum et terram esse creata a Deo, et pisces et aves esse productos ex aquis, et gressibilia animalia et plantas ex terra. Ergo caritas etiam se extendit ad creaturas irrationales.

SED CONTRA est quod dilectio caritatis solum se extendit ad Deum et proximum. Sed nomine proximi non potest intelligi creatura irrationalis, quia non communicat cum homine in vita rationali. Ergo caritas non se extendit ad creaturas irrationales.

RESPONDEO dicendum quod caritas, secundum praedicta, est amicitia quaedam. Per amicitiam autem amatur uno quidem modo, amicus ad quem amicitia habetur; et alio modo, bona quae amico optantur. Primo ergo modo nulla creatura irrationalis potest ex caritate amari. Et hoc triplici ratione. Quarum duae pertinent communiter ad amicitiam, quae ad creaturas irrationales haberi non potest. Primo quidem, quia amicitia ad eum habetur cui volumus bonum. Non autem proprie possum bonum velle creaturae irrationali, quia non est eius proprie habere bonum, sed solum creaturae rationalis, quae est domina utendi bono quod habet per liberum arbitrium. Et ideo philosophus dicit, in II Physic., quod huiusmodi rebus non dicimus aliquid bene vel male contingere nisi secundum similitudinem. Secundo, quia

OBJECTION 1: It would seem that irrational creatures also ought to be loved out of charity. For it is chiefly by charity that we are conformed to God. Now God loves irrational creatures out of charity, for He loves *all things that are* (Wis 11:25), and whatever He loves, He loves by Himself Who is charity. Therefore we also should love irrational creatures out of charity.

OBJ. 2: Further, charity is referred to God principally, and extends to other things as referable to God. Now just as the rational creature is referable to God, inasmuch as it bears the resemblance of image, so too, are the irrational creatures, inasmuch as they bear the resemblance of a trace. Therefore charity extends also to irrational creatures.

OBJ. 3: Further, just as the object of charity is God. so is the object of faith. Now faith extends to irrational creatures, since we believe that heaven and earth were created by God, that the fishes and birds were brought forth out of the waters, and animals that walk, and plants, out of the earth. Therefore charity extends also to irrational creatures.

ON THE CONTRARY, The love of charity extends to none but God and our neighbor. But the word neighbor cannot be extended to irrational creatures, since they have no fellowship with man in the rational life. Therefore charity does not extend to irrational creatures.

I ANSWER THAT, According to what has been stated above (Q. 13, A. 1) charity is a kind of friendship. Now the love of friendship is twofold: first, there is the love for the friend to whom our friendship is given, second, the love for those good things which we desire for our friend. With regard to the first, no irrational creature can be loved out of charity; and for three reasons. Two of these reasons refer in a general way to friendship, which cannot have an irrational creature for its object: first because friendship is towards one to whom we wish good things, while, properly speaking, we cannot wish good things to an irrational creature, because it is not competent, properly speaking, to possess good, this being proper to the rational creature which, through its free-will, is the master of its disposal of the good it possesses. Hence the Philosopher says (*Phys.* ii,

omnis amicitia fundatur super aliqua communicatione vitae, *nihil enim est ita proprium amicitiae sicut convivere*, ut patet per philosophum, VIII Ethic. Creaturae autem irrationales non possunt communicationem habere in vita humana, quae est secundum rationem. Unde nulla amicitia potest haberi ad creaturas irrationales, nisi forte secundum metaphoram. Tertia ratio est propria caritati, quia caritas fundatur super communicatione beatitudinis aeternae, cuius creatura irrationalis capax non est. Unde amicitia caritatis non potest haberi ad creaturam irrationalem.

Possunt tamen ex caritate diligi creaturae irrationales sicut bona quae aliis volumus, inquantum scilicet ex caritate volumus eas conservari ad honorem Dei et utilitatem hominum. Et sic etiam ex caritate Deus eas diligit.

**UNDE PATET** responsio ad primum.

**AD SECUNDUM** dicendum quod similitudo vestigii non causat capacitatem vitae aeternae, sicut similitudo imaginis. Unde non est similis ratio.

**AD TERTIUM** dicendum quod fides se potest extendere ad omnia quae sunt quocumque modo vera. Sed amicitia caritatis se extendit ad illa sola quae nata sunt habere bonum vitae aeternae. Unde non est simile.

6) that we do not speak of good or evil befalling such like things, except metaphorically. Second, because all friendship is based on some fellowship in life; since *nothing is so proper to friendship as to live together*, as the Philosopher proves (*Ethic.* viii, 5). Now irrational creatures can have no fellowship in human life which is regulated by reason. Hence friendship with irrational creatures is impossible, except metaphorically speaking. The third reason is proper to charity, for charity is based on the fellowship of everlasting happiness, to which the irrational creature cannot attain. Therefore we cannot have the friendship of charity towards an irrational creature.

Nevertheless we can love irrational creatures out of charity, if we regard them as the good things that we desire for others, insofar, to wit, as we wish for their preservation, to God's honor and man's use; thus too does God love them out of charity.

**WHEREFORE** the Reply to the First Objection is evident.

**REPLY OBJ. 2**: The likeness by way of trace does not confer the capacity for everlasting life, whereas the likeness of image does: and so the comparison fails.

**REPLY OBJ. 3**: Faith can extend to all that is in any way true, whereas the friendship of charity extends only to such things as have a natural capacity for everlasting life; wherefore the comparison fails.

# Article 4

*Whether a man ought to love himself out of charity?*

**AD QUARTUM SIC PROCEDITUR.** Videtur quod homo non diligat seipsum ex caritate. Dicit enim Gregorius, in quadam homilia, quod *caritas minus quam inter duos haberi non potest*. Ergo ad seipsum nullus habet caritatem.

**PRAETEREA**, amicitia de sui ratione importat reamationem et aequalitatem, ut patet in VIII Ethic., quae quidem non possunt esse homini ad seipsum. Sed caritas amicitia quaedam est, ut dictum est. Ergo ad seipsum aliquis caritatem habere non potest.

**PRAETEREA**, illud quod ad caritatem pertinet non potest esse vituperabile, quia *caritas non agit perperam*, ut dicitur I ad Cor. XIII. Sed amare seipsum est vituperabile, dicitur enim II ad Tim. III, *in novissimis diebus instabunt tempora periculosa, et erunt homines amantes seipsos*. Ergo homo non potest seipsum ex caritate diligere.

**SED CONTRA** est quod dicitur Levit. XIX, *diliges amicum tuum sicut teipsum*. Sed amicum ex caritate diligimus. Ergo et nosipsos ex caritate debemus diligere.

**OBJECTION 1**: It would seem that a man is bound to love himself out of charity. For Gregory says in a homily (*In Evang.* xvii) that there *can be no charity between less than two*. Therefore no man has charity towards himself.

**OBJ. 2**: Further, friendship, by its very nature, implies mutual love and equality (*Ethic.* viii, 2, 7), which cannot be of one man towards himself. But charity is a kind of friendship, as stated above (Q. 23, A. 1). Therefore a man cannot have charity towards himself.

**OBJ. 3**: Further, anything relating to charity cannot be blameworthy, since charity *dealeth not perversely* (1 Cor 23:4). Now a man deserves to be blamed for loving himself, since it is written (2 Tim 3:1, 2): *In the last days shall come dangerous times, men shall be lovers of themselves*. Therefore a man cannot love himself out of charity.

**ON THE CONTRARY**, It is written (Lev 19:18): *Thou shalt love thy friend as thyself*. Now we love our friends out of charity. Therefore we should love ourselves too out of charity.

RESPONDEO dicendum quod, cum caritas sit amicitia quaedam, sicut dictum est, dupliciter possumus de caritate loqui. Uno modo, sub communi ratione amicitiae. Et secundum hoc dicendum est quod amicitia proprie non habetur ad seipsum, sed aliquid maius amicitia, quia amicitia unionem quandam importat, dicit enim Dionysius quod amor est *virtus unitiva*; unicuique autem ad seipsum est unitas, quae est potior unione. Unde sicut unitas est principium unionis, ita amor quo quis diligit seipsum, est forma et radix amicitiae, in hoc enim amicitiam habemus ad alios, quod ad eos nos habemus sicut ad nosipsos; dicitur enim in IX Ethic. quod *amicabilia quae sunt ad alterum veniunt ex his quae sunt ad seipsum*. Sicut etiam de principiis non habetur scientia, sed aliquid maius, scilicet intellectus.

Alio modo possumus loqui de caritate secundum propriam rationem ipsius, prout scilicet est amicitia hominis ad Deum principaliter, et ex consequenti ad ea quae sunt Dei. Inter quae etiam est ipse homo qui caritatem habet. Et sic inter cetera quae ex caritate diligit quasi ad Deum pertinentia, etiam seipsum ex caritate diligit.

AD PRIMUM ergo dicendum quod Gregorius loquitur de caritate secundum communem amicitiae rationem.

ET SECUNDUM hoc etiam procedit secunda ratio.

AD TERTIUM dicendum quod amantes seipsos vituperantur inquantum amant se secundum naturam sensibilem, cui obtemperant. Quod non est vere amare seipsum secundum naturam rationalem, ut sibi velit ea bona quae pertinent ad perfectionem rationis. Et hoc modo praecipue ad caritatem pertinet diligere seipsum.

I ANSWER THAT, Since charity is a kind of friendship, as stated above (Q. 23, A. 1), we may consider charity from two standpoints: first, under the general notion of friendship, and in this way we must hold that, properly speaking, a man is not a friend to himself, but something more than a friend, since friendship implies union, for Dionysius says (*Div. Nom.* iv) that love is *a unitive force*, whereas a man is one with himself which is more than being united to another. Hence, just as unity is the principle of union, so the love with which a man loves himself is the form and root of friendship. For if we have friendship with others it is because we do unto them as we do unto ourselves, hence we read in *Ethic.* ix, 4, 8, that *the origin of friendly relations with others lies in our relations to ourselves.* Thus too with regard to principles we have something greater than science, namely understanding.

Second, we may speak of charity in respect of its specific nature, namely as denoting man's friendship with God in the first place, and, consequently, with the things of God, among which things is man himself who has charity. Hence, among these other things which he loves out of charity because they pertain to God, he loves also himself out of charity.

REPLY OBJ. 1: Gregory speaks there of charity under the general notion of friendship.

AND THE SECOND Objection is to be taken in the same sense.

REPLY OBJ. 3: Those who love themselves are to be blamed, insofar as they love themselves as regards their sensitive nature, which they humor. This is not to love oneself truly according to one's rational nature, so as to desire for oneself the good things which pertain to the perfection of reason: and in this way chiefly it is through charity that a man loves himself.

# Article 5

*Whether a man ought to love his body out of charity?*

AD QUINTUM SIC PROCEDITUR. Videtur quod homo non debeat corpus suum ex caritate diligere. Non enim diligimus illum cui convivere non volumus. Sed homines caritatem habentes refugiunt corporis convictum, secundum illud Rom. VII, *quis me liberabit de corpore mortis huius?* Et Philipp. I, *desiderium habens dissolvi et cum Christo esse.* Ergo corpus nostrum non est ex caritate diligendum.

PRAETEREA, amicitia caritatis fundatur super communicatione divinae fruitionis. Sed huius fruitionis corpus particeps esse non potest. Ergo corpus non est ex caritate diligendum.

OBJECTION 1: It would seem that a man ought not to love his body out of charity. For we do not love one with whom we are unwilling to associate. But those who have charity shun the society of the body, according to Rom. 7:24: *Who shall deliver me from the body of this death?* and Phil. 1:23: *Having a desire to be dissolved and to be with Christ.* Therefore our bodies are not to be loved out of charity.

OBJ. 2: Further, the friendship of charity is based on fellowship in the enjoyment of God. But the body can have no share in that enjoyment. Therefore the body is not to be loved out of charity.

PRAETEREA, caritas, cum sit amicitia quaedam, ad eos habetur qui reamare possunt. Sed corpus nostrum non potest nos ex caritate diligere. Ergo non est ex caritate diligendum.

SED CONTRA est quod Augustinus, in I de Doct. Christ., ponit quatuor ex caritate diligenda, inter quae unum est corpus proprium.

RESPONDEO dicendum quod corpus nostrum secundum duo potest considerari, uno modo, secundum eius naturam; alio modo, secundum corruptionem culpae et poenae.

Natura autem corporis nostri non est a malo principio creata, ut Manichaei fabulantur, sed est a Deo. Unde possumus eo uti ad servitium Dei, secundum illud Rom. VI, *exhibete membra vestra arma iustitiae Deo.* Et ideo ex dilectione caritatis qua diligimus Deum, debemus etiam corpus nostrum diligere. Sed infectionem culpae et corruptionem poenae in corpore nostro diligere non debemus, sed potius ad eius remotionem anhelare desiderio caritatis.

AD PRIMUM ergo dicendum quod apostolus non refugiebat corporis communionem quantum ad corporis naturam, immo secundum hoc nolebat ab eo spoliari, secundum illud II ad Cor. V, *nolumus expoliari, sed supervestiri.* Sed volebat carere infectione concupiscentiae, quae remanet in corpore; et corruptione ipsius, quae aggravat animam, ne possit Deum videre. Unde signanter dixit: *de corpore mortis huius.*

AD SECUNDUM dicendum quod corpus nostrum quamvis Deo frui non possit cognoscendo et amando ipsum, tamen per opera quae per corpus agimus ad perfectam Dei fruitionem possumus venire. Unde et ex fruitione animae redundat quaedam beatitudo ad corpus, scilicet *sanitatis et incorruptionis vigor*; ut Augustinus dicit, in epistola ad Diosc. Et ideo, quia corpus aliquo modo est particeps beatitudinis, potest dilectione caritatis amari.

AD TERTIUM dicendum quod reamatio habet locum in amicitia quae est ad alterum, non autem in amicitia quae est ad seipsum, vel secundum animam vel secundum corpus.

OBJ. 3: Further, since charity is a kind of friendship it is towards those who are capable of loving in return. But our body cannot love us out of charity. Therefore it should not be loved out of charity.

ON THE CONTRARY, Augustine says (*De Doctr. Christ.* i, 23, 26) that there are four things that we should love out of charity, and among them he reckons our own body.

I ANSWER THAT, Our bodies can be considered in two ways: first, in respect of their nature, second, in respect of the corruption of sin and its punishment.

Now the nature of our body was created, not by an evil principle, as the Manicheans pretend, but by God. Hence we can use it for God's service, according to Rom. 6:13: *Present . . . your members as instruments of justice unto God.* Consequently, out of the love of charity with which we love God, we ought to love our bodies also, but we ought not to love the evil effects of sin and the corruption of punishment; we ought rather, by the desire of charity, to long for the removal of such things.

REPLY OBJ. 1: The Apostle did not shrink from the society of his body, as regards the nature of the body, in fact in this respect he was loth to be deprived thereof, according to 2 Cor. 5:4: *We would not be unclothed, but clothed over.* He did, however, wish to escape from the taint of concupiscence, which remains in the body, and from the corruption of the body which weighs down the soul, so as to hinder it from seeing God. Hence he says expressly: *From the body of this death.*

REPLY OBJ. 2: Although our bodies are unable to enjoy God by knowing and loving Him, yet by the works which we do through the body, we are able to attain to the perfect knowledge of God. Hence from the enjoyment in the soul there overflows a certain happiness into the body, viz., *the flush of health and incorruption*, as Augustine states (*Ep. ad Dioscor.* cxviii). Hence, since the body has, in a fashion, a share of happiness, it can be loved with the love of charity.

REPLY OBJ. 3: Mutual love is found in the friendship which is for another, but not in that which a man has for himself, either in respect of his soul, or in respect of his body.

# Article 6

*Whether we ought to love sinners out of charity?*

AD SEXTUM SIC PROCEDITUR. Videtur quod peccatores non sint ex caritate diligendi. Dicitur enim in Psalm., *iniquos odio habui.* Sed David caritatem habebat. Ergo ex caritate magis sunt odiendi peccatores quam diligendi.

OBJECTION 1: It would seem that we ought not to love sinners out of charity. For it is written (Ps 118:113): *I have hated the unjust.* But David had perfect charity. Therefore sinners should be hated rather than loved, out of charity.

**PRAETEREA**, *probatio dilectionis exhibitio est operis*; ut Gregorius dicit, in homilia Pentecostes. Sed peccatoribus iusti non exhibent opera dilectionis, sed magis opera quae videntur esse odii, secundum illud Psalm., *in matutino interficiebam omnes peccatores terrae*. Et dominus praecepit, Exod. XXII, *maleficos non patieris vivere*. Ergo peccatores non sunt ex caritate diligendi.

**PRAETEREA**, ad amicitiam pertinet ut amicis velimus et optemus bona. Sed sancti ex caritate optant peccatoribus mala, secundum illud Psalm., *convertantur peccatores in Infernum*. Ergo peccatores non sunt ex caritate diligendi.

**PRAETEREA**, proprium amicorum est de eisdem gaudere et idem velle. Sed caritas non facit velle quod peccatores volunt, neque facit gaudere de hoc de quo peccatores gaudent; sed magis facit contrarium. Ergo peccatores non sunt ex caritate diligendi.

**PRAETEREA**, *proprium est amicorum simul convivere*, ut dicitur in VIII Ethic. Sed cum peccatoribus non est convivendum, secundum illud II ad Cor. VI, *recedite de medio eorum*. Ergo peccatores non sunt ex caritate diligendi.

**SED CONTRA** est quod Augustinus dicit, in I de Doct. Christ., quod cum dicitur, *diliges proximum tuum, manifestum est omnem hominem proximum esse deputandum*. Sed peccatores non desinunt esse homines, quia peccatum non tollit naturam. Ergo peccatores sunt ex caritate diligendi.

**RESPONDEO** dicendum quod in peccatoribus duo possunt considerari, scilicet natura, et culpa. Secundum naturam quidem, quam a Deo habent, capaces sunt beatitudinis, super cuius communicatione caritas fundatur, ut supra dictum est. Et ideo secundum naturam suam sunt ex caritate diligendi.

Sed culpa eorum Deo contrariatur, et est beatitudinis impedimentum. Unde secundum culpam, qua Deo adversantur, sunt odiendi quicumque peccatores, etiam pater et mater et propinqui, ut habetur Luc. XIV. Debemus enim in peccatoribus odire quod peccatores sunt, et diligere quod homines sunt beatitudinis capaces. Et hoc est eos vere ex caritate diligere propter Deum.

**AD PRIMUM** ergo dicendum quod iniquos propheta odio habuit inquantum iniqui sunt, habens odio iniquitatem ipsorum, quod est ipsorum malum. Et hoc est perfectum odium, de quo ipse dicit, *perfecto odio oderam illos*. Eiusdem autem rationis est odire malum alicuius et diligere bonum eius. Unde etiam istud odium perfectum ad caritatem pertinet.

**AD SECUNDUM** dicendum quod amicis peccantibus, sicut philosophus dicit, in IX Ethic., non sunt subtrahenda amicitiae beneficia, quousque habeatur spes sanationis eorum, sed magis est eis auxiliandum ad recuperationem virtutis quam ad recuperationem pecuniae,

**OBJ. 2**: Further, *love is proved by deeds* as Gregory says in a homily for Pentecost (*In Evang. xxx*). But good men do no works of the unjust: on the contrary, they do such as would appear to be works of hate, according to Ps. 100:8: *In the morning I put to death all the wicked of the land*: and God commanded (Exod 22:18): *Wizards thou shalt not suffer to live*. Therefore sinners should not be loved out of charity.

**OBJ. 3**: Further, it is part of friendship that one should desire and wish good things for one's friends. Now the saints, out of charity, desire evil things for the wicked, according to Ps. 9:18: *May the wicked be turned into hell*. Therefore sinners should not be loved out of charity.

**OBJ. 4**: Further, it is proper to friends to rejoice in, and will the same things. Now charity does not make us will what sinners will, nor to rejoice in what gives them joy, but rather the contrary. Therefore sinners should not be loved out of charity.

**OBJ. 5**: Further, *it is proper to friends to associate together*, according to *Ethic.* viii. But we ought not to associate with sinners, according to 2 Cor. 6:17: *Go ye out from among them*. Therefore we should not love sinners out of charity.

**ON THE CONTRARY**, Augustine says (*De Doctr. Christ.* i, 30) that *when it is said: 'Thou shalt love thy neighbor,' it is evident that we ought to look upon every man as our neighbor*. Now sinners do not cease to be men, for sin does not destroy nature. Therefore we ought to love sinners out of charity.

**I ANSWER THAT**, Two things may be considered in the sinner: his nature and his guilt. According to his nature, which he has from God, he has a capacity for happiness, on the fellowship of which charity is based, as stated above (A. 3; Q. 23, AA. 1, 5), wherefore we ought to love sinners, out of charity, in respect of their nature.

On the other hand their guilt is opposed to God, and is an obstacle to happiness. Wherefore, in respect of their guilt whereby they are opposed to God, all sinners are to be hated, even one's father or mother or kindred, according to Luke 12:26. For it is our duty to hate, in the sinner, his being a sinner, and to love in him, his being a man capable of bliss; and this is to love him truly, out of charity, for God's sake.

**REPLY OBJ. 1**: The prophet hated the unjust, as such, and the object of his hate was their injustice, which was their evil. Such hatred is perfect, of which he himself says (Ps 138:22): *I have hated them with a perfect hatred*. Now hatred of a person's evil is equivalent to love of his good. Hence also this perfect hatred belongs to charity.

**REPLY OBJ. 2**: As the Philosopher observes (*Ethic.* ix, 3), when our friends fall into sin, we ought not to deny them the amenities of friendship, so long as there is hope of their mending their ways, and we ought to help them more readily to regain virtue than to recover money, had

si eam amisissent, quanto virtus est magis amicitiae affinis quam pecunia. Sed quando in maximam malitiam incidunt et insanabiles fiunt, tunc non est eis amicitiae familiaritas exhibenda. Et ideo huiusmodi peccantes, de quibus magis praesumitur nocumentum aliorum quam eorum emendatio, secundum legem divinam et humanam praecipiuntur occidi. Et tamen hoc facit iudex non ex odio eorum, sed ex caritatis amore quo bonum publicum praefertur vitae singularis personae. Et tamen mors per iudicem inflicta peccatori prodest, sive convertatur, ad culpae expiationem; sive non convertatur, ad culpae terminationem, quia per hoc tollitur ei potestas amplius peccandi.

**AD TERTIUM** dicendum quod huiusmodi imprecationes quae in sacra Scriptura inveniuntur, tripliciter possunt intelligi. Uno modo, per modum praenuntiationis, non per modum optationis, ut sit sensus, *convertantur peccatores in Infernum*, idest *convertentur*. Alio modo, per modum optationis, ut tamen desiderium optantis non referatur ad poenam hominum, sed ad iustitiam punientis, secundum illud, *laetabitur iustus cum viderit vindictam*. Quia nec ipse Deus puniens *laetatur in perditione impiorum*, ut dicitur Sap. I, sed in sua iustitia, *quia iustus Dominus, et iustitias dilexit*. Tertio, ut desiderium referatur ad remotionem culpae, non ad ipsam poenam, ut scilicet peccata destruantur et homines remaneant.

**AD QUARTUM** dicendum quod ex caritate diligimus peccatores non quidem ut velimus quae ipsi volunt, vel gaudeamus de his de quibus ipsi gaudent, sed ut faciamus eos velle quod volumus, et gaudere de his de quibus gaudemus. Unde dicitur Ierem. XV, *ipsi convertentur ad te, et tu non converteris ad eos*.

**AD QUINTUM** dicendum quod convivere peccatoribus infirmis quidem est vitandum, propter periculum quod eis imminet ne ab eis subvertantur. Perfectis autem, de quorum corruptione non timetur, laudabile est quod cum peccatoribus conversentur, ut eos convertant. Sic enim dominus cum peccatoribus manducabat et bibebat, ut habetur Matth. IX. Convictus tamen peccatorum quantum ad consortium peccati vitandus est omnibus. Et sic dicitur II ad Cor. VI, *recedite de medio eorum, et immundum ne tetigeritis*, scilicet secundum peccati consensum.

they lost it, for as much as virtue is more akin than money to friendship. When, however, they fall into very great wickedness, and become incurable, we ought no longer to show them friendliness. It is for this reason that both Divine and human laws command such like sinners to be put to death, because there is greater likelihood of their harming others than of their mending their ways. Nevertheless the judge puts this into effect, not out of hatred for the sinners, but out of the love of charity, by reason of which he prefers the public good to the life of the individual. Moreover the death inflicted by the judge profits the sinner, if he be converted, unto the expiation of his crime; and, if he be not converted, it profits so as to put an end to the sin, because the sinner is thus deprived of the power to sin any more.

REPLY OBJ. 3: Such like imprecations which we come across in Holy Writ, may be understood in three ways: first, by way of prediction, not by way of wish, so that the sense is: *May the wicked be*, that is, *The wicked shall be, turned into hell*. Second, by way of wish, yet so that the desire of the wisher is not referred to the man's punishment, but to the justice of the punisher, according to Ps. 57:11: *The just shall rejoice when he shall see the revenge*, since, according to Wis. 1:13, not even God *hath pleasure in the destruction of the wicked* when He punishes them, but He rejoices in His justice, according to Ps. 10:8: *The Lord is just and hath loved justice*. Third, so that this desire is referred to the removal of the sin, and not to the punishment itself, to the effect, namely, that the sin be destroyed, but that the man may live.

REPLY OBJ. 4: We love sinners out of charity, not so as to will what they will, or to rejoice in what gives them joy, but so as to make them will what we will, and rejoice in what rejoices us. Hence it is written (Jer 15:19): *They shall be turned to thee, and thou shalt not to be turned to them*.

REPLY OBJ. 5: The weak should avoid associating with sinners, on account of the danger in which they stand of being perverted by them. But it is commendable for the perfect, of whose perversion there is no fear, to associate with sinners that they may convert them. For thus did Our Lord eat and drink with sinners as related by Matt. 9:11–13. Yet all should avoid the society of sinners, as regards fellowship in sin; in this sense it is written (2 Cor 6:17): *Go out from among them . . . and touch not the unclean thing*, i.e., by consenting to sin.

# Article 7

*Whether sinners love themselves?*

**AD SEPTIMUM SIC PROCEDITUR.** Videtur quod peccatores seipsos diligant. Illud enim quod est principium peccati maxime in peccatoribus invenitur. Sed amor sui est principium peccati, dicit enim Augustinus, XIV de Civ. Dei, quod *facit civitatem Babylonis.* Ergo peccatores maxime amant seipsos.

**PRAETEREA,** peccatum non tollit naturam. Sed hoc unicuique convenit ex sua natura quod diligat seipsum, unde etiam creaturae irrationales naturaliter appetunt proprium bonum, puta conservationem sui esse et alia huiusmodi. Ergo peccatores diligunt seipsos.

**PRAETEREA,** *omnibus est diligibile bonum*; ut Dionysius dicit, in IV cap. de Div. Nom. Sed multi peccatores reputant se bonos. Ergo multi peccatores seipsos diligunt.

**SED CONTRA** est quod dicitur in Psalm., *qui diligit iniquitatem, odit animam suam.*

**RESPONDEO** dicendum quod amare seipsum uno modo commune est omnibus; alio modo proprium est bonorum; tertio modo proprium est malorum. Quod enim aliquis amet id quod seipsum esse aestimat, hoc commune est omnibus. Homo autem dicitur esse aliquid dupliciter. Uno modo, secundum suam substantiam et naturam. Et secundum hoc omnes aestimant bonum commune se esse id quod sunt, scilicet ex anima et corpore compositos. Et sic etiam omnes homines, boni et mali, diligunt seipsos, inquantum diligunt sui ipsorum conservationem.

Alio modo dicitur esse homo aliquid secundum principalitatem, sicut princeps civitatis dicitur esse civitas; unde quod principes faciunt, dicitur civitas facere. Sic autem non omnes aestimant se esse id quod sunt. Principale enim in homine est mens rationalis, secundarium autem est natura sensitiva et corporalis, quorum primum apostolus nominat *interiorem hominem,* secundum *exteriorem,* ut patet II ad Cor. IV. Boni autem aestimant principale in seipsis rationalem naturam, sive interiorem hominem, unde secundum hoc aestimant se esse quod sunt. Mali autem aestimant principale in seipsis naturam sensitivam et corporalem, scilicet exteriorem hominem. Unde non recte cognoscentes seipsos, non vere diligunt seipsos, sed diligunt id quod seipsos esse reputant. Boni autem, vere cognoscentes seipsos, vere seipsos diligunt.

Et hoc probat Philosophus, in IX Ethic., per quinque quae sunt amicitiae propria. Unusquisque enim amicus primo quidem vult suum amicum esse et vivere; secundo, vult ei bona; tertio, operatur bona ad ipsum; quarto, convivit ei delectabiliter; quinto, concordat cum ipso,

**OBJECTION 1:** It would seem that sinners love themselves. For that which is the principle of sin, is most of all in the sinner. Now love of self is the principle of sin, since Augustine says (*De Civ. Dei* xiv, 28) that it *builds up the city of Babylon.* Therefore sinners most of all love themselves.

**OBJ. 2:** Further, sin does not destroy nature. Now it is in keeping with nature that every man should love himself: wherefore even irrational creatures naturally desire their own good, for instance, the preservation of their being, and so forth. Therefore sinners love themselves.

**OBJ. 3:** Further, *good is beloved by all,* as Dionysius states (*Div. Nom.* iv). Now many sinners reckon themselves to be good. Therefore many sinners love themselves.

**ON THE CONTRARY,** It is written (Ps 10:6): *He that loveth iniquity, hateth his own soul.*

**I ANSWER THAT,** Love of self is common to all, in one way; in another way it is proper to the good; in a third way, it is proper to the wicked. For it is common to all for each one to love what he thinks himself to be. Now a man is said to be a thing, in two ways: first, in respect of his substance and nature, and, this way all think themselves to be what they are, that is, composed of a soul and body. In this way too, all men, both good and wicked, love themselves, insofar as they love their own preservation.

Second, a man is said to be something in respect of some predominance, as the sovereign of a state is spoken of as being the state, and so, what the sovereign does, the state is said to do. In this way, all do not think themselves to be what they are. For the reasoning mind is the predominant part of man, while the sensitive and corporeal nature takes the second place, the former of which the Apostle calls the *inward man,* and the latter, the *outward man* (2 Cor 4:16). Now the good look upon their rational nature or the inward man as being the chief thing in them, wherefore in this way they think themselves to be what they are. On the other hand, the wicked reckon their sensitive and corporeal nature, or the outward man, to hold the first place. Wherefore, since they know not themselves aright, they do not love themselves aright, but love what they think themselves to be. But the good know themselves truly, and therefore truly love themselves.

The Philosopher proves this from five things that are proper to friendship. For in the first place, every friend wishes his friend to be and to live; second, he desires good things for him; third, he does good things to him; fourth, he takes pleasure in his company; fifth, he is of one mind with

quasi in iisdem delectatus et contristatus. Et secundum hoc boni diligunt seipsos quantum ad interiorem hominem, quia etiam volunt ipsum servari in sua integritate; et optant ei bona eius, quae sunt bona spiritualia; et etiam ad assequenda operam impendunt; et delectabiliter ad cor proprium redeunt, quia ibi inveniunt et bonas cogitationes in praesenti, et memoriam bonorum praeteritorum, et spem futurorum bonorum, ex quibus delectatio causatur; similiter etiam non patiuntur in seipsis voluntatis dissensionem, quia tota anima eorum tendit in unum.

E contrario autem mali non volunt conservari integritatem interioris hominis; neque appetunt spiritualia eius bona; neque ad hoc operantur; neque delectabile est eis secum convivere redeundo ad cor, quia inveniunt ibi mala et praesentia et praeterita et futura, quae abhorrent; neque etiam sibi ipsis concordant, propter conscientiam remordentem, secundum illud Psalm., *arguam te, et statuam contra faciem tuam.*

Et per eadem probari potest quod mali amant seipsos secundum corruptionem exterioris hominis. Sic autem boni non amant seipsos.

**AD PRIMUM** ergo dicendum quod amor sui qui est principium peccati, est ille qui est proprius malorum, perveniens *usque ad contemptum Dei,* ut ibi dicitur, quia mali sic etiam cupiunt exteriora bona quod spiritualia contemnunt.

**AD SECUNDUM** dicendum quod naturalis amor, etsi non totaliter tollatur a malis, tamen in eis pervertitur per modum iam dictum.

**AD TERTIUM** dicendum quod mali, inquantum aestimant se bonos, sic aliquid participant de amore sui. Nec tamen ista est vera sui dilectio, sed apparens. Quae etiam non est possibilis in his qui valde sunt mali.

him, rejoicing and sorrowing in almost the same things. In this way the good love themselves, as to the inward man, because they wish the preservation thereof in its integrity, they desire good things for him, namely spiritual goods, indeed they do their best to obtain them, and they take pleasure in entering into their own hearts, because they find there good thoughts in the present, the memory of past good, and the hope of future good, all of which are sources of pleasure. Likewise they experience no clashing of wills, since their whole soul tends to one thing.

On the other hand, the wicked have no wish to be preserved in the integrity of the inward man, nor do they desire spiritual goods for him, nor do they work for that end, nor do they take pleasure in their own company by entering into their own hearts, because whatever they find there, present, past and future, is evil and horrible; nor do they agree with themselves, on account of the gnawings of conscience, according to Ps. 49:21: *I will reprove thee and set before thy face.*

In the same manner it may be shown that the wicked love themselves, as regards the corruption of the outward man, whereas the good do not love themselves thus.

**REPLY OBJ. 1**: The love of self which is the principle of sin is that which is proper to the wicked, and reaches *to the contempt of God,* as stated in the passage quoted, because the wicked so desire external goods as to despise spiritual goods.

**REPLY OBJ. 2**: Although natural love is not altogether forfeited by wicked men, yet it is perverted in them, as explained above.

**REPLY OBJ. 3**: The wicked have some share of self-love, insofar as they think themselves good. Yet such love of self is not true but apparent: and even this is not possible in those who are very wicked.

# Article 8

*Whether charity requires that we should love our enemies?*

**AD OCTAVUM SIC PROCEDITUR**. Videtur quod non sit de necessitate caritatis ut inimici diligantur. Dicit enim Augustinus, in Enchirid., quod *hoc tam magnum bonum,* scilicet diligere inimicos, *non est tantae multitudinis quantam credimus exaudiri cum in oratione dicitur, dimitte nobis debita nostra.* Sed nulli dimittitur peccatum sine caritate, quia, ut dicitur Proverb. X, *universa delicta operit caritas.* Ergo non est de necessitate caritatis diligere inimicos.

**PRAETEREA**, caritas non tollit naturam. Sed unaquaeque res, etiam irrationalis, naturaliter odit suum

**OBJECTION 1**: It would seem that charity does not require us to love our enemies. For Augustine says (*Enchiridion* lxxiii) that *this great good,* namely, the love of our enemies, is *not so universal in its application, as the object of our petition when we say: Forgive us our trespasses.* Now no one is forgiven sin without he have charity, because, according to Prov. 10:12, *charity covereth all sins.* Therefore charity does not require that we should love our enemies.

**OBJ. 2**: Further, charity does not do away with nature. Now everything, even an irrational being, naturally hates its

contrarium, sicut ovis lupum, et aqua ignem. Ergo caritas non facit quod inimici diligantur.

**PRAETEREA**, *caritas non agit perperam*. Sed hoc videtur esse perversum quod aliquis diligat inimicos, sicut et quod aliquis odio habeat amicos, unde II Reg. XIX exprobrando dicit Ioab ad David, *diligis odientes te, et odio habes diligentes te*. Ergo caritas non facit ut inimici diligantur.

**SED CONTRA** est quod dominus dicit, Matth. V, *diligite inimicos vestros*.

**RESPONDEO** dicendum quod dilectio inimicorum tripliciter potest considerari. Uno quidem modo, ut inimici diligantur inquantum sunt inimici. Et hoc est perversum et caritati repugnans, quia hoc est diligere malum alterius.

Alio modo potest accipi dilectio inimicorum quantum ad naturam, sed in universali. Et sic dilectio inimicorum est de necessitate caritatis, ut scilicet aliquis diligens Deum et proximum ab illa generalitate dilectionis proximi inimicos suos non excludat.

Tertio modo potest considerari dilectio inimicorum in speciali, ut scilicet aliquis in speciali moveatur motu dilectionis ad inimicum. Et istud non est de necessitate caritatis absolute, quia nec etiam moveri motu dilectionis in speciali ad quoslibet homines singulariter est de necessitate caritatis, quia hoc esset impossibile. Est tamen de necessitate caritatis secundum praeparationem animi, ut scilicet homo habeat animum paratum ad hoc quod in singulari inimicum diligeret si necessitas occurreret. Sed quod absque articulo necessitatis homo etiam hoc actu impleat ut diligat inimicum propter Deum, hoc pertinet ad perfectionem caritatis. Cum enim ex caritate diligatur proximus propter Deum, quanto aliquis magis diligit Deum, tanto etiam magis ad proximum dilectionem ostendit, nulla inimicitia impediente. Sicut si aliquis multum diligeret aliquem hominem, amore ipsius filios eius amaret etiam sibi inimicos. Et secundum hunc modum loquitur Augustinus.

**UNDE PATET** responsio ad primum.

**AD SECUNDUM** dicendum quod unaquaeque res naturaliter odio habet id quod est sibi contrarium inquantum est sibi contrarium. Inimici autem sunt nobis contrarii inquantum sunt inimici. Unde hoc debemus in eis odio habere, debet enim nobis displicere quod nobis inimici sunt. Non autem sunt nobis contrarii inquantum homines sunt et beatitudinis capaces. Et secundum hoc debemus eos diligere.

**AD TERTIUM** dicendum quod diligere inimicos inquantum sunt inimici, hoc est vituperabile. Et hoc non facit caritas, ut dictum est.

contrary, as a lamb hates a wolf, and water fire. Therefore charity does not make us love our enemies.

**OBJ. 3**: Further, charity *doth nothing perversely* (1 Cor 13:4). Now it seems perverse to love one's enemies, as it would be to hate one's friends: hence Joab upbraided David by saying (2 Kgs 19:6): *Thou lovest them that hate thee, and thou hatest them that love thee.* Therefore charity does not make us love our enemies.

**ON THE CONTRARY**, Our Lord said (Matt 4:44): *Love your enemies.*

**I ANSWER THAT**, Love of one's enemies may be understood in three ways. First, as though we were to love our enemies as such: this is perverse, and contrary to charity, since it implies love of that which is evil in another.

Second love of one's enemies may mean that we love them as to their nature, but in general: and in this sense charity requires that we should love our enemies, namely, that in loving God and our neighbor, we should not exclude our enemies from the love given to our neighbor in general.

Third, love of one's enemies may be considered as specially directed to them, namely, that we should have a special movement of love towards our enemies. Charity does not require this absolutely, because it does not require that we should have a special movement of love to every individual man, since this would be impossible. Nevertheless charity does require this, in respect of our being prepared in mind, namely, that we should be ready to love our enemies individually, if the necessity were to occur. That man should actually do so, and love his enemy for God's sake, without it being necessary for him to do so, belongs to the perfection of charity. For since man loves his neighbor, out of charity, for God's sake, the more he loves God, the more does he put enmities aside and show love towards his neighbor: thus if we loved a certain man very much, we would love his children though they were unfriendly towards us. This is the sense in which Augustine speaks in the passage quoted.

**HENCE** the Reply to the first is evident.

**REPLY OBJ. 2**: Everything naturally hates its contrary as such. Now our enemies are contrary to us, as enemies, wherefore this itself should be hateful to us, for their enmity should displease us. They are not, however, contrary to us, as men and capable of happiness: and it is as such that we are bound to love them.

**REPLY OBJ. 3**: It is wrong to love one's enemies as such: charity does not do this, as stated above.

# Article 9

*Whether it is necessary for salvation that we should show our enemies the signs and effects of love?*

**AD NONUM SIC PROCEDITUR.** Videtur quod de necessitate caritatis sit quod aliquis homo signa vel effectus dilectionis inimico exhibeat. Dicitur enim I Ioan. III, *non diligamus verbo neque lingua, sed opere et veritate.* Sed opere diligit aliquis exhibendo ad eum quem diligit signa et effectus dilectionis. Ergo de necessitate caritatis est ut aliquis huiusmodi signa et effectus inimicis exhibeat.

**PRAETEREA,** Matth. V dominus simul dicit, *diligite inimicos vestros, et, benefacite his qui oderunt vos.* Sed diligere inimicos est de necessitate caritatis. Ergo et benefacere inimicis.

**PRAETEREA,** caritate amatur non solum Deus, sed etiam proximus. Sed Gregorius dicit, in homilia Pentecostes, quod *amor Dei non potest esse otiosus, magna enim operatur, si est; si desinit operari, amor non est.* Ergo caritas quae habetur ad proximum non potest esse sine operationis effectu. Sed de necessitate caritatis est ut omnis proximus diligatur, etiam inimicus. Ergo de necessitate caritatis est ut etiam ad inimicos signa et effectus dilectionis extendamus.

**SED CONTRA** est quod Matth. V, super illud, *benefacite his qui oderunt vos,* dicit Glossa quod *benefacere inimicis est cumulus perfectionis.* Sed id quod pertinet ad perfectionem caritatis non est de necessitate ipsius. Ergo non est de necessitate caritatis quod aliquis signa et effectus dilectionis inimicis exhibeat.

**RESPONDEO** dicendum quod effectus et signa caritatis ex interiori dilectione procedunt et ei proportionantur. Dilectio autem interior ad inimicum in communi quidem est de necessitate praecepti absolute; in speciali autem non absolute, sed secundum praeparationem animi, ut supra dictum est.

Sic igitur dicendum est de effectu vel signo dilectionis exterius exhibendo. Sunt enim quaedam beneficia vel signa dilectionis quae exhibentur proximis in communi, puta cum aliquis orat pro omnibus fidelibus vel pro toto populo, aut cum aliquod beneficium impendit aliquis toti communitati. Et talia beneficia vel dilectionis signa inimicis exhibere est de necessitate praecepti, si enim non exhiberentur inimicis, hoc pertineret ad livorem vindictae, contra id quod dicitur Levit. XIX, *non quaeres ultionem; et non eris memor iniuriae civium tuorum.* Alia vero sunt beneficia vel dilectionis signa quae quis exhibet particulariter aliquibus personis. Et talia beneficia vel dilectionis signa inimicis exhibere non est de necessitate salutis nisi secundum praeparationem animi, ut scilicet subveniatur eis in articulo necessitatis, secundum illud Proverb. XXV, *si esurierit inimicus tuus, ciba illum, si sitit, da illi potum.* Sed quod praeter articulum necessitatis

**OBJECTION 1**: It would seem that charity demands of a man to show his enemy the signs or effects of love. For it is written (1 John 3:18): *Let us not love in word nor in tongue, but in deed and in truth.* Now a man loves in deed by showing the one he loves signs and effects of love. Therefore charity requires that a man show his enemies such signs and effects of love.

**OBJ. 2**: Further, Our Lord said in the same breath (Matt 5:44): *Love your enemies,* and, *Do good to them that hate you.* Now charity demands that we love our enemies. Therefore it demands also that we should *do good to them.*

**OBJ. 3**: Further, not only God but also our neighbor is the object of charity. Now Gregory says in a homily for Pentecost (*In Evang. xxx*), that *love of God cannot be idle for wherever it is it does great things, and if it ceases to work, it is no longer love.* Hence charity towards our neighbor cannot be without producing works. But charity requires us to love our neighbor without exception, though he be an enemy. Therefore charity requires us to show the signs and effects of love towards our enemies.

**ON THE CONTRARY**, A gloss on Matt. 5:44, *Do good to them that hate you,* says: *To do good to one's enemies is the height of perfection.* Now charity does not require us to do that which belongs to its perfection. Therefore charity does not require us to show the signs and effects of love to our enemies.

**I ANSWER THAT**, The effects and signs of charity are the result of inward love, and are in proportion with it. Now it is absolutely necessary, for the fulfilment of the precept, that we should inwardly love our enemies in general, but not individually, except as regards the mind being prepared to do so, as explained above (A. 8).

We must accordingly apply this to the showing of the effects and signs of love. For some of the signs and favors of love are shown to our neighbors in general, as when we pray for all the faithful, or for a whole people, or when anyone bestows a favor on a whole community: and the fulfilment of the precept requires that we should show such like favors or signs of love towards our enemies. For if we did not so, it would be a proof of vengeful spite, and contrary to what is written (Lev 19:18): *Seek not revenge, nor be mindful of the injury of thy citizens.* But there are other favors or signs of love, which one shows to certain persons in particular: and it is not necessary for salvation that we show our enemies such like favors and signs of love, except as regards being ready in our minds, for instance to come to their assistance in a case of urgency, according to Prov. 25:21: *If thy enemy be hungry, give him to eat; if he thirst, give him . . . drink.* Outside cases of urgency, to show such like favors to an

huiusmodi beneficia aliquis inimicis exhibeat, pertinet ad perfectionem caritatis, per quam aliquis non solum cavet *vinci a malo*, quod necessitatis est, sed etiam vult *in bono vincere malum*, quod est etiam perfectionis, dum scilicet non solum cavet propter iniuriam sibi illatam detrahi ad odium; sed etiam propter sua beneficia inimicum intendit pertrahere ad suum amorem.

**ET PER HOC** patet responsio ad obiecta.

enemy belongs to the perfection of charity, whereby we not only beware, as in duty bound, of being overcome by evil, but also wish to overcome evil by good, which belongs to perfection: for then we not only beware of being drawn into hatred on account of the hurt done to us, but purpose to induce our enemy to love us on account of our kindliness.

**THIS SUFFICES** for the Replies to the Objections.

# Article 10

*Whether we ought to love the angels out of charity?*

**AD DECIMUM SIC PROCEDITUR.** Videtur quod Angelos non debeamus ex caritate diligere. Ut enim Augustinus dicit, in libro de Doct. Christ., *gemina est dilectio caritatis, scilicet Dei et proximi.* Sed dilectio Angelorum non continetur sub dilectione Dei, cum sint substantiae creatae, nec etiam videtur contineri sub dilectione proximi, cum non communicent nobiscum in specie. Ergo Angeli non sunt ex caritate diligendi.

**PRAETEREA,** magis conveniunt nobiscum bruta animalia quam Angeli, nam nos et bruta animalia sumus in eodem genere propinquo. Sed ad bruta animalia non habemus caritatem, ut supra dictum est. Ergo etiam neque ad Angelos.

**PRAETEREA,** *nihil est ita proprium amicorum sicut convivere*, ut dicitur in VIII Ethic. Sed Angeli non convivunt nobiscum, nec etiam eos videre possumus. Ergo ad eos caritatis amicitiam habere non valemus.

**SED CONTRA** est quod Augustinus dicit, in I de Doct. Christ., *iam vero si vel cui praebendum, vel a quo nobis praebendum est officium misericordiae, recte proximus dicitur; manifestum est praecepto quo iubemur diligere proximum, etiam sanctos Angelos contineri, a quibus multa nobis misericordiae impenduntur officia.*

**RESPONDEO** dicendum quod amicitia caritatis, sicut supra dictum est, fundatur super communicatione beatitudinis aeternae, in cuius participatione communicant cum Angelis homines, dicitur enim Matth. XXII quod *in resurrectione erunt homines sicut Angeli in caelo.* Et ideo manifestum est quod amicitia caritatis etiam ad Angelos se extendit.

**AD PRIMUM** ergo dicendum quod proximus non solum dicitur communicatione speciei, sed etiam communicatione beneficiorum pertinentium ad vitam aeternam; super qua communicatione amicitia caritatis fundatur.

**AD SECUNDUM** dicendum quod bruta animalia conveniunt nobiscum in genere propinquo ratione naturae sensitivae, secundum quam non sumus participes aeter-

**OBJECTION 1**: It would seem that we are not bound to love the angels out of charity. For, as Augustine says (*De Doctr. Christ.* i), *charity is a twofold love: the love of God and of our neighbor.* Now love of the angels is not contained in the love of God, since they are created substances; nor is it, seemingly, contained in the love of our neighbor, since they do not belong with us to a common species. Therefore we are not bound to love them out of charity.

**OBJ. 2**: Further, dumb animals have more in common with us than the angels have, since they belong to the same proximate genus as we do. But we have not charity towards dumb animals, as stated above (A. 3). Neither, therefore, have we towards the angels.

**OBJ. 3**: Further, *nothing is so proper to friends as companionship with one another* (*Ethic.* viii, 5). But the angels are not our companions; we cannot even see them. Therefore we are unable to give them the friendship of charity.

**ON THE CONTRARY**, Augustine says (*De Doctr. Christ.* i, 30): *If the name of neighbor is given either to those whom we pity, or to those who pity us, it is evident that the precept binding us to love our neighbor includes also the holy angels from whom we receive many merciful favors.*

**I ANSWER THAT**, As stated above (Q. 23, A. 1), the friendship of charity is founded upon the fellowship of everlasting happiness, in which men share in common with the angels. For it is written (Matt 22:30) that *in the resurrection . . . men shall be as the angels of God in heaven.* It is therefore evident that the friendship of charity extends also to the angels.

**REPLY OBJ. 1**: Our neighbor is not only one who is united to us in a common species, but also one who is united to us by sharing in the blessings pertaining to everlasting life, and it is on the latter fellowship that the friendship of charity is founded.

**REPLY OBJ. 2**: Dumb animals are united to us in the proximate genus, by reason of their sensitive nature; whereas we are partakers of everlasting happiness, by rea-

nae beatitudinis, sed secundum mentem rationalem; in qua communicamus cum Angelis.

**Ad tertium** dicendum quod Angeli non convivunt nobis exteriori conversatione, quae nobis est secundum sensitivam naturam. Convivimus tamen Angelis secundum mentem, imperfecte quidem in hac vita, perfecte autem in patria, sicut et supra dictum est.

son not of our sensitive nature but of our rational mind wherein we associate with the angels.

**Reply Obj. 3:** The companionship of the angels does not consist in outward fellowship, which we have in respect of our sensitive nature; it consists in a fellowship of the mind, imperfect indeed in this life, but perfect in heaven, as stated above (Q. 23, A. 1, ad 1).

# Article 11

*Whether we are bound to love the demons out of charity?*

**Ad undecimum sic proceditur.** Videtur quod Daemones ex caritate debeamus diligere. Angeli enim sunt nobis proximi inquantum communicamus cum eis in rationali mente. Sed etiam Daemones sic nobiscum communicant, quia data naturalia in eis manent integra, scilicet esse, vivere et intelligere, ut dicitur in IV cap. de Div. Nom. Ergo debemus Daemones ex caritate diligere.

**Praeterea,** Daemones differunt a beatis Angelis differentia peccati, sicut et peccatores homines a iustis. Sed iusti homines ex caritate diligunt peccatores. Ergo etiam ex caritate debent diligere Daemones.

**Praeterea,** illi a quibus beneficia nobis impenduntur debent a nobis ex caritate diligi tanquam proximi, sicut patet ex auctoritate Augustini supra inducta. Sed Daemones nobis in multis sunt utiles, dum *nos tentando nobis coronas fabricant,* sicut Augustinus dicit, XI de Civ. Dei. Ergo Daemones sunt ex caritate diligendi.

**Sed contra** est quod dicitur Isaiae XXVIII, *delebitur foedus vestrum cum morte, et pactum vestrum cum Inferno non stabit.* Sed perfectio pacis et foederis est per caritatem. Ergo ad Daemones, qui sunt Inferni incolae et mortis procuratores, caritatem habere non debemus.

**Respondeo** dicendum quod, sicut supra dictum est, in peccatoribus ex caritate debemus diligere naturam, peccatum odire. In nomine autem Daemonis significatur natura peccato deformata. Et ideo Daemones ex caritate non sunt diligendi. Et si non fiat vis in nomine, et quaestio referatur ad illos spiritus qui Daemones dicuntur, utrum sint ex caritate diligendi, respondendum est, secundum praemissa, quod aliquid ex caritate diligitur dupliciter. Uno modo, sicut ad quem amicitia habetur. Et sic ad illos spiritus caritatis amicitiam habere non possumus. Pertinet enim ad rationem amicitiae ut amicis nostris bonum velimus. Illud autem bonum vitae aeternae quod respicit caritas, spiritibus illis a Deo aeternaliter damnatis ex caritate velle non possumus, hoc

**Objection 1:** It would seem that we ought to love the demons out of charity. For the angels are our neighbors by reason of their fellowship with us in a rational mind. But the demons also share in our fellowship thus, since natural gifts, such as life and understanding, remain in them unimpaired, as Dionysius states (*Div. Nom.* iv). Therefore we ought to love the demons out of charity.

**Obj. 2:** Further, the demons differ from the blessed angels in the matter of sin, even as sinners from just men. Now the just man loves the sinner out of charity. Therefore he ought to love the demons also out of charity.

**Obj. 3:** Further, we ought, out of charity, to love, as being our neighbors, those from whom we receive favors, as appears from the passage of Augustine quoted above (A. 9). Now the demons are useful to us in many things, for *by tempting us they work crowns for us,* as Augustine says (*De Civ. Dei* xi, 17). Therefore we ought to love the demons out of charity.

**On the contrary,** It is written (Isa 28:18): *Your league with death shall be abolished, and your covenant with hell shall not stand.* Now the perfection of a peace and covenant is through charity. Therefore we ought not to have charity for the demons who live in hell and compass death.

**I answer that,** As stated above (A. 6), in the sinner, we are bound, out of charity, to love his nature, but to hate his sin. But the name of demon is given to designate a nature deformed by sin, wherefore demons should not be loved out of charity. Without however laying stress on the word, the question as to whether the spirits called demons ought to be loved out of charity, must be answered in accordance with the statement made above (AA. 2, 3), that a thing may be loved out of charity in two ways. First, a thing may be loved as the person who is the object of friendship, and thus we cannot have the friendship of charity towards the demons. For it is an essential part of friendship that one should be a well-wisher towards one's friend; and it is impossible for us, out of charity, to desire the good of

enim repugnaret caritati Dei, per quam eius iustitiam approbamus.

Alio modo diligitur aliquid sicut quod volumus permanere ut bonum alterius, per quem modum ex caritate diligimus irrationales creaturas, inquantum volumus eas permanere ad gloriam Dei et utilitatem hominum, ut supra dictum est. Et per hunc modum et naturam Daemonum etiam ex caritate diligere possumus, inquantum scilicet volumus illos spiritus in suis naturalibus conservari ad gloriam Dei.

**AD PRIMUM** ergo dicendum quod mens Angelorum non habet impossibilitatem ad aeternam beatitudinem habendam, sicut habet mens Daemonum. Et ideo amicitia caritatis, quae fundatur super communicatione vitae aeternae magis quam super communicatione naturae, habetur ad Angelos, non autem ad Daemones.

**AD SECUNDUM** dicendum quod homines peccatores in hac vita habent possibilitatem perveniendi ad beatitudinem aeternam. Quod non habent illi qui sunt in Inferno damnati; de quibus, quantum ad hoc, est eadem ratio sicut et de Daemonibus.

**AD TERTIUM** dicendum quod utilitas quae nobis ex Daemonibus provenit non est ex eorum intentione, sed ex ordinatione divinae providentiae. Et ideo ex hoc non inducimur ad habendum amicitiam eorum, sed ad hoc quod simus Deo amici, qui eorum perversam intentionem convertit in nostram utilitatem.

everlasting life, to which charity is referred, for those spirits whom God has condemned eternally, since this would be in opposition to our charity towards God whereby we approve of His justice.

Second, we love a thing as being that which we desire to be enduring as another's good. In this way we love irrational creatures out of charity, inasmuch as we wish them to endure, to give glory to God and be useful to man, as stated above (A. 3): and in this way too we can love the nature of the demons even out of charity, inasmuch as we desire those spirits to endure, as to their natural gifts, unto God's glory.

**REPLY OBJ. 1**: The possession of everlasting happiness is not impossible for the angelic mind as it is for the mind of a demon; consequently the friendship of charity which is based on the fellowship of everlasting life, rather than on the fellowship of nature, is possible towards the angels, but not towards the demons.

**REPLY OBJ. 2**: In this life, men who are in sin retain the possibility of obtaining everlasting happiness: not so those who are lost in hell, who, in this respect, are in the same case as the demons.

**REPLY OBJ. 3**: That the demons are useful to us is due not to their intention but to the ordering of Divine providence; hence this leads us to be friends, not with them, but with God, Who turns their perverse intention to our profit.

# Article 12

*Whether four things are rightly reckoned as to be loved out of charity:*
*God, our neighbor, our body, and ourselves?*

**AD DUODECIMUM SIC PROCEDITUR**. Videtur quod inconvenienter enumerentur quatuor ex caritate diligenda, scilicet Deus, proximus, corpus nostrum et nos ipsi. Ut enim Augustinus dicit, super Ioan., *qui non diligit Deum, nec seipsum diligit*. In Dei ergo dilectione includitur dilectio sui ipsius. Non ergo est alia dilectio sui ipsius, et alia dilectio Dei.

**PRAETEREA**, pars non debet dividi contra totum. Sed corpus nostrum est quaedam pars nostri. Non ergo debet dividi, quasi aliud diligibile, corpus nostrum a nobis ipsis.

**PRAETEREA**, sicut nos habemus corpus, ita etiam et proximus. Sicut ergo dilectio qua quis diligit proximum, distinguitur a dilectione qua quis diligit seipsum; ita dilectio qua quis diligit corpus proximi, debet distingui a dilectione qua quis diligit corpus suum. Non ergo convenienter distinguuntur quatuor ex caritate diligenda.

**OBJECTION 1**: It would seem that these four things are not rightly reckoned as to be loved out of charity, to wit: God, our neighbor, our body, and ourselves. For, as Augustine states (*Tract. super Joan.* lxxxiii), *he that loveth not God, loveth not himself*. Hence love of oneself is included in the love of God. Therefore love of oneself is not distinct from the love of God.

**OBJ. 2**: Further, a part ought not to be condivided with the whole. But our body is part of ourselves. Therefore it ought not to be condivided with ourselves as a distinct object of love.

**OBJ. 3**: Further, just as a man has a body, so has his neighbor. Since then the love with which a man loves his neighbor, is distinct from the love with which a man loves himself, so the love with which a man loves his neighbor's body, ought to be distinct from the love with which he loves his own body. Therefore these four things are not rightly distinguished as objects to be loved out of charity.

**SED CONTRA** est quod Augustinus dicit, in I de Doct. Christ., *quatuor sunt diligenda, unum quod supra nos est*, scilicet Deus; *alterum quod nos sumus; tertium quod iuxta nos est*, scilicet proximus; *quartum quod infra nos est*, scilicet proprium corpus.

**RESPONDEO** dicendum quod, sicut dictum est, amicitia caritatis super communicatione beatitudinis fundatur. In qua quidem communicatione unum quidem est quod consideratur ut principium influens beatitudinem, scilicet Deus; aliud est beatitudinem directe participans, scilicet homo et Angelus; tertium autem est id ad quod per quandam redundantiam beatitudo derivatur, scilicet corpus humanum.

Id quidem quod est beatitudinem influens est ea ratione diligibile quia est beatitudinis causa. Id autem quod est beatitudinem participans potest esse duplici ratione diligibile, vel quia est unum nobiscum; vel quia est nobis consociatum in beatitudinis participatione. Et secundum hoc sumuntur duo ex caritate diligibilia, prout scilicet homo diligit et seipsum et proximum.

**AD PRIMUM** ergo dicendum quod diversa habitudo diligentis ad diversa diligibilia facit diversam rationem diligibilitatis. Et secundum hoc, quia alia est habitudo hominis diligentis ad Deum et ad seipsum, propter hoc ponuntur duo diligibilia, cum dilectio unius sit causa dilectionis alterius. Unde, ea remota, alia removetur.

**AD SECUNDUM** dicendum quod subiectum caritatis est mens rationalis quae potest beatitudinis esse capax, ad quam corpus directe non attingit, sed solum per quandam redundantiam. Et ideo homo secundum rationalem mentem, quae est principalis in homine, alio modo se diligit secundum caritatem, et alio modo corpus proprium.

**AD TERTIUM** dicendum quod homo diligit proximum et secundum animam et secundum corpus ratione cuiusdam consociationis in beatitudine. Et ideo ex parte proximi est una tantum ratio dilectionis. Unde corpus proximi non ponitur speciale diligibile.

**ON THE CONTRARY**, Augustine says (*De Doctr. Christ.* i, 23): *There are four things to be loved; one which is above us*, namely God, *another, which is ourselves, a third which is nigh to us*, namely our neighbor, *and a fourth which is beneath us*, namely our own body.

**I ANSWER THAT**, As stated above (Q. 23, AA. 1, 5), the friendship of charity is based on the fellowship of happiness. Now, in this fellowship, one thing is considered as the principle from which happiness flows, namely God; a second is that which directly partakes of happiness, namely men and angels; a third is a thing to which happiness comes by a kind of overflow, namely the human body.

Now the source from which happiness flows is lovable by reason of its being the cause of happiness: that which is a partaker of happiness, can be an object of love for two reasons, either through being identified with ourselves, or through being associated with us in partaking of happiness, and in this respect, there are two things to be loved out of charity, inasmuch as man loves both himself and his neighbor.

**REPLY OBJ. 1**: The different relations between a lover and the various things loved make a different kind of lovableness. Accordingly, since the relation between the human lover and God is different from his relation to himself, these two are reckoned as distinct objects of love, for the love of the one is the cause of the love of the other, so that the former love being removed the latter is taken away.

**REPLY OBJ. 2**: The subject of charity is the rational mind that can be capable of obtaining happiness, to which the body does not reach directly, but only by a kind of overflow. Hence, by his reasonable mind which holds the first place in him, man, out of charity, loves himself in one way, and his own body in another.

**REPLY OBJ. 3**: Man loves his neighbor, both as to his soul and as to his body, by reason of a certain fellowship in happiness. Wherefore, on the part of his neighbor, there is only one reason for loving him; and our neighbor's body is not reckoned as a special object of love.

# QUESTION 26

## THE ORDER OF CHARITY

Deinde considerandum est de ordine caritatis. Et circa hoc quaeruntur tredecim.

Primo, utrum sit aliquis ordo in caritate.

Secundo, utrum homo debeat Deum diligere plus quam proximum.

Tertio, utrum plus quam seipsum.

Quarto, utrum se plus quam proximum.

Quinto, utrum homo debeat plus diligere proximum quam corpus proprium.

Sexto, utrum unum proximum plus quam alterum.

Septimo, utrum plus proximum meliorem, vel sibi magis coniunctum.

Octavo, utrum coniunctum sibi secundum carnis affinitatem, vel secundum alias necessitudines.

Nono, utrum ex caritate plus debeat diligere filium quam patrem.

Decimo, utrum magis debeat diligere matrem quam patrem.

Undecimo, utrum uxorem plus quam patrem vel matrem.

Duodecimo, utrum magis benefactorem quam beneficiatum.

Decimotertio, utrum ordo caritatis maneat in patria.

We must now consider the order of charity, under which head there are thirteen points of inquiry:

(1) Whether there is an order in charity?

(2) Whether man ought to love God more than his neighbor?

(3) Whether more than himself?

(4) Whether he ought to love himself more than his neighbor?

(5) Whether man ought to love his neighbor more than his own body?

(6) Whether he ought to love one neighbor more than another?

(7) Whether he ought to love more, a neighbor who is better, or one who is more closely united to him?

(8) Whether he ought to love more, one who is akin to him by blood, or one who is united to him by other ties?

(9) Whether, out of charity, a man ought to love his son more than his father?

(10) Whether he ought to love his mother more than his father?

(11) Whether he ought to love his wife more than his father or mother?

(12) Whether we ought to love those who are kind to us more than those whom we are kind to?

(13) Whether the order of charity endures in heaven?

# Article 1

*Whether there is order in charity?*

**AD PRIMUM SIC PROCEDITUR.** Videtur quod in caritate non sit aliquis ordo. Caritas enim quaedam virtus est. Sed in aliis virtutibus non assignatur aliquis ordo. Ergo neque in caritate aliquis ordo assignari debet.

**PRAETEREA,** sicuti fidei obiectum est prima veritas, ita caritatis obiectum est summa bonitas. Sed in fide non ponitur aliquis ordo, sed omnia aequaliter creduntur. Ergo nec in caritate debet poni aliquis ordo.

**PRAETEREA,** caritas in voluntate est. Ordinare autem non est voluntatis, sed rationis. Ergo ordo non debet attribui caritati.

**SED CONTRA** est quod dicitur Cant. II, *introduxit me rex in cellam vinariam; ordinavit in me caritatem.*

**OBJECTION 1**: It would seem that there is no order in charity. For charity is a virtue. But no order is assigned to the other virtues. Neither, therefore, should any order be assigned to charity.

**OBJ. 2**: Further, just as the object of faith is the First Truth, so is the object of charity the Sovereign Good. Now no order is appointed for faith, but all things are believed equally. Neither, therefore, ought there to be any order in charity.

**OBJ. 3**: Further, charity is in the will: whereas ordering belongs, not to the will, but to the reason. Therefore no order should be ascribed to charity.

**ON THE CONTRARY,** It is written (Song 2:4): *He brought me into the cellar of wine, he set in order charity in me.*

RESPONDEO dicendum quod, sicut Philosophus dicit, in V Metaphys., prius et posterius dicitur secundum relationem ad aliquod principium. Ordo autem includit in se aliquem modum prioris et posterioris. Unde oportet quod ubicumque est aliquod principium, sit etiam aliquis ordo. Dictum autem est supra quod dilectio caritatis tendit in Deum sicut in principium beatitudinis, in cuius communicatione amicitia caritatis fundatur. Et ideo oportet quod in his quae ex caritate diliguntur attendatur aliquis ordo, secundum relationem ad primum principium huius dilectionis, quod est Deus.

AD PRIMUM ergo dicendum quod caritas tendit in ultimum finem sub ratione finis ultimi, quod non convenit alicui alii virtuti, ut supra dictum est. Finis autem habet rationem principii in appetibilibus et in agendis, ut ex supradictis patet. Et ideo caritas maxime importat comparationem ad primum principium. Et ideo in ea maxime consideratur ordo secundum relationem ad primum principium.

AD SECUNDUM dicendum quod fides pertinet ad vim cognitivam, cuius operatio est secundum quod res cognitae sunt in cognoscente. Caritas autem est in vi affectiva, cuius operatio consistit in hoc quod anima tendit in ipsas res. Ordo autem principalius invenitur in ipsis rebus; et ex eis derivatur ad cognitionem nostram. Et ideo ordo magis appropriatur caritati quam fidei.

Licet etiam in fide sit aliquis ordo, secundum quod principaliter est de Deo, secundario autem de aliis quae referuntur ad Deum.

AD TERTIUM dicendum quod ordo pertinet ad rationem sicut ad ordinantem, sed ad vim appetitivam pertinet sicut ad ordinatam. Et hoc modo ordo in caritate ponitur.

I ANSWER THAT, As the Philosopher says (*Metaph.* v, text. 16), the terms *before* and *after* are used in reference to some principle. Now order implies that certain things are, in some way, before or after. Hence wherever there is a principle, there must needs be also order of some kind. But it has been said above (Q. 23, A. 1; Q. 25, A. 12) that the love of charity tends to God as to the principle of happiness, on the fellowship of which the friendship of charity is based. Consequently there must needs be some order in things loved out of charity, which order is in reference to the first principle of that love, which is God.

REPLY OBJ. 1: Charity tends towards the last end considered as last end: and this does not apply to any other virtue, as stated above (Q. 23, A. 6). Now the end has the character of principle in matters of appetite and action, as was shown above (Q. 23, A. 7, ad 2; I-II, A. 1, ad 1). Wherefore charity, above all, implies relation to the First Principle, and consequently, in charity above all, we find an order in reference to the First Principle.

REPLY OBJ. 2: Faith pertains to the cognitive power, whose operation depends on the thing known being in the knower. On the other hand, charity is in an appetitive power, whose operation consists in the soul tending to things themselves. Now order is to be found in things themselves, and flows from them into our knowledge. Hence order is more appropriate to charity than to faith.

And yet there is a certain order in faith, insofar as it is chiefly about God, and secondarily about things referred to God.

REPLY OBJ. 3: Order belongs to reason as the faculty that orders, and to the appetitive power as to the faculty which is ordered. It is in this way that order is stated to be in charity.

# Article 2

*Whether God ought to be loved more than our neighbor?*

AD SECUNDUM SIC PROCEDITUR. Videtur quod Deus non sit magis diligendus quam proximus. Dicitur enim I Ioan. IV, *qui non diligit fratrem suum, quem videt, Deum, quem non videt, quomodo potest diligere?* Ex quo videtur quod illud sit magis diligibile quod est magis visibile, nam et visio est principium amoris, ut dicitur IX Ethic. Sed Deus est minus visibilis quam proximus. Ergo etiam est minus ex caritate diligibilis.

PRAETEREA, similitudo est causa dilectionis, secundum illud Eccli. XIII, *omne animal diligit simile sibi.* Sed maior est similitudo hominis ad proximum suum quam ad Deum. Ergo homo ex caritate magis diligit proximum quam Deum.

OBJECTION 1: It would seem that God ought not to be loved more than our neighbor. For it is written (1 John 4:20): *He that loveth not his brother whom he seeth, how can he love God, Whom he seeth not?* Whence it seems to follow that the more a thing is visible the more lovable it is, since loving begins with seeing, according to *Ethic.* ix, 5, 12. Now God is less visible than our neighbor. Therefore He is less lovable, out of charity, than our neighbor.

OBJ. 2: Further, likeness causes love, according to Ecclus. 13:19: *Every beast loveth its like.* Now man bears more likeness to his neighbor than to God. Therefore man loves his neighbor, out of charity, more than he loves God.

**PRAETEREA**, illud quod in proximo caritas diligit, Deus est; ut patet per Augustinum, in I de Doct. Christ. Sed Deus non est maior in seipso quam in proximo. Ergo non est magis diligendus in seipso quam in proximo. Ergo non debet magis diligi Deus quam proximus.

**SED CONTRA**, illud magis est diligendum propter quod aliqua odio sunt habenda. Sed proximi sunt odio habendi propter Deum, si scilicet a Deo abducunt, secundum illud Luc. XIV, *si quis venit ad me et non odit patrem et matrem et uxorem et filios et fratres et sorores, non potest meus esse discipulus*. Ergo Deus est magis ex caritate diligendus quam proximus.

**RESPONDEO** dicendum quod unaquaeque amicitia respicit principaliter illud in quo principaliter invenitur illud bonum super cuius communicatione fundatur, sicut amicitia politica principalius respicit principem civitatis, a quo totum bonum commune civitatis dependet; unde et ei maxime debetur fides et obedientia a civibus. Amicitia autem caritatis fundatur super communicatione beatitudinis, quae consistit essentialiter in Deo sicut in primo principio, a quo derivatur in omnes qui sunt beatitudinis capaces.

Et ideo principaliter et maxime Deus est ex caritate diligendus, ipse enim diligitur sicut beatitudinis causa; proximus autem sicut beatitudinem simul nobiscum ab eo participans.

**AD PRIMUM** ergo dicendum quod dupliciter est aliquid causa dilectionis. Uno modo, sicut id quod est ratio diligendi. Et hoc modo bonum est causa diligendi, quia unumquodque diligitur inquantum habet rationem boni. Alio modo, quia est via quaedam ad acquirendum dilectionem. Et hoc modo visio est causa dilectionis, non quidem ita quod ea ratione sit aliquid diligibile quia est visibile; sed quia per visionem perducimur ad dilectionem non ergo oportet quod illud quod est magis visibile sit magis diligibile, sed quod prius occurrat nobis ad diligendum. Et hoc modo argumentatur apostolus. Proximus enim, quia est nobis magis visibilis, primo occurrit nobis diligendus, *ex his enim quae novit animus discit incognita amare*, ut Gregorius dicit, in quadam homilia. Unde si aliquis proximum non diligit, argui potest quod nec Deum diligit, non propter hoc quod proximus sit magis diligibilis; sed quia prius diligendus occurrit. Deus autem est magis diligibilis propter maiorem bonitatem.

**AD SECUNDUM** dicendum quod similitudo quam habemus ad Deum est prior et causa similitudinis quam habemus ad proximum, ex hoc enim quod participamus a Deo id quod ab ipso etiam proximus habet similes proximo efficimur. Et ideo ratione similitudinis magis debemus Deum quam proximum diligere.

**OBJ. 3**: Further, what charity loves in a neighbor, is God, according to Augustine (*De Doctr. Christ.* i, 22, 27). Now God is not greater in Himself than He is in our neighbor. Therefore He is not more to be loved in Himself than in our neighbor. Therefore we ought not to love God more than our neighbor.

**ON THE CONTRARY**, A thing ought to be loved more, if others ought to be hated on its account. Now we ought to hate our neighbor for God's sake, if, to wit, he leads us astray from God, according to Luke 14:26: *If any man come to Me and hate not his father, and mother, and wife, end children, and brethren, and sisters . . . he cannot be My disciple.* Therefore we ought to love God, out of charity, more than our neighbor.

**I ANSWER THAT**, Each kind of friendship regards chiefly the subject in which we chiefly find the good on the fellowship of which that friendship is based: thus civil friendship regards chiefly the ruler of the state, on whom the entire common good of the state depends; hence to him before all, the citizens owe fidelity and obedience. Now the friendship of charity is based on the fellowship of happiness, which consists essentially in God, as the First Principle, whence it flows to all who are capable of happiness.

Therefore God ought to be loved chiefly and before all out of charity: for He is loved as the cause of happiness, whereas our neighbor is loved as receiving together with us a share of happiness from Him.

**REPLY OBJ. 1**: A thing is a cause of love in two ways: first, as being the reason for loving. In this way good is the cause of love, since each thing is loved according to its measure of goodness. Second, a thing causes love, as being a way to acquire love. It is in this way that seeing is the cause of loving, not as though a thing were lovable according as it is visible, but because by seeing a thing we are led to love it. Hence it does not follow that what is more visible is more lovable, but that as an object of love we meet with it before others: and that is the sense of the Apostle's argument. For, since our neighbor is more visible to us, he is the first lovable object we meet with, because *the soul learns, from those things it knows, to love what it knows not*, as Gregory says in a homily (*In Evang. xi*). Hence it can be argued that, if any man loves not his neighbor, neither does he love God, not because his neighbor is more lovable, but because he is the first thing to demand our love: and God is more lovable by reason of His greater goodness.

**REPLY OBJ. 2**: The likeness we have to God precedes and causes the likeness we have to our neighbor: because from the very fact that we share along with our neighbor in something received from God, we become like to our neighbor. Hence by reason of this likeness we ought to love God more than we love our neighbor.

AD TERTIUM dicendum quod Deus, secundum substantiam suam consideratus, in quocumque sit, aequalis est, quia non minuitur per hoc quod est in aliquo. Sed tamen non aequaliter habet proximus bonitatem Dei sicut habet ipsam Deus, nam Deus habet ipsam essentialiter, proximus autem participative.

REPLY OBJ. 3: Considered in His substance, God is equally in all, in whomsoever He may be, for He is not lessened by being in anything. And yet our neighbor does not possess God's goodness equally with God, for God has it essentially, and our neighbor by participation.

# Article 3

*Whether out of charity, man is bound to love God more than himself?*

AD TERTIUM SIC PROCEDITUR. Videtur quod homo non debeat ex caritate plus Deum diligere quam seipsum. Dicit enim philosophus, in IX Ethic., quod *amicabilia quae sunt ad alterum veniunt ex amicabilibus quae sunt ad seipsum.* Sed causa est potior effectu. Ergo maior est amicitia hominis ad seipsum quam ad quemcumque alium. Ergo magis se debet diligere quam Deum.

PRAETEREA, unumquodque diligitur inquantum est proprium bonum. Sed id quod est ratio diligendi magis diligitur quam id quod propter hanc rationem diligitur, sicut principia, quae sunt ratio cognoscendi, magis cognoscuntur. Ergo homo magis diligit seipsum quam quodcumque aliud bonum dilectum. Non ergo magis diligit Deum quam seipsum.

PRAETEREA, quantum aliquis diligit Deum, tantum diligit frui eo. Sed quantum aliquis diligit frui Deo, tantum diligit seipsum, quia hoc est summum bonum quod aliquis sibi velle potest. Ergo homo non plus debet ex caritate Deum diligere quam seipsum.

SED CONTRA est quod Augustinus dicit, in I de Doct. Christ., *si teipsum non propter te debes diligere, sed propter ipsum ubi dilectionis tuae rectissimus finis est, non succenseat aliquis alius homo si et ipsum propter Deum diligas.* Sed propter quod unumquodque, illud magis. Ergo magis debet homo diligere Deum quam seipsum.

RESPONDEO dicendum quod a Deo duplex bonum accipere possumus, scilicet bonum naturae, et bonum gratiae. Super communicatione autem bonorum naturalium nobis a Deo facta fundatur amor naturalis, quo non solum homo in suae integritate naturae super omnia diligit Deum et plus quam seipsum, sed etiam quaelibet creatura suo modo, idest vel intellectuali vel rationali vel animali, vel saltem naturali amore, sicut lapides et alia quae cognitione carent, quia unaquaeque pars naturaliter plus amat commune bonum totius quam particulare bonum proprium. Quod manifestatur ex opere, quaelibet enim pars habet inclinationem principalem ad actionem communem utilitati totius. Apparet etiam hoc in politicis virtutibus, secundum quas cives pro bono communi et dispendia propriarum rerum

OBJECTION 1: It would seem that man is not bound, out of charity, to love God more than himself. For the Philosopher says (*Ethic.* ix, 8) that *a man's friendly relations with others arise from his friendly relations with himself.* Now the cause is stronger than its effect. Therefore man's friendship towards himself is greater than his friendship for anyone else. Therefore he ought to love himself more than God.

OBJ. 2: Further, one loves a thing insofar as it is one's own good. Now the reason for loving a thing is more loved than the thing itself which is loved for that reason, even as the principles which are the reason for knowing a thing are more known. Therefore man loves himself more than any other good loved by him. Therefore he does not love God more than himself.

OBJ. 3: Further, a man loves God as much as he loves to enjoy God. But a man loves himself as much as he loves to enjoy God; since this is the highest good a man can wish for himself. Therefore man is not bound, out of charity, to love God more than himself.

ON THE CONTRARY, Augustine says (*De Doctr. Christ.* i, 22): *If thou oughtest to love thyself, not for thy own sake, but for the sake of Him in Whom is the rightest end of thy love, let no other man take offense if him also thou lovest for God's sake.* Now *the cause of a thing being such is yet more so.* Therefore man ought to love God more than himself.

I ANSWER THAT, The good we receive from God is twofold, the good of nature, and the good of grace. Now the fellowship of natural goods bestowed on us by God is the foundation of natural love, in virtue of which not only man, so long as his nature remains unimpaired, loves God above all things and more than himself, but also every single creature, each in its own way, i.e., either by an intellectual, or by a rational, or by an animal, or at least by a natural love, as stones do, for instance, and other things bereft of knowledge, because each part naturally loves the common good of the whole more than its own particular good. This is evidenced by its operation, since the principal inclination of each part is towards common action conducive to the good of the whole. It may also be seen in civic virtues whereby sometimes the citizens suffer damage even to their

et personarum interdum sustinent. Unde multo magis hoc verificatur in amicitia caritatis, quae fundatur super communicatione donorum gratiae.

Et ideo ex caritate magis debet homo diligere Deum, qui est bonum commune omnium, quam seipsum, quia beatitudo est in Deo sicut in communi et fontali omnium principio qui beatitudinem participare possunt.

**AD PRIMUM** ergo dicendum quod Philosophus loquitur de amicabilibus quae sunt ad alterum in quo bonum quod est obiectum amicitiae invenitur secundum aliquem particularem modum, non autem de amicabilibus quae sunt ad alterum in quo bonum praedictum invenitur secundum rationem totius.

**AD SECUNDUM** dicendum quod bonum totius diligit quidem pars secundum quod est sibi conveniens, non autem ita quod bonum totius ad se referat, sed potius ita quod seipsam refert in bonum totius.

**AD TERTIUM** dicendum quod hoc quod aliquis velit frui Deo, pertinet ad amorem quo Deus amatur amore concupiscentiae. Magis autem amamus Deum amore amicitiae quam amore concupiscentiae, quia maius est in se bonum Dei quam participare possumus fruendo ipso. Et ideo simpliciter homo magis diligit Deum ex caritate quam seipsum.

own property and persons for the sake of the common good. Wherefore much more is this realized with regard to the friendship of charity which is based on the fellowship of the gifts of grace.

Therefore man ought, out of charity, to love God, Who is the common good of all, more than himself: since happiness is in God as in the universal and fountain principle of all who are able to have a share of that happiness.

**REPLY OBJ. 1**: The Philosopher is speaking of friendly relations towards another person in whom the good, which is the object of friendship, resides in some restricted way; and not of friendly relations with another in whom the aforesaid good resides in totality.

**REPLY OBJ. 2**: The part does indeed love the good of the whole, as becomes a part, not however so as to refer the good of the whole to itself, but rather itself to the good of the whole.

**REPLY OBJ. 3**: That a man wishes to enjoy God pertains to that love of God which is love of concupiscence. Now we love God with the love of friendship more than with the love of concupiscence, because the Divine good is greater in itself, than our share of good in enjoying Him. Hence, out of charity, man simply loves God more than himself.

# Article 4

*Whether out of charity, man ought to love himself more than his neighbor?*

**AD QUARTUM SIC PROCEDITUR**. Videtur quod homo ex caritate non magis debeat diligere seipsum quam proximum. Principale enim obiectum caritatis est Deus, ut supra dictum est. Sed quandoque homo habet proximum magis Deo coniunctum quam sit ipse. Ergo debet aliquis magis talem diligere quam seipsum.

**PRAETEREA**, detrimentum illius quem magis diligimus, magis vitamus. Sed homo ex caritate sustinet detrimentum pro proximo, secundum illud Proverb. XII, *qui negligit damnum propter amicum, iustus est*. Ergo homo debet ex caritate magis alium diligere quam seipsum.

**PRAETEREA**, I ad Cor. XIII dicitur quod caritas *non quaerit quae sua sunt*. Sed illud maxime amamus cuius bonum maxime quaerimus. Ergo per caritatem aliquis non amat seipsum magis quam proximum.

**SED CONTRA** est quod dicitur Levit. XIX, et Matth. XXII, *diliges proximum tuum sicut teipsum*, ex quo videtur quod dilectio hominis ad seipsum est sicut exemplar dilectionis quae habetur ad alterum. Sed exemplar potius est quam exemplatum. Ergo homo ex caritate magis debet diligere seipsum quam proximum.

**OBJECTION 1**: It would seem that a man ought not, out of charity, to love himself more than his neighbor. For the principal object of charity is God, as stated above (A. 2; Q. 25, AA. 1, 12). Now sometimes our neighbor is more closely united to God than we are ourselves. Therefore we ought to love such a one more than ourselves.

**OBJ. 2**: Further, the more we love a person, the more we avoid injuring him. Now a man, out of charity, submits to injury for his neighbor's sake, according to Prov. 12:26: *He that neglecteth a loss for the sake of a friend, is just*. Therefore a man ought, out of charity, to love his neighbor more than himself.

**OBJ. 3**: Further, it is written (1 Cor 13:5) *charity seeketh not its own*. Now the thing we love most is the one whose good we seek most. Therefore a man does not, out of charity, love himself more than his neighbor.

**ON THE CONTRARY**, It is written (Lev 19:18, Matt 22:39): *Thou shalt love thy neighbor as thyself*. Whence it seems to follow that man's love for himself is the model of his love for another. But the model exceeds the copy. Therefore, out of charity, a man ought to love himself more than his neighbor.

RESPONDEO dicendum quod in homine duo sunt, scilicet natura spiritualis, et natura corporalis. Per hoc autem homo dicitur diligere seipsum quod diligit se secundum naturam spiritualem, ut supra dictum est. Et secundum hoc debet homo magis se diligere, post Deum, quam quemcumque alium.

Et hoc patet ex ipsa ratione diligendi. Nam sicut supra dictum est, Deus diligitur ut principium boni super quo fundatur dilectio caritatis; homo autem seipsum diligit ex caritate secundum rationem qua est particeps praedicti boni; proximus autem diligitur secundum rationem societatis in isto bono. Consociatio autem est ratio dilectionis secundum quandam unionem in ordine ad Deum. Unde sicut unitas potior est quam unio, ita quod homo ipse participet bonum divinum est potior ratio diligendi quam quod alius associetur sibi in hac participatione. Et ideo homo ex caritate debet magis seipsum diligere quam proximum. Et huius signum est quod homo non debet subire aliquod malum peccati, quod contrariatur participationi beatitudinis, ut proximum liberet a peccato.

AD PRIMUM ergo dicendum quod dilectio caritatis non solum habet quantitatem a parte obiecti, quod est Deus; sed ex parte diligentis qui est ipse homo caritatem habens, sicut et quantitas cuiuslibet actionis dependet quodammodo ex ipso subiecto. Et ideo, licet proximus melior sit Deo propinquior, quia tamen non est ita propinquus caritatem habenti sicut ipse sibi, non sequitur quod magis debeat aliquis proximum quam seipsum diligere.

AD SECUNDUM dicendum quod detrimenta corporalia debet homo sustinere propter amicum, et in hoc ipso seipsum magis diligit secundum spiritualem mentem, quia hoc pertinet ad perfectionem virtutis, quae est bonum mentis. Sed in spiritualibus non debet homo pati detrimentum peccando ut proximum liberet a peccato, sicut dictum est.

AD TERTIUM dicendum quod, sicut Augustinus dicit, in regula, *quod dicitur, caritas non quaerit quae sua sunt, sic intelligitur quia communia propriis anteponit.* Semper autem commune bonum est magis amabile unicuique quam proprium bonum, sicut etiam ipsi parti est magis amabile bonum totius quam bonum partiale sui ipsius, ut dictum est.

I ANSWER THAT, There are two things in man, his spiritual nature and his corporeal nature. And a man is said to love himself by reason of his loving himself with regard to his spiritual nature, as stated above (Q. 25, A. 7): so that accordingly a man ought out of charity to love himself, after God, more than he loves anyone else.

This is evident from the very reason for loving: since, as stated above (Q. 25, AA. 1, 12), God is loved as the principle of good, on which the love of charity is founded; while man, out of charity, loves himself by reason of his being a partaker of the aforesaid good, and loves his neighbor by reason of his fellowship in that good. Now fellowship is a reason for love according to a certain union in relation to God. Wherefore just as unity surpasses union, the fact that man himself has a share of the Divine good, is a more potent reason for loving than that another should be a partner with him in that share. Therefore man, out of charity, ought to love himself more than his neighbor: in sign whereof, a man ought not to give way to any evil of sin, which counteracts his share of happiness, not even that he may free his neighbor from sin.

REPLY OBJ. 1: The love of charity takes its quantity not only from its object which is God, but also from the lover, who is the man that has charity, even as the quantity of any action depends in some way on the subject. Wherefore, though a better neighbor is nearer to God, yet because he is not as near to the man who has charity, as this man is to himself, it does not follow that a man is bound to love his neighbor more than himself.

REPLY OBJ. 2: A man ought to bear bodily injury for his friend's sake, and precisely in so doing he loves himself more as regards his spiritual mind, because it pertains to the perfection of virtue, which is a good of the mind. In spiritual matters, however, man ought not to suffer injury by sinning, in order to free his neighbor from sin, as stated above.

REPLY OBJ. 3: As Augustine says in his *Rule* (*Ep. ccxi*), the saying, '*charity seeks not her own*,' means that it prefers the common to the private good. Now the common good is always more lovable to the individual than his private good, even as the good of the whole is more lovable to the part, than the latter's own partial good, as stated above (A. 3).

# Article 5

*Whether a man ought to love his neighbor more than his own body?*

AD QUINTUM SIC PROCEDITUR. Videtur quod homo non magis debeat diligere proximum quam corpus proprium. In proximo enim intelligitur corpus nostri

OBJECTION 1: It would seem that a man is not bound to love his neighbor more than his own body. For his neighbor includes his neighbor's body. If therefore a man ought to

proximi. Si ergo debet homo diligere proximum plus quam corpus proprium, sequitur quod plus debeat diligere corpus proximi quam corpus proprium.

**PRAETEREA**, homo plus debet diligere animam propriam quam proximum, ut dictum est. Sed corpus proprium propinquius est animae nostrae quam proximus. Ergo plus debemus diligere corpus proprium quam proximum.

**PRAETEREA**, unusquisque exponit id quod minus amat pro eo quod magis amat. Sed non omnis homo tenetur exponere corpus proprium pro salute proximi, sed hoc est perfectorum, secundum illud Ioan. XV, *maiorem caritatem nemo habet quam ut animam suam ponat quis pro amicis suis*. Ergo homo non tenetur ex caritate plus diligere proximum quam corpus proprium.

**SED CONTRA** est quod Augustinus dicit, in I de Doct. Christ., quod *plus debemus diligere proximum quam corpus proprium*.

**RESPONDEO** dicendum quod illud magis est ex caritate diligendum quod habet pleniorem rationem diligibilis ex caritate, ut dictum est. Consociatio autem in plena participatione beatitudinis, quae est ratio diligendi proximum, est maior ratio diligendi quam participatio beatitudinis per redundantiam, quae est ratio diligendi proprium corpus. Et ideo proximum, quantum ad salutem animae, magis debemus diligere quam proprium corpus.

**AD PRIMUM** ergo dicendum quod quia, secundum Philosophum, in IX Ethic., unumquodque videtur esse id quod est praecipuum in ipso; cum dicitur proximus esse magis diligendus quam proprium corpus, intelligitur hoc quantum ad animam, quae est potior pars eius.

**AD SECUNDUM** dicendum quod corpus nostrum est propinquius animae nostrae quam proximus quantum ad constitutionem propriae naturae. Sed quantum ad participationem beatitudinis maior est consociatio animae proximi ad animam nostram quam etiam corporis proprii.

**AD TERTIUM** dicendum quod cuilibet homini imminet cura proprii corporis, non autem imminet cuilibet homini cura de salute proximi, nisi forte in casu. Et ideo non est de necessitate caritatis quod homo proprium corpus exponat pro salute proximi, nisi in casu quod tenetur eius saluti providere. Sed quod aliquis sponte ad hoc se offerat, pertinet ad perfectionem caritatis.

love his neighbor more than his own body, it follows that he ought to love his neighbor's body more than his own.

**OBJ. 2**: Further, a man ought to love his own soul more than his neighbor's, as stated above (A. 4). Now a man's own body is nearer to his soul than his neighbor. Therefore we ought to love our body more than our neighbor.

**OBJ. 3**: Further, a man imperils that which he loves less for the sake of what he loves more. Now every man is not bound to imperil his own body for his neighbor's safety: this belongs to the perfect, according to John 15:13: *Greater love than this no man hath, that a man lay down his life for his friends*. Therefore a man is not bound, out of charity, to love his neighbor more than his own body.

**ON THE CONTRARY**, Augustine says (*De Doctr. Christ.* i, 27) that *we ought to love our neighbor more than our own body*.

**I ANSWER THAT**, Out of charity we ought to love more that which has more fully the reason for being loved out of charity, as stated above (A. 2; Q. 25, A. 12). Now fellowship in the full participation of happiness which is the reason for loving one's neighbor, is a greater reason for loving, than the participation of happiness by way of overflow, which is the reason for loving one's own body. Therefore, as regards the welfare of the soul we ought to love our neighbor more than our own body.

**REPLY OBJ. 1**: According to the Philosopher (*Ethic.* ix, 8) a thing seems to be that which is predominant in it: so that when we say that we ought to love our neighbor more than our own body, this refers to his soul, which is his predominant part.

**REPLY OBJ. 2**: Our body is nearer to our soul than our neighbor, as regards the constitution of our own nature: but as regards the participation of happiness, our neighbor's soul is more closely associated with our own soul, than even our own body is.

**REPLY OBJ. 3**: Every man is immediately concerned with the care of his own body, but not with his neighbor's welfare, except perhaps in cases of urgency: wherefore charity does not necessarily require a man to imperil his own body for his neighbor's welfare, except in a case where he is under obligation to do so; and if a man of his own accord offer himself for that purpose, this belongs to the perfection of charity.

# Article 6

*Whether we ought to love one neighbor more than another?*

AD SEXTUM SIC PROCEDITUR. Videtur quod unus proximus non sit magis diligendus quam alius. Dicit enim Augustinus, in I de Doct. Christ., *omnes homines aeque diligendi sunt. Sed cum omnibus prodesse non possis, his potissimum consulendum est qui pro locorum et temporum vel quarumlibet rerum opportunitatibus, constrictius tibi quasi quadam sorte iunguntur.* Ergo proximorum unus non est magis diligendus quam alius.

PRAETEREA, ubi una et eadem est ratio diligendi diversos, non debet esse inaequalis dilectio. Sed una est ratio diligendi omnes proximos, scilicet Deus; ut patet per Augustinum, in I de Doct. Christ. Ergo omnes proximos aequaliter diligere debemus.

PRAETEREA, amare est velle bonum alicui; ut patet per Philosophum, in II Rhet. Sed omnibus proximis aequale bonum volumus, scilicet vitam aeternam. Ergo omnes proximos aequaliter debemus diligere.

SED CONTRA est quod tanto unusquisque magis debet diligi, quanto gravius peccat qui contra eius dilectionem operatur. Sed gravius peccat qui agit contra dilectionem aliquorum proximorum quam qui agit contra dilectionem aliorum, unde Levit. XX praecipitur quod *qui maledixerit patri aut matri, morte moriatur,* quod non praecipitur de his qui alios homines maledicunt. Ergo quosdam proximorum magis debemus diligere quam alios.

RESPONDEO dicendum quod circa hoc fuit duplex opinio. Quidam enim dixerunt quod omnes proximi sunt aequaliter ex caritate diligendi quantum ad affectum, sed non quantum ad exteriorem effectum; ponentes ordinem dilectionis esse intelligendum secundum exteriora beneficia, quae magis debemus impendere proximis quam alienis; non autem secundum interiorem affectum, quem aequaliter debemus impendere omnibus, etiam inimicis.

Sed hoc irrationabiliter dicitur. Non enim minus est ordinatus affectus caritatis, qui est inclinatio gratiae, quam appetitus naturalis, qui est inclinatio naturae, utraque enim inclinatio ex divina sapientia procedit. Videmus autem in naturalibus quod inclinatio naturalis proportionatur actui vel motui qui convenit naturae uniuscuiusque, sicut terra habet maiorem inclinationem gravitatis quam aqua, quia competit ei esse sub aqua. Oportet igitur quod etiam inclinatio gratiae, quae est affectus caritatis, proportionetur his quae sunt exterius agenda, ita scilicet ut ad eos intensiorem caritatis affectum habeamus quibus convenit nos magis beneficos esse.

OBJECTION 1: It would seem that we ought not to love one neighbor more than another. For Augustine says (*De Doctr. Christ.* i, 28): *One ought to love all men equally.* Since, however, one cannot do good to all, we ought to consider those chiefly who by reason of place, time or any other circumstance, by a kind of chance, are more closely united to us. Therefore one neighbor ought not to be loved more than another.

OBJ. 2: Further, where there is one and the same reason for loving several, there should be no inequality of love. Now there is one and the same reason for loving all one's neighbors, which reason is God, as Augustine states (*De Doctr. Christ.* i, 27). Therefore we ought to love all our neighbors equally.

OBJ. 3: Further, to love a man is to wish him good things, as the Philosopher states (*Rhet.* ii, 4). Now to all our neighbors we wish an equal good, viz. everlasting life. Therefore we ought to love all our neighbors equally.

ON THE CONTRARY, One's obligation to love a person is proportionate to the gravity of the sin one commits in acting against that love. Now it is a more grievous sin to act against the love of certain neighbors, than against the love of others. Hence the commandment (Lev 10:9), *He that curseth his father or mother, dying let him die,* which does not apply to those who cursed others than the above. Therefore we ought to love some neighbors more than others.

I ANSWER THAT, There have been two opinions on this question: for some have said that we ought, out of charity, to love all our neighbors equally, as regards our affection, but not as regards the outward effect. They held that the order of love is to be understood as applying to outward favors, which we ought to confer on those who are connected with us in preference to those who are unconnected, and not to the inward affection, which ought to be given equally to all including our enemies.

But this is unreasonable. For the affection of charity, which is the inclination of grace, is not less orderly than the natural appetite, which is the inclination of nature, for both inclinations flow from Divine wisdom. Now we observe in the physical order that the natural inclination in each thing is proportionate to the act or movement that is becoming to the nature of that thing: thus in earth the inclination of gravity is greater than in water, because it is becoming to earth to be beneath water. Consequently the inclination also of grace which is the effect of charity, must needs be proportionate to those actions which have to be performed outwardly, so that, to wit, the affection of our charity be more intense towards those to whom we ought to behave with greater kindness.

Et ideo dicendum est quod etiam secundum affectum oportet magis unum proximorum quam alium diligere. Et ratio est quia, cum principium dilectionis sit Deus et ipse diligens, necesse est quod secundum propinquitatem maiorem ad alterum istorum principiorum maior sit dilectionis affectus, sicut enim supra dictum est, in omnibus in quibus invenitur aliquod principium, ordo attenditur secundum comparationem ad illud principium.

AD PRIMUM ergo dicendum quod dilectio potest esse inaequalis dupliciter. Uno modo, ex parte eius boni quod amico optamus. Et quantum ad hoc, omnes homines aeque diligimus ex caritate, quia omnibus optamus bonum idem in genere, scilicet beatitudinem aeternam. Alio modo dicitur maior dilectio propter intensiorem actum dilectionis. Et sic non oportet omnes aeque diligere.

Vel aliter dicendum quod dilectio inaequaliter potest ad aliquos haberi dupliciter. Uno modo, ex eo quod quidam diliguntur et alii non diliguntur. Et hanc inaequalitatem oportet servare in beneficentia, quia non possumus omnibus prodesse, sed in benevolentia dilectionis talis inaequalitas haberi non debet. Alia vero est inaequalitas dilectionis ex hoc quod quidam plus aliis diliguntur. Augustinus ergo non intendit hanc excludere inaequalitatem, sed primam, ut patet ex his quae de beneficentia dicit.

AD SECUNDUM dicendum quod non omnes proximi aequaliter se habent ad Deum, sed quidam sunt ei propinquiores, propter maiorem bonitatem. Qui sunt magis diligendi ex caritate quam alii, qui sunt ei minus propinqui.

AD TERTIUM dicendum quod ratio illa procedit de quantitate dilectionis ex parte boni quod amicis optamus.

We must, therefore, say that, even as regards the affection we ought to love one neighbor more than another. The reason is that, since the principle of love is God, and the person who loves, it must needs be that the affection of love increases in proportion to the nearness to one or the other of those principles. For as we stated above (A. 1), wherever we find a principle, order depends on relation to that principle.

REPLY OBJ. 1: Love can be unequal in two ways: first on the part of the good we wish our friend. In this respect we love all men equally out of charity: because we wish them all one same generic good, namely everlasting happiness. Second love is said to be greater through its action being more intense: and in this way we ought not to love all equally.

Or we may reply that we have unequal love for certain persons in two ways: first, through our loving some and not loving others. As regards beneficence we are bound to observe this inequality, because we cannot do good to all: but as regards benevolence, love ought not to be thus unequal. The other inequality arises from our loving some more than others: and Augustine does not mean to exclude the latter inequality, but the former, as is evident from what he says of beneficence.

REPLY OBJ. 2: Our neighbors are not all equally related to God; some are nearer to Him, by reason of their greater goodness, and those we ought, out of charity, to love more than those who are not so near to Him.

REPLY OBJ. 3: This argument considers the quantity of love on the part of the good which we wish our friends.

# Article 7

*Whether we ought to love those who are better more than those who are more closely united to us?*

AD SEPTIMUM SIC PROCEDITUR. Videtur quod magis debeamus diligere meliores quam nobis coniunctiores. Illud enim videtur esse magis diligendum quod nulla ratione debet odio haberi, quam illud quod aliqua ratione est odiendum, sicut et albius est quod est nigro impermixtius. Sed personae nobis coniunctae sunt secundum aliquam rationem odiendae, secundum illud Luc. XIV, *si quis venit ad me et non odit patrem et matrem*, etc., homines autem boni nulla ratione sunt odiendi. Ergo videtur quod meliores sint magis amandi quam coniunctiores.

PRAETEREA, secundum caritatem homo maxime conformatur Deo. Sed Deus diligit magis meliorem. Er-

OBJECTION 1: It would seem that we ought to love those who are better more than those who are more closely united to us. For that which is in no way hateful seems more lovable than that which is hateful for some reason: just as a thing is all the whiter for having less black mixed with it. Now those who are connected with us are hateful for some reason, according to Luke 14:26: *If any man come to Me, and hate not his father*, etc. On the other hand good men are not hateful for any reason. Therefore it seems that we ought to love those who are better more than those who are more closely connected with us.

OBJ. 2: Further, by charity above all, man is likened to God. But God loves more the better man. Therefore man

go et homo per caritatem magis debet meliorem diligere quam sibi coniunctiorem.

PRAETEREA, secundum unamquamque amicitiam illud est magis amandum quod magis pertinet ad id supra quod amicitia fundatur, amicitia enim naturali magis diligimus eos qui sunt magis nobis secundum naturam coniuncti, puta parentes vel filios. Sed amicitia caritatis fundatur super communicatione beatitudinis, ad quam magis pertinent meliores quam nobis coniunctiores. Ergo ex caritate magis debemus diligere meliores quam nobis coniunctiores.

SED CONTRA est quod dicitur I ad Tim. V, *si quis suorum, et maxime domesticorum curam non habet, fidem negavit et est infideli deterior.* Sed interior caritatis affectio debet respondere exteriori effectui. Ergo caritas magis debet haberi ad propinquiores quam ad meliores.

RESPONDEO dicendum quod omnis actus oportet quod proportionetur et obiecto et agenti, sed ex obiecto habet speciem, ex virtute autem agentis habet modum suae intensionis; sicut motus habet speciem ex termino ad quem est, sed intensionem velocitatis habet ex dispositione mobilis et virtute moventis. Sic igitur dilectio speciem habet ex obiecto, sed intensionem habet ex parte ipsius diligentis.

Obiectum autem caritativae dilectionis Deus est; homo autem diligens est. Diversitas igitur dilectionis quae est secundum caritatem, quantum ad speciem est attendenda in proximis diligendis secundum comparationem ad Deum, ut scilicet ei qui est Deo propinquior maius bonum ex caritate velimus. Quia licet bonum quod omnibus vult caritas, scilicet beatitudo aeterna, sit unum secundum se, habet tamen diversos gradus secundum diversas beatitudinis participationes, et hoc ad caritatem pertinet, ut velit iustitiam Dei servari, secundum quam meliores perfectius beatitudinem participant. Et hoc pertinet ad speciem dilectionis, sunt enim diversae dilectionis species secundum diversa bona quae optamus his quos diligimus.

Sed intensio dilectionis est attendenda per comparationem ad ipsum hominem qui diligit. Et secundum hoc illos qui sunt sibi propinquiores intensiori affectu diligit homo ad illud bonum ad quod eos diligit, quam meliores ad maius bonum.

Est etiam ibi et alia differentia attendenda. Nam aliqui proximi sunt propinqui nobis secundum naturalem originem, a qua discedere non possunt, quia secundum eam sunt id quod sunt. Sed bonitas virtutis, secundum quam aliqui appropinquant Deo, potest accedere et recedere, augeri et minui, ut ex supradictis patet. Et ideo possum ex caritate velle quod iste qui est mihi coniunc-

also, out of charity, ought to love the better man more than one who is more closely united to him.

OBJ. 3: Further, in every friendship, that ought to be loved most which has most to do with the foundation of that friendship: for, by natural friendship we love most those who are connected with us by nature, our parents for instance, or our children. Now the friendship of charity is founded upon the fellowship of happiness, which has more to do with better men than with those who are more closely united to us. Therefore, out of charity, we ought to love better men more than those who are more closely connected with us.

ON THE CONTRARY, It is written (1 Tim 5:8): *If any man have not care of his own and especially of those of his house, he hath denied the faith, and is worse than an infidel.* Now the inward affection of charity ought to correspond to the outward effect. Therefore charity regards those who are nearer to us before those who are better.

I ANSWER THAT, Every act should be proportionate both to its object and to the agent. But from its object it takes its species, while, from the power of the agent it takes the mode of its intensity: thus movement has its species from the term to which it tends, while the intensity of its speed arises from the disposition of the thing moved and the power of the mover. Accordingly love takes its species from its object, but its intensity is due to the lover.

Now the object of charity's love is God, and man is the lover. Therefore the specific diversity of the love which is in accordance with charity, as regards the love of our neighbor, depends on his relation to God, so that, out of charity, we should wish a greater good to one who is nearer to God; for though the good which charity wishes to all, viz. everlasting happiness, is one in itself, yet it has various degrees according to various shares of happiness, and it belongs to charity to wish God's justice to be maintained, in accordance with which better men have a fuller share of happiness. And this regards the species of love; for there are different species of love according to the different goods that we wish for those whom we love.

On the other hand, the intensity of love is measured with regard to the man who loves, and accordingly man loves those who are more closely united to him, with more intense affection as to the good he wishes for them, than he loves those who are better as to the greater good he wishes for them.

Again a further difference must be observed here: for some neighbors are connected with us by their natural origin, a connection which cannot be severed, since that origin makes them to be what they are. But the goodness of virtue, wherein some are close to God, can come and go, increase and decrease, as was shown above (Q. 24, AA. 4, 10, 11). Hence it is possible for one, out of charity, to wish

tus sit melior alio, et sic ad maiorem beatitudinis gradum pervenire possit.

Est autem et alius modus quo plus diligimus ex caritate magis nobis coniunctos, quia pluribus modis eos diligimus. Ad eos enim qui non sunt nobis coniuncti non habemus nisi amicitiam caritatis. Ad eos vero qui sunt nobis coniuncti habemus aliquas alias amicitias, secundum modum coniunctionis eorum ad nos. Cum autem bonum super quod fundatur quaelibet alia amicitia honesta ordinetur sicut ad finem ad bonum super quod fundatur caritas, consequens est ut caritas imperet actui cuiuslibet alterius amicitiae, sicut ars quae est circa finem imperat arti quae est circa ea quae sunt ad finem. Et sic hoc ipsum quod est diligere aliquem quia consanguineus vel quia coniunctus est vel concivis, vel propter quodcumque huiusmodi aliud licitum ordinabile in finem caritatis, potest a caritate imperari. Et ita ex caritate eliciente cum imperante pluribus modis diligimus magis nobis coniunctos.

**AD PRIMUM** ergo dicendum quod in propinquis nostris non praecipimur odire quod propinqui nostri sunt; sed hoc solum quod impediunt nos a Deo. Et in hoc non sunt propinqui, sed inimici, secundum illud Mich. VII, *inimici hominis domestici eius.*

**AD SECUNDUM** dicendum quod caritas facit hominem conformari Deo secundum proportionem, ut scilicet ita se habeat homo ad id quod suum est, sicut Deus ad id quod suum est. Quaedam enim possumus ex caritate velle, quia sunt nobis convenientia, quae tamen Deus non vult, quia non convenit ei ut ea velit, sicut supra habitum est, cum de bonitate voluntatis ageretur.

**AD TERTIUM** dicendum quod caritas non solum elicit actum dilectionis secundum rationem obiecti, sed etiam secundum rationem diligentis, ut dictum est. Ex quo contingit quod magis coniunctus magis amatur.

this man who is more closely united to one, to be better than another, and so reach a higher degree of happiness.

Moreover there is yet another reason for which, out of charity, we love more those who are more nearly connected with us, since we love them in more ways. For, towards those who are not connected with us we have no other friendship than charity, whereas for those who are connected with us, we have certain other friendships, according to the way in which they are connected. Now since the good on which every other friendship of the virtuous is based, is directed, as to its end, to the good on which charity is based, it follows that charity commands each act of another friendship, even as the art which is about the end commands the art which is about the means. Consequently this very act of loving someone because he is akin or connected with us, or because he is a fellow-countryman or for any like reason that is referable to the end of charity, can be commanded by charity, so that, out of charity both eliciting and commanding, we love in more ways those who are more nearly connected with us.

**REPLY OBJ. 1**: We are commanded to hate, in our kindred, not their kinship, but only the fact of their being an obstacle between us and God. In this respect they are not akin but hostile to us, according to Micah 7:6: *A man's enemies are they of his own household.*

**REPLY OBJ. 2**: Charity conforms man to God proportionately, by making man comport himself towards what is his, as God does towards what is His. For we may, out of charity, will certain things as becoming to us which God does not will, because it becomes Him not to will them, as stated above (I-II, Q. 19, A. 10), when we were treating of the goodness of the will.

**REPLY OBJ. 3**: Charity elicits the act of love not only as regards the object, but also as regards the lover, as stated above. The result is that the man who is more nearly united to us is more loved.

# Article 8

*Whether we ought to love more those who are connected with us by ties of blood?*

**AD OCTAVUM SIC PROCEDITUR.** Videtur quod non sit maxime diligendus ille qui est nobis coniunctus secundum carnalem originem. Dicitur enim Proverb. XVIII, *vir amicabilis ad societatem magis erit amicus quam frater.* Et maximus Valerius dicit quod *amicitiae vinculum praevalidum est, neque ulla ex parte sanguinis viribus inferius. Hoc etiam certius et exploratius, quod illud nascendi sors fortuitum opus dedit; hoc uniuscuiusque solido iudicio incoacta voluntas contrahit.* Ergo illi qui sunt coniuncti sanguine non sunt magis amandi quam alii.

**OBJECTION 1**: It would seem that we ought not to love more those who are more closely united to us by ties of blood. For it is written (Prov 18:24): *A man amiable in society, shall be more friendly than a brother.* Again, Valerius Maximus says (*Fact. et Dict. Memor.* iv 7): *The ties of friendship are most strong and in no way yield to the ties of blood.* Moreover it is quite certain and undeniable, that as to the latter, the lot of birth is fortuitous, whereas we contract the former by an untrammelled will, and a solid pledge. Therefore we ought not to love more than others those who are united to us by ties of blood.

PRAETEREA, Ambrosius dicit, in I de Offic., *non minus vos diligo, quos in Evangelio genui, quam si in coniugio suscepissem. Non enim vehementior est natura ad diligendum quam gratia. Plus certe diligere debemus quos perpetuo nobiscum putamus futuros, quam quos in hoc tantum saeculo.* Non ergo consanguinei sunt magis diligendi his qui sunt aliter nobis coniuncti.

PRAETEREA, *probatio dilectionis est exhibitio operis;* ut Gregorius dicit, in homilia. Sed quibusdam magis debemus impendere dilectionis opera quam etiam consanguineis, sicut magis est obediendum in exercitu duci quam patri. Ergo illi qui sunt sanguine iuncti non sunt maxime diligendi.

SED CONTRA est quod in praeceptis Decalogi specialiter mandatur de honoratione parentum; ut patet Exod. XX. Ergo illi qui sunt nobis coniuncti secundum carnis originem sunt a nobis specialius diligendi.

RESPONDEO dicendum quod, sicut dictum est, illi qui sunt nobis magis coniuncti, sunt ex caritate magis diligendi, tum quia intensius diliguntur; tum etiam quia pluribus rationibus diliguntur. Intensio autem dilectionis est ex coniunctione dilecti ad diligentem. Et ideo diversorum dilectio est mensuranda secundum diversam rationem coniunctionis, ut scilicet unusquisque diligatur magis in eo quod pertinet ad illam coniunctionem secundum quam diligitur. Et ulterius comparanda est dilectio dilectioni secundum comparationem coniunctionis ad coniunctionem. Sic igitur dicendum est quod amicitia consanguineorum fundatur in coniunctione naturalis originis; amicitia autem concivium in communicatione civili; et amicitia commilitantium in communicatione bellica. Et ideo in his quae pertinent ad naturam plus debemus diligere consanguineos; in his autem quae pertinent ad civilem conversationem plus debemus diligere concives; et in bellicis plus commilitones. Unde et philosophus dicit, in IX Ethic., quod *singulis propria et congruentia est attribuendum. Sic autem et facere videntur. Ad nuptias quidem vocant cognatos, videbitur utique et nutrimento parentibus oportere maxime sufficere, et honorem paternum.*

Et simile etiam in aliis.

Si autem comparemus coniunctionem ad coniunctionem, constat quod coniunctio naturalis originis est prior et immobilior, quia est secundum id quod pertinet ad substantiam; aliae autem coniunctiones sunt supervenientes, et removeri possunt. Et ideo amicitia consanguineorum est stabilior. Sed aliae amicitiae possunt esse potiores secundum illud quod est proprium unicuique amicitiae.

AD PRIMUM ergo dicendum quod quia amicitia sociorum propria electione contrahitur in his quae sub nostra electione cadunt, puta in agendis, praeponde-

OBJ. 2: Further, Ambrose says (*De Officiis* i, 7): *I love not less you whom I have begotten in the Gospel, than if I had begotten you in wedlock, for nature is no more eager to love than grace.* Surely we ought to love those whom we expect to be with us for ever more than those who will be with us only in this world. Therefore we should not love our kindred more than those who are otherwise connected with us.

OBJ. 3: Further, *Love is proved by deeds,* as Gregory states (*Hom. in Evang. xxx*). Now we are bound to do acts of love to others than our kindred: thus in the army a man must obey his officer rather than his father. Therefore we are not bound to love our kindred most of all.

ON THE CONTRARY, The commandments of the decalogue contain a special precept about the honor due to our parents (Exod 20:12). Therefore we ought to love more specially those who are united to us by ties of blood.

I ANSWER THAT, As stated above (A. 7), we ought out of charity to love those who are more closely united to us more, both because our love for them is more intense, and because there are more reasons for loving them. Now intensity of love arises from the union of lover and beloved: and therefore we should measure the love of different persons according to the different kinds of union, so that a man is more loved in matters touching that particular union in respect of which he is loved. And, again, in comparing love to love we should compare one union with another. Accordingly we must say that friendship among blood relations is based upon their connection by natural origin, the friendship of fellow-citizens on their civic fellowship, and the friendship of those who are fighting side by side on the comradeship of battle. Wherefore in matters pertaining to nature we should love our kindred most, in matters concerning relations between citizens, we should prefer our fellow-citizens, and on the battlefield our fellow-soldiers. Hence the Philosopher says (*Ethic.* ix, 2) that *it is our duty to render to each class of people such respect as is natural and appropriate. This is in fact the principle upon which we seem to act, for we invite our relations to a wedding . . . It would seem to be a special duty to afford our parents the means of living . . . and to honor them.*

The same applies to other kinds of friendship.

If however we compare union with union, it is evident that the union arising from natural origin is prior to, and more stable than, all others, because it is something affecting the very substance, whereas other unions supervene and may cease altogether. Therefore the friendship of kindred is more stable, while other friendships may be stronger in respect of that which is proper to each of them.

REPLY OBJ. 1: inasmuch as the friendship of comrades originates through their own choice, love of this kind takes precedence of the love of kindred in matters where we are

rat haec dilectio dilectioni consanguineorum, ut scilicet magis cum illis consentiamus in agendis. Amicitia tamen consanguineorum est stabilior, utpote naturalior existens, et praevalet in his quae ad naturam spectant. Unde magis eis tenemur in provisione necessariorum.

**AD SECUNDUM** dicendum quod Ambrosius loquitur de dilectione quantum ad beneficia quae pertinent ad communicationem gratiae, scilicet de instructione morum. In hac enim magis debet homo subvenire filiis spiritualibus, quos spiritualiter genuit, quam filiis corporalibus, quibus tenetur magis providere in corporalibus subsidiis.

**AD TERTIUM** dicendum quod ex hoc quod duci exercitus magis obeditur in bello quam patri, non probatur quod simpliciter pater minus diligatur, sed quod minus diligatur secundum quid, idest secundum dilectionem bellicae communicationis.

free to do as we choose, for instance in matters of action. Yet the friendship of kindred is more stable, since it is more natural, and preponderates over others in matters touching nature: consequently we are more beholden to them in the providing of necessaries.

**REPLY OBJ. 2**: Ambrose is speaking of love with regard to favors respecting the fellowship of grace, namely, moral instruction. For in this matter, a man ought to provide for his spiritual children whom he has begotten spiritually, more than for the sons of his body, whom he is bound to support in bodily sustenance.

**REPLY OBJ. 3**: The fact that in the battle a man obeys his officer rather than his father proves, that he loves his father less, not simply relatively, i.e., as regards the love which is based on fellowship in battle.

# Article 9

*Whether a man ought, out of charity, to love his children more than his father?*

**AD NONUM SIC PROCEDITUR**. Videtur quod homo ex caritate magis debeat diligere filium quam patrem. Illum enim magis debemus diligere cui magis debemus benefacere. Sed magis debemus benefacere filiis quam parentibus, dicit enim apostolus, II ad Cor. XII, *non debent filii thesaurizare parentibus, sed parentes filiis*. Ergo magis sunt diligendi filii quam parentes.

**PRAETEREA**, gratia perficit naturam. Sed naturaliter parentes plus diligunt filios quam ab eis diligantur; ut Philosophus dicit, in VIII Ethic. Ergo magis debemus diligere filios quam parentes.

**PRAETEREA**, per caritatem affectus hominis Deo conformatur. Sed Deus magis diligit filios quam diligatur ab eis. Ergo etiam et nos magis debemus diligere filios quam parentes.

**SED CONTRA** est quod Ambrosius dicit, *primo Deus diligendus est, secundo parentes, inde filii, post domestici.*

**RESPONDEO** dicendum quod, sicut supra dictum est, gradus dilectionis ex duobus pensari potest. Uno modo, ex parte obiecti. Et secundum hoc id quod habet maiorem rationem boni est magis diligendum, et quod est Deo similius. Et sic pater est magis diligendus quam filius, quia scilicet patrem diligimus sub ratione principii, quod habet rationem eminentioris boni et Deo similioris.

Alio modo computantur gradus dilectionis ex parte ipsius diligentis. Et sic magis diligitur quod est coniunctius. Et secundum hoc filius est magis diligendus quam pater; ut Philosophus dicit, in VIII Ethic. Primo quidem,

**OBJECTION 1**: It seems that a man ought, out of charity, to love his children more than his father. For we ought to love those more to whom we are more bound to do good. Now we are more bound to do good to our children than to our parents, since the Apostle says (2 Cor 12:14): *Neither ought the children to lay up for the parents, but the parents for the children.* Therefore a man ought to love his children more than his parents.

**OBJ. 2**: Further, grace perfects nature. But parents naturally love their children more than these love them, as the Philosopher states (*Ethic.* viii, 12). Therefore a man ought to love his children more than his parents.

**OBJ. 3**: Further, man's affections are conformed to God by charity. But God loves His children more than they love Him. Therefore we also ought to love our children more than our parents.

**ON THE CONTRARY**, Ambrose says: *We ought to love God first, then our parents, then our children, and lastly those of our household.*

**I ANSWER THAT**, As stated above (A. 4, ad 1; A. 7), the degrees of love may be measured from two standpoints. First, from that of the object. In this respect the better a thing is, and the more like to God, the more is it to be loved: and in this way a man ought to love his father more than his children, because, to wit, he loves his father as his principle, in which respect he is a more exalted good and more like God.

Second, the degrees of love may be measured from the standpoint of the lover, and in this respect a man loves more that which is more closely connected with him, in which way a man's children are more lovable to him than his

quia parentes diligunt filios ut aliquid sui existentes; pater autem non est aliquid filii; et ideo dilectio secundum quam pater diligit filium similior est dilectioni qua quis diligit seipsum. Secundo, quia parentes magis sciunt aliquos esse suos filios quam e converso. Tertio, quia filius est magis propinquus parenti, utpote pars existens, quam pater filio, ad quem habet habitudinem principii. Quarto, quia parentes diutius amaverunt, nam statim pater incipit diligere filium; filius autem tempore procedente incipit diligere patrem. Dilectio autem quanto est diuturnior, tanto est fortior, secundum illud Eccli. IX, *non derelinquas amicum antiquum, novus enim non erit similis illi.*

**AD PRIMUM** ergo dicendum quod principio debetur subiectio reverentiae et honor, effectui autem proportionaliter competit recipere influentiam principii et provisionem ipsius. Et propter hoc parentibus a filiis magis debetur honor, filiis autem magis debetur cura provisionis.

**AD SECUNDUM** dicendum quod pater naturaliter plus diligit filium secundum rationem coniunctionis ad seipsum. Sed secundum rationem eminentioris boni filius naturaliter plus diligit patrem.

**AD TERTIUM** dicendum quod, sicut Augustinus dicit, in I de Doct. Christ., *Deus diligit nos ad nostram utilitatem et suum honorem.* Et ideo, quia pater comparatur ad nos in habitudine principii, sicut et Deus, ad patrem proprie pertinet ut ei a filiis honor impendatur, ad filium autem ut eius utilitati a parentibus provideatur. Quamvis in articulo necessitatis filius obligatus sit ex beneficiis susceptis, ut parentibus maxime provideat.

father, as the Philosopher states (*Ethic.* viii). First, because parents love their children as being part of themselves, whereas the father is not part of his son, so that the love of a father for his children, is more like a man's love for himself. Second, because parents know better that so and so is their child than vice versa. Third, because children are nearer to their parents, as being part of them, than their parents are to them to whom they stand in the relation of a principle. Fourth, because parents have loved longer, for the father begins to love his child at once, whereas the child begins to love his father after a lapse of time; and the longer love lasts, the stronger it is, according to Ecclus. 9:14: *Forsake not an old friend, for the new will not be like to him.*

**REPLY OBJ. 1:** The debt due to a principle is submission of respect and honor, whereas that due to the effect is one of influence and care. Hence the duty of children to their parents consists chiefly in honor: while that of parents to their children is especially one of care.

**REPLY OBJ. 2:** It is natural for a man as father to love his children more, if we consider them as closely connected with him: but if we consider which is the more exalted good, the son naturally loves his father more.

**REPLY OBJ. 3:** As Augustine says (*De Doctr. Christ.* i, 32), *God loves us for our good and for His honor.* Wherefore since our father is related to us as principle, even as God is, it belongs properly to the father to receive honor from his children, and to the children to be provided by their parents with what is good for them. Nevertheless in cases of necessity the child is bound out of the favors received to provide for his parents before all.

# Article 10

*Whether a man ought to love his mother more than his father?*

**AD DECIMUM SIC PROCEDITUR**. Videtur quod homo magis debeat diligere matrem quam patrem. Ut enim philosophus dicit, in I de Gen. Animal., *femina in generatione dat corpus.* Sed homo non habet animam a patre, sed per creationem a Deo, ut in primo dictum est. Ergo homo plus habet a matre quam a patre. Plus ergo debet diligere matrem quam patrem.

**PRAETEREA**, magis amantem debet homo magis diligere. Sed mater plus diligit filium quam pater, dicit enim philosophus, in IX Ethic., quod *matres magis sunt amatrices filiorum. Laboriosior enim est generatio matrum; et magis sciunt quoniam ipsarum sunt filii quam patres.* Ergo mater est magis diligenda quam pater.

**PRAETEREA**, ei debetur maior dilectionis affectus qui pro nobis amplius laboravit, secundum illud Rom.

**OBJECTION 1:** It would seem that a man ought to love his mother more than his father. For, as the Philosopher says (*De Gener. Animal.* i, 20), *the female produces the body in generation.* Now man receives his soul, not from his father, but from God by creation, as stated in the First Part (Q. 90, A. 2; Q. 118). Therefore a man receives more from his mother than from his father: and consequently he ought to love her more than him.

**OBJ. 2:** Further, where greater love is given, greater love is due. Now a mother loves her child more than the father does: for the Philosopher says (*Ethic.* ix, 7) that *mothers have greater love for their children. For the mother labors more in child-bearing, and she knows more surely than the father who are her children.*

**OBJ. 3:** Further, love should be more fond towards those who have labored for us more, according to Rom. 16:6:

ult., *salutate Mariam, quae multum laboravit in vobis.* Sed mater plus laborat in generatione et educatione quam pater, unde dicitur Eccli. VII, *gemitum matris tuae ne obliviscaris.* Ergo plus debet homo diligere matrem quam patrem.

**SED CONTRA** est quod Hieronymus dicit, super Ezech., quod *post Deum, omnium patrem, diligendus est pater*, et postea addit de matre.

**RESPONDEO** dicendum quod in istis comparationibus id quod dicitur est intelligendum per se, ut videlicet intelligatur esse quaesitum de patre inquantum est pater, an sit plus diligendus matre inquantum est mater. Potest enim in omnibus huiusmodi tanta esse distantia virtutis et malitiae ut amicitia solvatur vel minuatur; ut philosophus dicit, in VIII Ethic. Et ideo, ut Ambrosius dicit, *boni domestici sunt malis filiis praeponendi.*

Sed per se loquendo, pater magis est amandus quam mater. Amantur enim pater et mater ut principia quaedam naturalis originis. Pater autem habet excellentiorem rationem principii quam mater, quia pater est principium per modum agentis, mater autem magis per modum patientis et materiae. Et ideo, per se loquendo, pater est magis diligendus.

**AD PRIMUM** ergo dicendum quod in generatione hominis mater ministrat materiam corporis informem, formatur autem per virtutem formativam quae est in semine patris. Et quamvis huiusmodi virtus non possit creare animam rationalem, disponit tamen materiam corporalem ad huiusmodi formae susceptionem.

**AD SECUNDUM** dicendum quod hoc pertinet ad aliam rationem dilectionis, alia enim est species amicitiae qua diligimus amantem, et qua diligimus generantem. Nunc autem loquimur de amicitia quae debetur patri et matri secundum generationis rationem.

*Salute Mary, who hath labored much among you.* Now the mother labors more than the father in giving birth and education to her child; wherefore it is written (Sir 7:29): *Forget not the groanings of thy mother.* Therefore a man ought to love his mother more than his father.

**ON THE CONTRARY,** Jerome says on Ezech. 44:25 that *man ought to love God the Father of all, and then his own father*, and mentions the mother afterwards.

**I ANSWER THAT,** In making such comparisons as this, we must take the answer in the strict sense, so that the present question is whether the father as father, ought to be loved more than the mother as mother. The reason is that virtue and vice may make such a difference in such like matters, that friendship may be diminished or destroyed, as the Philosopher remarks (*Ethic.* viii, 7). Hence Ambrose says: *Good servants should be preferred to wicked children.*

Strictly speaking, however, the father should be loved more than the mother. For father and mother are loved as principles of our natural origin. Now the father is principle in a more excellent way than the mother, because he is the active principle, while the mother is a passive and material principle. Consequently, strictly speaking, the father is to be loved more.

**REPLY OBJ. 1:** In the begetting of man, the mother supplies the formless matter of the body; and the latter receives its form through the formative power that is in the semen of the father. And though this power cannot create the rational soul, yet it disposes the matter of the body to receive that form.

**REPLY OBJ. 2:** This applies to another kind of love. For the friendship between lover and lover differs specifically from the friendship between child and parent: while the friendship we are speaking of here, is that which a man owes his father and mother through being begotten of them. The Reply to the Third Objection is evident.

# Article 11

*Whether a man ought to love his wife more than his father and mother?*

**AD UNDECIMUM SIC PROCEDITUR.** Videtur quod homo plus debeat diligere uxorem quam patrem et matrem. Nullus enim dimittit rem aliquam nisi pro re magis dilecta. Sed Gen. II dicitur quod propter uxorem *relinquet homo patrem et matrem.* Ergo magis debet diligere uxorem quam patrem vel matrem.

**PRAETEREA,** apostolus dicit, ad Ephes. V, quod *viri debent diligere uxores sicut seipsos.* Sed homo magis debet diligere seipsum quam parentes. Ergo etiam magis debet diligere uxorem quam parentes.

**PRAETEREA,** ubi sunt plures rationes dilectionis, ibi debet esse maior dilectio. Sed in amicitia quae est ad

**OBJECTION 1:** It would seem that a man ought to love his wife more than his father and mother. For no man leaves a thing for another unless he love the latter more. Now it is written (Gen 2:24) that *a man shall leave father and mother* on account of his wife. Therefore a man ought to love his wife more than his father and mother.

**OBJ. 2:** Further, the Apostle says (Eph 5:33) that a husband should *love his wife as himself.* Now a man ought to love himself more than his parents. Therefore he ought to love his wife also more than his parents.

**OBJ. 3:** Further, love should be greater where there are more reasons for loving. Now there are more reasons for

uxorem sunt plures rationes dilectionis, dicit enim philosophus, in VIII Ethic., quod *in hac amicitia videtur esse utile et delectabile et propter virtutem, si virtuosi sint coniuges.* Ergo maior debet esse dilectio ad uxorem quam ad parentes.

**SED CONTRA** est quod *vir debet diligere uxorem suam sicut carnem suam,* ut dicitur ad Ephes. V. Sed corpus suum minus debet homo diligere quam proximum, ut supra dictum est. Inter proximos autem magis debemus diligere parentes. Ergo magis debemus diligere parentes quam uxorem.

**RESPONDEO** dicendum quod, sicut dictum est, gradus dilectionis attendi potest et secundum rationem boni, et secundum coniunctionem ad diligentem. Secundum igitur rationem boni, quod est obiectum dilectionis, magis sunt diligendi parentes quam uxores, quia diliguntur sub ratione principii et eminentioris cuiusdam boni.

Secundum autem rationem coniunctionis magis diligenda est uxor, quia uxor coniungitur viro ut una caro existens, secundum illud Matth. XIX, *itaque iam non sunt duo, sed una caro.* Et ideo intensius diligitur uxor, sed maior reverentia est parentibus exhibenda.

**AD PRIMUM** ergo dicendum quod non quantum ad omnia deseritur pater et mater propter uxorem, in quibusdam enim magis debet homo assistere parentibus quam uxori. Sed quantum ad unionem carnalis copulae et cohabitationis, relictis omnibus parentibus, homo adhaeret uxori.

**AD SECUNDUM** dicendum quod in verbis apostoli non est intelligendum quod homo debeat diligere uxorem suam aequaliter sibi ipsi, sed quia dilectio quam aliquis habet ad seipsum est ratio dilectionis quam quis habet ad uxorem sibi coniunctam.

**AD TERTIUM** dicendum quod etiam in amicitia paterna inveniuntur multae rationes dilectionis. Et quantum ad aliquid praeponderant rationi dilectionis quae habetur ad uxorem, secundum scilicet rationem boni, quamvis illae praeponderent secundum coniunctionis rationem.

**AD QUARTUM** dicendum quod illud etiam non est sic intelligendum quod ly *sicut* importet aequalitatem, sed rationem dilectionis. Diligit enim homo uxorem suam principaliter ratione carnalis coniunctionis.

love in the friendship of a man towards his wife. For the Philosopher says (*Ethic.* viii, 12) that *in this friendship there are the motives of utility, pleasure, and also of virtue, if husband and wife are virtuous.* Therefore a man's love for his wife ought to be greater than his love for his parents.

**ON THE CONTRARY,** According to Eph. 5:28, *men ought to love their wives as their own bodies.* Now a man ought to love his body less than his neighbor, as stated above (A. 5): and among his neighbors he should love his parents most. Therefore he ought to love his parents more than his wife.

**I ANSWER THAT,** As stated above (A. 9), the degrees of love may be taken from the good (which is loved), or from the union between those who love. On the part of the good which is the object loved, a man should love his parents more than his wife, because he loves them as his principles and considered as a more exalted good.

But on the part of the union, the wife ought to be loved more, because she is united with her husband, as one flesh, according to Matt. 19:6: *Therefore now they are not two, but one flesh.* Consequently a man loves his wife more intensely, but his parents with greater reverence.

**REPLY OBJ. 1:** A man does not in all respects leave his father and mother for the sake of his wife: for in certain cases a man ought to succor his parents rather than his wife. He does however leave all his kinsfolk, and cleaves to his wife as regards the union of carnal connection and cohabitation.

**REPLY OBJ. 2:** The words of the Apostle do not mean that a man ought to love his wife equally with himself, but that a man's love for himself is the reason for his love of his wife, since she is one with him.

**REPLY OBJ. 3:** There are also several reasons for a man's love for his father; and these, in a certain respect, namely, as regards good, are more weighty than those for which a man loves his wife; although the latter outweigh the former as regards the closeness of the union.

**AS TO THE ARGUMENT** in the contrary sense, it must be observed that in the words quoted, the particle *as* denotes not equality of love but the motive of love. For the principal reason why a man loves his wife is her being united to him in the flesh.

# Article 12

*Whether a man ought to love more his benefactor than one he has benefited?*

**AD DUODECIMUM SIC PROCEDITUR.** Videtur quod homo magis debeat diligere benefactorem quam beneficiatum. Quia ut dicit Augustinus, in libro de Catechiz.

**OBJECTION 1:** It would seem that a man ought to love his benefactor more than one he has benefited. For Augustine says (*De Catech. Rud.* iv): *Nothing will incite another*

Rud., *nulla est maior provocatio ad amandum quam praevenire amando, nimis enim durus est animus qui dilectionem, etsi non vult impendere, nolit rependere.* Sed benefactores praeveniunt nos in beneficio caritatis. Ergo benefactores maxime debemus diligere.

**PRAETEREA**, tanto aliquis est magis diligendus quanto gravius homo peccat si ab eius dilectione desistat, vel contra eam agat. Sed gravius peccat qui benefactorem non diligit, vel contra eum agit, quam si diligere desinat eum cui hactenus benefecit. Ergo magis sunt amandi benefactores quam hi quibus benefacimus.

**PRAETEREA**, inter omnia diligenda maxime diligendus est Deus et post eum pater, ut Hieronymus dicit. Sed isti sunt maximi benefactores. Ergo benefactor est maxime diligendus.

**SED CONTRA** est quod Philosophus dicit, in IX Ethic., quod *benefactores magis videntur amare beneficiatos quam e converso.*

**RESPONDEO** dicendum quod, sicut supra dictum est, aliquid magis diligitur dupliciter, uno quidem modo, quia habet rationem excellentioris boni; alio modo, ratione maioris coniunctionis. Primo quidem igitur modo benefactor est magis diligendus, quia, cum sit principium boni in beneficiato, habet excellentioris boni rationem; sicut et de patre dictum est.

Secundo autem modo magis diligimus beneficiatos, ut Philosophus probat, in IX Ethic., per quatuor rationes. Primo quidem, quia beneficiatus est quasi quoddam opus benefactoris, unde consuevit dici de aliquo, *iste est factura illius.* Naturale autem est cuilibet quod diligat opus suum, sicut videmus quod poetae diligunt poemata sua. Et hoc ideo quia unumquodque diligit suum esse et suum vivere, quod maxime manifestatur in suo agere. Secundo, quia unusquisque naturaliter diligit illud in quo inspicit suum bonum. Habet quidem igitur et benefactor in beneficiato aliquod bonum, et e converso, sed benefactor inspicit in beneficiato suum bonum honestum, beneficiatus in benefactore suum bonum utile. Bonum autem honestum delectabilius consideratur quam bonum utile, tum quia est diuturnius, utilitas enim cito transit, et delectatio memoriae non est sicut delectatio rei praesentis; tum etiam quia bona honesta magis cum delectatione recolimus quam utilitates quae nobis ab aliis provenerunt. Tertio, quia ad amantem pertinet agere, vult enim et operatur bonum amato, ad amatum autem pertinet pati. Et ideo excellentioris est amare. Et propter hoc ad benefactorem pertinet ut plus amet. Quarto, quia difficilius est beneficia impendere quam recipere. Ea vero in quibus laboramus magis diligimus; quae vero nobis de facili proveniunt quodammodo contemnimus.

more to love you than that you love him first: *for he must have a hard heart indeed, who not only refuses to love, but declines to return love already given.* Now a man's benefactor forestalls him in the kindly deeds of charity. Therefore we ought to love our benefactors above all.

**OBJ. 2**: Further, the more grievously we sin by ceasing to love a man or by working against him, the more ought we to love him. Now it is a more grievous sin to cease loving a benefactor or to work against him, than to cease loving one to whom one has hitherto done kindly actions. Therefore we ought to love our benefactors more than those to whom we are kind.

**OBJ. 3**: Further, of all things lovable, God is to be loved most, and then one's father, as Jerome says. Now these are our greatest benefactors. Therefore a benefactor should be loved above all others.

**ON THE CONTRARY**, The Philosopher says (*Ethic.* ix, 7), that *benefactors seem to love recipients of their benefactions, rather than vice versa.*

**I ANSWER THAT**, As stated above (AA. 9, 11), a thing is loved more in two ways: first because it has the character of a more excellent good, second by reason of a closer connection. In the first way we ought to love our benefactor most, because, since he is a principle of good to the man he has benefited, he has the character of a more excellent good, as stated above with regard to one's father (A. 9).

In the second way, however, we love those more who have received benefactions from us, as the Philosopher proves (*Ethic.* ix, 7) by four arguments. First because the recipient of benefactions is the handiwork of the benefactor, so that we are wont to say of a man: *He was made by so and so.* Now it is natural to a man to love his own work (thus it is to be observed that poets love their own poems): and the reason is that we love to be and to live, and these are made manifest in our action. Second, because we all naturally love that in which we see our own good. Now it is true that the benefactor has some good of his in the recipient of his benefaction, and the recipient some good in the benefactor; but the benefactor sees his virtuous good in the recipient, while the recipient sees his useful good in the benefactor. Now it gives more pleasure to see one's virtuous good than one's useful good, both because it is more enduring—for usefulness quickly flits by, and the pleasure of calling a thing to mind is not like the pleasure of having it present—and because it is more pleasant to recall virtuous goods than the profit we have derived from others. Third, because is it the lover's part to act, since he wills and works the good of the beloved, while the beloved takes a passive part in receiving good, so that to love surpasses being loved, for which reason the greater love is on the part of the benefactor. Fourth because it is more difficult to give than to receive favors: and we are most fond of things which have cost us most trouble, while we almost despise what comes easy to us.

AD PRIMUM ergo dicendum quod in benefactore est ut beneficiatus provocetur ad ipsum amandum. Benefactor autem diligit beneficiatum non quasi provocatus ab illo, sed ex seipso motus. Quod autem est ex se potius est eo quod est per aliud.

AD SECUNDUM dicendum quod amor beneficiati ad benefactorem est magis debitus, et ideo contrarium habet rationem maioris peccati. Sed amor benefactoris ad beneficiatum est magis spontaneus, et ideo habet maiorem promptitudinem.

AD TERTIUM dicendum quod Deus etiam plus nos diligit quam nos eum diligimus, et parentes plus diligunt filios quam ab eis diligantur. Nec tamen oportet quod quoslibet beneficiatos plus diligamus quibuslibet benefactoribus. Benefactores enim a quibus maxima beneficia recepimus, scilicet Deum et parentes, praeferimus his quibus aliqua minora beneficia impendimus.

REPLY OBJ. 1: It is some thing in the benefactor that incites the recipient to love him: whereas the benefactor loves the recipient, not through being incited by him, but through being moved thereto of his own accord: and what we do of our own accord surpasses what we do through another.

REPLY OBJ. 2: The love of the beneficiary for the benefactor is more of a duty, wherefore the contrary is the greater sin. On the other hand, the love of the benefactor for the beneficiary is more spontaneous, wherefore it is quicker to act.

REPLY OBJ. 3: God also loves us more than we love Him, and parents love their children more than these love them. Yet it does not follow that we love all who have received good from us, more than any of our benefactors. For we prefer such benefactors as God and our parents, from whom we have received the greatest favors, to those on whom we have bestowed lesser benefits.

# Article 13

*Whether the order of charity endures in heaven?*

AD TERTIUMDECIMUM SIC PROCEDITUR. Videtur quod ordo caritatis non remaneat in patria. Dicit enim Augustinus, in libro de vera Relig., *perfecta caritas est ut plus potiora bona, et minus minora diligamus.* Sed in patria erit perfecta caritas. Ergo plus diliget aliquis meliorem quam seipsum vel sibi coniunctum.

PRAETEREA, ille magis amatur cui maius bonum volumus. Sed quilibet in patria existens vult maius bonum ei qui plus bonum habet, alioquin voluntas eius non per omnia divinae voluntati conformaretur. Ibi autem plus bonum habet qui melior est. Ergo in patria quilibet magis diliget meliorem. Et ita magis alium quam seipsum, et extraneum quam propinquum.

PRAETEREA, tota ratio dilectionis in patria Deus erit, tunc enim implebitur quod dicitur I ad Cor. XV, *ut sit Deus omnia in omnibus.* Ergo magis diligitur qui est Deo propinquior. Et ita aliquis magis diliget meliorem quam seipsum, et extraneum quam coniunctum.

SED CONTRA est quia natura non tollitur per gloriam, sed perficitur. Ordo autem caritatis supra positus ex ipsa natura procedit. Omnia autem naturaliter plus se quam alia amant. Ergo iste ordo caritatis remanebit in patria.

RESPONDEO dicendum quod necesse est ordinem caritatis remanere in patria quantum ad hoc quod Deus est super omnia diligendus. Hoc enim simpliciter erit

OBJECTION 1: It would seem that the order of charity does not endure in heaven. For Augustine says (*De Vera Relig.* xlviii): *Perfect charity consists in loving greater goods more, and lesser goods less.* Now charity will be perfect in heaven. Therefore a man will love those who are better more than either himself or those who are connected with him.

OBJ. 2: Further, we love more him to whom we wish a greater good. Now each one in heaven wishes a greater good for those who have more good, else his will would not be conformed in all things to God's will: and there to be better is to have more good. Therefore in heaven each one loves more those who are better, and consequently he loves others more than himself, and one who is not connected with him, more than one who is.

OBJ. 3: Further, in heaven love will be entirely for God's sake, for then will be fulfilled the words of 1 Cor. 15:28: *That God may be all in all.* Therefore he who is nearer God will be loved more, so that a man will love a better man more than himself, and one who is not connected with him, more than one who is.

ON THE CONTRARY, Nature is not done away, but perfected, by glory. Now the order of charity given above (AA. 2, 3, 4) is derived from nature: since all things naturally love themselves more than others. Therefore this order of charity will endure in heaven.

I ANSWER THAT, The order of charity must needs remain in heaven, as regards the love of God above all things. For this will be realized simply when man shall enjoy God

tunc, quando homo perfecte eo fruetur. Sed de ordine sui ipsius ad alios distinguendum videtur. Quia sicut supra dictum est, dilectionis gradus distingui potest vel secundum differentiam boni quod quis alii exoptat; vel secundum intensionem dilectionis. Primo quidem modo plus diliget meliores quam seipsum, minus vero minus bonos. Volet enim quilibet beatus unumquemque habere quod sibi debetur secundum divinam iustitiam, propter perfectam conformitatem voluntatis humanae ad divinam. Nec tunc erit tempus proficiendi per meritum ad maius praemium, sicut nunc accidit, quando potest homo melioris et virtutem et praemium desiderare, sed tunc voluntas uniuscuiusque infra hoc sistet quod est determinatum divinitus. Secundo vero modo aliquis plus seipsum diliget quam proximum, etiam meliorem. Quia intensio actus dilectionis provenit ex parte subiecti diligentis, ut supra dictum est. Et ad hoc etiam donum caritatis unicuique confertur a Deo, ut primo quidem mentem suam in Deum ordinet, quod pertinet ad dilectionem sui ipsius; secundario vero ordinem aliorum in Deum velit, vel etiam operetur secundum suum modum.

Sed quantum ad ordinem proximorum ad invicem simpliciter quis magis diliget meliorem, secundum caritatis amorem. Tota enim vita beata consistit in ordinatione mentis ad Deum. Unde totus ordo dilectionis beatorum observabitur per comparationem ad Deum, ut scilicet ille magis diligatur et propinquior sibi habeatur ab unoquoque qui est Deo propinquior. Cessabit enim tunc provisio, quae est in praesenti vita necessaria, qua necesse est ut unusquisque magis sibi coniuncto, secundum quamcumque necessitudinem, provideat magis quam alieno; ratione cuius in hac vita ex ipsa inclinatione caritatis homo plus diligit magis sibi coniunctum, cui magis debet impendere caritatis effectum. Continget tamen in patria quod aliquis sibi coniunctum pluribus rationibus diliget, non enim cessabunt ab animo beati honestae dilectionis causae. Tamen omnibus istis rationibus praefertur incomparabiliter ratio dilectionis quae sumitur ex propinquitate ad Deum.

**AD PRIMUM** ergo dicendum quod quantum ad coniunctos sibi ratio illa concedenda est. Sed quantum ad seipsum oportet quod aliquis plus se quam alios diligat, tanto magis quanto perfectior est caritas, quia perfectio caritatis ordinat hominem perfecte in Deum quod pertinet ad dilectionem sui ipsius, ut dictum est.

**AD SECUNDUM** dicendum quod ratio illa procedit de ordine dilectionis secundum gradum boni quod aliquis vult amato.

**AD TERTIUM** dicendum quod unicuique erit Deus tota ratio diligendi eo quod Deus est totum hominis

perfectly. But, as regards the order between man himself and other men, a distinction would seem to be necessary, because, as we stated above (AA. 7, 9), the degrees of love may be distinguished either in respect of the good which a man desires for another, or according to the intensity of love itself. In the first way a man will love better men more than himself, and those who are less good, less than himself: because, by reason of the perfect conformity of the human to the Divine will, each of the blessed will desire everyone to have what is due to him according to Divine justice. Nor will that be a time for advancing by means of merit to a yet greater reward, as happens now while it is possible for a man to desire both the virtue and the reward of a better man, whereas then the will of each one will rest within the limits determined by God. But in the second way a man will love himself more than even his better neighbors, because the intensity of the act of love arises on the part of the person who loves, as stated above (AA. 7, 9). Moreover it is for this that the gift of charity is bestowed by God on each one, namely, that he may first of all direct his mind to God, and this pertains to a man's love for himself, and that, in the second place, he may wish other things to be directed to God, and even work for that end according to his capacity.

As to the order to be observed among our neighbors, a man will simply love those who are better, according to the love of charity. Because the entire life of the blessed consists in directing their minds to God, wherefore the entire ordering of their love will be ruled with respect to God, so that each one will love more and reckon to be nearer to himself those who are nearer to God. For then one man will no longer succor another, as he needs to in the present life, wherein each man has to succor those who are closely connected with him rather than those who are not, no matter what be the nature of their distress: hence it is that in this life, a man, by the inclination of charity, loves more those who are more closely united to him, for he is under a greater obligation to bestow on them the effect of charity. It will however be possible in heaven for a man to love in several ways one who is connected with him, since the causes of virtuous love will not be banished from the mind of the blessed. Yet all these reasons are incomparably surpassed by that which is taken from nighness to God.

**REPLY OBJ. 1**: This argument should be granted as to those who are connected together; but as regards man himself, he ought to love himself so much the more than others, as his charity is more perfect, since perfect entire reason of his love, for God is man's charity directs man to God perfectly, and this belongs to love of oneself, as stated above.

**REPLY OBJ. 2**: This argument considers the order of charity in respect of the degree of good one wills the person one loves.

**REPLY OBJ. 3**: God will be to each one the entire reason of his love, for God is man's entire good. For if we make the

bonum, dato enim, per impossibile, quod Deus non esset hominis bonum, non esset ei ratio diligendi. Et ideo in ordine dilectionis oportet quod post Deum homo maxime diligat seipsum.

impossible supposition that God were not man's good, He would not be man's reason for loving. Hence it is that in the order of love man should love himself more than all else after God.

# QUESTION 27

## THE PRINCIPAL ACT OF CHARITY, WHICH IS TO LOVE

Deinde considerandum est de actu caritatis. Et primo, de principali actu caritatis, qui est dilectio; secundo, de aliis actibus vel effectibus consequentibus.

Circa primum quaeruntur octo.

Primo, quid sit magis proprium caritatis, utrum amari vel amare.

Secundo, utrum amare, prout est actus caritatis, sit idem quod benevolentia.

Tertio, utrum Deus sit propter seipsum amandus.

Quarto, utrum possit in hac vita immediate amari.

Quinto, utrum possit amari totaliter.

Sexto, utrum eius dilectio habeat modum.

Septimo, quid sit melius, utrum diligere amicum vel diligere inimicum.

Octavo, quid sit melius, utrum diligere Deum vel diligere proximum.

We must now consider the act of charity, and (1) the principal act of charity, which is to love, (2) the other acts or effects which follow from that act.

Under the first head there are eight points of inquiry:

(1) Which is the more proper to charity, to love or to be loved?

(2) Whether to love considered as an act of charity is the same as goodwill?

(3) Whether God should be loved for His own sake?

(4) Whether God can be loved immediately in this life?

(5) Whether God can be loved wholly?

(6) Whether the love of God is according to measure?

(7) Which is the better, to love one's friend, or one's enemy?

(8) Which is the better, to love God, or one's neighbor?

# Article 1

*Whether to be loved is more proper to charity than to love?*

**AD PRIMUM SIC PROCEDITUR.** Videtur quod caritatis magis sit proprium amari quam amare. Caritas enim in melioribus melior invenitur. Sed meliores debent magis amari. Ergo caritatis magis est proprium amari.

**PRAETEREA,** illud quod in pluribus invenitur videtur esse magis conveniens naturae, et per consequens melius. Sed sicut dicit Philosophus, in VIII Ethic., *multi magis volunt amari quam amare, propter quod amatores adulationis sunt multi.* Ergo melius est amari quam amare, et per consequens magis conveniens caritati.

**PRAETEREA,** propter quod unumquodque, illud magis. Sed homines propter hoc quod amantur, amant, dicit enim Augustinus, in libro de Catechiz. Rud., quod *nulla est maior provocatio ad amandum quam praevenire amando.* Ergo caritas magis consistit in amari quam in amare.

**SED CONTRA** est quod philosophus dicit, in VIII Ethic., quod *magis existit amicitia in amare quam in amari.* Sed caritas est amicitia quaedam. Ergo caritas magis consistit in amare quam in amari.

**RESPONDEO** dicendum quod amare convenit caritati inquantum est caritas. Caritas enim, cum sit virtus quaedam, secundum suam essentiam habet inclinationem ad

**OBJECTION 1**: It would seem that it is more proper to charity to be loved than to love. For the better charity is to be found in those who are themselves better. But those who are better should be more loved. Therefore to be loved is more proper to charity.

**OBJ. 2**: Further, that which is to be found in more subjects seems to be more in keeping with nature, and, for that reason, better. Now, as the Philosopher says (*Ethic.* viii, 8), *many would rather be loved than love, and lovers of flattery always abound.* Therefore it is better to be loved than to love, and consequently it is more in keeping with charity.

**OBJ. 3**: Further, the cause of anything being such is yet more so. Now men love because they are loved, for Augustine says (*De Catech. Rud.* iv) that *nothing incites another more to love you than that you love him first.* Therefore charity consists in being loved rather than in loving.

**ON THE CONTRARY**, The Philosopher says (*Ethic.* viii, 8) that *friendship consists in loving rather than in being loved.* Now charity is a kind of friendship. Therefore it consists in loving rather than in being loved.

**I ANSWER THAT**, To love belongs to charity as charity. For, since charity is a virtue, by its very essence it has an inclination to its proper act. Now to be loved is not the act

proprium actum. Amari autem non est actus caritatis ipsius qui amatur, sed actus caritatis eius est amare; amari autem competit ei secundum communem rationem boni, prout scilicet ad eius bonum alius per actum caritatis movetur. Unde manifestum est quod caritati magis convenit amare quam amari, magis enim convenit unicuique quod convenit ei per se et substantialiter quam quod convenit ei per aliud. Et huius duplex est signum. Primum quidem, quia amici magis laudantur ex hoc quod amant quam ex hoc quod amantur, quinimmo si non amant et amentur, vituperantur. Secundo, quia matres, quae maxime amant, plus quaerunt amare quam amari, *quaedam enim*, ut Philosophus dicit, in eodem libro, *filios suos dant nutrici, et amant quidem, reamari autem non quaerunt, si non contingat.*

AD PRIMUM ergo dicendum quod meliores ex eo quod meliores sunt, sunt magis amabiles. Sed ex eo quod in eis est perfectior caritas, sunt magis amantes, secundum tamen proportionem amati. Non enim melior minus amat id quod infra ipsum est quam amabile sit, sed ille qui est minus bonus non attingit ad amandum meliorem quantum amabilis est.

AD SECUNDUM dicendum quod, sicut Philosophus dicit ibidem, homines volunt amari inquantum volunt honorari. Sicut enim honor exhibetur alicui ut quoddam testimonium boni in ipso qui honoratur, ita per hoc quod aliquis amatur ostenditur in ipso esse aliquod bonum, quia solum bonum amabile est. Sic igitur amari et honorari quaerunt homines propter aliud, scilicet ad manifestationem boni in amato existentis. Amare autem quaerunt caritatem habentes secundum se, quasi ipsum sit bonum caritatis, sicut et quilibet actus virtutis est bonum virtutis illius. Unde magis pertinet ad caritatem velle amare quam velle amari.

AD TERTIUM dicendum quod propter amari aliqui amant, non ita quod amari sit finis eius quod est amare, sed eo quod est via quaedam ad hoc inducens quod homo amet.

of the charity of the person loved; for this act is to love: and to be loved is competent to him as coming under the common notion of good, insofar as another tends towards his good by an act of charity. Hence it is clear that to love is more proper to charity than to be loved: for that which befits a thing by reason of itself and its essence is more competent to it than that which is befitting to it by reason of something else. This can be exemplified in two ways. First, in the fact that friends are more commended for loving than for being loved, indeed, if they be loved and yet love not, they are blamed. Second, because a mother, whose love is the greatest, seeks rather to love than to be loved: for *some women*, as the Philosopher observes (*Ethic.* viii, 8) *entrust their children to a nurse; they do love them indeed, yet seek not to be loved in return, if they happen not to be loved.*

REPLY OBJ. 1: A better man, through being better, is more lovable; but through having more perfect charity, loves more. He loves more, however, in proportion to the person he loves. For a better man does not love that which is beneath him less than it ought to be loved: whereas he who is less good fails to love one who is better, as much as he ought to be loved.

REPLY OBJ. 2: As the Philosopher says (*Ethic.* viii, 8), men wish to be loved inasmuch as they wish to be honored. For just as honor is bestowed on a man in order to bear witness to the good which is in him, so by being loved a man is shown to have some good, since good alone is lovable. Accordingly men seek to be loved and to be honored, for the sake of something else, viz. to make known the good which is in the person loved. On the other hand, those who have charity seek to love for the sake of loving, as though this were itself the good of charity, even as the act of any virtue is that virtue's good. Hence it is more proper to charity to wish to love than to wish to be loved.

REPLY OBJ. 3: Some love on account of being loved, not so that to be loved is the end of their loving, but because it is a kind of way leading a man to love.

# Article 2

*Whether to love, considered as an act of charity, is the same as goodwill?*

AD SECUNDUM SIC PROCEDITUR. Videtur quod amare, secundum quod est actus caritatis, nihil sit aliud quam benevolentia. Dicit enim philosophus, in II Rhet. *amare est velle alicui bona.* Sed hoc est benevolentia. Ergo nihil aliud est actus caritatis quam benevolentia.

PRAETEREA, cuius est habitus, eius est actus. Sed habitus caritatis est in potentia voluntatis, ut supra dictum est. Ergo etiam actus caritatis est actus voluntatis. Sed

OBJECTION 1: It would seem that to love, considered as an act of charity, is nothing else than goodwill. For the Philosopher says (*Rhet.* ii, 4) that *to love is to wish a person well*; and this is goodwill. Therefore the act of charity is nothing but goodwill.

OBJ. 2: Further, the act belongs to the same subject as the habit. Now the habit of charity is in the power of the will, as stated above (Q. 24, A. 1). Therefore the act of

non nisi in bonum tendens, quod est benevolentia. Ergo actus caritatis nihil est aliud quam benevolentia.

**PRAETEREA**, Philosophus, in IX Ethic., ponit quinque ad amicitiam pertinentia, quorum primum est quod homo *velit amico bonum*; secundum est quod *velit ei esse et vivere*; tertium est quod *ei convivat*; quartum est quod *eadem eligat*; quintum est quod *condoleat et congaudeat*. Sed prima duo ad benevolentiam pertinent. Ergo primus actus caritatis est benevolentia.

**SED CONTRA** est quod Philosophus dicit, in eodem libro, quod benevolentia neque est *amicitia* neque est *amatio*, sed est *amicitiae principium*. Sed caritas est amicitia, ut supra dictum est. Ergo benevolentia non est idem quod dilectio, quae est caritatis actus.

**RESPONDEO** dicendum quod benevolentia proprie dicitur actus voluntatis quo alteri bonum volumus. Hic autem voluntatis actus differt ab actuali amore tam secundum quod est in appetitu sensitivo, quam etiam secundum quod est in appetitu intellectivo, qui est voluntas. Amor enim qui est in appetitu sensitivo passio quaedam est. Omnis autem passio cum quodam impetu inclinat in suum obiectum. Passio autem amoris hoc habet quod non subito exoritur, sed per aliquam assiduam inspectionem rei amatae. Et ideo Philosophus, in IX Ethic., ostendens differentiam inter benevolentiam et amorem qui est passio, dicit quod benevolentia non habet distensionem et appetitum, idest aliquem impetum inclinationis, sed ex solo iudicio rationis homo vult bonum alicui. Similiter etiam talis amor est ex quadam consuetudine, benevolentia autem interdum oritur ex repentino, sicut accidit nobis de pugilibus qui pugnant, quorum alterum vellemus vincere. Sed amor qui est in appetitu intellectivo etiam differt a benevolentia. Importat enim quandam unionem secundum affectus amantis ad amatum, inquantum scilicet amans aestimat amatum quodammodo ut unum sibi, vel ad se pertinens, et sic movetur in ipsum. Sed benevolentia est simplex actus voluntatis quo volumus alicui bonum, etiam non praesupposita praedicta unione affectus ad ipsum. Sic igitur in dilectione, secundum quod est actus caritatis, includitur quidem benevolentia, sed dilectio sive amor addit unionem affectus. Et propter hoc Philosophus dicit ibidem quod *benevolentia est principium amicitiae*.

**AD PRIMUM** ergo dicendum quod Philosophus ibi definit amare non ponens totam rationem ipsius, sed aliquid ad rationem eius pertinens in quo maxime manifestatur dilectionis actus.

**AD SECUNDUM** dicendum quod dilectio est actus voluntatis in bonum tendens, sed cum quadam unione ad amatum, quae quidem in benevolentia non importatur.

**AD TERTIUM** dicendum quod intantum illa quae Philosophus ibi ponit ad amicitiam pertinent, inquan-

charity is also an act of the will. But it tends to good only, and this is goodwill. Therefore the act of charity is nothing else than goodwill.

OBJ. 3: Further, the Philosopher reckons five things pertaining to friendship (*Ethic.* ix, 4), the first of which is that a man should wish his friend well; the second, that he should wish him to be and to live; the third, that he should take pleasure in his company; the fourth, that he should make choice of the same things; the fifth, that he should grieve and rejoice with him. Now the first two pertain to goodwill. Therefore goodwill is the first act of charity.

ON THE CONTRARY, The Philosopher says (*Ethic.* ix, 5) that *goodwill is neither friendship nor love, but the beginning of friendship*. Now charity is friendship, as stated above (Q. 23, A. 1). Therefore goodwill is not the same as to love considered as an act of charity.

I ANSWER THAT, Goodwill properly speaking is that act of the will whereby we wish well to another. Now this act of the will differs from actual love, considered not only as being in the sensitive appetite but also as being in the intellective appetite or will. For the love which is in the sensitive appetite is a passion. Now every passion seeks its object with a certain eagerness. And the passion of love is not aroused suddenly, but is born of an earnest consideration of the object loved; wherefore the Philosopher, showing the difference between goodwill and the love which is a passion, says (*Ethic.* ix, 5) that goodwill does not imply impetuosity or desire, that is to say, has not an eager inclination, because it is by the sole judgment of his reason that one man wishes another well. Again such like love arises from previous acquaintance, whereas goodwill sometimes arises suddenly, as happens to us if we look on at a boxing-match, and we wish one of the boxers to win. But the love, which is in the intellective appetite, also differs from goodwill, because it denotes a certain union of affections between the lover and the beloved, inasmuch as the lover deems the beloved as somewhat united to him, or belonging to him, and so tends towards him. On the other hand, goodwill is a simple act of the will, whereby we wish a person well, even without presupposing the aforesaid union of the affections with him. Accordingly, to love, considered as an act of charity, includes goodwill, but such dilection or love adds union of affections, wherefore the Philosopher says (*Ethic.* ix, 5) that *goodwill is a beginning of friendship*.

REPLY OBJ. 1: The Philosopher, by thus defining *to love*, does not describe it fully, but mentions only that part of its definition in which the act of love is chiefly manifested.

REPLY OBJ. 2: To love is indeed an act of the will tending to the good, but it adds a certain union with the beloved, which union is not denoted by goodwill.

REPLY OBJ. 3: These things mentioned by the Philosopher belong to friendship because they arise from a man's

tum proveniunt ex amore quem quis habet ad seipsum, ut ibidem dicitur, ut scilicet haec omnia aliquis erga amicum agat sicut ad seipsum. Quod pertinet ad praedictam unionem affectus.

love for himself, as he says in the same passage, insofar as a man does all these things in respect of his friend, even as he does them to himself: and this belongs to the aforesaid union of the affections.

# Article 3

*Whether out of charity God ought to be loved for himself, or for the sake of something else?*

**AD TERTIUM SIC PROCEDITUR**. Videtur quod Deus non propter seipsum, sed propter aliud diligatur ex caritate. Dicit enim Gregorius, in quadam homilia, *ex his quae novit animus discit incognita amare*. Vocat autem incognita intelligibilia et divina, cognita autem sensibilia. Ergo Deus est propter alia diligendus.

**PRAETEREA**, amor sequitur cognitionem. Sed Deus per aliud cognoscitur, secundum illud Rom. I. *Invisibilia Dei per ea quae facta sunt intellecta conspiciuntur*. Ergo etiam propter aliud amatur, et non propter se.

**PRAETEREA**, *spes generat caritatem*, ut dicitur in Glossa Matth. I. *Timor etiam caritatem introducit*; ut Augustinus dicit, super Prim. Canonic. Ioan. Sed spes expectat aliquid adipisci a Deo, timor autem refugit aliquid quod a Deo infligi potest. Ergo videtur quod Deus propter aliquod bonum speratum, vel propter aliquod malum timendum sit amandus. Non ergo est amandus propter seipsum.

**SED CONTRA** est quod, sicut Augustinus dicit, in I de Doct. Christ., *frui est amore inhaerere alicui propter seipsum*. Sed Deo fruendum est, ut in eodem libro dicitur. Ergo Deus diligendus est propter seipsum.

**RESPONDEO** dicendum quod ly *propter* importat habitudinem alicuius causae. Est autem quadruplex genus causae, scilicet finalis, formalis, efficiens et materialis, ad quam reducitur etiam materialis dispositio, quae non est causa simpliciter, sed secundum quid. Et secundum haec quatuor genera causarum dicitur aliquid propter alterum diligendum. Secundum quidem genus causae finalis, sicut diligimus medicinam propter sanitatem. Secundum autem genus causae formalis, sicut diligimus hominem propter virtutem, quia scilicet virtute formaliter est bonus, et per consequens diligibilis. Secundum autem causam efficientem, sicut diligimus aliquos inquantum sunt filii talis patris. Secundum autem dispositionem, quae reducitur ad genus causae materialis, dicimur aliquid diligere propter id quod nos disposuit ad eius dilectionem, puta propter aliqua beneficia suscepta, quamvis postquam iam amare incipimus, non propter illa beneficia amemus amicum, sed propter eius virtutem. Primis igitur tribus modis Deum non diligimus propter aliud, sed propter seipsum. Non enim

**OBJECTION 1**: It would seem that God is loved out of charity, not for Himself but for the sake of something else. For Gregory says in a homily (*In Evang. xi*): *The soul learns from the things it knows, to love those it knows not*, where by things unknown he means the intelligible and the Divine, and by things known he indicates the objects of the senses. Therefore God is to be loved for the sake of something else.

**OBJ. 2**: Further, love follows knowledge. But God is known through something else, according to Rom. 1:20: *The invisible things of God are clearly seen, being understood by the things that are made*. Therefore He is also loved on account of something else and not for Himself.

**OBJ. 3**: Further, *hope begets charity* as a gloss says on Matt. 1:1, and *fear leads to charity*, according to Augustine in his commentary on the First Canonical Epistle of John (*In prim. canon. Joan. Tract. ix*). Now hope looks forward to obtain something from God, while fear shuns something which can be inflicted by God. Therefore it seems that God is to be loved on account of some good we hope for, or some evil to be feared. Therefore He is not to be loved for Himself.

**ON THE CONTRARY**, According to Augustine (*De Doctr. Christ. i*), to enjoy is to cleave to something for its own sake. Now *God is to be enjoyed* as he says in the same book. Therefore God is to be loved for Himself.

**I ANSWER THAT**, The preposition *for* denotes a relation of causality. Now there are four kinds of cause, viz., final, formal, efficient, and material, to which a material disposition also is to be reduced, though it is not a cause simply but relatively. According to these four different causes one thing is said to be loved for another. In respect of the final cause, we love medicine, for instance, for health; in respect of the formal cause, we love a man for his virtue, because, to wit, by his virtue he is formally good and therefore lovable; in respect of the efficient cause, we love certain men because, for instance, they are the sons of such and such a father; and in respect of the disposition which is reducible to the genus of a material cause, we speak of loving something for that which disposed us to love it, e.g., we love a man for the favors received from him, although after we have begun to love our friend, we no longer love him for his favors, but for his virtue. Accordingly, as regards the first three ways, we love God, not for anything else, but for Himself. For He is not directed to anything else as to an end, but is Himself the last end of all things; nor does He require to

ordinatur ad aliud sicut ad finem, sed ipse est finis ultimus omnium. Neque etiam informatur aliquo alio ad hoc quod sit bonus, sed eius substantia est eius bonitas, secundum quam exemplariter omnia bona sunt. Neque iterum ei ab altero bonitas inest, sed ab ipso omnibus aliis. Sed quarto modo potest diligi propter aliud, quia scilicet ex aliquibus aliis disponimur ad hoc quod in Dei dilectione proficiamus, puta per beneficia ab eo suscepta, vel etiam per praemia sperata, vel per poenas quas per ipsum vitare intendimus.

**AD PRIMUM** ergo dicendum quod *ex his quae animus novit discit incognita amare*, non quod cognita sint ratio diligendi ipsa incognita per modum causae formalis vel finalis vel efficientis, sed quia per hoc homo disponitur ad amandum incognita.

**AD SECUNDUM** dicendum quod cognitio Dei acquiritur quidem per alia, sed postquam iam cognoscitur, non per alia cognoscitur, sed per seipsum; secundum illud Ioan. IV. *Iam non propter tuam loquelam credimus, ipsi enim vidimus, et scimus quia hic est vere salvator mundi.*

**AD TERTIUM** dicendum quod spes et timor ducunt ad caritatem per modum dispositionis cuiusdam, ut ex supradictis patet.

receive any form in order to be good, for His very substance is His goodness, which is itself the exemplar of all other good things; nor again does goodness accrue to Him from aught else, but from Him to all other things. In the fourth way, however, He can be loved for something else, because we are disposed by certain things to advance in His love, for instance, by favors bestowed by Him, by the rewards we hope to receive from Him, or even by the punishments which we are minded to avoid through Him.

REPLY OBJ. 1: From the things it knows the soul learns to love what it knows not, not as though the things it knows were the reason for its loving things it knows not, through being the formal, final, or efficient cause of this love, but because this knowledge disposes man to love the unknown.

REPLY OBJ. 2: Knowledge of God is indeed acquired through other things, but after He is known, He is no longer known through them, but through Himself, according to John 4:42: *We now believe, not for thy saying: for we ourselves have heard Him, and know that this is indeed the Savior of the world.*

REPLY OBJ. 3: Hope and fear lead to charity by way of a certain disposition, as was shown above (Q. 17, A. 8; Q. 19, AA. 4, 7, 10).

# Article 4

*Whether God can be loved immediately in this life?*

**AD QUARTUM SIC PROCEDITUR.** Videtur quod Deus in hac vita non possit immediate amari. *Incognita* enim *amari non possunt*; ut Augustinus dicit, X de Trin. Sed Deum non cognoscimus immediate in hac vita, quia *videmus nunc per speculum in aenigmate*, ut dicitur I ad Cor. XIII. Ergo neque etiam eum immediate amamus.

**PRAETEREA**, qui non potest quod minus est non potest quod maius est. Sed maius est amare Deum quam cognoscere ipsum, *qui enim adhaeret Deo* per amorem *unus spiritus cum illo fit*, ut dicitur I ad Cor. VI. Sed homo non potest Deum cognoscere immediate. Ergo multo minus amare.

**PRAETEREA**, homo a Deo disiungitur per peccatum, secundum illud Isaiae LIX, *peccata vestra diviserunt inter vos et Deum vestrum*. Sed peccatum magis est in voluntate quam in intellectu. Ergo minus potest homo Deum diligere immediate quam immediate eum cognoscere.

**SED CONTRA** est quod cognitio Dei, quia est mediata, dicitur aenigmatica, et evacuatur in patria, ut patet I ad Cor. XIII. Sed *caritas non evacuatur*, ut dicitur I ad Cor. XIII. Ergo caritas viae immediate Deo adhaeret.

OBJECTION 1: It would seem that God cannot be loved immediately in this life. For the *unknown cannot be loved* as Augustine says (*De Trin.* x, 1). Now we do not know God immediately in this life, since *we see now through a glass, in a dark manner* (1 Cor 13:12). Neither, therefore, do we love Him immediately.

OBJ. 2: Further, he who cannot do what is less, cannot do what is more. Now it is more to love God than to know Him, since *he who is joined* to God by love, is *one spirit with Him* (1 Cor 6:17). But man cannot know God immediately. Therefore much less can he love Him immediately.

OBJ. 3: Further, man is severed from God by sin, according to Isa. 59:2: *Your iniquities have divided between you and your God.* Now sin is in the will rather than in the intellect. Therefore man is less able to love God immediately than to know Him immediately.

ON THE CONTRARY, Knowledge of God, through being mediate, is said to be *enigmatic*, and *falls away* in heaven, as stated in 1 Cor. 13:12. But charity *does not fall away* as stated in the same passage (1 Cor 13:12). Therefore the charity of the way adheres to God immediately.

**RESPONDEO** dicendum quod, sicut supra dictum est, actus cognitivae virtutis perficitur per hoc quod cognitum est in cognoscente, actus autem virtutis appetitivae perficitur per hoc quod appetitus inclinatur in rem ipsam. Et ideo oportet quod motus appetitivae virtutis sit in res secundum conditionem ipsarum rerum, actus autem cognitivae virtutis est secundum modum cognoscentis.

Est autem ipse ordo rerum talis secundum se quod Deus est propter seipsum cognoscibilis et diligibilis, utpote essentialiter existens ipsa veritas et bonitas, per quam alia et cognoscuntur et amantur. Sed quoad nos, quia nostra cognitio a sensu ortum habet, prius sunt cognoscibilia quae sunt sensui propinquiora; et ultimus terminus cognitionis est in eo quod est maxime a sensu remotum.

Secundum hoc ergo dicendum est quod dilectio, quae est appetitivae virtutis actus, etiam in statu viae tendit in Deum primo, et ex ipso derivatur ad alia, et secundum hoc caritas Deum immediate diligit, alia vero mediante Deo. In cognitione vero est e converso, quia scilicet per alia Deum cognoscimus, sicut causam per effectus, vel per modum eminentiae aut negationis ut patet per Dionysium, in libro de Div. Nom.

**AD PRIMUM** ergo dicendum quod quamvis incognita amari non possint, tamen non oportet quod sit idem ordo cognitionis et dilectionis. Nam dilectio est cognitionis terminus. Et ideo ubi desinit cognitio, scilicet in ipsa re quae per aliam cognoscitur, ibi statim dilectio incipere potest.

**AD SECUNDUM** dicendum quod quia dilectio Dei est maius aliquid quam eius cognitio, maxime secundum statum viae, ideo praesupponit ipsam. Et quia cognitio non quiescit in rebus creatis, sed per eas in aliud tendit, in illo dilectio incipit, et per hoc ad alia derivatur, per modum cuiusdam circulationis, dum cognitio, a creaturis incipiens, tendit in Deum; et dilectio, a Deo incipiens sicut ab ultimo fine, ad creaturas derivatur.

**AD TERTIUM** dicendum quod per caritatem tollitur aversio a Deo quae est per peccatum; non autem per solam cognitionem. Et ideo caritas est quae, diligendo, animam immediate Deo coniungit spiritualis vinculo unionis.

**I ANSWER THAT**, As stated above (I, Q. 82, A. 3; Q. 84, A. 7), the act of a cognitive power is completed by the thing known being in the knower, whereas the act of an appetitive power consists in the appetite being inclined towards the thing in itself. Hence it follows that the movement of the appetitive power is towards things in respect of their own condition, whereas the act of a cognitive power follows the mode of the knower.

Now in itself the very order of things is such, that God is knowable and lovable for Himself, since He is essentially truth and goodness itself, whereby other things are known and loved: but with regard to us, since our knowledge is derived through the senses, those things are knowable first which are nearer to our senses, and the last term of knowledge is that which is most remote from our senses.

Accordingly, we must assert that to love which is an act of the appetitive power, even in this state of life, tends to God first, and flows on from Him to other things, and in this sense charity loves God immediately, and other things through God. On the other hand, with regard to knowledge, it is the reverse, since we know God through other things, either as a cause through its effects, or by way of pre-eminence or negation as Dionysius states (*Div. Nom.* i; cf. I, Q. 12, A. 12).

**REPLY OBJ. 1:** Although the unknown cannot be loved, it does not follow that the order of knowledge is the same as the order of love, since love is the term of knowledge, and consequently, love can begin at once where knowledge ends, namely in the thing itself which is known through another thing.

**REPLY OBJ. 2:** Since to love God is something greater than to know Him, especially in this state of life, it follows that love of God presupposes knowledge of God. And because this knowledge does not rest in creatures, but, through them, tends to something else, love begins there, and thence goes on to other things by a circular movement so to speak; for knowledge begins from creatures, tends to God, and love begins with God as the last end, and passes on to creatures.

**REPLY OBJ. 3:** Aversion from God, which is brought about by sin, is removed by charity, but not by knowledge alone: hence charity, by loving God, unites the soul immediately to Him with a chain of spiritual union.

# Article 5

*Whether God can be loved wholly?*

**AD QUINTUM SIC PROCEDITUR.** Videtur quod Deus non possit totaliter amari. Amor enim sequitur cognitionem. Sed Deus non potest totaliter a nobis cognosci, quia hoc esset eum comprehendere. Ergo non potest a nobis totaliter amari.

**PRAETEREA,** amor est unio quaedam, ut patet per Dionysium, IV cap. de Div. Nom. Sed cor hominis non potest ad Deum uniri totaliter, quia *Deus est maior corde nostro*, ut dicitur I Ioan. III. Ergo Deus non potest totaliter amari.

**PRAETEREA,** Deus seipsum totaliter amat. Si igitur ab aliquo alio totaliter amatur, aliquis alius diligit Deum tantum quantum ipse se diligit. Hoc autem est inconveniens. Ergo Deus non potest totaliter diligi ab aliqua creatura.

**SED CONTRA** est quod dicitur Deut. VI, *diliges dominum Deum tuum ex toto corde tuo.*

**RESPONDEO** dicendum quod, cum dilectio intelligatur quasi medium inter amantem et amatum, cum quaeritur an Deus possit totaliter diligi, tripliciter potest intelligi. Uno modo, ut modus totalitatis referatur ad rem dilectam. Et sic Deus est totaliter diligendus, quia totum quod ad Deum pertinet homo diligere debet.

Alio modo potest intelligi ita quod totalitas referatur ad diligentem. Et sic etiam Deus totaliter diligi debet, quia ex toto posse suo debet homo diligere Deum, et quidquid habet ad Dei amorem ordinare, secundum illud Deut. VI, *diliges dominum Deum tuum ex toto corde tuo.*

Tertio modo potest intelligi secundum comparationem diligentis ad rem dilectam, ut scilicet modus diligentis adaequet modum rei dilectae. Et hoc non potest esse. Cum enim unumquodque intantum diligibile sit inquantum est bonum, Deus, cuius bonitas est infinita, est infinite diligibilis, nulla autem creatura potest Deum infinite diligere, quia omnis virtus creaturae, sive naturalis sive infusa, est finita.

**ET PER HOC** patet responsio ad obiecta. Nam primae tres obiectiones procedunt secundum hunc tertium sensum, ultima autem ratio procedit in sensu secundo.

**OBJECTION 1**: It would seem that God cannot be loved wholly. For love follows knowledge. Now God cannot be wholly known by us, since this would imply comprehension of Him. Therefore He cannot be wholly loved by us.

**OBJ. 2**: Further, love is a kind of union, as Dionysius shows (*Div. Nom.* iv). But the heart of man cannot be wholly united to God, because *God is greater than our heart* (1 John 3:20). Therefore God cannot be loved wholly.

**OBJ. 3**: Further, God loves Himself wholly. If therefore He be loved wholly by another, this one will love Him as much as God loves Himself. But this is unreasonable. Therefore God cannot be wholly loved by a creature.

**ON THE CONTRARY**, It is written (Deut 6:5): *Thou shalt love the Lord thy God with thy whole heart.*

**I ANSWER THAT**, Since love may be considered as something between lover and beloved, when we ask whether God can be wholly loved, the question may be understood in three ways, first so that the qualification *wholly* be referred to the thing loved, and thus God is to be loved wholly, since man should love all that pertains to God.

Second, it may be understood as though *wholly* qualified the lover: and thus again God ought to be loved wholly, since man ought to love God with all his might, and to refer all he has to the love of God, according to Deut. 6:5: *Thou shalt love the Lord thy God with thy whole heart.*

Third, it may be understood by way of comparison of the lover to the thing loved, so that the mode of the lover equal the mode of the thing loved. This is impossible: for, since a thing is lovable in proportion to its goodness, God is infinitely lovable, since His goodness is infinite. Now no creature can love God infinitely, because all power of creatures, whether it be natural or infused, is finite.

**THIS SUFFICES** for the Replies to the Objections, because the first three objections consider the question in this third sense, while the last takes it in the second sense.

# Article 6

*Whether in loving God we ought to observe any mode?*

**AD SEXTUM SIC PROCEDITUR.** Videtur quod divinae dilectionis sit aliquis modus habendus. Ratio enim boni consistit in *modo, specie* et *ordine*, ut patet per Augustinum, in libro de Nat. boni. Sed dilectio Dei est

**OBJECTION 1**: It would seem that we ought to observe some mode in loving God. For the notion of good consists in *mode, species* and *order*, as Augustine states (*De Nat. Boni* iii, iv). Now the love of God is the best thing in man,

optimum in homine, secundum illud ad Coloss. III, *super omnia caritatem habete*. Ergo dilectio Dei debet modum habere.

**PRAETEREA**, Augustinus dicit, in libro de Morib. Eccles., *dic mihi, quaeso te, quis sit diligendi modus. Vereor enim ne plus minusve quam oportet inflammer desiderio et amore domini mei* frustra autem quaereret modum nisi esset aliquis divinae dilectionis modus. Ergo est aliquis modus divinae dilectionis.

**PRAETEREA**, sicut Augustinus dicit, IV super Gen. ad Litt., *modus est quem unicuique propria mensura praefigit*. Sed mensura voluntatis humanae, sicut et actionis exterioris, est ratio. Ergo sicut in exteriori effectu caritatis oportet habere modum a ratione praestitum, secundum illud Rom. XII, *rationabile obsequium vestrum*; ita etiam ipsa interior dilectio Dei debet modum habere.

**SED CONTRA** est quod Bernardus dicit, in libro de diligendo Deum, *quod causa diligendi Deum Deus est; modus, sine modo diligere*.

**RESPONDEO** dicendum quod, sicut patet ex inducta auctoritate Augustini, modus importat quandam mensurae determinationem. Haec autem determinatio invenitur et in mensura et in mensurato, aliter tamen et aliter. In mensura enim invenitur essentialiter, quia mensura secundum seipsam est determinativa et modificativa aliorum, in mensuratis autem invenitur mensura secundum aliud, idest inquantum attingunt mensuram. Et ideo in mensura nihil potest accipi immodificatum, sed res mensurata est immodificata nisi mensuram attingat, sive deficiat sive excedat.

In omnibus autem appetibilibus et agibilibus mensura est finis, quia eorum quae appetimus et agimus oportet propriam rationem ex fine accipere, ut patet per Philosophum, in II Physic. Et ideo finis secundum seipsum habet modum, ea vero quae sunt ad finem habent modum ex eo quod sunt fini proportionata. Et ideo, sicut Philosophus dicit, in I Polit., *appetitus finis in omnibus artibus est absque fine et termino, eorum autem quae sunt ad finem est aliquis terminus*. Non enim medicus imponit aliquem terminum sanitati, sed facit eam perfectam quantumcumque potest, sed medicinae imponit terminum; non enim dat tantum de medicina quantum potest, sed secundum proportionem ad sanitatem; quam quidem proportionem si medicina excederet, vel ab ea deficeret, esset immoderata.

Finis autem omnium actionum humanarum et affectionum est Dei dilectio, per quam maxime attingimus ultimum finem, ut supra dictum est. Et ideo in dilectione Dei non potest accipi modus sicut in re mensurata, ut sit in ea accipere plus et minus, sed sicut invenitur modus in mensura, in qua non potest esse excessus, sed quanto plus attingitur regula, tanto melius est. Et ita quanto plus Deus diligitur, tanto est dilectio melior.

according to Col. 3:14: *Above all . . . things, have charity.* Therefore there ought to be a mode of the love of God.

**OBJ. 2**: Further, Augustine says (*De Morib.* Eccl. viii): *Prithee, tell me which is the mode of love. For I fear lest I burn with the desire and love of my Lord, more or less than I ought.* But it would be useless to seek the mode of the Divine love, unless there were one. Therefore there is a mode of the love of God.

**OBJ. 3**: Further, as Augustine says (*Gen ad lit.* iv, 3), *the measure which nature appoints to a thing, is its mode*. Now the measure of the human will, as also of external action, is the reason. Therefore just as it is necessary for the reason to appoint a mode to the exterior effect of charity, according to Rom. 12:1: *Your reasonable service*, so also the interior love of God requires a mode.

**ON THE CONTRARY**, Bernard says (*De Dilig. Deum* 1) that *God is the cause of our loving God; the measure is to love Him without measure.*

**I ANSWER THAT**, As appears from the words of Augustine quoted above (Obj. 3) mode signifies a determination of measure; which determination is to be found both in the measure and in the thing measured, but not in the same way. For it is found in the measure essentially, because a measure is of itself the determining and modifying rule of other things; whereas in the things measured, it is found relatively, that is insofar as they attain to the measure. Hence there can be nothing unmodified in the measure whereas the thing measured is unmodified if it fails to attain to the measure, whether by deficiency or by excess.

Now in all matters of appetite and action the measure is the end, because the proper reason for all that we desire or do should be taken from the end, as the Philosopher proves (*Phys.* ii, 9). Therefore the end has a mode by itself, while the means take their mode from being proportionate to the end. Hence, according to the Philosopher (*Polit.* i, 3), *in every art, the desire for the end is endless and unlimited,* whereas there is a limit to the means: thus the physician does not put limits to health, but makes it as perfect as he possibly can; but he puts a limit to medicine, for he does not give as much medicine as he can, but according as health demands so that if he give too much or too little, the medicine would be immoderate.

Again, the end of all human actions and affections is the love of God, whereby principally we attain to our last end, as stated above (Q. 23, A. 6), wherefore the mode in the love of God, must not be taken as in a thing measured where we find too much or too little, but as in the measure itself, where there cannot be excess, and where the more the rule is attained the better it is, so that the more we love God the better our love is.

**AD PRIMUM** ergo dicendum quod illud quod est per se potius est eo quod est per aliud. Et ideo bonitas mensurae, quae per se habet modum, potior est quam bonitas mensurati, quod habet modum per aliud. Et sic etiam caritas, quae habet modum sicut mensura, praeeminet aliis virtutibus, quae habent modum sicut mensuratae.

**AD SECUNDUM** dicendum quod Augustinus ibidem subiungit quod modus diligendi Deum est ut ex toto corde diligatur, idest ut diligatur quantumcumque potest diligi. Et hoc pertinet ad modum qui convenit mensurae.

**AD TERTIUM** dicendum quod affectio illa cuius obiectum subiacet iudicio rationis, est ratione mensuranda. Sed obiectum divinae dilectionis, quod est Deus, excedit iudicium rationis. Et ideo non mensuratur ratione, sed rationem excedit. Nec est simile de interiori actu caritatis et exterioribus actibus. Nam interior actus caritatis habet rationem finis, quia ultimum bonum hominis consistit in hoc quod anima Deo inhaereat, secundum illud Psalm., *mihi adhaerere Deo bonum est.* Exteriores autem actus sunt sicut ad finem. Et ideo sunt commensurandi et secundum caritatem et secundum rationem.

**REPLY OBJ. 1:** That which is so by its essence takes precedence of that which is so through another, wherefore the goodness of the measure which has the mode essentially, takes precedence of the goodness of the thing measured, which has its mode through something else; and so too, charity, which has a mode as a measure has, stands before the other virtues, which have a mode through being measured.

**REPLY OBJ. 2:** As Augustine adds in the same passage, the measure of our love for God is to love Him with our whole heart, that is to love Him as much as He can be loved, and this belongs to the mode which is proper to the measure.

**REPLY OBJ. 3:** An affection, whose object is subject to reason's judgment, should be measured by reason. But the object of the Divine love which is God surpasses the judgment of reason, wherefore it is not measured by reason but transcends it. Nor is there parity between the interior act and external acts of charity. For the interior act of charity has the character of an end, since man's ultimate good consists in his soul cleaving to God, according to Ps. 72:28: *It is good for me to adhere to my God*; whereas the exterior acts are as means to the end, and so have to be measured both according to charity and according to reason.

# Article 7

*Whether it is more meritorious to love an enemy than to love a friend?*

**AD SEPTIMUM SIC PROCEDITUR.** Videtur quod magis meritorium sit diligere inimicum quam amicum. Dicitur enim Matth. V, *si diligitis eos qui vos diligunt, quam mercedem habebitis?* Diligere ergo amicum non meretur mercedem. Sed diligere inimicum meretur mercedem, ut ibidem ostenditur. Ergo magis est meritorium diligere inimicos quam diligere amicos.

**PRAETEREA,** tanto aliquid est magis meritorium quanto ex maiori caritate procedit. Sed diligere inimicum est *perfectorum filiorum Dei*, ut Augustinus dicit, in Enchirid., diligere autem amicum est etiam caritatis imperfectae. Ergo maioris meriti est diligere inimicum quam diligere amicum.

**PRAETEREA,** ubi est maior conatus ad bonum, ibi videtur esse maius meritum, *quia unusquisque propriam mercedem accipiet secundum suum laborem,* ut dicitur I Cor. III. Sed maiori conatu indiget homo ad hoc quod diligat inimicum quam ad hoc quod diligat amicum, quia difficilius est. Ergo videtur quod diligere inimicum sit magis meritorium quam diligere amicum.

**SED CONTRA** est quia illud quod est melius est magis meritorium. Sed melius est diligere amicum, quia melius est diligere meliorem; amicus autem, qui amat, est me-

**OBJECTION 1:** It would seem more meritorious to love an enemy than to love a friend. For it is written (Matt 5:46): *If you love them that love you, what reward shall you have?* Therefore it is not deserving of reward to love one's friend: whereas, as the same passage proves, to love one's enemy is deserving of a reward. Therefore it is more meritorious to love one's enemy than to love one's friend.

**OBJ. 2:** Further, an act is the more meritorious through proceeding from a greater charity. But it belongs to the *perfect children of God* to love their enemies, as Augustine states, whereas those also who have imperfect charity love their friends. Therefore it is more meritorious to love one's enemy than to love one's friend.

**OBJ. 3:** Further, where there is more effort for good, there seems to be more merit, since *every man shall receive his own reward according to his own labor* (1 Cor 3:8). Now a man has to make a greater effort to love his enemy than to love his friend, because it is more difficult. Therefore it seems more meritorious to love one's enemy than to love one's friend.

**ON THE CONTRARY,** The better an action is, the more meritorious it is. Now it is better to love one's friend, since it is better to love a better man, and the friend who loves you

lior quam inimicus, qui odit. Ergo diligere amicum est magis meritorium quam diligere inimicum.

**RESPONDEO** dicendum quod ratio diligendi proximum ex caritate Deus est, sicut supra dictum est. Cum ergo quaeritur quid sit melius, vel magis meritorium, utrum diligere amicum vel inimicum, dupliciter istae dilectiones comparari possunt, uno modo, ex parte proximi qui diligitur; alio modo, ex parte rationis propter quam diligitur.

Primo quidem modo dilectio amici praeeminet dilectioni inimici. Quia amicus et melior est et magis coniunctus; unde est materia magis conveniens dilectioni; et propter hoc actus dilectionis super hanc materiam transiens melior est. Unde et eius oppositum est deterius, peius enim est odire amicum quam inimicum.

Secundo autem modo dilectio inimici praeeminet, propter duo. Primo quidem, quia dilectionis amici potest esse alia ratio quam Deus, sed dilectionis inimici solus Deus est ratio. Secundo quia, supposito quod uterque propter Deum diligatur, fortior ostenditur esse Dei dilectio quae animum hominis ad remotiora extendit, scilicet usque ad dilectionem inimicorum, sicut virtus ignis tanto ostenditur esse fortior quanto ad remotiora diffundit suum calorem. Tanto etiam ostenditur divina dilectio esse fortior quanto propter ipsam difficiliora implemus, sicut et virtus ignis tanto est fortior quanto comburere potest materiam minus combustibilem.

Sed sicut idem ignis in propinquiora fortius agit quam in remotiora, ita etiam caritas ferventius diligit coniunctos quam remotos. Et quantum ad hoc dilectio amicorum, secundum se considerata, est ferventior et melior quam dilectio inimicorum.

**AD PRIMUM** ergo dicendum quod verbum domini est per se intelligendum. Tunc enim dilectio amicorum apud Deum mercedem non habet, quando propter hoc solum amantur quia amici sunt, et hoc videtur accidere quando sic amantur amici quod inimici non diliguntur. Est tamen meritoria amicorum dilectio si propter Deum diligantur, et non solum quia amici sunt.

**AD ALIA** patet responsio per ea quae dicta sunt. Nam duae rationes sequentes procedunt ex parte rationis diligendi; ultima vero ex parte eorum qui diliguntur.

is better than the enemy who hates you. Therefore it is more meritorious to love one's friend than to love one's enemy.

**I ANSWER THAT**, God is the reason for our loving our neighbor out of charity, as stated above (Q. 25, A. 1). When therefore it is asked which is better or more meritorious, to love one's friend or one's enemy, these two loves may be compared in two ways, first, on the part of our neighbor whom we love, second, on the part of the reason for which we love him.

In the first way, love of one's friend surpasses love of one's enemy, because a friend is both better and more closely united to us, so that he is a more suitable matter of love and consequently the act of love that passes over this matter, is better, and therefore its opposite is worse, for it is worse to hate a friend than an enemy.

In the second way, however, it is better to love one's enemy than one's friend, and this for two reasons. First, because it is possible to love one's friend for another reason than God, whereas God is the only reason for loving one's enemy. Second, because if we suppose that both are loved for God, our love for God is proved to be all the stronger through carrying a man's affections to things which are furthest from him, namely, to the love of his enemies, even as the power of a furnace is proved to be the stronger, according as it throws its heat to more distant objects. Hence our love for God is proved to be so much the stronger, as the more difficult are the things we accomplish for its sake, just as the power of fire is so much the stronger, as it is able to set fire to a less inflammable matter.

Yet just as the same fire acts with greater force on what is near than on what is distant, so too, charity loves with greater fervor those who are united to us than those who are far removed; and in this respect the love of friends, considered in itself, is more ardent and better than the love of one's enemy.

**REPLY OBJ. 1**: The words of Our Lord must be taken in their strict sense: because the love of one's friends is not meritorious in God's sight when we love them merely because they are our friends: and this would seem to be the case when we love our friends in such a way that we love not our enemies. On the other hand the love of our friends is meritorious, if we love them for God's sake, and not merely because they are our friends.

**THE REPLY** to the other Objections is evident from what has been said in the article, because the two arguments that follow consider the reason for loving, while the last considers the question on the part of those who are loved.

# Article 8

*Whether it is more meritorious to love one's neighbor than to love God?*

AD OCTAVUM SIC PROCEDITUR. Videtur quod magis sit meritorium diligere proximum quam diligere Deum. Illud enim videtur esse magis meritorium quod apostolus magis elegit. Sed apostolus praeelegit dilectionem proximi dilectioni Dei, secundum illud ad Rom. IX, *optabam anathema esse a Christo pro fratribus meis.* Ergo magis est meritorium diligere proximum quam diligere Deum.

PRAETEREA, minus videtur esse meritorium aliquo modo diligere amicum, ut dictum est. Sed Deus maxime est amicus, *qui prior dilexit nos,* ut dicitur I Ioan. IV. Ergo diligere eum videtur esse minus meritorium.

PRAETEREA, illud quod est difficilius videtur esse virtuosius et magis meritorium, quia *virtus est circa difficile et bonum,* ut dicitur in II Ethic. Sed facilius est diligere Deum quam proximum, tum quia naturaliter omnia Deum diligunt; tum quia in Deo nihil occurrit quod non sit diligendum, quod circa proximum non contingit. Ergo magis est meritorium diligere proximum quam diligere Deum.

SED CONTRA, propter quod unumquodque, illud magis. Sed dilectio proximi non est meritoria nisi propter hoc quod proximus diligitur propter Deum. Ergo dilectio Dei est magis meritoria quam dilectio proximi.

RESPONDEO dicendum quod comparatio ista potest intelligi dupliciter. Uno modo, ut seorsum consideretur utraque dilectio. Et tunc non est dubium quod dilectio Dei est magis meritoria, debetur enim ei merces propter seipsam, quia ultima merces est frui Deo, in quem tendit divinae dilectionis motus. Unde et diligenti Deum merces promittitur, Ioan. XIV, *si quis diligit me, diligetur a patre meo, et manifestabo ei meipsum.* Alio modo potest attendi ista comparatio ut dilectio Dei accipiatur secundum quod solus diligitur; dilectio autem proximi accipiatur secundum quod proximus diligitur propter Deum. Et sic dilectio proximi includet dilectionem Dei, sed dilectio Dei non includet dilectionem proximi. Unde erit comparatio dilectionis Dei perfectae, quae extendit se etiam ad proximum, ad dilectionem Dei insufficientem et imperfectam, quia *hoc mandatum habemus a Deo, ut qui diligit Deum, diligat et fratrem suum.* Et in hoc sensu dilectio proximi praeeminet.

AD PRIMUM ergo dicendum quod secundum unam Glossae expositionem, hoc apostolus tunc non optabat quando erat in statu gratiae, ut scilicet separaretur a Christo pro fratribus suis, sed hoc optaverat quando erat in statu infidelitatis. Unde in hoc non est imitandus.

OBJECTION 1: It would seem that it is more meritorious to love one's neighbor than to love God. For the more meritorious thing would seem to be what the Apostle preferred. Now the Apostle preferred the love of our neighbor to the love of God, according to Rom. 9:3: *I wished myself to be an anathema from Christ for my brethren.* Therefore it is more meritorious to love one's neighbor than to love God.

OBJ. 2: Further, in a certain sense it seems to be less meritorious to love one's friend, as stated above (A. 7). Now God is our chief friend, since *He hath first loved us* (1 John 4:10). Therefore it seems less meritorious to love God.

OBJ. 3: Further, whatever is more difficult seems to be more virtuous and meritorious since *virtue is about that which is difficult and good* (*Ethic.* ii, 3). Now it is easier to love God than to love one's neighbor, both because all things love God naturally, and because there is nothing unlovable in God, and this cannot be said of one's neighbor. Therefore it is more meritorious to love one's neighbor than to love God.

ON THE CONTRARY, That on account of which a thing is such, is yet more so. Now the love of one's neighbor is not meritorious, except by reason of his being loved for God's sake. Therefore the love of God is more meritorious than the love of our neighbor.

I ANSWER THAT, This comparison may be taken in two ways. First, by considering both loves separately: and then, without doubt, the love of God is the more meritorious, because a reward is due to it for its own sake, since the ultimate reward is the enjoyment of God, to Whom the movement of the Divine love tends: hence a reward is promised to him that loves God (John 14:21): *He that loveth Me, shall be loved of My Father, and I will . . . manifest Myself to him.* Second, the comparison may be understood to be between the love of God alone on the one side, and the love of one's neighbor for God's sake, on the other. In this way love of our neighbor includes love of God, while love of God does not include love of our neighbor. Hence the comparison will be between perfect love of God, extending also to our neighbor, and inadequate and imperfect love of God, for *this commandment we have from God, that he, who loveth God, love also his brother* (1 John 4:21).

REPLY OBJ. 1: According to one gloss, the Apostle did not desire this, viz. to be severed from Christ for his brethren, when he was in a state of grace, but had formerly desired it when he was in a state of unbelief, so that we should not imitate him in this respect.

Vel potest dici, sicut dicit Chrysostomus, in libro de Compunct., quod per hoc non ostenditur quod apostolus plus diligeret proximum quam Deum, sed quod plus diligebat Deum quam seipsum. Volebat enim ad tempus privari fruitione divina, quod pertinet ad dilectionem sui, ad hoc quod honor Dei procuraretur in proximis, quod pertinet ad dilectionem Dei.

**AD SECUNDUM** dicendum quod dilectio amici pro tanto est quandoque minus meritoria quia amicus diligitur propter seipsum, et ita deficit a vera ratione amicitiae caritatis, quae Deus est. Et ideo quod Deus diligatur propter seipsum non diminuit meritum, sed hoc constituit totam meriti rationem.

**AD TERTIUM** dicendum quod plus facit ad rationem meriti et virtutis bonum quam difficile. Unde non oportet quod omne difficilius sit magis meritorium, sed quod sic est difficilius ut etiam sit melius.

We may also reply, with Chrysostom (*De Compunct.* i, 8) that this does not prove the Apostle to have loved his neighbor more than God, but that he loved God more than himself. For he wished to be deprived for a time of the Divine fruition which pertains to love of one self, in order that God might be honored in his neighbor, which pertains to the love of God.

**REPLY OBJ. 2**: A man's love for his friends is sometimes less meritorious insofar as he loves them for their sake, so as to fall short of the true reason for the friendship of charity, which is God. Hence that God be loved for His own sake does not diminish the merit, but is the entire reason for merit.

**REPLY OBJ. 3**: The good has, more than the difficult, to do with the reason of merit and virtue. Therefore it does not follow that whatever is more difficult is more meritorious, but only what is more difficult, and at the same time better.

# QUESTION 28

## JOY

Deinde considerandum est de effectibus consequentibus actum caritatis principalem, qui est dilectio. Et primo, de effectibus interioribus; secundo, de exterioribus. Circa primum tria consideranda sunt, primo, de gaudio; secundo, de pace; tertio, de misericordia.

Circa primum quaeruntur quatuor.

Primo, utrum gaudium sit effectus caritatis.

Secundo, utrum huiusmodi gaudium compatiatur secum tristitiam.

Tertio, utrum istud gaudium possit esse plenum.

Quarto, utrum sit virtus.

We must now consider the effects which result from the principal act of charity which is love, and (1) the interior effects, (2) the exterior effects. As to the first, three things have to be considered: (1) Joy, (2) Peace, (3) Mercy.

Under the first head there are four points of inquiry:

(1) Whether joy is an effect of charity?

(2) Whether this kind of joy is compatible with sorrow?

(3) Whether this joy can be full?

(4) Whether it is a virtue?

# Article 1

*Whether joy is effected in us by charity?*

**AD PRIMUM SIC PROCEDITUR.** Videtur quod gaudium non sit effectus caritatis in nobis. Ex absentia enim rei amatae magis sequitur tristitia quam gaudium. Sed Deus, quem per caritatem diligimus, est nobis absens, quandiu in hac vita vivimus, *quandiu enim sumus in corpore, peregrinamur a domino*, ut dicitur II ad Cor. V. Ergo caritas in nobis magis causat tristitiam quam gaudium.

**PRAETEREA,** per caritatem maxime meremur beatitudinem. Sed inter ea per quae beatitudinem meremur ponitur luctus, qui ad tristitiam pertinet, secundum illud Matth. V, *beati qui lugent, quoniam consolabuntur*. Ergo magis est effectus caritatis tristitia quam gaudium.

**PRAETEREA,** caritas est virtus distincta a spe, ut ex supradictis patet. Sed gaudium causatur ex spe, secundum illud Rom. XII, *spe gaudentes*. Non ergo causatur ex caritate.

**SED CONTRA** est quia, sicut dicitur Rom. V, *caritas Dei diffusa est in cordibus nostris per spiritum sanctum, qui datus est nobis.* Sed gaudium in nobis causatur ex spiritu sancto, secundum illud Rom. XIV, *non est regnum Dei esca et potus, sed iustitia et pax et gaudium in spiritu sancto.* Ergo caritas est causa gaudii.

**RESPONDEO** dicendum quod, sicut supra dictum est, cum de passionibus ageretur, ex amore procedit et gaudium et tristitia, sed contrario modo. Gaudium enim ex amore causatur vel propter praesentiam boni amati; vel etiam propter hoc quod ipsi bono amato proprium bonum inest et conservatur. Et hoc secundum maxime

**OBJECTION 1**: It would seem that joy is not effected in us by charity. For the absence of what we love causes sorrow rather than joy. But God, Whom we love by charity, is absent from us, so long as we are in this state of life, since *while we are in the body, we are absent from the Lord* (2 Cor 5:6). Therefore charity causes sorrow in us rather than joy.

**OBJ. 2**: Further, it is chiefly through charity that we merit happiness. Now mourning, which pertains to sorrow, is reckoned among those things whereby we merit happiness, according to Matt. 5:5: *Blessed are they that mourn, for they shall be comforted.* Therefore sorrow, rather than joy, is an effect of charity.

**OBJ. 3**: Further, charity is a virtue distinct from hope, as shown above (Q. 17, A. 6). Now joy is the effect of hope, according to Rom. 12:12: *Rejoicing in hope.* Therefore it is not the effect of charity.

**ON THE CONTRARY**, It is written (Rom 5:5): *The charity of God is poured forth in our hearts by the Holy Spirit, Who is given to us.* But joy is caused in us by the Holy Spirit according to Rom. 14:17: *The kingdom of God is not meat and drink, but justice and peace, and joy in the Holy Spirit.* Therefore charity is a cause of joy.

**I ANSWER THAT,** As stated above (I-II, Q. 25, AA. 1, 2, 3), when we were treating of the passions, joy and sorrow proceed from love, but in contrary ways. For joy is caused by love, either through the presence of the thing loved, or because the proper good of the thing loved exists and endures in it; and the latter is the case chiefly in the love of

pertinet ad amorem benevolentiae, per quem aliquis gaudet de amico prospere se habente, etiam si sit absens. E contrario autem ex amore sequitur tristitia vel propter absentiam amati; vel propter hoc quod cui volumus bonum suo bono privatur, aut aliquo malo deprimitur. Caritas autem est amor Dei, cuius bonum immutabile est, quia ipse est sua bonitas. Et ex hoc ipso quod amatur est in amante per nobilissimum sui effectum, secundum illud I Ioan. IV, *qui manet in caritate, in Deo manet et Deus in eo*. Et ideo spirituale gaudium, quod de Deo habetur, ex caritate causatur.

**AD PRIMUM** ergo dicendum quod quandiu sumus in corpore dicimur peregrinari a domino, in comparatione ad illam praesentiam qua quibusdam est praesens per speciei visionem, unde et apostolus subdit ibidem, *per fidem enim ambulamus, et non per speciem*. Est autem praesens etiam se amantibus etiam in hac vita per gratiae inhabitationem.

**AD SECUNDUM** dicendum quod luctus qui beatitudinem meretur est de his quae sunt beatitudini contraria. Unde eiusdem rationis est quod talis luctus ex caritate causetur, et gaudium spirituale de Deo, quia eiusdem rationis est gaudere de aliquo bono et tristari de his quae ei repugnant.

**AD TERTIUM** dicendum quod de Deo potest esse spirituale gaudium dupliciter, uno modo, secundum quod gaudemus de bono divino in se considerato; alio modo, secundum quod gaudemus de bono divino prout a nobis participatur. Primum autem gaudium melius est, et hoc procedit principaliter ex caritate. Sed secundum gaudium procedit etiam ex spe, per quam expectamus divini boni fruitionem. Quamvis etiam ipsa fruitio, vel perfecta vel imperfecta, secundum mensuram caritatis obtineatur.

benevolence, whereby a man rejoices in the well-being of his friend, though he be absent. On the other hand sorrow arises from love, either through the absence of the thing loved, or because the loved object to which we wish well, is deprived of its good or afflicted with some evil. Now charity is love of God, Whose good is unchangeable, since He is His goodness, and from the very fact that He is loved, He is in those who love Him by His most excellent effect, according to 1 John 4:16: *He that abideth in charity, abideth in God, and God in him*. Therefore spiritual joy, which is about God, is caused by charity.

**REPLY OBJ. 1**: So long as we are in the body, we are said to be *absent from the Lord*, in comparison with that presence whereby He is present to some by the vision of *sight*; wherefore the Apostle goes on to say (2 Cor 5:6): *For we walk by faith and not by sight*. Nevertheless, even in this life, He is present to those who love Him, by the indwelling of His grace.

**REPLY OBJ. 2**: The mourning that merits happiness, is about those things that are contrary to happiness. Wherefore it amounts to the same that charity causes this mourning, and this spiritual joy about God, since to rejoice in a certain good amounts to the same as to grieve for things that are contrary to it.

**REPLY OBJ. 3**: There can be spiritual joy about God in two ways. First, when we rejoice in the Divine good considered in itself; second, when we rejoice in the Divine good as participated by us. The former joy is the better, and proceeds from charity chiefly: while the latter joy proceeds from hope also, whereby we look forward to enjoy the Divine good, although this enjoyment itself, whether perfect or imperfect, is obtained according to the measure of one's charity.

# Article 2

*Whether the spiritual joy, which results from charity, is compatible with an admixture of sorrow?*

**AD SECUNDUM SIC PROCEDITUR**. Videtur quod gaudium spirituale quod ex caritate causatur recipiat admixtionem tristitiae. Congaudere enim bonis proximi ad caritatem pertinet, secundum illud I ad Cor. XIII, *caritas non gaudet super iniquitate, congaudet autem veritati*. Sed hoc gaudium recipit permixtionem tristitiae, secundum illud Rom. XII, *gaudere cum gaudentibus, flere cum flentibus*. Ergo gaudium spirituale caritatis admixtionem tristitiae patitur.

**PRAETEREA**, poenitentia, sicut dicit Gregorius, est *anteacta mala flere, et flenda iterum non committere*. Sed vera poenitentia non est sine caritate. Ergo gaudium caritatis habet tristitiae admixtionem.

**OBJECTION 1**: It would seem that the spiritual joy that results from charity is compatible with an admixture of sorrow. For it belongs to charity to rejoice in our neighbor's good, according to 1 Cor. 13:4, 6: *Charity... rejoiceth not in iniquity, but rejoiceth with the truth*. But this joy is compatible with an admixture of sorrow, according to Rom. 12:15: *Rejoice with them that rejoice, weep with them that weep*. Therefore the spiritual joy of charity is compatible with an admixture of sorrow.

**OBJ. 2**: Further, according to Gregory (*Hom. in Evang. xxxiv*), *penance consists in deploring past sins, and in not committing again those we have deplored*. But there is no true penance without charity. Therefore the joy of charity has an admixture of sorrow.

**PRAETEREA**, ex caritate contingit quod aliquis desiderat esse cum Christo, secundum illud Philipp. I, *desiderium habens dissolvi et esse cum Christo.* Sed ex isto desiderio sequitur in homine quaedam tristitia, secundum illud Psalm., *heu mihi, quia incolatus meus prolongatus est!* Ergo gaudium caritatis recipit admixtionem tristitiae.

**SED CONTRA** est quod gaudium caritatis est gaudium de divina sapientia. Sed huiusmodi gaudium non habet permixtionem tristitiae, secundum illud Sap. VIII, *non habet amaritudinem conversatio illius.* Ergo gaudium caritatis non patitur permixtionem tristitiae.

**RESPONDEO** dicendum quod ex caritate causatur duplex gaudium de Deo, sicut supra dictum est. Unum quidem principale, quod est proprium caritatis, quo scilicet gaudemus de bono divino secundum se considerato. Et tale gaudium caritatis permixtionem tristitiae non patitur, sicut nec illud bonum de quo gaudetur potest aliquam mali admixtionem habere. Et ideo apostolus dicit, ad Philipp. IV, *gaudete in domino semper.*

Aliud autem est gaudium caritatis quo gaudet quis de bono divino secundum quod participatur a nobis. Haec autem participatio potest impediri per aliquod contrarium. Et ideo ex hac parte gaudium caritatis potest habere permixtionem tristitiae, prout scilicet aliquis tristatur de eo quod repugnat participationi divini boni vel in nobis vel in proximis, quos tanquam nosipsos diligimus.

**AD PRIMUM** ergo dicendum quod fletus proximi non est nisi de aliquo malo. Omne autem malum importat defectum participationis summi boni. Et ideo intantum caritas facit condolere proximo inquantum participatio divini boni in eo impeditur.

**AD SECUNDUM** dicendum quod *peccata dividunt inter nos et Deum*, ut dicitur Isaiae LIX. Et ideo haec est ratio dolendi de peccatis praeteritis nostris, vel etiam aliorum, inquantum per ea impedimur a participatione divini boni.

**AD TERTIUM** dicendum quod, quamvis in incolatu huius miseriae aliquo modo participemus divinum bonum per cognitionem et amorem, tamen huius vitae miseria impedit a perfecta participatione divini boni, qualis erit in patria. Et ideo haec etiam tristitia qua quis luget de dilatione gloriae pertinet ad impedimentum participationis divini boni.

**OBJ. 3**: Further, it is through charity that man desires to be with Christ according to Phil. 1:23: *Having a desire to be dissolved and to be with Christ.* Now this desire gives rise, in man, to a certain sadness, according to Ps. 119:5: *Woe is me, that my sojourning is prolonged!* Therefore the joy of charity admits of a seasoning of sorrow.

**ON THE CONTRARY**, The joy of charity is joy about the Divine wisdom. Now such like joy has no admixture of sorrow, according to Wis. 8:16: *Her conversation hath no bitterness.* Therefore the joy of charity is incompatible with an admixture of sorrow.

**I ANSWER THAT**, As stated above (A. 1, ad 3), a twofold joy in God arises from charity. One, the more excellent, is proper to charity; and with this joy we rejoice in the Divine good considered in itself. This joy of charity is incompatible with an admixture of sorrow, even as the good which is its object is incompatible with any admixture of evil: hence the Apostle says (Phil 4:4): *Rejoice in the Lord always.*

The other is the joy of charity whereby we rejoice in the Divine good as participated by us. This participation can be hindered by anything contrary to it, wherefore, in this respect, the joy of charity is compatible with an admixture of sorrow, insofar as a man grieves for that which hinders the participation of the Divine good, either in us or in our neighbor, whom we love as ourselves.

**REPLY OBJ. 1**: Our neighbor does not weep save on account of some evil. Now every evil implies lack of participation in the sovereign good: hence charity makes us weep with our neighbor insofar as he is hindered from participating in the Divine good.

**REPLY OBJ. 2**: *Our sins divide between us and God*, according to Isa. 59:2; wherefore this is the reason why we grieve for our past sins, or for those of others, insofar as they hinder us from participating in the Divine good.

**REPLY OBJ. 3**: Although in this unhappy abode we participate, after a fashion, in the Divine good, by knowledge and love, yet the unhappiness of this life is an obstacle to a perfect participation in the Divine good: hence this very sorrow, whereby a man grieves for the delay of glory, is connected with the hindrance to a participation of the Divine good.

# Article 3

*Whether the spiritual joy, which proceeds from charity, can be filled?*

AD TERTIUM SIC PROCEDITUR. Videtur quod spirituale gaudium quod ex caritate causatur non possit in nobis impleri. Quanto enim maius gaudium de Deo habemus, tanto gaudium eius in nobis magis impletur. Sed nunquam possumus tantum de Deo gaudere quantum dignum est ut de eo gaudeatur, quia semper bonitas eius, quae est infinita, excedit gaudium creaturae, quod est finitum. Ergo gaudium de Deo nunquam potest impleri.

PRAETEREA, illud quod est impletum non potest esse maius. Sed gaudium etiam beatorum potest esse maius, quia unius gaudium est maius quam alterius. Ergo gaudium de Deo non potest in creatura impleri.

PRAETEREA, nihil aliud videtur esse comprehensio quam cognitionis plenitudo. Sed sicut vis cognoscitiva creaturae est finita, ita et vis appetitiva eiusdem. Cum ergo Deus non possit ab aliqua creatura comprehendi, videtur quod non possit alicuius creaturae gaudium de Deo impleri.

SED CONTRA est quod dominus discipulis dixit, Ioan. XV, *gaudium meum in vobis sit, et gaudium vestrum impleatur.*

RESPONDEO dicendum quod plenitudo gaudii potest intelligi dupliciter. Uno modo, ex parte rei de qua gaudetur, ut scilicet tantum gaudeatur de ea quantum est dignum de ea gauderi. Et sic solum Dei gaudium est plenum de seipso, quia gaudium eius est infinitum, et hoc est condignum infinitae bonitati Dei; cuiuslibet autem creaturae gaudium oportet esse finitum. Alio modo potest intelligi plenitudo gaudii ex parte gaudentis. Gaudium autem comparatur ad desiderium sicut quies ad motum; ut supra dictum est, cum de passionibus ageretur. Est autem quies plena cum nihil restat de motu. Unde tunc est gaudium plenum quando iam nihil desiderandum restat. Quandiu autem in hoc mundo sumus, non quiescit in nobis desiderii motus, quia adhuc restat quod Deo magis appropinquemus per gratiam, ut ex supradictis patet. Sed quando iam ad beatitudinem perfectam perventum fuerit, nihil desiderandum restabit, quia ibi erit plena Dei fruitio, in qua homo obtinebit quidquid etiam circa alia bona desideravit, secundum illud Psalm., *qui replet in bonis desiderium tuum.* Et ideo quiescet desiderium non solum quo desideramus Deum, sed etiam erit omnium desideriorum quies. Unde gaudium beatorum est perfecte plenum, et etiam superplenum, quia plus obtinebunt quam desiderare suffecerint; *non enim in cor hominis ascendit quae praeparavit Deus diligentibus se,* ut dicitur I ad Cor. II. Et hinc est quod dicitur Luc. VI, *mensuram bonam et supereffluentem dabunt in sinus vestros.* Quia tamen nulla creatura est capax gaudii de Deo ei condigni, inde est quod illud gaudium omnino

OBJECTION 1: It would seem that the spiritual joy which proceeds from charity cannot be filled. For the more we rejoice in God, the more is our joy in Him filled. But we can never rejoice in Him as much as it is meet that we should rejoice in God, since His goodness which is infinite, surpasses the creature's joy which is finite. Therefore joy in God can never be filled.

OBJ. 2: Further, that which is filled cannot be increased. But the joy, even of the blessed, can be increased, since one's joy is greater than another's. Therefore joy in God cannot be filled in a creature.

OBJ. 3: Further, comprehension seems to be nothing else than the fullness of knowledge. Now, just as the cognitive power of a creature is finite, so is its appetitive power. Since therefore God cannot be comprehended by any creature, it seems that no creature's joy in God can be filled.

ON THE CONTRARY, Our Lord said to His disciples (John 15:11): *That My joy may be in you, and your joy may be filled.*

I ANSWER THAT, Fullness of joy can be understood in two ways; first, on the part of the thing rejoiced in, so that one rejoice in it as much as it is meet that one should rejoice in it, and thus God's joy alone in Himself is filled, because it is infinite; and this is condignly due to the infinite goodness of God: but the joy of any creature must needs be finite. Second, fullness of joy may be understood on the part of the one who rejoices. Now joy is compared to desire, as rest to movement, as stated above (I-II, Q. 25, AA. 1, 2), when we were treating of the passions: and rest is full when there is no more movement. Hence joy is full, when there remains nothing to be desired. But as long as we are in this world, the movement of desire does not cease in us, because it still remains possible for us to approach nearer to God by grace, as was shown above (Q. 24, AA. 4, 7). When once, however, perfect happiness has been attained, nothing will remain to be desired, because then there will be full enjoyment of God, wherein man will obtain whatever he had desired, even with regard to other goods, according to Ps. 102:5: *Who satisfieth thy desire with good things.* Hence desire will be at rest, not only our desire for God, but all our desires: so that the joy of the blessed is full to perfection—indeed over-full, since they will obtain more than they were capable of desiring: for *neither hath it entered into the heart of man, what things God hath prepared for them that love Him* (1 Cor 2:9). This is what is meant by the words of Luke 6:38: *Good measure and pressed down, and shaken together, and running over shall they give into your bosom.* Yet, since no creature is capable of the joy condignly due to

plenum non capitur in homine, sed potius homo intrat in ipsum, secundum illud Matth. XXV, *intra in gaudium domini tui.*

**AD PRIMUM** ergo dicendum quod ratio illa procedit de plenitudine gaudii ex parte rei de qua gaudetur.

**AD SECUNDUM** dicendum quod cum perventum fuerit ad beatitudinem, unusquisque attinget terminum sibi praefixum ex praedestinatione divina, nec restabit ulterius aliquid quo tendatur, quamvis in illa terminatione unus perveniat ad maiorem propinquitatem Dei, alius ad minorem. Et ideo uniuscuiusque gaudium erit plenum ex parte gaudentis, quia uniuscuiusque desiderium plene quietabitur. Erit tamen gaudium unius maius quam alterius, propter pleniorem participationem divinae beatitudinis.

**AD TERTIUM** dicendum quod comprehensio importat plenitudinem cognitionis ex parte rei cognitae, ut scilicet tantum cognoscatur res quantum cognosci potest. Habet tamen etiam cognitio aliquam plenitudinem ex parte cognoscentis, sicut et de gaudio dictum est. Unde et apostolus dicit, ad Coloss. I, *impleamini agnitione voluntatis eius in omni sapientia et intellectu spirituali.*

God, it follows that this perfectly full joy is not taken into man, but, on the contrary, man enters into it, according to Matt. 25:21: *Enter into the joy of thy Lord.*

**REPLY OBJ. 1**: This argument takes the fullness of joy in reference to the thing in which we rejoice.

**REPLY OBJ. 2**: When each one attains to happiness he will reach the term appointed to him by Divine predestination, and nothing further will remain to which he may tend, although by reaching that term, some will approach nearer to God than others. Hence each one's joy will be full with regard to himself, because his desire will be fully set at rest; yet one's joy will be greater than another's, on account of a fuller participation of the Divine happiness.

**REPLY OBJ. 3**: Comprehension denotes fullness of knowledge in respect of the thing known, so that it is known as much as it can be. There is however a fullness of knowledge in respect of the knower, just as we have said of joy. Wherefore the Apostle says (Col 1:9): *That you may be filled with the knowledge of His will, in all wisdom and spiritual understanding.*

# Article 4

*Whether joy is a virtue?*

**AD QUARTUM SIC PROCEDITUR**. Videtur quod gaudium sit virtus. Vitium enim contrariatur virtuti. Sed tristitia ponitur vitium, ut patet de acedia et de invidia. Ergo etiam gaudium debet poni virtus.

**PRAETEREA**, sicut amor et spes sunt passiones quaedam quarum obiectum est bonum, ita et gaudium. Sed amor et spes ponuntur virtutes. Ergo et gaudium debet poni virtus.

**PRAETEREA**, praecepta legis dantur de actibus virtutum. Sed praecipitur nobis quod de Deo gaudeamus, secundum illud ad Philipp. IV, *gaudete in domino semper.* Ergo gaudium est virtus.

**SED CONTRA** est quod neque connumeratur inter virtutes theologicas, neque inter virtutes morales, neque inter virtutes intellectuales, ut ex supradictis patet.

**RESPONDEO** dicendum quod virtus, sicut supra habitum est, est habitus quidam operativus; et ideo secundum propriam rationem habet inclinationem ad aliquem actum. Est autem contingens ex uno habitu plures actus eiusdem rationis ordinatos provenire, quorum unus sequatur ex altero. Et quia posteriores actus non procedunt ab habitu virtutis nisi per actum priorem, inde est quod virtus non definitur nec denominatur nisi ab actu priori, quamvis etiam alii actus ab ea

**OBJECTION 1**: It would seem that joy is a virtue. For vice is contrary to virtue. Now sorrow is set down as a vice, as in the case of sloth and envy. Therefore joy also should be accounted a virtue.

**OBJ. 2**: Further, as love and hope are passions, the object of which is good, so also is joy. Now love and hope are reckoned to be virtues. Therefore joy also should be reckoned a virtue.

**OBJ. 3**: Further, the precepts of the Law are about acts of virtue. But we are commanded to rejoice in the Lord, according to Phil. 4:4: *Rejoice in the Lord always.* Therefore joy is a virtue.

**ON THE CONTRARY**, It is not numbered among the theological virtues, nor among the moral, nor among the intellectual virtues, as is evident from what has been said above (I-II, QQ. 57, 60, 62).

**I ANSWER THAT**, As stated above (I-II, Q. 55, AA. 2, 4), virtue is an operative habit, wherefore by its very nature it has an inclination to a certain act. Now it may happen that from the same habit there proceed several ordinate and homogeneous acts, each of which follows from another. And since the subsequent acts do not proceed from the virtuous habit except through the preceding act, hence it is that the virtue is defined and named in reference to that preceding act, although those other acts also proceed from

consequantur. Manifestum est autem ex his quae supra de passionibus dicta sunt, quod amor est prima affectio appetitivae potentiae, ex qua sequitur et desiderium et gaudium. Et ideo habitus virtutis idem est qui inclinat ad diligendum, et ad desiderandum bonum dilectum, et ad gaudendum de eo. Sed quia dilectio inter hos actus est prior, inde est quod virtus non denominatur a gaudio nec a desiderio, sed a dilectione, et dicitur caritas. Sic ergo gaudium non est aliqua virtus a caritate distincta, sed est quidam caritatis actus sive effectus. Et propter hoc connumeratur inter fructus, ut patet Gal. V.

**AD PRIMUM** ergo dicendum quod tristitia quae est vitium causatur ex inordinato amore sui, quod non est aliquod speciale vitium, sed quaedam generalis radix vitiorum, ut supra dictum est. Et ideo oportuit tristitias quasdam particulares ponere specialia vitia, quia non derivantur ab aliquo speciali vitio, sed a generali. Sed amor Dei ponitur specialis virtus, quae est caritas, ad quam reducitur gaudium, ut dictum est, sicut proprius actus eius.

**AD SECUNDUM** dicendum quod spes consequitur ex amore sicut et gaudium, sed spes addit ex parte obiecti quandam specialem rationem, scilicet arduum et possibile adipisci; et ideo ponitur specialis virtus. Sed gaudium ex parte obiecti nullam rationem specialem addit supra amorem quae possit causare specialem virtutem.

**AD TERTIUM** dicendum quod intantum datur praeceptum legis de gaudio inquantum est actus caritatis; licet non sit primus actus eius.

the virtue. Now it is evident from what we have said about the passions (I-II, Q. 25, AA. 2, 4) that love is the first affection of the appetitive power, and that desire and joy follow from it. Hence the same virtuous habit inclines us to love and desire the beloved good, and to rejoice in it. But inasmuch as love is the first of these acts, that virtue takes its name, not from joy, nor from desire, but from love, and is called charity. Hence joy is not a virtue distinct from charity, but an act, or effect, of charity: for which reason it is numbered among the Fruits (Gal 5:22).

**REPLY OBJ. 1**: The sorrow which is a vice is caused by inordinate self-love, and this is not a special vice, but a general source of the vices, as stated above (I-II, Q. 77, A. 4); so that it was necessary to account certain particular sorrows as special vices, because they do not arise from a special, but from a general vice. On the other hand love of God is accounted a special virtue, namely charity, to which joy must be referred, as its proper act, as stated above (here and A. 2).

**REPLY OBJ. 2**: Hope proceeds from love even as joy does, but hope adds, on the part of the object, a special character, viz. difficult, and possible to obtain; for which reason it is accounted a special virtue. On the other hand joy does not add to love any special aspect, that might cause a special virtue.

**REPLY OBJ. 3**: The Law prescribes joy, as being an act of charity, albeit not its first act.

# QUESTION 29

## PEACE

Deinde considerandum est de pace. Et circa hoc quaeruntur quatuor.

Primo, utrum pax sit idem quod concordia.

Secundo, utrum omnia appetant pacem.

Tertio, utrum pax sit effectus caritatis.

Quarto, utrum pax sit virtus.

We must now consider peace, under which head there are four points of inquiry:

(1) Whether peace is the same as concord?

(2) Whether all things desire peace?

(3) Whether peace is an effect of charity?

(4) Whether peace is a virtue?

## Article 1

*Whether peace is the same as concord?*

**AD PRIMUM SIC PROCEDITUR.** Videtur quod pax sit idem quod concordia. Dicit enim Augustinus, XIX de Civ. Dei, quod *pax hominum est ordinata concordia.* Sed non loquimur nunc nisi de pace hominum. Ergo pax est idem quod concordia.

**PRAETEREA,** concordia est quaedam unio voluntatum. Sed ratio pacis in tali unione consistit, dicit enim Dionysius, XI cap. de Div. Nom., quod *pax est omnium unitiva et consensus operativa.* Ergo pax est idem quod concordia.

**PRAETEREA,** quorum est idem oppositum, et ipsa sunt idem. Sed idem opponitur concordiae et paci, scilicet dissensio, unde dicitur, I ad Cor. XIV, *non est dissensionis Deus, sed pacis.* Ergo pax est idem quod concordia.

**SED CONTRA** est quod concordia potest esse aliquorum impiorum in malo. Sed *non est pax impiis,* ut dicitur Isaiae XLVIII. Ergo pax non est idem quod concordia.

**RESPONDEO** dicendum quod pax includit concordiam et aliquid addit. Unde ubicumque est pax, ibi est concordia, non tamen ubicumque est concordia, est pax, si nomen pacis proprie sumatur.

Concordia enim, proprie sumpta, est ad alterum, inquantum scilicet diversorum cordium voluntates simul in unum consensum conveniunt. Contingit etiam unius hominis cor tendere in diversa, et hoc dupliciter. Uno quidem modo, secundum diversas potentias appetitivas, sicut appetitus sensitivus plerumque tendit in contrarium rationalis appetitus, secundum illud ad Gal. V, *caro concupiscit adversus spiritum.* Alio modo, inquantum una et eadem vis appetitiva in diversa appetibilia tendit quae simul assequi non potest. Unde necesse est esse repugnantiam motuum appetitus. Unio autem horum motuum est quidem de ratione pacis, non enim homo habet pacatum cor quandiu, etsi habeat aliquid quod

**OBJECTION 1**: It would seem that peace is the same as concord. For Augustine says (*De Civ. Dei* xix, 13): *Peace among men is well ordered concord.* Now we are speaking here of no other peace than that of men. Therefore peace is the same as concord.

**OBJ. 2**: Further, concord is union of wills. Now the nature of peace consists in such like union, for Dionysius says (*Div. Nom.* xi) that *peace unites all, and makes them of one mind.* Therefore peace is the same as concord.

**OBJ. 3**: Further, things whose opposites are identical are themselves identical. Now the one same thing is opposed to concord and peace, viz. dissension; hence it is written (1 Cor 16:33): *God is not the God of dissension but of peace.* Therefore peace is the same as concord.

**ON THE CONTRARY**, There can be concord in evil between wicked men. But *there is no peace to the wicked* (Isa 48:22). Therefore peace is not the same as concord.

**I ANSWER THAT**, Peace includes concord and adds something thereto. Hence wherever peace is, there is concord, but there is not peace, wherever there is concord, if we give peace its proper meaning.

For concord, properly speaking, is between one man and another, insofar as the wills of various hearts agree together in consenting to the same thing. Now the heart of one man may happen to tend to diverse things, and this in two ways. First, in respect of the diverse appetitive powers: thus the sensitive appetite tends sometimes to that which is opposed to the rational appetite, according to Gal. 5:17: *The flesh lusteth against the spirit.* Second, insofar as one and the same appetitive power tends to diverse objects of appetite, which it cannot obtain all at the same time: so that there must needs be a clashing of the movements of the appetite. Now the union of such movements is essential to peace, because man's heart is not at peace, so long as he has

vult, tamen adhuc restat ei aliquid volendum quod simul habere non potest. Haec autem unio non est de ratione concordiae. Unde concordia importat unionem appetituum diversorum appetentium, pax autem, supra hanc unionem, importat etiam appetituum unius appetentis unionem.

AD PRIMUM ergo dicendum quod Augustinus loquitur ibi de pace quae est unius hominis ad alium. Et hanc pacem dicit esse concordiam, non quamlibet, sed *ordinatam*, ex eo scilicet quod unus homo concordat cum alio secundum illud quod utrique convenit. Si enim homo concordet cum alio non spontanea voluntate, sed quasi coactus timore alicuius mali imminentis, talis concordia non est vere pax, quia non servatur ordo utriusque concordantis, sed perturbatur ab aliquo timorem inferente. Et propter hoc praemittit quod *pax est tranquillitas ordinis*. Quae quidem tranquillitas consistit in hoc quod omnes motus appetitivi in uno homine conquiescunt.

AD SECUNDUM dicendum quod, si homo simul cum alio homine in idem consentiat, non tamen consensus eius est omnino unitus nisi etiam sibi invicem omnes motus appetitivi eius sint consentientes.

AD TERTIUM dicendum quod paci opponitur duplex dissensio, scilicet dissensio hominis ad seipsum, et dissensio hominis ad alterum. Concordiae vero opponitur haec sola secunda dissensio.

not what he wants, or if, having what he wants, there still remains something for him to want, and which he cannot have at the same time. On the other hand this union is not essential to concord: wherefore concord denotes union of appetites among various persons, while peace denotes, in addition to this union, the union of the appetites even in one man.

REPLY OBJ. 1: Augustine is speaking there of that peace which is between one man and another, and he says that this peace is concord, not indeed any kind of concord, but that which is *well ordered*, through one man agreeing with another in respect of something befitting to both of them. For if one man concord with another, not of his own accord, but through being forced, as it were, by the fear of some evil that besets him, such concord is not really peace, because the order of each concordant is not observed, but is disturbed by some fear-inspiring cause. For this reason he premises that *peace is tranquillity of order*, which tranquillity consists in all the appetitive movements in one man being set at rest together.

REPLY OBJ. 2: If one man consent to the same thing together with another man, his consent is nevertheless not perfectly united to himself, unless at the same time all his appetitive movements be in agreement.

REPLY OBJ. 3: A twofold dissension is opposed to peace, namely dissension between a man and himself, and dissension between one man and another. The latter alone is opposed to concord.

# Article 2

*Whether all things desire peace?*

AD SECUNDUM SIC PROCEDITUR. Videtur quod non omnia appetant pacem. Pax enim, secundum Dionysium, est *unitiva consensus*. Sed in his quae cognitione carent non potest uniri consensus. Ergo huiusmodi pacem appetere non possunt.

PRAETEREA, appetitus non fertur simul ad contraria. Sed multi sunt appetentes bella et dissensiones. Ergo non omnes appetunt pacem.

PRAETEREA, solum bonum est appetibile. Sed quaedam pax videtur esse mala, alioquin dominus non diceret, Matth. X, *non veni mittere pacem*. Ergo non omnia pacem appetunt.

PRAETEREA, illud quod omnia appetunt videtur esse summum bonum, quod est ultimus finis. Sed pax non est huiusmodi, quia etiam in statu viae habetur; alioquin frustra dominus mandaret, Marc. IX, *pacem habete inter vos*. Ergo non omnia pacem appetunt.

OBJECTION 1: It would seem that not all things desire peace. For, according to Dionysius (*Div. Nom.* xi), peace *unites consent*. But there cannot be unity of consent in things which are devoid of knowledge. Therefore such things cannot desire peace.

OBJ. 2: Further, the appetite does not tend to opposite things at the same time. Now many desire war and dissension. Therefore all men do not desire peace.

OBJ. 3: Further, good alone is an object of appetite. But a certain peace is, seemingly, evil, else Our Lord would not have said (Matt 10:34): *I came not to send peace*. Therefore all things do not desire peace.

OBJ. 4: Further, that which all desire is, seemingly, the sovereign good which is the last end. But this is not true of peace, since it is attainable even by a wayfarer; else Our Lord would vainly command (Mark 9:49): *Have peace among you*. Therefore all things do not desire peace.

S<small>ED CONTRA</small> est quod Augustinus dicit, XIX de Civ. Dei, quod omnia pacem appetunt. Et idem etiam dicit Dionysius, XI cap. de Div. Nom.

R<small>ESPONDEO</small> dicendum quod ex hoc ipso quod homo aliquid appetit, consequens est ipsum appetere eius quod appetit assecutionem, et per consequens remotionem eorum quae consecutionem impedire possunt. Potest autem impediri assecutio boni desiderati per contrarium appetitum vel sui ipsius vel alterius, et utrumque tollitur per pacem, sicut supra dictum est. Et ideo necesse est quod omne appetens appetat pacem, inquantum scilicet omne appetens appetit tranquille et sine impedimento pervenire ad id quod appetit, in quo consistit ratio pacis, quam Augustinus definit *tranquillitatem ordinis*.

A<small>D PRIMUM</small> ergo dicendum quod pax importat unionem non solum appetitus intellectualis seu rationalis aut animalis, ad quos potest pertinere consensus, sed etiam appetitus naturalis. Et ideo Dionysius dicit quod *pax est operativa et consensus et connaturalitatis*, ut in consensu importetur unio appetituum ex cognitione procedentium; per connaturalitatem vero importatur unio appetituum naturalium.

A<small>D SECUNDUM</small> dicendum quod illi etiam qui bella quaerunt et dissensiones non desiderant nisi pacem, quam se habere non aestimant. Ut enim dictum est, non est pax si quis cum alio concordet contra id quod ipse magis vellet. Et ideo homines quaerunt hanc concordiam rumpere bellando, tanquam defectum pacis habentem, ut ad pacem perveniant in qua nihil eorum voluntati repugnet. Et propter hoc omnes bellantes quaerunt per bella ad pacem aliquam pervenire perfectiorem quam prius haberent.

A<small>D TERTIUM</small> dicendum quod, quia pax consistit in quietatione et unione appetitus; sicut autem appetitus potest esse vel boni simpliciter vel boni apparentis, ita etiam et pax potest esse et vera et apparens, vera quidem pax non potest esse nisi circa appetitum veri boni; quia omne malum, etsi secundum aliquid appareat bonum, unde ex aliqua parte appetitum quietet, habet tamen multos defectus, ex quibus appetitus remanet inquietus et perturbatus. Unde pax vera non potest esse nisi in bonis et bonorum. Pax autem quae malorum est, est pax apparens et non vera. Unde dicitur Sap. XIV, *in magno viventes inscientiae bello, tot et tanta mala pacem arbitrati sunt*.

A<small>D QUARTUM</small> dicendum quod, cum vera pax non sit nisi de bono, sicut dupliciter habetur verum bonum, scilicet perfecte et imperfecte, ita est duplex pax vera. Una quidem perfecta, quae consistit in perfecta fruitione summi boni, per quam omnes appetitus uniuntur quietati in uno. Et hic est ultimus finis creaturae rationalis, secundum illud Psalm., *qui posuit fines tuos pacem*. Alia vero est pax imperfecta, quae habetur in hoc mundo.

O<small>N THE CONTRARY</small>, Augustine says (*De Civ. Dei* xix, 12, 14) that all things desire peace: and Dionysius says the same (*Div. Nom.* xi).

I <small>ANSWER THAT</small>, From the very fact that a man desires a certain thing it follows that he desires to obtain what he desires, and, in consequence, to remove whatever may be an obstacle to his obtaining it. Now a man may be hindered from obtaining the good he desires, by a contrary desire either of his own or of some other, and both are removed by peace, as stated above. Hence it follows of necessity that whoever desires anything desires peace, insofar as he who desires anything, desires to attain, with tranquillity and without hindrance, to that which he desires: and this is what is meant by peace which Augustine defines (*De Civ. Dei* xix, 13) *the tranquillity of order*.

R<small>EPLY OBJ</small>. 1: Peace denotes union not only of the intellective or rational appetite, or of the animal appetite, in both of which consent may be found, but also of the natural appetite. Hence Dionysius says that *peace is the cause of consent and of connaturalness*, where *consent* denotes the union of appetites proceeding from knowledge, and *connaturalness*, the union of natural appetites.

R<small>EPLY OBJ</small>. 2: Even those who seek war and dissension, desire nothing but peace, which they deem themselves not to have. For as we stated above, there is no peace when a man concords with another man counter to what he would prefer. Consequently men seek by means of war to break this concord, because it is a defective peace, in order that they may obtain peace, where nothing is contrary to their will. Hence all wars are waged that men may find a more perfect peace than that which they had heretofore.

R<small>EPLY OBJ</small>. 3: Peace gives calm and unity to the appetite. Now just as the appetite may tend to what is good simply, or to what is good apparently, so too, peace may be either true or apparent. There can be no true peace except where the appetite is directed to what is truly good, since every evil, though it may appear good in a way, so as to calm the appetite in some respect, has, nevertheless many defects, which cause the appetite to remain restless and disturbed. Hence true peace is only in good men and about good things. The peace of the wicked is not a true peace but a semblance thereof, wherefore it is written (Wis 14:22): *Whereas they lived in a great war of ignorance, they call so many and so great evils peace.*

R<small>EPLY OBJ</small>. 4: Since true peace is only about good things, as the true good is possessed in two ways, perfectly and imperfectly, so there is a twofold true peace. One is perfect peace. It consists in the perfect enjoyment of the sovereign good, and unites all one's desires by giving them rest in one object. This is the last end of the rational creature, according to Ps. 147:3: *Who hath placed peace in thy borders.* The other is imperfect peace, which may be had in

Quia etsi principalis animae motus quiescat in Deo, sunt tamen aliqua repugnantia et intus et extra quae perturbant hanc pacem.

this world, for though the chief movement of the soul finds rest in God, yet there are certain things within and without which disturb the peace.

# Article 3

*Whether peace is the proper effect of charity?*

AD TERTIUM SIC PROCEDITUR. Videtur quod pax non sit proprius effectus caritatis. Caritas enim non habetur sine gratia gratum faciente. Sed pax a quibusdam habetur qui non habent gratiam gratum facientem, sicut et gentiles aliquando habent pacem. Ergo pax non est effectus caritatis.

PRAETEREA, illud non est effectus caritatis cuius contrarium cum caritate esse potest. Sed dissensio, quae contrariatur paci, potest esse cum caritate, videmus enim quod etiam sacri doctores, ut Hieronymus et Augustinus, in aliquibus opinionibus dissenserunt; Paulus etiam et Barnabas dissensisse leguntur, Act. XV. Ergo videtur quod pax non sit effectus caritatis.

PRAETEREA, idem non est proprius effectus diversorum. Sed pax est effectus iustitiae, secundum illud Isaiae XXXII, *opus iustitiae pax*. Ergo non est effectus caritatis.

SED CONTRA est quod dicitur in Psalm., *pax multa diligentibus legem tuam.*

RESPONDEO dicendum quod duplex unio est de ratione pacis, sicut dictum est, quarum una est secundum ordinationem propriorum appetituum in unum; alia vero est secundum unionem appetitus proprii cum appetitu alterius. Et utramque unionem efficit caritas. Primam quidem unionem, secundum quod Deus diligitur ex toto corde, ut scilicet omnia referamus in ipsum, et sic omnes appetitus nostri in unum feruntur. Aliam vero, prout diligimus proximum sicut nosipsos, ex quo contingit quod homo vult implere voluntatem proximi sicut et sui ipsius. Et propter hoc inter amicabilia unum ponitur identitas electionis, ut patet in IX Ethic.; et Tullius dicit, in libro de amicitia, quod *amicorum est idem velle et nolle.*

AD PRIMUM ergo dicendum quod a gratia gratum faciente nullus deficit nisi propter peccatum, ex quo contingit quod homo sit aversus a fine debito, in aliquo indebito finem constituens. Et secundum hoc appetitus eius non inhaeret principaliter vero finali bono, sed apparenti. Et propter hoc sine gratia gratum faciente non potest esse vera pax, sed solum apparens.

AD SECUNDUM dicendum quod, sicut Philosophus dicit, in IX Ethic., ad amicitiam non pertinet concordia in opinionibus, sed concordia in bonis conferentibus ad vitam, et praecipue in magnis, quia dissentire in aliqui-

OBJECTION 1: It would seem that peace is not the proper effect of charity. For one cannot have charity without sanctifying grace. But some have peace who have not sanctifying grace, thus heathens sometimes have peace. Therefore peace is not the effect of charity.

OBJ. 2: Further, if a certain thing is caused by charity, its contrary is not compatible with charity. But dissension, which is contrary to peace, is compatible with charity, for we find that even holy doctors, such as Jerome and Augustine, dissented in some of their opinions. We also read that Paul and Barnabas dissented from one another (Acts 15). Therefore it seems that peace is not the effect of charity.

OBJ. 3: Further, the same thing is not the proper effect of different things. Now peace is the effect of justice, according to Isa. 32:17: *And the work of justice shall be peace.* Therefore it is not the effect of charity.

ON THE CONTRARY, It is written (Ps 118:165): *Much peace have they that love Thy Law.*

I ANSWER THAT, Peace implies a twofold union, as stated above (A. 1). The first is the result of one's own appetites being directed to one object; while the other results from one's own appetite being united with the appetite of another: and each of these unions is effected by charity—the first, insofar as man loves God with his whole heart, by referring all things to Him, so that all his desires tend to one object—the second, insofar as we love our neighbor as ourselves, the result being that we wish to fulfill our neighbor's will as though it were ours: hence it is reckoned a sign of friendship if people make choice of the same things (*Ethic.* ix, 4), and Tully says (*De Amicitia*) that friends *like and dislike the same things* (Sallust, *Catilin.*)

REPLY OBJ. 1: Without sin no one falls from a state of sanctifying grace, for it turns man away from his due end by making him place his end in something undue: so that his appetite does not cleave chiefly to the true final good, but to some apparent good. Hence, without sanctifying grace, peace is not real but merely apparent.

REPLY OBJ. 2: As the Philosopher says (*Ethic.* ix, 6) friends need not agree in opinion, but only upon such goods as conduce to life, and especially upon such as are important; because dissension in small matters is scarcely

bus parvis quasi videtur non esse dissensus. Et propter hoc nihil prohibet aliquos caritatem habentes in opinionibus dissentire. Nec hoc repugnat paci, quia opiniones pertinent ad intellectum, qui praecedit appetitum, qui per pacem unitur. Similiter etiam, existente concordia in principalibus bonis, dissensio in aliquibus parvis non est contra caritatem. Procedit enim talis dissensio ex diversitate opinionum, dum unus aestimat hoc de quo est dissensio pertinere ad illud bonum in quo conveniunt, et alius aestimat non pertinere. Et secundum hoc talis dissensio de minimis et de opinionibus repugnat quidem paci perfectae, in qua plene veritas cognoscetur et omnis appetitus complebitur, non tamen repugnat paci imperfectae, qualis habetur in via.

AD TERTIUM dicendum quod pax est opus iustitiae indirecte, inquantum scilicet removet prohibens. Sed est opus caritatis directe, quia secundum propriam rationem caritas pacem causat. Est enim amor *vis unitiva*, ut Dionysius dicit, IV cap. de Div. Nom. pax autem est unio appetitivarum inclinationum.

accounted dissension. Hence nothing hinders those who have charity from holding different opinions. Nor is this an obstacle to peace, because opinions concern the intellect, which precedes the appetite that is united by peace. In like manner if there be concord as to goods of importance, dissension with regard to some that are of little account is not contrary to charity: for such a dissension proceeds from a difference of opinion, because one man thinks that the particular good, which is the object of dissension, belongs to the good about which they agree, while the other thinks that it does not. Accordingly such like dissension about very slight matters and about opinions is inconsistent with a state of perfect peace, wherein the truth will be known fully, and every desire fulfilled; but it is not inconsistent with the imperfect peace of the wayfarer.

REPLY OBJ. 3: Peace is the *work of justice* indirectly, insofar as justice removes the obstacles to peace: but it is the work of charity directly, since charity, according to its very nature, causes peace. For love is *a unitive force* as Dionysius says (*Div. Nom.* iv): and peace is the union of the appetite's inclinations.

# Article 4

*Whether peace is a virtue?*

AD QUARTUM SIC PROCEDITUR. Videtur quod pax sit virtus. Praecepta enim non dantur nisi de actibus virtutum. Sed dantur praecepta de habendo pacem, ut patet Marc. IX, *pacem habete inter vos*. Ergo pax est virtus.

PRAETEREA, non meremur nisi actibus virtutum. Sed facere pacem est meritorium, secundum illud Matth. V, *beati pacifici, quoniam filii Dei vocabuntur*. Ergo pax est virtus.

PRAETEREA, vitia virtutibus opponuntur. Sed dissensiones, quae opponuntur paci, numerantur inter vitia; ut patet ad Gal. V. Ergo pax est virtus.

SED CONTRA, virtus non est finis ultimus, sed via in ipsum. Sed pax est quodammodo finis ultimus; ut Augustinus dicit, XIX de Civ. Dei. Ergo pax non est virtus.

RESPONDEO dicendum quod, sicut supra dictum est, cum omnes actus se invicem consequuntur, secundum eandem rationem ab agente procedentes, omnes huiusmodi actus ab una virtute procedunt, nec habent singuli singulas virtutes a quibus procedant. Ut patet in rebus corporalibus, quia enim ignis calefaciendo liquefacit et rarefacit, non est in igne alia virtus liquefactiva et alia rarefactiva, sed omnes actus hos operatur ignis per unam suam virtutem calefactivam.

OBJECTION 1: It would seem that peace is a virtue. For nothing is a matter of precept, unless it be an act of virtue. But there are precepts about keeping peace, for example: *Have peace among you* (Mark 9:49). Therefore peace is a virtue.

OBJ. 2: Further, we do not merit except by acts of virtue. Now it is meritorious to keep peace, according to Matt. 5:9: *Blessed are the peacemakers, for they shall be called the children of God*. Therefore peace is a virtue.

OBJ. 3: Further, vices are opposed to virtues. But dissensions, which are contrary to peace, are numbered among the vices (Gal 5:20). Therefore peace is a virtue.

ON THE CONTRARY, Virtue is not the last end, but the way thereto. But peace is the last end, in a sense, as Augustine says (*De Civ. Dei* xix, 11). Therefore peace is not a virtue.

I ANSWER THAT, As stated above (Q. 28, A. 4), when a number of acts all proceeding uniformly from an agent, follow one from the other, they all arise from the same virtue, nor do they each have a virtue from which they proceed, as may be seen in corporeal things. For, though fire by heating, both liquefies and rarefies, there are not two powers in fire, one of liquefaction, the other of rarefaction: and fire produces all such actions by its own power of calefaction.

Cum igitur pax causetur ex caritate secundum ipsam rationem dilectionis Dei et proximi, ut ostensum est, non est alia virtus cuius pax sit proprius actus nisi caritas, sicut et de gaudio dictum est.

AD PRIMUM ergo dicendum quod ideo praeceptum datur de pace habenda, quia est actus caritatis. Et propter hoc etiam est actus meritorius. Et ideo ponitur inter beatitudines, quae sunt actus virtutis perfectae, ut supra dictum est. Ponitur etiam inter fructus, inquantum est quoddam finale bonum spiritualem dulcedinem habens.

ET PER HOC patet solutio ad secundum.

AD TERTIUM dicendum quod uni virtuti multa vitia opponuntur, secundum diversos actus eius. Et secundum hoc caritati non solum opponitur odium, ratione actus dilectionis; sed etiam acedia vel invidia, ratione gaudii; et dissensio, ratione pacis.

Since then charity causes peace precisely because it is love of God and of our neighbor, as shown above (A. 3), there is no other virtue except charity whose proper act is peace, as we have also said in reference to joy (Q. 28, A. 4).

REPLY OBJ. 1: We are commanded to keep peace because it is an act of charity; and for this reason too it is a meritorious act. Hence it is placed among the beatitudes, which are acts of perfect virtue, as stated above (I-II, Q. 69, AA. 1, 3). It is also numbered among the fruits, insofar as it is a final good, having spiritual sweetness.

THIS SUFFICES for the Reply to the Second Objection.

REPLY OBJ. 3: Several vices are opposed to one virtue in respect of its various acts: so that not only is hatred opposed to charity, in respect of its act which is love, but also sloth and envy, in respect of joy, and dissension in respect of peace.

# QUESTION 30

## MERCY

Deinde considerandum est de misericordia. Et circa hoc quaeruntur quatuor.

Primo, utrum malum sit causa misericordiae ex parte eius cuius miseremur.

Secundo, quorum sit misereri.

Tertio, utrum misericordia sit virtus.

Quarto, utrum sit maxima virtutum.

We must now go on to consider Mercy, under which head there are four points of inquiry:

(1) Whether evil is the cause of mercy on the part of the person pitied?

(2) To whom does it belong to pity?

(3) Whether mercy is a virtue?

(4) Whether it is the greatest of virtues?

# Article 1

*Whether evil is properly the motive of mercy?*

AD PRIMUM SIC PROCEDITUR. Videtur quod malum non sit proprie motivum ad misericordiam. Ut enim supra ostensum est, culpa est magis malum quam poena. Sed culpa non est provocativum ad misericordiam, sed magis ad indignationem. Ergo malum non est misericordiae provocativum.

PRAETEREA, ea quae sunt crudelia seu dira videntur quendam excessum mali habere. Sed philosophus dicit, in II Rhet., quod *dirum est aliud a miserabili, et expulsivum miserationis*. Ergo malum, inquantum huiusmodi, non est motivum ad misericordiam.

PRAETEREA, signa malorum non vere sunt mala. Sed signa malorum provocant ad misericordiam; ut patet per philosophum, in II Rhet. Ergo malum non est proprie provocativum misericordiae.

SED CONTRA est quod Damascenus dicit, in II Lib., quod misericordia est species tristitiae. Sed motivum ad tristitiam est malum. Ergo motivum ad misericordiam est malum.

RESPONDEO dicendum quod, sicut Augustinus dicit, IX de Civ. Dei, *misericordia est alienae miseriae in nostro corde compassio, qua utique, si possumus, subvenire compellimur*, dicitur enim misericordia ex eo quod aliquis habet *miserum cor* super miseria alterius. Miseria autem felicitati opponitur. Est autem de ratione beatitudinis sive felicitatis ut aliquis potiatur eo quod vult, nam sicut Augustinus dicit, XIII de Trin., *beatus qui habet omnia quae vult, et nihil mali vult*. Et ideo e contrario ad miseriam pertinet ut homo patiatur quae non vult.

Tripliciter autem aliquis vult aliquid. Uno quidem modo, appetitu naturali, sicut omnes homines volunt esse et vivere. Alio modo homo vult aliquid per electionem ex aliqua praemeditatione. Tertio modo homo

OBJECTION 1: It would seem that, properly speaking, evil is not the motive of mercy. For, as shown above (Q. 19, A. 1; I-II, Q. 79, A. 1, ad 4; I, Q. 48, A. 6), fault is an evil rather than punishment. Now fault provokes indignation rather than mercy. Therefore evil does not excite mercy.

OBJ. 2: Further, cruelty and harshness seem to excel other evils. Now the Philosopher says (*Rhet.* ii, 8) that *harshness does not call for pity but drives it away*. Therefore evil, as such, is not the motive of mercy.

OBJ. 3: Further, signs of evils are not true evils. But signs of evils excite one to mercy, as the Philosopher states (*Rhet.* ii, 8). Therefore evil, properly speaking, is not an incentive to mercy.

ON THE CONTRARY, Damascene says (*De Fide Orth.* ii, 2) that mercy is a kind of sorrow. Now evil is the motive of sorrow. Therefore it is the motive of mercy.

I ANSWER THAT, As Augustine says (*De Civ. Dei* ix, 5), *mercy is heartfelt sympathy for another's distress, impelling us to succor him if we can*. For mercy takes its name *misericordia* from denoting a man's compassionate heart (*miserum cor*) for another's unhappiness. Now unhappiness is opposed to happiness: and it is essential to beatitude or happiness that one should obtain what one wishes; for, according to Augustine (*De Trin.* xiii, 5), *happy is he who has whatever he desires, and desires nothing amiss*. Hence, on the other hand, it belongs to unhappiness that a man should suffer what he wishes not.

Now a man wishes a thing in three ways: first, by his natural appetite; thus all men naturally wish to be and to live: second, a man wishes a thing from deliberate choice: third, a man wishes a thing, not in itself, but in its cause,

vult aliquid non secundum se, sed in causa sua, puta, qui vult comedere nociva, quodammodo dicimus eum velle infirmari.

Sic igitur motivum misericordiae est, tanquam ad miseriam pertinens, primo quidem illud quod contrariatur appetitui naturali volentis, scilicet mala corruptiva et contristantia, quorum contraria homines naturaliter appetunt. Unde philosophus dicit, in II Rhet., quod *misericordia est tristitia quaedam super apparenti malo corruptivo vel contristativo.* Secundo, huiusmodi magis efficiuntur ad misericordiam provocantia si sint contra voluntatem electionis. Unde et philosophus ibidem dicit quod illa mala sunt miserabilia *quorum fortuna est causa,* puta *cum aliquod malum eveniat unde sperabatur bonum.* Tertio autem, sunt adhuc magis miserabilia si sunt contra totam voluntatem, puta si aliquis semper sectatus est bona et eveniunt ei mala. Et ideo philosophus dicit, in eodem libro, quod *misericordia maxime est super malis eius qui indignus patitur.*

**AD PRIMUM** ergo dicendum quod de ratione culpae est quod sit voluntaria. Et quantum ad hoc non habet rationem miserabilis, sed magis rationem puniendi. Sed quia culpa potest esse aliquo modo poena, inquantum scilicet habet aliquid annexum quod est contra voluntatem peccantis, secundum hoc potest habere rationem miserabilis. Et secundum hoc miseremur et compatimur peccantibus, sicut Gregorius dicit, in quadam homilia, quod *vera iustitia non habet dedignationem,* scilicet ad peccatores, *sed compassionem.* Et Matth. IX dicitur, *videns Iesus turbas misertus est eis, quia erant vexati, et iacentes sicut oves non habentes pastorem.*

**AD SECUNDUM** dicendum quod quia misericordia est compassio miseriae alterius, proprie misericordia est ad alterum, non autem ad seipsum, nisi secundum quandam similitudinem, sicut et iustitia, secundum quod in homine considerantur diversae partes, ut dicitur in V Ethic. Et secundum hoc dicitur Eccli. XXX, *miserere animae tuae placens Deo.*

Sicut ergo misericordia non est proprie ad seipsum, sed dolor, puta cum patimur aliquid crudele in nobis; ita etiam, si sint aliquae personae ita nobis coniunctae ut sint quasi aliquid nostri, puta filii aut parentes, in eorum malis non miseremur, sed dolemus, sicut in vulneribus propriis. Et secundum hoc Philosophus dicit quod *dirum est expulsivum miserationis.*

**AD TERTIUM** dicendum quod sicut ex spe et memoria bonorum sequitur delectatio, ita ex spe et memoria malorum sequitur tristitia, non autem tam vehemens sicut ex sensu praesentium. Et ideo signa malorum, inquantum repraesentant nobis mala miserabilia sicut praesentia, commovent ad miserendum.

thus, if a man wishes to eat what is bad for him, we say that, in a way, he wishes to be ill.

Accordingly the motive of mercy, being something pertaining to misery, is, in the first way, anything contrary to the will's natural appetite, namely corruptive or distressing evils, the contrary of which man desires naturally, wherefore the Philosopher says (*Rhet.* ii, 8) that *pity is sorrow for a visible evil, whether corruptive or distressing.* Second, such like evils are yet more provocative of pity if they are contrary to deliberate choice, wherefore the Philosopher says (*Rhet.* ii, 8) that evil excites our pity *when it is the result of an accident, as when something turns out ill, whereas we hoped well of it.* Third, they cause yet greater pity, if they are entirely contrary to the will, as when evil befalls a man who has always striven to do well: wherefore the Philosopher says (*Rhet.* ii, 8) that *we pity most the distress of one who suffers undeservedly.*

**REPLY OBJ. 1**: It is essential to fault that it be voluntary; and in this respect it deserves punishment rather than mercy. Since, however, fault may be, in a way, a punishment, through having something connected with it that is against the sinner's will, it may, in this respect, call for mercy. It is in this sense that we pity and commiserate sinners. Thus Gregory says in a homily (*Hom. in Evang.* xxxiv) that *true godliness is not disdainful but compassionate,* and again it is written (Matt 9:36) that Jesus *seeing the multitudes, had compassion on them: because they were distressed, and lying like sheep that have no shepherd.*

**REPLY OBJ. 2**: Since pity is sympathy for another's distress, it is directed, properly speaking, towards another, and not to oneself, except figuratively, like justice, according as a man is considered to have various parts (*Ethic.* v, 11). Thus it is written (Sir 30:24): *Have pity on thy own soul, pleasing God.*

Accordingly just as, properly speaking, a man does not pity himself, but suffers in himself, as when we suffer cruel treatment in ourselves, so too, in the case of those who are so closely united to us, as to be part of ourselves, such as our children or our parents, we do not pity their distress, but suffer as for our own sores; in which sense the Philosopher says that *harshness drives pity away.*

**REPLY OBJ. 3**: Just as pleasure results from hope and memory of good things, so does sorrow arise from the prospect or the recollection of evil things; though not so keenly as when they are present to the senses. Hence the signs of evil move us to pity, insofar as they represent as present, the evil that excites our pity.

# Article 2

*Whether the reason for taking pity is a defect in the person who pities?*

**AD SECUNDUM SIC PROCEDITUR.** Videtur quod defectus non sit ratio miserendi ex parte miserentis. Proprium enim Dei est misereri, unde dicitur in Psalm., *miserationes eius super omnia opera eius.* Sed in Deo nullus est defectus. Ergo defectus non potest esse ratio miserendi.

**PRAETEREA**, si defectus est ratio miserendi, oportet quod illi qui maxime sunt cum defectu maxime miserentur. Sed hoc est falsum, dicit enim philosophus, in II Rhet., quod *qui ex toto perierunt non miserentur.* Ergo videtur quod defectus non sit ratio miserendi ex parte miserentis.

**PRAETEREA**, sustinere aliquam contumeliam ad defectum pertinet. Sed philosophus dicit ibidem quod *illi qui sunt in contumeliativa dispositione non miserentur.* Ergo defectus ex parte miserentis non est ratio miserendi.

**SED CONTRA** est quod misericordia est quaedam tristitia. Sed defectus est ratio tristitiae, unde infirmi facilius contristantur, ut supra dictum est. Ergo ratio miserendi est defectus miserentis.

**RESPONDEO** dicendum quod, cum misericordia sit compassio super miseria aliena, ut dictum est, ex hoc contingit quod aliquis misereatur ex quo contingit quod de miseria aliena doleat. Quia autem tristitia seu dolor est de proprio malo, intantum aliquis de miseria aliena tristatur aut dolet inquantum miseriam alienam apprehendit ut suam.

Hoc autem contingit dupliciter. Uno modo, secundum unionem affectus, quod fit per amorem. Quia enim amans reputat amicum tanquam seipsum, malum ipsius reputat tanquam suum malum, et ideo dolet de malo amici sicut de suo. Et inde est quod Philosophus, in IX Ethic., inter alia amicabilia ponit hoc quod est *condolere amico.* Et apostolus dicit, ad Rom. XII, *gaudere cum gaudentibus, flere cum flentibus.*

Alio modo contingit secundum unionem realem, utpote cum malum aliquorum propinquum est ut ab eis ad nos transeat. Et ideo philosophus dicit, in II Rhet., homines miserentur super illos qui sunt eis coniuncti et similes, quia per hoc fit eis aestimatio quod ipsi etiam possint similia pati. Et inde est etiam quod senes et sapientes, qui considerant se posse in mala incidere, et debiles et formidolosi magis sunt misericordes. E contrario autem alii, qui reputant se esse felices et intantum potentes quod nihil mali putant se posse pati, non ita miserentur.

**OBJECTION 1**: It would seem that the reason for taking pity is not a defect in the person who takes pity. For it is proper to God to be merciful, wherefore it is written (Ps 144:9): *His tender mercies are over all His works.* But there is no defect in God. Therefore a defect cannot be the reason for taking pity.

**OBJ. 2**: Further, if a defect is the reason for taking pity, those in whom there is most defect, must needs take most pity. But this is false: for the Philosopher says (*Rhet.* ii, 8) that *those who are in a desperate state are pitiless.* Therefore it seems that the reason for taking pity is not a defect in the person who pities.

**OBJ. 3**: Further, to be treated with contempt is to be defective. But the Philosopher says (*Rhet.* ii, 8) that *those who are disposed to contumely are pitiless.* Therefore the reason for taking pity, is not a defect in the person who pities.

**ON THE CONTRARY**, Pity is a kind of sorrow. But a defect is the reason of sorrow, wherefore those who are in bad health give way to sorrow more easily, as we shall say further on (Q. 35, A. 1, ad 2). Therefore the reason why one takes pity is a defect in oneself.

**I ANSWER THAT**, Since pity is grief for another's distress, as stated above (A. 1), from the very fact that a person takes pity on anyone, it follows that another's distress grieves him. And since sorrow or grief is about one's own ills, one grieves or sorrows for another's distress, insofar as one looks upon another's distress as one's own.

Now this happens in two ways: first, through union of the affections, which is the effect of love. For, since he who loves another looks upon his friend as another self, he counts his friend's hurt as his own, so that he grieves for his friend's hurt as though he were hurt himself. Hence the Philosopher (*Ethic.* ix, 4) reckons *grieving with one's friend* as being one of the signs of friendship, and the Apostle says (Rom 12:15): *Rejoice with them that rejoice, weep with them that weep.*

Second, it happens through real union, for instance when another's evil comes near to us, so as to pass to us from him. Hence the Philosopher says (*Rhet.* ii, 8) that men pity such as are akin to them, and the like, because it makes them realize that the same may happen to themselves. This also explains why the old and the wise who consider that they may fall upon evil times, as also feeble and timorous persons, are more inclined to pity: whereas those who deem themselves happy, and so far powerful as to think themselves in no danger of suffering any hurt, are not so inclined to pity.

Sic igitur semper defectus est ratio miserendi, vel inquantum aliquis defectum alicuius reputat suum, propter unionem amoris; vel propter possibilitatem similia patiendi.

**AD PRIMUM** ergo dicendum quod Deus non miseretur nisi propter amorem, inquantum amat nos tanquam aliquid sui.

**AD SECUNDUM** dicendum quod illi qui iam sunt in infimis malis non timent se ulterius pati aliquid, et ideo non miserentur. Similiter etiam nec illi qui valde timent, quia tantum intendunt propriae passioni quod non intendunt miseriae alienae.

**AD TERTIUM** dicendum quod illi qui sunt in contumeliativa dispositione, sive quia sint contumeliam passi, sive quia velint contumeliam inferre, provocantur ad iram et audaciam, quae sunt quaedam passiones virilitatis extollentes animum hominis ad arduum. Unde auferunt homini aestimationem quod sit aliquid in futurum passurus. Unde tales, dum sunt in hac dispositione, non miserentur, secundum illud Prov. XXVII, *ira non habet misericordiam, neque erumpens furor.* Et ex simili ratione superbi non miserentur, qui contemnunt alios et reputant eos malos. Unde reputant quod digne patiantur quidquid patiuntur. Unde et Gregorius dicit quod *falsa iustitia,* scilicet superborum, *non habet compassionem, sed dedignationem.*

Accordingly a defect is always the reason for taking pity, either because one looks upon another's defect as one's own, through being united to him by love, or on account of the possibility of suffering in the same way.

**REPLY OBJ. 1**: God takes pity on us through love alone, inasmuch as He loves us as belonging to Him.

**REPLY OBJ. 2**: Those who are already in infinite distress, do not fear to suffer more, wherefore they are without pity. In like manner this applies to those also who are in great fear, for they are so intent on their own passion, that they pay no attention to the suffering of others.

**REPLY OBJ. 3**: Those who are disposed to contumely, whether through having been contemned, or because they wish to contemn others, are incited to anger and daring, which are manly passions and arouse the human spirit to attempt difficult things. Hence they make a man think that he is going to suffer something in the future, so that while they are disposed in that way they are pitiless, according to Prov. 27:4: *Anger hath no mercy, nor fury when it breaketh forth.* For the same reason the proud are without pity, because they despise others, and think them wicked, so that they account them as suffering deservedly whatever they suffer. Hence Gregory says (*Hom. in Evang. xxxiv*) that *false godliness,* i.e., of the proud, *is not compassionate but disdainful.*

# Article 3

*Whether mercy is a virtue?*

**AD TERTIUM SIC PROCEDITUR**. Videtur quod misericordia non sit virtus. Principale enim in virtute est electio, ut patet per philosophum, in libro Ethic. Electio autem est *appetitus praeconsiliati,* ut in eodem libro dicitur. Illud ergo quod impedit consilium non potest dici virtus. Sed misericordia impedit consilium, secundum illud Sallustii, *omnes homines qui de rebus dubiis consultant ab ira et misericordia vacuos esse decet, non enim animus facile verum providet ubi ista officiunt.* Ergo misericordia non est virtus.

**PRAETEREA**, nihil quod est contrarium virtuti est laudabile. Sed Nemesis contrariatur misericordiae, ut philosophus dicit, in II Rhet. Nemesis autem est passio laudabilis, ut dicitur in II Ethic. Ergo misericordia non est virtus.

**PRAETEREA**, gaudium et pax non sunt speciales virtutes quia consequuntur ex caritate, ut supra dictum est. Sed etiam misericordia consequitur ex caritate, sic enim ex caritate *flemus cum flentibus* sicut *gaudemus cum gaudentibus.* Ergo misericordia non est specialis virtus.

**OBJECTION 1**: It would seem that mercy is not a virtue. For the chief part of virtue is choice as the Philosopher states (*Ethic.* ii, 5). Now choice is *the desire of what has been already counselled* (*Ethic.* iii, 2). Therefore whatever hinders counsel cannot be called a virtue. But mercy hinders counsel, according to the saying of Sallust (*Catilin.*): *All those that take counsel about matters of doubt, should be free from . . . anger . . . and mercy, because the mind does not easily see aright, when these things stand in the way.* Therefore mercy is not a virtue.

**OBJ. 2**: Further, nothing contrary to virtue is praiseworthy. But nemesis is contrary to mercy, as the Philosopher states (*Rhet.* ii, 9), and yet it is a praiseworthy passion (*Rhet.* ii, 9). Therefore mercy is not a virtue.

**OBJ. 3**: Further, joy and peace are not special virtues, because they result from charity, as stated above (Q. 28, A. 4; Q. 29, A. 4). Now mercy, also, results from charity; for it is out of charity that *we weep with them that weep,* as *we rejoice with them that rejoice.* Therefore mercy is not a special virtue.

**PRAETEREA**, cum misericordia ad vim appetitivam pertineat, non est virtus intellectualis. Nec est virtus theologica, cum non habeat Deum pro obiecto. Similiter etiam non est virtus moralis, quia nec est circa operationes, hoc enim pertinet ad iustitiam; nec est circa passiones, non enim reducitur ad aliquam duodecim medietatum quas Philosophus ponit, in II Ethic. Ergo misericordia non est virtus.

**SED CONTRA** est quod Augustinus dicit, in IX de Civ. Dei, *longe melius et humanius et piorum sensibus accommodatius Cicero in Caesaris laude locutus est, ubi ait, nulla de virtutibus tuis nec admirabilior nec gratior misericordia est.* Ergo misericordia est virtus.

**RESPONDEO** dicendum quod misericordia importat dolorem de miseria aliena. Iste autem dolor potest nominare, uno quidem modo, motum appetitus sensitivi. Et secundum hoc misericordia passio est, et non virtus. Alio vero modo potest nominare motum appetitus intellectivi, secundum quod alicui displicet malum alterius. Hic autem motus potest esse secundum rationem regulatus, et potest secundum hunc motum ratione regulatum regulari motus inferioris appetitus. Unde Augustinus dicit, in IX de Civ. Dei, quod *iste motus animi, scilicet misericordia, servit rationi quando ita praebetur misericordia ut iustitia conservetur, sive cum indigenti tribuitur, sive cum ignoscitur poenitenti.* Et quia ratio virtutis humanae consistit in hoc quod motus animi ratione reguletur, ut ex superioribus patet, consequens est misericordiam esse virtutem.

**AD PRIMUM** ergo dicendum quod auctoritas illa Sallustii intelligitur de misericordia secundum quod est passio ratione non regulata. Sic enim impedit consilium rationis, dum facit a iustitia discedere.

**AD SECUNDUM** dicendum quod Philosophus loquitur ibi de misericordia et Nemesi secundum quod utrumque est passio. Et habent quidem contrarietatem ex parte aestimationis quam habent de malis alienis, de quibus misericors dolet, inquantum aestimat aliquem indigna pati; Nemeseticus autem gaudet, inquantum aestimat aliquos digne pati, et tristatur si indignis bene accidat. Et *utrumque est laudabile, et ab eodem more descendens*, ut ibidem dicitur. Sed proprie misericordiae opponitur invidia, ut infra dicetur.

**AD TERTIUM** dicendum quod gaudium et pax nihil adiiciunt super rationem boni quod est obiectum caritatis, et ideo non requirunt alias virtutes quam caritatem. Sed misericordia respicit quandam specialem rationem, scilicet miseriam eius cuius misereretur.

**AD QUARTUM** dicendum quod misericordia, secundum quod est virtus, est moralis virtus circa passiones existens, et reducitur ad illam medietatem quae dicitur Nemesis, quia *ab eodem more procedunt*, ut in II Rhet.

**OBJ. 4**: Further, since mercy belongs to the appetitive power, it is not an intellectual virtue, and, since it has not God for its object, neither is it a theological virtue. Moreover it is not a moral virtue, because neither is it about operations, for this belongs to justice; nor is it about passions, since it is not reduced to one of the twelve means mentioned by the Philosopher (*Ethic.* ii, 7). Therefore mercy is not a virtue.

**ON THE CONTRARY**, Augustine says (*De Civ. Dei* ix, 5): *Cicero in praising Caesar expresses himself much better and in a fashion at once more humane and more in accordance with religious feeling, when he says: 'Of all thy virtues none is more marvelous or more graceful than thy mercy.'* Therefore mercy is a virtue.

**I ANSWER THAT**, Mercy signifies grief for another's distress. Now this grief may denote, in one way, a movement of the sensitive appetite, in which case mercy is not a virtue but a passion; whereas, in another way, it may denote a movement of the intellective appetite, inasmuch as one person's evil is displeasing to another. This movement may be ruled in accordance with reason, and in accordance with this movement regulated by reason, the movement of the lower appetite may be regulated. Hence Augustine says (*De Civ. Dei* ix, 5) that *this movement of the mind* (viz. mercy) *obeys the reason, when mercy is vouchsafed in such a way that justice is safeguarded, whether we give to the needy or forgive the repentant.* And since it is essential to human virtue that the movements of the soul should be regulated by reason, as was shown above (I-II, Q. 59, AA. 4, 5), it follows that mercy is a virtue.

**REPLY OBJ. 1**: The words of Sallust are to be understood as applying to the mercy which is a passion unregulated by reason: for thus it impedes the counselling of reason, by making it wander from justice.

**REPLY OBJ. 2**: The Philosopher is speaking there of pity and nemesis, considered, both of them, as passions. They are contrary to one another on the part of their respective estimation of another's evils, for which pity grieves, insofar as it esteems someone to suffer undeservedly, whereas nemesis rejoices, insofar as it esteems someone to suffer deservedly, and grieves, if things go well with the undeserving: *both of these are praiseworthy and come from the same disposition of character* (*Rhet.* ii, 9). Properly speaking, however, it is envy which is opposed to pity, as we shall state further on (Q. 36, A. 3).

**REPLY OBJ. 3**: Joy and peace add nothing to the aspect of good which is the object of charity, wherefore they do not require any other virtue besides charity. But mercy regards a certain special aspect, namely the misery of the person pitied.

**REPLY OBJ. 4**: Mercy, considered as a virtue, is a moral virtue having relation to the passions, and it is reduced to the mean called nemesis, because *they both proceed from the same character* (*Rhet.* ii, 9). Now the Philosopher proposes

dicitur. Has autem medietates Philosophus non ponit virtutes, sed passiones, quia etiam secundum quod sunt passiones, laudabiles sunt. Nihil tamen prohibet quin ab aliquo habitu electivo proveniant. Et secundum hoc assumunt rationem virtutis.

these means not as virtues, but as passions, because, even as passions, they are praiseworthy. Yet nothing prevents them from proceeding from some elective habit, in which case they assume the character of a virtue.

# Article 4

*Whether mercy is the greatest of the virtues?*

AD QUARTUM SIC PROCEDITUR. Videtur quod misericordia sit maxima virtutum. Maxime enim ad virtutem pertinere videtur cultus divinus. Sed misericordia cultui divino praefertur, secundum illud Osee VI et Matth. XII, *misericordiam volo, et non sacrificium.* Ergo misericordia est maxima virtus.

PRAETEREA, super illud I ad Tim. IV, *pietas ad omnia utilis est,* dicit Glossa Ambrosii, *omnis summa disciplinae Christianae in misericordia et pietate est.* Sed disciplina Christiana continet omnem virtutem. Ergo summa totius virtutis in misericordia consistit.

PRAETEREA, *virtus est quae bonum facit habentem.* Ergo tanto aliqua virtus est melior quanto facit hominem Deo similiorem, quia per hoc melior est homo quod Deo est similior. Sed hoc maxime facit misericordia, quia de Deo dicitur in Psalm. quod *miserationes eius sunt super omnia opera eius.* Unde et Luc. VI dominus dicit, *estote misericordes, sicut et pater vester misericors est.* Misericordia igitur est maxima virtutum.

SED CONTRA est quod apostolus, ad Coloss. III, cum dixisset, *induite vos, sicut dilecti Dei, viscera misericordiae* etc., postea subdit, *super omnia, caritatem habete.* Ergo misericordia non est maxima virtutum.

RESPONDEO dicendum quod aliqua virtus potest esse maxima dupliciter, uno modo, secundum se; alio modo, per comparationem ad habentem. Secundum se quidem misericordia maxima est. Pertinet enim ad misericordiam quod alii effundat; et, quod plus est, quod defectus aliorum sublevet; et hoc est maxime superioris. Unde et misereri ponitur proprium Deo, et in hoc maxime dicitur eius omnipotentia manifestari.

Sed quoad habentem, misericordia non est maxima, nisi ille qui habet sit maximus, qui nullum supra se habeat, sed omnes sub se. Ei enim qui supra se aliquem habet maius est et melius coniungi superiori quam supplere defectum inferioris. Et ideo quantum ad hominem, qui habet Deum superiorem, caritas, per quam Deo unitur, est potior quam misericordia, per quam defectus proximorum supplet. Sed inter omnes virtutes quae ad proximum pertinent potissima est misericordia, sicut etiam est potioris actus, nam supplere defectum alterius, inquantum huiusmodi, est superioris et melioris.

OBJECTION 1: It would seem that mercy is the greatest of the virtues. For the worship of God seems a most virtuous act. But mercy is preferred before the worship of God, according to Osee 6:6 and Matt. 12:7: *I have desired mercy and not sacrifice.* Therefore mercy is the greatest virtue.

OBJ. 2: Further, on the words of 1 Tim. 4:8: *Godliness is profitable to all things,* a gloss says: *The sum total of a Christian's rule of life consists in mercy and godliness.* Now the Christian rule of life embraces every virtue. Therefore the sum total of all virtues is contained in mercy.

OBJ. 3: Further, *Virtue is that which makes its subject good,* according to the Philosopher. Therefore the more a virtue makes a man like God, the better is that virtue: since man is the better for being more like God. Now this is chiefly the result of mercy, since of God is it said (Ps 144:9) that *His tender mercies are over all His works,* and (Luke 6:36) Our Lord said: *Be ye . . . merciful, as your Father also is merciful.* Therefore mercy is the greatest of virtues.

ON THE CONTRARY, The Apostle after saying (Col 3:12): *Put ye on . . . as the elect of God . . . the bowels of mercy,* etc., adds (Col 3:14): *Above all things have charity.* Therefore mercy is not the greatest of virtues.

I ANSWER THAT, A virtue may take precedence of others in two ways: first, in itself; second, in comparison with its subject. In itself, mercy takes precedence of other virtues, for it belongs to mercy to be bountiful to others, and, what is more, to succor others in their wants, which pertains chiefly to one who stands above. Hence mercy is accounted as being proper to God: and therein His omnipotence is declared to be chiefly manifested.

On the other hand, with regard to its subject, mercy is not the greatest virtue, unless that subject be greater than all others, surpassed by none and excelling all: since for him that has anyone above him it is better to be united to that which is above than to supply the defect of that which is beneath. . Hence, as regards man, who has God above him, charity which unites him to God, is greater than mercy, whereby he supplies the defects of his neighbor. But of all the virtues which relate to our neighbor, mercy is the greatest, even as its act surpasses all others, since it belongs to one who is higher and better to supply the defect of another, insofar as the latter is deficient.

**AD PRIMUM** ergo dicendum quod Deum non colimus per exteriora sacrificia aut munera propter ipsum, sed propter nos et propter proximos, non enim indiget sacrificiis nostris, sed vult ea sibi offerri propter nostram devotionem et proximorum utilitatem. Et ideo misericordia, qua subvenitur defectibus aliorum, est sacrificium ei magis acceptum, utpote propinquius utilitatem proximorum inducens, secundum illud Heb. ult., *beneficentiae et communionis nolite oblivisci, talibus enim hostiis promeretur Deus.*

**AD SECUNDUM** dicendum quod summa religionis Christianae in misericordia consistit quantum ad exteriora opera. Interior tamen affectio caritatis, qua coniungimur Deo, praeponderat et dilectioni et misericordiae in proximos.

**AD TERTIUM** dicendum quod per caritatem assimilamur Deo tanquam ei per affectum uniti. Et ideo potior est quam misericordia, per quam assimilamur Deo secundum similitudinem operationis.

**REPLY OBJ. 1**: We worship God by external sacrifices and gifts, not for His own profit, but for that of ourselves and our neighbor. For He needs not our sacrifices, but wishes them to be offered to Him, in order to arouse our devotion and to profit our neighbor. Hence mercy, whereby we supply others' defects is a sacrifice more acceptable to Him, as conducing more directly to our neighbor's well-being, according to Heb. 13:16: *Do not forget to do good and to impart, for by such sacrifices God's favor is obtained.*

**REPLY OBJ. 2**: The sum total of the Christian religion consists in mercy, as regards external works: but the inward love of charity, whereby we are united to God preponderates over both love and mercy for our neighbor.

**REPLY OBJ. 3**: Charity likens us to God by uniting us to Him in the bond of love: wherefore it surpasses mercy, which likens us to God as regards similarity of works.

# QUESTION 31

Deinde considerandum est de exterioribus actibus vel effectibus caritatis. Et primo, de beneficentia; secundo, de eleemosyna, quae est quaedam pars beneficentiae; tertio, de correctione fraterna, quae est quaedam eleemosyna.

Circa primum quaeruntur quatuor.

Primo, utrum beneficentia sit actus caritatis.

Secundo, utrum sit omnibus benefaciendum.

Tertio, utrum magis coniunctis sit magis benefaciendum.

Quarto, utrum beneficentia sit virtus specialis.

We must now consider the outward acts or effects of charity, (1) Beneficence, (2) Almsdeeds, which are a part of beneficence, (3) Fraternal correction, which is a kind of alms.

Under the first head there are four points of inquiry:

(1) Whether beneficence is an act of charity?

(2) Whether we ought to be beneficent to all?

(3) Whether we ought to be more beneficent to those who are more closely united to us?

(4) Whether beneficence is a special virtue?

# Article 1

*Whether beneficence is an act of charity?*

**AD PRIMUM SIC PROCEDITUR.** Videtur quod beneficentia non sit actus caritatis. Caritas enim maxime habetur ad Deum. Sed ad eum non possumus esse benefici, secundum illud Iob XXXV, *quid dabis ei? Aut quid de manu tua accipiet?* Ergo beneficentia non est actus caritatis.

**PRAETEREA,** beneficentia maxime consistit in collatione donorum. Sed hoc pertinet ad liberalitatem. Ergo beneficentia non est actus caritatis, sed liberalitatis.

**PRAETEREA,** omne quod quis dat, vel dat sicut debitum vel dat sicut non debitum. Sed beneficium quod impenditur tanquam debitum pertinet ad iustitiam, quod autem impenditur tanquam non debitum, gratis datur, et secundum hoc pertinet ad misericordiam. Ergo omnis beneficentia vel est actus iustitiae vel est actus misericordiae. Non est ergo actus caritatis.

**SED CONTRA,** caritas est amicitia quaedam, ut dictum est. Sed philosophus, in IX Ethic., inter alios amicitiae actus ponit hoc unum quod est *operari bonum ad amicos,* quod est amicis benefacere. Ergo beneficentia est actus caritatis.

**RESPONDEO** dicendum quod beneficentia nihil aliud importat quam facere bonum alicui. Potest autem hoc bonum considerari dupliciter. Uno modo, secundum communem rationem boni. Et hoc pertinet ad communem rationem beneficentiae. Et hoc est actus amicitiae, et per consequens caritatis. Nam in actu dilectionis includitur benevolentia, per quam aliquis vult bonum amico, ut supra habitum est. Voluntas autem est effectiva eorum quae vult, si facultas adsit. Et ideo ex consequenti

**OBJECTION 1:** It would seem that beneficence is not an act of charity. For charity is chiefly directed to God. Now we cannot benefit God, according to Job 35:7: *What shalt thou give Him? or what shall He receive of thy hand?* Therefore beneficence is not an act of charity.

**OBJ. 2:** Further, beneficence consists chiefly in making gifts. But this belongs to liberality. Therefore beneficence is an act of liberality and not of charity.

**OBJ. 3:** Further, what a man gives, he gives either as being due, or as not due. But a benefit conferred as being due belongs to justice while a benefit conferred as not due, is gratuitous, and in this respect is an act of mercy. Therefore every benefit conferred is either an act of justice, or an act of mercy. Therefore it is not an act of charity.

**ON THE CONTRARY,** Charity is a kind of friendship, as stated above (Q. 23, A. 1). Now the Philosopher reckons among the acts of friendship (*Ethic.* ix, 1) *doing good,* i.e., being beneficent, *to one's friends.* Therefore it is an act of charity to do good to others.

**I ANSWER THAT,** Beneficence simply means doing good to someone. This good may be considered in two ways, first under the general aspect of good, and this belongs to beneficence in general, and is an act of friendship, and, consequently, of charity: because the act of love includes goodwill whereby a man wishes his friend well, as stated above (Q. 23, A. 1; Q. 27, A. 2). Now the will carries into effect if possible, the things it wills, so that, consequently, the result of an act of love is that a man is beneficent to his

benefacere amico ex actu dilectionis consequitur. Et propter hoc beneficentia secundum communem rationem, est amicitiae vel caritatis actus.

Si autem bonum quod quis facit alteri accipiatur sub aliqua speciali ratione boni, sic beneficentia accipiet specialem rationem, et pertinebit ad aliquam specialem virtutem.

**AD PRIMUM** ergo dicendum quod, sicut Dionysius dicit, IV cap. de Div. Nom., *amor movet ordinata ad mutuam habitudinem, et inferiora convertit in superiora ut ab eis perficiantur, et superiora movet ad inferiorum provisionem.* Et quantum ad hoc beneficentia est effectus dilectionis. Et ideo nostrum non est Deo benefacere, sed eum honorare, nos ei subiiciendo, eius autem est ex sua dilectione nobis benefacere.

**AD SECUNDUM** dicendum quod in collatione donorum duo sunt attendenda, quorum unum est exterius datum; aliud autem est interior passio quam habet quis ad divitias, in eis delectatus. Ad liberalitatem autem pertinet moderari interiorem passionem, ut scilicet aliquis non superexcedat in concupiscendo et amando divitias, ex hoc enim efficietur homo facile emissivus donorum. Unde si homo det aliquod donum magnum, et tamen cum quadam concupiscentia retinendi, datio non est liberalis. Sed ex parte exterioris dati collatio beneficii pertinet in generali ad amicitiam vel caritatem. Unde hoc non derogat amicitiae, si aliquis rem quam concupiscit retinere det alicui propter amorem; sed magis ex hoc ostenditur amicitiae perfectio.

**AD TERTIUM** dicendum quod sicut amicitia seu caritas respicit in beneficio collato communem rationem boni, ita iustitia respicit ibi rationem debiti. Misericordia vero respicit ibi rationem relevantis miseriam vel defectum.

friend. Therefore beneficence in its general acceptation is an act of friendship or charity.

But if the good which one man does another, be considered under some special aspect of good, then beneficence will assume a special character and will belong to some special virtue.

**REPLY OBJ. 1:** According to Dionysius (*Div. Nom.* iv), *love moves those, whom it unites, to a mutual relationship: it turns the inferior to the superior to be perfected thereby; it moves the superior to watch over the inferior:* and in this respect beneficence is an effect of love. Hence it is not for us to benefit God, but to honor Him by obeying Him, while it is for Him, out of His love, to bestow good things on us.

**REPLY OBJ. 2:** Two things must be observed in the bestowal of gifts. One is the thing given outwardly, while the other is the inward passion that a man has in the delight of riches. It belongs to liberality to moderate this inward passion so as to avoid excessive desire and love for riches; for this makes a man more ready to part with his wealth. Hence, if a man makes some great gift, while yet desiring to keep it for himself, his is not a liberal giving. On the other hand, as regards the outward gift, the act of beneficence belongs in general to friendship or charity. Hence it does not detract from a man's friendship, if, through love, he give his friend something he would like to keep for himself; rather does this prove the perfection of his friendship.

**REPLY OBJ. 3:** Just as friendship or charity sees, in the benefit bestowed, the general aspect of good, so does justice see therein the aspect of debt, while pity considers the relieving of distress or defect.

# Article 2

*Whether we ought to do good to all?*

**AD SECUNDUM SIC PROCEDITUR.** Videtur quod non sit omnibus benefaciendum. Dicit enim Augustinus, in I de Doct. Christ., quod *omnibus prodesse non possumus.* Sed virtus non inclinat ad impossibile. Ergo non oportet omnibus benefacere.

**PRAETEREA,** Eccli. XII dicitur, *da iusto, et non recipias peccatorem.* Sed multi homines sunt peccatores. Non ergo omnibus est benefaciendum.

**PRAETEREA,** *caritas non agit perperam,* ut dicitur I ad Cor. XIII. Sed benefacere quibusdam est agere perperam, puta si aliquis benefaciat inimicis reipublicae; vel si benefaciat excommunicato, quia per hoc ei communicat.

**OBJECTION 1:** It would seem that we are not bound to do good to all. For Augustine says (*De Doctr. Christ.* i, 28) that we *are unable to do good to everyone.* Now virtue does not incline one to the impossible. Therefore it is not necessary to do good to all.

**OBJ. 2:** Further, it is written (Sir 12:5) *Give to the good, and receive not a sinner.* But many men are sinners. Therefore we need not do good to all.

**OBJ. 3:** Further, *Charity dealeth not perversely* (1 Cor 13:4). Now to do good to some is to deal perversely: for instance if one were to do good to an enemy of the common weal, or if one were to do good

Ergo, cum benefacere sit actus caritatis, non est omnibus benefaciendum.

SED CONTRA est quod apostolus dicit, ad Gal. ult., *dum tempus habemus, operemur bonum ad omnes.*

RESPONDEO dicendum quod, sicut supra dictum est, beneficentia consequitur amorem ex ea parte qua movet superiora ad provisionem inferiorum. Gradus autem in hominibus non sunt immutabiles, sicut in Angelis, quia homines possunt pati multiplices defectus; unde qui est superior secundum aliquid, vel est vel potest esse inferior secundum aliud. Et ideo, cum dilectio caritatis se extendat ad omnes, etiam beneficentia se debet extendere ad omnes, pro loco tamen et tempore, omnes enim actus virtutum sunt secundum debitas circumstantias limitandi.

AD PRIMUM ergo dicendum quod, simpliciter loquendo, non possumus omnibus benefacere in speciali, nullus tamen est de quo non possit occurrere casus in quo oporteat ei benefacere etiam in speciali. Et ideo caritas requirit ut homo, etsi non actu alicui benefaciat, habeat tamen hoc in sui animi praeparatione, ut benefaciat cuicumque si tempus adesset. Aliquod tamen beneficium est quod possumus omnibus impendere, si non in speciali saltem in generali, sicut cum oramus pro omnibus fidelibus et infidelibus.

AD SECUNDUM dicendum quod in peccatore duo sunt, scilicet culpa et natura. Est ergo subveniendum peccatori quantum ad sustentationem naturae, non est autem ei subveniendum ad fomentum culpae; hoc enim non esset benefacere, sed potius malefacere.

AD TERTIUM dicendum quod excommunicatis et reipublicae hostibus sunt beneficia subtrahenda inquantum per hoc arcentur a culpa. Si tamen immineret necessitas, ne natura deficeret, esset eis subveniendum, debito tamen modo, puta ne fame aut siti morerentur, aut aliquod huiusmodi dispendium, nisi secundum ordinem iustitiae, paterentur.

to an excommunicated person, since, by doing so, he would be holding communion with him. Therefore, since beneficence is an act of charity, we ought not to do good to all.

ON THE CONTRARY, The Apostle says (Gal 6:10): *Whilst we have time, let us work good to all men.*

I ANSWER THAT, As stated above (A. 1, ad 1), beneficence is an effect of love insofar as love moves the superior to watch over the inferior. Now degrees among men are not unchangeable as among angels, because men are subject to many failings, so that he who is superior in one respect, is or may be inferior in another. Therefore, since the love of charity extends to all, beneficence also should extend to all, but according as time and place require: because all acts of virtue must be modified with a view to their due circumstances.

REPLY OBJ. 1: Absolutely speaking it is impossible to do good to every single one: yet it is true of each individual that one may be bound to do good to him in some particular case. Hence charity binds us, though not actually doing good to someone, to be prepared in mind to do good to anyone if we have time to spare. There is however a good that we can do to all, if not to each individual, at least to all in general, as when we pray for all, for unbelievers as well as for the faithful.

REPLY OBJ. 2: In a sinner there are two things, his guilt and his nature. Accordingly we are bound to succor the sinner as to the maintenance of his nature, but not so as to abet his sin, for this would be to do evil rather than good.

REPLY OBJ. 3: The excommunicated and the enemies of the common weal are deprived of all beneficence, insofar as this prevents them from doing evil deeds. Yet if their nature be in urgent need of succor lest it fail, we are bound to help them: for instance, if they be in danger of death through hunger or thirst, or suffer some like distress, unless this be according to the order of justice.

# Article 3

*Whether we ought to do good to those rather who are more closely united to us?*

AD TERTIUM SIC PROCEDITUR. Videtur quod non sit magis benefaciendum his qui sunt nobis magis coniuncti. Dicitur enim Luc. XIV, *cum facis prandium aut cenam, noli vocare amicos tuos neque fratres neque cognatos.* Sed isti sunt maxime coniuncti. Ergo non est magis benefaciendum coniunctis, sed potius extraneis

OBJECTION 1: It would seem that we are not bound to do good to those rather who are more closely united to us. For it is written (Luke 14:12): *When thou makest a dinner or a supper, call not thy friends, nor thy brethren, nor thy kinsmen.* Now these are the most closely united to us. Therefore we are not bound to do good to those rather who

indigentibus, sequitur enim, *sed cum facis convivium, voca pauperes et debiles*, et cetera.

PRAETEREA, maximum beneficium est quod homo aliquem in bello adiuvet. Sed miles in bello magis debet iuvare extraneum commilitonem quam consanguineum hostem. Ergo beneficia non sunt magis exhibenda magis coniunctis.

PRAETEREA, prius sunt debita restituenda quam gratuita beneficia impendenda. Sed debitum est quod aliquis impendat beneficium ei a quo accepit. Ergo benefactoribus magis est benefaciendum quam propinquis.

PRAETEREA, magis sunt diligendi parentes quam filii, ut supra dictum est. Sed magis est benefaciendum filiis, quia *non debent filii thesaurizare parentibus*, ut dicitur II ad Cor. XII. Ergo non est magis benefaciendum magis coniunctis.

SED CONTRA est quod Augustinus dicit, in I de Doct. Christ., *cum omnibus prodesse non possis, his potissimum consulendum est qui, pro locorum et temporum vel quarumlibet rerum opportunitatibus, constrictius tibi, quasi quadam sorte, iunguntur.*

RESPONDEO dicendum quod gratia et virtus imitantur naturae ordinem, qui est ex divina sapientia institutus. Est autem talis ordo naturae ut unumquodque agens naturale per prius magis diffundat suam actionem ad ea quae sunt sibi propinquiora, sicut ignis magis calefacit rem sibi magis propinquam. Et similiter Deus in substantias sibi propinquiores per prius et copiosius dona suae bonitatis diffundit; ut patet per Dionysium, IV cap. Cael. Hier. Exhibitio autem beneficiorum est quaedam actio caritatis in alios. Et ideo oportet quod ad magis propinquos simus magis benefici.

Sed propinquitas unius hominis ad alium potest attendi secundum diversa in quibus sibi ad invicem homines communicant, ut consanguinei naturali communicatione, concives in civili, fideles in spirituali, et sic de aliis. Et secundum diversas coniunctiones sunt diversimode diversa beneficia dispensanda, nam unicuique est magis exhibendum beneficium pertinens ad illam rem secundum quam est magis nobis coniunctus, simpliciter loquendo. Tamen hoc potest variari secundum diversitatem locorum et temporum et negotiorum, nam in aliquo casu est magis subveniendum extraneo, puta si sit in extrema necessitate, quam etiam patri non tantam necessitatem patienti.

AD PRIMUM ergo dicendum quod dominus non prohibet simpliciter vocare amicos aut consanguineos ad convivium, sed vocare eos ea intentione quod *te ipsi reinvitent*. Hoc enim non erit caritatis, sed cupiditatis.

are more closely united to us, but preferably to strangers and to those who are in want: hence the text goes on: *But, when thou makest a feast, call the poor, the maimed*, etc.

OBJ. 2: Further, to help another in the battle is an act of very great goodness. But a soldier on the battlefield is bound to help a fellow-soldier who is a stranger rather than a kinsman who is a foe. Therefore in doing acts of kindness we are not bound to give the preference to those who are most closely united to us.

OBJ. 3: Further, we should pay what is due before conferring gratuitous favors. But it is a man's duty to be good to those who have been good to him. Therefore we ought to do good to our benefactors rather than to those who are closely united to us.

OBJ. 4: Further, a man ought to love his parents more than his children, as stated above (Q. 26, A. 9). Yet a man ought to be more beneficent to his children, since *neither ought the children to lay up for the parents*, according to 2 Cor. 12:14. Therefore we are not bound to be more beneficent to those who are more closely united to us.

ON THE CONTRARY, Augustine says (*De Doctr. Christ.* i, 28): *Since one cannot do good to all, we ought to consider those chiefly who by reason of place, time or any other circumstance, by a kind of chance are more closely united to us.*

I ANSWER THAT, Grace and virtue imitate the order of nature, which is established by Divine wisdom. Now the order of nature is such that every natural agent pours forth its activity first and most of all on the things which are nearest to it: thus fire heats most what is next to it. In like manner God pours forth the gifts of His goodness first and most plentifully on the substances which are nearest to Him, as Dionysius declares (*Coel. Hier.* vii). But the bestowal of benefits is an act of charity towards others. Therefore we ought to be most beneficent towards those who are most closely connected with us.

Now one man's connection with another may be measured in reference to the various matters in which men are engaged together; (thus the intercourse of kinsmen is in natural matters, that of fellow-citizens is in civic matters, that of the faithful is in spiritual matters, and so forth): and various benefits should be conferred in various ways according to these various connections, because we ought in preference to bestow on each one such benefits as pertain to the matter in which, speaking simply, he is most closely connected with us. And yet this may vary according to the various requirements of time, place, or matter in hand: because in certain cases one ought, for instance, to succor a stranger, in extreme necessity, rather than one's own father, if he is not in such urgent need.

REPLY OBJ. 1: Our Lord did not absolutely forbid us to invite our friends and kinsmen to eat with us, but to invite them so that *they may invite us in return*, since that would be an act not of charity but of cupidity. The case may

Potest tamen contingere quod extranei sint magis invitandi in aliquo casu, propter maiorem indigentiam. Intelligendum est enim quod magis coniunctis magis est, ceteris paribus, benefaciendum. Si autem duorum unus sit magis coniunctus et alter magis indigens, non potest universali regula determinari cui sit magis subveniendum, quia sunt diversi gradus et indigentiae et propinquitatis, sed hoc requirit prudentis iudicium.

AD SECUNDUM dicendum quod bonum commune multorum divinius est quam bonum unius. Unde pro bono communi reipublicae vel spiritualis vel temporalis virtuosum est quod aliquis etiam propriam vitam exponat periculo. Et ideo, cum communicatio in bellicis ordinetur ad conservationem reipublicae, in hoc miles impendens commilitoni auxilium, non impendit ei tanquam privatae personae, sed sicut totam rempublicam iuvans. Et ideo non est mirum si in hoc praefertur extraneus coniuncto secundum carnem.

AD TERTIUM dicendum quod duplex est debitum. Unum quidem quod non est numerandum in bonis eius qui debet, sed potius in bonis eius cui debetur. Puta si aliquis habet pecuniam aut rem aliam alterius vel furto sublatam vel mutuo acceptam sive depositam, vel aliquo alio simili modo, quantum ad hoc plus debet homo reddere debitum quam ex eo benefacere coniunctis. Nisi forte esset tantae necessitatis articulus in quo etiam liceret rem alienam accipere ad subveniendum necessitatem patienti. Nisi forte et ille cui res debetur in simili necessitate esset. In quo tamen casu pensanda esset utriusque conditio secundum alias conditiones, prudentis iudicio, quia in talibus non potest universalis regula dari, propter varietatem singulorum casuum, ut Philosophus dicit, in IX Ethic.

Aliud autem est debitum quod computatur in bonis eius qui debet, et non eius cui debetur, puta si debeatur non ex necessitate iustitiae, sed ex quadam morali aequitate, ut contingit in beneficiis gratis susceptis. Nullius autem benefactoris beneficium est tantum sicut parentum, et ideo parentes in recompensandis beneficiis sunt omnibus aliis praeferendi; nisi necessitas ex alia parte praeponderaret, vel aliqua alia conditio, puta communis utilitas Ecclesiae vel reipublicae. In aliis autem est aestimatio habenda et coniunctionis et beneficii suscepti. Quae similiter non potest communi regula determinari.

AD QUARTUM dicendum quod parentes sunt sicut superiores, et ideo amor parentum est ad benefaciendum, amor autem filiorum ad honorandum parentes. Et tamen in necessitatis extremae articulo magis liceret deserere filios quam parentes; quos nullo modo deserere

occur, however, that one ought rather to invite strangers, on account of their greater want. For it must be understood that, other things being equal, one ought to succor those rather who are most closely connected with us. And if of two, one be more closely connected, and the other in greater want, it is not possible to decide, by any general rule, which of them we ought to help rather than the other, since there are various degrees of want as well as of connection: and the matter requires the judgment of a prudent man.

REPLY OBJ. 2: The common good of many is more godlike than the good of an individual. Wherefore it is a virtuous action for a man to endanger even his own life, either for the spiritual or for the temporal common good of his country. Since therefore men engage together in warlike acts in order to safeguard the common weal, the soldier who with this in view succors his comrade, succors him not as a private individual, but with a view to the welfare of his country as a whole: wherefore it is not a matter for wonder if a stranger be preferred to one who is a blood relation.

REPLY OBJ. 3: A thing may be due in two ways. There is one which should be reckoned, not among the goods of the debtor, but rather as belonging to the person to whom it is due: for instance, a man may have another's goods, whether in money or in kind, either because he has stolen them, or because he has received them on loan or in deposit or in some other way. In this case a man ought to pay what he owes, rather than benefit his connections out of it, unless perchance the case be so urgent that it would be lawful for him to take another's property in order to relieve the one who is in need. Yet, again, this would not apply if the creditor were in equal distress: in which case, however, the claims on either side would have to be weighed with regard to such other conditions as a prudent man would take into consideration, because, on account of the different particular cases, as the Philosopher states (*Ethic.* ix, 2), it is impossible to lay down a general rule.

The other kind of due is one which is reckoned among the goods of the debtor and not of the creditor; for instance, a thing may be due, not because justice requires it, but on account of a certain moral equity, as in the case of benefits received gratis. Now no benefactor confers a benefit equal to that which a man receives from his parents: wherefore in paying back benefits received, we should give the first place to our parents before all others, unless, on the other side, there be such weightier motives, as need or some other circumstance, for instance the common good of the Church or state. In other cases we must take to account the connection and the benefit received; and here again no general rule can laid down.

REPLY OBJ. 4: Parents are like superiors, and so a parent's love tends to conferring benefits, while the children's love tends to honor their parents. Nevertheless in a case of extreme urgency it would be lawful to abandon one's children rather than one's parents, to abandon whom it is by

licet, propter obligationem beneficiorum susceptorum; ut patet per Philosophum, in VIII Ethic.

no means lawful, on account of the obligation we lie under towards them for the benefits we have received from them, as the Philosopher states (*Ethic.* iii, 14).

# Article 4

*Whether beneficence is a special virtue?*

AD QUARTUM SIC PROCEDITUR. Videtur quod beneficentia sit specialis virtus. Praecepta enim ad virtutes ordinantur, quia *legislatores intendunt facere homines virtuosos*, sicut dicitur in II Ethic. Sed seorsum datur praeceptum de beneficentia et de dilectione, dicitur enim Matth. V, *diligite inimicos vestros, benefacite his qui oderunt vos.* Ergo beneficentia est virtus distincta a caritate.

PRAETEREA, vitia virtutibus opponuntur. Sed beneficentiae opponuntur aliqua specialia vitia, per quae nocumentum proximo infertur, puta rapina, furtum et alia huiusmodi. Ergo beneficentia est specialis virtus.

PRAETEREA, caritas non distinguitur in multas species. Sed beneficentia videtur distingui in multas species, secundum diversas beneficiorum species. Ergo beneficentia est alia virtus a caritate.

SED CONTRA est quod actus interior et exterior non requirunt diversas virtutes. Sed beneficentia et benevolentia non differunt nisi sicut actus exterior et interior, quia beneficentia est executio benevolentiae. Ergo, sicut benevolentia non est alia virtus a caritate, ita nec beneficentia.

RESPONDEO dicendum quod virtutes diversificantur secundum diversas rationes obiecti. Eadem autem est ratio formalis obiecti caritatis et beneficentiae, nam utraque respicit communem rationem boni, ut ex praedictis patet. Unde beneficentia non est alia virtus a caritate, sed nominat quendam caritatis actum.

AD PRIMUM ergo dicendum quod praecepta non dantur de habitibus virtutum, sed de actibus. Et ideo diversitas praeceptorum non significat diversos habitus virtutum, sed diversos actus.

AD SECUNDUM dicendum quod sicut omnia beneficia proximo exhibita, inquantum considerantur sub communi ratione boni, reducuntur ad amorem; ita omnia nocumenta, inquantum considerantur secundum communem rationem mali, reducuntur ad odium. Prout autem considerantur secundum aliquas speciales rationes vel boni vel mali, reducuntur ad aliquas speciales virtutes vel vitia. Et secundum hoc etiam sunt diversae beneficiorum species.

UNDE PATET responsio ad tertium.

OBJECTION 1: It would seem that beneficence is a special virtue. For precepts are directed to virtue, since *lawgivers purpose to make men virtuous* (*Ethic.* i 9, 13; ii, 1). Now beneficence and love are prescribed as distinct from one another, for it is written (Matt 4:44): *Love your enemies, do good to them that hate you.* Therefore beneficence is a virtue distinct from charity.

OBJ. 2: Further, vices are opposed to virtues. Now there are opposed to beneficence certain vices whereby a hurt is inflicted on our neighbor, for instance, rapine, theft and so forth. Therefore beneficence is a special virtue.

OBJ. 3: Further, charity is not divided into several species: whereas there would seem to be several kinds of beneficence, according to the various kinds of benefits. Therefore beneficence is a distinct virtue from charity.

ON THE CONTRARY, The internal and the external act do not require different virtues. Now beneficence and goodwill differ only as external and internal act, since beneficence is the execution of goodwill. Therefore as goodwill is not a distinct virtue from charity, so neither is beneficence.

I ANSWER THAT, Virtues differ according to the different aspects of their objects. Now the formal aspect of the object of charity and of beneficence is the same, since both virtues regard the common aspect of good, as explained above (A. 1). Wherefore beneficence is not a distinct virtue from charity, but denotes an act of charity.

REPLY OBJ. 1: Precepts are given, not about habits but about acts of virtue: wherefore distinction of precept denotes distinction, not of habits, but of acts.

REPLY OBJ. 2: Even as all benefits conferred on our neighbor, if we consider them under the common aspect of good, are to be traced to love, so all hurts considered under the common aspect of evil, are to be traced to hatred. But if we consider these same things under certain special aspects of good or of evil, they are to be traced to certain special virtues or vices, and in this way also there are various kinds of benefits.

HENCE the Reply to the Third Objection is evident.

# QUESTION 32

## ALMSGIVING

Deinde considerandum est de eleemosyna. Et circa hoc quaeruntur decem.

Primo, utrum eleemosynae largitio sit actus caritatis.

Secundo, de distinctione eleemosynarum.

Tertio, quae sint potiores eleemosynae, utrum spirituales vel corporales.

Quarto, utrum corporales eleemosynae habeant effectum spiritualem.

Quinto, utrum dare eleemosynas sit in praecepto.

Sexto, utrum corporalis eleemosyna sit danda de necessario.

Septimo, utrum sit danda de iniuste acquisito.

Octavo, quorum sit dare eleemosynam.

Nono, quibus sit danda.

Decimo, de modo dandi eleemosynas.

We must now consider almsgiving, under which head there are ten points of inquiry:

(1) Whether almsgiving is an act of charity?

(2) Of the different kinds of alms;

(3) Which alms are of greater account, spiritual or corporal?

(4) Whether corporal alms have a spiritual effect?

(5) Whether the giving of alms is a matter of precept?

(6) Whether corporal alms should be given out of the things we need?

(7) Whether corporal alms should be given out of ill-gotten goods?

(8) Who can give alms?

(9) To whom should we give alms?

(10) How should alms be given?

# Article 1

*Whether almsgiving is an act of charity?*

**AD PRIMUM SIC PROCEDITUR.** Videtur quod dare eleemosynam non sit actus caritatis. Actus enim caritatis non potest esse sine caritate. Sed largitio eleemosynarum potest esse sine caritate, secundum illud I ad Cor. XIII, *si distribuero in cibos pauperum omnes facultates meas, caritatem autem non habuero.* Ergo dare eleemosynam non est actus caritatis.

**PRAETEREA,** eleemosyna computatur inter opera satisfactionis, secundum illud Dan. IV, *peccata tua eleemosynis redime.* Sed satisfactio est actus iustitiae. Ergo dare eleemosynam non est actus caritatis, sed iustitiae.

**PRAETEREA,** offerre hostiam Deo est actus latriae. Sed dare eleemosynam est offerre hostiam Deo, secundum illud ad Heb. ult., *beneficentiae et communionis nolite oblivisci, talibus enim hostiis promeretur Deus.* Ergo caritatis non est actus dare eleemosynam, sed magis latriae.

**PRAETEREA,** philosophus dicit, in IV Ethic., quod dare aliquid propter bonum est actus liberalitatis. Sed hoc maxime fit in largitione eleemosynarum. Ergo dare eleemosynam non est actus caritatis.

**SED CONTRA** est quod dicitur I Ioan. III, *qui habuerit substantiam huius mundi, et viderit fratrem suum necessitatem patientem, et clauserit viscera sua ab eo, quomodo caritas Dei manet in illo?*

**OBJECTION 1**: It would seem that almsgiving is not an act of charity. For without charity one cannot do acts of charity. Now it is possible to give alms without having charity, according to 1 Cor. 13:3: *If I should distribute all my goods to feed the poor . . . and have not charity, it profiteth me nothing.* Therefore almsgiving is not an act of charity.

**OBJ. 2**: Further, almsdeeds are reckoned among works of satisfaction, according to Dan. 4:24: *Redeem thou thy sins with alms.* Now satisfaction is an act of justice. Therefore almsgiving is an act of justice and not of charity.

**OBJ. 3**: Further, the offering of sacrifices to God is an act of religion. But almsgiving is offering a sacrifice to God, according to Heb. 13:16: *Do not forget to do good and to impart, for by such sacrifices God's favor is obtained.* Therefore almsgiving is not an act of charity, but of religion.

**OBJ. 4**: Further, the Philosopher says (*Ethic.* iv, 1) that to give for a good purpose is an act of liberality. Now this is especially true of almsgiving. Therefore almsgiving is not an act of charity.

**ON THE CONTRARY,** It is written 2 John 3:17: *He that hath the substance of this world, and shall see his brother in need, and shall put up his bowels from him, how doth the charity of God abide in him?*

RESPONDEO dicendum quod exteriores actus ad illam virtutem referuntur ad quam pertinet id quod est motivum ad agendum huiusmodi actus. Motivum autem ad dandum eleemosynas est ut subveniatur necessitatem patienti, unde quidam, definientes eleemosynam, dicunt quod eleemosyna est *opus quo datur aliquid indigenti ex compassione propter Deum.* Quod quidem motivum pertinet ad misericordiam, ut supra dictum est. Unde manifestum est quod dare eleemosynam proprie est actus misericordiae. Et hoc apparet ex ipso nomine, nam in Graeco a *misericordia* derivatur, sicut in Latino *miseratio.* Et quia misericordia est effectus caritatis, ut supra ostensum est, ex consequenti dare eleemosynam est actus caritatis, misericordia mediante.

AD PRIMUM ergo dicendum quod aliquid dicitur esse actus virtutis dupliciter. Uno modo, materialiter, sicut actus iustitiae est facere iusta. Et talis actus virtutis potest esse sine virtute, multi enim non habentes habitum iustitiae iusta operantur, vel ex naturali ratione, vel ex timore sive ex spe aliquid adipiscendi. Alio modo dicitur esse aliquid actus virtutis formaliter, sicut actus iustitiae est actio iusta eo modo quo iustus facit, scilicet prompte et delectabiliter. Et hoc modo actus virtutis non est sine virtute.

Secundum hoc ergo dare eleemosynas materialiter potest esse sine caritate, formaliter autem eleemosynas dare, idest propter Deum, delectabiliter et prompte et omni eo modo quo debet, non est sine caritate.

AD SECUNDUM dicendum quod nihil prohibet actum qui est proprie unius virtutis elicitive, attribui alteri virtuti sicut imperanti et ordinanti ad suum finem. Et hoc modo dare eleemosynam ponitur inter opera satisfactoria, inquantum miseratio in defectum patientis ordinatur ad satisfaciendum pro culpa. Secundum autem quod ordinatur ad placandum Deum, habet rationem sacrificii, et sic imperatur a latria.

UNDE PATET responsio ad tertium.

AD QUARTUM dicendum quod dare eleemosynam pertinet ad liberalitatem inquantum liberalitas aufert impedimentum huius actus, quod esse posset ex superfluo amore divitiarum, propter quem aliquis efficitur nimis retentivus earum.

I ANSWER THAT, External acts belong to that virtue which regards the motive for doing those acts. Now the motive for giving alms is to relieve one who is in need. Wherefore some have defined alms as being *a deed whereby something is given to the needy, out of compassion and for God's sake,* which motive belongs to mercy, as stated above (Q. 30, AA. 1, 2). Hence it is clear that almsgiving is, properly speaking, an act of mercy. This appears in its very name, for in Greek (*eleemosyne*) it is derived from having mercy (*eleein*) even as the Latin *miseratio* is. And since mercy is an effect of charity, as shown above (Q. 30, A. 2, A. 3, Obj. 3), it follows that almsgiving is an act of charity through the medium of mercy.

REPLY OBJ. 1: An act of virtue may be taken in two ways: first materially, thus an act of justice is to do what is just; and such an act of virtue can be without the virtue, since many, without having the habit of justice, do what is just, led by the natural light of reason, or through fear, or in the hope of gain. Second, we speak of a thing being an act of justice formally, and thus an act of justice is to do what is just, in the same way as a just man, i.e., with readiness and delight, and such an act of virtue cannot be without the virtue.

Accordingly almsgiving can be materially without charity, but to give alms formally, i.e., for God's sake, with delight and readiness, and altogether as one ought, is not possible without charity.

REPLY OBJ. 2: Nothing hinders the proper elicited act of one virtue being commanded by another virtue as commanding it and directing it to this other virtue's end. It is in this way that almsgiving is reckoned among works of satisfaction insofar as pity for the one in distress is directed to the satisfaction for his sin; and insofar as it is directed to placate God, it has the character of a sacrifice, and thus it is commanded by religion.

WHEREFORE the Reply to the Third Objection is evident.

REPLY OBJ. 4: Almsgiving belongs to liberality, insofar as liberality removes an obstacle to that act, which might arise from excessive love of riches, the result of which is that one clings to them more than one ought.

# Article 2

*Whether the different kinds of almsdeeds are suitably enumerated?*

AD SECUNDUM SIC PROCEDITUR. Videtur quod inconvenienter eleemosynarum genera distinguantur. Ponuntur enim septem eleemosynae corporales, scilicet pascere esurientem, potare sitientem, vestire nudum, recolligere hospitem, visitare infirmum, redimere capti-

OBJECTION 1: It would seem that the different kinds of almsdeeds are unsuitably enumerated. For we reckon seven corporal almsdeeds, namely, to feed the hungry, to give drink to the thirsty, to clothe the naked, to harbor the harborless, to visit the sick, to ransom the captive, to bury

vum, et sepelire mortuum; quae in hoc versu continentur, *visito, poto, cibo, redimo, tego, colligo, condo*.

Ponuntur etiam aliae septem eleemosynae spirituales, scilicet docere ignorantem, consulere dubitanti, consolari tristem, corrigere peccantem, remittere offendenti, portare onerosos et graves, et pro omnibus orare; quae etiam in hoc versu continentur, *consule, castiga, solare, remitte, fer, ora*; ita tamen quod sub eodem intelligatur consilium et doctrina.

Videtur autem quod inconvenienter huiusmodi eleemosynae distinguantur. Eleemosyna enim ordinatur ad subveniendum proximo. Sed per hoc quod proximus sepelitur, in nullo ei subvenitur, alioquin non esset verum quod dominus dicit, Matth. X, *nolite timere eos qui occidunt corpus, et post hoc non habent amplius quid faciant*. Unde et dominus, Matth. XXV, commemorans misericordiae opera, de sepultura mortuorum mentionem non facit. Ergo videtur quod inconvenienter huiusmodi eleemosynae distinguantur.

PRAETEREA, eleemosyna datur ad subveniendum necessitatibus proximi, sicut dictum est. Sed multae aliae sunt necessitates humanae vitae quam praedictae, sicut quod caecus indiget ductore, claudus sustentatione, pauper divitiis. Ergo inconvenienter praedictae eleemosynae enumerantur.

PRAETEREA, dare eleemosynam est actus misericordiae. Sed corrigere delinquentem magis videtur ad severitatem pertinere quam ad misericordiam. Ergo non debet computari inter eleemosynas spirituales.

PRAETEREA, eleemosyna ordinatur ad subveniendum defectui. Sed nullus est homo qui defectum ignorantiae non patiatur in aliquibus. Ergo videtur quod quilibet debeat quemlibet docere, si ignoret id quod ipse scit.

SED CONTRA est quod Gregorius dicit, in quadam homilia, *habens intellectum curet omnino ne taceat; habens rerum affluentiam vigilet ne a misericordiae largitate torpescat; habens artem qua regitur magnopere studeat ut usum atque utilitatem illius cum proximo partiatur; habens loquendi locum apud divitem damnationem pro retento talento timeat si, cum valet, non apud eum pro pauperibus intercedat*. Ergo praedictae eleemosynae convenienter distinguuntur secundum ea in quibus homines abundant et deficiunt.

RESPONDEO dicendum quod praedicta eleemosynarum distinctio convenienter sumitur secundum diversos defectus proximorum. Quorum quidam sunt ex parte animae, ad quos ordinantur spirituales eleemosynae; quidam vero ex parte corporis, ad quos ordinantur eleemosynae corporales. Defectus enim corporalis aut est in vita, aut est post vitam. Si quidem est in vita, aut est communis defectus respectu eorum quibus omnes indigent; aut est specialis propter aliquod accidens superveniens.

the dead; all of which are expressed in the following verse: *To visit, to quench, to feed, to ransom, clothe, harbor or bury*.

Again we reckon seven spiritual alms, namely, to instruct the ignorant, to counsel the doubtful, to comfort the sorrowful, to reprove the sinner, to forgive injuries, to bear with those who trouble and annoy us, and to pray for all, which are all contained in the following verse: *To counsel, reprove, console, to pardon, forbear, and to pray*, yet so that counsel includes both advice and instruction.

And it seems that these various almsdeeds are unsuitably enumerated. For the purpose of almsdeeds is to succor our neighbor. But a dead man profits nothing by being buried, else Our Lord would not have spoken truly when He said (Matt 10:28): *Be not afraid of them who kill the body, and after that have no more that they can do*. This explains why Our Lord, in enumerating the works of mercy, made no mention of the burial of the dead (Matt 25:35, 36). Therefore it seems that these almsdeeds are unsuitably enumerated.

OBJ. 2: Further, as stated above (A. 1), the purpose of giving alms is to relieve our neighbor's need. Now there are many needs of human life other than those mentioned above, for instance, a blind man needs a leader, a lame man needs someone to lean on, a poor man needs riches. Therefore these almsdeeds are unsuitably enumerated.

OBJ. 3: Further, almsgiving is a work of mercy. But the reproof of the wrong-doer savors, apparently, of severity rather than of mercy. Therefore it ought not to be reckoned among the spiritual almsdeeds.

OBJ. 4: Further, almsgiving is intended for the supply of a defect. But no man is without the defect of ignorance in some matter or other. Therefore, apparently, each one ought to instruct anyone who is ignorant of what he knows himself.

ON THE CONTRARY, Gregory says (*Nom. in Evang.* ix): *Let him that hath understanding beware lest he withhold his knowledge; let him that hath abundance of wealth, watch lest he slacken his merciful bounty; let him who is a servant to art be most solicitous to share his skill and profit with his neighbor; let him who has an opportunity of speaking with the wealthy, fear lest he be condemned for retaining his talent, if when he has the chance he plead not with him the cause of the poor*. Therefore the aforesaid almsdeeds are suitably enumerated in respect of those things whereof men have abundance or insufficiency.

I ANSWER THAT, The aforesaid distinction of almsdeeds is suitably taken from the various needs of our neighbor: some of which affect the soul, and are relieved by spiritual almsdeeds, while others affect the body, and are relieved by corporal almsdeeds. For corporal need occurs either during this life or afterwards. If it occurs during this life, it is either a common need in respect of things needed by all, or it is a special need occurring through some accident supervening. In the first case, the need is either internal or

Si primo modo, aut defectus est interior, aut exterior. Interior quidem est duplex, unus quidem cui subvenitur per alimentum siccum, scilicet fames, et secundum hoc ponitur pascere esurientem; alius autem est cui subvenitur per alimentum humidum, scilicet sitis, et secundum hoc dicitur potare sitientem. Defectus autem communis respectu exterioris auxilii est duplex, unus respectu tegumenti, et quantum ad hoc ponitur vestire nudum; alius est respectu habitaculi, et quantum ad hoc est suscipere hospitem. Similiter autem si sit defectus aliquis specialis, aut est ex causa intrinseca, sicut infirmitas, et quantum ad hoc ponitur visitare infirmum, aut ex causa extrinseca, et quantum ad hoc ponitur redemptio captivorum. Post vitam autem exhibetur mortuis sepultura.

Similiter autem spiritualibus defectibus spiritualibus actibus subvenitur dupliciter. Uno modo, poscendo auxilium a Deo, et quantum ad hoc ponitur oratio, qua quis pro aliis orat. Alio modo, impendendo humanum auxilium, et hoc tripliciter. Uno modo, contra defectum intellectus, et si quidem sit defectus speculativi intellectus, adhibetur ei remedium per doctrinam; si autem practici intellectus, adhibetur ei remedium per consilium. Alio modo est defectus ex passione appetitivae virtutis, inter quos est maximus tristitia, cui subvenitur per consolationem. Tertio modo, ex parte inordinati actus, qui quidem tripliciter considerari potest. Uno modo, ex parte ipsius peccantis, inquantum procedit ab eius inordinata voluntate, et sic adhibetur remedium per correctionem. Alio modo, ex parte eius in quem peccatur, et sic, si quidem sit peccatum in nos, remedium adhibemus remittendo offensam; si autem sit in Deum vel in proximum, *non est nostri arbitrii remittere*, ut Hieronymus dicit, super Matth. Tertio modo, ex parte sequelae ipsius actus inordinati, ex qua gravantur ei conviventes, etiam praeter peccantis intentionem, et sic remedium adhibetur supportando; maxime in his qui ex infirmitate peccant, secundum illud Rom. XV, *debemus nos firmiores infirmitates aliorum portare*. Et non solum secundum quod infirmi sunt graves ex inordinatis actibus, sed etiam quaecumque eorum onera sunt supportanda, secundum illud Galat. VI, *alter alterius onera portate*.

**AD PRIMUM** ergo dicendum quod sepultura mortui non confert ei quantum ad sensum quem corpus post mortem habeat. Et secundum hoc dominus dicit quod interficientes corpus non habent amplius quid faciant. Et propter hoc etiam dominus non commemorat sepulturam inter alia misericordiae opera, sed numerat solum illa quae sunt evidentioris necessitatis. Pertinet tamen ad defunctum quid de eius corpore agatur, tum quantum ad hoc quod vivit in memoriis hominum, cuius honor dehonestatur si insepultus remaneat; tum etiam

external. Internal need is twofold: one which is relieved by solid food, viz. hunger, in respect of which we have to feed the hungry; while the other is relieved by liquid food, viz. thirst, and in respect of this we have to give drink to the thirsty. The common need with regard to external help is twofold; one in respect of clothing, and as to this we have to clothe the naked: while the other is in respect of a dwelling place, and as to this we have to harbor the harborless. Again if the need be special, it is either the result of an internal cause, like sickness, and then we have to visit the sick, or it results from an external cause, and then we have to ransom the captive. After this life we give burial to the dead.

In like manner spiritual needs are relieved by spiritual acts in two ways, first by asking for help from God, and in this respect we have prayer, whereby one man prays for others; second, by giving human assistance, and this in three ways. First, in order to relieve a deficiency on the part of the intellect, and if this deficiency be in the speculative intellect, the remedy is applied by instructing, and if in the practical intellect, the remedy is applied by counselling. Second, there may be a deficiency on the part of the appetitive power, especially by way of sorrow, which is remedied by comforting. Third, the deficiency may be due to an inordinate act; and this may be the subject of a threefold consideration. First, in respect of the sinner, inasmuch as the sin proceeds from his inordinate will, and thus the remedy takes the form of reproof. Second, in respect of the person sinned against; and if the sin be committed against ourselves, we apply the remedy by pardoning the injury, while, if it be committed against God or our neighbor, *it is not in our power to pardon*, as Jerome observes (*Super Matth.* xviii, 15). Third, in respect of the result of the inordinate act, on account of which the sinner is an annoyance to those who live with him, even beside his intention; in which case the remedy is applied by bearing with him, especially with regard to those who sin out of weakness, according to Rom. 15:1: *We that are stronger, ought to bear the infirmities of the weak*, and not only as regards their being infirm and consequently troublesome on account of their unruly actions, but also by bearing any other burdens of theirs with them, according to Gal. 6:2: *Bear ye one another's burdens.*

**REPLY OBJ. 1:** Burial does not profit a dead man as though his body could be capable of perception after death. In this sense Our Lord said that those who kill the body have no more that they can do; and for this reason He did not mention the burial of the dead with the other works of mercy, but those only which are more clearly necessary. Nevertheless it does concern the deceased what is done with his body: both that he may live in the memory of man whose respect he forfeits if he remain without burial, and as regards a man's fondness for his own body while he was

quantum ad affectum quem adhuc vivens habebat de suo corpore, cui piorum affectus conformari debet post mortem ipsius. Et secundum hoc aliqui commendantur de mortuorum sepultura, ut Tobias et illi qui dominum sepelierunt; ut patet per Augustinum, in libro de cura pro mortuis agenda.

**AD SECUNDUM** dicendum quod omnes aliae necessitates ad has reducuntur. Nam et caecitas et claudicatio sunt infirmitates quaedam, unde dirigere caecum et sustentare claudum reducitur ad visitationem infirmorum. Similiter etiam subvenire homini contra quamcumque oppressionem illatam extrinsecus reducitur ad redemptionem captivorum. Divitiae autem, quibus paupertati subvenitur, non quaeruntur nisi ad subveniendum praedictis defectibus, et ideo non fuit specialis mentio de hoc defectu facienda.

**AD TERTIUM** dicendum quod correctio peccantium, quantum ad ipsam executionem actus, severitatem iustitiae continere videtur. Sed quantum ad intentionem corrigentis, qui vult hominem a malo culpae liberare, pertinet ad misericordiam et dilectionis affectum, secundum illud Prov. XXVII, *meliora sunt verbera diligentis quam fraudulenta oscula odientis.*

**AD QUARTUM** dicendum quod non quaelibet nescientia pertinet ad hominis defectum, sed solum ea qua quis nescit ea quae convenit eum scire, cui defectui per doctrinam subvenire ad eleemosynam pertinet. In quo tamen observandae sunt debitae circumstantiae personae et loci et temporis, sicut et in aliis actibus virtuosis.

yet living, a fondness which kindly persons should imitate after his death. It is thus that some are praised for burying the dead, as Tobias, and those who buried Our Lord; as Augustine says (*De Cura pro Mort.* iii).

**REPLY OBJ. 2**: All other needs are reduced to these, for blindness and lameness are kinds of sickness, so that to lead the blind, and to support the lame, come to the same as visiting the sick. In like manner to assist a man against any distress that is due to an extrinsic cause comes to the same as the ransom of captives. And the wealth with which we relieve the poor is sought merely for the purpose of relieving the aforesaid needs: hence there was no reason for special mention of this particular need.

**REPLY OBJ. 3**: The reproof of the sinner, as to the exercise of the act of reproving, seems to imply the severity of justice, but, as to the intention of the reprover, who wishes to free a man from the evil of sin, it is an act of mercy and lovingkindness, according to Prov. 27:6: *Better are the wounds of a friend, than the deceitful kisses of an enemy.*

**REPLY OBJ. 4**: Nescience is not always a defect, but only when it is about what one ought to know, and it is a part of almsgiving to supply this defect by instruction. In doing this however we should observe the due circumstances of persons, place and time, even as in other virtuous acts.

# Article 3

*Whether corporal alms are of more account than spiritual alms?*

**AD TERTIUM SIC PROCEDITUR.** Videtur quod eleemosynae corporales sint potiores quam spirituales. Laudabilius enim est magis indigenti eleemosynam facere, ex hoc enim eleemosyna laudem habet quod indigenti subvenit. Sed corpus, cui subvenitur per eleemosynas corporales, est indigentioris naturae quam spiritus, cui subvenitur per eleemosynas spirituales. Ergo eleemosynae corporales sunt potiores.

**PRAETEREA**, recompensatio beneficii laudem et meritum eleemosynae minuit, unde et dominus dicit, Luc. XIV, *cum facis prandium aut cenam, noli vocare vicinos divites, ne forte et ipsi te reinvitent.* Sed in eleemosynis spiritualibus semper est recompensatio, quia qui orat pro alio sibi proficit, secundum illud Psalm., *oratio mea in sinu meo convertetur*; qui etiam alium docet, ipse in scientia proficit. Quod non contingit in eleemosynis cor-

**OBJECTION 1**: It would seem that corporal alms are of more account than spiritual alms. For it is more praiseworthy to give an alms to one who is in greater want, since an almsdeed is to be praised because it relieves one who is in need. Now the body which is relieved by corporal alms, is by nature more needy than the spirit which is relieved by spiritual alms. Therefore corporal alms are of more account.

**OBJ. 2**: Further, an alms is less praiseworthy and meritorious if the kindness is compensated, wherefore Our Lord says (Luke 14:12): *When thou makest a dinner or a supper, call not thy neighbors who are rich, lest perhaps they also invite thee again.* Now there is always compensation in spiritual almsdeeds, since he who prays for another, profits thereby, according to Ps. 34:13: *My prayer shall be turned into my bosom*: and he who teaches another, makes progress

poralibus. Ergo eleemosynae corporales sunt potiores quam spirituales.

**PRAETEREA**, ad laudem eleemosynae pertinet quod pauper ex eleemosyna data consoletur, unde Iob XXXI dicitur, *si non benedixerunt mihi latera eius*; et ad Philemonem dicit apostolus, *viscera sanctorum requieverunt per te, frater*. Sed quandoque magis est grata pauperi eleemosyna corporalis quam spiritualis. Ergo eleemosyna corporalis potior est quam spiritualis.

**SED CONTRA** est quod Augustinus, in libro de Serm. Dom. in monte, super illud, *qui petit a te, da ei*, dicit, *dandum est quod nec tibi nec alteri noceat, et cum negaveris quod petit, indicanda est iustitia, ut non eum inanem dimittas. Et aliquando melius aliquid dabis, cum iniuste petentem correxeris*. Correctio autem est eleemosyna spiritualis. Ergo spirituales eleemosynae sunt corporalibus praeferendae.

**RESPONDEO** dicendum quod comparatio istarum eleemosynarum potest attendi dupliciter. Uno modo, simpliciter loquendo, et secundum hoc eleemosynae spirituales praeeminent, triplici ratione. Primo quidem quia id quod exhibetur nobilius est, scilicet donum spirituale, quod praeeminet corporali, secundum illud Prov. IV, *donum bonum tribuam vobis, legem meam ne derelinquatis*. Secundo, ratione eius cui subvenitur, quia spiritus nobilior est corpore. Unde sicut homo sibi ipsi magis debet providere quantum ad spiritum quam quantum ad corpus, ita et proximo, quem debet tanquam seipsum diligere. Tertio, quantum ad ipsos actus quibus subvenitur proximo, quia spirituales actus sunt nobiliores corporalibus, qui sunt quodammodo serviles.

Alio modo possunt comparari secundum aliquem particularem casum, in quo quaedam corporalis eleemosyna alicui spirituali praefertur. Puta, magis esset pascendum fame morientem quam docendum, sicut et *indigenti*, secundum philosophum, *melius est ditari quam philosophari*, quamvis hoc sit simpliciter melius.

**AD PRIMUM** ergo dicendum quod dare magis indigenti melius est, ceteris paribus. Sed si minus indigens sit melior, et melioribus indigeat, dare ei melius est. Et sic est in proposito.

**AD SECUNDUM** dicendum quod recompensatio non minuit meritum et laudem eleemosynae si non sit intenta, sicut etiam humana gloria, si non sit intenta, non minuit rationem virtutis; sicut et de Catone Sallustius dicit quod *quo magis gloriam fugiebat, eo magis eum gloria sequebatur*. Et ita contingit in clccmosynis spiritualibus.

Et tamen intentio bonorum spiritualium non minuit meritum, sicut intentio bonorum corporalium.

in knowledge, which cannot be said of corporal almsdeeds. Therefore corporal almsdeeds are of more account than spiritual almsdeeds.

**OBJ. 3**: Further, an alms is to be commended if the needy one is comforted by it: wherefore it is written (Job 31:20): *If his sides have not blessed me*, and the Apostle says to Philemon (verse 7): *The bowels of the saints have been refreshed by thee, brother*. Now a corporal alms is sometimes more welcome to a needy man than a spiritual alms. Therefore bodily almsdeeds are of more account than spiritual almsdeeds.

**ON THE CONTRARY**, Augustine says (*De Serm. Dom. in Monte* i, 20) on the words, *Give to him that asketh of thee* (Matt 5:42): *You should give so as to injure neither yourself nor another, and when you refuse what another asks you must not lose sight of the claims of justice, and send him away empty; at times indeed you will give what is better than what is asked for, if you reprove him that asks unjustly*. Now reproof is a spiritual alms. Therefore spiritual almsdeeds are preferable to corporal almsdeeds.

**I ANSWER THAT**, There are two ways of comparing these almsdeeds. First, simply; and in this respect, spiritual almsdeeds hold the first place, for three reasons. First, because the offering is more excellent, since it is a spiritual gift, which surpasses a corporal gift, according to Prov. 4:2: *I will give you a good gift, forsake not My Law*. Second, on account of the object succored, because the spirit is more excellent than the body, wherefore, even as a man in looking after himself, ought to look to his soul more than to his body, so ought he in looking after his neighbor, whom he ought to love as himself. Third, as regards the acts themselves by which our neighbor is succored, because spiritual acts are more excellent than corporal acts, which are, in a fashion, servile.

Second, we may compare them with regard to some particular case, when some corporal alms excels some spiritual alms: for instance, a man in hunger is to be fed rather than instructed, and as the Philosopher observes (*Topic*. iii, 2), for a needy man *money is better than philosophy*, although the latter is better simply.

**REPLY OBJ. 1**: It is better to give to one who is in greater want, other things being equal, but if he who is less needy is better, and is in want of better things, it is better to give to him: and it is thus in the case in point.

**REPLY OBJ. 2**: Compensation does not detract from merit and praise if it be not intended, even as human glory, if not intended, does not detract from virtue. Thus Sallust says of Cato (*Catilin*.), that *the less he sought fame, the more he became famous*: and thus it is with spiritual almsdeeds.

Nevertheless the intention of gaining spiritual goods does not detract from merit, as the intention of gaining corporal goods.

**AD TERTIUM** dicendum quod meritum dantis eleemosynam attenditur secundum id in quo debet rationabiliter requiescere voluntas accipientis, non in eo in quo requiescit si sit inordinata.

**REPLY OBJ. 3**: The merit of an almsgiver depends on that in which the will of the recipient rests reasonably, and not on that in which it rests when it is inordinate.

# Article 4

*Whether corporal almsdeeds have a spiritual effect?*

**AD QUARTUM SIC PROCEDITUR**. Videtur quod eleemosynae corporales non habeant effectum spiritualem. Effectus enim non est potior sua causa. Sed bona spiritualia sunt potiora corporalibus. Non ergo eleemosynae corporales habent spirituales effectus.

**PRAETEREA**, dare corporale pro spirituali vitium simoniae est. Sed hoc vitium est omnino vitandum. Non ergo sunt dandae eleemosynae ad consequendum spirituales effectus.

**PRAETEREA**, multiplicata causa, multiplicatur effectus. Si igitur eleemosyna corporalis causaret spiritualem effectum, sequeretur quod maior eleemosyna magis spiritualiter proficeret. Quod est contra illud quod legitur Luc. XXI de vidua mittente duo aera minuta in gazophylacium, quae, secundum sententiam domini, *plus omnibus misit*. Non ergo eleemosyna corporalis habet spiritualem effectum.

**SED CONTRA** est quod dicitur Eccli. XXIX, *eleemosyna viri gratiam hominis quasi pupillam conservabit*.

**RESPONDEO** dicendum quod eleemosyna corporalis tripliciter potest considerari. Uno modo, secundum suam substantiam. Et secundum hoc non habet nisi corporalem effectum, inquantum scilicet supplet corporales defectus proximorum. Alio modo potest considerari ex parte causae eius, inquantum scilicet aliquis eleemosynam corporalem dat propter dilectionem Dei et proximi. Et quantum ad hoc affert fructum spiritualem, secundum illud Eccli. XXIX, *perde pecuniam propter fratrem. Pone thesaurum in praeceptis altissimi, et proderit tibi magis quam aurum.*

Tertio modo, ex parte effectus. Et sic etiam habet spiritualem fructum, inquantum scilicet proximus, cui per corporalem eleemosynam subvenitur, movetur ad orandum pro benefactore. Unde et ibidem subditur, *conclude eleemosynam in sinu pauperis, et haec pro te exorabit ab omni malo.*

**AD PRIMUM** ergo dicendum quod ratio illa procedit de corporali eleemosyna secundum suam substantiam.

**AD SECUNDUM** dicendum quod ille qui dat eleemosynam non intendit emere aliquid spirituale per corporale, quia scit spiritualia in infinitum corporalibus

**OBJECTION 1**: It would seem that corporal almsdeeds have not a spiritual effect. For no effect exceeds its cause. But spiritual goods exceed corporal goods. Therefore corporal almsdeeds have no spiritual effect.

**OBJ. 2**: Further, the sin of simony consists in giving the corporal for the spiritual, and it is to be utterly avoided. Therefore one ought not to give alms in order to receive a spiritual effect.

**OBJ. 3**: Further, to multiply the cause is to multiply the effect. If therefore corporal almsdeeds cause a spiritual effect, the greater the alms, the greater the spiritual profit, which is contrary to what we read (Luke 21:3) of the widow who cast two brass mites into the treasury, and in Our Lord's own words *cast in more than . . . all*. Therefore bodily almsdeeds have no spiritual effect.

**ON THE CONTRARY**, It is written (Sir 17:18): *The alms of a man . . . shall preserve the grace of a man as the apple of the eye.*

**I ANSWER THAT**, Corporal almsdeeds may be considered in three ways. First, with regard to their substance, and in this way they have merely a corporal effect, inasmuch as they supply our neighbor's corporal needs. Second, they may be considered with regard to their cause, insofar as a man gives a corporal alms out of love for God and his neighbor, and in this respect they bring forth a spiritual fruit, according to Ecclus. 29:13, 14: *Lose thy money for thy brother . . . place thy treasure in the commandments of the Most High, and it shall bring thee more profit than gold.*

Third, with regard to the effect, and in this way again, they have a spiritual fruit, inasmuch as our neighbor, who is succored by a corporal alms, is moved to pray for his benefactor; wherefore the above text goes on (Sir 29:15): *Shut up alms in the heart of the poor, and it shall obtain help for thee from all evil.*

**REPLY OBJ. 1**: This argument considers corporal almsdeeds as to their substance.

**REPLY OBJ. 2**: He who gives an alms does not intend to buy a spiritual thing with a corporal thing, for he knows that spiritual things infinitely surpass corporal things, but

praeeminere, sed intendit per caritatis affectum spiritualem fructum promereri.

**AD TERTIUM** dicendum quod vidua, quae minus dedit secundum quantitatem, plus dedit secundum suam proportionem; ex quo pensatur in ipsa maior caritatis affectus, ex qua corporalis eleemosyna spiritualem efficaciam habet.

he intends to merit a spiritual fruit through the love of charity.

**REPLY OBJ. 3:** The widow who gave less in quantity, gave more in proportion; and thus we gather that the fervor of her charity, whence corporal almsdeeds derive their spiritual efficacy, was greater.

# Article 5

*Whether almsgiving is a matter of precept?*

**AD QUINTUM SIC PROCEDITUR.** Videtur quod dare eleemosynam non sit in praecepto. Consilia enim a praeceptis distinguuntur. Sed dare eleemosynam est consilium, secundum illud Dan. IV, *consilium meum regi placeat, peccata tua eleemosynis redime.* Ergo dare eleemosynam non est in praecepto.

**PRAETEREA,** cuilibet licet sua re uti et eam retinere. Sed retinendo rem suam aliquis eleemosynam non dabit. Ergo licitum est eleemosynam non dare. Non ergo dare eleemosynam est in praecepto.

**PRAETEREA,** omne quod cadit sub praecepto aliquo tempore obligat transgressores ad peccatum mortale, quia praecepta affirmativa obligant pro tempore determinato. Si ergo dare eleemosynam caderet sub praecepto, esset determinare aliquod tempus in quo homo peccaret mortaliter nisi eleemosynam daret. Sed hoc non videtur, quia semper probabiliter aestimari potest quod pauperi aliter subveniri possit; et quod id quod est in eleemosynas erogandum possit ei esse necessarium vel in praesenti vel in futuro. Ergo videtur quod dare eleemosynam non sit in praecepto.

**PRAETEREA,** omnia praecepta reducuntur ad praecepta Decalogi. Sed inter illa praecepta nihil continetur de datione eleemosynarum. Ergo dare eleemosynas non est in praecepto.

**SED CONTRA,** nullus punitur poena aeterna pro omissione alicuius quod non cadit sub praecepto. Sed aliqui puniuntur poena aeterna pro omissione eleemosynarum; ut patet Matth. XXV. Ergo dare eleemosynam est in praecepto.

**RESPONDEO** dicendum quod cum dilectio proximi sit in praecepto, necesse est omnia illa cadere sub praecepto sine quibus dilectio proximi non conservatur. Ad dilectionem autem proximi pertinet ut proximo non solum velimus bonum, sed etiam operemur, secundum illud I Ioan. III, *non diligamus verbo neque lingua, sed opere et veritate.* Ad hoc autem quod velimus et operemur bonum alicuius requiritur quod eius necessitati subveniamus, quod fit per eleemosynarum largitionem. Et ideo eleemosynarum largitio est in praecepto.

**OBJECTION 1:** It would seem that almsgiving is not a matter of precept. For the counsels are distinct from the precepts. Now almsgiving is a matter of counsel, according to Dan. 4:24: *Let my counsel be acceptable to the King; redeem thou thy sins with alms.* Therefore almsgiving is not a matter of precept.

**OBJ. 2:** Further, it is lawful for everyone to use and to keep what is his own. Yet by keeping it he will not give alms. Therefore it is lawful not to give alms: and consequently almsgiving is not a matter of precept.

**OBJ. 3:** Further, whatever is a matter of precept binds the transgressor at some time or other under pain of mortal sin, because positive precepts are binding for some fixed time. Therefore, if almsgiving were a matter of precept, it would be possible to point to some fixed time when a man would commit a mortal sin unless he gave an alms. But it does not appear how this can be so, because it can always be deemed probable that the person in need can be relieved in some other way, and that what we would spend in almsgiving might be needful to ourselves either now or in some future time. Therefore it seems that almsgiving is not a matter of precept.

**OBJ. 4:** Further, every commandment is reducible to the precepts of the Decalogue. But these precepts contain no reference to almsgiving. Therefore almsgiving is not a matter of precept.

**ON THE CONTRARY,** No man is punished eternally for omitting to do what is not a matter of precept. But some are punished eternally for omitting to give alms, as is clear from Matt. 25:41–43. Therefore almsgiving is a matter of precept.

**I ANSWER THAT,** As love of our neighbor is a matter of precept, whatever is a necessary condition to the love of our neighbor is a matter of precept also. Now the love of our neighbor requires that not only should we be our neighbor's well-wishers, but also his well-doers, according to 1 John 3:18: *Let us not love in word, nor in tongue, but in deed, and in truth.* And in order to be a person's well-wisher and well-doer, we ought to succor his needs: this is done by almsgiving. Therefore almsgiving is a matter of precept.

Sed quia praecepta dantur de actibus virtutum, necesse est quod hoc modo donum eleemosynae cadat sub praecepto, secundum quod actus est de necessitate virtutis, scilicet secundum quod recta ratio requirit. Secundum quam est aliquid considerandum ex parte dantis; et aliquid ex parte eius cui est eleemosyna danda. Ex parte quidem dantis considerandum est ut id quod est in eleemosynas erogandum sit ei superfluum, secundum illud Luc. XI, *quod superest date eleemosynam.* Et dico superfluum non solum respectu sui ipsius, quod est supra id quod est necessarium individuo; sed etiam respectu aliorum quorum cura sibi incumbit, quia prius oportet quod unusquisque sibi provideat et his quorum cura ei incumbit (respectu quorum dicitur necessarium personae secundum quod persona dignitatem importat), et postea de residuo aliorum necessitatibus subveniatur sicut et natura primo accipit sibi, ad sustentationem proprii corporis, quod est necessarium ministerio virtutis nutritivae; superfluum autem erogat ad generationem alterius per virtutem generativam.

Ex parte autem recipientis requiritur quod necessitatem habeat, alioquin non esset ratio quare eleemosyna ei daretur. Sed cum non possit ab aliquo uno omnibus necessitatem habentibus subveniri, non omnis necessitas obligat ad praeceptum, sed illa sola sine qua is qui necessitatem patitur sustentari non potest. In illo enim casu locum habet quod Ambrosius dicit, *pasce fame morientem. Si non paveris, occidisti.* Sic igitur dare eleemosynam de superfluo est in praecepto; et dare eleemosynam ei qui est in extrema necessitate. Alias autem eleemosynam dare est in consilio, sicut et de quolibet meliori bono dantur consilia.

**AD PRIMUM** ergo dicendum quod Daniel loquebatur regi qui non erat legi Dei subiectus. Et ideo ea etiam quae pertinent ad praeceptum legis, quam non profitebatur, erant ei proponenda per modum consilii. Vel potest dici quod loquebatur in casu illo in quo dare eleemosynam non est in praecepto.

**AD SECUNDUM** dicendum quod bona temporalia, quae homini divinitus conferuntur, eius quidem sunt quantum ad proprietatem, sed quantum ad usum non solum debent esse eius, sed etiam aliorum, qui ex eis sustentari possunt ex eo quod ei superfluit. Unde Basilius dicit, *si fateris ea tibi divinitus provenisse* (scilicet temporalia bona) *an iniustus est Deus inaequaliter res nobis distribuens? Cur tu abundas, ille vero mendicat, nisi ut tu bonae dispensationis merita consequaris, ille vero patientiae braviis decoretur? Est panis famelici quem tu tenes, nudi tunica quam in conclavi conservas, discalceati calceus qui penes te marcescit, indigentis argentum quod possides inhumatum. Quocirca tot iniuriaris quot dare valeres.* Et hoc idem dicit Ambrosius, in Decret., dist. XLVII.

Since, however, precepts are about acts of virtue, it follows that all almsgiving must be a matter of precept, insofar as it is necessary to virtue, namely, insofar as it is demanded by right reason. Now right reason demands that we should take into consideration something on the part of the giver, and something on the part of the recipient. On the part of the giver, it must be noted that he should give of his surplus, according to Luke 11:41: *That which remaineth, give alms.* This surplus is to be taken in reference not only to himself, so as to denote what is unnecessary to the individual, but also in reference to those of whom he has charge (in which case we have the expression *necessary to the person* taking the word *person* as expressive of dignity). Because each one must first of all look after himself and then after those over whom he has charge, and afterwards with what remains relieve the needs of others. Thus nature first, by its nutritive power, takes what it requires for the upkeep of one's own body, and afterwards yields the residue for the formation of another by the power of generation.

On the part of the recipient it is requisite that he should be in need, else there would be no reason for giving him alms: yet since it is not possible for one individual to relieve the needs of all, we are not bound to relieve all who are in need, but only those who could not be succored if we not did succor them. For in such cases the words of Ambrose apply, *Feed him that dies of hunger: if thou hast not fed him, thou hast slain him.* Accordingly we are bound to give alms of our surplus, as also to give alms to one whose need is extreme: otherwise almsgiving, like any other greater good, is a matter of counsel.

**REPLY OBJ. 1:** Daniel spoke to a king who was not subject to God's Law, wherefore such things as were prescribed by the Law which he did not profess, had to be counselled to him. Or he may have been speaking in reference to a case in which almsgiving was not a matter of precept.

**REPLY OBJ. 2:** The temporal goods which God grants us, are ours as to the ownership, but as to the use of them, they belong not to us alone but also to such others as we are able to succor out of what we have over and above our needs. Hence Basil says: *If you acknowledge them,* viz. your temporal goods, *as coming from God, is He unjust because He apportions them unequally? Why are you rich while another is poor, unless it be that you may have the merit of a good stewardship, and he the reward of patience? It is the hungry man's bread that you withhold, the naked man's cloak that you have stored away, the shoe of the barefoot that you have left to rot, the money of the needy that you have buried underground: and so you injure as many as you might help.* Ambrose expresses himself in the same way.

**AD TERTIUM** dicendum quod est aliquod tempus dare in quo mortaliter peccat si eleemosynam dare omittat, ex parte quidem recipientis, cum apparet evidens et urgens necessitas, nec apparet in promptu qui ei subveniat; ex parte vero dantis, cum habet superflua quae secundum statum praesentem non sunt sibi necessaria, prout probabiliter aestimari potest. Nec oportet quod consideret ad omnes casus qui possunt contingere in futurum, hoc enim esset *de crastino cogitare*, quod dominus prohibet, Matth. VI. Sed debet diiudicari superfluum et necessarium secundum ea quae probabiliter et ut in pluribus occurrunt.

**AD QUARTUM** dicendum quod omnis subventio proximi reducitur ad praeceptum de honoratione parentum. Sic enim et apostolus interpretatur, I ad Tim. IV, dicens, *pietas ad omnia utilis est, promissionem habens vitae quae nunc est et futurae*, quod dicit quia in praecepto de honoratione parentum additur promissio, ut sis longaevus super terram. Sub pietate autem comprehenditur omnis eleemosynarum largitio.

**REPLY OBJ. 3**: There is a time when we sin mortally if we omit to give alms; on the part of the recipient when we see that his need is evident and urgent, and that he is not likely to be succored otherwise—on the part of the giver, when he has superfluous goods, which he does not need for the time being, as far as he can judge with probability. Nor need he consider every case that may possibly occur in the future, for this would be *to think about the morrow*, which Our Lord forbade us to do (Matt 6:34), but he should judge what is superfluous and what necessary, according as things probably and generally occur.

**REPLY OBJ. 4**: All succor given to our neighbor is reduced to the precept about honoring our parents. For thus does the Apostle interpret it (1 Tim 4:8) where he says: *Dutifulness is profitable to all things, having promise of the life that now is, and of that which is to come*, and he says this because the precept about honoring our parents contains the promise, *that thou mayest be longlived upon the land* (Exod 20:12): and dutifulness comprises all kinds of almsgiving.

# Article 6

*Whether one ought to give alms out of what one needs?*

**AD SEXTUM SIC PROCEDITUR**. Videtur quod aliquis non debeat eleemosynam dare de necessario. Ordo enim caritatis non minus attenditur penes effectum beneficii quam penes interiorem affectum. Peccat autem qui praepostere agit in ordine caritatis, quia ordo caritatis est in praecepto. Cum ergo ex ordine caritatis plus debeat aliquis se quam proximum diligere, videtur quod peccet si subtrahat sibi necessaria ut alteri largiatur.

**PRAETEREA**, quicumque largitur de his quae sunt necessaria sibi est propriae substantiae dissipator, quod pertinet ad prodigum, ut patet per Philosophum, in IV Ethic. Sed nullum opus vitiosum est faciendum. Ergo non est danda eleemosyna de necessario.

**PRAETEREA**, apostolus dicit, I ad Tim. V, *si quis suorum, et maxime domesticorum curam non habet, fidem negavit et est infideli deterior*. Sed quod aliquis det de his quae sunt sibi necessaria vel suis videtur derogare curae quam quis debet habere de se et de suis. Ergo videtur quod quicumque de necessariis eleemosynam dat, quod graviter peccet.

**SED CONTRA** est quod dominus dicit, Matth. XIX, *si vis perfectus esse, vade et vende omnia quae habes, et da pauperibus*. Sed ille qui dat omnia quae habet pauperibus non solum dat superflua sed etiam necessaria. Ergo de necessariis potest homo eleemosynam dare.

**OBJECTION 1**: It would seem that one ought not to give alms out of what one needs. For the order of charity should be observed not only as regards the effect of our benefactions but also as regards our interior affections. Now it is a sin to contravene the order of charity, because this order is a matter of precept. Since, then, the order of charity requires that a man should love himself more than his neighbor, it seems that he would sin if he deprived himself of what he needed, in order to succor his neighbor.

**OBJ. 2**: Further, whoever gives away what he needs himself, squanders his own substance, and that is to be a prodigal, according to the Philosopher (*Ethic.* iv, 1). But no sinful deed should be done. Therefore we should not give alms out of what we need.

**OBJ. 3**: Further, the Apostle says (1 Tim 5:8): *If any man have not care of his own, and especially of those of his house, he hath denied the faith, and is worse than an infidel.* Now if a man gives of what he needs for himself or for his charge, he seems to detract from the care he should have for himself or his charge. Therefore it seems that whoever gives alms from what he needs, sins gravely.

**ON THE CONTRARY**, Our Lord said (Matt 19:21): *If thou wilt be perfect, go, sell what thou hast, and give to the poor.* Now he that gives all he has to the poor, gives not only what he needs not, but also what he needs. Therefore a man may give alms out of what he needs.

**RESPONDEO** dicendum quod necessarium dupliciter dicitur. Uno modo, sine quo aliquid esse non potest. Et de tali necessario omnino eleemosyna dari non debet, puta si aliquis in articulo necessitatis constitutus haberet solum unde posset sustentari, et filii sui vel alii ad eum pertinentes; de hoc enim necessario eleemosynam dare est sibi et suis vitam subtrahere. Sed hoc dico nisi forte talis casus immineret ubi, subtrahendo sibi, daret alicui magnae personae, per quam Ecclesia vel respublica sustentaretur, quia pro talis personae liberatione seipsum et suos laudabiliter periculo mortis exponeret, cum bonum commune sit proprio praeferendum.

Alio modo dicitur aliquid esse necessarium sine quo non potest convenienter vita transigi secundum conditionem vel statum personae propriae et aliarum personarum quarum cura ei incumbit. Huius necessarii terminus non est in indivisibili constitutus, sed multis additis, non potest diiudicari esse ultra tale necessarium; et multis subtractis, adhuc remanet unde possit convenienter aliquis vitam transigere secundum proprium statum. De huiusmodi ergo eleemosynam dare est bonum, et non cadit sub praecepto, sed sub consilio. Inordinatum autem esset si aliquis tantum sibi de bonis propriis subtraheret ut aliis largiretur, quod de residuo non posset vitam transigere convenienter secundum proprium statum et negotia occurrentia, nullus enim inconvenienter vivere debet. Sed ab hoc tria sunt excipienda. Quorum primum est quando aliquis statum mutat, puta per religionis ingressum. Tunc enim, omnia sua propter Christum largiens, opus perfectionis facit, se in alio statu ponendo. Secundo, quando ea quae sibi subtrahit, etsi sint necessaria ad convenientiam vitae, tamen de facili resarciri possunt, ut non sequatur maximum inconveniens. Tertio, quando occurreret extrema necessitas alicuius privatae personae, vel etiam aliqua magna necessitas reipublicae. In his enim casibus laudabiliter praetermitteret aliquis id quod ad decentiam sui status pertinere videretur, ut maiori necessitati subveniret.

**ET PER HOC** patet de facili responsio ad obiecta.

**I ANSWER THAT**, A thing is necessary in two ways: first, because without it something is impossible, and it is altogether wrong to give alms out of what is necessary to us in this sense; for instance, if a man found himself in the presence of a case of urgency, and had merely sufficient to support himself and his children, or others under his charge, he would be throwing away his life and that of others if he were to give away in alms, what was then necessary to him. Yet I say this without prejudice to such a case as might happen, supposing that by depriving himself of necessaries a man might help a great personage, and a support of the Church or State, since it would be a praiseworthy act to endanger one's life and the lives of those who are under our charge for the delivery of such a person, since the common good is to be preferred to one's own.

Second, a thing is said to be necessary, if a man cannot without it live in keeping with his social station, as regards either himself or those of whom he has charge. The *necessary* considered thus is not an invariable quantity, for one might add much more to a man's property, and yet not go beyond what he needs in this way, or one might take much from him, and he would still have sufficient for the decencies of life in keeping with his own position. Accordingly it is good to give alms of this kind of *necessary*; and it is a matter not of precept but of counsel. Yet it would be inordinate to deprive oneself of one's own, in order to give to others to such an extent that the residue would be insufficient for one to live in keeping with one's station and the ordinary occurrences of life: for no man ought to live unbecomingly. There are, however, three exceptions to the above rule. The first is when a man changes his state of life, for instance, by entering religion, for then he gives away all his possessions for Christ's sake, and does the deed of perfection by transferring himself to another state. Second, when that which he deprives himself of, though it be required for the decencies of life, can nevertheless easily be recovered, so that he does not suffer extreme inconvenience. Third, when he is in presence of extreme indigence in an individual, or great need on the part of the common weal. For in such cases it would seem praiseworthy to forego the requirements of one's station, in order to provide for a greater need.

**THE OBJECTIONS** may be easily solved from what has been said.

# Article 7

*Whether one may give alms out of ill-gotten goods?*

**AD SEPTIMUM SIC PROCEDITUR.** Videtur quod possit eleemosyna fieri de illicite acquisitis. Dicitur enim Luc. XVI, *facite vobis amicos de mammona iniquitatis.*

**OBJECTION 1**: It would seem that one may give alms out of ill-gotten goods. For it is written (Luke 16:9): *Make unto you friends of the mammon of iniquity.* Now mammon

Mammona autem significat divitias. Ergo de divitiis inique acquisitis potest sibi aliquis spirituales amicos facere, eleemosynas largiendo.

PRAETEREA, omne turpe lucrum videtur esse illicite acquisitum. Sed turpe lucrum est quod de meretricio acquiritur, unde et de huiusmodi sacrificium vel oblatio Deo offerri non debet, secundum illud Deut. XXIII, *non offeres mercedem prostibuli in domo Dei tui.* Similiter etiam turpiter acquiritur quod acquiritur per aleas, quia, ut Philosophus dicit, in IV Ethic., *tales ab amicis lucrantur, quibus oportet dare.* Turpissime etiam acquiritur aliquid per simoniam, per quam aliquis spiritui sancto iniuriam facit. Et tamen de huiusmodi eleemosyna fieri potest. Ergo de male acquisitis potest aliquis eleemosynam facere.

PRAETEREA, maiora mala sunt magis vitanda quam minora. Sed minus peccatum est detentio rei alienae quam homicidium, quod aliquis incurrit nisi alicui in ultima necessitate subveniat, ut patet per Ambrosium, qui dicit, *pasce fame morientem, quoniam si non paveris, occidisti.* Ergo aliquis potest eleemosynam facere in aliquo casu de male acquisitis.

SED CONTRA est quod Augustinus dicit, in libro de Verb. Dom., *de iustis laboribus facite eleemosynas. Non enim corrupturi estis iudicem Christum, ut non vos audiat cum pauperibus, quibus tollitis. Nolite velle eleemosynas facere de faenore et usuris. Fidelibus dico, quibus corpus Christi erogamus.*

RESPONDEO dicendum quod tripliciter potest esse aliquid illicite acquisitum. Uno enim modo id quod illicite ab aliquo acquiritur debetur ei a quo est acquisitum, nec potest ab eo retineri qui acquisivit, sicut contingit in rapina et furto et usuris. Et de talibus, cum homo teneatur ad restitutionem, eleemosyna fieri non potest.

Alio vero modo est aliquid illicite acquisitum quia ille quidem qui acquisivit retinere non potest, nec tamen debetur ei a quo acquisivit, quia scilicet contra iustitiam accepit, et alter contra iustitiam dedit, sicut contingit in simonia, in qua dans et accipiens contra iustitiam legis divinae agit. Unde non debet fieri restitutio ei qui dedit, sed debet in eleemosynas erogari. Et eadem ratio est in similibus, in quibus scilicet et datio et acceptio est contra legem.

Tertio modo est aliquid illicite acquisitum, non quidem quia ipsa acquisitio sit illicita, sed quia id ex quo acquiritur est illicitum, sicut patet de eo quod mulier acquirit per meretricium. Et hoc proprie vocatur *turpe lucrum.* Quod enim mulier meretricium exerceat, turpiter agit et contra legem Dei, sed in eo quod accipit non iniuste agit nec contra legem. Unde quod sic illicite acquisitum est retineri potest, et de eo eleemosyna fieri.

signifies riches. Therefore it is lawful to make unto oneself spiritual friends by giving alms out of ill-gotten riches.

**OBJ. 2**: Further, all filthy lucre seems to be ill-gotten. But the profits from whoredom are filthy lucre; wherefore it was forbidden (Deut 23:18) to offer therefrom sacrifices or oblations to God: *Thou shalt not offer the hire of a strumpet . . . in the house of . . . thy God.* In like manner gains from games of chance are ill-gotten, for, as the Philosopher says (*Ethic.* iv, 1), *we take such like gains from our friends to whom we ought rather to give.* And most of all are the profits from simony ill-gotten, since thereby the Holy Spirit is wronged. Nevertheless out of such gains it is lawful to give alms. Therefore one may give alms out of ill-gotten goods.

**OBJ. 3**: Further, greater evils should be avoided more than lesser evils. Now it is less sinful to keep back another's property than to commit murder, of which a man is guilty if he fails to succor one who is in extreme need, as appears from the words of Ambrose who says (Cf. *Canon Pasce*, dist. lxxxvi, whence the words, as quoted, are taken): *Feed him that dies of hunger, if thou hast not fed him, thou hast slain him.* Therefore, in certain cases, it is lawful to give alms of ill-gotten goods.

**ON THE CONTRARY**, Augustine says (*De Verb. Dom.* xxxv, 2): *Give alms from your just labors. For you will not bribe Christ your judge, not to hear you with the poor whom you rob . . . Give not alms from interest and usury: I speak to the faithful to whom we dispense the Body of Christ.*

**I ANSWER THAT**, A thing may be ill-gotten in three ways. In the first place a thing is ill-gotten if it be due to the person from whom it is gotten, and may not be kept by the person who has obtained possession of it; as in the case of rapine, theft and usury, and of such things a man may not give alms since he is bound to restore them.

Second, a thing is ill-gotten, when he that has it may not keep it, and yet he may not return it to the person from whom he received it, because he received it unjustly, while the latter gave it unjustly. This happens in simony, wherein both giver and receiver contravene the justice of the Divine Law, so that restitution is to be made not to the giver, but by giving alms. The same applies to all similar cases of illegal giving and receiving.

Third, a thing is ill-gotten, not because the taking was unlawful, but because it is the outcome of something unlawful, as in the case of a woman's profits from whoredom. This is *filthy lucre* properly so called, because the practice of whoredom is filthy and against the Law of God, yet the woman does not act unjustly or unlawfully in taking the money. Consequently it is lawful to keep and to give in alms what is thus acquired by an unlawful action.

**AD PRIMUM** ergo dicendum quod, sicut Augustinus dicit, in libro de Verb. Dom., *illud verbum domini quidam male intelligendo, rapiunt res alienas, et aliquid inde pauperibus largiuntur, et putant se facere quod praeceptum est. Intellectus iste corrigendus est. Sed omnes divitiae iniquitatis dicuntur,* ut dicit in libro de quaestionibus Evangelii, *quia non sunt divitiae nisi iniquis, qui in eis spem constituunt. Iniquum mammona dixit quia variis divitiarum illecebris nostros tentat affectus. Vel quia in pluribus praedecessoribus, quibus patrimonio succedis, aliquis reperitur qui iniuste usurpavit aliena, quamvis tu nescias* ut Basilius dicit. Vel omnes divitiae dicuntur iniquitatis, idest *inaequalitatis,* quia non aequaliter sunt omnibus distributae uno egente et alio superabundante.

**AD SECUNDUM** dicendum quod de acquisito per meretricium iam dictum est qualiter eleemosyna fieri possit. Non autem fit de eo sacrificium vel oblatio ad altare, tum propter scandalum; tum propter sacrorum reverentiam. De eo etiam quod est per simoniam acquisitum potest fieri eleemosyna, quia non est debitum ei qui dedit, sed meretur illud amittere. Circa illa vero quae per aleas acquiruntur videtur esse aliquid illicitum ex iure divino, scilicet quod aliquis lucretur ab his qui rem suam alienare non possunt, sicut sunt minores et furiosi et huiusmodi; et quod aliquis trahat alium ex cupiditate lucrandi ad ludum; et quod fraudulenter ab eo lucretur. Et in his casibus tenetur ad restitutionem, et sic de eo non potest eleemosynam facere. Aliquid autem videtur esse ulterius illicitum ex iure positivo civili, quod prohibet universaliter tale lucrum. Sed quia ius civile non obligat omnes, sed eos solos qui sunt his legibus subiecti; et iterum per dissuetudinem abrogari potest, ideo apud illos qui sunt huiusmodi legibus obstricti, tenentur universaliter ad restitutionem qui lucrantur; nisi forte contraria consuetudo praevaleat; aut nisi aliquis lucratus sit ab eo qui traxit eum ad ludum. In quo casu non teneretur restituere, quia ille qui amisit non est dignus recipere; nec potest licite retinere, tali iure positivo durante; unde debet de hoc eleemosynam facere in hoc casu.

**AD TERTIUM** dicendum quod in casu extremae necessitatis omnia sunt communia. Unde licet ei qui talem necessitatem patitur accipere de alieno ad sui sustentationem, si non inveniat qui sibi dare velit. Et eadem ratione licet habere aliquid de alieno et de hoc eleemosynam dare, quinimmo et accipere, si aliter subveniri non possit necessitatem patienti. Si tamen fieri potest sine periculo, debet requisita domini voluntate pauperi providere extremam necessitatem patienti.

**REPLY OBJ. 1**: As Augustine says (*De Verb. Dom.* 2), *Some have misunderstood this saying of Our Lord, so as to take another's property and give thereof to the poor, thinking that they are fulfilling the commandment by so doing. This interpretation must be amended. Yet all riches are called riches of iniquity,* as stated in *De Quaest. Ev.* ii, 34, *because riches are not unjust save for those who are themselves unjust, and put all their trust in them.* Or, according to Ambrose in his commentary on Luke 16:9, *Make unto yourselves friends,* etc., *He calls mammon unjust, because it draws our affections by the various allurements of wealth.* Or, because *among the many ancestors whose property you inherit, there is one who took the property of others unjustly, although you know nothing about it,* as Basil says in a homily (*Hom. super Luc.* A, 5). Or, all riches are styled riches *of iniquity,* i.e., of *inequality,* because they are not distributed equally among all, one being in need, and another in affluence.

**REPLY OBJ. 2**: We have already explained how alms may be given out of the profits of whoredom. Yet sacrifices and oblations were not made therefrom at the altar, both on account of the scandal, and through reverence for sacred things. It is also lawful to give alms out of the profits of simony, because they are not due to him who paid, indeed he deserves to lose them. But as to the profits from games of chance, there would seem to be something unlawful as being contrary to the Divine Law, when a man wins from one who cannot alienate his property, such as minors, lunatics and so forth, or when a man, with the desire of making money out of another man, entices him to play, and wins from him by cheating. In these cases he is bound to restitution, and consequently cannot give away his gains in alms. Then again there would seem to be something unlawful as being against the positive civil law, which altogether forbids any such profits. Since, however, a civil law does not bind all, but only those who are subject to that law, and moreover may be abrogated through desuetude, it follows that all such as are bound by these laws are bound to make restitution of such gains, unless perchance the contrary custom prevail, or unless a man win from one who enticed him to play, in which case he is not bound to restitution, because the loser does not deserve to be paid back: and yet he cannot lawfully keep what he has won, so long as that positive law is in force, wherefore in this case he ought to give it away in alms.

**REPLY OBJ. 3**: All things are common property in a case of extreme necessity. Hence one who is in such dire straits may take another's goods in order to succor himself, if he can find no one who is willing to give him something. For the same reason a man may retain what belongs to another, and give alms thereof; or even take something if there be no other way of succoring the one who is in need. If however this be possible without danger, he must ask the owner's consent, and then succor the poor man who is in extreme necessity.

# Article 8

*Whether one who is under another's power can give alms?*

AD OCTAVUM SIC PROCEDITUR. Videtur quod ille qui est in potestate alterius constitutus possit eleemosynam facere. Religiosi enim sunt in potestate eorum quibus obedientiam voverunt. Sed si eis non liceret eleemosynam facere, damnum reportarent ex statu religionis, quia sicut Ambrosius dicit, *summa Christianae religionis in pietate consistit,* quae maxime per eleemosynarum largitionem commendatur. Ergo illi qui sunt in potestate alterius constituti possunt eleemosynam facere.

PRAETEREA, uxor est *sub potestate viri,* ut dicitur Gen. III. Sed uxor potest eleemosynam facere, cum assumatur in viri societatem, unde et de beata Lucia dicitur quod, ignorante sponso, eleemosynas faciebat. Ergo per hoc quod aliquis est in potestate alterius constitutus, non impeditur quin possit eleemosynas facere.

PRAETEREA, naturalis quaedam subiectio est filiorum ad parentes, unde apostolus, ad Ephes. VI, dicit, *filii, obedite parentibus vestris in domino.* Sed filii, ut videtur, possunt de rebus patris eleemosynas dare, quia sunt quodammodo ipsorum, cum sint haeredes; et cum possint eis uti ad usum corporis, multo magis videtur quod possint eis uti, eleemosynas dando, ad remedium animae suae. Ergo illi qui sunt in potestate constituti possunt eleemosynas dare.

PRAETEREA, servi sunt sub potestate dominorum, secundum illud ad Tit. II, *servos dominis suis subditos esse.* Licet autem eis aliquid in utilitatem domini facere, quod maxime fit si pro eis eleemosynas largiantur. Ergo illi qui sunt in potestate constituti possunt eleemosynas facere.

SED CONTRA est quod eleemosynae non sunt faciendae de alieno, sed de iustis laboribus propriis unusquisque eleemosynam facere debet; ut Augustinus dicit, in libro de Verb. Dom. Sed si subiecti aliis eleemosynam facerent, hoc esset de alieno. Ergo illi qui sunt sub potestate aliorum non possunt eleemosynam facere.

RESPONDEO dicendum quod ille qui est sub potestate alterius constitutus, inquantum huiusmodi, secundum superioris potestatem regulari debet, hic est enim ordo naturalis, ut inferiora secundum superiora regulentur. Et ideo oportet quod ea in quibus inferior superiori subiicitur, dispenset non aliter quam ei sit a superiore commissum.

Sic igitur ille qui est sub potestate constitutus de re secundum quam superiori subiicitur eleemosynam facere non debet nisi quatenus ei a superiore fuerit permissum. Si quis vero habeat aliquid secundum quod potestati superioris non subsit, iam secundum hoc non

OBJECTION 1: It would seem that one who is under another's power can give alms. For religious are under the power of their prelates to whom they have vowed obedience. Now if it were unlawful for them to give alms, they would lose by entering the state of religion, for as Ambrose says on 1 Tim. 4:8: *'Dutifulness is profitable to all things': The sum total of the Christian religion consists in doing one's duty by all,* and the most creditable way of doing this is to give alms. Therefore those who are in another's power can give alms.

OBJ. 2: Further, a wife is *under her husband's power* (Gen 3:16). But a wife can give alms since she is her husband's partner; hence it is related of the Blessed Lucy that she gave alms without the knowledge of her betrothed Therefore a person is not prevented from giving alms, by being under another's power.

OBJ. 3: Further, the subjection of children to their parents is founded on nature, wherefore the Apostle says (*Eph 6:1*): *Children, obey your parents in the Lord.* But, apparently, children may give alms out of their parents' property. For it is their own, since they are the heirs; wherefore, since they can employ it for some bodily use, it seems that much more can they use it in giving alms so as to profit their souls. Therefore those who are under another's power can give alms.

OBJ. 4: Further, servants are under their master's power, according to Titus 2:9: *Exhort servants to be obedient to their masters.* Now they may lawfully do anything that will profit their masters: and this would be especially the case if they gave alms for them. Therefore those who are under another's power can give alms.

ON THE CONTRARY, Alms should not be given out of another's property; and each one should give alms out of the just profit of his own labor as Augustine says (*De Verb. Dom.* xxxv, 2). Now if those who are subject to anyone were to give alms, this would be out of another's property. Therefore those who are under another's power cannot give alms.

I ANSWER THAT, Anyone who is under another's power must, as such, be ruled in accordance with the power of his superior: for the natural order demands that the inferior should be ruled according to its superior. Therefore in those matters in which the inferior is subject to his superior, his ministrations must be subject to the superior's permission.

Accordingly he that is under another's power must not give alms of anything in respect of which he is subject to that other, except insofar as he has been commissioned by his superior. But if he has something in respect of which he is not under the power of his superior, he is no longer sub-

est potestati subiectus, quantum ad hoc proprii iuris existens. Et de hoc potest eleemosynam facere.

**AD PRIMUM** ergo dicendum quod monachus, si habet dispensationem a praelato commissam, potest facere eleemosynam de rebus monasterii, secundum quod sibi est commissum. Si vero non habet dispensationem, quia nihil proprium habet, tunc non potest facere eleemosynam sine licentia abbatis vel expresse habita vel probabiliter praesumpta, nisi forte in articulo extremae necessitatis, in quo licitum esset ei furari ut eleemosynam daret. Nec propter hoc efficitur peioris conditionis, quia sicut dicitur in libro de Eccles. Dogmat., *bonum est facultates cum dispensatione pauperibus erogare, sed melius est, pro intentione sequendi dominum, insimul donare, et, absolutum sollicitudine, egere cum Christo.*

**AD SECUNDUM** dicendum quod si uxor habeat alias res praeter dotem, quae ordinatur ad sustentanda onera matrimonii, vel ex proprio lucro vel quocumque alio licito modo, potest dare eleemosynas, etiam irrequisito assensu viri, moderatas tamen, ne ex earum superfluitate vir depauperetur. Alias autem non debet dare eleemosynas sine consensu viri vel expresso vel praesumpto, nisi in articulo necessitatis, sicut de monacho dictum est. Quamvis enim mulier sit aequalis in actu matrimonii, tamen in his quae ad dispositionem domus pertinent *vir caput est mulieris*, secundum apostolum, I ad Cor. XI. Beata autem Lucia sponsum habebat, non virum. Unde de consensu matris poterat eleemosynam facere.

**AD TERTIUM** dicendum quod ea quae sunt filiifamilias sunt patris. Et ideo non potest eleemosynam facere (nisi forte aliquam modicam, de qua potest praesumere quod patri placeat), nisi forte alicuius rei esset sibi a patre dispensatio commissa. Et idem dicendum de servis.

**UNDE PATET** solutio ad quartum.

ject to another in its regard, being independent in respect of that particular thing, and he can give alms therefrom.

**REPLY OBJ. 1:** If a monk be dispensed through being commissioned by his superior, he can give alms from the property of his monastery, in accordance with the terms of his commission; but if he has no such dispensation, since he has nothing of his own, he cannot give alms without his abbot's permission either express or presumed for some probable reason: except in a case of extreme necessity, when it would be lawful for him to commit a theft in order to give an alms. Nor does it follow that he is worse off than before, because, as stated in *De Eccles. Dogm.* lxxi, *it is a good thing to give one's property to the poor little by little, but it is better still to give all at once in order to follow Christ, and being freed from care, to be needy with Christ.*

**REPLY OBJ. 2:** A wife, who has other property besides her dowry which is for the support of the burdens of marriage, whether that property be gained by her own industry or by any other lawful means, can give alms, out of that property, without asking her husband's permission: yet such alms should be moderate, lest through giving too much she impoverish her husband. Otherwise she ought not to give alms without the express or presumed consent of her husband, except in cases of necessity as stated, in the case of a monk, in the preceding Reply. For though the wife be her husband's equal in the marriage act, yet in matters of housekeeping, *the head of the woman is the man*, as the Apostle says (1 Cor 11:3). As regards Blessed Lucy, she had a betrothed, not a husband, wherefore she could give alms with her mother's consent.

**REPLY OBJ. 3:** What belongs to the children belongs also to the father: wherefore the child cannot give alms, except in such small quantity that one may presume the father to be willing: unless, perchance, the father authorize his child to dispose of any particular property. The same applies to servants.

**HENCE** the Reply to the Fourth Objection is clear.

# Article 9

*Whether one ought to give alms to those rather who are more closely united to us?*

**AD NONUM SIC PROCEDITUR.** Videtur quod non sit magis propinquioribus eleemosyna facienda. Dicitur enim Eccli. XII, *da misericordi, et ne suscipias peccatorem, benefac humili, et non des impio.* Sed quandoque contingit quod propinqui nostri sunt peccatores et impii. Ergo non sunt eis magis eleemosynae faciendae.

**PRAETEREA**, eleemosynae sunt faciendae propter retributionem mercedis aeternae, secundum illud Matth. VI, *et pater tuus, qui videt in abscondito, reddet tibi.*

**OBJECTION 1:** It would seem that one ought not to give alms to those rather who are more closely united to us. For it is written (Sir 12:4, 6): *Give to the merciful and uphold not the sinner . . . Do good to the humble and give not to the ungodly.* Now it happens sometimes that those who are closely united to us are sinful and ungodly. Therefore we ought not to give alms to them in preference to others.

**OBJ. 2:** Further, alms should be given that we may receive an eternal reward in return, according to Matt. 6:18: *And thy Father Who seeth in secret, will repay thee.* Now the

Sed retributio aeterna maxime acquiritur ex eleemosynis quae sanctis erogantur, secundum illud Luc. XVI, *facite vobis amicos de mammona iniquitatis, ut, cum defeceritis, recipiant vos in aeterna tabernacula*; quod exponens Augustinus, in libro de Verb. Dom., dicit, *qui sunt qui habebunt aeterna habitacula nisi sancti Dei? Et qui sunt qui ab eis accipiendi sunt in tabernacula nisi qui eorum indigentiae serviunt?* Ergo magis sunt eleemosynae dandae sanctioribus quam propinquioribus.

**PRAETEREA**, maxime homo est sibi propinquus. Sed sibi non potest homo eleemosynam facere. Ergo videtur quod non sit magis facienda eleemosyna personae magis coniunctae.

**SED CONTRA** est quod apostolus dicit, I ad Tim. V, *si quis suorum, et maxime domesticorum curam non habet, fidem negavit et est infideli deterior.*

**RESPONDEO** dicendum quod, sicut Augustinus dicit, in I de Doct. Christ., illi qui sunt nobis magis coniuncti quasi quadam sorte nobis obveniunt, ut eis magis providere debemus. Est tamen circa hoc discretionis ratio adhibenda, secundum differentiam coniunctionis et sanctitatis et utilitatis. Nam multo sanctiori magis indigentiam patienti, et magis utili ad commune bonum, est magis eleemosyna danda quam personae propinquiori; maxime si non sit multum coniuncta, cuius cura specialis nobis immineat, et si magnam necessitatem non patiatur.

**AD PRIMUM** ergo dicendum quod peccatori non est subveniendum inquantum peccator est, idest ut per hoc in peccato foveatur, sed inquantum homo est, idest ut natura sustentetur.

**AD SECUNDUM** dicendum quod opus eleemosynae ad mercedem retributionis aeternae dupliciter valet. Uno quidem modo, ex radice caritatis. Et secundum hoc eleemosyna est meritoria prout in ea servatur ordo caritatis, secundum quem propinquioribus magis providere debemus, ceteris paribus. Unde Ambrosius dicit, in I de Offic., *est illa probanda liberalitas, ut proximos sanguinis tui non despicias, si egere cognoscas, melius est enim ut ipse subvenias tuis, quibus pudor est ab aliis sumptum deposcere.* Alio modo valet eleemosyna ad retributionem vitae aeternae ex merito eius cui donatur, qui orat pro eo qui eleemosynam dedit. Et secundum hoc loquitur ibi Augustinus.

**AD TERTIUM** dicendum quod, cum eleemosyna sit opus misericordiae, sicut misericordia non est proprie ad seipsum, sed per quandam similitudinem, ut supra dictum est; ita etiam, proprie loquendo, nullus sibi eleemosynam facit, nisi forte ex persona alterius. Puta, cum aliquis distributor ponitur eleemosynarum, potest et ipse sibi accipere, si indigeat, eo tenore quo et aliis ministrat.

eternal reward is gained chiefly by the alms which are given to the saints, according to Luke 16:9: *Make unto you friends of the mammon of iniquity, that when you shall fail, they may receive you into everlasting dwellings*, which passage Augustine expounds (*De Verb. Dom.* xxxv, 1): *Who shall have everlasting dwellings unless the saints of God? And who are they that shall be received by them into their dwellings, if not those who succor them in their needs?* Therefore alms should be given to the more holy persons rather than to those who are more closely united to us.

**OBJ. 3**: Further, man is more closely united to himself. But a man cannot give himself an alms. Therefore it seems that we are not bound to give alms to those who are most closely united to us.

**ON THE CONTRARY**, The Apostle says (1 Tim 5:8): *If any man have not care of his own, and especially of those of his house, he hath denied the faith, and is worse than an infidel.*

**I ANSWER THAT**, As Augustine says (*De Doctr. Christ.* i, 28), it falls to us by lot, as it were, to have to look to the welfare of those who are more closely united to us. Nevertheless in this matter we must employ discretion, according to the various degrees of connection, holiness and utility. For we ought to give alms to one who is much holier and in greater want, and to one who is more useful to the common weal, rather than to one who is more closely united to us, especially if the latter be not very closely united, and has no special claim on our care then and there, and who is not in very urgent need.

**REPLY OBJ. 1**: We ought not to help a sinner as such, that is by encouraging him to sin, but as man, that is by supporting his nature.

**REPLY OBJ. 2**: Almsdeeds deserve on two counts to receive an eternal reward. First because they are rooted in charity, and in this respect an almsdeed is meritorious insofar as it observes the order of charity, which requires that, other things being equal, we should, in preference, help those who are more closely connected with us. Wherefore Ambrose says (*De Officiis* i, 30): *It is with commendable liberality that you forget not your kindred, if you know them to be in need, for it is better that you should yourself help your own family, who would be ashamed to beg help from others.* Second, almsdeeds deserve to be rewarded eternally, through the merit of the recipient, who prays for the giver, and it is in this sense that Augustine is speaking.

**REPLY OBJ. 3**: Since almsdeeds are works of mercy, just as a man does not, properly speaking, pity himself, but only by a kind of comparison, as stated above (Q. 30, AA. 1, 2), so too, properly speaking, no man gives himself an alms, unless he act in another's person; thus when a man is appointed to distribute alms, he can take something for himself, if he be in want, on the same ground as when he gives to others.

# Article 10

*Whether alms should be given in abundance?*

AD DECIMUM SIC PROCEDITUR. Videtur quod eleemosyna non sit abundanter facienda. Eleemosyna enim maxime debet fieri coniunctioribus. Sed illis non debet sic dari *ut ditiores inde fieri velint*; sicut Ambrosius dicit, in I de Offic. Ergo nec aliis debet abundanter dari.

PRAETEREA, Ambrosius dicit ibidem, *non debent simul effundi opes, sed dispensari*. Sed abundantia eleemosynarum ad effusionem pertinet. Ergo eleemosyna non debet fieri abundanter.

PRAETEREA, II ad Cor. VIII dicit apostolus, *non ut aliis sit remissio*, idest ut alii de nostris otiose vivant; *vobis autem sit tribulatio*, idest paupertas. Sed hoc contingeret si eleemosyna daretur abundanter. Ergo non est abundanter eleemosyna largienda.

SED CONTRA est quod dicitur Tob. IV, *si multum tibi fuerit, abundanter tribue*.

RESPONDEO dicendum quod abundantia eleemosynae potest considerari et ex parte dantis, et ex parte recipientis. Ex parte quidem dantis cum scilicet aliquis dat quod est multum secundum proportionem propriae facultatis. Et sic laudabile est abundanter dare, unde et dominus, Luc. XXI, laudavit viduam, quae *ex eo quod deerat illi, omnem victum quem habuit misit*, observatis tamen his quae supra dicta sunt de eleemosyna facienda de necessariis.

Ex parte vero eius cui datur est abundans eleemosyna dupliciter. Uno modo, quod suppleat sufficienter eius indigentiam. Et sic laudabile est abundanter eleemosynam tribuere. Alio modo, ut superabundet ad superfluitatem. Et hoc non est laudabile, sed melius est pluribus indigentibus elargiri. Unde et apostolus dicit, I ad Cor. XIII, *si distribuero in cibos pauperum*; ubi Glossa dicit, *per hoc cautela eleemosynae docetur, ut non uni sed multis detur, ut pluribus prosit*.

AD PRIMUM ergo dicendum quod ratio illa procedit de abundantia superexcedente necessitatem recipientis eleemosynam.

AD SECUNDUM dicendum quod auctoritas illa loquitur de abundantia eleemosynae ex parte dantis. Sed intelligendum est quod Deus non vult simul effundi omnes opes, nisi in mutatione status. Unde subdit ibidem, *nisi forte ut Elisaeus boves suos occidit, et pavit pauperes ex eo quod habuit, ut nulla cura domestica teneretur*.

AD TERTIUM dicendum quod auctoritas inducta, quantum ad hoc quod dicit, non ut alii sit remissio vel refrigerium, loquitur de abundantia eleemosynae quae superexcedit necessitatem recipientis, cui non est danda eleemosyna ut inde luxurietur, sed ut inde sustente-

OBJECTION 1: It would seem that alms should not be given in abundance. For we ought to give alms to those chiefly who are most closely connected with us. But we ought not to give to them in such a way that *they are likely to become richer thereby*, as Ambrose says (*De Officiis* i, 30). Therefore neither should we give abundantly to others.

OBJ. 2: Further, Ambrose says (*De Officiis* i, 30): *We should not lavish our wealth on others all at once, we should dole it out by degrees*. But to give abundantly is to give lavishly. Therefore alms should not be given in abundance.

OBJ. 3: Further, the Apostle says (2 Cor 8:13): *Not that others should be eased*, i.e., should live on you without working themselves, *and you burdened*, i.e., impoverished. But this would be the result if alms were given in abundance. Therefore we ought not to give alms abundantly.

ON THE CONTRARY, It is written (Tob 4:93): *If thou have much, give abundantly*.

I ANSWER THAT, Alms may be considered abundant in relation either to the giver, or to the recipient: in relation to the giver, when that which a man gives is great as compared with his means. To give thus is praiseworthy, wherefore Our Lord (Luke 21:3, 4) commended the widow because *of her want, she cast in all the living that she had*. Nevertheless those conditions must be observed which were laid down when we spoke of giving alms out of one's necessary goods (A. 9).

On the part of the recipient, an alms may be abundant in two ways; first, by relieving his need sufficiently, and in this sense it is praiseworthy to give alms: second, by relieving his need more than sufficiently; this is not praiseworthy, and it would be better to give to several that are in need, wherefore the Apostle says (1 Cor 13:3): *If I should distribute . . . to feed the poor*, on which words a gloss comments: *Thus we are warned to be careful in giving alms, and to give, not to one only, but to many, that we may profit many*.

REPLY OBJ. 1: This argument considers abundance of alms as exceeding the needs of the recipient.

REPLY OBJ. 2: The passage quoted considers abundance of alms on the part of the giver; but the sense is that God does not wish a man to lavish all his wealth at once, except when he changes his state of life, wherefore he goes on to say: *Except we imitate Eliseus who slew his oxen and fed the poor with what he had, so that no household cares might keep him back* (3 Kgs 19:21).

REPLY OBJ. 3: In the passage quoted the words, *not that others should be eased or refreshed*, refer to that abundance of alms which surpasses the need of the recipient, to whom one should give alms not that he may have an easy life, but that he may have relief. Nevertheless we must bring

tur. Circa quod tamen est discretio adhibenda propter diversas conditiones hominum, quorum quidam, delicatioribus nutriti, indigent magis delicatis cibis aut vestibus. Unde et Ambrosius dicit, in libro de Offic., *consideranda est in largiendo aetas atque debilitas. Nonnunquam etiam verecundia, quae ingenuos prodit natales. Aut si quis ex divitiis in egestatem cecidit sine vitio suo.*

Quantum vero ad id quod subditur, *vobis autem tribulatio,* loquitur de abundantia ex parte dantis. Sed, sicut Glossa ibi dicit, *non hoc ideo dicit quin melius esset,* scilicet abundanter dare. *Sed de infirmis timet, quos sic dare monet ut egestatem non patiantur.*

discretion to bear on the matter, on account of the various conditions of men, some of whom are more daintily nurtured, and need finer food and clothing. Hence Ambrose says (*De Officiis* i, 30): *When you give an alms to a man, you should take into consideration his age and his weakness; and sometimes the shame which proclaims his good birth; and again that perhaps he has fallen from riches to indigence through no fault of his own.*

With regard to the words that follow, *and you burdened,* they refer to abundance on the part of the giver. Yet, as a gloss says on the same passage, *he says this, not because it would be better to give in abundance, but because he fears for the weak, and he admonishes them so to give that they lack not for themselves.*

# QUESTION 33

## FRATERNAL CORRECTION

Deinde considerandum est de correctione fraterna. Et circa hoc quaeruntur octo.

Primo, utrum fraterna correctio sit actus caritatis.

Secundo, utrum sit sub praecepto.

Tertio, utrum hoc praeceptum extendat se ad omnes, vel solum in praelatis.

Quarto, utrum subditi teneantur ex hoc praecepto praelatos corrigere.

Quinto, utrum peccator possit corrigere.

Sexto, utrum aliquis debeat corrigi qui ex correctione fit deterior.

Septimo, utrum secreta correctio debeat praecedere denuntiationem.

Octavo, utrum testium inductio debeat praecedere denuntiationem.

We must now consider Fraternal Correction, under which head there are eight points of inquiry:

(1) Whether fraternal correction is an act of charity?

(2) Whether it is a matter of precept?

(3) Whether this precept binds all, or only superiors?

(4) Whether this precept binds the subject to correct his superior?

(5) Whether a sinner may correct anyone?

(6) Whether one ought to correct a person who becomes worse through being corrected?

(7) Whether secret correction should precede denouncement?

(8) Whether witnesses should be called before denouncement?

# Article 1

*Whether fraternal correction is an act of charity?*

**AD PRIMUM SIC PROCEDITUR.** Videtur quod fraterna correctio non sit actus caritatis. Dicit enim Glossa Matth. XVIII, super illud, *si peccaverit in te frater tuus*, quod frater est arguendus *ex zelo iustitiae*. Sed iustitia est virtus distincta a caritate. Ergo correctio fraterna non est actus caritatis, sed iustitiae.

**PRAETEREA**, correctio fraterna fit per secretam admonitionem. Sed admonitio est consilium quoddam, quod pertinet ad prudentiam, prudentis enim est *esse bene consiliativum*, ut dicitur in VI Ethic. Ergo fraterna correctio non est actus caritatis, sed prudentiae.

**PRAETEREA**, contrarii actus non pertinent ad eandem virtutem. Sed supportare peccantem est actus caritatis, secundum illud ad Gal. VI, *alter alterius onera portate, et sic adimplebitis legem Christi*, quae est lex caritatis. Ergo videtur quod corrigere fratrem peccantem, quod est contrarium supportationi, non sit actus caritatis.

**SED CONTRA**, corripere delinquentem est quaedam eleemosyna spiritualis. Sed eleemosyna est actus caritatis, ut supra dictum est. Ergo et correctio fraterna est actus caritatis.

**RESPONDEO** dicendum quod correctio delinquentis est quoddam remedium quod debet adhiberi contra peccatum alicuius. Peccatum autem alicuius dupliciter considerari potest, uno quidem modo, inquantum est

**OBJECTION 1**: It would seem that fraternal correction is not an act of charity. For a gloss on Matt. 18:15, *If thy brother shall offend against thee*, says that a man should reprove his brother *out of zeal for justice*. But justice is a distinct virtue from charity. Therefore fraternal correction is an act, not of charity, but of justice.

**OBJ. 2**: Further, fraternal correction is given by secret admonition. Now admonition is a kind of counsel, which is an act of prudence, for a prudent man is one *who is of good counsel* (*Ethic.* vi, 5). Therefore fraternal correction is an act, not of charity, but of prudence.

**OBJ. 3**: Further, contrary acts do not belong to the same virtue. Now it is an act of charity to bear with a sinner, according to Gal. 6:2: *Bear ye one another's burdens, and so you shall fulfill the law of Christ*, which is the law of charity. Therefore it seems that the correction of a sinning brother, which is contrary to bearing with him, is not an act of charity.

**ON THE CONTRARY**, To correct the wrongdoer is a spiritual almsdeed. But almsdeeds are works of charity, as stated above (Q. 32, A. 1). Therefore fraternal correction is an act of charity.

**I ANSWER THAT**, The correction of the wrongdoer is a remedy which should be employed against a man's sin. Now a man's sin may be considered in two ways, first as being harmful to the sinner, second as conducing to the harm

331

nocivum ei qui peccat; alio modo, inquantum vergit in nocumentum aliorum, qui ex eius peccato laeduntur vel scandalizantur; et etiam inquantum est in nocumentum boni communis, cuius iustitia per peccatum hominis perturbatur.

Duplex ergo est correctio delinquentis. Una quidem quae adhibet remedium peccato inquantum est quoddam malum ipsius peccantis, et ista est proprie fraterna correctio, quae ordinatur ad emendationem delinquentis. Removere autem malum alicuius eiusdem rationis est et bonum eius procurare. Procurare autem fratris bonum pertinet ad caritatem, per quam volumus et operamur bonum amico. Unde etiam correctio fraterna est actus caritatis, quia per eam repellimus malum fratris, scilicet peccatum. Cuius remotio magis pertinet ad caritatem quam etiam remotio exterioris damni, vel etiam corporalis nocumenti, quanto contrarium bonum virtutis magis est affine caritati quam bonum corporis vel exteriorum rerum. Unde correctio fraterna magis est actus caritatis quam curatio infirmitatis corporalis, vel subventio qua excluditur exterior egestas. Alia vero correctio est quae adhibet remedium peccati delinquentis secundum quod est in malum aliorum, et etiam praecipue in nocumentum communis boni. Et talis correctio est actus iustitiae, cuius est conservare rectitudinem iustitiae unius ad alium.

**AD PRIMUM** ergo dicendum quod Glossa illa loquitur de secunda correctione, quae est actus iustitiae. Vel, si loquatur etiam de prima, iustitia ibi sumitur secundum quod est universalis virtus, ut infra dicetur, prout etiam *omne peccatum est iniquitas*, ut dicitur I Ioan. III, quasi contra iustitiam existens.

**AD SECUNDUM** dicendum quod, sicut philosophus dicit, in VI Ethic., *prudentia facit rectitudinem in his quae sunt ad finem*, de quibus est consilium et electio. Tamen cum per prudentiam aliquid recte agimus ad finem alicuius virtutis moralis, puta temperantiae vel fortitudinis, actus ille est principaliter illius virtutis ad cuius finem ordinatur. Quia ergo admonitio quae fit in correctione fraterna ordinatur ad amovendum peccatum fratris, quod pertinet ad caritatem; manifestum est quod talis admonitio principaliter est actus caritatis, quasi imperantis, prudentiae vero secundario, quasi exequentis et dirigentis actum.

**AD TERTIUM** dicendum quod correctio fraterna non opponitur supportationi infirmorum, sed magis ex ea consequitur. Intantum enim aliquis supportat peccantem inquantum contra eum non turbatur, sed benevolentiam ad eum servat. Et ex hoc contingit quod eum satagit emendare.

of others, by hurting or scandalizing them, or by being detrimental to the common good, the justice of which is disturbed by that man's sin.

Consequently the correction of a wrongdoer is twofold, one which applies a remedy to the sin considered as an evil of the sinner himself. This is fraternal correction properly so called, which is directed to the amendment of the sinner. Now to do away with anyone's evil is the same as to procure his good: and to procure a person's good is an act of charity, whereby we wish and do our friend well. Consequently fraternal correction also is an act of charity, because thereby we drive out our brother's evil, viz. sin, the removal of which pertains to charity rather than the removal of an external loss, or of a bodily injury, in so much as the contrary good of virtue is more akin to charity than the good of the body or of external things. Therefore fraternal correction is an act of charity rather than the healing of a bodily infirmity, or the relieving of an external bodily need. There is another correction which applies a remedy to the sin of the wrongdoer, considered as hurtful to others, and especially to the common good. This correction is an act of justice, whose concern it is to safeguard the rectitude of justice between one man and another.

**REPLY OBJ. 1**: This gloss speaks of the second correction which is an act of justice. Or if it speaks of the first correction, then it takes justice as denoting a general virtue, as we shall state further on (Q. 58, A. 5), in which sense again all *sin is iniquity* (1 John 3:4), through being contrary to justice.

**REPLY OBJ. 2**: According to the Philosopher (*Ethic.* vi, 12), *prudence regulates whatever is directed to the end*, about which things counsel and choice are concerned. Nevertheless when, guided by prudence, we perform some action aright which is directed to the end of some virtue, such as temperance or fortitude, that action belongs chiefly to the virtue to whose end it is directed. Since, then, the admonition which is given in fraternal correction is directed to the removal of a brother's sin, which removal pertains to charity, it is evident that this admonition is chiefly an act of charity, which virtue commands it, so to speak, but secondarily an act of prudence, which executes and directs the action.

**REPLY OBJ. 3**: Fraternal correction is not opposed to forbearance with the weak, on the contrary it results from it. For a man bears with a sinner, insofar as he is not disturbed against him, and retains his goodwill towards him: the result being that he strives to make him do better.

# Article 2

*Whether fraternal correction is a matter of precept?*

**AD SECUNDUM SIC PROCEDITUR.** Videtur quod correctio fraterna non sit in praecepto. Nihil enim quod est impossibile cadit sub praecepto, secundum illud Hieronymi, *maledictus qui dicit Deum aliquid impossibile praecepisse.* Sed Eccle. VII dicitur, *considera opera Dei, quod nemo possit corrigere quem ille despexerit.* Ergo correctio fraterna non est in praecepto.

**PRAETEREA,** omnia praecepta legis divinae ad praecepta Decalogi reducuntur. Sed correctio fraterna non cadit sub aliquo praeceptorum Decalogi. Ergo non cadit sub praecepto.

**PRAETEREA,** omissio praecepti divini est peccatum mortale, quod in sanctis viris non invenitur. Sed omissio fraternae correctionis invenitur in sanctis et in spiritualibus viris, dicit enim Augustinus, I de Civ. Dei, quod *non solum inferiores, verum etiam hi qui superiorem vitae gradum tenent ab aliorum reprehensione se abstinent, propter quaedam cupiditatis vincula, non propter officia caritatis.* Ergo correctio fraterna non est in praecepto.

**PRAETEREA,** illud quod est in praecepto habet rationem debiti. Si ergo correctio fraterna caderet sub praecepto, hoc fratribus deberemus ut eos peccantes corrigeremus. Sed ille qui debet alicui debitum corporale, puta pecuniam, non debet esse contentus ut ei occurrat creditor, sed debet eum quaerere ut debitum reddat. Oporteret ergo quod homo quaereret correctione indigentes ad hoc quod eos corrigeret. Quod videtur inconveniens, tum propter multitudinem peccantium, ad quorum correctionem unus homo non posset sufficere; tum etiam quia oporteret quod religiosi de claustris suis exirent ad homines corrigendos, quod est inconveniens. Non ergo fraterna correctio est in praecepto.

**SED CONTRA** est quod Augustinus dicit, in libro de Verb. Dom., *si neglexeris corrigere, peior eo factus es qui peccavit.* Sed hoc non esset nisi per huiusmodi negligentiam aliquis praeceptum omitteret. Ergo correctio fraterna est in praecepto.

**RESPONDEO** dicendum quod correctio fraterna cadit sub praecepto. Sed considerandum est quod sicut praecepta negativa legis prohibent actus peccatorum, ita praecepta affirmativa inducunt ad actus virtutum. Actus autem peccatorum sunt secundum se mali, et nullo modo bene fieri possunt, nec aliquo tempore aut loco, quia secundum se sunt coniuncti malo fini, ut dicitur in II Ethic. Et ideo praecepta negativa obligant semper et ad semper. Sed actus virtutum non quolibet modo fieri debent, sed observatis debitis circumstantiis quae requiruntur ad hoc quod sit actus virtuosus, ut scilicet fiat ubi debet, et quando debet, et secundum quod

**OBJECTION 1:** It would seem that fraternal correction is not a matter of precept. For nothing impossible is a matter of precept, according to the saying of Jerome: *Accursed be he who says that God has commanded anything impossible.* Now it is written (Eccl 7:14): *Consider the works of God, that no man can correct whom He hath despised.* Therefore fraternal correction is not a matter of precept.

**OBJ. 2:** Further, all the precepts of the Divine Law are reduced to the precepts of the Decalogue. But fraternal correction does not come under any precept of the Decalogue. Therefore it is not a matter of precept.

**OBJ. 3:** Further, the omission of a Divine precept is a mortal sin, which has no place in a holy man. Yet holy and spiritual men are found to omit fraternal correction: since Augustine says (*De Civ. Dei* i, 9): *Not only those of low degree, but also those of high position, refrain from reproving others, moved by a guilty cupidity, not by the claims of charity.* Therefore fraternal correction is not a matter of precept.

**OBJ. 4:** Further, whatever is a matter of precept is something due. If, therefore, fraternal correction is a matter of precept, it is due to our brethren that we correct them when they sin. Now when a man owes anyone a material due, such as the payment of a sum of money, he must not be content that his creditor come to him, but he should seek him out, that he may pay him his due. Hence we should have to go seeking for those who need correction, in order that we might correct them; which appears to be inconvenient, both on account of the great number of sinners, for whose correction one man could not suffice, and because religious would have to leave the cloister in order to reprove men, which would be unbecoming. Therefore fraternal correction is not a matter of precept.

**ON THE CONTRARY,** Augustine says (*De Verb. Dom.* xvi, 4): *You become worse than the sinner if you fail to correct him.* But this would not be so unless, by this neglect, one omitted to observe some precept. Therefore fraternal correction is a matter of precept.

**I ANSWER THAT,** Fraternal correction is a matter of precept. We must observe, however, that while the negative precepts of the Law forbid sinful acts, the positive precepts inculcate acts of virtue. Now sinful acts are evil in themselves, and cannot become good, no matter how, or when, or where, they are done, because of their very nature they are connected with an evil end, as stated in *Ethic.* ii, 6: wherefore negative precepts bind always and for all times. On the other hand, acts of virtue must not be done anyhow, but by observing the due circumstances, which are requisite in order that an act be virtuous; namely, that it be done where, when, and how it ought to be done.

debet. Et quia dispositio eorum quae sunt ad finem attenditur secundum rationem finis, in istis circumstantiis virtuosi actus praecipue attendenda est ratio finis, qui est bonum virtutis. Si ergo sit aliqua talis omissio alicuius circumstantiae circa virtuosum actum quae totaliter tollat bonum virtutis, hoc contrariatur praecepto. Si autem sit defectus alicuius circumstantiae quae non totaliter tollat virtutem, licet non perfecte attingat ad bonum virtutis, non est contra praeceptum. Unde et Philosophus dicit, in II Ethic., quod si parum discedatur a medio, non est contra virtutem, sed si multum discedatur, corrumpitur virtus in suo actu. Correctio autem fraterna ordinatur ad fratris emendationem. Et ideo hoc modo cadit sub praecepto, secundum quod est necessaria ad istum finem, non autem ita quod quolibet loco vel tempore frater delinquens corrigatur.

**AD PRIMUM** ergo dicendum quod in omnibus bonis agendis operatio hominis non est efficax nisi adsit auxilium divinum, et tamen homo debet facere quod in se est. Unde Augustinus dicit, in libro de Corr. et Grat., *nescientes quis pertineat ad praedestinatorum numerum et quis non pertineat, sic affici debemus caritatis affectu ut omnes velimus salvos fieri.* Et ideo omnibus debemus fraternae correctionis officium impendere sub spe divini auxilii.

**AD SECUNDUM** dicendum quod, sicut supra dictum est, omnia praecepta quae pertinent ad impendendum aliquod beneficium proximo reducuntur ad praeceptum de honoratione parentum.

**AD TERTIUM** dicendum quod correctio fraterna tripliciter omitti potest.

Uno quidem modo, meritorie, quando ex caritate aliquis correctionem omittit. Dicit enim Augustinus, in I de Civ. Dei, *si propterea quisque obiurgandis et corripiendis male agentibus parcit, quia opportunius tempus inquiritur; vel eisdem ipsis metuit ne deteriores ex hoc efficiantur, vel ad bonam vitam et piam erudiendos impediant alios infirmos et premant, atque avertant a fide; non videtur esse cupiditatis occasio, sed consilium caritatis.*

Alio modo praetermittitur fraterna correctio cum peccato mortali, quando scilicet *formidatur,* ut ibi dicitur, *iudicium vulgi et carnis excruciatio vel peremptio*; dum tamen haec ita dominentur in animo quod fraternae caritati praeponantur. Et hoc videtur contingere quando aliquis praesumit de aliquo delinquente probabiliter quod posset eum a peccato retrahere, et tamen propter timorem vel cupiditatem praetermittit.

Tertio modo huiusmodi omissio est peccatum veniale, quando timor et cupiditas tardiorem faciunt hominem ad corrigendum delicta fratris, non tamen ita quod, si ei constaret quod fratrem posset a peccato retrahere, propter timorem vel cupiditatem dimitteret,

And since the disposition of whatever is directed to the end depends on the formal aspect of the end, the chief of these circumstances of a virtuous act is this aspect of the end, which in this case is the good of virtue. If therefore such a circumstance be omitted from a virtuous act, as entirely takes away the good of virtue, such an act is contrary to a precept. If, however, the circumstance omitted from a virtuous act be such as not to destroy the virtue altogether, though it does not perfectly attain the good of virtue, it is not against a precept. Hence the Philosopher (*Ethic.* ii, 9) says that if we depart but little from the mean, it is not contrary to the virtue, whereas if we depart much from the mean virtue is destroyed in its act. Now fraternal correction is directed to a brother's amendment: so that it is a matter of precept, insofar as it is necessary for that end, but not so as we have to correct our erring brother at all places and times.

**REPLY OBJ. 1**: In all good deeds man's action is not efficacious without the Divine assistance: and yet man must do what is in his power. Hence Augustine says (*De Correp. et Gratia* xv): *Since we ignore who is predestined and who is not, charity should so guide our feelings, that we wish all to be saved.* Consequently we ought to do our brethren the kindness of correcting them, with the hope of God's help.

**REPLY OBJ. 2**: As stated above (Q. 32, A. 5, ad 4), all the precepts about rendering service to our neighbor are reduced to the precept about the honor due to parents.

**REPLY OBJ. 3**: Fraternal correction may be omitted in three ways.

First, meritoriously, when out of charity one omits to correct someone. For Augustine says (*De Civ. Dei* i, 9): *If a man refrains from chiding and reproving wrongdoers, because he awaits a suitable time for so doing, or because he fears lest, if he does so, they may become worse, or hinder, oppress, or turn away from the faith, others who are weak and need to be instructed in a life of goodness and virtue, this does not seem to result from covetousness, but to be counselled by charity.*

Second, fraternal correction may be omitted in such a way that one commits a mortal sin, namely, *when* (as he says in the same passage) *one fears what people may think, or lest one may suffer grievous pain or death*; provided, however, that the mind is so dominated by such things, that it gives them the preference to fraternal charity. This would seem to be the case when a man reckons that he might probably withdraw some wrongdoer from sin, and yet omits to do so, through fear or covetousness.

Third, such an omission is a venial sin, when through fear or covetousness, a man is loth to correct his brother's faults, and yet not to such a degree, that if he saw clearly that he could withdraw him from sin, he would still forbear from so doing, through fear or covetousness, because in

quibus in animo suo praeponit caritatem fraternam. Et hoc modo quandoque viri sancti negligunt corrigere delinquentes.

**AD QUARTUM** dicendum quod illud quod debetur alicui determinatae et certae personae, sive sit bonum corporale sive spirituale, oportet quod ei impendamus non expectantes quod nobis occurrat, sed debitam sollicitudinem habentes ut eum inquiramus. Unde sicut ille qui debet pecuniam creditori debet eum requirere cum tempus fuerit ut ei debitum reddat, ita qui habet spiritualiter curam alicuius debet eum quaerere ad hoc quod eum corrigat de peccato. Sed illa beneficia quae non debentur certae personae sed communiter omnibus proximis, sive sint corporalia sive spiritualia, non oportet nos quaerere quibus impendamus, sed sufficit quod impendamus eis qui nobis occurrunt, hoc enim *quasi pro quadam sorte* habendum est, ut Augustinus dicit, in I de Doct. Christ. Et propter hoc dicit, in libro de Verb. Dom., quod *admonet nos dominus noster non negligere invicem peccata nostra, non quaerendo quid reprehendas, sed videndo quid corrigas.* Alioquin efficeremur exploratores vitae aliorum, contra id quod dicitur Prov. XXIV, *ne quaeras impietatem in domo iusti, et non vastes requiem eius.* Unde patet quod nec religiosos oportet exire claustrum ad corrigendum delinquentes.

his own mind he prefers fraternal charity to these things. It is in this way that holy men sometimes omit to correct wrongdoers.

**REPLY OBJ. 4**: We are bound to pay that which is due to some fixed and certain person, whether it be a material or a spiritual good, without waiting for him to come to us, but by taking proper steps to find him. Wherefore just as he that owes money to a creditor should seek him, when the time comes, so as to pay him what he owes, so he that has spiritual charge of some person is bound to seek him out, in order to reprove him for a sin. On the other hand, we are not bound to seek someone on whom to bestow such favors as are due, not to any certain person, but to all our neighbors in general, whether those favors be material or spiritual goods, but it suffices that we bestow them when the opportunity occurs; because, as Augustine says (*De Doctr. Christ.* i, 28), *we must look upon this as a matter of chance.* For this reason he says (*De Verb. Dom.* xvi, 1) that *Our Lord warns us not to be listless in regard of one another's sins: not indeed by being on the lookout for something to denounce, but by correcting what we see*: else we should become spies on the lives of others, which is against the saying of Prov. 24:19: *Lie not in wait, nor seek after wickedness in the house of the just, nor spoil his rest.* It is evident from this that there is no need for religious to leave their cloister in order to rebuke evil-doers.

# Article 3

*Whether fraternal correction belongs only to prelates?*

**AD TERTIUM SIC PROCEDITUR**. Videtur quod correctio fraterna non pertineat nisi ad praelatos. Dicit enim Hieronymus, *sacerdotes studeant illud Evangelii implere, si peccaverit in te frater tuus*, et cetera. Sed nomine *sacerdotum* consueverunt significari praelati, qui habent curam aliorum. Ergo videtur quod ad solos praelatos pertineat fraterna correctio.

**PRAETEREA**, fraterna correctio est quaedam eleemosyna spiritualis. Sed corporalem eleemosynam facere pertinet ad eos qui sunt superiores in temporalibus, scilicet ad ditiores. Ergo etiam fraterna correctio pertinet ad eos qui sunt superiores in spiritualibus, scilicet ad praelatos.

**PRAETEREA**, ille qui corripit alium movet eum sua admonitione ad melius. Sed in rebus naturalibus inferiora moventur a superioribus. Ergo etiam secundum ordinem virtutis, qui sequitur ordinem naturae, ad solos praelatos pertinet inferiores corrigere.

**SED CONTRA** est quod dicitur XXIV, qu. III, *tam sacerdotes quam reliqui fideles omnes summam debent habere curam de his qui pereunt, quatenus eorum redar-*

**OBJECTION 1**: It would seem that fraternal correction belongs to prelates alone. For Jerome says: *Let priests endeavor to fulfill this saying of the Gospel: 'If thy brother sin against thee,' etc.* Now prelates having charge of others were usually designated under the name of *priests*. Therefore it seems that fraternal correction belongs to prelates alone.

**OBJ. 2**: Further, fraternal correction is a spiritual alms. Now corporal almsgiving belongs to those who are placed above others in temporal matters, i.e., to the rich. Therefore fraternal correction belongs to those who are placed above others in spiritual matters, i.e., to prelates.

**OBJ. 3**: Further, when one man reproves another he moves him by his rebuke to something better. Now in the physical order the inferior is moved by the superior. Therefore in the order of virtue also, which follows the order of nature, it belongs to prelates alone to correct inferiors.

**ON THE CONTRARY**, It is written (*Dist. xxiv, qu. 3, Can. Tam Sacerdotes*): *Both priests and all the rest of the faithful should be most solicitous for those who perish, so that their*

*gutione aut corrigantur a peccatis, aut, si incorrigibiles appareant, ab Ecclesia separentur.*

RESPONDEO dicendum quod, sicut dictum est, duplex est correctio. Una quidem quae est actus caritatis, qui specialiter tendit ad emendationem fratris delinquentis per simplicem admonitionem. Et talis correctio pertinet ad quemlibet caritatem habentem, sive sit subditus sive praelatus.

Est autem alia correctio quae est actus iustitiae, per quam intenditur bonum commune, quod non solum procuratur per admonitionem fratris, sed interdum etiam per punitionem, ut alii a peccato timentes desistant. Et talis correctio pertinet ad solos praelatos, qui non solum habent admonere, sed etiam corrigere puniendo.

AD PRIMUM ergo dicendum quod etiam in correctione fraterna, quae ad omnes pertinet, gravior est cura praelatorum; ut dicit Augustinus, in I de Civ. Dei. Sicut enim temporalia beneficia potius debet aliquis exhibere illis quorum curam temporalem habet, ita etiam beneficia spiritualia, puta correctionem, doctrinam et alia huiusmodi magis debet exhibere illis qui sunt suae spirituali curae commissi. Non ergo intendit Hieronymus dicere quod ad solos sacerdotes pertineat praeceptum de correctione fraterna, sed quod ad hos specialiter pertinet.

AD SECUNDUM dicendum quod sicut ille qui habet unde corporaliter subvenire possit quantum ad hoc dives est, ita ille qui habet sanum rationis iudicium, ex quo possit alterius delictum corrigere quantum ad hoc est superior habendus.

AD TERTIUM dicendum quod etiam in rebus naturalibus quaedam mutuo in se agunt, quia quantum ad aliquid sunt se invicem superiora, prout scilicet utrumque est quodammodo in potentia et quodammodo in actu respectu alterius. Et similiter aliquis, inquantum habet sanum rationis iudicium in hoc in quo alter delinquit, potest eum corrigere, licet non sit simpliciter superior.

*reproof may either correct their sinful ways, or, if they be incorrigible, cut them off from the Church.*

I ANSWER THAT, As stated above (A. 1), correction is twofold. One is an act of charity, which seeks in a special way the recovery of an erring brother by means of a simple warning: such like correction belongs to anyone who has charity, be he subject or prelate.

But there is another correction which is an act of justice purposing the common good, which is procured not only by warning one's brother, but also, sometimes, by punishing him, that others may, through fear, desist from sin. Such a correction belongs only to prelates, whose business it is not only to admonish, but also to correct by means of punishments.

REPLY OBJ. 1: Even as regards that fraternal correction which is common to all, prelates have a grave responsibility, as Augustine says (*De Civ. Dei* i, 9), for just as a man ought to bestow temporal favors on those especially of whom he has temporal care, so too ought he to confer spiritual favors, such as correction, teaching and the like, on those who are entrusted to his spiritual care. Therefore Jerome does not mean that the precept of fraternal correction concerns priests only, but that it concerns them chiefly.

REPLY OBJ. 2: Just as he who has the means wherewith to give corporal assistance is rich in this respect, so he whose reason is gifted with a sane judgment, so as to be able to correct another's wrong-doing, is, in this respect, to be looked on as a superior.

REPLY OBJ. 3: Even in the physical order certain things act mutually on one another, through being in some respect higher than one another, insofar as each is somewhat in act, and somewhat in potentiality with regard to another. In like manner one man can correct another insofar as he has a sane judgment in a matter wherein the other sins, though he is not his superior simply.

# Article 4

*Whether a man is bound to correct his prelate?*

AD QUARTUM SIC PROCEDITUR. Videtur quod aliquis non teneatur corrigere praelatum suum. Dicitur enim Exod. XIX, *bestia quae tetigerit montem lapidabitur*, et II Reg. VI dicitur quod Oza percussus est a domino quia tetigit arcam. Sed per montem et arcam significatur praelatus. Ergo praelati non sunt corrigendi a subditis.

OBJECTION 1: It would seem that no man is bound to correct his prelate. For it is written (Exod 19:12): *The beast that shall touch the mount shall be stoned*, and (2 Kgs 6:7) it is related that the Lord struck Oza for touching the ark. Now the mount and the ark signify our prelates. Therefore prelates should not be corrected by their subjects.

**PRAETEREA**, Gal. II, super illud, *in faciem ei restiti*, dicit Glossa, *ut par*. Ergo, cum subditus non sit par praelato, non debet eum corrigere.

**PRAETEREA**, Gregorius dicit, *sanctorum vitam corrigere non praesumat nisi qui de se meliora sentit*. Sed aliquis non debet de se meliora sentire quam de praelato suo. Ergo praelati non sunt corrigendi.

**SED CONTRA** est quod Augustinus dicit, in regula, *non solum vestri, sed etiam ipsius, idest praelati, miseremini, qui inter vos quanto in loco superiore, tanto in periculo maiore versatur*. Sed correctio fraterna est opus misericordiae. Ergo etiam praelati sunt corrigendi.

**RESPONDEO** dicendum quod correctio quae est actus iustitiae per coercionem poenae non competit subditis respectu praelati. Sed correctio fraterna, quae est actus caritatis, pertinet ad unumquemque respectu cuiuslibet personae ad quam caritatem debet habere, si in eo aliquid corrigibile inveniatur.

Actus enim ex aliquo habitu vel potentia procedens se extendit ad omnia quae continentur sub obiecto illius potentiae vel habitus, sicut visio ad omnia quae continentur sub obiecto visus. Sed quia actus virtuosus debet esse moderatus debitis circumstantiis, ideo in correctione qua subditi corrigunt praelatos debet modus congruus adhiberi, ut scilicet non cum protervia et duritia, sed cum mansuetudine et reverentia corrigantur. Unde apostolus dicit, I ad Tim. V, *seniorem ne increpaveris, sed obsecra ut patrem*. Et ideo Dionysius redarguit Demophilum monachum quia sacerdotem irreverenter correxerat, eum percutiens et de Ecclesia eiiciens.

**AD PRIMUM** ergo dicendum quod tunc praelatus inordinate tangi videtur quando irreverenter obiurgatur, vel etiam quando ei detrahitur. Et hoc significatur per contactum montis et arcae damnatum a Deo.

**AD SECUNDUM** dicendum quod *in faciem resistere coram omnibus* excedit modum fraternae correctionis, et ideo sic Paulus Petrum non reprehendisset nisi aliquo modo par esset, quantum ad fidei defensionem. Sed in occulto admonere et reverenter, hoc potest etiam ille qui non est par. Unde apostolus, ad Coloss. ult., scribit ut praelatum suum admoneant, cum dicit, *dicite Archippo, ministerium tuum imple*. Sciendum tamen est quod ubi immineret periculum fidei, etiam publice essent praelati a subditis arguendi. Unde et Paulus, qui erat subditus Petro, propter imminens periculum scandali circa fidem, Petrum publice arguit. Et sicut Glossa Augustini dicit, ad Gal. II, *ipse Petrus exemplum maioribus praebuit ut, sicubi forte rectum tramitem reliquissent, non dedignentur etiam a posterioribus corrigi*.

**AD TERTIUM** dicendum quod praesumere se esse simpliciter meliorem quam praelatus sit, videtur esse

**OBJ. 2**: Further, a gloss on Gal. 2:11, *I withstood him to the face*, adds: *as an equal*. Therefore, since a subject is not equal to his prelate, he ought not to correct him.

**OBJ. 3**: Further, Gregory says (*Moral.* xxiii, 8) that *one ought not to presume to reprove the conduct of holy men, unless one thinks better of oneself*. But one ought not to think better of oneself than of one's prelate. Therefore one ought not to correct one's prelate.

**ON THE CONTRARY**, Augustine says in his Rule: *Show mercy not only to yourselves, but also to him who, being in the higher position among you, is therefore in greater danger*. But fraternal correction is a work of mercy. Therefore even prelates ought to be corrected.

**I ANSWER THAT**, A subject is not competent to administer to his prelate the correction which is an act of justice through the coercive nature of punishment: but the fraternal correction which is an act of charity is within the competency of everyone in respect of any person towards whom he is bound by charity, provided there be something in that person which requires correction.

Now an act which proceeds from a habit or power extends to whatever is contained under the object of that power or habit: thus vision extends to all things comprised in the object of sight. Since, however, a virtuous act needs to be moderated by due circumstances, it follows that when a subject corrects his prelate, he ought to do so in a becoming manner, not with impudence and harshness, but with gentleness and respect. Hence the Apostle says (1 Tim 5:1): *An ancient man rebuke not, but entreat him as a father*. Wherefore Dionysius finds fault with the monk Demophilus (*Ep. viii*), for rebuking a priest with insolence, by striking and turning him out of the church.

**REPLY OBJ. 1**: It would seem that a subject touches his prelate inordinately when he upbraids him with insolence, as also when he speaks ill of him: and this is signified by God's condemnation of those who touched the mount and the ark.

**REPLY OBJ. 2**: *To withstand anyone in public* exceeds the mode of fraternal correction, and so Paul would not have withstood Peter then, unless he were in some way his equal as regards the defense of the faith. But one who is not an equal can reprove privately and respectfully. Hence the Apostle in writing to the Colossians (4:17) tells them to admonish their prelate: *Say to Archippus: Fulfill thy ministry*. It must be observed, however, that if the faith were endangered, a subject ought to rebuke his prelate even publicly. Hence Paul, who was Peter's subject, rebuked him in public, on account of the imminent danger of scandal concerning faith, and, as the gloss of Augustine says on Gal. 2:11, *Peter gave an example to superiors, that if at any time they should happen to stray from the straight path, they should not disdain to be reproved by their subjects*.

**REPLY OBJ. 3**: To presume oneself to be simply better than one's prelate, would seem to savor of presumptuous

praesumptuosae superbiae. Sed aestimare se meliorem quantum ad aliquid non est praesumptionis, quia nullus est in hac vita qui non habeat aliquem defectum. Et etiam considerandum est quod cum aliquis praelatum caritative monet, non propter hoc se maiorem existimat, sed auxilium impartitur ei qui, *quanto in loco superiori, tanto in periculo maiori versatur*, ut Augustinus dicit, in regula.

pride; but there is no presumption in thinking oneself better in some respect, because, in this life, no man is without some fault. We must also remember that when a man reproves his prelate charitably, it does not follow that he thinks himself any better, but merely that he offers his help to one who, *being in the higher position among you, is therefore in greater danger*, as Augustine observes in his Rule quoted above.

# Article 5

*Whether a sinner ought to reprove a wrongdoer?*

AD QUINTUM SIC PROCEDITUR. Videtur quod peccator corrigere debeat delinquentem. Nullus enim propter peccatum quod commisit a praecepto observando excusatur. Sed correctio fraterna cadit sub praecepto, ut dictum est. Ergo videtur quod propter peccatum quod quis commisit non debet praetermittere huiusmodi correctionem.

PRAETEREA, eleemosyna spiritualis est potior quam eleemosyna corporalis. Sed ille qui est in peccato non debet abstinere quin eleemosynam corporalem faciat. Ergo multo minus debet abstinere a correctione delinquentis propter peccatum praecedens.

PRAETEREA, I Ioan. I dicitur, *si dixerimus quia peccatum non habemus, nosipsos seducimus*. Si igitur propter peccatum aliquis impeditur a correctione fraterna, nullus erit qui possit corrigere delinquentem. Hoc autem est inconveniens. Ergo et primum.

SED CONTRA est quod Isidorus dicit, in libro de summo bono, *non debet vitia aliorum corrigere qui est vitiis subiectus*. Et Rom. II dicitur, *in quo alium iudicas, teipsum condemnas, eadem enim agis quae iudicas*.

RESPONDEO dicendum quod, sicut dictum est, correctio delinquentis pertinet ad aliquem inquantum viget in eo rectum iudicium rationis. Peccatum autem, ut supra dictum est, non tollit totum bonum naturae, quin remaneat in peccante aliquid de recto iudicio rationis. Et secundum hoc potest sibi competere alterius delictum arguere. Sed tamen per peccatum praecedens impedimentum quoddam huic correctioni affertur, propter tria. Primo quidem, quia ex peccato praecedenti indignus redditur ut alium corrigat. Et praecipue si maius peccatum commisit, non est dignus ut alium corrigat de minori peccato. Unde super illud Matth. VII, *quid vides festucam* etc., dicit Hieronymus, *de his loquitur qui, cum mortali crimine detineantur obnoxii, minora peccata fratribus non concedunt*.

Secundo, redditur indebita correctio propter scandalum, quod sequitur ex correctione si peccatum corri-

OBJECTION 1: It would seem that a sinner ought to reprove a wrongdoer. For no man is excused from obeying a precept by having committed a sin. But fraternal correction is a matter of precept, as stated above (A. 2). Therefore it seems that a man ought not to forbear from such like correction for the reason that he has committed a sin.

OBJ. 2: Further, spiritual almsdeeds are of more account than corporal almsdeeds. Now one who is in sin ought not to abstain from administering corporal alms. Much less therefore ought he, on account of a previous sin, to refrain from correcting wrongdoers.

OBJ. 3: Further, it is written (1 John 1:8): *If we say that we have no sin, we deceive ourselves*. Therefore if, on account of a sin, a man is hindered from reproving his brother, there will be none to reprove the wrongdoer. But the latter proposition is unreasonable: therefore the former is also.

ON THE CONTRARY, Isidore says (*De Summo Bono* iii, 32): *He that is subject to vice should not correct the vices of others*. Again it is written (Rom 2:1): *Wherein thou judgest another, thou condemnest thyself. For thou dost the same things which thou judgest*.

I ANSWER THAT, As stated above (A. 3, ad 2), to correct a wrongdoer belongs to a man, insofar as his reason is gifted with right judgment. Now sin, as stated above (I-II, Q. 85, AA. 1, 2), does not destroy the good of nature so as to deprive the sinner's reason of all right judgment, and in this respect he may be competent to find fault with others for committing sin. Nevertheless a previous sin proves somewhat of a hindrance to this correction, for three reasons. First because this previous sin renders a man unworthy to rebuke another; and especially is he unworthy to correct another for a lesser sin, if he himself has committed a greater. Hence Jerome says on the words, *Why seest thou the mote?* etc. (Matt 7:3): *He is speaking of those who, while they are themselves guilty of mortal sin, have no patience with the lesser sins of their brethren*.

Second, such like correction becomes unseemly, on account of the scandal which ensues therefrom, if the

pientis sit manifestum, quia videtur quod ille qui corrigit non corrigat ex caritate, sed magis ad ostentationem. Unde super illud Matth. VII, *quomodo dicis fratri tuo* etc., exponit Chrysostomus, *in quo proposito? Puta ex caritate, ut salves proximum tuum? Non, quia teipsum ante salvares. Vis ergo non alios salvare, sed per bonam doctrinam malos actus celare, et scientiae laudem ab hominibus quaerere.*

Tertio modo, propter superbiam corripientis, inquantum scilicet aliquis, propria peccata parvipendens, seipsum proximo praefert in corde suo, peccata eius austera severitate diiudicans, ac si ipse esset iustus. Unde Augustinus dicit, in libro de Serm. Dom. in monte, *accusare vitia officium est bonorum, quod cum mali faciunt, alienas partes agunt.* Et ideo, sicut Augustinus dicit in eodem, *cogitemus, cum aliquem reprehendere nos necessitas coegerit, utrum tale sit vitium quod nunquam habuimus, et tunc cogitemus nos homines esse, et habere potuisse. Vel tale quod habuimus et iam non habemus, et tunc tangat memoriam communis fragilitas, ut illam correctionem non odium sed misericordia praecedat. Si autem invenerimus nos in eodem vitio esse, non obiurgemus, sed congemiscamus et ad pariter poenitendum invitemus.* Ex his igitur patet quod peccator, si cum humilitate corripiat delinquentem, non peccat, nec sibi novam condemnationem acquirit; licet per hoc vel in conscientia fratris, vel saltem sua, pro peccato praeterito condemnabilem se esse ostendat.

**UNDE PATET** responsio ad obiecta.

corrector's sin be well known, because it would seem that he corrects, not out of charity, but more for the sake of ostentation. Hence the words of Matt. 7:4, *How sayest thou to thy brother?* etc. are expounded by Chrysostom thus: *That is—'With what object?' Out of charity, think you, that you may save your neighbor? No, because you would look after your own salvation first. What you want is, not to save others, but to hide your evil deeds with good teaching, and to seek to be praised by men for your knowledge.*

Third, on account of the rebuker's pride; when, for instance, a man thinks lightly of his own sins, and, in his own heart, sets himself above his neighbor, judging the latter's sins with harsh severity, as though he himself were a just man. Hence Augustine says (*De Serm. Dom. in Monte* ii, 19): *To reprove the faults of others is the duty of good and kindly men: when a wicked man rebukes anyone, his rebuke is the latter's acquittal.* And so, as Augustine says (*De Serm. Dom. in Monte* ii, 19): *When we have to find fault with anyone, we should think whether we were never guilty of his sin; and then we must remember that we are men, and might have been guilty of it; or that we once had it on our conscience, but have it no longer: and then we should bethink ourselves that we are all weak, in order that our reproof may be the outcome, not of hatred, but of pity. But if we find that we are guilty of the same sin, we must not rebuke him, but groan with him, and invite him to repent with us.* It follows from this that, if a sinner reprove a wrongdoer with humility, he does not sin, nor does he bring a further condemnation on himself, although thereby he proves himself deserving of condemnation, either in his brother's or in his own conscience, on account of his previous sin.

**HENCE** the Replies to the Objections are clear.

# Article 6

*Whether one ought to forbear from correcting someone, through fear lest he become worse?*

**AD SEXTUM SIC PROCEDITUR.** Videtur quod aliquis non debeat a correctione cessare propter timorem ne ille fiat deterior. Peccatum enim est quaedam infirmitas animae, secundum illud Psalm., *miserere mei, domine, quoniam infirmus sum.* Sed ille cui imminet cura infirmi etiam propter eius contradictionem vel contemptum non debet cessare, quia tunc imminet maius periculum, sicut patet circa furiosos. Ergo multo magis debet homo peccantem corrigere, quantumcumque graviter ferat.

**PRAETEREA,** secundum Hieronymum, *veritas vitae non est dimittenda propter scandalum.* Praecepta autem Dei pertinent ad veritatem vitae. Cum ergo correctio fraterna cadat sub praecepto, ut dictum est, videtur quod

**OBJECTION 1:** It would seem that one ought not to forbear from correcting someone through fear lest he become worse. For sin is weakness of the soul, according to Ps. 6:3: *Have mercy on me, O Lord, for I am weak.* Now he that has charge of a sick person, must not cease to take care of him, even if he be fractious or contemptuous, because then the danger is greater, as in the case of madmen. Much more, therefore should one correct a sinner, no matter how badly he takes it.

**OBJ. 2:** Further, according to Jerome *vital truths are not to be foregone on account of scandal.* Now God's commandments are vital truths. Since, therefore, fraternal correction is a matter of precept, as stated above (A. 2), it seems that it

non sit dimittenda propter scandalum eius qui corripitur.

PRAETEREA, secundum apostolum, ad Rom. III, *non sunt facienda mala ut veniant bona.* Ergo, pari ratione, non sunt praetermittenda bona ne veniant mala. Sed correctio fraterna est quoddam bonum. Ergo non est praetermittenda propter timorem ne ille qui corripitur fiat deterior.

SED CONTRA est quod dicitur Prov. IX, *noli arguere derisorem, ne oderit te,* ubi dicit Glossa, *non est timendum ne tibi derisor, cum arguitur, contumelias inferat, sed hoc potius providendum, ne, tractus ad odium, inde fiat peior.* Ergo cessandum est a correctione fraterna quando timetur ne fiat ille inde deterior.

RESPONDEO dicendum quod, sicut dictum est, duplex est correctio delinquentis. Una quidem pertinens ad praelatos, quae ordinatur ad bonum commune, et habet vim coactivam. Et talis correctio non est dimittenda propter turbationem eius qui corripitur. Tum quia, si propria sponte emendari non velit, cogendus est per poenas ut peccare desistat. Tum etiam quia, si incorrigibilis sit, per hoc providetur bono communi, dum servatur ordo iustitiae, et unius exemplo alii deterrentur. Unde iudex non praetermittit ferre sententiam condemnationis in peccantem propter timorem turbationis ipsius, vel etiam amicorum eius.

Alia vero est correctio fraterna, cuius finis est emendatio delinquentis, non habens coactionem sed simplicem admonitionem. Et ideo ubi probabiliter aestimatur quod peccator admonitionem non recipiat, sed ad peiora labatur, est ab huiusmodi correctione desistendum, quia ea quae sunt ad finem debent regulari secundum quod exigit ratio finis.

AD PRIMUM ergo dicendum quod medicus quadam coactione utitur in phreneticum, qui curam eius recipere non vult. Et huic similatur correctio praelatorum, quae habet vim coactivam, non autem simplex correctio fraterna.

AD SECUNDUM dicendum quod de correctione fraterna datur praeceptum secundum quod est actus virtutis. Hoc autem est secundum quod proportionatur fini. Et ideo quando est impeditiva finis, puta cum efficitur homo deterior, iam non pertinet ad veritatem vitae, nec cadit sub praecepto.

AD TERTIUM dicendum quod ea quae ordinantur ad finem habent rationem boni ex ordine ad finem. Et ideo correctio fraterna, quando est impeditiva finis, scilicet emendationis fratris, iam non habet rationem boni. Et ideo cum praetermittitur talis correctio, non praetermittitur bonum ne eveniat malum.

should not be foregone for fear of scandalizing the person to be corrected.

OBJ. 3: Further, according to the Apostle (Rom 3:8) *we should not do evil that good may come of it.* Therefore, in like manner, good should not be omitted lest evil befall. Now fraternal correction is a good thing. Therefore it should not be omitted for fear lest the person corrected become worse.

ON THE CONTRARY, It is written (Prov 9:8): *Rebuke not a scorner lest he hate thee,* where a gloss remarks: *You must not fear lest the scorner insult you when you rebuke him: rather should you bear in mind that by making him hate you, you may make him worse.* Therefore one ought to forego fraternal correction, when we fear lest we may make a man worse.

I ANSWER THAT, As stated above (A. 3) the correction of the wrongdoer is twofold. One, which belongs to prelates, and is directed to the common good, has coercive force. Such correction should not be omitted lest the person corrected be disturbed, both because if he is unwilling to amend his ways of his own accord, he should be made to cease sinning by being punished, and because, if he be incorrigible, the common good is safeguarded in this way, since the order of justice is observed, and others are deterred by one being made an example of. Hence a judge does not desist from pronouncing sentence of condemnation against a sinner, for fear of disturbing him or his friends.

The other fraternal correction is directed to the amendment of the wrongdoer, whom it does not coerce, but merely admonishes. Consequently when it is deemed probable that the sinner will not take the warning, and will become worse, such fraternal correction should be foregone, because the means should be regulated according to the requirements of the end.

REPLY OBJ. 1: The doctor uses force towards a madman, who is unwilling to submit to his treatment; and this may be compared with the correction administered by prelates, which has coercive power, but not with simple fraternal correction.

REPLY OBJ. 2: Fraternal correction is a matter of precept, insofar as it is an act of virtue, and it will be a virtuous act insofar as it is proportionate to the end. Consequently whenever it is a hindrance to the end, for instance when a man becomes worse through it, it is longer a vital truth, nor is it a matter of precept.

REPLY OBJ. 3: Whatever is directed to an end, becomes good through being directed to the end. Hence whenever fraternal correction hinders the end, namely the amendment of our brother, it is no longer good, so that when such a correction is omitted, good is not omitted lest evil should befall.

# Article 7

*Whether the precept of fraternal correction demands that a*
*private admonition should precede denunciation?*

**AD SEPTIMUM SIC PROCEDITUR.** Videtur quod in correctione fraterna non debeat, ex necessitate praecepti, admonitio secreta praecedere denuntiationem. Operibus enim caritatis praecipue debemus Deum imitari, secundum illud Ephes. V, *estote imitatores Dei, sicut filii carissimi, et ambulate in dilectione.* Deus autem interdum publice punit hominem pro peccato nulla secreta monitione praecedente. Ergo videtur quod non sit necessarium admonitionem secretam praecedere denuntiationem.

**PRAETEREA,** sicut Augustinus dicit, in libro contra mendacium, *ex gestis sanctorum intelligi potest qualiter sunt praecepta sacrae Scripturae intelligenda.* Sed in gestis sanctorum invenitur facta publica denuntiatio peccati occulti nulla secreta monitione praecedente, sicut legitur Gen. XXXVII quod Ioseph *accusavit fratres suos apud patrem crimine pessimo*; et Act. V dicitur quod Petrus Ananiam et Saphiram, occulte defraudantes de pretio agri, publice denuntiavit nulla secreta admonitione praemissa. Ipse etiam dominus non legitur secreto admonuisse Iudam antequam eum denuntiaret. Non ergo est de necessitate praecepti ut secreta admonitio praecedat publicam denuntiationem.

**PRAETEREA,** accusatio est gravior quam denuntiatio. Sed ad publicam accusationem potest aliquis procedere nulla admonitione secreta praecedente, determinatur enim in decretali quod *accusationem debet praecedere inscriptio.* Ergo videtur quod non sit de necessitate praecepti quod secreta admonitio praecedat publicam denuntiationem.

**PRAETEREA,** non videtur esse probabile quod ea quae sunt in communi consuetudine religiosorum sint contra praecepta Christi. Sed consuetum est in religionibus quod in capitulis aliqui proclamantur de culpis nulla secreta admonitione praemissa. Ergo videtur quod hoc non sit de necessitate praecepti.

**PRAETEREA,** religiosi tenentur suis praelatis obedire. Sed quandoque praelati praecipiunt, vel communiter omnibus vel alicui specialiter, ut si quid scit corrigendum, ei dicatur. Ergo videtur quod teneantur ei dicere etiam ante secretam admonitionem. Non ergo est de necessitate praecepti ut secreta admonitio praecedat publicam denuntiationem.

**SED CONTRA** est quod Augustinus dicit, in libro de verbis Dom., exponens illud, *corripe ipsum inter te et ipsum solum, studens correctioni, parcens pudori. Forte enim prae verecundia incipit defendere peccatum suum, et quem vis facere meliorem, facis peiorem.* Sed ad hoc

**OBJECTION 1**: It would seem that the precept of fraternal correction does not demand that a private admonition should precede denunciation. For, in works of charity, we should above all follow the example of God, according to Eph. 5:1, 2: *Be ye followers of God, as most dear children, and walk in love.* Now God sometimes punishes a man for a sin, without previously warning him in secret. Therefore it seems that there is no need for a private admonition to precede denunciation.

**OBJ. 2**: Further, according to Augustine (*De Mendacio* xv), *we learn from the deeds of holy men how we ought to understand the commandments of Holy Writ.* Now among the deeds of holy men we find that a hidden sin is publicly denounced, without any previous admonition in private. Thus we read (Gen 37:2) that *Joseph accused his brethren to his father of a most wicked crime*: and (Acts 5:4, 9) that Peter publicly denounced Ananias and Saphira who had secretly by fraud kept back the price of the land, without beforehand admonishing them in private: nor do we read that Our Lord admonished Judas in secret before denouncing him. Therefore the precept does not require that secret admonition should precede public denunciation.

**OBJ. 3**: Further, it is a graver matter to accuse than to denounce. Now one may go to the length of accusing a person publicly, without previously admonishing him in secret: for it is decided in the Decretal (*Cap. Qualiter*, xiv, *De Accusationibus*) that *nothing else need precede accusation except inscription.* Therefore it seems that the precept does not require that a secret admonition should precede public denunciation.

**OBJ. 4**: Further, it does not seem probable that the customs observed by religious in general are contrary to the precepts of Christ. Now it is customary among religious orders to proclaim this or that one for a fault, without any previous secret admonition. Therefore it seems that this admonition is not required by the precept.

**OBJ. 5**: Further, religious are bound to obey their prelates. Now a prelate sometimes commands either all in general, or someone in particular, to tell him if they know of anything that requires correction. Therefore it would seem that they are bound to tell them this, even before any secret admonition. Therefore the precept does not require secret admonition before public denunciation.

**ON THE CONTRARY**, Augustine says (*De Verb. Dom.* xvi, 4) on the words, *Rebuke him between thee and him alone* (Matt 18:15): *Aiming at his amendment, while avoiding his disgrace: since perhaps from shame he might begin to defend his sin; and him whom you thought to make a better*

tenemur per praeceptum caritatis ut caveamus ne frater deterior efficiatur. Ergo ordo correctionis fraternae cadit sub praecepto.

**RESPONDEO** dicendum quod circa publicam de-nuntiationem peccatorum distinguendum est. Aut enim peccata sunt publica, aut sunt occulta. Si quidem sint publica, non est tantum adhibendum remedium ei qui peccavit, ut melior fiat, sed etiam aliis, in quorum noti-tiam devenit, ut non scandalizentur. Et ideo talia peccata sunt publice arguenda, secundum illud apostoli, I ad Tim. V, *peccantem coram omnibus argue, ut ceteri timo-rem habeant*; quod intelligitur de peccatis publicis, ut Augustinus dicit, in libro de verbis Dom.

Si vero sint peccata occulta, sic videtur habere lo-cum quod dominus dicit, *si peccaverit in te frater tuus*, quando enim te offendit publice coram aliis, iam non solum in te peccat, sed etiam in alios, quos turbat. Sed quia etiam in occultis peccatis potest parari proximorum offensa, ideo adhuc distinguendum videtur. Quaedam enim peccata occulta sunt quae sunt in nocumentum proximorum vel corporale vel spirituale, puta si aliquis occulte tractet quomodo civitas tradatur hostibus; vel si haereticus privatim homines a fide avertat. Et quia hic ille qui occulte peccat non solum in te peccat, sed etiam in alios; oportet statim ad denuntiationem procedere, ut huiusmodi nocumentum impediatur, nisi forte aliquis firmiter aestimaret quod statim per secretam admoni-tionem posset huiusmodi mala impedire. Quaedam vero peccata sunt quae sunt solum in malum peccantis et tui, in quem peccatur vel quia a peccante laederis, vel saltem ex sola notitia. Et tunc ad hoc solum tendendum est ut fratri peccanti subveniatur. Et sicut medicus corpo-ralis sanitatem confert, si potest, sine alicuius membri abscissione; si autem non potest, abscindit membrum minus necessarium, ut vita totius conservetur, ita etiam ille qui studet emendationi fratris debet, si potest, sic emendare fratrem, quantum ad conscientiam, ut fama eius conservetur.

Quae quidem est utilis, primo quidem et ipsi pec-canti, non solum in temporalibus, in quibus quantum ad multa homo patitur detrimentum amissa fama; sed etiam quantum ad spiritualia, quia prae timore infamiae multi a peccato retrahuntur, unde quando se infamatos conspiciunt, irrefrenate peccant. Unde Hieronymus di-cit, *corripiendus est seorsum frater, ne, si semel pudorem aut verecundiam amiserit, permaneat in peccato*. Secun-do debet conservari fama fratris peccantis, tum quia, uno infamato, alii infamantur, secundum illud Augusti-ni, in Epist. ad plebem Hipponensem, *cum de aliquibus qui sanctum nomen profitentur aliquid criminis vel falsi sonuerit vel veri patuerit, instant, satagunt, ambiunt ut de*

*man, you make worse*. Now we are bound by the precept of charity to beware lest our brother become worse. Therefore the order of fraternal correction comes under the precept.

**I ANSWER THAT,** With regard to the public denuncia-tion of sins it is necessary to make a distinction: because sins may be either public or secret. In the case of public sins, a remedy is required not only for the sinner, that he may become better, but also for others, who know of his sin, lest they be scandalized. Wherefore such like sins should be denounced in public, according to the saying of the Apostle (1 Tim 5:20): *Them that sin reprove before all, that the rest also may have fear*, which is to be understood as referring to public sins, as Augustine states (*De Verb. Dom.* xvi, 7).

On the other hand, in the case of secret sins, the words of Our Lord seem to apply (Matt 18:15): *If thy brother shall offend against thee*, etc. For if he offend thee publicly in the presence of others, he no longer sins against thee alone, but also against others whom he disturbs. Since, however, a man's neighbor may take offense even at his secret sins, it seems that we must make yet a further dis-tinction. For certain secret sins are hurtful to our neighbor either in his body or in his soul, as, for instance, when a man plots secretly to betray his country to its enemies, or when a heretic secretly turns other men away from the faith. And since he that sins thus in secret, sins not only against you in particular, but also against others, it is necessary to take steps to denounce him at once, in order to prevent him doing such harm, unless by chance you were firmly persuaded that this evil result would be prevented by admonishing him secretly. On the other hand there are other sins which injure none but the sinner, and the person sinned against, either because he alone is hurt by the sinner, or at least because he alone knows about his sin, and then our one purpose should be to succor our sinning brother: and just as the physician of the body restores the sick man to health, if possible, without cutting off a limb, but, if this be unavoidable, cuts off a limb which is least indispensable, in order to preserve the life of the whole body, so too he who desires his brother's amendment should, if possible, so amend him as regards his conscience, that he keep his good name.

For a good name is useful, first of all to the sinner himself, not only in temporal matters wherein a man suffers many losses, if he lose his good name, but also in spir-itual matters, because many are restrained from sinning, through fear of dishonor, so that when a man finds his honor lost, he puts no curb on his sinning. Hence Jerome says on Matt. 18:15: *If he sin against thee, thou shouldst rebuke him in private, lest he persist in his sin if he should once become shameless or unabashed*. Second, we ought to safeguard our sinning brother's good name, both because the dishonor of one leads to the dishonor of others, ac-cording to the saying of Augustine (*Ep. ad pleb. Hipponens.* lxxviii): *When a few of those who bear a name for holiness*

*omnibus hoc credatur.* Tum etiam quia ex peccato unius publicato alii provocantur ad peccatum.

Sed quia conscientia praeferenda est famae, voluit dominus ut saltem cum dispendio famae fratris conscientia per publicam denuntiationem a peccato liberetur. Unde patet de necessitate praecepti esse quod secreta admonitio publicam denuntiationem praecedat.

**AD PRIMUM** ergo dicendum quod omnia occulta Deo sunt nota. Et ideo hoc modo se habent occulta peccata ad iudicium divinum sicut publica ad humanum. Et tamen plerumque Deus peccatores quasi secreta admonitione arguit interius inspirando, vel vigilanti vel dormienti, secundum illud Iob XXXIII, *per somnium in visione nocturna, quando irruit sopor super homines, tunc aperit aures virorum, et erudiens eos instruit disciplina, ut avertat hominem ab his quae fecit.*

**AD SECUNDUM** dicendum quod dominus peccatum Iudae, tanquam Deus, sicut publicum habebat. Unde statim poterat ad publicandum procedere. Tamen ipse non publicavit, sed obscuris verbis eum de peccato suo admonuit. Petrus autem publicavit peccatum occultum Ananiae et Saphirae tanquam executor Dei, cuius revelatione peccatum cognovit. De Ioseph autem credendum est quod fratres suos quandoque admonuerit, licet non sit scriptum. Vel potest dici quod peccatum publicum erat inter fratres, unde dicit pluraliter, *accusavit fratres suos.*

**AD TERTIUM** dicendum quod quando imminet periculum multitudinis, non habent ibi locum haec verba domini, quia tunc frater peccans non peccat in te tantum.

**AD QUARTUM** dicendum quod huiusmodi proclamationes quae in capitulis religiosorum fiunt sunt de aliquibus levibus, quae famae non derogant. Unde sunt quasi quaedam commemorationes potius oblitarum culparum quam accusationes vel denuntiationes. Si essent tamen talia de quibus frater infamaretur, contra praeceptum domini ageret qui per hunc modum peccatum fratris publicaret.

**AD QUINTUM** dicendum quod praelato non est obediendum contra praeceptum divinum, secundum illud Act. V, *obedire oportet Deo magis quam hominibus.* Et ideo quando praelatus praecipit ut sibi dicatur quod quis sciverit corrigendum, intelligendum est praeceptum sane, salvo ordine correctionis fraternae, sive praeceptum fiat communiter ad omnes, sive ad aliquem specialiter. Sed si praelatus expresse praeciperet contra hunc ordinem a domino constitutum, et ipse peccaret praecipiens et ei obediens, quasi contra praeceptum domini agens, unde non esset ei obediendum. Quia praelatus

*are reported falsely or proved in truth to have done anything wrong, people will seek by busily repeating it to make it believed of all*: and also because when one man's sin is made public others are incited to sin likewise.

Since, however, one's conscience should be preferred to a good name, Our Lord wished that we should publicly denounce our brother and so deliver his conscience from sin, even though he should forfeit his good name. Therefore it is evident that the precept requires a secret admonition to precede public denunciation.

**REPLY OBJ. 1**: Whatever is hidden, is known to God, wherefore hidden sins are to the judgment of God, just what public sins are to the judgment of man. Nevertheless God does rebuke sinners sometimes by secretly admonishing them, so to speak, with an inward inspiration, either while they wake or while they sleep, according to Job 33:15–17: *By a dream in a vision by night, when deep sleep falleth upon men . . . then He openeth the ears of men, and teaching instructeth them in what they are to learn, that He may withdraw a man from the things he is doing.*

**REPLY OBJ. 2**: Our Lord as God knew the sin of Judas as though it were public, wherefore He could have made it known at once. Yet He did not, but warned Judas of his sin in words that were obscure. The sin of Ananias and Saphira was denounced by Peter acting as God's executor, by Whose revelation he knew of their sin. With regard to Joseph it is probable that he warned his brethren, though Scripture does not say so. Or we may say that the sin was public with regard to his brethren, wherefore it is stated in the plural that he accused *his brethren.*

**REPLY OBJ. 3**: When there is danger to a great number of people, those words of Our Lord do not apply, because then thy brother does not sin against thee alone.

**REPLY OBJ. 4**: Proclamations made in the chapter of religious are about little faults which do not affect a man's good name, wherefore they are reminders of forgotten faults rather than accusations or denunciations. If, however, they should be of such a nature as to injure our brother's good name, it would be contrary to Our Lord's precept, to denounce a brother's fault in this manner.

**REPLY OBJ. 5**: A prelate is not to be obeyed contrary to a Divine precept, according to Acts 5:29: *We ought to obey God rather then men.* Therefore when a prelate commands anyone to tell him anything that he knows to need correction, the command rightly understood supports the safeguarding of the order of fraternal correction, whether the command be addressed to all in general, or to some particular individual. If, on the other hand, a prelate were to issue a command in express opposition to this order instituted by Our Lord, both would sin, the one commanding, and the one obeying him, as disobeying Our

non est iudex occultorum, sed solus Deus, unde non habet potestatem praecipiendi aliquid super occultis nisi inquantum per aliqua indicia manifestantur, puta per infamiam vel aliquas suspiciones; in quibus casibus potest praelatus praecipere eodem modo sicut et iudex saecularis vel ecclesiasticus potest exigere iuramentum de veritate dicenda.

Lord's command. Consequently he ought not to be obeyed, because a prelate is not the judge of secret things, but God alone is, wherefore he has no power to command anything in respect of hidden matters, except insofar as they are made known through certain signs, as by ill-repute or suspicion; in which cases a prelate can command just as a judge, whether secular or ecclesiastical, can bind a man under oath to tell the truth.

# Article 8

*Whether before the public denunciation witnesses ought to be brought forward?*

AD OCTAVUM SIC PROCEDITUR. Videtur quod testium inductio non debeat praecedere publicam denuntiationem. Peccata enim occulta non sunt aliis manifestanda, quia sic homo magis esset *proditor* criminis quam *corrector* fratris, ut Augustinus dicit. Sed ille qui inducit testes peccatum fratris alteri manifestat. Ergo in peccatis occultis non debet testium inductio praecedere publicam denuntiationem.

PRAETEREA, homo debet diligere proximum sicut seipsum. Sed nullus ad suum peccatum occultum inducit testes. Ergo neque ad peccatum occultum fratris debet inducere.

PRAETEREA, testes inducuntur ad aliquid probandum. Sed in occultis non potest fieri probatio per testes. Ergo frustra huiusmodi testes inducuntur.

PRAETEREA, Augustinus dicit, in regula, quod *prius praeposito debet ostendi quam testibus*. Sed ostendere praeposito sive praelato est dicere Ecclesiae. Non ergo testium inductio debet praecedere publicam denuntiationem.

SED CONTRA est quod dominus dicit, Matth. XVIII.

RESPONDEO dicendum quod de uno extremo ad aliud extremum convenienter transitur per medium. In correctione autem fraterna dominus voluit quod principium esset occultum, dum frater corriperet fratrem inter se et ipsum solum; finem autem voluit esse publicum, ut scilicet Ecclesiae denuntiaretur. Et ideo convenienter in medio ponitur testium inductio, ut primo paucis indicetur peccatum fratris, qui possint prodesse et non obesse, ut saltem sic sine multitudinis infamia emendetur.

AD PRIMUM ergo dicendum quod quidam sic intellexerunt ordinem fraternae correctionis esse servandum ut primo frater sit in secreto corripiendus, et si audierit, bene quidem. Si autem non audierit, si peccatum sit omnino occultum, dicebant non esse ulterius pro-

OBJECTION 1: It would seem that before the public denunciation witnesses ought not to be brought forward. For secret sins ought not to be made known to others, because by so doing a man would *betray* his brother's sins instead of *correcting* them, as Augustine says (*De Verb. Dom.* xvi, 7). Now by bringing forward witnesses one makes known a brother's sin to others. Therefore in the case of secret sins one ought not to bring witnesses forward before the public denunciation.

OBJ. 2: Further, man should love his neighbor as himself. Now no man brings in witnesses to prove his own secret sin. Neither therefore ought one to bring forward witnesses to prove the secret sin of our brother.

OBJ. 3: Further, witnesses are brought forward to prove something. But witnesses afford no proof in secret matters. Therefore it is useless to bring witnesses forward in such cases.

OBJ. 4: Further, Augustine says in his Rule that *before bringing it to the notice of witnesses . . . it should be put before the superior.* Now to bring a matter before a superior or a prelate is to tell the Church. Therefore witnesses should not be brought forward before the public denunciation.

ON THE CONTRARY, Our Lord said (Matt 18:16): *Take with thee one or two more, that in the mouth of two,* etc.

I ANSWER THAT, The right way to go from one extreme to another is to pass through the middle space. Now Our Lord wished the beginning of fraternal correction to be hidden, when one brother corrects another between this one and himself alone, while He wished the end to be public, when such a one would be denounced to the Church. Consequently it is befitting that a citation of witnesses should be placed between the two extremes, so that at first the brother's sin be indicated to a few, who will be of use without being a hindrance, and thus his sin be amended without dishonoring him before the public.

REPLY OBJ. 1: Some have understood the order of fraternal correction to demand that we should first of all rebuke our brother secretly, and that if he listens, it is well; but if he listen not, and his sin be altogether hidden, they say that we should go no further in the matter, whereas if

cedendum. Si autem incipit iam ad plurium notitiam devenire aliquibus indiciis, debet ulterius procedi, secundum quod dominus mandat. Sed hoc est contra id quod Augustinus dicit, in regula, quod peccatum fratris non debet occultari, *ne putrescat in corde*. Et ideo aliter dicendum est quod post admonitionem secretam semel vel pluries factam, quandiu spes probabiliter habetur de correctione, per secretam admonitionem procedendum est. Ex quo autem iam probabiliter cognoscere possumus quod secreta admonitio non valet, procedendum est ulterius, quantumcumque sit peccatum occultum, ad testium inductionem. Nisi forte probabiliter aestimaretur quod hoc ad emendationem fratris non proficeret, sed exinde deterior redderetur, quia propter hoc est totaliter a correctione cessandum, ut supra dictum est.

**Ad secundum** dicendum quod homo non indiget testibus ad emendationem sui peccati, quod tamen potest esse necessarium ad emendationem peccati fratris. Unde non est similis ratio.

**Ad tertium** dicendum quod testes possunt induci propter tria. Uno modo, ad ostendendum quod hoc sit peccatum de quo aliquis arguitur; ut Hieronymus dicit. Secundo, ad convincendum de actu, si actus iteretur; ut Augustinus dicit, in regula. Tertio, *ad testificandum quod frater admonens fecit quod in se fuit*; ut Chrysostomus dicit.

**Ad quartum** dicendum quod Augustinus intelligit quod prius dicatur praelato quam testibus secundum quod praelatus est quaedam singularis persona quae magis potest prodesse quam alii, non autem quod dicatur ei tanquam Ecclesiae, idest sicut in loco iudicis residenti.

it has already begun to reach the ears of several by various signs, we ought to prosecute the matter, according to Our Lord's command. But this is contrary to what Augustine says in his *Rule* that we are bound not to hide a brother's sin, *if it will cause a worse corruption in the heart*. Wherefore we must say otherwise that when the secret admonition has been given once or several times, as long as there is probable hope of his amendment, we must continue to admonish him in private, but as soon as we are able to judge with any probability that the secret admonition is of no avail, we must take further steps, however secret the sin may be, and call witnesses, unless perhaps it were thought probable that this would not conduce to our brother's amendment, and that he would become worse: because on that account one ought to abstain altogether from correcting him, as stated above (A. 6).

**Reply Obj. 2:** A man needs no witnesses that he may amend his own sin: yet they may be necessary that we may amend a brother's sin. Hence the comparison fails.

**Reply Obj. 3:** There may be three reasons for citing witnesses. First, to show that the deed in question is a sin, as Jerome says: second, to prove that the deed was done, if repeated, as Augustine says (loc. cit.): third, *to prove that the man who rebuked his brother, has done what he could*, as Chrysostom says (*Hom. in Matth. lx*).

**Reply Obj. 4:** Augustine means that the matter ought to be made known to the prelate before it is stated to the witnesses, insofar as the prelate is a private individual who is able to be of more use than others, but not that it is to be told him as to the Church, i.e., as holding the position of judge.

# QUESTION 34

## HATRED

Deinde considerandum est de vitiis oppositis caritati. Et primo, de odio, quod opponitur ipsi dilectioni; secundo, de acedia et invidia, quae opponuntur gaudio caritatis; tertio, de discordia et schismate, quae opponuntur paci; quarto, de offensione et scandalo, quae opponuntur beneficentiae et correctioni fraternae.

Circa primum quaeruntur sex,

Primo, utrum Deus possit odio haberi.

Secundo, utrum odium Dei sit maximum peccatorum.

Tertio, utrum odium proximi semper sit peccatum.

Quarto, utrum sit maximum inter peccata quae sunt in proximum.

Quinto, utrum sit vitium capitale.

Sexto, ex quo capitali vitio oriatur.

We must now consider the vices opposed to charity: (1) hatred, which is opposed to love; (2) sloth and envy, which are opposed to the joy of charity; (3) discord and schism, which are contrary to peace; (4) offense and scandal, which are contrary to beneficence and fraternal correction.

Under the first head there are six points of inquiry:
(1) Whether it is possible to hate God?
(2) Whether hatred of God is the greatest of sins?
(3) Whether hatred of one's neighbor is always a sin?
(4) Whether it is the greatest of all sins against our neighbor?
(5) Whether it is a capital sin?
(6) From what capital sin does it arise?

# Article 1

*Whether it is possible for anyone to hate God?*

**AD PRIMUM SIC PROCEDITUR.** Videtur quod Deum nullus odio habere possit. Dicit enim Dionysius, IV cap. de Div. Nom., quod *omnibus amabile et diligibile est ipsum bonum et pulchrum.* Sed Deus est ipsa bonitas et pulchritudo. Ergo a nullo odio habetur.

**PRAETEREA,** in apocryphis Esdrae dicitur quod *omnia invocant veritatem, et benignantur in operibus eius.* Sed Deus est ipsa veritas, ut dicitur Ioan. XIV. Ergo omnes diligunt Deum, et nullus eum odio habere potest.

**PRAETEREA,** odium est aversio quaedam. Sed sicut Dionysius dicit, in IV cap. de Div. Nom., Deus *omnia ad seipsum convertit.* Ergo nullus eum odio habere potest.

**SED CONTRA** est, quod dicitur in Psalm., *superbia eorum qui te oderunt ascendit semper*; et Ioan. XV, *nunc autem et viderunt et oderunt me et patrem meum.*

**RESPONDEO** dicendum quod, sicut ex supradictis patet, odium est quidam motus appetitivae potentiae, quae non movetur nisi ab aliquo apprehenso. Deus autem dupliciter ab homine apprehendi potest, uno modo, secundum seipsum, puta cum per essentiam videtur; alio modo, per effectus suos, cum scilicet *invisibilia Dei per ea quae facta sunt intellecta conspiciuntur.* Deus autem per essentiam suam est ipsa bonitas, quam nullus habere odio potest, quia de ratione boni est ut ametur.

**OBJECTION 1**: It would seem that no man can hate God. For Dionysius says (*Div. Nom.* iv) that *the first good and beautiful is an object of love and dilection to all.* But God is goodness and beauty itself. Therefore He is hated by none.

**OBJ. 2**: Further, in the Apocryphal books of 3 Esdras 4:36, 39 it is written that *all things call upon truth . . . and (all men) do well like of her works.* Now God is the very truth according to John 14:6. Therefore all love God, and none can hate Him.

**OBJ. 3**: Further, hatred is a kind of aversion. But according to Dionysius (*Div. Nom.* i) God draws all things to Himself. Therefore none can hate Him.

**ON THE CONTRARY**, It is written (Ps 73:23): *The pride of them that hate Thee ascendeth continually,* and (John 15:24): *But now they have both seen and hated both Me and My Father.*

**I ANSWER THAT,** As shown above (I-II, Q. 29, A. 1), hatred is a movement of the appetitive power, which power is not set in motion save by something apprehended. Now God can be apprehended by man in two ways; first, in Himself, as when He is seen in His Essence; second, in His effects, when, to wit, *the invisible things* of God . . . *are clearly seen, being understood by the things that are made* (Rom 1:20). Now God in His Essence is goodness itself, which no man can hate—for it is natural to good to be

Et ideo impossibile est quod aliquis videns Deum per essentiam eum odio habeat.

Sed effectus eius aliqui sunt qui nullo modo possunt esse contrarii voluntati humanae, quia esse, vivere et intelligere est appetibile et amabile omnibus, quae sunt quidam effectus Dei. Unde etiam secundum quod Deus apprehenditur ut auctor horum effectuum, non potest odio haberi. Sunt autem quidam effectus Dei qui repugnant inordinatae voluntati, sicut inflictio poenae; et etiam cohibitio peccatorum per legem divinam, quae repugnat voluntati depravatae per peccatum. Et quantum ad considerationem talium effectuum, ab aliquibus Deus odio haberi potest, inquantum scilicet apprehenditur peccatorum prohibitor et poenarum inflictor.

**AD PRIMUM** ergo dicendum quod ratio illa procedit quantum ad illos qui vident Dei essentiam, quae est ipsa essentia bonitatis.

**AD SECUNDUM** dicendum quod ratio illa procedit quantum ad hoc quod apprehenditur Deus ut causa illorum effectuum qui naturaliter ab hominibus amantur, inter quos sunt opera veritatis praebentis suam cognitionem hominibus.

**AD TERTIUM** dicendum quod Deus convertit omnia ad seipsum inquantum est essendi principium, quia omnia, inquantum sunt, tendunt in Dei similitudinem, qui est ipsum esse.

loved. Hence it is impossible for one who sees God in His Essence, to hate Him.

Moreover some of His effects are such that they can nowise be contrary to the human will, since to be, to live, to understand, which are effects of God, are desirable and lovable to all. Wherefore again God cannot be an object of hatred if we consider Him as the Author of such like effects. Some of God's effects, however, are contrary to an inordinate will, such as the infliction of punishment, and the prohibition of sin by the Divine Law. Such like effects are repugnant to a will debased by sin, and as regards the consideration of them, God may be an object of hatred to some, insofar as they look upon Him as forbidding sin, and inflicting punishment.

**REPLY OBJ. 1**: This argument is true of those who see God's Essence, which is the very essence of goodness.

**REPLY OBJ. 2**: This argument is true insofar as God is apprehended as the cause of such effects as are naturally beloved of all, among which are the works of Truth who reveals herself to men.

**REPLY OBJ. 3**: God draws all things to Himself, insofar as He is the source of being, since all things, inasmuch as they are, tend to be like God, Who is Being itself.

# Article 2

*Whether hatred of God is the greatest of sins?*

**AD SECUNDUM SIC PROCEDITUR**. Videtur quod odium Dei non sit maximum peccatorum. Gravissimum enim peccatum est peccatum in spiritum sanctum, quod est irremissibile, ut dicitur Matth. XII. Sed odium Dei non computatur inter species peccati in spiritum sanctum; ut ex supradictis patet. Ergo odium Dei non est gravissimum peccatorum.

**PRAETEREA**, peccatum consistit in elongatione a Deo. Sed magis videtur esse elongatus a Deo infidelis, qui nec Dei cognitionem habet, quam fidelis, qui saltem, quamvis Deum odio habet, eum tamen cognoscit. Ergo videtur quod gravius sit peccatum infidelitatis quam peccatum odii in Deum.

**PRAETEREA**, Deus habetur odio solum ratione suorum effectuum qui repugnant voluntati, inter quos praecipuum est poena. Sed odire poenam non est maximum peccatorum. Ergo odium Dei non est maximum peccatorum.

**SED CONTRA** est quod *optimo opponitur pessimum*; ut patet per Philosophum, in VIII Ethic. Sed odium Dei

**OBJECTION 1**: It would seem that hatred of God is not the greatest of sins. For the most grievous sin is the sin against the Holy Spirit, since it cannot be forgiven, according to Matt. 12:32. Now hatred of God is not reckoned among the various kinds of sin against the Holy Spirit, as may be seen from what has been said above (Q. 14, A. 2). Therefore hatred of God is not the most grievous sin.

**OBJ. 2**: Further, sin consists in withdrawing oneself from God. Now an unbeliever who has not even knowledge of God seems to be further away from Him than a believer, who though he hate God, nevertheless knows Him. Therefore it seems that the sin of unbelief is graver than the sin of hatred against God.

**OBJ. 3**: Further, God is an object of hatred, only by reason of those of His effects that are contrary to the will: the chief of which is punishment. But hatred of punishment is not the most grievous sin. Therefore hatred of God is not the most grievous sin.

**ON THE CONTRARY**, *The best is opposite to the worst*, according to the Philosopher (*Ethic.* viii, 10). But hatred

opponitur dilectioni Dei, in qua consistit optimum hominis. Ergo odium Dei est pessimum peccatum hominis.

**RESPONDEO** dicendum quod defectus peccati consistit in aversione a Deo, ut supra dictum est. Huiusmodi autem aversio rationem culpae non haberet nisi voluntaria esset. Unde ratio culpae consistit in voluntaria aversione a Deo.

Haec autem voluntaria aversio a Deo per se quidem importatur in odio Dei, in aliis autem peccatis quasi participative et secundum aliud. Sicut enim voluntas per se inhaeret ei quod amat, ita secundum se refugit id quod odit, unde quando aliquis odit Deum, voluntas eius secundum se ab eo avertitur. Sed in aliis peccatis, puta cum aliquis fornicatur, non avertitur a Deo secundum se, sed secundum aliud, inquantum scilicet appetit inordinatam delectationem, quae habet annexam aversionem a Deo. Semper autem id quod est per se est potius eo quod est secundum aliud. Unde odium Dei inter alia peccata est gravius.

**AD PRIMUM** ergo dicendum quod, sicut Gregorius dicit, XXV Moral., *aliud est bona non facere, aliud est bonorum odisse datorem, sicut aliud est ex praecipitatione, aliud ex deliberatione peccare* ex quo datur intelligi quod odire Deum, omnium bonorum datorem, sit ex deliberatione peccare, quod est peccatum in spiritum sanctum. Unde manifestum est quod odium Dei maxime est peccatum in spiritum sanctum, secundum quod peccatum in spiritum sanctum nominat aliquod genus speciale peccati. Ideo tamen non computatur inter species peccati in spiritum sanctum, quia generaliter invenitur in omni specie peccati in spiritum sanctum.

**AD SECUNDUM** dicendum quod ipsa infidelitas non habet rationem culpae nisi inquantum est voluntaria. Et ideo tanto est gravior quanto est magis voluntaria. Quod autem sit voluntaria provenit ex hoc quod aliquis odio habet veritatem quae proponitur. Unde patet quod ratio peccati in infidelitate sit ex odio Dei, circa cuius veritatem est fides. Et ideo, sicut causa est potior effectu, ita odium Dei est maius peccatum quam infidelitas.

**AD TERTIUM** dicendum quod non quicumque odit poenas odit Deum, poenarum auctorem, nam multi oderunt poenas qui tamen patienter eas ferunt ex reverentia divinae iustitiae. Unde et Augustinus dicit, X Confess., quod mala poenalia Deus *tolerare iubet, non amari.* Sed prorumpere in odium Dei punientis, hoc est habere odio ipsam Dei iustitiam, quod est gravissimum peccatum. Unde Gregorius dicit, XXV Moral., *sicut nonnunquam gravius est peccatum diligere quam perpetrare, ita nequius est odisse iustitiam quam non fecisse.*

of God is contrary to the love of God, wherein man's best consists. Therefore hatred of God is man's worst sin.

I ANSWER THAT, The defect in sin consists in its aversion from God, as stated above (Q. 10, A. 3): and this aversion would not have the character of guilt, were it not voluntary. Hence the nature of guilt consists in a voluntary aversion from God.

Now this voluntary aversion from God is directly implied in the hatred of God, but in other sins, by participation and indirectly. For just as the will cleaves directly to what it loves, so does it directly shun what it hates. Hence when a man hates God, his will is directly averted from God, whereas in other sins, fornication for instance, a man turns away from God, not directly, but indirectly, in so far, namely, as he desires an inordinate pleasure, to which aversion from God is connected. Now that which is so by itself, always takes precedence of that which is so by another. Wherefore hatred of God is more grievous than other sins.

REPLY OBJ. 1: According to Gregory (*Moral.* xxv, 11), *it is one thing not to do good things, and another to hate the giver of good things, even as it is one thing to sin indeliberately, and another to sin deliberately.* This implies that to hate God, the giver of all good things, is to sin deliberately, and this is a sin against the Holy Spirit. Hence it is evident that hatred of God is chiefly a sin against the Holy Spirit, insofar as the sin against the Holy Spirit denotes a special kind of sin: and yet it is not reckoned among the kinds of sin against the Holy Spirit, because it is universally found in every kind of that sin.

REPLY OBJ. 2: Even unbelief is not sinful unless it be voluntary: wherefore the more voluntary it is, the more it is sinful. Now it becomes voluntary by the fact that a man hates the truth that is proposed to him. Wherefore it is evident that unbelief derives its sinfulness from hatred of God, Whose truth is the object of faith; and hence just as a cause is greater than its effect, so hatred of God is a greater sin than unbelief.

REPLY OBJ. 3: Not everyone who hates his punishment, hates God the author of punishments. For many hate the punishments inflicted on them, and yet they bear them patiently out of reverence for the Divine justice. Wherefore Augustine says (*Confess.* x) that God commands us *to bear with penal evils, not to love them.* On the other hand, to break out into hatred of God when He inflicts those punishments, is to hate God's very justice, and that is a most grievous sin. Hence Gregory says (*Moral.* xxv, 11): *Even as sometimes it is more grievous to love sin than to do it, so is it more wicked to hate justice than not to have done it.*

# Article 3

*Whether hatred of one's neighbor is always a sin?*

**AD TERTIUM SIC PROCEDITUR**. Videtur quod non omne odium proximi sit peccatum. Nullum enim peccatum invenitur in praeceptis vel consiliis legis divinae, secundum illud Prov. VIII. *Recti sunt omnes sermones mei, non est in eis pravum quid nec perversum*. Sed Luc. XIV dicitur, *si quis venit ad me et non odit patrem et matrem, non potest meus esse discipulus*. Ergo non omne odium proximi est peccatum.

**PRAETEREA**, nihil potest esse peccatum secundum quod Deum imitamur. Sed imitando Deum quosdam odio habemus, dicitur enim Rom. I, *detractores, Deo odibiles*. Ergo possumus aliquos odio habere absque peccato.

**PRAETEREA**, nihil naturalium est peccatum, quia peccatum est *recessus ab eo quod est secundum naturam*, ut Damascenus dicit, in II libro. Sed naturale est unicuique rei quod odiat id quod est sibi contrarium et quod nitatur ad eius corruptionem. Ergo videtur non esse peccatum quod aliquis habeat odio inimicum suum.

**SED CONTRA** est quod dicitur I Ioan. II, *qui fratrem suum odit in tenebris est*. Sed tenebrae spirituales sunt peccata. Ergo odium proximi non potest esse sine peccato.

**RESPONDEO** dicendum quod odium amori opponitur, ut supra dictum est. Unde tantum habet odium de ratione mali quantum amor habet de ratione boni. Amor autem debetur proximo secundum id quod a Deo habet, idest secundum naturam et gratiam, non autem debetur ei amor secundum id quod habet a seipso et Diabolo, scilicet secundum peccatum et iustitiae defectum.

Et ideo licet habere odio in fratre peccatum et omne illud quod pertinet ad defectum divinae iustitiae, sed ipsam naturam et gratiam fratris non potest aliquis habere odio sine peccato. Hoc autem ipsum quod in fratre odimus culpam et defectum boni, pertinet ad fratris amorem, eiusdem enim rationis est quod velimus bonum alicuius et quod odimus malum ipsius. Unde, simpliciter accipiendo odium fratris, semper est cum peccato.

**AD PRIMUM** ergo dicendum quod parentes, quantum ad naturam et affinitatem qua nobis coniunguntur, sunt a nobis secundum praeceptum Dei honorandi, ut patet Exod. XX. Odiendi autem sunt quantum ad hoc quod impedimentum praestant nobis accedendi ad perfectionem divinae iustitiae.

**AD SECUNDUM** dicendum quod Deus in detractoribus odio habet culpam, non naturam. Et sic sine culpa possumus odio detractores habere.

**AD TERTIUM** dicendum quod homines secundum bona quae habent a Deo non sunt nobis contrarii, un-

**OBJECTION 1**: It would seem that hatred of one's neighbor is not always a sin. For no sin is commanded or counselled by God, according to Prov. 8:8: *All My words are just, there is nothing wicked nor perverse in them*. Now, it is written (Luke 14:26): *If any man come to Me, and hate not his father and mother . . . he cannot be My disciple*. Therefore hatred of one's neighbor is not always a sin.

**OBJ. 2**: Further, nothing wherein we imitate God can be a sin. But it is in imitation of God that we hate certain people: for it is written (Rom 1:30): *Detractors, hateful to God*. Therefore it is possible to hate certain people without committing a sin.

**OBJ. 3**: Further, nothing that is natural is a sin, for sin is a *wandering away from what is according to nature*, according to Damascene (*De Fide Orth.* ii, 4, 30; iv, 20). Now it is natural to a thing to hate whatever is contrary to it, and to aim at its undoing. Therefore it seems that it is not a sin to hate one's I enemy.

**ON THE CONTRARY**, It is written (1 John 2:9): *He that . . . hateth his brother, is in darkness*. Now spiritual darkness is sin. Therefore there cannot be hatred of one's neighbor without sin.

**I ANSWER THAT**, Hatred is opposed to love, as stated above (I-II, Q. 29, A. 2); so that hatred of a thing is evil according as the love of that thing is good. Now love is due to our neighbor in respect of what he holds from God, i.e., in respect of nature and grace, but not in respect of what he has of himself and from the devil, i.e., in respect of sin and lack of justice.

Consequently it is lawful to hate the sin in one's brother, and whatever pertains to the defect of Divine justice, but we cannot hate our brother's nature and grace without sin. Now it is part of our love for our brother that we hate the fault and the lack of good in him, since desire for another's good is equivalent to hatred of his evil. Consequently the hatred of one's brother, if we consider it simply, is always sinful.

**REPLY OBJ. 1**: By the commandment of God (Exod 20:12) we must honor our parents—as united to us in nature and kinship. But we must hate them insofar as they prove an obstacle to our attaining the perfection of Divine justice.

**REPLY OBJ. 2**: God hates the sin which is in the detractor, not his nature: so that we can hate detractors without committing a sin.

**REPLY OBJ. 3**: Men are not opposed to us in respect of the goods which they have received from God: wherefore,

de quantum ad hoc sunt amandi. Contrariantur autem nobis secundum quod contra nos inimicitias exercent, quod ad eorum culpam pertinet, et quantum ad hoc sunt odio habendi. Hoc enim in eis debemus habere odio, quod nobis sunt inimici.

in this respect, we should love them. But they are opposed to us, insofar as they show hostility towards us, and this is sinful in them. In this respect we should hate them, for we should hate in them the fact that they are hostile to us.

# Article 4

*Whether hatred of our neighbor is the most grievous sin against our neighbor?*

AD QUARTUM SIC PROCEDITUR. Videtur quod odium proximi sit gravissimum peccatum eorum quae in proximo committuntur. Dicitur enim I Ioan. III, *omnis qui odit fratrem suum homicida est*. Sed homicidium est gravissimum peccatorum quae committuntur in proximum. Ergo et odium.

PRAETEREA, *pessimum opponitur optimo*. Sed optimum eorum quae proximo exhibemus est amor, omnia enim alia ad dilectionem referuntur. Ergo et pessimum est odium.

SED CONTRA, malum dicitur *quod nocet*; secundum Augustinum, in Enchirid. Sed plus aliquis nocet proximo per alia peccata quam per odium, puta per furtum et homicidium et adulterium. Ergo odium non est gravissimum peccatum.

PRAETEREA, Chrysostomus, exponens illud Matth., *qui solverit unum de mandatis istis minimis*, dicit, *mandata Moysi, non occides, non adulterabis, in remuneratione modica sunt, in peccato autem magna, mandata autem Christi, idest non irascaris, non concupiscas, in remuneratione magna sunt, in peccato autem minima*. Odium autem pertinet ad interiorem motum, sicut et ira et concupiscentia. Ergo odium proximi est minus peccatum quam homicidium.

RESPONDEO dicendum quod peccatum quod committitur in proximum habet rationem mali ex duobus, uno quidem modo, ex deordinatione eius qui peccat; alio modo, ex nocumento quod infertur ei contra quem peccatur. Primo ergo modo odium est maius peccatum quam exteriores actus qui sunt in proximi nocumentum, quia scilicet per odium deordinatur voluntas hominis, quae est potissimum in homine, et ex qua est radix peccati. Unde etiam si exteriores actus inordinati essent absque inordinatione voluntatis, non essent peccata, puta cum aliquis ignoranter vel zelo iustitiae hominem occidit. Et si quid culpae est in exterioribus peccatis quae contra proximum committuntur, totum est ex interiori odio.

Sed quantum ad nocumentum quod proximo infertur peiora sunt exteriora peccata quam interius odium.

OBJECTION 1: It would seem that hatred of our neighbor is the most grievous sin against our neighbor. For it is written (1 John 3:15): *Whosoever hateth his brother is a murderer*. Now murder is the most grievous of sins against our neighbor. Therefore hatred is also.

OBJ. 2: Further, *worst is opposed to best*. Now the best thing we give our neighbor is love, since all other things are referable to love. Therefore hatred is the worst.

ON THE CONTRARY, A thing is said to be evil *because it hurts*, as Augustine observes (*Enchiridion* xii). Now there are sins by which a man hurts his neighbor more than by hatred, e.g., theft, murder and adultery. Therefore hatred is not the most grievous sin.

MOREOVER, Chrysostom commenting on Matt. 5:19, *He that shall break one of these least commandments*, says: *The commandments of Moses, Thou shalt not kill, Thou shalt not commit adultery, count for little in their reward, but they count for much if they be disobeyed. On the other hand the commandments of Christ such as, Thou shalt not be angry, Thou shalt not desire, are reckoned great in their reward, but little in the transgression*. Now hatred is an internal movement like anger and desire. Therefore hatred of one's brother is a less grievous sin than murder.

I ANSWER THAT, Sins committed against our neighbor are evil on two counts; first by reason of the disorder in the person who sins, second by reason of the hurt inflicted on the person sinned against. On the first count, hatred is a more grievous sin than external actions that hurt our neighbor, because hatred is a disorder of man's will, which is the chief part of man, and wherein is the root of sin, so that if a man's outward actions were to be inordinate, without any disorder in his will, they would not be sinful, for instance, if he were to kill a man, through ignorance or out of zeal for justice: and if there be anything sinful in a man's outward sins against his neighbor, it is all to be traced to his inward hatred.

On the other hand, as regards the hurt inflicted on his neighbor, a man's outward sins are worse than his inward hatred.

**ET PER HOC** patet responsio ad obiecta.

**THIS SUFFICES** for the Replies to the Objections.

# Article 5

*Whether hatred is a capital sin?*

**AD QUINTUM SIC PROCEDITUR.** Videtur quod odium sit vitium capitale. Odium enim directe opponitur caritati. Sed caritas est principalissima virtutum et mater aliarum. Ergo odium est maxime vitium capitale, et principium omnium aliorum.

**PRAETEREA**, peccata oriuntur in nobis secundum inclinationem passionum, secundum illud ad Rom. VII, *passiones peccatorum operabantur in membris nostris, ut fructificarent morti*. Sed in passionibus animae ex amore et odio videntur omnes aliae sequi, ut ex supradictis patet. Ergo odium debet poni inter vitia capitalia.

**PRAETEREA**, vitium est malum morale. Sed odium principalius respicit malum quam alia passio. Ergo videtur quod odium debet poni vitium capitale.

**SED CONTRA** est quod Gregorius, XXXI Moral., non enumerat odium inter septem vitia capitalia.

**RESPONDEO** dicendum quod, sicut supra dictum est, vitium capitale est ex quo ut frequentius alia vitia oriuntur. Vitium autem est contra naturam hominis inquantum est animal rationale. In his autem quae contra naturam fiunt paulatim id quod est naturae corrumpitur. Unde oportet quod primo recedatur ab eo quod est minus secundum naturam, et ultimo ab eo quod est maxime secundum naturam, quia id quod est primum in constructione est ultimum in resolutione. Id autem quod est maxime et primo naturale homini est quod diligat bonum, et praecipue bonum divinum et bonum proximi. Et ideo odium, quod huic dilectioni opponitur, non est primum in deletione virtutis, quae fit per vitia, sed ultimum. Et ideo odium non est vitium capitale.

**AD PRIMUM** ergo dicendum quod, sicut dicitur in VII Physic., *virtus uniuscuiusque rei consistit in hoc quod sit bene disposita secundum suam naturam*. Et ideo in virtutibus oportet esse primum et principale quod est primum et principale in ordine naturali. Et propter hoc caritas ponitur principalissima virtutum. Et eadem ratione odium non potest esse primum in vitiis, ut dictum est.

**AD SECUNDUM** dicendum quod odium mali quod contrariatur naturali bono est primum inter passiones animae, sicut et amor naturalis boni. Sed odium boni connaturalis non potest esse primum, sed habet rationem ultimi, quia tale odium attestatur corruptioni naturae iam factae, sicut et amor extranei boni.

**OBJECTION 1**: It would seem that hatred is a capital sin. For hatred is directly opposed to charity. Now charity is the foremost among the virtues, and the mother of all others. Therefore hatred is the chief of the capital sins, and the origin of all others.

**OBJ. 2**: Further, sins arise in us on account of the inclinations of our passions, according to Rom. 7:5: *The passions of sins . . . did work in our members to bring forth fruit unto death*. Now all other passions of the soul seem to arise from love and hatred, as was shown above (I-II, Q. 25, AA. 1, 2). Therefore hatred should be reckoned one of the capital sins.

**OBJ. 3**: Further, vice is a moral evil. Now hatred regards evil more than any other passion does. Therefore it seems that hatred should be reckoned a capital sin.

**ON THE CONTRARY**, Gregory (*Moral.* xxxi) does not reckon hatred among the seven capital sins.

**I ANSWER THAT**, As stated above (I-II, Q. 84, AA. 3, 4), a capital vice is one from which other vices arise most frequently. Now vice is contrary to man's nature, inasmuch as he is a rational animal: and when a thing acts contrary to its nature, that which is natural to it is corrupted little by little. Consequently it must first of all fail in that which is less in accordance with its nature, and last of all in that which is most in accordance with its nature, since what is first in construction is last in destruction. Now that which, first and foremost, is most natural to man, is the love of what is good, and especially love of the Divine good, and of his neighbor's good. Wherefore hatred, which is opposed to this love, is not the first but the last thing in the downfall of virtue resulting from vice: and therefore it is not a capital vice.

**REPLY OBJ. 1**: As stated in *Phys.* vii, text. 18, *the virtue of a thing consists in its being well disposed in accordance with its nature*. Hence what is first and foremost in the virtues must be first and foremost in the natural order. Hence charity is reckoned the foremost of the virtues, and for the same reason hatred cannot be first among the vices, as stated above.

**REPLY OBJ. 2**: Hatred of the evil that is contrary to one's natural good, is the first of the soul's passions, even as love of one's natural good is. But hatred of one's connatural good cannot be first, but is something last, because such like hatred is a proof of an already corrupted nature, even as love of an extraneous good.

**Ad tertium** dicendum quod duplex est malum. Quoddam verum, quia scilicet repugnat naturali bono, et huius mali odium potest habere rationem prioritatis inter passiones. Est autem aliud malum non verum, sed apparens, quod scilicet est verum bonum et connaturale, sed aestimatur ut malum propter corruptionem naturae. Et huiusmodi mali odium oportet quod sit in ultimo. Hoc autem odium est vitiosum, non autem primum.

**Reply Obj. 3**: Evil is twofold. One is a true evil, for the reason that it is incompatible with one's natural good, and the hatred of such an evil may have priority over the other passions. There is, however, another which is not a true, but an apparent evil, which, namely, is a true and connatural good, and yet is reckoned evil on account of the corruption of nature: and the hatred of such an evil must needs come last. This hatred is vicious, but the former is not.

# Article 6

### *Whether hatred arises from envy?*

**Ad sextum sic proceditur.** Videtur quod odium non oriatur ex invidia. Invidia enim est tristitia quaedam de alienis bonis. Odium autem non oritur ex tristitia, sed potius e converso, tristamur enim de praesentia malorum quae odimus. Ergo odium non oritur ex invidia.

**Praeterea**, odium dilectioni opponitur. Sed dilectio proximi refertur ad dilectionem Dei, ut supra habitum est. Ergo et odium proximi refertur ad odium Dei. Sed odium Dei non causatur ex invidia, non enim invidemus his qui maxime a nobis distant, sed his qui propinqui videntur, ut patet per philosophum, in II Rhet. Ergo odium non causatur ex invidia.

**Praeterea**, unius effectus una est causa. Sed odium causatur ex ira, dicit enim Augustinus, in regula, quod *ira crescit in odium*. Non ergo causatur odium ex invidia.

**Sed contra** est quod Gregorius dicit, XXXI Moral., quod *de invidia oritur odium*.

**Respondeo** dicendum quod, sicut dictum est, odium proximi est ultimum in progressu peccati, eo quod opponitur dilectioni qua naturaliter proximus diligitur. Quod autem aliquis recedat ab eo quod est naturale, contingit ex hoc quod intendit vitare aliquid quod est naturaliter fugiendum. Naturaliter autem omne animal fugit tristitiam, sicut et appetit delectationem; sicut patet per Philosophum, in VII et X Ethic. Et ideo sicut ex delectatione causatur amor, ita ex tristitia causatur odium, sicut enim movemur ad diligendum ea quae nos delectant, inquantum ex hoc ipso accipiuntur sub ratione boni; ita movemur ad odiendum ea quae nos contristant, inquantum ex hoc ipso accipiuntur sub ratione mali. Unde cum invidia sit tristitia de bono proximi, sequitur quod bonum proximi reddatur nobis odiosum. Et inde est quod ex invidia oritur odium.

**Ad primum** ergo dicendum quod quia vis appetitiva, sicut et apprehensiva, reflectitur super suos actus, sequitur quod in motibus appetitivae virtutis sit quaedam circulatio. Secundum igitur primum processum

**Objection 1**: It seems that hatred does not arise from envy. For envy is sorrow for another's good. Now hatred does not arise from sorrow, for, on the contrary, we grieve for the presence of the evil we hate. Therefore hatred does not arise from envy.

**Obj. 2**: Further, hatred is opposed to love. Now love of our neighbor is referred to our love of God, as stated above (Q. 25, A. 1; Q. 26, A. 2). Therefore hatred of our neighbor is referred to our hatred of God. But hatred of God does not arise from envy, for we do not envy those who are very far removed from us, but rather those who seem to be near us, as the Philosopher states (*Rhet.* ii). Therefore hatred does not arise from envy.

**Obj. 3**: Further, to one effect there is one cause. Now hatred is caused by anger, for Augustine says in his Rule that *anger grows into hatred*. Therefore hatred does not arise from envy.

**On the contrary**, Gregory says (*Moral.* xxxi, 45) that *out of envy cometh hatred*.

**I answer that**, As stated above (A. 5), hatred of his neighbor is a man's last step in the path of sin, because it is opposed to the love which he naturally has for his neighbor. Now if a man declines from that which is natural, it is because he intends to avoid that which is naturally an object to be shunned. Now every animal naturally avoids sorrow, just as it desires pleasure, as the Philosopher states (*Ethic.* vii, x). Accordingly just as love arises from pleasure, so does hatred arise from sorrow. For just as we are moved to love whatever gives us pleasure, inasmuch as for that very reason it assumes the aspect of good; so we are moved to hate whatever displeases us, insofar as for this very reason it assumes the aspect of evil. Wherefore, since envy is sorrow for our neighbor's good, it follows that our neighbor's good becomes hateful to us, so that *out of envy cometh hatred*.

**Reply Obj. 1**: Since the appetitive power, like the apprehensive power, reflects on its own acts, it follows that there is a kind of circular movement in the actions of the appetitive power. And so according to the first forward

appetitivi motus, ex amore consequitur desiderium, ex quo consequitur delectatio, cum quis consecutus fuerit quod desiderabat. Et quia hoc ipsum quod est delectari in bono amato habet quandam rationem boni, sequitur quod delectatio causet amorem. Et secundum eandem rationem sequitur quod tristitia causet odium.

AD SECUNDUM dicendum quod alia ratio est de dilectione et odio. Nam dilectionis obiectum est bonum, quod a Deo in creaturas derivatur, et ideo dilectio per prius est Dei, et per posterius est proximi. Sed odium est mali, quod non habet locum in ipso Deo, sed in eius effectibus, unde etiam supra dictum est quod Deus non habetur odio nisi inquantum apprehenditur secundum suos effectus. Et ideo per prius est odium proximi quam odium Dei. Unde, cum invidia ad proximum sit mater odii quod est ad proximum, fit per consequens causa odii quod est in Deum.

AD TERTIUM dicendum quod nihil prohibet secundum diversas rationes aliquid oriri ex diversis causis. Et secundum hoc odium potest oriri et ex ira et ex invidia. Directius tamen oritur ex invidia, per quam ipsum bonum proximi redditur contristabile et per consequens odibile. Sed ex ira oritur odium secundum quoddam augmentum. Nam primo per iram appetimus malum proximi secundum quandam mensuram, prout scilicet habet rationem vindictae, postea autem per continuitatem irae pervenitur ad hoc quod homo malum proximi absolute desideret, quod pertinet ad rationem odii. Unde patet quod odium ex invidia causatur formaliter secundum rationem obiecti; ex ira autem dispositive.

course of the appetitive movement, love gives rise to desire, whence follows pleasure when one has obtained what one desired. And since the very fact of taking pleasure in the good one loves is a kind of good, it follows that pleasure causes love. And in the same way sorrow causes hatred.

REPLY OBJ. 2: Love and hatred are essentially different, for the object of love is good, which flows from God to creatures, wherefore love is due to God in the first place, and to our neighbor afterwards. On the other hand, hatred is of evil, which has no place in God Himself, but only in His effects, for which reason it has been stated above (A. 1), that God is not an object of hatred, except insofar as He is considered in relation to His effects, and consequently hatred is directed to our neighbor before being directed to God. Therefore, since envy of our neighbor is the mother of hatred of our neighbor, it becomes, in consequence, the cause of hatred towards God.

REPLY OBJ. 3: Nothing prevents a thing arising from various causes in various respects, and accordingly hatred may arise both from anger and from envy. However it arises more directly from envy, which looks upon the very good of our neighbor as displeasing and therefore hateful, whereas hatred arises from anger by way of increase. For at first, through anger, we desire our neighbor's evil according to a certain measure, that is insofar as that evil has the aspect of vengeance: but afterwards, through the continuance of anger, man goes so far as absolutely to desire his neighbor's evil, which desire is part of hatred. Wherefore it is evident that hatred is caused by envy formally as regards the aspect of the object, but dispositively by anger.

# QUESTION 35

## SLOTH

Deinde considerandum est de vitiis oppositis gaudio caritatis. Quod quidem est et de bono divino, cui gaudio opponitur acedia; et de bono proximi, cui gaudio opponitur invidia. Unde primo considerandum est de acedia; secundo, de invidia.

Circa primum quaeruntur quatuor.

Primo, utrum acedia sit peccatum.

Secundo, utrum sit speciale vitium.

Tertio, utrum sit mortale peccatum.

Quarto, utrum sit vitium capitale.

We must now consider the vices opposed to the joy of charity. This joy is either about the Divine good, and then its contrary is sloth, or about our neighbor's good, and then its contrary is envy. Wherefore we must consider (1) Sloth and (2) Envy.

Under the first head there are four points of inquiry:

(1) Whether sloth is a sin?

(2) Whether it is a special vice?

(3) Whether it is a mortal sin?

(4) Whether it is a capital sin?

# Article 1

*Whether sloth is a sin?*

**AD PRIMUM SIC PROCEDITUR.** Videtur quod acedia non sit peccatum. *Passionibus* enim *non laudamur neque vituperamur*; secundum Philosophum, in II Ethic. Sed acedia est quaedam passio, est enim species tristitiae, ut Damascenus dicit, et supra habitum est. Ergo acedia non est peccatum.

**PRAETEREA,** nullus defectus corporalis qui statutis horis accidit habet rationem peccati. Sed acedia est huiusmodi, dicit enim Cassianus, in X Lib. de institutis monasteriorum, *maxime acedia circa horam sextam monachum inquietat, ut quaedam febris ingruens tempore praestituto, ardentissimos aestus accensionum suarum solitis ac statutis horis animae inferens aegrotanti.* Ergo acedia non est peccatum.

**PRAETEREA,** illud quod ex radice bona procedit non videtur esse peccatum. Sed acedia ex bona radice procedit, dicit enim Cassianus, in eodem libro, quod acedia provenit ex hoc quod aliquis *ingemiscit se fructum spiritualem non habere, et absentia longeque posita magnificat monasteria*; quod videtur ad humilitatem pertinere. Ergo acedia non est peccatum.

**PRAETEREA,** omne peccatum est fugiendum, secundum illud Eccli. XXI, *quasi a facie colubri, fuge peccatum.* Sed Cassianus dicit, in eodem libro, *experimento probatum est acediae impugnationem non declinando fugiendam, sed resistendo superandam.* Ergo acedia non est peccatum.

**SED CONTRA,** illud quod interdicitur in sacra Scriptura est peccatum. Sed acedia est huiusmodi, dicitur enim Eccli. VI, *subiice humerum tuum et porta illam,*

**OBJECTION 1**: It would seem that sloth is not a sin. For *we are neither praised nor blamed for our passions*, according to the Philosopher (*Ethic.* ii, 5). Now sloth is a passion, since it is a kind of sorrow, according to Damascene (*De Fide Orth.* ii, 14), and as we stated above (I-II, Q. 35, A. 8). Therefore sloth is not a sin.

**OBJ. 2**: Further, no bodily failing that occurs at fixed times is a sin. But sloth is like this, for Cassian says (*De Instit. Monast.* x, ): *The monk is troubled with sloth chiefly about the sixth hour: it is like an intermittent fever, and inflicts the soul of the one it lays low with burning fires at regular and fixed intervals.* Therefore sloth is not a sin.

**OBJ. 3**: Further, that which proceeds from a good root is, seemingly, no sin. Now sloth proceeds from a good root, for Cassian says (*De Instit. Monast.* x) that *sloth arises from the fact that we sigh at being deprived of spiritual fruit, and think that other monasteries and those which are a long way off are much better than the one we dwell in*: all of which seems to point to humility. Therefore sloth is not a sin.

**OBJ. 4**: Further, all sin is to be avoided, according to Ecclus. 21:2: *Flee from sins as from the face of a serpent.* Now Cassian says (*De Instit. Monast.* x): *Experience shows that the onslaught of sloth is not to be evaded by flight but to be conquered by resistance.* Therefore sloth is not a sin.

**ON THE CONTRARY,** Whatever is forbidden in Holy Writ is a sin. Now such is sloth (*acedia*): for it is written (Sir 6:26): *Bow down thy shoulder, and bear her,* namely

idest spiritualem sapientiam, *et non acedieris in vinculis eius*. Ergo acedia est peccatum.

**RESPONDEO** dicendum quod acedia, secundum Damascenum, est *quaedam tristitia aggravans*, quae scilicet ita deprimit animum hominis ut nihil ei agere libeat; sicuti ea quae sunt acida etiam frigida sunt. Et ideo acedia importat quoddam taedium operandi, ut patet per hoc quod dicitur in Glossa super illud Psalm., *omnem escam abominata est anima eorum*; et a quibusdam dicitur quod acedia est torpor mentis bona negligentis inchoare.

Huiusmodi autem tristitia semper est mala, quandoque quidem etiam secundum seipsam; quandoque vero secundum effectum. Tristitia enim secundum se mala est quae est de eo quod est apparens malum et vere bonum, sicut e contrario delectatio mala est quae est de eo quod est apparens bonum et vere malum. Cum igitur spirituale bonum sit vere bonum, tristitia quae est de spirituali bono est secundum se mala. Sed etiam tristitia quae est de vere malo mala est secundum effectum si sic hominem aggravet ut eum totaliter a bono opere retrahat, unde et apostolus, II ad Cor. II, non vult ut poenitens *maiori tristitia* de peccato *absorbeatur*.

Quia igitur acedia, secundum quod hic sumitur, nominat tristitiam spiritualis boni, est dupliciter mala, et secundum se et secundum effectum. Et ideo acedia est peccatum, malum enim in motibus appetitivis dicimus esse peccatum, ut ex supradictis patet.

**AD PRIMUM** ergo dicendum quod passiones secundum se non sunt peccata, sed secundum quod applicantur ad aliquod malum, vituperantur; sicut et laudantur ex hoc quod applicantur ad aliquod bonum. Unde tristitia secundum se non nominat nec aliquid laudabile nec vituperabile, sed tristitia de malo vero moderata nominat aliquid laudabile; tristitia autem de bono, et iterum tristitia immoderata, nominat aliquid vituperabile. Et secundum hoc acedia ponitur peccatum.

**AD SECUNDUM** dicendum quod passiones appetitus sensitivi et in se possunt esse peccata venialia, et inclinant animam ad peccatum mortale. Et quia appetitus sensitivus habet organum corporale, sequitur quod per aliquam corporalem transmutationem homo fit habilior ad aliquod peccatum. Et ideo potest contingere quod secundum aliquas transmutationes corporales certis temporibus provenientes aliqua peccata nos magis impugnent. Omnis autem corporalis defectus de se ad tristitiam disponit. Et ideo ieiunantes, circa meridiem, quando iam incipiunt sentire defectum cibi et urgeri ab aestibus solis, magis ab acedia impugnantur.

**AD TERTIUM** dicendum quod ad humilitatem pertinet ut homo, defectus proprios considerans, seipsum non extollat. Sed hoc non pertinet ad humilitatem, sed potius ad ingratitudinem, quod bona quae quis a Deo possidet contemnat. Et ex tali contemptu sequitur ace-

spiritual wisdom, *and be not grieved (acedieris) with her bands*. Therefore sloth is a sin.

**I ANSWER THAT**, Sloth, according to Damascene (*De Fide Orth.* ii, 14) is *an oppressive sorrow*, which, to wit, so weighs upon man's mind, that he wants to do nothing; thus acid things are also cold. Hence sloth implies a certain weariness of work, as appears from a gloss on Ps. 106:18, *Their soul abhorred all manner of meat*, and from the definition of some who say that sloth is a *sluggishness of the mind which neglects to begin good*.

Now this sorrow is always evil, sometimes in itself, sometimes in its effect. For sorrow is evil in itself when it is about that which is apparently evil but good in reality, even as, on the other hand, pleasure is evil if it is about that which seems to be good but is, in truth, evil. Since, then, spiritual good is a good in very truth, sorrow about spiritual good is evil in itself. And yet that sorrow also which is about a real evil, is evil in its effect, if it so oppresses man as to draw him away entirely from good deeds. Hence the Apostle (2 Cor 2:7) did not wish those who repented to be *swallowed up with overmuch sorrow*.

Accordingly, since sloth, as we understand it here, denotes sorrow for spiritual good, it is evil on two counts, both in itself and in point of its effect. Consequently it is a sin, for by sin we mean an evil movement of the appetite, as appears from what has been said above (Q. 10, A. 2; I-II, Q. 74, A. 4).

**REPLY OBJ. 1**: Passions are not sinful in themselves; but they are blameworthy insofar as they are applied to something evil, just as they deserve praise insofar as they are applied to something good. Wherefore sorrow, in itself, calls neither for praise nor for blame: whereas moderate sorrow for evil calls for praise, while sorrow for good, and again immoderate sorrow for evil, call for blame. It is in this sense that sloth is said to be a sin.

**REPLY OBJ. 2**: The passions of the sensitive appetite may either be venial sins in themselves, or incline the soul to mortal sin. And since the sensitive appetite has a bodily organ, it follows that on account of some bodily transmutation a man becomes apt to commit some particular sin. Hence it may happen that certain sins may become more insistent, through certain bodily transmutations occurring at certain fixed times. Now all bodily effects, of themselves, dispose one to sorrow; and thus it is that those who fast are harassed by sloth towards mid-day, when they begin to feel the want of food, and to be parched by the sun's heat.

**REPLY OBJ. 3**: It is a sign of humility if a man does not think too much of himself, through observing his own faults; but if a man contemns the good things he has received from God, this, far from being a proof of humility, shows him to be ungrateful: and from such like contempt

dia, de his enim tristamur quae quasi mala vel vilia reputamus. Sic igitur necesse est ut aliquis aliorum bona extollat quod tamen bona sibi divinitus provisa non contemnat, quia sic ei tristia redderentur.

**AD QUARTUM** dicendum quod peccatum semper est fugiendum, sed impugnatio peccati quandoque est vincenda fugiendo, quandoque resistendo. Fugiendo quidem, quando continua cogitatio auget peccati incentivum, sicut est in luxuria, unde dicitur I ad Cor. VI, *fugite fornicationem*. Resistendo autem, quando cogitatio perseverans tollit incentivum peccati, quod provenit ex aliqua levi apprehensione. Et hoc contingit in acedia, quia quanto magis cogitamus de bonis spiritualibus, tanto magis nobis placentia redduntur; ex quo cessat acedia.

results sloth, because we sorrow for things that we reckon evil and worthless. Accordingly we ought to think much of the goods of others, in such a way as not to disparage those we have received ourselves, because if we did they would give us sorrow.

**REPLY OBJ. 4**: Sin is ever to be shunned, but the assaults of sin should be overcome, sometimes by flight, sometimes by resistance; by flight when a continued thought increases the incentive to sin, as in lust; for which reason it is written (1 Cor 6:18): *Fly fornication*; by resistance, when perseverance in the thought diminishes the incentive to sin, which incentive arises from some trivial consideration. This is the case with sloth, because the more we think about spiritual goods, the more pleasing they become to us, and forthwith sloth dies away.

# Article 2

*Whether sloth is a special vice?*

**AD SECUNDUM SIC PROCEDITUR.** Videtur quod acedia non sit speciale vitium. Illud enim quod convenit omni vitio non constituit specialis vitii rationem. Sed quodlibet vitium facit hominem tristari de bono spirituali opposito, nam luxuriosus tristatur de bono continentiae, et gulosus de bono abstinentiae. Cum ergo acedia sit tristitia de bono spirituali, sicut dictum est, videtur quod acedia non sit speciale peccatum.

**PRAETEREA**, acedia, cum sit tristitia quaedam, gaudio opponitur. Sed gaudium non ponitur una specialis virtus. Ergo neque acedia debet poni speciale vitium.

**PRAETEREA**, spirituale bonum, cum sit quoddam commune obiectum quod virtus appetit et vitium refugit, non constituit specialem rationem virtutis aut vitii nisi per aliquid additum contrahatur. Sed nihil videtur quod contrahat ipsum ad acediam, si sit vitium speciale, nisi labor, ex hoc enim aliqui refugiunt spiritualia bona quia sunt laboriosa; unde et acedia taedium quoddam est. Refugere autem labores, et quaerere quietem corporalem, ad idem pertinere videtur, scilicet ad pigritiam. Ergo acedia nihil aliud esset quam pigritia. Quod videtur esse falsum, nam pigritia sollicitudini opponitur, acediae autem gaudium. Non ergo acedia est speciale vitium.

**SED CONTRA** est quod Gregorius, XXXI Moral., distinguit acediam ab aliis vitiis. Ergo est speciale peccatum.

**RESPONDEO** dicendum quod, cum acedia sit tristitia de spirituali bono, si accipiatur spirituale bonum communiter, non habebit acedia rationem specialis vitii, quia sicut dictum est, omne vitium refugit spirituale bonum virtutis oppositae. Similiter etiam non potest dici quod sit speciale vitium acedia inquantum refugit

**OBJECTION 1**: It would seem that sloth is not a special vice. For that which is common to all vices does not constitute a special kind of vice. But every vice makes a man sorrowful about the opposite spiritual good: for the lustful man is sorrowful about the good of continence, and the glutton about the good of abstinence. Since then sloth is sorrow for spiritual good, as stated above (A. 1), it seems that sloth is not a special sin.

**OBJ. 2**: Further, sloth, through being a kind of sorrow, is opposed to joy. Now joy is not accounted one special virtue. Therefore sloth should not be reckoned a special vice.

**OBJ. 3**: Further, since spiritual good is a general kind of object, which virtue seeks, and vice shuns, it does not constitute a special virtue or vice, unless it be determined by some addition. Now nothing, seemingly, except toil, can determine it to sloth, if this be a special vice; because the reason why a man shuns spiritual goods, is that they are toilsome, wherefore sloth is a kind of weariness: while dislike of toil, and love of bodily repose seem to be due to the same cause, viz. idleness. Hence sloth would be nothing but laziness, which seems untrue, for idleness is opposed to carefulness, whereas sloth is opposed to joy. Therefore sloth is not a special vice.

**ON THE CONTRARY**, Gregory (*Moral.* xxxi, 45) distinguishes sloth from the other vices. Therefore it is a special vice.

**I ANSWER THAT**, Since sloth is sorrow for spiritual good, if we take spiritual good in a general way, sloth will not be a special vice, because, as stated above (I-II, Q. 71, A. 1), every vice shuns the spiritual good of its opposite virtue. Again it cannot be said that sloth is a special vice, insofar as it shuns spiritual good, as toilsome,

spirituale bonum prout est laboriosum vel molestum corpori, aut delectationis eius impeditivum, quia hoc etiam non separaret acediam a vitiis carnalibus, quibus aliquis quietem et delectationem corporis quaerit.

Et ideo dicendum est quod in spiritualibus bonis est quidam ordo, nam omnia spiritualia bona quae sunt in actibus singularum virtutum ordinantur ad unum spirituale bonum quod est bonum divinum, circa quod est specialis virtus, quae est caritas. Unde ad quamlibet virtutem pertinet gaudere de proprio spirituali bono, quod consistit in proprio actu, sed ad caritatem pertinet specialiter illud gaudium spirituale quo quis gaudet de bono divino. Et similiter illa tristitia qua quis tristatur de bono spirituali quod est in actibus singularum virtutum non pertinet ad aliquod vitium speciale, sed ad omnia vitia. Sed tristari de bono divino, de quo caritas gaudet, pertinet ad speciale vitium, quod acedia vocatur.

ET PER HOC patet responsio ad obiecta.

or troublesome to the body, or as a hindrance to the body's pleasure, for this again would not sever sloth from carnal vices, whereby a man seeks bodily comfort and pleasure.

Wherefore we must say that a certain order exists among spiritual goods, since all the spiritual goods that are in the acts of each virtue are directed to one spiritual good, which is the Divine good, about which there is a special virtue, viz. charity. Hence it is proper to each virtue to rejoice in its own spiritual good, which consists in its own act, while it belongs specially to charity to have that spiritual joy whereby one rejoices in the Divine good. In like manner the sorrow whereby one is displeased at the spiritual good which is in each act of virtue, belongs, not to any special vice, but to every vice, but sorrow in the Divine good about which charity rejoices, belongs to a special vice, which is called sloth.

THIS SUFFICES for the Replies to the Objections.

# Article 3

### *Whether sloth is a mortal sin?*

AD TERTIUM SIC PROCEDITUR. Videtur quod acedia non sit peccatum mortale. Omne enim peccatum mortale contrariatur praecepto legis Dei. Sed acedia nulli praecepto contrariari videtur, ut patet discurrenti per singula praecepta Decalogi. Ergo acedia non est peccatum mortale.

PRAETEREA, peccatum operis in eodem genere non est minus quam peccatum cordis. Sed recedere opere ab aliquo spirituali bono in Deum ducente non est peccatum mortale, alioquin mortaliter peccaret quicumque consilia non observaret. Ergo recedere corde per tristitiam ab huiusmodi spiritualibus operibus non est peccatum mortale. Non ergo acedia est peccatum mortale.

PRAETEREA, nullum peccatum mortale in viris perfectis invenitur. Sed acedia invenitur in viris perfectis, dicit enim Cassianus, in Lib. X de institutis coenobiorum, quod *acedia est solitariis magis experta, et in eremo commorantibus infestior hostis ac frequens*. Ergo acedia non est peccatum mortale.

SED CONTRA est quod dicitur II ad Cor. VII, *tristitia saeculi mortem operatur*. Sed huiusmodi est acedia, non enim est *tristitia secundum Deum*, quae contra tristitiam saeculi dividitur, quae mortem operatur. Ergo est peccatum mortale.

RESPONDEO dicendum quod, sicut supra dictum est, peccatum mortale dicitur quod tollit spiritualem vitam, quae est per caritatem, secundum quam Deus nos inhabitat, unde illud peccatum ex suo genere est mortale quod de se, secundum propriam rationem, contrariatur

OBJECTION 1: It would seem that sloth is not a mortal sin. For every mortal sin is contrary to a precept of the Divine Law. But sloth seems contrary to no precept, as one may see by going through the precepts of the Decalogue. Therefore sloth is not a mortal sin.

OBJ. 2: Further, in the same genus, a sin of deed is no less grievous than a sin of thought. Now it is not a mortal sin to refrain in deed from some spiritual good which leads to God, else it would be a mortal sin not to observe the counsels. Therefore it is not a mortal sin to refrain in thought from such like spiritual works. Therefore sloth is not a mortal sin.

OBJ. 3: Further, no mortal sin is to be found in a perfect man. But sloth is to be found in a perfect man: for Cassian says (*De Instit. Coenob.* x, 1) that *sloth is well known to the solitary, and is a most vexatious and persistent foe to the hermit*. Therefore sloth is not always a mortal sin.

ON THE CONTRARY, It is written (2 Cor 7:20): *The sorrow of the world worketh death*. But such is sloth; for it is not *sorrow according to God*, which is contrasted with sorrow of the world. Therefore it is a mortal sin.

I ANSWER THAT, As stated above (I-II, Q. 88, AA. 1, 2), mortal sin is so called because it destroys the spiritual life which is the effect of charity, whereby God dwells in us. Wherefore any sin which by its very nature is contrary to charity is a mortal sin by reason of its genus. And such

caritati. Huiusmodi autem est acedia. Nam proprius effectus caritatis est gaudium de Deo, ut supra dictum est, acedia autem est tristitia de bono spirituali inquantum est bonum divinum. Unde secundum suum genus acedia est peccatum mortale. Sed considerandum est in omnibus peccatis quae sunt secundum suum genus mortalia quod non sunt mortalia nisi quando suam perfectionem consequuntur. Est autem consummatio peccati in consensu rationis, loquimur enim nunc de peccato humano, quod in actu humano consistit, cuius principium est ratio. Unde si sit inchoatio peccati in sola sensualitate, et non pertingat usque ad consensum rationis, propter imperfectionem actus est peccatum veniale. Sicut in genere adulterii concupiscentia quae consistit in sola sensualitate est peccatum veniale; si tamen pervenitur usque ad consensum rationis, est peccatum mortale. Ita etiam et motus acediae in sola sensualitate quandoque est, propter repugnantiam carnis ad spiritum, et tunc est peccatum veniale. Quandoque vero pertingit usque ad rationem, quae consentit in fugam et horrorem et detestationem boni divini, carne omnino contra spiritum praevalente. Et tunc manifestum est quod acedia est peccatum mortale.

**AD PRIMUM** ergo dicendum quod acedia contrariatur praecepto de sanctificatione sabbati, in quo, secundum quod est praeceptum morale, praecipitur quies mentis in Deo, cui contrariatur tristitia mentis de bono divino.

**AD SECUNDUM** dicendum quod acedia non est recessus mentalis a quocumque spirituali bono, sed a bono divino, cui oportet mentem inhaerere ex necessitate. Unde si aliquis contristetur de hoc quod aliquis cogit eum implere opera virtutis quae facere non tenetur, non est peccatum acediae, sed quando contristatur in his quae ei imminent facienda propter Deum.

**AD TERTIUM** dicendum quod in viris sanctis inveniuntur aliqui imperfecti motus acediae, qui tamen non pertingunt usque ad consensum rationis.

is sloth, because the proper effect of charity is joy in God, as stated above (Q. 28, A. 1), while sloth is sorrow about spiritual good inasmuch as it is a Divine good. Therefore sloth is a mortal sin in respect of its genus. But it must be observed with regard to all sins that are mortal in respect of their genus, that they are not mortal, save when they attain to their perfection. Because the consummation of sin is in the consent of reason: for we are speaking now of human sins consisting in human acts, the principle of which is the reason. Wherefore if the sin be a mere beginning of sin in the sensuality alone, without attaining to the consent of reason, it is a venial sin on account of the imperfection of the act. Thus in the genus of adultery, the concupiscence that goes no further than the sensuality is a venial sin, whereas if it reach to the consent of reason, it is a mortal sin. So too, the movement of sloth is sometimes in the sensuality alone, by reason of the opposition of the flesh to the spirit, and then it is a venial sin; whereas sometimes it reaches to the reason, which consents in the dislike, horror and detestation of the Divine good, on account of the flesh utterly prevailing over the spirit. In this case it is evident that sloth is a mortal sin.

**REPLY OBJ. 1**: Sloth is opposed to the precept about hallowing the Sabbath day. For this precept, insofar as it is a moral precept, implicitly commands the mind to rest in God: and sorrow of the mind about the Divine good is contrary thereto.

**REPLY OBJ. 2**: Sloth is not an aversion of the mind from any spiritual good, but from the Divine good, to which the mind is obliged to adhere. Wherefore if a man is sorry because someone forces him to do acts of virtue that he is not bound to do, this is not a sin of sloth; but when he is sorry to have to do something for God's sake.

**REPLY OBJ. 3**: Imperfect movements of sloth are to be found in holy men, but they do not reach to the consent of reason.

# Article 4

*Whether sloth should be accounted a capital vice?*

**AD QUARTUM SIC PROCEDITUR.** Videtur quod acedia non debeat poni vitium capitale. Vitium enim capitale dicitur quod movet ad actus peccatorum, ut supra habitum est. Sed acedia non movet ad agendum, sed magis retrahit ab agendo. Ergo non debet poni vitium capitale.

**PRAETEREA**, vitium capitale habet filias sibi deputatas. Assignat autem Gregorius, XXXI Moral., sex filias acediae, quae sunt *malitia, rancor, pusillanimitas, despe-*

**OBJECTION 1**: It would seem that sloth ought not to be accounted a capital vice. For a capital vice is one that moves a man to sinful acts, as stated above (Q. 34, A. 5). Now sloth does not move one to action, but on the contrary withdraws one from it. Therefore it should not be accounted a capital sin.

**OBJ. 2**: Further, a capital sin is one to which daughters are assigned. Now Gregory (*Moral.* xxxi, 45) assigns six daughters to sloth, viz. *malice, spite, faint-heartedness,*

ratio, *torpor circa praecepta, vagatio mentis circa illicita*, quae non videntur convenienter oriri ex acedia. Nam rancor idem esse videtur quod odium, quod oritur ex invidia, ut supra dictum est. Malitia autem est genus ad omnia vitia, et similiter vagatio mentis circa illicita, et in omnibus vitiis inveniuntur. Torpor autem circa praecepta idem videtur esse quod acedia. Pusillanimitas autem et desperatio ex quibuscumque peccatis oriri possunt. Non ergo convenienter ponitur acedia esse vitium capitale.

**Praeterea**, Isidorus, in libro de summo bono, distinguit vitium acediae a vitio tristitiae, dicens tristitiam esse inquantum recedit a graviori et laborioso ad quod tenetur; acediam inquantum se convertit ad quietem indebitam. Et dicit de tristitia oriri rancorem, pusillanimitatem, amaritudinem, desperationem, de acedia vero dicit oriri septem, quae sunt otiositas, somnolentia, importunitas mentis, inquietudo corporis, instabilitas, verbositas, curiositas. Ergo videtur quod vel a Gregorio vel ab Isidoro male assignetur acedia vitium capitale cum suis filiabus.

**Sed contra** est quod Gregorius dicit, XXXI Moral., acediam esse vitium capitale et habere praedictas filias.

**Respondeo** dicendum quod, sicut supra dictum est, vitium capitale dicitur ex quo promptum est ut alia vitia oriantur secundum rationem causae finalis. Sicut autem homines multa operantur propter delectationem, tum ut ipsam consequantur, tum etiam ex eius impetu ad aliquid agendum permoti; ita etiam propter tristitiam multa operantur, vel ut ipsam evitent, vel ex eius pondere in aliqua agenda proruentes. Unde cum acedia sit tristitia quaedam, ut supra dictum est, convenienter ponitur vitium capitale.

**Ad primum** ergo dicendum quod acedia, aggravando animum, impedit hominem ab illis operibus quae tristitiam causant. Sed tamen inducit animum ad aliqua agenda vel quae sunt tristitiae consona, sicut ad plorandum; vel etiam ad aliqua per quae tristitia evitatur.

**Ad secundum** dicendum quod Gregorius convenienter assignat filias acediae. Quia enim, ut Philosophus dicit, in VIII Ethic., *nullus diu absque delectatione potest manere cum tristitia*, necesse est quod ex tristitia aliquid dupliciter oriatur, uno modo, ut homo recedat a contristantibus; alio modo, ut ad alia transeat in quibus delectatur, sicut illi qui non possunt gaudere in spiritualibus delectationibus transferunt se ad corporales, secundum Philosophum, in X Ethic. In fuga autem tristitiae talis processus attenditur quod primo homo fugit contristantia; secundo, etiam impugnat ea quae tristitiam ingerunt. Spiritualia autem bona, de quibus tristatur acedia, sunt et finis et id quod est ad finem. Fuga autem finis fit per *desperationem*. Fuga autem bonorum quae sunt ad finem, quantum ad ardua, quae subsunt

*despair, sluggishness in regard to the commandments, wandering of the mind after unlawful things*. Now these do not seem in reality to arise from sloth. For *spite* is, seemingly the same as hatred, which arises from envy, as stated above (Q. 34, A. 6); *malice* is a genus which contains all vices, and, in like manner, a *wandering* of the mind after unlawful things is to be found in every vice; *sluggishness* about the commandments seems to be the same as sloth, while *faintheartedness* and *despair* may arise from any sin. Therefore sloth is not rightly accounted a capital sin.

**Obj. 3**: Further, Isidore distinguishes the vice of sloth from the vice of sorrow, saying (*De Summo Bono* ii, 37) that insofar as a man shirks his duty because it is distasteful and burdensome, it is sorrow, and insofar as he is inclined to undue repose, it is sloth: and of sorrow he says that it gives rise to *spite, faint-heartedness, bitterness, despair*, whereas he states that from sloth seven things arise, viz. *idleness, drowsiness, uneasiness of the mind, restlessness of the body, instability, loquacity, curiosity*. Therefore it seems that either Gregory or Isidore has wrongly assigned sloth as a capital sin together with its daughters.

**On the contrary**, The same Gregory (*Moral.* xxxi, 45) states that sloth is a capital sin, and has the daughters aforesaid.

**I answer that**, As stated above (I-II, Q. 84, AA. 3, 4), a capital vice is one which easily gives rise to others as being their final cause. Now just as we do many things on account of pleasure, both in order to obtain it, and through being moved to do something under the impulse of pleasure, so again we do many things on account of sorrow, either that we may avoid it, or through being exasperated into doing something under pressure thereof. Wherefore, since sloth is a kind of sorrow, as stated above (A. 2; I-II, Q. 85, A. 8), it is fittingly reckoned a capital sin.

**Reply Obj. 1**: Sloth by weighing on the mind, hinders us from doing things that cause sorrow: nevertheless it induces the mind to do certain things, either because they are in harmony with sorrow, such as weeping, or because they are a means of avoiding sorrow.

**Reply Obj. 2**: Gregory fittingly assigns the daughters of sloth. For since, according to the Philosopher (*Ethic.* viii, 5, 6) *no man can be a long time in company with what is painful and unpleasant*, it follows that something arises from sorrow in two ways: first, that man shuns whatever causes sorrow; second, that he passes to other things that give him pleasure: thus those who find no joy in spiritual pleasures, have recourse to pleasures of the body, according to the Philosopher (*Ethic.* x, 6). Now in the avoidance of sorrow the order observed is that man at first flies from unpleasant objects, and second he even struggles against such things as cause sorrow. Now spiritual goods which are the object of the sorrow of sloth, are both end and means. Avoidance of the end is the result of *despair*, while avoidance of those goods which are the means to the end,

consiliis, fit per *pusillanimitatem*; quantum autem ad ea quae pertinent ad communem iustitiam, fit per *torporem circa praecepta*. Impugnatio autem contristantium bonorum spiritualium quandoque quidem est contra homines qui ad bona spiritualia inducunt, et hoc est *rancor*; quandoque vero se extendit ad ipsa spiritualia bona, in quorum detestationem aliquis adducitur, et hoc proprie est *malitia*. Inquantum autem propter tristitiam a spiritualibus aliquis transfert se ad delectabilia exteriora, ponitur filia acediae *evagatio circa illicita*. Per quod patet responsio ad ea quae circa singulas filias obiiciebantur. Nam malitia non accipitur hic secundum quod est genus vitiorum, sed sicut dictum est. Rancor etiam non accipitur hic communiter pro odio, sed pro quadam indignatione, sicut dictum est. Et idem dicendum est de aliis.

**AD TERTIUM** dicendum quod etiam Cassianus, in libro de institutis Coenob., distinguit tristitiam ab acedia, sed convenientius Gregorius acediam tristitiam nominat. Quia sicut supra dictum est, tristitia non est vitium ab aliis distinctum secundum quod aliquis recedit a gravi et laborioso opere, vel secundum quascumque alias causas aliquis tristetur, sed solum secundum quod contristatur de bono divino. Quod pertinet ad rationem acediae, quae intantum convertit ad quietem indebitam inquantum aspernatur bonum divinum. Illa autem quae Isidorus ponit oriri ex tristitia et acedia reducuntur ad ea quae Gregorius ponit. Nam *amaritudo*, quam ponit Isidorus oriri ex tristitia, est quidam effectus rancoris. *Otiositas* autem et *somnolentia* reducuntur ad torporem circa praecepta, circa quae est aliquis otiosus, omnino ea praetermittens et somnolentus, ea negligenter implens. Omnia autem alia quinque quae ponit ex acedia oriri pertinent ad evagationem mentis circa illicita. Quae quidem secundum quod in ipsa arce mentis residet volentis importune ad diversa se diffundere, vocatur *importunitas mentis*; secundum autem quod pertinet ad cognitivam, dicitur *curiositas*; quantum autem ad locutionem, dicitur *verbositas*; quantum autem ad corpus in eodem loco non manens, dicitur *inquietudo corporis*, quando scilicet aliquis per inordinatos motus membrorum vagationem indicat mentis; quantum autem ad diversa loca, dicitur *instabilitas*. Vel potest accipi instabilitas secundum mutabilitatem propositi.

in matters of difficulty which come under the counsels, is the effect of *faint-heartedness*, and in matters of common righteousness, is the effect of *sluggishness about the commandments*. The struggle against spiritual goods that cause sorrow is sometimes with men who lead others to spiritual goods, and this is called *spite*; and sometimes it extends to the spiritual goods themselves, when a man goes so far as to detest them, and this is properly called *malice*. insofar as a man has recourse to eternal objects of pleasure, the daughter of sloth is called *wandering after unlawful things*. From this it is clear how to reply to the objections against each of the daughters: for *malice* does not denote here that which is generic to all vices, but must be understood as explained. Nor is *spite* taken as synonymous with hatred, but for a kind of indignation, as stated above: and the same applies to the others.

**REPLY OBJ. 3**: This distinction between sorrow and sloth is also given by Cassian (*De Instit. Coenob.* x, 1). But Gregory more fittingly (*Moral.* xxxi, 45) calls sloth a kind of sorrow, because, as stated above (A. 2), sorrow is not a distinct vice, insofar as a man shirks a distasteful and burdensome work, or sorrows on account of any other cause whatever, but only insofar as he is sorry on account of the Divine good, which sorrow belongs essentially to sloth; since sloth seeks undue rest insofar as it spurns the Divine good. Moreover the things which Isidore reckons to arise from sloth and sorrow, are reduced to those mentioned by Gregory: for *bitterness* which Isidore states to be the result of sorrow, is an effect of *spite*. *Idleness* and *drowsiness* are reduced to *sluggishness about the precepts*: for some are idle and omit them altogether, while others are drowsy and fulfill them with negligence. All the other five which he reckons as effects of sloth, belong to the *wandering of the mind after unlawful things*. This tendency to wander, if it reside in the mind itself that is desirous of rushing after various things without rhyme or reason, is called *uneasiness of the mind*, but if it pertains to the imaginative power, it is called *curiosity*; if it affect the speech it is called *loquacity*; and insofar as it affects a body that changes place, it is called *restlessness of the body*, when, to wit, a man shows the unsteadiness of his mind, by the inordinate movements of members of his body; while if it causes the body to move from one place to another, it is called *instability*; or *instability* may denote changeableness of purpose.

# QUESTION 36

## ENVY

Deinde considerandum est de invidia. Et circa hoc quaeruntur quatuor.

Primo, quid sit invidia.

Secundo, utrum sit peccatum.

Tertio, utrum sit peccatum mortale.

Quarto, utrum sit vitium capitale, et de filiabus eius.

We must now consider envy, and under this head there are four points of inquiry:

(1) What is envy?

(2) Whether it is a sin?

(3) Whether it is a mortal sin?

(4) Whether it is a capital sin, and which are its daughters?

# Article 1

*Whether envy is a kind of sorrow?*

**AD PRIMUM SIC PROCEDITUR.** Videtur quod invidia non sit tristitia. Obiectum enim tristitiae est malum. Sed obiectum invidiae est bonum, dicit enim Gregorius, in V Moral., de invido loquens, *tabescentem mentem sua poena sauciat, quam felicitas torquet aliena.* Ergo invidia non est tristitia.

**PRAETEREA,** similitudo non est causa tristitiae, sed magis delectationis. Sed similitudo est causa invidiae, dicit enim philosophus, in II Rhet., *invidebunt tales quibus sunt aliqui similes aut secundum genus, aut secundum cognationem, aut secundum staturam, aut secundum habitum, aut secundum opinionem.* Ergo invidia non est tristitia.

**PRAETEREA,** tristitia ex aliquo defectu causatur, unde illi qui sunt in magno defectu sunt ad tristitiam proni, ut supra dictum est, cum de passionibus ageretur. Sed illi *quibus modicum deficit, et qui sunt amatores honoris, et qui reputantur sapientes,* sunt invidi; ut patet per Philosophum, in II Rhet. Ergo invidia non est tristitia.

**PRAETEREA,** tristitia delectationi opponitur. Oppositorum autem non est eadem causa. Ergo, cum memoria bonorum habitorum sit causa delectationis, ut supra dictum est, non erit causa tristitiae. Est autem causa invidiae, dicit enim philosophus, in II Rhet., quod his aliqui invident *qui habent aut possederunt quae ipsis conveniebant aut quae ipsi quandoque possidebant.* Ergo invidia non est tristitia.

**SED CONTRA** est quod Damascenus, in II libro, ponit invidiam speciem tristitiae, et dicit quod invidia est *tristitia in alienis bonis.*

**RESPONDEO** dicendum quod obiectum tristitiae est malum proprium. Contingit autem id quod est alienum bonum apprehendi ut malum proprium. Et secundum

**OBJECTION 1**: It would seem that envy is not a kind of sorrow. For the object of envy is a good, for Gregory says (*Moral.* v, 46) of the envious man that *self-inflicted pain wounds the pining spirit, which is racked by the prosperity of another.* Therefore envy is not a kind of sorrow.

**OBJ. 2**: Further, likeness is a cause, not of sorrow but rather of pleasure. But likeness is a cause of envy: for the Philosopher says (*Rhet.* ii, 10): *Men are envious of such as are like them in genus, in knowledge, in stature, in habit, or in reputation.* Therefore envy is not a kind of sorrow.

**OBJ. 3**: Further, sorrow is caused by a defect, wherefore those who are in great defect are inclined to sorrow, as stated above (I-II, Q. 47, A. 3) when we were treating of the passions. Now *those who lack little, and who love honors, and who are considered wise,* are envious, according to the Philosopher (*Rhet.* ii, 10). Therefore envy is not a kind of sorrow.

**OBJ. 4**: Further, sorrow is opposed to pleasure. Now opposite effects have not one and the same cause. Therefore, since the recollection of goods once possessed is a cause of pleasure, as stated above (I-II, Q. 32, A. 3) it will not be a cause of sorrow. But it is a cause of envy; for the Philosopher says (*Rhet.* ii, 10) that *we envy those who have or have had things that befitted ourselves, or which we possessed at some time.* Therefore envy is not a kind of sorrow.

**ON THE CONTRARY,** Damascene (*De Fide Orth.* ii, 14) calls envy a species of sorrow, and says that *envy is sorrow for another's good.*

**I ANSWER THAT,** The object of a man's sorrow is his own evil. Now it may happen that another's good is apprehended as one's own evil, and in this way sorrow can be about

hoc de bono alieno potest esse tristitia. Sed hoc contingit dupliciter. Uno modo, quando quis tristatur de bono alicuius inquantum imminet sibi ex hoc periculum alicuius nocumenti, sicut cum homo tristatur de exaltatione inimici sui, timens ne eum laedat. Et talis tristitia non est invidia, sed magis timoris effectus; ut philosophus dicit, in II Rhet.

Alio modo bonum alterius aestimatur ut malum proprium inquantum est diminutivum propriae gloriae vel excellentiae. Et hoc modo de bono alterius tristatur invidia. Et ideo praecipue de illis bonis homines invident in quibus est gloria, et *in quibus homines amant honorari et in opinione esse*; ut Philosophus dicit, in II Rhet.

**AD PRIMUM** ergo dicendum quod nihil prohibet id quod est bonum uni apprehendi ut malum alteri. Et secundum hoc tristitia aliqua potest esse de bono, ut dictum est.

**AD SECUNDUM** dicendum quod quia invidia est de gloria alterius inquantum diminuit gloriam quam quis appetit, consequens est ut ad illos tantum invidia habeatur quibus homo vult se aequare vel praeferre in gloria. Hoc autem non est respectu multum a se distantium, nullus enim, nisi insanus, studet se aequare vel praeferre in gloria his qui sunt multo eo maiores, puta plebeius homo regi; vel etiam rex plebeio, quem multum excedit. Et ideo his qui multum distant vel loco vel tempore vel statu homo non invidet, sed his qui sunt propinqui, quibus se nititur aequare vel praeferre. Nam cum illi excedunt in gloria, accidit hoc contra nostram utilitatem, et inde causatur tristitia. Similitudo autem delectationem causat inquantum concordat voluntati.

**AD TERTIUM** dicendum quod nullus conatur ad ea in quibus est multum deficiens. Et ideo cum aliquis in hoc eum excedat, non invidet. Sed si modicum deficiat, videtur quod ad hoc pertingere possit, et sic ad hoc conatur. Unde si frustraretur eius conatus propter excessum gloriae alterius, tristatur. Et inde est quod amatores honoris sunt magis invidi. Et similiter etiam pusillanimes sunt invidi, quia omnia reputant magna, et quidquid boni alicui accidat, reputant se in magno superatos esse. Unde et Iob V dicitur, *parvulum occidit invidia*. Et dicit Gregorius, in V Moral., quod *invidere non possumus nisi eis quos nobis in aliquo meliores putamus.*

**AD QUARTUM** dicendum quod memoria praeteritorum bonorum, inquantum fuerunt habita, delectationem causat, sed inquantum sunt amissa, causant tristitiam. Et inquantum ab aliis habentur, causant invidiam, quia hoc maxime videtur gloriae propriae derogare. Et ideo dicit philosophus, in II Rhet., quod *senes invident iunioribus; et illi qui multa expenderunt*

another's good. But this happens in two ways: first, when a man is sorry about another's good, insofar as it threatens to be an occasion of harm to himself, as when a man grieves for his enemy's prosperity, for fear lest he may do him some harm: such like sorrow is not envy, but rather an effect of fear, as the Philosopher states (*Rhet.* ii, 9).

Second, another's good may be reckoned as being one's own evil, insofar as it conduces to the lessening of one's own good name or excellence. It is in this way that envy grieves for another's good: and consequently men are envious of those goods in which a good name consists, and *about which men like to be honored and esteemed*, as the Philosopher remarks (*Rhet.* ii, 10).

**REPLY OBJ. 1**: Nothing hinders what is good for one from being reckoned as evil for another: and in this way it is possible for sorrow to be about good, as stated above.

**REPLY OBJ. 2**: Since envy is about another's good name insofar as it diminishes the good name a man desires to have, it follows that a man is envious of those only whom he wishes to rival or surpass in reputation. But this does not apply to people who are far removed from one another: for no man, unless he be out of his mind, endeavors to rival or surpass in reputation those who are far above him. Thus a commoner does not envy the king, nor does the king envy a commoner whom he is far above. Wherefore a man envies not those who are far removed from him, whether in place, time, or station, but those who are near him, and whom he strives to rival or surpass. For it is against our will that these should be in better repute than we are, and that gives rise to sorrow. On the other hand, likeness causes pleasure insofar as it is in agreement with the will.

**REPLY OBJ. 3**: A man does not strive for mastery in matters where he is very deficient; so that he does not envy one who surpasses him in such matters, unless he surpass him by little, for then it seems to him that this is not beyond him, and so he makes an effort; wherefore, if his effort fails through the other's reputation surpassing his, he grieves. Hence it is that those who love to be honored are more envious; and in like manner the faint-hearted are envious, because all things are great to them, and whatever good may befall another, they reckon that they themselves have been bested in something great. Hence it is written (Job 5:2): *Envy slayeth the little one*, and Gregory says (*Moral.* v, 46) that *we can envy those only whom we think better in some respect than ourselves.*

**REPLY OBJ. 4**: Recollection of past goods insofar as we have had them, causes pleasure; insofar as we have lost them, causes sorrow; and insofar as others have them, causes envy, because that, above all, seems to belittle our reputation. Hence the Philosopher says (*Rhet.* ii) that *the old envy the young, and those who have spent much in order to get something, envy those who have got it by spending little,*

*ad aliquid consequendum invident his qui parvis expensis illud sunt consecuti*; dolent enim de amissione suorum bonorum, et de hoc quod alii consecuti sunt bona.

because they grieve that they have lost their goods, and that others have acquired goods.

# Article 2

*Whether envy is a sin?*

**AD SECUNDUM SIC PROCEDITUR.** Videtur quod invidia non sit peccatum. Dicit enim Hieronymus, ad Laetam, de Instruct. filiae, *habeat socias cum quibus discat, quibus invideat, quarum laudibus mordeatur.* Sed nullus est sollicitandus ad peccandum. Ergo invidia non est peccatum.

**PRAETEREA**, invidia est *tristitia de alienis bonis*, ut Damascenus dicit. Sed hoc quandoque laudabiliter fit, dicitur enim Prov. XXIX, *cum impii sumpserint principatum, gemet populus.* Ergo invidia non semper est peccatum.

**PRAETEREA**, invidia zelum quendam nominat. Sed zelus quidam est bonus, *zelus domus tuae comedit me.* Secundum illud Psalm., ergo invidia non semper est peccatum.

**PRAETEREA**, poena dividitur contra culpam. Sed invidia est quaedam poena, dicit enim Gregorius, V Moral., *cum devictum cor livoris putredo corruperit, ipsa quoque exteriora indicant quam graviter animum vesania instigat, color quippe pallore afficitur, oculi deprimuntur, mens accenditur, membra frigescunt, fit in cogitatione rabies, in dentibus stridor.* Ergo invidia non est peccatum.

**SED CONTRA** est quod dicitur ad Gal. V, *non efficiamur inanis gloriae cupidi, invicem provocantes, invicem invidentes.*

**RESPONDEO** dicendum quod, sicut dictum est, invidia est tristitia de alienis bonis. Sed haec tristitia potest contingere quatuor modis. Uno quidem modo, quando aliquis dolet de bono alicuius inquantum ex eo timetur nocumentum vel sibi ipsi vel etiam aliis bonis. Et talis tristitia non est invidia, ut dictum est; et potest esse sine peccato. Unde Gregorius, XXII Moral., ait, *evenire plerumque solet ut, non amissa caritate, et inimici nos ruina laetificet, et rursum eius gloria sine invidiae culpa contristet, cum et ruente eo quosdam bene erigi credimus, et proficiente illo plerosque iniuste opprimi formidamus.*

Alio modo potest aliquis tristari de bono alterius, non ex eo quod ipse habet bonum, sed ex eo quod nobis deest bonum illud quod ipse habet. Et hoc proprie est zelus; ut Philosophus dicit, in II Rhet. Et si iste zelus sit circa bona honesta, laudabilis est, secundum illud I ad Cor. XIV, *aemulamini spiritualia.* Si autem sit de bonis temporalibus, potest esse cum peccato, et sine peccato.

**OBJECTION 1**: It would seem that envy is not a sin. For Jerome says to Laeta about the education of her daughter (*Ep. cvii*): *Let her have companions, so that she may learn together with them, envy them, and be nettled when they are praised.* But no one should be advised to commit a sin. Therefore envy is not a sin.

**OBJECTION 2**: Further, Envy is *sorrow for another's good*, as Damascene says (*De Fide Orth.* ii, 14). But this is sometimes praiseworthy: for it is written (Prov 29:2): *When the wicked shall bear rule, the people shall mourn.* Therefore envy is not always a sin.

**OBJ. 3**: Further, envy denotes a kind of zeal. But there is a good zeal, according to Ps. 68:10: *The zeal of Thy house hath eaten me up.* Therefore envy is not always a sin.

**OBJ. 4**: Further, punishment is condivided with fault. But envy is a kind of punishment: for Gregory says (*Moral.* v, 46): *When the foul sore of envy corrupts the vanquished heart, the very exterior itself shows how forcibly the mind is urged by madness. For paleness seizes the complexion, the eyes are weighed down, the spirit is inflamed, while the limbs are chilled, there is frenzy in the heart, there is gnashing with the teeth.* Therefore envy is not a sin.

**ON THE CONTRARY**, It is written (Gal 5:26): *Let us not be made desirous of vainglory, provoking one another, envying one another.*

**I ANSWER THAT**, As stated above (A. 1), envy is sorrow for another's good. Now this sorrow may come about in four ways. First, when a man grieves for another's good, through fear that it may cause harm either to himself, or to some other goods. This sorrow is not envy, as stated above (A. 1), and may be void of sin. Hence Gregory says (*Moral.* xxii, 11): *It very often happens that without charity being lost, both the destruction of an enemy rejoices us, and again his glory, without any sin of envy, saddens us, since, when he falls, we believe that some are deservedly set up, and when he prospers, we dread lest many suffer unjustly.*

Second, we may grieve over another's good, not because he has it, but because the good which he has, we have not: and this, properly speaking, is zeal, as the Philosopher says (*Rhet.* ii, 9). And if this zeal be about virtuous goods, it is praiseworthy, according to 1 Cor. 14:1: *Be zealous for spiritual gifts*: while, if it be about temporal goods, it may be either sinful or sinless. Third, one may grieve over

Tertio modo aliquis tristatur de bono alterius inquantum ille cui accidit bonum est eo indignus. Quae quidem tristitia non potest oriri ex bonis honestis, ex quibus aliquis iustus efficitur; sed sicut Philosophus dicit, in II Rhet., est de divitiis et de talibus, quae possunt provenire dignis et indignis. Et haec tristitia, secundum ipsum, vocatur *nemesis*, et pertinet ad bonos mores. Sed hoc ideo dicit quia considerabat ipsa bona temporalia secundum se, prout possunt magna videri non respicientibus ad aeterna. Sed secundum doctrinam fidei, temporalia bona quae indignis proveniunt ex iusta Dei ordinatione disponuntur vel ad eorum correctionem vel ad eorum damnationem, et huiusmodi bona quasi nihil sunt in comparatione ad bona futura, quae servantur bonis. Et ideo huiusmodi tristitia prohibetur in Scriptura sacra, secundum illud Psalm., *noli aemulari in malignantibus, neque zelaveris facientes iniquitatem.* Et alibi, *pene effusi sunt gressus mei, quia zelavi super iniquos, pacem peccatorum videns.* Quarto aliquis tristatur de bonis alicuius inquantum alter excedit ipsum in bonis. Et hoc proprie est invidia. Et istud semper est pravum, ut etiam philosophus dicit, in II Rhet., quia dolet de eo de quo est gaudendum, scilicet de bono proximi.

**AD PRIMUM** ergo dicendum quod ibi sumitur invidia pro zelo quo quis debet incitari ad proficiendum cum melioribus.

**AD SECUNDUM** dicendum quod ratio illa procedit de tristitia alienorum bonorum secundum primum modum.

**AD TERTIUM** dicendum quod invidia differt a zelo, sicut dictum est. Unde zelus aliquis potest esse bonus, sed invidia semper est mala.

**AD QUARTUM** dicendum quod nihil prohibet aliquod peccatum, ratione alicuius adiuncti, poenale esse; ut supra dictum est, cum de peccatis ageretur.

another's good, because he who happens to have that good is unworthy of it. Such sorrow as this cannot be occasioned by virtuous goods, which make a man righteous, but, as the Philosopher states, is about riches, and those things which can accrue to the worthy and the unworthy; and he calls this sorrow *nemesis*, saying that it belongs to good morals. But he says this because he considered temporal goods in themselves, insofar as they may seem great to those who look not to eternal goods: whereas, according to the teaching of faith, temporal goods that accrue to those who are unworthy, are so disposed according to God's just ordinance, either for the correction of those men, or for their condemnation, and such goods are as nothing in comparison with the goods to come, which are prepared for good men. Wherefore sorrow of this kind is forbidden in Holy Writ, according to Ps. 36:1: *Be not emulous of evil doers, nor envy them that work iniquity,* and elsewhere (Ps 72:2, 3): *My steps had well nigh slipped, for I was envious of the wicked, when I saw the prosperity of sinners.* Fourth, we grieve over a man's good, insofar as his good surpasses ours; this is envy properly speaking, and is always sinful, as also the Philosopher states (*Rhet.* ii, 10), because to do so is to grieve over what should make us rejoice, viz. over our neighbor's good.

**REPLY OBJ. 1**: Envy there denotes the zeal with which we ought to strive to progress with those who are better than we are.

**REPLY OBJ. 2**: This argument considers sorrow for another's good in the first sense given above.

**REPLY OBJ. 3**: Envy differs from zeal, as stated above. Hence a certain zeal may be good, whereas envy is always evil.

**REPLY OBJ. 4**: Nothing hinders a sin from being penal accidentally, as stated above (I-II, Q. 87, A. 2) when we were treating of sins.

# Article 3

*Whether envy is a mortal sin?*

**AD TERTIUM SIC PROCEDITUR**. Videtur quod invidia non sit peccatum mortale. Invidia enim, cum sit tristitia, est passio appetitus sensitivi. Sed in sensualitate non est peccatum mortale, sed solum in ratione; ut patet per Augustinum, XII de Trin. Ergo invidia non est peccatum mortale.

**PRAETEREA**, in infantibus non potest esse peccatum mortale. Sed in eis potest esse invidia, dicit enim Augustinus, in I Confess., *vidi ego et expertus sum zelan-*

**OBJECTION 1**: It would seem that envy is not a mortal sin. For since envy is a kind of sorrow, it is a passion of the sensitive appetite. Now there is no mortal sin in the sensuality, but only in the reason, as Augustine declares (*De Trin.* xii, 12). Therefore envy is not a mortal sin.

**OBJ. 2**: Further, there cannot be mortal sin in infants. But envy can be in them, for Augustine says (*Confess.* i): *I myself have seen and known even a baby envious, it could*

*tem puerum, nondum loquebatur, et intuebatur pallidus amaro aspectu collactaneum suum.* Ergo invidia non est peccatum mortale.

**PRAETEREA**, omne peccatum mortale alicui virtuti contrariatur. Sed invidia non contrariatur alicui virtuti, sed Nemesi, quae est quaedam passio; ut patet per philosophum, in II Rhet. Ergo invidia non est peccatum mortale.

**SED CONTRA** est quod dicitur Iob V, *parvulum occidit invidia.* Nihil autem occidit spiritualiter nisi peccatum mortale. Ergo invidia est peccatum mortale.

**RESPONDEO** dicendum quod invidia ex genere suo est peccatum mortale. Genus enim peccati ex obiecto consideratur. Invidia autem, secundum rationem sui obiecti, contrariatur caritati, per quam est vita animae spiritualis, secundum illud I Ioan. III, *nos scimus quoniam translati sumus de morte ad vitam, quoniam diligimus fratres.* Utriusque enim obiectum, et caritatis et invidiae, est bonum proximi, sed secundum contrarium motum, nam caritas gaudet de bono proximi, invidia autem de eodem tristatur, ut ex dictis patet. Unde manifestum est quod invidia ex suo genere est peccatum mortale.

Sed sicut supra dictum est, in quolibet genere peccati mortalis inveniuntur aliqui imperfecti motus in sensualitate existentes qui sunt peccata venialia, sicut in genere adulterii primus motus concupiscentiae, et in genere homicidii primus motus irae. Ita etiam et in genere invidiae inveniuntur aliqui primi motus quandoque etiam in viris perfectis, qui sunt peccata venialia.

**AD PRIMUM** ergo dicendum quod motus invidiae secundum quod est passio sensualitatis, est quoddam imperfectum in genere actuum humanorum, quorum principium est ratio. Unde talis invidia non est peccatum mortale. Et similis est ratio de invidia parvulorum, in quibus non est usus rationis.

**UNDE PATET** responsio ad secundum.

**AD TERTIUM** dicendum quod invidia, secundum philosophum, in II Rhet. opponitur et Nemesi et misericordiae, sed secundum diversa. Nam misericordiae opponitur directe, secundum contrarietatem principalis obiecti, invidus enim tristatur de bono proximi; misericors autem tristatur de malo proximi. Unde invidi non sunt misericordes, sicut ibidem dicitur, nec e converso. Ex parte vero eius de cuius bono tristatur invidus, opponitur invidia Nemesi, Nemeseticus enim tristatur de bono indigne agentium, secundum illud Psalm., *zelavi super iniquos, pacem peccatorum videns;* invidus autem tristatur de bono eorum qui sunt digni. Unde patet quod prima contrarietas est magis directa quam secunda. Misericordia autem quaedam virtus est, et caritatis

not speak, yet it turned pale and looked bitterly on its foster-brother. Therefore envy is not a mortal sin.

**OBJ. 3**: Further, every mortal sin is contrary to some virtue. But envy is contrary, not to a virtue but to nemesis, which is a passion, according to the Philosopher (*Rhet.* ii, 9). Therefore envy is not a mortal sin.

**ON THE CONTRARY**, It is written (Job 5:2): *Envy slayeth the little one.* Now nothing slays spiritually, except mortal sin. Therefore envy is a mortal sin.

**I ANSWER THAT**, Envy is a mortal sin, in respect of its genus. For the genus of a sin is taken from its object; and envy according to the aspect of its object is contrary to charity, whence the soul derives its spiritual life, according to 1 John 3:14: *We know that we have passed from death to life, because we love the brethren.* Now the object both of charity and of envy is our neighbor's good, but by contrary movements, since charity rejoices in our neighbor's good, while envy grieves over it, as stated above (A. 1). Therefore it is evident that envy is a mortal sin in respect of its genus.

Nevertheless, as stated above (Q. 35, A. 4; I-II, Q. 72, A. 5, ad 1), in every kind of mortal sin we find certain imperfect movements in the sensuality, which are venial sins: such are the first movement of concupiscence, in the genus of adultery, and the first movement of anger, in the genus of murder, and so in the genus of envy we find sometimes even in perfect men certain first movements, which are venial sins.

**REPLY OBJ. 1**: The movement of envy insofar as it is a passion of the sensuality, is an imperfect thing in the genus of human acts, the principle of which is the reason, so that envy of that kind is not a mortal sin. The same applies to the envy of little children who have not the use of reason.

**WHEREFORE** the Reply to the Second Objection is manifest.

**REPLY OBJ. 3**: According to the Philosopher (*Rhet.* ii, 9), envy is contrary both to nemesis and to pity, but for different reasons. For it is directly contrary to pity, their principal objects being contrary to one another, since the envious man grieves over his neighbor's good, whereas the pitiful man grieves over his neighbor's evil, so that the envious have no pity, as he states in the same passage, nor is the pitiful man envious. On the other hand, envy is contrary to nemesis on the part of the man whose good grieves the envious man, for nemesis is sorrow for the good of the undeserving according to Ps. 72:3: *I was envious of the wicked, when I saw the prosperity of sinners,* whereas the envious grieves over the good of those who are deserving of it. Hence it is clear that the former contrariety is more direct

proprius effectus. Unde invidia misericordiae opponitur et caritati.

than the latter. Now pity is a virtue, and an effect proper to charity: so that envy is contrary to pity and charity.

# Article 4

*Whether envy is a capital vice?*

**AD QUARTUM SIC PROCEDITUR**. Videtur quod invidia non sit vitium capitale. Vitia enim capitalia distinguuntur contra filias capitalium vitiorum. Sed invidia est filia inanis gloriae, dicit enim philosophus, in II Rhet., quod *amatores honoris et gloriae magis invident*. Ergo invidia non est vitium capitale.

**PRAETEREA**, vitia capitalia videntur esse leviora quam alia quae ex eis oriuntur, dicit enim Gregorius, XXXI Moral., *prima vitia deceptae menti quasi sub quadam ratione se ingerunt, sed quae sequuntur, dum mentem ad omnem insaniam protrahunt, quasi bestiali clamore mentem confundunt*. Sed invidia videtur esse gravissimum peccatum, dicit enim Gregorius, V Moral., *quamvis per omne vitium quod perpetratur humano cordi antiqui hostis virus infunditur, in hac tamen nequitia tota sua viscera serpens concutit, et imprimendae malitiae pestem vomit*. Ergo invidia non est vitium capitale.

**PRAETEREA**, videtur quod inconvenienter eius filiae assignentur a Gregorio, XXXI Moral., ubi dicit quod *de invidia oritur odium, susurratio, detractio, exultatio in adversis proximi et afflictio in prosperis*. Exultatio enim in adversis proximi, et afflictio in prosperis, idem videtur esse quod invidia, ut ex praemissis patet. Non ergo ista debent poni ut filiae invidiae.

**SED CONTRA** est auctoritas Gregorii, XXXI Moral., qui ponit invidiam vitium capitale, et ei praedictas filias assignat.

**RESPONDEO** dicendum quod sicut acedia est tristitia de bono spirituali divino, ita invidia est tristitia de bono proximi. Dictum est autem supra acediam esse vitium capitale, ea ratione quia ex acedia homo impellitur ad aliqua facienda vel ut fugiat tristitiam vel ut tristitiae satisfaciat. Unde eadem ratione invidia ponitur vitium capitale.

**AD PRIMUM** ergo dicendum quod, sicut Gregorius dicit, in XXXI Moral. *capitalia vitia tanta sibi coniunctione coniunguntur ut non nisi unum de altero proferatur. Prima namque superbiae soboles inanis est gloria, quae dum oppressam mentem corruperit, mox invidiam gignit, quia dum vani nominis potentiam appetit, ne quis hanc alius adipisci valeat, tabescit*. Non est ergo contra rationem vitii capitalis quod ipsum ex alio oriatur, sed quod non habeat aliquam principalem rationem producendi

**OBJECTION 1**: It would seem that envy is not a capital vice. For the capital vices are distinct from their daughters. Now envy is the daughter of vainglory; for the Philosopher says (*Rhet.* ii, 10) that *those who love honor and glory are more envious*. Therefore envy is not a capital vice.

**OBJ. 2**: Further, the capital vices seem to be less grave than the other vices which arise from them. For Gregory says (*Moral.* xxxi, 45): *The leading vices seem to worm their way into the deceived mind under some kind of pretext, but those which follow them provoke the soul to all kinds of outrage, and confuse the mind with their wild outcry*. Now envy is seemingly a most grave sin, for Gregory says (*Moral.* v, 46): *Though in every evil thing that is done, the venom of our old enemy is infused into the heart of man, yet in this wickedness the serpent stirs his whole bowels and discharges the bane of spite fitted to enter deep into the mind*. Therefore envy is not a capital sin.

**OBJ. 3**: Further, it seems that its daughters are unfittingly assigned by Gregory (*Moral.* xxxi, 45), who says that from envy arise *hatred, tale-bearing, detraction, joy at our neighbor's misfortunes, and grief for his prosperity*. For joy at our neighbor's misfortunes and grief for his prosperity seem to be the same as envy, as appears from what has been said above (A. 3). Therefore these should not be assigned as daughters of envy.

**ON THE CONTRARY** stands the authority of Gregory (*Moral.* xxxi, 45) who states that envy is a capital sin and assigns the aforesaid daughters thereto.

**I ANSWER THAT**, Just as sloth is grief for a Divine spiritual good, so envy is grief for our neighbor's good. Now it has been stated above (Q. 35, A. 4) that sloth is a capital vice for the reason that it incites man to do certain things, with the purpose either of avoiding sorrow or of satisfying its demands. Wherefore envy is accounted a capital vice for the same reason.

**REPLY OBJ. 1**: As Gregory says (*Moral.* xxxi, 45), *the capital vices are so closely akin to one another that one springs from the other. For the first offspring of pride is vainglory, which by corrupting the mind it occupies begets envy, since while it craves for the power of an empty name, it repines for fear lest another should acquire that power*. Consequently the notion of a capital vice does not exclude its originating from another vice, but it demands that it should have some principal reason for being itself the origin of

ex se multa genera peccatorum. Forte tamen propter hoc quod invidia manifeste ex inani gloria nascitur, non ponitur vitium capitale neque ab Isidoro, in libro de summo bono, neque a Cassiano, in libro de Instit. Coenob.

**AD SECUNDUM** dicendum quod ex verbis illis non habetur quod invidia sit maximum peccatorum, sed quod quando Diabolus invidiam suggerit, ad hoc hominem inducit quod ipse principaliter in corde habet; quia sicut ibi inducitur consequenter, *invidia Diaboli mors introivit in orbem terrarum.*

Est tamen quaedam invidia quae inter gravissima peccata computatur, scilicet *invidentia fraternae gratiae,* secundum quod aliquis dolet de ipso augmento gratiae Dei, non solum de bono proximi. Unde ponitur peccatum in spiritum sanctum, quia per hanc invidentiam homo quodammodo invidet spiritui sancto, qui in suis operibus glorificatur.

**AD TERTIUM** dicendum quod numerus filiarum invidiae sic potest sumi. Quia in conatu invidiae est aliquid tanquam principium, et aliquid tanquam medium, et aliquid tanquam terminus. Principium quidem est ut aliquis diminuat gloriam alterius vel in occulto, et sic est *susurratio*; vel manifeste, et sic est *detractio.* Medium autem est quia aliquis intendens diminuere gloriam alterius aut potest, et sic est *exultatio in adversis*; aut non potest, et sic est *afflictio in prosperis.* Terminus autem est in ipso *odio,* quia sicut bonum delectans causat amorem, ita tristitia causat odium, ut supra dictum est. Afflictio autem in prosperis proximi uno modo est ipsa invidia, inquantum scilicet aliquis tristatur de prosperis alicuius secundum quod habent quandam gloriam. Alio vero modo est filia invidiae, secundum quod prospera proximi eveniunt contra conatum invidentis, qui nititur impedire. Exultatio autem in adversis non est directe idem quod invidia, sed ex ea sequitur, nam ex tristitia de bono proximi, quae est invidia, sequitur exultatio de malo eiusdem.

several kinds of sin. However it is perhaps because envy manifestly arises from vainglory, that it is not reckoned a capital sin, either by Isidore (*De Summo Bono*) or by Cassian (*De Instit. Coenob.* v, 1).

**REPLY OBJ. 2**: It does not follow from the passage quoted that envy is the greatest of sins, but that when the devil tempts us to envy, he is enticing us to that which has its chief place in his heart, for as quoted further on in the same passage, *by the envy of the devil, death came into the world* (Wis 2:24).

There is, however, a kind of envy which is accounted among the most grievous sins, viz. *envy of another's spiritual good,* which envy is a sorrow for the increase of God's grace, and not merely for our neighbor's good. Hence it is accounted a sin against the Holy Spirit, because thereby a man envies, as it were, the Holy Spirit Himself, Who is glorified in His works.

**REPLY OBJ. 3**: The number of envy's daughters may be understood for the reason that in the struggle aroused by envy there is something by way of beginning, something by way of middle, and something by way of term. The beginning is that a man strives to lower another's reputation, and this either secretly, and then we have *talebearing,* or openly, and then we have *detraction.* The middle consists in the fact that when a man aims at defaming another, he is either able to do so, and then we have *joy at another's misfortune,* or he is unable, and then we have *grief at another's prosperity.* The term is hatred itself, because just as good which delights causes love, so does sorrow cause *hatred,* as stated above (Q. 34, A. 6). Grief at another's prosperity is in one way the very same as envy, when, to wit, a man grieves over another's prosperity, insofar as it gives the latter a good name, but in another way it is a daughter of envy, insofar as the envious man sees his neighbor prosper notwithstanding his efforts to prevent it. On the other hand, joy at another's misfortune is not directly the same as envy, but is a result thereof, because grief over our neighbor's good which is envy, gives rise to joy in his evil.

# QUESTION 37

Deinde considerandum est de peccatis quae opponuntur paci. Et primo, de discordia, quae est in corde; secundo, de contentione, quae est in ore; tertio, de his quae pertinent ad opus, scilicet, de schismate, rixa et bello. Circa primum quaeruntur duo,

Primo, utrum discordia sit peccatum.

Secundo, utrum sit filia inanis gloriae.

We must now consider the sins contrary to peace, and first we shall consider discord which is in the heart, second contention, which is on the lips, third, those things which consist in deeds, viz. schism, quarrelling, war, and sedition. Under the first head there are two points of inquiry:

(1) Whether discord is a sin?

(2) Whether it is a daughter of vainglory?

## Article 1

*Whether discord is a sin?*

**AD PRIMUM SIC PROCEDITUR.** Videtur quod discordia non sit peccatum. Discordare enim ab aliquo est recedere ab alterius voluntate. Sed hoc non videtur esse peccatum, quia voluntas proximi non est regula voluntatis nostrae, sed sola voluntas divina. Ergo discordia non est peccatum.

**PRAETEREA,** quicumque inducit aliquem ad peccandum, et ipse peccat. Sed inducere inter aliquos discordiam non videtur esse peccatum, dicitur enim Act. XXIII, quod *sciens Paulus quia una pars esset Sadducaeorum et altera Pharisaeorum, exclamavit in Concilio, viri fratres, ego Pharisaeus sum, filius Pharisaeorum, de spe et resurrectione mortuorum ego iudicor. Et cum haec dixisset, facta est dissensio inter Pharisaeos et Sadducaeos.* Ergo discordia non est peccatum.

**PRAETEREA,** peccatum, praecipue mortale, in sanctis viris non invenitur. Sed in sanctis viris invenitur discordia, dicitur enim Act. XV, *facta est dissensio inter Paulum et Barnabam, ita ut discederent ab invicem.* Ergo discordia non est peccatum, et maxime mortale.

**SED CONTRA** est quod ad Gal. V dissensiones, idest discordiae, ponuntur inter opera carnis, de quibus subditur, *qui talia agunt, regnum Dei non consequuntur.* Nihil autem excludit a regno Dei nisi peccatum mortale. Ergo discordia est peccatum mortale.

**RESPONDEO** dicendum quod discordia concordiae opponitur. Concordia autem, ut supra dictum est, ex caritate causatur, inquantum scilicet caritas multorum corda coniungit in aliquid unum, quod est principaliter quidem bonum divinum, secundario autem bonum proximi. Discordia igitur ea ratione est peccatum, inquantum huiusmodi concordiae contrariatur.

**OBJECTION 1:** It would seem that discord is not a sin. For to disaccord with man is to sever oneself from another's will. But this does not seem to be a sin, because God's will alone, and not our neighbor's, is the rule of our own will. Therefore discord is not a sin.

**OBJ. 2:** Further, whoever induces another to sin, sins also himself. But it appears not to be a sin to incite others to discord, for it is written (Acts 23:6) that Paul, knowing that the one part were Sadducees, and the other Pharisees, cried out in the council: *Men brethren, I am a Pharisee, the son of Pharisees, concerning the hope and resurrection of the dead I am called in question. And when he had so said, there arose a dissension between the Pharisees and the Sadducees.* Therefore discord is not a sin.

**OBJ. 3:** Further, sin, especially mortal sin, is not to be found in a holy man. But discord is to be found even among holy men, for it is written (Acts 15:39): *There arose a* dissension *between Paul and Barnabas, so that they departed one from another.* Therefore discord is not a sin, and least of all a mortal sin.

**ON THE CONTRARY,** *Dissensions,* that is, discords, are reckoned among the works of the flesh (Gal 5:20), of which it is said afterwards (Gal 5:21) that *they who do such things shall not obtain the kingdom of God.* Now nothing, save mortal sin, excludes man from the kingdom of God. Therefore discord is a mortal sin.

**I ANSWER THAT,** Discord is opposed to concord. Now, as stated above (Q. 29, AA. 1, 3) concord results from charity, inasmuch as charity directs many hearts together to one thing, which is chiefly the Divine good, secondarily, the good of our neighbor. Wherefore discord is a sin, insofar as it is opposed to this concord.

Sed sciendum quod haec concordia per discordiam tollitur dupliciter, uno quidem modo, per se; alio vero modo, per accidens. Per se quidem in humanis actibus et motibus dicitur esse id quod est secundum intentionem. Unde per se discordat aliquis a proximo quando scienter et ex intentione dissentit a bono divino et a proximi bono, in quo debet consentire. Et hoc est peccatum mortale ex suo genere, propter contrarietatem ad caritatem, licet primi motus huius discordiae, propter imperfectionem actus, sint peccata venialia.

Per accidens autem in humanis actibus consideratur ex hoc quod aliquid est praeter intentionem. Unde cum intentio aliquorum est ad aliquod bonum quod pertinet ad honorem Dei vel utilitatem proximi, sed unus aestimat hoc esse bonum, alius autem habet contrariam opinionem, discordia tunc est per accidens contra bonum divinum vel proximi. Et talis discordia non est peccatum, nec repugnat caritati, nisi huiusmodi discordia sit vel cum errore circa ea quae sunt de necessitate salutis, vel pertinacia indebite adhibeatur, cum etiam supra dictum est quod concordia quae est caritatis effectus est unio voluntatum, non unio opinionum. Ex quo patet quod discordia quandoque est ex peccato unius tantum, puta cum unus vult bonum, cui alius scienter resistit, quandoque autem est cum peccato utriusque, puta cum uterque dissentit a bono alterius, et uterque diligit bonum proprium.

**AD PRIMUM** ergo dicendum quod voluntas unius hominis secundum se considerata non est regula voluntatis alterius. Sed inquantum voluntas proximi inhaeret voluntati Dei, fit per consequens regula regulata secundum primam regulam. Et ideo discordare a tali voluntate est peccatum, quia per hoc discordatur a regula divina.

**AD SECUNDUM** dicendum quod sicut voluntas hominis adhaerens Deo est quaedam regula recta, a qua peccatum est discordare; ita etiam voluntas hominis Deo contraria est quaedam perversa regula, a qua bonum est discordare. Facere ergo discordiam per quam tollitur bona concordia quam caritas facit, est grave peccatum, unde dicitur Prov. VI, *sex sunt quae odit dominus, et septimum detestatur anima eius*, et hoc septimum ponit *eum qui seminat inter fratres discordias*. Sed causare discordiam per quam tollitur mala concordia, scilicet in mala voluntate, est laudabile. Et hoc modo laudabile fuit quod Paulus dissensionem posuit inter eos qui erant concordes in malo, nam et dominus de se dicit, Matth. X, *non veni pacem mittere, sed gladium.*

**AD TERTIUM** dicendum quod discordia quae fuit inter Paulum et Barnabam fuit per accidens et non per se, uterque enim intendebat bonum, sed uni videbatur hoc esse bonum, alii aliud. Quod ad defectum humanum pertinebat, non enim erat talis controversia in his quae

But it must be observed that this concord is destroyed by discord in two ways: first, directly; second, accidentally. Now, human acts and movements are said to be direct when they are according to one's intention. Wherefore a man directly disaccords with his neighbor, when he knowingly and intentionally dissents from the Divine good and his neighbor's good, to which he ought to consent. This is a mortal sin in respect of its genus, because it is contrary to charity, although the first movements of such discord are venial sins by reason of their being imperfect acts.

The accidental in human acts is that which occurs beside the intention. Hence when several intend a good pertaining to God's honor, or our neighbor's profit, while one deems a certain thing good, and another thinks contrariwise, the discord is in this case accidentally contrary to the Divine good or that of our neighbor. Such like discord is neither sinful nor against charity, unless it be accompanied by an error about things necessary to salvation, or by undue obstinacy, since it has also been stated above (Q. 29, AA. 1, 3, ad 2) that the concord which is an effect of charity, is union of wills not of opinions. It follows from this that discord is sometimes the sin of one party only, for instance, when one wills a good which the other knowingly resists; while sometimes it implies sin in both parties, as when each dissents from the other's good, and loves his own.

**REPLY OBJ. 1**: One man's will considered in itself is not the rule of another man's will; but insofar as our neighbor's will adheres to God's will, it becomes in consequence, a rule regulated according to its proper measure. Wherefore it is a sin to disaccord with such a will, because by that very fact one disaccords with the Divine rule.

**REPLY OBJ. 2**: Just as a man's will that adheres to God is a right rule, to disaccord with which is a sin, so too a man's will that is opposed to God is a perverse rule, to disaccord with which is good. Hence to cause a discord, whereby a good concord resulting from charity is destroyed, is a grave sin: wherefore it is written (Prov 6:16): *Six things there are, which the Lord hateth, and the seventh His soul detesteth,* which seventh is stated (Prov 6:19) to be *him that soweth discord among brethren*. On the other hand, to arouse a discord whereby an evil concord (i.e., concord in an evil will) is destroyed, is praiseworthy. In this way Paul was to be commended for sowing discord among those who concorded together in evil, because Our Lord also said of Himself (Matt 10:34): *I came not to send peace, but the sword.*

**REPLY OBJ. 3**: The discord between Paul and Barnabas was accidental and not direct: because each intended some good, yet the one thought one thing good, while the other thought something else, which was owing to human deficiency: for that controversy was not about things necessary

sunt de necessitate salutis. Quamvis hoc ipsum fuerit ex divina providentia ordinatum, propter utilitatem inde consequentem.

to salvation. Moreover all this was ordained by Divine providence, on account of the good which would ensue.

# Article 2

*Whether discord is a daughter of vainglory?*

AD SECUNDUM SIC PROCEDITUR. Videtur quod discordia non sit filia inanis gloriae. Ira enim est aliud vitium ab inani gloria. Sed discordia videtur esse filia irae, secundum illud Prov. XV, *vir iracundus provocat rixas*. Ergo non est filia inanis gloriae.

PRAETEREA, Augustinus dicit, super Ioan., exponens illud quod habetur Ioan. VII, *nondum erat spiritus datus, livor separat, caritas iungit*. Sed discordia nihil est aliud quam quaedam separatio voluntatum. Ergo discordia procedit ex livore, idest invidia, magis quam ex inani gloria.

PRAETEREA, illud ex quo multa mala oriuntur videtur esse vitium capitale. Sed discordia est huiusmodi, quia super illud Matth. XII, *omne regnum contra se divisum desolabitur*, dicit Hieronymus, *quo modo concordia parvae res crescunt, sic discordia maximae dilabuntur*. Ergo ipsa discordia debet poni vitium capitale, magis quam filia inanis gloriae.

SED CONTRA est auctoritas Gregorii, XXXI Moral.

RESPONDEO dicendum quod discordia importat quandam disgregationem voluntatum, inquantum scilicet voluntas unius stat in uno, et voluntas alterius stat in altero. Quod autem voluntas alicuius in proprio sistat, provenit ex hoc quod aliquis ea quae sunt sua praefert his quae sunt aliorum. Quod cum inordinate fit, pertinet ad superbiam et inanem gloriam. Et ideo discordia, per quam unusquisque sequitur quod suum est et recedit ab eo quod est alterius, ponitur filia inanis gloriae.

AD PRIMUM ergo dicendum quod rixa non est idem quod discordia. Nam rixa consistit in exteriori opere, unde convenienter causatur ab ira, quae movet animum ad nocendum proximo. Sed discordia consistit in disiunctione motuum voluntatis, quam facit superbia vel inanis gloria, ratione iam dicta.

AD SECUNDUM dicendum quod in discordia consideratur quidem ut terminus a quo recessus a voluntate alterius, et quantum ad hoc causatur ex invidia. Ut terminus autem ad quem, accessus ad id quod est sibi proprium, et quantum ad hoc causatur ex inani gloria. Et quia in quolibet motu terminus ad quem est potior termino a quo (finis enim est potior principio), potius ponitur discordia filia inanis gloriae quam invidiae, licet

OBJECTION 1: It would seem that discord is not a daughter of vainglory. For anger is a vice distinct from vainglory. Now discord is apparently the daughter of anger, according to Prov. 15:18: *A passionate man stirreth up strifes*. Therefore it is not a daughter of vainglory.

OBJ. 2: Further, Augustine expounding the words of John 7:39, *As yet the Spirit was not given*, says (*Tract. xxxii*) *Malice severs, charity unites*. Now discord is merely a separation of wills. Therefore discord arises from malice, i.e., envy, rather than from vainglory.

OBJ. 3: Further, whatever gives rise to many evils, would seem to be a capital vice. Now such is discord, because Jerome in commenting on Matt. 12:25, *Every kingdom divided against itself shall be made desolate*, says: *Just as concord makes small things thrive, so discord brings the greatest things to ruin*. Therefore discord should itself be reckoned a capital vice, rather than a daughter of vainglory.

ON THE CONTRARY stands the authority of Gregory (*Moral.* xxxi, 45).

I ANSWER THAT, Discord denotes a certain disunion of wills, in so far, to wit, as one man's will holds fast to one thing, while the other man's will holds fast to something else. Now if a man's will holds fast to its own ground, this is due to the act that he prefers what is his own to that which belongs to others, and if he do this inordinately, it is due to pride and vainglory. Therefore discord, whereby a man holds to his own way of thinking, and departs from that of others, is reckoned to be a daughter of vainglory.

REPLY OBJ. 1: Strife is not the same as discord, for strife consists in external deeds, wherefore it is becoming that it should arise from anger, which incites the mind to hurt one's neighbor; whereas discord consists in a divergence in the movements of wills, which arises from pride or vainglory, for the reason given above.

REPLY OBJ. 2: In discord we may consider that which is the term wherefrom, i.e., another's will from which we recede, and in this respect it arises from envy; and again we may consider that which is the term whither, i.e., something of our own to which we cling, and in this respect it is caused by vainglory. And since in every moment the term whither is more important than the term wherefrom (because the end is of more account than the beginning), discord is

ex utraque oriri possit secundum diversas rationes, ut dictum est.

**AD TERTIUM** dicendum quod ideo concordia magnae res crescunt et per discordiam dilabuntur, quia virtus quanto est magis unita, tanto est fortior, et per separationem diminuitur; ut dicitur in libro de causis. Unde patet quod hoc pertinet ad proprium effectum discordiae, quae est divisio voluntatum, non autem pertinet ad originem diversorum vitiorum a discordia, per quod habeat rationem vitii capitalis.

accounted a daughter of vainglory rather than of envy, though it may arise from both for different reasons, as stated.

**REPLY OBJ. 3**: The reason why concord makes small things thrive, while discord brings the greatest to ruin, is because the more united a force is, the stronger it is, while the more disunited it is the weaker it becomes (*De Causis* xvii). Hence it is evident that this is part of the proper effect of discord which is a disunion of wills, and in no way indicates that other vices arise from discord, as though it were a capital vice.

# Question 38

## Contention

Deinde considerandum est de contentione. Et circa hoc quaeruntur duo.

Primo, utrum contentio sit peccatum mortale.

Secundo, utrum sit filia inanis gloriae.

We must now consider contention, in respect of which there are two points of inquiry:

(1) Whether contention is a mortal sin?

(2) Whether it is a daughter of vainglory?

## Article 1

### *Whether contention is a mortal sin?*

**Ad primum sic proceditur.** Videtur quod contentio non sit peccatum mortale. Peccatum enim mortale in viris spiritualibus non invenitur. In quibus tamen invenitur contentio, secundum illud Luc. XXII, *facta est contentio inter discipulos Iesu, quis eorum esset maior.* Ergo contentio non est peccatum mortale.

**Praeterea,** nulli bene disposito debet placere peccatum mortale in proximo. Sed dicit apostolus, ad Philipp. I, *quidam ex contentione Christum annuntiant*; et postea subdit, *et in hoc gaudeo, sed et gaudebo.* Ergo contentio non est peccatum mortale.

**Praeterea,** contingit quod aliqui vel in iudicio vel in disputatione contendunt non aliquo animo malignandi, sed potius intendentes ad bonum, sicut illi qui contra haereticos disputando contendunt. Unde super illud, I Reg. XIV, *accidit quadam die* etc., dicit Glossa, *Catholici contra haereticos contentiones commovent, ubi prius ad certamen convocantur.* Ergo contentio non est peccatum mortale.

**Praeterea,** Iob videtur cum Deo contendisse, secundum illud Iob XXXIX, *numquid qui contendit cum Deo tam facile conquiescit?* Et tamen Iob non peccavit mortaliter, quia dominus de eo dicit, *non estis locuti recte coram me, sicut servus meus Iob,* ut habetur Iob ult. Ergo contentio non semper est peccatum mortale.

**Sed contra** est quod contrariatur praecepto apostoli, qui dicit II ad Tim. II, *noli verbis contendere.* Et Gal. V contentio numeratur inter opera carnis, *quae qui agunt, regnum Dei non possident,* ut ibidem dicitur. Sed omne quod excludit a regno Dei, et quod contrariatur praecepto, est peccatum mortale. Ergo contentio est peccatum mortale.

**Respondeo** dicendum quod contendere est contra aliquem tendere. Unde sicut discordia contrarietatem quandam importat in voluntate, ita contentio contrarie-

**Objection 1:** It would seem that contention is not a mortal sin. For there is no mortal sin in spiritual men: and yet contention is to be found in them, according to Luke 22:24: *And there was also a strife amongst the disciples of Jesus, which of them should . . . be the greatest.* Therefore contention is not a mortal sin.

**Obj. 2:** Further, no well disposed man should be pleased that his neighbor commit a mortal sin. But the Apostle says (Phil 1:17): *Some out of contention preach Christ,* and afterwards he says (Phil 1:18): *In this also I rejoice, yea, and will rejoice.* Therefore contention is not a mortal sin.

**Obj. 3:** Further, it happens that people contend either in the courts or in disputations, without any spiteful purpose, and with a good intention, as, for example, those who contend by disputing with heretics. Hence a gloss on 1 Kings 14:1, *It came to pass one day,* etc. says: *Catholics do not raise contentions with heretics, unless they are first challenged to dispute.* Therefore contention is not a mortal sin.

**Obj. 4:** Further, Job seems to have contended with God, according to Job 39:32: *Shall he that contendeth with God be so easily silenced?* And yet Job was not guilty of mortal sin, since the Lord said of him (Job 42:7): *You have not spoken the thing that is right before me, as my servant Job hath.* Therefore contention is not always a mortal sin.

**On the contrary,** It is against the precept of the Apostle who says (2 Tim 2:14): *Contend not in words.* Moreover (Gal 5:20) contention is included among the works of the flesh, and as stated there (Gal 5:21) *they who do such things shall not obtain the kingdom of God.* Now whatever excludes a man from the kingdom of God and is against a precept, is a mortal sin. Therefore contention is a mortal sin.

**I answer that,** To contend is to tend against some one. Wherefore just as discord denotes a contrariety of wills, so contention signifies contrariety of speech. For this

tatem quandam importat in locutione. Et propter hoc etiam cum oratio alicuius per contraria se diffundit, vocatur contentio, quae ponitur unus color rhetoricus a Tullio, qui dicit, *contentio est cum ex contrariis rebus oratio efficitur, hoc pacto, habet assentatio iucunda principia, eadem exitus amarissimos affert.*

Contrarietas autem locutionis potest attendi dupliciter, uno modo, quantum ad intentionem contendentis; alio modo, quantum ad modum. In intentione quidem considerandum est utrum aliquis contrarietur veritati, quod est vituperabile, vel falsitati, quod est laudabile. In modo autem considerandum est utrum talis modus contrariandi conveniat et personis et negotiis, quia hoc est laudabile (unde et Tullius dicit, in III Rhet., *quod contentio est oratio acris ad confirmandum et confutandum accommodata*), vel excedat convenientiam personarum et negotiorum, et sic contentio est vituperabilis.

Si ergo accipiatur contentio secundum quod importat impugnationem veritatis et inordinatum modum, sic est peccatum mortale. Et hoc modo definit Ambrosius contentionem, dicens, *contentio est impugnatio veritatis cum confidentia clamoris.* Si autem contentio dicatur impugnatio falsitatis cum debito modo acrimoniae, sic contentio est laudabilis. Si autem accipiatur contentio secundum quod importat impugnationem falsitatis cum inordinato modo, sic potest esse peccatum veniale, nisi forte tanta inordinatio fiat in contendendo quod ex hoc generetur scandalum aliorum. Unde et apostolus, cum dixisset, II ad Tim. II, *noli verbis contendere,* subdit, *ad nihil enim utile est, nisi ad subversionem audientium.*

**AD PRIMUM** ergo dicendum quod in discipulis Christi non erat contentio cum intentione impugnandi veritatem, quia unusquisque defendebat quod sibi verum videbatur. Erat tamen in eorum contentione inordinatio, quia contendebant de quo non erat contendendum, scilicet de primatu honoris; nondum enim erant spirituales, sicut Glossa ibidem dicit. Unde et dominus eos consequenter compescuit.

**AD SECUNDUM** dicendum quod illi qui ex contentione Christum praedicabant reprehensibiles erant, quia quamvis non impugnarent veritatem fidei, sed eam praedicarent, impugnabant tamen veritatem quantum ad hoc quod putabant *se suscitare pressuram* apostolo veritatem fidei praedicanti. Unde apostolus non gaudebat de eorum contentione, sed de fructu qui ex hoc proveniebat, scilicet *quod Christus annuntiabatur,* quia ex malis etiam occasionaliter subsequuntur bona.

**AD TERTIUM** dicendum quod secundum completam rationem contentionis prout est peccatum mortale, ille in iudicio contendit qui impugnat veritatem iustitiae, et in disputatione contendit qui intendit impugnare veritatem doctrinae. Et secundum hoc Catholici non

reason when a man contrasts various contrary things in a speech, this is called contentio, which Tully calls one of the rhetorical colors (*De Rhet. ad Heren.* iv), where he says that *it consists in developing a speech from contrary things,* for instance: *Adulation has a pleasant beginning, and a most bitter end.*

Now contrariety of speech may be looked at in two ways: first with regard to the intention of the contentious party, second, with regard to the manner of contending. As to the intention, we must consider whether he contends against the truth, and then he is to be blamed, or against falsehood, and then he should be praised. As to the manner, we must consider whether his manner of contending is in keeping with the persons and the matter in dispute, for then it would be praiseworthy, hence Tully says (*De Rhet. ad Heren.* iii) that *contention is a sharp speech suitable for proof and refutation*—or whether it exceeds the demands of the persons and matter in dispute, in which case it is blameworthy.

Accordingly if we take contention as denoting a disclaimer of the truth and an inordinate manner, it is a mortal sin. Thus Ambrose defines contention: *Contention is a disclaimer of the truth with clamorous confidence.* If, however, contention denote a disavowal of what is false, with the proper measure of acrimony, it is praiseworthy: whereas, if it denote a disavowal of falsehood, together with an inordinate manner, it can be a venial sin, unless the contention be conducted so inordinately, as to give scandal to others. Hence the Apostle after saying (2 Tim 2:14): *Contend not in words,* adds, *for it is to no profit, but to the subverting of the hearers.*

**REPLY OBJ. 1**: The disciples of Christ contended together, not with the intention of disclaiming the truth, since each one stood up for what he thought was true. Yet there was inordinateness in their contention, because they contended about a matter which they ought not to have contended about, viz. the primacy of honor; for they were not spiritual men as yet, as a gloss says on the same passage; and for this reason Our Lord checked them.

**REPLY OBJ. 2**: Those who preached Christ *out of contention,* were to be blamed, because, although they did not gainsay the truth of faith, but preached it, yet they did gainsay the truth, by the fact that they thought they would *raise affliction* to the Apostle who was preaching the truth of faith. Hence the Apostle rejoiced not in their contention, but in the fruit that would result therefrom, namely *that Christ would be made known*—since evil is sometimes the occasion of good results.

**REPLY OBJ. 3**: Contention is complete and is a mortal sin when, in contending before a judge, a man gainsays the truth of justice, or in a disputation, intends to impugn the true doctrine. In this sense Catholics do not contend against heretics, but the reverse. But when, whether in court

contendunt contra haereticos, sed potius e converso. Si autem accipiatur contentio in iudicio vel disputatione secundum imperfectam rationem, scilicet secundum quod importat quandam acrimoniam locutionis, sic non semper est peccatum mortale.

AD QUARTUM dicendum quod contentio ibi sumitur communiter pro disputatione. Dixerat enim Iob, XIII cap., *ad omnipotentem loquar, et disputare cum Deo cupio*, non tamen intendens neque veritatem impugnare, sed exquirere; neque circa hanc inquisitionem aliqua inordinatione vel animi vel vocis uti.

or in a disputation, it is incomplete, i.e., in respect of the acrimony of speech, it is not always a mortal sin.

REPLY OBJ. 4: Contention here denotes an ordinary dispute. For Job had said (13:3): *I will speak to the Almighty, and I desire to reason with God*: yet he intended not to impugn the truth, but to defend it, and in seeking the truth thus, he had no wish to be inordinate in mind or in speech.

# Article 2

## *Whether contention is a daughter of vainglory?*

AD SECUNDUM SIC PROCEDITUR. Videtur quod contentio non sit filia inanis gloriae. Contentio enim affinitatem habet ad zelum, unde dicitur I ad Cor. III, *cum sit inter vos zelus et contentio, nonne carnales estis, et secundum hominem ambulatis?* Zelus autem ad invidiam pertinet. Ergo contentio magis ex invidia oritur.

PRAETEREA, contentio cum clamore quodam est. Sed clamor ex ira oritur; ut patet per Gregorium, XXXI Moral. Ergo etiam contentio oritur ex ira.

PRAETEREA, inter alia scientia praecipue videtur esse materia superbiae et inanis gloriae, secundum illud I ad Cor. VIII, *scientia inflat*. Sed contentio provenit plerumque ex defectu scientiae, per quam veritas cognoscitur, non impugnatur. Ergo contentio non est filia inanis gloriae.

SED CONTRA est auctoritas Gregorii, XXXI Moral.

RESPONDEO dicendum quod, sicut supra dictum est, discordia est filia inanis gloriae, eo quod discordantium uterque in suo proprio stat, et unus alteri non acquiescit; proprium autem superbiae est et inanis gloriae propriam excellentiam quaerere. Sicut autem discordantes aliqui sunt ex hoc quod stant corde in propriis, ita contendentes sunt aliqui ex hoc quod unusquisque verbo id quod sibi videtur defendit. Et ideo eadem ratione ponitur contentio filia inanis gloriae sicut et discordia.

AD PRIMUM ergo dicendum quod contentio, sicut et discordia, habet affinitatem cum invidia quantum ad recessum eius a quo aliquis discordat vel cum quo contendit. Sed quantum ad id in quo sistit ille qui contendit, habet convenientiam cum superbia et inani gloria, inquantum scilicet in proprio sensu statur, ut supra dictum est.

AD SECUNDUM dicendum quod clamor assumitur in contentione de qua loquimur ad finem impugnandae veritatis. Unde non est principale in contentione. Et ideo

OBJECTION 1: It would seem that contention is not a daughter of vainglory. For contention is akin to zeal, wherefore it is written (1 Cor 3:3): *Whereas there is among you zeal and contention, are you not carnal, and walk according to men?* Now zeal pertains to envy. Therefore contention arises rather from envy.

OBJ. 2: Further, contention is accompanied by raising of the voice. But the voice is raised on account of anger, as Gregory declares (*Moral.* xxxi, 14). Therefore contention too arises from anger.

OBJ. 3: Further, among other things knowledge seems to be the matter of pride and vainglory, according to 1 Cor. 8:1: *Knowledge puffeth up*. Now contention is often due to lack of knowledge, and by knowledge we do not impugn the truth, we know it. Therefore contention is not a daughter of vainglory.

ON THE CONTRARY stands the authority of Gregory (*Moral.* xxxi, 14).

I ANSWER THAT, As stated above (Q. 37, A. 2), discord is a daughter of vainglory, because each of the disaccording parties clings to his own opinion, rather than acquiesce with the other. Now it is proper to pride and vainglory to seek one's own glory. And just as people are discordant when they hold to their own opinion in their hearts, so are they contentious when each defends his own opinion by words. Consequently contention is reckoned a daughter of vainglory for the same reason as discord.

REPLY OBJ. 1: Contention, like discord, is akin to envy insofar as a man severs himself from the one with whom he is discordant, or with whom he contends, but insofar as a contentious man holds to something, it is akin to pride and vainglory, because, to wit, he clings to his own opinion, as stated above (Q. 37, A. 2, ad 1).

REPLY OBJ. 2: The contention of which we are speaking puts on a loud voice, for the purpose of impugning the truth, so that it is not the chief part of contention. Hence it

non oportet quod contentio ex eodem derivetur ex quo derivatur clamor.

**AD TERTIUM** dicendum quod superbia et inanis gloria occasionem sumunt praecipue a bonis, etiam sibi contrariis, puta cum de humilitate aliquis superbit, est enim huiusmodi derivatio non per se, sed per accidens, secundum quem modum nihil prohibet contrarium a contrario oriri. Et ideo nihil prohibet ea quae ex superbia vel inani gloria per se et directe oriuntur causari ex contrariis eorum ex quibus occasionaliter superbia oritur.

does not follow that contention arises from the same source as the raising of the voice.

**REPLY OBJ. 3**: Pride and vainglory are occasioned chiefly by goods even those that are contrary to them, for instance, when a man is proud of his humility: for when a thing arises in this way, it does so not directly but accidentally, in which way nothing hinders one contrary from arising out of another. Hence there is no reason why the per se and direct effects of pride or vainglory, should not result from the contraries of those things which are the occasion of pride.

# Question 39

## Schism

Deinde considerandum est de vitiis oppositis paci pertinentibus ad opus; quae sunt schisma, rixa, seditio et bellum. Primo ergo circa schisma quaeruntur quatuor.

Primo, utrum schisma sit speciale peccatum.
Secundo, utrum sit gravius infidelitate.
Tertio, de potestate schismaticorum.
Quarto, de poena eorum.

We must now consider the vices contrary to peace, which belong to deeds: such are schism, strife, sedition, and war. In the first place, then, about schism, there are four points of inquiry:

(1) Whether schism is a special sin?
(2) Whether it is graver than unbelief?
(3) Of the power exercised by schismatics;
(4) Of the punishment inflicted on them.

# Article 1

### Whether schism is a special sin?

**Ad primum sic proceditur.** Videtur quod schisma non sit peccatum speciale. Schisma enim, ut Pelagius Papa dicit, scissuram sonat. Sed omne peccatum scissuram quandam facit, secundum illud Isaiae LIX, *peccata vestra diviserunt inter vos et Deum vestrum.* Ergo schisma non est speciale peccatum.

**Praeterea,** illi videntur esse schismatici qui Ecclesiae non obediunt. Sed per omne peccatum fit homo inobediens praeceptis Ecclesiae, quia peccatum, secundum Ambrosium, est *caelestium inobedientia mandatorum.* Ergo omne peccatum est schisma.

**Praeterea,** haeresis etiam dividit hominem ab unitate fidei. Si ergo schismatis nomen divisionem importat, videtur quod non differat a peccato infidelitatis quasi speciale peccatum.

**Sed contra** est quod Augustinus, contra Faustum, distinguit inter schisma et haeresim, dicens quod *schisma est eadem opinantem atque eodem ritu colentem quo ceteri, solo congregationis delectari dissidio, haeresis vero diversa opinatur ab his quae Catholica credit Ecclesia.* Ergo schisma non est generale peccatum.

**Respondeo** dicendum quod, sicut Isidorus dicit, in libro Etymol., nomen schismatis a *scissura animorum* vocatum est. Scissio autem unitati opponitur. Unde peccatum schismatis dicitur quod directe et per se opponitur unitati, sicut enim in rebus naturalibus id quod est per accidens non constituit speciem, ita etiam nec in rebus moralibus. In quibus id quod est intentum est per se, quod autem sequitur praeter intentionem est quasi per accidens. Et ideo peccatum schismatis proprie est speciale peccatum ex eo quod intendit se ab unitate separare quam caritas facit. Quae non solum alteram

**Objection 1**: It would seem that schism is not a special sin. For *schism*, as Pope Pelagius I says (*Epist. ad Victor. et Pancrat.*), *denotes a division.* But every sin causes a division, according to Isa. 59: *Your sins have divided between you and your God.* Therefore schism is not a special sin.

**Obj. 2**: Further, a man is apparently a schismatic if he disobeys the Church. But every sin makes a man disobey the commandments of the Church, because sin, according to Ambrose (*De Parad.* viii) *is disobedience against the heavenly commandments.* Therefore every sin is a schism.

**Obj. 3**: Further, heresy also divides a man from the unity of faith. If, therefore, the word schism denotes a division, it would seem not to differ, as a special sin, from the sin of unbelief.

**On the contrary**, Augustine (*Contra Faust.* xx, 3; Contra Crescon. ii, 4) distinguishes between schism and heresy, for he says that a *schismatic is one who holds the same faith, and practises the same worship, as others, and takes pleasure in the mere disunion of the community, whereas a heretic is one who holds another faith from that of the Catholic Church.* Therefore schism is not a generic sin.

**I answer that,** As Isidore says (*Etym.* viii, 3), schism takes its name *from being a scission of minds,* and scission is opposed to unity. Wherefore the sin of schism is one that is directly and essentially opposed to unity. For in the moral, as in the physical order, the species is not constituted by that which is accidental. Now, in the moral order, the essential is that which is intended, and that which results beside the intention, is, as it were, accidental. Hence the sin of schism is, properly speaking, a special sin, for the reason that the schismatic intends to sever himself from that unity which is the effect of charity: because charity unites not only one

personam alteri unit spirituali dilectionis vinculo, sed etiam totam Ecclesiam in unitate spiritus.

Et ideo proprie schismatici dicuntur qui propria sponte et intentione se ab unitate Ecclesiae separant, quae est unitas principalis, nam unitas particularis aliquorum ad invicem ordinatur ad unitatem Ecclesiae, sicut compositio singulorum membrorum in corpore naturali ordinatur ad totius corporis unitatem. Ecclesiae autem unitas in duobus attenditur, scilicet in connexione membrorum Ecclesiae ad invicem, seu communicatione; et iterum in ordine omnium membrorum Ecclesiae ad unum caput; secundum illud ad Coloss. II, *inflatus sensu carnis suae, et non tenens caput, ex quo totum corpus, per nexus et coniunctiones subministratum et constructum, crescit in augmentum Dei.* Hoc autem caput est ipse Christus, cuius vicem in Ecclesia gerit summus pontifex. Et ideo schismatici dicuntur qui subesse renuunt summo pontifici, et qui membris Ecclesiae ei subiectis communicare recusant.

Ad primum ergo dicendum quod divisio hominis a Deo per peccatum non est intenta a peccante, sed praeter intentionem eius accidit ex inordinata conversione ipsius ad commutabile bonum. Et ideo non est schisma, per se loquendo.

Ad secundum dicendum quod non obedire praeceptis cum rebellione quadam constituit schismatis rationem. Dico autem cum rebellione, cum et pertinaciter praecepta Ecclesiae contemnit, et iudicium eius subire recusat. Hoc autem non facit quilibet peccator. Unde non omne peccatum est schisma.

Ad tertium dicendum quod haeresis et schisma distinguuntur secundum ea quibus utrumque per se et directe opponitur. Nam haeresis per se opponitur fidei, schisma autem per se opponitur unitati ecclesiasticae caritatis. Et ideo sicut fides et caritas sunt diversae virtutes, quamvis quicumque careat fide careat caritate; ita etiam schisma et haeresis sunt diversa vitia, quamvis quicumque est haereticus sit etiam schismaticus, sed non convertitur. Et hoc est quod Hieronymus dicit, in Epist. ad Gal., *inter schisma et haeresim hoc interesse arbitror, quod haeresis perversum dogma habet, schisma ab Ecclesia separat.* Et tamen sicut amissio caritatis est via ad amittendum fidem, secundum illud I ad Tim. I, *a quibus quidam aberrantes,* scilicet a caritate et aliis huiusmodi, *conversi sunt in vaniloquium*; ita etiam schisma est via ad haeresim. Unde Hieronymus ibidem subdit quod *schisma a principio aliqua in parte potest intelligi diversum ab haeresi, ceterum nullum schisma est, nisi sibi aliquam haeresim confingat, ut recte ab Ecclesia recessisse videatur.*

person to another with the bond of spiritual love, but also the whole Church in unity of spirit.

Accordingly schismatics properly so called are those who, wilfully and intentionally separate themselves from the unity of the Church; for this is the chief unity, and the particular unity of several individuals among themselves is subordinate to the unity of the Church, even as the mutual adaptation of each member of a natural body is subordinate to the unity of the whole body. Now the unity of the Church consists in two things; namely, in the mutual connection or communion of the members of the Church, and again in the subordination of all the members of the Church to the one head, according to Col. 2:18, 19: *Puffed up by the sense of his flesh, and not holding the Head, from which the whole body, by joints and bands, being supplied with nourishment and compacted, groweth unto the increase of God.* Now this Head is Christ Himself, Whose viceregent in the Church is the Sovereign Pontiff. Wherefore schismatics are those who refuse to submit to the Sovereign Pontiff, and to hold communion with those members of the Church who acknowledge his supremacy.

Reply Obj. 1: The division between man and God that results from sin is not intended by the sinner: it happens beside his intention as a result of his turning inordinately to a mutable good, and so it is not schism properly so called.

Reply Obj. 2: The essence of schism consists in rebelliously disobeying the commandments: and I say *rebelliously*, since a schismatic both obstinately scorns the commandments of the Church, and refuses to submit to her judgment. But every sinner does not do this, wherefore not every sin is a schism.

Reply Obj. 3: Heresy and schism are distinguished in respect of those things to which each is opposed essentially and directly. For heresy is essentially opposed to faith, while schism is essentially opposed to the unity of ecclesiastical charity. Wherefore just as faith and charity are different virtues, although whoever lacks faith lacks charity, so too schism and heresy are different vices, although whoever is a heretic is also a schismatic, but not conversely. This is what Jerome says in his commentary on the Epistle to the Galatians: *I consider the difference between schism and heresy to be that heresy holds false doctrine while schism severs a man from the Church.* Nevertheless, just as the loss of charity is the road to the loss of faith, according to 1 Tim. 1:6: *From which things,* i.e., charity and the like, *some going astray, are turned aside into vain babbling,* so too, schism is the road to heresy. Wherefore Jerome adds (In Ep. ad Tit. iii, 10) that *at the outset it is possible, in a certain respect, to find a difference between schism and heresy: yet there is no schism that does not devise some heresy for itself, that it may appear to have had a reason for separating from the Church.*

# Article 2

*Whether schism is a graver sin than unbelief?*

Aᴅ sᴇᴄᴜɴᴅᴜᴍ sɪᴄ ᴘʀᴏᴄᴇᴅɪᴛᴜʀ. Videtur quod schisma gravius peccatum sit quam infidelitas. Maius enim peccatum graviori poena punitur, secundum illud Deut. XXV, *pro mensura peccati erit et plagarum modus*. Sed peccatum schismatis gravius invenitur punitum quam etiam peccatum infidelitatis sive idololatriae. Legitur enim Exod. XXXII quod propter idololatriam sunt aliqui humana manu gladio interfecti, de peccato autem schismatis legitur Num. XVI, *si novam rem fecerit dominus, ut aperiens terra os suum deglutiat eos et omnia quae ad illos pertinent, descenderintque viventes in Infernum, scietis quod blasphemaverunt dominum*. Decem etiam tribus, quae vitio schismatis a regno David recesserunt, sunt gravissime punitae, ut habetur IV Reg. XVII. Ergo peccatum schismatis est gravius peccato infidelitatis.

Pʀᴀᴇᴛᴇʀᴇᴀ, *bonum multitudinis est maius et divinius quam bonum unius*; ut patet per philosophum, in I Ethic. Sed schisma est contra bonum multitudinis, idest contra ecclesiasticam unitatem, infidelitas autem est contra bonum particulare unius, quod est fides unius hominis singularis. Ergo videtur quod schisma sit gravius peccatum quam infidelitas.

Pʀᴀᴇᴛᴇʀᴇᴀ, maiori malo maius bonum opponitur; ut patet per philosophum, in VIII Ethic. Sed schisma opponitur caritati, quae est maior virtus quam fides, cui opponitur infidelitas, ut ex praemissis patet. Ergo schisma est gravius peccatum quam infidelitas.

Sᴇᴅ ᴄᴏɴᴛʀᴀ, quod se habet ex additione ad alterum potius est vel in bono vel in malo. Sed haeresis se habet per additionem ad schisma, addit enim perversum dogma, ut patet ex auctoritate Hieronymi supra inducta. Ergo schisma est minus peccatum quam infidelitas.

Rᴇsᴘᴏɴᴅᴇᴏ dicendum quod gravitas peccati dupliciter potest considerari, uno modo, secundum suam speciem; alio modo, secundum circumstantias. Et quia circumstantiae particulares sunt et infinitis modis variari possunt, cum quaeritur in communi de duobus peccatis quod sit gravius, intelligenda est quaestio de gravitate quae attenditur secundum genus peccati. Genus autem seu species peccati attenditur ex obiecto; sicut ex supradictis patet. Et ideo illud peccatum quod maiori bono contrariatur est ex suo genere gravius, sicut peccatum in Deum quam peccatum in proximum.

Manifestum est autem quod infidelitas est peccatum contra ipsum Deum, secundum quod in se est veritas prima, cui fides innititur. Schisma autem est con-

Oʙᴊᴇᴄᴛɪᴏɴ 1: It would seem that schism is a graver sin than unbelief. For the graver sin meets with a graver punishment, according to Deut. 25:2: *According to the measure of the sin shall the measure also of the stripes be*. Now we find the sin of schism punished more severely than even the sin of unbelief or idolatry: for we read (Exod 32:28) that some were slain by the swords of their fellow men on account of idolatry: whereas of the sin of schism we read (Num 16:30): *If the Lord do a new thing, and the earth opening her mouth swallow them down, and all things that belong to them, and they go down alive into hell, you shall know that they have blasphemed the Lord God*. Moreover the ten tribes who were guilty of schism in revolting from the rule of David were most severely punished (4 Kgs 17). Therefore the sin of schism is graver than the sin of unbelief.

Oʙᴊ. 2: Further, *The good of the multitude is greater and more godlike than the good of the individual*, as the Philosopher states (*Ethic.* i, 2). Now schism is opposed to the good of the multitude, namely, ecclesiastical unity, whereas unbelief is contrary to the particular good of one man, namely, the faith of an individual. Therefore it seems that schism is a graver sin than unbelief.

Oʙᴊ. 3: Further, a greater good is opposed to a greater evil, according to the Philosopher (*Ethic.* viii, 10). Now schism is opposed to charity, which is a greater virtue than faith to which unbelief is opposed, as shown above (Q. 10, A. 2; Q. 23, A. 6). Therefore schism is a graver sin than unbelief.

Oɴ ᴛʜᴇ ᴄᴏɴᴛʀᴀʀʏ, That which results from an addition to something else surpasses that thing either in good or in evil. Now heresy results from something being added to schism, for it adds corrupt doctrine, as Jerome declares in the passage quoted above (A. 1, ad 3). Therefore schism is a less grievous sin than unbelief.

I ᴀɴsᴡᴇʀ ᴛʜᴀᴛ, The gravity of a sin can be considered in two ways: first, according to the species of that sin, second, according to its circumstances. And since particular circumstances are infinite in number, so too they can be varied in an infinite number of ways: wherefore if one were to ask in general which of two sins is the graver, the question must be understood to refer to the gravity derived from the sin's genus. Now the genus or species of a sin is taken from its object, as shown above (I-II, Q. 72, A. 1; I-II, Q. 73, A. 3). Wherefore the sin which is opposed to the greater good is, in respect of its genus, more grievous, for instance a sin committed against God is graver than a sin committed against one's neighbor.

Now it is evident that unbelief is a sin committed against God Himself, according as He is Himself the First Truth, on which faith is founded; whereas schism is opposed to ec-

tra ecclesiasticam unitatem, quae est quoddam bonum participatum, et minus quam sit ipse Deus. Unde manifestum est quod peccatum infidelitatis ex suo genere est gravius quam peccatum schismatis, licet possit contingere quod aliquis schismaticus gravius peccet quam quidam infidelis, vel propter maiorem contemptum, vel propter maius periculum quod inducit, vel propter aliquid huiusmodi.

**AD PRIMUM** ergo dicendum quod populo illi manifestum erat iam per legem susceptam quod erat unus Deus et quod non erant alii dii colendi, et hoc erat apud eos per multiplicia signa confirmatum. Et ideo non oportebat quod peccantes contra hanc fidem per idololatriam punirentur inusitata aliqua et insolita poena, sed solum communi. Sed non erat sic notum apud eos quod Moyses deberet esse semper eorum princeps. Et ideo rebellantes eius principatui oportebat miraculosa et insueta poena puniri.

Vel potest dici quod peccatum schismatis quandoque gravius est punitum in populo illo quia erat ad seditiones et schismata promptus, dicitur enim I Esdr. IV, *civitas illa a diebus antiquis adversus regem rebellat, et seditiones et praelia concitantur in ea.* Poena autem maior quandoque infligitur pro peccato magis consueto, ut supra habitum est, nam poenae sunt medicinae quaedam ad arcendum homines a peccato; unde ubi est maior pronitas ad peccandum, debet severior poena adhiberi. Decem autem tribus non solum fuerunt punitae pro peccato schismatis, sed etiam pro peccato idololatriae, ut ibidem dicitur.

**AD SECUNDUM** dicendum quod sicut bonum multitudinis est maius quam bonum unius qui est de multitudine, ita est minus quam bonum extrinsecum ad quod multitudo ordinatur, sicut bonum ordinis exercitus est minus quam bonum ducis. Et similiter bonum ecclesiasticae unitatis, cui opponitur schisma, est minus quam bonum veritatis divinae, cui opponitur infidelitas.

**AD TERTIUM** dicendum quod caritas habet duo obiecta, unum principale, scilicet bonitatem divinam; et aliud secundarium, scilicet bonum proximi. Schisma autem et alia peccata quae fiunt in proximum opponuntur caritati quantum ad secundarium bonum, quod est minus quam obiectum fidei, quod est ipse Deus. Et ideo ista peccata sunt minora quam infidelitas. Sed odium Dei, quod opponitur caritati quantum ad principale obiectum, non est minus. Tamen inter peccata quae sunt in proximum, peccatum schismatis videtur esse maximum, quia est contra spirituale bonum multitudinis.

clesiastical unity, which is a participated good, and a lesser good than God Himself. Wherefore it is manifest that the sin of unbelief is generically more grievous than the sin of schism, although it may happen that a particular schismatic sins more grievously than a particular unbeliever, either because his contempt is greater, or because his sin is a source of greater danger, or for some similar reason.

**REPLY OBJ. 1:** It had already been declared to that people by the law which they had received that there was one God, and that no other God was to be worshipped by them; and the same had been confirmed among them by many kinds of signs. Consequently there was no need for those who sinned against this faith by falling into idolatry, to be punished in an unwonted manner: it was enough that they should be punished in the usual way. On the other hand, it was not so well known among them that Moses was always to be their ruler, and so it behooved those who rebelled against his authority to be punished in a miraculous and unwonted manner.

We may also reply by saying that the sin of schism was sometimes more severely punished in that people, because they were inclined to seditions and schisms. For it is written (1 Esdra 4:15): *This city since days gone by has rebelled against its kings: and seditions and wars were raised therein.* Now sometimes a more severe punishment is inflicted for an habitual sin (as stated above, I-II, Q. 105, A. 2, ad 9), because punishments are medicines intended to keep man away from sin: so that where there is greater proneness to sin, a more severe punishment ought to be inflicted. As regards the ten tribes, they were punished not only for the sin of schism, but also for that of idolatry as stated in the passage quoted.

**REPLY OBJ. 2:** Just as the good of the multitude is greater than the good of a unit in that multitude, so is it less than the extrinsic good to which that multitude is directed, even as the good of a rank in the army is less than the good of the commander-in-chief. In like manner the good of ecclesiastical unity, to which schism is opposed, is less than the good of Divine truth, to which unbelief is opposed.

**REPLY OBJ. 3:** Charity has two objects; one is its principal object and is the Divine goodness, the other is its secondary object and is our neighbor's good. Now schism and other sins against our neighbor, are opposed to charity in respect of its secondary good, which is less than the object of faith, for this is God Himself; and so these sins are less grievous than unbelief. On the other hand, hatred of God, which is opposed to charity in respect of its principal object, is not less grievous than unbelief. Nevertheless of all sins committed by man against his neighbor, the sin of schism would seem to be the greatest, because it is opposed to the spiritual good of the multitude.

# Article 3

*Whether schismatics have any power?*

**Ad tertium sic proceditur.** Videtur quod schismatici habeant aliquam potestatem. Dicit enim Augustinus, in libro contra Donatist., *sicut redeuntes ad Ecclesiam qui priusquam recederent baptizati sunt non rebaptizantur, ita redeuntes qui priusquam recederent ordinati sunt non utique rursus ordinantur.* Sed ordo est potestas quaedam. Ergo schismatici habent aliquam potestatem, quia retinent ordinem.

**Praeterea,** Augustinus dicit, in libro de Unic. Bapt., *potest sacramentum tradere separatus, sicut potest habere separatus.* Sed potestas tradendi sacramenta est maxima potestas. Ergo schismatici, qui sunt ab Ecclesia separati, habent potestatem spiritualem.

**Praeterea,** Urbanus Papa dicit quod *ab episcopis quondam Catholice ordinatis sed in schismate a Romana Ecclesia separatis qui consecrati sunt, eos, cum ad Ecclesiae unitatem redierint, servatis propriis ordinibus, misericorditer suscipi iubemus, si eos vita et scientia commendat.* Sed hoc non esset nisi spiritualis potestas apud schismaticos remaneret. Ergo schismatici habent spiritualem potestatem.

**Sed contra** est quod Cyprianus dicit in quadam epistola, et habetur VII, qu. I, Can. Novatianus: *qui nec unitatem,* inquit, *spiritus nec conventionis pacem observat, et se ab Ecclesiae vinculo atque a sacerdotum collegio separat, nec episcopi potestatem habere potest nec honorem.*

**Respondeo** dicendum quod duplex est spiritualis potestas, una quidem sacramentalis; alia iurisdictionalis. Sacramentalis quidem potestas est quae per aliquam consecrationem confertur. Omnes autem consecrationes Ecclesiae sunt immobiles, manente re quae consecratur, sicut patet etiam in rebus inanimatis, nam altare semel consecratum non consecratur iterum nisi fuerit dissipatum. Et ideo talis potestas secundum suam essentiam remanet in homine qui per consecrationem eam est adeptus quandiu vivit, sive in schisma sive in haeresim labatur, quod patet ex hoc quod rediens ad Ecclesiam non iterum consecratur. Sed quia potestas inferior non debet exire in actum nisi secundum quod movetur a potestate superiori, ut etiam in rebus naturalibus patet; inde est quod tales usum potestatis amittunt, ita scilicet quod non liceat eis sua potestate uti. Si tamen usi fuerint, eorum potestas effectum habet in sacramentalibus, quia in his homo non operatur nisi sicut instrumentum Dei; unde effectus sacramentales non excluduntur propter culpam quamcumque conferentis sacramentum.

Potestas autem iurisdictionalis est quae ex simplici iniunctione hominis confertur. Et talis potestas non

**Objection 1**: It would seem that schismatics have some power. For Augustine says (*Contra Donat.* i, 1): *Just as those who come back to the Church after being baptized, are not baptized again, so those who return after being ordained, are not ordained again.* Now Order is a kind of power. Therefore schismatics have some power since they retain their Orders.

**Obj. 2**: Further, Augustine says (*De Unico Bapt.*): *One who is separated can confer a sacrament even as he can have it.* But the power of conferring a sacrament is a very great power. Therefore schismatics who are separated from the Church, have a spiritual power.

**Obj. 3**: Further, Pope Urban II says: *We command that persons consecrated by bishops who were themselves consecrated according to the Catholic rite, but have separated themselves by schism from the Roman Church, should be received mercifully and that their Orders should be acknowledged, when they return to the unity of the Church, provided they be of commendable life and knowledge.* But this would not be so, unless spiritual power were retained by schismatics. Therefore schismatics have spiritual power.

**On the contrary**, Cyprian says in a letter (*Ep. lii*, quoted vii, qu. 1, can. *Novatianus*): *He who observes neither unity of spirit nor the concord of peace, and severs himself from the bonds of the Church, and from the fellowship of her priests, cannot have episcopal power or honor.*

**I answer that**, Spiritual power is twofold, the one sacramental, the other a power of jurisdiction. The sacramental power is one that is conferred by some kind of consecration. Now all the consecrations of the Church are immovable so long as the consecrated thing remains: as appears even in inanimate things, since an altar, once consecrated, is not consecrated again unless it has been broken up. Consequently such a power as this remains, as to its essence, in the man who has received it by consecration, as long as he lives, even if he fall into schism or heresy: and this is proved from the fact that if he come back to the Church, he is not consecrated anew. Since, however, the lower power ought not to exercise its act, except insofar as it is moved by the higher power, as may be seen also in the physical order, it follows that such persons lose the use of their power, so that it is not lawful for them to use it. Yet if they use it, this power has its effect in sacramental acts, because therein man acts only as God's instrument, so that sacramental effects are not precluded on account of any fault whatever in the person who confers the sacrament.

On the other hand, the power of jurisdiction is that which is conferred by a mere human appointment. Such a

immobiliter adhaeret. Unde in schismaticis et haereticis non manet. Unde non possunt nec absolvere nec excommunicare nec indulgentias facere, aut aliquid huiusmodi, quod si fecerint, nihil est actum.

Cum ergo dicitur tales non habere potestatem spiritualem, intelligendum est vel de potestate secunda, vel, si referatur ad primam potestatem, non est referendum ad ipsam essentiam potestatis, sed ad legitimum usum eius.

**ET PER HOC** patet responsio ad obiecta.

power as this does not adhere to the recipient immovably: so that it does not remain in heretics and schismatics; and consequently they neither absolve nor excommunicate, nor grant indulgence, nor do anything of the kind, and if they do, it is invalid.

Accordingly when it is said that such like persons have no spiritual power, it is to be understood as referring either to the second power, or if it be referred to the first power, not as referring to the essence of the power, but to its lawful use.

**THIS SUFFICES** for the Replies to the Objections.

# Article 4

*Whether schismatics are rightly punished with excommunication?*

**AD QUARTUM SIC PROCEDITUR.** Videtur quod poena schismaticorum non sit conveniens ut excommunicentur. Excommunicatio enim maxime separat hominem a communione sacramentorum. Sed Augustinus dicit, in libro contra Donatist., quod Baptisma potest recipi a schismatico. Ergo videtur quod excommunicatio non est conveniens poena schismatis.

**PRAETEREA,** ad fideles Christi pertinet ut eos qui sunt dispersi reducant, unde contra quosdam dicitur Ezech. XXXIV, *quod abiectum est non reduxistis, quod perierat non quaesistis.* Sed schismatici convenientius reducuntur per aliquos qui eis communicent. Ergo videtur quod non sint excommunicandi.

**PRAETEREA,** pro eodem peccato non infligitur duplex poena, secundum illud Nahum I, *non iudicabit Deus bis in idipsum.* Sed pro peccato schismatis aliqui poena temporali puniuntur, ut habetur XXIII, qu. V, ubi dicitur, *divinae et mundanae leges statuerunt ut ab Ecclesiae unitate divisi, et eius pacem perturbantes, a saecularibus potestatibus comprimantur.* Non ergo sunt puniendi per excommunicationem.

**SED CONTRA** est quod Num. XVI dicitur, *recedite a tabernaculis hominum impiorum,* qui scilicet schisma fecerant, *et nolite tangere quae ad eos pertinent, ne involvamini in peccatis eorum.*

**RESPONDEO** dicendum quod per quae peccat quis, per ea debet puniri, ut dicitur Sap. XI. Schismaticus autem, ut ex dictis patet, in duobus peccat. In uno quidem, quia separat se a communione membrorum Ecclesiae. Et quantum ad hoc conveniens poena schismaticorum est ut excommunicentur. In alio vero, quia subdi recusant capiti Ecclesiae. Et ideo, quia coerceri nolunt per

**OBJECTION 1:** It would seem that schismatics are not rightly punished with excommunication. For excommunication deprives a man chiefly of a share in the sacraments. But Augustine says (*Contra Donat.* vi, 5) that Baptism can be received from a schismatic. Therefore it seems that excommunication is not a fitting punishment for schismatics.

**OBJ. 2:** Further, it is the duty of Christ's faithful to lead back those who have gone astray, wherefore it is written against certain persons (Ezek 34:4): *That which was driven away you have not brought again, neither have you sought that which was lost.* Now schismatics are more easily brought back by such as may hold communion with them. Therefore it seems that they ought not to be excommunicated.

**OBJ. 3:** Further, a double punishment is not inflicted for one and the same sin, according to Nahum 1:9: *God will not judge the same twice.* Now some receive a temporal punishment for the sin of schism, according to 23, qu. 5, where it is stated: *Both divine and earthly laws have laid down that those who are severed from the unity of the Church, and disturb her peace, must be punished by the secular power.* Therefore they ought not to be punished with excommunication.

**ON THE CONTRARY,** It is written (Num 16:26): *Depart from the tents of these wicked men,* those, to wit, who had caused the schism, *and touch nothing of theirs, lest you be involved in their sins.*

**I ANSWER THAT,** According to Wis. 11:11, *By what things a man sinneth, by the same also he should be punished.* Now a schismatic, as shown above (A. 1), commits a twofold sin: first by separating himself from communion with the members of the Church, and in this respect the fitting punishment for schismatics is that they be excommunicated. Second, they refuse submission to the head

spiritualem potestatem Ecclesiae, iustum est ut potestate temporali coerceantur.

**AD PRIMUM** ergo dicendum quod Baptismum a schismaticis recipere non licet nisi in articulo necessitatis, quia melius est de hac vita cum signo Christi exire, a quocumque detur, etiam si sit Iudaeus vel Paganus, quam sine hoc signo, quod per Baptismum confertur.

**AD SECUNDUM** dicendum quod per excommunicationem non interdicitur illa communicatio per quam aliquis salubribus monitis divisos reducit ad Ecclesiae unitatem. Tamen et ipsa separatio quodammodo eos reducit, dum, de sua separatione confusi, quandoque ad poenitentiam adducuntur.

**AD TERTIUM** dicendum quod poenae praesentis vitae sunt medicinales; et ideo quando una poena non sufficit ad coercendum hominem, superadditur altera, sicut et medici diversas medicinas corporales apponunt quando una non est efficax et ita Ecclesia, quando aliqui per excommunicationem non sufficienter reprimuntur, adhibet coercionem brachii saecularis. Sed si una poena sit sufficiens, non debet alia adhiberi.

of the Church, wherefore, since they are unwilling to be controlled by the Church's spiritual power, it is just that they should be compelled by the secular power.

**REPLY OBJ. 1**: It is not lawful to receive Baptism from a schismatic, save in a case of necessity, since it is better for a man to quit this life, marked with the sign of Christ, no matter from whom he may receive it, whether from a Jew or a pagan, than deprived of that mark, which is bestowed in Baptism.

**REPLY OBJ. 2**: Excommunication does not forbid the intercourse whereby a person by salutary admonitions leads back to the unity of the Church those who are separated from her. Indeed this very separation brings them back somewhat, because through confusion at their separation, they are sometimes led to do penance.

**REPLY OBJ. 3**: The punishments of the present life are medicinal, and therefore when one punishment does not suffice to compel a man, another is added: just as physicians employ several body medicines when one has no effect. In like manner the Church, when excommunication does not sufficiently restrain certain men, employs the compulsion of the secular arm. If, however, one punishment suffices, another should not be employed.

# QUESTION 40

## WAR

Deinde considerandum est de bello. Et circa hoc quaeruntur quatuor.

Primo, utrum aliquod bellum sit licitum.

Secundo, utrum clericis sit licitum bellare.

Tertio, utrum liceat bellantibus uti insidiis.

Quarto, utrum liceat in diebus festis bellare.

We must now consider war, under which head there are four points of inquiry:

(1) Whether some kind of war is lawful?

(2) Whether it is lawful for clerics to fight?

(3) Whether it is lawful for belligerents to lay ambushes?

(4) Whether it is lawful to fight on holy days?

## Article 1

*Whether it is always sinful to wage war?*

**AD PRIMUM SIC PROCEDITUR.** Videtur quod bellare semper sit peccatum. Poena enim non infligitur nisi pro peccato. Sed bellantibus a domino indicitur poena, secundum illud Matth. XXVI, *omnis qui acceperit gladium gladio peribit.* Ergo omne bellum est illicitum.

**PRAETEREA,** quidquid contrariatur divino praecepto est peccatum. Sed bellare contrariatur divino praecepto, dicitur enim Matth. V, *ego dico vobis non resistere malo*; et Rom. XII dicitur, *non vos defendentes, carissimi, sed date locum irae.* Ergo bellare semper est peccatum.

**PRAETEREA,** nihil contrariatur actui virtutis nisi peccatum. Sed bellum contrariatur paci. Ergo bellum semper est peccatum.

**PRAETEREA,** omne exercitium ad rem licitam licitum est, sicut patet in exercitiis scientiarum. Sed exercitia bellorum, quae fiunt in torneamentis, prohibentur ab Ecclesia, quia morientes in huiusmodi tyrociniis ecclesiastica sepultura privantur. Ergo bellum videtur esse simpliciter peccatum.

**SED CONTRA** est quod Augustinus dicit, in sermone de puero centurionis, *si Christiana disciplina omnino bella culparet, hoc potius consilium salutis petentibus in Evangelio daretur, ut abiicerent arma, seque militiae omnino subtraherent. Dictum est autem eis, neminem concutiatis; estote contenti stipendiis vestris. Quibus proprium stipendium sufficere praecepit, militare non prohibuit.*

**RESPONDEO** dicendum quod ad hoc quod aliquod bellum sit iustum, tria requiruntur. Primo quidem, auctoritas principis, cuius mandato bellum est gerendum. Non enim pertinet ad personam privatam bellum movere, quia potest ius suum in iudicio superioris prosequi.

**OBJECTION 1**: It would seem that it is always sinful to wage war. Because punishment is not inflicted except for sin. Now those who wage war are threatened by Our Lord with punishment, according to Matt. 26:52: *All that take the sword shall perish with the sword.* Therefore all wars are unlawful.

**OBJ. 2**: Further, whatever is contrary to a Divine precept is a sin. But war is contrary to a Divine precept, for it is written (Matt 5:39): *But I say to you not to resist evil*; and (Rom 12:19): *Not revenging yourselves, my dearly beloved, but give place unto wrath.* Therefore war is always sinful.

**OBJ. 3**: Further, nothing, except sin, is contrary to an act of virtue. But war is contrary to peace. Therefore war is always a sin.

**OBJ. 4**: Further, the exercise of a lawful thing is itself lawful, as is evident in scientific exercises. But warlike exercises which take place in tournaments are forbidden by the Church, since those who are slain in these trials are deprived of ecclesiastical burial. Therefore it seems that war is a sin in itself.

**ON THE CONTRARY**, Augustine says in a sermon on the son of the centurion: *If the Christian Religion forbade war altogether, those who sought salutary advice in the Gospel would rather have been counselled to cast aside their arms, and to give up soldiering altogether. On the contrary, they were told: 'Do violence to no man . . . and be content with your pay.' If he commanded them to be content with their pay, he did not forbid soldiering.*

**I ANSWER THAT,** In order for a war to be just, three things are necessary. First, the authority of the sovereign by whose command the war is to be waged. For it is not the business of a private individual to declare war, because he can seek for redress of his rights from the tribunal of

387

Similiter etiam quia convocare multitudinem, quod in bellis oportet fieri, non pertinet ad privatam personam. Cum autem cura reipublicae commissa sit principibus, ad eos pertinet rem publicam civitatis vel regni seu provinciae sibi subditae tueri.

Et sicut licite defendunt eam materiali gladio contra interiores quidem perturbatores, dum malefactores puniunt, secundum illud apostoli, ad Rom. XIII, *non sine causa gladium portat, minister enim Dei est, vindex in iram ei qui male agit*; ita etiam gladio bellico ad eos pertinet rempublicam tueri ab exterioribus hostibus.

Unde et principibus dicitur in Psalm., *eripite pauperem, et egenum de manu peccatoris liberate*. Unde Augustinus dicit, contra Faust., *ordo naturalis, mortalium paci accommodatus, hoc poscit, ut suscipiendi belli auctoritas atque consilium penes principes sit*.

Secundo, requiritur causa iusta, ut scilicet illi qui impugnantur propter aliquam culpam impugnationem mereantur. Unde Augustinus dicit, in libro quaest., *iusta bella solent definiri quae ulciscuntur iniurias, si gens vel civitas plectenda est quae vel vindicare neglexerit quod a suis improbe factum est, vel reddere quod per iniuriam ablatum est*.

Tertio, requiritur ut sit intentio bellantium recta, qua scilicet intenditur vel ut bonum promoveatur, vel ut malum vitetur. Unde Augustinus, in libro de verbis Dom., *apud veros Dei cultores etiam illa bella pacata sunt quae non cupiditate aut crudelitate, sed pacis studio geruntur, ut mali coerceantur et boni subleventur*. Potest autem contingere quod etiam si sit legitima auctoritas indicentis bellum et causa iusta, nihilominus propter pravam intentionem bellum reddatur illicitum. Dicit enim Augustinus, in libro contra Faust., *nocendi cupiditas, ulciscendi crudelitas, implacatus et implacabilis animus, feritas rebellandi, libido dominandi, et si qua sunt similia, haec sunt quae in bellis iure culpantur*.

**AD PRIMUM** ergo dicendum quod, sicut Augustinus dicit, in II Lib. contra Manich., *ille accipit gladium qui, nulla superiori aut legitima potestate aut iubente vel concedente, in sanguinem alicuius armatur*. Qui vero ex auctoritate principis vel iudicis, si sit persona privata; vel ex zelo iustitiae, quasi ex auctoritate Dei, si sit persona publica, gladio utitur, non ipse accipit gladium, sed ab alio sibi commisso utitur. Unde ei poena non debetur. Nec tamen illi etiam qui cum peccato gladio utuntur semper gladio occiduntur. Sed ipso suo gladio semper

his superior. Moreover it is not the business of a private individual to summon together the people, which has to be done in wartime. And as the care of the common weal is committed to those who are in authority, it is their business to watch over the common weal of the city, kingdom or province subject to them.

And just as it is lawful for them to have recourse to the sword in defending that common weal against internal disturbances, when they punish evil-doers, according to the words of the Apostle (Rom 13:4): *He beareth not the sword in vain: for he is God's minister, an avenger to execute wrath upon him that doth evil*; so too, it is their business to have recourse to the sword of war in defending the common weal against external enemies.

Hence it is said to those who are in authority (Ps 81:4): *Rescue the poor: and deliver the needy out of the hand of the sinner*; and for this reason Augustine says (*Contra Faust.* xxii, 75): *The natural order conducive to peace among mortals demands that the power to declare and counsel war should be in the hands of those who hold the supreme authority.*

Second, a just cause is required, namely that those who are attacked, should be attacked because they deserve it on account of some fault. Wherefore Augustine says (*QQ. in Hept.*, qu. x, *super Jos.*): *A just war is wont to be described as one that avenges wrongs, when a nation or state has to be punished, for refusing to make amends for the wrongs inflicted by its subjects, or to restore what it has seized unjustly.*

Third, it is necessary that the belligerents should have a rightful intention, so that they intend the advancement of good, or the avoidance of evil. Hence Augustine says (*De Verb. Dom.*): *True religion looks upon as peaceful those wars that are waged not for motives of aggrandizement, or cruelty, but with the object of securing peace, of punishing evil-doers, and of uplifting the good*. For it may happen that the war is declared by the legitimate authority, and for a just cause, and yet be rendered unlawful through a wicked intention. Hence Augustine says (*Contra Faust.* xxii, 74): *The passion for inflicting harm, the cruel thirst for vengeance, an unpacific and relentless spirit, the fever of revolt, the lust of power, and such like things, all these are rightly condemned in war.*

**REPLY OBJ. 1**: As Augustine says (*Contra Faust.* xxii, 70): *To take the sword is to arm oneself in order to take the life of anyone, without the command or permission of superior or lawful authority*. On the other hand, to have recourse to the sword (as a private person) by the authority of the sovereign or judge, or (as a public person) through zeal for justice, and by the authority, so to speak, of God, is not to *take the sword*, but to use it as commissioned by another, wherefore it does not deserve punishment. And yet even those who make sinful use of the sword are not always slain with

pereunt, quia pro peccato gladii aeternaliter puniuntur, nisi poeniteant.

**AD SECUNDUM** dicendum quod huiusmodi praecepta, sicut Augustinus dicit, in libro de Serm. Dom. in monte, semper sunt servanda in praeparatione animi, ut scilicet semper homo sit paratus non resistere vel non se defendere si opus fuerit. Sed quandoque est aliter agendum propter commune bonum, et etiam illorum cum quibus pugnatur. Unde Augustinus dicit, in Epist. ad Marcellinum, *agenda sunt multa etiam cum invitis benigna quadam asperitate plectendis. Nam cui licentia iniquitatis eripitur, utiliter vincitur, quoniam nihil est infelicius felicitate peccantium, qua poenalis nutritur impunitas, et mala voluntas, velut hostis interior, roboratur.*

**AD TERTIUM** dicendum quod etiam illi qui iusta bella gerunt pacem intendunt. Et ita paci non contrariantur nisi malae, quam dominus *non venit mittere in terram,* ut dicitur Matth. X. Unde Augustinus dicit, ad Bonifacium, *non quaeritur pax ut bellum exerceatur, sed bellum geritur ut pax acquiratur. Esto ergo bellando pacificus, ut eos quos expugnas ad pacis utilitatem vincendo perducas.*

**AD QUARTUM** dicendum quod exercitia hominum ad res bellicas non sunt universaliter prohibita, sed inordinata exercitia et periculosa, ex quibus occisiones et depraedationes proveniunt. Apud antiquos autem exercitationes ad bella sine huiusmodi periculis erant, et ideo vocabantur *meditationes armorum,* vel *bella sine sanguine,* ut per Hieronymum patet, in quadam epistola.

the sword, yet they always perish with their own sword, because, unless they repent, they are punished eternally for their sinful use of the sword.

**REPLY OBJ. 2:** Such like precepts, as Augustine observes (*De Serm. Dom. in Monte* i, 19), should always be borne in readiness of mind, so that we be ready to obey them, and, if necessary, to refrain from resistance or self-defense. Nevertheless it is necessary sometimes for a man to act otherwise for the common good, or for the good of those with whom he is fighting. Hence Augustine says (*Ep. ad Marcellin. cxxxviii*): *Those whom we have to punish with a kindly severity, it is necessary to handle in many ways against their will. For when we are stripping a man of the lawlessness of sin, it is good for him to be vanquished, since nothing is more hopeless than the happiness of sinners, whence arises a guilty impunity, and an evil will, like an internal enemy.*

**REPLY OBJ. 3:** Those who wage war justly aim at peace, and so they are not opposed to peace, except to the evil peace, which Our Lord *came not to send upon earth* (Matt 10:34). Hence Augustine says (*Ep. ad Bonif. clxxxix*): *We do not seek peace in order to be at war, but we go to war that we may have peace. Be peaceful, therefore, in warring, so that you may vanquish those whom you war against, and bring them to the prosperity of peace.*

**REPLY OBJ. 4:** Manly exercises in warlike feats of arms are not all forbidden, but those which are inordinate and perilous, and end in slaying or plundering. In olden times warlike exercises presented no such danger, and hence they were called *exercises of arms* or *bloodless wars,* as Jerome states in an epistle.

# Article 2

*Whether it is lawful for clerics and bishops to fight?*

**AD SECUNDUM SIC PROCEDITUR.** Videtur quod clericis et episcopis liceat pugnare. Bella enim intantum sunt licita et iusta, sicut dictum est, inquantum tuentur pauperes et totam rempublicam ab hostium iniuriis. Sed hoc maxime videtur ad praelatos pertinere, dicit enim Gregorius, in quadam homilia, *lupus super oves venit, cum quilibet iniustus et raptor fideles quosque atque humiles opprimit. Sed is qui pastor videbatur esse et non erat, relinquit oves et fugit, quia dum sibi ab eo periculum metuit, resistere eius iniustitiae non praesumit.* Ergo praelatis et clericis licitum est pugnare.

**PRAETEREA,** XXIII, qu. VIII, Leo Papa scribit, *cum saepe adversa a Saracenorum partibus pervenerint nuntia, quidam in Romanorum portum Saracenos clam*

**OBJECTION 1:** It would seem lawful for clerics and bishops to fight. For, as stated above (A. 1), wars are lawful and just insofar as they protect the poor and the entire common weal from suffering at the hands of the foe. Now this seems to be above all the duty of prelates, for Gregory says (*Hom. in Ev. xiv*): *The wolf comes upon the sheep, when any unjust and rapacious man oppresses those who are faithful and humble. But he who was thought to be the shepherd, and was not, leaveth the sheep, and flieth, for he fears lest the wolf hurt him, and dares not stand up against his injustice.* Therefore it is lawful for prelates and clerics to fight.

**OBJ. 2:** Further, Pope Leo IV writes (xxiii, qu. 8, can. Igitur): *As untoward tidings had frequently come from the Saracen side, some said that the Saracens would come to*

*furtivique venturos esse dicebant. Pro quo nostrum congregari praecepimus populum, maritimumque ad littus descendere decrevimus.* Ergo episcopis licet ad bella procedere.

PRAETEREA, eiusdem rationis esse videtur quod homo aliquid faciat, et quod facienti consentiat, secundum illud Rom. I, *non solum digni sunt morte qui faciunt, sed et qui consentiunt facientibus.* Maxime autem consentit qui ad aliquid faciendum alios inducit. Licitum autem est episcopis et clericis inducere alios ad bellandum, dicitur enim XXIII, qu. VIII, quod *hortatu et precibus Adriani Romanae urbis episcopi, Carolus bellum contra Longobardos suscepit.* Ergo etiam eis licet pugnare.

PRAETEREA, illud quod est secundum se honestum et meritorium non est illicitum praelatis et clericis. Sed bellare est quandoque et honestum et meritorium, dicitur enim XXIII, qu. VIII, quod *si aliquis pro veritate fidei et salvatione patriae ac defensione Christianorum mortuus fuerit, a Deo caeleste praemium consequetur.* Ergo licitum est episcopis et clericis bellare.

SED CONTRA est quod Petro, in persona episcoporum et clericorum, dicitur Matth. XXVI, *converte gladium tuum in vaginam.* Non ergo licet eis pugnare.

RESPONDEO dicendum quod ad bonum societatis humanae plura sunt necessaria. Diversa autem a diversis melius et expeditius aguntur quam ab uno; ut patet per philosophum, in sua politica. Et quaedam negotia sunt adeo sibi repugnantia ut convenienter simul exerceri non possint. Et ideo illis qui maioribus deputantur prohibentur minora, sicut secundum leges humanas militibus, qui deputantur ad exercitia bellica, negotiationes interdicuntur.

Bellica autem exercitia maxime repugnant illis officiis quibus episcopi et clerici deputantur, propter duo. Primo quidem, generali ratione, quia bellica exercitia maximas inquietudines habent; unde multum impediunt animum a contemplatione divinorum et laude Dei et oratione pro populo, quae ad officium pertinent clericorum. Et ideo sicut negotiationes, propter hoc quod nimis implicant animum, interdicuntur clericis, ita et bellica exercitia, secundum illud II ad Tim. II, *nemo militans Deo implicat se saecularibus negotiis.* Secundo, propter specialem rationem. Nam omnes clericorum ordines ordinantur ad altaris ministerium, in quo sub sacramento repraesentatur passio Christi, secundum illud I ad Cor. XI, *quotiescumque manducabitis panem hunc et calicem bibetis, mortem domini annuntiabitis, donec veniat.* Et ideo non competit eis occidere vel effundere sanguinem, sed magis esse paratos ad propriam sanguinis effusionem pro Christo, ut imitentur opere quod gerunt ministerio. Et propter hoc est institutum ut

the port of Rome secretly and covertly; for which reason we commanded our people to gather together, and ordered them to go down to the seashore. Therefore it is lawful for bishops to fight.

OBJ. 3: Further, apparently, it comes to the same whether a man does a thing himself, or consents to its being done by another, according to Rom. 1:32: *They who do such things, are worthy of death, and not only they that do them, but they also that consent to them that do them.* Now those, above all, seem to consent to a thing, who induce others to do it. But it is lawful for bishops and clerics to induce others to fight: for it is written (xxiii, qu. 8, can. Hortatu) that Charles went to war with the Lombards at the instance and entreaty of Adrian, bishop of Rome. Therefore they also are allowed to fight.

OBJ. 4: Further, whatever is right and meritorious in itself, is lawful for prelates and clerics. Now it is sometimes right and meritorious to make war, for it is written (xxiii, qu. 8, can. Omni timore) that if *a man die for the true faith, or to save his country, or in defense of Christians, God will give him a heavenly reward.* Therefore it is lawful for bishops and clerics to fight.

ON THE CONTRARY, It was said to Peter as representing bishops and clerics (Matt 16:52): *Put up again thy sword into the scabbard.* Therefore it is not lawful for them to fight.

I ANSWER THAT, Several things are requisite for the good of a human society: and a number of things are done better and quicker by a number of persons than by one, as the Philosopher observes (*Polit.* i, 1), while certain occupations are so inconsistent with one another, that they cannot be fittingly exercised at the same time; wherefore those who are deputed to important duties are forbidden to occupy themselves with things of small importance. Thus according to human laws, soldiers who are deputed to warlike pursuits are forbidden to engage in commerce.

Now warlike pursuits are altogether incompatible with the duties of a bishop and a cleric, for two reasons. The first reason is a general one, because, to wit, warlike pursuits are full of unrest, so that they hinder the mind very much from the contemplation of Divine things, the praise of God, and prayers for the people, which belong to the duties of a cleric. Wherefore just as commercial enterprises are forbidden to clerics, because they unsettle the mind too much, so too are warlike pursuits, according to 2 Tim. 2:4: *No man being a soldier to God, entangleth himself with secular business.* The second reason is a special one, because, to wit, all the clerical Orders are directed to the ministry of the altar, on which the Passion of Christ is represented sacramentally, according to 1 Cor. 11:26: *As often as you shall eat this bread, and drink the chalice, you shall show the death of the Lord, until He come.* Wherefore it is unbecoming for them to slay or shed blood, and it is more fitting that they should be ready to shed their own blood for Christ, so as to imitate in deed what they portray in their ministry. For this reason it

effundentes sanguinem, etiam sine peccato, sint irregulares. Nulli autem qui est deputatus ad aliquod officium licet id per quod suo officio incongruus redditur. Unde clericis omnino non licet bella gerere, quae ordinantur ad sanguinis effusionem.

AD PRIMUM ergo dicendum quod praelati debent resistere non solum lupis qui spiritualiter interficiunt gregem, sed etiam raptoribus et tyrannis qui corporaliter vexant, non autem materialibus armis in propria persona utendo, sed spiritualibus; secundum illud apostoli, II ad Cor. X, *arma militiae nostrae non sunt carnalia, sed spiritualia.* Quae quidem sunt salubres admonitiones, devotae orationes, contra pertinaces excommunicationis sententia.

AD SECUNDUM dicendum quod praelati et clerici, ex auctoritate superioris, possunt interesse bellis, non quidem ut ipsi propria manu pugnent, sed ut iuste pugnantibus spiritualiter subveniant suis exhortationibus et absolutionibus et aliis huiusmodi spiritualibus subventionibus. Sicut et in veteri lege mandabatur, Ios. VI, quod sacerdotes sacris tubis in bellis clangerent. Et ad hoc primo fuit concessum quod episcopi vel clerici ad bella procederent. Quod autem aliqui propria manu pugnent, abusionis est.

AD TERTIUM dicendum quod, sicut supra habitum est, omnis potentia vel ars vel virtus ad quam pertinet finis habet disponere de his quae sunt ad finem. Bella autem carnalia in populo fideli sunt referenda, sicut ad finem, ad bonum spirituale divinum, cui clerici deputantur. Et ideo ad clericos pertinet disponere et inducere alios ad bellandum bella iusta. Non enim interdicitur eis bellare quia peccatum sit, sed quia tale exercitium eorum personae non congruit.

AD QUARTUM dicendum quod, licet exercere bella iusta sit meritorium, tamen illicitum redditur clericis propter hoc quod sunt ad opera magis meritoria deputati. Sicut matrimonialis actus potest esse meritorius, et tamen virginitatem voventibus damnabilis redditur, propter obligationem eorum ad maius bonum.

has been decreed that those who shed blood, even without sin, become irregular. Now no man who has a certain duty to perform, can lawfully do that which renders him unfit for that duty. Wherefore it is altogether unlawful for clerics to fight, because war is directed to the shedding of blood.

REPLY OBJ. 1: Prelates ought to withstand not only the wolf who brings spiritual death upon the flock, but also the pillager and the oppressor who work bodily harm; not, however, by having recourse themselves to material arms, but by means of spiritual weapons, according to the saying of the Apostle (2 Cor 10:4): *The weapons of our warfare are not carnal, but mighty through God.* Such are salutary warnings, devout prayers, and, for those who are obstinate, the sentence of excommunication.

REPLY OBJ. 2: Prelates and clerics may, by the authority of their superiors, take part in wars, not indeed by taking up arms themselves, but by affording spiritual help to those who fight justly, by exhorting and absolving them, and by other like spiritual helps. Thus in the Old Testament (Josh 6:4) the priests were commanded to sound the sacred trumpets in the battle. It was for this purpose that bishops or clerics were first allowed to go to the front: and it is an abuse of this permission, if any of them take up arms themselves.

REPLY OBJ. 3: As stated above (Q. 23, A. 4, ad 2) every power, art or virtue that regards the end, has to dispose that which is directed to the end. Now, among the faithful, carnal wars should be considered as having for their end the Divine spiritual good to which clerics are deputed. Wherefore it is the duty of clerics to dispose and counsel other men to engage in just wars. For they are forbidden to take up arms, not as though it were a sin, but because such an occupation is unbecoming their personality.

REPLY OBJ. 4: Although it is meritorious to wage a just war, nevertheless it is rendered unlawful for clerics, by reason of their being deputed to works more meritorious still. Thus the marriage act may be meritorious; and yet it becomes reprehensible in those who have vowed virginity, because they are bound to a yet greater good.

# Article 3

*Whether it is lawful to lay ambushes in war?*

AD TERTIUM SIC PROCEDITUR. Videtur quod non sit licitum in bellis uti insidiis. Dicitur enim Deut. XVI, *iuste quod iustum est exequeris.* Sed insidiae, cum sint fraudes quaedam, videntur ad iniustitiam pertinere. Ergo non est utendum insidiis etiam in bellis iustis.

PRAETEREA, insidiae et fraudes fidelitati videntur opponi, sicut et mendacia. Sed quia ad omnes fidem debemus servare, nulli homini est mentiendum; ut pa-

OBJECTION 1: It would seem that it is unlawful to lay ambushes in war. For it is written (Deut 16:20): *Thou shalt follow justly after that which is just.* But ambushes, since they are a kind of deception, seem to pertain to injustice. Therefore it is unlawful to lay ambushes even in a just war.

OBJ. 2: Further, ambushes and deception seem to be opposed to faithfulness even as lies are. But since we are bound to keep faith with all men, it is wrong to lie to

tet per Augustinum, in libro contra mendacium. Cum ergo *fides hosti* servanda sit, ut Augustinus dicit, ad Bonifacium, videtur quod non sit contra hostes insidiis utendum.

PRAETEREA, Matth. VII dicitur, *quae vultis ut faciant vobis homines, et vos facite illis*, et hoc est observandum ad omnes proximos. Inimici autem sunt proximi. Cum ergo nullus sibi velit insidias vel fraudes parari, videtur quod nullus ex insidiis debeat gerere bella.

SED CONTRA est quod Augustinus dicit, in libro quaest., *cum iustum bellum suscipitur, utrum aperte pugnet aliquis an ex insidiis, nihil ad iustitiam interest*. Et hoc probat auctoritate domini, qui mandavit Iosue ut insidias poneret habitatoribus civitatis hai, ut habetur Ios. VIII.

RESPONDEO dicendum quod insidiae ordinantur ad fallendum hostes. Dupliciter autem aliquis potest falli ex facto vel dicto alterius uno modo, ex eo quod ei dicitur falsum, vel non servatur promissum. Et istud semper est illicitum. Et hoc modo nullus debet hostes fallere, sunt enim quaedam iura bellorum et foedera etiam inter ipsos hostes servanda, ut Ambrosius dicit, in libro de officiis.

Alio modo potest aliquis falli ex dicto vel facto nostro, quia ei propositum aut intellectum non aperimus. Hoc autem semper facere non tenemur, quia etiam in doctrina sacra multa sunt occultanda, maxime infidelibus, ne irrideant, secundum illud Matth. VII, *nolite sanctum dare canibus*. Unde multo magis ea quae ad impugnandum inimicos paramus sunt eis occultanda. Unde inter cetera documenta rei militaris hoc praecipue ponitur de occultandis consiliis ne ad hostes perveniant; ut patet in libro stratagematum Frontini. Et talis occultatio pertinet ad rationem insidiarum quibus licitum est uti in bellis iustis.

Nec proprie huiusmodi insidiae vocantur fraudes; nec iustitiae repugnant; nec ordinatae voluntati, esset enim inordinata voluntas si aliquis vellet nihil sibi ab aliis occultari.

ET PER HOC patet responsio ad obiecta.

anyone, as Augustine states (*Contra Mend.* xv). Therefore, as one is bound *to keep faith with one's enemy*, as Augustine states (*Ep. ad Bonif. clxxxix*), it seems that it is unlawful to lay ambushes for one's enemies.

OBJ. 3: Further, it is written (Matt 7:12): *Whatsoever you would that men should do to you, do you also to them*: and we ought to observe this in all our dealings with our neighbor. Now our enemy is our neighbor. Therefore, since no man wishes ambushes or deceptions to be prepared for himself, it seems that no one ought to carry on war by laying ambushes.

ON THE CONTRARY, Augustine says (*QQ. in Hept. qu. x super Jos*): *Provided the war be just, it is no concern of justice whether it be carried on openly or by ambushes*: and he proves this by the authority of the Lord, Who commanded Joshua to lay ambushes for the city of Hai (Josh 8:2).

I ANSWER THAT, The object of laying ambushes is in order to deceive the enemy. Now a man may be deceived by another's word or deed in two ways. First, through being told something false, or through the breaking of a promise, and this is always unlawful. No one ought to deceive the enemy in this way, for there are certain rights of war and covenants, which ought to be observed even among enemies, as Ambrose states (*De Officiis* i).

Second, a man may be deceived by what we say or do, because we do not declare our purpose or meaning to him. Now we are not always bound to do this, since even in the Sacred Doctrine many things have to be concealed, especially from unbelievers, lest they deride it, according to Matt. 7:6: *Give not that which is holy, to dogs*. Wherefore much more ought the plan of campaign to be hidden from the enemy. For this reason among other things that a soldier has to learn is the art of concealing his purpose lest it come to the enemy's knowledge, as stated in the Book on Strategy by Frontinus. Such like concealment is what is meant by an ambush which may be lawfully employed in a just war.

Nor can these ambushes be properly called deceptions, nor are they contrary to justice or to a well-ordered will. For a man would have an inordinate will if he were unwilling that others should hide anything from him.

THIS SUFFICES for the Replies to the Objections.

# Article 4

*Whether it is lawful to fight on holy days?*

AD QUARTUM SIC PROCEDITUR. Videtur quod in diebus festis non liceat bellare. Festa enim sunt ordinata ad vacandum divinis, unde intelliguntur per observationem sabbati, quae praecipitur Exod. XX; *sabbatum* enim

OBJECTION 1: It would seem unlawful to fight on holy days. For holy days are instituted that we may give our time to the things of God. Hence they are included in the keeping of the Sabbath prescribed Ex. 20:8: for *sabbath* is

interpretatur *requies*. Sed bella maximam inquietudinem habent. Ergo nullo modo est in diebus festis pugnandum.

PRAETEREA, Isaiae LVIII reprehenduntur quidam quod in diebus ieiunii *repetunt debita et committunt lites, pugno percutientes*. Ergo multo magis in diebus festis illicitum est bellare.

PRAETEREA, nihil est inordinate agendum ad vitandum incommodum temporale. Sed bellare in die festo, hoc videtur esse secundum se inordinatum. Ergo pro nulla necessitate temporalis incommodi vitandi debet aliquis in die festo bellare.

SED CONTRA est quod I Machab. II dicitur, *cogitaverunt laudabiliter Iudaei, dicentes, omnis homo quicumque venerit ad nos in bello in die sabbatorum, pugnemus adversus eum*.

RESPONDEO dicendum quod observatio festorum non impedit ea quae ordinantur ad hominis salutem etiam corporalem. Unde dominus arguit Iudaeos, dicens, Ioan. VII, *mihi indignamini quia totum hominem salvum feci in sabbato?* Et inde est quod medici licite possunt medicari homines in die festo. Multo autem magis est conservanda salus reipublicae, per quam impediuntur occisiones plurimorum et innumera mala et temporalia et spiritualia, quam salus corporalis unius hominis. Et ideo pro tuitione reipublicae fidelium licitum est iusta bella exercere in diebus festis, si tamen hoc necessitas exposcat, hoc enim esset tentare Deum, si quis, imminente tali necessitate, a bello vellet abstinere.

Sed necessitate cessante, non est licitum bellare in diebus festis, propter rationes inductas.

ET PER HOC patet responsio ad obiecta.

interpreted *rest*. But wars are full of unrest. Therefore by no means is it lawful to fight on holy days.

OBJ. 2: Further, certain persons are reproached (Isa 58:3) because on fast-days *they exacted what was owing to them, and were guilty of strife and smiting with the fist*. Much more, therefore, is it unlawful to fight on holy days.

OBJ. 3: Further, no ill deed should be done to avoid temporal harm. But fighting on a holy day seems in itself to be an ill deed. Therefore no one should fight on a holy day even through the need of avoiding temporal harm.

ON THE CONTRARY, It is written (1 Macc 2:41): The Jews rightly determined . . . saying: *Whosoever shall come up against us to fight on the Sabbath-day, we will fight against him*.

I ANSWER THAT, The observance of holy days is no hindrance to those things which are ordained to man's safety, even that of his body. Hence Our Lord argued with the Jews, saying (John 7:23): *Are you angry at Me because I have healed the whole man on the Sabbath-day?* Hence physicians may lawfully attend to their patients on holy days. Now there is much more reason for safeguarding the common weal (whereby many are saved from being slain, and innumerable evils both temporal and spiritual prevented), than the bodily safety of an individual. Therefore, for the purpose of safeguarding the common weal of the faithful, it is lawful to carry on a war on holy days, provided there be need for doing so: because it would be to tempt God, if notwithstanding such a need, one were to choose to refrain from fighting.

However, as soon as the need ceases, it is no longer lawful to fight on a holy day, for the reasons given.

WHEREFORE this suffices for the Replies to the Objections.

# QUESTION 41

## STRIFE

Deinde considerandum est de rixa. Et circa hoc quaeruntur duo.

    Primo, utrum rixa sit peccatum.

    Secundo, utrum sit filia irae.

We must now consider strife, under which head there are two points of inquiry:

    (1) Whether strife is a sin?

    (2) Whether it is a daughter of anger?

# Article 1

### *Whether strife is always a sin?*

**AD PRIMUM SIC PROCEDITUR.** Videtur quod rixa non semper sit peccatum. Rixa enim videtur esse contentio quaedam, dicit enim Isidorus, in libro Etymol., quod *rixosus est a rictu canino dictus, semper enim ad contradicendum paratus est, et iurgio delectatur, et provocat contendentem.* Sed contentio non semper est peccatum. Ergo neque rixa.

**PRAETEREA,** Gen. XXVI dicitur quod *servi Isaac foderunt alium puteum, et pro illo quoque rixati sunt.* Sed non est credendum quod familia Isaac rixaretur publice, eo non contradicente, si hoc esset peccatum. Ergo rixa non est peccatum.

**PRAETEREA,** rixa videtur esse quoddam particulare bellum. Sed bellum non semper est peccatum. Ergo rixa non semper est peccatum.

**SED CONTRA** est quod ad Gal. V rixae ponuntur inter opera carnis, *quae qui agunt regnum Dei non consequuntur.* Ergo rixae non solum sunt peccata, sed etiam sunt peccata mortalia.

**RESPONDEO** dicendum quod sicut contentio importat quandam contradictionem verborum, ita etiam rixa importat quandam contradictionem in factis, unde super illud Gal. V dicit Glossa quod rixae sunt *quando ex ira invicem se percutiunt.* Et ideo rixa videtur esse quoddam privatum bellum, quod inter privatas personas agitur non ex aliqua publica auctoritate, sed magis ex inordinata voluntate. Et ideo rixa semper importat peccatum. Et in eo quidem qui alterum invadit iniuste est peccatum mortale, inferre enim nocumentum proximo etiam opere manuali non est absque mortali peccato. In eo autem qui se defendit potest esse sine peccato, et quandoque cum peccato veniali, et quandoque etiam cum mortali, secundum diversum motum animi eius, et diversum modum se defendendi. Nam si solo animo repellendi iniuriam illatam, et cum debita moderatione se defendat, non est peccatum, nec proprie potest dici rixa ex parte eius. Si vero cum animo vindictae vel

**OBJECTION 1**: It would seem that strife is not always a sin. For strife seems a kind of contention: hence Isidore says (*Etym.* x) that the word *rixosus is derived from the snarling of a dog, because the quarrelsome man is ever ready to contradict; he delights in brawling, and provokes contention.* Now contention is not always a sin. Neither, therefore, is strife.

**OBJ. 2**: Further, it is related (Gen 26:21) that the servants of Isaac *digged* another well, *and for that they quarrelled likewise.* Now it is not credible that the household of Isaac quarrelled publicly, without being reproved by him, supposing it were a sin. Therefore strife is not a sin.

**OBJ. 3**: Further, strife seems to be a war between individuals. But war is not always sinful. Therefore strife is not always a sin.

**ON THE CONTRARY**, Strifes are reckoned among the works of the flesh (Gal 5:20), and *they who do such things shall not obtain the kingdom of God.* Therefore strifes are not only sinful, but they are even mortal sins.

**I ANSWER THAT**, While contention implies a contradiction of words, strife denotes a certain contradiction of deeds. Wherefore a gloss on Gal. 5:20 says that *strifes are when persons strike one another through anger.* Hence strife is a kind of private war, because it takes place between private persons, being declared not by public authority, but rather by an inordinate will. Therefore strife is always sinful. In fact it is a mortal sin in the man who attacks another unjustly, for it is not without mortal sin that one inflicts harm on another even if the deed be done by the hands. But in him who defends himself, it may be without sin, or it may sometimes involve a venial sin, or sometimes a mortal sin; and this depends on his intention and on his manner of defending himself. For if his sole intention be to withstand the injury done to him, and he defend himself with due moderation, it is no sin, and one cannot say properly that there is strife on his part. But if, on the other hand, his self-defense be inspired by vengeance and hatred, it is always

odii, vel cum excessu debitae moderationis se defendat, semper est peccatum, sed veniale quidem quando aliquis levis motus odii vel vindictae se immiscet, vel cum non multum excedat moderatam defensionem; mortale autem quando obfirmato animo in impugnantem insurgit ad eum occidendum vel graviter laedendum.

**AD PRIMUM** ergo dicendum quod rixa non simpliciter nominat contentionem, sed tria in praemissis verbis Isidori ponuntur quae inordinationem rixae declarant. Primo quidem, promptitudinem animi ad contendendum, quod significat cum dicit, *semper ad contradicendum paratus*, scilicet sive alius bene aut male dicat aut faciat. Secundo, quia in ipsa contradictione delectatur, unde sequitur, et *in iurgio delectatur*. Tertio, quia ipse alios provocat ad contradictiones, unde sequitur, *et provocat contendentem*.

**AD SECUNDUM** dicendum quod ibi non intelligitur quod servi Isaac sint rixati, sed quod incolae terrae rixati sunt contra eos. Unde illi peccaverunt, non autem servi Isaac, qui calumniam patiebantur.

**AD TERTIUM** dicendum quod ad hoc quod iustum sit bellum, requiritur quod fiat auctoritate publicae potestatis, sicut supra dictum est. Rixa autem fit ex privato affectu irae vel odii. Si enim minister principis aut iudicis publica potestate aliquos invadat qui se defendant, non dicuntur ipsi rixari, sed illi qui publicae potestati resistunt. Et sic illi qui invadunt non rixantur neque peccant, sed illi qui se inordinate defendunt.

a sin. It is a venial sin, if a slight movement of hatred or vengeance obtrude itself, or if he does not much exceed moderation in defending himself: but it is a mortal sin if he makes for his assailant with the fixed intention of killing him, or inflicting grievous harm on him.

**REPLY OBJ. 1**: Strife is not just the same as contention: and there are three things in the passage quoted from Isidore, which express the inordinate nature of strife. First, the quarrelsome man is always ready to fight, and this is conveyed by the words, *ever ready to contradict*, that is to say, whether the other man says or does well or ill. Second, he delights in quarrelling itself, and so the passage proceeds, *and delights in brawling*. Third, *he* provokes others to quarrel, wherefore it goes on, *and provokes contention*.

**REPLY OBJ. 2**: The sense of the text is not that the servants of Isaac quarrelled, but that the inhabitants of that country quarrelled with them: wherefore these sinned, and not the servants of Isaac, who bore the calumny.

**REPLY OBJ. 3**: In order for a war to be just it must be declared by authority of the governing power, as stated above (Q. 40, A. 1); whereas strife proceeds from a private feeling of anger or hatred. For if the servants of a sovereign or judge, in virtue of their public authority, attack certain men and these defend themselves, it is not the former who are said to be guilty of strife, but those who resist the public authority. Hence it is not the assailants in this case who are guilty of strife and commit sin, but those who defend themselves inordinately.

# Article 2

### *Whether strife is a daughter of anger?*

**AD SECUNDUM SIC PROCEDITUR**. Videtur quod rixa non sit filia irae. Dicitur enim Iac. IV, *unde bella et lites in vobis? Nonne ex concupiscentiis quae militant in membris vestris?* Sed ira non pertinet ad concupiscibilem. Ergo rixa non est filia irae, sed magis concupiscentiae.

**PRAETEREA**, Prov. XXVIII dicitur, *qui se iactat et dilatat iurgia concitat*. Sed idem videtur esse rixa quod iurgium. Ergo videtur quod rixa sit filia superbiae vel inanis gloriae, ad quam pertinet se iactare et dilatare.

**PRAETEREA**, Prov. XVIII dicitur, *labia stulti immiscent se rixis*. Sed stultitia differt ab ira, non enim opponitur mansuetudini, sed magis sapientiae vel prudentiae. Ergo rixa non est filia irae.

**OBJECTION 1**: It would seem that strife is not a daughter of anger. For it is written (Jas 4:1): *Whence are wars and contentions? Are they not . . . from your concupiscences, which war in your members?* But anger is not in the concupiscible faculty. Therefore strife is a daughter, not of anger, but of concupiscence.

**OBJ. 2**: Further, it is written (Prov 28:25): *He that boasteth and puffeth up himself, stirreth up quarrels.* Now strife is apparently the same as quarrel. Therefore it seems that strife is a daughter of pride or vainglory which makes a man boast and puff himself up.

**OBJ. 3**: Further, it is written (Prov 18:6): *The lips of a fool intermeddle with strife.* Now folly differs from anger, for it is opposed, not to meekness, but to wisdom or prudence. Therefore strife is not a daughter of anger.

PRAETEREA, Prov. X dicitur, *odium suscitat rixas.* Sed *odium oritur ex invidia*; ut Gregorius dicit, XXXI Moral. Ergo rixa non est filia irae, sed invidiae.

PRAETEREA, Prov. XVII dicitur, *qui meditatur discordias seminat rixas.* Sed discordia est filia inanis gloriae, ut supra dictum est. Ergo et rixa.

SED CONTRA est quod Gregorius dicit, XXXI Moral., quod *ex ira oritur rixa.* Et Prov. XV et XXIX dicitur, *vir iracundus provocat rixas.*

RESPONDEO dicendum quod, sicut dictum est, rixa importat quandam contradictionem usque ad facta pervenientem, dum unus alterum laedere molitur. Dupliciter autem unus alium laedere intendit. Uno modo, quasi intendens absolute malum ipsius. Et talis laesio pertinet ad odium, cuius intentio est ad laedendum inimicum vel in manifesto vel in occulto. Alio modo aliquis intendit alium laedere eo sciente et repugnante, quod importatur nomine rixae. Et hoc proprie pertinet ad iram, quae est appetitus vindictae, non enim sufficit irato quod latenter noceat ei contra quem irascitur, sed vult quod ipse sentiat, et quod contra voluntatem suam aliquid patiatur in vindictam eius quod fecit, ut patet per ea quae supra dicta sunt de passione irae. Et ideo rixa proprie oritur ex ira.

AD PRIMUM ergo dicendum quod, sicut supra dictum est, omnes passiones irascibilis ex passionibus concupiscibilis oriuntur. Et secundum hoc, illud quod proxime oritur ex ira, oritur etiam ex concupiscentia sicut ex prima radice.

AD SECUNDUM dicendum quod iactatio et dilatatio sui, quae fit per superbiam vel inanem gloriam, non directe concitat iurgium aut rixam, sed occasionaliter, inquantum scilicet ex hoc concitatur ira, dum aliquis sibi ad iniuriam reputat quod alter ei se praeferat; et sic ex ira sequuntur iurgia et rixae.

AD TERTIUM dicendum quod ira, sicut supra dictum est, impedit iudicium rationis, unde habet similitudinem cum stultitia. Et ex hoc sequitur quod habeant communem effectum, ex defectu enim rationis contingit quod aliquis inordinate alium laedere molitur.

AD QUARTUM dicendum quod rixa, etsi quandoque ex odio oriatur, non tamen est proprius effectus odii. Quia praeter intentionem odientis est quod rixose et manifeste inimicum laedat, quandoque enim etiam occulte laedere quaerit; sed quando videt se praevalere cum rixa et iurgio laesionem intendit. Sed rixose aliquem laedere est proprius effectus irae, ratione iam dicta.

AD QUINTUM dicendum quod ex rixis sequitur odium et discordia in cordibus rixantium. Et ideo ille qui *meditatur*, idest qui intendit inter aliquos seminare

OBJ. 4: Further, it is written (Prov 10:12): *Hatred stirreth up strifes.* But *hatred arises from envy*, according to Gregory (*Moral.* xxxi, 17). Therefore strife is not a daughter of anger, but of envy.

OBJ. 5: Further, it is written (Prov 17:19): *He that studieth discords, soweth quarrels.* But discord is a daughter of vainglory, as stated above (Q. 37, A. 2). Therefore strife is also.

ON THE CONTRARY, Gregory says (*Moral.* xxxi, 17) that *anger gives rise to strife*; and it is written (Prov 15:18; 29:22): *A passionate man stirreth up strifes.*

I ANSWER THAT, As stated above (A. 1), strife denotes an antagonism extending to deeds, when one man designs to harm another. Now there are two ways in which one man may intend to harm another. In one way it is as though he intended absolutely the other's hurt, which in this case is the outcome of hatred, for the intention of hatred is directed to the hurt of one's enemy either openly or secretly. In another way a man intends to hurt another who knows and withstands his intention. This is what we mean by strife, and belongs properly to anger which is the desire of vengeance: for the angry man is not content to hurt secretly the object of his anger, he even wishes him to feel the hurt and know that what he suffers is in revenge for what he has done, as may be seen from what has been said above about the passion of anger (I-II, Q. 46, A. 6, ad 2). Therefore, properly speaking, strife arises from anger.

REPLY OBJ. 1: As stated above (I-II, Q. 25, AA. 1, 2), all the irascible passions arise from those of the concupiscible faculty, so that whatever is the immediate outcome of anger, arises also from concupiscence as from its first root.

REPLY OBJ. 2: Boasting and puffing up of self which are the result of anger or vainglory, are not the direct but the occasional cause of quarrels or strife, because, when a man resents another being preferred to him, his anger is aroused, and then his anger results in quarrel and strife.

REPLY OBJ. 3: Anger, as stated above (I-II, Q. 48, A. 3) hinders the judgment of the reason, so that it bears a likeness to folly. Hence they have a common effect, since it is due to a defect in the reason that a man designs to hurt another inordinately.

REPLY OBJ. 4: Although strife sometimes arises from hatred, it is not the proper effect thereof, because when one man hates another it is beside his intention to hurt him in a quarrelsome and open manner, since sometimes he seeks to hurt him secretly. When, however, he sees himself prevailing, he endeavors to harm him with strife and quarrel. But to hurt a man in a quarrel is the proper effect of anger, for the reason given above.

REPLY OBJ. 5: Strifes give rise to hatred and discord in the hearts of those who are guilty of strife, and so he that *studies*, i.e., intends to sow discord among others, causes

discordias, procurat quod ad invicem rixantur, sicut quodlibet peccatum potest imperare actum alterius peccati, ordinando illum in suum finem. Sed ex hoc non sequitur quod rixa sit filia inanis gloriae proprie et directe.

them to quarrel among themselves. Even so any sin may command the act of another sin, by directing it to its own end. This does not, however, prove that strife is the daughter of vainglory properly and directly.

# QUESTION 42

## SEDITION

Deinde considerandum est de seditione. Et circa hoc quaeruntur duo.

Primo, utrum sit speciale peccatum.

Secundo, utrum sit mortale peccatum.

We must now consider sedition, under which head there are two points of inquiry:

(1) Whether it is a special sin?

(2) Whether it is a mortal sin?

# Article 1

*Whether sedition is a special sin distinct from other sins?*

AD PRIMUM SIC PROCEDITUR. Videtur quod seditio non sit speciale peccatum ab aliis distinctum. Quia ut Isidorus dicit, in libro Etymol., *seditiosus est qui dissensionem animorum facit et discordias gignit.* Sed ex hoc quod aliquis aliquod peccatum procurat, non peccat alio peccati genere nisi illo quod procurat. Ergo videtur quod seditio non sit speciale peccatum a discordia distinctum.

PRAETEREA, seditio divisionem quandam importat. Sed nomen etiam schismatis sumitur a scissura, ut supra dictum est. Ergo peccatum seditionis non videtur esse distinctum a peccato schismatis.

PRAETEREA, omne peccatum speciale ab aliis distinctum vel est vitium capitale, aut ex aliquo vitio capitali oritur. Sed seditio neque computatur inter vitia capitalia, neque inter vitia quae ex capitalibus oriuntur, ut patet in XXXI Moral., ubi utraque vitia numerantur. Ergo seditio non est speciale peccatum ab aliis distinctum.

SED CONTRA est quod II ad Cor. XII seditiones ab aliis peccatis distinguuntur.

RESPONDEO dicendum quod seditio est quoddam peccatum speciale, quod quantum ad aliquid convenit cum bello et rixa, quantum autem ad aliquid differt ab eis. Convenit quidem cum eis in hoc quod importat quandam contradictionem. Differt autem ab eis in duobus. Primo quidem, quia bellum et rixa important mutuam impugnationem in actu, sed seditio potest dici sive fiat huiusmodi impugnatio in actu, sive sit praeparatio ad talem impugnationem. Unde Glossa II ad Cor. XII dicit quod seditiones sunt *tumultus ad pugnam*, cum scilicet aliqui se praeparant et intendunt pugnare. Secundo differunt, quia bellum proprie est contra extraneos et hostes, quasi multitudinis ad multitudinem; rixa autem est unius ad unum, vel paucorum ad paucos; seditio autem proprie est inter partes unius multitudinis inter se dissentientes, puta cum una pars civitatis excitatur in tumultum contra aliam. Et ideo seditio, quia habet spe-

OBJECTION 1: It would seem that sedition is not a special sin distinct from other sins. For, according to Isidore (*Etym.* x), *a seditious man is one who sows dissent among minds, and begets discord.* Now, by provoking the commission of a sin, a man sins by no other kind of sin than that which he provoked. Therefore it seems that sedition is not a special sin distinct from discord.

OBJ. 2: Further, sedition denotes a kind of division. Now schism takes its name from scission, as stated above (Q. 39, A. 1). Therefore, seemingly, the sin of sedition is not distinct from that of schism.

OBJ. 3: Further, every special sin that is distinct from other sins, is either a capital vice, or arises from some capital vice. Now sedition is reckoned neither among the capital vices, nor among those vices which arise from them, as appears from Moral. xxxi, 45, where both kinds of vice are enumerated. Therefore sedition is not a special sin, distinct from other sins.

ON THE CONTRARY, Seditions are mentioned as distinct from other sins (2 Cor 12:20).

I ANSWER THAT, Sedition is a special sin, having something in common with war and strife, and differing somewhat from them. It has something in common with them, insofar as it implies a certain antagonism, and it differs from them in two points. First, because war and strife denote actual aggression on either side, whereas sedition may be said to denote either actual aggression, or the preparation for such aggression. Hence a gloss on 2 Cor. 12:20 says that seditions are *tumults tending to fight,* when, to wit, a number of people make preparations with the intention of fighting. Second, they differ in that war is, properly speaking, carried on against external foes, being as it were between one people and another, whereas strife is between one individual and another, or between few people on one side and few on the other side, while sedition, in its proper sense, is between mutually dissentient parts of one people, as when one part of the state rises in tumult

ciale bonum cui opponitur, scilicet unitatem et pacem multitudinis, ideo est speciale peccatum.

AD PRIMUM ergo dicendum quod seditiosus dicitur qui seditionem excitat. Et quia seditio quandam discordiam importat, ideo seditiosus est qui discordiam facit non quamcumque, sed inter partes alicuius multitudinis. Peccatum autem seditionis non solum est in eo qui discordiam seminat, sed etiam in eis qui inordinate ab invicem dissentiunt.

AD SECUNDUM dicendum quod seditio differt a schismate in duobus. Primo quidem, quia schisma opponitur spirituali unitati multitudinis, scilicet unitati ecclesiasticae, seditio autem opponitur temporali vel saeculari multitudinis unitati, puta civitatis vel regni. Secundo, quia schisma non importat aliquam praeparationem ad pugnam corporalem, sed solum importat dissensionem spiritualem, seditio autem importat praeparationem ad pugnam corporalem.

AD TERTIUM dicendum quod seditio, sicut et schisma, sub discordia continetur. Utrumque enim est discordia quaedam, non unius ad unum, sed partium multitudinis ad invicem.

against another part. Wherefore, since sedition is opposed to a special kind of good, namely the unity and peace of a people, it is a special kind of sin.

REPLY OBJ. 1: A seditious man is one who incites others to sedition, and since sedition denotes a kind of discord, it follows that a seditious man is one who creates discord, not of any kind, but between the parts of a multitude. And the sin of sedition is not only in him who sows discord, but also in those who dissent from one another inordinately.

REPLY OBJ. 2: Sedition differs from schism in two respects. First, because schism is opposed to the spiritual unity of the multitude, viz. ecclesiastical unity, whereas sedition is contrary to the temporal or secular unity of the multitude, for instance of a city or kingdom. Second, schism does not imply any preparation for a material fight as sedition does, but only for a spiritual dissent.

REPLY OBJ. 3: Sedition, like schism, is contained under discord, since each is a kind of discord, not between individuals, but between the parts of a multitude.

# Article 2

*Whether sedition is always a mortal sin?*

AD SECUNDUM SIC PROCEDITUR. Videtur quod seditio non semper sit peccatum mortale. Seditio enim importat *tumultum ad pugnam*; ut patet per Glossam supra inductam. Sed pugna non semper est peccatum mortale, sed quandoque est iusta et licita, ut supra habitum est. Ergo multo magis seditio potest esse sine peccato mortali.

PRAETEREA, seditio est discordia quaedam, ut dictum est. Sed discordia potest esse sine peccato mortali, et quandoque etiam sine omni peccato. Ergo etiam seditio.

PRAETEREA, laudantur qui multitudinem a potestate tyrannica liberant. Sed hoc non de facili potest fieri sine aliqua dissensione multitudinis, dum una pars multitudinis nititur retinere tyrannum, alia vero nititur eum abiicere. Ergo seditio potest fieri sine peccato.

SED CONTRA est quod apostolus, II ad Cor. XII, prohibet seditiones inter alia quae sunt peccata mortalia. Ergo seditio est peccatum mortale.

RESPONDEO dicendum quod, sicut dictum est, seditio opponitur unitati multitudinis, idest populi, civitatis vel regni. Dicit autem Augustinus, II de Civ. Dei, quod *populum determinant sapientes non omnem coetum multitudinis, sed coetum iuris consensu et utilitatis*

OBJECTION 1: It would seem that sedition is not always a mortal sin. For sedition denotes *a tumult tending to fight*, according to the gloss quoted above (A. 1). But fighting is not always a mortal sin, indeed it is sometimes just and lawful, as stated above (Q. 40, A. 1). Much more, therefore, can sedition be without a mortal sin.

OBJ. 2: Further, sedition is a kind of discord, as stated above (A. 1, ad 3). Now discord can be without mortal sin, and sometimes without any sin at all. Therefore sedition can be also.

OBJ. 3: Further, it is praiseworthy to deliver a multitude from a tyrannical rule. Yet this cannot easily be done without some dissension in the multitude, if one part of the multitude seeks to retain the tyrant, while the rest strive to dethrone him. Therefore there can be sedition without mortal sin.

ON THE CONTRARY, The Apostle forbids seditions together with other things that are mortal sins (2 Cor 12:20).

I ANSWER THAT, As stated above (A. 1, ad 2), sedition is contrary to the unity of the multitude, viz. the people of a city or kingdom. Now Augustine says (De Civ. Dei ii, 21) that *wise men understand the word people to designate not any crowd of persons, but the assembly of those who*

*communione sociatum.* Unde manifestum est unitatem cui opponitur seditio esse unitatem iuris et communis utilitatis. Manifestum est ergo quod seditio opponitur et iustitiae et communi bono. Et ideo ex suo genere est peccatum mortale, et tanto gravius quanto bonum commune, quod impugnatur per seditionem, est maius quam bonum privatum, quod impugnatur per rixam.

Peccatum autem seditionis primo quidem et principaliter pertinet ad eos qui seditionem procurant, qui gravissime peccant. Secundo autem, ad eos qui eos sequuntur, perturbantes bonum commune. Illi vero qui bonum commune defendunt, eis resistentes, non sunt dicendi seditiosi, sicut nec illi qui se defendunt dicuntur rixosi, ut supra dictum est.

**AD PRIMUM** ergo dicendum quod pugna quae est licita fit pro communi utilitate, sicut supra dictum est. Sed seditio fit contra commune bonum multitudinis. Unde semper est peccatum mortale.

**AD SECUNDUM** dicendum quod discordia ab eo quod non est manifeste bonum potest esse sine peccato. Sed discordia ab eo quod est manifeste bonum non potest esse sine peccato. Et talis discordia est seditio, quae opponitur utilitati multitudinis, quae est manifeste bonum.

**AD TERTIUM** dicendum quod regimen tyrannicum non est iustum, quia non ordinatur ad bonum commune, sed ad bonum privatum regentis, ut patet per Philosophum, in III Polit. et in VIII Ethic. Et ideo perturbatio huius regiminis non habet rationem seditionis, nisi forte quando sic inordinate perturbatur tyranni regimen quod multitudo subiecta maius detrimentum patitur ex perturbatione consequenti quam ex tyranni regimine. Magis autem tyrannus seditiosus est, qui in populo sibi subiecto discordias et seditiones nutrit, ut tutius dominari possit. Hoc enim tyrannicum est, cum sit ordinatum ad bonum proprium praesidentis cum multitudinis nocumento.

*are united together in fellowship recognized by law and for the common good.* Wherefore it is evident that the unity to which sedition is opposed is the unity of law and common good: whence it follows manifestly that sedition is opposed to justice and the common good. Therefore by reason of its genus it is a mortal sin, and its gravity will be all the greater according as the common good which it assails surpasses the private good which is assailed by strife.

Accordingly the sin of sedition is first and chiefly in its authors, who sin most grievously; and second it is in those who are led by them to disturb the common good. Those, however, who defend the common good, and withstand the seditious party, are not themselves seditious, even as neither is a man to be called quarrelsome because he defends himself, as stated above (Q. 41, A. 1).

**REPLY OBJ. 1**: It is lawful to fight, provided it be for the common good, as stated above (Q. 40, A. 1). But sedition runs counter to the common good of the multitude, so that it is always a mortal sin.

**REPLY OBJ. 2**: Discord from what is not evidently good, may be without sin, but discord from what is evidently good, cannot be without sin: and sedition is discord of this kind, for it is contrary to the unity of the multitude, which is a manifest good.

**REPLY OBJ. 3**: A tyrannical government is not just, because it is directed, not to the common good, but to the private good of the ruler, as the Philosopher states (*Polit.* iii, 5; *Ethic.* viii, 10). Consequently there is no sedition in disturbing a government of this kind, unless indeed the tyrant's rule be disturbed so inordinately, that his subjects suffer greater harm from the consequent disturbance than from the tyrant's government. Indeed it is the tyrant rather that is guilty of sedition, since he encourages discord and sedition among his subjects, that he may lord over them more securely; for this is tyranny, being conducive to the private good of the ruler, and to the injury of the multitude.

# QUESTION 43

## SCANDAL

Deinde considerandum restat de vitiis quae beneficentiae opponuntur. Inter quae alia quidem pertinent ad rationem iustitiae, illa scilicet quibus aliquis iniuste proximum laedit, sed contra caritatem specialiter scandalum esse videtur. Et ideo considerandum est hic de scandalo. Circa quod quaeruntur octo.

Primo, quid sit scandalum.

Secundo, utrum scandalum sit peccatum.

Tertio, utrum sit peccatum speciale.

Quarto, utrum sit peccatum mortale.

Quinto, utrum perfectorum sit scandalizari.

Sexto, utrum eorum sit scandalizare.

Septimo, utrum spiritualia bona sint dimittenda propter scandalum.

Octavo, utrum sint propter scandalum temporalia dimittenda.

It remains for us to consider the vices which are opposed to beneficence, among which some come under the head of injustice, those, to wit, whereby one harms one's neighbor unjustly. But scandal seems to be specially opposed to charity. Accordingly we must here consider scandal, under which head there are eight points of inquiry:

(1) What is scandal?

(2) Whether scandal is a sin?

(3) Whether it is a special sin?

(4) Whether it is a mortal sin?

(5) Whether the perfect can be scandalized?

(6) Whether they can give scandal?

(7) Whether spiritual goods are to be foregone on account of scandal?

(8) Whether temporal things are to be foregone on account of scandal?

# Article 1

*Whether scandal is fittingly defined as: "something less rightly said or done that occasions spiritual downfall"?*

**AD PRIMUM SIC PROCEDITUR.** Videtur quod scandalum inconvenienter definiatur esse *dictum vel factum minus rectum praebens occasionem ruinae.* Scandalum enim peccatum est, ut post dicetur. Sed secundum Augustinum, XXII contra Faust., *peccatum est dictum vel factum vel concupitum contra legem Dei.* Ergo praedicta definitio est insufficiens, quia praetermittitur cogitatum sive concupitum.

**PRAETEREA,** cum inter actus virtuosos vel rectos unus sit virtuosior vel rectior altero, illud solum videtur non esse minus rectum quod est rectissimum. Si igitur scandalum sit dictum vel factum minus rectum, sequetur quod omnis actus virtuosus praeter optimum sit scandalum.

**PRAETEREA,** occasio nominat causam per accidens. Sed id quod est per accidens non debet poni in definitione, quia non dat speciem. Ergo inconvenienter in definitione scandali ponitur occasio.

**PRAETEREA,** ex quolibet facto alterius potest aliquis sumere occasionem ruinae, quia causae per accidens sunt indeterminatae. Si igitur scandalum est quod praebet alteri occasionem ruinae, quodlibet factum vel dictum poterit esse scandalum. Quod videtur inconveniens.

**OBJECTION 1:** It would seem that scandal is unfittingly defined as *something less rightly said or done that occasions spiritual downfall.* For scandal is a sin as we shall state further on (A. 2). Now, according to Augustine (*Contra Faust.* xxii, 27), a sin is a *word, deed, or desire contrary to the law of God.* Therefore the definition given above is insufficient, since it omits *thought* or *desire.*

**OBJ. 2:** Further, since among virtuous or right acts one is more virtuous or more right than another, that one alone which has perfect rectitude would not seem to be a *less* right one. If, therefore, scandal is something *less* rightly said or done, it follows that every virtuous act except the best of all, is a scandal.

**OBJ. 3:** Further, an occasion is an accidental cause. But nothing accidental should enter a definition, because it does not specify the thing defined. Therefore it is unfitting, in defining scandal, to say that it is an *occasion.*

**OBJ. 4:** Further, whatever a man does may be the occasion of another's spiritual downfall, because accidental causes are indeterminate. Consequently, if scandal is something that occasions another's spiritual downfall, any deed or word can be a scandal: and this seems unreasonable.

403

**PRAETEREA**, occasio ruinae datur proximo quando offenditur aut infirmatur. Sed scandalum dividitur contra offensionem et infirmitatem, dicit enim apostolus, ad Rom. XIV, *bonum est non manducare carnem et non bibere vinum, neque in quo frater tuus offenditur aut scandalizatur aut infirmatur.* Ergo praedicta definitio scandali non est conveniens.

**SED CONTRA** est quod Hieronymus, exponens illud quod habetur Matth. XV, *scis quia Pharisaei, audito hoc verbo*, etc., dicit, *quando legimus, quicumque scandalizaverit, hoc intelligimus, qui dicto vel facto occasionem ruinae dederit.*

**RESPONDEO** dicendum quod, sicut Hieronymus ibidem dicit, *quod Graece scandalon dicitur, nos offensionem vel ruinam et impactionem pedis possumus dicere.* Contingit enim quod quandoque aliquis obex ponitur alicui in via corporali, cui impingens disponitur ad ruinam, et talis obex dicitur scandalum.

**ET SIMILITER** in processu viae spiritualis contingit aliquem disponi ad ruinam spiritualem per dictum vel factum alterius, inquantum scilicet aliquis sua admonitione vel inductione aut exemplo alterum trahit ad peccandum. Et hoc proprie dicitur scandalum.

Nihil autem secundum propriam rationem disponit ad spiritualem ruinam nisi quod habet aliquem defectum rectitudinis, quia id quod est perfecte rectum magis munit hominem contra casum quam ad ruinam inducat. Et ideo convenienter dicitur quod *dictum vel factum minus rectum praebens occasionem ruinae sit scandalum.*

**AD PRIMUM** ergo dicendum quod cogitatio vel concupiscentia mali latet in corde, unde non proponitur alteri ut obex disponens ad ruinam. Et propter hoc non potest habere scandali rationem.

**AD SECUNDUM** dicendum quod minus rectum hic non dicitur quod ab aliquo alio superatur in rectitudine, sed quod habet aliquem rectitudinis defectum, vel quia est secundum se malum, sicut peccata; vel quia habet speciem mali, sicut cum aliquis recumbit in idolio. Quamvis enim hoc secundum se non sit peccatum, si aliquis hoc non corrupta intentione faciat; tamen quia habet quandam speciem vel similitudinem venerationis idoli, potest alteri praebere occasionem ruinae. Et ideo apostolus monet, I ad Thess. V, *ab omni specie mala abstinete vos.* Et ideo convenienter dicitur *minus rectum*, ut comprehendantur tam illa quae sunt secundum se peccata, quam illa quae habent speciem mali.

**AD TERTIUM** dicendum quod, sicut supra habitum est, nihil potest esse homini sufficiens causa peccati, quod est spiritualis ruina, nisi propria voluntas. Et ideo dicta vel facta alterius hominis possunt esse solum causa imperfecta, aliqualiter inducens ad ruinam. Et propter hoc non dicitur, *dans causam ruinae*, sed, *dans occasionem*, quod significat causam imperfectam, et non

**OBJ. 5**: Further, a man occasions his neighbor's spiritual downfall when he offends or weakens him. Now scandal is condivided with offense and weakness, for the Apostle says (Rom 14:21): *It is good not to eat flesh, and not to drink wine, nor anything whereby thy brother is offended or scandalized, or weakened.* Therefore the aforesaid definition of scandal is unfitting.

**ON THE CONTRARY**, Jerome in expounding Matt. 15:12, *Dost thou know that the Pharisees, when they heard this word*, etc. says: *When we read 'Whosoever shall scandalize,' the sense is 'Whosoever shall, by deed or word, occasion another's spiritual downfall.'*

**I ANSWER THAT,** As Jerome observes, *the Greek skandalon may be rendered offense, downfall, or a stumbling against something.* For when a body, while moving along a path, meets with an obstacle, it may happen to stumble against it, and be disposed to fall down: such an obstacle is a skandalon.

**IN LIKE MANNER**, while going along the spiritual way, a man may be disposed to a spiritual downfall by another's word or deed, in so far, to wit, as one man by his injunction, inducement or example, moves another to sin; and this is scandal properly so called.

Now nothing by its very nature disposes a man to spiritual downfall, except that which has some lack of rectitude, since what is perfectly right, secures man against a fall, instead of conducing to his downfall. Scandal is, therefore, fittingly defined as *something less rightly done or said, that occasions another's spiritual downfall.*

**REPLY OBJ. 1**: The thought or desire of evil lies hidden in the heart, wherefore it does not suggest itself to another man as an obstacle conducing to his spiritual downfall: hence it cannot come under the head of scandal.

**REPLY OBJ. 2**: A thing is said to be less right, not because something else surpasses it in rectitude, but because it has some lack of rectitude, either through being evil in itself, such as sin, or through having an appearance of evil. Thus, for instance, if a man were to sit at meat in the idol's temple (1 Cor 8:10), though this is not sinful in itself, provided it be done with no evil intention, yet, since it has a certain appearance of evil, and a semblance of worshipping the idol, it might occasion another man's spiritual downfall. Hence the Apostle says (1 Thess 5:22): *From all appearance of evil refrain yourselves.* Scandal is therefore fittingly described as something done *less rightly*, so as to comprise both whatever is sinful in itself, and all that has an appearance of evil.

**REPLY OBJ. 3**: As stated above (I-II, Q. 75, AA. 2, 3; I-II, Q. 80, A. 1), nothing can be a sufficient cause of a man's spiritual downfall, which is sin, save his own will. Wherefore another man's words or deeds can only be an imperfect cause, conducing somewhat to that downfall. For this reason scandal is said to afford not a *cause*, but an *occasion*, which is an imperfect, and not always an accidental cause.

semper causam per accidens. Et tamen nihil prohibet in quibusdam definitionibus poni id quod est per accidens, quia id quod est secundum accidens uni potest per se alteri convenire, sicut in definitione fortunae ponitur causa per accidens, in II Physic.

AD QUARTUM dicendum quod dictum vel factum alterius potest esse alteri causa peccandi dupliciter, uno modo, per se; alio modo, per accidens. Per se quidem, quando aliquis suo malo verbo vel facto intendit alium ad peccandum inducere; vel, etiam si ipse hoc non intendat, ipsum factum est tale quod de sui ratione habet ut sit inductivum ad peccandum, puta quod aliquis publice facit peccatum vel quod habet similitudinem peccati. Et tunc ille qui huiusmodi actum facit proprie dat occasionem ruinae, unde vocatur *scandalum activum*. Per accidens autem aliquod verbum vel factum unius est alteri causa peccandi, quando etiam praeter intentionem operantis, et praeter conditionem operis, aliquis male dispositus ex huiusmodi opere inducitur ad peccandum, puta cum aliquis invidet bonis aliorum. Et tunc ille qui facit huiusmodi actum rectum non dat occasionem, quantum in se est, sed alius sumit occasionem, secundum illud ad Rom. VII, *occasione autem accepta*, et cetera. Et ideo hoc est *scandalum passivum* sine activo, quia ille qui recte agit, quantum est de se, non dat occasionem ruinae quam alter patitur. Quandoque ergo contingit quod et sit simul scandalum activum in uno et passivum in altero, puta cum ad inductionem unius alius peccat. Quandoque vero est scandalum activum sine passivo, puta cum aliquis inducit verbo vel facto alium ad peccandum, et ille non consentit. Quandoque vero est scandalum passivum sine activo, sicut iam dictum est.

AD QUINTUM dicendum quod *infirmitas* nominat promptitudinem ad scandalum; *offensio* autem nominat indignationem alicuius contra eum qui peccat, quae potest esse quandoque sine ruina; *scandalum* autem importat ipsam impactionem ad ruinam.

Nor is there any reason why certain definitions should not make mention of things that are accidental, since what is accidental to one, may be proper to something else: thus the accidental cause is mentioned in the definition of chance (*Phys.* ii, 5).

REPLY OBJ. 4: Another's words or deed may be the cause of another's sin in two ways, directly and accidentally. Directly, when a man either intends, by his evil word or deed, to lead another man into sin, or, if he does not so intend, when his deed is of such a nature as to lead another into sin: for instance, when a man publicly commits a sin or does something that has an appearance of sin. In this case he that does such an act does, properly speaking, afford an occasion of another's spiritual downfall, wherefore his act is called *active scandal*. One man's word or deed is the accidental cause of another's sin, when he neither intends to lead him into sin, nor does what is of a nature to lead him into sin, and yet this other one, through being ill-disposed, is led into sin, for instance, into envy of another's good, and then he who does this righteous act, does not, so far as he is concerned, afford an occasion of the other's downfall, but it is this other one who takes the occasion according to Rom. 7:8: *Sin taking occasion by the commandment wrought in me all manner of concupiscence.* Wherefore this is *passive*, without *active scandal*, since he that acts rightly does not, for his own part, afford the occasion of the other's downfall. Sometimes therefore it happens that there is active scandal in the one together with passive scandal in the other, as when one commits a sin being induced thereto by another; sometimes there is active without passive scandal, for instance when one, by word or deed, provokes another to sin, and the latter does not consent; and sometimes there is passive without active scandal, as we have already said.

REPLY OBJ. 5: *Weakness* denotes proneness to scandal; while *offense* signifies resentment against the person who commits a sin, which resentment may be sometimes without spiritual downfall; and *scandal* is the stumbling that results in downfall.

# Article 2

*Whether scandal is a sin?*

AD SECUNDUM SIC PROCEDITUR. Videtur quod scandalum non sit peccatum. Peccata enim non eveniunt ex necessitate, quia omne peccatum est voluntarium, ut supra habitum est. Sed Matth. XVIII dicitur, *necesse est ut veniant scandala*. Ergo scandalum non est peccatum.

PRAETEREA, nullum peccatum procedit ex pietatis affectu, quia *non potest arbor bona fructus malos facere*, ut dicitur Matth. VII. Sed aliquod scandalum est ex pietatis affectu, dicit enim dominus Petro, Matth. XVI, *scandalum mihi es*; ubi dicit Hieronymus quod *error*

OBJECTION 1: It would seem that scandal is not a sin. For sins do not occur from necessity, since all sin is voluntary, as stated above (I-II, Q. 74, AA. 1, 2). Now it is written (Matt 18:7): *It must needs be that scandals come.* Therefore scandal is not a sin.

OBJ. 2: Further, no sin arises from a sense of dutifulness, because *a good tree cannot bring forth evil fruit* (Matt 7:18). But scandal may come from a sense of dutifulness, for Our Lord said to Peter (Matt 16:23): *Thou art a scandal unto Me*, in reference to which words Jerome says

*apostoli, de pietatis affectu veniens, nunquam incentivum videtur esse Diaboli.* Ergo non omne scandalum est peccatum.

**PRAETEREA**, scandalum impactionem quandam importat. Sed non quicumque impingit, cadit. Ergo scandalum potest esse sine peccato, quod est spiritualis casus.

**SED CONTRA** est quod scandalum est *dictum vel factum minus rectum.* Ex hoc autem habet aliquid rationem peccati quod a rectitudine deficit. Ergo scandalum semper est cum peccato.

**RESPONDEO** dicendum quod, sicut iam supra dictum est, duplex est scandalum, scilicet passivum, in eo qui scandalizatur; et activum, in eo qui scandalizat, dans occasionem ruinae. Scandalum igitur passivum semper est peccatum in eo qui scandalizatur, non enim scandalizatur nisi inquantum aliqualiter ruit spirituali ruina, quae est peccatum.

Potest tamen esse scandalum passivum sine peccato eius ex cuius facto aliquis scandalizatur, sicut cum aliquis scandalizatur de his quae alius bene facit. Similiter etiam scandalum activum semper est peccatum in eo qui scandalizat. Quia vel ipsum opus quod facit est peccatum, vel etiam, si habeat speciem peccati, dimittendum est semper propter proximi caritatem, ex qua unusquisque conatur saluti proximi providere; et sic qui non dimittit contra caritatem agit.

Potest tamen esse scandalum activum sine peccato alterius qui scandalizatur, sicut supra dictum est.

**AD PRIMUM** ergo dicendum quod hoc quod dicitur, *necesse est ut veniant scandala,* non est intelligendum de necessitate absoluta, sed de necessitate conditionali, qua scilicet necesse est praescita vel praenuntiata a Deo evenire, si tamen coniunctim accipiatur, ut in primo libro dictum est.

Vel necesse est evenire scandala necessitate finis, quia utilia sunt ad hoc quod *qui probati sunt manifesti fiant.*

Vel necesse est evenire scandala secundum conditionem hominum, qui sibi a peccatis non cavent. Sicut si aliquis medicus, videns aliquos indebita diaeta utentes, dicat, *necesse est tales infirmari,* quod intelligendum est sub hac conditione, si diaetam non mutent. Et similiter necesse est evenire scandala si homines conversationem malam non mutent.

**AD SECUNDUM** dicendum quod scandalum ibi large ponitur pro quolibet impedimento. Volebat enim Petrus Christi passionem impedire, quodam pietatis affectu ad Christum.

**AD TERTIUM** dicendum quod nullus impingit spiritualiter nisi retardetur aliqualiter a processu in via Dei, quod fit saltem per peccatum veniale.

that *the Apostle's error was due to his sense of dutifulness, and such is never inspired by the devil.* Therefore scandal is not always a sin.

**OBJ. 3**: Further, scandal denotes a stumbling. But he that stumbles does not always fall. Therefore scandal, which is a spiritual fall, can be without sin.

**ON THE CONTRARY**, Scandal is *something less rightly said or done.* Now anything that lacks rectitude is a sin. Therefore scandal is always with sin.

**I ANSWER THAT**, As already said (A. 1, ad 4), scandal is of two kinds, passive scandal in the person scandalized, and active scandal in the person who gives scandal, and so occasions a spiritual downfall. Accordingly passive scandal is always a sin in the person scandalized; for he is not scandalized except insofar as he succumbs to a spiritual downfall, and that is a sin.

Yet there can be passive scandal, without sin on the part of the person whose action has occasioned the scandal, as for instance, when a person is scandalized at another's good deed. In like manner active scandal is always a sin in the person who gives scandal, since either what he does is a sin, or if it only have the appearance of sin, it should always be left undone out of that love for our neighbor which binds each one to be solicitous for his neighbor's spiritual welfare; so that if he persist in doing it he acts against charity.

Yet there can be active scandal without sin on the part of the person scandalized, as stated above (A. 1, ad 4).

**REPLY OBJ. 1**: These words, *It must needs be that scandals come,* are to be understood to convey, not the absolute, but the conditional necessity of scandal; in which sense it is necessary that whatever God foresees or foretells must happen, provided it be taken conjointly with such foreknowledge, as explained in the First Part (Q. 14, A. 13, ad 3; Q. 23, A. 6, ad 2).

Or we may say that the necessity of scandals occurring is a necessity of end, because they are useful in order that *they . . . who are reproved may be made manifest* (1 Cor 11:19).

Or scandals must needs occur, seeing the condition of man who fails to shield himself from sin. Thus a physician on seeing a man partaking of unsuitable food might say that such a man *must needs injure his health,* which is to be understood on the condition that he does not change his diet. In like manner it must needs be that scandals come, so long as men fail to change their evil mode of living.

**REPLY OBJ. 2**: In that passage scandal denotes any kind of hindrance: for Peter wished to hinder Our Lord's Passion out of a sense of dutifulness towards Christ.

**REPLY OBJ. 3**: No man stumbles spiritually, without being kept back somewhat from advancing in God's way, and that is at least a venial sin.

# Article 3

*Whether scandal is a special sin?*

AD TERTIUM SIC PROCEDITUR. Videtur quod scandalum non sit speciale peccatum. Scandalum enim est dictum vel factum minus rectum. Sed omne peccatum est huiusmodi. Ergo omne peccatum est scandalum. Non ergo scandalum est speciale peccatum.

PRAETEREA, omne speciale peccatum, sive omnis specialis iniustitia, invenitur separatim ab aliis; ut dicitur in V Ethic. Sed scandalum non invenitur separatim ab aliis peccatis. Ergo scandalum non est speciale peccatum.

PRAETEREA, omne speciale peccatum constituitur secundum aliquid quod dat speciem morali actui. Sed ratio scandali constituitur per hoc quod coram aliis peccatur. In manifesto autem peccare, etsi sit circumstantia aggravans, non videtur constituere peccati speciem. Ergo scandalum non est speciale peccatum.

SED CONTRA, speciali virtuti speciale peccatum opponitur. Sed scandalum opponitur speciali virtuti, scilicet caritati, dicitur enim Rom. XIV, *si propter cibum frater tuus contristatur, iam non secundum caritatem ambulas*. Ergo scandalum est speciale peccatum.

RESPONDEO dicendum quod, sicut supra dictum est, duplex est scandalum, activum scilicet, et passivum. Passivum quidem scandalum non potest esse speciale peccatum, quia ex dicto vel facto alterius aliquem ruere contingit secundum quodcumque genus peccati; nec hoc ipsum quod est occasionem peccandi sumere ex dicto vel facto alterius specialem rationem peccati constituit, quia non importat specialem deformitatem speciali virtuti oppositam.

Scandalum autem activum potest accipi dupliciter, per se scilicet, et per accidens. Per accidens quidem, quando est praeter intentionem agentis, ut puta cum aliquis suo facto vel verbo inordinato non intendit alteri dare occasionem ruinae, sed solum suae satisfacere voluntati. Et sic etiam scandalum activum non est peccatum speciale, quia quod est per accidens non constituit speciem.

Per se autem est activum scandalum quando aliquis suo inordinato dicto vel facto intendit alium trahere ad peccatum. Et sic ex intentione specialis finis sortitur rationem specialis peccati, finis enim dat speciem in moralibus, ut supra dictum est. Unde sicut furtum est speciale peccatum, aut homicidium, propter speciale nocumentum proximi quod intenditur; ita etiam scandalum est speciale peccatum, propter hoc quod intenditur speciale proximi nocumentum. Et opponitur

OBJECTION 1: It would seem that scandal is not a special sin. For scandal is *something said or done less rightly*. But this applies to every kind of sin. Therefore every sin is a scandal, and consequently, scandal is not a special sin.

OBJ. 2: Further, every special kind of sin, or every special kind of injustice, may be found separately from other kinds, as stated in *Ethic.* v, 3, 5. But scandal is not to be found separately from other sins. Therefore it is not a special kind of sin.

OBJ. 3: Further, every special sin is constituted by something which specifies the moral act. But the notion of scandal consists in its being something done in the presence of others: and the fact of a sin being committed openly, though it is an aggravating circumstance, does not seem to constitute the species of a sin. Therefore scandal is not a special sin.

ON THE CONTRARY, A special virtue has a special sin opposed to it. But scandal is opposed to a special virtue, viz. charity. For it is written (Rom 14:15): *If, because of thy meat, thy brother be grieved, thou walkest not now according to charity.* Therefore scandal is a special sin.

I ANSWER THAT, As stated above (A. 2), scandal is twofold, active and passive. Passive scandal cannot be a special sin, because through another's word or deed a man may fall into any kind of sin: and the fact that a man takes occasion to sin from another's word or deed, does not constitute a special kind of sin, because it does not imply a special deformity in opposition to a special virtue.

On the other hand, active scandal may be understood in two ways, directly and accidentally. The scandal is accidental when it is beside the agent's intention, as when a man does not intend, by his inordinate deed or word, to occasion another's spiritual downfall, but merely to satisfy his own will. In such a case even active scandal is not a special sin, because a species is not constituted by that which is accidental.

Active scandal is direct when a man intends, by his inordinate word or deed, to draw another into sin, and then it becomes a special kind of sin on account of the intention of a special kind of end, because moral actions take their species from their end, as stated above (I-II, Q. 1, A. 3; Q. 18, AA. 4, 6). Hence, just as theft and murder are special kinds of sin, on account of their denoting the intention of doing a special injury to one's neighbor: so too, scandal is a special kind of sin, because thereby a man intends a special

directe correctioni fraternae, in qua attenditur specialis nocumenti remotio.

AD PRIMUM ergo dicendum quod omne peccatum potest materialiter se habere ad scandalum activum. Sed formalem rationem specialis peccati potest habere ex intentione finis, ut dictum est.

AD SECUNDUM dicendum quod scandalum activum potest inveniri separatim ab aliis peccatis, ut puta cum aliquis proximum scandalizat facto quod de se non est peccatum, sed habet speciem mali.

AD TERTIUM dicendum quod scandalum non habet rationem specialis peccati ex praedicta circumstantia, sed ex intentione finis, ut dictum est.

harm to his neighbor, and it is directly opposed to fraternal correction, whereby a man intends the removal of a special kind of harm.

REPLY OBJ. 1: Any sin may be the matter of active scandal, but it may derive the formal aspect of a special sin from the end intended, as stated above.

REPLY OBJ. 2: Active scandal can be found separate from other sins, as when a man scandalizes his neighbor by a deed which is not a sin in itself, but has an appearance of evil.

REPLY OBJ. 3: Scandal does not derive the species of a special sin from the circumstance in question, but from the intention of the end, as stated above.

# Article 4

## Whether scandal is a mortal sin?

AD QUARTUM SIC PROCEDITUR. Videtur quod scandalum sit peccatum mortale. Omne enim peccatum quod contrariatur caritati est peccatum mortale, ut supra dictum est. Sed scandalum contrariatur caritati, ut dictum est. Ergo scandalum est peccatum mortale.

PRAETEREA, nulli peccato debetur poena damnationis aeternae nisi mortali. Sed scandalo debetur poena damnationis aeternae, secundum illud Matth. XVIII, *qui scandalizaverit unum de pusillis istis qui in me credunt, expedit ei ut suspendatur mola asinaria in collo eius et demergatur in profundum maris.* Quia, ut dicit Hieronymus, *multo melius est pro culpa brevem recipere poenam quam aeternis servari cruciatibus.* Ergo scandalum est peccatum mortale.

PRAETEREA, omne peccatum quod in Deum committitur est peccatum mortale, quia solum peccatum mortale avertit hominem a Deo. Sed scandalum est peccatum in Deum, dicit enim apostolus, I ad Cor. VIII, *percutientes conscientiam fratrum infirmam, in Christum peccatis.* Ergo scandalum semper est peccatum mortale.

SED CONTRA, inducere aliquem ad peccandum venialiter potest esse peccatum veniale. Sed hoc pertinet ad rationem scandali. Ergo scandalum potest esse peccatum veniale.

RESPONDEO dicendum quod, sicut supra dictum est, scandalum importat impactionem quandam, per quam aliquis disponitur ad ruinam. Et ideo scandalum passivum quandoque quidem potest esse peccatum veniale, quasi habens impactionem tantum, puta cum aliquis ex inordinato dicto vel facto alterius commovetur motu venialis peccati. Quandoque vero est peccatum mortale, quasi habens cum impactione ruinam, puta cum aliquis ex inordinato dicto vel facto alterius procedit usque ad peccatum mortale.

OBJECTION 1: It would seem that scandal is a mortal sin. For every sin that is contrary to charity is a mortal sin, as stated above (Q. 24, A. 12; Q. 35, A. 3). But scandal is contrary to charity, as stated above (AA. 2, 3). Therefore scandal is a mortal sin.

OBJ. 2: Further, no sin, save mortal sin, deserves the punishment of eternal damnation. But scandal deserves the punishment of eternal damnation, according to Matt. 18:6: *He that shall scandalize one of these little ones, that believe in Me, it were better for him that a mill-stone should be hanged about his neck, and that he should be drowned in the depth of the sea.* For, as Jerome says on this passage, *it is much better to receive a brief punishment for a fault, than to await everlasting torments.* Therefore scandal is a mortal sin.

OBJ. 3: Further, every sin committed against God is a mortal sin, because mortal sin alone turns man away from God. Now scandal is a sin against God, for the Apostle says (1 Cor 8:12): *When you wound the weak conscience of the brethren, you sin against Christ.* Therefore scandal is always a mortal sin.

ON THE CONTRARY, It may be a venial sin to lead a person into venial sin: and yet this would be to give scandal. Therefore scandal may be a venial sin.

I ANSWER THAT, As stated above (A. 1), scandal denotes a stumbling whereby a person is disposed to a spiritual downfall. Consequently passive scandal may sometimes be a venial sin, when it consists in a stumbling and nothing more; for instance, when a person is disturbed by a movement of venial sin occasioned by another's inordinate word or deed: while sometimes it is a mortal sin, when the stumbling results in a downfall, for instance, when a person goes so far as to commit a mortal sin through another's inordinate word or deed.

Scandalum autem activum, si sit quidem per accidens, potest esse quandoque quidem peccatum veniale, puta cum aliquis vel actum peccati venialis committit; vel actum qui non est secundum se peccatum sed habet aliquam speciem mali, cum aliqua levi indiscretione. Quandoque vero est peccatum mortale, sive quia committit actum peccati mortalis; sive quia contemnit salutem proximi, ut pro ea conservanda non praetermittat aliquis facere quod sibi libuerit. Si vero scandalum activum sit per se, puta cum intendit inducere alium ad peccandum, si quidem intendat inducere ad peccandum mortaliter, est peccatum mortale. Et similiter si intendat inducere ad peccandum venialiter per actum peccati mortalis. Si vero intendat inducere proximum ad peccandum venialiter per actum peccati venialis, est peccatum veniale.

**ET PER HOC** patet responsio ad obiecta.

Active scandal, if it be accidental, may sometimes be a venial sin; for instance, when, through a slight indiscretion, a person either commits a venial sin, or does something that is not a sin in itself, but has some appearance of evil. On the other hand, it is sometimes a mortal sin, either because a person commits a mortal sin, or because he has such contempt for his neighbor's spiritual welfare that he declines, for the sake of procuring it, to forego doing what he wishes to do. But in the case of active direct scandal, as when a person intends to lead another into sin, if he intends to lead him into mortal sin, his own sin will be mortal; and in like manner if he intends by committing a mortal sin himself, to lead another into venial sin; whereas if he intends, by committing a venial sin, to lead another into venial sin, there will be a venial sin of scandal.

**AND THIS SUFFICES** for the Replies to the Objections.

# Article 5

*Whether passive scandal may happen even to the perfect?*

**AD QUINTUM SIC PROCEDITUR**. Videtur quod scandalum passivum possit etiam in perfectos cadere. Christus enim fuit maxime perfectus. Sed ipse dixit Petro, *scandalum mihi es*. Ergo multo magis alii perfecti possunt scandalum pati.

**PRAETEREA**, scandalum importat impedimentum aliquod quod alicui opponitur in vita spirituali. Sed etiam perfecti viri in processibus spiritualis vitae impediri possunt, secundum illud I ad Thess. II, *voluimus venire ad vos, ego quidem Paulus, semel et iterum, sed impedivit nos Satanas*. Ergo etiam perfecti viri possunt scandalum pati.

**PRAETEREA**, etiam in perfectis viris peccata venialia inveniri possunt, secundum illud I Ioan. I, *si dixerimus quoniam peccatum non habemus, ipsi nos seducimus*. Sed scandalum passivum non semper est peccatum mortale, sed quandoque veniale, ut dictum est. Ergo scandalum passivum potest in perfectis viris inveniri.

**SED CONTRA** est quod super illud Matth. XVIII, *qui scandalizaverit unum de pusillis istis*, dicit Hieronymus, *nota quod qui scandalizatur parvulus est, maiores enim scandala non recipiunt*.

**RESPONDEO** dicendum quod scandalum passivum importat quandam commotionem animi a bono in eo qui scandalum patitur. Nullus autem commovetur qui rei immobili firmiter inhaeret. Maiores autem, sive perfecti, soli Deo inhaerent, cuius est immutabilis bonitas, quia etsi inhaereant suis praelatis, non inhaerent eis nisi inquantum illi inhaerent Christo, secundum illud I ad Cor. IV, *imitatores mei estote, sicut et ego Christi*. Un-

**OBJECTION 1**: It would seem that passive scandal may happen even to the perfect. For Christ was supremely perfect: and yet He said to Peter (Matt 16:23): *Thou art a scandal to Me*. Much more therefore can other perfect men suffer scandal.

**OBJ. 2**: Further, scandal denotes an obstacle which is put in a person's spiritual way. Now even perfect men can be hindered in their progress along the spiritual way, according to 1 Thess. 2:18: *We would have come to you, I Paul indeed, once and again; but Satan hath hindered us.* Therefore even perfect men can suffer scandal.

**OBJ. 3**: Further, even perfect men are liable to venial sins, according to 1 John 1:8: *If we say that we have no sin, we deceive ourselves.* Now passive scandal is not always a mortal sin, but is sometimes venial, as stated above (A. 4). Therefore passive scandal may be found in perfect men.

**ON THE CONTRARY**, Jerome, in commenting on Matt. 18:6, *He that shall scandalize one of these little ones*, says: *Observe that it is the little one that is scandalized, for the elders do not take scandal.*

**I ANSWER THAT**, Passive scandal implies that the mind of the person who takes scandal is unsettled in its adherence to good. Now no man can be unsettled, who adheres firmly to something immovable. The elders, i.e., the perfect, adhere to God alone, Whose goodness is unchangeable, for though they adhere to their superiors, they do so only insofar as these adhere to Christ, according to 1 Cor. 4:16: *Be ye followers of me, as I also am of Christ.* Wherefore, however

de quantumcumque videant alios inordinate se habere dictis vel factis, ipsi a sua rectitudine non recedunt, secundum illud Psalm., *qui confidunt in domino, sicut mons Sion, non commovebitur in aeternum qui habitat in Ierusalem.* Et ideo in his qui perfecte Deo adhaerent per amorem scandalum non invenitur, secundum illud Psalm., *pax multa diligentibus legem tuam, et non est illis scandalum.*

**AD PRIMUM** ergo dicendum quod, sicut supra dictum est, scandalum large ponitur ibi pro quolibet impedimento. Unde dominus Petro dicit, *scandalum mihi es,* quia nitebatur eius propositum impedire circa passionem subeundam.

**AD SECUNDUM** dicendum quod in exterioribus actibus perfecti viri possunt impediri. Sed in interiori voluntate per dicta vel facta aliorum non impediuntur quominus tendant in Deum, secundum illud Rom. VIII, *neque mors neque vita poterit nos separare a caritate Dei.*

**AD TERTIUM** dicendum quod perfecti viri ex infirmitate carnis incidunt interdum in aliqua peccata venialia, non autem ex aliorum dictis vel factis scandalizantur secundum veram scandali rationem. Sed potest esse in eis quaedam appropinquatio ad scandalum, secundum illud Psalm., *mei pene moti sunt pedes.*

much others may appear to them to conduct themselves ill in word or deed, they themselves do not stray from their righteousness, according to Ps. 124:1: *They that trust in the Lord shall be as Mount Zion: he shall not be moved for ever that dwelleth in Jerusalem.* Therefore scandal is not found in those who adhere to God perfectly by love, according to Ps. 118:165: *Much peace have they that love Thy law, and to them there is no stumbling-block (scandalum).*

**REPLY OBJ. 1:** As stated above (A. 2, ad 2), in this passage, scandal is used in a broad sense, to denote any kind of hindrance. Hence Our Lord said to Peter: *Thou art a scandal to Me,* because he was endeavoring to weaken Our Lord's purpose of undergoing His Passion.

**REPLY OBJ. 2:** Perfect men may be hindered in the performance of external actions. But they are not hindered by the words or deeds of others, from tending to God in the internal acts of the will, according to Rom. 8:38, 39: *Neither death, nor life . . . shall be able to separate us from the love of God.*

**REPLY OBJ. 3:** Perfect men sometimes fall into venial sins through the weakness of the flesh; but they are not scandalized (taking scandal in its true sense), by the words or deeds of others, although there can be an approach to scandal in them, according to Ps. 72:2: *My feet were almost moved.*

# Article 6

*Whether active scandal can be found in the perfect?*

**AD SEXTUM SIC PROCEDITUR.** Videtur quod scandalum activum possit inveniri in viris perfectis. Passio enim est effectus actionis. Sed ex dictis vel factis perfectorum aliqui passive scandalizantur, secundum illud Matth. XV, *scis quia Pharisaei, audito hoc verbo, scandalizati sunt?* Ergo in perfectis viris potest inveniri scandalum activum.

**PRAETEREA,** Petrus post acceptum spiritum sanctum in statu perfectorum erat. Sed postea gentiles scandalizavit, dicitur enim ad Gal. II, *cum vidissem quod non recte ambularent ad veritatem Evangelii, dixi Cephae,* idest Petro, *coram omnibus, si tu cum Iudaeus sis, gentiliter et non Iudaice vivis, quomodo gentes cogis iudaizare?* Ergo scandalum activum potest esse in viris perfectis.

**PRAETEREA,** scandalum activum quandoque est peccatum veniale. Sed peccata venialia possunt etiam esse in viris perfectis. Ergo scandalum activum potest esse in viris perfectis.

**SED CONTRA,** plus repugnat perfectioni scandalum activum quam passivum. Sed scandalum passivum non

**OBJECTION 1:** It would seem that active scandal can be found in the perfect. For passion is the effect of action. Now some are scandalized passively by the words or deeds of the perfect, according to Matt. 15:12: *Dost thou know that the Pharisees, when they heard this word, were scandalized?* Therefore active scandal can be found in the perfect.

**OBJ. 2:** Further, Peter, after receiving the Holy Spirit, was in the state of the perfect. Yet afterwards he scandalized the gentiles: for it is written (Gal 2:14): *When I saw that they walked not uprightly unto the truth of the Gospel, I said to Cephas,* i.e., Peter, *before them all: If thou being a Jew, livest after the manner of the gentiles, and not as the Jews do, how dost thou compel the gentiles to live as do the Jews?* Therefore active scandal can be in the perfect.

**OBJ. 3:** Further, active scandal is sometimes a venial sin. But venial sins may be in perfect men. Therefore active scandal may be in perfect men.

**ON THE CONTRARY,** Active scandal is more opposed to perfection, than passive scandal. But passive scandal cannot

potest esse in viris perfectis. Ergo multo minus scandalum activum.

**RESPONDEO** dicendum quod scandalum activum proprie est cum aliquis tale aliquid dicit vel facit quod de se tale est ut alterum natum sit inducere ad ruinam, quod quidem est solum id quod inordinate fit vel dicitur. Ad perfectos autem pertinet ea quae agunt secundum regulam rationis ordinare, secundum illud I ad Cor. XIV, *omnia honeste et secundum ordinem fiant in vobis.* Et praecipue hanc cautelam adhibent in his in quibus non solum ipsi offenderent, sed etiam aliis offensionem pararent. Et si quidem in eorum manifestis dictis vel factis aliquid ab hac moderatione desit, hoc provenit ex infirmitate humana, secundum quam a perfectione deficiunt. Non tamen intantum deficiunt ut multum ab ordine rationis recedatur, sed modicum et leviter, quod non est tam magnum ut ex hoc rationabiliter possit ab alio sumi peccandi occasio.

**AD PRIMUM** ergo dicendum quod scandalum passivum semper ab aliquo activo causatur, sed non semper ab aliquo scandalo activo alterius, sed eiusdem qui scandalizatur; quia scilicet ipse seipsum scandalizat.

**AD SECUNDUM** dicendum quod Petrus peccavit quidem, et reprehensibilis fuit, secundum sententiam Augustini et ipsius Pauli, subtrahens se a gentilibus ut vitaret scandalum Iudaeorum, quia hoc incaute aliqualiter faciebat, ita quod ex hoc gentiles ad fidem conversi scandalizabantur. Non tamen factum Petri erat tam grave peccatum quod merito possent alii scandalizari. Unde patiebantur scandalum passivum, non autem erat in Petro scandalum activum.

**AD TERTIUM** dicendum quod peccata venialia perfectorum praecipue consistunt in subitis motibus, qui, cum sint occulti, scandalizare non possunt. Si qua vero etiam in exterioribus dictis vel factis venialia peccata committant, tam levia sunt ut de se scandalizandi virtutem non habeant.

be in the perfect. Much less, therefore, can active scandal be in them.

**I ANSWER THAT,** Active scandal, properly so called, occurs when a man says or does a thing which in itself is of a nature to occasion another's spiritual downfall, and that is only when what he says or does is inordinate. Now it belongs to the perfect to direct all their actions according to the rule of reason, as stated in 1 Cor. 14:40: *Let all things be done decently and according to order*; and they are careful to do this in those matters chiefly wherein not only would they do wrong, but would also be to others an occasion of wrongdoing. And if indeed they fail in this moderation in such words or deeds as come to the knowledge of others, this has its origin in human weakness wherein they fall short of perfection. Yet they do not fall short so far as to stray far from the order of reason, but only a little and in some slight matter: and this is not so grave that anyone can reasonably take therefrom an occasion for committing sin.

**REPLY OBJ. 1:** Passive scandal is always due to some active scandal; yet this active scandal is not always in another, but in the very person who is scandalized, because, to wit, he scandalizes himself.

**REPLY OBJ. 2:** In the opinion of Augustine (*Ep. xxviii, xl, lxxxii*) and of Paul also, Peter sinned and was to be blamed, in withdrawing from the gentiles in order to avoid the scandal of the Jews, because he did this somewhat imprudently, so that the gentiles who had been converted to the faith were scandalized. Nevertheless Peter's action was not so grave a sin as to give others sufficient ground for scandal. Hence they were guilty of passive scandal, while there was no active scandal in Peter.

**REPLY OBJ. 3:** The venial sins of the perfect consist chiefly in sudden movements, which being hidden cannot give scandal. If, however, they commit any venial sins even in their external words or deeds, these are so slight as to be insufficient in themselves to give scandal.

# Article 7

*Whether spiritual goods should be foregone on account of scandal?*

**AD SEPTIMUM SIC PROCEDITUR.** Videtur quod bona spiritualia sint propter scandalum dimittenda. Augustinus enim, in libro contra epistolam Parmen., docet quod ubi schismatis periculum timetur, a punitione peccatorum cessandum est. Sed punitio peccatorum est quoddam spirituale, cum sit actus iustitiae. Ergo bonum spirituale est propter scandalum dimittendum.

**PRAETEREA,** sacra doctrina maxime videtur esse spiritualis. Sed ab ea est cessandum propter scandalum, secundum illud Matth. VII, *nolite sanctum dare canibus, neque margaritas vestras spargatis ante porcos,*

**OBJECTION 1:** It would seem that spiritual goods ought to be foregone on account of scandal. For Augustine (*Contra Ep. Parmen.* iii, 2) teaches that punishment for sin should cease, when the peril of schism is feared. But punishment of sins is a spiritual good, since it is an act of justice. Therefore a spiritual good is to be foregone on account of scandal.

**OBJ. 2:** Further, sacred doctrine is a most spiritual thing. Yet one ought to desist therefrom on account of scandal, according to Matt. 7:6: *Give not that which is holy to dogs, neither cast ye your pearls before swine lest . . . turning*

*ne conversi dirumpant vos.* Ergo bonum spirituale est dimittendum propter scandalum.

**Praeterea,** correctio fraterna, cum sit actus caritatis, est quoddam spirituale bonum. Sed interdum ex caritate dimittitur, ad vitandum scandalum aliorum; ut Augustinus dicit, in I de Civ. Dei. Ergo bonum spirituale est propter scandalum dimittendum.

**Praeterea,** Hieronymus dicit quod dimittendum est propter scandalum omne quod potest praetermitti salva triplici veritate, scilicet *vitae, iustitiae et doctrinae.* Sed impletio consiliorum, et largitio eleemosynarum, multoties potest praetermitti salva triplici veritate praedicta, alioquin semper peccarent omnes qui praetermittunt. Et tamen haec sunt maxima inter spiritualia opera. Ergo spiritualia opera debent praetermitti propter scandalum.

**Praeterea,** vitatio cuiuslibet peccati est quoddam spirituale bonum, quia quodlibet peccatum affert peccanti aliquod spirituale detrimentum. Sed videtur quod pro scandalo proximi vitando debeat aliquis quandoque peccare venialiter, puta cum peccando venialiter impedit peccatum mortale alterius, debet enim homo impedire damnationem proximi quantum potest sine detrimento propriae salutis, quae non tollitur per peccatum veniale. Ergo aliquod bonum spirituale debet homo praetermittere propter scandalum vitandum.

**Sed contra** est quod Gregorius dicit, super Ezech., *si de veritate scandalum sumitur, utilius nasci permittitur scandalum quam veritas relinquatur.* Sed bona spiritualia maxime pertinent ad veritatem. Ergo bona spiritualia non sunt propter scandalum dimittenda.

**Respondeo** dicendum quod, cum duplex sit scandalum, activum scilicet et passivum, quaestio ista non habet locum de scandalo activo, quia cum scandalum activum sit dictum vel factum minus rectum, nihil est cum scandalo activo faciendum. Habet autem locum quaestio si intelligatur de scandalo passivo. Considerandum est igitur quid sit dimittendum ne alius scandalizetur. Est autem in spiritualibus bonis distinguendum. Nam quaedam horum sunt de necessitate salutis, quae praetermitti non possunt sine peccato mortali. Manifestum est autem quod nullus debet mortaliter peccare ut alterius peccatum impediat, quia secundum ordinem caritatis plus debet homo suam salutem spiritualem diligere quam alterius. Et ideo ea quae sunt de necessitate salutis praetermitti non debent propter scandalum vitandum.

In his autem spiritualibus bonis quae non sunt de necessitate salutis videtur distinguendum. Quia scandalum quod ex eis oritur quandoque ex malitia procedit, cum scilicet aliqui volunt impedire huiusmodi spiritualia bona, scandala concitando, et hoc est scandalum Pharisaeorum, qui de doctrina domini scandalizabantur. Quod esse contemnendum dominus docet, Matth. XV. Quandoque vero scandalum procedit ex infirmitate

*upon you, they tear you.* Therefore a spiritual good should be foregone on account of scandal.

**Obj. 3:** Further, since fraternal correction is an act of charity, it is a spiritual good. Yet sometimes it is omitted out of charity, in order to avoid giving scandal to others, as Augustine observes (*De Civ. Dei* i, 9). Therefore a spiritual good should be foregone on account of scandal.

**Obj. 4:** Further, Jerome says that in order to avoid scandal we should forego whatever it is possible to omit without prejudice to the threefold truth, i.e., *the truth of life, of justice and of doctrine.* Now the observance of the counsels, and the bestowal of alms may often be omitted without prejudice to the aforesaid threefold truth, else whoever omitted them would always be guilty of sin, and yet such things are the greatest of spiritual works. Therefore spiritual works should be omitted on account of scandal.

**Obj. 5:** Further, the avoidance of any sin is a spiritual good, since any sin brings spiritual harm to the sinner. Now it seems that one ought sometimes to commit a venial sin in order to avoid scandalizing one's neighbor, for instance, when by sinning venially, one would prevent someone else from committing a mortal sin: because one is bound to hinder the damnation of one's neighbor as much as one can without prejudice to one's own salvation, which is not precluded by a venial sin. Therefore one ought to forego a spiritual good in order to avoid scandal.

**On the contrary,** Gregory says (*Hom. Super Ezech.* vii): *If people are scandalized at the truth, it is better to allow the birth of scandal, than to abandon the truth.* Now spiritual goods belong, above all others, to the truth. Therefore spiritual goods are not to be foregone on account of scandal.

**I answer that,** Whereas scandal is twofold, active and passive, the present question does not apply to active scandal, for since active scandal is *something said or done less rightly,* nothing ought to be done that implies active scandal. The question does, however, apply to passive scandal, and accordingly we have to see what ought to be foregone in order to avoid scandal. Now a distinction must be made in spiritual goods. For some of them are necessary for salvation, and cannot be foregone without mortal sin: and it is evident that no man ought to commit a mortal sin, in order to prevent another from sinning, because according to the order of charity, a man ought to love his own spiritual welfare more than another's. Therefore one ought not to forego that which is necessary for salvation, in order to avoid giving scandal.

Again a distinction seems necessary among spiritual things which are not necessary for salvation: because the scandal which arises from such things sometimes proceeds from malice, for instance when a man wishes to hinder those spiritual goods by stirring up scandal. This is the *scandal of the Pharisees,* who were scandalized at Our Lord's teaching: and Our Lord teaches (Matt 15:14) that we ought to treat such like scandal with contempt. Sometimes scan-

vel ignorantia, et huiusmodi est scandalum pusillorum. Propter quod sunt spiritualia opera vel occultanda, vel etiam interdum differenda, ubi periculum non imminet, quousque, reddita ratione, huiusmodi scandalum cesset. Si autem post redditam rationem huiusmodi scandalum duret, iam videtur ex malitia esse, et sic propter ipsum non sunt huiusmodi spiritualia opera dimittenda.

**AD PRIMUM** ergo dicendum quod poenarum inflictio non est propter se expetenda, sed poenae infliguntur ut medicinae quaedam ad cohibendum peccata. Et ideo intantum habent rationem iustitiae inquantum per eas peccata cohibentur. Si autem per inflictionem poenarum manifestum sit plura et maiora peccata sequi, tunc poenarum inflictio non continebitur sub iustitia. Et in hoc casu loquitur Augustinus, quando scilicet ex excommunicatione aliquorum imminet periculum schismatis, tunc enim excommunicationem ferre non pertineret ad veritatem iustitiae.

**AD SECUNDUM** dicendum quod circa doctrinam duo sunt consideranda, scilicet veritas quae docetur; et ipse actus docendi. Quorum primum est de necessitate salutis, ut scilicet contrarium veritati non doceat, sed veritatem secundum congruentiam temporis et personarum proponat ille cui incumbit docendi officium. Et ideo propter nullum scandalum quod sequi videatur debet homo, praetermissa veritate, falsitatem docere. Sed ipse actus docendi inter spirituales eleemosynas computatur, ut supra dictum est. Et ideo eadem ratio est de doctrina et de aliis misericordiae operibus, de quibus postea dicetur.

**AD TERTIUM** dicendum quod correctio fraterna, sicut supra dictum est, ordinatur ad emendationem fratris. Et ideo intantum computanda est inter spiritualia bona inquantum hoc consequi potest. Quod non contingit si ex correctione frater scandalizetur. Et ideo si propter scandalum correctio dimittatur, non dimittitur spirituale bonum.

**AD QUARTUM** dicendum quod in veritate *vitae, doctrinae et iustitiae* non solum comprehenditur id quod est de necessitate salutis, sed etiam id per quod perfectius pervenitur ad salutem, secundum illud I ad Cor. XII, *aemulamini charismata meliora.* Unde etiam consilia non sunt simpliciter praetermittenda, nec etiam misericordiae opera, propter scandalum, sed sunt interdum occultanda vel differenda propter scandalum pusillorum, ut dictum est. Quandoque tamen consiliorum observatio et impletio operum misericordiae sunt de necessitate salutis. Quod patet in his qui iam voverunt consilia; et in his quibus ex debito imminet defectibus aliorum subvenire, vel in temporalibus, puta pascendo esurientem, vel in spiritualibus, puta docendo igno-

dal proceeds from weakness or ignorance, and such is the *scandal of little ones*. In order to avoid this kind of scandal, spiritual goods ought to be either concealed, or sometimes even deferred (if this can be done without incurring immediate danger), until the matter being explained the scandal cease. If, however, the scandal continue after the matter has been explained, it would seem to be due to malice, and then it would no longer be right to forego that spiritual good in order to avoid such like scandal.

**REPLY OBJ. 1**: In the infliction of punishment it is not the punishment itself that is the end in view, but its medicinal properties in checking sin; wherefore punishment partakes of the nature of justice, insofar as it checks sin. But if it is evident that the infliction of punishment will result in more numerous and more grievous sins being committed, the infliction of punishment will no longer be a part of justice. It is in this sense that Augustine is speaking, when, to wit, the excommunication of a few threatens to bring about the danger of a schism, for in that case it would be contrary to the truth of justice to pronounce excommunication.

**REPLY OBJ. 2**: With regard to a man's doctrine two points must be considered, namely, the truth which is taught, and the act of teaching. The first of these is necessary for salvation, to wit, that he whose duty it is to teach should not teach what is contrary to the truth, and that he should teach the truth according to the requirements of times and persons: wherefore on no account ought he to suppress the truth and teach error in order to avoid any scandal that might ensue. But the act itself of teaching is one of the spiritual almsdeeds, as stated above (Q. 32, A. 2), and so the same is to be said of it as of the other works of mercy, of which we shall speak further on (ad 4).

**REPLY OBJ. 3**: As stated above (Q. 33, A. 1), fraternal correction aims at the correction of a brother, wherefore it is to be reckoned among spiritual goods insofar as this end can be obtained, which is not the case if the brother be scandalized through being corrected. And so, if the correction be omitted in order to avoid scandal, no spiritual good is foregone.

**REPLY OBJ. 4**: The truth *of life, of doctrine, and of justice* comprises not only whatever is necessary for salvation, but also whatever is a means of obtaining salvation more perfectly, according to 1 Cor. 12:31: *Be zealous for the better gifts.* Wherefore neither the counsels nor even the works of mercy are to be altogether omitted in order to avoid scandal; but sometimes they should be concealed or deferred, on account of the scandal of the little ones, as stated above. Sometimes, however, the observance of the counsels and the fulfilment of the works of mercy are necessary for salvation. This may be seen in the case of those who have vowed to keep the counsels, and of those whose duty it is to relieve the wants of others, either in temporal matters (as by feeding the hungry), or in spiritual matters (as by

rantem; sive huiusmodi fiant debita propter iniunctum officium, ut patet in praelatis, sive propter necessitatem indigentis. Et tunc eadem ratio est de huiusmodi sicut de aliis quae sunt de necessitate salutis.

**AD QUINTUM** dicendum quod quidam dixerunt quod peccatum veniale est committendum propter vitandum scandalum. Sed hoc implicat contraria, si enim faciendum est, iam non est malum neque peccatum; nam peccatum non potest esse eligibile. Contingit tamen aliquid propter aliquam circumstantiam non esse peccatum veniale quod, illa circumstantia sublata, peccatum veniale esset, sicut verbum iocosum est peccatum veniale quando absque utilitate dicitur; si autem ex causa rationabili proferatur, non est otiosum neque peccatum. Quamvis autem per peccatum veniale gratia non tollatur, per quam est hominis salus; inquantum tamen veniale disponit ad mortale, vergit in detrimentum salutis.

instructing the ignorant), whether such duties arise from their being enjoined as in the case of prelates, or from the need on the part of the person in want; and then the same applies to these things as to others that are necessary for salvation.

**REPLY OBJ. 5**: Some have said that one ought to commit a venial sin in order to avoid scandal. But this implies a contradiction, since if it ought to be done, it is no longer evil or sinful, for a sin cannot be a matter of choice. It may happen however that, on account of some circumstance, something is not a venial sin, though it would be were it not for that circumstance: thus an idle word is a venial sin, when it is uttered uselessly; yet if it be uttered for a reasonable cause, it is neither idle nor sinful. And though venial sin does not deprive a man of grace which is his means of salvation, yet, insofar as it disposes him to mortal sin, it tends to the loss of salvation.

# Article 8

*Whether temporal goods should be foregone on account of scandal?*

**AD OCTAVUM SIC PROCEDITUR.** Videtur quod temporalia sint dimittenda propter scandalum. Magis enim debemus diligere spiritualem salutem proximi, quae impeditur per scandalum, quam quaecumque temporalia bona. Sed id quod minus diligimus dimittimus propter id quod magis diligimus. Ergo temporalia magis debemus dimittere ad vitandum scandalum proximorum.

**PRAETEREA**, secundum regulam Hieronymi, omnia quae possunt praetermitti salva triplici veritate, sunt propter scandalum dimittenda. Sed temporalia possunt praetermitti salva triplici veritate. Ergo sunt propter scandalum dimittenda.

**PRAETEREA**, in temporalibus bonis nihil est magis necessarium quam cibus. Sed cibus est praetermittendus propter scandalum, secundum illud Rom. XIV, *noli cibo tuo illum perdere pro quo Christus mortuus est.* Ergo multo magis omnia alia temporalia sunt propter scandalum dimittenda.

**PRAETEREA**, temporalia nullo convenientiori modo conservare aut recuperare possumus quam per iudicium. Sed iudiciis uti non licet, et praecipue cum scandalo, dicitur enim Matth. V, *ei qui vult tecum in iudicio contendere et tunicam tuam tollere, dimitte ei et pallium*; et I ad Cor. VI, *iam quidem omnino delictum est in vobis quod iudicia habetis inter vos. Quare non magis iniuriam accipitis? Quare non magis fraudem patimini?*

**OBJECTION 1**: It would seem that temporal goods should be foregone on account of scandal. For we ought to love our neighbor's spiritual welfare which is hindered by scandal, more than any temporal goods whatever. But we forego what we love less for the sake of what we love more. Therefore we should forego temporal goods in order to avoid scandalizing our neighbor.

**OBJ. 2**: Further, according to Jerome's rule, whatever can be foregone without prejudice to the threefold truth, should be omitted in order to avoid scandal. Now temporal goods can be foregone without prejudice to the threefold truth. Therefore they should be foregone in order to avoid scandal.

**OBJ. 3**: Further, no temporal good is more necessary than food. But we ought to forego taking food on account of scandal, according to Rom. 14:15: *Destroy not him with thy meat for whom Christ died.* Much more therefore should all other temporal goods be foregone on account of scandal.

**OBJ. 4**: Further, the most fitting way of safeguarding and recovering temporal goods is the court of justice. But it is unlawful to have recourse to justice, especially if scandal ensues: for it is written (Matt 5:40): *If a man will contend with thee in judgment, and take away thy coat, let go thy cloak also unto him*; and (1 Cor 6:7): *Already indeed there is plainly a fault among you, that you have lawsuits one with another. Why do you not rather take wrong? why do*

Ergo videtur quod temporalia sint propter scandalum dimittenda.

PRAETEREA, inter omnia temporalia minus videntur dimittenda quae sunt spiritualibus annexa. Sed ista sunt propter scandalum dimittenda, apostolus enim, seminans spiritualia, temporalia stipendia non accepit, *ne offendiculum daret Evangelio Christi*, ut patet I ad Cor. IX; et ex simili causa Ecclesia in aliquibus terris non exigit decimas, propter scandalum vitandum. Ergo multo magis alia temporalia sunt propter scandalum dimittenda.

SED CONTRA est quod beatus Thomas Cantuariensis repetiit res Ecclesiae cum scandalo regis.

RESPONDEO dicendum quod circa temporalia bona distinguendum est. Aut enim sunt nostra, aut sunt nobis ad conservandum pro aliis commissa; sicut bona Ecclesiae committuntur praelatis, et bona communia quibuscumque reipublicae rectoribus. Et talium conservatio, sicut et depositorum, imminet his quibus sunt commissa ex necessitate. Et ideo non sunt propter scandalum dimittenda, sicut nec alia quae sunt de necessitate salutis.

Temporalia vero quorum nos sumus domini dimittere, ea tribuendo si penes nos ea habeamus, vel non repetendo si apud alios sint, propter scandalum quandoque quidem debemus, quandoque autem non. Si enim scandalum ex hoc oriatur propter ignorantiam vel infirmitatem aliorum, quod supra diximus esse scandalum pusillorum; tunc vel totaliter dimittenda sunt temporalia; vel aliter scandalum sedandum, scilicet per aliquam admonitionem.

Unde Augustinus dicit, in libro de Serm. Dom. in monte, *dandum est quod nec tibi nec alteri noceat, quantum ab homine credi potest. Et cum negaveris quod petit, indicanda est ei iustitia, et melius ei aliquid dabis, cum petentem iniuste correxeris.* Aliquando vero scandalum nascitur ex malitia, quod est scandalum Pharisaeorum. Et propter eos qui sic scandala concitant non sunt temporalia dimittenda, quia hoc et noceret bono communi, daretur enim malis rapiendi occasio; et noceret ipsis rapientibus, qui retinendo aliena in peccato remanerent. Unde Gregorius dicit, in Moral., *quidam, dum temporalia nobis rapiunt, solummodo sunt tolerandi, quidam vero, servata aequitate, prohibendi; non sola cura ne no-*

*you not rather suffer yourselves to be defrauded?* Therefore it seems that we ought to forego temporal goods on account of scandal.

OBJ. 5: Further, we ought, seemingly, to forego least of all those temporal goods which are connected with spiritual goods: and yet we ought to forego them on account of scandal. For the Apostle while sowing spiritual things did not accept a temporal stipend lest he *should give any hindrance to the Gospel of Christ* as we read 1 Cor. 9:12. For a like reason the Church does not demand tithes in certain countries, in order to avoid scandal. Much more, therefore, ought we to forego other temporal goods in order to avoid scandal.

ON THE CONTRARY, Blessed Thomas of Canterbury demanded the restitution of Church property, notwithstanding that the king took scandal from his doing so.

I ANSWER THAT, A distinction must be made in temporal goods: for either they are ours, or they are consigned to us to take care of them for someone else; thus the goods of the Church are consigned to prelates, and the goods of the community are entrusted to all such persons as have authority over the common weal. In this latter case the care of such things (as of things held in deposit) devolves of necessity on those persons to whom they are entrusted, wherefore, even as other things that are necessary for salvation, they are not to be foregone on account of scandal.

On the other hand, as regards those temporalities of which we have the dominion, sometimes, on account of scandal, we are bound to forego them, and sometimes we are not so bound, whether we forego them by giving them up, if we have them in our possession, or by omitting to claim them, if they are in the possession of others. For if the scandal arise therefrom through the ignorance or weakness of others (in which case, as stated above, A. 7, it is scandal of the little ones) we must either forego such temporalities altogether, or the scandal must be abated by some other means, namely, by some kind of admonition.

Hence Augustine says (*De Serm. Dom. in Monte* i, 20): *Thou shouldst give so as to injure neither thyself nor another, as much as thou canst lend, and if thou refusest what is asked, thou must yet be just to him, indeed thou wilt give him something better than he asks, if thou reprove him that asks unjustly.* Sometimes, however, scandal arises from malice. This is scandal of the Pharisees: and we ought not to forego temporal goods for the sake of those who stir up scandals of this kind, for this would both be harmful to the common good, since it would give wicked men an opportunity of plunder, and would be injurious to the plunderers themselves, who would remain in sin as long as they were in possession of another's property. Hence

*stra subtrahantur, sed ne rapientes non sua semetipsos perdant.*

**ET PER HOC** patet solutio ad primum.

**AD SECUNDUM** dicendum quod si passim permitteretur malis hominibus ut aliena raperent, vergeret hoc in detrimentum veritatis vitae et iustitiae. Et ideo non oportet propter quodcumque scandalum temporalia dimitti.

**AD TERTIUM** dicendum quod non est de intentione apostoli monere quod cibus totaliter propter scandalum dimittatur, quia sumere cibum est de necessitate salutis. Sed talis cibus est propter scandalum dimittendus, secundum illud I ad Cor. VIII, *non manducabo carnem in aeternum, ne fratrem meum scandalizem.*

**AD QUARTUM** dicendum quod secundum Augustinum, in libro de Serm. Dom. in monte, illud praeceptum domini est intelligendum secundum praeparationem animi, ut scilicet homo sit paratus prius pati iniuriam vel fraudem quam iudicium subire, si hoc expediat. Quandoque tamen non expedit, ut dictum est. Et similiter intelligendum est verbum apostoli.

**AD QUINTUM** dicendum quod scandalum quod vitabat apostolus ex ignorantia procedebat gentilium, qui hoc non consueverant. Et ideo ad tempus abstinendum erat, ut prius instruerentur hoc esse debitum. Et ex simili causa Ecclesia abstinet de decimis exigendis in terris in quibus non est consuetum decimas solvere.

Gregory says (*Moral.* xxxi, 13): *Sometimes we ought to suffer those who rob us of our temporalities, while sometimes we should resist them, as far as equity allows, in the hope not only that we may safeguard our property, but also lest those who take what is not theirs may lose themselves.*

**THIS SUFFICES** for the Reply to the First Objection.

**REPLY OBJ. 2**: If it were permissible for wicked men to rob other people of their property, this would tend to the detriment of the truth of life and justice. Therefore we are not always bound to forego our temporal goods in order to avoid scandal.

**REPLY OBJ. 3**: The Apostle had no intention of counselling total abstinence from food on account of scandal, because our welfare requires that we should take food: but he intended to counsel abstinence from a particular kind of food, in order to avoid scandal, according to 1 Cor. 8:13: *I will never eat flesh, lest I should scandalize my brother.*

**REPLY OBJ. 4**: According to Augustine (*De Serm. Dom. in Monte* i, 19) this precept of Our Lord is to be understood of the preparedness of the mind, namely, that man should be prepared, if it be expedient, to suffer being harmed or defrauded, rather than go to law. But sometimes it is not expedient, as stated above (ad 2). The same applies to the saying of the Apostle.

**REPLY OBJ. 5**: The scandal which the Apostle avoided, arose from an error of the gentiles who were not used to this payment. Hence it behooved him to forego it for the time being, so that they might be taught first of all that such a payment was a duty. For a like reason the Church refrains from demanding tithes in those countries where it is not customary to pay them.

# QUESTION 44

## THE PRECEPTS OF CHARITY

Deinde considerandum est de praeceptis caritatis. Et circa hoc quaeruntur octo.

Primo, utrum de caritate sint danda praecepta.

Secundo, utrum unum tantum, vel duo.

Tertio, utrum duo sufficiant.

Quarto, utrum convenienter praecipiatur ut Deus ex toto corde diligatur.

Quinto, utrum convenienter addatur, ex tota mente et cetera.

Sexto, utrum praeceptum hoc possit in vita ista impleri.

Septimo, de hoc praecepto, diliges proximum tuum sicut teipsum.

Octavo, utrum ordo caritatis cadat sub praecepto.

We must now consider the Precepts of Charity, under which there are eight points of inquiry:

(1) Whether precepts should be given about charity?

(2) Whether there should be one or two?

(3) Whether two suffice?

(4) Whether it is fittingly prescribed that we should love God, *with thy whole heart*?

(5) Whether it is fittingly added: *With thy whole mind,* etc.?

(6) Whether it is possible to fulfill this precept in this life?

(7) Of the precept: *Thou shalt love thy neighbor as thyself*;

(8) Whether the order of charity is included in the precept?

# Article 1

*Whether any precept should be given about charity?*

**Ad primum sic proceditur.** Videtur quod de caritate non debeat dari aliquod praeceptum. Caritas enim imponit modum actibus omnium virtutum, de quibus dantur praecepta, cum sit forma virtutum, ut supra dictum est. Sed modus non est in praecepto, ut communiter dicitur. Ergo de caritate non sunt danda praecepta.

**Praeterea,** caritas, quae *in cordibus nostris per spiritum sanctum diffunditur,* facit nos liberos, *quia ubi spiritus domini, ibi libertas,* ut dicitur II ad Cor. III. Sed obligatio, quae ex praeceptis nascitur, libertati opponitur, quia necessitatem imponit. Ergo de caritate non sunt danda praecepta.

**Praeterea,** caritas est praecipua inter omnes virtutes, ad quas ordinantur praecepta, ut ex supradictis patet. Si igitur de caritate dantur aliqua praecepta, deberent poni inter praecipua praecepta, quae sunt praecepta Decalogi. Non autem ponuntur. Ergo nulla praecepta sunt de caritate danda.

**Sed contra,** illud quod Deus requirit a nobis cadit sub praecepto. Requirit autem Deus ab homine *ut diligat eum,* ut dicitur Deut. X. Ergo de dilectione caritatis, quae est dilectio Dei, sunt danda praecepta.

**Objection 1:** It would seem that no precept should be given about charity. For charity imposes the mode on all acts of virtue, since it is the form of the virtues as stated above (Q. 23, A. 8), while the precepts are about the virtues themselves. Now, according to the common saying, the mode is not included in the precept. Therefore no precepts should be given about charity.

**Obj. 2:** Further, charity, which *is poured forth in our hearts by the Holy Spirit* (Rom 5:5), makes us free, since *where the Spirit of the Lord is, there is liberty* (2 Cor 3:17). Now the obligation that arises from a precept is opposed to liberty, since it imposes a necessity. Therefore no precept should be given about charity.

**Obj. 3:** Further, charity is the foremost among all the virtues, to which the precepts are directed, as shown above (I-II, Q. 90, A. 2; Q. 100, A. 9). If, therefore, any precepts were given about charity, they should have a place among the chief precepts which are those of the decalogue. But they have no place there. Therefore no precepts should be given about charity.

**On the contrary,** Whatever God requires of us is included in a precept. Now God requires that man *should love Him,* according to Deut. 10:12. Therefore it behooved precepts to be given about the love of charity, which is the love of God.

417

**RESPONDEO** dicendum quod, sicut supra dictum est, praeceptum importat rationem debiti. Intantum ergo aliquid cadit sub praecepto inquantum habet rationem debiti. Est autem aliquid debitum dupliciter, uno modo, per se; alio modo, propter aliud. Per se quidem debitum est in unoquoque negotio id quod est finis, quia habet rationem per se boni; propter aliud autem est debitum id quod ordinatur ad finem, sicut medico per se debitum est ut sanet; propter aliud autem, ut det medicinam ad sanandum.

Finis autem spiritualis vitae est ut homo uniatur Deo, quod fit per caritatem, et ad hoc ordinantur, sicut ad finem, omnia quae pertinent ad spiritualem vitam. Unde et apostolus dicit, I ad Tim. I, *finis praecepti est caritas de corde puro et conscientia bona et fide non ficta.*

Omnes enim virtutes, de quarum actibus dantur praecepta, ordinantur vel ad purificandum cor a turbinibus passionum, sicut virtutes quae sunt circa passiones; vel saltem ad habendam bonam conscientiam, sicut virtutes quae sunt circa operationes; vel ad habendam rectam fidem, sicut illa quae pertinent ad divinum cultum. Et haec tria requiruntur ad diligendum Deum, nam cor impurum a Dei dilectione abstrahitur propter passionem inclinantem ad terrena; conscientia vero mala facit horrere divinam iustitiam propter timorem poenae; fides autem ficta trahit affectum in id quod de Deo fingitur, separans a Dei veritate. In quolibet autem genere id quod est per se potius est eo quod est propter aliud. Et ideo *maximum praeceptum* est de caritate, ut dicitur Matth. XXII.

**AD PRIMUM** ergo dicendum quod, sicut supra dictum est cum de praeceptis ageretur, modus dilectionis non cadit sub illis praeceptis quae dantur de aliis actibus virtutum, puta sub hoc praecepto, *honora patrem tuum et matrem tuam*, non cadit quod hoc ex caritate fiat. Cadit tamen actus dilectionis sub praeceptis specialibus.

**AD SECUNDUM** dicendum quod obligatio praecepti non opponitur libertati nisi in eo cuius mens aversa est ab eo quod praecipitur sicut patet in his qui ex solo timore praecepta custodiunt. Sed praeceptum dilectionis non potest impleri nisi ex propria voluntate. Et ideo libertati non repugnat.

**AD TERTIUM** dicendum quod omnia praecepta Decalogi ordinantur ad dilectionem Dei et proximi. Et ideo praecepta caritatis non fuerunt connumeranda inter praecepta Decalogi, sed in omnibus includuntur.

**I ANSWER THAT,** As stated above (Q. 16, A. 1; I-II, Q. 99, A. 1), a precept implies the notion of something due. Hence a thing is a matter of precept, insofar as it is something due. Now a thing is due in two ways, for its own sake, and for the sake of something else. In every affair, it is the end that is due for its own sake, because it has the character of a good for its own sake: while that which is directed to the end is due for the sake of something else: thus for a physician, it is due for its own sake, that he should heal, while it is due for the sake of something else that he should give a medicine in order to heal.

Now the end of the spiritual life is that man be united to God, and this union is effected by charity, while all things pertaining to the spiritual life are ordained to this union, as to their end. Hence the Apostle says (1 Tim 1:5): *The end of the commandment is charity from a pure heart, and a good conscience, and an unfeigned faith.*

For all the virtues, about whose acts the precepts are given, are directed either to the freeing of the heart from the turbulence of the passions—such are the virtues that regulate the passions—or at least to the possession of a good conscience—such are the virtues that regulate operations—or to the having of a right faith—such are those which pertain to the worship of God: and these three things are required of man that he may love God. For an impure heart is withdrawn from loving God, on account of the passion that inclines it to earthly things; an evil conscience gives man a horror for God's justice, through fear of His punishments; and an untrue faith draws man's affections to an untrue representation of God, and separates him from the truth of God. Now in every genus that which is for its own sake takes precedence of that which is for the sake of another, wherefore *the greatest precept* is that of charity, as stated in Matt. 22:39.

**REPLY OBJ. 1**: As stated above (I-II, Q. 100, A. 10) when we were treating of the commandments, the mode of love does not come under those precepts which are about the other acts of virtue: for instance, this precept, *Honor thy father and thy mother*, does not prescribe that this should be done out of charity. The act of love does, however, fall under special precepts.

**REPLY OBJ. 2**: The obligation of a precept is not opposed to liberty, except in one whose mind is averted from that which is prescribed, as may be seen in those who keep the precepts through fear alone. But the precept of love cannot be fulfilled save of one's own will, wherefore it is not opposed to charity.

**REPLY OBJ. 3**: All the precepts of the decalogue are directed to the love of God and of our neighbor: and therefore the precepts of charity had not to be enumerated among the precepts of the decalogue, since they are included in all of them.

# Article 2

*Whether there should have been given two precepts of charity?*

**AD SECUNDUM SIC PROCEDITUR**. Videtur quod de caritate non fuerint danda duo praecepta. Praecepta enim legis ordinantur ad virtutem, ut supra dictum est. Sed caritas est una virtus, ut ex supradictis patet. Ergo de caritate non fuit dandum nisi unum praeceptum.

**PRAETEREA**, sicut Augustinus dicit, in I de Doct. Christ., caritas in proximo non diligit nisi Deum. Sed ad diligendum Deum sufficienter ordinamur per hoc praeceptum, *diliges dominum Deum tuum*. Ergo non oportuit addere aliud praeceptum de dilectione proximi.

**PRAETEREA**, diversa peccata diversis praeceptis opponuntur. Sed non peccat aliquis praetermittens dilectionem proximi, si non praetermittat dilectionem Dei, quinimmo dicitur Luc. XIV, *si quis venit ad me et non odit patrem suum et matrem suam, non potest meus esse discipulus*. Ergo non est aliud praeceptum de dilectione Dei et de dilectione proximi.

**PRAETEREA**, apostolus dicit, ad Rom. XIII, *qui diligit proximum legem implevit*. Sed non impletur lex nisi per observantiam omnium praeceptorum. Ergo omnia praecepta includuntur in dilectione proximi. Sufficit ergo hoc unum praeceptum de dilectione proximi. Non ergo debent esse duo praecepta caritatis.

**SED CONTRA** est quod dicitur I Ioan. IV, *hoc mandatum habemus a Deo, ut qui diligit Deum diligat et fratrem suum*.

**RESPONDEO** dicendum quod, sicut supra dictum est cum de praeceptis ageretur, hoc modo se habent praecepta in lege sicut propositiones in scientiis speculativis. In quibus conclusiones virtute continentur in primis principiis, unde qui perfecte cognosceret principia secundum totam suam virtutem, non opus haberet ut ei conclusiones seorsum proponerentur. Sed quia non omnes qui cognoscunt principia sufficiunt considerare quidquid in principiis virtute continetur, necesse est propter eos ut in scientiis ex principiis conclusiones deducantur. In operabilibus autem, in quibus praecepta legis nos dirigunt, finis habet rationem principii, ut supra dictum est. Dilectio autem Dei finis est, ad quem dilectio proximi ordinatur. Et ideo non solum oportet dari praeceptum de dilectione Dei, sed etiam de dilectione proximi, propter minus capaces, qui non de facili considerarent unum horum praeceptorum sub alio contineri.

**AD PRIMUM** ergo dicendum quod, si caritas sit una virtus, habet tamen duos actus, quorum unus ordinatur

**OBJECTION 1**: It would seem that there should not have been given two precepts of charity. For the precepts of the Law are directed to virtue, as stated above (A. 1, Obj. 3). Now charity is one virtue, as shown above (Q. 33, A. 5). Therefore only one precept of charity should have been given.

**OBJ. 2**: Further, as Augustine says (*De Doctr. Christ.* i, 22, 27), charity loves none but God in our neighbor. Now we are sufficiently directed to love God by the precept, *Thou shalt love the Lord thy God*. Therefore there was no need to add the precept about loving our neighbor.

**OBJ. 3**: Further, different sins are opposed to different precepts. But it is not a sin to put aside the love of our neighbor, provided we put not aside the love of God; indeed, it is written (Luke 15:26): *If any man come to Me, and hate not his father, and mother . . . he cannot be My disciple*. Therefore the precept of the love of God is not distinct from the precept of the love of our neighbor.

**OBJ. 4**: Further, the Apostle says (Rom 13:8): *He that loveth his neighbor hath fulfilled the Law*. But a law is not fulfilled unless all its precepts be observed. Therefore all the precepts are included in the love of our neighbor: and consequently the one precept of the love of our neighbor suffices. Therefore there should not be two precepts of charity.

**ON THE CONTRARY**, It is written (1 John 4:21): *This commandment we have from God, that he who loveth God, love also his brother*.

**I ANSWER THAT**, As stated above (I-II, Q. 91, A. 3; Q. 94, A. 2) when we were treating of the commandments, the precepts are to the Law what propositions are to speculative sciences, for in these latter, the conclusions are virtually contained in the first principles. Hence whoever knows the principles as to their entire virtual extent has no need to have the conclusions put separately before him. Since, however, some who know the principles are unable to consider all that is virtually contained therein, it is necessary, for their sake, that scientific conclusions should be traced to their principles. Now in practical matters wherein the precepts of the Law direct us, the end has the character of principle, as stated above (Q. 23, A. 7, ad 2; Q. 26, A. 1, ad 1): and the love of God is the end to which the love of our neighbor is directed. Therefore it behooved us to receive precepts not only of the love of God but also of the love of our neighbor, on account of those who are less intelligent, who do not easily understand that one of these precepts is included in the other.

**REPLY OBJ. 1**: Although charity is one virtue, yet it has two acts, one of which is directed to the other as to its end.

ad alium sicut ad finem. Praecepta autem dantur de actibus virtutum. Et ideo oportuit esse plura praecepta caritatis.

AD SECUNDUM dicendum quod Deus diligitur in proximo sicut finis in eo quod est ad finem. Et tamen oportuit de utroque explicite dari praecepta, ratione iam dicta.

AD TERTIUM dicendum quod id quod est ad finem habet rationem boni ex ordine ad finem. Et secundum hoc etiam recedere ab eo habet rationem mali, et non aliter.

AD QUARTUM dicendum quod in dilectione proximi includitur dilectio Dei sicut finis in eo quod est ad finem, et e converso. Et tamen oportuit utrumque praeceptum explicite dari, ratione iam dicta.

Now precepts are given about acts of virtue, and so there had to be several precepts of charity.

REPLY OBJ. 2: God is loved in our neighbor, as the end is loved in that which is directed to the end; and yet there was need for an explicit precept about both, for the reason given above.

REPLY OBJ. 3: The means derive their goodness from their relation to the end, and accordingly aversion from the means derives its malice from the same source and from no other.

REPLY OBJ. 4: Love of our neighbor includes love of God, as the end is included in the means, and vice versa: and yet it behooved each precept to be given explicitly, for the reason given above.

# Article 3

### Whether two precepts of charity suffice?

AD TERTIUM SIC PROCEDITUR. Videtur quod non sufficiant duo praecepta caritatis. Praecepta enim dantur de actibus virtutum. Actus autem secundum obiecta distinguuntur. Cum igitur quatuor homo debeat ex caritate diligere, scilicet Deum, seipsum, proximum et corpus proprium, ut ex supradictis patet; videtur quod quatuor debeant esse caritatis praecepta. Et sic duo non sufficiunt.

PRAETEREA, caritatis actus non solum est dilectio, sed gaudium, pax, beneficentia. Sed de actibus virtutum sunt danda praecepta. Ergo duo praecepta caritatis non sufficiunt.

PRAETEREA, sicut ad virtutem pertinet facere bonum, ita et declinare a malo. Sed ad faciendum bonum inducimur per praecepta affirmativa, ad declinandum a malo per praecepta negativa. Ergo de caritate fuerunt danda praecepta non solum affirmativa, sed etiam negativa. Et sic praedicta duo praecepta caritatis non sufficiunt.

SED CONTRA est quod dominus dicit, Matth. XXII, in his duobus mandatis tota lex pendet et prophetae.

RESPONDEO dicendum quod caritas, sicut supra dictum est, est amicitia quaedam. Amicitia autem ad alterum est. Unde Gregorius dicit, in quadam homilia, caritas minus quam inter duos haberi non potest. Quomodo autem ex caritate aliquis seipsum diligat, supra dictum est. Cum autem dilectio et amor sit boni, bonum autem sit vel finis vel id quod est ad finem, convenienter de caritate duo praecepta sufficiunt, unum quidem quo inducimur ad Deum diligendum sicut finem; aliud

OBJECTION 1: It would seem that two precepts of charity do not suffice. For precepts are given about acts of virtue. Now acts are distinguished by their objects. Since, then, man is bound to love four things out of charity, namely, God, himself, his neighbor and his own body, as shown above (Q. 25, A. 12; Q. 26), it seems that there ought to be four precepts of charity, so that two are not sufficient.

OBJ. 2: Further, love is not the only act of charity, but also joy, peace and beneficence. But precepts should be given about the acts of the virtues. Therefore two precepts of charity do not suffice.

OBJ. 3: Further, virtue consists not only in doing good but also in avoiding evil. Now we are led by the positive precepts to do good, and by the negative precepts to avoid evil. Therefore there ought to have been not only positive, but also negative precepts about charity; and so two precepts of charity are not sufficient.

ON THE CONTRARY, Our Lord said (Matt 22:40): On these two commandments dependeth the whole Law and the prophets.

I ANSWER THAT, Charity, as stated above (Q. 23, A. 1), is a kind of friendship. Now friendship is between one person and another, wherefore Gregory says (Hom. in Ev. xvii): Charity is not possible between less than two: and it has been explained how one may love oneself out of charity (Q. 25, A. 4). Now since good is the object of dilection and love, and since good is either an end or a means, it is fitting that there should be two precepts of charity, one whereby we are induced to love God as our end, and

autem quo inducimur ad diligendum proximum propter Deum sicut propter finem.

**AD PRIMUM** ergo dicendum quod, sicut Augustinus dicit, in I de Doct. Christ., *cum quatuor sint ex caritate diligenda*, de secundo et quarto, idest de dilectione sui et corporis proprii, *nulla praecepta danda erant, quantumlibet enim homo excidat a veritate, remanet illi dilectio sui et dilectio corporis sui.* Modus autem diligendi praecipiendus est homini, ut scilicet se ordinate diligat et corpus proprium. Quod quidem fit per hoc quod homo diligit Deum et proximum.

**AD SECUNDUM** dicendum quod alii actus caritatis consequuntur ex actu dilectionis sicut effectus ex causa, ut ex supradictis patet. Unde in praeceptis dilectionis virtute includuntur praecepta de aliis actibus. Et tamen propter tardiores inveniuntur de singulis explicite praecepta tradita, de gaudio quidem, Philipp. IV, *gaudete in domino semper*; de pace autem, ad Heb. ult., *pacem sequimini cum omnibus*; de beneficentia autem, ad Gal. ult., *dum tempus habemus, operemur bonum ad omnes.* De singulis beneficentiae partibus inveniuntur praecepta tradita in sacra Scriptura, ut patet diligenter consideranti.

**AD TERTIUM** dicendum quod plus est operari bonum quam vitare malum. Et ideo in praeceptis affirmativis virtute includuntur praecepta negativa. Et tamen explicite inveniuntur praecepta data contra vitia caritati opposita. Nam contra odium dicitur Lev. XIX, *ne oderis fratrem tuum in corde tuo* contra acediam dicitur Eccli. VI, *ne acedieris in vinculis eius*; contra invidiam, Gal. V, *non efficiamur inanis gloriae cupidi, invicem provocantes, invicem invidentes*; contra discordiam vero, I ad Cor. I, *idipsum dicatis omnes, et non sint in vobis schismata*; contra scandalum autem, ad Rom. XIV, *ne ponatis offendiculum fratri vel scandalum.*

another whereby we are led to love our neighbor for God's sake, as for the sake of our end.

**REPLY OBJ. 1**: As Augustine says (*De Doctr. Christ.* i, 23), *though four things are to be loved out of charity, there was no need of a precept as regards the second and fourth*, i.e., love of oneself and of one's own body. *For however much a man may stray from the truth, the love of himself and of his own body always remains in him.* And yet the mode of this love had to be prescribed to man, namely, that he should love himself and his own body in an ordinate manner, and this is done by his loving God and his neighbor.

**REPLY OBJ. 2**: As stated above (Q. 28, A. 4; Q. 29, A. 3), the other acts of charity result from the act of love as effects from their cause. Hence the precepts of love virtually include the precepts about the other acts. And yet we find that, for the sake of the laggards, special precepts were given about each act—about joy (Phil 4:4): *Rejoice in the Lord always*—about peace (Heb 12:14): *Follow peace with all men*—about beneficence (Gal 6:10): *Whilst we have time, let us work good to all men*—and Holy Writ contains precepts about each of the parts of beneficence, as may be seen by anyone who considers the matter carefully.

**REPLY OBJ. 3**: To do good is more than to avoid evil, and therefore the positive precepts virtually include the negative precepts. Nevertheless we find explicit precepts against the vices contrary to charity: for, against hatred it is written (Lev 12:17): *Thou shalt not hate thy brother in thy heart*; against sloth (Sir 6:26): *Be not grieved with her bands*; against envy (Gal 5:26): *Let us not be made desirous of vainglory, provoking one another, envying one another*; against discord (1 Cor 1:10): *That you all speak the same thing, and that there be no schisms among you*; and against scandal (Rom 14:13): *That you put not a stumbling-block or a scandal in your brother's way.*

# Article 4

*Whether it is fittingly commanded that man should love God with his whole heart?*

**AD QUARTUM SIC PROCEDITUR.** Videtur quod inconvenienter mandetur quod Deus diligatur ex toto corde. Modus enim virtuosi actus non est in praecepto, ut ex supradictis patet. Sed hoc quod dicitur ex toto corde, importat modum divinae dilectionis. Ergo inconvenienter praecipitur quod Deus ex toto corde diligatur.

**PRAETEREA**, *totum et perfectum est cui nihil deest*; ut dicitur in III Physic. Si igitur in praecepto cadit quod Deus ex toto corde diligatur, quicumque facit aliquid quod non pertinet ad Dei dilectionem agit contra praeceptum, et per consequens peccat mortaliter. Sed

**OBJECTION 1**: It would seem that it is unfittingly commanded that man should love God with his whole heart. For the mode of a virtuous act is not a matter of precept, as shown above (A. 1, ad 1; I-II, Q. 100, A. 9). Now the words *with thy whole heart* signify the mode of the love of God. Therefore it is unfittingly commanded that man should love God with his whole heart.

**OBJ. 2**: Further, *A thing is whole and perfect when it lacks nothing* (*Phys.* iii, 6). If therefore it is a matter of precept that God be loved with the whole heart, whoever does something not pertaining to the love of God, acts counter to the precept, and consequently sins mortally. Now a venial

peccatum veniale non pertinet ad Dei dilectionem. Ergo peccatum veniale erit mortale. Quod est inconveniens.

PRAETEREA, diligere Deum ex toto corde est perfectionis, quia secundum philosophum, totum et perfectum idem sunt. Sed ea quae sunt perfectionis non cadunt sub praecepto, sed sub consilio. Ergo non debet praecipi quod Deus ex toto corde diligatur.

SED CONTRA est quod dicitur Deut. VI, *diliges dominum Deum tuum ex toto corde tuo.*

RESPONDEO dicendum quod, cum praecepta dentur de actibus virtutum, hoc ergo modo aliquis actus cadit sub praecepto, secundum quod est actus virtutis. Requiritur autem ad actum virtutis non solum quod cadat super debitam materiam, sed etiam quod vestiatur debitis circumstantiis, quibus sit proportionatus tali materiae. Deus autem est diligendus sicut finis ultimus, ad quem omnia sunt referenda. Et ideo totalitas quaedam fuit designanda circa praeceptum de dilectione Dei.

AD PRIMUM ergo dicendum quod sub praecepto quod datur de actu alicuius virtutis non cadit modus quem habet ille actus ex alia superiori virtute. Cadit tamen sub praecepto modus ille qui pertinet ad rationem propriae virtutis. Et talis modus significatur cum dicitur, ex toto corde.

AD SECUNDUM dicendum quod dupliciter contingit ex toto corde Deum diligere. Uno quidem modo, in actu, idest ut totum cor hominis semper actualiter in Deum feratur. Et ista est perfectio patriae. Alio modo, ut habitualiter totum cor hominis in Deum feratur, ita scilicet quod nihil contra Dei dilectionem cor hominis recipiat. Et haec est perfectio viae. Cui non contrariatur peccatum veniale, quia non tollit habitum caritatis, cum non tendat in oppositum obiectum; sed solum impedit caritatis usum.

AD TERTIUM dicendum quod perfectio caritatis ad quam ordinantur consilia est media inter duas perfectiones praedictas, ut scilicet homo, quantum possibile est, se abstrahat a rebus temporalibus etiam licitis, quae, occupando animum, impediunt actualem motum cordis in Deum.

sin does not pertain to the love of God. Therefore a venial sin is a mortal sin, which is absurd.

OBJ. 3: Further, to love God with one's whole heart belongs to perfection, since according to the Philosopher (*Phys.* iii, text. 64), to be whole is to be perfect. But that which belongs to perfection is not a matter of precept, but a matter of counsel. Therefore we ought not to be commanded to love God with our whole heart.

ON THE CONTRARY, It is written (Deut 6:5): *Thou shalt love the Lord thy God with thy whole heart.*

I ANSWER THAT, Since precepts are given about acts of virtue, an act is a matter of precept according as it is an act of virtue. Now it is requisite for an act of virtue that not only should it fall on its own matter, but also that it should be endued with its due circumstances, whereby it is adapted to that matter. But God is to be loved as the last end, to which all things are to be referred. Therefore some kind of totality was to be indicated in connection with the precept of the love of God.

REPLY OBJ. 1: The commandment that prescribes an act of virtue does not prescribe the mode which that virtue derives from another and higher virtue, but it does prescribe the mode which belongs to its own proper virtue, and this mode is signified in the words *with thy whole heart.*

REPLY OBJ. 2: To love God with one's whole heart has a twofold signification. First, actually, so that a man's whole heart be always actually directed to God: this is the perfection of heaven. Second, in the sense that a man's whole heart be habitually directed to God, so that it consent to nothing contrary to the love of God, and this is the perfection of the way. Venial sin is not contrary to this latter perfection, because it does not destroy the habit of charity, since it does not tend to a contrary object, but merely hinders the use of charity.

REPLY OBJ. 3: That perfection of charity to which the counsels are directed, is between the two perfections mentioned in the preceding reply: and it consists in man renouncing, as much as possible, temporal things, even such as are lawful, because they occupy the mind and hinder the actual movement of the heart towards God.

# Article 5

*Whether to the words, "thou shalt love the Lord thy God with thy whole heart," it was fitting to add "and with thy whole soul, and with thy whole strength"?*

AD QUINTUM SIC PROCEDITUR. Videtur quod inconvenienter, Deut. VI, super hoc quod dicitur, *diliges dominum Deum tuum ex toto corde tuo,* addatur, *et ex tota anima tua et ex tota fortitudine tua.* Non enim accipitur hic cor pro membro corporali, quia diligere Deum non est corporis actus. Oportet igitur quod cor

OBJECTION 1: It would seem that it was unfitting to the words, *Thou shalt love the Lord thy God, with thy whole heart,* to add, *and with thy whole soul, and with thy whole strength* (Deut 6:5). For heart does not mean here a part of the body, since to love God is not a bodily action: and therefore heart is to be taken here in a spiritual sense. Now

accipiatur spiritualiter. Cor autem spiritualiter acceptum vel est ipsa anima vel aliquid animae. Superfluum igitur fuit utrumque ponere.

**PRAETEREA**, fortitudo hominis praecipue dependet ex corde, sive spiritualiter hoc accipiatur, sive corporaliter. Ergo postquam dixerat, *diliges dominum Deum tuum ex toto corde tuo*, superfluum fuit addere, *ex tota fortitudine tua*.

**PRAETEREA**, Matth. XXII dicitur, *in tota mente tua*, quod hic non ponitur. Ergo videtur quod inconvenienter hoc praeceptum detur Deut. VI.

**SED CONTRA** est auctoritas Scripturae.

**RESPONDEO** dicendum quod hoc praeceptum diversimode invenitur traditum in diversis locis. Nam sicut dictum est, Deut. VI ponuntur tria, scilicet *ex toto corde*, et *ex tota anima*, et *ex tota fortitudine*. Matth. XXII ponuntur duo horum, scilicet *ex toto corde* et *ex tota anima*, et omittitur *ex tota fortitudine*, sed additur *in tota mente*. Sed Marc. XII ponuntur quatuor, scilicet *ex toto corde*, et *ex tota anima*, et *ex tota mente*, et *ex tota virtute*, quae est idem *fortitudini*. Et haec etiam quatuor tanguntur Luc. X, nam loco *fortitudinis* seu *virtutis* ponitur *ex omnibus viribus tuis*.

Et ideo horum quatuor est ratio assignanda, nam quod alicubi unum horum omittitur, hoc est quia unum intelligitur ex aliis. Est igitur considerandum quod dilectio est actus voluntatis, quae hic significatur per *cor*, nam sicut cor corporale est principium omnium corporalium motuum, ita etiam voluntas, et maxime quantum ad intentionem finis ultimi, quod est obiectum caritatis, est principium omnium spiritualium motuum. Tria autem sunt principia factuum quae moventur a voluntate, scilicet intellectus, qui significatur per *mentem*; vis appetitiva inferior, quae significatur per *animam*; et vis executiva exterior, quae significatur per *fortitudinem* seu *virtutem* sive *vires*. Praecipitur ergo nobis ut tota nostra intentio feratur in Deum, quod est *ex toto corde*; et quod intellectus noster subdatur Deo, quod est *ex tota mente*; et quod appetitus noster reguletur secundum Deum, quod est *ex tota anima*; et quod exterior actus noster obediat Deo, quod est *ex tota fortitudine* vel *virtute* vel *viribus* Deum diligere.

Chrysostomus tamen, super Matth., accipit e contrario *cor* et *animam* quam dictum sit. Augustinus vero, in I de Doct. Christ., refert *cor* ad cogitationes, et *animam* ad vitam, *mentem* ad intellectum. Quidam autem dicunt, *ex toto corde*, idest intellectu; *anima*, idest voluntate; *mente*, idest memoria. Vel, secundum Gregorium Nyssenum, per *cor* significat animam vegetabilem, per *animam* sensitivam, per *mentem* intellectivam, quia hoc quod nutrimur, sentimus et intelligimus, debemus ad Deum referre.

the heart understood spiritually is either the soul itself or part of the soul. Therefore it is superfluous to mention both heart and soul.

**OBJ. 2**: Further, a man's strength whether spiritual or corporal depends on the heart. Therefore after the words, *Thou shalt love the Lord thy God with thy whole heart*, it was unnecessary to add, *with all thy strength*.

**OBJ. 3**: Further, in Matt. 22:37 we read: *With all thy mind*, which words do not occur here. Therefore it seems that this precept is unfittingly worded in Deut. 6.

**ON THE CONTRARY** stands the authority of Scripture.

**I ANSWER THAT**, This precept is differently worded in various places: for, as we said in the first objection, in Deut. 6 three points are mentioned: *with thy whole heart*, and *with thy whole soul*, and *with thy whole strength*. In Matt. 22 we find two of these mentioned, viz. *with thy whole heart* and *with thy whole soul*, while *with thy whole strength* is omitted, but *with thy whole mind* is added. Yet in Mark 12 we find all four, viz. *with thy whole heart*, and *with thy whole soul*, and *with thy whole mind*, and *with thy whole force* which is the same as *strength*. Moreover, these four are indicated in Luke 10, where in place of *strength* or *force* we read *with all thy might*.

Accordingly these four have to be explained, since the fact that one of them is omitted here or there is due to one implying another. We must therefore observe that love is an act of the will which is here denoted by the *heart*, because just as the bodily heart is the principle of all the movements of the body, so too the will, especially as regards the intention of the last end which is the object of charity, is the principle of all the movements of the soul. Now there are three principles of action that are moved by the will, namely, the intellect which is signified by *the mind*, the lower appetitive power, signified by *the soul*; and the exterior executive power signified by *strength*, *force* or *might*. Accordingly we are commanded to direct our whole intention to God, and this is signified by the words *with thy whole heart*; to submit our intellect to God, and this is expressed in the words *with thy whole mind*; to regulate our appetite according to God, in the words *with thy whole soul*; and to obey God in our external actions, and this is to love God with our whole *strength*, *force* or *might*.

Chrysostom, on the other hand, takes *heart* and *soul* in the contrary sense; and Augustine (*De Doctr. Christ.* i, 22) refers *heart* to the thought, *soul* to the manner of life, and *mind* to the intellect. Again some explain *with thy whole heart* as denoting the intellect, *with thy whole soul* as signifying the will, *with thy mind* as pointing to the memory. And again, according to Gregory of Nyssa (*De Hom. Opif. viii*), *heart* signifies the vegetative soul, *soul* the sensitive, and *mind* the intellective soul, because our nourishment, sensation, and understanding ought all to be referred by us to God.

**ET PER HOC** patet responsio ad obiecta.

**THIS SUFFICES** for the Replies to the Objections.

# Article 6

*Whether it is possible in this life to fulfill this precept of the love of God?*

**AD SEXTUM SIC PROCEDITUR.** Videtur quod hoc praeceptum de dilectione Dei possit servari in via. Quia secundum Hieronymum, in Expos. Cathol. Fid., *maledictus qui dicit Deum aliquid impossibile praecepisse.* Sed Deus hoc praeceptum dedit, ut patet Deut. VI. Ergo hoc praeceptum potest in via impleri.

**PRAETEREA,** quicumque non implet praeceptum peccat mortaliter, quia secundum Ambrosium, peccatum nihil est aliud quam *transgressio legis divinae et caelestium inobedientia mandatorum.* Si ergo hoc praeceptum non potest in via servari, sequitur quod nullus possit esse in vita ista sine peccato mortali. Quod est contra id quod apostolus dicit, I ad Cor. I, *confirmabit vos usque in finem sine crimine*; et I ad Tim. III, *ministrent nullum crimen habentes.*

**PRAETEREA,** praecepta dantur ad dirigendos homines in viam salutis, secundum illud Psalm., *praeceptum domini lucidum, illuminans oculos.* Sed frustra dirigitur aliquis ad impossibile. Non ergo impossibile est hoc praeceptum in vita ista servari.

**SED CONTRA** est quod Augustinus dicit, in libro de Perfect. Iustit. *quod in plenitudine caritatis patriae praeceptum illud implebitur diliges dominum Deum tuum, et cetera. Nam cum adhuc est aliquid carnalis concupiscentiae quod continendo frenetur, non omnino ex tota anima diligitur Deus.*

**RESPONDEO** dicendum quod praeceptum aliquod dupliciter impleri potest, uno modo, perfecte; alio modo, imperfecte. Perfecte quidem impletur praeceptum quando pervenitur ad finem quem intendit praecipiens, impletur autem, sed imperfecte, quando, etsi non pertingat ad finem praecipientis, non tamen receditur ab ordine ad finem. Sicut si dux exercitus praecipiat militibus ut pugnent, ille perfecte implet praeceptum qui pugnando hostem vincit, quod dux intendit, ille autem implet, sed imperfecte, cuius pugna ad victoriam non pertingit, non tamen contra disciplinam militarem agit. Intendit autem Deus per hoc praeceptum ut homo Deo totaliter uniatur, quod fiet in patria, quando *Deus erit omnia in omnibus,* ut dicitur I ad Cor. XV. Et ideo plene et perfecte in patria implebitur hoc praeceptum. In via vero impletur, sed imperfecte. Et tamen in via tanto

**OBJECTION 1:** It would seem that in this life it is possible to fulfill this precept of the love of God. For according to Jerome *accursed is he who says that God has commanded anything impossible.* But God gave this commandment, as is clear from Deut. 6:5. Therefore it is possible to fulfill this precept in this life.

**OBJ. 2:** Further, whoever does not fulfill a precept sins mortally, since according to Ambrose (*De Parad.* viii) sin is nothing else than *a transgression of the Divine Law, and disobedience of the heavenly commandments.* If therefore this precept cannot be fulfilled by wayfarers, it follows that in this life no man can be without mortal sin, and this is against the saying of the Apostle (1 Cor 1:8): *(Who also) will confirm you unto the end without crime,* and (1 Tim 3:10): *Let them minister, having no crime.*

**OBJ. 3:** Further, precepts are given in order to direct man in the way of salvation, according to Ps. 18:9: *The commandment of the Lord is lightsome, enlightening the eyes.* Now it is useless to direct anyone to what is impossible. Therefore it is not impossible to fulfill this precept in this life.

**ON THE CONTRARY,** Augustine says (*De Perfect. Justit.* viii): *In the fullness of heavenly charity this precept will be fulfilled: Thou shalt love the Lord thy God, etc.* For as long as any carnal concupiscence remains, that can be restrained by continence, man cannot love God with all his heart.

**I ANSWER THAT,** A precept can be fulfilled in two ways; perfectly, and imperfectly. A precept is fulfilled perfectly, when the end intended by the author of the precept is reached; yet it is fulfilled, imperfectly however, when although the end intended by its author is not reached, nevertheless the order to that end is not departed from. Thus if the commander of an army order his soldiers to fight, his command will be perfectly obeyed by those who fight and conquer the foe, which is the commander's intention; yet it is fulfilled, albeit imperfectly, by those who fight without gaining the victory, provided they do nothing contrary to military discipline. Now God intends by this precept that man should be entirely united to Him, and this will be realized in heaven, when God will be *all in all,* according to 1 Cor. 15:28. Hence this precept will be observed fully and perfectly in heaven; yet it is fulfilled, though imperfectly,

unus alio perfectius implet, quanto magis accedit per quandam similitudinem ad patriae perfectionem.

on the way. Nevertheless on the way one man will fulfill it more perfectly than another, and so much the more, as he approaches by some kind of likeness to the perfection of heaven.

**AD PRIMUM** ergo dicendum quod ratio illa probat quod aliquo modo potest impleri in via, licet non perfecte.

**REPLY OBJ. 1**: This argument proves that the precept can be fulfilled after a fashion on the way, but not perfectly.

**AD SECUNDUM** dicendum quod sicut miles qui legitime pugnat, licet non vincat, non inculpatur nec poenam meretur; ita etiam qui in via hoc praeceptum implet nihil contra divinam dilectionem agens, non peccat mortaliter.

**REPLY OBJ. 2**: Even as the soldier who fights legitimately without conquering is not blamed nor deserves to be punished for this, so too he that does not fulfill this precept on the way, but does nothing against the love of God, does not sin mortally.

**AD TERTIUM** dicendum quod, sicut Augustinus dicit, in libro de Perfect. Iustit., *cur non praeciperetur homini ista perfectio, quamvis eam in hac vita nemo habeat? Non enim recte curritur, si quo currendum est nesciatur. Quomodo autem sciretur, si nullis praeceptis ostenderetur?*

**REPLY OBJ. 3**: As Augustine says (*De Perfect. Justit.* viii), *why should not this perfection be prescribed to man, although no man attains it in this life? For one cannot run straight unless one knows whither to run. And how would one know this if no precept pointed it out.*

# Article 7

*Whether the precept of love of our neighbor is fittingly expressed?*

**AD SEPTIMUM SIC PROCEDITUR**. Videtur quod inconvenienter detur praeceptum de dilectione proximi. Dilectio enim caritatis ad omnes homines extenditur, etiam ad inimicos; ut patet Matth. V. Sed nomen proximi importat quandam propinquitatem, quae non videtur haberi ad omnes homines. Ergo videtur quod inconvenienter detur hoc praeceptum.

**OBJECTION 1**: It would seem that the precept of the love of our neighbor is unfittingly expressed. For the love of charity extends to all men, even to our enemies, as may be seen in Matt. 5:44. But the word *neighbor* denotes a kind of *nighness* which does not seem to exist towards all men. Therefore it seems that this precept is unfittingly expressed.

**PRAETEREA**, secundum philosophum, in IX Ethic., *amicabilia quae sunt ad alterum venerunt ex amicabilibus quae sunt ad seipsum*, ex quo videtur quod dilectio sui ipsius sit principium dilectionis proximi. Sed principium potius est eo quod est ex principio. Ergo non debet homo diligere proximum sicut seipsum.

**OBJ. 2**: Further, according to the Philosopher (*Ethic.* ix, 8) *the origin of our friendly relations with others lies in our relation to ourselves*, whence it seems to follow that love of self is the origin of one's love for one's neighbor. Now the principle is greater than that which results from it. Therefore man ought not to love his neighbor as himself.

**PRAETEREA**, homo seipsum diligit naturaliter, non autem proximum. Inconvenienter igitur mandatur quod homo diligat proximum sicut seipsum.

**OBJ. 3**: Further, man loves himself, but not his neighbor, naturally. Therefore it is unfitting that he should be commanded to love his neighbor as himself.

**SED CONTRA** est quod dicitur Matth. XXII, *secundum praeceptum est simile huic, diliges proximum tuum sicut teipsum.*

**ON THE CONTRARY**, It is written (Matt 22:39): *The second commandment is like to this: Thou shalt love thy neighbor as thyself.*

**RESPONDEO** dicendum quod hoc praeceptum convenienter traditur, tangitur enim in eo et diligendi ratio et dilectionis modus. Ratio quidem diligendi tangitur ex eo quod *proximus* nominatur, propter hoc enim ex caritate debemus alios diligere, quia sunt nobis proximi et secundum naturalem Dei imaginem et secundum capacitatem gloriae. Nec refert utrum dicatur *proximus* vel *frater*, ut habetur I Ioan. IV; vel *amicus*, ut habetur Lev. XIX, quia per omnia haec eadem affinitas designatur.

**I ANSWER THAT**, This precept is fittingly expressed, for it indicates both the reason for loving and the mode of love. The reason for loving is indicated in the word *neighbor*, because the reason why we ought to love others out of charity is because they are nigh to us, both as to the natural image of God, and as to the capacity for glory. Nor does it matter whether we say *neighbor*, or *brother* according to 1 John 4:21, or *friend*, according to Lev. 19:18, because all these words express the same affinity.

Modus autem dilectionis tangitur cum dicitur, *sicut teipsum*. Quod non est intelligendum quantum ad hoc

The mode of love is indicated in the words *as thyself*. This does not mean that a man must love his neighbor

quod aliquis proximum aequaliter sibi diligat; sed similiter sibi. Et hoc tripliciter. Primo quidem, ex parte finis, ut scilicet aliquis diligat proximum propter Deum, sicut et seipsum propter Deum debet diligere; ut sic sit dilectio proximi *sancta*. Secundo, ex parte regulae dilectionis, ut scilicet aliquis non condescendat proximo in aliquo malo, sed solum in bonis, sicut et suae voluntati satisfacere debet homo solum in bonis; ut sic sit dilectio proximi *iusta*. Tertio, ex parte rationis dilectionis, ut scilicet non diligat aliquis proximum propter propriam utilitatem vel delectationem, sed ea ratione quod velit proximo bonum, sicut vult bonum sibi ipsi; ut sic dilectio proximi sit *vera*. Nam cum quis diligit proximum propter suam utilitatem vel delectationem, non vere diligit proximum, sed seipsum.

**ET PER HOC** patet responsio ad obiecta.

equally as himself, but in like manner as himself, and this in three ways. First, as regards the end, namely, that he should love his neighbor for God's sake, even as he loves himself for God's sake, so that his love for his neighbor is a *holy* love. Second, as regards the rule of love, namely, that a man should not give way to his neighbor in evil, but only in good things, even as he ought to gratify his will in good things alone, so that his love for his neighbor may be a *righteous* love. Third, as regards the reason for loving, namely, that a man should love his neighbor, not for his own profit, or pleasure, but in the sense of wishing his neighbor well, even as he wishes himself well, so that his love for his neighbor may be a *true* love: since when a man loves his neighbor for his own profit or pleasure, he does not love his neighbor truly, but loves himself.

**THIS SUFFICES** for the Replies to the Objections.

# Article 8

*Whether the order of charity is included in the precept?*

**AD OCTAVUM SIC PROCEDITUR**. Videtur quod ordo caritatis non cadat sub praecepto. Quicumque enim transgreditur praeceptum iniuriam facit. Sed si aliquis diligat aliquem quantum debet, et alterum quemcumque plus diligat, nulli facit iniuriam. Ergo non transgreditur praeceptum. Ordo ergo caritatis non cadit sub praecepto.

**PRAETEREA**, ea quae cadunt sub praecepto sufficienter nobis traduntur in sacra Scriptura. Sed ordo caritatis qui supra positus est nusquam traditur nobis in sacra Scriptura. Ergo non cadit sub praecepto.

**PRAETEREA**, ordo distinctionem quandam importat. Sed indistincte praecipitur dilectio proximi, cum dicitur, *diliges proximum tuum sicut teipsum*. Ergo ordo caritatis non cadit sub praecepto.

**SED CONTRA** est quod illud quod Deus in nobis facit per gratiam, instruit per legis praecepta, secundum illud Ierem. XXXI, *dabo legem meam in cordibus eorum*. Sed Deus causat in nobis ordinem caritatis, secundum illud Cant. II, *ordinavit in me caritatem*. Ergo ordo caritatis sub praecepto legis cadit.

**RESPONDEO** dicendum quod, sicut dictum est, modus qui pertinet ad rationem virtuosi actus cadit sub praecepto quod datur de actu virtutis. Ordo autem caritatis pertinet ad ipsam rationem virtutis, cum accipiatur secundum proportionem dilectionis ad diligibile, ut ex supradictis patet. Unde manifestum est quod ordo caritatis debet cadere sub praecepto.

**AD PRIMUM** ergo dicendum quod homo plus satisfacit ei quem plus diligit. Et ita, si minus diligeret aliquis

**OBJECTION 1**: It would seem that the order of charity is not included in the precept. For whoever transgresses a precept does a wrong. But if man loves some one as much as he ought, and loves any other man more, he wrongs no man. Therefore he does not transgress the precept. Therefore the order of charity is not included in the precept.

**OBJ. 2**: Further, whatever is a matter of precept is sufficiently delivered to us in Holy Writ. Now the order of charity which was given above (Q. 26) is nowhere indicated in Holy Writ. Therefore it is not included in the precept.

**OBJ. 3**: Further, order implies some kind of distinction. But the love of our neighbor is prescribed without any distinction, in the words, *Thou shalt love thy neighbor as thyself*. Therefore the order of charity is not included in the precept.

**ON THE CONTRARY**, Whatever God works in us by His grace, He teaches us first of all by His Law, according to Jer. 31:33: *I will give My Law in their heart*. Now God causes in us the order of charity, according to Cant. 2:4: *He set in order charity in me*. Therefore the order of charity comes under the precept of the Law.

**I ANSWER THAT**, As stated above (A. 4, ad 1), the mode which is essential to an act of virtue comes under the precept which prescribes that virtuous act. Now the order of charity is essential to the virtue, since it is based on the proportion of love to the thing beloved, as shown above (Q. 25, A. 12; Q. 26, AA. 1, 2). It is therefore evident that the order of charity must come under the precept.

**REPLY OBJ. 1**: A man gratifies more the person he loves more, so that if he loved less one whom he ought to love

eum quem plus debet diligere, plus vellet satisfacere illi cui minus satisfacere debet. Et sic fieret iniuria illi quem plus debet diligere.

Ad secundum dicendum quod ordo quatuor diligendorum ex caritate in sacra Scriptura exprimitur. Nam cum mandatur quod Deum ex toto corde diligamus, datur intelligi quod Deum super omnia debemus diligere. Cum autem mandatur quod aliquis diligat proximum sicut seipsum, praefertur dilectio sui ipsius dilectioni proximi. Similiter etiam cum mandatur, I Ioan. III, quod *debemus pro fratribus animam ponere*, idest vitam corporalem, datur intelligi quod proximum plus debemus diligere quam corpus proprium. Similiter etiam cum mandatur, ad Gal. ult., quod *maxime operemur bonum ad domesticos fidei*; et I ad Tim. V vituperatur *qui non habet curam suorum, et maxime domesticorum*; datur intelligi quod inter proximos, meliores et magis propinquos magis debemus diligere.

Ad tertium dicendum quod ex ipso quod dicitur, *diliges proximum tuum*, datur consequenter intelligi quod illi qui sunt magis proximi sunt magis diligendi.

more, he would wish to gratify more one whom he ought to gratify less, and so he would do an injustice to the one he ought to love more.

Reply Obj. 2: The order of those four things we have to love out of charity is expressed in Holy Writ. For when we are commanded to love God with our *whole heart*, we are given to understand that we must love Him above all things. When we are commanded to love our neighbor *as ourselves*, the love of self is set before love of our neighbor. In like manner where we are commanded (1 John 3:16) *to lay down our souls*, i.e., the life of our bodies, *for the brethren*, we are given to understand that a man ought to love his neighbor more than his own body; and again when we are commanded (Gal 6:10) to *work good . . . especially to those who are of the household of the faith*, and when a man is blamed (1 Tim 5:8) if he *have not care of his own, and especially of those of his house*, it means that we ought to love most those of our neighbors who are more virtuous or more closely united to us.

Reply Obj. 3: It follows from the very words, *Thou shalt love thy neighbor* that those who are nearer to us are to be loved more.

# QUESTION 45

## THE GIFT OF WISDOM

Deinde considerandum est de dono sapientiae, quod respondet caritati. Et primo, de ipsa sapientia; secundo, de vitio opposito. Circa primum quaeruntur sex.

Primo, utrum sapientia debeat numerari inter dona spiritus sancti.

Secundo, in quo sit sicut in subiecto.

Tertio, utrum sapientia sit speculativa tantum, vel etiam practica.

Quarto, utrum sapientia quae est donum possit esse cum peccato mortali.

Quinto, utrum sit in omnibus habentibus gratiam gratum facientem.

Sexto, quae beatitudo ei respondeat.

We must now consider the gift of wisdom which corresponds to charity; and first, wisdom itself, second, the opposite vice. Under the first head there are six points of inquiry:

(1) Whether wisdom should be reckoned among the gifts of the Holy Spirit?

(2) What is its subject?

(3) Whether wisdom is only speculative or also practical?

(4) Whether the wisdom that is a gift is compatible with mortal sin?

(5) Whether it is in all those who have sanctifying grace?

(6) Which beatitude corresponds to it?

# Article 1

*Whether wisdom should be reckoned among the gifts of the Holy Spirit?*

**AD PRIMUM SIC PROCEDITUR.** Videtur quod sapientia non debeat inter dona spiritus sancti computari. Dona enim sunt perfectiora virtutibus, ut supra dictum est. Sed virtus se habet solum ad bonum, unde et Augustinus dicit, in libro de Lib. Arb., quod *nullus virtutibus male utitur.* Ergo multo magis dona spiritus sancti se habent solum ad bonum. Sed sapientia se habet etiam ad malum, dicitur enim Iac. III quaedam sapientia esse *terrena, animalis, diabolica.* Ergo sapientia non debet poni inter dona spiritus sancti.

**PRAETEREA,** sicut Augustinus dicit, XIV de Trin., *sapientia est divinarum rerum cognitio.* Sed cognitio divinarum rerum quam homo potest per sua naturalia habere, pertinet ad sapientiam quae est virtus intellectualis, cognitio autem divinorum supernaturalis pertinet ad fidem quae est virtus theologica, ut ex supradictis patet. Ergo sapientia magis debet dici virtus quam donum.

**PRAETEREA,** Iob XXVIII dicitur, *ecce timor domini ipsa est sapientia,* habetur, ecce, pietas ipsa est sapientia. Ubi secundum litteram Septuaginta, qua utitur Augustinus, habetur, *ecce, pietas ipsa est sapientia.* Sed tam timor quam pietas ponuntur dona spiritus sancti. Ergo sapientia non debet numerari inter dona spiritus sancti quasi donum ab aliis distinctum.

**OBJECTION 1:** It would seem that wisdom ought not to be reckoned among the gifts of the Holy Spirit. For the gifts are more perfect than the virtues, as stated above (I-II, Q. 68, A. 8). Now virtue is directed to the good alone, wherefore Augustine says (*De Lib. Arb.* ii, 19) that *no man makes bad use of the virtues.* Much more therefore are the gifts of the Holy Spirit directed to the good alone. But wisdom is directed to evil also, for it is written (Jas 3:15) that a certain wisdom is *earthly, sensual, devilish.* Therefore wisdom should not be reckoned among the gifts of the Holy Spirit.

**OBJ. 2:** Further, according to Augustine (*De Trin.* xii, 14) *wisdom is the knowledge of Divine things.* Now that knowledge of Divine things which man can acquire by his natural endowments, belongs to the wisdom which is an intellectual virtue, while the supernatural knowledge of Divine things belongs to faith which is a theological virtue, as explained above (Q. 4, A. 5; I-II, Q. 62, A. 3). Therefore wisdom should be called a virtue rather than a gift.

**OBJ. 3:** Further, it is written (Job 28:28): *Behold the fear of the Lord, that is wisdom, and to depart from evil, that is understanding.* And in this passage according to the rendering of the Septuagint which Augustine follows (*De Trin.* xii, 14; xiv, 1) we read: *Behold piety, that is wisdom.* Now both fear and piety are gifts of the Holy Spirit. Therefore wisdom should not be reckoned among the gifts of the Holy Spirit, as though it were distinct from the others.

**Sed contra** est quod Isaiae XI dicitur, *requiescet super eum spiritus domini, sapientiae et intellectus*, et cetera.

**Respondeo** dicendum quod secundum Philosophum, in principio Metaphys., ad sapientem pertinet considerare causam altissimam, per quam de aliis certissime iudicatur, et secundum quam omnia ordinari oportet. Causa autem altissima dupliciter accipi potest, vel simpliciter, vel in aliquo genere. Ille igitur qui cognoscit causam altissimam in aliquo genere et per eam potest de omnibus quae sunt illius generis iudicare et ordinare, dicitur esse sapiens in illo genere, ut in medicina vel architectura, secundum illud I ad Cor. III, *ut sapiens architectus fundamentum posui*. Ille autem qui cognoscit causam altissimam simpliciter, quae est Deus, dicitur sapiens simpliciter, inquantum per regulas divinas omnia potest iudicare et ordinare.

Huiusmodi autem iudicium consequitur homo per spiritum sanctum, secundum illud I ad Cor. II, *spiritualis iudicat omnia*; quia, sicut ibidem dicitur, *spiritus omnia scrutatur, etiam profunda Dei*. Unde manifestum est quod sapientia est donum spiritus sancti.

**Ad primum** ergo dicendum quod bonum dicitur dupliciter. Uno modo, quod vere est bonum et simpliciter perfectum. Alio modo dicitur aliquid esse bonum, secundum quandam similitudinem, quod est in malitia perfectum, sicut dicitur *bonus latro* vel *perfectus latro*, ut patet per Philosophum, in V Metaphys. Et sicut circa ea quae sunt vere bona invenitur aliqua altissima causa, quae est summum bonum, quod est ultimus finis, per cuius cognitionem homo dicitur vere sapiens; ita etiam in malis est invenire aliquid ad quod alia referuntur sicut ad ultimum finem, per cuius cognitionem homo dicitur esse sapiens ad male agendum; secundum illud Ierem. IV, *sapientes sunt ut faciant mala, bene autem facere nescierunt*. Quicumque enim avertitur a fine debito, necesse est quod aliquem finem indebitum sibi praestituat, quia omne agens agit propter finem. Unde si praestituat sibi finem in bonis exterioribus terrenis, vocatur *sapientia terrena*; si autem in bonis corporalibus, vocatur *sapientia animalis*; si autem in aliqua excellentia, vocatur *sapientia diabolica*, propter imitationem superbiae Diaboli, de quo dicitur Iob XLI, *ipse est rex super universos filios superbiae*.

**Ad secundum** dicendum quod sapientia quae ponitur donum differt ab ea quae ponitur virtus intellectualis acquisita. Nam illa acquiritur studio humano, haec autem est *de sursum descendens*, ut dicitur Iac. III. Similiter et differt a fide. Nam fides assentit veritati divinae secundum seipsam, sed iudicium quod est secundum veritatem divinam pertinet ad donum sapientiae. Et ideo

**On the contrary,** It is written (Isa 11:2): *The Spirit of the Lord shall rest upon Him; the spirit of wisdom and of understanding.*

**I answer that,** According to the Philosopher (*Metaph.* i: 2), it belongs to wisdom to consider the highest cause. By means of that cause we are able to form a most certain judgment about other causes, and according thereto all things should be set in order. Now the highest cause may be understood in two ways, either simply or in some particular genus. Accordingly he that knows the highest cause in any particular genus, and by its means is able to judge and set in order all the things that belong to that genus, is said to be wise in that genus, for instance in medicine or architecture, according to 1 Cor. 3:10: *As a wise architect, I have laid a foundation.* On the other hand, he who knows the cause that is simply the highest, which is God, is said to be wise simply, because he is able to judge and set in order all things according to Divine rules.

Now man obtains this judgment through the Holy Spirit, according to 1 Cor. 2:15: *The spiritual man judgeth all things*, because as stated in the same chapter (1 Cor 2:10), *the Spirit searcheth all things, yea the deep things of God.* Wherefore it is evident that wisdom is a gift of the Holy Spirit.

**Reply Obj. 1:** A thing is said to be good in two senses: first in the sense that it is truly good and simply perfect, second, by a kind of likeness, being perfect in wickedness; thus we speak of a *good* or a *perfect thief*, as the Philosopher observes (*Metaph.* v, text. 21). And just as with regard to those things which are truly good, we find a highest cause, namely the sovereign good which is the last end, by knowing which, man is said to be truly wise, so too in evil things something is to be found to which all others are to be referred as to a last end, by knowing which, man is said to be wise unto evil doing, according to Jer. 4:22: *They are wise to do evils, but to do good they have no knowledge.* Now whoever turns away from his due end, must needs fix on some undue end, since every agent acts for an end. Wherefore, if he fixes his end in external earthly things, his *wisdom* is called *earthly*, if in the goods of the body, it is called *sensual wisdom*, if in some excellence, it is called *devilish wisdom* because it imitates the devil's pride, of which it is written (Job 41:25): *He is king over all the children of pride.*

**Reply Obj. 2:** The wisdom which is called a gift of the Holy Spirit, differs from that which is an acquired intellectual virtue, for the latter is attained by human effort, whereas the former is *descending from above* (Jas 3:15). In like manner it differs from faith, since faith assents to the Divine truth in itself, whereas it belongs to the gift of wisdom to judge according to the Divine truth. Hence the

donum sapientiae praesupponit fidem, quia *unusquisque bene iudicat quae cognoscit*, ut dicitur in I Ethic.

**AD TERTIUM** dicendum quod sicut pietas, quae pertinet ad cultum Dei, est manifestativa fidei, inquantum per cultum Dei protestamur fidem; ita etiam pietas manifestat sapientiam. Et propter hoc dicitur quod *pietas est sapientia*. Et eadem ratione timor. Per hoc enim ostenditur quod homo rectum habet iudicium de divinis, quod Deum timet et colit.

gift of wisdom presupposes faith, because *a man judges well what he knows* (Ethic. i, 3).

**REPLY OBJ. 3**: Just as piety which pertains to the worship of God is a manifestation of faith, insofar as we make profession of faith by worshipping God, so too, piety manifests wisdom. For this reason *piety* is stated to be *wisdom*, and so is fear, for the same reason, because if a man fear and worship God, this shows that he has a right judgment about Divine things.

# Article 2

### Whether wisdom is in the intellect as its subject?

**AD SECUNDUM SIC PROCEDITUR**. Videtur quod sapientia non sit in intellectu sicut in subiecto. Dicit enim Augustinus, in libro de gratia novi Test., quod *sapientia est caritas Dei*. Sed caritas est sicut in subiecto in voluntate, non in intellectu, ut supra habitum est. Ergo sapientia non est in intellectu sicut in subiecto.

**PRAETEREA**, Eccli. VI dicitur, *sapientia doctrinae secundum nomen eius est*. Dicitur autem sapientia quasi *sapida scientia*, quod videtur ad affectum pertinere, ad quem pertinet experiri spirituales delectationes sive dulcedines. Ergo sapientia non est in intellectu, sed magis in affectu.

**PRAETEREA**, potentia intellectiva sufficienter perficitur per donum intellectus. Sed ad id quod potest fieri per unum superfluum esset plura ponere. Ergo non est in intellectu.

**SED CONTRA** est quod Gregorius dicit, in II Moral., quod sapientia contrariatur stultitiae. Sed stultitia est in intellectu. Ergo et sapientia.

**RESPONDEO** dicendum quod, sicut supra dictum est, sapientia importat quandam rectitudinem iudicii secundum rationes divinas. Rectitudo autem iudicii potest contingere dupliciter, uno modo, secundum perfectum usum rationis; alio modo, propter connaturalitatem quandam ad ea de quibus iam est iudicandum. Sicut de his quae ad castitatem pertinent per rationis inquisitionem recte iudicat ille qui didicit scientiam moralem, sed per quandam connaturalitatem ad ipsa recte iudicat de eis ille qui habet habitum castitatis.

Sic igitur circa res divinas ex rationis inquisitione rectum iudicium habere pertinet ad sapientiam quae est virtus intellectualis, sed rectum iudicium habere de eis secundum quandam connaturalitatem ad ipsa pertinet ad sapientiam secundum quod donum est spiritus sancti, sicut Dionysius dicit, in II cap. de Div. Nom., quod Hierotheus est perfectus in divinis *non solum discens, sed et patiens divina*.

**OBJECTION 1**: It would seem that wisdom is not in the intellect as its subject. For Augustine says (*Ep. cxx*) that *wisdom is the charity of God*. Now charity is in the will as its subject, and not in the intellect, as stated above (Q. 24, A. 1). Therefore wisdom is not in the intellect as its subject.

**OBJ. 2**: Further, it is written (Sir 6:23): *The wisdom of doctrine is according to her name*, for wisdom (*sapientia*) may be described as *sweet-tasting science (sapida scientia)*, and this would seem to regard the appetite, to which it belongs to taste spiritual pleasure or sweetness. Therefore wisdom is in the appetite rather than in the intellect.

**OBJ. 3**: Further, the intellective power is sufficiently perfected by the gift of understanding. Now it is superfluous to require two things where one suffices for the purpose. Therefore wisdom is not in the intellect.

**ON THE CONTRARY**, Gregory says (*Moral.* ii, 49) that wisdom is contrary to folly. But folly is in the intellect. Therefore wisdom is also.

**I ANSWER THAT**, As stated above (A. 1), wisdom denotes a certain rectitude of judgment according to the Eternal Law. Now rectitude of judgment is twofold: first, on account of perfect use of reason, second, on account of a certain connaturality with the matter about which one has to judge. Thus, about matters of chastity, a man after inquiring with his reason forms a right judgment, if he has learnt the science of morals, while he who has the habit of chastity judges of such matters by a kind of connaturality.

Accordingly it belongs to the wisdom that is an intellectual virtue to pronounce right judgment about Divine things after reason has made its inquiry, but it belongs to wisdom as a gift of the Holy Spirit to judge aright about them on account of connaturality with them: thus Dionysius says (*Div. Nom.* ii) that Hierotheus is perfect in divine things, *for he not only learns, but is patient of, divine things*.

Huiusmodi autem compassio sive connaturalitas ad res divinas fit per caritatem, quae quidem unit nos Deo, secundum illud I ad Cor. VI, *qui adhaeret Deo unus spiritus est.* Sic igitur sapientia quae est donum causam quidem habet in voluntate, scilicet caritatem, sed essentiam habet in intellectu, cuius actus est recte iudicare, ut supra habitum est.

**AD PRIMUM** ergo dicendum quod Augustinus loquitur de sapientia quantum ad suam causam. Ex qua etiam sumitur nomen sapientiae, secundum quod *saporem* quendam importat.

**UNDE PATET** responsio ad secundum. Si tamen iste sit intellectus illius auctoritatis. Quod non videtur, quia talis expositio non convenit nisi secundum nomen quod habet sapientia in Latina lingua. In Graeco autem non competit; et forte nec in aliis linguis. Unde potius videtur *nomen* sapientiae ibi accipi pro eius fama, qua a cunctis commendatur.

**AD TERTIUM** dicendum quod intellectus habet duos actus, scilicet percipere, et iudicare. Ad quorum primum ordinatur donum intellectus, ad secundum autem, secundum rationes divinas, donum sapientiae; sed secundum rationes humanas, donum scientiae.

Now this sympathy or connaturality for Divine things is the result of charity, which unites us to God, according to 1 Cor. 6:17: *He who is joined to the Lord, is one spirit.* Consequently wisdom which is a gift, has its cause in the will, which cause is charity, but it has its essence in the intellect, whose act is to judge aright, as stated above (I-II, Q. 14, A. 1).

**REPLY OBJ. 1**: Augustine is speaking of wisdom as to its cause, whence also wisdom (*sapientia*) takes its name, insofar as it denotes a certain sweetness (*saporem*).

**HENCE** the Reply to the Second Objection is evident, that is if this be the true meaning of the text quoted. For, apparently this is not the case, because such an exposition of the text would only fit the Latin word for wisdom, whereas it does not apply to the Greek and perhaps not in other languages. Hence it would seem that in the text quoted wisdom stands for the renown of doctrine, for which it is praised by all.

**REPLY OBJ. 3**: The intellect exercises a twofold act, perception and judgment. The gift of understanding regards the former; the gift of wisdom regards the latter according to the Divine ideas, the gift of knowledge, according to human ideas.

# Article 3

*Whether wisdom is merely speculative, or practical also?*

**AD TERTIUM SIC PROCEDITUR.** Videtur quod sapientia non sit practica, sed speculativa tantum. Donum enim sapientiae est excellentius quam sapientia secundum quod est intellectualis virtus. Sed sapientia secundum quod est intellectualis virtus est speculativa tantum. Ergo multo magis sapientia quae est donum est speculativa, et non practica.

**PRAETEREA**, practicus intellectus est circa operabilia, quae sunt contingentia. Sed sapientia est circa divina, quae sunt aeterna et necessaria. Ergo sapientia non potest esse practica.

**PRAETEREA**, Gregorius dicit, in VI Moral., quod *in contemplatione principium, quod Deus est, quaeritur, in operatione autem sub gravi necessitatis fasce laboratur.* Sed ad sapientiam pertinet divinorum visio, ad quam non pertinet sub aliquo fasce laborare, quia ut dicitur Sap. VIII, *non habet amaritudinem conversatio eius, nec taedium convictus illius.* Ergo sapientia est contemplativa tantum, non autem practica sive activa.

**SED CONTRA** est quod dicitur ad Coloss. IV, *in sapientia ambulate ad eos qui foris sunt.* Hoc autem pertinet ad actionem. Ergo sapientia non solum est speculativa, sed etiam practica.

**OBJECTION 1**: It would seem that wisdom is not practical but merely speculative. For the gift of wisdom is more excellent than the wisdom which is an intellectual virtue. But wisdom, as an intellectual virtue, is merely speculative. Much more therefore is wisdom, as a gift, speculative and not practical.

**OBJ. 2**: Further, the practical intellect is about matters of operation which are contingent. But wisdom is about Divine things which are eternal and necessary. Therefore wisdom cannot be practical.

**OBJ. 3**: Further, Gregory says (*Moral.* vi, 37) that *in contemplation we seek the Beginning which is God, but in action we labor under a mighty bundle of wants.* Now wisdom regards the vision of Divine things, in which there is no toiling under a load, since according to Wis. 8:16, *her conversation hath no bitterness, nor her company any tediousness.* Therefore wisdom is merely contemplative, and not practical or active.

**ON THE CONTRARY**, It is written (Col 4:5): *Walk with wisdom towards them that are without.* Now this pertains to action. Therefore wisdom is not merely speculative, but also practical.

**RESPONDEO** dicendum quod, sicut Augustinus dicit, in XII de Trin., superior pars rationis sapientiae deputatur, inferior autem scientiae. Superior autem ratio, ut ipse in eodem libro dicit, intendit *rationibus supernis*, scilicet divinis, *et conspiciendis et consulendis*, conspiciendis quidem, secundum quod divina in seipsis contemplatur; consulendis autem, secundum quod per divina iudicat de humanis, per divinas regulas dirigens actus humanos.

Sic igitur sapientia, secundum quod est donum, non solum est speculativa, sed etiam practica.

**AD PRIMUM** ergo dicendum quod quanto aliqua virtus est altior, tanto ad plura se extendit; ut habetur in libro de causis. Unde ex hoc ipso quod sapientia quae est donum est excellentior quam sapientia quae est virtus intellectualis, utpote magis de propinquo Deum attingens, per quandam scilicet unionem animae ad ipsum, habet quod non solum dirigat in contemplatione, sed etiam in actione.

**AD SECUNDUM** dicendum quod divina in se quidem sunt necessaria et aeterna, sunt tamen regulae contingentium, quae humanis actibus subsunt.

**AD TERTIUM** dicendum quod prius est considerare aliquid in seipso quam secundum quod ad alterum comparatur. Unde ad sapientiam per prius pertinet contemplatio divinorum, quae est *visio principii*; et posterius dirigere actus humanos secundum rationes divinas. Nec tamen in actibus humanis ex directione sapientiae provenit amaritudo aut labor, sed potius amaritudo propter sapientiam vertitur in dulcedinem, et labor in requiem.

**I ANSWER THAT,** As Augustine says (*De Trin.* xii, 14), the higher part of the reason is the province of wisdom, while the lower part is the domain of knowledge. Now the higher reason according to the same authority (*De Trin.* xii, 7) *is intent on the consideration and consultation of the heavenly*, i.e., Divine, *types*; it considers them, insofar as it contemplates Divine things in themselves, and it consults them, insofar as it judges of human acts by Divine things, and directs human acts according to Divine rules.

Accordingly wisdom as a gift, is not merely speculative but also practical.

**REPLY OBJ. 1:** The higher a virtue is, the greater the number of things to which it extends, as stated in De Causis, prop. x, xvii. Wherefore from the very fact that wisdom as a gift is more excellent than wisdom as an intellectual virtue, since it attains to God more intimately by a kind of union of the soul with Him, it is able to direct us not only in contemplation but also in action.

**REPLY OBJ. 2:** Divine things are indeed necessary and eternal in themselves, yet they are the rules of the contingent things which are the subject-matter of human actions.

**REPLY OBJ. 3:** A thing is considered in itself before being compared with something else. Wherefore to wisdom belongs first of all contemplation which is the *vision of the Beginning*, and afterwards the direction of human acts according to the Divine rules. Nor from the direction of wisdom does there result any bitterness or toil in human acts; on the contrary the result of wisdom is to make the bitter sweet, and labor a rest.

# Article 4

*Whether wisdom can be without grace, and with mortal sin?*

**AD QUARTUM SIC PROCEDITUR.** Videtur quod sapientia possit esse sine gratia, cum peccato mortali. De his enim quae cum peccato mortali haberi non possunt praecipue sancti gloriantur, secundum illud II ad Cor. I, *gloria nostra haec est, testimonium conscientiae nostrae.* Sed de sapientia non debet aliquis gloriari, secundum illud Ierem. IX, *non glorietur sapiens in sapientia sua.* Ergo sapientia potest esse sine gratia, cum peccato mortali.

**PRAETEREA**, sapientia importat cognitionem divinorum, ut dictum est. Sed aliqui cum peccato mortali possunt habere cognitionem veritatis divinae, secundum illud Rom. I, *veritatem Dei in iniustitia detinent.* Ergo sapientia potest esse cum peccato mortali.

**PRAETEREA**, Augustinus dicit, in XV de Trin., de caritate loquens, *nullum est isto Dei dono excellentius, solum est quod dividit inter filios regni aeterni et filios perditionis aeternae.* Sed sapientia differt a caritate. Ergo

**OBJECTION 1:** It would seem that wisdom can be without grace and with mortal sin. For saints glory chiefly in such things as are incompatible with mortal sin, according to 2 Cor. 1:12: *Our glory is this, the testimony of our conscience.* Now one ought not to glory in one's wisdom, according to Jer. 9:23: *Let not the wise man glory in his wisdom.* Therefore wisdom can be without grace and with mortal sin.

**OBJ. 2:** Further, wisdom denotes knowledge of Divine things, as stated above (A. 1). Now one in mortal sin may have knowledge of the Divine truth, according to Rom. 1:18: *(Those men that) detain the truth of God in injustice.* Therefore wisdom is compatible with mortal sin.

**OBJ. 3:** Further, Augustine says (*De Trin.* xv, 18) while speaking of charity: *Nothing surpasses this gift of God, it is this alone that divides the children of the eternal kingdom from the children of eternal perdition.* But wisdom is distinct

non dividit inter filios regni et filios perditionis. Ergo potest esse cum peccato mortali.

**Sed contra** est quod dicitur Sap. I, *in malevolam animam non introibit sapientia, nec habitabit in corpore subdito peccatis.*

**Respondeo** dicendum quod sapientia quae est donum spiritus sancti, sicut dictum est, facit rectitudinem iudicii circa res divinas, vel per regulas divinas de aliis, ex quadam connaturalitate sive unione ad divina. Quae quidem est per caritatem, ut dictum est. Et ideo sapientia de qua loquimur praesupponit caritatem. Caritas autem non potest esse cum peccato mortali, ut ex supradictis patet. Unde relinquitur quod sapientia de qua loquimur non potest esse cum peccato mortali.

**Ad primum** ergo dicendum quod illud intelligendum est de sapientia in rebus mundanis; sive etiam in rebus divinis per rationes humanas. De qua sancti non gloriantur, sed eam se fatentur non habere, secundum illud Prov. XXX, *sapientia hominum non est mecum.* Gloriantur autem de sapientia divina, secundum illud I ad Cor. I, *factus est nobis sapientia a Deo.*

**Ad secundum** dicendum quod ratio illa procedit de cognitione divinorum quae habetur per studium et inquisitionem rationis. Quae potest haberi cum peccato mortali, non autem illa sapientia de qua loquimur.

**Ad tertium** dicendum quod sapientia, etsi differat a caritate, tamen praesupponit eam; et ex hoc ipso dividit inter filios perditionis et regni.

from charity. Therefore it does not divide the children of the kingdom from the children of perdition. Therefore it is compatible with mortal sin.

**On the contrary,** It is written (Wis 1:4): *Wisdom will not enter into a malicious soul, nor dwell in a body subject to sins.*

**I answer that,** The wisdom which is a gift of the Holy Spirit, as stated above (A. 1), enables us to judge aright of Divine things, or of other things according to Divine rules, by reason of a certain connaturalness or union with Divine things, which is the effect of charity, as stated above (A. 2; Q. 23, A. 5). Hence the wisdom of which we are speaking presupposes charity. Now charity is incompatible with mortal sin, as shown above (Q. 24, A. 12). Therefore it follows that the wisdom of which we are speaking cannot be together with mortal sin.

**Reply Obj. 1:** These words are to be understood as referring to worldly wisdom, or to wisdom in Divine things acquired through human reasons. In such wisdom the saints do not glory, according to Prov. 30:2: *The wisdom of men is not with Me*: But they do glory in Divine wisdom according to 1 Cor. 1:30: *(Who) of God is made unto us wisdom.*

**Reply Obj. 2:** This argument considers, not the wisdom of which we speak but that which is acquired by the study and research of reason, and is compatible with mortal sin.

**Reply Obj. 3:** Although wisdom is distinct from charity, it presupposes it, and for that very reason divides the children of perdition from the children of the kingdom.

# Article 5

*Whether wisdom is in all who have grace?*

**Ad quintum sic proceditur.** Videtur quod sapientia non sit in omnibus habentibus gratiam. Maius enim est sapientiam habere quam sapientiam audire. Sed solum perfectorum est sapientiam audire, secundum illud I ad Cor. II, *sapientiam loquimur inter perfectos.* Cum ergo non omnes habentes gratiam sint perfecti, videtur quod multo minus omnes habentes gratiam sapientiam habeant.

**Praeterea,** *sapientis est ordinare*; ut Philosophus dicit, in principio Metaphys. Et Iac. III dicitur quod est *iudicans sine simulatione.* Sed non omnium habentium gratiam est de aliis iudicare aut alios ordinare, sed solum praelatorum. Ergo non omnium habentium gratiam est habere sapientiam.

**Praeterea,** sapientia datur contra stultitiam; ut Gregorius dicit, in II Moral. Sed multi habentes gratiam sunt naturaliter stulti, ut patet de amentibus baptizatis,

**Objection 1:** It would seem that wisdom is not in all who have grace. For it is more to have wisdom than to hear wisdom. Now it is only for the perfect to hear wisdom, according to 1 Cor. 2:6: *We speak wisdom among the perfect.* Since then not all who have grace are perfect, it seems that much less all who have grace have wisdom.

**Obj. 2:** Further, *The wise man sets things in order*, as the Philosopher states (*Metaph.* i, 2): and it is written (Jas 3:17) that the wise man *judges without dissimulation.* Now it is not for all that have grace, to judge, or put others in order, but only for those in authority. Therefore wisdom is not in all that have grace.

**Obj. 3:** Further, Wisdom is a remedy against folly, as Gregory says (*Moral.* ii, 49). Now many that have grace are naturally foolish, for instance madmen who are baptized or

vel qui postmodum sine peccato in amentiam incidunt. Ergo non in omnibus habentibus gratiam est sapientia.

**SED CONTRA** est quod quicumque qui est sine peccato mortali diligitur a Deo, quia caritatem habet, qua Deum diligit; Deus autem *diligentes se diligit*, ut dicitur Prov. VIII. Sed Sap. VII dicitur quod *neminem diligit Deus nisi eum qui cum sapientia inhabitat.* Ergo in omnibus habentibus gratiam, sine peccato mortali existentibus, est sapientia.

**RESPONDEO** dicendum quod sapientia de qua loquimur, sicut dictum est, importat quandam rectitudinem iudicii circa divina et conspicienda et consulenda. Et quantum ad utrumque, ex unione ad divina secundum diversos gradus aliqui sapientiam sortiuntur. Quidam enim tantum sortiuntur de recto iudicio, tam in contemplatione divinorum quam etiam in ordinatione rerum humanarum secundum divinas regulas, quantum est necessarium ad salutem. Et hoc nulli deest sine peccato mortali existenti per gratiam gratum facientem, quia si natura non deficit in necessariis, multo minus gratia. Unde dicitur I Ioan. II, *unctio docet vos de omnibus.*

Quidam autem altiori gradu percipiunt sapientiae donum, et quantum ad contemplationem divinorum, inquantum scilicet altiora quaedam mysteria et cognoscunt et aliis manifestare possunt; et etiam quantum ad directionem humanorum secundum regulas divinas, inquantum possunt secundum eas non solum seipsos, sed etiam alios ordinare. Et iste gradus sapientiae non est communis omnibus habentibus gratiam gratum facientem, sed magis pertinet ad gratias gratis datas, quas Spiritus Sanctus *distribuit prout vult*, secundum illud I ad Cor. XII, *alii datur per spiritum sermo sapientiae*, et cetera.

**AD PRIMUM** ergo dicendum quod apostolus loquitur ibi de sapientia secundum quod se extendit ad occulta mysteria divinorum, sicut et ibidem dicitur, *loquimur Dei sapientiam in mysterio absconditam.*

**AD SECUNDUM** dicendum quod quamvis ordinare alios homines et de eis iudicare pertineat ad solos praelatos, tamen ordinare proprios actus et de eis iudicare pertinet ad unumquemque; ut patet per Dionysium, in epistola ad Demophilum.

**AD TERTIUM** dicendum quod amentes baptizati, sicut et pueri, habent quidem habitum sapientiae, secundum quod est donum spiritus sancti, sed non habent actum, propter impedimentum corporale quo impeditur in eis usus rationis.

those who without being guilty of mortal sin have become insane. Therefore wisdom is not in all that have grace.

**ON THE CONTRARY,** Whoever is without mortal sin, is beloved of God; since he has charity, whereby he loves God, and *God loves them that love Him* (Prov 8:17). Now it is written (Wis 7:28) that *God loveth none but him that dwelleth with wisdom.* Therefore wisdom is in all those who have charity and are without mortal sin.

**I ANSWER THAT,** The wisdom of which we are speaking, as stated above (A. 4), denotes a certain rectitude of judgment in the contemplation and consultation of Divine things, and as to both of these men obtain various degrees of wisdom through union with Divine things. For the measure of right judgment attained by some, whether in the contemplation of Divine things or in directing human affairs according to Divine rules, is no more than suffices for their salvation. This measure is wanting to none who is without mortal sin through having sanctifying grace, since if nature does not fail in necessaries, much less does grace fail: wherefore it is written (1 John 2:27): *(His) unction teacheth you of all things.*

Some, however, receive a higher degree of the gift of wisdom, both as to the contemplation of Divine things (by both knowing more exalted mysteries and being able to impart this knowledge to others) and as to the direction of human affairs according to Divine rules (by being able to direct not only themselves but also others according to those rules). This degree of wisdom is not common to all that have sanctifying grace, but belongs rather to the gratuitous graces, which the Holy Spirit *dispenses as He will*, according to 1 Cor. 12:8: *To one indeed by the Spirit is given the word of wisdom*, etc.

**REPLY OBJ. 1:** The Apostle speaks there of wisdom, as extending to the hidden mysteries of Divine things, as indeed he says himself (2 Cor 1:7): *We speak the wisdom of God in a mystery, a wisdom which is hidden.*

**REPLY OBJ. 2:** Although it belongs to those alone who are in authority to direct and judge other men, yet every man is competent to direct and judge his own actions, as Dionysius declares (*Ep. ad Demophil.*).

**REPLY OBJ. 3:** Baptized idiots, like little children, have the habit of wisdom, which is a gift of the Holy Spirit, but they have not the act, on account of the bodily impediment which hinders the use of reason in them.

# Article 6

*Whether the seventh beatitude corresponds to the gift of wisdom?*

AD SEXTUM SIC PROCEDITUR. Videtur quod septima beatitudo non respondeat dono sapientiae. Septima enim beatitudo est, *beati pacifici, quoniam filii Dei vocabuntur*. Utrumque autem horum pertinet immediate ad caritatem. Nam de pace dicitur in Psalm., *pax multa diligentibus legem tuam*. Et ut apostolus dicit, Rom. V, *caritas Dei diffusa est in cordibus nostris per spiritum sanctum, qui datus est nobis*; qui quidem est spiritus adoptionis filiorum, in quo clamamus, abba, pater, ut dicitur Rom. VIII. Ergo septima beatitudo magis debet attribui caritati quam sapientiae.

PRAETEREA, unumquodque magis manifestatur per proximum effectum quam per remotum. Sed proximus effectus sapientiae videtur esse caritas, secundum illud Sap. VII, *per nationes in animas sanctas se transfert, amicos Dei et prophetas constituit*, pax autem et adoptio filiorum videntur esse remoti effectus, cum procedant ex caritate, ut dictum est. Ergo beatitudo sapientiae respondens deberet magis determinari secundum dilectionem caritatis quam secundum pacem.

PRAETEREA, Iac. III dicitur, *quae desursum est sapientia primo quidem pudica est, deinde autem pacifica, modesta, suadibilis, bonis consentiens, plena misericordia et fructibus bonis, iudicans sine simulatione*. Beatitudo ergo correspondens sapientiae non magis debuit accipi secundum pacem quam secundum alios effectus caelestis sapientiae.

SED CONTRA est quod Augustinus dicit, in libro de Serm. Dom. in monte, quod *sapientia convenit pacificis, in quibus nullus motus est rebellis, sed obtemperans rationi*.

RESPONDEO dicendum quod septima beatitudo congrue adaptatur dono sapientiae et quantum ad meritum et quantum ad praemium. Ad meritum quidem pertinet quod dicitur, *beati pacifici*. Pacifici autem dicuntur quasi pacem facientes vel in seipsis vel etiam in aliis. Quorum utrumque contingit per hoc quod ea in quibus pax constituitur ad debitum ordinem rediguntur, nam pax est *tranquillitas ordinis*, ut Augustinus dicit, XIX de Civ. Dei. Ordinare autem pertinet ad sapientiam; ut patet per philosophum, in principio Metaphys. Et ideo esse pacificum convenienter attribuitur sapientiae. Ad praemium autem pertinet quod dicitur, *filii Dei vocabuntur*. Dicuntur autem aliqui filii Dei inquantum participant similitudinem filii unigeniti et naturalis, secundum illud Rom. VIII, *quos praescivit conformes fieri imaginis filii sui*, qui quidem est sapientia genita. Et ideo percipiendo donum sapientiae, ad Dei filiationem homo pertingit.

OBJECTION 1: It seems that the seventh beatitude does not correspond to the gift of wisdom. For the seventh beatitude is: *Blessed are the peacemakers, for they shall be called the children of God*. Now both these things belong to charity: since of peace it is written (Ps 118:165): *Much peace have they that love Thy law*, and, as the Apostle says (Rom 5:5), *the charity of God is poured forth in our hearts by the Holy Spirit Who is given to us*, and Who is *the Spirit of adoption of sons, whereby we cry: Abba* (Rom 8:15). Therefore the seventh beatitude ought to be ascribed to charity rather than to wisdom.

OBJ. 2: Further, a thing is declared by its proximate effect rather than by its remote effect. Now the proximate effect of wisdom seems to be charity, according to Wis. 7:27: *Through nations she conveyeth herself into holy souls; she maketh the friends of God and prophets*: whereas peace and the adoption of sons seem to be remote effects, since they result from charity, as stated above (Q. 29, A. 3). Therefore the beatitude corresponding to wisdom should be determined in respect of the love of charity rather than in respect of peace.

OBJ. 3: Further, it is written (Jas 3:17): *The wisdom, that is from above, first indeed is chaste, then peaceable, modest, easy to be persuaded, consenting to the good, full of mercy and good fruits, judging without dissimulation*. Therefore the beatitude corresponding to wisdom should not refer to peace rather than to the other effects of heavenly wisdom.

ON THE CONTRARY, Augustine says (*De Serm. Dom. in Monte* i, 4) that *wisdom is becoming to peacemakers, in whom there is no movement of rebellion, but only obedience to reason*.

I ANSWER THAT, The seventh beatitude is fittingly ascribed to the gift of wisdom, both as to the merit and as to the reward. The merit is denoted in the words, *Blessed are the peacemakers*. Now a peacemaker is one who makes peace, either in himself, or in others: and in both cases this is the result of setting in due order those things in which peace is established, for *peace is the tranquillity of order*, according to Augustine (*De Civ. Dei* xix, 13). Now it belongs to wisdom to set things in order, as the Philosopher declares (*Metaph.* i, 2), wherefore peaceableness is fittingly ascribed to wisdom. The reward is expressed in the words, *they shall be called the children of God*. Now men are called the children of God insofar as they participate in the likeness of the only-begotten and natural Son of God, according to Rom. 8:29, *Whom He foreknew . . . to be made conformable to the image of His Son*, Who is Wisdom Begotten. Hence by participating in the gift of wisdom, man attains to the sonship of God.

**Ad primum** ergo dicendum quod caritatis est habere pacem, sed facere pacem est sapientiae ordinantis. Similiter etiam Spiritus Sanctus intantum dicitur *spiritus adoptionis* inquantum per eum datur nobis similitudo filii naturalis, qui est genita sapientia.

**Ad secundum** dicendum quod illud est intelligendum de sapientia increata, quae prima se nobis unit per donum caritatis, et ex hoc revelat nobis mysteria, quorum cognitio est sapientia infusa. Et ideo sapientia infusa, quae est donum, non est causa caritatis, sed magis effectus.

**Ad tertium** dicendum quod, sicut iam dictum est, ad sapientiam, secundum quod est donum, pertinet non solum contemplari divina, sed etiam regulare humanos actus. In qua quidem directione primo occurrit remotio a malis quae contrariantur sapientiae, unde et timor dicitur esse *initium sapientiae*, inquantum facit recedere a malis. Ultimum autem est, sicut finis, quod omnia ad debitum ordinem redigantur, quod pertinet ad rationem pacis. Et ideo convenienter Iacobus dicit quod *sapientia quae desursum est*, quae est donum spiritus sancti, *primum est pudica*, quasi vitans corruptelas peccati; *deinde autem pacifica*, quod est finalis effectus sapientiae, propter quod ponitur beatitudo. Iam vero omnia quae sequuntur manifestant ea per quae sapientia ad pacem perducit, et ordine congruo. Nam homini per pudicitiam a corruptelis recedenti primo occurrit quod quantum ex se potest, modum in omnibus teneat, et quantum ad hoc dicitur, *modesta*. Secundo, ut in his in quibus ipse sibi non sufficit, aliorum monitis acquiescat, et quantum ad hoc subdit, *suadibilis*. Et haec duo pertinent ad hoc quod homo consequatur pacem in seipso. Sed ulterius, ad hoc quod homo sit pacificus etiam aliis, primo requiritur ut bonis eorum non repugnet, et hoc est quod dicit, *bonis consentiens*. Secundo, quod defectibus proximi et compatiatur in affectu et subveniat in effectu, et hoc est quod dicitur, *plena misericordia et fructibus bonis*. Tertio requiritur ut caritative emendare peccata satagat, et hoc est quod dicit, *iudicans sine simulatione*, ne scilicet, correctionem praetendens, odium intendat explere.

**Reply Obj. 1**: It belongs to charity to be at peace, but it belongs to wisdom to make peace by setting things in order. Likewise the Holy Spirit is called the *Spirit of adoption* insofar as we receive from Him the likeness of the natural Son, Who is the Begotten Wisdom.

**Reply Obj. 2**: These words refer to the Uncreated Wisdom, which in the first place unites itself to us by the gift of charity, and consequently reveals to us the mysteries the knowledge of which is infused wisdom. Hence, the infused wisdom which is a gift, is not the cause but the effect of charity.

**Reply Obj. 3**: As stated above (A. 3) it belongs to wisdom, as a gift, not only to contemplate Divine things, but also to regulate human acts. Now the first thing to be effected in this direction of human acts is the removal of evils opposed to wisdom: wherefore fear is said to be *the beginning of wisdom*, because it makes us shun evil, while the last thing is like an end, whereby all things are reduced to their right order; and it is this that constitutes peace. Hence James said with reason that *the wisdom that is from above* (and this is the gift of the Holy Spirit) *first indeed is chaste*, because it avoids the corruption of sin, and *then peaceable*, wherein lies the ultimate effect of wisdom, for which reason peace is numbered among the beatitudes. As to the things that follow, they declare in becoming order the means whereby wisdom leads to peace. For when a man, by chastity, avoids the corruption of sin, the first thing he has to do is, as far as he can, to be moderate in all things, and in this respect wisdom is said to be modest. Second, in those matters in which he is not sufficient by himself, he should be guided by the advice of others, and as to this we are told further that wisdom is *easy to be persuaded*. These two are conditions required that man may be at peace with himself. But in order that man may be at peace with others it is furthermore required, first that he should not be opposed to their good; this is what is meant by *consenting to the good*. Second, that he should bring to his neighbor's deficiencies, sympathy in his heart, and succor in his actions, and this is denoted by the words *full of mercy and good fruits*. Third, he should strive in all charity to correct the sins of others, and this is indicated by the words *judging without dissimulation*, lest he should purpose to sate his hatred under cover of correction.

## FOLLY

Deinde considerandum est de stultitia, quae opponitur sapientiae. Et circa hoc quaeruntur tria.

Primo, utrum stultitia opponatur sapientiae.

Secundo, utrum stultitia sit peccatum.

Tertio, ad quod vitium capitale reducatur.

We must now consider folly which is opposed to wisdom; and under this head there are three points of inquiry:

(1) Whether folly is contrary to wisdom?

(2) Whether folly is a sin?

(3) To which capital sin is it reducible?

# Article 1

*Whether folly is contrary to wisdom?*

**AD PRIMUM SIC PROCEDITUR.** Videtur quod stultitia non opponatur sapientiae. sapientiae enim directe videtur opponi insipientia. Sed stultitia non videtur esse idem quod insipientia, quia insipientia videtur esse solum circa divina, sicut et sapientia; stultitia autem se habet et circa divina et circa humana. Ergo sapientiae non opponitur stultitia.

**PRAETEREA,** unum oppositorum non est via perveniendi ad aliud. Sed stultitia est via perveniendi ad sapientiam, dicitur enim I ad Cor. III, *si quis videtur inter vos sapiens esse in hoc saeculo, stultus fiat, ut sit sapiens.* Ergo sapientiae non opponitur stultitia.

**PRAETEREA,** unum oppositorum non est causa alterius. Sapientia autem est causa stultitiae, dicitur enim Ierem. X, *stultus factus est omnis homo a scientia sua;* sapientia autem quaedam scientia est. Et Isaiae XLVII dicitur, *sapientia tua et scientia tua, haec decepit te,* decipi autem ad stultitiam pertinet. Ergo sapientiae non opponitur stultitia.

**PRAETEREA,** Isidorus dicit, in libro Etymol., quod *stultus est qui per ignominiam non commovetur ad dolorem, et qui non movetur iniuria.* Sed hoc pertinet ad sapientiam spiritualem; ut Gregorius dicit, in X Moral. Ergo sapientiae non opponitur stultitia.

**SED CONTRA** est quod Gregorius dicit, in II Moral., quod donum sapientiae datur contra stultitiam.

**RESPONDEO** dicendum quod nomen stultitiae a stupore videtur esse sumptum, unde Isidorus dicit, in libro Etymol., *stultus est qui propter stuporem non movetur.* Et differt stultitia a fatuitate, sicut ibidem dicitur, quia stultitia importat hebetudinem cordis et obtusionem sensuum; fatuitas autem importat totaliter spiritualis sensus privationem. Et ideo convenienter stultitia sapientiae opponitur.

*Sapiens* enim, ut ibidem Isidorus dicit, *dictus est a sapore, quia sicut gustus est aptus ad discretionem saporis*

**OBJECTION 1:** It would seem that folly is not contrary to wisdom. For seemingly unwisdom is directly opposed to wisdom. But folly does not seem to be the same as unwisdom, for the latter is apparently about Divine things alone, whereas folly is about both Divine and human things. Therefore folly is not contrary to wisdom.

**OBJ. 2:** Further, one contrary is not the way to arrive at the other. But folly is the way to arrive at wisdom, for it is written (1 Cor 3:18): *If any man among you seem to be wise in this world, let him become a fool, that he may be wise.* Therefore folly is not opposed to wisdom.

**OBJ. 3:** Further, one contrary is not the cause of the other. But wisdom is the cause of folly; for it is written (Jer 10:14): *Every man is become a fool for knowledge,* and wisdom is a kind of knowledge. Moreover, it is written (Isa 47:10): *Thy wisdom and thy knowledge, this hath deceived thee.* Now it belongs to folly to be deceived. Therefore folly is not contrary to wisdom.

**OBJ. 4:** Further, Isidore says (*Etym.* x, under the letter S) that *a fool is one whom shame does not incite to sorrow, and who is unconcerned when he is injured.* But this pertains to spiritual wisdom, according to Gregory (*Moral.* x, 49). Therefore folly is not opposed to wisdom.

**ON THE CONTRARY,** Gregory says (*Moral.* ii, 26) that the gift of wisdom is given as a remedy against folly.

**I ANSWER THAT,** *Stultitia* (Folly) seems to take its name from stupor; wherefore Isidore says (loc. cit.): *A fool is one who through stupor remains unmoved.* And folly differs from fatuity, according to the same authority (*Etym.* x), in that folly implies apathy in the heart and dullness in the senses, while fatuity denotes entire privation of the spiritual sense. Therefore folly is fittingly opposed to wisdom.

For *sapiens* (wise) as Isidore says (*Etym.* x) *is so named from* sapor *(savor), because just as the taste is quick to*

*ciborum, sic sapiens ad dignoscentiam rerum atque causarum.* Unde patet quod stultitia opponitur sapientiae sicut contrarium; fatuitas autem sicut pura negatio. Nam fatuus caret sensu iudicandi; stultus autem habet, sed hebetatum; sapiens autem subtilem ac perspicacem.

AD PRIMUM ergo dicendum quod, sicut Isidorus ibidem dicit, *insipiens contrarius est sapienti, eo quod est sine sapore discretionis et sensus.* Unde idem videtur esse insipientia cum stultitia. Praecipue autem videtur aliquis esse stultus quando patitur defectum in sententia iudicii quae attenditur secundum causam altissimam, nam si deficiat in iudicio circa aliquid modicum, non ex hoc vocatur aliquis stultus.

AD SECUNDUM dicendum quod sicut est quaedam sapientia mala, ut supra dictum est, quae dicitur *sapientia saeculi,* quia accipit pro causa altissima et fine ultimo aliquod terrenum bonum; ita etiam est aliqua stultitia bona, huic sapientiae malae opposita, per quam aliquis terrena contemnit. Et de hac stultitia loquitur apostolus.

AD TERTIUM dicendum quod sapientia saeculi est quae decipit et facit esse *stultum apud Deum,* ut patet per apostolum, I ad Cor. III.

AD QUARTUM dicendum quod non moveri iniuriis quandoque quidem contingit ex hoc quod homini non sapiunt terrena, sed sola caelestia. Unde hoc pertinet ad stultitiam mundi, sed ad sapientiam Dei, ut Gregorius ibidem dicit. Quandoque autem contingit ex hoc quod homo est simpliciter circa omnia stupidus, ut patet in amentibus, qui non discernunt quid sit iniuria. Et hoc pertinet ad stultitiam simpliciter.

*distinguish between savors of meats,* so is a wise man in discerning things and causes. Wherefore it is manifest that folly is opposed to wisdom as its contrary, while fatuity is opposed to it as a pure negation: since the fatuous man lacks the sense of judgment, while the fool has the sense, though dulled, whereas the wise man has the sense acute and penetrating.

REPLY OBJ. 1: According to Isidore (*Etym.* x), *unwisdom is contrary to wisdom because it lacks the savor of discretion and sense;* so that unwisdom is seemingly the same as folly. Yet a man would appear to be a fool chiefly through some deficiency in the verdict of that judgment, which is according to the highest cause, for if a man fails in judgment about some trivial matter, he is not for that reason called a fool.

REPLY OBJ. 2: Just as there is an evil wisdom, as stated above (Q. 45, A. 1, ad 1), called *worldly wisdom,* because it takes for the highest cause and last end some worldly good, so too there is a good folly opposed to this evil wisdom, whereby man despises worldly things: and it is of this folly that the Apostle speaks.

REPLY OBJ. 3: It is the wisdom of the world that deceives and makes us foolish in God's sight, as is evident from the Apostle's words (1 Cor 3:19).

REPLY OBJ. 4: To be unconcerned when one is injured is sometimes due to the fact that one has no taste for worldly things, but only for heavenly things. Hence this belongs not to worldly but to Divine wisdom, as Gregory declares (*Moral.* x, 49). Sometimes however it is the result of a man's being simply stupid about everything, as may be seen in idiots, who do not discern what is injurious to them, and this belongs to folly simply.

# Article 2

### *Whether folly is a sin?*

AD SECUNDUM SIC PROCEDITUR. Videtur quod stultitia non sit peccatum. Nullum enim peccatum provenit in nobis a natura. Sed quidam sunt stulti naturaliter. Ergo stultitia non est peccatum.

PRAETEREA, omne peccatum est voluntarium, ut Augustinus dicit. Sed stultitia non est voluntaria. Ergo non est peccatum.

PRAETEREA, omne peccatum opponitur alicui praecepto divino. Sed stultitia nulli praecepto opponitur. Ergo stultitia non est peccatum.

SED CONTRA est quod dicitur Prov. I, *prosperitas stultorum perdet eos.* Sed nullus perditur nisi pro peccato. Ergo stultitia est peccatum.

RESPONDEO dicendum quod stultitia, sicut dictum est, importat quendam stuporem sensus in iudicando,

OBJECTION 1: It would seem that folly is not a sin. For no sin arises in us from nature. But some are fools naturally. Therefore folly is not a sin.

OBJ. 2: Further, every sin is voluntary, according to Augustine (*De Vera Relig.* xiv). But folly is not voluntary. Therefore it is not a sin.

OBJ. 3: Further, every sin is contrary to a Divine precept. But folly is not contrary to any precept. Therefore folly is not a sin.

ON THE CONTRARY, It is written (Prov 1:32): *The prosperity of fools shall destroy them.* But no man is destroyed save for sin. Therefore folly is a sin.

I ANSWER THAT, Folly, as stated above (A. 1), denotes dullness of sense in judging, and chiefly as regards the high-

et praecipue circa altissimam causam, quae est finis ultimus et summum bonum. Circa quod aliquis potest pati stuporem in iudicando dupliciter. Uno modo, ex indispositione naturali, sicut patet in amentibus. Et talis stultitia non est peccatum. Alio modo, inquantum immergit homo sensum suum rebus terrenis, ex quo redditur eius sensus ineptus ad percipiendum divina, secundum illud I ad Cor. II, *animalis homo non percipit ea quae sunt spiritus Dei*, sicut etiam homini habenti gustum infectum malo humore non sapiunt dulcia. Et talis stultitia est peccatum.

**ET PER HOC** patet responsio ad primum.

**AD SECUNDUM** dicendum quod quamvis stultitiam nullus velit, vult tamen ea ad quae consequitur esse stultum, scilicet abstrahere sensum suum a spiritualibus et immergere terrenis. Et idem etiam contingit in aliis peccatis. Nam luxuriosus vult delectationem sine qua non est peccatum, quamvis non simpliciter velit peccatum, vellet enim frui delectatione sine peccato.

**AD TERTIUM** dicendum quod stultitia opponitur praeceptis quae dantur de contemplatione veritatis; de quibus supra habitum est cum de scientia et intellectu ageretur.

est cause, which is the last end and the sovereign good. Now a man may in this respect contract dullness in judgment in two ways. First, from a natural indisposition, as in the case of idiots, and such like folly is no sin. Second, by plunging his sense into earthly things, whereby his sense is rendered incapable of perceiving Divine things, according to 1 Cor. 2:14, *The sensual man perceiveth not these things that are of the Spirit of God*, even as sweet things have no savor for a man whose taste is infected with an evil humor: and such like folly is a sin.

**THIS SUFFICES** for the Reply to the First Objection.

**REPLY OBJ. 2**: Though no man wishes to be a fool, yet he wishes those things of which folly is a consequence, viz. to withdraw his sense from spiritual things and to plunge it into earthly things. The same thing happens in regard to other sins; for the lustful man desires pleasure, without which there is no sin, although he does not desire sin simply, for he would wish to enjoy the pleasure without sin.

**REPLY OBJ. 3**: Folly is opposed to the precepts about the contemplation of truth, of which we have spoken above (Q. 16) when we were treating of knowledge and understanding.

# Article 3

*Whether folly is a daughter of lust?*

**AD TERTIUM SIC PROCEDITUR**. Videtur quod stultitia non sit filia luxuriae. Gregorius enim, XXXI Moral., enumerat luxuriae filias; inter quas tamen non continetur stultitia. Ergo stultitia non procedit ex luxuria.

**PRAETEREA**, apostolus dicit, I ad Cor. III, *sapientia huius mundi stultitia est apud Deum*. Sed sicut Gregorius dicit, X Moral., *sapientia mundi est cor machinationibus tegere*, quod pertinet ad duplicitatem. Ergo stultitia est magis filia duplicitatis quam luxuriae.

**PRAETEREA**, ex ira aliqui praecipue vertuntur in furorem et insaniam, quae pertinent ad stultitiam. Ergo stultitia magis oritur ex ira quam ex luxuria.

**SED CONTRA** est quod dicitur Prov. VII, *statim eam sequitur*, scilicet meretricem, *ignorans quod ad vincula stultus trahatur*.

**RESPONDEO** dicendum quod, sicut iam dictum est, stultitia, secundum quod est peccatum, provenit ex hoc quod sensus spiritualis hebetatus est, ut non sit aptus ad spiritualia diiudicanda. Maxime autem sensus hominis immergitur ad terrena per luxuriam, quae est circa maximas delectationes, quibus anima maxime absorbetur. Et ideo stultitia quae est peccatum maxime nascitur ex luxuria.

**OBJECTION 1**: It would seem that folly is not a daughter of lust. For Gregory (*Moral.* xxxi, 45) enumerates the daughters of lust, among which however he makes no mention of folly. Therefore folly does not proceed from lust.

**OBJ. 2**: Further, the Apostle says (1 Cor 3:19): *The wisdom of this world is foolishness with God*. Now, according to Gregory (*Moral.* x, 29) *the wisdom of this world consists in covering the heart with crafty devices*; and this savors of duplicity. Therefore folly is a daughter of duplicity rather than of lust.

**OBJ. 3**: Further, anger especially is the cause of fury and madness in some persons; and this pertains to folly. Therefore folly arises from anger rather than from lust.

**ON THE CONTRARY**, It is written (Prov 7:22): *Immediately he followeth her*, i.e., the harlot . . . *not knowing that he is drawn like a fool to bonds*.

**I ANSWER THAT**, As already stated (A. 2), folly, insofar as it is a sin, is caused by the spiritual sense being dulled, so as to be incapable of judging spiritual things. Now man's sense is plunged into earthly things chiefly by lust, which is about the greatest of pleasures; and these absorb the mind more than any others. Therefore the folly which is a sin, arises chiefly from lust.

**AD PRIMUM** ergo dicendum quod ad stultitiam pertinet quod homo habeat fastidium de Deo et de donis ipsius. Unde Gregorius duo numerat inter filias luxuriae quae pertinent ad stultitiam, scilicet *odium Dei* et *desperationem futuri saeculi*, quasi dividens stultitiam in duas partes.

**AD SECUNDUM** dicendum quod verbum illud apostoli non est intelligendum causaliter, sed essentialiter, quia scilicet ipsa sapientia mundi est stultitia apud Deum. Unde non oportet quod quaecumque pertinent ad sapientiam mundi sint causa huius stultitiae.

**AD TERTIUM** dicendum quod ira, ut supra dictum est, sua acuitate maxime immutat corporis naturam. Unde maxime causat stultitiam quae provenit ex impedimento corporali. Sed stultitia quae provenit ex impedimento spirituali, scilicet ex immersione mentis ad terrena, maxime provenit ex luxuria, ut dictum est.

**REPLY OBJ. 1**: It is part of folly that a man should have a distaste for God and His gifts. Hence Gregory mentions two daughters of lust, pertaining to folly, namely, *hatred of God* and *despair of the life to come*; thus he divides folly into two parts as it were.

**REPLY OBJ. 2**: These words of the Apostle are to be understood, not causally but essentially, because, to wit, worldly wisdom itself is folly with God. Hence it does not follow that whatever belongs to worldly wisdom, is a cause of this folly.

**REPLY OBJ. 3**: Anger by reason of its keenness, as stated above (I-II, Q. 48, AA. 2, 3, 4), produces a great change in the nature of the body, wherefore it conduces very much to the folly which results from a bodily impediment. On the other hand the folly which is caused by a spiritual impediment, viz. by the mind being plunged into earthly things, arises chiefly from lust, as stated above.

# QUESTION 47

## PRUDENCE, CONSIDERED IN ITSELF

Consequenter, post virtutes theologicas, primo considerandum est, circa virtutes cardinales, de prudentia. Et primo, de prudentia secundum se; secundo, de partibus eius; tertio, de dono ei correspondente; quarto, de vitiis oppositis; quinto, de praeceptis ad hoc pertinentibus.

Circa primum quaeruntur sexdecim.

Primo, utrum prudentia sit in voluntate, vel in ratione.

Secundo, si est in ratione, utrum in practica tantum, vel etiam in speculativa.

Tertio, utrum sit cognoscitiva singularium.

Quarto, utrum sit virtus.

Quinto, utrum sit virtus specialis.

Sexto, utrum praestituat finem virtutibus moralibus.

Septimo, utrum constituat medium in eis.

Octavo, utrum praecipere sit proprius actus eius.

Nono, utrum sollicitudo vel vigilantia pertineat ad prudentiam.

Decimo, utrum prudentia se extendat ad regimen multitudinis.

Undecimo, utrum prudentia quae est respectu boni proprii sit eadem specie cum ea quae se extendit ad bonum commune

duodecimo, utrum prudentia sit in subditis, an solum in principibus.

Tertiodecimo, utrum inveniatur in malis.

Quartodecimo, utrum inveniatur in omnibus bonis.

Quintodecimo, utrum insit nobis a natura.

Sextodecimo, utrum perdatur per oblivionem.

After treating of the theological virtues, we must in due sequence consider the cardinal virtues. In the first place we shall consider prudence in itself; second, its parts; third, the corresponding gift; fourth, the contrary vices; fifth, the precepts concerning prudence.

Under the first head there are sixteen points of inquiry:

(1) Whether prudence is in the will or in the reason?

(2) If in the reason, whether it is only in the practical, or also in the speculative reason?

(3) Whether it takes cognizance of singulars?

(4) Whether it is virtue?

(5) Whether it is a special virtue?

(6) Whether it appoints the end to the moral virtues?

(7) Whether it fixes the mean in the moral virtues?

(8) Whether its proper act is command?

(9) Whether solicitude or watchfulness belongs to prudence?

(10) Whether prudence extends to the governing of many?

(11) Whether the prudence which regards private good is the same in species as that which regards the common good?

(12) Whether prudence is in subjects, or only in their rulers?

(13) Whether prudence is in the wicked?

(14) Whether prudence is in all good men?

(15) Whether prudence is in us naturally?

(16) Whether prudence is lost by forgetfulness?

# Article 1

*Whether prudence is in the cognitive or in the appetitive faculty?*

**AD PRIMUM SIC PROCEDITUR.** Videtur quod prudentia non sit in vi cognoscitiva, sed in appetitiva. Dicit enim Augustinus, in libro de moribus Eccle., *prudentia est amor ea quibus adiuvatur ab eis quibus impeditur sagaciter eligens.* Sed amor non est in cognoscitiva, sed in appetitiva. Ergo prudentia est in vi appetitiva.

**PRAETEREA,** sicut ex praedicta definitione apparet, ad prudentiam pertinet *eligere sagaciter.* Sed electio est actus appetitivae virtutis, ut supra habitum est. Ergo prudentia non est in vi cognoscitiva, sed in appetitiva.

**OBJECTION 1**: It would seem that prudence is not in the cognitive but in the appetitive faculty. For Augustine says (*De Morib. Eccl.* xv): *Prudence is love choosing wisely between the things that help and those that hinder.* Now love is not in the cognitive, but in the appetitive faculty. Therefore prudence is in the appetitive faculty.

**OBJ. 2**: Further, as appears from the foregoing definition it belongs to prudence *to choose wisely.* But choice is an act of the appetitive faculty, as stated above (I-II, Q. 13, A. 1). Therefore prudence is not in the cognitive but in the appetitive faculty.

**PRAETEREA**, philosophus dicit, in VI Ethic., quod *in arte quidem volens peccans eligibilior est, circa prudentiam autem, minus, quemadmodum et circa virtutes.* Sed virtutes morales, de quibus ibi loquitur, sunt in parte appetitiva, ars autem in ratione. Ergo prudentia magis est in parte appetitiva quam in ratione.

**SED CONTRA** est quod Augustinus dicit, in libro Octoginta trium Quaest., *prudentia est cognitio rerum appetendarum et fugiendarum.*

**RESPONDEO** dicendum quod, sicut Isidorus dicit, in libro Etymol., *prudens dicitur quasi porro videns, perspicax enim est, et incertorum videt casus.* Visio autem non est virtutis appetitivae, sed cognoscitivae. Unde manifestum est quod prudentia directe pertinet ad vim cognoscitivam. Non autem ad vim sensitivam, quia per eam cognoscuntur solum ea quae praesto sunt et sensibus offeruntur. Cognoscere autem futura ex praesentibus vel praeteritis, quod pertinet ad prudentiam, proprie rationis est, quia hoc per quandam collationem agitur. Unde relinquitur quod prudentia proprie sit in ratione.

**AD PRIMUM** ergo dicendum quod, sicut supra dictum est, voluntas movet omnes potentias ad suos actus. Primus autem actus appetitivae virtutis est amor, ut supra dictum est. Sic igitur prudentia dicitur esse amor non quidem essentialiter, sed inquantum amor movet ad actum prudentiae. Unde et postea subdit Augustinus quod *prudentia est amor bene discernens ea quibus adiuvetur ad tendendum in Deum ab his quibus impediri potest.* Dicitur autem amor discernere, inquantum movet rationem ad discernendum.

**AD SECUNDUM** dicendum quod prudens considerat ea quae sunt procul inquantum ordinantur ad adiuvandum vel impediendum ea quae sunt praesentialiter agenda. Unde patet quod ea quae considerat prudentia ordinantur ad alia sicut ad finem. Eorum autem quae sunt ad finem est consilium in ratione et electio in appetitu. Quorum duorum consilium magis proprie pertinet ad prudentiam, dicit enim philosophus, in VI Ethic., quod prudens est *bene consiliativus.* Sed quia electio praesupponit consilium, est enim *appetitus praeconsiliati,* ut dicitur in III Ethic.; ideo etiam eligere potest attribui prudentiae consequenter, inquantum scilicet electionem per consilium dirigit.

**AD TERTIUM** dicendum quod laus prudentiae non consistit in sola consideratione, sed in applicatione ad opus, quod est finis practicae rationis. Et ideo si in hoc defectus accidat, maxime est contrarium prudentiae, quia sicut finis est potissimus in unoquoque, ita et defectus qui est circa finem est pessimus. Unde ibidem philosophus subdit quod *prudentia non est solum cum*

**OBJ. 3**: Further, the Philosopher says (*Ethic.* vi, 5) that *in art it is better to err voluntarily than involuntarily, whereas in the case of prudence, as of the virtues, it is worse.* Now the moral virtues, of which he is treating there, are in the appetitive faculty, whereas art is in the reason. Therefore prudence is in the appetitive rather than in the rational faculty.

**ON THE CONTRARY**, Augustine says (*83 Questions*, Q. 61): *Prudence is the knowledge of what to seek and what to avoid.*

**I ANSWER THAT**, As Isidore says (*Etym.* x): *A prudent man is one who sees as it were from afar, for his sight is keen, and he foresees the event of uncertainties.* Now sight belongs not to the appetitive but to the cognitive faculty. Wherefore it is manifest that prudence belongs directly to the cognitive, and not to the sensitive faculty, because by the latter we know nothing but what is within reach and offers itself to the senses: while to obtain knowledge of the future from knowledge of the present or past, which pertains to prudence, belongs properly to the reason, because this is done by a process of comparison. It follows therefore that prudence, properly speaking, is in the reason.

**REPLY OBJ. 1**: As stated above (I, Q. 82, A. 4) the will moves all the faculties to their acts. Now the first act of the appetitive faculty is love, as stated above (I-II, Q. 25, AA. 1, 2). Accordingly prudence is said to be love, not indeed essentially, but insofar as love moves to the act of prudence. Wherefore Augustine goes on to say that *prudence is love discerning aright that which helps from that which hinders us in tending to God.* Now love is said to discern because it moves the reason to discern.

**REPLY OBJ. 2**: The prudent man considers things afar off, insofar as they tend to be a help or a hindrance to that which has to be done at the present time. Hence it is clear that those things which prudence considers stand in relation to this other, as in relation to the end. Now of those things that are directed to the end there is counsel in the reason, and choice in the appetite, of which two, counsel belongs more properly to prudence, since the Philosopher states (*Ethic.* vi, 5, 7, 9) that a prudent man *takes good counsel.* But as choice presupposes counsel, since it is *the desire for what has been already counselled* (*Ethic.* iii, 2), it follows that choice can also be ascribed to prudence indirectly, in so far, to wit, as prudence directs the choice by means of counsel.

**REPLY OBJ. 3**: The worth of prudence consists not in thought merely, but in its application to action, which is the end of the practical reason. Wherefore if any defect occur in this, it is most contrary to prudence, since, the end being of most import in everything, it follows that a defect which touches the end is the worst of all. Hence the Philosopher goes on to say (*Ethic.* vi, 5) that prudence is *something more*

*ratione*, sicut ars, habet enim, ut dictum est, applicationem ad opus, quod fit per voluntatem.

*than a merely rational habit*, such as art is, since, as stated above (I-II, Q. 57, A. 4) it includes application to action, which application is an act of the will.

# Article 2

*Whether prudence belongs to the practical reason alone or also to the speculative reason?*

AD SECUNDUM SIC PROCEDITUR. Videtur quod prudentia non solum pertineat ad rationem practicam, sed etiam ad speculativam. Dicitur enim Prov. X, *sapientia est viro prudentia*. Sed sapientia principalius consistit in contemplatione. Ergo et prudentia.

PRAETEREA, Ambrosius dicit, in I de officiis, *prudentia in veri investigatione versatur, et scientiae plenioris infundit cupiditatem*. Sed hoc pertinet ad rationem speculativam. Ergo prudentia consistit etiam in ratione speculativa.

PRAETEREA, in eadem parte animae ponitur a Philosopho ars et prudentia; ut patet in VI Ethic. Sed ars non solum invenitur practica, sed etiam speculativa, ut patet in artibus liberalibus. Ergo etiam prudentia invenitur et practica et speculativa.

SED CONTRA est quod Philosophus dicit, in VI Ethic., quod prudentia est recta ratio agibilium. Sed hoc non pertinet nisi ad rationem practicam. Ergo prudentia non est nisi in ratione practica.

RESPONDEO dicendum quod, sicut Philosophus dicit, in VI Ethic., *prudentis est bene posse consiliari*. Consilium autem est de his quae sunt per nos agenda in ordine ad finem aliquem. Ratio autem eorum quae sunt agenda propter finem est ratio practica. Unde manifestum est quod prudentia non consistit nisi in ratione practica.

AD PRIMUM ergo dicendum quod, sicut supra dictum est, sapientia considerat causam altissimam simpliciter. Unde consideratio causae altissimae in quolibet genere pertinet ad sapientiam in illo genere. In genere autem humanorum actuum causa altissima est finis communis toti vitae humanae. Et hunc finem intendit prudentia, dicit enim Philosophus, in VI Ethic., quod sicut ille qui ratiocinatur bene ad aliquem finem particularem, puta ad victoriam, dicitur esse prudens non simpliciter, sed in hoc genere, scilicet in rebus bellicis; ita ille qui bene ratiocinatur ad totum bene vivere dicitur prudens simpliciter. Unde manifestum est quod prudentia est sapientia in rebus humanis, non autem sapientia simpliciter, quia non est circa causam altissimam simpliciter; est enim circa bonum humanum, homo autem non est optimum eorum quae sunt. Et ideo signanter dicitur quod prudentia est *sapientia viro*, non autem sapientia simpliciter.

OBJECTION 1: It would seem that prudence belongs not only to the practical, but also to the speculative reason. For it is written (Prov 10:23): *Wisdom is prudence to a man*. Now wisdom consists chiefly in contemplation. Therefore prudence does also.

OBJ. 2: Further, Ambrose says (*De Offic.* i, 24): *Prudence is concerned with the quest of truth, and fills us with the desire of fuller knowledge*. Now this belongs to the speculative reason. Therefore prudence resides also in the speculative reason.

OBJ. 3: Further, the Philosopher assigns art and prudence to the same part of the soul (*Ethic.* vi, 1). Now art may be not only practical but also speculative, as in the case of the liberal arts. Therefore prudence also is both practical and speculative.

ON THE CONTRARY, The Philosopher says (*Ethic.* vi, 5) that prudence is right reason applied to action. Now this belongs to none but the practical reason. Therefore prudence is in the practical reason only.

I ANSWER THAT, According to the Philosopher (*Ethic.* vi, 5) *a prudent man is one who is capable of taking good counsel*. Now counsel is about things that we have to do in relation to some end: and the reason that deals with things to be done for an end is the practical reason. Hence it is evident that prudence resides only in the practical reason.

REPLY OBJ. 1: As stated above (Q. 45, AA. 1, 3), wisdom considers the absolutely highest cause: so that the consideration of the highest cause in any particular genus belongs to wisdom in that genus. Now in the genus of human acts the highest cause is the common end of all human life, and it is this end that prudence intends. For the Philosopher says (*Ethic.* vi, 5) that just as he who reasons well for the realization of a particular end, such as victory, is said to be prudent, not absolutely, but in a particular genus, namely warfare, so he that reasons well with regard to right conduct as a whole, is said to be prudent absolutely. Wherefore it is clear that prudence is wisdom about human affairs: but not wisdom absolutely, because it is not about the absolutely highest cause, for it is about human good, and this is not the best thing of all. And so it is stated significantly that *prudence is wisdom for man*, but not wisdom absolutely.

**AD SECUNDUM** dicendum quod Ambrosius et etiam Tullius nomen prudentiae largius sumunt pro qualibet cognitione humana tam speculativa quam practica. Quamvis dici possit quod ipse actus speculativae rationis, secundum quod est voluntarius, cadit sub electione et consilio quantum ad suum exercitium, et per consequens cadit sub ordinatione prudentiae. Sed quantum ad suam speciem, prout comparatur ad obiectum, quod est verum necessarium, non cadit sub consilio nec sub prudentia.

**AD TERTIUM** dicendum quod omnis applicatio rationis rectae ad aliquid factibile pertinet ad artem. Sed ad prudentiam non pertinet nisi applicatio rationis rectae ad ea de quibus est consilium. Et huiusmodi sunt in quibus non sunt viae determinatae perveniendi ad finem; ut dicitur in III Ethic. Quia igitur ratio speculativa quaedam facit, puta syllogismum, propositionem et alia huiusmodi, in quibus proceditur secundum certas et determinatas vias; inde est quod respectu horum potest salvari ratio artis, non autem ratio prudentiae. Et ideo invenitur aliqua ars speculativa, non autem aliqua prudentia.

**REPLY OBJ. 2**: Ambrose, and Tully also (*De Invent.* ii, 53) take the word prudence in a broad sense for any human knowledge, whether speculative or practical. And yet it may also be replied that the act itself of the speculative reason, insofar as it is voluntary, is a matter of choice and counsel as to its exercise; and consequently comes under the direction of prudence. On the other hand, as regards its specification in relation to its object which is the *necessary true*, it comes under neither counsel nor prudence.

**REPLY OBJ. 3**: Every application of right reason in the work of production belongs to art: but to prudence belongs only the application of right reason in matters of counsel, which are those wherein there is no fixed way of obtaining the end, as stated in *Ethic.* iii, 3. Since then, the speculative reason makes things such as syllogisms, propositions and the like, wherein the process follows certain and fixed rules, consequently in respect of such things it is possible to have the essentials of art, but not of prudence; and so we find such a thing as a speculative art, but not a speculative prudence.

# Article 3

*Whether prudence takes cognizance of singulars?*

**AD TERTIUM SIC PROCEDITUR**. Videtur quod prudentia non sit cognoscitiva singularium. Prudentia enim est in ratione, ut dictum est. Sed *ratio est universalium*, ut dicitur in I Physic. Ergo prudentia non est cognoscitiva nisi universalium.

**PRAETEREA**, singularia sunt infinita. Sed infinita non possunt comprehendi a ratione. Ergo prudentia, quae est ratio recta, non est singularium.

**PRAETEREA**, particularia per sensum cognoscuntur. Sed prudentia non est in sensu, multi enim habentes sensus exteriores perspicaces non sunt prudentes. Ergo prudentia non est singularium.

**SED CONTRA** est quod philosophus dicit, in VI Ethic., quod *prudentia non est universalium solum, sed oportet et singularia cognoscere*.

**RESPONDEO** dicendum quod, sicut supra dictum est, ad prudentiam pertinet non solum consideratio rationis, sed etiam applicatio ad opus, quae est finis practicae rationis. Nullus autem potest convenienter aliquid alteri applicare nisi utrumque cognoscat, scilicet et id quod applicandum est et id cui applicandum est. Operationes autem sunt in singularibus. Et ideo necesse est quod prudens et cognoscat universalia principia rationis, et cognoscat singularia, circa quae sunt operationes.

**OBJECTION 1**: It would seem that prudence does not take cognizance of singulars. For prudence is in the reason, as stated above (AA. 1, 2). But *reason deals with universals*, according to *Phys.* i, 5. Therefore prudence does not take cognizance except of universals.

**OBJ. 2**: Further, singulars are infinite in number. But the reason cannot comprehend an infinite number of things. Therefore prudence which is right reason, is not about singulars.

**OBJ. 3**: Further, particulars are known by the senses. But prudence is not in a sense, for many persons who have keen outward senses are devoid of prudence. Therefore prudence does not take cognizance of singulars.

**ON THE CONTRARY**, The Philosopher says (*Ethic.* vi, 7) that *prudence does not deal with universals only, but needs to take cognizance of singulars also.*

**I ANSWER THAT**, As stated above (A. 1, ad 3), to prudence belongs not only the consideration of the reason, but also the application to action, which is the end of the practical reason. But no man can conveniently apply one thing to another, unless he knows both the thing to be applied, and the thing to which it has to be applied. Now actions are in singular matters: and so it is necessary for the prudent man to know both the universal principles of reason, and the singulars about which actions are concerned.

**AD PRIMUM** ergo dicendum quod ratio primo quidem et principaliter est universalium, potest tamen universales rationes ad particularia applicare (unde syllogismorum conclusiones non solum sunt universales, sed etiam particulares); quia intellectus per quandam reflexionem se ad materiam extendit, ut dicitur in III de anima.

**AD SECUNDUM** dicendum quod quia infinitas singularium non potest ratione humana comprehendi, inde est quod sunt *incertae providentiae nostrae*, ut dicitur Sap. IX. Tamen per experientiam singularia infinita reducuntur ad aliqua finita quae ut in pluribus accidunt, quorum cognitio sufficit ad prudentiam humanam.

**AD TERTIUM** dicendum quod, sicut philosophus dicit, in VI Ethic., prudentia non consistit in sensu exteriori, quo cognoscimus sensibilia propria, sed in sensu interiori, qui perficitur per memoriam et experimentum ad prompte iudicandum de particularibus expertis. Non tamen ita quod prudentia sit in sensu interiori sicut in subiecto principali, sed principaliter quidem est in ratione, per quandam autem applicationem pertingit ad huiusmodi sensum.

**REPLY OBJ. 1**: Reason first and chiefly is concerned with universals, and yet it is able to apply universal rules to particular cases: hence the conclusions of syllogisms are not only universal, but also particular, because the intellect by a kind of reflection extends to matter, as stated in *De Anima* iii.

**REPLY OBJ. 2**: It is because the infinite number of singulars cannot be comprehended by human reason, that *our counsels are uncertain* (Wis 9:14). Nevertheless experience reduces the infinity of singulars to a certain finite number which occur as a general rule, and the knowledge of these suffices for human prudence.

**REPLY OBJ. 3**: As the Philosopher says (*Ethic.* vi, 8), prudence does not reside in the external senses whereby we know sensible objects, but in the interior sense, which is perfected by memory and experience so as to judge promptly of particular cases. This does not mean however that prudence is in the interior sense as in its principle subject, for it is chiefly in the reason, yet by a kind of application it extends to this sense.

# Article 4

### Whether prudence is a virtue?

**AD QUARTUM SIC PROCEDITUR.** Videtur quod prudentia non sit virtus. Dicit enim Augustinus, in I de Lib. Arb., quod *prudentia est appetendarum et vitandarum rerum scientia*. Sed scientia contra virtutem dividitur; ut patet in praedicamentis. Ergo prudentia non est virtus.

**PRAETEREA**, virtutis non est virtus. Sed *artis est virtus*; ut Philosophus dicit, in VI Ethic. Ergo ars non est virtus. Sed in arte est prudentia, dicitur enim II Paral. II de Hiram quod *sciebat caelare omnem sculpturam, et adinvenire prudenter quodcumque in opere necessarium est*. Ergo prudentia non est virtus.

**PRAETEREA**, nulla virtus potest esse immoderata. Sed prudentia est immoderata, alioquin frustra diceretur in Prov. XXIII, *prudentiae tuae pone modum*. Ergo prudentia non est virtus.

**SED CONTRA** est quod Gregorius, in II Moral., prudentiam, temperantiam, fortitudinem et iustitiam dicit esse quatuor virtutes.

**RESPONDEO** dicendum quod, sicut supra dictum est cum de virtutibus in communi ageretur, *virtus est quae bonum facit habentem et opus eius bonum reddit*. Bonum autem potest dici dupliciter, uno modo, materialiter, pro eo quod est bonum; alio modo, formaliter, secundum rationem boni. Bonum autem, inquantum huiusmodi, est obiectum appetitivae virtutis. Et ideo si qui habitus

**OBJECTION 1**: It would seem that prudence is not a virtue. For Augustine says (*De Lib. Arb.* i, 13) that *prudence is the science of what to desire and what to avoid*. Now science is condivided with virtue, as appears in the Predicaments (vi). Therefore prudence is not a virtue.

**OBJ. 2**: Further, there is no virtue of a virtue: but *there is a virtue of art*, as the Philosopher states (*Ethic.* vi, 5): wherefore art is not a virtue. Now there is prudence in art, for it is written (2 Chr 2:14) concerning Hiram, that he knew *to grave all sort of graving, and to devise ingeniously (prudenter) all that there may be need of in the work*. Therefore prudence is not a virtue.

**OBJ. 3**: Further, no virtue can be immoderate. But prudence is immoderate, else it would be useless to say (Prov 23:4): *Set bounds to thy prudence*. Therefore prudence is not a virtue.

**ON THE CONTRARY**, Gregory states (*Moral.* ii, 49) that prudence, temperance, fortitude and justice are four virtues.

**I ANSWER THAT**, As stated above (I-II, Q. 55, A. 3; Q. 56, A. 1) when we were treating of virtues in general, *virtue is that which makes its possessor good, and his work good likewise*. Now good may be understood in a twofold sense: first, materially, for the thing that is good, second, formally, under the aspect of good. Good, under the aspect of good, is the object of the appetitive power. Hence if any

sunt qui faciant rectam considerationem rationis non habito respectu ad rectitudinem appetitus, minus habent de ratione virtutis, tanquam ordinantes ad bonum materialiter, idest ad id quod est bonum non sub ratione boni, plus autem habent de ratione virtutis habitus illi qui respiciunt rectitudinem appetitus, quia respiciunt bonum non solum materialiter, sed etiam formaliter, idest id quod est bonum sub ratione boni.

Ad prudentiam autem pertinet, sicut dictum est, applicatio rectae rationis ad opus, quod non fit sine appetitu recto. Et ideo prudentia non solum habet rationem virtutis quam habent aliae virtutes intellectuales; sed etiam habet rationem virtutis quam habent virtutes morales, quibus etiam connumeratur.

**Ad primum** ergo dicendum quod Augustinus ibi large accepit scientiam pro qualibet recta ratione.

**Ad secundum** dicendum quod philosophus dicit artis esse virtutem, quia non importat rectitudinem appetitus, et ideo ad hoc quod homo recte utatur arte, requiritur quod habeat virtutem, quae faciat rectitudinem appetitus. Prudentia autem non habet locum in his quae sunt artis, tum quia ars ordinatur ad aliquem particularem finem; tum quia ars habet determinata media per quae pervenitur ad finem. Dicitur tamen aliquis prudenter operari in his quae sunt artis per similitudinem quandam, in quibusdam enim artibus, propter incertitudinem eorum quibus pervenitur ad finem, necessarium est consilium, sicut in medicinali et in navigatoria, ut dicitur in III Ethic.

**Ad tertium** dicendum quod illud dictum sapientis non est sic intelligendum quasi ipsa prudentia sit moderanda, sed quia secundum prudentiam est aliis modus imponendus.

habits rectify the consideration of reason, without regarding the rectitude of the appetite, they have less of the nature of a virtue since they direct man to good materially, that is to say, to the thing which is good, but without considering it under the aspect of good. On the other hand those virtues which regard the rectitude of the appetite, have more of the nature of virtue, because they consider the good not only materially, but also formally, in other words, they consider that which is good under the aspect of good.

Now it belongs to prudence, as stated above (A. 1, ad 3; A. 3) to apply right reason to action, and this is not done without a right appetite. Hence prudence has the nature of virtue not only as the other intellectual virtues have it, but also as the moral virtues have it, among which virtues it is enumerated.

**Reply Obj. 1**: Augustine there takes science in the broad sense for any kind of right reason.

**Reply Obj. 2**: The Philosopher says that there is a virtue of art, because art does not require rectitude of the appetite; wherefore in order that a man may make right use of his art, he needs to have a virtue which will rectify his appetite. Prudence however has nothing to do with the matter of art, because art is both directed to a particular end, and has fixed means of obtaining that end. And yet, by a kind of comparison, a man may be said to act prudently in matters of art. Moreover in certain arts, on account of the uncertainty of the means for obtaining the end, there is need for counsel, as for instance in the arts of medicine and navigation, as stated in *Ethic*. iii, 3.

**Reply Obj. 3**: This saying of the wise man does not mean that prudence itself should be moderate, but that moderation must be imposed on other things according to prudence.

# Article 5

*Whether prudence is a special virtue?*

**Ad quintum sic proceditur**. Videtur quod prudentia non sit specialis virtus. Nulla enim specialis virtus ponitur in communi definitione virtutis. Sed prudentia ponitur in communi definitione virtutis, quia in II Ethic. definitur virtus *habitus electivus in medietate existens determinata ratione quoad nos, prout sapiens determinabit*; recta autem ratio intelligitur secundum prudentiam, ut dicitur in VI Ethic. Ergo prudentia non est specialis virtus.

**Praeterea**, philosophus dicit, in VI Ethic., quod *virtus moralis recte facit operari finem, prudentia autem ea quae sunt ad finem*. Sed in qualibet virtute sunt aliqua

**Objection 1**: It would seem that prudence is not a special virtue. For no special virtue is included in the definition of virtue in general, since virtue is defined (*Ethic*. ii, 6) *an elective habit that follows a mean appointed by reason in relation to ourselves, even as a wise man decides*. Now right reason is reason in accordance with prudence, as stated in *Ethic*. vi, 13. Therefore prudence is not a special virtue.

**Obj. 2**: Further, the Philosopher says (*Ethic*. vi, 13) that *the effect of moral virtue is right action as regards the end, and that of prudence, right action as regards the means*.

operanda propter finem. Ergo prudentia est in qualibet virtute. Non est ergo virtus specialis.

**Praeterea**, specialis virtus habet speciale obiectum. Sed prudentia non habet speciale obiectum, est enim recta ratio agibilium, ut dicitur in VI Ethic.; agibilia autem sunt omnia opera virtutum. Ergo prudentia non est specialis virtus.

**Sed contra** est quod condividitur et connumeratur aliis virtutibus, dicitur enim Sap. VIII. *Sobrietatem et prudentiam docet, iustitiam et virtutem.*

**Respondeo** dicendum quod cum actus et habitus recipiant speciem ex obiectis, ut ex supradictis patet, necesse est quod habitus cui respondet speciale obiectum ab aliis distinctum specialis sit habitus, et si est bonus, est specialis virtus. Speciale autem obiectum dicitur non secundum materialem considerationem ipsius, sed magis secundum rationem formalem, ut ex supradictis patet, nam una et eadem res cadit sub actu diversorum habituum, et etiam diversarum potentiarum, secundum rationes diversas. Maior autem diversitas obiecti requiritur ad diversitatem potentiae quam ad diversitatem habitus, cum plures habitus inveniantur in una potentia, ut supra dictum est. Diversitas ergo rationis obiecti quae diversificat potentiam, multo magis diversificat habitum.

Sic igitur dicendum est quod cum prudentia sit in ratione, ut dictum est, diversificatur quidem ab aliis virtutibus intellectualibus secundum materialem diversitatem obiectorum. Nam sapientia, scientia et intellectus sunt circa necessaria; ars autem et prudentia circa contingentia; sed ars circa factibilia, quae scilicet in exteriori materia constituuntur, sicut domus, cultellus et huiusmodi; prudentia autem est circa agibilia, quae scilicet in ipso operante consistunt, ut supra habitum est. Sed a virtutibus moralibus distinguitur prudentia secundum formalem rationem potentiarum distinctivam, scilicet intellectivi, in quo est prudentia; et appetitivi, in quo est virtus moralis. Unde manifestum est prudentiam esse specialem virtutem ab omnibus aliis virtutibus distinctam.

**Ad primum** ergo dicendum quod illa definitio non datur de virtute in communi, sed de virtute morali. In cuius definitione convenienter ponitur virtus intellectualis communicans in materia cum ipsa, scilicet prudentia, quia sicut virtutis moralis subiectum est aliquid participans ratione, ita virtus moralis habet rationem virtutis inquantum participat virtutem intellectualem.

**Ad secundum** dicendum quod ex illa ratione habetur quod prudentia adiuvet omnes virtutes, et in omnibus operetur. Sed hoc non sufficit ad ostendendum

Now in every virtue certain things have to be done as means to the end. Therefore prudence is in every virtue, and consequently is not a special virtue.

**Obj. 3**: Further, a special virtue has a special object. But prudence has not a special object, for it is right reason applied to action (*Ethic.* vi, 5); and all works of virtue are actions. Therefore prudence is not a special virtue.

**On the contrary**, It is distinct from and numbered among the other virtues, for it is written (Wis 8:7): *She teacheth temperance and prudence, justice and fortitude.*

**I answer that**, Since acts and habits take their species from their objects, as shown above (I-II, Q. 1, A. 3; Q. 18, A. 2; Q. 54, A. 2), any habit that has a corresponding special object, distinct from other objects, must needs be a special habit, and if it be a good habit, it must be a special virtue. Now an object is called special, not merely according to the consideration of its matter, but rather according to its formal aspect, as explained above (I-II, Q. 54, A. 2, ad 1). Because one and the same thing is the subject matter of the acts of different habits, and also of different powers, according to its different formal aspects. Now a yet greater difference of object is requisite for a difference of powers than for a difference of habits, since several habits are found in the same power, as stated above (I-II, Q. 54, A. 1). Consequently any difference in the aspect of an object, that requires a difference of powers, will a fortiori require a difference of habits.

Accordingly we must say that since prudence is in the reason, as stated above (A. 2), it is differentiated from the other intellectual virtues by a material difference of objects. Wisdom, knowledge and understanding are about necessary things, whereas art and prudence are about contingent things, art being concerned with things made, that is, with things produced in external matter, such as a house, a knife and so forth; and prudence, being concerned with things done, that is, with things that have their being in the doer himself, as stated above (I-II, Q. 57, A. 4). On the other hand prudence is differentiated from the moral virtues according to a formal aspect distinctive of powers, i.e., the intellective power, wherein is prudence, and the appetitive power, wherein is moral virtue. Hence it is evident that prudence is a special virtue, distinct from all other virtues.

**Reply Obj. 1**: This is not a definition of virtue in general, but of moral virtue, the definition of which fittingly includes an intellectual virtue, viz., prudence, which has the same matter in common with moral virtue; because, just as the subject of moral virtue is something that partakes of reason, so moral virtue has the aspect of virtue, insofar as it partakes of intellectual virtue.

**Reply Obj. 2**: This argument proves that prudence helps all the virtues, and works in all of them; but this does not suffice to prove that it is not a special virtue; for nothing

quod non sit virtus specialis, quia nihil prohibet in aliquo genere esse aliquam speciem quae aliqualiter operetur in omnibus speciebus eiusdem generis; sicut sol aliqualiter influit in omnia corpora.

**Ad tertium** dicendum quod agibilia sunt quidem materia prudentiae secundum quod sunt obiectum rationis, scilicet sub ratione veri. Sunt autem materia moralium virtutum secundum quod sunt obiectum virtutis appetitivae, scilicet sub ratione boni.

prevents a certain genus from containing a species which is operative in every other species of that same genus, even as the sun has an influence over all bodies.

**Reply Obj. 3**: Things done are indeed the matter of prudence, insofar as they are the object of reason, that is, considered as true: but they are the matter of the moral virtues, insofar as they are the object of the appetitive power, that is, considered as good.

# Article 6

*Whether prudence appoints the end to moral virtues?*

**Ad sextum sic proceditur**. Videtur quod prudentia praestituat finem virtutibus moralibus. Cum enim prudentia sit in ratione, virtus autem moralis in vi appetitiva, videtur quod hoc modo se habeat prudentia ad virtutem moralem sicut ratio ad vim appetitivam. Sed ratio praestituit finem potentiae appetitivae. Ergo prudentia praestituit finem virtutibus moralibus.

**Praeterea**, homo excedit res irrationales secundum rationem, sed secundum alia cum eis communicat. Sic igitur se habent aliae partes hominis ad rationem sicut se habent creaturae irrationales ad hominem. Sed homo est finis creaturarum irrationalium ut dicitur in I Politic. ergo omnes aliae partes hominis ordinantur ad rationem sicut ad finem. Sed prudentia est recta ratio agibilium, ut dictum est. Ergo omnia agibilia ordinantur ad prudentiam sicut ad finem. Ipsa ergo praestituit finem omnibus virtutibus moralibus.

**Praeterea**, proprium est virtutis vel artis seu potentiae ad quam pertinet finis ut praecipiat aliis virtutibus seu artibus ad quas pertinent ea quae sunt ad finem. Sed prudentia disponit de aliis virtutibus moralibus et praecipit eis. Ergo praestituit eis finem.

**Sed contra** est quod philosophus dicit, in VI Ethic., quod *virtus moralis intentionem finis facit rectam, prudentia autem quae ad hanc*. Ergo ad prudentiam non pertinet praestituere finem virtutibus moralibus, sed solum disponere de his quae sunt ad finem.

**Respondeo** dicendum quod finis virtutum moralium est bonum humanum. Bonum autem humanae animae est secundum rationem esse; ut patet per Dionysium, IV cap. de Div. Nom. Unde necesse est quod fines moralium virtutum praeexistant in ratione.

Sicut autem in ratione speculativa sunt quaedam ut naturaliter nota, quorum est intellectus; et quaedam quae per illa innotescunt, scilicet conclusiones, quarum est scientia, ita in ratione practica praeexistunt quaedam ut principia naturaliter nota, et huiusmodi sunt fines virtutum moralium, quia finis se habet in operabilibus

**Objection 1**: It would seem that prudence appoints the end to moral virtues. Since prudence is in the reason, while moral virtue is in the appetite, it seems that prudence stands in relation to moral virtue, as reason to the appetite. Now reason appoints the end to the appetitive power. Therefore prudence appoints the end to the moral virtues.

**Obj. 2**: Further, man surpasses irrational beings by his reason, but he has other things in common with them. Accordingly the other parts of man are in relation to his reason, what man is in relation to irrational creatures. Now man is the end of irrational creatures, according to *Polit.* i, 3. Therefore all the other parts of man are directed to reason as to their end. But prudence is *right reason applied to action*, as stated above (A. 2). Therefore all actions are directed to prudence as their end. Therefore prudence appoints the end to all moral virtues.

**Obj. 3**: Further, it belongs to the virtue, art, or power that is concerned about the end, to command the virtues or arts that are concerned about the means. Now prudence disposes of the other moral virtues, and commands them. Therefore it appoints their end to them.

**On the contrary**, The Philosopher says (*Ethic.* vi, 12) that *moral virtue ensures the rectitude of the intention of the end, while prudence ensures the rectitude of the means.* Therefore it does not belong to prudence to appoint the end to moral virtues, but only to regulate the means.

**I answer that**, The end of moral virtues is human good. Now the good of the human soul is to be in accord with reason, as Dionysius declares (*Div. Nom.* iv). Wherefore the ends of moral virtue must of necessity pre-exist in the reason.

Now, just as, in the speculative reason, there are certain things naturally known, about which is understanding, and certain things of which we obtain knowledge through them, viz. conclusions, about which is science, so in the practical reason, certain things pre-exist, as naturally known principles, and such are the ends of the moral

sicut principium in speculativis, ut supra habitum est; et quaedam sunt in ratione practica ut conclusiones, et huiusmodi sunt ea quae sunt ad finem, in quae pervenimus ex ipsis finibus. Et horum est prudentia, applicans universalia principia ad particulares conclusiones operabilium. Et ideo ad prudentiam non pertinet praestituere finem virtutibus moralibus, sed solum disponere de his quae sunt ad finem.

**AD PRIMUM** ergo dicendum quod virtutibus moralibus praestituit finem ratio naturalis quae dicitur synderesis, ut in primo habitum est, non autem prudentia, ratione iam dicta.

**ET PER HOC** etiam patet responsio ad secundum.

**AD TERTIUM** dicendum quod finis non pertinet ad virtutes morales tanquam ipsae praestituant finem, sed quia tendunt in finem a ratione naturali praestitutum. Ad quod iuvantur per prudentiam, quae eis viam parat, disponendo ea quae sunt ad finem. Unde relinquitur quod prudentia sit nobilior virtutibus moralibus, et moveat eas. Sed synderesis movet prudentiam, sicut intellectus principiorum scientiam.

virtues, since the end is in practical matters what principles are in speculative matters, as stated above (Q. 23, A. 7, ad 2; I-II, Q. 13, A. 3); while certain things are in the practical reason by way of conclusions, and such are the means which we gather from the ends themselves. About these is prudence, which applies universal principles to the particular conclusions of practical matters. Consequently it does not belong to prudence to appoint the end to moral virtues, but only to regulate the means.

**REPLY OBJ. 1**: Natural reason known by the name of synderesis appoints the end to moral virtues, as stated above (I, Q. 79, A. 12): but prudence does not do this for the reason given above.

**THIS SUFFICES** for the Reply to the Second Objection.

**REPLY OBJ. 3**: The end concerns the moral virtues, not as though they appointed the end, but because they tend to the end which is appointed by natural reason. In this they are helped by prudence, which prepares the way for them, by disposing the means. Hence it follows that prudence is more excellent than the moral virtues, and moves them: yet synderesis moves prudence, just as the understanding of principles moves science.

# Article 7

*Whether it belongs to prudence to find the mean in moral virtues?*

**AD SEPTIMUM SIC PROCEDITUR.** Videtur quod ad prudentiam non pertineat invenire medium in virtutibus moralibus. Consequi enim medium est finis moralium virtutum. Sed prudentia non praestituit finem moralibus virtutibus, ut ostensum est. Ergo non invenit in eis medium.

**PRAETEREA**, illud quod est per se non videtur causam habere, sed ipsum esse est sui ipsius causa, quia unumquodque dicitur esse per causam suam. Sed existere in medio convenit virtuti morali per se, quasi positum in eius definitione, ut ex dictis patet. Non ergo prudentia causat medium in virtutibus moralibus.

**PRAETEREA**, prudentia operatur secundum modum rationis. Sed virtus moralis tendit ad medium per modum naturae, quia ut Tullius dicit, in II Rhet., *virtus est habitus per modum naturae rationi consentaneus.* Ergo prudentia non praestituit medium virtutibus moralibus.

**SED CONTRA** est quod in supraposita definitione virtutis moralis dicitur quod *est in medietate existens determinata ratione prout sapiens determinabit.*

**RESPONDEO** dicendum quod hoc ipsum quod est conformari rationi rectae est finis proprius cuiuslibet moralis virtutis, temperantia enim hoc intendit, ne prop-

**OBJECTION 1**: It would seem that it does not belong to prudence to find the mean in moral virtues. For the achievement of the mean is the end of moral virtues. But prudence does not appoint the end to moral virtues, as shown above (A. 6). Therefore it does not find the mean in them.

**OBJ. 2**: Further, that which of itself has being, would seem to have no cause, but its very being is its cause, since a thing is said to have being by reason of its cause. Now *to follow the mean* belongs to moral virtue by reason of itself, as part of its definition, as shown above (A. 5, Obj. 1). Therefore prudence does not cause the mean in moral virtues.

**OBJ. 3**: Further, prudence works after the manner of reason. But moral virtue tends to the mean after the manner of nature, because, as Tully states (*De Invent. Rhet.* ii, 53), *virtue is a habit like a second nature in accord with reason.* Therefore prudence does not appoint the mean to moral virtues.

**ON THE CONTRARY**, In the foregoing definition of moral virtue (A. 5, Obj. 1) it is stated that it *follows a mean appointed by reason . . . even as a wise man decides.*

**I ANSWER THAT**, The proper end of each moral virtue consists precisely in conformity with right reason. For temperance intends that man should not stray from reason for

ter concupiscentias homo divertat a ratione; et similiter fortitudo ne a recto iudicio rationis divertat propter timorem vel audaciam. Et hic finis praestitutus est homini secundum naturalem rationem, naturalis enim ratio dictat unicuique ut secundum rationem operetur.

Sed qualiter et per quae homo in operando attingat medium rationis pertinet ad dispositionem prudentiae. Licet enim attingere medium sit finis virtutis moralis, tamen per rectam dispositionem eorum quae sunt ad finem medium invenitur.

ET PER HOC patet responsio ad primum.

AD SECUNDUM dicendum quod sicut agens naturale facit ut forma sit in materia, non tamen facit ut formae conveniant ea quae per se ei insunt; ita etiam prudentia medium constituit in passionibus et operationibus, non tamen facit quod medium quaerere conveniat virtuti.

AD TERTIUM dicendum quod virtus moralis per modum naturae intendit pervenire ad medium. Sed quia medium non eodem modo invenitur in omnibus, ideo inclinatio naturae, quae semper eodem modo operatur, ad hoc non sufficit, sed requiritur ratio prudentiae.

the sake of his concupiscences; fortitude, that he should not stray from the right judgment of reason through fear or daring. Moreover this end is appointed to man according to natural reason, since natural reason dictates to each one that he should act according to reason.

But it belongs to the ruling of prudence to decide in what manner and by what means man shall obtain the mean of reason in his deeds. For though the attainment of the mean is the end of a moral virtue, yet this mean is found by the right disposition of these things that are directed to the end.

THIS SUFFICES for the Reply to the First Objection.

REPLY OBJ. 2: Just as a natural agent makes form to be in matter, yet does not make that which is essential to the form to belong to it, so too, prudence appoints the mean in passions and operations, and yet does not make the searching of the mean to belong to virtue.

REPLY OBJ. 3: Moral virtue after the manner of nature intends to attain the mean. Since, however, the mean as such is not found in all matters after the same manner, it follows that the inclination of nature which ever works in the same manner, does not suffice for this purpose, and so the ruling of prudence is required.

# Article 8

*Whether command is the chief act of prudence?*

AD OCTAVUM SIC PROCEDITUR. Videtur quod praecipere non sit principalis actus prudentiae. Praecipere enim pertinet ad bona quae sunt fienda. Sed Augustinus, XIV de Trin., ponit actum prudentiae *praecavere insidias*. Ergo praecipere non est principalis actus prudentiae.

PRAETEREA, Philosophus dicit, in VI Ethic., quod *prudentis videtur esse bene consiliari*. Sed alius actus videtur esse consiliari et praecipere, ut ex supradictis patet. Ergo prudentiae principalis actus non est praecipere.

PRAETEREA, praecipere, vel imperare, videtur pertinere ad voluntatem, cuius obiectum est finis et quae movet alias potentias animae. Sed prudentia non est in voluntate, sed in ratione. Ergo prudentiae actus non est praecipere.

SED CONTRA est quod Philosophus dicit, in VI Ethic., quod *prudentia praeceptiva est*.

RESPONDEO dicendum quod prudentia est *recta ratio agibilium*, ut supra dictum est. Unde oportet quod ille sit praecipuus actus prudentiae qui est praecipuus actus rationis agibilium. Cuius quidem sunt tres actus. Quorum primus est consiliari, quod pertinet ad inventionem, nam consiliari est quaerere, ut supra habitum

OBJECTION 1: It would seem that command is not the chief act of prudence. For command regards the good to be ensued. Now Augustine (*De Trin.* xiv, 9) states that it is an act of prudence *to avoid ambushes*. Therefore command is not the chief act of prudence.

OBJ. 2: Further, the Philosopher says (*Ethic.* vi, 5) that *the prudent man takes good counsel*. Now to take counsel and to command seem to be different acts, as appears from what has been said above (I-II, Q. 57, A. 6). Therefore command is not the chief act of prudence.

OBJ. 3: Further, it seems to belong to the will to command and to rule, since the will has the end for its object, and moves the other powers of the soul. Now prudence is not in the will, but in the reason. Therefore command is not an act of prudence.

ON THE CONTRARY, The Philosopher says (*Ethic.* vi, 10) that *prudence commands*.

I ANSWER THAT, Prudence is *right reason applied to action*, as stated above (A. 2). Hence that which is the chief act of reason in regard to action must needs be the chief act of prudence. Now there are three such acts. The first is to take counsel, which belongs to discovery, for counsel is an act of inquiry, as stated above (I-II, Q. 14, A. 1). The

est. Secundus actus est iudicare de inventis, et hic sistit speculativa ratio. Sed practica ratio, quae ordinatur ad opus, procedit ulterius et est tertius actus eius praecipere, qui quidem actus consistit in applicatione consiliatorum et iudicatorum ad operandum. Et quia iste actus est propinquior fini rationis practicae, inde est quod iste est principalis actus rationis practicae, et per consequens prudentiae.

Et huius signum est quod perfectio artis consistit in iudicando, non autem in praecipiendo. Ideo reputatur melior artifex qui volens peccat in arte, quasi habens rectum iudicium, quam qui peccat nolens, quod videtur esse ex defectu iudicii. Sed in prudentia est e converso, ut dicitur in VI Ethic., imprudentior enim est qui volens peccat, quasi deficiens in principali actu prudentiae, qui est praecipere, quam qui peccat nolens.

**AD PRIMUM** ergo dicendum quod actus praecipiendi se extendit et ad bona prosequenda et ad mala cavenda. Et tamen *praecavere insidias* non attribuit Augustinus prudentiae quasi principalem actum ipsius, sed quia iste actus prudentiae non manet in patria.

**AD SECUNDUM** dicendum quod bonitas consilii requiritur ut ea quae sunt bene inventa applicentur ad opus. Et ideo praecipere pertinet ad prudentiam, quae est bene consiliativa.

**AD TERTIUM** dicendum quod movere absolute pertinet ad voluntatem. Sed praecipere importat motionem cum quadam ordinatione. Et ideo est actus rationis, ut supra dictum est.

second act is to judge of what one has discovered, and this is an act of the speculative reason. But the practical reason, which is directed to action, goes further, and its third act is to command, which act consists in applying to action the things counselled and judged. And since this act approaches nearer to the end of the practical reason, it follows that it is the chief act of the practical reason, and consequently of prudence.

In confirmation of this we find that the perfection of art consists in judging and not in commanding: wherefore he who sins voluntarily against his craft is reputed a better craftsman than he who does so involuntarily, because the former seems to do so from right judgment, and the latter from a defective judgment. On the other hand it is the reverse in prudence, as stated in *Ethic.* vi, 5, for it is more imprudent to sin voluntarily, since this is to be lacking in the chief act of prudence, viz. command, than to sin involuntarily.

**REPLY OBJ. 1**: The act of command extends both to the ensuing of good and to the avoidance of evil. Nevertheless Augustine ascribes *the avoidance of ambushes* to prudence, not as its chief act, but as an act of prudence that does not continue in heaven.

**REPLY OBJ. 2**: Good counsel is required in order that the good things discovered may be applied to action: wherefore command belongs to prudence which takes good counsel.

**REPLY OBJ. 3**: Simply to move belongs to the will: but command denotes motion together with a kind of ordering, wherefore it is an act of the reason, as stated above (I-II, Q. 17, A. 1).

# Article 9

*Whether solicitude belongs to prudence?*

**AD NONUM SIC PROCEDITUR.** Videtur quod sollicitudo non pertineat ad prudentiam. Sollicitudo enim inquietudinem quandam importat, dicit enim Isidorus, in libro Etymol., quod *sollicitus dicitur qui est inquietus.* Sed motio maxime pertinet ad vim appetitivam. Ergo et sollicitudo. Sed prudentia non est in vi appetitiva, sed in ratione, ut supra habitum est. Ergo sollicitudo non pertinet ad prudentiam.

**PRAETEREA,** sollicitudini videtur opponi certitudo veritatis, unde dicitur I Reg. IX quod Samuel dixit ad Saul, *de asinis quas nudiustertius perdidisti ne sollicitus sis, quia inventae sunt.* Sed certitudo veritatis pertinet ad prudentiam, cum sit virtus intellectualis. Ergo sollicitudo opponitur prudentiae, magis quam ad eam pertineat.

**OBJECTION 1**: It would seem that solicitude does not belong to prudence. For solicitude implies disquiet, wherefore Isidore says (*Etym.* x) that *a solicitous man is a restless man.* Now motion belongs chiefly to the appetitive power: wherefore solicitude does also. But prudence is not in the appetitive power, but in the reason, as stated above (A. 1). Therefore solicitude does not belong to prudence.

**OBJ. 2**: Further, the certainty of truth seems opposed to solicitude, wherefore it is related (1 Kgs 9:20) that Samuel said to Saul: *As for the asses which were lost three days ago, be not solicitous, because they are found.* Now the certainty of truth belongs to prudence, since it is an intellectual virtue. Therefore solicitude is in opposition to prudence rather than belonging to it.

PRAETEREA, philosophus dicit, in IV Ethic., quod ad magnanimum pertinet *pigrum esse et otiosum.* Pigritiae autem opponitur sollicitudo. Cum ergo prudentia non opponatur magnanimitati, quia bonum non est bono contrarium, ut dicitur in Praedic.; videtur quod sollicitudo non pertineat ad prudentiam.

SED CONTRA est quod dicitur I Pet. IV, *estote prudentes, et vigilate in orationibus.* Sed vigilantia est idem sollicitudini. Ergo sollicitudo pertinet ad prudentiam.

RESPONDEO dicendum quod, sicut dicit Isidorus, in libro Etymol., *sollicitus dicitur quasi solers citus,* inquantum scilicet aliquis ex quadam solertia animi velox est ad prosequendum ea quae sunt agenda. Hoc autem pertinet ad prudentiam, cuius praecipuus actus est circa agenda praecipere de praeconsiliatis et iudicatis. Unde philosophus dicit, in VI Ethic., quod *oportet operari quidem velociter consiliata, consiliari autem tarde.* Et inde est quod sollicitudo proprie ad prudentiam pertinet. Et propter hoc Augustinus dicit, in libro de moribus Eccles., quod *prudentiae sunt excubiae atque diligentissima vigilantia ne, subrepente paulatim mala suasione, fallamur.*

AD PRIMUM ergo dicendum quod motus pertinet quidem ad vim appetitivam sicut ad principium movens, tamen secundum directionem et praeceptum rationis, in quo consistit ratio sollicitudinis.

AD SECUNDUM dicendum quod, secundum philosophum, in I Ethic., *certitudo non est similiter quaerenda in omnibus, sed in unaquaque materia secundum proprium modum.* Quia vero materiae prudentiae sunt singularia contingentia, circa quae sunt operationes humanae, non potest certitudo prudentiae tanta esse quod omnino sollicitudo tollatur.

AD TERTIUM dicendum quod magnanimus dicitur esse piger et otiosus, non quia de nullo sit sollicitus, sed quia non est superflue sollicitus de multis, sed confidit in his de quibus confidendum est, et circa illa non superflue sollicitatur. Superfluitas enim timoris et diffidentiae facit superfluitatem sollicitudinis, quia timor facit consiliativos, ut supra dictum est cum de passione timoris ageretur.

OBJ. 3: Further, the Philosopher says (*Ethic.* iv, 3) the magnanimous man is *slow and leisurely.* Now slowness is contrary to solicitude. Since then prudence is not opposed to magnanimity, for *good is not opposed to good,* as stated in the Predicaments (viii) it would seem that solicitude does not belong to prudence.

ON THE CONTRARY, It is written (1 Pet 4:7): *Be prudent . . . and watch in prayers.* But watchfulness is the same as solicitude. Therefore solicitude belongs to prudence.

I ANSWER THAT, According to Isidore (*Etym.* x), a man *is said to be solicitous through being shrewd (solers) and alert (citus),* insofar as a man through a certain shrewdness of mind is on the alert to do whatever has to be done. Now this belongs to prudence, whose chief act is a command about what has been already counselled and judged in matters of action. Hence the Philosopher says (*Ethic.* vi, 9) that *one should be quick in carrying out the counsel taken, but slow in taking counsel.* Hence it is that solicitude belongs properly to prudence, and for this reason Augustine says (*De Morib. Eccl.* xxiv) that *prudence keeps most careful watch and ward, lest by degrees we be deceived unawares by evil counsel.*

REPLY OBJ. 1: Movement belongs to the appetitive power as to the principle of movement, in accordance however, with the direction and command of reason, wherein solicitude consists.

REPLY OBJ. 2: According to the Philosopher (*Ethic.* i, 3), *equal certainty should not be sought in all things, but in each matter according to its proper mode.* And since the matter of prudence is the contingent singulars about which are human actions, the certainty of prudence cannot be so great as to be devoid of all solicitude.

REPLY OBJ. 3: The magnanimous man is said to be *slow and leisurely* not because he is solicitous about nothing, but because he is not over-solicitous about many things, and is trustful in matters where he ought to have trust, and is not over-solicitous about them: for over-much fear and distrust are the cause of over-solicitude, since fear makes us take counsel, as stated above (I-II, Q. 44, A. 2) when we were treating of the passion of fear.

# Article 10

*Whether prudence extends to the governing of many?*

AD DECIMUM SIC PROCEDITUR. Videtur quod prudentia non se extendat ad regimen multitudinis, sed solum ad regimen sui ipsius. Dicit enim philosophus, in V Ethic., quod virtus relata ad bonum commune est iustitia. Sed prudentia differt a iustitia. Ergo prudentia non refertur ad bonum commune.

OBJECTION 1: It would seem that prudence does not extend to the governing of many, but only to the government of oneself. For the Philosopher says (*Ethic.* v, 1) that virtue directed to the common good is justice. But prudence differs from justice. Therefore prudence is not directed to the common good.

PRAETEREA, ille videtur esse prudens qui sibi ipsi bonum quaerit et operatur. Sed frequenter illi qui quaerunt bona communia negligunt sua. Ergo non sunt prudentes.

PRAETEREA, prudentia dividitur contra temperantiam et fortitudinem. Sed temperantia et fortitudo videntur dici solum per comparationem ad bonum proprium. Ergo etiam et prudentia.

SED CONTRA est quod dominus dicit, Matth. XXIV, *quis, putas, est fidelis servus et prudens, quem constituit dominus super familiam suam?*

RESPONDEO dicendum quod, sicut philosophus dicit, in VI Ethic., quidam posuerunt quod prudentia non se extendit ad bonum commune, sed solum ad bonum proprium. Et hoc ideo quia existimabant quod non oportet hominem quaerere nisi bonum proprium. Sed haec aestimatio repugnat caritati, quae *non quaerit quae sua sunt,* ut dicitur I ad Cor. XIII. Unde et apostolus de seipso dicit, I ad Cor. X, *non quaerens quod mihi utile sit, sed quod multis, ut salvi fiant.* Repugnat etiam rationi rectae, quae hoc iudicat, quod bonum commune sit melius quam bonum unius.

Quia igitur ad prudentiam pertinet recte consiliari, iudicare et praecipere de his per quae pervenitur ad debitum finem, manifestum est quod prudentia non solum se habet ad bonum privatum unius hominis, sed etiam ad bonum commune multitudinis.

AD PRIMUM ergo dicendum quod philosophus ibi loquitur de virtute morali. Sicut autem omnis virtus moralis relata ad bonum commune dicitur legalis iustitia, ita prudentia relata ad bonum commune vocatur *politica,* ut sic se habeat politica ad iustitiam legalem, sicut se habet prudentia simpliciter dicta ad virtutem moralem.

AD SECUNDUM dicendum quod ille qui quaerit bonum commune multitudinis ex consequenti etiam quaerit bonum suum, propter duo. Primo quidem, quia bonum proprium non potest esse sine bono communi vel familiae vel civitatis aut regni. Unde et maximus Valerius dicit de antiquis Romanis quod *malebant esse pauperes in divite imperio quam divites in paupere imperio.* Secundo quia, cum homo sit pars domus et civitatis, oportet quod homo consideret quid sit sibi bonum ex hoc quod est prudens circa bonum multitudinis, bona enim dispositio partis accipitur secundum habitudinem ad totum; quia ut Augustinus dicit, in libro Confess., *turpis est omnis pars suo toti non congruens.*

AD TERTIUM dicendum quod etiam temperantia et fortitudo possunt referri ad bonum commune, unde de actibus earum dantur praecepta legis, ut dicitur in V Ethic. Magis tamen prudentia et iustitia, quae pertinent ad partem rationalem, ad quam directe pertinent communia, sicut ad partem sensitivam pertinent singularia.

OBJ. 2: Further, he seems to be prudent, who seeks and does good for himself. Now those who seek the common good often neglect their own. Therefore they are not prudent.

OBJ. 3: Further, prudence is specifically distinct from temperance and fortitude. But temperance and fortitude seem to be related only to a man's own good. Therefore the same applies to prudence.

ON THE CONTRARY, Our Lord said (Matt 24:45): *Who, thinkest thou, is a faithful and prudent servant whom his lord hath appointed over his family?*

I ANSWER THAT, According to the Philosopher (*Ethic.* vi, 8) some have held that prudence does not extend to the common good, but only to the good of the individual, and this because they thought that man is not bound to seek other than his own good. But this opinion is opposed to charity, which *seeketh not her own* (1 Cor 13:5): wherefore the Apostle says of himself (1 Cor 10:33): *Not seeking that which is profitable to myself, but to many, that they may be saved.* Moreover it is contrary to right reason, which judges the common good to be better than the good of the individual.

Accordingly, since it belongs to prudence rightly to counsel, judge, and command concerning the means of obtaining a due end, it is evident that prudence regards not only the private good of the individual, but also the common good of the multitude.

REPLY OBJ. 1: The Philosopher is speaking there of moral virtue. Now just as every moral virtue that is directed to the common good is called *legal* justice, so the prudence that is directed to the common good is called *political* prudence, for the latter stands in the same relation to legal justice, as prudence simply so called to moral virtue.

REPLY OBJ. 2: He that seeks the good of the many, seeks in consequence his own good, for two reasons. First, because the individual good is impossible without the common good of the family, state, or kingdom. Hence Valerius Maximus says of the ancient Romans that *they would rather be poor in a rich empire than rich in a poor empire.* Second, because, since man is a part of the home and state, he must needs consider what is good for him by being prudent about the good of the many. For the good disposition of parts depends on their relation to the whole; thus Augustine says (*Confess.* iii, 8) that *any part which does not harmonize with its whole, is offensive.*

REPLY OBJ. 3: Even temperance and fortitude can be directed to the common good, hence there are precepts of law concerning them as stated in *Ethic.* v, 1: more so, however, prudence and justice, since these belong to the rational faculty which directly regards the universal, just as the sensitive part regards singulars.

# Article 11

*Whether prudence about one's own good is specifically the same*
*as that which extends to the common good?*

AD UNDECIMUM SIC PROCEDITUR. Videtur quod prudentia quae est respectu boni proprii sit eadem specie cum ea quae se extendit ad bonum commune. Dicit enim philosophus, in VI Ethic., quod *politica et prudentia idem habitus est, esse autem non idem ipsis.*

PRAETEREA, philosophus dicit, in III Polit., quod *eadem est virtus boni viri et boni principis.* Sed politica maxime est in principe, in quo est sicut architectonica. Cum ergo prudentia sit virtus boni viri, videtur quod sit idem habitus prudentia et politica.

PRAETEREA, ea quorum unum ordinatur ad aliud non diversificant speciem aut substantiam habitus. Sed bonum proprium, quod pertinet ad prudentiam simpliciter dictam, ordinatur ad bonum commune, quod pertinet ad politicam. Ergo politica et prudentia neque differunt specie, neque secundum habitus substantiam.

SED CONTRA est quod diversae scientiae sunt politica, quae ordinatur ad bonum commune civitatis; et oeconomica, quae est de his quae pertinent ad bonum commune domus vel familiae; et monastica, quae est de his quae pertinent ad bonum unius personae. Ergo pari ratione et prudentiae sunt species diversae secundum hanc diversitatem materiae.

RESPONDEO dicendum quod, sicut supra dictum est, species habituum diversificantur secundum diversitatem obiecti quae attenditur penes rationem formalem ipsius. Ratio autem formalis omnium quae sunt ad finem attenditur ex parte finis; sicut ex supradictis patet. Et ideo necesse est quod ex relatione ad diversos fines diversificentur species habitus. Diversi autem fines sunt bonum proprium unius, et bonum familiae, et bonum civitatis et regni. Unde necesse est quod et prudentiae differant specie secundum differentiam horum finium, ut scilicet una sit prudentia simpliciter dicta, quae ordinatur ad bonum proprium; alia autem oeconomica, quae ordinatur ad bonum commune domus vel familiae; et tertia politica, quae ordinatur ad bonum commune civitatis vel regni.

AD PRIMUM ergo dicendum quod Philosophus non intendit dicere quod politica sit idem secundum substantiam habitus cuilibet prudentiae, sed prudentiae quae ordinatur ad bonum commune. Quae quidem prudentia dicitur secundum communem rationem prudentiae, prout scilicet est quaedam recta ratio agibilium, dicitur autem politica secundum ordinem ad bonum commune.

OBJECTION 1: It seems that prudence about one's own good is the same specifically as that which extends to the common good. For the Philosopher says (*Ethic.* vi, 8) that *political prudence, and prudence are the same habit, yet their essence is not the same.*

OBJ. 2: Further, the Philosopher says (*Polit.* iii, 2) that *virtue is the same in a good man and in a good ruler.* Now political prudence is chiefly in the ruler, in whom it is architectonic, as it were. Since then prudence is a virtue of a good man, it seems that prudence and political prudence are the same habit.

OBJ. 3: Further, a habit is not diversified in species or essence by things which are subordinate to one another. But the particular good, which belongs to prudence simply so called, is subordinate to the common good, which belongs to political prudence. Therefore prudence and political prudence differ neither specifically nor essentially.

ON THE CONTRARY, *Political prudence,* which is directed to the common good of the state, *domestic economy* which is of such things as relate to the common good of the household or family, and *monastic economy* which is concerned with things affecting the good of one person, are all distinct sciences. Therefore in like manner there are different kinds of prudence, corresponding to the above differences of matter.

I ANSWER THAT, As stated above (A. 5; Q. 54, A. 2, ad 1), the species of habits differ according to the difference of object considered in its formal aspect. Now the formal aspect of all things directed to the end, is taken from the end itself, as shown above (I-II, Prolog.; Q. 102, A. 1), wherefore the species of habits differ by their relation to different ends. Again the individual good, the good of the family, and the good of the city and kingdom are different ends. Wherefore there must needs be different species of prudence corresponding to these different ends, so that one is *prudence* simply so called, which is directed to one's own good; another, *domestic prudence* which is directed to the common good of the home; and a third, *political prudence,* which is directed to the common good of the state or kingdom.

REPLY OBJ. 1: The Philosopher means, not that political prudence is substantially the same habit as any kind of prudence, but that it is the same as the prudence which is directed to the common good. This is called *prudence* in respect of the common notion of prudence, i.e., as being right reason applied to action, while it is called *political,* as being directed to the common good.

**Ad secundum** dicendum quod, sicut Philosophus ibidem dicit, *ad bonum virum pertinet posse bene principari et bene subiici.* Et ideo in virtute boni viri includitur etiam virtus principis. Sed virtus principis et subditi differt specie, sicut etiam virtus viri et mulieris, ut ibidem dicitur.

**Ad tertium** dicendum quod etiam diversi fines quorum unus ordinatur ad alium diversificant speciem habitus, sicut equestris et militaris et civilis differunt specie, licet finis unius ordinetur ad finem alterius. Et similiter, licet bonum unius ordinetur ad bonum multitudinis, tamen hoc non impedit quin talis diversitas faciat habitus differre specie. Sed ex hoc sequitur quod habitus qui ordinatur ad finem ultimum sit principalior, et imperet aliis habitibus.

**Reply Obj. 2**: As the Philosopher declares (*Polit.* iii, 2), *it belongs to a good man to be able to rule well and to obey well*, wherefore the virtue of a good man includes also that of a good ruler. Yet the virtue of the ruler and of the subject differs specifically, even as the virtue of a man and of a woman, as stated by the same authority (*Polit.* iii, 2).

**Reply Obj. 3**: Even different ends, one of which is subordinate to the other, diversify the species of a habit, thus for instance, habits directed to riding, soldiering, and civic life, differ specifically although their ends are subordinate to one another. In like manner, though the good of the individual is subordinate to the good of the many, that does not prevent this difference from making the habits differ specifically; but it follows that the habit which is directed to the last end is above the other habits and commands them.

# Article 12

*Whether prudence is in subjects, or only in their rulers?*

**Ad duodecimum sic proceditur.** Videtur quod prudentia non sit in subditis, sed solum in principibus. Dicit enim Philosophus, in III Polit., quod *prudentia sola est propria virtus principis, aliae autem virtutes sunt communes subditorum et principum. Subditi autem non est virtus prudentia, sed opinio vera.*

**Praeterea**, in I Polit. dicitur quod *servus omnino non habet quid consiliativum.* Sed *prudentia facit bene consiliativos*; ut dicitur in VI Ethic. Ergo prudentia non competit servis, seu subditis.

**Praeterea**, prudentia est praeceptiva, ut supra dictum est. Sed praecipere non pertinet ad servos vel subditos, sed solum ad principes. Ergo prudentia non est in subditis, sed solum in principibus.

**Sed contra** est quod Philosophus dicit, in VI Ethic., quod prudentiae politicae sunt duae species, una quae est *legum positiva*, quae pertinet ad principes; alia quae *retinet commune nomen politicae*, quae est *circa singularia.* Huiusmodi autem singularia peragere pertinet etiam ad subditos. Ergo prudentia non solum est principum, sed etiam subditorum.

**Respondeo** dicendum quod prudentia in ratione est. Regere autem et gubernare proprie rationis est. Et ideo unusquisque inquantum participat de regimine et gubernatione, intantum convenit sibi habere rationem et prudentiam. Manifestum est autem quod subditi inquantum est subditus, et servi inquantum est servus, non est regere et gubernare, sed magis regi et gubernari. Et ideo prudentia non est virtus servi inquantum est servus, nec subditi inquantum est subditus.

Sed quia quilibet homo, inquantum est rationalis, participat aliquid de regimine secundum arbitrium ra-

**Objection 1**: It would seem that prudence is not in subjects but only in their rulers. For the Philosopher says (*Polit.* iii, 2) that *prudence alone is the virtue proper to a ruler, while other virtues are common to subjects and rulers, and the prudence of the subject is not a virtue but a true opinion.*

**Obj. 2**: Further, it is stated in *Polit.* i, 5 that *a slave is not competent to take counsel.* But *prudence makes a man take good counsel* (*Ethic.* vi, 5). Therefore prudence is not befitting slaves or subjects.

**Obj. 3**: Further, prudence exercises command, as stated above (A. 8). But command is not in the competency of slaves or subjects but only of rulers. Therefore prudence is not in subjects but only in rulers.

**On the contrary**, The Philosopher says (*Ethic.* vi, 8) that there are two kinds of political prudence, one of which is *legislative* and belongs to rulers, while the other *retains the common name political*, and is about *individual actions.* Now it belongs also to subjects to perform these individual actions. Therefore prudence is not only in rulers but also in subjects.

**I answer that**, Prudence is in the reason. Now ruling and governing belong properly to the reason; and therefore it is proper to a man to reason and be prudent insofar as he has a share in ruling and governing. But it is evident that the subject as subject, and the slave as slave, are not competent to rule and govern, but rather to be ruled and governed. Therefore prudence is not the virtue of a slave as slave, nor of a subject as subject.

Since, however, every man, for as much as he is rational, has a share in ruling according to the judgment of reason,

tionis, intantum convenit ei prudentiam habere. Unde manifestum est quod prudentia quidem in principe est *ad modum artis architectonicae*, ut dicitur in VI Ethic., in subditis autem *ad modum artis manu operantis*.

**AD PRIMUM** ergo dicendum quod verbum Philosophi est intelligendum per se loquendo, quia scilicet virtus prudentiae non est virtus subditi inquantum huiusmodi.

**AD SECUNDUM** dicendum quod servus non habet consiliativum inquantum est servus, sic enim est instrumentum domini. Est tamen consiliativus inquantum est animal rationale.

**AD TERTIUM** dicendum quod per prudentiam homo non solum praecipit aliis, sed etiam sibi ipsi, prout scilicet ratio dicitur praecipere inferioribus viribus.

he is proportionately competent to have prudence. Wherefore it is manifest that prudence is in the ruler *after the manner of a mastercraft* (*Ethic.* vi, 8), but in the subjects, *after the manner of a handicraft*.

REPLY OBJ. 1: The saying of the Philosopher is to be understood strictly, namely, that prudence is not the virtue of a subject as such.

REPLY OBJ. 2: A slave is not capable of taking counsel, insofar as he is a slave (for thus he is the instrument of his master), but he does take counsel insofar as he is a rational animal.

REPLY OBJ. 3: By prudence a man commands not only others, but also himself, insofar as the reason is said to command the lower powers.

# Article 13

*Whether prudence can be in sinners?*

**AD DECIMUMTERTIUM SIC PROCEDITUR.** Videtur quod prudentia possit esse in peccatoribus. Dicit enim dominus, Luc. XVI, *filii huius saeculi prudentiores filiis lucis in generatione sua sunt*. Sed filii huius saeculi sunt peccatores. Ergo in peccatoribus potest esse prudentia.

**PRAETEREA**, fides est nobilior virtus quam prudentia. Sed fides potest esse in peccatoribus. Ergo et prudentia.

**PRAETEREA**, *prudentis hoc opus maxime dicimus, bene consiliari*; ut dicitur in VI Ethic. Sed multi peccatores sunt boni consilii. Ergo multi peccatores habent prudentiam.

**SED CONTRA** est quod philosophus dicit, in VI Ethic., *impossibile prudentem esse non entem bonum*. Sed nullus peccator est bonus. Ergo nullus peccator est prudens.

**RESPONDEO** dicendum quod prudentia dicitur tripliciter. Est enim quaedam prudentia falsa, vel per similitudinem dicta. Cum enim prudens sit qui bene disponit ea quae sunt agenda propter aliquem bonum finem, ille qui propter malum finem aliqua disponit congruentia illi fini habet falsam prudentiam, inquantum illud quod accipit pro fine non est vere bonum, sed secundum similitudinem, sicut dicitur aliquis bonus latro. Hoc enim modo potest secundum similitudinem dici prudens latro qui convenientes vias adinvenit ad latrocinandum. Et huiusmodi est prudentia de qua apostolus dicit, ad Rom. VIII, *prudentia carnis mors est*, quae scilicet finem ultimum constituit in delectatione carnis.

Secunda autem prudentia est quidem vera, quia adinvenit vias accommodatas ad finem vere bonum; sed est imperfecta, duplici ratione. Uno modo, quia illud bo-

OBJECTION 1: It would seem that there can be prudence in sinners. For our Lord said (Luke 16:8): *The children of this world are more prudent in their generation than the children of light*. Now the children of this world are sinners. Therefore there be prudence in sinners.

OBJ. 2: Further, faith is a more excellent virtue than prudence. But there can be faith in sinners. Therefore there can be prudence also.

OBJ. 3: Further, according to *Ethic.* vi, 7, *we say that to be of good counsel is the work of prudent man especially*. Now many sinners can take good counsel. Therefore sinners can have prudence.

ON THE CONTRARY, The Philosopher declares (*Ethic.* vi, 12) that *it is impossible for a man be prudent unless he be good*. Now no sinner is a good man. Therefore no sinner is prudent.

I ANSWER THAT, Prudence is threefold. There is a false prudence, which takes its name from its likeness to true prudence. For since a prudent man is one who disposes well of the things that have to be done for a good end, whoever disposes well of such things as are fitting for an evil end, has false prudence, in far as that which he takes for an end, is good, not in truth but in appearance. Thus man is called *a good robber*, and in this way may speak of *a prudent robber*, by way of similarity, because he devises fitting ways of committing robbery. This is the prudence of which the Apostle says (Rom 8:6): *The prudence of the flesh is death*, because, to wit, it places its ultimate end in the pleasures of the flesh.

The second prudence is indeed true prudence, because it devises fitting ways of obtaining a good end; and yet it is imperfect, from a twofold source. First, because the good

num quod accipit pro fine non est communis finis totius humanae vitae, sed alicuius specialis negotii, puta cum aliquis adinvenit vias accommodatas ad negotiandum vel ad navigandum, dicitur prudens negotiator vel nauta. Alio modo, quia deficit in principali actu prudentiae, puta cum aliquis bene consiliatur et recte iudicat etiam de his quae pertinent ad totam vitam, sed non efficaciter praecipit.

Tertia autem prudentia est et vera et perfecta, quae ad bonum finem totius vitae recte consiliatur, iudicat et praecipit. Et haec sola dicitur prudentia simpliciter. Quae in peccatoribus esse non potest. Prima autem prudentia est in solis peccatoribus. Prudentia autem imperfecta est communis bonis et malis, maxime illa quae est imperfecta propter finem particularem. Nam illa quae est imperfecta propter defectum principalis actus etiam non est nisi in malis.

**AD PRIMUM** ergo dicendum quod illud verbum domini intelligitur de prima prudentia. Unde non dicitur simpliciter quod sint prudentes; sed quod sint prudentes *in generatione sua*.

**AD SECUNDUM** dicendum quod fides in sui ratione non importat aliquam conformitatem ad appetitum rectorum operum, sed ratio fidei consistit in sola cognitione. Sed prudentia importat ordinem ad appetitum rectum. Tum quia principia prudentiae sunt fines operabilium, de quibus aliquis habet rectam aestimationem per habitus virtutum moralium, quae faciunt appetitum rectum, unde prudentia non potest esse sine virtutibus moralibus, ut supra ostensum est. Tum etiam quia prudentia est praeceptiva rectorum operum, quod non contingit nisi existente appetitu recto. Unde fides licet sit nobilior quam prudentia propter obiectum, tamen prudentia secundum sui rationem magis repugnat peccato, quod procedit ex perversitate appetitus.

**AD TERTIUM** dicendum quod peccatores possunt quidem esse bene consiliativi ad aliquem finem malum, vel ad aliquod particulare bonum, ad finem autem bonum totius vitae non sunt bene consiliativi perfecte, quia consilium ad effectum non perducunt. Unde non est in eis prudentia, quae se habet solum ad bonum, sed sicut philosophus dicit, in VI Ethic., est in talibus *deinotica*, idest naturalis industria, quae se habet ad bonum et ad malum; vel *astutia*, quae se habet solum ad malum, quam supra diximus falsam prudentiam vel prudentiam carnis.

which it takes for an end, is not the common end of all human life, but of some particular affair; thus when a man devises fitting ways of conducting business or of sailing a ship, he is called a prudent businessman, or a prudent sailor; second, because he fails in the chief act of prudence, as when a man takes counsel aright, and forms a good judgment, even about things concerning life as a whole, but fails to make an effective command.

The third prudence is both true and perfect, for it takes counsel, judges and commands aright in respect of the good end of man's whole life: and this alone is prudence simply so-called, and cannot be in sinners, whereas the first prudence is in sinners alone, while imperfect prudence is common to good and wicked men, especially that which is imperfect through being directed to a particular end, since that which is imperfect on account of a failing in the chief act, is only in the wicked.

**REPLY OBJ. 1:** This saying of our Lord is to be understood of the first prudence, wherefore it is not said that they are prudent absolutely, but that they are prudent in *their generation*.

**REPLY OBJ. 2:** The nature of faith consists not in conformity with the appetite for certain right actions, but in knowledge alone. On the other hand prudence implies a relation to a right appetite. First because its principles are the ends in matters of action; and of such ends one forms a right estimate through the habits of moral virtue, which rectify the appetite: wherefore without the moral virtues there is no prudence, as shown above (I-II, Q. 58, A. 5); second because prudence commands right actions, which does not happen unless the appetite be right. Wherefore though faith on account of its object is more excellent than prudence, yet prudence, by its very nature, is more opposed to sin, which arises from a disorder of the appetite.

**REPLY OBJ. 3:** Sinners can take good counsel for an evil end, or for some particular good, but they do not perfectly take good counsel for the end of their whole life, since they do not carry that counsel into effect. Hence they lack prudence which is directed to the good only; and yet in them, according to the Philosopher (*Ethic.* vi, 12) there is *cleverness*, i.e., natural diligence which may be directed to both good and evil; or *cunning*, which is directed only to evil, and which we have stated above, to be *false prudence* or *prudence of the flesh*.

# Article 14

*Whether prudence is in all who have grace?*

AD DECIMUMQUARTUM SIC PROCEDITUR. Videtur quod prudentia non sit in omnibus habentibus gratiam. Ad prudentiam enim requiritur industria quaedam, per quam sciant bene providere quae agenda sunt. Sed multi habentes gratiam carent tali industria. Ergo non omnes habentes gratiam habent prudentiam.

PRAETEREA, prudens dicitur qui est bene consiliativus, ut dictum est. Sed multi habent gratiam qui non sunt bene consiliativi, sed necesse habent regi consilio alieno. Ergo non omnes habentes gratiam habent prudentiam.

PRAETEREA, philosophus dicit, in III Topic., quod *iuvenes non constat esse prudentes*. Sed multi iuvenes habent gratiam. Ergo prudentia non invenitur in omnibus gratiam habentibus.

SED CONTRA est quod nullus habet gratiam nisi sit virtuosus. Sed nullus potest esse virtuosus nisi habeat prudentiam, dicit enim Gregorius, in II Moral., quod *ceterae virtutes, nisi ea quae appetunt prudenter agant, virtutes esse nequaquam possunt.* Ergo omnes habentes gratiam habent prudentiam.

RESPONDEO dicendum quod necesse est virtutes esse connexas, ita ut qui unam habet omnes habeat, ut supra ostensum est. Quicumque autem habet gratiam habet caritatem. Unde necesse est quod habeat omnes alias virtutes. Et ita, cum prudentia sit virtus, ut ostensum est, necesse est quod habeat prudentiam.

AD PRIMUM ergo dicendum quod duplex est industria. Una quidem quae est sufficiens ad ea quae sunt de necessitate salutis. Et talis industria datur omnibus habentibus gratiam, quos *unctio docet de omnibus*, ut dicitur I Ioan. II. Est autem alia industria plenior, per quam aliquis sibi et aliis potest providere, non solum de his quae sunt necessaria ad salutem sed etiam de quibuscumque pertinentibus ad humanam vitam. Et talis industria non est in omnibus habentibus gratiam.

AD SECUNDUM dicendum quod illi qui indigent regi consilio alieno saltem in hoc sibi ipsis consulere sciunt, si gratiam habent, ut aliorum requirant consilia, et discernant consilia bona a malis.

AD TERTIUM dicendum quod prudentia acquisita causatur ex exercitio actuum, unde *indiget ad sui generationem experimento et tempore*, ut dicitur in II Ethic. Unde non potest esse in iuvenibus nec secundum habitum nec secundum actum. Sed prudentia gratuita causatur ex infusione divina. Unde in pueris baptizatis nondum habentibus usum rationis est prudentia secundum habitum, sed non secundum actum, sicut et in amentibus. In his autem qui iam habent usum rationis est etiam secundum actum quantum ad ea quae sunt de

OBJECTION 1: It would seem that prudence is not in all who have grace. Prudence requires diligence, that one may foresee aright what has to be done. But many who have grace have not this diligence. Therefore not all who have grace have prudence.

OBJ. 2: Further, a prudent man is one who takes good counsel, as stated above (A. 8, Obj. 2; A. 13, Obj. 3). Yet many have grace who do not take good counsel, and need to be guided by the counsel of others. Therefore not all who have grace, have prudence.

OBJ. 3: Further, the Philosopher says (*Topic.* iii, 2) that *young people are not obviously prudent.* Yet many young people have grace. Therefore prudence is not to be found in all who have grace.

ON THE CONTRARY, No man has grace unless he be virtuous. Now no man can be virtuous without prudence, for Gregory says (*Moral.* ii, 46) that *the other virtues cannot be virtues at all unless they effect prudently what they desire to accomplish.* Therefore all who have grace have prudence.

I ANSWER THAT, The virtues must needs be connected together, so that whoever has one has all, as stated above (I-II, Q. 65, A. 1). Now whoever has grace has charity, so that he must needs have all the other virtues, and hence, since prudence is a virtue, as shown above (A. 4), he must, of necessity, have prudence also.

REPLY OBJ. 1: Diligence is twofold: one is merely sufficient with regard to things necessary for salvation; and such diligence is given to all who have grace, whom *His unction teacheth of all things* (1 John 2:27). There is also another diligence which is more than sufficient, whereby a man is able to make provision both for himself and for others, not only in matters necessary for salvation, but also in all things relating to human life; and such diligence as this is not in all who have grace.

REPLY OBJ. 2: Those who require to be guided by the counsel of others, are able, if they have grace, to take counsel for themselves in this point at least, that they require the counsel of others and can discern good from evil counsel.

REPLY OBJ. 3: Acquired prudence is caused by the exercise of acts, wherefore *its acquisition demands experience and time* (*Ethic.* ii, 1), hence it cannot be in the young, neither in habit nor in act. On the other hand gratuitous prudence is caused by divine infusion. Wherefore, in children who have been baptized but have not come to the use of reason, there is prudence as to habit but not as to act, even as in idiots; whereas in those who have come to the use of reason, it is also as to act, with regard to things necessary for salvation. This by practice merits increase,

necessitate salutis, sed per exercitium meretur augmentum quousque perficiatur, sicut et ceterae virtutes. Unde et apostolus dicit, ad Heb. V, quod *perfectorum est solidus cibus, qui pro consuetudine exercitatos habent sensus ad discretionem boni et mali.*

until it becomes perfect, even as the other virtues. Hence the Apostle says (Heb 5:14) that *strong meat is for the perfect, for them who by custom have their senses exercised to the discerning of good and evil.*

# Article 15

## Whether prudence is in us by nature?

**AD DECIMUMQUINTUM SIC PROCEDITUR.** Videtur quod prudentia insit nobis a natura. Dicit enim Philosophus, in VI Ethic., quod ea quae pertinent ad prudentiam *naturalia videntur esse*, scilicet synesis, gnome et huiusmodi, non autem ea quae pertinent ad sapientiam speculativam. Sed eorum quae sunt unius generis eadem est originis ratio. Ergo etiam prudentia inest nobis a natura.

**PRAETEREA**, aetatum variatio est secundum naturam. Sed prudentia consequitur aetates, secundum illud Iob XII, *in antiquis est sapientia, et in multo tempore prudentia.* Ergo prudentia est naturalis.

**PRAETEREA**, prudentia magis convenit naturae humanae quam naturae brutorum animalium. Sed bruta animalia habent quasdam naturales prudentias; ut patet per Philosophum, in VIII de Historiis animal. Ergo prudentia est naturalis.

**SED CONTRA** est quod Philosophus dicit, in II Ethic., quod *virtus intellectualis plurimum ex doctrina habet et generationem et augmentum, ideo experimento indiget et tempore.* Sed prudentia est virtus intellectualis, ut supra habitum est. Ergo prudentia non inest nobis a natura, sed ex doctrina et experimento.

**RESPONDEO** dicendum quod, sicut ex praemissis patet, prudentia includit cognitionem et universalium et singularium operabilium, ad quae prudens universalia principia applicat. Quantum igitur ad universalem cognitionem, eadem ratio est de prudentia et de scientia speculativa. Quia utriusque prima principia universalia sunt naturaliter nota, ut ex supradictis patet, nisi quod principia communia prudentiae sunt magis connaturalia homini; ut enim philosophus dicit, in X Ethic., *vita quae est secundum speculationem est melior quam quae est secundum hominem.* Sed alia principia universalia posteriora, sive sint rationis speculativae sive practicae, non habentur per naturam, sed per inventionem secundum viam experimenti, vel per disciplinam.

Quantum autem ad particularem cognitionem eorum circa quae operatio consistit est iterum distinguendum. Quia operatio consistit circa aliquid vel sicut circa finem; vel sicut circa ea quae sunt ad finem. Fines autem recti humanae vitae sunt determinati. Et ideo potest esse naturalis inclinatio respectu horum finium, sicut supra

**OBJECTION 1**: It would seem that prudence is in us by nature. The Philosopher says that things connected with prudence *seem to be natural*, namely *synesis, gnome* and the like, but not those which are connected with speculative wisdom. Now things belonging to the same genus have the same kind of origin. Therefore prudence also is in us from nature.

**OBJ. 2**: Further, the changes of age are according to nature. Now prudence results from age, according to Job 12:12: *In the ancient is wisdom, and in length of days prudence.* Therefore prudence is natural.

**OBJ. 3**: Further, prudence is more consistent with human nature than with that of dumb animals. Now there are instances of a certain natural prudence in dumb animals, according to the Philosopher (*De Hist. Anim.* viii, 1). Therefore prudence is natural.

**ON THE CONTRARY**, The Philosopher says (*Ethic.* ii, 1) that *intellectual virtue is both originated and fostered by teaching; it therefore demands experience and time.* Now prudence is an intellectual virtue, as stated above (A. 4). Therefore prudence is in us, not by nature, but by teaching and experience.

**I ANSWER THAT**, As shown above (A. 3), prudence includes knowledge both of universals, and of the singular matters of action to which prudence applies the universal principles. Accordingly, as regards the knowledge of universals, the same is to be said of prudence as of speculative science, because the primary universal principles of either are known naturally, as shown above (A. 6): except that the common principles of prudence are more connatural to man; for as the Philosopher remarks (*Ethic.* x, 7) *the life which is according to the speculative reason is better than that which is according to man*: whereas the secondary universal principles, whether of the speculative or of the practical reason, are not inherited from nature, but are acquired by discovery through experience, or through teaching.

On the other hand, as regards the knowledge of particulars which are the matter of action, we must make a further distinction, because this matter of action is either an end or the means to an end. Now the right ends of human life are fixed; wherefore there can be a natural inclination in respect of these ends; thus it has been stated above (I-

dictum est quod quidam habent ex naturali dispositione quasdam virtutes quibus inclinantur ad rectos fines, et per consequens etiam habent naturaliter rectum iudicium de huiusmodi finibus.

Sed ea quae sunt ad finem in rebus humanis non sunt determinata, sed multipliciter diversificantur secundum diversitatem personarum et negotiorum. Unde quia inclinatio naturae semper est ad aliquid determinatum, talis cognitio non potest homini inesse naturaliter, licet ex naturali dispositione unus sit aptior ad huiusmodi discernenda quam alius; sicut etiam accidit circa conclusiones speculativarum scientiarum. Quia igitur prudentia non est circa fines, sed circa ea quae sunt ad finem, ut supra habitum est; ideo prudentia non est naturalis.

AD PRIMUM ergo dicendum quod philosophus ibi loquitur de pertinentibus ad prudentiam secundum quod ordinantur ad fines, unde supra praemiserat quod *principia sunt eius quod est cuius gratia*, idest finis. Et propter hoc non facit mentionem de eubulia, quae est consiliativa eorum quae sunt ad finem.

AD SECUNDUM dicendum quod prudentia magis est in senibus non solum propter naturalem dispositionem, quietatis motibus passionum sensibilium, sed etiam propter experientiam longi temporis.

AD TERTIUM dicendum quod in brutis animalibus sunt determinatae viae perveniendi ad finem, unde videmus quod omnia animalia eiusdem speciei similiter operantur. Sed hoc non potest esse in homine, propter rationem eius, quae, cum sit cognoscitiva universalium, ad infinita singularia se extendit.

II, Q. 51, A. 1; Q. 63, A. 1) that some, from a natural inclination, have certain virtues whereby they are inclined to right ends; and consequently they also have naturally a right judgment about such like ends.

But the means to the end, in human concerns, far from being fixed, are of manifold variety according to the variety of persons and affairs. Wherefore since the inclination of nature is ever to something fixed, the knowledge of those means cannot be in man naturally, although, by reason of his natural disposition, one man has a greater aptitude than another in discerning them, just as it happens with regard to the conclusions of speculative sciences. Since then prudence is not about the ends, but about the means, as stated above (A. 6; I-II, Q. 57, A. 5), it follows that prudence is not from nature.

REPLY OBJ. 1: The Philosopher is speaking there of things relating to prudence, insofar as they are directed to ends. Wherefore he had said before (*Ethic.* vi, 5, 11) that *they are the principles of the 'ou heneka'*, namely, the end; and so he does not mention euboulia among them, because it takes counsel about the means.

REPLY OBJ. 2: Prudence is rather in the old, not only because their natural disposition calms the movement of the sensitive passions, but also because of their long experience.

REPLY OBJ. 3: Even in dumb animals there are fixed ways of obtaining an end, wherefore we observe that all the animals of a same species act in like manner. But this is impossible in man, on account of his reason, which takes cognizance of universals, and consequently extends to an infinity of singulars.

# Article 16

*Whether prudence can be lost through forgetfulness?*

AD DECIMUMSEXTUM SIC PROCEDITUR. Videtur quod prudentia possit amitti per oblivionem. Scientia enim, cum sit necessariorum, est certior quam prudentia, quae est contingentium operabilium. Sed scientia amittitur per oblivionem. Ergo multo magis prudentia.

PRAETEREA, sicut philosophus dicit, in II Ethic., *virtus ex eisdem generatur et corrumpitur contrario modo factis.* Sed ad generationem prudentiae necessarium est experimentum, quod fit *ex multis memoriis*, ut dicitur in principio Metaphys. Ergo, cum oblivio memoriae opponatur, videtur quod prudentia per oblivionem possit amitti.

PRAETEREA, prudentia non est sine cognitione universalium. Sed universalium cognitio potest per oblivionem amitti. Ergo et prudentia.

OBJECTION 1: It would seem that prudence can be lost through forgetfulness. For since science is about necessary things, it is more certain than prudence which is about contingent matters of action. But science is lost by forgetfulness. Much more therefore is prudence.

OBJ. 2: Further, as the Philosopher says (*Ethic.* ii, 3) *the same things, but by a contrary process, engender and corrupt virtue.* Now the engendering of prudence requires experience which is made up *of many memories*, as he states at the beginning of his Metaphysics (i, 1). Therefore since forgetfulness is contrary to memory, it seems that prudence can be lost through forgetfulness.

OBJ. 3: Further, there is no prudence without knowledge of universals. But knowledge of universals can be lost through forgetfulness. Therefore prudence can also.

**Sed contra** est quod philosophus dicit, in VI Ethic., quod *oblivio est artis, et non prudentiae.*

**Respondeo** dicendum quod oblivio respicit cognitionem tantum. Et ideo per oblivionem potest aliquis artem totaliter perdere, et similiter scientiam, quae in ratione consistunt. Sed prudentia non consistit in sola cognitione, sed etiam in appetitu, quia ut dictum est, principalis eius actus est praecipere, quod est applicare cognitionem habitam ad appetendum et operandum. Et ideo prudentia non directe tollitur per oblivionem, sed magis corrumpitur per passiones, dicit enim philosophus, in VI Ethic., quod *delectabile et triste pervertit existimationem prudentiae.* Unde Dan. XIII dicitur, *species decepit te, et concupiscentia subvertit cor tuum*; et Exod. XXIII dicitur, *ne accipias munera, quae excaecant etiam prudentes.*

Oblivio tamen potest impedire prudentiam, inquantum procedit ad praecipiendum ex aliqua cognitione, quae per oblivionem tolli potest.

**Ad primum** ergo dicendum quod scientia est in sola ratione. Unde de ea est alia ratio, ut supra dictum est.

**Ad secundum** dicendum quod experimentum prudentiae non acquiritur ex sola memoria, sed ex exercitio recte praecipiendi.

**Ad tertium** dicendum quod prudentia principaliter consistit non in cognitione universalium, sed in applicatione ad opera, ut dictum est. Et ideo oblivio universalis cognitionis non corrumpit id quod est principale in prudentia, sed aliquid impedimentum ei affert, ut dictum est.

**On the contrary,** The Philosopher says (*Ethic.* vi, 5) that *forgetfulness is possible to art but not to prudence.*

**I answer that,** Forgetfulness regards knowledge only, wherefore one can forget art and science, so as to lose them altogether, because they belong to the reason. But prudence consists not in knowledge alone, but also in an act of the appetite, because as stated above (A. 8), its principal act is one of command, whereby a man applies the knowledge he has, to the purpose of appetition and operation. Hence prudence is not taken away directly by forgetfulness, but rather is corrupted by the passions. For the Philosopher says (*Ethic.* vi, 5) that *pleasure and sorrow pervert the estimate of prudence*: wherefore it is written (Dan 13:56): *Beauty hath deceived thee, and lust hath subverted thy heart,* and (Exod 23:8): *Neither shalt thou take bribes which blind even the prudent.*

Nevertheless forgetfulness may hinder prudence, insofar as the latter's command depends on knowledge which may be forgotten.

**Reply Obj. 1**: Science is in the reason only: hence the comparison fails, as stated above.

**Reply Obj. 2**: The experience required by prudence results not from memory alone, but also from the practice of commanding aright.

**Reply Obj. 3**: Prudence consists chiefly, not in the knowledge of universals, but in applying them to action, as stated above (A. 3). Wherefore forgetting the knowledge of universals does not destroy the principal part of prudence, but hinders it somewhat, as stated above.

# QUESTION 48

## THE PARTS OF PRUDENCE

Deinde considerandum est de partibus prudentiae. Et circa hoc quaeruntur quatuor, primo, quae sint partes prudentiae; secundo, de partibus quasi integralibus eius; tertio, de partibus subiectivis eius; quarto, de partibus potentialibus.

We must now consider the parts of prudence, under which head there are four points of inquiry: (1) Which are the parts of prudence? (2) Of its integral parts; (3) Of its subjective parts; (4) Of its potential parts.

# Article 1

*Whether three parts of prudence are fittingly assigned?*

**AD PRIMUM SIC PROCEDITUR.** Videtur quod inconvenienter assignentur partes prudentiae. Tullius enim, in II Rhet., ponit tres partes prudentiae, scilicet *memoriam, intelligentiam* et *providentiam*. Macrobius autem, secundum sententiam Plotini, attribuit prudentiae sex, scilicet *rationem, intellectum, circumspectionem, providentiam, docilitatem* et *cautionem*. Aristoteles autem, in VI Ethic., dicit ad prudentiam pertinere *eubuliam, synesim* et *gnomen*. Facit etiam mentionem circa prudentiam de *eustochia* et *solertia, sensu* et *intellectu*. Quidam autem alius philosophus Graecus dicit quod ad prudentiam decem pertinent, scilicet *eubulia, solertia, providentia, regnativa, militaris, politica, oeconomica, dialectica, rhetorica, physica*. Ergo videtur quod vel una assignatio sit superflua, vel alia diminuta.

**PRAETEREA,** prudentia dividitur contra scientiam. Sed politica, oeconomica, dialectica, rhetorica, physica sunt quaedam scientiae. Non ergo sunt partes prudentiae.

**PRAETEREA,** partes non excedunt totum. Sed memoria intellectiva, vel intelligentia, ratio, sensus et docilitas non solum pertinent ad prudentiam, sed etiam ad omnes habitus cognoscitivos. Ergo non debent poni partes prudentiae.

**PRAETEREA,** sicut consiliari et iudicare et praecipere sunt actus rationis practicae, ita etiam et uti, sicut supra habitum est. Sicut ergo eubulia adiungitur prudentiae, quae pertinet ad consilium, et synesis et gnome, quae pertinent ad iudicium; ita etiam debuit poni aliquid pertinens ad usum.

**PRAETEREA,** sollicitudo ad prudentiam pertinet, sicut supra habitum est. Ergo etiam inter partes prudentiae sollicitudo poni debuit.

**RESPONDEO** dicendum quod triplex est pars, scilicet *integralis*, ut paries, tectum et fundamentum sunt partes domus; *subiectiva*, sicut bos et leo sunt partes anima-

**OBJECTION 1**: It would seem that the parts of prudence are assigned unfittingly. Tully (*De Invent. Rhet.* ii, 53) assigns three parts of prudence, namely, *memory, understanding* and *foresight*. Macrobius (*In Somn. Scip.* i) following the opinion of Plotinus ascribes to prudence six parts, namely, *reasoning, understanding, circumspection, foresight, docility* and *caution*. Aristotle says (*Ethic.* vi, 9, 10, 11) that *good counsel, synesis* and *gnome* belong to prudence. Again under the head of prudence he mentions *conjecture, shrewdness, sense* and *understanding*. And another Greek philosopher says that ten things are connected with prudence, namely, *good counsel, shrewdness, foresight, regnative, military, political* and *domestic prudence, dialectics, rhetoric* and *physics*. Therefore it seems that one or the other enumeration is either excessive or deficient.

**OBJ. 2**: Further, prudence is specifically distinct from science. But politics, economics, logic, rhetoric, physics are sciences. Therefore they are not parts of prudence.

**OBJ. 3**: Further, the parts do not exceed the whole. Now the intellective memory or intelligence, reason, sense and docility, belong not only to prudence but also to all the cognitive habits. Therefore they should not be set down as parts of prudence.

**OBJ. 4**: Further, just as counselling, judging and commanding are acts of the practical reason, so also is using, as stated above (I-II, Q. 16, A. 1). Therefore, just as *eubulia* which refers to counsel, is connected with prudence, and *synesis* and *gnome* which refer to judgment, so also ought something to have been assigned corresponding to use.

**OBJ. 5**: Further, solicitude pertains to prudence, as stated above (Q. 47, A. 9). Therefore solicitude also should have been mentioned among the parts of prudence.

**I ANSWER THAT**, Parts are of three kinds, namely, *integral*, as wall, roof, and foundations are parts of a house; *subjective*, as ox and lion are parts of animal; and *potential*,

lis; et *potentialis*, sicut nutritivum et sensitivum sunt partes animae. Tribus ergo modis possunt assignari partes alicui virtuti. Uno modo, ad similitudinem partium integralium, ut scilicet illa dicantur esse partes virtutis alicuius quae necesse est concurrere ad perfectum actum virtutis illius. Et sic ex omnibus enumeratis possunt accipi octo partes prudentiae, scilicet sex quas enumerat Macrobius; quibus addenda est septima, scilicet *memoria*, quam ponit Tullius; et *eustochia* sive *solertia*, quam ponit Aristoteles (nam *sensus* prudentiae etiam *intellectus* dicitur, unde Philosophus dicit, in VI Ethic., *horum igitur oportet habere sensum, hic autem est intellectus*). Quorum octo quinque pertinent ad prudentiam secundum id quod est cognoscitiva, scilicet *memoria, ratio, intellectus, docilitas* et *solertia*, tria vero alia pertinent ad eam secundum quod est praeceptiva, applicando cognitionem ad opus, scilicet *providentia, circumspectio* et *cautio*. Quorum diversitatis ratio patet ex hoc quod circa cognitionem tria sunt consideranda. Primo quidem, ipsa cognitio. Quae si sit praeteritorum, est *memoria*, si autem praesentium, sive contingentium sive necessariorum, vocatur *intellectus* sive *intelligentia*. Secundo, ipsa cognitionis acquisitio. Quae fit vel per disciplinam, et ad hoc pertinet *docilitas*, vel per inventionem, et ad hoc pertinet *eustochia*, quae est *bona coniecturatio*. Huius autem pars, ut dicitur in VI Ethic., est *solertia*, quae est velox *coniecturatio medii*, ut dicitur in I Poster. Tertio considerandus est usus cognitionis, secundum scilicet quod ex cognitis aliquis procedit ad alia cognoscenda vel iudicanda. Et hoc pertinet ad *rationem*. Ratio autem, ad hoc quod recte praecipiat, tria debet habere. Primo quidem, ut ordinet aliquid accommodum ad finem, et hoc pertinet ad *providentiam*. Secundo, ut attendat circumstantias negotii, quod pertinet ad *circumspectionem*. Tertio, ut vitet impedimenta, quod pertinet ad *cautionem*.

Partes autem subiectivae virtutis dicuntur species eius diversae. Et hoc modo partes prudentiae, secundum quod proprie sumuntur, sunt prudentia per quam aliquis regit seipsum, et prudentia per quam aliquis regit multitudinem, quae differunt specie, ut dictum est, et iterum prudentia quae est multitudinis regitiva dividitur in diversas species secundum diversas species multitudinis. Est autem quaedam multitudo adunata ad aliquod speciale negotium, sicut exercitus congregatur ad pugnandum, cuius regitiva est prudentia *militaris*. Quaedam vero multitudo est adunata ad totam vitam, sicut multitudo unius domus vel familiae, cuius regitiva est prudentia *oeconomica*; et multitudo unius civitatis vel regni, cuius quidem directiva est in principe *regnativa*, in subditis autem *politica* simpliciter dicta.

Si vero prudentia sumatur large, secundum quod includit etiam scientiam speculativam, ut supra dictum est;

as the nutritive and sensitive powers are parts of the soul. Accordingly, parts can be assigned to a virtue in three ways. First, in likeness to integral parts, so that the things which need to concur for the perfect act of a virtue, are called the parts of that virtue. In this way, out of all the things mentioned above, eight may be taken as parts of prudence, namely, the six assigned by Macrobius; with the addition of a seventh, viz. *memory* mentioned by Tully; and *eustochia* or *shrewdness* mentioned by Aristotle. For the *sense* of prudence is also called *understanding*: wherefore the Philosopher says (*Ethic*. vi, 11): *Of such things one needs to have the sense, and this is understanding*. Of these eight, five belong to prudence as a cognitive virtue, namely, *memory, reasoning, understanding, docility* and *shrewdness*: while the three others belong thereto, as commanding and applying knowledge to action, namely, *foresight, circumspection* and *caution*. The reason of their difference is seen from the fact that three things may be observed in reference to knowledge. In the first place, knowledge itself, which, if it be of the past, is called *memory*, if of the present, whether contingent or necessary, is called *understanding* or *intelligence*. Second, the acquiring of knowledge, which is caused either by teaching, to which pertains *docility*, or by discovery, and to this belongs to *eustochia*, i.e., *a happy conjecture*, of which *shrewdness* is a part, which is a *quick conjecture of the middle term*, as stated in *Poster*. i, 9. Third, the use of knowledge, inasmuch as we proceed from things known to knowledge or judgment of other things, and this belongs to *reasoning*. And the reason, in order to command aright, requires to have three conditions. First, to order that which is befitting the end, and this belongs to *foresight*; second, to attend to the circumstances of the matter in hand, and this belongs to *circumspection*; third, to avoid obstacles, and this belongs to *caution*.

The subjective parts of a virtue are its various species. In this way the parts of prudence, if we take them properly, are the prudence whereby a man rules himself, and the prudence whereby a man governs a multitude, which differ specifically as stated above (Q. 47, A. 11). Again, the prudence whereby a multitude is governed, is divided into various species according to the various kinds of multitude. There is the multitude which is united together for some particular purpose; thus an army is gathered together to fight, and the prudence that governs this is called *military*. There is also the multitude that is united together for the whole of life; such is the multitude of a home or family, and this is ruled by *domestic* prudence: and such again is the multitude of a city or kingdom, the ruling principle of which is *regnative* prudence in the ruler, and *political* prudence, simply so called, in the subjects.

If, however, prudence be taken in a wide sense, as including also speculative knowledge, as stated above (Q. 47,

tunc etiam partes eius ponuntur dialectica, rhetorica et physica, secundum tres modos procedendi in scientiis. Quorum unus est per demonstrationem ad scientiam causandam, quod pertinet ad *physicam*; ut sub physica intelligantur omnes scientiae demonstrativae. Alius modus est ex probabilibus ad opinionem faciendam, quod pertinet ad *dialecticam*. Tertius modus est ex quibusdam coniecturis ad suspicionem inducendam, vel ad aliqualiter persuadendum, quod pertinet ad *rhetoricam*. Potest tamen dici quod haec tria pertinent ad prudentiam etiam proprie dictam, quae ratiocinatur interdum quidem ex necessariis, interdum ex probabilibus, interdum autem ex quibusdam coniecturis.

Partes autem potentiales alicuius virtutis dicuntur virtutes adiunctae quae ordinantur ad aliquos secundarios actus vel materias, quasi non habentes totam potentiam principalis virtutis. Et secundum hoc ponuntur partes prudentiae *eubulia*, quae est circa consilium; et *synesis*, quae est circa iudicium eorum quae communiter accidunt; et *gnome*, quae est circa iudicium eorum in quibus oportet quandoque a communi lege recedere. Prudentia vero est circa principalem actum, qui est praecipere.

**AD PRIMUM** ergo dicendum quod diversae assignationes differunt secundum quod diversa genera partium ponuntur; vel secundum quod sub una parte unius assignationis includuntur multae partes alterius assignationis. Sicut Tullius sub *providentia* includit cautionem et circumspectionem; sub *intelligentia* autem rationem, docilitatem et solertiam.

**AD SECUNDUM** dicendum quod oeconomica et politica non accipiuntur hic secundum quod sunt scientiae; sed secundum quod sunt prudentiae quaedam. De aliis autem tribus patet responsio ex dictis.

**AD TERTIUM** dicendum quod omnia illa ponuntur partes prudentiae non secundum suam communitatem; sed secundum quod se habent ad ea quae pertinent ad prudentiam.

**AD QUARTUM** dicendum quod recte praecipere et recte uti semper se comitantur, quia ad praeceptum rationis sequitur obedientia inferiorum virium, quae pertinent ad usum.

**AD QUINTUM** dicendum quod sollicitudo includitur in ratione providentiae.

A. 2, ad 2) then its parts include dialectics, rhetoric and physics, according to three methods of prudence in the sciences. The first of these is the attaining of science by demonstration, which belongs to *physics* (if physics be understood to comprise all demonstrative sciences). The second method is to arrive at an opinion through probable premises, and this belongs to *dialectics*. The third method is to employ conjectures in order to induce a certain suspicion, or to persuade somewhat, and this belongs to *rhetoric*. It may be said, however, that these three belong also to prudence properly so called, since it argues sometimes from necessary premises, sometimes from probabilities, and sometimes from conjectures.

The potential parts of a virtue are the virtues connected with it, which are directed to certain secondary acts or matters, not having, as it were, the whole power of the principal virtue. In this way the parts of prudence are *good counsel*, which concerns counsel, *synesis*, which concerns judgment in matters of ordinary occurrence, and *gnome*, which concerns judgment in matters of exception to the law: while prudence is about the chief act, viz. that of commanding.

**REPLY OBJ. 1**: The various enumerations differ, either because different kinds of parts are assigned, or because that which is mentioned in one enumeration includes several mentioned in another enumeration. Thus Tully includes *caution* and *circumspection* under *foresight*, and *reasoning*, *docility* and *shrewdness* under *understanding*.

**REPLY OBJ. 2**: Here domestic and civic prudence are not to be taken as sciences, but as kinds of prudence. As to the other three, the reply may be gathered from what has been said.

**REPLY OBJ. 3**: All these things are reckoned parts of prudence, not by taking them altogether, but insofar as they are connected with things pertaining to prudence.

**REPLY OBJ. 4**: Right command and right use always go together, because the reason's command is followed by obedience on the part of the lower powers, which pertain to use.

**REPLY OBJ. 5**: Solicitude is included under foresight.

# QUESTION 49

## EACH QUASI-INTEGRAL PART OF PRUDENCE

Deinde considerandum est de singulis prudentiae partibus quasi integralibus. Et circa hoc quaeruntur octo.

Primo, de memoria.
Secundo, de intellectu vel intelligentia.
Tertio, de docilitate.
Quarto, de solertia.
Quinto, de ratione.
Sexto, de providentia.
Septimo, de circumspectione.
Octavo, de cautione.

We must now consider each quasi-integral part of prudence, and under this head there are eight points of inquiry:

(1) Memory;
(2) Understanding or Intelligence;
(3) Docility;
(4) Shrewdness;
(5) Reason;
(6) Foresight;
(7) Circumspection;
(8) Caution.

# Article 1

### Whether memory is a part of prudence?

**AD PRIMUM SIC PROCEDITUR**. Videtur quod memoria non sit pars prudentiae. Memoria enim, ut probat philosophus, est in parte animae sensitiva. Prudentia autem est in ratiocinativa; ut patet in VI Ethic. Ergo memoria non est pars prudentiae.

**PRAETEREA**, prudentia per exercitium acquiritur et proficit. Sed memoria inest nobis a natura. Ergo memoria non est pars prudentiae.

**PRAETEREA**, memoria est praeteritorum. Prudentia autem futurorum operabilium, de quibus est consilium, ut dicitur in VI Ethic. Ergo memoria non est pars prudentiae.

**SED CONTRA** est quod Tullius, in II Rhet., ponit memoriam inter partes prudentiae.

**RESPONDEO** dicendum quod prudentia est circa contingentia operabilia, sicut dictum est. In his autem non potest homo dirigi per ea quae sunt simpliciter et ex necessitate vera, sed ex his quae ut in pluribus accidunt, oportet enim principia conclusionibus esse proportionata, et ex talibus talia concludere, ut dicitur in VI Ethic. Quid autem in pluribus sit verum oportet per experimentum considerare, unde et in II Ethic. Philosophus dicit quod *virtus intellectualis habet generationem et augmentum ex experimento et tempore*. Experimentum autem est ex pluribus memoriis; ut patet in I Metaphys. Unde consequens est quod ad prudentiam requiritur plurium memoriam habere. Unde convenienter memoria ponitur pars prudentiae.

**AD PRIMUM** ergo dicendum quod quia, sicut dictum est, prudentia applicat universalem cognitionem ad particularia, quorum est sensus, inde multa quae pertinent

**OBJECTION 1**: It would seem that memory is not a part of prudence. For memory, as the Philosopher proves (*De Memor. et Remin.* i), is in the sensitive part of the soul: whereas prudence is in the rational part (*Ethic.* vi, 5). Therefore memory is not a part of prudence.

**OBJ. 2**: Further, prudence is acquired and perfected by experience, whereas memory is in us from nature. Therefore memory is not a part of prudence.

**OBJ. 3**: Further, memory regards the past, whereas prudence regards future matters of action, about which counsel is concerned, as stated in *Ethic.* vi, 2, 7. Therefore memory is not a part of prudence.

**ON THE CONTRARY**, Tully (*De Invent. Rhet.* ii, 53) places memory among the parts of prudence.

**I ANSWER THAT**, Prudence regards contingent matters of action, as stated above (Q. 47, A. 5). Now in such like matters a man can be directed, not by those things that are simply and necessarily true, but by those which occur in the majority of cases: because principles must be proportionate to their conclusions, and like must be concluded from like (*Ethic.* vi ). But we need experience to discover what is true in the majority of cases: wherefore the Philosopher says (*Ethic.* ii, 1) that *intellectual virtue is engendered and fostered by experience and time*. Now experience is the result of many memories as stated in *Metaph.* i, 1, and therefore prudence requires the memory of many things. Hence memory is fittingly accounted a part of prudence.

**REPLY OBJ. 1**: As stated above (Q. 47, AA. 3, 6), prudence applies universal knowledge to particulars which are objects of sense: hence many things belonging to the

ad partem sensitivam requiruntur ad prudentiam. Inter quae est memoria.

**AD SECUNDUM** dicendum quod sicut prudentia aptitudinem quidem habet ex natura, sed eius complementum est ex exercitio vel gratia ita etiam, ut Tullius dicit, in sua rhetorica, memoria non solum a natura proficiscitur, sed etiam habet plurimum artis et industriae.

Et sunt quatuor per quae homo proficit in bene memorando. Quorum primum est ut eorum quae vult memorari quasdam similitudines assumat convenientes, nec tamen omnino consuetas, quia ea quae sunt inconsueta magis miramur, et sic in eis animus magis et vehementius detinetur; ex quo fit quod eorum quae in pueritia vidimus magis memoremur. Ideo autem necessaria est huiusmodi similitudinum vel imaginum adinventio, quia intentiones simplices et spirituales facilius ex anima elabuntur nisi quibusdam similitudinibus corporalibus quasi alligentur, quia humana cognitio potentior est circa sensibilia. Unde et memorativa ponitur in parte sensitiva. Secundo, oportet ut homo ea quae memoriter vult tenere sua consideratione ordinate disponat, ut ex uno memorato facile ad aliud procedatur. Unde philosophus dicit, in libro de Mem., *a locis videntur reminisci aliquando, causa autem est quia velociter ab alio in aliud veniunt.* Tertio, oportet ut homo sollicitudinem apponat et affectum adhibeat ad ea quae vult memorari, quia quo aliquid magis fuerit impressum animo, eo minus elabitur. Unde et Tullius dicit, in sua rhetorica, quod *sollicitudo conservat integras simulacrorum figuras.* Quarto, oportet quod ea frequenter meditemur quae volumus memorari. Unde philosophus dicit, in libro de Mem., quod *meditationes memoriam salvant,* quia, ut in eodem libro dicitur, *consuetudo est quasi natura*; unde quae multoties intelligimus cito reminiscimur, quasi naturali quodam ordine ab uno ad aliud procedentes.

**AD TERTIUM** dicendum quod ex praeteritis oportet nos quasi argumentum sumere de futuris. Et ideo memoria praeteritorum necessaria est ad bene consiliandum de futuris.

sensitive faculties are requisite for prudence, and memory is one of them.

**REPLY OBJ. 2**: Just as aptitude for prudence is in our nature, while its perfection comes through practice or grace, so too, as Tully says in his Rhetoric, memory not only arises from nature, but is also aided by art and diligence.

There are four things whereby a man perfects his memory. First, when a man wishes to remember a thing, he should take some suitable yet somewhat unwonted illustration of it, since the unwonted strikes us more, and so makes a greater and stronger impression on the mind; the mind; and this explains why we remember better what we saw when we were children. Now the reason for the necessity of finding these illustrations or images, is that simple and spiritual impressions easily slip from the mind, unless they be tied as it were to some corporeal image, because human knowledge has a greater hold on sensible objects. For this reason memory is assigned to the sensitive part of the soul. Second, whatever a man wishes to retain in his memory he must carefully consider and set in order, so that he may pass easily from one memory to another. Hence the Philosopher says (*De Memor. et Remin.* ii): *Sometimes a place brings memories back to us: the reason being that we pass quickly from the one to the other.* Third, we must be anxious and earnest about the things we wish to remember, because the more a thing is impressed on the mind, the less it is liable to slip out of it. Wherefore Tully says in his *Rhetoric* that *anxiety preserves the figures of images entire.* Fourth, we should often reflect on the things we wish to remember. Hence the Philosopher says (*De Memoria* i) that *reflection preserves memories*, because as he remarks (*De Memoria* ii) *custom is a second nature*: wherefore when we reflect on a thing frequently, we quickly call it to mind, through passing from one thing to another by a kind of natural order.

**REPLY OBJ. 3**: It behooves us to argue, as it were, about the future from the past; wherefore memory of the past is necessary in order to take good counsel for the future.

# Article 2

*Whether understanding is a part of prudence?*

**AD SECUNDUM SIC PROCEDITUR.** Videtur quod intellectus non sit pars prudentiae. Eorum enim quae ex opposito dividuntur unum non est pars alterius. Sed intellectus ponitur virtus intellectualis condivisa prudentiae, ut patet in VI Ethic. Ergo intellectus non debet poni pars prudentiae.

**PRAETEREA,** intellectus ponitur inter dona spiritus sancti, et correspondet fidei, ut supra habitum est. Sed

**OBJECTION 1**: It would seem that understanding is not a part of prudence. When two things are members of a division, one is not part of the other. But intellectual virtue is divided into understanding and prudence, according to *Ethic.* vi, 3. Therefore understanding should not be reckoned a part of prudence.

**OBJ. 2**: Further, understanding is numbered among the gifts of the Holy Spirit, and corresponds to faith, as stated

prudentia est alia virtus a fide, ut per supradicta patet. Ergo intellectus non pertinet ad prudentiam.

PRAETEREA, prudentia est singularium operabilium, ut dicitur in VI Ethic. Sed intellectus est universalium cognoscitivus et immaterialium; ut patet in III de anima. Ergo intellectus non est pars prudentiae.

SED CONTRA est quod Tullius ponit intelligentiam partem prudentiae, et Macrobius intellectum, quod in idem redit.

RESPONDEO dicendum quod intellectus non sumitur hic pro potentia intellectiva, sed prout importat quandam rectam aestimationem alicuius extremi principii quod accipitur ut per se notum, sicut et prima demonstrationum principia intelligere dicimur. Omnis autem deductio rationis ab aliquibus procedit quae accipiuntur ut prima. Unde oportet quod omnis processus rationis ab aliquo intellectu procedat. Quia igitur prudentia est recta ratio agibilium, ideo necesse est quod totus processus prudentiae ab intellectu derivetur. Et propter hoc intellectus ponitur pars prudentiae.

AD PRIMUM ergo dicendum quod ratio prudentiae terminatur, sicut ad conclusionem quandam, ad particulare operabile, ad quod applicat universalem cognitionem, ut ex dictis patet. Conclusio autem singularis syllogizatur ex universali et singulari propositione. Unde oportet quod ratio prudentiae ex duplici intellectu procedat. Quorum unus est qui est cognoscitivus universalium. Quod pertinet ad intellectum qui ponitur virtus intellectualis, quia naturaliter nobis cognita sunt non solum universalia principia speculativa, sed etiam practica, sicut *nulli esse malefaciendum*, ut ex dictis patet. Alius autem intellectus est qui, ut dicitur in VI Ethic., est cognoscitivus *extremi*, idest alicuius primi singularis et contingentis operabilis, propositionis scilicet minoris, quam oportet esse singularem in syllogismo prudentiae, ut dictum est. Hoc autem primum singulare est aliquis singularis finis, ut ibidem dicitur. Unde intellectus qui ponitur pars prudentiae est quaedam recta aestimatio de aliquo particulari fine.

AD SECUNDUM dicendum quod intellectus qui ponitur donum spiritus sancti est quaedam acuta perspectio divinorum, ut ex supradictis patet. Aliter autem ponitur intellectus pars prudentiae, ut dictum est.

AD TERTIUM dicendum quod ipsa recta aestimatio de fine particulari et *intellectus* dicitur, inquantum est alicuius principii; et *sensus*, inquantum est particularis. Et hoc est quod Philosophus dicit, in VI Ethic., *horum*, scilicet singularium, *oportet habere sensum, hic autem est intellectus*. Non autem hoc est intelligendum de sensu particulari quo cognoscimus propria sensibilia, sed de sensu interiori quo de particulari iudicamus.

above (Q. 8, AA. 1, 8). But prudence is a virtue other than faith, as is clear from what has been said above (Q. 4, A. 8; I-II, Q. 62, A. 2). Therefore understanding does not pertain to prudence.

OBJ. 3: Further, prudence is about singular matters of action (*Ethic.* vi, 7): whereas understanding takes cognizance of universal and immaterial objects (*De Anima* iii, 4). Therefore understanding is not a part of prudence.

ON THE CONTRARY, Tully accounts *intelligence* a part of prudence, and Macrobius mentions *understanding*, which comes to the same.

I ANSWER THAT, Understanding denotes here, not the intellectual power, but the right estimate about some final principle, which is taken as self-evident: thus we are said to understand the first principles of demonstrations. Now every deduction of reason proceeds from certain statements which are taken as primary: wherefore every process of reasoning must needs proceed from some understanding. Therefore since prudence is right reason applied to action, the whole process of prudence must needs have its source in understanding. Hence it is that understanding is reckoned a part of prudence.

REPLY OBJ. 1: The reasoning of prudence terminates, as in a conclusion, in the particular matter of action, to which, as stated above (Q. 47, AA. 3, 6), it applies the knowledge of some universal principle. Now a singular conclusion is argued from a universal and a singular proposition. Wherefore the reasoning of prudence must proceed from a twofold understanding. The one is cognizant of universals, and this belongs to the understanding which is an intellectual virtue, whereby we know naturally not only speculative principles, but also practical universal principles, such as *One should do evil to no man*, as shown above (Q. 47, A. 6). The other understanding, as stated in *Ethic.* vi, 11, is cognizant of an *extreme*, i.e., of some primary singular and contingent practical matter, viz. the minor premiss, which must needs be singular in the syllogism of prudence, as stated above (Q. 47, AA. 3, 6). Now this primary singular is some singular end, as stated in the same place. Wherefore the understanding which is a part of prudence is a right estimate of some particular end.

REPLY OBJ. 2: The understanding which is a gift of the Holy Spirit, is a quick insight into divine things, as shown above (Q. 8, AA. 1, 2). It is in another sense that it is accounted a part of prudence, as stated above.

REPLY OBJ. 3: The right estimate about a particular end is called both *understanding*, insofar as its object is a principle, and *sense*, insofar as its object is a particular. This is what the Philosopher means when he says (*Ethic.* v, 11): *Of such things we need to have the sense, and this is understanding*. But this is to be understood as referring, not to the particular sense whereby we know proper sensibles, but to the interior sense, whereby we judge of a particular.

# Article 3

*Whether docility should be accounted a part of prudence?*

**AD TERTIUM SIC PROCEDITUR**. Videtur quod docilitas non debeat poni pars prudentiae. Illud enim quod requiritur ad omnem virtutem intellectualem non debet appropriari alicui earum. Sed docilitas necessaria est ad quamlibet virtutem intellectualem. Ergo non debet poni pars prudentiae.

**PRAETEREA**, ea quae ad virtutes humanas pertinent sunt in nobis, quia secundum ea quae in nobis sunt laudamur vel vituperamur. Sed non est in potestate nostra quod dociles simus, sed hoc ex naturali dispositione quibusdam contingit. Ergo non est pars prudentiae.

**PRAETEREA**, docilitas ad discipulum pertinet. Sed prudentia, cum sit praeceptiva, magis videtur ad magistros pertinere, qui etiam praeceptores dicuntur. Ergo docilitas non est pars prudentiae.

**SED CONTRA** est quod Macrobius, secundum sententiam Plotini, ponit docilitatem inter partes prudentiae.

**RESPONDEO** dicendum quod, sicut supra dictum est, prudentia consistit circa particularia operabilia. In quibus cum sint quasi infinitae diversitates, non possunt ab uno homine sufficienter omnia considerari, nec per modicum tempus, sed per temporis diuturnitatem. Unde in his quae ad prudentiam pertinent maxime indiget homo ab alio erudiri, et praecipue ex senibus, qui sanum intellectum adepti sunt circa fines operabilium. Unde philosophus dicit, in VI Ethic., *oportet attendere expertorum et seniorum et prudentium indemonstrabilibus enuntiationibus et opinionibus non minus quam demonstrationibus, propter experientiam enim vident principia.* Unde et Prov. III dicitur, *ne innitaris prudentiae tuae*; et Eccli. VI dicitur, *in multitudine presbyterorum*, idest seniorum, *prudentium sta, et sapientiae illorum ex corde coniungere.* Hoc autem pertinet ad docilitatem, ut aliquis sit bene disciplinae susceptivus. Et ideo convenienter ponitur docilitas pars prudentiae.

**AD PRIMUM** ergo dicendum quod etsi docilitas utilis sit ad quamlibet virtutem intellectualem, praecipue tamen ad prudentiam, ratione iam dicta.

**AD SECUNDUM** dicendum quod docilitas, sicut et alia quae ad prudentiam pertinent, secundum aptitudinem quidem est a natura, sed ad eius consummationem plurimum valet humanum studium, dum scilicet homo sollicite, frequenter et reverenter applicat animum suum documentis maiorum, non negligens ea propter ignaviam, nec contemnens propter superbiam.

**AD TERTIUM** dicendum quod per prudentiam aliquis praecipit non solum aliis, sed etiam sibi ipsi, ut dictum est. Unde etiam in subditis locum habet, ut supra

**OBJECTION 1**: It would seem that docility should not be accounted a part of prudence. For that which is a necessary condition of every intellectual virtue, should not be appropriated to one of them. But docility is requisite for every intellectual virtue. Therefore it should not be accounted a part of prudence.

**OBJ. 2**: Further, that which pertains to a human virtue is in our power, since it is for things that are in our power that we are praised or blamed. Now it is not in our power to be docile, for this is befitting to some through their natural disposition. Therefore it is not a part of prudence.

**OBJ. 3**: Further, docility is in the disciple: whereas prudence, since it makes precepts, seems rather to belong to teachers, who are also called *preceptors*. Therefore docility is not a part of prudence.

**ON THE CONTRARY**, Macrobius following the opinion of Plotinus places docility among the parts of prudence.

**I ANSWER THAT**, As stated above (A. 2, ad 1; Q. 47, A. 3) prudence is concerned with particular matters of action, and since such matters are of infinite variety, no one man can consider them all sufficiently; nor can this be done quickly, for it requires length of time. Hence in matters of prudence man stands in very great need of being taught by others, especially by old folk who have acquired a sane understanding of the ends in practical matters. Wherefore the Philosopher says (*Ethic.* vi, 11): *It is right to pay no less attention to the undemonstrated assertions and opinions of such persons as are experienced, older than we are, and prudent, than to their demonstrations, for their experience gives them an insight into principles.* Thus it is written (Prov 3:5): *Lean not on thy own prudence*, and (Sir 6:35): *Stand in the multitude of the ancients* (i.e., the old men), *that are wise, and join thyself from thy heart to their wisdom.* Now it is a mark of docility to be ready to be taught: and consequently docility is fittingly reckoned a part of prudence.

**REPLY OBJ. 1**: Although docility is useful for every intellectual virtue, yet it belongs to prudence chiefly, for the reason given above.

**REPLY OBJ. 2**: Man has a natural aptitude for docility even as for other things connected with prudence. Yet his own efforts count for much towards the attainment of perfect docility: and he must carefully, frequently and reverently apply his mind to the teachings of the learned, neither neglecting them through laziness, nor despising them through pride.

**REPLY OBJ. 3**: By prudence man makes precepts not only for others, but also for himself, as stated above (Q. 47, A. 12, ad 3). Hence as stated (*Ethic.* vi, 11), even in subjects,

dictum est, ad quorum prudentiam pertinet docilitas. Quamvis etiam ipsos maiores oportet dociles quantum ad aliqua esse, quia nullus in his quae subsunt prudentiae sibi quantum ad omnia sufficit, ut dictum est.

there is place for prudence; to which docility pertains. And yet even the learned should be docile in some respects, since no man is altogether self-sufficient in matters of prudence, as stated above.

# Article 4

*Whether shrewdness is part of prudence?*

AD QUARTUM SIC PROCEDITUR. Videtur quod solertia non sit pars prudentiae. Solertia enim se habet ad facile invenienda media in demonstrationibus; ut patet in I Poster. Sed ratio prudentiae non est demonstrativa, cum sit contingentium. Ergo ad prudentiam non pertinet solertia.

PRAETEREA, ad prudentiam pertinet bene consiliari, ut dicitur in VI Ethic. Sed in bene consiliando non habet locum solertia, quae est *eustochia quaedam*, idest *bona coniecturatio*, quae est *sine ratione et velox; oportet autem consiliari tarde*; ut dicitur in VI Ethic. Ergo solertia non debet poni pars prudentiae.

PRAETEREA, solertia, ut dictum est, est *quaedam bona coniecturatio*. Sed coniecturis uti est proprie rhetorum. Ergo solertia magis pertinet ad rhetoricam quam ad prudentiam.

SED CONTRA est quod Isidorus dicit, in libro Etymol., *sollicitus dicitur quasi solers et citus*. Sed sollicitudo ad prudentiam pertinet, ut supra dictum est. Ergo et solertia.

RESPONDEO dicendum quod prudentis est rectam aestimationem habere de operandis. Recta autem aestimatio sive opinio acquiritur in operativis, sicut in speculativis, dupliciter, uno quidem modo, per se inveniendo; alio modo, ab alio addiscendo. Sicut autem docilitas ad hoc pertinet ut homo bene se habeat in acquirendo rectam opinionem ab alio; ita solertia ad hoc pertinet ut homo bene se habeat in acquirendo rectam existimationem per seipsum. Ita tamen ut solertia accipiatur pro *eustochia*, cuius est pars. Nam Eustochia est bene coniecturativa de quibuscumque, solertia autem est *facilis et prompta coniecturatio circa inventionem medii*, ut dicitur in I Poster. Tamen ille Philosophus qui ponit solertiam partem prudentiae, accipit eam communiter pro omni Eustochia, unde dicit quod *solertia est habitus qui provenit ex repentino, inveniens quod convenit*.

AD PRIMUM ergo dicendum quod solertia non solum se habet circa inventionem medii in demonstrativis, sed etiam in operativis, puta cum aliquis videns aliquos amicos factos coniecturat eos esse inimicos eiusdem, ut ibidem Philosophus dicit. Et hoc modo solertia pertinet ad prudentiam.

OBJECTION 1: It would seem that shrewdness is not a part of prudence. For shrewdness consists in easily finding the middle term for demonstrations, as stated in *Poster.* i, 34. Now the reasoning of prudence is not a demonstration since it deals with contingencies. Therefore shrewdness does not pertain to prudence.

OBJ. 2: Further, good counsel pertains to prudence according to *Ethic.* vi, 5, 7, 9. Now there is no place in good counsel for shrewdness which is a kind of eustochia, i.e., *a happy conjecture*: for the latter is *unreasoning and rapid*, whereas *counsel needs to be slow*, as stated in *Ethic.* vi, 9. Therefore shrewdness should not be accounted a part of prudence.

OBJ. 3: Further, shrewdness as stated above (Q. 48) is a *happy conjecture*. Now it belongs to rhetoricians to make use of conjectures. Therefore shrewdness belongs to rhetoric rather than to prudence.

ON THE CONTRARY, Isidore says (*Etym.* x): *A solicitous man is one who is shrewd and alert (solers citus)*. But solicitude belongs to prudence, as stated above (Q. 47, A. 9). Therefore shrewdness does also.

I ANSWER THAT, Prudence consists in a right estimate about matters of action. Now a right estimate or opinion is acquired in two ways, both in practical and in speculative matters, first by discovering it oneself, second by learning it from others. Now just as docility consists in a man being well disposed to acquire a right opinion from another man, so shrewdness is an apt disposition to acquire a right estimate by oneself, yet so that shrewdness be taken for eustochia, of which it is a part. For *eustochia* is a happy conjecture about any matter, while shrewdness is *an easy and rapid conjecture in finding the middle term* (*Poster.* i, 34). Nevertheless the philosopher who calls shrewdness a part of prudence, takes it for eustochia, in general, hence he says: *Shrewdness is a habit whereby congruities are discovered rapidly.*

REPLY OBJ. 1: Shrewdness is concerned with the discovery of the middle term not only in demonstrative, but also in practical syllogisms, as, for instance, when two men are seen to be friends they are reckoned to be enemies of a third one, as the Philosopher says (*Poster.* i, 34). In this way shrewdness belongs to prudence.

**AD SECUNDUM** dicendum quod Philosophus veram rationem inducit in VI Ethic. ad ostendendum quod euboulia, quae est bene consiliativa, non est Eustochia, cuius laus est in veloci consideratione eius quod oportet, potest autem esse aliquis bene consiliativus etiam si diutius consilietur vel tardius. Nec tamen propter hoc excluditur quin bona coniecturatio ad bene consiliandum valeat. Et quandoque necessaria est, quando scilicet ex improviso occurrit aliquid agendum. Et ideo solertia convenienter ponitur pars prudentiae.

**AD TERTIUM** dicendum quod rhetorica etiam ratiocinatur circa operabilia. Unde nihil prohibet idem ad rhetoricam et prudentiam pertinere. Et tamen coniecturatio hic non sumitur solum secundum quod pertinet ad coniecturas quibus utuntur rhetores, sed secundum quod in quibuscumque dicitur homo coniicere veritatem.

**REPLY OBJ. 2**: The Philosopher adduces the true reason (*Ethic.* vi, 9) to prove that euboulia, i.e., good counsel, is not eustochia, which is commended for grasping quickly what should be done. Now a man may take good counsel, though he be long and slow in so doing, and yet this does not discount the utility of a happy conjecture in taking good counsel: indeed it is sometimes a necessity, when, for instance, something has to be done without warning. It is for this reason that shrewdness is fittingly reckoned a part of prudence.

**REPLY OBJ. 3**: Rhetoric also reasons about practical matters, wherefore nothing hinders the same thing belonging both to rhetoric and prudence. Nevertheless, conjecture is taken here not only in the sense in which it is employed by rhetoricians, but also as applicable to all matters whatsoever wherein man is said to conjecture the truth.

# Article 5

*Whether reason should be reckoned a part of prudence?*

**AD QUINTUM SIC PROCEDITUR.** Videtur quod ratio non debeat poni pars prudentiae. Subiectum enim accidentis non est pars eius. Sed prudentia est in ratione sicut in subiecto, ut dicitur in VI Ethic. Ergo ratio non debet poni pars prudentiae.

**PRAETEREA,** illud quod est multis commune non debet alicuius eorum poni pars, vel, si ponatur, debet poni pars eius cui potissime convenit. Ratio autem necessaria est in omnibus virtutibus intellectualibus, et praecipue in sapientia et scientia, quae utuntur ratione demonstrativa. Ergo ratio non debet poni pars prudentiae.

**PRAETEREA,** ratio non differt per essentiam potentiae ab intellectu, ut prius habitum est. Si ergo intellectus ponitur pars prudentiae, superfluum fuit addere rationem.

**SED CONTRA** est quod Macrobius, secundum sententiam Plotini, rationem numerat inter partes prudentiae.

**RESPONDEO** dicendum quod opus prudentis est esse bene consiliativum, ut dicitur in VI Ethic. Consilium autem est inquisitio quaedam ex quibusdam ad alia procedens. Hoc autem est opus rationis. Unde ad prudentiam necessarium est quod homo sit bene ratiocinativus. Et quia ea quae exiguntur ad perfectionem prudentiae dicuntur exigitivae vel quasi integrales partes prudentiae, inde est quod ratio inter partes prudentiae connumerari debet.

**AD PRIMUM** ergo dicendum quod ratio non sumitur hic pro ipsa potentia rationis, sed pro eius bono usu.

**OBJECTION 1**: It would seem that reason should not be reckoned a part of prudence. For the subject of an accident is not a part thereof. But prudence is in the reason as its subject (*Ethic.* vi, 5). Therefore reason should not be reckoned a part of prudence.

**OBJ. 2**: Further, that which is common to many, should not be reckoned a part of any one of them; or if it be so reckoned, it should be reckoned a part of that one to which it chiefly belongs. Now reason is necessary in all the intellectual virtues, and chiefly in wisdom and science, which employ a demonstrative reason. Therefore reason should not be reckoned a part of prudence

**OBJ. 3**: Further, reason as a power does not differ essentially from the intelligence, as stated above (I, Q. 79, A. 8). If therefore intelligence be reckoned a part of prudence, it is superfluous to add reason.

**ON THE CONTRARY**, Macrobius, following the opinion of Plotinus, numbers reason among the parts of prudence.

**I ANSWER THAT**, The work of prudence is to take good counsel, as stated in *Ethic.* vi, 7. Now counsel is a research proceeding from certain things to others. But this is the work of reason. Wherefore it is requisite for prudence that man should be an apt reasoner. And since the things required for the perfection of prudence are called requisite or quasi-integral parts of prudence, it follows that reason should be numbered among these parts.

**REPLY OBJ. 1**: Reason denotes here, not the power of reason, but its good use.

AD SECUNDUM dicendum quod certitudo rationis est ex intellectu, sed necessitas rationis est ex defectu intellectus, illa enim in quibus vis intellectiva plenarie viget ratione non indigent, sed suo simplici intuitu veritatem comprehendunt, sicut Deus et Angeli. Particularia autem operabilia, in quibus prudentia dirigit, recedunt praecipue ab intelligibilium conditione, et tanto magis quanto minus sunt certa seu determinata. Ea enim quae sunt artis, licet sint singularia, tamen sunt magis determinata et certa, unde in pluribus eorum non est consilium, propter certitudinem, ut dicitur in III Ethic. Et ideo quamvis in quibusdam aliis virtutibus intellectualibus sit certior ratio quam prudentia, tamen ad prudentiam maxime requiritur quod sit homo bene ratiocinativus, ut possit bene applicare universalia principia ad particularia, quae sunt varia et incerta.

AD TERTIUM dicendum quod etsi intellectus et ratio non sunt diversae potentiae, tamen denominantur ex diversis actibus, nomen enim intellectus sumitur ab intima penetratione veritatis; nomen autem rationis ab inquisitione et discursu. Et ideo utrumque ponitur pars prudentiae, ut ex dictis patet.

REPLY OBJ. 2: The certitude of reason comes from the intellect. Yet the need of reason is from a defect in the intellect, since those things in which the intellective power is in full vigor, have no need for reason, for they comprehend the truth by their simple insight, as do God and the angels. On the other hand particular matters of action, wherein prudence guides, are very far from the condition of things intelligible, and so much the farther, as they are less certain and fixed. Thus matters of art, though they are singular, are nevertheless more fixed and certain, wherefore in many of them there is no room for counsel on account of their certitude, as stated in *Ethic.* iii, 3. Hence, although in certain other intellectual virtues reason is more certain than in prudence, yet prudence above all requires that man be an apt reasoner, so that he may rightly apply universals to particulars, which latter are various and uncertain.

REPLY OBJ. 3: Although intelligence and reason are not different powers, yet they are named after different acts. For intelligence takes its name from being an intimate penetration of the truth, while reason is so called from being inquisitive and discursive. Hence each is accounted a part of reason as explained above (A. 2; Q. 47, A. 2, 3).

# Article 6

*Whether foresight should be accounted a part of prudence?*

AD SEXTUM SIC PROCEDITUR. Videtur quod providentia non debeat poni pars prudentiae. Nihil enim est pars sui ipsius. Sed providentia videtur idem esse quod prudentia, quia ut Isidorus dicit, in libro Etymol., *prudens dicitur quasi porro videns*, et ex hoc etiam nomen providentiae sumitur, ut Boetius dicit, in fine de Consol. Ergo providentia non est pars prudentiae.

PRAETEREA, prudentia est solum practica. Sed providentia potest etiam esse speculativa, quia visio, ex qua sumitur nomen providentiae, magis pertinet ad speculativam quam ad operativam. Ergo providentia non est pars prudentiae.

PRAETEREA, principalis actus prudentiae est praecipere, secundarii autem iudicare et consiliari. Sed nihil horum videtur importari proprie per nomen providentiae. Ergo providentia non est pars prudentiae.

SED CONTRA est auctoritas Tullii et Macrobii, qui ponunt providentiam partem prudentiae, ut ex dictis patet.

RESPONDEO dicendum quod, sicut supra dictum est, prudentia proprie est circa ea quae sunt ad finem; et hoc ad eius officium proprie pertinet, ut ad finem debite ordinentur. Et quamvis aliqua necessaria sint propter finem quae subiiciuntur divinae providentiae, humanae

OBJECTION 1: It would seem that foresight should not be accounted a part of prudence. For nothing is part of itself. Now foresight seems to be the same as prudence, because according to Isidore (*Etym.* x), *a prudent man is one who sees from afar (porro videns)*: and this is also the derivation of *providentia* (foresight), according to Boethius (*De Consol.* v). Therefore foresight is not a part of prudence.

OBJ. 2: Further, prudence is only practical, whereas foresight may be also speculative, because seeing, whence we have the word *to foresee*, has more to do with speculation than operation. Therefore foresight is not a part of prudence.

OBJ. 3: Further, the chief act of prudence is to command, while its secondary act is to judge and to take counsel. But none of these seems to be properly implied by foresight. Therefore foresight is not part of prudence.

ON THE CONTRARY stands the authority of Tully and Macrobius, who number foresight among the parts of prudence, as stated above (Q. 48).

I ANSWER THAT, As stated above (Q. 47, A. 1, ad 2, AA. 6, 13), prudence is properly about the means to an end, and its proper work is to set them in due order to the end. And although certain things are necessary for an end, which are subject to divine providence, yet nothing is

tamen prudentiae non subiiciuntur nisi contingentia operabilia quae per hominem possunt fieri propter finem. Praeterita autem in necessitatem quandam transeunt, quia impossibile est non esse quod factum est. Similiter etiam praesentia, inquantum huiusmodi, necessitatem quandam habent, necesse est enim Socratem sedere dum sedet.

Unde consequens est quod contingentia futura, secundum quod sunt per hominem in finem humanae vitae ordinabilia, pertineant ad prudentiam. Utrumque autem horum importatur in nomine providentiae, importat enim providentia respectum quendam alicuius distantis, ad quod ea quae in praesenti occurrunt ordinanda sunt. Unde providentia est pars prudentiae.

**AD PRIMUM** ergo dicendum quod quandocumque multa requiruntur ad unum, necesse est unum eorum esse principale, ad quod omnia alia ordinantur. Unde et in quolibet toto necesse est esse unam partem formalem et praedominantem, a qua totum unitatem habet. Et secundum hoc providentia est principalior inter omnes partes prudentiae, quia omnia alia quae requiruntur ad prudentiam ad hoc necessaria sunt ut aliquid recte ordinetur ad finem. Et ideo nomen ipsius prudentiae sumitur a providentia, sicut a principaliori sua parte.

**AD SECUNDUM** dicendum quod speculatio est circa universalia et circa necessaria, quae secundum se non sunt procul, cum sint ubique et semper, etsi sint procul quoad nos, inquantum ab eorum cognitione deficimus. Unde providentia non proprie dicitur in speculativis, sed solum in practicis.

**AD TERTIUM** dicendum quod in recta ordinatione ad finem, quae includitur in ratione providentiae, importatur rectitudo consilii et iudicii et praecepti, sine quibus recta ordinatio ad finem esse non potest.

subject to human providence except the contingent matters of actions which can be done by man for an end. Now the past has become a kind of necessity, since what has been done cannot be undone. In like manner, the present as such, has a kind of necessity, since it is necessary that Socrates sit, so long as he sits.

Consequently, future contingents, insofar as they can be directed by man to the end of human life, are the matter of prudence: and each of these things is implied in the word foresight, for it implies the notion of something distant, to which that which occurs in the present has to be directed. Therefore foresight is part of prudence.

**REPLY OBJ. 1**: Whenever many things are requisite for a unity, one of them must needs be the principal to which all the others are subordinate. Hence in every whole one part must be formal and predominant, whence the whole has unity. Accordingly foresight is the principal of all the parts of prudence, since whatever else is required for prudence, is necessary precisely that some particular thing may be rightly directed to its end. Hence it is that the very name of prudence is taken from foresight (*providentia*) as from its principal part.

**REPLY OBJ. 2**: Speculation is about universal and necessary things, which, in themselves, are not distant, since they are everywhere and always, though they are distant from us, insofar as we fail to know them. Hence foresight does not apply properly to speculative, but only to practical matters.

**REPLY OBJ. 3**: Right order to an end which is included in the notion of foresight, contains rectitude of counsel, judgment and command, without which no right order to the end is possible.

# Article 7

*Whether circumspection can be a part of prudence?*

**AD SEPTIMUM SIC PROCEDITUR.** Videtur quod circumspectio non possit esse pars prudentiae. Circumspectio enim videtur esse consideratio quaedam eorum quae circumstant. Huiusmodi autem sunt infinita, quae non possunt comprehendi ratione, in qua est prudentia. Ergo circumspectio non debet poni pars prudentiae.

**PRAETEREA**, circumstantiae magis videntur pertinere ad virtutes morales quam ad prudentiam. Sed circumspectio nihil aliud esse videtur quam respectus circumstantiarum. Ergo circumspectio magis videtur pertinere ad morales virtutes quam ad prudentiam.

**PRAETEREA**, qui potest videre quae procul sunt multo magis potest videre quae circa sunt. Sed per

**OBJECTION 1**: It would seem that circumspection cannot be a part of prudence. For circumspection seems to signify looking at one's surroundings. But these are of infinite number, and cannot be considered by the reason wherein is prudence. Therefore circumspection should not be reckoned a part of prudence.

**OBJ. 2**: Further, circumstances seem to be the concern of moral virtues rather than of prudence. But circumspection seems to denote nothing but attention to circumstances. Therefore circumspection apparently belongs to the moral virtues rather than to prudence.

**OBJ. 3**: Further, whoever can see things afar off can much more see things that are near. Now foresight enables

providentiam homo est potens prospicere quae procul sunt. Ergo ipsa sufficit ad considerandum ea quae circumstant. Non ergo oportuit, praeter providentiam, ponere circumspectionem partem prudentiae.

**SED CONTRA** est auctoritas Macrobii, ut supra dictum est.

**RESPONDEO** dicendum quod ad prudentiam, sicut dictum est, praecipue pertinet recte ordinare aliquid in finem. Quod quidem recte non fit nisi et finis sit bonus, et id quod ordinatur in finem sit etiam bonum et conveniens fini.

Sed quia prudentia, sicut dictum est, est circa singularia operabilia, in quibus multa concurrunt, contingit aliquid secundum se consideratum esse bonum et conveniens fini, quod tamen ex aliquibus concurrentibus redditur vel malum vel non opportunum ad finem. Sicut ostendere signa amoris alicui, secundum se consideratum, videtur esse conveniens ad alliciendum eius animum ad amorem, sed si contingat in animo illius superbia vel suspicio adulationis, non erit hoc conveniens ad finem. Et ideo necessaria est circumspectio ad prudentiam, ut scilicet homo id quod ordinatur in finem comparet etiam cum his quae circumstant.

**AD PRIMUM** ergo dicendum quod licet ea quae possunt circumstare sint infinita, tamen ea quae circumstant in actu non sunt infinita, sed pauca quaedam sunt quae immutant iudicium rationis in agendis.

**AD SECUNDUM** dicendum quod circumstantiae pertinent ad prudentiam quidem sicut ad determinandum eas, ad virtutes autem morales inquantum per circumstantiarum determinationem perficiuntur.

**AD TERTIUM** dicendum quod sicut ad providentiam pertinet prospicere id quod est per se conveniens fini, ita ad circumspectionem pertinet considerare an sit conveniens fini secundum ea quae circumstant. Utrumque autem horum habet specialem difficultatem. Et ideo utrumque eorum seorsum ponitur pars prudentiae.

a man to look on distant things. Therefore there is no need to account circumspection a part of prudence in addition to foresight.

**ON THE CONTRARY** stands the authority of Macrobius, quoted above (Q. 48).

**I ANSWER THAT**, As stated above (A. 6), it belongs to prudence chiefly to direct something aright to an end; and this is not done aright unless both the end be good, and the means good and suitable.

Since, however, prudence, as stated above (Q. 47, A. 3) is about singular matters of action, which contain many combinations of circumstances, it happens that a thing is good in itself and suitable to the end, and nevertheless becomes evil or unsuitable to the end, by reason of some combination of circumstances. Thus to show signs of love to someone seems, considered in itself, to be a fitting way to arouse love in his heart, yet if pride or suspicion of flattery arise in his heart, it will no longer be a means suitable to the end. Hence the need of circumspection in prudence, viz. of comparing the means with the circumstances.

**REPLY OBJ. 1**: Though the number of possible circumstances be infinite, the number of actual circumstances is not; and the judgment of reason in matters of action is influenced by things which are few in number.

**REPLY OBJ. 2**: Circumstances are the concern of prudence, because prudence has to fix them; on the other hand they are the concern of moral virtues, insofar as moral virtues are perfected by the fixing of circumstances.

**REPLY OBJ. 3**: Just as it belongs to foresight to look on that which is by its nature suitable to an end, so it belongs to circumspection to consider whether it be suitable to the end in view of the circumstances. Now each of these presents a difficulty of its own, and therefore each is reckoned a distinct part of prudence.

# Article 8

*Whether caution should be reckoned a part of prudence?*

**AD OCTAVUM SIC PROCEDITUR.** Videtur quod cautio non debeat poni pars prudentiae. In his enim in quibus non potest malum esse non est necessaria cautio. Sed *virtutibus nemo male utitur*, ut dicitur in libro de Lib. Arb. Ergo cautio non pertinet ad prudentiam, quae est directiva virtutum.

**PRAETEREA**, eiusdem est providere bona et cavere mala, sicut eiusdem artis est facere sanitatem et curare aegritudinem. Sed providere bona pertinet ad providen-

**OBJECTION 1**: It would seem that caution should not be reckoned a part of prudence. For when no evil is possible, no caution is required. Now *no man makes evil use of virtue*, as Augustine declares (*De Lib. Arb.* ii, 19). Therefore caution does not belong to prudence which directs the virtues.

**OBJ. 2**: Further, to foresee good and to avoid evil belong to the same faculty, just as the same art gives health and cures ill-health. Now it belongs to foresight to foresee

tiam. Ergo etiam cavere mala. Non ergo cautio debet poni alia pars prudentiae a providentia.

**PRAETEREA**, nullus prudens conatur ad impossibile. Sed nullus potest praecavere omnia mala quae possunt contingere. Ergo cautio non pertinet ad prudentiam.

**SED CONTRA** est quod apostolus dicit, ad Ephes. V, *videte quomodo caute ambuletis.*

**RESPONDEO** dicendum quod ea circa quae est prudentia sunt contingentia operabilia, in quibus, sicut verum potest admisceri falso, ita et malum bono, propter multiformitatem huiusmodi operabilium, in quibus bona plerumque impediuntur a malis, et mala habent speciem boni. Et ideo necessaria est cautio ad prudentiam, ut sic accipiantur bona quod vitentur mala.

**AD PRIMUM** ergo dicendum quod cautio non est necessaria in moralibus actibus ut aliquis sibi caveat ab actibus virtutum, sed ut sibi caveat ab eis per quae actus virtutum impediri possunt.

**AD SECUNDUM** dicendum quod opposita mala cavere eiusdem rationis est et prosequi bona. Sed vitare aliqua impedimenta extrinseca, hoc pertinet ad aliam rationem. Et ideo cautio distinguitur a providentia, quamvis utrumque pertineat ad unam virtutem prudentiae.

**AD TERTIUM** dicendum quod malorum quae homini vitanda occurrunt quaedam sunt quae ut in pluribus accidere solent. Et talia comprehendi ratione possunt. Et contra haec ordinatur cautio, ut totaliter vitentur, vel ut minus noceant. Quaedam vero sunt quae ut in paucioribus et casualiter accidunt. Et haec, cum sint infinita, ratione comprehendi non possunt, nec sufficienter homo potest ea praecavere, quamvis per officium prudentiae homo contra omnes fortunae insultus disponere possit ut minus laedatur.

good, and consequently, also to avoid evil. Therefore caution should not be accounted a part of prudence, distinct from foresight.

**OBJ. 3**: Further, no prudent man strives for the impossible. But no man can take precautions against all possible evils. Therefore caution does not belong to prudence.

**ON THE CONTRARY**, The Apostle says (*Eph 5:15*): *See how you walk cautiously.*

**I ANSWER THAT**, The things with which prudence is concerned, are contingent matters of action, wherein, even as false is found with true, so is evil mingled with good, on account of the great variety of these matters of action, wherein good is often hindered by evil, and evil has the appearance of good. Wherefore prudence needs caution, so that we may have such a grasp of good as to avoid evil.

**REPLY OBJ. 1**: Caution is required in moral acts, that we may be on our guard, not against acts of virtue, but against the hindrance of acts of virtue.

**REPLY OBJ. 2**: It is the same in idea, to ensue good and to avoid the opposite evil, but the avoidance of outward hindrances is different in idea. Hence caution differs from foresight, although they both belong to the one virtue of prudence.

**REPLY OBJ. 3**: Of the evils which man has to avoid, some are of frequent occurrence; the like can be grasped by reason, and against them caution is directed, either that they may be avoided altogether, or that they may do less harm. Others there are that occur rarely and by chance, and these, since they are infinite in number, cannot be grasped by reason, nor is man able to take precautions against them, although by exercising prudence he is able to prepare against all the surprises of chance, so as to suffer less harm thereby.

# QUESTION 50

## THE SUBJECTIVE PARTS OF PRUDENCE

Deinde considerandum est de partibus subiectivis prudentiae. Et quia de prudentia per quam aliquis regit seipsum iam dictum est, restat dicendum de speciebus prudentiae quibus multitudo gubernatur. Circa quas quaeruntur quatuor.

Primo, utrum legispositiva debeat poni species prudentiae.
Secundo, utrum politica. Tertio, utrum oeconomica.

Quarto, utrum militaris.

We must, in due sequence, consider the subjective parts of prudence. And since we have already spoken of the prudence with which a man rules himself (Q. 47, seqq.), it remains for us to discuss the species of prudence whereby a multitude is governed. Under this head there are four points of inquiry:

(1) Whether a species of prudence is regnative?

(2) Whether political and (3) domestic economy are species of prudence?

(4) Whether military prudence is?

# Article 1

*Whether a species of prudence is regnative?*

**Ad primum sic proceditur.** Videtur quod regnativa non debeat poni species prudentiae. Regnativa enim ordinatur ad iustitiam conservandam, dicitur enim in V Ethic. quod *princeps est custos iusti*. Ergo regnativa magis pertinet ad iustitiam quam ad prudentiam.

**Praeterea,** secundum Philosophum, in III Polit., regnum est una sex politiarum. Sed nulla species prudentiae sumitur secundum alias quinque politias, quae sunt aristocratia, politia (quae alio nomine dicitur timocratia), tyrannis, oligarchia, democratia. Ergo nec secundum regnum debet sumi regnativa.

**Praeterea,** leges condere non solum pertinet ad reges, sed etiam ad quosdam alios principatus, et etiam ad populum; ut patet per Isidorum, in libro Etymol. Sed Philosophus, in VI Ethic., ponit legispositivam partem prudentiae. Inconvenienter igitur loco eius ponitur regnativa.

**Sed contra** est quod philosophus dicit, in III Polit., quod *prudentia est propria virtus principis*. Ergo specialis prudentia debet esse regnativa.

**Respondeo** dicendum quod sicut ex supradictis patet, ad prudentiam pertinet regere et praecipere. Et ideo ubi invenitur specialis ratio regiminis et praecepti in humanis actibus, ibi etiam invenitur specialis ratio prudentiae. Manifestum est autem quod in eo qui non solum seipsum habet regere, sed etiam communitatem perfectam civitatis vel regni, invenitur specialis et perfecta ratio regiminis, tanto enim regimen perfectius est quanto est universalius, ad plura se extendens et ulteriorem finem

**Objection 1:** It would seem that regnative should not be reckoned a species of prudence. For regnative prudence is directed to the preservation of justice, since according to *Ethic.* v, 6 the prince is the guardian of justice. Therefore regnative prudence belongs to justice rather than to prudence.

**Obj. 2:** Further, according to the Philosopher (*Polit.* iii, 5) a kingdom (*regnum*) is one of six species of government. But no species of prudence is ascribed to the other five forms of government, which are *aristocracy*, *polity*, also called *timocracy*, *tyranny*, *oligarchy* and *democracy*. Therefore neither should a regnative species be ascribed to a kingdom.

**Obj. 3:** Further, lawgiving belongs not only to kings, but also to certain others placed in authority, and even to the people, according to Isidore (*Etym.* v). Now the Philosopher (*Ethic.* vi, 8) reckons a part of prudence to be *legislative*. Therefore it is not becoming to substitute regnative prudence in its place.

**On the contrary,** The Philosopher says (*Polit.* iii, 11) that *prudence is a virtue which is proper to the prince.* Therefore a special kind of prudence is regnative.

**I answer that,** As stated above (Q. 47, AA. 8, 10), it belongs to prudence to govern and command, so that wherever in human acts we find a special kind of governance and command, there must be a special kind of prudence. Now it is evident that there is a special and perfect kind of governance in one who has to govern not only himself but also the perfect community of a city or kingdom; because a government is the more perfect according as it is more universal, extends to more matters, and attains a higher

attingens. Et ideo regi, ad quem pertinet regere civitatem vel regnum, prudentia competit secundum specialem et perfectissimam sui rationem. Et propter hoc regnativa ponitur species prudentiae.

**AD PRIMUM** ergo dicendum quod omnia quae sunt virtutum moralium pertinent ad prudentiam sicut ad dirigentem, unde et ratio recta prudentiae ponitur in definitione virtutis moralis, ut supra dictum est. Et ideo etiam executio iustitiae, prout ordinatur ad bonum commune, quae pertinet ad officium regis, indiget directione prudentiae. Unde istae duae virtutes sunt maxime propriae regi, scilicet prudentia et iustitia, secundum illud Ierem. XXIII, *regnabit rex, et sapiens erit et faciet iudicium et iustitiam in terra.* Quia tamen dirigere magis pertinet ad regem, exequi vero ad subditos, ideo regnativa magis ponitur species prudentiae, quae est directiva, quam iustitiae, quae est executiva.

**AD SECUNDUM** dicendum quod regnum inter alias politias est optimum regimen, ut dicitur in VIII Ethic. Et ideo species prudentiae magis debuit denominari a regno. Ita tamen quod sub regnativa comprehendantur omnia alia regimina recta, non autem perversa, quae virtuti opponuntur, unde non pertinent ad prudentiam.

**AD TERTIUM** dicendum quod philosophus denominat regnativam a principali actu regis, qui est leges ponere. Quod etsi conveniat aliis, non convenit eis nisi secundum quod participant aliquid de regimine regis.

end. Hence prudence in its special and most perfect sense, belongs to a king who is charged with the government of a city or kingdom: for which reason a species of prudence is reckoned to be regnative.

**REPLY OBJ. 1**: All matters connected with moral virtue belong to prudence as their guide, wherefore *right reason in accord with prudence* is included in the definition of moral virtue, as stated above (Q. 47, A. 5, ad 1; I-II, Q. 58, A. 2, ad 4). For this reason also the execution of justice insofar as it is directed to the common good, which is part of the kingly office, needs the guidance of prudence. Hence these two virtues—prudence and justice—belong most properly to a king, according to Jer. 23:5: *A king shall reign and shall be wise, and shall execute justice and judgment in the earth.* Since, however, direction belongs rather to the king, and execution to his subjects, regnative prudence is reckoned a species of prudence which is directive, rather than to justice which is executive.

**REPLY OBJ. 2**: A kingdom is the best of all governments, as stated in *Ethic.* viii, 10: wherefore the species of prudence should be denominated rather from a kingdom, yet so as to comprehend under regnative all other rightful forms of government, but not perverse forms which are opposed to virtue, and which, accordingly, do not pertain to prudence.

**REPLY OBJ. 3**: The Philosopher names regnative prudence after the principal act of a king which is to make laws, and although this applies to the other forms of government, this is only insofar as they have a share of kingly government.

# Article 2

*Whether political prudence is fittingly accounted a part of prudence?*

**AD SECUNDUM SIC PROCEDITUR.** Videtur quod politica inconvenienter ponatur pars prudentiae. Regnativa enim est pars politicae prudentiae, ut dictum est. Sed pars non debet dividi contra totum. Ergo politica non debet poni alia species prudentiae.

**PRAETEREA**, species habituum distinguuntur secundum diversa obiecta. Sed eadem sunt quae oportet regnantem praecipere et subditum exequi. Ergo politica, secundum quod pertinet ad subditos, non debet poni species prudentiae distincta a regnativa.

**PRAETEREA**, unusquisque subditorum est singularis persona. Sed quaelibet singularis persona seipsam sufficienter dirigere potest per prudentiam communiter dictam. Ergo non oportet poni aliam speciem prudentiae quae dicatur politica.

**OBJECTION 1**: It would seem that political prudence is not fittingly accounted a part of prudence. For regnative is a part of political prudence, as stated above (A. 1). But a part should not be reckoned a species with the whole. Therefore political prudence should not be reckoned a part of prudence.

**OBJ. 2**: Further, the species of habits are distinguished by their various objects. Now what the ruler has to command is the same as what the subject has to execute. Therefore political prudence as regards the subjects, should not be reckoned a species of prudence distinct from regnative prudence.

**OBJ. 3**: Further, each subject is an individual person. Now each individual person can direct himself sufficiently by prudence commonly so called. Therefore there is no need of a special kind of prudence called political.

**SED CONTRA** est quod philosophus dicit, in VI Ethic., *eius autem quae circa civitatem haec quidem ut architectonica prudentia legispositiva; haec autem commune nomen habet politica, circa singularia existens.*

**RESPONDEO** dicendum quod servus per imperium movetur a domino et subditus a principante, aliter tamen quam irrationalia et inanimata moveantur a suis motoribus. Nam inanimata et irrationalia aguntur solum ab alio, non autem ipsa agunt seipsa quia non habent dominium sui actus per liberum arbitrium. Et ideo rectitudo regiminis ipsorum non est in ipsis, sed solum in motoribus. Sed homines servi, vel quicumque subditi, ita aguntur ab aliis per praeceptum quod tamen agunt seipsos per liberum arbitrium. Et ideo requiritur in eis quaedam rectitudo regiminis per quam seipsos dirigant in obediendo principatibus. Et ad hoc pertinet species prudentiae quae politica vocatur.

**AD PRIMUM** ergo dicendum quod sicut dictum est, regnativa est perfectissima species prudentiae. Et ideo prudentia subditorum, quae deficit a prudentia regnativa, retinet sibi nomen commune, ut politica dicatur, sicut in logicis convertibile quod non significat essentiam retinet sibi commune nomen *proprii.*

**AD SECUNDUM** dicendum quod diversa ratio obiecti diversificat habitum secundum speciem, ut ex supradictis patet. Eadem autem agenda considerantur quidem a rege secundum universaliorem rationem quam considerentur a subdito, qui obedit, uni enim regi in diversis officiis multi obediunt. Et ideo regnativa comparatur ad hanc politicam de qua loquimur sicut ars architectonica ad eam quae manu operatur.

**AD TERTIUM** dicendum quod per prudentiam communiter dictam regit homo seipsum in ordine ad proprium bonum, per politicam autem de qua loquimur, in ordine ad bonum commune.

**ON THE CONTRARY,** The Philosopher says (*Ethic.* vi, 8) that *of the prudence which is concerned with the state one kind is a master-prudence and is called legislative; another kind bears the common name political, and deals with individuals.*

**I ANSWER THAT,** A slave is moved by his master, and a subject by his ruler, by command, but otherwise than as irrational and inanimate beings are set in motion by their movers. For irrational and inanimate beings are moved only by others and do not put themselves in motion, since they have no free-will whereby to be masters of their own actions, wherefore the rectitude of their government is not in their power but in the power of their movers. On the other hand, men who are slaves or subjects in any sense, are moved by the commands of others in such a way that they move themselves by their free-will; wherefore some kind of rectitude of government is required in them, so that they may direct themselves in obeying their superiors; and to this belongs that species of prudence which is called political.

**REPLY OBJ. 1:** As stated above, regnative is the most perfect species of prudence, wherefore the prudence of subjects, which falls short of regnative prudence, retains the common name of political prudence, even as in logic a convertible term which does not denote the essence of a thing retains the name of *proper.*

**REPLY OBJ. 2:** A different aspect of the object diversifies the species of a habit, as stated above (Q. 47, A. 5). Now the same actions are considered by the king, but under a more general aspect, as by his subjects who obey: since many obey one king in various departments. Hence regnative prudence is compared to this political prudence of which we are speaking, as mastercraft to handicraft.

**REPLY OBJ. 3:** Man directs himself by prudence commonly so called, in relation to his own good, but by political prudence, of which we speak, he directs himself in relation to the common good.

# Article 3

*Whether a part of prudence should be reckoned to be domestic?*

**AD TERTIUM SIC PROCEDITUR.** Videtur quod oeconomica non debeat poni species prudentiae. Quia ut Philosophus dicit, in VI Ethic., prudentia ordinatur *ad bene vivere totum.* Sed oeconomica ordinatur ad aliquem particularem finem, scilicet ad divitias, ut dicitur in I Ethic. Ergo oeconomica non est species prudentiae.

**PRAETEREA,** sicut supra habitum est, prudentia non est nisi bonorum. Sed oeconomica potest esse etiam malorum, multi enim peccatores providi sunt in gu-

**OBJECTION 1:** It would seem that domestic should not be reckoned a part of prudence. For, according to the Philosopher (*Ethic.* vi, 5) *prudence is directed to a good life in general*: whereas domestic prudence is directed to a particular end, viz. wealth, according to *Ethic.* i, 1. Therefore a species of prudence is not domestic.

**OBJ. 2:** Further, as stated above (Q. 47, A. 13) prudence is only in good people. But domestic prudence may be also in wicked people, since many sinners are provident in

bernatione familiae. Ergo oeconomica non debet poni species prudentiae.

PRAETEREA, sicut in regno invenitur principans et subiectum, ita etiam in domo. Si ergo oeconomica est species prudentiae sicut et politica, deberet etiam paterna prudentia poni, sicut et regnativa. Non autem ponitur. Ergo nec oeconomica debet poni species prudentiae.

SED CONTRA est quod Philosophus dicit, in VI Ethic., quod *illarum*, scilicet prudentiarum quae se habent ad regimen multitudinis, *haec quidem oeconomica, haec autem legispositiva, haec autem politica.*

RESPONDEO dicendum quod ratio obiecti diversificata secundum universale et particulare, vel secundum totum et partem, diversificat artes et virtutes, secundum quam diversitatem una est principalis respectu alterius. Manifestum est autem quod domus medio modo se habet inter unam singularem personam et civitatem vel regnum, nam sicut una singularis persona est pars domus, ita una domus est pars civitatis vel regni. Et ideo sicut prudentia communiter dicta, quae est regitiva unius, distinguitur a politica prudentia, ita oportet quod oeconomica distinguatur ab utraque.

AD PRIMUM ergo dicendum quod divitiae comparantur ad oeconomicam non sicut finis ultimus, sed sicut instrumenta quaedam, ut dicitur in I Polit. Finis autem ultimus oeconomicae est totum bene vivere secundum domesticam conversationem. Philosophus autem I Ethic. ponit exemplificando divitias finem oeconomicae secundum studium plurimorum.

AD SECUNDUM dicendum quod ad aliqua particularia quae sunt in domo disponenda possunt aliqui peccatores provide se habere, sed non ad ipsum totum bene vivere domesticae conversationis, ad quod praecipue requiritur vita virtuosa.

AD TERTIUM dicendum quod pater in domo habet quandam similitudinem regii principatus, ut dicitur in VIII Ethic., non tamen habet perfectam potestatem regiminis sicut rex. Et ideo non ponitur separatim paterna species prudentiae, sicut regnativa.

governing their household. Therefore domestic prudence should not be reckoned a species of prudence.

OBJ. 3: Further, just as in a kingdom there is a ruler and subject, so also is there in a household. If therefore domestic like political is a species of prudence, there should be a paternal corresponding to regnative prudence. Now there is no such prudence. Therefore neither should domestic prudence be accounted a species of prudence.

ON THE CONTRARY, The Philosopher states (*Ethic.* vi, 8) that there are various kinds of prudence in the government of a multitude, *one of which is domestic, another legislative, and another political.*

I ANSWER THAT, Different aspects of an object, in respect of universality and particularity, or of totality and partiality, diversify arts and virtues; and in respect of such diversity one act of virtue is principal as compared with another. Now it is evident that a household is a mean between the individual and the city or kingdom, since just as the individual is part of the household, so is the household part of the city or kingdom. And therefore, just as prudence commonly so called which governs the individual, is distinct from political prudence, so must domestic prudence be distinct from both.

REPLY OBJ. 1: Riches are compared to domestic prudence, not as its last end, but as its instrument, as stated in *Polit.* i, 3. On the other hand, the end of political prudence is a good life in general as regards the conduct of the household. In *Ethic.* i, 1 the Philosopher speaks of riches as the end of political prudence, by way of example and in accordance with the opinion of many.

REPLY OBJ. 2: Some sinners may be provident in certain matters of detail concerning the disposition of their household, but not in regard to a good life in general as regards the conduct of the household, for which above all a virtuous life is required.

REPLY OBJ. 3: The father has in his household an authority like that of a king, as stated in *Ethic.* viii, 10, but he has not the full power of a king, wherefore paternal government is not reckoned a distinct species of prudence, like regnative prudence.

# Article 4

*Whether military prudence should be reckoned a part of prudence?*

AD QUARTUM SIC PROCEDITUR. Videtur quod militaris non debeat poni species prudentiae. Prudentia enim contra artem dividitur, ut dicitur in VI Ethic. Sed militaris videtur esse quaedam ars in rebus bellicis; sicut patet per philosophum, in III Ethic. Ergo militaris non debet poni species prudentiae.

OBJECTION 1: It would seem that military prudence should not be reckoned a part of prudence. For prudence is distinct from art, according to *Ethic.* vi, 3. Now military prudence seems to be the art of warfare, according to the Philosopher (*Ethic.* iii, 8). Therefore military prudence should not be accounted a species of prudence.

**PRAETEREA**, sicut militare negotium continetur sub politico, ita etiam et plura alia negotia, sicut mercatorum, artificum et aliorum huiusmodi. Sed secundum alia negotia quae sunt in civitate non accipiuntur aliquae species prudentiae. Ergo etiam neque secundum militare negotium.

**PRAETEREA**, in rebus bellicis plurimum valet militum fortitudo. Ergo militaris magis pertinet ad fortitudinem quam ad prudentiam.

**SED CONTRA** est quod dicitur Prov. XXIV, *cum dispositione initur bellum, et erit salus ubi sunt multa consilia.* Sed consiliari pertinet ad prudentiam. Ergo in rebus bellicis maxime necessaria est aliqua species prudentiae quae militaris dicitur.

**RESPONDEO** dicendum quod ea quae secundum artem et rationem aguntur conformia esse oportet his quae sunt secundum naturam, quae a ratione divina sunt instituta. Natura autem ad duo intendit primo quidem, ad regendum unamquamque rem in seipsa; secundo vero, ad resistendum extrinsecis impugnantibus et corruptivis. Et propter hoc non solum dedit animalibus vim concupiscibilem, per quam moveantur ad ea quae sunt saluti eorum accommoda; sed etiam vim irascibilem, per quam animal resistit impugnantibus. Unde et in his quae sunt secundum rationem non solum oportet esse prudentiam politicam, per quam convenienter disponantur ea quae pertinent ad bonum commune; sed etiam militarem, per quam hostium insultus repellantur.

**AD PRIMUM** ergo dicendum quod militaris potest esse ars secundum quod habet quasdam regulas recte utendi quibusdam exterioribus rebus, puta armis et equis, sed secundum quod ordinatur ad bonum commune, habet magis rationem prudentiae.

**AD SECUNDUM** dicendum quod alia negotia quae sunt in civitate ordinantur ad aliquas particulares utilitates, sed militare negotium ordinatur ad tuitionem totius boni communis.

**AD TERTIUM** dicendum quod executio militiae pertinet ad fortitudinem, sed directio ad prudentiam, et praecipue secundum quod est in duce exercitus.

**OBJ. 2**: Further, just as military business is contained under political affairs, so too are many other matters, such as those of tradesmen, craftsmen, and so forth. But there are no species of prudence corresponding to other affairs in the state. Neither therefore should any be assigned to military business.

**OBJ. 3**: Further, the soldiers' bravery counts for a great deal in warfare. Therefore military prudence pertains to fortitude rather than to prudence.

**ON THE CONTRARY**, It is written (Prov 24:6): *War is managed by due ordering, and there shall be safety where there are many counsels.* Now it belongs to prudence to take counsel. Therefore there is great need in warfare for that species of prudence which is called *military*.

**I ANSWER THAT**, Whatever things are done according to art or reason, should be made to conform to those which are in accordance with nature, and are established by the Divine Reason. Now nature has a twofold tendency: first, to govern each thing in itself, second, to withstand outward assailants and corruptives: and for this reason she has provided animals not only with the concupiscible faculty, whereby they are moved to that which is conducive to their well-being, but also with the irascible power, whereby the animal withstands an assailant. Therefore in those things also which are in accordance with reason, there should be not only *political* prudence, which disposes in a suitable manner such things as belong to the common good, but also a *military* prudence, whereby hostile attacks are repelled.

**REPLY OBJ. 1**: Military prudence may be an art, insofar as it has certain rules for the right use of certain external things, such as arms and horses, but insofar as it is directed to the common good, it belongs rather to prudence.

**REPLY OBJ. 2**: Other matters in the state are directed to the profit of individuals, whereas the business of soldiering is directed to the service belongs to fortitude, but the direction, protection of the entire common good.

**REPLY OBJ. 3**: The execution of military service belongs to fortitude, but the direction, especially insofar as it concerns the commander-in-chief, belongs to prudence.

# QUESTION 51

## THE VIRTUES WHICH ARE CONNECTED WITH PRUDENCE

Deinde considerandum est de virtutibus adiunctis prudentiae, quae sunt quasi partes potentiales ipsius. Et circa hoc quaeruntur quatuor.

Primo, utrum eubulia sit virtus.

Secundo, utrum sit specialis virtus a prudentia distincta.

Tertio, utrum synesis sit specialis virtus.

Quarto, utrum gnome sit specialis virtus.

In due sequence, we must consider the virtues that are connected with prudence, and which are its quasi-potential parts. Under this head there are four points of inquiry:

(1) Whether euboulia is a virtue?

(2) Whether it is a special virtue, distinct from prudence?

(3) Whether synesis is a special virtue?

(4) Whether gnome is a special virtue?

# Article 1

### Whether euboulia is a virtue?

**AD PRIMUM SIC PROCEDITUR.** Videtur quod eubulia non sit virtus. Quia secundum Augustinum, in libro de Lib. Arb., *virtutibus nullus male utitur*. Sed eubulia, quae est bene consiliativa, aliqui male utuntur, vel quia astuta consilia excogitant ad malos fines consequendos; aut quia etiam ad bonos fines consequendos aliqua peccata ordinant, puta qui furatur ut eleemosynam det. Ergo eubulia non est virtus.

**PRAETEREA,** *virtus perfectio quaedam est*, ut dicitur in VII Phys. Sed eubulia circa consilium consistit, quod importat dubitationem et inquisitionem, quae imperfectionis sunt. Ergo eubulia non est virtus.

**PRAETEREA,** virtutes sunt connexae ad invicem, ut supra habitum est. Sed eubulia non est connexa aliis virtutibus multi enim peccatores sunt bene consiliativi, et multi iusti sunt in consiliis tardi. Ergo eubulia non est virtus.

**SED CONTRA** est quod eubulia est *rectitudo consilii*, ut philosophus dicit, in VI Ethic. Sed recta ratio perficit rationem virtutis. Ergo eubulia est virtus.

**RESPONDEO** dicendum quod, sicut supra dictum est, de ratione virtutis humanae est quod faciat actum hominis bonum. Inter ceteros autem actus hominis proprium est ei consiliari, quia hoc importat quandam rationis inquisitionem circa agenda, in quibus consistit vita humana; nam vita speculativa est supra hominem, ut dicitur in X Ethic. Eubulia autem importat bonitatem consilii, dicitur enim ab *eu*, quod est *bonum*, et *boule*, quod est *consilium*, quasi *bona consiliatio*, vel *potius bene consiliativa*. Unde manifestum est quod eubulia est virtus humana.

**OBJECTION 1:** It would seem that euboulia is not a virtue. For, according to Augustine (*De Lib. Arb.* ii, 18, 19) *no man makes evil use of virtue*. Now some make evil use of euboulia or good counsel, either through devising crafty counsels in order to achieve evil ends, or through committing sin in order that they may achieve good ends, as those who rob that they may give alms. Therefore euboulia is not a virtue.

**OBJ. 2:** Further, *virtue is a perfection*, according to *Phys.* vii. But euboulia is concerned with counsel, which implies doubt and research, and these are marks of imperfection. Therefore euboulia is not a virtue.

**OBJ. 3:** Further, virtues are connected with one another, as stated above (I-II, Q. 65). Now euboulia is not connected with the other virtues, since many sinners take good-counsel, and many godly men are slow in taking counsel. Therefore euboulia is not a virtue.

**ON THE CONTRARY,** According to the Philosopher (*Ethic.* vi, 9) euboulia *is a right counselling*. Now the perfection of virtue consists in right reason. Therefore euboulia is a virtue.

**I ANSWER THAT,** As stated above (Q. 47, A. 4) the nature of a human virtue consists in making a human act good. Now among the acts of man, it is proper to him to take counsel, since this denotes a research of the reason about the actions he has to perform and whereof human life consists, for the speculative life is above man, as stated in *Ethic.* x. But euboulia signifies goodness of counsel, for it is derived from the *eu*, good, and *boule*, counsel, being *a good counsel* or rather *a disposition to take good counsel*. Hence it is evident that euboulia is a human virtue.

**AD PRIMUM** ergo dicendum quod non est bonum consilium sive aliquis malum finem sibi in consiliando praestituat, sive etiam ad bonum finem malas vias adinveniat. Sicut etiam in speculativis non est bona ratiocinatio sive aliquis falsum concludat, sive etiam concludat verum ex falsis, quia non utitur convenienti medio. Et ideo utrumque praedictorum est contra rationem eubuliae, ut Philosophus dicit, in VI Ethic.

**AD SECUNDUM** dicendum quod etsi virtus sit essentialiter perfectio quaedam, non tamen oportet quod omne illud quod est materia virtutis perfectionem importet. Oportet enim circa omnia humana perfici per virtutes, et non solum circa actus rationis, inter quos est consilium; sed etiam circa passiones appetitus sensitivi, quae adhuc sunt multo imperfectiores.

Vel potest dici quod virtus humana est perfectio secundum modum hominis, qui non potest per certitudinem comprehendere veritatem rerum simplici intuitu; et praecipue in agibilibus, quae sunt contingentia.

**AD TERTIUM** dicendum quod in nullo peccatore, inquantum huiusmodi, invenitur eubulia. Omne enim peccatum est contra bonam consiliationem. Requiritur enim ad bene consiliandum non solum adinventio vel excogitatio eorum quae sunt opportuna ad finem, sed etiam aliae circumstantiae, scilicet tempus congruum, ut nec nimis tardus nec nimis velox sit in consiliis; et modus consiliandi, ut scilicet sit firmus in suo consilio; et aliae huiusmodi debitae circumstantiae, quae peccator peccando non observat. Quilibet autem virtuosus est bene consiliativus in his quae ordinantur ad finem virtutis, licet forte in aliquibus particularibus negotiis non sit bene consiliativus, puta in mercationibus vel in rebus bellicis vel in aliquo huiusmodi.

**REPLY OBJ. 1**: There is no good counsel either in deliberating for an evil end, or in discovering evil means for attaining a good end, even as in speculative matters, there is no good reasoning either in coming to a false conclusion, or in coming to a true conclusion from false premises through employing an unsuitable middle term. Hence both the aforesaid processes are contrary to euboulia, as the Philosopher declares (*Ethic.* vi, 9).

**REPLY OBJ. 2**: Although virtue is essentially a perfection, it does not follow that whatever is the matter of a virtue implies perfection. For man needs to be perfected by virtues in all his parts, and this not only as regards the acts of reason, of which counsel is one, but also as regards the passions of the sensitive appetite, which are still more imperfect.

It may also be replied that human virtue is a perfection according to the mode of man, who is unable by simple insight to comprehend with certainty the truth of things, especially in matters of action which are contingent.

**REPLY OBJ. 3**: In no sinner as such is euboulia to be found: since all sin is contrary to taking good counsel. For good counsel requires not only the discovery or devising of fit means for the end, but also other circumstances. Such are suitable time, so that one be neither too slow nor too quick in taking counsel, and the mode of taking counsel, so that one be firm in the counsel taken, and other like due circumstances, which sinners fail to observe when they sin. On the other hand, every virtuous man takes good counsel in those things which are directed to the end of virtue, although perhaps he does not take good counsel in other particular matters, for instance in matters of trade, or warfare, or the like.

# Article 2

*Whether euboulia is a special virtue, distinct from prudence?*

**AD SECUNDUM SIC PROCEDITUR.** Videtur quod eubulia non sit virtus distincta a prudentia. Quia ut philosophus dicit, in VI Ethic., *videtur prudentis esse bene consiliari.* Sed hoc pertinet ad eubuliam, ut dictum est. Ergo eubulia non distinguitur a prudentia.

**PRAETEREA**, humani actus, ad quos ordinantur humanae virtutes, praecipue specificantur ex fine, ut supra habitum est. Sed ad eundem finem ordinantur eubulia et prudentia, ut dicitur VI Ethic., idest non ad quendam particularem finem, sed ad communem finem totius vitae. Ergo eubulia non est virtus distincta a prudentia.

**OBJECTION 1**: It would seem that euboulia is not a distinct virtue from prudence. For, according to the Philosopher (*Ethic.* vi, 5), the *prudent man is, seemingly, one who takes good counsel.* Now this belongs to euboulia as stated above. Therefore euboulia is not distinct from prudence.

**OBJ. 2**: Further, human acts to which human virtues are directed, are specified chiefly by their end, as stated above (I-II, Q. 1, A. 3; Q. 18, AA. 4, 6). Now euboulia and prudence are directed to the same end, as stated in *Ethic.* vi, 9, not indeed to some particular end, but to the common end of all life. Therefore euboulia is not a distinct virtue from prudence.

**PRAETEREA**, in scientiis speculativis ad eandem scientiam pertinet inquirere et determinare. Ergo pari ratione in operativis hoc pertinet ad eandem virtutem. Sed inquirere pertinet ad eubuliam, determinare autem ad prudentiam. Ergo eubulia non est alia virtus a prudentia.

**SED CONTRA**, *prudentia est praeceptiva*, ut dicitur in VI Ethic. Hoc autem non convenit eubuliae. Ergo eubulia est alia virtus a prudentia.

**RESPONDEO** dicendum quod, sicut dictum est supra, virtus proprie ordinatur ad actum, quem reddit bonum. Et ideo oportet secundum differentiam actuum esse diversas virtutes, et maxime quando non est eadem ratio bonitatis in actibus. Si enim esset eadem ratio bonitatis in eis, tunc ad eandem virtutem pertinerent diversi actus, sicut ex eodem dependet bonitas amoris, desiderii et gaudii, et ideo omnia ista pertinent ad eandem virtutem caritatis.

Actus autem rationis ordinati ad opus sunt diversi, nec habent eandem rationem bonitatis, ex alia enim efficitur homo bene consiliativus, et bene iudicativus, et bene praeceptivus; quod patet ex hoc quod ista aliquando ab invicem separantur. Et ideo oportet aliam esse virtutem eubuliam, per quam homo est bene consiliativus; et aliam prudentiam, per quam homo est bene praeceptivus. Et sicut consiliari ordinatur ad praecipere tanquam ad principalius, ita etiam eubulia ordinatur ad prudentiam tanquam ad principaliorem virtutem; sine qua nec virtus esset, sicut nec morales virtutes sine prudentia, nec ceterae virtutes sine caritate.

**AD PRIMUM** ergo dicendum quod ad prudentiam pertinet bene consiliari imperative, ad eubuliam autem elicitive.

**AD SECUNDUM** dicendum quod ad unum finem ultimum, quod est *bene vivere totum*, ordinantur diversi actus secundum quendam gradum, nam praecedit consilium, sequitur iudicium, et ultimum est praeceptum, quod immediate se habet ad finem ultimum, alii autem duo actus remote se habent. Qui tamen habent quosdam proximos fines, consilium quidem inventionem eorum quae sunt agenda; iudicium autem certitudinem. Unde ex hoc non sequitur quod eubulia et prudentia non sint diversae virtutes, sed quod eubulia ordinetur ad prudentiam sicut virtus secundaria ad principalem.

**AD TERTIUM** dicendum quod etiam in speculativis alia rationalis scientia est dialectica, quae ordinatur ad inquisitionem inventivam; et alia scientia demonstrativa, quae est veritatis determinativa.

**OBJ. 3**: Further, in speculative sciences, research and decision belong to the same science. Therefore in like manner these belong to the same virtue in practical matters. Now research belongs to euboulia, while decision belongs to prudence. There euboulia is not a distinct virtue from prudence.

**ON THE CONTRARY**, *Prudence is preceptive*, according to *Ethic.* vi, 10. But this does not apply to euboulia. Therefore euboulia is a distinct virtue from prudence.

**I ANSWER THAT**, As stated above (A. 1), virtue is properly directed to an act which it renders good; and consequently virtues must differ according to different acts, especially when there is a different kind of goodness in the acts. For, if various acts contained the same kind of goodness, they would belong to the same virtue: thus the goodness of love, desire and joy depends on the same, wherefore all these belong to the same virtue of charity.

Now acts of the reason that are ordained to action are diverse, nor have they the same kind of goodness: since it is owing to different causes that a man acquires good counsel, good judgment, or good command, inasmuch as these are sometimes separated from one another. Consequently euboulia which makes man take good counsel must needs be a distinct virtue from prudence, which makes man command well. And since counsel is directed to command as to that which is principal, so euboulia is directed to prudence as to a principal virtue, without which it would be no virtue at all, even as neither are the moral virtues without prudence, nor the other virtues without charity.

**REPLY OBJ. 1**: It belongs to prudence to take good counsel by commanding it, to euboulia by eliciting it.

**REPLY OBJ. 2**: Different acts are directed in different degrees to the one end which is *a good life in general*: for counsel comes first, judgment follows, and command comes last. The last named has an immediate relation to the last end: whereas the other two acts are related thereto remotely. Nevertheless these have certain proximate ends of their own, the end of counsel being the discovery of what has to be done, and the end of judgment, certainty. Hence this proves not that euboulia is not a distinct virtue from prudence, but that it is subordinate thereto, as a secondary to a principal virtue.

**REPLY OBJ. 3**: Even in speculative matters the rational science of dialectics, which is directed to research and discovery, is distinct from demonstrative science, which decides the truth.

# Article 3

*Whether synesis is a virtue?*

**AD TERTIUM SIC PROCEDITUR.** Videtur quod synesis non sit virtus. Virtutes enim *non insunt nobis a natura*, ut dicitur in II Ethic. Sed synesis inest aliquibus a natura, ut dicit philosophus, in VI Ethic. Ergo synesis non est virtus.

**PRAETEREA,** synesis, ut in eodem libro dicitur, *est solum iudicativa*. Sed iudicium solum, sine praecepto, potest esse etiam in malis. Cum ergo virtus sit solum in bonis, videtur quod synesis non sit virtus.

**PRAETEREA,** nunquam est defectus in praecipiendo nisi sit aliquis defectus in iudicando, saltem in particulari operabili, in quo omnis malus errat. Si ergo synesis ponitur virtus ad bene iudicandum, videtur quod non sit necessaria alia virtus ad bene praecipiendum. Et ideo prudentia erit superflua, quod est inconveniens. Non ergo synesis est virtus.

**SED CONTRA,** iudicium est perfectius quam consilium. Sed eubulia, quae est bene consiliativa, est virtus. Ergo multo magis synesis, quae est bene iudicativa, est virtus.

**RESPONDEO** dicendum quod synesis importat iudicium rectum non quidem circa speculabilia, sed circa particularia operabilia, circa quae etiam est prudentia. Unde secundum synesim dicuntur in Graeco aliqui *syneti*, idest sensati, vel *eusyneti*, idest homines boni sensus, sicut e contrario qui carent hac virtute dicuntur *asyneti*, idest insensati.

Oportet autem quod secundum differentiam actuum qui non reducuntur in eandem causam sit etiam diversitas virtutum. Manifestum est autem quod bonitas consilii et bonitas iudicii non reducuntur in eandem causam, multi enim sunt bene consiliativi qui tamen non sunt bene sensati, quasi recte iudicantes. Sicut etiam in speculativis aliqui sunt bene inquirentes, propter hoc quod ratio eorum prompta est ad discurrendum per diversa, quod videtur provenire ex dispositione imaginativae virtutis, quae de facili potest formare diversa phantasmata, et tamen huiusmodi quandoque non sunt boni iudicii, quod est propter defectum intellectus, qui maxime contingit ex mala dispositione communis sensus non bene iudicantis. Et ideo oportet praeter eubuliam esse aliam virtutem quae est bene iudicativa. Et haec dicitur synesis.

**AD PRIMUM** ergo dicendum quod rectum iudicium in hoc consistit quod vis cognoscitiva apprehendat rem aliquam secundum quod in se est. Quod quidem provenit ex recta dispositione virtutis apprehensivae, sicut in speculo, si fuerit bene dispositum, imprimuntur formae corporum secundum quod sunt; si vero fuerit specu-

**OBJECTION 1**: It would seem that synesis is not a virtue. Virtues are *not in us by nature*, according to *Ethic.* ii, 1. But synesis is natural to some, as the Philosopher states (*Ethic.* vi, 11). Therefore synesis is not a virtue.

**OBJ. 2**: Further, as stated in the same book (10), synesis is nothing but *a faculty of judging*. But judgment without command can be even in the wicked. Since then virtue is only in the good, it seems that synesis is not a virtue.

**OBJ. 3**: Further, there is never a defective command, unless there be a defective judgment, at least in a particular matter of action; for it is in this that every wicked man errs. If therefore synesis be reckoned a virtue directed to good judgment, it seems that there is no need for any other virtue directed to good command: and consequently prudence would be superfluous, which is not reasonable. Therefore synesis is not a virtue.

**ON THE CONTRARY**, Judgment is more perfect than counsel. But euboulia, or good counsel, is a virtue. Much more, therefore, is synesis a virtue, as being good judgment.

**I ANSWER THAT**, synesis signifies a right judgment, not indeed about speculative matters, but about particular practical matters, about which also is prudence. Hence in Greek some, in respect of synesis are said to be *synetoi*, i.e., persons of sense, or *eusynetoi*, i.e., men of good sense, just as on the other hand, those who lack this virtue are called *asynetoi*, i.e., senseless.

Now, different acts which cannot be ascribed to the same cause, must correspond to different virtues. And it is evident that goodness of counsel and goodness of judgment are not reducible to the same cause, for many can take good counsel, without having good sense so as to judge well. Even so, in speculative matters some are good at research, through their reason being quick at arguing from one thing to another (which seems to be due to a disposition of their power of imagination, which has a facility in forming phantasms), and yet such persons sometimes lack good judgment (and this is due to a defect in the intellect arising chiefly from a defective disposition of the common sense which fails to judge aright). Hence there is need, besides euboulia, for another virtue, which judges well, and this is called synesis.

**REPLY OBJ. 1**: Right judgment consists in the cognitive power apprehending a thing just as it is in reality, and this is due to the right disposition of the apprehensive power. Thus if a mirror be well disposed the forms of bodies are reflected in it just as they are, whereas if it be ill disposed, the images therein appear distorted and misshapen. Now that

lum male dispositum, apparent ibi imagines distortae et prave se habentes. Quod autem virtus cognoscitiva sit bene disposita ad recipiendum res secundum quod sunt, contingit quidem radicaliter ex natura, consummative autem ex exercitio vel ex munere gratiae. Et hoc dupliciter. Uno modo, directe ex parte ipsius cognoscitivae virtutis, puta quia non est imbuta pravis conceptionibus, sed veris et rectis, et hoc pertinet ad synesim secundum quod est specialis virtus. Alio modo, indirecte, ex bona dispositione appetitivae virtutis, ex qua sequitur quod homo bene iudicet de appetibilibus. Et sic bonum virtutis iudicium consequitur habitus virtutum moralium, sed circa fines, synesis autem est magis circa ea quae sunt ad finem.

**AD SECUNDUM** dicendum quod in malis potest quidem iudicium rectum esse in universali, sed in particulari agibili semper eorum iudicium corrumpitur, ut supra habitum est.

**AD TERTIUM** dicendum quod contingit quandoque id quod bene iudicatum est differri, vel negligenter agi aut inordinate. Et ideo post virtutem quae est bene iudicativa necessaria est finalis virtus principalis quae sit bene praeceptiva, scilicet prudentia.

the cognitive power be well disposed to receive things just as they are in reality, is radically due to nature, but, as to its consummation, is due to practice or to a gift of grace, and this in two ways. First directly, on the part of the cognitive power itself, for instance, because it is imbued, not with distorted, but with true and correct ideas: this belongs to synesis which in this respect is a special virtue. Second indirectly, through the good disposition of the appetitive power, the result being that one judges well of the objects of appetite: and thus a good judgment of virtue results from the habits of moral virtue; but this judgment is about the ends, whereas synesis is rather about the means.

**REPLY OBJ. 2:** In wicked men there may be right judgment of a universal principle, but their judgment is always corrupt in the particular matter of action, as stated above (Q. 47, A. 13).

**REPLY OBJ. 3:** Sometimes after judging aright we delay to execute or execute negligently or inordinately. Hence after the virtue which judges aright there is a further need of a final and principal virtue, which commands aright, and this is prudence.

# Article 4

*Whether gnome is a special virtue distinct from synesis?*

**AD QUARTUM SIC PROCEDITUR.** Videtur quod gnome non sit specialis virtus a synesi distincta. Quia secundum synesim dicitur aliquis bene iudicativus. Sed nullus potest dici bene iudicativus nisi in omnibus bene iudicet. Ergo synesis se extendit ad omnia diiudicanda. Non est ergo aliqua alia virtus bene iudicativa quae gnome vocatur.

**PRAETEREA**, iudicium medium est inter consilium et praeceptum. Sed una tantum virtus est bene consiliativa, scilicet eubulia; et una tantum virtus est bene praeceptiva, scilicet prudentia. Ergo una tantum est virtus bene iudicativa, scilicet synesis.

**PRAETEREA**, ea quae raro accidunt, in quibus oportet a communibus legibus discedere, videntur praecipue casualia esse, quorum non est ratio, ut dicitur in II Phys. Omnes autem virtutes intellectuales pertinent ad rationem rectam. Ergo circa praedicta non est aliqua virtus intellectualis.

**SED CONTRA** est quod Philosophus determinat, in VI Ethic., gnomen esse specialem virtutem.

**RESPONDEO** dicendum quod habitus cognoscitivi distinguuntur secundum altiora vel inferiora principia, sicut sapientia in speculativis altiora principia considerat quam scientia, et ideo ab ea distinguitur. Et ita etiam

**OBJECTION 1:** It would seem that gnome is not a special virtue distinct from synesis. For a man is said, in respect of synesis, to have good judgment. Now no man can be said to have good judgment, unless he judge aright in all things. Therefore synesis extends to all matters of judgment, and consequently there is no other virtue of good judgment called gnome.

**OBJ. 2:** Further, judgment is midway between counsel and precept. Now there is only one virtue of good counsel, viz. euboulia, and only one virtue of good command, viz. prudence. Therefore there is only one virtue of good judgment, viz. synesis.

**OBJ. 3:** Further, rare occurrences wherein there is need to depart from the common law, seem for the most part to happen by chance, and with such things reason is not concerned, as stated in *Phys.* ii, 5. Now all the intellectual virtues depend on right reason. Therefore there is no intellectual virtue about such matters.

**ON THE CONTRARY,** The Philosopher concludes (*Ethic.* vi, 11) that gnome is a special virtue.

**I ANSWER THAT** cognitive habits differ according to higher and lower principles: thus in speculative matters wisdom considers higher principles than science does, and consequently is distinguished from it; and so must it be also

oportet esse in activis. Manifestum est autem quod illa quae sunt praeter ordinem inferioris principii sive causae reducuntur quandoque in ordinem altioris principii, sicut monstruosi partus animalium sunt praeter ordinem virtutis activae in semine, tamen cadunt sub ordine altioris principii, scilicet caelestis corporis, vel ulterius providentiae divinae. Unde ille qui consideraret virtutem activam in semine non posset iudicium certum ferre de huiusmodi monstris, de quibus tamen potest iudicari secundum considerationem divinae providentiae.

Contingit autem quandoque aliquid esse faciendum praeter communes regulas agendorum, puta cum impugnatori patriae non est depositum reddendum, vel aliquid aliud huiusmodi. Et ideo oportet de huiusmodi iudicare secundum aliqua altiora principia quam sint regulae communes, secundum quas iudicat synesis. Et secundum illa altiora principia exigitur altior virtus iudicativa, quae vocatur gnome, quae importat quandam perspicacitatem iudicii.

**AD PRIMUM** ergo dicendum quod synesis est vere iudicativa de omnibus quae secundum communes regulas fiunt. Sed praeter communes regulas sunt quaedam alia diiudicanda, ut iam dictum est.

**AD SECUNDUM** dicendum quod iudicium debet sumi ex propriis principiis rei, inquisitio autem fit etiam per communia. Unde etiam in speculativis dialectica, quae est inquisitiva, procedit ex communibus, demonstrativa autem, quae est iudicativa, procedit ex propriis. Et ideo eubulia, ad quam pertinet inquisitio consilii, est una de omnibus, non autem synesis, quae est iudicativa. Praeceptum autem respicit in omnibus unam rationem boni. Et ideo etiam prudentia non est nisi una.

**AD TERTIUM** dicendum quod omnia illa quae praeter communem cursum contingere possunt considerare pertinet ad solam providentiam divinam, sed inter homines ille qui est magis perspicax potest plura horum sua ratione diiudicare. Et ad hoc pertinet gnome, quae importat quandam perspicacitatem iudicii.

in practical matters. Now it is evident that what is beside the order of a lower principle or cause, is sometimes reducible to the order of a higher principle; thus monstrous births of animals are beside the order of the active seminal force, and yet they come under the order of a higher principle, namely, of a heavenly body, or higher still, of Divine Providence. Hence by considering the active seminal force one could not pronounce a sure judgment on such monstrosities, and yet this is possible if we consider Divine Providence.

Now it happens sometimes that something has to be done which is not covered by the common rules of actions, for instance in the case of the enemy of one's country, when it would be wrong to give him back his deposit, or in other similar cases. Hence it is necessary to judge of such matters according to higher principles than the common laws, according to which synesis judges: and corresponding to such higher principles it is necessary to have a higher virtue of judgment, which is called gnome, and which denotes a certain discrimination in judgment.

**REPLY OBJ. 1**: Synesis judges rightly about all actions that are covered by the common rules: but certain things have to be judged beside these common rules, as stated above.

**REPLY OBJ. 2**: Judgment about a thing should be formed from the proper principles thereof, whereas research is made by employing also common principles. Wherefore also in speculative matters, dialectics which aims at research proceeds from common principles; while demonstration which tends to judgment, proceeds from proper principles. Hence euboulia to which the research of counsel belongs is one for all, but not so synesis whose act is judicial. Command considers in all matters the one aspect of good, wherefore prudence also is only one.

**REPLY OBJ. 3**: It belongs to Divine Providence alone to consider all things that may happen beside the common course. On the other hand, among men, he who is most discerning can judge a greater number of such things by his reason: this belongs to gnome, which denotes a certain discrimination in judgment.

# QUESTION 52

## THE GIFT OF COUNSEL

Deinde considerandum est de dono consilii, quod respondet prudentiae. Et circa hoc quaeruntur quatuor.

Primo, utrum consilium debeat poni inter septem dona spiritus sancti.

Secundo, utrum donum consilii respondeat virtuti prudentiae.

Tertio, utrum donum consilii maneat in patria.

Quarto, utrum quinta beatitudo, quae est, beati misericordes, respondeat dono consilii.

We must now consider the gift of counsel which corresponds to prudence. Under this head there are four points of inquiry:

(1) Whether counsel should be reckoned among the seven gifts of the Holy Spirit?

(2) Whether the gift of counsel corresponds to prudence?

(3) Whether the gift of counsel remains in heaven?

(4) Whether the fifth beatitude, *Blessed are the merciful*, etc. corresponds to the gift of counsel?

# Article 1

*Whether counsel should be reckoned among the gifts of the Holy Spirit?*

**AD PRIMUM SIC PROCEDITUR.** Videtur quod consilium non debeat poni inter dona spiritus sancti. Dona enim spiritus sancti in adiutorium virtutum dantur; ut patet per Gregorium, in II Moral. Sed ad consiliandum homo sufficienter perficitur per virtutem prudentiae, vel etiam eubuliae, ut ex dictis patet. Ergo consilium non debet poni inter dona spiritus sancti.

**PRAETEREA,** haec videtur esse differentia inter septem dona spiritus sancti et gratias gratis datas, quod gratiae gratis datae non dantur omnibus, sed distribuuntur diversis; dona autem spiritus sancti dantur omnibus habentibus spiritum sanctum. Sed consilium videtur esse de his quae specialiter aliquibus a spiritu sancto dantur, secundum illud I Machab. II, *ecce Simon, frater vester, ipse vir consilii est.* Ergo consilium magis debet poni inter gratias gratis datas quam inter septem dona spiritus sancti.

**PRAETEREA,** Rom. VIII dicitur, *qui spiritu Dei aguntur, hi filii Dei sunt.* Sed his qui ab alio aguntur non competit consilium. Cum igitur dona spiritus sancti maxime competant filiis Dei, qui *acceperunt spiritum adoptionis filiorum*, videtur quod consilium inter dona spiritus sancti poni non debeat.

**SED CONTRA** est quod Isaiae XI dicitur, *requiescet super eum spiritus consilii et fortitudinis.*

**RESPONDEO** dicendum quod dona spiritus sancti, ut supra dictum est, sunt quaedam dispositiones quibus anima redditur bene mobilis a spiritu sancto. Deus au-

**OBJECTION 1**: It would seem that counsel should not be reckoned among the gifts of the Holy Spirit. The gifts of the Holy Spirit are given as a help to the virtues, according to Gregory (*Moral.* ii, 49). Now for the purpose of taking counsel, man is sufficiently perfected by the virtue of prudence, or even of euboulia, as is evident from what has been said (Q. 47, A. 1, ad 2; Q. 51, AA. 1, 2). Therefore counsel should not be reckoned among the gifts of the Holy Spirit.

**OBJ. 2**: Further, the difference between the seven gifts of the Holy Spirit and the gratuitous graces seems to be that the latter are not given to all, but are divided among various people, whereas the gifts of the Holy Spirit are given to all who have the Holy Spirit. But counsel seems to be one of those things which are given by the Holy Spirit specially to certain persons, according to 1 Macc. 2:65: *Behold . . . your brother Simon is a man of counsel.* Therefore counsel should be numbered among the gratuitous graces rather than among the seven gifts of the Holy Spirit.

**OBJ. 3**: Further, it is written (Rom 8:14): *Whosoever are led by the Spirit of God, they are the sons of God.* But counselling is not consistent with being led by another. Since then the gifts of the Holy Spirit are most befitting the children of God, who *have received the spirit of adoption of sons*, it would seem that counsel should not be numbered among the gifts of the Holy Spirit.

**ON THE CONTRARY**, It is written (Isa 11:2): *(The Spirit of the Lord) shall rest upon him . . . the spirit of counsel, and of fortitude.*

**I ANSWER THAT**, As stated above (I-II, Q. 68, A. 1), the gifts of the Holy Spirit are dispositions whereby the soul is rendered amenable to the motion of the Holy Spirit. Now

tem movet unumquodque secundum modum eius quod movetur, sicut *creaturam corporalem movet per tempus et locum, creaturam autem spiritualem per tempus et non per locum,* ut Augustinus dicit, VIII super Gen. ad Litt. Est autem proprium rationali creaturae quod per inquisitionem rationis moveatur ad aliquid agendum, quae quidem inquisitio consilium dicitur. Et ideo Spiritus Sanctus per modum consilii creaturam rationalem movet. Et propter hoc consilium ponitur inter dona spiritus sancti.

AD PRIMUM ergo dicendum quod prudentia vel eubulia, sive sit acquisita sive infusa, dirigit hominem in inquisitione consilii secundum ea quae ratio comprehendere potest, unde homo per prudentiam vel eubuliam fit bene consilians vel sibi vel alii. Sed quia humana ratio non potest comprehendere singularia et contingentia quae occurrere possunt, fit quod *cogitationes mortalium sunt timidae, et incertae providentiae nostrae,* ut dicitur Sap. IX. Et ideo indiget homo in inquisitione consilii dirigi a Deo, qui omnia comprehendit. Quod fit per donum consilii, per quod homo dirigitur quasi consilio a Deo accepto. Sicut etiam in rebus humanis qui sibi ipsis non sufficiunt in inquisitione consilii a sapientioribus consilium requirunt.

AD SECUNDUM dicendum quod hoc potest pertinere ad gratiam gratis datam quod aliquis sit ita boni consilii quod aliis consilium praebeat. Sed quod aliquis a Deo consilium habeat quid fieri oporteat in his quae sunt necessaria ad salutem, hoc est commune omnium sanctorum.

AD TERTIUM dicendum quod filii Dei aguntur a spiritu sancto secundum modum eorum, salvato scilicet libero arbitrio, quae est *facultas voluntatis et rationis.* Et sic inquantum ratio a spiritu sancto instruitur de agendis, competit filiis Dei donum consilii.

God moves everything according to the mode of the thing moved: thus *He moves the corporeal creature through time and place, and the spiritual creature through time, but not through place,* as Augustine declares (*Gen ad lit.* viii, 20, 22). Again, it is proper to the rational creature to be moved through the research of reason to perform any particular action, and this research is called counsel. Hence the Holy Spirit is said to move the rational creature by way of counsel, wherefore counsel is reckoned among the gifts of the Holy Spirit.

REPLY OBJ. 1: Prudence or euboulia, whether acquired or infused, directs man in the research of counsel according to principles that the reason can grasp; hence prudence or euboulia makes man take good counsel either for himself or for another. Since, however, human reason is unable to grasp the singular and contingent things which may occur, the result is that *the thoughts of mortal men are fearful, and our counsels uncertain* (Wis 9:14). Hence in the research of counsel, man requires to be directed by God who comprehends all things: and this is done through the gift of counsel, whereby man is directed as though counseled by God, just as, in human affairs, those who are unable to take counsel for themselves, seek counsel from those who are wiser.

REPLY OBJ. 2: That a man be of such good counsel as to counsel others, may be due to a gratuitous grace; but that a man be counselled by God as to what he ought to do in matters necessary for salvation is common to all holy persons.

REPLY OBJ. 3: The children of God are moved by the Holy Spirit according to their mode, without prejudice to their free-will which is the *faculty of will and reason.* Accordingly the gift of counsel is befitting the children of God insofar as the reason is instructed by the Holy Spirit about what we have to do.

# Article 2

*Whether the gift of counsel corresponds to the virtue of prudence?*

AD SECUNDUM SIC PROCEDITUR. Videtur quod donum consilii non respondeat convenienter virtuti prudentiae. Inferius enim in suo supremo attingit id quod est superius, ut patet per Dionysium, VII cap. de Div. Nom., sicut homo attingit Angelum secundum intellectum. Sed virtus cardinalis est inferior dono, ut supra habitum est. Cum ergo consilium sit primus et infimus actus prudentiae, supremus autem actus eius est praecipere, medius autem iudicare; videtur quod donum respondens prudentiae non sit consilium, sed magis iudicium vel praeceptum.

OBJECTION 1: It would seem that the gift of counsel does not fittingly correspond to the virtue of prudence. For the highest point of that which is underneath touches that which is above, as Dionysius observes (*Div. Nom.* vii), even as a man comes into contact with the angel in respect of his intellect. Now cardinal virtues are inferior to the gifts, as stated above (I-II, Q. 68, A. 8). Since, then, counsel is the first and lowest act of prudence, while command is its highest act, and judgment comes between, it seems that the gift corresponding to prudence is not counsel, but rather a gift of judgment or command.

**PRAETEREA**, uni virtuti sufficienter auxilium praebetur per unum donum, quia quanto aliquid est superius tanto est magis unitum, ut probatur in libro de causis. Sed prudentiae auxilium praebetur per donum scientiae, quae non solum est speculativa, sed etiam practica, ut supra habitum est. Ergo donum consilii non respondet virtuti prudentiae.

**PRAETEREA**, ad prudentiam proprie pertinet dirigere, ut supra habitum est. Sed ad donum consilii pertinet quod homo dirigatur a Deo, sicut dictum est. Ergo donum consilii non pertinet ad virtutem prudentiae.

**SED CONTRA** est quod donum consilii est circa ea quae sunt agenda propter finem. Sed circa haec etiam est prudentia. Ergo sibi invicem correspondent.

**RESPONDEO** dicendum quod principium motivum inferius praecipue adiuvatur et perficitur per hoc quod movetur a superiori motivo principio, sicut corpus in hoc quod movetur a spiritu. Manifestum est autem quod rectitudo rationis humanae comparatur ad rationem divinam sicut principium motivum inferius ad superius, ratio enim aeterna est suprema regula omnis humanae rectitudinis. Et ideo prudentia, quae importat rectitudinem rationis, maxime perficitur et iuvatur secundum quod regulatur et movetur a spiritu sancto. Quod pertinet ad donum consilii, ut dictum est. Unde donum consilii respondet prudentiae, sicut ipsam adiuvans et perficiens.

**AD PRIMUM** ergo dicendum quod iudicare et praecipere non est moti, sed moventis. Et quia in donis spiritus sancti mens humana non se habet ut movens, sed magis ut mota, ut supra dictum est; inde est quod non fuit conveniens quod donum correspondens prudentiae praeceptum diceretur vel iudicium, sed consilium, per quod potest significari motio mentis consiliatae ab alio consiliante.

**AD SECUNDUM** dicendum quod scientiae donum non directe respondet prudentiae, cum sit in speculativa, sed secundum quandam extensionem eam adiuvat. Donum autem consilii directe respondet prudentiae, sicut circa eadem existens.

**AD TERTIUM** dicendum quod movens motum ex hoc quod movetur movet. Unde mens humana ex hoc ipso quod dirigitur a spiritu sancto, fit potens dirigere se et alios.

**OBJ. 2**: Further, one gift suffices to help one virtue, since the higher a thing is the more one it is, as proved in De Causis. Now prudence is helped by the gift of knowledge, which is not only speculative but also practical, as shown above (Q. 9, A. 3). Therefore the gift of counsel does not correspond to the virtue of prudence.

**OBJ. 3**: Further, it belongs properly to prudence to direct, as stated above (Q. 47, A. 8). But it belongs to the gift of counsel that man should be directed by God, as stated above (A. 1). Therefore the gift of counsel does not correspond to the virtue of prudence.

**ON THE CONTRARY**, The gift of counsel is about what has to be done for the sake of the end. Now prudence is about the same matter. Therefore they correspond to one another.

**I ANSWER THAT**, A lower principle of movement is helped chiefly, and is perfected through being moved by a higher principle of movement, as a body through being moved by a spirit. Now it is evident that the rectitude of human reason is compared to the Divine Reason, as a lower motive principle to a higher: for the Eternal Reason is the supreme rule of all human rectitude. Consequently prudence, which denotes rectitude of reason, is chiefly perfected and helped through being ruled and moved by the Holy Spirit, and this belongs to the gift of counsel, as stated above (A. 1). Therefore the gift of counsel corresponds to prudence, as helping and perfecting it.

**REPLY OBJ. 1**: To judge and command belongs not to the thing moved, but to the mover. Wherefore, since in the gifts of the Holy Spirit, the position of the human mind is of one moved rather than of a mover, as stated above (A. 1; I-II, Q. 68, A. 1), it follows that it would be unfitting to call the gift corresponding to prudence by the name of command or judgment rather than of counsel whereby it is possible to signify that the counselled mind is moved by another counselling it.

**REPLY OBJ. 2**: The gift of knowledge does not directly correspond to prudence, since it deals with speculative matters: yet by a kind of extension it helps it. On the other hand the gift of counsel corresponds to prudence directly, because it is concerned about the same things.

**REPLY OBJ. 3**: The mover that is moved, moves through being moved. Hence the human mind, from the very fact that it is directed by the Holy Spirit, is enabled to direct itself and others.

# Article 3

*Whether the gift of counsel remains in heaven?*

**AD TERTIUM SIC PROCEDITUR**. Videtur quod donum consilii non maneat in patria. Consilium enim est eorum quae sunt agenda propter finem. Sed in patria nihil erit agendum propter finem, quia ibi homines ultimo fine potiuntur. Ergo in patria non est donum consilii.

**PRAETEREA**, consilium dubitationem importat, in his enim quae manifesta sunt ridiculum est consiliari, sicut patet per philosophum, in III Ethic. In patria autem tolletur omnis dubitatio. Ergo in patria non erit consilium.

**PRAETEREA**, in patria sancti maxime Deo conformantur, secundum illud I Ioan. III, *cum apparuerit, similes ei erimus*. Sed Deo non convenit consilium, secundum illud Rom. XI, *quis consiliarius eius fuit?* Ergo etiam neque sanctis in patria competit donum consilii.

**SED CONTRA** est quod dicit Gregorius, XVII Moral., *cumque uniuscuiusque gentis vel culpa vel iustitia ad supernae curiae consilium ducitur, eiusdem gentis praepositus vel obtinuisse in certamine vel non obtinuisse perhibetur*.

**RESPONDEO** dicendum quod, sicut dictum est, dona spiritus sancti ad hoc pertinent quod creatura rationalis movetur a Deo. Circa motionem autem humanae mentis a Deo duo considerari oportet. Primo quidem, quod alia est dispositio eius quod movetur dum movetur; et alia dum est in termino motus. Et quidem quando movens est solum principium movendi, cessante motu cessat actio moventis super mobile, quod iam pervenit ad terminum, sicut domus, postquam aedificata est, non aedificatur ulterius ab aedificatore. Sed quando movens non solum est causa movendi, sed etiam est causa ipsius formae ad quam est motus, tunc non cessat actio moventis etiam post adeptionem formae, sicut sol illuminat aerem etiam postquam est illuminatus. Et hoc modo Deus causat in nobis et virtutem et cognitionem non solum quando primo acquirimus, sed etiam quandiu in eis perseveramus. Et sic cognitionem agendorum causat Deus in beatis, non quasi in ignorantibus, sed quasi continuando in eis cognitionem eorum quae agenda sunt.

Tamen quaedam sunt quae beati, vel Angeli vel homines, non cognoscunt, quae non sunt de essentia beatitudinis, sed pertinent ad gubernationem rerum secundum divinam providentiam. Et quantum ad hoc est aliud considerandum, scilicet quod mens beatorum aliter movetur a Deo, et aliter mens viatorum. Nam mens viatorum movetur a Deo in agendis per hoc quod

**OBJECTION 1**: It would seem that the gift of counsel does not remain in heaven. For counsel is about what has to be done for the sake of an end. But in heaven nothing will have to be done for the sake of an end, since there man possesses the last end. Therefore the gift of counsel is not in heaven.

**OBJ. 2**: Further, counsel implies doubt, for it is absurd to take counsel in matters that are evident, as the Philosopher observes (*Ethic.* iii, 3). Now all doubt will cease in heaven. Therefore there is no counsel in heaven.

**OBJ. 3**: Further, the saints in heaven are most conformed to God, according to 1 John 3:2, *When He shall appear, we shall be like to Him*. But counsel is not becoming to God, according to Rom. 11:34, *Who hath been His counsellor?* Therefore neither to the saints in heaven is the gift of counsel becoming.

**ON THE CONTRARY**, Gregory says (*Moral.* xvii, 12): *When either the guilt or the righteousness of each nation is brought into the debate of the heavenly Court, the guardian of that nation is said to have won in the conflict, or not to have won.*

**I ANSWER THAT**, As stated above (A. 2; I-II, Q. 68, A. 1), the gifts of the Holy Spirit are connected with the motion of the rational creature by God. Now we must observe two points concerning the motion of the human mind by God. First, that the disposition of that which is moved, differs while it is being moved from its disposition when it is in the term of movement. Indeed if the mover is the principle of the movement alone, when the movement ceases, the action of the mover ceases as regards the thing moved, since it has already reached the term of movement, even as a house, after it is built, ceases being built by the builder. On the other hand, when the mover is cause not only of the movement, but also of the form to which the movement tends, then the action of the mover does not cease even after the form has been attained: thus the sun lightens the air even after it is lightened. In this way, then, God causes in us virtue and knowledge, not only when we first acquire them, but also as long as we persevere in them: and it is thus that God causes in the blessed a knowledge of what is to be done, not as though they were ignorant, but by continuing that knowledge in them.

Nevertheless there are things which the blessed, whether angels or men, do not know: such things are not essential to blessedness, but concern the government of things according to Divine Providence. As regards these, we must make a further observation, namely, that God moves the mind of the blessed in one way, and the mind of the wayfarer, in another. For God moves the mind of the

sedatur anxietas dubitationis in eis praecedens. In mente vero beatorum circa ea quae non cognoscunt est simplex nescientia, a qua etiam Angeli purgantur, secundum Dionysium, VI cap. Eccl. Hier., non autem praecedit in eis inquisitio dubitationis, sed simplex conversio ad Deum. Et hoc est Deum consulere, sicut Augustinus dicit, V super Gen. ad Litt., quod Angeli *de inferioribus Deum consulunt*. Unde et instructio qua super hoc a Deo instruuntur consilium dicitur.

Et secundum hoc donum consilii est in beatis, inquantum in eis a Deo continuatur cognitio eorum quae sciunt; et inquantum illuminantur de his quae nesciunt circa agenda.

**Ad primum** ergo dicendum quod etiam in beatis sunt aliqui actus ordinati ad finem, vel quasi procedentes ex consecutione finis, sicut quod Deum laudant; vel quibus alios pertrahunt ad finem quem ipsi sunt consecuti, sicut sunt ministeria Angelorum et orationes sanctorum. Et quantum ad hoc habet in eis locum donum consilii.

**Ad secundum** dicendum quod dubitatio pertinet ad consilium secundum statum vitae praesentis, non autem pertinet secundum quod est consilium in patria. Sicut etiam virtutes cardinales non habent omnino eosdem actus in patria et in via.

**Ad tertium** dicendum quod consilium non est in Deo sicut in recipiente, sed sicut in dante. Hoc autem modo conformantur Deo sancti in patria, sicut recipiens influenti.

wayfarer in matters of action, by soothing the pre-existing anxiety of doubt; whereas there is simple nescience in the mind of the blessed as regards the things they do not know. From this nescience the angel's mind is cleansed, according to Dionysius (*Coel. Hier.* vii), nor does there precede in them any research of doubt, for they simply turn to God; and this is to take counsel of God, for as Augustine says (*Gen ad lit.* v, 19) *the angels take counsel of God about things beneath them*: wherefore the instruction which they receive from God in such matters is called *counsel*.

Accordingly the gift of counsel is in the blessed, insofar as God preserves in them the knowledge that they have, and enlightens them in their nescience of what has to be done.

**Reply Obj. 1**: Even in the blessed there are acts directed to an end, or resulting, as it were, from their attainment of the end, such as the acts of praising God, or of helping on others to the end which they themselves have attained, for example the ministrations of the angels, and the prayers of the saints. In this respect the gift of counsel finds a place in them.

**Reply Obj. 2**: Doubt belongs to counsel according to the present state of life, but not to that counsel which takes place in heaven. Even so neither have the theological virtues quite the same acts in heaven as on the way thither.

**Reply Obj. 3**: Counsel is in God, not as receiving but as giving it: and the saints in heaven are conformed to God, as receivers to the source whence they receive.

# Article 4

*Whether the fifth beatitude, which is that of mercy, corresponds to the gift of counsel?*

**Ad quartum sic proceditur.** Videtur quod quinta beatitudo, quae est de misericordia, non respondeat dono consilii. Omnes enim beatitudines sunt quidam actus virtutum, ut supra habitum est. Sed per consilium in omnibus virtutum actibus dirigimur. Ergo consilio non respondet magis quinta beatitudo quam alia.

**Praeterea,** praecepta dantur de his quae sunt de necessitate salutis, consilium autem datur de his quae non sunt de necessitate salutis. Misericordia autem est de necessitate salutis, secundum illud Iac. II, *iudicium sine misericordia ei qui non fecit misericordiam*, paupertas autem non est de necessitate salutis, sed pertinet ad perfectionem vitae, ut patet Matth. XIX. Ergo dono consilii magis respondet beatitudo paupertatis quam beatitudo misericordiae.

**Praeterea,** fructus consequuntur ad beatitudines, important enim delectationem quandam spiritualem

**Objection 1**: It would seem that the fifth beatitude, which is that of mercy, does not correspond to the gift of counsel. For all the beatitudes are acts of virtue, as stated above (I-II, Q. 69, A. 1). Now we are directed by counsel in all acts of virtue. Therefore the fifth beatitude does not correspond more than any other to counsel.

**Obj. 2**: Further, precepts are given about matters necessary for salvation, while counsel is given about matters which are not necessary for salvation. Now mercy is necessary for salvation, according to James 2:13, *Judgment without mercy to him that hath not done mercy*. On the other hand poverty is not necessary for salvation, but belongs to the life of perfection, according to Matt. 19:21. Therefore the beatitude of poverty corresponds to the gift of counsel, rather than to the beatitude of mercy.

**Obj. 3**: Further, the fruits result from the beatitudes, for they denote a certain spiritual delight resulting from

quae consequitur perfectos actus virtutum. Sed inter fructus non ponitur aliquid respondens dono consilii, ut patet Gal. V. Ergo etiam beatitudo misericordiae non respondet dono consilii.

**SED CONTRA** est quod Augustinus dicit, in libro de Serm. Dom. in monte, *consilium convenit misericordibus, quia unicum remedium est de tantis malis erui, dimittere aliis et dare.*

**RESPONDEO** dicendum quod consilium proprie est de his quae sunt utilia ad finem. Unde ea quae maxime sunt utilia ad finem maxime debent correspondere dono consilii. Hoc autem est misericordia, secundum illud I ad Tim. IV, *pietas ad omnia utilis est.* Et ideo specialiter dono consilii respondet beatitudo misericordiae, non sicut elicienti, sed sicut dirigenti.

**AD PRIMUM** ergo dicendum quod etsi consilium dirigat in omnibus actibus virtutum, specialiter tamen dirigit in operibus misericordiae, ratione iam dicta.

**AD SECUNDUM** dicendum quod consilium, secundum quod est donum spiritus sancti, dirigit nos in omnibus quae ordinantur in finem vitae aeternae, sive sint de necessitate salutis sive non. Et tamen non omne opus misericordiae est de necessitate salutis.

**AD TERTIUM** dicendum quod fructus importat quoddam ultimum. In practicis autem non est ultimum in cognitione, sed in operatione, quae est finis. Et ideo inter fructus nihil ponitur quod pertineat ad cognitionem practicam, sed solum ea quae pertinent ad operationes, in quibus cognitio practica dirigit. Inter quae ponitur bonitas et benignitas, quae respondent misericordiae.

perfect acts of virtue. Now none of the fruits correspond to the gift of counsel, as appears from Gal. 5:22, 23. Therefore neither does the beatitude of mercy correspond to the gift of counsel.

**ON THE CONTRARY,** Augustine says (*De Serm. Dom.* iv): *Counsel is befitting the merciful, because the one remedy is to be delivered from evils so great, to pardon, and to give.*

**I ANSWER THAT,** Counsel is properly about things useful for an end. Hence such things as are of most use for an end, should above all correspond to the gift of counsel. Now such is mercy, according to 1 Tim. 4:8, *Godliness is profitable to all things.* Therefore the beatitude of mercy specially corresponds to the gift of counsel, not as eliciting but as directing mercy.

**REPLY OBJ. 1:** Although counsel directs in all the acts of virtue, it does so in a special way in works of mercy, for the reason given above.

**REPLY OBJ. 2:** Counsel considered as a gift of the Holy Spirit guides us in all matters that are directed to the end of eternal life whether they be necessary for salvation or not, and yet not every work of mercy is necessary for salvation.

**REPLY OBJ. 3:** Fruit denotes something ultimate. Now the ultimate in practical matters consists not in knowledge but in an action which is the end. Hence nothing pertaining to practical knowledge is numbered among the fruits, but only such things as pertain to action, in which practical knowledge is the guide. Among these we find *goodness* and *benignity* which correspond to mercy.

# Question 53

## Imprudence

Deinde considerandum est de vitiis oppositis prudentiae. Dicit autem Augustinus, in IV contra Iulian., quod *omnibus virtutibus non solum sunt vitia manifesta discretione contraria, sicut prudentiae temeritas, verum etiam vicina quodammodo, nec veritate, sed quadam specie fallente similia, sicut ipsi prudentiae astutia.*

Primo ergo considerandum est de vitiis quae manifeste contrarietatem habent ad prudentiam, quae scilicet vitia proveniunt ex defectu prudentiae vel eorum quae ad prudentiam requiruntur; secundo, de vitiis quae habent quandam similitudinem falsam cum prudentia quae scilicet contingunt per abusum eorum quae ad prudentiam requiruntur. Quia vero sollicitudo ad prudentiam pertinet, circa primum consideranda sunt duo, primo quidem, de imprudentia; secundo, de negligentia, quae sollicitudini opponitur.

Circa primum quaeruntur sex.

Primo, de imprudentia, utrum sit peccatum.

Secundo, utrum sit speciale peccatum.

Tertio, de praecipitatione, sive temeritate.

Quarto, de inconsideratione.

Quinto, de inconstantia.

Sexto, de origine horum vitiorum.

We must now consider the vices opposed to prudence. For Augustine says (*Contra Julian.* iv, 3): *There are vices opposed to every virtue, not only vices that are in manifest opposition to virtue, as temerity is opposed to prudence, but also vices which have a kind of kinship and not a true but a spurious likeness to virtue; thus in opposition to prudence we have craftiness.*

Accordingly we must consider first of all those vices which are in evident opposition to prudence, those namely which are due to a defect either of prudence or of those things which are requisite for prudence, and second those vices which have a false resemblance to prudence, those namely which are due to abuse of the things required for prudence. And since solicitude pertains to prudence, the first of these considerations will be twofold: (1) Of imprudence; (2) Of negligence which is opposed to solicitude.

Under the first head there are six points of inquiry:

(1) Concerning imprudence, whether it is a sin?

(2) Whether it is a special sin?

(3) Of precipitation or temerity;

(4) Of thoughtlessness;

(5) Of inconstancy;

(6) Concerning the origin of these vices.

# Article 1

*Whether imprudence is a sin?*

**Ad primum sic proceditur.** Videtur quod imprudentia non sit peccatum. Omne enim peccatum est voluntarium, ut Augustinus dicit. Imprudentia autem non est aliquid voluntarium, nullus enim vult esse imprudens. Ergo imprudentia non est peccatum.

**Praeterea,** nullum peccatum nascitur cum homine nisi originale. Sed imprudentia nascitur cum homine, unde et iuvenes imprudentes sunt. Nec est originale peccatum, quod opponitur originali iustitiae. Ergo imprudentia non est peccatum.

**Praeterea,** omne peccatum per poenitentiam tollitur. Sed imprudentia non tollitur per poenitentiam. Ergo imprudentia non est peccatum.

**Sed contra,** spiritualis thesaurus gratiae non tollitur nisi per peccatum. Tollitur autem per imprudentiam, secundum illud Prov. XXI, *thesaurus desiderabilis et*

**Objection 1**: It would seem that imprudence is not a sin. For every sin is voluntary, according to Augustine ; whereas imprudence is not voluntary, since no man wishes to be imprudent. Therefore imprudence is not a sin.

**Obj. 2**: Further, none but original sin comes to man with his birth. But imprudence comes to man with his birth, wherefore the young are imprudent; and yet it is not original sin which is opposed to original justice. Therefore imprudence is not a sin.

**Obj. 3**: Further, every sin is taken away by repentance. But imprudence is not taken away by repentance. Therefore imprudence is not a sin.

**On the contrary**, The spiritual treasure of grace is not taken away save by sin. But it is taken away by imprudence, according to Prov. 21:20, *There is a treasure*

*oleum in habitaculo iusti, et homo imprudens dissipabit illud.*

**RESPONDEO** dicendum quod imprudentia dupliciter accipi potest, uno modo, privative; alio modo, contrarie. Negative autem non proprie dicitur, ita scilicet quod importet solam carentiam prudentiae, quae potest esse sine peccato. Privative quidem imprudentia dicitur inquantum aliquis caret prudentia quam natus est et debet habere. Et secundum hoc imprudentia est peccatum ratione negligentiae, qua quis non adhibet studium ad prudentiam habendam.

Contrarie vero accipitur imprudentia secundum quod ratio contrario modo movetur vel agit prudentiae. Puta, si recta ratio prudentiae agit consiliando, imprudens consilium spernit, et sic de aliis quae in actu prudentis observanda sunt. Et hoc modo imprudentia est peccatum secundum rationem propriam prudentiae. Non enim potest hoc contingere quod homo contra prudentiam agat, nisi divertens a regulis quibus ratio prudentiae rectificatur. Unde si hoc contingat per aversionem a regulis divinis, est peccatum mortale, puta cum quis quasi contemnens et repudians divina documenta, praecipitanter agit. Si vero praeter eas agat absque contemptu, et absque detrimento eorum quae sunt de necessitate salutis, est peccatum veniale.

**AD PRIMUM** ergo dicendum quod deformitatem imprudentiae nullus vult, sed actum imprudentiae vult temerarius, qui vult praecipitanter agere. Unde et philosophus dicit, VI Ethic., quod *ille qui circa prudentiam peccat volens, minus acceptatur.*

**AD SECUNDUM** dicendum quod ratio illa procedit de imprudentia secundum quod sumitur negative. Sciendum tamen quod carentia prudentiae et cuiuslibet virtutis includitur in carentia originalis iustitiae, quae totam animam perficiebat. Et secundum hoc omnes isti defectus virtutum possunt reduci ad originale peccatum.

**AD TERTIUM** dicendum quod per poenitentiam restituitur prudentia infusa, et sic cessat carentia huius prudentiae. Non tamen restituitur prudentia acquisita quantum ad habitum, sed tollitur actus contrarius, in quo proprie consistit peccatum imprudentiae.

*to be desired, and oil in the dwelling of the just, and the imprudent man shall spend it.* Therefore imprudence is a sin.

**I ANSWER THAT**, Imprudence may be taken in two ways, first, as a privation, second, as a contrary. Properly speaking it is not taken as a negation, so as merely to signify the absence of prudence, for this can be without any sin. Taken as a privation, imprudence denotes lack of that prudence which a man can and ought to have, and in this sense imprudence is a sin by reason of a man's negligence in striving to have prudence.

Imprudence is taken as a contrary, insofar as the movement or act of reason is in opposition to prudence: for instance, whereas the right reason of prudence acts by taking counsel, the imprudent man despises counsel, and the same applies to the other conditions which require consideration in the act of prudence. In this way imprudence is a sin in respect of prudence considered under its proper aspect, since it is not possible for a man to act against prudence, except by infringing the rules on which the right reason of prudence depends. Wherefore, if this should happen through aversion from the Divine Law, it will be a mortal sin, as when a man acts precipitately through contempt and rejection of the Divine teaching: whereas if he act beside the Law and without contempt, and without detriment to things necessary for salvation, it will be a venial sin.

**REPLY OBJ. 1**: No man desires the deformity of imprudence, but the rash man wills the act of imprudence, because he wishes to act precipitately. Hence the Philosopher says (*Ethic.* vi, 5) that *he who sins willingly against prudence is less to be commended.*

**REPLY OBJ. 2**: This argument takes imprudence in the negative sense. It must be observed however that lack of prudence or of any other virtue is included in the lack of original justice which perfected the entire soul. Accordingly all such lack of virtue may be ascribed to original sin.

**REPLY OBJ. 3**: Repentance restores infused prudence, and thus the lack of this prudence ceases; but acquired prudence is not restored as to the habit, although the contrary act is taken away, wherein properly speaking the sin of imprudence consists.

# Article 2

*Whether imprudence is a special sin?*

**AD SECUNDUM SIC PROCEDITUR.** Videtur quod imprudentia non sit speciale peccatum. Quicumque enim peccat agit contra rationem rectam, quae est prudentia.

**OBJECTION 1**: It would seem that imprudence is not a special sin. For whoever sins, acts against right reason, i.e., against prudence. But imprudence consists in acting

Sed imprudentia consistit in hoc quod aliquis agit contra prudentiam, ut dictum est. Ergo imprudentia non est speciale peccatum.

**PRAETEREA**, prudentia magis est affinis moralibus actibus quam scientia. Sed ignorantia, quae opponitur scientiae, ponitur inter generales causas peccati. Ergo multo magis imprudentia.

**PRAETEREA**, peccata contingunt ex hoc quod virtutum circumstantiae corrumpuntur, unde et Dionysius dicit, IV cap. de Div. Nom., quod *malum contingit ex singularibus defectibus*. Sed multa requiruntur ad prudentiam, sicut ratio, intellectus, docilitas, et cetera quae supra posita sunt. Ergo multae sunt imprudentiae species. Ergo non est peccatum speciale.

**SED CONTRA**, imprudentia est contrarium prudentiae, ut dictum est. Sed prudentia est una virtus specialis. Ergo imprudentia est unum vitium speciale.

**RESPONDEO** dicendum quod aliquod vitium vel peccatum potest dici generale dupliciter, uno modo, absolute, quia scilicet est generale respectu omnium peccatorum; alio modo, quia est generale respectu quorundam vitiorum quae sunt species eius. Primo autem modo potest dici aliquod vitium generale dupliciter. Uno modo, per essentiam, quia scilicet praedicatur de omnibus peccatis. Et hoc modo imprudentia non est generale peccatum, sicut nec prudentia generalis virtus, cum sint circa actus speciales, scilicet circa ipsos actus rationis. Alio modo, per participationem. Et hoc modo imprudentia est generale peccatum. Sicut enim prudentia participatur quodammodo in omnibus virtutibus, inquantum est directiva earum, ita et imprudentia in omnibus vitiis et peccatis, nullum enim peccatum accidere potest nisi sit defectus in aliquo actu rationis dirigentis, quod pertinet ad imprudentiam.

Si vero dicatur peccatum generale non simpliciter, sed secundum aliquod genus, quia scilicet continet sub se multas species; sic imprudentia est generale peccatum. Continet enim sub se diversas species tripliciter. Uno quidem modo, per oppositum ad diversas partes subiectivas prudentiae. Sicut enim distinguitur prudentia in monasticam, quae est regitiva unius, et in alias species prudentiae quae sunt multitudinis regitivae, ut supra habitum est; ita etiam imprudentia. Alio modo, secundum partes quasi potentiales prudentiae, quae sunt virtutes adiunctae, et accipiuntur secundum diversos actus rationis. Et hoc modo, quantum ad defectum consilii, circa quod est eubulia, est *praecipitatio*, sive *temeritas*, imprudentiae species. Quantum vero ad defectum iudicii, circa quod sunt synesis et gnome, est *inconsideratio*. Quantum vero ad ipsum praeceptum, quod est proprius actus prudentiae, est *inconstantia* et *negligentia*. Tertio modo possunt sumi per oppositum ad ea quae requiruntur ad prudentiam, quae sunt quasi partes integrales

against prudence, as stated above (A. 1). Therefore imprudence is not a special sin.

**OBJ. 2**: Further, prudence is more akin to moral action than knowledge is. But ignorance which is opposed to knowledge, is reckoned one of the general causes of sin. Much more therefore should imprudence be reckoned among those causes.

**OBJ. 3**: Further, sin consists in the corruption of the circumstances of virtue, wherefore Dionysius says (*Div. Nom.* iv) that *evil results from each single defect*. Now many things are requisite for prudence; for instance, reason, intelligence, docility, and so on, as stated above (QQ. 48, 49). Therefore there are many species of imprudence, so that it is not a special sin.

**ON THE CONTRARY**, Imprudence is opposed to prudence, as stated above (A. 1). Now prudence is a special virtue. Therefore imprudence too is one special vice.

**I ANSWER THAT**, A vice or sin may be styled general in two ways; first, absolutely, because, to wit, it is general in respect of all sins; second, because it is general in respect of certain vices, which are its species. In the first way, a vice may be said to be general on two counts: first, essentially, because it is predicated of all sins: and in this way imprudence is not a general sin, as neither is prudence a general virtue: since it is concerned with special acts, namely the very acts of reason: second, by participation; and in this way imprudence is a general sin: for, just as all the virtues have a share of prudence, insofar as it directs them, so have all vices and sins a share of imprudence, because no sin can occur, without some defect in an act of the directing reason, which defect belongs to imprudence.

If, on the other hand, a sin be called general, not simply but in some particular genus, that is, as containing several species of sin, then imprudence is a general sin. For it contains various species in three ways. First, by opposition to the various subjective parts of prudence, for just as we distinguish the prudence that guides the individual, from other kinds that govern communities, as stated above (Q. 48; Q. 50, A. 7), so also we distinguish various kinds of imprudence. Second, in respect of the quasi-potential parts of prudence, which are virtues connected with it, and correspond to the several acts of reason. Thus, by defect of *counsel* to which euboulia corresponds, *precipitation* or *temerity* is a species of imprudence; by defect of *judgment*, to which synesis (judging well according to common law) and gnome (judging well according to general law) refer, there is *thoughtlessness*; while *inconstancy* and *negligence* correspond to the *command* which is the proper act of prudence. Third, this may be taken by opposition to those things which are requisite for prudence, which

prudentiae. Sed quia omnia illa ordinantur ad dirigendum praedictos tres rationis actus, inde est quod omnes defectus oppositi reducuntur ad quatuor praedictas partes. Sicut incautela et incircumspectio includitur sub inconsideratione. Quod autem aliquis deficiat a docilitate vel memoria vel ratione, pertinet ad praecipitationem. Improvidentia vero et defectus intelligentiae et solertiae pertinent ad negligentiam et inconstantiam.

**AD PRIMUM** ergo dicendum quod ratio illa procedit de generalitate quae est secundum participationem.

**AD SECUNDUM** dicendum quod quia scientia est magis remota a moralibus quam prudentia secundum propriam rationem utriusque, inde est quod ignorantia non habet de se rationem peccati moralis, sed solum ratione negligentiae praecedentis vel effectus sequentis. Et propter hoc ponitur inter generales causas peccati. Sed imprudentia secundum propriam rationem importat vitium morale. Et ideo magis potest poni speciale peccatum.

**AD TERTIUM** dicendum quod quando corruptio diversarum circumstantiarum habet idem motivum, non diversificatur peccati species, sicut eiusdem speciei est peccatum ut aliquis accipiat non sua ubi non debet, et quando non debet. Sed si sint diversa motiva, tunc essent diversae species, puta si unus acciperet unde non deberet ut faceret iniuriam loco sacro, quod faceret speciem sacrilegii; alius quando non debet propter solum superfluum appetitum habendi, quod esset simplex avaritia. Et ideo defectus eorum quae requiruntur ad prudentiam non diversificant species nisi quatenus ordinantur ad diversos actus rationis, ut dictum est.

are the quasi-integral parts of prudence. Since however all these things are intended for the direction of the aforesaid three acts of reason, it follows that all the opposite defects are reducible to the four parts mentioned above. Thus incautiousness and incircumspection are included in *thoughtlessness*; lack of docility, memory, or reason is referable to *precipitation*; improvidence, lack of intelligence and of shrewdness, belong to *negligence* and *inconstancy*.

**REPLY OBJ. 1**: This argument considers generality by participation.

**REPLY OBJ. 2**: Since knowledge is further removed from morality than prudence is, according to their respective proper natures, it follows that ignorance has the nature of mortal sin, not of itself, but on account either of a preceding negligence, or of the consequent result, and for this reason it is reckoned one of the general causes of sin. On the other hand imprudence, by its very nature, denotes a moral vice; and for this reason it can be called a special sin.

**REPLY OBJ. 3**: When various circumstances are corrupted for the same motive, the species of sin is not multiplied: thus it is the same species of sin to take what is not one's own, where one ought not, and when one ought not. If, however, there be various motives, there are various species: for instance, if one man were to take another's property from where he ought not, so as to wrong a sacred place, this would constitute the species called sacrilege, while if another were to take another's property when he ought not, merely through the lust of possession, this would be a case of simple avarice. Hence the lack of those things which are requisite for prudence, does not constitute a diversity of species, except insofar as they are directed to different acts of reason, as stated above.

# Article 3

*Whether precipitation is a sin included in imprudence?*

**AD TERTIUM SIC PROCEDITUR**. Videtur quod praecipitatio non sit peccatum sub imprudentia contentum. Imprudentia enim opponitur virtuti prudentiae. Sed praecipitatio opponitur dono consilii, dicit enim Gregorius, in II Moral., quod donum consilii datur contra praecipitationem. Ergo praecipitatio non est peccatum sub imprudentia contentum.

**PRAETEREA**, praecipitatio videtur ad temeritatem pertinere. Temeritas autem praesumptionem importat, quae pertinet ad superbiam. Ergo praecipitatio non est vitium sub imprudentia contentum.

**PRAETEREA**, praecipitatio videtur importare quandam inordinatam festinationem. Sed in consiliando non solum contingit esse peccatum per hoc quod aliquis est festinus, sed etiam si sit nimis tardus, ita quod praetereat

**OBJECTION 1**: It would seem that precipitation is not a sin included in imprudence. Imprudence is opposed to the virtue of prudence; whereas precipitation is opposed to the gift of counsel, according to Gregory, who says (*Moral.* ii, 49) that the gift of counsel is given as a remedy to precipitation. Therefore precipitation is not a sin contained under imprudence.

**OBJ. 2**: Further, precipitation seemingly pertains to rashness. Now rashness implies presumption, which pertains to pride. Therefore precipitation is not a vice contained under imprudence.

**OBJ. 3**: Further, precipitation seems to denote inordinate haste. Now sin happens in counselling not only through being over hasty but also through being over slow, so that the opportunity for action passes by, and through

opportunitas operis; et etiam secundum inordinationes aliarum circumstantiarum, ut dicitur in VI Ethic. Ergo non magis praecipitatio debet poni peccatum sub imprudentia contentum quam tarditas, aut aliqua alia huiusmodi ad inordinationem consilii pertinentia.

**SED CONTRA** est quod dicitur Prov. IV, *via impiorum tenebrosa, nesciunt ubi corruant.* Tenebrae autem viae impietatis pertinent ad imprudentiam. Ergo corruere, sive praecipitari, ad imprudentiam pertinet.

**RESPONDEO** dicendum quod praecipitatio in actibus animae metaphorice dicitur secundum similitudinem a corporali motu acceptam. Dicitur autem praecipitari secundum corporalem motum quod a superiori in ima pervenit secundum impetum quendam proprii motus vel alicuius impellentis, non ordinate incedendo per gradus. Summum autem animae est ipsa ratio. Imum autem est operatio per corpus exercita. Gradus autem medii, per quos oportet ordinate descendere, sunt memoria praeteritorum, intelligentia praesentium, solertia in considerandis futuris eventibus, ratiocinatio conferens unum alteri, docilitas, per quam aliquis acquiescit sententiis maiorum, per quos quidem gradus aliquis ordinate descendit recte consiliando. Si quis autem feratur ad agendum per impetum voluntatis vel passionis, pertransitis huiusmodi gradibus, erit praecipitatio. Cum ergo inordinatio consilii ad imprudentiam pertineat, manifestum est quod vitium praecipitationis sub imprudentia continetur.

**AD PRIMUM** ergo dicendum quod consilii rectitudo pertinet ad donum consilii et ad virtutem prudentiae, licet diversimode, ut supra dictum est. Et ideo praecipitatio utrique contrariatur.

**AD SECUNDUM** dicendum quod illa dicuntur fieri temere quae ratione non reguntur. Quod quidem potest contingere dupliciter. Uno modo, ex impetu voluntatis vel passionis. Alio modo, ex contemptu regulae dirigentis, et hoc proprie importat temeritas. Unde videtur ex radice superbiae provenire, quae refugit subesse regulae alienae. Praecipitatio autem se habet ad utrumque. Unde temeritas sub praecipitatione continetur, quamvis praecipitatio magis respiciat primum.

**AD TERTIUM** dicendum quod in inquisitione consilii multa particularia sunt consideranda, et ideo philosophus dicit, in VI Ethic., *oportet consiliari tarde.* Unde praecipitatio directius opponitur rectitudini consilii quam tarditas superflua, quae habet quandam similitudinem recti consilii.

corruption of other circumstances, as stated in *Ethic.* vi, 9. Therefore there is no reason for reckoning precipitation as a sin contained under imprudence, rather than slowness, or something else of the kind pertaining to inordinate counsel.

**ON THE CONTRARY,** It is written (Prov 4:19): *The way of the wicked is darksome, they know not where they fall.* Now the darksome ways of ungodliness belong to imprudence. Therefore imprudence leads a man to fall or to be precipitate.

**I ANSWER THAT,** Precipitation is ascribed metaphorically to acts of the soul, by way of similitude to bodily movement. Now a thing is said to be precipitated as regards bodily movement, when it is brought down from above by the impulse either of its own movement or of another's, and not in orderly fashion by degrees. Now the summit of the soul is the reason, and the base is reached in the action performed by the body; while the steps that intervene by which one ought to descend in orderly fashion are memory of the past, intelligence of the present, shrewdness in considering the future outcome, reasoning which compares one thing with another, docility in accepting the opinions of others. He that takes counsel descends by these steps in due order, whereas if a man is rushed into action by the impulse of his will or of a passion, without taking these steps, it will be a case of precipitation. Since then inordinate counsel pertains to imprudence, it is evident that the vice of precipitation is contained under imprudence.

**REPLY OBJ. 1:** Rectitude of counsel belongs to the gift of counsel and to the virtue of prudence; albeit in different ways, as stated above (Q. 52, A. 2), and consequently precipitation is opposed to both.

**REPLY OBJ. 2:** Things are said to be done rashly when they are not directed by reason: and this may happen in two ways; first through the impulse of the will or of a passion, second through contempt of the directing rule; and this is what is meant by rashness properly speaking, wherefore it appears to proceed from that root of pride, which refuses to submit to another's ruling. But precipitation refers to both, so that rashness is contained under precipitation, although precipitation refers rather to the first.

**REPLY OBJ. 3:** Many things have to be considered in the research of reason; hence the Philosopher declares (*Ethic.* vi, 9) that *one should be slow in taking counsel.* Hence precipitation is more directly opposed to rectitude of counsel than over slowness is, for the latter bears a certain likeness to right counsel.

# Article 4

*Whether thoughtlessness is a special sin included in imprudence?*

AD QUARTUM SIC PROCEDITUR. Videtur quod inconsideratio non sit peccatum speciale sub imprudentia contentum. Lex enim divina ad nullum peccatum nos inducit, secundum illud Psalm., *lex domini immaculata*. Inducit autem ad non considerandum, secundum illud Matth. X, *nolite cogitare quomodo aut quid loquamini*. Ergo inconsideratio non est peccatum.

PRAETEREA, quicumque consiliatur oportet quod multa consideret. Sed per defectum consilii est praecipitatio; et per consequens ex defectu considerationis. Ergo praecipitatio sub inconsideratione continetur. Non ergo inconsideratio est speciale peccatum.

PRAETEREA, prudentia consistit in actibus rationis practicae, qui sunt consiliari, iudicare de consiliatis, et praecipere. Sed considerare praecedit omnes istos actus, quia pertinet etiam ad intellectum speculativum. Ergo inconsideratio non est speciale peccatum sub imprudentia contentum.

SED CONTRA est quod dicitur Prov. IV, *oculi tui videant recta, et palpebrae tuae praecedant gressus tuos*, quod pertinet ad prudentiam. Sed contrarium huius agitur per inconsiderationem. Ergo inconsideratio est speciale peccatum sub imprudentia contentum.

RESPONDEO dicendum quod consideratio importat actum intellectus veritatem rei intuentis. Sicut autem inquisitio pertinet ad rationem, ita iudicium pertinet ad intellectum, unde et in speculativis demonstrativa scientia dicitur iudicativa, inquantum per resolutionem in prima principia intelligibilia de veritate inquisitorum diiudicatur. Et ideo consideratio maxime pertinet ad iudicium. Unde et defectus recti iudicii ad vitium inconsiderationis pertinet, prout scilicet aliquis in recte iudicando deficit ex hoc quod contemnit vel negligit attendere ea ex quibus rectum iudicium procedit. Unde manifestum est quod inconsideratio est peccatum.

AD PRIMUM ergo dicendum quod dominus non prohibet considerare ea quae sunt agenda vel dicenda, quando homo habet opportunitatem. Sed dat fiduciam discipulis in verbis inductis ut, deficiente sibi opportunitate vel propter imperitiam vel quia subito praeoccupantur, in solo divino confidant consilio, quia *cum ignoramus quid agere debeamus, hoc solum habemus residui, ut oculos nostros dirigamus ad Deum*, sicut dicitur II Paral. XX. Alioquin, si homo praetermittat facere quod potest, solum divinum auxilium expectans, videtur tentare Deum.

AD SECUNDUM dicendum quod tota consideratio eorum quae in consilio attenduntur ordinatur ad recte iudicandum, et ideo consideratio in iudicio perficitur.

OBJECTION 1: It would seem that thoughtlessness is not a special sin included in imprudence. For the Divine law does not incite us to any sin, according to Ps. 18:8, *The law of the Lord is unspotted*; and yet it incites us to be thoughtless, according to Matt. 10:19, *Take no thought how or what to speak*. Therefore thoughtlessness is not a sin.

OBJ. 2: Further, whoever takes counsel must needs give thought to many things. Now precipitation is due to a defect of counsel and therefore to a defect of thought. Therefore precipitation is contained under thoughtlessness: and consequently thoughtlessness is not a special sin.

OBJ. 3: Further, prudence consists in acts of the practical reason, viz. counsel, judgment about what has been counselled, and command. Now thought precedes all these acts, since it belongs also to the speculative intellect. Therefore thoughtlessness is not a special sin contained under imprudence.

ON THE CONTRARY, It is written (Prov 4:25): *Let thy eyes look straight on, and let thine eye-lids go before thy steps*. Now this pertains to prudence, while the contrary pertains to thoughtlessness. Therefore thoughtlessness is a special sin contained under imprudence.

I ANSWER THAT, Thought signifies the act of the intellect in considering the truth about something. Now just as research belongs to the reason, so judgment belongs to the intellect. Wherefore in speculative matters a demonstrative science is said to exercise judgment, insofar as it judges the truth of the results of research by tracing those results back to the first indemonstrable principles. Hence thought pertains chiefly to judgment; and consequently the lack of right judgment belongs to the vice of thoughtlessness, in so far, to wit, as one fails to judge rightly through contempt or neglect of those things on which a right judgment depends. It is therefore evident that thoughtlessness is a sin.

REPLY OBJ. 1: Our Lord did not forbid us to take thought, when we have the opportunity, about what we ought to do or say, but, in the words quoted, He encourages His disciples, so that when they had no opportunity of taking thought, either through lack of knowledge or through a sudden call, they should trust in the guidance of God alone, because *as we know not what to do, we can only turn our eyes to God*, according to 2 Paral. 20:12: else if man, instead of doing what he can, were to be content with awaiting God's assistance, he would seem to tempt God.

REPLY OBJ. 2: All thought about those things of which counsel takes cognizance, is directed to the formation of a right judgment, wherefore this thought is perfected in judg-

Unde etiam inconsideratio maxime opponitur rectitudini iudicii.

**AD TERTIUM** dicendum quod inconsideratio hic accipitur secundum determinatam materiam, idest secundum agibilia humana, in quibus plura sunt attendenda ad recte iudicandum quam etiam in speculativis; quia operationes sunt in singularibus.

ment. Consequently thoughtlessness is above all opposed to the rectitude of judgment.

**REPLY OBJ. 3**: Thoughtlessness is to be taken here in relation to a determinate matter, namely, that of human action, wherein more things have to be thought about for the purpose of right judgment, than in speculative matters, because actions are about singulars.

# Article 5

*Whether inconstancy is a vice contained under imprudence?*

**AD QUINTUM SIC PROCEDITUR**. Videtur quod inconstantia non sit vitium sub imprudentia contentum. Inconstantia enim videtur in hoc consistere quod homo non persistat in aliquo difficili. Sed persistere in difficilibus pertinet ad fortitudinem. Ergo inconstantia magis opponitur fortitudini quam prudentiae.

**PRAETEREA**, Iac. III dicitur, *ubi zelus et contentio, ibi inconstantia et omne opus pravum*. Sed zelus ad invidiam pertinet. Ergo inconstantia non pertinet ad imprudentiam, sed magis ad invidiam.

**PRAETEREA**, ille videtur esse inconstans qui non perseverat in eo quod proposuerat. Quod quidem pertinet in delectationibus ad *incontinentem*, in tristitiis autem ad *mollem* sive *delicatum*, ut dicitur VII Ethic. Ergo inconstantia non pertinet ad imprudentiam.

**SED CONTRA** est quod ad prudentiam pertinet praeferre maius bonum minus bono. Ergo desistere a meliori pertinet ad imprudentiam. Sed hoc est inconstantia. Ergo inconstantia pertinet ad imprudentiam.

**RESPONDEO** dicendum quod inconstantia importat recessum quendam a bono proposito definito. Huiusmodi autem recessus principium quidem habet a vi appetitiva, non enim aliquis recedit a priori bono proposito nisi propter aliquid quod sibi inordinate placet. Sed iste recessus non consummatur nisi per defectum rationis, quae fallitur in hoc quod repudiat id quod recte acceptaverat, et quia, cum possit resistere impulsui passionis, si non resistat, hoc est ex debilitate ipsius, quae non tenet se firmiter in bono concepto. Et ideo inconstantia, quantum ad sui consummationem, pertinet ad defectum rationis. Sicut autem omnis rectitudo rationis practicae pertinet aliqualiter ad prudentiam, ita omnis defectus eiusdem pertinet ad imprudentiam. Et ideo inconstantia, secundum sui consummationem, ad imprudentiam pertinet. Et sicut praecipitatio est ex defectu circa actum consilii, et inconsideratio circa actum iudicii, ita inconstantia circa actum praecepti, ex hoc enim dicitur aliquis esse inconstans quod ratio deficit in praecipiendo ea quae sunt consiliata et iudicata.

**OBJECTION 1**: It would seem that inconstancy is not a vice contained under imprudence. For inconstancy consists seemingly in a lack of perseverance in matters of difficulty. But perseverance in difficult matters belongs to fortitude. Therefore inconstancy is opposed to fortitude rather than to prudence.

**OBJ. 2**: Further, it is written (Jas 3:16): *Where jealousy and contention are, there are inconstancy and every evil work*. But jealousy pertains to envy. Therefore inconstancy pertains not to imprudence but to envy.

**OBJ. 3**: Further, a man would seem to be inconstant who fails to persevere in what he has proposed to do. Now this is a mark of *incontinency* in pleasurable matters, and of *effeminacy* or *squeamishness* in unpleasant matters, according to *Ethic.* vii, 1. Therefore inconstancy does not pertain to imprudence.

**ON THE CONTRARY**, It belongs to prudence to prefer the greater good to the lesser. Therefore to forsake the greater good belongs to imprudence. Now this is inconstancy. Therefore inconstancy belongs to imprudence.

**I ANSWER THAT**, Inconstancy denotes withdrawal from a definite good purpose. Now the origin of this withdrawal is in the appetite, for a man does not withdraw from a previous good purpose, except on account of something being inordinately pleasing to him: nor is this withdrawal completed except through a defect of reason, which is deceived in rejecting what before it had rightly accepted. And since it can resist the impulse of the passions, if it fail to do this, it is due to its own weakness in not standing to the good purpose it has conceived; hence inconstancy, as to its completion, is due to a defect in the reason. Now just as all rectitude of the practical reason belongs in some degree to prudence, so all lack of that rectitude belongs to imprudence. Consequently inconstancy, as to its completion, belongs to imprudence. And just as precipitation is due to a defect in the act of counsel, and thoughtlessness to a defect in the act of judgment, so inconstancy arises from a defect in the act of command. For a man is stated to be inconstant because his reason fails in commanding what has been counselled and judged.

**AD PRIMUM** ergo dicendum quod bonum prudentiae participatur in omnibus virtutibus moralibus, et secundum hoc persistere in bono pertinet ad omnes virtutes morales. Praecipue tamen ad fortitudinem, quae patitur maiorem impulsum ad contrarium.

**AD SECUNDUM** dicendum quod invidia et ira, quae est contentionis principium, faciunt inconstantiam ex parte appetitivae virtutis, ex qua est principium inconstantiae, ut dictum est.

**AD TERTIUM** dicendum quod continentia et perseverantia non videntur esse in vi appetitiva, sed solum in ratione. Continens enim patitur quidem perversas concupiscentias, et perseverans graves tristitias, quod designat defectum appetitivae virtutis, sed ratio firmiter persistit, continentis quidem contra concupiscentias, perseverantis autem contra tristitias. Unde continentia et perseverantia videntur esse species constantiae ad rationem pertinentis, ad quam etiam pertinet inconstantia.

**REPLY OBJ. 1:** The good of prudence is shared by all the moral virtues, and accordingly perseverance in good belongs to all moral virtues, chiefly, however, to fortitude, which suffers a greater impulse to the contrary.

**REPLY OBJ. 2:** Envy and anger, which are the source of contention, cause inconstancy on the part of the appetite, to which power the origin of inconstancy is due, as stated above.

**REPLY OBJ. 3:** Continency and perseverance seem to be not in the appetitive power, but in the reason. For the continent man suffers evil concupiscences, and the persevering man suffers grievous sorrows (which points to a defect in the appetitive power); but reason stands firm, in the continent man, against concupiscence, and in the persevering man, against sorrow. Hence continency and perseverance seem to be species of constancy which pertains to reason; and to this power inconstancy pertains also.

# Article 6

*Whether the aforesaid vices arise from lust?*

**AD SEXTUM SIC PROCEDITUR.** Videtur quod praedicta vitia non oriantur ex luxuria. Inconstantia enim oritur ex invidia, ut dictum est. Sed invidia est vitium distinctum a luxuria. Ergo praedicta vitia non oriuntur ex luxuria.

**PRAETEREA,** Iac. I dicitur, *vir duplex animo inconstans est in omnibus viis suis.* Sed duplicitas non videtur ad luxuriam pertinere, sed magis ad dolositatem, quae est filia avaritiae, secundum Gregorium, XXXI Moral. Ergo praedicta vitia non oriuntur ex luxuria.

**PRAETEREA,** praedicta vitia pertinent ad defectum rationis. Sed vitia spiritualia propinquiora sunt rationi quam vitia carnalia. Ergo praedicta vitia magis oriuntur ex vitiis spiritualibus quam ex vitiis carnalibus.

**SED CONTRA** est quod Gregorius, XXXI Moral., ponit praedicta vitia ex luxuria oriri.

**RESPONDEO** dicendum quod, sicut philosophus dicit, in VI Ethic., *delectatio maxime corrumpit existimationem prudentiae,* et praecipue delectatio quae est in venereis, quae totam animam absorbet et trahit ad sensibilem delectationem; perfectio autem prudentiae, et cuiuslibet intellectualis virtutis, consistit in abstractione a sensibilibus. Unde cum praedicta vitia pertineant ad defectum prudentiae et rationis practicae, sicut habitum est, sequitur quod ex luxuria maxime oriantur.

**AD PRIMUM** ergo dicendum quod invidia et ira causant inconstantiam pertrahendo rationem ad aliud, sed luxuria causat inconstantiam totaliter extinguendo iu-

**OBJECTION 1:** It would seem that the aforesaid vices do not arise from lust. For inconstancy arises from envy, as stated above (A. 5, ad 2). But envy is a distinct vice from lust.

**OBJ. 2:** Further, it is written (Jas 1:8): *A double-minded man is inconstant in all his ways.* Now duplicity does not seem to pertain to lust, but rather to deceitfulness, which is a daughter of covetousness, according to Gregory (*Moral.* xxxi, 45). Therefore the aforesaid vices do not arise from lust.

**OBJ. 3:** Further, the aforesaid vices are connected with some defect of reason. Now spiritual vices are more akin to the reason than carnal vices. Therefore the aforesaid vices arise from spiritual vices rather than from carnal vices.

**ON THE CONTRARY,** Gregory declares (*Moral.* xxxi, 45) that the aforesaid vices arise from lust.

**I ANSWER THAT,** As the Philosopher states (*Ethic.* vi, 5) *pleasure above all corrupts the estimate of prudence,* and chiefly sexual pleasure which absorbs the mind, and draws it to sensible delight. Now the perfection of prudence and of every intellectual virtue consists in abstraction from sensible objects. Wherefore, since the aforesaid vices involve a defect of prudence and of the practical reason, as stated above (AA. 2, 5), it follows that they arise chiefly from lust.

**REPLY OBJ. 1:** Envy and anger cause inconstancy by drawing away the reason to something else; whereas lust causes inconstancy by destroying the judgment of reason

dicium rationis. Unde philosophus dicit, in VII Ethic., quod *incontinens irae audit quidem rationem, sed non perfecte, incontinens autem concupiscentiae totaliter eam non audit.*

**AD SECUNDUM** dicendum quod etiam duplicitas animi est quoddam consequens ad luxuriam, sicut et inconstantia, prout duplicitas animi importat vertibilitatem animi ad diversa. Unde et Terentius dicit, in eunucho, quod *in amore est bellum, et rursus pax et indutiae.*

**AD TERTIUM** dicendum quod vitia carnalia intantum magis extinguunt iudicium rationis inquantum longius abducunt a ratione.

entirely. Hence the Philosopher says (*Ethic.* vii, 6) that *the man who is incontinent through anger listens to reason, yet not perfectly, whereas he who is incontinent through lust does not listen to it at all.*

**REPLY OBJ. 2:** Duplicity also is something resulting from lust, just as inconstancy is, if by duplicity we understand fluctuation of the mind from one thing to another. Hence Terence says (*Eunuch.* act 1, sc. 1) that *love leads to war, and likewise to peace and truce.*

**REPLY OBJ. 3:** Carnal vices destroy the judgment of reason so much the more as they lead us away from reason.

# QUESTION 54

Deinde considerandum est de negligentia. Et circa hoc quaeruntur tria.

Primo, utrum negligentia sit peccatum speciale.

Secundo, cui virtuti opponatur.

Tertio, utrum negligentia sit peccatum mortale.

We must now consider negligence, under which head there are three points of inquiry:

(1) Whether negligence is a special sin?

(2) To which virtue is it opposed?

(3) Whether negligence is a mortal sin?

## Article 1

*Whether negligence is a special sin?*

**AD PRIMUM SIC PROCEDITUR.** Videtur quod negligentia non sit peccatum speciale. Negligentia enim diligentiae opponitur. Sed diligentia requiritur in qualibet virtute, sicut et eligentia. Ergo negligentia non est peccatum speciale.

**PRAETEREA,** illud quod invenitur in quolibet peccato non est speciale peccatum. Sed negligentia invenitur in quolibet peccato, quia omnis qui peccat negligit ea per quae a peccato retraheretur; et qui in peccato perseverat negligit conteri de peccato. Ergo negligentia non est speciale peccatum.

**PRAETEREA,** omne peccatum speciale habet materiam determinatam. Sed negligentia non videtur habere determinatam materiam, neque enim est circa mala aut indifferentia, quia ea praetermittere nulli ad negligentiam deputatur; similiter etiam non est circa bona, quia si negligenter aguntur, iam non sunt bona. Ergo videtur quod negligentia non sit vitium speciale.

**SED CONTRA** est quod peccata quae committuntur ex negligentia distinguuntur contra peccata quae committuntur ex contemptu.

**RESPONDEO** dicendum quod negligentia importat defectum debitae sollicitudinis. Omnis autem defectus debiti actus habet rationem peccati. Unde manifestum est quod negligentia habet rationem peccati, et eo modo quo sollicitudo est specialis virtutis actus, necesse est quod negligentia sit speciale peccatum. Sunt enim aliqua peccata specialia quia sunt circa aliquam materiam specialem, sicut luxuria est circa venerea, quaedam autem sunt vitia specialia propter specialitatem actus se extendentis ad omnem materiam. Et huiusmodi sunt omnia vitia quae sunt circa actum rationis, nam quilibet actus

**OBJECTION 1:** It would seem that negligence is not a special sin. For negligence is opposed to diligence. But diligence is required in every virtue. Therefore negligence is not a special sin.

**OBJ. 2:** Further, that which is common to every sin is not a special sin. Now negligence is common to every sin, because he who sins neglects that which withdraws him from sin, and he who perseveres in sin neglects to be contrite for his sin. Therefore negligence is not a special sin.

**OBJ. 3:** Further, every special sin has a determinate matter. But negligence seems to have no determinate matter: since it is neither about evil or indifferent things (for no man is accused of negligence if he omit them), nor about good things, for if these be done negligently, they are no longer good. Therefore it seems that negligence is not a special vice.

**ON THE CONTRARY,** Sins committed through negligence are distinguished from those which are committed through contempt.

**I ANSWER THAT,** Negligence denotes lack of due solicitude. Now every lack of a due act is sinful: wherefore it is evident that negligence is a sin, and that it must needs have the character of a special sin according as solicitude is the act of a special virtue. For certain sins are special through being about a special matter, as lust is about sexual matters, while some vices are special on account of their having a special kind of act which extends to all kinds of matter, and such are all vices affecting an act of reason, since every act of reason extends to any kind of moral matter. Since then solicitude is a special act of reason, as stated above

507

rationis se extendit ad quamlibet materiam moralem. Et ideo, cum sollicitudo sit quidam specialis actus rationis, ut supra habitum est, consequens est quod negligentia, quae importat defectum sollicitudinis, sit speciale peccatum.

AD PRIMUM ergo dicendum quod diligentia videtur esse idem sollicitudini, quia in his quae diligimus maiorem sollicitudinem adhibemus. Unde diligentia, sicut et sollicitudo, requiritur ad quamlibet virtutem, inquantum in qualibet virtute requiruntur debiti actus rationis.

AD SECUNDUM dicendum quod in quolibet peccato necesse est esse defectum circa aliquem actum rationis, puta defectum consilii et aliorum huiusmodi. Unde sicut praecipitatio est speciale peccatum propter specialem actum rationis qui praetermittitur, scilicet consilium, quamvis possit inveniri in quolibet genere peccatorum; ita negligentia est speciale peccatum propter defectum specialis actus rationis qui est sollicitudo, quamvis inveniatur aliqualiter in omnibus peccatis.

AD TERTIUM dicendum quod materia negligentiae proprie sunt bona quae quis agere debet, non quod ipsa sunt bona cum negligenter aguntur; sed quia per negligentiam accidit defectus bonitatis in eis, sive praetermittatur totaliter actus debitus propter defectum sollicitudinis, sive etiam aliqua debita circumstantia actus.

(Q. 47, A. 9), it follows that negligence, which denotes lack of solicitude, is a special sin.

REPLY OBJ. 1: Diligence seems to be the same as solicitude, because the more we love (*diligimus*) a thing the more solicitous are we about it. Hence diligence, no less than solicitude, is required for every virtue, insofar as due acts of reason are requisite for every virtue.

REPLY OBJ. 2: In every sin there must needs be a defect affecting an act of reason, for instance a defect in counsel or the like. Hence just as precipitation is a special sin on account of a special act of reason which is omitted, namely counsel, although it may be found in any kind of sin; so negligence is a special sin on account of the lack of a special act of reason, namely solicitude, although it is found more or less in all sins.

REPLY OBJ. 3: Properly speaking the matter of negligence is a good that one ought to do, not that it is a good when it is done negligently, but because on account of negligence it incurs a lack of goodness, whether a due act be entirely omitted through lack of solicitude, or some due circumstance be omitted.

# Article 2

*Whether negligence is opposed to prudence?*

AD SECUNDUM SIC PROCEDITUR. Videtur quod negligentia non opponatur prudentiae. Negligentia enim videtur esse idem quod pigritia vel torpor, qui pertinet ad acediam, ut patet per Gregorium, XXXI Moral. Acedia autem non opponitur prudentiae, sed magis caritati, ut supra dictum est. Ergo negligentia non opponitur prudentiae.

PRAETEREA, ad negligentiam videtur pertinere omne peccatum omissionis. Sed peccatum omissionis non opponitur prudentiae, sed magis virtutibus moralibus executivis. Ergo negligentia non opponitur prudentiae.

PRAETEREA, imprudentia est circa aliquem actum rationis. Sed negligentia non importat defectum neque circa consilium, in quo deficit praecipitatio; neque circa iudicium, in quo deficit inconsideratio; neque circa praeceptum, in quo deficit inconstantia. Ergo negligentia non pertinet ad imprudentiam.

PRAETEREA, dicitur Eccle. VII, *qui timet Deum nihil negligit.* Sed unumquodque peccatum praecipue excluditur per virtutem oppositam. Ergo negligentia magis opponitur timori quam prudentiae.

OBJECTION 1: It would seem that negligence is not opposed to prudence. For negligence seems to be the same as idleness or laziness, which belongs to sloth, according to Gregory (*Moral.* xxxi, 45). Now sloth is not opposed to prudence, but to charity, as stated above (Q. 35, A. 3). Therefore negligence is not opposed to prudence.

OBJ. 2: Further, every sin of omission seems to be due to negligence. But sins of omission are not opposed to prudence, but to the executive moral virtues. Therefore negligence is not opposed to prudence.

OBJ. 3: Further, imprudence relates to some act of reason. But negligence does not imply a defect of counsel, for that is precipitation, nor a defect of judgment, since that is thoughtlessness, nor a defect of command, because that is inconstancy. Therefore negligence does not pertain to imprudence.

OBJ. 4: Further, it is written (Eccl 7:19): *He that feareth God, neglecteth nothing.* But every sin is excluded by the opposite virtue. Therefore negligence is opposed to fear rather than to prudence.

**SED CONTRA** est quod dicitur Eccli. XX, *lascivus et imprudens non observant tempus*. Sed hoc pertinet ad negligentiam. Ergo negligentia opponitur prudentiae.

**RESPONDEO** dicendum quod negligentia directe opponitur sollicitudini. Sollicitudo autem ad rationem pertinet, et rectitudo sollicitudinis ad prudentiam. Unde, per oppositum, negligentia ad imprudentiam pertinet. Et hoc etiam ex ipso nomine apparet. Quia sicut Isidorus dicit, in libro Etymol., *negligens dicitur quasi nec eligens*. Electio autem recta eorum quae sunt ad finem ad prudentiam pertinet. Unde negligentia pertinet ad imprudentiam.

**AD PRIMUM** ergo dicendum quod negligentia consistit in defectu interioris actus, ad quem pertinet etiam electio. Pigritia autem et torpor magis pertinent ad executionem, ita tamen quod pigritia importat tarditatem ad exequendum; torpor remissionem quandam importat in ipsa executione. Et ideo convenienter torpor ex acedia nascitur, quia acedia est *tristitia aggravans*, idest impediens animum ab operando.

**AD SECUNDUM** dicendum quod omissio pertinet ad exteriorem actum, est enim omissio quando praetermittitur aliquis actus debitus. Et ideo opponitur iustitiae. Et est effectus negligentiae, sicut etiam executio iusti operis est effectus rationis rectae.

**AD TERTIUM** dicendum quod negligentia est circa actum praecipiendi ad quem etiam pertinet sollicitudo. Aliter tamen circa hunc actum deficit negligens, et aliter inconstans. Inconstans enim deficit in praecipiendo quasi ab aliquo impeditus, negligens autem per defectum promptae voluntatis.

**AD QUARTUM** dicendum quod timor Dei operatur ad vitationem cuiuslibet peccati, quia ut dicitur Prov. XV, *per timorem domini declinat omnis a malo*. Et ideo timor facit negligentiam vitare. Non tamen ita quod directe negligentia timori opponatur, sed inquantum timor excitat hominem ad actus rationis. Unde etiam supra habitum est, cum de passionibus ageretur, quod timor facit consiliativos.

**ON THE CONTRARY**, It is written (Sir 20:7): *A babbler and a fool (imprudens) will regard no time*. Now this is due to negligence. Therefore negligence is opposed to prudence.

**I ANSWER THAT**, Negligence is directly opposed to solicitude. Now solicitude pertains to the reason, and rectitude of solicitude to prudence. Hence, on the other hand, negligence pertains to imprudence. This appears from its very name, because, as Isidore observes (*Etym.* x) *a negligent man is one who fails to choose (nec eligens)*: and the right choice of the means belongs to prudence. Therefore negligence pertains to imprudence.

**REPLY OBJ. 1**: Negligence is a defect in the internal act, to which choice also belongs: whereas idleness and laziness denote slowness of execution, yet so that idleness denotes slowness in setting about the execution, while laziness denotes remissness in the execution itself. Hence it is becoming that laziness should arise from sloth, which is *an oppressive sorrow*, i.e., hindering, the mind from action.

**REPLY OBJ. 2**: Omission regards the external act, for it consists in failing to perform an act which is due. Hence it is opposed to justice, and is an effect of negligence, even as the execution of a just deed is the effect of right reason.

**REPLY OBJ. 3**: Negligence regards the act of command, which solicitude also regards. Yet the negligent man fails in regard to this act otherwise than the inconstant man: for the inconstant man fails in commanding, being hindered as it were, by something, whereas the negligent man fails through lack of a prompt will.

**REPLY OBJ. 4**: The fear of God helps us to avoid all sins, because according to Prov. 15:27, *by the fear of the Lord everyone declineth from evil*. Hence fear makes us avoid negligence, yet not as though negligence were directly opposed to fear, but because fear incites man to acts of reason. Wherefore also it has been stated above (I-II, Q. 44, A. 2) when we were treating of the passions, that fear makes us take counsel.

# Article 3

*Whether negligence can be a mortal sin?*

**AD TERTIUM SIC PROCEDITUR.** Videtur quod negligentia non possit esse peccatum mortale. Quia super illud Iob IX, *verebar opera mea* etc., dicit Glossa Gregorii quod illam, scilicet negligentiam, *minor amor Dei exaggerat*. Sed ubicumque est peccatum mortale, totaliter tollitur amor Dei. Ergo negligentia non est peccatum mortale.

**PRAETEREA**, super illud Eccli. VII, *de negligentia purga te cum paucis*, dicit Glossa, *quamvis oblatio parva*

**OBJECTION 1**: It would seem that negligence cannot be a mortal sin. For a gloss of Gregory on Job 9:28, *I feared all my works*, etc. says that *too little love of God aggravates the former*, viz. negligence. But wherever there is mortal sin, the love of God is done away with altogether. Therefore negligence is not a mortal sin.

**OBJ. 2**: Further, a gloss on Ecclus. 7:34, *For thy negligences purify thyself with a few*, says: *Though the offering*

*sit, multorum delictorum purgat negligentias.* Sed hoc non esset si negligentia esset peccatum mortale. Ergo negligentia non est peccatum mortale.

PRAETEREA, in lege fuerunt statuta sacrificia pro peccatis mortalibus, sicut patet in Levitico. Sed nullum fuit statutum sacrificium pro negligentia. Ergo negligentia non est peccatum mortale.

SED CONTRA est quod habetur Prov. XIX, *qui negligit vitam suam mortificabitur.*

RESPONDEO dicendum quod, sicut supra dictum est, negligentia provenit ex quadam remissione voluntatis, per quam contingit quod ratio non sollicitatur ut praecipiat ea quae debet vel eo modo quo debet. Potest ergo dupliciter contingere quod negligentia sit peccatum mortale. Uno modo, ex parte eius quod praetermittitur per negligentiam. Quod quidem si sit de necessitate salutis, sive sit actus sive circumstantia, erit peccatum mortale. Alio modo, ex parte causae. Si enim voluntas intantum sit remissa circa ea quae sunt Dei ut totaliter a Dei caritate deficiat, talis negligentia est peccatum mortale. Et hoc praecipue contingit quando negligentia sequitur ex contemptu.

Alioquin, si negligentia consistat in praetermissione alicuius actus vel circumstantiae quae non sit de necessitate salutis; nec hoc fiat ex contemptu, sed ex aliquo defectu fervoris, qui impeditur interdum per aliquod veniale peccatum, tunc negligentia non est peccatum mortale, sed veniale.

AD PRIMUM ergo dicendum quod minor amor Dei potest intelligi dupliciter. Uno modo, per defectum fervoris caritatis, et sic causatur negligentia quae est peccatum veniale. Alio modo, per defectum ipsius caritatis, sicut dicitur minor amor Dei quando aliquis diligit Deum solum amore naturali. Et tunc causatur negligentia quae est peccatum mortale.

AD SECUNDUM dicendum quod *parva oblatio cum humili mente et pura dilectione facta,* ut ibi dicitur, non solum purgat peccata venialia, sed etiam mortalia.

AD TERTIUM dicendum quod quando negligentia consistit in praetermissione eorum quae sunt de necessitate salutis, tunc trahitur ad aliud genus peccati magis manifestum. Peccata enim quae consistunt in interioribus actibus sunt magis occulta. Et ideo pro eis certa sacrificia non iniungebantur in lege, quia sacrificiorum oblatio erat quaedam publica protestatio peccati, quae non est facienda de peccato occulto.

be small it cleanses the negligences of many sins. Now this would not be, if negligence were a mortal sin. Therefore negligence is not a mortal sin.

OBJ. 3: Further, under the law certain sacrifices were prescribed for mortal sins, as appears from the book of Leviticus. Yet no sacrifice was prescribed for negligence. Therefore negligence is not a mortal sin.

ON THE CONTRARY, It is written (Prov 19:16): *He that neglecteth his own life shall die.*

I ANSWER THAT, As stated above (A. 2, ad 3), negligence arises out of a certain remissness of the will, the result being a lack of solicitude on the part of the reason in commanding what it should command, or as it should command. Accordingly negligence may happen to be a mortal sin in two ways. First on the part of that which is omitted through negligence. If this be either an act or a circumstance necessary for salvation, it will be a mortal sin. Second on the part of the cause: for if the will be so remiss about Divine things, as to fall away altogether from the charity of God, such negligence is a mortal sin, and this is the case chiefly when negligence is due to contempt.

But if negligence consists in the omission of an act or circumstance that is not necessary for salvation, it is not a mortal but a venial sin, provided the negligence arise, not from contempt, but from some lack of fervor, to which venial sin is an occasional obstacle.

REPLY OBJ. 1: Man may be said to love God less in two ways. First through lack of the fervor of charity, and this causes the negligence that is a venial sin: second through lack of charity itself, in which sense we say that a man loves God less when he loves Him with a merely natural love; and this causes the negligence that is a mortal sin.

REPLY OBJ. 2: According to the same authority (gloss), a *small offering made with a humble mind and out of pure love,* cleanses man not only from venial but also from mortal sin.

REPLY OBJ. 3: When negligence consists in the omission of that which is necessary for salvation, it is drawn to the other more manifest genus of sin. Because those sins that consist of inward actions, are more hidden, wherefore no special sacrifices were prescribed for them in the Law, since the offering of sacrifices was a kind of public confession of sin, whereas hidden sins should not be confessed in public.

# QUESTION 55

## VICES OPPOSED TO PRUDENCE BY WAY OF RESEMBLANCE

Deinde considerandum est de vitiis oppositis prudentiae quae habent similitudinem cum ipsa. Et circa hoc quaeruntur octo.

Primo, utrum prudentia carnis sit peccatum.

Secundo, utrum sit peccatum mortale.

Tertio, utrum astutia sit peccatum speciale.

Quarto, de dolo.

Quinto, de fraude.

Sexto, de sollicitudine temporalium rerum.

Septimo, de sollicitudine futurorum.

Octavo, de origine horum vitiorum.

We must now consider those vices opposed to prudence, which have a resemblance thereto. Under this head there are eight points of inquiry:

(1) Whether prudence of the flesh is a sin?

(2) Whether it is a mortal sin?

(3) Whether craftiness is a special sin?

(4) Of guile;

(5) Of fraud;

(6) Of solicitude about temporal things;

(7) Of solicitude about the future;

(8) Of the origin of these vices.

# Article 1

*Whether prudence of the flesh is a sin?*

**AD PRIMUM SIC PROCEDITUR.** Videtur quod prudentia carnis non sit peccatum. Prudentia enim est nobilior virtus quam aliae virtutes morales, utpote omnium regitiva. Sed nulla iustitia vel temperantia est peccatum. Ergo etiam neque aliqua prudentia est peccatum.

**PRAETEREA,** prudenter operari ad finem qui licite amatur non est peccatum. Sed caro licite amatur, *nemo enim unquam carnem suam odio habuit,* ut habetur ad Ephes. V. Ergo prudentia carnis non est peccatum.

**PRAETEREA,** sicut homo tentatur a carne, ita etiam tentatur a mundo, et etiam a Diabolo. Sed non ponitur inter peccata aliqua prudentia mundi, vel etiam Diaboli. Ergo neque debet poni inter peccata aliqua prudentia carnis.

**SED CONTRA,** nullus est inimicus Deo nisi propter iniquitatem, secundum illud Sap. XIV, *simul odio sunt Deo impius et impietas eius.* Sed sicut dicitur ad Rom. VIII, *prudentia carnis inimica est Deo.* Ergo prudentia carnis est peccatum.

**RESPONDEO** dicendum quod, sicut supra dictum est, prudentia est circa ea quae sunt ad finem totius vitae. Et ideo prudentia carnis proprie dicitur secundum quod aliquis bona carnis habet ut ultimum finem suae vitae. Manifestum est autem quod hoc est peccatum, per hoc enim homo deordinatur circa ultimum finem, qui non consistit in bonis corporis, sicut supra habitum est. Et ideo prudentia carnis est peccatum.

**OBJECTION 1:** It would seem that prudence of the flesh is not a sin. For prudence is more excellent than the other moral virtues, since it governs them all. But no justice or temperance is sinful. Neither therefore is any prudence a sin.

**OBJ. 2:** Further, it is not a sin to act prudently for an end which it is lawful to love. But it is lawful to love the flesh, *for no man ever hated his own flesh (Eph 5:29).* Therefore prudence of the flesh is not a sin.

**OBJ. 3:** Further, just as man is tempted by the flesh, so too is he tempted by the world and the devil. But no prudence of the world, or of the devil is accounted a sin. Therefore neither should any prudence of the flesh be accounted among sins.

**ON THE CONTRARY,** No man is an enemy to God save for wickedness according to Wis. 14:9, *To God the wicked and his wickedness are hateful alike.* Now it is written (Rom 8:7): *The prudence of the flesh is an enemy to God.* Therefore prudence of the flesh is a sin.

**I ANSWER THAT,** As stated above (Q. 47, A. 13), prudence regards things which are directed to the end of life as a whole. Hence prudence of the flesh signifies properly the prudence of a man who looks upon carnal goods as the last end of his life. Now it is evident that this is a sin, because it involves a disorder in man with respect to his last end, which does not consist in the goods of the body, as stated above (I-II, Q. 2, A. 5). Therefore prudence of the flesh is a sin.

**AD PRIMUM** ergo dicendum quod iustitia et temperantia in sui ratione important id unde virtus laudatur, scilicet aequalitatem et concupiscentiarum refrenationem, et ideo nunquam accipiuntur in malo. Sed nomen prudentiae sumitur a providendo, sicut supra dictum est, quod potest etiam ad mala extendi. Et ideo, licet prudentia simpliciter dicta in bono accipiatur, aliquo tamen addito potest accipi in malo. Et secundum hoc dicitur prudentia carnis esse peccatum.

**AD SECUNDUM** dicendum quod caro est propter animam sicut materia propter formam et instrumentum propter principale agens. Et ideo sic licite diligitur caro ut ordinetur ad bonum animae sicut ad finem. Si autem in ipso bono carnis constituatur ultimus finis, erit inordinata et illicita dilectio. Et hoc modo ad amorem carnis ordinatur prudentia carnis.

**AD TERTIUM** dicendum quod Diabolus nos tentat non per modum appetibilis, sed per modum suggerentis. Et ideo, cum prudentia importet ordinem ad aliquem finem appetibilem, non ita dicitur *prudentia Diaboli* sicut prudentia respectu alicuius mali finis, sub cuius ratione tentat nos mundus et caro, inquantum scilicet proponuntur nobis ad appetendum bona mundi vel carnis. Et ideo dicitur *prudentia carnis*, et etiam *prudentia mundi*, secundum illud Luc. XVI, *filii huius saeculi prudentiores sunt in generatione sua* et cetera. Apostolus autem totum comprehendit sub prudentia carnis, quia etiam exteriores res mundi appetimus propter carnem.

Potest tamen dici quod quia prudentia quodammodo dicitur *sapientia*, ut supra dictum est, ideo secundum tres tentationes potest intelligi triplex prudentia. Unde dicitur Iac. III sapientia esse *terrena, animalis, diabolica*, ut supra expositum est cum de sapientia ageretur.

**REPLY OBJ. 1**: Justice and temperance include in their very nature that which ranks them among the virtues, viz. equality and the curbing of concupiscence; hence they are never taken in a bad sense. On the other hand prudence is so called from foreseeing (providendo), as stated above (Q. 47, A. 1; Q. 49, A. 6), which can extend to evil things also. Therefore, although prudence is taken simply in a good sense, yet, if something be added, it may be taken in a bad sense: and it is thus that prudence of the flesh is said to be a sin.

**REPLY OBJ. 2**: The flesh is on account of the soul, as matter is on account of the form, and the instrument on account of the principal agent. Hence the flesh is loved lawfully, if it be directed to the good of the soul as its end. If, however, a man place his last end in a good of the flesh, his love will be inordinate and unlawful, and it is thus that the prudence of the flesh is directed to the love of the flesh.

**REPLY OBJ. 3**: The devil tempts us, not through the good of the appetible object, but by way of suggestion. Wherefore, since prudence implies direction to some appetible end, we do not speak of *prudence of the devil*, as of a prudence directed to some evil end, which is the aspect under which the world and the flesh tempt us, insofar as worldly or carnal goods are proposed to our appetite. Hence we speak of *carnal* and again of *worldly* prudence, according to Luke 16:8, *The children of this world are more prudent in their generation*, etc. The Apostle includes all in the *prudence of the flesh*, because we covet the external things of the world on account of the flesh.

We may also reply that since prudence is in a certain sense called *wisdom*, as stated above (Q. 47, A. 2, ad 1), we may distinguish a threefold prudence corresponding to the three kinds of temptation. Hence it is written (Jas 3:15) that there is a wisdom which is *earthly, sensual and devilish*, as explained above (Q. 45, A. 1, ad 1), when we were treating of wisdom.

# Article 2

*Whether prudence of the flesh is a mortal sin?*

**AD SECUNDUM SIC PROCEDITUR**. Videtur quod prudentia carnis sit peccatum mortale. Rebellare enim divinae legi est peccatum mortale quia per hoc dominus contemnitur. Sed *prudentia carnis non est subiecta legi Dei*, ut habetur Rom. VIII. Ergo prudentia carnis est peccatum mortale.

**PRAETEREA**, omne peccatum in spiritum sanctum est peccatum mortale. Sed prudentia carnis videtur esse peccatum in spiritum sanctum, *non enim potest esse subiecta legi Dei*, ut dicitur Rom. VIII; et ita videtur esse

**OBJECTION 1**: It would seem that prudence of the flesh is a mortal sin. For it is a mortal sin to rebel against the Divine law, since this implies contempt of God. Now *the prudence of the flesh . . . is not subject to the law of God* (Rom 8:7). Therefore prudence of the flesh is a mortal sin.

**OBJ. 2**: Further, every sin against the Holy Spirit is a mortal sin. Now prudence of the flesh seems to be a sin against the Holy Spirit, for *it cannot be subject to the law of God* (Rom 8:7), and so it seems to be an unpardonable sin,

peccatum irremissibile, quod est proprium peccati in spiritum sanctum. Ergo prudentia carnis est peccatum mortale.

PRAETEREA, maximo bono opponitur maximum malum; ut patet in VIII Ethic. Sed prudentia carnis opponitur prudentiae quae est praecipua inter virtutes morales. Ergo prudentia carnis est praecipuum inter peccata moralia. Et ita est peccatum mortale.

SED CONTRA, illud quod diminuit peccatum non importat de se rationem peccati mortalis. Sed caute prosequi ea quae pertinent ad curam carnis, quod videtur ad prudentiam carnis pertinere, diminuit peccatum. Ergo prudentia carnis de sui ratione non importat peccatum mortale.

RESPONDEO dicendum quod, sicut supra dictum est, prudens dicitur aliquis dupliciter, uno modo, simpliciter, scilicet in ordine ad finem totius vitae; alio modo, secundum quid, scilicet in ordine ad finem aliquem particularem, puta sicut dicitur aliquis prudens in negotiatione vel in aliquo huiusmodi. Si ergo prudentia carnis accipiatur secundum absolutam prudentiae rationem, ita scilicet quod in cura carnis constituatur ultimus finis totius vitae, sic est peccatum mortale, quia per hoc homo avertitur a Deo, cum impossibile sit esse plures fines ultimos, ut supra habitum est.

Si vero prudentia carnis accipiatur secundum rationem particularis prudentiae, sic prudentia carnis est peccatum veniale. Contingit enim quandoque quod aliquis inordinate afficitur ad aliquod delectabile carnis absque hoc quod avertatur a Deo per peccatum mortale, unde non constituit finem totius vitae in delectatione carnis. Et sic adhibere studium ad hanc delectationem consequendam est peccatum veniale, quod pertinet ad prudentiam carnis. Si vero aliquis actu curam carnis referat in finem honestum, puta cum aliquis studet comestioni propter corporis sustentationem, non vocatur prudentia carnis, quia sic utitur homo cura carnis ut ad finem.

AD PRIMUM ergo dicendum quod apostolus loquitur de prudentia carnis secundum quod finis totius vitae humanae constituitur in bonis carnis. Et sic est peccatum mortale.

AD SECUNDUM dicendum quod prudentia carnis non importat peccatum in spiritum sanctum. Quod enim dicitur quod *non potest esse subiecta legi Dei*, non sic est intelligendum quasi ille qui habet prudentiam carnis non possit converti et subiici legi Dei, sed quia ipsa prudentia carnis legi Dei non potest esse subiecta, sicut nec iniustitia potest esse iusta, nec calor potest esse frigidus, quamvis calidum posset esse frigidum.

AD TERTIUM dicendum quod omne peccatum opponitur prudentiae, sicut et prudentia participatur in omni

which is proper to the sin against the Holy Spirit. Therefore prudence of the flesh is a mortal sin.

OBJ. 3: Further, the greatest evil is opposed to the greatest good, as stated in *Ethic.* viii, 10. Now prudence of the flesh is opposed to that prudence which is the chief of the moral virtues. Therefore prudence of the flesh is chief among mortal sins, so that it is itself a mortal sin.

ON THE CONTRARY, That which diminishes a sin has not of itself the nature of a mortal sin. Now the thoughtful quest of things pertaining to the care of the flesh, which seems to pertain to carnal prudence, diminishes sin. Therefore prudence of the flesh has not of itself the nature of a mortal sin.

I ANSWER THAT, As stated above (Q. 47, A. 2, ad 1; A. 13), a man is said to be prudent in two ways. First, simply, i.e., in relation to the end of life as a whole. Second, relatively, i.e., in relation to some particular end; thus a man is said to be prudent in business or something else of the kind. Accordingly if prudence of the flesh be taken as corresponding to prudence in its absolute signification, so that a man place the last end of his whole life in the care of the flesh, it is a mortal sin, because he turns away from God by so doing, since he cannot have several last ends, as stated above (I-II, Q. 1, A. 5).

If, on the other hand, prudence of the flesh be taken as corresponding to particular prudence, it is a venial sin. For it happens sometimes that a man has an inordinate affection for some pleasure of the flesh, without turning away from God by a mortal sin; in which case he does not place the end of his whole life in carnal pleasure. To apply oneself to obtain this pleasure is a venial sin and pertains to prudence of the flesh. But if a man actually refers the care of the flesh to a good end, as when one is careful about one's food in order to sustain one's body, this is no longer prudence of the flesh, because then one uses the care of the flesh as a means to an end.

REPLY OBJ. 1: The Apostle is speaking of that carnal prudence whereby a man places the end of his whole life in the goods of the flesh, and this is a mortal sin.

REPLY OBJ. 2: Prudence of the flesh does not imply a sin against the Holy Spirit. For when it is stated that *it cannot be subject to the law of God*, this does not mean that he who has prudence of the flesh, cannot be converted and submit to the law of God, but that carnal prudence itself cannot be subject to God's law, even as neither can injustice be just, nor heat cold, although that which is hot may become cold.

REPLY OBJ. 3: Every sin is opposed to prudence, just as prudence is shared by every virtue. But it does not follow

virtute. Sed ideo non oportet quod quodlibet peccatum prudentiae oppositum sit gravissimum, sed solum quando opponitur prudentiae in aliquo maximo.

that every sin opposed to prudence is most grave, but only when it is opposed to prudence in some very grave matter.

# Article 3

*Whether craftiness is a special sin?*

AD TERTIUM SIC PROCEDITUR. Videtur quod astutia non sit speciale peccatum. Verba enim sacrae Scripturae non inducunt aliquem ad peccatum. Inducunt autem ad astutiam, secundum illud Prov. I, *ut detur parvulis astutia*. Ergo astutia non est peccatum.

PRAETEREA, Prov. XIII dicitur, *astutus omnia agit cum consilio*. Aut ergo ad finem bonum; aut ad finem malum. Si ad finem bonum, non videtur esse peccatum. Si autem ad finem malum, videtur pertinere ad prudentiam carnis vel saeculi. Ergo astutia non est speciale peccatum a prudentia carnis distinctum.

PRAETEREA, Gregorius, X Moral., exponens illud Iob XII, *deridetur iusti simplicitas*, dicit, *sapientia huius mundi est cor machinationibus tegere, sensum verbis velare, quae falsa sunt vera ostendere, quae vera sunt falsa demonstrare*. Et postea subdit, *haec prudentia usu a iuvenibus scitur, a pueris pretio discitur*. Sed ea quae praedicta sunt videntur ad astutiam pertinere. Ergo astutia non distinguitur a prudentia carnis vel mundi; et ita non videtur esse speciale peccatum.

SED CONTRA est quod apostolus dicit, II ad Cor. IV, *abdicamus occulta dedecoris, non ambulantes in astutia, neque adulterantes verbum Dei*. Ergo astutia est quoddam peccatum.

RESPONDEO dicendum quod prudentia est recta ratio agibilium, sicut scientia est recta ratio scibilium. Contingit autem contra rectitudinem scientiae dupliciter peccari in speculativis, uno quidem modo, quando ratio inducitur ad aliquam conclusionem falsam quae apparet vera; alio modo, ex eo quod ratio procedit ex aliquibus falsis quae videntur esse vera, sive sint ad conclusionem veram sive ad conclusionem falsam. Ita etiam aliquod peccatum potest esse contra prudentiam habens aliquam similitudinem eius dupliciter. Uno modo, quia studium rationis ordinatur ad finem qui non est vere bonus sed apparens, et hoc pertinet ad prudentiam carnis. Alio modo, inquantum aliquis ad finem aliquem consequendum, vel bonum vel malum, utitur non veris viis, sed simulatis et apparentibus, et hoc pertinet ad peccatum astutiae. Unde est quoddam peccatum prudentiae oppositum a prudentia carnis distinctum.

AD PRIMUM ergo dicendum quod, sicut Augustinus dicit, in IV contra Iulian., sicut prudentia abusive quan-

OBJECTION 1: It would seem that craftiness is not a special sin. For the words of Holy Writ do not induce anyone to sin; and yet they induce us to be crafty, according to Prov. 1:4, *To give craftiness to little ones*. Therefore craftiness is not a sin.

OBJ. 2: Further, it is written (Prov 13:16): *The crafty man doth all things with counsel*. Therefore, he does so either for a good or for an evil end. If for a good end, there is no sin seemingly, and if for an evil end, it would seem to pertain to carnal or worldly prudence. Therefore craftiness is not a special sin distinct from prudence of the flesh.

OBJ. 3: Further, Gregory expounding the words of Job 12, *The simplicity of the just man is laughed to scorn*, says (*Moral*. x, 29): *The wisdom of this world is to hide one's thoughts by artifice, to conceal one's meaning by words, to represent error as truth, to make out the truth to be false*, and further on he adds: *This prudence is acquired by the young, it is learnt at a price by children*. Now the above things seem to belong to craftiness. Therefore craftiness is not distinct from carnal or worldly prudence, and consequently it seems not to be a special sin.

ON THE CONTRARY, The Apostle says (2 Cor 4:2): *We renounce the hidden things of dishonesty, not walking in craftiness, nor adulterating the word of God*. Therefore craftiness is a sin.

I ANSWER THAT, Prudence is right reason applied to action, just as science is right reason applied to knowledge. In speculative matters one may sin against rectitude of knowledge in two ways: in one way when the reason is led to a false conclusion that appears to be true; in another way when the reason proceeds from false premises, that appear to be true, either to a true or to a false conclusion. Even so a sin may be against prudence, through having some resemblance thereto, in two ways. First, when the purpose of the reason is directed to an end which is good not in truth but in appearance, and this pertains to prudence of the flesh; second, when, in order to obtain a certain end, whether good or evil, a man uses means that are not true but fictitious and counterfeit, and this belongs to the sin of craftiness. This is consequently a sin opposed to prudence, and distinct from prudence of the flesh.

REPLY OBJ. 1: As Augustine observes (*Contra Julian*. iv, 3) just as prudence is sometimes improperly taken in a

doque in malo accipitur, ita etiam astutia quandoque in bono, et hoc propter similitudinem unius ad alterum. Proprie tamen astutia in malo accipitur; sicut et philosophus dicit, in VI Ethic.

**Ad secundum** dicendum quod astutia potest consiliari et ad finem bonum et ad finem malum, nec oportet ad finem bonum falsis viis pervenire et simulatis, sed veris. Unde etiam astutia si ordinetur ad bonum finem, est peccatum.

**Ad tertium** dicendum quod Gregorius sub *prudentia mundi* accepit omnia quae possunt ad falsam prudentiam pertinere. Unde etiam sub hac comprehenditur astutia.

bad sense, so is craftiness sometimes taken in a good sense, and this on account of their mutual resemblance. Properly speaking, however, craftiness is taken in a bad sense, as the Philosopher states in *Ethic.* vi, 12.

**Reply Obj. 2:** Craftiness can take counsel both for a good end and for an evil end: nor should a good end be pursued by means that are false and counterfeit but by such as are true. Hence craftiness is a sin if it be directed to a good end.

**Reply Obj. 3:** Under *worldly prudence* Gregory included everything that can pertain to false prudence, so that it comprises craftiness also.

# Article 4

*Whether guile is a sin pertaining to craftiness?*

**Ad quartum sic proceditur.** Videtur quod dolus non sit peccatum ad astutiam pertinens. Peccatum enim in perfectis viris non invenitur, praecipue mortale. Invenitur autem in eis aliquis dolus, secundum illud II ad Cor. XII, *cum essem astutus, dolo vos cepi.* Ergo dolus non est semper peccatum.

**Praeterea,** dolus maxime ad linguam pertinere videtur, secundum illud Psalm., *linguis suis dolose agebant.* Astutia autem, sicut et prudentia, est in ipso actu rationis. Ergo dolus non pertinet ad astutiam.

**Praeterea,** Prov. XII dicitur, *dolus in corde cogitantium mala.* Sed non omnis malorum cogitatio pertinet ad astutiam. Ergo dolus non videtur ad astutiam pertinere.

**Sed contra** est quod astutia ad circumveniendum ordinatur, secundum illud apostoli, ad Ephes. IV, *in astutia ad circumventionem erroris.* Ad quod etiam dolus ordinatur. Ergo dolus pertinet ad astutiam.

**Respondeo** dicendum quod, sicut supra dictum est, ad astutiam pertinet assumere vias non veras, sed simulatas et apparentes, ad aliquem finem prosequendum vel bonum vel malum. Assumptio autem harum viarum potest dupliciter considerari. Uno quidem modo, in ipsa excogitatione viarum huiusmodi, et hoc proprie pertinet ad astutiam, sicut etiam excogitatio rectarum viarum ad debitum finem pertinet ad prudentiam. Alio modo potest considerari talium viarum assumptio secundum executionem operis, et secundum hoc pertinet ad dolum. Et ideo dolus importat quandam executionem astutiae. Et secundum hoc ad astutiam pertinet.

**Ad primum** ergo dicendum quod sicut astutia proprie accipitur in malo, abusive autem in bono; ita etiam et dolus, qui est astutiae executio.

**Ad secundum** dicendum quod executio astutiae ad decipiendum primo quidem et principaliter fit per verba,

**Objection 1:** It would seem that guile is not a sin pertaining to craftiness. For sin, especially mortal, has no place in perfect men. Yet a certain guile is to be found in them, according to 2 Cor. 12:16, *Being crafty I caught you by guile.* Therefore guile is not always a sin.

**Obj. 2:** Further, guile seems to pertain chiefly to the tongue, according to Ps. 5:11, *They dealt deceitfully with their tongues.* Now craftiness like prudence is in the very act of reason. Therefore guile does not pertain to craftiness.

**Obj. 3:** Further, it is written (Prov 12:20): *Guile is in the heart of them that think evil things.* But the thought of evil things does not always pertain to craftiness. Therefore guile does not seem to belong to craftiness.

**On the contrary,** Craftiness aims at lying in wait, according to Eph. 4:14, *By cunning craftiness by which they lie in wait to deceive*: and guile aims at this also. Therefore guile pertains to craftiness.

**I answer that,** As stated above (A. 3), it belongs to craftiness to adopt ways that are not true but counterfeit and apparently true, in order to attain some end either good or evil. Now the adopting of such ways may be subjected to a twofold consideration; first, as regards the process of thinking them out, and this belongs properly to craftiness, even as thinking out right ways to a due end belongs to prudence. Second the adopting of such like ways may be considered with regard to their actual execution, and in this way it belongs to guile. Hence guile denotes a certain execution of craftiness, and accordingly belongs thereto.

**Reply Obj. 1:** Just as craftiness is taken properly in a bad sense, and improperly in a good sense, so too is guile which is the execution of craftiness.

**Reply Obj. 2:** The execution of craftiness with the purpose of deceiving, is effected first and foremost by words,

quae praecipuum locum tenent inter signa quibus homo significat aliquid alteri, ut patet per Augustinum, in libro de Doct. Christ. Et ideo dolus maxime attribuitur locutioni. Contingit tamen esse dolum et in factis, secundum illud Psalm., *et dolum facerent in servos eius*. Est etiam et dolus in corde, secundum illud Eccli. XIX. *Interiora eius plena sunt dolo*. Sed hoc est secundum quod aliquis dolos excogitat, secundum illud Psalm., *dolos tota die meditabantur*.

**Ad tertium** dicendum quod quicumque cogitant aliquod malum facere, necesse est quod excogitent aliquas vias ad hoc quod suum propositum impleant, et ut plurimum excogitant vias dolosas, quibus facilius propositum consequantur. Quamvis contingat quandoque quod absque astutia et dolo aliqui aperte et per violentiam malum operentur. Sed hoc, quia difficilius fit, in paucioribus accidit.

which hold the chief place among those signs whereby a man signifies something to another man, as Augustine states (*De Doctr. Christ.* ii, 3), hence guile is ascribed chiefly to speech. Yet guile may happen also in deeds, according to Ps. 104:25, *And to deal deceitfully with his servants.* Guile is also in the heart, according to Ecclus. 19:23, *His interior is full of deceit*, but this is to devise deceits, according to Ps. 37:13: *They studied deceits all the day long.*

**Reply Obj. 3**: Whoever purposes to do some evil deed, must needs devise certain ways of attaining his purpose, and for the most part he devises deceitful ways, whereby the more easily to obtain his end. Nevertheless it happens sometimes that evil is done openly and by violence without craftiness and guile; but as this is more difficult, it is of less frequent occurrence.

# Article 5

*Whether fraud pertains to craftiness?*

**Ad quintum sic proceditur**. Videtur quod fraus ad astutiam non pertineat. Non enim est laudabile quod aliquis decipi se patiatur, ad quod astutia tendit. Est autem laudabile quod aliquis patiatur fraudem, secundum illud I ad Cor. VI, *quare non magis fraudem patimini?* Ergo fraus non pertinet ad astutiam.

**Praeterea**, fraus pertinere videtur ad illicitam acceptionem vel receptionem exteriorum rerum, dicitur enim Act. V quod *vir quidam nomine Ananias, cum Saphira uxore sua, vendidit agrum et fraudavit de pretio agri*. Sed illicite usurpare vel retinere res exteriores pertinet ad iniustitiam vel illiberalitatem. Ergo fraus non pertinet ad astutiam, quae opponitur prudentiae.

**Praeterea**, nullus astutia utitur contra seipsum. Sed aliquorum fraudes sunt contra seipsos, dicitur enim Prov. I de quibusdam quod *moliuntur fraudes contra animas suas*. Ergo fraus non pertinet ad astutiam.

**Sed contra**, fraus ad deceptionem ordinatur, secundum illud Iob XIII, *numquid decipietur ut homo vestris fraudulentiis?* Ad idem etiam ordinatur astutia. Ergo fraus ad astutiam pertinet.

**Respondeo** dicendum quod sicut dolus consistit in executione astutiae, ita etiam et fraus, sed in hoc differre videntur quod dolus pertinet universaliter ad executionem astutiae, sive fiat per verba sive per facta; fraus autem magis proprie pertinet ad executionem astutiae secundum quod fit per facta.

**Objection 1**: It would seem that fraud does not pertain to craftiness. For a man does not deserve praise if he allows himself to be deceived, which is the object of craftiness; and yet a man deserves praise for allowing himself to be defrauded, according to 1 Cor. 6:1, *Why do you not rather suffer yourselves to be defrauded?* Therefore fraud does not belong to craftiness.

**Obj. 2**: Further, fraud seems to consist in unlawfully taking or receiving external things, for it is written (Acts 5:1) that *a certain man named Ananias with Saphira his wife, sold a piece of land, and by fraud kept back part of the price of the land*. Now it pertains to injustice or illiberality to take possession of or retain external things unjustly. Therefore fraud does not belong to craftiness which is opposed to prudence.

**Obj. 3**: Further, no man employs craftiness against himself. But the frauds of some are against themselves, for it is written (Prov 1:18) concerning some *that they practice frauds against their own souls*. Therefore fraud does not belong to craftiness.

**On the contrary**, The object of fraud is to deceive, according to Job 13:9, *Shall he be deceived as a man, with your fraudulent dealings?* Now craftiness is directed to the same object. Therefore fraud pertains to craftiness.

**I answer that**, Just as guile consists in the execution of craftiness, so also does fraud. But they seem to differ in the fact that guile belongs in general to the execution of craftiness, whether this be effected by words, or by deeds, whereas fraud belongs more properly to the execution of craftiness by deeds.

**Ad primum** ergo dicendum quod apostolus non inducit fideles ad hoc quod decipiantur in cognoscendo, sed ad hoc quod effectum deceptionis patienter tolerent in sustinendis iniuriis fraudulenter illatis.

**Ad secundum** dicendum quod executio astutiae potest fieri per aliquod aliud vitium, sicut et executio prudentiae fit per virtutes. Et hoc modo nihil prohibet defraudationem pertinere ad avaritiam vel illiberalitatem.

**Ad tertium** dicendum quod illi qui fraudes faciunt ex eorum intentione non moliuntur aliquid contra seipsos vel contra animas suas, sed ex iusto Dei iudicio provenit ut id quod contra alios moliuntur contra eos retorqueatur; secundum illud Psalm., *incidit in foveam quam fecit.*

**Reply Obj. 1**: The Apostle does not counsel the faithful to be deceived in their knowledge, but to bear patiently the effect of being deceived, and to endure wrongs inflicted on them by fraud.

**Reply Obj. 2**: The execution of craftiness may be carried out by another vice, just as the execution of prudence by the virtues: and accordingly nothing hinders fraud from pertaining to covetousness or illiberality.

**Reply Obj. 3**: Those who commit frauds, do not design anything against themselves or their own souls; it is through God's just judgment that what they plot against others, recoils on themselves, according to Ps. 7:16, *He is fallen into the hole he made.*

# Article 6

*Whether it is lawful to be solicitous about temporal matters?*

**Ad sextum sic proceditur**. Videtur quod licitum sit sollicitudinem habere de temporalibus rebus. Ad praesidentem enim pertinet sollicitum esse de his quibus praeest, secundum illud Rom. XII, *qui praeest in sollicitudine.* Sed homo praeest ex divina ordinatione temporalibus rebus, secundum illud Psalm., *omnia subiecisti sub pedibus eius, oves et boves* et cetera. Ergo homo debet habere sollicitudinem de temporalibus rebus.

**Praeterea**, unusquisque sollicitus est de fine propter quem operatur. Sed licitum est hominem operari propter temporalia, quibus vitam sustentet, unde apostolus dicit, II ad Thess. III, *si quis non vult operari, non manducet.* Ergo licitum est sollicitari de rebus temporalibus.

**Praeterea**, sollicitudo de operibus misericordiae laudabilis est, secundum illud II ad Tim. I, *cum Romam venisset, sollicite me quaesivit.* Sed sollicitudo temporalium rerum quandoque pertinet ad opera misericordiae, puta cum quis sollicitudinem adhibet ad procurandum negotia pupillorum et pauperum. Ergo sollicitudo temporalium rerum non est illicita.

**Sed contra** est quod dominus dicit, Matth. VI, *nolite solliciti esse, dicentes, quid manducabimus aut quid bibemus, aut quo operiemur?* Quae tamen sunt maxime necessaria.

**Respondeo** dicendum quod sollicitudo importat studium quoddam adhibitum ad aliquid consequendum. Manifestum est autem quod maius studium adhibetur ubi est timor deficiendi, et ideo ubi est securitas consequendi, minor intervenit sollicitudo. Sic ergo sollicitudo temporalium rerum tripliciter potest esse illicita.

**Objection 1**: It would seem lawful to be solicitous about temporal matters. Because a superior should be solicitous for his subjects, according to Rom. 12:8, *He that ruleth, with solicitude.* Now according to the Divine ordering, man is placed over temporal things, according to Ps. 8:8, *Thou hast subjected all things under his feet*, etc. Therefore man should be solicitous about temporal things.

**Obj. 2**: Further, everyone is solicitous about the end for which he works. Now it is lawful for a man to work for the temporal things whereby he sustains life, wherefore the Apostle says (2 Thess 3:10): *If any man will not work, neither let him eat.* Therefore it is lawful to be solicitous about temporal things.

**Obj. 3**: Further, solicitude about works of mercy is praiseworthy, according to 2 Tim. 1:17, *When he was come to Rome, he carefully sought me.* Now solicitude about temporal things is sometimes connected with works of mercy; for instance, when a man is solicitous to watch over the interests of orphans and poor persons. Therefore solicitude about temporal things is not unlawful.

**On the contrary**, Our Lord said (Matt 6:31): *Be not solicitous . . . saying, What shall we eat, or what shall we drink, or wherewith shall we be clothed?* And yet such things are very necessary.

**I answer that**, Solicitude denotes an earnest endeavor to obtain something. Now it is evident that the endeavor is more earnest when there is fear of failure, so that there is less solicitude when success is assured. Accordingly solicitude about temporal things may be unlawful in three ways. First on the part of the object of solicitude; that

Uno quidem modo, ex parte eius de quo sollicitamur, si scilicet temporalia tanquam finem quaeramus. Unde et Augustinus dicit, in libro de operibus Monach., *cum dominus dicit, nolite solliciti esse etc., hoc dicit ut non ista intueantur, et propter ista faciant quidquid in Evangelii praedicatione facere iubentur.* Alio modo potest esse temporalium sollicitudo illicita propter superfluum studium quod apponitur ad temporalia procuranda, propter quod homo a spiritualibus, quibus principalius inservire debet, retrahitur. Et ideo dicitur Matth. XIII quod *sollicitudo saeculi suffocat verbum.* Tertio modo, ex parte timoris superflui, quando scilicet aliquis timet ne, faciendo quod debet, necessaria sibi deficiant. Quod dominus tripliciter excludit. Primo, propter maiora beneficia homini praestita divinitus praeter suam sollicitudinem, scilicet corpus et animam. Secundo, propter subventionem qua Deus animalibus et plantis subvenit absque opere humano, secundum proportionem suae naturae. Tertio, ex divina providentia, propter cuius ignorantiam gentiles circa temporalia bona quaerenda principalius sollicitantur. Et ideo concludit quod principaliter nostra sollicitudo esse debet de spiritualibus bonis, sperantes quod etiam temporalia nobis provenient ad necessitatem, si fecerimus quod debemus.

**AD PRIMUM** ergo dicendum quod temporalia bona subiecta sunt homini ut eis utatur ad necessitatem, non ut in eis finem constituat, et superflue circa ea sollicitetur.

**AD SECUNDUM** dicendum quod sollicitudo eius qui corporali labore panem acquirit non est superflua, sed moderata. Et ideo Hieronymus dicit quod *labor exercendus est, sollicitudo tollenda,* superflua scilicet, animum inquietans.

**AD TERTIUM** dicendum quod sollicitudo temporalium in operibus misericordiae ordinatur ad finem caritatis. Et ideo non est illicita, nisi sit superflua.

is, if we seek temporal things as an end. Hence Augustine says (*De Operibus Monach.* xxvi): *When Our Lord said: 'Be not solicitous,' etc. . . . He intended to forbid them either to make such things their end, or for the sake of these things to do whatever they were commanded to do in preaching the Gospel.* Second, solicitude about temporal things may be unlawful, through too much earnestness in endeavoring to obtain temporal things, the result being that a man is drawn away from spiritual things which ought to be the chief object of his search, wherefore it is written (Matt 13:22) that *the care of this world . . . chokes up the word.* Third, through over much fear, when, to wit, a man fears to lack necessary things if he do what he ought to do. Now our Lord gives three motives for laying aside this fear. First, on account of the yet greater favors bestowed by God on man, independently of his solicitude, viz. his body and soul (Matt 6:26); second, on account of the care with which God watches over animals and plants without the assistance of man, according to the requirements of their nature; third, because of Divine providence, through ignorance of which the gentiles are solicitous in seeking temporal goods before all others. Consequently He concludes that we should be solicitous most of all about spiritual goods, hoping that temporal goods also may be granted us according to our needs, if we do what we ought to do.

**REPLY OBJ. 1**: Temporal goods are subjected to man that he may use them according to his needs, not that he may place his end in them and be over solicitous about them.

**REPLY OBJ. 2**: The solicitude of a man who gains his bread by bodily labor is not superfluous but proportionate; hence Jerome says on Matt. 6:31, *Be not solicitous,* that *labor is necessary, but solicitude must be banished,* namely superfluous solicitude which unsettles the mind.

**REPLY OBJ. 3**: In the works of mercy solicitude about temporal things is directed to charity as its end, wherefore it is not unlawful, unless it be superfluous.

# Article 7

*Whether we should be solicitous about the future?*

**AD SEPTIMUM SIC PROCEDITUR**. Videtur quod aliquis debeat esse sollicitus in futurum. Dicitur enim Prov. VI, *vade ad formicam, o piger, et considera vias eius, et disce sapientiam, quae cum non habeat ducem nec praeceptorem, parat in aestate cibum sibi, et congregat in messe quod comedat.* Sed hoc est in futurum sollicitari. Ergo laudabilis est sollicitudo futurorum.

**PRAETEREA**, sollicitudo ad prudentiam pertinet. Sed prudentia praecipue est futurorum, praecipua enim

**OBJECTION 1**: It would seem that we should be solicitous about the future. For it is written (Prov 6:6–8): *Go to the ant, O sluggard, and consider her ways and learn wisdom; which, although she hath no guide, nor master . . . provideth her meat for herself in the summer, and gathereth her food in the harvest.* Now this is to be solicitous about the future. Therefore solicitude about the future is praiseworthy.

**OBJ. 2**: Further, solicitude pertains to prudence. But prudence is chiefly about the future, since its principal part

pars eius est *providentia futurorum*, ut supra dictum est. Ergo virtuosum est sollicitari de futuris.

**Praeterea**, quicumque reponit aliquid in posterum conservandum sollicitus est in futurum. Sed ipse Christus legitur, Ioan. XII, loculos habuisse ad aliquid conservandum, quos Iudas deferebat. Apostoli etiam conservabant pretia praediorum, quae ante pedes eorum ponebantur, ut legitur Act. IV. Ergo licitum est in futurum sollicitari.

**Sed contra** est quod dominus dicit, Matth. VI, *nolite solliciti esse in crastinum*. Cras autem ibi ponitur pro *futuro*, sicut dicit Hieronymus.

**Respondeo** dicendum quod nullum opus potest esse virtuosum nisi debitis circumstantiis vestiatur; inter quas una est debitum tempus, secundum illud Eccle. VIII, *omni negotio tempus est et opportunitas*. Quod non solum in exterioribus operibus, sed etiam in interiori sollicitudine locum habet. Unicuique enim tempori competit propria sollicitudo, sicut tempori aestatis competit sollicitudo metendi, tempori autumni sollicitudo vindemiae. Si quis ergo tempore aestatis de vindemia iam esset sollicitus, superflue praeoccuparet futuri temporis sollicitudinem. Unde huiusmodi sollicitudinem tanquam superfluam dominus prohibet, dicens, *nolite solliciti esse in crastinum*. Unde subdit, *crastinus enim dies sollicitus erit sibi ipsi*, idest, suam propriam sollicitudinem habebit, quae sufficiet ad animum affligendum. Et hoc est quod subdit, *sufficit diei malitia sua*, idest afflictio sollicitudinis.

**Ad primum** ergo dicendum quod formica habet sollicitudinem congruam tempori, et hoc nobis imitandum proponitur.

**Ad secundum** dicendum quod ad prudentiam pertinet providentia debita futurorum. Esset autem inordinata futurorum providentia vel sollicitudo si quis temporalia, in quibus dicitur praeteritum et futurum, tanquam fines quaereret; vel si superflua quaereret ultra praesentis vitae necessitatem; vel si tempus sollicitudinis praeoccuparet.

**Ad tertium** dicendum quod, sicut Augustinus dicit, in libro de Serm. Dom. in monte, *cum viderimus aliquem servum Dei providere ne ista necessaria sibi desint, non iudicemus eum de crastino sollicitum esse. Nam et ipse dominus propter exemplum loculos habere dignatus est; et in actibus apostolorum scriptum est ea quae ad victum sunt necessaria procurata esse in futurum propter imminentem famem. Non ergo dominus improbat si quis humano more ista procuret, sed si quis propter ista militet Deo.*

is *foresight of future things*, as stated above (Q. 49, A. 6, ad 1). Therefore it is virtuous to be solicitous about the future.

**Obj. 3**: Further, whoever puts something by that he may keep it for the morrow, is solicitous about the future. Now we read (John 12:6) that Christ had a bag for keeping things in, which Judas carried, and (Acts 4:34–37) that the Apostles kept the price of the land, which had been laid at their feet. Therefore it is lawful to be solicitous about the future.

**On the contrary**, Our Lord said (Matt 6:34): *Be not ... solicitous for tomorrow*; where *tomorrow* stands for the *future*, as Jerome says in his commentary on this passage.

**I answer that**, No work can be virtuous, unless it be vested with its due circumstances, and among these is the due time, according to Eccles. 8:6, *There is a time and opportunity for every business*; which applies not only to external deeds but also to internal solicitude. For every time has its own fitting proper solicitude; thus solicitude about the crops belongs to the summer time, and solicitude about the vintage to the time of autumn. Accordingly if a man were solicitous about the vintage during the summer, he would be needlessly forestalling the solicitude belonging to a future time. Hence Our Lord forbids such like excessive solicitude, saying: *Be ... not solicitous for tomorrow*, wherefore He adds, *for the morrow will be solicitous for itself*, that is to say, the morrow will have its own solicitude, which will be burden enough for the soul. This is what He means by adding: *Sufficient for the day is the evil thereof*, namely, the burden of solicitude.

**Reply Obj. 1**: The ant is solicitous at a befitting time, and it is this that is proposed for our example.

**Reply Obj. 2**: Due foresight of the future belongs to prudence. But it would be an inordinate foresight or solicitude about the future, if a man were to seek temporal things, to which the terms *past* and *future* apply, as ends, or if he were to seek them in excess of the needs of the present life, or if he were to forestall the time for solicitude.

**Reply Obj. 3**: As Augustine says (*De Serm. Dom. in Monte* ii, 17), *when we see a servant of God taking thought lest he lack these needful things, we must not judge him to be solicitous for the morrow, since even Our Lord deigned for our example to have a purse, and we read in the Acts of the Apostles that they procured the necessary means of livelihood in view of the future on account of a threatened famine. Hence Our Lord does not condemn those who according to human custom, provide themselves with such things, but those who oppose themselves to God for the sake of these things.*

# Article 8

*Whether these vices arise from covetousness?*

AD OCTAVUM SIC PROCEDITUR. Videtur quod huiusmodi vitia non oriantur ex avaritia. Quia sicut dictum est, per luxuriam maxime ratio patitur defectum in sua rectitudine. Sed huiusmodi vitia opponuntur rationi rectae, scilicet prudentiae. Ergo huiusmodi vitia maxime ex luxuria oriuntur, praesertim cum philosophus dicat, in VII Ethic., quod *Venus est dolosa, et eius corrigia est varia*, et quod *ex insidiis agit incontinens concupiscentiae*.

PRAETEREA, praedicta vitia habent quandam similitudinem prudentiae, ut dictum est. Sed ad prudentiam, cum sit in ratione, maiorem propinquitatem habere videntur vitia magis spiritualia, sicut superbia et inanis gloria. Ergo huiusmodi vitia magis videntur ex superbia oriri quam ex avaritia.

PRAETEREA, homo insidiis utitur non solum in diripiendis bonis alienis, sed etiam in machinando aliorum caedes, quorum primum pertinet ad avaritiam, secundum ad iram. Sed insidiis uti pertinet ad astutiam, dolum et fraudem. Ergo praedicta vitia non solum oriuntur ex avaritia, sed etiam ex ira.

SED CONTRA est quod Gregorius, XXXI Moral., ponit fraudem filiam avaritiae.

RESPONDEO dicendum quod, sicut dictum est, prudentia carnis et astutia, cum dolo et fraude, quandam similitudinem habent cum prudentia in aliquali usu rationis. Praecipue autem inter alias virtutes morales usus rationis rectae apparet in iustitia, quae est in appetitu rationali. Et ideo usus rationis indebitus etiam maxime apparet in vitiis oppositis iustitiae. Opponitur autem sibi maxime avaritia. Et ideo praedicta vitia maxime ex avaritia oriuntur.

AD PRIMUM ergo dicendum quod luxuria, propter vehementiam delectationis et concupiscentiae, totaliter opprimit rationem, ne prodeat in actum. In praedictis autem vitiis aliquis usus rationis est, licet inordinatus. Unde praedicta vitia non oriuntur directe ex luxuria. Quod autem philosophus Venerem dolosam appellat, hoc dicitur secundum quandam similitudinem, inquantum scilicet subito hominem surripit, sicut et in dolis agitur; non tamen per astutias, sed magis per violentiam concupiscentiae et delectationis. Unde et subdit quod *Venus furatur intellectum multum sapientis*.

AD SECUNDUM dicendum quod ex insidiis agere ad quandam pusillanimitatem pertinere videtur, magnanimus enim in omnibus vult manifestus esse, ut philosophus dicit, in IV Ethic. Et ideo quia superbia quandam similitudinem magnanimitatis habet vel fingit, inde est quod non directe ex superbia huiusmodi vitia

OBJECTION 1: It would seem that these vices do not arise from covetousness. As stated above (Q. 43, A. 6) lust is the chief cause of lack of rectitude in the reason. Now these vices are opposed to right reason, i.e., to prudence. Therefore they arise chiefly from lust; especially since the Philosopher says (*Ethic.* vii, 6) that *Venus is full of guile and her girdle is many colored* and that *he who is incontinent in desire acts with cunning*.

OBJ. 2: Further, these vices bear a certain resemblance to prudence, as stated above (Q. 47, A. 13). Now, since prudence is in the reason, the more spiritual vices seem to be more akin thereto, such as pride and vainglory. Therefore the aforesaid vices seem to arise from pride rather than from covetousness.

OBJ. 3: Further, men make use of stratagems not only in laying hold of other people's goods, but also in plotting murders, the former of which pertains to covetousness, and the latter to anger. Now the use of stratagems pertains to craftiness, guile, and fraud. Therefore the aforesaid vices arise not only from covetousness, but also from anger.

ON THE CONTRARY, Gregory (*Moral.* xxxi, 45) states that fraud is a daughter of covetousness.

I ANSWER THAT, As stated above (A. 3; Q. 47, A. 13), carnal prudence and craftiness, as well as guile and fraud, bear a certain resemblance to prudence in some kind of use of the reason. Now among all the moral virtues it is justice wherein the use of right reason appears chiefly, for justice is in the rational appetite. Hence the undue use of reason appears chiefly in the vices opposed to justice, the chief of which is covetousness. Therefore the aforesaid vices arise chiefly from covetousness.

REPLY OBJ. 1: On account of the vehemence of pleasure and of concupiscence, lust entirely suppresses the reason from exercising its act: whereas in the aforesaid vices there is some use of reason, albeit inordinate. Hence these vices do not arise directly from lust. When the Philosopher says that *Venus is full of guile*, he is referring to a certain resemblance, insofar as she carries man away suddenly, just as he is moved in deceitful actions, yet not by means of craftiness but rather by the vehemence of concupiscence and pleasure; wherefore he adds that *Venus doth cozen the wits of the wisest man*.

REPLY OBJ. 2: To do anything by stratagem seems to be due to pusillanimity: because a magnanimous man wishes to act openly, as the Philosopher says (*Ethic.* iv, 3). Wherefore, as pride resembles or apes magnanimity, it follows that the aforesaid vices which make use of fraud and guile, do not arise directly from pride, but rather from

oriuntur, quae utuntur fraude et dolis. Magis autem hoc pertinet ad avaritiam, quae utilitatem quaerit, parvipendens excellentiam.

**AD TERTIUM** dicendum quod ira habet subitum motum, unde praecipitanter agit et absque consilio; quo utuntur praedicta vitia, licet inordinate. Quod autem aliqui insidiis utantur ad caedes aliorum, non provenit ex ira, sed magis ex odio, quia iracundus appetit esse manifestus in nocendo, ut dicit philosophus, in II Rhet.

covetousness, which seeks its own profit and sets little by excellence.

**REPLY OBJ. 3**: Anger's movement is sudden, hence it acts with precipitation, and without counsel, contrary to the use of the aforesaid vices, though these use counsel inordinately. That men use stratagems in plotting murders, arises not from anger but rather from hatred, because the angry man desires to harm manifestly, as the Philosopher states (*Rhet.* ii, 2, 3).

# QUESTION 56

## THE PRECEPTS RELATING TO PRUDENCE

Deinde considerandum est de praeceptis ad pruden-tiam pertinentibus. Et circa hoc quaeruntur duo.

Primo, de praeceptis pertinentibus ad prudentiam.

Secundo, de praeceptis pertinentibus ad vitia opposita.

We must now consider the precepts relating to pru-dence, under which head there are two points of inquiry:

(1) The precepts of prudence;

(2) The precepts relating to the opposite vices.

# Article 1

*Whether the precepts of the decalogue should have included a precept of prudence?*

AD PRIMUM SIC PROCEDITUR. Videtur quod de prudentia fuerit dandum aliquod praeceptum inter praecepta Decalogi. De principaliori enim virtute principaliora praecepta dari debent. Sed principaliora praecepta legis sunt praecepta Decalogi. Cum ergo prudentia sit principalior inter virtutes morales, videtur quod de prudentia fuerit dandum aliquod praeceptum inter praecepta Decalogi.

PRAETEREA, in doctrina evangelica continetur lex maxime quantum ad praecepta Decalogi. Sed in doctri-na evangelica datur praeceptum de prudentia, ut patet Matth. X, *estote prudentes sicut serpentes.* Ergo inter praecepta Decalogi debuit praecipi actus prudentiae.

PRAETEREA, alia documenta veteris testamenti ad praecepta Decalogi ordinantur, unde et Malach. ult. dici-tur, *mementote legis Moysi, servi mei, quam mandavi ei in Horeb.* Sed in aliis documentis veteris testamenti dantur praecepta de prudentia, sicut Prov. III, *ne innitaris pru-dentiae tuae;* et infra, IV cap., *palpebrae tuae praecedant gressus tuos.* Ergo et in lege debuit aliquod praeceptum de prudentia dari, et praecipue inter praecepta Decalogi.

SED CONTRARIUM patet enumeranti praecepta De-calogi.

RESPONDEO dicendum quod, sicut supra dictum est cum de praeceptis ageretur, praecepta Decalogi, sicut data sunt omni populo, ita etiam cadunt in aestimatio-ne omnium, quasi ad naturalem rationem pertinentia. Praecipue autem sunt de dictamine rationis naturalis fines humanae vitae, qui se habent in agendis sicut prin-cipia naturaliter cognita in speculativis, ut ex supradictis patet. Prudentia autem non est circa finem, sed circa ea quae sunt ad finem, ut supra dictum est. Et ideo non fuit conveniens ut inter praecepta Decalogi aliquod praeceptum poneretur ad prudentiam directe pertinens.

OBJECTION 1: It would seem that the precepts of the decalogue should have included a precept of prudence. For the chief precepts should include a precept of the chief virtue. Now the chief precepts are those of the decalogue. Since then prudence is the chief of the moral virtues, it seems that the precepts of the decalogue should have in-cluded a precept of prudence.

OBJ. 2: Further, the teaching of the Gospel contains the Law especially with regard to the precepts of the decalogue. Now the teaching of the Gospel contains a precept of pru-dence (Matt 10:16): *Be ye . . . prudent as serpents.* Therefore the precepts of the decalogue should have included a pre-cept of prudence.

OBJ. 3: Further, the other lessons of the Old Testament are directed to the precepts of the decalogue: wherefore it is written (Mal 4:4): *Remember the law of Moses My servant, which I commanded him in Horeb.* Now the other lessons of the Old Testament include precepts of prudence; for instance (Prov 3:5): *Lean not upon thy own prudence;* and further on (Prov 4:25): *Let thine eyelids go before thy steps.* Therefore the Law also should have contained a precept of prudence, especially among the precepts of the decalogue.

THE CONTRARY however appears to anyone who goes through the precepts of the decalogue.

I ANSWER THAT, As stated above (I-II, Q. 100, A. 3; A. 5, ad 1) when we were treating of precepts, the command-ments of the decalogue being given to the whole people, are a matter of common knowledge to all, as coming under the purview of natural reason. Now foremost among the things dictated by natural reason are the ends of human life, which are to the practical order what naturally known principles are to the speculative order, as shown above (Q. 47, A. 6). Now prudence is not about the end, but about the means, as stated above (Q. 47, A. 6). Hence it was not fitting that the precepts of the decalogue should include a precept

Ad quam tamen omnia praecepta Decalogi pertinent secundum quod ipsa est directiva omnium virtuosorum actuum.

**Ad primum** ergo dicendum quod licet prudentia sit simpliciter principalior virtus aliis virtutibus moralibus, iustitia tamen principalius respicit rationem debiti, quod requiritur ad praeceptum, ut supra dictum est. Et ideo principalia praecepta legis, quae sunt praecepta Decalogi, magis debuerunt ad iustitiam quam ad prudentiam pertinere.

**Ad secundum** dicendum quod doctrina evangelica est doctrina perfectionis, et ideo oportuit quod in ipsa perfecte instrueretur homo de omnibus quae pertinent ad rectitudinem vitae, sive sint fines sive ea quae sunt ad finem. Et propter hoc oportuit in doctrina evangelica etiam de prudentia praecepta dari.

**Ad tertium** dicendum quod sicut alia doctrina veteris testamenti ordinatur ad praecepta Decalogi ut ad finem, ita etiam conveniens fuit ut in subsequentibus documentis veteris testamenti homines instruerentur de actu prudentiae, qui est circa ea quae sunt ad finem.

relating directly to prudence. And yet all the precepts of the decalogue are related to prudence, insofar as it directs all virtuous acts.

**Reply Obj. 1**: Although prudence is simply foremost among all the moral virtues, yet justice, more than any other virtue, regards its object under the aspect of something due, which is a necessary condition for a precept, as stated above (Q. 44, A. 1; I-II, Q. 99, AA. 1, 5). Hence it behooved the chief precepts of the Law, which are those of the decalogue, to refer to justice rather than to prudence.

**Reply Obj. 2**: The teaching of the Gospel is the doctrine of perfection. Therefore it needed to instruct man perfectly in all matters relating to right conduct, whether ends or means: wherefore it behooved the Gospel teaching to contain precepts also of prudence.

**Reply Obj. 3**: Just as the rest of the teaching of the Old Testament is directed to the precepts of the decalogue as its end, so it behooved man to be instructed by the subsequent lessons of the Old Testament about the act of prudence which is directed to the means.

# Article 2

*Whether the prohibitive precepts relating to the vices opposed to prudence are fittingly propounded in the Old Law?*

**Ad secundum sic proceditur.** Videtur quod in veteri lege fuerint inconvenienter praecepta prohibitiva proposita de vitiis oppositis prudentiae. Opponuntur enim prudentiae non minus illa quae habent directam oppositionem ad ipsam, sicut imprudentia et partes eius, quam illa quae cum ipsa similitudinem habent, sicut astutia et quae ad ipsam pertinent. Sed haec vitia prohibentur in lege, dicitur enim Lev. XIX, *non facies calumniam proximo tuo*; et Deut. XXV, *non habebis in sacculo tuo diversa pondera, maius et minus*. Ergo et de illis vitiis quae directe opponuntur prudentiae aliqua praecepta prohibitiva dari debuerunt.

**Praeterea**, in multis aliis rebus potest fraus fieri quam in emptione et venditione. Inconvenienter igitur fraudem in sola emptione et venditione lex prohibuit.

**Praeterea**, eadem ratio est praecipiendi actum virtutis et prohibendi actum vitii oppositi. Sed actus prudentiae non inveniuntur in lege praecepti. Ergo nec aliqua opposita vitia debuerunt in lege prohiberi.

**Sed contrarium** patet per praecepta legis inducta.

**Respondeo** dicendum quod, sicut supra dictum est, iustitia maxime respicit rationem debiti, quod requiritur ad praeceptum, quia iustitia est ad reddendum debitum

**Objection 1**: It would seem that the prohibitive precepts relating to the vices opposed to prudence are unfittingly propounded in the Old Law. For such vices as imprudence and its parts which are directly opposed to prudence are not less opposed thereto, than those which bear a certain resemblance to prudence, such as craftiness and vices connected with it. Now the latter vices are forbidden in the Law: for it is written (Lev 19:13): *Thou shalt not calumniate thy neighbor*, and (Deut 25:13): *Thou shalt not have diverse weights in thy bag, a greater and a less*. Therefore there should have also been prohibitive precepts about the vices directly opposed to prudence.

**Obj. 2**: Further, there is room for fraud in other things than in buying and selling. Therefore the Law unfittingly forbade fraud solely in buying and selling.

**Obj. 3**: Further, there is the same reason for prescribing an act of virtue as for prohibiting the act of a contrary vice. But acts of prudence are not prescribed in the Law. Therefore neither should any contrary vices have been forbidden in the Law.

**The contrary**, however, appears from the precepts of the Law which are quoted in the first objection.

**I answer that**, As stated above (A. 1), justice, above all, regards the aspect of something due, which is a necessary condition for a precept, because justice tends to

alteri, ut infra dicetur. Astutia autem quantum ad executionem maxime committitur in his circa quae est iustitia, ut dictum est. Et ideo conveniens fuit ut praecepta prohibitiva darentur in lege de executione astutiae inquantum ad iniustitiam pertinet, sicut cum dolo vel fraude aliquis alicui calumniam ingerit, vel eius bona surripit.

**Ad primum** ergo dicendum quod illa vitia quae directe opponuntur prudentiae manifesta contrarietate non ita pertinent ad iniustitiam sicut executio astutiae. Et ideo non ita prohibentur in lege sicut fraus et dolus, quae ad iniustitiam pertinent.

**Ad secundum** dicendum quod omnis fraus vel dolus commissa in his quae ad iustitiam pertinent potest intelligi esse prohibita, Lev. XIX, in prohibitione calumniae. Praecipue autem solet fraus exerceri et dolus in emptione et venditione, secundum illud Eccli. XXVI, *non iustificabitur caupo a peccato labiorum.* Propter hoc specialiter praeceptum prohibitivum datur in lege de fraude circa emptiones et venditiones commissa.

**Ad tertium** dicendum quod omnia praecepta de actibus iustitiae in lege data pertinent ad executionem prudentiae, sicut et praecepta prohibitiva data de furto, calumnia et fraudulenta venditione pertinent ad executionem astutiae.

render that which is due to another, as we shall state further on (Q. 58, A. 2). Now craftiness, as to its execution, is committed chiefly in matters of justice, as stated above (Q. 55, A. 8): and so it was fitting that the Law should contain precepts forbidding the execution of craftiness, insofar as this pertains to injustice, as when a man uses guile and fraud in calumniating another or in stealing his goods.

**Reply Obj. 1:** Those vices that are manifestly opposed to prudence, do not pertain to injustice in the same way as the execution of craftiness, and so they are not forbidden in the Law, as fraud and guile are, which latter pertain to injustice.

**Reply Obj. 2:** All guile and fraud committed in matters of injustice, can be understood to be forbidden in the prohibition of calumny (Lev 19:13). Yet fraud and guile are wont to be practiced chiefly in buying and selling, according to Ecclus. 26:28, *A huckster shall not be justified from the sins of the lips*: and it is for this reason that the Law contained a special precept forbidding fraudulent buying and selling.

**Reply Obj. 3:** All the precepts of the Law that relate to acts of justice pertain to the execution of prudence, even as the precepts prohibitive of stealing, calumny and fraudulent selling pertain to the execution of craftiness.

# QUESTION 57

## RIGHT

Consequenter post prudentiam considerandum est de iustitia. Circa quam quadruplex consideratio occurrit, prima est de iustitia; secunda, de partibus eius; tertia, de dono ad hoc pertinente; quarta, de praeceptis ad iustitiam pertinentibus.

Circa iustitiam vero consideranda sunt quatuor, primo quidem, de iure; secundo, de ipsa iustitia; tertio, de iniustitia; quarto, de iudicio.

Circa primum quaeruntur quatuor.

Primo, utrum ius sit obiectum iustitiae.

Secundo, utrum ius convenienter dividatur in ius naturale et positivum.

Tertio, utrum ius gentium sit ius naturale.

Quarto, utrum ius dominativum et paternum debeat specialiter distingui.

After considering prudence we must in due sequence consider justice, the consideration of which will be fourfold: (1) Of justice; (2) Of its parts; (3) Of the corresponding gift; (4) Of the precepts relating to justice.

Four points will have to be considered about justice: (1) Right; (2) Justice itself; (3) Injustice; (4) Judgment.

Under the first head there are four points of inquiry:
(1) Whether right is the object of justice?
(2) Whether right is fittingly divided into natural and positive right?
(3) Whether the right of nations is the same as natural right?
(4) Whether right of dominion and paternal right are distinct species?

# Article 1

## *Whether right is the object of justice?*

**AD PRIMUM SIC PROCEDITUR**. Videtur quod ius non sit obiectum iustitiae. Dicit enim celsus iurisconsultus quod *ius est ars boni et aequi*. Ars autem non est obiectum iustitiae, sed est per se virtus intellectualis. Ergo ius non est obiectum iustitiae.

**PRAETEREA**, *lex*, sicut Isidorus dicit, in libro Etymol., *iuris est species*. Lex autem non est obiectum iustitiae, sed magis prudentiae, unde et philosophus *legispositivam* partem prudentiae ponit. Ergo ius non est obiectum iustitiae.

**PRAETEREA**, iustitia principaliter subiicit hominem Deo, dicit enim Augustinus, libro de moribus Eccles., quod *iustitia est amor Deo tantum serviens, et ob hoc bene imperans ceteris, quae homini subiecta sunt*. Sed ius non pertinet ad divina, sed solum ad humana, dicit enim Isidorus, in libro Etymol., quod *fas lex divina est, ius autem lex humana*. Ergo ius non est obiectum iustitiae.

**SED CONTRA** est quod Isidorus dicit, in eodem, quod *ius dictum est quia est iustum*. Sed iustum est obiectum iustitiae, dicit enim philosophus, in V Ethic., quod *omnes talem habitum volunt dicere iustitiam a quo operativi iustorum sunt*. Ergo ius est obiectum iustitiae.

**RESPONDEO** dicendum quod iustitiae proprium est inter alias virtutes ut ordinet hominem in his quae sunt ad alterum. Importat enim aequalitatem quandam, ut

**OBJECTION 1**: It would seem that right is not the object of justice. For the jurist Celsus says that *right is the art of goodness and equality*. Now art is not the object of justice, but is by itself an intellectual virtue. Therefore right is not the object of justice.

**OBJ. 2**: Further, *Law*, according to Isidore (*Etym.* v, 3), *is a kind of right*. Now law is the object not of justice but of prudence, wherefore the Philosopher reckons *legislative* as one of the parts of prudence. Therefore right is not the object of justice.

**OBJ. 3**: Further, justice, before all, subjects man to God: for Augustine says (*De Moribus Eccl.* xv) that *justice is love serving God alone, and consequently governing aright all things subject to man*. Now right (jus) does not pertain to Divine things, but only to human affairs, for Isidore says (*Etym.* v, 2) that *fas is the Divine law, and jus, the human law*. Therefore right is not the object of justice.

**ON THE CONTRARY**, Isidore says (*Etym.* v, 2) that *right (jus) is so called because it is just*. Now the just is the object of justice, for the Philosopher declares (*Ethic.* v, 1) that *all are agreed in giving the name of justice to the habit which makes men capable of doing just actions*.

**I ANSWER THAT**, It is proper to justice, as compared with the other virtues, to direct man in his relations with others: because it denotes a kind of equality, as its very

ipsum nomen demonstrat, dicuntur enim vulgariter ea quae adaequantur iustari. Aequalitas autem ad alterum est. Aliae autem virtutes perficiunt hominem solum in his quae ei conveniunt secundum seipsum. Sic igitur illud quod est rectum in operibus aliarum virtutum, ad quod tendit intentio virtutis quasi in proprium obiectum, non accipitur nisi per comparationem ad agentem. Rectum vero quod est in opere iustitiae, etiam praeter comparationem ad agentem, constituitur per comparationem ad alium, illud enim in opere nostro dicitur esse iustum quod respondet secundum aliquam aequalitatem alteri, puta recompensatio mercedis debitae pro servitio impenso. Sic igitur iustum dicitur aliquid, quasi habens rectitudinem iustitiae, ad quod terminatur actio iustitiae, etiam non considerato qualiter ab agente fiat. Sed in aliis virtutibus non determinatur aliquid rectum nisi secundum quod aliqualiter fit ab agente. Et propter hoc specialiter iustitiae prae aliis virtutibus determinatur secundum se obiectum, quod vocatur iustum. Et hoc quidem est ius. Unde manifestum est quod ius est obiectum iustitiae.

**Ad primum** ergo dicendum quod consuetum est quod nomina a sui prima impositione detorqueantur ad alia significanda, sicut nomen *medicinae* impositum est primo ad significandum remedium quod praestatur infirmo ad sanandum, deinde tractum est ad significandum artem qua hoc fit. Ita etiam hoc nomen ius primo impositum est ad significandum ipsam rem iustam; postmodum autem derivatum est ad artem qua cognoscitur quid sit iustum; et ulterius ad significandum locum in quo ius redditur, sicut dicitur aliquis comparere *in iure*; et ulterius dicitur etiam ius quod redditur ab eo ad cuius officium pertinet iustitiam facere, licet etiam id quod decernit sit iniquum.

**Ad secundum** dicendum quod sicut eorum quae per artem exterius fiunt quaedam ratio in mente artificis praeexistit, quae dicitur regula artis; ita etiam illius operis iusti quod ratio determinat quaedam ratio praeexistit in mente, quasi quaedam prudentiae regula. Et hoc si in scriptum redigatur, vocatur lex, est enim lex, secundum Isidorum, *constitutio scripta*. Et ideo lex non est ipsum ius, proprie loquendo, sed aliqualis ratio iuris.

**Ad tertium** dicendum quod quia iustitia aequalitatem importat, Deo autem non possumus aequivalens recompensare, inde est quod iustum, secundum perfectam rationem, non possumus reddere Deo. Et propter hoc non dicitur proprie ius lex divina, sed *fas*, quia videlicet sufficit Deo ut impleamus quod possumus. Iustitia tamen ad hoc tendit ut homo, quantum potest, Deo recompenset, totaliter animam ei subiiciens.

name implies; indeed we are wont to say that things are adjusted when they are made equal, for equality is in reference of one thing to some other. On the other hand the other virtues perfect man in those matters only which befit him in relation to himself. Accordingly that which is right in the works of the other virtues, and to which the intention of the virtue tends as to its proper object, depends on its relation to the agent only, whereas the right in a work of justice, besides its relation to the agent, is set up by its relation to others. Because a man's work is said to be just when it is related to some other by way of some kind of equality, for instance the payment of the wage due for a service rendered. And so a thing is said to be just, as having the rectitude of justice, when it is the term of an act of justice, without taking into account the way in which it is done by the agent: whereas in the other virtues nothing is declared to be right unless it is done in a certain way by the agent. For this reason justice has its own special proper object over and above the other virtues, and this object is called the just, which is the same as right. Hence it is evident that right is the object of justice.

**Reply Obj. 1:** It is usual for words to be distorted from their original signification so as to mean something else: thus the word *medicine* was first employed to signify a remedy used for curing a sick person, and then it was drawn to signify the art by which this is done. In like manner the word right (*jus*) was first of all used to denote the just thing itself, but afterwards it was transferred to designate the art whereby it is known what is just, and further to denote the place where justice is administered, thus a man is said to appear *in jure*, and yet further, we say even that a man, who has the office of exercising justice, administers the jus even if his sentence be unjust.

**Reply Obj. 2:** Just as there pre-exists in the mind of the craftsman an expression of the things to be made externally by his craft, which expression is called the rule of his craft, so too there pre-exists in the mind an expression of the particular just work which the reason determines, and which is a kind of rule of prudence. If this rule be expressed in writing it is called a *law*, which according to Isidore (*Etym.* v, 1) is *a written decree*: and so law is not the same as right, but an expression of right.

**Reply Obj. 3:** Since justice implies equality, and since we cannot offer God an equal return, it follows that we cannot make Him a perfectly just repayment. For this reason the Divine law is not properly called *jus* but *fas*, because, to wit, God is satisfied if we accomplish what we can. Nevertheless justice tends to make man repay God as much as he can, by subjecting his mind to Him entirely.

# Article 2

*Whether right is fittingly divided into natural right and positive right?*

**Ad secundum sic proceditur.** Videtur quod ius non convenienter dividatur in ius naturale et ius positivum. Illud enim quod est naturale est immutabile, et idem apud omnes. Non autem invenitur in rebus humanis aliquid tale, quia omnes regulae iuris humani in aliquibus casibus deficiunt, nec habent suam virtutem ubique. Ergo non est aliquod ius naturale.

**Praeterea,** illud dicitur esse positivum quod ex voluntate humana procedit. Sed non ideo aliquid est iustum quia a voluntate humana procedit, alioquin voluntas hominis iniusta esse non posset. Ergo, cum iustum sit idem quod ius, videtur quod nullum sit ius positivum.

**Praeterea,** ius divinum non est ius naturale, cum excedat naturam humanam. Similiter etiam non est ius positivum, quia non innititur auctoritati humanae, sed auctoritati divinae. Ergo inconvenienter dividitur ius per naturale et positivum.

**Sed contra** est quod philosophus dicit, in V Ethic., quod *politici iusti hoc quidem naturale est, hoc autem legale,* idest lege positum.

**Respondeo** dicendum quod, sicut dictum est, ius, sive iustum, est aliquod opus adaequatum alteri secundum aliquem aequalitatis modum. Dupliciter autem potest alicui homini aliquid esse adaequatum. Uno quidem modo, ex ipsa natura rei, puta cum aliquis tantum dat ut tantundem recipiat. Et hoc vocatur ius naturale. Alio modo aliquid est adaequatum vel commensuratum alteri ex condicto, sive ex communi placito, quando scilicet aliquis reputat se contentum si tantum accipiat. Quod quidem potest fieri dupliciter. Uno modo, per aliquod privatum condictum, sicut quod firmatur aliquo pacto inter privatas personas. Alio modo, ex condicto publico, puta cum totus populus consentit quod aliquid habeatur quasi adaequatum et commensuratum alteri; vel cum hoc ordinat princeps, qui curam populi habet et eius personam gerit. Et hoc dicitur ius positivum.

**Ad primum** ergo dicendum quod illud quod est naturale habenti naturam immutabilem, oportet quod sit semper et ubique tale. Natura autem hominis est mutabilis. Et ideo id quod naturale est homini potest aliquando deficere. Sicut naturalem aequalitatem habet ut deponenti depositum reddatur, et si ita esset quod natura humana semper esset recta, hoc esset semper servandum. Sed quia quandoque contingit quod voluntas hominis depravatur, est aliquis casus in quo depositum non est reddendum, ne homo perversam voluntatem habens male eo utatur, ut puta si furiosus vel hostis reipublicae arma deposita reposcat.

**Objection 1**: It would seem that right is not fittingly divided into natural right and positive right. For that which is natural is unchangeable, and is the same for all. Now nothing of the kind is to be found in human affairs, since all the rules of human right fail in certain cases, nor do they obtain force everywhere. Therefore there is no such thing as natural right.

**Obj. 2**: Further, a thing is called *positive* when it proceeds from the human will. But a thing is not just, simply because it proceeds from the human will, else a man's will could not be unjust. Since then the *just* and the *right* are the same, it seems that there is no positive right.

**Obj. 3**: Further, Divine right is not natural right, since it transcends human nature. In like manner, neither is it positive right, since it is based not on human, but on Divine authority. Therefore right is unfittingly divided into natural and positive.

**On the contrary,** The Philosopher says (*Ethic.* v, 7) that *political justice is partly natural and partly legal,* i.e., established by law.

**I answer that,** As stated above (A. 1) the *right* or the *just* is a work that is adjusted to another person according to some kind of equality. Now a thing can be adjusted to a man in two ways: first by its very nature, as when a man gives so much that he may receive equal value in return, and this is called *natural right.* In another way a thing is adjusted or commensurated to another person, by agreement, or by common consent, when, to wit, a man deems himself satisfied, if he receive so much. This can be done in two ways: first by private agreement, as that which is confirmed by an agreement between private individuals; second, by public agreement, as when the whole community agrees that something should be deemed as though it were adjusted and commensurated to another person, or when this is decreed by the prince who is placed over the people, and acts in its stead, and this is called *positive right.*

**Reply Obj. 1**: That which is natural to one whose nature is unchangeable, must needs be such always and everywhere. But man's nature is changeable, wherefore that which is natural to man may sometimes fail. Thus the restitution of a deposit to the depositor is in accordance with natural equality, and if human nature were always right, this would always have to be observed; but since it happens sometimes that man's will is unrighteous there are cases in which a deposit should not be restored, lest a man of unrighteous will make evil use of the thing deposited: as when a madman or an enemy of the common weal demands the return of his weapons.

**AD SECUNDUM** dicendum quod voluntas humana ex communi condicto potest aliquid facere iustum in his quae secundum se non habent aliquam repugnantiam ad naturalem iustitiam. Et in his habet locum ius positivum. Unde philosophus dicit, in V Ethic., quod legale iustum est *quod ex principio quidem nihil differt sic vel aliter, quando autem ponitur, differt.* Sed si aliquid de se repugnantiam habeat ad ius naturale, non potest voluntate humana fieri iustum, puta si statuatur quod liceat furari vel adulterium committere. Unde dicitur Isaiae X, *vae qui condunt leges iniquas.*

**AD TERTIUM** dicendum quod ius divinum dicitur quod divinitus promulgatur. Et hoc quidem partim est de his quae sunt naturaliter iusta, sed tamen eorum iustitia homines latet, partim autem est de his quae fiunt iusta institutione divina. Unde etiam ius divinum per haec duo distingui potest, sicut et ius humanum. Sunt enim in lege divina quaedam praecepta quia bona, et prohibita quia mala, quaedam vero bona quia praecepta, et mala quia prohibita.

**REPLY OBJ. 2**: The human will can, by common agreement, make a thing to be just provided it be not, of itself, contrary to natural justice, and it is in such matters that positive right has its place. Hence the Philosopher says (*Ethic.* v, 7) that *in the case of the legal just, it does not matter in the first instance whether it takes one form or another, it only matters when once it is laid down.* If, however, a thing is, of itself, contrary to natural right, the human will cannot make it just, for instance by decreeing that it is lawful to steal or to commit adultery. Hence it is written (Isa 10:1): *Woe to them that make wicked laws.*

**REPLY OBJ. 3**: The Divine right is that which is promulgated by God. Such things are partly those that are naturally just, yet their justice is hidden to man, and partly are made just by God's decree. Hence also Divine right may be divided in respect of these two things, even as human right is. For the Divine law commands certain things because they are good, and forbids others, because they are evil, while others are good because they are prescribed, and others evil because they are forbidden.

# Article 3

*Whether the right of nations is the same as the natural right?*

**AD TERTIUM SIC PROCEDITUR**. Videtur quod ius gentium sit idem cum iure naturali. Non enim omnes homines conveniunt nisi in eo quod est eis naturale. Sed in iure gentium omnes homines conveniunt, dicit enim iurisconsultus quod *ius gentium est quo gentes humanae utuntur.* Ergo ius gentium est ius naturale.

**PRAETEREA**, servitus inter homines est naturalis, quidam enim sunt naturaliter servi, ut philosophus probat, in I Polit. Sed *servitutes pertinent ad ius gentium*, ut Isidorus dicit. Ergo ius gentium est ius naturale.

**PRAETEREA**, ius, ut dictum est, dividitur per ius naturale et positivum. Sed ius gentium non est ius positivum, non enim omnes gentes unquam convenerunt ut ex communi condicto aliquid statuerent. Ergo ius gentium est ius naturale.

**SED CONTRA** est quod Isidorus dicit, quod *ius aut naturale est, aut civile, aut gentium.* Et ita ius gentium distinguitur a iure naturali.

**RESPONDEO** dicendum quod, sicut dictum est, ius sive iustum naturale est quod ex sui natura est adaequatum vel commensuratum alteri. Hoc autem potest contingere dupliciter. Uno modo, secundum absolutam sui considerationem, sicut masculus ex sui ratione habet commensurationem ad feminam ut ex ea generet, et parens ad filium ut eum nutriat. Alio modo aliquid est naturaliter alteri commensuratum non secundum absolutam sui rationem, sed secundum aliquid quod

**OBJECTION 1**: It would seem that the right of nations is the same as the natural right. For all men do not agree save in that which is natural to them. Now all men agree in the right of nations; since the jurist says: *the right of nations is that which is in use among all nations.* Therefore the right of nations is the natural right.

**OBJ. 2**: Further, slavery among men is natural, for some are naturally slaves according to the Philosopher (*Polit.* i, 2). Now *slavery belongs to the right of nations*, as Isidore states (*Etym.* v, 4). Therefore the right of nations is a natural right.

**OBJ. 3**: Further, right as stated above (A. 2) is divided into natural and positive. Now the right of nations is not a positive right, since all nations never agreed to decree anything by common agreement. Therefore the right of nations is a natural right.

**ON THE CONTRARY**, Isidore says (*Etym.* v, 4) that *right is either natural, or civil, or right of nations*, and consequently the right of nations is distinct from natural right.

**I ANSWER THAT**, As stated above (A. 2), the natural right or just is that which by its very nature is adjusted to or commensurate with another person. Now this may happen in two ways; first, according as it is considered absolutely: thus a male by very nature is commensurate with the female to beget offspring by her, and a parent is commensurate with the offspring to nourish it. Second a thing is naturally commensurate with another person, not according as it is considered absolutely, but according to something resultant

ex ipso consequitur, puta proprietas possessionum. Si enim consideretur iste ager absolute, non habet unde magis sit huius quam illius, sed si consideretur quantum ad opportunitatem colendi et ad pacificum usum agri, secundum hoc habet quandam commensurationem ad hoc quod sit unius et non alterius, ut patet per philosophum, in II Polit.

Absolute autem apprehendere aliquid non solum convenit homini, sed etiam aliis animalibus. Et ideo ius quod dicitur naturale secundum primum modum, commune est nobis et aliis animalibus. *A iure autem naturali* sic dicto recedit ius gentium, ut iurisconsultus dicit, *quia illud omnibus animalibus, hoc solum hominibus inter se commune est.* Considerare autem aliquid comparando ad id quod ex ipso sequitur, est proprium rationis. Et ideo hoc quidem est naturale homini secundum rationem naturalem, quae hoc dictat. Et ideo dicit Gaius iurisconsultus, *quod naturalis ratio inter omnes homines constituit, id apud omnes gentes custoditur, vocaturque ius gentium.*

ET PER HOC patet responsio ad primum.

AD SECUNDUM dicendum quod hunc hominem esse servum, absolute considerando, magis quam alium, non habet rationem naturalem, sed solum secundum aliquam utilitatem consequentem, inquantum utile est huic quod regatur a sapientiori, et illi quod ab hoc iuvetur, ut dicitur in I Polit. Et ideo servitus pertinens ad ius gentium est naturalis secundo modo, sed non primo.

AD TERTIUM dicendum quod quia ea quae sunt iuris gentium naturalis ratio dictat, puta ex propinquo habentia aequitatem; inde est quod non indigent aliqua speciali institutione, sed ipsa naturalis ratio ea instituit, ut dictum est in auctoritate inducta.

from it, for instance the possession of property. For if a particular piece of land be considered absolutely, it contains no reason why it should belong to one man more than to another, but if it be considered in respect of its adaptability to cultivation, and the unmolested use of the land, it has a certain commensuration to be the property of one and not of another man, as the Philosopher shows (*Polit.* ii, 2).

Now it belongs not only to man but also to other animals to apprehend a thing absolutely: wherefore the right which we call natural, is common to us and other animals according to the first kind of commensuration. But the right of nations falls short of natural right in this sense, as the jurist says because *the latter is common to all animals, while the former is common to men only.* On the other hand to consider a thing by comparing it with what results from it, is proper to reason, wherefore this same is natural to man in respect of natural reason which dictates it. Hence the jurist Gaius says (*Digest.* i, 1; *De Just. et Jure* i, 9): *whatever natural reason decrees among all men, is observed by all equally, and is called the right of nations.*

THIS SUFFICES for the Reply to the First Objection.

REPLY OBJ. 2: Considered absolutely, the fact that this particular man should be a slave rather than another man, is based, not on natural reason, but on some resultant utility, in that it is useful to this man to be ruled by a wiser man, and to the latter to be helped by the former, as the Philosopher states (*Polit.* i, 2). Wherefore slavery which belongs to the right of nations is natural in the second way, but not in the first.

REPLY OBJ. 3: Since natural reason dictates matters which are according to the right of nations, as implying a proximate equality, it follows that they need no special institution, for they are instituted by natural reason itself, as stated by the authority quoted above.

# Article 4

*Whether paternal right and right of dominion should be distinguished as special species?*

AD QUARTUM SIC PROCEDITUR. Videtur quod non debeat specialiter distingui ius paternum et dominativum. Ad iustitiam enim pertinet *reddere unicuique quod suum est*; ut dicit Ambrosius, in I de officiis. Sed ius est obiectum iustitiae, sicut dictum est. Ergo ius ad unumquemque aequaliter pertinet. Et sic non debet distingui specialiter ius patris et domini.

PRAETEREA, ratio iusti est lex, ut dictum est. Sed lex respicit commune bonum civitatis et regni, ut supra habitum est, non autem respicit bonum privatum unius personae, aut etiam unius familiae. Non ergo debet esse aliquod speciale ius vel iustum dominativum vel pater-

OBJECTION 1: It would seem that *paternal right* and *right of dominion* should not be distinguished as special species. For it belongs to justice to render to each one what is his, as Ambrose states (*De Offic.* i, 24). Now right is the object of justice, as stated above (A. 1). Therefore right belongs to each one equally; and we ought not to distinguish the rights of fathers and masters as distinct species.

OBJ. 2: Further, the law is an expression of what is just, as stated above (A. 1, ad 2). Now a law looks to the common good of a city or kingdom, as stated above (I-II, Q. 90, A. 2), but not to the private good of an individual or even of one household. Therefore there is no need for a special right of

num, cum dominus et pater pertineant ad domum, ut dicitur in I Polit.

**PRAETEREA**, multae aliae sunt differentiae graduum in hominibus, ut puta quod quidam sunt milites, quidam sacerdotes, quidam principes. Ergo ad eos debet aliquod speciale iustum determinari.

**SED CONTRA** est quod philosophus, in V Ethic., specialiter a iusto politico distinguit dominativum et paternum, et alia huiusmodi.

**RESPONDEO** dicendum quod ius, sive iustum dicitur per commensurationem ad alterum. Alterum autem potest dici dupliciter. Uno modo, quod simpliciter est alterum, sicut quod est omnino distinctum, sicut apparet in duobus hominibus quorum unus non est sub altero, sed ambo sunt sub uno principe civitatis. Et inter tales, secundum philosophum, in V Ethic., est simpliciter iustum. Alio modo dicitur aliquid alterum non simpliciter, sed quasi aliquid eius existens. Et hoc modo in rebus humanis filius est aliquid patris, quia quodammodo est pars eius, ut dicitur in VIII Ethic.; et servus est aliquid domini, quia est instrumentum eius, ut dicitur in I Polit. Et ideo patris ad filium non est comparatio sicut ad simpliciter alterum, et propter hoc non est ibi simpliciter iustum, sed quoddam iustum, scilicet paternum. Et eadem ratione nec inter dominum et servum, sed est inter eos dominativum iustum. Uxor autem, quamvis sit aliquid viri, quia comparatur ad eam sicut ad proprium corpus, ut patet per apostolum, ad Ephes. V; tamen magis distinguitur a viro quam filius a patre vel servus a domino, assumitur enim in quandam socialem vitam matrimonii. Et ideo, ut philosophus dicit, inter virum et uxorem plus est de ratione iusti quam inter patrem et filium, vel dominum et servum. Quia tamen vir et uxor habent immediatam relationem ad domesticam communitatem, ut patet in I Polit.; ideo inter eos non est etiam simpliciter politicum iustum, sed magis iustum oeconomicum.

**AD PRIMUM** ergo dicendum quod ad iustitiam pertinet reddere ius suum unicuique, supposita tamen diversitate unius ad alterum, si quis enim sibi det quod sibi debetur, non proprie vocatur hoc iustum. Et quia quod est filii est patris, et quod est servi est domini, ideo non est proprie iustitia patris ad filium, vel domini ad servum.

**AD SECUNDUM** dicendum quod filius, inquantum filius, est aliquid patris; et similiter servus, inquantum servus, est aliquid domini. Uterque tamen prout consideratur ut quidam homo, est aliquid secundum se subsistens ab aliis distinctum. Et ideo inquantum uterque est homo, aliquo modo ad eos est iustitia. Et propter hoc etiam aliquae leges dantur de his quae sunt

dominion or paternal right, since the master and the father pertain to a household, as stated in *Polit.* i, 2.

**OBJ. 3**: Further, there are many other differences of degrees among men, for instance some are soldiers, some are priests, some are princes. Therefore some special kind of right should be allotted to them.

**ON THE CONTRARY**, The Philosopher (*Ethic.* v, 6) distinguishes right of dominion, paternal right and so on as species distinct from civil right.

**I ANSWER THAT**, Right or just depends on commensuration with another person. Now *another* has a twofold signification. First, it may denote something that is other simply, as that which is altogether distinct; as, for example, two men neither of whom is subject to the other, and both of whom are subjects of the ruler of the state; and between these according to the Philosopher (*Ethic.* v, 6) there is the *just* simply. Second a thing is said to be other from something else, not simply, but as belonging in some way to that something else: and in this way, as regards human affairs, a son belongs to his father, since he is part of him somewhat, as stated in *Ethic.* viii, 12, and a slave belongs to his master, because he is his instrument, as stated in *Polit.* i, 2. Hence a father is not compared to his son as to another simply, and so between them there is not the just simply, but a kind of just, called *paternal*. In like manner neither is there the just simply, between master and servant, but that which is called *dominative*. A wife, though she is something belonging to the husband, since she stands related to him as to her own body, as the Apostle declares (*Eph 5:28*), is nevertheless more distinct from her husband, than a son from his father, or a slave from his master: for she is received into a kind of social life, that of matrimony, wherefore according to the Philosopher (*Ethic.* v, 6) there is more scope for justice between husband and wife than between father and son, or master and slave, because, as husband and wife have an immediate relation to the community of the household, as stated in *Polit.* i, 2, 5, it follows that between them there is *domestic justice* rather than *civic*.

**REPLY OBJ. 1**: It belongs to justice to render to each one his right, the distinction between individuals being presupposed: for if a man gives himself his due, this is not strictly called *just*. And since what belongs to the son is his father's, and what belongs to the slave is his master's, it follows that properly speaking there is not justice of father to son, or of master to slave.

**REPLY OBJ. 2**: A son, as such, belongs to his father, and a slave, as such, belongs to his master; yet each, considered as a man, is something having separate existence and distinct from others. Hence insofar as each of them is a man, there is justice towards them in a way: and for this reason too there are certain laws regulating the relations of father to his son, and of a master to his slave; but insofar as each

patris ad filium, vel domini ad servum. Sed inquantum uterque est aliquid alterius, secundum hoc deficit ibi perfecta ratio iusti vel iuris.

**AD TERTIUM** dicendum quod omnes aliae diversitates personarum quae sunt in civitate, habent immediatam relationem ad communitatem civitatis et ad principem ipsius. Et ideo ad eos est iustum secundum perfectam rationem iustitiae. Distinguitur tamen istud iustum secundum diversa officia. Unde et dicitur ius militare vel ius magistratuum aut sacerdotum, non propter defectum a simpliciter iusto, sicut dicitur ius paternum et dominativum, sed propter hoc quod unicuique conditioni personae secundum proprium officium aliquid proprium debetur.

is something belonging to another, the perfect idea of *right* or *just* is wanting to them.

**REPLY OBJ. 3**: All other differences between one person and another in a state, have an immediate relation to the community of the state and to its ruler, wherefore there is just towards them in the perfect sense of justice. This *just* however is distinguished according to various offices, hence when we speak of *military*, or *magisterial*, or *priestly* right, it is not as though such rights fell short of the simply right, as when we speak of *paternal* right, or right of *dominion*, but for the reason that something proper is due to each class of person in respect of his particular office.

# QUESTION 58

## JUSTICE

Deinde considerandum est de iustitia. Circa quam quaeruntur duodecim.

Primo, quid sit iustitia.

Secundo, utrum iustitia semper sit ad alterum.

Tertio, utrum sit virtus.

Quarto, utrum sit in voluntate sicut in subiecto.

Quinto, utrum sit virtus generalis.

Sexto, utrum secundum quod est generalis, sit idem in essentia cum omni virtute.

Septimo, utrum sit aliqua iustitia particularis.

Octavo, utrum iustitia particularis habeat propriam materiam.

Nono, utrum sit circa passiones, vel circa operationes tantum.

Decimo, utrum medium iustitiae sit medium rei.

Undecimo, utrum actus iustitiae sit reddere unicuique quod suum est.

Duodecimo, utrum iustitia sit praecipua inter alias virtutes morales.

We must now consider justice. Under this head there are twelve points of inquiry:

(1) What is justice?

(2) Whether justice is always towards another?

(3) Whether it is a virtue?

(4) Whether it is in the will as its subject?

(5) Whether it is a general virtue?

(6) Whether, as a general virtue, it is essentially the same as every virtue?

(7) Whether there is a particular justice?

(8) Whether particular justice has a matter of its own?

(9) Whether it is about passions, or about operations only?

(10) Whether the mean of justice is the real mean?

(11) Whether the act of justice is to render to everyone his own?

(12) Whether justice is the chief of the moral virtues?

# Article 1

*Whether justice is fittingly defined as being "the perpetual and constant will to render to each one his right"?*

**AD PRIMUM SIC PROCEDITUR.** Videtur quod inconvenienter definiatur a iurisperitis quod *iustitia est constans et perpetua voluntas ius suum unicuique tribuens. Iustitia enim,* secundum Philosophum, in V Ethic., *est habitus a quo sunt aliqui operativi iustorum, et a quo operantur et volunt iusta.* Sed voluntas nominat potentiam, vel etiam actum. Ergo inconvenienter iustitia dicitur esse voluntas.

**PRAETEREA,** rectitudo voluntatis non est voluntas, alioquin, si voluntas esset sua rectitudo, sequeretur quod nulla voluntas esset perversa. Sed secundum Anselmum, in libro de veritate, *iustitia est rectitudo.* Ergo iustitia non est voluntas.

**PRAETEREA,** sola Dei voluntas est perpetua. Si ergo iustitia est perpetua voluntas, in solo Deo erit iustitia.

**PRAETEREA,** omne perpetuum est constans, quia est immutabile. Superflue ergo utrumque ponitur in definitione iustitiae, et *perpetuum* et *constans.*

**OBJECTION 1:** It would seem that lawyers have unfittingly defined justice as being *the perpetual and constant will to render to each one his right.* For, according to the Philosopher (*Ethic.* v, 1), justice is a habit which makes a man *capable of doing what is just, and of being just in action and in intention.* Now *will* denotes a power, or also an act. Therefore justice is unfittingly defined as being a will.

**OBJ. 2:** Further, rectitude of the will is not the will; else if the will were its own rectitude, it would follow that no will is unrighteous. Yet, according to Anselm (*De Veritate* xii), *justice is rectitude.* Therefore justice is not the will.

**OBJ. 3:** Further, no will is perpetual save God's. If therefore justice is a perpetual will, in God alone will there be justice.

**OBJ. 4:** Further, whatever is perpetual is constant, since it is unchangeable. Therefore it is needless in defining justice, to say that it is both *perpetual* and *constant.*

535

**Praeterea**, reddere ius unicuique pertinet ad principem. Si igitur iustitia sit ius suum unicuique tribuens, sequetur quod iustitia non sit nisi in principe. Quod est inconveniens.

**Praeterea**, Augustinus dicit, in libro de moribus Eccles., quod *iustitia est amor Deo tantum serviens*. Non ergo reddit unicuique quod suum est.

**Respondeo** dicendum quod praedicta iustitiae definitio conveniens est, si recte intelligatur. Cum enim omnis virtus sit habitus qui est principium boni actus, necesse est quod virtus definiatur per actum bonum circa propriam materiam virtutis. Est autem iustitia circa ea quae ad alterum sunt sicut circa propriam materiam, ut infra patebit. Et ideo actus iustitiae per comparationem ad propriam materiam et obiectum tangitur cum dicitur, *ius suum unicuique tribuens*, quia, ut Isidorus dicit, in libro Etymol., *iustus dicitur quia ius custodit*.

Ad hoc autem quod aliquis actus circa quamcumque materiam sit virtuosus, requiritur quod sit voluntarius, et quod sit stabilis et firmus, quia philosophus dicit, in II Ethic., quod ad virtutis actum requiritur primo quidem quod *operetur sciens*, secundo autem quod *eligens et propter debitum finem*, tertio quod *immobiliter operetur*. Primum autem horum includitur in secundo, quia quod *per ignorantiam agitur est involuntarium*, ut dicitur in III Ethic. Et ideo in definitione iustitiae primo ponitur *voluntas*, ad ostendendum quod actus iustitiae debet esse voluntarius. Additur autem de *constantia* et *perpetuitate*, ad designandum actus firmitatem.

Et ideo praedicta definitio est completa definitio iustitiae, nisi quod actus ponitur pro habitu, qui per actum specificatur, habitus enim ad actum dicitur. Et si quis vellet in debitam formam definitionis reducere, posset sic dicere, quod iustitia est habitus secundum quem aliquis constanti et perpetua voluntate ius suum unicuique tribuit. Et quasi est eadem definitio cum ea quam philosophus ponit, in V Ethic., dicens quod *iustitia est habitus secundum quem aliquis dicitur operativus secundum electionem iusti*.

**Ad primum** ergo dicendum quod voluntas hic nominat actum, non potentiam. Est autem consuetum quod apud auctores habitus per actus definiantur, sicut Augustinus dicit, super Ioan., quod *fides est credere quod non vides*.

**Ad secundum** dicendum quod neque etiam iustitia est essentialiter rectitudo, sed causaliter tantum, est enim habitus secundum quem aliquis recte operatur et vult.

**Ad tertium** dicendum quod voluntas potest dici perpetua dupliciter. Uno modo, ex parte ipsius actus, qui perpetuo durat. Et sic solius Dei voluntas est perpetua. Alio modo, ex parte obiecti, quia scilicet aliquis vult perpetuo facere aliquid. Et hoc requiritur ad rationem

**Obj. 5**: Further, it belongs to the sovereign to give each one his right. Therefore, if justice gives each one his right, it follows that it is in none but the sovereign: which is absurd.

**Obj. 6**: Further, Augustine says (*De Moribus Eccl.* xv) that *justice is love serving God alone*. Therefore it does not render to each one his right.

**I answer that**, The aforesaid definition of justice is fitting if understood aright. For since every virtue is a habit that is the principle of a good act, a virtue must needs be defined by means of the good act bearing on the matter proper to that virtue. Now the proper matter of justice consists of those things that belong to our intercourse with other men, as shall be shown further on (A. 2). Hence the act of justice in relation to its proper matter and object is indicated in the words, *Rendering to each one his right*, since, as Isidore says (*Etym.* x), *a man is said to be just because he respects the rights (jus) of others*.

Now in order that an act bearing upon any matter whatever be virtuous, it requires to be voluntary, stable, and firm, because the Philosopher says (*Ethic.* ii, 4) that in order for an act to be virtuous it needs first of all to be done *knowingly*, second to be done *by choice*, and *for a due end*, third to be done *immovably*. Now the first of these is included in the second, since *what is done through ignorance is involuntary* (*Ethic.* iii, 1). Hence the definition of justice mentions first the *will*, in order to show that the act of justice must be voluntary; and mention is made afterwards of its *constancy* and *perpetuity* in order to indicate the firmness of the act.

Accordingly, this is a complete definition of justice; save that the act is mentioned instead of the habit, which takes its species from that act, because habit implies relation to act. And if anyone would reduce it to the proper form of a definition, he might say that *justice is a habit whereby a man renders to each one his due by a constant and perpetual will*: and this is about the same definition as that given by the Philosopher (*Ethic.* v, 5) who says that *justice is a habit whereby a man is said to be capable of doing just actions in accordance with his choice*.

**Reply Obj. 1**: Will here denotes the act, not the power: and it is customary among writers to define habits by their acts: thus Augustine says (*Tract. in Joan.* xl) that *faith is to believe what one sees not*.

**Reply Obj. 2**: Justice is the same as rectitude, not essentially but causally; for it is a habit which rectifies the deed and the will.

**Reply Obj. 3**: The will may be called perpetual in two ways. First on the part of the will's act which endures for ever, and thus God's will alone is perpetual. Second on the part of the subject, because, to wit, a man wills to do a certain thing always, and this is a necessary condition of

iustitiae. Non enim sufficit ad rationem iustitiae quod aliquis velit ad horam in aliquo negotio servare iustitiam, quia vix invenitur aliquis qui velit in omnibus iniuste agere, sed requiritur quod homo habeat voluntatem perpetuo et in omnibus iustitiam conservandi.

**AD QUARTUM** dicendum quod quia perpetuum non accipitur secundum durationem perpetuam actus voluntatis, non superflue additur *constans*, ut sicut per hoc quod dicitur *perpetua voluntas* designatur quod aliquis gerat in proposito perpetuo iustitiam conservandi, ita etiam per hoc quod dicitur *constans* designatur quod in hoc proposito firmiter perseveret.

**AD QUINTUM** dicendum quod iudex reddit quod suum est per modum imperantis et dirigentis, quia *iudex est iustum animatum*, et *princeps est custos iusti*, ut dicitur in V Ethic. Sed subditi reddunt quod suum est unicuique per modum executionis.

**AD SEXTUM** dicendum quod sicut in dilectione Dei includitur dilectio proximi, ut supra dictum est; ita etiam in hoc quod homo servit Deo includitur quod unicuique reddat quod debet.

justice. For it does not satisfy the conditions of justice that one wish to observe justice in some particular matter for the time being, because one could scarcely find a man willing to act unjustly in every case; and it is requisite that one should have the will to observe justice at all times and in all cases.

**REPLY OBJ. 4**: Since *perpetual* does not imply perpetuity of the act of the will, it is not superfluous to add *constant*: for while the *perpetual will* denotes the purpose of observing justice always, *constant* signifies a firm perseverance in this purpose.

**REPLY OBJ. 5**: A judge renders to each one what belongs to him, by way of command and direction, because *a judge is the personification of justice*, and *the sovereign is its guardian* (*Ethic.* v, 4). On the other hand, the subjects render to each one what belongs to him, by way of execution.

**REPLY OBJ. 6**: Just as love of God includes love of our neighbor, as stated above (Q. 25, A. 1), so too the service of God includes rendering to each one his due.

# Article 2

### Whether justice is always towards another?

**AD SECUNDUM SIC PROCEDITUR.** Videtur quod iustitia non semper sit ad alterum. Dicit enim apostolus, ad Rom. III, quod *iustitia Dei est per fidem Iesu Christi*. Sed fides non dicitur per comparationem unius hominis ad alterum. Ergo neque iustitia.

**PRAETEREA,** secundum Augustinum, in libro de moribus Eccles., ad iustitiam pertinet, ob hoc quod servit Deo, *bene imperare ceteris, quae homini sunt subiecta.* Sed appetitus sensitivus est homini subiectus, ut patet Gen. IV, ubi dicitur, *subter te erit appetitus eius*, scilicet peccati, *et tu dominaberis illius*. Ergo ad iustitiam pertinet dominari proprio appetitui. Et sic erit iustitia ad seipsum.

**PRAETEREA,** iustitia Dei est aeterna. Sed nihil aliud fuit Deo coaeternum. Ergo de ratione iustitiae non est quod sit ad alterum.

**PRAETEREA,** sicut operationes quae sunt ad alterum indigent rectificari, ita etiam operationes quae sunt ad seipsum. Sed per iustitiam rectificantur operationes, secundum illud Prov. XI, *iustitia simplicis dirigit viam eius*. Ergo iustitia non solum est circa ea quae sunt ad alterum, sed etiam circa ea quae sunt ad seipsum.

**SED CONTRA** est quod Tullius dicit, in I de Offic., quod *iustitiae ea ratio est qua societas hominum inter ipsos, et vitae communitas continetur*. Sed hoc importat

**OBJECTION 1**: It would seem that justice is not always towards another. For the Apostle says (Rom 3:22) that *the justice of God is by faith of Jesus Christ*. Now faith does not concern the dealings of one man with another. Neither therefore does justice.

**OBJ. 2**: Further, according to Augustine (*De Moribus Eccl.* xv), *it belongs to justice that man should direct to the service of God his authority over the things that are subject to him*. Now the sensitive appetite is subject to man, according to Gen. 4:7, where it is written: *The lust thereof*, viz. of sin, *shall be under thee, and thou shalt have dominion over it*. Therefore it belongs to justice to have dominion over one's own appetite: so that justice is towards oneself.

**OBJ. 3**: Further, the justice of God is eternal. But nothing else is co-eternal with God. Therefore justice is not essentially towards another.

**OBJ. 4**: Further, man's dealings with himself need to be rectified no less than his dealings with another. Now man's dealings are rectified by justice, according to Prov. 11:5, *The justice of the upright shall make his way prosperous*. Therefore justice is about our dealings not only with others, but also with ourselves.

**ON THE CONTRARY**, Tully says (*De Officiis* i, 7) that *the object of justice is to keep men together in society and mutual intercourse*. Now this implies relationship of one

respectum ad alterum. Ergo iustitia est solum circa ea quae sunt ad alterum.

**Respondeo** dicendum quod, sicut supra dictum est, cum nomen iustitiae aequalitatem importet, ex sua ratione iustitia habet quod sit ad alterum, nihil enim est sibi aequale, sed alteri. Et quia ad iustitiam pertinet actus humanos rectificare, ut dictum est, necesse est quod alietas ista quam requirit iustitia, sit diversorum agere potentium. Actiones autem sunt suppositorum et totorum, non autem, proprie loquendo, partium et formarum, seu potentiarum, non enim proprie dicitur quod manus percutiat, sed homo per manum; neque proprie dicitur quod calor calefaciat, sed ignis per calorem. Secundum tamen similitudinem quandam haec dicuntur. Iustitia ergo proprie dicta requirit diversitatem suppositorum, et ideo non est nisi unius hominis ad alium. Sed secundum similitudinem accipiuntur in uno et eodem homine diversa principia actionum quasi diversa agentia, sicut ratio et irascibilis et concupiscibilis. Et ideo metaphorice in uno et eodem homine dicitur esse iustitia, secundum quod ratio imperat irascibili et concupiscibili, et secundum quod hae obediunt rationi, et universaliter secundum quod unicuique parti hominis attribuitur quod ei convenit. Unde philosophus, in V Ethic., hanc iustitiam appellat *secundum metaphoram* dictam.

**Ad primum** ergo dicendum quod iustitia quae fit per fidem in nobis, est per quam iustificatur impius, quae quidem in ipsa debita ordinatione partium animae consistit, sicut supra dictum est, cum de iustificatione impii ageretur. Hoc autem pertinet ad iustitiam metaphorice dictam, quae potest inveniri etiam in aliquo solitariam vitam agente.

**Et per hoc** patet responsio ad secundum.

**Ad tertium** dicendum quod iustitia Dei est ab aeterno secundum voluntatem et propositum aeternum, et in hoc praecipue iustitia consistit. Quamvis secundum effectum non sit ab aeterno, quia nihil est Deo coaeternum.

**Ad quartum** dicendum quod actiones quae sunt hominis ad seipsum sufficienter rectificantur rectificatis passionibus per alias virtutes morales. Sed actiones quae sunt ad alterum indigent speciali rectificatione, non solum per comparationem ad agentem, sed etiam per comparationem ad eum ad quem sunt. Et ideo circa eas est specialis virtus, quae est iustitia.

man to another. Therefore justice is concerned only about our dealings with others.

**I answer that,** As stated above (Q. 57, A. 1) since justice by its name implies equality, it denotes essentially relation to another, for a thing is equal, not to itself, but to another. And forasmuch as it belongs to justice to rectify human acts, as stated above (Q. 57, A. 1; I-II, Q. 113, A. 1) this otherness which justice demands must needs be between beings capable of action. Now actions belong to supposits and wholes and, properly speaking, not to parts and forms or powers, for we do not say properly that the hand strikes, but a man with his hand, nor that heat makes a thing hot, but fire by heat, although such expressions may be employed metaphorically. Hence, justice properly speaking demands a distinction of supposits, and consequently is only in one man towards another. Nevertheless in one and the same man we may speak metaphorically of his various principles of action such as the reason, the irascible, and the concupiscible, as though they were so many agents: so that metaphorically in one and the same man there is said to be justice insofar as the reason commands the irascible and concupiscible, and these obey reason; and in general insofar as to each part of man is ascribed what is becoming to it. Hence the Philosopher (*Ethic.* v, 11) calls this *metaphorical justice.*

**Reply Obj. 1:** The justice which faith works in us, is that whereby the ungodly is justified: it consists in the due coordination of the parts of the soul, as stated above (I-II, Q. 113, A. 1) where we were treating of the justification of the ungodly. Now this belongs to metaphorical justice, which may be found even in a man who lives all by himself.

**This suffices** for the Reply to the Second Objection.

**Reply Obj. 3:** God's justice is from eternity in respect of the eternal will and purpose (and it is chiefly in this that justice consists); although it is not eternal as regards its effect, since nothing is co-eternal with God.

**Reply Obj. 4:** Man's dealings with himself are sufficiently rectified by the rectification of the passions by the other moral virtues. But his dealings with others need a special rectification, not only in relation to the agent, but also in relation to the person to whom they are directed. Hence about such dealings there is a special virtue, and this is justice.

# Article 3

*Whether justice is a virtue?*

**AD TERTIUM SIC PROCEDITUR.** Videtur quod iustitia non sit virtus. Dicitur enim Luc. XVII, *cum feceritis omnia quae praecepta sunt vobis, dicite, servi inutiles sumus, quod debuimus facere fecimus.* Sed non est inutile facere opus virtutis, dicit enim Ambrosius, in II de Offic., *utilitatem non pecuniarii lucri aestimationem dicimus, sed acquisitionem pietatis.* Ergo facere quod quis debet facere non est opus virtutis. Est autem opus iustitiae. Ergo iustitia non est virtus.

**PRAETEREA,** quod fit ex necessitate non est meritorium. Sed reddere alicui quod suum est, quod pertinet ad iustitiam, est necessitatis. Ergo non est meritorium. Actibus autem virtutum meremur. Ergo iustitia non est virtus.

**PRAETEREA,** omnis virtus moralis est circa agibilia. Ea autem quae exterius constituuntur non sunt agibilia, sed factibilia, ut patet per philosophum, in IX Metaphys. Cum igitur ad iustitiam pertineat exterius facere aliquod opus secundum se iustum, videtur quod iustitia non sit virtus moralis.

**SED CONTRA** est quod Gregorius dicit, in II Moral., quod *in quatuor virtutibus,* scilicet temperantia, prudentia, fortitudine et iustitia, *tota boni operis structura consurgit.*

**RESPONDEO** dicendum quod virtus humana est quae bonum reddit actum humanum, et ipsum hominem bonum facit. Quod quidem convenit iustitiae. Actus enim hominis bonus redditur ex hoc quod attingit regulam rationis, secundum quam humani actus rectificantur. Unde cum iustitia operationes humanas rectificet, manifestum est quod opus hominis bonum reddit. Et ut Tullius dicit, in I de Offic., *ex iustitia praecipue viri boni nominantur.* Unde, sicut ibidem dicit, *in ea virtutis splendor est maximus.*

**AD PRIMUM** ergo dicendum quod cum aliquis facit quod debet, non affert utilitatem lucri ei cui facit quod debet, sed solum abstinet a damno eius. Sibi tamen facit utilitatem, inquantum spontanea et prompta voluntate facit illud quod debet, quod est virtuose agere. Unde dicitur Sap. VIII quod sapientia Dei *sobrietatem et iustitiam docet, prudentiam et virtutem*; quibus in vita nihil est utilius hominibus, scilicet virtuosis.

**AD SECUNDUM** dicendum quod duplex est necessitas. Una coactionis, et haec, quia repugnat voluntati, tollit rationem meriti. Alia autem est necessitas ex obligatione praecepti, sive ex necessitate finis, quando scilicet aliquis non potest consequi finem virtutis nisi hoc faciat. Et talis necessitas non excludit rationem

**OBJECTION 1:** It would seem that justice is not a virtue. For it is written (Luke 17:10): *When you shall have done all these things that are commanded you, say: We are unprofitable servants; we have done that which we ought to do.* Now it is not unprofitable to do a virtuous deed: for Ambrose says (*De Officiis* ii, 6): *We look to a profit that is estimated not by pecuniary gain but by the acquisition of godliness.* Therefore to do what one ought to do, is not a virtuous deed. And yet it is an act of justice. Therefore justice is not a virtue.

**OBJ. 2:** Further, that which is done of necessity, is not meritorious. But to render to a man what belongs to him, as justice requires, is of necessity. Therefore it is not meritorious. Yet it is by virtuous actions that we gain merit. Therefore justice is not a virtue.

**OBJ. 3:** Further, every moral virtue is about matters of action. Now those things which are wrought externally are not things concerning behavior but concerning handicraft, according to the Philosopher (*Metaph.* ix). Therefore since it belongs to justice to produce externally a deed that is just in itself, it seems that justice is not a moral virtue.

**ON THE CONTRARY,** Gregory says (*Moral.* ii, 49) that *the entire structure of good works is built on four virtues,* viz. temperance, prudence, fortitude and justice.

**I ANSWER THAT,** A human virtue is one which renders a human act and man himself good, and this can be applied to justice. For a man's act is made good through attaining the rule of reason, which is the rule whereby human acts are regulated. Hence, since justice regulates human operations, it is evident that it renders man's operations good, and, as Tully declares (*De Officiis* i, 7), good men are so called chiefly from their justice, wherefore, as he says again (*De Officiis* i, 7) *the luster of virtue appears above all in justice.*

**REPLY OBJ. 1:** When a man does what he ought, he brings no gain to the person to whom he does what he ought, but only abstains from doing him a harm. He does however profit himself, insofar as he does what he ought, spontaneously and readily, and this is to act virtuously. Hence it is written (Wis 8:7) that Divine wisdom *teacheth temperance, and prudence, and justice, and fortitude, which are such things as men (i.e., virtuous men) can have nothing more profitable in life.*

**REPLY OBJ. 2:** Necessity is twofold. One arises from constraint, and this removes merit, since it runs counter to the will. The other arises from the obligation of a command, or from the necessity of obtaining an end, when, to wit, a man is unable to achieve the end of virtue without doing some particular thing. The latter necessity does not

meriti, inquantum aliquis hoc quod sic est necessarium voluntarie agit. Excludit tamen gloriam supererogationis, secundum illud I ad Cor. IX, *si evangelizavero, non est mihi gloria, necessitas enim mihi incumbit.*

**AD TERTIUM** dicendum quod iustitia non consistit circa exteriores res quantum ad facere, quod pertinet ad artem, sed quantum ad hoc quod utitur eis ad alterum.

remove merit, when a man does voluntarily that which is necessary in this way. It does however exclude the credit of supererogation, according to 1 Cor. 9:16, *If I preach the Gospel, it is no glory to me, for a necessity lieth upon me.*

**REPLY OBJ. 3**: Justice is concerned about external things, not by making them, which pertains to art, but by using them in our dealings with other men.

# Article 4

*Whether justice is in the will as its subject?*

**AD QUARTUM SIC PROCEDITUR**. Videtur quod iustitia non sit in voluntate sicut in subiecto. Iustitia enim quandoque veritas dicitur. Sed veritas non est voluntatis, sed intellectus. Ergo iustitia non est in voluntate sicut in subiecto.

**PRAETEREA**, iustitia est circa ea quae sunt ad alterum. Sed ordinare aliquid ad alterum est rationis. Iustitia ergo non est in voluntate sicut in subiecto, sed magis in ratione.

**PRAETEREA**, iustitia non est virtus intellectualis, cum non ordinetur ad cognitionem. Unde relinquitur quod sit virtus moralis. Sed subiectum virtutis moralis est *rationale per participationem*, quod est irascibilis et concupiscibilis, ut patet per philosophum, in I Ethic. Ergo iustitia non est in voluntate sicut in subiecto, sed magis in irascibili et concupiscibili.

**SED CONTRA** est quod Anselmus dicit, quod *iustitia est rectitudo voluntatis propter se servata.*

**RESPONDEO** dicendum quod illa potentia est subiectum virtutis ad cuius potentiae actum rectificandum virtus ordinatur. Iustitia autem non ordinatur ad dirigendum aliquem actum cognoscitivum, non enim dicimur iusti ex hoc quod recte aliquid cognoscimus. Et ideo subiectum iustitiae non est intellectus vel ratio, quae est potentia cognoscitiva. Sed quia iusti dicimur in hoc quod aliquid recte agimus; proximum autem principium actus est vis appetitiva; necesse est quod iustitia sit in aliqua vi appetitiva sicut in subiecto.

Est autem duplex appetitus, scilicet voluntas, quae est in ratione; et appetitus sensitivus consequens apprehensionem sensus, qui dividitur per irascibilem et concupiscibilem, ut in primo habitum est. Reddere autem unicuique quod suum est non potest procedere ex appetitu sensitivo, quia apprehensio sensitiva non se extendit ad hoc quod considerare possit proportionem unius ad alterum, sed hoc est proprium rationis. Unde iustitia non potest esse sicut in subiecto in irascibili vel concupiscibili, sed solum in voluntate. Et ideo philosophus definit iustitiam per actum voluntatis, ut ex supradictis patet.

**OBJECTION 1**: It would seem that justice is not in the will as its subject. For justice is sometimes called truth. But truth is not in the will, but in the intellect. Therefore justice is not in the will as its subject.

**OBJ. 2**: Further, justice is about our dealings with others. Now it belongs to the reason to direct one thing in relation to another. Therefore justice is not in the will as its subject but in the reason.

**OBJ. 3**: Further, justice is not an intellectual virtue, since it is not directed to knowledge; wherefore it follows that it is a moral virtue. Now the subject of moral virtue is the faculty which is *rational by participation*, viz. the irascible and the concupiscible, as the Philosopher declares (*Ethic.* i, 13). Therefore justice is not in the will as its subject, but in the irascible and concupiscible.

**ON THE CONTRARY**, Anselm says (De Verit. xii) that *justice is rectitude of the will observed for its own sake.*

**I ANSWER THAT**, The subject of a virtue is the power whose act that virtue aims at rectifying. Now justice does not aim at directing an act of the cognitive power, for we are not said to be just through knowing something aright. Hence the subject of justice is not the intellect or reason which is a cognitive power. But since we are said to be just through doing something aright, and because the proximate principle of action is the appetitive power, justice must needs be in some appetitive power as its subject.

Now the appetite is twofold; namely, the will which is in the reason and the sensitive appetite which follows on sensitive apprehension, and is divided into the irascible and the concupiscible, as stated in the First Part (Q. 81, A. 2). Again the act of rendering his due to each man cannot proceed from the sensitive appetite, because sensitive apprehension does not go so far as to be able to consider the relation of one thing to another; but this is proper to the reason. Therefore justice cannot be in the irascible or concupiscible as its subject, but only in the will: hence the Philosopher (*Ethic.* v, 1) defines justice by an act of the will, as may be seen above (A. 1).

**AD PRIMUM** ergo dicendum quod quia voluntas est appetitus rationalis, ideo rectitudo rationis, quae veritas dicitur, voluntati impressa, propter propinquitatem ad rationem, nomen retinet veritatis. Et inde est quod quandoque iustitia veritas vocatur.

**AD SECUNDUM** dicendum quod voluntas fertur in suum obiectum consequenter ad apprehensionem rationis. Et ideo, quia ratio ordinat in alterum, voluntas potest velle aliquid in ordine ad alterum, quod pertinet ad iustitiam.

**AD TERTIUM** dicendum quod rationale per participationem non solum est irascibilis et concupiscibilis, sed *omnino appetitivum*, ut dicitur in I Ethic., quia omnis appetitus obedit rationi. Sub appetitivo autem comprehenditur voluntas. Et ideo voluntas potest esse subiectum virtutis moralis.

**REPLY OBJ. 1:** Since the will is the rational appetite, when the rectitude of the reason which is called truth is imprinted on the will on account of its nighness to the reason, this imprint retains the name of truth; and hence it is that justice sometimes goes by the name of truth.

**REPLY OBJ. 2:** The will is borne towards its object consequently on the apprehension of reason: wherefore, since the reason directs one thing in relation to another, the will can will one thing in relation to another, and this belongs to justice.

**REPLY OBJ. 3:** Not only the irascible and concupiscible parts are rational by participation, but the entire appetitive faculty, as stated in *Ethic.* i, 13, because all appetite is subject to reason. Now the will is contained in the appetitive faculty, wherefore it can be the subject of moral virtue.

# Article 5

*Whether justice is a general virtue?*

**AD QUINTUM SIC PROCEDITUR.** Videtur quod iustitia non sit virtus generalis. Iustitia enim condividitur aliis virtutibus, ut patet Sap. VIII, *sobrietatem et iustitiam docet, prudentiam et virtutem.* Sed generale non condividitur seu connumeratur speciebus sub illo generali contentis. Ergo iustitia non est virtus generalis.

**PRAETEREA**, sicut iustitia ponitur virtus cardinalis, ita etiam temperantia et fortitudo. Sed temperantia vel fortitudo non ponitur virtus generalis. Ergo neque iustitia debet aliquo modo poni virtus generalis.

**PRAETEREA**, iustitia est semper ad alterum, ut supra dictum est. Sed peccatum quod est in proximum non est peccatum generale, sed dividitur contra peccatum quo peccat homo contra seipsum. Ergo etiam neque iustitia est virtus generalis.

**SED CONTRA** est quod philosophus dicit, in V Ethic., quod *iustitia est omnis virtus.*

**RESPONDEO** dicendum quod iustitia, sicut dictum est, ordinat hominem in comparatione ad alium. Quod quidem potest esse dupliciter. Uno modo, ad alium singulariter consideratum. Alio modo, ad alium in communi, secundum scilicet quod ille qui servit alicui communitati servit omnibus hominibus qui sub communitate illa continentur. Ad utrumque igitur se potest habere iustitia secundum propriam rationem. Manifestum est autem quod omnes qui sub communitate aliqua continentur comparantur ad communitatem sicut partes ad totum. Pars autem id quod est totius est, unde et quodlibet bonum partis est ordinabile in bonum totius. Secundum hoc igitur bonum cuiuslibet virtutis, sive ordinantis aliquem hominem ad seipsum sive ordinantis

**OBJECTION 1:** It would seem that justice is not a general virtue. For justice is specified with the other virtues, according to Wis. 8:7, *She teacheth temperance and prudence, and justice, and fortitude.* Now the *general* is not specified or reckoned together with the species contained under the same *general.* Therefore justice is not a general virtue.

**OBJ. 2:** Further, as justice is accounted a cardinal virtue, so are temperance and fortitude. Now neither temperance nor fortitude is reckoned to be a general virtue. Therefore neither should justice in any way be reckoned a general virtue.

**OBJ. 3:** Further, justice is always towards others, as stated above (A. 2). But a sin committed against one's neighbor cannot be a general sin, because it is condivided with sin committed against oneself. Therefore neither is justice a general virtue.

**ON THE CONTRARY**, The Philosopher says (*Ethic.* v, 1) that *justice is every virtue.*

**I ANSWER THAT**, Justice, as stated above (A. 2) directs man in his relations with other men. Now this may happen in two ways: first as regards his relation with individuals, second as regards his relations with others in general, insofar as a man who serves a community, serves all those who are included in that community. Accordingly justice in its proper acceptation can be directed to another in both these senses. Now it is evident that all who are included in a community, stand in relation to that community as parts to a whole; while a part, as such, belongs to a whole, so that whatever is the good of a part can be directed to the good of the whole. It follows therefore that the good of any virtue, whether such virtue direct man in relation to himself, or in relation to certain other individual persons, is referable to

ipsum ad aliquas alias personas singulares, est referibile ad bonum commune, ad quod ordinat iustitia. Et secundum hoc actus omnium virtutum possunt ad iustitiam pertinere, secundum quod ordinat hominem ad bonum commune. Et quantum ad hoc iustitia dicitur virtus generalis. Et quia ad legem pertinet ordinare in bonum commune, ut supra habitum est, inde est quod talis iustitia, praedicto modo generalis, dicitur iustitia legalis, quia scilicet per eam homo concordat legi ordinanti actus omnium virtutum in bonum commune.

**AD PRIMUM** ergo dicendum quod iustitia condividitur seu connumeratur aliis virtutibus non inquantum est generalis, sed inquantum est specialis virtus, ut infra dicetur.

**AD SECUNDUM** dicendum quod temperantia et fortitudo sunt in appetitu sensitivo, idest in concupiscibili et irascibili. Huiusmodi autem vires sunt appetitivae quorundam bonorum particularium, sicut et sensus est particularium cognoscitivus. Sed iustitia est sicut in subiecto in appetitu intellectivo, qui potest esse universalis boni, cuius intellectus est apprehensivus. Et ideo iustitia magis potest esse virtus generalis quam temperantia vel fortitudo.

**AD TERTIUM** dicendum quod illa quae sunt ad seipsum sunt ordinabilia ad alterum, praecipue quantum ad bonum commune. Unde et iustitia legalis, secundum quod ordinat ad bonum commune, potest dici virtus generalis; et eadem ratione iniustitia potest dici peccatum commune, unde dicitur I Ioan. III quod *omne peccatum est iniquitas*.

the common good, to which justice directs: so that all acts of virtue can pertain to justice, insofar as it directs man to the common good. It is in this sense that justice is called a general virtue. And since it belongs to the law to direct to the common good, as stated above (I-II, Q. 90, A. 2), it follows that the justice which is in this way styled general, is called *legal justice*, because thereby man is in harmony with the law which directs the acts of all the virtues to the common good.

**REPLY OBJ. 1**: Justice is specified or enumerated with the other virtues, not as a general but as a special virtue, as we shall state further on (AA. 7, 12).

**REPLY OBJ. 2**: Temperance and fortitude are in the sensitive appetite, viz. in the concupiscible and irascible. Now these powers are appetitive of certain particular goods, even as the senses are cognitive of particulars. On the other hand justice is in the intellective appetite as its subject, which can have the universal good as its object, knowledge whereof belongs to the intellect. Hence justice can be a general virtue rather than temperance or fortitude.

**REPLY OBJ. 3**: Things referable to oneself are referable to another, especially in regard to the common good. Wherefore legal justice, insofar as it directs to the common good, may be called a general virtue: and in like manner injustice may be called a general sin; hence it is written (1 John 3:4) that *all sin is iniquity*.

# Article 6

*Whether justice, as a general virtue, is essentially the same as all virtue?*

**AD SEXTUM SIC PROCEDITUR.** Videtur quod iustitia, secundum quod est generalis, sit idem per essentiam cum omni virtute. Dicit enim philosophus, in V Ethic., quod virtus et iustitia legalis *est eadem omni virtuti, esse autem non est idem*. Sed illa quae differunt solum secundum esse, vel secundum rationem, non differunt secundum essentiam. Ergo iustitia est idem per essentiam cum omni virtute.

**PRAETEREA**, omnis virtus quae non est idem per essentiam cum omni virtute, est pars virtutis. Sed iustitia praedicta, ut ibidem philosophus dicit, *non est pars virtutis, sed tota virtus*. Ergo praedicta iustitia est idem essentialiter cum omni virtute.

**PRAETEREA**, per hoc quod aliqua virtus ordinat actum suum ad altiorem finem, non diversificatur secundum essentiam habitus, sicut idem est essentialiter habitus temperantiae, etiam si actus eius ordinetur ad

**OBJECTION 1**: It would seem that justice, as a general virtue, is essentially the same as all virtue. For the Philosopher says (*Ethic.* v, 1) that *virtue and legal justice are the same as all virtue, but differ in their mode of being*. Now things that differ merely in their mode of being or logically do not differ essentially. Therefore justice is essentially the same as every virtue.

**OBJ. 2**: Further, every virtue that is not essentially the same as all virtue is a part of virtue. Now the aforesaid justice, according to the Philosopher (*Ethic.* v. 1) *is not a part but the whole of virtue*. Therefore the aforesaid justice is essentially the same as all virtue.

**OBJ. 3**: Further, the essence of a virtue does not change through that virtue directing its act to some higher end even as the habit of temperance remains essentially the same even though its act be directed to a Divine good. Now

bonum divinum. Sed ad iustitiam legalem pertinet quod actus omnium virtutum ordinentur ad altiorem finem, idest ad bonum commune multitudinis, quod praeeminet bono unius singularis personae. Ergo videtur quod iustitia legalis essentialiter sit omnis virtus.

**Praeterea**, omne bonum partis ordinabile est ad bonum totius, unde si non ordinetur in illud, videtur esse vanum et frustra. Sed illud quod est secundum virtutem non potest esse huiusmodi. Ergo videtur quod nullus actus possit esse alicuius virtutis qui non pertineat ad iustitiam generalem, quae ordinat in bonum commune. Et sic videtur quod iustitia generalis sit idem in essentia cum omni virtute.

**Sed contra** est quod philosophus dicit, in V Ethic., quod *multi in propriis quidem possunt virtute uti, in his autem quae ad alterum non possunt*. Et in III Polit. dicit quod *non est simpliciter eadem virtus boni viri et boni civis*. Sed virtus boni civis est iustitia generalis, per quam aliquis ordinatur ad bonum commune. Ergo non est eadem iustitia generalis cum virtute communi, sed una potest sine alia haberi.

**Respondeo** dicendum quod generale dicitur aliquid dupliciter. Uno modo, per praedicationem, sicut *animal* est generale ad hominem et equum et ad alia huiusmodi. Et hoc modo generale oportet quod sit idem essentialiter cum his ad quae est generale, quia genus pertinet ad essentiam speciei et cadit in definitione eius. Alio modo dicitur aliquid generale secundum virtutem, sicut causa universalis est generalis ad omnes effectus, ut sol ad omnia corpora, quae illuminantur vel immutantur per virtutem ipsius. Et hoc modo generale non oportet quod sit idem in essentia cum his ad quae est generale, quia non est eadem essentia causae et effectus. Hoc autem modo, secundum praedicta, iustitia legalis dicitur esse virtus generalis, inquantum scilicet ordinat actus aliarum virtutum ad suum finem, quod est movere per imperium omnes alias virtutes. Sicut enim caritas potest dici virtus generalis inquantum ordinat actus omnium virtutum ad bonum divinum, ita etiam iustitia legalis inquantum ordinat actus omnium virtutum ad bonum commune. Sicut ergo caritas, quae respicit bonum divinum ut proprium obiectum, est quaedam specialis virtus secundum suam essentiam; ita etiam iustitia legalis est specialis virtus secundum suam essentiam, secundum quod respicit commune bonum ut proprium obiectum. Et sic est in principe principaliter, et quasi architectonice; in subditis autem secundario et quasi ministrative.

Potest tamen quaelibet virtus, secundum quod a praedicta virtute, speciali quidem in essentia, generali autem secundum virtutem, ordinatur ad bonum commune, dici iustitia legalis. Et hoc modo loquendi iustitia

it belongs to legal justice that the acts of all the virtues are directed to a higher end, namely the common good of the multitude, which transcends the good of one single individual. Therefore it seems that legal justice is essentially all virtue.

**Obj. 4**: Further, every good of a part can be directed to the good of the whole, so that if it be not thus directed it would seem without use or purpose. But that which is in accordance with virtue cannot be so. Therefore it seems that there can be no act of any virtue, that does not belong to general justice, which directs to the common good; and so it seems that general justice is essentially the same as all virtue.

**On the contrary**, The Philosopher says (*Ethic.* v, 1) that *many are able to be virtuous in matters affecting themselves, but are unable to be virtuous in matters relating to others*, and (*Polit.* iii, 2) that *the virtue of the good man is not strictly the same as the virtue of the good citizen*. Now the virtue of a good citizen is general justice, whereby a man is directed to the common good. Therefore general justice is not the same as virtue in general, and it is possible to have one without the other.

**I answer that**, A thing is said to be *general* in two ways. First, by predication: thus *animal* is general in relation to man and horse and the like: and in this sense that which is general must needs be essentially the same as the things in relation to which it is general, for the reason that the genus belongs to the essence of the species, and forms part of its definition. Second a thing is said to be general virtually; thus a universal cause is general in relation to all its effects, the sun, for instance, in relation to all bodies that are illumined, or transmuted by its power; and in this sense there is no need for that which is *general* to be essentially the same as those things in relation to which it is general, since cause and effect are not essentially the same. Now it is in the latter sense that, according to what has been said (A. 5), legal justice is said to be a general virtue, in as much, to wit, as it directs the acts of the other virtues to its own end, and this is to move all the other virtues by its command; for just as charity may be called a general virtue insofar as it directs the acts of all the virtues to the Divine good, so too is legal justice, insofar as it directs the acts of all the virtues to the common good. Accordingly, just as charity which regards the Divine good as its proper object, is a special virtue in respect of its essence, so too legal justice is a special virtue in respect of its essence, insofar as it regards the common good as its proper object. And thus it is in the sovereign principally and by way of a mastercraft, while it is secondarily and administratively in his subjects.

However the name of legal justice can be given to every virtue, insofar as every virtue is directed to the common good by the aforesaid legal justice, which though special essentially is nevertheless virtually general. Speaking in this

legalis est idem in essentia cum omni virtute, differt autem ratione. Et hoc modo loquitur philosophus.

**UNDE PATET** responsio ad primum et secundum.

**AD TERTIUM** dicendum quod etiam illa ratio secundum hunc modum procedit de iustitia legali, secundum quod virtus imperata a iustitia legali iustitia legalis dicitur.

**AD QUARTUM** dicendum quod quaelibet virtus secundum propriam rationem ordinat actum suum ad proprium finem illius virtutis. Quod autem ordinetur ad ulteriorem finem, sive semper sive aliquando, hoc non habet ex propria ratione, sed oportet esse aliam superiorem virtutem a qua in illum finem ordinetur. Et sic oportet esse unam virtutem superiorem quae ordinet omnes virtutes in bonum commune, quae est iustitia legalis, et est alia per essentiam ab omni virtute.

way, legal justice is essentially the same as all virtue, but differs therefrom logically: and it is in this sense that the Philosopher speaks.

**WHEREFORE** the Replies to the First and Second Objections are manifest.

**REPLY OBJ. 3**: This argument again takes legal justice for the virtue commanded by legal justice.

**REPLY OBJ. 4**: Every virtue strictly speaking directs its act to that virtue's proper end: that it should happen to be directed to a further end either always or sometimes, does not belong to that virtue considered strictly, for it needs some higher virtue to direct it to that end. Consequently there must be one supreme virtue essentially distinct from every other virtue, which directs all the virtues to the common good; and this virtue is legal justice.

# Article 7

*Whether there is a particular besides a general justice?*

**AD SEPTIMUM SIC PROCEDITUR.** Videtur quod non sit aliqua iustitia particularis praeter iustitiam generalem. In virtutibus enim nihil est superfluum, sicut nec in natura. Sed iustitia generalis sufficienter ordinat hominem circa omnia quae ad alterum sunt. Ergo non est necessaria aliqua iustitia particularis.

**PRAETEREA,** unum et multa non diversificant speciem virtutis. Sed iustitia legalis ordinat hominem ad alium secundum ea quae ad multitudinem pertinent, ut ex praedictis patet. Ergo non est alia species iustitiae quae ordinet hominem ad alterum in his quae pertinent ad unam singularem personam.

**PRAETEREA,** inter unam singularem personam et multitudinem civitatis media est multitudo domestica. Si ergo est iustitia alia particularis per comparationem ad unam personam praeter iustitiam generalem, pari ratione debet esse alia iustitia oeconomica, quae ordinet hominem ad bonum commune unius familiae. Quod quidem non dicitur. Ergo nec aliqua particularis iustitia est praeter iustitiam legalem.

**SED CONTRA** est quod Chrysostomus dicit, super illud Matth. V, *beati qui esuriunt et sitiunt iustitiam, iustitiam autem dicit vel universalem virtutem, vel particularem avaritiae contrariam.*

**RESPONDEO** dicendum quod, sicut dictum est, iustitia legalis non est essentialiter omnis virtus, sed oportet praeter iustitiam legalem, quae ordinat hominem immediate ad bonum commune, esse alias virtutes quae

**OBJECTION 1**: It would seem that there is not a particular besides a general justice. For there is nothing superfluous in the virtues, as neither is there in nature. Now general justice directs man sufficiently in all his relations with other men. Therefore there is no need for a particular justice.

**OBJ. 2**: Further, the species of a virtue does not vary according to *one* and *many*. But legal justice directs one man to another in matters relating to the multitude, as shown above (AA. 5, 6). Therefore there is not another species of justice directing one man to another in matters relating to the individual.

**OBJ. 3**: Further, between the individual and the general public stands the household community. Consequently, if in addition to general justice there is a particular justice corresponding to the individual, for the same reason there should be a domestic justice directing man to the common good of a household: and yet this is not the case. Therefore neither should there be a particular besides a legal justice.

**ON THE CONTRARY**, Chrysostom in his commentary on Matt. 5:6, *Blessed are they that hunger and thirst after justice*, says (*Hom. xv in Matth.*): *By justice He signifies either the general virtue, or the particular virtue which is opposed to covetousness.*

**I ANSWER THAT**, As stated above (A. 6), legal justice is not essentially the same as every virtue, and besides legal justice which directs man immediately to the common good, there is a need for other virtues to direct him im-

immediate ordinant hominem circa particularia bona. Quae quidem possunt esse vel ad seipsum, vel ad alteram singularem personam. Sicut ergo praeter iustitiam legalem oportet esse aliquas virtutes particulares quae ordinant hominem in seipso, puta temperantiam et fortitudinem; ita etiam praeter iustitiam legalem oportet esse particularem quandam iustitiam, quae ordinet hominem circa ea quae sunt ad alteram singularem personam.

**AD PRIMUM** ergo dicendum quod iustitia legalis sufficienter quidem ordinat hominem in his quae sunt ad alterum, quantum ad commune quidem bonum, immediate; quantum autem ad bonum unius singularis personae, mediate. Et ideo oportet esse aliquam particularem iustitiam, quae immediate ordinet hominem ad bonum alterius singularis personae.

**AD SECUNDUM** dicendum quod bonum commune civitatis et bonum singulare unius personae non differunt solum secundum multum et paucum, sed secundum formalem differentiam, alia enim est ratio boni communis et boni singularis, sicut et alia est ratio totius et partis. Et ideo philosophus, in I Polit., dicit quod *non bene dicunt qui dicunt civitatem et domum et alia huiusmodi differre solum multitudine et paucitate, et non specie.*

**AD TERTIUM** dicendum quod domestica multitudo, secundum philosophum, in I Polit., distinguitur secundum tres coniugationes, scilicet uxoris et viri, patris et filii, domini et servi, quarum personarum una est quasi aliquid alterius. Et ideo ad huiusmodi personam non est simpliciter iustitia, sed quaedam iustitiae species, scilicet oeconomica, ut dicitur in V Ethic.

mediately in matters relating to particular goods: and these virtues may be relative to himself or to another individual person. Accordingly, just as in addition to legal justice there is a need for particular virtues to direct man in relation to himself, such as temperance and fortitude, so too besides legal justice there is need for particular justice to direct man in his relations to other individuals.

**REPLY OBJ. 1**: Legal justice does indeed direct man sufficiently in his relations towards others. As regards the common good it does so immediately, but as to the good of the individual, it does so mediately. Wherefore there is need for particular justice to direct a man immediately to the good of another individual.

**REPLY OBJ. 2**: The common good of the realm and the particular good of the individual differ not only in respect of the many and the few, but also under a formal aspect. For the aspect of the common good differs from the aspect of the individual good, even as the aspect of whole differs from that of part. Wherefore the Philosopher says (*Polit.* i, 1) that *they are wrong who maintain that the State and the home and the like differ only as many and few and not specifically.*

**REPLY OBJ. 3**: The household community, according to the Philosopher (*Polit.* i, 2), differs in respect of a threefold fellowship; namely *of husband and wife, father and son, master and slave,* in each of which one person is, as it were, part of the other. Wherefore between such persons there is not justice simply, but a species of justice, viz. domestic justice, as stated in *Ethic.* v, 6.

# Article 8

*Whether particular justice has a special matter?*

**AD OCTAVUM SIC PROCEDITUR.** Videtur quod iustitia particularis non habeat materiam specialem. Quia super illud Gen. II, *fluvius quartus ipse est Euphrates,* dicit Glossa, *Euphrates frugifer interpretatur. Nec dicitur contra quod vadat, quia iustitia ad omnes animae partes pertinet.* Hoc autem non esset si haberet materiam specialem, quia quaelibet materia specialis ad aliquam specialem potentiam pertinet. Ergo iustitia particularis non habet materiam specialem.

**PRAETEREA**, Augustinus, in libro Octoginta trium Quaest., dicit quod *quatuor sunt animae virtutes, quibus in hac vita spiritualiter vivitur, scilicet prudentia, temperantia, fortitudo, iustitia,* et dicit quod quarta est iustitia, *quae per omnes diffunditur.* Ergo iustitia particularis, quae est una de quatuor virtutibus cardinalibus, non habet specialem materiam.

**OBJECTION 1**: It would seem that particular justice has no special matter. Because a gloss on Gen. 2:14, *The fourth river is Euphrates,* says: *Euphrates signifies 'fruitful'; nor is it stated through what country it flows, because justice pertains to all the parts of the soul.* Now this would not be the case, if justice had a special matter, since every special matter belongs to a special power. Therefore particular justice has no special matter.

**OBJ. 2**: Further, Augustine says (*83 Questions*, Q. 61) that *the soul has four virtues whereby, in this life, it lives spiritually, viz. temperance, prudence, fortitude and justice;* and he says that *the fourth is justice, which pervades all the virtues.* Therefore particular justice, which is one of the four cardinal virtues, has no special matter.

**PRAETEREA**, iustitia dirigit hominem sufficienter in his quae sunt ad alterum. Sed per omnia quae sunt huius vitae homo potest ordinari ad alterum. Ergo materia iustitiae est generalis, non specialis.

**SED CONTRA** est quod philosophus, in V Ethic., ponit iustitiam particularem circa ea specialiter quae pertinent ad communicationem vitae.

**RESPONDEO** dicendum quod omnia quaecumque rectificari possunt per rationem sunt materia virtutis moralis, quae definitur per rationem rectam, ut patet per philosophum, in II Ethic. Possunt autem per rationem rectificari et interiores animae passiones, et exteriores actiones, et res exteriores quae in usum hominis veniunt, sed tamen per exteriores actiones et per exteriores res, quibus sibi invicem homines communicare possunt, attenditur ordinatio unius hominis ad alium; secundum autem interiores passiones consideratur rectificatio hominis in seipso. Et ideo, cum iustitia ordinetur ad alterum, non est circa totam materiam virtutis moralis, sed solum circa exteriores actiones et res secundum quandam rationem obiecti specialem, prout scilicet secundum eas unus homo alteri coordinatur.

**AD PRIMUM** ergo dicendum quod iustitia pertinet quidem essentialiter ad unam partem animae, in qua est sicut in subiecto, scilicet ad voluntatem, quae quidem movet per suum imperium omnes alias animae partes. Et sic iustitia non directe, sed quasi per quandam redundantiam ad omnes animae partes pertinet.

**AD SECUNDUM** dicendum quod, sicut supra dictum est, virtutes cardinales dupliciter accipiuntur. Uno modo, secundum quod sunt speciales virtutes habentes determinatas materias. Alio modo, secundum quod significant quosdam generales modos virtutis. Et hoc modo loquitur ibi Augustinus. Dicit enim quod prudentia est *cognitio rerum appetendarum et fugiendarum*; temperantia est *refrenatio cupiditatis ab his quae temporaliter delectant*; fortitudo est *firmitas animi adversus ea quae temporaliter molesta sunt*; iustitia est, *quae per ceteras diffunditur, dilectio Dei et proximi*, quae scilicet est communis radix totius ordinis ad alterum.

**AD TERTIUM** dicendum quod passiones interiores, quae sunt pars materiae moralis, secundum se non ordinantur ad alterum, quod pertinet ad specialem rationem iustitiae, sed earum effectus sunt ad alterum ordinabiles, scilicet operationes exteriores. Unde non sequitur quod materia iustitiae sit generalis.

**OBJ. 3**: Further, justice directs man sufficiently in matters relating to others. Now a man can be directed to others in all matters relating to this life. Therefore the matter of justice is general and not special.

**ON THE CONTRARY**, The Philosopher reckons (*Ethic.* v, 2) particular justice to be specially about those things which belong to social life.

**I ANSWER THAT**, Whatever can be rectified by reason is the matter of moral virtue, for this is defined in reference to right reason, according to the Philosopher (*Ethic.* ii, 6). Now the reason can rectify not only the internal passions of the soul, but also external actions, and also those external things of which man can make use. And yet it is in respect of external actions and external things by means of which men can communicate with one another, that the relation of one man to another is to be considered; whereas it is in respect of internal passions that we consider man's rectitude in himself. Consequently, since justice is directed to others, it is not about the entire matter of moral virtue, but only about external actions and things, under a certain special aspect of the object, insofar as one man is related to another through them.

**REPLY OBJ. 1**: It is true that justice belongs essentially to one part of the soul, where it resides as in its subject; and this is the will which moves by its command all the other parts of the soul; and accordingly justice belongs to all the parts of the soul, not directly but by a kind of diffusion.

**REPLY OBJ. 2**: As stated above (I-II, Q. 61, AA. 3, 4), the cardinal virtues may be taken in two ways: first as special virtues, each having a determinate matter; second, as certain general modes of virtue. In this latter sense Augustine speaks in the passage quoted: for he says that prudence is *knowledge of what we should seek and avoid*, temperance is *the curb on the lust for fleeting pleasures*, fortitude is *strength of mind in bearing with passing trials*, justice is *the love of God and our neighbor which pervades the other virtues*, that is to say, is the common principle of the entire order between one man and another.

**REPLY OBJ. 3**: A man's internal passions which are a part of moral matter, are not in themselves directed to another man, which belongs to the specific nature of justice; yet their effects, i.e., external actions, are capable of being directed to another man. Consequently it does not follow that the matter of justice is general.

# Article 9

*Whether justice is about the passions?*

AD NONUM SIC PROCEDITUR. Videtur quod iustitia sit circa passiones. Dicit enim philosophus, in II Ethic., quod *circa voluptates et tristitias est moralis virtus*. Voluptas autem, idest delectatio, et tristitia sunt passiones quaedam; ut supra habitum est, cum de passionibus ageretur. Ergo iustitia, cum sit virtus moralis, erit circa passiones.

PRAETEREA, per iustitiam rectificantur operationes quae sunt ad alterum. Sed operationes huiusmodi rectificari non possunt nisi passiones sint rectificatae, quia ex inordinatione passionum provenit inordinatio in praedictis operationibus; propter concupiscentiam enim venereorum proceditur ad adulterium, et propter superfluum amorem pecuniae proceditur ad furtum. Ergo oportet quod iustitia sit circa passiones.

PRAETEREA, sicut iustitia particularis est ad alterum, ita etiam et iustitia legalis. Sed iustitia legalis est circa passiones, alioquin non se extenderet ad omnes virtutes, quarum quaedam manifeste sunt circa passiones. Ergo iustitia est circa passiones.

SED CONTRA est quod philosophus dicit, in V Ethic., quod est circa operationes.

RESPONDEO dicendum quod huius quaestionis veritas ex duobus apparet. Primo quidem, ex ipso subiecto iustitiae, quod est voluntas cuius motus vel actus non sunt passiones, ut supra habitum est; sed solum motus appetitus sensitivi passiones dicuntur. Et ideo iustitia non est circa passiones, sicut temperantia et fortitudo, quae sunt irascibilis et concupiscibilis, sunt circa passiones. Alio modo, ex parte materiae. Quia iustitia est circa ea quae sunt ad alterum. Non autem per passiones interiores immediate ad alterum ordinamur. Et ideo iustitia circa passiones non est.

AD PRIMUM ergo dicendum quod non quaelibet virtus moralis est circa voluptates et tristitias sicut circa materiam, nam fortitudo est circa timores et audacias. Sed omnis virtus moralis ordinatur ad delectationem et tristitiam sicut ad quosdam fines consequentes, quia, ut philosophus dicit, in VII Ethic., *delectatio et tristitia est finis principalis, ad quem respicientes unumquodque hoc quidem malum, hoc quidem bonum dicimus*. Et hoc modo etiam pertinent ad iustitiam, quia *non est iustus qui non gaudet iustis operationibus*, ut dicitur in I Ethic.

AD SECUNDUM dicendum quod operationes exteriores mediae sunt quodammodo inter res exteriores, quae sunt earum materia, et inter passiones interiores, quae sunt earum principia. Contingit autem quandoque esse defectum in uno eorum sine hoc quod sit defectus in alio, sicut si aliquis surripiat rem alterius non cupiditate habendi, sed voluntate nocendi; vel e converso si

OBJECTION 1: It would seem that justice is about the passions. For the Philosopher says (*Ethic.* ii, 3) that *moral virtue is about pleasure and pain*. Now pleasure or delight, and pain are passions, as stated above when we were treating of the passions. Therefore justice, being a moral virtue, is about the passions.

OBJ. 2: Further, justice is the means of rectifying a man's operations in relation to another man. Now such like operations cannot be rectified unless the passions be rectified, because it is owing to disorder of the passions that there is disorder in the aforesaid operations: thus sexual lust leads to adultery, and overmuch love of money leads to theft. Therefore justice must needs be about the passions.

OBJ. 3: Further, even as particular justice is towards another person so is legal justice. Now legal justice is about the passions, else it would not extend to all the virtues, some of which are evidently about the passions. Therefore justice is about the passions.

ON THE CONTRARY, The Philosopher says (*Ethic.* v, 1) that justice is about operations.

I ANSWER THAT, The true answer to this question may be gathered from a twofold source. First from the subject of justice, i.e., from the will, whose movements or acts are not passions, as stated above (I-II, Q. 22, A. 3; Q. 59, A. 4), for it is only the sensitive appetite whose movements are called passions. Hence justice is not about the passions, as are temperance and fortitude, which are in the irascible and concupiscible parts. Second, on he part of the matter, because justice is about man's relations with another, and we are not directed immediately to another by the internal passions. Therefore justice is not about the passions.

REPLY OBJ. 1: Not every moral virtue is about pleasure and pain as its proper matter, since fortitude is about fear and daring: but every moral virtue is directed to pleasure and pain, as to ends to be acquired, for, as the Philosopher says (*Ethic.* vii, 11), *pleasure and pain are the principal end in respect of which we say that this is an evil, and that a good*: and in this way too they belong to justice, since *a man is not just unless he rejoice in just actions* (*Ethic.* i, 8).

REPLY OBJ. 2: External operations are as it were between external things, which are their matter, and internal passions, which are their origin. Now it happens sometimes that there is a defect in one of these, without there being a defect in the other. Thus a man may steal another's property, not through the desire to have the thing, but through the will to hurt the man; or vice versa, a man may covet

aliquis alterius rem concupiscat, quam tamen surripere non velit. Rectificatio ergo operationum secundum quod ad exteriora terminantur, pertinet ad iustitiam, sed rectificatio earum secundum quod a passionibus oriuntur, pertinet ad alias virtutes morales, quae sunt circa passiones. Unde surreptionem alienae rei iustitia impedit inquantum est contra aequalitatem in exterioribus constituendam, liberalitas vero inquantum procedit ab immoderata concupiscentia divitiarum. Sed quia operationes exteriores non habent speciem ab interioribus passionibus, sed magis a rebus exterioribus, sicut ex obiectis; ideo, per se loquendo, operationes exteriores magis sunt materia iustitiae quam aliarum virtutum moralium.

**AD TERTIUM** dicendum quod bonum commune est finis singularum personarum in communitate existentium, sicut bonum totius finis est cuiuslibet partium. Bonum autem unius personae singularis non est finis alterius. Et ideo iustitia legalis, quae ordinatur ad bonum commune, magis se potest extendere ad interiores passiones, quibus homo aliqualiter disponitur in seipso, quam iustitia particularis, quae ordinatur ad bonum alterius singularis personae. Quamvis iustitia legalis principalius se extendat ad alias virtutes quantum ad exteriores operationes earum, inquantum scilicet *praecipit lex fortis opera facere, et quae temperati, et quae mansueti,* ut dicitur in V Ethic.

another's property without wishing to steal it. Accordingly the directing of operations insofar as they tend towards external things, belongs to justice, but insofar as they arise from the passions, it belongs to the other moral virtues which are about the passions. Hence justice hinders theft of another's property, insofar as stealing is contrary to the equality that should be maintained in external things, while liberality hinders it as resulting from an immoderate desire for wealth. Since, however, external operations take their species, not from the internal passions but from external things as being their objects, it follows that, external operations are essentially the matter of justice rather than of the other moral virtues.

**REPLY OBJ. 3**: The common good is the end of each individual member of a community, just as the good of the whole is the end of each part. On the other hand the good of one individual is not the end of another individual: wherefore legal justice which is directed to the common good, is more capable of extending to the internal passions whereby man is disposed in some way or other in himself, than particular justice which is directed to the good of another individual: although legal justice extends chiefly to other virtues in the point of their external operations, in so far, to wit, as *the law commands us to perform the actions of a courageous person . . . the actions of a temperate person . . . and the actions of a gentle person* (*Ethic.* v, 5).

# Article 10

*Whether the mean of justice is the real mean?*

**AD DECIMUM SIC PROCEDITUR.** Videtur quod medium iustitiae non sit medium rei. Ratio enim generis salvatur in omnibus speciebus. Sed virtus moralis in II Ethic. definitur esse *habitus electivus in medietate existens determinata ratione quoad nos.* Ergo et in iustitia est medium rationis, et non rei.

**PRAETEREA**, in his quae *simpliciter sunt bona* non est accipere superfluum et diminutum, et per consequens nec medium, sicut patet de virtutibus, ut dicitur in II Ethic. Sed iustitia est circa simpliciter bona, ut dicitur in V Ethic. Ergo in iustitia non est medium rei.

**PRAETEREA**, in aliis virtutibus ideo dicitur esse medium rationis et non rei, quia diversimode accipitur per comparationem ad diversas personas, quia quod uni est multum, alteri est parum, ut dicitur in II Ethic. Sed hoc etiam observatur in iustitia, non enim eadem poena punitur qui percutit principem, et qui percutit privatam personam. Ergo etiam iustitia non habet medium rei, sed medium rationis.

**OBJECTION 1**: It would seem that the mean of justice is not the real mean. For the generic nature remains entire in each species. Now moral virtue is defined (*Ethic.* ii, 6) to be *an elective habit which observes the mean fixed, in our regard, by reason.* Therefore justice observes the rational and not the real mean.

**OBJ. 2**: Further, in things that are *good simply*, there is neither excess nor defect, and consequently neither is there a mean; as is clearly the case with the virtues, according to *Ethic.* ii, 6. Now justice is about things that are good simply, as stated in *Ethic.* v. Therefore justice does not observe the real mean.

**OBJ. 3**: Further, the reason why the other virtues are said to observe the rational and not the real mean, is because in their case the mean varies according to different persons, since what is too much for one is too little for another (*Ethic.* ii, 6). Now this is also the case in justice: for one who strikes a prince does not receive the same punishment as one who strikes a private individual. Therefore justice also observes, not the real, but the rational mean.

**SED CONTRA** est quod philosophus, in V Ethic., assignat medium iustitiae secundum proportionalitatem *arithmeticam*, quod est medium rei.

**RESPONDEO** dicendum quod, sicut supra dictum est, aliae virtutes morales consistunt principaliter circa passiones, quarum rectificatio non attenditur nisi secundum comparationem ad ipsum hominem cuius sunt passiones, secundum scilicet quod irascitur et concupiscit prout debet secundum diversas circumstantias. Et ideo medium talium virtutum non accipitur secundum proportionem unius rei ad alteram, sed solum secundum comparationem ad ipsum virtuosum. Et propter hoc in ipsis est medium solum secundum rationem quoad nos.

Sed materia iustitiae est exterior operatio secundum quod ipsa, vel res cuius est usus, debitam proportionem habet ad aliam personam. Et ideo medium iustitiae consistit in quadam proportionis aequalitate rei exterioris ad personam exteriorem. Aequale autem est realiter medium inter maius et minus, ut dicitur in X Metaphys. Unde iustitia habet medium rei.

**AD PRIMUM** ergo dicendum quod hoc medium rei est etiam medium rationis. Et ideo in iustitia salvatur ratio virtutis moralis.

**AD SECUNDUM** dicendum quod bonum simpliciter dupliciter dicitur. Uno modo, quod est omnibus modis bonum, sicut virtutes sunt bonae. Et sic in his quae sunt bona simpliciter non est accipere medium et extrema. Alio modo dicitur aliquid simpliciter bonum quia est absolute bonum, scilicet secundum suam naturam consideratum, quamvis per abusum possit fieri malum, sicut patet de divitiis et honoribus. Et in talibus potest accipi superfluum, diminutum et medium quantum ad homines, qui possunt eis uti vel bene vel male. Ei sic circa simpliciter bona dicitur esse iustitia.

**AD TERTIUM** dicendum quod iniuria illata aliam proportionem habet ad principem, et aliam ad personam privatam. Et ideo oportet aliter adaequare utramque iniuriam per vindictam. Quod pertinet ad diversitatem rei, et non solum ad diversitatem rationis.

**ON THE CONTRARY**, The Philosopher says (*Ethic.* ii, 6; v, 4) that the mean of justice is to be taken according to *arithmetical* proportion, so that it is the real mean.

**I ANSWER THAT**, As stated above (A. 9; I-II, Q. 59, A. 4), the other moral virtues are chiefly concerned with the passions, the regulation of which is gauged entirely by a comparison with the very man who is the subject of those passions, insofar as his anger and desire are vested with their various due circumstances. Hence the mean in such like virtues is measured not by the proportion of one thing to another, but merely by comparison with the virtuous man himself, so that with them the mean is only that which is fixed by reason in our regard.

On the other hand, the matter of justice is external operation, insofar as an operation or the thing used in that operation is duly proportionate to another person, wherefore the mean of justice consists in a certain proportion of equality between the external thing and the external person. Now equality is the real mean between greater and less, as stated in *Metaph.* x: wherefore justice observes the real mean.

**REPLY OBJ. 1**: This real mean is also the rational mean, wherefore justice satisfies the conditions of a moral virtue.

**REPLY OBJ. 2**: We may speak of a thing being good simply in two ways. First a thing may be good in every way: thus the virtues are good; and there is neither mean nor extremes in things that are good simply in this sense. Second a thing is said to be good simply through being good absolutely i.e., in its nature, although it may become evil through being abused. Such are riches and honors; and in the like it is possible to find excess, deficiency and mean, as regards men who can use them well or ill: and it is in this sense that justice is about things that are good simply.

**REPLY OBJ. 3**: The injury inflicted bears a different proportion to a prince from that which it bears to a private person: wherefore each injury requires to be equalized by vengeance in a different way: and this implies a real and not merely a rational diversity.

# Article 11

*Whether the act of justice is to render to each one his own?*

**AD UNDECIMUM SIC PROCEDITUR**. Videtur quod actus iustitiae non sit reddere unicuique quod suum est. Augustinus enim, XIV de Trin., attribuit iustitiae *subvenire miseris*. Sed in subveniendo miseris non tribuimus eis quae sunt eorum, sed magis quae sunt nostra. Ergo iustitiae actus non est tribuere unicuique quod suum est.

**OBJECTION 1**: It would seem that the act of justice is not to render to each one his own. For Augustine (*De Trin.* xiv, 9) ascribes to justice the act of *succoring the needy*. Now in succoring the needy we give them what is not theirs but ours. Therefore the act of justice does not consist in rendering to each one his own.

PRAETEREA, Tullius, in I de Offic., dicit quod *beneficentia, quam benignitatem vel liberalitatem appellari licet, ad iustitiam pertinet.* Sed liberalitatis est de proprio dare alicui, non de eo quod est eius. Ergo iustitiae actus non est reddere unicuique quod suum est.

PRAETEREA, ad iustitiam pertinet non solum res dispensare debito modo, sed etiam iniuriosas actiones cohibere, puta homicidia, adulteria et alia huiusmodi. Sed reddere quod suum est videtur solum ad dispensationem rerum pertinere. Ergo non sufficienter per hoc notificatur actus iustitiae quod dicitur actus eius esse reddere unicuique quod suum est.

SED CONTRA est quod Ambrosius dicit, in I de Offic., *iustitia est quae unicuique quod suum est tribuit, alienum non vindicat, utilitatem propriam negligit ut communem aequitatem custodiat.*

RESPONDEO dicendum quod, sicut dictum est, materia iustitiae est operatio exterior secundum quod ipsa, vel res qua per eam utimur, proportionatur alteri personae, ad quam per iustitiam ordinamur. Hoc autem dicitur esse suum uniuscuiusque personae quod ei secundum proportionis aequalitatem debetur. Et ideo proprius actus iustitiae nihil est aliud quam reddere unicuique quod suum est.

AD PRIMUM ergo dicendum quod iustitiae, cum sit virtus cardinalis, quaedam aliae virtutes secundariae adiunguntur, sicut misericordia, liberalitas et aliae huiusmodi virtutes, ut infra patebit. Et ideo subvenire miseris, quod pertinet ad misericordiam sive pietatem, et liberaliter benefacere, quod pertinet ad liberalitatem, per quandam reductionem attribuitur iustitiae, sicut principali virtuti.

ET PER HOC patet responsio ad secundum.

AD TERTIUM dicendum quod, sicut philosophus dicit, in V Ethic., omne superfluum in his quae ad iustitiam pertinent *lucrum*, extenso nomine, vocatur, sicut et omne quod minus est vocatur *damnum*. Et hoc ideo, quia iustitia prius est exercita, et communius exercetur in voluntariis commutationibus rerum, puta emptione et venditione, in quibus proprie haec nomina dicuntur; et exinde derivantur haec nomina ad omnia circa quae potest esse iustitia. Et eadem ratio est de hoc quod est reddere unicuique quod suum est.

OBJ. 2: Further, Tully says (*De Offic.* i, 7) that *beneficence which we may call kindness or liberality, belongs to justice.* Now it pertains to liberality to give to another of one's own, not of what is his. Therefore the act of justice does not consist in rendering to each one his own.

OBJ. 3: Further, it belongs to justice not only to distribute things duly, but also to repress injurious actions, such as murder, adultery and so forth. But the rendering to each one of what is his seems to belong solely to the distribution of things. Therefore the act of justice is not sufficiently described by saying that it consists in rendering to each one his own.

ON THE CONTRARY, Ambrose says (*De Offic.* i, 24): *It is justice that renders to each one what is his, and claims not another's property; it disregards its own profit in order to preserve the common equity.*

I ANSWER THAT, As stated above (AA. 8, 10), the matter of justice is an external operation insofar as either it or the thing we use by it is made proportionate to some other person to whom we are related by justice. Now each man's own is that which is due to him according to equality of proportion. Therefore the proper act of justice is nothing else than to render to each one his own.

REPLY OBJ. 1: Since justice is a cardinal virtue, other secondary virtues, such as mercy, liberality and the like are connected with it, as we shall state further on (Q. 80, A. 1). Wherefore to succor the needy, which belongs to mercy or pity, and to be liberally beneficent, which pertains to liberality, are by a kind of reduction ascribed to justice as to their principal virtue.

THIS SUFFICES for the Reply to the Second Objection.

REPLY OBJ. 3: As the Philosopher states (*Ethic.* v, 4), in matters of justice, the name of *profit* is extended to whatever is excessive, and whatever is deficient is called *loss*. The reason for this is that justice is first of all and more commonly exercised in voluntary interchanges of things, such as buying and selling, wherein those expressions are properly employed; and yet they are transferred to all other matters of justice. The same applies to the rendering to each one of what is his own.

# Article 12

*Whether justice stands foremost among all moral virtues?*

AD DUODECIMUM SIC PROCEDITUR. Videtur quod iustitia non praemineat inter omnes virtutes morales. Ad iustitiam enim pertinet reddere alteri quod suum est.

OBJECTION 1: It would seem that justice does not stand foremost among all the moral virtues. Because it belongs to justice to render to each one what is his, whereas it belongs

Ad liberalitatem autem pertinet de proprio dare, quod virtuosius est. Ergo liberalitas est maior virtus quam iustitia.

**Praeterea**, nihil ornatur nisi per aliquid dignius se. Sed *magnanimitas est ornamentum* et iustitiae et *omnium virtutum*, ut dicitur in IV Ethic. Ergo magnanimitas est nobilior quam iustitia.

**Praeterea**, virtus est circa *difficile* et *bonum*, ut dicitur in II Ethic. Sed fortitudo est circa magis difficilia quam iustitia, idest circa *pericula* mortis, ut dicitur in III Ethic. Ergo fortitudo est nobilior iustitia.

**Sed contra** est quod Tullius dicit, in I de Offic., *in iustitia virtutis splendor est maximus, ex qua boni viri nominantur.*

**Respondeo** dicendum quod si loquamur de iustitia legali, manifestum est quod ipsa est praeclarior inter omnes virtutes morales, inquantum bonum commune praeeminet bono singulari unius personae. Et secundum hoc philosophus, in V Ethic., dicit quod *praeclarissima virtutum videtur esse iustitia, et neque est Hesperus neque Lucifer ita admirabilis.* Sed etiam si loquamur de iustitia particulari, praecellit inter alias virtutes morales, duplici ratione. Quarum prima potest sumi ex parte subiecti, quia scilicet est in nobiliori parte animae, idest in appetitu rationali, scilicet voluntate; aliis virtutibus moralibus existentibus in appetitu sensitivo, ad quem pertinent passiones, quae sunt materia aliarum virtutum moralium. Secunda ratio sumitur ex parte obiecti. Nam aliae virtutes laudantur solum secundum bonum ipsius virtuosi. Iustitia autem laudatur secundum quod virtuosus ad alium bene se habet, et sic iustitia quodammodo est bonum alterius, ut dicitur in V Ethic. Et propter hoc philosophus dicit, in I Rhet., *necesse est maximas esse virtutes eas quae sunt aliis honestissimae, siquidem est virtus potentia benefactiva. Propter hoc fortes et iustos maxime honorant, quoniam fortitudo est utilis aliis in bello, iustitia autem et in bello et in pace.*

**Ad primum** ergo dicendum quod liberalitas, etsi de suo det, tamen hoc facit inquantum in hoc considerat propriae virtutis bonum. Iustitia autem dat alteri quod suum est quasi considerans bonum commune. Et praeterea iustitia observatur ad omnes, liberalitas autem ad omnes se extendere non potest. Et iterum liberalitas, quae de suo dat, supra iustitiam fundatur, per quam conservatur unicuique quod suum est.

**Ad secundum** dicendum quod magnanimitas, inquantum supervenit iustitiae, auget eius bonitatem. Quae tamen sine iustitia nec virtutis rationem haberet.

**Ad tertium** dicendum quod fortitudo consistit circa difficiliora, non tamen est circa meliora, cum sit

---

to liberality to give of one's own, and this is more virtuous. Therefore liberality is a greater virtue than justice.

**Obj. 2**: Further, nothing is adorned by a less excellent thing than itself. Now magnanimity is the ornament both of justice and of all the virtues, according to *Ethic.* iv, 3. Therefore magnanimity is more excellent than justice.

**Obj. 3**: Further, virtue is about that which is *difficult* and *good*, as stated in *Ethic.* ii, 3. But fortitude is about more difficult things than justice is, since it is about dangers of death, according to *Ethic.* iii, 6. Therefore fortitude is more excellent than justice.

**On the contrary**, Tully says (*De Offic.* i, 7): *Justice is the most resplendent of the virtues, and gives its name to a good man.*

**I answer that**, If we speak of legal justice, it is evident that it stands foremost among all the moral virtues, for as much as the common good transcends the individual good of one person. In this sense the Philosopher declares (*Ethic.* v, 1) that *the most excellent of the virtues would seem to be justice, and more glorious than either the evening or the morning star.* But, even if we speak of particular justice, it excels the other moral virtues for two reasons. The first reason may be taken from the subject, because justice is in the more excellent part of the soul, viz. the rational appetite or will, whereas the other moral virtues are in the sensitive appetite, whereunto appertain the passions which are the matter of the other moral virtues. The second reason is taken from the object, because the other virtues are commendable in respect of the sole good of the virtuous person himself, whereas justice is praiseworthy in respect of the virtuous person being well disposed towards another, so that justice is somewhat the good of another person, as stated in *Ethic.* v, 1. Hence the Philosopher says (*Rhet.* i, 9): *The greatest virtues must needs be those which are most profitable to other persons, because virtue is a faculty of doing good to others. For this reason the greatest honors are accorded the brave and the just, since bravery is useful to others in warfare, and justice is useful to others both in warfare and in time of peace.*

**Reply Obj. 1**: Although the liberal man gives of his own, yet he does so insofar as he takes into consideration the good of his own virtue, while the just man gives to another what is his, through consideration of the common good. Moreover justice is observed towards all, whereas liberality cannot extend to all. Again liberality which gives of a man's own is based on justice, whereby one renders to each man what is his.

**Reply Obj. 2**: When magnanimity is added to justice it increases the latter's goodness; and yet without justice it would not even be a virtue.

**Reply Obj. 3**: Although fortitude is about the most difficult things, it is not about the best, for it is only useful in

---

solum in bello utilis, iustitia autem et in pace et in bello, sicut dictum est.

warfare, whereas justice is useful both in war and in peace, as stated above.

# QUESTION 59

## Injustice

Deinde considerandum est de iniustitia. Et circa hoc quaeruntur quatuor.

Primo, utrum iniustitia sit speciale vitium.

Secundo, utrum iniusta agere sit proprium iniusti.

Tertio, utrum aliquis possit iniustum pati volens.

Quarto, utrum iniustitia ex suo genere sit peccatum mortale.

We must now consider injustice, under which head there are four points of inquiry:

(1) Whether injustice is a special vice?

(2) Whether it is proper to the unjust man to do unjust deeds?

(3) Whether one can suffer injustice willingly?

(4) Whether injustice is a mortal sin according to its genus?

# Article 1

*Whether injustice is a special vice?*

**Ad primum sic proceditur.** Videtur quod iniustitia non sit vitium speciale. Dicitur enim 1 Ioan. III, *omne peccatum est iniquitas.* Sed iniquitas videtur idem esse quod iniustitia, quia iustitia est aequalitas quaedam, unde iniustitia idem videtur esse quod inaequalitas, sive iniquitas. Ergo iniustitia non est speciale peccatum.

**Praeterea,** nullum speciale peccatum opponitur omnibus virtutibus. Sed iniustitia opponitur omnibus virtutibus, nam quantum ad adulterium, opponitur castitati; quantum ad homicidium, opponitur mansuetudini; et sic de aliis. Ergo iniustitia non est speciale peccatum.

**Praeterea,** iniustitia iustitiae opponitur, quae in voluntate est. Sed *omne peccatum est in voluntate,* ut Augustinus dicit. Ergo iniustitia non est speciale peccatum.

**Sed contra,** iniustitia iustitiae opponitur. Sed iustitia est specialis virtus. Ergo iniustitia est speciale vitium.

**Respondeo** dicendum quod iniustitia est duplex. Una quidem illegalis, quae opponitur legali iustitiae. Et haec quidem secundum essentiam est speciale vitium, inquantum respicit speciale obiectum, scilicet bonum commune, quod contemnit. Sed quantum ad intentionem est vitium generale, quia per contemptum boni communis potest homo ad omnia peccata deduci. Sicut etiam omnia vitia, inquantum repugnant bono communi, iniustitiae rationem habent, quasi ab iniustitia derivata, sicut et supra de iustitia dictum est. Alio modo dicitur iniustitia secundum inaequalitatem quandam ad alterum, prout scilicet homo vult habere plus de bonis, puta divitiis et honoribus; et minus de malis, puta

**Objection 1:** It would seem that injustice is not a special vice. For it is written (1 John 3:4): *All sin is iniquity.* Now iniquity would seem to be the same as injustice, because justice is a kind of equality, so that injustice is apparently the same as inequality or iniquity. Therefore injustice is not a special sin.

**Obj. 2:** Further, no special sin is contrary to all the virtues. But injustice is contrary to all the virtues: for as regards adultery it is opposed to chastity, as regards murder it is opposed to meekness, and in like manner as regards the other sins. Therefore injustice is not a special sin.

**Obj. 3:** Further, injustice is opposed to justice which is in the will. But *every sin is in the will,* as Augustine declares (*De Duabus Anim.* x). Therefore injustice is not a special sin.

**On the contrary,** Injustice is contrary to justice. But justice is a special virtue. Therefore injustice is a special vice.

**I answer that,** Injustice is twofold. First there is illegal injustice which is opposed to legal justice: and this is essentially a special vice, insofar as it regards a special object, namely the common good which it contemns; and yet it is a general vice, as regards the intention, since contempt of the common good may lead to all kinds of sin. Thus too all vices, as being repugnant to the common good, have the character of injustice, as though they arose from injustice, in accord with what has been said above about justice (Q. 58, AA. 5, 6). Second we speak of injustice in reference to an inequality between one person and another, when one man wishes to have more goods, riches for example, or honors, and less evils, such as toil and losses, and

laboribus et damnis. Et sic iniustitia habet materiam specialem, et est particulare vitium iustitiae particulari oppositum.

AD PRIMUM ergo dicendum quod sicut iustitia legalis dicitur per comparationem ad bonum commune humanum, ita iustitia divina dicitur per comparationem ad bonum divinum, cui repugnat omne peccatum. Et secundum hoc omne peccatum dicitur iniquitas.

AD SECUNDUM dicendum quod iniustitia etiam particularis opponitur indirecte omnibus virtutibus, inquantum scilicet exteriores etiam actus pertinent et ad iustitiam et ad alias virtutes morales, licet diversimode, sicut supra dictum est.

AD TERTIUM dicendum quod voluntas, sicut et ratio, se extendit ad materiam totam moralem, idest ad passiones et ad operationes exteriores quae sunt ad alterum. Sed iustitia perficit voluntatem solum secundum quod se extendit ad operationes quae sunt ad alterum. Et similiter iniustitia.

thus injustice has a special matter and is a particular vice opposed to particular justice.

REPLY OBJ. 1: Even as legal justice is referred to human common good, so Divine justice is referred to the Divine good, to which all sin is repugnant, and in this sense all sin is said to be iniquity.

REPLY OBJ. 2: Even particular justice is indirectly opposed to all the virtues; in so far, to wit, as even external acts pertain both to justice and to the other moral virtues, although in different ways as stated above (Q. 58, A. 9, ad 2).

REPLY OBJ. 3: The will, like the reason, extends to all moral matters, i.e., passions and those external operations that relate to another person. On the other hand justice perfects the will solely in the point of its extending to operations that relate to another: and the same applies to injustice.

# Article 2

*Whether a man is called unjust through doing an unjust thing?*

AD SECUNDUM SIC PROCEDITUR. Videtur quod aliquis dicatur iniustus ex hoc quod facit iniustum. Habitus enim specificantur per obiecta, ut ex supradictis patet. Sed proprium obiectum iustitiae est iustum, et proprium obiectum iniustitiae est iniustum. Ergo et iustus dicendus est aliquis ex hoc quod facit iustum, et iniustus ex hoc quod facit iniustum.

PRAETEREA, philosophus dicit, in V Ethic., falsam esse opinionem quorundam qui aestimant in potestate hominis esse ut statim faciat iniustum, et quod iustus non minus possit facere iniustum quam iniustus. Hoc autem non esset nisi facere iniustum esset proprium iniusti. Ergo aliquis iudicandus est iniustus ex hoc quod facit iniustum.

PRAETEREA, eodem modo se habet omnis virtus ad proprium actum, et eadem ratio est de vitiis oppositis. Sed quicumque facit aliquid intemperatum dicitur intemperatus. Ergo quicumque facit aliquid iniustum dicitur iniustus.

SED CONTRA est quod philosophus dicit, in V Ethic., quod *aliquis facit iniustum et iniustus non est.*

RESPONDEO dicendum quod sicut obiectum iustitiae est aliquid aequale in rebus exterioribus, ita etiam obiectum iniustitiae est aliquid inaequale, prout scilicet alicui attribuitur plus vel minus quam sibi competat. Ad hoc autem obiectum comparatur habitus iniustitiae mediante proprio actu, qui vocatur iniustificatio. Potest

OBJECTION 1: It would seem that a man is called unjust through doing an unjust thing. For habits are specified by their objects, as stated above (I-II, Q. 54, A. 2). Now the proper object of justice is the just, and the proper object of injustice is the unjust. Therefore a man should be called just through doing a just thing, and unjust through doing an unjust thing.

OBJ. 2: Further, the Philosopher declares (*Ethic.* v, 9) that they hold a false opinion who maintain that it is in a man's power to do suddenly an unjust thing, and that a just man is no less capable of doing what is unjust than an unjust man. But this opinion would not be false unless it were proper to the unjust man to do what is unjust. Therefore a man is to be deemed unjust from the fact that he does an unjust thing.

OBJ. 3: Further, every virtue bears the same relation to its proper act, and the same applies to the contrary vices. But whoever does what is intemperate, is said to be intemperate. Therefore whoever does an unjust thing, is said to be unjust.

ON THE CONTRARY, The Philosopher says (*Ethic.* v, 6) that *a man may do an unjust thing without being unjust.*

I ANSWER THAT, Even as the object of justice is something equal in external things, so too the object of injustice is something unequal, through more or less being assigned to some person than is due to him. To this object the habit of injustice is compared by means of its proper act which is called an injustice. Accordingly it may happen in two

ergo contingere quod qui facit iniustum non est iniustus, dupliciter. Uno modo, propter defectum comparationis operationis ad proprium obiectum, quae quidem recipit speciem et nomen a per se obiecto, non autem ab obiecto per accidens. In his autem quae sunt propter finem, per se dicitur aliquid quod est intentum, per accidens autem quod est praeter intentionem. Et ideo si aliquis faciat aliquid quod est iniustum non intendens iniustum facere, puta cum hoc facit per ignorantiam, non existimans se iniustum facere; tunc non facit iniustum per se et formaliter loquendo, sed solum per accidens, et quasi materialiter faciens id quod est iniustum. Et talis operatio non denominatur iniustificatio. Alio modo potest contingere propter defectum comparationis ipsius operationis ad habitum. Potest enim iniustificatio procedere quandoque quidem ex aliqua passione, puta irae vel concupiscentiae, quandoque autem ex electione, quando scilicet ipsa iniustificatio per se placet; et tunc proprie procedit ab habitu, quia unicuique habenti aliquem habitum est secundum se acceptum quod convenit illi habitui. Facere ergo iniustum ex intentione et electione est proprium iniusti, secundum quod iniustus dicitur qui habet iniustitiae habitum. Sed facere iniustum praeter intentionem, vel ex passione, potest aliquis absque habitu iniustitiae.

AD PRIMUM ergo dicendum quod obiectum per se et formaliter acceptum specificat habitum, non autem prout accipitur materialiter et per accidens.

AD SECUNDUM dicendum quod non est facile cuicumque facere iniustum ex electione, quasi aliquid per se placens et non propter aliud, sed hoc proprium est habentis habitum, ut ibidem philosophus dicit.

AD TERTIUM dicendum quod obiectum temperantiae non est aliquid exterius constitutum, sicut obiectum iustitiae, sed obiectum temperantiae, idest temperatum, accipitur solum in comparatione ad ipsum hominem. Et ideo quod est per accidens et praeter intentionem non potest dici temperatum nec materialiter nec formaliter, et similiter neque intemperatum. Et quantum ad hoc est dissimile in iustitia et in aliis virtutibus moralibus. Sed quantum ad comparationem operationis ad habitum, in omnibus similiter se habet.

ways that a man who does an unjust thing, is not unjust: first, on account of a lack of correspondence between the operation and its proper object. For the operation takes its species and name from its direct and not from its indirect object: and in things directed to an end the direct is that which is intended, and the indirect is what is beside the intention. Hence if a man do that which is unjust, without intending to do an unjust thing, for instance if he do it through ignorance, being unaware that it is unjust, properly speaking he does an unjust thing, not directly, but only indirectly, and, as it were, doing materially that which is unjust: hence such an operation is not called an injustice. Second, this may happen on account of a lack of proportion between the operation and the habit. For an injustice may sometimes arise from a passion, for instance, anger or desire, and sometimes from choice, for instance when the injustice itself is the direct object of one's complacency. In the latter case properly speaking it arises from a habit, because whenever a man has a habit, whatever befits that habit is, of itself, pleasant to him. Accordingly, to do what is unjust intentionally and by choice is proper to the unjust man, in which sense the unjust man is one who has the habit of injustice: but a man may do what is unjust, unintentionally or through passion, without having the habit of injustice.

REPLY OBJ. 1: A habit is specified by its object in its direct and formal acceptation, not in its material and indirect acceptation.

REPLY OBJ. 2: It is not easy for any man to do an unjust thing from choice, as though it were pleasing for its own sake and not for the sake of something else: this is proper to one who has the habit, as the Philosopher declares (*Ethic.* v, 9).

REPLY OBJ. 3: The object of temperance is not something established externally, as is the object of justice: the object of temperance, i.e., the temperate thing, depends entirely on proportion to the man himself. Consequently what is accidental and unintentional cannot be said to be temperate either materially or formally. In like manner neither can it be called intemperate: and in this respect there is dissimilarity between justice and the other moral virtues; but as regards the proportion between operation and habit, there is similarity in all respects.

# Article 3

*Whether we can suffer injustice willingly?*

AD TERTIUM SIC PROCEDITUR. Videtur quod aliquis possit pati iniustum volens. Iniustum enim est inaequale, ut dictum est. Sed aliquis laedendo seipsum recedit ab aequalitate, sicut et laedendo alium. Ergo

OBJECTION 1: It would seem that one can suffer injustice willingly. For injustice is inequality, as stated above (A. 2). Now a man by injuring himself, departs from equality, even as by injuring another. Therefore a man can do an

aliquis potest sibi ipsi facere iniustum, sicut et alteri. Sed quicumque facit iniustum volens facit. Ergo aliquis volens potest pati iniustum, maxime a seipso.

**Praeterea**, nullus secundum legem civilem punitur nisi propter hoc quod facit aliquam iniustitiam. Sed illi qui interimunt seipsos puniuntur secundum leges civitatum, in hoc quod privabantur antiquitus honore sepulturae; ut patet per philosophum, in V Ethic. Ergo aliquis potest sibi ipsi facere iniustum. Et ita contingit quod aliquis iniustum patiatur volens.

**Praeterea**, nullus facit iniustum nisi alicui patienti iniustum. Sed contingit quod aliquis faciat iniustum alicui hoc volenti, puta si vendat ei rem carius quam valeat. Ergo contingit aliquem volentem iniustum pati.

**Sed contra** est quod iniustum pati oppositum est ei quod est iniustum facere. Sed nullus facit iniustum nisi volens. Ergo, per oppositum, nullus patitur iniustum nisi nolens.

**Respondeo** dicendum quod actio, de sui ratione, procedit ab agente; passio autem, secundum propriam rationem, est ab alio, unde non potest esse idem, secundum idem, agens et patiens, ut dicitur in III et VIII Physic. Principium autem proprium agendi in hominibus est voluntas. Et ideo illud proprie et per se homo facit quod volens facit, et e contrario illud proprie homo patitur quod praeter voluntatem suam patitur; quia inquantum est volens, principium est ex ipso, et ideo, inquantum est huiusmodi, magis est agens quam patiens. Dicendum est ergo quod iniustum, per se et formaliter loquendo, nullus potest facere nisi volens, nec pati nisi nolens. Per accidens autem et quasi materialiter loquendo, potest aliquis id quod est de se iniustum vel facere nolens, sicut cum quis praeter intentionem operatur; vel pati volens, sicut cum quis plus alteri dat sua voluntate quam debeat.

**Ad primum** ergo dicendum quod cum aliquis sua voluntate dat alicui id quod ei non debet, non facit nec iniustitiam nec inaequalitatem. Homo enim per suam voluntatem possidet res, et ita non est praeter proportionem si aliquid ei subtrahatur secundum propriam voluntatem, vel a seipso vel ab alio.

**Ad secundum** dicendum quod aliqua persona singularis dupliciter potest considerari. Uno modo, secundum se. Et sic, si sibi aliquod nocumentum inferat, potest quidem habere rationem alterius peccati, puta intemperantiae vel imprudentiae, non tamen rationem iniustitiae, quia sicut iustitia semper est ad alterum, ita et iniustitia. Alio modo potest considerari aliquis homo inquantum est aliquid civitatis, scilicet pars; vel inquantum est aliquid Dei, scilicet creatura et imago. Et sic qui occidit seipsum iniuriam quidem facit non sibi, sed civitati et Deo. Et ideo punitur tam secundum

injustice to himself, even as to another. But whoever does himself an injustice, does so involuntarily. Therefore a man can voluntarily suffer injustice especially if it be inflicted by himself.

**Obj. 2**: Further, no man is punished by the civil law, except for having committed some injustice. Now suicides were formerly punished according to the law of the state by being deprived of an honorable burial, as the Philosopher declares (*Ethic.* v, 11). Therefore a man can do himself an injustice, and consequently it may happen that a man suffers injustice voluntarily.

**Obj. 3**: Further, no man does an injustice save to one who suffers that injustice. But it may happen that a man does an injustice to one who wishes it, for instance if he sell him a thing for more than it is worth. Therefore a man may happen to suffer an injustice voluntarily.

**On the contrary**, To suffer an injustice and to do an injustice are contraries. Now no man does an injustice against his will. Therefore on the other hand no man suffers an injustice except against his will.

**I answer that**, Action by its very nature proceeds from an agent, whereas passion as such is from another: wherefore the same thing in the same respect cannot be both agent and patient, as stated in *Phys.* iii, 1; viii, 5. Now the proper principle of action in man is the will, wherefore man does properly and essentially what he does voluntarily, and on the other hand a man suffers properly what he suffers against his will, since insofar as he is willing, he is a principle in himself, and so, considered thus, he is active rather than passive. Accordingly we must conclude that properly and strictly speaking no man can do an injustice except voluntarily, nor suffer an injustice save involuntarily; but that accidentally and materially so to speak, it is possible for that which is unjust in itself either to be done involuntarily (as when a man does anything unintentionally), or to be suffered voluntarily (as when a man voluntarily gives to another more than he owes him).

**Reply Obj. 1**: When one man gives voluntarily to another that which he does not owe him, he causes neither injustice nor inequality. For a man's ownership depends on his will, so there is no disproportion if he forfeit something of his own free-will, either by his own or by another's action.

**Reply Obj. 2**: An individual person may be considered in two ways. First, with regard to himself; and thus, if he inflict an injury on himself, it may come under the head of some other kind of sin, intemperance for instance or imprudence, but not injustice; because injustice no less than justice, is always referred to another person. Second, this or that man may be considered as belonging to the State as part thereof, or as belonging to God, as His creature and image; and thus a man who kills himself, does an injury not indeed to himself, but to the State and to God. Wherefore he is punished in accordance with both Divine and human

legem divinam quam secundum legem humanam, sicut et de fornicatore apostolus dicit, *si quis templum Dei violaverit, disperdet ipsum Deus.*

**AD TERTIUM** dicendum quod passio est effectus actionis exterioris. In hoc autem quod est facere et pati iniustum, id quod materialiter est attenditur secundum id quod exterius agitur, prout in se consideratur, ut dictum est, id autem quod est ibi formale et per se, attenditur secundum voluntatem agentis et patientis, ut ex dictis patet. Dicendum est ergo quod aliquem facere iniustum, et alium pati iniustum, materialiter loquendo, semper se concomitantur. Sed si formaliter loquamur, potest aliquis facere iniustum, intendens iniustum facere, tamen alius non patietur iniustum, quia volens patietur. Et e converso potest aliquis pati iniustum, si nolens id quod est iniustum patiatur, et tamen ille qui hoc facit ignorans, non faciet iniustum formaliter, sed materialiter tantum.

law, even as the Apostle declares in respect of the fornicator (1 Cor 3:17): *If any man violate the temple of God, him shall God destroy.*

**REPLY OBJ. 3**: Suffering is the effect of external action. Now in the point of doing and suffering injustice, the material element is that which is done externally, considered in itself, as stated above (A. 2), and the formal and essential element is on the part of the will of agent and patient, as stated above (A. 2). Accordingly we must reply that injustice suffered by one man and injustice done by another man always accompany one another, in the material sense. But if we speak in the formal sense a man can do an injustice with the intention of doing an injustice, and yet the other man does not suffer an injustice, because he suffers voluntarily; and on the other hand a man can suffer an injustice if he suffer an injustice against his will, while the man who does the injury unknowingly, does an injustice, not formally but only materially.

# Article 4

*Whether whoever does an injustice sins mortally?*

**AD QUARTUM SIC PROCEDITUR**. Videtur quod non quicumque facit iniustum peccet mortaliter. Peccatum enim veniale mortali opponitur. Sed quandoque veniale peccatum est quod aliquis faciat iniustum, dicit enim philosophus, in V Ethic., de iniusta agentibus loquens, *quaecumque non solum ignorantes, sed et propter ignorantiam peccant, venialia sunt.* Ergo non quicumque facit iniustum mortaliter peccat.

**PRAETEREA**, qui in aliquo parvo iniustitiam facit, parum a medio declinat. Sed hoc videtur esse tolerabile, et inter minima malorum computandum, ut patet per philosophum, in II Ethic. Non ergo quicumque facit iniustum peccat mortaliter.

**PRAETEREA**, caritas est *mater omnium virtutum*, ex cuius contrarietate aliquod peccatum dicitur mortale. Sed non omnia peccata opposita aliis virtutibus sunt mortalia. Ergo etiam neque facere iniustum semper est peccatum mortale.

**SED CONTRA**, quidquid est contra legem Dei est peccatum mortale. Sed quicumque facit iniustum facit contra praeceptum legis Dei, quia vel reducitur ad furtum, vel ad adulterium, vel ad homicidium; vel ad aliquid huiusmodi, ut ex sequentibus patebit. Ergo quicumque facit iniustum peccat mortaliter.

**RESPONDEO** dicendum quod, sicut supra dictum est cum de differentia peccatorum ageretur, peccatum mortale est quod contrariatur caritati, per quam est animae vita. Omne autem nocumentum alteri illatum ex se caritati repugnat, quae movet ad volendum bonum alterius.

**OBJECTION 1**: It would seem that not everyone who does an injustice sins mortally. For venial sin is opposed to mortal sin. Now it is sometimes a venial sin to do an injury: for the Philosopher says (*Ethic.* v, 8) in reference to those who act unjustly: *Whatever they do not merely in ignorance but through ignorance is a venial matter.* Therefore not everyone that does an injustice sins mortally.

**OBJ. 2**: Further, he who does an injustice in a small matter, departs but slightly from the mean. Now this seems to be insignificant and should be accounted among the least of evils, as the Philosopher declares (*Ethic.* ii, 9). Therefore not everyone that does an injustice sins mortally.

**OBJ. 3**: Further, charity is the *mother of all the virtues*, and it is through being contrary thereto that a sin is called mortal. But not all the sins contrary to the other virtues are mortal. Therefore neither is it always a mortal sin to do an injustice.

**ON THE CONTRARY**, Whatever is contrary to the law of God is a mortal sin. Now whoever does an injustice does that which is contrary to the law of God, since it amounts either to theft, or to adultery, or to murder, or to something of the kind, as will be shown further on (Q. 64, seqq.). Therefore whoever does an injustice sins mortally.

**I ANSWER THAT**, As stated above (I-II, Q. 12, A. 5), when we were treating of the distinction of sins, a mortal sin is one that is contrary to charity which gives life to the soul. Now every injury inflicted on another person is of itself contrary to charity, which moves us to will the good

Et ideo, cum iniustitia semper consistat in nocumento alterius, manifestum est quod facere iniustum ex genere suo est peccatum mortale.

**Ad primum** ergo dicendum quod verbum philosophi intelligitur de ignorantia facti, quam ipse vocat *ignorantiam particularium circumstantiarum*, quae meretur veniam, non autem de ignorantia iuris, quae non excusat. Qui autem ignorans facit iniustum, non facit iniustum nisi per accidens, ut supra dictum est.

**Ad secundum** dicendum quod ille qui in parvis facit iniustitiam, deficit a perfecta ratione eius quod est iniustum facere, inquantum potest reputari non esse omnino contra voluntatem eius qui hoc patitur, puta si auferat aliquis alicui unum pomum vel aliquid tale, de quo probabile sit quod ille inde non laedatur, nec ei displiceat.

**Ad tertium** dicendum quod peccata quae sunt contra alias virtutes non semper sunt in nocumentum alterius, sed important inordinationem quandam circa passiones humanas. Unde non est similis ratio.

of another. And so since injustice always consists in an injury inflicted on another person, it is evident that to do an injustice is a mortal sin according to its genus.

**Reply Obj. 1**: This saying of the Philosopher is to be understood as referring to ignorance of fact, which he calls ignorance of particular circumstances, and which deserves pardon, and not to ignorance of the law which does not excuse: and he who does an injustice through ignorance, does no injustice except accidentally, as stated above (A. 2)

**Reply Obj. 2**: He who does an injustice in small matters falls short of the perfection of an unjust deed, insofar as what he does may be deemed not altogether contrary to the will of the person who suffers therefrom: for instance, if a man take an apple or some such thing from another man, in which case it is probable that the latter is not hurt or displeased.

**Reply Obj. 3**: The sins which are contrary to the other virtues are not always hurtful to another person, but imply a disorder affecting human passions; hence there is no comparison.

# QUESTION 60

## JUDGMENT

Deinde considerandum est de iudicio. Et circa hoc quaeruntur sex.

Primo, utrum iudicium sit actus iustitiae.

Secundo, utrum sit licitum iudicare.

Tertio, utrum per suspiciones sit iudicandum.

Quarto, utrum dubia sint in meliorem partem interpretanda.

Quinto, utrum iudicium semper sit secundum leges scriptas proferendum.

Sexto, utrum iudicium per usurpationem pervertatur.

In due sequence we must consider judgment, under which head there are six points of inquiry:

(1) Whether judgment is an act of justice?

(2) Whether it is lawful to judge?

(3) Whether judgment should be based on suspicions?

(4) Whether doubts should be interpreted favorably?

(5) Whether judgment should always be given according to the written law?

(6) Whether judgment is perverted by being usurped?

# Article 1

*Whether judgment is an act of justice?*

**AD PRIMUM SIC PROCEDITUR.** Videtur quod iudicium non sit actus iustitiae. Dicit enim philosophus, in I Ethic., quod *unusquisque bene iudicat quae cognoscit*, et sic iudicium ad vim cognoscitivam pertinere videtur. Vis autem cognoscitiva per prudentiam perficitur. Ergo iudicium magis pertinet ad prudentiam quam ad iustitiam, quae est in voluntate, ut dictum est.

**PRAETEREA,** apostolus dicit, I ad Cor. II, *spiritualis iudicat omnia.* Sed homo maxime efficitur spiritualis per virtutem caritatis, quae *diffunditur in cordibus nostris per spiritum sanctum, qui datus est nobis,* ut dicitur Rom. V. Ergo iudicium magis pertinet ad caritatem quam ad iustitiam.

**PRAETEREA,** ad unamquamque virtutem pertinet rectum iudicium circa propriam materiam, quia *virtuosus in singulis est regula et mensura,* secundum philosophum, in libro Ethic. Non ergo iudicium magis pertinet ad iustitiam quam ad alias virtutes morales.

**PRAETEREA,** iudicium videtur ad solos iudices pertinere. Actus autem iustitiae invenitur in omnibus iustis. Cum igitur non soli iudices sint iusti, videtur quod iudicium non sit actus proprius iustitiae.

**SED CONTRA** est quod in Psalm. dicitur, *quoadusque iustitia convertatur in iudicium.*

**RESPONDEO** dicendum quod iudicium proprie nominat actum iudicis inquantum est iudex. Iudex autem dicitur quasi *ius dicens.* Ius autem est obiectum iustitiae, ut supra habitum est. Et ideo iudicium importat, secundum primam nominis impositionem, definitionem vel determinationem iusti sive iuris. Quod autem aliquis be-

**OBJECTION 1**: It would seem that judgment is not an act of justice. The Philosopher says (*Ethic.* i, 3) that *everyone judges well of what he knows,* so that judgment would seem to belong to the cognitive faculty. Now the cognitive faculty is perfected by prudence. Therefore judgment belongs to prudence rather than to justice, which is in the will, as stated above (Q. 58, A. 4).

**OBJ. 2**: Further, the Apostle says (1 Cor 2:15): *The spiritual man judgeth all things.* Now man is made spiritual chiefly by the virtue of charity, which *is poured forth in our hearts by the Holy Spirit Who is given to us* (Rom 5:5). Therefore judgment belongs to charity rather than to justice.

**OBJ. 3**: Further, it belongs to every virtue to judge aright of its proper matter, because *the virtuous man is the rule and measure in everything,* according to the Philosopher (*Ethic.* iii, 4). Therefore judgment does not belong to justice any more than to the other moral virtues.

**OBJ. 4**: Further, judgment would seem to belong only to judges. But the act of justice is to be found in every just man. Since then judges are not the only just men, it seems that judgment is not the proper act of justice.

**ON THE CONTRARY**, It is written (Ps 93:15): *Until justice be turned into judgment.*

**I ANSWER THAT,** Judgment properly denotes the act of a judge as such. Now a judge (*judex*) is so called because he asserts the right (jus dicens) and right is the object of justice, as stated above (Q. 57, A. 1). Consequently the original meaning of the word *judgment* is a statement or decision of the just or right. Now to decide rightly about virtuous

ne definiat aliquid in operibus virtuosis proprie procedit ex habitu virtutis, sicut castus recte determinat ea quae pertinent ad castitatem. Et ideo iudicium, quod importat rectam determinationem eius quod est iustum, proprie pertinet ad iustitiam. Propter quod philosophus dicit, in V Ethic., quod *homines ad iudicem confugiunt sicut ad quandam iustitiam animatam.*

**AD PRIMUM** ergo dicendum quod nomen iudicii, quod secundum primam impositionem significat rectam determinationem iustorum, ampliatum est ad significandum rectam determinationem in quibuscumque rebus, tam in speculativis quam in practicis. In omnibus tamen ad rectum iudicium duo requiruntur. Quorum unum est ipsa virtus proferens iudicium. Et sic iudicium est actus rationis, dicere enim vel definire aliquid rationis est. Aliud autem est dispositio iudicantis, ex qua habet idoneitatem ad recte iudicandum. Et sic in his quae ad iustitiam pertinent iudicium procedit ex iustitia, sicut et in his quae ad fortitudinem pertinent ex fortitudine. Sic ergo iudicium est quidam actus iustitiae sicut inclinantis ad recte iudicandum, prudentiae autem sicut iudicium proferentis. Unde et synesis, ad prudentiam pertinens, dicitur bene iudicativa, ut supra habitum est.

**AD SECUNDUM** dicendum quod homo spiritualis ex habitu caritatis habet inclinationem ad recte iudicandum de omnibus secundum regulas divinas, ex quibus iudicium per donum sapientiae pronuntiat, sicut iustus per virtutem prudentiae pronuntiat iudicium ex regulis iuris.

**AD TERTIUM** dicendum quod aliae virtutes ordinant hominem in seipso, sed iustitia ordinat hominem ad alium, ut ex dictis patet. Homo autem est dominus eorum quae ad ipsum pertinent, non autem est dominus eorum quae ad alium pertinent. Et ideo in his quae sunt secundum alias virtutes non requiritur nisi iudicium virtuosi, extenso tamen nomine iudicii, ut dictum est. Sed in his quae pertinent ad iustitiam requiritur ulterius iudicium alicuius superioris, *qui utrumque valeat arguere, et ponere manum suam in ambobus.* Et propter hoc iudicium specialius pertinet ad iustitiam quam ad aliquam aliam virtutem.

**AD QUARTUM** dicendum quod iustitia in principe quidem est sicut virtus architectonica, quasi imperans et praecipiens quod iustum est, in subditis autem est tanquam virtus executiva et ministrans. Et ideo iudicium, quod importat definitionem iusti, pertinet ad iustitiam secundum quod est principaliori modo in praesidente.

deeds proceeds, properly speaking, from the virtuous habit; thus a chaste person decides rightly about matters relating to chastity. Therefore judgment, which denotes a right decision about what is just, belongs properly to justice. For this reason the Philosopher says (*Ethic.* v, 4) that *men have recourse to a judge as to one who is the personification of justice.*

**REPLY OBJ. 1**: The word *judgment*, from its original meaning of a right decision about what is just, has been extended to signify a right decision in any matter whether speculative or practical. Now a right judgment in any matter requires two things. The first is the virtue itself that pronounces judgment: and in this way, judgment is an act of reason, because it belongs to the reason to pronounce or define. The other is the disposition of the one who judges, on which depends his aptness for judging aright. In this way, in matters of justice, judgment proceeds from justice, even as in matters of fortitude, it proceeds from fortitude. Accordingly judgment is an act of justice insofar as justice inclines one to judge aright, and of prudence insofar as prudence pronounces judgment: wherefore synesis which belongs to prudence is said to *judge rightly*, as stated above (Q. 51, A. 3).

**REPLY OBJ. 2**: The spiritual man, by reason of the habit of charity, has an inclination to judge aright of all things according to the Divine rules; and it is in conformity with these that he pronounces judgment through the gift of wisdom: even as the just man pronounces judgment through the virtue of prudence conformably with the ruling of the law.

**REPLY OBJ. 3**: The other virtues regulate man in himself, whereas justice regulates man in his dealings with others, as shown above (Q. 58, A. 2). Now man is master in things concerning himself, but not in matters relating to others. Consequently where the other virtues are in question, there is no need for judgment other than that of a virtuous man, taking judgment in its broader sense, as explained above (ad 1). But in matters of justice, there is further need for the judgment of a superior, who is *able to reprove both, and to put his hand between both.* Hence judgment belongs more specifically to justice than to any other virtue.

**REPLY OBJ. 4**: Justice is in the sovereign as a master-virtue, commanding and prescribing what is just; while it is in the subjects as an executive and administrative virtue. Hence judgment, which denotes a decision of what is just, belongs to justice, considered as existing chiefly in one who has authority.

# Article 2

*Whether it is lawful to judge?*

**AD SECUNDUM SIC PROCEDITUR**. Videtur quod non sit licitum iudicare. Non enim infligitur poena nisi pro illicito. Sed iudicantibus imminet poena, quam non iudicantes effugiunt, secundum illud Matth. VII, *nolite iudicare, ut non iudicemini*. Ergo iudicare est illicitum.

**PRAETEREA**, Rom. XIV dicitur, *tu quis es, qui iudicas alienum servum? Suo domino stat aut cadit*. Dominus autem omnium Deus est. Ergo nulli homini licet iudicare.

**PRAETEREA**, nullus homo est sine peccato, secundum illud I Ioan. I, *si dixerimus quia peccatum non habemus, nosipsos seducimus*. Sed peccanti non licet iudicare, secundum illud Rom. II, *inexcusabilis es, o homo omnis qui iudicas, in quo enim alterum iudicas, teipsum condemnas; eadem enim agis quae iudicas*. Ergo nulli est licitum iudicare.

**SED CONTRA** est quod dicitur Deut. XVI, *iudices et magistros constitues in omnibus portis tuis, ut iudicent populum iusto iudicio*.

**RESPONDEO** dicendum quod iudicium intantum est licitum inquantum est iustitiae actus. Sicut autem ex praedictis patet, ad hoc quod iudicium sit actus iustitiae tria requiruntur, primo quidem, ut procedat ex inclinatione iustitiae; secundo, quod procedat ex auctoritate praesidentis; tertio, quod proferatur secundum rectam rationem prudentiae. Quodcumque autem horum defuerit, est iudicium vitiosum et illicitum. Uno quidem modo, quando est contra rectitudinem iustitiae, et sic dicitur iudicium *perversum* vel *iniustum*. Alio modo, quando homo iudicat in his in quibus non habet auctoritatem, et sic dicitur iudicium *usurpatum*. Tertio modo, quando deest certitudo rationis, puta cum aliquis de his iudicat quae sunt dubia vel occulta per aliquas leves coniecturas, et sic dicitur iudicium *suspiciosum* vel *temerarium*.

**AD PRIMUM** ergo dicendum quod dominus ibi prohibet iudicium temerarium, quod est de intentione cordis vel de aliis incertis, ut Augustinus dicit, in libro de Serm. Dom. in monte. Vel prohibet ibi iudicium de rebus divinis, de quibus, cum sint supra nos, non debemus iudicare, sed simpliciter ea credere, ut Hilarius dicit, super Matth. Vel prohibet iudicium quod non sit ex benevolentia, sed ex animi amaritudine, ut Chrysostomus dicit.

**AD SECUNDUM** dicendum quod iudex constituitur ut minister Dei. Unde dicitur Deut. I, *quod iustum est iudicate*; et postea subdit, *quia Dei est iudicium*.

**AD TERTIUM** dicendum quod illi qui sunt in gravibus peccatis non debent iudicare eos qui sunt in eisdem

**OBJECTION 1**: It would seem unlawful to judge. For nothing is punished except what is unlawful. Now those who judge are threatened with punishment, which those who judge not will escape, according to Matt. 7:1, *Judge not, and ye shall not be judged*. Therefore it is unlawful to judge.

**OBJ. 2**: Further, it is written (Rom 14:4): *Who art thou that judgest another man's servant To his own lord he standeth or falleth*. Now God is the Lord of all. Therefore to no man is it lawful to judge.

**OBJ. 3**: Further, no man is sinless, according to 1 John 1:8, *If we say that we have no sin, we deceive ourselves*. Now it is unlawful for a sinner to judge, according to Rom. 2:1, *Thou art inexcusable, O man, whosoever thou art, that judgest; for wherein thou judgest another, thou condemnest thyself, for thou dost the same things which thou judgest*. Therefore to no man is it lawful to judge.

**ON THE CONTRARY**, It is written (Deut 16:18): *Thou shalt appoint judges and magistrates in all thy gates . . . that they may judge the people with just judgment*.

**I ANSWER THAT**, Judgment is lawful insofar as it is an act of justice. Now it follows from what has been stated above (A. 1, ad 1, 3) that three conditions are requisite for a judgment to be an act of justice: first, that it proceed from the inclination of justice; second, that it come from one who is in authority; third, that it be pronounced according to the right ruling of prudence. If any one of these be lacking, the judgment will be faulty and unlawful. First, when it is contrary to the rectitude of justice, and then it is called *perverted* or *unjust*: second, when a man judges about matters wherein he has no authority, and this is called judgment *by usurpation*: third, when the reason lacks certainty, as when a man, without any solid motive, forms a judgment on some doubtful or hidden matter, and then it is called judgment by *suspicion* or *rash* judgment.

**REPLY OBJ. 1**: In these words our Lord forbids rash judgment which is about the inward intention, or other uncertain things, as Augustine states (*De Serm. Dom. in Monte* ii, 18). Or else He forbids judgment about Divine things, which we ought not to judge, but simply believe, since they are above us, as Hilary declares in his commentary on Matt. 5. Or again according to Chrysostom, He forbids the judgment which proceeds not from benevolence but from bitterness of heart.

**REPLY OBJ. 2**: A judge is appointed as God's servant; wherefore it is written (Deut 1:16): *Judge that which is just*, and further on (Deut 1:17), *because it is the judgment of God*.

**REPLY OBJ. 3**: Those who stand guilty of grievous sins should not judge those who are guilty of the same or lesser

peccatis vel minoribus, ut Chrysostomus dicit, super illud Matth. VII, *nolite iudicare*. Et praecipue est hoc intelligendum quando illa peccata sunt publica, quia ex hoc generatur scandalum in cordibus aliorum. Si autem non sunt publica, sed occulta, et necessitas iudicandi immineat propter officium, potest cum humilitate et timore vel arguere vel iudicare. Unde Augustinus dicit, in libro de Serm. Dom. in monte, *si invenerimus nos in eodem vitio esse, congemiscamus, et ad pariter conandum invitemus*. Nec tamen propter hoc homo sic seipsum condemnat ut novum condemnationis meritum sibi acquirat, sed quia, condemnans alium, ostendit se similiter condemnabilem esse, propter idem peccatum vel simile.

sins, as Chrysostom says on the words of Matt. 7:1, *Judge not*. Above all does this hold when such sins are public, because there would be an occasion of scandal arising in the hearts of others. If however they are not public but hidden, and there be an urgent necessity for the judge to pronounce judgment, because it is his duty, he can reprove or judge with humility and fear. Hence Augustine says (*De Serm. Dom. in Monte* ii, 19): *If we find that we are guilty of the same sin as another man, we should groan together with him, and invite him to strive against it together with us.* And yet it is not through acting thus that a man condemns himself so as to deserve to be condemned once again, but when, in condemning another, he shows himself to be equally deserving of condemnation on account of another or a like sin.

# Article 3

*Whether it is unlawful to form a judgment from suspicions?*

**AD TERTIUM SIC PROCEDITUR.** Videtur quod iudicium ex suspicione procedens non sit illicitum. Suspicio enim videtur esse opinio incerta de aliquo malo, unde et philosophus, in VI Ethic., ponit quod suspicio se habet et ad verum et ad falsum. Sed de singularibus contingentibus non potest haberi opinio nisi incerta. Cum igitur iudicium humanum sit circa humanos actus, qui sunt in singularibus et contingentibus, videtur quod nullum iudicium esset licitum, si ex suspicione iudicare non liceret.

**PRAETEREA**, per iudicium illicitum fit aliqua iniuria proximo. Sed suspicio mala in sola opinione hominis consistit, et sic non videtur ad iniuriam alterius pertinere. Ergo suspicionis iudicium non est illicitum.

**PRAETEREA**, si sit illicitum, oportet quod ad iniustitiam reducatur, quia iudicium est actus iustitiae, ut dictum est. Sed iniustitia ex suo genere semper est peccatum mortale, ut supra habitum est. Ergo suspicionis iudicium semper esset peccatum mortale, si esset illicitum. Sed hoc est falsum, quia *suspiciones vitare non possumus*, ut dicit Glossa Augustini super illud I ad Cor. IV, *nolite ante tempus iudicare*. Ergo iudicium suspiciosum non videtur esse illicitum.

**SED CONTRA** est quod Chrysostomus, super illud Matth. VII, *nolite iudicare* etc., dicit, *dominus hoc mandato non prohibet Christianos ex benevolentia alios corripere, sed ne per iactantiam iustitiae suae Christiani Christianos despiciant, ex solis plerumque suspicionibus odientes ceteros et condemnantes.*

**RESPONDEO** dicendum quod, sicut Tullius dicit, suspicio importat opinionem mali quando ex levibus

**OBJECTION 1**: It would seem that it is not unlawful to form a judgment from suspicions. For suspicion is seemingly an uncertain opinion about an evil, wherefore the Philosopher states (*Ethic.* vi, 3) that suspicion is about both the true and the false. Now it is impossible to have any but an uncertain opinion about contingent singulars. Since then human judgment is about human acts, which are about singular and contingent matters, it seems that no judgment would be lawful, if it were not lawful to judge from suspicions.

**OBJ. 2**: Further, a man does his neighbor an injury by judging him unlawfully. But an evil suspicion consists in nothing more than a man's opinion, and consequently does not seem to pertain to the injury of another man. Therefore judgment based on suspicion is not unlawful.

**OBJ. 3**: Further, if it is unlawful, it must needs be reducible to an injustice, since judgment is an act of justice, as stated above (A. 1). Now an injustice is always a mortal sin according to its genus, as stated above (Q. 59, A. 4). Therefore a judgment based on suspicion would always be a mortal sin, if it were unlawful. But this is false, because *we cannot avoid suspicions*, according to a gloss of Augustine (*Tract. xc in Joan.*) on 1 Cor. 4:5, Judge not before the time. Therefore a judgment based on suspicion would seem not to be unlawful.

**ON THE CONTRARY**, Chrysostom in comment on the words of Matt. 7:1, *Judge not*, etc., says: *By this commandment our Lord does not forbid Christians to reprove others from kindly motives, but that Christian should despise Christian by boasting his own righteousness, by hating and condemning others for the most part on mere suspicion.*

**I ANSWER THAT**, As Tully says (*De Invent. Rhet.* ii), suspicion denotes evil thinking based on slight indications,

indiciis procedit. Et contingit ex tribus. Uno quidem modo, ex hoc quod aliquis in seipso malus est, et ex hoc ipso, quasi conscius suae malitiae, faciliter de aliis malum opinatur, secundum illud Eccle. X, *in via stultus ambulans, cum ipse sit insipiens, omnes stultos aestimat.* Alio modo provenit ex hoc quod aliquis male afficitur ad alterum. Cum enim aliquis contemnit vel odit aliquem, aut irascitur vel invidet ei, ex levibus signis opinatur mala de ipso, quia unusquisque faciliter credit quod appetit. Tertio modo provenit ex longa experientia, unde philosophus dicit, in II Rhet., quod *senes sunt maxime suspiciosi, quia multoties experti sunt aliorum defectus.* Primae autem duae suspicionis causae manifeste pertinent ad perversitatem affectus. Tertia vero causa diminuit rationem suspicionis, inquantum experientia ad certitudinem proficit, quae est contra rationem suspicionis. Et ideo suspicio vitium quoddam importat, et quanto magis procedit suspicio, tanto magis est vitiosum.

Est autem triplex gradus suspicionis. Primus quidem gradus est ut homo ex levibus indiciis de bonitate alicuius dubitare incipiat. Et hoc est veniale et leve peccatum, *pertinet* enim *ad tentationem humanam, sine qua vita ista non ducitur,* ut habetur in Glossa super illud I ad Cor. IV, *nolite ante tempus iudicare.* Secundus gradus est cum aliquis pro certo malitiam alterius aestimat ex levibus indiciis. Et hoc, si sit de aliquo gravi, est peccatum mortale, inquantum non est sine contemptu proximi, unde Glossa ibidem subdit, *etsi ergo suspiciones vitare non possumus, quia homines sumus, iudicia tamen, idest definitivas firmasque sententias, continere debemus.* Tertius gradus est cum aliquis iudex ex suspicione procedit ad aliquem condemnandum. Et hoc directe ad iniustitiam pertinet. Unde est peccatum mortale.

**AD PRIMUM** ergo dicendum quod in humanis actibus invenitur aliqua certitudo, non quidem sicut in demonstrativis, sed secundum quod convenit tali materiae, puta cum aliquid per idoneos testes probatur.

**AD SECUNDUM** dicendum quod ex hoc ipso quod aliquis malam opinionem habet de alio sine causa sufficienti, indebite contemnit ipsum. Et ideo iniuriatur ei.

**AD TERTIUM** dicendum quod quia iustitia et iniustitia est circa exteriores operationes, ut dictum est, tunc iudicium suspiciosum directe ad iniustitiam pertinet quando ad actum exteriorem procedit. Et tunc est peccatum mortale, ut dictum est. Iudicium autem interius pertinet ad iustitiam secundum quod comparatur ad exterius iudicium ut actus interior ad exteriorem, sicut concupiscentia ad fornicationem, et ira ad homicidium.

and this is due to three causes. First, from a man being evil in himself, and from this very fact, as though conscious of his own wickedness, he is prone to think evil of others, according to Eccles. 10:3, *The fool when he walketh in the way, whereas he himself is a fool, esteemeth all men fools.* Second, this is due to a man being ill-disposed towards another: for when a man hates or despises another, or is angry with or envious of him, he is led by slight indications to think evil of him, because everyone easily believes what he desires. Third, this is due to long experience: wherefore the Philosopher says (*Rhet.* ii, 13) that *old people are very suspicious, for they have often experienced the faults of others.* The first two causes of suspicion evidently connote perversity of the affections, while the third diminishes the nature of suspicion, inasmuch as experience leads to certainty which is contrary to the nature of suspicion. Consequently suspicion denotes a certain amount of vice, and the further it goes, the more vicious it is.

Now there are three degrees of suspicion. The first degree is when a man begins to doubt of another's goodness from slight indications. This is a venial and a light sin; for *it belongs to human temptation without which no man can go through this life,* according to a gloss on 1 Cor. 4:5, *Judge not before the time.* The second degree is when a man, from slight indications, esteems another man's wickedness as certain. This is a mortal sin, if it be about a grave matter, since it cannot be without contempt of one's neighbor. Hence the same gloss goes on to say: *If then we cannot avoid suspicions, because we are human, we must nevertheless restrain our judgment, and refrain from forming a definite and fixed opinion.* The third degree is when a judge goes so far as to condemn a man on suspicion: this pertains directly to injustice, and consequently is a mortal sin.

**REPLY OBJ. 1**: Some kind of certainty is found in human acts, not indeed the certainty of a demonstration, but such as is befitting the matter in point, for instance when a thing is proved by suitable witnesses.

**REPLY OBJ. 2**: From the very fact that a man thinks evil of another without sufficient cause, he despises him unduly, and therefore does him an injury.

**REPLY OBJ. 3**: Since justice and injustice are about external operations, as stated above (Q. 58, AA. 8, 10, 11; Q. 59, A. 1, ad 3), the judgment of suspicion pertains directly to injustice when it is betrayed by external action, and then it is a mortal sin, as stated above. The internal judgment pertains to justice, insofar as it is related to the external judgment, even as the internal to the external act, for instance as desire is related to fornication, or anger to murder.

# Article 4

*Whether doubts should be interpreted for the best?*

AD QUARTUM SIC PROCEDITUR. Videtur quod dubia non sint in meliorem partem interpretanda. Iudicium enim magis esse debet de eo quod ut in pluribus accidit. Sed in pluribus accidit quod aliqui male agant, *quia stultorum infinitus est numerus*, ut dicitur Eccle. I; *proni enim sunt sensus hominis ad malum ab adolescentia sua*, ut dicitur Gen. VIII. Ergo dubia magis debemus interpretari in malum quam in bonum.

PRAETEREA, Augustinus dicit quod *ille pie et iuste vivit qui rerum integer est aestimator, in neutram partem declinando*. Sed ille qui interpretatur in melius quod dubium est declinat in alteram partem. Ergo hoc non est faciendum.

PRAETEREA, homo debet diligere proximum sicut seipsum. Sed circa seipsum homo debet dubia interpretari in peiorem partem, secundum illud Iob IX, *verebar omnia opera mea*. Ergo videtur quod ea quae sunt dubia circa proximos sint in peiorem partem interpretanda.

SED CONTRA est quod Rom. XIV, super illud, *qui non manducat manducantem non iudicet*, dicit Glossa, *dubia in meliorem partem sunt interpretanda*.

RESPONDEO dicendum quod, sicut dictum est, ex hoc ipso quod aliquis habet malam opinionem de alio absque sufficienti causa, iniuriatur ei et contemnit ipsum. Nullus autem debet alium contemnere, vel nocumentum quodcumque inferre, absque causa cogente. Et ideo ubi non apparent manifesta indicia de malitia alicuius, debemus eum ut bonum habere, in meliorem partem interpretando quod dubium est.

AD PRIMUM ergo dicendum quod potest contingere quod ille qui in meliorem partem interpretatur, frequentius fallitur. Sed melius est quod aliquis frequenter fallatur habens bonam opinionem de aliquo malo homine, quam quod rarius fallatur habens malam opinionem de aliquo bono, quia ex hoc fit iniuria alicui, non autem ex primo.

AD SECUNDUM dicendum quod aliud est iudicare de rebus, et aliud de hominibus. In iudicio enim quo de rebus iudicamus non attenditur bonum vel malum ex parte ipsius rei de qua iudicamus, cui nihil nocet qualitercumque iudicemus de ipsa, sed attenditur ibi solum bonum iudicantis si vere iudicet, vel malum si falso; *quia verum est bonum intellectus, falsum autem est malum ipsius*, ut dicitur in VI Ethic. Et ideo unusquisque debet niti ad hoc quod de rebus iudicet secundum quod sunt. Sed in iudicio quo iudicamus de hominibus praecipue attenditur bonum et malum ex parte eius de quo iudicatur, qui in hoc ipso honorabilis habetur quod bonus iudicatur, et contemptibilis si iudicetur malus.

OBJECTION 1: It would seem that doubts should not be interpreted for the best. Because we should judge from what happens for the most part. But it happens for the most part that evil is done, since *the number of fools is infinite* (Eccl 1:15), *for the imagination and thought of man's heart are prone to evil from his youth* (Gen 8:21). Therefore doubts should be interpreted for the worst rather than for the best.

OBJ. 2: Further, Augustine says (*De Doctr. Christ.* i, 27) that *he leads a godly and just life who is sound in his estimate of things, and turns neither to this side nor to that*. Now he who interprets a doubtful point for the best, turns to one side. Therefore this should not be done.

OBJ. 3: Further, man should love his neighbor as himself. Now with regard to himself, a man should interpret doubtful matters for the worst, according to Job 9:28, *I feared all my works*. Therefore it seems that doubtful matters affecting one's neighbor should be interpreted for the worst.

ON THE CONTRARY, A gloss on Rom. 14:3, *He that eateth not, let him not judge him that eateth*, says: *Doubts should be interpreted in the best sense*.

I ANSWER THAT, As stated above (A. 3, ad 2), from the very fact that a man thinks ill of another without sufficient cause, he injures and despises him. Now no man ought to despise or in any way injure another man without urgent cause: and, consequently, unless we have evident indications of a person's wickedness, we ought to deem him good, by interpreting for the best whatever is doubtful about him.

REPLY OBJ. 1: He who interprets doubtful matters for the best, may happen to be deceived more often than not; yet it is better to err frequently through thinking well of a wicked man, than to err less frequently through having an evil opinion of a good man, because in the latter case an injury is inflicted, but not in the former.

REPLY OBJ. 2: It is one thing to judge of things and another to judge of men. For when we judge of things, there is no question of the good or evil of the thing about which we are judging, since it will take no harm no matter what kind of judgment we form about it; but there is question of the good of the person who judges, if he judge truly, and of his evil if he judge falsely because *the true is the good of the intellect, and the false is its evil*, as stated in *Ethic.* vi, 2, wherefore everyone should strive to make his judgment accord with things as they are. On the other hand when we judge of men, the good and evil in our judgment is considered chiefly on the part of the person about whom judgment is being formed; for he is deemed worthy of

Et ideo ad hoc potius tendere debemus in tali iudicio quod hominem iudicemus bonum, nisi manifesta ratio in contrarium appareat. Ipsi autem homini iudicanti, falsum iudicium quo bene iudicat de alio non pertinet ad malum intellectus ipsius, sicut nec ad eius perfectionem pertinet secundum se cognoscere veritatem singularium contingentium, sed magis pertinet ad bonum affectum.

honor from the very fact that he is judged to be good, and deserving of contempt if he is judged to be evil. For this reason we ought, in this kind of judgment, to aim at judging a man good, unless there is evident proof of the contrary. And though we may judge falsely, our judgment in thinking well of another pertains to our good feeling and not to the evil of the intellect, even as neither does it pertain to the intellect's perfection to know the truth of contingent singulars in themselves.

**Ad tertium** dicendum quod interpretari aliquid in deteriorem vel meliorem partem contingit dupliciter. Uno modo, per quandam suppositionem. Et sic, cum debemus aliquibus malis adhibere remedium, sive nostris sive alienis, expedit ad hoc ut securius remedium apponatur, quod supponatur id quod deterius est, quia remedium quod est efficax contra maius malum, multo magis est efficax contra minus malum. Alio modo interpretamur aliquid in bonum vel malum definiendo sive determinando. Et sic in rerum iudicio debet aliquis niti ad hoc ut interpretetur unumquodque secundum quod est, in iudicio autem personarum, ut interpretetur in melius, sicut dictum est.

**Reply Obj. 3**: One may interpret something for the worst or for the best in two ways. First, by a kind of supposition; and thus, when we have to apply a remedy to some evil, whether our own or another's, in order for the remedy to be applied with greater certainty of a cure, it is expedient to take the worst for granted, since if a remedy be efficacious against a worse evil, much more is it efficacious against a lesser evil. Second we may interpret something for the best or for the worst, by deciding or determining, and in this case when judging of things we should try to interpret each thing according as it is, and when judging of persons, to interpret things for the best as stated above.

# Article 5

*Whether we should always judge according to the written law?*

**Ad quintum sic proceditur.** Videtur quod non sit semper secundum leges scriptas iudicandum. Semper enim vitandum est iniustum iudicium. Sed quandoque leges scriptae iniustitiam continent, secundum illud Isaiae X, *vae qui condunt leges iniquas, et scribentes iniustitias scripserunt.* Ergo non semper est secundum leges scriptas iudicandum.

**Praeterea**, iudicium oportet esse de singularibus eventibus. Sed nulla lex scripta potest omnes singulares eventus comprehendere, ut patet per philosophum, in V Ethic. Ergo videtur quod non semper sit secundum leges scriptas iudicandum.

**Praeterea**, lex ad hoc scribitur ut sententia legislatoris manifestetur. Sed quandoque contingit quod si ipse lator legis praesens esset, aliter iudicaret. Ergo non est semper secundum legem scriptam iudicandum.

**Sed contra** est quod Augustinus dicit, in libro de vera Relig., *in istis temporalibus legibus, quanquam de his homines iudicent cum eas instituerint, tamen cum fuerint institutae et firmatae, non licebit iudicibus de ipsis iudicare, sed secundum ipsas.*

**Respondeo** dicendum quod, sicut dictum est, iudicium nihil est aliud nisi quaedam definitio vel determinatio eius quod iustum est. Fit autem aliquid iustum dupliciter, uno modo, ex ipsa natura rei, quod dicitur ius

**Objection 1**: It would seem that we ought not always to judge according to the written law. For we ought always to avoid judging unjustly. But written laws sometimes contain injustice, according to Isa. 10:1, *Woe to them that make wicked laws, and when they write, write injustice.* Therefore we ought not always to judge according to the written law.

**Obj. 2**: Further, judgment has to be formed about individual happenings. But no written law can cover each and every individual happening, as the Philosopher declares (*Ethic.* v, 10). Therefore it seems that we are not always bound to judge according to the written law.

**Obj. 3**: Further, a law is written in order that the lawgiver's intention may be made clear. But it happens sometimes that even if the lawgiver himself were present he would judge otherwise. Therefore we ought not always to judge according to the written law.

**On the contrary**, Augustine says (*De Vera Relig.* xxxi): *In these earthly laws, though men judge about them when they are making them, when once they are established and passed, the judges may judge no longer of them, but according to them.*

**I answer that**, As stated above (A. 1), judgment is nothing else but a decision or determination of what is just. Now a thing becomes just in two ways: first by the very nature of the case, and this is called *natural right*, second

naturale; alio modo, ex quodam condicto inter homines, quod dicitur ius positivum, ut supra habitum est. Leges autem scribuntur ad utriusque iuris declarationem, aliter tamen et aliter. Nam legis Scriptura ius quidem naturale continet, sed non instituit, non enim habet robur ex lege, sed ex natura. Ius autem positivum Scriptura legis et continet et instituit, dans ei auctoritatis robur.

Et ideo necesse est quod iudicium fiat secundum legis Scripturam, alioquin iudicium deficeret vel a iusto naturali, vel a iusto positivo.

**AD PRIMUM** ergo dicendum quod lex scripta, sicut non dat robur iuri naturali, ita nec potest eius robur minuere vel auferre, quia nec voluntas hominis potest immutare naturam. Et ideo si Scriptura legis contineat aliquid contra ius naturale, iniusta est, nec habet vim obligandi, ibi enim ius positivum locum habet ubi quantum ad ius naturale *nihil differt utrum sic vel aliter fiat*, sicut supra habitum est. Et ideo nec tales Scripturae leges dicuntur, sed potius legis corruptiones, ut supra dictum est. Et ideo secundum eas non est iudicandum.

**AD SECUNDUM** dicendum quod sicut leges iniquae secundum se contrariantur iuri naturali, vel semper vel ut in pluribus; ita etiam leges quae sunt recte positae in aliquibus casibus deficiunt, in quibus si servarentur, esset contra ius naturale. Et ideo in talibus non est secundum litteram legis iudicandum, sed recurrendum ad aequitatem, quam intendit legislator. Unde iurisperitus dicit, *nulla ratio iuris aut aequitatis benignitas patitur ut quae salubriter pro utilitate hominum introducuntur, ea nos duriore interpretatione contra ipsorum commodum producamus ad severitatem*. Et in talibus etiam legislator aliter iudicaret, et, si considerasset, lege determinasset.

**ET PER HOC** patet responsio ad tertium.

by some agreement between men, and this is called *positive right*, as stated above (Q. 57, A. 2). Now laws are written for the purpose of manifesting both these rights, but in different ways. For the written law does indeed contain natural right, but it does not establish it, for the latter derives its force, not from the law but from nature: whereas the written law both contains positive right, and establishes it by giving it force of authority.

Hence it is necessary to judge according to the written law, else judgment would fall short either of the natural or of the positive right.

**REPLY OBJ. 1:** Just as the written law does not give force to the natural right, so neither can it diminish or annul its force, because neither can man's will change nature. Hence if the written law contains anything contrary to the natural right, it is unjust and has no binding force. For positive right has no place except where *it matters not*, according to the natural right, *whether a thing be done in one way or in another*; as stated above (Q. 57, A. 2, ad 2). Wherefore such documents are to be called, not laws, but rather corruptions of law, as stated above (I-II, Q. 95, A. 2): and consequently judgment should not be delivered according to them.

**REPLY OBJ. 2:** Even as unjust laws by their very nature are, either always or for the most part, contrary to the natural right, so too laws that are rightly established, fail in some cases, when if they were observed they would be contrary to the natural right. Wherefore in such cases judgment should be delivered, not according to the letter of the law, but according to equity which the lawgiver has in view. Hence the jurist says: *By no reason of law, or favor of equity, is it allowable for us to interpret harshly, and render burdensome, those useful measures which have been enacted for the welfare of man.* In such cases even the lawgiver himself would decide otherwise; and if he had foreseen the case, he might have provided for it by law.

**THIS SUFFICES** for the Reply to the Third Objection.

# Article 6

### Whether judgment is rendered perverse by being usurped?

**AD SEXTUM SIC PROCEDITUR.** Videtur quod iudicium per usurpationem non reddatur perversum. Iustitia enim est quaedam rectitudo in agendis. Sed nihil deperit veritati a quocumque dicatur, sed a quocumque est accipienda. Ergo etiam nihil deperit iustitiae, a quocumque iustum determinetur, quod pertinet ad rationem iudicii.

**PRAETEREA**, peccata punire ad iudicium pertinet. Sed aliqui laudabiliter leguntur peccata punisse qui tamen auctoritatem non habebant super illos quos puniebant, sicut Moyses occidendo Aegyptium, ut habetur

**OBJECTION 1:** It would seem that judgment is not rendered perverse by being usurped. For justice is rectitude in matters of action. Now truth is not impaired, no matter who tells it, but it may suffer from the person who ought to accept it. Therefore again justice loses nothing, no matter who declares what is just, and this is what is meant by judgment.

**OBJ. 2:** Further, it belongs to judgment to punish sins. Now it is related to the praise of some that they punished sins without having authority over those whom they punished; such as Moses in slaying the Egyptian (Exod 2:12),

Exod. II; et Phinees, filius Eleazari, Zambri, filium Salomi, ut legitur Num. XXV, *et reputatum est ei ad iustitiam*, ut dicitur in Psalm. Ergo usurpatio iudicii non pertinet ad iniustitiam.

**PRAETEREA**, potestas spiritualis distinguitur a temporali. Sed quandoque praelati habentes spiritualem potestatem intromittunt se de his quae pertinent ad potestatem saecularem. Ergo usurpatum iudicium non est illicitum.

**PRAETEREA**, sicut ad recte iudicandum requiritur auctoritas, ita etiam et iustitia iudicantis et scientia, ut ex supradictis patet. Sed non dicitur iudicium esse iniustum si aliquis iudicet non habens habitum iustitiae, vel non habens scientiam iuris. Ergo neque etiam iudicium usurpatum, quod fit per defectum auctoritatis, semper erit iniustum.

**SED CONTRA** est quod dicitur Rom. XIV, *tu quis es, qui iudicas alienum servum?*

**RESPONDEO** dicendum quod, cum iudicium sit ferendum secundum leges scriptas, ut dictum est, ille qui iudicium fert legis dictum quodammodo interpretatur, applicando ipsum ad particulare negotium. Cum autem eiusdem auctoritatis sit legem interpretari et legem condere, sicut lex condi non potest nisi publica auctoritate, ita nec iudicium ferri potest nisi publica auctoritate, quae quidem se extendit ad eos qui communitati subduntur. Et ideo sicut iniustum esset ut aliquis constringeret alium ad legem servandam quae non esset publica auctoritate sancita, ita etiam iniustum est si aliquis aliquem compellat ferre iudicium quod publica auctoritate non fertur.

**AD PRIMUM** ergo dicendum quod pronuntiatio veritatis non importat compulsionem ad hoc quod suscipiatur, sed liberum est unicuique eam recipere vel non recipere prout vult. Sed iudicium importat quandam impulsionem. Et ideo iniustum est quod aliquis iudicetur ab eo qui publicam auctoritatem non habet.

**AD SECUNDUM** dicendum quod Moyses videtur Aegyptium occidisse quasi ex inspiratione divina auctoritatem adeptus, ut videtur per hoc quod dicitur Act. VII, quod, *percusso Aegyptio, aestimabat Moyses intelligere fratres suos quoniam dominus per manum ipsius daret salutem Israel*. Vel potest dici quod Moyses occidit Aegyptium defendendo eum qui iniuriam patiebatur cum moderamine inculpatae tutelae. Unde Ambrosius dicit, in libro de Offic., quod *qui non repellit iniuriam a socio cum potest, tam est in vitio quam ille qui facit*; et inducit exemplum Moysi. Vel potest dici, sicut dicit Augustinus, in quaestionibus Exod., quod *sicut terra, ante utilia semina, herbarum inutilium fertilitate laudatur; sic illud Moysi factum vitiosum quidem fuit, sed magnae fertilitatis signum gerebat*, inquantum scilicet erat signum virtutis eius qua populum liberaturus erat.

and Phinees the son of Eleazar in slaying Zambri the son of Salu (Num 25:7–14), and *it was reputed to him unto justice* (Ps 105:31). Therefore usurpation of judgment pertains not to injustice.

**OBJ. 3**: Further, spiritual power is distinct from temporal. Now prelates having spiritual power sometimes interfere in matters concerning the secular power. Therefore usurped judgment is not unlawful.

**OBJ. 4**: Further, even as the judge requires authority in order to judge aright, so also does he need justice and knowledge, as shown above (A. 1, ad 1, 3; A. 2). But a judgment is not described as unjust, if he who judges lacks the habit of justice or the knowledge of the law. Neither therefore is it always unjust to judge by usurpation, i.e., without authority.

**ON THE CONTRARY**, It is written (Rom 14:4): *Who art thou that judgest another man's servant?*

**I ANSWER THAT**, Since judgment should be pronounced according to the written law, as stated above (A. 5), he that pronounces judgment, interprets, in a way, the letter of the law, by applying it to some particular case. Now since it belongs to the same authority to interpret and to make a law, just as a law cannot be made save by public authority, so neither can a judgment be pronounced except by public authority, which extends over those who are subject to the community. Wherefore even as it would be unjust for one man to force another to observe a law that was not approved by public authority, so too it is unjust, if a man compels another to submit to a judgment that is pronounced by other than the public authority.

**REPLY OBJ. 1**: When the truth is declared there is no obligation to accept it, and each one is free to receive it or not, as he wishes. On the other hand judgment implies an obligation, wherefore it is unjust for anyone to be judged by one who has no public authority.

**REPLY OBJ. 2**: Moses seems to have slain the Egyptian by authority received as it were, by divine inspiration; this seems to follow from Acts 7:24, 25, where it is said that *striking the Egyptian . . . he thought that his brethren understood that God by his hand would save Israel* . Or it may be replied that Moses slew the Egyptian in order to defend the man who was unjustly attacked, without himself exceeding the limits of a blameless defense. Wherefore Ambrose says (*De Offic.* i, 36) that *whoever does not ward off a blow from a fellow man when he can, is as much in fault as the striker*; and he quotes the example of Moses. Again we may reply with Augustine (*QQ. Exod.* qu. 2) that just as *the soil gives proof of its fertility by producing useless herbs before the useful seeds have grown, so this deed of Moses was sinful although it gave a sign of great fertility*, in so far, to wit, as it was a sign of the power whereby he was to deliver his people.

De Phinee autem dicendum est quod ex inspiratione divina, zelo Dei commotus, hoc fecit. Vel quia, licet nondum esset summus sacerdos, erat tamen filius summi sacerdotis, et ad eum hoc iudicium pertinebat, sicut et ad alios iudices, quibus hoc erat praeceptum.

**AD TERTIUM** dicendum quod potestas saecularis subditur spirituali sicut corpus animae. Et ideo non est usurpatum iudicium si spiritualis praelatus se intromittat de temporalibus quantum ad ea in quibus subditur ei saecularis potestas, vel quae ei a saeculari potestate relinquuntur.

**AD QUARTUM** dicendum quod habitus scientiae et iustitiae sunt perfectiones singularis personae, et ideo per eorum defectum non dicitur usurpatum iudicium, sicut per defectum publicae auctoritatis, ex qua iudicium vim coactivam habet.

With regard to Phinees the reply is that he did this out of zeal for God by Divine inspiration; or because though not as yet high-priest, he was nevertheless the high-priest's son, and this judgment was his concern as of the other judges, to whom this was commanded.

**REPLY OBJ. 3**: The secular power is subject to the spiritual, even as the body is subject to the soul. Consequently the judgment is not usurped if the spiritual authority interferes in those temporal matters that are subject to the spiritual authority or which have been committed to the spiritual by the temporal authority.

**REPLY OBJ. 4**: The habits of knowledge and justice are perfections of the individual, and consequently their absence does not make a judgment to be usurped, as in the absence of public authority which gives a judgment its coercive force.

# QUESTION 61

## THE PARTS OF JUSTICE

Deinde considerandum est de partibus iustitiae. Et primo, de partibus subiectivis, quae sunt species iustitiae, scilicet distributiva et commutativa; secundo, de partibus quasi integralibus; tertio, de partibus quasi potentialibus, scilicet de virtutibus adiunctis. Circa primum occurrit duplex consideratio, prima, de ipsis iustitiae partibus; secunda, de vitiis oppositis. Et quia restitutio videtur esse actus commutativae iustitiae, primo considerandum est de distinctione iustitiae commutativae et distributivae, secundo, de restitutione.

Circa primum quaeruntur quatuor.

Primo, utrum sint duae species iustitiae, iustitia distributiva et commutativa.

Secundo, utrum eodem modo in eis medium accipiatur.

Tertio, utrum sit earum uniformis vel multiplex materia.

Quarto, utrum secundum aliquam earum specierum iustum sit idem quod *contrapassum*.

We must now consider the parts of justice; (1) the subjective parts, which are the species of justice, i.e., distributive and commutative justice; (2) the quasi-integral parts; (3) the quasi-potential parts, i.e., the virtues connected with justice. The first consideration will be twofold: (1) The parts of justice; (2) their opposite vices. And since restitution would seem to be an act of commutative justice, we must consider (1) the distinction between commutative and distributive justice; (2) restitution.

Under the first head there are four points of inquiry:

(1) Whether there are two species of justice, viz. distributive and commutative?

(2) Whether in either case the mean is take in the same way?

(3) Whether their matter is uniform or manifold?

(4) Whether in any of these species the just is the same as counter-passion?

# Article 1

*Whether two species of justice are suitably assigned, as commutative and distributive?*

**AD PRIMUM SIC PROCEDITUR**. Videtur quod inconvenienter ponantur duae species iustitiae, iustitia distributiva et commutativa. Non enim potest esse iustitiae species quod multitudini nocet, cum iustitia ad bonum commune ordinetur. Sed distribuere bona communia in multos nocet bono communi multitudinis, tum quia exhauriuntur opes communes; tum etiam quia mores hominum corrumpuntur; dicit enim Tullius, in libro de Offic., *fit deterior qui accipit, et ad idem semper expectandum paratior*. Ergo distributio non pertinet ad aliquam iustitiae speciem.

**PRAETEREA**, iustitiae actus est reddere unicuique quod suum est, ut supra habitum est. Sed in distributione non redditur alicui quod suum erat, sed de novo appropriatur sibi id quod erat commune. Ergo hoc ad iustitiam non pertinet.

**PRAETEREA**, iustitia non solum est in principe, sed etiam in subiectis, ut supra habitum est. Sed distribuere semper pertinet ad principem. Ergo distributiva non pertinet ad iustitiam.

**OBJECTION 1**: It would seem that the two species of justice are unsuitably assigned, viz. distributive and commutative. That which is hurtful to the many cannot be a species of justice, since justice is directed to the common good. Now it is hurtful to the common good of the many, if the goods of the community are distributed among many, both because the goods of the community would be exhausted, and because the morals of men would be corrupted. For Tully says (*De Offic.* ii, 15): *He who receives becomes worse, and the more ready to expect that he will receive again*. Therefore distribution does not belong to any species of justice.

**OBJ. 2**: Further, the act of justice is to render to each one what is his own, as stated above (Q. 58, A. 2). But when things are distributed, a man does not receive what was his, but becomes possessed of something which belonged to the community. Therefore this does not pertain to justice.

**OBJ. 3**: Further, justice is not only in the sovereign, but also in the subject, as stated above (Q. 58, A. 6). But it belongs exclusively to the sovereign to distribute. Therefore distribution does not always belong to justice.

PRAETEREA, *distributivum iustum est bonorum communium*, ut dicitur in V Ethic. sed communia pertinent ad iustitiam legalem. Ergo iustitia distributiva non est species iustitiae particularis, sed iustitiae legalis.

PRAETEREA, unum et multa non diversificant speciem virtutis. Sed iustitia commutativa consistit in hoc quod aliquid redditur uni; iustitia vero distributiva in hoc quod aliquid datur multis. Ergo non sunt diversae species iustitiae.

SED CONTRA est quod philosophus, in V Ethic., ponit duas partes iustitiae, et dicit quod *una est directiva in distributionibus, alia in commutationibus*.

RESPONDEO dicendum quod, sicut dictum est, iustitia particularis ordinatur ad aliquam privatam personam, quae comparatur ad communitatem sicut pars ad totum. Potest autem ad aliquam partem duplex ordo attendi. Unus quidem partis ad partem, cui similis est ordo unius privatae personae ad aliam. Et hunc ordinem dirigit commutativa iustitia, quae consistit in his quae mutuo fiunt inter duas personas ad invicem. Alius ordo attenditur totius ad partes, et huic ordini assimilatur ordo eius quod est commune ad singulas personas. Quem quidem ordinem dirigit iustitia distributiva, quae est distributiva communium secundum proportionalitatem. Et ideo duae sunt iustitiae species, scilicet commutativa et distributiva.

AD PRIMUM ergo dicendum quod sicut in largitionibus privatarum personarum commendatur moderatio, effusio vero culpatur; ita etiam in distributione communium bonorum est moderatio servanda, in quo dirigit iustitia distributiva.

AD SECUNDUM dicendum quod sicut pars et totum quodammodo sunt idem, ita id quod est totius quodammodo est partis. Et ita cum ex bonis communibus aliquid in singulos distribuitur, quilibet aliquo modo recipit quod suum est.

AD TERTIUM dicendum quod actus distributionis quae est communium bonorum pertinet solum ad praesidentem communibus bonis, sed tamen iustitia distributiva est et in subditis, quibus distribuitur, inquantum scilicet sunt contenti iusta distributione. Quamvis etiam distributio quandoque fiat bonorum communium non quidem civitati, sed uni familiae, quorum distributio fieri potest auctoritate alicuius privatae personae.

AD QUARTUM dicendum quod motus accipiunt speciem a termino ad quem. Et ideo ad iustitiam legalem pertinet ordinare ea quae sunt privatarum personarum in bonum commune, sed ordinare e converso bonum commune ad personas particulares per distributionem est iustitiae particularis.

AD QUINTUM dicendum quod iustitia distributiva et commutativa non solum distinguuntur secundum unum et multa, sed secundum diversam rationem debiti, alio

OBJ. 4: Further, *Distributive justice regards common goods* (*Ethic.* v, 4). Now matters regarding the community pertain to legal justice. Therefore distributive justice is a part, not of particular, but of legal justice.

OBJ. 5: Further, unity or multitude do not change the species of a virtue. Now commutative justice consists in rendering something to one person, while distributive justice consists in giving something to many. Therefore they are not different species of justice.

ON THE CONTRARY, The Philosopher assigns two parts to justice and says (*Ethic.* v, 2) that *one directs distributions, the other, commutations.*

I ANSWER THAT, As stated above (Q. 58, AA. 7, 8), particular justice is directed to the private individual, who is compared to the community as a part to the whole. Now a twofold order may be considered in relation to a part. In the first place there is the order of one part to another, to which corresponds the order of one private individual to another. This order is directed by commutative justice, which is concerned about the mutual dealings between two persons. In the second place there is the order of the whole towards the parts, to which corresponds the order of that which belongs to the community in relation to each single person. This order is directed by distributive justice, which distributes common goods proportionately. Hence there are two species of justice, distributive and commutative.

REPLY OBJ. 1: Just as a private individual is praised for moderation in his bounty, and blamed for excess therein, so too ought moderation to be observed in the distribution of common goods, wherein distributive justice directs.

REPLY OBJ. 2: Even as part and whole are somewhat the same, so too that which pertains to the whole, pertains somewhat to the part also: so that when the goods of the community are distributed among a number of individuals each one receives that which, in a way, is his own.

REPLY OBJ. 3: The act of distributing the goods of the community, belongs to none but those who exercise authority over those goods; and yet distributive justice is also in the subjects to whom those goods are distributed insofar as they are contented by a just distribution. Moreover distribution of common goods is sometimes made not to the state but to the members of a family, and such distribution can be made by authority of a private individual.

REPLY OBJ. 4: Movement takes its species from the term whereunto. Hence it belongs to legal justice to direct to the common good those matters which concern private individuals: whereas on the contrary it belongs to particular justice to direct the common good to particular individuals by way of distribution.

REPLY OBJ. 5: Distributive and commutative justice differ not only in respect of unity and multitude, but also in respect of different kinds of due: because common property

enim modo debetur alicui id quod est commune, alio modo id quod est proprium.

is due to an individual in one way, and his personal property in another way.

# Article 2

*Whether the mean is to be observed in the same way in distributive as in commutative justice?*

**AD SECUNDUM SIC PROCEDITUR.** Videtur quod medium eodem modo accipiatur in iustitia distributiva et commutativa. Utraque enim sub iustitia particulari continetur, ut dictum est. Sed in omnibus temperantiae vel fortitudinis partibus accipitur uno modo medium. Ergo etiam eodem modo est accipiendum medium in iustitia distributiva et commutativa.

**PRAETEREA**, forma virtutis moralis in medio consistit quod secundum rationem determinatur. Cum ergo unius virtutis sit una forma, videtur quod in utraque sit eodem modo medium accipiendum.

**PRAETEREA**, in iustitia distributiva accipitur medium attendendo diversam dignitatem personarum. Sed dignitas personarum attenditur etiam in commutativa iustitia, sicut in punitionibus, plus enim punitur qui percussit principem quam qui percussit privatam personam. Ergo eodem modo accipitur medium in utraque iustitia.

**SED CONTRA** est quod philosophus dicit, in V Ethic., quod in iustitia distributiva accipitur medium secundum *geometricam proportionalitatem*, in commutativa autem secundum *arithmeticam*.

**RESPONDEO** dicendum quod, sicut dictum est, in distributiva iustitia datur aliquid alicui privatae personae inquantum id quod est totius est debitum parti. Quod quidem tanto maius est quanto ipsa pars maiorem principalitatem habet in toto. Et ideo in distributiva iustitia tanto plus alicui de bonis communibus datur quanto illa persona maiorem principalitatem habet in communitate. Quae quidem principalitas in aristocratica communitate attenditur secundum virtutem, in oligarchica secundum divitias, in democratica secundum libertatem, et in aliis aliter. Et ideo in iustitia distributiva non accipitur medium secundum aequalitatem rei ad rem, sed secundum proportionem rerum ad personas, ut scilicet, sicut una persona excedit aliam, ita etiam res quae datur uni personae excedit rem quae datur alii. Et ideo dicit philosophus quod tale medium est secundum *geometricam proportionalitatem*, in qua attenditur aequale non secundum quantitatem, sed secundum proportionem. Sicut si dicamus quod sicut se habent sex ad quatuor, ita se habent tria ad duo, quia utrobique est sesquialtera proportio, in qua maius habet totum minus et mediam partem eius, non autem

**OBJECTION 1**: It would seem that the mean in distributive justice is to be observed in the same way as in commutative justice. For each of these is a kind of particular justice, as stated above (A. 1). Now the mean is taken in the same way in all the parts of temperance or fortitude. Therefore the mean should also be observed in the same way in both distributive and commutative justice.

**OBJ. 2**: Further, the form of a moral virtue consists in observing the mean which is determined in accordance with reason. Since, then, one virtue has one form, it seems that the mean for both should be the same.

**OBJ. 3**: Further, in order to observe the mean in distributive justice we have to consider the various deserts of persons. Now a person's deserts are considered also in commutative justice, for instance, in punishments; thus a man who strikes a prince is punished more than one who strikes a private individual. Therefore the mean is observed in the same way in both kinds of justice.

**ON THE CONTRARY**, The Philosopher says (*Ethic.* v, 3, 4) that the mean in distributive justice is observed according to *geometrical proportion*, whereas in commutative justice it follows *arithmetical proportion*.

**I ANSWER THAT**, As stated above (A. 1), in distributive justice something is given to a private individual, insofar as what belongs to the whole is due to the part, and in a quantity that is proportionate to the importance of the position of that part in respect of the whole. Consequently in distributive justice a person receives all the more of the common goods, according as he holds a more prominent position in the community. This prominence in an aristocratic community is gauged according to virtue, in an oligarchy according to wealth, in a democracy according to liberty, and in various ways according to various forms of community. Hence in distributive justice the mean is observed, not according to equality between thing and thing, but according to proportion between things and persons: in such a way that even as one person surpasses another, so that which is given to one person surpasses that which is allotted to another. Hence the Philosopher says (*Ethic.* v, 3, 4) that the mean in the latter case follows *geometrical proportion*, wherein equality depends not on quantity but on proportion. For example we say that 6 is to 4 as 3 is to 2, because in either case the proportion equals 1½; since the greater number is the sum of the lesser plus its half: whereas

est aequalitas excessus secundum quantitatem, quia sex excedunt quatuor in duobus, tria vero excedunt duo in uno.

Sed in commutationibus redditur aliquid alicui singulari personae propter rem eius quae accepta est, ut maxime patet in emptione et venditione, in quibus primo invenitur ratio commutationis. Et ideo oportet adaequare rem rei, ut quanto iste plus habet quam suum sit de eo quod est alterius, tantundem restituat ei cuius est. Et sic fit aequalitas secundum *arithmeticam* medietatem, quae attenditur secundum parem quantitatis excessum, sicut quinque est medium inter sex et quatuor, in unitate enim excedit et exceditur. Si ergo a principio uterque habebat quinque, et unus eorum accepit unum de eo quod est alterius; unus, scilicet accipiens, habebit sex, et alii relinquentur quatuor. Erit ergo iustitia si uterque reducatur ad medium, ut accipiatur unum ab eo qui habet sex, et detur ei qui habet quatuor, sic enim uterque habebit quinque, quod est medium.

AD PRIMUM ergo dicendum quod in aliis virtutibus moralibus accipitur medium secundum rationem, et non secundum rem. Sed in iustitia accipitur medium rei, et ideo secundum diversitatem rerum diversimode medium accipitur.

AD SECUNDUM dicendum quod generalis forma iustitiae est aequalitas, in qua convenit iustitia distributiva cum commutativa. In una tamen invenitur aequalitas secundum proportionalitatem geometricam, in alia secundum arithmeticam.

AD TERTIUM dicendum quod in actionibus et passionibus conditio personae facit ad quantitatem rei, maior enim est iniuria si percutiatur princeps quam si percutiatur privata persona. Et ita conditio personae in distributiva iustitia attenditur secundum se, in commutativa autem secundum quod per hoc diversificatur res.

the equality of excess is not one of quantity, because 6 exceeds 4 by 2, while 3 exceeds 2 by 1.

On the other hand in commutations something is paid to an individual on account of something of his that has been received, as may be seen chiefly in selling and buying, where the notion of commutation is found primarily. Hence it is necessary to equalize thing with thing, so that the one person should pay back to the other just so much as he has become richer out of that which belonged to the other. The result of this will be equality according to the *arithmetical mean* which is gauged according to equal excess in quantity. Thus 5 is the mean between 6 and 4, since it exceeds the latter and is exceeded by the former, by 1. Accordingly if, at the start, both persons have 5, and one of them receives 1 out of the other's belongings, the one that is the receiver, will have 6, and the other will be left with 4: and so there will be justice if both be brought back to the mean, 1 being taken from him that has 6, and given to him that has 4, for then both will have 5 which is the mean.

REPLY OBJ. 1: In the other moral virtues the rational, not the real mean, is to be followed: but justice follows the real mean; wherefore the mean, in justice, depends on the diversity of things.

REPLY OBJ. 2: Equality is the general form of justice, wherein distributive and commutative justice agree: but in one we find equality of geometrical proportion, whereas in the other we find equality of arithmetical proportion.

REPLY OBJ. 3: In actions and passions a person's station affects the quantity of a thing: for it is a greater injury to strike a prince than a private person. Hence in distributive justice a person's station is considered in itself, whereas in commutative justice it is considered insofar as it causes a diversity of things.

# Article 3

*Whether there is a different matter for both kinds of justice?*

AD TERTIUM SIC PROCEDITUR. Videtur quod materia utriusque iustitiae non sit diversa. Diversitas enim materiae facit diversitatem virtutis, ut patet in temperantia et fortitudine. Si igitur distributivae iustitiae et commutativae sit diversa materia, videtur quod non contineantur sub una virtute, scilicet sub iustitia.

PRAETEREA, distributio, quae pertinet ad distributivam iustitiam, *est pecuniae vel honoris vel aliorum quaecumque dispertiri possunt inter eos qui communitate communicant*; ut dicitur in V Ethic. Quorum etiam est commutatio inter personas ad invicem, quae pertinet ad

OBJECTION 1: It would seem that there is not a different matter for both kinds of justice. Diversity of matter causes diversity of virtue, as in the case of fortitude and temperance. Therefore, if distributive and commutative justice have different matters, it would seem that they are not comprised under the same virtue, viz. justice.

OBJ. 2: Further, the distribution that has to do with distributive justice is one of *wealth or of honors, or of whatever can be distributed among the members of the community* (*Ethic.* v, 2), which very things are the subject matter of commutations between one person and another, and this

commutativam iustitiam. Ergo non est diversa materia distributivae et commutativae iustitiae.

**Praeterea**, si sit alia materia distributivae iustitiae et alia materia commutativae propter hoc quod differunt specie, ubi non erit differentia speciei, non debebit esse materiae diversitas. Sed philosophus ponit unam speciem commutativae iustitiae, quae tamen habet multiplicem materiam. Non ergo videtur esse multiplex materia harum specierum.

**In contrarium** est quod dicitur in V Ethic., quod *una species iustitiae est directiva in distributionibus, alia in commutationibus.*

**Respondeo** dicendum quod, sicut supra dictum est, iustitia est circa quasdam operationes exteriores, scilicet distributionem et commutationem, quae quidem sunt usus quorundam exteriorum, vel rerum vel personarum vel etiam operum, rerum quidem, sicut cum aliquis vel aufert vel restituit alteri suam rem; personarum autem, sicut cum aliquis in ipsam personam hominis iniuriam facit, puta percutiendo vel conviciando, aut etiam cum reverentiam exhibet; operum autem, sicut cum quis iuste ab alio exigit vel alteri reddit aliquod opus. Si igitur accipiamus ut materiam utriusque iustitiae ea quorum operationes sunt usus, eadem est materia distributivae et commutativae iustitiae, nam et res distribui possunt a communi in singulos, et commutari de uno in alium; et etiam est quaedam distributio laboriosorum operum, et recompensatio.

Si autem accipiamus ut materiam utriusque iustitiae actiones ipsas principales quibus utimur personis, rebus et operibus, sic invenitur utrobique alia materia. Nam distributiva iustitia est directiva distributionis, commutativa vero iustitia est directiva commutationum quae attendi possunt inter duas personas. Quarum quaedam sunt involuntariae; quaedam vero voluntariae.

Involuntariae quidem, quando aliquis utitur re alterius vel persona vel opere, eo invito. Quod quidem contingit quandoque occulte per fraudem; quandoque etiam manifeste per violentiam. Utrumque autem contingit aut in rem aut in personam propriam, aut in personam coniunctam. In rem quidem, si occulte unus rem alterius accipiat, vocatur furtum; si autem manifeste, vocatur rapina. In personam autem propriam, vel quantum ad ipsam consistentiam personae; vel quantum ad dignitatem ipsius. Si autem quantum ad consistentiam personae, sic laeditur aliquis occulte per dolosam occisionem seu percussionem, et per veneni exhibitionem; manifeste autem per occisionem manifestam, aut per incarcerationem aut verberationem seu membri mutilationem. Quantum autem ad dignitatem personae, laeditur aliquis occulte quidem per falsa testimonia seu detractiones, quibus aliquis aufert famam suam, et per

belongs to commutative justice. Therefore the matters of distributive and commutative justice are not distinct.

**Obj. 3**: Further, if the matter of distributive justice differs from that of commutative justice, for the reason that they differ specifically, where there is no specific difference, there ought to be no diversity of matter. Now the Philosopher (*Ethic.* v, 2) reckons commutative justice as one species, and yet this has many kinds of matter. Therefore the matter of these species of justice is, seemingly, not of many kinds.

**On the contrary**, It is stated in *Ethic.* v, 2 that *one kind of justice directs distributions, and another commutations.*

**I answer that**, As stated above (Q. 51, AA. 8, 10), justice is about certain external operations, namely distribution and commutation. These consist in the use of certain externals, whether things, persons or even works: of things, as when one man takes from or restores to another that which is his; of persons, as when a man does an injury to the very person of another, for instance by striking or insulting him, or even by showing respect for him; and of works, as when a man justly exacts a work of another, or does a work for him. Accordingly, if we take for the matter of each kind of justice the things themselves of which the operations are the use, the matter of distributive and commutative justice is the same, since things can be distributed out of the common property to individuals, and be the subject of commutation between one person and another; and again there is a certain distribution and payment of laborious works.

If, however, we take for the matter of both kinds of justice the principal actions themselves, whereby we make use of persons, things, and works, there is then a difference of matter between them. For distributive justice directs distributions, while commutative justice directs commutations that can take place between two persons. Of these some are involuntary, some voluntary.

They are involuntary when anyone uses another man's chattel, person, or work against his will, and this may be done secretly by fraud, or openly by violence. In either case the offense may be committed against the other man's chattel or person, or against a person connected with him. If the offense is against his chattel and this be taken secretly, it is called *theft*, if openly, it is called *robbery*. If it be against another man's person, it may affect either the very substance of his person, or his dignity. If it be against the substance of his person, a man is injured secretly if he is treacherously slain, struck or poisoned, and openly, if he is publicly slain, imprisoned, struck or maimed. If it be against his personal dignity, a man is injured secretly by false witness, detractions and so forth, whereby he is deprived of his good name, and openly, by being accused in a court of law, or by public insult. If it be against a personal connection, a man is injured in the person of his

alia huiusmodi; manifeste autem per accusationem in iudicio, seu per convicii illationem. Quantum autem ad personam coniunctam, laeditur aliquis in uxore, ut in pluribus occulte, per adulterium; in servo autem, cum aliquis servum seducit, ut a domino discedat; et haec etiam manifeste fieri possunt. Et eadem ratio est de aliis personis coniunctis, in quas etiam possunt omnibus modis iniuriae committi sicut et in personam principalem. Sed adulterium et servi seductio sunt proprie iniuriae circa has personas, tamen, quia servus est possessio quaedam, hoc refertur ad furtum.

Voluntariae autem commutationes dicuntur quando aliquis voluntarie transfert rem suam in alterum. Et si quidem simpliciter in alterum transferat rem suam absque debito, sicut in donatione, non est actus iustitiae, sed liberalitatis. Intantum autem ad iustitiam voluntaria translatio pertinet inquantum est ibi aliquid de ratione debiti. Quod quidem contingit tripliciter. Uno modo, quando aliquis transfert simpliciter rem suam in alterum pro recompensatione alterius rei, sicut accidit in venditione et emptione. Secundo modo, quando aliquis tradit rem suam alteri concedens ei usum rei cum debito recuperandi rem. Et si quidem gratis concedit usum rei, vocatur ususfructus in rebus quae aliquid fructificant; vel simpliciter mutuum seu accommodatum in rebus quae non fructificant, sicut sunt denarii, vasa et huiusmodi. Si vero nec ipse usus gratis conceditur, vocatur locatio et conductio. Tertio modo aliquis tradit rem suam ut recuperandam, non ratione usus, sed vel ratione conservationis, sicut in deposito; vel ratione obligationis, sicut cum quis rem suam pignori obligat, seu cum aliquis pro alio fideiubet. In omnibus autem huiusmodi actionibus, sive voluntariis sive involuntariis, est eadem ratio accipiendi medium secundum aequalitatem recompensationis. Et ideo omnes istae actiones ad unam speciem iustitiae pertinent, scilicet ad commutativam.

**ET PER HOC** patet responsio ad obiecta.

wife, secretly (for the most part) by adultery, in the person of his slave, if the latter be induced to leave his master: which things can also be done openly. The same applies to other personal connections, and whatever injury may be committed against the principal, may be committed against them also. Adultery, however, and inducing a slave to leave his master are properly injuries against the person; yet the latter, since a slave is his master's chattel, is referred to theft.

Voluntary commutations are when a man voluntarily transfers his chattel to another person. And if he transfer it simply so that the recipient incurs no debt, as in the case of gifts, it is an act, not of justice but of liberality. A voluntary transfer belongs to justice insofar as it includes the notion of debt, and this may occur in many ways. First when one man simply transfers his thing to another in exchange for another thing, as happens in selling and buying. Second when a man transfers his thing to another, that the latter may have the use of it with the obligation of returning it to its owner. If he grant the use of a thing gratuitously, it is called *usufruct* in things that bear fruit; and simply *borrowing* on *loan* in things that bear no fruit, such as money, pottery, etc.; but if not even the use is granted gratis, it is called *letting* or *hiring*. Third, a man transfers his thing with the intention of recovering it, not for the purpose of its use, but that it may be kept safe, as in a *deposit*, or under some obligation, as when a man pledges his property, or when one man stands security for another. In all these actions, whether voluntary or involuntary, the mean is taken in the same way according to the equality of repayment. Hence all these actions belong to the one same species of justice, namely commutative justice.

**AND THIS SUFFICES** for the Replies to the Objections.

# Article 4

*Whether the just is absolutely the same as retaliation?*

**AD QUARTUM SIC PROCEDITUR.** Videtur quod iustum sit simpliciter idem quod *contrapassum*. Iudicium enim divinum est simpliciter iustum. Sed haec est forma divini iudicii, ut secundum quod aliquis fecit, patiatur, secundum illud Matth. VII, *in quo iudicio iudicaveritis, iudicabimini, et in qua mensura mensi fueritis, remetietur vobis.* Ergo iustum est simpliciter idem quod contrapassum.

**PRAETEREA,** in utraque iustitiae specie datur aliquid alicui secundum quandam aequalitatem, in respectu

**OBJECTION 1**: It would seem that the just is absolutely the same as *retaliation*. For the judgment of God is absolutely just. Now the judgment of God is such that a man has to suffer in proportion with his deeds, according to Matt. 7:2: *With what measure you judge, you shall be judged: and with what measure you mete, it shall be measured to you again.* Therefore the just is absolutely the same as retaliation.

**OBJ. 2**: Further, in either kind of justice something is given to someone according to a kind of equality. In

quidem ad dignitatem personae in iustitia distributiva, quae quidem personae dignitas maxime videtur attendi secundum opera quibus aliquis communitati servivit; in respectu autem ad rem in qua quis damnificatus est, in iustitia commutativa. Secundum autem utramque aequalitatem aliquis contrapatitur secundum quod fecit. Ergo videtur quod iustum simpliciter sit idem quod contrapassum.

**PRAETEREA**, maxime videtur quod non oporteat aliquem contrapati secundum quod fecit, propter differentiam voluntarii et involuntarii, qui enim involuntarie fecit iniuriam, minus punitur. Sed voluntarium et involuntarium, quae accipiuntur ex parte nostra, non diversificant medium iustitiae, quod est medium rei et non quoad nos. Ergo iustum simpliciter idem esse videtur quod contrapassum.

**SED CONTRA** est quod philosophus, in V Ethic., probat non quodlibet iustum esse *contrapassum*.

**RESPONDEO** dicendum quod hoc quod dicitur *contrapassum* importat aequalem recompensationem passionis ad actionem praecedentem. Quod quidem propriissime dicitur in passionibus iniuriosis quibus aliquis personam proximi laedit, puta, si percutit, quod repercutiatur. Et hoc quidem iustum determinatur in lege, Exod. XXI, *reddet animam pro anima, oculum pro oculo*, et cetera. Et quia etiam auferre rem alterius est quoddam facere, ideo secundario etiam in his dicitur contrapassum, prout scilicet aliquis qui damnum intulit, in re sua ipse etiam damnificatur. Et hoc etiam iustum continetur in lege, Exod. XXII, *si quis furatus fuerit bovem aut ovem, et occiderit vel vendiderit, quinque boves pro uno bove restituet, et quatuor oves pro una ove.* Tertio vero transfertur nomen contrapassi ad voluntarias commutationes, in quibus utrinque est actio et passio, sed voluntarium diminuit de ratione passionis, ut dictum est.

In omnibus autem his debet fieri, secundum rationem iustitiae commutativae, recompensatio secundum aequalitatem, ut scilicet passio recompensata sit aequalis actioni. Non autem semper esset aequalis si idem specie aliquis pateretur quod fecit. Nam primo quidem, cum quis iniuriose laedat alterius personam maiorem, maior est actio quam passio eiusdem speciei quam ipse pateretur. Et ideo ille qui percutit principem non solum repercutitur, sed multo gravius punitur. Similiter etiam cum quis aliquem involuntarium in re sua damnificat, maior est actio quam esset passio si sibi sola res illa auferretur, quia ipse qui damnificavit alium, in re sua nihil damnificaretur. Et ideo punitur in hoc quod multiplicius restituat, quia etiam non solum damnificavit personam privatam, sed rempublicam, eius tutelae securitatem infringendo. Similiter etiam nec in commutationibus voluntariis semper esset aequalis passio si aliquis daret rem suam, accipiens rem alterius, quia forte

distributive justice this equality regards personal dignity, which would seem to depend chiefly on what a person has done for the good of the community; while in commutative justice it regards the thing in which a person has suffered loss. Now in respect of either equality there is retaliation in respect of the deed committed. Therefore it would seem that the just is absolutely the same as retaliation.

**OBJ. 3**: Further, the chief argument against retaliation is based on the difference between the voluntary and the involuntary; for he who does an injury involuntarily is less severely punished. Now voluntary and involuntary taken in relation to ourselves, do not diversify the mean of justice since this is the real mean and does not depend on us. Therefore it would seem that the just is absolutely the same as retaliation.

**ON THE CONTRARY**, The Philosopher proves (*Ethic.* v, 5) that the just is not always the same as *retaliation*.

**I ANSWER THAT**, Retaliation (*contrapassum*) denotes equal passion repaid for previous action; and the expression applies most properly to injurious passions and actions, whereby a man harms the person of his neighbor; for instance if a man strike, that he be struck back. This kind of just is laid down in the Law (Exod 21:23, 24): *He shall render life for life, eye for eye*, etc. And since also to take away what belongs to another is to do an unjust thing, it follows that second retaliation consists in this also, that whosoever causes loss to another, should suffer loss in his belongings. This just loss is also found in the Law (Exod 22:1): *If any man steal an ox or a sheep, and kill or sell it, he shall restore five oxen for one ox and four sheep for one sheep.* Third retaliation is transferred to voluntary commutations, where action and passion are on both sides, although voluntariness detracts from the nature of passion, as stated above (Q. 59, A. 3).

In all these cases, however, repayment must be made on a basis of equality according to the requirements of commutative justice, namely that the meed of passion be equal to the action. Now there would not always be equality if passion were in the same species as the action. Because, in the first place, when a person injures the person of one who is greater, the action surpasses any passion of the same species that he might undergo, wherefore he that strikes a prince, is not only struck back, but is much more severely punished. In like manner when a man despoils another of his property against the latter's will, the action surpasses the passion if he be merely deprived of that thing, because the man who caused another's loss, himself would lose nothing, and so he is punished by making restitution several times over, because not only did he injure a private individual, but also the common weal, the security of whose protection he has infringed. Nor again would there be equality of passion in voluntary commutations, were

res alterius est multo maior quam sua. Et ideo oportet secundum quandam proportionatam commensurationem adaequare passionem actioni in commutationibus, ad quod inventa sunt numismata. Et sic contrapassum est commutativum iustum. In distributiva autem iustitia locum non habet. Quia in distributiva iustitia non attenditur aequalitas secundum proportionem rei ad rem, vel passionis ad actionem, unde dicitur contrapassum, sed secundum proportionalitatem rerum ad personas, ut supra dictum est.

AD PRIMUM ergo dicendum quod illa forma divini iudicii attenditur secundum rationem commutativae iustitiae, prout scilicet recompensat praemia meritis et supplicia peccatis.

AD SECUNDUM dicendum quod si alicui qui communitati servisset retribueretur aliquid pro servitio impenso, non esset hoc distributivae iustitiae, sed commutativae. In distributiva enim iustitia non attenditur aequalitas eius quod quis accipit ad id quod ipse impendit, sed ad id quod alius accipit, secundum modum utriusque personae.

AD TERTIUM dicendum quod quando actio iniuriosa est voluntaria, excedit iniuria, et sic accipitur ut maior res. Unde oportet maiorem poenam ei recompensari non secundum differentiam quoad nos, sed secundum differentiam rei.

one always to exchange one's chattel for another man's, because it might happen that the other man's chattel is much greater than our own: so that it becomes necessary to equalize passion and action in commutations according to a certain proportionate commensuration, for which purpose money was invented. Hence retaliation is in accordance with commutative justice: but there is no place for it in distributive justice, because in distributive justice we do not consider the equality between thing and thing or between passion and action (whence the expression contrapassum), but according to proportion between things and persons, as stated above (A. 2).

REPLY OBJ. 1: This form of the Divine judgment is in accordance with the conditions of commutative justice, insofar as rewards are apportioned to merits, and punishments to sins.

REPLY OBJ. 2: When a man who has served the community is paid for his services, this is to be referred to commutative, not distributive, justice. Because distributive justice considers the equality, not between the thing received and the thing done, but between the thing received by one person and the thing received by another according to the respective conditions of those persons.

REPLY OBJ. 3: When the injurious action is voluntary, the injury is aggravated and consequently is considered as a greater thing. Hence it requires a greater punishment in repayment, by reason of a difference, not on our part, but on the part of the thing.

# QUESTION 62

## RESTITUTION

Deinde considerandum est de restitutione. Et circa hoc quaeruntur octo.

Primo, cuius actus sit.

Secundo, utrum necesse sit ad salutem omne ablatum restitui.

Tertio, utrum oporteat multiplicatum illud restituere.

Quarto, utrum oporteat restitui id quod quis non accepit.

Quinto, utrum oporteat restitui ei a quo acceptum est.

Sexto, utrum oporteat restituere eum qui accepit.

Septimo, utrum aliquem alium.

Octavo, utrum sit statim restituendum.

We must now consider restitution, under which head there are eight points of inquiry:

(1) Of what is it an act?

(2) Whether it is always of necessity for salvation to restore what one has taken away?

(3) Whether it is necessary to restore more than has been taken away?

(4) Whether it is necessary to restore what one has not taken away?

(5) Whether it is necessary to make restitution to the person from whom something has been taken?

(6) Whether the person who has taken something away is bound to restore it?

(7) Whether any other person is bound to restitution?

(8) Whether one is bound to restore at once?

# Article 1

*Whether restitution is an act of commutative justice?*

**AD PRIMUM SIC PROCEDITUR.** Videtur quod restitutio non sit actus iustitiae commutativae. Iustitia enim respicit rationem debiti. Sed sicut donatio potest esse eius quod non debetur, ita etiam et restitutio. Ergo restitutio non est actus alicuius partis iustitiae.

**PRAETEREA,** illud quod iam transiit et non est, restitui non potest. Sed iustitia et iniustitia sunt circa quasdam actiones et passiones, quae non manent, sed transeunt. Ergo restitutio non videtur esse actus alicuius partis iustitiae.

**PRAETEREA,** restitutio est quasi quaedam recompensatio eius quod subtractum est. Sed aliquid potest homini subtrahi non solum in commutatione, sed etiam in distributione, puta cum aliquis distribuens minus dat alicui quam debeat habere. Ergo restitutio non magis est actus commutativae iustitiae quam distributivae.

**SED CONTRA,** restitutio ablationi opponitur. Sed ablatio rei alienae est actus iniustitiae circa commutationes. Ergo restitutio eius est actus iustitiae quae est in commutationibus directiva.

**RESPONDEO** dicendum quod restituere nihil aliud esse videtur quam iterato aliquem statuere in possessionem vel dominium rei suae. Et ita in restitutione attenditur aequalitas iustitiae secundum recompensationem rei ad rem, quae pertinet ad iustitiam commutativam. Et ideo restitutio est actus commutativae iustitiae, quando

**OBJECTION 1:** It would seem that restitution is not an act of commutative justice. For justice regards the notion of what is due. Now one may restore, even as one may give, that which is not due. Therefore restitution is not the act of any part of justice.

**OBJ. 2:** Further, that which has passed away and is no more cannot be restored. Now justice and injustice are about certain actions and passions, which are unenduring and transitory. Therefore restitution would not seem to be the act of a part of justice.

**OBJ. 3:** Further, restitution is repayment of something taken away. Now something may be taken away from a man not only in commutation, but also in distribution, as when, in distributing, one gives a man less than his due. Therefore restitution is not more an act of commutative than of distributive justice.

**ON THE CONTRARY,** Restitution is opposed to taking away. Now it is an act of commutative injustice to take away what belongs to another. Therefore to restore it is an act of that justice which directs commutations.

**I ANSWER THAT,** To restore is seemingly the same as to reinstate a person in the possession or dominion of his thing, so that in restitution we consider the equality of justice attending the payment of one thing for another, and this belongs to commutative justice. Hence restitution is an act of commutative justice, occasioned by one person

scilicet res unius ab alio habetur, vel per voluntatem eius, sicut in mutuo vel deposito; vel contra voluntatem eius, sicut in rapina vel furto.

**AD PRIMUM** ergo dicendum quod illud quod alteri non debetur non est, proprie loquendo, eius, etsi aliquando eius fuerit. Et ideo magis videtur esse nova donatio quam restitutio cum quis alteri reddit quod ei non debet. Habet tamen aliquam similitudinem restitutionis, quia res materialiter est eadem. Non tamen est eadem secundum formalem rationem quam respicit iustitia, quod est esse suum alicuius. Unde nec proprie restitutio dicitur.

**AD SECUNDUM** dicendum quod nomen restitutionis, inquantum importat iterationem quandam, supponit rei identitatem. Et ideo secundum primam impositionem nominis, restitutio videtur locum habere praecipue in rebus exterioribus, quae manentes eaedem et secundum substantiam et secundum ius dominii, ab uno possunt ad alium devenire. Sed sicut ab huiusmodi rebus nomen commutationis translatum est ad actiones vel passiones quae pertinent ad reverentiam vel iniuriam alicuius personae, seu nocumentum vel profectum; ita etiam nomen restitutionis ad haec derivatur quae, licet realiter non maneant, tamen manent in effectu, vel corporali, puta cum ex percussione laeditur corpus; vel qui est in opinione hominum, sicut cum aliquis verbo opprobrioso remanet homo infamatus, vel etiam minoratus in suo honore.

**AD TERTIUM** dicendum quod recompensatio quam facit distribuens ei cui dedit minus quam debuit, fit secundum comparationem rei ad rem, ut si quanto minus habuit quam debuit, tanto plus ei detur. Et ideo iam pertinet ad iustitiam commutativam.

having what belongs to another, either with his consent, for instance on loan or deposit, or against his will, as in robbery or theft.

**REPLY OBJ. 1**: That which is not due to another is not his properly speaking, although it may have been his at some time: wherefore it is a mere gift rather than a restitution, when anyone renders to another what is not due to him. It is however somewhat like a restitution, since the thing itself is materially the same; yet it is not the same in respect of the formal aspect of justice, which considers that thing as belonging to this particular man: and so it is not restitution properly so called.

**REPLY OBJ. 2**: insofar as the word restitution denotes something done over again, it implies identity of object. Hence it would seem originally to have applied chiefly to external things, which can pass from one person to another, since they remain the same both substantially and in respect of the right of dominion. But, even as the term *commutation* has passed from such like things to those actions and passions which confer reverence or injury, harm or profit on another person, so too the term *restitution* is applied, to things which though they be transitory in reality, yet remain in their effect; whether this touch his body, as when the body is hurt by being struck, or his reputation, as when a man remains defamed or dishonored by injurious words.

**REPLY OBJ. 3**: Compensation is made by the distributor to the man to whom less was given than his due, by comparison of thing with thing, when the latter receives so much the more according as he received less than his due: and consequently it pertains to commutative justice.

# Article 2

*Whether restitution of what has been taken away is necessary for salvation?*

**AD SECUNDUM SIC PROCEDITUR**. Videtur quod non sit necessarium ad salutem quod fiat restitutio eius quod ablatum est. Quod enim est impossibile non est de necessitate salutis. Sed aliquando impossibile est restituere id quod est ablatum, puta cum aliquis abstulit alicui membrum vel vitam. Ergo non videtur esse de necessitate salutis quod aliquis restituat quod alteri abstulit.

**PRAETEREA**, committere aliquod peccatum non est de necessitate salutis, quia sic homo esset perplexus. Sed quandoque illud quod aufertur non potest restitui sine peccato, puta cum aliquis alicui famam abstulit verum dicendo. Ergo restituere ablatum non est de necessitate salutis.

**OBJECTION 1**: It would seem that it is not necessary to restore what has been taken away. For that which is impossible is not necessary for salvation. But sometimes it is impossible to restore what has been taken, as when a man has taken limb or life. Therefore it does not seem necessary for salvation to restore what one has taken from another.

**OBJ. 2**: Further, the commission of a sin is not necessary for salvation, for then a man would be in a dilemma. But sometimes it is impossible, without sin, to restore what has been taken, as when one has taken away another's good name by telling the truth. Therefore it is not necessary for salvation to restore what one has taken from another.

PRAETEREA, quod factum est non potest fieri ut factum non fuerit. Sed aliquando alicui aufertur honor suae personae ex hoc ipso quod passus est aliquo iniuste eum vituperante. Ergo non potest sibi restitui quod ablatum est. Et ita non est de necessitate salutis restituere ablatum.

PRAETEREA, ille qui impedit aliquem ab aliquo bono consequendo videtur ei auferre, quia *quod modicum deest, quasi nihil deesse videtur*, ut philosophus dicit, in II Physic. Sed cum aliquis impedit aliquem ne consequatur praebendam vel aliquid huiusmodi, non videtur quod teneatur ei ad restitutionem praebendae, quia quandoque non posset. Non ergo restituere ablatum est de necessitate salutis.

SED CONTRA est quod Augustinus dicit, *non dimittitur peccatum, nisi restituatur ablatum.*

RESPONDEO dicendum quod restitutio, sicut dictum est, est actus iustitiae commutativae, quae in quadam aequalitate consistit. Et ideo restituere importat redditionem illius rei quae iniuste ablata est, sic enim per iteratam eius exhibitionem aequalitas reparatur. Si vero iuste ablatum sit, inaequalitas erit ut ei restituatur, quia iustitia in aequalitate consistit. Cum igitur servare iustitiam sit de necessitate salutis, consequens est quod restituere id quod iniuste ablatum est alicui, sit de necessitate salutis.

AD PRIMUM ergo dicendum quod in quibus non potest recompensari aequivalens, sufficit quod recompensetur quod possibile est, sicut patet *de honoribus qui sunt ad Deum et ad parentes*, ut philosophus dicit, in VIII Ethic. Et ideo quando id quod est ablatum non est restituibile per aliquid aequale, debet fieri recompensatio qualis possibilis est. Puta, cum aliquis alicui abstulit membrum, debet ei recompensare vel in pecunia vel in aliquo honore, considerata conditione utriusque personae, secundum arbitrium probi viri.

AD SECUNDUM dicendum quod aliquis potest alicui famam tripliciter auferre. Uno modo, verum dicendo et iuste, puta cum aliquis crimen alicuius prodit ordine debito servato. Et tunc non tenetur ad restitutionem famae. Alio modo, falsum dicendo et iniuste. Et tunc tenetur restituere famam confitendo se falsum dixisse. Tertio modo, verum dicendo sed iniuste, puta cum aliquis prodit crimen alterius contra ordinem debitum. Et tunc tenetur ad restitutionem famae quantum potest, sine mendacio tamen, utpote quod dicat se male dixisse, vel quod iniuste eum diffamaverit. Vel, si non possit famam restituere, debet ei aliter recompensare, sicut et in aliis dictum est.

AD TERTIUM dicendum quod actio contumeliam inferentis non potest fieri ut non fuerit. Potest tamen

OBJ. 3: Further, what is done cannot be undone. Now sometimes a man loses his personal honor by being unjustly insulted. Therefore that which has been taken from him cannot be restored to him: so that it is not necessary for salvation to restore what one has taken.

OBJ. 4: Further, to prevent a person from obtaining a good thing is seemingly the same as to take it away from him, since *to lack little is almost the same as to lack nothing at all*, as the Philosopher says (*Phys.* ii, 5). Now when anyone prevents a man from obtaining a benefice or the like, seemingly he is not bound to restore the benefice, since this would be sometimes impossible. Therefore it is not necessary for salvation to restore what one has taken.

ON THE CONTRARY, Augustine says (*Ep. ad Maced.* cxliii): *Unless a man restore what he has purloined, his sin is not forgiven.*

I ANSWER THAT, Restitution as stated above (A. 1) is an act of commutative justice, and this demands a certain equality. Wherefore restitution denotes the return of the thing unjustly taken; since it is by giving it back that equality is reestablished. If, however, it be taken away justly, there will be equality, and so there will be no need for restitution, for justice consists in equality. Since therefore the safeguarding of justice is necessary for salvation, it follows that it is necessary for salvation to restore what has been taken unjustly.

REPLY OBJ. 1: When it is impossible to repay the equivalent, it suffices to repay what one can, as in the case of honor due to God and our parents, as the Philosopher states (*Ethic.* viii, 14). Wherefore when that which has been taken cannot be restored in equivalent, compensation should be made as far as possible: for instance if one man has deprived another of a limb, he must make compensation either in money or in honor, the condition of either party being duly considered according to the judgment of a good man.

REPLY OBJ. 2: There are three ways in which one may take away another's good name. First, by saying what is true, and this justly, as when a man reveals another's sin, while observing the right order of so doing, and then he is not bound to restitution. Second, by saying what is untrue and unjustly, and then he is bound to restore that man's good name, by confessing that he told an untruth. Third, by saying what is true, but unjustly, as when a man reveals another's sin contrarily to the right order of so doing, and then he is bound to restore his good name as far as he can, and yet without telling an untruth; for instance by saying that he spoke ill, or that he defamed him unjustly; or if he be unable to restore his good name, he must compensate him otherwise, the same as in other cases, as stated above (ad 1).

REPLY OBJ. 3: The action of the man who has defamed another cannot be undone, but it is possible, by showing

fieri ut eius effectus, scilicet diminutio dignitatis personae in opinione hominum, reparetur per exhibitionem reverentiae.

**AD QUARTUM** dicendum quod aliquis potest impedire aliquem ne habeat praebendam, multipliciter. Uno modo, iuste, puta si, intendens honorem Dei vel utilitatem Ecclesiae, procuret quod detur alicui personae digniori. Et tunc nullo modo tenetur ad restitutionem vel ad aliquam recompensationem faciendam. Alio modo, iniuste, puta si intendat eius nocumentum quem impedit, propter odium vel vindictam aut aliquid huiusmodi. Et tunc, si impedit ne praebenda detur digno, consulens quod non detur, antequam sit firmatum quod ei detur; tenetur quidem ad aliquam recompensationem, pensatis conditionibus personarum et negotii, secundum arbitrium sapientis; non tamen tenetur ad aequale, quia ille nondum fuerat adeptus et poterat multipliciter impediri. Si vero iam firmatum sit quod alicui detur praebenda, et aliquis propter causam indebitam procuret quod revocetur, idem est ac si iam habitam ei auferret. Et ideo tenetur ad restitutionem aequalis, tamen secundum suam facultatem.

him deference, to undo its effect, viz. the lowering of the other man's personal dignity in the opinion of other men.

**REPLY OBJ. 4**: There are several ways of preventing a man from obtaining a benefice. First, justly: for instance, if having in view the honor of God or the good of the Church, one procures its being conferred on a more worthy subject, and then there is no obligation whatever to make restitution or compensation. Second, unjustly, if the intention is to injure the person whom one hinders, through hatred, revenge or the like. In this case, if before the benefice has been definitely assigned to anyone, one prevents its being conferred on a worthy subject by counseling that it be not conferred on him, one is bound to make some compensation, after taking account of the circumstances of persons and things according to the judgment of a prudent person: but one is not bound in equivalent, because that man had not obtained the benefice and might have been prevented in many ways from obtaining it. If, on the other hand, the benefice had already been assigned to a certain person, and someone, for some undue cause procures its revocation, it is the same as though he had deprived a man of what he already possessed, and consequently he would be bound to compensation in equivalent, in proportion, however, to his means.

# Article 3

*Whether it suffices to restore the exact amount taken?*

**AD TERTIUM SIC PROCEDITUR**. Videtur quod non sufficiat restituere simplum quod iniuste ablatum est. Dicitur enim Exod. XXII, *si quis furatus fuerit bovem aut ovem, et occiderit vel vendiderit, quinque boves pro uno bove restituet, et quatuor oves pro una ove.* Sed quilibet tenetur mandatum divinae legis observare. Ergo ille qui furatur tenetur restituere quadruplum vel quintuplum.

**PRAETEREA**, *ea quae scripta sunt, ad nostram doctrinam scripta sunt*, ut dicitur ad Rom. XV. Sed Luc. XIX Zachaeus dicit ad dominum, *si quem defraudavi, reddo quadruplum.* Ergo homo debet restituere multiplicatum id quod iniuste accepit.

**PRAETEREA**, nulli potest iuste auferri id quod dare non debet. Sed iudex iuste aufert ab eo qui furatus est plus quam furatus est, pro emenda. Ergo homo debet illud solvere. Et ita non sufficit reddere simplum.

**SED CONTRA** est quia restitutio reducit ad aequalitatem quod inaequaliter ablatum est. Sed aliquis reddendo quod accepit simplum, reducit ad aequalitatem. Ergo solum tenetur tantum restituere quantum accepit.

**OBJECTION 1**: It would seem that it is not sufficient to restore the exact amount taken. For it is written (Exod 22:1): *If a man shall steal an ox or a sheep and kill or sell it, he shall restore five oxen for one ox, and four sheep for one sheep.* Now everyone is bound to keep the commandments of the Divine law. Therefore a thief is bound to restore four- or fivefold.

**OBJ. 2**: Further, *What things soever were written, were written for our learning* (Rom 15:4). Now Zachaeus said (Luke 19:8) to our Lord: *If I have wronged any man of any thing, I restore him fourfold.* Therefore a man is bound to restore several times over the amount he has taken unjustly.

**OBJ. 3**: Further, no one can be unjustly deprived of what he is not bound to give. Now a judge justly deprives a thief of more than the amount of his theft, under the head of damages. Therefore a man is bound to pay it, and consequently it is not sufficient to restore the exact amount.

**ON THE CONTRARY**, Restitution re-establishes equality where an unjust taking has caused inequality. Now equality is restored by repaying the exact amount taken. Therefore there is no obligation to restore more than the exact amount taken.

**Respondeo** dicendum quod cum aliquis iniuste accipit rem alienam, duo sunt ibi. Quorum unum est inaequalitas ex parte rei, quae quandoque est sine iniustitia, ut patet in mutuis. Aliud autem est iniustitiae culpa, quae potest esse etiam cum aequalitate rei, puta cum aliquis intendat inferre violentiam sed non praevalet.

Quantum ergo ad primum adhibetur remedium per restitutionem, inquantum per eam aequalitas reparatur, ad quod sufficit quod restituat tantum quantum habuit de alieno. Sed quantum ad culpam adhibetur remedium per poenam, cuius inflictio pertinet ad iudicem. Et ideo antequam sit condemnatus per iudicium non tenetur plus restituere quam accepit, sed postquam condemnatus est, tenetur poenam solvere.

**Et per hoc** patet responsio ad primum, quia lex illa determinativa est poenae per iudicem infligendae. Et quamvis ad observantiam iudicialis praecepti nullus teneatur post Christi adventum, ut supra habitum est; potest tamen idem vel simile statui in lege humana, de qua erit eadem ratio.

**Ad secundum** dicendum quod Zachaeus id dixit quasi supererogare volens. Unde et praemiserat, *ecce dimidium bonorum meorum do pauperibus.*

**Ad tertium** dicendum quod iudex, condemnando, iuste potest accipere aliquid amplius, loco emendae, quod tamen, antequam condemnaretur, non debebat.

**I answer that,** When a man takes another's thing unjustly, two things must be considered. One is the inequality on the part of the thing, which inequality is sometimes void of injustice, as is the case in loans. The other is the sin of injustice, which is consistent with equality on the part of the thing, as when a person intends to use violence but fails.

As regards the first, the remedy is applied by making restitution, since thereby equality is re-established; and for this it is enough that a man restore just so much as he has belonging to another. But as regards the sin, the remedy is applied by punishment, the infliction of which belongs to the judge: and so, until a man is condemned by the judge, he is not bound to restore more than he took, but when once he is condemned, he is bound to pay the penalty.

**Hence** it is clear how to answer the First Objection: because this law fixes the punishment to be inflicted by the judge. Nor is this commandment to be kept now, because since the coming of Christ no man is bound to keep the judicial precepts, as stated above (I-II, Q. 104, A. 3). Nevertheless the same might be determined by human law, and then the same answer would apply.

**Reply Obj. 2:** Zachaeus said this being willing to do more than he was bound to do; hence he had said already: *Behold . . . the half of my goods I give to the poor.*

**Reply Obj. 3:** By condemning the man justly, the judge can exact more by way of damages; and yet this was not due before the sentence.

# Article 4

*Whether a man is bound to restore what he has not taken?*

**Ad quartum sic proceditur.** Videtur quod aliquis debeat restituere quod non abstulit. Ille enim qui damnum alicui infert tenetur damnum removere. Sed quandoque aliquis damnificat aliquem ultra id quod accepit, puta cum aliquis effodit semina, damnificat eum qui seminavit in tota messe futura; et sic videtur quod teneatur ad eius restitutionem. Ergo aliquis tenetur ad restitutionem eius quod non abstulit.

**Praeterea**, ille qui detinet pecuniam creditoris ultra terminum praefixum videtur eum damnificare in toto eo quod lucrari de pecunia posset. Quod tamen ipse non aufert. Ergo videtur quod aliquis teneatur restituere quod non abstulit.

**Praeterea**, iustitia humana derivatur a iustitia divina. Sed Deo debet aliquis restituere plus quam ab eo accepit, secundum illud Matth. XXV, *sciebas quod meto ubi non semino, et congrego ubi non sparsi.* Ergo iustum est ut etiam restituat homini aliquid quod non accepit.

**Objection 1:** It would seem that a man is bound to restore what he has not taken. For he that has inflicted a loss on a man is bound to remove that loss. Now it happens sometimes that the loss sustained is greater than the thing taken: for instance, if you dig up a man's seeds, you inflict on the sower a loss equal to the coming harvest, and thus you would seem to be bound to make restitution accordingly. Therefore a man is bound to restore what he has not taken.

**Obj. 2:** Further, he who retains his creditor's money beyond the stated time, would seem to occasion his loss of all his possible profits from that money, and yet he does not really take them. Therefore it seems that a man is bound to restore what he did not take.

**Obj. 3:** Further, human justice is derived from Divine justice. Now a man is bound to restore to God more than he has received from Him, according to Matt. 25:26, *Thou knewest that I reap where I sow not, and gather where I have not strewed.* Therefore it is just that one should restore to a man also, something that one has not taken.

**Sed contra** est quod recompensatio ad iustitiam pertinet inquantum aequalitatem facit. Sed si aliquis restitueret quod non accepit, hoc non esset aequale. Ergo talis restitutio non est iustum quod fiat.

**Respondeo** dicendum quod quicumque damnificat aliquem videtur ei auferre id in quo ipsum damnificat, damnum enim dicitur ex eo quod aliquis minus habet quam debet habere, secundum philosophum, in V Ethic. Et ideo homo tenetur ad restitutionem eius in quo aliquem damnificavit.

Sed aliquis damnificatur dupliciter. Uno modo, quia aufertur ei id quod actu habebat. Et tale damnum semper est restituendum secundum recompensationem aequalis, puta si aliquis damnificet aliquem diruens domum eius, tenetur ad tantum quantum valet domus. Alio modo damnificat aliquis aliquem impediendo ne adipiscatur quod erat in via habendi. Et tale damnum non oportet recompensare ex aequo. Quia minus est habere aliquid virtute quam habere actu. Qui autem est in via adipiscendi aliquid habet illud solum secundum virtutem vel potentiam. Et ideo si redderetur ei ut haberet hoc in actu, restitueretur ei quod est ablatum non simplum, sed multiplicatum, quod non est de necessitate restitutionis, ut dictum est. Tenetur tamen aliquam recompensationem facere, secundum conditionem personarum et negotiorum.

**Et per hoc** patet responsio ad primum et secundum. Nam ille qui semen sparsit in agro nondum habet messem in actu, sed solum in virtute; et similiter ille qui habet pecuniam nondum habet lucrum in actu, sed solum virtute; et utrumque potest multipliciter impediri.

**Ad tertium** dicendum quod Deus nihil requirit ab homine nisi bonum quod ipse in nobis seminavit. Et ideo verbum illud vel intelligitur secundum pravam existimationem servi pigri, qui existimavit se ab alio non accepisse. Vel intelligitur quantum ad hoc quod Deus requirit a nobis fructus donorum, qui sunt et ab eo et a nobis, quamvis ipsa dona a Deo sint sine nobis.

**On the contrary,** Restitution belongs to justice, because it re-establishes equality. But if one were to restore what one did not take, there would not be equality. Therefore it is not just to make such a restitution.

**I answer that,** Whoever brings a loss upon another person, seemingly, takes from him the amount of the loss, since, according to the Philosopher (*Ethic.* v, 4) loss is so called from a man having less than his due. Therefore a man is bound to make restitution according to the loss he has brought upon another.

Now a man suffers a loss in two ways. First, by being deprived of what he actually has; and a loss of this kind is always to be made good by repayment in equivalent: for instance if a man damnifies another by destroying his house he is bound to pay him the value of the house. Second, a man may damnify another by preventing him from obtaining what he was on the way to obtain. A loss of this kind need not be made good in equivalent; because to have a thing virtually is less than to have it actually, and to be on the way to obtain a thing is to have it merely virtually or potentially, and so were he to be indemnified by receiving the thing actually, he would be paid, not the exact value taken from him, but more, and this is not necessary for salvation, as stated above. However he is bound to make some compensation, according to the condition of persons and things.

**From this** we see how to answer the First and Second Objections: because the sower of the seed in the field, has the harvest, not actually but only virtually. In like manner he that has money has the profit not yet actually but only virtually: and both may be hindered in many ways.

**Reply Obj. 3:** God requires nothing from us but what He Himself has sown in us. Hence this saying is to be understood as expressing either the shameful thought of the lazy servant, who deemed that he had received nothing from the other, or the fact that God expects from us the fruit of His gifts, which fruit is from Him and from us, although the gifts themselves are from God without us.

# Article 5

*Whether restitution must always be made to the person from whom a thing has been taken?*

**Ad quintum sic proceditur.** Videtur quod non oporteat restitutionem facere semper ei a quo acceptum est aliquid. Nulli enim debemus nocere. Sed aliquando esset in nocumentum hominis si redderetur quod ab eo acceptum est; vel etiam in nocumentum aliorum, puta si aliquis redderet gladium depositum furioso. Ergo non semper est restituendum ei a quo acceptum est.

**Objection 1:** It would seem that restitution need not always be made to the person from whom a thing has been taken. For it is not lawful to injure anyone. Now it would sometimes be injurious to the man himself, or to others, were one to restore to him what has been taken from him; if, for instance, one were to return a madman his sword. Therefore restitution need not always be made to the person from whom a thing has been taken.

PRAETEREA, ille qui illicite aliquid dedit non meretur illud recuperare. Sed quandoque aliquis illicite dat quod alius etiam illicite accipit, sicut apparet in dante et recipiente aliquid simoniace. Ergo non semper restituendum est ei a quo acceptum est.

PRAETEREA, nullus tenetur ad impossibile. Sed quandoque est impossibile restituere ei a quo acceptum est, vel quia est mortuus, vel quia nimis distat, vel quia est ignotus. Ergo non semper facienda est restitutio ei a quo acceptum est.

PRAETEREA, magis debet homo recompensare ei a quo maius beneficium accepit. Sed ab aliis personis homo plus accepit beneficii quam ab illo qui mutuavit vel deposuit, sicut a parentibus. Ergo magis subveniendum est quandoque alicui personae alteri quam restituendum ei a quo est acceptum.

PRAETEREA, vanum est restituere illud quod ad manum restituentis per restitutionem pervenit. Sed si praelatus iniuste aliquid Ecclesiae subtraxit et ei restituat, ad manus eius deveniet, quia ipse est rerum Ecclesiae conservator. Ergo non debet restituere Ecclesiae a qua abstulit. Et sic non semper restituendum est ei a quo est ablatum.

SED CONTRA est quod dicitur Rom. XIII, *reddite omnibus debita, cui tributum, tributum; cui vectigal, vectigal.*

RESPONDEO dicendum quod per restitutionem fit reductio ad aequalitatem commutativae iustitiae, quae consistit in rerum adaequatione, sicut dictum est. Huiusmodi autem rerum adaequatio fieri non posset nisi ei qui minus habet quam quod suum est, suppleretur quod deest. Et ad hanc suppletionem faciendam necesse est ut ei fiat restitutio a quo acceptum est.

AD PRIMUM ergo dicendum quod quando res restituenda apparet esse graviter noxia ei cui restitutio facienda est vel alteri, non ei debet tunc restitui, quia restitutio ordinatur ad utilitatem eius cui restituitur; omnia enim quae possidentur sub ratione utilis cadunt. Nec tamen debet ille qui detinet rem alienam, sibi appropriare, sed vel reservare ut congruo tempore restituat, vel etiam alibi tradere tutius conservandam.

AD SECUNDUM dicendum quod aliquis dupliciter aliquid illicite dat uno modo, quia ipsa datio est illicita et contra legem, sicut patet in eo qui simoniace aliquid dedit. Talis meretur amittere quod dedit, unde non debet ei restitutio fieri de his. Et quia etiam ille qui accepit contra legem accepit, non debet sibi retinere, sed debet in pios usus convertere. Alio modo aliquis illicite dat quia propter rem illicitam dat, licet ipsa datio non sit illi-

OBJ. 2: Further, if a man has given a thing unlawfully, he does not deserve to recover it. Now sometimes a man gives unlawfully that which another accepts unlawfully, as in the case of the giver and receiver who are guilty of simony. Therefore it is not always necessary to make restitution to the person from whom one has taken something.

OBJ. 3: Further, no man is bound to do what is impossible. Now it is sometimes impossible to make restitution to the person from whom a thing has been taken, either because he is dead, or because he is too far away, or because he is unknown to us. Therefore restitution need not always be made to the person from whom a thing has been taken.

OBJ. 4: Further, we owe more compensation to one from whom we have received a greater favor. Now we have received greater favors from others (our parents for instance) than from a lender or depositor. Therefore sometimes we ought to succor some other person rather than make restitution to one from whom we have taken something.

OBJ. 5: Further, it is useless to restore a thing which reverts to the restorer by being restored. Now if a prelate has unjustly taken something from the Church and makes restitution to the Church, it reverts into his hands, since he is the guardian of the Church's property. Therefore he ought not to restore to the Church from whom he has taken: and so restitution should not always be made to the person from whom something has been taken away.

ON THE CONTRARY, It is written (Rom 13:7): *Render ... to all men their dues; tribute to whom tribute is due, custom to whom custom.*

I ANSWER THAT, Restitution re-establishes the equality of commutative justice, which equality consists in the equalizing of thing to thing, as stated above (A. 2; Q. 58, A. 10). Now this equalizing of things is impossible, unless he that has less than his due receive what is lacking to him: and for this to be done, restitution must be made to the person from whom a thing has been taken.

REPLY OBJ. 1: When the thing to be restored appears to be grievously injurious to the person to whom it is to be restored, or to some other, it should not be restored to him there and then, because restitution is directed to the good of the person to whom it is made, since all possessions come under the head of the useful. Yet he who retains another's property must not appropriate it, but must either reserve it, that he may restore it at a fitting time, or hand it over to another to keep it more securely.

REPLY OBJ. 2: A person may give a thing unlawfully in two ways. First through the giving itself being illicit and against the law, as is the case when a man gives a thing simoniacally. Such a man deserves to lose what he gave, wherefore restitution should not be made to him: and, since the receiver acted against the law in receiving, he must not retain the price, but must use it for some pious object. Second a man gives unlawfully, through giving for an un-

cita, sicut cum quis dat meretrici propter fornicationem. Unde et mulier potest sibi retinere quod ei datum est, et si superflue aliquid per fraudem vel dolum extorsisset, tenetur eidem restituere.

AD TERTIUM dicendum quod si ille cui debet fieri restitutio sit omnino ignotus, debet homo restituere secundum quod potest, scilicet dando in eleemosynas pro salute ipsius, sive sit mortuus sive sit vivus; praemissa tamen diligenti inquisitione de persona eius cui est restitutio facienda. Si vero sit mortuus ille cui est restitutio facienda, debet restitui heredi eius, qui computatur quasi una persona cum ipso. Si vero sit multum distans, debet sibi transmitti quod ei debetur, et praecipue si sit res magni valoris, et possit commode transmitti. Alioquin debet in aliquo loco tuto deponi ut pro eo conservetur, et domino significari.

AD QUARTUM dicendum quod aliquis de hoc quod est sibi proprium debet magis satisfacere parentibus vel his a quibus accepit maiora beneficia. Non autem debet aliquis recompensare benefactori de alieno, quod contingeret si quod debet uni alteri restitueret, nisi forte in casu extremae necessitatis, in quo posset et deberet aliquis etiam auferre aliena ut patri subveniret.

AD QUINTUM dicendum quod praelatus potest rem Ecclesiae surripere tripliciter. Uno modo, si rem Ecclesiae non sibi deputatam, sed alteri, sibi usurparet, puta si episcopus usurparet sibi rem capituli. Et tunc planum est quod debet restituere ponendo in manus eorum ad quos de iure pertinet. Alio modo, si rem Ecclesiae suae custodiae deputatam in alterius dominium transferat, puta consanguinei vel amici. Et tunc debet Ecclesiae restituere, et sub sua cura habere ut ad successorem perveniat. Alio modo potest praelatus surripere rem Ecclesiae solo animo, dum scilicet incipit habere animum possidendi eam ut suam, et non nomine Ecclesiae. Et tunc debet restituere talem animum deponendo.

lawful purpose, albeit the giving itself is not unlawful, as when a woman receives payment for fornication: wherefore she may keep what she has received. If, however, she has extorted overmuch by fraud or deceit, she would be bound to restitution.

REPLY OBJ. 3: If the person to whom restitution is due is unknown altogether, restitution must be made as far as possible, for instance by giving an alms for his spiritual welfare (whether he be dead or living): but not without previously making a careful inquiry about his person. If the person to whom restitution is due be dead, restitution should be made to his heir, who is looked upon as one with him. If he be very far away, what is due to him should be sent to him, especially if it be of great value and can easily be sent: else it should be deposited in a safe place to be kept for him, and the owner should be advised of the fact.

REPLY OBJ. 4: A man is bound, out of his own property, to succor his parents, or those from whom he has received greater benefits; but he ought not to compensate a benefactor out of what belongs to others; and he would be doing this if he were to compensate one with what is due to another. Exception must be made in cases of extreme need, for then he could and should even take what belongs to another in order to succor a parent.

REPLY OBJ. 5: There are three ways in which a prelate can rob the Church of her property. First by laying hands on Church property which is committed, not to him but to another; for instance, if a bishop appropriates the property of the chapter. In such a case it is clear that he is bound to restitution, by handing it over to those who are its lawful owners. Second by transferring to another person (for instance a relative or a friend) Church property committed to himself: in which case he must make restitution to the Church, and have it under his own care, so as to hand it over to his successor. Third, a prelate may lay hands on Church property, merely in intention, when, to wit, he begins to have a mind to hold it as his own and not in the name of the Church: in which case he must make restitution by renouncing his intention.

# Article 6

*Whether he that has taken a thing is always bound to restitution?*

AD SEXTUM SIC PROCEDITUR. Videtur quod non teneatur semper restituere ille qui accepit. Per restitutionem enim reparatur aequalitas iustitiae, quae consistit in hoc quod subtrahatur ei qui plus habet et detur ei qui minus habet. Sed contingit quandoque quod ille qui rem aliquam subtraxit alicui non habet eam, sed devenit

OBJECTION 1: It would seem that he who has taken a thing is not always bound to restore it. Restitution re-establishes the equality of justice, by taking away from him that has more and giving to him that has less. Now it happens sometimes that he who has taken that which belongs to another, no longer has it, through its having

ad manus alterius. Ergo non tenetur ille restituere qui accepit, sed alius qui rem habet.

PRAETEREA, nullus tenetur crimen suum detegere. Sed aliquando aliquis restitutionem faciendo crimen suum detegit, ut patet in furto. Ergo non semper tenetur ille qui abstulit restituere.

PRAETEREA, eiusdem rei non est multoties restitutio facienda. Sed quandoque multi simul aliquam rem surripiunt et unus eorum eam integre restituit. Ergo non semper ille qui accepit tenetur ad restituendum.

SED CONTRA, ille qui peccavit tenetur satisfacere. Sed restitutio ad satisfactionem pertinet. Ergo ille qui abstulit tenetur restituere.

RESPONDEO dicendum quod circa illum qui rem alienam accepit duo sunt consideranda, scilicet ipsa res accepta, et ipsa acceptio. Ratione autem rei tenetur eam restituere quandiu eam apud se habet, quia quod habet ultra id quod suum est, debet ei subtrahi et dari ei cui deest, secundum formam commutativae iustitiae. Sed ipsa acceptio rei alienae potest tripliciter se habere. Quandoque enim est iniuriosa, scilicet contra voluntatem existens eius qui est rei dominus, ut patet in furto et rapina. Et tunc tenetur ad restitutionem non solum ratione rei, sed etiam ratione iniuriosae actionis, etiam si res apud ipsum non remaneat. Sicut enim qui percutit aliquem tenetur recompensare iniuriam passo, quamvis nihil apud ipsum maneat; ita etiam qui furatur vel rapit tenetur ad recompensationem damni illati, etiam si nihil inde habeat; et ulterius pro iniuria illata debet puniri.

Alio modo aliquis accipit rem alterius in utilitatem suam absque iniuria, cum voluntate scilicet eius cuius est res, sicut patet in mutuis. Et tunc ille qui accepit tenetur ad restitutionem eius quod accepit non solum ratione rei, sed etiam ratione acceptionis, etiam si rem amiserit, tenetur enim recompensare ei qui gratiam fecit, quod non fiet si per hoc damnum incurrat. Tertio modo aliquis accipit rem alterius absque iniuria non pro sua utilitate, sicut patet in depositis. Et ideo ille qui sic accepit in nullo tenetur ratione acceptionis, quinimmo accipiendo impendit obsequium, tenetur autem ratione rei. Et propter hoc, si ei subtrahatur res absque sua culpa, non tenetur ad restitutionem. Secus autem esset si cum magna sua culpa rem depositam amitteret.

AD PRIMUM ergo dicendum quod restitutio non ordinatur principaliter ad hoc quod ille qui plus habet quam debet, habere desinat, sed ad hoc quod illi qui minus habet suppleatur. Unde in his rebus quae unus potest ab alio accipere sine eius detrimento, non habet locum restitutio, puta cum aliquis accipit lumen a can-

passed into another's hands. Therefore it should be restored, not by the person that took it, but by the one that has it.

OBJ. 2: Further, no man is bound to reveal his own crime. But by making restitution a man would sometimes reveal his crime, as in the case of theft. Therefore he that has taken a thing is not always bound to restitution.

OBJ. 3: Further, the same thing should not be restored several times. Now sometimes several persons take a thing at the same time, and one of them restores it in its entirety. Therefore he that takes a thing is not always bound to restitution.

ON THE CONTRARY, He that has sinned is bound to satisfaction. Now restitution belongs to satisfaction. Therefore he that has taken a thing is bound to restore it.

I ANSWER THAT, With regard to a man who has taken another's property, two points must be considered: the thing taken, and the taking. By reason of the thing taken, he is bound to restore it as long as he has it in his possession, since the thing that he has in addition to what is his, should be taken away from him, and given to him who lacks it according to the form of commutative justice. On the other hand, the taking of the thing that is another's property, may be threefold. For sometimes it is injurious, i.e., against the will of the owner, as in theft and robbery: in which case the thief is bound to restitution not only by reason of the thing, but also by reason of the injurious action, even though the thing is no longer in his possession. For just as a man who strikes another, though he gain nothing thereby, is bound to compensate the injured person, so too he that is guilty of theft or robbery, is bound to make compensation for the loss incurred, although he be no better off; and in addition he must be punished for the injustice committed.

Second, a man takes another's property for his own profit but without committing an injury, i.e., with the consent of the owner, as in the case of a loan: and then, the taker is bound to restitution, not only by reason of the thing, but also by reason of the taking, even if he has lost the thing: for he is bound to compensate the person who has done him a favor, and he would not be doing so if the latter were to lose thereby. Third, a man takes another's property without injury to the latter or profit to himself, as in the case of a deposit; wherefore he that takes a thing thus, incurs no obligation on account of the taking, in fact by taking he grants a favor; but he is bound to restitution on account of the thing taken. Consequently if this thing be taken from him without any fault on his part, he is not bound to restitution, although he would be, if he were to lose the thing through a grievous fault on his part.

REPLY OBJ. 1: The chief end of restitution is, not that he who has more than his due may cease to have it, but that he who has less than his due may be compensated. Wherefore there is no place for restitution in those things which one man may receive from another without loss to the latter, as when a person takes a light from another's candle.

dela alterius. Et ideo quamvis ille qui abstulit non habeat id quod accepit, sed in alium sit translatum; quia tamen alter privatur re sua, tenetur ei ad restitutionem et ille qui rem abstulit, ratione iniuriosae actionis; et ille qui rem habet, ratione ipsius rei.

AD SECUNDUM dicendum quod homo, etsi non teneatur crimen suum detegere hominibus, tenetur tamen crimen suum detegere Deo in confessione. Et ita per sacerdotem cui confitetur potest restitutionem facere rei alienae.

AD TERTIUM dicendum quod quia restitutio principaliter ordinatur ad removendum damnum eius a quo est aliquid iniuste ablatum, ideo postquam ei restitutio sufficiens facta est per unum, alii non tenentur ei ulterius restituere, sed magis refusionem facere ei qui restituit, qui tamen potest condonare.

Consequently although he that has taken something from another, may have ceased to have what he took, through having transferred it to another, yet since that other is deprived of what is his, both are bound to restitution, he that took the thing, on account of the injurious taking, and he that has it, on account of the thing.

REPLY OBJ. 2: Although a man is not bound to reveal his crime to other men, yet is he bound to reveal it to God in confession; and so he may make restitution of another's property through the priest to whom he confesses.

REPLY OBJ. 3: Since restitution is chiefly directed to the compensation for the loss incurred by the person from whom a thing has been taken unjustly, it stands to reason that when he has received sufficient compensation from one, the others are not bound to any further restitution in his regard: rather ought they to refund the person who has made restitution, who, nevertheless, may excuse them from so doing.

# Article 7

*Whether restitution is binding on those who have not taken?*

AD SEPTIMUM SIC PROCEDITUR. Videtur quod illi qui non acceperunt non teneantur restituere. Restitutio enim quaedam poena est accipientis. Sed nullus debet puniri nisi qui peccavit. Ergo nullus debet restituere nisi qui accepit.

PRAETEREA, iustitia non obligat aliquem ad hoc quod rem alterius augeat. Sed si ad restitutionem teneretur non solum ille qui accepit, sed etiam illi qui qualitercumque cooperantur, augeretur ex hoc res illius cui est aliquid subtractum, tum quia sibi multoties restitutio fieret; tum etiam quia quandoque aliqui operam dant ad hoc quod aliqua res alicui auferatur, quae tamen ei non aufertur. Ergo non tenentur alii ad restitutionem.

PRAETEREA, nullus tenetur se periculo exponere ad hoc quod rem alterius salvet. Sed aliquando, manifestando latronem vel ei resistendo, aliquis periculo mortis se exponeret. Non ergo tenetur aliquis ad restitutionem propter hoc quod non manifestat latronem, vel non ei resistit.

SED CONTRA est quod dicitur Rom. I, *digni sunt morte non solum qui faciunt, sed etiam qui consentiunt facientibus.* Ergo, pari ratione, etiam consentientes debent restituere.

RESPONDEO dicendum quod, sicut dictum est, ad restitutionem tenetur aliquis non solum ratione rei alienae quam accepit, sed etiam ratione iniuriosae acceptionis.

OBJECTION 1: It would seem that restitution is not binding on those who have not taken. For restitution is a punishment of the taker. Now none should be punished except the one who sinned. Therefore none are bound to restitution save the one who has taken.

OBJ. 2: Further, justice does not bind one to increase another's property. Now if restitution were binding not only on the man who takes a thing but also on all those who cooperate with him in any way whatever, the person from whom the thing was taken would be the gainer, both because he would receive restitution many times over, and because sometimes a person cooperates towards a thing being taken away from someone, without its being taken away in effect. Therefore the others are not bound to restitution.

OBJ. 3: Further, no man is bound to expose himself to danger, in order to safeguard another's property. Now sometimes a man would expose himself to the danger of death, were he to betray a thief, or withstand him. Therefore one is not bound to restitution, through not betraying or withstanding a thief.

ON THE CONTRARY, It is written (Rom 1:32): *They who do such things are worthy of death, and not only they that do them, but also they that consent to them that do them.* Therefore in like manner they that consent are bound to restitution.

I ANSWER THAT, As stated above (A. 6), a person is bound to restitution not only on account of someone else's property which he has taken, but also on account of the in-

Et ideo quicumque est causa iniustae acceptionis tenetur ad restitutionem quod quidem contingit dupliciter, directe scilicet, et indirecte. Directe quidem, quando inducit aliquis alium ad accipiendum. Et hoc quidem tripliciter. Primo quidem, movendo ad ipsam acceptionem, quod quidem fit praecipiendo, consulendo, consentiendo expresse, et laudando aliquem quasi strenuum de hoc quod aliena accipit. Alio modo, ex parte ipsius accipientis, quia scilicet eum receptat, vel qualitercumque ei auxilium fert. Tertio modo, ex parte rei acceptae, quia scilicet est particeps furti vel rapinae, quasi socius maleficii. Indirecte vero, quando aliquis non impedit, cum possit et debeat impedire, vel quia subtrahit praeceptum sive consilium impediens furtum sive rapinam; vel quia subtrahit suum auxilium, quo posset obsistere; vel quia occultat post factum.

Quae his versibus comprehenduntur, *iussio, consilium, consensus, palpo, recursus, participans, mutus, non obstans, non manifestans.*

Sciendum tamen quod quinque praemissorum semper obligant ad restitutionem. Primo, iussio, quia scilicet ille qui iubet est principaliter movens; unde ipse principaliter tenetur ad restituendum. Secundo, consensus, in eo scilicet sine quo rapina fieri non potest. Tertio, recursus, quando scilicet aliquis est receptator latronum et eis patrocinium praestat. Quarto, participatio, quando scilicet aliquis participat in crimine latrocinii et in praeda. Quinto, tenetur ille qui non obstat, cum obstare teneatur, sicut principes, qui tenentur custodire iustitiam in terra, si per eorum defectum latrones increscant, ad restitutionem tenentur; quia redditus quos habent sunt quasi stipendia ad hoc instituta ut iustitiam conservent in terra.

In aliis autem casibus enumeratis non semper obligatur aliquis ad restituendum. Non enim semper consilium vel adulatio, vel aliquid huiusmodi, est efficax causa rapinae. Unde tunc solum tenetur consiliator aut palpo, idest adulator, ad restitutionem, quando probabiliter aestimari potest quod ex huiusmodi causis fuerit iniusta acceptio subsecuta.

**AD PRIMUM** ergo dicendum quod non solum peccat ille qui peccatum exequitur, sed etiam qui quocumque modo peccati est causa sive consiliando, sive praecipiendo, sive quovis alio modo.

**AD SECUNDUM** dicendum quod principaliter tenetur restituere ille qui est principalis in facto, principaliter quidem praecipiens, secundario exequens, et consequenter alii per ordinem. Uno tamen restituente illi qui passus est damnum, alius eidem restituere non tenetur, sed illi qui sunt principales in facto, et ad quos res pervenit, tenentur aliis restituere qui restituerunt. Quando autem aliquis praecipit iniustam acceptionem quae non subsequitur, non est restitutio facienda, cum

jurious taking. Hence whoever is cause of an unjust taking is bound to restitution. This happens in two ways, directly and indirectly. Directly, when a man induces another to take, and this in three ways. First, on the part of the taking, by moving a man to take, either by express command, counsel, or consent, or by praising a man for his courage in thieving. Second, on the part of the taker, by giving him shelter or any other kind of assistance. Third, on the part of the thing taken, by taking part in the theft or robbery, as a fellow evil-doer. Indirectly, when a man does not prevent another from evil-doing (provided he be able and bound to prevent him), either by omitting the command or counsel which would hinder him from thieving or robbing, or by omitting to do what would have hindered him, or by sheltering him after the deed.

All these are expressed as follows: *By command, by counsel, by consent, by flattery, by receiving, by participation, by silence, by not preventing, by not denouncing.*

It must be observed, however, that in five of these cases the cooperator is always bound to restitution. First, in the case of command: because he that commands is the chief mover, wherefore he is bound to restitution principally. Second, in the case of consent; namely of one without whose consent the robbery cannot take place. Third, in the case of receiving; when, to wit, a man is a receiver of thieves, and gives them assistance. Fourth, in the case of participation; when a man takes part in the theft and in the booty. Fifth, he who does not prevent the theft, whereas he is bound to do so; for instance, persons in authority who are bound to safeguard justice on earth, are bound to restitution, if by their neglect thieves prosper, because their salary is given to them in payment of their preserving justice here below.

In the other cases mentioned above, a man is not always bound to restitution: because counsel and flattery are not always the efficacious cause of robbery. Hence the counsellor or flatterer is bound to restitution, only when it may be judged with probability that the unjust taking resulted from such causes.

**REPLY OBJ. 1:** Not only is he bound to restitution who commits the sin, but also he who is in any way cause of the sin, whether by counselling, or by commanding, or in any other way whatever.

**REPLY OBJ. 2:** He is bound chiefly to restitution, who is the principal in the deed; first of all, the commander; second, the executor, and in due sequence, the others: yet so that, if one of them make restitution, another is not bound to make restitution to the same person. Yet those who are principals in the deed, and who took possession of the thing, are bound to compensate those who have already made restitution. When a man commands an unjust taking that does not follow, no restitution has to be made, since its

restitutio principaliter ordinetur ad reintegrandam rem eius qui iniuste est damnificatus.

**AD TERTIUM** dicendum quod non semper ille qui non manifestat latronem tenetur ad restitutionem, aut qui non obstat, vel qui non reprehendit, sed solum quando incumbit alicui ex officio, sicut principibus terrae. Quibus ex hoc non multum imminet periculum, propter hoc enim potestate publica potiuntur, ut sint iustitiae custodes.

end is chiefly to restore the property of the person who has been unjustly injured.

**REPLY OBJ. 3**: He that fails to denounce a thief or does not withstand or reprehend him is not always bound to restitution, but only when he is obliged, in virtue of his office, to do so: as in the case of earthly princes who do not incur any great danger thereby; for they are invested with public authority, in order that they may maintain justice.

# Article 8

*Whether a man is bound to immediate restitution, or may he put it off?*

**AD OCTAVUM SIC PROCEDITUR.** Videtur quod non teneatur aliquis statim restituere, sed potius licite possit restitutionem differre. Praecepta enim affirmativa non obligant ad semper. Sed necessitas restituendi imminet ex praecepto affirmativo. Ergo non obligatur homo ad statim restituendum.

**PRAETEREA,** nullus tenetur ad impossibile. Sed quandoque aliquis non potest statim restituere. Ergo nullus tenetur ad statim restituendum.

**PRAETEREA,** restitutio est quidam actus virtutis, scilicet iustitiae. Tempus autem est una de circumstantiis quae requiruntur ad actus virtutum. Cum igitur aliae circumstantiae non sint determinatae in actibus virtutum, sed determinabiles secundum rationem prudentiae; videtur quod nec in restitutione sit tempus determinatum, ut scilicet aliquis teneatur ad statim restituendum.

**SED CONTRA** est quod eadem ratio esse videtur in omnibus quae sunt restituenda. Sed ille qui conducit opera mercenarii non potest differre restitutionem, ut patet per illud quod habetur Levit. XIX *non morabitur opus mercenarii tui apud te usque mane.* Ergo neque in aliis restitutionibus faciendis potest fieri dilatio, sed statim restituere oportet.

**RESPONDEO** dicendum quod sicut accipere rem alienam est peccatum contra iustitiam, ita etiam detinere eam, quia per hoc quod aliquis detinet rem alienam invito domino, impedit eum ab usu rei suae, et sic ei facit iniuriam. Manifestum est autem quod nec per modicum tempus licet in peccato morari, sed quilibet tenetur statim peccatum deserere, secundum illud Eccli. XXI, *quasi a facie colubri fuge peccatum.* Et ideo quilibet tenetur statim restituere, vel petere dilationem ab eo qui potest usum rei concedere.

**AD PRIMUM** ergo dicendum quod praeceptum de restitutione facienda, quamvis secundum formam sit affirmativum, implicat tamen in se negativum praeceptum, quo prohibemur rem alterius detinere.

**OBJECTION 1**: It would seem that a man is not bound to immediate restitution, and can lawfully delay to restore. For affirmative precepts do not bind for always. Now the necessity of making restitution is binding through an affirmative precept. Therefore a man is not bound to immediate restitution.

**OBJ. 2**: Further, no man is bound to do what is impossible. But it is sometimes impossible to make restitution at once. Therefore no man is bound to immediate restitution.

**OBJ. 3**: Further, restitution is an act of virtue, viz. of justice. Now time is one of the circumstances requisite for virtuous acts. Since then the other circumstances are not determinate for acts of virtue, but are determinable according to the dictate of prudence, it seems that neither in restitution is there any fixed time, so that a man be bound to restore at once.

**ON THE CONTRARY**, All matters of restitution seem to come under one head. Now a man who hires the services of a wage-earner, must not delay compensation, as appears from Lev. 19:13, *The wages of him that hath been hired by thee shall not abide with thee until the morning.* Therefore neither is it lawful, in other cases of restitution, to delay, and restitution should be made at once.

**I ANSWER THAT**, Even as it is a sin against justice to take another's property, so also is it to withhold it, since, to withhold the property of another against the owner's will, is to deprive him of the use of what belongs to him, and to do him an injury. Now it is clear that it is wrong to remain in sin even for a short time; and one is bound to renounce one's sin at once, according to Ecclus. 21:2, *Flee from sin as from the face of a serpent.* Consequently one is bound to immediate restitution, if possible, or to ask for a respite from the person who is empowered to grant the use of the thing.

**REPLY OBJ. 1**: Although the precept about the making of restitution is affirmative in form, it implies a negative precept forbidding us to withhold another's property.

**Ad secundum** dicendum quod quando aliquis non potest statim restituere, ipsa impotentia absolvit eum ab instanti restitutione facienda, sicut etiam totaliter a restitutione absolvitur si omnino sit impotens. Debet tamen remissionem vel dilationem petere ab eo cui debet, aut per se aut per alium.

**Ad tertium** dicendum quod cuiuscumque circumstantiae omissio contrariatur virtuti, pro determinata est habenda, et oportet illam circumstantiam observare. Et quia per dilationem restitutionis committitur peccatum iniustae detentionis, quod iustitiae opponitur, ideo necesse est tempus esse determinatum, ut statim restitutio fiat.

**Reply Obj. 2:** When one is unable to restore at once, this very inability excuses one from immediate restitution: even as a person is altogether excused from making restitution if he is altogether unable to make it. He is, however, bound either himself or through another to ask the person to whom he owes compensation to grant him a remission or a respite.

**Reply Obj. 3:** Whenever the omission of a circumstance is contrary to virtue that circumstance must be looked upon as determinate, and we are bound to observe it: and since delay of restitution involves a sin of unjust detention which is opposed to just detention, it stands to reason that the time is determinate in the point of restitution being immediate.

# QUESTION 63

## RESPECT OF PERSONS

Deinde considerandum est de vitiis oppositis prae-dictis iustitiae partibus. Et primo, de acceptione perso-narum, quae opponitur iustitiae distributivae; secundo, de peccatis quae opponuntur iustitiae commutativae.

Circa primum quaeruntur quatuor.

Primo, utrum personarum acceptio sit peccatum.

Secundo, utrum habeat locum in dispensatione spiritualium.

Tertio, utrum in exhibitione honorum.

Quarto, utrum in iudiciis.

We must now consider the vices opposed to the afore-said parts of justice. First we shall consider respect of persons which is opposed to distributive justice; second we shall consider the vices opposed to commutative justice.

Under the first head there are four points of inquiry:

(1) Whether respect of persons is a sin?

(2) Whether it takes place in the dispensation of spiritualities?

(3) Whether it takes place in showing honor?

(4) Whether it takes place in judicial sentences?

## Article 1

### Whether respect of persons is a sin?

AD PRIMUM SIC PROCEDITUR. Videtur quod personarum acceptio non sit peccatum. In nomine enim *personae* intelligitur personae dignitas. Sed considerare dignitates personarum pertinet ad distributivam iusti-tiam. Ergo personarum acceptio non est peccatum.

PRAETEREA, in rebus humanis personae sunt princi-paliores quam res, quia res sunt propter personas, et non e converso. Sed rerum acceptio non est peccatum. Ergo multo minus acceptio personarum.

PRAETEREA, apud Deum nulla potest esse iniquitas vel peccatum. Sed Deus videtur personas accipere, quia interdum duorum hominum unius conditionis unum assumit per gratiam, et alterum relinquit in peccato, secundum illud Matth. XXIV, *duo erunt in lecto, unus assumetur et alius relinquetur.* Ergo acceptio personarum non est peccatum.

SED CONTRA, nihil prohibetur in lege divina nisi peccatum. Sed personarum acceptio prohibetur Deut. I, ubi dicitur, *non accipietis cuiusquam personam.* Ergo personarum acceptio est peccatum.

RESPONDEO dicendum quod personarum acceptio opponitur distributivae iustitiae. Consistit enim ae-qualitas distributivae iustitiae in hoc quod diversis personis diversa tribuuntur secundum proportionem ad dignitates personarum. Si ergo aliquis consideret illam proprietatem personae propter quam id quod ei confertur est ei debitum, non erit acceptio personae, sed causae, unde Glossa, super illud ad Ephes. VI, *non est personarum acceptio apud Deum,* dicit quod iudex iustus causas discernit, non personas. Puta si aliquis promoveat aliquem ad magisterium propter sufficientiam scientiae,

OBJECTION 1: It would seem that respect of persons is not a sin. For the word *person* includes a reference to personal dignity. Now it belongs to distributive justice to consider personal dignity. Therefore respect of persons is not a sin.

OBJ. 2: Further, in human affairs persons are of more importance than things, since things are for the benefit of persons and not conversely. But respect of things is not a sin. Much less, therefore, is respect of persons.

OBJ. 3: Further, no injustice or sin can be in God. Yet God seems to respect persons, since of two men circum-stanced alike He sometimes upraises one by grace, and leaves the other in sin, according to Matt. 24:40: *Two shall be in a bed, one shall be taken, and one shall be left.* Therefore respect of persons is not a sin.

ON THE CONTRARY, Nothing but sin is forbidden in the Divine law. Now respect of persons is forbidden, Deut. 1:17: *Neither shall you respect any man's person.* Therefore respect of persons is a sin.

I ANSWER THAT, Respect of persons is opposed to distributive justice. For the equality of distributive justice consists in allotting various things to various persons in proportion to their personal dignity. Accordingly, if one considers that personal property by reason of which the thing allotted to a particular person is due to him, this is respect not of the person but of the cause. Hence a gloss on Eph. 6:9, *There is no respect of persons with God,* says that *a just judge regards causes, not persons.* For instance if you promote a man to a professorship on account of his having sufficient knowledge, you consider the due cause,

hic attenditur causa debita, non persona, si autem aliquis consideret in eo cui aliquid confert, non id propter quod id quod ei datur esset ei proportionatum vel debitum, sed solum hoc quod est iste homo, puta Petrus vel Martinus, est hic acceptio personae, quia non attribuitur ei aliquid propter aliquam causam quae faciat eum dignum, sed simpliciter attribuitur personae. Ad personam autem refertur quaecumque conditio non faciens ad causam propter quam sit dignus hoc dono, puta si aliquis promoveat aliquem ad praelationem vel magisterium quia est dives, vel quia est consanguineus suus, est acceptio personae. Contingit tamen aliquam conditionem personae facere eam dignam respectu unius rei, et non respectu alterius, sicut consanguinitas facit aliquem dignum ad hoc quod instituatur heres patrimonii, non autem ad hoc quod conferatur ei praelatio ecclesiastica. Et ideo eadem conditio personae in uno negotio considerata facit acceptionem personae, in alio autem non facit. Sic ergo patet quod personarum acceptio opponitur iustitiae distributivae in hoc quod praeter proportionem agitur. Nihil autem opponitur virtuti nisi peccatum. Unde consequens est quod personarum acceptio sit peccatum.

**Ad primum** ergo dicendum quod in distributiva iustitia considerantur conditiones personarum quae faciunt ad causam dignitatis vel debiti. Sed in acceptione personarum considerantur conditiones quae non faciunt ad causam, ut dictum est.

**Ad secundum** dicendum quod personae proportionantur et dignae redduntur aliquibus quae eis distribuuntur, propter aliquas res quae pertinent ad conditionem personae, et ideo huiusmodi conditiones sunt attendendae tanquam propriae causae. Cum autem considerantur ipsae personae, attenditur non causa ut causa. Et ideo patet quod, quamvis personae sint digniores simpliciter, non tamen sunt digniores quoad hoc.

**Ad tertium** dicendum quod duplex est datio. Una quidem pertinens ad iustitiam, qua scilicet aliquis dat alicui quod ei debetur. Et circa tales dationes attenditur personarum acceptio. Alia est datio ad liberalitatem pertinens, qua scilicet gratis datur alicui quod ei non debetur. Et talis est collatio munerum gratiae, per quae peccatores assumuntur a Deo. Et in hac donatione non habet locum personarum acceptio, quia quilibet potest absque iniustitia de suo dare quantum vult et cui vult, secundum illud Matth. XX, *an non licet mihi quod volo facere? Tolle quod tuum est, et vade.*

not the person; but if, in conferring something on someone, you consider in him not the fact that what you give him is proportionate or due to him, but the fact that he is this particular man (e.g., Peter or Martin), then there is respect of the person, since you give him something not for some cause that renders him worthy of it, but simply because he is this person. And any circumstance that does not amount to a reason why this man be worthy of this gift, is to be referred to his person: for instance if a man promote someone to a prelacy or a professorship, because he is rich or because he is a relative of his, it is respect of persons. It may happen, however, that a circumstance of person makes a man worthy as regards one thing, but not as regards another: thus consanguinity makes a man worthy to be appointed heir to an estate, but not to be chosen for a position of ecclesiastical authority: wherefore consideration of the same circumstance of person will amount to respect of persons in one matter and not in another. It follows, accordingly, that respect of persons is opposed to distributive justice in that it fails to observe due proportion. Now nothing but sin is opposed to virtue: and therefore respect of persons is a sin.

**Reply Obj. 1:** In distributive justice we consider those circumstances of a person which result in dignity or right, whereas in respect of persons we consider circumstances that do not so result.

**Reply Obj. 2:** Persons are rendered proportionate to and worthy of things which are distributed among them, by reason of certain things pertaining to circumstances of person, wherefore such conditions ought to be considered as the proper cause. But when we consider the persons themselves, that which is not a cause is considered as though it were; and so it is clear that although persons are more worthy, absolutely speaking, yet they are not more worthy in this regard.

**Reply Obj. 3:** There is a twofold giving. One belongs to justice, and occurs when we give a man his due: in such like givings respect of persons takes place. The other giving belongs to liberality, when one gives gratis that which is not a man's due: such is the bestowal of the gifts of grace, whereby sinners are chosen by God. In such a giving there is no place for respect of persons, because anyone may, without injustice, give of his own as much as he will, and to whom he will, according to Matt. 20:14, 15, *Is it not lawful for me to do what I will? . . . Take what is thine, and go thy way.*

# Article 2

*Whether respect of persons takes place in the dispensation of spiritual goods?*

AD SECUNDUM SIC PROCEDITUR. Videtur quod in dispensatione spiritualium locum non habeat personarum acceptio. Conferre enim dignitatem ecclesiasticam seu beneficium alicui propter consanguinitatem videtur ad acceptionem personarum pertinere, quia consanguinitas non est causa faciens hominem dignum ecclesiastico beneficio. Sed hoc non videtur esse peccatum, cum hoc ex consuetudine praelati Ecclesiae faciant. Ergo peccatum personarum acceptionis non videtur locum habere in dispensatione spiritualium.

PRAETEREA, praeferre divitem pauperi videtur ad acceptionem personarum pertinere, ut patet Iac. II. Sed facilius dispensatur cum divitibus et potentibus quod contrahant matrimonium in gradu prohibito, quam cum aliis. Ergo peccatum personarum acceptionis non videtur locum habere circa dispensationem spiritualium.

PRAETEREA, secundum iura sufficit eligere bonum, non autem requiritur quod aliquis eligat meliorem. Sed eligere minus bonum ad aliquid altius videtur ad acceptionem personarum pertinere. Ergo personarum acceptio non est peccatum in spiritualibus.

PRAETEREA, secundum statuta Ecclesiae eligendus est aliquis *de gremio Ecclesiae*. Sed hoc videtur ad acceptionem personarum pertinere, quia quandoque sufficientiores alibi invenirentur. Ergo personarum acceptio non est peccatum in spiritualibus.

SED CONTRA est quod dicitur Iac. II, *nolite in personarum acceptione habere fidem domini nostri Iesu Christi.* Ubi dicit Glossa Augustini, *quis ferat si quis divitem eligat ad sedem honoris Ecclesiae, contempto paupere instructiore et sanctiore?*

RESPONDEO dicendum quod, sicut dictum est, acceptio personarum est peccatum inquantum contrariatur iustitiae. Quanto autem in maioribus aliquis iustitiam transgreditur, tanto gravius peccat. Unde cum spiritualia sint temporalibus potiora, gravius peccatum est personas accipere in dispensatione spiritualium quam in dispensatione temporalium. Et quia personarum acceptio est cum aliquid personae attribuitur praeter proportionem dignitatis ipsius, considerare oportet quod dignitas alicuius personae potest attendi dupliciter. Uno modo, simpliciter et secundum se, et sic maioris dignitatis est ille qui magis abundat in spiritualibus gratiae donis. Alio modo, per comparationem ad bonum commune, contingit enim quandoque quod ille qui est minus sanctus et minus sciens, potest maius conferre ad bonum commune, propter potentiam vel industriam

OBJECTION 1: It would seem that respect of persons does not take place in the dispensation of spiritual goods. For it would seem to savor of respect of persons if a man confers ecclesiastical dignity or benefice on account of consanguinity, since consanguinity is not a cause whereby a man is rendered worthy of an ecclesiastical benefice. Yet this apparently is not a sin, for ecclesiastical prelates are wont to do so. Therefore the sin of respect of persons does not take place in the conferring of spiritual goods.

OBJ. 2: Further, to give preference to a rich man rather than to a poor man seems to pertain to respect of persons (according to James 2:2–3). Nevertheless dispensations to marry within forbidden degrees are more readily granted to the rich and powerful than to others. Therefore the sin of respect of persons seems not to take place in the dispensation of spiritual goods.

OBJ. 3: Further, according to jurists it suffices to choose a good man, and it is not requisite that one choose the better man. But it would seem to savor of respect of persons to choose one who is less good for a higher position. Therefore respect of persons is not a sin in spiritual matters.

OBJ. 4: Further, according to the law of the Church (*Cap. Cum dilectus.*) the person to be chosen should be *a member of the flock*. Now this would seem to imply respect of persons, since sometimes more competent persons would be found elsewhere. Therefore respect of persons is not a sin in spiritual matters.

ON THE CONTRARY, It is written (Jas 2:1): *Have not the faith of our Lord Jesus Christ . . . with respect of persons.* On these words a gloss of Augustine says: *Who is there that would tolerate the promotion of a rich man to a position of honor in the Church, to the exclusion of a poor man more learned and holier?*

I ANSWER THAT, As stated above (A. 1), respect of persons is a sin, insofar as it is contrary to justice. Now the graver the matter in which justice is transgressed, the more grievous the sin: so that, spiritual things being of greater import than temporal, respect of persons is a more grievous sin in dispensing spiritualities than in dispensing temporalities. And since it is respect of persons when something is allotted to a person out of proportion to his deserts, it must be observed that a person's worthiness may be considered in two ways. First, simply and absolutely: and in this way the man who abounds the more in the spiritual gifts of grace is the more worthy. Second, in relation to the common good; for it happens at times that the less holy and less learned man may conduce more to the common good, on account of worldly authority or activity, or something of the kind. And since the dispensation of spiritualities is directed

saecularem, vel propter aliquid huiusmodi. Et quia dispensationes spiritualium principalius ordinantur ad utilitatem communem, secundum illud I ad Cor. XII, *unicuique datur manifestatio spiritus ad utilitatem*; ideo quandoque absque acceptione personarum in dispensatione spiritualium illi qui sunt simpliciter minus boni, melioribus praeferuntur, sicut etiam et Deus gratias gratis datas quandoque concedit minus bonis.

**AD PRIMUM** ergo dicendum quod circa consanguineos praelati distinguendum est. Quia quandoque sunt minus digni et simpliciter, et per respectum ad bonum commune. Et sic si dignioribus praeferantur, est peccatum personarum acceptionis in dispensatione spiritualium, quorum praelatus ecclesiasticus non est dominus, ut possit ea dare pro libito, sed dispensator, secundum illud I ad Cor. IV, *sic nos existimet homo ut ministros Christi, et dispensatores mysteriorum Dei*. Quandoque vero consanguinei praelati ecclesiastici sunt aeque digni ut alii. Et sic licite potest, absque personarum acceptione, consanguineos suos praeferre, quia saltem in hoc praeeminent, quod de ipsis magis confidere potest ut unanimiter secum negotia Ecclesiae tractent. Esset tamen hoc propter scandalum dimittendum, si ex hoc aliqui exemplum sumerent, etiam praeter dignitatem, bona Ecclesiae consanguineis dandi.

**AD SECUNDUM** dicendum quod dispensatio matrimonii contrahendi principaliter fieri consuevit propter foedus pacis firmandum, quod quidem magis est necessarium communi utilitati circa personas excellentes. Ideo cum eis facilius dispensatur absque peccato acceptionis personarum.

**AD TERTIUM** dicendum quod quantum ad hoc quod electio impugnari non possit in foro iudiciali, sufficit eligere bonum, nec oportet eligere meliorem, quia sic omnis electio posset habere calumniam. Sed quantum ad conscientiam eligentis, necesse est eligere meliorem vel simpliciter, vel in comparatione ad bonum commune. Quia si potest haberi aliquis magis idoneus erga aliquam dignitatem et alius praeferatur, oportet quod hoc sit propter aliquam causam. Quae quidem si pertineat ad negotium, quantum ad hoc erit ille qui eligitur magis idoneus. Si vero non pertineat ad negotium id quod consideratur ut causa, erit manifeste acceptio personae.

**AD QUARTUM** dicendum quod ille qui de gremio Ecclesiae assumitur, ut in pluribus consuevit esse utilior quantum ad bonum commune, quia magis diligit Ecclesiam in qua est nutritus. Et propter hoc etiam mandatur Deut. XVII, *non poteris alterius gentis facere regem, qui non sit frater tuus.*

chiefly to the common good, according to 1 Cor. 12:7, *The manifestation of the Spirit is given to every man unto profit*, it follows that in the dispensation of spiritualities the simply less good are sometimes preferred to the better, without respect of persons, just as God sometimes bestows gratuitous graces on the less worthy.

**REPLY OBJ. 1:** We must make a distinction with regard to a prelate's kinsfolk: for sometimes they are less worthy, both absolutely speaking, and in relation to the common good: and then if they are preferred to the more worthy, there is a sin of respect of persons in the dispensation of spiritual goods, whereof the ecclesiastical superior is not the owner, with power to give them away as he will, but the dispenser, according to 1 Cor. 4:1, *Let a man so account of us as of the ministers of Christ, and the dispensers of the mysteries of God*. Sometimes however the prelate's kinsfolk are as worthy as others, and then without respect of persons he can lawfully give preference to his kindred since there is at least this advantage, that he can trust the more in their being of one mind with him in conducting the business of the Church. Yet he would have to forego so doing for fear of scandal, if anyone might take an example from him and give the goods of the Church to their kindred without regard to their deserts.

**REPLY OBJ. 2:** Dispensations for contracting marriage came into use for the purpose of strengthening treaties of peace: and this is more necessary for the common good in relation to persons of standing, so that there is no respect of persons in granting dispensations more readily to such persons.

**REPLY OBJ. 3:** In order that an election be not rebutted in a court of law, it suffices to elect a good man, nor is it necessary to elect the better man, because otherwise every election might have a flaw. But as regards the conscience of an elector, it is necessary to elect one who is better, either absolutely speaking, or in relation to the common good. For if it is possible to have one who is more competent for a post, and yet another be preferred, it is necessary to have some cause for this. If this cause have anything to do with the matter in point, he who is elected will, in this respect, be more competent; and if that which is taken for cause have nothing to do with the matter, it will clearly be respect of persons.

**REPLY OBJ. 4:** The man who is taken from among the members of a particular Church, is generally speaking more useful as regards the common good, since he loves more the Church wherein he was brought up. For this reason it was commanded (Deut 17:15): *Thou mayest not make a man of another nation king, who is not thy brother.*

# Article 3

*Whether the sin of respect of persons takes place in showing honor and respect?*

AD TERTIUM SIC PROCEDITUR. Videtur quod in exhibitione honoris et reverentiae non habeat locum peccatum acceptionis personarum. Honor enim nihil aliud esse videtur quam *reverentia quaedam alicui exhibita in testimonium virtutis*, ut patet per philosophum, in I Ethic. Sed praelati et principes sunt honorandi, etiam si sint mali; sicut etiam et parentes, de quibus mandatur Exod. XX, honora patrem tuum et matrem tuam; et etiam domini sunt a servis honorandi, etiam si sint mali, secundum illud I ad Tim. VI, *quicumque sunt sub iugo servi, dominos suos honore dignos arbitrentur.* Ergo videtur quod acceptio personae non sit peccatum in exhibitione honoris.

PRAETEREA, Levit. XIX praecipitur, *coram cano capite consurge, et honora personam senis.* Sed hoc videtur ad acceptionem personarum pertinere, quia quandoque senes non sunt virtuosi, secundum illud Dan. XIII, *egressa est iniquitas a senioribus populi.* Ergo acceptio personarum non est peccatum in exhibitione honoris.

PRAETEREA, super illud Iac. II, *nolite in personarum acceptione habere* etc., dicit Glossa Augustini, *si hoc quod Iacobus dicit, si introierit in conventum vestrum vir habens anulum aureum* etc., *intelligatur de quotidianis consessibus quis hic non peccat, si tamen peccat?* Sed haec est acceptio personarum, divites propter divitias honorare, dicit enim Gregorius, in quadam homilia, *superbia nostra retunditur, quia in hominibus non naturam, qua ad imaginem Dei facti sunt, sed divitias honoramus*; et sic, cum divitiae non sint debita causa honoris, pertinebit hoc ad personarum acceptionem. Ergo personarum acceptio non est peccatum circa exhibitionem honoris.

SED CONTRA est quod dicitur in Glossa Iac. II, *quicumque divitem propter divitias honorat, peccat.* Et pari ratione, si aliquis honoretur propter alias causas quae non faciunt dignum honore, quod pertinet ad acceptionem personarum. Ergo acceptio personarum in exhibitione honoris est peccatum.

RESPONDEO dicendum quod honor est quoddam testimonium de virtute eius qui honoratur, et ideo sola virtus est debita causa honoris. Sciendum tamen quod aliquis potest honorari non solum propter virtutem propriam, sed etiam propter virtutem alterius. Sicut principes et praelati honorantur etiam si sint mali, inquantum gerunt personam Dei et communitatis cui praeficiuntur, secundum illud Prov. XXVI, *sicut qui immittit lapides in acervum Mercurii, ita qui tribuit insipienti honorem.* Quia gentiles rationem attribuebant Mercurio, acervus Mercurii dicitur cumulus ratiocinii, in quo mercator quandoque mittit unum lapillum loco centum marcarum, ita etiam honoratur insipiens, quia

OBJECTION 1: It would seem that respect of persons does not take place in showing honor and respect. For honor is apparently nothing else than *reverence shown to a person in recognition of his virtue*, as the Philosopher states (*Ethic.* i, 5). Now prelates and princes should be honored although they be wicked, even as our parents, of whom it is written (Exod 20:12): *Honor thy father and thy mother.* Again masters, though they be wicked, should be honored by their servants, according to 1 Tim. 6:1: *Whoever are servants under the yoke, let them count their masters worthy of all honor.* Therefore it seems that it is not a sin to respect persons in showing honor.

OBJ. 2: Further, it is commanded (Lev 19:32): *Rise up before the hoary head, and, honor the person of the aged man.* But this seems to savor of respect of persons, since sometimes old men are not virtuous; according to Dan. 13:5: *Iniquity came out from the ancients of the people.* Therefore it is not a sin to respect persons in showing honor.

OBJ. 3: Further, on the words of James 2:1, *Have not the faith . . . with respect of persons*, a gloss of Augustine says: *If the saying of James, 'If there shall come into your assembly a man having a golden ring,' etc., refer to our daily meetings, who sins not here, if however he sin at all?* Yet it is respect of persons to honor the rich for their riches, for Gregory says in a homily (*xxviii in Evang.*): *Our pride is blunted, since in men we honor, not the nature wherein they are made to God's image, but wealth*, so that, wealth not being a due cause of honor, this will savor of respect of persons. Therefore it is not a sin to respect persons in showing honor.

ON THE CONTRARY, A gloss on James 2:1, says: *Whoever honors the rich for their riches, sins*, and in like manner, if a man be honored for other causes that do not render him worthy of honor. Now this savors of respect of persons. Therefore it is a sin to respect persons in showing honor.

I ANSWER THAT, To honor a person is to recognize him as having virtue, wherefore virtue alone is the due cause of a person being honored. Now it is to be observed that a person may be honored not only for his own virtue, but also for another's: thus princes and prelates, although they be wicked, are honored as standing in God's place, and as representing the community over which they are placed, according to Prov. 26:8, *As he that casteth a stone into the heap of Mercury, so is he that giveth honor to a fool.* For, since the gentiles ascribed the keeping of accounts to Mercury, *the heap of Mercury* signifies the casting up of an account, when a merchant sometimes substitutes a pebble for one hundred marks. So too, is a fool honored if he stand

ponitur loco Dei et loco totius communitatis. Et eadem ratione parentes et domini sunt honorandi, propter participationem divinae dignitatis, qui est omnium pater et dominus. Senes autem sunt honorandi propter signum virtutis, quod est senectus, licet hoc signum quandoque deficiat. Unde, ut dicitur Sap. IV, *senectus vere honoranda est non diuturna neque annorum numero computata, cani autem sunt sensus hominis, et aetas senectutis vita est immaculata.* Divites autem honorandi sunt propter hoc quod maiorem locum in communitatibus obtinent. Si autem solum intuitu divitiarum honorentur, erit peccatum acceptionis personarum.

ET PER HOC patet responsio ad obiecta.

in God's place or represent the whole community: and in the same way parents and masters should be honored, on account of their having a share of the dignity of God Who is the Father and Lord of all. The aged should be honored, because old age is a sign of virtue, though this sign fail at times: wherefore, according to Wis. 4:8, 9, *venerable old age is not that of long time, nor counted by the number of years; but the understanding of a man is gray hairs, and a spotless life is old age.* The rich ought to be honored by reason of their occupying a higher position in the community: but if they be honored merely for their wealth, it will be the sin of respect of persons.

HENCE the Replies to the Objections are clear.

# Article 4

*Whether the sin of respect of persons takes place in judicial sentences?*

AD QUARTUM SIC PROCEDITUR. Videtur quod in iudiciis locum non habeat peccatum acceptionis personarum. Acceptio enim personarum opponitur distributivae iustitiae, ut dictum est. Sed iudicia maxime videntur ad iustitiam commutativam pertinere. Ergo personarum acceptio non habet locum in iudiciis.

PRAETEREA, poenae secundum aliquod iudicium infliguntur. Sed in poenis accipiuntur personae absque peccato, quia gravius puniuntur qui inferunt iniuriam in personas principum quam qui in personas aliorum. Ergo personarum acceptio non habet locum in iudiciis.

PRAETEREA, Eccli. IV dicitur, *in iudicando esto pupillis misericors.* Sed hoc videtur accipere personam pauperis. Ergo acceptio personae in iudiciis non est peccatum.

SED CONTRA est quod dicitur Prov. XVIII, *accipere personam in iudicio non est bonum.*

RESPONDEO dicendum quod, sicut supra dictum est, iudicium est actus iustitiae, prout iudex ad aequalitatem iustitiae reducit ea quae inaequalitatem oppositam facere possunt. Personarum autem acceptio inaequalitatem quandam habet, inquantum attribuitur alicui personae praeter proportionem suam, in qua consistit aequalitas iustitiae. Et ideo manifestum est quod per personarum acceptionem iudicium corrumpitur.

AD PRIMUM ergo dicendum quod iudicium dupliciter potest considerari. Uno modo, quantum ad ipsam rem iudicatam. Et sic iudicium se habet communiter ad commutativam et ad distributivam iustitiam, potest enim iudicio definiri qualiter aliquid commune sit distribuendum in multos, et qualiter unus alteri restituat quod ab eo accepit. Alio modo potest considerari quantum ad ipsam formam iudicii, prout scilicet iudex, etiam

OBJECTION 1: It would seem that the sin of respect of persons does not take place in judicial sentences. For respect of persons is opposed to distributive justice, as stated above (A. 1): whereas judicial sentences seem to pertain chiefly to commutative justice. Therefore respect of persons does not take place in judicial sentences.

OBJ. 2: Further, penalties are inflicted according to a sentence. Now it is not a sin to respect persons in pronouncing penalties, since a heavier punishment is inflicted on one who injures the person of a prince than on one who injures the person of others. Therefore respect of persons does not take place in judicial sentences.

OBJ. 3: Further, it is written (Sir 4:10): *In judging be merciful to the fatherless.* But this seems to imply respect of the person of the needy. Therefore in judicial sentences respect of persons is not a sin.

ON THE CONTRARY, It is written (Prov 18:5): *It is not good to accept the person in judgment.*

I ANSWER THAT, As stated above (Q. 60, A. 1), judgment is an act of justice, inasmuch as the judge restores to the equality of justice, those things which may cause an opposite inequality. Now respect of persons involves a certain inequality, insofar as something is allotted to a person out of that proportion to him in which the equality of justice consists. Wherefore it is evident that judgment is rendered corrupt by respect of persons.

REPLY OBJ. 1: A judgment may be looked at in two ways. First, in view of the thing judged, and in this way judgment is common to commutative and distributive justice: because it may be decided by judgment how some common good is to be distributed among many, and how one person is to restore to another what he has taken from him. Second, it may be considered in view of the form of judgment, inasmuch as, even in commutative justice, the

in ipsa commutativa iustitia, ab uno accipit et alteri dat. Et hoc pertinet ad distributivam iustitiam. Et secundum hoc in quolibet iudicio locum habere potest personarum acceptio.

**AD SECUNDUM** dicendum quod cum punitur gravius aliquis propter iniuriam in maiorem personam commissam, non est personarum acceptio, quia ipsa diversitas personae facit, quantum ad hoc, diversitatem rei, ut supra dictum est.

**AD TERTIUM** dicendum quod homo in iudicio debet pauperi subvenire quantum fieri potest, tamen sine laesione iustitiae. Alioquin habet locum illud quod dicitur Exod. XXIII, *pauperis quoque non misereberis in iudicio.*

judge takes from one and gives to another, and this belongs to distributive justice. In this way respect of persons may take place in any judgment.

**REPLY OBJ. 2**: When a person is more severely punished on account of a crime committed against a greater person, there is no respect of persons, because the very difference of persons causes, in that case, a diversity of things, as stated above (Q. 58, A. 10, ad 3; Q. 61, A. 2, ad 3).

**REPLY OBJ. 3**: In pronouncing judgment one ought to succor the needy as far as possible, yet without prejudice to justice: else the saying of Ex. 23:3 would apply: *Neither shalt thou favor a poor man in judgment.*

# QUESTION 64

## MURDER

Deinde considerandum est de vitiis oppositis commutativae iustitiae. Et primo considerandum est de peccatis quae committuntur circa involuntarias commutationes; secundo, de peccatis quae committuntur circa commutationes voluntarias. Committuntur autem peccata circa involuntarias commutationes per hoc quod aliquod nocumentum proximo infertur contra eius voluntatem, quod quidem potest fieri dupliciter, scilicet facto, et verbo. Facto quidem, cum proximus laeditur vel in persona propria; vel in persona coniuncta; vel in propriis rebus.

De his ergo per ordinem considerandum est. Et primo, de homicidio, per quod maxime nocetur proximo. Et circa hoc quaeruntur octo.

Primo, utrum occidere animalia bruta, vel etiam plantas, sit peccatum.

Secundo, utrum occidere peccatorem sit licitum.

Tertio, utrum hoc liceat privatae personae, vel solum publicae.

Quarto, utrum hoc liceat clerico.

Quinto, utrum liceat alicui occidere seipsum.

Sexto, utrum liceat occidere hominem iustum.

Septimo, utrum liceat alicui occidere hominem seipsum defendendo.

Octavo, utrum homicidium casuale sit peccatum mortale.

In due sequence we must consider the vices opposed to commutative justice. We must consider (1) those sins that are committed in relation to involuntary commutations; (2) those that are committed with regard to voluntary commutations. Sins are committed in relation to involuntary commutations by doing an injury to one's neighbor against his will: and this can be done in two ways, namely by deed or by word. By deed when one's neighbor is injured either in his own person, or in a person connected with him, or in his possessions.

We must therefore consider these points in due order, and in the first place we shall consider murder whereby a man inflicts the greatest injury on his neighbor. Under this head there are eight points of inquiry:

(1) Whether it is a sin to kill dumb animals or even plants?

(2) Whether it is lawful to kill a sinner?

(3) Whether this is lawful to a private individual, or to a public person only?

(4) Whether this is lawful to a cleric?

(5) Whether it is lawful to kill oneself?

(6) Whether it is lawful to kill a just man?

(7) Whether it is lawful to kill a man in self-defense?

(8) Whether accidental homicide is a mortal sin?

# Article 1

### Whether it is unlawful to kill any living thing?

**AD PRIMUM SIC PROCEDITUR.** Videtur quod occidere quaecumque viventia sit illicitum. Dicit enim apostolus, ad Rom. XIII, *qui ordinationi Dei resistit, ipse sibi damnationem acquirit.* Sed per ordinationem divinae providentiae omnia viventia conservantur, secundum illud Psalm., *qui producit in montibus faenum, et dat iumentis escam ipsorum.* Ergo mortificare quaecumque viventia videtur esse illicitum.

**PRAETEREA,** homicidium est peccatum ex eo quod homo privatur vita. Sed vita communis est omnibus animalibus et plantis. Ergo eadem ratione videtur esse peccatum occidere bruta animalia et plantas.

**PRAETEREA,** in lege divina non determinatur specialis poena nisi peccato. Sed occidenti ovem vel bovem

**OBJECTION 1**: It would seem unlawful to kill any living thing. For the Apostle says (Rom 13:2): *They that resist the ordinance of God purchase to themselves damnation.* Now Divine providence has ordained that all living things should be preserved, according to Ps. 146:8, 9, *Who maketh grass to grow on the mountains . . . Who giveth to beasts their food.* Therefore it seems unlawful to take the life of any living thing.

**OBJ. 2**: Further, murder is a sin because it deprives a man of life. Now life is common to all animals and plants. Hence for the same reason it is apparently a sin to slay dumb animals and plants.

**OBJ. 3**: Further, in the Divine law a special punishment is not appointed save for a sin. Now a special punishment

599

alterius statuitur poena determinata in lege divina, ut patet Exod. XXII. Ergo occisio brutorum animalium est peccatum.

**SED CONTRA** est quod Augustinus dicit, in I de Civ. Dei, *cum audimus, non occides, non accipimus hoc dictum esse de fructetis, quia nullus eis est sensus, nec de irrationalibus animalibus, quia nulla nobis ratione sociantur. Restat ergo ut de homine intelligamus quod dictum est, non occides.*

**RESPONDEO** dicendum quod nullus peccat ex hoc quod utitur re aliqua ad hoc ad quod est. In rerum autem ordine imperfectiora sunt propter perfectiora, sicut etiam in generationis via natura ab imperfectis ad perfecta procedit. Et inde est quod sicut in generatione hominis prius est vivum, deinde animal, ultimo autem homo; ita etiam ea quae tantum vivunt, ut plantae, sunt communiter propter omnia animalia, et animalia sunt propter hominem. Et ideo si homo utatur plantis ad utilitatem animalium, et animalibus ad utilitatem hominum, non est illicitum, ut etiam per philosophum patet, in I Polit.

Inter alios autem usus maxime necessarius esse videtur ut animalia plantis utantur in cibum, et homines animalibus, quod sine mortificatione eorum fieri non potest. Et ideo licitum est et plantas mortificare in usum animalium, et animalia in usum hominum, ex ipsa ordinatione divina, dicitur enim Gen. I, *ecce, dedi vobis omnem herbam et universa ligna, ut sint vobis in escam et cunctis animantibus.* Et Gen. IX dicitur, *omne quod movetur et vivit, erit vobis in cibum.*

**AD PRIMUM** ergo dicendum quod ex ordinatione divina conservatur vita animalium et plantarum non propter seipsam, sed propter hominem. Unde ut Augustinus dicit, in I de Civ. Dei, *iustissima ordinatione creatoris et vita et mors eorum nostris usibus subditur.*

**AD SECUNDUM** dicendum quod animalia bruta et plantae non habent vitam rationalem, per quam a seipsis agantur, sed semper aguntur quasi ab alio, naturali quodam impulsu. Et hoc est signum quod sunt naturaliter serva, et aliorum usibus accommodata.

**AD TERTIUM** dicendum quod ille qui occidit bovem alterius peccat quidem, non quia occidit bovem, sed quia damnificat hominem in re sua. Unde non continetur sub peccato homicidii, sed sub peccato furti vel rapinae.

had to be inflicted, according to the Divine law, on one who killed another man's ox or sheep (Exod 22:1). Therefore the slaying of dumb animals is a sin.

**ON THE CONTRARY**, Augustine says (*De Civ. Dei* i, 20): *When we hear it said, 'Thou shalt not kill,' we do not take it as referring to trees, for they have no sense, nor to irrational animals, because they have no fellowship with us. Hence it follows that the words, 'Thou shalt not kill' refer to the killing of a man.*

**I ANSWER THAT**, There is no sin in using a thing for the purpose for which it is. Now the order of things is such that the imperfect are for the perfect, even as in the process of generation nature proceeds from imperfection to perfection. Hence it is that just as in the generation of a man there is first a living thing, then an animal, and lastly a man, so too things, like the plants, which merely have life, are all alike for animals, and all animals are for man. Wherefore it is not unlawful if man use plants for the good of animals, and animals for the good of man, as the Philosopher states (*Polit.* i, 3).

Now the most necessary use would seem to consist in the fact that animals use plants, and men use animals, for food, and this cannot be done unless these be deprived of life: wherefore it is lawful both to take life from plants for the use of animals, and from animals for the use of men. In fact this is in keeping with the commandment of God Himself: for it is written (Gen 1:29, 30): *Behold I have given you every herb . . . and all trees . . . to be your meat, and to all beasts of the earth*: and again (Gen 9:3): *Everything that moveth and liveth shall be meat to you.*

**REPLY OBJ. 1**: According to the Divine ordinance the life of animals and plants is preserved not for themselves but for man. Hence, as Augustine says (*De Civ. Dei* i, 20), *by a most just ordinance of the Creator, both their life and their death are subject to our use.*

**REPLY OBJ. 2**: Dumb animals and plants are devoid of the life of reason whereby to set themselves in motion; they are moved, as it were by another, by a kind of natural impulse, a sign of which is that they are naturally enslaved and accommodated to the uses of others.

**REPLY OBJ. 3**: He that kills another's ox, sins, not through killing the ox, but through injuring another man in his property. Wherefore this is not a species of the sin of murder but of the sin of theft or robbery.

# Article 2

*Whether it is lawful to kill sinners?*

**Ad secundum sic proceditur.** Videtur quod non sit licitum occidere homines peccatores. Dominus enim, Matth. XIII, in parabola, prohibuit extirpare zizania, qui sunt *filii nequam*, ut ibidem dicitur. Sed omne quod est prohibitum a Deo est peccatum. Ergo occidere peccatorem est peccatum.

**Praeterea**, iustitia humana conformatur iustitiae divinae. Sed secundum divinam iustitiam peccatores ad poenitentiam reservantur, secundum illud Ezech. XVIII, *nolo mortem peccatoris, sed ut convertatur et vivat*. Ergo videtur esse omnino iniustum quod peccatores occidantur.

**Praeterea**, illud quod est secundum se malum nullo bono fine fieri licet, ut patet per Augustinum, in libro contra mendacium, et per philosophum, in II Ethic. Sed occidere hominem secundum se est malum, quia ad omnes homines debemus caritatem habere; *amicos autem volumus vivere et esse*, ut dicitur in IX Ethic. Ergo nullo modo licet hominem peccatorem interficere.

**Sed contra** est quod dicitur Exod. XXII, *maleficos non patieris vivere*; et in Psalm., *in matutino interficiebam omnes peccatores terrae*.

**Respondeo** dicendum quod, sicut dictum est, licitum est occidere animalia bruta inquantum ordinantur naturaliter ad hominum usum, sicut imperfectum ordinatur ad perfectum. Omnis autem pars ordinatur ad totum ut imperfectum ad perfectum. Et ideo omnis pars naturaliter est propter totum. Et propter hoc videmus quod si saluti totius corporis humani expediat praecisio alicuius membri, puta cum est putridum et corruptivum aliorum, laudabiliter et salubriter absciditur. Quaelibet autem persona singularis comparatur ad totam communitatem sicut pars ad totum. Et ideo si aliquis homo sit periculosus communitati et corruptivus ipsius propter aliquod peccatum, laudabiliter et salubriter occiditur, ut bonum commune conservetur, *modicum* enim *fermentum totam massam corrumpit*, ut dicitur I ad Cor. V.

**Ad primum** ergo dicendum quod dominus abstinendum mandavit ab eradicatione zizaniorum ut tritico parceretur, idest bonis. Quod quidem fit quando non possunt occidi mali quin simul occidantur et boni, vel quia latent inter bonos; vel quia habent multos sequaces, ita quod sine bonorum periculo interfici non possunt; ut Augustinus dicit, contra Parmen. Unde dominus docet magis esse sinendum malos vivere, et ultionem reservandum usque ad extremum iudicium, quam quod boni simul occidantur. Quando vero ex occisione malorum non imminet periculum bonis, sed magis tutela et salus, tunc licite possunt mali occidi.

**Objection 1**: It would seem unlawful to kill men who have sinned. For our Lord in the parable (Matt 13) forbade the uprooting of the cockle which denotes *wicked men* according to a gloss. Now whatever is forbidden by God is a sin. Therefore it is a sin to kill a sinner.

**Obj. 2**: Further, human justice is conformed to Divine justice. Now according to Divine justice sinners are kept back for repentance, according to Ezech. 33:11, *I desire not the death of the wicked, but that the wicked turn from his way and live*. Therefore it seems altogether unjust to kill sinners.

**Obj. 3**: Further, it is not lawful, for any good end whatever, to do that which is evil in itself, according to Augustine (*Contra Mendac.* vii) and the Philosopher (*Ethic.* ii, 6). Now to kill a man is evil in itself, since we are bound to have charity towards all men, and *we wish our friends to live and to exist*, according to *Ethic.* ix, 4. Therefore it is nowise lawful to kill a man who has sinned.

**On the contrary**, It is written (Exod 22:18): *Wizards thou shalt not suffer to live*; and (Ps 100:8): *In the morning I put to death all the wicked of the land*.

**I answer that**, As stated above (A. 1), it is lawful to kill dumb animals, insofar as they are naturally directed to man's use, as the imperfect is directed to the perfect. Now every part is directed to the whole, as imperfect to perfect, wherefore every part is naturally for the sake of the whole. For this reason we observe that if the health of the whole body demands the excision of a member, through its being decayed or infectious to the other members, it will be both praiseworthy and advantageous to have it cut away. Now every individual person is compared to the whole community, as part to whole. Therefore if a man be dangerous and infectious to the community, on account of some sin, it is praiseworthy and advantageous that he be killed in order to safeguard the common good, since *a little leaven corrupteth the whole lump* (1 Cor 5:6).

**Reply Obj. 1**: Our Lord commanded them to forbear from uprooting the cockle in order to spare the wheat, i.e., the good. This occurs when the wicked cannot be slain without the good being killed with them, either because the wicked lie hidden among the good, or because they have many followers, so that they cannot be killed without danger to the good, as Augustine says (*Contra Parmen.* iii, 2). Wherefore our Lord teaches that we should rather allow the wicked to live, and that vengeance is to be delayed until the last judgment, rather than that the good be put to death together with the wicked. When, however, the good incur no danger, but rather are protected and saved by the slaying of the wicked, then the latter may be lawfully put to death.

**AD SECUNDUM** dicendum quod Deus, secundum ordinem suae sapientiae, quandoque statim peccatores occidit, ad liberationem bonorum; quandoque autem eis poenitendi tempus concedit; secundum quod ipse novit suis electis expedire. Et hoc etiam humana iustitia imitatur pro posse, illos enim qui sunt perniciosi in alios, occidit; eos vero qui peccant aliis graviter non nocentes, ad poenitentiam reservat.

**AD TERTIUM** dicendum quod homo peccando ab ordine rationis recedit, et ideo decidit a dignitate humana, prout scilicet homo est naturaliter liber et propter seipsum existens, et incidit quodammodo in servitutem bestiarum, ut scilicet de ipso ordinetur secundum quod est utile aliis; secundum illud Psalm., *homo, cum in honore esset, non intellexit, comparatus est iumentis insipientibus, et similis factus est illis*; et Prov. XI dicitur, *qui stultus est serviet sapienti*. Et ideo quamvis hominem in sua dignitate manentem occidere sit secundum se malum, tamen hominem peccatorem occidere potest esse bonum, sicut occidere bestiam, peior enim est malus homo bestia, et plus nocet, ut philosophus dicit, in I Polit. et in VII Ethic.

**REPLY OBJ. 2**: According to the order of His wisdom, God sometimes slays sinners forthwith in order to deliver the good, whereas sometimes He allows them time to repent, according as He knows what is expedient for His elect. This also does human justice imitate according to its powers; for it puts to death those who are dangerous to others, while it allows time for repentance to those who sin without grievously harming others.

**REPLY OBJ. 3**: By sinning man departs from the order of reason, and consequently falls away from the dignity of his manhood, insofar as he is naturally free, and exists for himself, and he falls into the slavish state of the beasts, by being disposed of according as he is useful to others. This is expressed in Ps. 48:21: *Man, when he was in honor, did not understand; he hath been compared to senseless beasts, and made like to them*, and Prov. 11:29: *The fool shall serve the wise*. Hence, although it be evil in itself to kill a man so long as he preserve his dignity, yet it may be good to kill a man who has sinned, even as it is to kill a beast. For a bad man is worse than a beast, and is more harmful, as the Philosopher states (*Polit.* i, 1 and *Ethic.* vii, 6).

# Article 3

*Whether it is lawful for a private individual to kill a man who has sinned?*

**AD TERTIUM SIC PROCEDITUR**. Videtur quod occidere hominem peccatorem liceat privatae personae. In lege enim divina nihil illicitum mandatur. Sed Exod. XXXII praecepit Moyses, *occidat unusquisque proximum suum, fratrem et amicum suum*, pro peccato vituli conflatilis. Ergo etiam privatis personis licet peccatorem occidere.

**PRAETEREA**, homo propter peccatum bestiis comparatur, ut dictum est. Sed occidere bestiam sylvestrem, maxime nocentem, cuilibet privatae personae licet. Ergo, pari ratione, occidere hominem peccatorem.

**PRAETEREA**, laudabile est quod homo, etiam si sit privata persona, operetur quod est utile bono communi. Sed occisio maleficorum est utilis bono communi, ut dictum est. Ergo laudabile est si etiam privatae personae malefactores occidant.

**SED CONTRA** est quod Augustinus dicit, in I de Civ. Dei, *qui sine aliqua publica administratione maleficum interfecerit, velut homicida iudicabitur, et tanto amplius quanto sibi potestatem a Deo non concessam usurpare non timuit*.

**RESPONDEO** dicendum quod, sicut dictum est, occidere malefactorem licitum est inquantum ordinatur ad salutem totius communitatis. Et ideo ad illum solum pertinet cui committitur cura communitatis conservan-

**OBJECTION 1**: It would seem lawful for a private individual to kill a man who has sinned. For nothing unlawful is commanded in the Divine law. Yet, on account of the sin of the molten calf, Moses commanded (Exod 32:27): *Let every man kill his brother, and friend, and neighbor*. Therefore it is lawful for private individuals to kill a sinner.

**OBJ. 2**: Further, as stated above (A. 2, ad 3), man, on account of sin, is compared to the beasts. Now it is lawful for any private individual to kill a wild beast, especially if it be harmful. Therefore for the same reason, it is lawful for any private individual to kill a man who has sinned.

**OBJ. 3**: Further, a man, though a private individual, deserves praise for doing what is useful for the common good. Now the slaying of evildoers is useful for the common good, as stated above (A. 2). Therefore it is deserving of praise if even private individuals kill evil-doers.

**ON THE CONTRARY**, Augustine says (*De Civ. Dei* i): *A man who, without exercising public authority, kills an evildoer, shall be judged guilty of murder, and all the more, since he has dared to usurp a power which God has not given him*.

**I ANSWER THAT**, As stated above (A. 2), it is lawful to kill an evildoer insofar as it is directed to the welfare of the whole community, so that it belongs to him alone who has charge of the community's welfare. Thus it belongs to

dae, sicut ad medicum pertinet praecidere membrum putridum quando ei commissa fuerit cura salutis totius corporis. Cura autem communis boni commissa est principibus habentibus publicam auctoritatem. Et ideo eis solum licet malefactores occidere, non autem privatis personis.

**AD PRIMUM** ergo dicendum quod ille aliquid facit cuius auctoritate fit, ut patet per Dionysium, XIII cap. Cael. Hier. Et ideo, ut Augustinus dicit, in I de Civ. Dei, *non ipse occidit qui ministerium debet iubenti sicut adminiculum gladius utenti.* Unde illi qui occiderunt proximos et amicos ex mandato domini, non hoc fecisse ipsi videntur, sed potius ille cuius auctoritate fecerunt, sicut et miles interficit hostem auctoritate principis, et minister latronem auctoritate iudicis.

**AD SECUNDUM** dicendum quod bestia naturaliter est distincta ab homine. Unde super hoc non requiritur aliquod iudicium an sit occidenda, si sit sylvestris. Si vero sit domestica, requiretur iudicium non propter ipsam, sed propter damnum domini. Sed homo peccator non est naturaliter distinctus ab hominibus iustis. Et ideo indiget publico iudicio, ut discernatur an sit occidendus propter communem salutem.

**AD TERTIUM** dicendum quod facere aliquid ad utilitatem communem quod nulli nocet, hoc est licitum cuilibet privatae personae. Sed si sit cum nocumento alterius, hoc non debet fieri nisi secundum iudicium eius ad quem pertinet existimare quid sit subtrahendum partibus pro salute totius.

a physician to cut off a decayed limb, when he has been entrusted with the care of the health of the whole body. Now the care of the common good is entrusted to persons of rank having public authority: wherefore they alone, and not private individuals, can lawfully put evildoers to death.

**REPLY OBJ. 1**: The person by whose authority a thing is done really does the thing as Dionysius declares (*Coel. Hier. iii*). Hence according to Augustine (*De Civ. Dei i, 21*), *He slays not who owes his service to one who commands him, even as a sword is merely the instrument to him that wields it.* Wherefore those who, at the Lord's command, slew their neighbors and friends, would seem not to have done this themselves, but rather He by whose authority they acted thus: just as a soldier slays the foe by the authority of his sovereign, and the executioner slays the robber by the authority of the judge.

**REPLY OBJ. 2**: A beast is by nature distinct from man, wherefore in the case of a wild beast there is no need for an authority to kill it; whereas, in the case of domestic animals, such authority is required, not for their sake, but on account of the owner's loss. On the other hand a man who has sinned is not by nature distinct from good men; hence a public authority is requisite in order to condemn him to death for the common good.

**REPLY OBJ. 3**: It is lawful for any private individual to do anything for the common good, provided it harm nobody: but if it be harmful to some other, it cannot be done, except by virtue of the judgment of the person to whom it pertains to decide what is to be taken from the parts for the welfare of the whole.

# Article 4

*Whether it is lawful for clerics to kill evil-doers?*

**AD QUARTUM SIC PROCEDITUR.** Videtur quod occidere malefactores liceat clericis. Clerici enim praecipue debent implere quod apostolus dicit, I ad Cor. IV, *imitatores mei estote, sicut et ego Christi*, per quod nobis indicitur ut Deum et sanctos eius imitemur. Sed ipse Deus, quem colimus, occidit malefactores, secundum illud Psalm., *qui percussit Aegyptum cum primogenitis eorum.* Moyses etiam a Levitis fecit interfici viginti tria millia hominum propter adorationem vituli, ut habetur Exod. XXXII. Et Phinees, sacerdos, interfecit Israelitem coeuntem cum Madianitide, ut habetur Num. XXV. Samuel etiam interfecit Agag, regem Amalec; et Elias sacerdotes Baal; et Mathathias eum qui ad sacrificandum accesserat; et in novo testamento, Petrus Ananiam et Saphiram. Ergo videtur quod etiam clericis liceat occidere malefactores.

**OBJECTION 1**: It would seem lawful for clerics to kill evil-doers. For clerics especially should fulfill the precept of the Apostle (1 Cor 4:16): *Be ye followers of me as I also am of Christ*, whereby we are called upon to imitate God and His saints. Now the very God whom we worship puts evildoers to death, according to Ps. 135:10, *Who smote Egypt with their firstborn*. Again Moses made the Levites slay twenty-three thousand men on account of the worship of the calf (Exod 32), the priest Phinees slew the Israelite who went in to the woman of Madian (Num 25), Samuel killed Agag king of Amalec (1 Kgs 15), Elias slew the priests of Baal (3 Kgs 18), Mathathias killed the man who went up to the altar to sacrifice (1 Macc 2); and, in the New Testament, Peter killed Ananias and Saphira (Acts 5). Therefore it seems that even clerics may kill evil-doers.

PRAETEREA, potestas spiritualis est maior quam temporalis, et Deo coniunctior. Sed potestas temporalis licite malefactores occidit tanquam *Dei minister*, ut dicitur Rom. XIII. Ergo multo magis clerici, qui sunt Dei ministri spiritualem potestatem habentes, licite possunt malefactores occidere.

PRAETEREA, quicumque licite suscipit aliquod officium, licite potest ea exercere quae ad officium illud pertinent. Sed officium principis terrae est malefactores occidere, ut dictum est. Ergo clerici qui sunt terrarum principes, licite possunt occidere malefactores.

SED CONTRA est quod dicitur I ad Tim. III, *oportet episcopum sine crimine esse, non vinolentum, non percussorem.*

RESPONDEO dicendum quod non licet clericis occidere, duplici ratione. Primo quidem, quia sunt electi ad altaris ministerium, in quo repraesentatur passio Christi occisi, *qui cum percuteretur, non repercutiebat*, ut dicitur I Pet. II. Et ideo non competit ut clerici sint percussores aut occisores, debent enim ministri suum dominum imitari, secundum illud Eccli. X, *secundum iudicem populi, sic et ministri eius*. Alia ratio est quia clericis committitur ministerium novae legis, in qua non determinatur poena occisionis vel mutilationis corporalis. Et ideo, ut sint *idonei ministri novi testamenti*, debent a talibus abstinere.

AD PRIMUM ergo dicendum quod Deus universaliter in omnibus operatur quae recta sunt, in unoquoque tamen secundum eius congruentiam. Et ideo unusquisque debet Deum imitari in hoc quod sibi specialiter congruit. Unde licet Deus corporaliter etiam malefactores occidat, non tamen oportet quod omnes in hoc eum imitentur. Petrus autem non propria auctoritate vel manu Ananiam et Saphiram interfecit, sed magis divinam sententiam de eorum morte promulgavit. Sacerdotes autem vel Levitae veteris testamenti erant ministri veteris legis, secundum quam poenae corporales infligebantur, et ideo etiam eis occidere propria manu congruebat.

AD SECUNDUM dicendum quod ministerium clericorum est in melioribus ordinatum quam sint corporales occisiones, scilicet in his quae pertinent ad salutem spiritualem. Et ideo non congruit eis quod minoribus se ingerant.

AD TERTIUM dicendum quod praelati Ecclesiarum accipiunt officia principum terrae non ut ipsi iudicium sanguinis exerceant per seipsos, sed quod eorum auctoritate per alios exerceatur.

OBJ. 2: Further, spiritual power is greater than the secular and is more united to God. Now the secular power as *God's minister* lawfully puts evil-doers to death, according to Rom. 13:4. Much more therefore may clerics, who are God's ministers and have spiritual power, put evil-doers to death.

OBJ. 3: Further, whosoever lawfully accepts an office, may lawfully exercise the functions of that office. Now it belongs to the princely office to slay evildoers, as stated above (A. 3). Therefore those clerics who are earthly princes may lawfully slay malefactors.

ON THE CONTRARY, It is written (1 Tim 3:2, 3): *It behooveth . . . a bishop to be without crime . . . not given to wine, no striker.*

I ANSWER THAT, It is unlawful for clerics to kill, for two reasons. First, because they are chosen for the ministry of the altar, whereon is represented the Passion of Christ slain *Who, when He was struck did not strike* (1 Pet 2:23). Therefore it becomes not clerics to strike or kill: for ministers should imitate their master, according to Ecclus. 10:2, *As the judge of the people is himself, so also are his ministers.* The other reason is because clerics are entrusted with the ministry of the New Law, wherein no punishment of death or of bodily maiming is appointed: wherefore they should abstain from such things in order that they may be *fitting ministers of the New Testament.*

REPLY OBJ. 1: God works in all things without exception whatever is right, yet in each one according to its mode. Wherefore everyone should imitate God in that which is specially becoming to him. Hence, though God slays evildoers even corporally, it does not follow that all should imitate Him in this. As regards Peter, he did not put Ananias and Saphira to death by his own authority or with his own hand, but published their death sentence pronounced by God. The Priests or Levites of the Old Testament were the ministers of the Old Law, which appointed corporal penalties, so that it was fitting for them to slay with their own hands.

REPLY OBJ. 2: The ministry of clerics is concerned with better things than corporal slayings, namely with things pertaining to spiritual welfare, and so it is not fitting for them to meddle with minor matters.

REPLY OBJ. 3: Ecclesiastical prelates accept the office of earthly princes, not that they may inflict capital punishment themselves, but that this may be carried into effect by others in virtue of their authority.

# Article 5

*Whether it is lawful to kill oneself?*

**AD QUINTUM SIC PROCEDITUR.** Videtur quod alicui liceat seipsum occidere. Homicidium enim est peccatum inquantum iustitiae contrariatur. Sed nullus potest sibi ipsi iniustitiam facere, ut probatur in V Ethic. Ergo nullus peccat occidendo seipsum.

**PRAETEREA,** occidere malefactores licet habenti publicam potestatem. Sed quandoque ille qui habet publicam potestatem est malefactor. Ergo licet ei occidere seipsum.

**PRAETEREA,** licitum est quod aliquis spontanee minus periculum subeat ut maius periculum vitet, sicut licitum est quod aliquis etiam sibi ipsi amputet membrum putridum ut totum corpus salvetur. Sed quandoque aliquis per occisionem sui ipsius vitat maius malum, vel miseram vitam vel turpitudinem alicuius peccati. Ergo licet alicui occidere seipsum.

**PRAETEREA,** Samson seipsum interfecit, ut habetur Iudic. XVI, qui tamen connumeratur inter sanctos, ut patet Heb. XI. Ergo licitum est alicui occidere seipsum.

**PRAETEREA,** II Machab. XIV dicitur quod Razias quidam seipsum interfecit, *eligens nobiliter mori potius quam subditus fieri peccatoribus et contra natales suos iniuriis agi.* Sed nihil quod nobiliter fit et fortiter, est illicitum. Ergo occidere seipsum non est illicitum.

**SED CONTRA** est quod Augustinus dicit, in I de Civ. Dei, *restat ut de homine intelligamus quod dictum est, non occides. Nec alterum ergo, nec te. Neque enim aliud quam hominem occidit qui seipsum occidit.*

**RESPONDEO** dicendum quod seipsum occidere est omnino illicitum triplici ratione. Primo quidem, quia naturaliter quaelibet res seipsam amat, et ad hoc pertinet quod quaelibet res naturaliter conservat se in esse et corrumpentibus resistit quantum potest. Et ideo quod aliquis seipsum occidat est contra inclinationem naturalem, et contra caritatem, qua quilibet debet seipsum diligere. Et ideo occisio sui ipsius semper est peccatum mortale, utpote contra naturalem legem et contra caritatem existens. Secundo, quia quaelibet pars id quod est, est totius. Quilibet autem homo est pars communitatis, et ita id quod est, est communitatis. Unde in hoc quod seipsum interficit, iniuriam communitati facit, ut patet per philosophum, in V Ethic. Tertio, quia vita est quoddam donum divinitus homini attributum, et eius potestati subiectum qui *occidit et vivere facit.* Et ideo qui seipsum vita privat in Deum peccat, sicut qui alienum servum interficit peccat in dominum cuius est servus; et sicut peccat ille qui usurpat sibi iudicium de re sibi non commissa. Ad solum enim Deum pertinet iudicium mortis et vitae, secundum illud Deut. XXXII, *ego occidam, et vivere faciam.*

**OBJECTION 1:** It would seem lawful for a man to kill himself. For murder is a sin insofar as it is contrary to justice. But no man can do an injustice to himself, as is proved in *Ethic.* v, 11. Therefore no man sins by killing himself.

**OBJ. 2:** Further, it is lawful, for one who exercises public authority, to kill evil-doers. Now he who exercises public authority is sometimes an evil-doer. Therefore he may lawfully kill himself.

**OBJ. 3:** Further, it is lawful for a man to suffer spontaneously a lesser danger that he may avoid a greater: thus it is lawful for a man to cut off a decayed limb even from himself, that he may save his whole body. Now sometimes a man, by killing himself, avoids a greater evil, for example an unhappy life, or the shame of sin. Therefore a man may kill himself.

**OBJ. 4:** Further, Samson killed himself, as related in Judges 16, and yet he is numbered among the saints (Heb 11). Therefore it is lawful for a man to kill himself.

**OBJ. 5:** Further, it is related (2 Macc 14:42) that a certain Razias killed himself, *choosing to die nobly rather than to fall into the hands of the wicked, and to suffer abuses unbecoming his noble birth.* Now nothing that is done nobly and bravely is unlawful. Therefore suicide is not unlawful.

**ON THE CONTRARY,** Augustine says (*De Civ. Dei* i, 20): *Hence it follows that the words 'Thou shalt not kill' refer to the killing of a man—not another man; therefore, not even thyself. For he who kills himself, kills nothing else than a man.*

**I ANSWER THAT,** It is altogether unlawful to kill oneself, for three reasons. First, because everything naturally loves itself, the result being that everything naturally keeps itself in being, and resists corruptions so far as it can. Wherefore suicide is contrary to the inclination of nature, and to charity whereby every man should love himself. Hence suicide is always a mortal sin, as being contrary to the natural law and to charity. Second, because every part, as such, belongs to the whole. Now every man is part of the community, and so, as such, he belongs to the community. Hence by killing himself he injures the community, as the Philosopher declares (*Ethic.* v, 11). Third, because life is God's gift to man, and is subject to His power, Who *kills and makes to live.* Hence whoever takes his own life, sins against God, even as he who kills another's slave, sins against that slave's master, and as he who usurps to himself judgment of a matter not entrusted to him. For it belongs to God alone to pronounce sentence of death and life, according to Deut. 32:39, *I will kill and I will make to live.*

**AD PRIMUM** ergo dicendum quod homicidium est peccatum non solum quia contrariatur iustitiae, sed etiam quia contrariatur caritati quam habere debet aliquis ad seipsum. Et ex hac parte occisio sui ipsius est peccatum per comparationem ad seipsum. Per comparationem autem ad communitatem et ad Deum, habet rationem peccati etiam per oppositionem ad iustitiam.

**AD SECUNDUM** dicendum quod ille qui habet publicam potestatem potest licite malefactorem occidere per hoc quod potest de ipso iudicare. Nullus autem est iudex sui ipsius. Unde non licet habenti publicam potestatem seipsum occidere propter quodcumque peccatum. Licet tamen ei se committere iudicio aliorum.

**AD TERTIUM** dicendum quod homo constituitur dominus sui ipsius per liberum arbitrium. Et ideo licite potest homo de seipso disponere quantum ad ea quae pertinent ad hanc vitam, quae hominis libero arbitrio regitur. Sed transitus de hac vita ad aliam feliciorem non subiacet libero arbitrio hominis, sed potestati divinae. Et ideo non licet homini seipsum interficere ut ad feliciorem transeat vitam. Similiter etiam nec ut miserias quaslibet praesentis vitae evadat. Quia *ultimum* malorum huius vitae et *maxime terribile* est mors, ut patet per philosophum, in III Ethic. Et ita inferre sibi mortem ad alias huius vitae miserias evadendas est maius malum assumere ad minoris mali vitationem. Similiter etiam non licet seipsum occidere propter aliquod peccatum commissum. Tum quia in hoc sibi maxime nocet quod sibi adimit necessarium poenitentiae tempus. Tum etiam quia malefactorem occidere non licet nisi per iudicium publicae potestatis. Similiter etiam non licet mulieri seipsam occidere ne ab alio corrumpatur. Quia non debet in se committere crimen maximum, quod est sui ipsius occisio, ut vitet minus crimen alienum (non enim est crimen mulieris per violentiam violatae, si consensus non adsit, quia *non inquinatur corpus nisi de consensu mentis*, ut Lucia dixit). Constat autem minus esse peccatum fornicationem vel adulterium quam homicidium, et praecipue sui ipsius, quod est gravissimum, quia sibi ipsi nocet, cui maximam dilectionem debet. Est etiam periculosissimum, quia non restat tempus ut per poenitentiam expietur. Similiter etiam nulli licet seipsum occidere ob timorem ne consentiat in peccatum. Quia *non sunt facienda mala ut veniant bona*, vel ut vitentur mala, praesertim minora et minus certa. Incertum enim est an aliquis in futurum consentiat in peccatum, potens est enim Deus hominem, quacumque tentatione superveniente, liberare a peccato.

**AD QUARTUM** dicendum quod, sicut Augustinus dicit, in I de Civ. Dei, *nec Samson aliter excusatur quod seipsum cum hostibus ruina domus oppressit, nisi quia latenter spiritus hoc iusserat, qui per illum miracula faciebat.* Et eandem rationem assignat de quibusdam sanctis

**REPLY OBJ. 1:** Murder is a sin, not only because it is contrary to justice, but also because it is opposed to charity which a man should have towards himself: in this respect suicide is a sin in relation to oneself. In relation to the community and to God, it is sinful, by reason also of its opposition to justice.

**REPLY OBJ. 2:** One who exercises public authority may lawfully put to death an evil-doer, since he can pass judgment on him. But no man is judge of himself. Wherefore it is not lawful for one who exercises public authority to put himself to death for any sin whatever: although he may lawfully commit himself to the judgment of others.

**REPLY OBJ. 3:** Man is made master of himself through his free-will: wherefore he can lawfully dispose of himself as to those matters which pertain to this life which is ruled by man's free-will. But the passage from this life to another and happier one is subject not to man's free-will but to the power of God. Hence it is not lawful for man to take his own life that he may pass to a happier life, nor that he may escape any unhappiness whatsoever of the present life, because the *ultimate* and *most fearsome* evil of this life is death, as the Philosopher states (*Ethic.* iii, 6). Therefore to bring death upon oneself in order to escape the other afflictions of this life, is to adopt a greater evil in order to avoid a lesser. In like manner it is unlawful to take one's own life on account of one's having committed a sin, both because by so doing one does oneself a very great injury, by depriving oneself of the time needful for repentance, and because it is not lawful to slay an evildoer except by the sentence of the public authority. Again it is unlawful for a woman to kill herself lest she be violated, because she ought not to commit on herself the very great sin of suicide, to avoid the lesser sin of another. For she commits no sin in being violated by force, provided she does not consent, since *without consent of the mind there is no stain on the body*, as the Blessed Lucy declared. Now it is evident that fornication and adultery are less grievous sins than taking a man's, especially one's own, life: since the latter is most grievous, because one injures oneself, to whom one owes the greatest love. Moreover it is most dangerous since no time is left wherein to expiate it by repentance. Again it is not lawful for anyone to take his own life for fear he should consent to sin, because *evil must not be done that good may come* (Rom 3:8) or that evil may be avoided especially if the evil be of small account and an uncertain event, for it is uncertain whether one will at some future time consent to a sin, since God is able to deliver man from sin under any temptation whatever.

**REPLY OBJ. 4:** As Augustine says (*De Civ. Dei* i, 21), *not even Samson is to be excused that he crushed himself together with his enemies under the ruins of the house, except the Holy Spirit, Who had wrought many wonders through him, had secretly commanded him to do this.* He assigns the

feminis quae tempore persecutionis seipsas occiderunt, quarum memoria in Ecclesia celebratur.

**AD QUINTUM** dicendum quod ad fortitudinem pertinet quod aliquis ab alio mortem pati non refugiat propter bonum virtutis, et ut vitet peccatum. Sed quod aliquis sibi ipsi inferat mortem ut vitet mala poenalia, habet quidem quandam speciem fortitudinis, propter quod quidam seipsos interfecerunt aestimantes se fortiter agere, de quorum numero Razias fuit, non tamen est vera fortitudo, sed magis quaedam mollities animi non valentis mala poenalia sustinere, ut patet per philosophum, in III Ethic., et per Augustinum, in I de Civ. Dei.

same reason in the case of certain holy women, who at the time of persecution took their own lives, and who are commemorated by the Church.

**REPLY OBJ. 5**: It belongs to fortitude that a man does not shrink from being slain by another, for the sake of the good of virtue, and that he may avoid sin. But that a man take his own life in order to avoid penal evils has indeed an appearance of fortitude (for which reason some, among whom was Razias, have killed themselves thinking to act from fortitude), yet it is not true fortitude, but rather a weakness of soul unable to bear penal evils, as the Philosopher (*Ethic.* iii, 7) and Augustine (*De Civ. Dei* 22, 23) declare.

# Article 6

*Whether it is lawful in any case to kill the innocent?*

**AD SEXTUM SIC PROCEDITUR.** Videtur quod liceat in aliquo casu interficere innocentem. Divinus enim timor non manifestatur per peccatum, quin magis *timor domini expellit peccatum*, ut dicitur Eccli. I. Sed Abraham commendatus est quod timuerit dominum, quia voluit interficere filium innocentem. Ergo potest aliquis innocentem interficere sine peccato.

**PRAETEREA**, in genere peccatorum quae contra proximum committuntur, tanto videtur aliquid esse maius peccatum quanto maius nocumentum infertur ei in quem peccatur. Sed occisio plus nocet peccatori quam innocenti, qui de miseria huius vitae ad caelestem gloriam transit per mortem. Cum ergo liceat in aliquo casu peccatorem occidere, multo magis licet occidere innocentem vel iustum.

**PRAETEREA**, illud quod fit secundum ordinem iustitiae non est peccatum. Sed quandoque cogitur aliquis secundum ordinem iustitiae occidere innocentem, puta cum iudex, qui debet secundum allegata iudicare, condemnat ad mortem eum quem scit innocentem, per falsos testes convictum; et similiter minister qui iniuste condemnatum occidit obediens iudici. Ergo absque peccato potest aliquis occidere innocentem.

**SED CONTRA** est quod dicitur Exod. XXIII, *innocentem et iustum non occides.*

**RESPONDEO** dicendum quod aliquis homo dupliciter considerari potest, uno modo, secundum se; alio modo, per comparationem ad aliud. Secundum se quidem considerando hominem, nullum occidere licet, quia in quolibet, etiam peccatore, debemus amare naturam, quam Deus fecit, quae per occisionem corrumpitur. Sed sicut supra dictum est, occisio peccatoris fit licita per comparationem ad bonum commune, quod per pecca-

**OBJECTION 1**: It would seem that in some cases it is lawful to kill the innocent. The fear of God is never manifested by sin, since on the contrary *the fear of the Lord driveth out sin* (Sir 1:27). Now Abraham was commended in that he feared the Lord, since he was willing to slay his innocent son. Therefore one may, without sin, kill an innocent person.

**OBJ. 2**: Further, among those sins that are committed against one's neighbor, the more grievous seem to be those whereby a more grievous injury is inflicted on the person sinned against. Now to be killed is a greater injury to a sinful than to an innocent person, because the latter, by death, passes forthwith from the unhappiness of this life to the glory of heaven. Since then it is lawful in certain cases to kill a sinful man, much more is it lawful to slay an innocent or a righteous person.

**OBJ. 3**: Further, what is done in keeping with the order of justice is not a sin. But sometimes a man is forced, according to the order of justice, to slay an innocent person: for instance, when a judge, who is bound to judge according to the evidence, condemns to death a man whom he knows to be innocent but who is convicted by false witnesses; and again the executioner, who in obedience to the judge puts to death the man who has been unjustly sentenced.

**ON THE CONTRARY**, It is written (Exod 23:7): *The innocent and just person thou shalt not put to death.*

**I ANSWER THAT**, An individual man may be considered in two ways: first, in himself; second, in relation to something else. If we consider a man in himself, it is unlawful to kill any man, since in every man though he be sinful, we ought to love the nature which God has made, and which is destroyed by slaying him. Nevertheless, as stated above (A. 2) the slaying of a sinner becomes lawful in relation to the common good, which is corrupted by sin. On the

tum corrumpitur. Vita autem iustorum est conservativa et promotiva boni communis, quia ipsi sunt principalior pars multitudinis. Et ideo nullo modo licet occidere innocentem.

AD PRIMUM ergo dicendum quod Deus habet dominium mortis et vitae, eius enim ordinatione moriuntur et peccatores et iusti. Et ideo ille qui mandato Dei occidit innocentem, talis non peccat, sicut nec Deus, cuius est executor, et ostenditur Deum timere, eius mandatis obediens.

AD SECUNDUM dicendum quod in pensanda gravitate peccati magis est considerandum illud quod est per se quam illud quod est per accidens. Unde ille qui occidit iustum gravius peccat quam ille qui occidit peccatorem. Primo quidem, quia nocet ei quem plus debet diligere, et ita magis contra caritatem agit. Secundo, quia iniuriam infert ei qui est minus dignus, et ita magis contra iustitiam agit. Tertio, quia privat communitatem maiori bono. Quarto, quia magis Deum contemnit, secundum illud Luc. X, *qui vos spernit, me spernit*. Quod autem iustus occisus ad gloriam perducatur a Deo, per accidens se habet ad occisionem.

AD TERTIUM dicendum quod iudex, si scit aliquem esse innocentem qui falsis testibus convincitur, debet diligentius examinare testes, ut inveniat occasionem liberandi innoxium, sicut Daniel fecit. Si autem hoc non potest, debet eum ad superiorem remittere iudicandum. Si autem nec hoc potest, non peccat secundum allegata sententiam ferens, quia non ipse occidit innocentem, sed illi qui eum asserunt nocentem. Minister autem iudicis condemnantis innocentem, si sententia intolerabilem errorem contineat, non debet obedire, alias excusarentur carnifices qui martyres occiderunt. Si vero non contineat manifestam iniustitiam, non peccat praeceptum exequendo, quia ipse non habet discutere superioris sententiam; nec ipse occidit innocentem, sed iudex, cui ministerium adhibet.

other hand the life of righteous men preserves and forwards the common good, since they are the chief part of the community. Therefore it is in no way lawful to slay the innocent.

REPLY OBJ. 1: God is Lord of death and life, for by His decree both the sinful and the righteous die. Hence he who at God's command kills an innocent man does not sin, as neither does God Whose behest he executes: indeed his obedience to God's commands is a proof that he fears Him.

REPLY OBJ. 2: In weighing the gravity of a sin we must consider the essential rather than the accidental. Wherefore he who kills a just man, sins more grievously than he who slays a sinful man: first, because he injures one whom he should love more, and so acts more in opposition to charity: second, because he inflicts an injury on a man who is less deserving of one, and so acts more in opposition to justice: third, because he deprives the community of a greater good: fourth, because he despises God more, according to Luke 10:16, *He that despiseth you despiseth Me*. On the other hand it is accidental to the slaying that the just man whose life is taken be received by God into glory.

REPLY OBJ. 3: If the judge knows that a man who has been convicted by false witnesses, is innocent he must, like Daniel, examine the witnesses with great care, so as to find a motive for acquitting the innocent: but if he cannot do this he should remit him for judgment by a higher tribunal. If even this is impossible, he does not sin if he pronounce sentence in accordance with the evidence, for it is not he that puts the innocent man to death, but they who stated him to be guilty. He that carries out the sentence of the judge who has condemned an innocent man, if the sentence contains an inexcusable error, he should not obey, else there would be an excuse for the executions of the martyrs: if however it contain no manifest injustice, he does not sin by carrying out the sentence, because he has no right to discuss the judgment of his superior; nor is it he who slays the innocent man, but the judge whose minister he is.

# Article 7

*Whether it is lawful to kill a man in self-defense?*

AD SEPTIMUM SIC PROCEDITUR. Videtur quod nulli liceat occidere aliquem se defendendo. Dicit enim Augustinus, ad Publicolam, *de occidendis hominibus ne ab eis quisquam occidatur, non mihi placet consilium, nisi forte sit miles, aut publica functione teneatur, ut non pro se hoc faciat sed pro aliis, accepta legitima potestate, si eius congruat personae*. Sed ille qui se defendendo occidit aliquem, ad hoc eum occidit ne ipse ab eo occidatur. Ergo hoc videtur esse illicitum.

OBJECTION 1: It would seem that nobody may lawfully kill a man in self-defense. For Augustine says to Publicola (*Ep. xlvii*): *I do not agree with the opinion that one may kill a man lest one be killed by him; unless one be a soldier, exercise a public office, so that one does it not for oneself but for others, having the power to do so, provided it be in keeping with one's person*. Now he who kills a man in self-defense, kills him lest he be killed by him. Therefore this would seem to be unlawful.

**Praeterea**, in I de Lib. Arb. dicitur, *quomodo apud divinam providentiam a peccato liberi sunt qui pro his rebus quas contemni oportet, humana caede polluti sunt?* Eas autem res dicit esse contemnendas *quas homines inviti amittere possunt*, ut ex praemissis patet. Horum autem est vita corporalis. Ergo pro conservanda vita corporali nulli licitum est hominem occidere.

**Praeterea**, Nicolaus Papa dicit, et habetur in decretis, dist. l, *de clericis pro quibus consuluisti, scilicet qui se defendendo Paganum occiderunt, si postea per poenitentiam possent ad pristinum statum redire aut ad altiorem ascendere, scito nos nullam occasionem dare, nec ullam tribuere licentiam eis quemlibet hominem quolibet modo occidendi.* Sed ad praecepta moralia servanda tenentur communiter clerici et laici. Ergo etiam laicis non est licitum occidere aliquem se defendendo.

**Praeterea**, homicidium est gravius peccatum quam simplex fornicatio vel adulterium. Sed nulli licet committere simplicem fornicationem vel adulterium, vel quodcumque aliud peccatum mortale, pro conservatione propriae vitae, quia vita spiritualis praeferenda est corporali. Ergo nulli licet, defendendo seipsum, alium occidere ut propriam vitam conservet.

**Praeterea**, si arbor est mala, et fructus, ut dicitur Matth. VII. Sed ipsa defensio sui videtur esse illicita, secundum illud Rom. XII, *non vos defendentes, carissimi.* Ergo et occisio hominis exinde procedens est illicita.

**Sed contra** est quod Exod. XXII dicitur, *si effringens fur domum sive suffodiens fuerit inventus, et, accepto vulnere, mortuus fuerit, percussor non erit reus sanguinis.* Sed multo magis licitum est defendere propriam vitam quam propriam domum. Ergo etiam si aliquis occidat aliquem pro defensione vitae suae, non erit reus homicidii.

**Respondeo** dicendum quod nihil prohibet unius actus esse duos effectus, quorum alter solum sit in intentione, alius vero sit praeter intentionem. Morales autem actus recipiunt speciem secundum id quod intenditur, non autem ab eo quod est praeter intentionem, cum sit per accidens, ut ex supradictis patet. Ex actu igitur alicuius seipsum defendentis duplex effectus sequi potest, unus quidem conservatio propriae vitae; alius autem occisio invadentis. Actus igitur huiusmodi ex hoc quod intenditur conservatio propriae vitae, non habet rationem illiciti, cum hoc sit cuilibet naturale quod se conservet in esse quantum potest. Potest tamen aliquis actus ex bona intentione proveniens illicitus reddi si non sit proportionatus fini. Et ideo si aliquis ad defendendum propriam vitam utatur maiori violentia quam oporteat, erit illicitum. Si vero moderate violentiam repellat, erit licita defensio, nam secundum iura, *vim vi repellere licet cum moderamine inculpatae tutelae.* Nec est

**Obj. 2**: Further, he says (*De Lib. Arb.* i, 5): *How are they free from sin in sight of Divine providence, who are guilty of taking a man's life for the sake of these contemptible things?* Now among contemptible things he reckons *those which men may forfeit unwillingly*, as appears from the context (*De Lib. Arb.* i, 5): and the chief of these is the life of the body. Therefore it is unlawful for any man to take another's life for the sake of the life of his own body.

**Obj. 3**: Further, Pope Nicolas says in the Decretals: *Concerning the clerics about whom you have consulted Us, those, namely, who have killed a pagan in self-defense, as to whether, after making amends by repenting, they may return to their former state, or rise to a higher degree; know that in no case is it lawful for them to kill any man under any circumstances whatever.* Now clerics and laymen are alike bound to observe the moral precepts. Therefore neither is it lawful for laymen to kill anyone in self-defense.

**Obj. 4**: Further, murder is a more grievous sin than fornication or adultery. Now nobody may lawfully commit simple fornication or adultery or any other mortal sin in order to save his own life; since the spiritual life is to be preferred to the life of the body. Therefore no man may lawfully take another's life in self-defense in order to save his own life.

**Obj. 5**: Further, if the tree be evil, so is the fruit, according to Matt. 7:17. Now self-defense itself seems to be unlawful, according to Rom. 12:19: *Not defending yourselves, my dearly beloved.* Therefore its result, which is the slaying of a man, is also unlawful.

**On the contrary**, It is written (Exod 22:2): *If a thief be found breaking into a house or undermining it, and be wounded so as to die; he that slew him shall not be guilty of blood.* Now it is much more lawful to defend one's life than one's house. Therefore neither is a man guilty of murder if he kill another in defense of his own life.

**I answer that**, Nothing hinders one act from having two effects, only one of which is intended, while the other is beside the intention. Now moral acts take their species according to what is intended, and not according to what is beside the intention, since this is accidental as explained above (Q. 43, A. 3; I-II, Q. 12, A. 1). Accordingly the act of self-defense may have two effects, one is the saving of one's life, the other is the slaying of the aggressor. Therefore this act, since one's intention is to save one's own life, is not unlawful, seeing that it is natural to everything to keep itself in being, as far as possible. And yet, though proceeding from a good intention, an act may be rendered unlawful, if it be out of proportion to the end. Wherefore if a man, in self-defense, uses more than necessary violence, it will be unlawful: whereas if he repel force with moderation his defense will be lawful, because according to the jurists, *it is lawful to repel force by force, provided one does not exceed the limits of a blameless defense.* Nor is it necessary for salvation

necessarium ad salutem ut homo actum moderatae tutelae praetermittat ad evitandum occisionem alterius, quia plus tenetur homo vitae suae providere quam vitae alienae. Sed quia occidere hominem non licet nisi publica auctoritate propter bonum commune, ut ex supradictis patet; illicitum est quod homo intendat occidere hominem ut seipsum defendat, nisi ei qui habet publicam auctoritatem, qui, intendens hominem occidere ad sui defensionem, refert hoc ad publicum bonum, ut patet in milite pugnante contra hostes, et in ministro iudicis pugnante contra latrones. Quamvis et isti etiam peccent si privata libidine moveantur.

**AD PRIMUM** ergo dicendum quod auctoritas Augustini intelligenda est in eo casu quo quis intendit occidere hominem ut seipsum a morte liberet.

**IN QUO** etiam casu intelligitur auctoritas inducta ex libro de libero arbitrio. Unde signanter dicitur, *pro his rebus*, in quo designatur intentio. Et per hoc patet responsio ad secundum.

**AD TERTIUM** dicendum quod irregularitas consequitur actum homicidii etiam si sit absque peccato, ut patet in iudice qui iuste aliquem condemnat ad mortem. Et propter hoc clericus, etiam si se defendendo interficiat aliquem, irregularis est, quamvis non intendat occidere, sed seipsum defendere.

**AD QUARTUM** dicendum quod actus fornicationis vel adulterii non ordinatur ad conservationem propriae vitae ex necessitate, sicut actus ex quo quandoque sequitur homicidium.

**AD QUINTUM** dicendum quod ibi prohibetur defensio quae est cum livore vindictae. Unde Glossa dicit, *non vos defendentes, idest, non sitis referientes adversarios.*

that a man omit the act of moderate self-defense in order to avoid killing the other man, since one is bound to take more care of one's own life than of another's. But as it is unlawful to take a man's life, except for the public authority acting for the common good, as stated above (A. 3), it is not lawful for a man to intend killing a man in self-defense, except for such as have public authority, who while intending to kill a man in self-defense, refer this to the public good, as in the case of a soldier fighting against the foe, and in the minister of the judge struggling with robbers, although even these sin if they be moved by private animosity.

REPLY OBJ. 1: The words quoted from Augustine refer to the case when one man intends to kill another to save himself from death.

THE PASSAGE quoted in the Second Objection is to be understood in the same sense. Hence he says pointedly, *for the sake of these things*, whereby he indicates the intention. This suffices for the Reply to the Second Objection.

REPLY OBJ. 3: Irregularity results from the act though sinless of taking a man's life, as appears in the case of a judge who justly condemns a man to death. For this reason a cleric, though he kill a man in self-defense, is irregular, albeit he intends not to kill him, but to defend himself.

REPLY OBJ. 4: The act of fornication or adultery is not necessarily directed to the preservation of one's own life, as is the act whence sometimes results the taking of a man's life.

REPLY OBJ. 5: The defense forbidden in this passage is that which comes from revengeful spite. Hence a gloss says: *Not defending yourselves—that is, not striking your enemy back.*

# Article 8

*Whether one is guilty of murder through killing someone by chance?*

**AD OCTAVUM SIC PROCEDITUR.** Videtur quod aliquis casualiter occidens hominem incurrat homicidii reatum. Legitur enim Gen. IV quod Lamech, credens interficere bestiam, interfecit hominem, et reputatum est ei ad homicidium. Ergo reatum homicidii incurrit qui casualiter hominem occidit.

**PRAETEREA,** Exod. XXI dicitur quod *si quis percusserit mulierem praegnantem et aborsum fecerit, si mors eius fuerit subsecuta, reddet animam pro anima.* Sed hoc potest fieri absque intentione occisionis. Ergo homicidium casuale habet homicidii reatum.

**PRAETEREA,** in decretis, dist. l, inducuntur plures canones in quibus casualia homicidia puniuntur. Sed

OBJECTION 1: It would seem that one is guilty of murder through killing someone by chance. For we read (Gen 4:23, 24) that Lamech slew a man in mistake for a wild beast, and that he was accounted guilty of murder. Therefore one incurs the guilt of murder through killing a man by chance.

OBJ. 2: Further, it is written (Exod 21:22): *If . . . one strike a woman with child, and she miscarry indeed . . . if her death ensue thereupon, he shall render life for life.* Yet this may happen without any intention of causing her death. Therefore one is guilty of murder through killing someone by chance.

OBJ. 3: Further, the Decretals contain several canons prescribing penalties for unintentional homicide. Now

poena non debetur nisi culpae. Ergo ille qui casualiter occidit hominem, incurrit homicidii culpam.

**SED CONTRA** est quod Augustinus dicit, ad Publicolam, *absit ut ea quae propter bonum ac licitum facimus, si quid per haec, praeter nostram voluntatem, cuiquam mali acciderit, nobis imputetur.* Sed contingit quandoque ut propter bonum aliquid facientibus homicidium consequatur casualiter. Ergo non imputatur facienti ad culpam.

**RESPONDEO** dicendum quod, secundum philosophum, in II Physic., casus est causa agens praeter intentionem. Et ideo ea quae casualia sunt, simpliciter loquendo, non sunt intenta neque voluntaria. Et quia omne peccatum est voluntarium, secundum Augustinum, consequens est quod casualia, inquantum huiusmodi, non sunt peccata.

Contingit tamen id quod non est actu et per se volitum vel intentum, esse per accidens volitum et intentum, secundum quod causa per accidens dicitur *removens prohibens.* Unde ille qui non removet ea ex quibus sequitur homicidium, si debeat removere, erit quodammodo homicidium voluntarium. Hoc autem contingit dupliciter, uno modo, quando dans operam rebus illicitis, quas vitare debebat, homicidium incurrit; alio modo, quando non adhibet debitam sollicitudinem. Et ideo secundum iura, si aliquis det operam rei licitae, debitam diligentiam adhibens, et ex hoc homicidium sequatur, non incurrit homicidii reatum, si vero det operam rei illicitae, vel etiam det operam rei licitae non adhibens diligentiam debitam, non evadit homicidii reatum si ex eius opere mors hominis consequatur.

**AD PRIMUM** ergo dicendum quod Lamech non adhibuit sufficientem diligentiam ad homicidium vitandum, et ideo reatum homicidii non evasit.

**AD SECUNDUM** dicendum quod ille qui percutit mulierem praegnantem dat operam rei illicitae. Et ideo si sequatur mors vel mulieris vel puerperii animati, non effugiet homicidii crimen, praecipue cum ex tali percussione in promptu sit quod mors sequatur.

**AD TERTIUM** dicendum quod secundum canones imponitur poena his qui casualiter occidunt dantes operam rei illicitae, vel non adhibentes diligentiam debitam.

penalty is not due save for guilt. Therefore he who kills a man by chance, incurs the guilt of murder.

**ON THE CONTRARY,** Augustine says to Publicola (*Ep. xlvii*): *When we do a thing for a good and lawful purpose, if thereby we unintentionally cause harm to anyone, it should by no means be imputed to us.* Now it sometimes happens by chance that a person is killed as a result of something done for a good purpose. Therefore the person who did it is not accounted guilty.

**I ANSWER THAT,** According to the Philosopher (*Phys.* ii, 6) chance is a cause that acts beside one's intention. Hence chance happenings, strictly speaking, are neither intended nor voluntary. And since every sin is voluntary, according to Augustine (*De Vera Relig.* xiv) it follows that chance happenings, as such, are not sins.

Nevertheless it happens that what is not actually and directly voluntary and intended, is voluntary and intended accidentally, according as that which *removes an obstacle* is called an accidental cause. Wherefore he who does not remove something whence homicide results whereas he ought to remove it, is in a sense guilty of voluntary homicide. This happens in two ways: first when a man causes another's death through occupying himself with unlawful things which he ought to avoid: second, when he does not take sufficient care. Hence, according to jurists, if a man pursue a lawful occupation and take due care, the result being that a person loses his life, he is not guilty of that person's death: whereas if he be occupied with something unlawful, or even with something lawful, but without due care, he does not escape being guilty of murder, if his action results in someone's death.

**REPLY OBJ. 1:** Lamech did not take sufficient care to avoid taking a man's life: and so he was not excused from being guilty of homicide.

**REPLY OBJ. 2:** He that strikes a woman with child does something unlawful: wherefore if there results the death either of the woman or of the animated fetus, he will not be excused from homicide, especially seeing that death is the natural result of such a blow.

**REPLY OBJ. 3:** According to the canons a penalty is inflicted on those who cause death unintentionally, through doing something unlawful, or failing to take sufficient care.

# QUESTION 65

## OTHER INJURIES COMMITTED ON THE PERSON

Deinde considerandum est de peccatis aliarum iniuriarum quae in personam committuntur. Et circa hoc quaeruntur quatuor.

Primo, de mutilatione membrorum.

Secundo, de verberatione.

Tertio, de incarceratione.

Quarto, utrum peccatum huiusmodi iniuriarum aggravetur ex hoc quod committitur in personam coniunctam aliis.

We must now consider other sinful injuries committed on the person. Under this head there are four points of inquiry:

(1) The mutilation of members;

(2) Blows;

(3) Imprisonment;

(4) Whether the sins that consist in inflicting such like injuries are aggravated through being perpetrated on persons connected with others?

## Article 1

*Whether in some cases it may be lawful to maim anyone?*

**AD PRIMUM SIC PROCEDITUR**. Videtur quod mutilare aliquem membro in nullo casu possit esse licitum. Damascenus enim dicit, in II libro, quod peccatum committitur per hoc quod receditur *ab eo quod est secundum naturam in id quod est contra naturam*. Sed secundum naturam a Deo institutam est quod corpus hominis sit integrum membris; contra naturam autem est quod sit membro diminutum. Ergo mutilare aliquem membro semper videtur esse peccatum.

**PRAETEREA**, sicut se habet tota anima ad totum corpus, ita se habent partes animae ad partes corporis, ut dicitur in II de anima. Sed non licet aliquem privare anima occidendo ipsum, nisi publica potestate. Ergo etiam non licet aliquem mutilare membro, nisi forte secundum publicam potestatem.

**PRAETEREA**, salus animae praeferenda est saluti corporali. Sed non licet aliquem mutilare se membro propter salutem animae, puniuntur enim secundum statuta Nicaeni Concilii qui se castraverunt propter castitatem servandam. Ergo propter nullam aliam causam licet aliquem membro mutilare.

**SED CONTRA** est quod dicitur Exod. XXI, *oculum pro oculo, dentem pro dente, manum pro manu, pedem pro pede.*

**RESPONDEO** dicendum quod cum membrum aliquod sit pars totius humani corporis, est propter totum, sicut imperfectum propter perfectum. Unde disponendum est de membro humani corporis secundum quod expedit toti. Membrum autem humani corporis per se quidem utile est ad bonum totius corporis, per accidens tamen potest contingere quod sit nocivum, puta cum membrum putridum est totius corporis corruptivum.

**OBJECTION 1**: It would seem that in no case can it be lawful to maim anyone. For Damascene says (*De Fide Orth.* iv, 20) that *sin consists in departing from what is according to nature, towards that which is contrary to nature.* Now according to nature it is appointed by God that a man's body should be entire in its members, and it is contrary to nature that it should be deprived of a member. Therefore it seems that it is always a sin to maim a person.

**OBJ. 2**: Further, as the whole soul is to the whole body, so are the parts of the soul to the parts of the body (*De Anima* ii, 1). But it is unlawful to deprive a man of his soul by killing him, except by public authority. Therefore neither is it lawful to maim anyone, except perhaps by public authority.

**OBJ. 3**: Further, the welfare of the soul is to be preferred to the welfare of the body. Now it is not lawful for a man to maim himself for the sake of the soul's welfare: since the council of Nicea punished those who castrated themselves that they might preserve chastity. Therefore it is not lawful for any other reason to maim a person.

**ON THE CONTRARY**, It is written (Exod 21:24): *Eye for eye, tooth for tooth, hand for hand, foot for foot.*

**I ANSWER THAT**, Since a member is part of the whole human body, it is for the sake of the whole, as the imperfect for the perfect. Hence a member of the human body is to be disposed of according as it is expedient for the body. Now a member of the human body is of itself useful to the good of the whole body, yet, accidentally it may happen to be hurtful, as when a decayed member is a source of corruption to the whole body. Accordingly so long as a member is

Si ergo membrum sanum fuerit et in sua naturali dispositione consistens, non potest praecidi absque totius hominis detrimento. Sed quia ipse totus homo ordinatur ut ad finem ad totam communitatem cuius est pars, ut supra dictum est; potest contingere quod abscisio membri, etsi vergat in detrimentum totius corporis, ordinatur tamen ad bonum communitatis, inquantum alicui infertur in poenam ad cohibitionem peccatorum. Et ideo sicut per publicam potestatem aliquis licite privatur totaliter vita propter aliquas maiores culpas, ita etiam privatur membro propter aliquas culpas minores. Hoc autem non est licitum alicui privatae personae, etiam volente illo cuius est membrum, quia per hoc fit iniuria communitati, cuius est ipse homo et omnes partes eius. Si vero membrum propter putredinem sit totius corporis corruptivum, tunc licitum est, de voluntate eius cuius est membrum, putridum membrum praescindere propter salutem totius corporis, quia unicuique commissa est cura propriae salutis. Et eadem ratio est si fiat voluntate eius ad quem pertinet curare de salute eius qui habet membrum corruptum. Aliter autem aliquem membro mutilare est omnino illicitum.

**AD PRIMUM** ergo dicendum quod nihil prohibet id quod est contra particularem naturam esse secundum naturam universalem, sicut mors et corruptio in rebus naturalibus est contra particularem naturam eius quod corrumpitur, cum tamen sit secundum naturam universalem. Et similiter mutilare aliquem membro, etsi sit contra naturam particularem corporis eius qui mutilatur, est tamen secundum naturalem rationem in comparatione ad bonum commune.

**AD SECUNDUM** dicendum quod totius hominis vita non ordinatur ad aliquid proprium ipsius hominis, sed ad ipsam potius omnia quae sunt hominis ordinantur. Et ideo privare aliquem vita in nullo casu pertinet ad aliquem nisi ad publicam potestatem, cui committitur procuratio boni communis. Sed praecisio membri potest ordinari ad propriam salutem unius hominis. Et ideo in aliquo casu potest ad ipsum pertinere.

**AD TERTIUM** dicendum quod membrum non est praecidendum propter corporalem salutem totius nisi quando aliter toti subveniri non potest. Saluti autem spirituali semper potest aliter subveniri quam per membri praecisionem, quia peccatum subiacet voluntati. Et ideo in nullo casu licet membrum praecidere propter quodcumque peccatum vitandum. Unde Chrysostomus, exponens illud Matth. XIX, *sunt eunuchi qui seipsos castraverunt propter regnum caelorum, dicit, non membrorum abscisionem, sed malarum cogitationum interemptionem. Maledictioni enim est obnoxius qui membrum abscidit, etenim quae homicidarum sunt talis praesumit. Et postea subdit, neque concupiscentia*

healthy and retains its natural disposition, it cannot be cut off without injury to the whole body. But as the whole of man is directed as to his end to the whole of the community of which he is a part, as stated above (Q. 61, A. 1; Q. 64, AA. 2, 5), it may happen that although the removal of a member may be detrimental to the whole body, it may nevertheless be directed to the good of the community, insofar as it is applied to a person as a punishment for the purpose of restraining sin. Hence just as by public authority a person is lawfully deprived of life altogether on account of certain more heinous sins, so is he deprived of a member on account of certain lesser sins. But this is not lawful for a private individual, even with the consent of the owner of the member, because this would involve an injury to the community, to whom the man and all his parts belong. If, however, the member be decayed and therefore a source of corruption to the whole body, then it is lawful with the consent of the owner of the member, to cut away the member for the welfare of the whole body, since each one is entrusted with the care of his own welfare. The same applies if it be done with the consent of the person whose business it is to care for the welfare of the person who has a decayed member: otherwise it is altogether unlawful to maim anyone.

**REPLY OBJ. 1**: Nothing prevents that which is contrary to a particular nature from being in harmony with universal nature: thus death and corruption, in the physical order, are contrary to the particular nature of the thing corrupted, although they are in keeping with universal nature. In like manner to maim anyone, though contrary to the particular nature of the body of the person maimed, is nevertheless in keeping with natural reason in relation to the common good.

**REPLY OBJ. 2**: The life of the entire man is not directed to something belonging to man; on the contrary whatever belongs to man is directed to his life. Hence in no case does it pertain to a person to take anyone's life, except to the public authority to whom is entrusted the procuring of the common good. But the removal of a member can be directed to the good of one man, and consequently in certain cases can pertain to him.

**REPLY OBJ. 3**: A member should not be removed for the sake of the bodily health of the whole, unless otherwise nothing can be done to further the good of the whole. Now it is always possible to further one's spiritual welfare otherwise than by cutting off a member, because sin is always subject to the will: and consequently in no case is it allowable to maim oneself, even to avoid any sin whatever. Hence Chrysostom, in his exposition on Matt. 19:12 (*Hom. lxii in Matth.*), *There are eunuchs who have made themselves eunuchs for the kingdom of heaven*, says: *Not by maiming themselves, but by destroying evil thoughts, for a man is accursed who maims himself, since they are murderers who do such things*. And further on he says: *Nor is lust tamed*

*mansuetior ita fit, sed molestior. Aliunde enim habet fontes sperma quod in nobis est, et praecipue a proposito incontinenti et mente negligente, nec ita abscisio membri comprimit tentationes, ut cogitationis frenum.*

thereby, on the contrary it becomes more importunate, for the seed springs in us from other sources, and chiefly from an incontinent purpose and a careless mind: and temptation is curbed not so much by cutting off a member as by curbing one's thoughts.

# Article 2

*Whether it is lawful for parents to strike their children, or masters their slaves?*

**AD SECUNDUM SIC PROCEDITUR**. Videtur quod non liceat patribus verberare filios, aut dominis servos. Dicit enim apostolus, ad Ephes. VI, *vos, patres, nolite ad iracundiam provocare filios vestros*. Et infra subdit, *et vos, domini, eadem facite servis, remittentes minas*. Sed propter verbera aliqui ad iracundiam provocantur. Sunt etiam minis graviora. Ergo neque patres filios, neque domini servos debent verberare.

**PRAETEREA**, philosophus dicit, in X Ethic., quod *sermo paternus habet solum monitionem, non autem coactionem*. Sed quaedam coactio est per verbera. Ergo parentibus non licet filios verberare.

**PRAETEREA**, unicuique licet alteri disciplinam impendere, hoc enim pertinet ad eleemosynas spirituales, ut supra dictum est. Si ergo parentibus licet propter disciplinam filios verberare, pari ratione cuilibet licebit quemlibet verberare. Quod patet esse falsum. Ergo et primum.

**SED CONTRA** est quod dicitur Prov. XIII, *qui parcit virgae, odit filium suum*; et infra XXIII, *noli subtrahere a puero disciplinam. Si enim percusseris eum virga, non morietur, tu virga percuties eum, et animam eius de Inferno liberabis*. Et Eccli. XXXIII dicitur, *servo malevolo tortura et compedes*.

**RESPONDEO** dicendum quod per verberationem nocumentum quoddam infertur corpori eius qui verberatur, aliter tamen quam in mutilatione, nam mutilatio tollit corporis integritatem, verberatio vero tantummodo afficit sensum dolore. Unde multo minus nocumentum est quam membri mutilatio. Nocumentum autem inferre alicui non licet nisi per modum poenae propter iustitiam. Nullus autem iuste punit aliquem nisi sit eius ditioni subiectus. Et ideo verberare aliquem non licet nisi habenti potestatem aliquam super illum qui verberatur. Et quia filius subditur potestati patris, et servus potestati domini, licite potest verberare pater filium et dominus servum, causa correctionis et disciplinae.

**AD PRIMUM** ergo dicendum quod, cum ira sit appetitus vindictae, praecipue concitatur ira cum aliquis se reputat laesum iniuste, ut patet per philosophum, in II Rhet. Et ideo per hoc quod patribus interdicitur ne filios

**OBJECTION 1**: It would seem unlawful for parents to strike their children, or masters their slaves. For the Apostle says (*Eph 6:4*): *You, fathers, provoke not your children to anger*; and further on (*Eph 9:6*): *And you, masters, do the same thing to your slaves, forbearing threatenings*. Now some are provoked to anger by blows, and become more troublesome when threatened. Therefore neither should parents strike their children, nor masters their slaves.

**OBJ. 2**: Further, the Philosopher says (*Ethic. x, 9*) that *a father's words are admonitory and not coercive*. Now blows are a kind of coercion. Therefore it is unlawful for parents to strike their children.

**OBJ. 3**: Further, everyone is allowed to impart correction, for this belongs to the spiritual almsdeeds, as stated above (Q. 32, A. 2). If, therefore, it is lawful for parents to strike their children for the sake of correction, for the same reason it will be lawful for any person to strike anyone, which is clearly false. Therefore the same conclusion follows.

**ON THE CONTRARY**, It is written (Prov 13:24): *He that spareth the rod hateth his son*, and further on (Prov 23:13): *Withhold not correction from a child, for if thou strike him with the rod, he shall not die. Thou shalt beat him with the rod, and deliver his soul from hell*. Again it is written (Sir 33:28): *Torture and fetters are for a malicious slave*.

**I ANSWER THAT**, Harm is done a body by striking it, yet not so as when it is maimed: since maiming destroys the body's integrity, while a blow merely affects the sense with pain, wherefore it causes much less harm than cutting off a member. Now it is unlawful to do a person a harm, except by way of punishment in the cause of justice. Again, no man justly punishes another, except one who is subject to his jurisdiction. Therefore it is not lawful for a man to strike another, unless he have some power over the one whom he strikes. And since the child is subject to the power of the parent, and the slave to the power of his master, a parent can lawfully strike his child, and a master his slave that instruction may be enforced by correction.

**REPLY OBJ. 1**: Since anger is a desire for vengeance, it is aroused chiefly when a man deems himself unjustly injured, as the Philosopher states (*Rhet. ii*). Hence when parents are forbidden to provoke their children to anger,

ad iracundiam provocent, non prohibetur quin filios verberent causa disciplinae, sed quod non immoderate eos affligant verberibus. Quod vero inducitur dominis quod remittant minas, potest dupliciter intelligi. Uno modo, ut remisse minis utantur, quod pertinet ad moderationem disciplinae. Alio modo, ut aliquis non semper impleat quod comminatus est, quod pertinet ad hoc quod iudicium quo quis comminatus est poenam, quandoque per remissionis misericordiam temperetur.

**AD SECUNDUM** dicendum quod maior potestas maiorem debet habere coactionem. Sicut autem civitas est perfecta communitas, ita princeps civitatis habet perfectam potestatem coercendi, et ideo potest infligere poenas irreparabiles, scilicet occisionis vel mutilationis. Pater autem et dominus, qui praesunt familiae domesticae, quae est imperfecta communitas, habent imperfectam potestatem coercendi secundum leviores poenas, quae non inferunt irreparabile nocumentum. Et huiusmodi est verberatio.

**AD TERTIUM** dicendum quod exhibere disciplinam volenti cuilibet licet. Sed disciplinam nolenti adhibere est solum eius cui alterius cura committitur. Et ad hoc pertinet aliquem verberibus castigare.

they are not prohibited from striking their children for the purpose of correction, but from inflicting blows on them without moderation. The command that masters should forbear from threatening their slaves may be understood in two ways. First that they should be slow to threaten, and this pertains to the moderation of correction; second, that they should not always carry out their threats, that is that they should sometimes by a merciful forgiveness temper the judgment whereby they threatened punishment.

**REPLY OBJ. 2**: The greater power should exercise the greater coercion. Now just as a city is a perfect community, so the governor of a city has perfect coercive power: wherefore he can inflict irreparable punishments such as death and mutilation. On the other hand the father and the master who preside over the family household, which is an imperfect community, have imperfect coercive power, which is exercised by inflicting lesser punishments, for instance by blows, which do not inflict irreparable harm.

**REPLY OBJ. 3**: It is lawful for anyone to impart correction to a willing subject. But to impart it to an unwilling subject belongs to those only who have charge over him. To this pertains chastisement by blows.

# Article 3

*Whether it is lawful to imprison a man?*

**AD TERTIUM SIC PROCEDITUR**. Videtur quod non liceat aliquem hominem incarcerare. Actus enim est malus ex genere qui cadit supra indebitam materiam, ut supra dictum est. Sed homo, habens naturalem arbitrii libertatem, est indebita materia incarcerationis, quae libertati repugnat. Ergo illicitum est aliquem incarcerare.

**PRAETEREA**, humana iustitia regulari debet ex divina. Sed sicut dicitur Eccli. XV, *Deus reliquit hominem in manu consilii sui*. Ergo videtur quod non est aliquis coercendus vinculis vel carcere.

**PRAETEREA**, nullus est cohibendus nisi ab opere malo, a quo quilibet licite potest alium impedire. Si ergo incarcerare aliquem esset licitum ad hoc quod cohiberetur a malo, cuilibet esset licitum aliquem incarcerare. Quod patet esse falsum. Ergo et primum.

**SED CONTRA** est quod Levit. XXIV legitur quendam missum fuisse in carcerem propter peccatum blasphemiae.

**RESPONDEO** dicendum quod in bonis corporis tria per ordinem considerantur. Primo quidem, integritas corporalis substantiae, cui detrimentum affertur per occisionem vel mutilationem. Secundo, delectatio vel quies sensus, cui opponitur verberatio, vel quidlibet sensum

**OBJECTION 1**: It would seem unlawful to imprison a man. An act which deals with undue matter is evil in its genus, as stated above (I-II, Q. 18, A. 2). Now man, having a free-will, is undue matter for imprisonment which is inconsistent with free-will. Therefore it is unlawful to imprison a man.

**OBJ. 2**: Further, human justice should be ruled by Divine justice. Now according to Ecclus. 15:14, *God left man in the hand of his own counsel*. Therefore it seems that a man ought not to be coerced by chains or prisons.

**OBJ. 3**: Further, no man should be forcibly prevented except from doing an evil deed; and any man can lawfully prevent another from doing this. If, therefore, it were lawful to imprison a man, in order to restrain him from evil deeds, it would be lawful for anyone to put a man in prison; and this is clearly false. Therefore the same conclusion follows.

**ON THE CONTRARY**, We read in Lev. 24 that a man was imprisoned for the sin of blasphemy.

**I ANSWER THAT**, In the goods of the body three things may be considered in due order. First, the substantial integrity of the body, and this is injured by death or maiming. Second, pleasure or rest of the senses, and to this striking or anything causing a sense of pain is opposed. Third, the

dolore afficiens. Tertio, motus et usus membrorum, qui impeditur per ligationem vel incarcerationem, seu quamcumque detentionem.

Et ideo incarcerare aliquem, vel qualitercumque detinere, est illicitum nisi fiat secundum ordinem iustitiae, aut in poenam aut ad cautelam alicuius mali vitandi.

**Ad primum** ergo dicendum quod homo qui abutitur potestate sibi data, meretur eam amittere. Et ideo homo qui peccando abusus est libero usu suorum membrorum, conveniens est incarcerationis materia.

**Ad secundum** dicendum quod Deus quandoque, secundum ordinem suae sapientiae, peccatores cohibet ne possint peccata implere, secundum illud Iob V, *qui dissipat cogitationes malignorum, ne possint implere manus eorum quod coeperant.* Quandoque vero eos permittit quod volunt agere. Et similiter secundum humanam iustitiam non pro qualibet culpa homines incarcerantur, sed pro aliquibus.

**Ad tertium** dicendum quod detinere hominem ad horam ab aliquo opere illicito statim perpetrando, cuilibet licet, sicut cum aliquis detinet aliquem ne se praecipitet, vel ne alium feriat. Sed simpliciter aliquem includere vel ligare ad eum solum pertinet qui habet disponere universaliter de actibus et vita alterius, quia per hoc impeditur non solum a malis, sed etiam a bonis agendis.

movement or use of the members, and this is hindered by binding or imprisoning or any kind of detention.

Therefore it is unlawful to imprison or in any way detain a man, unless it be done according to the order of justice, either in punishment, or as a measure of precaution against some evil.

**Reply Obj. 1**: A man who abuses the power entrusted to him deserves to lose it, and therefore when a man by sinning abuses the free use of his members, he becomes a fitting matter for imprisonment.

**Reply Obj. 2**: According to the order of His wisdom God sometimes restrains a sinner from accomplishing a sin, according to Job 5:12: *Who bringeth to naught the designs of the malignant, so that their hand cannot accomplish what they had begun, while sometimes He allows them to do what they will.* In like manner, according to human justice, men are imprisoned, not for every sin but for certain ones.

**Reply Obj. 3**: It is lawful for anyone to restrain a man for a time from doing some unlawful deed there and then: as when a man prevents another from throwing himself over a precipice, or from striking another. But to him alone who has the right of disposing in general of the actions and of the life of another does it belong primarily to imprison or fetter, because by so doing he hinders him from doing not only evil but also good deeds.

# Article 4

*Whether the sin is aggravated by the fact that the aforesaid injuries are perpetrated on those who are connected with others?*

**Ad quartum sic proceditur.** Videtur quod peccatum non aggravetur ex hoc quod praedictae iniuriae inferuntur in personas aliis coniunctas. Huiusmodi enim iniuriae habent rationem peccati prout nocumentum alicui infertur contra eius voluntatem. Sed magis est contra hominis voluntatem malum quod in personam propriam infertur quam quod infertur in personam coniunctam. Ergo iniuria illata in personam coniunctam est minor.

**Praeterea**, in sacra Scriptura praecipue reprehenduntur qui pupillis et viduis iniurias inferunt, unde dicitur Eccli. XXXV, *non despiciet preces pupilli, nec viduam, si effundat loquelam gemitus.* Sed vidua et pupillus non sunt personae aliis coniunctae. Ergo ex hoc quod infertur iniuria personis coniunctis non aggravatur peccatum.

**Praeterea**, persona coniuncta habet propriam voluntatem, sicut et principalis persona. Potest ergo aliquid ei esse voluntarium quod est contra voluntatem princi-

**Objection 1**: It would seem that the sin is not aggravated by the fact that the aforesaid injuries are perpetrated on those who are connected with others. Such like injuries take their sinful character from inflicting an injury on another against his will. Now the evil inflicted on a man's own person is more against his will than that which is inflicted on a person connected with him. Therefore an injury inflicted on a person connected with another is less grievous.

**Obj. 2**: Further, Holy Writ reproves those especially who do injuries to orphans and widows: hence it is written (Sir 35:17): *He will not despise the prayers of the fatherless, nor the widow when she poureth out her complaint.* Now the widow and the orphan are not connected with other persons. Therefore the sin is not aggravated through an injury being inflicted on one who is connected with others.

**Obj. 3**: Further, the person who is connected has a will of his own just as the principal person has, so that something may be voluntary for him and yet against the

palis personae, ut patet in adulterio, quod placet uxori et displicet viro. Sed huiusmodi iniuriae habent rationem peccati prout consistunt in involuntaria commutatione. Ergo huiusmodi iniuriae minus habent de ratione peccati.

**SED CONTRA** est quod Deut. XXVIII, ad quandam exaggerationem dicitur, *filii tui et filiae tuae tradentur alteri populo videntibus oculis tuis.*

**RESPONDEO** dicendum quod quanto aliqua iniuria in plures redundat, ceteris paribus, tanto gravius est peccatum. Et inde est quod gravius est peccatum si aliquis percutiat principem quam personam privatam, quia redundat in iniuriam totius multitudinis, ut supra dictum est. Cum autem infertur iniuria in aliquam personam coniunctam alteri qualitercumque, iniuria illa pertinet ad duas personas. Et ideo, ceteris paribus, ex hoc ipso aggravatur peccatum. Potest tamen contingere quod secundum aliquas circumstantias sit gravius peccatum quod fit contra personam nulli coniunctam, vel propter dignitatem personae, vel propter magnitudinem nocumenti.

**AD PRIMUM** ergo dicendum quod iniuria illata in personam coniunctam minus est nociva personae cui coniungitur quam si in ipsam immediate inferretur, et ex hac parte est minus peccatum. Sed hoc totum quod pertinet ad iniuriam personae cui coniungitur, superadditur peccato quod quis incurrit ex eo quod aliam personam secundum se laedit.

**AD SECUNDUM** dicendum quod iniuriae illatae in viduas et pupillos magis exaggerantur, tum quia magis opponuntur misericordiae. Tum quia idem nocumentum huiusmodi personis inflictum est eis gravius, quia non habent relevantem.

**AD TERTIUM** dicendum quod per hoc quod uxor voluntarie consentit in adulterium, minoratur quidem peccatum et iniuria ex parte ipsius mulieris, gravius enim esset si adulter violenter eam opprimeret. Non tamen per hoc tollitur iniuria ex parte viri, quia *uxor non habet potestatem sui corporis, sed vir,* ut dicitur I ad Cor. VII. Et eadem ratio est de similibus. De adulterio tamen, quod non solum iustitiae, sed etiam castitati opponitur, erit locus infra agendi in tractatu de temperantia.

will of the principal person, as in the case of adultery which pleases the woman but not the husband. Now these injuries are sinful insofar as they consist in an involuntary commutation. Therefore such like injuries are of a less sinful nature.

**ON THE CONTRARY**, It is written (Deut 28:32) as though indicating an aggravating circumstance: *Thy sons and thy daughters shall be given to another people, thy eyes looking on.*

**I ANSWER THAT**, Other things being equal, an injury is a more grievous sin according as it affects more persons; and hence it is that it is a more grievous sin to strike or injure a person in authority than a private individual, because it conduces to the injury of the whole community, as stated above (I-II, Q. 73, A. 9). Now when an injury is inflicted on one who is connected in any way with another, that injury affects two persons, so that, other things being equal, the sin is aggravated by this very fact. It may happen, however, that in view of certain circumstances, a sin committed against one who is not connected with any other person, is more grievous, on account of either the dignity of the person, or the greatness of the injury.

**REPLY OBJ. 1**: An injury inflicted on a person connected with others is less harmful to the persons with whom he is connected, than if it were perpetrated immediately on them, and from this point of view it is a less grievous sin. But all that belongs to the injury of the person with whom he is connected, is added to the sin of which a man is guilty through injuring the other one in himself.

**REPLY OBJ. 2**: Injuries done to widows and orphans are more insisted upon both through being more opposed to mercy, and because the same injury done to such persons is more grievous to them since they have no one to turn to for relief.

**REPLY OBJ. 3**: The fact that the wife voluntarily consents to the adultery, lessens the sin and injury, so far as the woman is concerned, for it would be more grievous, if the adulterer oppressed her by violence. But this does not remove the injury as affecting her husband, since *the wife hath not power of her own body; but the husband* (1 Cor 7:4). The same applies to similar cases. Of adultery, however, as it is opposed not only to justice but also to chastity, we shall speak in the treatise on Temperance (Q. 154, A. 8).

# QUESTION 66

Deinde considerandum est de peccatis iustitiae oppositis per quae infertur nocumentum proximo in rebus, scilicet de furto et rapina.

Et circa hoc quaeruntur novem.

Primo, utrum naturalis sit homini possessio exteriorum rerum.

Secundo, utrum licitum sit quod aliquis rem aliquam possideat quasi propriam.

Tertio, utrum furtum sit occulta acceptio rei alienae.

Quarto, utrum rapina sit peccatum specie differens a furto.

Quinto, utrum omne furtum sit peccatum.

Sexto, utrum furtum sit peccatum mortale.

Septimo, utrum liceat furari in necessitate.

Octavo, utrum omnis rapina sit peccatum mortale.

Nono, utrum rapina sit gravius peccatum quam furtum.

We must now consider the sins opposed to justice, whereby a man injures his neighbor in his belongings; namely theft and robbery.

Under this head there are nine points of inquiry:

(1) Whether it is natural to man to possess external things?

(2) Whether it is lawful for a man to possess something as his own?

(3) Whether theft is the secret taking of another's property?

(4) Whether robbery is a species of sin distinct from theft?

(5) Whether every theft is a sin?

(6) Whether theft is a mortal sin?

(7) Whether it is lawful to thieve in a case of necessity?

(8) Whether every robbery is a mortal sin?

(9) Whether robbery is a more grievous sin than theft?

# Article 1

*Whether it is natural for man to possess external things?*

**AD PRIMUM SIC PROCEDITUR.** Videtur quod non sit naturalis homini possessio exteriorum rerum. Nullus enim debet sibi attribuere quod Dei est. Sed dominium omnium creaturarum est proprie Dei, secundum illud Psalm., *domini est terra* et cetera. Ergo non est naturalis homini rerum possessio.

**PRAETEREA,** Basilius, exponens verbum divitis dicentis, Luc. XII, *congregabo omnia quae nata sunt mihi et bona mea*, dicit, *dic mihi, quae tua? Unde ea sumens in vitam tulisti?* Sed illa quae homo possidet naturaliter, potest aliquis convenienter dicere esse sua. Ergo homo non possidet naturaliter exteriora bona.

**PRAETEREA,** sicut Ambrosius dicit, in libro de Trin., *dominus nomen est potestatis.* Sed homo non habet potestatem super res exteriores, nihil enim potest circa earum naturam immutare. Ergo possessio exteriorum rerum non est homini naturalis.

**SED CONTRA** est quod dicitur in Psalm., *omnia subiecisti sub pedibus eius*, scilicet hominis.

**RESPONDEO** dicendum quod res exterior potest dupliciter considerari. Uno modo, quantum ad eius naturam, quae non subiacet humanae potestati, sed

**OBJECTION 1**: It would seem that it is not natural for man to possess external things. For no man should ascribe to himself that which is God's. Now the dominion over all creatures is proper to God, according to Ps. 23:1, *The earth is the Lord's*, etc. Therefore it is not natural for man to possess external things.

**OBJ. 2**: Further, Basil in expounding the words of the rich man (Luke 12:18), *I will gather all things that are grown to me, and my goods*, says: *Tell me: which are thine? where did you take them from and bring them into being?* Now whatever man possesses naturally, he can fittingly call his own. Therefore man does not naturally possess external things.

**OBJ. 3**: Further, according to Ambrose (*De Trin.* i ) *dominion denotes power*. But man has no power over external things, since he can work no change in their nature. Therefore the possession of external things is not natural to man.

**ON THE CONTRARY**, It is written (Ps 8:8): *Thou hast subjected all things under his feet*, namely, man.

**I ANSWER THAT**, External things can be considered in two ways. First, as regards their nature, and this is not subject to the power of man, but only to the power of

solum divinae, cui omnia ad nutum obediunt. Alio modo, quantum ad usum ipsius rei. Et sic habet homo naturale dominium exteriorum rerum, quia per rationem et voluntatem potest uti rebus exterioribus ad suam utilitatem, quasi propter se factis; semper enim imperfectiora sunt propter perfectiora, ut supra habitum est. Et ex hac ratione philosophus probat, in I Polit., quod possessio rerum exteriorum est homini naturalis. Hoc autem naturale dominium super ceteras creaturas, quod competit homini secundum rationem, in qua imago Dei consistit, manifestatur in ipsa hominis creatione, Gen. I, ubi dicitur, *faciamus hominem ad similitudinem et imaginem nostram, et praesit piscibus maris*, et cetera.

**AD PRIMUM** ergo dicendum quod Deus habet principale dominium omnium rerum. Et ipse secundum suam providentiam ordinavit res quasdam ad corporalem hominis sustentationem. Et propter hoc homo habet naturale rerum dominium quantum ad potestatem utendi ipsis.

**AD SECUNDUM** dicendum quod dives ille reprehenditur ex hoc quod putabat exteriora bona esse principaliter sua, quasi non accepisset ea ab alio, scilicet a Deo.

**AD TERTIUM** dicendum quod ratio illa procedit de dominio exteriorum rerum quantum ad naturas ipsarum, quod quidem dominium soli Deo convenit, ut dictum est.

God Whose mere will all things obey. Second, as regards their use, and in this way, man has a natural dominion over external things, because, by his reason and will, he is able to use them for his own profit, as they were made on his account: for the imperfect is always for the sake of the perfect, as stated above (Q. 64, A. 1). It is by this argument that the Philosopher proves (*Polit.* i, 3) that the possession of external things is natural to man. Moreover, this natural dominion of man over other creatures, which is competent to man in respect of his reason wherein God's image resides, is shown forth in man's creation (Gen 1:26) by the words: *Let us make man to our image and likeness: and let him have dominion over the fishes of the sea*, etc.

**REPLY OBJ. 1**: God has sovereign dominion over all things: and He, according to His providence, directed certain things to the sustenance of man's body. For this reason man has a natural dominion over things, as regards the power to make use of them.

**REPLY OBJ. 2**: The rich man is reproved for deeming external things to belong to him principally, as though he had not received them from another, namely from God.

**REPLY OBJ. 3**: This argument considers the dominion over external things as regards their nature. Such a dominion belongs to God alone, as stated above.

# Article 2

*Whether it is lawful for a man to possess a thing as his own?*

**AD SECUNDUM SIC PROCEDITUR**. Videtur quod non liceat alicui rem aliquam quasi propriam possidere. Omne enim quod est contra ius naturale est illicitum. Sed secundum ius naturale omnia sunt communia, cui quidem communitati contrariatur possessionum proprietas. Ergo illicitum est cuilibet homini appropriare sibi aliquam rem exteriorem.

**PRAETEREA**, Basilius dicit, exponens praedictum verbum divitis, *sicut qui, praeveniens ad spectacula, prohiberet advenientes, sibi appropriando quod ad communem usum ordinatur; similes sunt divites qui communia, quae praeoccupaverunt, aestimant sua esse*. Sed illicitum esset praecludere viam aliis ad potiendum communibus bonis. Ergo illicitum est appropriare sibi aliquam rem communem.

**PRAETEREA**, Ambrosius dicit, et habetur in decretis, dist. XLVII, Can. sicut hi, *proprium nemo dicat quod est commune*. Appellat autem communes res exteriores, sicut patet ex his quae praemittit. Ergo videtur illicitum

**OBJECTION 1**: It would seem unlawful for a man to possess a thing as his own. For whatever is contrary to the natural law is unlawful. Now according to the natural law all things are common property: and the possession of property is contrary to this community of goods. Therefore it is unlawful for any man to appropriate any external thing to himself.

**OBJ. 2**: Further, Basil in expounding the words of the rich man quoted above (A. 1, Obj. 2), says: *The rich who deem as their own property the common goods they have seized upon, are like to those who by going beforehand to the play prevent others from coming, and appropriate to themselves what is intended for common use*. Now it would be unlawful to prevent others from obtaining possession of common goods. Therefore it is unlawful to appropriate to oneself what belongs to the community.

**OBJ. 3**: Further, Ambrose says, and his words are quoted in the *Decretals*: *Let no man call his own that which is common property*: and by *common* he means external things, as is clear from the context. Therefore it seems

esse quod aliquis appropriet sibi aliquam rem exteriorem.

**Sed contra** est quod Augustinus dicit, in libro de Haeres., *apostolici dicuntur qui se hoc nomine arrogantissime vocaverunt, eo quod in suam communionem non acciperent utentes coniugibus, et res proprias possidentes, quales habet Catholica Ecclesia et monachos et clericos plurimos.* Sed ideo isti haeretici sunt quoniam, se ab Ecclesia separantes, nullam spem putant eos habere qui utuntur his rebus, quibus ipsi carent. Est ergo erroneum dicere quod non liceat homini propria possidere.

**Respondeo** dicendum quod circa rem exteriorem duo competunt homini. Quorum unum est potestas procurandi et dispensandi. Et quantum ad hoc licitum est quod homo propria possideat. Et est etiam necessarium ad humanam vitam, propter tria. Primo quidem, quia magis sollicitus est unusquisque ad procurandum aliquid quod sibi soli competit quam aliquid quod est commune omnium vel multorum, quia unusquisque, laborem fugiens, relinquit alteri id quod pertinet ad commune; sicut accidit in multitudine ministrorum. Alio modo, quia ordinatius res humanae tractantur si singulis immineat propria cura alicuius rei procurandae, esset autem confusio si quilibet indistincte quaelibet procuraret. Tertio, quia per hoc magis pacificus status hominum conservatur, dum unusquisque re sua contentus est. Unde videmus quod inter eos qui communiter et ex indiviso aliquid possident, frequentius iurgia oriuntur.

Aliud vero quod competit homini circa res exteriores est usus ipsarum. Et quantum ad hoc non debet homo habere res exteriores ut proprias, sed ut communes, ut scilicet de facili aliquis ea communicet in necessitates aliorum. Unde apostolus dicit, I ad Tim. ult., *divitibus huius saeculi praecipe facile tribuere, communicare.*

**Ad primum** ergo dicendum quod communitas rerum attribuitur iuri naturali, non quia ius naturale dictet omnia esse possidenda communiter et nihil esse quasi proprium possidendum, sed quia secundum ius naturale non est distinctio possessionum, sed magis secundum humanum condictum, quod pertinet ad ius positivum, ut supra dictum est. Unde proprietas possessionum non est contra ius naturale; sed iuri naturali superadditur per adinventionem rationis humanae.

**Ad secundum** dicendum quod ille qui, praeveniens ad spectacula, praepararet aliis viam, non illicite ageret, sed ex hoc illicite agit quod alios prohibet. Et similiter dives non illicite agit si, praeoccupans possessionem rei quae a principio erat communis, aliis communicat, peccat autem si alios ab usu illius rei indiscrete prohibeat.

unlawful for a man to appropriate an external thing to himself.

**On the contrary,** Augustine says (*De Haeres.*, haer. 40): *The 'Apostolici' are those who with extreme arrogance have given themselves that name, because they do not admit into their communion persons who are married or possess anything of their own, such as both monks and clerics who in considerable number are to be found in the Catholic Church.* Now the reason why these people are heretics was because severing themselves from the Church, they think that those who enjoy the use of the above things, which they themselves lack, have no hope of salvation. Therefore it is erroneous to maintain that it is unlawful for a man to possess property.

**I answer that,** Two things are competent to man in respect of exterior things. One is the power to procure and dispense them, and in this regard it is lawful for man to possess property. Moreover this is necessary to human life for three reasons. First because every man is more careful to procure what is for himself alone than that which is common to many or to all: since each one would shirk the labor and leave to another that which concerns the community, as happens where there is a great number of servants. Second, because human affairs are conducted in more orderly fashion if each man is charged with taking care of some particular thing himself, whereas there would be confusion if everyone had to look after any one thing indeterminately. Third, because a more peaceful state is ensured to man if each one is contented with his own. Hence it is to be observed that quarrels arise more frequently where there is no division of the things possessed.

The second thing that is competent to man with regard to external things is their use. In this respect man ought to possess external things, not as his own, but as common, so that, to wit, he is ready to communicate them to others in their need. Hence the Apostle says (1 Tim 6:17, 18): *Charge the rich of this world . . . to give easily, to communicate to others,* etc.

**Reply Obj. 1:** Community of goods is ascribed to the natural law, not that the natural law dictates that all things should be possessed in common and that nothing should be possessed as one's own: but because the division of possessions is not according to the natural law, but rather arose from human agreement which belongs to positive law, as stated above (Q. 57, AA. 2, 3). Hence the ownership of possessions is not contrary to the natural law, but an addition thereto devised by human reason.

**Reply Obj. 2:** A man would not act unlawfully if by going beforehand to the play he prepared the way for others: but he acts unlawfully if by so doing he hinders others from going. In like manner a rich man does not act unlawfully if he anticipates someone in taking possession of something which at first was common property, and gives others a

Unde Basilius ibidem dicit, *cur tu abundas, ille vero mendicat, nisi ut tu bonae dispensationis merita consequaris, ille vero patientiae praemiis coronetur?*

**AD TERTIUM** dicendum quod cum dicit Ambrosius, *nemo proprium dicat quod est commune,* loquitur de proprietate quantum ad usum. Unde subdit, *plus quam sufficeret sumptui, violenter obtentum est.*

share: but he sins if he excludes others indiscriminately from using it. Hence Basil says (*Hom. in Luc.* xii, 18): *Why are you rich while another is poor, unless it be that you may have the merit of a good stewardship, and he the reward of patience?*

**REPLY OBJ. 3**: When Ambrose says: *Let no man call his own that which is common,* he is speaking of ownership as regards use, wherefore he adds: *He who spends too much is a robber.*

# Article 3

*Whether the essence of theft consists in taking another's thing secretly?*

**AD TERTIUM SIC PROCEDITUR.** Videtur quod non sit de ratione furti occulte accipere rem alienam. Illud enim quod diminuit peccatum non videtur ad rationem peccati pertinere. Sed in occulto peccare pertinet ad diminutionem peccati, sicut e contrario ad exaggerandum peccatum quorundam dicitur Isaiae III, *peccatum suum quasi Sodoma praedicaverunt, nec absconderunt.* Ergo non est de ratione furti occulta acceptio rei alienae.

**PRAETEREA,** Ambrosius dicit, et habetur in decretis, dist. XLVII, *neque minus est criminis habenti tollere quam, cum possis et abundas, indigentibus denegare.* Ergo sicut furtum consistit in acceptione rei alienae, ita et in detentione ipsius.

**PRAETEREA,** homo potest furtim ab alio accipere etiam quod suum est puta rem quam apud alium deposuit, vel quae est ab eo iniuste ablata. Non est ergo de ratione furti quod sit occulta acceptio rei alienae.

**SED CONTRA** est quod Isidorus dicit, in libro Etymol., *fur a furvo dictus est, idest a fusco, nam noctis utitur tempore.*

**RESPONDEO** dicendum quod ad rationem furti tria concurrunt. Quorum primum convenit sibi secundum quod contrariatur iustitiae, quae unicuique tribuit quod suum est. Et ex hoc competit ei quod usurpat alienum. Secundum vero pertinet ad rationem furti prout distinguitur a peccatis quae sunt contra personam, sicut ab homicidio et adulterio. Et secundum hoc competit furto quod sit circa rem possessam. Si quis enim accipiat id quod est alterius non quasi possessio, sed quasi pars, sicut si amputet membrum; vel sicut persona coniuncta, ut si auferat filiam vel uxorem, non habet proprie rationem furti. Tertia differentia est quae complet furti rationem, ut scilicet occulte usurpetur alienum. Et secundum hoc propria ratio furti est ut sit occulta acceptio rei alienae.

**OBJECTION 1**: It would seem that it is not essential to theft to take another's thing secretly. For that which diminishes a sin, does not, apparently, belong to the essence of a sin. Now to sin secretly tends to diminish a sin, just as, on the contrary, it is written as indicating an aggravating circumstance of the sin of some (Isa 3:9): *They have proclaimed abroad their sin as Sodom, and they have not hid it.* Therefore it is not essential to theft that it should consist in taking another's thing secretly.

**OBJ. 2**: Further, Ambrose says: and his words are embodied in the Decretals: *It is no less a crime to take from him that has, than to refuse to succor the needy when you can and are well off.* Therefore just as theft consists in taking another's thing, so does it consist in keeping it back.

**OBJ. 3**: Further, a man may take by stealth from another, even that which is his own, for instance a thing that he has deposited with another, or that has been taken away from him unjustly. Therefore it is not essential to theft that it should consist in taking another's thing secretly.

**ON THE CONTRARY**, Isidore says (*Etym.* x): *Fur (thief) is derived from furvus and so from fuscus (dark), because he takes advantage of the night.*

**I ANSWER THAT**, Three things combine together to constitute theft. The first belongs to theft as being contrary to justice, which gives to each one that which is his, so that it belongs to theft to take possession of what is another's. The second thing belongs to theft as distinct from those sins which are committed against the person, such as murder and adultery, and in this respect it belongs to theft to be about a thing possessed: for if a man takes what is another's not as a possession but as a part (for instance, if he amputates a limb), or as a person connected with him (for instance, if he carry off his daughter or his wife), it is not strictly speaking a case of theft. The third difference is that which completes the nature of theft, and consists in a thing being taken secretly: and in this respect it belongs properly to theft that it consists in taking another's thing secretly.

AD PRIMUM ergo dicendum quod occultatio quandoque quidem est causa peccati, puta cum quis utitur occultatione ad peccandum, sicut accidit in fraude et dolo. Et hoc modo non diminuit, sed constituit speciem peccati. Et ita est in furto. Alio modo occultatio est simplex circumstantia peccati. Et sic diminuit peccatum, tum quia est signum verecundiae; tum quia tollit scandalum.

AD SECUNDUM dicendum quod detinere id quod alteri debetur eandem rationem nocumenti habet cum acceptione. Et ideo sub iniusta acceptione intelligitur etiam iniusta detentio.

AD TERTIUM dicendum quod nihil prohibet id quod est simpliciter unius, secundum quid esse alterius. Sicut res deposita est simpliciter quidem deponentis, sed est eius apud quem deponitur quantum ad custodiam. Et id quod est per rapinam ablatum est rapientis, non simpliciter, sed quantum ad detentionem.

REPLY OBJ. 1: Secrecy is sometimes a cause of sin, as when a man employs secrecy in order to commit a sin, for instance in fraud and guile. In this way it does not diminish sin, but constitutes a species of sin: and thus it is in theft. In another way secrecy is merely a circumstance of sin, and thus it diminishes sin, both because it is a sign of shame, and because it removes scandal.

REPLY OBJ. 2: To keep back what is due to another, inflicts the same kind of injury as taking a thing unjustly: wherefore an unjust detention is included in an unjust taking.

REPLY OBJ. 3: Nothing prevents that which belongs to one person simply, from belonging to another in some respect: thus a deposit belongs simply to the depositor, but with regard to its custody it is the depositary's, and the thing stolen is the thief's, not simply, but as regards its custody.

# Article 4

*Whether theft and robbery are sins of different species?*

AD QUARTUM SIC PROCEDITUR. Videtur quod furtum et rapina non sint peccata differentia specie. Furtum enim et rapina differunt secundum occultum et manifestum, furtum enim importat occultam acceptionem, rapina vero violentam et manifestam. Sed in aliis generibus peccatorum occultum et manifestum non diversificant speciem. Ergo furtum et rapina non sunt peccata specie diversa.

PRAETEREA, moralia recipiunt speciem a fine, ut supra dictum est. Sed furtum et rapina ordinantur ad eundem finem, scilicet ad habendum aliena. Ergo non differunt specie.

PRAETEREA, sicut rapitur aliquid ad possidendum, ita rapitur mulier ad delectandum, unde et Isidorus dicit, in libro Etymol., quod *raptor dicitur corruptor, et rapta corrupta*. Sed raptus dicitur sive mulier auferatur publice, sive occulte. Ergo et res possessa rapi dicitur sive occulte, sive publice rapiatur. Ergo non differunt furtum et rapina.

SED CONTRA est quod philosophus, in V Ethic., distinguit furtum a rapina, ponens furtum occultum, rapinam vero violentam.

RESPONDEO dicendum quod furtum et rapina sunt vitia iustitiae opposita, inquantum aliquis alter facit iniustum. *Nullus* autem *patitur iniustum volens*, ut probatur in V Ethic. Et ideo furtum et rapina ex hoc habent

OBJECTION 1: It would seem that theft and robbery are not sins of different species. For theft and robbery differ as *secret* and *manifest*: because theft is taking something secretly, while robbery is to take something violently and openly. Now in the other kinds of sins, the secret and the manifest do not differ specifically. Therefore theft and robbery are not different species of sin.

OBJ. 2: Further, moral actions take their species from the end, as stated above (I-II, Q. 1, A. 3; Q. 18, A. 6). Now theft and robbery are directed to the same end, viz. the possession of another's property. Therefore they do not differ specifically.

OBJ. 3: Further, just as a thing is taken by force for the sake of possession, so is a woman taken by force for pleasure: wherefore Isidore says (*Etym.* x) that *he who commits a rape is called a corrupter, and the victim of the rape is said to be corrupted*. Now it is a case of rape whether the woman be carried off publicly or secretly. Therefore the thing appropriated is said to be taken by force, whether it be done secretly or publicly. Therefore theft and robbery do not differ.

ON THE CONTRARY, The Philosopher (*Ethic.* v, 2) distinguishes theft from robbery, and states that theft is done in secret, but that robbery is done openly.

I ANSWER THAT, Theft and robbery are vices contrary to justice, inasmuch as one man does another an injustice. Now *no man suffers an injustice willingly*, as stated in *Ethic.* v, 9. Wherefore theft and robbery derive their

rationem peccati quod acceptio est involuntaria ex parte eius cui aliquid subtrahitur. Involuntarium autem dupliciter dicitur, scilicet per ignorantiam, et violentiam, ut habetur in III Ethic. Et ideo aliam rationem peccati habet rapina, et aliam furtum. Et propter hoc differunt specie.

AD PRIMUM ergo dicendum quod in aliis generibus peccatorum non attenditur ratio peccati ex aliquo involuntario, sicut attenditur in peccatis oppositis iustitiae. Et ideo ubi occurrit diversa ratio involuntarii, est diversa species peccati.

AD SECUNDUM dicendum quod finis remotus est idem rapinae et furti, sed hoc non sufficit ad identitatem speciei, quia est diversitas in finibus proximis. Raptor enim vult per propriam potestatem obtinere, fur vero per astutiam.

AD TERTIUM dicendum quod raptus mulieris non potest esse occultus ex parte mulieris quae rapitur. Et ideo etiam si sit occultus ex parte aliorum, quibus rapitur, adhuc remanet ratio rapinae ex parte mulieris, cui violentia infertur.

sinful nature, through the taking being involuntary on the part of the person from whom something is taken. Now the involuntary is twofold, namely, through violence and through ignorance, as stated in *Ethic.* iii, 1. Therefore the sinful aspect of robbery differs from that of theft: and consequently they differ specifically.

REPLY OBJ. 1: In the other kinds of sin the sinful nature is not derived from something involuntary, as in the sins opposed to justice: and so where there is a different kind of involuntary, there is a different species of sin.

REPLY OBJ. 2: The remote end of robbery and theft is the same. But this is not enough for identity of species, because there is a difference of proximate ends, since the robber wishes to take a thing by his own power, but the thief, by cunning.

REPLY OBJ. 3: The robbery of a woman cannot be secret on the part of the woman who is taken: wherefore even if it be secret as regards the others from whom she is taken, the nature of robbery remains on the part of the woman to whom violence is done.

# Article 5

### Whether theft is always a sin?

AD QUINTUM SIC PROCEDITUR. Videtur quod furtum non semper sit peccatum. Nullum enim peccatum cadit sub praecepto divino, dicitur enim Eccli. XV, *nemini mandavit impie agere.* Sed Deus invenitur praecepisse furtum, dicitur enim Exod. XII, *fecerunt filii Israel sicut praeceperat dominus Moysi, et expoliaverunt Aegyptios.* Ergo furtum non semper est peccatum.

PRAETEREA, ille qui invenit rem non suam, si eam accipiat, videtur furtum committere, quia accipit rem alienam. Sed hoc videtur esse licitum secundum naturalem aequitatem; ut iuristae dicunt. Ergo videtur quod furtum non semper sit peccatum.

PRAETEREA, ille qui accipit rem suam non videtur peccare, cum non agat contra iustitiam, cuius aequalitatem non tollit. Sed furtum committitur etiam si aliquis rem suam occulte accipiat ab altero detentam vel custoditam. Ergo videtur quod furtum non semper sit peccatum.

SED CONTRA est quod dicitur Exod. XX, *non furtum facies.*

RESPONDEO dicendum quod si quis consideret furti rationem, duas rationes peccati in eo inveniet. Primo quidem, propter contrarietatem ad iustitiam, quae reddit unicuique quod suum est. Et sic furtum iustitiae opponitur, inquantum furtum est acceptio rei alienae. Secundo, ratione doli seu fraudis, quam fur committit occulte et

OBJECTION 1: It would seem that theft is not always a sin. For no sin is commanded by God, since it is written (Sir 15:21): *He hath commanded no man to do wickedly.* Yet we find that God commanded theft, for it is written (Exod 12:35, 36): *And the children of Israel did as the Lord had commanded Moses . . . and they stripped the Egyptians.* Therefore theft is not always a sin.

OBJ. 2: Further, if a man finds a thing that is not his and takes it, he seems to commit a theft, for he takes another's property. Yet this seems lawful according to natural equity, as the jurists hold. Therefore it seems that theft is not always a sin.

OBJ. 3: Further, he that takes what is his own does not seem to sin, because he does not act against justice, since he does not destroy its equality. Yet a man commits a theft even if he secretly take his own property that is detained by or in the safe-keeping of another. Therefore it seems that theft is not always a sin.

ON THE CONTRARY, It is written (Exod 20:15): *Thou shalt not steal.*

I ANSWER THAT, If anyone consider what is meant by theft, he will find that it is sinful on two counts. First, because of its opposition to justice, which gives to each one what is his, so that for this reason theft is contrary to justice, through being a taking of what belongs to another. Second, because of the guile or fraud committed by the thief, by

quasi ex insidiis rem alienam usurpando. Unde manifestum est quod omne furtum est peccatum.

**AD PRIMUM** ergo dicendum quod accipere rem alienam vel occulte vel manifeste auctoritate iudicis hoc decernentis, non est furtum, quia iam fit sibi debitum per hoc quod sententialiter sibi est adiudicatum. Unde multo minus furtum fuit quod filii Israel tulerunt spolia Aegyptiorum de praecepto domini hoc decernentis pro afflictionibus quibus Aegyptii eos sine causa afflixerant. Et ideo signanter dicitur Sap. X, *iusti tulerunt spolia impiorum.*

**AD SECUNDUM** dicendum quod circa res inventas est distinguendum. Quaedam enim sunt quae nunquam fuerunt in bonis alicuius, sicut lapilli et gemmae quae inveniuntur in littore maris, et talia occupanti conceduntur. Et eadem ratio est de thesauris antiquo tempore sub terra occultatis, quorum non est aliquis possessor, nisi quod secundum leges civiles tenetur inventor medietatem dare domino agri, si in alieno agro invenerit; propter quod in parabola Evangelii dicitur, Matth. XIII, de inventore *thesauri absconditi in agro*, quod *emit agrum*, quasi ut haberet ius possidendi totum thesaurum. Quaedam vero res inventae fuerunt de propinquo in alicuius bonis. Et tunc, si quis eas accipiat non animo retinendi, sed animo restituendi domino, qui eas pro derelictis non habet, non committit furtum. Et similiter si pro derelictis habeantur, et hoc credat inventor, licet sibi retineat, non committit furtum. Alias autem committitur peccatum furti. Unde Augustinus dicit, in quadam homilia, et habetur XIV, qu. V, *si quid invenisti et non reddidisti, rapuisti.*

**AD TERTIUM** dicendum quod ille qui furtim accipit rem suam apud alium depositam, gravat depositarium, quia tenetur ad restituendum, vel ad ostendendum se esse innoxium. Unde manifestum est quod peccat, et tenetur ad relevandum gravamen depositarii. Qui vero furtim accipit rem suam apud alium iniuste detentam, peccat quidem, non quia gravet eum qui detinet, et ideo non tenetur ad restituendum aliquid vel ad recompensandum, sed peccat contra communem iustitiam, dum ipse sibi usurpat suae rei iudicium, iuris ordine praetermisso. Et ideo tenetur Deo satisfacere, et dare operam ut scandalum proximorum, si inde exortum fuerit, sedetur.

laying hands on another's property secretly and cunningly. Wherefore it is evident that every theft is a sin.

**REPLY OBJ. 1:** It is no theft for a man to take another's property either secretly or openly by order of a judge who has commanded him to do so, because it becomes his due by the very fact that it is adjudicated to him by the sentence of the court. Hence still less was it a theft for the Israelites to take away the spoils of the Egyptians at the command of the Lord, Who ordered this to be done on account of the ill-treatment accorded to them by the Egyptians without any cause: wherefore it is written significantly (Wis 10:19): *The just took the spoils of the wicked.*

**REPLY OBJ. 2:** With regard to treasure-trove a distinction must be made. For some there are that were never in anyone's possession, for instance precious stones and jewels, found on the seashore, and such the finder is allowed to keep. The same applies to treasure hidden underground long since and belonging to no man, except that according to civil law the finder is bound to give half to the owner of the land, if the treasure trove be in the land of another person. Hence in the parable of the Gospel (Matt 13:44) it is said of the finder of the treasure hidden in a field that he bought the field, as though he purposed thus to acquire the right of possessing the whole treasure. On the other Land the treasure-trove may be nearly in someone's possession: and then if anyone take it with the intention, not of keeping it but of returning it to the owner who does not look upon such things as unappropriated, he is not guilty of theft. In like manner if the thing found appears to be unappropriated, and if the finder believes it to be so, although he keep it, he does not commit a theft. In any other case the sin of theft is committed: wherefore Augustine says in a homily (*Serm.* clxxviii; *De Verb. Apost.*): *If thou hast found a thing and not returned it, thou hast stolen it* (*Dig.* xiv, 5, can. *Si quid invenisti*).

**REPLY OBJ. 3:** He who by stealth takes his own property which is deposited with another man burdens the depositary, who is bound either to restitution, or to prove himself innocent. Hence he is clearly guilty of sin, and is bound to ease the depositary of his burden. On the other hand he who, by stealth, takes his own property, if this be unjustly detained by another, he sins indeed; yet not because he burdens the retainer, and so he is not bound to restitution or compensation: but he sins against general justice by disregarding the order of justice and usurping judgment concerning his own property. Hence he must make satisfaction to God and endeavor to allay whatever scandal he may have given his neighbor by acting this way.

# Article 6

*Whether theft is a mortal sin?*

**AD SEXTUM SIC PROCEDITUR.** Videtur quod furtum non sit peccatum mortale. Dicitur enim Prov. VI, *non grandis est culpae cum quis furatus fuerit.* Sed omne peccatum mortale est grandis culpae. Ergo furtum non est peccatum mortale.

**PRAETEREA,** peccato mortali mortis poena debetur. Sed pro furto non infligitur in lege poena mortis, sed solum poena damni, secundum illud Exod. XXII, *si quis furatus fuerit bovem aut ovem, quinque boves pro uno bove restituet, et quatuor oves pro una ove.* Ergo furtum non est peccatum mortale.

**PRAETEREA,** furtum potest committi in parvis rebus, sicut et in magnis. Sed inconveniens videtur quod pro furto alicuius parvae rei, puta unius acus vel unius pennae, aliquis puniatur morte aeterna. Ergo furtum non est peccatum mortale.

**SED CONTRA** est quod nullus damnatur secundum divinum iudicium nisi pro peccato mortali. Condemnatur autem aliquis pro furto, secundum illud Zach. V, *haec est maledictio quae egreditur super faciem omnis terrae, quia omnis fur sicut ibi scriptum est condemnatur.* Ergo furtum est peccatum mortale.

**RESPONDEO** dicendum quod, sicut supra habitum est, peccatum mortale est quod contrariatur caritati, secundum quam est spiritualis animae vita. Caritas autem consistit quidem principaliter in dilectione Dei, secundario vero in dilectione proximi, ad quam pertinet ut proximo bonum velimus et operemur. Per furtum autem homo infert nocumentum proximo in suis rebus, et si passim homines sibi invicem furarentur, periret humana societas. Unde furtum, tanquam contrarium caritati, est peccatum mortale.

**AD PRIMUM** ergo dicendum quod furtum dicitur non esse grandis culpae duplici ratione. Primo quidem, propter necessitatem inducentem ad furandum, quae diminuit vel totaliter tollit culpam, ut infra patebit. Unde subdit, *furatur enim ut esurientem impleat animam.* Alio modo dicitur furtum non esse grandis culpae per comparationem ad reatum adulterii, quod punitur morte. Unde subditur de fure quod *deprehensus reddet septuplum, qui autem adulter est, perdet animam suam.*

**AD SECUNDUM** dicendum quod poenae praesentis vitae magis sunt medicinales quam retributivae, retributio enim reservatur divino iudicio, quod est *secundum veritatem* in peccantes. Et ideo secundum iudicium praesentis vitae non pro quolibet peccato mortali infligitur poena mortis, sed solum pro illis quae inferunt irreparabile nocumentum, vel etiam pro illis quae habent aliquam horribilem deformitatem. Et ideo pro

**OBJECTION 1:** It would seem that theft is not a mortal sin. For it is written (Prov 6:30): *The fault is not so great when a man hath stolen.* But every mortal sin is a great fault. Therefore theft is not a mortal sin.

**OBJ. 2:** Further, mortal sin deserves to be punished with death. But in the Law theft is punished not by death but by indemnity, according to Ex. 22:1, *If any man steal an ox or a sheep . . . he shall restore have oxen for one ox, and four sheep for one sheep.* Therefore theft is not a mortal sin.

**OBJ. 3:** Further, theft can be committed in small even as in great things. But it seems unreasonable for a man to be punished with eternal death for the theft of a small thing such as a needle or a quill. Therefore theft is not a mortal sin.

**ON THE CONTRARY,** No man is condemned by the Divine judgment save for a mortal sin. Yet a man is condemned for theft, according to Zech. 5:3, *This is the curse that goeth forth over the face of the earth; for every thief shall be judged as is there written.* Therefore theft is a mortal sin.

**I ANSWER THAT,** As stated above (Q. 59, A. 4; I-II, Q. 72, A. 5), a mortal sin is one that is contrary to charity as the spiritual life of the soul. Now charity consists principally in the love of God, and secondarily in the love of our neighbor, which is shown in our wishing and doing him well. But theft is a means of doing harm to our neighbor in his belongings; and if men were to rob one another habitually, human society would be undone. Therefore theft, as being opposed to charity, is a mortal sin.

**REPLY OBJ. 1:** The statement that theft is not a great fault is in view of two cases. First, when a person is led to thieve through necessity. This necessity diminishes or entirely removes sin, as we shall show further on (A. 7). Hence the text continues: *For he stealeth to fill his hungry soul.* Second, theft is stated not to be a great fault in comparison with the guilt of adultery, which is punished with death. Hence the text goes on to say of the thief that *if he be taken, he shall restore sevenfold . . . but he that is an adulterer . . . shall destroy his own soul.*

**REPLY OBJ. 2:** The punishments of this life are medicinal rather than retributive. For retribution is reserved to the Divine judgment which is pronounced against sinners *according to truth* (Rom 2:2). Wherefore, according to the judgment of the present life the death punishment is inflicted, not for every mortal sin, but only for such as inflict an irreparable harm, or again for such as contain some horrible deformity. Hence according to the present

furto, quod reparabile damnum infert, non infligitur secundum praesens iudicium poena mortis, nisi furtum aggravetur per aliquam gravem circumstantiam, sicut patet de sacrilegio, quod est furtum rei sacrae, et de peculatu, quod est furtum rei communis, ut patet per Augustinum, super Ioan.; et de plagio, quod est furtum hominis, pro quo quis morte punitur, ut patet Exod. XXI.

**Ad tertium** dicendum quod illud quod modicum est ratio apprehendit quasi nihil. Et ideo in his quae minima sunt homo non reputat sibi nocumentum inferri, et ille qui accipit potest praesumere hoc non esse contra voluntatem eius cuius est res. Et pro tanto si quis furtive huiusmodi res minimas accipiat, potest excusari a peccato mortali. Si tamen habeat animum furandi et inferendi nocumentum proximo, etiam in talibus minimis potest esse peccatum mortale, sicut et in solo cogitatu per consensum.

judgment the pain of death is not inflicted for theft which does not inflict an irreparable harm, except when it is aggravated by some grave circumstance, as in the case of sacrilege which is the theft of a sacred thing, of peculation, which is theft of common property, as Augustine states (*Tract. 1, Super Joan.*), and of kidnaping which is stealing a man, for which the pain of death is inflicted (Exod 21:16).

**Reply Obj. 3**: Reason accounts as nothing that which is little: so that a man does not consider himself injured in very little matters: and the person who takes such things can presume that this is not against the will of the owner. And if a person take such like very little things, he may be proportionately excused from mortal sin. Yet if his intention is to rob and injure his neighbor, there may be a mortal sin even in these very little things, even as there may be through consent in a mere thought.

# Article 7

*Whether it is lawful to steal through stress of need?*

**Ad septimum sic proceditur.** Videtur quod non liceat alicui furari propter necessitatem. Non enim imponitur poenitentia nisi peccanti. Sed extra, de furtis, dicitur, *si quis per necessitatem famis aut nuditatis furatus fuerit cibaria, vestem vel pecus, poeniteat hebdomadas tres.* Ergo non licet furari propter necessitatem.

**Praeterea,** philosophus dicit, in II Ethic., quod *quaedam confestim nominata convoluta sunt cum malitia,* inter quae ponit furtum. Sed illud quod est secundum se malum non potest propter aliquem bonum finem bonum fieri. Ergo non potest aliquis licite furari ut necessitati suae subveniat.

**Praeterea,** homo debet diligere proximum sicut seipsum. Sed non licet furari ad hoc quod aliquis per eleemosynam proximo subveniat; ut Augustinus dicit, in libro contra mendacium. Ergo etiam non licet furari ad subveniendum propriae necessitati.

**Sed contra** est quod in necessitate sunt omnia communia. Et ita non videtur esse peccatum si aliquis rem alterius accipiat, propter necessitatem sibi factam communem.

**Respondeo** dicendum quod ea quae sunt iuris humani non possunt derogare iuri naturali vel iuri divino. Secundum autem naturalem ordinem ex divina providentia institutum, res inferiores sunt ordinatae ad hoc quod ex his subveniatur hominum necessitati. Et ideo per rerum divisionem et appropriationem, de iure humano procedentem, non impeditur quin hominis necessitati sit subveniendum ex huiusmodi rebus. Et ideo res quas aliqui superabundanter habent, ex naturali

**Objection 1**: It would seem unlawful to steal through stress of need. For penance is not imposed except on one who has sinned. Now it is stated (*Extra, De furtis*, Cap. *Si quis*): *If anyone, through stress of hunger or nakedness, steal food, clothing or beast, he shall do penance for three weeks.* Therefore it is not lawful to steal through stress of need.

**Obj. 2**: Further, the Philosopher says (*Ethic.* ii, 6) that *there are some actions whose very name implies wickedness,* and among these he reckons theft. Now that which is wicked in itself may not be done for a good end. Therefore a man cannot lawfully steal in order to remedy a need.

**Obj. 3**: Further, a man should love his neighbor as himself. Now, according to Augustine (*Contra Mendac.* vii), it is unlawful to steal in order to succor one's neighbor by giving him an alms. Therefore neither is it lawful to steal in order to remedy one's own needs.

**On the contrary,** In cases of need all things are common property, so that there would seem to be no sin in taking another's property, for need has made it common.

**I answer that,** Things which are of human right cannot derogate from natural right or Divine right. Now according to the natural order established by Divine Providence, inferior things are ordained for the purpose of succoring man's needs by their means. Wherefore the division and appropriation of things which are based on human law, do not preclude the fact that man's needs have to be remedied by means of these very things. Hence whatever certain people have in superabundance is due, by natural

iure debentur pauperum sustentationi. Unde Ambrosius dicit, et habetur in decretis, dist. XLVII, *esurientium panis est quem tu detines; nudorum indumentum est quod tu recludis; miserorum redemptio et absolutio est pecunia quam tu in terram defodis.*

Sed quia multi sunt necessitatem patientes, et non potest ex eadem re omnibus subveniri, committitur arbitrio uniuscuiusque dispensatio propriarum rerum, ut ex eis subveniat necessitatem patientibus. Si tamen adeo sit urgens et evidens necessitas ut manifestum sit instanti necessitati de rebus occurrentibus esse subveniendum, puta cum imminet personae periculum et aliter subveniri non potest; tunc licite potest aliquis ex rebus alienis suae necessitati subvenire, sive manifeste sive occulte sublatis. Nec hoc proprie habet rationem furti vel rapinae.

**AD PRIMUM** ergo dicendum quod decretalis illa loquitur in casu in quo non est urgens necessitas.

**AD SECUNDUM** dicendum quod uti re aliena occulte accepta in casu necessitatis extremae non habet rationem furti, proprie loquendo. Quia per talem necessitatem efficitur suum illud quod quis accipit ad sustentandam propriam vitam.

**AD TERTIUM** dicendum quod in casu similis necessitatis etiam potest aliquis occulte rem alienam accipere ut subveniat proximo sic indigenti.

law, to the purpose of succoring the poor. For this reason Ambrose says, and his words are embodied in the Decretals (Dist. xlvii, can. Sicut ii): *It is the hungry man's bread that you withhold, the naked man's cloak that you store away, the money that you bury in the earth is the price of the poor man's ransom and freedom.*

Since, however, there are many who are in need, while it is impossible for all to be succored by means of the same thing, each one is entrusted with the stewardship of his own things, so that out of them he may come to the aid of those who are in need. Nevertheless, if the need be so manifest and urgent, that it is evident that the present need must be remedied by whatever means be at hand (for instance when a person is in some imminent danger, and there is no other possible remedy), then it is lawful for a man to succor his own need by means of another's property, by taking it either openly or secretly: nor is this properly speaking theft or robbery.

**REPLY OBJ. 1**: This decretal considers cases where there is no urgent need.

**REPLY OBJ. 2**: It is not theft, properly speaking, to take secretly and use another's property in a case of extreme need: because that which he takes for the support of his life becomes his own property by reason of that need.

**REPLY OBJ. 3**: In a case of a like need a man may also take secretly another's property in order to succor his neighbor in need.

# Article 8

*Whether robbery may be committed without sin?*

**AD OCTAVUM SIC PROCEDITUR.** Videtur quod rapina possit fieri sine peccato. Praeda enim per violentiam accipitur; quod videtur ad rationem rapinae pertinere, secundum praedicta. Sed praedam accipere ab hostibus licitum est, dicit enim Ambrosius, in libro de patriarchis, *cum praeda fuerit in potestate victoris, decet militarem disciplinam ut regi serventur omnia,* scilicet ad distribuendum. Ergo rapina in aliquo casu est licita.

**PRAETEREA,** licitum est auferre ab aliquo id quod non est eius. Sed res quas infideles habent non sunt eorum, dicit enim Augustinus, in epistola ad Vinc. Donatist., *res falso appellatis vestras, quas nec iuste possidetis, et secundum leges terrenorum regum amittere iussi estis.* Ergo videtur quod ab infidelibus aliquis licite rapere posset.

**PRAETEREA,** terrarum principes multa a suis subditis violenter extorquent; quod videtur ad rationem rapinae pertinere. Grave autem videtur dicere quod in

**OBJECTION 1**: It would seem that robbery may be committed without sin. For spoils are taken by violence, and this seems to belong to the essence of robbery, according to what has been said (A. 4). Now it is lawful to take spoils from the enemy; for Ambrose says (*De Patriarch.* 4 ): *When the conqueror has taken possession of the spoils, military discipline demands that all should be reserved for the sovereign,* in order, to wit, that he may distribute them. Therefore in certain cases robbery is lawful.

**OBJ. 2**: Further, it is lawful to take from a man what is not his. Now the things which unbelievers have are not theirs, for Augustine says (*Ep. ad Vincent. Donat.* xciii.): *You falsely call things your own, for you do not possess them justly, and according to the laws of earthly kings you are commanded to forfeit them.* Therefore it seems that one may lawfully rob unbelievers.

**OBJ. 3**: Further, earthly princes violently extort many things from their subjects: and this seems to savor of robbery. Now it would seem a grievous matter to say that they

hoc peccent, quia sic fere omnes principes damnarentur. Ergo rapina in aliquo casu est licita.

**Sed contra** est quod de quolibet licite accepto potest fieri Deo sacrificium vel oblatio. Non autem potest fieri de rapina, secundum illud Isaiae LXI, *ego dominus diligens iudicium, et odio habens rapinam in holocaustum*. Ergo per rapinam aliquid accipere non est licitum.

**Respondeo** dicendum quod rapina quandam violentiam et coactionem importat per quam, contra iustitiam, alicui aufertur quod suum est. In societate autem hominum nullus habet coactionem nisi per publicam potestatem. Et ideo quicumque per violentiam aliquid alteri aufert, si sit privata persona non utens publica potestate, illicite agit et rapinam committit, sicut patet in latronibus. Principibus vero publica potestas committitur ad hoc quod sint iustitiae custodes. Et ideo non licet eis violentia et coactione uti nisi secundum iustitiae tenorem, et hoc vel contra hostes pugnando, vel contra cives malefactores puniendo. Et quod per talem violentiam aufertur non habet rationem rapinae, cum non sit contra iustitiam. Si vero contra iustitiam aliqui per publicam potestatem violenter abstulerint res aliorum, illicite agunt et rapinam committunt, et ad restitutionem tenentur.

**Ad primum** ergo dicendum quod circa praedam distinguendum est. Quia si illi qui depraedantur hostes habeant bellum iustum, ea quae per violentiam in bello acquirunt eorum efficiuntur. Et hoc non habet rationem rapinae, unde nec ad restitutionem tenentur. Quamvis possint in acceptione praedae iustum bellum habentes peccare per cupiditatem ex prava intentione, si scilicet non propter iustitiam, sed propter praedam principaliter pugnent, dicit enim Augustinus, in libro de Verb. Dom., quod *propter praedam militare peccatum est*. Si vero illi qui praedam accipiunt habeant bellum iniustum, rapinam committunt, et ad restitutionem tenentur.

**Ad secundum** dicendum quod intantum aliqui infideles iniuste res suas possident, inquantum eas *secundum leges terrenorum principum amittere iussi sunt*. Et ideo ab eis possunt per violentiam subtrahi, non privata auctoritate, sed publica.

**Ad tertium** dicendum quod si principes a subditis exigant quod eis secundum iustitiam debetur propter bonum commune conservandum, etiam si violentia adhibeatur, non est rapina. Si vero aliquid principes indebite extorqueant per violentiam, rapina est, sicut et latrocinium. Unde dicit Augustinus, in IV de Civ. Dei, *remota iustitia, quid sunt regna nisi magna latrocinia? Quia et latrocinia quid sunt nisi parva regna?* Et Ezech. XXII dicitur, *principes eius in medio eius quasi lupi rapientes praedam*. Unde et ad restitutionem tenentur, sicut et latrones. Et tanto gravius peccant quam latrones,

sin in acting thus, for in that case nearly every prince would be damned. Therefore in some cases robbery is lawful.

**On the contrary,** Whatever is taken lawfully may be offered to God in sacrifice and oblation. Now this cannot be done with the proceeds of robbery, according to Isa. 61:8, *I am the Lord that love judgment, and hate robbery in a holocaust.* Therefore it is not lawful to take anything by robbery.

**I answer that,** Robbery implies a certain violence and coercion employed in taking unjustly from a man that which is his. Now in human society no man can exercise coercion except through public authority: and, consequently, if a private individual not having public authority takes another's property by violence, he acts unlawfully and commits a robbery, as burglars do. As regards princes, the public power is entrusted to them that they may be the guardians of justice: hence it is unlawful for them to use violence or coercion, save within the bounds of justice—either by fighting against the enemy, or against the citizens, by punishing evil-doers: and whatever is taken by violence of this kind is not the spoils of robbery, since it is not contrary to justice. On the other hand to take other people's property violently and against justice, in the exercise of public authority, is to act unlawfully and to be guilty of robbery; and whoever does so is bound to restitution.

**Reply Obj. 1:** A distinction must be made in the matter of spoils. For if they who take spoils from the enemy, are waging a just war, such things as they seize in the war become their own property. This is no robbery, so that they are not bound to restitution. Nevertheless even they who are engaged in a just war may sin in taking spoils through cupidity arising from an evil intention, if, to wit, they fight chiefly not for justice but for spoil. For Augustine says (*De Verb. Dom.* xix; *Serm. lxxxii*) that *it is a sin to fight for booty.* If, however, those who take the spoil, are waging an unjust war, they are guilty of robbery, and are bound to restitution.

**Reply Obj. 2:** Unbelievers possess their goods unjustly insofar as they are ordered by *the laws of earthly princes to forfeit those goods.* Hence these may be taken violently from them, not by private but by public authority.

**Reply Obj. 3:** It is no robbery if princes exact from their subjects that which is due to them for the safeguarding of the common good, even if they use violence in so doing: but if they extort something unduly by means of violence, it is robbery even as burglary is. Hence Augustine says (*De Civ. Dei* iv, 4): *If justice be disregarded, what is a king but a mighty robber? since what is a robber but a little king?* And it is written (Ezek 22:27): *Her princes in the midst of her, are like wolves ravening the prey.* Wherefore they are bound to restitution, just as robbers are, and by so much do they sin more grievously than robbers, as their actions are

quanto periculosius et communius contra publicam iustitiam agunt, cuius custodes sunt positi.

fraught with greater and more universal danger to public justice whose wardens they are.

# Article 9

*Whether theft is a more grievous sin than robbery?*

**AD NONUM SIC PROCEDITUR.** Videtur quod furtum sit gravius peccatum quam rapina. Furtum enim, super acceptionem rei alienae, habet adiunctam fraudem et dolum, quod non est in rapina. Sed fraus et dolus de se habent rationem peccati, ut supra habitum est. Ergo furtum videtur esse gravius peccatum quam rapina.

**PRAETEREA,** verecundia est timor de turpi actu, ut dicitur in IV Ethic. Sed magis verecundantur homines de furto quam de rapina. Ergo furtum est turpius quam rapina.

**PRAETEREA,** quanto aliquod peccatum pluribus nocet, tanto gravius esse videtur. Sed per furtum potest nocumentum inferri et magnis et parvis, per rapinam autem solum impotentibus, quibus potest violentia inferri. Ergo gravius videtur esse peccatum furti quam rapinae.

**SED CONTRA** est quod secundum leges gravius punitur rapina quam furtum.

**RESPONDEO** dicendum quod rapina et furtum habent rationem peccati, sicut supra dictum est, propter involuntarium quod est ex parte eius cui aliquid aufertur; ita tamen quod in furto est involuntarium per ignorantiam, in rapina autem involuntarium per violentiam. Magis est autem aliquid involuntarium per violentiam quam per ignorantiam, quia violentia directius opponitur voluntati quam ignorantia. Et ideo rapina est gravius peccatum quam furtum. Est et alia ratio. Quia per rapinam non solum infertur alicui damnum in rebus, sed etiam vergit in quandam personae ignominiam sive iniuriam. Et hoc praeponderat fraudi vel dolo, quae pertinent ad furtum.

**UNDE PATET** responsio ad primum.

**AD SECUNDUM** dicendum quod homines sensibilibus inhaerentes magis gloriantur de virtute exteriori, quae manifestatur in rapina, quam de virtute interiori, quae tollitur per peccatum. Et ideo minus verecundantur de rapina quam de furto.

**AD TERTIUM** dicendum quod licet pluribus possit noceri per furtum quam per rapinam, tamen graviora nocumenta possunt inferri per rapinam quam per furtum. Unde ex hoc etiam rapina est detestabilior.

**OBJECTION 1**: It would seem that theft is a more grievous sin than robbery. For theft adds fraud and guile to the taking of another's property: and these things are not found in robbery. Now fraud and guile are sinful in themselves, as stated above (Q. 55, AA. 4, 5). Therefore theft is a more grievous sin than robbery.

**OBJ. 2**: Further, shame is fear about a wicked deed, as stated in *Ethic.* iv, 9. Now men are more ashamed of theft than of robbery. Therefore theft is more wicked than robbery.

**OBJ. 3**: Further, the more persons a sin injures the more grievous it would seem to be. Now the great and the lowly may be injured by theft: whereas only the weak can be injured by robbery, since it is possible to use violence towards them. Therefore the sin of theft seems to be more grievous than the sin of robbery.

**ON THE CONTRARY**, According to the laws robbery is more severely punished than theft.

**I ANSWER THAT**, Robbery and theft are sinful, as stated above (AA. 4, 6), on account of the involuntariness on the part of the person from whom something is taken: yet so that in theft the involuntariness is due to ignorance, whereas in robbery it is due to violence. Now a thing is more involuntary through violence than through ignorance, because violence is more directly opposed to the will than ignorance. Therefore robbery is a more grievous sin than theft. There is also another reason, since robbery not only inflicts a loss on a person in his things, but also conduces to the ignominy and injury of his person, and this is of graver import than fraud or guile which belong to theft.

**HENCE** the Reply to the First Objection is evident.

**REPLY OBJ. 2**: Men who adhere to sensible things think more of external strength which is evidenced in robbery, than of internal virtue which is forfeit through sin: wherefore they are less ashamed of robbery than of theft.

**REPLY OBJ. 3**: Although more persons may be injured by theft than by robbery, yet more grievous injuries may be inflicted by robbery than by theft: for which reason also robbery is more odious.

# QUESTION 67

## THE INJUSTICE OF A JUDGE, IN JUDGING

Deinde considerandum est de vitiis oppositis commutativae iustitiae quae consistunt in verbis in quibus laeditur proximus. Et primo, de his quae pertinent ad iudicium; secundo, de nocumentis verborum quae fiunt extra iudicium.

Circa primum quinque consideranda occurrunt, primo quidem, de iniustitia iudicis in iudicando; secundo, de iniustitia accusatoris in accusando; tertio, de iniustitia ex parte rei in sua defensione; quarto, de iniustitia testis in testificando; quinto, de iniustitia advocati in patrocinando.

Circa primum quaeruntur quatuor. Primo, utrum aliquis possit iuste iudicare eum qui non est sibi subditus.

    Secundo, utrum liceat iudicium ferre contra veritatem quam novit, propter ea quae sibi proponuntur.

    Tertio, utrum iudex possit aliquem iuste condemnare non accusatum.

    Quarto, utrum licite possit poenam relaxare.

We must now consider those vices opposed to commutative justice, that consist in words injurious to our neighbors. We shall consider (1) those which are connected with judicial proceedings, and (2) injurious words uttered extra-judicially.

Under the first head five points occur for our consideration: (1) The injustice of a judge in judging; (2) The injustice of the prosecutor in accusing; (3) The injustice of the defendant in defending himself; (4) The injustice of the witnesses in giving evidence; (5) The injustice of the advocate in defending.

Under the first head there are four points of inquiry: (1) Whether a man can justly judge one who is not his subject?

    (2) Whether it is lawful for a judge, on account of the evidence, to deliver judgment in opposition to the truth which is known to him?

    (3) Whether a judge can justly sentence a man who is not accused?

    (4) Whether he can justly remit the punishment?

# Article 1

*Whether a man can justly judge one who is not subject to his jurisdiction?*

**AD PRIMUM SIC PROCEDITUR.** Videtur quod aliquis possit iuste iudicare eum qui non est sibi subditus. Dicitur enim Dan. XIII quod Daniel seniores de falso testimonio convictos suo iudicio condemnavit. Sed illi seniores non erant subditi Danieli, quinimmo ipsi erant iudices populi. Ergo aliquis potest licite iudicare sibi non subditum.

**PRAETEREA,** Christus non erat alicuius hominis subditus, quinimmo ipse erat *rex regum et dominus dominantium.* Sed ipse exhibuit se iudicio hominis. Ergo videtur quod aliquis licite possit iudicare aliquem qui non est subditus eius.

**PRAETEREA,** secundum iura quilibet sortitur forum secundum rationem delicti. Sed quandoque ille qui delinquit non est subditus eius ad quem pertinet forum illius loci, puta cum est alterius dioecesis, vel cum est exemptus. Ergo videtur quod aliquis possit iudicare eum qui non est sibi subditus.

**SED CONTRA** est quod Gregorius dicit, super illud Deut. XXIII, *si intraveris segetem et cetera. Falcem iudicii*

**OBJECTION 1:** It would seem that a man can justly judge one who is not subject to his jurisdiction. For it is stated (Dan 13) that Daniel sentenced the ancients who were convicted of bearing false witness. But these ancients were not subject to Daniel; indeed they were judges of the people. Therefore a man may lawfully judge one that is not subject to his jurisdiction.

**OBJ. 2:** Further, Christ was no man's subject, indeed He was *King of kings and Lord of lords* (Rev 19:16). Yet He submitted to the judgment of a man. Therefore it seems that a man may lawfully judge one that is not subject to his jurisdiction.

**OBJ. 3:** Further, according to the law a man is tried in this or that court according to his kind of offense. Now sometimes the defendant is not the subject of the man whose business it is to judge in that particular place, for instance when the defendant belongs to another diocese or is exempt. Therefore it seems that a man may judge one that is not his subject.

**ON THE CONTRARY,** Gregory in commenting on Deut. 23:25, *If thou go into thy friend's corn,* etc. says: *Thou*

*mittere non potest in eam rem quae alteri videtur esse commissa.*

**RESPONDEO** dicendum quod sententia iudicis est quasi quaedam particularis lex in aliquo particulari facto. Et ideo sicut lex generalis debet habere vim coactivam, ut patet per philosophum, in X Ethic.; ita etiam et sententia iudicis debet habere vim coactivam, per quam constringatur utraque pars ad servandam sententiam iudicis, alioquin iudicium non esset efficax. Potestatem autem coactivam non habet licite in rebus humanis nisi ille qui fungitur publica potestate. Et qui ea funguntur superiores reputantur respectu eorum in quos, sicut in subditos, potestatem accipiunt, sive habeant ordinarie, sive per commissionem. Et ideo manifestum est quod nullus potest iudicare aliquem nisi sit aliquo modo subditus eius, vel per commissionem vel per potestatem ordinariam.

**AD PRIMUM** ergo dicendum quod Daniel accepit potestatem ad iudicandum illos seniores quasi commissam ex instinctu divino. Quod significatur per hoc quod ibi dicitur, quod *suscitavit dominus spiritum pueri iunioris.*

**AD SECUNDUM** dicendum quod in rebus humanis aliqui propria sponte possunt se subiicere aliorum iudicio, quamvis non sint eis superiores, sicut patet in his qui compromittunt in aliquos arbitros. Et inde est quod necesse est arbitrium poena vallari, quia arbitri, qui non sunt superiores, non habent de se plenam potestatem coercendi. Sic igitur et Christus propria sponte humano iudicio se subdidit, sicut etiam et Leo Papa iudicio imperatoris se subdidit.

**AD TERTIUM** dicendum quod episcopus in cuius dioecesi aliquis delinquit, efficitur superior eius ratione delicti, etiam si sit exemptus, nisi forte delinquat in re aliqua exempta, puta in administratione bonorum alicuius monasterii exempti. Sed si aliquis exemptus committat furtum vel homicidium vel aliquid huiusmodi, potest per ordinarium iuste condemnari.

*mayest not put the sickle of judgment to the corn that is entrusted to another.*

**I ANSWER THAT,** A judge's sentence is like a particular law regarding some particular fact. Wherefore just as a general law should have coercive power, as the Philosopher states (*Ethic.* x, 9), so too the sentence of a judge should have coercive power, whereby either party is compelled to comply with the judge's sentence; else the judgment would be of no effect. Now coercive power is not exercised in human affairs, save by those who hold public authority: and those who have this authority are accounted the superiors of those over whom they preside whether by ordinary or by delegated authority. Hence it is evident that no man can judge others than his subjects and this in virtue either of delegated or of ordinary authority.

**REPLY OBJ. 1:** In judging those ancients Daniel exercised an authority delegated to him by Divine instinct. This is indicated where it is said (Dan 13:45) that *the Lord raised up the . . . spirit of a young boy.*

**REPLY OBJ. 2:** In human affairs a man may submit of his own accord to the judgment of others although these be not his superiors, an example of which is when parties agree to a settlement by arbitrators. Wherefore it is necessary that the arbitrator should be upheld by a penalty, since the arbitrators through not exercising authority in the case, have not of themselves full power of coercion. Accordingly in this way did Christ of his own accord submit to human judgment: and thus too did Pope Leo submit to the judgment of the emperor.

**REPLY OBJ. 3:** The bishop of the defendant's diocese becomes the latter's superior as regards the fault committed, even though he be exempt: unless perchance the defendant offend in a matter exempt from the bishop's authority, for instance in administering the property of an exempt monastery. But if an exempt person commits a theft, or a murder or the like, he may be justly condemned by the ordinary.

# Article 2

*Whether it is lawful for a judge to pronounce judgment against the truth that he knows, on account of evidence to the contrary?*

**AD SECUNDUM SIC PROCEDITUR.** Videtur quod iudici non liceat iudicare contra veritatem quam novit, propter ea quae in contrarium proponuntur. Dicitur enim Deut. XVII, *venies ad sacerdotes levitici generis, et ad iudicem qui fuerit in illo tempore, quaeresque ab eis, qui indicabunt tibi iudicii veritatem.* Sed quandoque aliqua proponuntur contra veritatem, sicut cum aliquid

**OBJECTION 1:** It would seem unlawful for a judge to pronounce judgment against the truth that he knows, on account of evidence to the contrary. For it is written (Deut 17:9): *Thou shalt come to the priests of the Levitical race, and to the judge that shall be at that time; and thou shalt ask of them, and they shall show thee the truth of the judgment.* Now sometimes certain things are alleged

per falsos testes probatur. Ergo non licet iudici iudicare secundum ea quae proponuntur et probantur, contra veritatem quam ipse novit.

**PRAETEREA**, homo in iudicando debet divino iudicio conformari, quia *Dei iudicium est*, ut dicitur Deut. I. Sed *iudicium Dei est secundum veritatem*, ut dicitur Rom. II, et Isaiae XI praedicitur de Christo, *non secundum visionem oculorum iudicabit, neque secundum auditum aurium arguet, sed iudicabit in iustitia pauperes, et arguet in aequitate pro mansuetis terrae*. Ergo iudex non debet, secundum ea quae coram ipso probantur, sententiam ferre contra ea quae ipse novit.

**PRAETEREA**, idcirco in iudicio probationes requiruntur ut fides fiat iudici de rei veritate, unde in his quae sunt notoria non requiritur iudicialis ordo, secundum illud I ad Tim. V, *quorundam hominum peccata manifesta sunt, praecedentia ad iudicium*. Si ergo iudex per se cognoscat veritatem, non debet attendere ad ea quae probantur, sed sententiam ferre secundum veritatem quam novit.

**PRAETEREA**, nomen conscientiae importat applicationem scientiae ad aliquid agibile, ut in primo habitum est. Sed facere contra conscientiam est peccatum. Ergo iudex peccat si sententiam ferat, secundum allegata, contra conscientiam veritatis quam habet.

**SED CONTRA** est quod Augustinus dicit, super Psalt., *bonus iudex nihil ex arbitrio suo facit, sed secundum leges et iura pronuntiat*. Sed hoc est iudicare secundum ea quae in iudicio proponuntur et probantur. Ergo iudex debet secundum huiusmodi iudicare, et non secundum proprium arbitrium.

**RESPONDEO** dicendum quod, sicut dictum est, iudicare pertinet ad iudicem secundum quod fungitur publica potestate. Et ideo informari debet in iudicando non secundum id quod ipse novit tanquam privata persona, sed secundum id quod sibi innotescit tanquam personae publicae. Hoc autem innotescit sibi et in communi, et in particulari. In communi quidem, per leges publicas vel divinas vel humanas, contra quas nullas probationes admittere debet. In particulari autem negotio aliquo, per instrumenta et testes et alia huiusmodi legitima documenta, quae debet sequi in iudicando magis quam id quod ipse novit tanquam privata persona. Ex quo tamen ad hoc adiuvari potest ut districtius discutiat probationes inductas, ut possit earum defectum investigare. Quod si eas non possit de

against the truth, as when something is proved by means of false witnesses. Therefore it is unlawful for a judge to pronounce judgment according to what is alleged and proved in opposition to the truth which he knows.

**OBJ. 2**: Further, in pronouncing judgment a man should conform to the Divine judgment, since *it is the judgment of God* (Deut 1:17). Now *the judgment of God is according to the truth* (Rom 2:2), and it was foretold of Christ (Isa 11:3, 4): *He shall not judge according to the sight of the eyes, nor reprove according to the hearing of the ears. But He shall judge the poor with justice, and shall reprove with equity for the meek of the earth*. Therefore the judge ought not to pronounce judgment according to the evidence before him if it be contrary to what he knows himself.

**OBJ. 3**: Further, the reason why evidence is required in a court of law, is that the judge may have a faithful record of the truth of the matter, wherefore in matters of common knowledge there is no need of judicial procedure, according to 1 Tim. 5:24, *Some men's sins are manifest, going before to judgment*. Consequently, if the judge by his personal knowledge is aware of the truth, he should pay no heed to the evidence, but should pronounce sentence according to the truth which he knows.

**OBJ. 4**: Further, the word *conscience* denotes application of knowledge to a matter of action as stated in the First Part (Q. 79, A. 13). Now it is a sin to act contrary to one's knowledge. Therefore a judge sins if he pronounces sentence according to the evidence but against his conscience of the truth.

**ON THE CONTRARY**, Augustine says in his commentary on the Psalter: *A good judge does nothing according to his private opinion but pronounces sentence according to the law and the right*. Now this is to pronounce judgment according to what is alleged and proved in court. Therefore a judge ought to pronounce judgment in accordance with these things, and not according to his private opinion.

**I ANSWER THAT**, As stated above (A. 1; Q. 60, AA. 2, 6) it is the duty of a judge to pronounce judgment inasmuch as he exercises public authority, wherefore his judgment should be based on information acquired by him, not from his knowledge as a private individual, but from what he knows as a public person. Now the latter knowledge comes to him both in general and in particular—in general through the public laws, whether Divine or human, and he should admit no evidence that conflicts therewith—in some particular matter, through documents and witnesses, and other legal means of information, which in pronouncing his sentence, he ought to follow rather than the information he has acquired as a private individual. And yet this same information may be of use to him, so that he can more rigorously sift the evidence brought forward,

iure repellere, debet, sicut dictum est, eas in iudicando sequi.

**AD PRIMUM** ergo dicendum quod ideo praemittitur in verbis illis de quaestione iudicibus facienda, ut intelligatur quod iudices debent veritatem iudicare secundum ea quae fuerunt sibi proposita.

**AD SECUNDUM** dicendum quod Deo competit iudicare secundum propriam potestatem. Et ideo in iudicando informatur secundum veritatem quam ipse cognoscit, non secundum hoc quod ab aliis accipit. Et eadem ratio est de Christo, qui est verus Deus et homo. Alii autem iudices non iudicant secundum propriam potestatem. Et ideo non est similis ratio.

**AD TERTIUM** dicendum quod apostolus loquitur in casu quando aliquid non solum est manifestum iudici, sed sibi et aliis, ita quod reus nullo modo crimen infitiari potest, sed statim ex ipsa evidentia facti convincitur. Si autem sit manifestum iudici et non aliis, vel aliis et non iudici, tunc est necessaria iudicii discussio.

**AD QUARTUM** dicendum quod homo in his quae ad propriam personam pertinent, debet informare conscientiam suam ex propria scientia. Sed in his quae pertinent ad publicam potestatem, debet informare conscientiam suam secundum ea quae in publico iudicio sciri possunt, et cetera.

and discover its weak points. If, however, he is unable to reject that evidence juridically, he must, as stated above, follow it in pronouncing sentence.

**REPLY OBJ. 1:** The reason why, in the passage quoted, it is stated that the judges should first of all be asked their reasons, is to make it clear that the judges ought to judge the truth in accordance with the evidence.

**REPLY OBJ. 2:** To judge belongs to God in virtue of His own power: wherefore His judgment is based on the truth which He Himself knows, and not on knowledge imparted by others: the same is to be said of Christ, Who is true God and true man: whereas other judges do not judge in virtue of their own power, so that there is no comparison.

**REPLY OBJ. 3:** The Apostle refers to the case where something is well known not to the judge alone, but both to him and to others, so that the guilty party can by no means deny his guilt (as in the case of notorious criminals), and is convicted at once from the evidence of the fact. If, on the other hand, it be well known to the judge, but not to others, or to others, but not to the judge, then it is necessary for the judge to sift the evidence.

**REPLY OBJ. 4:** In matters touching his own person, a man must form his conscience from his own knowledge, but in matters concerning the public authority, he must form his conscience in accordance with the knowledge attainable in the public judicial procedure.

# Article 3

*Whether a judge may pass sentence on a man who is not accused?*

**AD TERTIUM SIC PROCEDITUR.** Videtur quod iudex possit aliquem iudicare etiam si non sit alius accusator. Humana enim iustitia derivatur a iustitia divina. Sed Deus peccatores iudicat etiam si nullus sit accusator. Ergo videtur quod homo possit in iudicio alium condemnare etiam si non adsit accusator.

**PRAETEREA,** accusator requiritur in iudicio ad hoc quod deferat crimen ad iudicem. Sed quandoque potest crimen ad iudicem devenire alio modo quam per accusationem, sicut per denuntiationem vel per infamiam, vel etiam si ipse iudex videat. Ergo iudex potest aliquem condemnare absque accusatore.

**PRAETEREA,** facta sanctorum in Scripturis narrantur quasi quaedam exemplaria humanae vitae. Sed Daniel simul fuit accusator et iudex contra iniquos senes, ut patet Dan. XIII. Ergo non est contra iustitiam si aliquis aliquem damnet tanquam iudex, et ipsemet sit accusator.

**OBJECTION 1:** It would seem that a judge may pass sentence on a man who is not accused. For human justice is derived from Divine justice. Now God judges the sinner even though there be no accuser. Therefore it seems that a man may pass sentence of condemnation on a man even though there be no accuser.

**OBJ. 2:** Further, an accuser is required in judicial procedure in order that he may relate the crime to the judge. Now sometimes the crime may come to the judge's knowledge otherwise than by accusation; for instance, by denunciation, or by evil report, or through the judge himself being an eye-witness. Therefore a judge may condemn a man without there being an accuser.

**OBJ. 3:** Further, the deeds of holy persons are related in Holy Writ, as models of human conduct. Now Daniel was at the same time the accuser and the judge of the wicked ancients (Dan 13). Therefore it is not contrary to justice for a man to condemn anyone as judge while being at the same time his accuser.

**SED CONTRA** est quod, I ad Cor. V, Ambrosius, exponens sententiam apostoli de fornicatore, dicit quod *iudicis non est sine accusatore damnare, quia dominus Iudam, cum fuisset fur, quia non est accusatus, minime abiecit.*

**RESPONDEO** dicendum quod iudex est interpres iustitiae, unde sicut philosophus dicit, in V Ethic., *ad iudicem confugiunt sicut ad quandam iustitiam animatam.* Iustitia autem, sicut supra habitum est, non est ad seipsum, sed ad alterum. Et ideo oportet quod iudex inter aliquos duos diiudicet, quod quidem fit cum unus est actor et alius est reus. Et ideo in criminibus non potest aliquem iudicio condemnare iudex nisi habeat accusatorem, secundum illud Act. XXV, *non est consuetudo Romanis damnare aliquem hominem prius quam is qui accusatur praesentes habeat accusatores, locumque defendendi accipiat ad abluenda crimina quae ei obiiciebantur.*

**AD PRIMUM** ergo dicendum quod Deus in suo iudicio utitur conscientia peccantis quasi accusatore, secundum illud Rom. II, *inter se invicem cogitationum accusantium, aut etiam defendentium.* Vel etiam evidentia facti quantum ad ipsum, secundum illud Gen. IV *vox sanguinis fratris tui Abel clamat ad me de terra.*

**AD SECUNDUM** dicendum quod publica infamia habet locum accusatoris. Unde super illud Gen. IV, *vox sanguinis fratris tui* etc., dicit Glossa, *evidentia patrati sceleris accusatore non eget.* In denuntiatione vero, sicut supra dictum est, non intenditur punitio peccantis, sed emendatio, et ideo nihil agitur contra eum cuius peccatum denuntiatur, sed pro eo. Et ideo non est ibi necessarius accusator. Poena autem infertur propter rebellionem ad Ecclesiam, quae, quia est manifesta, tenet locum accusatoris. Ex eo autem quod ipse iudex videt, non potest procedere ad sententiam ferendam, nisi secundum ordinem publici iudicii.

**AD TERTIUM** dicendum quod Deus in suo iudicio procedit ex propria notitia veritatis, non autem homo, ut supra dictum est. Et ideo homo non potest esse simul accusator, iudex et testis, sicut Deus. Daniel autem accusator fuit simul et iudex quasi divini iudicii executor, cuius instinctu movebatur, ut dictum est.

**ON THE CONTRARY**, Ambrose in his commentary on 1 Cor. 5:2, expounding the Apostle's sentence on the fornicator, says that *a judge should not condemn without an accuser, since our Lord did not banish Judas, who was a thief, yet was not accused.*

**I ANSWER THAT**, A judge is an interpreter of justice. Wherefore, as the Philosopher says (*Ethic.* v, 4), *men have recourse to a judge as to one who is the personification of justice.* Now, as stated above (Q. 58, A. 2), justice is not between a man and himself but between one man and another. Hence a judge must needs judge between two parties, which is the case when one is the prosecutor, and the other the defendant. Therefore in criminal cases the judge cannot sentence a man unless the latter has an accuser, according to Acts 25:16: *It is not the custom of the Romans to condemn any man, before that he who is accused have his accusers present, and have liberty to make his answer, to clear himself of the crimes* of which he is accused.

**REPLY OBJ. 1**: God, in judging man, takes the sinner's conscience as his accuser, according to Rom. 2:15, *Their thoughts between themselves accusing, or also defending one another*; or again, He takes the evidence of the fact as regards the deed itself, according to Gen. 4:10, *The voice of thy brother's blood crieth to Me from the earth.*

**REPLY OBJ. 2**: Public disgrace takes the place of an accuser. Hence a gloss on Gen. 4:10, *The voice of thy brother's blood*, etc. says: *There is no need of an accuser when the crime committed is notorious.* In a case of denunciation, as stated above (Q. 33, A. 7), the amendment, not the punishment, of the sinner is intended: wherefore when a man is denounced for a sin, nothing is done against him, but for him, so that no accuser is required. The punishment that is inflicted is on account of his rebellion against the Church, and since this rebellion is manifest, it stands instead of an accuser. The fact that the judge himself was an eye-witness, does not authorize him to proceed to pass sentence, except according to the order of judicial procedure.

**REPLY OBJ. 3**: God, in judging man, proceeds from His own knowledge of the truth, whereas man does not, as stated above (A. 2). Hence a man cannot be accuser, witness and judge at the same time, as God is. Daniel was at once accuser and judge, because he was the executor of the sentence of God, by whose instinct he was moved, as stated above (A. 1, ad 1).

# Article 4

*Whether the judge can lawfully remit the punishment?*

AD QUARTUM SIC PROCEDITUR. Videtur quod iudex licite possit poenam relaxare. Dicitur enim Iac. II, *iudicium sine misericordia ei qui non facit misericordiam.* Sed nullus punitur propter hoc quod non facit illud quod licite facere non potest. Ergo quilibet iudex potest licite misericordiam facere, relaxando poenam.

PRAETEREA, iudicium humanum debet imitari iudicium divinum. Sed Deus poenitentibus relaxat poenam, quia *non vult mortem peccatoris,* ut dicitur Ezech. XVIII. Ergo etiam homo iudex potest poenitenti licite laxare poenam.

PRAETEREA, unicuique licet facere quod alicui prodest et nulli nocet. Sed absolvere reum a poena prodest ei et nulli nocet. Ergo iudex licite potest reum a poena absolvere.

SED CONTRA est quod dicitur Deut. XIII de eo qui persuadet servire diis alienis, *non parcat ei oculus tuus ut miserearis et occultes eum, sed statim interficies eum.* Et de homicida dicitur Deut. XIX, *morietur, nec misereberis eius.*

RESPONDEO dicendum quod, sicut ex dictis patet, duo sunt, quantum ad propositum pertinet, circa iudicem consideranda, quorum unum est quod ipse habet iudicare inter accusatorem et reum; aliud autem est quod ipse non fert iudicii sententiam quasi ex propria, sed quasi ex publica potestate. Duplici ergo ratione impeditur iudex ne reum a poena absolvere possit. Primo quidem, ex parte accusatoris, ad cuius ius quandoque pertinet ut reus puniatur, puta propter aliquam iniuriam in ipsum commissam, cuius relaxatio non est in arbitrio alicuius iudicis, quia quilibet iudex tenetur ius suum reddere unicuique. Alio modo impeditur ex parte reipublicae, cuius potestate fungitur, ad cuius bonum pertinet quod malefactores puniantur.

Sed tamen quantum ad hoc differt inter inferiores iudices et supremum iudicem, scilicet principem, cui est plenarie potestas publica commissa. Iudex enim inferior non habet potestatem absolvendi reum a poena, contra leges a superiore sibi impositas. Unde super illud Ioan. XIX, *non haberes adversum me potestatem ullam,* dicit Augustinus, *talem Deus dederat Pilato potestatem ut esset sub Caesaris potestate, ne ei omnino liberum esset accusatum absolvere.* Sed princeps, qui habet plenariam potestatem in republica, si ille qui passus est iniuriam

OBJECTION 1: It would seem that the judge can lawfully remit the punishment. For it is written (Jas 2:13): *Judgment without mercy* shall be done *to him that hath not done mercy.* Now no man is punished for not doing what he cannot do lawfully. Therefore any judge can lawfully do mercy by remitting the punishment.

OBJ. 2: Further, human judgment should imitate the Divine judgment. Now God remits the punishment to sinners, because *He desires not the death of the sinner,* according to Ezech. 18:23. Therefore a human judge also may lawfully remit the punishment to one who repents.

OBJ. 3: Further, it is lawful for anyone to do what is profitable to some one and harmful to none. Now the remission of his punishment profits the guilty man and harms nobody. Therefore the judge can lawfully loose a guilty man from his punishment.

ON THE CONTRARY, It is written (Deut 13:8, 9) concerning anyone who would persuade a man to serve strange gods: *Neither let thy eye spare him to pity and conceal him, but thou shalt presently put him to death:* and of the murderer it is written (Deut 19:12, 13): *He shall die. Thou shalt not pity him.*

I ANSWER THAT, As may be gathered from what has been said (AA. 2, 3), with regard to the question in point, two things may be observed in connection with a judge. One is that he has to judge between accuser and defendant, while the other is that he pronounces the judicial sentence, in virtue of his power, not as a private individual but as a public person. Accordingly on two counts a judge is hindered from loosing a guilty person from his punishment. First on the part of the accuser, whose right it sometimes is that the guilty party should be punished—for instance on account of some injury committed against the accuser—because it is not in the power of a judge to remit such punishment, since every judge is bound to give each man his right. Second, he finds a hindrance on the part of the commonwealth, whose power he exercises, and to whose good it belongs that evil-doers should be punished.

Nevertheless in this respect there is a difference between judges of lower degree and the supreme judge, i.e., the sovereign, to whom the entire public authority is entrusted. For the inferior judge has no power to exempt a guilty man from punishment against the laws imposed on him by his superior. Wherefore Augustine in commenting on John 19:11, *Thou shouldst not have any power against Me,* says (*Tract. cxvi in Joan.*): *The power which God gave Pilate was such that he was under the power of Caesar, so that he was by no means free to acquit the person accused.* On

velit eam remittere, poterit reum licite absolvere, si hoc publicae utilitati viderit non esse nocivum.

**AD PRIMUM** ergo dicendum quod misericordia iudicis habet locum in his quae arbitrio iudicis relinquuntur, in quibus *boni viri est ut sit diminutivus poenarum*, sicut philosophus dicit, in V Ethic. In his autem quae sunt determinata secundum legem divinam vel humanam, non est suum misericordiam facere.

**AD SECUNDUM** dicendum quod Deus habet supremam potestatem iudicandi, et ad ipsum pertinet quidquid contra aliquem peccatur. Et ideo liberum est ei poenam remittere, praecipue cum peccato ex hoc poena maxime debeatur quod est contra ipsum. Non tamen remittit poenam nisi secundum quod decet suam bonitatem, quae est omnium legum radix.

**AD TERTIUM** dicendum quod iudex, si inordinate poenam remitteret, nocumentum inferret et communitati, cui expedit ut maleficia puniantur, ad hoc quod peccata vitentur, unde Deut. XIII, post poenam seductoris, subditur, *ut omnis Israel, audiens, timeat, et nequaquam ultra faciat quispiam huius rei simile.* Nocet etiam personae cui est illata iniuria, quae recompensationem accipit per quandam restitutionem honoris in poena iniuriantis.

the other hand the sovereign who has full authority in the commonwealth, can lawfully remit the punishment to a guilty person, provided the injured party consent to the remission, and that this do not seem detrimental to the public good.

**REPLY OBJ. 1**: There is a place for the judge's mercy in matters that are left to the judge's discretion, because in like matters a good man is slow to punish as the Philosopher states (*Ethic.* v, 10). But in matters that are determined in accordance with Divine or human laws, it is not left to him to show mercy.

**REPLY OBJ. 2**: God has supreme power of judging, and it concerns Him whatever is done sinfully against anyone. Therefore He is free to remit the punishment, especially since punishment is due to sin chiefly because it is done against Him. He does not, however, remit the punishment, except insofar as it becomes His goodness, which is the source of all laws.

**REPLY OBJ. 3**: If the judge were to remit punishment inordinately, he would inflict an injury on the community, for whose good it behooves ill-deeds to be punished, in order that men may avoid sin. Hence the text, after appointing the punishment of the seducer, adds (Deut 13:11): *That all Israel hearing may fear, and may do no more anything like this.* He would also inflict harm on the injured person; who is compensated by having his honor restored in the punishment of the man who has injured him.

# QUESTION 68

## MATTERS CONCERNING UNJUST ACCUSATION

Deinde considerandum est de his quae pertinent ad iniustam accusationem. Et circa hoc quaeruntur quatuor.

Primo, utrum homo accusare teneatur.

Secundo, utrum accusatio sit facienda in scriptis.

Tertio, quomodo accusatio sit vitiosa.

Quarto, qualiter male accusantes sint puniendi.

We must now consider matters pertaining to unjust accusation. Under this head there are four points of inquiry:

(1) Whether a man is bound to accuse?

(2) Whether the accusation should be made in writing?

(3) How is an accusation vitiated?

(4) How should those be punished who have accused a man wrongfully?

# Article 1

*Whether a man is bound to accuse?*

**AD PRIMUM SIC PROCEDITUR.** Videtur quod homo non teneatur accusare. Nullus enim excusatur ab impletione divini praecepti propter peccatum, quia iam ex suo peccato commodum reportaret. Sed aliqui propter peccatum redduntur inhabiles ad accusandum, sicut excommunicati, infames, et illi qui sunt de maioribus criminibus accusati prius quam innoxii demonstrentur. Ergo homo non tenetur ex praecepto divino ad accusandum.

**PRAETEREA**, omne debitum ex caritate dependet, quae est *finis praecepti*, unde dicitur Rom. XIII, *nemini quidquam debeatis, nisi ut invicem diligatis*. Sed illud quod est caritatis homo debet omnibus, maioribus et minoribus, subditis et praelatis. Cum igitur subditi non debeant praelatos accusare, nec minores suos maiores, ut per plura capitula probatur II, qu. VII; videtur quod nullus ex debito teneatur accusare.

**PRAETEREA**, nullus tenetur contra fidelitatem agere quam debet amico, quia non debet alteri facere quod sibi non vult fieri. Sed accusare aliquem quandoque est contra fidelitatem quam quis debet amico, dicitur enim Prov. XI, *qui ambulat fraudulenter revelat arcana, qui autem fidelis est celat amici commissum*. Ergo homo non tenetur ad accusandum.

**SED CONTRA** est quod dicitur Levit. V, *si peccaverit anima, et audierit vocem iurantis, testisque fuerit quod aut ipse vidit aut conscius est, nisi indicaverit, portabit iniquitatem suam*.

**RESPONDEO** dicendum quod, sicut supra dictum est, haec est differentia inter denuntiationem et accusationem, quod in denuntiatione attenditur emendatio

**OBJECTION 1**: It would seem that a man is not bound to accuse. For no man is excused on account of sin from fulfilling a Divine precept, since he would thus profit by his sin. Yet on account of sin some are disqualified from accusing, such as those who are excommunicate or of evil fame, or who are accused of grievous crimes and are not yet proved to be innocent. Therefore a man is not bound by a Divine precept to accuse.

**OBJ. 2**: Further, every duty depends on charity which is *the end of the precept*: wherefore it is written (Rom 13:8): *Owe no man anything, but to love one another*. Now that which belongs to charity is a duty that man owes to all both of high and of low degree, both superiors and inferiors. Since therefore subjects should not accuse their superiors, nor persons of lower degree, those of a higher degree, as shown in several chapters (*Decret*. II, qu. vii), it seems that it is no man's duty to accuse.

**OBJ. 3**: Further, no man is bound to act against the fidelity which he owes his friend; because he ought not to do to another what he would not have others do to him. Now to accuse anyone is sometimes contrary to the fidelity that one owes a friend; for it is written (Prov 11:13): *He that walketh deceitfully, revealeth secrets; but he that is faithful, concealeth the thing committed to him by his friend*. Therefore a man is not bound to accuse.

**ON THE CONTRARY**, It is written (Lev 5:1): *If any one sin, and hear the voice of one swearing, and is a witness either because he himself hath seen, or is privy to it: if he do not utter it, he shall bear his iniquity*.

**I ANSWER THAT**, As stated above (Q. 33, AA. 6, 7; Q. 67, A. 3, ad 2), the difference between denunciation and accusation is that in denunciation we aim at a brother's

fratris, in accusatione autem attenditur punitio criminis. Poenae autem praesentis vitae non per se expetuntur, quia non est hic ultimum retributionis tempus, sed inquantum sunt medicinales, conferentes vel ad emendationem personae peccantis, vel ad bonum reipublicae, cuius quies procuratur per punitionem peccantium. Quorum primum intenditur in denuntiatione, ut dictum est, secundum autem proprie pertinet ad accusationem. Et ideo si crimen fuerit tale quod vergat in detrimentum reipublicae, tenetur homo ad accusationem, dummodo sufficienter possit probare, quod pertinet ad officium accusatoris, puta cum peccatum alicuius vergit in multitudinis corruptelam corporalem seu spiritualem. Si autem non fuerit tale peccatum quod in multitudinem redundet, vel etiam si sufficientem probationem adhibere non possit, non tenetur ad intentandum accusationem, quia ad hoc nullus tenetur quod non potest debito modo perficere.

**AD PRIMUM** ergo dicendum quod nihil prohibet per peccatum reddi aliquem impotentem ad ea quae homines facere tenentur, sicut ad merendum vitam aeternam, et ad assumendum ecclesiastica sacramenta. Nec tamen ex hoc homo reportat commodum, quinimmo deficere ab his quae tenetur facere est gravissima poena, quia virtuosi actus sunt quaedam hominis perfectiones.

**AD SECUNDUM** dicendum quod subditi praelatos suos accusare prohibentur *qui non affectione caritatis, sed sua pravitate vitam eorum diffamare et reprehendere quaerunt*; vel etiam si subditi accusare volentes, fuerint criminosi; ut habetur II, qu. VII. Alioquin, si fuerint alias idonei ad accusandum, licet subditis ex caritate suos praelatos accusare.

**AD TERTIUM** dicendum quod revelare secreta in malum personae, est contra fidelitatem, non autem si revelentur propter bonum commune, quod semper praeferendum est bono privato. Et ideo contra bonum commune nullum secretum licet recipere. Nec tamen est omnino secretum quod per sufficientes testes potest probari.

amendment, whereas in accusation we intend the punishment of his crime. Now the punishments of this life are sought, not for their own sake, because this is not the final time of retribution, but in their character of medicine, conducing either to the amendment of the sinner, or to the good of the commonwealth whose calm is ensured by the punishment of evil-doers. The former of these is intended in denunciation, as stated, whereas the second regards properly accusation. Hence in the case of a crime that conduces to the injury of the commonwealth, a man is bound to accusation, provided he can offer sufficient proof, since it is the accuser's duty to prove: as, for example, when anyone's sin conduces to the bodily or spiritual corruption of the community. If, however, the sin be not such as to affect the community, or if he cannot offer sufficient proof, a man is not bound to attempt to accuse, since no man is bound to do what he cannot duly accomplish.

**REPLY OBJ. 1**: Nothing prevents a man being debarred by sin from doing what men are under an obligation to do: for instance from meriting eternal life, and from receiving the sacraments of the Church. Nor does a man profit by this: indeed it is a most grievous fault to fail to do what one is bound to do, since virtuous acts are perfections of man.

**REPLY OBJ. 2**: Subjects are debarred from accusing their superiors, *if it is not the affection of charity but their own wickedness that leads them to defame and disparage the conduct of their superiors*—or again if the subject who wishes to accuse his superior is himself guilty of crime. Otherwise, provided they be in other respects qualified to accuse, it is lawful for subjects to accuse their superiors out of charity.

**REPLY OBJ. 3**: It is contrary to fidelity to make known secrets to the injury of a person; but not if they be revealed for the good of the community, which should always be preferred to a private good. Hence it is unlawful to receive any secret in detriment to the common good: and yet a thing is scarcely a secret when there are sufficient witnesses to prove it.

# Article 2

*Whether it is necessary for the accusation to be made in writing?*

**AD SECUNDUM SIC PROCEDITUR.** Videtur quod non sit necessarium accusationem in scriptis fieri. Scriptura enim adinventa est ad subveniendum humanae memoriae circa praeterita. Sed accusatio in praesenti agitur. Ergo accusatio Scriptura non indiget.

**PRAETEREA**, II, qu. VIII, dicitur, *nullus absens accusare potest, nec ab aliquo accusari*. Sed Scriptura ad hoc

**OBJECTION 1**: It would seem unnecessary for the accusation to be made in writing. For writing was devised as an aid to the human memory of the past. But an accusation is made in the present. Therefore the accusation needs not to be made in writing.

**OBJ. 2**: Further, it is laid down (*Decret.* II, qu. viii, can. *Per scripta*) that *no man may accuse or be accused in his*

videtur esse utilis ut absentibus aliquid significetur, ut patet per Augustinum, X de Trin. Ergo in accusatione non est necessaria Scriptura, praesertim cum canon dicat quod *per scripta nullius accusatio suscipiatur.*

**PRAETEREA**, sicut crimen alicuius manifestatur per accusationem, ita per denuntiationem. Sed in denuntiatione non est Scriptura necessaria. Ergo videtur quod neque etiam in accusatione.

**SED CONTRA** est quod dicitur II, qu. VIII, *accusatorum personae sine scripto nunquam recipiantur.*

**RESPONDEO** dicendum quod, sicut supra dictum est, quando in criminibus per modum accusationis agitur, accusator constituitur pars, ita quod iudex inter accusatorem et eum qui accusatur medius constituitur ad examen iustitiae, in quo oportet, quantum possibile est, secundum certitudinem procedere. Quia vero ea quae verbotenus dicuntur facile labuntur a memoria, non posset iudici esse certum quid et qualiter dictum sit, cum debet proferre sententiam, nisi esset in scriptis redactum. Et ideo rationabiliter institutum est ut accusatio, sicut et alia quae in iudicio aguntur, redigantur in scriptis.

**AD PRIMUM** ergo dicendum quod difficile est singula verba, propter eorum multitudinem et varietatem, retinere, cuius signum est quod multi, eadem verba audientes, si interrogentur, non referent ea similiter etiam post modicum tempus. Et tamen modica verborum differentia sensum variat. Et ideo, etiam si post modicum tempus debeat iudicis sententia promulgari, expedit tamen ad certitudinem iudicii ut accusatio redigatur in scriptis.

**AD SECUNDUM** dicendum quod Scriptura non solum necessaria est propter absentiam personae quae significat vel cui est aliquid significandum, sed etiam propter dilationem temporis, ut dictum est. Et ideo cum dicit canon, *per scripta nullius accusatio suscipiatur,* intelligendum est ab absente, qui per epistolam accusationem mittat. Non tamen excluditur quin, si praesens fuerit, necessaria sit Scriptura.

**AD TERTIUM** dicendum quod denuntiator non obligat se ad probandum, unde nec punitur si probare nequiverit. Et propter hoc in denuntiatione non est necessaria Scriptura, sed sufficit si aliquis verbo denuntiet Ecclesiae, quae ex officio suo procedet ad fratris emendationem.

*absence.* Now writing seems to be useful in the fact that it is a means of notifying something to one who is absent, as Augustine declares (*De Trin.* x, 1). Therefore the accusation need not be in writing: and all the more that the canon declares that *no accusation in writing should be accepted.*

**OBJ. 3**: Further, a man's crime is made known by denunciation, even as by accusation. Now writing is unnecessary in denunciation. Therefore it is seemingly unnecessary in accusation.

**ON THE CONTRARY**, It is laid down (*Decret.* II, qu. viii, can. Accusatorum) that *the role of accuser must never be sanctioned without the accusation be in writing.*

**I ANSWER THAT**, As stated above (Q. 67, A. 3), when the process in a criminal case goes by way of accusation, the accuser is in the position of a party, so that the judge stands between the accuser and the accused for the purpose of the trial of justice, wherein it behooves one to proceed on certainties, as far as possible. Since however verbal utterances are apt to escape one's memory, the judge would be unable to know for certain what had been said and with what qualifications, when he comes to pronounce sentence, unless it were drawn up in writing. Hence it has with reason been established that the accusation, as well as other parts of the judicial procedure, should be put into writing.

**REPLY OBJ. 1**: Words are so many and so various that it is difficult to remember each one. A proof of this is the fact that if a number of people who have heard the same words be asked what was said, they will not agree in repeating them, even after a short time. And since a slight difference of words changes the sense, even though the judge's sentence may have to be pronounced soon afterwards, the certainty of judgment requires that the accusation be drawn up in writing.

**REPLY OBJ. 2**: Writing is needed not only on account of the absence of the person who has something to notify, or of the person to whom something is notified, but also on account of the delay of time as stated above (ad 1). Hence when the canon says, *Let no accusation be accepted in writing* it refers to the sending of an accusation by one who is absent: but it does not exclude the necessity of writing when the accuser is present.

**REPLY OBJ. 3**: The denouncer does not bind himself to give proofs: wherefore he is not punished if he is unable to prove. For this reason writing is unnecessary in a denunciation: and it suffices that the denunciation be made verbally to the Church, who will proceed, in virtue of her office, to the correction of the brother.

# Article 3

*Whether an accusation is rendered unjust by calumny, collusion, or evasion?*

AD TERTIUM SIC PROCEDITUR. Videtur quod accusatio non reddatur iniusta per calumniam, praevaricationem et tergiversationem. Quia sicut dicitur II, qu. III, *calumniari est falsa crimina intendere.* Sed quandoque aliquis alteri falsum crimen obiicit ex ignorantia facti, quae excusat. Ergo videtur quod non semper reddatur iniusta accusatio si sit calumniosa.

PRAETEREA, ibidem dicitur quod *praevaricari est vera crimina abscondere.* Sed hoc non videtur esse illicitum, quia homo non tenetur ad omnia crimina detegenda, ut supra dictum est. Ergo videtur quod accusatio non reddatur iniusta ex praevaricatione.

PRAETEREA, sicut ibidem dicitur, *tergiversari est in universo ab accusatione desistere.* Sed hoc absque iniustitia fieri potest, dicitur enim ibidem, *si quem poenituerit criminaliter accusationem et inscriptionem fecisse de eo quod probare non potuerit, si ei cum accusato innocente convenerit, invicem se absolvant.* Ergo accusatio non redditur iniusta per tergiversationem.

SED CONTRA est quod ibidem dicitur, *accusatorum temeritas tribus modis detegitur, aut enim calumniantur, aut praevaricantur, aut tergiversantur.*

RESPONDEO dicendum quod, sicut dictum est, accusatio ordinatur ad bonum commune, quod intenditur per cognitionem criminis. Nullus autem debet alicui nocere iniuste ut bonum commune promoveat. Et ideo in accusatione duplici ratione contingit esse peccatum. Uno modo, ex eo quod iniuste agit contra eum qui accusatur, falsa crimina ei imponendo, quod est *calumniari.* Alio modo, ex parte reipublicae, cuius bonum principaliter intenditur in accusatione, dum aliquis impedit malitiose punitionem peccati. Quod iterum dupliciter contingit. Uno modo, fraudem in accusatione adhibendo. Et hoc pertinet ad *praevaricationem,* nam *praevaricator est quasi varicator, qui adversam partem adiuvat, prodita causa sua.* Alio modo, totaliter ab accusatione desistendo. Quod est *tergiversari,* in hoc enim quod desistit ab hoc quod coeperat, quasi *tergum vertere* videtur.

AD PRIMUM ergo dicendum quod homo non debet ad accusationem procedere nisi de re sibi omnino certa, in quo ignorantia facti locum non habeat. Nec tamen qui falsum crimen alicui imponit calumniatur, sed solum qui ex malitia in falsam accusationem prorumpit. Contingit enim quandoque ex animi levitate ad accusationem procedere, quia scilicet aliquis nimis faciliter credit quod audivit, et hoc temeritatis est. Aliquando

OBJECTION 1: It would seem that an accusation is not rendered unjust by calumny, collusion or evasion. For according to *Decret.* II, qu. iii, *calumny consists in falsely charging a person with a crime.* Now sometimes one man falsely accuses another of a crime through ignorance of fact which excuses him. Therefore it seems that an accusation is not always rendered unjust through being slanderous.

OBJ. 2: Further, it is stated by the same authority that *collusion consists in hiding the truth about a crime.* But seemingly this is not unlawful, because one is not bound to disclose every crime, as stated above (A. 1; Q. 33, A. 7). Therefore it seems that an accusation is not rendered unjust by collusion.

OBJ. 3: Further, it is stated by the same authority that *evasion consists in withdrawing altogether from an accusation.* But this can be done without injustice: for it is stated there also: *If a man repent of having made a wicked accusation and inscription in a matter which he cannot prove, and come to an understanding with the innocent party whom he has accused, let them acquit one another.* Therefore evasion does not render an accusation unjust.

ON THE CONTRARY, It is stated by the same authority: *The rashness of accusers shows itself in three ways. For they are guilty either of calumny, or of collusion, or of evasion.*

I ANSWER THAT, As stated above (A. 1), accusation is ordered for the common good which it aims at procuring by means of knowledge of the crime. Now no man ought to injure a person unjustly, in order to promote the common good. Wherefore a man may sin in two ways when making an accusation: first through acting unjustly against the accused, by charging him falsely with the commission of a crime, i.e., by *calumniating* him; second, on the part of the commonwealth, whose good is intended chiefly in an accusation, when anyone with wicked intent hinders a sin being punished. This again happens in two ways: first by having recourse to fraud in making the accusation. This belongs to collusion (*praevaricatio*) for *he that is guilty of collusion is like one who rides astraddle* (variator), *because he helps the other party, and betrays his own side.* Second by withdrawing altogether from the accusation. This is evasion (*tergiversatio*) for by desisting from what he had begun he seems to turn his back (*tergum vertere*).

REPLY OBJ. 1: A man ought not to proceed to accuse except of what he is quite certain about, wherein ignorance of fact has no place. Yet he who falsely charges another with a crime is not a calumniator unless he gives utterance to false accusations out of malice. For it happens sometimes that a man through levity of mind proceeds to accuse someone, because he believes too readily what he hears, and this pertains to rashness; while, on the other hand

autem ex iusto errore movetur aliquis ad accusandum. Quae omnia secundum prudentiam iudicis debent discerni, ut non prorumpat eum calumniatum fuisse qui vel ex levitate animi vel ex iusto errore in falsam accusationem prorupit.

**AD SECUNDUM** dicendum quod non quicumque abscondit vera crimina praevaricatur, sed solum si fraudulenter abscondit ea de quibus accusationem proponit, colludens cum reo, proprias probationes dissimulando, et falsas excusationes admittendo.

**AD TERTIUM** dicendum quod tergiversari est ab accusatione desistere omnino animum accusandi deponendo, non qualitercumque, sed inordinate. Contingit autem aliquem ab accusatione desistere ordinate absque vitio, dupliciter. Uno modo, si in ipso accusationis processu cognoverit falsum esse id de quo accusabat, et si pari consensu se absolvunt accusator et reus. Alio modo, si princeps, ad quem pertinet cura boni communis, quod per accusationem intenditur, accusationem aboleverit.

sometimes a man is led to make an accusation on account of an error for which he is not to blame. All these things must be weighed according to the judge's prudence, lest he should declare a man to have been guilty of calumny, who through levity of mind or an error for which he is not to be blamed has uttered a false accusation.

REPLY OBJ. 2: Not everyone who hides the truth about a crime is guilty of collusion, but only he who deceitfully hides the matter about which he makes the accusation, by collusion with the defendant, dissembling his proofs, and admitting false excuses.

REPLY OBJ. 3: Evasion consists in withdrawing altogether from the accusation, by renouncing the intention of accusing, not anyhow, but inordinately. There are two ways, however, in which a man may rightly desist from accusing without committing a sin—in one way, in the very process of accusation, if it come to his knowledge that the matter of his accusation is false, and then by mutual consent the accuser and the defendant acquit one another—in another way, if the accusation be quashed by the sovereign to whom belongs the care of the common good, which it is intended to procure by the accusation.

# Article 4

*Whether an accuser who fails to prove his indictment is bound to the punishment of retaliation?*

**AD QUARTUM SIC PROCEDITUR.** Videtur quod accusator qui in probatione defecerit non teneatur ad poenam talionis. Contingit enim quandoque aliquem ex iusto errore ad accusationem procedere, in quo casu iudex accusatorem absolvit, ut dicitur II, qu. III. Non ergo accusator qui in probatione defecerit tenetur ad poenam talionis.

**PRAETEREA**, si poena talionis ei qui iniuste accusat sit iniungenda, hoc erit propter iniuriam in aliquem commissam. Sed non propter iniuriam commissam in personam accusati, quia sic princeps non posset hanc poenam remittere. Nec etiam propter iniuriam illatam in rempublicam, quia sic accusatus non posset eum absolvere. Ergo poena talionis non debetur ei qui in accusatione defecerit.

**PRAETEREA**, eidem peccato non debetur duplex poena, secundum illud Nahum I, *non iudicabit Deus bis in idipsum*. Sed ille qui in probatione deficit incurrit poenam infamiae, quam etiam Papa non videtur posse remittere, secundum illud Gelasii Papae, *quanquam animas per poenitentiam salvare possumus, infamiam tamen abolere non possumus*. Non ergo tenetur ad poenam talionis.

OBJECTION 1: It would seem that the accuser who fails to prove his indictment is not bound to the punishment of retaliation. For sometimes a man is led by a just error to make an accusation, in which case the judge acquit the accuser, as stated in Decret. II, qu. iii. Therefore the accuser who fails to prove his indictment is not bound to the punishment of retaliation.

OBJ. 2: Further, if the punishment of retaliation ought to be inflicted on one who has accused unjustly, this will be on account of the injury he has done to someone—but not on account of any injury done to the person of the accused, for in that case the sovereign could not remit this punishment, nor on account of an injury to the commonwealth, because then the accused could not acquit him. Therefore the punishment of retaliation is not due to one who has failed to prove his accusation.

OBJ. 3: Further, the one same sin does not deserve a twofold punishment, according to Nahum 1:9: *God shall not judge the same thing a second time.* But he who fails to prove his accusation, incurs the punishment due to defamation, which punishment even the Pope seemingly cannot remit, according to a statement of Pope Gelasius: *Although we are able to save souls by Penance, we are unable to remove the defamation.* Therefore he is not bound to suffer the punishment of retaliation.

**SED CONTRA** est quod Hadrianus Papa dicit, qui *non probaverit quod obiecit, poenam quam intulerit ipse patiatur.*

**RESPONDEO** dicendum quod, sicut supra dictum est, accusator in causa accusationis constituitur pars intendens ad poenam accusati. Ad iudicem autem pertinet ut inter eos iustitiae aequalitatem constituat. Iustitiae autem aequalitas hoc requirit, ut nocumentum quod quis alteri intentat, ipse patiatur, secundum illud Exod. XXI, *oculum pro oculo, dentem pro dente.* Et ideo iustum est ut ille qui per accusationem aliquem in periculum gravis poenae inducit, ipse etiam similem poenam patiatur.

**AD PRIMUM** ergo dicendum quod, sicut philosophus dicit, in V Ethic., in iustitia non semper competit contrapassum simpliciter, quia multum differt an aliquis voluntarie an involuntarie alium laedat. Voluntarium autem meretur poenam, sed involuntario debetur venia. Et ideo quando iudex cognoverit aliquem de falso accusasse non voluntate nocendi, sed involuntarie propter ignorantiam ex iusto errore, non imponit poenam talionis.

**AD SECUNDUM** dicendum quod ille qui male accusat peccat et contra personam accusati, et contra rempublicam. Unde propter utrumque punitur. Et hoc est quod dicitur Deut. XIX, *cumque, diligentissime perscrutantes, invenerint falsum testem dixisse contra fratrem suum mendacium, reddent ei sicut fratri suo facere cogitavit,* quod pertinet ad iniuriam personae, et postea, quantum ad iniuriam reipublicae, subditur, *et auferes malum de medio tui, ut audientes ceteri timorem habeant, et nequaquam talia audeant facere.* Specialiter tamen personae accusati facit iniuriam si de falso accuset, et ideo accusatus, si innocens fuerit, potest ei iniuriam suam remittere; maxime si non calumniose accusaverit, sed ex animi levitate. Si vero ab accusatione innocentis desistat propter aliquam collusionem cum adversario, facit iniuriam reipublicae, et hoc non potest ei remitti ab eo qui accusatur, sed potest ei remitti per principem, qui curam reipublicae gerit.

**AD TERTIUM** dicendum quod poenam talionis meretur accusator in recompensationem nocumenti quod proximo inferre intentat, sed poena infamiae ei debetur propter malitiam ex qua calumniose alium accusat. Et quandoque quidem princeps remittit poenam, et non abolet infamiam, quandoque autem etiam infamiam abolet. Unde et Papa potest huiusmodi infamiam abolere, et quod dicit Papa Gelasius, *infamiam abolere non possumus,* intelligendum est vel de infamia facti, vel quia eam abolere aliquando non expedit. Vel etiam loquitur

**ON THE CONTRARY,** Pope Hadrian I says (Cap. lii): *He that fails to prove his accusation, must himself suffer the punishment which his accusation inferred.*

**I ANSWER THAT,** As stated above (A. 2), in a case, where the procedure is by way of accusation, the accuser holds the position of a party aiming at the punishment of the accused. Now the duty of the judge is to establish the equality of justice between them: and the equality of justice requires that a man should himself suffer whatever harm he has intended to be inflicted on another, according to Ex. 21:24, *Eye for eye, tooth for tooth.* Consequently it is just that he who by accusing a man has put him in danger of being punished severely, should himself suffer a like punishment.

**REPLY OBJ. 1:** As the Philosopher says (*Ethic.* v, 5) justice does not always require counterpassion, because it matters considerably whether a man injures another voluntarily or not. Voluntary injury deserves punishment, involuntary deserves forgiveness. Hence when the judge becomes aware that a man has made a false accusation, not with a mind to do harm, but involuntarily through ignorance or a just error, he does not impose the punishment of retaliation.

**REPLY OBJ. 2:** He who accuses wrongfully sins both against the person of the accused and against the commonwealth; wherefore he is punished on both counts. This is the meaning of what is written (Deut 19:18–20): *And when after most diligent inquisition, they shall find that the false witness hath told a lie against his brother: they shall render to him as he meant to do to his brother,* and this refers to the injury done to the person: and afterwards, referring to the injury done to the commonwealth, the text continues: *And thou shalt take away the evil out of the midst of thee, that others hearing may fear, and may not dare to do such things.* Specially, however, does he injure the person of the accused, if he accuse him falsely. Wherefore the accused, if innocent, may condone the injury done to himself, particularly if the accusation were made not calumniously but out of levity of mind. But if the accuser desist from accusing an innocent man, through collusion with the latter's adversary, he inflicts an injury on the commonwealth: and this cannot be condoned by the accused, although it can be remitted by the sovereign, who has charge of the commonwealth.

**REPLY OBJ. 3:** The accuser deserves the punishment of retaliation in compensation for the harm he attempts to inflict on his neighbor: but the punishment of disgrace is due to him for his wickedness in accusing another man calumniously. Sometimes the sovereign remits the punishment, and not the disgrace, and sometimes he removes the disgrace also: wherefore the Pope also can remove this disgrace. When Pope Gelasius says: *We cannot remove the disgrace,* he may mean either the disgrace attaching to the deed (*infamia facti*), or that sometimes it is not expedient

de infamia irrogata per iudicem civilem, sicut dicit Gratianus.

to remove it, or again he may be referring to the disgrace inflicted by the civil judge, as Gratian states (*Callist. I, Epist. ad omn. Gall. episc.*).

# QUESTION 69

## SINS COMMITTED AGAINST JUSTICE ON THE PART OF THE DEFENDANT

Deinde considerandum est de peccatis quae sunt contra iustitiam ex parte rei. Et circa hoc quaeruntur quatuor.

Primo, utrum peccet aliquis mortaliter veritatem negando per quam condemnaretur.

Secundo, utrum liceat alicui se calumniose defendere.

Tertio, utrum liceat alicui iudicium subterfugere appellando.

Quarto, utrum liceat alicui condemnato per violentiam se defendere, si adsit facultas.

We must now consider those sins which are committed against justice on the part of the defendant. Under this head there are four points of inquiry:

(1) Whether it is a mortal sin to deny the truth which would lead to one's condemnation?

(2) Whether it is lawful to defend oneself with calumnies?

(3) Whether it is lawful to escape condemnation by appealing?

(4) Whether it is lawful for one who has been condemned to defend himself by violence if he be able to do so?

# Article 1

*Whether one can, without a mortal sin, deny the truth which would lead to one's condemnation?*

AD PRIMUM SIC PROCEDITUR. Videtur quod absque peccato mortali possit accusatus veritatem negare per quam condemnaretur. Dicit enim Chrysostomus, *non tibi dico ut te prodas in publicum, neque apud alium accuses.* Sed si veritatem confiteretur in iudicio accusatus, seipsum proderet et accusaret. Non ergo tenetur veritatem dicere. Et ita non peccat mortaliter si in iudicio mentiatur.

PRAETEREA, sicut mendacium officiosum est quando aliquis mentitur ut alium a morte liberet, ita mendacium officiosum esse videtur quando aliquis mentitur ut se liberet a morte, quia plus sibi tenetur quam alteri. Mendacium autem officiosum non ponitur esse peccatum mortale, sed veniale. Ergo si accusatus veritatem in iudicio neget ut se a morte liberet, non peccat mortaliter.

PRAETEREA, omne peccatum mortale est contra caritatem, ut supra dictum est. Sed quod accusatus mentiatur excusando se a peccato sibi imposito, non contrariatur caritati, neque quantum ad dilectionem Dei neque quantum ad dilectionem proximi. Ergo huiusmodi mendacium non est peccatum mortale.

SED CONTRA, omne quod est contrarium divinae gloriae est peccatum mortale, quia ex praecepto tenemur *omnia in gloriam Dei facere,* ut patet I ad Cor. X. Sed quod reus id quod contra se est confiteatur, pertinet ad gloriam Dei, ut patet per id quod Iosue dixit ad Achar, *fili mi, da gloriam domino Deo Israel, et confitere*

OBJECTION 1: It would seem one can, without a mortal sin, deny the truth which would lead to one's condemnation. For Chrysostom says (*Hom. xxxi super Ep. ad Heb.*): *I do not say that you should lay bare your guilt publicly, nor accuse yourself before others.* Now if the accused were to confess the truth in court, he would lay bare his guilt and be his own accuser. Therefore he is not bound to tell the truth: and so he does not sin mortally if he tell a lie in court.

OBJ. 2: Further, just as it is an officious lie when one tells a lie in order to rescue another man from death, so is it an officious lie when one tells a lie in order to free oneself from death, since one is more bound towards oneself than towards another. Now an officious lie is considered not a mortal but a venial sin. Therefore if the accused denies the truth in court, in order to escape death, he does not sin mortally.

OBJ. 3: Further, every mortal sin is contrary to charity, as stated above (Q. 24, A. 12). But that the accused lie by denying himself to be guilty of the crime laid to his charge is not contrary to charity, neither as regards the love we owe God, nor as to the love due to our neighbor. Therefore such a lie is not a mortal sin.

ON THE CONTRARY, Whatever is opposed to the glory of God is a mortal sin, because we are bound by precept to *do all to the glory of God* (1 Cor 10:31). Now it is to the glory of God that the accused confess that which is alleged against him, as appears from the words of Josue to Achan, *My son, give glory to the Lord God of Israel, and confess*

647

atque indica mihi quid feceris, ne abscondas, ut habetur Iosue VII. Ergo mentiri ad excusandum peccatum est peccatum mortale.

**RESPONDEO** dicendum quod quicumque facit contra debitum iustitiae, mortaliter peccat, sicut supra dictum est. Pertinet autem ad debitum iustitiae quod aliquis obediat suo superiori in his ad quae ius praelationis se extendit. Iudex autem, ut supra dictum est, superior est respectu eius qui iudicatur. Et ideo ex debito tenetur accusatus iudici veritatem exponere quam ab eo secundum formam iuris exigit. Et ideo si confiteri noluerit veritatem quam dicere tenetur, vel si eam mendaciter negaverit, mortaliter peccat. Si vero iudex hoc exquirat quod non potest secundum ordinem iuris, non tenetur ei accusatus respondere, sed potest vel per appellationem vel aliter licite subterfugere, mendacium tamen dicere non licet.

**AD PRIMUM** ergo dicendum quod quando aliquis secundum ordinem iuris a iudice interrogatur, non ipse se prodit, sed ab alio proditur, dum ei necessitas respondendi imponitur per eum cui obedire tenetur.

**AD SECUNDUM** dicendum quod mentiri ad liberandum aliquem a morte cum iniuria alterius, non est mendacium simpliciter officiosum, sed habet aliquid de pernicioso admixtum. Cum autem aliquis mentitur in iudicio ad excusationem sui, iniuriam facit ei cui obedire tenetur, dum sibi denegat quod ei debet, scilicet confessionem veritatis.

**AD TERTIUM** dicendum quod ille qui mentitur in iudicio se excusando, facit et contra dilectionem Dei, cuius est iudicium; et contra dilectionem proximi, tum ex parte iudicis, cui debitum negat; tum ex parte accusatoris, qui punitur si in probatione deficiat. Unde et in Psalm. dicitur, *ne declines cor meum in verba malitiae, ad excusandas excusationes in peccatis*, ubi dicit Glossa, *haec est consuetudo impudentium, ut deprehensi per aliqua falsa se excusent.* Et Gregorius, XXII Moral., exponens illud Iob XXXI, si abscondi quasi homo peccatum meum, dicit, *usitatum humani generis vitium est et latendo peccatum committere, et commissum negando abscondere, et convictum defendendo multiplicare.*

and tell me what thou hast done, hide it not (Josh 7:19). Therefore it is a mortal sin to lie in order to cover one's guilt.

**I ANSWER THAT,** Whoever acts against the due order of justice, sins mortally, as stated above (Q. 59, A. 4). Now it belongs to the order of justice that a man should obey his superior in those matters to which the rights of his authority extend. Again, the judge, as stated above (Q. 67, A. 1), is the superior in relation to the person whom he judges. Therefore the accused is in duty bound to tell the judge the truth which the latter exacts from him according to the form of law. Hence if he refuse to tell the truth which he is under obligation to tell, or if he mendaciously deny it, he sins mortally. If, on the other hand, the judge asks of him that which he cannot ask in accordance with the order of justice, the accused is not bound to satisfy him, and he may lawfully escape by appealing or otherwise: but it is not lawful for him to lie.

**REPLY OBJ. 1:** When a man is examined by the judge according to the order of justice, he does not lay bare his own guilt, but his guilt is unmasked by another, since the obligation of answering is imposed on him by one whom he is bound to obey.

**REPLY OBJ. 2:** To lie, with injury to another person, in order to rescue a man from death is not a purely officious lie, for it has an admixture of the pernicious lie: and when a man lies in court in order to exculpate himself, he does an injury to one whom he is bound to obey, since he refuses him his due, namely an avowal of the truth.

**REPLY OBJ. 3:** He who lies in court by denying his guilt, acts both against the love of God to whom judgment belongs, and against the love of his neighbor, and this not only as regards the judge, to whom he refuses his due, but also as regards his accuser, who is punished if he fail to prove his accusation. Hence it is written (Ps 140:4): *Incline not my heart to evil words, to make excuses in sins*: on which words a gloss says: *Shameless men are wont by lying to deny their guilt when they have been found out.* And Gregory in expounding Job 31:33, *If as a man I have hid my sin*, says (*Moral.* xxii, 15): *It is a common vice of mankind to sin in secret, by lying to hide the sin that has been committed, and when convicted to aggravate the sin by defending oneself.*

# Article 2

*Whether it is lawful for the accused to defend himself with calumnies?*

**AD SECUNDUM SIC PROCEDITUR.** Videtur quod accusato liceat calumniose se defendere. Quia secundum iura civilia, in causa sanguinis licitum est cuilibet adversarium corrumpere. Sed hoc maxime est calumniose se

**OBJECTION 1:** It would seem lawful for the accused to defend himself with calumnies. Because, according to civil law (*Cod. II, iv, De transact. 18*), when a man is on trial for his life it is lawful for him to bribe his adversary. Now

defendere. Ergo non peccat accusatus in causa sanguinis si calumniose se defendat.

**PRAETEREA**, *accusator cum accusato colludens poenam recipit legibus constitutam*, ut habetur, II, qu. III, non autem imponitur poena accusato propter hoc quod cum accusatore colludit. Ergo videtur quod liceat accusato calumniose se defendere.

**PRAETEREA**, Prov. XIV dicitur, *sapiens timet et declinat a malo, stultus transilit et confidit.* Sed illud quod fit per sapientiam non est peccatum. Ergo si aliquis qualitercumque se liberet a malo, non peccat.

**SED CONTRA** est quod etiam in causa criminali iuramentum de calumnia est praestandum, ut habetur extra, de iuramento Calum., inhaerentes. Quod non esset si calumniose defendere se liceret. Ergo non est licitum accusato calumniose se defendere.

**RESPONDEO** dicendum quod aliud est veritatem tacere, aliud est falsitatem proponere. Quorum primum in aliquo casu licet. Non enim aliquis tenetur omnem veritatem confiteri, sed illam solum quam ab eo potest et debet requirere iudex secundum ordinem iuris, puta cum praecessit infamia super aliquo crimine, vel aliqua expressa indicia apparuerunt, vel etiam cum praecessit probatio semiplena. Falsitatem tamen proponere in nullo casu licet alicui.

Ad id autem quod licitum est potest aliquis procedere vel per vias licitas et fini intento accommodas, quod pertinet ad prudentiam, vel per aliquas vias illicitas et proposito fini incongruas, quod pertinet ad astutiam, quae exercetur per fraudem et dolum, ut ex supradictis patet. Quorum primum est laudabile; secundum vero vitiosum. Sic igitur reo qui accusatur licet se defendere veritatem occultando quam confiteri non tenetur, per aliquos convenientes modos, puta quod non respondeat ad quae respondere non tenetur. Hoc autem non est calumniose se defendere, sed magis prudenter evadere. Non autem licet ei vel falsitatem dicere, vel veritatem tacere quam confiteri tenetur; neque etiam aliquam fraudem vel dolum adhibere, quia fraus et dolus vim mendacii habent. Et hoc est calumniose se defendere.

**AD PRIMUM** ergo dicendum quod multa secundum leges humanas impunita relinquuntur quae secundum divinum iudicium sunt peccata, sicut patet in simplici fornicatione, quia lex humana non exigit ab homine omnimodam virtutem, quae paucorum est, et non potest inveniri in tanta multitudine populi quantam lex humana sustinere habet necesse. Quod autem aliquis non velit aliquod peccatum committere ut mortem corporalem evadat, cuius periculum in causa sanguinis imminet reo,

this is done chiefly by defending oneself with calumnies. Therefore the accused who is on trial for his life does not sin if he defend himself with calumnies.

**OBJ. 2**: Further, an accuser who is guilty of collusion with the accused, is punishable by law (*Decret.* II, qu. iii, can. *Si quem poenit*). Yet no punishment is imposed on the accused for collusion with the accuser. Therefore it would seem lawful for the accused to defend himself with calumnies.

**OBJ. 3**: Further, it is written (Prov 14:16): *A wise man feareth and declineth from evil, the fool leapeth over and is confident.* Now what is done wisely is no sin. Therefore no matter how a man declines from evil, he does not sin.

**ON THE CONTRARY**, In criminal cases an oath has to be taken against calumnious allegations (Extra, *De juramento calumniae*, cap. *Inhaerentes*): and this would not be the case if it were lawful to defend oneself with calumnies. Therefore it is not lawful for the accused to defend himself with calumnies.

**I ANSWER THAT**, It is one thing to withhold the truth, and another to utter a falsehood. The former is lawful sometimes, for a man is not bound to divulge all truth, but only such as the judge can and must require of him according to the order of justice; as, for instance, when the accused is already disgraced through the commission of some crime, or certain indications of his guilt have already been discovered, or again when his guilt is already more or less proven. On the other hand it is never lawful to make a false declaration.

As regards what he may do lawfully, a man can employ either lawful means, and such as are adapted to the end in view, which belongs to prudence; or he can use unlawful means, unsuitable to the proposed end, and this belongs to craftiness, which is exercised by fraud and guile, as shown above (Q. 55, AA. 3, seqq.). His conduct in the former case is praiseworthy, in the latter sinful. Accordingly it is lawful for the accused to defend himself by withholding the truth that he is not bound to avow, by suitable means, for instance by not answering such questions as he is not bound to answer. This is not to defend himself with calumnies, but to escape prudently. But it is unlawful for him, either to utter a falsehood, or to withhold a truth that he is bound to avow, or to employ guile or fraud, because fraud and guile have the force of a lie, and so to use them would be to defend oneself with calumnies.

**REPLY OBJ. 1**: Human laws leave many things unpunished, which according to the Divine judgment are sins, as, for example, simple fornication; because human law does not exact perfect virtue from man, for such virtue belongs to few and cannot be found in so great a number of people as human law has to direct. That a man is sometimes unwilling to commit a sin in order to escape from the death of the body, the danger of which threatens the accused who is on trial for his life, is an act of perfect virtue, since

est perfectae virtutis, quia *omnium temporalium maxime terribile est mors*, ut dicitur in III Ethic. Et ideo si reus in causa sanguinis corrumpat adversarium suum, peccat quidem inducendo eum ad illicitum, non autem huic peccato lex civilis adhibet poenam. Et pro tanto licitum esse dicitur.

**AD SECUNDUM** dicendum quod accusator, si colludat cum reo qui noxius, est, poenam incurrit, ex quo patet quod peccat. Unde, cum inducere aliquem ad peccandum sit peccatum, vel qualitercumque peccati participem esse, cum apostolus dicat dignos morte eos qui peccantibus consentiunt, manifestum est quod etiam reus peccat cum adversario colludendo. Non tamen secundum leges humanas imponitur sibi poena, propter rationem iam dictam.

**AD TERTIUM** dicendum quod sapiens non abscondit se calumniose, sed prudenter.

death is the most fearful of all temporal things (*Ethic.* iii, 6). Wherefore if the accused, who is on trial for his life, bribes his adversary, he sins indeed by inducing him to do what is unlawful, yet the civil law does not punish this sin, and in this sense it is said to be lawful.

**REPLY OBJ. 2**: If the accuser is guilty of collusion with the accused and the latter is guilty, he incurs punishment, and so it is evident that he sins. Wherefore, since it is a sin to induce a man to sin, or to take part in a sin in any way—for the Apostle says (Rom 1:32), that they are worthy of death that consent to those who sin—it is evident that the accused also sins if he is guilty of collusion with his adversary. Nevertheless according to human laws no punishment is inflicted on him, for the reason given above.

**REPLY OBJ. 3**: The wise man hides himself not by slandering others but by exercising prudence.

# Article 3

*Whether it is lawful for the accused to escape judgment by appealing?*

**AD TERTIUM SIC PROCEDITUR.** Videtur quod reo non liceat iudicium declinare per appellationem. Dicit enim apostolus, Rom. XIII, *omnis anima potestatibus sublimioribus subdita sit.* Sed reus appellando recusat subiici potestati superiori, scilicet iudici. Ergo peccat.

**PRAETEREA**, maius est vinculum ordinariae potestatis quam propriae electionis. Sed sicut legitur II, qu. VI, *a iudicibus quos communis consensus elegerit non liceat provocari.* Ergo multo minus licet appellare a iudicibus ordinariis.

**PRAETEREA**, illud quod semel est licitum, semper est licitum. Sed non est licitum appellare post decimum diem, neque tertio super eodem. Ergo videtur quod appellatio non sit secundum se licita.

**SED CONTRA** est quod Paulus Caesarem appellavit, ut habetur Act. XXV.

**RESPONDEO** dicendum quod duplici de causa contingit aliquem appellare. Uno quidem modo, confidentia iustae causae, quia videlicet iniuste a iudice gravatur. Et sic licitum est appellare, hoc enim est prudenter evadere. Unde II, qu. VI, dicitur, *omnis oppressus libere sacerdotum si voluerit appellet iudicium, et a nullo prohibeatur.* Alio modo aliquis appellat causa afferendae morae, ne contra eum iusta sententia proferatur. Et hoc est calumniose se defendere, quod est illicitum, sicut dictum est, facit enim iniuriam et iudici, cuius officium impedit, et adversario suo, cuius iustitiam, quantum potest, pertur-

**OBJECTION 1**: It would seem unlawful for the accused to escape judgment by appealing. The Apostle says (Rom 13:1): *Let every soul be subject to the higher powers.* Now the accused by appealing refuses to be subject to a higher power, viz. the judge. Therefore he commits a sin.

**OBJ. 2**: Further, ordinary authority is more binding than that which we choose for ourselves. Now according to the Decretals (II, qu. vi, cap. *A judicibus*) it is unlawful to *appeal from the judges chosen by common consent.* Much less therefore is it lawful to appeal from ordinary judges.

**OBJ. 3**: Further, whatever is lawful once is always lawful. But it is not lawful to appeal after the tenth day, nor a third time on the same point. Therefore it would seem that an appeal is unlawful in itself.

**ON THE CONTRARY**, Paul appealed to Caesar (Acts 25).

**I ANSWER THAT,** There are two motives for which a man appeals. First through confidence in the justice of his cause, seeing that he is unjustly oppressed by the judge, and then it is lawful for him to appeal, because this is a prudent means of escape. Hence it is laid down (*Decret.* II, qu. vi, can. Omnis oppressus): *All those who are oppressed are free, if they so wish, to appeal to the judgment of the priests, and no man may stand in their way.* Second, a man appeals in order to cause a delay, lest a just sentence be pronounced against him. This is to defend oneself calumniously, and is unlawful as stated above (A. 2). For he inflicts an injury both on the

bat. Et ideo sicut dicitur II, qu. VI, *omni modo puniendus est cuius iniusta appellatio pronuntiatur.*

**AD PRIMUM** ergo dicendum quod potestati inferiori intantum aliquis subiici debet inquantum ordinem superioris servat, a quo si exorbitaverit, ei subiici non oportet, puta *si aliud iusserit proconsul, et aliud imperator,* ut patet per Glossam Rom. XIII. Cum autem iudex iniuste aliquem gravat, quantum ad hoc relinquit ordinem superioris potestatis, secundum quam necessitas sibi iuste iudicandi imponitur. Et ideo licitum est ei qui contra iustitiam gravatur, ad directionem superioris potestatis recurrere appellando, vel ante sententiam vel post. Et quia non praesumitur esse rectitudo ubi vera fides non est, ideo non licet Catholico ad infidelem iudicem appellare, secundum illud II, qu. VI, *Catholicus qui causam suam, sive iustam sive iniustam, ad iudicium alterius fidei iudicis provocaverit, excommunicetur.* Nam et apostolus arguit eos qui iudicio contendebant apud infideles.

**AD SECUNDUM** dicendum quod ex proprio defectu vel negligentia procedit quod aliquis sua sponte se alterius iudicio subiiciat de cuius iustitia non confidit. Levis etiam animi esse videtur ut quis non permaneat in eo quod semel approbavit. Et ideo rationabiliter denegatur subsidium appellationis a iudicibus arbitrariis, qui non habent potestatem nisi ex consensu litigantium. Sed potestas iudicis ordinarii non dependet ex consensu illius qui eius iudicio subditur, sed ex auctoritate regis et principis, qui eum instituit. Et ideo contra eius iniustum gravamen lex tribuit appellationis subsidium, ita quod, etiam si sit simul ordinarius et arbitrarius iudex, potest ab eo appellari; quia videtur ordinaria potestas occasio fuisse quod arbiter eligeretur; nec debet ad defectum imputari eius qui consensit sicut in arbitrum in eum quem princeps iudicem ordinarium dedit.

**AD TERTIUM** dicendum quod aequitas iuris ita subvenit uni parti quod altera non gravetur. Et ideo tempus decem dierum concessit ad appellandum, quod sufficiens aestimavit ad deliberandum an expediat appellare. Si vero non esset determinatum tempus in quo appellare liceret, semper certitudo iudicii remaneret in suspenso, et ita pars altera damnaretur. Ideo autem non est concessum ut tertio aliquis appellet super eodem, quia non est probabile toties iudices a recto iudicio declinare.

judge, whom he hinders in the exercise of his office, and on his adversary, whose justice he disturbs as far as he is able. Hence it is laid down (II, qu. vi, can. *Omnino puniendus*): *Without doubt a man should be punished if his appeal be declared unjust.*

**REPLY OBJ. 1**: A man should submit to the lower authority insofar as the latter observes the order of the higher authority. If the lower authority departs from the order of the higher, we ought not to submit to it, for instance *if the proconsul order one thing and the emperor another,* according to a gloss on Rom. 13:2. Now when a judge oppresses anyone unjustly, in this respect he departs from the order of the higher authority, whereby he is obliged to judge justly. Hence it is lawful for a man who is oppressed unjustly, to have recourse to the authority of the higher power, by appealing either before or after sentence has been pronounced. And since it is to be presumed that there is no rectitude where true faith is lacking, it is unlawful for a Catholic to appeal to an unbelieving judge (*Decret.* II, qu. vi, can. *Catholicus*): *The Catholic who appeals to the decision of a judge of another faith shall be excommunicated, whether his case be just or unjust.* Hence the Apostle also rebuked those who went to law before unbelievers (1 Cor 6:6).

**REPLY OBJ. 2**: It is due to a man's own fault or neglect that, of his own accord, he submits to the judgment of one in whose justice he has no confidence. Moreover it would seem to point to levity of mind for a man not to abide by what he has once approved of. Hence it is with reason that the law refuses us the faculty of appealing from the decision of judges of our own choice, who have no power save by virtue of the consent of the litigants. On the other hand the authority of an ordinary judge depends, not on the consent of those who are subject to his judgment, but on the authority of the king or prince who appointed him. Hence, as a remedy against his unjust oppression, the law allows one to have recourse to appeal, so that even if the judge be at the same time ordinary and chosen by the litigants, it is lawful to appeal from his decision, since seemingly his ordinary authority occasioned his being chosen as arbitrator. Nor is it to be imputed as a fault to the man who consented to his being arbitrator, without adverting to the fact that he was appointed ordinary judge by the prince.

**REPLY OBJ. 3**: The equity of the law so guards the interests of the one party that the other is not oppressed. Thus it allows ten days for appeal to be made, this being considered sufficient time for deliberating on the expediency of an appeal. If on the other hand there were no fixed time limit for appealing, the certainty of judgment would ever be in suspense, so that the other party would suffer an injury. The reason why it is not allowed to appeal a third time on the same point, is that it is not probable that the judges would fail to judge justly so many times.

# Article 4

*Whether a man who is condemned to death may lawfully defend himself if he can?*

**AD QUARTUM SIC PROCEDITUR.** Videtur quod liceat condemnato ad mortem se defendere, si possit. Illud enim ad quod natura inclinat semper est licitum, quasi de iure naturali existens. Sed naturae inclinatio est ad resistendum corrumpentibus, non solum in hominibus et animalibus, sed etiam in insensibilibus rebus. Ergo licet reo condemnato resistere, si potest, ne tradatur in mortem.

**PRAETEREA,** sicut aliquis sententiam mortis contra se latam subterfugit resistendo, ita etiam fugiendo. Sed licitum esse videtur quod aliquis se a morte per fugam liberet, secundum illud Eccli. IX, *longe esto ab homine potestatem habente occidendi et non vivificandi.* Ergo etiam licitum est resistere.

**PRAETEREA,** Prov. XXIV dicitur, *erue eos qui ducuntur ad mortem, et eos qui trahuntur ad interitum liberare ne cesses.* Sed plus tenetur aliquis sibi quam alteri. Ergo licitum est quod aliquis condemnatus seipsum defendat ne in mortem tradatur.

**SED CONTRA** est quod dicit apostolus, Rom. XIII, *qui potestati resistit, Dei ordinationi resistit, et ipse sibi damnationem acquirit.* Sed condemnatus se defendendo potestati resistit quantum ad hoc in quo est divinitus instituta *ad vindictam malefactorum, laudem vero bonorum.* Ergo peccat se defendendo.

**RESPONDEO** dicendum quod aliquis damnatur ad mortem dupliciter. Uno modo, iuste. Et sic non licet condemnato se defendere, licitum enim est iudici eum resistentem impugnare; unde relinquitur quod ex parte eius sit bellum iniustum. Unde indubitanter peccat.

Alio modo condemnatur aliquis iniuste. Et tale iudicium simile est violentiae latronum, secundum illud Ezech. XXII, *principes eius in medio eius quasi lupi rapientes praedam ad effundendum sanguinem.* Et ideo sicut licet resistere latronibus, ita licet resistere in tali casu malis principibus, nisi forte propter scandalum vitandum, cum ex hoc aliqua gravis turbatio timeretur.

**AD PRIMUM** ergo dicendum quod ideo homini data est ratio, ut ea ad quae natura inclinat non passim, sed secundum rationis ordinem exequatur. Et ideo non quaelibet defensio sui est licita, sed quae fit cum debito moderamine.

**AD SECUNDUM** dicendum quod nullus ita condemnatur quod ipse sibi inferat mortem, sed quod ipse mortem patiatur. Et ideo non tenetur facere id unde mors sequatur, quod est manere in loco unde ducatur ad mortem. Tenetur tamen non resistere agenti, quin patiatur quod iustum est eum pati. Sicut etiam si aliquis

**OBJECTION 1**: It would seem that a man who is condemned to death may lawfully defend himself if he can. For it is always lawful to do that to which nature inclines us, as being of natural right, so to speak. Now, to resist corruption is an inclination of nature not only in men and animals but also in things devoid of sense. Therefore if he can do so, the accused, after condemnation, may lawfully resist being put to death.

**OBJ. 2**: Further, just as a man, by resistance, escapes the death to which he has been condemned, so does he by flight. Now it is lawful seemingly to escape death by flight, according to Ecclus. 9:18, *Keep thee far from the man that hath power to kill.* Therefore it is also lawful for the accused to resist.

**OBJ. 3**: Further, it is written (Prov 24:11): *Deliver them that are led to death: and those that are drawn to death forbear not to deliver.* Now a man is under greater obligation to himself than to another. Therefore it is lawful for a condemned man to defend himself from being put to death.

**ON THE CONTRARY**, The Apostle says (Rom 13:2): *He that resisteth the power, resisteth the ordinance of God: and they that resist, purchase to themselves damnation.* Now a condemned man, by defending himself, resists the power in the point of its being ordained by God *for the punishment of evil-doers, and for the praise of the good.* Therefore he sins in defending himself.

**I ANSWER THAT**, A man may be condemned to death in two ways. First justly, and then it is not lawful for the condemned to defend himself, because it is lawful for the judge to combat his resistance by force, so that on his part the fight is unjust, and consequently without any doubt he sins.

Second a man is condemned unjustly: and such a sentence is like the violence of robbers, according to Ezech. 22:21, *Her princes in the midst of her are like wolves ravening the prey to shed blood.* Wherefore even as it is lawful to resist robbers, so is it lawful, in a like case, to resist wicked princes; except perhaps in order to avoid scandal, whence some grave disturbance might be feared to arise.

**REPLY OBJ. 1**: Reason was given to man that he might ensue those things to which his nature inclines, not in all cases, but in accordance with the order of reason. Hence not all self-defense is lawful, but only such as is accomplished with due moderation.

**REPLY OBJ. 2**: When a man is condemned to death, he has not to kill himself, but to suffer death: wherefore he is not bound to do anything from which death would result, such as to stay in the place whence he would be led to execution. But he may not resist those who lead him to death, in order that he may not suffer what is just for

652

sit condemnatus ut fame moriatur, non peccat si cibum sibi occulte ministratum sumat, quia non sumere esset seipsum occidere.

**AD TERTIUM** dicendum quod per illud dictum sapientis non inducitur aliquis ad liberandum alium a morte contra ordinem iustitiae. Unde nec seipsum contra iustitiam resistendo aliquis debet liberare a morte.

him to suffer. Even so, if a man were condemned to die of hunger, he does not sin if he partakes of food brought to him secretly, because to refrain from taking it would be to kill himself.

**REPLY OBJ. 3**: This saying of the wise man does not direct that one should deliver a man from death in opposition to the order of justice: wherefore neither should a man deliver himself from death by resisting against justice.

# QUESTION 70

## INJUSTICE WITH REGARD TO THE PERSON OF THE WITNESS

Deinde considerandum est de iniustitia pertinente ad personam testis. Et circa hoc quaeruntur quatuor.

Primo, utrum homo teneatur ad testimonium ferendum.

Secundo, utrum duorum vel trium testimonium sufficiat.

Tertio, utrum alicuius testimonium repellatur absque eius culpa.

Quarto, utrum perhibere falsum testimonium sit peccatum mortale.

We must now consider injustice with regard to the person of the witness. Under this head there are four points of inquiry:

(1) Whether a man is bound to give evidence?

(2) Whether the evidence of two or three witnesses suffices?

(3) Whether a man's evidence may be rejected without any fault on his part?

(4) Whether it is a mortal sin to bear false witness?

# Article 1

### *Whether a man is bound to give evidence?*

**AD PRIMUM SIC PROCEDITUR.** Videtur quod homo non teneatur ad testimonium ferendum. Dicit enim Augustinus, in quaest. Gen., quod Abraham dicens de uxore sua, *soror mea est*, veritatem celari voluit, non mendacium dici. Sed veritatem celando aliquis a testificando abstinet. Ergo non tenetur aliquis ad testificandum.

**PRAETEREA,** nullus tenetur fraudulenter agere. Sed Prov. XI dicitur, *qui ambulat fraudulenter revelat arcana, qui autem fidelis est celat amici commissum.* Ergo non tenetur homo semper ad testificandum, praesertim super his quae sunt sibi in secreto ab amico commissa.

**PRAETEREA,** ad ea quae sunt de necessitate salutis maxime tenentur clerici et sacerdotes. Sed clericis et sacerdotibus prohibetur ferre testimonium in causa sanguinis. Ergo testificari non est de necessitate salutis.

**SED CONTRA** est quod Augustinus dicit, *qui veritatem occultat, et qui prodit mendacium, uterque reus est, ille quia prodesse non vult, iste quia nocere desiderat.*

**RESPONDEO** dicendum quod in testimonio ferendo distinguendum est. Quia aliquando requiritur testimonium alicuius, aliquando non requiritur. Si requiritur testimonium alicuius subditi auctoritate superioris cui in his quae ad iustitiam pertinent obedire tenetur, non est dubium quin teneatur testimonium ferre in his in quibus secundum ordinem iuris testimonium ab eo exigitur, puta in manifestis, et in his de quibus infamia

**OBJECTION 1**: It would seem that a man is not bound to give evidence. Augustine says (QQ. Gen. 1:26), that when Abraham said of his wife (Gen 20:2), *She is my sister*, he wished the truth to be concealed and not a lie be told. Now, by hiding the truth a man abstains from giving evidence. Therefore a man is not bound to give evidence.

**OBJ. 2**: Further, no man is bound to act deceitfully. Now it is written (Prov 11:13): *He that walketh deceitfully revealeth secrets, but he that is faithful concealeth the thing committed to him by his friend.* Therefore a man is not always bound to give evidence, especially on matters committed to him as a secret by a friend.

**OBJ. 3**: Further, clerics and priests, more than others, are bound to those things that are necessary for salvation. Yet clerics and priests are forbidden to give evidence when a man is on trial for his life. Therefore it is not necessary for salvation to give evidence.

**ON THE CONTRARY,** Augustine says: *Both he who conceals the truth and he who tells a lie are guilty, the former because he is unwilling to do good, the latter because he desires to hurt.*

**I ANSWER THAT,** We must make a distinction in the matter of giving evidence: because sometimes a certain man's evidence is necessary, and sometimes not. If the necessary evidence is that of a man subject to a superior whom, in matters pertaining to justice, he is bound to obey, without doubt he is bound to give evidence on those points which are required of him in accordance with the order of justice, for instance on manifest things or when ill-report

praecessit. Si autem exigatur ab eo testimonium in aliis, puta in occultis et de quibus infamia non praecessit, non tenetur ad testificandum. Si vero requiratur eius testimonium non auctoritate superioris cui obedire tenetur, tunc distinguendum est. Quia si testimonium requiratur ad liberandum hominem vel ab iniusta morte seu poena quacumque, vel a falsa infamia, vel etiam ab iniquo damno, tunc tenetur homo ad testificandum. Et si eius testimonium non requiratur, tenetur facere quod in se est ut veritatem denuntiet alicui qui ad hoc possit prodesse. Dicitur enim in Psalm., *eripite pauperem, et egenum de manu peccatoris liberate*; et Prov. XXIV, *erue eos qui dicuntur ad mortem*. Et Rom. I dicitur, *digni sunt morte non solum qui faciunt, sed etiam qui consentiunt facientibus*, ubi dicit Glossa, *consentire est tacere, cum possis redarguere*. Super his vero quae pertinent ad condemnationem alicuius, non tenetur aliquis ferre testimonium nisi cum a superiori compellitur secundum ordinem iuris. Quia si circa hoc veritas occultetur, nulli ex hoc speciale damnum nascitur. Vel, si immineat periculum accusatori, non est curandum, quia ipse se in hoc periculum sponte ingessit. Alia autem ratio est de reo, cui periculum imminet eo nolente.

**AD PRIMUM** ergo dicendum quod Augustinus loquitur de occultatione veritatis in casu illo quando aliquis non compellitur superioris auctoritate veritatem propalare; et quando occultatio veritatis nulli specialiter est damnosa.

**AD SECUNDUM** dicendum quod de illis quae homini sunt commissa in secreto per confessionem, nullo modo debet testimonium ferre, quia huiusmodi non scit ut homo, sed tanquam Dei minister, et maius est vinculum sacramenti quolibet hominis praecepto. Circa ea vero quae aliter homini sub secreto committuntur, distinguendum est. Quandoque enim sunt talia quae, statim cum ad notitiam hominis venerint, homo ea manifestare tenetur, puta si pertineret ad corruptionem multitudinis spiritualem vel corporalem, vel in grave damnum alicuius personae, vel si quid aliud est huiusmodi, quod quis propalare tenetur vel testificando vel denuntiando. Et contra hoc debitum obligari non potest per secreti commissum, quia in hoc frangeret fidem quam alteri debet. Quandoque vero sunt talia quae quis prodere non tenetur. Unde potest obligari ex hoc quod sibi sub secreto committuntur. Et tunc nullo modo tenetur ea prodere, etiam ex praecepto superioris, quia servare fidem est de iure naturali; nihil autem potest praecipi homini contra id quod est de iure naturali.

**AD TERTIUM** dicendum quod operari vel cooperari ad occisionem hominis non competit ministris altaris,

has preceded. If however he is required to give evidence on other points, for instance secret matters, and those of which no ill report has preceded, he is not bound to give evidence. On the other hand, if his evidence be required by authority of a superior whom he is bound to obey, we must make a distinction: because if his evidence is required in order to deliver a man from an unjust death or any other penalty, or from false defamation, or some loss, in such cases he is bound to give evidence. Even if his evidence is not demanded, he is bound to do what he can to declare the truth to someone who may profit thereby. For it is written (Ps 81:4): *Rescue the poor, and deliver the needy from the hand of the sinner*; and (Prov 24:11): *Deliver them that are led to death*; and (Rom 1:32): *They are worthy of death, not only they that do them, but they also that consent to them that do them*, on which words a gloss says: *To be silent when one can disprove is to consent*. In matters pertaining to a man's condemnation, one is not bound to give evidence, except when one is constrained by a superior in accordance with the order of justice; since if the truth of such a matter be concealed, no particular injury is inflicted on anyone. Or, if some danger threatens the accuser, it matters not since he risked the danger of his own accord: whereas it is different with the accused, who incurs the danger against his will.

**REPLY OBJ. 1**: Augustine is speaking of concealment of the truth in a case when a man is not compelled by his superior's authority to declare the truth, and when such concealment is not specially injurious to any person.

**REPLY OBJ. 2**: A man should by no means give evidence on matters secretly committed to him in confession, because he knows such things, not as man but as God's minister: and the sacrament is more binding than any human precept. But as regards matters committed to man in some other way under secrecy, we must make a distinction. Sometimes they are of such a nature that one is bound to make them known as soon as they come to our knowledge, for instance if they conduce to the spiritual or corporal corruption of the community, or to some grave personal injury, in short any like matter that a man is bound to make known either by giving evidence or by denouncing it. Against such a duty a man cannot be obliged to act on the plea that the matter is committed to him under secrecy, for he would break the faith he owes to another. On the other hand sometimes they are such as one is not bound to make known, so that one may be under obligation not to do so on account of their being committed to one under secrecy. In such a case one is by no means bound to make them known, even if the superior should command; because to keep faith is of natural right, and a man cannot be commanded to do what is contrary to natural right.

**REPLY OBJ. 3**: It is unbecoming for ministers of the altar to slay a man or to cooperate in his slaying, as stated

ut supra dictum est. Et ideo secundum iuris ordinem compelli non possunt ad ferendum testimonium in causa sanguinis.

above (Q. 64, A. 4); hence according to the order of justice they cannot be compelled to give evidence when a man is on trial for his life.

# Article 2

*Whether the evidence of two or three persons suffices?*

**AD SECUNDUM SIC PROCEDITUR**. Videtur quod non sufficiat duorum vel trium testimonium. Iudicium enim certitudinem requirit. Sed non habetur certitudo veritatis per dictum duorum testium, legitur enim III Reg. XXI quod Naboth ad dictum duorum testium falso condemnatus est. Ergo duorum vel trium testimonium non sufficit.

**PRAETEREA**, testimonium, ad hoc quod sit credibile, debet esse concors. Sed plerumque duorum vel trium testimonium in aliquo discordat. Ergo non est efficax ad veritatem in iudicio probandam.

**PRAETEREA**, II, qu. IV, dicitur, *praesul non damnetur nisi in septuaginta duobus testibus. Presbyter autem cardinalis nisi quadraginta quatuor testibus non deponatur. Diaconus cardinalis urbis Romae nisi in viginti octo testibus non condemnabitur. Subdiaconus, acolythus, exorcista, lector, ostiarius, nisi in septem testibus non condemnabitur.* Sed magis est periculosum peccatum eius qui in maiori dignitate constitutus est, et ita minus est tolerandum. Ergo nec in aliorum condemnatione sufficit duorum vel trium testimonium.

**SED CONTRA** est quod dicitur Deut. XVII, *in ore duorum vel trium testium peribit qui interficietur*; et infra, XIX, *in ore duorum vel trium testium stabit omne verbum*.

**RESPONDEO** dicendum quod, secundum philosophum, in I Ethic., *certitudo non est similiter quaerenda in omni materia*. In actibus enim humanis, super quibus constituuntur iudicia et exiguntur testimonia, non potest haberi certitudo demonstrativa, eo quod sunt circa contingentia et variabilia. Et ideo sufficit probabilis certitudo, quae ut in pluribus veritatem attingat, etsi in paucioribus a veritate deficiat. Est autem probabile quod magis veritatem contineat dictum multorum quam dictum unius. Et ideo, cum reus sit unus qui negat, sed multi testes asserunt idem cum actore, rationabiliter institutum est, iure divino et humano, quod dicto testium stetur. Omnis autem multitudo in tribus comprehenditur, scilicet principio, medio et fine, unde secundum philosophum, in I de coelo, *omne et totum in tribus ponimus*. Ternarius quidem constituitur asserentium, cum duo testes conveniunt cum actore. Et ideo requiritur binarius testium, vel, ad maiorem certitudinem, ut sit

**OBJECTION 1**: It would seem that the evidence of two or three persons is not sufficient. For judgment requires certitude. Now certitude of the truth is not obtained by the assertions of two or three witnesses, for we read that Naboth was unjustly condemned on the evidence of two witnesses (3 Kgs 21). Therefore the evidence of two or three witnesses does not suffice.

**OBJ. 2**: Further, in order for evidence to be credible it must agree. But frequently the evidence of two or three disagrees in some point. Therefore it is of no use for proving the truth in court.

**OBJ. 3**: Further, it is laid down (*Decret.* II, qu. iv, can. Praesul.): *A bishop shall not be condemned save on the evidence of seventy-two witnesses; nor a cardinal priest of the Roman Church, unless there be sixty-four witnesses. Nor a cardinal deacon of the Roman Church, unless there be twenty-seven witnesses; nor a subdeacon, an acolyte, an exorcist, a reader or a doorkeeper without seven witnesses.* Now the sin of one who is of higher dignity is more grievous, and consequently should be treated more severely. Therefore neither is the evidence of two or three witnesses sufficient for the condemnation of other persons.

**ON THE CONTRARY**, It is written (Deut 17:6): *By the mouth of two or three witnesses shall he die that is to be slain*, and further on (Deut 19:15): *In the mouth of two or three witnesses every word shall stand*.

**I ANSWER THAT**, According to the Philosopher (*Ethic.* i, 3), *we must not expect to find certitude equally in every matter*. For in human acts, on which judgments are passed and evidence required, it is impossible to have demonstrative certitude, because they are about things contingent and variable. Hence the certitude of probability suffices, such as may reach the truth in the greater number of cases, although it fail in the minority. Now it is probable that the assertion of several witnesses contains the truth rather than the assertion of one: and since the accused is the only one who denies, while several witness affirm the same as the prosecutor, it is reasonably established both by Divine and by human law, that the assertion of several witnesses should be upheld. Now all multitude is comprised of three elements, the beginning, the middle and the end. Wherefore, according to the Philosopher (*De Caelo* i, 1), *we reckon 'all' and 'whole' to consist of three parts*. Now we have a triple voucher when two agree with the prosecutor:

ternarius, qui est multitudo perfecta, in ipsis testibus. Unde et Eccle. IV dicitur, *funiculus triplex difficile rumpitur.* Augustinus autem, super illud Ioan. VIII, *duorum hominum testimonium verum est,* dicit quod *in hoc est Trinitas secundum mysterium commendata,* in qua est perpetua firmitas veritatis.

**AD PRIMUM** ergo dicendum quod, quantacumque multitudo testium determinaretur, posset quandoque testimonium esse iniquum, cum scriptum sit Exod. XXIII, *ne sequaris turbam ad faciendum malum.* Nec tamen, quia non potest in talibus infallibilis certitudo haberi, debet negligi certitudo quae probabiliter haberi potest per duos vel tres testes, ut dictum est.

**AD SECUNDUM** dicendum quod discordia testium in aliquibus principalibus circumstantiis, quae variant substantiam facti, puta in tempore vel loco vel in personis de quibus principaliter agitur, aufert efficaciam testimonii, quia si discordant in talibus, videntur singulares esse in suis testimoniis, et de diversis factis loqui; puta si unus dicat hoc factum esse tali tempore vel loco, alius alio tempore vel loco, non videntur de eodem facto loqui.

Non tamen praeiudicatur testimonio si unus dicat se non recordari, et alius asserat determinatum tempus vel locum. Et si in talibus omnino discordaverint testes actoris et rei, si sint aequales numero et pares dignitate, statur pro reo, quia facilior debet esse iudex ad absolvendum quam ad condemnandum; nisi forte in causis favorabilibus, sicut est causa libertatis et huiusmodi.

Si vero testes eiusdem partis dissenserint, debet iudex ex motu sui animi percipere cui parti sit standum, vel ex numero testium, vel ex dignitate eorum, vel ex favorabilitate causae, vel ex conditione negotii et dictorum. Multo autem magis testimonium unius repellitur si sibi ipsi dissideat interrogatus de visu et scientia. Non autem si dissideat interrogatus de opinione et fama, quia potest secundum diversa visa et audita diversimode motus esse ad respondendum.

Si vero sit discordia testimonii in aliquibus circumstantiis non pertinentibus ad substantiam facti, puta si tempus fuerit nubilosum vel serenum, vel si domus fuerit picta aut non, aut aliquid huiusmodi, talis discordia non praeiudicat testimonio, quia homines non consueverunt circa talia multum sollicitari, unde facile a memoria elabuntur. Quinimmo aliqua discordia in talibus facit testimonium credibilius, ut Chrysostomus dicit, super Matth., quia si in omnibus

hence two witnesses are required; or for the sake of greater certitude three, which is the perfect number. Wherefore it is written (Eccl 4:12): *A threefold cord is not easily broken*: and Augustine, commenting on John 8:17, *The testimony of two men is true,* says (*Tract. xxxvi*) that *there is here a mystery by which we are given to understand that Trinity wherein is perpetual stability of truth.*

**REPLY OBJ. 1**: No matter how great a number of witnesses may be determined, the evidence might sometimes be unjust, since is written (Exod 23:2): *Thou shalt not follow the multitude to do evil.* And yet the fact that in so many it is not possible to have certitude without fear of error, is no reason why we should reject the certitude which can probably be had through two or three witnesses, as stated above.

**REPLY OBJ. 2**: If the witnesses disagree in certain principal circumstances which change the substance of the fact, for instance in time, place, or persons, which are chiefly in question, their evidence is of no weight, because if they disagree in such things, each one would seem to be giving distinct evidence and to be speaking of different facts. For instance, one say that a certain thing happened at such and such a time or place, while another says it happened at another time or place, they seem not to be speaking of the same event.

The evidence is not weakened if one witness says that he does not remember, while the other attests to a determinate time or place. And if on such points as these the witness for prosecution and defense disagree altogether, and if they be equal in number on either side, and of equal standing, the accused should have the benefit of the doubt, because the judge ought to be more inclined to acquit than to condemn, except perhaps in favorable suits, such as a pleading for liberty and the like.

If, however, the witnesses for the same side disagree, the judge ought to use his own discretion in discerning which side to favor, by considering either the number of witnesses, or their standing, or the favorableness of the suit, or the nature of the business and of the evidence. Much more ought the evidence of one witness to be rejected if he contradict himself when questioned about what he has seen and about what he knows; not, however, if he contradict himself when questioned about matters of opinion and report, since he may be moved to answer differently according to the different things he has seen and heard.

On the other hand if there be discrepancy of evidence in circumstances not touching the substance of the fact, for instance, whether the weather were cloudy or fine, whether the house were painted or not, or such like matters, such discrepancy does not weaken the evidence, because men are not wont to take much notice of such things, wherefore they easily forget them. Indeed, a discrepancy of this kind renders the evidence more credible, as Chrysostom states (*Hom. i in Matth.*), because if the witnesses agreed in every

concordarent, etiam in minimis, viderentur ex condicto eundem sermonem proferre. Quod tamen prudentiae iudicis relinquitur discernendum.

**AD TERTIUM** dicendum quod illud locum habet specialiter in episcopis, presbyteris, diaconibus et clericis Ecclesiae Romanae, propter eius dignitatem. Et hoc triplici ratione. Primo quidem, quia in ea tales institui debent quorum sanctitati plus credatur quam multis testibus. Secundo, quia homines qui habent de aliis iudicare, saepe, propter iustitiam, multos adversarios habent. Unde non est passim credendum testibus contra eos, nisi magna multitudo conveniat. Tertio, quia ex condemnatione alicuius eorum derogaretur in opinione hominum dignitati illius Ecclesiae et auctoritati. Quod est periculosius quam in ea tolerare aliquem peccatorem, nisi valde publicum et manifestum, de quo grave scandalum oriretur.

point, even in the minutest of details, they would seem to have conspired together to say the same thing: but this must be left to the prudent discernment of the judge.

**REPLY OBJ. 3**: This passage refers specially to the bishops, priests, deacons and clerics of the Roman Church, on account of its dignity: and this for three reasons. First because in that Church those men ought to be promoted whose sanctity makes their evidence of more weight than that of many witnesses. Second, because those who have to judge other men, often have many opponents on account of their justice, wherefore those who give evidence against them should not be believed indiscriminately, unless they be very numerous. Third, because the condemnation of any one of them would detract in public opinion from the dignity and authority of that Church, a result which would be more fraught with danger than if one were to tolerate a sinner in that same Church, unless he were very notorious and manifest, so that a grave scandal would arise if he were tolerated.

# Article 3

*Whether a man's evidence can be rejected without any fault of his?*

**AD TERTIUM SIC PROCEDITUR**. Videtur quod alicuius testimonium non sit repellendum nisi propter culpam. Quibusdam enim in poenam infligitur quod ad testimonium non admittantur, sicut patet in his qui infamia notantur. Sed poena non est inferenda nisi pro culpa. Ergo videtur quod nullius testimonium debeat repelli nisi propter culpam.

**PRAETEREA**, *de quolibet praesumendum est bonum, nisi appareat contrarium*. Sed ad bonitatem hominis pertinet quod verum testimonium dicat. Cum ergo non possit constare de contrario nisi propter aliquam culpam, videtur quod nullius testimonium debeat repelli nisi propter culpam.

**PRAETEREA**, ad ea quae sunt de necessitate salutis nullus redditur non idoneus nisi propter peccatum. Sed testificari veritatem est de necessitate salutis, ut supra dictum est. Ergo nullus debet excludi a testificando nisi propter culpam.

**SED CONTRA** est quod Gregorius dicit, et habetur II, qu. I, *quia a servis suis accusatus est episcopus, sciendum est quod minime audiri debuerunt.*

**RESPONDEO** dicendum quod testimonium, sicut dictum est, non habet infallibilem certitudinem, sed probabilem. Et ideo quidquid est quod probabilitatem afferat in contrarium, reddit testimonium inefficax. Redditur autem probabile quod aliquis in veritate testificanda non sit firmus, quandoque quidem propter

**OBJECTION 1**: It would seem that a man's evidence ought not to be rejected except on account of some fault. For it is inflicted as a penalty on some that their evidence is inadmissible, as in the case of those who are branded with infamy. Now a penalty must not be inflicted save for a fault. Therefore it would seem that no man's evidence ought to be rejected save on account of a fault.

**OBJ. 2**: Further, *Good is to be presumed of every one, unless the contrary appear*. Now it pertains to a man's goodness that he should give true evidence. Since therefore there can be no proof of the contrary, unless there be some fault of his, it would seem that no man's evidence should be rejected save for some fault.

**OBJ. 3**: Further, no man is rendered unfit for things necessary for salvation except by some sin. But it is necessary for salvation to give true evidence, as stated above (A. 1). Therefore no man should be excluded from giving evidence save for some fault.

**ON THE CONTRARY**, Gregory says (*Regist.* xiii, 44): *As to the bishop who is said to have been accused by his servants, you are to know that they should by no means have been heard*: which words are embodied in the Decretals (II, qu. 1, can. Imprimis).

**I ANSWER THAT**, As stated above (A. 2), the authority of evidence is not infallible but probable; and consequently the evidence for one side is weakened by whatever strengthens the probability of the other. Now the reliability of a person's evidence is weakened, sometimes indeed on account of some fault of his, as in the case of unbelievers and

culpam, sicut infideles, infames, item illi qui publico crimine rei sunt, qui nec accusare possunt, quandoque autem absque culpa. Et hoc vel ex defectu rationis, sicut patet in pueris, amentibus et mulieribus; vel ex affectu, sicut patet de inimicis et de personis coniunctis et domesticis; vel etiam ex exteriori conditione, sicut sunt pauperes, servi et illi quibus imperari potest, de quibus probabile est quod facile possint induci ad testimonium ferendum contra veritatem.

Et sic patet quod testimonium alicuius repellitur et propter culpam, et absque culpa.

**AD PRIMUM** ergo dicendum quod repellere aliquem a testimonio magis pertinet ad cautelam falsi testimonii vitandi quam ad poenam. Unde ratio non sequitur.

**AD SECUNDUM** dicendum quod de quolibet praesumendum est bonum nisi appareat contrarium, dummodo non vergat in periculum alterius. Quia tunc est adhibenda cautela, ut non de facili unicuique credatur, secundum illud I Ioan. IV, *nolite credere omni spiritui.*

**AD TERTIUM** dicendum quod testificari est de necessitate salutis, supposita testis idoneitate et ordine iuris. Unde nihil prohibet aliquos excusari a testimonio ferendo, si non reputentur idonei secundum iura.

persons of evil repute, as well as those who are guilty of a public crime and who are not allowed even to accuse; sometimes, without any fault on his part, and this owing either to a defect in the reason, as in the case of children, imbeciles and women, or to personal feeling, as in the case of enemies, or persons united by family or household ties, or again owing to some external condition, as in the case of poor people, slaves, and those who are under authority, concerning whom it is to be presumed that they might easily be induced to give evidence against the truth.

Thus it is manifest that a person's evidence may be rejected either with or without some fault of his.

**REPLY OBJ. 1:** If a person is disqualified from giving evidence this is done as a precaution against false evidence rather than as a punishment. Hence the argument does not prove.

**REPLY OBJ. 2:** Good is to be presumed of everyone unless the contrary appear, provided this does not threaten injury to another: because, in that case, one ought to be careful not to believe everyone readily, according to 1 John 4:1: *Believe not every spirit.*

**REPLY OBJ. 3:** To give evidence is necessary for salvation, provided the witness be competent, and the order of justice observed. Hence nothing hinders certain persons being excused from giving evidence, if they be considered unfit according to law.

# Article 4

*Whether it is always a mortal sin to give false evidence?*

**AD QUARTUM SIC PROCEDITUR.** Videtur quod falsum testimonium non semper sit peccatum mortale. Contingit enim aliquem falsum testimonium ferre ex ignorantia facti. Sed talis ignorantia excusat a peccato mortali. Ergo testimonium falsum non semper est peccatum mortale.

**PRAETEREA**, mendacium quod alicui prodest et nulli nocet, est officiosum, quod non est peccatum mortale. Sed quandoque in falso testimonio est tale mendacium, puta cum aliquis falsum testimonium perhibet ut aliquem a morte liberet, vel ab iniusta sententia quae intentatur per alios falsos testes vel per iudicis perversitatem. Ergo tale falsum testimonium non est peccatum mortale.

**PRAETEREA**, iuramentum a teste requiritur ut timeat peccare mortaliter deierando. Hoc autem non esset necessarium si ipsum falsum testimonium esset peccatum mortale. Ergo falsum testimonium non semper est peccatum mortale.

**SED CONTRA** est quod dicitur Prov. XIX, *falsus testis non erit impunitus.*

**OBJECTION 1:** It would seem that it is not always a mortal sin to give false evidence. For a person may happen to give false evidence, through ignorance of fact. Now such ignorance excuses from mortal sin. Therefore the giving of false evidence is not always a mortal sin.

**OBJ. 2:** Further, a lie that benefits someone and hurts no man is officious, and this is not a mortal sin. Now sometimes a lie of this kind occurs in false evidence, as when a person gives false evidence in order to save a man from death, or from an unjust sentence which threatens him through other false witnesses or a perverse judge. Therefore in such cases it is not a mortal sin to give false evidence.

**OBJ. 3:** Further, a witness is required to take an oath in order that he may fear to commit a mortal sin of perjury. But this would not be necessary, if it were already a mortal sin to give false evidence. Therefore the giving of false evidence is not always mortal sin.

**ON THE CONTRARY,** It is written (Prov 19:5): *A false witness shall not be unpunished.*

**RESPONDEO** dicendum quod falsum testimonium habet triplicem deformitatem. Uno modo, ex periurio, quia testes non admittuntur nisi iurati. Et ex hoc semper est peccatum mortale. Alio modo, ex violatione iustitiae. Et hoc modo est peccatum mortale in suo genere, sicut et quaelibet iniustitia. Et ideo in praecepto Decalogi sub hac forma interdicitur falsum testimonium, cum dicitur Exod. XX, *non loquaris contra proximum tuum falsum testimonium*, non enim contra aliquem facit qui eum ab iniuria facienda impedit, sed solum qui ei suam iustitiam tollit. Tertio modo, ex ipsa falsitate, secundum quod omne mendacium est peccatum. Et ex hoc non habet falsum testimonium quod semper sit peccatum mortale.

**AD PRIMUM** ergo dicendum quod in testimonio ferendo non debet homo pro certo asserere, quasi sciens, id de quo certus non est, sed dubium debet sub dubio proferre, et id de quo certus est pro certo asserere. Sed quia contingit ex labilitate humanae memoriae quod reputat se homo quandoque certum esse de eo quod falsum est, si aliquis, cum debita sollicitudine recogitans, existimet se certum esse de eo quod falsum est, non peccat mortaliter hoc asserens, quia non dicit falsum testimonium per se et ex intentione, sed per accidens, contra id quod intendit.

**AD SECUNDUM** dicendum quod iniustum iudicium iudicium non est. Et ideo ex vi iudicii falsum testimonium in iniusto iudicio prolatum ad iniustitiam impediendam, non habet rationem peccati mortalis, sed solum ex iuramento violato.

**AD TERTIUM** dicendum quod homines maxime abhorrent peccata quae sunt contra Deum, quasi gravissima, inter quae est periurium. Non autem ita abhorrent peccata quae sunt contra proximum. Et ideo ad maiorem certitudinem testimonii, requiritur testis iuramentum.

**I ANSWER THAT,** False evidence has a threefold deformity. The first is owing to perjury, since witnesses are admitted only on oath and on this count it is always a mortal sin. Second, owing to the violation of justice, and on this account it is a mortal sin generically, even as any kind of injustice. Hence the prohibition of false evidence by the precept of the decalogue is expressed in this form when it is said (Exod 20:16), *Thou shalt not bear false witness against thy neighbor.* For one does nothing against a man by preventing him from doing someone an injury, but only by taking away his justice. Third, owing to the falsehood itself, by reason of which every lie is a sin: on this account, the giving of false evidence is not always a mortal sin.

**REPLY OBJ. 1:** In giving evidence a man ought not to affirm as certain, as though he knew it, that about which he is not certain; and he should confess his doubt in doubtful terms, and that which he is certain about, in terms of certainty. Owing however to the frailty of the human memory, a man sometimes thinks he is certain about something that is not true; and then if after thinking over the matter with due care he deems himself certain about that false thing, he does not sin mortally if he asserts it, because the evidence which he gives is not directly and intentionally, but accidentally contrary to what he intends.

**REPLY OBJ. 2:** An unjust judgment is not a judgment, wherefore the false evidence given in an unjust judgment, in order to prevent injustice is not a mortal sin by virtue of the judgment, but only by reason of the oath violated.

**REPLY OBJ. 3:** Men abhor chiefly those sins that are against God, as being most grievous; and among them is perjury: whereas they do not abhor so much sins against their neighbor. Consequently, for the greater certitude of evidence, the witness is required to take a oath.

# QUESTION 71

## INJUSTICE IN JUDGMENT ON THE PART OF COUNSEL

Deinde considerandum est de iniustitia quae fit in iudicio ex parte advocatorum. Et circa hoc quaeruntur quatuor.

Primo, utrum advocatus teneatur praestare patrocinium causae pauperum.

Secundo, utrum aliquis debeat arceri ab officio advocati.

Tertio, utrum advocatus peccet iniustam causam defendendo.

Quarto, utrum peccet pecuniam accipiendo pro suo patrocinio.

We must now consider the injustice which takes place in judgment on the part of counsel, and under this head there are four points of inquiry:

(1) Whether an advocate is bound to defend the suits of the poor?

(2) Whether certain persons should be prohibited from exercising the office of advocate?

(3) Whether an advocate sins by defending an unjust cause?

(4) Whether he sins if he accept a fee for defending a suit?

# Article 1

*Whether an advocate is bound to defend the suits of the poor?*

**AD PRIMUM SIC PROCEDITUR.** Videtur quod advocatus teneatur patrocinium praestare causae pauperum. Dicitur enim Exod. XXIII, *si videris asinum odientis te iacere sub onere, non pertransibis, sed sublevabis cum eo.* Sed non minus periculum imminet pauperi si eius causa contra iustitiam opprimatur, quam si eius asinus iaceat sub onere. Ergo advocatus tenetur praestare patrocinium causae pauperum.

**PRAETEREA,** Gregorius dicit, in quadam homilia, *habens intellectum curet omnino ne taceat; habens rerum affluentiam a misericordia non torpescat; habens artem qua regitur, usum illius cum proximo partiatur; habens loquendi locum apud divitem, pro pauperibus intercedat, talenti enim nomine cuilibet reputabitur quod vel minimum accepit.* Sed talentum commissum non abscondere, sed fideliter dispensare quilibet tenetur, quod patet ex poena servi abscondentis talentum, Matth. XXV. Ergo advocatus tenetur pro pauperibus loqui.

**PRAETEREA,** praeceptum de misericordiae operibus adimplendis, cum sit affirmativum, obligat pro loco et tempore, quod est maxime in necessitate. Sed tempus necessitatis videtur esse quando alicuius pauperis causa opprimitur. Ergo in tali casu videtur quod advocatus teneatur pauperibus patrocinium praestare.

**SED CONTRA,** non minor necessitas est indigentis cibo quam indigentis advocato. Sed ille qui habet potestatem cibandi non semper tenetur pauperem cibare.

**OBJECTION 1**: It would seem that an advocate is bound to defend the suits of the poor. For it is written (Exod 23:5): *If thou see the ass of him that hateth thee lie underneath his burden, thou shalt not pass by, but shall lift him up with him.* Now no less a danger threatens the poor man whose suit is being unjustly prejudiced, than if his ass were to lie underneath its burden. Therefore an advocate is bound to defend the suits of the poor.

**OBJ. 2**: Further, Gregory says in a homily (ix in Evang.): *Let him that hath understanding beware lest he withhold his knowledge; let him that hath abundance of wealth watch lest he slacken his merciful bounty; let him who is a servant to art share his skill with his neighbor; let him who has an opportunity of speaking with the wealthy plead the cause of the poor: for the slightest gift you have received will be reputed a talent.* Now every man is bound, not to hide but faithfully to dispense the talent committed to him; as evidenced by the punishment inflicted on the servant who hid his talent (Matt 25:30). Therefore an advocate is bound to plead for the poor.

**OBJ. 3**: Further, the precept about performing works of mercy, being affirmative, is binding according to time and place, and this is chiefly in cases of need. Now it seems to be a case of need when the suit of a poor man is being prejudiced. Therefore it seems that in such a case an advocate is bound to defend the poor man's suit.

**ON THE CONTRARY**, He that lacks food is no less in need than he that lacks an advocate. Yet he that is able to give food is not always bound to feed the needy. Therefore

Ergo nec advocatus semper tenetur causae pauperum patrocinium praestare.

**RESPONDEO** dicendum quod cum praestare patrocinium causae pauperum ad opus misericordiae pertineat, idem est hic dicendum quod et supra de aliis misericordiae operibus dictum est. Nullus enim sufficit omnibus indigentibus misericordiae opus impendere. Et ideo sicut Augustinus dicit, in I de Doct. Christ., *cum omnibus prodesse non possis, his potissime consulendum est qui pro locorum et temporum vel quarumlibet rerum opportunitatibus, constrictius tibi, quasi quadam sorte, iunguntur.* Dicit, *pro locorum opportunitatibus,* quia non tenetur homo per mundum quaerere indigentes quibus subveniat, sed sufficit si eis qui sibi occurrunt misericordiae opus impendat. Unde dicitur Exod. XXIII, *si occurreris bovi inimici tui aut asino erranti, reduc ad eum.* Addit autem, *et temporum,* quia non tenetur homo futurae necessitati alterius providere, sed sufficit si praesenti necessitati succurrat. Unde dicitur I Ioan. III, *qui viderit fratrem suum necessitatem patientem, et clauserit viscera sua ab eo,* et cetera. Subdit autem, *vel quarumlibet rerum,* quia homo sibi coniunctis quacumque necessitudine maxime debet curam impendere; secundum illud I ad Tim. V, *si quis suorum, et maxime domesticorum curam non habet, fidem negavit.*

Quibus tamen concurrentibus, considerandum restat utrum aliquis tantam necessitatem patiatur quod non in promptu appareat quomodo ei possit aliter subveniri. Et in tali casu tenetur ei opus misericordiae impendere. Si autem in promptu appareat quomodo ei aliter subveniri possit, vel per seipsum vel per aliam personam magis coniunctam aut maiorem facultatem habentem, non tenetur ex necessitate indigenti subvenire, ita quod non faciendo peccet, quamvis, si subvenerit absque tali necessitate, laudabiliter faciat. Unde advocatus non tenetur semper causae pauperum patrocinium praestare, sed solum concurrentibus conditionibus praedictis. Alioquin oporteret eum omnia alia negotia praetermittere, et solis causis pauperum iuvandis intendere. Et idem dicendum est de medico, quantum ad curationem pauperum.

**AD PRIMUM** ergo dicendum quod quando asinus iacet sub onere, non potest ei aliter subveniri in casu isto nisi per advenientes subveniatur, et ideo tenentur iuvare. Non autem tenerentur si posset aliunde remedium afferri.

**AD SECUNDUM** dicendum quod homo talentum sibi creditum tenetur utiliter dispensare, servata opportunitate locorum et temporum et aliarum rerum, ut dictum est.

**AD TERTIUM** dicendum quod non quaelibet necessitas causat debitum subveniendi, sed solum illa quae est dicta.

neither is an advocate always bound to defend the suits of the poor.

**I ANSWER THAT**, Since defense of the poor man's suit belongs to the works of mercy, the answer to this inquiry is the same as the one given above with regard to the other works of mercy (Q. 32, AA. 5, 9). Now no man is sufficient to bestow a work of mercy on all those who need it. Wherefore, as Augustine says (*De Doctr. Christ.* i, 28), *since one cannot do good to all, we ought to consider those chiefly who by reason of place, time, or any other circumstance, by a kind of chance are more closely united to us.* He says *by reason of place,* because one is not bound to search throughout the world for the needy that one may succor them; and it suffices to do works of mercy to those one meets with. Hence it is written (Exod 23:4): *If thou meet thy enemy's ass going astray, bring it back to him.* He says also *by reason of time,* because one is not bound to provide for the future needs of others, and it suffices to succor present needs. Hence it is written (1 John 3:17): *He that . . . shall see his brother in need, and shall put up his bowels from him, how doth the charity of God abide in him?* Lastly he says, *or any other circumstance,* because one ought to show kindness to those especially who are by any tie whatever united to us, according to 1 Tim. 5:8, *If any man have not care of his own, and especially of those of his house, he hath denied the faith and is worse than an infidel.*

It may happen however that these circumstances concur, and then we have to consider whether this particular man stands in such a need that it is not easy to see how he can be succored otherwise, and then one is bound to bestow the work of mercy on him. If, however, it is easy to see how he can be otherwise succored, either by himself, or by some other person still more closely united to him, or in a better position to help him, one is not bound so strictly to help the one in need that it would be a sin not to do so: although it would be praiseworthy to do so where one is not bound to. Therefore an advocate is not always bound to defend the suits of the poor, but only when the aforesaid circumstances concur, else he would have to put aside all other business, and occupy himself entirely in defending the suits of poor people. The same applies to a physician with regard to attendance on the sick.

**REPLY OBJ. 1**: So long as the ass lies under the burden, there is no means of help in this case, unless those who are passing along come to the man's aid, and therefore they are bound to help. But they would not be so bound if help were possible from another quarter.

**REPLY OBJ. 2**: A man is bound to make good use of the talent bestowed on him, according to the opportunities afforded by time, place, and other circumstances, as stated above.

**REPLY OBJ. 3**: Not every need is such that it is one's duty to remedy it, but only such as we have stated above.

# Article 2

*Whether it is fitting that the law should debar certain persons from the office of advocate?*

**AD SECUNDUM SIC PROCEDITUR.** Videtur quod inconvenienter aliqui secundum iura arceantur ab officio advocandi. Ab operibus enim misericordiae nullus debet arceri. Sed patrocinium praestare in causis ad opera misericordiae pertinet, ut dictum est. Ergo nullus debet ab hoc officio arceri.

**PRAETEREA,** contrariarum causarum non videtur esse idem effectus. Sed esse deditum rebus divinis, et esse deditum peccatis, est contrarium. Inconvenienter igitur excluduntur ab officio advocati quidam propter religionem, ut monachi et clerici; quidam autem propter culpam, ut infames et haeretici.

**PRAETEREA,** homo debet diligere proximum sicut seipsum. Sed ad effectum dilectionis pertinet quod aliquis advocatus causae alicuius patrocinetur. Inconvenienter ergo aliqui quibus conceditur pro seipsis auctoritas advocationis, prohibentur patrocinari causis aliorum.

**SED CONTRA** est quod III, qu. VII, multae personae arcentur ab officio postulandi.

**RESPONDEO** dicendum quod aliquis impeditur ab aliquo actu duplici ratione, uno modo, propter impotentiam; alio modo, propter indecentiam. Sed impotentia simpliciter excludit aliquem ab actu, indecentia autem non excludit omnino, quia necessitas indecentiam tollere potest.

Sic igitur ab officio advocatorum prohibentur quidam propter impotentiam, eo quod deficiunt sensu, vel interiori, sicut furiosi et impuberes; vel exteriori, sicut surdi et muti. Est enim necessaria advocato et interior peritia, qua possit convenienter iustitiam assumptae causae ostendere, et iterum loquela cum auditu, ut possit et pronuntiare et audire quod ei dicitur. Unde qui in his defectum patiuntur omnino prohibentur ne sint advocati, nec pro se nec pro aliis.

Decentia autem huius officii exercendi tollitur dupliciter. Uno modo, ex hoc quod aliquis est rebus maioribus obligatus. Unde monachos et presbyteros non decet in quacumque causa advocatos esse, neque clericos in iudicio saeculari, quia huiusmodi personae sunt rebus divinis adstrictae. Alio modo, propter personae defectum, vel corporalem, ut patet de caecis, qui convenienter iudici adstare non possent; vel spiritualem, non enim decet ut alterius iustitiae patronus existat qui in seipso iustitiam contempsit. Et ideo infames, infideles et damnati de gravibus criminibus non decenter sunt advocati.

**OBJECTION 1:** It would seem unfitting for the law to debar certain persons from the office of advocate. For no man should be debarred from doing works of mercy. Now it belongs to the works of mercy to defend a man's suit, as stated above (A. 1). Therefore no man should be debarred from this office.

**OBJ. 2:** Further, contrary causes have not, seemingly, the same effect. Now to be busy with Divine things and to be busy about sin are contrary to one another. Therefore it is unfitting that some should be debarred from the office of advocate, on account of religion, as monks and clerics, while others are debarred on account of sin, as persons of ill-repute and heretics.

**OBJ. 3:** Further, a man should love his neighbor as himself. Now it is a duty of love for an advocate to plead a person's cause. Therefore it is unfitting that certain persons should be debarred from pleading the cause of others, while they are allowed to advocate their own cause.

**ON THE CONTRARY,** According to *Decret.* III, qu. vii, can. *Infames*, many persons are debarred from the office of advocate.

**I ANSWER THAT,** In two ways a person is debarred from performing a certain act: first because it is impossible to him, second because it is unbecoming to him: but, whereas the man to whom a certain act is impossible, is absolutely debarred from performing it, he to whom an act is unbecoming is not debarred altogether, since necessity may do away with its unbecomingness.

Accordingly some are debarred from the office of advocate because it is impossible to them through lack of sense—either interior, as in the case of madmen and minors—or exterior, as in the case of the deaf and dumb. For an advocate needs to have both interior skill so that he may be able to prove the justice of the cause he defends, and also speech and hearing, that he may speak and hear what is said to him. Consequently those who are defective in these points, are altogether debarred from being advocates either in their own or in another's cause.

The becomingness of exercising this office is removed in two ways. First, through a man being engaged in higher things. Wherefore it is unfitting that monks or priests should be advocates in any cause whatever, or that clerics should plead in a secular court, because such persons are engaged in Divine things. Second, on account of some personal defect, either of body (for instance a blind man whose attendance in a court of justice would be unbecoming) or of soul, for it ill becomes one who has disdained to be just himself, to plead for the justice of another. Wherefore it is unbecoming that persons of ill repute, unbelievers,

Tamen huiusmodi indecentiae necessitas praefertur. Et propter hoc huiusmodi personae possunt pro seipsis, vel pro personis sibi coniunctis, uti officio advocati. Unde et clerici pro Ecclesiis suis possunt esse advocati, et monachi pro causa monasterii sui, si abbas praeceperit.

**AD PRIMUM** ergo dicendum quod ab operibus misericordiae interdum aliqui propter impotentiam, interdum etiam propter indecentiam impediuntur. Non enim omnia opera misericordiae omnes decent, sicut stultos non decet consilium dare, neque ignorantes docere.

**AD SECUNDUM** dicendum quod sicut virtus corrumpitur per superabundantiam et defectum, ita aliquis fit indecens et per maius et per minus. Et propter hoc quidam arcentur a patrocinio praestando in causis quia sunt maiores tali officio, sicut religiosi et clerici, quidam vero quia sunt minores quam ut eis hoc officium competat, sicut infames et infideles.

**AD TERTIUM** dicendum quod non ita imminet homini necessitas patrocinari causis aliorum sicut propriis, quia alii possunt sibi aliter subvenire. Unde non est similis ratio.

and those who have been convicted of grievous crimes should be advocates. Nevertheless this unbecomingness is outweighed by necessity: and for this reason such persons can plead either their own cause or that of persons closely connected with them. Moreover, clerics can be advocates in the cause of their own church, and monks in the cause of their own monastery, if the abbot direct them to do so.

**REPLY OBJ. 1:** Certain persons are sometimes debarred by unbecomingness, and others by inability from performing works of mercy: for not all the works of mercy are becoming to all persons: thus it ill becomes a fool to give counsel, or the ignorant to teach.

**REPLY OBJ. 2:** Just as virtue is destroyed by *too much* and *too little*, so does a person become incompetent by *more* and *less*. For this reason some, like religious and clerics, are debarred from pleading in causes, because they are above such an office; and others because they are less than competent to exercise it, such as persons of ill-repute and unbelievers.

**REPLY OBJ. 3:** The necessity of pleading the causes of others is not so pressing as the necessity of pleading one's own cause, because others are able to help themselves otherwise: hence the comparison fails.

# Article 3

*Whether an advocate sins by defending an unjust cause?*

**AD TERTIUM SIC PROCEDITUR.** Videtur quod advocatus non peccet si iniustam causam defendat. Sicut enim ostenditur peritia medici si infirmitatem desperatam sanet, ita etiam ostenditur peritia advocati si etiam iniustam causam defendere possit. Sed medicus laudatur si infirmitatem desperatam sanet. Ergo etiam advocatus non peccat, sed magis laudandus est, si iniustam causam defendat.

**PRAETEREA,** a quolibet peccato licet desistere. Sed advocatus punitur si causam suam prodiderit, ut habetur II, qu. III. Ergo advocatus non peccat iniustam causam defendendo, si eam defendendam susceperit.

**PRAETEREA,** maius videtur esse peccatum si iniustitia utatur ad iustam causam defendendam, puta producendo falsos testes vel allegando falsas leges, quam iniustam causam defendendo, quia hoc est peccatum in forma, illud in materia. Sed videtur advocato licere talibus astutiis uti, sicut militi licet ex insidiis pugnare. Ergo videtur quod advocatus non peccat si iniustam causam defendat.

**SED CONTRA** est quod dicitur II Paralip. XIX, *impio praebes auxilium, et idcirco iram domini merebaris.* Sed

**OBJECTION 1:** It would seem that an advocate does not sin by defending an unjust cause. For just as a physician proves his skill by healing a desperate disease, so does an advocate prove his skill, if he can defend an unjust cause. Now a physician is praised if he heals a desperate malady. Therefore an advocate also commits no sin, but ought to be praised, if he defends an unjust cause.

**OBJ. 2:** Further, it is always lawful to desist from committing a sin. Yet an advocate is punished if he throws up his brief (*Decret.* II, qu. iii, can. *Si quem poenit.*). Therefore an advocate does not sin by defending an unjust cause, when once he has undertaken its defense.

**OBJ. 3:** Further, it would seem to be a greater sin for an advocate to use unjust means in defense of a just cause (e.g., by producing false witnesses, or alleging false laws), than to defend an unjust cause, since the former is a sin against the form, the latter against the matter of justice. Yet it is seemingly lawful for an advocate to make use of such underhand means, even as it is lawful for a soldier to lay ambushes in a battle. Therefore it would seem that an advocate does not sin by defending an unjust cause.

**ON THE CONTRARY,** It is said (2 Chr 19:2): *Thou helpest the ungodly . . . and therefore thou didst deserve . . . the wrath*

advocatus defendens causam iniustam impio praebet auxilium. Ergo, peccando, iram domini meretur.

**Respondeo** dicendum quod illicitum est alicui cooperari ad malum faciendum sive consulendo, sive adiuvando, sive qualitercumque consentiendo, quia consilians et coadiuvans quodammodo est faciens; et apostolus dicit, ad Rom. I, quod *digni sunt morte non solum qui faciunt peccatum, sed etiam qui consentiunt facientibus.* Unde et supra dictum est quod omnes tales ad restitutionem tenentur. Manifestum est autem quod advocatus et auxilium et consilium praestat ei cuius causae patrocinatur. Unde si scienter iniustam causam defendit, absque dubio graviter peccat; et ad restitutionem tenetur eius damni quod contra iustitiam per eius auxilium altera pars incurrit. Si autem ignoranter iniustam causam defendit, putans esse iustam, excusatur, secundum modum quo ignorantia excusare potest.

**Ad primum** ergo dicendum quod medicus accipiens in cura infirmitatem desperatam nulli facit iniuriam. Advocatus autem suscipiens causam iniustam iniuste laedit cum contra quem patrocinium praestat. Et ideo non est similis ratio. Quamvis enim laudabilis videatur quantum ad peritiam artis, tamen peccat quantum ad iniustitiam voluntatis, qua abutitur arte ad malum.

**Ad secundum** dicendum quod advocatus, si in principio credidit causam iustam esse et postea in processu appareat eam esse iniustam, non debet eam prodere, ut scilicet aliam partem iuvet, vel secreta suae causae alteri parti revelet. Potest tamen et debet causam deserere; vel eum cuius causam agit ad cedendum inducere, sive ad componendum, sine adversarii damno.

**Ad tertium** dicendum quod, sicut supra dictum est, militi vel duci exercitus licet in bello iusto ex insidiis agere ea quae facere debet prudenter occultando, non autem falsitatem fraudulenter faciendo, quia *etiam hosti fidem servare oportet,* sicut Tullius dicit, in III de Offic. Unde et advocato defendenti causam iustam licet prudenter occultare ea quibus impediri posset processus eius, non autem licet ei aliqua falsitate uti.

*of the Lord.* Now an advocate by defending an unjust cause, helps the ungodly. Therefore he sins and deserves the wrath of the Lord.

**I answer that,** It is unlawful to cooperate in an evil deed, by counseling, helping, or in any way consenting, because to counsel or assist an action is, in a way, to do it, and the Apostle says (Rom 1:32) that *they . . . are worthy of death, not only they that do a sin, but they also that consent to them that do* it. Hence it was stated above (Q. 62, A. 7), that all such are bound to restitution. Now it is evident that an advocate provides both assistance and counsel to the party for whom he pleads. Wherefore, if knowingly he defends an unjust cause, without doubt he sins grievously, and is bound to restitution of the loss unjustly incurred by the other party by reason of the assistance he has provided. If, however, he defends an unjust cause unknowingly, thinking it just, he is to be excused according to the measure in which ignorance is excusable.

**Reply Obj. 1:** The physician injures no man by undertaking to heal a desperate malady, whereas the advocate who accepts service in an unjust cause, unjustly injures the party against whom he pleads unjustly. Hence the comparison fails. For though he may seem to deserve praise for showing skill in his art, nevertheless he sins by reason of injustice in his will, since he abuses his art for an evil end.

**Reply Obj. 2:** If an advocate believes from the outset that the cause is just, and discovers afterwards while the case is proceeding that it is unjust, he ought not to throw up his brief in such a way as to help the other side, or so as to reveal the secrets of his client to the other party. But he can and must give up the case, or induce his client to give way, or make some compromise without prejudice to the opposing party.

**Reply Obj. 3:** As stated above (Q. 40, A. 3), it is lawful for a soldier, or a general to lay ambushes in a just war, by prudently concealing what he has a mind to do, but not by means of fraudulent falsehoods, since *we should keep faith even with a foe,* as Tully says (*De offic.* iii, 29). Hence it is lawful for an advocate, in defending his case, prudently to conceal whatever might hinder its happy issue, but it is unlawful for him to employ any kind of falsehood.

# Article 4

*Whether it is lawful for an advocate to take a fee for pleading?*

**Ad quartum sic proceditur.** Videtur quod advocato non liceat pro suo patrocinio pecuniam accipere. Opera enim misericordiae non sunt intuitu humanae remunerationis facienda, secundum illud Luc. XIV, *cum facis prandium aut cenam, noli vocare amicos tuos neque vicinos divites, ne forte et ipsi te reinvitent, et fiat*

**Objection 1:** It would seem unlawful for an advocate to take a fee for pleading. Works of mercy should not be done with a view to human remuneration, according to Luke 14:12, *When thou makest a dinner or a supper, call not thy friends . . . nor thy neighbors who are rich: lest perhaps they also invite thee again, and a recompense be made to thee.*

*tibi retributio.* Sed praestare patrocinium causae alicuius pertinet ad opera misericordiae, ut dictum est. Ergo non licet advocato accipere retributionem pecuniae pro patrocinio praestito.

PRAETEREA, spirituale non est pro temporali commutandum. Sed patrocinium praestitum videtur esse quiddam spirituale, cum sit usus scientiae iuris. Ergo non licet advocato pro patrocinio praestito pecuniam accipere.

PRAETEREA, sicut ad iudicium concurrit persona advocati, ita etiam persona iudicis et persona testis. Sed secundum Augustinum, ad Macedonium, *non debet iudex vendere iustum iudicium, nec testis verum testimonium.* Ergo nec advocatus poterit vendere iustum patrocinium.

SED CONTRA est quod Augustinus dicit ibidem, quod *advocatus licite vendit iustum patrocinium, et iurisperitus verum consilium.*

RESPONDEO dicendum quod ea quae quis non tenetur alteri exhibere, iuste potest pro eorum exhibitione recompensationem accipere. Manifestum est autem quod advocatus non semper tenetur patrocinium praestare aut consilium dare causis aliorum. Et ideo si vendat suum patrocinium sive consilium, non agit contra iustitiam. Et eadem ratio est de medico opem ferente ad sanandum, et de omnibus aliis huiusmodi personis, dum tamen moderate accipiant, considerata conditione personarum et negotiorum et laboris, et consuetudine patriae. Si autem per improbitatem aliquid immoderate extorqueat, peccat contra iustitiam. Unde Augustinus dicit, ad Macedonium, quod *ab his extorta per immoderatam improbitatem repeti solent, data per tolerabilem consuetudinem non solent.*

AD PRIMUM ergo dicendum quod non semper quae homo potest misericorditer facere, tenetur facere gratis, alioquin nulli liceret aliquam rem vendere, quia quamlibet rem potest homo misericorditer impendere. Sed quando eam misericorditer impendit, non humanam, sed divinam remunerationem quaerere debet. Et similiter advocatus, quando causae pauperum misericorditer patrocinatur, non debet intendere remunerationem humanam, sed divinam, non tamen semper tenetur gratis patrocinium impendere.

AD SECUNDUM dicendum quod etsi scientia iuris sit quiddam spirituale, tamen usus eius fit opere corporali. Et ideo pro eius recompensatione licet pecuniam accipere, alioquin nulli artifici liceret de arte sua lucrari.

AD TERTIUM dicendum quod iudex et testis communes sunt utrique parti, quia iudex tenetur iustam sententiam dare, et testis tenetur verum testimonium dicere; iustitia autem et veritas non declinant in unam partem magis quam in aliam. Et ideo iudicibus de publico sunt stipendia laboris statuta; et testes accipiunt, non

Now it is a work of mercy to plead another's cause, as stated above (A. 1). Therefore it is not lawful for an advocate to take payment in money for pleading.

OBJ. 2: Further, spiritual things are not to be bartered with temporal things. But pleading a person's cause seems to be a spiritual good since it consists in using one's knowledge of law. Therefore it is not lawful for an advocate to take a fee for pleading.

OBJ. 3: Further, just as the person of the advocate concurs towards the pronouncement of the verdict, so do the persons of the judge and of the witness. Now, according to Augustine (*Ep. cliii ad Macedon.*), *the judge should not sell a just sentence, nor the witness true evidence.* Therefore neither can an advocate sell a just pleading.

ON THE CONTRARY, Augustine says (*Ep. cliii ad Macedon.*) that *an advocate may lawfully sell his pleading, and a lawyer his advice.*

I ANSWER THAT, A man may justly receive payment for granting what he is not bound to grant. Now it is evident that an advocate is not always bound to consent to plead, or to give advice in other people's causes. Wherefore, if he sell his pleading or advice, he does not act against justice. The same applies to the physician who attends on a sick person to heal him, and to all like persons; provided, however, they take a moderate fee, with due consideration for persons, for the matter in hand, for the labor entailed, and for the custom of the country. If, however, they wickedly extort an immoderate fee, they sin against justice. Hence Augustine says (*Ep. cliii ad Macedon.*) that *it is customary to demand from them restitution of what they have extorted by a wicked excess, but not what has been given to them in accordance with a commendable custom.*

REPLY OBJ. 1: Man is not bound to do gratuitously whatever he can do from motives of mercy: else no man could lawfully sell anything, since anything may be given from motives of mercy. But when a man does give a thing out of mercy, he should seek, not a human, but a Divine reward. In like manner an advocate, when he mercifully pleads the cause of a poor man, should have in view not a human but a Divine meed; and yet he is not always bound to give his services gratuitously.

REPLY OBJ. 2: Though knowledge of law is something spiritual, the use of that knowledge is accomplished by the work of the body: hence it is lawful to take money in payment of that use, else no craftsman would be allowed to make profit by his art.

REPLY OBJ. 3: The judge and witnesses are common to either party, since the judge is bound to pronounce a just verdict, and the witness to give true evidence. Now justice and truth do not incline to one side rather than to the other: and consequently judges receive out of the public funds a fixed pay for their labor; and witnesses receive their

quasi pretium testimonii, sed quasi stipendium laboris, expensas vel ab utraque parte, vel ab ea a qua inducuntur, quia *nemo militat stipendiis suis unquam*, ut dicitur I ad Cor. IX. Sed advocatus alteram partem tantum defendit. Et ideo licite potest pretium accipere a parte quam adiuvat.

expenses (not as payment for giving evidence, but as a fee for their labor) either from both parties or from the party by whom they are adduced, because *no man serveth as a soldier at any time at his own charge* (1 Cor 9:7). On the other hand an advocate defends one party only, and so he may lawfully accept fee from the party he assists.

# QUESTION 72

## REVILING

Deinde considerandum est de iniuriis verborum quae inferuntur extra iudicium. Et primo, de contumelia; secundo, de detractione; tertio, de susurratione; quarto, de derisione; quinto, de maledictione.

Circa primum quaeruntur quatuor.

Primo, quid sit contumelia.

Secundo, utrum omnis contumelia sit peccatum mortale.

Tertio, utrum oporteat contumeliosos reprimere.

Quarto, de origine contumeliae.

We must now consider injuries inflicted by words uttered extrajudicially. We shall consider (1) reviling, (2) backbiting, (3) tale bearing, (4) derision, (5) cursing.

Under the first head there are four points of inquiry:

(1) What is reviling?

(2) Whether every reviling is a mortal sin?

(3) Whether one ought to check revilers?

(4) Of the origin of reviling.

## Article 1

### *Whether reviling consists in words?*

**AD PRIMUM SIC PROCEDITUR.** Videtur quod contumelia non consistat in verbis. Contumelia enim importat quoddam nocumentum proximo illatum, cum pertineat ad iniustitiam. Sed verba nullum nocumentum videntur inferre proximo, nec in rebus nec in persona. Ergo contumelia non consistit in verbis.

**PRAETEREA,** contumelia videtur ad quandam dehonorationem pertinere. Sed magis aliquis potest inhonorari seu vituperari factis quam verbis. Ergo videtur quod contumelia non consistit in verbis, sed magis in factis.

**PRAETEREA,** dehonoratio quae fit in verbis dicitur convicium vel improperium. Sed contumelia videtur differre a convicio et improperio. Ergo contumelia non consistit in verbis.

**SED CONTRA,** nihil auditu percipitur nisi verbum. Sed contumelia auditu percipitur, secundum illud Ierem. XX, *audivi contumelias in circuitu.* Ergo contumelia est in verbis.

**RESPONDEO** dicendum quod contumelia importat dehonorationem alicuius. Quod quidem contingit dupliciter. Cum enim honor aliquam excellentiam consequatur, uno modo aliquis alium dehonorat cum privat eum excellentia propter quam habebat honorem. Quod quidem fit per peccata factorum, de quibus supra dictum est. Alio modo, cum aliquis id quod est contra honorem alicuius deducit in notitiam eius et aliorum. Et hoc proprie pertinet ad contumeliam. Quod quidem fit per aliqua signa. Sed sicut Augustinus dicit, in II de Doct. Christ., *omnia signa, verbis comparata, paucissima sunt, verba enim inter homines obtinuerunt principatum significandi quaecumque animo concipiuntur.* Et ideo

**OBJECTION 1:** It would seem that reviling does not consist in words. Reviling implies some injury inflicted on one's neighbor, since it is a kind of injustice. But words seem to inflict no injury on one's neighbor, either in his person, or in his belongings. Therefore reviling does not consist in words.

**OBJ. 2:** Further, reviling seems to imply dishonor. But a man can be dishonored or slighted by deeds more than by words. Therefore it seems that reviling consists, not in words but in deeds.

**OBJ. 3:** Further, a dishonor inflicted by words is called a railing or a taunt. But reviling seems to differ from railing or taunt. Therefore reviling does not consist in words.

**ON THE CONTRARY,** Nothing, save words, is perceived by the hearing. Now reviling is perceived by the hearing according to Jer. 20:10, *I heard reviling on every side.* Therefore reviling consists in words.

**I ANSWER THAT,** Reviling denotes the dishonoring of a person, and this happens in two ways: for since honor results from excellence, one person dishonors another, first, by depriving him of the excellence for which he is honored. This is done by sins of deed, whereof we have spoken above (Q. 64, seqq.). Second, when a man publishes something against another's honor, thus bringing it to the knowledge of the latter and of other men. This reviling properly so called, and is done by some kind of signs. Now, according to Augustine (*De Doctr. Christ.* ii, 3), *compared with words all other signs are very few, for words have obtained the chief place among men for the purpose of expressing whatever the mind conceives.* Hence reviling, properly speaking,

671

contumelia, proprie loquendo, in verbis consistit. Unde Isidorus dicit, in libro Etymol., quod contumeliosus dicitur aliquis *quia velox est et tumet verbis iniuriae.* Quia tamen etiam per facta aliqua significatur aliquid, quae in hoc quod significant habent vim verborum significantium; inde est quod contumelia, extenso nomine, etiam in factis dicitur. Unde Rom. I, super illud, *contumeliosos, superbos,* dicit Glossa quod *contumeliosi sunt qui dictis vel factis contumelias et turpia inferunt.*

AD PRIMUM ergo dicendum quod verba secundum suam essentiam, idest inquantum sunt quidam soni audibiles, nullum nocumentum alteri inferunt, nisi forte gravando auditum, puta cum aliquis nimis alte loquitur. Inquantum vero sunt signa repraesentantia aliquid in notitiam aliorum, sic possunt multa damna inferre. Inter quae unum est quod homo damnificatur quantum ad detrimentum honoris sui vel reverentiae sibi ab aliis exhibendae. Et ideo maior est contumelia si aliquis alicui defectum suum dicat coram multis. Et tamen si sibi soli dicat, potest esse contumelia, inquantum ipse qui loquitur contra audientis reverentiam agit.

AD SECUNDUM dicendum quod intantum aliquis aliquem factis dehonorat inquantum illa facta vel faciunt vel significant illud quod est contra honorem alicuius. Quorum primum non pertinet ad contumeliam, sed ad alias iniustitiae species, de quibus supra dictum est. Secundum vero pertinet ad contumeliam inquantum facta habent vim verborum in significando.

AD TERTIUM dicendum quod convicium et improperium consistunt in verbis, sicut et contumelia, quia per omnia haec repraesentatur aliquis defectus alicuius in detrimentum honoris ipsius. Huiusmodi autem defectus est triplex. Scilicet defectus culpae, qui repraesentatur per verba contumeliosa. Et defectus generaliter culpae et poenae, qui repraesentatur per *convicium,* quia *vitium* consuevit dici non solum animae, sed etiam corporis. Unde si quis alicui iniuriose dicat eum esse caecum, convicium quidem dicit, sed non contumeliam, si quis autem dicat alteri quod sit fur, non solum convicium, sed etiam contumeliam infert. Quandoque vero repraesentat aliquis alicui defectum minorationis sive indigentiae, qui etiam derogat honori consequenti quamcumque excellentiam. Et hoc fit per verbum *improperii,* quod proprie est quando aliquis iniuriose alteri ad memoriam reducit auxilium quod contulit ei necessitatem patienti. Unde dicitur Eccli. XX, *exigua dabit, et multa improperabit.* Quandoque tamen unum istorum pro alio ponitur.

consists in words: wherefore, Isidore says (*Etym.* x) that a reviler (*contumeliosus*) *is hasty and bursts out (tumet) in injurious words.* Since, however, things are also signified by deeds, which on this account have the same significance as words, it follows that reviling in a wider sense extends also to deeds. Wherefore a gloss on Rom. 1:30, *contumelious, proud,* says: *The contumelious are those who by word or deed revile and shame others.*

REPLY OBJ. 1: Our words, if we consider them in their essence, i.e., as audible sounds, injure no man, except perhaps by jarring of the ear, as when a person speaks too loud. But, considered as signs conveying something to the knowledge of others, they may do many kinds of harm. Such is the harm done to a man to the detriment of his honor, or of the respect due to him from others. Hence the reviling is greater if one man reproach another in the presence of many: and yet there may still be reviling if he reproach him by himself, insofar as the speaker acts unjustly against the respect due to the hearer.

REPLY OBJ. 2: One man slights another by deeds insofar as such deeds cause or signify that which is against that other man's honor. In the former case it is not a matter of reviling but of some other kind of injustice, of which we have spoken above (QQ. 64, 65, 66): where as in the latter case there is reviling, insofar as deeds have the significant force of words.

REPLY OBJ. 3: Railing and taunts consist in words, even as reviling, because by all of them a man's faults are exposed to the detriment of his honor. Such faults are of three kinds. First, there is the fault of guilt, which is exposed by reviling words. Second, there is the fault of both guilt and punishment, which is exposed by taunts (*convicium*), because *vice* is commonly spoken of in connection with not only the soul but also the body. Hence if one man says spitefully to another that he is blind, he taunts but does not revile him: whereas if one man calls another a thief, he not only taunts but also reviles him. Third, a man reproaches another for his inferiority or indigence, so as to lessen the honor due to him for any kind of excellence. This is done by *upbraiding* words, and properly speaking, occurs when one spitefully reminds a man that one has succored him when he was in need. Hence it is written (Sir 20:15): *He will give a few things and upbraid much.* Nevertheless these terms are sometimes employed one for the other.

# Article 2

*Whether reviling or railing is a mortal sin?*

**AD SECUNDUM SIC PROCEDITUR.** Videtur quod contumelia, vel convicium, non sit peccatum mortale. Nullum enim peccatum mortale est actus alicuius virtutis. Sed conviciari est actus alicuius virtutis, scilicet eutrapeliae, ad quam pertinet bene conviciari, secundum philosophum, in IV Ethic. Ergo convicium, sive contumelia, non est peccatum mortale.

**PRAETEREA,** peccatum mortale non invenitur in viris perfectis. Qui tamen aliquando convicia vel contumelias dicunt, sicut patet de apostolo, qui, ad Gal. III, dixit, *o insensati Galatae.* Et dominus dicit, Luc. ult., *o stulti, et tardi corde ad credendum.* Ergo convicium, sive contumelia, non est peccatum mortale.

**PRAETEREA,** quamvis id quod est peccatum veniale ex genere possit fieri mortale, non tamen peccatum quod ex genere est mortale potest esse veniale, ut supra habitum est. Si ergo dicere convicium vel contumeliam esset peccatum mortale ex genere suo, sequeretur quod semper esset peccatum mortale. Quod videtur esse falsum, ut patet in eo qui leviter et ex subreptione, vel ex levi ira dicit aliquod verbum contumeliosum. Non ergo contumelia vel convicium ex genere suo est peccatum mortale.

**SED CONTRA,** nihil meretur poenam aeternam Inferni nisi peccatum mortale. Sed convicium vel contumelia meretur poenam Inferni, secundum illud Matth. V, *qui dixerit fratri suo, fatue, reus erit Gehennae ignis.* Ergo convicium vel contumelia est peccatum mortale.

**RESPONDEO** dicendum quod, sicut supra dictum est, verba inquantum sunt soni quidam, non sunt in nocumentum aliorum, sed inquantum significant aliquid. Quae quidem significatio ex interiori affectu procedit. Et ideo in peccatis verborum maxime considerandum videtur ex quo affectu aliquis verba proferat. Cum igitur convicium, seu contumelia, de sui ratione importet quandam dehonorationem, si intentio proferentis ad hoc feratur ut aliquis per verba quae profert honorem alterius auferat, hoc proprie et per se est dicere convicium vel contumeliam. Et hoc est peccatum mortale, non minus quam furtum vel rapina, non enim homo minus amat suum honorem quam rem possessam. Si vero aliquis verbum convicii vel contumeliae alteri dixerit, non tamen animo dehonorandi, sed forte propter correctionem vel propter aliquid huiusmodi, non dicit convicium vel contumeliam formaliter et per se, sed per accidens et materialiter, inquantum scilicet dicit id quod potest esse convicium, vel contumelia. Unde hoc potest esse quandoque peccatum veniale; quandoque autem absque omni peccato. In quo tamen necessaria est discretio,

**OBJECTION 1:** It would seem that reviling or railing is not a mortal sin. For no mortal sin is an act of virtue. Now railing is the act of a virtue, viz. of wittiness (eutrapelia) to which it pertains to rail well, according to the Philosopher (*Ethic.* iv, 8). Therefore railing or reviling is not a mortal sin.

**OBJ. 2:** Further, mortal sin is not to be found in perfect men; and yet these sometimes give utterance to railing or reviling. Thus the Apostle says (Gal 3:1): *O senseless Galatians!*, and our Lord said (Luke 24:25): *O foolish and slow of heart to believe!* Therefore railing or reviling is not a mortal sin.

**OBJ. 3:** Further, although that which is a venial sin by reason of its genus may become mortal, that which is mortal by reason of its genus cannot become venial, as stated above (I-II, Q. 88, AA. 4, 6). Hence if by reason of its genus it were a mortal sin to give utterance to railing or reviling, it would follow that it is always a mortal sin. But this is apparently untrue, as may be seen in the case of one who utters a reviling word indeliberately or through slight anger. Therefore reviling or railing is not a mortal sin, by reason of its genus.

**ON THE CONTRARY,** Nothing but mortal sin deserves the eternal punishment of hell. Now railing or reviling deserves the punishment of hell, according to Matt. 5:22, *Whosoever shall say to his brother . . . Thou fool, shall be in danger of hell fire.* Therefore railing or reviling is a mortal sin.

**I ANSWER THAT,** As stated above (A. 1), words are injurious to other persons, not as sounds, but as signs, and this signification depends on the speaker's inward intention. Hence, in sins of word, it seems that we ought to consider with what intention the words are uttered. Since then railing or reviling essentially denotes a dishonoring, if the intention of the utterer is to dishonor the other man, this is properly and essentially to give utterance to railing or reviling: and this is a mortal sin no less than theft or robbery, since a man loves his honor no less than his possessions. If, on the other hand, a man says to another a railing or reviling word, yet with the intention, not of dishonoring him, but rather perhaps of correcting him or with some like purpose, he utters a railing or reviling not formally and essentially, but accidentally and materially, in so far to wit as he says that which might be a railing or reviling. Hence this may be sometimes a venial sin, and sometimes without any sin at all. Nevertheless there is need of discretion in such matters, and one should use such words with moderation, because the railing might be so grave that being uttered inconsiderately it might dishonor

ut moderate homo talibus verbis utatur. Quia posset esse ita grave convicium quod, per incautelam prolatum, auferret honorem eius contra quem proferretur. Et tunc posset homo peccare mortaliter etiam si non intenderet dehonorationem alterius. Sicut etiam si aliquis, incaute alium ex ludo percutiens, graviter laedat, culpa non caret.

**AD PRIMUM** ergo dicendum quod ad eutrapelum pertinet dicere aliquod leve convicium, non ad dehonorationem vel ad contristationem eius in quem dicitur, sed magis causa delectationis et ioci. Et hoc potest esse sine peccato, si debitae circumstantiae observantur. Si vero aliquis non reformidet contristare eum in quem profertur huiusmodi iocosum convicium, dummodo aliis risum excitet, hoc est vitiosum, ut ibidem dicitur.

**AD SECUNDUM** dicendum quod sicut licitum est aliquem verberare vel in rebus damnificare causa disciplinae, ita etiam et causa disciplinae potest aliquis alteri, quem debet corrigere, verbum aliquod conviciosum dicere. Et hoc modo dominus discipulos vocavit stultos, et apostolus Galatas insensatos. Tamen, sicut dicit Augustinus, in libro de Serm. Dom. in monte, *raro, et ex magna necessitate obiurgationes sunt adhibendae, in quibus non nobis, sed ut domino serviatur, instemus.*

**AD TERTIUM** dicendum quod, cum peccatum convicii vel contumeliae ex animo dicentis dependeat, potest contingere quod sit peccatum veniale, si sit leve convicium, non multum hominem dehonestans, et proferatur ex aliqua animi levitate, vel ex levi ira, absque firmo proposito aliquem dehonestandi, puta cum aliquis intendit aliquem per huiusmodi verbum leviter contristare.

the person against whom it is uttered. In such a case a man might commit a mortal sin, even though he did not intend to dishonor the other man: just as were a man incautiously to injure grievously another by striking him in fun, he would not be without blame.

**REPLY OBJ. 1:** It belongs to wittiness to utter some slight mockery, not with intent to dishonor or pain the person who is the object of the mockery, but rather with intent to please and amuse: and this may be without sin, if the due circumstances be observed. On the other hand if a man does not shrink from inflicting pain on the object of his witty mockery, so long as he makes others laugh, this is sinful, as stated in the passage quoted.

**REPLY OBJ. 2:** Just as it is lawful to strike a person, or damnify him in his belongings for the purpose of correction, so too, for the purpose of correction, may one say a mocking word to a person whom one has to correct. It is thus that our Lord called the disciples *foolish*, and the Apostle called the Galatians *senseless*. Yet, as Augustine says (*De Serm. Dom. in Monte* ii, 19), *seldom and only when it is very necessary should we have recourse to invectives, and then so as to urge God's service, not our own.*

**REPLY OBJ. 3:** Since the sin of railing or reviling depends on the intention of the utterer, it may happen to be a venial sin, if it be a slight railing that does not inflict much dishonor on a man, and be uttered through lightness of heart or some slight anger, without the fixed purpose of dishonoring him, for instance when one intends by such a word to give but little pain.

# Article 3

*Whether one ought to suffer oneself to be reviled?*

**AD TERTIUM SIC PROCEDITUR.** Videtur quod aliquis non debeat contumelias sibi illatas sustinere. Qui enim sustinet contumeliam sibi illatam, audaciam nutrit conviciantis. Sed hoc non est faciendum. Ergo homo non debet sustinere contumeliam sibi illatam, sed magis convicianti respondere.

**PRAETEREA,** homo debet plus se diligere quam alium. Sed aliquis non debet sustinere quod alteri convicium inferatur, unde dicitur Prov. XXVI, *qui imponit stulto silentium, iras mitigat.* Ergo etiam aliquis non debet sustinere contumelias illatas sibi.

**PRAETEREA,** non licet alicui vindicare seipsum, secundum illud, *mihi vindictam, et ego retribuam.* Sed aliquis non resistendo contumeliae se vindicat, secundum illud Chrysostomi, *si vindicare vis, sile, et funestam*

**OBJECTION 1:** It would seem that one ought not to suffer oneself to be reviled. For he that suffers himself to be reviled, encourages the reviler. But one ought not to do this. Therefore one ought not to suffer oneself to be reviled, but rather reply to the reviler.

**OBJ. 2:** Further, one ought to love oneself more than another. Now one ought not to suffer another to be reviled, wherefore it is written (Prov 26:10): *He that putteth a fool to silence appeaseth anger.* Therefore neither should one suffer oneself to be reviled.

**OBJ. 3:** Further, a man is not allowed to revenge himself, for it is said: *Vengeance belongeth to Me, I will repay.* Now by submitting to be reviled a man revenges himself, according to Chrysostom (*Hom. xxii, in Ep. ad Rom.*): *If thou wilt*

*ei dedisti plagam.* Ergo aliquis non debet, silendo, sustinere verba contumeliosa, sed magis respondere.

**Sed contra** est quod dicitur in Psalm., *qui inquirebant mala mihi, locuti sunt vanitates*; et postea subdit, *ego autem tanquam surdus non audiebam, et sicut mutus non aperiens os suum.*

**Respondeo** dicendum quod sicut patientia necessaria est in his quae contra nos fiunt, ita etiam in his quae contra nos dicuntur. Praecepta autem patientiae in his quae contra nos fiunt, sunt in praeparatione animae habenda, sicut Augustinus, in libro de Serm. Dom. in monte, exponit illud praeceptum domini, *si quis percusserit te in una maxilla, praebe ei et aliam*, ut scilicet homo sit paratus hoc facere, si opus fuerit; non tamen hoc semper tenetur facere actu, quia nec ipse dominus hoc fecit, sed, cum suscepisset alapam, dixit, *quid me caedis?* Ut habetur Ioan. XVIII. Et ideo etiam circa verba contumeliosa quae contra nos dicuntur, est idem intelligendum. Tenemur enim habere animum paratum ad contumelias tolerandas si expediens fuerit. Quandoque tamen oportet ut contumeliam illatam repellamus, maxime propter duo. Primo quidem, propter bonum eius qui contumeliam infert, ut videlicet eius audacia reprimatur, et de cetero talia non attentet; secundum illud Prov. XXVI, *responde stulto iuxta stultitiam suam, ne sibi sapiens videatur.* Alio modo, propter bonum multorum, quorum profectus impeditur per contumelias nobis illatas. Unde Gregorius dicit, super Ezech., Homil. IX, *hi quorum vita in exemplo imitationis est posita, debent, si possunt, detrahentium sibi verba compescere, ne eorum praedicationem non audiant qui audire poterant, et in pravis moribus remanentes, bene vivere contemnant.*

**Ad primum** ergo dicendum quod audaciam conviciantis contumeliosi debet aliquis moderate reprimere, scilicet propter officium caritatis, non propter cupiditatem privati honoris. Unde dicitur Prov. XXVI, *ne respondeas stulto iuxta stultitiam suam, ne ei similis efficiaris.*

**Ad secundum** dicendum quod in hoc quod aliquis alienas contumelias reprimit, non ita timetur cupiditas privati honoris sicut cum aliquis repellit contumelias proprias, magis autem videtur hoc provenire ex caritatis affectu.

**Ad tertium** dicendum quod si aliquis hoc animo taceret ut tacendo contumeliantem ad iracundiam provocaret, pertineret hoc ad vindictam. Sed si aliquis taceat volens dare locum irae, hoc est laudabile. Unde dicitur Eccli. VIII, *non litiges cum homine linguato, et non struas in ignem illius ligna.*

be revenged, be silent; thou hast dealt him a fatal blow. Therefore one ought not by silence to submit to reviling words, but rather answer back.

**On the contrary,** It is written (Ps 37:13): *They that sought evils to me spoke vain things*, and afterwards (Ps 37:14) he says: *But I as a deaf man, heard not; and as a dumb man not opening his mouth.*

**I answer that,** Just as we need patience in things done against us, so do we need it in those said against us. Now the precepts of patience in those things done against us refer to the preparedness of the mind, according to Augustine's (*De Serm. Dom. in Monte* i, 19) exposition on our Lord's precept, *If one strike thee on thy right cheek, turn to him also the other*: that is to say, a man ought to be prepared to do so if necessary. But he is not always bound to do this actually: since not even did our Lord do so, for when He received a blow, He said: *Why strikest thou Me?* (John 18:23). Consequently the same applies to the reviling words that are said against us. For we are bound to hold our minds prepared to submit to be reviled, if it should be expedient. Nevertheless it sometimes behooves us to withstand against being reviled, and this chiefly for two reasons. First, for the good of the reviler; namely, that his daring may be checked, and that he may not repeat the attempt, according to Prov. 26:5, *Answer a fool according to his folly, lest he imagine himself to be wise.* Second, for the good of many who would be prevented from progressing in virtue on account of our being reviled. Hence Gregory says (*Hom. ix, Super Ezech.*): *Those who are so placed that their life should be an example to others, ought, if possible, to silence their detractors, lest their preaching be not heard by those who could have heard it, and they continue their evil conduct through contempt of a good life.*

**Reply Obj. 1:** The daring of the railing reviler should be checked with moderation, i.e., as a duty of charity, and not through lust for one's own honor. Hence it is written (Prov 26:4): *Answer not a fool according to his folly, lest thou be like him.*

**Reply Obj. 2:** When one man prevents another from being reviled there is not the danger of lust for one's own honor as there is when a man defends himself from being reviled: indeed rather would it seem to proceed from a sense of charity.

**Reply Obj. 3:** It would be an act of revenge to keep silence with the intention of provoking the reviler to anger, but it would be praiseworthy to be silent, in order to give place to anger. Hence it is written (Sir 8:4): *Strive not with a man that is full of tongue, and heap not wood upon his fire.*

# Article 4

*Whether reviling arises from anger?*

**AD QUARTUM SIC PROCEDITUR**. Videtur quod contumelia non oriatur ex ira. Quia dicitur Prov. XI, *ubi superbia, ibi contumelia*. Sed ira est vitium distinctum a superbia. Ergo contumelia non oritur ex ira.

**PRAETEREA**, Prov. XX dicitur, *omnes stulti miscentur contumeliis*. Sed stultitia est vitium oppositum sapientiae, ut supra habitum est, ira autem opponitur mansuetudini. Ergo contumelia non oritur ex ira.

**PRAETEREA**, nullum peccatum diminuitur ex sua causa. Sed peccatum contumeliae diminuitur si ex ira proferatur, gravius enim peccat qui ex odio contumeliam infert quam qui ex ira. Ergo contumelia non oritur ex ira.

**SED CONTRA** est quod Gregorius dicit, XXXI Moral., quod ex ira oriuntur contumeliae.

**RESPONDEO** dicendum quod, cum unum peccatum possit ex diversis oriri, ex illo tamen dicitur principalius habere originem ex quo frequentius procedere consuevit, propter propinquitatem ad finem ipsius. Contumelia autem magnam habet propinquitatem ad finem irae, qui est vindicta, nulla enim vindicta est irato magis in promptu quam inferre contumeliam alteri. Et ideo contumelia maxime oritur ex ira.

**AD PRIMUM** ergo dicendum quod contumelia non ordinatur ad finem superbiae, qui est celsitudo, et ideo non directe contumelia oritur ex superbia. Disponit tamen superbia ad contumeliam, inquantum illi qui se superiores aestimant, facilius alios contemnunt et iniurias eis irrogant. Facilius etiam irascuntur, utpote reputantes indignum quidquid contra eorum voluntatem agitur.

**AD SECUNDUM** dicendum quod, secundum philosophum, in VII Ethic., *ira non perfecte audit rationem*, et sic iratus patitur rationis defectum, in quo convenit cum stultitia. Et propter hoc ex stultitia oritur contumelia, secundum affinitatem quam habet cum ira.

**AD TERTIUM** dicendum quod, secundum philosophum, in II Rhet., *iratus intendit manifestam offensam, quod non curat odiens*. Et ideo contumelia, quae importat manifestam iniuriam, magis pertinet ad iram quam ad odium.

**OBJECTION 1**: It would seem that reviling does not arise from anger. For it is written (Prov 11:2): *Where pride is, there shall also be reviling*. But anger is a vice distinct from pride. Therefore reviling does not arise from anger.

**OBJ. 2**: Further, it is written (Prov 20:3): *All fools are meddling with revilings*. Now folly is a vice opposed to wisdom, as stated above (Q. 46, A. 1); whereas anger is opposed to meekness. Therefore reviling does not arise from anger.

**OBJ. 3**: Further, no sin is diminished by its cause. But the sin of reviling is diminished if one gives vent to it through anger: for it is a more grievous sin to revile out of hatred than out of anger. Therefore reviling does not arise from anger.

**ON THE CONTRARY**, Gregory says (*Moral.* xxxi, 45) that anger gives rise to revilings.

**I ANSWER THAT**, While one sin may arise from various causes, it is nevertheless said to have its source chiefly in that one from which it is wont to arise most frequently, through being closely connected with its end. Now reviling is closely connected with anger's end, which is revenge: since the easiest way for the angry man to take revenge on another is to revile him. Therefore reviling arises chiefly from anger.

**REPLY OBJ. 1**: Reviling is not directed to the end of pride which is excellency. Hence reviling does not arise directly from pride. Nevertheless pride disposes a man to revile, insofar as those who think themselves to excel, are more prone to despise others and inflict injuries on them, because they are more easily angered, through deeming it an affront to themselves whenever anything is done against their will.

**REPLY OBJ. 2**: According to the Philosopher (*Ethic.* vii, 6) *anger listens imperfectly to reason*: wherefore an angry man suffers a defect of reason, and in this he is like the foolish man. Hence reviling arises from folly on account of the latter's kinship with anger.

**REPLY OBJ. 3**: According to the Philosopher (*Rhet.* ii, 4) *an angry man seeks an open offense, but he who hates does not worry about this*. Hence reviling which denotes a manifest injury belongs to anger rather than to hatred.

# QUESTION 73

## BACKBITING

Deinde considerandum est de detractione. Et circa hoc quaeruntur quatuor.

Primo, quid sit detractio.

Secundo, utrum sit peccatum mortale.

Tertio, de comparatione eius ad alia peccata.

Quarto, utrum peccet aliquis audiendo detractionem.

We must now consider backbiting, under which head there are four points of inquiry:

(1) What is backbiting?

(2) Whether it is a mortal sin?

(3) Of its comparison with other sins;

(4) Whether it is a sin to listen to backbiting?

# Article 1

*Whether backbiting is suitably defined as the blackening of another's character by secret words?*

**AD PRIMUM SIC PROCEDITUR.** Videtur quod detractio non sit *denigratio alienae famae per occulta verba*, ut a quibusdam definitur. Occultum enim et manifestum sunt circumstantiae non constituentes speciem peccati, accidit enim peccato quod a multis sciatur vel a paucis. Sed illud quod non constituit speciem peccati non pertinet ad rationem ipsius, nec debet poni in eius definitione. Ergo ad rationem detractionis non pertinet quod fiat per occulta verba.

**PRAETEREA,** ad rationem famae pertinet publica notitia. Si igitur per detractionem denigretur fama alicuius, non poterit hoc fieri per verba occulta, sed per verba in manifesto dicta.

**PRAETEREA,** ille detrahit qui aliquid subtrahit vel diminuit de eo quod est. Sed quandoque denigratur fama alicuius etiam si nihil subtrahatur de veritate, puta cum aliquis vera crimina alicuius pandit. Ergo non omnis denigratio famae est detractio.

**SED CONTRA** est quod dicitur Eccle. X, *si mordeat serpens in silentio, nihil eo minus habet qui occulte detrahit.* Ergo occulte mordere famam alicuius est detrahere.

**RESPONDEO** dicendum quod sicut facto aliquis alteri nocet dupliciter, manifeste quidem sicut in rapina vel quacumque violentia illata, occulte autem sicut in furto et dolosa percussione; ita etiam verbo aliquis dupliciter aliquem laedit, uno modo, in manifesto, et hoc fit per contumeliam, ut supra dictum est; alio modo, occulte, et hoc fit per detractionem. Ex hoc autem quod aliquis manifeste verba contra alium profert, videtur eum parvipendere, unde ex hoc ipso exhonoratur, et ideo contumelia detrimentum affert honori eius in quem profertur. Sed qui verba contra aliquem profert in occulto, videtur eum vereri magis quam parvipendere, unde non

**OBJECTION 1**: It would seem that backbiting is not as defined by some, *the blackening of another's good name by words uttered in secret.* For *secretly* and *openly* are circumstances that do not constitute the species of a sin, because it is accidental to a sin that it be known by many or by few. Now that which does not constitute the species of a sin, does not belong to its essence, and should not be included in its definition. Therefore it does not belong to the essence of backbiting that it should be done by secret words.

**OBJ. 2**: Further, the notion of a good name implies something known to the public. If, therefore, a person's good name is blackened by backbiting, this cannot be done by secret words, but by words uttered openly.

**OBJ. 3**: Further, to detract is to subtract, or to diminish something already existing. But sometimes a man's good name is blackened, even without subtracting from the truth: for instance, when one reveals the crimes which a man has in truth committed. Therefore not every blackening of a good name is backbiting.

**ON THE CONTRARY**, It is written (Eccl 10:11): *If a serpent bite in silence, he is nothing better that backbiteth.*

**I ANSWER THAT,** Just as one man injures another by deed in two ways—openly, as by robbery or by doing him any kind of violence—and secretly, as by theft, or by a crafty blow, so again one man injures another by words in two ways—in one way, openly, and this is done by reviling him, as stated above (Q. 72, A. 1)—and in another way secretly, and this is done by backbiting. Now from the fact that one man openly utters words against another man, he would appear to think little of him, so that for this reason he dishonors him, so that reviling is detrimental to the honor of the person reviled. On the other hand, he that speaks against another secretly, seems to respect

directe infert detrimentum honori, sed famae; inquantum, huiusmodi verba occulte proferens, quantum in ipso est, eos qui audiunt facit malam opinionem habere de eo contra quem loquitur. Hoc enim intendere videtur, et ad hoc conatur detrahens, ut eius verbis credatur. Unde patet quod detractio differt a contumelia dupliciter. Uno modo, quantum ad modum proponendi verba, quia scilicet contumeliosus manifeste contra aliquem loquitur, detractor autem occulte. Alio modo, quantum ad finem intentum, sive quantum ad nocumentum illatum, quia scilicet contumeliosus derogat honori, detractor famae.

**AD PRIMUM** ergo dicendum quod in involuntariis commutationibus, ad quas reducuntur omnia nocumenta proximo illata verbo vel facto, diversificat rationem peccati occultum et manifestum, quia alia est ratio involuntarii per violentiam, et per ignorantiam, ut supra dictum est.

**AD SECUNDUM** dicendum quod verba detractionis dicuntur occulta non simpliciter, sed per comparationem ad eum de quo dicuntur, quia eo absente et ignorante, dicuntur. Sed contumeliosus in faciem contra hominem loquitur. Unde si aliquis de alio male loquatur coram multis, eo absente, detractio est, si autem eo solo praesente, contumelia est. Quamvis etiam si uni soli aliquis de absente malum dicat, corrumpit famam eius, non in toto, sed in parte.

**AD TERTIUM** dicendum quod aliquis dicitur detrahere non quia diminuat de veritate, sed quia diminuit famam eius. Quod quidem quandoque fit directe, quandoque indirecte. Directe quidem, quadrupliciter, uno modo, quando falsum imponit alteri; secundo, quando peccatum adauget suis verbis; tertio, quando occultum revelat; quarto, quando id quod est bonum dicit mala intentione factum. Indirecte autem, vel negando bonum alterius; vel malitiose reticendo.

rather than slight him, so that he injures directly, not his honor but his good name, insofar as by uttering such words secretly, he, for his own part, causes his hearers to have a bad opinion of the person against whom he speaks. For the backbiter apparently intends and aims at being believed. It is therefore evident that backbiting differs from reviling in two points: first, in the way in which the words are uttered, the reviler speaking openly against someone, and the backbiter secretly; second, as to the end in view, i.e., as regards the injury inflicted, the reviler injuring a man's honor, the backbiter injuring his good name.

**REPLY OBJ. 1**: In involuntary commutations, to which are reduced all injuries inflicted on our neighbor, whether by word or by deed, the kind of sin is differentiated by the circumstances *secretly* and *openly*, because involuntariness itself is diversified by violence and by ignorance, as stated above (Q. 65, A. 4; I-II, Q. 6, AA. 5, 8).

**REPLY OBJ. 2**: The words of a backbiter are said to be secret, not altogether, but in relation to the person of whom they are said, because they are uttered in his absence and without his knowledge. On the other hand, the reviler speaks against a man to his face. Wherefore if a man speaks ill of another in the presence of several, it is a case of backbiting if he be absent, but of reviling if he alone be present: although if a man speak ill of an absent person to one man alone, he destroys his good name not altogether but partly.

**REPLY OBJ. 3**: A man is said to backbite (detrahere) another, not because he detracts from the truth, but because he lessens his good name. This is done sometimes directly, sometimes indirectly. Directly, in four ways: first, by saying that which is false about him; second, by stating his sin to be greater than it is; third, by revealing something unknown about him; fourth, by ascribing his good deeds to a bad intention. Indirectly, this is done either by gainsaying his good, or by maliciously concealing it, or by diminishing it.

# Article 2

### *Whether backbiting is a mortal sin?*

**AD SECUNDUM SIC PROCEDITUR.** Videtur quod detractio non sit peccatum mortale. Nullus enim actus virtutis est peccatum mortale. Sed revelare peccatum occultum, quod, sicut dictum est, ad detractionem pertinet, est actus virtutis, vel caritatis, dum aliquis fratris peccatum denuntiat eius emendationem intendens; vel etiam est actus iustitiae, dum aliquis fratrem accusat. Ergo detractio non est peccatum mortale.

**PRAETEREA**, super illud Prov. XXIV, *cum detractoribus non commiscearis*, dicit Glossa, *hoc specialiter*

**OBJECTION 1**: It would seem that backbiting is not a mortal sin. For no act of virtue is a mortal sin. Now, to reveal an unknown sin, which pertains to backbiting, as stated above (A. 1, ad 3), is an act of the virtue of charity, whereby a man denounces his brother's sin in order that he may amend: or else it is an act of justice, whereby a man accuses his brother. Therefore backbiting is not a mortal sin.

**OBJ. 2**: Further, a gloss on Prov. 24:21, *Have nothing to do with detractors*, says: *The whole human race is in peril*

*vitio periclitatur totum genus humanum.* Sed nullum peccatum mortale in toto humano genere invenitur, quia multi abstinent a peccato mortali, peccata autem venialia sunt quae in omnibus inveniuntur. Ergo detractio est peccatum veniale.

**PRAETEREA**, Augustinus, in homilia de igne Purg., inter *peccata minuta* ponit, *quando cum omni facilitate vel temeritate maledicimus,* quod pertinet ad detractionem. Ergo detractio est peccatum veniale.

**SED CONTRA** est quod Rom. I dicitur, *detractores, Deo odibiles,* quod ideo additur, ut dicit Glossa, *ne leve putetur propter hoc quod consistit in verbis.*

**RESPONDEO** dicendum quod, sicut supra dictum est, peccata verborum maxime sunt ex intentione dicentis diiudicanda. Detractio autem, secundum suam rationem, ordinatur ad denigrandam famam alicuius. Unde ille, per se loquendo, detrahit qui ad hoc de aliquo obloquitur, eo absente, ut eius famam denigret. Auferre autem alicui famam valde grave est, quia inter res temporales videtur fama esse pretiosior, per cuius defectum homo impeditur a multis bene agendis. Propter quod dicitur Eccli. XLI, *curam habe de bono nomine, hoc enim magis permanebit tibi quam mille thesauri magni et pretiosi.* Et ideo detractio, per se loquendo, est peccatum mortale. Contingit tamen quandoque quod aliquis dicit aliqua verba per quae diminuitur fama alicuius, non hoc intendens, sed aliquid aliud hoc autem non est detrahere per se et formaliter loquendo, sed solum materialiter et quasi per accidens. Et si quidem verba per quae fama alterius diminuitur proferat aliquis propter aliquod bonum vel necessarium, debitis circumstantiis observatis, non est peccatum, nec potest dici detractio. Si autem proferat ex animi levitate, vel propter aliquid non necessarium, non est peccatum mortale, nisi forte verbum quod dicitur sit adeo grave quod notabiliter famam alicuius laedat, et praecipue in his quae pertinent ad honestatem vitae; quia hoc ex ipso genere verborum habet rationem peccati mortalis. Et tenetur aliquis ad restitutionem famae, sicut ad restitutionem cuiuslibet rei subtractae, eo modo quo supra dictum est, cum de restitutione ageretur.

**AD PRIMUM** ergo dicendum quod revelare peccatum occultum alicuius propter eius emendationem denuntiando, vel propter bonum publicae iustitiae accusando, non est detrahere, ut dictum est.

**AD SECUNDUM** dicendum quod Glossa illa non dicit quod detractio in toto genere humano inveniatur, sed addit, *paene.* Tum quia *stultorum infinitus est numerus,* et pauci sunt qui ambulant per viam salutis. Tum etiam quia pauci vel nulli sunt qui non aliquando ex animi levitate aliquid dicunt unde in aliquo, vel leviter, alterius fama minoratur, quia, ut dicitur Iac. III, *si quis in verbo non offendit, hic perfectus est vir.*

*from this vice.* But no mortal sin is to be found in the whole of mankind, since many refrain from mortal sin: whereas they are venial sins that are found in all. Therefore backbiting is a venial sin.

**OBJ. 3**: Further, Augustine in a homily on the *Fire of Purgatory* reckons it a slight sin *to speak ill without hesitation or forethought.* But this pertains to backbiting. Therefore backbiting is a venial sin.

**ON THE CONTRARY**, It is written (Rom 1:30): *Backbiters, hateful to God,* which epithet, according to a gloss, is inserted, *lest it be deemed a slight sin because it consists in words.*

**I ANSWER THAT**, As stated above (Q. 72, A. 2), sins of word should be judged chiefly from the intention of the speaker. Now backbiting by its very nature aims at blackening a man's good name. Wherefore, properly speaking, to backbite is to speak ill of an absent person in order to blacken his good name. Now it is a very grave matter to blacken a man's good name, because of all temporal things a man's good name seems the most precious, since for lack of it he is hindered from doing many things well. For this reason it is written (Sir 41:15): *Take care of a good name, for this shall continue with thee, more than a thousand treasures precious and great.* Therefore backbiting, properly speaking, is a mortal sin. Nevertheless it happens sometimes that a man utters words, whereby someone's good name is tarnished, and yet he does not intend this, but something else. This is not backbiting strictly and formally speaking, but only materially and accidentally as it were. And if such defamatory words be uttered for the sake of some necessary good, and with attention to the due circumstances, it is not a sin and cannot be called backbiting. But if they be uttered out of lightness of heart or for some unnecessary motive, it is not a mortal sin, unless perchance the spoken word be of such a grave nature, as to cause a notable injury to a man's good name, especially in matters pertaining to his moral character, because from the very nature of the words this would be a mortal sin. And one is bound to restore a man his good name, no less than any other thing one has taken from him, in the manner stated above (Q. 62, A. 2) when we were treating of restitution.

**REPLY OBJ. 1**: As stated above, it is not backbiting to reveal a man's hidden sin in order that he may mend, whether one denounce it, or accuse him for the good of public justice.

**REPLY OBJ. 2**: This gloss does not assert that backbiting is to be found throughout the whole of mankind, but *almost,* both because *the number of fools is infinite,* and few are they that walk in the way of salvation, and because there are few or none at all who do not at times speak from lightness of heart, so as to injure someone's good name at least slightly, for it is written (Jas 3:2): *If any man offend not in word, the same is a perfect man.*

**AD TERTIUM** dicendum quod Augustinus loquitur in casu illo quo aliquis dicit aliquod leve malum de alio non ex intentione nocendi, sed ex animi levitate vel ex lapsu linguae.

**REPLY OBJ. 3:** Augustine is referring to the case when a man utters a slight evil about someone, not intending to injure him, but through lightness of heart or a slip of the tongue.

# Article 3

*Whether backbiting is the gravest of all sins committed against one's neighbor?*

**AD TERTIUM SIC PROCEDITUR.** Videtur quod detractio sit gravius omnibus peccatis quae in proximum committuntur. Quia super illud Psalm., *pro eo ut me diligerent, detrahebant mihi,* dicit Glossa, *plus nocent in membris detrahentes Christo, quia animas crediturorum interficiunt, quam qui eius carnem, mox resurrecturam, peremerunt.* Ex quo videtur quod detractio sit gravius peccatum quam homicidium, quanto gravius est occidere animam quam occidere corpus. Sed homicidium est gravius inter cetera peccata quae in proximum committuntur. Ergo detractio est simpliciter inter omnia gravior.

**PRAETEREA,** detractio videtur esse gravius peccatum quam contumelia quia contumeliam potest homo repellere, non autem detractionem latentem. Sed contumelia videtur esse maius peccatum quam adulterium, per hoc quod adulterium unit duos in unam carnem, contumelia autem unitos in multa dividit. Ergo detractio est maius peccatum quam adulterium, quod tamen, inter alia peccata quae sunt in proximum, magnam gravitatem habet.

**PRAETEREA,** contumelia oritur ex ira, detractio autem ex invidia, ut patet per Gregorium, XXXI Moral. Sed invidia est maius peccatum quam ira. Ergo et detractio est maius peccatum quam contumelia. Et sic idem quod prius.

**PRAETEREA,** tanto aliquod peccatum est gravius quanto graviorem defectum inducit. Sed detractio inducit gravissimum defectum, scilicet excaecationem mentis, dicit enim Gregorius, *quid aliud detrahentes faciunt nisi quod in pulverem sufflant et in oculos suos terram excitant, ut unde plus detractionis perflant, inde minus veritatis videant?* Ergo detractio est gravissimum peccatum inter ea quae committuntur in proximum.

**SED CONTRA,** gravius est peccare facto quam verbo. Sed detractio est peccatum verbi, adulterium autem et homicidium et furtum sunt peccata in factis. Ergo detractio non est gravius ceteris peccatis quae sunt in proximum.

**RESPONDEO** dicendum quod peccata quae committuntur in proximum sunt pensanda per se quidem secundum nocumenta quae proximo inferuntur, quia ex hoc habent rationem culpae. Tanto autem est maius nocumentum quanto maius bonum demitur. Cum au-

**OBJECTION 1:** It would seem that backbiting is the gravest of all sins committed against one's neighbor. Because a gloss on Ps. 108:4, *Instead of making me a return of love they detracted me,* a gloss says: *Those who detract Christ in His members and slay the souls of future believers are more guilty than those who killed the flesh that was soon to rise again.* From this it seems to follow that backbiting is by so much a graver sin than murder, as it is a graver matter to kill the soul than to kill the body. Now murder is the gravest of the other sins that are committed against one's neighbor. Therefore backbiting is absolutely the gravest of all.

**OBJ. 2:** Further, backbiting is apparently a graver sin than reviling, because a man can withstand reviling, but not a secret backbiting. Now backbiting is seemingly a graver sin than adultery, because adultery unites two persons in one flesh, whereas reviling severs utterly those who were united. Therefore backbiting is more grievous than adultery: and yet of all other sins a man commits against his neighbor, adultery is most grave.

**OBJ. 3:** Further, reviling arises from anger, while backbiting arises from envy, according to Gregory (*Moral.* xxxi, 45). But envy is a graver sin than anger. Therefore backbiting is a graver sin than reviling; and so the same conclusion follows as before.

**OBJ. 4:** Further, the gravity of a sin is measured by the gravity of the defect that it causes. Now backbiting causes a most grievous defect, viz. blindness of mind. For Gregory says (*Regist.* xi, Ep. 2): *What else do backbiters but blow on the dust and stir up the dirt into their eyes, so that the more they breathe of detraction, the less they see of the truth?* Therefore backbiting is the most grievous sin committed against one's neighbor.

**ON THE CONTRARY,** It is more grievous to sin by deed than by word. But backbiting is a sin of word, while adultery, murder, and theft are sins of deed. Therefore backbiting is not graver than the other sins committed against one's neighbor.

**I ANSWER THAT,** The essential gravity of sins committed against one's neighbor must be weighed by the injury they inflict on him, since it is thence that they derive their sinful nature. Now the greater the good taken away, the greater the injury. And while man's good is threefold,

tem sit triplex bonum hominis, scilicet bonum animae et bonum corporis et bonum exteriorum rerum, bonum animae, quod est maximum, non potest alicui ab alio tolli nisi occasionaliter, puta per malam persuasionem, quae necessitatem non infert, sed alia duo bona, scilicet corporis et exteriorum rerum, possunt ab alio violenter auferri. Sed quia bonum corporis praeeminet bono exteriorum rerum, graviora sunt peccata quibus infertur nocumentum corpori quam ea quibus infertur nocumentum exterioribus rebus. Unde inter cetera peccata quae sunt in proximum, homicidium gravius est, per quod tollitur vita proximi iam actu existens, consequenter autem adulterium, quod est contra debitum ordinem generationis humanae, per quam est introitus ad vitam. Consequenter autem sunt exteriora bona. Inter quae, fama praeeminet divitiis, eo quod propinquior est spiritualibus bonis, unde dicitur Prov. XXII, *melius est nomen bonum quam divitiae multae*. Et ideo detractio, secundum suum genus, est maius peccatum quam furtum, minus tamen quam homicidium vel adulterium. Potest tamen esse alius ordo propter circumstantias aggravantes vel diminuentes

Per accidens autem gravitas peccati attenditur ex parte peccantis, qui gravius peccat si ex deliberatione peccet quam si peccet ex infirmitate vel incautela. Et secundum hoc peccata locutionis habent aliquam levitatem, inquantum de facili ex lapsu linguae proveniunt, absque magna praemeditatione.

**AD PRIMUM** ergo dicendum quod illi qui detrahunt Christo impedientes fidem membrorum ipsius, derogant divinitati eius, cui fides innititur. Unde non est simplex detractio, sed blasphemia.

**AD SECUNDUM** dicendum quod gravius peccatum est contumelia quam detractio, inquantum habet maiorem contemptum proximi, sicut et rapina est gravius peccatum quam furtum, ut supra dictum est. Contumelia tamen non est gravius peccatum quam adulterium, non enim gravitas adulterii pensatur ex coniunctione corporum, sed ex deordinatione generationis humanae. Contumeliosus autem non sufficienter causat inimicitiam in alio, sed occasionaliter tantum dividit unitos, inquantum scilicet per hoc quod mala alterius promit, alios, quantum in se est, ab eius amicitia separat, licet ad hoc per eius verba non cogantur. Sic etiam et detractor occasionaliter est homicida, inquantum scilicet per sua verba dat alteri occasionem ut proximum odiat vel contemnat. Propter quod in epistola Clementis dicitur *detractores esse homicidas*, scilicet occasionaliter, *quia qui odit fratrem suum, homicida est*, ut dicitur I Ioan. III.

**AD TERTIUM** dicendum quod quia *ira quaerit in manifesto vindictam inferre*, ut philosophus dicit, in II Rhet., ideo detractio, quae est in occulto, non est filia irae, sicut contumelia; sed magis invidiae, quae nititur

namely the good of his soul, the good of his body, and the good of external things; the good of the soul, which is the greatest of all, cannot be taken from him by another save as an occasional cause, for instance by an evil persuasion, which does not induce necessity. On the other hand the two latter goods, viz. of the body and of external things, can be taken away by violence. Since, however, the goods of the body excel the goods of external things, those sins which injure a man's body are more grievous than those which injure his external things. Consequently, among other sins committed against one's neighbor, murder is the most grievous, since it deprives man of the life which he already possesses: after this comes adultery, which is contrary to the right order of human generation, whereby man enters upon life. In the last place come external goods, among which a man's good name takes precedence of wealth because it is more akin to spiritual goods, wherefore it is written (Prov 22:1): *A good name is better than great riches*. Therefore backbiting according to its genus is a more grievous sin than theft, but is less grievous than murder or adultery. Nevertheless the order may differ by reason of aggravating or extenuating circumstances.

The accidental gravity of a sin is to be considered in relation to the sinner, who sins more grievously, if he sins deliberately than if he sins through weakness or carelessness. In this respect sins of word have a certain levity, insofar as they are apt to occur through a slip of the tongue, and without much forethought.

**REPLY OBJ. 1**: Those who detract Christ by hindering the faith of His members, disparage His Godhead, which is the foundation of our faith. Wherefore this is not simple backbiting but blasphemy.

**REPLY OBJ. 2**: Reviling is a more grievous sin than backbiting, inasmuch as it implies greater contempt of one's neighbor: even as robbery is a graver sin than theft, as stated above (Q. 66, A. 9). Yet reviling is not a more grievous sin than adultery. For the gravity of adultery is measured, not from its being a union of bodies, but from being a disorder in human generation. Moreover the reviler is not the sufficient cause of unfriendliness in another man, but is only the occasional cause of division among those who were united, in so far, to wit, as by declaring the evils of another, he for his own part severs that man from the friendship of other men, though they are not forced by his words to do so. Accordingly a backbiter is a murderer occasionally, since by his words he gives another man an occasion for hating or despising his neighbor. For this reason it is stated in the Epistle of Clement that *backbiters are murderers*, i.e., occasionally; because *he that hateth his brother is a murderer* (1 John 3:15).

**REPLY OBJ. 3**: *Anger seeks openly to be avenged*, as the Philosopher states (*Rhet.* ii, 2): wherefore backbiting which takes place in secret, is not the daughter of anger, as reviling is, but rather of envy, which strives by any means to lessen

qualitercumque minuere gloriam proximi. Nec tamen sequitur propter hoc quod detractio sit gravior quam contumelia, quia ex minori vitio potest oriri maius peccatum, sicut ex ira nascitur homicidium et blasphemia. Origo enim peccatorum attenditur secundum inclinationem ad finem, quod est ex parte conversionis, gravitas autem peccati magis attenditur ex parte aversionis.

**AD QUARTUM** dicendum quod quia *homo laetatur in sententia oris sui*, ut dicitur Prov. XV, inde est quod ille qui detrahit incipit magis amare et credere quod dicit; et per consequens proximum magis odire; et sic magis recedere a cognitione veritatis. Iste tamen effectus potest sequi etiam ex aliis peccatis quae pertinent ad odium proximi.

one's neighbor's glory. Nor does it follow from this that backbiting is more grievous than reviling: since a lesser vice can give rise to a greater sin, just as anger gives birth to murder and blasphemy. For the origin of a sin depends on its inclination to an end, i.e., on the thing to which the sin turns, whereas the gravity of a sin depends on what it turns away from.

**REPLY OBJ. 4**: Since *a man rejoiceth in the sentence of his mouth* (Prov 15:23), it follows that a backbiter more and more loves and believes what he says, and consequently more and more hates his neighbor, and thus his knowledge of the truth becomes less and less. This effect however may also result from other sins pertaining to hate of one's neighbor.

# Article 4

### Whether it is a grave sin for the listener to suffer the backbiter?

**AD QUARTUM SIC PROCEDITUR**. Videtur quod audiens qui tolerat detrahentem non graviter peccet. Non enim aliquis magis tenetur alteri quam sibi ipsi. Sed laudabile est si patienter homo suos detractores toleret, dicit enim Gregorius, super Ezech. Homil. IX, *linguas detrahentium, sicut nostro studio non debemus excitare, ne ipsi pereant; ita per suam malitiam excitatas debemus aequanimiter tolerare, ut nobis meritum crescat.* Ergo non peccat aliquis si detractionibus aliorum non resistat.

**PRAETEREA**, Eccli. IV dicitur, *non contradicas verbo veritatis ullo modo.* Sed quandoque aliquis detrahit verba veritatis dicendo, ut supra dictum est. Ergo videtur quod non semper teneatur homo detractionibus resistere.

**PRAETEREA**, nullus debet impedire id quod est in utilitatem aliorum. Sed detractio frequenter est in utilitatem eorum contra quos detrahitur, dicit enim pius Papa, *nonnunquam detractio adversus bonos excitatur, ut quos vel domestica adulatio vel aliorum favor in altum extulerat, detractio humiliet.* Ergo aliquis non debet detractiones impedire.

**SED CONTRA** est quod Hieronymus dicit, *cave ne linguam aut aures habeas prurientes, aut aliis detrahas, aut alios audias detrahentes.*

**RESPONDEO** dicendum quod, secundum apostolum, ad Rom. I, *digni sunt morte non solum qui peccata faciunt, sed etiam qui facientibus peccata consentiunt.* Quod quidem contingit dupliciter. Uno modo, directe, quando scilicet quis inducit alium ad peccatum, vel ei placet peccatum. Alio modo, indirecte, quando scilicet non resistit, cum resistere possit, et hoc contingit quan-

**OBJECTION 1**: It would seem that the listener who suffers a backbiter does not sin grievously. For a man is not under greater obligations to others than to himself. But it is praiseworthy for a man to suffer his own backbiters: for Gregory says (*Hom. ix, super Ezech*): *Just as we ought not to incite the tongue of backbiters, lest they perish, so ought we to suffer them with equanimity when they have been incited by their own wickedness, in order that our merit may be the greater.* Therefore a man does not sin if he does not withstand those who backbite others.

**OBJ. 2**: Further, it is written (Sir 4:30): *In no wise speak against the truth.* Now sometimes a person tells the truth while backbiting, as stated above (A. 1, ad 3). Therefore it seems that one is not always bound to withstand a backbiter.

**OBJ. 3**: Further, no man should hinder what is profitable to others. Now backbiting is often profitable to those who are backbitten: for Pope Pius says: *Not unfrequently backbiting is directed against good persons, with the result that those who have been unduly exalted through the flattery of their kindred, or the favor of others, are humbled by backbiting.* Therefore one ought not to withstand backbiters.

**ON THE CONTRARY**, Jerome says (*Ep. ad Nepot. lii*): *Take care not to have an itching tongue, nor tingling ears, that is, neither detract others nor listen to backbiters.*

**I ANSWER THAT**, According to the Apostle (Rom 1:32), they *are worthy of death . . . not only they that commit sins, but they also that consent to them that do them.* Now this happens in two ways. First, directly, when, to wit, one man induces another to sin, or when the sin is pleasing to him: second, indirectly, that is, if he does not withstand him when he might do so, and this happens sometimes, not

doque non quia peccatum placeat, sed propter aliquem humanum timorem.

Dicendum est ergo quod si aliquis detractiones audiat absque resistentia, videtur detractori consentire, unde fit particeps peccati eius. Et si quidem inducat eum ad detrahendum, vel saltem placeat ei detractio, propter odium eius cui detrahitur, non minus peccat quam detrahens, et quandoque magis. Unde Bernardus dicit, *detrahere, aut detrahentem audire, quid horum damnabilius sit, non facile dixerim.* Si vero non placeat ei peccatum, sed ex timore vel negligentia vel etiam verecundia quadam omittat repellere detrahentem, peccat quidem, sed multo minus quam detrahens, et plerumque venialiter. Quandoque etiam hoc potest esse peccatum mortale, vel propter hoc quod alicui ex officio incumbit detrahentem corrigere; vel propter aliquod periculum consequens; vel propter radicem, qua timor humanus quandoque potest esse peccatum mortale, ut supra habitum est.

**AD PRIMUM** ergo dicendum quod detractiones suas nullus audit, quia scilicet mala quae dicuntur de aliquo eo audiente, non sunt detractiones, proprie loquendo, sed contumeliae, ut dictum est. Possunt tamen ad notitiam alicuius detractiones contra ipsum factae aliorum relationibus pervenire. Et tunc sui arbitrii est detrimentum suae famae pati, nisi hoc vergat in periculum aliorum, ut supra dictum est. Et ideo in hoc potest commendari eius patientia quod patiehter proprias detractiones sustinet. Non autem est sui arbitrii quod patiatur detrimentum famae alterius. Et ideo in culpam ei vertitur si non resistit, cum possit resistere, eadem ratione qua tenetur aliquis *sublevare asinum alterius iacentem sub onere,* ut praecipitur Deut. XXII.

**AD SECUNDUM** dicendum quod non semper debet aliquis resistere detractori arguendo eum de falsitate, maxime si quis sciat verum esse quod dicitur. Sed debet eum verbis redarguere de hoc quod peccat fratri detrahendo, vel saltem ostendere quod ei detractio displiceat per tristitiam faciei; quia, ut dicitur Prov. XXV, *ventus Aquilo dissipat pluvias, et facies tristis linguam detrahentem.*

**AD TERTIUM** dicendum quod utilitas quae ex detractione provenit non est ex intentione detrahentis, sed ex Dei ordinatione, qui ex quolibet malo elicit bonum. Et ideo nihilo minus est detractoribus resistendum, sicut et raptoribus vel oppressoribus aliorum, quamvis ex hoc oppressis vel spoliatis per patientiam meritum crescat.

because the sin is pleasing to him, but on account of some human fear.

Accordingly we must say that if a man listens to backbiting without resisting it, he seems to consent to the backbiter, so that he becomes a participator in his sin. And if he induces him to backbite, or at least if the detraction be pleasing to him on account of his hatred of the person detracted, he sins no less than the detractor, and sometimes more. Wherefore Bernard says (*De Consid.* ii, 13): *It is difficult to say which is the more to be condemned the backbiter or he that listens to backbiting.* If however the sin is not pleasing to him, and he fails to withstand the backbiter, through fear, negligence, or even shame, he sins indeed, but much less than the backbiter, and, as a rule venially. Sometimes too this may be a mortal sin, either because it is his official duty to correct the backbiter, or by reason of some consequent danger; or on account of the radical reason for which human fear may sometimes be a mortal sin, as stated above (Q. 19, A. 3).

**REPLY OBJ. 1**: No man hears himself backbitten, because when a man is spoken evil of in his hearing, it is not backbiting, properly speaking, but reviling, as stated above (A. 1, ad 2). Yet it is possible for the detractions uttered against a person to come to his knowledge through others telling him, and then it is left to his discretion whether he will suffer their detriment to his good name, unless this endanger the good of others, as stated above (Q. 72, A. 3). Wherefore his patience may deserve commendation for as much as he suffers patiently being detracted himself. But it is not left to his discretion to permit an injury to be done to another's good name, hence he is accounted guilty if he fails to resist when he can, for the same reason whereby a man is bound *to raise another man's ass lying underneath his burden,* as commanded in Deut. 21:4.

**REPLY OBJ. 2**: One ought not always to withstand a backbiter by endeavoring to convince him of falsehood, especially if one knows that he is speaking the truth: rather ought one to reprove him with words, for that he sins in backbiting his brother, or at least by our pained demeanor show him that we are displeased with his backbiting, because according to Prov. 25:23, *the north wind driveth away rain, as doth a sad countenance a backbiting tongue.*

**REPLY OBJ. 3**: The profit one derives from being backbitten is due, not to the intention of the backbiter, but to the ordinance of God Who produces good out of every evil. Hence we should nonetheless withstand backbiters, just as those who rob or oppress others, even though the oppressed and the robbed may gain merit by patience.

# QUESTION 74

## TALE-BEARING

Deinde considerandum est de susurratione. Et circa hoc quaeruntur duo.

Primo, utrum susurratio sit peccatum distinctum a detractione.

Secundo, quod horum sit gravius.

We must now consider tale-bearing: under which head there are two points of inquiry:

(1) Whether tale-bearing is a sin distinct from backbiting?

(2) Which of the two is the more grievous?

# Article 1

*Whether tale-bearing is a sin distinct from backbiting?*

**AD PRIMUM SIC PROCEDITUR.** Videtur quod susurratio non sit peccatum distinctum a detractione. Dicit enim Isidorus, in libro Etymol., *susurro de sono locutionis appellatur, quia non in facie alicuius, sed in aure loquitur, detrahendo.* Sed loqui de altero detrahendo ad detractionem pertinet. Ergo susurratio non est peccatum distinctum a detractione.

**PRAETEREA,** Levit. XIX dicitur, *non eris criminator nec susurro in populis.* Sed criminator idem videtur esse quod detractor. Ergo etiam susurratio a detractione non differt.

**PRAETEREA,** Eccli. XXVIII dicitur, *susurro et bilinguis maledictus erit.* Sed bilinguis videtur idem esse quod detractor, quia detractorum est duplici lingua loqui, aliter scilicet in absentia et aliter in praesentia. Ergo susurro est idem quod detractor.

**SED CONTRA** est quod, Rom. I, super illud, *susurrones, detractores,* dicit Glossa, *susurrones, inter amicos discordiam seminantes; detractores, qui aliorum bona negant vel minuunt.*

**RESPONDEO** dicendum quod susurratio et detractio in materia conveniunt, et etiam in forma, sive in modo loquendi, quia uterque malum occulte de proximo dicit. Propter quam similitudinem interdum unum pro alio ponitur, unde Eccli. V, super illud, *non appelleris susurro,* dicit Glossa, *idest detractor.* Differunt autem in fine. Quia detractor intendit denigrare famam proximi, unde illa mala de proximo praecipue profert ex quibus proximus infamari possit, vel saltem diminui eius fama. Susurro autem intendit amicitiam separare, ut patet per Glossam inductam, et per id quod dicitur Prov. XXVI, *susurrone subtracto, iurgia conquiescunt.* Et ideo susurro talia mala profert de proximo quae possunt contra ipsum commovere animum audientis, secundum illud Eccli.

**OBJECTION 1:** It would seem that tale-bearing is not a distinct sin from backbiting. Isidore says (*Etym.* x): *The tale-bearer* (susurro) *takes his name from the sound of his speech, for he speaks disparagingly not to the face but into the ear.* But to speak of another disparagingly belongs to backbiting. Therefore tale-bearing is not a distinct sin from backbiting.

**OBJ. 2:** Further, it is written (Lev 19:16): *Thou shalt not be an informer nor a tale-bearer among the people.* But an informer is apparently the same as a backbiter. Therefore neither does tale-bearing differ from backbiting.

**OBJ. 3:** Further, it is written (Sir 28:15): *The tale-bearer and the double-tongued is accursed.* But a double-tongued man is apparently the same as a backbiter, because a backbiter speaks with a double tongue, with one in your absence, with another in your presence. Therefore a tale-bearer is the same as a backbiter.

**ON THE CONTRARY,** A gloss on Rom. 1:29, 30, *Tale-bearers, backbiters* says: *Tale-bearers sow discord among friends; backbiters deny or disparage others' good points.*

**I ANSWER THAT,** The tale-bearer and the backbiter agree in matter, and also in form or mode of speaking, since they both speak evil secretly of their neighbor: and for this reason these terms are sometimes used one for the other. Hence a gloss on Ecclus. 5:16, *Be not called a tale-bearer* says: i.e., *a backbiter.* They differ however in end, because the backbiter intends to blacken his neighbor's good name, wherefore he brings forward those evils especially about his neighbor which are likely to defame him, or at least to depreciate his good name: whereas a tale-bearer intends to sever friendship, as appears from the gloss quoted above and from the saying of Prov. 26:20, *Where the tale-bearer is taken away, contentions shall cease.* Hence it is that a tale-bearer speaks such ill about his neighbors as may stir his

XXVIII, *vir peccator conturbabit amicos, et in medio pacem habentium immittit inimicitiam.*

**AD PRIMUM** ergo dicendum quod susurro, inquantum dicit malum de alio, dicitur detrahere. In hoc tamen differt a detractore, quia non intendit simpliciter malum dicere; sed quidquid sit illud quod possit animum unius turbare contra alium, etiam si sit simpliciter bonum, et tamen apparens malum, inquantum displicet ei cui dicitur.

**AD SECUNDUM** dicendum quod criminator differt et a susurrone et a detractore. Quia criminator est qui publice aliis crimina imponit, vel accusando vel conviciando, quod non pertinet ad detractorem et susurronem.

**AD TERTIUM** dicendum quod bilinguis proprie dicitur susurro. Cum enim amicitia sit inter duos, nititur susurro ex utraque parte amicitiam rumpere, et ideo duabus linguis utitur ad duos, uni dicens malum de alio. Propter quod dicitur Eccli. XXVIII, *susurro et bilinguis maledictus,* et subditur, *multos enim turbant pacem habentes.*

hearer's mind against them, according to Ecclus. 28:11, *A sinful man will trouble his friends, and bring in debate in the midst of them that are at peace.*

**REPLY OBJ. 1**: A tale-bearer is called a backbiter insofar as he speaks ill of another; yet he differs from a backbiter since he intends not to speak ill as such, but to say anything that may stir one man against another, though it be good simply, and yet has a semblance of evil through being unpleasant to the hearer.

**REPLY OBJ. 2**: An informer differs from a tale-bearer and a backbiter, for an informer is one who charges others publicly with crimes, either by accusing or by railing them, which does not apply to a backbiter or tale-bearer.

**REPLY OBJ. 3**: A double-tongued person is properly speaking a tale-bearer. For since friendship is between two, the tale-bearer strives to sever friendship on both sides. Hence he employs a double tongue towards two persons, by speaking ill of one to the other: wherefore it is written (Sir 28:15): *The tale-bearer and the double-tongued is accursed,* and then it is added, *for he hath troubled many that were peace.*

# Article 2

*Whether backbiting is a graver sin than tale-bearing?*

**AD SECUNDUM SIC PROCEDITUR.** Videtur quod detractio sit gravius peccatum quam susurratio. Peccata enim oris consistunt in hoc quod aliquis mala dicit. Sed detractor dicit de proximo ea quae sunt mala simpliciter, quia ex talibus oritur infamia vel diminuitur fama, susurro autem non curat dicere nisi mala apparentia, quae scilicet displiceant audienti. Ergo gravius peccatum est detractio quam susurratio.

**PRAETEREA,** quicumque aufert alicui famam, aufert ei non solum unum amicum, sed multos, quia unusquisque refugit amicitiam infamium personarum; unde contra quendam dicitur, II Paralip. XIX, *his qui oderunt dominum amicitia iungeris.* Susurratio autem aufert unum solum amicum. Gravius ergo peccatum est detractio quam susurratio.

**PRAETEREA,** Iac. IV dicitur, *qui detrahit fratri suo, detrahit legi*; et per consequens Deo, qui est legislator, et sic peccatum detractionis videtur esse peccatum in Deum, quod est gravissimum, ut supra habitum est. Peccatum autem susurrationis est in proximum. Ergo peccatum detractionis est gravius quam peccatum susurrationis.

**OBJECTION 1**: It would seem that backbiting is a graver sin than tale-bearing. For sins of word consist in speaking evil. Now a backbiter speaks of his neighbor things that are evil simply, for such things lead to the loss or depreciation of his good name: whereas a tale-bearer is only intent on saying what is apparently evil, because to wit they are unpleasant to the hearer. Therefore backbiting is a graver sin than tale-bearing.

**OBJ. 2**: Further, he that deprives a man of his good name, deprives him not merely of one friend, but of many, because everyone is minded to scorn the friendship of a person with a bad name. Hence it is reproached against a certain individual (2 Paralip. 19:2): *Thou art joined in friendship with them that hate the Lord.* But tale-bearing deprives one of only one friend. Therefore backbiting is a graver sin than tale-bearing.

**OBJ. 3**: Further, it is written (Jas 4:11): *He that backbiteth his brother . . . detracteth the law,* and consequently God the giver of the law. Wherefore the sin of backbiting seems to be a sin against God, which is most grievous, as stated above (Q. 20, A. 3; I-II, Q. 73, A. 3). On the other hand the sin of tale-bearing is against one's neighbor. Therefore the sin of backbiting is graver than the sin of tale-bearing.

**SED CONTRA** est quod dicitur Eccli. V, *denotatio pessima super bilinguem, susurratori autem odium et inimicitia et contumelia.*

**RESPONDEO** dicendum quod, sicut supra dictum est, peccatum in proximum tanto est gravius quanto per ipsum maius nocumentum proximo infertur, nocumentum autem tanto maius est quanto maius est bonum quod tollitur. Inter cetera vero exteriora bona praeeminet amicus, quia *sine amicis nullus vivere posset*, ut patet per philosophum, in VIII Ethic. Unde dicitur Eccli. VI, *amico fideli nulla est comparatio*, quia et optima fama, quae per detractionem tollitur, ad hoc maxime necessaria est ut homo idoneus ad amicitiam habeatur. Et ideo susurratio est maius peccatum quam detractio, et etiam quam contumelia, quia *amicus est melior quam honor, et amari quam honorari*, ut in VIII Ethic. philosophus dicit.

**AD PRIMUM** ergo dicendum quod species et gravitas peccati magis attenditur ex fine quam ex materiali obiecto. Et ideo ratione finis susurratio est gravior, quamvis detractor quandoque peiora dicat.

**AD SECUNDUM** dicendum quod fama est dispositio ad amicitiam, et infamia ad inimicitiam. Dispositio autem deficit ab eo ad quod disponit. Et ideo ille qui operatur ad aliquid quod est dispositio ad inimicitiam, minus peccat quam ille qui directe operatur ad inimicitiam inducendam.

**AD TERTIUM** dicendum quod ille qui detrahit fratri intantum videtur detrahere legi inquantum contemnit praeceptum de dilectione proximi. Contra quod directius agit qui amicitiam disrumpere nititur. Unde hoc peccatum maxime contra Deum est, quia *Deus dilectio est*, ut dicitur I Ioan. IV. Et propter hoc dicitur Prov. VI, *sex sunt quae odit dominus, et septimum detestatur anima eius*, et hoc septimum ponit *eum qui seminat inter fratres discordiam.*

**ON THE CONTRARY,** It is written (Sir 5:17): *An evil mark of disgrace is upon the double-tongued; but to the tale-bearer hatred, and enmity, and reproach.*

**I ANSWER THAT,** As stated above (Q. 73, A. 3; I-II, Q. 73, A. 8), sins against one's neighbor are the more grievous, according as they inflict a greater injury on him: and an injury is so much the greater, according to the greatness of the good which it takes away. Now of all one's external goods a friend takes the first place, since *no man can live without friends*, as the Philosopher declares (*Ethic.* viii, 1). Hence it is written (Sir 6:15): *Nothing can be compared to a faithful friend*. Again, a man's good name whereof backbiting deprives him, is most necessary to him that he may be fitted for friendship. Therefore tale-bearing is a greater sin than backbiting or even reviling, because *a friend is better than honor, and to be loved is better than to be honored*, according to the Philosopher (*Ethic.* viii).

**REPLY OBJ. 1:** The species and gravity of a sin depend on the end rather than on the material object, wherefore, by reason of its end, tale-bearing is worse than backbiting, although sometimes the backbiter says worse things.

**REPLY OBJ. 2:** A good name is a disposition for friendship, and a bad name is a disposition for enmity. But a disposition falls short of the thing for which it disposes. Hence to do anything that leads to a disposition for enmity is a less grievous sin than to do what conduces directly to enmity.

**REPLY OBJ. 3:** He that backbites his brother, seems to detract the law, insofar as he despises the precept of love for one's neighbor: while he that strives to sever friendship seems to act more directly against this precept. Hence the latter sin is more specially against God, because *God is charity* (1 John 4:16), and for this reason it is written (Prov 6:16): *Six things there are, which the Lord hateth, and the seventh His soul detesteth*, and the seventh is (Prov 6:19) *he that soweth discord among brethren.*

# QUESTION 75

## DERISION

Deinde considerandum est de derisione. Et circa hoc quaeruntur duo.

Primo, utrum derisio sit peccatum speciale distinctum ab aliis peccatis quibus per verba nocumentum proximo infertur.

Secundo, utrum derisio sit peccatum mortale.

We must now speak of derision, under which head there are two points of inquiry:

(1) Whether derision is a special sin distinct from the other sins whereby one's neighbor is injured by words?

(2) Whether derision is a mortal sin?

# Article 1

### Whether derision is a special sin?

**AD PRIMUM SIC PROCEDITUR.** Videtur quod derisio non sit speciale peccatum ab aliis praemissis distinctum. Subsannatio enim videtur idem esse quod derisio. Sed subsannatio ad contumeliam videtur pertinere. Ergo derisio non videtur distingui a contumelia.

**PRAETEREA,** nullus irridetur nisi de aliquo turpi, ex quo homo erubescit. Huiusmodi autem sunt peccata, quae si manifeste de aliquo dicuntur, pertinent ad contumeliam; si autem occulte, pertinent ad detractionem sive susurrationem. Ergo derisio non est vitium a praemissis distinctum.

**PRAETEREA,** huiusmodi peccata distinguuntur secundum nocumenta quae proximo inferuntur. Sed per derisionem non infertur aliud nocumentum proximo quam in honore vel fama vel detrimento amicitiae. Ergo derisio non est peccatum distinctum a praemissis.

**SED CONTRA** est quod irrisio fit ludo, unde et *illusio* nominatur. Nullum autem praemissorum ludo agitur, sed serio. Ergo derisio ab omnibus praedictis differt.

**RESPONDEO** dicendum quod, sicut supra dictum est, peccata verborum praecipue pensanda sunt secundum intentionem proferentis. Et ideo secundum diversa quae quis intendit contra alium loquens, huiusmodi peccata distinguuntur. Sicut autem aliquis conviciando intendit conviciati honorem deprimere, et detrahendo diminuere famam, et susurrando tollere amicitiam; ita etiam irridendo aliquis intendit quod ille qui irridetur erubescat. Et quia hic finis est distinctus ab aliis, ideo etiam peccatum derisionis distinguitur a praemissis peccatis.

**AD PRIMUM** ergo dicendum quod subsannatio et irrisio conveniunt in fine, sed differunt in modo, quia *irrisio fit ore,* idest verbo et cachinnis; subsannatio autem naso rugato, ut dicit Glossa super illud Psalm., *qui habitat in caelis irridebit eos.* Talis tamen differentia non

**OBJECTION 1:** It would seem that derision is not a special sin distinct from those mentioned above. For laughing to scorn is apparently the same as derision. But laughing to scorn pertains to reviling. Therefore derision would seem not to differ from reviling.

**OBJ. 2:** Further, no man is derided except for something reprehensible which puts him to shame. Now such are sins; and if they be imputed to a person publicly, it is a case of reviling, if privately, it amounts to backbiting or tale-bearing. Therefore derision is not distinct from the foregoing vices.

**OBJ. 3:** Further, sins of this kind are distinguished by the injury they inflict on one's neighbor. Now the injury inflicted on a man by derision affects either his honor, or his good name, or is detrimental to his friendship. Therefore derision is not a sin distinct from the foregoing.

**ON THE CONTRARY,** Derision is done in jest, wherefore it is described as *making fun.* Now all the foregoing are done seriously and not in jest. Therefore derision differs from all of them.

**I ANSWER THAT,** As stated above (Q. 72, A. 2), sins of word should be weighed chiefly by the intention of the speaker, wherefore these sins are differentiated according to the various intentions of those who speak against another. Now just as the railer intends to injure the honor of the person he rails, the backbiter to depreciate a good name, and the tale-bearer to destroy friendship, so too the derider intends to shame the person he derides. And since this end is distinct from the others, it follows that the sin of derision is distinct from the foregoing sins.

**REPLY OBJ. 1:** Laughing to scorn and derision agree as to the end but differ in mode, because derision is done with the *mouth,* i.e., by words and laughter, while laughing to scorn is done by wrinkling the nose, as a gloss says on Ps. 2:4, *He that dwelleth in heaven shall laugh at them:* and

689

diversificat speciem. Utrumque tamen differt a contumelia, sicut erubescentia a dehonoratione, est enim erubescentia *timor dehonorationis*, sicut Damascenus dicit.

**AD SECUNDUM** dicendum quod de opere virtuoso aliquis apud alios et reverentiam meretur et famam; apud seipsum bonae conscientiae gloriam, secundum illud II ad Cor. I, *gloria nostra haec est, testimonium conscientiae nostrae*. Unde e contrario de actu turpi, idest vitioso, apud alios quidem tollitur hominis honor et fama, et ad hoc contumeliosus et detractor turpia de alio dicunt. Apud seipsum autem per turpia quae dicuntur aliquis perdit conscientiae gloriam per quandam confusionem et erubescentiam, et ad hoc turpia dicit derisor. Et sic patet quod derisor communicat cum praedictis vitiis in materia, differt autem in fine.

**AD TERTIUM** dicendum quod securitas conscientiae et quies illius magnum bonum est, secundum illud Prov. XV, *secura mens quasi iuge convivium*. Et ideo qui conscientiam alicuius inquietat confundendo ipsum, aliquod speciale nocumentum ei infert. Unde derisio est peccatum speciale.

such a distinction does not differentiate the species. Yet they both differ from reviling, as being shamed differs from being dishonored: for to be ashamed is *to fear dishonor*, as Damascene states (*De Fide Orth.* ii, 15).

**REPLY OBJ. 2**: For doing a virtuous deed a man deserves both respect and a good name in the eyes of others, and in his own eyes the glory of a good conscience, according to 2 Cor. 1:12, *Our glory is this, the testimony of our conscience.* Hence, on the other hand, for doing a reprehensible, i.e., a vicious action, a man forfeits his honor and good name in the eyes of others—and for this purpose the reviler and the backbiter speak of another person—while in his own eyes, he loses the glory of his conscience through being confused and ashamed at reprehensible deeds being imputed to him—and for this purpose the derider speaks ill of him. It is accordingly evident that derision agrees with the foregoing vices as the matter but differs as to the end.

**REPLY OBJ. 3**: A secure and calm conscience is a great good, according to Prov. 15:15, *A secure mind is like a continual feast.* Wherefore he that disturbs another's conscience by confounding him inflicts a special injury on him: hence derision is a special kind of sin.

# Article 2

*Whether derision can be a mortal sin?*

**AD SECUNDUM SIC PROCEDITUR.** Videtur quod derisio non possit esse peccatum mortale. Omne enim peccatum mortale contrariatur caritati. Sed derisio non videtur contrariari caritati, agitur enim ludo quandoque inter amicos; unde et *delusio* nominatur. Ergo derisio non potest esse peccatum mortale.

**PRAETEREA**, derisio illa videtur esse maxima quae fit in iniuriam Dei. Sed non omnis derisio quae vergit in iniuriam Dei est peccatum mortale. Alioquin quicumque recidivat in aliquod peccatum veniale de quo poenituit, peccaret mortaliter, dicit enim Isidorus quod *irrisor est, et non poenitens, qui adhuc agit quod poenitet*. Similiter etiam sequeretur quod omnis simulatio esset peccatum mortale, quia sicut Gregorius dicit, in Moral., per *struthionem* significatur simulator, qui deridet *equum*, idest hominem iustum, et *ascensorem*, idest Deum. Ergo derisio non est peccatum mortale.

**PRAETEREA**, contumelia et detractio videntur esse graviora peccata quam derisio, quia maius est facere aliquid serio quam ioco. Sed non omnis detractio vel contumelia est peccatum mortale. Ergo multo minus derisio.

**SED CONTRA** est quod dicitur Prov. III, *ipse deridet illusores*. Sed deridere Dei est aeternaliter punire pro peccato mortali, ut patet per id quod dicitur in Psalm.,

**OBJECTION 1**: It would seem that derision cannot be a mortal sin. Every mortal sin is contrary to charity. But derision does not seem contrary to charity, for sometimes it takes place in jest among friends, wherefore it is known as *making fun*. Therefore derision cannot be a mortal sin.

**OBJ. 2**: Further, the greatest derision would appear to be that which is done as an injury to God. But derision is not always a mortal sin when it tends to the injury of God: else it would be a mortal sin to relapse into a venial sin of which one has repented. For Isidore says (*De Sum. Bon.* ii, 16) that *he who continues to do what he has repented of, is a derider and not a penitent.* It would likewise follow that all hypocrisy is a mortal sin, because, according to Gregory (*Moral.* xxxi, 15) *the ostrich* signifies the *hypocrite*, who derides *the horse*, i.e., the just man, and *his rider*, i.e., God. Therefore derision is not a mortal sin.

**OBJ. 3**: Further, reviling and backbiting seem to be graver sins than derision, because it is more grievous to do a thing seriously than in jest. But not all backbiting or reviling is a mortal sin. Much less therefore is derision a mortal sin.

**ON THE CONTRARY**, It is written (Prov 3:34): *He derideth the scorners.* But God's derision is eternal punishment for mortal sin, as appears from the words of Ps. 2:4,

*qui habitat in caelis irridebit eos.* Ergo derisio est peccatum mortale.

**RESPONDEO** dicendum quod irrisio non fit nisi de aliquo malo vel defectu. Malum autem si sit magnum, non pro ludo accipitur, sed seriose. Unde si in lusum vel risum vertatur (ex quo *irrisionis* vel *illusionis* nomen sumitur), hoc est quia accipitur ut parvum. Potest autem aliquod malum accipi ut parvum, dupliciter, uno modo, secundum se; alio modo, ratione personae. Cum autem aliquis alterius personae malum vel defectum in ludum vel risum ponit quia secundum se parvum malum est, est veniale et leve peccatum secundum suum genus. Cum autem accipitur quasi parvum ratione personae, sicut defectus puerorum et stultorum parum ponderare solemus, sic aliquem illudere vel irridere est eum omnino parvipendere, et eum tam vilem aestimare ut de eius malo non sit curandum, sed sit quasi pro ludo habendum. Et sic derisio est peccatum mortale. Et gravius quam contumelia, quae similiter est in manifesto, quia contumeliosus videtur accipere malum alterius seriose, illusor autem in ludum; et ita videtur esse maior contemptus et dehonoratio. Et secundum hoc, illusio est grave peccatum, et tanto gravius quanto maior reverentia debetur personae quae illuditur.

Unde gravissimum est irridere Deum et ea quae Dei sunt, secundum illud Isaiae XXXVII, *cui exprobrasti? Et quem blasphemasti? Et super quem exaltasti vocem tuam? Et postea subditur, ad sanctum Israel.* Deinde secundum locum tenet irrisio parentum. Unde dicitur Prov. XXX, *oculum qui subsannat patrem et despicit partum matris suae, effodiant eum corvi de torrentibus, et comedant eum filii aquilae.* Deinde iustorum derisio gravis est, quia *honor est virtutis praemium.* Et contra hoc dicitur Iob XII, *deridetur iusti simplicitas.* Quae quidem derisio valde nociva est, quia per hoc homines a bene agendo impediuntur; secundum illud Gregorii, *qui in aliorum actibus exoriri bona conspiciunt, mox ea manu pestiferae exprobrationis evellunt.*

**AD PRIMUM** ergo dicendum quod ludus non importat aliquid contrarium caritati respectu eius cum quo luditur, potest tamen importare aliquid contrarium caritati respectu eius de quo luditur, propter contemptum, ut dictum est.

**AD SECUNDUM** dicendum quod ille qui recidivat in peccatum de quo poenituit, et ille qui simulat, non expresse Deum irridet, sed quasi interpretative, inquantum scilicet ad modum deridentis se habet. Nec tamen venialiter peccando aliquis simpliciter recidivat vel simulat, sed dispositive et imperfecte.

**AD TERTIUM** dicendum quod derisio, secundum suam rationem, levius aliquid est quam detractio vel

*He that dwelleth in heaven shall laugh at them.* Therefore derision is a mortal sin.

**I ANSWER THAT,** The object of derision is always some evil or defect. Now when an evil is great, it is taken, not in jest, but seriously: consequently if it is taken in jest or turned to ridicule (whence the terms *derision* and *jesting*), this is because it is considered to be slight. Now an evil may be considered to be slight in two ways: first, in itself, second, in relation to the person. When anyone makes game or fun of another's evil or defect, because it is a slight evil in itself, this is a venial sin by reason of its genus. On the other hand this defect may be considered as a slight evil in relation to the person, just as we are wont to think little of the defects of children and imbeciles: and then to make game or fun of a person, is to scorn him altogether, and to think him so despicable that his misfortune troubles us not one whit, but is held as an object of derision. In this way derision is a mortal sin, and more grievous than reviling, which is also done openly: because the reviler would seem to take another's evil seriously; whereas the derider does so in fun, and so would seem the more to despise and dishonor the other man. Wherefore, in this sense, derision is a grievous sin, and all the more grievous according as a greater respect is due to the person derided.

Consequently it is an exceedingly grievous sin to deride God and the things of God, according to Isa. 37:23, *Whom hast thou reproached, and whom hast thou blasphemed, and against whom hast thou exalted thy voice?* and he replies: *Against the Holy One of Israel.* In the second place comes derision of one's parents, wherefore it is written (Prov 30:17): *The eye that mocketh at his father, and that despiseth the labor of his mother in bearing him, let the ravens of the brooks pick it out, and the young eagles eat it.* Further, the derision of good persons is grievous, because *honor is the reward of virtue,* and against this it is written (Job 12:4): *The simplicity of the just man is laughed to scorn.* Such like derision does very much harm: because it turns men away from good deeds, according to Gregory (*Moral.* xx, 14), *Who when they perceive any good points appearing in the acts of others, directly pluck them up with the hand of a mischievous reviling.*

**REPLY OBJ. 1:** Jesting implies nothing contrary to charity in relation to the person with whom one jests, but it may imply something against charity in relation to the person who is the object of the jest, on account of contempt, as stated above.

**REPLY OBJ. 2:** Neither he that relapses into a sin of which he has repented, nor a hypocrite, derides God explicitly, but implicitly, insofar as either's behavior is like a derider's. Nor is it true that to commit a venial sin is to relapse or dissimulate altogether, but only dispositively and imperfectly.

**REPLY OBJ. 3:** Derision considered in itself is less grievous than backbiting or reviling, because it does not

contumelia, quia non importat contemptum, sed ludum. Quandoque tamen habet maiorem contemptum quam etiam contumelia, ut supra dictum est. Et tunc est grave peccatum.

imply contempt, but jest. Sometimes however it includes greater contempt than reviling does, as stated above, and then it is a grave sin.

# QUESTION 76

## CURSING

Deinde considerandum est de maledictione. Et circa hoc quaeruntur quatuor.

Primo, utrum licite possit aliquis maledicere homini.

Secundo, utrum licite possit aliquis maledicere irrationali creaturae.

Tertio, utrum maledictio sit peccatum mortale.

Quarto, de comparatione eius ad alia peccata.

We must now consider cursing. Under this head there are four points of inquiry:

(1) Whether one may lawfully curse another?

(2) Whether one may lawfully curse an irrational creature?

(3) Whether cursing is a mortal sin?

(4) Of its comparison with other sins.

# Article 1

*Whether it is lawful to curse anyone?*

**AD PRIMUM SIC PROCEDITUR.** Videtur quod non liceat maledicere aliquem. Non est enim licitum praeterire mandatum apostoli, in quo Christus loquebatur, ut dicitur II ad Cor. XIII. Sed ipse praecipit, Rom. XII, *benedicite, et nolite maledicere.* Ergo non licet aliquem maledicere.

**PRAETEREA,** omnes tenentur Deum benedicere, secundum illud Dan. III, *benedicite, filii hominum, domino.* Sed non potest ex ore eodem procedere benedictio Dei et maledictio hominis, ut probatur Iac. III. Ergo nulli licet aliquem maledicere.

**PRAETEREA,** ille qui aliquem maledicit, videtur optare eius malum culpae vel poenae, quia maledictio videtur esse imprecatio quaedam. Sed non licet desiderare malum alterius, quinimmo orare oportet pro omnibus ut liberentur a malo. Ergo nulli licet maledicere.

**PRAETEREA,** Diabolus per obstinationem maxime subiectus est malitiae. Sed non licet alicui maledicere Diabolum, sicut nec seipsum, dicitur enim Eccli. XXI, *cum maledicit impius Diabolum, maledicit ipse animam suam.* Ergo multo minus licet maledicere hominem.

**PRAETEREA,** Num. XXIII, super illud, *quomodo maledicam cui non maledixit dominus?* Dicit Glossa, *non potest esse iusta maledicendi causa ubi peccantis ignoratur affectus.* Sed homo non potest scire affectum alterius hominis, nec etiam utrum sit maledictus a Deo. Ergo nulli licet aliquem hominem maledicere.

**SED CONTRA** est quod Deut. XXVII dicitur, *maledictus qui non permanet in sermonibus legis huius.* Elisaeus etiam pueris sibi illudentibus maledixit, ut habetur IV Reg. II.

**OBJECTION 1:** It would seem unlawful to curse anyone. For it is unlawful to disregard the command of the Apostle in whom Christ spoke, according to 2 Cor. 13:3. Now he commanded (Rom 12:14), *Bless and curse not.* Therefore it is not lawful to curse anyone.

**OBJ. 2:** Further, all are bound to bless God, according to Dan. 3:82, *O ye sons of men, bless the Lord.* Now the same mouth cannot both bless God and curse man, as proved in the third chapter of James. Therefore no man may lawfully curse another man.

**OBJ. 3:** Further, he that curses another would seem to wish him some evil either of fault or of punishment, since a curse appears to be a kind of imprecation. But it is not lawful to wish ill to anyone, indeed we are bound to pray that all may be delivered from evil. Therefore it is unlawful for any man to curse.

**OBJ. 4:** Further, the devil exceeds all in malice on account of his obstinacy. But it is not lawful to curse the devil, as neither is it lawful to curse oneself; for it is written (Sir 21:30): *While the ungodly curseth the devil, he curseth his own soul.* Much less therefore is it lawful to curse a man.

**OBJ. 5:** Further, a gloss on Num. 23:8, *How shall I curse whom God hath not cursed?* says: *There cannot be a just cause for cursing a sinner if one be ignorant of his sentiments.* Now one man cannot know another man's sentiments, nor whether he is cursed by God. Therefore no man may lawfully curse another.

**ON THE CONTRARY,** It is written (Deut 27:26): *Cursed be he that abideth not in the words of this law.* Moreover Eliseus cursed the little boys who mocked him (4 Kgs 2:24).

693

RESPONDEO dicendum quod maledicere idem est quod *malum dicere*. Dicere autem tripliciter se habet ad id quod dicitur. Uno modo, per modum enuntiationis, sicut aliquis exprimitur modo indicativo. Et sic maledicere nihil est aliud quam malum alterius referre, quod pertinet ad detractionem. Unde quandoque maledici detractores dicuntur. Alio modo dicere se habet ad id quod dicitur per modum causae. Et hoc quidem primo et principaliter competit Deo, qui omnia suo verbo fecit, secundum illud Psalm, *dixit, et facta sunt*. Consequenter autem competit hominibus, qui verbo suo alios movent per imperium ad aliquid faciendum. Et ad hoc instituta sunt verba imperativi modi. Tertio modo ipsum dicere se habet ad id quod dicitur quasi expressio quaedam affectus desiderantis id quod verbo exprimitur. Et ad hoc instituta sunt verba optativi modi.

Praetermisso igitur primo modo maledictionis, qui est per simplicem enuntiationem mali, considerandum est de aliis duobus. Ubi scire oportet quod facere aliquid et velle illud se consequuntur in bonitate et malitia, ut ex supradictis patet. Unde in istis duobus modis, quibus malum dicitur per modum imperantis vel per modum optantis, eadem ratione est aliquid licitum et illicitum. Si enim aliquis imperet vel optet malum alterius inquantum est malum, quasi ipsum malum intendens, sic maledicere utroque modo erit illicitum. Et hoc est maledicere per se loquendo. Si autem aliquis imperet vel optet malum alterius sub ratione boni, sic est licitum. Nec erit maledictio per se loquendo, sed per accidens, quia principalis intentio dicentis non fertur ad malum, sed ad bonum.

Contingit autem malum aliquod dici imperando vel optando sub ratione duplicis boni. Quandoque quidem sub ratione iusti. Et sic iudex licite maledicit illum cui praecipit iustam poenam inferri. Et sic etiam Ecclesia maledicit anathematizando. Sic etiam prophetae quandoque imprecantur mala peccatoribus, quasi conformantes voluntatem suam divinae iustitiae (licet huiusmodi imprecationes possint etiam per modum praenuntiationis intelligi). Quandoque vero dicitur aliquod malum sub ratione utilis, puta cum aliquis optat aliquem peccatorem pati aliquam aegritudinem, aut aliquod impedimentum, vel ut ipse melior efficiatur, vel ut saltem ab aliorum nocumento cesset.

AD PRIMUM ergo dicendum quod apostolus prohibet maledicere per se loquendo, cum intentione mali.

ET SIMILITER dicendum ad secundum.

AD TERTIUM dicendum quod optare alicui malum sub ratione boni non contrariatur affectui quo quis simpliciter alicui optat bonum, sed magis habet conformitatem ad ipsum.

I ANSWER THAT, To curse (*maledicere*) is the same as to speak ill (*malum dicere*). Now *speaking* has a threefold relation to the thing spoken. First, by way of assertion, as when a thing is expressed in the indicative mood: in this way *maledicere* signifies simply to tell someone of another's evil, and this pertains to backbiting, wherefore tellers of evil (*maledici*) are sometimes called backbiters. Second, speaking is related to the thing spoken, by way of cause, and this belongs to God first and foremost, since He made all things by His word, according to Ps. 32:9, *He spoke and they were made*; while secondarily it belongs to man, who, by his word, commands others and thus moves them to do something: it is for this purpose that we employ verbs in the imperative mood. Third, *speaking* is related to the thing spoken by expressing the sentiments of one who desires that which is expressed in words; and for this purpose we employ the verb in the optative mood.

Accordingly we may omit the first kind of evil speaking which is by way of simple assertion of evil, and consider the other two kinds. And here we must observe that to do something and to will it are consequent on one another in the matter of goodness and wickedness, as shown above (I-II, Q. 20, A. 3). Hence in these two ways of evil speaking, by way of command and by way of desire, there is the same aspect of lawfulness and unlawfulness, for if a man commands or desires another's evil, as evil, being intent on the evil itself, then evil speaking will be unlawful in both ways, and this is what is meant by cursing. On the other hand if a man commands or desires another's evil under the aspect of good, it is lawful; and it may be called cursing, not strictly speaking, but accidentally, because the chief intention of the speaker is directed not to evil but to good.

Now evil may be spoken, by commanding or desiring it, under the aspect of a twofold good. Sometimes under the aspect of just, and thus a judge lawfully curses a man whom he condemns to a just penalty: thus too the Church curses by pronouncing anathema. In the same way the prophets in the Scriptures sometimes call down evils on sinners, as though conforming their will to Divine justice, although such like imprecation may be taken by way of foretelling. Sometimes evil is spoken under the aspect of useful, as when one wishes a sinner to suffer sickness or hindrance of some kind, either that he may himself reform, or at least that he may cease from harming others.

REPLY OBJ. 1: The Apostle forbids cursing strictly so called with an evil intent.

AND SIMILARLY this ought to be said to the second objection.

REPLY OBJ. 3: To wish another man evil under the aspect of good, is not opposed to the sentiment whereby one wishes him good simply, in fact rather is it in conformity therewith.

**AD QUARTUM** dicendum quod in Diabolo est considerare naturam, et culpam. Natura quidem eius bona est, et a Deo, nec eam maledicere licet. Culpa autem eius est maledicenda, secundum illud Iob III, *maledicant ei qui maledicunt diei.* Cum autem peccator maledicit Diabolum propter culpam, seipsum simili ratione iudicat maledictione dignum. Et secundum hoc dicitur maledicere animam suam.

**AD QUINTUM** dicendum quod affectus peccantis, etsi in se non videatur, potest tamen percipi ex aliquo manifesto peccato, pro quo poena est infligenda. Similiter etiam, quamvis sciri non possit quem Deus maledicit secundum finalem reprobationem, potest tamen sciri quis sit maledictus a Deo secundum reatum praesentis culpae.

**REPLY OBJ. 4:** In the devil both nature and guilt must be considered. His nature indeed is good and is from God nor is it lawful to curse it. On the other hand his guilt is deserving of being cursed, according to Job 3:8, *Let them curse it who curse the day.* Yet when a sinner curses the devil on account of his guilt, for the same reason he judges himself worthy of being cursed; and in this sense he is said to curse his own soul.

**REPLY OBJ. 5:** Although the sinner's sentiments cannot be perceived in themselves, they can be perceived through some manifest sin, which has to be punished. Likewise although it is not possible to know whom God curses in respect of final reprobation, it is possible to know who is accursed of God in respect of being guilty of present sin.

# Article 2

*Whether it is lawful to curse an irrational creature?*

**AD SECUNDUM SIC PROCEDITUR.** Videtur quod non liceat creaturam irrationalem maledicere. Maledictio enim praecipue videtur esse licita inquantum respicit poenam. Sed creatura irrationalis non est susceptiva nec culpae nec poenae. Ergo eam maledicere non licet.

**PRAETEREA**, in creatura irrationali nihil invenitur nisi natura, quam Deus fecit. Hanc autem maledicere non licet, etiam in Diabolo, ut dictum est. Ergo creaturam irrationalem nullo modo licet maledicere.

**PRAETEREA**, creatura irrationalis aut est permanens, sicut corpora; aut est transiens, sicut tempora. Sed sicut Gregorius dicit, in IV Moral., *otiosum est maledicere non existenti; vitiosum vero si existeret.* Ergo nullo modo licet maledicere creaturae irrationali.

**SED CONTRA** est quod dominus maledixit ficulneae, ut habetur Matth. XXI; et Iob maledixit diei suo, ut habetur Iob III.

**RESPONDEO** dicendum quod benedictio vel maledictio ad illam rem proprie pertinet cui potest aliquid bene vel male contingere, scilicet rationali creaturae. Creaturis autem irrationalibus bonum vel malum dicitur contingere in ordine ad creaturam rationalem, propter quam sunt. Ordinantur autem ad eam multipliciter. Uno quidem modo, per modum subventionis, inquantum scilicet ex creaturis irrationalibus subvenitur humanae necessitati. Et hoc modo dominus homini dixit, Gen. III, *maledicta terra in opere tuo,* ut scilicet per eius sterilitatem homo puniretur. Et ita etiam intelligitur quod habetur Deut. XXVIII, *benedicta horrea tua,* et infra, *maledictum horreum tuum.* Sic etiam David maledixit montes Gelboe, secundum Gregorii expositionem. Alio modo creatura irrationalis ordinatur ad rationalem

**OBJECTION 1:** It would seem that it is unlawful to curse an irrational creature. Cursing would seem to be lawful chiefly in its relation to punishment. Now irrational creatures are not competent subjects either of guilt or of punishment. Therefore it is unlawful to curse them.

**OBJ. 2:** Further, in an irrational creature there is nothing but the nature which God made. But it is unlawful to curse this even in the devil, as stated above (A. 1). Therefore it is nowise lawful to curse an irrational creature.

**OBJ. 3:** Further, irrational creatures are either stable, as bodies, or transient, as the seasons. Now, according to Gregory (*Moral.* iv, 2), *it is useless to curse what does not exist, and wicked to curse what exists.* Therefore it is nowise lawful to curse an irrational creature.

**ON THE CONTRARY,** our Lord cursed the fig tree, as related in Matt. 21:19; and Job cursed his day, according to Job 3:1.

**I ANSWER THAT,** Benediction and malediction, properly speaking, regard things to which good or evil may happen, viz. rational creatures: while good and evil are said to happen to irrational creatures in relation to the rational creature for whose sake they are. Now they are related to the rational creature in several ways. First by way of ministration, insofar as irrational creatures minister to the needs of man. In this sense the Lord said to man (Gen 3:17): *Cursed is the earth in thy work,* so that its barrenness would be a punishment to man. Thus is understood what is said in Deut. 28, *blessed be your barns,* and further, *cursed be your barns.* Thus also David cursed the mountains of Gelboe, according to Gregory's expounding (*Moral.* iv, 3). Again the irrational creature is related to the rational creature by way of signification: and thus our Lord cursed the fig

per modum significationis. Et sic dominus maledixit ficulneam, in significationem Iudaeae. Tertio modo ordinatur creatura irrationalis ad rationalem per modum continentis, scilicet temporis vel loci. Et sic maledixit Iob diei nativitatis suae, propter culpam originalem, quam nascendo contraxit, et propter sequentes poenalitates. Et propter hoc etiam potest intelligi David maledixisse montibus Gelboe, ut legitur II Reg. I, scilicet propter caedem populi quae in eis contigerat.

Maledicere autem rebus irrationalibus inquantum sunt creaturae Dei, est peccatum blasphemiae. Maledicere autem eis secundum se consideratis, est otiosum et vanum, et per consequens illicitum.

**ET PER HOC** patet responsio ad obiecta.

tree in signification of Judea. Third, the irrational creature is related to rational creatures as something containing them, namely by way of time or place: and thus Job cursed the day of his birth, on account of the original sin which he contracted in birth, and on account of the consequent penalties. In this sense also we may understand David to have cursed the mountains of Gelboe, as we read in 2 Kings 1:21, namely on account of the people slaughtered there.

But to curse irrational beings, considered as creatures of God, is a sin of blasphemy; while to curse them considered in themselves is idle and vain and consequently unlawful.

**FROM THIS** the Replies to the objections may easily be gathered.

# Article 3

*Whether cursing is a mortal sin?*

**AD TERTIUM SIC PROCEDITUR.** Videtur quod maledicere non sit peccatum mortale. Augustinus enim, in homilia de igne Purgatorio, numerat maledictionem inter levia peccata. Haec autem sunt venialia. Ergo maledictio non est peccatum mortale, sed veniale.

**PRAETEREA,** ea quae ex levi motu mentis procedunt non videntur esse peccata mortalia. Sed interdum maledictio ex levi motu procedit. Ergo maledictio non est peccatum mortale.

**PRAETEREA,** gravius est male facere quam maledicere. Sed male facere non semper est peccatum mortale. Ergo multo minus maledicere.

**SED CONTRA,** nihil excludit a regno Dei nisi peccatum mortale. Sed maledictio excludit a regno Dei, secundum illud I ad Cor. VI, *neque maledici neque rapaces regnum Dei possidebunt.* Ergo maledictio est peccatum mortale.

**RESPONDEO** dicendum quod maledictio de qua nunc loquimur, est per quam pronuntiatur malum contra aliquem vel imperando vel optando. Velle autem, vel imperio movere ad malum alterius, secundum se repugnat caritati, qua diligimus proximum volentes bonum ipsius. Et ita secundum suum genus est peccatum mortale. Et tanto gravius quanto personam cui maledicimus magis amare et revereri tenemur, unde dicitur Levit. XX, *qui maledixerit patri suo et matri, morte moriatur.*

Contingit tamen verbum maledictionis prolatum esse peccatum veniale, vel propter parvitatem mali quod quis alteri, maledicendo, imprecatur, vel etiam propter affectum eius qui profert maledictionis verba, dum ex levi motu, vel ex ludo, aut ex subreptione aliqua talia

**OBJECTION 1:** It would seem that cursing is not a mortal sin. For Augustine in a homily on the Fire of Purgatory reckons cursing among slight sins. But such sins are venial. Therefore cursing is not a mortal but a venial Sin.

**OBJ. 2:** Further, that which proceeds from a slight movement of the mind does not seem to be generically a mortal sin. But cursing sometimes arises from a slight movement. Therefore cursing is not a mortal sin.

**OBJ. 3:** Further, evil deeds are worse than evil words. But evil deeds are not always mortal sins. Much less therefore is cursing a mortal sin.

**ON THE CONTRARY,** Nothing save mortal sin excludes one from the kingdom of God. But cursing excludes from the kingdom of God, according to 1 Cor. 6:10, *Nor cursers, nor extortioners shall possess the kingdom of God.* Therefore cursing is a mortal sin.

**I ANSWER THAT,** The evil words of which we are speaking now are those whereby evil is uttered against someone by way of command or desire. Now to wish evil to another man, or to conduce to that evil by commanding it, is, of its very nature, contrary to charity whereby we love our neighbor by desiring his good. Consequently it is a mortal sin, according to its genus, and so much the graver, as the person whom we curse has a greater claim on our love and respect. Hence it is written (Lev 20:9): *He that curseth his father, or mother, dying let him die.*

It may happen however that the word uttered in cursing is a venial sin either through the slightness of the evil invoked on another in cursing him, or on account of the sentiments of the person who utters the curse; because he may say such words through some slight movement, or in

verba profert; quia peccata verborum maxime ex affectu pensantur, ut supra dictum est.

**ET PER HOC** patet responsio ad obiecta.

jest, or without deliberation, and sins of word should be weighed chiefly with regard to the speaker's intention, as stated above (Q. 72, A. 2).

**FROM THIS** the Replies to the Objections may be easily gathered.

# Article 4

*Whether cursing is a graver sin than backbiting?*

**AD QUARTUM SIC PROCEDITUR.** Videtur quod maledictio sit gravius peccatum quam detractio. Maledictio enim videtur esse blasphemia quaedam, ut patet per id quod dicitur in canonica Iudae, quod *cum Michael Archangelus, cum Diabolo disputans, altercaretur de Moysi corpore, non est ausus iudicium inferre blasphemiae*; et accipitur ibi blasphemia pro maledictione, secundum Glossam. Blasphemia autem est gravius peccatum quam detractio. Ergo maledictio est gravior detractione.

**PRAETEREA,** homicidium est detractione gravius, ut supra dictum est. Sed maledictio est par peccato homicidii, dicit enim Chrysostomus, super Matth., *cum dixeris, maledic ei, et domum everte, et omnia perire fac, nihil ab homicida differs.* Ergo maledictio est gravior quam detractio.

**PRAETEREA,** causa praeeminet signo. Sed ille qui maledicit causat malum suo imperio, ille autem qui detrahit solum significat malum iam existens. Gravius ergo peccat maledicus quam detractor.

**SED CONTRA** est quod detractio non potest bene fieri. Maledictio autem fit bene et male, ut ex dictis patet. Ergo gravior est detractio quam maledictio.

**RESPONDEO** dicendum quod, sicut in primo habitum est, duplex est malum, scilicet culpae, et poenae. Malum autem culpae peius est, ut ibidem ostensum est. Unde dicere malum culpae peius est quam dicere malum poenae, dummodo sit idem modus dicendi. Ad contumeliosum igitur, susurronem et detractorem, et etiam derisorem, pertinet dicere malum culpae, sed ad maledicentem, prout nunc loquimur, pertinet dicere malum poenae, non autem malum culpae nisi forte sub ratione poenae. Non tamen est idem modus dicendi. Nam ad praedicta quatuor vitia pertinet dicere malum culpae solum enuntiando, per maledictionem vero dicitur malum poenae vel causando per modum imperii, vel optando. Ipsa autem enuntiatio culpae peccatum est inquantum aliquod nocumentum ex hoc proximo infertur. Gravius autem est nocumentum inferre quam nocumentum desiderare, ceteris paribus.

Unde detractio, secundum communem rationem, gravius peccatum est quam maledictio simplex deside-

**OBJECTION 1:** It would seem that cursing is a graver sin than backbiting. Cursing would seem to be a kind of blasphemy, as implied in the canonical epistle of Jude (verse 9) where it is said that *when Michael the archangel, disputing with the devil, contended about the body of Moses, he durst not bring against him the judgment of blasphemy,* where blasphemy stands for cursing, according to a gloss. Now blasphemy is a graver sin than backbiting. Therefore cursing is a graver sin than backbiting.

**OBJ. 2:** Further, murder is more grievous than backbiting, as stated above (Q. 73, A. 3). But cursing is on a par with the sin of murder; for Chrysostom says (*Hom. xix, super Matth.*): *When thou sayest: 'Curse him down with his house, away with everything,' you are no better than a murderer.* Therefore cursing is graver than backbiting.

**OBJ. 3:** Further, to cause a thing is more than to signify it. But the curser causes evil by commanding it, whereas the backbiter merely signifies an evil already existing. Therefore the curser sins more grievously than the backbiter.

**ON THE CONTRARY,** It is impossible to do well in backbiting, whereas cursing may be either a good or an evil deed, as appears from what has been said (A. 1). Therefore backbiting is graver than cursing.

**I ANSWER THAT,** As stated in the First Part (Q. 48, A. 5), evil is twofold, evil of fault, and evil of punishment; and of the two, evil of fault is the worse (I, Q. 48, A. 6). Hence to speak evil of fault is worse than to speak evil of punishment, provided the mode of speaking be the same. Accordingly it belongs to the reviler, the tale-bearer, the backbiter and the derider to speak evil of fault, whereas it belongs to the evil-speaker, as we understand it here, to speak evil of punishment, and not evil of fault except under the aspect of punishment. But the mode of speaking is not the same, for in the case of the four vices mentioned above, evil of fault is spoken by way of assertion, whereas in the case of cursing evil of punishment is spoken, either by causing it in the form of a command, or by wishing it. Now the utterance itself of a person's fault is a sin, inasmuch as it inflicts an injury on one's neighbor, and it is more grievous to inflict an injury, than to wish to inflict it, other things being equal.

Hence backbiting considered in its generic aspect is a graver sin than the cursing which expresses a mere desire;

rium exprimens. Maledictio vero quae fit per modum imperii, cum habeat rationem causae, potest esse detractione gravior, si maius nocumentum inferat quam sit denigratio famae; vel levior, si minus. Et haec quidem accipienda sunt secundum ea quae per se pertinent ad rationem horum vitiorum. Possunt autem et alia per accidens considerari quae praedicta vitia vel augent vel minuunt.

**AD PRIMUM** ergo dicendum quod maledictio creaturae inquantum creatura est, redundat in Deum, et sic per accidens habet rationem blasphemiae, non autem si maledicatur creatura propter culpam. Et eadem ratio est de detractione.

**AD SECUNDUM** dicendum quod, sicut dictum est, maledictio uno modo includit desiderium mali. Unde si ille qui maledicit velit malum occisionis alterius, desiderio non differt ab homicida. Differt tamen inquantum actus exterior aliquid adiicit voluntati.

**AD TERTIUM** dicendum quod ratio illa procedit de maledictione secundum quod importat imperium.

while the cursing which is expressed by way of command, since it has the aspect of a cause, will be more or less grievous than backbiting, according as it inflicts an injury more or less grave than the blackening of a man's good name. Moreover this must be taken as applying to these vices considered in their essential aspects: for other accidental points might be taken into consideration, which would aggravate or extenuate the aforesaid vices.

**REPLY OBJ. 1**: To curse a creature, as such, reflects on God, and thus accidentally it has the character of blasphemy; not so if one curse a creature on account of its fault: and the same applies to backbiting.

**REPLY OBJ. 2**: As stated above (A. 3), cursing, in one way, includes the desire for evil, where if the curser desire the evil of another's violent death, he does not differ, in desire, from a murderer, but he differs from him insofar as the external act adds something to the act of the will.

**REPLY OBJ. 3**: This argument considers cursing by way of command.

# QUESTION 77

## CHEATING

Deinde considerandum est de peccatis quae sunt circa voluntarias commutationes. Et primo, de fraudulentia quae committitur in emptionibus et venditionibus; secundo, de usura, quae fit in mutuis. Circa alias enim commutationes voluntarias non invenitur aliqua species peccati quae distinguatur a rapina vel furto.

Circa primum quaeruntur quatuor.

Primo, de iniusta venditione ex parte pretii, scilicet, utrum liceat aliquid vendere plus quam valeat.

Secundo, de iniusta venditione ex parte rei venditae.

Tertio, utrum teneatur venditor dicere vitium rei venditae.

Quarto, utrum licitum sit aliquid, negotiando, plus vendere quam emptum sit.

We must now consider those sins which relate to voluntary commutations. First, we shall consider cheating, which is committed in buying and selling: second, we shall consider usury, which occurs in loans. In connection with the other voluntary commutations no special kind of sin is to be found distinct from rapine and theft.

Under the first head there are four points of inquiry:

(1) Of unjust sales as regards the price; namely, whether it is lawful to sell a thing for more than its worth?

(2) Of unjust sales on the part of the thing sold;

(3) Whether the seller is bound to reveal a fault in the thing sold?

(4) Whether it is lawful in trading to sell a thing at a higher price than was paid for it?

# Article 1

*Whether it is lawful to sell a thing for more than its worth?*

**AD PRIMUM SIC PROCEDITUR.** Videtur quod aliquis licite possit vendere rem plus quam valeat. Iustum enim in commutationibus humanae vitae secundum leges civiles determinatur. Sed secundum eas licitum est emptori et venditori ut se invicem decipiant, quod quidem fit inquantum venditor plus vendit rem quam valeat, emptor autem minus quam valeat. Ergo licitum est quod aliquis vendat rem plus quam valeat.

**PRAETEREA**, illud quod est omnibus commune videtur esse naturale et non esse peccatum. Sed sicut Augustinus refert, XIII de Trin., dictum cuiusdam mimi fuit ab omnibus acceptatum, *vili vultis emere, et care vendere*. Cui etiam consonat quod dicitur Prov. XX, *malum est, malum est, dicit omnis emptor, et cum recesserit, gloriatur*. Ergo licitum est aliquid carius vendere et vilius emere quam valeat.

**PRAETEREA**, non videtur esse illicitum si ex conventione agatur id quod fieri debet ex debito honestatis. Sed secundum philosophum, in VIII Ethic., in amicitia utilis recompensatio fieri debet secundum utilitatem quam consecutus est ille qui beneficium suscepit, quae quidem quandoque excedit valorem rei datae; sicut contingit cum aliquis multum re aliqua indiget, vel ad periculum evitandum vel ad aliquod commodum consequendum. Ergo licet in contractu emptionis et venditionis aliquid dare pro maiori pretio quam valeat.

**OBJECTION 1**: It would seem that it is lawful to sell a thing for more than its worth. In the commutations of human life, civil laws determine that which is just. Now according to these laws it is just for buyer and seller to deceive one another (*Cod.* IV, xliv, *De Rescind. Vend.* 8, 15): and this occurs by the seller selling a thing for more than its worth, and the buyer buying a thing for less than its worth. Therefore it is lawful to sell a thing for more than its worth.

**OBJ. 2**: Further, that which is common to all would seem to be natural and not sinful. Now Augustine relates that the saying of a certain jester was accepted by all, *You wish to buy for a song and to sell at a premium*, which agrees with the saying of Prov. 20:14, *It is naught, it is naught, saith every buyer: and when he is gone away, then he will boast*. Therefore it is lawful to sell a thing for more than its worth.

**OBJ. 3**: Further, it does not seem unlawful if that which honesty demands be done by mutual agreement. Now, according to the Philosopher (*Ethic.* viii, 13), in the friendship which is based on utility, the amount of the recompense for a favor received should depend on the utility accruing to the receiver: and this utility sometimes is worth more than the thing given, for instance if the receiver be in great need of that thing, whether for the purpose of avoiding a danger, or of deriving some particular benefit. Therefore, in contracts of buying and selling, it is lawful to give a thing in return for more than its worth.

**SED CONTRA** est quod dicitur Matth. VII, *omnia quaecumque vultis ut faciant vobis homines, et vos facite illis.* Sed nullus vult sibi rem vendi carius quam valeat. Ergo nullus debet alteri vendere rem carius quam valeat.

**RESPONDEO** dicendum quod fraudem adhibere ad hoc quod aliquid plus iusto pretio vendatur, omnino peccatum est, inquantum aliquis decipit proximum in damnum ipsius. Unde et Tullius dicit, in libro de Offic., *tollendum est ex rebus contrahendis omne mendacium, non licitatorem venditor, non qui contra se licitetur emptor apponet.*

Si autem fraus deficit, tunc de emptione et venditione dupliciter loqui possumus. Uno modo, secundum se. Et secundum hoc emptio et venditio videtur esse introducta pro communi utilitate utriusque, dum scilicet unus indiget re alterius et e converso, sicut patet per philosophum, in I Polit. Quod autem pro communi utilitate est inductum, non debet esse magis in gravamen unius quam alterius. Et ideo debet secundum aequalitatem rei inter eos contractus institui. Quantitas autem rerum quae in usum hominis veniunt mensuratur secundum pretium datum, ad quod est inventum numisma, ut dicitur in V Ethic. Et ideo si vel pretium excedat quantitatem valoris rei, vel e converso res excedat pretium, tolletur iustitiae aequalitas. Et ideo carius vendere aut vilius emere rem quam valeat est secundum se iniustum et illicitum.

Alio modo possumus loqui de emptione et venditione secundum quod per accidens cedit in utilitatem unius et detrimentum alterius, puta cum aliquis multum indiget habere rem aliquam, et alius laeditur si ea careat. Et in tali casu iustum pretium erit ut non solum respiciatur ad rem quae venditur, sed ad damnum quod venditor ex venditione incurrit. Et sic licite poterit aliquid vendi plus quam valeat secundum se, quamvis non vendatur plus quam valeat habenti. Si vero aliquis multum iuvetur ex re alterius quam accepit, ille vero qui vendidit non damnificatur carendo re illa, non debet eam supervendere. Quia utilitas quae alteri accrescit non est ex vendente, sed ex conditione ementis, nullus autem debet vendere alteri quod non est suum, licet possit ei vendere damnum quod patitur.

Ille tamen qui ex re alterius accepta multum iuvatur, potest propria sponte aliquid vendenti supererogare, quod pertinet ad eius honestatem.

**AD PRIMUM** ergo dicendum quod, sicut supra dictum est, lex humana populo datur, in quo sunt multi a virtute deficientes, non autem datur solis virtuosis. Et ideo lex humana non potuit prohibere quidquid est contra virtutem, sed ei sufficit ut prohibeat ea quae

**ON THE CONTRARY,** It is written (Matt 7:12): *All things . . . whatsoever you would that men should do to you, do you also to them.* But no man wishes to buy a thing for more than its worth. Therefore no man should sell a thing to another man for more than its worth.

**I ANSWER THAT,** It is altogether sinful to have recourse to deceit in order to sell a thing for more than its just price, because this is to deceive one's neighbor so as to injure him. Hence Tully says (*De Offic.* iii, 15): *Contracts should be entirely free from double-dealing: the seller must not impose upon the bidder, nor the buyer upon one that bids against him.*

But, apart from fraud, we may speak of buying and selling in two ways. First, as considered in themselves, and from this point of view, buying and selling seem to be established for the common advantage of both parties, one of whom requires that which belongs to the other, and vice versa, as the Philosopher states (*Polit.* i, 3). Now whatever is established for the common advantage, should not be more of a burden to one party than to another, and consequently all contracts between them should observe equality of thing and thing. Again, the quality of a thing that comes into human use is measured by the price given for it, for which purpose money was invented, as stated in *Ethic.* v, 5. Therefore if either the price exceed the quantity of the thing's worth, or, conversely, the thing exceed the price, there is no longer the equality of justice: and consequently, to sell a thing for more than its worth, or to buy it for less than its worth, is in itself unjust and unlawful.

Second we may speak of buying and selling, considered as accidentally tending to the advantage of one party, and to the disadvantage of the other: for instance, when a man has great need of a certain thing, while another man will suffer if he be without it. In such a case the just price will depend not only on the thing sold, but on the loss which the sale brings on the seller. And thus it will be lawful to sell a thing for more than it is worth in itself, though the price paid be not more than it is worth to the owner. Yet if the one man derive a great advantage by becoming possessed of the other man's property, and the seller be not at a loss through being without that thing, the latter ought not to raise the price, because the advantage accruing to the buyer, is not due to the seller, but to a circumstance affecting the buyer. Now no man should sell what is not his, though he may charge for the loss he suffers.

On the other hand if a man find that he derives great advantage from something he has bought, he may, of his own accord, pay the seller something over and above: and this pertains to his honesty.

**REPLY OBJ. 1:** As stated above (I-II, Q. 96, A. 2) human law is given to the people among whom there are many lacking virtue, and it is not given to the virtuous alone. Hence human law was unable to forbid all that is contrary to virtue; and it suffices for it to prohibit whatever

destruunt hominum convictum; alia vero habeat quasi licita, non quia ea approbet, sed quia ea non punit. Sic igitur habet quasi licitum, poenam non inducens, si absque fraude venditor rem suam supervendat aut emptor vilius emat, nisi sit nimius excessus, quia tunc etiam lex humana cogit ad restituendum, puta si aliquis sit deceptus ultra dimidiam iusti pretii quantitatem.

Sed lex divina nihil impunitum relinquit quod sit virtuti contrarium. Unde secundum divinam legem illicitum reputatur si in emptione et venditione non sit aequalitas iustitiae observata. Et tenetur ille qui plus habet recompensare ei qui damnificatus est, si sit notabile damnum. Quod ideo dico quia iustum pretium rerum quandoque non est punctaliter determinatum, sed magis in quadam aestimatione consistit, ita quod modica additio vel minutio non videtur tollere aequalitatem iustitiae.

**Aᴅ sᴇᴄᴜɴᴅᴜᴍ** dicendum quod, sicut Augustinus ibidem dicit, *mimus ille vel seipsum intuendo, vel alios experiendo vili velle emere et care vendere, omnibus id credidit esse commune. Sed quoniam revera vitium est, potest quisque adipisci huiusmodi iustitiam qua huic resistat et vincat.* Et ponit exemplum de quodam qui modicum pretium de quodam libro propter ignorantiam postulanti iustum pretium dedit. Unde patet quod illud commune desiderium non est naturae, sed vitii. Et ideo commune est multis, qui per latam viam vitiorum incedunt.

**Aᴅ ᴛᴇʀᴛɪᴜᴍ** dicendum quod in iustitia commutativa consideratur principaliter aequalitas rei. Sed in amicitia utilis consideratur aequalitas utilitatis, et ideo recompensatio fieri debet secundum utilitatem perceptam. In emptione vero, secundum aequalitatem rei.

is destructive of human intercourse, while it treats other matters as though they were lawful, not by approving of them, but by not punishing them. Accordingly, if without employing deceit the seller disposes of his goods for more than their worth, or the buyer obtain them for less than their worth, the law looks upon this as licit, and provides no punishment for so doing, unless the excess be too great, because then even human law demands restitution to be made, for instance if a man be deceived in regard to more than half the amount of the just price of a thing.

On the other hand the Divine law leaves nothing unpunished that is contrary to virtue. Hence, according to the Divine law, it is reckoned unlawful if the equality of justice be not observed in buying and selling: and he who has received more than he ought must make compensation to him that has suffered loss, if the loss be considerable. I add this condition, because the just price of things is not fixed with mathematical precision, but depends on a kind of estimate, so that a slight addition or subtraction would not seem to destroy the equality of justice.

**Rᴇᴘʟʏ Oʙᴊ. 2:** As Augustine says *this jester, either by looking into himself or by his experience of others, thought that all men are inclined to wish to buy for a song and sell at a premium. But since in reality this is wicked, it is in every man's power to acquire that justice whereby he may resist and overcome this inclination.* And then he gives the example of a man who gave the just price for a book to a man who through ignorance asked a low price for it. Hence it is evident that this common desire is not from nature but from vice, wherefore it is common to many who walk along the broad road of sin.

**Rᴇᴘʟʏ Oʙᴊ. 3:** In commutative justice we consider chiefly real equality. On the other hand, in friendship based on utility we consider equality of usefulness, so that the recompense should depend on the usefulness accruing, whereas in buying it should be equal to the thing bought.

# Article 2

*Whether a sale is rendered unlawful through a fault in the thing sold?*

**Aᴅ sᴇᴄᴜɴᴅᴜᴍ sɪᴄ ᴘʀᴏᴄᴇᴅɪᴛᴜʀ.** Videtur quod venditio non reddatur iniusta et illicita propter defectum rei venditae. Minus enim cetera sunt pensanda in re quam rei species substantialis. Sed propter defectum speciei substantialis non videtur reddi venditio rei illicita, puta si aliquis vendat argentum vel aurum alchimicum pro vero, quod est utile ad omnes humanos usus ad quos necessarium est argentum et aurum, puta ad vasa et ad alia huiusmodi. Ergo multo minus erit illicita venditio si sit defectus in aliis.

**Oʙᴊᴇᴄᴛɪᴏɴ 1:** It would seem that a sale is not rendered unjust and unlawful through a fault in the thing sold. For less account should be taken of the other parts of a thing than of what belongs to its substance. Yet the sale of a thing does not seem to be rendered unlawful through a fault in its substance: for instance, if a man sell instead of the real metal, silver or gold produced by some chemical process, which is adapted to all the human uses for which silver and gold are necessary, for instance in the making of vessels and the like. Much less therefore will it be an unlawful sale if the thing be defective in other ways.

PRAETEREA, defectus ex parte rei qui est secundum quantitatem maxime videtur iustitiae contrariari, quae in aequalitate consistit. Quantitas autem per mensuram cognoscitur. Mensurae autem rerum quae in usum hominum veniunt non sunt determinatae, sed alicubi maiores, alicubi minores, ut patet per philosophum, in V Ethic. Ergo non potest evitari defectus ex parte rei venditae. Et ita videtur quod ex hoc venditio non reddatur illicita.

PRAETEREA, ad defectum rei pertinet si ei conveniens qualitas deest. Sed ad qualitatem rei cognoscendam requiritur magna scientia, quae plerisque venditoribus deest. Ergo non redditur venditio illicita propter rei defectum.

SED CONTRA est quod Ambrosius dicit, in libro de Offic., *regula iustitiae manifesta est quod a vero non declinare virum deceat bonum, nec damno iniusto afficere quemquam, nec aliquid dolo annectere rei suae.*

RESPONDEO dicendum quod circa rem quae venditur triplex defectus considerari potest. Unus quidem secundum speciem rei. Et hunc quidem defectum si venditor cognoscat in re quam vendit, fraudem committit in venditione, unde venditio illicita redditur. Et hoc est quod dicitur contra quosdam Isaiae I, *argentum tuum versum est in scoriam; vinum tuum mixtum est aqua,* quod enim permixtum est patitur defectum quantum ad speciem.

Alius autem defectus est secundum quantitatem, quae per mensuram cognoscitur. Et ideo si quis scienter utatur deficienti mensura in vendendo, fraudem committit, et est illicita venditio. Unde dicitur Deut. XXV, *non habebis in sacculo diversa pondera, maius et minus, nec erit in domo tua modius maior et minor*; et postea subditur, *abominatur enim dominus eum qui facit haec, et adversatur omnem iniustitiam.*

Tertius defectus est ex parte qualitatis, puta si aliquod animal infirmum vendat quasi sanum. Quod si quis scienter fecerit, fraudem committit in venditione, unde est illicita venditio.

Et in omnibus talibus non solum aliquis peccat iniustam venditionem faciendo, sed etiam ad restitutionem tenetur. Si vero eo ignorante aliquis praedictorum defectuum in re vendita fuerit, venditor quidem non peccat, quia facit iniustum materialiter, non tamen eius operatio est iniusta, ut ex supradictis patet, tenetur tamen, cum ad eius notitiam pervenerit, damnum recompensare emptori. Et quod dictum est de venditore, etiam intelligendum est ex parte emptoris. Contingit enim quandoque venditorem credere suam rem esse minus pretiosam quantum ad speciem, sicut si aliquis vendat aurum loco aurichalci, emptor, si id cognoscat, iniuste emit, et ad restitutionem tenetur. Et eadem ratio est de defectu qualitatis et quantitatis.

**OBJ. 2**: Further, any fault in the thing, affecting the quantity, would seem chiefly to be opposed to justice which consists in equality. Now quantity is known by being measured: and the measures of things that come into human use are not fixed, but in some places are greater, in others less, as the Philosopher states (*Ethic.* v, 7). Therefore just as it is impossible to avoid defects on the part of the thing sold, it seems that a sale is not rendered unlawful through the thing sold being defective.

**OBJ. 3**: Further, the thing sold is rendered defective by lacking a fitting quality. But in order to know the quality of a thing, much knowledge is required that is lacking in most buyers. Therefore a sale is not rendered unlawful by a fault (in the thing sold).

**ON THE CONTRARY**, Ambrose says (*De Offic.* iii, 11): *It is manifestly a rule of justice that a good man should not depart from the truth, nor inflict an unjust injury on anyone, nor have any connection with fraud.*

**I ANSWER THAT**, A threefold fault may be found pertaining to the thing which is sold. One, in respect of the thing's substance: and if the seller be aware of a fault in the thing he is selling, he is guilty of a fraudulent sale, so that the sale is rendered unlawful. Hence we find it written against certain people (Isa 1:22), *Thy silver is turned into dross, thy wine is mingled with water*: because that which is mixed is defective in its substance.

Another defect is in respect of quantity which is known by being measured: wherefore if anyone knowingly make use of a faulty measure in selling, he is guilty of fraud, and the sale is illicit. Hence it is written (Deut 25:13, 14): *Thou shalt not have diverse weights in thy bag, a greater and a less: neither shall there be in thy house a greater bushel and a less,* and further on (Deut 25:16): *For the Lord . . . abhorreth him that doth these things, and He hateth all injustice.*

A third defect is on the part of the quality, for instance, if a man sell an unhealthy animal as being a healthy one: and if anyone do this knowingly he is guilty of a fraudulent sale, and the sale, in consequence, is illicit.

In all these cases not only is the man guilty of a fraudulent sale, but he is also bound to restitution. But if any of the foregoing defects be in the thing sold, and he knows nothing about this, the seller does not sin, because he does that which is unjust materially, nor is his deed unjust, as shown above (Q. 59, A. 2). Nevertheless he is bound to compensate the buyer, when the defect comes to his knowledge. Moreover what has been said of the seller applies equally to the buyer. For sometimes it happens that the seller thinks his goods to be specifically of lower value, as when a man sells gold instead of copper, and then if the buyer be aware of this, he buys it unjustly and is bound to restitution: and the same applies to a defect in quantity as to a defect in quality.

**AD PRIMUM** ergo dicendum quod aurum et argentum non solum cara sunt propter utilitatem vasorum quae ex eis fabricantur, aut aliorum huiusmodi, sed etiam propter dignitatem et puritatem substantiae ipsorum. Et ideo si aurum vel argentum ab alchimicis factum veram speciem non habeat auri et argenti, est fraudulenta et iniusta venditio. Praesertim cum sint aliquae utilitates auri et argenti veri, secundum naturalem operationem ipsorum, quae non conveniunt auro per alchimiam sophisticato, sicut quod habet proprietatem laetificandi, et contra quasdam infirmitates medicinaliter iuvat. Frequentius etiam potest poni in operatione, et diutius in sua puritate permanet aurum verum quam aurum sophisticatum. Si autem per alchimiam fieret aurum verum, non esset illicitum ipsum pro vero vendere, quia nihil prohibet artem uti aliquibus naturalibus causis ad producendum naturales et veros effectus; sicut Augustinus dicit, in III de Trin., de his quae arte Daemonum fiunt.

**AD SECUNDUM** dicendum quod mensuras rerum venalium necesse est in diversis locis esse diversas, propter diversitatem copiae et inopiae rerum, quia ubi res magis abundant, consueverunt esse maiores mensurae. In unoquoque tamen loco ad rectores civitatis pertinet determinare quae sunt iustae mensurae rerum venalium, pensatis conditionibus locorum et rerum. Et ideo has mensuras publica auctoritate vel consuetudine institutas praeterire non licet.

**AD TERTIUM** dicendum quod, sicut Augustinus dicit, in XI de Civ. Dei, pretium rerum venalium non consideratur secundum gradum naturae, cum quandoque pluris vendatur unus equus quam unus servus, sed consideratur secundum quod res in usum hominis veniunt. Et ideo non oportet quod venditor vel emptor cognoscat occultas rei venditae qualitates, sed illas solum per quas redditur humanis usibus apta, puta quod equus sit fortis et bene currat, et similiter in ceteris. Has autem qualitates de facili venditor et emptor cognoscere possunt.

**REPLY OBJ. 1**: Gold and silver are costly not only on account of the usefulness of the vessels and other like things made from them, but also on account of the excellence and purity of their substance. Hence if the gold or silver produced by alchemists has not the true specific nature of gold and silver, the sale thereof is fraudulent and unjust, especially as real gold and silver can produce certain results by their natural action, which the counterfeit gold and silver of alchemists cannot produce. Thus the true metal has the property of making people joyful, and is helpful medicinally against certain maladies. Moreover real gold can be employed more frequently, and lasts longer in its condition of purity than counterfeit gold. If however real gold were to be produced by alchemy, it would not be unlawful to sell it for the genuine article, for nothing prevents art from employing certain natural causes for the production of natural and true effects, as Augustine says (*De Trin.* iii, 8) of things produced by the art of the demons.

**REPLY OBJ. 2**: The measures of salable commodities must needs be different in different places, on account of the difference of supply: because where there is greater abundance, the measures are wont to be larger. However in each place those who govern the state must determine the just measures of things salable, with due consideration for the conditions of place and time. Hence it is not lawful to disregard such measures as are established by public authority or custom.

**REPLY OBJ. 3**: As Augustine says (*De Civ. Dei* xi, 16) the price of things salable does not depend on their degree of nature, since at times a horse fetches a higher price than a slave; but it depends on their usefulness to man. Hence it is not necessary for the seller or buyer to be cognizant of the hidden qualities of the thing sold, but only of such as render the thing adapted to man's use, for instance, that the horse be strong, run well and so forth. Such qualities the seller and buyer can easily discover.

# Article 3

*Whether the seller is bound to state the defects of the thing sold?*

**AD TERTIUM SIC PROCEDITUR.** Videtur quod venditor non teneatur dicere vitium rei venditae. Cum enim venditor emptorem ad emendum non cogat, videtur eius iudicio rem quam vendit supponere. Sed ad eundem pertinet iudicium et cognitio rei. Non ergo videtur imputandum venditori si emptor in suo iudicio decipitur,

**OBJECTION 1**: It would seem that the seller is not bound to state the defects of the thing sold. Since the seller does not bind the buyer to buy, he would seem to leave it to him to judge of the goods offered for sale. Now judgment about a thing and knowledge of that thing belong to the same person. Therefore it does not seem imputable to the

praecipitanter emendo, absque diligenti inquisitione de conditionibus rei.

**PRAETEREA**, stultum videtur quod aliquis id faciat unde eius operatio impediatur. Sed si aliquis vitia rei vendendae indicet, impedit suam venditionem, ut enim Tullius, in libro de Offic., inducit quendam dicentem, *quid tam absurdum quam si, domini iussu, ita praeco praediceret, domum pestilentem vendo?* Ergo venditor non tenetur dicere vitia rei venditae.

**PRAETEREA**, magis necessarium est homini ut cognoscat viam virtutis quam ut cognoscat vitia rerum quae venduntur. Sed homo non tenetur cuilibet consilium dare et veritatem dicere de his quae pertinent ad virtutem, quamvis nulli debeat dicere falsitatem. Ergo multo minus tenetur venditor vitia rei venditae dicere, quasi consilium dando emptori.

**PRAETEREA**, si aliquis teneatur dicere defectum rei venditae, hoc non est nisi ut minuatur de pretio. Sed quandoque diminueretur de pretio etiam sine vitio rei venditae, propter aliquid aliud, puta si venditor deferens triticum ad locum ubi est carestia frumenti, sciat multos posse venire qui deferant; quod si sciretur ab ementibus, minus pretium darent. Huiusmodi autem non oportet dicere venditorem, ut videtur. Ergo, pari ratione, nec vitia rei venditae.

**SED CONTRA** est quod Ambrosius dicit, in III de Offic., *in contractibus vitia eorum quae veneunt prodi iubentur, ac nisi intimaverit venditor, quamvis in ius emptoris transierint, doli actione vacuantur.*

**RESPONDEO** dicendum quod dare alicui occasionem periculi vel damni semper est illicitum, quamvis non sit necessarium quod homo alteri semper det auxilium vel consilium pertinens ad eius qualemcumque promotionem, sed hoc solum est necessarium in aliquo casu determinato, puta cum alius eius curae subdatur, vel cum non potest ei per alium subveniri. Venditor autem, qui rem vendendam proponit, ex hoc ipso dat emptori damni vel periculi occasionem quod rem vitiosam ei offert, si ex eius vitio damnum vel periculum incurrere possit, damnum quidem, si propter huiusmodi vitium res quae vendenda proponitur minoris sit pretii, ipse vero propter huiusmodi vitium nihil de pretio subtrahat; periculum autem, puta si propter huiusmodi vitium usus rei reddatur impeditus vel noxius, puta si aliquis alicui vendat equum claudicantem pro veloci, vel ruinosam domum pro firma, vel cibum corruptum sive venenosum pro bono. Unde si huiusmodi vitia sint occulta et ipse non detegat, erit illicita et dolosa venditio, et tenetur venditor ad damni recompensationem.

seller if the buyer be deceived in his judgment, and be hurried into buying a thing without carefully inquiring into its condition.

**OBJ. 2**: Further, it seems foolish for anyone to do what prevents him carrying out his work. But if a man states the defects of the goods he has for sale, he prevents their sale: wherefore Tully (*De Offic.* iii, 13) pictures a man as saying: *Could anything be more absurd than for a public crier, instructed by the owner, to cry: 'I offer this unhealthy horse for sale?'* Therefore the seller is not bound to state the defects of the thing sold.

**OBJ. 3**: Further, man needs more to know the road of virtue than to know the faults of things offered for sale. Now one is not bound to offer advice to all or to tell them the truth about matters pertaining to virtue, though one should not tell anyone what is false. Much less therefore is a seller bound to tell the faults of what he offers for sale, as though he were counseling the buyer.

**OBJ. 4**: Further, if one were bound to tell the faults of what one offers for sale, this would only be in order to lower the price. Now sometimes the price would be lowered for some other reason, without any defect in the thing sold: for instance, if the seller carry wheat to a place where wheat fetches a high price, knowing that many will come after him carrying wheat; because if the buyers knew this they would give a lower price. But apparently the seller need not give the buyer this information. Therefore, in like manner, neither need he tell him the faults of the goods he is selling.

**ON THE CONTRARY**, Ambrose says (*De Offic.* iii, 10): *In all contracts the defects of the salable commodity must be stated; and unless the seller make them known, although the buyer has already acquired a right to them, the contract is voided on account of the fraudulent action.*

**I ANSWER THAT**, It is always unlawful to give anyone an occasion of danger or loss, although a man need not always give another the help or counsel which would be for his advantage in any way; but only in certain fixed cases, for instance when someone is subject to him, or when he is the only one who can assist him. Now the seller who offers goods for sale, gives the buyer an occasion of loss or danger, by the very fact that he offers him defective goods, if such defect may occasion loss or danger to the buyer—loss, if, by reason of this defect, the goods are of less value, and he takes nothing off the price on that account—danger, if this defect either hinder the use of the goods or render it hurtful, for instance, if a man sells a lame for a fleet horse, a tottering house for a safe one, rotten or poisonous food for wholesome. Wherefore if such like defects be hidden, and the seller does not make them known, the sale will be illicit and fraudulent, and the seller will be bound to compensation for the loss incurred.

Si vero vitium sit manifestum, puta cum equus est monoculus; vel cum usus rei, etsi non competat venditori, potest tamen esse conveniens aliis; et si ipse propter huiusmodi vitium subtrahat quantum oportet de pretio, non tenetur ad manifestandum vitium rei. Quia forte propter huiusmodi vitium emptor vellet plus subtrahi de pretio quam esset subtrahendum. Unde potest licite venditor indemnitati suae consulere, vitium rei reticendo.

**AD PRIMUM** ergo dicendum quod iudicium non potest fieri nisi de re manifesta, *unusquisque* enim *iudicat quae cognoscit*, ut dicitur in I Ethic. Unde si vitia rei quae vendenda proponitur sint occulta, nisi per venditorem manifestentur, non sufficienter committitur emptori iudicium. Secus autem esset si essent vitia manifesta.

**AD SECUNDUM** dicendum quod non oportet quod aliquis per praeconem vitium rei vendendae praenuntiet, quia si praediceret vitium, exterrerentur emptores ab emendo, dum ignorarent alias conditiones rei, secundum quas est bona et utilis. Sed singulariter est dicendum vitium ei qui ad emendum accedit, qui potest simul omnes conditiones ad invicem comparare, bonas et malas, nihil enim prohibet rem in aliquo vitiosam, in multis aliis utilem esse.

**AD TERTIUM** dicendum quod quamvis homo non teneatur simpliciter omni homini dicere veritatem de his quae pertinent ad virtutes, teneretur tamen in casu illo de his dicere veritatem quando ex eius facto alteri periculum immineret in detrimentum virtutis nisi diceret veritatem. Et sic est in proposito.

**AD QUARTUM** dicendum quod vitium rei facit rem in praesenti esse minoris valoris quam videatur, sed in casu praemisso, in futurum res expectatur esse minoris valoris per superventum negotiatorum, qui ab ementibus ignoratur. Unde venditor qui vendit rem secundum pretium quod invenit, non videtur contra iustitiam facere si quod futurum est non exponat. Si tamen exponeret, vel de pretio subtraheret, abundantioris esset virtutis, quamvis ad hoc non videatur teneri ex iustitiae debito.

On the other hand, if the defect be manifest, for instance if a horse have but one eye, or if the goods thought useless to the buyer, be useful to someone else, provided the seller take as much as he ought from the price, he is not bound to state the defect of the goods, since perhaps on account of that defect the buyer might want him to allow a greater rebate than he need. Wherefore the seller may look to his own indemnity, by withholding the defect of the goods.

**REPLY OBJ. 1**: Judgment cannot be pronounced save on what is manifest: for *a man judges of what he knows* (*Ethic.* i, 3). Hence if the defects of the goods offered for sale be hidden, judgment of them is not sufficiently left with the buyer unless such defects be made known to him. The case would be different if the defects were manifest.

**REPLY OBJ. 2**: There is no need to publish beforehand by the public crier the defects of the goods one is offering for sale, because if he were to begin by announcing its defects, the bidders would be frightened to buy, through ignorance of other qualities that might render the thing good and serviceable. Such defect ought to be stated to each individual that offers to buy: and then he will be able to compare the various points one with the other, the good with the bad: for nothing prevents that which is defective in one respect being useful in many others.

**REPLY OBJ. 3**: Although a man is not bound strictly speaking to tell everyone the truth about matters pertaining to virtue, yet he is so bound in a case when, unless he tells the truth, his conduct would endanger another man in detriment to virtue: and so it is in this case.

**REPLY OBJ. 4**: The defect in a thing makes it of less value now than it seems to be: but in the case cited, the goods are expected to be of less value at a future time, on account of the arrival of other merchants, which was not foreseen by the buyers. Wherefore the seller, since he sells his goods at the price actually offered him, does not seem to act contrary to justice through not stating what is going to happen. If however he were to do so, or if he lowered his price, it would be exceedingly virtuous on his part: although he does not seem to be bound to do this as a debt of justice.

# Article 4

*Whether, in trading, it is lawful to sell a thing at a higher price than what was paid for it?*

**AD QUARTUM SIC PROCEDITUR.** Videtur quod non liceat, negotiando, aliquid carius vendere quam emere. Dicit enim Chrysostomus, super Matth. XXI, *quicumque rem comparat ut, integram et immutatam vendendo, lucretur, ille est mercator qui de templo Dei eiicitur.* Et idem dicit Cassiodorus, super illud Psalm., *quoniam non*

**OBJECTION 1**: It would seem that it is not lawful, in trading, to sell a thing for a higher price than we paid for it. For Chrysostom says on Matt. 21:12: *He that buys a thing in order that he may sell it, entire and unchanged, at a profit, is the trader who is cast out of God's temple.* Cassiodorus speaks in the same sense in his commentary on Ps. 70:15,

*cognovi litteraturam*, vel negotiationem secundum aliam litteram, *quid, inquit, est aliud negotiatio nisi vilius comparare et carius velle distrahere?* Et subdit, *negotiatores tales dominus eiecit de templo.* Sed nullus eiicitur de templo nisi propter aliquod peccatum. Ergo talis negotiatio est peccatum.

**PRAETEREA**, contra iustitiam est quod aliquis rem carius vendat quam valeat, vel vilius emat, ut ex dictis apparet. Sed ille qui, negotiando, rem carius vendit quam emerit, necesse est quod vel vilius emerit quam valeat, vel carius vendat. Ergo hoc sine peccato fieri non potest.

**PRAETEREA**, Hieronymus dicit, *negotiatorem clericum, ex inope divitem, ex ignobili gloriosum, quasi quandam pestem fuge.* Non autem negotiatio clericis interdicenda esse videtur nisi propter peccatum. Ergo negotiando aliquid vilius emere et carius vendere est peccatum.

**SED CONTRA** est quod Augustinus dicit, super illud Psalm., *quoniam non cognovi litteraturam, negotiator avidus acquirendi pro damno blasphemat, pro pretiis rerum mentitur et peierat. Sed haec vitia hominis sunt, non artis, quae sine his vitiis agi potest.* Ergo negotiari secundum se non est illicitum.

**RESPONDEO** dicendum quod ad negotiatores pertinet commutationibus rerum insistere. Ut autem philosophus dicit, in I *Polit.*, duplex est rerum commutatio. Una quidem quasi naturalis et necessaria, per quam scilicet fit commutatio rei ad rem, vel rerum et denariorum, propter necessitatem vitae. Et talis commutatio non proprie pertinet ad negotiatores, sed magis ad oeconomicos vel politicos, qui habent providere vel domui vel civitati de rebus necessariis ad vitam. Alia vero commutationis species est vel denariorum ad denarios, vel quarumcumque rerum ad denarios, non propter res necessarias vitae, sed propter lucrum quaerendum. Et haec quidem negotiatio proprie videtur ad negotiatores pertinere. Secundum philosophum autem, prima commutatio laudabilis est, quia deservit naturali necessitati. Secunda autem iuste vituperatur, quia, quantum est de se, deservit cupiditati lucri, quae terminum nescit sed in infinitum tendit. Et ideo negotiatio, secundum se considerata, quandam turpitudinem habet, inquantum non importat de sui ratione finem honestum vel necessarium. Lucrum tamen, quod est negotiationis finis, etsi in sui ratione non importet aliquid honestum vel necessarium, nihil tamen importat in sui ratione vitiosum vel virtuti contrarium. Unde nihil prohibet lucrum ordinari ad aliquem finem necessarium, vel etiam honestum. Et sic negotiatio licita reddetur. Sicut cum aliquis lucrum moderatum, quod negotiando quaerit, ordinat ad domus suae sustentationem, vel etiam ad subveniendum indigentibus, vel etiam cum aliquis negotiationi intendit propter publicam utili-

*Because I have not known learning, or trading* according to another version: *What is trade,* says he, *but buying at a cheap price with the purpose of retailing at a higher price?* and he adds: *Such were the tradesmen whom Our Lord cast out of the temple.* Now no man is cast out of the temple except for a sin. Therefore such like trading is sinful.

**OBJ. 2**: Further, it is contrary to justice to sell goods at a higher price than their worth, or to buy them for less than their value, as shown above (A. 1). Now if you sell a thing for a higher price than you paid for it, you must either have bought it for less than its value, or sell it for more than its value. Therefore this cannot be done without sin.

**OBJ. 3**: Further, Jerome says (*Ep. ad Nepot.* lii): *Shun, as you would the plague, a cleric who from being poor has become wealthy, or who, from being a nobody has become a celebrity.* Now trading would net seem to be forbidden to clerics except on account of its sinfulness. Therefore it is a sin in trading, to buy at a low price and to sell at a higher price.

**ON THE CONTRARY**, Augustine commenting on Ps. 70:15, *Because I have not known learning,* says: *The greedy tradesman blasphemes over his losses; he lies and perjures himself over the price of his wares. But these are vices of the man, not of the craft, which can be exercised without these vices.* Therefore trading is not in itself unlawful.

**I ANSWER THAT**, A tradesman is one whose business consists in the exchange of things. According to the Philosopher (*Polit.* i, 3), exchange of things is twofold; one, natural as it were, and necessary, whereby one commodity is exchanged for another, or money taken in exchange for a commodity, in order to satisfy the needs of life. Such like trading, properly speaking, does not belong to tradesmen, but rather to housekeepers or civil servants who have to provide the household or the state with the necessaries of life. The other kind of exchange is either that of money for money, or of any commodity for money, not on account of the necessities of life, but for profit, and this kind of exchange, properly speaking, regards tradesmen, according to the Philosopher (*Polit.* i, 3). The former kind of exchange is commendable because it supplies a natural need: but the latter is justly deserving of blame, because, considered in itself, it satisfies the greed for gain, which knows no limit and tends to infinity. Hence trading, considered in itself, has a certain debasement attaching thereto, insofar as, by its very nature, it does not imply a virtuous or necessary end. Nevertheless gain which is the end of trading, though not implying, by its nature, anything virtuous or necessary, does not, in itself, connote anything sinful or contrary to virtue: wherefore nothing prevents gain from being directed to some necessary or even virtuous end, and thus trading becomes lawful. Thus, for instance, a man may intend the moderate gain which he seeks to acquire by trading for the upkeep of his household, or for the assistance of the needy: or again, a man may take to trade

tatem, ne scilicet res necessariae ad vitam patriae desint, et lucrum expetit non quasi finem, sed quasi stipendium laboris.

**AD PRIMUM** ergo dicendum quod verbum Chrysostomi est intelligendum de negotiatione secundum quod ultimum finem in lucro constituit, quod praecipue videtur quando aliquis rem non immutatam carius vendit. Si enim rem immutatam carius vendat, videtur praemium sui laboris accipere. Quamvis et ipsum lucrum possit licite intendi, non sicut ultimus finis, sed propter alium finem necessarium vel honestum, ut dictum est.

**AD SECUNDUM** dicendum quod non quicumque carius vendit aliquid quam emerit, negotiatur, sed solum qui ad hoc emit ut carius vendat. Si autem emit rem non ut vendat, sed ut teneat, et postmodum propter aliquam causam eam vendere velit, non est negotiatio, quamvis carius vendat. Potest enim hoc licite facere, vel quia in aliquo rem melioravit; vel quia pretium rei est mutatum, secundum diversitatem loci vel temporis; vel propter periculum cui se exponit transferendo rem de loco ad locum, vel eam ferri faciendo. Et secundum hoc, nec emptio nec venditio est iniusta.

**AD TERTIUM** dicendum quod clerici non solum debent abstinere ab his quae sunt secundum se mala, sed etiam ab his quae habent speciem mali. Quod quidem in negotiatione contingit, tum propter hoc quod est ordinata ad lucrum terrenum, cuius clerici debent esse contemptores; tum etiam propter frequentia negotiatorum vitia, quia *difficiliter exuitur negotiator a peccatis labiorum*, ut dicitur Eccli. XXVI. Est et alia causa, quia negotiatio nimis implicat animum saecularibus curis, et per consequens a spiritualibus retrahit, unde apostolus dicit, II ad Tim. II, *nemo militans Deo implicat se negotiis saecularibus*. Licet tamen clericis uti prima commutationis specie, quae ordinatur ad necessitatem vitae, emendo vel vendendo.

for some public advantage, for instance, lest his country lack the necessaries of life, and seek gain, not as an end, but as payment for his labor.

**REPLY OBJ. 1:** The saying of Chrysostom refers to the trading which seeks gain as a last end. This is especially the case where a man sells something at a higher price without its undergoing any change. For if he sells at a higher price something that has changed for the better, he would seem to receive the reward of his labor. Nevertheless the gain itself may be lawfully intended, not as a last end, but for the sake of some other end which is necessary or virtuous, as stated above.

**REPLY OBJ. 2:** Not everyone that sells at a higher price than he bought is a tradesman, but only he who buys that he may sell at a profit. If, on the contrary, he buys not for sale but for possession, and afterwards, for some reason wishes to sell, it is not a trade transaction even if he sell at a profit. For he may lawfully do this, either because he has bettered the thing, or because the value of the thing has changed with the change of place or time, or on account of the danger he incurs in transferring the thing from one place to another, or again in having it carried by another. In this sense neither buying nor selling is unjust.

**REPLY OBJ. 3:** Clerics should abstain not only from things that are evil in themselves, but even from those that have an appearance of evil. This happens in trading, both because it is directed to worldly gain, which clerics should despise, and because trading is open to so many vices, since *a merchant is hardly free from sins of the lips* (Sir 26:28). There is also another reason, because trading engages the mind too much with worldly cares, and consequently withdraws it from spiritual cares; wherefore the Apostle says (2 Tim 2:4): *No man being a soldier to God entangleth himself with secular businesses*. Nevertheless it is lawful for clerics to engage in the first mentioned kind of exchange, which is directed to supply the necessaries of life, either by buying or by selling.

# QUESTION 78

## THE SIN OF USURY

Deinde considerandum est de peccato usurae, quod committitur in mutuis. Et circa hoc quaeruntur quatuor.

Primo, utrum sit peccatum accipere pecuniam in pretium pro pecunia mutuata, quod est accipere usuram.

Secundo, utrum liceat pro eodem quamcumque utilitatem accipere quasi in recompensationem mutui.

Tertio, utrum aliquis restituere teneatur id quod de pecunia usuraria iusto lucro lucratus est.

Quarto, utrum liceat accipere mutuo pecuniam sub usura.

We must now consider the sin of usury, which is committed in loans: and under this head there are four points of inquiry:

(1) Whether it is a sin to take money as a price for money lent, which is to receive usury?

(2) Whether it is lawful to lend money for any other kind of consideration, by way of payment for the loan?

(3) Whether a man is bound to restore just gains derived from money taken in usury?

(4) Whether it is lawful to borrow money under a condition of usury?

# Article 1

*Whether it is a sin to take usury for money lent?*

**AD PRIMUM SIC PROCEDITUR.** Videtur quod accipere usuram pro pecunia mutuata non sit peccatum. Nullus enim peccat ex hoc quod sequitur exemplum Christi. Sed dominus de seipso dicit, Luc. XIX, *ego veniens cum usuris exegissem illam*, scilicet pecuniam mutuatam. Ergo non est peccatum accipere usuram pro mutuo pecuniae.

**PRAETEREA,** sicut dicitur in Psalm., *lex domini immaculata*, quia scilicet peccatum prohibet. Sed in lege divina conceditur aliqua usura, secundum illud Deut. XXIII, *non faenerabis fratri tuo ad usuram pecuniam, nec fruges nec quamlibet aliam rem, sed alieno*. Et, quod plus est, etiam in praemium repromittitur pro lege servata, secundum illud Deut. XXVIII, *faenerabis gentibus multis; et ipse a nullo faenus accipies*. Ergo accipere usuram non est peccatum.

**PRAETEREA,** in rebus humanis determinatur iustitia per leges civiles. Sed secundum eas conceditur usuras accipere. Ergo videtur non esse illicitum.

**PRAETEREA,** praetermittere consilia non obligat ad peccatum. Sed Luc. VI inter alia consilia ponitur, *date mutuum, nihil inde sperantes*. Ergo accipere usuram non est peccatum.

**PRAETEREA,** pretium accipere quo eo quod quis facere non tenetur, non videtur esse secundum se peccatum. Sed non in quolibet casu tenetur pecuniam habens eam proximo mutuare. Ergo licet ei aliquando pro mutuo accipere pretium.

**OBJECTION 1:** It would seem that it is not a sin to take usury for money lent. For no man sins through following the example of Christ. But Our Lord said of Himself (Luke 19:23): *At My coming I might have exacted it*, i.e., the money lent, *with usury*. Therefore it is not a sin to take usury for lending money.

**OBJ. 2:** Further, according to Ps. 18:8, *The law of the Lord is unspotted*, because, to wit, it forbids sin. Now usury of a kind is allowed in the Divine law, according to Deut. 23:19, 20: *Thou shalt not fenerate to thy brother money, nor corn, nor any other thing, but to the stranger*: nay more, it is even promised as a reward for the observance of the Law, according to Deut. 28:12: *Thou shalt fenerate to many nations, and shalt not borrow of any one.* Therefore it is not a sin to take usury.

**OBJ. 3:** Further, in human affairs justice is determined by civil laws. Now civil law allows usury to be taken. Therefore it seems to be lawful.

**OBJ. 4:** Further, the counsels are not binding under sin. But, among other counsels we find (Luke 6:35): *Lend, hoping for nothing thereby.* Therefore it is not a sin to take usury.

**OBJ. 5:** Further, it does not seem to be in itself sinful to accept a price for doing what one is not bound to do. But one who has money is not bound in every case to lend it to his neighbor. Therefore it is lawful for him sometimes to accept a price for lending it.

**Praeterea**, argentum monetatum, et in vasa formatum, non differt specie. Sed licet accipere pretium pro vasis argenteis accommodatis. Ergo etiam licet accipere pretium pro mutuo argenti monetati. Usura ergo non est secundum se peccatum.

**Praeterea**, quilibet potest licite accipere rem quam ei dominus rei voluntarie tradit. Sed ille qui accipit mutuum voluntarie tradit usuram. Ergo ille qui mutuat licite potest accipere.

**Sed contra** est quod dicitur Exod. XXII, *si pecuniam mutuam dederis populo meo pauperi qui habitat tecum, non urgebis eum quasi exactor, nec usuris opprimes.*

**Respondeo** dicendum quod accipere usuram pro pecunia mutuata est secundum se iniustum, quia venditur id quod non est, per quod manifeste inaequalitas constituitur, quae iustitiae contrariatur. Ad cuius evidentiam, sciendum est quod quaedam res sunt quarum usus est ipsarum rerum consumptio, sicut vinum consumimus eo utendo ad potum, et triticum consumimus eo utendo ad cibum. Unde in talibus non debet seorsum computari usus rei a re ipsa, sed cuicumque conceditur usus, ex hoc ipso conceditur res. Et propter hoc in talibus per mutuum transfertur dominium. Si quis ergo seorsum vellet vendere vinum et seorsum vellet vendere usum vini, venderet eandem rem bis, vel venderet id quod non est. Unde manifeste per iniustitiam peccaret. Et simili ratione, iniustitiam committit qui mutuat vinum aut triticum petens sibi duas recompensationes, unam quidem restitutionem aequalis rei, aliam vero pretium usus, quod *usura* dicitur.

Quaedam vero sunt quorum usus non est ipsa rei consumptio, sicut usus domus est inhabitatio, non autem dissipatio. Et ideo in talibus seorsum potest utrumque concedi, puta cum aliquis tradit alteri dominium domus, reservato sibi usu ad aliquod tempus; vel e converso cum quis concedit alicui usum domus, reservato sibi eius dominio. Et propter hoc licite potest homo accipere pretium pro usu domus, et praeter hoc petere domum commodatam, sicut patet in conductione et locatione domus.

Pecunia autem, secundum philosophum, in V Ethic. et in I Polit., principaliter est inventa ad commutationes faciendas, et ita proprius et principalis pecuniae usus est ipsius consumptio sive distractio, secundum quod in commutationes expenditur. Et propter hoc secundum se est illicitum pro usu pecuniae mutuatae accipere pretium, quod dicitur usura. Et sicut alia iniuste acquisita tenetur homo restituere, ita pecuniam quam per usuram accepit.

**Ad primum** ergo dicendum quod usura ibi metaphorice accipitur pro superexcrescentia bonorum spiritualium, quam exigit Deus volens ut in bonis acceptis ab

**Obj. 6**: Further, silver made into coins does not differ specifically from silver made into a vessel. But it is lawful to accept a price for the loan of a silver vessel. Therefore it is also lawful to accept a price for the loan of a silver coin. Therefore usury is not in itself a sin.

**Obj. 7**: Further, anyone may lawfully accept a thing which its owner freely gives him. Now he who accepts the loan, freely gives the usury. Therefore he who lends may lawfully take the usury.

**On the contrary**, It is written (Exod 22:25): *If thou lend money to any of thy people that is poor, that dwelleth with thee, thou shalt not be hard upon them as an extortioner, nor oppress them with usuries.*

**I answer that**, To take usury for money lent is unjust in itself, because this is to sell what does not exist, and this evidently leads to inequality which is contrary to justice. In order to make this evident, we must observe that there are certain things the use of which consists in their consumption: thus we consume wine when we use it for drink and we consume wheat when we use it for food. Wherefore in such like things the use of the thing must not be reckoned apart from the thing itself, and whoever is granted the use of the thing, is granted the thing itself and for this reason, to lend things of this kind is to transfer the ownership. Accordingly if a man wanted to sell wine separately from the use of the wine, he would be selling the same thing twice, or he would be selling what does not exist, wherefore he would evidently commit a sin of injustice. In like manner he commits an injustice who lends wine or wheat, and asks for double payment, viz. one, the return of the thing in equal measure, the other, the price of the use, which is called *usury*.

On the other hand, there are things the use of which does not consist in their consumption: thus to use a house is to dwell in it, not to destroy it. Wherefore in such things both may be granted: for instance, one man may hand over to another the ownership of his house while reserving to himself the use of it for a time, or vice versa, he may grant the use of the house, while retaining the ownership. For this reason a man may lawfully make a charge for the use of his house, and, besides this, revendicate the house from the person to whom he has granted its use, as happens in renting and letting a house.

Now money, according to the Philosopher (*Ethic.* v, 5; *Polit.* i, 3) was invented chiefly for the purpose of exchange: and consequently the proper and principal use of money is its consumption or alienation whereby it is sunk in exchange. Hence it is by its very nature unlawful to take payment for the use of money lent, which payment is known as usury: and just as a man is bound to restore other ill-gotten goods, so is he bound to restore the money which he has taken in usury.

**Reply Obj. 1**: In this passage usury must be taken figuratively for the increase of spiritual goods which God exacts from us, for He wishes us ever to advance in the

eo semper proficiamus. Quod est ad utilitatem nostram, non eius.

**AD SECUNDUM** dicendum quod Iudaeis prohibitum fuit accipere usuram *a fratribus suis*, scilicet Iudaeis, per quod datur intelligi quod accipere usuram a quocumque homine est simpliciter malum; debemus enim omnem hominem habere *quasi proximum et fratrem*, praecipue in statu Evangelii, ad quod omnes vocantur. Unde in Psalm. absolute dicitur, *qui pecuniam suam non dedit ad usuram*; et Ezech. XVIII, *qui usuram non acceperit*. Quod autem ab extraneis usuram acciperent, non fuit eis concessum quasi licitum, sed permissum ad maius malum vitandum, ne scilicet a Iudaeis, Deum colentibus, usuras acciperent, propter avaritiam, cui dediti erant, ut habetur Isaiae LVI.

Quod autem in praemium promittitur, *faenerabis gentibus multis, etc.*, faenus ibi large accipitur pro mutuo, sicut et Eccli. XXIX dicitur, *multi non causa nequitiae non faenerati sunt*, idest non mutuaverunt. Promittitur ergo in praemium Iudaeis abundantia divitiarum, ex qua contingit quod aliis mutuare possint.

**AD TERTIUM** dicendum quod leges humanae dimittunt aliqua peccata impunita propter conditiones hominum imperfectorum, in quibus multae utilitates impedirentur si omnia peccata districte prohiberentur poenis adhibitis. Et ideo usuras lex humana concessit, non quasi existimans eas esse secundum iustitiam, sed ne impedirentur utilitates multorum. Unde in ipso iure civili dicitur quod *res quae usu consumuntur neque ratione naturali neque civili recipiunt usumfructum, et quod senatus non fecit earum rerum usumfructum, nec enim poterat; sed quasi usumfructum constituit*, concedens scilicet usuras. Et philosophus, naturali ratione ductus, dicit, in I Polit., quod *usuraria acquisitio pecuniarum est maxime praeter naturam*.

**AD QUARTUM** dicendum quod dare mutuum non semper tenetur homo, et ideo quantum ad hoc ponitur inter consilia. Sed quod homo lucrum de mutuo non quaerat, hoc cadit sub ratione praecepti. Potest tamen dici consilium per comparationem ad dicta Pharisaeorum, qui putabant usuram aliquam esse licitam, sicut et dilectio inimicorum est consilium. Vel loquitur ibi non de spe usurarii lucri, sed de spe quae ponitur in homine. Non enim debemus mutuum dare, vel quodcumque bonum facere, propter spem hominis, sed propter spem Dei.

**AD QUINTUM** dicendum quod ille qui mutuare non tenetur recompensationem potest accipere eius quod fecit, sed non amplius debet exigere. Recompensatur autem sibi secundum aequalitatem iustitiae si tantum ei reddatur quantum mutuavit. Unde si amplius exigat

goods which we receive from Him: and this is for our own profit not for His.

**REPLY OBJ. 2:** The Jews were forbidden to take usury *from their brethren*, i.e., from other Jews. By this we are given to understand that to take usury from any man is evil simply, because we ought to treat every man *as our neighbor and brother*, especially in the state of the Gospel, whereto all are called. Hence it is said without any distinction in Ps. 14:5: *He that hath not put out his money to usury*, and (Ezek 18:8): *Who hath not taken usury*. They were permitted, however, to take usury from foreigners, not as though it were lawful, but in order to avoid a greater evil, lest, to wit, through avarice to which they were prone according to Isa. 56:11, they should take usury from the Jews who were worshippers of God.

Where we find it promised to them as a reward, *Thou shalt fenerate to many nations*, etc., fenerating is to be taken in a broad sense for lending, as in Ecclus. 29:10, where we read: *Many have refused to fenerate, not out of wickedness*, i.e., they would not lend. Accordingly the Jews are promised in reward an abundance of wealth, so that they would be able to lend to others.

**REPLY OBJ. 3:** Human laws leave certain things unpunished, on account of the condition of those who are imperfect, and who would be deprived of many advantages, if all sins were strictly forbidden and punishments appointed for them. Wherefore human law has permitted usury, not that it looks upon usury as harmonizing with justice, but lest the advantage of many should be hindered. Hence it is that in civil law it is stated that *those things according to natural reason and civil law which are consumed by being used, do not admit of usufruct, and that the senate did not (nor could it) appoint a usufruct to such things, but established a quasi-usufruct*, namely by permitting usury. Moreover the Philosopher, led by natural reason, says (*Polit.* i, 3) that *to make money by usury is exceedingly unnatural*.

**REPLY OBJ. 4:** A man is not always bound to lend, and for this reason it is placed among the counsels. Yet it is a matter of precept not to seek profit by lending: although it may be called a matter of counsel in comparison with the maxims of the Pharisees, who deemed some kinds of usury to be lawful, just as love of one's enemies is a matter of counsel. Or again, He speaks here not of the hope of usurious gain, but of the hope which is put in man. For we ought not to lend or do any good deed through hope in man, but only through hope in God.

**REPLY OBJ. 5:** He that is not bound to lend, may accept repayment for what he has done, but he must not exact more. Now he is repaid according to equality of justice if he is repaid as much as he lent. Wherefore if he exacts more for the usufruct of a thing which has no other use

pro usufructu rei quae alium usum non habet nisi consumptionem substantiae, exigit pretium eius quod non est. Et ita est iniusta exactio.

**AD SEXTUM** dicendum quod usus principalis vasorum argenteorum non est ipsa eorum consumptio, et ideo usus eorum potest vendi licite, servato dominio rei. Usus autem principalis pecuniae argenteae est distractio pecuniae in commutationes. Unde non licet eius usum vendere cum hoc quod aliquis velit eius restitutionem quod mutuo dedit. Sciendum tamen quod secundarius usus argenteorum vasorum posset esse commutatio. Et talem usum eorum vendere non liceret. Et similiter potest esse aliquis alius secundarius usus pecuniae argenteae, ut puta si quis concederet pecuniam signatam ad ostentationem, vel ad ponendum loco pignoris. Et talem usum pecuniae licite homo vendere potest.

**AD SEPTIMUM** dicendum quod ille qui dat usuram non simpliciter voluntarie dat, sed cum quadam necessitate, inquantum indiget pecuniam accipere mutuo, quam ille qui habet non vult sine usura mutuare.

but the consumption of its substance, he exacts a price of something non-existent: and so his exaction is unjust.

**REPLY OBJ. 6**: The principal use of a silver vessel is not its consumption, and so one may lawfully sell its use while retaining one's ownership of it. On the other hand the principal use of silver money is sinking it in exchange, so that it is not lawful to sell its use and at the same time expect the restitution of the amount lent. It must be observed, however, that the secondary use of silver vessels may be an exchange, and such use may not be lawfully sold. In like manner there may be some secondary use of silver money; for instance, a man might lend coins for show, or to be used as security. And a man can licitly buy such a use of money.

**REPLY OBJ. 7**: He who gives usury does not give it voluntarily simply, but under a certain necessity, insofar as he needs to borrow money which the owner is unwilling to lend without usury.

# Article 2

*Whether it is lawful to ask for any other kind of consideration for money lent?*

**AD SECUNDUM SIC PROCEDITUR.** Videtur quod aliquis possit pro pecunia mutuata aliquam aliam commoditatem expetere. Unusquisque enim licite potest suae indemnitati consulere. Sed quandoque damnum aliquis patitur ex hoc quod pecuniam mutuat. Ergo licitum est ei, supra pecuniam mutuatam, aliquid aliud pro damno expetere, vel etiam exigere.

**PRAETEREA**, unusquisque tenetur ex quodam debito honestatis *aliquid recompensare ei qui sibi gratiam fecit*, ut dicitur in V Ethic. Sed ille qui alicui in necessitate constituto pecuniam mutuat, gratiam facit, unde et gratiarum actio ei debetur. Ergo ille qui recipit tenetur naturali debito aliquid recompensare. Sed non videtur esse illicitum obligare se ad aliquid ad quod quis ex naturali iure tenetur. Ergo non videtur esse illicitum si aliquis, pecuniam alteri mutuans, in obligationem deducat aliquam recompensationem.

**PRAETEREA**, sicut est quoddam *munus a manu*, ita est *munus a lingua*, et *ab obsequio*, ut dicit Glossa Isaiae XXXIII, *beatus qui excutit manus suas ab omni munere*. Sed licet accipere servitium, vel etiam laudem, ab eo cui quis pecuniam mutuavit. Ergo, pari ratione, licet quodcumque aliud munus accipere.

**PRAETEREA**, eadem videtur esse comparatio dati ad datum et mutuati ad mutuatum. Sed licet pecuniam

**OBJECTION 1**: It would seem that one may ask for some other kind of consideration for money lent. For everyone may lawfully seek to indemnify himself. Now sometimes a man suffers loss through lending money. Therefore he may lawfully ask for or even exact something else besides the money lent.

**OBJ. 2**: Further, as stated in *Ethic.* v, 5, one is in duty bound by a point of honor, to repay anyone who has done us a favor. Now to lend money to one who is in straits is to do him a favor for which he should be grateful. Therefore the recipient of a loan, is bound by a natural debt to repay something. Now it does not seem unlawful to bind oneself to an obligation of the natural law. Therefore it is not unlawful, in lending money to anyone, to demand some sort of compensation as condition of the loan.

**OBJ. 3**: Further, just as there is real remuneration, so is there verbal remuneration, and remuneration by service, as a gloss says on Isa. 33:15, *Blessed is he that shaketh his hands from all bribes*. Now it is lawful to accept service or praise from one to whom one has lent money. Therefore in like manner it is lawful to accept any other kind of remuneration.

**OBJ. 4**: Further, seemingly the relation of gift to gift is the same as of loan to loan. But it is lawful to accept money

accipere pro alia pecunia data. Ergo licet accipere recompensationem alterius mutui pro pecunia mutuata.

**PRAETEREA**, magis a se pecuniam alienat qui, eam mutuando, dominium transfert, quam qui eam mercatori vel artifici committit. Sed licet lucrum accipere de pecunia commissa mercatori vel artifici. Ergo licet etiam lucrum accipere de pecunia mutuata.

**PRAETEREA**, pro pecunia mutuata potest homo pignus accipere, cuius usus posset aliquo pretio vendi, sicut cum impignoratur ager vel domus quae inhabitatur. Ergo licet aliquod lucrum habere de pecunia mutuata.

**PRAETEREA**, contingit quandoque quod aliquis carius vendit res suas ratione mutui; aut vilius emit quod est alterius; vel etiam pro dilatione pretium auget, vel pro acceleratione diminuit, in quibus omnibus videtur aliqua recompensatio fieri quasi pro mutuo pecuniae. Hoc autem non manifeste apparet illicitum. Ergo videtur licitum esse aliquod commodum de pecunia mutuata expectare, vel etiam exigere.

**SED CONTRA** est quod Ezech. XVIII dicitur, inter alia quae ad virum iustum requiruntur, *usuram et superabundantiam non acceperit*.

**RESPONDEO** dicendum quod, secundum philosophum, in IV Ethic., omne illud pro pecunia habetur *cuius pretium potest pecunia mensurari*. Et ideo sicut si aliquis pro pecunia mutuata, vel quacumque alia re quae ex ipso usu consumitur, pecuniam accipit ex pacto tacito vel expresso, peccat contra iustitiam, ut dictum est; ita etiam quicumque ex pacto tacito vel expresso quodcumque aliud acceperit cuius pretium pecunia mensurari potest, simile peccatum incurrit. Si vero accipiat aliquid huiusmodi non quasi exigens, nec quasi ex aliqua obligatione tacita vel expressa, sed sicut gratuitum donum, non peccat, quia etiam antequam pecuniam mutuasset, licite poterat aliquod donum gratis accipere, nec peioris conditionis efficitur per hoc quod mutuavit.

Recompensationem vero eorum quae pecunia non mensurantur licet pro mutuo exigere, puta benevolentiam et amorem eius qui mutuavit, vel aliquid huiusmodi.

**AD PRIMUM** ergo dicendum quod ille qui mutuum dat potest absque peccato in pactum deducere cum eo qui mutuum accipit recompensationem damni per quod subtrahitur sibi aliquid quod debet habere, hoc enim non est vendere usum pecuniae, sed damnum vitare. Et potest esse quod accipiens mutuum maius damnum evitet quam dans incurret, unde accipiens mutuum cum sua utilitate damnum alterius recompensat. Recompensationem vero damni quod consideratur in hoc quod de pecunia non lucratur, non potest in pactum deducere, quia non debet vendere id quod nondum habet et potest impediri multipliciter ab habendo.

for money given. Therefore it is lawful to accept repayment by loan in return for a loan granted.

**OBJ. 5**: Further, the lender, by transferring his ownership of a sum of money removes the money further from himself than he who entrusts it to a merchant or craftsman. Now it is lawful to receive interest for money entrusted to a merchant or craftsman. Therefore it is also lawful to receive interest for money lent.

**OBJ. 6**: Further, a man may accept a pledge for money lent, the use of which pledge he might sell for a price: as when a man mortgages his land or the house wherein he dwells. Therefore it is lawful to receive interest for money lent.

**OBJ. 7**: Further, it sometimes happens that a man raises the price of his goods under guise of loan, or buys another's goods at a low figure; or raises his price through delay in being paid, and lowers his price that he may be paid the sooner. Now in all these cases there seems to be payment for a loan of money: nor does it appear to be manifestly illicit. Therefore it seems to be lawful to expect or exact some consideration for money lent.

**ON THE CONTRARY**, Among other conditions requisite in a just man it is stated (Ezek 18:17) that he *hath not taken usury and increase*.

**I ANSWER THAT**, According to the Philosopher (*Ethic.* iv, 1), a thing is reckoned as money *if its value can be measured by money*. Consequently, just as it is a sin against justice, to take money, by tacit or express agreement, in return for lending money or anything else that is consumed by being used, so also is it a like sin, by tacit or express agreement to receive anything whose price can be measured by money. Yet there would be no sin in receiving something of the kind, not as exacting it, nor yet as though it were due on account of some agreement tacit or expressed, but as a gratuity: since, even before lending the money, one could accept a gratuity, nor is one in a worse condition through lending.

On the other hand it is lawful to exact compensation for a loan, in respect of such things as are not appreciated by a measure of money, for instance, benevolence, and love for the lender, and so forth.

**REPLY OBJ. 1**: A lender may without sin enter an agreement with the borrower for compensation for the loss he incurs of something he ought to have, for this is not to sell the use of money but to avoid a loss. It may also happen that the borrower avoids a greater loss than the lender incurs, wherefore the borrower may repay the lender with what he has gained. But the lender cannot enter an agreement for compensation, through the fact that he makes no profit out of his money: because he must not sell that which he has not yet and may be prevented in many ways from having.

Ad secundum dicendum quod recompensatio alicuius beneficii dupliciter fieri potest. Uno quidem modo, ex debito iustitiae, ad quod aliquis ex certo pacto obligari potest. Et hoc debitum attenditur secundum quantitatem beneficii quod quis accepit. Et ideo ille qui accipit mutuum pecuniae, vel cuiuscumque similis rei cuius usus est eius consumptio, non tenetur ad plus recompensandum quam mutuo acceperit. Unde contra iustitiam est si ad plus reddendum obligetur. Alio modo tenetur aliquis ad recompensandum beneficium ex debito amicitiae, in quo magis consideratur affectus ex quo aliquis beneficium contulit quam etiam quantitas eius quod fecit. Et tali debito non competit civilis obligatio, per quam inducitur quaedam necessitas, ut non spontanea recompensatio fiat.

Ad tertium dicendum quod si aliquis ex pecunia mutuata expectet vel exigat, quasi per obligationem pacti taciti vel expressi, recompensationem muneris ab obsequio vel lingua, perinde est ac si expectaret vel exigeret munus a manu, quia utrumque pecunia aestimari potest, ut patet in his qui locant operas suas, quas manu vel lingua exercent. Si vero munus ab obsequio vel lingua non quasi ex obligatione rei exhibeat, sed ex benevolentia, quae sub aestimatione pecuniae non cadit, licet hoc accipere et exigere et expectare.

Ad quartum dicendum quod pecunia non potest vendi pro pecunia ampliori quam sit quantitas pecuniae mutuatae, quae restituenda est, nec ibi aliquid est exigendum aut expectandum nisi benevolentiae affectus, qui sub aestimatione pecuniae non cadit, ex quo potest procedere spontanea mutuatio. Repugnat autem ei obligatio ad mutuum in posterum faciendum, quia etiam talis obligatio pecunia aestimari posset. Et ideo licet simul mutuanti unum aliquid aliud mutuare, non autem licet eum obligare ad mutuum in posterum faciendum.

Ad quintum dicendum quod ille qui mutuat pecuniam transfert dominium pecuniae in eum cui mutuat. Unde ille cui pecunia mutuatur sub suo periculo tenet eam, et tenetur integre restituere. Unde non debet amplius exigere ille qui mutuavit. Sed ille qui committit pecuniam suam vel mercatori vel artifici per modum societatis cuiusdam, non transfert dominium pecuniae suae in illum, sed remanet eius, ita quod cum periculo ipsius mercator de ea negotiatur vel artifex operatur. Et ideo licite potest partem lucri inde provenientis expetere, tanquam de re sua.

Ad sextum dicendum quod si quis pro pecunia sibi mutuata obliget rem aliquam cuius usus pretio aestimari potest, debet usum illius rei ille qui mutuavit computare in restitutionem eius quod mutuavit. Alioquin, si usum illius rei quasi gratis sibi superaddi velit, idem est ac si pecuniam acciperet pro mutuo, quod est usurarium, nisi

Reply Obj. 2: Repayment for a favor may be made in two ways. In one way, as a debt of justice; and to such a debt a man may be bound by a fixed contract; and its amount is measured according to the favor received. Wherefore the borrower of money or any such thing the use of which is its consumption is not bound to repay more than he received in loan: and consequently it is against justice if he be obliged to pay back more. In another way a man's obligation to repayment for favor received is based on a debt of friendship, and the nature of this debt depends more on the feeling with which the favor was conferred than on the greatness of the favor itself. This debt does not carry with it a civil obligation, involving a kind of necessity that would exclude the spontaneous nature of such a repayment.

Reply Obj. 3: If a man were, in return for money lent, as though there had been an agreement tacit or expressed, to expect or exact repayment in the shape of some remuneration of service or words, it would be the same as if he expected or exacted some real remuneration, because both can be priced at a money value, as may be seen in the case of those who offer for hire the labor which they exercise by work or by tongue. If on the other hand the remuneration by service or words be given not as an obligation, but as a favor, which is not to be appreciated at a money value, it is lawful to take, exact, and expect it.

Reply Obj. 4: Money cannot be sold for a greater sum than the amount lent, which has to be paid back: nor should the loan be made with a demand or expectation of aught else but of a feeling of benevolence which cannot be priced at a pecuniary value, and which can be the basis of a spontaneous loan. Now the obligation to lend in return at some future time is repugnant to such a feeling, because again an obligation of this kind has its pecuniary value. Consequently it is lawful for the lender to borrow something else at the same time, but it is unlawful for him to bind the borrower to grant him a loan at some future time.

Reply Obj. 5: He who lends money transfers the ownership of the money to the borrower. Hence the borrower holds the money at his own risk and is bound to pay it all back: wherefore the lender must not exact more. On the other hand he that entrusts his money to a merchant or craftsman so as to form a kind of society, does not transfer the ownership of his money to them, for it remains his, so that at his risk the merchant speculates with it, or the craftsman uses it for his craft, and consequently he may lawfully demand as something belonging to him, part of the profits derived from his money.

Reply Obj. 6: If a man in return for money lent to him pledges something that can be valued at a price, the lender must allow for the use of that thing towards the repayment of the loan. Else if he wishes the gratuitous use of that thing in addition to repayment, it is the same as if he took money for lending, and that is usury, unless perhaps it were such a

forte esset talis res cuius usus sine pretio soleat concedi inter amicos, sicut patet de libro accommodato.

**AD SEPTIMUM** dicendum quod si aliquis carius velit vendere res suas quam sit iustum pretium, ut de pecunia solvenda emptorem expectet, usura manifeste committitur, quia huiusmodi expectatio pretii solvendi habet rationem mutui; unde quidquid ultra iustum pretium pro huiusmodi expectatione exigitur, est quasi pretium mutui, quod pertinet ad rationem usurae. Similiter etiam si quis emptor velit rem emere vilius quam sit iustum pretium, eo quod pecuniam ante solvit quam possit ei tradi, est peccatum usurae, quia etiam ista anticipatio solutionis pecuniae habet mutui rationem, cuius quoddam pretium est quod diminuitur de iusto pretio rei emptae. Si vero aliquis de iusto pretio velit diminuere ut pecuniam prius habeat, non peccat peccato usurae.

thing as friends are wont to lend to one another gratis, as in the case of the loan of a book.

**REPLY OBJ. 7**: If a man wish to sell his goods at a higher price than that which is just, so that he may wait for the buyer to pay, it is manifestly a case of usury: because this waiting for the payment of the price has the character of a loan, so that whatever he demands beyond the just price in consideration of this delay, is like a price for a loan, which pertains to usury. In like manner if a buyer wishes to buy goods at a lower price than what is just, for the reason that he pays for the goods before they can be delivered, it is a sin of usury; because again this anticipated payment of money has the character of a loan, the price of which is the rebate on the just price of the goods sold. On the other hand if a man wishes to allow a rebate on the just price in order that he may have his money sooner, he is not guilty of the sin of usury.

# Article 3

*Whether a man is bound to restore whatever profits he has made out of money gotten by usury?*

**AD TERTIUM SIC PROCEDITUR.** Videtur quod quidquid aliquis de pecunia usuraria lucratus fuerit, reddere teneatur. Dicit enim apostolus, ad Rom. XI, *si radix sancta, et rami.* Ergo, eadem ratione, si radix infecta, et rami. Sed radix fuit usuraria. Ergo et quidquid ex ea acquisitum est, est usurarium. Ergo tenetur ad restitutionem illius.

**PRAETEREA**, sicut dicitur extra, de usuris, in illa decretali, *cum tu sicut asseris, possessiones quae de usuris sunt comparatae debent vendi, et ipsarum pretia his a quibus sunt extorta restitui.* Ergo, eadem ratione, quidquid aliud ex pecunia usuraria acquiritur debet restitui.

**PRAETEREA**, illud quod aliquis emit de pecunia usuraria debetur sibi ratione pecuniae quam dedit. Non ergo habet maius ius in re quam acquisivit quam in pecunia quam dedit. Sed pecuniam usurariam tenebatur restituere. Ergo et illud quod ex ea acquirit tenetur restituere.

**SED CONTRA**, quilibet potest licite tenere id quod legitime acquisivit. Sed id quod acquiritur per pecuniam usurariam interdum legitime acquiritur. Ergo licite potest retineri.

**RESPONDEO** dicendum quod, sicut supra dictum est, res quaedam sunt quarum usus est ipsarum rerum consumptio, quae non habent usumfructum, secundum iura. Et ideo si talia fuerint per usuram extorta, puta denarii, triticum, vinum aut aliquid huiusmodi, non tenetur homo ad restituendum nisi id quod accepit, quia id quod de tali re est acquisitum non est fructus huius rei, sed humanae industriae. Nisi forte per detentionem

**OBJECTION 1**: It would seem that a man is bound to restore whatever profits he has made out of money gotten by usury. For the Apostle says (Rom 11:16): *If the root be holy, so are the branches.* Therefore likewise if the root be rotten so are the branches. But the root was infected with usury. Therefore whatever profit is made therefrom is infected with usury. Therefore he is bound to restore it.

**OBJ. 2**: Further, it is laid down (Extra, *De Usuris,* in the *Decretal: Cum tu sicut asseris*): *Property accruing from usury must be sold, and the price repaid to the persons from whom the usury was extorted.* Therefore, likewise, whatever else is acquired from usurious money must be restored.

**OBJ. 3**: Further, that which a man buys with the proceeds of usury is due to him by reason of the money he paid for it. Therefore he has no more right to the thing purchased than to the money he paid. But he was bound to restore the money gained through usury. Therefore he is also bound to restore what he acquired with it.

**ON THE CONTRARY**, A man may lawfully hold what he has lawfully acquired. Now that which is acquired by the proceeds of usury is sometimes lawfully acquired. Therefore it may be lawfully retained.

**I ANSWER THAT**, As stated above (A. 1), there are certain things whose use is their consumption, and which do not admit of usufruct, according to law (ibid., ad 3). Wherefore if such like things be extorted by means of usury, for instance money, wheat, wine and so forth, the lender is not bound to restore more than he received (since what is acquired by such things is the fruit not of the thing but of human industry), unless indeed the other party by

talis rei alter sit damnificatus, amittendo aliquid de bonis suis, tunc enim tenetur ad recompensationem nocumenti.

Quaedam vero res sunt quarum usus non est earum consumptio, et talia habent usumfructum, sicut domus et ager et alia huiusmodi. Et ideo si quis domum alterius vel agrum per usuram extorsisset, non solum teneretur restituere domum vel agrum, sed etiam fructus inde perceptos, quia sunt fructus rerum quarum alius est dominus, et ideo ei debentur.

**AD PRIMUM** ergo dicendum quod radix non solum habet rationem materiae, sicut pecunia usuraria, sed habet etiam aliqualiter rationem causae activae, inquantum administrat nutrimentum. Et ideo non est simile.

**AD SECUNDUM** dicendum quod possessiones quae de usuris sunt comparatae non sunt eorum quorum fuerunt usurae, sed illorum qui eas emerunt. Sunt tamen obligatae illis a quibus fuerunt usurae acceptae, sicut et alia bona usurarii. Et ideo non praecipitur quod assignentur illae possessiones his a quibus fuerunt acceptae usurae, quia forte plus valent quam usurae quas dederunt, sed praecipitur quod vendantur possessiones et earum pretia restituantur, scilicet secundum quantitatem usurae acceptae.

**AD TERTIUM** dicendum quod illud quod acquiritur de pecunia usuraria debetur quidem acquirenti propter pecuniam usurariam datam sicut propter causam instrumentalem, sed propter suam industriam sicut propter causam principalem. Et ideo plus iuris habet in re acquisita de pecunia usuraria quam in ipsa pecunia usuraria.

losing some of his own goods be injured through the lender retaining them: for then he is bound to make good the loss.

On the other hand, there are certain things whose use is not their consumption: such things admit of usufruct, for instance house or land property and so forth. Wherefore if a man has by usury extorted from another his house or land, he is bound to restore not only the house or land but also the fruits accruing to him therefrom, since they are the fruits of things owned by another man and consequently are due to him.

**REPLY OBJ. 1**: The root has not only the character of matter, as money made by usury has; but has also somewhat the character of an active cause, insofar as it administers nourishment. Hence the comparison fails.

**REPLY OBJ. 2**: Further, property acquired from usury does not belong to the person who paid usury, but to the person who bought it. Yet he that paid usury has a certain claim on that property just as he has on the other goods of the usurer. Hence it is not prescribed that such property should be assigned to the persons who paid usury, since the property is perhaps worth more than what they paid in usury, but it is commanded that the property be sold, and the price be restored, of course according to the amount taken in usury.

**REPLY OBJ. 3**: The proceeds of money taken in usury are due to the person who acquired them not by reason of the usurious money as instrumental cause, but on account of his own industry as principal cause. Wherefore he has more right to the goods acquired with usurious money than to the usurious money itself.

# Article 4

*Whether it is lawful to borrow money under a condition of usury?*

**AD QUARTUM SIC PROCEDITUR.** Videtur quod non liceat pecuniam accipere mutuo sub usura. Dicit enim apostolus, Rom. I, quod *digni sunt morte non solum qui faciunt peccata, sed etiam qui consentiunt facientibus.* Sed ille qui accipit pecuniam mutuo sub usuris consentit usurario in suo peccato, et praebet ei occasionem peccandi. Ergo etiam ipse peccat.

**PRAETEREA,** pro nullo commodo temporali debet aliquis alteri quamcumque occasionem praebere peccandi, hoc enim pertinet ad rationem scandali activi, quod semper est peccatum, ut supra dictum est. Sed ille qui petit mutuum ab usurario expresse dat ei occasionem peccandi. Ergo pro nullo commodo temporali excusatur.

**PRAETEREA,** non minor videtur esse necessitas quandoque deponendi pecuniam suam apud usurarium

**OBJECTION 1**: It would seem that it is not lawful to borrow money under a condition of usury. For the Apostle says (Rom 1:32) that they *are worthy of death . . . not only they that do* these sins, *but they also that consent to them that do them.* Now he that borrows money under a condition of usury consents in the sin of the usurer, and gives him an occasion of sin. Therefore he sins also.

**OBJ. 2**: Further, for no temporal advantage ought one to give another an occasion of committing a sin: for this pertains to active scandal, which is always sinful, as stated above (Q. 43, A. 2). Now he that seeks to borrow from a usurer gives him an occasion of sin. Therefore he is not to be excused on account of any temporal advantage.

**OBJ. 3**: Further, it seems no less necessary sometimes to deposit one's money with a usurer than to borrow from

quam mutuum accipiendi ab ipso. Sed deponere pecuniam apud usurarium videtur esse omnino illicitum, sicut illicitum esset deponere gladium apud furiosum, vel virginem committere luxurioso, seu cibum guloso. Ergo neque licitum est accipere mutuum ab usurario.

**SED CONTRA**, ille qui iniuriam patitur non peccat, secundum philosophum, in V Ethic., unde iustitia non est media inter duo vitia, ut ibidem dicitur. Sed usurarius peccat inquantum facit iniustitiam accipienti mutuum sub usuris. Ergo ille qui accipit mutuum sub usuris non peccat.

**RESPONDEO** dicendum quod inducere hominem ad peccandum nullo modo licet, uti tamen peccato alterius ad bonum licitum est, quia et Deus utitur omnibus peccatis ad aliquod bonum, ex quolibet enim malo elicit aliquod bonum, ut dicitur in Enchiridio. Et ideo Augustinus Publicolae quaerenti utrum liceret uti iuramento eius qui per falsos deos iurat, in quo manifeste peccat eis reverentiam divinam adhibens, respondit quod *qui utitur fide illius qui per falsos deos iurat, non ad malum sed ad bonum, non peccato illius se sociat, quo per Daemonia iuravit, sed pacto bono eius, quo fidem servavit.* Si tamen induceret eum ad iurandum per falsos deos, peccaret.

Ita etiam in proposito dicendum est quod nullo modo licet inducere aliquem ad mutuandum sub usuris, licet tamen ab eo qui hoc paratus est facere et usuras exercet, mutuum accipere sub usuris, propter aliquod bonum, quod est subventio suae necessitatis vel alterius. Sicut etiam licet ei qui incidit in latrones manifestare bona quae habet, quae latrones diripiendo peccant, ad hoc quod non occidatur, exemplo decem virorum qui dixerunt ad Ismahel, *noli occidere nos, quia habemus thesaurum in agro,* ut dicitur Ierem. XLI.

**AD PRIMUM** ergo dicendum quod ille qui accipit pecuniam mutuo sub usuris non consentit in peccatum usurarii, sed utitur eo. Nec placet ei usurarum acceptio, sed mutuatio, quae est bona.

**AD SECUNDUM** dicendum quod ille qui accipit pecuniam mutuo sub usuris non dat usurario occasionem usuras accipiendi, sed mutuandi, ipse autem usurarius sumit occasionem peccandi ex malitia cordis sui. Unde scandalum passivum est ex parte sua, non autem activum ex parte petentis mutuum. Nec tamen propter huiusmodi scandalum passivum debet alius a mutuo petendo desistere, si indigeat, quia huiusmodi passivum scandalum non provenit ex infirmitate vel ignorantia, sed ex malitia.

**AD TERTIUM** dicendum quod si quis committeret pecuniam suam usurario non habenti alias unde usuras exerceret; vel hac intentione committeret ut inde copiosius per usuram lucraretur; daret materiam peccanti. Unde et ipse esset particeps culpae. Si autem aliquis

---

him. Now it seems altogether unlawful to deposit one's money with a usurer, even as it would be unlawful to deposit one's sword with a madman, a maiden with a libertine, or food with a glutton. Neither therefore is it lawful to borrow from a usurer.

**ON THE CONTRARY**, He that suffers injury does not sin, according to the Philosopher (*Ethic.* v, 11), wherefore justice is not a mean between two vices, as stated in the same book (ch. 5). Now a usurer sins by doing an injury to the person who borrows from him under a condition of usury. Therefore he that accepts a loan under a condition of usury does not sin.

**I ANSWER THAT**, It is by no means lawful to induce a man to sin, yet it is lawful to make use of another's sin for a good end, since even God uses all sin for some good, since He draws some good from every evil as stated in the *Enchiridion* (xi). Hence when Publicola asked whether it were lawful to make use of an oath taken by a man swearing by false gods (which is a manifest sin, for he gives Divine honor to them) Augustine (*Ep. xlvii*) answered that *he who uses, not for a bad but for a good purpose, the oath of a man that swears by false gods, is a party, not to his sin of swearing by demons, but to his good compact whereby he kept his word.* If however he were to induce him to swear by false gods, he would sin.

Accordingly we must also answer to the question in point that it is by no means lawful to induce a man to lend under a condition of usury: yet it is lawful to borrow for usury from a man who is ready to do so and is a usurer by profession; provided the borrower have a good end in view, such as the relief of his own or another's need. Thus too it is lawful for a man who has fallen among thieves to point out his property to them (which they sin in taking) in order to save his life, after the example of the ten men who said to Ismahel (Jer 41:8): *Kill us not: for we have stores in the field.*

**REPLY OBJ. 1**: He who borrows for usury does not consent to the usurer's sin but makes use of it. Nor is it the usurer's acceptance of usury that pleases him, but his lending, which is good.

**REPLY OBJ. 2**: He who borrows for usury gives the usurer an occasion, not for taking usury, but for lending; it is the usurer who finds an occasion of sin in the malice of his heart. Hence there is passive scandal on his part, while there is no active scandal on the part of the person who seeks to borrow. Nor is this passive scandal a reason why the other person should desist from borrowing if he is in need, since this passive scandal arises not from weakness or ignorance but from malice.

**REPLY OBJ. 3**: If one were to entrust one's money to a usurer lacking other means of practising usury; or with the intention of making a greater profit from his money by reason of the usury, one would be giving a sinner matter for sin, so that one would be a participator in his guilt. If,

usurario alias habenti unde usuras exerceat, pecuniam suam committat ut tutius servetur, non peccat, sed utitur homine peccatore ad bonum.

on the other hand, the usurer to whom one entrusts one's money has other means of practising usury, there is no sin in entrusting it to him that it may be in safer keeping, since this is to use a sinner for a good purpose.

# QUESTION 79

## THE QUASI-INTEGRAL PARTS OF JUSTICE

Deinde considerandum est de partibus quasi integralibus iustitiae quae sunt facere bonum et declinare a malo, et de vitiis oppositis. Circa quod quaeruntur quatuor.

Primo, utrum duo praedicta sint partes iustitiae.

Secundo, utrum transgressio sit speciale peccatum.

Tertio, utrum omissio sit speciale peccatum.

Quarto, de comparatione omissionis ad transgressionem.

We must now consider the quasi-integral parts of justice, which are to do good, and to decline from evil, and the opposite vices. Under this head there are four points of inquiry:

(1) Whether these two are parts of justice?

(2) Whether transgression is a special sin?

(3) Whether omission is a special sin?

(4) Of the comparison between omission and transgression.

## Article 1

*Whether to decline from evil and to do good are parts of justice?*

**AD PRIMUM SIC PROCEDITUR.** Videtur quod declinare a malo et facere bonum non sint partes iustitiae. Ad quamlibet enim virtutem pertinet facere bonum opus et vitare malum. Sed partes non excedunt totum. Ergo declinare a malo et facere bonum non debent poni partes iustitiae, quae est quaedam virtus specialis.

**PRAETEREA,** super illud Psalm., *diverte a malo et fac bonum,* dicit Glossa, *illud vitat culpam,* scilicet divertere a malo; *hoc meretur vitam et palmam,* scilicet facere bonum. Sed quaelibet pars virtutis meretur vitam et palmam. Ergo declinare a malo non est pars iustitiae.

**PRAETEREA,** quaecumque ita se habent quod unum includitur in alio, non distinguuntur ab invicem sicut partes alicuius totius. Sed declinare a malo includitur in hoc quod est facere bonum, nullus enim simul facit malum et bonum. Ergo declinare a malo et facere bonum non sunt partes iustitiae.

**SED CONTRA** est quod Augustinus, in libro de Correp. et Grat., ponit ad iustitiam legis pertinere *declinare a malo et facere bonum.*

**RESPONDEO** dicendum quod si loquamur de bono et malo in communi, facere bonum et vitare malum pertinet ad omnem virtutem. Et secundum hoc non possunt poni partes iustitiae, nisi forte iustitia accipiatur prout est *omnis virtus.* Quamvis etiam iustitia hoc modo accepta respiciat quandam rationem boni specialem, prout scilicet est debitum in ordine ad legem divinam vel humanam.

Sed iustitia secundum quod est specialis virtus, respicit bonum sub ratione debiti ad proximum. Et secundum hoc ad iustitiam specialem pertinet facere bonum sub ratione debiti in comparatione ad proximum, et vitare

**OBJECTION 1:** It would seem that to decline from evil and to do good are not parts of justice. For it belongs to every virtue to perform a good deed and to avoid an evil one. But parts do not exceed the whole. Therefore to decline from evil and to do good should not be reckoned parts of justice, which is a special kind of virtue.

**OBJ. 2:** Further, a gloss on Ps. 33:15, *Turn away from evil and do good,* says: *The former,* i.e., to turn away from evil, *avoids sin, the latter,* i.e., to do good, *deserves the life and the palm.* But any part of a virtue deserves the life and the palm. Therefore to decline from evil is not a part of justice.

**OBJ. 3:** Further, things that are so related that one implies the other, are not mutually distinct as parts of a whole. Now declining from evil is implied in doing good: since no one does evil and good at the same time. Therefore declining from evil and doing good are not parts of justice.

**ON THE CONTRARY,** Augustine (*De Correp. et Grat.* i) declares that *declining from evil and doing good* belong to the justice of the law.

**I ANSWER THAT,** If we speak of good and evil in general, it belongs to every virtue to do good and to avoid evil: and in this sense they cannot be reckoned parts of justice, except justice be taken in the sense of *all virtue.* And yet even if justice be taken in this sense it regards a certain special aspect of good; namely, the good as due in respect of Divine or human law.

On the other hand justice considered as a special virtue regards good as due to one's neighbor. And in this sense it belongs to special justice to do good considered as due to one's neighbor, and to avoid the opposite evil, that, namely,

719

malum oppositum, scilicet quod est nocivum proximo. Ad iustitiam vero generalem pertinet facere bonum debitum in ordine ad communitatem vel ad Deum, et vitare malum oppositum.

Dicuntur autem haec duo partes iustitiae generalis vel specialis quasi integrales, quia utrumque eorum requiritur ad perfectum actum iustitiae. Ad iustitiam enim pertinet aequalitatem constituere in his quae sunt ad alterum, ut ex supradictis patet. Eiusdem autem est aliquid constituere, et constitutum conservare. Constituit autem aliquis aequalitatem iustitiae faciendo bonum, idest reddendo alteri quod ei debetur. Conservat autem aequalitatem iustitiae iam constitutae declinando a malo, idest nullum nocumentum proximo inferendo.

**AD PRIMUM** ergo dicendum quod bonum et malum hic accipiuntur sub quadam speciali ratione, per quam appropriantur iustitiae. Ideo autem haec duo ponuntur partes iustitiae secundum aliquam propriam rationem boni et mali, non autem alterius alicuius virtutis moralis, quia aliae virtutes morales consistunt circa passiones, in quibus bonum facere est venire ad medium, quod est declinare ab extremis quasi a malis, et sic in idem redit quantum ad alias virtutes, facere bonum et declinare a malo. Sed iustitia consistit circa operationes et res exteriores, in quibus aliud est facere aequalitatem, et aliud est factam non corrumpere.

**AD SECUNDUM** dicendum quod declinare a malo, secundum quod ponitur pars iustitiae, non importat negationem puram, quod est non facere malum, hoc enim non meretur palmam, sed solum vitat poenam. Importat autem motum voluntatis repudiantis malum, ut ipsum nomen *declinationis* ostendit. Et hoc est meritorium, praecipue quando aliquis impugnatur ut malum faciat, et resistit.

**AD TERTIUM** dicendum quod facere bonum est actus completivus iustitiae, et quasi pars principalis eius. Declinare autem a malo est actus imperfectior, et secundaria pars eius. Et ideo est quasi pars materialis, sine qua non potest esse pars formalis completiva.

which is hurtful to one's neighbor; while it belongs to general justice to do good in relation to the community or in relation to God, and to avoid the opposite evil.

Now these two are said to be quasi-integral parts of general or of special justice, because each is required for the perfect act of justice. For it belongs to justice to establish equality in our relations with others, as shown above (Q. 58, A. 2): and it pertains to the same cause to establish and to preserve that which it has established. Now a person establishes the equality of justice by doing good, i.e., by rendering to another his due: and he preserves the already established equality of justice by declining from evil, that is by inflicting no injury on his neighbor.

**REPLY OBJ. 1**: Good and evil are here considered under a special aspect, by which they are appropriated to justice. The reason why these two are reckoned parts of justice under a special aspect of good and evil, while they are not reckoned parts of any other moral virtue, is that the other moral virtues are concerned with the passions wherein to do good is to observe the mean, which is the same as to avoid the extremes as evils: so that doing good and avoiding evil come to the same, with regard to the other virtues. On the other hand justice is concerned with operations and external things, wherein to establish equality is one thing, and not to disturb the equality established is another.

**REPLY OBJ. 2**: To decline from evil, considered as a part of justice, does not denote a pure negation, viz. *not to do evil*; for this does not deserve the palm, but only avoids the punishment. But it implies a movement of the will in repudiating evil, as the very term *decline* shows. This is meritorious; especially when a person resists against an instigation to do evil.

**REPLY OBJ. 3**: Doing good is the completive act of justice, and the principal part, so to speak, thereof. Declining from evil is a more imperfect act, and a secondary part of that virtue. Hence it is a material part, so to speak, thereof, and a necessary condition of the formal and completive part.

# Article 2

*Whether transgression is a special sin?*

**AD SECUNDUM SIC PROCEDITUR.** Videtur quod transgressio non sit speciale peccatum. Nulla enim species ponitur in definitione generis. Sed transgressio ponitur in communi definitione peccati, dicit enim Ambrosius quod peccatum est *transgressio legis divinae.* Ergo transgressio non est species peccati.

**OBJECTION 1**: It would seem that transgression is not a special sin. For no species is included in the definition of its genus. Now transgression is included in the definition of sin; because Ambrose says (*De Parad.* viii) that sin is *a transgression of the Divine law.* Therefore transgression is not a species of sin.

**PRAETEREA**, nulla species excedit suum genus. Sed transgressio excedit peccatum, quia peccatum est *dictum vel factum vel concupitum contra legem Dei*, ut patet per Augustinum, XXII contra Faust.; transgressio est etiam contra naturam vel consuetudinem. Ergo transgressio non est species peccati.

**PRAETEREA**, nulla species continet sub se omnes partes in quas dividitur genus. Sed peccatum transgressionis se extendit ad omnia vitia capitalia, et etiam ad peccata cordis, oris et operis. Ergo transgressio non est speciale peccatum.

**SED CONTRA** est quod opponitur speciali virtuti, scilicet iustitiae.

**RESPONDEO** dicendum quod nomen transgressionis a corporalibus motibus ad morales actus derivatum est. Dicitur autem aliquis secundum corporalem motum transgredi ex eo quod *graditur trans* terminum sibi praefixum. Terminus autem praefigitur homini, ut ultra non transeat, in moralibus per praeceptum negativum. Et ideo transgressio proprie dicitur ex eo quod aliquis agit aliquid contra praeceptum negativum.

Quod quidem materialiter potest esse commune omnibus speciebus peccatorum, quia per quamlibet speciem peccati mortalis homo transgreditur aliquod praeceptum divinum. Sed si accipiatur formaliter, scilicet secundum hanc specialem rationem quod est facere contra praeceptum negativum, sic est speciale peccatum dupliciter. Uno quidem modo, secundum quod opponitur ad genera peccatorum opposita aliis virtutibus, sicut enim ad propriam rationem iustitiae legalis pertinet attendere debitum praecepti, ita ad propriam rationem transgressionis pertinet attendere contemptum praecepti. Alio modo, secundum quod distinguitur ab omissione, quae contrariatur praecepto affirmativo.

**AD PRIMUM** ergo dicendum quod sicut iustitia legalis est *omnis virtus* subiecto et quasi materialiter, ita etiam iniustitia legalis est materialiter omne peccatum. Et hoc modo peccatum definivit Ambrosius, secundum scilicet rationem iniustitiae legalis.

**AD SECUNDUM** dicendum quod inclinatio naturae pertinet ad praecepta legis naturalis. Consuetudo etiam honesta habet vim praecepti, quia ut Augustinus dicit, in epistola de ieiunio sabbati *mos populi Dei pro lege habendus est*. Et ideo tam peccatum quam transgressio potest esse contra consuetudinem honestam et contra inclinationem naturalem.

**AD TERTIUM** dicendum quod omnes enumeratae species peccatorum possunt habere transgressionem non secundum proprias rationes, sed secundum quandam specialem rationem, ut dictum est. Peccatum tamen omissionis omnino a transgressione distinguitur.

**OBJ. 2**: Further, no species is more comprehensive than its genus. But transgression is more comprehensive than sin, because sin is a *word, deed or desire against the law of God*, according to Augustine (*Contra Faust.* xxii, 27), while transgression is also against nature, or custom. Therefore transgression is not a species of sin.

**OBJ. 3**: Further, no species contains all the parts into which its genus is divided. Now the sin of transgression extends to all the capital vices, as well as to sins of thought, word and deed. Therefore transgression is not a special sin.

**ON THE CONTRARY**, It is opposed to a special virtue, namely justice.

**I ANSWER THAT**, The term transgression is derived from bodily movement and applied to moral actions. Now a person is said to transgress in bodily movement, when he steps (*graditur*) beyond (*trans*) a fixed boundary—and it is a negative precept that fixes the boundary that man must not exceed in his moral actions. Wherefore to transgress, properly speaking, is to act against a negative precept.

Now materially considered this may be common to all the species of sin, because man transgresses a Divine precept by any species of mortal sin. But if we consider it formally, namely under its special aspect of an act against a negative precept, it is a special sin in two ways. First, insofar as it is opposed to those kinds of sin that are opposed to the other virtues: for just as it belongs properly to legal justice to consider a precept as binding, so it belongs properly to a transgression to consider a precept as an object of contempt. Second, insofar as it is distinct from omission which is opposed to an affirmative precept.

**REPLY OBJ. 1**: Even as legal justice is *all virtue* (Q. 58, A. 5) as regards its subject and matter, so legal injustice is materially all sin. It is in this way that Ambrose defined sin, considering it from the point of view of legal injustice.

**REPLY OBJ. 2**: The natural inclination concerns the precepts of the natural law. Again, a laudable custom has the force of a precept; since as Augustine says in an epistle on the Fast of the Sabbath (*Ep. xxxvi*), *a custom of God's people should be looked upon as law*. Hence both sin and transgression may be against a laudable custom and against a natural inclination.

**REPLY OBJ. 3**: All these species of sin may include transgression, if we consider them not under their proper aspects, but under a special aspect, as stated above. The sin of omission, however, is altogether distinct from the sin of transgression.

# Article 3

*Whether omission is a special sin?*

**AD TERTIUM SIC PROCEDITUR**. Videtur quod omissio non sit speciale peccatum. Omne enim peccatum aut est originale aut actuale. Sed omissio non est originale peccatum, quia non contrahitur per originem. Nec est actuale, quia potest esse absque omni actu, ut supra habitum est, cum de peccatis in communi ageretur. Ergo omissio non est speciale peccatum.

**PRAETEREA**, omne peccatum est voluntarium. Sed omissio quandoque non est voluntaria, sed necessaria, puta cum mulier corrupta est quae virginitatem vovit; vel cum aliquis amittit rem quam restituere tenetur; vel cum sacerdos tenetur celebrare et habet aliquod impedimentum. Ergo omissio non semper est peccatum.

**PRAETEREA**, cuilibet speciali peccato est determinare aliquod tempus quando incipit esse. Sed hoc non est determinare in omissione, quia quandocumque non facit similiter se habet, nec tamen semper peccat. Ergo omissio non est speciale peccatum.

**PRAETEREA**, omne peccatum speciale speciali virtuti opponitur. Sed non est dare aliquam specialem virtutem cui omissio opponitur. Tum quia bonum cuiuslibet virtutis omitti potest. Tum quia iustitia, cui specialius videtur opponi, semper requirit aliquem actum, etiam in declinatione a malo, ut dictum est, omissio autem potest esse absque omni actu. Ergo omissio non est speciale peccatum.

**SED CONTRA** est quod dicitur Iac. IV, *scienti bonum et non facienti, peccatum est illi.*

**RESPONDEO** dicendum quod omissio importat praetermissionem boni, non autem cuiuscumque, sed boni debiti. Bonum autem sub ratione debiti pertinet proprie ad iustitiam, ad legalem quidem, si debitum accipiatur in ordine ad legem divinam vel humanam; ad specialem autem iustitiam, secundum quod debitum consideratur in ordine ad proximum. Unde eo modo quo iustitia est specialis virtus, ut supra habitum est, et omissio est speciale peccatum distinctum a peccatis quae opponuntur aliis virtutibus. Eo vero modo quo facere bonum, cui opponitur omissio, est quaedam specialis pars iustitiae distincta a declinatione mali, cui opponitur transgressio, etiam omissio a transgressione distinguitur.

**AD PRIMUM** ergo dicendum quod omissio non est peccatum originale, sed actuale, non quia habeat aliquem actum sibi essentialem; sed secundum quod negatio actus reducitur ad genus actus. Et secundum hoc non agere accipitur ut agere quoddam, sicut supra dictum est.

**AD SECUNDUM** dicendum quod omissio, sicut dictum est, non est nisi boni debiti, ad quod aliquis tenetur. Nullus autem tenetur ad impossibile. Unde nullus, si

**OBJECTION 1**: It would seem that omission is not a special sin. For every sin is either original or actual. Now omission is not original sin, for it is not contracted through origin; nor is it actual sin, for it may be altogether without act, as stated above (I-II, Q. 71, A. 5) when we were treating of sins in general. Therefore omission is not a special sin.

**OBJ. 2**: Further, every sin is voluntary. Now omission sometimes is not voluntary but necessary, as when a woman is violated after taking a vow of virginity, or when one lose that which one is under an obligation to restore, or when a priest is bound to say Mass, and is prevented from doing so. Therefore omission is not always a sin.

**OBJ. 3**: Further, it is possible to fix the time when any special sin begins. But this is not possible in the case of omission, since one is not altered by not doing a thing, no matter when the omission occurs, and yet the omission is not always sinful. Therefore omission is not a special sin.

**OBJ. 4**: Further, every special sin is opposed to a special virtue. But it is not possible to assign any special virtue to which omission is opposed, both because the good of any virtue can be omitted, and because justice to which it would seem more particularly opposed, always requires an act, even in declining from evil, as stated above (A. 1, ad 2), while omission may be altogether without act. Therefore omission is not a special sin.

**ON THE CONTRARY**, It is written (Jas 4:17): *To him . . . who knoweth to do good and doth it not, to him it is sin.*

**I ANSWER THAT**, omission signifies the non-fulfilment of a good, not indeed of any good, but of a good that is due. Now good under the aspect of due belongs properly to justice; to legal justice, if the thing due depends on Divine or human law; to special justice, if the due is something in relation to one's neighbor. Wherefore, in the same way as justice is a special virtue, as stated above (Q. 58, AA. 6, 7), omission is a special sin distinct from the sins which are opposed to the other virtues; and just as doing good, which is the opposite of omitting it, is a special part of justice, distinct from avoiding evil, to which transgression is opposed, so too is omission distinct from transgression.

**REPLY OBJ. 1**: Omission is not original but actual sin, not as though it had some act essential to it, but for as much as the negation of an act is reduced to the genus of act, and in this sense non-action is a kind of action, as stated above (I-II, Q. 71, A. 6, ad 1).

**REPLY OBJ. 2**: Omission, as stated above, is only of such good as is due and to which one is bound. Now no man is bound to the impossible: wherefore no man sins by

non facit id quod facere non potest, peccat per omissionem. Mulier ergo corrupta quae virginitatem vovit, non omittit virginitatem non habendo, sed non poenitendo de peccato praeterito, vel non faciendo quod potest ad votum adimplendum per continentiae observantiam. Sacerdos etiam non tenetur dicere Missam nisi supposita debita opportunitate, quae si desit, non omittit. Et similiter aliquis tenetur ad restitutionem, supposita facultate, quam si non habet nec habere potest, non omittit, dummodo faciat quod potest. Et idem dicendum est in aliis.

**AD TERTIUM** dicendum quod sicut peccatum transgressionis opponitur praeceptis negativis, quae pertinent ad declinandum a malo, ita peccatum omissionis opponitur praeceptis affirmativis, quae pertinent ad faciendum bonum. Praecepta autem affirmativa non obligant ad semper, sed ad tempus determinatum. Et pro illo tempore peccatum omissionis incipit esse. Potest tamen contingere quod aliquis tunc sit impotens ad faciendum quod debet. Quod quidem si sit praeter eius culpam, non omittit, ut dictum est. Si vero sit propter eius culpam praecedentem, puta cum aliquis de sero se inebriavit et non potest surgere ad matutinas ut debet, dicunt quidam quod tunc incoepit peccatum omissionis quando aliquis applicat se ad actum illicitum et incompossibilem cum illo actu ad quem tenetur. Sed hoc non videtur verum. Quia, dato quod excitaretur per violentiam et iret ad matutinas, non omitteret. Unde patet quod praecedens inebriatio non fuit omissio, sed omissionis causa. Unde dicendum est quod omissio incipit ei imputari ad culpam quando fuit tempus operandi, tamen propter causam praecedentem, ex qua omissio sequens redditur voluntaria.

**AD QUARTUM** dicendum quod omissio directe opponitur iustitiae, ut dictum est, non enim est omissio boni alicuius virtutis nisi sub ratione debiti, quod pertinet ad iustitiam. Plus autem requiritur ad actum virtutis meritorium quam ad demeritum culpae, quia *bonum est ex integra causa, malum autem ex singularibus defectibus*. Et ideo ad iustitiae meritum requiritur actus, non autem ad omissionem.

omission, if he does not do what he cannot. Accordingly she who is violated after vowing virginity, is guilty of an omission, not through not having virginity, but through not repenting of her past sin, or through not doing what she can to fulfill her vow by observing continence. Again a priest is not bound to say Mass, except he have a suitable opportunity, and if this be lacking, there is no omission. And in like manner, a person is bound to restitution, supposing he has the wherewithal; if he has not and cannot have it, he is not guilty of an omission, provided he does what he can. The same applies to other similar cases.

**REPLY OBJ. 3**: Just as the sin of transgression is opposed to negative precepts which regard the avoidance of evil, so the sin of omission is opposed to affirmative precepts, which regard the doing of good. Now affirmative precepts bind not for always, but for a fixed time, and at that time the sin of omission begins. But it may happen that then one is unable to do what one ought, and if this inability is without any fault on his part, he does not omit his duty, as stated above (ad 2; I-II, Q. 71, A. 5). On the other hand if this inability is due to some previous fault of his (for instance, if a man gets drunk at night, and cannot get up for matins, as he ought to), some say that the sin of omission begins when he engages in an action that is illicit and incompatible with the act to which he is bound. But this does not seem to be true, for supposing one were to rouse him by violence and that he went to matins, he would not omit to go, so that, evidently, the previous drunkenness was not an omission, but the cause of an omission. Consequently, we must say that the omission begins to be imputed to him as a sin, when the time comes for the action; and yet this is on account of a preceding cause by reason of which the subsequent omission becomes voluntary.

**REPLY OBJ. 4**: Omission is directly opposed to justice, as stated above; because it is a non-fulfilment of a good of virtue, but only under the aspect of due, which pertains to justice. Now more is required for an act to be virtuous and meritorious than for it to be sinful and demeritorious, because *good results from an entire cause, whereas evil arises from each single defect*. Wherefore the merit of justice requires an act, whereas an omission does not.

# Article 4

*Whether a sin of omission is more grievous than a sin of transgression?*

**AD QUARTUM SIC PROCEDITUR**. Videtur quod peccatum omissionis sit gravius quam peccatum transgressionis. Delictum enim videtur idem esse quod *derelictum*, et sic per consequens videtur idem esse omissioni. Sed delictum est gravius quam peccatum transgressionis, quia maiori expiatione indigebat, ut pa-

**OBJECTION 1**: It would seem that a sin of omission is more grievous than a sin of transgression. For *delictum* would seem to signify the same as *derelictum*, and therefore is seemingly the same as an omission. But delictum denotes a more grievous offense than transgression, because it deserves more expiation as appears from Lev. 5. Therefore the

tet Levit. V. Ergo peccatum omissionis est gravius quam peccatum transgressionis.

PRAETEREA, maiori bono maius malum opponitur, ut patet per philosophum, in VIII Ethic. Sed facere bonum, cui opponitur omissio, est nobilior pars iustitiae quam declinare a malo, cui opponitur transgressio, ut ex supradictis patet. Ergo omissio est gravius peccatum quam transgressio.

PRAETEREA, peccatum commissionis potest esse et veniale et mortale. Sed peccatum omissionis videtur esse semper mortale, quia opponitur praecepto affirmativo. Ergo omissio videtur esse gravius peccatum quam sit transgressio.

PRAETEREA, maior poena est poena damni, scilicet carentia visionis divinae, quae debetur peccato omissionis, quam poena sensus, quae debetur peccato transgressionis, ut patet per Chrysostomum super Matth. Sed poena proportionatur culpae. Ergo gravius est peccatum omissionis quam transgressionis.

SED CONTRA est quod facilius est abstinere a malo faciendo quam implere bonum. Ergo gravius peccat qui non abstinet a malo faciendo, quod est transgredi, quam qui non implet bonum, quod est omittere.

RESPONDEO dicendum quod peccatum intantum est grave inquantum a virtute distat. Contrarietas autem est maxima distantia, ut dicitur in X Metaphys. unde contrarium magis distat a suo contrario quam simplex eius negatio, sicut nigrum plus distat ab albo quam simpliciter non album; omne enim nigrum est non album, sed non convertitur. Manifestum est autem quod transgressio contrariatur actui virtutis, omissio autem importat negationem ipsius, puta peccatum omissionis est si quis parentibus debitam reverentiam non exhibeat, peccatum autem transgressionis si contumeliam vel quamcumque iniuriam eis inferat. Unde manifestum est quod, simpliciter et absolute loquendo, transgressio est gravius peccatum quam omissio, licet aliqua omissio possit esse gravior aliqua transgressione.

AD PRIMUM ergo dicendum quod delictum communiter sumptum significat quamcumque omissionem. Quandoque tamen stricte accipitur pro eo quod omittitur aliquid de his quae pertinent ad Deum, vel quando scienter et quasi cum quodam contemptu derelinquit homo id quod facere debet. Et sic habet quandam gravitatem, ratione cuius maiori expiatione indiget.

AD SECUNDUM dicendum quod ei quod est facere bonum opponitur et non facere bonum, quod est omittere, et facere malum, quod est transgredi, sed primum contradictorie, secundum contrarie, quod importat maiorem distantiam. Et ideo transgressio est gravius peccatum.

AD TERTIUM dicendum quod sicut omissio opponitur praeceptis affirmativis, ita transgressio opponitur

sin of omission is more grievous than the sin of transgression.

OBJ. 2: Further, the greater evil is opposed to the greater good, as the Philosopher declares (*Ethic.* viii, 10). Now to do good is a more excellent part of justice, than to decline from evil, to which transgression is opposed, as stated above (A. 1, ad 3). Therefore omission is a graver sin than transgression.

OBJ. 3: Further, sins of transgression may be either venial or mortal. But sins of omission seem to be always mortal, since they are opposed to an affirmative precept. Therefore omission would seem to be a graver sin than transgression.

OBJ. 4: Further, the pain of loss which consists in being deprived of seeing God and is inflicted for the sin of omission, is a greater punishment than the pain of sense, which is inflicted for the sin of transgression, as Chrysostom states (*Hom. xxiii super Matth.*). Now punishment is proportionate to fault. Therefore the sin of omission is graver than the sin of transgression.

ON THE CONTRARY, It is easier to refrain from evil deeds than to accomplish good deeds. Therefore it is a graver sin not to refrain from an evil deed, i.e., to transgress, than not to accomplish a good deed, which is to omit.

I ANSWER THAT, The gravity of a sin depends on its remoteness from virtue. Now contrariety is the greatest remoteness, according to *Metaph.* x. Wherefore a thing is further removed from its contrary than from its simple negation; thus black is further removed from white than not-white is, since every black is not-white, but not conversely. Now it is evident that transgression is contrary to an act of virtue, while omission denotes the negation thereof: for instance it is a sin of omission, if one fail to give one's parents due reverence, while it is a sin of transgression to revile them or injure them in any way. Hence it is evident that, simply and absolutely speaking, transgression is a graver sin than omission, although a particular omission may be graver than a particular transgression.

REPLY OBJ. 1: *Delictum* in its widest sense denotes any kind of omission; but sometimes it is taken strictly for the omission of something concerning God, or for a man's intentional and as it were contemptuous dereliction of duty: and then it has a certain gravity, for which reason it demands a greater expiation.

REPLY OBJ. 2: The opposite of doing good is both not doing good, which is an omission, and doing evil, which is a transgression: but the first is opposed by contradiction, the second by contrariety, which implies greater remoteness: wherefore transgression is the more grievous sin.

REPLY OBJ. 3: Just as omission is opposed to affirmative precepts, so is transgression opposed to negative precepts:

praeceptis negativis. Et ideo utrumque, si proprie accipiatur, importat rationem peccati mortalis. Potest autem large dici transgressio vel omissio ex eo quod aliquid sit praeter praecepta affirmativa vel negativa, disponens ad oppositum ipsorum. Et sic utrumque, large accipiendo, potest esse peccatum veniale.

**AD QUARTUM** dicendum quod peccato transgressionis respondet et poena damni, propter aversionem a Deo; et poena sensus, propter inordinatam conversionem ad bonum commutabile. Similiter etiam omissioni non solum debetur poena damni, sed etiam poena sensus, secundum illud Matth. VII, *omnis arbor quae non facit fructum bonum, excidetur et in ignem mittetur*. Et hoc propter radicem ex qua procedit, licet non habeat ex necessitate actualem conversionem ad aliquod bonum commutabile.

wherefore both, strictly speaking, have the character of mortal sin. Transgression and omission, however, may be taken broadly for any infringement of an affirmative or negative precept, disposing to the opposite of such precept: and so taking both in a broad sense they may be venial sins.

**REPLY OBJ. 4**: To the sin of transgression there correspond both the pain of loss on account of the aversion from God, and the pain of sense, on account of the inordinate conversion to a mutable good. In like manner omission deserves not only the pain of loss, but also the pain of sense, according to Matt. 7:19, *Every tree that bringeth not forth good fruit shall be cut down, and shall be cast into the fire*; and this on account of the root from which it grows, although it does not necessarily imply conversion to any mutable good.

## THE POTENTIAL PARTS OF JUSTICE

Deinde considerandum est de partibus potentialibus iustitiae, idest de virtutibus ei annexis. Et circa hoc duo sunt consideranda primo quidem, quae virtutes iustitiae annectantur; secundo, considerandum est de singulis virtutibus iustitiae annexis.

We must now consider the potential parts of justice, namely the virtues annexed thereto; under which head there are two points of consideration: (1) What virtues are annexed to justice? (2) The individual virtues annexed to justice.

# Article 1

*Whether the virtues annexed to justice are suitably enumerated?*

**AD PRIMUM SIC PROCEDITUR.** Videtur quod inconvenienter assignentur virtutes iustitiae annexae. Tullius enim enumerat sex, scilicet *religionem, pietatem, gratiam, vindicationem, observantiam, veritatem.* Vindicatio autem videtur species esse commutativae iustitiae, secundum quam illatis iniuriis vindicta rependitur, ut ex supradictis patet. Non ergo debet poni inter virtutes iustitiae annexas.

**PRAETEREA,** Macrobius, super somnium Scipionis, ponit septem, scilicet *innocentiam, amicitiam, concordiam, pietatem, religionem, affectum, humanitatem*; quarum plures a Tullio praetermittuntur. Ergo videtur insufficienter enumeratas esse virtutes iustitiae adiunctas.

**PRAETEREA,** a quibusdam aliis ponuntur quinque partes iustitiae, scilicet *obedientia* respectu superioris, *disciplina* respectu inferioris, *aequitas* respectu aequalium, *fides* et *veritas* respectu omnium; de quibus a Tullio non ponitur nisi *veritas.* Ergo videtur insufficienter numerasse virtutes iustitiae annexas.

**PRAETEREA,** Andronicus Peripateticus ponit novem partes iustitiae annexas, *scilicet liberalitatem, benignitatem, vindicativam, eugnomosynam, eusebiam, Eucharistiam, sanctitatem, bonam commutationem, legispositivam*; ex quibus etiam Tullius manifeste non ponit nisi vindicativam. Ergo videtur insufficienter enumerasse.

**PRAETEREA,** Aristoteles, in V Ethic., ponit *epieikeiam* iustitiae adiunctam, de qua in nulla praemissarum assignationum videtur mentio esse facta. Ergo insufficienter sunt enumeratae virtutes iustitiae annexae.

**RESPONDEO** dicendum quod in virtutibus quae adiunguntur alicui principali virtuti duo sunt consideranda, primo quidem, quod virtutes illae in aliquo cum principali virtute conveniant; secundo, quod in aliquo deficiant a perfecta ratione ipsius. Quia vero iustitia ad

**OBJECTION 1**: It would seem that the virtues annexed to justice are unsuitably enumerated. Tully reckons six, viz. *religion, piety, gratitude, revenge, observance, truth.* Now revenge is seemingly a species of commutative justice whereby revenge is taken for injuries inflicted, as stated above (Q. 61, A. 4). Therefore it should not be reckoned among the virtues annexed to justice.

**OBJ. 2**: Further, Macrobius (*Super Somn. Scip.* i, 8) reckons seven, viz. *innocence, friendship, concord, piety, religion, affection, humanity,* several of which are omitted by Tully. Therefore the virtues annexed to justice would seem to be insufficiently enumerated.

**OBJ. 3**: Further, others reckon five parts of justice, viz. *obedience* in respect of one's superiors, *discipline* with regard to inferiors, *equity* as regards equals, *fidelity* and *truthfulness* towards all; and of these *truthfulness* alone is mentioned by Tully. Therefore he would seem to have enumerated insufficiently the virtues annexed to justice.

**OBJ. 4**: Further, the peripatetic Andronicus reckons nine parts annexed to justice viz. *liberality, kindliness, revenge, commonsense, piety, gratitude, holiness, just exchange* and *just lawgiving*; and of all these it is evident that Tully mentions none but *revenge.* Therefore he would appear to have made an incomplete enumeration.

**OBJ. 5**: Further, Aristotle (*Ethic.* v, 10) mentions *epieikeia* as being annexed to justice: and yet seemingly it is not included in any of the foregoing enumerations. Therefore the virtues annexed to justice are insufficiently enumerated.

**I ANSWER THAT,** Two points must be observed about the virtues annexed to a principal virtue. The first is that these virtues have something in common with the principal virtue; and the second is that in some respect they fall short of the perfection of that virtue. Accordingly since justice

alterum est, ut ex supradictis patet, omnes virtutes quae ad alterum sunt possunt ratione convenientiae iustitiae annecti. Ratio vero iustitiae consistit in hoc quod alteri reddatur quod ei debetur secundum aequalitatem, ut ex supradictis patet. Dupliciter igitur aliqua virtus ad alterum existens a ratione iustitiae deficit, uno quidem modo, inquantum deficit a ratione aequalis; alio modo, inquantum deficit a ratione debiti. Sunt enim quaedam virtutes quae debitum quidem alteri reddunt, sed non possunt reddere aequale. Et primo quidem, quidquid ab homine Deo redditur, debitum est, non tamen potest esse aequale, ut scilicet tantum ei homo reddat quantum debet; secundum illud Psalm., *quid retribuam domino pro omnibus quae retribuit mihi?* Et secundum hoc adiungitur iustitiae religio, quae, ut Tullius dicit, *superioris cuiusdam naturae, quam divinam vocant, curam caeremoniamque vel cultum affert.* Secundo, parentibus non potest secundum aequalitatem recompensari quod eis debetur, ut patet per philosophum, in VIII Ethic. Et sic adiungitur iustitiae *pietas, per quam,* ut Tullius dicit, *sanguine iunctis patriaeque benevolis officium et diligens tribuitur cultus.* Tertio, non potest secundum aequale praemium recompensari ab homine virtuti, ut patet per philosophum, in IV Ethic. Et sic adiungitur iustitiae *observantia, per quam,* ut Tullius dicit, *homines aliqua dignitate antecedentes quodam cultu et honore dignantur.*

A ratione vero debiti iustitiae defectus potest attendi secundum quod est duplex debitum, scilicet morale et legale, unde et philosophus, in VIII Ethic., secundum hoc duplex iustum assignat. Debitum quidem legale est ad quod reddendum aliquis lege adstringitur, et tale debitum proprie attendit iustitia quae est principalis virtus. Debitum autem morale est quod aliquis debet ex honestate virtutis. Et quia debitum necessitatem importat, ideo tale debitum habet duplicem gradum. Quoddam enim est sic necessarium ut sine eo honestas morum conservari non possit, et hoc habet plus de ratione debiti. Et potest hoc debitum attendi ex parte ipsius debentis. Et sic ad hoc debitum pertinet quod homo talem se exhibeat alteri in verbis et factis qualis est. Et ita adiungitur iustitiae *veritas, per quam,* ut Tullius dicit, *immutata ea quae sunt aut fuerunt aut futura sunt, dicuntur.* Potest etiam attendi ex parte eius cui debetur, prout scilicet aliquis recompensat alicui secundum ea quae fecit. Quandoque quidem in bonis. Et sic adiungitur iustitiae *gratia, in qua,* ut Tullius dicit, *amicitiarum et officiorum alterius memoria, remunerandi voluntas continetur alterius.* Quandoque vero in malis. Et sic adiungitur iustitiae *vindicatio, per quam,* ut Tullius dicit, *vis aut*

is of one man to another as stated above (Q. 58, A. 2), all the virtues that are directed to another person may by reason of this common aspect be annexed to justice. Now the essential character of justice consists in rendering to another his due according to equality, as stated above (Q. 58, A. 11). Wherefore in two ways may a virtue directed to another person fall short of the perfection of justice: first, by falling short of the aspect of equality; second, by falling short of the aspect of due. For certain virtues there are which render another his due, but are unable to render the equal due. In the first place, whatever man renders to God is due, yet it cannot be equal, as though man rendered to God as much as he owes Him, according to Ps. 115:12, *What shall I render to the Lord for all the things that He hath rendered to me?* In this respect religion is annexed to justice since, according to Tully (*De invent.* ii, 53), it consists in offering service and ceremonial rites or worship to *some superior nature that men call divine.* Second, it is not possible to make to one's parents an equal return of what one owes to them, as the Philosopher declares (*Ethic.* viii, 14); and thus *piety* is annexed to justice, *for thereby,* as Tully says (*De invent.* ii, 53), a man *renders service and constant deference to his kindred and the well-wishers of his country.* Third, according to the Philosopher (*Ethic.* iv, 3), man is unable to offer an equal meed for virtue, and thus *observance* is annexed to justice, *consisting,* according to Tully (*De invent.* ii, 53), in the *deference and honor rendered to those who excel in worth.*

A falling short of the just due may be considered in respect of a twofold due, moral or legal: wherefore the Philosopher (*Ethic.* viii, 13) assigns a corresponding twofold just. The legal due is that which one is bound to render by reason of a legal obligation; and this due is chiefly the concern of justice, which is the principal virtue. On the other hand, the moral due is that to which one is bound in respect of the rectitude of virtue: and since a due implies necessity, this kind of due has two degrees. For one due is so necessary that without it moral rectitude cannot be ensured: and this has more of the character of due. Moreover this due may be considered from the point of view of the debtor, and in this way it pertains to this kind of due that a man represent himself to others just as he is, both in word and deed. Wherefore to justice is annexed *truth, whereby,* as Tully says (*De invent.* ii, 53), *present, past and future things are told without perversion.* It may also be considered from the point of view of the person to whom it is due, by comparing the reward he receives with what he has done—sometimes in good things; and then annexed to justice we have *gratitude,* which *consists in recollecting the friendship and kindliness shown by others, and in desiring to pay them back,* as Tully states (*De invent.* ii, 53)—and

*iniuria, et omnino quidquid obscurum est, defendendo aut ulciscendo propulsatur.*

Aliud vero debitum est necessarium sicut conferens ad maiorem honestatem, sine quo tamen honestas conservari potest. Quod quidem debitum attendit *liberalitas, affabilitas* sive *amicitia*, et alia huiusmodi. Quae Tullius praetermittit in praedicta enumeratione, quia parum habent de ratione debiti.

**AD PRIMUM** ergo dicendum quod vindicta quae fit auctoritate publicae potestatis secundum sententiam iudicis, pertinet ad iustitiam commutativam. Sed vindicta quam quis facit proprio motu, non tamen contra legem, vel quam quis a iudice requirit, pertinet ad virtutem iustitiae adiunctam.

**AD SECUNDUM** dicendum quod Macrobius videtur attendisse ad duas partes integrales iustitiae, scilicet declinare a malo, ad quod pertinet *innocentia*; et facere bonum, ad quod pertinent sex alia. Quorum duo videntur pertinere ad aequales, scilicet *amicitia* in exteriori convictu, et *concordia* interius. Duo vero pertinent ad superiores, *pietas* ad parentes, et *religio* ad Deum. Duo vero ad inferiores, scilicet *affectus*, inquantum placent bona eorum; et *humanitas*, per quam subvenitur eorum defectibus. Dicit enim Isidorus, in libro Etymol., quod *humanus dicitur aliquis quia habeat circa hominem amorem et miserationis affectum, unde humanitas dicta est qua nos invicem tuemur.* Et secundum hoc amicitia sumitur prout ordinat exteriorem convictum, sicut de ea philosophus tractat in IV Ethic. Potest etiam *amicitia* sumi secundum quod proprie respicit affectum, prout determinatur a philosopho in VIII et in IX Ethic. Et sic ad amicitiam pertinent tria, scilicet benevolentia, quae hic dicitur *affectus*; et *concordia*; et *beneficentia*, quae hic vocatur humanitas. Haec autem Tullius praetermisit, quia parum habent de ratione debiti, ut dictum est.

**AD TERTIUM** dicendum quod *obedientia* includitur in *observantia*, quam Tullius ponit, nam praecellentibus personis debetur et reverentia honoris et obedientia. *Fides* autem, *per quam fiunt dicta*, includitur in *veritate*, quantum ad observantiam promissorum. Veritas autem in plus se habet, ut infra patebit. *Disciplina* autem non debetur ex debito necessitatis, quia inferiori non est aliquis obligatus, inquantum est inferior (potest tamen aliquis superiori obligari ut inferioribus provideat, secundum illud Matth. XXIV, *fidelis servus et prudens, quem constituit dominus super familiam suam*). Et ideo a Tullio praetermittitur. Potest autem contineri sub *humanitate*, quam Macrobius ponit. *Aequitas* vero sub *epieikeia*, vel *amicitia*.

sometimes in evil things, and then to justice is annexed *revenge*, whereby, as Tully states (*De invent.* ii, 53), *we resist force, injury or anything obscure by taking vengeance or by self-defense.*

There is another due that is necessary in the sense that it conduces to greater rectitude, although without it rectitude may be ensured. This due is the concern of *liberality, affability* or *friendship*, or the like, all of which Tully omits in the aforesaid enumeration because there is little of the nature of anything due in them.

**REPLY OBJ. 1**: The revenge taken by authority of a public power, in accordance with a judge's sentence, belongs to commutative justice: whereas the revenge which a man takes on his own initiative, though not against the law, or which a man seeks to obtain from a judge, belongs to the virtue annexed to justice.

**REPLY OBJ. 2**: Macrobius appears to have considered the two integral parts of justice, namely, declining from evil, to which *innocence* belongs, and doing good, to which the six others belong. Of these, two would seem to regard relations between equals, namely, *friendship* in the external conduct and *concord* internally; two regard our relations toward superiors, namely, *piety* to parents, and *religion* to God; while two regard our relations towards inferiors, namely, *condescension*, insofar as their good pleases us, and *humanity*, whereby we help them in their needs. For Isidore says (*Etym.* x) that a man is said to be *humane, through having a feeling of love and pity towards men: this gives its name to humanity whereby we uphold one another.* In this sense friendship is understood as directing our external conduct towards others, from which point of view the Philosopher treats of it in *Ethic.* iv, 6. *Friendship* may also be taken as regarding properly the affections, and as the Philosopher describes it in *Ethic.* viii and ix. In this sense three things pertain to friendship, namely, benevolence which is here called *affection*; *concord*, and beneficence which is here called *humanity*. These three, however, are omitted by Tully, because, as stated above, they have little of the nature of a due.

**REPLY OBJ. 3**: *Obedience* is included in *observance*, which Tully mentions, because both reverential honor and obedience are due to persons who excel. *Faithfulness whereby a man's acts agree with his words*, is contained in *truthfulness* as to the observance of one's promises: yet truthfulness covers a wider ground, as we shall state further on (Q. 109, AA. 1, 3). *Discipline* is not due as a necessary duty, because one is under no obligation to an inferior as such, although a superior may be under an obligation to watch over his inferiors, according to Matt. 24:45, *A faithful and wise servant, whom his lord hath appointed over his family*: and for this reason it is omitted by Tully. It may, however, be included in *humanity* mentioned by Macrobius; and *equity* under *epieikeia* or under *friendship*.

**AD QUARTUM** dicendum quod in illa enumeratione ponuntur quaedam pertinentia ad veram iustitiam. Ad particularem quidem, *bona commutatio*, de qua dicit quod est *habitus in commutationibus aequalitatem custodiens*. Ad legalem autem iustitiam, quantum ad ea quae communiter sunt observanda, ponitur *legispositiva*, quae, ut ipse dicit, est *scientia commutationum politicarum ad communitatem relatarum*. Quantum vero ad ea quae quandoque particulariter agenda occurrunt praeter communes leges, ponitur *eugnomosyna*, quasi *bona gnome*, quae est in talibus directiva, ut supra habitum est in tractatu de prudentia. Et ideo dicit de ea quod est *voluntaria iustificatio*, quia scilicet ex proprio arbitrio id quod iustum est homo secundum eam servat, non secundum legem scriptam. Attribuuntur autem haec duo prudentiae secundum directionem, iustitiae vero secundum executionem. *Eusebia* vero dicitur quasi *bonus cultus*. Unde est idem quod *religio*. Ideo de ea dicit quod est *scientia Dei famulatus* (et loquitur secundum modum quo Socrates dicebat omnes virtutes esse scientias). Et ad idem reducitur sanctitas, ut post dicetur. *Eucharistia* autem est idem quod *bona gratia*, quam Tullius ponit, sicut et *vindicativam*. *Benignitas* autem videtur esse idem cum affectu, quem ponit Macrobius. Unde et Isidorus dicit, in libro Etymol., quod *benignus est vir sponte ad benefaciendum paratus, et dulcis ad eloquium*. Et ipse Andronicus dicit quod *benignitas est habitus voluntarie benefactivus*. Liberalitas autem videtur ad *humanitatem* pertinere.

**AD QUINTUM** dicendum quod *epieikeia* non adiungitur iustitiae particulari, sed legali. Et videtur esse idem cum ea quae dicta est *eugnomosyna*.

**REPLY OBJ. 4:** This enumeration contains some belonging to true justice. To particular justice belongs *justice of exchange*, which he describes as *the habit of observing equality in commutations*. To legal justice, as regards things to be observed by all, he ascribes *legislative justice*, which he describes as *the science of political commutations relating to the community*. As regards things which have to be done in particular cases beside the general laws, he mentions *common sense* or *good judgment*, which is our guide in such like matters, as stated above (Q. 51, A. 4) in the treatise on prudence: wherefore he says that it is a *voluntary justification*, because by his own free will man observes what is just according to his judgment and not according to the written law. These two are ascribed to prudence as their director, and to justice as their executor. *Eusebeia* (piety) means *good worship* and consequently is the same as *religion*, wherefore he says that it is the science of *the service of God* (he speaks after the manner of Socrates who said that 'all the virtues are sciences'): and holiness comes to the same, as we shall state further on (Q. 81, A. 8). *Eucharistia* (gratitude) means *good thanksgiving*, and is mentioned by Macrobius: wherefore Isidore says (*Etym.* x) that *a kind man is one who is ready of his own accord to do good, and is of gentle speech*: and Andronicus too says that *kindliness is a habit of voluntary beneficence*. Liberality would seem to pertain to *humanity*.

**REPLY OBJ. 5:** *Epieikeia* is annexed, not to particular but to legal justice, and apparently is the same as that which goes by the name of *eugnomosyne* (common sense).

# QUESTION 81

Deinde considerandum est de singulis praedictarum virtutum, quantum ad praesentem intentionem pertinet. Et primo considerandum est de religione; secundo, de pietate; tertio, de observantia; quarto, de gratia; quinto, de vindicta; sexto, de veritate; septimo, de amicitia; octavo, de liberalitate; nono, de epieikeia. De aliis autem hic enumeratis supra dictum est, partim in tractatu de caritate, scilicet de concordia et aliis huiusmodi; partim in hoc tractatu de iustitia, sicut de bona commutatione et innocentia; de legispositiva autem in tractatu de prudentia.

Circa religionem vero tria consideranda occurrunt, primo quidem, de ipsa religione secundum se; secundo, de actibus eius; tertio, de vitiis oppositis.

Circa primum quaeruntur octo.

Primo, utrum religio consistat tantum in ordine ad Deum.

Secundo, utrum religio sit virtus.

Tertio, utrum religio sit una virtus.

Quarto, utrum religio sit specialis virtus.

Quinto, utrum religio sit virtus theologica.

Sexto, utrum religio sit praeferenda aliis virtutibus moralibus.

Septimo, utrum religio habeat exteriores actus.

Octavo, utrum religio sit eadem sanctitati.

We must now consider each of the foregoing virtues, insofar as our present scope demands. We shall consider (1) religion, (2) piety, (3) observance, (4) gratitude, (5) revenge, (6) truth, (7) friendship, (8) liberality, (9) epieikeia. Of the other virtues that have been mentioned we have spoken partly in the treatise on charity, viz. of concord and the like, and partly in this treatise on justice, for instance, of right commutations and of innocence. Of legislative justice we spoke in the treatise on prudence.

Religion offers a threefold consideration: (1) Religion considered in itself; (2) its acts; (3) the opposite vices.

Under the first head there are eight points of inquiry:

(1) Whether religion regards only our relation to God?

(2) Whether religion is a virtue?

(3) Whether religion is one virtue?

(4) Whether religion is a special virtue?

(5) Whether religion is a theological virtue?

(6) Whether religion should be preferred to the other moral virtues?

(7) Whether religion has any external actions?

(8) Whether religion is the same as holiness?

# Article 1

*Whether religion directs man to God alone?*

**AD PRIMUM SIC PROCEDITUR.** Videtur quod religio non ordinet hominem solum ad Deum. Dicitur enim Iac. I, *religio munda et immaculata apud Deum et patrem haec est, visitare pupillos et viduas in tribulatione eorum, et immaculatum se custodire ab hoc saeculo.* Sed visitare pupillos et viduas dicitur secundum ordinem ad proximum, quod autem dicit *immaculatum se custodire ab hoc saeculo*, pertinet ad ordinem quo ordinatur homo in seipso. Ergo religio non solum dicitur in ordine ad Deum.

**PRAETEREA,** Augustinus dicit, in X de Civ. Dei, *quia Latina loquendi consuetudine, non imperitorum, verum etiam doctissimorum, cognationibus humanis atque affinitatibus et quibuscumque necessitudinibus dicitur exhibenda religio; non eo vocabulo vitatur ambiguum cum de cultu deitatis vertitur quaestio, ut fidenter dicere*

**OBJECTION 1:** It would seem that religion does not direct man to God alone. It is written (Jas 1:27): *Religion clean and undefiled before God and the Father is this, to visit the fatherless and widows in their tribulation, and to keep oneself unspotted from this world.* Now *to visit the fatherless and widows* indicates an order between oneself and one's neighbor, and *to keep oneself unspotted from this world* belongs to the order of a man within himself. Therefore religion does not imply order to God alone.

**OBJ. 2:** Further, Augustine says (*De Civ. Dei* x, 1) that since in speaking Latin not only unlettered but even most cultured persons ere wont to speak of religion as being exhibited, to our human kindred and relations as also to those who are linked with us by any kind of tie, that term does not escape ambiguity when it is a question of Divine worship, so that

*valeamus religionem non esse nisi cultum Dei. Ergo religio dicitur non solum in ordine ad Deum, sed etiam in ordine ad propinquos.*

**Praeterea**, ad religionem videtur latria pertinere. *Latria* autem *interpretatur servitus*, ut Augustinus dicit, in X de Civ. Dei. Servire autem debemus non solum Deo, sed etiam proximis, secundum illud Gal. V, *per caritatem spiritus servite invicem.* Ergo religio importat etiam ordinem ad proximum.

**Praeterea**, ad religionem pertinet cultus. Sed homo dicitur non solum colere Deum, sed etiam proximum, secundum illud Catonis, *cole parentes.* Ergo etiam religio nos ordinat ad proximum, et non solum ad Deum.

**Praeterea**, omnes in statu salutis existentes Deo sunt subiecti. Non autem dicuntur religiosi omnes qui sunt in statu salutis, sed solum illi qui quibusdam votis et observantiis et ad obediendum aliquibus hominibus se adstringunt. Ergo religio non videtur importare ordinem subiectionis hominis ad Deum.

**Sed contra** est quod Tullius dicit, II Rhet., quod *religio est quae superioris naturae, quam divinam vocant, curam caeremoniamque affert.*

**Respondeo** dicendum quod, sicut Isidorus dicit, in libro Etymol., *religiosus, ut ait Cicero, a religione appellatus, qui retractat et tanquam relegit ea quae ad cultum divinum pertinent.* Et sic religio videtur dicta a religendo ea quae sunt divini cultus, quia huiusmodi sunt frequenter in corde revolvenda, secundum illud Prov. III, *in omnibus viis tuis cogita illum.* Quamvis etiam possit intelligi religio ex hoc dicta quod *Deum reeligere debemus, quem amiseramus negligentes,* sicut Augustinus dicit, X de Civ. Dei. Vel potest intelligi religio a religando dicta, unde Augustinus dicit, in libro de vera Relig., *religet nos religio uni omnipotenti Deo.* Sive autem religio dicatur a frequenti lectione, sive ex iterata electione eius quod negligenter amissum est, sive a religatione, religio proprie importat ordinem ad Deum. Ipse enim est cui principaliter alligari debemus, tanquam indeficienti principio; ad quem etiam nostra electio assidue dirigi debet, sicut in ultimum finem; quem etiam negligenter peccando amittimus, et credendo et fidem protestando recuperare debemus.

**Ad primum** ergo dicendum quod religio habet duplices actus. Quosdam quidem proprios et immediatos, quos elicit, per quos homo ordinatur ad solum Deum, sicut sacrificare, adorare et alia huiusmodi. Alios autem actus habet quos producit mediantibus virtutibus quibus imperat, ordinans eos in divinam reverentiam, quia scilicet virtus ad quam pertinet finis, imperat virtutibus ad quas pertinent ea quae sunt ad finem. Et secundum hoc actus religionis per modum imperii ponitur esse *visitare*

*we be able to say without hesitation that religion is nothing else but the worship of God.* Therefore religion signifies a relation not only to God but also to our kindred.

**Obj. 3**: Further, seemingly latria pertains to religion. Now *latria signifies servitude*, as Augustine states (*De Civ. Dei* x, 1). And we are bound to serve not only God, but also our neighbor, according to Gal. 5:13, *By charity of the spirit serve one another.* Therefore religion includes a relation to one's neighbor also.

**Obj. 4**: Further, worship belongs to religion. Now man is said to worship not only God, but also his neighbor, according to the saying of Cato, *Worship thy parents.* Therefore religion directs us also to our neighbor, and not only to God.

**Obj. 5**: Further, all those who are in the state of grace are subject to God. Yet not all who are in a state of grace are called religious, but only those who bind themselves by certain vows and observances, and to obedience to certain men. Therefore religion seemingly does not denote a relation of subjection of man to God.

**On the contrary,** Tully says (*Rhet.* ii, 53) that *religion consists in offering service and ceremonial rites to a superior nature that men call divine.*

**I answer that,** as Isidore says (*Etym.* x), *according to Cicero, a man is said to be religious from religio, because he often ponders over, and, as it were, reads again (relegit), the things which pertain to the worship of God,* so that religion would seem to take its name from reading over those things which belong to Divine worship because we ought frequently to ponder over such things in our hearts, according to Prov. 3:6, *In all thy ways think on Him.* According to Augustine (*De Civ. Dei* x, 3) it may also take its name from the fact that *we ought to seek God again, whom we had lost by our neglect.* Or again, religion may be derived from *religare* (to bind together), wherefore Augustine says (*De Vera Relig.* 55): *May religion bind us to the one Almighty God.* However, whether religion take its name from frequent reading, or from a repeated choice of what has been lost through negligence, or from being a bond, it denotes properly a relation to God. For it is He to Whom we ought to be bound as to our unfailing principle; to Whom also our choice should be resolutely directed as to our last end; and Whom we lose when we neglect Him by sin, and should recover by believing in Him and confessing our faith.

**Reply Obj. 1**: Religion has two kinds of acts. Some are its proper and immediate acts, which it elicits, and by which man is directed to God alone, for instance, sacrifice, adoration and the like. But it has other acts, which it produces through the medium of the virtues which it commands, directing them to the honor of God, because the virtue which is concerned with the end, commands the virtues which are concerned with the means. Accordingly *to visit the fatherless and widows in their tribulation* is an act

*pupillos et viduas in tribulatione eorum*, quod est actus elicitus a misericordia, *immaculatum* autem *custodire se ab hoc saeculo* imperative quidem est religionis, elicitive autem temperantiae vel alicuius huiusmodi virtutis.

AD SECUNDUM dicendum quod religio refertur ad ea quae exhibentur cognationibus humanis, extenso nomine religionis, non autem secundum quod religio proprie dicitur. Unde Augustinus, parum ante verba inducta, praemittit, *religio distinctius non quemlibet, sed Dei cultum significare videtur.*

AD TERTIUM dicendum quod cum servus dicatur ad dominum, necesse est quod ubi est propria et specialis ratio dominii, ibi sit specialis et propria ratio servitutis. Manifestum est autem quod dominium convenit Deo secundum propriam et singularem quandam rationem, quia scilicet ipse omnia fecit, et quia summum in omnibus rebus obtinet principatum. Et ideo specialis ratio servitutis ei debetur. Et talis servitus nomine latriae designatur apud Graecos. Et ideo ad religionem proprie pertinet.

AD QUARTUM dicendum quod colere dicimus homines quos honorificatione, vel recordatione, vel praesentia frequentamus. Et etiam aliqua quae nobis subiecta sunt coli a nobis dicuntur, sicut agricolae dicuntur ex eo quod *colunt* agros, et incolae dicuntur ex eo quod *colunt* loca quae inhabitant. Quia tamen specialis honor debetur Deo, tanquam primo omnium principio, etiam specialis ratio cultus ei debetur, quae Graeco nomine vocatur *eusebia* vel *theosebia*, ut patet per Augustinum, X de Civ. Dei.

AD QUINTUM dicendum quod quamvis religiosi dici possint communiter omnes qui Deum colunt, specialiter tamen religiosi dicuntur qui totam vitam suam divino cultui dedicant, a mundanis negotiis se abstrahentes. Sicut etiam contemplativi dicuntur non qui contemplantur, sed qui contemplationi totam vitam suam deputant. Huiusmodi autem non se subiiciunt homini propter hominem sed propter Deum, secundum illud apostoli, Gal. IV, *sicut Angelum Dei excepistis me, sicut Christum Iesum.*

of religion as commanding, and an act of mercy as eliciting; and *to keep oneself unspotted from this world* is an act of religion as commanding, but of temperance or of some similar virtue as eliciting.

REPLY OBJ. 2: Religion is referred to those things one exhibits to one's human kindred, if we take the term religion in a broad sense, but not if we take it in its proper sense. Hence, shortly before the passage quoted, Augustine says: *In a stricter sense religion seems to denote, not any kind of worship, but the worship of God.*

REPLY OBJ. 3: Since servant implies relation to a lord, wherever there is a special kind of lordship there must needs be a special kind of service. Now it is evident that lordship belongs to God in a special and singular way, because He made all things, and has supreme dominion over all. Consequently a special kind of service is due to Him, which is known as latria in Greek; and therefore it belongs to religion.

REPLY OBJ. 4: We are said to worship those whom we honor, and to cultivate a man's memory or presence: we even speak of cultivating things that are beneath us, thus a farmer (*agricola*) is one who cultivates the land, and an inhabitant (*incola*) is one who cultivates the place where he dwells. Since, however, special honor is due to God as the first principle of all things, to Him also is due a special kind of worship, which in Greek is *Eusebeia* or *Theosebeia*, as Augustine states (*De Civ. Dei* x, 1).

REPLY OBJ. 5: Although the name *religious* may be given to all in general who worship God, yet in a special way religious are those who consecrate their whole life to the Divine worship, by withdrawing from human affairs. Thus also the term *contemplative* is applied, not to those who contemplate, but to those who give up their whole lives to contemplation. Such men subject themselves to man, not for man's sake but for God's sake, according to the word of the Apostle (Gal 4:14), *You . . . received me as an angel of God, even as Christ Jesus.*

# Article 2

*Whether religion is a virtue?*

AD SECUNDUM SIC PROCEDITUR. Videtur quod religio non sit virtus. Ad religionem enim pertinere videtur Deo reverentiam exhibere. Sed revereri est actus timoris, qui est donum, ut ex supradictis patet. Ergo religio non est virtus, sed donum.

PRAETEREA, omnis virtus in libera voluntate consistit, unde dicitur *habitus electivus*, vel voluntarius. Sed

OBJECTION 1: It would seem that religion is not a virtue. Seemingly it belongs to religion to pay reverence to God. But reverence is an act of fear which is a gift, as stated above (Q. 19, A. 9). Therefore religion is not a virtue but a gift.

OBJ. 2: Further, every virtue is a free exercise of the will, wherefore it is described as an *elective* or voluntary *habit*.

sicut dictum est, ad religionem pertinet latria, quae servitutem quandam importat. Ergo religio non est virtus.

**PRAETEREA**, sicut dicitur in II Ethic., aptitudo virtutum inest nobis a natura, unde ea quae pertinent ad virtutes sunt de dictamine rationis naturalis. Sed ad religionem pertinet *caeremoniam divinae naturae afferre*. Caeremonialia autem, ut supra dictum est, non sunt de dictamine rationis naturalis. Ergo religio non est virtus.

**SED CONTRA** est quia connumeratur aliis virtutibus, ut ex praemissis patet.

**RESPONDEO** dicendum quod, sicut supra dictum est, *virtus est quae bonum facit habentem et opus eius bonum reddit*. Et ideo necesse est dicere omnem actum bonum ad virtutem pertinere. Manifestum est autem quod reddere debitum alicui habet rationem boni, quia per hoc quod aliquis alteri debitum reddit, etiam constituitur in proportione convenienti respectu ipsius, quasi convenienter ordinatus ad ipsum; ordo autem ad rationem boni pertinet, sicut et modus et species, ut per Augustinum patet, in libro de natura boni. Cum igitur ad religionem pertineat reddere honorem debitum alicui, scilicet Deo, manifestum est quod religio virtus est.

**AD PRIMUM** ergo dicendum quod revereri Deum est actus doni timoris. Ad religionem autem pertinet facere aliqua propter divinam reverentiam. Unde non sequitur quod religio sit idem quod donum timoris, sed quod ordinetur ad ipsum sicut ad aliquid principalius. Sunt enim dona principaliora virtutibus moralibus, ut supra habitum est.

**AD SECUNDUM** dicendum quod etiam servus potest voluntarie domino suo exhibere quod debet, et sic *facit de necessitate virtutem*, debitum voluntarie reddens. Et similiter etiam exhibere Deo debitam servitutem potest esse actus virtutis, secundum quod homo voluntarie hoc facit.

**AD TERTIUM** dicendum quod de dictamine rationis naturalis est quod homo aliqua faciat ad reverentiam divinam, sed quod haec determinate faciat vel illa, istud non est de dictamine rationis naturalis, sed de institutione iuris divini vel humani.

Now, as stated above (A. 1, ad 3) latria belongs to religion, and latria denotes a kind of servitude. Therefore religion is not a virtue.

**OBJ. 3**: Further, according to *Ethic.* ii, 1, aptitude for virtue is in us by nature, wherefore things pertaining to virtue belong to the dictate of natural reason. Now, it belongs to religion *to offer ceremonial worship to the Godhead*, and ceremonial matters, as stated above (I-II, Q. 99, A. 3, ad 2; Q. 101), do not belong to the dictate of natural reason. Therefore religion is not a virtue.

**ON THE CONTRARY**, It is enumerated with the other virtues, as appears from what has been said above (Q. 80).

**I ANSWER THAT**, As stated above (Q. 58, A. 3; I-II, Q. 55, AA. 3, 4) *a virtue is that which makes its possessor good, and his act good likewise*, wherefore we must needs say that every good act belongs to a virtue. Now it is evident that to render anyone his due has the aspect of good, since by rendering a person his due, one becomes suitably proportioned to him, through being ordered to him in a becoming manner. But order comes under the aspect of good, just as mode and species, according to Augustine (*De Nat. Boni* iii). Since then it belongs to religion to pay due honor to someone, namely, to God, it is evident that religion is a virtue.

**REPLY OBJ. 1**: To pay reverence to God is an act of the gift of fear. Now it belongs to religion to do certain things through reverence for God. Hence it follows, not that religion is the same as the gift of fear, but that it is referred thereto as to something more excellent; for the gifts are more excellent than the moral virtues, as stated above (Q. 9, A. 1, ad 3; I-II, Q. 68, A. 8).

**REPLY OBJ. 2**: Even a slave can voluntarily do his duty by his master, and so *he makes a virtue of necessity*, by doing his duty voluntarily. In like manner, to render due service to God may be an act of virtue, insofar as man does so voluntarily.

**REPLY OBJ. 3**: It belongs to the dictate of natural reason that man should do something through reverence for God. But that he should do this or that determinate thing does not belong to the dictate of natural reason, but is established by Divine or human law.

# Article 3

*Whether religion is one virtue?*

**AD TERTIUM SIC PROCEDITUR**. Videtur quod religio non sit una virtus. Per religionem enim ordinamur ad Deum, ut dictum est. In Deo autem est accipere tres personas, et iterum multa attributa, quae saltem ratione differunt. Diversa autem ratio obiecti sufficit ad

**OBJECTION 1**: It would seem that religion is not one virtue. Religion directs us to God, as stated above (A. 1). Now in God there are three Persons; and also many attributes, which differ at least logically from one another. Now a logical difference in the object suffices for a differ-

diversificandum virtutes, ut ex supradictis patet. Ergo religio non est una virtus.

**PRAETEREA**, unius virtutis unus videtur esse actus, habitus enim distinguuntur secundum actus. Religionis autem multi sunt actus, sicut colere et servire, vovere, orare, sacrificare, et multa huiusmodi. Ergo religio non est una virtus.

**PRAETEREA**, adoratio ad religionem pertinet. Sed adoratio alia ratione adhibetur imaginibus, et alia ipsi Deo. Cum ergo diversa ratio distinguat virtutes, videtur quod religio non sit una virtus.

**SED CONTRA** est quod dicitur Ephes. IV, *unus Deus, una fides.* Sed vera religio protestatur fidem unius Dei. Ergo religio est una virtus.

**RESPONDEO** dicendum quod, sicut supra habitum est, habitus distinguuntur secundum diversam rationem obiecti. Ad religionem autem pertinet exhibere reverentiam uni Deo secundum unam rationem, inquantum scilicet est primum principium creationis et gubernationis rerum, unde ipse dicit, Malach. I, *si ego pater, ubi honor meus?* Patris enim est et producere et gubernare Et ideo manifestum est quod religio est una virtus.

**AD PRIMUM** ergo dicendum quod tres personae divinae sunt unum principium creationis et gubernationis rerum, et ideo eis una religione servitur. Diversae autem rationes attributorum concurrunt ad rationem primi principii, quia Deus producit omnia et gubernat sapientia, voluntate et potentia bonitatis suae. Et ideo religio est una virtus.

**AD SECUNDUM** dicendum quod eodem actu homo servit Deo et colit ipsum, nam cultus respicit Dei excellentiam, cui reverentia debetur; servitus autem respicit subiectionem hominis, qui ex sua conditione obligatur ad exhibendum reverentiam Deo. Et ad haec duo pertinent omnes actus qui religioni attribuuntur, quia per omnes homo protestatur divinam excellentiam et subiectionem sui ad Deum, vel exhibendo aliquid ei, vel iterum assumendo aliquid divinum.

**AD TERTIUM** dicendum quod imaginibus non exhibetur religionis cultus secundum quod in seipsis considerantur, quasi res quaedam, sed secundum quod sunt imagines ducentes in Deum incarnatum. Motus autem qui est in imaginem prout est imago, non sistit in ipsa, sed tendit in id cuius est imago. Et ideo ex hoc quod imaginibus Christi exhibetur religionis cultus, non diversificatur ratio latriae, nec virtus religionis.

ence of virtue, as stated above (Q. 50, A. 2, ad 2). Therefore religion is not one virtue.

**OBJ. 2:** Further, of one virtue there is seemingly one act, since habits are distinguished by their acts. Now there are many acts of religion, for instance to worship, to serve, to vow, to pray, to sacrifice and many such like. Therefore religion is not one virtue.

**OBJ. 3:** Further, adoration belongs to religion. Now adoration is paid to images under one aspect, and under another aspect to God Himself. Since, then, a difference of aspect distinguishes virtues, it would seem that religion is not one virtue.

**ON THE CONTRARY,** It is written (*Eph 4:5*): *One God, one faith.* Now true religion professes faith in one God. Therefore religion is one virtue.

**I ANSWER THAT,** As stated above (I-II, Q. 54, A. 2, ad 1), habits are differentiated according to a different aspect of the object. Now it belongs to religion to show reverence to one God under one aspect, namely, as the first principle of the creation and government of things. Wherefore He Himself says (Mal 1:6): *If . . . I be a father, where is My honor?* For it belongs to a father to beget and to govern. Therefore it is evident that religion is one virtue.

**REPLY OBJ. 1:** The three Divine Persons are the one principle of the creation and government of things, wherefore they are served by one religion. The different aspects of the attributes concur under the aspect of first principle, because God produces all things, and governs them by the wisdom, will and power of His goodness. Wherefore religion is one virtue.

**REPLY OBJ. 2:** By the one same act man both serves and worships God, for worship regards the excellence of God, to Whom reverence is due: while service regards the subjection of man who, by his condition, is under an obligation of showing reverence to God. To these two belong all acts ascribed to religion, because, by them all, man bears witness to the Divine excellence and to his own subjection to God, either by offering something to God, or by assuming something Divine.

**REPLY OBJ. 3:** The worship of religion is paid to images, not as considered in themselves, nor as things, but as images leading us to God incarnate. Now movement to an image as image does not stop at the image, but goes on to the thing it represents. Hence neither latria nor the virtue of religion is differentiated by the fact that religious worship is paid to the images of Christ.

# Article 4

*Whether religion is a special virtue, distinct from the others?*

**Ad quartum sic proceditur**. Videtur quod religio non sit specialis virtus ab aliis distincta. Dicit enim Augustinus, X de Civ. Dei, *verum sacrificium est omne opus quod geritur ut sancta societate Deo iungamur.* Sed sacrificium pertinet ad religionem. Ergo omne opus virtutis ad religionem pertinet. Et sic non est specialis virtus.

**Praeterea**, apostolus dicit, I ad Cor. X, *omnia in gloriam Dei facite.* Sed ad religionem pertinet aliqua facere ad Dei reverentiam, ut supra dictum est. Ergo religio non est specialis virtus.

**Praeterea**, caritas qua diligitur Deus non est virtus distincta a caritate qua diligitur proximus. Sed sicut dicitur in VIII Ethic., *honorari propinquum est ei quod est amari.* Ergo religio, qua honoratur Deus, non est virtus specialiter distincta ab observantia vel dulia vel pietate, quibus honoratur proximus. Ergo non est virtus specialis.

**Sed contra** est quod ponitur pars iustitiae ab aliis eius partibus distincta.

**Respondeo** dicendum quod cum virtus ordinetur ad bonum, ubi est specialis ratio boni, ibi oportet esse specialem virtutem. Bonum autem ad quod ordinatur religio est exhibere Deo debitum honorem. Honor autem debetur alicui ratione excellentiae. Deo autem competit singularis excellentia, inquantum omnia in infinitum transcendit secundum omnimodum excessum. Unde ei debetur specialis honor, sicut in rebus humanis videmus quod diversis excellentiis personarum diversus honor debetur, alius quidem patri, alius regi, et sic de aliis. Unde manifestum est quod religio est specialis virtus.

**Ad primum** ergo dicendum quod omne opus virtutis dicitur esse sacrificium inquantum ordinatur ad Dei reverentiam. Unde ex hoc non habetur quod religio sit generalis virtus, sed quod imperet omnibus aliis virtutibus, sicut supra dictum est.

**Ad secundum** dicendum quod omnia, secundum quod in gloriam Dei fiunt, pertinent ad religionem non quasi ad elicientem, sed quasi ad imperantem. Illa autem pertinent ad religionem elicientem quae secundum rationem suae speciei pertinent ad reverentiam Dei.

**Ad tertium** dicendum quod obiectum amoris est bonum, obiectum autem honoris vel reverentiae est aliquid excellens. Bonitas autem Dei communicatur creaturae, non autem excellentia bonitatis eius. Et ideo caritas qua diligitur Deus non est virtus distincta a caritate qua diligitur proximus, religio autem, qua honoratur Deus, distinguitur a virtutibus quibus honoratur proximus.

**Objection 1**: It would seem that religion is not a special virtue distinct from the others. Augustine says (*De Civ. Dei* x, 6): *Any action whereby we are united to God in holy fellowship, is a true sacrifice.* But sacrifice belongs to religion. Therefore every virtuous deed belongs to religion; and consequently religion is not a special virtue.

**Obj. 2**: Further, the Apostle says (1 Cor 10:31): *Do all to the glory of God.* Now it belongs to religion to do anything in reverence of God, as stated above (A. 1, ad 2; A. 2). Therefore religion is not a special virtue.

**Obj. 3**: Further, the charity whereby we love God is not distinct from the charity whereby we love our neighbor. But according to *Ethic.* viii, 8 *to be honored is almost to be loved.* Therefore the religion whereby we honor God is not a special virtue distinct from observance, or dulia, or piety whereby we honor our neighbor. Therefore religion is not a special virtue.

**On the contrary**, It is reckoned a part of justice, distinct from the other parts.

**I answer that**, Since virtue is directed to the good, wherever there is a special aspect of good, there must be a special virtue. Now the good to which religion is directed, is to give due honor to God. Again, honor is due to someone under the aspect of excellence: and to God a singular excellence is competent, since He infinitely surpasses all things and exceeds them in every way. Wherefore to Him is special honor due: even as in human affairs we see that different honor is due to different personal excellences, one kind of honor to a father, another to the king, and so on. Hence it is evident that religion is a special virtue.

**Reply Obj. 1**: Every virtuous deed is said to be a sacrifice, insofar as it is done out of reverence of God. Hence this does not prove that religion is a general virtue, but that it commands all other virtues, as stated above (A. 1, ad 1).

**Reply Obj. 2**: Every deed, insofar as it is done in God's honor, belongs to religion, not as eliciting but as commanding: those belong to religion as eliciting which pertain to the reverence of God by reason of their specific character.

**Reply Obj. 3**: The object of love is the good, but the object of honor and reverence is something excellent. Now God's goodness is communicated to the creature, but the excellence of His goodness is not. Hence the charity whereby God is loved is not distinct from the charity whereby our neighbor is loved; whereas the religion whereby God is honored, is distinct from the virtues whereby we honor our neighbor.

# Article 5

*Whether religion is a theological virtue?*

AD QUINTUM SIC PROCEDITUR. Videtur quod religio sit virtus theologica. Dicit enim Augustinus, in Enchirid., quod *Deus colitur fide, spe et caritate*, quae sunt virtutes theologicae. Sed *cultum Deo afferre* pertinet ad religionem. Ergo religio est virtus theologica.

PRAETEREA, virtus theologica dicitur quae habet Deum pro obiecto. Religio autem habet Deum pro obiecto, quia ad solum Deum ordinat, ut dictum est. Ergo religio est virtus theologica.

PRAETEREA, omnis virtus vel est theologica, vel intellectualis, vel moralis, ut ex supradictis patet. Manifestum est autem quod religio non est virtus intellectualis, quia eius perfectio non attenditur secundum considerationem veri. Similiter etiam non est virtus moralis, cuius proprium est tenere medium inter superfluum et diminutum, non enim aliquis potest superflue Deum colere, secundum illud Eccli. XLIII, *benedicentes dominum, exaltate illum quantum potestis, maior enim est omni laude.* Ergo relinquitur quod sit virtus theologica.

SED CONTRA est quod ponitur pars iustitiae, quae est virtus moralis.

RESPONDEO dicendum quod, sicut dictum est, religio est quae Deo debitum cultum affert. Duo igitur in religione considerantur. Unum quidem quod religio Deo affert, cultus scilicet, et hoc se habet per modum materiae et obiecti ad religionem. Aliud autem est id cui affertur, scilicet Deus. Cui cultus exhibetur non quasi actus quibus Deus colitur ipsum Deum attingunt, sicut cum credimus Deo, credendo Deum attingimus (propter quod supra dictum est quod Deus est fidei obiectum non solum inquantum credimus Deum, sed inquantum credimus Deo), affertur autem Deo debitus cultus inquantum actus quidam, quibus Deus colitur, in Dei reverentiam fiunt, puta sacrificiorum oblationes et alia huiusmodi.

Unde manifestum est quod Deus non comparatur ad virtutem religionis sicut materia vel obiectum, sed sicut finis. Et ideo religio non est virtus theologica, cuius obiectum est ultimus finis, sed est virtus moralis, cuius est esse circa ea quae sunt ad finem.

AD PRIMUM ergo dicendum quod semper potentia vel virtus quae operatur circa finem, per imperium movet potentiam vel virtutem operantem ea quae ordinantur in finem illum. Virtutes autem theologicae, scilicet fides, spes et caritas, habent actum circa Deum sicut circa proprium obiectum. Et ideo suo imperio causant actum religionis, quae operatur quaedam in ordine ad Deum. Et ideo Augustinus dicit quod *Deus colitur fide, spe et caritate.*

OBJECTION 1: It would seem that religion is a theological virtue. Augustine says (*Enchiridion* iii) that *God is worshiped by faith, hope and charity*, which are theological virtues. Now it belongs to religion *to pay worship to God*. Therefore religion is a theological virtue.

OBJ. 2: Further, a theological virtue is one that has God for its object. Now religion has God for its object, since it directs us to God alone, as stated above (A. 1). Therefore religion is a theological virtue.

OBJ. 3: Further, every virtue is either theological, or intellectual, or moral, as is clear from what has been said (I-II, QQ. 57, 58, 62). Now it is evident that religion is not an intellectual virtue, because its perfection does not depend on the consideration of truth: nor is it a moral virtue, which consists properly in observing the mean between too much and too little, for one cannot worship God too much, according to Ecclus. 43:33, *Blessing the Lord, exalt Him as much as you can; for He is above all praise.* Therefore it remains that it is a theological virtue.

ON THE CONTRARY, It is reckoned a part of justice which is a moral virtue.

I ANSWER THAT, As stated above (A. 4) religion pays due worship to God. Hence two things are to be considered in religion: first that which it offers to God, viz. worship, and this is by way of matter and object in religion; second, that to which something is offered, viz. God, to Whom worship is paid. And yet the acts whereby God is worshiped do not reach out to God himself, as when we believe God we reach out to Him by believing; for which reason it was stated (Q. 1, AA. 1, 2, 4) that God is the object of faith, not only because we believe in a God, but because we believe God. Now due worship is paid to God, insofar as certain acts whereby God is worshiped, such as the offering of sacrifices and so forth, are done out of reverence for God.

Hence it is evident that God is related to religion not as matter or object, but as end: and consequently religion is not a theological virtue whose object is the last end, but a moral virtue which is properly about things referred to the end.

REPLY OBJ. 1: The power or virtue whose action deals with an end, moves by its command the power or virtue whose action deals with matters directed to that end. Now the theological virtues, faith, hope and charity have an act in reference to God as their proper object: wherefore, by their command, they cause the act of religion, which performs certain deeds directed to God: and so Augustine says that *God is worshipped by faith, hope and charity.*

**Ad secundum** dicendum quod religio ordinat hominem in Deum non sicut in obiectum, sed sicut in finem.

**Ad tertium** dicendum quod religio non est virtus theologica neque intellectualis, sed moralis, cum sit pars iustitiae. Et medium in ipsa accipitur non quidem inter passiones, sed secundum quandam aequalitatem inter operationes quae sunt ad Deum. Dico autem aequalitatem non absolute, quia Deo non potest tantum exhiberi quantum ei debetur, sed secundum considerationem humanae facultatis et divinae acceptationis.

Superfluum autem in his quae ad divinum cultum pertinent esse potest, non secundum circumstantiam *quanti*, sed secundum alias circumstantias, puta quia cultus divinus exhibetur cui non debet exhiberi, vel quando non debet, vel secundum alias circumstantias prout non debet.

**Reply Obj. 2**: Religion directs man to God not as its object but as its end.

**Reply Obj. 3**: Religion is neither a theological nor an intellectual, but a moral virtue, since it is a part of justice, and observes a mean, not in the passions, but in actions directed to God, by establishing a kind of equality in them. And when I say *equality*, I do not mean absolute equality, because it is not possible to pay God as much as we owe Him, but equality in consideration of man's ability and God's acceptance.

And it is possible to have too much in matters pertaining to the Divine worship, not as regards the circumstance of *quantity*, but as regards other circumstances, as when Divine worship is paid to whom it is not due, or when it is not due, or unduly in respect of some other circumstance.

# Article 6

*Whether religion should be preferred to the other moral virtues?*

**Ad sextum sic proceditur.** Videtur quod religio non sit praeferenda aliis virtutibus moralibus. Perfectio enim virtutis moralis consistit in hoc quod attingit medium, ut patet in II Ethic. Sed religio deficit in attingendo medium iustitiae, quia non reddit Deo omnino aequale. Ergo religio non est potior aliis virtutibus moralibus.

**Praeterea**, in his quae hominibus exhibentur, tanto videtur aliquid esse laudabilius quanto magis indigenti exhibetur, unde dicitur Isaiae LVIII, *frange esurienti panem tuum*. Sed Deus non indiget aliquo quod ei a nobis exhibeatur, secundum illud Psalm., *dixi, Deus meus es tu, quoniam bonorum meorum non eges*. Ergo religio videtur minus laudabilis aliis virtutibus, per quas hominibus subvenitur.

**Praeterea**, quanto aliquid fit ex maiori necessitate, tanto minus est laudabile, secundum illud I ad Cor. IX, *si evangelizavero, non est mihi gloria, necessitas mihi incumbit*. Ubi autem est maius debitum, ibi est maior necessitas. Cum igitur Deo maxime sit debitum quod ei ab homine exhibetur, videtur quod religio sit minus laudabilis inter virtutes humanas.

**Sed contra** est quod Exod. XX ponuntur primo praecepta ad religionem pertinentia, tanquam praecipua. Ordo autem praeceptorum proportionatur ordini virtutum, quia praecepta legis dantur de actibus virtutum. Ergo religio est praecipua inter virtutes morales.

**Respondeo** dicendum quod ea quae sunt ad finem sortiuntur bonitatem ex ordine in finem, et ideo quanto sunt fini propinquiora, tanto sunt meliora. Virtutes autem morales, ut supra habitum est, sunt circa

**Objection 1**: It would seem that religion should not be preferred to the other moral virtues. The perfection of a moral virtue consists in its observing the mean, as stated in *Ethic.* ii, 6. But religion fails to observe the mean of justice, since it does not render an absolute equal to God. Therefore religion is not more excellent than the other moral virtues.

**Obj. 2**: Further, what is offered by one man to another is the more praiseworthy, according as the person it is offered to is in greater need: wherefore it is written (Isa 57:7): *Deal thy bread to the hungry*. But God needs nothing that we can offer Him, according to Ps. 15:2, *I have said: Thou art my God, for Thou hast no need of my goods*. Therefore religion would seem less praiseworthy than the other virtues whereby man's needs are relieved.

**Obj. 3**: Further, the greater the obligation to do a thing, the less praise does it deserve, according to 1 Cor. 9:16, *If I preach the Gospel, it is no glory to me: a necessity lieth upon me*. Now the more a thing is due, the greater the obligation of paying it. Since, then, what is paid to God by man is in the highest degree due to Him, it would seem that religion is less praiseworthy than the other human virtues.

**On the contrary**, The precepts pertaining to religion are given precedence (Exod 20) as being of greatest importance. Now the order of precepts is proportionate to the order of virtues, since the precepts of the Law prescribe acts of virtue. Therefore religion is the chief of the moral virtues.

**I answer that**, Whatever is directed to an end takes its goodness from being ordered to that end; so that the nearer it is to the end the better it is. Now moral virtues, as stated above (A. 5; Q. 4, A. 7), are about matters that

ea quae ordinantur in Deum sicut in finem. Religio autem magis de propinquo accedit ad Deum quam aliae virtutes morales, inquantum operatur ea quae directe et immediate ordinantur in honorem divinum. Et ideo religio praeeminet inter alias virtutes morales.

**AD PRIMUM** ergo dicendum quod laus virtutis in voluntate consistit, non autem in potestate. Et ideo deficere ab aequalitate, quae est medium iustitiae, propter defectum potestatis, non diminuit laudem virtutis, si non fuerit defectus ex parte voluntatis.

**AD SECUNDUM** dicendum quod in his quae exhibentur alteri propter eorum utilitatem, est exhibitio laudabilior quae fit magis indigenti, quia est utilior. Deo autem non exhibetur aliquid propter eius utilitatem, sed propter eius gloriam, nostram autem utilitatem.

**AD TERTIUM** dicendum quod ubi est necessitas, tollitur gloria supererogationis, non autem excluditur meritum virtutis, si adsit voluntas. Et propter hoc ratio non sequitur.

are ordered to God as their end. And religion approaches nearer to God than the other moral virtues, insofar as its actions are directly and immediately ordered to the honor of God. Hence religion excels among the moral virtues.

**REPLY OBJ. 1**: Virtue is praised because of the will, not because of the ability: and therefore if a man fall short of equality which is the mean of justice, through lack of ability, his virtue deserves no less praise, provided there be no failing on the part of his will.

**REPLY OBJ. 2**: In offering a thing to a man on account of its usefulness to him, the more needy the man the more praiseworthy the offering, because it is more useful: whereas we offer a thing to God not on account of its usefulness to Him, but for the sake of His glory, and on account of its usefulness to us.

**REPLY OBJ. 3**: Where there is an obligation to do a thing it loses the luster of supererogation, but not the merit of virtue, provided it be done voluntarily. Hence the argument proves nothing.

# Article 7

*Whether religion has an external act?*

**AD SEPTIMUM SIC PROCEDITUR**. Videtur quod latria non habeat aliquem exteriorem actum. Dicitur enim Ioan. IV, *Deus spiritus est, et eos qui adorant eum, in spiritu et veritate adorare oportet*. Sed exteriores actus non pertinent ad spiritum, sed magis ad corpus. Ergo religio, ad quam pertinet adoratio, non habet exteriores actus, sed interiores.

**PRAETEREA**, religionis finis est Deo reverentiam et honorem exhibere. Sed videtur ad irreverentiam alicuius excellentis pertinere si ea sibi exhibeantur quae proprie ad inferiores pertinent. Cum igitur ea quae exhibet homo corporalibus actibus proprie videantur ad indigentias hominum ordinari, vel ad reverentiam inferiorum creaturarum; non videtur quod congrue possunt assumi in divinam reverentiam.

**PRAETEREA**, Augustinus, in VI de Civ. Dei, commendat Senecam de hoc quod vituperat quosdam qui idolis ea exhibebant quae solent hominibus exhiberi, quia scilicet immortalibus non conveniunt ea quae sunt mortalium. Sed haec multo minus conveniunt Deo vero, qui est excelsus *super omnes deos*. Ergo videtur reprehensibile esse quod aliquis corporalibus actibus Deum colat. Non ergo habet religio corporales actus.

**SED CONTRA** est quod in Psalm. dicitur, *cor meum et caro mea exultaverunt in Deum vivum*. Sed sicut interiores actus pertinent ad cor, ita exteriores actus pertinent

**OBJECTION 1**: It would seem that religion has not an external act. It is written (John 4:24): *God is a spirit, and they that adore Him, must adore Him in spirit and in truth.* Now external acts pertain, not to the spirit but to the body. Therefore religion, to which adoration belongs, has acts that are not external but internal.

**OBJ. 2**: Further, the end of religion is to pay God reverence and honor. Now it would savor of irreverence towards a superior, if one were to offer him that which properly belongs to his inferior. Since then whatever man offers by bodily actions, seems to be directed properly to the relief of human needs, or to the reverence of inferior creatures, it would seem unbecoming to employ them in showing reverence to God.

**OBJ. 3**: Further, Augustine (*De Civ. Dei* vi, 10) commends Seneca for finding fault with those who offered to idols those things that are wont to be offered to men, because, to wit, that which befits mortals is unbecoming to immortals. But such things are much less becoming to the true God, Who is *exalted above all gods*. Therefore it would seem wrong to worship God with bodily actions. Therefore religion has no bodily actions.

**ON THE CONTRARY**, It is written (Ps 83:3): *My heart and my flesh have rejoiced in the living God.* Now just as internal actions belong to the heart, so do external actions

ad membra carnis. Ergo videtur quod Deus sit colendus non solum interioribus actibus, sed etiam exterioribus.

**RESPONDEO** dicendum quod Deo reverentiam et honorem exhibemus non propter ipsum, qui in seipso est gloria plenus, cui nihil a creatura adiici potest, sed propter nos, quia videlicet per hoc quod Deum reveremur et honoramus, mens nostra ei subiicitur, et in hoc eius perfectio consistit; quaelibet enim res perficitur per hoc quod subditur suo superiori, sicut corpus per hoc quod vivificatur ab anima, et aer per hoc quod illuminatur a sole. Mens autem humana indiget ad hoc quod coniungatur Deo, sensibilium manuductione, quia *invisibilia per ea quae facta sunt, intellecta, conspiciuntur*, ut apostolus dicit, ad Rom. Et ideo in divino cultu necesse est aliquibus corporalibus uti, ut eis, quasi signis quibusdam, mens hominis excitetur ad spirituales actus, quibus Deo coniungitur. Et ideo religio habet quidem interiores actus quasi principales et per se ad religionem pertinentes, exteriores vero actus quasi secundarios, et ad interiores actus ordinatos.

**AD PRIMUM** ergo dicendum quod dominus loquitur quantum ad id quod est principale et per se intentum in cultu divino.

**AD SECUNDUM** dicendum quod huiusmodi exteriora non exhibentur Deo quasi his indigeat, secundum illud Psalm., *numquid manducabo carnes taurorum, aut sanguinem hircorum potabo?* Sed exhibentur Deo tanquam signa quaedam interiorum et spiritualium operum, quae per se Deus acceptat. Unde Augustinus dicit, in X de Civ. Dei, *sacrificium visibile invisibilis sacrificii sacramentum, idest sacrum signum, est.*

**AD TERTIUM** dicendum quod idololatrae deridentur ex hoc quod ea quae ad homines pertinent idolis exhibebant non tanquam signa excitantia eos ad aliqua spiritualia, sed tanquam per se eis accepta. Et praecipue quia erant vana et turpia.

belong to the members of the flesh. Therefore it seems that God ought to be worshiped not only by internal but also by external actions.

**I ANSWER THAT,** We pay God honor and reverence, not for His sake (because He is of Himself full of glory to which no creature can add anything), but for our own sake, because by the very fact that we revere and honor God, our mind is subjected to Him; wherein its perfection consists, since a thing is perfected by being subjected to its superior, for instance the body is perfected by being quickened by the soul, and the air by being enlightened by the sun. Now the human mind, in order to be united to God, needs to be guided by the sensible world, since *invisible things . . . are clearly seen, being understood by the things that are made*, as the Apostle says (Rom 1:20). Wherefore in the Divine worship it is necessary to make use of corporeal things, that man's mind may be aroused thereby, as by signs, to the spiritual acts by means of which he is united to God. Therefore the internal acts of religion take precedence of the others and belong to religion essentially, while its external acts are secondary, and subordinate to the internal acts.

**REPLY OBJ. 1:** Our Lord is speaking of that which is most important and directly intended in the worship of God.

**REPLY OBJ. 2:** These external things are offered to God, not as though He stood in need of them, according to Ps. 49:13, *Shall I eat the flesh of bullocks? or shall I drink the blood of goats?* but as signs of the internal and spiritual works, which are of themselves acceptable to God. Hence Augustine says (*De Civ. Dei* x, 5): *The visible sacrifice is the sacrament or sacred sign of the invisible sacrifice.*

**REPLY OBJ. 3:** Idolaters are ridiculed for offering to idols things pertaining to men, not as signs arousing them to certain spiritual things, but as though they were of themselves acceptable to the idols; and still more because they were foolish and wicked.

# Article 8

*Whether religion is the same as sanctity?*

**AD OCTAVUM SIC PROCEDITUR.** Videtur quod religio non sit idem sanctitati. Religio enim est quaedam specialis virtus, ut habitum est. Sanctitas autem dicitur esse generalis virtus, est enim *faciens fideles et servantes ea quae ad Deum sunt iusta*, ut Andronicus dicit. Ergo sanctitas non est idem religioni.

**PRAETEREA**, sanctitas munditiam importare videtur, dicit enim Dionysius, XII cap. de Div. Nom., quod *sanctitas est ab omni immunditia libera et perfecta et*

**OBJECTION 1:** It would seem that religion is not the same as sanctity. Religion is a special virtue, as stated above (A. 4): whereas sanctity is a general virtue, because *it makes us faithful, and fulfill our just obligations to God*, according to Andronicus. Therefore sanctity is not the same as religion.

**OBJ. 2:** Further, sanctity seems to denote a kind of purity. For Dionysius says (*Div. Nom.* xii) that *sanctity is free from all uncleanness, and is perfect and altogether unspotted*

*omnino immaculata munditia.* Munditia autem maxime videtur pertinere ad temperantiam, quae turpitudines corporales excludit. Cum igitur religio ad iustitiam pertineat, videtur quod sanctitas non sit idem religioni.

**PRAETEREA**, ea quae dividuntur ex opposito non sunt idem. Sed in quadam enumeratione partium iustitiae sanctitas condividitur religioni, ut supra habitum est. Ergo sanctitas non est idem quod religio.

**SED CONTRA** est quod dicitur Luc. I, *serviamus illi in sanctitate et iustitia.* Sed servire Deo pertinet ad religionem, ut supra habitum est. Ergo religio est idem sanctitati.

**RESPONDEO** dicendum quod nomen sanctitatis duo videtur importare. Uno quidem modo, munditiam, et huic significationi competit nomen Graecum, dicitur enim *agios* quasi *sine terra.* Alio modo importat firmitatem, unde apud antiquos *sancta* dicebantur quae legibus erant munita ut violari non deberent; unde et dicitur esse aliquid *sancitum* quia est lege firmatum. Potest etiam secundum Latinos hoc nomen *sanctus* ad munditiam pertinere, ut intelligatur sanctus quasi *sanguine tinctus, eo quod antiquitus illi qui purificari volebant sanguine hostiae tingebantur,* ut Isidorus dicit, in libro Etymol. Et utraque significatio competit, ut sanctitas attribuatur his quae divino cultui applicantur, ita quod non solum homines, sed etiam templum et vasa et alia huiusmodi sanctificari dicantur ex hoc quod cultui divino applicantur. Munditia enim necessaria est ad hoc quod mens Deo applicetur. Quia mens humana inquinatur ex hoc quod inferioribus rebus immergitur, sicut quaelibet res ex immixtione peioris sordescit, ut argentum ex immixtione plumbi. Oportet autem quod mens ab inferioribus rebus abstrahatur, ad hoc quod supremae rei possit coniungi. Et ideo mens sine munditia Deo applicari non potest. Unde ad Heb. ult. dicitur, *pacem sequimini cum omnibus, et sanctimoniam, sine qua nemo videbit Deum.* Firmitas etiam exigitur ad hoc quod mens Deo applicetur. Applicatur enim ei sicut ultimo fini et primo principio, huiusmodi autem oportet maxime immobilia esse. Unde dicebat apostolus, Rom. VIII, *certus sum quod neque mors neque vita separabit me a caritate Dei.*

Sic igitur sanctitas dicitur per quam mens hominis seipsam et suos actus applicat Deo. Unde non differt a religione secundum essentiam, sed solum ratione. Nam religio dicitur secundum quod exhibet Deo debitum famulatum in his quae pertinent specialiter ad cultum divinum, sicut in sacrificiis, oblationibus et aliis huiusmodi, sanctitas autem dicitur secundum quod homo non solum haec, sed aliarum virtutum opera refert in Deum, vel secundum quod homo se disponit per bona opera ad cultum divinum.

*purity.* Now purity would seem above all to pertain to temperance which repels bodily uncleanness. Since then religion belongs to justice, it would seem that sanctity is not the same as religion.

**OBJ. 3**: Further, things that are opposite members of a division are not identified with one another. But in an enumeration given above (Q. 80, ad 4) of the parts of justice, sanctity is reckoned as distinct from religion. Therefore sanctity is not the same as religion.

**ON THE CONTRARY**, It is written (Luke 1:74, 75): *That . . . we may serve Him . . . in holiness and justice.* Now, *to serve God* belongs to religion, as stated above (A. 1, ad 3; A. 3, ad 2). Therefore religion is the same as sanctity.

**I ANSWER THAT**, The word *sanctity* seems to have two significations. In one way it denotes purity; and this signification fits in with the Greek, for *hagios* means *unsoiled.* In another way it denotes firmness, wherefore in olden times the term *sancta* was applied to such things as were upheld by law and were not to be violated. Hence a thing is said to be sacred (*sancitum*) when it is ratified by law. Again, in Latin, this word *sanctus* may be connected with purity, if it be resolved into *sanguine tinctus, since, in olden times, those who wished to be purified were sprinkled with the victim's blood,* according to Isidore (*Etym.* x). In either case the signification requires sanctity to be ascribed to those things that are applied to the Divine worship; so that not only men, but also the temple, vessels and such like things are said to be sanctified through being applied to the worship of God. For purity is necessary in order that the mind be applied to God, since the human mind is soiled by contact with inferior things, even as all things depreciate by admixture with baser things, for instance, silver by being mixed with lead. Now in order for the mind to be united to the Supreme Being it must be withdrawn from inferior things: and hence it is that without purity the mind cannot be applied to God. Wherefore it is written (Heb 12:14): *Follow peace with all men, and holiness, without which no man shall see God.* Again, firmness is required for the mind to be applied to God, for it is applied to Him as its last end and first beginning, and such things must needs be most immovable. Hence the Apostle said (Rom 8:38, 39): *I am sure that neither death, nor life . . . shall separate me from the love of God.*

Accordingly, it is by sanctity that the human mind applies itself and its acts to God: so that it differs from religion not essentially but only logically. For it takes the name of religion according as it gives God due service in matters pertaining specially to the Divine worship, such as sacrifices, oblations, and so forth; while it is called sanctity, according as man refers to God not only these but also the works of the other virtues, or according as man by means of certain good works disposes himself to the worship of God.

**AD PRIMUM** ergo dicendum quod sanctitas est quaedam specialis virtus secundum essentiam, et secundum hoc est quodammodo eadem religioni. Habet autem quandam generalitatem, secundum quod omnes virtutum actus per imperium ordinat in bonum divinum, sicut et iustitia legalis dicitur generalis virtus, inquantum ordinat omnium virtutum actus in bonum commune.

**AD SECUNDUM** dicendum quod temperantia munditiam quidem operatur, non tamen ita quod habeat rationem sanctitatis nisi referatur in Deum. Unde de ipsa virginitate dicit Augustinus, in libro de virginitate, quod *non quia virginitas est, sed quia Deo dicata est, honoratur.*

**AD TERTIUM** dicendum quod sanctitas distincta est a religione propter differentiam praedictam, non quia differat re, sed ratione tantum, ut dictum est.

**REPLY OBJ. 1**: Sanctity is a special virtue according to its essence; and in this respect it is in a way identified with religion. But it has a certain generality, insofar as by its command it directs the acts of all the virtues to the Divine good, even as legal justice is said to be a general virtue, insofar as it directs the acts of all the virtues to the common good.

**REPLY OBJ. 2**: Temperance practices purity, yet not so as to have the character of sanctity unless it be referred to God. Hence of virginity itself Augustine says (*De Virgin.* viii) that *it is honored not for what it is, but for being consecrated to God.*

**REPLY OBJ. 3**: Sanctity differs from religion as explained above, not really but logically.

# QUESTION 82

Deinde considerandum est de actibus religionis. Et primo, de actibus interioribus, qui, secundum praedicta, sunt principaliores; secundo, de actibus exterioribus, qui sunt secundarii. Interiores autem actus religionis videntur esse devotio et oratio. Primo ergo de devotione agendum est; secundo, de oratione.

Circa primum quaeruntur quatuor.

Primo, utrum devotio sit specialis actus.

Secundo, utrum sit actus religionis.

Tertio, de causa devotionis.

Quarto, de eius effectu.

We must now consider the acts of religion. First, we shall consider the interior acts, which, as stated above, are its principal acts; second, we shall consider its exterior acts, which are secondary. The interior acts of religion are seemingly devotion and prayer. Accordingly we shall treat first of devotion, and afterwards of prayer.

Under the first head there are four points of inquiry:

(1) Whether devotion is a special act?

(2) Whether it is an act of religion?

(3) Of the cause of devotion?

(4) Of its effect?

# Article 1

*Whether devotion is a special act?*

AD PRIMUM SIC PROCEDITUR. Videtur quod devotio non sit specialis actus. Illud enim quod pertinet ad modum aliorum actuum non videtur esse specialis actus. Sed devotio videtur pertinere ad modum aliorum actuum, dicitur enim II Paral. XXIX, *obtulit universa multitudo hostias et laudes et holocausta mente devota.* Ergo devotio non est specialis actus.

PRAETEREA, nullus specialis actus invenitur in diversis generibus actuum. Sed devotio invenitur in diversis generibus actuum, scilicet in actibus corporalibus et etiam in spiritualibus, dicitur enim aliquis et devote meditari et devote genu flectere. Ergo devotio non est specialis actus.

PRAETEREA, omnis actus specialis aut est appetitivae aut cognoscitivae virtutis. Sed devotio neutri earum appropriatur, ut patet discurrenti per singulas species actuum utriusque partis, quae supra enumeratae sunt. Ergo devotio non est specialis actus.

SED CONTRA est quod actibus meremur, ut supra habitum est. Sed devotio habet specialem rationem merendi. Ergo devotio est specialis actus.

RESPONDEO dicendum quod devotio dicitur a *devovendo*, unde *devoti* dicuntur qui seipsos quodammodo Deo devovent, ut ei se totaliter subdant. Propter quod et olim apud gentiles devoti dicebantur qui seipsos idolis devovebant in mortem pro sui salute exercitus, sicut de duobus Deciis Titus Livius narrat. Unde devotio nihil aliud esse videtur quam voluntas quaedam prompte tradendi se ad ea quae pertinent ad Dei famulatum. Unde

OBJECTION 1: It would seem that devotion is not a special act. That which qualifies other acts is seemingly not a special act. Now devotion seems to qualify other acts, for it is written (2 Chr 29:31): *All the multitude offered victims, and praises, and holocausts with a devout mind.* Therefore devotion is not a special act.

OBJ. 2: Further, no special kind of act is common to various genera of acts. But devotion is common to various genera of acts, namely, corporal and spiritual acts: for a person is said to meditate devoutly and to genuflect devoutly. Therefore devotion is not a special act.

OBJ. 3: Further, every special act belongs either to an appetitive or to a cognitive virtue or power. But devotion belongs to neither, as may be seen by going through the various species of acts of either faculty, as enumerated above (I, QQ. 78, seqq.; I-II, Q. 23, A. 4). Therefore devotion is not a special act.

ON THE CONTRARY, Merits are acquired by acts as stated above (I-II, Q. 21, AA. 34). But devotion has a special reason for merit. Therefore devotion is a special act.

I ANSWER THAT, Devotion is derived from *devote* ; wherefore those persons are said to be *devout* who, in a way, devote themselves to God, so as to subject themselves wholly to Him. Hence in olden times among the heathens a devotee was one who vowed to his idols to suffer death for the safety of his army, as Livy relates of the two Decii (*Decad.* I, viii, 9; x, 28). Hence devotion is apparently nothing else but the will to give oneself readily

Exod. XXXV dicitur quod *multitudo filiorum Israel obtulit mente promptissima atque devota primitias domino.* Manifestum est autem quod voluntas prompte faciendi quod ad Dei servitium pertinet est quidam specialis actus. Unde devotio est specialis actus voluntatis.

**AD PRIMUM** ergo dicendum quod movens imponit modum motui mobilis. Voluntas autem movet alias vires animae ad suos actus, et voluntas secundum quod est finis, movet seipsam ad ea quae sunt ad finem, ut supra habitum est. Et ideo, cum devotio sit actus voluntatis hominis offerentis seipsum Deo ad ei serviendum, qui est ultimus finis, consequens est quod devotio imponat modum humanis actibus, sive sint ipsius voluntatis circa ea quae sunt ad finem, sive etiam sint aliarum potentiarum quae a voluntate moventur.

**AD SECUNDUM** dicendum quod devotio invenitur in diversis generibus actuum non sicut species illorum generum, sed sicut motio moventis invenitur virtute in motibus mobilium.

**AD TERTIUM** dicendum quod devotio est actus appetitivae partis animae, et est quidam motus voluntatis, ut dictum est.

to things concerning the service of God. Wherefore it is written (Exod 35:20, 21) that *the multitude of the children of Israel . . . offered first-fruits to the Lord with a most ready and devout mind.* Now it is evident that the will to do readily what concerns the service of God is a special kind of act. Therefore devotion is a special act of the will.

**REPLY OBJ. 1:** The mover prescribes the mode of the movement of the thing moved. Now the will moves the other powers of the soul to their acts, and the will, insofar as it regards the end, moves both itself and whatever is directed to the end, as stated above (I-II, Q. 9, A. 3). Wherefore, since devotion is an act of the will whereby a man offers himself for the service of God Who is the last end, it follows that devotion prescribes the mode to human acts, whether they be acts of the will itself about things directed to the end, or acts of the other powers that are moved by the will.

**REPLY OBJ. 2:** Devotion is to be found in various genera of acts, not as a species of those genera, but as the motion of the mover is found virtually in the movements of the things moved.

**REPLY OBJ. 3:** Devotion is an act of the appetitive part of the soul, and is a movement of the will, as stated above.

# Article 2

*Whether devotion is an act of religion?*

**AD SECUNDUM SIC PROCEDITUR.** Videtur quod devotio non sit actus religionis. Devotio enim, ut dictum est, ad hoc pertinet quod aliquis Deo se tradat. Sed hoc maxime fit per caritatem, quia, ut Dionysius dicit, IV cap. de Div. Nom., *divinus amor extasim facit, non sinens amantes sui ipsorum esse, sed eorum quae amant.* Ergo devotio magis est actus caritatis quam religionis.

**PRAETEREA,** caritas praecedit religionem. Devotio autem videtur praecedere caritatem, quia caritas in Scripturis significatur per ignem, devotio vero per pinguedinem, quae est ignis materia. Ergo devotio non est actus religionis.

**PRAETEREA,** per religionem homo ordinatur solum ad Deum, ut dictum est. Sed devotio etiam habetur ad homines, dicuntur enim aliqui esse devoti aliquibus sanctis viris; et etiam subditi dicuntur esse devoti dominis suis, sicut Leo Papa dicit quod Iudaei, *quasi devoti Romanis legibus,* dixerunt, *non habemus regem nisi Caesarem.* Ergo devotio non est actus religionis.

**SED CONTRA** est quod devotio dicitur a devovendo, ut dictum est. Sed votum est actus religionis. Ergo et devotio.

**RESPONDEO** dicendum quod ad eandem virtutem pertinet velle facere aliquid, et promptam voluntatem

**OBJECTION 1:** It would seem that devotion is not an act of religion. Devotion, as stated above (A. 1), consists in giving oneself up to God. But this is done chiefly by charity, since according to Dionysius (*Div. Nom.* iv) *the Divine love produces ecstasy, for it takes the lover away from himself and gives him to the beloved.* Therefore devotion is an act of charity rather than of religion.

**OBJ. 2:** Further, charity precedes religion; and devotion seems to precede charity; since, in the Scriptures, charity is represented by fire, while devotion is signified by fatness which is the material of fire. Therefore devotion is not an act of religion.

**OBJ. 3:** Further, by religion man is directed to God alone, as stated above (Q. 81, A. 1). But devotion is directed also to men; for we speak of people being devout to certain holy men, and subjects are said to be devoted to their masters; thus Pope Leo says that the Jews *out of devotion to the Roman laws,* said: *We have no king but Caesar.* Therefore devotion is not an act of religion.

**ON THE CONTRARY,** Devotion is derived from devovere, as stated (A. 1). But a vow is an act of religion. Therefore devotion is also an act of religion.

**I ANSWER THAT,** It belongs to the same virtue, to will to do something, and to have the will ready to do it, be-

habere ad illud faciendum, quia utriusque actus est idem obiectum. Propter quod philosophus dicit, in V Ethic., *iustitia est qua volunt homines et operantur iusta.* Manifestum est autem quod operari ea quae pertinent ad divinum cultum seu famulatum pertinet proprie ad religionem, ut ex praedictis patet. Unde etiam ad eam pertinet habere promptam voluntatem ad huiusmodi exequenda, quod est esse devotum. Et sic patet quod devotio est actus religionis.

AD PRIMUM ergo dicendum quod ad caritatem pertinet immediate quod homo tradat seipsum Deo adhaerendo ei per quandam spiritus unionem. Sed quod homo tradat seipsum Deo ad aliqua opera divini cultus, hoc immediate pertinet ad religionem, mediate autem ad caritatem, quae est religionis principium.

AD SECUNDUM dicendum quod pinguedo corporalis et generatur per calorem naturalem digerentem; et ipsum naturalem calorem conservat quasi eius nutrimentum. Et similiter caritas et devotionem causat, inquantum ex amore aliquis redditur promptus ad serviendum amico; et etiam per devotionem caritas nutritur, sicut et quaelibet amicitia conservatur et augetur per amicabilium operum exercitium et meditationem.

AD TERTIUM dicendum quod devotio quae habetur ad sanctos Dei, mortuos vel vivos, non terminatur ad ipsos, sed transit in Deum, inquantum scilicet in ministris Dei Deum veneramur. Devotio autem quam subditi dicuntur habere ad dominos temporales alterius est rationis, sicut et temporalibus dominis famulari differt a famulatu divino.

cause both acts have the same object. For this reason the Philosopher says (*Ethic.* v, 1): *It is justice whereby men both will end do just actions.* Now it is evident that to do what pertains to the worship or service of God, belongs properly to religion, as stated above (Q. 81). Wherefore it belongs to that virtue to have the will ready to do such things, and this is to be devout. Hence it is evident that devotion is an act of religion.

REPLY OBJ. 1: It belongs immediately to charity that man should give himself to God, adhering to Him by a union of the spirit; but it belongs immediately to religion, and, through the medium of religion, to charity which is the principle of religion, that man should give himself to God for certain works of Divine worship.

REPLY OBJ. 2: Bodily fatness is produced by the natural heat in the process of digestion, and at the same time the natural heat thrives, as it were, on this fatness. In like manner charity both causes devotion (inasmuch as love makes one ready to serve one's friend) and feeds on devotion. Even so all friendship is safeguarded and increased by the practice and consideration of friendly deeds.

REPLY OBJ. 3: Devotion to God's holy ones, dead or living, does not terminate in them, but passes on to God, insofar as we honor God in His servants. But the devotion of subjects to their temporal masters is of another kind, just as service of a temporal master differs from the service of God.

# Article 3

*Whether contemplation, or meditation, is the cause of devotion?*

AD TERTIUM SIC PROCEDITUR. Videtur quod contemplatio, seu meditatio, non sit devotionis causa. Nulla enim causa impedit suum effectum. Sed subtiles meditationes intelligibilium multoties devotionem impediunt. Ergo contemplatio, seu meditatio, non est devotionis causa.

PRAETEREA, si contemplatio esset propria et per se devotionis causa, oporteret quod ea quae sunt altioris contemplationis magis devotionem excitarent. Huius autem contrarium apparet, frequenter enim maior devotio excitatur ex consideratione passionis Christi, et aliis mysteriis humanitatis ipsius, quam ex consideratione divinae magnitudinis. Ergo contemplatio non est propria devotionis causa.

PRAETEREA, si contemplatio esset propria causa devotionis, oporteret quod illi qui sunt magis apti ad contemplationem essent etiam magis apti ad devotionem. Huius autem contrarium videmus, quia devotio

OBJECTION 1: It would seem that contemplation or meditation is not the cause of devotion. No cause hinders its effect. But subtle considerations about abstract matters are often a hindrance to devotion. Therefore contemplation or meditation is not the cause of devotion.

OBJ. 2: Further, if contemplation were the proper and essential cause of devotion, the higher objects of contemplation would arouse greater devotion. But the contrary is the case: since frequently we are urged to greater devotion by considering Christ's Passion and other mysteries of His humanity than by considering the greatness of His Godhead. Therefore contemplation is not the proper cause of devotion.

OBJ. 3: Further, if contemplation were the proper cause of devotion, it would follow that those who are most apt for contemplation, are also most apt for devotion. Yet the contrary is to be noticed, for devotion is frequently found

frequenter magis invenitur in quibusdam simplicibus viris et in femineo sexu, in quibus invenitur contemplationis defectus. Ergo contemplatio non est propria causa devotionis.

**Sed contra** est quod in Psalm dicitur, *in meditatione mea exardescet ignis.* Sed ignis spiritualis causat devotionem. Ergo meditatio est devotionis causa.

**Respondeo** dicendum quod causa devotionis extrinseca et principalis Deus est; de quo dicit Ambrosius, super Luc., quod *Deus quos dignatur vocat, et quem vult religiosum facit, et si voluisset, Samaritanos ex indevotis devotos fecisset.* Causa autem intrinseca ex parte nostra, oportet quod sit meditatio seu contemplatio. Dictum est enim quod devotio est quidam voluntatis actus ad hoc quod homo prompte se tradat ad divinum obsequium. Omnis autem actus voluntatis ex aliqua consideratione procedit, eo quod bonum intellectum est obiectum voluntatis, unde et Augustinus dicit, in libro de Trin., quod voluntas oritur ex intelligentia. Et ideo necesse est quod meditatio sit devotionis causa, inquantum scilicet per meditationem homo concipit quod se tradat divino obsequio. Ad quod quidem inducit duplex consideratio. Una quidem quae est ex parte divinae bonitatis et beneficiorum ipsius, secundum illud Psalm., *mihi adhaerere Deo bonum est, ponere in domino Deo spem meam.* Et haec consideratio excitat dilectionem, quae est proxima devotionis causa. Alia vero est ex parte hominis considerantis suos defectus, ex quibus indiget ut Deo innitatur, secundum illud Psalm., *levavi oculos meos in montes, unde veniet auxilium mihi. Auxilium meum a domino, qui fecit caelum et terram.* Et haec consideratio excludit praesumptionem, per quam aliquis impeditur ne Deo se subiiciat, dum suae virtuti innititur.

**Ad primum** ergo dicendum quod consideratio eorum quae nata sunt dilectionem Dei excitare, devotionem causant. Consideratio vero quorumcumque ad hoc non pertinentium, sed ab his mentem distrahentium, impedit devotionem.

**Ad secundum** dicendum quod ea quae sunt divinitatis sunt secundum se maxime excitantia dilectionem, et per consequens devotionem, quia Deus est super omnia diligendus. Sed ex debilitate mentis humanae est quod sicut indiget manuduci ad cognitionem divinorum, ita ad dilectionem, per aliqua sensibilia nobis nota. Inter quae praecipuum est humanitas Christi, secundum quod in praefatione dicitur, *ut dum visibiliter Deum cognoscimus, per hunc in invisibilium amorem rapiamur.* Et ideo ea quae pertinent ad Christi humanitatem, per modum cuiusdam manuductionis, maxime devotionem excitant, cum tamen devotio principaliter circa ea quae sunt divinitatis consistat.

**Ad tertium** dicendum quod scientia, et quidquid aliud ad magnitudinem pertinet, occasio est quod homo

in men of simplicity and members of the female sex, who are defective in contemplation. Therefore contemplation is not the proper cause of devotion.

**On the contrary,** It is written (Ps 38:4): *In my meditation a fire shall flame out.* But spiritual fire causes devotion. Therefore meditation is the cause of devotion.

**I answer that,** The extrinsic and chief cause of devotion is God, of Whom Ambrose, commenting on Luke 9:55, says that *God calls whom He deigns to call, and whom He wills He makes religious: the profane Samaritans, had He so willed, He would have made devout.* But the intrinsic cause on our part must needs be meditation or contemplation. For it was stated above (A. 1) that devotion is an act of the will to the effect that man surrenders himself readily to the service of God. Now every act of the will proceeds from some consideration, since the object of the will is a good understood. Wherefore Augustine says (*De Trin.* ix, 12; xv, 23) that the will arises from the intelligence. Consequently meditation must needs be the cause of devotion, insofar as through meditation man conceives the thought of surrendering himself to God's service. Indeed a twofold consideration leads him thereto. The one is the consideration of God's goodness and loving kindness, according to Ps. 72:28, *It is good for me to adhere to my God, to put my hope in the Lord God*: and this consideration wakens love which is the proximate cause of devotion. The other consideration is that of man's own shortcomings, on account of which he needs to lean on God, according to Ps. 120:1, 2, *I have lifted up my eyes to the mountains, from whence help shall come to me: my help is from the Lord, Who made heaven and earth*; and this consideration shuts out presumption whereby man is hindered from submitting to God, because he leans on His strength.

**Reply Obj. 1:** The consideration of such things as are of a nature to awaken our love of God, causes devotion; whereas the consideration of foreign matters that distract the mind from such things is a hindrance to devotion.

**Reply Obj. 2:** Matters concerning the Godhead are, in themselves, the strongest incentive to love and consequently to devotion, because God is supremely lovable. Yet such is the weakness of the human mind that it needs a guiding hand, not only to the knowledge, but also to the love of Divine things by means of certain sensible objects known to us. Chief among these is the humanity of Christ, according to the words of the Preface, *that through knowing God visibly, we may be caught up to the love of things invisible.* Wherefore matters relating to Christ's humanity are the chief incentive to devotion, leading us thither as a guiding hand, although devotion itself has for its object matters concerning the Godhead.

**Reply Obj. 3:** Science and anything else conducive to greatness, is to man an occasion of self-confidence, so that

confidat de seipso, et ideo non totaliter se Deo tradat. Et inde est quod huiusmodi quandoque occasionaliter devotionem impediunt, et in simplicibus et mulieribus devotio abundat, elationem comprimendo. Si tamen scientiam, et quamcumque aliam perfectionem, homo perfecte Deo subdat, ex hoc ipso devotio augetur.

he does not wholly surrender himself to God. The result is that such like things sometimes occasion a hindrance to devotion; while in simple souls and women devotion abounds by repressing pride. If, however, a man perfectly submits to God his science or any other perfection, by this very fact his devotion is increased.

# Article 4

*Whether joy is an effect of devotion?*

**AD QUARTUM SIC PROCEDITUR.** Videtur quod laetitia non sit devotionis effectus. Quia, ut dictum est, passio Christi praecipue ad devotionem excitat. Sed ex eius consideratione consequitur in anima quaedam afflictio, secundum illud Thren. III, *recordare paupertatis meae, absinthii et fellis*, quod pertinet ad passionem; et subditur, *memoria memor ero, et tabescet in me anima mea*. Ergo delectatio, sive gaudium, non est devotionis effectus.

**PRAETEREA,** devotio praecipue consistit in interiori sacrificio spiritus. Sed in Psalm. dicitur, *sacrificium Deo spiritus contribulatus*. Ergo afflictio magis est devotionis effectus quam iucunditas sive gaudium.

**PRAETEREA,** Gregorius Nyssenus dicit, in libro de homine, quod *sicut risus procedit ex gaudio, ita lacrimae et gemitus sunt signa tristitiae*. Sed ex devotione contingit quod aliqui prorumpant in lacrimas. Ergo laetitia, vel gaudium, non est devotionis effectus.

**SED CONTRA** est quod in collecta dicitur, *quos ieiunia votiva castigant, ipsa quoque devotio sancta laetificet*.

**RESPONDEO** dicendum quod devotio per se quidem et principaliter spiritualem laetitiam mentis causat, ex consequenti autem et per accidens causat tristitiam. Dictum est enim quod devotio ex duplici consideratione procedit. Principaliter quidem ex consideratione divinae bonitatis, quia ista consideratio pertinet quasi ad terminum motus voluntatis tradentis se Deo. Et ex ista consideratione per se quidem sequitur delectatio, secundum illud Psalm., *memor fui Dei, et delectatus sum*, sed per accidens haec consideratio tristitiam quandam causat in his qui nondum plene Deo fruuntur, secundum illud Psalm., *sitivit anima mea ad Deum vivum*, et postea sequitur, *fuerunt mihi lacrimae meae*, etc. Secundario vero causatur devotio, ut dictum est, ex consideratione propriorum defectuum, nam haec consideratio pertinet ad terminum a quo homo per motum voluntatis devotae recedit, ut scilicet non in se existat, sed Deo se subdat. Haec autem consideratio e converso se habet ad primam. Nam per se quidem nata est tristitiam causare, recogitando proprios defectus, per accidens autem laetitiam, scilicet propter spem divinae subventionis. Et sic patet

**OBJECTION 1:** It would seem that joy is not an effect of devotion. As stated above (A. 3, ad 2), Christ's Passion is the chief incentive to devotion. But the consideration thereof causes an affliction of the soul, according to Lam. 3:19, *Remember my poverty . . . the wormwood and the gall*, which refers to the Passion, and afterwards (Lam 3:20) it is said: *I will be mindful and remember, and my soul shall languish within me*. Therefore delight or joy is not the effect of devotion.

**OBJ. 2:** Further, devotion consists chiefly in an interior sacrifice of the spirit. But it is written (Ps 50:19): *A sacrifice to God is an afflicted spirit*. Therefore affliction is the effect of devotion rather than gladness or joy.

**OBJ. 3:** Further, Gregory of Nyssa says (*De Homine* xii) that *just as laughter proceeds from joy, so tears and groans are signs of sorrow*. But devotion makes some people shed tears. Therefore gladness or joy is not the effect of devotion.

**ON THE CONTRARY,** We say in the Collect: *That we who are punished by fasting may be comforted by a holy devotion.*

**I ANSWER THAT,** The direct and principal effect of devotion is the spiritual joy of the mind, though sorrow is its secondary and indirect effect. For it has been stated (A. 3) that devotion is caused by a twofold consideration: chiefly by the consideration of God's goodness, because this consideration belongs to the term, as it were, of the movement of the will in surrendering itself to God, and the direct result of this consideration is joy, according to Ps. 76:4, *I remembered God, and was delighted*; but accidentally this consideration causes a certain sorrow in those who do not yet enjoy God fully, according to Ps. 41:3, *My soul hath thirsted after the strong living God*, and afterwards it is said (Ps 41:4): *My tears have been my bread*, etc. Secondarily devotion is caused as stated (A. 3), by the consideration of one's own failings; for this consideration regards the term from which man withdraws by the movement of his devout will, in that he trusts not in himself, but subjects himself to God. This consideration has an opposite tendency to the first: for it is of a nature to cause sorrow directly (when one thinks over one's own failings), and joy accidentally, namely, through hope of the Divine assistance. It is accord-

quod ad devotionem primo et per se consequitur delectatio, secundario autem et per accidens *tristitia quae est secundum Deum.*

**AD PRIMUM** ergo dicendum quod in consideratione passionis Christi est aliquid quod contristet, scilicet defectus humanus, propter quem tollendum *Christum pati oportuit,* et est aliquid quod laetificet, scilicet Dei erga nos benignitas, quae nobis de tali liberatione providit.

**AD SECUNDUM** dicendum quod spiritus qui ex una parte contribulatur propter praesentis vitae defectus, ex alia parte condelectatur ex consideratione divinae bonitatis et ex spe divini auxilii.

**AD TERTIUM** dicendum quod lacrimae prorumpunt non solum ex tristitia, sed etiam ex quadam affectus teneritudine, praecipue cum consideratur aliquid delectabile cum permixtione alicuius tristabilis; sicut solent homines lacrimari ex pietatis affectu cum recuperant filios vel caros amicos quos aestimaverant se perdidisse. Et per hunc modum lacrimae ex devotione procedunt.

ingly evident that the first and direct effect of devotion is joy, while the secondary and accidental effect is that *sorrow which is according to God.*

**REPLY OBJ. 1:** In the consideration of Christ's Passion there is something that causes sorrow, namely, the human defect, the removal of which made it *necessary for Christ to suffer*; and there is something that causes joy, namely, God's loving-kindness to us in giving us such a deliverance.

**REPLY OBJ. 2:** The spirit which on the one hand is afflicted on account of the defects of the present life, on the other hand is rejoiced, by the consideration of God's goodness, and by the hope of the Divine help.

**REPLY OBJ. 3:** Tears are caused not only through sorrow, but also through a certain tenderness of the affections, especially when one considers something that gives joy mixed with pain. Thus men are wont to shed tears through a sentiment of piety, when they recover their children or dear friends, whom they thought to have lost. In this way tears arise from devotion.

# QUESTION 83

## PRAYER

Deinde considerandum est de oratione. Et circa hoc quaeruntur decem et septem.

Primo, utrum oratio sit actus appetitivae virtutis vel cognitivae.

Secundo, utrum conveniens sit orare.

Tertio, utrum oratio sit actus religionis.

Quarto, utrum solus Deus sit orandus.

Quinto, utrum in oratione sit aliquid determinate petendum.

Sexto, utrum orando debeamus temporalia petere.

Septimo, utrum pro aliis orare debeamus.

Octavo, utrum debeamus orare pro inimicis.

Nono, de septem petitionibus orationis dominicae.

Decimo, utrum orare sit proprium rationalis creaturae.

Undecimo, utrum sancti in patria orent pro nobis.

Duodecimo, utrum, oratio debeat esse vocalis.

Tertiodecimo, utrum attentio requiratur ad orationem.

Quartodecimo, utrum oratio debeat esse diuturna.

Quintodecimo, utrum oratio sit efficax ad impetrandum quod petitur.

Sextodecimo, utrum sit meritoria.

Septimodecimo, de speciebus orationis.

We must now consider prayer, under which head there are seventeen points of inquiry:

(1) Whether prayer is an act of the appetitive or of the cognitive power?

(2) Whether it is fitting to pray to God?

(3) Whether prayer is an act of religion?

(4) Whether we ought to pray to God alone?

(5) Whether we ought to ask for something definite when we pray?

(6) Whether we ought to ask for temporal things when we pray?

(7) Whether we ought to pray for others?

(8) Whether we ought to pray for our enemies?

(9) Of the seven petitions of the Lord's Prayer;

(10) Whether prayer is proper to the rational creature?

(11) Whether the saints in heaven pray for us?

(12) Whether prayer should be vocal?

(13) Whether attention is requisite in prayer?

(14) Whether prayer should last a long time?

(15) Whether prayer is meritorious?

(16) Whether sinners impetrate anything from God by praying?

(17) of the different kinds of prayer.

# Article 1

*Whether prayer is an act of the appetitive power?*

**AD PRIMUM SIC PROCEDITUR.** Videtur quod oratio sit actus appetitivae virtutis. Orationis enim est exaudiri. Sed desiderium est quod exauditur a Deo, secundum illud Psalm., *desiderium pauperum exaudivit dominus.* Ergo oratio est desiderium. Sed desiderium est actus appetitivae virtutis. Ergo et oratio.

**PRAETEREA,** Dionysius dicit, in III cap. de Div. Nom., *ante omnia ab oratione incipere est utile, sicut Deo nosipsos tradentes et unientes.* Sed unio ad Deum per amorem fit, qui pertinet ad vim appetitivam. Ergo oratio ad vim appetitivam pertinet.

**PRAETEREA,** philosophus, in III de anima, ponit duas operationes intellectivae partis, quarum prima est *indivisibilium intelligentia,* per quam scilicet appre-

**OBJECTION 1:** It would seem that prayer is an act of the appetitive power. It belongs to prayer to be heard. Now it is the desire that is heard by God, according to Ps. 9:38, *The Lord hath heard the desire of the poor.* Therefore prayer is desire. But desire is an act of the appetitive power: and therefore prayer is also.

**OBJ. 2:** Further, Dionysius says (*Div. Nom.* iii): *It is useful to begin everything with prayer, because thereby we surrender ourselves to God and unite ourselves to Him.* Now union with God is effected by love which belongs to the appetitive power. Therefore prayer belongs to the appetitive power.

**OBJ. 3:** Further, the Philosopher states (*De Anima* iii, 6) that there are two operations of the intellective part. Of these the first is *the understanding of indivisibles,* by which

hendimus de unoquoque quid est; secunda vero est *compositio et divisio*, per quam scilicet apprehenditur aliquid esse vel non esse. Quibus tertia additur *ratiocinari*, procedendo scilicet de notis ad ignota. Sed oratio ad nullam istarum operationum reducitur. Ergo non est actus intellectivae virtutis, sed appetitivae.

**SED CONTRA** est quod Isidorus dicit, in libro Etymol., quod *orare idem est quod dicere*. Sed dictio pertinet ad intellectum. Ergo oratio non est actus appetitivae virtutis, sed intellectivae.

**RESPONDEO** dicendum quod, secundum Cassiodorum, *oratio dicitur quasi oris ratio*. Ratio autem speculativa et practica in hoc differunt quod ratio speculativa est apprehensiva solum rerum; ratio vero practica est non solum apprehensiva, sed etiam causativa. Est autem aliquid alterius causa dupliciter. Uno quidem modo, perfecte, necessitatem inducendo, et hoc contingit quando effectus totaliter subditur potestati causae. Alio vero modo, imperfecte, solum disponendo, quando scilicet effectus non subditur totaliter potestati causae. Sic igitur et ratio dupliciter est causa aliquorum. Uno quidem modo, sicut necessitatem imponens, et hoc modo ad rationem pertinet imperare non solum inferioribus potentiis et membris corporis, sed etiam hominibus subiectis, quod quidem fit imperando. Alio modo, sicut inducens et quodammodo disponens, et hoc modo ratio petit aliquid fieri ab his qui ei non subiiciuntur, sive sint aequales sive sint superiores. Utrumque autem horum, scilicet imperare et petere sive deprecari, ordinationem quandam important, prout scilicet homo disponit aliquid per aliud esse faciendum. Unde pertinent ad rationem, cuius est ordinare, propter quod philosophus dicit, in I Ethic., quod *ad optima deprecatur ratio*.

Sic autem nunc loquimur de oratione, prout significat quandam deprecationem vel petitionem, secundum quod Augustinus dicit, in libro de Verb. Dom., quod *oratio petitio quaedam est*; et Damascenus dicit, in III libro, quod *oratio est petitio decentium a Deo*. Sic ergo patet quod oratio de qua nunc loquimur, est rationis actus.

**AD PRIMUM** ergo dicendum quod desiderium pauperum dicitur dominus exaudire, vel quia desiderium est causa petendi, cum petitio sit quodammodo desiderii interpres. Vel hoc dicitur ad ostendendum exauditionis velocitatem, quia scilicet dum adhuc aliquid in desiderio pauperum est, Deus exaudit, antequam orationem proponant; secundum illud Isaiae LXV, *eritque, antequam clament, ego exaudiam*.

**AD SECUNDUM** dicendum quod, sicut supra dictum est, voluntas movet rationem ad suum finem. Unde nihil prohibet, movente voluntate, actum rationis tendere in finem caritatis, qui est Deo uniri. Tendit autem oratio

operation we apprehend what a thing is: while the second is *synthesis* and *analysis*, whereby we apprehend that a thing is or is not. To these a third may be added, namely, *reasoning*, whereby we proceed from the known to the unknown. Now prayer is not reducible to any of these operations. Therefore it is an operation, not of the intellective, but of the appetitive power.

**ON THE CONTRARY,** Isidore says (*Etym.* x) that *to pray is to speak*. Now speech belongs to the intellect. Therefore prayer is an act, not of the appetitive, but of the intellective power.

**I ANSWER THAT,** According to Cassiodorus *prayer (oratio) is spoken reason (oris ratio)*. Now the speculative and practical reason differ in this, that the speculative merely apprehends its object, whereas the practical reason not only apprehends but causes. Now one thing is the cause of another in two ways: first perfectly, when it necessitates its effect, and this happens when the effect is wholly subject to the power of the cause; second imperfectly, by merely disposing to the effect, for the reason that the effect is not wholly subject to the power of the cause. Accordingly in this way the reason is cause of certain things in two ways: first, by imposing necessity; and in this way it belongs to reason, to command not only the lower powers and the members of the body, but also human subjects, which indeed is done by commanding; second, by leading up to the effect, and, in a way, disposing to it, and in this sense the reason asks for something to be done by things not subject to it, whether they be its equals or its superiors. Now both of these, namely, to command and to ask or beseech, imply a certain ordering, seeing that man proposes something to be effected by something else, wherefore they pertain to the reason to which it belongs to set in order. For this reason the Philosopher says (*Ethic.* i, 13) that the *reason exhorts us to do what is best*.

Now in the present instance we are speaking of prayer as signifying a beseeching or petition, in which sense Augustine: says (*De Verb. Dom.*) that *prayer is a petition*, and Damascene states (*De Fide Orth.* iii, 24) that *to pray is to ask becoming things of God*. Accordingly it is evident that prayer, as we speak of it now, is an act of reason.

**REPLY OBJ. 1:** The Lord is said to hear the desire of the poor, either because desire is the cause of their petition, since a petition is like the interpreter of a desire, or in order to show how speedily they are heard, since no sooner do the poor desire something than God hears them before they put up a prayer, according to the saying of Isa. 65:24, *And it shall come to pass, that before they call, I will hear.*

**REPLY OBJ. 2:** As stated above (I, Q. 82, A. 4; I-II, Q. 9, A. 1, ad 3), the will moves the reason to its end: wherefore nothing hinders the act of reason, under the motion of the will, from tending to an end such as charity which is union

in Deum quasi a voluntate caritatis mota, dupliciter. Uno quidem modo, ex parte eius quod petitur, quia hoc praecipue est in oratione petendum, ut Deo uniamur; secundum illud Psalm., *unam petii a domino, hanc requiram, ut inhabitem in domo domini omnibus diebus vitae meae.* Alio modo, ex parte ipsius petentis, quem oportet accedere ad eum a quo petit, vel loco, sicut ad hominem; vel mente, sicut ad Deum. Unde dicit ibidem quod, *quando orationibus invocamus Deum, revelata mente adsumus ipsi.* Et secundum hoc etiam Damascenus dicit quod *oratio est ascensus intellectus in Deum.*

**AD TERTIUM** dicendum quod illi tres actus pertinent ad rationem speculativam. Sed ulterius ad rationem practicam pertinet causare aliquid per modum imperii vel per modum petitionis, ut dictum est.

with God. Now prayer tends to God through being moved by the will of charity, as it were, and this in two ways. First, on the part of the object of our petition, because when we pray we ought principally to ask to be united to God, according to Ps. 26:4, *One thing I have asked of the Lord, this will I seek after, that I may dwell in the house of the Lord all the days of my life.* Second, on the part of the petitioner, who ought to approach the person whom he petitions, either locally, as when he petitions a man, or mentally, as when he petitions God. Hence Dionysius says (*Div. Nom.* iii) that *when we call upon God in our prayers, we unveil our mind in His presence*: and in the same sense Damascene says (*De Fide Orth.* iii, 24) that *prayer is the raising up of the mind to God.*

**REPLY OBJ. 3**: These three acts belong to the speculative reason, but to the practical reason it belongs in addition to cause something by way of command or of petition, as stated above.

# Article 2

*Whether it is becoming to pray?*

**AD SECUNDUM SIC PROCEDITUR.** Videtur quod non sit conveniens orare. Oratio enim videtur esse necessaria ad hoc quod intimemus ei a quo petimus id quo indigemus. Sed, sicut dicitur Matth. VI, *scit pater vester quia his indigetis.* Ergo non est conveniens Deum orare.

**PRAETEREA**, per orationem flectitur animus eius qui oratur ut faciat quod ab eo petitur. Sed animus Dei est immutabilis et inflexibilis, secundum illud I Reg. XV, *porro triumphator in Israel non parcet, nec poenitudine flectetur.* Ergo non est conveniens quod Deum oremus.

**PRAETEREA**, liberalius est dare aliquid non petenti quam dare petenti, quia, sicut Seneca dicit, *nulla res carius emitur quam quae precibus empta est.* Sed Deus est liberalissimus. Ergo non videtur esse conveniens quod Deum oremus.

**SED CONTRA** est quod dicitur Luc. XVIII, *oportet orare, et non deficere.*

**RESPONDEO** dicendum quod triplex fuit circa orationem antiquorum error. Quidam enim posuerunt quod res humanae non reguntur divina providentia. Ex quo sequitur quod vanum sit orare, et omnino Deum colere. Et de his dicitur Malach. III, *dixistis, vanus est qui servit Deo.* Secunda fuit opinio ponentium omnia, etiam in rebus humanis, ex necessitate contingere, sive ex immutabilitate divinae providentiae, sive ex necessitate stellarum, sive ex connexione causarum. Et secundum hos etiam excluditur orationis utilitas. Tertia fuit opinio

**OBJECTION 1**: It would seem that it is unbecoming to pray. Prayer seems to be necessary in order that we may make our needs known to the person to whom we pray. But according to Matt. 6:32, *Your Father knoweth that you have need of all these things.* Therefore it is not becoming to pray to God.

**OBJ. 2**: Further, by prayer we bend the mind of the person to whom we pray, so that he may do what is asked of him. But God's mind is unchangeable and inflexible, according to 1 Kings 15:29, *But the Triumpher in Israel will not spare, and will not be moved to repentance.* Therefore it is not fitting that we should pray to God.

**OBJ. 3**: Further, it is more liberal to give to one that asks not, than to one who asks because, according to Seneca (*De Benefic.* ii, 1), *nothing is bought more dearly than what is bought with prayers.* But God is supremely liberal. Therefore it would seem unbecoming to pray to God.

**ON THE CONTRARY**, It is written (Luke 18:1): *We ought always to pray, and not to faint.*

**I ANSWER THAT**, Among the ancients there was a threefold error concerning prayer. Some held that human affairs are not ruled by Divine providence; whence it would follow that it is useless to pray and to worship God at all: of these it is written (Mal 3:14): *You have said: He laboreth in vain that serveth God.* Another opinion held that all things, even in human affairs, happen of necessity, whether by reason of the unchangeableness of Divine providence, or through the compelling influence of the stars, or on account of the connection of causes: and this opinion also excluded

ponentium quidem res humanas divina providentia regi, et quod res humanae non proveniunt ex necessitate, sed dicebant similiter dispositionem divinae providentiae variabilem esse, et quod orationibus et aliis quae ad divinum cultum pertinent dispositio divinae providentiae immutatur. Haec autem omnia in primo libro improbata sunt. Et ideo oportet sic inducere orationis utilitatem ut neque rebus humanis, divinae providentiae subiectis, necessitatem imponamus; neque etiam divinam dispositionem mutabilem aestimemus.

Ad huius ergo evidentiam, considerandum est quod ex divina providentia non solum disponitur qui effectus fiant, sed etiam ex quibus causis et quo ordine proveniant. Inter alias autem causas sunt etiam quorundam causae actus humani. Unde oportet homines agere aliqua, non ut per suos actus divinam dispositionem immutent, sed ut per actus suos impleant quosdam effectus secundum ordinem a Deo dispositum. Et idem etiam est in naturalibus causis. Et simile est etiam de oratione. Non enim propter hoc oramus ut divinam dispositionem immutemus, sed ut id impetremus quod Deus disposuit per orationes sanctorum esse implendum; ut scilicet homines *postulando mereantur accipere quod eis omnipotens Deus ante saecula disposuit donare*, ut Gregorius dicit, in libro dialogorum.

**AD PRIMUM** ergo dicendum quod non est necessarium nos Deo preces porrigere ut ei nostras indigentias vel desideria manifestemus, sed ut nosipsi consideremus in his ad divinum auxilium esse recurrendum.

**AD SECUNDUM** dicendum quod, sicut dictum est, oratio nostra non ordinatur ad immutationem divinae dispositionis, sed ut obtineatur nostris precibus quod Deus disposuit.

**AD TERTIUM** dicendum quod Deus multa nobis praestat ex sua liberalitate etiam non petita. Sed quod aliqua vult praestare nobis petentibus, hoc est propter nostram utilitatem, ut scilicet fiduciam quandam accipiamus recurrendi ad Deum, et ut recognoscamus eum esse bonorum nostrorum auctorem. Unde Chrysostomus dicit, *considera quanta est tibi concessa felicitas, quanta gloria attributa, orationibus fabulari cum Deo, cum Christo miscere colloquia, optare quod velis, quod desideras postulare.*

the utility of prayer. There was a third opinion of those who held that human affairs are indeed ruled by Divine providence, and that they do not happen of necessity; yet they deemed the disposition of Divine providence to be changeable, and that it is changed by prayers and other things pertaining to the worship of God. All these opinions were disproved in the First Part (Q. 19, AA. 7, 8; Q. 22, AA. 2, 4; Q. 115, A. 6; Q. 116). Wherefore it behooves us so to account for the utility of prayer as neither to impose necessity on human affairs subject to Divine providence, nor to imply changeableness on the part of the Divine disposition.

In order to throw light on this question we must consider that Divine providence disposes not only what effects shall take place, but also from what causes and in what order these effects shall proceed. Now among other causes human acts are the causes of certain effects. Wherefore it must be that men do certain actions, not that thereby they may change the Divine disposition, but that by those actions they may achieve certain effects according to the order of the Divine disposition: and the same is to be said of natural causes. And so is it with regard to prayer. For we pray not that we may change the Divine disposition, but that we may impetrate that which God has disposed to be fulfilled by our prayers, in other words *that by asking, men may deserve to receive what Almighty God from eternity has disposed to give*, as Gregory says (*Dial.* i, 8).

**REPLY OBJ. 1**: We need to pray to God, not in order to make known to Him our needs or desires but that we ourselves may be reminded of the necessity of having recourse to God's help in these matters.

**REPLY OBJ. 2**: As stated above, our motive in praying is, not that we may change the Divine disposition, but that, by our prayers, we may obtain what God has appointed.

**REPLY OBJ. 3**: God bestows many things on us out of His liberality, even without our asking for them: but that He wishes to bestow certain things on us at our asking, is for the sake of our good, namely, that we may acquire confidence in having recourse to God, and that we may recognize in Him the Author of our goods. Hence Chrysostom says: *Think what happiness is granted thee, what honor bestowed on thee, when thou conversest with God in prayer, when thou talkest with Christ, when thou askest what thou wilt, whatever thou desirest.*

# Article 3

### Whether prayer is an act of religion?

**Ad tertium sic proceditur.** Videtur quod oratio non sit actus religionis. Religio enim, cum sit pars iustitiae, est in voluntate sicut in subiecto. Sed oratio pertinet ad partem intellectivam, ut ex supradictis patet. Ergo oratio non videtur esse actus religionis, sed doni intellectus, per quod mens ascendit in Deum.

**Praeterea,** actus latriae cadit sub necessitate praecepti. Sed oratio non videtur cadere sub necessitate praecepti, sed ex mera voluntate procedere, cum nihil aliud sit quam volitorum petitio. Ergo oratio non videtur esse religionis actus.

**Praeterea,** ad religionem pertinere videtur ut quis *divinae naturae cultum caeremoniamque afferat.* Sed oratio non videtur aliquid Deo afferre, sed magis aliquid obtinendum ab eo petere. Ergo oratio non est religionis actus.

**Sed contra** est quod dicitur in Psalm., *dirigatur oratio mea sicut incensum in conspectu tuo,* ubi dicit Glossa quod *in huius figuram, in veteri lege incensum dicebatur offerri in odorem suavem domino.* Sed hoc pertinet ad religionem. Ergo oratio est religionis actus.

**Respondeo** dicendum quod, sicut supra dictum est, ad religionem proprie pertinet reverentiam et honorem Deo exhibere. Et ideo omnia illa per quae Deo reverentia exhibetur pertinent ad religionem. Per orationem autem homo Deo reverentiam exhibet, inquantum scilicet se ei subiicit, et profitetur orando se eo indigere sicut auctore suorum bonorum. Unde manifestum est quod oratio est proprie religionis actus.

**Ad primum** ergo dicendum quod voluntas movet alias potentias animae in suum finem, sicut supra dictum est. Et ideo religio, quae est in voluntate, ordinat actus aliarum potentiarum ad Dei reverentiam. Inter alias autem potentias animae, intellectus altior est et voluntati propinquior. Et ideo post devotionem, quae pertinet ad ipsam voluntatem, oratio, quae pertinet ad partem intellectivam, est praecipua inter actus religionis, per quam religio intellectum hominis movet in Deum.

**Ad secundum** dicendum quod non solum petere quae desideramus, sed etiam recte aliquid desiderare sub praecepto cadit. Sed desiderare quidem cadit sub praecepto caritatis, petere autem sub praecepto religionis. Quod quidem praeceptum ponitur Matth. VII, ubi dicitur, *petite, et accipietis.*

**Ad tertium** dicendum quod orando tradit homo mentem suam Deo, quam ei per reverentiam subiicit et quodammodo praesentat, ut patet ex auctoritate Dionysii prius inducta. Et ideo sicut mens humana praeeminet exterioribus vel corporalibus membris, vel exterioribus

**Objection 1:** It would seem that prayer is not an act of religion. Since religion is a part of justice, it resides in the will as in its subject. But prayer belongs to the intellective part, as stated above (A. 1). Therefore prayer seems to be an act, not of religion, but of the gift of understanding whereby the mind ascends to God.

**Obj. 2:** Further, the act of latria falls under a necessity of precept. But prayer does not seem to come under a necessity of precept, but to come from the mere will, since it is nothing else than a petition for what we will. Therefore prayer seemingly is not an act of religion.

**Obj. 3:** Further, it seems to belong to religion that one *offers worship and ceremonial rites to the Godhead.* But prayer seems not to offer anything to God, but to ask to obtain something from Him. Therefore prayer is not an act of religion.

**On the contrary,** It is written (Ps 140:2): *Let my prayer be directed as incense in Thy sight:* and a gloss on the passage says that *it was to signify this that under the Old Law incense was said to be offered for a sweet smell to the Lord.* Now this belongs to religion. Therefore prayer is an act of religion.

**I answer that,** As stated above (Q. 81, AA. 2, 4), it belongs properly to religion to show honor to God, wherefore all those things through which reverence is shown to God, belong to religion. Now man shows reverence to God by means of prayer, insofar as he subjects himself to Him, and by praying confesses that he needs Him as the Author of his goods. Hence it is evident that prayer is properly an act of religion.

**Reply Obj. 1:** The will moves the other powers of the soul to its end, as stated above (Q. 82, A. 1, ad 1), and therefore religion, which is in the will, directs the acts of the other powers to the reverence of God. Now among the other powers of the soul the intellect is the highest, and the nearest to the will; and consequently after devotion which belongs to the will, prayer which belongs to the intellective part is the chief of the acts of religion, since by it religion directs man's intellect to God.

**Reply Obj. 2:** It is a matter of precept not only that we should ask for what we desire, but also that we should desire aright. But to desire comes under a precept of charity, whereas to ask comes under a precept of religion, which precept is expressed in Matt. 7:7, where it is said: *Ask and ye shall receive.*

**Reply Obj. 3:** By praying man surrenders his mind to God, since he subjects it to Him with reverence and, so to speak, presents it to Him, as appears from the words of Dionysius quoted above (A. 1, Obj. 2). Wherefore just as the human mind excels exterior things, whether bodily

rebus quae ad Dei servitium applicantur, ita etiam oratio praeeminet aliis actibus religionis.

members, or those external things that are employed for God's service, so too, prayer surpasses other acts of religion.

# Article 4

*Whether we ought to pray to God alone?*

AD QUARTUM SIC PROCEDITUR. Videtur quod solus Deus debeat orari. Oratio enim est actus religionis, ut dictum est. Sed solus Deus est religione colendus. Ergo solus Deus est orandus.

PRAETEREA, frustra porrigitur oratio ad eum qui orationem non cognoscit. Sed solius Dei est orationem cognoscere. Tum quia plerumque oratio magis agitur interiori actu, quem solus Deus cognoscit, quam voce, secundum illud quod apostolus dicit, I ad Cor. XIV, *orabo spiritu, orabo et mente*. Tum etiam quia, ut Augustinus dicit, in libro de cura pro mortuis agenda, *nesciunt mortui, etiam sancti, quid agant vivi, etiam eorum filii*. Ergo oratio non est nisi Deo porrigenda.

PRAETEREA, si aliquibus sanctis orationem porrigimus, hoc non est nisi inquantum sunt Deo coniuncti. Sed quidam in hoc mundo viventes, vel etiam in Purgatorio existentes, sunt multum Deo coniuncti per gratiam. Ad eos autem non porrigitur oratio. Ergo nec ad sanctos qui sunt in Paradiso debemus orationem porrigere.

SED CONTRA est quod dicitur Iob V, *voca, si est qui tibi respondeat, et ad aliquem sanctorum convertere*.

RESPONDEO dicendum quod oratio porrigitur alicui dupliciter, uno modo, quasi per ipsum implenda; alio modo, sicut per ipsum impetranda. Primo quidem modo soli Deo orationem porrigimus, quia omnes orationes nostrae ordinari debent ad gratiam et gloriam consequendam, quae solus Deus dat, secundum illud Psalm., *gratiam et gloriam dabit dominus*. Sed secundo modo orationem porrigimus sanctis Angelis et hominibus, non ut per eos Deus nostras petitiones cognoscat, sed ut eorum precibus et meritis orationes nostrae sortiantur effectum. Et ideo dicitur Apoc. VIII quod *ascendit fumus aromatum, idest orationes sanctorum, de manu Angeli coram domino*. Et hoc etiam patet ex ipso modo quo Ecclesia utitur in orando. Nam a sancta Trinitate petimus ut nostri misereatur, ab aliis autem sanctis quibuscumque petimus ut orent pro nobis.

AD PRIMUM ergo dicendum quod illi soli impendimus orando religionis cultum a quo quaerimus obtinere quod oramus, quia in hoc protestamur eum bonorum nostrorum auctorem, non autem eis quos requirimus quasi interpellatores nostros apud Deum.

OBJECTION 1: It would seem that we ought to pray to God alone. Prayer is an act of religion, as stated above (A. 3). But God alone is to be worshiped by religion. Therefore we should pray to God alone.

OBJ. 2: Further, it is useless to pray to one who is ignorant of the prayer. But it belongs to God alone to know one's prayer, both because frequently prayer is uttered by an interior act which God alone knows, rather than by words, according to the saying of the Apostle (1 Cor 14:15), *I will pray with the spirit, I will pray also with the understanding*: and again because, as Augustine says (*De Cura pro mortuis* xiii) the *dead, even the saints, know not what the living, even their own children, are doing*. Therefore we ought to pray to God alone.

OBJ. 3: Further, if we pray to any of the saints, this is only because they are united to God. Now some yet living in this world, or even some who are in Purgatory, are closely united to God by grace, and yet we do not pray to them. Therefore neither should we pray to the saints who are in Paradise.

ON THE CONTRARY, It is written (Job 5:1), *Call . . . if there be any that will answer thee, and turn to some of the saints.*

I ANSWER THAT, Prayer is offered to a person in two ways: first, as to be fulfilled by him, second, as to be obtained through him. In the first way we offer prayer to God alone, since all our prayers ought to be directed to the acquisition of grace and glory, which God alone gives, according to Ps. 83:12, *The Lord will give grace and glory*. But in the second way we pray to the saints, whether angels or men, not that God may through them know our petitions, but that our prayers may be effective through their prayers and merits. Hence it is written (Rev 8:4) that *the smoke of the incense*, namely *the prayers of the saints ascended up before God*. This is also clear from the very style employed by the Church in praying: since we beseech the Blessed Trinity *to have mercy on us*, while we ask any of the saints *to pray for us*.

REPLY OBJ. 1: To Him alone do we offer religious worship when praying, from Whom we seek to obtain what we pray for, because by so doing we confess that He is the Author of our goods: but not to those whom we call upon as our advocates in God's presence.

**Ad secundum** dicendum quod mortui ea quae in hoc mundo aguntur, considerata eorum naturali conditione, non cognoscunt, et praecipue interiores motus cordis. Sed beatis, ut Gregorius dicit, in XII Moral., in verbo manifestatur illud quod decet eos cognoscere de eis quae circa nos aguntur, etiam quantum ad interiores motus cordis. Maxime autem eorum excellentiam decet ut cognoscant petitiones ad eos factas vel voce vel corde. Et ideo petitiones quas ad eos dirigimus, Deo manifestante, cognoscunt.

**Ad tertium** dicendum quod illi qui sunt in hoc mundo aut in Purgatorio, nondum fruuntur visione verbi, ut possint cognoscere ea quae nos cogitamus vel dicimus. Et ideo eorum suffragia non imploramus orando, sed a vivis petimus colloquendo.

**Reply Obj. 2**: The dead, if we consider their natural condition, do not know what takes place in this world, especially the interior movements of the heart. Nevertheless, according to Gregory (*Moral.* xii, 21), whatever it is fitting the blessed should know about what happens to us, even as regards the interior movements of the heart, is made known to them in the Word: and it is most becoming to their exalted position that they should know the petitions we make to them by word or thought; and consequently the petitions which we raise to them are known to them through Divine manifestation.

**Reply Obj. 3**: Those who are in this world or in Purgatory, do not yet enjoy the vision of the Word, so as to be able to know what we think or say. Wherefore we do not seek their assistance by praying to them, but ask it of the living by speaking to them.

# Article 5

*Whether we ought to ask for something definite when we pray?*

**Ad quintum sic proceditur.** Videtur quod in oratione nihil determinate a Deo petere debeamus. Quia, ut Damascenus dicit, *oratio est petitio decentium a Deo.* Unde inefficax est oratio per quam petitur id quod non expedit, secundum illud Iac. IV, *petitis et non accipitis, eo quod male petatis.* Sed sicut dicitur Rom. VIII. *Nam quid oremus sicut oportet, nescimus.* Ergo non debemus aliquid orando determinate petere.

**Praeterea,** quicumque aliquid determinate ab alio petit, nititur voluntatem ipsius inclinare ad faciendum id quod ipse vult. Non autem ad hoc tendere debemus ut Deus velit quod nos volumus, sed magis ut nos velimus quod Deus vult, ut dicit Glossa, super illud Psalm., *exultate, iusti, in domino.* Ergo non debemus aliquid determinatum a Deo petere.

**Praeterea,** mala a Deo petenda non sunt, ad bona autem Deus ipse nos invitat. Frustra autem ab aliquo petitur ad quod accipiendum invitatur. Ergo non est determinate aliquid a Deo in oratione petendum.

**Sed contra** est quod dominus, Matth. VI et Luc. XI, docuit discipulos determinate petere ea quae continentur in petitionibus orationis dominicae.

**Respondeo** dicendum quod, sicut maximus Valerius refert, *Socrates nihil ultra petendum a diis immortalibus arbitrabatur quam ut bona tribuerent, quia hi demum scirent quid unicuique esset utile; nos autem plerumque id votis expetere quod non impetrasse melius foret.* Quae quidem sententia aliqualiter vera est, quantum ad illa quae possunt malum eventum habere, quibus etiam homo potest male et bene uti, sicut divitiae, quae, ut

**Objection 1**: It would seem that we ought not to ask for anything definite when we pray to God. According to Damascene (*De Fide Orth.* iii, 24), *to pray is to ask becoming things of God;* wherefore it is useless to pray for what is inexpedient, according to James 4:3, *You ask, and receive not: because you ask amiss.* Now according to Rom. 8:26, *we know not what we should pray for as we ought.* Therefore we ought not to ask for anything definite when we pray.

**Obj. 2**: Further, those who ask another person for something definite strive to incline his will to do what they wish themselves. But we ought not to endeavor to make God will what we will; on the contrary, we ought to strive to will what He wills, according to a gloss on Ps. 32:1, *Rejoice in the Lord, O ye just.* Therefore we ought not to ask God for anything definite when we pray.

**Obj. 3**: Further, evil things are not to be sought from God; and as to good things, God Himself invites us to take them. Now it is useless to ask a person to give you what he invites you to take. Therefore we ought not to ask God for anything definite in our prayers.

**On the contrary**, our Lord (Matt 6 and Luke 11) taught His disciples to ask definitely for those things which are contained in the petitions of the Lord's Prayer.

**I answer that**, According to Valerius Maximus, *Socrates deemed that we should ask the immortal gods for nothing else but that they should grant us good things, because they at any rate know what is good for each one whereas when we pray we frequently ask for what it had been better for us not to obtain.* This opinion is true to a certain extent, as to those things which may have an evil result, and which man may use ill or well, such as *riches, by which,* as

ibidem dicitur, *multis exitio fuere; honores, qui complures pessumdederunt; regna, quorum exitus saepe miserabiles cernuntur; splendida coniugia, quae nonnunquam funditus domos evertunt.* Sunt tamen quaedam bona quibus homo male uti non potest, quae scilicet malum eventum habere non possunt. Haec autem sunt quibus beatificamur et quibus beatitudinem meremur. Quae quidem sancti orando absolute petunt, secundum illud, *ostende faciem tuam, et salvi erimus*; et iterum, *deduc me in semitam mandatorum tuorum.*

**AD PRIMUM** ergo dicendum quod licet homo ex se scire non possit quid orare debeat, *spiritus tamen*, ut ibidem dicitur, *in hoc adiuvat infirmitatem nostram quod*, inspirando nobis sancta desideria, recte postulare nos facit. Unde dominus dicit, Ioan. IV, quod *veros adoratores adorare oportet in spiritu et veritate.*

**AD SECUNDUM** dicendum quod cum orando petimus aliqua quae pertinent ad nostram salutem, conformamus voluntatem nostram voluntati Dei, de quo dicitur, I ad Tim. II, quod *vult omnes homines salvos fieri.*

**AD TERTIUM** dicendum quod sic ad bona Deus nos invitat quod ad ea non passibus corporis, sed piis desideriis et devotis orationibus accedamus.

stated by the same authority (*Fact. et Dict. Memor.* vii, 2), *many have come to an evil end; honors, which have ruined many; power, of which we frequently witness the unhappy results; splendid marriages, which sometimes bring about the total wreck of a family.* Nevertheless there are certain goods which man cannot ill use, because they cannot have an evil result. Such are those which are the object of beatitude and whereby we merit it: and these the saints seek absolutely when they pray, as in Ps. 79:4, *Show us Thy face, and we shall be saved*, and again in Ps. 118:35, *Lead me into the path of Thy commandments.*

**REPLY OBJ. 1**: Although man cannot by himself know what he ought to pray for, *the Spirit*, as stated in the same passage, *helpeth our infirmity*, since by inspiring us with holy desires, He makes us ask for what is right. Hence our Lord said (John 4:24) that true adorers *must adore . . . in spirit and in truth.*

**REPLY OBJ. 2**: When in our prayers we ask for things concerning our salvation, we conform our will to God's, of Whom it is written (1 Tim 2:4) that *He will have all men to be saved.*

**REPLY OBJ. 3**: God so invites us to take good things, that we may approach to them not by the steps of the body, but by pious desires and devout prayers.

# Article 6

*Whether man ought to ask God for temporal things when he prays?*

**AD SEXTUM SIC PROCEDITUR.** Videtur quod homo non debeat temporalia petere a Deo orando. Quae enim orando petimus, quaerimus. Sed temporalia non debemus quaerere, dicitur enim Matth. VI, *primum quaerite regnum Dei et iustitiam eius, et haec omnia adiicientur vobis*, scilicet temporalia; quae non quaerenda dicit, sed adiicienda quaesitis. Ergo temporalia non sunt in oratione a Deo petenda.

**PRAETEREA**, nullus petit nisi ea de quibus est sollicitus. Sed de temporalibus sollicitudinem habere non debemus, secundum quod dicitur Matth. VI, *nolite solliciti esse animae vestrae, quid manducetis.* Ergo temporalia petere orando non debemus.

**PRAETEREA**, per orationem nostram mens debet elevari in Deum. Sed petendo temporalia descendit ad ea quae infra se sunt, contra id quod apostolus dicebat, II ad Cor. IV, *non contemplantibus nobis quae videntur, sed quae non videntur, quae enim videntur, temporalia sunt; quae autem non videntur, aeterna.* Ergo non debet homo temporalia in oratione a Deo petere.

**OBJECTION 1**: It would seem that man ought not to ask God for temporal things when he prays. We seek what we ask for in prayer. But we should not seek for temporal things, for it is written (Matt 6:33): *Seek ye . . . first the kingdom of God, and His justice: and all these things shall be added unto you*, that is to say, temporal things, which, says He, we are not to seek, but they will be added to what we seek. Therefore temporal things are not to be asked of God in prayer.

**OBJ. 2**: Further, no one asks save for that which he is solicitous about. Now we ought not to have solicitude for temporal things, according to the saying of Matt. 6:25, *Be not solicitous for your life, what you shall eat.* Therefore we ought not to ask for temporal things when we pray.

**OBJ. 3**: Further, by prayer our mind should be raised up to God. But by asking for temporal things, it descends to things beneath it, against the saying of the Apostle (2 Cor 4:18), *While we look not at the things which are seen, but at the things which are not seen. For the things which are seen are temporal, but the things which are not seen are eternal.* Therefore man ought not to ask God for temporal things when he prays.

**PRAETEREA**, homo non debet petere a Deo nisi bona et utilia. Sed quandoque temporalia habita sunt nociva, non solum spiritualiter, sed etiam temporaliter. Ergo non sunt a Deo in oratione petenda.

**SED CONTRA** est quod dicitur Prov. XXX, *tribue tantum victui meo necessaria.*

**RESPONDEO** dicendum quod, sicut Augustinus dicit, ad Probam, de orando Deum, *hoc licet orare quod licet desiderare.* Temporalia autem licet desiderare, non quidem principaliter, ut in eis finem constituamus; sed sicut quaedam adminicula quibus adiuvamur ad tendendum in beatitudinem, inquantum scilicet per ea vita corporalis sustentatur, et inquantum nobis organice deserviunt ad actus virtutum, ut etiam philosophus dicit, in I Ethic. Et ideo pro temporalibus licet orare. Et hoc est quod Augustinus dicit, ad Probam, *sufficientiam vitae non indecenter vult quisquis eam vult et non amplius. Quae quidem non appetitur propter seipsam, sed propter salutem corporis et congruentem habitum personae hominis, ut non sit inconveniens eis cum quibus vivendum est. Ista ergo, cum habentur, ut teneantur, cum non habentur, ut habeantur, orandum est.*

**AD PRIMUM** ergo dicendum quod temporalia non sunt quaerenda principaliter, sed secundario. Unde Augustinus dicit, in libro de Serm. Dom. in monte, *cum dixit, illud primo quaerendum est*, scilicet regnum Dei, *significavit quia hoc*, scilicet temporale bonum, *posterius quaerendum est, non tempore, sed dignitate, illud tanquam bonum nostrum, hoc tanquam necessarium nostrum.*

**AD SECUNDUM** dicendum quod non quaelibet sollicitudo rerum temporalium est prohibita, sed superflua et inordinata, ut supra habitum est.

**AD TERTIUM** dicendum quod quando mens nostra intendit temporalibus rebus ut in eis quiescat, remanet in eis depressa. Sed quando intendit eis in ordine ad beatitudinem consequendam, non ab eis deprimitur, sed magis ea elevat sursum.

**AD QUARTUM** dicendum quod ex quo non petimus temporalia tanquam principaliter quaesita, sed in ordine ad aliud, eo tenore a Deo petimus ipsa ut nobis concedantur secundum quod expediunt ad salutem.

**OBJ. 4**: Further, man ought not to ask of God other than good and useful things. But sometimes temporal things, when we have them, are harmful, not only in a spiritual sense, but also in a material sense. Therefore we should not ask God for them in our prayers.

**ON THE CONTRARY**, It is written (Prov 30:8): *Give me only the necessaries of life.*

**I ANSWER THAT**, As Augustine says (*ad Proba, de orando Deum, Ep.* cxxx, 12): *It is lawful to pray for what it is lawful to desire.* Now it is lawful to desire temporal things, not indeed principally, by placing our end therein, but as helps whereby we are assisted in tending towards beatitude, in so far, to wit, as they are the means of supporting the life of the body, and are of service to us as instruments in performing acts of virtue, as also the Philosopher states (*Ethic.* i, 8). Augustine too says the same to Proba (*ad Probam, de orando Deum, Ep.* cxxx, 6, 7) when he states that *it is not unbecoming for anyone to desire enough for a livelihood, and no more; for this sufficiency is desired, not for its own sake, but for the welfare of the body, or that we should desire to be clothed in a way befitting one's station, so as not to be out of keeping with those among whom we have to live. Accordingly we ought to pray that we may keep these things if we have them, and if we have them not, that we may gain possession of them.*

**REPLY OBJ. 1**: We should seek temporal things not in the first but in the second place. Hence Augustine says (*De Serm. Dom. in Monte* ii, 16): *When He says that this* (i.e., the kingdom of God) *is to be sought first*, He implies that the other (i.e., temporal goods) *is to be sought afterwards, not in time but in importance, this as being our good, the other as our need.*

**REPLY OBJ. 2**: Not all solicitude about temporal things is forbidden, but that which is superfluous and inordinate, as stated above (Q. 55, A. 6).

**REPLY OBJ. 3**: When our mind is intent on temporal things in order that it may rest in them, it remains immersed therein; but when it is intent on them in relation to the acquisition of beatitude, it is not lowered by them, but raises them to a higher level.

**REPLY OBJ. 4**: From the very fact that we ask for temporal things not as the principal object of our petition, but as subordinate to something else, we ask God for them in the sense that they may be granted to us insofar as they are expedient for salvation.

# Article 7

*Whether we ought to pray for others?*

AD SEPTIMUM SIC PROCEDITUR. Videtur quod non debeamus pro aliis orare. In orando enim sequi debemus formam quam dominus tradidit. Sed in oratione dominica petitiones pro nobis facimus, non pro aliis, dicentes, *panem nostrum quotidianum da nobis hodie*, et cetera huiusmodi. Ergo non debemus pro aliis orare.

PRAETEREA, ad hoc oratio fit quod exaudiatur. Sed una de conditionibus quae requiruntur ad hoc quod oratio sit audibilis, est ut aliquis oret pro seipso, unde super illud Ioan. XVI, *si quid petieritis patrem in nomine meo, dabit vobis*, Augustinus dicit, *exaudiuntur omnes pro seipsis, non autem pro omnibus. Unde non utcumque dictum est, dabit, sed, dabit vobis.* Ergo videtur quod non debeamus pro aliis orare, sed solum pro nobis.

PRAETEREA, pro aliis, si sunt mali, prohibemur orare, secundum illud Ierem. VII, *tu ergo noli orare pro populo hoc, et non obsistas mihi, quia non exaudiam te.* Pro bonis autem non oportet orare, quia ipsi pro seipsis orantes exaudiuntur. Ergo videtur quod non debeamus pro aliis orare.

SED CONTRA est quod dicitur Iac. V, *orate pro invicem, ut salvemini.*

RESPONDEO dicendum quod, sicut dictum est, illud debemus orando petere quod debemus desiderare. Desiderare autem debemus bona non solum nobis, sed etiam aliis, hoc enim pertinet ad rationem dilectionis, quam proximis debemus impendere, ut ex supradictis patet. Et ideo caritas hoc requirit, ut pro aliis oremus. Unde Chrysostomus dicit, super Matth., *pro se orare necessitas cogit, pro altero autem, caritas fraternitatis hortatur. Dulcior autem ante Deum est oratio, non quam necessitas transmittit, sed quam caritas fraternitatis commendat.*

AD PRIMUM ergo dicendum quod, sicut Cyprianus dicit, in libro de Orat. dominica, *ideo non dicimus, pater meus, sed noster; nec, da mihi, sed, da nobis, quia unitatis magister noluit privatim precem fieri, ut scilicet quis pro se tantum precetur. Unum enim orare pro omnibus voluit, quo modo in uno omnes ipse portavit.*

AD SECUNDUM dicendum quod pro se orare ponitur conditio orationis, non quidem necessaria ad effectum merendi, sed sicut necessaria ad indeficientiam impetrandi. Contingit enim quandoque quod oratio pro alio facta non impetrat, etiam si fiat pie et perseveranter et de pertinentibus ad salutem, propter impedimentum quod est ex parte eius pro quo oratur, secundum illud Ierem. XV, *si steterit Moyses et Samuel coram me, non est anima mea ad populum istum.* Nihilominus tamen oratio meritoria erit oranti, qui ex caritate orat, secundum illud

OBJECTION 1: It would seem that we ought not to pray for others. In praying we ought to conform to the pattern given by our Lord. Now in the Lord's Prayer we make petitions for ourselves, not for others; thus we say: *Give us this day our daily bread*, etc. Therefore we should not pray for others.

OBJ. 2: Further, prayer is offered that it may be heard. Now one of the conditions required for prayer that it may be heard is that one pray for oneself, wherefore Augustine in commenting on John 16:23, *If you ask the Father anything in My name He will give it you*, says (*Tract. cii*): *Everyone is heard when he prays for himself, not when he prays for all; wherefore He does not say simply 'He will give it,' but 'He will give it you.'* Therefore it would seem that we ought not to pray for others, but only for ourselves.

OBJ. 3: Further, we are forbidden to pray for others, if they are wicked, according to Jer. 7:16, *Therefore do not then pray for this people . . . and do not withstand Me, for I will not hear thee.* On the other hand we are not bound to pray for the good, since they are heard when they pray for themselves. Therefore it would seem that we ought not to pray for others.

ON THE CONTRARY, It is written (Jas 5:16): *Pray one for another, that you may be saved.*

I ANSWER THAT, As stated above (A. 6), when we pray we ought to ask for what we ought to desire. Now we ought to desire good things not only for ourselves, but also for others: for this is essential to the love which we owe to our neighbor, as stated above (Q. 25, AA. 1, 12; Q. 27, A. 2; Q. 31, A. 1). Therefore charity requires us to pray for others. Hence Chrysostom says (*Hom. xiv in Matth.*): *Necessity binds us to pray for ourselves, fraternal charity urges us to pray for others: and the prayer that fraternal charity proffers is sweeter to God than that which is the outcome of necessity.*

REPLY OBJ. 1: As Cyprian says (*De Orat. Dom.*), *We say 'Our Father' and not 'My Father,' 'Give us' and not 'Give me,' because the Master of unity did not wish us to pray privately, that is for ourselves alone, for He wished each one to pray for all, even as He Himself bore all in one.*

REPLY OBJ. 2: It is a condition of prayer that one pray for oneself: not as though it were necessary in order that prayer be meritorious, but as being necessary in order that prayer may not fail in its effect of impetration. For it sometimes happens that we pray for another with piety and perseverance, and ask for things relating to his salvation, and yet it is not granted on account of some obstacle on the part of the person we are praying for, according to Jer. 15:1, *If Moses and Samuel shall stand before Me, My soul is not towards this people.* And yet the prayer will be meritorious

Psalm., *oratio mea in sinu meo convertetur*, Glossa, idest, *etsi non eis profuit, ego tamen non sum frustratus mea mercede.*

**AD TERTIUM** dicendum quod etiam pro peccatoribus orandum est, ut convertantur, et pro iustis, ut perseverent et proficiant. Orantes tamen non pro omnibus peccatoribus exaudiuntur, sed pro quibusdam, exaudiuntur enim pro praedestinatis, non autem pro praescitis ad mortem. Sicut etiam correctio qua fratres corrigimus, effectum habet in praedestinatis, non in reprobatis, secundum illud Eccle. VII, *nemo potest corrigere quem Deus despexerit.* Et ideo dicitur I Ioan. V, *qui scit fratrem suum peccare peccato non ad mortem, petat, et dabitur ei vita peccanti peccatum non ad mortem.* Sed sicut nulli, quandiu hic vivit, subtrahendum est correctionis beneficium, quia non possumus distinguere praedestinatos a reprobatis, ut Augustinus dicit, in libro de Corr. et gratia; ita etiam nulli est denegandum orationis suffragium.

Pro iustis etiam est orandum, triplici ratione. Primo quidem, quia multorum preces facilius exaudiuntur. Unde Rom. XV, super illud, *adiuvetis me in orationibus vestris*, dicit Glossa, *bene rogat apostolus minores pro se orare. Multi enim minimi, dum congregantur unanimes, fiunt magni, et multorum preces impossibile est quod non impetrent, illud scilicet quod est impetrabile.* Secundo, ut ex multis gratia agatur Deo de beneficiis quae confert iustis, quae etiam in utilitatem multorum vergunt, ut patet per apostolum, II ad Cor. I. Tertio, ut maiores non superbiant, dum considerant se minorum suffragiis indigere.

for the person who prays thus out of charity, according to Ps. 34:13, *My prayer shall be turned into my bosom, i.e., though it profit them not, I am not deprived of my reward*, as the gloss expounds it.

**REPLY OBJ. 3**: We ought to pray even for sinners, that they may be converted, and for the just that they may persevere and advance in holiness. Yet those who pray are heard not for all sinners but for some: since they are heard for the predestined, but not for those who are foreknown to death; even as the correction whereby we correct the brethren, has an effect in the predestined but not in the reprobate, according to Eccles. 7:14, *No man can correct whom God hath despised.* Hence it is written (1 John 5:16): *He that knoweth his brother to sin a sin which is not to death, let him ask, and life shall be given to him, who sinneth not to death.* Now just as the benefit of correction must not be refused to any man so long as he lives here below, because we cannot distinguish the predestined from the reprobate, as Augustine says (*De Correp. et Grat.* xv), so too no man should be denied the help of prayer.

We ought also to pray for the just for three reasons: First, because the prayers of a multitude are more easily heard, wherefore a gloss on Rom. 15:30, *Help me in your prayers*, says: *The Apostle rightly tells the lesser brethren to pray for him, for many lesser ones, if they be united together in one mind, become great, and it is impossible for the prayers of a multitude not to obtain* that which is possible to be obtained by prayer. Second, that many may thank God for the graces conferred on the just, which graces conduce to the profit of many, according to the Apostle (2 Cor 1:11). Third, that the more perfect may not wax proud, seeing that they find that they need the prayers of the less perfect.

# Article 8

*Whether we ought to pray for our enemies?*

**AD OCTAVUM SIC PROCEDITUR.** Videtur quod non debeamus pro inimicis orare. Quia, ut dicitur Rom. XV, *quaecumque scripta sunt, ad nostram doctrinam scripta sunt.* Sed in sacra Scriptura inducuntur multae imprecationes contra inimicos, dicitur enim in Psalm., *erubescant et conturbentur omnes inimici mei, erubescant et conturbentur valde velociter.* Ergo et nos debemus orare contra inimicos, magis quam pro eis.

**PRAETEREA**, vindicari de inimicis in malum inimicorum cedit. Sed sancti vindictam de inimicis petunt, secundum illud Apoc. VI, *usquequo non vindicas sanguinem nostrum de his qui habitant in terra?* Unde et de vindicta impiorum laetantur, secundum illud Psalm.,

**OBJECTION 1**: It would seem that we ought not to pray for our enemies. According to Rom. 15:4, *what things soever were written, were written for our learning.* Now Holy Writ contains many imprecations against enemies; thus it is written (Ps 6:11): *Let all my enemies be ashamed and be . . . troubled, let them be ashamed and be troubled very speedily.* Therefore we too should pray against rather than for our enemies.

**OBJ. 2**: Further, to be revenged on one's enemies is harmful to them. But holy men seek vengeance of their enemies according to Apoc. 6:10, *How long . . . dost Thou not . . . revenge our blood on them that dwell on earth?* Wherefore they rejoice in being revenged on their enemies,

*laetabitur iustus cum viderit vindictam.* Ergo non est orandum pro inimicis, sed magis contra eos.

**Praeterea**, operatio hominis et eius oratio non debent esse contraria. Sed homines quandoque licite impugnant inimicos, alioquin omnia bella essent illicita, quod est contra supradicta. Ergo non debemus orare pro inimicis.

**Sed contra** est quod dicitur Matth. V, *orate pro persequentibus et calumniantibus vos.*

**Respondeo** dicendum quod orare pro alio caritatis est, sicut dictum est. Unde eodem modo quo tenemur diligere inimicos, tenemur pro inimicis orare. Qualiter autem teneamur inimicos diligere supra habitum est, in tractatu de caritate, ut scilicet in eis diligamus naturam, non culpam; et quod diligere inimicos in generali est in praecepto, in speciali autem non est in praecepto nisi secundum praeparationem animi, ut scilicet homo esset paratus etiam specialiter inimicum diligere et eum iuvare in necessitatis articulo, vel si veniam peteret; sed in speciali absolute inimicos diligere et eos iuvare perfectionis est.

Et similiter necessitatis est ut in communibus nostris orationibus quas pro aliis facimus, inimicos non excludamus. Quod autem pro eis specialiter oremus, perfectionis est, non necessitatis, nisi in aliquo casu speciali.

**Ad primum** ergo dicendum quod imprecationes quae in sacra Scriptura ponuntur quadrupliciter possunt intelligi. Uno modo, secundum quod *prophetae solent figura imprecantis futura praedicere*, ut Augustinus dicit, in libro de Serm. Dom. in monte. Secundo, prout quaedam temporalia mala peccatoribus quandoque a Deo ad correctionem immittuntur. Tertio, quia intelliguntur petere non contra ipsos homines, sed contra regnum peccati, ut scilicet correctione hominum peccatum destruatur. Quarto, conformando voluntatem suam divinae iustitiae circa damnationem perseverantium in peccato.

**Ad secundum** dicendum quod, sicut in eodem libro Augustinus dicit, *vindicta martyrum est ut evertatur regnum peccati, quo regnante tanta perpessi sunt.* Vel, sicut dicitur in libro de quaest. Vet. et novi Test., *postulant se vindicari non voce, sed ratione, sicut sanguis Abel clamavit de terra.* Laetantur autem de vindicta non propter eam, sed propter divinam iustitiam.

**Ad tertium** dicendum quod licitum est impugnare inimicos ut compescantur a peccatis, quod cedit in bonum eorum et aliorum. Et sic etiam licet orando petere

according to Ps. 57:11, *The just shall rejoice when he shall see the revenge.* Therefore we should not pray for our enemies, but against them.

**Obj. 3**: Further, man's deed should not be contrary to his prayer. Now sometimes men lawfully attack their enemies, else all wars would be unlawful, which is opposed to what we have said above (Q. 40, A. 1). Therefore we should not pray for our enemies.

**On the contrary**, It is written (Matt 5:44): *Pray for them that persecute and calumniate you.*

**I answer that**, To pray for another is an act of charity, as stated above (A. 7). Wherefore we are bound to pray for our enemies in the same manner as we are bound to love them. Now it was explained above in the treatise on charity (Q. 25, AA. 8, 9), how we are bound to love our enemies, namely, that we must love in them their nature, not their sin, and that to love our enemies in general is a matter of precept, while to love them in the individual is not a matter of precept, except in the preparedness of the mind, so that a man must be prepared to love his enemy even in the individual and to help him in a case of necessity, or if his enemy should beg his forgiveness. But to love one's enemies absolutely in the individual, and to assist them, is an act of perfection.

In like manner it is a matter of obligation that we should not exclude our enemies from the general prayers which we offer up for others: but it is a matter of perfection, and not of obligation, to pray for them individually, except in certain special cases.

**Reply Obj. 1**: The imprecations contained in Holy Writ may be understood in four ways. First, according to the custom of the prophets *to foretell the future under the veil of an imprecation*, as Augustine states. Second, in the sense that certain temporal evils are sometimes inflicted by God on the wicked for their correction. Third, because they are understood to be pronounced, not against the men themselves, but against the kingdom of sin, with the purpose, to wit, of destroying sin by the correction of men. Fourth, by way of conformity of our will to the Divine justice with regard to the damnation of those who are obstinate in sin.

**Reply Obj. 2**: As Augustine states in the same book (*De Serm. Dom. in Monte* i, 22), *the martyrs' vengeance is the overthrow of the kingdom of sin, because they suffered so much while it reigned*: or as he says again (*QQ. Vet. et Nov. Test.* lxviii), *their prayer for vengeance is expressed not in words but in their minds, even as the blood of Abel cried from the earth.* They rejoice in vengeance not for its own sake, but for the sake of Divine justice.

**Reply Obj. 3**: It is lawful to attack one's enemies, that they may be restrained from sin: and this is for their own good and for the good of others. Consequently it is even

aliqua temporalia mala inimicorum ut corrigantur. Et sic oratio et operatio non erunt contraria.

lawful in praying to ask that temporal evils be inflicted on our enemies in order that they may mend their ways. Thus prayer and deed will not be contrary to one another.

# Article 9

*Whether the seven petitions of the Lord's Prayer are fittingly assigned?*

AD NONUM SIC PROCEDITUR. Videtur quod inconvenienter septem petitiones orationis dominicae assignentur. Vanum enim est petere illud quod semper est. Sed nomen Dei semper est sanctum, secundum illud Luc. I, *sanctum nomen eius*. Regnum etiam eius est sempiternum, secundum illud Psalmo, *regnum tuum, domine, regnum omnium saeculorum*. Voluntas etiam Dei semper impletur, secundum illud Isaiae XLVI, *omnis voluntas mea fiet*. Vanum ergo est petere quod *nomen Dei sanctificetur*, quod *regnum eius adveniat*, et quod *eius voluntas fiat*.

PRAETEREA, prius est recedere a malo quam consequi bonum. Inconvenienter igitur videntur praeordinari petitiones quae pertinent ad consequendum bonum, petitionibus quae pertinent ad amotionem mali.

PRAETEREA, ad hoc aliquid petitur ut donetur. Sed praecipuum donum Dei est Spiritus Sanctus, et ea quae nobis per ipsum dantur. Ergo videntur inconvenienter proponi petitiones, cum non respondeant donis spiritus sancti.

PRAETEREA, secundum Lucam in oratione dominica ponuntur solum quinque petitiones, ut patet Luc. XI. Superfluum igitur fuit quod secundum Matthaeum septem petitiones ponuntur.

PRAETEREA, in vanum videtur captare benevolentiam eius qui benevolentia sua nos praevenit. Sed Deus nos sua benevolentia praevenit, quia *ipse prior dilexit nos*, ut dicitur I Ioan. IV. Superflue ergo praemittitur petitionibus, *pater noster, qui es in caelis*, quod videtur ad benevolentiam captandam pertinere.

SED IN CONTRARIUM sufficit auctoritas Christi orationem instituentis.

RESPONDEO dicendum quod oratio dominica perfectissima est, quia, sicut Augustinus dicit, ad Probam, *si recte et congruenter oramus, nihil aliud dicere possumus quam quod in ista oratione dominica positum est*. Quia enim oratio est quodammodo desiderii nostri interpres apud Deum, illa solum recte orando petimus quae recte desiderare valemus. In oratione autem dominica non solum petuntur omnia quae recte desiderare possumus, sed etiam eo ordine quo desideranda sunt, ut sic haec oratio non solum instruat postulare, sed etiam sit informativa totius nostri affectus. Manifestum est autem quod primo cadit in desiderio finis; deinde ea quae sunt ad

OBJECTION 1: It would seem that the seven petitions of the Lord's Prayer are not fittingly assigned. It is useless to ask for that to be hallowed which is always holy. But the name of God is always holy, according to Luke 1:49, *Holy is His name*. Again, His kingdom is everlasting, according to Ps. 144:13, *Thy kingdom is a kingdom of all ages*. Again, God's will is always fulfilled, according to Isa 46:10, *All My will shall be done*. Therefore it is useless to ask for *the name of God to be hallowed*, for *His kingdom to come*, and for *His will to be done*.

OBJ. 2: Further, one must withdraw from evil before attaining good. Therefore it seems unfitting for the petitions relating to the attainment of good to be set forth before those relating to the removal of evil.

OBJ. 3: Further, one asks for a thing that it may be given to one. Now the chief gift of God is the Holy Spirit, and those gifts that we receive through Him. Therefore the petitions seem to be unfittingly assigned, since they do not correspond to the gifts of the Holy Spirit.

OBJ. 4: Further, according to Luke, only five petitions are mentioned in the Lord's Prayer, as appears from the eleventh chapter. Therefore it was superfluous for Matthew to mention seven.

OBJ. 5: Further, it seems useless to seek to win the benevolence of one who forestalls us by his benevolence. Now God forestalls us by His benevolence, since *He first hath loved us* (1 John 4:19). Therefore it is useless to preface the petitions with the words our *Father Who art in heaven*, which seem to indicate a desire to win God's benevolence.

ON THE CONTRARY, The authority of Christ, who composed this prayer, suffices.

I ANSWER THAT, The Lord's Prayer is most perfect, because, as Augustine says (*ad Probam Ep. cxxx*, 12), *if we pray rightly and fittingly, we can say nothing else but what is contained in this prayer of our Lord*. For since prayer interprets our desires, as it were, before God, then alone is it right to ask for something in our prayers when it is right that we should desire it. Now in the Lord's Prayer not only do we ask for all that we may rightly desire, but also in the order wherein we ought to desire them, so that this prayer not only teaches us to ask, but also directs all our affections. Thus it is evident that the first thing to be the object of our desire is the end, and afterwards whatever is directed to the

finem. Finis autem noster Deus est. In quem noster affectus tendit dupliciter, uno quidem modo, prout volumus gloriam Dei; alio modo, secundum quod volumus frui gloria eius. Quorum primum pertinet ad dilectionem qua Deum in seipso diligimus, secundum vero pertinet ad dilectionem qua diligimus nos in Deo. Et ideo prima petitio ponitur, *sanctificetur nomen tuum*, per quam petimus gloriam Dei. Secunda vero ponitur, *adveniat regnum tuum*, per quam petimus ad gloriam regni eius pervenire.

Ad finem autem praedictum ordinat nos aliquid dupliciter, uno modo, per se; alio modo, per accidens. Per se quidem, bonum quod est utile in finem. Est autem aliquid utile in finem beatitudinis dupliciter. Uno modo, directe et principaliter, secundum meritum quo beatitudinem meremur Deo obediendo. Et quantum ad hoc ponitur, *fiat voluntas tua, sicut in caelo, et in terra*. Alio modo, instrumentaliter, et quasi coadiuvans nos ad merendum. Et ad hoc pertinet quod dicitur, *panem nostrum quotidianum da nobis hodie*, sive hoc intelligatur de pane sacramentali, cuius quotidianus usus proficit homini, in quo etiam intelliguntur omnia alia sacramenta; sive etiam intelligatur de pane corporali, ut per panem intelligatur *omnis sufficientia victus*, sicut dicit Augustinus, ad Probam; quia et Eucharistia est praecipuum sacramentum, et panis est praecipuus cibus, unde et in Evangelio Matthaei scriptum est, *supersubstantialem*, idest *praecipuum*, ut Hieronymus exponit.

Per accidens autem ordinamur in beatitudinem per remotionem prohibentis. Tria autem sunt quae nos a beatitudine prohibent. Primo quidem, peccatum, quod directe excludit a regno, secundum illud I ad Cor. VI, *neque fornicarii, neque idolis servientes, etc., regnum Dei possidebunt*. Et ad hoc pertinet quod dicitur, *dimitte nobis debita nostra*. Secundo, tentatio, quae nos impedit ab observantia divinae voluntatis. Et ad hoc pertinet quod dicitur, *et ne nos inducas in tentationem*, per quod non petimus ut non tentemur, sed ut a tentatione non vincamur, quod est in tentationem induci. Tertio, poenalitas praesens, quae impedit sufficientiam vitae. Et quantum ad hoc dicitur, *libera nos a malo*.

**AD PRIMUM** ergo dicendum quod, sicut Augustinus dicit, in libro de Serm. Dom. in monte, cum dicimus, sanctificetur nomen tuum, *non hoc petitur quasi non sit sanctum Dei nomen, sed ut sanctum ab hominibus habeatur*; quod pertinet ad Dei gloriam in hominibus propagandam. Quod autem dicitur, adveniat regnum tuum, *non ita dictum est quasi Deus nunc non regnet*, sed, sicut Augustinus dicit, ad Probam, *desiderium nostrum ad illud regnum excitamus, ut nobis veniat, atque in eo regnemus*. Quod autem dicitur, fiat voluntas tua, *recte intelligitur, obediatur praeceptis tuis. Sicut in caelo et in terra, idest, sicut ab Angelis, ita ab hominibus*. Unde hae

end. Now our end is God towards Whom our affections tend in two ways: first, by our willing the glory of God, second, by willing to enjoy His glory. The first belongs to the love whereby we love God in Himself, while the second belongs to the love whereby we love ourselves in God. Wherefore the first petition is expressed thus: *Hallowed be Thy name*, and the second thus: *Thy kingdom come*, by which we ask to come to the glory of His kingdom.

To this same end a thing directs us in two ways: in one way, by its very nature, in another way, accidentally. Of its very nature the good which is useful for an end directs us to that end. Now a thing is useful in two ways to that end which is beatitude: in one way, directly and principally, according to the merit whereby we merit beatitude by obeying God, and in this respect we ask: *Thy will be done on earth as it is in heaven*; in another way instrumentally, and as it were helping us to merit, and in this respect we say: *Give us this day our daily bread*, whether we understand this of the sacramental Bread, the daily use of which is profitable to man, and in which all the other sacraments are contained, or of the bread of the body, so that it denotes *all sufficiency of food*, as Augustine says (*ad Probam, Ep. cxxx*, 11), since the Eucharist is the chief sacrament, and bread is the chief food: thus in the Gospel of Matthew we read, *supersubstantial*, i.e., *principal*, as Jerome expounds it.

We are directed to beatitude accidentally by the removal of obstacles. Now there are three obstacles to our attainment of beatitude. First, there is sin, which directly excludes a man from the kingdom, according to 1 Cor. 6:9, 10, *Neither fornicators, nor idolaters, etc., shall possess the kingdom of God*; and to this refer the words, *Forgive us our trespasses*. Second, there is temptation which hinders us from keeping God's will, and to this we refer when we say: *And lead us not into temptation*, whereby we do not ask not to be tempted, but not to be conquered by temptation, which is to be led into temptation. Third, there is the present penal state which is a kind of obstacle to a sufficiency of life, and to this we refer in the words, *Deliver us from evil*.

**REPLY OBJ. 1**: As Augustine says (*De Serm. Dom. in Monte* ii, 5), when we say, *Hallowed be Thy name*, we do not mean that God's name is not holy, but we ask that men may treat it as a holy thing, and this pertains to the diffusion of God's glory among men. When we say, *Thy kingdom come*, we do not imply that God is not reigning now, but we excite in ourselves the desire for that kingdom, that it may come to us, and that we may reign therein, as Augustine says (*ad Probam, Ep. cxxx*, 11). The words, *Thy will be done* rightly signify, 'May Thy commandments be obeyed' on earth as in heaven, i.e., by men as well as by angels (*De Serm. Dom. in Monte* ii, 6). Hence these three petitions will be perfectly

tres petitiones perfecte complebuntur in vita futura, aliae vero quatuor pertinent ad necessitatem vitae praesentis, sicut Augustinus dicit, in Enchiridio.

AD SECUNDUM dicendum quod, cum oratio sit interpres desiderii, ordo petitionum non respondet ordini executionis, sed ordini desiderii sive intentionis, in quo prius est finis quam ea quae sunt ad finem, et consecutio boni quam remotio mali.

AD TERTIUM dicendum quod Augustinus, in libro de Serm. Dom. in monte, adaptat septem petitiones donis et beatitudinibus, dicens, *si timor Dei est quo beati sunt pauperes spiritu, petamus ut sanctificetur in hominibus nomen Dei timore casto. Si pietas est qua beati sunt mites, petamus ut veniat regnum eius, ut mitescamus, nec ei resistamus. Si scientia est qua beati sunt qui lugent, oremus ut fiat voluntas eius, quia sic non lugebimus. Si fortitudo est qua beati sunt qui esuriunt, oremus ut panis noster quotidianus detur nobis. Si consilium est quo beati sunt misericordes, debita dimittamus, ut nobis nostra dimittantur. Si intellectus est quo beati sunt mundo corde, oremus ne habeamus duplex cor, temporalia sectando, de quibus tentationes fiunt in nobis. Si sapientia est qua beati sunt pacifici quoniam filii Dei vocabuntur, oremus ut liberemur a malo, ipsa enim liberatio liberos nos faciet filios Dei.*

AD QUARTUM dicendum quod, sicut Augustinus dicit, in Enchirid., *Lucas in oratione dominica petitiones non septem, sed quinque complexus est. Ostendens enim tertiam petitionem duarum praemissarum esse quodammodo repetitionem, praetermittendo eam facit intelligi, quia scilicet ad hoc praecipue voluntas Dei tendit ut eius sanctitatem cognoscamus, et cum ipso regnemus. Quod etiam Matthaeus in ultimo posuit, libera nos a malo, Lucas non posuit, ut sciat unusquisque in eo se liberari a malo quod non infertur in tentationem.*

AD QUINTUM dicendum quod oratio non porrigitur Deo ut ipsum flectamus, sed ut in nobis ipsis fiduciam excitemus postulandi. Quae quidem praecipue excitatur in nobis considerando eius caritatem ad nos, qua bonum nostrum vult, et ideo dicimus, *pater noster*; et eius excellentiam, qua potest, et ideo dicimus, *qui es in caelis.*

fulfilled in the life to come; while the other four, according to Augustine (*Enchiridion* cxv), belong to the needs of the present life.

REPLY OBJ. 2: Since prayer is the interpreter of desire, the order of the petitions corresponds with the order, not of execution, but of desire or intention, where the end precedes the things that are directed to the end, and attainment of good precedes removal of evil.

REPLY OBJ. 3: Augustine (*De Serm. Dom. in Monte* ii, 11) adapts the seven petitions to the gifts and beatitudes. He says: *If it is fear of God whereby blessed are the poor in spirit, let us ask that God's name be hallowed among men with a chaste fear. If it is piety whereby blessed are the meek, let us ask that His kingdom may come, so that we become meek and no longer resist Him. If it is knowledge whereby blessed are they that mourn, let us pray that His will be done, for thus we shall mourn no more. If it is fortitude whereby blessed ere they that hunger, let us pray that our daily bread be given to us. If it is counsel whereby blessed are the merciful, let us forgive the trespasses of others that our own may be forgiven. If it is understanding whereby blessed are the pure in heart, let us pray lest we have a double heart by seeking after worldly things which ere the occasion of our temptations. If it is wisdom whereby blessed are the peacemakers for they shall be called the children of God, let us pray to be delivered from evil: for if we be delivered we shall by that very fact become the free children of God.*

REPLY OBJ. 4: According to Augustine (*Enchiridion* cxvi), *Luke included not seven but five petitions in the Lord's Prayer, for by omitting it, he shows that the third petition is a kind of repetition of the two that precede, and thus helps us to understand it*; because, to wit, the will of God tends chiefly to this—that we come to the knowledge of His holiness and to reign together with Him. *Again the last petition mentioned by Matthew, Deliver us from evil, is omitted by Luke, so that each one may know himself to be delivered from evil if he be not led into temptation.*

REPLY OBJ. 5: Prayer is offered up to God, not that we may bend Him, but that we may excite in ourselves the confidence to ask: which confidence is excited in us chiefly by the consideration of His charity in our regard, whereby he wills our good—wherefore we say: *Our Father*; and of His excellence, whereby He is able to fulfill it—wherefore we say: *Who art in heaven.*

# Article 10

*Whether prayer is proper to the rational creature?*

AD DECIMUM SIC PROCEDITUR. Videtur quod orare non sit proprium rationalis creaturae. Eiusdem enim videtur esse petere et accipere. Sed accipere convenit etiam

OBJECTION 1: It would seem that prayer is not proper to the rational creature. Asking and receiving apparently belong to the same subject. But receiving is becoming also

personis increatis, scilicet filio et spiritui sancto. Ergo etiam eis convenit orare, nam et filius dicit, Ioan. XIV, *ego rogabo patrem*; et de spiritu sancto dicit apostolus, *spiritus postulat pro nobis*.

**PRAETEREA**, Angeli sunt supra rationales creaturas, cum sint intellectuales substantiae. Sed ad Angelos pertinet orare, unde in Psalm. dicitur, *adorate eum, omnes Angeli eius*. Ergo orare non est proprium rationalis creaturae.

**PRAETEREA**, eiusdem est orare cuius est invocare Deum, quod praecipue fit orando. Sed brutis animalibus convenit invocare Deum secundum illud Psalm., *qui dat iumentis escam ipsorum, et pullis corvorum invocantibus eum*. Ergo orare non est proprium rationalis creaturae.

**SED CONTRA**, oratio est actus rationis, ut supra habitum est. Sed rationalis creatura a ratione dicitur. Ergo orare est proprium rationalis creaturae.

**RESPONDEO** dicendum quod, sicut ex supradictis patet, oratio est actus rationis per quem aliquis superiorem deprecatur, sicut imperium est actus rationis quo inferior ad aliquid ordinatur. Illi ergo proprie competit orare cui convenit rationem habere, et superiorem quem deprecari possit. Divinis autem personis nihil est superius, bruta autem animalia non habent rationem. Unde neque divinis personis neque brutis animalibus convenit orare, sed proprium est rationalis creaturae.

**AD PRIMUM** ergo dicendum quod divinis personis convenit accipere per naturam, orare autem est accipientis per gratiam. Dicitur autem filius rogare, vel orare, secundum naturam assumptam, scilicet humanam, non secundum divinam. Spiritus autem sanctus dicitur postulare, quia postulantes nos facit.

**AD SECUNDUM** dicendum quod ratio et intellectus in nobis non sunt diversae potentiae, ut in primo habitum est, differunt autem secundum perfectum et imperfectum. Et ideo quandoque intellectuales creaturae, quae sunt Angeli, distinguuntur a rationalibus, quandoque autem sub rationalibus comprehenduntur. Et hoc modo dicitur oratio esse proprium rationalis creaturae.

**AD TERTIUM** dicendum quod pulli corvorum dicuntur Deum invocare, propter naturale desiderium quo omnia suo modo desiderant consequi bonitatem divinam. Sic etiam bruta animalia dicuntur Deo obedire, propter naturalem instinctum quo a Deo moventur.

to uncreated Persons, viz. the Son and Holy Spirit. Therefore it is competent to them to pray: for the Son said (John 14:16): *I will ask My Father*, and the Apostle says of the Holy Spirit (Rom 8:26): *The Spirit . . . asketh for us*.

**OBJ. 2**: Angels are above rational creatures, since they are intellectual substances. Now prayer is becoming to the angels, wherefore we read in the Ps. 96:7: *Adore Him, all you His angels*. Therefore prayer is not proper to the rational creature.

**OBJ. 3**: Further, the same subject is fitted to pray as is fitted to call upon God, since this consists chiefly in prayer. But dumb animals are fitted to call upon God, according to Ps. 146:9, *Who giveth to beasts their food and to the young ravens that call upon Him*. Therefore prayer is not proper to the rational creatures.

**ON THE CONTRARY**, Prayer is an act of reason, as stated above (A. 1). But the rational creature is so called from his reason. Therefore prayer is proper to the rational creature.

**I ANSWER THAT**, As stated above (A. 1) prayer is an act of reason, and consists in beseeching a superior; just as command is an act of reason, whereby an inferior is directed to something. Accordingly prayer is properly competent to one to whom it is competent to have reason, and a superior whom he may beseech. Now nothing is above the Divine Persons; and dumb animals are devoid of reason. Therefore prayer is unbecoming both the Divine Persons and dumb animals, and it is proper to the rational creature.

**REPLY OBJ. 1**: Receiving belongs to the Divine Persons in respect of their nature, whereas prayer belongs to one who receives through grace. The Son is said to ask or pray in respect of His assumed, i.e., His human, nature and not in respect of His Godhead: and the Holy Spirit is said to ask, because He makes us ask.

**REPLY OBJ. 2**: As stated in the First Part (Q. 79, A. 8), intellect and reason are not distinct powers in us: but they differ as the perfect from the imperfect. Hence intellectual creatures which are the angels are distinct from rational creatures, and sometimes are included under them. In this sense prayer is said to be proper to the rational creature.

**REPLY OBJ. 3**: The young ravens are said to call upon God, on account of the natural desire whereby all things, each in its own way, desire to attain the Divine goodness. Thus too dumb animals are said to obey God, on account of the natural instinct whereby they are moved by God.

# Article 11

*Whether the saints in heaven pray for us?*

**Ad undecimum sic proceditur.** Videtur quod sancti qui sunt in patria non orent pro nobis. Actus enim alicuius magis est meritorius sibi quam aliis. Sed sancti qui sunt in patria non merentur sibi, nec pro se orant, quia iam sunt in termino constituti. Ergo etiam neque pro nobis orant.

**Praeterea,** sancti perfecte suam voluntatem Deo conformant, ut non velint nisi quod Deus vult. Sed illud quod Deus vult semper impletur. Ergo frustra sancti pro nobis orarent.

**Praeterea,** sicut sancti qui sunt in patria sunt superiores nobis, ita et illi qui sunt in Purgatorio, quia iam peccare non possunt. Sed illi qui sunt in Purgatorio non orant pro nobis, sed magis nos pro eis. Ergo nec sancti qui sunt in patria pro nobis orant.

**Praeterea,** si sancti qui sunt in patria pro nobis orarent, superiorum sanctorum esset efficacior oratio. Non ergo deberet implorari suffragium orationum sanctorum inferiorum, sed solum superiorum.

**Praeterea,** anima Petri non est Petrus. Si ergo animae sanctorum pro nobis orarent quandiu sunt a corpore separatae, non deberemus interpellare sanctum Petrum ad orandum pro nobis, sed animam eius. Cuius contrarium Ecclesia facit. Non ergo sancti, ad minus ante resurrectionem, pro nobis orant.

**Sed contra** est quod dicitur II Mach. ult., *hic est qui multum orat pro populo et universa sancta civitate, Ieremias, propheta Dei.*

**Respondeo** dicendum quod, sicut Hieronymus dicit, *Vigilantii error fuit quod, dum vivimus, mutuo pro nobis orare possumus; postquam autem mortui fuerimus, nullius sit pro alio exaudienda oratio, praesertim cum martyres, ultionem sui sanguinis obsecrantes, impetrare nequiverint.* Sed hoc est omnino falsum. Quia cum oratio pro aliis facta ex caritate proveniat, ut dictum est, quanto sancti qui sunt in patria sunt perfectioris caritatis, tanto magis orant pro viatoribus, qui orationibus iuvari possunt, et quanto sunt Deo coniunctiores, tanto eorum orationes sunt magis efficaces. Habet enim hoc divinus ordo, ut ex superiorum excellentia in inferiora refundatur, sicut ex claritate solis in aerem. Unde et de Christo dicitur, Heb. VII, *accedens per semetipsum ad Deum ad interpellandum pro nobis.* Et propter hoc Hieronymus, contra Vigilantium, dicit, *si apostoli et martyres adhuc in corpore constituti possunt orare pro ceteris, quando pro se adhuc debent esse solliciti; quanto magis post coronas, victorias et triumphos.*

**Ad primum** ergo dicendum quod sanctis qui sunt in patria, cum sint beati, nihil deest nisi gloria corporis, pro qua orant. Orant autem pro nobis, quibus deest

**Objection 1:** It would seem that the saints in heaven do not pray for us. A man's action is more meritorious for himself than for others. But the saints in heaven do not merit for themselves, neither do they pray for themselves, since they are already established in the term. Neither therefore do they pray for us.

**Obj. 2:** Further, the saints conform their will to God perfectly, so that they will only what God wills. Now what God wills is always fulfilled. Therefore it would be useless for the saints to pray for us.

**Obj. 3:** Further, just as the saints in heaven are above, so are those in Purgatory, for they can no longer sin. Now those in Purgatory do not pray for us, on the contrary we pray for them. Therefore neither do the saints in heaven pray for us.

**Obj. 4:** Further, if the saints in heaven pray for us, the prayers of the higher saints would be more efficacious; and so we ought not to implore the help of the lower saints' prayers but only of those of the higher saints.

**Obj. 5:** Further, the soul of Peter is not Peter. If therefore the souls of the saints pray for us, so long as they are separated from their bodies, we ought not to call upon Saint Peter, but on his soul, to pray for us: yet the Church does the contrary. The saints therefore do not pray for us, at least before the resurrection.

**On the contrary,** It is written (2 Macc 15:14): *This is . . . he that prayeth much for the people, and for all the holy city, Jeremias the prophet of God.*

**I answer that,** As Jerome says (*Cont. Vigilant.* 6), the error of Vigilantius consisted in saying that *while we live, we can pray one for another; but that after we are dead, none of our prayers for others can be heard, seeing that not even the martyrs' prayers are granted when they pray for their blood to be avenged.* But this is absolutely false, because, since prayers offered for others proceed from charity, as stated above (AA. 7, 8), the greater the charity of the saints in heaven, the more they pray for wayfarers, since the latter can be helped by prayers: and the more closely they are united to God, the more are their prayers efficacious: for the Divine order is such that lower beings receive an overflow of the excellence of the higher, even as the air receives the brightness of the sun. Wherefore it is said of Christ (Heb 7:25): *Going to God by His own power . . . to make intercession for us.* Hence Jerome says (*Cont. Vigilant.* 6): *If the apostles and martyrs while yet in the body and having to be solicitous for themselves, can pray for others, how much more now that they have the crown of victory and triumph.*

**Reply Obj. 1:** The saints in heaven, since they are blessed, have no lack of bliss, save that of the body's glory, and for this they pray. But they pray for us who lack the

beatitudinis ultima perfectio. Et eorum orationes habent efficaciam impetrandi ex praecedentibus eorum meritis, et ex divina acceptatione.

**AD SECUNDUM** dicendum quod sancti impetrant illud quod Deus vult fieri per orationes eorum. Et hoc petunt quod aestimant eorum orationibus implendum secundum Dei voluntatem.

**AD TERTIUM** dicendum quod illi qui sunt in Purgatorio, etsi sint superiores nobis propter impeccabilitatem, sunt tamen inferiores quantum ad poenas quas patiuntur. Et secundum hoc non sunt in statu orandi, sed magis ut oretur pro eis.

**AD QUARTUM** dicendum quod Deus vult inferiora per omnia superiora iuvari. Et ideo oportet non solum superiores, sed etiam inferiores sanctos implorare. Alioquin esset solius Dei misericordia imploranda. Contingit tamen quandoque quod imploratio inferioris sancti efficacior est, vel quia devotius implorantur; vel quia Deus vult eorum sanctitatem declarare.

**AD QUINTUM** dicendum quod quia sancti viventes meruerunt ut pro nobis orarent, ideo eos invocamus nominibus quibus hic vocabantur, quibus etiam nobis magis innotescunt. Et iterum propter fidem resurrectionis insinuandam, sicut legitur Exod. III, *ego sum Deus Abraham*, etc.

ultimate perfection of bliss: and their prayers are efficacious in impetrating through their previous merits and through God's acceptance.

**REPLY OBJ. 2**: The saints impetrate what ever God wishes to take place through their prayers: and they pray for that which they deem will be granted through their prayers according to God's will.

**REPLY OBJ. 3**: Those who are in Purgatory though they are above us on account of their impeccability, yet they are below us as to the pains which they suffer: and in this respect they are not in a condition to pray, but rather in a condition that requires us to pray for them.

**REPLY OBJ. 4**: It is God's will that inferior beings should be helped by all those that are above them, wherefore we ought to pray not only to the higher but also to the lower saints; else we should have to implore the mercy of God alone. Nevertheless it happens sometime that prayers addressed to a saint of lower degree are more efficacious, either because he is implored with greater devotion, or because God wishes to make known his sanctity.

**REPLY OBJ. 5**: It is because the saints while living merited to pray for us, that we invoke them under the names by which they were known in this life, and by which they are better known to us: and also in order to indicate our belief in the resurrection, according to the saying of Ex. 3:6, *I am the God of Abraham*, etc.

# Article 12

*Whether prayer should be vocal?*

**AD DUODECIMUM SIC PROCEDITUR**. Videtur quod oratio non debeat esse vocalis. Oratio enim, sicut ex dictis patet, principaliter Deo porrigitur. Deus autem locutionem cordis cognoscit. Frustra igitur vocalis oratio adhibetur.

**PRAETEREA**, per orationem mens hominis debet in Deum ascendere, ut dictum est. Sed voces retrahunt homines ab ascensu contemplationis in Deum, sicut et alia sensibilia. Ergo in oratione non est vocibus utendum.

**PRAETEREA**, oratio debet offerri Deo in occulto, secundum illud Matth. VI, *tu autem cum oraveris, intra in cubiculum, et clauso ostio, ora patrem tuum in abscondito.* Sed per vocem oratio publicatur. Ergo non debet oratio esse vocalis.

**SED CONTRA** est quod dicitur in Psalm., *voce mea ad dominum clamavi, voce mea ad dominum deprecatus sum.*

**RESPONDEO** dicendum quod duplex est oratio, communis, et singularis. Communis quidem oratio est quae per ministros Ecclesiae in persona totius fidelis populi Deo offertur. Et ideo oportet quod talis oratio innotescat

**OBJECTION 1**: It would seem that prayer ought not to be vocal. As stated above (A. 4), prayer is addressed chiefly to God. Now God knows the language of the heart. Therefore it is useless to employ vocal prayer.

**OBJ. 2**: Further, prayer should lift man's mind to God, as stated above (A. 1, ad 2). But words, like other sensible objects, prevent man from ascending to God by contemplation. Therefore we should not use words in our prayers.

**OBJ. 3**: Further, prayer should be offered to God in secret, according to Matt. 6:6, *But thou, when thou shalt pray, enter into thy chamber, and having shut the door, pray to thy Father in secret.* But prayer loses its secrecy by being expressed vocally. Therefore prayer should not be vocal.

**ON THE CONTRARY**, It is written (Ps 141:2): *I cried to the Lord with my voice, with my voice I made supplication to the Lord.*

**I ANSWER THAT**, Prayer is twofold, common and individual. Common prayer is that which is offered to God by the ministers of the Church representing the body of the faithful: wherefore such like prayer should come to

toti populo, pro quo profertur. Quod non posset fieri nisi esset vocalis. Et ideo rationabiliter institutum est ut ministri Ecclesiae huiusmodi orationes etiam alta voce pronuntient, ut ad notitiam omnium possit pervenire.

Oratio vero singularis est quae offertur a singulari persona cuiuscumque sive pro se sive pro aliis orantis. Et de huiusmodi orationis necessitate non est quod sit vocalis. Adiungitur tamen vox tali orationi triplici ratione. Primo quidem, ad excitandum interiorem devotionem, qua mens orantis elevetur in Deum. Quia per exteriora signa, sive vocum sive etiam aliquorum factorum, movetur mens hominis et secundum apprehensionem, et per consequens secundum affectionem. Unde Augustinus dicit, ad Probam, quod *verbis et aliis signis ad augendum sanctum desiderium nosipsos acrius excitamus.* Et ideo in singulari oratione tantum est vocibus et huiusmodi signis utendum quantum proficit ad excitandum interius mentem. Si vero mens per hoc distrahatur, vel qualitercumque impediatur, est a talibus cessandum. Quod praecipue contingit in illis quorum mens sine huiusmodi signis est sufficienter ad devotionem parata. Unde Psalmista dicebat, *tibi dixit cor meum, exquisivit te facies mea*; et de Anna legitur, I Reg. I, quod *loquebatur in corde suo.* Secundo, adiungitur vocalis oratio quasi ad redditionem debiti, ut scilicet homo Deo serviat secundum totum illud quod ex Deo habet, idest non solum mente, sed etiam corpore. Quod praecipue competit orationi secundum quod est satisfactoria. Unde dicitur Osee ult., *omnem aufer iniquitatem, et accipe bonum, et reddemus vitulos labiorum nostrorum.* Tertio, adiungitur vocalis oratio ex quadam redundantia ab anima in corpus ex vehementi affectione, secundum illud Psalm., *laetatum est cor meum, et exultavit lingua mea.*

**AD PRIMUM** ergo dicendum quod vocalis oratio non profertur ad hoc quod aliquid ignotum Deo manifestetur, sed ad hoc quod mens orantis vel aliorum excitetur in Deum.

**AD SECUNDUM** dicendum quod verba ad aliud pertinentia distrahunt mentem, et impediunt devotionem orantis. Sed verba significantia aliquid ad devotionem pertinens excitant mentes, praecipue minus devotas.

**AD TERTIUM** dicendum quod, sicut Chrysostomus dicit, super Matth., *eo proposito dominus vetat in conventu orare ut a conventu videatur. Unde orans nihil novum facere debet quod aspiciant homines, vel clamando vel pectus percutiendo vel manus expandendo. Nec tamen,* ut Augustinus dicit, in libro de Serm. Dom. in monte, *videri ab hominibus nefas est, sed ideo haec agere ut ab hominibus videaris.*

the knowledge of the whole people for whom it is offered: and this would not be possible unless it were vocal prayer. Therefore it is reasonably ordained that the ministers of the Church should say these prayers even in a loud voice, so that they may come to the knowledge of all.

On the other hand individual prayer is that which is offered by any single person, whether he pray for himself or for others; and it is not essential to such a prayer as this that it be vocal. And yet the voice is employed in such like prayers for three reasons. First, in order to excite interior devotion, whereby the mind of the person praying is raised to God, because by means of external signs, whether of words or of deeds, the human mind is moved as regards apprehension, and consequently also as regards the affections. Hence Augustine says (*ad Probam.* Ep. cxxx, 9) that *by means of words and other signs we arouse ourselves more effectively to an increase of holy desires.* Hence then alone should we use words and such like signs when they help to excite the mind internally. But if they distract or in any way impede the mind we should abstain from them; and this happens chiefly to those whose mind is sufficiently prepared for devotion without having recourse to those signs. Wherefore the Psalmist (Ps 26:8) said: *My heart hath said to Thee: 'My face hath sought Thee,'* and we read of Anna (1 Kgs 1:13) that *she spoke in her heart.* Second, the voice is used in praying as though to pay a debt, so that man may serve God with all that he has from God, that is to say, not only with his mind, but also with his body: and this applies to prayer considered especially as satisfactory. Hence it is written (Hos 14:3): *Take away all iniquity, and receive the good: and we will render the calves of our lips.* Third, we have recourse to vocal prayer, through a certain overflow from the soul into the body, through excess of feeling, according to Ps. 15:9, *My heart hath been glad, and my tongue hath rejoiced.*

**REPLY OBJ. 1**: Vocal prayer is employed, not in order to tell God something He does not know, but in order to lift up the mind of the person praying or of other persons to God.

**REPLY OBJ. 2**: Words about other matters distract the mind and hinder the devotion of those who pray: but words signifying some object of devotion lift up the mind, especially one that is less devout.

**REPLY OBJ. 3**: As Chrysostom says, *Our Lord forbids one to pray in presence of others in order that one may be seen by others. Hence when you pray, do nothing strange to draw men's attention, either by shouting so as to be heard by others, or by openly striking the heart, or extending the hands, so as to be seen by many.* And yet, according to Augustine (*De Serm. Dom. in Monte* ii, 3), *it is not wrong to be seen by men, but to do this or that in order to be seen by men.*

# Article 13

*Whether attention is a necessary condition of prayer?*

AD TERTIUMDECIMUM SIC PROCEDITUR. Videtur quod de necessitate orationis sit quod sit attenta. Dicitur enim Ioan. IV, *spiritus est Deus, et eos qui adorant eum, in spiritu et veritate adorare oportet.* Sed oratio non est in spiritu si non sit attenta. Ergo de necessitate orationis est quod sit attenta.

PRAETEREA, oratio est *ascensus intellectus in Deum.* Sed quando oratio non est attenta, intellectus non ascendit in Deum. Ergo de necessitate orationis est quod sit attenta.

PRAETEREA, de necessitate orationis est quod careat omni peccato. Sed non est absque peccato quod aliquis orando evagationem mentis patiatur, videtur eum deridere Deum, sicut et si alicui homini loqueretur et non attenderet ad ea quae ipse proferret. Unde Basilius dicit, *est divinum auxilium implorandum non remisse, nec mente huc illuc evagante, eo quod talis non solum non impetrabit quod petit, sed et magis Deum irritabit.* Ergo de necessitate orationis esse videtur quod sit attenta.

SED CONTRA est quod etiam sancti viri quandoque orantes evagationem mentis patiuntur, secundum illud Psalm., *cor meum dereliquit me.*

RESPONDEO dicendum quod quaestio haec praecipue locum habet in oratione vocali. Circa quam sciendum est quod necessarium dicitur aliquid dupliciter. Uno modo, per quod melius pervenitur ad finem. Et sic attentio absolute orationi necessaria est. Alio modo dicitur aliquid necessarium sine quo res non potest consequi suum effectum. Est autem triplex effectus orationis. Primus quidem communis omnibus actibus caritate informatis, quod est mereri. Et ad hunc effectum non ex necessitate requiritur quod attentio adsit orationi per totum, sed vis primae intentionis qua aliquis ad orandum accedit, reddit totam orationem meritoriam, sicut in aliis meritoriis actibus accidit. Secundus autem effectus orationis est ei proprius, quod est impetrare. Et ad hunc etiam effectum sufficit prima intentio, quam Deus principaliter attendit. Si autem prima intentio desit, oratio nec meritoria est nec impetrativa, *illam enim orationem Deus non audit cui ille qui orat non intendit,* ut Gregorius dicit. Tertius autem effectus orationis est quem praesentialiter efficit, scilicet quaedam spiritualis refectio mentis. Et ad hoc de necessitate requiritur in oratione attentio. Unde dicitur I Cor. XIV, *si orem lingua, mens mea sine fructu est.*

Sciendum tamen quod est triplex attentio quae orationi vocali potest adhiberi. Una quidem qua attenditur ad verba, ne quis in eis erret. Secunda qua attenditur ad

OBJECTION 1: It would seem that attention is a necessary condition of prayer. It is written (John 4:24): *God is a spirit, and they that adore Him must adore Him in spirit and in truth.* But prayer is not in spirit unless it be attentive. Therefore attention is a necessary condition of prayer.

OBJ. 2: Further, prayer is *the ascent of the mind to God.* But the mind does not ascend to God if the prayer is inattentive. Therefore attention is a necessary condition of prayer.

OBJ. 3: Further, it is a necessary condition of prayer that it should be altogether sinless. Now if a man allows his mind to wander while praying he is not free of sin, for he seems to make light of God; even as if he were to speak to another man without attending to what he was saying. Hence Basil says that the *Divine assistance is to be implored, not lightly, nor with a mind wandering hither and thither: because he that prays thus not only will not obtain what he asks, nay rather will he provoke God to anger.* Therefore it would seem a necessary condition of prayer that it should be attentive.

ON THE CONTRARY, Even holy men sometimes suffer from a wandering of the mind when they pray, according to Ps. 39:13, *My heart hath forsaken me.*

I ANSWER THAT, This question applies chiefly to vocal prayer. Accordingly we must observe that a thing is necessary in two ways. First, a thing is necessary because thereby the end is better obtained: and thus attention is absolutely necessary for prayer. Second, a thing is said to be necessary when without it something cannot obtain its effect. Now the effect of prayer is threefold. The first is an effect which is common to all acts quickened by charity, and this is merit. In order to realize this effect, it is not necessary that prayer should be attentive throughout; because the force of the original intention with which one sets about praying renders the whole prayer meritorious, as is the case with other meritorious acts. The second effect of prayer is proper thereto, and consists in impetration: and again the original intention, to which God looks chiefly, suffices to obtain this effect. But if the original intention is lacking, prayer lacks both merit and impetration: because, as Gregory says, *God hears not the prayer of those who pay no attention to their prayer.* The third effect of prayer is that which it produces at once; this is the spiritual refreshment of the mind, and for this effect attention is a necessary condition: wherefore it is written (1 Cor 14:14): *If I pray in a tongue . . . my understanding is without fruit.*

It must be observed, however, that there are three kinds of attention that can be brought to vocal prayer: one which attends to the words, lest we say them wrong, another

sensum verborum. Tertia qua attenditur ad finem orationis, scilicet ad Deum et ad rem pro qua oratur, quae quidem est maxime necessaria. Et hanc etiam possunt habere idiotae. Et quandoque intantum abundat haec intentio, qua mens fertur in Deum, ut etiam omnium aliorum mens obliviscatur, sicut dicit Hugo de sancto Victore.

**A D PRIMUM** ergo dicendum quod in spiritu et veritate orat qui ex instinctu spiritus ad orandum accedit, etiam si ex aliqua infirmitate mens postmodum evagetur.

**A D SECUNDUM** dicendum quod mens humana, propter infirmitatem naturae, diu in alto stare non potest, pondere enim infirmitatis humanae deprimitur anima ad inferiora. Et ideo contingit quod quando mens orantis ascendit in Deum per contemplationem, subito evagetur ex quadam infirmitate.

**A D TERTIUM** dicendum quod si quis ex proposito in oratione mente evagetur, hoc peccatum est, et impedit orationis fructum. Et contra hoc Augustinus dicit, in regula, *Psalmis et hymnis cum oratis Deum, hoc versetur in corde quod profertur in ore.* Evagatio vero mentis quae fit praeter propositum, orationis fructum non tollit. Unde Basilius dicit, *si vero, debilitatus a peccato, fixe nequis orare, quantumcumque potes teipsum cohibeas, et Deus ignoscit, eo quod non ex negligentia, sed ex fragilitate non potes, ut oportet, assistere coram eo.*

which attends to the sense of the words, and a third, which attends to the end of prayer, namely, God, and to the thing we are praying for. That last kind of attention is most necessary, and even idiots are capable of it. Moreover this attention, whereby the mind is fixed on God, is sometimes so strong that the mind forgets all other things, as Hugh of St. Victor states.

**REPLY OBJ. 1**: To pray in spirit and in truth is to set about praying through the instigation of the Spirit, even though afterwards the mind wander through weakness.

**REPLY OBJ. 2**: The human mind is unable to remain aloft for long on account of the weakness of nature, because human weakness weighs down the soul to the level of inferior things: and hence it is that when, while praying, the mind ascends to God by contemplation, of a sudden it wanders off through weakness.

**REPLY OBJ. 3**: Purposely to allow one's mind to wander in prayer is sinful and hinders the prayer from having fruit. It is against this that Augustine says in his *Rule (Ep. ccxi)*: *When you pray God with psalms and hymns, let your mind attend to that which your lips pronounce.* But to wander in mind unintentionally does not deprive prayer of its fruit. Hence Basil says (*De Constit. Monach.* i): *If you are so truly weakened by sin that you are unable to pray attentively, strive as much as you can to curb yourself, and God will pardon you, seeing that you are unable to stand in His presence in a becoming manner, not through negligence but through frailty.*

# Article 14

*Whether prayer should last a long time?*

**A D QUARTUMDECIMUM SIC PROCEDITUR.** Videtur quod oratio non debeat esse diuturna. Dicitur enim Matth. VI, *orantes nolite multum loqui.* Sed oportet multum loqui diu orantem, praesertim si oratio sit vocalis. Ergo non debet esse oratio diuturna.

**PRAETEREA**, oratio est explicativa desiderii. Sed desiderium tanto est sanctius quanto magis ad unum restringitur, secundum illud Psalm., *unam petii a domino, hanc requiram.* Ergo et oratio tanto est Deo acceptior quanto est brevior.

**PRAETEREA**, illicitum videtur esse quod homo transgreditur terminos a Deo praefixos, praecipue in his quae pertinent ad cultum divinum, secundum illud Exod. XIX, *contestare populum, ne forte velit transcendere propositos terminos ad videndum dominum, et pereat ex eis plurima multitudo.* Sed a Deo praefixus est nobis terminus orandi per institutionem orationis dominicae, ut patet Matth. VI. Ergo non licet ultra orationem protendere.

**OBJECTION 1**: It would seem that prayer should not be continual. It is written (Matt 6:7): *When you are praying, speak not much.* Now one who prays a long time needs to speak much, especially if his be vocal prayer. Therefore prayer should not last a long time.

**OBJ. 2**: Further, prayer expresses the desire. Now a desire is all the holier according as it is centered on one thing, according to Ps. 26:4, *One thing I have asked of the Lord, this will I seek after.* Therefore the shorter prayer is, the more is it acceptable to God.

**OBJ. 3**: Further, it seems to be wrong to transgress the limits fixed by God, especially in matters concerning Divine worship, according to Ex. 19:21: *Charge the people, lest they should have a mind to pass the limits to see the Lord, and a very great multitude of them should perish.* But God has fixed for us the limits of prayer by instituting the Lord's Prayer (Matt 6). Therefore it is not right to prolong our prayer beyond its limits.

**SED CONTRA**, videtur quod continue sit orandum. Quia dominus dicit, Luc. XVIII, *oportet semper orare, et non deficere.* Et I ad Thess. V, *sine intermissione orate.*

**RESPONDEO** dicendum quod de oratione dupliciter loqui possumus, uno modo, secundum seipsam; alio modo, secundum causam suam. Causa autem orationis est desiderium caritatis, ex quo procedere debet oratio. Quod quidem in nobis debet esse continuum vel actu vel virtute, manet enim virtus huius desiderii in omnibus quae ex caritate facimus; *omnia* autem debemus *in gloriam Dei facere,* ut dicitur I ad Cor. X. Et secundum hoc oratio debet esse continua. Unde Augustinus dicit, ad Probam, *in ipsa fide, spe et caritate continuato desiderio semper oramus.* Sed ipsa oratio secundum se considerata non potest esse assidua, quia oportet aliis operibus occupari. *Sed,* sicut Augustinus ibidem dicit, *ideo per certa intervalla horarum et temporum etiam verbis rogamus Deum, ut illis rerum signis nosipsos admoneamus; quantumque in hoc desiderio profecerimus, nobis ipsis innotescamus; et ad hoc agendum nosipsos acrius excitemus.* Uniuscuiusque autem rei quantitas debet esse proportionata fini, sicut quantitas potionis sanitati. Unde et conveniens est ut oratio tantum duret quantum est utile ad excitandum interioris desiderii fervorem. Cum vero hanc mensuram excedit, ita quod sine taedio durare non possit, non est ulterius oratio protendenda. Unde Augustinus dicit, ad Probam, *dicuntur fratres in Aegypto crebras quidem habere orationes, sed eas tamen brevissimas, et raptim quodammodo iaculatas, ne illa vigilanter erecta, quae oranti plurimum necessaria est, per productiores moras evanescat atque hebetetur intentio. Ac per hoc etiam ipsi satis ostendunt hanc intentionem, sicut non esse obtundendam si perdurare non potest, ita, si perduraverit, non cito esse rumpendam.* Et sicut hoc est attendendum in oratione singulari per comparationem ad intentionem orantis, ita etiam in oratione communi per comparationem ad populi devotionem.

**AD PRIMUM** ergo dicendum quod, sicut Augustinus dicit, ad Probam, *non est hoc orare in multiloquio, si diutius oretur. Aliud est sermo multus; aliud diuturnus affectus. Nam et de ipso domino scriptum est quod pernoctaverit in orando, et quod prolixius oraverit, ut nobis praeberet exemplum.* Et postea subdit, *absit ab oratione multa locutio, sed non desit multa precatio, si fervens perseverat intentio. Nam multum loqui est in orando rem necessariam superfluis agere verbis. Plerumque autem hoc negotium plus gemitibus quam sermonibus agitur.*

**AD SECUNDUM** dicendum quod prolixitas orationis non consistit in hoc quod multa petantur, sed in hoc quod affectus continuetur ad unum desiderandum.

**OBJ. 4**: On the contrary, It would seem that we ought to pray continually. For our Lord said (Luke 18:1): *We ought always to pray, and not to faint*: and it is written (1 Thess 5:17): *Pray without ceasing.*

**I ANSWER THAT**, We may speak about prayer in two ways: first, by considering it in itself; second, by considering it in its cause. The cause of prayer is the desire of charity, from which prayer ought to arise: and this desire ought to be in us continually, either actually or virtually, for the virtue of this desire remains in whatever we do out of charity; and we ought to *do all things to the glory of God* (1 Cor 10:31). From this point of view prayer ought to be continual: wherefore Augustine says (*ad Probam, Ep. cxxx*, 9): *Faith, hope and charity are by themselves a prayer of continual longing.* But prayer, considered in itself, cannot be continual, because we have to be busy about other works, and, as Augustine says (*ad Probam. Ep. cxxx*, 9), *we pray to God with our lips at certain intervals and seasons, in order to admonish ourselves by means of such like signs, to take note of the amount of our progress in that desire, and to arouse ourselves more eagerly to an increase thereof.* Now the quantity of a thing should be commensurate with its end, for instance the quantity of the dose should be commensurate with health. And so it is becoming that prayer should last long enough to arouse the fervor of the interior desire: and when it exceeds this measure, so that it cannot be continued any longer without causing weariness, it should be discontinued. Wherefore Augustine says (*ad Probam. Ep. cxxx*): *It is said that the brethren in Egypt make frequent but very short prayers, rapid ejaculations, as it were, lest that vigilant and erect attention which is so necessary in prayer slacken and languish, through the strain being prolonged. By so doing they make it sufficiently clear not only that this attention must not be forced if we are unable to keep it up, but also that if we are able to continue, it should not be broken off too soon.* And just as we must judge of this in private prayers by considering the attention of the person praying, so too, in public prayers we must judge of it by considering the devotion of the people.

**REPLY OBJ. 1**: As Augustine says (*ad Probam. Ep. cxxx*), *to pray with many words is not the same as to pray long; to speak long is one thing, to be devout long is another. For it is written that our Lord passed the whole night in prayer, and that He 'prayed the longer' in order to set us an example.* Further on he says: *When praying say little, yet pray much so long as your attention is fervent. For to say much in prayer is to discuss your need in too many words: whereas to pray much is to knock at the door of Him we pray, by the continuous and devout clamor of the heart. Indeed this business is frequently done with groans rather than with words, with tears rather than with speech.*

**REPLY OBJ. 2**: Length of prayer consists, not in praying for many things, but in the affections persisting in the desire of one thing.

**AD TERTIUM** dicendum quod dominus non instituit hanc orationem ut his solis verbis uti debeamus in orando, sed quia ad haec sola impetranda debet tendere nostrae orationis intentio, qualitercumque ea proferamus vel cogitemus.

**AD QUARTUM** dicendum quod aliquis continue orat, vel propter continuitatem desiderii, ut dictum est. Vel quia non intermittit quin temporibus statutis oret. Vel propter effectum, sive in ipso orante, qui etiam post orationem remanet magis devotus; sive etiam in alio, puta cum aliquis suis beneficiis provocat alium ut pro se oret, etiam quando ipse ab orando quiescit.

**REPLY OBJ. 3**: Our Lord instituted this prayer, not that we might use no other words when we pray, but that in our prayers we might have none but these things in view, no matter how we express them or think of them.

**REPLY OBJ. 4**: One may pray continually, either through having a continual desire, as stated above; or through praying at certain fixed times, though interruptedly; or by reason of the effect, whether in the person who prays—because he remains more devout even after praying, or in some other person—as when by his kindness a man incites another to pray for him, even after he himself has ceased praying.

# Article 15

*Whether prayer is meritorious?*

**AD QUINTUMDECIMUM SIC PROCEDITUR.** Videtur quod oratio non sit meritoria. Omne enim meritum procedit a gratia. Sed oratio praecedit gratiam, quia etiam ipsa gratia per orationem impetratur, secundum illud Luc. XI, *pater vester de caelo dabit spiritum bonum petentibus se.* Ergo oratio non est actus meritorius.

**PRAETEREA**, si oratio aliquid meretur, maxime videtur mereri illud quod orando petitur. Sed hoc non semper meretur, quia multoties etiam sanctorum orationes non exaudiuntur; sicut Paulus non est exauditus petens removeri a se stimulum carnis. Ergo oratio non est actus meritorius.

**PRAETEREA**, oratio praecipue fidei innititur, secundum illud Iac. I, *postulet autem in fide, nihil haesitans.* Fides autem non sufficit ad merendum, ut patet in his qui habent fidem informem. Ergo oratio non est actus meritorius.

**SED CONTRA** est quod super illud Psalm., *oratio mea in sinu meo convertetur,* dicit Glossa, *etsi eis non profuit, ego tamen non sum frustratus mea mercede.* Merces autem non debetur nisi merito. Ergo oratio habet rationem meriti.

**RESPONDEO** dicendum quod, sicut dictum est, oratio, praeter effectum spiritualis consolationis quam praesentialiter affert, duplicem habet virtutem respectu futuri effectus, scilicet virtutem merendi, et virtutem impetrandi. Oratio autem, sicut et quilibet alius actus virtutis, habet efficaciam merendi inquantum procedit ex radice caritatis, cuius proprium obiectum est bonum aeternum, cuius fruitionem meremur. Procedit tamen oratio a caritate mediante religione, cuius est actus oratio ut dictum est; concomitantibus etiam quibusdam aliis virtutibus quae ad bonitatem orationis requiruntur, scilicet humilitate et fide. Ad religionem enim pertinet

**OBJECTION 1**: It would seem that prayer is not meritorious. All merit proceeds from grace. But prayer precedes grace, since even grace is obtained by means of prayer according to Luke 11:13, *(How much more) will your Father from heaven give the good Spirit to them that ask Him!* Therefore prayer is not a meritorious act.

**OBJ. 2**: Further, if prayer merits anything, this would seem to be chiefly that which is besought in prayer. Yet it does not always merit this, because even the saints' prayers are frequently not heard; thus Paul was not heard when he besought the sting of the flesh to be removed from him. Therefore prayer is not a meritorious act.

**OBJ. 3**: Further, prayer is based chiefly on faith, according to James 1:6, *But let him ask in faith, nothing wavering.* Now faith is not sufficient for merit, as instanced in those who have lifeless faith. Therefore prayer is not a meritorious act.

**ON THE CONTRARY**, A gloss on the words of Ps. 34:13, *My prayer shall be turned into my bosom,* explains them as meaning, *if my prayer does not profit them, yet shall not I be deprived of my reward.* Now reward is not due save to merit. Therefore prayer is meritorious.

**I ANSWER THAT**, As stated above (A. 13) prayer, besides causing spiritual consolation at the time of praying, has a twofold efficacy in respect of a future effect, namely, efficacy in meriting and efficacy in impetrating. Now prayer, like any other virtuous act, is efficacious in meriting, because it proceeds from charity as its root, the proper object of which is the eternal good that we merit to enjoy. Yet prayer proceeds from charity through the medium of religion, of which prayer is an act, as stated above (A. 3), and with the concurrence of other virtues requisite for the goodness of prayer, viz. humility and faith. For the offering of prayer itself to God belongs to religion, while the desire for the thing

ipsam orationem Deo offerre. Ad caritatem vero pertinet desiderium rei cuius complementum oratio petit. Fides autem est necessaria ex parte Dei, quem oramus, ut scilicet credamus ab eo nos posse obtinere quod petimus. Humilitas autem est necessaria ex parte ipsius petentis, qui suam indigentiam recognoscit. Est etiam et devotio necessaria, sed haec ad religionem pertinet, cuius est primus actus, necessarius ad omnes consequentes, ut supra dictum est.

Efficaciam autem impetrandi habet ex gratia Dei, quem oramus, qui etiam nos ad orandum inducit. Unde Augustinus dicit, in libro de Verb. Dom., *non nos hortaretur ut peteremus, nisi dare vellet.* Et Chrysostomus dicit, *nunquam oranti beneficia denegat qui ut orantes non deficiant sua pietate instigat.*

**AD PRIMUM** ergo dicendum quod oratio quae est sine gratia gratum faciente meritoria non est, sicut nec aliquis alius actus virtuosus. Et tamen etiam oratio quae impetrat gratiam gratum facientem procedit ex aliqua gratia, quasi ex gratuito dono, quia ipsum orare est quoddam *donum Dei,* ut Augustinus dicit, in libro de perseverantia.

**AD SECUNDUM** dicendum quod ad aliud principaliter respicit meritum orationis quandoque quam ad id quod petitur, meritum enim praecipue ordinatur ad beatitudinem; sed petitio orationis directe se extendit quandoque ad aliqua alia, ut ex dictis patet. Si ergo illud aliud quod petit aliquis pro seipso, non sit ei ad beatitudinem utile, non meretur illud, sed quandoque hoc petendo et desiderando meritum amittit, puta si petat a Deo complementum alicuius peccati, quod est non pie orare.

Quandoque vero non est necessarium ad salutem, nec manifeste saluti contrarium. Et tunc, licet orans possit orando mereri vitam aeternam, non tamen meretur illud obtinere quod petit. Unde Augustinus dicit, in libro sententiarum prosperi, *fideliter supplicans Deo pro necessitatibus huius vitae, et misericorditer auditur, et misericorditer non auditur. Quid enim infirmo sit utile magis novit medicus quam aegrotus.* Et propter hoc etiam Paulus non est exauditus petens amoveri stimulum carnis, quia non expediebat.

Si vero id quod petitur sit utile ad beatitudinem hominis, quasi pertinens ad eius salutem, meretur illud non solum orando, sed etiam alia bona opera faciendo. Et ideo indubitanter accipit quod petit, sed quando debet accipere, *quaedam enim non negantur, sed ut congruo dentur tempore, differuntur,* ut Augustinus dicit, super Ioan. Quod tamen potest impediri, si in petendo non perseveret. Et propter hoc dicit Basilius, *ideo quandoque*

that we pray to be accomplished belongs to charity. Faith is necessary in reference to God to Whom we pray; that is, we need to believe that we can obtain from Him what we seek. Humility is necessary on the part of the person praying, because he recognizes his neediness. Devotion too is necessary: but this belongs to religion, for it is its first act and a necessary condition of all its secondary acts, as stated above (Q. 82, AA. 1, 2).

As to its efficacy in impetrating, prayer derives this from the grace of God to Whom we pray, and Who instigates us to pray. Wherefore Augustine says (*De Verb. Dom.,* Serm. cv, 1): *He would not urge us to ask, unless He were willing to give;* and Chrysostom says: *He never refuses to grant our prayers, since in His loving-kindness He urged us not to faint in praying.*

**REPLY OBJ. 1:** Neither prayer nor any other virtuous act is meritorious without sanctifying grace. And yet even that prayer which impetrates sanctifying grace proceeds from some grace, as from a gratuitous gift, since the very act of praying is *a gift of God,* as Augustine states (*De Persever.* xxiii).

**REPLY OBJ. 2:** Sometimes the merit of prayer regards chiefly something distinct from the object of one's petition. For the chief object of merit is beatitude, whereas the direct object of the petition of prayer extends sometimes to certain other things, as stated above (AA. 6, 7). Accordingly if this other thing that we ask for ourselves be not useful for our beatitude, we do not merit it; and sometimes by asking for and desiring such things we lose merit for instance if we ask of God the accomplishment of some sin, which would be an impious prayer.

And sometimes it is not necessary for salvation, nor yet manifestly contrary thereto; and then although he who prays may merit eternal life by praying, yet he does not merit to obtain what he asks for. Hence Augustine says (*Liber Sentent. Prosperi* sent. ccxii): *He who faithfully prays God for the necessaries of this life, is both mercifully heard, and mercifully not heard. For the physician knows better than the sick man what is good for the disease.* For this reason, too, Paul was not heard when he prayed for the removal of the sting in his flesh, because this was not expedient.

If, however, we pray for something that is useful for our beatitude, through being conducive to salvation, we merit it not only by praying, but also by doing other good deeds: therefore without any doubt we receive what we ask for, yet when we ought to receive it: *since certain things are not denied us, but are deferred that they may be granted at a suitable time,* according to Augustine (*Tract. cii in Joan.*): and again this may be hindered if we persevere not in

*petis et non accipis, quia perperam postulasti, vel infideliter vel leviter, vel non conferentia tibi, vel destitisti.*

Quia vero homo non potest alii mereri vitam aeternam ex condigno, ut supra dictum est; ideo per consequens nec ea quae ad vitam aeternam pertinent potest aliquando aliquis ex condigno alteri mereri. Et propter hoc non semper ille auditur qui pro alio orat, ut supra habitum est. Et ideo ponuntur quatuor conditiones, quibus concurrentibus, semper aliquis impetrat quod petit, ut scilicet *pro se* petat, *necessaria ad salutem, pie* et *perseveranter.*

**AD TERTIUM** dicendum quod oratio innititur principaliter fidei non quantum ad efficaciam merendi, quia sic innititur principaliter caritati, sed quantum ad efficaciam impetrandi. Quia per fidem habet homo notitiam omnipotentiae divinae et misericordiae, ex quibus oratio impetrat quod petit.

asking for it. Wherefore Basil says (*De Constit. Monast.* i): *The reason why sometimes thou hast asked and not received, is because thou hast asked amiss, either inconsistently, or lightly, or because thou hast asked for what was not good for thee, or because thou hast ceased asking.*

Since, however, a man cannot condignly merit eternal life for another, as stated above (I-II, Q. 114, A. 6), it follows that sometimes one cannot condignly merit for another things that pertain to eternal life. For this reason we are not always heard when we pray for others, as stated above (A. 7, ad 2, 3). Hence it is that four conditions are laid down; namely, to ask—*for ourselves—things necessary for salvation—piously—perseveringly*; when all these four concur, we always obtain what we ask for.

**REPLY OBJ. 3**: Prayer depends chiefly on faith, not for its efficacy in meriting, because thus it depends chiefly on charity, but for its efficacy in impetrating, because it is through faith that man comes to know of God's omnipotence and mercy, which are the source whence prayer impetrates what it asks for.

# Article 16

*Whether sinners impetrate anything from God by their prayers?*

**AD SEXTUMDECIMUM SIC PROCEDITUR.** Videtur quod peccatores orando non impetrent aliquid a Deo. Dicitur enim Ioan. IX, *scimus quia peccatores Deus non audit.* Quod consonat ei quod dicitur Prov. XXVIII, *qui declinat aures suas ne audiat legem, oratio eius erit execrabilis,* oratio autem execrabilis non impetrat aliquid a Deo. Ergo peccatores non impetrant aliquid a Deo.

**PRAETEREA**, iusti impetrant a Deo illud quod merentur, ut supra habitum est. Sed peccatores nihil possunt mereri, quia gratia carent, et etiam caritate, quae est *virtus pietatis*, ut dicit Glossa, II ad Tim. III, super illud, *habentes quidem speciem pietatis, virtutem autem eius abnegantes*; et ita non pie orant, quod requiritur ad hoc quod oratio impetret, ut supra dictum est. Ergo peccatores nihil impetrant orando.

**PRAETEREA**, Chrysostomus dicit, super Matth., *pater non libenter exaudit orationem quam filius non dictavit.* Sed in oratione quam Christus dictavit dicitur, *dimitte nobis debita nostra, sicut et nos dimittimus debitoribus nostris,* quod peccatores non faciunt. Ergo vel mentiuntur hoc dicentes, et sic non sunt exauditione digni, vel, si non dicant, non exaudiuntur, quia formam orandi a Christo institutam non servant.

**SED CONTRA** est quod Augustinus dicit, super Ioan., *si peccatores non exaudiret Deus, frustra publicanus dixisset, domine, propitius esto mihi peccatori.* Et Chryso-

**OBJECTION 1**: It would seem that sinners impetrate nothing from God by their prayers. It is written (John 9:31): *We know that God doth not hear sinners*; and this agrees with the saying of Prov. 28:9, *He that turneth away his ears from hearing the law, his prayer shall be an abomination.* Now an abominable prayer impetrates nothing from God. Therefore sinners impetrate nothing from God.

**OBJ. 2**: Further, the just impetrate from God what they merit, as stated above (A. 15, ad 2). But sinners cannot merit anything since they lack grace and charity which is the *power of godliness*, according to a gloss on 2 Tim. 3:5, *Having an appearance indeed of godliness, but denying the power thereof.* and so their prayer is impious, and yet piety is required in order that prayer may be impetrative, as stated above (A. 15, ad 2). Therefore sinners impetrate nothing by their prayers.

**OBJ. 3**: Further, Chrysostom says: *The Father is unwilling to hear the prayer which the Son has not inspired.* Now in the prayer inspired by Christ we say: *Forgive us our trespasses as we forgive them that trespass against us*: and sinners do not fulfill this. Therefore either they lie in saying this, and so are unworthy to be heard, or, if they do not say it, they are not heard, because they do not observe the form of prayer instituted by Christ.

**ON THE CONTRARY**, Augustine says (*Tract. xliv, super Joan.*): *If God were not to hear sinners, the publican would have vainly said: Lord, be merciful to me a sinner*; and

stomus dicit, super Matth., *omnis qui petit accipit, idest, sive iustus sit sive peccator.*

**RESPONDEO** dicendum quod in peccatore duo sunt consideranda, scilicet natura, quam diligit Deus; et culpa, quam odit. Si ergo peccator orando aliquid petit inquantum peccator, idest secundum desiderium peccati, hoc a Deo non auditur ex misericordia, sed quandoque auditur ad vindictam, dum Deus permittit peccatorem adhuc amplius ruere in peccata, *Deus* enim *quaedam negat propitius quae concedit iratus,* ut Augustinus dicit. Orationem vero peccatoris ex bono naturae desiderio procedentem Deus audit, non quasi ex iustitia, quia peccator hoc non meretur, sed ex pura misericordia, observatis tamen quatuor praemissis conditionibus, ut scilicet pro se petat, necessaria ad salutem, pie et perseveranter.

**AD PRIMUM** ergo dicendum quod, sicut Augustinus dicit, super Ioan., illud verbum est caeci *adhuc inuncti,* idest nondum perfecte illuminati. Et ideo non est ratum. Quamvis possit verificari si intelligatur de peccatore inquantum est peccator. Per quem etiam modum oratio eius dicitur execrabilis.

**AD SECUNDUM** dicendum quod peccator non potest pie orare quasi eius oratio ex habitu virtutis informetur. Potest tamen eius oratio esse pia quantum ad hoc quod petit aliquid ad pietatem pertinens, sicut ille qui non habet habitum iustitiae, potest aliquid iustum velle, ut ex supradictis patet. Et quamvis eius oratio non sit meritoria, potest tamen esse impetrativa, quia meritum innititur iustitiae, sed impetratio gratiae.

**AD TERTIUM** dicendum quod, sicut dictum est, oratio dominica profertur ex persona communi totius Ecclesiae. Et ideo si aliquis nolens dimittere debita proximo dicat orationem dominicam, non mentitur, quamvis hoc quod dicit non sit verum quantum ad suam personam, est enim verum quantum ad personam Ecclesiae. Extra quam est merito, et ideo fructu orationis caret. Quandoque tamen aliqui peccatores parati sunt debitoribus suis remittere. Et ideo ipsi orantes exaudiuntur, secundum illud Eccli. XXVIII, *relinque proximo tuo nocenti te, et tunc deprecanti tibi peccata solventur.*

Chrysostom says: *Everyone that asketh shall receive, that is to say whether he be righteous or sinful.*

**I ANSWER THAT,** In the sinner, two things are to be considered: his nature which God loves, and the sin which He hates. Accordingly when a sinner prays for something as sinner, i.e., in accordance with a sinful desire, God hears him not through mercy but sometimes through vengeance when He allows the sinner to fall yet deeper into sin. For *God refuses in mercy what He grants in anger,* as Augustine declares (*Tract. lxxiii in Joan.*). On the other hand God hears the sinner's prayer if it proceed from a good natural desire, not out of justice, because the sinner does not merit to be heard, but out of pure mercy, provided however he fulfill the four conditions given above, namely, that he beseech for himself things necessary for salvation, piously and perseveringly.

**REPLY OBJ. 1:** As Augustine states (*Tract. xliv super Joan.*), these words were spoken by the blind man *before being anointed,* i.e., perfectly enlightened, and consequently lack authority. And yet there is truth in the saying if it refers to a sinner as such, in which sense also the sinner's prayer is said to be an abomination.

**REPLY OBJ. 2:** There can be no godliness in the sinner's prayer as though his prayer were quickened by a habit of virtue: and yet his prayer may be godly insofar as he asks for something pertaining to godliness. Even so a man who has not the habit of justice is able to will something just, as stated above (Q. 59, A. 2). And though his prayer is not meritorious, it can be impetrative, because merit depends on justice, whereas impetration rests on grace.

**REPLY OBJ. 3:** As stated above (A. 7, ad 1) the Lord's Prayer is pronounced in the common person of the whole Church: and so if anyone say the Lord's Prayer while unwilling to forgive his neighbor's trespasses, he lies not, although his words do not apply to him personally: for they are true as referred to the person of the Church, from which he is excluded by merit, and consequently he is deprived of the fruit of his prayer. Sometimes, however, a sinner is prepared to forgive those who have trespassed against him, wherefore his prayers are heard, according to Ecclus. 28:2, *Forgive thy neighbor if he hath hurt thee, and then shall thy sins be forgiven to thee when thou prayest.*

# Article 17

*Whether the parts of prayer are fittingly described as supplications, prayers, intercessions, and thanksgivings?*

**AD SEPTIMUMDECIMUM SIC PROCEDITUR.** Videtur quod inconvenienter dicantur esse orationis partes *obsecrationes, orationes, postulationes, gratiarum actiones.* Obsecratio enim videtur esse quaedam adiuratio. Sed,

**OBJECTION 1**: It would seem that the parts of prayer are unfittingly described as *supplications, prayers, intercessions,* and *thanksgivings.* Supplication would seem to be a kind of adjuration. Yet, according to Origen (*Super Matth. Tract.*

sicut Origenes dicit, super Matth., *non oportet ut vir qui vult secundum Evangelium vivere, adiuret alium, si enim iurare non licet, nec adiurare.* Ergo inconvenienter ponitur obsecratio orationis pars.

**PRAETEREA**, oratio, secundum Damascenum, est *petitio decentium a Deo.* Inconvenienter ergo orationes contra postulationes dividuntur.

**PRAETEREA**, gratiarum actiones pertinent ad praeterita, alia vero ad futura. Sed praeterita sunt priora futuris. Inconvenienter ergo gratiarum actiones post alia ponuntur.

**IN CONTRARIUM** est auctoritas apostoli, I ad Tim. II.

**RESPONDEO** dicendum quod ad orationem tria requiruntur. Quorum primum est ut orans accedat ad Deum, quem orat. Quod significatur nomine *orationis*, quia oratio est *ascensus intellectus in Deum.* Secundo, requiritur petitio, quae significatur nomine *postulationis*, sive petitio proponatur determinate, quod quidem nominant quidam proprie *postulationem*; sive indeterminate, ut cum quis petit iuvari a Deo, quod nominant *supplicationem*; sive solum factum narretur, secundum illud Ioan. XI, *ecce, quem amas infirmatur,* quod vocant *insinuationem.* Tertio, requiritur ratio impetrandi quod petitur. Et hoc vel ex parte Dei, vel ex parte petentis. Ratio quidem impetrandi ex parte Dei est eius sanctitas, propter quam petimus exaudiri, secundum illud Dan. IX, *propter temetipsum inclina, Deus meus, aurem tuam.* Et ad hoc pertinet *obsecratio*, quae est *per sacra contestatio*, sicut cum dicimus, *per nativitatem tuam, libera nos, domine.* Ratio vero impetrandi ex parte petentis est *gratiarum actio*, quia de acceptis beneficiis gratias agentes, meremur accipere potiora, ut in collecta dicitur. Et ideo dicit Glossa, I ad Tim. II, quod *in Missa obsecrationes sunt quae praecedunt consecrationem, in quibus quaedam sacra commemorantur; orationes sunt in ipsa consecratione, in qua mens maxime debet elevari in Deum; postulationes autem sunt in sequentibus petitionibus; gratiarum actiones in fine.*

In pluribus etiam Ecclesiae collectis haec quatuor possunt attendi. Sicut in collecta Trinitatis, quod dicitur, *omnipotens, sempiterne Deus*, pertinet ad orationis ascensum in Deum; quod dicitur, *qui dedisti famulis tuis* etc., pertinet ad gratiarum actionem; quod dicitur, *praesta, quaesumus* etc., pertinet ad postulationem; quod in fine ponitur, *per dominum nostrum* etc., pertinet ad obsecrationem.

In Collationibus autem Patrum dicitur quod *obsecratio est imploratio pro peccatis; oratio, cum aliquid Deo vovemus; postulatio, cum pro aliis petimus.* Sed primum melius est.

xxxv), *a man who wishes to live according to the gospel need not adjure another, for if it be unlawful to swear, it is also unlawful to adjure.* Therefore supplication is unfittingly reckoned a part of prayer.

**OBJ. 2**: Further, according to Damascene (*De Fide Orth.* iii, 24), *to pray is to ask becoming things of God.* Therefore it is unfitting to distinguish *prayers* from *intercessions.*

**OBJ. 3**: Further, thanksgivings regard the past, while the others regard the future. But the past precedes the future. Therefore thanksgivings are unfittingly placed after the others.

**ON THE CONTRARY**, suffices the authority of the Apostle (1 Tim 2:1).

**I ANSWER THAT**, Three conditions are requisite for prayer. First, that the person who prays should approach God Whom he prays: this is signified in the word *prayer*, because prayer is *the raising up of one's mind to God.* The second is that there should be a petition, and this is signified in the word *intercession.* In this case sometimes one asks for something definite, and then some say it is *intercession* properly so called, or we may ask for some thing indefinitely, for instance to be helped by God, or we may simply indicate a fact, as in John 11:3, *Behold, he whom Thou lovest is sick*, and then they call it *insinuation.* The third condition is the reason for impetrating what we ask for: and this either on the part of God, or on the part of the person who asks. The reason of impetration on the part of God is His sanctity, on account of which we ask to be heard, according to Dan. 9:17, 18, *For Thy own sake, incline, O God, Thy ear*; and to this pertains *supplication* (*obsecratio*) which means a pleading through sacred things, as when we say, *Through Thy nativity, deliver us, O Lord.* The reason for impetration on the part of the person who asks is *thanksgiving*; since *through giving thanks for benefits received we merit to receive yet greater benefits*, as we say in the collect. Hence a gloss on 1 Tim. 2:1 says that *in the Mass, the consecration is preceded by supplication*, in which certain sacred things are called to mind; that *prayers are in the consecration itself*, in which especially the mind should be raised up to God; and that *intercessions are in the petitions that follow, and thanksgivings at the end.*

We may notice these four things in several of the Church's collects. Thus in the collect of Trinity Sunday the words, *Almighty eternal God* belong to the offering up of prayer to God; the words, *Who hast given to Thy servants*, etc. belong to thanksgiving; the words, *grant, we beseech Thee*, belong to intercession; and the words at the end, *Through Our Lord*, etc. belong to supplication.

In the Conferences of the Fathers (ix, cap. 11, seqq.) we read: *Supplication is bewailing one's sins; prayer is vowing something to God; intercession is praying for others; thanksgiving is offered by the mind to God in ineffable ecstasy.* The first explanation, however, is the better.

**AD PRIMUM** ergo dicendum quod obsecratio non est adiuratio ad compellendum, quae prohibetur, sed ad misericordiam implorandum.

**AD SECUNDUM** dicendum quod oratio communiter sumpta includit omnia quae hic dicuntur. Sed secundum quod contra alia dividitur, importat proprie ascensum in Deum.

**AD TERTIUM** dicendum quod in diversis praeterita praecedunt futura, sed aliquid unum et idem prius est futurum quam sit praeteritum. Et ideo gratiarum actio de aliis beneficiis praecedit postulationem aliorum beneficiorum, sed idem beneficium prius postulatur, et ultimo, cum acceptum fuerit, de eo gratiae aguntur. Postulationem autem praecedit oratio, per quam acceditur ad eum a quo petimus. Orationem autem praecedit obsecratio, quia ex consideratione divinae bonitatis ad eum audemus accedere.

**REPLY OBJ. 1**: *Supplication* is an adjuration not for the purpose of compelling, for this is forbidden, but in order to implore mercy.

**REPLY OBJ. 2**: *Prayer* in the general sense includes all the things mentioned here; but when distinguished from the others it denotes properly the ascent to God.

**REPLY OBJ. 3**: Among things that are diverse the past precedes the future; but the one and same thing is future before it is past. Hence thanksgiving for other benefits precedes intercession: but one and the same benefit is first sought, and finally, when it has been received, we give thanks for it. Intercession is preceded by prayer whereby we approach Him of Whom we ask: and prayer is preceded by supplication, whereby through the consideration of God's goodness we dare approach Him.

# QUESTION 84

Deinde considerandum est de exterioribus actibus latriae. Et primo, de adoratione, per quam aliquis suum corpus ad Deum venerandum exhibet; secundo, de illis actibus quibus aliquid de rebus exterioribus Deo offertur; tertio, de actibus quibus ea quae Dei sunt assumuntur.

Circa primum quaeruntur tria.

Primo, utrum adoratio sit actus latriae.

Secundo, utrum adoratio importet actum interiorem, vel exteriorem.

Tertio, utrum adoratio requirat determinationem loci.

In due sequence we must consider the external acts of latria, and in the first place, adoration whereby one uses one's body to reverence God; second, those acts whereby some external thing is offered to God; third, those acts whereby something belonging to God is assumed.

Under the first head there are three points of inquiry:

(1) Whether adoration is an act of latria?

(2) Whether adoration denotes an internal or an external act?

(3) Whether adoration requires a definite place?

# Article 1

*Whether adoration is an act of latria, or religion?*

**AD PRIMUM SIC PROCEDITUR.** Videtur quod adoratio non sit actus latriae sive religionis. Cultus enim religionis soli Deo debetur. Sed adoratio non debetur soli Deo, legitur enim Gen. XVIII quod Abraham adoravit Angelos; et III Reg. I dicitur quod Nathan propheta, ingressus ad regem David, *adoravit eum pronus in terram*. Ergo adoratio non est actus religionis.

**PRAETEREA**, religionis cultus debetur Deo prout in ipso beatificamur, ut patet per Augustinum, in X de Civ. Dei. Sed adoratio debetur ei ratione maiestatis, quia super illud Psalm., *adorate dominum in atrio sancto eius*, dicit Glossa, *de his atriis venitur in atrium ubi maiestas adoratur*. Ergo adoratio non est actus latriae.

**PRAETEREA**, unius religionis cultus tribus personis debetur. Non autem una adoratione adoramus tres personas, sed ad invocationem trium personarum singulariter genu flectimus. Ergo adoratio non est actus latriae.

**SED CONTRA** est quod Matth. IV inducitur, *dominum Deum tuum adorabis, et illi soli servies*.

**RESPONDEO** dicendum quod adoratio ordinatur in reverentiam eius qui adoratur. Manifestum est autem ex dictis quod religionis proprium est reverentiam Deo exhibere. Unde adoratio qua Deus adoratur est religionis actus.

**AD PRIMUM** ergo dicendum quod Deo debetur reverentia propter eius excellentiam, quae aliquibus creaturis

**OBJECTION 1**: It would seem that adoration is not an act of latria or religion. The worship of religion is due to God alone. But adoration is not due to God alone: since we read (Gen 18:2) that Abraham adored the angels; and (3 Kgs 1:23) that the prophet Nathan, when he was come in to king David, *worshiped him bowing down to the ground*. Therefore adoration is not an act of religion.

**OBJ. 2**: Further, the worship of religion is due to God as the object of beatitude, according to Augustine (*De Civ. Dei* x, 3): whereas adoration is due to Him by reason of His majesty, since a gloss on Ps. 28:2, *Adore ye the Lord in His holy court*, says: *We pass from these courts into the court where we adore His majesty*. Therefore adoration is not an act of latria.

**OBJ. 3**: Further, the worship of one same religion is due to the three Persons. But we do not adore the three Persons with one adoration, for we genuflect at each separate invocation of Them. Therefore adoration is not an act of latria.

**ON THE CONTRARY**, are the words quoted Matt. 4:10: *The Lord thy God shalt thou adore and Him only shalt thou serve.*

**I ANSWER THAT**, Adoration is directed to the reverence of the person adored. Now it is evident from what we have said (Q. 81, AA. 2, 4) that it is proper to religion to show reverence to God. Hence the adoration whereby we adore God is an act of religion.

**REPLY OBJ. 1**: Reverence is due to God on account of His excellence, which is communicated to certain creatures

communicatur non secundum aequalitatem, sed secundum quandam participationem. Et ideo alia veneratione veneramur Deum, quod pertinet ad latriam, et alia veneratione quasdam excellentes creaturas, quod pertinet ad duliam, de qua post dicetur. Et quia ea quae exterius aguntur signa sunt interioris reverentiae, quaedam exteriora ad reverentiam pertinentia exhibentur excellentibus creaturis, inter quae maximum est adoratio, sed aliquid est quod soli Deo exhibetur, scilicet sacrificium. Unde Augustinus dicit, in X de Civ. Dei, *multa de cultu divino usurpata sunt quae honoribus deferrentur humanis, sive humilitate nimia sive adulatione pestifera, ita tamen ut quibus ea deferrentur, homines haberentur, qui dicuntur colendi et venerandi; si autem multum eis additur, et adorandi. Quis vero sacrificandum censuit nisi ei quem Deum aut scivit, aut putavit, aut finxit?* Secundum reverentiam igitur quae creaturae excellenti debetur, Nathan adoravit David. Secundum autem reverentiam quae Deo debetur, Mardochaeus noluit adorare Aman, *timens ne honorem Dei transferret ad hominem*, ut dicitur Esther XIII.

Et similiter secundum reverentiam debitam creaturae excellenti, Abraham adoravit Angelos; et etiam Iosue, ut legitur Iosue V. Quamvis possit intelligi quod adoraverint adoratione latriae Deum, qui in persona Angeli apparebat et loquebatur. Secundum autem reverentiam quae debetur Deo, prohibitus est Ioannes Angelum adorare, Apoc. ult. Tum ad ostendendum dignitatem hominis, quam adeptus est per Christum, ut Angelis aequetur, unde ibi subditur, *conservus tuus sum et fratrum tuorum*. Tum etiam ad excludendum idololatriae occasionem, unde subditur, *Deum adora*.

**AD SECUNDUM** dicendum quod sub maiestate divina intelligitur omnis Dei excellentia, ad quam pertinet quod in ipso, sicut in summo bono, beatificamur.

**AD TERTIUM** dicendum quod quia una est excellentia trium personarum, unus honor et reverentia eis debetur, et per consequens una adoratio. In cuius figuram, cum legatur de Abraham, Gen. XVIII, quod tres viri ei apparuerunt, adorans unum alloquitur. Dicens, *domine, si inveni gratiam*, etc. Trina autem genuflexio signum est ternarii personarum, non autem diversitatis adorationum.

not in equal measure, but according to a measure of proportion; and so the reverence which we pay to God, and which belongs to latria, differs from the reverence which we pay to certain excellent creatures; this belongs to dulia, and we shall speak of it further on (Q. 103). And since external actions are signs of internal reverence, certain external tokens significative of reverence are offered to creatures of excellence, and among these tokens the chief is adoration: yet there is one thing which is offered to God alone, and that is sacrifice. Hence Augustine says (*De Civ. Dei* x, 4): *Many tokens of Divine worship are employed in doing honor to men, either through excessive humility, or through pernicious flattery; yet so that those to whom these honors are given are recognized as being men to whom we owe esteem and reverence and even adoration if they be far above us. But who ever thought it his duty to sacrifice to any other than one whom he either knew or deemed or pretended to be a God?* Accordingly it was with the reverence due to an excellent creature that Nathan adored David; while it was the reverence due to God with which Mardochai refused to adore Aman fearing *lest he should transfer the honor of his God to a man* (Esther 13:14).

Again with the reverence due to an excellent creature Abraham adored the angels, as did also Josue (Josh 5:15): though we may understand them to have adored, with the adoration of latria, God Who appeared and spoke to them in the guise of an angel. It was with the reverence due to God that John was forbidden to adore the angel (Rev 22:9), both to indicate the dignity which he had acquired through Christ, whereby man is made equal to an angel: wherefore the same text goes on: *I am thy fellow-servant and of thy brethren*; as also to exclude any occasion of idolatry, wherefore the text continues: *Adore God*.

**REPLY OBJ. 2**: Every Divine excellency is included in His majesty: to which it pertains that we should be made happy in Him as in the sovereign good.

**REPLY OBJ. 3**: Since there is one excellence of the three Divine Persons, one honor and reverence is due to them and consequently one adoration. It is to represent this that where it is related (Gen 18:2) that three men appeared to Abraham, we are told that he addressed one, saying: *Lord, if I have found favor in thy sight*, etc. The triple genuflection represents the Trinity of Persons, not a difference of adoration.

# Article 2

*Whether adoration denotes an action of the body?*

**AD SECUNDUM SIC PROCEDITUR.** Videtur quod adoratio non importet actum corporalem. Dicitur enim Ioan. IV, *veri adoratores adorabunt patrem in spiritu et veritate*. Sed id quod fit in spiritu non pertinet ad cor-

**OBJECTION 1**: It would seem that adoration does not denote an act of the body. It is written (John 4:23): *The true adorers shall adore the Father in spirit and in truth*. Now what is done in spirit has nothing to do with an act of the

poralem actum. Ergo adoratio non importat corporalem actum.

**PRAETEREA**, nomen adorationis ab oratione sumitur. Sed oratio principaliter consistit in interiori actu, secundum illud I ad Cor. XIV, *orabo spiritu, orabo et mente*. Ergo adoratio maxime importat spiritualem actum.

**PRAETEREA**, corporales actus ad sensibilem cognitionem pertinent. Deum autem non attingimus sensu corporis, sed mentis. Ergo adoratio non importat corporalem actum.

**SED CONTRA** est quod super illud Exod. XX, *non adorabis ea, neque coles*, dicit Glossa, *nec affectu colas, nec specie adores*.

**RESPONDEO** dicendum quod, sicut Damascenus dicit, in IV libro, *quia ex duplici natura compositi sumus, intellectuali scilicet et sensibili, duplicem adorationem Deo offerimus*, scilicet spiritualem, quae consistit in interiori mentis devotione; et corporalem, quae consistit in exteriori corporis humiliatione. Et quia in omnibus actibus latriae id quod est exterius refertur ad id quod est interius sicut ad principalius, ideo ipsa exterior adoratio fit propter interiorem, ut videlicet per signa humilitatis quae corporaliter exhibemus, excitetur noster affectus ad subiiciendum se Deo; quia connaturale est nobis ut per sensibilia ad intelligibilia procedamus.

**AD PRIMUM** ergo dicendum quod etiam adoratio corporalis in spiritu fit, inquantum ex spirituali devotione procedit, et ad eam ordinatur.

**AD SECUNDUM** dicendum quod sicut oratio primordialiter quidem est in mente, secundario autem verbis exprimitur, ut supra dictum est; ita etiam adoratio principaliter quidem in interiori Dei reverentia consistit, secundario autem in quibusdam corporalibus humilitatis signis, sicut genu flectimus nostram infirmitatem significantes in comparatione ad Deum; prosternimus autem nos quasi profitentes nos nihil esse ex nobis.

**AD TERTIUM** dicendum quod etsi per sensum Deum attingere non possumus, per sensibilia tamen signa mens nostra provocatur ut tendat in Deum.

body. Therefore adoration does not denote an act of the body.

**OBJ. 2**: Further, the word adoration is taken from *oratio* (prayer). But prayer consists chiefly in an interior act, according to 1 Cor. 14:15, *I will pray with the spirit, I will pray also with the understanding*. Therefore adoration denotes chiefly a spiritual act.

**OBJ. 3**: Further, acts of the body pertain to sensible knowledge: whereas we approach God not by bodily but by spiritual sense. Therefore adoration does not denote an act of the body.

**ON THE CONTRARY**, A gloss on Ex. 20:5, *Thou shalt not adore them, nor serve them*, says: *Thou shalt neither worship them in mind, nor adore them outwardly*.

**I ANSWER THAT**, As Damascene says (*De Fide Orth.* iv, 12), since we are composed of a twofold nature, intellectual and sensible, we offer God a twofold adoration; namely, a spiritual adoration, consisting in the internal devotion of the mind; and a bodily adoration, which consists in an exterior humbling of the body. And since in all acts of latria that which is without is referred to that which is within as being of greater import, it follows that exterior adoration is offered on account of interior adoration, in other words we exhibit signs of humility in our bodies in order to incite our affections to submit to God, since it is connatural to us to proceed from the sensible to the intelligible.

**REPLY OBJ. 1**: Even bodily adoration is done in spirit, insofar as it proceeds from and is directed to spiritual devotion.

**REPLY OBJ. 2**: Just as prayer is primarily in the mind, and secondarily expressed in words, as stated above (Q. 83, A. 12), so too adoration consists chiefly in an interior reverence of God, but secondarily in certain bodily signs of humility; thus when we genuflect we signify our weakness in comparison with God, and when we prostrate ourselves we profess that we are nothing of ourselves.

**REPLY OBJ. 3**: Though we cannot reach God with the senses, our mind is urged by sensible signs to approach God.

# Article 3

*Whether adoration requires a definite place?*

**AD TERTIUM SIC PROCEDITUR**. Videtur quod adoratio non requirat determinatum locum. Dicitur enim Ioan. IV, *venit hora quando neque in monte hoc, neque in Ierosolymis adorabitis patrem*. Eadem autem ratio videtur esse et de aliis locis. Ergo determinatus locus non requiritur ad adorandum.

**OBJECTION 1**: It would seem that adoration does not require a definite place. It is written (John 4:21): *The hour cometh, when you shall neither on this mountain, nor in Jerusalem, adore the Father*; and the same reason seems to apply to other places. Therefore a definite place is not necessary for adoration.

**PRAETEREA**, adoratio exterior ordinatur ad interiorem. Sed interior adoratio fit ad Deum ut ubique existentem. Ergo exterior adoratio non requirit determinatum locum.

**PRAETEREA**, idem Deus est qui in novo et veteri testamento adoratur. Sed in veteri testamento fiebat adoratio ad occidentem, nam ostium tabernaculi respiciebat ad orientem, ut habetur Exod. XXVI. Ergo, eadem ratione, etiam nunc debemus adorare ad occidentem, si aliquis locus determinatus requiritur ad adorandum.

**SED CONTRA** est quod dicitur Isaiae LVI, et inducitur Ioan. II, *domus mea domus orationis vocabitur.*

**RESPONDEO** dicendum quod, sicut dictum est, in adoratione principalior est interior devotio mentis, secundarium autem est quod pertinet exterius ad corporalia signa. Mens autem interius apprehendit Deum quasi non comprehensum aliquo loco, sed corporalia signa necesse est quod in determinato loco et situ sint. Et ideo determinatio loci non requiritur ad adorationem principaliter, quasi sit de necessitate ipsius, sed secundum quandam decentiam, sicut et alia corporalia signa.

**AD PRIMUM** ergo dicendum quod dominus per illa verba praenuntiat cessationem adorationis tam secundum ritum Iudaeorum adorantium in Ierusalem, quam etiam secundum ritum Samaritanorum adorantium in monte Garizim. Uterque enim ritus cessavit veniente spirituali Evangelii veritate, secundum quam *in omni loco Deo sacrificatur,* ut dicitur Malach. I.

**AD SECUNDUM** dicendum quod determinatus locus eligitur ad adorandum, non propter Deum, qui adoratur, quasi loco concludatur, sed propter ipsos adorantes. Et hoc triplici ratione. Primo quidem, propter loci consecrationem, ex qua spiritualem devotionem concipiunt orantes, ut magis exaudiantur, sicut patet ex adoratione Salomonis, III Reg. VIII. Secundo, propter sacra mysteria et alia sanctitatis signa quae ibi continentur. Tertio, propter concursum multorum adorantium, ex quo fit oratio magis exaudibilis, secundum illud Matth. XVIII, *ubi sunt duo vel tres congregati in nomine meo, ibi sum ego in medio eorum.*

**AD TERTIUM** dicendum quod secundum quandam decentiam adoramus versus orientem. Primo quidem, propter divinae maiestatis indicium quod nobis manifestatur in motu caeli, qui est ab oriente secundo, propter Paradisum in oriente constitutum, ut legitur Gen. II, secundum litteram Septuaginta, quasi quaeramus ad Paradisum redire. Tertio, propter Christum, qui est *lux mundi* et oriens nominatur, Zach. VI; et *qui ascendit super caelum caeli ad orientem*; et *ab oriente etiam expectatur venturus,* secundum illud Matth. XXIV, *sicut fulgur exit ab oriente et paret usque ad occidentem, ita erit adventus filii hominis.*

**OBJ. 2**: Further, exterior adoration is directed to interior adoration. But interior adoration is shown to God as existing everywhere. Therefore exterior adoration does not require a definite place.

**OBJ. 3**: Further, the same God is adored in the New as in the Old Testament. Now in the Old Testament they adored towards the west, because the door of the Tabernacle looked to the east (Exod 26:18 seqq.). Therefore for the same reason we ought now to adore towards the west, if any definite place be requisite for adoration.

**ON THE CONTRARY**, It is written (Isa 56:7): *My house shall be called the house of prayer,* which words are also quoted (John 2:16).

**I ANSWER THAT**, As stated above (A. 2), the chief part of adoration is the internal devotion of the mind, while the secondary part is something external pertaining to bodily signs. Now the mind internally apprehends God as not comprised in a place; while bodily signs must of necessity be in some definite place and position. Hence a definite place is required for adoration, not chiefly, as though it were essential thereto, but by reason of a certain fittingness, like other bodily signs.

**REPLY OBJ. 1**: By these words our Lord foretold the cessation of adoration, both according to the rite of the Jews who adored in Jerusalem, and according to the rite of the Samaritans who adored on Mount Garizim. For both these rites ceased with the advent of the spiritual truth of the Gospel, according to which *a sacrifice is offered to God in every place,* as stated in Malach. 1:11.

**REPLY OBJ. 2**: A definite place is chosen for adoration, not on account of God Who is adored, as though He were enclosed in a place, but on account of the adorers; and this for three reasons. First, because the place is consecrated, so that those who pray there conceive a greater devotion and are more likely to be heard, as may be seen in the prayer of Solomon (3 Kgs 8). Second, on account of the sacred mysteries and other signs of holiness contained therein. Third, on account of the concourse of many adorers, by reason of which their prayer is more likely to be heard, according to Matt. 18:20, *Where there are two or three gathered together in My name, there am I in the midst of them.*

**REPLY OBJ. 3**: There is a certain fittingness in adoring towards the east. First, because the Divine majesty is indicated in the movement of the heavens which is from the east. Second, because Paradise was situated in the east according to the Septuagint version of Gen. 2:8, and so we signify our desire to return to Paradise. Third, on account of Christ Who is *the light of the world,* and is called *the Orient* (Zech 6:12); *Who mounteth above the heaven of heavens to the east* (Ps 67:34), and is expected to come from the east, according to Matt. 24:27, *As lightning cometh out of the east, and appeareth even into the west; so shall also the coming of the Son of Man be.*

# QUESTION 85

## SACRIFICES

Deinde considerandum est de actibus quibus aliquae res exteriores Deo offeruntur. Circa quos occurrit duplex consideratio, primo quidem, de his quae Deo a fidelibus dantur; secundo, de votis, quibus ei aliqua promittuntur.

Circa primum, considerandum est de sacrificiis, oblationibus, primitiis et decimis. Circa sacrificia quaeruntur quatuor.

Primo, utrum offerre Deo sacrificium sit de lege naturae.

Secundo, utrum soli Deo sit sacrificium offerendum.

Tertio, utrum offerre sacrificium sit specialis actus virtutis.

Quarto, utrum omnes teneantur ad sacrificium offerendum.

In due sequence we must consider those acts whereby external things are offered to God. These give rise to a twofold consideration: (1) Of things given to God by the faithful; (2) Of vows, whereby something is promised to Him.

Under the first head we shall consider sacrifices, oblations, first-fruits, and tithes. About sacrifices there are four points of inquiry:

(1) Whether offering a sacrifice to God is of the law of nature?

(2) Whether sacrifice should be offered to God alone?

(3) Whether the offering of a sacrifice is a special act of virtue?

(4) Whether all are bound to offer sacrifice?

## Article 1

*Whether offering a sacrifice to God is of the law of nature?*

**AD PRIMUM SIC PROCEDITUR.** Videtur quod offerre sacrificium Deo non sit de lege naturae. Ea enim quae sunt iuris naturalis communia sunt apud omnes. Non autem hoc contingit circa sacrificia, nam quidam leguntur obtulisse in sacrificium panem et vinum, sicut de Melchisedech dicitur, Gen. XIV; et quidam haec, quidam illa animalia. Ergo oblatio sacrificiorum non est de iure naturali.

**PRAETEREA,** ea quae sunt iuris naturalis omnes iusti servaverunt. Sed non legitur de Isaac quod sacrificium obtulerit, neque etiam de Adam, de quo tamen dicitur, Sap. X, quod *sapientia eduxit eum a delicto suo*. Ergo oblatio sacrificii non est de iure naturali.

**PRAETEREA,** Augustinus dicit, X de Civ. Dei, quod sacrificia in quadam significantia offeruntur. Voces autem, quae sunt praecipua inter signa, sicut idem dicit, in libro de Doct. Christ., *non significant naturaliter, sed ad placitum*, secundum Philosophum. Ergo sacrificia non sunt de lege naturali.

**SED CONTRA** est quod in qualibet aetate, et apud quaslibet hominum nationes, semper fuit aliqua sacrificiorum oblatio. Quod autem est apud omnes, videtur naturale esse. Ergo et oblatio sacrificii est de iure naturali.

**OBJECTION 1**: It would seem that offering a sacrifice to God is not of the natural law. Things that are of the natural law are common among all men. Yet this is not the case with sacrifices: for we read of some, e.g., Melchisedech (Gen 14:18), offering bread and wine in sacrifice, and of certain animals being offered by some, and others by others. Therefore the offering of sacrifices is not of the natural law.

**OBJ. 2**: Further, things that are of the natural law were observed by all just men. Yet we do not read that Isaac offered sacrifice; nor that Adam did so, of whom nevertheless it is written (Wis 10:2) that wisdom *brought him out of his sin*. Therefore the offering of sacrifice is not of the natural law.

**OBJ. 3**: Further, Augustine says (*De Civ. Dei* x, 5, 19) that sacrifices are offered in signification of something. Now words which are chief among signs, as he again says (*De Doctr. Christ.* ii, 3), *signify, not by nature but by convention*, according to the Philosopher (*Peri Herm.* i, 2). Therefore sacrifices are not of the natural law.

**ON THE CONTRARY**, At all times and among all nations there has always been the offering of sacrifices. Now that which is observed by all is seemingly natural. Therefore the offering of sacrifices is of the natural law.

781

RESPONDEO dicendum quod naturalis ratio dictat homini quod alicui superiori subdatur, propter defectus quos in seipso sentit, in quibus ab aliquo superiori eget adiuvari et dirigi. Et quidquid illud sit, hoc est quod apud omnes dicitur Deus. Sicut autem in rebus naturalibus naturaliter inferiora superioribus subduntur, ita etiam naturalis ratio dictat homini secundum naturalem inclinationem ut ei quod est supra hominem subiectionem et honorem exhibeat secundum suum modum. Est autem modus conveniens homini ut sensibilibus signis utatur ad aliqua exprimenda, quia ex sensibilibus cognitionem accipit. Et ideo ex naturali ratione procedit quod homo quibusdam sensibilibus rebus utatur offerens eas Deo, in signum debitae subiectionis et honoris, secundum similitudinem eorum qui dominis suis aliqua offerunt in recognitionem dominii. Hoc autem pertinet ad rationem sacrificii. Et ideo oblatio sacrificii pertinet ad ius naturale.

AD PRIMUM ergo dicendum quod, sicut supra dictum est, aliqua in communi sunt de iure naturali quorum determinationes sunt de iure positivo, sicut quod malefactores puniantur habet lex naturalis, sed quod tali poena vel tali puniantur est ex institutione divina vel humana. Similiter etiam oblatio sacrificii in communi est de lege naturae, et ideo in hoc omnes conveniunt. Sed determinatio sacrificiorum est ex institutione humana vel divina, et ideo in hoc differunt.

AD SECUNDUM dicendum quod Adam et Isaac, sicut et alii iusti, Deo sacrificium obtulerunt secundum sui temporis congruentiam, ut patet per Gregorium, qui dicit quod apud antiquos per sacrificiorum oblationes remittebatur pueris originale peccatum. Non tamen de omnibus iustorum sacrificiis fit mentio in Scriptura, sed solum de illis circa quae aliquid speciale accidit. Potest tamen esse ratio quare Adam non legitur sacrificium obtulisse, ne, quia in ipso notatur origo peccati, simul etiam in eo sanctificationis origo significaretur. Isaac vero significavit Christum inquantum ipse oblatus est in sacrificium. Unde non oportebat ut significaret quasi sacrificium offerens.

AD TERTIUM dicendum quod significare conceptus suos est homini naturale, sed determinatio signorum est secundum humanum placitum.

I ANSWER THAT, Natural reason tells man that he is subject to a higher being, on account of the defects which he perceives in himself, and in which he needs help and direction from someone above him: and whatever this superior being may be, it is known to all under the name of God. Now just as in natural things the lower are naturally subject to the higher, so too it is a dictate of natural reason in accordance with man's natural inclination that he should tender submission and honor, according to his mode, to that which is above man. Now the mode befitting to man is that he should employ sensible signs in order to signify anything, because he derives his knowledge from sensibles. Hence it is a dictate of natural reason that man should use certain sensibles, by offering them to God in sign of the subjection and honor due to Him, like those who make certain offerings to their lord in recognition of his authority. Now this is what we mean by a sacrifice, and consequently the offering of sacrifice is of the natural law.

REPLY OBJ. 1: As stated above (I-II, Q. 95, A. 2), certain things belong generically to the natural law, while their determination belongs to the positive law; thus the natural law requires that evildoers should be punished; but that this or that punishment should be inflicted on them is a matter determined by God or by man. In like manner the offering of sacrifice belongs generically to the natural law, and consequently all are agreed on this point, but the determination of sacrifices is established by God or by man, and this is the reason for their difference.

REPLY OBJ. 2: Adam, Isaac and other just men offered sacrifice to God in a manner befitting the times in which they lived, according to Gregory, who says (Moral. iv, 3) that in olden times original sin was remitted through the offering of sacrifices. Nor does Scripture mention all the sacrifices of the just, but only those that have something special connected with them. Perhaps the reason why we read of no sacrifice being offered by Adam may be that, as the origin of sin is ascribed to him, the origin of sanctification ought not to be represented as typified in him. Isaac was a type of Christ, being himself offered in sacrifice; and so there was no need that he should be represented as offering a sacrifice.

REPLY OBJ. 3: It is natural to man to express his ideas by signs, but the determination of those signs depends on man's pleasure.

# Article 2

*Whether sacrifice should be offered to the most high God alone?*

AD SECUNDUM SIC PROCEDITUR. Videtur quod non soli summo Deo sit sacrificium offerendum. Cum enim sacrificium Deo offerri debeat, videtur quod omnibus

OBJECTION 1: It would seem that sacrifice should not be offered to the most high God alone. Since sacrifice ought to be offered to God, it would seem that it ought

illis sit sacrificium offerendum qui divinitatis consortes fiunt. Sed etiam sancti homines *efficiuntur divinae naturae consortes*, ut dicitur II Petri I, unde et de eis in Psalm. dicitur, *ego dixi, dii estis*. Angeli etiam *filii Dei* nominantur, ut patet Iob I. Ergo omnibus his debet sacrificium offerri.

**Praeterea**, quanto aliquis maior est, tanto ei maior honor debet exhiberi. Sed Angeli et sancti sunt multo maiores quibuscumque terrenis principibus, quibus tamen eorum subditi multo maiorem honorem impendunt, se coram eis prosternentes et munera offerentes, quam sit oblatio alicuius animalis vel rei alterius in sacrificium. Ergo multo magis Angelis et sanctis potest sacrificium offerri.

**Praeterea**, templa et altaria instituuntur ad sacrificia offerenda. Sed templa et altaria instituuntur Angelis et sanctis. Ergo etiam sacrificia possunt eis offerri.

**Sed contra** est quod dicitur Exod. XXII, *qui immolat diis, occidetur, praeter domino soli*.

**Respondeo** dicendum quod, sicut dictum est, oblatio sacrificii fit ad aliquid significandum. Significat autem sacrificium quod offertur exterius, interius spirituale sacrificium, quo anima seipsam offert Deo, secundum illud Psalm., *sacrificium Deo spiritus contribulatus*, quia, sicut supra dictum est, exteriores actus religionis ad interiores ordinantur. Anima autem se offert Deo in sacrificium sicut principio suae creationis et sicut fini suae beatificationis. Secundum autem veram fidem solus Deus est creator animarum nostrarum, ut in primo habitum est. In solo etiam eo animae nostrae beatitudo consistit, ut supra dictum est. Et ideo sicut soli Deo summo debemus sacrificium spirituale offerre, ita etiam soli ei debemus offerre exteriora sacrificia, sicut etiam, *orantes atque laudantes, ad eum dirigimus significantes voces cui res ipsas in corde quas significamus, offerimus*, ut Augustinus dicit, X de Civ. Dei. Hoc etiam videmus in omni republica observari, quod summum rectorem aliquo signo singulari honorant, quod cuicumque alteri deferretur, esset crimen laesae maiestatis. Et ideo in lege divina statuitur poena mortis his qui divinum honorem aliis exhibent.

**Ad primum** ergo dicendum quod nomen divinitatis communicatur aliquibus non per aequalitatem, sed per participationem. Et ideo nec aequalis honor eis debetur.

**Ad secundum** dicendum quod in oblatione sacrificii non pensatur pretium occisi pecoris, sed significatio, qua hoc fit in honorem summi rectoris totius universi. Unde, sicut Augustinus dicit, X de Civ. Dei, *Daemones non cadaverinis nidoribus, sed divinis honoribus gaudent*.

**Ad tertium** dicendum quod, sicut Augustinus dicit, VIII de Civ. Dei, *non constituimus martyribus templa,*

to be offered to all such as are partakers of the Godhead. Now holy men are made *partakers of the Divine nature*, according to 2 Pet. 1:4; wherefore of them is it written (Ps 81:6): *I have said, You are gods*: and angels too are called *sons of God*, according to Job 1:6. Thus sacrifice should be offered to all these.

**Obj. 2**: Further, the greater a person is the greater the honor due to him from man. Now the angels and saints are far greater than any earthly princes: and yet the subjects of the latter pay them much greater honor, by prostrating before them, and offering them gifts, than is implied by offering an animal or any other thing in sacrifice. Much more therefore may one offer sacrifice to the angels and saints.

**Obj. 3**: Further, temples and altars are raised for the offering of sacrifices. Yet temples and altars are raised to angels and saints. Therefore sacrifices also may be offered to them.

**On the contrary**, It is written (Exod 22:20): *He that sacrificeth to gods shall be put to death, save only to the Lord.*

**I answer that**, As stated above (A. 1), a sacrifice is offered in order that something may be represented. Now the sacrifice that is offered outwardly represents the inward spiritual sacrifice, whereby the soul offers itself to God according to Ps. 50:19, *A sacrifice to God is an afflicted spirit*, since, as stated above (Q. 81, A. 7; Q. 84, A. 2), the outward acts of religion are directed to the inward acts. Again the soul offers itself in sacrifice to God as its beginning by creation, and its end by beatification: and according to the true faith God alone is the creator of our souls, as stated in the First Part (QQ. 90, A. 3; 118, A. 2), while in Him alone the beatitude of our soul consists, as stated above (I-II, Q. 1, A. 8; Q. 2, A. 8; Q. 3, AA. 1, 7, 8). Wherefore just as to God alone ought we to offer spiritual sacrifice, so too ought we to offer outward sacrifices to Him alone: even so *in our prayers and praises we proffer significant words to Him to Whom in our hearts we offer the things which we designate thereby*, as Augustine states (*De Civ. Dei* x, 19). Moreover we find that in every country the people are wont to show the sovereign ruler some special sign of honor, and that if this be shown to anyone else, it is a crime of high-treason. Therefore, in the Divine law, the death punishment is assigned to those who offer Divine honor to another than God.

**Reply Obj. 1**: The name of the Godhead is communicated to certain ones, not equally with God, but by participation; hence neither is equal honor due to them.

**Reply Obj. 2**: The offering of a sacrifice is measured not by the value of the animal killed, but by its signification, for it is done in honor of the sovereign Ruler of the whole universe. Wherefore, as Augustine says (*De Civ. Dei* x, 19), *the demons rejoice, not in the stench of corpses, but in receiving divine honors*.

**Reply Obj. 3**: As Augustine says (*De Civ. Dei* viii, 19), *we do not raise temples and priesthoods to the martyrs,*

*sacerdotia, quoniam non ipsi, sed Deus eorum nobis est Deus. Unde sacerdos non dicit, offero tibi sacrificium, Petre, vel Paule. Sed Deo de illorum victoriis gratias agimus, et nos ad imitationem eorum adhortamur.*

*because not they but their God is our God. Wherefore the priest says not: I offer sacrifice to thee, Peter or Paul. But we give thanks to God for their triumphs, and urge ourselves to imitate them.*

# Article 3

*Whether the offering of sacrifice is a special act of virtue?*

**AD TERTIUM SIC PROCEDITUR**. Videtur quod oblatio sacrificii non sit specialis actus virtutis. Dicit enim Augustinus, X de Civ. Dei, *verum sacrificium est omne opus quod agitur ut sancta societate inhaereamus Deo.* Sed omne opus bonum non est specialis actus alicuius determinatae virtutis. Ergo oblatio sacrificii non est specialis actus determinatae virtutis.

**PRAETEREA**, maceratio corporis quae fit per ieiunium, pertinet ad abstinentiam; quae autem fit per continentiam, pertinet ad castitatem; quae autem est in martyrio, pertinet ad fortitudinem. Quae omnia videntur comprehendi sub sacrificii oblatione, secundum illud Rom. XII, *exhibeatis corpora vestra hostiam viventem.* Dicit etiam apostolus, ad Heb. ult., *beneficentiae et communionis nolite oblivisci, talibus enim hostiis promeretur Deus,* beneficentia autem et communio pertinent ad caritatem, misericordiam et liberalitatem. Ergo sacrificii oblatio non est specialis actus determinatae virtutis.

**PRAETEREA**, sacrificium videtur quod Deo exhibetur. Sed multa sunt quae Deo exhibentur, sicut devotio, oratio, decimae, primitiae, oblationes et holocausta. Ergo sacrificium non videtur esse aliquis specialis actus determinatae virtutis.

**SED CONTRA** est quod in lege specialia praecepta de sacrificiis dantur, ut patet in principio Levitici.

**RESPONDEO** dicendum quod, sicut supra habitum est, quando actus unius virtutis ordinatur ad finem alterius virtutis, participat quodammodo speciem eius, sicut cum quis furatur ut fornicetur, ipsum furtum accipit quodammodo fornicationis deformitatem, ita quod si etiam alias non esset peccatum, ex hoc iam peccatum esset quod ad fornicationem ordinatur. Sic igitur sacrificium est quidam specialis actus laudem habens ex hoc quod in divinam reverentiam fit. Propter quod ad determinatam virtutem pertinet, scilicet ad religionem. Contingit autem etiam ea quae secundum alias virtutes fiunt, in divinam reverentiam ordinari, puta cum aliquis eleemosynam facit de rebus propriis propter Deum, vel cum aliquis proprium corpus alicui afflictioni subiicit propter divinam reverentiam. Et secundum hoc etiam actus aliarum virtutum sacrificia dici possunt. Sunt ta-

**OBJECTION 1**: It would seem that the offering of sacrifice is not a special act of virtue. Augustine says (*De Civ. Dei* x, 6): *A true sacrifice is any work done that we may cleave to God in holy fellowship*. But not every good work is a special act of some definite virtue. Therefore the offering of sacrifice is not a special act of a definite virtue.

**OBJ. 2**: Further, the mortification of the body by fasting belongs to abstinence, by continence belongs to chastity, by martyrdom belongs to fortitude. Now all these things seem to be comprised in the offering of sacrifice, according to Rom. 12:1, *Present your bodies a living sacrifice*. Again the Apostle says (Heb 13:16): *Do not forget to do good and to impart, for by such sacrifices God's favor is obtained*. Now it belongs to charity, mercy and liberality to do good and to impart. Therefore the offering of sacrifice is not a special act of a definite virtue.

**OBJ. 3**: Further, a sacrifice is apparently anything offered to God. Now many things are offered to God, such as devotion, prayer, tithes, first-fruits, oblations, and holocausts. Therefore sacrifice does not appear to be a special act of a definite virtue.

**ON THE CONTRARY**, The law contains special precepts about sacrifices, as appears from the beginning of Leviticus.

**I ANSWER THAT**, As stated above (I-II, Q. 18, AA. 6, 7), where an act of one virtue is directed to the end of another virtue it partakes somewhat of its species; thus when a man thieves in order to commit fornication, his theft assumes, in a sense, the deformity of fornication, so that even though it were not a sin otherwise, it would be a sin from the very fact that it was directed to fornication. Accordingly, sacrifice is a special act deserving of praise in that it is done out of reverence for God; and for this reason it belongs to a definite virtue, viz. religion. But it happens that the acts of the other virtues are directed to the reverence of God, as when a man gives alms of his own things for God's sake, or when a man subjects his own body to some affliction out of reverence for God; and in this way the acts also of other virtues may be called sacrifices. On the other hand there are acts that are not deserving of praise save through being

men quidam actus qui non habent ex alio laudem nisi quia fiunt propter reverentiam divinam. Et isti actus proprie sacrificia dicuntur, et pertinent ad virtutem religionis.

AD PRIMUM ergo dicendum quod hoc ipsum quod Deo quadam spirituali societate volumus inhaerere, ad divinam reverentiam pertinet. Et ideo cuiuscumque virtutis actus rationem sacrificii accipit ex hoc quod agitur ut sancta societate Deo inhaereamus.

AD SECUNDUM dicendum quod triplex est hominis bonum. Primum quidem est bonum animae, quod Deo offertur interiori quodam sacrificio per devotionem et orationem et alios huiusmodi interiores actus. Et hoc est principale sacrificium. Secundum est bonum corporis, quod Deo quodammodo offertur per martyrium, et abstinentiam seu continentiam. Tertium est bonum exteriorum rerum, de quo sacrificium offertur Deo, directe quidem, quando immediate res nostras Deo offerimus; mediate autem, quando eas communicamus proximis propter Deum.

AD TERTIUM dicendum quod sacrificia proprie dicuntur quando circa res Deo oblatas aliquid fit, sicut quod animalia occidebantur, quod panis frangitur et comeditur et benedicitur. Et hoc ipsum nomen sonat, nam sacrificium dicitur ex hoc quod homo *facit* aliquid *sacrum*. *Oblatio* autem directe dicitur cum Deo aliquid offertur, etiam si nihil circa ipsum fiat, sicut dicuntur offerri denarii vel panes in altari, circa quos nihil fit. Unde omne sacrificium est oblatio, sed non convertitur. *Primitiae* autem oblationes sunt, quia Deo offerebantur, ut legitur Deut. XXVI, non autem sunt sacrificia, quia nihil sacrum circa eas fiebat. *Decimae* autem, proprie loquendo, non sunt neque sacrificia neque oblationes, quia non immediate Deo, sed ministris divini cultus exhibentur.

done out of reverence for God: such acts are properly called sacrifices, and belong to the virtue of religion.

REPLY OBJ. 1: The very fact that we wish to cling to God in a spiritual fellowship pertains to reverence for God: and consequently the act of any virtue assumes the character of a sacrifice through being done in order that we may cling to God in holy fellowship.

REPLY OBJ. 2: Man's good is threefold. There is first his soul's good which is offered to God in a certain inward sacrifice by devotion, prayer and other like interior acts: and this is the principal sacrifice. The second is his body's good, which is, so to speak, offered to God in martyrdom, and abstinence or continency. The third is the good which consists of external things: and of these we offer a sacrifice to God, directly when we offer our possession to God immediately, and indirectly when we share them with our neighbor for God's sake.

REPLY OBJ. 3: A *sacrifice*, properly speaking, requires that something be done to the thing which is offered to God, for instance animals were slain and burnt, the bread is broken, eaten, blessed. The very word signifies this, since *sacrifice* is so called because a man does something sacred (*facit sacrum*). On the other hand an *oblation* is properly the offering of something to God even if nothing be done thereto, thus we speak of offering money or bread at the altar, and yet nothing is done to them. Hence every sacrifice is an oblation, but not conversely. *First-fruits* are oblations, because they were offered to God, according to Deut. 26, but they are not a sacrifice, because nothing sacred was done to them. *Tithes*, however, are neither a sacrifice nor an oblation, properly speaking, because they are not offered immediately to God, but to the ministers of Divine worship.

# Article 4

*Whether all are bound to offer sacrifices?*

AD QUARTUM SIC PROCEDITUR. Videtur quod non omnes teneantur ad sacrificia offerenda. Dicit enim apostolus, Rom. III, *quaecumque lex loquitur, his qui sunt in lege loquitur.* Sed lex de sacrificiis non fuit omnibus data, sed soli populo Hebraeorum. Ergo non omnes ad sacrificia tenebantur.

PRAETEREA, sacrificia Deo offeruntur ad aliquid significandum. Sed non est omnium huiusmodi significationes intelligere. Ergo non omnes tenentur ad sacrificia offerenda.

OBJECTION 1: It would seem that all are not bound to offer sacrifices. The Apostle says (Rom 3:19): *What things soever the Law speaketh, it speaketh to them that are in the Law.* Now the law of sacrifices was not given to all, but only to the Hebrew people. Therefore all are not bound to offer sacrifices.

OBJ. 2: Further, sacrifices are offered to God in order to signify something. But not everyone is capable of understanding these significations. Therefore not all are bound to offer sacrifices.

**PRAETEREA**, ex hoc sacerdotes dicuntur quod Deo sacrificium offerunt. Sed non omnes sunt sacerdotes. Ergo non omnes tenentur ad sacrificia offerenda.

**SED CONTRA** est quod sacrificium offerre est de lege naturae, ut supra habitum est. Ad ea autem quae sunt legis naturae omnes tenentur. Ergo omnes tenentur ad sacrificium Deo offerendum.

**RESPONDEO** dicendum quod duplex est sacrificium, sicut dictum est. Quorum primum et principale est sacrificium interius, ad quod omnes tenentur, omnes enim tenentur Deo devotam mentem offerre. Aliud autem est sacrificium exterius. Quod in duo dividitur. Nam quoddam est quod ex hoc solum laudem habet quod Deo aliquid exterius offertur in protestationem divinae subiectionis. Et ad hoc aliter tenentur illi qui sunt sub lege nova vel veteri, aliter illi qui non sunt sub lege. Nam illi qui sunt sub lege, tenentur ad determinata sacrificia offerenda secundum legis praecepta. Illi vero qui non erant sub lege, tenebantur ad aliqua exterius facienda in honorem divinum, secundum condecentiam ad eos inter quos habitabant, non autem determinate ad haec vel ad illa. Aliud vero est exterius sacrificium quando actus exteriores aliarum virtutum in divinam reverentiam assumuntur. Quorum quidam cadunt sub praecepto, ad quos omnes tenentur, quidam vero sunt supererogationis, ad quos non omnes tenentur.

**AD PRIMUM** ergo dicendum quod ad illa determinata sacrificia quae in lege erant praecepta, non omnes tenebantur, tenebantur tamen ad aliqua sacrificia interiora vel exteriora, ut dictum est.

**AD SECUNDUM** dicendum quod quamvis non omnes sciant explicite virtutem sacrificiorum, sciunt tamen implicite, sicut et habent fidem implicitam, ut supra habitum est.

**AD TERTIUM** dicendum quod sacerdotes offerunt sacrificia quae sunt specialiter ordinata ad cultum divinum, non solum pro se, sed etiam pro aliis. Quaedam vero sunt alia sacrificia quae quilibet potest pro se Deo offerre, ut ex supradictis patet.

**OBJ. 3**: Further, priests are so called because they offer sacrifice to God. But all are not priests. Therefore not all are bound to offer sacrifices.

**ON THE CONTRARY**, The offering of sacrifices is of the natural law, as stated above (A. 1). Now all are bound to do that which is of the natural law. Therefore all are bound to offer sacrifice to God.

**I ANSWER THAT**, Sacrifice is twofold, as stated above (A. 2). The first and principal is the inward sacrifice, which all are bound to offer, since all are obliged to offer to God a devout mind. The other is the outward sacrifice, and this again is twofold. There is a sacrifice which is deserving of praise merely through being offered to God in protestation of our subjection to God: and the obligation of offering this sacrifice was not the same for those under the New or the Old Law, as for those who were not under the Law. For those who are under the Law are bound to offer certain definite sacrifices according to the precepts of the Law, whereas those who were not under the Law were bound to perform certain outward actions in God's honor, as became those among whom they dwelt, but not definitely to this or that action. The other outward sacrifice is when the outward actions of the other virtues are performed out of reverence for God; some of which are a matter of precept; and to these all are bound, while others are works of supererogation, and to these all are not bound.

**REPLY OBJ. 1**: All were not bound to offer those particular sacrifices which were prescribed in the Law: but they were bound to some sacrifices inward or outward, as stated above.

**REPLY OBJ. 2**: Though all do not know explicitly the power of the sacrifices, they know it implicitly, even as they have implicit faith, as stated above (Q. 2, AA. 6, 7).

**REPLY OBJ. 3**: The priests offer those sacrifices which are specially directed to the Divine worship, not only for themselves but also for others. But there are other sacrifices, which anyone can offer to God for himself as explained above (AA. 2, 3).

# QUESTION 86

## OBLATIONS AND FIRST-FRUITS

Deinde considerandum est de oblationibus et primitiis. Et circa hoc quaeruntur quatuor.

Primo, utrum aliquae oblationes sint de necessitate praecepti.

Secundo, quibus oblationes debeantur.

Tertio, de quibus rebus fieri debeant.

Quarto, specialiter de oblationibus primitiarum, utrum ad eas homines ex necessitate teneantur.

We must next consider oblations and first-fruits. Under this head there are four points of inquiry:

(1) Whether any oblations are necessary as a matter of precept?

(2) To whom are oblations due?

(3) of what things they should be made?

(4) In particular, as to first-fruits, whether men are bound to offer them?

# Article 1

*Whether men are under a necessity of precept to make oblations?*

**AD PRIMUM SIC PROCEDITUR.** Videtur quod homines non tenentur ad oblationes ex necessitate praecepti. Non enim homines tempore Evangelii tenentur ad observanda caeremonialia praecepta veteris legis, ut supra habitum est. Sed oblationes offerre ponitur inter caeremonialia praecepta veteris legis, dicitur enim Exod. XXIII, *tribus vicibus per singulos annos mihi festa celebrabitis*, et postea subditur, *non apparebis in conspectu meo vacuus*. Ergo ad oblationes non tenentur nunc homines ex necessitate praecepti.

**PRAETEREA,** oblationes, antequam fiant, in voluntate hominis consistunt, ut videtur per hoc quod dominus dicit, Matth. V, *si offers munus tuum ad altare*, quasi hoc arbitrio offerentium relinquatur. Postquam autem oblationes sunt factae, non restat locus iterato eas offerendi. Ergo nullo modo aliquis ex necessitate praecepti ad oblationes tenetur.

**PRAETEREA,** quicumque aliquid tenetur reddere Ecclesiae, si non reddat, potest ad id compelli per subtractionem ecclesiasticorum sacramentorum. Sed illicitum videtur his qui offerre noluerint ecclesiastica sacramenta denegare, secundum illud decretum sextae synodi quod habetur I, qu. I, *nullus qui sacram communionem dispensat, a percipiente gratiam aliquid exigat, si vero exegerit, deponatur*. Ergo non tenentur homines ex necessitate ad oblationes.

**SED CONTRA** est quod Gregorius dicit, *omnis Christianus procuret ad Missarum solemnia aliquid Deo offerre*.

**RESPONDEO** dicendum quod, sicut dictum est, nomen oblationis commune est ad omnes res quae in cultum Dei exhibentur. Ita quod si aliquid exhibeatur in cultum divinum quasi in aliquod sacrum quod inde

**OBJECTION 1**: It would seem that men are not bound by precept to make oblations. Men are not bound, at the time of the Gospel, to observe the ceremonial precepts of the Old Law, as stated above (I-II, Q. 103, AA. 3, 4). Now the offering of oblations is one of the ceremonial precepts of the Old Law, since it is written (Exod 23:14): *Three times every year you shall celebrate feasts with Me*, and further on (Exod 23:15): *Thou shalt not appear empty before Me*. Therefore men are not now under a necessity of precept to make oblations.

**OBJ. 2**: Further, before they are made, oblations depend on man's will, as appears from our Lord's saying (Matt 5:23), *If . . . thou offer thy gift at the altar*, as though this were left to the choice of the offerer: and when once oblations have been made, there is no way of offering them again. Therefore in no way is a man under a necessity of precept to make oblations.

**OBJ. 3**: Further, if anyone is bound to give a certain thing to the Church, and fails to give it, he can be compelled to do so by being deprived of the Church's sacraments. But it would seem unlawful to refuse the sacraments of the Church to those who refuse to make oblations according to a decree of the sixth council: *Let none who dispense Holy Communion exact anything of the recipient, and if they exact anything let them be deposed*. Therefore it is not necessary that men should make oblations.

**ON THE CONTRARY**, Gregory says: *Let every Christian take care that he offer something to God at the celebration of Mass*.

**I ANSWER THAT**, As stated above (Q. 85, A. 3, ad 3), the term *oblation* is common to all things offered for the Divine worship, so that if a thing be offered to be destroyed in worship of God, as though it were being made into something

fieri debeat consumendum, et oblatio est et sacrificium, unde dicitur Exod. XXIX, *offeres totum arietem in incensum super altare, oblatio est domino, odor suavissimus victimae Dei*; et Levit. II dicitur, *anima cum obtulerit oblationem sacrificii domino, simila erit eius oblatio*. Si vero sic exhibeatur ut integrum maneat, divino cultui deputandum vel in usus ministrorum expendendum, erit oblatio et non sacrificium. Huiusmodi ergo oblationes de sui ratione habent quod voluntarie offerantur, secundum illud Exod. XXV, *ab homine qui offert ultroneus, accipietis eas*. Potest tamen contingere quod aliquis ad oblationes teneatur quadruplici ratione. Primo quidem, ex praecedenti conventione, sicut cum alicui conceditur aliquis fundus Ecclesiae, ut certis temporibus certas oblationes faciat. Quod tamen habet rationem census. Secundo, propter praecedentem deputationem sive promissionem, sicut cum aliquis offert donationem inter vivos vel cum relinquit in testamento Ecclesiae aliquam rem, mobilem vel immobilem, in posterum solvendam. Tertio modo, propter Ecclesiae necessitatem, puta si ministri Ecclesiae non haberent unde sustentarentur. Quarto modo, propter consuetudinem, tenentur enim fideles in aliquibus solemnitatibus ad aliquas oblationes consuetas. Tamen in his duobus ultimis casibus remanet oblatio quodammodo voluntaria, scilicet quantum ad quantitatem vel speciem rei oblatae.

**AD PRIMUM** ergo dicendum quod in nova lege homines non tenentur ad oblationem causa solemnitatum legalium, ut in Exodo dicitur, sed ex quibusdam aliis causis, ut dictum est.

**AD SECUNDUM** dicendum quod ad oblationes faciendas tenentur aliqui et antequam fiant, sicut in primo et tertio et quarto modo, et etiam postquam eas fecerint per deputationem sive promissionem; tenentur enim realiter exhibere quod est Ecclesiae per modum deputationis oblatum.

**AD TERTIUM** dicendum quod illi qui debitas oblationes non reddunt possunt puniri per subtractionem sacramentorum, non per ipsum sacerdotem cui sunt oblationes faciendae, ne videatur pro sacramentorum exhibitione aliquid exigere, sed per superiorem aliquem.

holy, it is both an oblation and a sacrifice. Wherefore it is written (Exod 29:18): *Thou shalt offer the whole ram for a burnt-offering upon the altar; it is an oblation to the Lord, a most sweet savor of the victim of the Lord*; and (Lev 2:1): *When anyone shall offer an oblation of sacrifice to the Lord, his offering shall be of fine flour*. If, on the other hand, it be offered with a view to its remaining entire and being deputed to the worship of God or to the use of His ministers, it will be an oblation and not a sacrifice. Accordingly it is essential to oblations of this kind that they be offered voluntarily, according to Ex. 25:2, of *every man that offereth of his own accord you shall take them*. Nevertheless it may happen in four ways that one is bound to make oblations. First, on account of a previous agreement: as when a person is granted a portion of Church land, that he may make certain oblations at fixed times, although this has the character of rent. Second, by reason of a previous assignment or promise; as when a man offers a gift among the living, or by will bequeaths to the Church something whether movable or immovable to be delivered at some future time. Third, on account of the need of the Church, for instance if her ministers were without means of support. Fourth, on account of custom; for the faithful are bound at certain solemn feasts to make certain customary oblations. In the last two cases, however, the oblation remains voluntary, as regards, to wit, the quantity or kind of the thing offered.

**REPLY OBJ. 1**: Under the New Law men are not bound to make oblations on account of legal solemnities, as stated in Exodus, but on account of certain other reasons, as stated above.

**REPLY OBJ. 2**: Some are bound to make oblations, both before making them, as in the first, third, and fourth cases, and after they have made them by assignment or promise: for they are bound to offer in reality that which has been already offered to the Church by way of assignment.

**REPLY OBJ. 3**: Those who do not make the oblations they are bound to make may be punished by being deprived of the sacraments, not by the priest himself to whom the oblations should be made, lest he seem to exact, something for bestowing the sacraments, but by someone superior to him.

# Article 2

*Whether oblations are due to priests alone?*

**AD SECUNDUM SIC PROCEDITUR.** Videtur quod oblationes non solum sacerdotibus debeantur. Inter oblationes enim praecipue videmus esse quae hostiarum sacrificiis deputantur. Sed ea quae pauperibus dantur in Scripturis hostiae dicuntur, secundum illud Heb. ult.,

**OBJECTION 1**: It would seem that oblations are not due to priests alone. For chief among oblations would seem to be those that are deputed to the sacrifices of victims. Now whatever is given to the poor is called a victim in Scripture according to Heb. 13:16, *Do not forget to do good and to*

*beneficentiae et communionis nolite oblivisci, talibus enim hostiis promeretur Deus.* Ergo multo magis oblationes pauperibus debentur.

PRAETEREA, in multis parochiis monachi de oblationibus partem habent. *Alia* autem *est causa clericorum, alia monachorum,* ut Hieronymus dicit. Ergo non solum sacerdotibus oblationes debentur.

PRAETEREA, laici de voluntate Ecclesiae emunt oblationes, ut panes et huiusmodi. Sed non nisi ut haec in suos usus convertant. Ergo oblationes possunt etiam ad laicos pertinere.

SED CONTRA est quod dicit canon Damasi Papae, et habetur X, qu. I, *oblationes quae intra sanctam Ecclesiam offeruntur, tantummodo sacerdotibus, qui quotidie domino servire videntur, licet comedere et bibere. Quia in veteri testamento prohibuit dominus panes sanctos comedere filiis Israel, nisi tantummodo Aaron et filiis eius.*

RESPONDEO dicendum quod sacerdos quodammodo constituitur *sequester et medius* inter populum et Deum, sicut de Moyse legitur Deut. V. Et ideo ad eum pertinet divina dogmata et sacramenta exhibere populo, et iterum ea quae sunt populi, puta preces et sacrificia et oblationes, per eum domino debent exhiberi; secundum illud apostoli, ad Heb. V, *omnis pontifex ex hominibus assumptus pro hominibus constituitur in his quae sunt ad Deum, ut offerat dona et sacrificia pro peccatis.* Et ideo oblationes quae a populo Deo exhibentur ad sacerdotes pertinent, non solum ut eas in suos usus convertant, verum etiam ut fideliter eas dispensent, partim quidem expendendo eas in his quae pertinent ad cultum divinum; partim vero in his quae pertinent ad proprium victum, quia *qui altari deserviunt cum altari participantur,* ut dicitur I ad Cor. IX; partim etiam in usus pauperum, qui sunt, quantum fieri potest, de rebus Ecclesiae sustentandi; quia et dominus in usum pauperum loculos habebat, ut Hieronymus dicit, super Matth.

AD PRIMUM ergo dicendum quod ea quae pauperibus dantur, sicut non proprie sunt sacrificia, dicuntur tamen sacrificia inquantum eis dantur propter Deum, ita etiam secundum eandem rationem oblationes dici possunt, tamen non proprie, quia non immediate Deo offeruntur. Oblationes vero proprie dictae in usum pauperum cedunt non per dispensationem offerentium, sed per dispensationem sacerdotum.

AD SECUNDUM dicendum quod monachi sive alii religiosi possunt oblationes recipere tripliciter. Uno modo, sicut pauperes, per dispensationem sacerdotis vel ordinationem Ecclesiae. Alio modo, si sint ministri altaris. Et tunc possunt accipere oblationes sponte oblatas. Tertio, si parochiae sint eorum. Et tunc ex debito possunt accipere, tanquam Ecclesiae rectores.

impart, for by such victims God's favor is obtained. Much more therefore are oblations due to the poor.

OBJ. 2: Further, in many parishes monks have a share in the oblations. Now *the case of clerics is distinct from the case of monks,* as Jerome states. Therefore oblations art not due to priests alone.

OBJ. 3: Further, lay people with the consent of the Church buy oblations such as loaves and so forth, and they do so for no other reason than that they may make use thereof themselves. Therefore oblations may have reference to the laity.

ON THE CONTRARY, A canon of Pope Damasus quoted X, qu. i, says: *None but the priests whom day by day we see serving the Lord may eat and drink of the oblations which are offered within the precincts of the Holy Church: because in the Old Testament the Lord forbade the children of Israel to eat the sacred loaves, with the exception of Aaron and his sons* (Lev 24:8, 9).

I ANSWER THAT, The priest is appointed mediator and stands, so to speak, between the people and God, as we read of Moses (Deut 5:5), wherefore it belongs to him to set forth the Divine teachings and sacraments before the people; and besides to offer to the Lord things appertaining to the people, their prayers, for instance, their sacrifices and oblations. Thus the Apostle says (Heb 5:1): *Every high priest taken from among men is ordained for men in the things that appertain to God, that he may offer up gifts and sacrifices for sins.* Hence the oblations which the people offer to God concern the priests, not only as regards their turning them to their own use, but also as regards the faithful dispensation thereof, by spending them partly on things appertaining to the Divine worship, partly on things touching their own livelihood (since *they that serve the altar partake with the altar,* according to 1 Cor. 9:13), and partly for the good of the poor, who, as far as possible, should be supported from the possessions of the Church: for our Lord had a purse for the use of the poor, as Jerome observes on Matt. 17:26, that we may not scandalize them.

REPLY OBJ. 1: Whatever is given to the poor is not a sacrifice properly speaking; yet it is called a sacrifice insofar as it is given to them for God's sake. In like manner, and for the same reason, it can be called an oblation, though not properly speaking, since it is not given immediately to God. Oblations properly so called fall to the use of the poor, not by the dispensation of the offerers, but by the dispensation of the priests.

REPLY OBJ. 2: Monks or other religious may receive oblations under three counts. First, as poor, either by the dispensation of the priests, or by ordination of the Church; second, through being ministers of the altar, and then they can accept oblations that are freely offered; third, if the parishes belong to them, and they can accept oblations, having a right to them as rectors of the Church.

**AD TERTIUM** dicendum quod oblationes, postquam fuerint consecratae, non possunt cedere in usum laicorum, sicut vasa et vestimenta sacra. Et hoc modo intelligitur dictum Damasi Papae. Illa vero quae non sunt consecrata, possunt in usum laicorum cedere ex dispensatione sacerdotum, sive per modum donationis sive per modum venditionis.

**REPLY OBJ. 3**: Oblations when once they are consecrated, such as sacred vessels and vestments, cannot be granted to the use of the laity: and this is the meaning of the words of Pope Damasus. But those which are unconsecrated may be allowed to the use of layfolk by permission of the priests, whether by way of gift or by way of sale.

# Article 3

*Whether a man may make oblations of whatever he lawfully possesses?*

**AD TERTIUM SIC PROCEDITUR**. Videtur quod non possit homo oblationes facere de omnibus rebus licite possessis. Quia secundum iura humana, *turpiter facit meretrix in hoc quod est meretrix, non tamen turpiter accipit*, et ita licite possidet. Sed non licet de eo facere oblationem, secundum illud Deut. XXIII, *non offeres mercedem prostibuli in domo domini Dei tui*. Ergo non licet facere oblationem de omnibus licite possessis.

**PRAETEREA**, ibidem prohibetur quod *pretium canis* non offeratur in domo Dei. Sed manifestum est quod pretium canis iuste venditi iuste possidetur. Ergo non licet de omnibus iuste possessis oblationem facere.

**PRAETEREA**, Malach. I dicitur, *si offeratur claudum et languidum, nonne malum est?* Sed claudum et languidum est animal iuste possessum. Ergo videtur quod non de omni iuste possesso possit oblatio fieri.

**SED CONTRA** est quod dicitur Prov. III, *honora dominum de tua substantia*. Ad substantiam autem hominis pertinet quidquid iuste possidet. Ergo de omnibus iuste possessis potest oblatio fieri.

**RESPONDEO** dicendum quod, sicut Augustinus dicit, in libro de Verb. Dom., *si depraedareris aliquem invalidum et de spoliis eius dares alicui iudici si pro te iudicaret, tanta vis est iustitiae ut et tibi displiceret. Non est talis Deus tuus qualis non debes esse nec tu*. Et ideo dicitur Eccli. XXXIV, *immolantis ex iniquo oblatio est maculata*. Unde patet quod de iniuste acquisitis et possessis non potest oblatio fieri. In veteri autem lege, in qua figurae serviebatur, quaedam propter significationem reputabantur immunda, quae offerre non licebat. Sed in nova lege omnis creatura Dei reputatur munda, ut dicitur ad Tit. I. Et ideo, quantum est de se, de quolibet licite possesso potest oblatio fieri. Per accidens tamen contingit quod de aliquo licite possesso oblatio fieri non potest, puta si vergat in detrimentum alterius, ut si filius aliquis offerat Deo id unde debet patrem nutrire, quod dominus

**OBJECTION 1**: It would seem that a man may not make oblations of whatever he lawfully possesses. According to human law *the whore's is a shameful trade in what she does but not in what she takes*, and consequently what she takes she possesses lawfully. Yet it is not lawful for her to make an oblation with her gains, according to Deut. 23:18, *Thou shalt not offer the hire of a strumpet . . . in the house of the Lord thy God*. Therefore it is not lawful to make an oblation of whatever one possesses lawfully.

**OBJ. 2**: Further, in the same passage it is forbidden to offer *the price of a dog* in the house of God. But it is evident that a man possesses lawfully the price of a dog he has lawfully sold. Therefore it is not lawful to make an oblation of whatever we possess lawfully.

**OBJ. 3**: Further, it is written (Mal 1:8): *If you offer the lame and the sick, is it not evil?* Yet an animal though lame or sick is a lawful possession. Therefore it would seem that not of every lawful possession may one make an oblation.

**ON THE CONTRARY**, It is written (Prov 3:9): *Honor the Lord with thy substance*. Now whatever a man possesses lawfully belongs to his substance. Therefore he may make oblations of whatever he possesses lawfully.

**I ANSWER THAT**, As Augustine says (*De Verb. Dom.* Serm. cxiii), *shouldst thou plunder one weaker than thyself and give some of the spoil to the judge, if he should pronounce in thy favor, such is the force of justice that even thou wouldst not be pleased with him: and if this should not please thee, neither does it please thy God*. Hence it is written (Sir 34:21): *The offering of him that sacrificeth of a thing wrongfully gotten is stained*. Therefore it is evident that an oblation must not be made of things unjustly acquired or possessed. In the Old Law, however, wherein the figure was predominant, certain things were reckoned unclean on account of their signification, and it was forbidden to offer them. But in the New Law all God's creatures are looked upon as clean, as stated in Titus 1:15: and consequently anything that is lawfully possessed, considered in itself, may be offered in oblation. But it may happen accidentally that one may

improbat Matth. XV; vel propter scandalum, vel propter contemptum, vel aliquid aliud huiusmodi.

**Ad primum** ergo dicendum quod in veteri lege prohibebatur oblatio de mercede prostibuli propter immunditiam. In nova autem lege propter scandalum, ne videatur Ecclesia favere peccato, si de lucro peccati oblationem recipiat.

**Ad secundum** dicendum quod canis secundum legem reputabatur animal immundum. Alia tamen animalia immunda redimebantur, et eorum pretium poterat offerri, secundum illud Levit. ult., *si immundum animal est, redimet qui obtulerit.* Sed canis nec offerebatur nec redimebatur, tum quia idololatrae canibus utebantur in sacrificiis idolorum; tum etiam quia significant rapacitatem, de qua non potest fieri oblatio. Sed haec prohibitio cessat in nova lege.

**Ad tertium** dicendum quod oblatio animalis caeci vel claudi reddebatur illicita tripliciter. Uno modo, ratione eius ad quod offerebatur. Unde dicitur Malach. I, *si offeratis caecum ad immolandum, nonne malum est?* Sacrificia autem oportebat esse immaculata. Secundo, ex contemptu. Unde ibidem subditur, *vos polluistis nomen meum in eo quod dicitis, mensa domini contaminata est, et quod superponitur contemptibile est.* Tertio modo, ex voto praecedenti, ex quo obligatur homo ut integrum reddat quod voverat. Unde ibidem subditur, *maledictus dolosus qui habet in grege suo masculum, et votum faciens immolat debile domino.* Et eaedem causae manent in lege nova. Quibus tamen cessantibus, non est illicitum.

not make an oblation of what one possesses lawfully; for instance if it be detrimental to another person, as in the case of a son who offers to God the means of supporting his father (which our Lord condemns, Matt. 15:5), or if it give rise to scandal or contempt, or the like.

**Reply Obj. 1:** In the Old Law it was forbidden to make an offering of the hire of a strumpet on account of its uncleanness, and in the New Law, on account of scandal, lest the Church seem to favor sin if she accept oblations from the profits of sin.

**Reply Obj. 2:** According to the Law, a dog was deemed an unclean animal. Yet other unclean animals were redeemed and their price could be offered, according to Lev. 27:27, *If it be an unclean animal, he that offereth it shall redeem it.* But a dog was neither offered nor redeemed, both because idolaters used dogs in sacrifices to their idols, and because they signify robbery, the proceeds of which cannot be offered in oblation. However, this prohibition ceased under the New Law.

**Reply Obj. 3:** The oblation of a blind or lame animal was declared unlawful for three reasons. First, on account of the purpose for which it was offered, wherefore it is written (Mal 1:8): *If you offer the blind in sacrifice, is it not evil?* and it behooved sacrifices to be without blemish. Second, on account of contempt, wherefore the same text goes on (Mal 1:12): *You have profaned My name, in that you say: The table of the Lord is defiled and that which is laid thereupon is contemptible.* Third, on account of a previous vow, whereby a man has bound himself to offer without blemish whatever he has vowed: hence the same text says further on (Mal 1:14): *Cursed is the deceitful man that hath in his flock a male, and making a vow offereth in sacrifice that which is feeble to the Lord.* The same reasons avail still in the New Law, but when they do not apply the unlawfulness ceases.

# Article 4

*Whether men are bound to pay first-fruits?*

**Ad quartum sic proceditur.** Videtur quod ad primitias solvendas homines non teneantur. Quia Exod. XIII, data lege primogenitorum, subditur, *erit quasi signum in manu tua,* et ita videtur esse praeceptum caeremoniale. Sed praecepta caeremonialia non sunt servanda in lege nova. Ergo neque primitiae sunt solvendae.

**Praeterea,** primitiae offerebantur domino pro speciali beneficio illi populo exhibito, unde dicitur Deut. XXVI, *tolles de cunctis frugibus tuis primitias, accedesque ad sacerdotem qui fuerit in diebus illis, et dices ad eum, profiteor hodie coram domino Deo tuo quod ingressus sum*

**Objection 1:** It would seem that men are not bound to pay first-fruits. After giving the law of the first-born the text continues (Exod 13:9): *It shall be as a sign in thy hand,* so that, apparently, it is a ceremonial precept. But ceremonial precepts are not to be observed in the New Law. Neither therefore ought first-fruits to be paid.

**Obj. 2:** Further, first-fruits were offered to the Lord for a special favor conferred on that people, wherefore it is written (Deut 26:2, 3): *Thou shalt take the first of all thy fruits . . . and thou shalt go to the priest that shall be in those days, and say to him: I profess this day before the Lord thy*

*terram pro qua iuravit patribus nostris ut daret eam nobis.* Ergo aliae nationes non tenentur ad primitias solvendas.

**PRAETEREA**, illud ad quod aliquis tenetur debet esse determinatum. Sed non invenitur nec in nova lege nec in veteri determinata quantitas primitiarum. Ergo ad eas solvendas non tenentur homines ex necessitate.

**SED CONTRA** est quod dicitur XVI, qu. VII, *oportet decimas et primitias, quas iure sacerdotum esse sancimus, ab omni populo accipere.*

**RESPONDEO** dicendum quod primitiae ad quoddam genus oblationum pertinent, quia Deo exhibentur cum quadam professione, ut habetur Deut. XXVI. Unde et ibidem subditur, *suscipiens sacerdos cartallum,* scilicet primitiarum, *de manu eius qui defert primitias, et ponet ante altare domini Dei tui;* et postea mandatur ei quod dicat, idcirco *nunc offero primitias frugum terrae, quas dominus dedit mihi.* Offerebantur autem primitiae ex speciali causa, scilicet in recognitionem divini beneficii, quasi aliquis profiteatur se a Deo fructus terrae percipere, et ideo se teneri ad aliquid de huiusmodi Deo exhibendum, secundum illud I Paral. ult., *quae de manu tua accepimus, dedimus tibi.* Et quia Deo debemus exhibere id quod praecipuum est, ideo primitias, quasi praecipuum aliquid de fructibus terrae, praeceptum fuit Deo offerre. Et quia sacerdos constituitur populo in his quae sunt ad Deum, ideo primitiae a populo oblatae in usum sacerdotum cedebant, unde dicitur Num. XVIII, *locutus est dominus ad Aaron, ecce, dedi tibi custodiam primitiarum mearum.* Pertinet autem ad ius naturale ut homo ex rebus sibi datis a Deo aliquid exhibeat ad eius honorem. Sed quod talibus personis exhibeatur, aut de primis fructibus, aut in tali quantitate, hoc quidem fuit in veteri lege iure divino determinatum, in nova autem lege definitur per determinationem Ecclesiae, ex qua homines obligantur ut primitias solvant secundum consuetudinem patriae et indigentiam ministrorum Ecclesiae.

**AD PRIMUM** ergo dicendum quod caeremonialia proprie erant in signum futuri, et ideo ad praesentiam veritatis significatae cessaverunt. Oblatio autem primitiarum fuit in signum praeteriti beneficii, ex quo etiam debitum recognitionis causatur secundum dictamen rationis naturalis. Et ideo in generali huiusmodi obligatio manet.

**AD SECUNDUM** dicendum quod primitiae offerebantur in veteri lege non solum propter beneficium terrae promissionis datae a Deo, sed etiam propter beneficium fructuum terrae a Deo datorum. Unde dicitur Deut. XXVI, *offero primitias frugum terrae, quas dominus Deus dedit mihi.* Et haec secunda causa apud omnes est communis. Potest etiam dici quod sicut speciali quadam

*God, that I am come into the land, for which He swore to our fathers, that He would give it us.* Therefore other nations are not bound to pay first-fruits.

**OBJ. 3**: That which one is bound to do should be something definite. But neither in the New Law nor in the Old do we find mention of a definite amount of first-fruits. Therefore one is not bound of necessity to pay them.

**ON THE CONTRARY**, It is laid down (16, qu. vii, can. Decimas): *We confirm the right of priests to tithes and first-fruits, and everybody must pay them.*

**I ANSWER THAT**, First-fruits are a kind of oblation, because they are offered to God with a certain profession (Deut 26); where the same passage continues: *The priest taking the basket containing the first-fruits from the hand of him that bringeth the first-fruits, shall set it before the altar of the Lord thy God,* and further on (Deut 26:10) he is commanded to say: *Therefore now I offer the first-fruits of the land, which the Lord hath given me.* Now the first-fruits were offered for a special reason, namely, in recognition of the divine favor, as though man acknowledged that he had received the fruits of the earth from God, and that he ought to offer something to God in return, according to 1 Paral 29:14, *We have given Thee what we received of Thy hand.* And since what we offer God ought to be something special, hence it is that man was commanded to offer God his first-fruits, as being a special part of the fruits of the earth: and since a priest is *ordained for the people in the things that appertain to God* (Heb 5:1), the first-fruits offered by the people were granted to the priest's use. Wherefore it is written (Num 18:8): *The Lord said to Aaron: Behold I have given thee the charge of My first-fruits.* Now it is a point of natural law that man should make an offering in God's honor out of the things he has received from God, but that the offering should be made to any particular person, or out of his first-fruits, or in such or such a quantity, was indeed determined in the Old Law by divine command; but in the New Law it is fixed by the declaration of the Church, in virtue of which men are bound to pay first-fruits according to the custom of their country and the needs of the Church's ministers.

**REPLY OBJ. 1**: The ceremonial observances were properly speaking signs of the future, and consequently they ceased when the foreshadowed truth was actually present. But the offering of first-fruits was for a sign of a past favor, whence arises the duty of acknowledgment in accordance with the dictate of natural reason. Hence taken in a general sense this obligation remains.

**REPLY OBJ. 2**: First-fruits were offered in the Old Law, not only on account of the favor of the promised land given by God, but also on account of the favor of the fruits of the earth, which were given by God. Hence it is written (Deut 26:10): *I offer the first-fruits of the land which the Lord hath given me,* which second motive is common among all people. We may also reply that just as God granted the land

beneficio terram promissionis contulit Deus, ita generali beneficio toti humano generi contulit terrae dominium, secundum illud Psalm., *terram dedit filiis hominum.*

**Ad tertium** dicendum quod, sicut Hieronymus dicit, *ex maiorum traditione introductum est quod qui plurimum, quadragesimam partem dabant sacerdotibus loco primitiarum; qui minimum, sexagesimam.* Unde videtur quod inter hos terminos sint primitiae offerendae, secundum consuetudinem patriae. Rationabiliter tamen primitiarum quantitas non fuit determinata in lege, quia, sicut dictum est, primitiae dantur per modum oblationis, de cuius ratione est quod sint voluntariae.

of promise to the Jews by a special favor, so by a general favor He bestowed the lordship of the earth on the whole of mankind, according to Ps. 113:24, *The earth He has given to the children of men.*

**Reply Obj. 3**: As Jerome says: *According to the tradition of the ancients the custom arose for those who had most to give the priests a fortieth part, and those who had least, one sixtieth, in lieu of first-fruits.* Hence it would seem that first-fruits should vary between these limits according to the custom of one's country. And it was reasonable that the amount of first-fruits should not be fixed by law, since, as stated above, first-fruits are offered by way of oblation, a condition of which is that it should be voluntary.

# QUESTION 87

## TITHES

Deinde considerandum est de decimis. Et circa hoc quaeruntur quatuor.

Primo, utrum homines teneantur ad solvendas decimas ex necessitate praecepti.

Secundo, de quibus rebus sint decimae dandae.

Tertio, quibus debeant dari.

Quarto, quibus competat eas dare.

Next we must consider tithes, under which head there are four points of inquiry:

(1) Whether men are bound by precept to pay tithes?

(2) Of what things ought tithes to be paid?

(3) To whom ought they to be paid?

(4) Who ought to pay tithes?

# Article 1

*Whether men are bound to pay tithes under a necessity of precept?*

**AD PRIMUM SIC PROCEDITUR.** Videtur quod homines non teneantur dare decimas ex necessitate praecepti. Praeceptum enim de solutione decimarum in lege veteri datur, ut patet Levit. XXVII, *omnes decimae terrae, sive de frugibus sive de pomis arborum, domini sunt*; et infra, *omnium decimarum ovis et bovis et caprae, quae sub pastoris virga transeunt, quidquid decimum venerit, sanctificabitur domino.* Non autem potest computari hoc inter praecepta moralia, quia ratio naturalis non magis dictat quod decima pars debeat magis dari quam nona vel undecima. Ergo vel est praeceptum iudiciale, vel caeremoniale. Sed sicut supra habitum est, tempore gratiae non obligantur homines neque ad praecepta caeremonialia neque ad iudicialia veteris legis. Ergo homines nunc non obligantur ad solutionem decimarum.

**PRAETEREA,** illa sola homines observare tenentur tempore gratiae quae a Christo per apostolos sunt mandata, secundum illud Matth. ult., *docentes eos servare omnia quaecumque mandavi vobis*; et Paulus dicit, Act. XX, *non enim subterfugi quominus annuntiarem vobis omne consilium Dei.* Sed neque in doctrina Christi neque in doctrina apostolorum aliquid continetur de solutione decimarum, nam quod dominus de decimis dicit, Matth. XXIII, *haec oportuit facere*, ad tempus praeteritum legalis observantiae referendum videtur; ut dicit Hilarius, super Matth., *decimatio illa olerum, quae in praefigurationem futurorum erat utilis, non debebat omitti.* Ergo homines tempore gratiae non tenentur ad decimarum solutionem.

**PRAETEREA,** homines tempore gratiae non magis tenentur ad observantiam legalium quam ante legem. Sed ante legem non dabantur decimae ex praecepto, sed solum ex voto, legitur enim Gen. XXVIII quod Iacob *vovit votum dicens, si fuerit Deus mecum et custodierit*

**OBJECTION 1**: It would seem that men are not bound by precept to pay tithes. The commandment to pay tithes is contained in the Old Law (Lev 27:30), *All tithes of the land, whether of corn or of the fruits of trees, are the Lord's*, and further on (Lev 27:32): *Of all the tithes of oxen and sheep and goats, that pass under the shepherd's rod, every tenth that cometh shall be sanctified to the Lord.* This cannot be reckoned among the moral precepts, because natural reason does not dictate that one ought to give a tenth part, rather than a ninth or eleventh. Therefore it is either a judicial or a ceremonial precept. Now, as stated above (I-II, Q. 103, A. 3; Q. 104, A. 3), during the time of grace men are bound neither to the ceremonial nor to the judicial precepts of the Old Law. Therefore men are not bound now to pay tithes.

**OBJ. 2**: Further, during the time of grace men are bound only to those things which were commanded by Christ through the Apostles, according to Matt. 28:20, *Teaching them to observe all things whatsoever I have commanded you*; and Paul says (Acts 20:27): *I have not spared to declare unto you all the counsel of God.* Now neither in the teaching of Christ nor in that of the apostles is there any mention of the paying of tithes: for the saying of our Lord about tithes (Matt 23:23), *These things you ought to have done* seems to refer to the past time of legal observance: thus Hilary says (*Super Matth.* can. xxiv): *The tithing of herbs, which was useful in foreshadowing the future, was not to be omitted.* Therefore during the time of grace men are not bound to pay tithes.

**OBJ. 3**: Further, during the time of grace, men are not more bound to the legal observances than before the Law. But before the Law tithes were given, by reason not of a precept but of a vow. For we read (Gen 28:20, 22) that Jacob *made a vow* saying: *If God shall be with me, and shall keep*

me in via qua ambulo, etc., cunctorum quae dederis mihi decimas offeram tibi. Ergo etiam neque tempore gratiae tenentur homines ad decimarum solutionem.

PRAETEREA, in veteri lege tenebantur homines ad triplices decimas solvendas. Quarum quasdam solvebant Levitis, dicitur enim Num. XVIII, *Levitae decimarum oblatione contenti erunt, quas in usus eorum et necessaria separavi*. Erant quoque et aliae decimae, de quibus legitur Deut. XIV, *decimam partem separabis de cunctis fructibus tuis qui nascuntur in terra per annos singulos, et comedes in conspectu domini Dei tui in loco quem elegerit Deus*. Erant quoque et aliae decimae, de quibus ibidem subditur, *anno tertio separabis aliam decimam ex omnibus quae nascuntur tibi eo tempore, et repones intra ianuas tuas, venietque Levites, qui aliam non habet partem neque possessionem tecum, et peregrinus ac pupillus et vidua qui intra portas tuas sunt, et comedent et saturabuntur*. Sed ad secundas et tertias decimas homines non tenentur tempore gratiae. Ergo neque ad primas.

PRAETEREA, quod sine determinatione temporis debetur, nisi statim solvatur, obligat ad peccatum. Si ergo homines tempore gratiae obligarentur ex necessitate praecepti ad decimas solvendas, in terris in quibus decimae non solvuntur omnes essent in peccato mortali, et per consequens etiam ministri Ecclesiae dissimulando, quod videtur inconveniens. Non ergo homines tempore gratiae ex necessitate tenentur ad solutionem decimarum.

SED CONTRA est quod Augustinus dicit, et habetur XVI, qu. I, *decimae ex debito requiruntur, et qui eas dare noluerint, res alienas invadunt*.

RESPONDEO dicendum quod decimae in veteri lege dabantur ad sustentationem ministrorum Dei, unde dicitur Malach. III, *inferte omnem decimationem in horreum meum, ut sit cibus in domo mea*. Unde praeceptum de solutione decimarum partim quidem erat morale, inditum naturali rationi, partim autem erat iudiciale, ex divina institutione robur habens. Quod enim eis qui divino cultui ministrabant ad salutem populi totius, populus necessaria victus ministraret, ratio naturalis dictat, sicut et his qui communi utilitati invigilant, scilicet principibus et militibus et aliis huiusmodi, stipendia victus debentur a populo. Unde et apostolus hoc probat, I ad Cor. IX, per humanas consuetudines, dicens, *quis militat suis stipendiis unquam? Quis plantat vineam et de fructibus eius non edit?* Sed determinatio certae partis exhibendae ministris divini cultus non est de iure naturali, sed est introducta institutione divina secundum conditionem illius populi cui lex dabatur; qui cum in duodecim tribus esset divisus, duodecima tribus, scilicet levitica, quae tota erat divinis ministeriis mancipata, possessiones non habebat, unde convenienter institutum est ut reliquae undecim tribus decimam partem suorum

me in the way by which I walk . . . of all the things that Thou shalt give to me, I will offer tithes to Thee. Neither, therefore, during the time of grace are men bound to pay tithes.

OBJ. 4: Further, in the Old Law men were bound to pay three kinds of tithe. For it is written (Num 18:23, 24): *The sons of Levi . . . shall . . . be content with the oblation of tithes, which I have separated for their uses and necessities.* Again, there were other tithes of which we read (Deut 14:22, 23): *Every year thou shalt set aside the tithes of all thy fruits, that the earth bringeth forth year by year; and thou shalt eat before the Lord thy God in the place which He shall choose.* And there were yet other tithes, of which it is written (Deut 14:28): *The third year thou shalt separate another tithe of all things that grow to thee at that time, and shalt lay it up within thy gates. And the Levite that hath no other part nor possession with thee, and the stranger, and the fatherless, and the widow, that are within thy gates, shall . . . eat and be filled.* Now during the time of grace men are not bound to pay the second and third tithes. Neither therefore are they bound to pay the first.

OBJ. 5: Further, a debt that is due without any time being fixed for its payment, must be paid at once under pain of sin. Accordingly if during the time of grace men are bound, under necessity of precept, to pay tithes in those countries where tithes are not paid, they would all be in a state of mortal sin, and so would also be the ministers of the Church for dissembling. But this seems unreasonable. Therefore during the time of grace men are not bound under necessity of precept to pay tithes.

ON THE CONTRARY, Augustine, whose words are quoted 16, qu. i, says: *It is a duty to pay tithes, and whoever refuses to pay them takes what belongs to another.*

I ANSWER THAT, In the Old Law tithes were paid for the sustenance of the ministers of God. Hence it is written (Mal 3:10): *Bring all the tithes into My store-house that there may be meat in My house.* Hence the precept about the paying of tithes was partly moral and instilled in the natural reason; and partly judicial, deriving its force from its divine institution. Because natural reason dictates that the people should administer the necessaries of life to those who minister the divine worship for the welfare of the whole people even as it is the people's duty to provide a livelihood for their rulers and soldiers and so forth. Hence the Apostle proves this from human custom, saying (1 Cor 9:7): *Who serveth as a soldier at any time at his own charge? Who planteth a vineyard and eateth not of the fruit thereof?* But the fixing of the proportion to be offered to the ministers of divine worship does not belong to the natural law, but was determined by divine institution, in accordance with the condition of that people to whom the law was being given. For they were divided into twelve tribes, and the twelfth tribe, namely that of Levi, was engaged exclusively in the divine ministry and had no possessions whence to derive a livelihood: and so it was becomingly ordained

proventuum Levitis darent, ut honorabilius viverent, et quia etiam aliqui per negligentiam erant transgressores futuri unde quantum ad determinationem decimae partis, erat iudiciale, sicut et alia multa specialiter in illo populo instituta erant ad aequalitatem inter homines ad invicem conservandam secundum populi illius conditionem, quae iudicialia praecepta dicuntur; licet ex consequenti aliquid significarent in futurum, sicut et omnia eorum facta, secundum illud I ad Cor. X, *omnia in figuram contingebant illis*; in quo conveniebant cum caeremonialibus praeceptis, quae principaliter instituta erant ad significandum aliquid futurum. Unde et praeceptum de decimis persolvendis hic significat aliquid in futurum, qui enim decimam dat, quae est perfectionis signum (eo quod denarius est quodammodo numerus perfectus, quasi primus limes numerorum, ultra quem numerum non procedunt, sed reiterantur ab uno), novem sibi partibus reservatis, protestatur quasi in quodam signo ad se pertinere imperfectionem, perfectionem vero, quae erat futura per Christum, esse expectandam a Deo. Nec tamen propter hoc est caeremoniale praeceptum, sed iudiciale, ut dictum est.

Est autem haec differentia inter caeremonialia et iudicialia legis praecepta, ut supra diximus, quod caeremonialia illicitum est observare tempore legis novae, iudicialia vero, etsi non obligent tempore gratiae, tamen possunt observari absque peccato, et ad eorum observantiam aliqui obligantur si statuatur auctoritate eorum quorum est condere legem. Sicut praeceptum iudiciale veteris legis est quod *qui furatus fuerit ovem, reddat quatuor oves*, ut legitur Exod. XXII, quod, si ab aliquo rege statuatur, tenentur eius subditi observare. Ita etiam determinatio decimae partis solvendae est auctoritate Ecclesiae tempore novae legis instituta secundum quandam humanitatem, ut scilicet non minus populus novae legis ministris novi testamenti exhiberet quam populus veteris legis ministris veteris testamenti exhibebat; cum tamen populus novae legis ad maiora obligetur, secundum illud Matth. V, *nisi abundaverit iustitia vestra plus quam Scribarum et Pharisaeorum, non intrabitis in regnum caelorum*; et cum ministri novi testamenti sint maioris dignitatis quam ministri veteris testamenti, ut probat apostolus, II ad Cor. III.

Sic ergo patet quod ad solutionem decimarum homines tenentur, partim quidem ex iure naturali, partim etiam ex institutione Ecclesiae, quae tamen, pensatis opportunitatibus temporum et personarum, posset aliam partem determinare solvendam.

ET PER HOC patet responsio ad primum.

AD SECUNDUM dicendum quod praeceptum de solutione decimarum, quantum ad id quod erat morale,

that the remaining eleven tribes should give one-tenth part of their revenues to the Levites that the latter might live respectably; and also because some, through negligence, would disregard this precept. Hence, so far as the tenth part was fixed, the precept was judicial, since all institutions established among this people for the special purpose of preserving equality among men, in accordance with this people's condition, are called *judicial precepts*. Nevertheless by way of consequence these institutions foreshadowed something in the future, even as everything else connected with them, according to 1 Cor. 12, *All these things happened to them in figure*. In this respect they had something in common with the ceremonial precepts, which were instituted chiefly that they might be signs of the future. Hence the precept about paying tithes foreshadowed something in the future. For ten is, in a way, the perfect number (being the first numerical limit, since the figures do not go beyond ten but begin over again from one), and therefore he that gave a tenth, which is the sign of perfection, reserving the nine other parts for himself, acknowledged by a sign that imperfection was his part, and that the perfection which was to come through Christ was to be hoped for from God. Yet this proves it to be, not a ceremonial but a judicial precept, as stated above.

There is this difference between the ceremonial and judicial precepts of the Law, as we stated above (I-II, Q. 104, A. 3), that it is unlawful to observe the ceremonial precepts at the time of the New Law, whereas there is no sin in keeping the judicial precepts during the time of grace although they are not binding. Indeed they are bound to be observed by some, if they be ordained by the authority of those who have power to make laws. Thus it was a judicial precept of the Old Law that *he who stole a sheep should restore four sheep* (Exod 22:1), and if any king were to order this to be done his subjects would be bound to obey. In like manner during the time of the New Law the authority of the Church has established the payment of tithe; thus showing a certain kindliness, lest the people of the New Law should give less to the ministers of the New Testament than did the people of the Old Law to the ministers of the Old Testament; for the people of the New Law are under greater obligations, according to Matt. 5:20, *Unless your justice abound more than that of the Scribes and Pharisees, you shall not enter into the kingdom of heaven*, and, moreover, the ministers of the New Testament are of greater dignity than the ministers of the Old Testament, as the Apostle shows (2 Cor 3:7, 8).

Accordingly it is evident that man's obligation to pay tithes arises partly from natural law, partly from the institution of the Church; who, nevertheless, in consideration of the requirements of time and persons might ordain the payment of some other proportion.

THIS SUFFICES for the Reply to the First Objection.

REPLY OBJ. 2: The precept about paying tithes, insofar as it was a moral precept, was given in the Gospel by our

datum est in Evangelio a domino ubi dicit, Matth. X, *dignus est operarius mercede sua*; et etiam ab apostolo, ut patet I ad Cor. IX. Sed determinatio certae partis est reservata ordinationi Ecclesiae.

**AD TERTIUM** dicendum quod ante tempus veteris legis non erant determinati ministri divini cultus, sed dicitur quod primogeniti erant sacerdotes, qui duplicem portionem accipiebant. Et ideo etiam non erat determinata aliqua pars exhibenda ministris divini cultus, sed ubi aliquis occurrebat, unusquisque dabat ei propria sponte quod sibi videbatur. Sicut Abraham quodam prophetico instinctu dedit decimas Melchisedech, sacerdoti Dei summi, ut dicitur Gen. XIV. Et similiter etiam Iacob decimas vovit se daturum, quamvis non videatur decimas vovisse quasi aliquibus ministris exhibendas, sed in divinum cultum, puta ad sacrificiorum consummationem; unde signanter dicit, *decimas offeram tibi*.

**AD QUARTUM** dicendum quod secundae decimae, quae reservabantur ad sacrificia offerenda, locum in nova lege non habent, cessantibus legalibus victimis. Tertiae vero decimae, quas cum pauperibus comedere debebant, in nova lege augentur, per hoc quod dominus non solum decimam partem, sed omnia superflua pauperibus iubet exhiberi, secundum illud Luc. XI, *quod superest, date eleemosynam*. Ipsae etiam decimae quae ministris Ecclesiae dantur, per eos debent in usus pauperum dispensari.

**AD QUINTUM** dicendum quod ministri Ecclesiae maiorem curam debent habere spiritualium bonorum in populo promovendorum quam temporalium colligendorum. Et ideo apostolus noluit uti potestate sibi a domino tradita, ut scilicet acciperet stipendia victus ab his quibus Evangelium praedicabat, ne daretur aliquod impedimentum Evangelio Christi. Nec tamen peccabant illi qui ei non subveniebant, alioquin apostolus eos corrigere non omisisset. Et similiter laudabiliter ministri Ecclesiae decimas Ecclesiae non requirunt, ubi sine scandalo requiri non possent, propter dissuetudinem vel propter aliquam aliam causam. Nec tamen sunt in statu damnationis qui non solvunt, in locis illis in quibus Ecclesia non petit, nisi forte propter obstinationem animi, habentes voluntatem non solvendi etiam si ab eis peterentur.

Lord when He said (Matt 10:10): *The workman is worthy of his hire*, and the Apostle says the same (1 Cor 9:4 seqq.). But the fixing of the particular proportion is left to the ordinance of the Church.

**REPLY OBJ. 3**: Before the time of the Old Law the ministry of the divine worship was not entrusted to any particular person; although it is stated that the first-born were priests, and that they received a double portion. For this very reason no particular portion was directed to be given to the ministers of the divine worship: but when they met with one, each man of his own accord gave him what he deemed right. Thus Abraham by a kind of prophetic instinct gave tithes to Melchisedech, the priest of the Most High God, according to Gen. 14:20, and again Jacob made a vow to give tithes, although he appears to have vowed to do so, not by paying them to ministers, but for the purpose of the divine worship, for instance for the fulfilling of sacrifices, hence he said significantly: *I will offer tithes to Thee*.

**REPLY OBJ. 4**: The second kind of tithe, which was reserved for the offering of sacrifices, has no place in the New Law, since the legal victims had ceased. But the third kind of tithe which they had to eat with the poor, is increased in the New Law, for our Lord commanded us to give to the poor not merely the tenth part, but all our surplus, according to Luke 11:41: *That which remaineth, give alms*. Moreover the tithes that are given to the ministers of the Church should be dispensed by them for the use of the poor.

**REPLY OBJ. 5**: The ministers of the Church ought to be more solicitous for the increase of spiritual goods in the people, than for the amassing of temporal goods: and hence the Apostle was unwilling to make use of the right given him by the Lord of receiving his livelihood from those to whom he preached the Gospel, lest he should occasion a hindrance to the Gospel of Christ. Nor did they sin who did not contribute to his upkeep, else the Apostle would not have omitted to reprove them. In like manner the ministers of the Church rightly refrain from demanding the Church's tithes, when they could not demand them without scandal, on account of their having fallen into desuetude, or for some other reason. Nevertheless those who do not give tithes in places where the Church does not demand them are not in a state of damnation, unless they be obstinate, and unwilling to pay even if tithes were demanded of them.

# Article 2

*Whether men are bound to pay tithes of all things?*

AD SECUNDUM SIC PROCEDITUR. Videtur quod non de omnibus teneantur homines decimas dare. Solutio enim decimarum videtur esse ex veteri lege introducta. Sed in veteri lege nullum praeceptum datur de personalibus decimis, quae scilicet solvuntur de his quae aliquis acquirit ex proprio actu, puta de mercationibus vel de militia. Ergo de talibus decimas solvere nullus tenetur.

PRAETEREA, de male acquisitis non debet fieri oblatio, ut supra dictum est. Sed oblationes, quae immediate Deo exhibentur, videntur magis pertinere ad divinum cultum quam decimae, quae exhibentur ministris. Ergo etiam nec decimae de male acquisitis sunt solvendae.

PRAETEREA, Levit. ult. non mandatur solvi decima nisi *de frugibus et pomis arborum, et animalibus quae transeunt sub virga pastoris.* Sed praeter haec sunt quaedam alia minuta quae homini proveniunt, sicut herbae quae nascuntur in horto, et alia huiusmodi. Ergo nec de illis homo decimas dare tenetur.

PRAETEREA, homo non potest solvere nisi id quod est in eius potestate. Sed non omnia quae proveniunt homini de fructibus agrorum aut animalium remanent in eius potestate, quia quaedam aliquando subtrahuntur per furtum vel rapinam; quaedam vero quandoque in alium transferuntur per venditionem; quaedam etiam aliis debentur, sicut principibus debentur tributa et operariis debentur mercedes. Ergo de his non tenetur aliquis decimas dare.

SED CONTRA est quod dicitur Gen. XXVIII, cunctorum quae dederis mihi decimas offeram tibi. Sed omnia quae homo habet sunt ei data divinitus. Ergo de omnibus debet decimas dare.

RESPONDEO dicendum quod de unaquaque re praecipue est iudicandum secundum eius radicem. Radix autem solutionis decimarum est debitum quo seminantibus spiritualia debentur carnalia, secundum illud apostoli, I ad Cor. IX, *si nos vobis spiritualia seminavimus, magnum est si carnalia vestra metamus?* Super hoc enim debitum fundavit Ecclesia determinationem solutionis decimarum. Omnia autem quaecumque homo possidet sub carnalibus continentur. Et ideo de omnibus possessis decimae sunt solvendae.

AD PRIMUM ergo dicendum quod specialis ratio fuit quare in veteri lege non fuit datum praeceptum de personalibus decimis, secundum conditionem populi illius, quia omnes aliae tribus certas possessiones habebant, de quibus poterant sufficienter providere Levitis, qui carebant possessionibus; non autem interdicebatur eis quin de aliis operibus honestis lucrarentur, sicut et alii

OBJECTION 1: It would seem that men are not bound to give tithes of all things. The paying of tithes seems to be an institution of the Old Law. Now the Old Law contains no precept about personal tithes, viz. those that are payable on property acquired by one's own act, for instance by commerce or soldiering. Therefore no man is bound to pay tithes on such things.

OBJ. 2: Further, it is not right to make oblations of that which is ill-gotten, as stated above (Q. 86, A. 3). Now oblations, being offered to God immediately, seem to be more closely connected with the divine worship than tithes which are offered to the ministers. Therefore neither should tithes be paid on ill-gotten goods.

OBJ. 3: Further, in the last chapter of Leviticus (30, 32) the precept of paying tithes refers only to *corn, fruits of trees, and animals that pass under the shepherd's rod.* But man derives a revenue from other smaller things, such as the herbs that grow in his garden and so forth. Therefore neither on these things is a man bound to pay tithes.

OBJ. 4: Further, man cannot pay except what is in his power. Now a man does not always remain in possession of all his profit from land and stock, since sometimes he loses them by theft or robbery; sometimes they are transferred to another person by sale; sometimes they are due to some other person, thus taxes are due to princes, and wages due to workmen. Therefore one ought not to pay tithes on such like things.

ON THE CONTRARY, It is written (Gen 28:22): *Of all things that Thou shalt give to me, I will offer tithes to Thee.*

I ANSWER THAT, In judging about a thing we should look to its principle. Now the principle of the payment of tithes is the debt whereby carnal things are due to those who sow spiritual things, according to the saying of the Apostle (1 Cor 9:11), *If we have sown unto you spiritual things, is it a great matter if we reap your carnal things?* For this debt is the principle on which is based the commandment of the Church about the payment of tithes. Now whatever man possesses comes under the designation of carnal things. Therefore tithes must be paid on whatever one possesses.

REPLY OBJ. 1: In accordance with the condition of that people there was a special reason why the Old Law did not include a precept about personal tithes; because, to wit, all the other tribes had certain possessions wherewith they were able to provide a sufficient livelihood for the Levites who had no possessions, but were not forbidden to make a profit out of other lawful occupations as the

Iudaei. Sed populus novae legis est ubique per mundum diffusus, quorum plurimi possessiones non habent, sed de aliquibus negotiis vivunt, qui nihil conferrent ad subsidium ministrorum Dei, si de eorum negotiis decimas non solverent. Ministris etiam novae legis arctius interdicitur ne se ingerant negotiis lucrativis, secundum illud II ad Tim. II, *nemo militans Deo implicat se saecularibus negotiis*. Et ideo in nova lege tenentur homines ad decimas personales, secundum consuetudinem patriae et indigentiam ministrorum. Unde Augustinus dicit, et habetur XVI qu. I, cap. decimae, *de militia, de negotio et de artificio redde decimas*.

AD SECUNDUM dicendum quod aliqua male acquiruntur dupliciter. Uno modo, quia ipsa acquisitio est iniusta, puta quae acquiruntur per rapinam aut usuram, quae homo tenetur restituere, non autem de eis decimas dare. Tamen si ager aliquis sit emptus de usura, de fructu eius tenetur usurarius decimas dare, quia fructus illi non sunt ex usura, sed ex Dei munere. Quaedam vero dicuntur male acquisita quia acquiruntur ex turpi causa, sicut de meretricio, de histrionatu, et aliis huiusmodi, quae non tenentur restituere. Unde de talibus tenentur decimas dare secundum modum aliarum personalium decimarum. Tamen Ecclesia non debet eas recipere quandiu sunt in peccato, ne videatur eorum peccatis communicare, sed postquam poenituerint, possunt ab eis de his recipi decimae.

AD TERTIUM dicendum quod ea quae ordinantur in finem sunt iudicanda secundum quod competunt fini. Decimarum autem solutio est debita non propter se, sed propter ministros, quorum honestati non convenit ut etiam minima exacta diligentia requirant, hoc enim in vitium computatur, ut patet per philosophum, in IV Ethic. Et ideo lex vetus non determinavit ut de huiusmodi minutis rebus decimae dentur, sed relinquit hoc arbitrio dare volentium, quia minima quasi nihil computantur. Unde Pharisaei, quasi perfectam legis iustitiam sibi adscribentes, etiam de his minutis decimas solvebant. Nec de hoc reprehenduntur a domino, sed solum de hoc quod maiora, idest spiritualia praecepta, contemnebant. Magis autem de hoc eos secundum se commendabiles esse ostendit, dicens, *haec oportuit facere*, scilicet tempore legis, ut Chrysostomus exponit. Quod etiam videtur magis in quandam decentiam sonare quam in obligationem. Unde et nunc de huiusmodi minutis non tenentur homines decimas dare, nisi forte propter consuetudinem patriae.

AD QUARTUM dicendum quod de his quae furto vel rapina tolluntur ille a quo auferuntur decimas solvere non tenetur antequam recuperet, nisi forte propter cul-

other Jews did. On the other hand the people of the New Law are spread abroad throughout the world, and many of them have no possessions, but live by trade, and these would contribute nothing to the support of God's ministers if they did not pay tithes on their trade profits. Moreover the ministers of the New Law are more strictly forbidden to occupy themselves in money-making trades, according to 2 Tim. 2:4, *No man being a soldier to God, entangleth himself with secular business*. Wherefore in the New Law men are bound to pay personal tithes, according to the custom of their country and the needs of the ministers: hence Augustine, whose words are quoted 16, qu. 1, cap. Decimae, says: *Tithes must be paid on the profits of soldiering, trade or craft*.

REPLY OBJ. 2: Things are ill-gotten in two ways. First, because the getting itself was unjust: such, for instance, are things gotten by robbery, theft or usury: and these a man is bound to restore, and not to pay tithes on them. If, however, a field be bought with the profits of usury, the usurer is bound to pay tithes on the produce, because the latter is not gotten usuriously but given by God. On the other hand certain things are said to be ill-gotten, because they are gotten of a shameful cause, for instance of whoredom or stage-playing, and the like. Such things a man is not bound to restore, and consequently he is bound to pay tithes on them in the same way as other personal tithes. Nevertheless the Church must not accept the tithe so long as those persons remain in sin, lest she appear to have a share in their sins: but when they have done penance, tithes may be accepted from them on these things.

REPLY OBJ. 3: Things directed to an end must be judged according to their fittingness to the end. Now the payment of tithes is due not for its own sake, but for the sake of the ministers, to whose dignity it is unbecoming that they should demand minute things with careful exactitude, for this is reckoned sinful according to the Philosopher (*Ethic.* iv, 2). Hence the Old Law did not order the payment of tithes on such like minute things, but left it to the judgment of those who are willing to pay, because minute things are counted as nothing. Wherefore the Pharisees who claimed for themselves the perfect justice of the Law, paid tithes even on these minute things: nor are they reproved by our Lord on that account, but only because they despised greater, i.e., spiritual, precepts; and rather did He show them to be deserving of praise in this particular, when He said (Matt 23:23): *These things you ought to have done*, i.e., during the time of the Law, according to Chrysostom's commentary. This also seems to denote fittingness rather than obligation. Therefore now too men are not bound to pay tithes on such minute things, except perhaps by reason of the custom of one's country.

REPLY OBJ. 4: A man is not bound to pay tithes on what he has lost by theft or robbery, before he recovers his property: unless he has incurred the loss through his own

pam vel negligentiam suam damnum incurrerit; quia ex hoc Ecclesia non debet damnificari. Si vero vendat triticum non decimatum, potest Ecclesia decimas exigere et ab emptore, quia habet rem Ecclesiae debitam; et a venditore, qui, quantum est de se, fraudavit Ecclesiam. Uno tamen solvente, alius non tenetur. Debentur autem decimae de fructibus terrae inquantum proveniunt ex divino munere. Et ideo decimae non cadunt sub tributo, nec etiam sunt obnoxiae mercedi operariorum. Et ideo non debent prius deduci tributa et pretium operariorum quam solvantur decimae, sed ante omnia debent decimae solvi ex integris fructibus.

fault or neglect, because the Church ought not to be the loser on that account. If he sell wheat that has not been tithed, the Church can command the tithes due to her, both from the buyer who has a thing due to the Church, and from the seller, because so far as he is concerned he has defrauded the Church: yet if one pays, the other is not bound. Tithes are due on the fruits of the earth, insofar as these fruits are the gift of God. Wherefore tithes do not come under a tax, nor are they subject to workmen's wages. Hence it is not right to deduct one's taxes and the wages paid to workmen, before paying tithes: but tithes must be paid before anything else on one's entire produce.

# Article 3

### *Whether tithes should be paid to the clergy?*

AD TERTIUM SIC PROCEDITUR. Videtur quod decimae non sint clericis dandae. Levitis enim in veteri testamento decimae dabantur quia non habebant aliquam partem in possessionibus populi, ut habetur Num. XVIII. Sed clerici in novo testamento habent possessiones, et patrimoniales interdum, et ecclesiasticas. Recipiunt insuper primitias, et oblationes pro vivis et mortuis. Superfluum igitur est quod eis decimae dentur.

PRAETEREA, contingit quandoque quod aliquis habet domicilium in una parochia, et colit agros in alia; vel aliquis pastor ducit gregem per unam partem anni in terminis unius parochiae, et alia parte anni in terminis alterius; vel habet ovile in una parochia, et pascit oves in alia, in quibus et similibus casibus non videtur posse distingui quibus clericis sint decimae solvendae. Ergo non videtur quod aliquibus clericis determinate sint solvendae decimae.

PRAETEREA, generalis consuetudo habet in quibusdam terris quod milites decimas ab Ecclesia in feudum tenent. Religiosi etiam quidam decimas accipiunt. Non ergo videtur quod solum clericis curam animarum habentibus decimae debentur.

SED CONTRA est quod dicitur Num. XVIII, *filiis levi dedi omnes decimas Israel in possessionem, pro ministerio quo serviunt mihi in tabernaculo.* Sed filiis levi succedunt clerici in novo testamento. Ergo solis clericis decimae debentur.

RESPONDEO dicendum quod circa decimas duo sunt consideranda, scilicet ipsum ius accipiendi decimas; et ipsae res quae nomine decimae dantur. Ius autem accipiendi decimas spirituale est, consequitur enim illud debitum quo ministris altaris debentur sumptus de ministerio, et quo *seminantibus spiritualia debentur temporalia;* quod ad solos clericos pertinet habentes

OBJECTION 1: It would seem that tithes should not be paid to the clergy. Tithes were paid to the Levites in the Old Testament, because they had no portion in the people's possessions, according to Num. 18:23, 24. But in the New Testament the clergy have possessions not only ecclesiastical, but sometimes also patrimonial: moreover they receive first-fruits, and oblations for the living and the dead. Therefore it is unnecessary to pay tithes to them.

OBJ. 2: Further, it sometimes happens that a man dwells in one parish, and farms in another; or a shepherd may take his flock within the bounds of one parish during one part of the year, and within the bounds of another parish during the other part of the year; or he may have his sheepfold in one parish, and graze the sheep in another. Now in all these and similar cases it seems impossible to decide to which clergy the tithes ought to be paid. Therefore it would seem that no fixed tithe ought to be paid to the clergy.

OBJ. 3: Further, it is the general custom in certain countries for the soldiers to hold the tithes from the Church in fee; and certain religious receive tithes. Therefore seemingly tithes are not due only to those of the clergy who have care of souls.

ON THE CONTRARY, It is written (Num 18:21): *I have given to the sons of Levi all the tithes of Israel for a possession, for the ministry wherewith they serve Me in the Tabernacle.* Now the clergy are the successors of the sons of Levi in the New Testament. Therefore tithes are due to the clergy alone.

I ANSWER THAT, Two things have to be considered with regard to tithes: namely, the right to receive tithes, and the things given in the name of tithes. The right to receive tithes is a spiritual thing, for it arises from the debt in virtue of which the ministers of the altar have a right to the expenses of their ministry, and *temporal things are due to those who sow spiritual things.* This debt concerns none but the clergy

curam animarum. Et ideo eis solum competit hoc ius habere.

Res autem quae nomine decimarum dantur, corporales sunt. Unde possunt in usum quorumlibet cedere. Et sic possunt etiam ad laicos pervenire.

**AD PRIMUM** ergo dicendum quod in veteri lege, sicut dictum est, speciales quaedam decimae deputabantur subventioni pauperum. Sed in nova lege decimae clericis dantur non solum propter sui sustentationem, sed etiam ut ex eis subveniant pauperibus. Et ideo non superfluunt, sed ad hoc necessariae sunt et possessiones ecclesiasticae et oblationes et primitiae, simul cum decimis.

**AD SECUNDUM** dicendum quod decimae personales debentur Ecclesiae in cuius parochia homo habitat. Decimae vero praediales rationabiliter magis videntur pertinere ad Ecclesiam in cuius terminis praedia sita sunt. Tamen iura determinant quod in hoc servetur consuetudo diu obtenta. Pastor autem qui diversis temporibus in duabus parochiis gregem pascit, debet proportionaliter utrique Ecclesiae decimas solvere. Et quia ex pascuis fructus gregis proveniunt, magis debetur decima gregis Ecclesiae in cuius territorio grex pascitur, quam illi in cuius territorio ovile locatur.

**AD TERTIUM** dicendum quod sicut res nomine decimae acceptas potest Ecclesia alicui laico tradere, ita etiam potest ei concedere ut dandas decimas ipsi accipiant, iure accipiendi ministris Ecclesiae reservato, sive pro necessitate Ecclesiae, sicut quibusdam militibus decimae dicuntur in feudum per Ecclesiam concessae; sive etiam ad subventionem pauperum, sicut quibusdam religiosis laicis vel non habentibus curam animarum aliquae decimae sunt concessae per modum eleemosynae. Quibusdam tamen religiosis competit accipere decimas ex eo quod habent curam animarum.

who have care of souls, and so they alone are competent to have this right.

On the other hand the things given in the name of tithes are material, wherefore they may come to be used by anyone, and thus it is that they fall into the hands of the laity.

**REPLY OBJ. 1**: In the Old Law, as stated above (A. 1, ad 4), special tithes were earmarked for the assistance of the poor. But in the New Law the tithes are given to the clergy, not only for their own support, but also that the clergy may use them in assisting the poor. Hence they are not unnecessary; indeed Church property, oblations and first-fruits as well as tithes are all necessary for this same purpose.

**REPLY OBJ. 2**: Personal tithes are due to the church in whose parish a man dwells, while predial tithes seem more reasonably to belong to the church within whose bounds the land is situated. The law, however, prescribes that in this matter a custom that has obtained for a long time must be observed. The shepherd who grazes his flock at different seasons in two parishes, should pay tithe proportionately to both churches. And since the fruit of the flock is derived from the pasture, the tithe of the flock is due to the church in whose lands the flock grazes, rather than to the church on whose land the fold is situated.

**REPLY OBJ. 3**: Just as the Church can hand over to a layman the things she receives under the title of tithe, so too can she allow him to receive tithes that are yet to be paid, the right of receiving being reserved to the ministers of the Church. The motive may be either the need of the Church, as when tithes are due to certain soldiers through being granted to them in fee by the Church, or it may be the succoring of the poor; thus certain tithes have been granted by way of alms to certain lay religious, or to those that have no care of souls. Some religious, however, are competent to receive tithes, because they have care of souls.

# Article 4

*Whether the clergy also are bound to pay tithes?*

**AD QUARTUM SIC PROCEDITUR**. Videtur quod etiam clerici teneantur decimas dare. Quia de iure communi Ecclesia parochialis debet recipere decimas praediorum quae in territorio eius sunt. Contingit autem quandoque quod clerici habent in territorio alicuius parochialis Ecclesiae aliqua praedia propria. Vel etiam aliqua alia Ecclesia habet ibi possessiones ecclesiasticas. Ergo videtur quod clerici teneantur dare praediales decimas.

**PRAETEREA**, aliqui religiosi sunt clerici. Qui tamen tenentur dare decimas Ecclesiis ratione praediorum

**OBJECTION 1**: It would seem that clerics also are bound to pay tithes. By common law the parish church should receive the tithes on the lands which are in its territory. Now it happens sometimes that the clergy have certain lands of their own on the territory of some parish church, or that one church has ecclesiastical property on the territory of another. Therefore it would seem that the clergy are bound to pay predial tithes.

**OBJ. 2**: Further, some religious are clerics; and yet they are bound to pay tithes to churches on account of the lands

quae etiam manibus propriis excolunt. Ergo videtur quod clerici non sint immunes a solutione decimarum.

**Praeterea**, sicut Num. XVIII praecipitur quod Levitae a populo decimas accipiant, ita etiam praecipitur quod ipsi dent decimas summo sacerdoti. Ergo, qua ratione laici debent dare decimas clericis, eadem ratione clerici debent dare decimas summo pontifici.

**Praeterea**, sicut decimae debent cedere in sustentationem clericorum, ita etiam debent cedere in subventionem pauperum. Si ergo clerici excusantur a solutione decimarum, pari ratione excusantur et pauperes. Hoc autem est falsum. Ergo et primum.

**Sed contra** est quod dicit decretalis paschalis Papae, *novum genus exactionis est ut clerici a clericis decimas exigant.*

**Respondeo** dicendum quod idem non potest esse causa dandi et recipiendi, sicut nec causa agendi et patiendi, contingit autem ex diversis causis, et respectu diversorum, eundem esse dantem et recipientem, sicut agentem et patientem. Clericis autem inquantum sunt ministri altaris spiritualia populo seminantes, decimae a fidelibus debentur. Unde tales clerici, inquantum clerici sunt, idest inquantum possessiones habent ecclesiasticas, decimas solvere non tenentur. Ex alia vero causa, scilicet propter hoc quod possident proprio iure, vel ex successione parentum, vel ex emptione, vel quocumque huiusmodi modo, sunt ad decimas solvendas obligati.

**Unde patet** responsio ad primum. Quia clerici de propriis praediis tenentur solvere decimas parochiali Ecclesiae sicut et alii, etiam si ipsi sint eiusdem Ecclesiae clerici, quia aliud est habere aliquid ut proprium, aliud ut commune. Praedia vero Ecclesiae non sunt ad decimas solvendas obligata, etiam si sint infra terminos alterius parochiae.

**Ad secundum** dicendum quod religiosi qui sunt clerici, si habeant curam animarum spiritualia populo dispensantes, non tenentur decimas dare, sed possunt eas recipere. De aliis vero religiosis, etiam si sint clerici, qui non dispensant populo spiritualia, est alia ratio. Ipsi enim tenentur de iure communi decimas dare, habent tamen aliquam immunitatem secundum diversas concessiones eis a sede apostolica factas.

**Ad tertium** dicendum quod in veteri lege primitiae debebantur sacerdotibus, decimae autem Levitis, et quia sub sacerdotibus Levitae erant, dominus mandavit ut ipsi, loco primitiarum, solverent summo sacerdoti decimam decimae. Unde nunc, eadem ratione, tenentur clerici summo pontifici decimam dare, si exigeret. Naturalis enim ratio dictat ut illi qui habet curam de

which they cultivate even with their own hands. Therefore it would seem that the clergy are not immune from the payment of tithes.

**Obj. 3**: Further, in the eighteenth chapter of Numbers (26, 28), it is prescribed not only that the Levites should receive tithes from the people, but also that they should themselves pay tithes to the high-priest. Therefore the clergy are bound to pay tithes to the Sovereign Pontiff, no less than the laity are bound to pay tithes to the clergy.

**Obj. 4**: Further, tithes should serve not only for the support of the clergy, but also for the assistance of the poor. Therefore, if the clergy are exempt from paying tithes, so too are the poor. Yet the latter is not true. Therefore the former is false.

**On the contrary**, A decretal of Pope Paschal says: *It is a new form of exaction when the clergy demand tithes from the clergy.*

**I answer that**, The cause of giving cannot be the cause of receiving, as neither can the cause of action be the cause of passion; yet it happens that one and the same person is giver and receiver, even as agent and patient, on account of different causes and from different points of view. Now tithes are due to the clergy as being ministers of the altar and sowers of spiritual things among the people. Wherefore those members of the clergy as such, i.e., as having ecclesiastical property, are not bound to pay tithes; whereas from some other cause through holding property in their own right, either by inheriting it from their kindred, or by purchase, or in any other similar manner, they are bound to the payment of tithes.

**Hence** the Reply to the First Objection is clear, because the clergy like anyone else are bound to pay tithes on their own lands to the parish church, even though they be the clergy of that same church, because to possess a thing as one's private property is not the same as possessing it in common. But church lands are not tithable, even though they be within the boundaries of another parish.

**Reply Obj. 2**: Religious who are clerics, if they have care of souls, and dispense spiritual things to the people, are not bound to pay tithes, but they may receive them. Another reason applies to other religious, who though clerics do not dispense spiritual things to the people; for according to the ordinary law they are bound to pay tithes, but they are somewhat exempt by reason of various concessions granted by the Apostolic See.

**Reply Obj. 3**: In the Old Law first-fruits were due to the priests, and tithes to the Levites; and since the Levites were below the priests, the Lord commanded that the former should pay the high-priest the tenth part of the tenth instead of first-fruits: wherefore for the same reason the clergy are bound now to pay tithes to the Sovereign Pontiff, if he demanded them. For natural reason dictates that he

communi multitudinis statu, provideatur unde possit exequi ea quae pertinent ad communem salutem.

**Ad quartum** dicendum quod decimae debent cedere in subventionem pauperum per dispensationem clericorum. Et ideo pauperes non habent causam accipiendi decimas, sed tenentur eas dare.

who has charge of the common estate of a multitude should be provided with all goods, so that he may be able to carry out whatever is necessary for the common welfare.

**Reply Obj. 4**: Tithes should be employed for the assistance of the poor, through the dispensation of the clergy. Hence the poor have no reason for accepting tithes, but they are bound to pay them.

# QUESTION 88

## Vows

Deinde considerandum est de voto, per quod aliquid Deo promittitur. Et circa hoc quaeruntur duodecim.

Primo, quid sit votum.

Secundo, quid cadat sub voto.

Tertio, de obligatione voti.

Quarto, de utilitate vovendi.

Quinto, cuius virtutis sit actus.

Sexto, utrum magis meritorium sit facere aliquid ex voto quam sine voto.

Septimo, de solemnitate voti.

Octavo, utrum possint vovere qui sunt potestati alterius subiecti.

Nono, utrum pueri possint voto obligari ad religionis ingressum.

Decimo, utrum votum sit dispensabile vel commutabile.

Undecimo, utrum in solemni voto continentiae possit dispensari.

Duodecimo, utrum requiratur in dispensatione voti superioris auctoritas.

We must now consider vows, whereby something is promised to God. Under this head there are twelve points of inquiry:

(1) What is a vow?

(2) What is the matter of a vow?

(3) Of the obligation of vows;

(4) Of the use of taking vows;

(5) Of what virtue is it an act?

(6) Whether it is more meritorious to do a thing from a vow, than without a vow?

(7) Of the solemnizing of a vow;

(8) Whether those who are under another's power can take vows?

(9) Whether children may be bound by vow to enter religion?

(10) Whether a vow is subject to dispensation or commutation?

(11) Whether a dispensation can be granted in a solemn vow of continence?

(12) Whether the authority of a superior is required in a dispensation from a vow?

# Article 1

*Whether a vow consists in a mere purpose of the will?*

**AD PRIMUM SIC PROCEDITUR.** Videtur quod votum consistat in solo proposito voluntatis. Quia secundum quosdam, *votum est conceptio boni propositi, animi deliberatione firmata, qua quis ad aliquid faciendum vel non faciendum se Deo obligat.* Sed conceptio boni propositi, cum omnibus quae adduntur, potest in solo motu voluntatis consistere. Ergo votum in solo proposito voluntatis consistit.

**PRAETEREA,** ipsum nomen *voti* videtur a *voluntate* assumptum, dicitur enim aliquis proprio voto facere quae voluntarie facit. Sed propositum est actus voluntatis, promissio autem rationis. Ergo votum in solo actu voluntatis consistit.

**PRAETEREA,** dominus dicit, Luc. IX, *nemo mittens manum ad aratrum et aspiciens retro aptus est regno Dei.* Sed aliquis ex hoc ipso quod habet propositum bene faciendi mittit manum ad aratrum. Ergo, si aspiciat retro, desistens a bono proposito, non est aptus regno Dei. Ex solo igitur bono proposito aliquis obligatur apud Deum,

**OBJECTION 1:** It would seem that a vow consists in nothing but a purpose of the will. According to some, *a vow is a conception of a good purpose after a firm deliberation of the mind, whereby a man binds himself before God to do or not to do a certain thing.* But the conception of a good purpose and so forth, may consist in a mere movement of the will. Therefore a vow consists in a mere purpose of the will.

**OBJ. 2:** Further, the very word *vow* seems to be derived from *voluntas* (will), for one is said to do a thing *proprio voto* (by one's own vow) when one does it voluntarily. Now to purpose is an act of the will, while to promise is an act of the reason. Therefore a vow consists in a mere act of the will.

**OBJ. 3:** Further, our Lord said (Luke 9:62): *No man putting his hand to the plough, and looking back, is fit for the kingdom of God.* Now from the very fact that a man has a purpose of doing good, he puts his hand to the plough. Consequently, if he look back by desisting from his good purpose, he is not fit for the kingdom of God. Therefore

etiam nulla promissione facta. Et ita videtur quod in solo proposito voluntatis votum consistat.

**Sed contra** est quod dicitur Eccle. V, *si quid vovisti Deo, ne moreris reddere, displicet enim ei infidelis et stulta promissio.* Ergo vovere est promittere, et votum est promissio.

**Respondeo** dicendum quod votum quandam obligationem importat ad aliquid faciendum vel dimittendum. Obligat autem homo se homini ad aliquid per modum promissionis, quae est rationis actus, ad quam pertinet ordinare, sicut enim homo imperando vel deprecando ordinat quodammodo quid sibi ab aliis fiat, ita promittendo ordinat quid ipse pro alio facere debeat. Sed promissio quae ab homine fit homini, non potest fieri nisi per verba vel quaecumque exteriora signa. Deo autem potest fieri promissio per solam interiorem cogitationem, quia ut dicitur I Reg. XVI, *homines vident ea quae parent, sed Deus intuetur cor.* Exprimuntur tamen quandoque verba exteriora vel ad sui ipsius excitationem, sicut circa orationem dictum est, vel ad alios contestandum, ut non solum desistat a fractione voti propter timorem Dei, sed etiam propter reverentiam hominum. Promissio autem procedit ex proposito faciendi. Propositum autem aliquam deliberationem praeexigit, cum sit actus voluntatis deliberatae. Sic igitur ad votum tria ex necessitate requiruntur, primo quidem, deliberatio; secundo, propositum voluntatis; tertio, promissio, in qua perficitur ratio voti. Superadduntur vero quandoque et alia duo, ad quandam voti confirmationem, scilicet pronuntiatio oris, secundum illud Psalm., *reddam tibi vota mea, quae distinxerunt labia mea*; et iterum testimonium aliorum. Unde Magister dicit, XXXVIII dist. IV Lib. Sent., quod *votum est testificatio quaedam promissionis spontaneae, quae Deo et de his quae sunt Dei fieri debet*, quamvis testificatio possit ad interiorem testificationem proprie referri.

**Ad primum** ergo dicendum quod conceptio boni propositi non firmatur ex animi deliberatione nisi promissione deliberationem consequente.

**Ad secundum** dicendum quod voluntas movet rationem ad promittendum aliquid circa ea quae eius voluntati subduntur. Et pro tanto votum a voluntate accepit nomen quasi a primo movente.

**Ad tertium** dicendum quod ille qui mittit manum ad aratrum iam facit aliquid. Sed ille qui solum proponit nondum aliquid facit. Sed quando promittit, iam incipit se exhibere ad faciendum, licet nondum impleat quod promittit, sicut ille qui ponit manum ad aratrum nondum arat, iam tamen apponit manum ad arandum.

by a mere good purpose a man is bound before God, even without making a promise; and consequently it would seem that a vow consists in a mere purpose of the will.

**On the contrary,** It is written (Eccl 5:3): *If thou hast vowed anything to God, defer not to pay it, for an unfaithful and foolish promise displeaseth Him.* Therefore to vow is to promise, and a vow is a promise.

**I answer that,** A vow denotes a binding to do or omit some particular thing. Now one man binds himself to another by means of a promise, which is an act of the reason to which faculty it belongs to direct. For just as a man by commanding or praying, directs, in a fashion, what others are to do for him, so by promising he directs what he himself is to do for another. Now a promise between man and man can only be expressed in words or any other outward signs; whereas a promise can be made to God by the mere inward thought, since according to 1 Kings 16:7, *Man seeth those things that appear, but the Lord beholdeth the heart.* Yet we express words outwardly sometimes, either to arouse ourselves, as was stated above with regard to prayer (Q. 83, A. 12), or to call others to witness, so that one may refrain from breaking the vow, not only through fear of God, but also through respect of men. Now a promise is the outcome from a purpose of doing something: and a purpose presupposes deliberation, since it is the act of a deliberate will. Accordingly three things are essential to a vow: the first is deliberation; the second is a purpose of the will; and the third is a promise, wherein is completed the nature of a vow. Sometimes, however, two other things are added as a sort of confirmation of the vow, namely, pronouncement by word of mouth, according to Ps. 65:13, *I will pay Thee my vows which my lips have uttered*; and the witnessing of others. Hence the Master says (*Sent.* iv, D, 38) that a vow is *the witnessing of a spontaneous promise and ought to be made to God and about things relating to God*: although the *witnessing* may strictly refer to the inward protestation.

**Reply Obj. 1:** The conceiving of a good purpose is not confirmed by the deliberation of the mind, unless the deliberation lead to a promise.

**Reply Obj. 2:** Man's will moves the reason to promise something relating to things subject to his will, and a vow takes its name from the will forasmuch as it proceeds from the will as first mover.

**Reply Obj. 3:** He that puts his hand to the plough does something already; while he that merely purposes to do something does nothing so far. When, however, he promises, he already sets about doing, although he does not yet fulfill his promise: even so, he that puts his hand to the plough does not plough yet, nevertheless he stretches out his hand for the purpose of ploughing.

# Article 2

*Whether a vow should always be about a better good?*

**AD SECUNDUM SIC PROCEDITUR**. Videtur quod votum non semper debeat fieri de meliori bono. Dicitur enim melius bonum quod ad supererogationem pertinet. Sed votum non solum fit de his quae sunt supererogationis, sed etiam de his quae pertinent ad salutem. Nam et *in Baptismo vovent homines abrenuntiare Diabolo et pompis eius, et fidem servare*, ut dicit Glossa, super illud Psalm., *vovete et reddite domino Deo vestro*. Iacob etiam vovit quod esset ei dominus in Deum, ut habetur Gen. XXVIII, hoc autem est maxime de necessitate salutis. Ergo votum non solum fit de meliori bono.

**PRAETEREA**, Iephte in catalogo sanctorum ponitur, ut patet Heb. XI. Sed ipse filiam innocentem occidit propter votum, ut habetur Iudic. XI. Cum igitur occisio innocentis non sit melius bonum, sed sit secundum se illicitum, videtur quod votum fieri possit non solum de meliori bono, sed etiam de illicitis.

**PRAETEREA**, ea quae redundant in detrimentum personae, vel quae ad nihil sunt utilia, non habent rationem melioris boni. Sed quandoque fiunt aliqua vota de immoderatis vigiliis et ieiuniis, quae vergunt in periculum personae. Quandoque etiam fiunt aliqua vota de aliquibus indifferentibus et ad nihil valentibus. Ergo non semper votum est melioris boni.

**SED CONTRA** est quod dicitur Deut. XXIII, *si nolueris polliceri, absque peccato eris*.

**RESPONDEO** dicendum quod, sicut dictum est, votum est promissio Deo facta. Promissio autem est alicuius quod quis pro aliquo voluntarie facit. Non enim esset promissio, sed comminatio, si quis diceret se contra aliquem facturum. Similiter vana esset promissio si aliquis alicui promitteret id quod ei non esset acceptum. Et ideo, cum omne peccatum sit contra Deum; nec aliquod opus sit Deo acceptum nisi sit virtuosum, consequens est quod de nullo illicito, nec de aliquo indifferenti debeat fieri votum, sed solum de aliquo actu virtutis. Sed quia votum promissionem voluntariam importat, necessitas autem voluntatem excludit, id quod est absolute necessarium esse vel non esse nullo modo cadit sub voto, stultum enim esset si quis voveret se esse moriturum, vel se non esse volaturum.

Illud vero quod non habet absolutam necessitatem, sed necessitatem finis, puta quia sine eo non potest esse salus, cadit quidem sub voto inquantum voluntarie fit, non autem inquantum est necessitatis. Illud autem quod neque cadit sub necessitate absoluta neque sub necessitate finis, omnino est voluntarium. Et ideo hoc propriissime cadit sub voto. Hoc autem dicitur esse maius bonum in comparatione ad bonum quod commu-

**OBJECTION 1**: It would seem that a vow need not be always about a better good. A greater good is one that pertains to supererogation. But vows are not only about matters of supererogation, but also about matters of salvation: thus *in Baptism men vow to renounce the devil and his pomps, and to keep the faith*, as a gloss observes on Ps. 75:12, *Vow ye, and pay to the Lord your God*; and Jacob vowed (Gen 28:21) that the Lord should be his God. Now this above all is necessary for salvation. Therefore vows are not only about a better good.

**OBJ. 2**: Further, Jephte is included among the saints (Heb 11:32). Yet he killed his innocent daughter on account of his vow (Judg 11). Since, then, the slaying of an innocent person is not a better good, but is in itself unlawful, it seems that a vow may be made not only about a better good, but also about something unlawful.

**OBJ. 3**: Further, things that tend to be harmful to the person, or that are quite useless, do not come under the head of a better good. Yet sometimes vows are made about immoderate vigils or fasts which tend to injure the person: and sometimes vows are about indifferent matters and such as are useful to no purpose. Therefore a vow is not always about a better good.

**ON THE CONTRARY**, It is written (Deut 23:22): *If thou wilt not promise thou shalt be without sin.*

**I ANSWER THAT**, As stated above (A. 1), a vow is a promise made to God. Now a promise is about something that one does voluntarily for someone else: since it would be not a promise but a threat to say that one would do something against someone. In like manner it would be futile to promise anyone something unacceptable to him. Wherefore, as every sin is against God, and since no work is acceptable to God unless it be virtuous, it follows that nothing unlawful or indifferent, but only some act of virtue, should be the matter of a vow. But as a vow denotes a voluntary promise, while necessity excludes voluntariness, whatever is absolutely necessary, whether to be or not to be, can nowise be the matter of a vow. For it would be foolish to vow that one would die or that one would not fly.

On the other hand, if a thing be necessary, not absolutely but on the supposition of an end—for instance if salvation be unattainable without it—it may be the matter of a vow insofar as it is done voluntarily, but not insofar as there is a necessity for doing it. But that which is not necessary, neither absolutely, nor on the supposition of an end, is altogether voluntary, and therefore is most properly the matter of a vow. And this is said to be a greater good

niter est de necessitate salutis. Et ideo, proprie loquendo, votum dicitur esse de bono meliori.´

AD PRIMUM ergo dicendum quod hoc modo sub voto baptizatorum cadit abrenuntiare pompis Diaboli et fidem Christi servare, quia voluntarie fit, licet sit de necessitate salutis. Et similiter potest dici de voto Iacob. Quamvis etiam possit intelligi quod Iacob vovit se habere dominum in Deum per specialem cultum, ad quem non tenebatur, sicut per decimarum oblationem, et alia huiusmodi quae ibi subduntur.

AD SECUNDUM dicendum quod quaedam sunt quae in omnem eventum sunt bona, sicut opera virtutis et alia quae absolute possunt cadere sub voto. Quaedam vero in omnem eventum sunt mala, sicut ea quae secundum se sunt peccata. Et haec nullo modo possunt sub voto cadere. Quaedam vero sunt quidem in se considerata bona, et secundum hoc possunt cadere sub voto, possunt tamen habere malum eventum, in quo non sunt observanda. Et sic accidit in voto Iephte, qui ut dicitur Iudic. XI, *votum vovit domino, dicens, si tradideris filios Ammon in manus meas, quicumque primus egressus fuerit de foribus domus meae mihique occurrerit revertenti in pace, eum offeram holocaustum domino.* Hoc enim poterat malum eventum habere, si occurreret ei aliquod animal non immolativum, sicut asinus vel homo, quod et accidit. Unde, ut Hieronymus dicit, *in vovendo fuit stultus, quia discretionem non adhibuit, et in reddendo impius.* Praemittitur tamen ibidem *quod factus est super eum spiritus domini,* quia fides et devotio ipsius, ex qua motus est ad vovendum, fuit a spiritu sancto. Propter quod ponitur in catalogo sanctorum, et propter victoriam quam obtinuit; et quia probabile est eum poenituisse de facto iniquo, quod tamen aliquod bonum figurabat.

AD TERTIUM dicendum quod maceratio proprii corporis, puta per vigilias et ieiunia, non est Deo accepta nisi inquantum est opus virtutis, quod quidem est inquantum cum debita discretione fit, ut scilicet concupiscentia refrenetur et natura non nimis gravetur. Et sub tali tenore possunt huiusmodi sub voto cadere. Propter quod et apostolus, Rom. XII, postquam dixerat, *exhibeatis corpora vestra hostiam viventem, sanctam, Deo placentem,* addidit, *rationabile obsequium vestrum.* Sed quia in his quae ad seipsum pertinent de facili fallitur homo in iudicando, talia vota congruentius secundum arbitrium superioris sunt vel servanda vel praetermittenda. Ita tamen quod si ex observatione talis voti magnum et manifestum gravamen sentiret, et non esset facultas ad superiorem recurrendi, non debet homo tale votum servare. Vota vero quae sunt de rebus vanis et inutilibus sunt magis deridenda quam servanda.

in comparison with that which is universally necessary for salvation. Therefore, properly speaking, a vow is said to be about a better good.

REPLY OBJ. 1: Renouncing the devil's pomps and keeping the faith of Christ are the matter of baptismal vows, insofar as these things are done voluntarily, although they are necessary for salvation. The same answer applies to Jacob's vow: although it may also be explained that Jacob vowed that he would have the Lord for his God, by giving Him a special form of worship to which he was not bound, for instance by offering tithes and so forth as mentioned further on in the same passage.

REPLY OBJ. 2: Certain things are good, whatever be their result; such are acts of virtue, and these can be, absolutely speaking, the matter of a vow: some are evil, whatever their result may be; as those things which are sins in themselves, and these can nowise be the matter of a vow: while some, considered in themselves, are good, and as such may be the matter of a vow, yet they may have an evil result, in which case the vow must not be kept. It was thus with the vow of Jephte, who as related in Judges 11:30, 31, *made a vow to the Lord, saying: If Thou wilt deliver the children of Ammon into my hands, whosoever shall first come forth out of the doors of my house, and shall meet me when I return in peace . . . the same will I offer a holocaust to the Lord.* For this could have an evil result if, as indeed happened, he were to be met by some animal which it would be unlawful to sacrifice, such as an ass or a human being. Hence Jerome says: *In vowing he was foolish, through lack of discretion, and in keeping his vow he was wicked.* Yet it is premised (Judg 11:29) that *the Spirit of the Lord came upon him,* because his faith and devotion, which moved him to make that vow, were from the Holy Spirit; and for this reason he is reckoned among the saints, as also by reason of the victory which he obtained, and because it is probable that he repented of his sinful deed, which nevertheless foreshadowed something good.

REPLY OBJ. 3: The mortification of one's own body, for instance by vigils and fasting, is not acceptable to God except insofar as it is an act of virtue; and this depends on its being done with due discretion, namely, that concupiscence be curbed without overburdening nature. On this condition such things may be the matter of a vow. Hence the Apostle after saying (Rom 12:1), *Present your bodies a living sacrifice, holy, pleasing to God,* adds, *your reasonable service.* Since, however, man is easily mistaken in judging of matters concerning himself, such vows as these are more fittingly kept or disregarded according to the judgment of a superior, yet so that, should a man find that without doubt he is seriously burdened by keeping such a vow, and should he be unable to appeal to his superior, he ought not to keep it. As to vows about vain and useless things they should be ridiculed rather than kept.

# Article 3

*Whether all vows are binding?*

**AD TERTIUM SIC PROCEDITUR.** Videtur quod non omne votum obliget ad sui observationem. Homo enim magis indiget his quae per alium hominem fiunt quam Deus, qui bonorum nostrorum non eget. Sed promissio simplex homini facta non obligat ad servandum, secundum institutionem legis humanae, quod videtur esse institutum propter mutabilitatem humanae voluntatis. Ergo multo minus simplex promissio Deo facta, quae dicitur votum, obligat ad observandum.

**PRAETEREA,** nullus obligatur ad impossibile. Sed quandoque illud quod quis vovit fit ei impossibile, vel quia dependet ex alieno arbitrio, sicut cum quis vovet aliquod monasterium intrare cuius monachi eum nolunt recipere; vel propter emergentem defectum, sicut mulier quae vovit virginitatem servare et postea corrumpitur, vel vir qui vovet pecuniam dare et postea amittit pecuniam. Ergo non semper votum est obligatorium.

**PRAETEREA,** illud ad cuius solutionem est aliquis obligatus, statim solvere tenetur. Sed aliquis non statim solvere tenetur illud quod vovit, praecipue cum sub conditione futura vovet. Ergo votum non semper est obligatorium.

**SED CONTRA** est quod dicitur Eccle. V, *quodcumque voveris, redde. Multoque melius est non vovere quam post votum promissa non reddere.*

**RESPONDEO** dicendum quod ad fidelitatem hominis pertinet ut solvat id quod promisit, unde secundum Augustinum, *fides dicitur ex hoc quod fiunt dicta.* Maxime autem debet homo Deo fidelitatem, tum ratione dominii; tum etiam ratione beneficii suscepti. Et ideo maxime obligatur homo ad hoc quod impleat vota Deo facta, hoc enim pertinet ad fidelitatem quam homo debet Deo, fractio autem voti est quaedam infidelitatis species. Unde Salomon rationem assignat quare sint vota reddenda, quia *displicet Deo infidelis promissio.*

**AD PRIMUM** ergo dicendum quod secundum honestatem ex qualibet promissione homo homini obligatur, et haec est obligatio iuris naturalis. Sed ad hoc quod aliquis obligetur ex aliqua promissione obligatione civili, quaedam alia requiruntur. Deus autem etsi bonis nostris non egeat, ei tamen maxime obligamur. Et ita votum ei factum est maxime obligatorium.

**AD SECUNDUM** dicendum quod si illud quod quis vovit ex quacumque causa impossibile reddatur, debet homo facere quod in se est, ut saltem habeat promptam voluntatem faciendi quod potest. Unde ille qui vovit monasterium aliquod intrare debet dare operam quam potest ut ibi recipiatur. Et si quidem intentio sua fuit

**OBJECTION 1**: It would seem that vows are not all binding. For man needs things that are done by another, more than God does, since He has no need for our goods (Ps 15:2). Now according to the prescription of human laws a simple promise made to a man is not binding; and this seems to be prescribed on account of the changeableness of the human will. Much less binding therefore is a simple promise made to God, which we call a vow.

**OBJ. 2**: Further, no one is bound to do what is impossible. Now sometimes that which a man has vowed becomes impossible to him, either because it depends on another's decision, as when, for instance, a man vows to enter a monastery, the monks of which refuse to receive him: or on account of some defect arising, for instance when a woman vows virginity, and afterwards is deflowered; or when a man vows to give a sum of money, and afterwards loses it. Therefore a vow is not always binding.

**OBJ. 3**: Further, if a man is bound to pay something, he must do so at once. But a man is not bound to pay his vow at once, especially if it be taken under a condition to be fulfilled in the future. Therefore a vow is not always binding.

**ON THE CONTRARY**, It is written (Eccl 5:3, 4): *Whatsoever thou hast vowed, pay it; and it is much better not to vow, than after a vow not to perform the things promised.*

**I ANSWER THAT,** For one to be accounted faithful one must keep one's promises. Wherefore, according to Augustine faith takes its name *from a man's deed agreeing with his word.* Now man ought to be faithful to God above all, both on account of God's sovereignty, and on account of the favors he has received from God. Hence man is obliged before all to fulfill the vows he has made to God, since this is part of the fidelity he owes to God. On the other hand, the breaking of a vow is a kind of infidelity. Wherefore Solomon gives the reason why vows should be paid to God, because *an unfaithful . . . promise displeaseth Him.*

**REPLY OBJ. 1**: Honesty demands that a man should keep any promise he makes to another man, and this obligation is based on the natural law. But for a man to be under a civil obligation through a promise he has made, other conditions are requisite. And although God needs not our goods, we are under a very great obligation to Him: so that a vow made to Him is most binding.

**REPLY OBJ. 2**: If that which a man has vowed becomes impossible to him through any cause whatsoever, he must do what he can, so that he have at least a will ready to do what he can. Hence if a man has vowed to enter a monastery, he must endeavor to the best of his power to be received there. And if his intention was chiefly to bind

se obligare ad religionis ingressum principaliter, et ex consequenti elegit hanc religionem vel hunc locum quasi sibi magis congruentem, tenetur, si non potest ibi recipi, aliam religionem intrare. Si autem principaliter intendit se obligare ad hanc religionem vel ad hunc locum, propter specialem complacentiam huius religionis vel loci, non tenetur aliam religionem intrare si illi eum recipere nolunt. Si vero incidit in impossibilitatem implendi votum ex propria culpa, tenetur insuper de propria culpa praeterita poenitentiam agere. Sicut mulier quae vovit virginitatem, si postea corrumpatur, non solum debet servare quod potest, scilicet perpetuam continentiam, sed etiam de eo quod admisit peccando poenitere.

Ad tertium dicendum quod obligatio voti ex propria voluntate et intentione causatur, unde dicitur Deut. XXIII, quod *semel egressum est de labiis tuis, observabis, et facies sicut promisisti domino Deo tuo, et propria voluntate et ore tuo locutus es.* Et ideo si in intentione et voluntate voventis est obligare se ad statim solvendum, tenetur statim solvere. Si autem ad certum tempus, vel sub certa conditione, non tenetur statim solvere. Sed nec debet tardare ultra quam intendit se obligare, dicitur enim ibidem, *cum votum voveris domino Deo tuo, non tardabis reddere, quia requiret illud dominus Deus tuus; et si moratus fueris, reputabitur tibi in peccatum.*

himself to enter the religious life, so that, in consequence, he chose this particular form of religious life, or this place, as being most agreeable to him, he is bound, should he be unable to be received there, to enter the religious life elsewhere. But if his principal intention is to bind himself to this particular kind of religious life, or to this particular place, because the one or the other pleases him in some special way, he is not bound to enter another religious house, if they are unwilling to receive him into this particular one. On the other hand, if he be rendered incapable of fulfilling his vow through his own fault, he is bound over and above to do penance for his past fault: thus if a woman has vowed virginity and is afterwards violated, she is bound not only to observe what is in her power, namely, perpetual continency, but also to repent of what she has lost by sinning.

REPLY OBJ. 3: The obligation of a vow is caused by our own will and intention, wherefore it is written (Deut 23:23): *That which is once gone out of thy lips, thou shalt observe, and shalt do as thou hast promised to the Lord thy God, and hast spoken with thy own will and with thy own mouth.* Wherefore if in taking a vow, it is one's intention and will to bind oneself to fulfill it at once, one is bound to fulfill it immediately. But if one intend to fulfill it at a certain time, or under a certain condition, one is not bound to immediate fulfilment. And yet one ought not to delay longer than one intended to bind oneself, for it is written (Deut 23:21): *When thou hast made a vow to the Lord thy God thou shalt not delay to pay it: because the Lord thy God will require it; and if thou delay, it shall be imputed to thee for a sin.*

# Article 4

### Whether it is expedient to take vows?

AD QUARTUM SIC PROCEDITUR. Videtur quod non expediat aliquid vovere. Non enim alicui expedit ut privet se bono quod ei Deus donavit. Sed libertas est unum de maximis bonis quae homini Deus dedit, qua videtur privari per necessitatem quam votum imponit. Ergo non videtur expediens homini quod aliquid voveat.

PRAETEREA, nullus debet se periculis iniicere. Sed quicumque vovet se periculo iniicit, quia quod ante votum sine periculo poterat praeteriri, si non servetur post votum, periculosum est. Unde Augustinus dicit, in epistola ad Armentarium et Paulinam, *quia iam vovisti, iam te obstrinxisti, aliud tibi facere non licet. Non talis eris si non feceris quod vovisti, qualis mansisses si nihil tale vovisses. Minor enim tunc esses, non peior. Modo autem,*

OBJECTION 1: It would seem that it is not expedient to take vows. It is not expedient to anyone to deprive himself of the good that God has given him. Now one of the greatest goods that God has given man is liberty whereof he seems to be deprived by the necessity implicated in a vow. Therefore it would seem inexpedient for man to take vows.

OBJ. 2: Further, no one should expose himself to danger. But whoever takes a vow exposes himself to danger, since that which, before taking a vow, he could omit without danger, becomes a source of danger to him if he should not fulfill it after taking the vow. Hence Augustine says (*Ep. cxxvii, ad Arment. et Paulin.*): *Since thou hast vowed, thou hast bound thyself, thou canst not do otherwise. If thou dost not what thou hast vowed thou wilt not be as thou*

*tanto, quod absit, miserior si fidem Deo fregeris, quanto beatior si persolveris.* Ergo non expedit aliquid vovere.

**PRAETEREA**, apostolus dicit, I ad Cor. IV, *imitatores mei estote, sicut et ego Christi.* Sed non legitur neque Christum aliquid vovisse, nec apostolos. Ergo videtur quod non expediat aliquid vovere.

**SED CONTRA** est quod dicitur in Psalm., *vovete et reddite domino Deo vestro.*

**RESPONDEO** dicendum quod, sicut dictum est, votum est promissio Deo facta. Alia autem ratione promittitur aliquid homini, et alia ratione Deo. Homini quidem promittimus aliquid propter eius utilitatem, cui utile est et quod ei aliquid exhibeamus, et quod eum de futura exhibitione prius certificemus. Sed promissionem Deo facimus non propter eius utilitatem, sed propter nostram. Unde Augustinus dicit, in praedicta epistola, *benignus exactor est, non egenus, et qui non crescat ex redditis, sed in se crescere faciat redditores.* Et sicut id quod damus Deo non est ei utile, sed nobis, quia *quod ei redditur reddenti additur,* ut Augustinus ibidem dicit; ita etiam promissio qua Deo aliquid vovemus, non cedit in eius utilitatem, qui a nobis certificari non indiget; sed ad utilitatem nostram, inquantum vovendo voluntatem nostram immobiliter firmamus ad id quod expedit facere. Et ideo expediens est vovere.

**AD PRIMUM** ergo dicendum quod sicut non posse peccare non diminuit libertatem, ita etiam necessitas firmatae voluntatis in bonum non diminuit libertatem, ut patet in Deo et in beatis. Et talis est necessitas voti, similitudinem quandam habens cum confirmatione beatorum. Unde Augustinus in eadem epistola dicit quod *felix necessitas est quae in meliora compellit.*

**AD SECUNDUM** dicendum quod quando periculum nascitur ex ipso facto, tunc illud factum non est expediens, puta quod aliquis per pontem ruinosum transeat fluvium. Sed si periculum immineat ex hoc quod homo deficit ab illo facto, non desinit propter hoc esse expediens, sicut expediens est ascendere equum, quamvis periculum immineat cadenti de equo. Alioquin oporteret ab omnibus bonis cessare quae per accidens ex aliquo eventu possunt esse periculosa. Unde dicitur Eccle. XI, *qui observat ventum non seminat, et qui considerat nubes nunquam metet.* Periculum autem voventi non imminet ex ipso voto, sed ex culpa hominis, qui voluntatem mutat transgrediens votum. Unde Augustinus dicit in eadem epistola, *non te vovisse poeniteat. Immo gaude iam tibi sic non licere quod cum tuo detrimento licuisset.*

wouldst have been hadst thou not vowed. For then thou wouldst have been less great, not less good: whereas now if thou breakest faith with God (which God forbid) thou art the more unhappy, as thou wouldst have been happier, hadst thou kept thy vow.* Therefore it is not expedient to take vows.

**OBJ. 3**: Further, the Apostle says (1 Cor 4:16): *Be ye followers of me, as I also am of Christ.* But we do not read that either Christ or the Apostles took any vows. Therefore it would seem inexpedient to take vows.

**ON THE CONTRARY**, It is written (Ps 75:12): *Vow ye and pay to the Lord your God.*

**I ANSWER THAT**, As stated above (AA. 1, 2), a vow is a promise made to God. Now one makes a promise to a man under one aspect, and to God under another. Because we promise something to a man for his own profit; since it profits him that we should be of service to him, and that we should at first assure him of the future fulfilment of that service: whereas we make promises to God not for His but for our own profit. Hence Augustine says (*Ep. cxxvii, ad Arment. et Paulin.*): *He is a kind and not a needy exactor, for he does not grow rich on our payments, but makes those who pay Him grow rich in Him.* And just as what we give God is useful not to Him but to us, since *what is given Him is added to the giver,* as Augustine says (*Ep. cxxvii, ad Arment. et Paulin.*), so also a promise whereby we vow something to God, does not conduce to His profit, nor does He need to be assured by us, but it conduces to our profit, insofar as by vowing we fix our wills immovably on that which it is expedient to do. Hence it is expedient to take vows.

**REPLY OBJ. 1**: Even as one's liberty is not lessened by one being unable to sin, so, too, the necessity resulting from a will firmly fixed to good does not lessen the liberty, as instanced in God and the blessed. Such is the necessity implied by a vow, bearing a certain resemblance to the confirmation of the blessed. Hence, Augustine says (*Ep. cxxvii, ad Arment. et Paulin.*) that *happy is the necessity that compels us to do the better things.*

**REPLY OBJ. 2**: When danger arises from the deed itself, this deed is not expedient, for instance that one cross a river by a tottering bridge: but if the danger arise through man's failure in the deed, the latter does not cease to be expedient: thus it is expedient to mount on horseback, though there be the danger of a fall from the horse: else it would behoove one to desist from all good things, that may become dangerous accidentally. Wherefore it is written (Eccl 11:4): *He that observeth the wind shall not sow, and he that considereth the clouds shall never reap.* Now a man incurs danger, not from the vow itself, but from his fault, when he changes his mind by breaking his vow. Hence, Augustine says (*Ep. cxxvii, ad Arment. et Paulin.*): *Repent not of thy vow: thou shouldst rather rejoice that thou canst no longer do what thou mightest lawfully have done to thy detriment.*

**AD TERTIUM** dicendum quod Christo secundum se non competebat vovere. Tum quia Deus erat. Tum etiam quia, inquantum homo, habebat firmatam voluntatem in bono, quasi comprehensor existens. Quamvis per quandam similitudinem ex persona eius dicatur in Psalm., secundum Glossam, *vota mea reddam in conspectu timentium eum*, loquitur autem pro corpore suo, quod est Ecclesia.

Apostoli autem intelliguntur vovisse pertinentia ad perfectionis statum quando Christum, *relictis omnibus, sunt secuti.*

**REPLY OBJ. 3**: It was incompetent for Christ, by His very nature, to take a vow, both because He was God, and because, as man, His will was firmly fixed on the good, since He was a comprehensor. By a kind of similitude, however, He is represented as saying (Ps 21:26): *I will pay my vows in the sight of them that fear Him*, when He is speaking of His body, which is the Church.

The apostles are understood to have vowed things pertaining to the state of perfection when *they left all things and followed Christ.*

# Article 5

*Whether a vow is an act of latria or religion?*

**AD QUINTUM SIC PROCEDITUR.** Videtur quod votum non sit actus latriae sive religionis. Omne enim opus virtutis cadit sub voto. Sed ad eandem virtutem pertinere videtur promittere aliquid et facere illud. Ergo votum pertinet ad quamlibet virtutem, et non specialiter ad religionem.

**PRAETEREA**, secundum Tullium, ad religionem pertinet *cultum et caeremoniam Deo offerre*. Sed ille qui vovet nondum aliquid Deo offert, sed solum promittit. Ergo votum non est actus religionis.

**PRAETEREA**, cultus religionis non debet exhiberi nisi Deo. Sed votum non solum fit Deo, sed etiam sanctis et praelatis, quibus religiosi profitentes obedientiam vovent. Ergo votum non est religionis actus.

**SED CONTRA** est quod dicitur Isaiae XIX, *colent eum in hostiis et muneribus, et vota vovebunt domino et solvent*. Sed colere Deum est proprie religionis sive latriae. Ergo votum est actus latriae sive religionis.

**RESPONDEO** dicendum quod, sicut supra dictum est, omne opus virtutis ad religionem seu latriam pertinet per modum imperii, secundum quod ad divinam reverentiam ordinatur, quod est proprius finis latriae. Ordinare autem alios actus in manifestum est autem ex praedictis quod votum est quaedam imperatas. Et ideo ipsa ordinatio actuum cuiuscumque virtutis in servitium Dei est proprius actus latriae.

Manifestum est autem ex praedictis quod votum est quaedam promissio Deo facta, et quod promissio nihil est aliud quam ordinatio quaedam eius quod promittitur in eum cui promittitur. Unde votum est ordinatio quaedam eorum quae quis vovet in divinum cultum seu obsequium. Et sic patet quod vovere proprie est actus latriae seu religionis.

**OBJECTION 1**: It would seem that a vow is not an act of latria or religion. Every act of virtue is matter for a vow. Now it would seem to pertain to the same virtue to promise a thing and to do it. Therefore a vow pertains to any virtue and not to religion especially.

**OBJ. 2**: Further, according to Tully (*De Invent.* ii, 53) it belongs to religion *to offer God worship and ceremonial rites*. But he who takes a vow does not yet offer something to God, but only promises it. Therefore, a vow is not an act of religion.

**OBJ. 3**: Further, religious worship should be offered to none but God. But a vow is made not only to God, but also to the saints and to one's superiors, to whom religious vow obedience when they make their profession. Therefore, a vow is not an act of religion.

**ON THE CONTRARY**, It is written (Isa 19:21): *(The Egyptians) shall worship Him with sacrifices and offerings and they shall make vows to the Lord, and perform them.* Now, the worship of God is properly the act of religion or latria. Therefore, a vow is an act of latria or religion.

**I ANSWER THAT**, As stated above (Q. 81, A. 1, ad 1), every act of virtue belongs to religion or latria by way of command, insofar as it is directed to the reverence of God which is the proper end of latria. Now the direction of other actions to their end belongs to the commanding virtue, not to those which are commanded. Therefore the direction of the acts of any virtue to the service of God is the proper act of latria.

Now, it is evident from what has been said above (AA. 1, 2) that a vow is a promise made to God, and that a promise is nothing else than a directing of the thing promised to the person to whom the promise is made. Hence a vow is a directing of the thing vowed to the worship or service of God. And thus it is clear that to take a vow is properly an act of latria or religion.

AD PRIMUM ergo dicendum quod illud quod cadit sub voto quandoque quidem est actus alterius virtutis, sicut ieiunare, continentiam servare; quandoque vero est actus religionis, sicut sacrificium offerre vel orare. Utrorumque tamen promissio Deo facta ad religionem pertinet, ratione iam dicta. Unde patet quod votorum quoddam pertinet ad religionem ratione solius promissionis Deo factae, quae est essentia voti, quandoque etiam ratione rei promissae, quae est voti materia.

AD SECUNDUM dicendum quod ille qui promittit, inquantum se obligat ad dandum, iam quodammodo dat, sicut dicitur fieri aliquid cum fit causa eius, quia effectus virtute continetur in causa. Et inde est quod non solum danti, sed etiam promittenti gratiae aguntur.

AD TERTIUM dicendum quod votum soli Deo fit, sed promissio potest etiam fieri homini, et ipsa promissio boni quae fit homini potest cadere sub voto, inquantum est quoddam opus virtuosum. Et per hunc modum intelligendum est votum quo quis vovet aliquid sanctis vel praelatis, ut ipsa promissio facta sanctis vel praelatis cadat sub voto materialiter, inquantum scilicet homo vovet Deo se impleturum quod sanctis vel praelatis promittit.

REPLY OBJ. 1: The matter of a vow is sometimes the act of another virtue, as, for instance, keeping the fast or observing continency; while sometimes it is an act of religion, as offering a sacrifice or praying. But promising either of them to God belongs to religion, for the reason given above. Hence it is evident that some vows belong to religion by reason only of the promise made to God, which is the essence of a vow, while others belong thereto by reason also of the thing promised, which is the matter of the vow.

REPLY OBJ. 2: He who promises something gives it already in as far as he binds himself to give it: even as a thing is said to be made when its cause is made, because the effect is contained virtually in its cause. This is why we thank not only a giver, but also one who promises to give.

REPLY OBJ. 3: A vow is made to God alone, whereas a promise may be made to a man also: and this very promise of good, which is made to a man, may be the matter of a vow, and insofar as it is a virtuous act. This is how we are to understand vows whereby we vow something to the saints or to one's superiors: so that the promise made to the saints or to one's superiors is the matter of the vow, insofar as one vows to God to fulfill what one has promised to the saints or one's superiors.

# Article 6

*Whether it is more praiseworthy and meritorious to do something in fulfilment of a vow, than without a vow?*

AD SEXTUM SIC PROCEDITUR. Videtur quod magis sit laudabile et meritorium facere aliquid sine voto quam cum voto. Dicit enim prosper, in II de vita Contempl., sic *abstinere vel ieiunare debemus ut non nos necessitati ieiunandi subdamus, ne iam non devoti, sed inviti rem voluntariam faciamus.* Sed ille qui vovet ieiunium subdit se necessitati ieiunandi. Ergo melius esset si ieiunaret sine voto.

PRAETEREA, apostolus dicit, II Cor. IX, *unusquisque prout destinavit in corde suo, non ex tristitia aut ex necessitate, hilarem enim datorem diligit Deus.* Sed quidam ea quae vovent ex tristitia faciunt, et hoc videtur procedere ex necessitate quam votum imponit, quia necessitas contristans est, ut dicitur V Metaphys. Ergo melius est aliquid facere sine voto quam cum voto.

PRAETEREA, votum necessarium est ad hoc quod firmetur voluntas hominis ad rem quam vovet, ut supra habitum est. Sed non magis potest firmari voluntas ad aliquid faciendum quam cum actu facit illud. Ergo non melius est facere aliquid cum voto quam sine voto.

SED CONTRA est quod super illud Psalm, *vovete et reddite,* dicit Glossa, *vovere voluntati consulitur.* Sed con-

OBJECTION 1: It would seem that it is more praiseworthy and meritorious to do a thing without a vow than in fulfilment of a vow. Prosper says (*De Vita Contempl.* ii): *We should abstain or fast without putting ourselves under the necessity of fasting, lest that which we are free to do be done without devotion and unwillingly.* Now he who vows to fast puts himself under the necessity of fasting. Therefore it would be better for him to fast without taking the vow.

OBJ. 2: Further, the Apostle says (2 Cor 9:7): *Everyone as he hath determined in his heart, not with sadness, or of necessity: for God loveth a cheerful giver.* Now some fulfill sorrowfully what they have vowed: and this seems to be due to the necessity arising from the vow, for necessity is a cause of sorrow according to *Metaph.* v. Therefore, it is better to do something without a vow, than in fulfilment of a vow.

OBJ. 3: Further, a vow is necessary for the purpose of fixing the will on that which is vowed, as stated above (A. 4). But the will cannot be more fixed on a thing than when it actually does that thing. Therefore it is no better to do a thing in fulfilment of a vow than without a vow.

ON THE CONTRARY, A gloss on the words of Ps. 75:12, *Vow ye and pay,* says: *Vows are counseled to the will.* But

silium non est nisi de meliori bono. Ergo melius est facere aliquod melius opus ex voto quam sine voto, quia qui facit sine voto, implet tantum unum consilium, scilicet de faciendo; qui autem facit cum voto, implet duo consilia, scilicet et vovendo et faciendo.

**RESPONDEO** dicendum quod triplici ratione facere idem opus cum voto est melius et magis meritorium quam facere sine voto. Primo quidem, quia vovere, sicut dictum est, est actus latriae, quae est praecipua inter virtutes morales. Nobilioris autem virtutis est opus melius et magis meritorium. Unde actus inferioris virtutis est melior et magis meritorius ex hoc quod imperatur a superiori virtute, cuius actus fit per imperium, sicut actus fidei vel spei melior est si imperetur a caritate. Et ideo actus aliarum virtutum moralium, puta ieiunare, quod est actus abstinentiae, et continere, quod est actus castitatis, sunt meliora et magis meritoria si fiant ex voto, quia sic iam pertinent ad divinum cultum, quasi quaedam Dei sacrificia. Unde Augustinus dicit, in libro de virginitate, quod *neque ipsa virginitas quia virginitas est, sed quia Deo dicata est, honoratur; quam fovet et servat continentia pietatis.*

Secundo, quia ille qui vovet aliquid et facit, plus se Deo subiicit quam ille qui solum facit. Subiicit enim se Deo non solum quantum ad actum sed etiam quantum ad potestatem, quia de cetero, non potest aliud facere, sicut plus daret homini qui daret ei arborem cum fructibus quam qui daret ei fructus tantum, ut dicit Anselmus, in libro de Similitud. Et inde est quod etiam promittentibus gratiae aguntur, ut dictum est.

Tertio, quia per votum immobiliter voluntas firmatur in bonum. Facere autem aliquid ex voluntate firmata in bonum pertinet ad perfectionem virtutis, ut patet per Philosophum, in II Ethic., sicut etiam peccare mente obstinata aggravat peccatum, et dicitur peccatum in spiritum sanctum, ut supra dictum est.

**AD PRIMUM** ergo dicendum quod auctoritas illa est intelligenda de necessitate coactionis, quae involuntarium causat et devotionem excludit. Unde signanter dicit, *ne iam non devoti, sed inviti rem voluntariam faciamus.* Necessitas autem voti est per immutabilitatem voluntatis, unde et voluntatem confirmat et devotionem auget. Et ideo ratio non sequitur.

**AD SECUNDUM** dicendum quod necessitas coactionis, inquantum est contraria voluntati, tristitiam causat, secundum philosophum. Necessitas autem voti in his qui sunt bene dispositi, inquantum voluntatem confirmat, non causat tristitiam, sed gaudium. Unde Augustinus dicit, in epistola ad Armentarium et Paulinam, *non te vovisse poeniteat, immo gaude iam tibi sic non licere quod cum tuo detrimento licuisset.* Si tamen ipsum opus,

a counsel is about none but a better good. Therefore it is better to do a deed in fulfilment of a vow than without a vow: since he that does it without a vow fulfils only one counsel, viz. the counsel to do it, whereas he that does it with a vow, fulfils two counsels, viz. the counsel to vow and the counsel to do it.

**I ANSWER THAT,** For three reasons it is better and more meritorious to do one and the same deed with a vow than without. First, because to vow, as stated above (A. 5) is an act of religion which is the chief of the moral virtues. Now the more excellent the virtue the better and more meritorious the deed. Wherefore the act of an inferior virtue is the better and more meritorious for being commanded by a superior virtue, whose act it becomes through being commanded by it, just as the act of faith or hope is better if it be commanded by charity. Hence the works of the other moral virtues (for instance, fasting, which is an act of abstinence; and being continent, which is an act of chastity) are better and more meritorious, if they be done in fulfilment of a vow, since thus they belong to the divine worship, being like sacrifices to God. Wherefore Augustine says (*De Virg.* viii) that *not even is virginity honorable as such, but only when it is consecrated to God, and cherished by godly continence.*

Second, because he that vows something and does it, subjects himself to God more than he that only does it; for he subjects himself to God not only as to the act, but also as to the power, since in future he cannot do something else. Even so he gives more who gives the tree with its fruit, than he that gives the fruit only, as Anselm observes (*De Simil.* viii). For this reason, we thank even those who promise, as stated above (A. 5, ad 2).

Third, because a vow fixes the will on the good immovably and to do anything of a will that is fixed on the good belongs to the perfection of virtue, according to the Philosopher (*Ethic.* ii, 4), just as to sin with an obstinate mind aggravates the sin, and is called a sin against the Holy Spirit, as stated above (Q. 14, A. 2).

**REPLY OBJ. 1:** The passage quoted should be understood as referring to necessity of coercion which causes an act to be involuntary and excludes devotion. Hence he says pointedly: *Lest that which we are free to do be done without devotion and unwillingly.* On the other hand the necessity resulting from a vow is caused by the immobility of the will, wherefore it strengthens the will and increases devotion. Hence the argument does not conclude.

**REPLY OBJ. 2:** According to the Philosopher, necessity of coercion, insofar as it is opposed to the will, causes sorrow. But the necessity resulting from a vow, in those who are well disposed, insofar as it strengthens the will, causes not sorrow but joy. Hence Augustine says (*Ep. ad Arment. et Paulin.* cxxcii): *Repent not of thy vow: thou shouldst rather rejoice that thou canst no longer do what thou mightest lawfully have done to thy detriment.* If, however, the very

secundum se consideratum, triste et involuntarium redderetur post votum, dum tamen remaneat voluntas votum implendi, adhuc est magis meritorium quam si fieret sine voto, quia impletio voti est actus religionis, quae est potior virtus quam abstinentia, cuius actus est ieiunare.

**AD TERTIUM** dicendum quod ille qui facit aliquid sine voto habet immobilem voluntatem respectu illius operis singularis quod facit, et tunc quando facit, non autem manet voluntas eius omnino firmata in futurum, sicut voventis, qui suam voluntatem obligavit ad aliquid faciendum et antequam faceret illud singulare opus, et fortasse ad pluries faciendum.

deed, considered in itself, were to become disagreeable and involuntary after one has taken the vow, the will to fulfill it remaining withal, it is still more meritorious than if it were done without the vow, since the fulfilment of a vow is an act of religion which is a greater virtue than abstinence, of which fasting is an act.

**REPLY OBJ. 3**: He who does something without having vowed it has an immovable will as regards the individual deed which he does and at the time when he does it; but his will does not remain altogether fixed for the time to come, as does the will of one who makes a vow: for the latter has bound his will to do something, both before he did that particular deed, and perchance to do it many times.

# Article 7

*Whether a vow is solemnized by the reception of holy orders, and by the profession of a certain rule?*

**AD SEPTIMUM SIC PROCEDITUR**. Videtur quod votum non solemnizetur per susceptionem sacri ordinis, et per professionem ad certam regulam. Votum enim, ut dictum est, promissio Deo facta est. Ea vero quae exterius aguntur ad solemnitatem pertinentia non videntur ordinari ad Deum, sed ad homines. Ergo per accidens se habent ad votum. Non ergo solemnitas talis est propria conditio voti.

**PRAETEREA**, illud quod pertinet ad conditionem alicuius rei, videtur posse competere omnibus illis in quibus res illa invenitur. Sed multa possunt sub voto cadere quae non pertinent neque ad sacrum ordinem, neque pertinent ad aliquam certam regulam, sicut cum quis vovet peregrinationem, aut aliquid huiusmodi. Ergo solemnitas quae fit in susceptione sacri ordinis vel in promissione certae regulae, non pertinet ad conditionem voti.

**PRAETEREA**, votum solemne idem videtur esse quod votum publicum. Sed multa alia vota possunt fieri in publico quam votum quod emittitur in susceptione sacri ordinis vel professione certae regulae, et huiusmodi etiam vota possunt fieri in occulto. Ergo non solum huiusmodi vota sunt solemnia.

**SED CONTRA** est quod solum huiusmodi vota impediunt matrimonium contrahendum et dirimunt iam contractum; quod est effectus voti solemnis, ut infra dicetur in tertia huius operis parte.

**RESPONDEO** dicendum quod unicuique rei solemnitas adhibetur secundum illius rei conditionem, sicut alia est solemnitas novae militiae, scilicet in quodam apparatu equorum et armorum et concursu militum; et alia solemnitas nuptiarum, quae consistit in apparatu sponsi et sponsae et conventu propinquorum. Votum autem est promissio Deo facta. Unde solemnitas voti attenditur

**OBJECTION 1**: It would seem that a vow is not solemnized by the reception of holy orders and by the profession of a certain rule. As stated above (A. 1), a vow is a promise made to God. Now external actions pertaining to solemnity seem to be directed, not to God, but to men. Therefore they are related to vows accidentally: and consequently a solemnization of this kind is not a proper circumstance of a vow.

**OBJ. 2**: Further, whatever belongs to the condition of a thing, would seem to be applicable to all in which that thing is found. Now many things may be the subject of a vow, which have no connection either with holy orders, or to any particular rule: as when a man vows a pilgrimage, or something of the kind. Therefore the solemnization that takes place in the reception of holy orders or in the profession of a certain rule does not belong to the condition of a vow.

**OBJ. 3**: Further, a solemn vow seems to be the same as a public vow. Now many other vows may be made in public besides that which is pronounced in receiving holy orders or in professing a certain rule; which latter, moreover, may be made in private. Therefore not only these vows are solemn.

**ON THE CONTRARY**, These vows alone are an impediment to the contract of marriage, and annul marriage if it be contracted, which is the effect of a solemn vow, as we shall state further on in the Third Part of this work.

**I ANSWER THAT**, The manner in which a thing is solemnized depends on its nature (*conditio*): thus when a man takes up arms he solemnizes the fact in one way, namely, with a certain display of horses and arms and a concourse of soldiers, while a marriage is solemnized in another way, namely, the array of the bridegroom and bride and the gathering of their kindred. Now a vow is

secundum aliquid spirituale, quod ad Deum pertineat, idest secundum aliquam spiritualem benedictionem vel consecrationem, quae ex institutione apostolorum adhibetur in professione certae regulae, secundo gradu post sacri ordinis susceptionem, ut Dionysius dicit, VI cap. Eccles. Hier. Et huius ratio est quia solemnitates non consueverunt adhiberi nisi quando aliquis totaliter mancipatur alicui rei, non enim solemnitas nuptialis adhibetur nisi in celebratione matrimonii, quando uterque coniugum sui corporis potestatem alteri tradit. Et similiter voti solemnitas adhibetur quando aliquis per susceptionem sacri ordinis divino ministerio applicatur; et in professione certae regulae, quando per abrenuntiationem saeculi et propriae voluntatis aliquis statum perfectionis assumit.

AD PRIMUM ergo dicendum quod huiusmodi solemnitas pertinet non solum ad homines, sed ad Deum, inquantum habet aliquam spiritualem consecrationem seu benedictionem, cuius Deus est auctor, etsi homo sit minister, secundum illud Num. VI, *invocabunt nomen meum super filios Israel, et ego benedicam eis.* Et ideo votum solemne habet fortiorem obligationem apud Deum quam votum simplex; et gravius peccat qui illud transgreditur. Quod autem dicitur quod *votum simplex non minus obligat apud Deum quam solemne*, intelligendum est quantum ad hoc quod utriusque transgressor peccat mortaliter.

AD SECUNDUM dicendum quod particularibus actibus non consuevit solemnitas adhiberi, sed assumptioni novi status, ut dictum est. Et ideo cum quis vovet aliqua particularia opera, sicut aliquam peregrinationem vel aliquod speciale ieiunium, tali voto non congruit solemnitas, sed solum voto quo aliquis totaliter se subiicit divino ministerio seu famulatui; in quo tamen voto, quasi universali, multa particularia opera comprehenduntur.

AD TERTIUM dicendum quod vota ex hoc quod fiunt in publico possunt habere quandam solemnitatem humanam, non autem solemnitatem spiritualem et divinam, sicut habent vota praemissa, etiam si coram paucis fiant. Unde aliud est votum esse publicum, et aliud esse solemne.

a promise made to God: wherefore, the solemnization of a vow consists in something spiritual pertaining to God; i.e., in some spiritual blessing or consecration which, in accordance with the institution of the apostles, is given when a man makes profession of observing a certain rule, in the second degree after the reception of holy orders, as Dionysius states (*Eccl. Hier.* vi). The reason of this is that solemnization is not wont to be employed, save when a man gives himself up entirely to some particular thing. For the nuptial solemnization takes place only when the marriage is celebrated, and when the bride and bridegroom mutually deliver the power over their bodies to one another. In like manner a vow is solemnized when a man devotes himself to the divine ministry by receiving holy orders, or embraces the state of perfection by renouncing the world and his own will by the profession of a certain rule.

REPLY OBJ. 1: This kind of solemnization regards not only men but also God insofar as it is accompanied by a spiritual consecration or blessing, of which God is the author, though man is the minister, according to Num. 6:27, *They shall invoke My name upon the children of Israel, and I will bless them.* Hence a solemn vow is more binding with God than a simple vow, and he who breaks a solemn vow sins more grievously. When it is said that *a simple vow is no less binding than a solemn vow*, this refers to the fact that the transgressor of either commits a mortal sin.

REPLY OBJ. 2: It is not customary to solemnize particular acts, but the embracing of a new state, as we have said above. Hence when a man vows particular deeds, such as a pilgrimage, or some special fast, such a vow is not competent to be solemnized, but only such as the vow whereby a man entirely devotes himself to the divine ministry or service: and yet many particular works are included under this vow as under a universal.

REPLY OBJ. 3: Through being pronounced in public vows may have a certain human solemnity, but not a spiritual and divine solemnity, as the aforesaid vows have, even when they are pronounced before a few persons. Hence the publicity of a vow differs from its solemnization.

# Article 8

*Whether those who are subject to another's power are hindered from taking vows?*

AD OCTAVUM SIC PROCEDITUR. Videtur quod illi qui sunt alterius potestati subiecti non impediantur a vovendo. Minus enim vinculum superatur a maiori. Sed obligatio qua quis subiicitur homini est minus vinculum quam votum, per quod aliquis obligatur Deo. Ergo illi

OBJECTION 1: It would seem that those who are subject to another's power are not hindered from taking vows. The lesser bond is surpassed by the greater. Now the obligation of one man subject to another is a lesser bond than a vow whereby one is under an obligation to God. Therefore those

qui sunt alienae potestati subiecti non impediuntur a vovendo.

**PRAETEREA,** filii sunt in potestate patris. Sed filii possunt profiteri in aliqua religione etiam sine voluntate parentum. Ergo non impeditur aliquis a vovendo per hoc quod est subiectus potestati alterius.

**PRAETEREA,** maius est facere quam promittere. Sed religiosi qui sunt sub potestate praelatorum possunt aliqua facere sine licentia suorum praelatorum, puta dicere aliquos Psalmos, vel facere aliquas abstinentias. Ergo videtur quod multo magis possunt huiusmodi vovendo Deo promittere.

**PRAETEREA,** quicumque facit quod de iure facere non potest, peccat. Sed subditi non peccant vovendo, quia hoc nunquam invenitur prohibitum. Ergo videtur quod de iure possunt vovere.

**SED CONTRA** est quod Num. XXX mandatur quod, *si mulier in domo patris sui, et adhuc in puellari aetate, aliquid voverit,* non tenetur rea voti nisi pater eius consenserit. Et idem dicit de muliere habente virum. Ergo, pari ratione, nec aliae personae alterius potestati subiectae possunt se voto obligare.

**RESPONDEO** dicendum quod, sicut supra dictum est, votum est promissio quaedam Deo facta. Nullus autem potest per promissionem se firmiter obligare ad id quod est in potestate alterius, sed solum ad id quod est omnino in sua potestate. Quicumque autem est subiectus alicui, quantum ad id in quo est subiectus, non est suae potestatis facere quod vult, sed dependet ex voluntate alterius. Et ideo non potest se per votum firmiter obligare, in his in quibus alteri subiicitur, sine consensu sui superioris.

**AD PRIMUM** ergo dicendum quod sub promissione Deo facta non cadit nisi quod est virtuosum, ut supra dictum est. Est autem contra virtutem ut id quod est alterius homo offerat Deo, ut supra dictum est. Et ideo non potest omnino salvari ratio voti, cum quis in potestate constitutus vovet id quod est in potestate alterius, nisi sub conditione si ille ad cuius potestatem pertinet non contradicat.

**AD SECUNDUM** dicendum quod ex quo homo venit ad annos pubertatis, si sit liberae conditionis, est suae potestatis quantum ad ea quae pertinent ad suam personam, puta quod obliget se religioni per votum, vel quod matrimonium contrahat. Non autem est suae potestatis quantum ad dispensationem domesticam. Unde circa hoc non potest aliquid vovere quod sit ratum, sine consensu patris.

Servus autem, quia est in potestate domini etiam quantum ad personales operationes, non potest se voto obligare ad religionem, per quam ab obsequio domini sui abstraheretur.

who are subject to another's power are not hindered from taking vows.

**OBJ. 2:** Further, children are under their parents' power. Yet children may make religious profession even without the consent of their parents. Therefore one is not hindered from taking vows, through being subject to another's power.

**OBJ. 3:** Further, to do is more than to promise. But religious who are under the power of their superiors can do certain things such as to say some psalms, or abstain from certain things. Much more therefore seemingly can they promise such things to God by means of vows.

**OBJ. 4:** Further, whoever does what he cannot do lawfully sins. But subjects do not sin by taking vows, since nowhere do we find this forbidden. Therefore it would seem that they can lawfully take vows.

**ON THE CONTRARY,** It is commanded (Num 30:4–6) that *if a woman vow any thing... being in her father's house, and yet but a girl in age,* she is not bound by the vow, unless her father consent: and the same is said there (Num 30:7–9) of the woman that has a husband. Therefore in like manner other persons that are subject to another's power cannot bind themselves by vow.

**I ANSWER THAT,** As stated above (A. 1), a vow is a promise made to God. Now no man can firmly bind himself by a promise to do what is in another's power, but only to that which is entirely in his own power. Now whoever is subject to another, as to the matter wherein he is subject to him, it does not lie in his power to do as he will, but it depends on the will of the other. And therefore without the consent of his superior he cannot bind himself firmly by a vow in those matters wherein he is subject to another.

**REPLY OBJ. 1:** Nothing but what is virtuous can be the subject of a promise made to God, as stated above (A. 2). Now it is contrary to virtue for a man to offer to God that which belongs to another, as stated above (Q. 86, A. 3). Hence the conditions necessary for a vow are not altogether ensured, when a man who is under another's power vows that which is in that other's power, except under the condition that he whose power it concerns does not gainsay it.

**REPLY OBJ. 2:** As soon as a man comes of age, if he be a freeman he is in his own power in all matters concerning his person, for instance with regard to binding himself by vow to enter religion, or with regard to contracting marriage. But he is not in his own power as regards the arrangements of the household, so that in these matters he cannot vow anything that shall be valid without the consent of his father.

A slave, through being in his master's power, even as regards his personal deeds, cannot bind himself by vow to enter religion, since this would withdraw him from his master's service.

**AD TERTIUM** dicendum quod religiosus subditus est praelato quantum ad suas operationes secundum professionem regulae. Et ideo etiam si aliquis ad horam aliquid facere possit quando ad alia non occupatur a praelato, quia tamen nullum tempus est exceptum in quo praelatus non possit eum circa aliquid occupare, nullum votum religiosi est firmum nisi sit de consensu praelati. Sicut nec votum puellae existentis in domo, nisi sit de consensu patris, nec uxoris, nisi de consensu viri.

**AD QUARTUM** dicendum quod licet votum eorum qui sunt alterius potestati subiecti non sit firmum sine consensu eorum quibus subiiciuntur, non tamen peccant vovendo, quia in eorum voto intelligitur debita conditio, scilicet si suis superioribus placuerit, vel non renitantur.

**REPLY OBJ. 3**: A religious is subject to his superior as to his actions connected with his profession of his rule. Wherefore even though one may be able to do something now and then, when one is not being occupied with other things by one's superior, yet since there is no time when his superior cannot occupy him with something, no vow of a religious stands without the consent of his superior, as neither does the vow of a girl while in (her father's) house without his consent; nor of a wife, without the consent of her husband.

**REPLY OBJ. 4**: Although the vow of one who is subject to another's power does not stand without the consent of the one to whom he is subject, he does not sin by vowing; because his vow is understood to contain the requisite condition, providing, namely, that his superior approve or do not gainsay it.

# Article 9

*Whether children can bind themselves by vow to enter religion?*

**AD NONUM SIC PROCEDITUR.** Videtur quod pueri non possint voto se obligare ad religionis ingressum. Cum enim ad votum requiratur animi deliberatio, non competit vovere nisi illis qui habent usum rationis. Sed hoc deficit in pueris, sicut et in amentibus vel furiosis. Sicut ergo amentes et furiosi non possunt se ad aliquid voto adstringere, ita etiam nec pueri, ut videtur, possunt se voto obligare religioni.

**PRAETEREA**, illud quod rite potest ab aliquo fieri, non potest ab alio irritari. Sed votum religionis a puero vel puella factum ante annos pubertatis potest a parentibus revocari, vel a tutore, ut habetur XX, qu. II, cap. puella. Ergo videtur quod puer vel puella, ante quatuordecim annos, non possit rite vovere.

**PRAETEREA**, religionem intrantibus annus probationis conceditur, secundum regulam beati Benedicti et secundum statutum Innocentii IV, ad hoc quod probatio obligationem voti praecedat. Ergo illicitum videtur esse quod pueri voto obligentur ad religionem ante probationis annum.

**SED CONTRA**, illud quod non est rite factum non est validum, etiam si a nullo revocetur. Sed votum puellae, etiam ante annos pubertatis emissum, validum est si infra annum a parentibus non revocetur, ut habetur XX, qu. II, cap. puella. Ergo licite et rite possunt pueri voto obligari ad religionem, etiam ante annos pubertatis.

**RESPONDEO** dicendum quod, sicut ex praedictis patet, duplex est votum, scilicet simplex, et solemne. Et quia solemnitas voti in quadam spirituali benedictione et consecratione consistit, ut dictum est, quae fit

**OBJECTION 1**: It would seem that children cannot bind themselves by vow to enter religion. Since a vow requires deliberation of the mind, it is fitting that those alone should vow who have the use of reason. But this is lacking in children just as in imbeciles and madmen. Therefore just as imbeciles and madmen cannot bind themselves to anything by vow, so neither, seemingly, can children bind themselves by vow to enter religion.

**OBJ. 2**: Further, that which can be validly done by one cannot be annulled by another. Now a vow to enter religion made by a boy or girl before the age of puberty can be revoked by the parents or guardian (20, qu. ii, cap. *Puella*). Therefore it seems that a boy or girl cannot validly make a vow before the age of fourteen.

**OBJ. 3**: Further, according to the rule of Blessed Benedict and a statute of Innocent IV, a year's probation is granted to those who enter religion, so that probation may precede the obligation of the vow. Therefore it seems unlawful, before the year of probation, for children to be bound by vow to enter religion.

**ON THE CONTRARY**, That which is not done aright is invalid without being annulled by anyone. But the vow pronounced by a maiden, even before attaining the age of puberty, is valid, unless it be annulled by her parents within a year (20, qu. ii, cap. *Puella*). Therefore even before attaining to puberty children can lawfully and validly be bound by a vow to enter religion.

**I ANSWER THAT**, As may be gathered from what has been said above (A. 7), vows are of two kinds, simple and solemn. And since, as stated in the same article, the solemnization of a vow consists in a spiritual blessing and

per ministerium Ecclesiae; ideo solemnizatio voti sub dispensatione Ecclesiae cadit. Votum autem simplex efficaciam habet ex deliberatione animi, qua quis se obligare intendit. Quod autem talis obligatio robur non habeat, dupliciter potest contingere. Uno quidem modo, propter defectum rationis, sicut patet in furiosis et amentibus, qui se voto non possunt obligare ad aliquid, dum sunt in furia vel amentia. Alio modo, quia ille qui vovet est alterius potestati subiectus, ut supra dictum est. Et ista duo concurrunt in pueris ante annos pubertatis, quia et patiuntur rationis defectum, ut in pluribus; et sunt naturaliter sub cura parentum, vel tutorum, qui sunt eis loco parentum. Et ideo eorum vota ex duplici causa robur non habent. Contingit tamen, propter naturae dispositionem, quae legibus humanis non subditur, in aliquibus, licet paucis, accelerari rationis usum, qui ob hoc dicuntur *doli capaces*. Nec tamen propter hoc in aliquo eximuntur a cura parentum, quae subiacet legi humanae respicienti ad id quod frequentius accidit.

Est ergo dicendum quod si puer vel puella, ante pubertatis annos, nondum habeat usum rationis, nullo modo potest se ad aliquid voto obligare. Si vero ante annos pubertatis attigerit usum rationis, potest quidem, quantum in ipso est, se obligare, sed votum eius potest irritari per parentes, quorum curae remanet adhuc subiectus.

Quantumcumque tamen sit doli capax, ante annos pubertatis non potest obligari voto solemni religionis, propter Ecclesiae statutum, quod respicit id quod in pluribus accidit. Post annos autem pubertatis, possunt iam se voto religionis obligare, vel simplici vel solemni, absque voluntate parentum.

**AD PRIMUM** ergo dicendum quod ratio illa procedit de pueris qui nondum attigerunt usum rationis, quorum vota sunt invalida, ut dictum est.

**AD SECUNDUM** dicendum quod vota eorum qui sunt in potestate aliorum habent conditionem implicitam, scilicet si non revocentur a superiori, ex qua licita redduntur, et valida si conditio extat, ut dictum est.

**AD TERTIUM** dicendum quod ratio illa procedit de voto solemni quod fit per professionem.

consecration bestowed through the ministry of the Church, it follows that it comes under the Church's dispensation. Now a simple vow takes its efficacy from the deliberation of the mind, whereby one intends to put oneself under an obligation. That such an obligation be of no force may happen in two ways. First, through defect of reason, as in madmen and imbeciles, who cannot bind themselves by vow so long as they remain in a state of madness or imbecility. Second, through the maker of a vow being subject to another's power, as stated above (A. 8). Now these two circumstances concur in children before the age of puberty, because in most instances they are lacking in reason, and besides are naturally under the care of their parents, or guardians in place of their parents: wherefore in both events their vows are without force. It happens, however, through a natural disposition which is not subject to human laws, that the use of reason is accelerated in some, albeit few, who on this account are said to be *capable of guile*: and yet they are not, for this reason, exempt in any way from the care of their parents; for this care is subject to human law, which takes into account that which is of most frequent occurrence.

Accordingly we must say that boys or girls who have not reached the years of puberty and have not attained the use of reason can nowise bind themselves to anything by vow. If, however, they attain the use of reason, before reaching the years of puberty, they can for their own part, bind themselves by vow; but their vows can be annulled by their parents, under whose care they are still subject.

Yet no matter how much they be capable of guile before the years of puberty, they cannot be bound by a solemn religious vow, on account of the Church's decree which considers the majority of cases. But after the years of puberty have been reached, they can bind themselves by religious vows, simple or solemn, without the consent of their parents.

**REPLY OBJ. 1:** This argument avails in the case of children who have not yet reached the use of reason: for their vows then are invalid, as stated above.

**REPLY OBJ. 2:** The vows of persons subject to another's power contain an implied condition, namely, that they be not annulled by the superior. This condition renders them licit and valid if it be fulfilled, as stated above.

**REPLY OBJ. 3:** This argument avails in the case of solemn vows which are taken in profession.

# Article 10

*Whether vows admit of dispensation?*

**AD DECIMUM SIC PROCEDITUR.** Videtur quod in voto dispensari non possit. Minus enim est commutari votum quam in eo dispensari. Sed votum non potest commutari, dicitur enim Levit. XXVII, *animal quod immolari potest domino, si quis voverit, sanctum erit, et mutari non poterit, nec melius malo nec peius bono.* Ergo multo minus potest dispensari in voto.

**PRAETEREA,** in his quae sunt de lege naturae et in praeceptis divinis non potest per hominem dispensari, et praecipue in praeceptis primae tabulae, quae ordinantur directe ad dilectionem Dei, quae est ultimus praeceptorum finis. Sed implere votum est de lege naturae; et est etiam praeceptum legis divinae, ut ex supra dictis patet; et pertinet ad praecepta primae tabulae, cum sit actus latriae. Ergo in voto dispensari non potest.

**PRAETEREA,** obligatio voti fundatur super fidelitatem quam homo debet Deo, ut dictum est. Sed in hac nullus potest dispensare. Ergo nec in voto.

**SED CONTRA,** maioris firmitatis esse videtur quod procedit ex communi voluntate quam quod procedit ex singulari voluntate alicuius personae. Sed in lege, quae habet robur ex communi voluntate, potest per hominem dispensari. Ergo videtur quod etiam in voto per hominem dispensari possit.

**RESPONDEO** dicendum quod dispensatio voti intelligenda est ad modum dispensationis quae fit in observantia alicuius legis. Quia, ut supra dictum est, lex ponitur respiciendo ad id quod est ut in pluribus bonum, sed quia contingit huiusmodi in aliquo casu non esse bonum, oportuit per aliquem determinari in illo particulari casu legem non esse servandam. Et hoc proprie est dispensare in lege, nam dispensatio videtur importare commensuratam quandam distributionem vel applicationem communis alicuius ad ea quae sub ipso continentur, per quem modum dicitur aliquis dispensare cibum familiae.

Similiter autem ille qui vovet quodammodo sibi statuit legem, obligans se ad aliquid quod est secundum se et in pluribus bonum. Potest tamen contingere quod in aliquo casu sit vel simpliciter malum, vel inutile, vel maioris boni impeditivum, quod est contra rationem eius quod cadit sub voto, ut ex praedictis patet. Et ideo necesse est quod determinetur in tali casu votum non esse servandum. Et si quidem absolute determinetur aliquod votum non esse servandum, dicitur esse *dispensatio* voti. Si autem pro hoc quod servandum erat aliquid aliud imponatur, dicitur *commutatio* voti. Unde minus

**OBJECTION 1**: It would seem that vows are not subject to dispensation. It is less to have a vow commuted than to be dispensed from keeping it. But a vow cannot be commuted, according to Lev. 27:9, 10, *A beast that may be sacrificed to the Lord, if anyone shall vow, shall be holy, and cannot be changed, neither a better for a worse, nor a worse for a better.* Much less, therefore, do vows admit of dispensation.

**OBJ. 2**: Further, no man can grant a dispensation in matters concerning the natural law and in the Divine precepts, especially those of the First Table, since these aim directly at the love of God, which is the last end of the precepts. Now the fulfilment of a vow is a matter of the natural law, and is commanded by the Divine law, as shown above (A. 3), and belongs to the precepts of the First Table since it is an act of religion. Therefore vows do not admit of dispensation.

**OBJ. 3**: Further, the obligation of a vow is based on the fidelity which a man owes to God, as stated above (A. 3). But no man can dispense in such a matter as this. Neither, therefore, can any one grant a dispensation from a vow.

**ON THE CONTRARY**, That which proceeds from the common will of many has apparently greater stability than that which proceeds from the individual will of some one person. Now the law which derives its force from the common will admits of dispensation by a man. Therefore it seems that vows also admit of dispensation by a man.

**I ANSWER THAT**, The dispensation from a vow is to be taken in the same sense as a dispensation given in the observance of a law because, as stated above (I-II, Q. 96, A. 6; Q. 97, A. 4), a law is made with an eye to that which is good in the majority of instances. But since in certain cases this is not good, there is need for someone to decide that in that particular case the law is not to be observed. This is properly speaking to dispense in the law: for a dispensation would seem to denote a commensurate distribution or application of some common thing to those that are contained under it, in the same way as a person is said to dispense food to a household.

In like manner a person who takes a vow makes a law for himself as it were, and binds himself to do something which in itself and in the majority of cases is a good. But it may happen that in some particular case this is simply evil, or useless, or a hindrance to a greater good: and this is essentially contrary to that which is the matter of a vow, as is clear from what has been said above (A. 2). Therefore it is necessary, in such a case, to decide that the vow is not to be observed. And if it be decided absolutely that a particular vow is not to be observed, this is called a *dispensation* from that vow; but if some other obligation be imposed in lieu

est votum commutare quam in voto dispensare. Utrumque tamen in potestate Ecclesiae consistit.

**Ad primum** ergo dicendum quod animal quod immolari poterat, ex hoc ipso quod vovebatur, sanctum reputabatur, quasi divino cultui mancipatum, et haec erat ratio quare non poterat commutari; sicut nec modo posset aliquis rem quam vovit, iam consecratam, puta calicem vel domum, commutare in melius vel in peius. Animal autem quod non poterat sanctificari quia non erat immolatitium, redimi poterat et debebat, sicut ibidem lex dicit. Et ita etiam nunc commutari possunt vota si consecratio non interveniat.

**Ad secundum** dicendum quod sicut ex iure naturali et praecepto divino tenetur homo implere votum, ita etiam tenetur ex eisdem obedire superiorum legi vel mandato. Et tamen cum dispensatur in aliqua lege humana, non fit ut legi humanae non obediatur, quod est contra legem naturae et mandatum divinum, sed fit ut hoc quod erat lex, non sit lex in hoc casu. Ita etiam auctoritate superioris dispensantis fit ut hoc quod continebatur sub voto, non contineatur, inquantum determinatur in hoc casu hoc non esse congruam materiam voti. Et ideo cum praelatus Ecclesiae dispensat in voto, non dispensat in praecepto iuris naturalis vel divini, sed determinat id quod cadebat sub obligatione deliberationis humanae, quae non potuit omnia circumspicere.

**Ad tertium** dicendum quod ad fidelitatem Deo debitam non pertinet quod homo faciat id quod ad vovendum est malum, vel inutile, vel maioris boni impeditivum, ad quod tendit voti dispensatio. Et ideo dispensatio voti non est contra fidelitatem Deo debitam.

of that which was to have been observed, the vow is said to be *commuted*. Hence it is less to commute a vow than to dispense from a vow: both, however, are in the power of the Church.

**Reply Obj. 1**: An animal that could be lawfully sacrificed was deemed holy from the very moment that it was the subject of a vow, being, as it were, dedicated to the worship of God: and for this reason it could not be changed: even so neither may one now exchange for something better, or worse, that which one has vowed, if it be already consecrated, e.g., a chalice or a house. On the other hand, an animal that could not be sacrificed, through not being the lawful matter of a sacrifice, could and had to be bought back, as the law requires. Even so, vows can be commuted now, if no consecration has intervened.

**Reply Obj. 2**: Even as man is bound by natural law and Divine precept to fulfill his vow, so, too, is he bound under the same heads to obey the law or commands of his superiors. And yet when he is dispensed from keeping a human law, this does not involve disobedience to that human law, for this would be contrary to the natural law and the Divine command, but it amounts to this—that what was law is not law in this particular case. Even so, when a superior grants a dispensation, that which was contained under a vow is by his authority no longer so contained, insofar as he decides that in this case such and such a thing is not fitting matter for a vow. Consequently when an ecclesiastical superior dispenses someone from a vow, he does not dispense him from keeping a precept of the natural or of the Divine law, but he pronounces a decision on a matter to which a man had bound himself of his own accord, and of which he was unable to consider every circumstance.

**Reply Obj. 3**: The fidelity we owe to God does not require that we fulfill that which it would be wrong or useless to vow, or which would be an obstacle to the greater good whereunto the dispensation from that vow would conduce. Hence the dispensation from a vow is not contrary to the fidelity due to God.

# Article 11

*Whether it is possible to be dispensed from a solemn vow of continency?*

**Ad undecimum sic proceditur**. Videtur quod in voto solemni continentiae possit fieri dispensatio. Una enim ratio dispensandi in voto est si sit impeditivum melioris boni, sicut dictum est. Sed votum continentiae, etiam si sit solemne, potest esse impeditivum melioris boni, nam *bonum commune est divinius quam bonum unius*; potest autem per continentiam alicuius impediri bonum totius multitudinis, puta si quando per

**Objection 1**: It would seem that it is possible to be dispensed from a solemn vow of continency. As stated above, one reason for granting a dispensation from a vow is if it be an obstacle to a greater good. But a vow of continency, even though it be solemn, may be an obstacle to a greater good, since *the common good is more God-like than the good of an individual*. Now one man's continency may be an obstacle to the good of the whole community,

contractum matrimonii aliquarum personarum quae continentiam voverunt, posset pax patriae procurari. Ergo videtur quod in solemni voto continentiae possit dispensari.

PRAETEREA, latria est nobilior virtus quam castitas. Sed si quis voveat aliquem actum latriae, puta offerre Deo sacrificium, potest in illo voto dispensari. Ergo multo magis potest dispensari in voto continentiae, quod est de actu castitatis.

PRAETEREA, sicut votum abstinentiae observatum potest vergere in periculum personae, ita etiam observatio voti continentiae. Sed in voto abstinentiae, si vergat in corporale periculum voventis, potest fieri dispensatio. Ergo etiam, pari ratione, in voto continentiae potest dispensari.

PRAETEREA, sicut sub professione religionis, ex qua votum solemnizatur, continetur votum continentiae, ita etiam et votum paupertatis et obedientiae. Sed in voto paupertatis et obedientiae potest dispensari, sicut patet in illis qui post professionem ad episcopatum assumuntur. Ergo videtur quod in solemni voto continentiae possit dispensari.

SED CONTRA est quod dicitur Eccli. XXVI, *omnis ponderatio non est digna animae continentis.*

PRAETEREA, extra, de statu Monach., in fine illius Decretalis, *Cum ad monasterium*, dicitur, abdicatio proprietatis, *sicut etiam custodia castitatis, adeo est annexa regulae monachali ut contra eam nec summus pontifex possit indulgere.*

RESPONDEO dicendum quod in solemni voto continentiae tria possunt considerari, primo quidem, materia voti, scilicet ipsa continentia; secundo, perpetuitas voti, cum scilicet aliquis voto se adstringit ad perpetuam observantiam continentiae; tertio, ipsa solemnitas voti. Dicunt ergo quidam quod votum solemne est indispensabile ratione ipsius continentiae, quae non recipit condignam recompensationem, ut patet ex auctoritate inducta. Cuius rationem quidam assignant quia per continentiam homo triumphat de domestico inimico, vel quia per continentiam homo perfecte conformatur Christo, secundum puritatem animae et corporis. Sed hoc non videtur efficaciter dici. Quia bona animae, utpote contemplatio et oratio, sunt multo meliora bonis corporis, et magis nos Deo conformant, et tamen potest dispensari in voto orationis vel contemplationis. Unde non videtur esse ratio quare non possit dispensari in voto continentiae, si respiciatur absolute ad ipsam continentiae dignitatem. Praesertim cum apostolus, I ad Cor. VII, ad continentiam inducat propter contemplationem, dicens quod *mulier innupta cogitat quae Dei sunt,* finis autem potior est his quae sunt ad finem.

for instance, in the case where, if certain persons who have vowed continency were to marry, the peace of their country might be procured. Therefore it seems that it is possible to be dispensed even from a solemn vow of continency.

OBJ. 2: Further, religion is a more excellent virtue than chastity. Now if a man vows an act of religion, e.g., to offer sacrifice to God he can be dispensed from that vow. Much more, therefore, can he be dispensed from the vow of continency which is about an act of chastity.

OBJ. 3: Further, just as the observance of a vow of abstinence may be a source of danger to the person, so too may be the observance of a vow of continency. Now one who takes a vow of abstinence can be dispensed from that vow if it prove a source of danger to his body. Therefore for the same reason one may be dispensed from a vow of continency.

OBJ. 4: Further, just as the vow of continency is part of the religious profession, whereby the vow is solemnized, so also are the vows of poverty and obedience. But it is possible to be dispensed from the vows of poverty and obedience, as in the case of those who are appointed bishops after making profession. Therefore it seems that it is possible to be dispensed from a solemn vow of continency.

ON THE CONTRARY, It is written (Sir 26:20): *No price is worthy of a continent soul.*

FURTHER, (*Extra, De Statu Monach.*) at the end of the Decretal, *Cum ad monasterium*, it is stated that the *renouncing of property, like the keeping of chastity, is so bound up with the monastic rule, that not even the Sovereign Pontiff can disperse from its observance.*

I ANSWER THAT, Three things may be considered in a solemn vow of continency: first, the matter of the vow, namely, continency; second, the perpetuity of the vow, namely, when a person binds himself by vow to the perpetual observance of chastity: third, the solemnity of the vow. Accordingly, some say that the solemn vow cannot be a matter of dispensation, on account of the continency itself for which no worthy price can be found, as is stated by the authority quoted above. The reason for this is assigned by some to the fact that by continency man overcomes a foe within himself, or to the fact that by continency man is perfectly conformed to Christ in respect of purity of both body and soul. But this reason does not seem to be cogent since the goods of the soul, such as contemplation and prayer, far surpass the goods of the body and still more conform us to God, and yet one may be dispensed from a vow of prayer or contemplation. Therefore, continency itself absolutely considered seems no reason why the solemn vow thereof cannot be a matter of dispensation; especially seeing that the Apostle (1 Cor 7:34) exhorts us to be continent on account of contemplation, when he says that *the unmarried woman . . . thinketh on the things of God,* and since the end is of more account than the means.

Et ideo alii rationem huius assignant ex perpetuitate et universalitate huius voti. Dicunt enim quod votum continentiae non potest praetermitti nisi per id quod est omnino contrarium, quod nunquam licet in aliquo voto. Sed hoc est manifeste falsum. Quia sicut uti carnali copula est continentiae contrarium, ita comedere carnes vel bibere vinum est contrarium abstinentiae a talibus, et tamen in huiusmodi votis potest dispensari.

Et ideo aliis videtur quod in voto solemni continentiae possit dispensari propter aliquam communem utilitatem seu necessitatem, ut patet in exemplo praemisso de pacificatione terrarum ex aliquo matrimonio contrahendo. Sed quia decretalis inducta expresse dicit quod nec summus pontifex potest contra custodiam castitatis monacho licentiam dare, ideo aliter videtur dicendum, quod, sicut supra dictum est, et habetur Levit. ult., illud quod semel sanctificatum est domino, non potest in alios usus commutari. Non autem potest facere aliquis Ecclesiae praelatus ut id quod est sanctificatum sanctificationem amittat, etiam in rebus inanimatis, puta quod calix consecratus desinat esse consecratus, si maneat integer. Unde multo minus hoc potest facere aliquis praelatus, ut homo Deo consecratus, quandiu vivit, consecratus esse desistat. Solemnitas autem voti consistit in quadam consecratione seu benedictione voventis, ut dictum est. Et ideo non potest fieri per aliquem praelatum Ecclesiae quod ille qui votum solemne emisit desistat ab eo ad quod est consecratus, puta quod ille qui est sacerdos non sit sacerdos, licet possit praelatus ob aliquam causam executionem ordinis inhibere. Et simili ratione, Papa non potest facere quod ille qui est professus religionem non sit religiosus, licet quidam iuristae ignoranter contrarium dicant.

Est ergo considerandum utrum continentia sit essentialiter annexa ei ad quod votum solemnizatur, quia si non est ei essentialiter annexa, potest manere solemnitas consecrationis sine debito continentiae; quod non potest contingere si sit essentialiter annexum ei ad quod votum solemnizatur. Non est autem essentialiter annexum debitum continentiae ordini sacro, sed ex statuto Ecclesiae. Unde videtur quod per Ecclesiam possit dispensari in voto continentiae solemnizato per susceptionem sacri ordinis. Est autem debitum continentiae essentiale statui religionis, per quem homo abrenuntiat saeculo, totaliter Dei servitio mancipatus; quod non potest simul stare cum matrimonio, in quo incumbit necessitas procurandae uxoris et prolis et familiae, et rerum quae ad hoc requiruntur. Unde apostolus dicit, I ad Cor. VII, quod *qui est cum uxore sollicitus est quae sunt mundi, quomodo placeat uxori, et divisus est.* Unde nomen monachi ab unitate sumitur, per oppositum ad divisionem praedictam. Et ideo in voto solemnizato per professionem

Consequently others find the reason for this in the perpetuity and universality of this vow. For they assert that the vow of continency cannot be canceled, save by something altogether contrary thereto, which is never lawful in any vow. But this is evidently false, because just as the practice of carnal intercourse is contrary to continency, so is eating flesh or drinking wine contrary to abstinence from such things, and yet these latter vows may be a matter for dispensation.

For this reason others maintain that one may be dispensed even from a solemn vow of continency, for the sake of some common good or common need, as in the case of the example given above (Obj. 1), of a country being restored to peace through a certain marriage to be contracted. Yet since the *Decretal* quoted says explicitly that not even the Sovereign Pontiff can dispense a monk from keeping chastity, it follows seemingly, that we must maintain that, as stated above (A. 10, ad 1; cf. Lev. 27:9, 10, 28), whatsoever has once been sanctified to the Lord cannot be put to any other use. For no ecclesiastical prelate can make that which is sanctified to lose its consecration, not even though it be something inanimate, for instance a consecrated chalice to be not consecrated, so long as it remains entire. Much less, therefore, can a prelate make a man that is consecrated to God cease to be consecrated, so long as he lives. Now the solemnity of a vow consists in a kind of consecration or blessing of the person who takes the vow, as stated above (A. 7). Hence no prelate of the Church can make a man, who has pronounced a solemn vow, to be quit of that to which he was consecrated, e.g., one who is a priest, to be a priest no more, although a prelate may, for some particular reason, inhibit him from exercising his order. In like manner the Pope cannot make a man who has made his religious profession cease to be a religious, although certain jurists have ignorantly held the contrary.

We must therefore consider whether continency is essentially bound up with the purpose for which the vow is solemnized. Because if not, the solemnity of the consecration can remain without the obligation of continency, but not if continency is essentially bound up with that for which the vow is solemnized. Now the obligation of observing continency is connected with Holy Orders, not essentially but by the institution of the Church; wherefore it seems that the Church can grant a dispensation from the vow of continency solemnized by the reception of Holy Orders. On the other hand the obligation of observing continency is an essential condition of the religious state, whereby a man renounces the world and binds himself wholly to God's service, for this is incompatible with matrimony, in which state a man is under the obligation of taking to himself a wife, of begetting children, of looking after his household, and of procuring whatever is necessary for these purposes. Wherefore the Apostle says (1 Cor 7:33) that *he that is with a wife, is solicitous for the things of the*

religionis non potest per Ecclesiam dispensari, et rationem assignat decretalis, quia *castitas est annexa regulae monachali*.

**AD PRIMUM** ergo dicendum quod periculis rerum humanarum est obviandum per res humanas, non autem per hoc quod res divinae convertantur in usum humanum. Professi autem religionem mortui sunt mundo et vivunt Deo. Unde non sunt revocandi ad vitam humanam occasione cuiuscumque eventus.

**AD SECUNDUM** dicendum quod in voto temporalis continentiae dispensari potest, sicut et in voto temporalis orationis vel temporalis abstinentiae. Sed quod in voto continentiae per professionem solemnizato non possit dispensari, hoc non est inquantum est actus castitatis, sed inquantum incipit ad latriam pertinere per professionem religionis.

**AD TERTIUM** dicendum quod cibus directe ordinatur ad conservationem personae, et ideo abstinentia cibi directe potest vergere in periculum personae. Unde ex hac ratione recipit votum abstinentiae dispensationem. Sed coitus non ordinatur directe ad conservationem personae, sed ad conservationem speciei. Unde nec directe abstinentia coitus per continentiam vergit in periculum personae. Sed si per accidens ex ea aliquod periculum personale accidat, potest aliter subveniri, scilicet per abstinentiam, vel alia corporalia remedia.

**AD QUARTUM** dicendum quod religiosus qui fit episcopus, sicut non absolvitur a voto continentiae, ita nec a voto paupertatis, quia nihil debet habere tanquam proprium, sed sicut dispensator communium bonorum Ecclesiae. Similiter etiam non absolvitur a voto obedientiae, sed per accidens obedire non tenetur, si superiorem non habeat, sicut et abbas monasterii, qui tamen non est a voto obedientiae absolutus.

**AUCTORITAS** vero Ecclesiastici quae in contrarium obiicitur, intelligenda est quantum ad hoc quod nec fecunditas carnis, nec aliquod corporale bonum est comparandum continentiae, quae inter bona animae computatur, ut Augustinus dicit, in libro de sancta virginitate. Unde signanter dicitur, *animae continentis*, non, *carnis continentis*.

*world, how he may please his wife; and he is divided.* Hence the *monk* takes his name from *unity* in contrast with this division. For this reason the Church cannot dispense from a vow solemnized by the religious profession; and the reason assigned by the *Decretal* is because *chastity is bound up with the monastic rule*.

**REPLY OBJ. 1:** Perils occasioned by human affairs should be obviated by human means, not by turning divine things to a human use. Now a professed religious is dead to the world and lives to God, and so he must not be called back to the human life on the pretext of any human contingency.

**REPLY OBJ. 2:** A vow of temporal continency can be a matter of dispensation, as also a vow of temporal prayer or of temporal abstinence. But the fact that no dispensation can be granted from a vow of continency solemnized by profession is due, not to its being an act of chastity, but because through the religious profession it is already an act of religion.

**REPLY OBJ. 3:** Food is directly ordered to the upkeep of the person, therefore abstinence from food may be a direct source of danger to the person: and so on this count a vow of abstinence is a matter of dispensation. On the other hand sexual intercourse is directly ordered to the upkeep not of the person but of the species, wherefore to abstain from such intercourse by continency does not endanger the person. And if indeed accidentally it prove a source of danger to the person, this danger may be obviated by some other means, for instance by abstinence, or other corporal remedies.

**REPLY OBJ. 4:** A religious who is made a bishop is no more absolved from his vow of poverty than from his vow of continency, since he must have nothing of his own and must hold himself as being the dispenser of the common goods of the Church. In like manner neither is he dispensed from his vow of obedience; it is an accident that he is not bound to obey if he have no superior; just as the abbot of a monastery, who nevertheless is not dispensed from his vow of obedience.

**THE PASSAGE** of Ecclesiasticus, which is put forward in the contrary sense, should be taken as meaning that neither fruitfulness of the flesh nor any bodily good is to be compared with continency, which is reckoned one of the goods of the soul, as Augustine declares (*De Sanct. Virg.* viii). Wherefore it is said pointedly *of a continent soul*, not *of a continent body*.

# Article 12

*Whether the authority of a prelate is required for the commutation or the dispensation of a vow?*

**AD DUODECIMUM SIC PROCEDITUR.** Videtur quod ad commutationem vel dispensationem voti non requiratur praelati auctoritas. Aliquis enim potest intrare religionem absque auctoritate alicuius superioris praelati. Sed per introitum religionis absolvitur homo a votis in saeculo factis, etiam a voto terrae sanctae. Ergo voti commutatio vel dispensatio potest esse absque auctoritate superioris praelati.

**PRAETEREA,** dispensatio voti in hoc consistere videtur quod determinatur in quo casu votum non sit observandum. Sed si praelatus male determinet, non videtur esse vovens absolutus a voto, quia nullus praelatus potest dispensare contra praeceptum divinum de implendo voto, ut dictum est. Similiter etiam si aliquis propria auctoritate recte determinet in quo casu votum non sit implendum, non videtur voto teneri, quia votum non obligat in casu in quo habet peiorem eventum, ut dictum est. Ergo dispensatio voti non requirit auctoritatem alicuius praelati.

**PRAETEREA,** si dispensare in voto pertinet ad potestatem praelatorum, pari ratione pertineret ad omnes. Sed non pertinet ad omnes dispensare in quolibet voto. Ergo non pertinet ad potestatem praelatorum dispensatio voti.

**SED CONTRA,** sicut lex obligat ad aliquid faciendum, ita et votum. Sed ad dispensandum in praecepto legis requiritur superioris auctoritas, ut supra dictum est. Ergo, pari ratione, etiam in dispensatione voti.

**RESPONDEO** dicendum quod, sicut supra dictum est, votum est promissio Deo facta de aliquo quod sit Deo acceptum. Quid sit autem in aliqua promissione acceptum ei cui promittitur, ex eius pendet arbitrio. Praelatus autem in Ecclesia gerit vicem Dei. Et ideo in commutatione vel dispensatione votorum requiritur praelati auctoritas, quae in persona Dei determinat quid sit Deo acceptum, secundum illud II ad Cor. II, *nam et ego propter vos donavi in persona Christi.* Et signanter dicit, *propter vos,* quia omnis dispensatio petita a praelato debet fieri ad honorem Christi, in cuius persona dispensat; vel ad utilitatem Ecclesiae, quae est eius corpus.

**AD PRIMUM** ergo dicendum quod omnia alia vota sunt quorundam particularium operum, sed per religionem homo totam vitam suam Dei obsequio deputat. Particulare autem in universali includitur. Et ideo decretalis dicit quod *reus fracti voti non habetur qui temporale obsequium in perpetuam religionis observantiam commutat.* Nec tamen in religionem ingrediens tenetur implere

**OBJECTION 1:** It would seem that the authority of a prelate is not required for the commutation or dispensation of a vow. A person may enter religion without the authority of a superior prelate. Now by entering religion one is absolved from the vows he made in the world, even from the vow of making a pilgrimage to the Holy Land. Therefore the commutation or dispensation of a vow is possible without the authority of a superior prelate.

**OBJ. 2:** Further, to dispense anyone from a vow seems to consist in deciding in what circumstances he need not keep that vow. But if the prelate is at fault in his decision, the person who took the vow does not seem to be absolved from his vow, since no prelate can grant a dispensation contrary to the divine precept about keeping one's vows, as stated above (A. 10, ad 2; A. 11). Likewise, when anyone rightly determines of his own authority that in his case a vow is not to be kept, he would seem not to be bound; since a vow need not be kept if it have an evil result (A. 2, ad 2). Therefore the Authority of a prelate is not required that one may be dispensed from a vow.

**OBJ. 3:** Further, if it belongs to a prelate's power to grant dispensations from vows, on the same count it is competent to all prelates, but it does not belong to all to dispense from every vow. Therefore it does not belong to the power of a prelate to dispense from vows.

**ON THE CONTRARY,** A vow binds one to do something, even as a law does. Now the superior's authority is requisite for a dispensation from a precept of the law, as stated above (I-II, Q. 96, A. 6; Q. 97, A. 4). Therefore it is likewise required in a dispensation from a vow.

**I ANSWER THAT,** As stated above (AA. 1, 2), a vow is a promise made to God about something acceptable to Him. Now if you promise something to anyone it depends on his decision whether he accept what you promise. Again in the Church a prelate stands in God's place. Therefore a commutation or dispensation of vows requires the authority of a prelate who in God's stead declares what is acceptable to God, according to 2 Cor. 2:10: *For . . . have pardoned . . . for your sakes . . . in the person of Christ.* And he says significantly *for your sakes,* since whenever we ask a prelate for a dispensation we should do so to honor Christ in Whose person he dispenses, or to promote the interests of the Church which is His Body.

**REPLY OBJ. 1:** All other vows are about some particular works, whereas by the religious life a man consecrates his whole life to God's service. Now the particular is included in the universal, wherefore a *Decretal* says that *a man is not deemed a vow-breaker if he exchange a temporal service for the perpetual service of religion.* And yet a man who enters religion is not bound to fulfill the vows, whether of fasting

vota vel ieiuniorum vel orationum vel aliorum huius-modi, quae existens in saeculo fecit, quia religionem ingrediens moritur priori vitae; et etiam singulares observantiae religioni non competunt; et religionis onus satis hominem onerat, ut alia superaddere non oporteat.

**AD SECUNDUM** dicendum quod quidam dixerunt quod praelati possunt in votis pro libito dispensare, quia in quolibet voto includitur conditionaliter voluntas praelati superioris, sicut supra dictum est quod in votis subditorum, puta servi vel filii, intelligitur conditio, *si placuerit patri vel domino*, vel, *si non renitantur*. Et sic subditus absque omni remorsu conscientiae posset votum praetermittere, quandocumque sibi a praelato diceretur.

Sed praedicta positio falso innititur. Quia cum potestas praelati spiritualis, qui non est dominus sed dispensator, sit *in aedificationem data, et non in destructionem*, ut patet II ad Cor. X; sicut praelatus non potest imperare ea quae secundum se Deo displicent, scilicet peccata, ita non potest prohibere ea quae secundum se Deo placent, scilicet virtutis opera. Et ideo absolute potest homo ea vovere. Ad praelatum tamen pertinet diiudicare quid sit magis virtuosum et Deo magis acceptum. Et ideo in manifestis dispensatio praelati non excusaret a culpa, puta si praelatus dispensaret cum aliquo super voto de ingressu religionis, nulla apparenti causa obstante. Si autem esset causa apparens, per quam saltem in dubium verteretur, posset stare iudicio praelati dispensantis vel commutantis. Non tamen iudicio proprio, quia ipse non gerit vicem Dei, nisi forte in casu in quo id quod vovit esset manifeste illicitum, et non posset opportune ad superiorem recurrere.

**AD TERTIUM** dicendum quod quia summus pontifex gerit plenarie vicem Christi in tota Ecclesia, ipse habet plenitudinem potestatis dispensandi in omnibus dispensabilibus votis. Aliis autem inferioribus praelatis committitur dispensatio in votis quae communiter fiunt et indigent frequenti dispensatione, ut habeant de facili homines ad quem recurrant, sicut sunt vota peregrinationum et ieiuniorum et aliorum huiusmodi. Vota vero maiora, puta continentiae et peregrinationis terrae sanctae, reservantur summo pontifici.

or of praying or the like, which he made when in the world, because by entering religion he dies to his former life, and it is unsuitable to the religious life that each one should have his own observances, and because the burden of religion is onerous enough without requiring the addition of other burdens.

**REPLY OBJ. 2**: Some have held that prelates can dispense from vows at their will, for the reason that every vow supposes as a condition that the superior prelate be willing; thus it was stated above (A. 8) that the vow of a subject, e.g., of a slave or a son, supposes this condition, if *the father or master consent*, or *does not dissent*. And thus a subject might break his vow without any remorse of conscience, whenever his superior tells him to.

But this opinion is based on a false supposition: because a spiritual prelate being, not a master, but a dispenser, his power is given *unto edification, not for destruction* (2 Cor 10:8), and consequently, just as he cannot command that which is in itself displeasing to God, namely, sin, so neither can he forbid what is in itself pleasing to God, namely, works of virtue. Therefore absolutely speaking man can vow them. But it does belong to a prelate to decide what is the more virtuous and the more acceptable to God. Consequently in matters presenting no difficulty, the prelate's dispensation would not excuse one from sin: for instance, if a prelate were to dispense a person from a vow to enter the religious life, without any apparent cause to prevent him from fulfilling his vow. But if some cause were to appear, giving rise, at least, to doubt, he could hold to the prelate's decision whether of commutation or of dispensation. He could not, however, follow his own judgment in the matter, because he does not stand in the place of God; except perhaps in the case when the thing he has vowed is clearly unlawful, and he is unable to have recourse to the prelate.

**REPLY OBJ. 3**: Since the Sovereign Pontiff holds the place of Christ throughout the whole Church, he exercises absolute power of dispensing from all vows that admit of dispensation. To other and inferior prelates is the power committed of dispensing from those vows that are commonly made and frequently require dispensation, in order that men may easily have recourse to someone; such are the vows of pilgrimage (*Cap. de Peregrin., de Voto et Voti redempt.*), fasting and the like, and of pilgrimage to the Holy Land, are reserved to the Sovereign Pontiff.

# QUESTION 89

Deinde considerandum est de actibus exterioribus latriae quibus aliquid divinum ab hominibus assumitur, quod est vel sacramentum aliquod, vel ipsum nomen divinum. Sed de sacramenti assumptione locus erit tractandi in tertia huius operis parte. De assumptione autem nominis divini nunc agendum est. Assumitur autem divinum nomen ab homine tripliciter, uno modo, per modum iuramenti, ad propria verba confirmanda; alio modo, per modum adiurationis, ad alios inducendum; tertio modo, per modum invocationis, ad orandum vel laudandum. Primo ergo de iuramento agendum est. Circa quod quaeruntur decem.

Primo, quid sit iuramentum.

Secundo, utrum sit licitum.

Tertio, qui sint comites iuramenti

Quarto, cuius virtutis sit actus.

Quinto, utrum sit appetendum et frequentandum, tanquam utile et bonum.

Sexto, utrum liceat iurare per creaturam.

Septimo, utrum iuramentum sit obligatorium.

Octavo, quae sit maior obligatio, utrum iuramenti vel voti.

Nono, utrum in iuramento possit dispensari.

Decimo, quibus et quando liceat iurare.

We must now consider those external acts of religion, whereby something divine is taken by man: and this is either a sacrament or the name of God. The place for treating of the taking of a sacrament will be in the Third Part of this work: of the taking of God's name we shall treat now. The name of God is taken by man in three ways. First, by way oath in order to confirm one's own assertion: second, by way of adjuration as an inducement to others: third, by way of invocation for the purpose of prayer or praise. Accordingly we must first treat of oaths: and under this head there are ten points of inquiry:

(1) What is an oath?

(2) Whether it is lawful?

(3) What are the accompanying conditions of an oath?

(4) Of what virtue is it an act?

(5) Whether oaths are desirable, and to be employed frequently as something useful and good?

(6) Whether it is lawful to swear by a creature?

(7) Whether an oath is binding?

(8) Which is more binding, an oath or a vow?

(9) Whether an oath is subject to dispensation?

(10) Who may lawfully swear, and when?

# Article 1

*Whether to swear is to call God to witness?*

**AD PRIMUM SIC PROCEDITUR.** Videtur quod iurare non sit testem Deum invocare. Quicumque enim inducit auctoritatem sacrae Scripturae inducit Deum in testimonium, cuius verba proponuntur in sacra Scriptura. Si ergo iurare est testem Deum invocare, quicumque inducit auctoritatem sacrae Scripturae iuraret. Hoc autem est falsum. Ergo et primum.

**PRAETEREA,** ex hoc quod aliquis inducit aliquem in testem, nihil ei reddit. Sed ille qui per Deum iurat aliquid Deo reddit, dicitur enim Matth. V, *reddes domino iuramenta tua*; et Augustinus dicit quod iurare est *ius veritatis Deo reddere*. Ergo iurare non est Deum testem invocare.

**PRAETEREA,** aliud est officium iudicis, et aliud testis, ut ex supradictis patet. Sed quandoque iurando implorat homo divinum iudicium, secundum illud Psalm., *si red-*

**OBJECTION 1:** It would seem that to swear is not to call God to witness. Whoever invokes the authority of Holy Writ calls God to witness, since it is His word that Holy Writ contains. Therefore, if to swear is to call God to witness, whoever invoked the authority of Holy Writ would swear. But this is false. Therefore the antecedent is false also.

**OBJ. 2:** Further, one does not pay anything to a person by calling him to witness. But he who swears by God pays something to Him for it is written (Matt 5:33): *Thou shall pay thy oaths to the Lord*; and Augustine says that to swear (*jurare*) is *to pay the right (jus reddere) of truth to God*. Therefore to swear is not to call God to witness.

**OBJ. 3:** Further, the duties of a judge differ from the duties of a witness, as shown above (QQ. 67, 70). Now sometimes a man, by swearing, implores the Divine judg-

*didi retribuentibus mihi mala, decidam merito ab inimicis meis inanis.* Ergo iurare non est testem Deum invocare.

**SED CONTRA** est quod Augustinus dicit, in quodam sermone de periurio, *quid est, per Deum, nisi, testis est Deus?*

**RESPONDEO** dicendum quod, sicut apostolus dicit, ad Heb. VI, iuramentum *ad confirmationem* ordinatur. Confirmatio autem in scibilibus per rationem fit, quae procedit ex aliquibus naturaliter notis, quae sunt infallibiliter vera. Sed particularia facta contingentia hominum non possunt per rationem necessariam confirmari. Et ideo ea quae de his dicuntur solent confirmari per testes. Sed humanum testimonium non est sufficiens ad huiusmodi confirmandum, propter duo. Primo quidem, propter defectum veritatis humanae, quia plurimi in mendacium labuntur, secundum illud Psalm., *os eorum locutum est mendacium.* Secundo, propter defectum cognitionis, quia homines non possunt cognoscere neque futura, neque cordium occulta, vel etiam absentia; de quibus tamen homines loquuntur, et expedit rebus humanis ut certitudo aliqua de his habeatur. Et ideo necessarium fuit recurrere ad divinum testimonium, quia Deus neque mentiri potest, neque eum aliquid latet. Assumere autem Deum in testem dicitur iurare, quia quasi pro *iure* introductum est ut quod sub invocatione divini testimonii dicitur pro vero habeatur. Divinum autem testimonium quandoque inducitur ad asserendum praesentia vel praeterita, et hoc dicitur iuramentum *assertorium.* Quandoque autem inducitur divinum testimonium ad confirmandum aliquid futurum, et hoc dicitur iuramentum *promissorium.* Ad ea vero quae sunt necessaria et per rationem investiganda non inducitur iuramentum, derisibile enim videretur si quis in disputatione alicuius scientiae vellet propositum per iuramentum probare.

**AD PRIMUM** ergo dicendum quod aliud est testimonio Dei uti iam dato, quod fit cum aliquis auctoritatem sacrae Scripturae inducit, et aliud est testimonium Dei implorare ut exhibendum, quod fit in iuramento.

**AD SECUNDUM** dicendum quod dicitur aliquis reddere iuramenta Deo ex hoc quod implet illud quod iurat. Vel quia in hoc ipso quod invocat Deum testem, recognoscit eum habere omnium cognitionem et infallibilem veritatem.

**AD TERTIUM** dicendum quod alicuius testimonium invocatur ad hoc quod testis invocatus veritatem manifestet circa ea quae dicuntur. Deus autem manifestat an verum sit quod dicitur, dupliciter. Uno modo, simpliciter revelando veritatem, vel per internam inspirationem; vel etiam per facti denudationem, dum scilicet producit in publicum ea quae erant occulta. Alio modo, per poenam mentientis, et tunc simul est iudex et testis, dum puniendo mendacem manifestat mendacium. Et ideo

ment, according to Ps. 7:5, *If I have rendered to them that repaid me evils, let me deservedly fall empty before my enemies.* Therefore to swear is not to call God to witness.

**ON THE CONTRARY,** Augustine says in a sermon on perjury (*Serm.* clxxx): *When a man says: 'By God,' what else does he mean but that God is his witness?*

**I ANSWER THAT,** As the Apostle says (Heb 6:16), oaths are taken *for the purpose of confirmation.* Now speculative propositions receive confirmation from reason, which proceeds from principles known naturally and infallibly true. But particular contingent facts regarding man cannot be confirmed by a necessary reason, wherefore propositions regarding such things are wont to be confirmed by witnesses. Now a human witness does not suffice to confirm such matters for two reasons. First, on account of man's lack of truth, for many give way to lying, according to Ps. 16:10, *Their mouth hath spoken lies.* Second, on account of lack of knowledge, since he can know neither the future, nor secret thoughts, nor distant things: and yet men speak about such things, and our everyday life requires that we should have some certitude about them. Hence the need to have recourse to a Divine witness, for neither can God lie, nor is anything hidden from Him. Now to call God to witness is named jurare (to swear) because it is established as though it were a principle of law (*jure*) that what a man asserts under the invocation of God as His witness should be accepted as true. Now sometimes God is called to witness when we assert present or past events, and this is termed a *declaratory oath*; while sometimes God is called to witness in confirmation of something future, and this is termed a *promissory oath.* But oaths are not employed in order to substantiate necessary matters, and such as come under the investigation of reason; for it would seem absurd in a scientific discussion to wish to prove one's point by an oath.

**REPLY OBJ. 1:** It is one thing to employ a Divine witness already given, as when one adduces the authority of Holy Scripture; and another to implore God to bear witness, as in an oath.

**REPLY OBJ. 2:** A man is said to pay his oaths to God because he performs what he swears to do, or because, from the very fact that he calls upon God to witness, he recognizes Him as possessing universal knowledge and unerring truth.

**REPLY OBJ. 3:** A person is called to give witness, in order that he may make known the truth about what is alleged. Now there are two ways in which God makes known whether the alleged facts are true or not. In one way He reveals the truth simply, either by inward inspiration, or by unveiling the facts, namely, by making public what was hitherto secret: in another way by punishing the lying witness, and then He is at once judge and witness, since by punishing the liar He makes known his lie. Hence oaths are

duplex est modus iurandi. Unus quidem per simplicem Dei *contestationem*, sicut cum aliquis dicit, *est mihi Deus testis*; vel, *coram Deo loquor*; vel, *per Deum*, quod idem est, ut dicit Augustinus. Alius modus iurandi est per *execrationem*, dum scilicet aliquis se, vel aliquid ad se pertinens, ad poenam obligat nisi sit verum quod dicitur.

of two kinds: one is a simple contestation of God, as when a man says *God is my witness*, or, *I speak before God*, or, *By God*, which has the same meaning, as Augustine states; the other is by *cursing*, and consists in a man binding himself or something of his to punishment if what is alleged be not true.

# Article 2

## *Whether it is lawful to swear?*

AD SECUNDUM SIC PROCEDITUR. Videtur quod non sit licitum iurare. Nihil enim quod prohibetur in lege divina est licitum. Sed iuramentum prohibetur Matth. V, *ego dico vobis, non iurare omnino*, et Iac. V dicitur, *ante omnia, fratres mei, nolite iurare*. Ergo iuramentum est illicitum.

PRAETEREA, id quod est a malo videtur esse illicitum, quia, ut dicitur Matth. VII, *non potest arbor mala fructus bonos facere*. Sed iuramentum est a malo, dicitur enim Matth. V, *sit autem sermo vester, est, est; non, non. Quod autem his abundantius est a malo est*. Ergo iuramentum videtur esse illicitum.

PRAETEREA, exquirere signum divinae providentiae est tentare Deum, quod est omnino illicitum, secundum illud Deut. VI, *non tentabis dominum Deum tuum*. Sed ille qui iurat videtur exquirere signum divinae providentiae, dum petit divinum testimonium, quod est per aliquem evidentem effectum. Ergo videtur quod iuramentum sit omnino illicitum.

SED CONTRA est quod dicitur Deut. VI, *dominum Deum tuum timebis, et per nomen eius iurabis*.

RESPONDEO dicendum quod nihil prohibet aliquid esse secundum se bonum quod tamen cedit in malum eius qui non utitur eo convenienter, sicut sumere Eucharistiam est bonum, et tamen qui indigne sumit *sibi iudicium manducat et bibit*, ut dicitur I ad Cor. XI. Sic ergo in proposito dicendum est quod iuramentum secundum se est licitum et honestum. Quod patet ex origine et ex fine. Ex origine quidem, quia iuramentum est introductum ex fide qua homines credunt Deum habere infallibilem veritatem et universalem omnium cognitionem et provisionem. Ex fine autem, quia iuramentum inducitur ad iustificandum homines, et ad finiendum controversias, ut dicitur ad Heb. VI.

Sed iuramentum cedit in malum alicui ex eo quod male utitur eo, idest sine necessitate et cautela debita. Videtur enim parvam reverentiam habere ad Deum qui eum ex levi causa testem inducit, quod non praesumeret etiam de aliquo viro honesto. Imminet etiam periculum periurii, quia de facili homo in verbo delinquit, secundum illud Iac. III, *si quis in verbo non offendit, hic*

OBJECTION 1: It would seem that it is not lawful to swear. Nothing forbidden in the Divine Law is lawful. Now swearing is forbidden (Matt 5:34), *But I say to you not to swear at all*; and (Jas 5:12), *Above all things, my brethren, swear not*. Therefore swearing is unlawful.

OBJ. 2: Further, whatever comes from an evil seems to be unlawful, because according to Matt. 7:18, *neither can an evil tree bring forth good fruit*. Now swearing comes from an evil, for it is written (Matt 5:37): *But let your speech be: Yea, yea: No, no. And that which is over and above these is of evil*. Therefore swearing is apparently unlawful.

OBJ. 3: Further, to seek a sign of Divine Providence is to tempt God, and this is altogether unlawful, according to Deut. 6:16, *Thou shalt not tempt the Lord thy God*. Now he that swears seems to seek a sign of Divine Providence, since he asks God to bear witness, and this must be by some evident effect. Therefore it seems that swearing is altogether unlawful.

ON THE CONTRARY, It is written (Deut 6:13): *Thou shalt fear the Lord thy God . . . and shalt swear by His name*.

I ANSWER THAT, Nothing prevents a thing being good in itself, and yet becoming a source of evil to one who makes use thereof unbecomingly: thus to receive the Eucharist is good, and yet he that receives it *unworthily, eateth and drinketh judgment to himself* (1 Cor 11:29). Accordingly in answer to the question in point it must be stated that an oath is in itself lawful and commendable. This is proved from its origin and from its end. From its origin, because swearing owes its introduction to the faith whereby man believes that God possesses unerring truth and universal knowledge and foresight of all things: and from its end, since oaths are employed in order to justify men, and to put an end to controversy (Heb 6:16).

Yet an oath becomes a source of evil to him that makes evil use of it, that is who employs it without necessity and due caution. For if a man calls God as witness, for some trifling reason, it would seemingly prove him to have but little reverence for God, since he would not treat even a good man in this manner. Moreover, he is in danger of committing perjury, because man easily offends in words,

*perfectus est vir.* Unde et Eccli. XXIII dicitur, *iurationi non assuescat os tuum, multi enim casus in illa.*

Ad primum ergo dicendum quod Hieronymus, super Matth., dicit, *considera quod salvator non per Deum iurare prohibuerit, sed per caelum et terram. Hanc enim per elementa iurandi pessimam consuetudinem habere Iudaei noscuntur.* Se ista responsio non sufficit, quia Iacobus addit, *neque per aliud quodcumque iuramentum.* Et ideo dicendum est quod, sicut Augustinus dicit, in libro de mendacio, quod *apostolus, in epistolis suis iurans, ostendit quomodo accipiendum esset quod dictum est, dico vobis non iurare omnino, ne scilicet iurando ad facilitatem iurandi veniatur, ex facilitate iurandi ad consuetudinem, a consuetudine in periurium decidatur. Et ideo non invenitur iurasse nisi scribens, ubi consideratio cautior non habet linguam praecipitem.*

Ad secundum dicendum quod, sicut Augustinus dicit, in libro de Serm. Dom. in monte, *si iurare cogeris, scias de necessitate venire infirmitatis eorum quibus aliquid suades, quae utique infirmitas malum est. Itaque non dixit, quod amplius est malum est; tu enim non malum facis qui bene uteris iuratione, ut alteri persuadeas quod utiliter persuades, sed, a malo est illius cuius infirmitate iurare cogeris.*

Ad tertium dicendum quod ille qui iurat non tentat Deum, quia non implorat divinum auxilium absque utilitate et necessitate; et praeterea non exponit se alicui periculo si Deus testimonium adhibere noluerit in praesenti. Adhibebit autem pro certo testimonium in futuro, quando *illuminabit abscondita tenebrarum et manifestabit consilia cordium*, ut dicitur I ad Cor. IV. Et illud testimonium nulli iuranti deficiet, vel pro eo vel contra eum.

according to James 3:2, *If any man offend not in word, the same is a perfect man.* Wherefore it is written (Sir 23:9): *Let not thy mouth be accustomed to swearing, for in it there are many falls.*

Reply Obj. 1: Jerome, commenting on Matt. 5:34, says: *Observe that our Savior forbade us to swear, not by God, but by heaven and earth. For it is known that the Jews have this most evil custom of swearing by the elements.* Yet this answer does not suffice, because James adds, *nor by any other oath.* Wherefore we must reply that, as Augustine states (*De Mendacio* xv), *when the Apostle employs an oath in his epistles, he shows how we are to understand the saying, 'I say to you, not to swear at all'; lest, to wit, swearing lead us to swear easily and from swearing easily, we contract the habit, and, from swearing habitually, we fall into perjury. Hence we find that he swore only when writing, because thought brings caution and avoids hasty words.*

Reply Obj. 2: According to Augustine (*De Serm. Dom. in Monte* i. 17): *If you have to swear, note that the necessity arises from the infirmity of those whom you convince, which infirmity is indeed an evil.* Accordingly He did not say: 'That which is over and above is evil,' but 'is of evil.' For you do no evil; since you make good use of swearing, by persuading another to a useful purpose: yet it 'comes of the evil' of the person by whose infirmity you are forced to swear.

Reply Obj. 3: He who swears tempts not God, because it is not without usefulness and necessity that he implores the Divine assistance. Moreover, he does not expose himself to danger, if God be unwilling to bear witness there and then: for He certainly will bear witness at some future time, when He *will bring to light the hidden things of darkness, and will make manifest the counsels of hearts* (1 Cor 4:5). And this witness will be lacking to none who swears, neither for nor against him.

# Article 3

*Whether three accompanying conditions of an oath are suitably assigned, namely, justice, judgment, and truth?*

Ad tertium sic proceditur. Videtur quod inconvenienter ponantur tres comites iuramenti iustitia, iudicium et veritas. Ea enim quorum unum includitur in altero non sunt connumeranda tanquam diversa. Sed horum trium unum includitur in altero, quia veritas pars iustitiae est, secundum Tullium; iudicium autem est actus iustitiae, ut supra habitum est. Ergo inconvenienter numerantur tres comites iuramenti.

Praeterea, multa alia requiruntur ad iuramentum, scilicet devotio, et fides, per quam credamus Deum

Objection 1: It would seem that justice, judgment and truth are unsuitably assigned as the conditions accompanying an oath. Things should not be enumerated as diverse, if one of them includes the other. Now of these three, one includes another, since truth is a part of justice, according to Tully (*De Invent. Rhet.* ii, 53): and judgment is an act of justice, as stated above (Q. 60, A. 1). Therefore the three accompanying conditions of an oath are unsuitably assigned.

Obj. 2: Further, many other things are required for an oath, namely, devotion, and faith whereby we believe

omnia scire et mentiri non posse. Ergo videtur quod insufficienter enumerentur tres comites iuramenti.

**PRAETEREA**, haec tria in quolibet opere humano inquirenda sunt, nihil enim debet fieri contra iustitiam aut veritatem, aut sine iudicio, secundum illud I ad Tim. V, *nihil facias sine praeiudicio*, idest sine praecedenti iudicio. Ergo haec tria non magis debent associari iuramento quam aliis humanis actibus.

**SED CONTRA** est quod dicitur Ierem. IV, *iurabis, vivit dominus, in veritate, in iudicio et in iustitia*, quod exponens Hieronymus dicit, *animadvertendum est quod iusiurandum hos habet comites, scilicet veritatem, iudicium et iustitiam.*

**RESPONDEO** dicendum quod, sicut supra dictum est, iuramentum non est bonum nisi ei qui bene utitur iuramento. Ad bonum autem usum iuramenti duo requiruntur. Primo quidem, quod aliquis non leviter, sed ex necessaria causa et discrete iuret. Et quantum ad hoc, requiritur iudicium, scilicet discretionis ex parte iurantis. Secundo, quantum ad id quod per iuramentum confirmatur, ut scilicet neque sit falsum, neque sit aliquid illicitum. Et quantum ad hoc, requiritur veritas, per quam aliquis iuramento confirmat quod verum est; et iustitia, per quam confirmat quod licitum est. Iudicio autem caret iuramentum *incautum*; veritate autem iuramentum *mendax*; iustitia autem iuramentum *iniquum* sive *illicitum*.

**AD PRIMUM** ergo dicendum quod iudicium non sumitur hic pro executione iustitiae, sed pro iudicio discretionis, ut dictum est. Neque etiam veritas hic accipitur secundum quod est pars iustitiae, sed secundum quod est quaedam conditio locutionis.

**AD SECUNDUM** dicendum quod et devotio et fides, et omnia huiusmodi quae exiguntur ad debitum modum iurandi, intelliguntur in iudicio. Alia enim duo pertinent ad rem de qua iuratur, ut dictum est. Quamvis posset dici quod iustitia pertinet ad causam pro qua iuratur.

**AD TERTIUM** dicendum quod in iuramento est magnum periculum, tum propter Dei magnitudinem, cuius testimonium invocatur; tum etiam propter labilitatem linguae humanae, cuius verba iuramento confirmantur. Et ideo huiusmodi magis requiruntur ad iuramentum quam ad alios humanos actus.

that God knows all things and cannot lie. Therefore the accompanying conditions of an oath are insufficiently enumerated.

**OBJ. 3**: Further, these three are requisite in man's every deed: since he ought to do nothing contrary to justice and truth, or without judgment, according to 1 Tim. 5:21, *Do nothing without prejudice*, i.e., without previous judgment. Therefore these three should not be associated with an oath any more than with other human actions.

**ON THE CONTRARY**, It is written (Jer 4:2): *Thou shalt swear: As the Lord liveth, in truth, and in judgment, and in justice*: which words Jerome expounds, saying: *Observe that an oath must be accompanied by these conditions, truth, judgment and justice.*

**I ANSWER THAT**, As stated above (A. 2), an oath is not good except for one who makes good use of it. Now two conditions are required for the good use of an oath. First, that one swear, not for frivolous, but for urgent reasons, and with discretion; and this requires judgment or discretion on the part of the person who swears. Second, as regards the point to be confirmed by oath, that it be neither false, nor unlawful, and this requires both truth, so that one employ an oath in order to confirm what is true, and justice, so that one confirm what is lawful. A *rash* oath lacks judgment, a *false* oath lacks truth, and a *wicked* or *unlawful* oath lacks justice.

**REPLY OBJ. 1**: Judgment does not signify here the execution of justice, but the judgment of discretion, as stated above. Nor is truth here to be taken for the part of justice, but for a condition of speech.

**REPLY OBJ. 2**: Devotion, faith and like conditions requisite for the right manner of swearing are implied by judgment: for the other two regard the things sworn to as stated above. We might also reply that justice regards the reason for swearing.

**REPLY OBJ. 3**: There is great danger in swearing, both on account of the greatness of God Who is called upon to bear witness, and on account of the frailty of the human tongue, the words of which are confirmed by oath. Hence these conditions are more requisite for an oath than for other human actions.

# Article 4

*Whether an oath is an act of religion or latria?*

**AD QUARTUM SIC PROCEDITUR**. Videtur quod iuramentum non sit actus religionis sive latriae. Actus enim latriae sunt circa aliqua sacra et divina. Sed iuramenta

**OBJECTION 1**: It would seem that an oath is not an act of religion, or latria. Acts of religion are about holy and divine things. But oaths are employed in connection

adhibentur circa controversias humanas, ut apostolus dicit, ad Heb. VI. Ergo iurare non est actus religionis seu latriae.

**PRAETEREA**, ad religionem pertinet *cultum Deo offerre*, ut Tullius dicit. Sed ille qui iurat nihil Deo offert, sed Deum inducit in testem. Ergo iurare non est actus religionis.

**PRAETEREA**, finis religionis seu latriae est reverentiam Deo exhibere. Hoc autem non est finis iuramenti, sed potius aliquod verbum confirmare. Ergo iurare non est actus religionis.

**SED CONTRA** est quod dicitur Deut. VI, *dominum Deum tuum timebis, et ipsi soli servies, ac per nomen illius iurabis*. Loquitur autem ibi de servitute latriae. Ergo iurare est actus latriae.

**RESPONDEO** dicendum quod, sicut ex dictis patet, ille qui iurat invocat divinum testimonium ad confirmandum ea quae dicit. Nihil autem confirmatur nisi per aliquid quod certius est et potius. Et ideo in hoc ipso quod homo per Deum iurat, profitetur Deum potiorem, utpote cuius veritas est indefectibilis et cognitio universalis, et sic aliquo modo Deo reverentiam exhibet. Unde et apostolus dicit, ad Heb. VI, quod *homines per maiores se iurant*. Et Hieronymus dicit, super Matth., quod *qui iurat, aut veneratur aut diligit eum per quem iurat*. Philosophus etiam dicit, in I Metaphys., quod *iuramentum est honorabilissimum*. Exhibere autem reverentiam Deo pertinet ad religionem sive latriam. Unde manifestum est quod iuramentum est actus religionis sive latriae.

**AD PRIMUM** ergo dicendum quod in iuramento duo considerantur, scilicet testimonium quod inducitur, et hoc est divinum; et id super quo inducitur testimonium, vel quod facit necessitatem testimonium inducendi, et hoc est humanum. Pertinet ergo iuramentum ad religionem ratione primi, non autem ratione secundi.

**AD SECUNDUM** dicendum quod in hoc ipso quod aliquis assumit Deum in testem per modum iuramenti, profitetur eum maiorem, quod pertinet ad Dei reverentiam. Et sic aliquid offert Deo, scilicet reverentiam et honorem.

**AD TERTIUM** dicendum quod omnia quae facimus debemus in Dei reverentiam facere. Et ideo nihil prohibet si in hoc ipso quod intendimus hominem certificare, Deo reverentiam exhibeamus. Sic enim debemus aliquid in Dei reverentiam facere ut ex hoc utilitas proximis proveniat, quia etiam Deus operatur ad suam gloriam et nostram utilitatem.

with human disputes, as the Apostle declares (Heb 6:16). Therefore swearing is not an act of religion or latria.

**OBJ. 2**: Further, it belongs to religion *to give worship to God*, as Tully says (*De Invent. Rhet.* ii, 53). But he who swears offers nothing to God, but calls God to be his witness. Therefore swearing is not an act of religion or latria.

**OBJ. 3**: Further, the end of religion or latria is to show reverence to God. But the end of an oath is not this, but rather the confirmation of some assertion. Therefore swearing is not an act of religion.

**ON THE CONTRARY**, It is written (Deut 6:13): *Thou shalt fear the Lord thy God, and shalt serve Him only, and thou shalt swear by His name*. Now he speaks there of the servitude of religion. Therefore swearing is an act of religion.

**I ANSWER THAT**, As appears from what has been said above (A. 1), he that swears calls God to witness in confirmation of what he says. Now nothing is confirmed save by what is more certain and more powerful. Therefore in the very fact that a man swears by God, he acknowledges God to be more powerful, by reason of His unfailing truth and His universal knowledge; and thus in a way he shows reverence to God. For this reason the Apostle says (Heb 6:16) that *men swear by one greater than themselves*, and Jerome commenting on Matt. 5:34, says that *he who swears either reveres or loves the person by whom he swears*. The Philosopher, too, states (*Metaph.* i, 3) that *to swear is to give very great honor*. Now to show reverence to God belongs to religion or latria. Wherefore it is evident that an oath is an act of religion or latria.

**REPLY OBJ. 1**: Two things may be observed in an oath. The witness adduced, and this is Divine: and the thing witnessed to, or that which makes it necessary to call the witness, and this is human. Accordingly an oath belongs to religion by reason of the former, and not of the latter.

**REPLY OBJ. 2**: In the very fact that a man takes God as witness by way of an oath, he acknowledges Him to be greater: and this pertains to the reverence and honor of God, so that he offers something to God, namely, reverence and honor.

**REPLY OBJ. 3**: Whatsoever we do, we should do it in honor of God: wherefore there is no hindrance, if by intending to assure a man, we show reverence to God. For we ought so to perform our actions in God's honor that they may conduce to our neighbor's good, since God also works for His own glory and for our good.

# Article 5

*Whether oaths are desirable and to be used frequently as something useful and good?*

**AD QUINTUM SIC PROCEDITUR.** Videtur quod iuramentum sit appetendum et frequentandum, tanquam utile et bonum. Sicut enim votum est actus latriae, ita et iuramentum. Sed facere aliquid ex voto est laudabilius et magis meritorium quia votum est actus latriae, ut supra dictum est. Ergo, pari ratione, facere vel dicere aliquid cum iuramento est laudabilius. Et sic iuramentum est appetendum tanquam per se bonum.

**PRAETEREA,** Hieronymus dicit, super Matth., quod *qui iurat, veneratur aut diligit eum per quem iurat.* Sed venerari aut diligere Deum est appetendum tanquam per se bonum. Ergo et iuramentum.

**PRAETEREA,** iuramentum ordinatur ad confirmationem seu certificationem. Sed quod homo suum dictum confirmet, bonum est. Ergo iuramentum est appetendum tanquam bonum.

**SED CONTRA** est quod dicitur Eccli. XXIII, *vir multum iurans replebitur iniquitate.* Et Augustinus dicit, in libro de mendacio, quod praeceptum domini de prohibitione iuramenti *ad hoc positum est ut, quantum in te est, non affectes, non, quasi pro bono, cum aliqua delectatione appetas iusiurandum.*

**RESPONDEO** dicendum quod id quod non quaeritur nisi ad subveniendum alicui defectui, non numeratur inter ea quae sunt per se appetenda, sed inter ea quae sunt necessaria, sicut patet de medicina, quae quaeritur ad subveniendum infirmitati. Iuramentum autem quaeritur ad subveniendum alicui defectui, quo scilicet unus homo alteri discredit. Et ideo iuramentum est habendum non inter ea quae sunt per se appetenda, sed inter ea quae sunt huic vitae necessaria, quibus indebite utitur quicumque eis utitur ultra terminos necessitatis. Unde Augustinus dicit, in libro de Serm. Dom. in monte, *qui intelligit non in bonis, idest per se appetendis, sed in necessariis iurationem habendam, refrenat se quantum potest, ut non ea utatur nisi necessitas cogat.*

**AD PRIMUM** ergo dicendum quod alia ratio est de voto, et de iuramento. Nam per votum aliquid in Dei reverentiam ordinamus, unde ex hoc ipso fit religionis actus. Sed in iuramento e converso reverentia divini nominis assumitur ad promissi confirmationem. Et ideo illud quod iuramento confirmatur non propter hoc fit religionis actus, quia secundum finem morales actus species sortiuntur.

**AD SECUNDUM** dicendum quod ille qui iurat utitur quidem veneratione aut dilectione eius per quem iurat, non autem ordinat iuramentum ad venerandum aut di-

**OBJECTION 1:** It would seem that oaths are desirable and to be used frequently as something useful and good. Just as a vow is an act of religion, so is an oath. Now it is commendable and more meritorious to do a thing by vow, because a vow is an act of religion, as stated above (Q. 88, A. 5). Therefore for the same reason, to do or say a thing with an oath is more commendable, and consequently oaths are desirable as being good essentially.

**OBJ. 2:** Further, Jerome, commenting on Matt. 5:34, says that *he who swears either reveres or loves the person by whom he swears.* Now reverence and love of God are desirable as something good essentially. Therefore swearing is also.

**OBJ. 3:** Further, swearing is directed to the purpose of confirming or assuring. But it is a good thing for a man to confirm his assertion. Therefore an oath is desirable as a good thing.

**ON THE CONTRARY,** It is written (Sir 23:12): *A man that sweareth much shall be filled with iniquity*: and Augustine says (*De Mendacio* xv) that *the Lord forbade swearing, in order that for your own part you might not be fond of it, and take pleasure in seeking occasions of swearing, as though it were a good thing.*

**I ANSWER THAT,** Whatever is required merely as a remedy for an infirmity or a defect, is not reckoned among those things that are desirable for their own sake, but among those that are necessary: this is clear in the case of medicine which is required as a remedy for sickness. Now an oath is required as a remedy to a defect, namely, some man's lack of belief in another man. Wherefore an oath is not to be reckoned among those things that are desirable for their own sake, but among those that are necessary for this life; and such things are used unduly whenever they are used outside the bounds of necessity. For this reason Augustine says (*De Serm. Dom. in Monte* i, 17): *He who understands that swearing is not to be held as a good thing,* i.e., desirable for its own sake, *restrains himself as far as he can from uttering oaths, unless there be urgent need.*

**REPLY OBJ. 1:** There is no parity between a vow and an oath: because by a vow we direct something to the honor of God, so that for this very reason a vow is an act of religion. On the other hand, in an oath reverence for the name of God is taken in confirmation of a promise. Hence what is confirmed by oath does not, for this reason, become an act of religion, since moral acts take their species from the end.

**REPLY OBJ. 2:** He who swears does indeed make use of his reverence or love for the person by whom he swears: he does not, however, direct his oath to the reverence or love

ligendum eum per quem iurat, sed ad aliquid aliud quod est necessarium praesenti vitae.

**AD TERTIUM** dicendum quod sicut medicina est utilis ad sanandum, et tamen quanto est virtuosior, tanto maius nocumentum inducit si non debite sumatur; ita etiam iuramentum utile quidem est ad confirmationem, tamen quanto est magis venerandum, tanto est magis periculosum nisi debite inducatur. Quia, ut dicitur Eccli. XXIII, *si frustraverit*, idest deceperit fratrem, *delictum illius supra ipsum erit; et si dissimulaverit*, quasi per simulationem iurando falsum, *delinquit dupliciter* (quia scilicet *simulata aequitas est duplex iniquitas*); *et si in vanum iuraverit*, idest sine debita causa et necessitate, *non iustificabitur*.

of that person, but to something else that is necessary for the present life.

**REPLY OBJ. 3**: Even as a medicine is useful for healing, and yet, the stronger it is, the greater harm it does if it be taken unduly, so too an oath is useful indeed as a means of confirmation, yet the greater the reverence it demands the more dangerous it is, unless it be employed aright; for, as it is written (Sir 23:13), *if he make it void*, i.e., if he deceive his brother, *his sin shall be upon him: and if he dissemble it*, by swearing falsely, and with dissimulation, *he offendeth double*, (because, to wit, *pretended equity is a twofold iniquity*, as Augustine declares): *and if he swear in vain*, i.e., without due cause and necessity, *he shall not be justified*.

# Article 6

*Whether it is lawful to swear by creatures?*

**AD SEXTUM SIC PROCEDITUR.** Videtur quod non liceat per creaturas iurare. Dicitur enim Matth. V, *ego dico vobis, non iurare omnino, neque per caelum, neque per terram, neque per Ierosolymam, neque per caput tuum*, quod exponens Hieronymus dicit, *considera quod hic salvator non per Deum iurare prohibuerit, sed per caelum et terram*, et cetera.

**PRAETEREA**, poena non debetur nisi culpae. Sed iuranti per creaturas adhibetur poena, dicitur enim XXII, qu. I, *clericum per creaturam iurantem acerrime obiurgandum, si perstiterit in vitio, excommunicandum placuit.* Ergo illicitum est per creaturas iurare.

**PRAETEREA**, iuramentum est actus latriae, sicut dictum est. Sed cultus latriae non debetur alicui creaturae, ut patet Rom. I. Ergo non licet iurare per aliquam creaturam.

**SED CONTRA** est quod Ioseph iuravit *per salutem Pharaonis*, ut legitur Gen. XLII. Ex consuetudine etiam iuratur per Evangelium, et per reliquias, et per sanctos.

**RESPONDEO** dicendum quod, sicut supra dictum est, duplex est iuramentum. Unum quidem quod fit per simplicem contestationem, inquantum scilicet Dei testimonium invocatur. Et hoc iuramentum innititur divinae veritati, sicut et fides. Fides autem est per se quidem et principaliter de Deo, qui est ipsa veritas; secundario autem de creaturis, in quibus veritas Dei relucet, ut supra habitum est. Et similiter iuramentum principaliter refertur ad ipsum Deum, cuius testimonium invocatur, secundario autem assumuntur ad iuramentum aliquae creaturae non secundum se, sed inquantum in eis divi-

**OBJECTION 1**: It would seem that it is not lawful to swear by creatures. It is written (Matt 5:34–36): *I say to you not to swear at all, neither by heaven . . . nor by the earth . . . nor by Jerusalem . . . nor by thy head*: and Jerome, expounding these words, says: *Observe that the Savior does not forbid swearing by God, but by heaven and earth*, etc.

**OBJ. 2**: Further, punishment is not due save for a fault. Now a punishment is appointed for one who swears by creatures: for it is written (22, qu. i, can. *Clericum*): *If a cleric swears by creatures he must be very severely rebuked: and if he shall persist in this vicious habit we wish that he be excommunicated.* Therefore it is unlawful to swear by creatures.

**OBJ. 3**: Further, an oath is an act of religion, as stated above (A. 4). But religious worship is not due to any creature, according to Rom. 1:23, 25. Therefore it is not lawful to swear by a creature.

**ON THE CONTRARY**, Joseph swore *by the health of Pharaoh* (Gen 42:16). Moreover it is customary to swear by the Gospel, by relics, and by the saints.

**I ANSWER THAT**, As stated above (A. 1, ad 3), there are two kinds of oath. One is uttered as a simple contestation or calling God as witness: and this kind of oath, like faith, is based on God's truth. Now faith is essentially and chiefly about God Who is the very truth, and secondarily about creatures in which God's truth is reflected, as stated above (Q. 1, A. 1). In like manner an oath is chiefly referred to God Whose testimony is invoked; and secondarily an appeal by oath is made to certain creatures considered, not in themselves, but as reflecting the Divine truth. Thus we swear by the Gospel, i.e., by God Whose truth is made

na veritas manifestatur; sicut iuramus per Evangelium, idest per Deum, cuius veritas in Evangelio manifestatur; et per sanctos, qui hanc veritatem crediderunt et observaverunt.

Alius autem modus iurandi est per execrationem. Et in hoc iuramento inducitur creatura aliqua ut in qua divinum iudicium exerceatur. Et sic solet homo iurare per caput suum, vel per filium suum, aut per aliquam aliam rem quam diligit. Sicut et apostolus iuravit, II ad Cor. I, dicens, *ego testem Deum invoco in animam meam.*

Quod autem Ioseph per salutem Pharaonis iuravit, utroque modo potest intelligi, vel per modum execrationis, quasi salutem Pharaonis obligaverit Deo; vel per modum contestationis, quasi contestando veritatem divinae iustitiae, ad cuius executionem principes terrae constituuntur.

**Ad primum** ergo dicendum quod dominus prohibuit iurare per creaturas ita quod eis adhibeatur reverentia divina. Unde Hieronymus ibidem subdit quod *Iudaei, per Angelos,* et cetera huiusmodi, *iurantes, creaturas venerabantur Dei honore.*

Et eadem ratione punitur secundum canones clericus per creaturam iurans, quod ad blasphemiam infidelitatis pertinet. Unde in sequenti capitulo dicitur, *si quis per capillum Dei vel caput iuraverit, vel alio modo blasphemia contra Deum usus fuerit, si in ecclesiastico ordine est, deponatur.*

**Et per hoc** patet responsio ad secundum.

**Ad tertium** dicendum quod cultus latriae adhibetur ei cuius testimonium iurando invocatur. Et ideo praecipitur Exod. XXIII, *per nomen externorum deorum non iurabitis.* Non autem exhibetur cultus latriae creaturis quae in iuramento assumuntur secundum modos praedictos.

known in the Gospel; and by the saints who believed this truth and kept it.

The other way of swearing is by cursing and in this kind of oath a creature is adduced that the judgment of God may be wrought therein. Thus a man is wont to swear by his head, or by his son, or by some other thing that he loves, even as the Apostle swore (2 Cor 1:23), saying: *I call God to witness upon my soul.*

As to Joseph's oath by the health of Pharaoh this may be understood in both ways: either by way of a curse, as though he pledged Pharaoh's health to God; or by way of contestation, as though he appealed to the truth of God's justice which the princes of the earth are appointed to execute.

**Reply Obj. 1**: Our Lord forbade us to swear by creatures so as to give them the reverence due to God. Hence Jerome adds that *the Jews, through swearing by the angels and the like, worshipped creatures with a Divine honor.*

In the same sense a cleric is punished, according to the canons (22, qu. i, can. *Clericum*, Obj. 2), for swearing by a creature, for this savors of the blasphemy of unbelief. Hence in the next chapter, it is said: *If any one swears by God's hair or head, or otherwise utter blasphemy against God, and he be in ecclesiastical orders, let him be degraded.*

**This suffices** for the Reply to the Second Objection.

**Reply Obj. 3**: Religious worship is shown to one whose testimony is invoked by oath: hence the prohibition (Exod 23:13): *By the name of strange gods you shall not swear.* But religious worship is not given to creatures employed in an oath in the ways mentioned above.

# Article 7

*Whether an oath has a binding force?*

**Ad septimum sic proceditur.** Videtur quod iuramentum non habeat vim obligandi. Inducitur enim iuramentum ad confirmandum veritatem eius quod dicitur. Sed quando aliquis dicit aliquid de futuro, verum dicit etiam si non eveniat quod dicit, sicut Paulus, quamvis non iverit Corinthum, sicut dixerat, non tamen est mentitus, ut patet II Cor. I. Ergo videtur quod iuramentum non sit obligatorium.

**Praeterea,** virtus non est virtuti contraria, ut dicitur in praedicamentis. Sed iuramentum est actus virtutis, ut dictum est. Quandoque autem esset contra virtutem, aut in aliquod eius impedimentum, si quis servaret id quod iuravit, sicut cum aliquis iurat se facere aliquod

**Objection 1**: It would seem that an oath has no binding force. An oath is employed in order to confirm the truth of an assertion. But when a person makes an assertion about the future his assertion is true, though it may not be verified. Thus Paul lied not (2 Cor 1:15, seqq.) though he went not to Corinth, as he had said he would (1 Cor 16:5). Therefore it seems that an oath is not binding.

**Obj. 2**: Further, virtue is not contrary to virtue (*Categ.* viii, 22). Now an oath is an act of virtue, as stated above (A. 4). But it would sometimes be contrary to virtue, or an obstacle thereto, if one were to fulfill what one has sworn to do: for instance, if one were to swear to commit a sin, or to

peccatum, vel cum iurat desistere ab aliquo opere virtutis. Ergo iuramentum non semper est obligatorium.

PRAETEREA, quandoque aliquis invitus compellitur ad hoc quod sub iuramento aliquid promittat. Sed *tales a iuramenti nexibus sunt per Romanos pontifices absoluti*, ut habetur extra, de iureiurando, cap. *Verum in ea quaestione*, etc. Ergo iuramentum non semper est obligatorium.

PRAETEREA, nullus potest obligari ad duo opposita. Sed quandoque oppositum est quod intendit iurans, et quod intendit ille cui iuramentum praestatur. Ergo iuramentum non potest semper esse obligatorium.

SED CONTRA est quod dicitur Matth. V, *reddes domino iuramenta tua.*

RESPONDEO dicendum quod obligatio refertur ad aliquid quod est faciendum vel dimittendum. Unde non videtur respicere iuramentum assertorium, quod est de praesenti vel de praeterito; neque etiam iuramentum de his quae sunt per alias causas fienda, sicut si quis iuramento assereret quod cras pluvia esset futura; sed solum in his quae sunt fienda per illum qui iurat.

Sicut autem iuramentum assertorium, quod est de praeterito vel de praesenti, debet habere veritatem, ita etiam et iuramentum de his quae sunt fienda a nobis in futurum. Et ideo utrumque iuramentum habet quandam obligationem, diversimode tamen. Quia in iuramento quod est de praeterito vel praesenti, obligatio est non respectu rei quae iam fuit vel est, sed respectu ipsius actus iurandi, ut scilicet iuret id quod iam verum est vel fuit. Sed in iuramento quod praestatur de his quae sunt fienda a nobis, obligatio cadit e converso super rem quam aliquis iuramento firmavit. Tenetur enim aliquis ut faciat verum esse id quod iuravit, alioquin deest veritas iuramento.

Si autem est talis res quae in eius potestate non fuit, deest iuramento discretionis iudicium, nisi forte quod erat ei possibile quando iuravit, ei reddatur impossibile per aliquem eventum; puta cum aliquis iuravit se pecuniam soluturum, quae ei postmodum vi vel furto subtrahitur. Tunc enim videtur excusatus esse a faciendo quod iuravit, licet teneatur facere quod in se est, sicut etiam supra circa obligationem voti diximus. Si vero sit quidem possibile fieri, sed fieri non debeat, vel quia est per se malum, vel quia est boni impeditivum, tunc iuramento deest iustitia. Et ideo iuramentum non est servandum in eo casu quo est peccatum vel boni impeditivum, secundum enim utrumque horum *vergit in deteriorem exitum.*

Sic ergo dicendum est quod quicumque iurat aliquid se facturum, obligatur ad id faciendum, ad hoc quod veritas impleatur, si tamen alii duo comites adsint, scilicet iudicium et iustitia.

AD PRIMUM ergo dicendum quod aliud est de simplici verbo, aliud de iuramento, in quo divinum

desist from some virtuous action. Therefore an oath is not always binding.

OBJ. 3: Further, sometimes a man is compelled against his will to promise something under oath. Now, *such a person is loosed by the Roman Pontiffs from the bond of his oath* (Extra, *De Jurejur.*, cap. *Verum in ea quaest.*, etc.). Therefore an oath is not always binding.

OBJ. 4: Further, no person can be under two opposite obligations. Yet sometimes the person who swears and the person to whom he swears have opposite intentions. Therefore an oath cannot always be binding.

ON THE CONTRARY, It is written (Matt 5:33): *Thou shalt perform thy oaths to the Lord.*

I ANSWER THAT, An obligation implies something to be done or omitted; so that apparently it regards neither the declaratory oath (which is about something present or past), nor such oaths as are about something to be effected by some other cause (as, for example, if one were to swear that it would rain tomorrow), but only such as are about things to be done by the person who swears.

Now just as a declaratory oath, which is about the future or the present, should contain the truth, so too ought the oath which is about something to be done by us in the future. Yet there is a difference: since, in the oath that is about the past or present, this obligation affects, not the thing that already has been or is, but the action of the swearer, in the point of his swearing to what is or was already true; whereas, on the contrary, in the oath that is made about something to be done by us, the obligation falls on the thing guaranteed by oath. For a man is bound to make true what he has sworn, else his oath lacks truth.

Now if this thing be such as not to be in his power, his oath is lacking in judgment of discretion: unless perchance what was possible when he swore become impossible to him through some mishap, as when a man swore to pay a sum of money, which is subsequently taken from him by force or theft. For then he would seem to be excused from fulfilling his oath, although he is bound to do what he can, as, in fact, we have already stated with regard to the obligation of a vow (Q. 88, A. 3, ad 2). If, on the other hand, it be something that he can do, but ought not to, either because it is essentially evil, or because it is a hindrance to a good, then his oath is lacking in justice: wherefore an oath must not be kept when it involves a sin or a hindrance to good. For in either case *its result is evil*

Accordingly we must conclude that whoever swears to do something is bound to do what he can for the fulfilment of truth; provided always that the other two accompanying conditions be present, namely, judgment and justice.

REPLY OBJ. 1: It is not the same with a simple assertion, and with an oath wherein God is called to witness: because

testimonium imploratur. Sufficit enim ad veritatem verbi quod aliquis dicat id quod proponit se facturum, quia hoc iam verum est in sua causa, scilicet in proposito facientis. Sed iuramentum adhiberi non debet nisi in re de qua aliquis firmiter certus est. Et ideo si iuramentum adhibeatur, propter reverentiam divini testimonii quod invocatur, obligatur homo ut faciat esse verum id quod iuravit, secundum suam possibilitatem, nisi in deteriorem exitum vergat, ut dictum est.

AD SECUNDUM dicendum quod iuramentum potest vergere in deteriorem exitum dupliciter. Uno modo, quia ab ipso principio habet peiorem exitum. Vel quia est secundum se malum, sicut cum aliquis iurat se adulterium patraturum. Sive quia est maioris boni impeditivum, puta cum aliquis iurat se non intraturum religionem, vel quod non fiet clericus, aut quod non accipiet praelationem in casu in quo expedit eum accipere, vel si quid aliud est huiusmodi. Huiusmodi enim iuramentum a principio est illicitum, differenter tamen. Quia si quis iuret se facturum aliquod peccatum, et peccat iurando, et peccat iuramentum servando. Si quis autem iurat se non facturum aliquod melius bonum, quod tamen facere non tenetur, peccat quidem iurando, inquantum ponit obicem spiritui sancto, qui est boni propositi inspirator, non tamen peccat iuramentum servando, sed multo melius facit si non servet.

Alio modo vergit in deteriorem exitum propter aliquid quod de novo emerserat, quod fuit impraemeditatum, sicut patet in iuramento Herodis, qui iuravit puellae saltanti se daturum quod petisset. Hoc enim iuramentum poterat esse a principio licitum, intellecta debita conditione, scilicet si peteret quod dare deceret, sed impletio iuramenti fuit illicita. Unde Ambrosius dicit, in I de officiis, *est contra officium nonnunquam promissum solvere sacramentum, sicut Herodes, qui necem Ioannis praestavit ne promissum negaret.*

AD TERTIUM dicendum quod in iuramento quod quis coactus facit, duplex est obligatio. Una quidem qua obligatur homini cui aliquid promittit. Et talis obligatio tollitur per coactionem, quia ille qui vim intulit hoc meretur, ut ei promissum non servetur. Alia autem est obligatio qua quis Deo obligatur ut impleat quod per nomen eius promisit. Et talis obligatio non tollitur in foro conscientiae, quia magis debet damnum temporale sustinere quam iuramentum violare. Potest tamen repetere in iudicio quod solvit, vel praelato denuntiare, non obstante si contrarium iuravit, quia tale iuramentum vergeret in deteriorem exitum, esset enim contra iustitiam publicam. Romani autem pontifices ab huiusmodi iuramentis homines absolverunt non quasi decernentes huiusmodi iuramenta non esse obligatoria, sed quasi huiusmodi obligationes ex iusta causa relaxantes.

it suffices for the truth of an assertion, that a person say what he proposes to do, since it is already true in its cause, namely, the purpose of the doer. But an oath should not be employed, save in a matter about which one is firmly certain: and, consequently, if a man employ an oath, he is bound, as far as he can, to make true what he has sworn, through reverence of the Divine witness invoked, unless it leads to an evil result, as stated.

REPLY OBJ. 2: An oath may lead to an evil result in two ways. First, because from the very outset it has an evil result, either through being evil of its very nature (as, if a man were to swear to commit adultery), or through being a hindrance to a greater good, as if a man were to swear not to enter religion, or not to become a cleric, or that he would not accept a prelacy, supposing it would be expedient for him to accept, or in similar cases. For oaths of this kind are unlawful from the outset: yet with a difference: because if a man swear to commit a sin, he sinned in swearing, and sins in keeping his oath: whereas if a man swear not to perform a greater good, which he is not bound to do withal, he sins indeed in swearing (through placing an obstacle to the Holy Spirit, Who is the inspirer of good purposes), yet he does not sin in keeping his oath, though he does much better if he does not keep it.

Second, an oath leads to an evil result through some new and unforeseen emergency. An instance is the oath of Herod, who swore to the damsel, who danced before him, that he would give her what she would ask of him. For this oath could be lawful from the outset, supposing it to have the requisite conditions, namely, that the damsel asked what it was right to grant, but the fulfilment of the oath was unlawful. Hence Ambrose says (*De Officiis* i, 50): *Sometimes it is wrong to fulfill a promise, and to keep an oath; as Herod, who granted the slaying of John, rather than refuse what he had promised.*

REPLY OBJ. 3: There is a twofold obligation in the oath which a man takes under compulsion: one, whereby he is beholden to the person to whom he promises something; and this obligation is cancelled by the compulsion, because he that used force deserves that the promise made to him should not be kept. The other is an obligation whereby a man is beholden to God, in virtue of which he is bound to fulfill what he has promised in His name. This obligation is not removed in the tribunal of conscience, because that man ought rather to suffer temporal loss, than violate his oath. He can, however, seek in a court of justice to recover what he has paid, or denounce the matter to his superior even if he has sworn to the contrary, because such an oath would lead to evil results since it would be contrary to public justice. The Roman Pontiffs, in absolving men from oaths of this kind, did not pronounce such oaths to be unbinding, but relaxed the obligation for some just cause.

AD QUARTUM dicendum quod quando non est eadem iurantis intentio et eius cui iurat, si hoc provenit ex dolo iurantis, debet iuramentum servari secundum sanum intellectum eius cui iuramentum praestatur. Unde Isidorus dicit, *quacumque arte verborum quis iuret, Deus tamen, qui conscientiae testis est, ita hoc accipit sicut ille cui iuratur intelligit.* Et quod hoc intelligatur de doloso iuramento, patet per id quod subditur, dupliciter reus fit *qui et nomen Dei in vanum assumit, et proximum dolo capit.* Si autem iurans dolum non adhibeat, obligatur secundum intentionem iurantis. Unde Gregorius dicit, XXVI Moral., *humanae aures talia verba nostra iudicant qualia foris sonant, divina vero iudicia talia foris audiunt qualia ex intimis proferuntur.*

REPLY OBJ. 4: When the intention of the swearer is not the same as the intention of the person to whom he swears, if this be due to the swearer's guile, he must keep his oath in accordance with the sound understanding of the person to whom the oath is made. Hence Isidore says (*De Summo Bono* ii, 31): *However artful a man may be in wording his oath, God Who witnesses his conscience accepts his oath as understood by the person to whom it is made.* And that this refers to the deceitful oath is clear from what follows: *He is doubly guilty who both takes God's name in vain, and tricks his neighbor by guile.* If, however, the swearer uses no guile, he is bound in accordance with his own intention. Wherefore Gregory says (*Moral.* xxvi, 7): *The human ear takes such like words in their natural outward sense, but the Divine judgment interprets them according to our inward intention.*

# Article 8

*Whether an oath is more binding than a vow?*

AD OCTAVUM SIC PROCEDITUR. Videtur quod maior sit obligatio iuramenti quam voti. Votum enim est simplex promissio. Sed iuramentum supra promissionem adhibet divinum testimonium. Ergo maior est obligatio iuramenti quam voti.

PRAETEREA, debilius solet per fortius confirmari. Sed votum interdum confirmatur iuramento. Ergo iuramentum est fortius quam votum.

PRAETEREA, obligatio voti causatur ex animi deliberatione, ut supra dictum est. Obligatio autem iuramenti causatur ex divina veritate, cuius testimonium invocatur. Cum ergo veritas Dei excedat deliberationem humanam, videtur quod obligatio iuramenti sit fortior quam obligatio voti.

SED CONTRA, per votum obligatur aliquis Deo, per iuramentum obligatur interdum homini. Magis autem obligatur homo Deo quam homini. Ergo maior est obligatio voti quam iuramenti.

RESPONDEO dicendum quod utraque obligatio, scilicet voti et iuramenti, causatur ex aliquo divino, aliter tamen et aliter. Nam obligatio voti causatur ex fidelitate quam Deo debemus, ut scilicet ei promissum solvamus. Obligatio autem iuramenti causatur ex reverentia quam debemus ei, ex qua tenemur quod verificemus id quod per nomen eius promittimus. Omnis autem infidelitas irreverentiam continet, sed non convertitur, videtur enim infidelitas subiecti ad dominum esse maxima irreverentia. Et ideo votum ex ratione sua magis est obligatorium quam iuramentum.

AD PRIMUM ergo dicendum quod votum est promissio non quaecumque, sed Deo facta, cui infidelem esse gravissimum est.

OBJECTION 1: It would seem that an oath is more binding than a vow. A vow is a simple promise: whereas an oath includes, besides a promise, an appeal to God as witness. Therefore an oath is more binding than a vow.

OBJ. 2: Further, the weaker is wont to be confirmed by the stronger. Now a vow is sometimes confirmed by an oath. Therefore an oath is stronger than a vow.

OBJ. 3: Further, the obligation of a vow arises from the deliberation of the mind, a stated above (Q. 88, A. 1); while the obligation of an oath results from the truth of God Whose testimony is invoked. Since therefore God's truth is something greater than human deliberation, it seems that the obligation of an oath is greater than that of a vow.

ON THE CONTRARY, A vow binds one to God while an oath sometimes binds one to man. Now one is more bound to God than to man. Therefore a vow is more binding than an oath.

I ANSWER THAT, The obligation both of vow and of an oath arises from something Divine; but in different ways. For the obligation of a vow arises from the fidelity we owe God, which binds us to fulfill our promises to Him. On the other hand, the obligation of an oath arises from the reverence we owe Him which binds us to make true what we promise in His name. Now every act of infidelity includes an irreverence, but not conversely, because the infidelity of a subject to his lord would seem to be the greatest irreverence. Hence a vow by its very nature is more binding than an oath.

REPLY OBJ. 1: A vow is not any kind of promise, but a promise made to God; and to be unfaithful to God is most grievous.

AD SECUNDUM dicendum quod iuramentum non adhibetur voto quasi aliquid firmius, sed ut *per duas res immobiles* maior firmitas adhibeatur.

AD TERTIUM dicendum quod deliberatio animi dat firmitatem voto quantum ex parte voventis est. Habet tamen maiorem firmitatis causam ex parte Dei, cui votum offertur.

REPLY OBJ. 2: An oath is added to a vow not because it is more stable, but because greater stability results from *two immutable things.*

REPLY OBJ. 3: Deliberation of the mind gives a vow its stability, on the part of the person who takes the vow: but it has a greater cause of stability on the part of God, to Whom the vow is offered.

# Article 9

### Whether anyone can dispense from an oath?

AD NONUM SIC PROCEDITUR. Videtur quod nullus possit dispensare in iuramento. Sicut enim veritas requiritur ad iuramentum assertorium, quod est de praeterito vel praesenti, ita ad iuramentum promissorium, quod est de futuro. Sed nullus potest cum aliquo dispensare quod de praeteritis vel praesentibus iuret contra veritatem. Ergo etiam nullus potest dispensare quod non faciat aliquis esse verum id quod cum iuramento in futurum promisit.

PRAETEREA, iuramentum promissorium inducitur ad utilitatem eius cui fit promissio. Sed ille, ut videtur, non potest relaxare, quia est contra divinam reverentiam. Ergo multo minus per aliquem potest super hoc dispensari.

PRAETEREA, in voto quilibet episcopus potest dispensare, exceptis quibusdam votis quae soli Papae reservantur, ut supra habitum est. Ergo, pari ratione, in iuramento, si esset dispensabile, quilibet episcopus posset dispensare. Quod tamen videtur esse contra iura. Non ergo videtur quod in iuramento possit dispensari.

SED CONTRA est quod votum est maioris obligationis quam iuramentum, ut supra dictum est. Sed in voto potest dispensari. Ergo in iuramento.

RESPONDEO dicendum quod, sicut supra dictum est, necessitas dispensationis tam in lege quam in voto est propter hoc quod id quod in se, vel universaliter consideratum, est utile et honestum, secundum aliquem particularem eventum potest esse inhonestum et nocivum, quod non potest cadere nec sub lege nec sub voto. Quod autem aliquid sit inhonestum vel noxium, repugnat his quae debent attendi in iuramento, nam si sit inhonestum, repugnat iustitiae; si sit noxium, repugnat iudicio. Et ideo, pari ratione, etiam in iuramento dispensari potest.

AD PRIMUM ergo dicendum quod dispensatio quae fit in iuramento non se extendit ad hoc quod aliquid contra iuramentum fiat, hoc enim est impossibile, cum observatio iuramenti cadat sub praecepto divino, quod est indispensabile. Sed ad hoc se extendit dispensatio

OBJECTION 1: It would seem that no one can dispense from an oath. Just as truth is required for a declaratory oath, which is about the past or the present, so too is it required for a promissory oath, which is about the future. Now no one can dispense a man from swearing to the truth about present or past things. Therefore neither can anyone dispense a man from making truth that which he has promised by oath to do in the future.

OBJ. 2: Further, a promissory oath is used for the benefit of the person to whom the promise is made. But, apparently, he cannot release the other from his oath, since it would be contrary to the reverence of God. Much less therefore can a dispensation from this oath be granted by anyone.

OBJ. 3: Further, any bishop can grant a dispensation from a vow, except certain vows reserved to the Pope alone, as stated above (Q. 88, A. 12, ad 3). Therefore in like manner, if an oath admits of dispensation, any bishop can dispense from an oath. And yet seemingly this is to be against the law. Therefore it would seem that an oath does not admit of dispensation.

ON THE CONTRARY, A vow is more binding than an oath, as stated above (A. 8). But a vow admits of dispensation and therefore an oath does also.

I ANSWER THAT, As stated above (Q. 88, A. 10), the necessity of a dispensation both from the law and from a vow arises from the fact that something which is useful and morally good in itself and considered in general, may be morally evil and hurtful in respect of some particular emergency: and such a case comes under neither law nor vow. Now anything morally evil or hurtful is incompatible with the matter of an oath: for if it be morally evil it is opposed to justice, and if it be hurtful it is contrary to judgment. Therefore an oath likewise admits of dispensation.

REPLY OBJ. 1: A dispensation from an oath does not imply a permission to do anything against the oath: for this is impossible, since the keeping of an oath comes under a Divine precept, which does not admit of dispensation: but it implies that what hitherto came under an oath no longer

iuramenti ut id quod sub iuramento cadebat, sub iuramento non cadat, quasi non existens debita materia iuramenti, sicut et de voto supra diximus. Materia autem iuramenti assertorii, quod est de praeterito vel praesenti, in quandam necessitatem iam transiit, et immutabilis facta est, et ideo dispensatio non referretur ad materiam, sed referretur ad ipsum actum iuramenti; unde talis dispensatio directe esset contra praeceptum divinum. Sed materia iuramenti promissorii est aliquid futurum, quod variari potest, ita scilicet quod in aliquo eventu potest esse illicitum vel nocivum, et per consequens non esse debita materia iuramenti. Et ideo dispensari potest in iuramento promissorio, quia talis dispensatio respicit materiam iuramenti, et non contrariatur praecepto divino de iuramenti observatione.

**AD SECUNDUM** dicendum quod homo potest alteri promittere aliquid sub iuramento dupliciter. Uno modo, quasi pertinens ad utilitatem ipsius, puta si sub iuramento promittat se serviturum ei, vel pecuniam daturum. Et a tali promissione potest absolvere ille cui promissio facta est, intelligitur enim iam ei solvisse promissum quando facit de eo secundum eius voluntatem. Alio modo promittit aliquis alteri quod pertinet ad honorem Dei vel utilitatem aliorum, puta si aliquis iuramento promittat alicui se intraturum religionem, vel aliquod opus pietatis facturum. Et tunc ille cui promittitur non potest absolvere promittentem, quia promissio non est facta ei principaliter, sed Deo, nisi forte sit interposita conditio, scilicet, *si illi videbitur cui promittit*, vel aliquid aliud tale.

**AD TERTIUM** dicendum quod quandoque illud quod cadit sub iuramento promissorio est manifeste repugnans iustitiae, vel quia est peccatum, sicut cum aliquis iurat se facturum homicidium; vel quia est maioris boni impeditivum, sicut cum aliquis iurat se non intraturum religionem. Et tale iuramentum dispensatione non indiget, sed in primo casu tenetur aliquis tale iuramentum non servare; in secundo autem casu licitum est et servare et non servare, ut supra dictum est. Quandoque vero aliquid sub iuramento promittitur de quo dubium est utrum sit licitum vel illicitum, proficuum vel nocivum, aut simpliciter aut in aliquo casu. Et in hoc potest quilibet episcopus dispensare quandoque vero sub iuramento promittitur aliquid quod est manifeste licitum et utile. Et in tali iuramento non videtur habere locum dispensatio, sed commutatio, si aliquid melius faciendum occurrat ad communem utilitatem, quod maxime videtur pertinere ad potestatem Papae, qui habet curam universalis Ecclesiae; vel etiam absoluta relaxatio, quod etiam ad Papam pertinet, in omnibus generaliter quae ad dispensationem rerum ecclesiasticarum pertinent, super quas habet plenitudinem potestatis; sicut et ad unumquemque pertinet irritare iuramentum quod a sibi subditis factum est circa

comes under it, as not being due matter for an oath, just as we have said with regard to vows (Q. 88, A. 10, ad 2). Now the matter of a declaratory oath, which is about something past or present, has already acquired a certain necessity, and has become unchangeable, wherefore the dispensation will regard not the matter but the act itself of the oath: so that such a dispensation would be directly contrary to the Divine precept. On the other hand, the matter of a promissory oath is something future, which admits of change, so that, to wit, in certain emergencies, it may be unlawful or hurtful, and consequently undue matter for an oath. Therefore a promissory oath admits of dispensation, since such dispensation regards the matter of an oath, and is not contrary to the Divine precept about the keeping of oaths.

**REPLY OBJ. 2**: One man may promise something under oath to another in two ways. First, when he promises something for his benefit: for instance, if he promise to serve him, or to give him money: and from such a promise he can be released by the person to whom he made it: for he is understood to have already kept his promise to him when he acts towards him according to his will. Second, one man promises another something pertaining to God's honor or to the benefit of others: for instance, if a man promise another under oath that he will enter religion, or perform some act of kindness. In this case the person to whom the promise is made cannot release him that made the promise, because it was made principally not to him but to God: unless perchance it included some condition, for instance, *provided he give his consent* or some such like condition.

**REPLY OBJ. 3**: Sometimes that which is made the matter of a promissory oath is manifestly opposed to justice, either because it is a sin, as when a man swears to commit a murder, or because it is an obstacle to a greater good, as when a man swears not to enter religion: and such an oath requires no dispensation. But in the former case a man is bound not to keep such an oath, while in the latter it is lawful for him to keep or not to keep the oath, as stated above (A. 7, ad 2). Sometimes what is promised on oath is doubtfully right or wrong, useful or harmful, either in itself or under the circumstance. In this case any bishop can dispense. Sometimes, however, that which is promised under oath is manifestly lawful and beneficial. An oath of this kind seemingly admits not of dispensation but of commutation, when there occurs something better to be done for the common good, in which case the matter would seem to belong chiefly to the power of the Pope, who has charge over the whole Church; and even of absolute relaxation, for this too belongs in general to the Pope in all matters regarding the administration of things ecclesiastical. Thus it is competent to any man to cancel an oath made by one of his subjects in matters that come under his authority: for instance, a father may annul his daughter's oath, and a

ea quae eius potestati subduntur; sicut pater potest irritare iuramentum puellae et vir uxoris, ut dicitur Num. XXX, sicut et supra de voto dictum est.

husband his wife's (Num 30:6, seqq.), as stated above with regard to vows (Q. 88, AA. 8, 9).

# Article 10

*Whether an oath is voided by a condition of person or time?*

**AD DECIMUM SIC PROCEDITUR.** Videtur quod iuramentum non impediatur per aliquam conditionem personae vel temporis. Iuramentum enim *ad confirmationem* inducitur, ut patet per apostolum, ad Heb. VI. Sed cuilibet convenit confirmare dictum suum, et quolibet tempore. Ergo videtur quod iuramentum non impediatur propter aliquam conditionem personae vel temporis.

**PRAETEREA,** maius est iurare per Deum quam per Evangelia, unde Chrysostomus dicit, *si aliqua causa fuerit, modicum videtur facere qui iurat per Deum, qui autem iurat per Evangelium, maius aliquid fecisse videtur. Quibus dicendum est, stulti, Scripturae propter Deum factae sunt, non Deus propter Scripturas.* Sed cuiuslibet conditionis personae, et quolibet tempore, in communi locutione consueverunt iurare per Deum. Ergo multo magis licitum est eis iurare per Evangelia.

**PRAETEREA,** idem non causatur ex contrariis causis, quia contrariae causae sunt contrariorum. Sed aliqui excluduntur a iuramento propter defectum personae, sicut pueri ante quatuordecim annos, et etiam illi qui semel fuerunt periuri. Non ergo videtur quod aliqui prohibeantur iurare vel propter dignitatem, sicut clerici; aut etiam propter temporis solemnitatem.

**PRAETEREA,** nullus homo vivens in hoc mundo est tantae dignitatis sicut Angeli, dicitur enim Matth. XI quod *qui minor est in regno caelorum maior est illo,* scilicet Ioanne Baptista adhuc in mundo vivente. Sed Angelo convenit iurare, dicitur enim Apoc. X quod *Angelus iuravit per viventem in saecula saeculorum.* Ergo nullus homo propter dignitatem debet excusari a iuramento.

**SED CONTRA** est quod habetur II, qu. V, *presbyter, vice iuramenti, per sanctam consecrationem interrogetur.* Et XXII, qu. V, dicitur, *nullus ex ecclesiastico ordine cuiquam laico quidquam super sancta Evangelia iurare praesumat.*

**RESPONDEO** dicendum quod in iuramento duo sunt consideranda. Unum quidem ex parte Dei, cuius testimonium inducitur. Et quantum ad hoc, debetur iuramento maxima reverentia. Et propter hoc a iuramento excluduntur et pueri ante annos pubertatis, qui non coguntur ad iurandum, quia nondum habent

**OBJECTION 1**: It would seem that an oath is not voided by a condition of person or time. An oath, according to the Apostle (Heb 6:16), is employed *for the purpose of confirmation.* Now it is competent to anyone to confirm his assertion, and at any time. Therefore it would seem that an oath is not voided by a condition of person or time.

**OBJ. 2**: Further, to swear by God is more than to swear by the Gospels: wherefore Chrysostom says: *If there is a reason for swearing, it seems a small thing to swear by God, but a great thing to swear by the Gospels. To those who think thus, it must be said: Nonsense! the Scriptures were made for God's sake, not God for the sake of the Scriptures.* Now men of all conditions and at all times are wont to swear by God. Much more, therefore, is it lawful to swear by the Gospels.

**OBJ. 3**: Further, the same effect does not proceed from contrary causes, since contrary causes produce contrary effects. Now some are debarred from swearing on account of some personal defect; children, for instance, before the age of fourteen, and persons who have already committed perjury. Therefore it would seem that a person ought not to be debarred from swearing either on account of his dignity, as clerics, or on account of the solemnity of the time.

**OBJ. 4**: Further, in this world no living man is equal in dignity to an angel: for it is written (Matt 11:11) that *he that is the lesser in the kingdom of heaven is greater than he,* namely than John the Baptist, while yet living. Now an angel is competent to swear, for it is written (Rev 10:6) that the angel *swore by Him that liveth for ever and ever.* Therefore no man ought to be excused from swearing, on account of his dignity.

**ON THE CONTRARY**, It is stated (II, qu. v, can. *Si quis presbyter): Let a priest be examined 'by his sacred consecration,' instead of being put on his oath*: and (22, qu. v, can. *Nullus): Let no one in ecclesiastical orders dare to swear on the Holy Gospels to a layman.*

**I ANSWER THAT,** Two things are to be considered in an oath. One is on the part of God, whose testimony is invoked, and in this respect we should hold an oath in the greatest reverence. For this reason children before the age of puberty are debarred from taking oaths, and are not called upon to swear, because they have not yet attained the

perfectum usum rationis, quo possint cum reverentia debita iuramentum praestare, et iterum periuri, qui ad iuramentum non admittuntur, quia ex retroactis praesumitur quod debitam reverentiam iuramento non exhibebunt. Et propter hoc etiam, ut iuramento debita reverentia exhibeatur, dicitur XXII, qu. V, *honestum est ut qui in sanctis audet iurare, hoc ieiunus faciat, cum omni honestate et timore Dei.*

Aliud autem est considerandum ex parte hominis, cuius dictum iuramento confirmatur. Non enim indiget dictum hominis confirmatione nisi quia de eo dubitatur. Hoc autem derogat dignitati personae, ut dubitetur de veritate eorum quae dicit. Et ideo personis magnae dignitatis non convenit iurare. Propter quod dicitur II, qu. V, cap. si quis presbyter, quod *sacerdotes ex levi causa iurare non debent.* Tamen pro aliqua necessitate, vel magna utilitate, licitum est eis iurare, et praecipue pro spiritualibus negotiis. Pro quibus etiam iuramenta competit praestare in solemnibus diebus, quibus est spiritualibus rebus vacandum, non autem tunc sunt iuramenta praestanda pro rebus temporalibus, nisi forte ex magna necessitate.

**AD PRIMUM** ergo dicendum quod quidam sunt qui dictum suum confirmare non possunt propter eorum defectum, et quidam sunt quorum dictum adeo debet esse certum quod confirmatione non egeat.

**AD SECUNDUM** dicendum quod iuramentum, secundum se consideratum, tanto sanctius est et magis obligat quanto maius est id per quod iuratur, ut Augustinus dicit, ad Publicolam. Et secundum hoc, maius est iurare per Deum quam per Evangelia. Sed potest esse e converso propter modum iurandi, utpote si iuramentum quod fit per Evangelia, fiat cum quadam deliberatione et solemnitate; iuramentum autem quod fit per Deum, fiat leviter et absque deliberatione.

**AD TERTIUM** dicendum quod nihil prohibet aliquid tolli ex contrariis causis per modum superabundantiae et defectus. Et hoc modo aliqui impediuntur a iuramento quia sunt maioris auctoritatis quam quod eos iurare deceat, aliqui vero quia sunt minoris auctoritatis quam quod eorum iuramento stetur.

**AD QUARTUM** dicendum quod iuramentum Angeli inducitur non propter defectum ipsius, quasi non sit eius simplici dicto credendum, sed ad ostendendum id quod dicitur ex infallibili Dei dispositione procedere. Sicut etiam et Deus aliquando in Scripturis iurans inducitur, ad ostendendum immobilitatem eius quod dicitur, sicut apostolus dicit, ad Heb. VI.

perfect use of reason, so as to be able to take a oath with due reverence. Perjurers also are debarred from taking an oath, because it is presumed from their antecedents that they will not treat an oath with the reverence due to it. For this same reason, in order that oaths might be treated with due reverence the law says (22, qu. v, can. *Honestum*): *It is becoming that he who ventures to swear on holy things should do so fasting, with all propriety and fear of God.*

The other thing to be considered is on the part of the man, whose assertion is confirmed by oath. For a man's assertion needs no confirmation save because there is a doubt about it. Now it derogates from a person's dignity that one should doubt about the truth of what he says, wherefore *it becomes not persons of great dignity to swear.* For this reason the law says (II, qu. v, can. *Si quis presbyter*) that *priests should not swear for trifling reasons.* Nevertheless it is lawful for them to swear if there be need for it, or if great good may result therefrom. Especially is this the case in spiritual affairs, when moreover it is becoming that they should take oath on days of solemnity, since they ought then to devote themselves to spiritual matters. Nor should they on such occasions take oaths temporal matters, except perhaps in cases grave necessity.

**REPLY OBJ. 1**: Some are unable to confirm their own assertions on account of their own defect: and some there are whose words should be so certain that they need no confirmation.

**REPLY OBJ. 2**: The greater the thing sworn by, the holier and the more binding is the oath, considered in itself, as Augustine states (*Ad Public., Ep. xlvii*): and accordingly it is a graver matter to swear by God than the Gospels. Yet the contrary may be the case on account of the manner of swearing for instance, an oath by the Gospels might be taken with deliberation and solemnity, and an oath by God frivolously and without deliberation.

**REPLY OBJ. 3**: Nothing prevents the same thing from arising out of contrary causes, by way of superabundance and defect. It is in this way that some are debarred from swearing, through being of so great authority that it is unbecoming for them to swear; while others are of such little authority that their oaths have no standing.

**REPLY OBJ. 4**: The angel's oath is adduced not on account of any defect in the angel, as though one ought not to credit his mere word, but in order to show that the statement made issues from God's infallible disposition. Thus too God is sometimes spoken of by Scripture as swearing, in order to express the immutability of His word, as the Apostle declares (Heb 6:17).

# QUESTION 90

## THE TAKING OF GOD'S NAME BY WAY OF ADJURATION

Deinde considerandum est de assumptione divini nominis per modum adiurationis. Et circa hoc quaeruntur tria.

Primo, utrum liceat adiurare homines.

Secundo, utrum liceat adiurare Daemones.

Tertio, utrum liceat adiurare irrationales creaturas.

We must now consider the taking of God's name by way of adjuration: under which head there are three points of inquiry:

(1) Whether it is lawful to adjure a man?

(2) Whether it is lawful to adjure the demons?

(3) Whether it is lawful to adjure irrational creatures?

# Article 1

*Whether it is lawful to adjure a man?*

**AD PRIMUM SIC PROCEDITUR.** Videtur quod non liceat hominem adiurare. Dicit enim Origenes, super Matth., *aestimo quoniam non oportet ut vir qui vult secundum Evangelium vivere, adiuret alterum. Si enim iurare non licet, quantum ad evangelicum Christi mandatum, notum est quia nec adiurare alterum licet. Propterea manifestum est quoniam princeps sacerdotum Iesum illicite adiuravit per Deum vivum.*

**PRAETEREA,** quicumque adiurat aliquem, quodammodo ipsum compellit. Sed non licet alium invitum cogere. Ergo videtur quod nec liceat aliquem adiurare.

**PRAETEREA,** adiurare est aliquem *ad iurandum* inducere. Sed inducere aliquem ad iurandum est superiorum, qui inferioribus iuramenta imponunt. Ergo inferiores superiores suos non possunt adiurare.

**SED CONTRA** est quod etiam Deum obsecramus per aliqua sacra eum obtestantes. Apostolus etiam fideles *obsecrat per misericordia Dei,* ut patet Rom. XII, quod videtur ad quandam adiurationem pertinere. Ergo licitum est alios adiurare.

**RESPONDEO** dicendum quod ille qui iurat iuramento promissorio, per reverentiam divini nominis, quod ad confirmationem suae promissionis inducit, seipsum obligat ad faciendum quod promittit, quod est seipsum immobiliter ordinare ad aliquid agendum. Sicut autem homo seipsum ordinare potest ad aliquid agendum, ita etiam et alios, superiores quidem deprecando, inferiores autem imperando, ut ex supradictis patet. Cum igitur utraque ordinatio per aliquod divinum confirmatur, est adiuratio. In hoc tamen differt, quod homo est suorum actuum dominus, non autem est dominus eorum quae sunt ab alio agenda. Et ideo sibi ipsi potest necessitatem imponere per divini nominis invocationem, non autem

**OBJECTION 1:** It would seem that it is not lawful to adjure a man. Origen says (*Tract. xxxv super Matth.*): *I deem that a man who wishes to live according to the Gospel should not adjure another man. For if, according to the Gospel mandate of Christ, it be unlawful to swear, it is evident that neither is it lawful to adjure: and consequently it is manifest that the high-priest unlawfully adjured Jesus by the living God.*

**OBJ. 2:** Further, whoever adjures a man, compels him after a fashion. But it is unlawful to compel a man against his will. Therefore seemingly it is also unlawful to adjure a man.

**OBJ. 3:** Further, to adjure is to induce a person *to swear.* Now it belongs to man's superior to induce him to swear, for the superior imposes an oath on his subject. Therefore subjects cannot adjure their superiors.

**ON THE CONTRARY,** Even when we pray God we implore Him by certain holy things: and the Apostle too besought the faithful *by the mercy of God* (Rom 12:1): and this seems to be a kind of adjuration. Therefore it is lawful to adjure.

**I ANSWER THAT,** A man who utters a promissory oath, swearing by his reverence for the Divine name, which he invokes in confirmation of his promise, binds himself to do what he has undertaken, and so orders himself unchangeably to do a certain thing. Now just as a man can order himself to do a certain thing, so too can he order others, by beseeching his superiors, or by commanding his inferiors, as stated above (Q. 83, A. 1). Accordingly when either of these orderings is confirmed by something Divine it is an adjuration. Yet there is this difference between them, that man is master of his own actions but not of those of others; wherefore he can put himself under an obligation by invoking the Divine name, whereas he cannot put others

843

hanc necessitatem potest aliis imponere, nisi subditis, quos potest ex debito praestiti iuramenti compellere.

Si igitur aliquis per invocationem divini nominis, vel cuiuscumque rei sacrae, alicui non sibi subdito adiurando necessitatem agendi aliquid imponere intendat, sicut imponit sibi ipsi iurando, talis adiuratio illicita est, quia usurpat potestatem in alium quam non habet. Tamen propter aliquam necessitatem superiores suos inferiores tali genere adiurationis constringere possunt.

Si vero intendat solummodo per reverentiam divini nominis, vel alicuius rei sacrae, aliquid ab alio obtinere absque necessitatis impositione, talis adiuratio licita est respectu quorumlibet.

AD PRIMUM ergo dicendum quod Origenes loquitur de adiuratione qua aliquis alicui necessitatem imponere intendit, sicut imponit sibi ipsi iurando, sic enim princeps sacerdotum praesumpsit dominum Iesum Christum adiurare.

AD SECUNDUM dicendum quod illa ratio procedit de adiuratione quae necessitatem imponit.

AD TERTIUM dicendum quod adiurare non est aliquem ad iurandum inducere, sed per quandam similitudinem iuramenti a se inducti, alium ad aliquid agendum provocare.

Aliter tamen adiuratione utimur ad hominem, et aliter ad Deum. Nam adiurando hominis voluntatem per reverentiam rei sacrae immutare intendimus, quod quidem non intendimus circa Deum, cuius voluntas est immutabilis; sed quod a Deo per aeternam eius voluntatem aliquid obtineamus, non est ex meritis nostris, sed ex eius bonitate.

under such an obligation unless they be his subjects, whom he can compel on the strength of the oath they have taken.

Therefore, if a man by invoking the name of God, or any holy thing, intends by this adjuration to put one who is not his subject under an obligation to do a certain thing, in the same way as he would bind himself by oath, such an adjuration is unlawful, because he usurps over another a power which he has not. But superiors may bind their inferiors by this kind of adjuration, if there be need for it.

If, however, he merely intend, through reverence of the Divine name or of some holy thing, to obtain something from the other man without putting him under any obligation, such an adjuration may be lawfully employed in respect of anyone.

REPLY OBJ. 1: Origen is speaking of an adjuration whereby a man intends to put another under an obligation, in the same way as he would bind himself by oath: for thus did the high-priest presume to adjure our Lord Jesus Christ.

REPLY OBJ. 2: This argument considers the adjuration which imposes an obligation.

REPLY OBJ. 3: To adjure is not to induce a man to swear, but to employ terms resembling an oath in order to provoke another to do a certain thing.

Moreover, we adjure God in one way and man in another; because when we adjure a man we intend to alter his will by appealing to his reverence for a holy thing: and we cannot have such an intention in respect of God Whose will is immutable. If we obtain something from God through His eternal will, it is due, not to our merits, but to His goodness.

# Article 2

*Whether it is lawful to adjure the demons?*

AD SECUNDUM SIC PROCEDITUR. Videtur quod non liceat Daemones adiurare. Dicit enim Origenes, super Matth., *non est secundum potestatem datam a salvatore adiurare Daemonia, Iudaicum enim est hoc.* Non autem debemus Iudaeorum ritus imitari, sed potius uti potestate a Christo data. Ergo non est licitum Daemones adiurare.

PRAETEREA, multi nigromanticis incantationibus Daemones per aliquid divinum invocant, quod est adiurare. Si igitur licitum est Daemones adiurare, licitum est nigromanticis incantationibus uti. Quod patet esse falsum. Ergo et primum.

PRAETEREA, quicumque adiurat aliquem, ex hoc ipso aliquam societatem cum ipso facit. Sed non licet cum

OBJECTION 1: It would seem unlawful to adjure the demons. Origen says (*Tract. xxxv, super Matth.*): *To adjure the demons is not accordance with the power given by our Savior: for this is a Jewish practice.* Now rather than imitate the rites of the Jews, we should use the power given by Christ. Therefore it is not lawful to adjure the demons.

OBJ. 2: Further, many make use of necromantic incantations when invoking the demons by something Divine: and this is an adjuration. Therefore, if it be lawful to adjure the demons, it is lawful to make use of necromantic incantations, which is evidently false. Therefore the antecedent is false also.

OBJ. 3: Further, whoever adjures a person, by that very fact associates himself with him. Now it is not lawful to have

Daemonibus societatem facere, secundum illud I Cor. X, *nolo vos socios fieri Daemoniorum*. Ergo non licet Daemones adiurare.

**SED CONTRA** est quod dicitur Marc. ult., *in nomine meo Daemonia eiicient*. Sed inducere alium ad aliquid agendum propter nomen divinum, hoc est adiurare. Ergo licitum est Daemones adiurare.

**RESPONDEO** dicendum quod, sicut dictum est, duplex est adiurandi modus, unus quidem per modum deprecationis vel inductionis ob reverentiam alicuius sacri; alius autem per modum compulsionis. Primo autem modo non licet Daemones adiurare, quia ille modus adiurandi videtur ad quandam benevolentiam vel amicitiam pertinere, qua non licet ad Daemones uti. Secundo autem adiurationis modo, qui est per compulsionem, licet nobis ad aliquid uti, et ad aliquid non licet. Daemones enim in cursu huius vitae nobis adversarii constituuntur, non autem eorum actus nostrae dispositioni subduntur, sed dispositioni divinae et sanctorum Angelorum; quia, ut Augustinus dicit, in III de Trin., *spiritus desertor regitur per spiritum iustum*. Possumus ergo Daemones, adiurando, per virtutem divini nominis tanquam inimicos repellere, ne nobis noceant vel spiritualiter vel corporaliter, secundum potestatem datam a Christo, secundum illud Luc. X, *ecce, dedi vobis potestatem calcandi supra serpentes et scorpiones, et supra omnem virtutem inimici, et nihil vobis nocebit*.

Non tamen licitum est eos adiurare ad aliquid ab eis addiscendum, vel etiam ad aliquid per eos obtinendum, quia hoc pertineret ad aliquam societatem cum ipsis habendam, nisi forte ex speciali instinctu vel revelatione divina, aliqui sancti ad aliquos effectus Daemonum operatione utantur; sicut legitur de beato Iacobo quod per Daemones fecit Hermogenem ad se adduci.

**AD PRIMUM** ergo dicendum quod Origenes loquitur de adiuratione quae non fit protestative per modum compulsionis, sed magis per modum cuiusdam benevolae deprecationis.

**AD SECUNDUM** dicendum quod nigromantici utuntur adiurationibus et invocationibus Daemonum ad aliquid ab eis adipiscendum vel addiscendum, et hoc est illicitum, ut dictum est. Unde Chrysostomus dicit, Marc. I, exponens illud verbum domini, quod spiritui immundo dixit, *obmutesce, et exi de homine, salutiferum hic nobis dogma datur, ne credamus Daemonibus, quantumcumque denuntient veritatem*.

**AD TERTIUM** dicendum quod ratio illa procedit de adiuratione qua imploratur auxilium Daemonum ad aliquid agendum vel cognoscendum, hoc enim videtur ad quandam societatem pertinere. Sed quod aliquis adiurando Daemones repellat, hoc est ab eorum societate recedere.

fellowship with the demons, according to 1 Cor. 10:20, *I would not that you should be made partakers with devils*. Therefore it is not lawful to adjure the demons.

**ON THE CONTRARY,** It is written (Mark 16:17): *In My name they shall cast out devils*. Now to induce anyone to do a certain thing for the sake of God's name is to adjure. Therefore it is lawful to adjure the demons.

**I ANSWER THAT,** As stated in the preceding article, there are two ways of adjuring: one by way of prayer or inducement through reverence of some holy thing: the other by way of compulsion. In the first way it is not lawful to adjure the demons because such a way seems to savor of benevolence or friendship, which it is unlawful to bear towards the demons. As to the second kind of adjuration, which is by compulsion, we may lawfully use it for some purposes, and not for others. For during the course of this life the demons are our adversaries: and their actions are not subject to our disposal but to that of God and the holy angels, because, as Augustine says (*De Trin.* iii, 4), *the rebel spirit is ruled by the just spirit*. Accordingly we may repulse the demons, as being our enemies, by adjuring them through the power of God's name, lest they do us harm of soul or body, in accord with the Divine power given by Christ, as recorded by Luke 10:19: *Behold, I have given you power to tread upon serpents and scorpions, and upon all the power of the enemy: and nothing shall hurt you.*

It is not, however, lawful to adjure them for the purpose of learning something from them, or of obtaining something through them, for this would amount to holding fellowship with them: except perhaps when certain holy men, by special instinct or Divine revelation, make use of the demons' actions in order to obtain certain results: thus we read of the Blessed James that he caused Hermogenes to be brought to him, by the instrumentality of the demons.

**REPLY OBJ. 1:** Origen is speaking of adjuration made, not authoritatively by way of compulsion, but rather by way of a friendly appeal.

**REPLY OBJ. 2:** Necromancers adjure and invoke the demons in order to obtain or learn something from them: and this is unlawful, as stated above. Wherefore Chrysostom, commenting on our Lord's words to the unclean spirit (Mark 1:25), *Speak no more, and go out of the man*, says: *A salutary teaching is given us here, lest we believe the demons, however much they speak the truth.*

**REPLY OBJ. 3:** This argument considers the adjuration whereby the demon's help is besought in doing or learning something: for this savors of fellowship with them. On the other hand, to repulse the demons by adjuring them, is to sever oneself from their fellowship.

# Article 3

*Whether it is lawful to adjure an irrational creature?*

**AD TERTIUM SIC PROCEDITUR.** Videtur quod non liceat adiurare irrationalem creaturam. Adiuratio enim fit per locutionem. Sed frustra sermo dirigitur ad eum qui non intelligit, qualis est irrationalis creatura. Ergo vanum est et illicitum irrationalem creaturam adiurare.

**PRAETEREA,** ad eum videtur competere adiuratio ad quem pertinet iuratio. Sed iuratio non pertinet ad creaturam irrationalem. Ergo videtur quod ad eam non liceat adiuratione uti.

**PRAETEREA,** duplex est adiurationis modus, ut ex supradictis patet. Unus quidem per modum deprecationis, quo non possumus uti ad irrationalem creaturam, quae non est domina sui actus. Alia autem est adiuratio per modum compulsionis, qua etiam, ut videtur, ad eam uti non possumus; quia non est nostrum creaturis irrationalibus imperare, sed solum illius de quo dicitur, Matth. VIII, *quia venti et mare obediunt ei.* Ergo nullo modo, ut videtur, licet uti adiuratione ad irrationales creaturas.

**SED CONTRA** est quod Simon et Iudas leguntur adiurasse dracones, et eis praecepisse ut in desertum locum discederent.

**RESPONDEO** dicendum quod creaturae irrationales ab alio aguntur ad proprias operationes. Eadem autem actio est eius quod agitur et movetur, et eius quod agit et movet, sicut motus sagittae est etiam quaedam operatio sagittantis. Et ideo operatio irrationalis creaturae non solum ipsi attribuitur, sed principaliter Deo, cuius dispositione omnia moventur. Pertinet etiam ad Diabolum, qui, permissione divina, utitur aliquibus irrationalibus creaturis ad nocendum hominibus.

Sic ergo adiuratio qua quis utitur ad irrationalem creaturam, potest intelligi dupliciter. Uno modo, ut adiuratio referatur ad ipsam creaturam irrationalem secundum se. Et sic vanum esset irrationalem creaturam adiurare. Alio modo, ut referatur ad eum a quo irrationalis creatura agitur et movetur. Et sic dupliciter adiuratur irrationalis creatura. Uno quidem modo, per modum deprecationis ad Deum directae, quod pertinet ad eos qui divina invocatione miracula faciunt. Alio modo, per modum compulsionis, quae refertur ad Diabolum, qui in nocumentum nostrum utitur irrationabilibus creaturis, et talis est modus adiurandi in Ecclesiae exorcismis, per quos Daemonum potestas excluditur ab irrationalibus creaturis. Adiurare autem Daemones ab eis auxilium implorando, non licet.

**ET PER HOC** patet responsio ad obiecta.

**OBJECTION 1**: It would seem unlawful to adjure an irrational creature. An adjuration consists of spoken words. But it is useless to speak to one that understands not, such as an irrational creature. Therefore it is vain and unlawful to adjure an irrational creature.

**OBJ. 2**: Further, seemingly wherever adjuration is admissible, swearing is also admissible. But swearing is not consistent with an irrational creature. Therefore it would seem unlawful to employ adjuration towards one.

**OBJ. 3**: Further, there are two ways of adjuring, as explained above (AA. 1, 2). One is by way of appeal; and this cannot be employed towards irrational creatures, since they are not masters of their own actions. The other kind of adjuration is by way of compulsion: and, seemingly, neither is it lawful to use this towards them, because we have not the power to command irrational creatures, but only He of Whom it was said (Matt 8:27): *For the winds and the sea obey Him.* Therefore in no way, apparently, is it lawful to adjure irrational creatures.

**ON THE CONTRARY**, Simon and Jude are related to have adjured dragons and to have commanded them to withdraw into the desert.

**I ANSWER THAT,** Irrational creatures are directed to their own actions by some other agent. Now the action of what is directed and moved is also the action of the director and mover: thus the movement of the arrow is an operation of the archer. Wherefore the operation of the irrational creature is ascribed not only to it, but also and chiefly to God, Who disposes the movements of all things. It is also ascribed to the devil, who, by God's permission, makes use of irrational creatures in order to inflict harm on man.

Accordingly the adjuration of an irrational creature may be of two kinds. First, so that the adjuration is referred to the irrational creature in itself: and in this way it would be vain to adjure an irrational creature. Second, so that it be referred to the director and mover of the irrational creature, and in this sense a creature of this kind may be adjured in two ways. First, by way of appeal made to God, and this relates to those who work miracles by calling on God: second, by way of compulsion, which relates to the devil, who uses the irrational creature for our harm. This is the kind of adjuration used in the exorcisms of the Church, whereby the power of the demons is expelled from an irrational creature. But it is not lawful to adjure the demons by beseeching them to help us.

**THIS SUFFICES** for the Replies to the Objections.

# Question 91

## Taking the Divine Name for the Purpose of Praise

Deinde considerandum est de assumptione divini nominis ad invocandum per orationem vel laudem. Et de oratione quidem iam dictum est. Unde nunc de laude restat dicendum. Circa quam quaeruntur duo.

Primo, utrum Deus sit ore laudandus.
Secundo, utrum in laudibus Dei sint cantus adhibendi.

We must now consider the taking of the Divine name for the purpose of invoking it by prayer or praise. Of prayer we have already spoken (Q. 83). Wherefore we must speak now of praise. Under this head there are two points of inquiry:

(1) Whether God should be praised with the lips?
(2) Whether God should be praised with song?

# Article 1

*Whether God should be praised with the lips?*

**Ad primum sic proceditur.** Videtur quod Deus non sit ore laudandus. Dicit enim philosophus, in I Ethic., *optimorum non est laus, sed maius aliquid et melius.* Sed Deus est super omnia optima. Ergo Deo non debetur laus, sed aliquid maius laude. Unde et Eccli. XLIII dicitur quod Deus *maior est omni laude.*

**Praeterea,** laus Dei ad cultum ipsius pertinet, est enim religionis actus. Sed Deus mente colitur magis quam ore, unde dominus, Matth. XV, contra quosdam inducit illud Isaiae, *populus hic labiis me honorat, cor autem eorum longe est a me.* Ergo laus Dei magis consistit in corde quam in ore.

**Praeterea,** homines ad hoc ore laudantur ut ad meliora provocentur. Sicut enim mali ex suis laudibus superbiunt, ita boni ex suis laudibus ad meliora provocantur, unde dicitur Prov. XXVII, *quomodo probatur in conflatorio argentum, sic probatur homo ore laudantium.* Sed Deus per verba hominum non provocatur ad meliora, tum quia immutabilis est; tum quia summe bonus est, et non habet quo crescat. Ergo Deus non est laudandus ore.

**Sed contra** est quod dicitur in Psalm., *labiis exultationis laudabit os meum.*

**Respondeo** dicendum quod verbis alia ratione utimur ad Deum, et alia ratione ad hominem. Ad hominem enim utimur verbis ut conceptum nostri cordis, quem non potest cognoscere, verbis nostris ei exprimamus. Et ideo laude oris ad hominem utimur ut vel ei vel aliis innotescat quod bonam opinionem de laudato habemus, ut per hoc et ipsum qui laudatur ad meliora provocemus; et alios, apud quos laudatur, in bonam opinionem et

**Objection 1.** It would seem that God should not be praised with the lips. The Philosopher says (*Ethic.* 1, 12): *The best of men ere accorded not praise, but something greater.* But God transcends the very best of all things. Therefore God ought to be given, not praise, but something greater than praise: wherefore He is said (Sir 43:33) to be *above all praise.*

**Obj. 2:** Further, divine praise is part of divine worship, for it is an act of religion. Now God is worshiped with the mind rather than with the lips: wherefore our Lord quoted against certain ones the words of Isa. 29:13, *This people . . . honors Me with their lips, but their heart is far from Me.* Therefore the praise of God lies in the heart rather than on the lips.

**Obj. 3:** Further, men are praised with the lips that they may be encouraged to do better: since just as being praised makes the wicked proud, so does it incite the good to better things. Wherefore it is written (Prov 27:21): *As silver is tried in the fining-pot . . . so a man is tried by the mouth of him that praiseth.* But God is not incited to better things by man's words, both because He is unchangeable, and because He is supremely good, and it is not possible for Him to grow better. Therefore God should not be praised with the lips.

**On the contrary,** It is written (Ps 62:6): *My mouth shall praise Thee with joyful lips.*

**I answer that,** We use words, in speaking to God, for one reason, and in speaking to man, for another reason. For when speaking to man we use words in order to tell him our thoughts which are unknown to him. Wherefore we praise a man with our lips, in order that he or others may learn that we have a good opinion of him: so that in consequence we may incite him to yet better things; and that we may induce others, who hear him praised, to

reverentiam et imitationem ipsius inducamus. Sed ad Deum verbis utimur non quidem ut ei, qui est inspector cordium, nostros conceptus manifestemus, sed ut nos ipsos et alios audientes ad eius reverentiam inducamus.

Et ideo necessaria est laus oris, non quidem propter Deum, sed propter ipsum laudantem, cuius affectus excitatur in Deum ex laude ipsius, secundum illud Psalm., *sacrificium laudis honorificabit me, et illic iter quo ostendam illi salutare Dei.* Et inquantum homo per divinam laudem affectu ascendit in Deum, intantum per hoc retrahitur ab his quae sunt contra Deum, secundum illud Isaiae XLVIII, *laude mea infrenabo te, ne intereas.* Proficit etiam laus oris ad hoc quod aliorum affectus provocetur in Deum. Unde dicitur in Psalm., *semper laus eius in ore meo,* et postea subditur, *audiant mansueti, et laetentur. Magnificate dominum mecum.*

**Ad primum** ergo dicendum quod de Deo dupliciter possumus loqui. Uno modo, quantum ad eius essentiam. Et sic, cum sit incomprehensibilis et ineffabilis, maior est omni laude. Debetur autem ei secundum hanc comparationem reverentia et latriae honor. Unde in Psalterio Hieronymi dicitur, *tibi silet laus,* Deus, quantum ad primum; et, *tibi reddetur votum,* quantum ad secundum. Alio modo, secundum effectus ipsius, qui in nostram utilitatem ordinantur. Et secundum hoc debetur Deo laus. Unde dicitur Isaiae LXIII, *miserationum domini recordabor, laudem domini super omnibus quae reddidit nobis dominus.* Et Dionysius dicit, I cap. de Div. Nom., *omnem sanctum theologorum hymnum,* idest divinam laudem, *invenies ad bonos thearchiae,* idest divinitatis, *processus manifestative et laudative Dei nominationes dividentem.*

**Ad secundum** dicendum quod laus oris inutilis est laudanti si sit sine laude cordis, quod loquitur Deo laudem dum *magnalia eius operum* recogitat cum affectu. Valet tamen exterior laus oris ad excitandum interiorem affectum laudantis, et ad provocandum alios ad Dei laudem, sicut dictum est.

**Ad tertium** dicendum quod Deum non laudamus propter utilitatem suam, sed propter utilitatem nostram, ut dictum est.

think well of him, to reverence him, and to imitate him. On the other hand we employ words, in speaking to God, not indeed to make known our thoughts to Him Who is the searcher of hearts, but that we may bring ourselves and our hearers to reverence Him.

Consequently we need to praise God with our lips, not indeed for His sake, but for our own sake; since by praising Him our devotion is aroused towards Him, according to Ps. 49:23: *The sacrifice of praise shall glorify Me, and there is the way by which I will show him the salvation of God.* And forasmuch as man, by praising God, ascends in his affections to God, by so much is he withdrawn from things opposed to God, according to Isa. 48:9, *For My praise I will bridle thee lest thou shouldst perish.* The praise of the lips is also profitable to others by inciting their affections towards God, wherefore it is written (Ps 33:2): *His praise shall always be in my mouth,* and farther on: *Let the meek hear and rejoice. O magnify the Lord with me.*

**Reply Obj. 1**: We may speak of God in two ways. First, with regard to His essence; and thus, since He is incomprehensible and ineffable, He is above all praise. In this respect we owe Him reverence and the honor of latria; wherefore Ps. 64:2 is rendered by Jerome in his Psalter: *Praise to Thee is speechless, O God,* as regards the first, and as to the second, *A vow shall be paid to Thee.* Second, we may speak of God as to His effects which are ordained for our good. In this respect we owe Him praise; wherefore it is written (Isa 63:7): *I will remember the tender mercies of the Lord, the praise of the Lord for all the things that the Lord hath bestowed upon us.* Again, Dionysius says (*Div. Nom.* 1): *Thou wilt find that all the sacred hymns,* i.e., divine praises *of the sacred writers, are directed respectively to the Blessed Processions of the Thearchy,* i.e., of the Godhead, *showing forth and praising the names of God.*

**Reply Obj. 2**: It profits one nothing to praise with the lips if one praise not with the heart. For the heart speaks God's praises when it fervently recalls *the glorious things of His works.* Yet the outward praise of the lips avails to arouse the inward fervor of those who praise, and to incite others to praise God, as stated above.

**Reply Obj. 3**: We praise God, not for His benefit, but for ours as stated.

# Article 2

*Whether God should be praised with song?*

**Ad secundum sic proceditur.** Videtur quod cantus non sint assumendi ad laudem divinam. Dicit enim apostolus, ad Coloss. III, *docentes et commonentes vosmetipsos in Psalmis et hymnis et canticis spiritualibus.* Sed nihil assumere debemus in divinum cultum praeter

**Objection 1**: It would seem that God should not be praised with song. For the Apostle says (Col 3:16): *Teaching and admonishing one another in psalms, hymns and spiritual canticles.* Now we should employ nothing in the divine worship, save what is delivered to us on the authority of

ea quae nobis auctoritate Scripturae traduntur. Ergo videtur quod non debemus uti in divinis laudibus canticis corporalibus, sed solum spiritualibus.

PRAETEREA, Hieronymus, super illud ad Ephes. V, *cantantes et psallentes in cordibus vestris domino*, dicit, *audiant haec adolescentuli quibus in Ecclesia est psallendi officium, Deo non voce, sed corde cantandum, nec in tragoediarum modum guttur et fauces medicamine liniendae sunt, ut in Ecclesia theatrales moduli audiantur et cantica.* Non ergo in laudes Dei sunt cantus assumendi.

PRAETEREA, laudare Deum convenit parvis et magnis, secundum illud Apoc. XIX, *laudem dicite Deo nostro, omnes servi eius et qui timetis illum, pusilli et magni.* Sed maiores qui sunt in Ecclesia non decet cantare, dicit enim Gregorius, et habetur in decretis, dist. XCII, cap. *in sancta Romana Ecclesia, praesenti decreto constituo ut in sede hac sacri altaris ministri cantare non debeant.* Ergo cantus non conveniunt divinis laudibus.

PRAETEREA, in veteri lege laudabatur Deus in musicis instrumentis et humanis cantibus, secundum illud Psalm., *confitemini domino in cithara; in Psalterio decem chordarum psallite illi; cantate ei canticum novum.* Sed instrumenta musica, sicut citharas et Psalteria, non assumit Ecclesia in divinas laudes, ne videatur iudaizare. Ergo, pari ratione, nec cantus in divinas laudes sunt assumendi.

PRAETEREA, principalior est laus mentis quam laus oris. Sed laus mentis impeditur per cantus, tum quia cantantium intentio abstrahitur a consideratione eorum quae cantant, dum circa cantum student; tum etiam quia ea quae cantantur minus ab aliis intelligi possunt quam si sine cantu proferrentur. Ergo cantus non sunt divinis laudibus adhibendi.

SED CONTRA est quod beatus Ambrosius in Ecclesia Mediolanensi cantus instituit, ut Augustinus refert, in IX Confess.

RESPONDEO dicendum quod, sicut dictum est, laus vocalis ad hoc necessaria est ut affectus hominis provocetur in Deum. Et ideo quaecumque ad hoc utilia esse possunt, in divinas laudes congruenter assumuntur. Manifestum est autem quod secundum diversas melodias sonorum animi hominum diversimode disponuntur, ut patet per philosophum, in VIII Polit., et per Boetium, in prologo musicae. Et ideo salubriter fuit institutum ut in divinas laudes cantus assumerentur, ut animi infirmorum magis provocarentur ad devotionem. Unde Augustinus dicit, in X Confess., *adducor cantandi consuetudinem approbare in Ecclesia, ut per oblectamenta aurium infirmorum animus in affectum pietatis assurgat.* Et de seipso dicit, in IX Confess., *flevi in hymnis et can-*

Scripture. Therefore it would seem that, in praising God, we should employ, not corporal but spiritual canticles.

OBJ. 2: Further, Jerome in his commentary on Eph. 5:19, *Singing and making melody in your hearts to the Lord*, says: *Listen, young men whose duty it is to recite the office in church: God is to be sung not with the voice but with the heart. Nor should you, like play-actors, ease your throat and jaws with medicaments, and make the church resound with theatrical measures and airs.* Therefore God should not be praised with song.

OBJ. 3: Further, the praise of God is competent to little and great, according to Apoc. 14, *Give praise to our God, all ye His servants; and you that fear Him, little and great.* But the great, who are in the church, ought not to sing: for Gregory says (*Regist.* iv, ep. 44): *I hereby ordain that in this See the ministers of the sacred altar must not sing* (Cf. *Decret.*, dist. xcii., cap. *In sancta Romana Ecclesia*). Therefore singing is unsuitable to the divine praises.

OBJ. 4: Further, in the Old Law God was praised with musical instruments and human song, according to Ps. 32:2, 3. *Give praise to the Lord on the harp, sing to Him with the psaltery, the instrument of ten strings. Sing to Him a new canticle.* But the Church does not make use of musical instruments such as harps and psalteries, in the divine praises, for fear of seeming to imitate the Jews. Therefore in like manner neither should song be used in the divine praises.

OBJ. 5: Further, the praise of the heart is more important than the praise of the lips. But the praise of the heart is hindered by singing, both because the attention of the singers is distracted from the consideration of what they are singing, so long as they give all their attention to the chant, and because others are less able to understand the things that are sung than if they were recited without chant. Therefore chants should not be employed in the divine praises.

ON THE CONTRARY, Blessed Ambrose established singing in the Church of Milan, as Augustine relates (*Confess.* ix).

I ANSWER THAT, As stated above (A. 1), the praise of the voice is necessary in order to arouse man's devotion towards God. Wherefore whatever is useful in conducing to this result is becomingly adopted in the divine praises. Now it is evident that the human soul is moved in various ways according to various melodies of sound, as the Philosopher state (*Polit.* viii, 5), and also Boethius (*De Musica*, prologue). Hence the use of music in the divine praises is a salutary institution, that the souls of the faint-hearted may be the more incited to devotion. Wherefore Augustine say (*Confess.* x, 33): *I am inclined to approve of the usage of singing in the church, that so by the delight of the ears the faint-hearted may rise to the feeling of devotion*: and he says of himself (*Confess.* ix, 6): *I wept in Thy hymns and*

*ticis tuis, suave sonantis Ecclesiae tuae vocibus commotus acriter.*

**AD PRIMUM** ergo dicendum quod cantica spiritualia possunt dici non solum ea quae interius canuntur in spiritu, sed etiam ea quae exterius ore cantantur, inquantum per huiusmodi cantica spiritualis devotio provocatur.

**AD SECUNDUM** dicendum quod Hieronymus non vituperat simpliciter cantum, sed reprehendit eos qui in Ecclesia cantant more theatrico, non propter devotionem excitandam, sed propter ostentationem vel delectationem provocandam. Unde Augustinus dicit, in X Confess., *cum mihi accidit ut me amplius cantus quam res quae canitur moveat, poenaliter me peccare confiteor, et tunc mallem non audire cantantem.*

**AD TERTIUM** dicendum quod nobilior modus est provocandi homines ad devotionem per doctrinam et praedicationem quam per cantum. Et ideo diaconi et praelati, quibus competit per praedicationem et doctrinam animos hominum provocare in Deum, non debent cantibus insistere, ne per hoc a maioribus retrahantur. Unde ibidem Gregorius dicit, *consuetudo est valde reprehensibilis ut in diaconatus ordine constituti modulationi vocis inserviant, quos ad praedicationis officium et eleemosynarum studium vacare congruebat.*

**AD QUARTUM** dicendum quod, sicut philosophus dicit, in VIII Polit., *neque fistulas ad disciplinam est adducendum, neque aliquod aliud artificiale organum, puta citharam et si quid tale alterum est, sed quaecumque faciunt auditores bonos.* Huiusmodi enim musica instrumenta magis animum movent ad delectationem quam per ea formetur interius bona dispositio. In veteri autem testamento usus erat talium instrumentorum, tum quia populus erat magis durus et carnalis, unde erat per huiusmodi instrumenta provocandus, sicut et per promissiones terrenas. Tum etiam quia huiusmodi instrumenta corporalia aliquid figurabant.

**AD QUINTUM** dicendum quod per cantum quo quis studiose ad delectandum utitur, abstrahitur animus a consideratione eorum quae cantantur. Sed si aliquis cantet propter devotionem, attentius considerat quae dicuntur, tum quia diutius moratur super eodem; tum quia, ut Augustinus dicit, in X Confess., *omnes affectus spiritus nostri pro sua diversitate habent proprios modos in voce atque cantu, quorum occulta familiaritate excitantur.* Et eadem est ratio de audientibus, in quibus, etsi aliquando non intelligant quae cantantur, intelligunt tamen propter quid cantantur, scilicet ad laudem Dei; et hoc sufficit ad devotionem excitandam.

*canticles, touched to the quick by the voices of Thy sweet-attuned Church.*

**REPLY OBJ. 1:** The name of spiritual canticle may be given not only to those that are sung inwardly in spirit, but also to those that are sung outwardly with the lips, inasmuch as such like canticles arouse spiritual devotion.

**REPLY OBJ. 2:** Jerome does not absolutely condemn singing, but reproves those who sing theatrically in church not in order to arouse devotion, but in order to show off, or to provoke pleasure. Hence Augustine says (*Confess.* x, 33): *When it befalls me to be more moved by the voice than by the words sung, I confess to have sinned penally, and then had rather not hear the singer.*

**REPLY OBJ. 3:** To arouse men to devotion by teaching and preaching is a more excellent way than by singing. Wherefore deacons and prelates, whom it becomes to incite men's minds towards God by means of preaching and teaching, ought not to be instant in singing, lest thereby they be withdrawn from greater things. Hence Gregory says (*Regist.* iv, ep. 44): *It is a most discreditable custom for those who have been raised to the diaconate to serve as choristers, for it behooves them to give their whole time to the duty of preaching and to taking charge of the alms.*

**REPLY OBJ. 4:** As the Philosopher says (*Polit.* viii, 6), *Teaching should not be accompanied with a flute or any artificial instrument such as the harp or anything else of this kind: but only with such things as make good hearers.* For such like musical instruments move the soul to pleasure rather than create a good disposition within it. In the Old Testament instruments of this description were employed, both because the people were more coarse and carnal—so that they needed to be aroused by such instruments as also by earthly promises—and because these material instruments were figures of something else.

**REPLY OBJ. 5:** The soul is distracted from that which is sung by a chant that is employed for the purpose of giving pleasure. But if the singer chant for the sake of devotion, he pays more attention to what he says, both because he lingers more thereon, and because, as Augustine remarks (*Confess.* x, 33), *each affection of our spirit, according to its variety, has its own appropriate measure in the voice, and singing, by some hidden correspondence wherewith it is stirred.* The same applies to the hearers, for even if some of them understand not what is sung, yet they understand why it is sung, namely, for God's glory: and this is enough to arouse their devotion.